Bill James presents. . .

STATS™
Minor League Handbook
1998

STATS, Inc.
and
Howe Sportsdata International

Published by STATS Publishing
A Division of Sports Team Analysis & Tracking Systems, Inc.

Cover by Ron Freer

Photo by Larry Goren

First Edition: November, 1997

Printed in the United States of America

ISBN 1-884064-43-4

Acknowledgments

A monk wrote this book by candlelight with a quill and ink. Although he's fantastically productive, our resident monk tends to be a little pubilicity-shy, so for his sake, the rest of us here at STATS, Inc. are going to take credit for this book. Under the leadership of John Dewan, President and CEO, STATS, Inc. continues to grow and prosper. He is assisted by Heather Schwarze, who has the daunting task of keeping up with John's hectic agenda.

Without our Systems Department, headed by Sue Dewan, Mike Canter and Art Ashley, we'd be at the complete mercy of our vast and powerful computer system. You can thank Andrew Bernstein, Dave Carlson, Drew Faust, Kevin Goldstein, Mike Hammer, Stefan Kretschmann, Steve Moyer, Brent Osland, Dean Peterson, Dave Pinto, Pat Quinn, Jeff Schinski, Allan Spear and Kevin Thomas for the considerable amount of data they manage to sort out, especially for this book. Special thanks go to Stefan, who served as chief programmer for both of our Handbooks.

Before our Systems staff can work its magic on the data, the Operations Department must first compile it. Doug Abel, our Operations Manager, heads up a team including Jeff Chernow, Brian Cousins, Jason Kinsey, Jim Osborne, John Sasman, Matt Senter, Joseph Weindel and Peter Woelflein that oversees our nationwide reporter network.

Don Zminda, STATS Vice President of Publications, supervises the production of the book and ensures that each STATS product is of the highest quality. The All-Prose Publications Department staff includes: Jim Callis, Ethan Cooperson, Kevin Fullam, Jim Henzler, Tony Nistler, and the guy who cashes all my paychecks, Mat Olkin.

Steve Byrd heads up the Marketing Department with help from Marc Elman, Ron Freer, Corey Roberts and Walter Lis. Jim Capuano leads the Sales team with the assistance of Kristen Beauregard, Leena Sheth and Lori Smith.

Bob Meyerhoff always has his hands full; he heads the Finances and Administration Department. His support group includes Steve Drago, Angela Gabe, Mark Hong, Betty Moy, Carol Savier and Taasha Schroeder. Stephanie Seburn leads our Human Resources Department with help from Tracy Lickton, and Susan Zamechek heads the Administrative staff, which includes Grant Blair, Ken Gilbert, Sherlinda Johnson, Antionette Kelly and Kacey Schueler Poulos.

Howe Sportsdata International is responsible for the collection and compilation of our minor league statistics. We'd like to offer our thanks to President Jay Virshbo and the following people: Tom Graham, Jim Keller, Mike Walczak, John Foley, Vin Vitro, Paul La Rocca, Brian Joura, Bob Chaban, Walter Kent, Marshall Wright and William Weiss. Special thanks goes to Chris Pollari, who, as usual, was particularly helpful in the production of this year's edition of the Handbook.

One more thing—the monk asked us to thank you profusely for reading. After all, the guy's got a monastery to feed.

—Mat Olkin

This book is dedicated to
STATS' 1997 Rookies of the Year:

Charlotte Marie Byrd
Ryan Christopher Callis
Brittany Briana Murphy
Reginald Murphy II
Christopher Gabriel Palacios
Darby Nicole Thomas
Siena Elizabeth Thomas

Table of Contents

Introduction

Welcome to the seventh edition of the *STATS Minor League Handbook*. We like to think we keep making the book better each year, adding new features for your enjoyment.

The *Minor League Handbook* begins with career stats for every player who appeared in Double-A or Triple-A in 1997. The exceptions are players who appeared in the major leagues in 1997. They can be found in our companion book, the *STATS Major League Handbook*. For players in Class A and Rookie leagues, we present their complete 1997 statistical lines in the section after the career register.

It wouldn't be a STATS publication if we simply presented you with the raw numbers. We also offer the totals for each minor league team and league. You can see, for instance, why a 20-homer season is much more significant in the Florida State League than in the California League, though both are high Class A circuits. We also list the individual leaders for Double-A and Triple-A combined, offering further perspective.

That's only the beginning. We have detailed ballpark data, so you can separate the bandboxes from the pitchers' parks. We've expanded our section on player splits, going from a Triple-A lefty/righty comparison in last year's book to lefty/righty and home/road numbers this time around.

Last and certainly not least, we reveal the major league equivalencies for the top Double-A and Triple-A hitters in each organization. The MLEs, developed by Bill James more than a decade ago, translate a hitter's minor league numbers into what they would have looked like in the majors, adjusting for home park (both major and minor league), league and level of competition. This can help you find the next Nomar Garciaparra or Scott Rolen.

Enjoy the best *Minor League Handbook* ever. We're committed to improving the book every year, so please let us know if you think something is missing or can be improved.

—Jim Callis

Career Statistics

Any player who appeared in Double-A or Triple-A in 1997 gets a profile in this section. The exception is if he also played in the major leagues, in which case his statistics are in our companion book, the *STATS Major League Handbook*.

The profiles have complete major and minor league records for all qualifying players. A player's age is as of July 1, 1998 and represents the age at which he'll play most of the 1998 season.

There are a few statistical categories which may not be immediately recognizable:

TBB — Total bases on balls

IBB — Intentional bases on balls

SB% — Stolen-base percentage (SB divided by SBA)

OBP — On-base percentage (H+TBB+HBP divided by AB+TBB+HBP+SF)

SLG — Slugging percentage (TB divided by AB)

BFP — Batters facing pitcher

Bk — Balks

ShO — Shutouts

Class A (A+, A, A-) and Rookie (R+, R) have separate classifications to distinguish the level of competition.

Andy Abad

Bats: Left **Throws:** Left **Pos:** 1B-OF

Ht: 6'1" **Wt:** 185 **Born:** 8/25/72 **Age:** 25

					BATTING												BASERUNNING				PERCENTAGES		
Year Team	Lg Org	G	AB	H	2B	3B	HR	TB	R	RBI	TBB	IBB	SO	HBP	SH	SF	SB	CS	SB%	GDP	Avg	OBP	SLG
1993 Red Sox	R Bos	59	230	57	9	2	1	73	24	28	25	0	27	2	2	4	2	2	.50	2	.248	.322	.317
1994 Sarasota	A+ Bos	111	354	102	20	0	2	128	39	35	42	4	58	5	5	5	2	12	.14	9	.288	.367	.362
1995 Trenton	AA Bos	89	287	69	14	3	4	101	29	32	36	2	58	3	6	3	5	7	.42	6	.240	.328	.352
Sarasota	A+ Bos	18	59	17	3	0	0	20	5	10	6	0	13	0	0	0	4	3	.57	0	.288	.354	.339
1996 Sarasota	A+ Bos	58	202	58	15	1	2	81	28	41	37	1	28	3	2	2	10	3	.77	6	.287	.402	.401
Trenton	AA Bos	65	213	59	22	1	4	95	33	39	33	2	41	0	0	3	5	3	.63	4	.277	.369	.446
1997 Trenton	AA Bos	45	165	50	13	0	8	87	37	24	33	3	27	2	0	1	2	4	.33	2	.303	.423	.527
Pawtucket	AAA Bos	68	227	62	7	0	9	96	28	32	36	1	47	2	1	1	3	2	.60	4	.273	.376	.423
5 Min. YEARS		513	1737	474	103	7	30	681	223	241	248	13	299	17	16	19	33	36	.48	33	.273	.366	.392

Paul Abbott

Pitches: Right **Bats:** Right **Pos:** P

Ht: 6'3" **Wt:** 194 **Born:** 9/15/67 **Age:** 30

		HOW MUCH HE PITCHED						WHAT HE GAVE UP										THE RESULTS					
Year Team	Lg Org	G	GS	CG	GF	IP	BFP	H	R	ER	HR	SH	SF	HB	TBB	IBB	SO	WP	Bk	W	L	Pct.	ShO	Sv	ERA
1985 Elizabethtn	R+ Min	10	10	1	0	35	172	33	32	27	3	1	0	0	32	0	34	7	1	1	5	.167	0	0	6.94
1986 Kenosha	A Min	25	15	1	7	98	462	102	62	49	13	3	2	2	73	3	73	7	0	6	10	.375	0	0	4.50
1987 Kenosha	A Min	26	25	1	0	145.1	620	102	76	59	11	5	6	3	103	0	138	11	2	13	6	.684	0	0	3.65
1988 Visalia	A+ Min	28	28	4	0	172.1	799	141	95	80	9	8	6	4	143	5	205	12	9	11	9	.550	2	0	4.18
1989 Orlando	AA Min	17	17	1	0	90.2	389	71	48	44	6	2	1	0	48	0	102	7	7	9	3	.750	0	0	4.37
1990 Portland	AAA Min	23	23	4	0	128.1	568	110	75	65	9	3	3	1	82	0	129	8	5	5	14	.263	1	0	4.56
1991 Portland	AAA Min	8	8	1	0	44	193	36	19	19	2	0	1	3	28	0	40	1	0	2	3	.400	1	0	3.89
1992 Portland	AAA Min	7	7	0	0	46.1	191	30	13	12	2	0	0	0	31	0	46	0	0	4	1	.800	0	0	2.33
1993 Charlotte	AAA Cle	4	4	0	0	19	91	25	16	14	4	3	1	0	7	0	12	3	0	0	1	.000	0	0	6.63
Canton-Akm	AA Cle	13	12	1	0	75.1	315	71	34	34	4	1	0	1	28	2	86	6	0	4	5	.444	0	0	4.06
1994 Omaha	AAA KC	15	10	0	4	57.1	262	57	32	31	8	1	0	2	45	0	48	3	0	4	1	.800	0	0	4.87
1995 Iowa	AAA ChN	46	11	0	7	115.1	498	104	50	47	12	4	1	0	64	4	127	12	9	7	7	.500	0	0	3.67
1996 Las Vegas	AAA SD	28	0	0	14	28	124	27	14	13	4	3	1	1	12	4	37	4	0	4	2	.667	0	7	4.18
1997 Mariners	R Sea	3	3	0	0	9.2	35	0	2	1	0	0	1	0	7	0	13	3	0	0	0	.000	0	0	0.93
Tacoma	AAA Sea	17	14	3	0	93.2	391	80	48	43	11	3	2	6	29	1	117	6	0	8	4	.667	1	0	4.13
1990 Minnesota	AL	7	7	0	0	34.2	162	37	24	23	0	1	1	1	28	0	25	1	0	0	5	.000	0	0	5.97
1991 Minnesota	AL	15	3	0	1	47.1	210	38	27	25	5	7	3	0	36	1	43	5	0	3	1	.750	0	0	4.75
1992 Minnesota	AL	6	0	0	5	11	50	12	4	4	1	0	1	1	5	0	13	1	0	0	0	.000	0	0	3.27
1993 Cleveland	AL	5	5	0	0	18.1	84	19	15	13	5	0	0	1	11	1	7	1	0	0	1	.000	0	0	6.38
13 Min. YEARS		270	187	17	32	1158.1	5110	989	616	538	98	37	25	23	732	19	1207	90	24	78	71	.523	4	7	4.18
4 Mai. YEARS		33	15	0	6	111.1	506	106	70	65	11	8	5	2	80	2	88	8	0	3	7	.300	0	0	5.25

Sharnol Adriana

Bats: Right **Throws:** Right **Pos:** 2B

Ht: 6'1" **Wt:** 185 **Born:** 11/13/70 **Age:** 27

					BATTING												BASERUNNING				PERCENTAGES		
Year Team	Lg Org	G	AB	H	2B	3B	HR	TB	R	RBI	TBB	IBB	SO	HBP	SH	SF	SB	CS	SB%	GDP	Avg	OBP	SLG
1991 St. Cathrns	A- Tor	51	170	35	8	0	5	58	27	20	26	0	33	5	1	4	9	4	.69	6	.206	.322	.341
1992 Dunedin	A+ Tor	69	210	58	6	3	0	70	25	18	31	1	43	0	4	0	9	4	.69	5	.276	.369	.333
1993 Knoxville	AA Tor	64	177	38	3	1	0	43	19	18	24	2	59	2	2	2	8	8	.53	4	.215	.312	.243
1994 Syracuse	AAA Tor	17	30	4	2	0	0	6	2	0	6	0	8	0	1	0	1	0	1.00	1	.133	.278	.200
Knoxville	AA Tor	69	189	47	7	1	3	65	28	21	31	1	39	2	3	1	7	7	.50	5	.249	.359	.344
1995 Knoxville	AA Tor	75	261	74	11	1	3	102	33	33	32	1	64	4	2	2	12	13	.48	6	.284	.368	.391
1996 Syracuse	AAA Tor	90	292	82	12	5	10	134	48	37	24	1	72	8	2	0	18	7	.72	5	.281	.352	.459
1997 Knoxville	AA Tor	99	314	74	11	1	6	105	50	39	47	2	66	5	5	4	9	7	.56	11	.236	.341	.334
7 Min. YEARS		534	1643	412	66	12	27	583	232	186	221	8	384	26	20	13	74	50	.60	43	.251	.346	.355

Benny Agbayani

Bats: Right **Throws:** Right **Pos:** OF

Ht: 5'11" **Wt:** 175 **Born:** 12/28/71 **Age:** 26

					BATTING												BASERUNNING				PERCENTAGES		
Year Team	Lg Org	G	AB	H	2B	3B	HR	TB	R	RBI	TBB	IBB	SO	HBP	SH	SF	SB	CS	SB%	GDP	Avg	OBP	SLG
1993 Pittsfield	A- NYN	51	167	42	6	3	2	60	26	22	20	0	43	0	0	0	7	2	.78	4	.251	.332	.359
1994 St. Lucie	A+ NYN	119	411	115	13	5	5	153	72	63	58	2	67	10	1	5	8	6	.57	9	.280	.378	.372
1995 St. Lucie	A+ NYN	44	155	48	9	3	2	69	24	29	26	1	27	5	1	4	8	3	.73	4	.310	.416	.445
Binghamton	AA NYN	88	295	81	11	2	1	99	38	26	39	0	51	5	1	1	12	6	.67	8	.275	.368	.336
1996 Binghamton	AA NYN	21	53	9	1	0	2	16	7	8	11	0	13	1	1	1	1	0	1.00	2	.170	.318	.302
Norfolk	AAA NYN	99	331	92	13	9	7	144	43	56	30	3	57	3	3	5	14	5	.74	5	.278	.339	.435
1997 Norfolk	AAA NYN	127	468	145	24	2	11	206	90	51	67	0	106	6	0	3	29	14	.67	13	.310	.401	.440
5 Min. YEARS		549	1880	532	77	24	30	747	300	255	251	6	364	30	7	19	79	33	.71	43	.283	.373	.397

Pat Ahearne

Pitches: Right **Bats:** Right **Pos:** P

Ht: 6'3" **Wt:** 195 **Born:** 12/10/69 **Age:** 28

		HOW MUCH HE PITCHED						WHAT HE GAVE UP										THE RESULTS					
Year Team	Lg Org	G	GS	CG	GF	IP	BFP	H	R	ER	HR	SH	SF	HB	TBB	IBB	SO	WP	Bk	W	L	Pct.	ShO	Sv	ERA
1992 Lakeland	A+ Det	1	1	0	0	4.2	17	4	2	1	0	0	0	0	0	0	4	0	0	0	0	.000	0	0	1.93
1993 Lakeland	A+ Det	25	24	2	0	147.1	650	160	87	73	8	7	4	6	48	0	51	3	1	6	15	.286	0	0	4.46
1994 Trenton	AA Det	30	13	2	3	108.2	467	126	55	48	8	1	6	5	25	1	57	5	0	7	5	.583	0	0	3.98
1995 Toledo	AAA Det	25	23	1	0	139.2	599	165	83	73	11	2	5	5	37	3	54	2	0	7	9	.438	1	0	4.70
1996 Norfolk	AAA NYN	5	4	0	0	25.1	108	26	14	13	1	3	0	1	9	0	14	0	1	1	2	.333	0	0	4.62
Duluth-Sup.	IND —	1	1	0	0	4.1	24	10	6	6	3	0	0	0	1	0	6	0	0	0	0	.000	0	0	12.46
San Antonio	AA LA	8	8	0	0	45.1	208	59	34	29	3	2	2	1	18	0	21	4	0	2	4	.333	0	0	5.76

Year Team	Lg Org	G	GS	CG	GF	IP	BFP	H	R	ER	HR	SH	SF	HB	TBB	IBB	SO	WP	Bk	W	L	Pct.	ShO	Sv	ERA
						HOW MUCH HE PITCHED			WHAT HE GAVE UP											THE RESULTS					
Vero Beach	A+ LA	6	6	1	0	47	179	38	16	11	1	2	1	1	5	0	26	2	0	3	2	.600	0	0	2.11
1997 Albuquerque	AAA LA	20	8	0	3	60.2	280	82	43	33	9	4	2	1	20	1	44	2	0	2	4	.333	0	0	4.90
San Antonio	AA LA	14	14	3	0	84	364	109	48	42	1	6	2	2	13	0	45	4	0	5	4	.444	0	0	4.50
1995 Detroit	AL	4	3	0	0	10	55	20	13	13	2	0	0	0	5	1	4	1	0	0	2	.000	0	0	11.70
6 Min. YEARS		135	102	9	6	667	2896	779	388	329	45	27	22	22	176	6	317	23	2	32	46	.410	2	0	4.44

Israel Alcantara

Bats: Right Throws: Right Pos: 3B　　　　Ht: 6'2" Wt: 165 Born: 5/6/73 Age: 25

Year Team	Lg Org	G	AB	H	2B	3B	HR	TB	R	RBI	TBB	IBB	SO	HBP	SH	SF	SB	CS	SB%	GDP	Avg	OBP	SLG
					BATTING												BASERUNNING				PERCENTAGES		
1992 Expos	R Mon	59	224	62	14	2	3	89	29	37	17	4	35	1	0	2	6	5	.55	8	.277	.328	.397
1993 Burlington	A Mon	126	470	115	26	3	18	201	65	73	20	2	125	7	1	5	6	7	.46	5	.245	.283	.428
1994 Wst Plm Bch	A+ Mon	125	471	134	26	4	15	213	65	69	26	0	130	3	1	3	9	3	.75	6	.285	.324	.452
1995 Harrisburg	AA Mon	71	237	50	12	2	10	96	25	29	21	1	81	2	1	1	1	1	.50	5	.211	.280	.405
Wst Plm Bch	A+ Mon	39	134	37	7	2	3	57	16	22	9	0	35	2	2	1	3	0	1.00	0	.276	.329	.425
1996 Harrisburg	AA Mon	62	218	46	5	0	8	75	26	19	14	0	62	1	0	1	1	1	.50	5	.211	.261	.344
Expos	R Mon	7	30	9	2	0	2	17	4	10	3	2	6	0	0	0	0	1	.00	1	.300	.364	.567
Wst Plm Bch	A+ Mon	15	61	19	2	0	4	33	11	14	3	0	13	1	0	1	0	0	.00	1	.311	.348	.541
1997 Harrisburg	AA Mon	89	301	85	9	2	27	179	48	68	29	1	84	3	0	3	4	5	.44	5	.282	.348	.595
6 Min. YEARS		593	2146	557	103	15	90	960	289	341	142	10	571	20	5	17	30	23	.57	36	.260	.309	.447

Mike Aldrete

Bats: Left Throws: Left Pos: 1B　　　　Ht: 5'11" Wt: 185 Born: 1/29/61 Age: 37

Year Team	Lg Org	G	AB	H	2B	3B	HR	TB	R	RBI	TBB	IBB	SO	HBP	SH	SF	SB	CS	SB%	GDP	Avg	OBP	SLG
					BATTING												BASERUNNING				PERCENTAGES		
1983 Great Falls	R+ SF	38	132	55	11	2	4	82	30	31	31	3	22	1	0	3	7	2	.78	-	.417	.521	.621
Fresno	A+ SF	20	68	14	4	0	1	21	5	12	11	1	17	2	0	1	2	0	1.00	-	.206	.329	.309
1984 Fresno	A+ SF	136	457	155	28	3	12	225	89	72	109	5	77	1	1	4	14	5	.74	5	.339	.464	.492
1985 Shreveport	AA SF	127	441	147	32	1	15	226	80	77	94	9	57	0	2	4	16	7	.70	11	.333	.447	.512
Phoenix	AAA SF	3	8	1	1	0	0	2	0	1	0	0	3	0	0	0	0	0	.00	0	.125	.125	.250
1986 Phoenix	AAA SF	47	159	59	14	0	6	91	36	35	36	3	24	0	1	4	0	0	.00	1	.371	.477	.572
1989 Indianapolis	AAA Mon	10	31	4	1	0	0	5	4	2	8	0	10	0	0	0	0	1	.00	1	.129	.308	.161
1991 Colo Spngs	AAA Cle	23	76	22	5	0	0	27	4	8	8	1	17	0	0	0	0	0	.00	2	.289	.357	.355
1992 Colo Spngs	AAA Cle	128	463	149	42	2	8	219	69	84	65	8	113	3	1	4	1	0	1.00	7	.322	.406	.473
1993 Tacoma	AAA Oak	37	122	39	11	2	7	75	20	21	26	5	22	0	1	2	2	2	.50	6	.320	.439	.615
1997 Syracuse	AAA Tor	27	74	22	5	0	2	27	8	8	17	0	15	0	1	1	0	0	.00	2	.297	.424	.365
1986 San Francisco	NL	84	216	54	18	3	2	84	27	25	33	4	34	2	4	1	1	3	.25	3	.250	.353	.389
1987 San Francisco	NL	126	357	116	18	2	9	165	50	51	43	5	50	0	4	2	6	0	1.00	6	.325	.396	.462
1988 San Francisco	NL	139	389	104	15	0	3	128	44	50	56	13	65	0	1	3	6	5	.55	10	.267	.357	.329
1989 Montreal	NL	76	136	30	8	1	1	43	12	12	19	0	30	1	1	1	1	3	.25	4	.221	.316	.316
1990 Montreal	NL	96	161	39	7	1	1	51	22	18	37	2	31	1	0	1	1	2	.33	2	.242	.385	.317
1991 San Diego	NL	12	15	0	0	0	0	0	2	1	3	0	4	0	0	0	0	1	.00	1	.000	.167	.000
Cleveland	AL	85	183	48	6	1	1	59	22	19	36	1	37	0	1	2	1	2	.33	0	.262	.380	.322
1993 Oakland	AL	95	255	68	13	1	10	113	40	33	34	2	45	0	3	0	1	1	.50	7	.267	.353	.443
1994 Oakland	AL	76	178	43	5	0	4	60	23	18	20	1	35	0	0	3	2	0	1.00	4	.242	.313	.337
1995 Oakland	AL	60	125	34	8	0	4	54	18	21	19	1	23	1	0	2	0	0	.00	3	.272	.367	.432
California	AL	18	24	6	0	0	0	6	1	3	5	0	8	0	0	1	0	0	.00	3	.250	.240	.250
1996 California	AL	31	40	6	1	0	3	16	5	8	5	0	4	0	0	0	0	0	.00	3	.150	.239	.400
New York	AL	32	68	17	5	0	3	31	11	12	9	0	15	0	0	0	0	1	.00	1	.250	.338	.456
9 Min. YEARS		596	2031	667	154	10	53	1000	345	351	405	31	377	7	7	21	42	17	.71	34	.328	.438	.492
10 Maj. YEARS		930	2147	565	104	9	41	810	277	271	314	29	381	5	14	18	19	18	.51	43	.263	.356	.377

Chad Allen

Bats: Right Throws: Right Pos: OF　　　　Ht: 6'1" Wt: 190 Born: 2/6/75 Age: 23

Year Team	Lg Org	G	AB	H	2B	3B	HR	TB	R	RBI	TBB	IBB	SO	HBP	SH	SF	SB	CS	SB%	GDP	Avg	OBP	SLG
					BATTING												BASERUNNING				PERCENTAGES		
1996 Ft. Wayne	A Min	7	21	9	0	0	0	9	2	2	3	1	2	0	0	1	1	1	.50	0	.429	.480	.429
1997 Ft. Myers	A+ Min	105	401	124	18	4	3	159	66	45	40	2	51	2	2	2	27	15	.64	9	.309	.373	.397
New Britain	AA Min	30	115	29	9	1	4	52	20	18	9	0	21	0	1	1	2	0	1.00	3	.252	.304	.452
2 Min. YEARS		142	537	162	27	5	7	220	88	65	52	3	74	2	3	4	30	16	.65	12	.302	.363	.410

Dusty Allen

Bats: Right Throws: Right Pos: 1B-OF　　　　Ht: 6'4" Wt: 215 Born: 8/9/72 Age: 25

Year Team	Lg Org	G	AB	H	2B	3B	HR	TB	R	RBI	TBB	IBB	SO	HBP	SH	SF	SB	CS	SB%	GDP	Avg	OBP	SLG
					BATTING												BASERUNNING				PERCENTAGES		
1995 Idaho Falls	R+ SD	29	104	34	7	0	4	53	21	24	21	0	19	0	0	2	1	2	.33	2	.327	.433	.510
Clinton	A SD	36	139	37	12	1	5	66	25	31	12	1	29	1	0	0	1	0	1.00	3	.266	.329	.475
1996 Clinton	A SD	77	243	65	10	3	10	111	46	46	67	1	59	4	0	3	4	7	.36	7	.267	.429	.457
Rancho Cuca	A+ SD	55	208	62	15	1	10	109	41	45	38	1	65	2	0	3	3	2	.60	3	.298	.406	.524
1997 Mobile	AA SD	131	475	120	28	4	17	207	85	75	81	0	116	0	0	3	1	4	.20	12	.253	.360	.436
3 Min. YEARS		328	1169	318	72	9	46	546	218	221	219	3	288	7	0	11	10	15	.40	27	.272	.387	.467

Marlon Allen

Bats: Right **Throws:** Right **Pos:** 1B   **Ht:** 6'6" **Wt:** 228 **Born:** 3/28/73 **Age:** 25

		BATTING															BASERUNNING				PERCENTAGES		
Year Team	Lg Org	G	AB	H	2B	3B	HR	TB	R	RBI	TBB	IBB	SO	HBP	SH	SF	SB	CS	SB%	GDP	Avg	OBP	SLG
1994 Princeton	R+ Cin	20	64	16	2	0	6	36	15	17	9	0	21	2	0	1	0	0	.00	0	.250	.355	.563
1995 Chston-WV	A Cin	117	396	107	26	0	9	160	47	76	42	3	108	13	0	6	2	2	.50	10	.270	.354	.404
1996 Winston-Sal	A+ Cin	121	426	101	19	1	17	173	57	82	32	2	133	5	1	12	8	2	.80	3	.237	.291	.406
1997 Burlington	A Cin	69	242	75	20	1	12	133	42	52	36	2	61	3	0	2	5	3	.63	5	.310	.403	.550
Chattanooga	AA Cin	62	196	50	15	2	4	81	27	23	26	1	39	3	0	4	0	1	.00	2	.255	.345	.413
4 Min. YEARS		389	1324	349	82	4	48	583	188	250	145	8	362	26	1	25	15	8	.65	20	.264	.342	.440

Chris Allison

Bats: Right **Throws:** Right **Pos:** 2B   **Ht:** 5'10" **Wt:** 165 **Born:** 10/22/71 **Age:** 26

		BATTING															BASERUNNING				PERCENTAGES		
Year Team	Lg Org	G	AB	H	2B	3B	HR	TB	R	RBI	TBB	IBB	SO	HBP	SH	SF	SB	CS	SB%	GDP	Avg	OBP	SLG
1994 Utica	A- Bos	39	144	48	4	3	0	58	19	16	10	0	16	1	4	2	11	3	.79	3	.333	.376	.403
1995 Michigan	A Bos	87	298	94	8	4	0	110	46	22	52	1	39	7	4	0	36	4	.90	5	.315	.429	.369
1996 Trenton	AA Bos	109	357	82	7	1	0	91	49	22	28	0	61	3	4	0	14	11	.56	7	.230	.291	.255
1997 Sarasota	A+ Bos	109	365	101	10	7	2	137	51	52	32	2	28	5	7	4	13	11	.54	10	.293	.355	.375
Pawtucket	AAA Bos	8	25	7	2	0	0	9	2	1	1	0	0	0	0	0	0	1	.00	1	.280	.308	.360
4 Min. YEARS		352	1189	338	31	15	2	405	167	113	123	3	144	16	19	6	74	30	.71	26	.284	.358	.341

Richard Almanzar

Bats: Right **Throws:** Right **Pos:** 2B   **Ht:** 5'10" **Wt:** 155 **Born:** 4/3/76 **Age:** 22

		BATTING															BASERUNNING				PERCENTAGES		
Year Team	Lg Org	G	AB	H	2B	3B	HR	TB	R	RBI	TBB	IBB	SO	HBP	SH	SF	SB	CS	SB%	GDP	Avg	OBP	SLG
1995 Lakeland	A+ Det	42	140	43	9	0	1	55	29	14	18	0	20	4	5	0	11	9	.55	5	.307	.401	.393
Fayetteville	A Det	80	308	76	12	1	0	90	47	16	29	0	32	7	9	0	39	15	.72	5	.247	.326	.292
1996 Lakeland	A+ Det	124	471	144	22	2	1	173	81	36	49	0	49	8	12	3	53	19	.74	5	.306	.379	.367
1997 Jacksnville	AA Det	103	387	94	20	2	5	133	55	35	37	0	43	3	11	0	20	6	.77	11	.243	.314	.344
3 Min. YEARS		349	1306	357	63	5	7	451	212	101	133	0	144	22	37	3	123	49	.72	26	.273	.350	.345

Greg Almond

Bats: Right **Throws:** Right **Pos:** C   **Ht:** 6'0" **Wt:** 195 **Born:** 4/14/71 **Age:** 27

		BATTING															BASERUNNING				PERCENTAGES		
Year Team	Lg Org	G	AB	H	2B	3B	HR	TB	R	RBI	TBB	IBB	SO	HBP	SH	SF	SB	CS	SB%	GDP	Avg	OBP	SLG
1993 Glens Falls	A- StL	68	239	61	17	1	2	86	33	30	31	1	47	2	1	1	4	5	.44	5	.255	.344	.360
1994 Madison	A StL	97	303	71	15	1	4	100	37	30	29	1	76	2	1	3	1	3	.25	5	.234	.303	.330
1995 Savannah	A StL	18	56	9	2	0	0	11	2	3	8	0	16	1	0	0	0	1	.00	0	.161	.277	.196
1996 Peoria	A StL	90	273	63	14	0	2	83	28	41	26	0	75	0	5	5	2	1	.00	8	.231	.293	.304
1997 Pr William	A+ StL	18	52	17	7	0	1	27	5	2	5	1	11	0	0	1	1	2	.33	2	.327	.379	.519
Arkansas	AA StL	69	158	32	4	1	0	38	23	16	29	1	38	1	4	2	0	0	.00	2	.203	.326	.241
5 Min. YEARS		360	1081	253	59	3	9	345	128	122	128	4	263	6	11	12	8	11	.42	22	.234	.315	.319

Wady Almonte

Bats: Right **Throws:** Right **Pos:** OF   **Ht:** 6'0" **Wt:** 180 **Born:** 4/20/75 **Age:** 23

		BATTING															BASERUNNING				PERCENTAGES		
Year Team	Lg Org	G	AB	H	2B	3B	HR	TB	R	RBI	TBB	IBB	SO	HBP	SH	SF	SB	CS	SB%	GDP	Avg	OBP	SLG
1994 Orioles	R Bal	42	120	24	2	0	2	32	11	9	8	0	22	1	1	0	1	2	.33	0	.200	.256	.267
1995 Bluefield	R+ Bal	51	189	58	12	1	6	90	37	30	9	2	49	1	0	2	6	5	.55	4	.307	.338	.476
1996 Orioles	R Bal	1	3	1	0	0	0	1	2	1	0	0	0	0	0	0	1	0	1.00	0	.333	.500	.333
Frederick	A+ Bal	85	287	82	12	2	12	134	45	44	21	2	59	6	4	1	1	5	.17	12	.286	.346	.467
1997 Bowie	AA Bal	69	222	46	7	2	6	75	25	25	27	0	64	5	0	1	2	4	.33	6	.207	.306	.338
Frederick	A+ Bal	57	202	52	13	2	10	99	34	36	16	4	59	4	1	3	4	1	.80	8	.257	.320	.490
4 Min. YEARS		305	1023	263	46	7	36	431	154	145	82	8	253	17	6	7	15	17	.47	30	.257	.321	.421

Clemente Alvarez

Bats: Right **Throws:** Right **Pos:** C   **Ht:** 5'11" **Wt:** 180 **Born:** 5/18/68 **Age:** 30

		BATTING															BASERUNNING				PERCENTAGES		
Year Team	Lg Org	G	AB	H	2B	3B	HR	TB	R	RBI	TBB	IBB	SO	HBP	SH	SF	SB	CS	SB%	GDP	Avg	OBP	SLG
1987 White Sox	R ChA	25	55	10	1	0	1	14	8	4	7	0	8	0	0	0	1	1	.50	1	.182	.274	.255
1988 South Bend	A ChA	15	41	3	0	0	0	3	0	1	3	0	19	0	0	0	0	0	.00	0	.073	.136	.073
Utica	A- ChA	53	132	31	5	1	0	38	15	14	11	0	36	2	4	1	5	2	.71	2	.235	.301	.288
1989 South Bend	A ChA	86	230	51	15	0	0	66	22	22	16	0	59	0	9	1	4	1	.80	6	.222	.271	.287
1990 Sarasota	A+ ChA	37	119	19	4	1	1	28	9	9	8	0	24	0	2	0	0	0	.00	0	.160	.213	.235
South Bend	A ChA	48	127	30	5	0	2	41	14	12	20	0	38	1	5	2	2	1	.67	1	.236	.340	.323
1991 Sarasota	A+ ChA	71	194	40	10	2	1	57	14	22	20	0	41	4	7	1	3	2	.60	6	.206	.292	.294
1992 Birmingham	AA ChA	57	169	24	8	0	1	35	7	10	10	0	52	2	3	0	1	1	.50	5	.142	.199	.207
1993 White Sox	R ChA	2	5	0	0	0	0	0	0	0	1	0	2	0	0	0	0	0	.00	0	.000	.167	.000
Nashville	AAA ChA	11	29	6	0	0	0	6	1	2	1	0	4	0	2	0	0	0	.00	0	.207	.233	.207
Birmingham	AA ChA	35	111	25	4	0	1	32	8	8	11	0	28	1	1	1	0	4	.00	3	.225	.298	.288
1994 Nashville	AAA ChA	87	223	48	8	1	3	67	18	14	17	0	48	2	12	2	0	2	.00	2	.215	.275	.300
1995 Ottawa	AAA Mon	50	143	33	7	0	4	52	15	20	10	1	34	2	3	0	0	0	.00	2	.231	.290	.364
1997 Winston-Sal	A+ ChA	2	4	1	0	0	0	1	0	1	0	0	2	1	0	0	0	0	.00		.400	.250	.250
Birmingham	AA ChA	79	242	49	10	1	3	70	29	23	27	0	49	5	3	1	0	0	.00	17	.202	.295	.289
10 Min. YEARS		658	1824	370	77	6	17	510	160	162	162	1	444	20	51	9	16	15	.52	52	.203	.274	.280

Gabe Alvarez

Bats: Right **Throws:** Right **Pos:** 3B   **Ht:** 6'1" **Wt:** 185 **Born:** 3/6/74 **Age:** 24

		BATTING															BASERUNNING				PERCENTAGES		
Year Team	Lg Org	G	AB	H	2B	3B	HR	TB	R	RBI	TBB	IBB	SO	HBP	SH	SF	SB	CS	SB%	GDP	Avg	OBP	SLG
1995 Rancho Cuca	A+ SD	59	212	73	17	2	6	112	41	36	29	0	30	5	0	2	1	0	1.00	3	.344	.431	.528
Memphis	AA SD	2	9	5	1	0	0	6	0	4	1	0	1	0	0	0	0		.00	0	.556	.600	.667
1996 Memphis	AA SD	104	368	91	23	1	8	140	58	40	64	1	87	3	0	3	2	3	.40	10	.247	.361	.380
1997 Mobile	AA SD	114	427	128	28	2	14	202	71	78	51	2	64	5	0	6	1	1	.50	21	.300	.376	.473
3 Min. YEARS		279	1016	297	69	5	28	460	170	158	145	3	182	13	0	11	4	4	.50	34	.292	.384	.453

Juan Alvarez

Pitches: Left **Bats:** Left **Pos:** P   **Ht:** 6'1" **Wt:** 180 **Born:** 8/9/73 **Age:** 24

		HOW MUCH HE PITCHED						WHAT HE GAVE UP												THE RESULTS					
Year Team	Lg Org	G	GS	CG	GF	IP	BFP	H	R	ER	HR	SH	SF	HB	TBB	IBB	SO	WP	Bk	W	L	Pct.	ShO	Sv	ERA
1995 Boise	A- Ana	9	0	0	2	11.2	47	12	1	1	0	0	0	0	2	0	11	0	0	0	0	.000	0	0	0.77
1996 Cedar Rapds	A Ana	40	0	0	14	53	238	50	25	20	0	3	1	7	30	1	53	4	0	1	2	.333	0	3	3.40
1997 Lk Elsinore	A+ Ana	27	0	0	10	51.1	196	33	9	8	2	2	1	4	13	2	46	2	0	2	2	.667	0	3	1.40
Midland	AA Ana	24	0	0	6	37	199	63	42	34	5	0	1	3	22	1	27	0	3	4	1	.800	0	0	8.27
3 Min. YEARS		100	0	0	32	153	680	158	77	63	7	5	3	15	67	4	137	6	5	9	5	.643	0	6	3.71

Rafael Alvarez

Bats: Left **Throws:** Left **Pos:** OF   **Ht:** 5'11" **Wt:** 165 **Born:** 1/22/77 **Age:** 21

		BATTING															BASERUNNING				PERCENTAGES		
Year Team	Lg Org	G	AB	H	2B	3B	HR	TB	R	RBI	TBB	IBB	SO	HBP	SH	SF	SB	CS	SB%	GDP	Avg	OBP	SLG
1994 Twins	R Min	32	101	32	5	0	2	43	15	10	18	0	14	1	2	0	4	2	.67	4	.317	.425	.426
1995 Ft. Wayne	A Min	99	374	106	17	5	5	148	62	36	34	1	53	2	2	4	15	11	.58	5	.283	.343	.396
1996 Ft. Myers	A+ Min	6	22	3	0	0	0	3	1	1	1	0	7	0	0	0	1	0	1.00	0	.136	.167	.136
Ft. Wayne	A Min	119	473	143	30	7	4	199	61	58	43	5	55	3	2	1	11	9	.55	5	.302	.363	.421
1997 Salt Lake	AAA Min	17	48	13	1	1	0	16	10	5	6	0	9	0	1	0	5	0	1.00	1	.271	.352	.333
New Britain	AA Min	16	47	12	0	0	2	18	5	7	5	0	9	1	1	0	1	4	.20	0	.255	.340	.383
Ft. Myers	A+ Min	47	122	33	9	1	1	47	13	15	17	0	27	0	3	1	6	2	.75	1	.270	.357	.385
4 Min. YEARS		336	1187	342	62	14	14	474	167	132	124	6	174	7	11	7	42	29	.59	16	.288	.357	.399

Tavo Alvarez

Pitches: Right **Bats:** Right **Pos:** P   **Ht:** 6'3" **Wt:** 235 **Born:** 11/25/71 **Age:** 26

		HOW MUCH HE PITCHED						WHAT HE GAVE UP												THE RESULTS					
Year Team	Lg Org	G	GS	CG	GF	IP	BFP	H	R	ER	HR	SH	SF	HB	TBB	IBB	SO	WP	Bk	W	L	Pct.	ShO	Sv	ERA
1990 Expos	R Mon	11	10	0	0	52	214	42	17	15	0	1	3	1	16	0	47	1	0	5	2	.714	0	0	2.60
1991 Sumter	A Mon	25	25	3	0	152.2	663	152	68	55	6	4	3	11	58	0	158	3	6	12	10	.545	1	0	3.24
1992 Wst Plm Bch	A+ Mon	19	19	7	0	139	542	124	30	23	0	2	1	3	24	0	83	2	0	13	4	.765	4	0	1.49
Harrisburg	AA Mon	7	7	2	0	47.1	191	48	15	15	3	1	1	2	9	0	42	0	0	4	1	.800	1	0	2.85
1993 Ottawa	AAA Mon	25	25	1	0	140.2	636	163	80	66	10	5	7	4	55	2	77	6	0	7	10	.412	0	0	4.22
1995 Harrisburg	AA Mon	3	3	0	0	16	70	17	8	4	0	0	0	0	5	0	14	0	0	2	1	.667	0	0	2.25
Ottawa	AAA Mon	3	3	0	0	21.2	83	17	6	6	1	0	0	1	5	0	11	1	0	2	1	.667	0	0	2.49
1996 Ottawa	AAA Mon	20	20	2	0	113	485	128	66	59	12	3	0	2	25	1	86	5	0	4	9	.308	1	0	4.70
1997 Ottawa	AAA Mon	37	13	0	6	106.1	470	123	61	57	11	6	3	3	42	3	86	6	0	4	8	.333	0	0	4.82
1995 Montreal	NL	8	8	0	0	37.1	173	46	30	28	2	1	0	3	14	0	17	1	0	1	5	.167	0	0	6.75
1996 Montreal	NL	11	5	0	3	21	96	19	10	7	0	2	0	1	12	1	9	0	0	2	1	.667	0	0	3.00
7 Min. YEARS		150	125	15	6	788.2	3354	814	351	300	43	22	18	27	239	6	604	24	6	53	46	.535	7	0	3.42
2 Maj. YEARS		19	13	0	3	58.1	269	65	40	35	2	3	0	4	26	1	26	1	0	3	6	.333	0	0	5.40

Manuel Amador

Bats: Both **Throws:** Right **Pos:** 3B   **Ht:** 6'0" **Wt:** 165 **Born:** 11/21/75 **Age:** 22

		BATTING															BASERUNNING				PERCENTAGES		
Year Team	Lg Org	G	AB	H	2B	3B	HR	TB	R	RBI	TBB	IBB	SO	HBP	SH	SF	SB	CS	SB%	GDP	Avg	OBP	SLG
1993 Martinsville	R+ Phi	61	234	55	7	1	9	91	38	35	26	0	49	1	1	1	5	1	.83	4	.235	.313	.389
1994 Spartanburg	A Phi	91	341	85	14	3	6	123	54	42	30	2	65	8	3	2	5	3	.63	4	.249	.323	.361
1995 Piedmont	A Phi	1	4	0	0	0	0	0	0	0	0	0	0	1	0	0	0	1	.00	0	.000	.200	.000
Clearwater	A+ Phi	96	330	92	19	4	6	137	45	47	22	0	38	6	1	0	5	2	.71	6	.279	.335	.415
1996 Reading	AA Phi	10	18	5	2	0	1	10	5	3	5	0	4	0	0	0	0	0	.00	1	.278	.435	.556
Clearwater	A+ Phi	52	172	47	10	0	5	72	24	21	19	0	46	2	2	1	1	1	.50	5	.273	.351	.419
1997 Scranton-WB	AAA Phi	23	70	24	5	0	1	32	12	9	6	0	11	1	0	0	0	0	.00	2	.343	.392	.457
Reading	AA Phi	63	169	41	9	1	2	58	17	22	20	1	29	4	2	2	0	0	.00	5	.243	.333	.343
5 Min. YEARS		397	1338	349	66	9	30	523	195	179	128	3	242	23	9	8	16	8	.67	27	.261	.334	.391

Bill Anderson

Pitches: Right **Bats:** Right **Pos:** P   **Ht:** 6'0" **Wt:** 190 **Born:** 9/23/71 **Age:** 26

		HOW MUCH HE PITCHED						WHAT HE GAVE UP												THE RESULTS					
Year Team	Lg Org	G	GS	CG	GF	IP	BFP	H	R	ER	HR	SH	SF	HB	TBB	IBB	SO	WP	Bk	W	L	Pct.	ShO	Sv	ERA
1994 Rancho Cuca	A+ SD	22	2	0	5	62.1	265	64	36	31	2	2	0	3	24	0	70	2	4	7	0	1.000	0	1	4.48
1997 Mobile	AA SD	7	0	0	3	9.2	43	8	3	2	0	0	0	2	6	0	6	1	0	0	0	.000	0	0	1.86
Rancho Cuca	A+ SD	29	14	0	6	101	429	78	53	45	9	2	2	6	51	0	118	6	2	8	4	.667	0	1	4.01
2 Min. YEARS		58	16	0	14	173	737	150	92	78	11	4	2	11	81	0	194	9	6	15	4	.789	0	2	4.06

Jimmy Anderson
Pitches: Left **Bats:** Left **Pos:** P **Ht:** 6'1" **Wt:** 180 **Born:** 1/22/76 **Age:** 22

Year Team	Lg Org	G	GS	CG	GF	IP	BFP	H	R	ER	HR	SH	SF	HB	TBB	IBB	SO	WP	Bk	W	L	Pct.	ShO	Sv	ERA
1994 Pirates	R Pit	10	10	0	0	56.1	230	35	21	10	1	2	1	2	27	0	66	5	1	5	1	.833	0	0	1.60
1995 Augusta	A Pit	14	14	0	0	76.2	305	51	15	13	1	1	0	4	31	0	75	9	1	4	2	.667	0	0	1.53
Lynchburg	A+ Pit	10	9	0	1	52.1	231	56	29	24	1	4	1	5	21	1	32	7	3	1	5	.167	0	0	4.13
1996 Lynchburg	A+ Pit	11	11	1	0	65.1	267	51	25	14	2	2	0	2	21	0	56	1	0	5	3	.625	0	0	1.93
Carolina	AA Pit	17	16	0	0	97	411	92	40	36	3	1	0	3	44	3	79	13	5	8	3	.727	0	0	3.34
1997 Carolina	AA Pit	4	4	0	0	24.2	98	16	4	4	1	0	0	2	9	0	23	1	0	2	1	.667	0	0	1.46
Calgary	AAA Pit	21	21	0	0	103	486	124	78	65	9	6	5	5	64	3	71	9	4	7	6	.538	0	0	5.68
4 Min. YEARS		87	85	1	1	475.1	2028	425	214	166	18	16	7	23	217	7	402	45	14	32	21	.604	1	0	3.14

Marlon Anderson
Bats: Left **Throws:** Right **Pos:** 2B **Ht:** 5'10" **Wt:** 190 **Born:** 1/3/74 **Age:** 24

Year Team	Lg Org	G	AB	H	2B	3B	HR	TB	R	RBI	TBB	IBB	SO	HBP	SH	SF	SB	CS	SB%	GDP	Avg	OBP	SLG
1995 Batavia	A- Phi	74	312	92	13	4	3	122	52	40	15	2	20	4	2	4	22	8	.73	2	.295	.331	.391
1996 Clearwater	A+ Phi	60	257	70	10	3	2	92	37	22	14	1	18	2	4	0	26	1	.96	4	.272	.315	.358
Reading	AA Phi	75	314	86	14	3	3	115	38	28	26	2	44	1	3	1	17	9	.65	5	.274	.330	.366
1997 Reading	AA Phi	137	553	147	18	6	10	207	88	62	42	1	77	10	9	1	27	15	.64	8	.266	.328	.374
3 Min. YEARS		346	1436	395	55	16	18	536	215	152	97	6	159	17	18	6	92	33	.74	19	.275	.327	.373

Mike Anderson
Pitches: Right **Bats:** Right **Pos:** P **Ht:** 6'3" **Wt:** 200 **Born:** 7/30/66 **Age:** 31

Year Team	Lg Org	G	GS	CG	GF	IP	BFP	H	R	ER	HR	SH	SF	HB	TBB	IBB	SO	WP	Bk	W	L	Pct.	ShO	Sv	ERA
1988 Reds	R Cin	2	2	0	0	7.1	34	6	7	4	0	0	0	0	5	0	11	3	4	0	1	.000	0	0	4.91
Billings	R+ Cin	17	4	0	12	44.1	192	36	17	16	1	0	4	2	21	1	52	4	0	3	1	.750	0	2	3.25
1989 Greensboro	A Cin	25	25	4	0	154.1	647	117	64	49	7	2	3	8	72	0	154	9	2	11	6	.647	2	0	2.86
1990 Cedar Rapds	A Cin	23	23	2	0	138.1	613	134	67	52	6	8	7	5	62	0	101	10	0	10	5	.667	0	0	3.38
1991 Chattanooga	AA Cin	28	26	3	1	155.1	698	142	94	76	8	4	4	8	93	2	115	17	1	10	9	.526	3	0	4.40
1992 Chattanooga	AA Cin	28	26	4	1	171.2	716	155	59	48	4	0	3	7	61	1	149	15	3	13	7	.650	4	0	2.52
1993 Chattanooga	AA Cin	2	2	1	0	15	54	10	3	2	0	1	1	0	1	0	14	0	0	1	1	.500	1	0	1.20
Indianapols	AAA Cin	23	23	2	0	151	647	150	73	63	10	7	7	4	56	5	111	8	0	10	6	.625	1	0	3.75
1994 Iowa	AAA ChN	40	14	0	9	110	510	132	90	75	6	6	7	5	57	6	78	12	0	4	8	.333	0	0	6.14
1995 Iowa	AAA ChN	27	27	3	0	171.2	715	156	71	66	23	3	3	12	69	3	123	7	1	7	9	.438	1	0	3.46
1996 Okla City	AAA Tex	11	4	0	3	32.2	154	45	32	23	7	1	1	0	11	1	21	2	0	3	4	.429	0	0	6.34
1997 Albuquerque	AAA LA	6	0	0	2	10	49	18	12	12	2	0	0	1	9	0	9	0	0	0	0	.000	0	1	10.80
San Berndno	A+ LA	4	0	0	1	9	39	7	5	4	1	1	0	0	5	0	13	1	0	1	0	1.000	0	0	4.00
San Antonio	AA LA	19	2	0	8	42.2	185	47	31	30	6	3	3	0	13	0	30	4	0	4	2	.667	0	0	6.33
1993 Cincinnati	NL	3	0	0	0	5.1	30	12	11	11	3	0	0	0	3	0	4	0	0	0	0	.000	0	0	18.56
10 Min. YEARS		255	178	19	37	1213.1	5253	1155	625	520	81	36	43	51	527	19	981	92	11	77	59	.566	11	3	3.86

Alex Andreopoulos
Bats: Left **Throws:** Right **Pos:** C **Ht:** 5'10" **Wt:** 190 **Born:** 8/19/72 **Age:** 25

Year Team	Lg Org	G	AB	H	2B	3B	HR	TB	R	RBI	TBB	IBB	SO	HBP	SH	SF	SB	CS	SB%	GDP	Avg	OBP	SLG
1995 Helena	R+ Mil	3	9	5	0	0	2	11	3	7	4	0	0	0	0	0	0	0	.00	0	.556	.692	1.222
Beloit	A Mil	60	163	49	9	0	1	61	32	20	35	1	16	3	3	1	5	3	.63	2	.301	.431	.374
1996 Stockton	A+ Mil	87	291	88	17	2	5	124	52	41	40	2	33	5	2	4	10	3	.77	5	.302	.391	.426
1997 El Paso	AA Mil	7	26	4	1	0	0	5	1	3	1	0	2	0	0	0	0	0	.00	1	.154	.185	.192
Tucson	AAA Mil	10	15	6	1	0	0	7	3	1	0	0	1	0	0	0	0	0	.00	0	.400	.400	.467
3 Min. YEARS		167	504	152	28	2	8	208	91	72	80	3	52	8	5	5	15	6	.71	8	.302	.402	.413

Doug Angeli
Bats: Right **Throws:** Right **Pos:** SS-3B **Ht:** 5'11" **Wt:** 183 **Born:** 1/7/71 **Age:** 27

Year Team	Lg Org	G	AB	H	2B	3B	HR	TB	R	RBI	TBB	IBB	SO	HBP	SH	SF	SB	CS	SB%	GDP	Avg	OBP	SLG
1993 Batavia	A- Phi	75	252	55	7	3	0	68	20	15	18	0	33	1	7	1	5	6	.45	5	.218	.272	.270
1994 Spartanburg	A Phi	43	165	40	8	0	0	48	16	14	15	0	29	0	0	1	5	3	.63	5	.242	.304	.291
Clearwater	A+ Phi	77	265	69	14	2	1	90	25	26	23	0	39	0	5	0	2	2	.50	6	.260	.319	.340
1995 Clearwater	A+ Phi	16	47	9	3	0	0	12	4	3	3	0	13	1	2	1	0	1	.00	0	.191	.250	.255
1996 Reading	AA Phi	56	187	44	9	0	8	77	24	29	20	3	43	2	6	2	3	2	.60	1	.235	.313	.412
1997 Reading	AA Phi	42	148	33	5	1	5	55	25	19	16	2	28	2	3	1	1	2	.33	3	.223	.305	.372
Scranton-WB	AAA Phi	78	241	54	11	2	2	75	24	19	27	3	53	1	3	3	0	3	.00	4	.224	.301	.311
5 Min. YEARS		387	1305	304	57	8	16	425	138	125	122	8	238	7	26	9	16	19	.46	24	.233	.300	.326

Matt Apana
Pitches: Right **Bats:** Right **Pos:** P **Ht:** 6'0" **Wt:** 195 **Born:** 1/16/71 **Age:** 27

Year Team	Lg Org	G	GS	CG	GF	IP	BFP	H	R	ER	HR	SH	SF	HB	TBB	IBB	SO	WP	Bk	W	L	Pct.	ShO	Sv	ERA
1993 Bellingham	A- Sea	14	14	0	0	61	282	50	38	30	7	5	1	4	43	0	59	7	2	5	3	.625	0	0	4.43
1994 Riverside	A+ Sea	26	26	3	0	165.1	694	142	63	52	8	5	3	4	70	0	137	5	0	14	4	.778	3	0	2.83
1995 Tacoma	AAA Sea	21	20	0	0	103.2	481	121	72	57	9	3	6	5	61	0	58	6	0	8	8	.500	0	0	4.95
Port City	AA Sea	6	6	0	0	33.1	154	34	24	16	4	1	0	2	24	1	28	2	0	1	3	.250	0	0	4.32
1996 Port City	AA Sea	18	18	0	0	96.1	431	86	58	57	8	2	6	4	69	0	55	13	0	3	8	.273	0	0	5.33

			HOW MUCH HE PITCHED						WHAT HE GAVE UP									THE RESULTS					
Year Team	Lg Org	G	GS	CG	GF	IP	BFP	H	R	ER	HR	SH	SF	HB	TBB	IBB	SO	WP	Bk	W	L	Pct.	ShO	Sv	ERA
1997 Lancaster	A+ Sea	3	3	0	0	11.2	54	13	7	7	3	0	2	1	8	0	7	0	0	1	1	.500	0	0	5.40
Memphis	AA Sea	17	16	1	0	80.1	365	78	59	52	14	1	2	6	47	0	45	6	0	3	9	.250	0	0	5.83
5 Min. YEARS		105	103	4	0	551.2	2461	524	321	271	53	17	20	26	322	1	389	39	2	35	36	.493	3	0	4.42

Danny Ardoin

Bats: Right **Throws:** Right **Pos:** C   **Ht:** 6'0" **Wt:** 195 **Born:** 7/8/74 **Age:** 23

					BATTING												BASERUNNING			PERCENTAGES		
Year Team	Lg Org	G	AB	H	2B	3B	HR	TB	R	RBI	TBB	IBB	SO	HBP	SH	SF	SB	CS	SB%	GDP	Avg	OBP	SLG
1995 Sou. Oregon	A- Oak	58	175	41	9	1	2	58	28	23	31	0	50	9	5	4	2	1	.67	2	.234	.370	.331
1996 Modesto	A+ Oak	91	317	83	13	3	6	120	55	34	47	0	81	9	3	2	5	7	.42	9	.262	.371	.379
1997 Huntsville	AA Oak	57	208	48	10	1	4	72	26	23	17	0	38	3	0	2	2	3	.40	7	.231	.296	.346
Visalia	A+ Oak	43	145	34	7	1	3	52	16	19	21	0	39	4	1	0	0	1	.00	3	.234	.347	.359
3 Min. YEARS		249	845	206	39	6	15	302	125	99	116	0	208	25	9	8	9	12	.43	21	.244	.349	.357

Jamie Arnold

Pitches: Right **Bats:** Right **Pos:** P   **Ht:** 6'2" **Wt:** 188 **Born:** 3/24/74 **Age:** 24

				HOW MUCH HE PITCHED						WHAT HE GAVE UP									THE RESULTS					
Year Team	Lg Org	G	GS	CG	GF	IP	BFP	H	R	ER	HR	SH	SF	HB	TBB	IBB	SO	WP	Bk	W	L	Pct.	ShO	Sv	ERA
1992 Braves	R Atl	7	5	0	2	20	85	16	12	9	0	0	2	4	6	0	22	0	2	0	1	.000	0	0	4.05
1993 Macon	A Atl	27	27	1	0	164.1	692	142	67	57	5	3	4	16	56	0	124	13	2	8	9	.471	0	0	3.12
1994 Durham	A+ Atl	25	25	0	0	145	656	144	96	75	26	3	1	14	79	4	91	8	4	7	7	.500	0	0	4.66
1995 Durham	A+ Atl	15	14	0	1	80	347	86	42	35	5	4	1	9	21	0	44	4	0	4	8	.333	0	0	3.94
Greenville	AA Atl	10	10	0	0	56.2	266	76	42	40	8	0	2	7	25	1	19	6	0	1	5	.167	0	0	6.35
1996 Greenville	AA Atl	23	23	2	0	128	573	149	79	70	17	0	5	10	44	1	64	6	1	7	7	.500	0	0	4.92
1997 Braves	R Atl	5	5	0	0	19	74	13	6	6	1	0	0	0	6	0	21	0	0	1	0	1.000	0	0	2.84
Durham	A+ Atl	5	5	0	0	24.1	115	25	21	16	2	2	0	1	13	0	21	2	0	2	2	.500	0	0	5.92
Greenville	AA Atl	1	1	0	0	4.2	27	10	6	6	3	0	0	1	2	0	3	1	0	0	1	.000	0	0	11.57
6 Min. YEARS		118	115	4	2	642	2835	661	371	314	67	12	15	62	252	6	409	40	9	30	40	.429	0	0	4.40

Matt Arrandale

Pitches: Right **Bats:** Right **Pos:** P   **Ht:** 6'0" **Wt:** 165 **Born:** 12/14/70 **Age:** 27

				HOW MUCH HE PITCHED						WHAT HE GAVE UP									THE RESULTS					
Year Team	Lg Org	G	GS	CG	GF	IP	BFP	H	R	ER	HR	SH	SF	HB	TBB	IBB	SO	WP	Bk	W	L	Pct.	ShO	Sv	ERA
1993 Glens Falls	A- StL	12	12	0	0	68.2	298	77	42	35	6	1	1	2	14	0	53	4	2	3	4	.429	0	0	4.59
St. Pete	A+ StL	2	2	0	0	14	49	8	2	2	1	0	0	0	3	0	11	1	0	1	0	1.000	0	0	1.29
1994 Savannah	A StL	19	19	5	0	133.1	519	112	36	26	2	1	2	4	21	1	121	3	0	15	3	.833	0	0	1.76
St. Pete	A+ StL	9	9	0	0	59	244	65	26	22	0	2	1	2	11	0	29	2	1	3	4	.429	0	0	3.36
1995 Arkansas	AA StL	47	3	0	23	68.2	296	72	28	25	1	2	2	1	22	4	28	1	0	3	5	.375	0	2	3.28
1996 Louisville	AAA StL	63	0	0	22	79	351	83	51	42	6	0	2	4	33	9	38	4	0	5	4	.556	0	3	4.78
1997 Louisville	AAA StL	56	1	0	15	83.1	360	84	38	34	9	5	2	3	38	9	32	5	0	2	6	.250	0	1	3.67
5 Min. YEARS		208	46	5	60	506	2117	501	223	186	25	11	10	16	142	23	312	20	3	32	26	.552	0	6	3.31

Luis Arroyo

Pitches: Left **Bats:** Left **Pos:** P   **Ht:** 6'0" **Wt:** 175 **Born:** 9/29/73 **Age:** 24

				HOW MUCH HE PITCHED						WHAT HE GAVE UP									THE RESULTS					
Year Team	Lg Org	G	GS	CG	GF	IP	BFP	H	R	ER	HR	SH	SF	HB	TBB	IBB	SO	WP	Bk	W	L	Pct.	ShO	Sv	ERA
1992 Padres	R SD	17	9	0	3	57.2	259	65	45	27	0	1	6	2	21	0	55	4	12	4	4	.500	0	0	4.21
1993 Waterloo	A SD	17	16	1	0	95.2	424	99	59	48	11	7	6	6	46	1	59	5	3	5	7	.417	0	0	4.52
1994 Springfield	A SD	16	16	1	0	99.2	434	86	50	38	8	5	2	1	47	4	76	4	4	8	2	.800	0	0	3.43
Rancho Cuca	A+ SD	10	10	0	0	54.1	243	62	33	29	6	1	1	3	30	0	34	2	0	3	4	.429	0	0	4.80
1995 Rancho Cuca	A+ SD	26	24	0	0	128.2	599	158	97	75	9	8	6	12	62	6	102	7	3	7	10	.412	0	0	5.25
1996 St. Lucie	A+ NYN	22	0	0	4	42	170	36	17	14	1	0	3	1	15	1	28	3	0	1	0	1.000	0	2	3.00
1997 Binghamton	AA NYN	7	0	0	1	14.2	60	14	6	5	2	2	1	0	6	0	9	0	1	0	0	.000	0	0	3.07
St. Lucie	A+ NYN	36	2	0	11	56	231	37	21	13	2	3	1	3	23	2	57	1	3	3	3	.500	0	0	2.09
6 Min. YEARS		151	77	2	20	548.2	2420	557	328	249	39	27	26	28	250	14	420	26	26	31	30	.508	0	2	4.08

Mike Asche

Bats: Right **Throws:** Right **Pos:** OF   **Ht:** 6'2" **Wt:** 190 **Born:** 2/13/72 **Age:** 26

					BATTING												BASERUNNING			PERCENTAGES		
Year Team	Lg Org	G	AB	H	2B	3B	HR	TB	R	RBI	TBB	IBB	SO	HBP	SH	SF	SB	CS	SB%	GDP	Avg	OBP	SLG
1994 Welland	A- Pit	55	204	49	5	1	4	68	22	25	13	0	30	1	3	0	6	3	.67	2	.240	.289	.333
1995 Augusta	A Pit	106	376	100	17	6	6	147	62	59	35	1	60	5	3	3	21	5	.81	6	.266	.334	.391
1996 Lynchburg	A+ Pit	129	498	147	25	6	7	205	79	54	38	1	92	2	8	7	26	5	.84	11	.295	.343	.412
1997 Carolina	AA Pit	15	42	9	1	1	0	12	2	2	4	0	6	0	1	0	0	0	.00	0	.214	.283	.286
Lynchburg	A+ Pit	107	409	125	34	4	11	200	70	70	41	0	77	4	1	8	33	3	.92	5	.306	.368	.489
4 Min. YEARS		412	1529	430	82	18	28	632	235	210	131	2	265	12	16	18	86	16	.84	24	.281	.339	.413

Chris Ashby

Bats: Right **Throws:** Right **Pos:** 1B   **Ht:** 6'3" **Wt:** 185 **Born:** 12/15/74 **Age:** 23

					BATTING												BASERUNNING			PERCENTAGES		
Year Team	Lg Org	G	AB	H	2B	3B	HR	TB	R	RBI	TBB	IBB	SO	HBP	SH	SF	SB	CS	SB%	GDP	Avg	OBP	SLG
1993 Yankees	R NYA	49	175	37	12	0	0	49	24	23	32	0	45	6	0	2	5	3	.63	6	.211	.349	.280
Greensboro	A NYA	1	4	3	0	0	0	3	2	0	0	0	0	1	0	0	0	0	.00	0	.750	.800	.750
1994 Yankees	R NYA	45	163	55	8	1	5	80	28	38	21	0	20	1	1	3	2	0	1.00	4	.337	.410	.491

BATTING

Year Team	Lg Org	G	AB	H	2B	3B	HR	TB	R	RBI	TBB	IBB	SO	HBP	SH	SF	SB	CS	SB%	GDP	Avg	OBP	SLG
Greensboro	A NYA	6	16	2	1	0	0	3	0	2	2	0	6	0	0	0	0	0	.00	1	.125	.222	.188
1995 Greensboro	A NYA	88	288	79	23	1	9	131	45	45	61	2	68	6	2	2	3	3	.50	9	.274	.409	.455
1996 Tampa	A+ NYA	100	325	80	28	0	6	126	55	46	71	1	78	6	1	1	16	4	.80	5	.246	.388	.388
1997 Norwich	AA NYA	136	457	114	20	1	24	208	92	82	80	2	95	6	0	3	10	7	.59	14	.249	.366	.455
5 Min. YEARS		425	1428	370	92	3	44	600	246	236	267	5	312	25	4	11	36	17	.68	39	.259	.382	.420

Justin Atchley

Pitches: Left Bats: Left Pos: P Ht: 6'2" Wt: 205 Born: 9/5/73 Age: 24

		HOW MUCH HE PITCHED						WHAT HE GAVE UP												THE RESULTS					
Year Team	Lg Org	G	GS	CG	GF	IP	BFP	H	R	ER	HR	SH	SF	HB	TBB	IBB	SO	WP	Bk	W	L	Pct.	ShO	Sv	ERA
1995 Billings	R+ Cin	13	13	0	0	77	327	91	33	30	4	2	1	2	20	2	65	2	1	10	0	1.000	0	0	3.51
1996 Chston-WV	A Cin	17	16	0	1	91	392	98	42	35	7	4	2	1	23	0	78	0	1	3	3	.500	0	1	3.46
Winston-Sal	A+ Cin	12	12	0	0	69	290	74	48	39	13	3	3	2	16	0	50	2	0	3	3	.500	0	0	5.09
1997 Chattanooga	AA Cin	13	13	1	0	67	289	75	45	35	8	2	5	1	14	0	48	5	0	4	2	.667	0	0	4.70
3 Min. YEARS		55	54	1	1	304	1298	338	168	139	32	11	11	6	73	2	241	9	2	20	8	.714	0	1	4.12

Derek Aucoin

Pitches: Right Bats: Right Pos: P Ht: 6'7" Wt: 235 Born: 3/27/70 Age: 28

		HOW MUCH HE PITCHED						WHAT HE GAVE UP												THE RESULTS					
Year Team	Lg Org	G	GS	CG	GF	IP	BFP	H	R	ER	HR	SH	SF	HB	TBB	IBB	SO	WP	Bk	W	L	Pct.	ShO	Sv	ERA
1989 Expos	R Mon	7	3	0	1	23.2	106	24	10	7	2	1	0	0	12	0	27	3	1	2	1	.667	0	1	2.66
1990 Jamestown	A- Mon	8	8	1	0	36.1	152	28	20	18	3	1	1	1	18	0	27	6	0	1	3	.250	0	0	4.46
1991 Sumter	A Mon	41	4	0	8	90.1	408	85	55	43	5	4	2	10	44	3	70	6	1	3	6	.333	0	1	4.28
1992 Rockford	A Mon	39	2	0	17	69	289	48	32	23	2	1	2	4	34	2	65	6	3	3	2	.600	0	3	3.00
1993 Wst Plm Bch	A+ Mon	38	6	0	6	87.1	387	89	48	41	5	6	2	0	44	3	62	8	2	4	4	.500	0	1	4.23
1994 Wst Plm Bch	A+ Mon	7	0	0	5	7.1	26	3	0	0	0	0	0	0	2	0	10	0	0	0	0	.000	0	2	0.00
Harrisburg	AA Mon	31	0	0	12	47	208	36	19	17	4	1	0	2	29	0	48	3	0	3	4	.429	0	1	3.26
1995 Harrisburg	AA Mon	29	0	0	10	52.2	242	52	34	29	3	0	5	8	28	2	48	2	0	2	4	.333	0	1	4.96
1996 Ottawa	AAA Mon	52	0	0	24	75	351	74	37	33	6	2	2	7	53	4	69	11	1	3	5	.375	0	3	3.96
1997 Ottawa	AAA Mon	8	0	0	0	6.1	54	5	16	16	0	0	1	10	21	0	5	2	0	0	1	.000	0	0	22.74
Wst Plm Bch	A+ Mon	17	0	0	9	19	102	13	17	16	1	2	1	6	27	0	27	15	0	0	1	.000	0	0	7.58
1996 Montreal	NL	2	0	0	0	2.2	12	3	1	1	0	0	0	0	1	0	1	0	0	0	0	.000	0	0	3.38
9 Min. YEARS		277	23	1	92	514	2325	457	288	243	31	18	16	48	312	14	452	62	8	21	30	.412	0	16	4.25

Rich Aude

Bats: Right Throws: Right Pos: 1B Ht: 6'5" Wt: 215 Born: 7/13/71 Age: 26

		BATTING												BASERUNNING							PERCENTAGES		
Year Team	Lg Org	G	AB	H	2B	3B	HR	TB	R	RBI	TBB	IBB	SO	HBP	SH	SF	SB	CS	SB%	GDP	Avg	OBP	SLG
1989 Pirates	R Pit	24	88	19	3	0	0	22	13	7	5	0	17	3	0	1	2	0	1.00	1	.216	.278	.250
1990 Augusta	A Pit	128	475	111	23	1	6	154	48	61	41	1	133	7	0	4	3	1	.75	11	.234	.302	.324
1991 Salem	A+ Pit	103	366	97	12	2	3	122	45	43	27	5	72	9	0	0	3	0	1.00	7	.265	.331	.333
1992 Salem	A+ Pit	122	447	128	26	4	9	189	63	60	50	2	79	8	0	1	11	2	.85	10	.286	.368	.423
Carolina	AA Pit	6	20	4	1	0	2	11	4	3	1	0	3	0	0	0	0	0	.00	0	.200	.238	.550
1993 Buffalo	AAA Pit	21	64	24	9	0	4	45	17	16	10	0	15	1	0	1	0	0	.00	1	.375	.461	.703
Carolina	AA Pit	120	422	122	25	3	18	207	66	73	50	1	79	12	1	6	8	4	.67	6	.289	.376	.491
1994 Buffalo	AAA Pit	138	520	146	38	4	15	237	66	79	41	3	83	11	0	2	9	5	.64	14	.281	.345	.456
1995 Calgary	AAA Pit	50	195	65	14	2	9	110	34	42	12	1	30	4	0	5	3	2	.60	11	.333	.375	.564
1996 Calgary	AAA Pit	103	394	115	29	0	17	195	69	81	26	2	69	4	0	5	4	4	.50	10	.292	.338	.495
1997 Syracuse	AAA Tor	100	350	99	23	2	15	171	48	59	26	2	88	11	0	3	3	0	1.00	9	.283	.349	.489
1993 Pittsburgh	NL	13	26	3	1	0	0	4	1	4	1	0	7	0	0	0	0	0	.00	0	.115	.148	.154
1995 Pittsburgh	NL	42	109	27	8	0	2	41	10	19	6	0	20	0	0	0	1	2	.33	4	.248	.287	.376
1996 Pittsburgh	NL	7	16	4	0	0	0	4	0	1	0	0	8	0	0	0	0	0	.00	0	.250	.250	.250
9 Min. YEARS		915	3341	930	203	18	98	1463	473	524	289	23	668	70	1	28	46	18	.72	80	.278	.346	.438
3 Maj. YEARS		62	151	34	9	0	2	49	11	24	7	0	35	0	0	0	1	2	.33	4	.225	.259	.325

Joe Ausanio

Pitches: Right Bats: Right Pos: P Ht: 6'1" Wt: 205 Born: 12/9/65 Age: 32

		HOW MUCH HE PITCHED						WHAT HE GAVE UP												THE RESULTS					
Year Team	Lg Org	G	GS	CG	GF	IP	BFP	H	R	ER	HR	SH	SF	HB	TBB	IBB	SO	WP	Bk	W	L	Pct.	ShO	Sv	ERA
1988 Watertown	A- Pit	28	0	0	23	47.2	200	29	10	7	1	6	1	3	27	5	56	3	0	2	4	.333	0	13	1.32
1989 Salem	A+ Pit	54	0	0	51	89	368	51	29	21	9	7	2	3	44	6	97	5	0	5	4	.556	0	20	2.12
1990 Harrisburg	AA Pit	43	0	0	38	54	211	36	15	11	2	6	1	2	16	4	49	4	0	3	2	.600	0	15	1.83
1991 Carolina	AA Pit	3	0	0	3	3	9	0	0	0	0	0	0	0	0	0	2	0	0	0	0	.000	0	2	0.00
Buffalo	AAA Pit	22	0	0	14	30.1	144	33	17	13	5	1	3	0	19	3	26	2	1	2	2	.500	0	3	3.86
1992 Buffalo	AAA Pit	53	0	0	39	83.2	352	64	35	27	5	6	2	1	40	6	66	4	0	6	4	.600	0	15	2.90
1993 Expos	R Mon	5	0	0	0	5	18	3	1	0	0	1	0	0	1	0	6	0	0	0	0	.000	0	0	0.00
Harrisburg	AA Mon	19	0	0	15	22.1	86	16	3	3	1	0	0	0	4	1	30	0	0	2	0	1.000	0	6	1.21
1994 Columbus	AAA NYA	44	0	0	29	60.1	243	45	21	16	5	2	6	1	16	1	69	3	0	3	3	.500	0	13	2.39
1995 Columbus	AAA NYA	11	0	0	9	12	53	12	5	5	1	0	1	2	5	0	20	1	0	1	0	1.000	0	3	7.50
1996 Norfolk	AAA NYN	35	0	0	17	43	197	38	31	28	8	2	4	2	29	1	40	2	0	3	3	.500	0	4	5.86
Colo Spmgs	AAA Col	13	1	0	6	18.2	84	18	10	9	2	0	2	0	10	2	18	2	0	1	1	.500	0	4	4.34
1997 Colo Spmgs	AAA Col	3	0	0	0	3.2	28	14	13	12	3	0	0	0	3	0	3	0	0	0	0	.000	0	0	29.45
1994 New York	AL	13	0	0	5	15.2	69	16	9	9	3	0	0	0	6	0	15	0	0	2	1	.667	0	1	5.17
1995 New York	AL	28	0	0	10	37.2	173	42	24	24	9	1	2	0	23	0	36	3	0	2	0	1.000	0	1	5.73
10 Min. YEARS		333	1	0	245	472.2	1993	359	195	157	42	32	23	13	214	29	482	26	1	28	23	.549	0	94	2.99
2 Maj. YEARS		41	0	0	15	53.1	242	58	33	33	12	1	2	0	29	0	51	3	0	4	1	.800	0	1	5.57

Joe Ayrault

Bats: Right **Throws:** Right **Pos:** C **Ht:** 6'3" **Wt:** 190 **Born:** 10/8/71 **Age:** 26

Year Team	Lg Org	G	AB	H	2B	3B	HR	TB	R	RBI	TBB	IBB	SO	HBP	SH	SF	SB	CS	SB%	GDP	Avg	OBP	SLG
1990 Braves	R Atl	30	87	24	2	2	0	30	8	12	9	0	14	1	2	0	1	1	.50	1	.276	.351	.345
1991 Pulaski	R+ Atl	55	202	52	12	0	3	73	22	27	13	0	49	0	2	0	0	0	.00	4	.257	.302	.361
1992 Macon	A Atl	90	297	77	12	0	6	107	24	24	24	0	68	4	2	1	1	1	.50	7	.259	.322	.360
1993 Durham	A+ Atl	119	390	99	21	0	6	138	45	52	23	0	103	7	8	3	1	4	.20	8	.254	.305	.354
1994 Greenville	AA Atl	107	350	80	24	0	6	122	38	40	19	1	74	7	6	4	2	2	.50	6	.229	.279	.349
1995 Greenville	AA Atl	89	302	74	20	0	7	115	27	42	13	5	70	3	7	3	2	4	.33	4	.245	.280	.381
1996 Richmond	AAA Atl	98	314	72	15	0	5	102	23	34	26	4	57	3	2	4	1	1	.50	12	.229	.291	.325
1997 Greenville	AA Atl	13	33	8	2	0	2	16	6	4	6	0	8	0	1	1	0	0	.00	0	.242	.350	.485
Richmond	AAA Atl	18	56	16	2	0	3	27	11	5	4	0	17	0	1	0	0	0	.00	0	.286	.333	.482
1996 Atlanta	NL	7	5	1	0	0	0	1	0	0	0	0	1	1	0	0	0	0	.00	1	.200	.333	.200
8 Min. YEARS		619	2031	502	110	2	38	730	204	240	137	10	460	25	31	16	8	13	.38	46	.247	.301	.359

Jesus Azuaje

Bats: Right **Throws:** Right **Pos:** 2B **Ht:** 5'10" **Wt:** 170 **Born:** 1/16/73 **Age:** 25

Year Team	Lg Org	G	AB	H	2B	3B	HR	TB	R	RBI	TBB	IBB	SO	HBP	SH	SF	SB	CS	SB%	GDP	Avg	OBP	SLG
1993 Burlington	R+ Cle	62	254	71	10	1	7	104	46	41	22	0	53	0	1	3	19	2	.90	4	.280	.333	.409
Kinston	A+ Cle	3	11	5	2	0	0	7	1	0	2	0	1	0	0	0	0	2	.00	0	.455	.538	.636
1994 Columbus	A Cle	118	450	127	20	1	7	170	77	57	69	0	72	5	6	0	21	7	.75	6	.282	.384	.378
1995 Norfolk	AAA NYN	5	14	6	1	0	0	7	1	0	2	0	2	0	0	0	1	1	.50	0	.429	.500	.500
Binghamton	AA NYN	24	86	17	5	0	0	22	10	8	11	0	25	2	3	0	1	1	.50	1	.198	.303	.256
St. Lucie	A+ NYN	91	306	73	5	1	2	86	35	20	36	1	55	7	11	0	14	9	.61	5	.239	.332	.281
1996 Capital City	A NYN	1	3	2	1	0	0	3	1	1	0	0	0	0	1	1	0	0	.00	0	.667	.500	1.000
Binghamton	AA NYN	86	249	59	16	0	2	81	36	26	45	1	33	1	3	1	5	6	.45	5	.237	.355	.325
1997 Binghamton	AA NYN	100	331	92	15	1	6	127	50	37	45	1	42	8	8	4	11	9	.55	13	.278	.374	.384
Norfolk	AAA NYN	22	49	15	3	0	1	21	11	6	7	1	8	2	0	0	1	0	1.00	2	.306	.414	.429
5 Min. YEARS		512	1753	467	78	4	25	628	268	196	239	4	291	25	33	9	73	37	.66	36	.266	.361	.358

Mike Badorek

Pitches: Right **Bats:** Right **Pos:** P **Ht:** 6'5" **Wt:** 230 **Born:** 5/15/69 **Age:** 29

Year Team	Lg Org	G	GS	CG	GF	IP	BFP	H	R	ER	HR	SH	SF	HB	TBB	IBB	SO	WP	Bk	W	L	Pct.	ShO	Sv	ERA
1991 Hamilton	A- StL	13	11	1	1	63.1	282	56	33	19	2	1	1	3	30	0	48	9	0	2	5	.286	0	0	2.70
1992 Springfield	A StL	29	28	2	1	187.1	780	175	74	61	6	3	4	9	39	1	119	10	0	17	8	.680	0	0	2.93
1993 St. Pete	A+ StL	29	28	2	1	170	712	170	76	65	6	4	5	4	53	1	60	3	0	15	7	.682	0	0	3.44
1994 Arkansas	AA StL	40	15	2	4	123.1	528	119	61	43	8	5	2	3	36	4	95	4	0	8	8	.500	0	0	3.14
1995 Arkansas	AA StL	18	17	4	1	101.1	446	119	61	49	4	4	5	3	30	0	50	2	0	7	5	.583	2	1	4.35
1996 Louisville	AAA StL	20	6	0	6	49.1	216	52	34	29	3	4	2	4	18	2	22	1	0	0	4	.000	0	0	5.29
1997 Louisville	AAA StL	1	0	0	0	2	12	4	4	4	2	0	0	0	2	0	3	0	0	0	0	.000	0	0	18.00
Madison	IND —	13	13	4	0	100	412	92	44	35	4	1	1	7	22	2	63	9	0	6	5	.545	1	0	3.15
Akron	AA Cle	4	4	0	0	25	122	40	22	17	0	2	3	0	6	1	15	3	0	1	2	.333	0	0	6.12
7 Min. YEARS		167	122	15	13	821.2	3510	827	409	322	35	24	23	33	236	11	475	41	0	56	44	.560	3	1	3.53

Edward Bady

Bats: Both **Throws:** Right **Pos:** OF **Ht:** 5'11" **Wt:** 170 **Born:** 2/5/73 **Age:** 25

Year Team	Lg Org	G	AB	H	2B	3B	HR	TB	R	RBI	TBB	IBB	SO	HBP	SH	SF	SB	CS	SB%	GDP	Avg	OBP	SLG
1994 Vermont	A- Mon	44	141	35	5	5	2	56	19	21	12	0	51	2	5	0	11	6	.65	3	.248	.316	.397
1995 Vermont	A- Mon	72	295	97	15	3	2	124	51	25	24	3	52	5	2	0	34	19	.64	3	.329	.389	.420
1996 Wst Plm Bch	A+ Mon	128	484	136	9	3	1	154	62	34	42	0	93	10	12	3	42	17	.71	2	.281	.349	.318
1997 Harrisburg	AA Mon	97	267	56	8	4	1	75	36	22	21	3	62	1	10	0	15	5	.75	3	.210	.270	.281
4 Min. YEARS		341	1187	324	37	15	6	409	168	102	99	6	258	18	29	3	102	47	.68	11	.273	.337	.345

Benito Baez

Pitches: Left **Bats:** Left **Pos:** P **Ht:** 6'0" **Wt:** 180 **Born:** 5/6/77 **Age:** 21

Year Team	Lg Org	G	GS	CG	GF	IP	BFP	H	R	ER	HR	SH	SF	HB	TBB	IBB	SO	WP	Bk	W	L	Pct.	ShO	Sv	ERA
1995 Athletics	R Oak	14	11	0	0	70	303	64	35	26	2	2	2	4	28	0	83	2	0	5	1	.833	0	0	3.34
1996 W Michigan	A Oak	32	20	0	4	129.2	557	123	60	50	6	5	6	2	52	1	92	4	1	8	4	.667	0	4	3.47
1997 Visalia	A+ Oak	16	15	1	0	96.2	393	83	40	38	8	1	2	3	28	0	87	0	1	5	5	.500	0	0	3.54
Huntsville	AA Oak	15	7	0	2	42.1	206	64	47	43	8	2	4	1	22	1	27	3	2	2	4	.333	0	0	9.14
3 Min. YEARS		77	53	2	6	338.2	1459	334	182	157	24	10	14	10	130	2	289	9	4	20	14	.588	0	4	4.17

Kevin Baez

Bats: Right **Throws:** Right **Pos:** SS **Ht:** 5'11" **Wt:** 175 **Born:** 1/10/67 **Age:** 31

Year Team	Lg Org	G	AB	H	2B	3B	HR	TB	R	RBI	TBB	IBB	SO	HBP	SH	SF	SB	CS	SB%	GDP	Avg	OBP	SLG
1988 Little Fall	A- NYN	70	218	58	7	1	1	70	23	19	32	1	30	2	2	3	7	3	.70	3	.266	.361	.321
1989 Columbia	A NYN	123	426	108	25	1	5	150	59	44	58	3	53	6	9	3	11	9	.55	5	.254	.349	.352
1990 Jackson	AA NYN	106	327	76	11	0	2	93	29	29	37	4	44	2	11	2	3	4	.43	7	.232	.313	.284
1991 Tidewater	AAA NYN	65	210	36	8	0	0	44	18	13	12	1	32	4	5	4	0	1	.00	5	.171	.226	.210
1992 Tidewater	AAA NYN	109	352	83	16	1	2	107	30	33	31	6	57	4	5	5	1	1	.50	9	.236	.267	.304
1993 Norfolk	AAA NYN	63	209	54	11	1	2	73	23	21	20	1	29	1	2	1	0	2	.00	3	.258	.325	.349

Year Team	Lg Org	G	AB	H	2B	3B	HR	TB	R	RBI	TBB	IBB	SO	HBP	SH	SF	SB	CS	SB%	GDP	Avg	OBP	SLG
1994 Rochester	AAA Bal	110	359	85	17	1	2	110	50	42	40	0	52	2	5	5	2	7	.22	13	.237	.313	.306
1995 Toledo	AAA Det	116	376	87	13	2	4	116	30	37	22	1	57	1	10	2	1	6	.14	13	.231	.274	.309
1996 Toledo	AAA Det	98	302	74	12	3	11	125	34	44	24	0	53	2	5	4	3	0	1.00	6	.245	.301	.414
1997 Salt Lake	AAA Min	112	383	105	25	3	5	151	38	54	29	0	74	4	3	6	3	4	.43	7	.274	.327	.394
1990 New York	NL	5	12	2	1	0	0	3	0	0	0	0	0	0	0	0	0	0	.00	2	.167	.167	.250
1992 New York	NL	6	13	2	0	0	0	2	0	0	0	0	0	0	0	0	0	0	.00	1	.154	.154	.154
1993 New York	NL	52	126	23	9	0	0	32	10	7	13	1	17	0	4	0	0	0	.00	1	.183	.259	.254
10 Min. YEARS		972	3162	766	145	13	34	1039	334	336	287	12	481	28	57	35	31	37	.46	71	.242	.308	.329
3 Maj. YEARS		63	151	27	10	0	0	37	10	7	13	1	17	0	4	0	0	0	.00	4	.179	.244	.245

Scott Baker

Pitches: Left **Bats:** Left **Pos:** P   **Ht:** 6' 2" **Wt:** 175 **Born:** 5/18/70 **Age:** 28

Year Team	Lg Org	G	GS	CG	GF	IP	BFP	H	R	ER	HR	SH	SF	HB	TBB	IBB	SO	WP	Bk	W	L	Pct.	ShO	Sv	ERA
1990 Johnson Cty	R+ StL	32	0	0	7	51.1	223	44	21	12	2	1	3	0	29	2	62	6	3	4	2	.667	0	0	2.10
1991 Savannah	A StL	8	8	0	0	46.2	200	42	27	15	1	1	3	1	25	0	41	2	0	2	3	.400	0	0	2.89
St. Pete	A+ StL	19	16	1	2	93.2	401	98	47	45	2	4	6	3	42	0	50	5	0	3	9	.250	1	0	4.32
1992 St. Pete	A+ StL	24	24	0	0	151.2	610	123	48	33	3	9	4	6	54	0	125	11	8	10	9	.526	1	0	1.96
1993 Huntsville	AA Oak	25	25	1	0	130.1	589	141	73	60	7	3	1	4	84	0	97	8	4	10	4	.714	1	0	4.14
1994 Huntsville	AA Oak	30	14	3	5	111	453	86	28	22	4	7	2	0	46	2	67	4	2	10	4	.714	2	2	1.78
1995 Edmonton	AAA Oak	22	20	1	0	107.1	474	123	69	63	9	2	2	3	46	4	56	4	0	4	7	.364	0	0	5.28
1997 Akron	AA Cle	4	4	1	0	26.1	108	25	11	10	2	2	3	0	4	0	12	0	0	2	1	.667	0	0	3.42
1995 Oakland	AL	1	0	0	0	3.2	22	5	4	4	0	0	1	1	5	0	3	0	0	0	0	.000	0	0	9.82
7 Min. YEARS		164	111	7	14	718.1	3058	682	324	260	30	29	24	16	330	8	510	40	17	45	39	.536	3	2	3.26

Paul Bako

Bats: Left **Throws:** Right **Pos:** C   **Ht:** 6'2" **Wt:** 205 **Born:** 6/20/72 **Age:** 26

Year Team	Lg Org	G	AB	H	2B	3B	HR	TB	R	RBI	TBB	IBB	SO	HBP	SH	SF	SB	CS	SB%	GDP	Avg	OBP	SLG
1993 Billings	R+ Cin	57	194	61	11	0	4	84	34	30	22	0	37	1	1	3	5	1	.83	5	.314	.382	.433
1994 Winston-Sal	A+ Cin	90	289	59	9	1	3	79	29	26	35	0	81	4	8	0	2	2	.50	6	.204	.299	.273
1995 Winston-Sal	A+ Cin	82	249	71	11	2	7	107	29	27	42	6	66	1	6	1	3	1	.75	6	.285	.389	.430
1996 Chattanooga	AA Cin	110	360	106	27	0	8	157	53	48	48	5	93	5	2	4	1	0	1.00	5	.294	.381	.436
1997 Indianapolis	AAA Cin	104	321	78	14	1	8	118	34	43	34	3	81	2	1	4	0	5	.00	7	.243	.316	.368
5 Min. YEARS		443	1413	375	72	4	30	545	179	174	181	14	358	13	18	12	11	9	.55	29	.265	.351	.386

Jeff Ball

Bats: Right **Throws:** Right **Pos:** 3B   **Ht:** 5'10" **Wt:** 185 **Born:** 4/17/69 **Age:** 29

Year Team	Lg Org	G	AB	H	2B	3B	HR	TB	R	RBI	TBB	IBB	SO	HBP	SH	SF	SB	CS	SB%	GDP	Avg	OBP	SLG
1990 Auburn	A- Hou	70	264	76	18	1	5	111	40	38	22	1	35	4	3	5	20	5	.80	4	.289	.347	.422
1991 Osceola	A+ Hou	118	392	96	15	3	5	132	53	51	49	4	74	10	3	4	20	8	.71	9	.245	.341	.337
1992 Jackson	AA Hou	93	278	53	14	1	5	84	27	24	20	1	58	10	2	1	5	3	.63	9	.191	.269	.302
1993 Quad City	A Hou	112	389	114	28	2	14	188	68	76	58	3	63	7	1	5	40	19	.68	11	.293	.390	.483
1994 Jackson	AA Hou	111	358	113	30	3	13	188	65	57	34	3	74	5	5	3	9	8	.53	9	.316	.380	.525
1995 Tucson	AAA Hou	110	362	106	25	2	4	147	58	56	25	3	66	7	4	5	11	5	.69	13	.293	.346	.406
1996 Tucson	AAA Hou	116	429	139	31	2	19	231	64	73	34	1	83	1	0	1	10	8	.56	12	.324	.374	.538
1997 Phoenix	AAA SF	126	470	151	38	3	18	249	90	103	58	5	84	5	1	7	10	4	.71	12	.321	.396	.530
8 Min. YEARS		856	2941	848	199	17	83	1330	465	478	300	21	537	49	19	31	125	60	.68	79	.288	.360	.452

Juan Ballara

Bats: Right **Throws:** Right **Pos:** C   **Ht:** 6'2" **Wt:** 150 **Born:** 3/30/72 **Age:** 26

Year Team	Lg Org	G	AB	H	2B	3B	HR	TB	R	RBI	TBB	IBB	SO	HBP	SH	SF	SB	CS	SB%	GDP	Avg	OBP	SLG
1991 Cardinals	R StL	53	185	41	7	5	3	67	25	26	20	1	62	2	0	0	1	2	.33	2	.222	.304	.362
Savannah	A StL	3	7	0	0	0	0	0	0	0	0	0	3	0	0	0	0	0	.00	0	.000	.000	.000
1992 Johnson Cty	R+ StL	26	81	15	5	2	1	27	9	11	11	0	27	0	1	1	0	1	.00	1	.185	.280	.333
1993 Springfield	A StL	60	195	48	8	1	5	73	24	29	12	0	42	2	1	2	1	1	.50	7	.246	.294	.374
1994 St. Pete	A+ StL	71	226	46	12	5	5	83	33	15	18	1	60	2	1	2	0	1	1.00	5	.204	.266	.367
1995 Peoria	A StL	86	243	62	12	6	8	110	33	27	17	1	53	2	0	0	3	3	.63	5	.255	.309	.453
1997 Orlando	AA ChN	15	31	6	0	0	0	6	2	2	5	0	10	0	0	1	2	0	1.00	0	.194	.297	.194
6 Min. YEARS		314	968	218	44	19	22	366	126	110	83	3	257	8	3	6	10	7	.59	15	.225	.290	.378

Travis Baptist

Pitches: Left **Bats:** Left **Pos:** P   **Ht:** 6'0" **Wt:** 190 **Born:** 12/30/71 **Age:** 26

Year Team	Lg Org	G	GS	CG	GF	IP	BFP	H	R	ER	HR	SH	SF	HB	TBB	IBB	SO	WP	Bk	W	L	Pct.	ShO	Sv	ERA
1991 Medicne Hat	R+ Tor	14	14	1	0	85.1	379	100	52	39	5	2	2	1	21	0	48	4	1	4	4	.500	1	0	4.11
1992 Myrtle Bch	A Tor	19	19	2	0	118	455	81	24	19	2	6	2	4	22	0	97	5	4	11	2	.846	1	0	1.45
1993 Knoxville	AA Tor	7	7	0	0	33	139	37	17	15	2	2	3	2	7	0	24	3	0	1	3	.250	0	0	4.09
1994 Syracuse	AAA Tor	24	22	1	0	122.2	539	145	80	62	20	3	4	0	33	2	42	6	2	8	8	.500	0	0	4.55
1995 Syracuse	AAA Tor	15	13	0	0	79	356	83	56	38	12	2	3	2	32	2	52	4	1	3	4	.429	0	0	4.33
1996 Syracuse	AAA Tor	30	21	2	0	141	633	187	91	85	15	5	10	2	48	2	77	7	2	7	6	.538	0	0	5.43
1997 New Britain	AA Min	36	3	0	7	60.2	247	49	27	23	6	8	1	2	26	2	50	4	0	5	6	.455	0	0	3.41
Salt Lake	AAA Min	7	6	1	0	47.2	194	47	16	11	2	1	1	1	9	0	28	2	1	4	1	.800	1	0	2.08

HOW MUCH HE PITCHED								WHAT HE GAVE UP												THE RESULTS					
Year Team	Lg Org	G	GS	CG	GF	IP	BFP	H	R	ER	HR	SH	SF	HB	TBB	IBB	SO	WP	Bk	W	L	Pct.	ShO	Sv	ERA
7 Min. YEARS		152	105	7	8	687.1	2942	729	363	292	65	28	26	14	198	8	418	35	11	43	34	.558	3	0	3.82

Joe Barbao

Pitches: Right **Bats:** Right **Pos:** P **Ht:** 6'1" **Wt:** 190 **Born:** 4/18/72 **Age:** 26

HOW MUCH HE PITCHED								WHAT HE GAVE UP												THE RESULTS					
Year Team	Lg Org	G	GS	CG	GF	IP	BFP	H	R	ER	HR	SH	SF	HB	TBB	IBB	SO	WP	Bk	W	L	Pct.	ShO	Sv	ERA
1994 Batavia	A- Phi	22	0	0	18	31.1	131	35	12	9	0	3	0	0	4	2	26	0	0	2	2	.500	0	6	2.59
1995 Piedmont	A Phi	43	0	0	14	66.2	288	70	34	25	2	4	5	7	12	1	24	2	1	8	4	.667	0	0	3.38
1996 Piedmont	A Phi	17	0	0	4	34	137	30	7	4	1	0	0	1	8	0	32	4	1	2	0	1.000	0	0	1.06
Clearwater	A+ Phi	28	0	0	10	40.1	170	49	19	15	0	2	2	1	5	2	14	0	0	4	2	.667	0	1	3.35
1997 Reading	AA Phi	52	0	0	16	75.2	359	101	53	44	12	6	1	8	28	3	33	3	0	2	3	.400	0	2	5.23
4 Min. YEARS		162	0	0	62	248	1085	285	125	97	15	15	8	17	57	8	129	9	2	18	11	.621	0	10	3.52

Brian Barber

Pitches: Right **Bats:** Right **Pos:** P **Ht:** 6'1" **Wt:** 175 **Born:** 3/4/73 **Age:** 25

HOW MUCH HE PITCHED								WHAT HE GAVE UP												THE RESULTS					
Year Team	Lg Org	G	GS	CG	GF	IP	BFP	H	R	ER	HR	SH	SF	HB	TBB	IBB	SO	WP	Bk	W	L	Pct.	ShO	Sv	ERA
1991 Johnson Cty	R+ StL	14	13	0	0	73.1	325	62	48	44	5	1	1	5	38	0	84	4	6	4	6	.400	0	0	5.40
1992 Springfield	A StL	8	8	0	0	50.2	215	39	21	21	7	2	0	1	24	0	56	2	1	3	4	.429	0	0	3.73
St. Pete	A+ StL	19	19	1	0	113.1	473	99	51	41	7	1	2	5	46	0	102	4	0	5	5	.500	0	0	3.26
1993 Arkansas	AA StL	24	24	1	0	143.1	625	154	70	64	19	7	4	4	56	2	126	10	2	9	8	.529	0	0	4.02
Louisville	AAA StL	1	1	0	0	5.2	25	4	3	3	0	1	0	0	4	0	5	0	1	0	1	.000	0	0	4.76
1994 Arkansas	AA StL	6	6	0	0	36	152	31	15	13	4	1	0	0	16	2	54	2	0	1	3	.250	0	0	3.25
Louisville	AAA StL	19	18	0	1	85.1	376	79	58	51	7	4	3	5	46	1	95	7	0	4	7	.364	0	1	5.38
1995 Louisville	AAA StL	20	19	0	0	107.1	465	105	67	56	14	2	6	4	40	1	94	1	0	6	5	.545	0	0	4.70
1996 Louisville	AAA StL	11	11	1	0	49.2	222	49	37	31	12	0	1	3	26	1	33	2	0	0	6	.000	0	0	5.62
1997 Pr William	A+ StL	2	2	0	0	11	44	10	5	5	3	0	0	0	5	0	13	0	0	1	1	.500	0	0	4.09
Arkansas	AA StL	3	3	0	0	16.1	80	28	19	19	2	0	2	3	5	0	15	0	1	0	1	.000	0	0	10.47
Louisville	AAA StL	18	18	0	0	92.2	431	111	80	71	20	2	4	3	44	1	74	5	0	4	8	.333	0	0	6.90
1995 St. Louis	NL	9	4	0	2	29.1	130	31	17	17	4	0	3	0	16	0	27	3	0	2	1	.667	0	0	5.22
1996 St. Louis	NL	1	1	0	0	3	20	4	5	5	0	0	2	1	6	0	1	0	0	0	0	.000	0	0	15.00
7 Min. YEARS		145	142	3	1	784.2	3433	771	474	419	100	21	23	33	350	8	751	37	11	37	55	.402	0	1	4.81
2 Maj. YEARS		10	5	0	2	32.1	150	35	22	22	4	0	5	1	22	0	28	3	0	2	1	.667	0	0	6.12

Lorenzo Barcelo

Pitches: Right **Bats:** Right **Pos:** P **Ht:** 6'4" **Wt:** 180 **Born:** 8/10/77 **Age:** 20

HOW MUCH HE PITCHED								WHAT HE GAVE UP												THE RESULTS					
Year Team	Lg Org	G	GS	CG	GF	IP	BFP	H	R	ER	HR	SH	SF	HB	TBB	IBB	SO	WP	Bk	W	L	Pct.	ShO	Sv	ERA
1995 Bellingham	A- SF	12	11	0	0	47	198	43	23	18	3	0	1	2	19	0	34	1	1	3	2	.600	0	0	3.45
1996 Burlington	A SF	26	26	1	0	152.2	633	138	70	60	19	5	5	5	46	0	139	5	1	12	10	.545	0	0	3.54
1997 San Jose	A+ SF	16	16	1	0	89	378	91	45	39	13	1	3	1	30	2	89	1	2	5	4	.556	1	0	3.94
Shreveport	AA SF	5	5	0	0	31.1	132	30	19	14	4	1	0	0	8	0	20	0	2	2	0	1.000	0	0	4.02
Birmingham	AA ChA	6	6	0	0	33.1	147	36	20	18	2	0	1	4	9	0	29	1	0	2	1	.667	0	0	4.86
3 Min. YEARS		65	64	2	0	353.1	1488	338	177	149	41	7	10	12	112	2	311	8	10	24	17	.585	1	0	3.80

Marc Barcelo

Pitches: Right **Bats:** Right **Pos:** P **Ht:** 6'3" **Wt:** 210 **Born:** 1/10/72 **Age:** 26

HOW MUCH HE PITCHED								WHAT HE GAVE UP												THE RESULTS					
Year Team	Lg Org	G	GS	CG	GF	IP	BFP	H	R	ER	HR	SH	SF	HB	TBB	IBB	SO	WP	Bk	W	L	Pct.	ShO	Sv	ERA
1993 Ft. Myers	A+ Min	7	3	0	3	23	89	18	10	7	1	0	1	1	4	0	24	1	0	1	1	.500	0	0	2.74
Nashville	AA Min	2	2	0	0	9.1	42	9	5	4	2	1	1	1	5	0	5	1	1	1	0	1.000	0	0	3.86
1994 Nashville	AA Min	29	28	4	0	183.1	760	167	74	54	11	5	2	9	45	0	153	8	0	11	6	.647	0	0	2.65
1995 Salt Lake	AAA Min	28	28	2	0	143	684	214	131	112	19	5	5	6	59	2	63	4	2	8	13	.381	0	0	7.05
1996 Salt Lake	AAA Min	12	9	0	1	59.1	267	82	45	43	8	4	3	3	17	1	34	6	0	2	2	.500	0	0	6.52
Hardware City	AA Min	14	13	3	1	80	377	98	53	45	7	2	5	4	38	0	59	5	0	3	8	.273	1	0	5.06
1997 New Britain	AA Min	7	4	0	1	23	118	27	22	22	2	1	3	1	28	0	9	4	0	0	1	.000	0	1	8.61
Daytona	A+ ChN	23	3	0	5	42.2	200	45	35	26	5	5	6	3	27	5	30	6	0	3	3	.500	0	1	5.48
5 Min. YEARS		122	90	9	11	563.2	2537	660	375	313	55	23	26	28	223	8	377	33	3	29	34	.460	1	2	5.00

John Barfield

Pitches: Left **Bats:** Left **Pos:** P **Ht:** 6'1" **Wt:** 195 **Born:** 10/15/64 **Age:** 33

HOW MUCH HE PITCHED								WHAT HE GAVE UP												THE RESULTS					
Year Team	Lg Org	G	GS	CG	GF	IP	BFP	H	R	ER	HR	SH	SF	HB	TBB	IBB	SO	WP	Bk	W	L	Pct.	ShO	Sv	ERA
1986 Daytona Bch	A+ Tex	3	3	0	0	17.1	69	14	9	8	0	0	0	1	1	0	13	0	0	1	1	.500	0	0	4.15
Salem	A+ Tex	13	11	0	0	56	250	71	43	31	7	2	0	1	22	0	39	3	1	2	5	.286	0	0	4.98
1987 Charlotte	A+ Tex	25	25	3	0	153.2	654	145	75	63	3	1	8	3	55	0	79	6	3	10	7	.588	2	0	3.69
1988 Tulsa	AA Tex	24	24	5	0	169	702	159	69	54	8	6	2	3	66	2	125	13	2	9	9	.500	0	0	2.88
1989 Okla City	AAA Tex	28	28	7	0	175.1	739	178	93	79	14	6	6	2	68	2	58	11	1	10	8	.556	3	0	4.06
1990 Okla City	AAA Tex	19	3	0	2	43.1	182	44	21	17	3	6	0	1	21	3	25	0	1	1	6	.143	0	1	3.53
1992 Charlotte	A+ Tex	3	0	0	2	7	30	10	7	6	0	0	0	0	1	0	4	0	0	0	1	.000	0	1	7.71
Okla City	AAA Tex	42	0	0	12	71.2	306	75	39	33	6	4	0	2	26	0	26	1	3	7	1	.875	0	2	4.14
1993 Birmingham	AA ChA	13	5	1	5	42	185	57	24	18	1	2	1	1	5	0	18	0	1	5	2	.714	1	1	3.86
Nashville	AAA ChA	14	4	0	4	35	147	36	19	16	3	1	1	1	11	2	15	3	0	3	1	.750	0	1	4.11
1994 San Antonio	AA LA	51	0	0	24	73.1	298	63	27	22	3	8	2	3	24	6	45	4	2	6	5	.545	0	3	2.70
1995 Okla City	AAA Tex	4	0	0	1	7.1	26	4	2	0	0	0	0	0	1	0	2	0	0	0	0	.000	0	1	0.00

		HOW MUCH HE PITCHED				WHAT HE GAVE UP				THE RESULTS						
Year Team	Lg Org	G GS CG GF	IP	BFP	H R ER	HR SH SF HB	TBB IBB	SO	WP Bk	W L	Pct.	ShO	Sv	ERA
1997 Buffalo	AAA Cle	1 0 0 0	1	6	3 3 3	1 0 0 0	0 0	1	0 0	0 1	.000	0 0	27.00
1989 Texas	AL	4 2 0 1	11.2	52	15 10 8	0 1 0 0	4 0	9	1 0	0 1	.000	0 0	6.17
1990 Texas	AL	33 0 0 10	44.1	178	42 25 23	2 3 4 1	13 3	17	1 1	4 3	.571	0 1	4.67
1991 Texas	AL	28 9 0 4	83.1	361	96 51 42	11 3 4 0	22 3	27	0 2	4 4	.500	0 1	4.54
10 Min. YEARS		240 103 16 50	852	3594	859 431 350	49 36 20 18	301 15	450	41 15	54 47	.535	6 10	3.70
3 Maj. YEARS		65 11 0 15	139.1	591	153 86 73	13 7 8 1	39 6	53	2 3	8 8	.500	0 2	4.72

Glen Barker

Bats: Right **Throws:** Right **Pos:** OF   **Ht:** 5'10" **Wt:** 180 **Born:** 5/10/71 **Age:** 27

		BATTING														BASERUNNING				PERCENTAGES		
Year Team	Lg Org	G	AB	H	2B	3B	HR	TB	R	RBI	TBB	IBB	SO	HBP	SH	SF	SB	CS	SB%	GDP	Avg	OBP	SLG
1993 Niagara Fal	A- Det	72	253	55	11	4	5	89	49	23	24	0	71	4	2	3	37	12	.76	1	.217	.292	.352
1994 Fayettevlle	A Det	74	267	61	13	5	1	87	38	30	33	0	79	9	2	1	41	13	.76	5	.228	.332	.326
Lakeland	A+ Det	28	104	19	5	1	2	32	10	6	4	0	34	2	0	0	5	3	.63	2	.183	.227	.308
1995 Jacksnville	AA Det	133	507	121	26	4	10	185	74	49	33	0	143	9	12	1	39	16	.71	1	.239	.296	.365
1996 Fayettevlle	A Det	37	132	38	1	0	1	42	23	9	16	1	34	3	3	0	20	6	.77	2	.288	.377	.318
Toledo	AAA Det	24	80	20	2	1	0	24	13	2	9	0	25	0	2	0	6	6	.50	1	.250	.326	.300
Jacksnville	AA Det	43	120	19	2	1	0	23	9	8	8	0	36	0	2	0	6	4	.60	2	.158	.211	.192
1997 Toledo	AAA Det	21	47	9	1	0	1	13	9	3	5	0	15	1	2	0	6	2	.75	0	.191	.283	.277
Lakeland	A+ Det	13	57	18	4	0	1	25	9	11	4	0	17	0	3	0	7	1	.88	0	.316	.361	.439
Jacksnville	AA Det	69	257	72	8	4	6	106	47	29	29	0	72	5	8	3	17	8	.68	4	.280	.361	.412
5 Min. YEARS		514	1824	432	73	20	27	626	281	170	165	1	526	33	36	8	184	71	.72	18	.237	.310	.343

Kevin Barker

Bats: Left **Throws:** Left **Pos:** 1B   **Ht:** 6'3" **Wt:** 205 **Born:** 7/26/75 **Age:** 22

		BATTING														BASERUNNING				PERCENTAGES		
Year Team	Lg Org	G	AB	H	2B	3B	HR	TB	R	RBI	TBB	IBB	SO	HBP	SH	SF	SB	CS	SB%	GDP	Avg	OBP	SLG
1996 Ogden	R+ Mil	71	281	89	19	4	9	143	61	56	46	4	54	3	0	5	4	2	.00	4	.317	.412	.509
1997 Stockton	A+ Mil	70	267	81	20	5	13	150	47	45	25	4	60	0	0	1	4	3	.57	6	.303	.362	.562
El Paso	AA Mil	65	238	66	15	6	10	123	37	63	28	0	40	2	0	5	3	3	.50	5	.277	.352	.517
2 Min. YEARS		206	786	236	54	15	32	416	145	164	99	8	154	5	0	11	7	8	.47	15	.300	.377	.529

Richie Barker

Pitches: Right **Bats:** Right **Pos:** P   **Ht:** 6'2" **Wt:** 195 **Born:** 10/29/72 **Age:** 25

		HOW MUCH HE PITCHED				WHAT HE GAVE UP				THE RESULTS						
Year Team	Lg Org	G GS CG GF	IP	BFP	H R ER	HR SH SF HB	TBB IBB	SO	WP Bk	W L	Pct.	ShO	Sv	ERA
1994 Huntington	R+ ChN	17 0 0 6	39.1	187	36 35 26	3 2 2 7	25 0	22	2 3	2 4	.333	0 0	5.95
1995 Rockford	A ChN	32 0 0 15	43.2	196	45 20 18	2 1 0 2	20 1	23	5 0	2 0	1.000	0 1	3.71
1996 Daytona	A+ ChN	17 0 0 7	27	135	34 23 17	0 2 1 2	18 0	14	10 0	4 0	1.000	0 0	5.67
Rockford	A ChN	19 0 0 9	33	156	42 24 19	2 1 4 0	15 0	23	3 0	1 1	.500	0 1	5.18
1997 Daytona	A+ ChN	29 1 0 10	51	220	49 27 19	3 2 1 3	15 1	38	7 1	2 1	.667	0 1	3.35
Orlando	AA ChN	19 0 0 7	30	121	25 17 11	5 0 1 2	7 0	19	2 0	0 1	.000	0 2	3.30
4 Min. YEARS		133 1 0 54	224	1015	231 146 110	15 8 9 16	100 2	139	29 4	11 7	.611	0 5	4.42

Tim Barker

Bats: Right **Throws:** Right **Pos:** 2B   **Ht:** 6'0" **Wt:** 175 **Born:** 6/30/68 **Age:** 30

		BATTING														BASERUNNING				PERCENTAGES		
Year Team	Lg Org	G	AB	H	2B	3B	HR	TB	R	RBI	TBB	IBB	SO	HBP	SH	SF	SB	CS	SB%	GDP	Avg	OBP	SLG
1989 Great Falls	R+ LA	59	201	63	9	6	5	99	54	36	37	0	55	2	1	4	25	9	.74	2	.313	.423	.493
1990 Bakersfield	A+ LA	125	443	120	22	6	8	178	83	62	71	1	116	6	5	4	33	14	.70	7	.271	.375	.402
1991 San Antonio	AA LA	119	401	117	20	4	2	151	70	46	80	2	61	6	8	5	32	13	.71	6	.292	.413	.377
1992 San Antonio	AA LA	97	350	95	17	3	1	121	47	26	33	2	91	5	6	1	25	9	.74	2	.271	.342	.346
1993 Harrisburg	AA Mon	49	185	57	10	1	4	81	40	16	30	0	32	2	6	2	7	4	.64	1	.308	.406	.438
Ottawa	AAA Mon	51	167	38	5	1	2	51	25	14	26	0	42	3	7	1	5	3	.63	3	.228	.340	.305
1994 New Orleans	AAA Mil	128	436	115	25	7	5	169	71	44	76	2	97	6	10	1	41	17	.71	6	.264	.380	.388
1995 New Orleans	AAA Mil	80	264	68	9	5	1	90	44	24	29	0	39	4	8	1	10	8	.56	2	.258	.339	.341
1996 Columbus	AAA NYA	116	402	107	27	8	2	156	71	45	56	1	57	2	2	4	24	8	.75	3	.266	.356	.388
1997 Columbus	AAA NYA	65	208	58	10	2	5	87	36	30	32	0	41	0	0	0	14	6	.70	5	.279	.375	.418
9 Min. YEARS		889	3057	838	154	43	35	1183	541	343	470	8	631	35	52	20	216	91	.70	37	.274	.375	.387

Andy Barkett

Bats: Left **Throws:** Left **Pos:** 1B   **Ht:** 6'1" **Wt:** 205 **Born:** 9/5/74 **Age:** 23

		BATTING														BASERUNNING				PERCENTAGES		
Year Team	Lg Org	G	AB	H	2B	3B	HR	TB	R	RBI	TBB	IBB	SO	HBP	SH	SF	SB	CS	SB%	GDP	Avg	OBP	SLG
1995 Butte	R+ Tex	45	162	54	11	5	5	90	33	51	33	2	39	3	0	4	1	0	1.00	1	.333	.446	.556
Chston-SC	A Tex	21	78	17	6	0	0	23	7	12	10	0	27	0	0	3	0	3	.00	3	.218	.297	.295
1996 Charlotte	A+ Tex	115	392	112	22	3	6	158	57	54	57	2	59	5	0	4	3	1	.75	6	.286	.380	.403
1997 Tulsa	AA Tex	130	471	141	34	8	8	215	82	65	63	2	86	5	1	2	1	3	.25	15	.299	.386	.456
3 Min. YEARS		311	1103	324	73	16	19	486	179	182	163	6	211	13	1	13	5	7	.42	25	.294	.387	.441

Brian Barkley

Pitches: Left **Bats:** Left **Pos:** P **Ht:** 6'2" **Wt:** 170 **Born:** 12/8/75 **Age:** 22

Year Team	Lg Org	G	GS	CG	GF	IP	BFP	H	R	ER	HR	SH	SF	HB	TBB	IBB	SO	WP	Bk	W	L	Pct.	ShO	Sv	ERA
1994 Red Sox	R Bos	4	3	0	0	18.2	71	11	7	2	1	1	0	0	4	0	14	2	1	0	1	.000	0	0	0.96
1995 Sarasota	A+ Bos	24	24	2	0	146.2	611	147	66	53	5	2	3	5	37	3	70	4	1	8	10	.444	2	0	3.25
1996 Trenton	AA Bos	22	21	0	0	119.2	535	126	79	76	17	6	5	5	56	4	89	7	2	8	8	.500	0	0	5.72
1997 Trenton	AA Bos	29	29	4	0	178.2	797	208	113	98	18	3	6	3	79	0	121	3	2	12	9	.571	0	0	4.94
4 Min. YEARS		79	77	6	0	463.2	2014	492	265	229	41	12	14	13	176	7	294	16	6	28	28	.500	2	0	4.45

Brian Barnes

Pitches: Left **Bats:** Left **Pos:** P **Ht:** 5'9" **Wt:** 170 **Born:** 3/25/67 **Age:** 31

Year Team	Lg Org	G	GS	CG	GF	IP	BFP	H	R	ER	HR	SH	SF	HB	TBB	IBB	SO	WP	Bk	W	L	Pct.	ShO	Sv	ERA
1989 Jamestown	A- Mon	2	2	0	0	9	33	4	1	1	0	0	0	0	3	0	15	1	1	1	0	1.000	0	0	1.00
Wst Plm Bch	A+ Mon	7	7	4	0	50	187	25	9	4	0	3	1	0	16	0	67	4	0	4	3	.571	3	0	0.72
Indianapolis	AAA Mon	1	1	0	0	6	24	5	1	1	0	0	0	0	2	0	5	0	0	1	0	1.000	0	0	1.50
1990 Jacksnville	AA Mon	29	28	3	0	201.1	828	144	78	62	12	7	5	9	87	2	213	8	1	13	7	.650	1	0	2.77
1991 Wst Plm Bch	A+ Mon	2	2	0	0	7	27	3	0	0	0	0	0	0	4	0	6	3	0	0	0	.000	0	0	0.00
Indianapolis	AAA Mon	2	2	0	0	11	44	6	2	2	0	1	0	1	8	0	10	0	0	2	0	1.000	0	0	1.64
1992 Indianapolis	AAA Mon	13	13	2	0	83	338	69	35	34	8	1	2	1	30	1	77	2	2	4	4	.500	1	0	3.69
1994 Charlotte	AAA Cle	13	0	0	2	18.1	80	17	10	8	2	0	0	1	8	2	23	1	0	1	0	1.000	0	0	3.93
Albuquerque	AAA LA	9	9	0	0	47	221	57	38	33	9	0	1	1	23	2	44	1	0	5	1	.833	0	1	6.32
1995 Pawtucket	AAA Bos	21	18	2	0	106.1	454	107	62	50	12	0	2	4	30	0	90	5	1	7	5	.583	0	0	4.23
1996 Jacksnville	AA Det	13	12	1	0	74.2	320	74	37	31	8	6	1	4	25	1	74	3	0	4	6	.400	1	0	3.74
Toledo	AAA Det	14	13	2	0	88	373	85	49	39	8	0	1	4	29	0	70	6	1	6	6	.500	0	0	3.99
1997 Toledo	AAA Det	32	18	0	0	115.1	540	143	100	86	16	2	8	7	57	6	86	9	0	7	10	.412	0	0	6.71
1990 Montreal	NL	4	4	1	0	28	115	25	10	9	2	2	0	0	7	0	23	2	0	1	1	.500	0	0	2.89
1991 Montreal	NL	28	27	1	0	160	684	135	82	75	16	9	5	6	84	2	117	5	1	5	8	.385	0	0	4.22
1992 Montreal	NL	21	17	0	2	100	417	77	34	33	9	5	1	3	46	1	65	1	2	6	6	.500	0	0	2.97
1993 Montreal	NL	52	8	0	8	100	442	105	53	49	9	8	3	0	48	2	60	5	1	2	6	.250	0	3	4.41
1994 Cleveland	AL	6	0	0	2	13.1	67	12	10	8	2	0	1	0	15	2	5	0	0	0	1	.000	0	0	5.40
Los Angeles	NL	5	0	0	1	5	29	10	4	4	1	0	0	0	4	1	5	2	0	0	0	.000	0	0	7.20
8 Min. YEARS		158	125	14	6	817	3469	739	422	351	75	20	21	32	322	14	780	43	6	54	43	.557	6	1	3.87
5 Maj. YEARS		116	56	2	13	406.1	1754	364	193	178	39	24	10	9	204	8	275	15	4	14	22	.389	0	3	3.94

Jim Baron

Pitches: Left **Bats:** Left **Pos:** P **Ht:** 6'3" **Wt:** 230 **Born:** 2/22/74 **Age:** 24

Year Team	Lg Org	G	GS	CG	GF	IP	BFP	H	R	ER	HR	SH	SF	HB	TBB	IBB	SO	WP	Bk	W	L	Pct.	ShO	Sv	ERA
1992 Padres	R SD	14	0	0	3	25	117	24	28	23	0	1	4	1	25	0	18	10	6	2	0	1.000	0	0	8.28
1993 Padres	R SD	13	8	1	2	48.2	220	38	33	24	0	1	3	6	38	0	36	5	1	1	3	.250	0	0	4.44
1994 Springfield	A SD	25	23	0	0	105.2	515	121	83	75	14	2	3	7	76	2	73	14	3	6	6	.500	0	1	6.39
1995 Rancho Cuca	A+ SD	3	0	0	1	2.2	12	7	8	5	1	1	0	0	6	0	3	2	0	0	0	.000	0	0	16.88
Clinton	A SD	11	9	1	1	50.2	232	65	42	35	4	3	2	1	16	2	31	4	0	0	8	.000	0	0	6.22
Idaho Falls	R+ SD	27	1	0	5	43	201	51	31	27	2	0	2	1	19	1	43	8	0	2	3	.400	0	0	5.65
1996 Rancho Cuca	A+ SD	54	0	0	17	87	383	87	44	29	9	2	3	1	35	0	85	7	2	6	3	.667	0	0	3.00
1997 Las Vegas	AAA SD	4	0	0	2	4	21	8	5	5	2	0	0	0	3	0	3	0	0	0	0	.000	0	0	11.25
Mobile	AA SD	19	1	0	4	33.2	152	35	21	17	3	2	0	0	13	1	30	3	0	2	4	.333	0	0	4.54
Rancho Cuca	A+ SD	14	14	0	0	85.1	371	89	50	32	2	4	7	2	28	1	64	4	1	1	7	.125	0	0	3.38
6 Min. YEARS		184	56	2	35	485.2	2234	525	345	272	37	16	24	22	259	7	386	57	13	20	34	.370	0	2	5.04

Jeff Barry

Bats: Both **Throws:** Right **Pos:** OF **Ht:** 6'0" **Wt:** 200 **Born:** 9/22/68 **Age:** 29

Year Team	Lg Org	G	AB	H	2B	3B	HR	TB	R	RBI	TBB	IBB	SO	HBP	SH	SF	SB	CS	SB%	GDP	Avg	OBP	SLG
1990 Jamestown	A- Mon	51	197	62	6	1	4	82	30	23	17	2	25	0	2	0	25	5	.83	1	.315	.369	.416
1991 Wst Plm Bch	A+ Mon	116	437	92	16	3	4	126	47	31	34	4	67	4	2	2	20	14	.59	7	.211	.273	.288
1992 St. Lucie	A+ NYN	3	9	3	2	0	0	5	0	1	0	0	0	0	0	0	0	0	.00	1	.333	.333	.556
Mets	R NYN	8	23	4	1	0	0	5	5	2	6	1	2	0	0	0	2	0	1.00	1	.174	.345	.217
1993 St. Lucie	A+ NYN	114	420	108	17	5	4	147	68	50	49	4	37	5	2	6	17	14	.55	7	.257	.338	.350
1994 Binghamton	AA NYN	110	388	118	24	3	9	175	48	69	35	4	62	6	1	6	10	11	.48	10	.304	.364	.451
1995 Norfolk	AAA NYN	12	41	9	2	0	0	11	3	6	3	0	6	1	0	2	0	0	.00	2	.220	.277	.268
Binghamton	AA NYN	80	290	78	17	6	11	140	49	53	31	6	61	9	0	9	4	1	.80	4	.269	.348	.483
1996 Las Vegas	AAA SD	4	12	1	0	0	0	1	1	0	3	0	0	1	0	0	0	0	.00	0	.083	.267	.083
Memphis	AA SD	91	226	55	7	0	3	71	29	25	29	5	48	1	1	6	3	7	.30	6	.243	.324	.314
1997 New Haven	AA Col	40	146	32	4	0	5	51	21	12	4	0	34	3	1	1	3	2	.60	3	.219	.253	.349
Colo Sprngs	AAA Col	81	273	82	13	3	13	140	46	70	30	2	45	4	0	2	5	0	1.00	5	.300	.375	.513
1995 New York	NL	15	15	2	1	0	0	3	2	0	1	0	8	0	0	0	0	0	.00	0	.133	.188	.200
8 Min. YEARS		710	2462	644	109	21	53	954	347	342	241	28	387	33	9	36	89	54	.62	46	.262	.331	.387

Blake Barthol

Bats: Right **Throws:** Right **Pos:** C **Ht:** 6'0" **Wt:** 200 **Born:** 4/7/73 **Age:** 25

Year Team	Lg Org	G	AB	H	2B	3B	HR	TB	R	RBI	TBB	IBB	SO	HBP	SH	SF	SB	CS	SB%	GDP	Avg	OBP	SLG
1995 Portland	A- Col	56	191	45	10	2	1	62	20	25	22	0	32	4	1	3	5	2	.71	5	.236	.323	.325
1996 Salem	A+ Col	109	375	107	17	2	13	167	58	67	36	0	48	12	6	1	12	5	.71	5	.285	.366	.445
1997 New Haven	AA Col	109	325	79	12	2	6	113	42	39	31	0	76	10	11	2	5	3	.63	6	.243	.326	.348

14

		BATTING															BASERUNNING				PERCENTAGES		
Year Team	Lg Org	G	AB	H	2B	3B	HR	TB	R	RBI	TBB	IBB	SO	HBP	SH	SF	SB	CS	SB%	GDP	Avg	OBP	SLG
3 Min. YEARS		274	891	231	39	6	20	342	120	131	89	0	156	26	18	6	22	10	.69	16	.259	.342	.384

Kevin Bass

Bats: Both Throws: Right Pos: OF   Ht: 6' 0" Wt: 190 Born: 5/12/59 Age: 39

		BATTING															BASERUNNING				PERCENTAGES		
Year Team	Lg Org	G	AB	H	2B	3B	HR	TB	R	RBI	TBB	IBB	SO	HBP	SH	SF	SB	CS	SB%	GDP	Avg	OBP	SLG
1977 Newark	A- Mil	48	189	56	11	7	1	84	30	33	19	-	17	3	1	1	11	9	.55	-	.296	.368	.444
1978 Burlington	A Mil	129	499	132	27	5	18	223	81	69	40	-	63	10	1	7	36	10	.78	-	.265	.327	.447
1979 Holyoke	AA Mil	135	490	129	15	4	8	176	69	54	37	-	77	4	7	3	17	10	.63	-	.263	.318	.359
1980 Holyoke	AA Mil	136	490	147	31	7	4	204	79	51	41	-	59	7	5	2	35	16	.69	-	.300	.361	.416
1981 Vancouver	AAA Mil	97	339	87	10	5	2	113	40	30	43	-	36	2	6	3	29	12	.71	-	.257	.341	.333
1982 Vancouver	AAA Mil	102	413	130	23	7	17	218	70	65	44	-	44	2	1	2	23	16	.59	-	.315	.382	.528
1989 Tucson	AAA Hou	6	17	5	1	0	0	6	1	2	1	0	2	0	0	1	0	0	.00	0	.294	.316	.353
1990 San Jose	A+ SF	6	22	8	1	0	0	9	2	4	0	0	1	1	0	0	1	0	1.00	0	.364	.391	.409
Phoenix	AAA SF	8	33	8	2	0	0	10	2	4	0	0	4	0	0	0	1	1	.50	3	.242	.242	.303
1991 San Jose	A+ SF	5	19	2	2	0	0	4	1	1	2	1	3	1	0	0	2	0	1.00	0	.105	.227	.211
Phoenix	AAA SF	10	41	13	3	1	2	24	8	7	2	0	4	0	0	0	1	0	1.00	0	.317	.341	.585
1997 Vancouver	AAA Ana	4	12	4	0	0	1	7	4	1	3	1	2	0	0	0	0	1	.00	0	.333	.467	.583
1982 Milwaukee	AL	18	9	0	0	0	0	0	4	0	1	0	1	0	1	0	0	0	.00	0	.000	.100	.000
Houston	NL	12	24	1	0	0	0	1	2	1	0	0	8	0	0	0	0	0	.00	0	.042	.042	.042
1983 Houston	NL	88	195	46	7	3	2	65	25	18	6	1	27	0	4	1	2	2	.50	2	.236	.257	.333
1984 Houston	NL	121	331	86	17	5	2	119	33	29	6	1	57	3	2	0	5	5	.50	2	.260	.279	.360
1985 Houston	NL	150	539	145	27	5	16	230	72	68	31	1	63	6	4	2	19	8	.70	10	.269	.315	.427
1986 Houston	NL	157	591	184	33	5	20	287	83	79	38	11	72	6	1	4	22	13	.63	15	.311	.357	.486
1987 Houston	NL	157	592	168	31	5	19	266	83	85	53	13	77	4	0	5	21	8	.72	15	.284	.344	.449
1988 Houston	NL	157	541	138	27	2	14	211	57	72	42	10	65	6	3	3	31	6	.84	16	.255	.314	.390
1989 Houston	NL	87	313	94	19	4	5	136	42	44	29	3	44	1	1	4	11	4	.73	2	.300	.357	.435
1990 San Francisco	NL	61	214	54	9	1	7	86	25	32	14	3	26	2	2	1	2	2	.50	1	.252	.303	.402
1991 San Francisco	NL	124	361	84	10	4	10	132	43	40	36	8	56	4	2	3	7	4	.64	12	.233	.307	.366
1992 San Francisco	NL	89	265	71	11	3	7	109	25	30	16	1	53	1	1	2	7	7	.50	6	.268	.310	.411
New York	NL	46	137	37	12	2	2	59	15	9	7	2	17	0	0	1	7	2	.78	4	.270	.303	.431
1993 Houston	NL	111	229	65	18	0	3	92	31	37	26	3	31	1	2	0	7	1	.88	4	.284	.359	.402
1994 Houston	NL	82	203	63	15	1	6	98	37	35	28	6	24	1	1	2	2	3	.40	2	.310	.393	.483
1995 Baltimore	AL	111	295	72	12	0	5	99	32	32	24	0	47	2	4	2	8	5	.50	15	.244	.303	.336
10 Min. YEARS		686	2564	721	126	36	53	1078	387	321	232	2	312	30	21	20	156	75	.68	3	.281	.345	.420
14 Maj. YEARS		1571	4839	1308	248	40	118	1990	609	611	357	63	668	37	28	30	151	73	.67	112	.270	.323	.411

Fletcher Bates

Bats: Both Throws: Right Pos: OF   Ht: 6'1" Wt: 193 Born: 3/24/74 Age: 24

		BATTING															BASERUNNING				PERCENTAGES		
Year Team	Lg Org	G	AB	H	2B	3B	HR	TB	R	RBI	TBB	IBB	SO	HBP	SH	SF	SB	CS	SB%	GDP	Avg	OBP	SLG
1994 Mets	R NYN	52	183	39	5	3	5	65	23	29	33	0	49	0	1	4	4	3	.57	1	.213	.327	.355
St. Lucie	A+ NYN	7	24	6	1	1	1	12	2	4	1	0	5	0	0	0	0	0	.00	0	.250	.280	.500
1995 Pittsfield	A- NYN	75	276	90	14	9	6	140	52	37	41	0	72	4	1	3	17	9	.65	1	.326	.417	.507
Binghamton	AA NYN	2	8	0	0	0	0	0	1	0	1	0	6	0	0	0	0	0	.00	0	.000	.111	.000
1996 Capital City	A NYN	132	491	127	21	13	15	219	84	72	64	4	162	3	4	3	16	6	.73	3	.259	.346	.446
1997 St. Lucie	A+ NYN	70	253	76	19	11	11	150	49	38	33	6	66	4	0	2	7	6	.54	4	.300	.387	.593
Binghamton	AA NYN	68	245	63	14	2	12	117	44	34	26	0	71	1	1	2	9	3	.75	2	.257	.328	.478
4 Min. YEARS		406	1480	401	74	39	50	703	255	214	199	10	431	12	7	14	53	27	.66	11	.271	.359	.475

Allen Battle

Bats: Right Throws: Right Pos: OF   Ht: 6' 0" Wt: 170 Born: 11/29/68 Age: 29

		BATTING															BASERUNNING				PERCENTAGES		
Year Team	Lg Org	G	AB	H	2B	3B	HR	TB	R	RBI	TBB	IBB	SO	HBP	SH	SF	SB	CS	SB%	GDP	Avg	OBP	SLG
1991 Johnson Cty	R+ StL	17	62	24	6	1	0	32	26	7	14	0	6	1	1	0	7	1	.88	2	.387	.506	.516
Savannah	A StL	48	169	42	7	1	0	51	27	20	27	0	34	1	0	2	12	3	.80	0	.249	.352	.302
1992 Springfield	A StL	67	235	71	10	4	4	101	49	24	41	0	34	10	1	2	22	12	.65	2	.302	.424	.430
St. Pete	A+ StL	60	222	71	9	2	1	87	34	15	35	2	38	4	4	2	21	11	.66	2	.320	.418	.392
1993 Arkansas	AA StL	108	390	107	24	12	3	164	71	40	45	0	75	6	2	3	20	12	.63	4	.274	.356	.421
1994 Louisville	AAA StL	132	520	163	44	7	6	239	104	69	59	2	82	6	1	7	23	8	.74	14	.313	.385	.460
1995 Louisville	AAA StL	47	164	46	12	1	3	69	28	18	28	0	32	1	5	0	7	1	.88	3	.280	.389	.421
1996 Edmonton	AAA Oak	62	224	68	12	4	3	97	53	33	37	0	37	3	6	2	9	3	.75	2	.304	.406	.433
1997 Nashville	AAA ChA	11	27	6	1	0	2	13	6	5	5	0	7	0	0	0	0	0	.00	0	.222	.344	.481
1995 St. Louis	NL	61	118	32	5	0	0	37	13	2	15	0	26	1	3	0	3	3	.50	0	.271	.358	.314
1996 Oakland	AL	47	130	25	3	0	1	31	20	5	17	1	26	2	1	1	10	2	.83	3	.192	.293	.238
7 Min. YEARS		552	2013	598	125	32	22	853	398	231	291	4	345	32	20	18	121	51	.70	31	.297	.391	.424
2 Maj. YEARS		108	248	57	8	0	1	68	33	7	32	1	52	3	4	1	13	5	.72	3	.230	.324	.274

Howard Battle

Bats: Right Throws: Right Pos: 3B   Ht: 6' 0" Wt: 197 Born: 3/25/72 Age: 26

		BATTING															BASERUNNING				PERCENTAGES		
Year Team	Lg Org	G	AB	H	2B	3B	HR	TB	R	RBI	TBB	IBB	SO	HBP	SH	SF	SB	CS	SB%	GDP	Avg	OBP	SLG
1990 Medicine Hat	R+ Tor	61	233	62	17	1	5	96	25	32	16	2	38	2	0	5	5	2	.71	2	.266	.316	.412
1991 Myrtle Bch	A Tor	138	520	147	33	4	20	248	82	86	49	2	88	3	0	4	15	7	.68	1	.283	.345	.477
1992 Dunedin	A+ Tor	136	520	132	27	3	17	216	76	85	49	3	89	5	1	5	6	8	.43	5	.254	.321	.415
1993 Knoxville	AA Tor	141	521	145	21	5	7	197	66	70	45	3	94	7	1	9	12	9	.57	8	.278	.342	.378
1994 Syracuse	AAA Tor	139	517	143	26	8	14	227	72	75	40	4	82	3	1	7	26	2	.93	15	.277	.328	.439

			BATTING														BASERUNNING				PERCENTAGES		
Year Team	Lg Org	G	AB	H	2B	3B	HR	TB	R	RBI	TBB	IBB	SO	HBP	SH	SF	SB	CS	SB%	GDP	Avg	OBP	SLG
1995 Syracuse	AAA Tor	118	443	111	17	4	8	160	43	48	39	2	73	3	1	2	10	11	.48	7	.251	.314	.361
1996 Scranton-WB	AAA Phi	115	391	89	24	1	8	139	37	44	21	0	53	2	2	6	3	8	.27	15	.228	.267	.355
1997 San Antonio	AA LA	16	33	8	1	0	0	9	2	1	0	0	7	2	1	0	0	0	.00	0	.242	.286	.273
Albuquerque	AAA LA	50	139	33	3	2	3	49	14	16	6	0	23	0	0	2	1	2	.33	3	.237	.265	.353
1995 Toronto	AL	9	15	3	0	0	0	3	3	0	4	0	8	0	0	0	1	0	1.00	0	.200	.368	.200
1996 Philadelphia	NL	5	5	0	0	0	0	0	0	0	0	0	2	0	0	0	0	0	.00	0	.000	.000	.000
8 Min. YEARS		914	3317	870	169	28	82	1341	417	457	264	16	547	27	7	29	78	49	.61	56	.262	.319	.404
2 Maj. YEARS		14	20	3	0	0	0	3	3	0	4	0	10	0	0	0	1	0	1.00	0	.150	.292	.150

Juan Bautista

Bats: Right **Throws:** Right **Pos:** SS   **Ht:** 6'1" **Wt:** 185 **Born:** 6/24/75 **Age:** 23

			BATTING														BASERUNNING				PERCENTAGES		
Year Team	Lg Org	G	AB	H	2B	3B	HR	TB	R	RBI	TBB	IBB	SO	HBP	SH	SF	SB	CS	SB%	GDP	Avg	OBP	SLG
1993 Albany	A Bal	98	295	70	17	2	0	91	24	28	14	0	72	7	3	4	11	3	.79	11	.237	.284	.308
1994 Orioles	R Bal	21	65	10	2	2	0	16	4	3	2	0	19	1	1	0	3	1	.75	3	.154	.191	.246
1995 Bowie	AA Bal	13	38	4	2	0	0	6	3	0	3	0	5	2	1	0	1	0	1.00	3	.105	.209	.158
High Desert	A+ Bal	99	374	98	13	4	11	152	54	51	18	0	74	7	6	3	22	9	.71	8	.262	.306	.406
1996 Bowie	AA Bal	129	441	103	18	3	3	136	35	33	21	1	102	5	8	2	15	12	.56	6	.234	.275	.308
1997 Orioles	R Bal	3	9	1	0	0	0	1	3	0	1	0	2	2	0	0	1	1	.50	0	.111	.333	.111
Bowie	AA Bal	21	68	17	1	0	0	18	9	3	5	0	17	0	1	1	1	2	.33	2	.250	.297	.265
Birmingham	AA ChA	12	46	11	3	0	0	14	6	4	3	0	15	0	1	0	0	1	.00	2	.239	.286	.304
5 Min. YEARS		396	1336	314	56	11	14	434	138	122	67	1	306	24	21	10	54	29	.65	35	.235	.282	.325

Bob Baxter

Pitches: Left **Bats:** Right **Pos:** P   **Ht:** 6'1" **Wt:** 180 **Born:** 2/17/69 **Age:** 29

		HOW MUCH HE PITCHED						WHAT HE GAVE UP										THE RESULTS					
Year Team	Lg Org	G	GS	CG	GF	IP	BFP	H	R	ER	HR	SH	SF	HB	TBB	IBB	SO	WP	Bk	W	L	Pct.	ShO	Sv	ERA
1990 Jamestown	A- Mon	13	13	2	0	74.1	321	85	44	32	4	2	1	0	25	1	67	4	0	5	4	.556	0	0	3.87
1991 Rockford	A Mon	45	0	0	39	65	262	56	20	18	1	4	1	1	16	6	52	2	0	6	5	.545	0	19	2.49
Wst Plm Bch	A+ Mon	1	0	0	0	1.1	8	4	3	3	0	0	0	0	0	0	1	0	0	0	0	.000	0	0	20.25
1992 Wst Plm Bch	A+ Mon	42	0	0	27	63.2	231	46	12	10	1	2	1	0	9	1	54	2	0	6	2	.750	0	7	1.41
1993 Wst Plm Bch	A+ Mon	33	0	0	18	59.1	232	55	20	15	1	4	4	0	5	1	29	2	1	2	2	.500	0	6	2.28
1994 Harrisburg	AA Mon	40	11	0	6	105	451	107	61	49	10	3	3	0	32	0	56	4	0	11	3	.786	0	6	4.20
1995 Ottawa	AAA Mon	39	13	0	10	101	426	125	51	44	6	4	5	0	25	1	39	3	0	5	5	.500	0	3	3.92
1996 Ottawa	AAA Mon	54	2	0	23	81.2	362	104	55	50	8	1	3	3	23	2	60	5	0	3	3	.500	0	3	5.51
1997 Ottawa	AAA Mon	4	0	0	1	6.1	35	11	10	9	1	1	1	1	3	1	4	0	0	0	0	.000	0	0	12.79
Huntsville	AA Oak	6	0	0	3	4.2	32	15	10	6	0	2	0	0	3	1	3	1	0	1	1	.500	0	0	11.57
8 Min. YEARS		277	39	2	127	562.1	2360	608	286	236	32	23	19	5	141	14	365	23	1	39	25	.609	0	35	3.78

Tony Beasley

Bats: Right **Throws:** Right **Pos:** 2B   **Ht:** 5'8" **Wt:** 165 **Born:** 12/5/66 **Age:** 31

			BATTING														BASERUNNING				PERCENTAGES		
Year Team	Lg Org	G	AB	H	2B	3B	HR	TB	R	RBI	TBB	IBB	SO	HBP	SH	SF	SB	CS	SB%	GDP	Avg	OBP	SLG
1989 Erie	A- Bal	65	247	69	12	2	1	88	39	14	25	0	31	4	5	0	19	4	.83	4	.279	.355	.356
1990 Frederick	A+ Bal	124	399	100	14	6	1	129	57	31	30	1	68	7	12	2	10	9	.53	6	.251	.313	.323
1991 Frederick	A+ Bal	124	387	96	11	10	1	130	50	34	27	0	74	6	6	3	29	8	.78	6	.248	.305	.336
1992 Salem	A+ Pit	72	237	62	10	2	1	97	34	25	16	0	44	3	2	1	12	4	.75	5	.262	.315	.409
Carolina	AA Pit	49	158	41	5	3	1	55	12	13	8	0	33	0	1	1	13	8	.62	0	.259	.293	.348
1993 Buffalo	AAA Pit	30	95	18	3	0	0	21	9	8	4	0	17	2	4	1	1	0	1.00	6	.189	.235	.221
Carolina	AA Pit	82	252	51	7	3	4	76	39	13	23	2	52	0	3	1	11	6	.65	10	.202	.268	.302
1995 Carolina	AA Pit	105	335	94	16	4	2	124	59	34	31	2	44	4	4	6	20	4	.83	6	.281	.343	.370
1996 Carolina	AA Pit	96	269	84	17	5	4	123	40	30	30	4	33	2	2	4	10	9	.53	5	.312	.380	.457
1997 Calgary	AAA Pit	75	220	60	7	5	1	80	36	28	25	0	23	2	1	2	11	6	.65	4	.273	.349	.364
Carolina	AA Pit	31	117	32	5	0	0	37	15	12	7	1	16	1	0	0	2	1	.67	3	.274	.317	.316
8 Min. YEARS		853	2716	707	107	40	22	960	390	242	226	10	435	31	40	22	138	59	.70	49	.260	.322	.353

Blaine Beatty

Pitches: Left **Bats:** Left **Pos:** P   **Ht:** 6'2" **Wt:** 185 **Born:** 4/25/64 **Age:** 34

		HOW MUCH HE PITCHED						WHAT HE GAVE UP										THE RESULTS					
Year Team	Lg Org	G	GS	CG	GF	IP	BFP	H	R	ER	HR	SH	SF	HB	TBB	IBB	SO	WP	Bk	W	L	Pct.	ShO	Sv	ERA
1986 Newark	A- Bal	15	15	8	0	119.1	475	98	37	28	6	5	2	1	30	3	93	6	0	11	3	.786	3	0	2.11
1987 Hagerstown	A+ Bal	13	13	4	0	100	389	81	32	28	7	3	1	1	11	0	65	6	0	11	1	.917	1	0	2.52
Charlotte	AA Bal	15	15	3	0	105.2	438	110	38	36	2	1	4	1	20	2	57	4	0	6	5	.545	1	0	3.07
1988 Jackson	AA NYN	30	28	12	1	208.2	824	191	64	57	13	12	6	0	34	3	103	3	7	16	8	.667	5	0	2.46
1989 Tidewater	AAA NYN	27	27	6	0	185	764	173	86	68	14	4	8	1	43	0	90	3	2	12	10	.545	1	0	3.31
1991 Tidewater	AAA NYN	28	28	3	0	175.1	750	192	86	80	8	7	4	6	43	6	74	0	1	12	9	.571	1	0	4.11
1992 Indianapols	AAA Mon	26	12	2	3	94	412	109	52	45	8	4	4	1	24	3	54	4	1	7	5	.583	0	0	4.31
1993 Carolina	AA Pit	17	13	2	1	94.1	378	87	42	30	8	3	0	2	35	0	67	4	0	7	3	.700	0	0	2.86
Buffalo	AAA Pit	20	4	0	5	36	168	51	25	22	2	2	2	2	8	0	14	3	0	2	3	.400	0	1	5.50
1994 Chattanooga	AA Cin	27	26	6	1	196.1	770	146	66	52	15	6	3	8	43	0	162	4	0	14	7	.667	4	0	2.38
1995 Indianapols	AAA Cin	20	8	1	0	67.1	293	80	33	27	7	4	1	2	16	0	37	3	2	7	1	.875	0	0	3.61
Chattanooga	AA Cin	8	8	1	0	52	225	60	22	20	2	3	3	1	17	2	34	2	1	3	2	.600	0	0	3.46
1996 Carolina	AA Pit	23	22	1	0	145	594	135	58	53	15	3	3	4	34	6	117	3	2	11	5	.688	1	0	3.29
1997 Calgary	AAA Pit	3	2	0	0	5.1	37	18	14	14	3	0	0	1	3	0	2	0	0	1	2	.333	0	0	23.63
Pirates	R Pit	4	3	1	1	23.2	96	23	8	4	0	0	0	1	2	0	14	2	0	1	0	1.000	0	0	1.52
Carolina	AA Pit	19	9	1	0	82	366	104	61	49	12	2	3	3	27	4	41	4	0	0	5	.000	0	0	5.38
1989 New York	NL	2	1	0	0	6	25	5	1	1	0	0	0	0	2	0	3	0	0	0	0	.000	0	0	1.50

16

Year Team	Lg Org	HOW MUCH HE PITCHED						WHAT HE GAVE UP												THE RESULTS					
		G	GS	CG	GF	IP	BFP	H	R	ER	HR	SH	SF	HB	TBB	IBB	SO	WP	Bk	W	L	Pct.	ShO	Sv	ERA
1991 New York	NL	5	0	0	1	9.2	42	9	3	3	0	1	1	0	4	1	7	1	0	0	0	.000	0	0	2.79
11 Min. YEARS		295	233	49	18	1690	6979	1638	724	613	132	59	44	34	390	29	1024	50	16	121	69	.637	19	1	3.26
2 Maj. YEARS		7	1	0	1	15.2	67	14	4	4	1	1	1	0	6	1	10	1	0	0	0	.000	0	0	2.30

Matt Beaumont

Pitches: Left **Bats:** Left **Pos:** P **Ht:** 6'3" **Wt:** 210 **Born:** 4/22/73 **Age:** 25

Year Team	Lg Org	HOW MUCH HE PITCHED						WHAT HE GAVE UP												THE RESULTS					
		G	GS	CG	GF	IP	BFP	H	R	ER	HR	SH	SF	HB	TBB	IBB	SO	WP	Bk	W	L	Pct.	ShO	Sv	ERA
1994 Boise	A- Ana	12	10	0	0	64	268	52	27	25	2	4	2	7	22	1	77	3	0	3	3	.500	0	0	3.52
1995 Lk Elsinore	A+ Ana	27	26	0	0	175.1	724	162	80	64	15	1	6	7	57	1	149	1	1	16	9	.640	0	0	3.29
1996 Midland	AA Ana	28	28	2	0	161.2	746	198	124	105	20	4	6	12	71	0	132	5	0	7	16	.304	0	0	5.85
1997 Midland	AA Ana	4	3	0	0	9.2	62	24	27	27	5	0	0	0	10	0	11	1	0	0	2	.000	0	0	25.14
Lk Elsinore	A+ Ana	1	1	0	0	1.1	7	2	1	1	0	0	0	0	1	0	1	0	0	0	1	.000	0	0	6.75
4 Min. YEARS		72	68	2	0	412	1807	438	259	222	42	9	14	26	161	2	370	10	2	26	30	.464	0	0	4.85

Chris Beck

Pitches: Right **Bats:** Right **Pos:** P **Ht:** 6'3" **Wt:** 205 **Born:** 6/11/72 **Age:** 26

Year Team	Lg Org	HOW MUCH HE PITCHED						WHAT HE GAVE UP												THE RESULTS					
		G	GS	CG	GF	IP	BFP	H	R	ER	HR	SH	SF	HB	TBB	IBB	SO	WP	Bk	W	L	Pct.	ShO	Sv	ERA
1994 Bellingham	A- Sea	15	11	0	1	59.1	268	66	46	36	3	3	2	2	26	1	57	10	2	2	4	.333	0	0	5.46
1995 Wisconsin	A Sea	28	19	2	6	130	553	113	62	56	13	3	3	4	61	2	119	10	1	12	8	.600	2	2	3.88
1996 Lancaster	A+ Sea	23	11	0	4	86.2	381	90	45	34	7	3	4	2	43	3	57	5	1	6	5	.545	0	1	3.53
1997 Memphis	AA Sea	5	1	0	1	9.1	48	8	3	2	0	0	0	1	10	0	2	1	0	0	0	.000	0	0	1.93
Lancaster	A+ Sea	8	7	0	0	33	171	53	37	33	8	3	1	3	15	0	23	3	0	1	4	.200	0	0	9.00
4 Min. YEARS		79	49	2	12	318.1	1421	330	193	161	31	12	10	12	155	6	258	29	4	21	21	.500	2	3	4.55

Greg Beck

Pitches: Right **Bats:** Right **Pos:** P **Ht:** 6'4" **Wt:** 215 **Born:** 10/21/72 **Age:** 25

Year Team	Lg Org	HOW MUCH HE PITCHED						WHAT HE GAVE UP												THE RESULTS					
		G	GS	CG	GF	IP	BFP	H	R	ER	HR	SH	SF	HB	TBB	IBB	SO	WP	Bk	W	L	Pct.	ShO	Sv	ERA
1994 Helena	R+ Mil	18	2	0	11	43.2	191	42	26	21	4	3	2	2	20	1	41	3	0	4	3	.571	0	4	4.33
1995 Beloit	A Mil	35	5	0	12	74.1	331	73	46	39	2	1	6	2	35	2	91	7	2	5	2	.714	0	2	4.72
1996 Stockton	A+ Mil	28	28	0	0	152.1	695	197	119	104	18	8	7	12	53	1	96	7	0	9	11	.450	0	0	6.14
1997 Stockton	A+ Mil	27	1	0	11	55	222	33	16	15	4	2	1	3	23	2	46	2	0	4	4	.500	0	0	2.45
El Paso	AA Mil	18	6	0	3	48.1	232	75	46	35	8	2	3	5	15	2	37	5	1	1	5	.167	0	0	6.52
4 Min. YEARS		126	42	0	37	373.2	1671	420	253	214	36	16	19	24	146	8	311	24	3	23	25	.479	0	6	5.15

Kevin Beirne

Pitches: Right **Bats:** Left **Pos:** P **Ht:** 6'4" **Wt:** 210 **Born:** 1/1/74 **Age:** 24

Year Team	Lg Org	HOW MUCH HE PITCHED						WHAT HE GAVE UP												THE RESULTS					
		G	GS	CG	GF	IP	BFP	H	R	ER	HR	SH	SF	HB	TBB	IBB	SO	WP	Bk	W	L	Pct.	ShO	Sv	ERA
1995 White Sox	R ChA	2	0	0	2	3.2	15	2	2	1	0	0	0	1	1	0	3	0	0	0	0	.000	0	2	2.45
Bristol	R+ ChA	9	0	0	7	9	35	4	0	0	0	0	0	0	4	0	12	0	0	1	0	1.000	0	2	0.00
Hickory	A ChA	3	0	0	1	4	16	7	2	2	0	0	0	0	0	0	4	0	0	0	0	.000	0	0	4.50
1996 South Bend	A ChA	26	25	1	0	145.1	627	153	85	67	5	5	5	9	60	0	110	12	3	4	11	.267	0	0	4.15
1997 Winston-Sal	A+ ChA	13	13	1	0	82.2	338	66	38	28	7	1	2	7	28	1	75	5	0	4	4	.500	0	0	3.05
Birmingham	AA ChA	13	12	0	1	75	336	76	51	41	4	2	3	4	41	0	49	2	1	6	4	.600	0	0	4.92
3 Min. YEARS		66	50	2	11	319.2	1367	308	178	139	16	8	10	21	134	1	253	19	4	15	19	.441	0	4	3.91

Tim Belk

Bats: Right **Throws:** Right **Pos:** 1B **Ht:** 6'3" **Wt:** 200 **Born:** 4/6/70 **Age:** 28

Year Team	Lg Org	BATTING															BASERUNNING				PERCENTAGES		
		G	AB	H	2B	3B	HR	TB	R	RBI	TBB	IBB	SO	HBP	SH	SF	SB	CS	SB%	GDP	Avg	OBP	SLG
1992 Billings	R+ Cin	73	273	78	13	0	12	127	60	56	35	0	33	4	0	6	15	2	.88	6	.286	.368	.465
1993 Winston-Sal	A+ Cin	134	509	156	23	3	14	227	89	65	48	3	76	6	2	2	9	7	.56	8	.306	.372	.446
1994 Indianapols	AAA Cin	6	18	2	1	0	0	3	1	0	1	0	5	0	1	0	0	1	.00	1	.111	.158	.167
Chattanooga	AA Cin	118	411	127	35	3	10	198	64	86	60	5	41	3	0	11	13	8	.62	7	.309	.392	.482
1995 Indianapols	AAA Cin	57	193	58	11	0	4	81	30	18	16	0	30	2	1	0	5	5	.29	9	.301	.360	.420
1996 Indianapols	AAA Cin	120	436	125	27	3	15	203	63	63	27	1	72	2	1	6	5	2	.71	7	.287	.327	.466
1997 Indianapols	AAA Cin	90	255	74	18	1	8	118	37	38	26	1	45	1	3	4	5	3	.63	1	.290	.353	.463
1996 Cincinnati	NL	7	15	3	0	0	0	3	2	0	1	0	2	0	0	0	0	0	.00	0	.200	.250	.200
6 Min. YEARS		598	2095	620	128	10	63	957	344	326	213	10	302	18	8	29	49	28	.64	39	.296	.361	.457

Jason Bell

Pitches: Right **Bats:** Right **Pos:** P **Ht:** 6'3" **Wt:** 208 **Born:** 9/30/74 **Age:** 23

Year Team	Lg Org	HOW MUCH HE PITCHED						WHAT HE GAVE UP												THE RESULTS					
		G	GS	CG	GF	IP	BFP	H	R	ER	HR	SH	SF	HB	TBB	IBB	SO	WP	Bk	W	L	Pct.	ShO	Sv	ERA
1995 Ft. Wayne	A Min	9	6	0	0	34.1	139	26	11	5	0	3	0	1	6	0	40	6	2	3	1	.750	0	0	1.31
1996 Ft. Myers	A+ Min	13	13	0	0	90.1	350	61	20	17	1	4	2	6	22	0	83	3	0	6	3	.667	0	0	1.69
Hardware City	AA Min	16	16	2	0	94	410	93	54	46	13	5	2	5	38	1	94	6	1	2	6	.250	0	0	4.40
1997 New Britain	AA Min	28	28	3	0	164.2	700	163	71	62	19	3	2	5	64	0	142	13	2	11	9	.550	1	0	3.39
3 Min. YEARS		66	63	5	2	383.1	1599	343	156	130	33	15	6	17	130	1	359	28	5	22	19	.537	2	0	3.05

Mike Bell

Bats: Right Throws: Right Pos: 3B-2B Ht: 6'2" Wt: 185 Born: 12/7/74 Age: 23

Year Team	Lg Org	G	AB	H	2B	3B	HR	TB	R	RBI	TBB	IBB	SO	HBP	SH	SF	SB	CS	SB%	GDP	Avg	OBP	SLG
1993 Rangers	R Tex	60	230	73	13	6	3	107	48	34	27	0	23	4	1	2	9	2	.82	2	.317	.395	.465
1994 Chston-SC	A Tex	120	475	125	22	6	6	177	58	58	47	1	76	3	1	6	16	12	.57	14	.263	.330	.373
1995 Charlotte	A+ Tex	129	470	122	20	1	5	159	49	52	48	0	72	0	3	2	9	8	.53	11	.260	.327	.338
1996 Tulsa	AA Tex	128	484	129	31	3	16	214	62	59	42	1	75	3	4	0	3	1	.75	13	.267	.329	.442
1997 Okla City	AAA Tex	93	328	77	18	2	5	114	35	38	29	0	78	4	0	3	4	2	.67	10	.235	.302	.348
Tulsa	AA Tex	33	123	35	11	0	8	70	17	23	15	0	28	4	2	2	0	1	.00	2	.285	.375	.569
5 Min. YEARS		563	2110	561	115	18	43	841	269	264	208	2	352	18	11	15	41	26	.61	52	.266	.335	.399

Ron Belliard

Bats: Right Throws: Right Pos: 2B Ht: 5'8" Wt: 180 Born: 4/7/75 Age: 23

Year Team	Lg Org	G	AB	H	2B	3B	HR	TB	R	RBI	TBB	IBB	SO	HBP	SH	SF	SB	CS	SB%	GDP	Avg	OBP	SLG
1994 Brewers	R Mil	39	143	42	7	3	0	55	32	27	14	1	25	3	2	1	7	0	1.00	3	.294	.366	.385
1995 Beloit	A Mil	130	461	137	28	5	13	214	76	76	36	2	67	4	2	1	16	12	.57	10	.297	.356	.464
1996 El Paso	AA Mil	109	416	116	20	8	3	161	73	57	60	1	51	4	4	3	26	10	.72	11	.279	.373	.387
1997 Tucson	AAA Mil	118	443	125	35	4	4	180	80	55	61	1	69	11	3	5	10	7	.59	13	.282	.379	.406
4 Min. YEARS		396	1463	420	90	20	20	610	261	215	171	5	212	25	11	10	59	29	.67	37	.287	.369	.417

Clay Bellinger

Bats: Right Throws: Right Pos: 3B Ht: 6'3" Wt: 195 Born: 11/18/68 Age: 29

Year Team	Lg Org	G	AB	H	2B	3B	HR	TB	R	RBI	TBB	IBB	SO	HBP	SH	SF	SB	CS	SB%	GDP	Avg	OBP	SLG
1989 Everett	A- SF	51	185	37	8	1	4	59	29	16	19	0	47	1	1	0	3	2	.60	4	.200	.278	.319
1990 Clinton	A SF	109	382	83	17	4	10	138	52	48	28	0	102	7	5	3	13	6	.68	5	.217	.281	.361
1991 San Jose	A+ SF	105	368	95	29	2	8	152	65	62	53	3	88	11	7	6	13	4	.76	3	.258	.363	.413
1992 Shreveport	AA SF	126	433	90	18	3	13	153	45	50	36	1	82	3	4	4	7	8	.47	15	.208	.271	.353
1993 Phoenix	AAA SF	122	407	104	20	3	6	148	50	49	38	4	81	4	7	5	7	7	.50	8	.256	.322	.364
1994 Phoenix	AAA SF	106	337	90	15	1	7	128	48	50	18	0	56	7	2	3	6	1	.86	8	.267	.315	.380
1995 Phoenix	AAA SF	97	277	76	16	1	2	100	34	32	27	1	52	2	2	3	3	2	.60	5	.274	.340	.361
1996 Rochester	AAA Bal	125	459	138	34	4	15	225	68	78	33	0	90	6	1	11	8	4	.67	6	.301	.348	.490
1997 Columbus	AAA NYA	111	416	114	31	3	12	187	55	59	34	2	74	7	2	1	10	4	.71	10	.274	.338	.450
9 Min. YEARS		952	3264	827	188	22	77	1290	446	444	286	11	672	48	31	36	70	38	.65	64	.253	.319	.395

Lou Benbow

Bats: Right Throws: Right Pos: 1B Ht: 6'0" Wt: 167 Born: 1/12/71 Age: 27

Year Team	Lg Org	G	AB	H	2B	3B	HR	TB	R	RBI	TBB	IBB	SO	HBP	SH	SF	SB	CS	SB%	GDP	Avg	OBP	SLG
1991 St. Cathrns	A- Tor	54	147	26	0	0	0	26	13	4	18	0	40	6	9	0	6	7	.46	1	.177	.292	.177
1992 St. Cathrns	A- Tor	50	171	29	10	0	0	39	8	5	11	0	43	1	2	1	1	0	1.00	4	.170	.223	.228
1993 Hagerstown	A Tor	71	193	32	5	2	1	44	22	12	13	0	47	2	2	2	2	1	.67	4	.166	.224	.228
1994 Dunedin	A+ Tor	28	69	8	3	0	0	11	7	5	6	0	17	2	1	0	1	2	.33	4	.116	.208	.159
St. Lucie	A+ NYN	15	34	9	1	0	0	10	2	3	10	0	10	1	2	0	1	2	.33	0	.265	.444	.294
1995 Binghamton	AA NYN	3	1	1	0	0	0	1	0	0	1	0	0	0	0	0	0	1	.00	0	1.000	1.000	1.000
St. Lucie	A+ NYN	12	33	12	2	0	0	14	4	2	1	0	7	1	1	0	0	1	.00	1	.364	.400	.424
Durham	A+ Atl	82	245	54	7	0	4	73	20	17	11	0	53	3	3	0	2	3	.40	8	.220	.263	.298
1996 Richmond	AAA Atl	91	250	58	8	0	1	69	21	23	16	1	65	0	1	3	3	4	.43	6	.232	.275	.276
1997 Greenville	AA Atl	117	315	73	14	1	9	116	39	34	34	1	80	3	4	2	4	8	.33	7	.232	.311	.368
7 Min. YEARS		523	1458	302	50	3	15	403	136	105	121	2	362	19	25	8	20	28	.42	34	.207	.275	.276

Bill Bene

Pitches: Right Bats: Right Pos: P Ht: 6'4" Wt: 205 Born: 11/21/67 Age: 30

Year Team	Lg Org	G	GS	CG	GF	IP	BFP	H	R	ER	HR	SH	SF	HB	TBB	IBB	SO	WP	Bk	W	L	Pct.	ShO	Sv	ERA
1988 Great Falls	R+ LA	13	12	0	0	65.1	302	53	43	33	3	1	5	5	45	0	56	14	4	5	0	1.000	0	0	4.55
1989 Bakersfield	A+ LA	7	5	0	2	13.1	82	14	20	17	1	0	0	2	29	0	11	8	0	0	2	.000	0	0	11.48
Salem	A- LA	7	4	0	0	13.2	85	13	18	14	1	0	1	3	27	0	13	10	0	0	2	.000	0	0	9.22
1990 Vero Beach	A+ LA	17	14	0	2	56.2	307	49	55	44	3	1	2	6	96	0	34	23	1	1	10	.091	0	0	6.99
1991 Vero Beach	A+ LA	31	1	0	12	52	267	39	37	24	0	3	3	2	65	1	57	21	0	1	1	.500	0	0	4.15
1992 San Antonio	AA LA	18	1	0	5	32	144	19	15	11	1	2	1	0	34	1	25	10	1	0	2	.000	0	0	3.09
Vero Beach	A+ LA	18	0	0	12	18	82	11	4	4	0	1	1	1	16	0	30	5	0	2	2	.500	0	0	2.00
1993 San Antonio	AA LA	46	0	0	12	70.2	313	50	43	38	3	3	5	4	53	1	82	15	2	5	6	.455	0	1	4.84
1994 Albuquerque	AAA LA	9	0	0	3	13.1	74	18	17	15	4	0	1	1	16	0	6	5	0	0	1	.000	0	0	10.13
San Antonio	AA LA	20	0	0	5	37.1	176	34	23	19	4	3	0	2	33	3	34	7	1	1	0	1.000	0	0	4.58
1995 Chattanooga	AA Cin	4	0	0	1	4	27	7	6	6	2	0	0	0	9	0	4	1	0	0	0	.000	0	0	13.50
Palm Spring	IND —	18	12	0	3	70.2	333	61	55	36	1	0	2	9	54	0	80	15	0	3	4	.429	0	0	4.58
1997 Vancouver	AAA Ana	19	0	0	8	27.1	141	28	25	22	6	1	1	3	26	0	29	10	0	0	1	.000	0	0	7.24
Midland	AA Ana	25	0	0	5	41.1	202	42	33	29	5	1	4	2	40	0	41	11	0	0	3	.000	0	0	6.31
9 Min. YEARS		252	49	0	70	515.2	2535	438	394	312	34	16	26	40	543	6	502	155	9	18	34	.346	0	1	5.45

Bob Bennett

Pitches: Right Bats: Right Pos: P   Ht: 6'4" Wt: 205 Born: 12/30/70 Age: 27

Year Team	Lg Org	G	GS	CG	GF	IP	BFP	H	R	ER	HR	SH	SF	HB	TBB	IBB	SO	WP	Bk	W	L	Pct.	ShO	Sv	ERA
1992 Sou. Oregon	A- Oak	17	6	0	3	48	222	60	41	31	4	1	0	2	20	0	41	4	1	2	6	.250	0	2	5.81
1993 Madison	A Oak	26	17	0	3	107	435	103	45	39	7	0	1	1	23	3	102	4	1	7	8	.467	0	1	3.28
1994 W Michigan	A Oak	6	4	0	1	24.2	103	23	8	6	1	2	0	2	6	0	23	0	0	0	2	.000	0	1	2.19
Modesto	A+ Oak	20	10	0	4	80.2	332	75	31	27	2	1	0	1	25	0	71	5	1	8	2	.800	0	0	3.01
1995 Huntsville	AA Oak	23	21	0	0	117.1	482	119	62	55	13	4	3	3	28	0	70	3	1	10	7	.588	0	0	4.22
1996 Huntsville	AA Oak	38	2	0	12	83.2	380	92	55	49	10	6	1	4	36	7	83	4	0	5	3	.625	0	0	5.27
1997 Huntsville	AA Oak	23	1	0	3	42.2	204	64	38	34	7	0	3	0	15	2	32	3	0	4	3	.571	0	1	7.17
6 Min. YEARS		153	61	0	26	504	2158	536	280	241	44	14	8	13	153	12	422	23	4	36	31	.537	0	5	4.30

Chris Bennett

Pitches: Right Bats: Right Pos: P   Ht: 6'6" Wt: 205 Born: 9/8/65 Age: 32

Year Team	Lg Org	G	GS	CG	GF	IP	BFP	H	R	ER	HR	SH	SF	HB	TBB	IBB	SO	WP	Bk	W	L	Pct.	ShO	Sv	ERA
1990 Jacksnville	AA Mon	37	0	0	24	50	210	45	23	18	2	4	0	2	13	6	45	0	3	3	4	.429	0	9	3.24
Indianapols	AAA Mon	23	0	0	13	35	163	36	24	19	6	2	0	1	24	1	15	2	1	2	7	.222	0	2	4.89
1991 Indianapols	AAA Mon	6	0	0	1	11.1	45	12	10	10	3	0	1	1	1	0	5	0	1	1	0	1.000	0	0	7.94
Harrisburg	AA Mon	28	9	0	7	74	320	82	36	26	5	1	5	2	22	1	35	3	1	5	6	.455	0	1	3.16
1993 Indianapols	AAA Cin	3	2	0	0	13	61	21	8	7	1	0	1	0	1	0	10	0	1	0	0	.000	0	0	4.85
1995 Calgary	AAA Pit	4	0	0	1	7	35	11	7	4	0	0	2	0	1	0	7	0	0	0	0	.000	0	0	5.14
Carolina	AA Pit	18	0	0	5	27	128	42	22	20	2	2	0	0	9	2	13	3	0	0	1	.000	0	1	6.67
1997 Bowie	AA Bal	10	0	0	3	18.2	79	15	9	6	1	0	0	1	11	2	9	0	0	2	1	.667	0	2	2.89
Rochester	AAA Bal	25	0	0	7	40.2	166	40	17	16	0	3	4	2	7	1	28	1	0	4	2	.667	0	1	3.54
5 Min. YEARS		154	11	0	61	276.2	1207	304	156	126	20	12	13	9	89	13	167	9	7	17	21	.447	0	15	4.10

Erik Bennett

Pitches: Right Bats: Right Pos: P   Ht: 6'2" Wt: 205 Born: 9/13/68 Age: 29

Year Team	Lg Org	G	GS	CG	GF	IP	BFP	H	R	ER	HR	SH	SF	HB	TBB	IBB	SO	WP	Bk	W	L	Pct.	ShO	Sv	ERA
1989 Bend	A- Ana	15	15	2	0	96	422	96	58	37	4	3	2	3	36	0	96	0	6	6	8	.429	0	0	3.47
1990 Quad City	A Ana	18	18	3	0	108.1	453	91	48	36	9	5	6	4	37	0	100	2	4	7	7	.500	1	0	2.99
1991 Palm Spring	A+ Ana	8	8	1	0	43	192	41	15	12	2	3	0	3	27	0	31	0	0	2	3	.400	0	0	2.51
1992 Quad City	A Ana	8	8	1	0	57.1	238	46	20	17	0	3	5	4	22	0	59	3	1	3	3	.500	1	0	2.67
Palm Spring	A+ Ana	6	6	1	0	42	171	27	19	17	0	2	1	4	15	0	33	2	1	4	2	.667	0	0	3.64
Midland	AA Ana	7	7	0	0	46	195	47	22	20	3	3	2	7	16	0	36	1	0	1	3	.250	0	0	3.91
1993 Midland	AA Ana	11	11	0	0	69.1	308	87	57	50	12	2	6	6	17	1	33	1	0	5	4	.556	0	0	6.49
Vancouver	AAA Ana	18	12	0	1	80.1	353	101	57	54	10	1	0	4	21	0	51	3	0	6	6	.500	0	0	6.05
1994 Vancouver	AAA Ana	45	1	0	14	89.2	375	71	32	28	9	2	4	10	28	2	83	8	2	1	4	.200	0	3	2.81
1995 Vancouver	AAA Ana	28	0	0	12	50.2	206	44	24	24	5	0	2	3	18	2	39	4	1	6	0	1.000	0	2	4.26
Tucson	AAA Hou	14	1	0	4	22.2	110	27	17	12	1	0	3	2	14	2	14	0	0	3	1	.750	0	0	4.76
1996 Salt Lake	AAA Min	17	0	0	4	24	114	27	17	17	4	0	2	2	14	1	10	0	0	3	1	.750	0	0	6.38
1997 Akron	AA Cle	11	1	0	5	24.1	107	26	13	13	1	0	0	1	9	1	20	1	1	2	3	.400	0	0	4.81
1995 California	AL	1	0	0	1	0.1	1	0	0	0	0	0	0	0	0	0	0	0	0	0	0	.000	0	0	0.00
1996 Minnesota	AL	24	0	0	10	27.1	130	33	24	24	7	3	1	2	16	1	13	1	0	2	0	1.000	0	1	7.90
9 Min. YEARS		206	88	8	40	753.2	3244	731	399	337	60	24	33	53	274	9	615	33	16	49	45	.521	2	7	4.02
2 Maj. YEARS		25	0	0	11	27.2	131	33	24	24	7	3	1	2	16	1	13	1	0	2	0	1.000	0	1	7.81

Gary Bennett

Bats: Right Throws: Right Pos: C   Ht: 6'0" Wt: 190 Born: 4/17/72 Age: 26

Year Team	Lg Org	G	AB	H	2B	3B	HR	TB	R	RBI	TBB	IBB	SO	HBP	SH	SF	SB	CS	SB%	GDP	Avg	OBP	SLG
1990 Martinsvlle	R+ Phi	16	52	14	2	1	0	18	3	10	4	0	15	0	0	0	0	1	.00	0	.269	.316	.346
1991 Martinsvlle	R+ Phi	41	136	32	7	0	1	42	15	16	17	0	26	5	1	1	0	1	.00	5	.235	.340	.309
1992 Batavia	A- Phi	47	146	30	2	0	0	32	22	12	15	0	27	2	3	0	2	1	.67	2	.205	.288	.219
1993 Spartanburg	A Phi	42	126	32	4	1	0	38	18	15	12	0	22	1	2	1	0	0	.00	0	.254	.321	.302
Clearwater	A+ Phi	17	55	18	0	0	1	21	5	6	3	0	10	1	2	0	1	0	.00	1	.327	.373	.382
1994 Clearwater	A+ Phi	19	55	13	3	0	0	16	6	10	8	0	6	0	1	0	0	0	.00	0	.236	.328	.291
Reading	AA Phi	63	208	48	9	0	3	66	13	22	14	0	26	0	3	3	0	1	.00	6	.231	.276	.317
1995 Reading	AA Phi	86	271	64	11	0	4	87	27	40	22	1	36	3	3	2	0	1	.00	12	.236	.299	.321
Scranton-WB	AAA Phi	7	20	3	0	0	0	3	1	1	2	1	2	0	1	0	0	0	.00	0	.150	.227	.150
1996 Scranton-WB	AAA Phi	91	286	71	15	1	8	112	37	37	24	2	43	3	3	3	1	0	1.00	10	.248	.310	.392
1997 Pawtucket	AAA Bos	71	224	48	7	1	4	69	16	22	18	0	39	2	1	1	1		.50	10	.214	.278	.308
1995 Philadelphia	NL	1	1	0	0	0	0	0	0	0	0	0	1	0	0	0	0	0	.00	0	.000	.000	.000
1996 Philadelphia	NL	6	16	4	0	0	0	4	0	2	1	1	6	0	0	0	0	0	.00	0	.250	.333	.250
8 Min. YEARS		500	1579	373	60	4	21	504	163	191	139	4	252	17	19	13	4	8	.33	48	.236	.303	.319
2 Maj. YEARS		7	17	4	0	0	0	4	0	1	2	1	7	0	0	0	0	0	.00	0	.235	.316	.235

Joel Bennett

Pitches: Right Bats: Right Pos: P   Ht: 6'1" Wt: 160 Born: 1/31/70 Age: 28

Year Team	Lg Org	G	GS	CG	GF	IP	BFP	H	R	ER	HR	SH	SF	HB	TBB	IBB	SO	WP	Bk	W	L	Pct.	ShO	Sv	ERA
1991 Red Sox	R Bos	2	2	0	0	10	38	6	2	2	0	0	1	0	4	0	8	2	1	0	0	.000	0	0	1.80
Elmira	A- Bos	13	12	1	0	81	325	60	29	22	3	3	1	6	30	0	75	7	0	5	3	.625	1	0	2.44
1992 Winter Havn	A+ Bos	26	26	4	0	161.2	690	161	86	76	7	7	5	7	55	2	154	7	3	7	11	.389	0	0	4.23
1993 Lynchburg	A+ Bos	29	29	3	0	181	754	151	93	77	7	7	9	4	67	6	221	18	0	7	12	.368	1	0	3.83

Year Team	Lg Org	G	GS	CG	GF	IP	BFP	H	R	ER	HR	SH	SF	HB	TBB	IBB	SO	WP	Bk	W	L	Pct.	ShO	Sv	ERA
		HOW MUCH HE PITCHED						WHAT HE GAVE UP												THE RESULTS					
1994 New Britain	AA Bos	23	23	1	0	130.2	560	119	65	59	9	2	2	4	56	0	130	10	0	11	7	.611	1	0	4.06
Pawtucket	AAA Bos	4	4	0	0	21	91	19	16	16	8	0	0	1	12	0	24	1	0	1	3	.250	0	0	6.86
1995 Pawtucket	AAA Bos	20	13	0	2	77	357	91	57	50	6	0	4	3	45	3	50	6	0	2	4	.333	0	0	5.84
1996 Trenton	AA Bos	3	0	0	1	4.1	18	3	4	4	2	0	0	0	2	0	8	0	0	1	0	1.000	0	0	8.31
Newburgh	IND —	9	9	2	0	57	211	18	8	5	2	0	1	2	16	0	82	3	0	6	0	1.000	2	0	0.79
Bowie	AA Bal	10	8	0	0	54.2	211	36	21	20	5	0	0	1	17	0	48	0	0	2	3	.400	0	0	3.29
1997 Bowie	AA Bal	44	10	0	12	113.1	461	89	45	40	12	6	3	4	40	6	146	2	1	6	8	.429	0	4	3.18
7 Min. YEARS		183	136	11	15	891.2	3716	753	426	371	71	25	26	33	344	17	946	56	5	48	51	.485	5	4	3.74

Kris Benson

Pitches: Right **Bats:** Right **Pos:** P **Ht:** 6'4" **Wt:** 190 **Born:** 11/7/74 **Age:** 23

Year Team	Lg Org	G	GS	CG	GF	IP	BFP	H	R	ER	HR	SH	SF	HB	TBB	IBB	SO	WP	Bk	W	L	Pct.	ShO	Sv	ERA
		HOW MUCH HE PITCHED						WHAT HE GAVE UP												THE RESULTS					
1997 Lynchburg	A+ Pit	10	10	0	0	59.1	241	49	20	17	1	3	1	2	13	0	72	3	1	5	2	.714	0	0	2.58
Carolina	AA Pit	14	14	0	0	68.2	316	81	49	38	11	0	2	2	32	1	66	2	0	3	5	.375	0	0	4.98
1 Min. YEARS		24	24	0	0	128	557	130	69	55	12	3	3	4	45	1	138	5	1	8	7	.533	0	0	3.87

Jacob Benz

Pitches: Left **Bats:** Left **Pos:** P **Ht:** 5'9" **Wt:** 162 **Born:** 2/27/72 **Age:** 26

Year Team	Lg Org	G	GS	CG	GF	IP	BFP	H	R	ER	HR	SH	SF	HB	TBB	IBB	SO	WP	Bk	W	L	Pct.	ShO	Sv	ERA
		HOW MUCH HE PITCHED						WHAT HE GAVE UP												THE RESULTS					
1994 Vermont	A- Mon	28	0	0	12	46	188	24	11	8	1	1	2	4	19	3	36	1	0	4	1	.800	0	3	1.57
1995 Wst Plm Bch	A+ Mon	44	0	0	38	54	220	44	13	7	0	3	2	3	18	3	48	4	1	0	2	.000	0	22	1.17
1996 Harrisburg	AA Mon	34	0	0	20	37.2	181	42	30	25	7	3	2	2	27	3	25	4	0	1	4	.200	0	4	5.97
Wst Plm Bch	A+ Mon	17	0	0	9	20.1	93	19	10	5	0	4	0	0	11	1	14	7	0	2	4	.333	0	2	2.21
1997 Wst Plm Bch	A+ Mon	14	0	0	3	24	94	18	9	7	1	1	1	2	6	0	28	3	0	0	2	.000	0	2	2.63
Harrisburg	AA Mon	23	0	0	9	38.2	168	39	12	10	0	3	1	1	20	0	36	4	0	4	1	.800	0	2	2.33
4 Min. YEARS		160	0	0	91	220.2	944	186	85	62	9	15	8	12	101	10	187	23	1	11	14	.440	0	33	2.53

Dave Berg

Bats: Right **Throws:** Right **Pos:** SS **Ht:** 5'11" **Wt:** 185 **Born:** 9/3/70 **Age:** 27

Year Team	Lg Org	G	AB	H	2B	3B	HR	TB	R	RBI	TBB	IBB	SO	HBP	SH	SF	SB	CS	SB%	GDP	Avg	OBP	SLG
		BATTING															BASERUNNING				PERCENTAGES		
1993 Elmira	A- Fla	75	281	74	13	1	4	101	37	28	35	1	37	8	4	3	6	4	.60	8	.263	.358	.359
1994 Kane County	A Fla	121	437	117	27	4	9	187	80	53	54	0	80	8	15	6	8	6	.57	10	.268	.354	.428
1995 Brevard Cty	A+ Fla	114	382	114	18	1	3	143	71	39	68	1	61	8	7	9	9	4	.69	5	.298	.407	.374
1996 Portland	AA Fla	109	414	125	28	5	9	190	64	73	42	1	60	5	8	6	17	7	.71	10	.302	.368	.459
1997 Charlotte	AAA Fla	117	424	125	26	6	9	190	76	47	55	1	71	3	10	3	16	7	.70	13	.295	.377	.448
5 Min. YEARS		536	1938	555	112	21	34	811	328	240	254	4	309	32	44	27	56	28	.67	46	.286	.374	.418

Steve Bernhardt

Bats: Right **Throws:** Right **Pos:** 2B **Ht:** 6'0" **Wt:** 180 **Born:** 10/9/70 **Age:** 27

Year Team	Lg Org	G	AB	H	2B	3B	HR	TB	R	RBI	TBB	IBB	SO	HBP	SH	SF	SB	CS	SB%	GDP	Avg	OBP	SLG
		BATTING															BASERUNNING				PERCENTAGES		
1993 Bend	A- Col	54	162	31	7	0	1	41	16	9	19	1	24	2	3	2	5	3	.63	1	.191	.281	.253
1994 Central Val	A+ Col	68	204	52	9	0	0	61	23	14	23	0	21	0	3	1	1	3	.25	3	.255	.329	.299
1995 Salem	A+ Col	59	180	39	3	2	4	58	18	16	8	0	38	5	5	2	2	3	.40	5	.217	.267	.322
1996 Salem	A+ Col	63	203	61	12	2	1	80	17	19	12	0	23	2	5	1	4	4	.50	4	.300	.344	.394
New Haven	AA Col	32	84	24	3	0	0	27	5	10	4	1	14	2	1	2	0	2	.00	1	.286	.326	.321
1997 New Haven	AA Col	101	315	67	14	0	6	99	35	38	27	0	46	3	8	5	2	2	.50	5	.213	.277	.314
5 Min. YEARS		377	1148	274	48	4	12	366	114	106	93	2	166	14	25	13	14	17	.45	19	.239	.300	.319

Mike Berry

Bats: Right **Throws:** Right **Pos:** 3B **Ht:** 5'10" **Wt:** 185 **Born:** 8/12/70 **Age:** 27

Year Team	Lg Org	G	AB	H	2B	3B	HR	TB	R	RBI	TBB	IBB	SO	HBP	SH	SF	SB	CS	SB%	GDP	Avg	OBP	SLG
		BATTING															BASERUNNING				PERCENTAGES		
1993 Burlington	A Mon	31	92	22	2	0	1	27	15	6	20	0	22	0	3	0	0	0	.00	0	.239	.375	.293
1994 Burlington	A Mon	94	334	105	18	1	10	155	67	45	53	0	59	1	1	1	7	3	.70	7	.314	.409	.464
1995 Wst Plm Bch	A+ Mon	24	79	13	3	1	1	21	16	2	13	0	16	0	0	0	0	1	.00	1	.165	.283	.266
Visalia	A+ Mon	98	368	113	28	4	9	176	69	61	57	1	70	5	1	3	12	6	.67	9	.307	.404	.478
1996 Frederick	A+ Bal	3	8	1	0	0	0	1	4	2	1	4	0	2	0	0	0	0	.00	1	.125	.417	.500
Bowie	AA Bal	2	7	1	0	0	0	1	1	2	0	0	4	0	0	1	0	0	.00	0	.143	.125	.143
High Desert	A+ Bal	121	463	167	44	5	13	260	109	113	99	3	67	7	0	3	7	4	.64	9	.361	.477	.562
1997 Bowie	AA Bal	53	204	47	10	0	8	81	34	30	24	0	53	3	1	2	1	1	.50	6	.230	.318	.397
Rochester	AAA Bal	54	177	53	11	3	1	73	23	19	13	0	31	1	0	1	1	1	.50	4	.299	.349	.412
5 Min. YEARS		480	1732	522	116	14	44	798	336	279	283	4	324	17	6	11	28	17	.62	41	.301	.402	.461

Andres Berumen

Pitches: Right **Bats:** Right **Pos:** P **Ht:** 6'2" **Wt:** 205 **Born:** 4/5/71 **Age:** 27

Year Team	Lg Org	G	GS	CG	GF	IP	BFP	H	R	ER	HR	SH	SF	HB	TBB	IBB	SO	WP	Bk	W	L	Pct.	ShO	Sv	ERA
		HOW MUCH HE PITCHED						WHAT HE GAVE UP												THE RESULTS					
1989 Royals	R KC	12	10	0	0	49	223	57	29	26	2	2	2	4	17	1	24	6	0	2	4	.333	0	0	4.78
1990 Royals	R KC	5	4	0	1	22.2	95	24	9	6	0	0	1	0	8	1	18	0	0	0	2	.000	0	1	2.38
Baseball Cy	A+ KC	9	9	1	0	44	197	30	27	21	0	2	5	4	28	0	35	2	1	3	5	.375	1	0	4.30

Year Team	Lg Org	G	GS	CG	GF	IP	BFP	H	R	ER	HR	SH	SF	HB	TBB	IBB	SO	WP	Bk	W	L	Pct.	ShO	Sv	ERA
1991 Baseball Cy	A+ KC	7	7	0	0	37	161	34	18	17	0	1	0	4	18	0	24	5	0	0	5	.000	0	0	4.14
Appleton	A KC	13	13	0	0	56.1	254	55	33	22	0	3	4	3	26	0	49	2	1	2	6	.250	0	0	3.51
1992 Appleton	A KC	46	0	0	38	57.2	245	50	25	17	3	1	3	1	23	2	52	3	0	5	2	.714	0	13	2.65
1993 High Desert	A+ Fla	14	13	1	0	92	396	85	45	37	8	0	4	7	36	1	74	6	1	9	2	.818	0	0	3.62
Wichita	AA SD	7	7	0	0	26.2	120	35	17	17	2	1	1	1	11	2	17	3	0	3	1	.750	0	0	5.74
1994 Las Vegas	AAA SD	43	6	0	14	75.2	375	93	70	55	5	2	2	5	57	1	49	6	1	4	7	.364	0	1	6.54
1995 Las Vegas	AAA SD	3	0	0	0	3.1	16	4	2	2	0	0	0	1	2	0	3	0	0	0	0	.000	0	0	5.40
Rancho Cuca	A+ SD	4	0	0	1	7.1	28	6	2	2	1	0	0	0	1	0	11	0	0	0	0	.000	0	1	2.45
1996 Las Vegas	AAA SD	50	0	0	20	70.2	342	73	53	48	4	4	3	6	58	9	59	17	0	4	7	.364	0	0	6.11
1997 Las Vegas	AAA SD	18	1	0	2	33	164	49	26	20	2	0	0	1	16	1	35	6	0	2	0	1.000	0	0	5.45
Tacoma	AAA Sea	16	15	0	0	80.2	363	78	45	42	11	2	1	6	48	0	79	7	2	7	4	.636	0	0	4.69
1995 San Diego	NL	37	0	0	17	44.1	207	37	29	28	3	1	3	3	36	3	42	6	0	2	3	.400	0	1	5.68
1996 San Diego	NL	3	0	0	1	3.1	16	3	2	2	1	0	0	1	2	1	4	0	0	0	0	.000	0	0	5.40
9 Min. YEARS		247	85	2	76	656	2979	673	401	332	38	18	26	43	349	18	529	63	6	41	45	.477	1	17	4.55
2 Maj. YEARS		40	0	0	18	47.2	223	40	31	30	4	1	3	4	38	4	46	6	0	2	3	.400	0	1	5.66

Johnny Bess

Bats: Both Throws: Right Pos: C Ht: 6'1" Wt: 190 Born: 4/6/70 Age: 28

Year Team	Lg Org	G	AB	H	2B	3B	HR	TB	R	RBI	TBB	IBB	SO	HBP	SH	SF	SB	CS	SB%	GDP	Avg	OBP	SLG
1992 Princeton	R+ Cin	48	173	36	9	1	2	53	22	21	15	2	55	4	1	0	3	2	.60	0	.208	.286	.306
1993 Winston-Sal	A+ Cin	11	33	8	0	0	2	14	4	7	6	1	7	0	0	0	2	1	.67	0	.242	.359	.424
Chston-WV	A Cin	106	358	82	16	7	5	127	35	67	47	2	107	6	2	2	10	5	.67	4	.229	.327	.355
1994 Winston-Sal	A+ Cin	58	186	56	7	0	8	87	41	29	34	1	51	2	3	2	8	6	.57	1	.301	.411	.468
Chattanooga	AA Cin	37	103	21	5	1	0	28	9	9	13	0	34	2	2	2	1	1	.50	1	.204	.300	.272
1995 Winston-Sal	A+ Cin	88	246	46	10	2	4	72	35	21	30	4	83	8	2	0	12	4	.75	4	.187	.296	.293
Indianapolis	AAA Cin	2	5	0	0	0	0	0	0	0	0	0	2	0	0	0	0	0	.00	0	.000	.000	.000
1996 Burlington	A SF	15	43	6	1	0	3	16	5	11	10	0	12	2	0	0	0	1	.00	0	.140	.327	.372
Shreveport	AA SF	57	175	43	10	3	7	80	25	30	19	1	63	2	1	3	1	1	.50	1	.246	.322	.457
1997 San Jose	A+ SF	44	155	37	9	1	5	63	29	26	15	2	41	2	1	2	4	2	.67	3	.239	.310	.406
Shreveport	AA SF	12	28	4	3	0	0	7	1	6	3	0	5	1	0	0	0	0	.00	2	.143	.250	.250
Wst Plm Bch	A+ Mon	23	62	9	0	0	0	9	2	2	3	1	21	0	0	1	1	1	.50	0	.145	.185	.145
6 Min. YEARS		501	1567	348	70	15	36	556	208	229	195	14	481	29	13	11	42	24	.64	16	.222	.317	.355

Randy Betten

Bats: Right Throws: Right Pos: OF Ht: 5'11" Wt: 170 Born: 7/28/71 Age: 26

Year Team	Lg Org	G	AB	H	2B	3B	HR	TB	R	RBI	TBB	IBB	SO	HBP	SH	SF	SB	CS	SB%	GDP	Avg	OBP	SLG
1995 Boise	A- Ana	2	8	3	0	0	0	3	2	2	1	0	2	0	0	0	0	0	.00	0	.375	.444	.375
Cedar Rapds	A Ana	36	60	14	2	0	0	16	8	4	13	0	8	0	0	1	6	2	.75	0	.233	.365	.267
1996 Lk Elsinore	A+ Ana	74	274	71	15	3	3	101	32	34	22	1	49	3	3	1	11	3	.79	6	.259	.320	.369
Midland	AA Ana	28	82	14	2	0	0	16	5	5	5	0	19	0	1	0	3	1	.75	2	.171	.218	.195
1997 Lk Elsinore	A+ Ana	35	116	40	5	2	2	55	18	27	16	1	29	3	4	0	7	5	.58	1	.345	.437	.474
Midland	AA Ana	57	220	64	13	3	3	92	39	24	22	0	45	1	4	1	7	3	.70	5	.291	.357	.418
Vancouver	AAA Ana	23	61	17	4	0	1	24	9	12	7	0	21	0	3	0	1	1	.50	1	.279	.353	.393
3 Min. YEARS		255	821	223	41	8	9	307	113	108	86	2	173	7	15	3	35	15	.70	15	.272	.345	.374

Rick Betti

Pitches: Left Bats: Right Pos: P Ht: 5'11" Wt: 170 Born: 9/16/73 Age: 24

Year Team	Lg Org	G	GS	CG	GF	IP	BFP	H	R	ER	HR	SH	SF	HB	TBB	IBB	SO	WP	Bk	W	L	Pct.	ShO	Sv	ERA
1993 Braves	R Atl	9	2	0	5	20.1	78	10	5	2	1	0	0	1	8	0	27	1	0	1	0	1.000	0	0	0.89
Danville	R+ Atl	11	5	0	1	34.1	140	20	13	8	0	0	1	2	19	0	28	1	0	2	1	.667	0	0	2.10
1995 Red Sox	R Bos	3	1	0	2	7.1	30	7	3	2	0	0	0	1	3	0	13	1	0	1	0	1.000	0	1	2.45
Utica	A- Bos	12	0	0	5	17.2	65	9	2	2	1	0	0	0	2	0	25	1	0	2	1	.667	0	2	1.02
Michigan	A Bos	1	0	0	0	2	7	0	0	0	0	0	0	0	1	0	1	0	0	0	0	.000	0	0	0.00
1996 Sarasota	A+ Bos	13	0	0	13	15.2	70	13	6	5	0	0	1	3	7	2	21	0	0	0	2	.000	0	7	2.87
Trenton	AA Bos	31	8	0	10	81	361	70	39	33	7	2	1	3	44	5	65	5	0	9	1	.900	0	1	3.67
1997 Red Sox	R Bos	4	0	0	3	9	31	4	1	1	0	0	0	1	0	0	14	0	0	1	0	1.000	0	0	1.00
Trenton	AA Bos	30	0	0	14	39.2	179	42	29	28	7	1	1	3	17	0	30	3	0	2	0	1.000	0	3	6.35
4 Min. YEARS		114	16	0	53	227	961	175	98	81	16	3	4	14	101	7	224	12	0	18	5	.783	0	16	3.21

Todd Betts

Bats: Left Throws: Right Pos: 3B Ht: 6'0" Wt: 190 Born: 6/24/73 Age: 25

Year Team	Lg Org	G	AB	H	2B	3B	HR	TB	R	RBI	TBB	IBB	SO	HBP	SH	SF	SB	CS	SB%	GDP	Avg	OBP	SLG
1993 Burlington	R+ Cle	56	168	39	9	0	7	69	40	27	32	2	26	3	0	1	6	1	.86	4	.232	.363	.411
1994 Watertown	A- Cle	65	227	74	18	2	10	126	49	53	54	2	29	4	1	2	3	2	.60	1	.326	.460	.555
1995 Kinston	A+ Cle	109	331	90	15	3	9	138	52	44	88	2	56	6	1	4	2	3	.40	5	.272	.429	.417
1996 Canton-Akrn	AA Cle	77	238	60	13	0	1	76	35	26	38	2	51	5	0	4	0	1	.00	6	.252	.361	.319
1997 Akron	AA Cle	128	439	108	25	1	20	195	65	69	73	8	97	4	1	5	1	3	.25	6	.246	.355	.444
5 Min. YEARS		435	1403	371	80	6	47	604	241	219	285	16	259	22	3	16	12	10	.55	22	.264	.393	.431

Jim Betzsold

Bats: Right Throws: Right Pos: OF Ht: 6'3" Wt: 210 Born: 8/7/72 Age: 25

							BATTING											BASERUNNING				PERCENTAGES		
Year Team	Lg Org	G	AB	H	2B	3B	HR	TB	R	RBI	TBB	IBB	SO	HBP	SH	SF	SB	CS	SB%	GDP	Avg	OBP	SLG
1994 Watertown	A- Cle	66	212	61	18	0	12	115	48	46	53	1	68	15	1	2	3	3	.50	2	.288	.457	.542
1995 Kinston	A+ Cle	126	455	122	22	2	25	223	77	71	55	3	137	10	0	4	3	5	.38	4	.268	.357	.490
1996 Canton-Akm	AA Cle	84	268	64	11	5	3	94	35	35	30	1	74	6	1	1	4	1	.80	3	.239	.328	.351
1997 Akron	AA Cle	118	434	115	21	5	19	203	76	79	60	2	119	10	0	2	4	5	.44	12	.265	.366	.468
4 Min. YEARS		394	1369	362	72	12	59	635	236	231	198	7	398	41	2	9	14	14	.50	21	.264	.372	.464

Jay Beverlin

Pitches: Right Bats: Left Pos: P Ht: 6'5" Wt: 230 Born: 11/27/73 Age: 24

				HOW MUCH HE PITCHED					WHAT HE GAVE UP										THE RESULTS					
Year Team	Lg Org	G	GS	CG	GF	IP	BFP	H	R	ER	HR	SH	SF	HB	TBB	IBB	SO	WP	Bk	W	L	Pct.	ShO	Sv	ERA
1994 W Michigan	A Oak	17	1	0	5	41	168	32	12	8	0	1	0	2	14	0	48	3	4	3	2	.600	0	1	1.76
1995 W Michigan	A Oak	22	14	0	1	89	392	76	51	40	4	3	3	8	40	0	84	5	5	3	9	.250	0	0	4.04
Greensboro	A NYA	7	7	1	0	51	198	49	15	15	1	0	0	0	6	0	31	4	0	2	4	.333	1	0	2.65
1996 Norwich	AA NYA	16	0	0	1	16	81	25	21	15	2	0	2	0	6	1	17	0	0	0	3	.000	0	0	8.44
Tampa	A+ NYA	25	1	0	6	46.1	194	43	22	18	5	1	1	1	17	2	38	4	1	1	0	1.000	0	0	3.50
1997 Norwich	AA NYA	25	0	0	8	41.2	203	50	38	36	10	0	0	6	24	0	42	3	0	1	0	1.000	0	0	7.78
Tampa	A+ NYA	7	6	0	0	41.1	167	37	26	22	4	2	2	4	13	1	24	6	0	1	3	.250	0	0	4.79
4 Min. YEARS		111	33	1	21	326.1	1403	312	185	154	26	7	8	21	120	4	284	25	10	12	21	.364	1	2	4.25

Kurt Bierek

Bats: Left Throws: Right Pos: OF Ht: 6'4" Wt: 200 Born: 9/13/72 Age: 25

							BATTING											BASERUNNING				PERCENTAGES		
Year Team	Lg Org	G	AB	H	2B	3B	HR	TB	R	RBI	TBB	IBB	SO	HBP	SH	SF	SB	CS	SB%	GDP	Avg	OBP	SLG
1993 Oneonta	A- NYA	70	274	64	6	6	5	97	36	37	19	2	49	3	1		4	4	.50	4	.234	.290	.354
1994 Greensboro	A NYA	133	467	118	24	6	14	196	78	73	69	2	101	8	2	3	8	1	.89	10	.253	.356	.420
1995 Tampa	A+ NYA	126	447	111	16	2	4	143	60	53	61	3	73	4	2	2	3	4	.43	11	.248	.342	.320
1996 Tampa	A+ NYA	88	320	97	14	2	11	148	48	55	41	3	40	6	0	3	6	3	.67	5	.303	.389	.463
1997 Norwich	AA NYA	133	473	128	32	2	18	218	77	78	56	2	89	7	0	2	4	4	.50	8	.271	.355	.461
5 Min. YEARS		550	1981	518	92	18	52	802	299	296	246	12	352	28	5	11	25	16	.61	38	.261	.350	.405

Ty Bilderback

Bats: Left Throws: Left Pos: OF-DH Ht: 6'2" Wt: 180 Born: 10/29/73 Age: 24

							BATTING											BASERUNNING				PERCENTAGES		
Year Team	Lg Org	G	AB	H	2B	3B	HR	TB	R	RBI	TBB	IBB	SO	HBP	SH	SF	SB	CS	SB%	GDP	Avg	OBP	SLG
1995 Boise	A- Ana	61	177	57	11	2	3	81	35	25	29	0	29	3	0	1	10	5	.67	4	.322	.424	.458
1996 Lk Elsinore	A+ Ana	42	150	40	10	0	3	59	21	22	17	1	38	4	0	1	4	2	.67	1	.267	.355	.393
1997 Lk Elsinore	A+ Ana	62	209	66	13	3	2	91	38	30	36	2	42	4	0	1	11	5	.69	4	.316	.424	.435
Midland	AA Ana	21	66	15	5	0	0	20	7	5	6	1	17	0	0	0	1	3	.25	2	.227	.292	.303
3 Min. YEARS		186	602	178	39	5	8	251	101	82	88	4	126	11	0	3	26	15	.63	9	.296	.393	.417

Brian Blair

Bats: Left Throws: Left Pos: OF Ht: 6'0" Wt: 180 Born: 4/9/72 Age: 26

							BATTING											BASERUNNING				PERCENTAGES		
Year Team	Lg Org	G	AB	H	2B	3B	HR	TB	R	RBI	TBB	IBB	SO	HBP	SH	SF	SB	CS	SB%	GDP	Avg	OBP	SLG
1993 Erie	A- Tex	65	233	58	11	2	5	88	33	26	24	0	47	5	2	3	11	4	.73	4	.249	.328	.378
1994 Chston-SC	A Tex	121	411	102	21	4	7	144	65	38	53	1	90	3	2	1	30	8	.79	7	.248	.335	.350
1995 Charlotte	A+ Tex	69	264	59	5	3	0	70	34	9	34	3	42	1	2	1	14	6	.70	4	.223	.313	.265
1996 Tulsa	AA Tex	113	379	93	28	3	3	136	47	29	45	2	86	2	6	1	7	8	.47	6	.245	.328	.359
1997 Tulsa	AA Tex	86	260	68	9	3	4	95	46	28	49	2	64	1	1	3	11	2	.85	4	.262	.377	.365
5 Min. YEARS		454	1547	380	74	11	19	533	225	130	205	8	329	12	13	12	73	28	.72	25	.246	.336	.345

Mike Blais

Pitches: Right Bats: Right Pos: P Ht: 6'5" Wt: 226 Born: 10/2/71 Age: 26

				HOW MUCH HE PITCHED					WHAT HE GAVE UP										THE RESULTS					
Year Team	Lg Org	G	GS	CG	GF	IP	BFP	H	R	ER	HR	SH	SF	HB	TBB	IBB	SO	WP	Bk	W	L	Pct.	ShO	Sv	ERA
1993 Red Sox	R Bos	22	0	0	17	26	99	15	6	4	0	1	2	2	8	0	22	2	0	3	1	.750	0	4	1.38
Ft. Laud	A+ Bos	3	0	0	3	6	26	4	1	1	0	1	0	0	3	1	7	0	0	1	1	.500	0	0	1.50
1994 Lynchburg	A+ Bos	25	10	0	6	77.1	354	99	66	57	12	2	2	1	18	0	46	3	1	1	6	.143	0	1	6.63
1995 Michigan	A Bos	32	0	0	26	46	184	34	12	10	0	3	4	1	11	3	35	4	0	2	1	.667	0	10	1.96
Trenton	AA Bos	13	0	0	7	25	96	19	8	7	1	1	2	1	7	0	20	0	0	2	0	1.000	0	0	2.52
1996 Trenton	AA Bos	53	0	0	27	77.2	323	74	37	34	10	5	1	2	23	4	52	3	0	10	3	.769	0	5	3.94
1997 Pawtucket	AAA Bos	10	0	0	7	13	64	10	15	12	3	2	0	3	10	1	10	3	0	1	4	.200	0	0	8.31
Red Sox	R Bos	3	1	0	2	5	17	2	0	0	0	0	0	0	0	0	5	0	0	1	0	1.000	0	0	0.00
Trenton	AA Bos	18	0	0	14	21.2	104	26	11	8	1	0	0	1	12	0	14	4	0	2	0	1.000	0	5	3.32
5 Min. YEARS		179	11	0	109	297.2	1267	283	156	133	27	15	11	11	92	9	211	19	1	23	16	.590	0	25	4.02

Alberto Blanco

Pitches: Left Bats: Left Pos: P Ht: 6'1" Wt: 170 Born: 6/27/76 Age: 22

				HOW MUCH HE PITCHED					WHAT HE GAVE UP										THE RESULTS					
Year Team	Lg Org	G	GS	CG	GF	IP	BFP	H	R	ER	HR	SH	SF	HB	TBB	IBB	SO	WP	Bk	W	L	Pct.	ShO	Sv	ERA
1993 Astros	R Hou	9	1	0	1	18	80	15	4	4	0	0	1	1	11	0	32	2	0	0	1	.000	0	1	2.00
1994 Quad City	A Hou	27	19	0	3	117	520	118	70	61	13	4	4	5	66	0	101	11	3	7	9	.438	0	0	4.69

Year Team	Lg Org	HOW MUCH HE PITCHED G GS CG GF	IP	BFP	WHAT HE GAVE UP H R ER HR SH SF HB	TBB IBB SO WP Bk	THE RESULTS W L Pct. ShO Sv ERA
1995 Quad City	A Hou	11 11 1 0	54.2	231	47 22 19 2 0 3 1	19 0 58 3 0	3 3 .500 1 0 3.13
1996 Quad City	A Hou	11 11 0 0	46.2	198	42 25 18 3 0 2 3	15 0 58 3 0	2 2 .500 0 0 3.47
1997 Jackson	AA Hou	1 1 0 0	7	30	5 2 2 1 0 0 1	3 0 4 0 0	1 0 1.000 0 0 2.57
Astros	R Hou	2 2 0 0	5	19	1 0 0 0 0 0 1	1 0 11 0 0	0 0 .000 0 0 0.00
Kissimmee	A+ Hou	19 19 1 0	114.1	467	83 45 36 4 5 4 11	45 0 95 6 2	7 4 .636 1 0 2.83
5 Min. YEARS		80 64 2 4	362.2	1545	311 168 140 23 9 14 23	160 0 359 25 5	20 19 .513 2 1 3.47

Nate Bland

Pitches: Left   Bats: Left   Pos: P   **Ht: 6'5"   Wt: 195   Born: 12/27/74   Age: 23**

Year Team	Lg Org	HOW MUCH HE PITCHED G GS CG GF	IP	BFP	WHAT HE GAVE UP H R ER HR SH SF HB	TBB IBB SO WP Bk	THE RESULTS W L Pct. ShO Sv ERA
1993 Yakima	A- LA	16 13 0 1	63.1	272	53 34 20 2 0 1 0	29 1 43 3 1	4 6 .400 0 0 2.84
1994 Great Falls	R+ LA	2 1 0 1	9.1	37	6 2 1 0 1 0 1	3 0 12 1 0	0 0 .000 0 0 0.96
Bakersfield	A+ LA	12 9 0 0	50.1	228	58 31 30 10 3 0 1	27 0 19 2 1	2 6 .250 0 0 5.36
1995 Bakersfield	A+ LA	27 23 0 1	122.1	562	155 89 71 13 5 3 1	55 0 46 12 2	4 9 .308 0 0 5.22
1996 Savannah	A LA	5 5 0 0	27.2	115	24 8 5 0 0 1 1	10 0 24 2 0	1 0 1.000 0 0 1.63
Vero Beach	A+ LA	17 17 0 0	96	414	99 42 33 3 4 2 4	35 0 69 5 0	10 4 .714 0 0 3.09
1997 San Antonio	AA LA	10 8 0 1	41	190	47 34 32 5 3 1 3	24 0 30 3 1	3 2 .600 0 0 7.02
Vero Beach	A+ LA	17 14 0 0	82.2	356	85 35 31 7 4 3 1	38 0 67 5 0	7 7 .500 0 0 3.38
5 Min. YEARS		106 90 0 4	492.2	2174	527 275 223 40 20 11 12	221 1 310 33 5	31 34 .477 0 0 4.07

Ben Blomdahl

Pitches: Right   Bats: Right   Pos: P   **Ht: 6'2"   Wt: 185   Born: 12/30/70   Age: 27**

Year Team	Lg Org	HOW MUCH HE PITCHED G GS CG GF	IP	BFP	WHAT HE GAVE UP H R ER HR SH SF HB	TBB IBB SO WP Bk	THE RESULTS W L Pct. ShO Sv ERA
1991 Niagara Fal	A- Det	16 13 0 2	78.2	344	72 43 39 2 1 3 2	50 0 30 7 6	6 6 .500 0 0 4.46
1992 Fayetteville	A Det	17 17 2 0	103.1	423	94 46 31 5 2 0 4	26 0 65 6 3	10 4 .714 2 0 2.70
Lakeland	A+ Det	10 10 2 0	62	264	77 35 32 3 2 1 3	5 0 41 2 0	5 3 .625 0 0 4.65
1993 London	AA Det	17 17 3 0	119	498	108 58 49 7 4 6 7	42 1 72 4 3	6 6 .500 0 0 3.71
Toledo	AAA Det	11 10 0 0	62.2	264	67 34 34 8 1 4 2	19 0 27 4 0	3 4 .429 0 0 4.88
1994 Toledo	AAA Det	28 28 0 0	165.1	729	192 92 82 18 6 10 7	47 3 83 5 0	11 11 .500 0 0 4.46
1995 Toledo	AAA Det	41 0 0 23	56	232	55 24 22 6 1 1 2	13 4 39 3 0	5 4 .556 0 3 3.54
1996 Toledo	AAA Det	53 0 0 27	59.1	271	77 42 41 9 1 1 1	18 1 34 9 0	2 6 .250 0 2 6.22
1997 Buffalo	AAA Cle	29 13 1 4	104	447	110 64 55 20 1 6 2	31 0 60 1 1	7 8 .467 0 0 4.76
1995 Detroit	AL	14 0 0 5	24.1	115	36 21 21 5 1 0 0	13 0 15 2 0	0 0 .000 0 1 7.77
7 Min. YEARS		222 108 8 56	810.1	3472	852 438 385 78 19 32 30	251 9 451 41 13	55 52 .514 2 5 4.28

Darin Blood

Pitches: Right   Bats: Both   Pos: P   **Ht: 6'2"   Wt: 205   Born: 8/31/74   Age: 23**

Year Team	Lg Org	HOW MUCH HE PITCHED G GS CG GF	IP	BFP	WHAT HE GAVE UP H R ER HR SH SF HB	TBB IBB SO WP Bk	THE RESULTS W L Pct. ShO Sv ERA
1995 Bellingham	A- SF	14 13 0 0	74.1	315	63 26 21 2 4 0 3	32 0 78 6 1	6 3 .667 0 0 2.54
1996 San Jose	A+ SF	27 25 2 0	170	717	140 59 50 4 5 2 10	71 0 193 26 2	17 6 .739 2 0 2.65
1997 Shreveport	AA SF	27 27 0 0	156	698	152 89 75 12 7 8 8	83 0 90 14 2	8 10 .444 0 0 4.33
3 Min. YEARS		68 65 2 0	400.1	1730	355 174 146 18 16 10 21	186 0 361 46 5	31 19 .620 2 0 3.28

Greg Blosser

Bats: Left   Throws: Left   Pos: OF   **Ht: 6'3"   Wt: 215   Born: 6/26/71   Age: 27**

Year Team	Lg Org	BATTING G AB H 2B 3B HR TB R RBI TBB IBB SO HBP SH SF	BASERUNNING SB CS SB% GDP	PERCENTAGES Avg OBP SLG
1989 Red Sox	R Bos	40 146 42 7 3 2 61 17 20 25 1 19 1 0 2	3 0 1.00 7	.288 .391 .418
Winter Havn	A+ Bos	28 94 24 1 1 2 33 6 14 8 0 14 1 0 1	1 0 1.00 1	.255 .317 .351
1990 Lynchburg	A+ Bos	119 447 126 23 1 18 205 63 62 55 3 99 1 0 1	5 4 .56 13	.282 .361 .459
1991 New Britain	AA Bos	134 452 98 21 3 8 149 48 46 63 0 114 1 0 4	9 4 .69 16	.217 .312 .330
1992 New Britain	AA Bos	129 434 105 23 4 22 202 59 71 64 9 122 1 0 7	0 2 .00 7	.242 .339 .465
Pawtucket	AAA Bos	1 0 0 0 0 0 0 1 0 1 0 0 0 0 0	0 0 .00 0	.000 1.000 .000
1993 Pawtucket	AAA Bos	130 478 109 22 2 23 204 66 66 58 5 139 2 1 4	3 3 .50 4	.228 .312 .427
1994 Pawtucket	AAA Bos	97 350 91 21 1 17 165 52 54 44 5 97 0 0 1	11 3 .79 4	.260 .342 .471
1995 Pawtucket	AAA Bos	17 50 10 0 0 1 13 5 4 5 0 13 0 0 1	0 0 .00 0	.200 .268 .260
Trenton	AA Bos	49 179 44 13 0 11 90 25 34 13 0 42 0 1 3	3 2 .60 4	.246 .292 .503
1996 Rochester	AAA Bal	38 115 27 6 1 2 41 11 12 12 0 29 0 0 0	2 1 .67 3	.235 .307 .357
1997 St. Pete	A+ TB	52 189 59 9 2 12 108 40 32 35 5 42 0 0 2	7 9 .44 3	.312 .416 .571
Okla City	AAA TB	54 178 54 11 1 12 103 33 27 27 0 46 0 0 2	6 2 .75 2	.303 .391 .579
1993 Boston	AL	17 28 2 1 0 0 3 1 1 2 0 7 0 0 0	1 0 1.00 0	.071 .133 .107
1994 Boston	AL	5 11 1 0 0 0 1 2 1 4 0 4 0 0 0	0 0 .00 0	.091 .333 .091
9 Min. YEARS		888 3112 789 157 19 130 1374 426 442 410 28 776 7 2 24	50 30 .63 69	.254 .339 .442
2 Maj. YEARS		22 39 3 1 0 0 4 3 2 6 0 11 0 0 0	1 0 1.00 0	.077 .200 .103

Geoff Blum

Bats: Both   Throws: Right   Pos: 2B   **Ht: 6'3"   Wt: 193   Born: 4/26/73   Age: 25**

Year Team	Lg Org	BATTING G AB H 2B 3B HR TB R RBI TBB IBB SO HBP SH SF	BASERUNNING SB CS SB% GDP	PERCENTAGES Avg OBP SLG
1994 Vermont	A- Mon	63 241 83 15 1 3 109 48 38 33 0 21 3 1 1	5 5 .50 4	.344 .428 .452
1995 Wst Plm Bch	A+ Mon	125 457 120 20 2 1 147 54 62 34 1 61 3 1 7	6 5 .55 12	.263 .313 .322
1996 Harrisburg	AA Mon	120 396 95 22 2 1 124 47 41 59 2 51 3 11 3	6 7 .46 11	.240 .341 .313

23

		BATTING															BASERUNNING				PERCENTAGES		
Year Team	Lg Org	G	AB	H	2B	3B	HR	TB	R	RBI	TBB	IBB	SO	HBP	SH	SF	SB	CS	SB%	GDP	Avg	OBP	SLG
1997 Ottawa	AAA Mon	118	407	101	21	2	3	135	59	35	52	1	73	3	12	6	14	6	.70	6	.248	.333	.332
4 Min. YEARS		426	1501	399	78	7	8	515	208	176	178	4	206	12	25	17	31	23	.57	33	.266	.345	.343

Hiram Bocachica

Bats: Right **Throws:** Right **Pos:** SS   **Ht:** 5'11" **Wt:** 165 **Born:** 3/4/76 **Age:** 22

		BATTING															BASERUNNING				PERCENTAGES		
Year Team	Lg Org	G	AB	H	2B	3B	HR	TB	R	RBI	TBB	IBB	SO	HBP	SH	SF	SB	CS	SB%	GDP	Avg	OBP	SLG
1994 Expos	R Mon	43	168	47	9	0	5	71	31	16	15	0	42	2	2	0	11	4	.73	1	.280	.346	.423
1995 Albany	A Mon	96	380	108	20	10	2	154	65	30	52	3	78	3	3	1	47	17	.73	4	.284	.381	.405
1996 Expos	R Mon	9	32	8	3	0	0	11	11	2	5	1	3	1	0	0	2	1	.67	0	.250	.368	.344
Wst Plm Bch	A+ Mon	71	267	90	17	5	2	123	50	26	34	0	47	6	3	3	21	3	.88	6	.337	.419	.461
1997 Harrisburg	AA Mon	119	443	123	19	3	11	181	82	35	41	1	98	13	1	3	29	12	.71	3	.278	.354	.409
4 Min. YEARS		338	1290	376	68	18	20	540	239	109	147	5	268	30	9	7	110	37	.75	14	.291	.375	.419

Joe Boever

Pitches: Right **Bats:** Right **Pos:** P   **Ht:** 6'1" **Wt:** 205 **Born:** 10/4/60 **Age:** 37

		HOW MUCH HE PITCHED						WHAT HE GAVE UP										THE RESULTS					
Year Team	Lg Org	G	GS	CG	GF	IP	BFP	H	R	ER	HR	SH	SF	HB	TBB	IBB	SO	WP	Bk	W	L	Pct.	ShO	Sv	ERA
1982 Erie	A- StL	19	0	0	19	32.2	—	20	8	7	0	—	—	1	12	5	63	0	0	2	3	.400	0	9	1.93
Springfield	A StL	3	0	0	1	4	—	3	1	1	0	—	—	0	2	0	7	0	0	0	0	.000	0	0	2.25
St. Pete	A+ StL	53	0	0	46	80.1	—	61	29	27	2	—	—	3	37	12	57	1	1	5	6	.455	0	26	3.02
1984 Arkansas	AA StL	8	0	0	8	11	56	10	11	10	1	0	0	0	12	0	12	1	0	0	1	.000	0	3	8.18
St. Pete	A+ StL	48	0	0	38	77.2	325	52	31	26	2	1	2	1	45	5	81	1	1	6	4	.600	0	14	3.01
1985 Arkansas	AA StL	27	0	0	20	37.2	151	21	5	5	1	3	1	0	23	4	45	2	0	3	1	.750	0	1	1.19
Louisville	AAA StL	21	0	0	13	35.1	156	28	11	8	0	0	1	0	22	0	37	3	1	3	2	.600	0	1	2.04
1986 Louisville	AAA StL	51	0	0	26	88	375	71	25	22	1	7	5	2	48	6	75	10	1	4	5	.444	0	5	2.25
1987 Louisville	AAA StL	43	0	0	36	59	263	52	22	22	7	1	3	1	27	2	79	1	0	3	2	.600	0	21	3.36
Richmond	AAA Atl	6	0	0	4	9	38	8	1	1	0	0	0	1	4	1	8	0	0	1	0	1.000	0	1	1.00
1988 Richmond	AAA Atl	48	0	0	43	71.1	279	47	17	17	5	2	2	1	22	4	71	2	3	6	3	.667	0	22	2.14
1996 Carolina	AA Pit	1	0	0	1	1	3	0	0	0	0	0	0	0	0	0	1	0	0	0	0	.000	0	0	0.00
Calgary	AAA Pit	44	0	0	12	83.2	341	78	24	20	1	5	0	0	19	2	66	2	0	12	1	.923	0	4	2.15
1997 Calgary	AAA Pit	36	0	0	31	46.2	217	59	28	26	5	1	2	0	19	3	55	2	0	4	5	.444	0	8	5.01
Edmonton	AAA Oak	17	3	0	5	45.1	191	53	26	25	8	0	5	0	4	0	26	0	0	6	3	.667	0	1	4.96
1985 St. Louis	NL	13	0	0	5	16.1	69	17	8	8	3	1	1	0	4	1	20	1	0	0	0	.000	0	0	4.41
1986 St. Louis	NL	11	0	0	4	21.2	93	19	5	4	2	0	0	0	11	0	8	1	0	0	1	.000	0	0	1.66
1987 Atlanta	NL	14	0	0	10	18.1	93	29	15	15	4	1	1	0	12	1	18	1	0	1	0	1.000	0	0	7.36
1988 Atlanta	NL	16	0	0	13	20.1	70	12	4	4	1	2	0	1	1	0	7	0	0	0	2	.000	0	1	1.77
1989 Atlanta	NL	66	0	0	53	82.1	349	78	37	36	6	5	0	1	34	5	68	5	0	4	11	.267	0	21	3.94
1990 Atlanta	NL	33	0	0	21	42.1	198	40	23	22	6	2	2	0	35	10	35	2	0	1	3	.250	0	8	4.68
Philadelphia	NL	34	0	0	13	46	190	37	12	11	0	2	0	0	16	2	40	1	2	2	3	.400	0	6	2.15
1991 Philadelphia	NL	68	0	0	27	98.1	431	90	45	42	10	3	6	0	54	11	89	6	1	3	5	.375	0	0	3.84
1992 Houston	NL	81	0	0	26	111.1	479	103	38	31	3	10	4	4	45	9	67	4	0	3	6	.333	0	2	2.51
1993 Oakland	AL	42	0	0	19	79.1	353	87	40	34	8	2	3	4	33	4	49	1	0	4	2	.667	0	3	3.86
Detroit	AL	19	0	0	3	23	96	14	10	7	1	3	4	0	11	3	14	0	0	2	1	.667	0	0	2.74
1994 Detroit	AL	46	0	0	27	81.1	349	80	40	36	12	4	2	2	37	12	49	4	0	9	2	.818	0	3	3.98
1995 Detroit	AL	60	0	0	27	98.2	463	128	74	70	17	7	8	3	44	12	71	1	1	5	7	.417	0	3	6.39
1996 Pittsburgh	NL	13	0	0	9	15	68	17	11	9	2	2	0	1	6	0	3	0	0	0	2	.000	0	2	5.40
9 Min. YEARS		425	3	0	303	682.2	2395	563	239	217	33	20	21	10	296	44	683	25	7	55	36	.604	0	124	2.86
12 Maj. YEARS		516	0	0	257	754.1	3301	751	362	329	75	44	31	16	343	70	541	30	4	34	45	.430	0	49	3.93

Robert Boggs

Pitches: Right **Bats:** Right **Pos:** P   **Ht:** 6'4" **Wt:** 225 **Born:** 8/30/74 **Age:** 23

		HOW MUCH HE PITCHED						WHAT HE GAVE UP										THE RESULTS					
Year Team	Lg Org	G	GS	CG	GF	IP	BFP	H	R	ER	HR	SH	SF	HB	TBB	IBB	SO	WP	Bk	W	L	Pct.	ShO	Sv	ERA
1995 Elizabethtn	R+ Min	12	12	0	0	60.1	276	77	53	39	2	2	4	2	20	0	55	6	0	3	5	.375	0	0	5.82
1996 Ft. Wayne	A Min	28	27	1	1	150	660	153	81	67	8	6	7	13	64	0	134	4	0	9	12	.429	1	0	4.02
1997 Chston-WV	A Cin	15	1	0	7	34.1	165	44	30	28	5	0	5	4	20	0	25	1	0	1	1	.500	0	1	7.34
Chattanooga	AA Cin	9	9	0	0	40.1	193	53	36	34	6	2	0	5	21	1	35	2	0	1	3	.250	0	0	7.59
3 Min. YEARS		64	49	1	8	285	1294	327	200	168	21	10	16	24	125	1	249	13	0	14	21	.400	1	1	5.31

Bryan Bogle

Bats: Right **Throws:** Right **Pos:** OF   **Ht:** 6'1" **Wt:** 205 **Born:** 5/18/73 **Age:** 25

		BATTING															BASERUNNING				PERCENTAGES		
Year Team	Lg Org	G	AB	H	2B	3B	HR	TB	R	RBI	TBB	IBB	SO	HBP	SH	SF	SB	CS	SB%	GDP	Avg	OBP	SLG
1994 Huntington	R+ ChN	46	140	39	7	1	5	63	17	20	8	1	41	3	0	2	8	2	.80	2	.279	.327	.450
1995 Rockford	A ChN	36	97	20	3	0	2	29	13	11	8	0	20	0	0	1	4	1	.80	2	.206	.264	.299
Butte	R+ ChN	2	9	3	1	0	0	4	0	2	1	0	4	0	0	0	0	0	.00	0	.333	.400	.444
Bluefield	R+ Bal	10	31	14	2	0	1	19	11	4	4	0	2	2	0	1	1	0	1.00	1	.452	.526	.613
High Desert	A+ Bal	19	64	11	2	1	0	15	7	4	8	0	18	0	0	0	3	1	.75	1	.172	.264	.234
1996 High Desert	A+ Bal	126	495	157	32	6	22	267	86	92	36	0	142	5	2	8	14	9	.61	7	.317	.364	.539
1997 Bowie	AA Bal	102	384	98	17	0	13	154	50	58	27	1	92	5	1	4	3	4	.43	15	.255	.310	.401
4 Min. YEARS		341	1220	342	64	8	43	551	184	191	92	2	319	15	3	16	33	17	.66	28	.280	.334	.452

Kurt Bogott

Pitches: Left Bats: Left Pos: P Ht: 6'4" Wt: 195 Born: 9/30/72 Age: 25

		HOW MUCH HE PITCHED						WHAT HE GAVE UP												THE RESULTS				
Year Team	Lg Org	G	GS	CG	GF	IP	BFP	H	R	ER	HR	SH	SF	HB	TBB	IBB	SO	WP	Bk	W	L	Pct.	ShO	Sv	ERA
1993 Red Sox	R Bos	3	2	0	0	15	57	10	3	3	1	0	0	2	4	0	20	3	0	0	1	.000	0	0	1.80
Utica	A- Bos	13	10	0	0	56.2	260	64	37	28	4	2	1	3	23	0	53	8	3	1	7	.125	0	0	4.45
1994 Red Sox	R Bos	3	2	0	0	13.2	49	7	1	1	0	0	0	1	3	0	12	2	0	1	0	1.000	0	0	0.66
Lynchburg	A+ Bos	6	6	0	0	26.1	127	32	23	18	1	1	1	1	14	0	14	2	0	2	3	.400	0	0	6.15
1995 Sarasota	A+ Bos	41	9	0	15	88.2	388	89	44	30	3	4	1	4	41	0	62	8	3	6	4	.600	0	0	3.05
Trenton	AA Bos	2	0	0	2	3.1	13	3	1	1	1	0	0	0	1	0	2	0	0	0	1	.000	0	0	2.70
1996 Knoxville	AA Tor	33	0	0	9	54	256	64	34	32	2	0	2	5	29	2	56	12	1	2	2	.500	0	3	5.33
Dunedin	A+ Tor	19	0	0	8	30.1	133	22	16	6	2	0	0	3	20	1	41	8	0	1	1	.500	0	1	1.78
1997 Syracuse	AAA Tor	16	0	0	6	21.2	106	23	20	19	2	2	2	3	15	1	16	1	0	1	3	.250	0	0	7.89
Knoxville	AA Tor	35	1	0	14	64.2	284	66	32	28	10	1	3	6	25	2	77	6	1	2	1	.667	0	2	3.90
5 Min. YEARS		171	30	0	54	374.1	1673	380	211	166	26	10	10	28	175	6	353	50	8	16	23	.410	0	9	3.99

Matt Bokemeier

Bats: Both Throws: Right Pos: SS Ht: 6'2" Wt: 190 Born: 8/7/72 Age: 25

		BATTING														BASERUNNING				PERCENTAGES		
Year Team	Lg Org	G	AB	H	2B	3B	HR	TB	R	RBI	TBB	IBB	SO	HBP	SH	SF	SB	CS	SB%	GDP	Avg	OBP	SLG
1994 Hudson Vall	A- Tex	72	262	54	12	0	1	69	24	24	11	0	50	2	0	2	4	5	.44	5	.206	.242	.263
1995 Charlotte	A+ Tex	105	385	91	16	1	8	133	42	34	26	1	76	2	4	0	7	7	.50	11	.236	.288	.345
1996 Charlotte	A+ Tex	131	503	138	31	4	2	183	74	62	28	6	81	3	3	7	18	2	.90	15	.274	.312	.364
1997 Tulsa	AA Tex	105	394	91	18	3	5	130	51	43	37	2	73	0	3	3	1	6	.14	7	.231	.295	.330
4 Min. YEARS		413	1544	374	77	8	16	515	191	163	102	9	280	7	10	12	30	20	.60	38	.242	.290	.334

Frank Bolick

Bats: Both Throws: Right Pos: DH Ht: 5'9" Wt: 190 Born: 6/28/66 Age: 32

		BATTING														BASERUNNING				PERCENTAGES		
Year Team	Lg Org	G	AB	H	2B	3B	HR	TB	R	RBI	TBB	IBB	SO	HBP	SH	SF	SB	CS	SB%	GDP	Avg	OBP	SLG
1987 Helena	R+ Mil	52	156	39	8	1	10	79	41	28	41	1	44	3	1	0	4	0	1.00	3	.250	.415	.506
1988 Beloit	A Mil	55	180	41	14	1	2	63	28	16	43	0	49	1	1	0	3	3	.50	3	.228	.379	.350
Brewers	R Mil	23	80	30	9	3	1	48	20	20	22	0	8	0	0	3	1	0	1.00	0	.375	.495	.600
Helena	R+ Mil	40	131	39	10	1	10	81	35	28	32	2	31	1	1	2	5	1	.83	2	.298	.434	.618
1989 Beloit	A Mil	88	299	90	23	0	9	140	44	41	47	5	52	6	0	2	9	6	.60	3	.301	.404	.468
1990 Stockton	A+ Mil	50	164	51	9	1	8	86	39	36	38	1	33	2	0	5	5	3	.63	0	.311	.435	.524
San Berndno	A+ Sea	78	277	92	24	4	10	154	61	66	53	6	53	2	0	8	3	6	.33	2	.332	.432	.556
1991 Jacksnville	AA Sea	136	468	119	19	0	16	186	69	73	84	3	115	5	2	7	5	4	.56	7	.254	.369	.397
1992 Jacksnville	AA Sea	63	224	60	9	0	13	108	32	42	42	1	38	1	0	4	1	4	.20	3	.268	.380	.482
Calgary	AAA Sea	78	274	79	18	6	14	151	35	54	39	2	52	1	1	4	4	4	.50	4	.288	.374	.551
1993 Ottawa	AAA Mon	2	8	1	0	0	0	1	0	0	0	0	0	0	0	0	0	0	.00	0	.125	.125	.125
1994 Buffalo	AAA Pit	35	95	25	6	0	2	37	18	8	27	3	29	2	1	2	0	1	.00	0	.263	.429	.389
New Haven	AA Col	85	301	76	13	0	21	152	53	63	41	3	57	3	1	2	2	2	.50	10	.252	.346	.505
1995 Colo Spmgs	AAA Col	23	68	16	3	1	2	27	8	7	8	0	14	0	0	0	0	0	.00	0	.235	.316	.397
Lubbock	IND —	59	214	76	17	1	7	116	42	56	46	7	33	1	0	5	1	1	.50	5	.355	.462	.542
Buffalo	AAA Cle	20	65	16	6	0	3	31	11	10	3	0	13	1	0	0	1	0	1.00	3	.246	.290	.477
1996 Lubbock	IND —	33	125	47	15	1	6	82	22	35	19	2	14	0	0	2	0	0	.00	1	.376	.452	.656
1997 Midland	AA Ana	28	97	32	5	1	8	63	26	27	26	0	18	1	0	0	0	0	.00	1	.330	.476	.649
Vancouver	AAA Ana	102	362	110	27	4	16	193	61	66	46	4	70	1	1	2	4	1	.80	12	.304	.382	.533
1993 Montreal	NL	95	213	45	13	0	4	70	25	24	23	2	37	4	0	2	1	0	1.00	4	.211	.298	.329
11 Min. YEARS		1050	3588	1039	235	25	158	1798	645	676	657	40	723	31	9	48	47	37	.56	60	.290	.399	.501

Rodney Bolton

Pitches: Right Bats: Right Pos: P Ht: 6'2" Wt: 190 Born: 9/23/68 Age: 29

		HOW MUCH HE PITCHED						WHAT HE GAVE UP												THE RESULTS				
Year Team	Lg Org	G	GS	CG	GF	IP	BFP	H	R	ER	HR	SH	SF	HB	TBB	IBB	SO	WP	Bk	W	L	Pct.	ShO	Sv	ERA
1990 Utica	A- ChA	6	6	1	0	44	168	27	4	2	0	1	0	3	11	0	45	0	0	5	1	.833	1	0	0.41
South Bend	A ChA	7	7	3	0	51	196	34	14	11	0	1	1	1	12	1	50	1	1	5	1	.833	1	0	1.94
1991 Sarasota	A+ ChA	15	15	5	0	103.2	412	81	29	22	2	5	1	2	23	0	77	3	1	7	6	.538	2	0	1.91
Birmingham	AA ChA	12	12	3	0	89	360	73	26	16	3	0	2	8	21	1	57	3	0	8	4	.667	2	0	1.62
1992 Vancouver	AAA ChA	27	27	3	0	187.1	781	174	72	61	9	9	4	1	59	2	111	9	2	11	9	.550	2	0	2.93
1993 Nashville	AAA ChA	18	16	1	1	115.2	486	108	40	37	10	2	3	3	37	2	75	11	0	10	1	.909	0	1	2.88
1994 Nashville	AAA ChA	17	17	1	0	116	480	108	43	33	4	6	1	4	35	2	63	2	0	7	5	.583	0	0	2.56
1995 Nashville	AAA ChA	20	20	3	0	131.1	534	127	44	42	13	2	2	7	23	1	76	2	0	14	3	.824	1	0	2.88
1997 Indianapolis	AAA Cin	28	27	1	0	169.2	730	185	96	81	21	6	4	3	47	0	108	16	2	9	8	.529	1	0	4.30
1993 Chicago	AL	9	8	0	0	42.1	197	55	40	35	4	1	4	1	16	0	17	4	0	2	6	.250	0	0	7.44
1995 Chicago	AL	8	3	0	2	22	109	33	23	20	4	0	1	0	14	1	10	1	0	0	2	.000	0	0	8.18
7 Min. YEARS		150	147	21	1	1007.2	4147	917	368	305	62	32	18	32	268	9	662	47	6	76	38	.667	10	1	2.72
2 Maj. YEARS		17	11	0	2	64.1	306	88	63	55	8	1	5	1	30	1	27	5	0	2	8	.200	0	0	7.69

Tom Bolton

Pitches: Left Bats: Left Pos: P Ht: 6'2" Wt: 185 Born: 5/6/62 Age: 36

		HOW MUCH HE PITCHED						WHAT HE GAVE UP												THE RESULTS				
Year Team	Lg Org	G	GS	CG	GF	IP	BFP	H	R	ER	HR	SH	SF	HB	TBB	IBB	SO	WP	Bk	W	L	Pct.	ShO	Sv	ERA
1980 Elmira	A- Bos	23	1	1	15	56	237	43	26	15	4	1	0	0	22	0	43	0	0	6	2	.750	1	5	2.41
1981 Wintr Haven	A+ Bos	24	0	0	3	92	420	125	62	46	5	2	3	3	41	0	47	7	1	2	3	.400	0	0	4.50
1982 Wintr Haven	A+ Bos	28	25	4	1	163	682	161	67	54	3	6	4	2	63	0	77	7	4	9	8	.529	0	0	2.98
1983 New Britain	AA Bos	16	16	2	0	99.2	416	93	36	32	7	1	0	1	41	0	62	5	0	7	3	.700	1	0	2.89

Year Team	Lg Org	G	GS	CG	GF	IP	BFP	H	R	ER	HR	SH	SF	HB	TBB	IBB	SO	WP	Bk	W	L	Pct.	ShO	Sv	ERA
Pawtucket	AAA Bos	6	6	0	0	29	144	33	26	21	4	1	0	1	25	0	20	1	1	0	5	.000	0	0	6.52
1984 New Britain	AA Bos	33	9	0	11	87	380	87	54	40	5	2	3	4	34	3	66	6	2	4	5	.444	0	1	4.14
1985 New Britain	AA Bos	34	10	1	14	101	437	106	53	48	3	5	3	2	40	1	74	3	2	6	6	.455	0	1	4.28
1986 Pawtucket	AAA Bos	29	7	1	11	86	356	80	30	26	6	9	2	0	25	2	58	1	1	3	4	.429	0	2	2.72
1987 Pawtucket	AAA Bos	5	4	0	1	21.2	93	25	14	13	0	0	1	0	12	1	8	1	0	2	1	.667	0	0	5.40
1988 Pawtucket	AAA Bos	18	1	0	8	19.1	87	17	7	6	0	0	0	0	10	0	15	2	0	3	0	1.000	0	0	2.79
1989 Pawtucket	AAA Bos	25	22	5	2	143.1	606	140	57	46	13	6	1	4	47	2	99	0	1	12	5	.706	2	1	2.89
1990 Pawtucket	AAA Bos	4	2	0	1	11.2	50	9	6	5	2	0	1	0	7	0	8	2	0	1	0	1.000	0	0	3.86
1994 Rochester	AAA Bal	16	0	0	7	20	76	13	5	5	1	0	0	0	8	0	16	2	1	2	0	1.000	0	2	2.25
1995 Nashville	AAA ChA	19	17	1	1	101.2	433	106	52	50	10	0	1	3	31	0	82	3	2	5	7	.417	1	0	4.43
1996 Calgary	AAA Pit	40	14	0	11	116.1	517	121	64	52	7	4	2	7	47	5	92	6	0	12	5	.706	0	2	4.02
1997 Calgary	AAA Pit	8	8	0	0	38	188	67	38	35	6	3	1	3	12	1	29	0	0	2	6	.250	0	0	8.29
Columbia	IND —	4	4	1	0	27	105	22	2	1	0	1	0	0	10	0	14	1	0	2	0	1.000	1	0	0.33
Tucson	AAA Mil	15	7	0	1	57	255	75	42	38	5	2	0	0	20	1	42	4	0	3	4	.429	0	0	6.00
1987 Boston	AL	29	0	0	5	61.2	287	83	33	30	5	3	3	2	27	2	49	3	0	1	0	1.000	0	0	4.38
1988 Boston	AL	28	0	0	8	30.1	140	35	17	16	1	2	1	0	14	1	21	2	1	1	3	.250	0	1	4.75
1989 Boston	AL	4	4	0	0	17.1	83	21	18	16	1	0	1	0	10	1	9	1	0	0	4	.000	0	0	8.31
1990 Boston	AL	21	16	3	2	119.2	501	111	46	45	6	3	5	3	47	3	65	1	1	10	5	.667	0	0	3.38
1991 Boston	AL	25	19	0	4	110	499	136	72	64	16	2	4	1	51	2	64	3	0	8	9	.471	0	0	5.24
1992 Boston	AL	21	1	0	6	29	135	34	11	11	0	0	0	2	14	1	23	2	1	1	2	.333	0	0	3.41
Cincinnati	NL	16	8	0	3	46.1	210	52	28	27	9	1	1	2	23	2	27	3	1	3	3	.500	0	0	5.24
1993 Detroit	AL	43	8	0	9	102.2	462	113	57	51	5	7	2	7	45	10	66	5	1	6	6	.500	0	0	4.47
1994 Baltimore	AL	22	0	0	3	23.1	109	29	15	14	3	1	1	0	13	1	12	1	0	1	2	.333	0	0	5.40
15 Min. YEARS		347	153	16	87	1269.2	5476	1323	641	533	81	43	23	30	495	16	852	51	15	80	64	.556	6	14	3.78
8 Maj. YEARS		209	56	3	40	540.1	2426	614	297	274	46	19	18	17	244	23	336	21	5	31	34	.477	0	1	4.56

Rob Bonanno

Pitches: Right **Bats:** Left **Pos:** P   **Ht:** 6'0" **Wt:** 195 **Born:** 1/5/71 **Age:** 27

Year Team	Lg Org	G	GS	CG	GF	IP	BFP	H	R	ER	HR	SH	SF	HB	TBB	IBB	SO	WP	Bk	W	L	Pct.	ShO	Sv	ERA
1994 Boise	A- Ana	6	6	0	0	39.2	155	23	11	6	1	0	0	2	10	0	41	2	0	5	0	1.000	0	0	1.36
Cedar Rapds	A Ana	9	9	0	0	51	219	56	25	25	4	1	2	4	16	1	40	6	1	3	2	.600	0	0	4.41
1995 Midland	AA Ana	3	3	0	0	13.1	68	24	16	14	5	0	1	0	6	0	6	0	0	1	1	.500	0	0	9.45
Lk Elsinore	A+ Ana	17	17	4	0	112	455	112	49	38	10	2	4	3	16	0	72	0	0	8	4	.667	2	0	3.05
1996 Midland	AA Ana	23	6	1	7	64.1	289	79	44	38	8	1	1	3	23	1	52	5	0	3	2	.333	0	2	5.32
Lk Elsinore	A+ Ana	13	2	0	9	32.2	131	34	11	8	0	1	1	1	10	1	34	1	0	3	2	.600	0	1	2.20
1997 Midland	AA Ana	21	21	3	0	125.1	536	125	83	64	9	5	10	8	34	0	64	5	0	5	10	.333	1	0	4.60
4 Min. YEARS		92	64	8	16	438.1	1853	453	239	193	37	10	19	21	115	3	309	19	1	26	21	.553	2	3	3.96

Bobby Bonds

Bats: Right **Throws:** Right **Pos:** DH-OF   **Ht:** 6'4" **Wt:** 180 **Born:** 3/7/70 **Age:** 28

Year Team	Lg Org	G	AB	H	2B	3B	HR	TB	R	RBI	TBB	IBB	SO	HBP	SH	SF	SB	CS	SB%	GDP	Avg	OBP	SLG
1992 Padres	R SD	12	41	13	2	2	0	19	10	2	7	0	11	0	0	0	5	0	1.00	2	.317	.417	.463
Spokane	A- SD	25	84	15	2	2	0	21	15	5	13	0	37	0	2	0	13	2	.87	1	.179	.289	.250
1993 Waterloo	A SD	102	359	89	12	3	4	119	44	35	30	0	124	4	4	3	30	11	.73	6	.248	.311	.331
1994 Las Vegas	AAA SD	4	4	0	0	0	0	0	0	0	0	0	1	0	0	0	0	0	.00	0	.000	.000	.000
Rancho Cuca	A+ SD	37	103	18	5	3	1	32	14	6	7	0	36	1	2	0	5	0	1.00	0	.175	.234	.311
Springfield	A SD	46	163	45	8	4	2	67	35	23	26	0	46	2	0	0	10	3	.77	1	.276	.382	.411
1995 Visalia	A+ KC	109	373	83	12	6	11	140	56	30	42	1	114	4	3	1	26	12	.68	5	.223	.307	.375
1996 San Jose	A+ SF	110	420	104	16	5	11	163	65	51	43	0	126	2	1	3	21	5	.81	15	.248	.318	.388
1997 San Jose	A+ SF	79	268	85	12	3	5	118	46	44	48	0	55	5	2	2	17	10	.63	7	.317	.427	.440
Phoenix	AAA SF	1	1	0	0	0	0	0	0	0	0	0	0	0	0	0	0	0	.00	0	.000	.000	.000
6 Min. YEARS		525	1816	452	69	28	34	679	285	196	216	1	550	18	14	9	127	43	.75	37	.249	.333	.374

Ken Bonifay

Bats: Left **Throws:** Right **Pos:** 3B-1B   **Ht:** 6'1" **Wt:** 185 **Born:** 9/1/70 **Age:** 27

Year Team	Lg Org	G	AB	H	2B	3B	HR	TB	R	RBI	TBB	IBB	SO	HBP	SH	SF	SB	CS	SB%	GDP	Avg	OBP	SLG
1991 Pirates	R Pit	20	64	22	1	0	1	26	13	9	14	0	8	1	0	1	4	1	.80	3	.344	.463	.406
Welland	A- Pit	37	140	33	5	3	2	50	17	13	11	1	38	0	0	0	2	1	.67	6	.236	.291	.357
1992 Augusta	A Pit	15	47	12	2	0	2	20	8	9	11	2	10	2	0	2	2	0	1.00	1	.255	.403	.426
Salem	A+ Pit	71	209	42	6	0	1	51	20	20	28	0	36	3	1	2	1	2	.33	4	.201	.302	.244
1993 Salem	A+ Pit	100	361	100	19	1	18	175	59	60	42	1	63	4	0	6	12	2	.86	3	.277	.354	.485
1994 Carolina	AA Pit	95	290	64	21	2	6	107	36	28	32	3	58	4	2	2	3	1	.75	4	.221	.305	.369
1995 Lynchburg	A+ Pit	116	375	92	22	2	10	148	57	54	63	4	88	11	0	4	3	5	.38	6	.245	.366	.395
1996 Carolina	AA Pit	95	272	66	18	2	6	106	43	42	41	2	68	4	2	0	4	3	.57	4	.243	.350	.390
1997 Carolina	AA Pit	22	68	12	4	1	1	21	11	7	17	1	23	0	0	0	1	1	1.00	0	.176	.341	.309
7 Min. YEARS		571	1826	443	98	11	47	704	254	242	259	14	392	29	5	17	32	15	.68	27	.243	.343	.386

James Bonnici

Bats: Right **Throws:** Right **Pos:** 1B   **Ht:** 6'4" **Wt:** 230 **Born:** 1/21/72 **Age:** 26

Year Team	Lg Org	G	AB	H	2B	3B	HR	TB	R	RBI	TBB	IBB	SO	HBP	SH	SF	SB	CS	SB%	GDP	Avg	OBP	SLG
1991 Mariners	R Sea	51	178	59	2	4	0	69	36	38	44	0	31	6	0	5	8	2	.80	1	.331	.468	.388
1992 Bellingham	A- Sea	53	168	44	6	1	4	64	13	20	22	2	54	2	1	0	5	2	.71	3	.262	.354	.381
1993 Riverside	A+ Sea	104	375	115	21	1	9	165	69	58	58	2	72	9	3	1	0	0	.00	7	.307	.411	.440

Year Team	Lg Org	G	AB	H	2B	3B	HR	TB	R	RBI	TBB	IBB	SO	HBP	SH	SF	SB	CS	SB%	GDP	Avg	OBP	SLG
1994 Riverside	A+ Sea	113	397	111	23	3	10	170	71	71	58	0	81	18	0	3	1	2	.33	14	.280	.393	.428
1995 Port City	AA Sea	138	508	144	36	3	20	246	75	91	76	15	97	9	0	3	2	2	.50	14	.283	.384	.484
1996 Tacoma	AAA Sea	139	497	145	25	0	26	248	76	74	59	4	100	2	1	3	1	3	.25	13	.292	.367	.499
1997 Tacoma	AAA Sea	1	4	1	0	0	0	1	0	1	1	0	1	0	0	0	0	0	.00	0	.250	.400	.250
7 Min. YEARS		599	2127	619	113	12	69	963	340	353	318	23	436	46	5	15	17	11	.61	52	.291	.392	.453

Richie Borrero

Bats: Right **Throws:** Right **Pos:** C   **Ht:** 6'1" **Wt:** 195 **Born:** 1/5/73 **Age:** 25

Year Team	Lg Org	G	AB	H	2B	3B	HR	TB	R	RBI	TBB	IBB	SO	HBP	SH	SF	SB	CS	SB%	GDP	Avg	OBP	SLG
1990 Red Sox	R Bos	34	109	23	6	0	1	32	13	10	16	1	28	0	0	1	0	2	.00	1	.211	.310	.294
1991 Red Sox	R Bos	35	118	26	3	1	1	34	11	16	2	1	23	1	0	2	4	2	.67	1	.220	.236	.288
1992 Red Sox	R Bos	34	99	18	5	2	1	30	9	12	14	0	24	1	1	1	2	1	.67	1	.182	.287	.303
1993 Utica	A- Bos	44	120	19	2	0	2	27	10	14	11	0	39	1	1	3	3	1	.75	2	.158	.230	.225
1994 Sarasota	A+ Bos	44	145	28	8	0	3	45	15	14	9	0	50	4	1	0	0	1	.00	2	.193	.259	.310
1995 Sarasota	A+ Bos	34	98	20	5	0	0	25	9	4	5	0	22	2	1	2	0	1	.00	1	.204	.252	.255
Michigan	A Bos	23	70	16	4	1	2	28	8	6	6	0	17	4	0	0	0	1	.00	2	.229	.325	.400
1996 Michigan	A Bos	11	30	5	1	0	0	6	3	1	2	0	5	0	0	0	0	1	.00	1	.167	.219	.200
Sarasota	A+ Bos	27	92	23	5	0	3	37	15	13	6	0	17	1	1	0	1	1	.50	3	.250	.303	.402
Trenton	AA Bos	26	71	22	5	2	3	40	12	26	8	0	16	0	1	0	2	1	.67	2	.310	.380	.563
1997 Pawtucket	AAA Bos	15	51	13	1	0	2	20	4	6	1	0	17	0	1	1	0	1	.00	0	.255	.264	.392
Trenton	AA Bos	57	203	51	12	1	3	74	31	23	13	0	46	3	2	1	2	1	.50	7	.251	.305	.365
8 Min. YEARS		384	1206	264	57	7	21	398	140	145	93	2	304	17	9	11	14	15	.48	27	.219	.282	.330

Heath Bost

Pitches: Right **Bats:** Right **Pos:** P   **Ht:** 6'4" **Wt:** 200 **Born:** 10/13/74 **Age:** 23

Year Team	Lg Org	G	GS	CG	GF	IP	BFP	H	R	ER	HR	SH	SF	HB	TBB	IBB	SO	WP	Bk	W	L	Pct.	ShO	Sv	ERA
1995 Portland	A- Col	10	0	0	1	16	63	15	6	6	1	0	0	0	0	0	25	1	0	1	0	1.000	0	0	3.38
Asheville	A Col	9	2	0	4	23.2	90	20	6	4	1	0	0	1	3	0	17	1	2	4	1	.800	0	0	1.52
1996 New Haven	AA Col	4	0	0	2	6	24	5	1	1	0	0	0	0	2	0	7	0	0	1	0	1.000	0	0	1.50
Asheville	A Col	41	0	0	29	76	293	45	13	11	3	6	0	1	19	5	102	2	0	5	2	.714	0	15	1.30
1997 Salem	A+ Col	13	0	0	10	15	57	9	4	4	1	0	2	0	2	0	9	0	0	1	0	1.000	0	3	2.40
Colo Sprngs	AAA Col	2	0	0	0	3	21	10	8	7	1	0	1	0	1	0	3	0	0	0	1	.000	0	0	21.00
New Haven	AA Col	38	0	0	32	43	180	44	18	17	3	0	0	0	10	1	45	5	0	2	2	.500	0	20	3.56
3 Min. YEARS		117	2	0	78	182.2	728	148	56	50	10	7	1	2	37	6	208	9	2	14	6	.700	0	38	2.46

D.J. Boston

Bats: Left **Throws:** Left **Pos:** 1B   **Ht:** 6'7" **Wt:** 230 **Born:** 9/6/71 **Age:** 26

Year Team	Lg Org	G	AB	H	2B	3B	HR	TB	R	RBI	TBB	IBB	SO	HBP	SH	SF	SB	CS	SB%	GDP	Avg	OBP	SLG
1991 Medcine Hat	R+ Tor	59	207	58	12	0	1	73	34	25	33	0	33	2	1	1	4	8	.33	5	.280	.383	.353
1992 St. Cathms	A- Tor	72	256	60	7	1	5	84	25	36	36	4	41	2	0	3	20	3	.87	5	.234	.330	.328
1993 Hagerstown	A Tor	127	464	146	35	4	13	228	76	92	54	6	77	4	0	3	31	11	.74	10	.315	.389	.491
1994 Dunedin	A+ Tor	119	433	125	20	1	7	168	59	52	55	2	65	0	2	5	19	9	.68	8	.289	.365	.388
1995 Knoxville	AA Tor	132	479	117	27	1	11	179	51	71	47	1	100	2	2	3	12	8	.60	12	.244	.313	.374
1996 Syracuse	AAA Tor	26	85	21	7	0	4	40	12	12	14	0	23	0	0	1	0	1	.00	3	.247	.350	.471
Carolina	AA Pit	93	321	90	16	4	8	138	47	48	49	3	61	3	0	4	5	3	.63	7	.280	.377	.430
1997 Visalia	A+ Oak	14	49	11	3	0	1	17	7	4	5	0	13	1	0	0	0	0	.00	0	.224	.309	.347
New Haven	AA Col	83	293	84	14	2	7	123	53	49	49	2	63	0	0	4	1	5	.17	5	.287	.384	.420
Colo Sprngs	AAA Col	2	6	2	0	0	0	2	1	0	0	0	3	0	0	0	0	0	.00	0	.333	.333	.333
7 Min. YEARS		727	2593	714	141	13	57	1052	365	389	342	18	479	14	5	24	92	48	.66	52	.275	.360	.406

Steve Bourgeois

Pitches: Right **Bats:** Right **Pos:** P   **Ht:** 6'1" **Wt:** 220 **Born:** 8/4/74 **Age:** 23

Year Team	Lg Org	G	GS	CG	GF	IP	BFP	H	R	ER	HR	SH	SF	HB	TBB	IBB	SO	WP	Bk	W	L	Pct.	ShO	Sv	ERA
1993 Everett	A- SF	15	15	0	0	77	337	62	44	36	7	0	3	7	44	0	77	4	1	5	3	.625	0	0	4.21
1994 Clinton	A SF	20	20	0	0	106.1	464	97	57	43	16	4	2	7	54	0	88	11	0	8	5	.615	0	0	3.64
San Jose	A+ SF	7	7	0	0	36.2	167	40	22	22	4	1	1	1	22	0	21	5	0	4	0	1.000	0	0	5.40
1995 Shreveport	AA SF	22	22	2	0	145.1	604	140	50	46	8	4	5	4	53	1	91	11	1	12	3	.800	2	0	2.85
Phoenix	AAA SF	6	5	0	0	34.2	153	38	18	13	2	0	4	0	13	0	23	4	1	1	1	.500	0	0	3.38
1996 Phoenix	AAA SF	20	18	2	0	97	435	112	50	39	6	2	4	6	42	1	65	5	1	8	6	.571	1	0	3.62
1997 Colo Sprngs	AAA Col	33	18	2	5	121.2	571	154	96	81	18	2	3	5	66	3	86	7	0	9	7	.563	2	0	5.99
1996 San Francisco	NL	15	5	0	4	40	198	60	35	28	4	2	2	4	21	4	17	4	0	1	3	.250	0	0	6.30
5 Min. YEARS		123	105	6	5	618.2	2731	643	337	280	61	13	18	32	294	5	457	47	4	47	25	.653	5	0	4.07

Ryan Bowen

Pitches: Right **Bats:** Right **Pos:** P   **Ht:** 6'0" **Wt:** 185 **Born:** 2/10/68 **Age:** 30

Year Team	Lg Org	G	GS	CG	GF	IP	BFP	H	R	ER	HR	SH	SF	HB	TBB	IBB	SO	WP	Bk	W	L	Pct.	ShO	Sv	ERA
1987 Asheville	A Hou	26	26	6	0	160.1	704	143	86	72	12	7	4	5	78	1	126	8	2	12	5	.706	2	0	4.04
1988 Osceola	A+ Hou	4	4	0	0	13.2	65	12	8	6	0	1	0	1	10	0	12	2	0	1	0	1.000	0	0	3.95
1989 Columbus	AA Hou	27	27	1	0	139.2	655	123	83	66	11	7	4	8	116	0	136	12	0	8	6	.571	1	0	4.25
1990 Tucson	AAA Hou	10	7	0	0	34.2	177	41	36	36	5	2	0	0	38	1	29	0	0	1	3	.250	0	0	9.35

		HOW MUCH HE PITCHED				WHAT HE GAVE UP								THE RESULTS					
Year Team	Lg Org	G	GS	CG	GF	IP	BFP	H	R	ER	HR	SH	SF	HB	TBB	IBB	SO	WP	Bk	W	L	Pct.	ShO	Sv	ERA
Columbus	AA Hou	18	18	2	0	113	491	103	59	47	7	4	6	0	49	0	109	5	1	8	4	.667	2	0	3.74
1991 Tucson	AAA Hou	18	18	2	0	98.2	450	114	56	48	3	3	0	3	56	2	78	9	0	5	5	.500	2	0	4.38
1992 Tucson	AAA Hou	21	20	1	0	122.1	555	128	68	56	7	6	2	5	64	1	94	8	0	7	6	.538	1	0	4.12
1994 Edmonton	AAA Fla	5	5	0	0	19	85	22	13	13	3	0	1	0	11	0	13	1	0	1	0	1.000	0	0	6.16
Brevard Cty	A+ Fla	2	1	0	0	6.2	28	4	3	3	0	0	0	2	3	0	5	0	0	0	1	.000	0	0	4.05
1995 Brevard Cty	A+ Fla	3	3	0	0	11	43	6	3	3	1	0	0	0	6	0	10	0	0	0	2	.000	0	0	2.45
Charlotte	AAA Fla	1	1	0	0	4.2	22	5	5	5	1	0	0	0	4	0	3	0	0	0	1	.000	0	0	9.64
1996 New Orleans	AAA Mil	6	6	0	0	27.1	125	27	18	15	4	0	1	1	19	0	23	3	0	2	2	.500	0	0	4.94
1997 Tampa	A+ NYA	4	4	0	0	15.2	66	17	7	7	1	0	0	1	5	0	15	1	1	0	2	.000	0	0	4.02
Columbus	AAA NYA	2	2	0	0	10	49	15	10	10	1	1	3	1	5	0	7	0	0	0	1	.000	0	0	9.00
1991 Houston	NL	14	13	0	0	71.2	319	73	43	41	4	2	6	3	36	1	49	8	1	6	4	.600	0	0	5.15
1992 Houston	NL	11	9	0	2	33.2	179	48	43	41	8	3	0	2	30	3	22	5	0	0	7	.000	0	0	10.96
1993 Florida	NL	27	27	2	0	156.2	693	156	83	77	11	5	4	3	87	7	98	10	4	8	12	.400	1	0	4.42
1994 Florida	NL	8	8	1	0	47.1	208	50	28	26	9	2	2	2	19	0	32	2	0	1	5	.167	0	0	4.94
1995 Florida	NL	4	3	0	0	16.2	85	23	11	7	3	1	2	0	12	2	15	0	0	2	0	1.000	0	0	3.78
10 Min. YEARS		147	142	12	0	776.2	3515	760	455	387	56	31	21	27	464	5	660	49	4	45	38	.542	8	0	4.48
5 Maj. YEARS		64	60	3	2	326	1484	350	208	192	35	13	14	10	184	13	216	25	5	17	28	.378	1	0	5.30

Brent Bowers

Bats: Left **Throws:** Right **Pos:** OF   **Ht:** 6'3" **Wt:** 200 **Born:** 5/2/71 **Age:** 27

		BATTING														BASERUNNING				PERCENTAGES		
Year Team	Lg Org	G	AB	H	2B	3B	HR	TB	R	RBI	TBB	IBB	SO	HBP	SH	SF	SB	CS	SB%	GDP	Avg	OBP	SLG
1989 Medicne Hat	R+ Tor	54	207	46	2	2	0	52	16	13	19	0	55	0	0	1	6	2	.75	5	.222	.286	.251
1990 Medicne Hat	R+ Tor	60	212	58	7	3	3	80	30	27	31	0	35	1	1	0	19	8	.70	2	.274	.369	.377
1991 Myrtle Bch	A Tor	120	402	101	8	4	2	123	53	44	31	1	76	2	9	4	35	12	.74	11	.251	.305	.306
1992 Dunedin	A+ Tor	128	524	133	10	3	3	158	74	46	34	0	99	3	8	1	31	15	.67	4	.254	.302	.302
1993 Knoxville	AA Tor	141	577	143	23	4	5	189	63	43	21	1	121	3	13	0	36	19	.65	5	.248	.278	.328
1994 Knoxville	AA Tor	127	472	129	18	11	4	181	52	49	20	4	75	1	7	2	15	8	.65	8	.273	.303	.383
1995 Syracuse	AAA Tor	111	305	77	16	5	5	118	38	26	10	0	57	1	1	1	5	1	.83	3	.252	.278	.387
1996 Bowie	AA Bal	58	228	71	11	1	9	111	37	25	17	2	40	2	3	0	10	4	.71	1	.311	.364	.487
Rochester	AAA Bal	49	206	67	8	4	4	95	40	19	14	0	41	0	3	0	9	3	.75	1	.325	.368	.461
1997 Scranton-WB	AAA Phi	39	110	28	2	0	3	39	15	7	8	0	28	1	0	1	1	1	.50	1	.255	.308	.355
1996 Baltimore	AL	21	39	12	2	0	0	14	6	3	0	0	7	0	0	0	0	0	.00	1	.308	.308	.359
9 Min. YEARS		887	3243	853	105	37	38	1146	418	299	205	8	627	14	45	10	167	73	.70	41	.263	.309	.353

Jim Bowie

Bats: Left **Throws:** Left **Pos:** DH   **Ht:** 6'0" **Wt:** 205 **Born:** 2/17/65 **Age:** 33

		BATTING														BASERUNNING				PERCENTAGES		
Year Team	Lg Org	G	AB	H	2B	3B	HR	TB	R	RBI	TBB	IBB	SO	HBP	SH	SF	SB	CS	SB%	GDP	Avg	OBP	SLG
1986 Bellingham	A- Sea	72	274	76	12	1	5	105	47	68	38	1	53	2	0	11	4	1	.80	6	.277	.357	.383
1987 Wausau	A Sea	127	448	119	26	0	10	175	56	66	56	3	67	3	3	5	8	3	.73	14	.266	.348	.391
1988 San Berndno	A+ Sea	139	529	154	28	0	15	227	76	102	58	5	84	1	1	10	8	5	.62	14	.291	.356	.429
1989 Calgary	AAA Sea	100	336	90	12	0	4	114	28	37	17	0	45	2	0	4	2	2	.50	6	.268	.304	.339
Williamsprt	AA Sea	11	42	11	5	0	0	16	3	1	5	0	7	0	0	0	0	0	.00	0	.262	.340	.381
1990 Williamsprt	AA Sea	128	446	122	18	0	5	155	45	48	51	6	47	3	1	3	0	2	.00	15	.274	.350	.348
1991 Jacksnville	AA Sea	123	448	139	25	0	10	194	51	67	36	2	67	0	1	6	3	3	.50	16	.310	.357	.433
Calgary	AAA Sea	14	50	17	3	0	1	23	9	7	2	0	8	0	0	0	0	0	.00	1	.340	.365	.460
1992 Calgary	AAA Sea	49	172	41	6	0	1	50	17	17	21	3	25	1	0	3	3	1	.75	6	.238	.320	.291
Jacksnville	AA Sea	80	276	79	16	0	10	125	36	43	41	2	40	3	1	2	0	1	.00	8	.286	.382	.453
1993 Huntsville	AA Oak	138	501	167	33	1	14	244	77	101	56	8	52	0	1	8	8	3	.73	17	.333	.395	.487
1994 Tacoma	AAA Oak	109	411	129	24	2	6	181	66	66	51	5	38	2	0	6	2	2	.50	17	.314	.387	.440
1995 Edmonton	AAA Oak	141	531	142	26	2	3	181	69	70	54	7	51	2	4	6	4	1	.80	21	.267	.334	.341
1997 Mobile	AA SD	32	54	13	2	0	1	18	4	10	10	2	5	1	0	2	0	0	.00	3	.241	.358	.333
1994 Oakland	AL	6	14	3	0	0	0	3	0	0	0	0	2	0	1	0	0	0	.00	1	.214	.214	.214
11 Min. YEARS		1263	4518	1299	236	6	87	1808	584	703	496	44	589	20	12	66	42	24	.64	144	.288	.356	.400

Micah Bowie

Pitches: Left **Bats:** Left **Pos:** P   **Ht:** 6'4" **Wt:** 185 **Born:** 11/10/74 **Age:** 23

		HOW MUCH HE PITCHED						WHAT HE GAVE UP												THE RESULTS					
Year Team	Lg Org	G	GS	CG	GF	IP	BFP	H	R	ER	HR	SH	SF	HB	TBB	IBB	SO	WP	Bk	W	L	Pct.	ShO	Sv	ERA
1994 Braves	R Atl	6	6	0	1	29.2	124	27	14	10	1	0	2	1	5	0	35	1	0	0	3	.000	0	0	3.03
Danville	R+ Atl	7	5	0	0	32.2	141	28	16	13	4	2	3	3	13	1	38	2	0	3	1	.750	0	0	3.58
1995 Macon	A Atl	5	5	0	0	27.2	104	9	8	7	1	0	0	3	11	0	36	1	0	4	1	.800	0	0	2.28
Durham	A+ Atl	23	23	1	0	130.1	561	119	65	52	8	13	3	8	61	3	91	4	3	4	11	.267	0	0	3.59
1996 Durham	A+ Atl	14	13	0	0	66.1	283	55	29	27	4	6	3	7	33	0	65	2	0	3	6	.333	0	0	3.66
1997 Durham	A+ Atl	9	6	0	0	39.1	167	29	16	16	2	0	2	0	27	0	44	2	0	2	2	.500	0	0	3.66
Greenville	AA Atl	8	7	0	0	43.2	193	34	19	17	3	1	2	3	26	1	41	2	0	3	2	.600	0	0	3.50
4 Min. YEARS		72	64	1	1	369.2	1573	301	167	142	23	22	15	25	176	5	350	14	3	19	26	.422	0	0	3.46

Jason Boyd

Pitches: Right **Bats:** Right **Pos:** P   **Ht:** 6'2" **Wt:** 165 **Born:** 2/23/73 **Age:** 25

		HOW MUCH HE PITCHED						WHAT HE GAVE UP												THE RESULTS					
Year Team	Lg Org	G	GS	CG	GF	IP	BFP	H	R	ER	HR	SH	SF	HB	TBB	IBB	SO	WP	Bk	W	L	Pct.	ShO	Sv	ERA
1994 Martinsvlle	R+ Phi	14	13	1	0	69	306	65	46	32	6	0	1	4	32	0	45	7	6	3	7	.300	0	0	4.17
1995 Piedmont	A Phi	26	24	1	0	151	638	151	77	60	8	5	3	4	44	0	129	18	2	6	8	.429	0	0	3.58
1996 Clearwater	A+ Phi	26	26	2	0	161.2	674	160	75	70	12	3	6	3	49	1	120	7	1	11	8	.579	0	0	3.90
1997 Reading	AA Phi	48	7	0	9	115.2	509	113	65	62	16	2	3	3	64	7	98	1	2	10	6	.625	0	0	4.82

			HOW MUCH HE PITCHED						WHAT HE GAVE UP												THE RESULTS					
Year Team	Lg Org	G	GS	CG	GF	IP	BFP	H	R	ER	HR	SH	SF	HB	TBB	IBB	SO	WP	Bk		W	L	Pct.	ShO	Sv	ERA
4 Min. YEARS		114	70	4	10	497.1	2127	489	263	224	42	10	13	14	189	8	392	33	11		30	29	.508	0	0	4.05

Marshall Boze

Pitches: Right **Bats:** Right **Pos:** P   **Ht:** 6' 1" **Wt:** 214 **Born:** 5/23/71 **Age:** 27

			HOW MUCH HE PITCHED						WHAT HE GAVE UP											THE RESULTS					
Year Team	Lg Org	G	GS	CG	GF	IP	BFP	H	R	ER	HR	SH	SF	HB	TBB	IBB	SO	WP	Bk	W	L	Pct.	ShO	Sv	ERA
1990 Brewers	R Mil	15	0	0	5	20.2	104	28	22	17	0	0	0	3	13	1	17	3	0	1	0	1.000	0	3	7.40
1991 Beloit	A Mil	3	1	0	2	6.1	34	8	4	4	0	0	0	0	7	0	4	0	1	0	1	.000	0	0	5.68
Helena	R+ Mil	16	8	0	1	56	271	59	49	43	3	2	3	3	47	0	64	6	2	3	3	.500	0	0	6.91
1992 Beloit	A Mil	26	22	4	4	146.1	635	117	59	46	6	6	2	12	82	4	126	18	1	13	7	.650	1	0	2.83
1993 Stockton	A+ Mil	14	14	0	0	88.1	379	82	36	26	4	2	4	7	41	2	54	6	0	7	2	.778	0	0	2.65
El Paso	AA Mil	13	13	1	0	86.1	357	78	36	26	5	0	3	4	32	2	48	6	0	10	3	.769	0	0	2.71
1994 New Orleans	AAA Mil	29	29	2	0	171.1	746	182	101	90	18	9	4	10	74	2	81	16	1	6	10	.375	0	0	4.73
1995 New Orleans	AAA Mil	23	19	1	1	111.2	495	134	65	53	10	2	2	2	45	1	47	6	1	3	9	.250	0	1	4.27
1996 New Orleans	AAA Mil	25	2	0	12	38.2	180	35	22	21	6	3	1	2	29	5	32	2	0	4	3	.571	0	3	4.89
1997 Las Vegas	AAA SD	14	8	0	2	52	252	68	51	44	11	1	4	1	29	2	44	2	0	0	7	.000	0	0	7.62
1996 Milwaukee	AL	25	0	0	8	32.1	165	47	29	28	5	3	1	6	25	4	19	3	0	0	2	.000	0	1	7.79
8 Min. YEARS		178	116	8	27	777.2	3453	791	445	370	63	25	23	44	399	19	517	65	6	47	45	.511	1	7	4.28

Bert Bradley

Pitches: Right **Bats:** Right **Pos:** P   **Ht:** 6'1" **Wt:** 190 **Born:** 12/23/56 **Age:** 41

			HOW MUCH HE PITCHED						WHAT HE GAVE UP											THE RESULTS					
Year Team	Lg Org	G	GS	CG	GF	IP	BFP	H	R	ER	HR	SH	SF	HB	TBB	IBB	SO	WP	Bk	W	L	Pct.	ShO	Sv	ERA
1997 Huntsville	AA Oak	1	0	0	1	1	2	0	0	0	0	0	0	0	0	0	0	0	0	0	0	.000	0	0	0.00

Terry Bradshaw

Bats: Left **Throws:** Right **Pos:** OF   **Ht:** 6' 0" **Wt:** 195 **Born:** 2/3/69 **Age:** 29

			BATTING														BASERUNNING				PERCENTAGES		
Year Team	Lg Org	G	AB	H	2B	3B	HR	TB	R	RBI	TBB	IBB	SO	HBP	SH	SF	SB	CS	SB%	GDP	Avg	OBP	SLG
1990 Hamilton	A- StL	68	236	55	5	1	3	71	37	13	24	1	60	1	2	1	15	3	.83	4	.233	.305	.301
1991 Savannah	A StL	132	443	105	17	1	7	145	90	42	99	1	117	10	4	5	64	15	.81	6	.237	.384	.327
1993 St. Pete	A+ StL	125	461	134	25	6	5	186	84	51	82	1	60	7	7	5	43	17	.72	8	.291	.402	.403
1994 Arkansas	AA StL	114	425	119	25	8	10	190	65	52	50	4	69	7	2	4	13	10	.57	5	.280	.362	.447
Louisville	AAA StL	22	80	20	4	0	4	36	16	8	6	0	10	2	1	0	5	1	.83	2	.250	.318	.450
1995 Louisville	AAA StL	111	389	110	24	8	8	174	65	42	53	0	60	3	7	1	20	7	.74	4	.283	.372	.447
1996 Louisville	AAA StL	102	389	118	23	1	12	179	56	44	42	1	64	2	0	2	21	9	.70	6	.303	.372	.460
1997 Louisville	AAA StL	130	453	113	17	6	8	166	79	43	61	1	79	9	1	0	26	10	.72	12	.249	.350	.366
1995 St. Louis	NL	19	44	10	1	1	0	13	6	2	2	0	10	0	0	0	1	2	.33	4	.227	.261	.295
1996 St. Louis	NL	15	21	7	1	0	0	8	4	3	3	0	2	0	1	0	0	1	.00	0	.333	.417	.381
7 Min. YEARS		804	2876	774	140	31	57	1147	492	295	417	9	519	41	24	18	207	72	.74	47	.269	.368	.399
2 Maj. YEARS		34	65	17	2	1	0	21	10	5	5	0	12	0	1	0	1	3	.25	0	.262	.314	.323

Doug Brady

Bats: Both **Throws:** Right **Pos:** 2B   **Ht:** 5'11" **Wt:** 165 **Born:** 11/23/69 **Age:** 28

			BATTING														BASERUNNING				PERCENTAGES		
Year Team	Lg Org	G	AB	H	2B	3B	HR	TB	R	RBI	TBB	IBB	SO	HBP	SH	SF	SB	CS	SB%	GDP	Avg	OBP	SLG
1991 Utica	A- ChA	65	226	53	6	3	2	71	37	31	31	0	31	1	3	4	21	6	.78	5	.235	.324	.314
1992 South Bend	A ChA	24	92	27	5	1	0	34	12	7	17	1	13	0	2	1	16	3	.84	0	.293	.400	.370
White Sox	R ChA	3	8	1	0	0	0	1	2	1	0	1	0	0	0	2	0	0	.00	0	.125	.182	.125
Sarasota	A+ ChA	56	184	50	6	0	2	62	21	27	25	1	33	3	6	2	5	7	.42	4	.272	.364	.337
1993 Sarasota	A+ ChA	115	449	113	16	6	5	156	75	44	55	2	54	6	4	5	26	9	.74	4	.252	.338	.347
Nashville	AAA ChA	2	3	0	0	0	0	0	0	0	0	0	0	0	0	0	0	0	.00	0	.000	.000	.000
1994 Birmingham	AA ChA	127	516	128	18	8	4	174	59	47	38	1	59	1	6	5	34	12	.74	4	.248	.298	.337
1995 Nashville	AAA ChA	125	450	134	15	6	5	176	71	27	31	3	76	0	4	3	32	6	.84	4	.298	.341	.391
1996 Nashville	AAA ChA	115	427	103	18	7	6	153	59	42	31	1	61	2	6	2	20	6	.77	4	.241	.294	.358
1997 Nashville	AAA ChA	106	370	88	12	3	7	127	43	36	18	0	47	2	8	1	13	4	.76	4	.238	.276	.343
1995 Chicago	AL	12	21	4	1	0	0	5	4	3	2	0	4	0	0	0	1	0	.00	1	.190	.261	.238
7 Min. YEARS		738	2725	697	96	34	31	954	378	263	247	9	375	15	39	25	167	53	.76	29	.256	.318	.350

Derek Brandow

Pitches: Right **Bats:** Right **Pos:** P   **Ht:** 6'1" **Wt:** 200 **Born:** 1/25/70 **Age:** 28

			HOW MUCH HE PITCHED						WHAT HE GAVE UP											THE RESULTS					
Year Team	Lg Org	G	GS	CG	GF	IP	BFP	H	R	ER	HR	SH	SF	HB	TBB	IBB	SO	WP	Bk	W	L	Pct.	ShO	Sv	ERA
1992 St. Cathms	A- Tor	22	2	0	9	58.1	249	51	23	16	6	3	3	2	26	0	74	5	1	5	2	.714	0	3	2.47
1993 Hagerstown	A Tor	40	1	0	27	76.1	340	76	38	31	5	2	2	4	34	1	62	6	0	4	5	.444	0	6	3.66
1994 Dunedin	A+ Tor	29	21	0	3	140.1	593	122	50	50	6	4	5	2	58	0	123	11	1	7	6	.538	0	1	3.21
1995 Knoxville	AA Tor	25	21	1	1	107	466	95	60	51	13	1	8	6	50	1	106	9	0	5	6	.455	0	1	4.29
1996 Knoxville	AA Tor	5	1	0	3	11.2	50	11	10	10	3	2	2	0	5	0	6	2	1	1	2	.333	0	2	7.71
Syracuse	AAA Tor	24	20	2	0	124	539	118	64	59	14	4	5	3	57	0	103	8	0	8	7	.533	0	0	4.28
1997 Syracuse	AAA Tor	31	25	1	0	143	677	161	103	86	14	5	12	11	91	1	120	10	1	7	11	.389	0	0	5.41
6 Min. YEARS		176	91	4	43	660.2	2914	634	357	303	61	21	37	28	321	3	594	51	4	37	39	.487	0	13	4.13

Ryan Brannan

Pitches: Right Bats: Right Pos: P   Ht: 6'3" Wt: 210 Born: 4/27/75 Age: 23

		HOW MUCH HE PITCHED						WHAT HE GAVE UP											THE RESULTS				
Year Team	Lg Org	G	GS	CG	GF	IP	BFP	H	R	ER	HR	SH	SF	HB	TBB	IBB	SO	WP	Bk	W	L	Pct.	ShO	Sv	ERA
1997 Clearwater	A+ Phi	21	0	0	18	27.1	108	20	2	1	0	5	0	0	8	0	25	2	2	0	0	.000	0	10	0.33
Reading	AA Phi	45	0	0	41	52.1	223	52	18	18	2	7	1	5	20	2	39	3	2	4	2	.667	0	20	3.10
1 Min. YEARS		66	0	0	59	79.2	331	72	20	19	2	12	1	5	28	2	64	5	4	4	2	.667	0	30	2.15

Russell Branyan

Bats: Left Throws: Right Pos: 3B   Ht: 6'3" Wt: 195 Born: 12/19/75 Age: 22

		BATTING													BASERUNNING				PERCENTAGES		
Year Team	Lg Org	G	AB	H	2B	3B	HR	TB	R	RBI	TBB	IBB	SO	HBP	SH	SF	SB	CS	SB%	GDP	Avg	OBP	SLG
1994 Burlington	R+ Cle	55	171	36	10	0	5	61	21	13	25	2	64	4	0	1	4	2	.67	3	.211	.323	.357
1995 Columbus	A Cle	76	277	71	8	6	19	148	46	55	27	2	120	3	0	3	1	1	.50	6	.256	.326	.534
1996 Columbus	A Cle	130	482	129	20	4	40	277	102	106	62	5	166	5	0	3	7	4	.64	4	.268	.355	.575
1997 Kinston	A+ Cle	83	297	86	26	2	27	197	59	75	52	4	94	5	0	5	3	1	.75	9	.290	.398	.663
Akron	AA Cle	41	137	32	4	0	12	72	26	30	28	1	56	2	0	1	0	0	.00	1	.234	.369	.526
4 Min. YEARS		385	1364	354	68	12	103	755	254	279	194	14	500	19	0	13	15	8	.65	23	.260	.357	.554

Scott Bream

Bats: Both Throws: Right Pos: 2B   Ht: 6'1" Wt: 170 Born: 11/4/70 Age: 27

		BATTING													BASERUNNING				PERCENTAGES		
Year Team	Lg Org	G	AB	H	2B	3B	HR	TB	R	RBI	TBB	IBB	SO	HBP	SH	SF	SB	CS	SB%	GDP	Avg	OBP	SLG
1989 Padres	R SD	28	97	17	3	1	0	22	15	8	18	0	22	1	0	0	9	5	.64	2	.175	.310	.227
1990 Chston-SC	A SD	4	14	1	0	0	0	1	2	0	4	0	7	0	1	0	1	0	1.00	0	.071	.278	.071
1991 Chston-SC	A SD	52	174	24	2	1	0	28	17	7	20	0	61	1	1	1	10	6	.63	1	.138	.230	.161
Spokane	A- SD	68	262	56	4	5	0	70	37	26	25	1	57	5	3	3	16	7	.70	5	.214	.292	.267
1992 Waterloo	A SD	124	392	90	8	6	1	114	50	29	33	0	126	2	4	0	17	9	.65	4	.230	.293	.291
1993 Rancho Cuca	A+ SD	113	405	114	15	6	4	153	70	52	74	3	85	2	4	3	30	14	.68	10	.281	.393	.378
1994 Wichita	AA SD	109	333	100	8	3	5	129	40	35	42	4	81	3	3	2	18	8	.69	4	.300	.382	.387
1995 Las Vegas	AAA SD	87	303	73	7	1	0	82	33	15	35	1	59	3	2	0	7	5	.58	7	.241	.326	.271
Iowa	AAA ChN	29	82	13	1	0	2	20	10	9	11	0	20	1	0	3	1	0	1.00	1	.159	.258	.244
1996 Jacksnville	AA Det	36	108	26	3	1	3	40	18	12	10	0	31	1	3	0	2	1	.67	0	.241	.311	.370
1997 Lakeland	A+ Det	11	37	8	1	1	0	11	5	6	3	0	11	0	1	1	0	0	.00	1	.216	.268	.297
Jacksnville	AA Det	19	55	15	1	0	2	22	12	3	14	0	12	0	1	0	1	0	1.00	1	.273	.420	.400
Toledo	AAA Det	30	91	21	1	0	0	22	11	0	13	0	31	0	0	0	0	1	.00	2	.231	.327	.242
9 Min. YEARS		710	2353	558	55	25	17	714	320	202	302	9	603	18	26	10	112	56	.67	38	.237	.327	.303

Rod Brewer

Bats: Left Throws: Left Pos: 1B   Ht: 6'3" Wt: 218 Born: 2/24/66 Age: 32

		BATTING													BASERUNNING				PERCENTAGES		
Year Team	Lg Org	G	AB	H	2B	3B	HR	TB	R	RBI	TBB	IBB	SO	HBP	SH	SF	SB	CS	SB%	GDP	Avg	OBP	SLG
1987 Johnson Cty	R+ StL	67	238	60	11	2	10	105	33	42	36	5	40	3	0	2	2	2	.50	4	.252	.355	.441
1988 Springfield	A StL	133	457	136	25	2	8	189	57	64	63	7	52	5	1	2	6	4	.60	22	.298	.386	.414
1989 Arkansas	AA StL	128	470	130	25	2	10	189	71	93	46	3	46	7	0	3	2	3	.40	8	.277	.348	.402
1990 Louisville	AAA StL	144	514	129	15	5	12	190	60	83	54	7	62	9	0	6	0	2	.00	9	.251	.329	.370
1991 Louisville	AAA StL	104	382	86	21	1	8	133	39	52	35	1	57	6	0	1	4	0	1.00	10	.225	.300	.348
1992 Louisville	AAA StL	120	423	122	20	2	18	200	57	86	49	6	60	5	0	1	3	0	.00	8	.288	.368	.473
1995 Phoenix	AAA SF	15	45	11	4	0	1	18	8	8	3	0	10	5	0	1	1	1	.50	1	.244	.345	.400
Charlotte	AAA Fla	69	236	76	15	1	9	120	31	55	33	3	45	5	0	5	0	0	.00	3	.322	.409	.508
1996 Abilene	IND —	95	348	113	23	3	19	199	67	87	50	6	53	4	0	7	10	1	.91	12	.325	.408	.572
1997 Buffalo	AAA Cle	10	31	5	1	0	2	12	3	5	8	1	9	0	0	1	0	0	.00	1	.161	.325	.387
Amarillo	IND —	86	294	94	18	2	18	170	73	73	64	8	38	9	0	7	18	6	.75	5	.320	.447	.578
1990 St. Louis	NL	14	25	6	1	0	0	7	4	2	0	0	4	0	0	0	0	0	.00	1	.240	.240	.280
1991 St. Louis	NL	19	13	1	0	0	0	1	0	1	0	0	5	0	0	0	0	0	.00	0	.077	.077	.077
1992 St. Louis	NL	29	103	31	6	0	0	37	11	10	8	0	12	1	0	1	0	1	.00	0	.301	.354	.359
1993 St. Louis	NL	110	147	42	8	0	2	56	15	20	17	5	26	1	2	2	1	0	1.00	5	.286	.359	.381
9 Min. YEARS		971	3438	962	178	20	115	1525	499	648	441	47	472	58	1	39	43	22	.66	83	.280	.367	.444
4 Maj. YEARS		172	288	80	15	0	2	101	30	33	25	5	47	2	2	3	1	1	.50	7	.278	.336	.351

Jamie Brewington

Pitches: Right Bats: Right Pos: P   Ht: 6'4" Wt: 190 Born: 9/28/71 Age: 26

		HOW MUCH HE PITCHED						WHAT HE GAVE UP											THE RESULTS				
Year Team	Lg Org	G	GS	CG	GF	IP	BFP	H	R	ER	HR	SH	SF	HB	TBB	IBB	SO	WP	Bk	W	L	Pct.	ShO	Sv	ERA
1992 Everett	A- SF	15	11	1	0	68.2	317	65	40	33	2	0	3	5	47	2	63	9	1	5	2	.714	0	0	4.33
1993 Clinton	A SF	26	25	1	0	133.2	580	126	78	71	20	1	3	5	61	1	111	19	2	13	5	.722	0	0	4.78
1994 Clinton	A SF	10	10	0	0	53	226	46	29	29	5	1	3	2	24	0	62	7	1	2	4	.333	0	0	4.92
San Jose	A+ SF	13	13	0	0	76	310	61	38	27	3	2	2	2	25	0	65	7	1	7	3	.700	0	0	3.20
1995 Shreveport	AA SF	16	16	1	0	88.1	376	72	39	30	8	2	7	0	55	0	74	4	0	8	3	.727	1	0	3.06
1996 Phoenix	AAA SF	35	17	0	7	110.1	526	130	93	86	14	5	3	6	72	1	75	15	0	6	9	.400	0	1	7.02
1997 Omaha	AAA KC	7	4	0	0	21.2	98	21	21	20	10	0	1	1	13	0	20	1	1	2	2	.500	0	0	8.31
Wichita	AA KC	10	10	0	0	51	245	68	43	38	12	0	1	4	28	0	31	2	0	2	5	.286	0	0	6.71
Tucson	AAA Mil	6	5	0	0	20.1	112	33	26	23	2	0	1	2	17	0	13	0	0	1	3	.250	0	0	10.18
1995 San Francisco	NL	13	13	0	0	75.1	334	68	38	38	8	4	4	4	45	6	45	3	0	6	4	.600	0	0	4.54
6 Min. YEARS		138	111	3	8	623	2790	622	407	357	76	11	24	27	342	4	514	64	6	46	36	.561	2	1	5.16

Kary Bridges

Bats: Left **Throws:** Right **Pos:** 2B **Ht:** 5'10" **Wt:** 165 **Born:** 10/27/71 **Age:** 26

Year Team	Lg Org	G	AB	H	2B	3B	HR	TB	R	RBI	TBB	IBB	SO	HBP	SH	SF	SB	CS	SB%	GDP	Avg	OBP	SLG
1993 Quad City	A Hou	65	263	74	9	0	3	92	37	24	31	1	18	2	1	3	15	10	.60	7	.281	.358	.350
1994 Quad City	A Hou	117	447	135	20	4	1	166	66	53	38	3	29	3	8	4	14	11	.56	9	.302	.354	.371
1995 Jackson	AA Hou	118	418	126	22	4	3	165	56	43	49	3	17	0	6	4	10	12	.45	12	.301	.372	.395
1996 Jackson	AA Hou	87	338	110	12	2	4	138	51	33	32	1	14	1	7	3	4	5	.44	11	.325	.382	.408
Tucson	AAA Hou	42	140	44	9	1	1	58	24	21	9	1	8	1	0	2	1	3	.25	3	.314	.355	.414
1997 New Orleans	AAA Hou	23	64	11	1	2	0	16	6	3	5	0	9	1	0	1	1	0	1.00	0	.172	.239	.250
Carolina	AA Pit	66	283	95	17	1	3	123	43	29	9	0	10	0	3	2	9	5	.64	7	.336	.354	.435
Calgary	AAA Pit	33	95	25	4	0	0	29	9	6	7	1	6	0	1	0	1	0	1.00	3	.263	.314	.305
5 Min. YEARS		551	2048	620	94	14	15	787	292	212	180	10	111	8	26	19	55	46	.54	52	.303	.358	.384

Anthony Briggs

Pitches: Right **Bats:** Right **Pos:** P **Ht:** 6'1" **Wt:** 162 **Born:** 9/14/73 **Age:** 24

Year Team	Lg Org	G	GS	CG	GF	IP	BFP	H	R	ER	HR	SH	SF	HB	TBB	IBB	SO	WP	Bk	W	L	Pct.	ShO	Sv	ERA
1994 Braves	R Atl	1	0	0	1	4	14	1	0	0	0	0	0	0	1	0	1	0	0	0	0	.000	0	0	0.00
Idaho Falls	R+ Atl	20	0	0	5	49.2	227	58	30	22	1	2	2	2	21	2	45	6	0	2	3	.400	0	1	3.99
1995 Macon	A Atl	29	24	1	1	147.1	635	145	76	49	12	2	1	4	56	1	114	9	0	8	5	.615	1	0	2.99
1996 Durham	A+ Atl	31	18	1	3	124.2	548	131	84	61	10	7	9	3	60	1	76	9	1	9	10	.474	0	0	4.40
1997 Durham	A+ Atl	17	0	0	10	30	129	27	16	15	2	1	1	0	13	2	25	3	0	1	2	.333	0	3	4.50
Greenville	AA Atl	19	13	0	0	94.1	413	91	64	57	11	4	2	0	43	0	59	4	2	6	3	.667	0	0	5.44
4 Min. YEARS		117	55	2	20	450	1966	453	270	204	36	16	15	9	194	6	320	31	3	26	23	.531	1	4	4.08

Stoney Briggs

Bats: Right **Throws:** Right **Pos:** OF **Ht:** 6'3" **Wt:** 215 **Born:** 12/26/71 **Age:** 26

Year Team	Lg Org	G	AB	H	2B	3B	HR	TB	R	RBI	TBB	IBB	SO	HBP	SH	SF	SB	CS	SB%	GDP	Avg	OBP	SLG
1991 Medicne Hat	R+ Tor	64	236	70	8	0	8	102	45	29	18	0	62	2	0	2	9	5	.64	2	.297	.349	.432
1992 Myrtle Bch	A Tor	136	514	123	18	5	11	184	75	41	43	0	156	8	6	2	33	14	.70	6	.239	.307	.358
1993 Waterloo	A SD	125	421	108	15	5	9	160	57	55	30	1	103	12	4	5	21	8	.72	3	.257	.321	.380
1994 Rancho Cuca	A+ SD	121	417	112	22	2	17	189	63	76	54	1	124	9	2	7	14	13	.52	7	.269	.359	.453
1995 Memphis	AA SD	118	385	95	14	7	8	147	60	46	40	5	133	10	1	3	17	8	.68	13	.247	.331	.382
1996 Memphis	AA SD	133	452	124	24	6	12	196	72	80	62	4	123	4	4	3	28	11	.72	18	.274	.365	.434
1997 Las Vegas	AAA SD	119	435	117	21	5	11	181	58	57	28	1	122	6	0	4	18	12	.60	10	.269	.319	.416
7 Min. YEARS		816	2860	749	122	30	76	1159	430	384	275	12	823	51	17	26	140	71	.66	59	.262	.335	.405

Darryl Brinkley

Bats: Right **Throws:** Right **Pos:** OF **Ht:** 5'11" **Wt:** 205 **Born:** 12/23/68 **Age:** 29

Year Team	Lg Org	G	AB	H	2B	3B	HR	TB	R	RBI	TBB	IBB	SO	HBP	SH	SF	SB	CS	SB%	GDP	Avg	OBP	SLG
1994 Winnipeg	IND —	72	294	86	18	3	8	134	48	44	21	0	31	6	3	1	32	13	.71	5	.293	.351	.456
1995 Winnipeg	IND —	30	131	44	2	1	4	60	22	19	8	1	13	3	1	2	6	4	.60	4	.336	.382	.458
1996 Rancho Cuca	A+ SD	65	259	94	28	2	9	153	52	59	23	2	37	2	0	6	18	10	.64	13	.363	.410	.591
Memphis	AA SD	60	203	60	9	0	9	96	36	29	22	2	33	3	1	1	13	5	.72	2	.296	.371	.473
1997 Mobile	AA SD	55	215	66	14	1	5	97	41	33	26	1	30	5	0	0	10	9	.53	6	.307	.394	.451
4 Min. YEARS		282	1102	350	71	7	35	540	199	184	100	6	144	19	5	10	79	41	.66	30	.318	.381	.490

Josh Brinkley

Bats: Right **Throws:** Right **Pos:** 3B **Ht:** 5'10" **Wt:** 175 **Born:** 8/5/73 **Age:** 24

Year Team	Lg Org	G	AB	H	2B	3B	HR	TB	R	RBI	TBB	IBB	SO	HBP	SH	SF	SB	CS	SB%	GDP	Avg	OBP	SLG
1993 Expos	R Mon	16	63	17	2	0	0	19	6	4	2	0	8	2	0	1	0	1	.00	0	.270	.309	.302
1994 Wst Plm Bch	A+ Mon	2	5	0	0	0	0	0	0	0	0	0	1	0	0	0	0	0	.00	0	.000	.000	.000
Expos	R Mon	8	27	3	0	0	0	3	3	1	1	0	5	2	0	0	0	0	.00	0	.111	.200	.111
Vermont	A- Mon	7	19	5	1	0	0	6	5	1	1	0	5	0	0	0	0	0	.00	0	.263	.300	.316
Burlington	A Mon	11	30	7	0	0	0	7	2	2	3	0	7	4	1	0	0	0	.00	0	.233	.368	.233
1995 Albany	A Mon	22	69	12	3	0	1	18	8	5	3	0	11	3	0	0	2	2	.50	1	.174	.240	.261
Vermont	A- Mon	38	122	27	2	0	0	29	14	11	14	0	26	6	0	2	6	1	.86	4	.221	.326	.238
1996 Wst Plm Bch	A+ Mon	87	268	70	11	2	5	100	34	27	26	0	44	14	5	3	1	2	.33	6	.261	.354	.373
1997 Harrisburg	AA Mon	22	54	17	2	0	2	25	8	6	1	0	12	0	0	1	0	1	.00	1	.315	.321	.463
Wst Plm Bch	A+ Mon	69	227	59	12	2	3	84	24	20	9	1	44	3	0	2	3	1	.75	6	.260	.295	.370
5 Min. YEARS		282	884	217	33	4	11	291	104	77	60	1	163	34	6	10	12	8	.60	18	.245	.315	.329

John Briscoe

Pitches: Right **Bats:** Right **Pos:** P **Ht:** 6'3" **Wt:** 190 **Born:** 9/22/67 **Age:** 30

Year Team	Lg Org	G	GS	CG	GF	IP	BFP	H	R	ER	HR	SH	SF	HB	TBB	IBB	SO	WP	Bk	W	L	Pct.	ShO	Sv	ERA
1988 Athletics	R Oak	7	6	0	0	25.2	105	26	14	10	1	0	1	1	6	0	23	3	3	1	1	.500	0	0	3.51
1989 Madison	A Oak	21	20	1	1	117.2	524	121	66	55	7	10	9	9	57	0	69	11	1	7	5	.583	0	0	4.21
1990 Modesto	A+ Oak	29	12	1	12	86.1	373	72	50	44	12	4	1	2	52	0	66	6	0	3	6	.333	0	4	4.59
Huntsville	AA Oak	3	0	0	0	4.2	30	9	7	7	1	0	0	0	7	0	7	1	0	0	0	.000	0	0	13.50
1991 Huntsville	AA Oak	2	0	0	2	4.1	19	1	2	0	0	0	0	0	2	0	6	0	0	2	0	1.000	0	0	0.00
Tacoma	AAA Oak	22	9	0	6	76.1	342	73	35	31	7	2	2	5	44	1	66	3	0	3	5	.375	0	1	3.66
1992 Tacoma	AAA Oak	33	6	0	11	78	368	78	62	51	7	5	2	1	68	5	66	6	0	2	5	.286	0	0	5.88

Year Team	Lg Org	G	GS	CG	GF	IP	BFP	H	R	ER	HR	SH	SF	HB	TBB	IBB	SO	WP	Bk	W	L	Pct.	ShO	Sv	ERA
						HOW MUCH HE PITCHED				WHAT HE GAVE UP												THE RESULTS			
1993 Huntsville	AA Oak	30	0	0	28	38.2	158	28	14	13	3	3	0	1	16	1	62	0	0	4	0	1.000	0	16	3.03
Tacoma	AAA Oak	9	0	0	8	12.1	59	13	5	4	1	2	0	0	9	3	16	1	0	1	1	.500	0	6	2.92
1994 Modesto	A+ Oak	2	2	0	0	3	12	2	0	0	0	0	0	0	0	0	9	0	0	0	0	.000	0	0	0.00
1995 Modesto	A+ Oak	4	4	0	0	5.2	22	5	1	1	0	0	0	0	2	0	5	0	0	0	0	.000	0	0	1.59
Edmonton	AAA Oak	3	3	0	0	6	26	5	2	2	0	0	0	0	5	0	3	0	0	0	0	.000	0	0	3.00
1996 Edmonton	AAA Oak	30	1	0	10	54.2	256	69	33	29	6	2	2	2	23	3	62	5	1	5	2	.714	0	1	4.77
1997 Calgary	AAA Pit	4	0	0	2	7.1	41	18	11	10	1	0	1	0	2	1	7	2	0	0	0	.000	0	0	12.27
Akron	AA Cle	33	0	0	26	32	145	41	19	14	7	1	0	2	12	2	28	4	0	0	1	.000	0	5	3.94
1991 Oakland	AL	11	0	0	9	14	62	12	11	11	3	0	1	0	10	0	9	3	0	0	0	.000	0	0	7.07
1992 Oakland	AL	2	2	0	0	7	40	12	6	5	0	1	0	0	9	0	4	2	0	0	1	.000	0	0	6.43
1993 Oakland	AL	17	0	0	6	24.2	122	26	25	22	2	0	2	0	26	3	24	5	0	1	0	1.000	0	0	8.03
1994 Oakland	AL	37	0	0	0	49.1	210	31	24	22	7	1	1	1	39	2	45	8	1	4	2	.667	0	1	4.01
1995 Oakland	AL	16	0	0	7	18.1	99	25	17	17	4	2	2	0	21	1	19	1	0	0	0	.000	0	0	8.35
1996 Oakland	AL	17	0	0	8	26.1	116	18	11	11	2	2	2	0	24	1	14	3	0	0	1	.000	0	1	3.76
10 Min. YEARS		232	63	2	106	552.2	2480	561	321	271	53	29	18	23	305	16	495	42	5	28	27	.509	0	33	4.41
6 Maj. YEARS		100	2	0	38	139.2	649	124	94	88	18	6	8	3	129	8	115	22	1	5	5	.500	0	2	5.67

Jorge Brito

Bats: Right **Throws:** Right **Pos:** C   **Ht:** 6' 1" **Wt:** 190 **Born:** 6/22/66 **Age:** 32

Year Team	Lg Org	G	AB	H	2B	3B	HR	TB	R	RBI	TBB	IBB	SO	HBP	SH	SF	SB	CS	SB%	GDP	Avg	OBP	SLG
				BATTING													BASERUNNING				PERCENTAGES		
1986 Medford	A- Oak	21	59	9	2	0	0	11	4	5	4	0	17	2	0	1	0	2	.00	3	.153	.227	.186
1987 Medford	A- Oak	40	110	20	1	0	1	24	7	15	12	0	54	1	1	2	0	0	.00	3	.182	.264	.218
1988 Modesto	A+ Oak	96	300	65	15	0	5	95	38	27	47	0	104	8	3	3	0	0	.00	6	.217	.335	.317
1989 Modesto	A+ Oak	16	54	13	2	0	1	18	8	6	5	0	14	1	1	0	0	0	.00	2	.241	.317	.333
Tacoma	AAA Oak	5	15	3	1	0	0	4	2	0	2	0	6	0	0	0	0	1	.00	2	.200	.294	.267
Huntsville	AA Oak	24	73	16	2	2	0	22	13	8	20	0	23	0	2	0	1	1	.50	2	.219	.387	.301
Madison	A Oak	43	143	30	4	1	3	45	20	14	22	1	46	2	1	0	1	0	1.00	9	.210	.323	.315
1990 Huntsville	AA Oak	57	164	44	6	1	2	58	17	20	30	1	49	3	3	1	0	1	.00	6	.268	.389	.354
1991 Tacoma	AAA Oak	22	73	17	2	0	1	22	6	3	4	0	20	0	0	0	0	0	.00	1	.233	.273	.301
Huntsville	AA Oak	65	203	41	11	0	1	55	26	23	28	0	50	4	2	1	0	1	.00	6	.202	.309	.271
1992 Tacoma	AAA Oak	18	35	5	2	0	0	7	4	1	2	0	17	0	0	0	0	0	.00	0	.143	.189	.200
Huntsville	AA Oak	33	72	15	2	0	2	23	6	13	6	0	21	1	3	0	0	2	1.00	1	.208	.337	.319
1993 Huntsville	AA Oak	18	36	10	3	0	4	25	6	11	10	1	10	2	0	1	0	0	.00	0	.278	.449	.694
1994 New Haven	AA Col	63	200	46	11	1	5	74	18	25	18	3	59	2	1	2	2	0	1.00	6	.230	.297	.370
Colo Spmgs	AAA Col	21	64	24	5	0	3	38	13	19	7	1	14	0	1	0	0	0	.00	3	.375	.437	.594
1995 Colo Spmgs	AAA Col	32	96	22	4	1	2	34	9	15	2	0	20	1	1	2	0	0	.00	3	.229	.248	.354
1996 Colo Spmgs	AAA Col	53	159	54	17	0	7	92	32	31	24	1	37	4	0	1	0	0	.00	7	.340	.436	.579
1997 Syracuse	AAA Tor	8	30	7	3	0	2	16	3	4	3	0	10	2	2	0	1	0	1.00	1	.233	.343	.533
1995 Colorado	NL	18	51	11	3	0	0	14	5	7	2	0	17	1	1	0	1	0	1.00	1	.216	.259	.275
1996 Colorado	NL	8	14	1	0	0	0	1	1	0	1	0	8	2	1	0	0	0	.00	0	.071	.235	.071
12 Min. YEARS		635	1886	441	93	6	39	663	236	233	253	8	571	33	21	14	7	7	.50	61	.234	.333	.352
2 Maj. YEARS		26	65	12	3	0	0	15	6	7	3	0	25	3	2	0	1	0	1.00	1	.185	.254	.231

Luis Brito

Bats: Both **Throws:** Right **Pos:** SS   **Ht:** 6'0" **Wt:** 155 **Born:** 4/12/71 **Age:** 27

Year Team	Lg Org	G	AB	H	2B	3B	HR	TB	R	RBI	TBB	IBB	SO	HBP	SH	SF	SB	CS	SB%	GDP	Avg	OBP	SLG
				BATTING													BASERUNNING				PERCENTAGES		
1989 Martinsvlle	R+ Phi	9	16	5	0	0	0	5	1	1	0	0	3	0	0	0	0	0	.00	0	.313	.313	.313
1990 Princeton	R+ Phi	27	95	23	2	0	0	25	15	4	2	0	11	2	1	0	4	2	.67	1	.242	.273	.263
1991 Martinsvlle	R+ Phi	31	123	33	5	0	0	38	17	9	5	0	21	2	1	0	5	2	.71	3	.268	.303	.309
Batavia	A- Phi	22	76	24	2	1	0	28	13	10	6	0	8	0	2	0	9	3	.75	1	.316	.366	.368
1992 Spartanburg	A Phi	34	105	23	1	0	0	26	11	9	4	0	17	0	1	0	7	8	.47	1	.219	.248	.248
Clearwater	A+ Phi	65	188	41	4	0	0	45	18	11	5	0	21	1	6	1	4	7	.36	0	.218	.241	.239
1993 Spartanburg	A Phi	127	467	146	16	4	0	170	56	33	11	0	47	1	8	3	9	12	.43	12	.313	.328	.364
1994 Clearwater	A+ Phi	31	108	35	4	3	1	48	18	13	2	0	3	0	1	1	2	1	.67	4	.324	.333	.444
Reading	AA Phi	86	284	63	6	2	3	82	33	21	13	0	38	2	4	2	4	4	.50	4	.222	.259	.289
1995 Reading	AA Phi	2	3	1	0	0	0	1	1	1	0	0	0	0	0	0	1	0	1.00	0	.333	.333	.333
Clearwater	A+ Phi	109	383	105	14	3	3	134	42	41	17	0	35	1	5	3	12	5	.71	14	.274	.304	.350
1996 Greenville	AA Atl	19	43	5	0	0	0	5	4	4	1	0	6	0	2	0	1	1	.50	2	.116	.136	.116
Durham	A+ Atl	81	315	90	16	1	3	117	35	34	10	0	33	3	6	1	6	3	.67	5	.286	.313	.371
1997 Greenville	AA Atl	97	336	97	12	0	1	112	35	36	15	1	25	0	6	3	4	5	.44	11	.289	.316	.333
9 Min. YEARS		740	2542	691	82	15	11	836	299	227	91	1	268	12	43	16	68	53	.56	58	.272	.298	.329

Dusty Brixey

Pitches: Right **Bats:** Right **Pos:** P   **Ht:** 6'4" **Wt:** 190 **Born:** 10/16/73 **Age:** 24

Year Team	Lg Org	G	GS	CG	GF	IP	BFP	H	R	ER	HR	SH	SF	HB	TBB	IBB	SO	WP	Bk	W	L	Pct.	ShO	Sv	ERA
						HOW MUCH HE PITCHED				WHAT HE GAVE UP												THE RESULTS			
1993 Royals	R KC	14	1	0	6	31	137	30	22	16	0	0	3	3	17	0	11	4	0	2	1	.667	0	2	4.65
1994 Royals	R KC	18	1	0	6	31	130	26	12	8	0	1	0	1	13	0	18	4	1	3	0	1.000	0	2	2.32
1995 Springfield	A KC	36	8	0	6	102	438	101	51	43	3	3	6	7	40	0	44	6	0	4	5	.444	0	2	3.79
1996 Wilmington	A+ KC	34	12	1	8	115	490	109	58	44	4	7	6	8	41	3	38	4	0	10	5	.667	0	1	3.44
1997 Wichita	AA KC	5	3	0	2	19.1	92	23	15	15	1	2	1	4	9	1	5	1	1	0	4	.000	0	0	6.98
Wilmington	A+ KC	24	0	0	9	42.1	192	49	29	18	1	2	1	2	22	7	22	5	0	0	4	.000	0	1	3.83
5 Min. YEARS		131	25	1	37	340.2	1479	338	187	144	9	15	17	25	142	11	138	24	2	19	19	.500	0	7	3.80

Donald Broach

Bats: **Right** Throws: **Right** Pos: **OF**   Ht: **6'0"** Wt: **185** Born: **7/18/71** Age: **26**

Year Team	Lg Org	G	AB	H	2B	3B	HR	TB	R	RBI	TBB	IBB	SO	HBP	SH	SF	SB	CS	SB%	GDP	Avg	OBP	SLG
1993 Princeton	R+ Cin	55	181	42	5	1	1	52	29	19	15	0	31	4	2	1	8	3	.73	0	.232	.303	.287
1994 Billings	R+ Cin	63	270	84	11	1	3	106	55	38	24	0	40	7	3	1	17	12	.59	7	.311	.381	.393
1995 Winston-Sal	A+ Cin	117	460	120	23	4	8	175	74	34	50	2	73	5	5	2	16	14	.53	9	.261	.338	.380
1996 Chattanooga	AA Cin	110	349	91	10	2	6	123	58	37	39	2	51	11	5	1	20	9	.69	7	.261	.353	.352
1997 Chston-WV	A Cin	18	60	18	0	0	0	18	15	8	11	0	9	5	0	2	8	1	.89	1	.300	.436	.300
Chattanooga	AA Cin	105	402	110	15	4	0	133	62	31	35	1	47	6	4	2	12	15	.44	6	.274	.339	.331
5 Min. YEARS		468	1722	465	64	12	18	607	293	167	174	5	251	38	19	9	81	54	.60	30	.270	.348	.352

Troy Brohawn

Pitches: **Left** Bats: **Left** Pos: **P**   Ht: **6'1"** Wt: **190** Born: **1/14/73** Age: **25**

Year Team	Lg Org	G	GS	CG	GF	IP	BFP	H	R	ER	HR	SH	SF	HB	TBB	IBB	SO	WP	Bk	W	L	Pct.	ShO	Sv	ERA
1994 San Jose	A+ SF	4	4	0	0	16.2	80	27	15	13	2	1	0	2	5	0	13	1	0	0	2	.000	0	0	7.02
1995 San Jose	A+ SF	11	10	0	1	65.1	246	45	14	12	4	1	1	1	20	0	57	5	1	7	3	.700	0	0	1.65
1996 Shreveport	AA SF	28	28	0	0	156.2	668	163	99	80	30	7	3	6	49	0	82	8	3	9	10	.474	0	0	4.60
1997 Shreveport	AA SF	26	26	1	0	169	695	148	57	48	10	3	1	2	64	0	98	4	3	13	5	.722	1	0	2.56
4 Min. YEARS		69	68	1	1	407.2	1689	383	185	153	46	12	5	11	138	0	250	18	7	29	20	.592	1	0	3.38

Antone Brooks

Pitches: **Left** Bats: **Left** Pos: **P**   Ht: **6'0"** Wt: **176** Born: **12/20/73** Age: **24**

Year Team	Lg Org	G	GS	CG	GF	IP	BFP	H	R	ER	HR	SH	SF	HB	TBB	IBB	SO	WP	Bk	W	L	Pct.	ShO	Sv	ERA
1995 Eugene	A- Atl	15	0	0	5	17	67	9	5	1	1	0	0	0	8	1	26	0	0	2	0	1.000	0	0	0.53
1996 Macon	A Atl	43	0	0	26	80.1	334	57	24	20	5	2	2	5	36	4	101	8	0	9	4	.692	0	10	2.24
Durham	A+ Atl	2	0	0	1	3	10	1	0	0	0	0	0	0	0	0	6	0	0	0	0	.000	0	0	0.00
1997 Greenville	AA Atl	14	0	0	3	20.2	93	21	14	11	3	0	2	2	8	1	10	1	0	1	0	1.000	0	0	4.79
3 Min. YEARS		74	0	0	35	121	504	88	43	32	9	2	4	7	52	6	143	9	0	12	4	.750	0	10	2.38

Rayme Brooks

Bats: **Right** Throws: **Right** Pos: **C**   Ht: **6'2"** Wt: **180** Born: **4/12/70** Age: **28**

Year Team	Lg Org	G	AB	H	2B	3B	HR	TB	R	RBI	TBB	IBB	SO	HBP	SH	SF	SB	CS	SB%	GDP	Avg	OBP	SLG
1990 Eugene	A- KC	10	29	3	2	0	1	8	4	2	7	0	8	0	0	0	0	0	.00	1	.103	.278	.276
1991 Eugene	A- KC	38	110	23	6	1	3	40	12	17	14	2	33	0	0	1	0	1	.00	2	.209	.296	.364
1992 Eugene	A- KC	50	160	41	10	2	3	64	20	18	20	0	34	0	0	2	1	5	.17	5	.256	.335	.400
1993 Rockford	A KC	120	415	106	34	2	15	189	74	65	60	1	91	7	1	3	14	5	.74	9	.255	.357	.455
1994 High Desert	A+ KC	95	326	89	20	3	20	175	55	76	45	0	102	7	0	4	2	3	.40	3	.273	.369	.537
1995 Wilmington	A+ KC	94	326	71	16	0	8	111	41	30	25	1	82	6	1	1	2	1	.67	7	.218	.285	.340
1996 Wilmington	A+ KC	111	363	91	24	2	15	164	54	66	45	0	80	0	2	7	4	3	.57	10	.251	.328	.452
1997 Wichita	AA KC	56	140	32	5	0	4	49	19	16	19	0	45	4	0	1	2	2	.50	2	.229	.335	.350
Omaha	AAA KC	3	9	0	0	0	0	0	0	0	0	0	4	0	0	0	0	0	.00	0	.000	.000	.000
8 Min. YEARS		577	1878	456	117	10	69	800	279	290	235	4	479	24	4	19	25	20	.56	39	.243	.332	.426

Jason Brosnan

Pitches: **Left** Bats: **Left** Pos: **P**   Ht: **6'1"** Wt: **190** Born: **1/26/68** Age: **30**

Year Team	Lg Org	G	GS	CG	GF	IP	BFP	H	R	ER	HR	SH	SF	HB	TBB	IBB	SO	WP	Bk	W	L	Pct.	ShO	Sv	ERA
1989 Great Falls	R+ LA	13	13	0	0	67	294	41	24	19	1	1	1	3	55	0	89	10	4	6	2	.750	0	0	2.55
1990 Bakersfield	A+ LA	26	25	0	0	136	607	113	63	47	4	3	4	7	91	1	157	7	2	12	4	.750	0	0	3.11
1991 San Antonio	AA LA	2	2	0	0	7.2	49	15	15	15	2	0	0	0	11	0	8	0	0	0	1	.000	0	0	17.61
Vero Beach	A+ LA	11	9	0	0	36.1	164	34	27	23	2	1	2	2	21	0	25	5	0	1	2	.333	0	0	5.70
1992 Albuquerque	AAA LA	8	0	0	3	8.2	44	13	9	8	2	1	0	1	4	0	12	2	0	0	0	.000	0	1	8.31
San Antonio	AA LA	8	8	0	0	32.1	163	44	33	28	9	2	2	1	21	1	27	4	0	1	7	.125	0	0	7.79
Vero Beach	A+ LA	18	8	2	3	58	255	69	32	30	2	2	1	2	26	2	51	11	1	3	4	.429	0	0	4.66
1993 Vero Beach	A+ LA	23	0	0	9	25.2	127	30	22	13	1	1	1	1	19	2	32	4	0	0	2	.000	0	1	4.56
Bakersfield	A+ LA	9	6	0	1	36.1	161	36	20	14	2	1	1	2	15	0	34	4	0	4	1	.800	0	0	3.47
San Antonio	AA LA	3	3	0	0	20.1	83	21	11	10	1	0	0	0	7	0	10	1	0	0	2	.000	0	0	4.43
1994 San Antonio	AA LA	17	1	0	8	30.2	141	34	16	12	3	1	0	2	12	1	29	3	0	2	3	.400	0	1	3.52
Albuquerque	AAA LA	24	7	0	5	61.2	275	75	36	36	4	2	1	0	30	0	43	3	2	2	4	.333	0	1	5.25
1995 Albuquerque	AAA LA	23	1	0	11	31	128	30	16	15	3	0	2	0	9	1	18	0	1	2	0	1.000	0	2	4.35
San Antonio	AA LA	19	0	0	7	22.2	94	24	9	9	1	1	0	0	4	0	21	1	0	1	0	1.000	0	2	3.57
1996 Tacoma	AAA Sea	12	2	0	3	31.2	125	19	14	10	2	1	1	3	15	1	26	2	0	3	1	.750	0	0	2.84
Port City	AA Sea	30	9	1	7	77	327	71	33	31	8	2	2	2	32	1	76	2	0	5	6	.455	1	1	3.62
1997 Memphis	AA Sea	40	0	0	21	53.1	213	44	16	15	7	2	1	4	11	1	62	2	1	2	3	.400	0	5	2.53
9 Min. YEARS		286	94	3	78	736.1	3250	713	396	335	54	20	20	29	383	11	720	61	11	44	42	.512	1	15	4.09

Scott Brow

Pitches: **Right** Bats: **Right** Pos: **P**   Ht: **6'3"** Wt: **200** Born: **3/17/69** Age: **29**

Year Team	Lg Org	G	GS	CG	GF	IP	BFP	H	R	ER	HR	SH	SF	HB	TBB	IBB	SO	WP	Bk	W	L	Pct.	ShO	Sv	ERA
1990 St. Cathms	A- Tor	9	7	0	0	39.2	165	34	18	10	2	2	0	2	11	0	39	4	0	3	1	.750	0	0	2.27
1991 Dunedin	A+ Tor	15	12	0	1	69.2	306	73	50	37	5	3	3	2	28	1	31	2	5	3	7	.300	0	0	4.78
1992 Dunedin	A+ Tor	25	25	3	0	170.2	690	143	53	46	8	4	5	7	44	2	107	3	3	14	2	.875	1	0	2.43

Year Team	Lg Org	G	GS	CG	GF	IP	BFP	H	R	ER	HR	SH	SF	HB	TBB	IBB	SO	WP	Bk	W	L	Pct.	ShO	Sv	ERA
		HOW MUCH HE PITCHED						**WHAT HE GAVE UP**												**THE RESULTS**					
1993 Knoxville	AA Tor	3	3	1	0	19	74	13	8	7	3	1	1	0	9	0	12	2	0	1	2	.333	0	0	3.32
Syracuse	AAA Tor	20	19	2	0	121.1	510	119	63	59	8	3	8	6	37	1	64	4	0	6	8	.429	0	0	4.38
1994 Syracuse	AAA Tor	14	13	1	0	79.1	346	77	45	38	9	1	2	3	38	0	30	2	0	5	3	.625	1	0	4.31
1995 Syracuse	AAA Tor	11	5	0	1	31	164	52	39	31	7	2	3	1	18	1	14	1	0	1	5	.167	0	0	9.00
1996 Syracuse	AAA Tor	18	11	0	2	76.2	331	84	49	42	6	0	3	0	26	1	52	1	0	5	4	.556	0	0	4.93
1997 Richmond	AAA Atl	61	1	0	50	83	369	89	48	41	12	1	1	2	35	2	62	6	1	5	9	.357	0	18	4.45
1993 Toronto	AL	6	3	0	1	18	83	19	15	12	2	1	2	1	10	1	7	0	0	1	1	.500	0	0	6.00
1994 Toronto	AL	18	0	0	9	29	141	34	27	19	4	1	2	1	19	2	15	6	0	0	3	.000	0	2	5.90
1996 Toronto	AL	18	0	0	9	38.2	180	45	25	24	5	1	1	0	25	1	23	2	1	1	0	1.000	0	0	5.59
8 Min. YEARS		176	96	7	54	690.1	2955	684	373	311	60	17	26	23	246	8	411	25	11	43	41	.512	2	18	4.05
3 Maj. YEARS		42	4	0	19	85.2	404	98	67	55	11	3	5	2	54	4	45	8	1	2	4	.333	0	2	5.78

Jim Brower

Pitches: Right **Bats:** Right **Pos:** P **Ht:** 6'2" **Wt:** 205 **Born:** 12/29/72 **Age:** 25

Year Team	Lg Org	G	GS	CG	GF	IP	BFP	H	R	ER	HR	SH	SF	HB	TBB	IBB	SO	WP	Bk	W	L	Pct.	ShO	Sv	ERA
		HOW MUCH HE PITCHED						**WHAT HE GAVE UP**												**THE RESULTS**					
1994 Hudson Vall	A- Tex	4	4	1	0	19.2	83	14	10	7	0	0	2	1	6	0	15	0	1	2	1	.667	0	0	3.20
Chston-SC	A Tex	12	12	3	0	78.2	312	52	18	15	2	1	1	5	26	1	84	6	0	7	3	.700	2	0	1.72
1995 Charlotte	A+ Tex	27	27	2	0	173.2	740	170	93	75	16	3	3	8	62	1	110	11	0	7	10	.412	1	0	3.89
1996 Charlotte	A+ Tex	23	21	2	2	145	607	148	67	61	11	5	4	4	40	0	86	7	2	9	8	.529	0	0	3.79
Tulsa	AA Tex	5	5	1	0	33.1	146	35	16	14	4	0	1	1	10	0	16	1	0	3	2	.600	1	0	3.78
1997 Tulsa	AA Tex	23	23	1	0	140	602	156	99	81	13	4	7	3	42	1	103	15	1	5	12	.294	0	0	5.21
Okla City	AAA Tex	4	3	0	0	18.2	92	30	17	15	3	0	2	1	8	0	7	3	0	2	1	.667	0	0	7.23
4 Min. YEARS		98	95	10	2	609	2576	605	320	268	49	13	20	23	194	3	421	43	4	35	37	.486	4	0	3.96

Alvin Brown

Pitches: Right **Bats:** Right **Pos:** P **Ht:** 6'1" **Wt:** 200 **Born:** 9/2/70 **Age:** 27

Year Team	Lg Org	G	GS	CG	GF	IP	BFP	H	R	ER	HR	SH	SF	HB	TBB	IBB	SO	WP	Bk	W	L	Pct.	ShO	Sv	ERA
		HOW MUCH HE PITCHED						**WHAT HE GAVE UP**												**THE RESULTS**					
1993 Bristol	R+ Det	15	6	0	4	39	182	27	30	27	2	0	1	4	47	0	30	14	0	2	2	.500	0	1	6.23
1994 Lakeland	A+ Det	4	0	0	3	7	40	11	8	7	0	0	0	0	7	0	9	1	0	0	0	.000	0	0	9.00
Fayettevlle	A Det	33	12	1	11	97.2	441	61	60	47	3	4	0	7	83	0	109	27	2	6	7	.462	1	0	4.33
1995 Lakeland	A+ Det	9	9	0	0	46.2	202	35	23	22	1	1	1	4	33	0	35	9	1	2	3	.400	0	0	4.24
1996 San Berndno	A+ LA	42	0	0	16	68.2	306	43	40	29	2	5	2	2	62	0	84	17	1	2	4	.333	0	2	3.80
1997 San Antonio	AA LA	16	16	2	0	96.1	406	83	48	40	9	2	2	5	33	0	67	9	2	6	5	.545	1	0	3.74
Albuquerque	AAA LA	12	11	0	0	61.2	291	74	50	42	9	4	2	1	35	0	43	6	1	4	6	.400	1	0	6.13
5 Min. YEARS		131	56	4	34	417	1868	334	259	214	26	16	8	23	300	0	377	83	7	22	27	.449	3	3	4.62

Armann Brown

Bats: Right **Throws:** Right **Pos:** OF **Ht:** 6'1" **Wt:** 163 **Born:** 9/10/72 **Age:** 25

Year Team	Lg Org	G	AB	H	2B	3B	HR	TB	R	RBI	TBB	IBB	SO	HBP	SH	SF	SB	CS	SB%	GDP	Avg	OBP	SLG
		BATTING															**BASERUNNING**				**PERCENTAGES**		
1992 Twins	R Min	20	77	21	1	0	0	22	13	4	12	0	11	0	0	0	4	1	.80	0	.273	.371	.286
1993 Ft. Wayne	A Min	41	124	24	3	0	0	27	11	10	18	0	27	5	0	0	13	1	.93	2	.194	.320	.218
Elizabethtn	R+ Min	50	182	49	8	2	3	70	31	21	19	0	41	2	0	1	7	3	.70	4	.269	.343	.385
1994 Ft. Wayne	A Min	10	38	10	2	0	0	12	8	4	2	0	12	2	2	1	3	1	.75	0	.263	.326	.316
Twins	R Min	5	16	2	1	0	0	3	1	0	1	0	4	1	0	0	0	0	.00	0	.125	.222	.188
1995 Ft. Myers	A+ Min	23	63	12	2	3	0	20	6	9	3	0	15	1	0	1	1	0	1.00	1	.190	.235	.317
Ft. Wayne	A Min	78	253	59	9	2	1	75	35	25	30	0	57	8	2	0	26	7	.79	8	.233	.333	.296
1996 Ft. Myers	A+ Min	112	403	100	14	8	3	139	75	27	65	0	75	5	7	3	36	15	.71	5	.248	.357	.345
1997 New Britain	AA Min	14	46	7	3	0	0	10	4	1	9	0	13	0	0	0	1	2	.33	0	.152	.291	.217
Adirondack	IND —	1	5	0	0	0	0	0	0	0	0	0	3	0	0	0	0	0	.00	0	.000	.000	.000
6 Min. YEARS		354	1207	284	43	15	7	378	184	101	159	0	258	24	11	6	91	30	.75	20	.235	.335	.313

Chad Brown

Pitches: Left **Bats:** Left **Pos:** P **Ht:** 6'0" **Wt:** 185 **Born:** 12/9/71 **Age:** 26

Year Team	Lg Org	G	GS	CG	GF	IP	BFP	H	R	ER	HR	SH	SF	HB	TBB	IBB	SO	WP	Bk	W	L	Pct.	ShO	Sv	ERA
		HOW MUCH HE PITCHED						**WHAT HE GAVE UP**												**THE RESULTS**					
1992 Medicne Hat	R+ Tor	37	0	0	9	37	180	46	28	18	4	0	0	1	21	1	28	7	1	3	3	.500	0	1	4.38
1993 St. Cathms	A- Tor	18	0	0	18	20.2	71	7	4	4	2	0	0	0	5	0	23	0	0	1	0	1.000	0	10	1.74
1994 Dunedin	A+ Tor	52	0	0	20	78	326	59	29	28	1	4	3	0	41	1	56	3	2	6	7	.462	0	4	3.23
1995 Knoxville	AA Tor	40	0	0	14	41.1	181	38	23	21	2	1	1	1	22	1	35	5	0	1	3	.250	0	1	4.57
Syracuse	AAA Tor	11	0	0	3	22	106	21	11	8	1	2	2	0	20	3	14	4	0	1	1	.500	0	0	3.27
1996 Knoxville	AA Tor	46	0	0	23	64.1	285	72	33	29	2	1	1	1	23	1	63	6	1	2	4	.333	0	7	4.06
1997 Syracuse	AAA Tor	22	0	0	14	38.1	178	41	32	27	5	1	1	1	26	0	26	1	0	0	0	.000	0	0	6.34
Knoxville	AA Tor	32	0	0	14	55.2	231	46	25	23	4	5	1	2	16	0	40	2	0	6	4	.600	0	4	3.72
6 Min. YEARS		242	0	0	117	357.1	1558	330	185	158	21	14	9	6	174	7	285	28	4	21	25	.457	0	27	3.98

Darold Brown

Pitches: Left **Bats:** Left **Pos:** P **Ht:** 6'0" **Wt:** 175 **Born:** 8/16/73 **Age:** 24

Year Team	Lg Org	G	GS	CG	GF	IP	BFP	H	R	ER	HR	SH	SF	HB	TBB	IBB	SO	WP	Bk	W	L	Pct.	ShO	Sv	ERA
		HOW MUCH HE PITCHED						**WHAT HE GAVE UP**												**THE RESULTS**					
1993 Danville	R+ Atl	11	1	0	3	19	88	12	8	3	0	0	1	1	19	0	19	1	2	1	0	1.000	0	0	1.42
1994 Idaho Falls	R+ Atl	14	14	0	0	71	307	70	35	29	4	0	1	5	34	2	58	5	0	4	7	.364	0	0	3.68
1995 Eugene	A- Atl	3	3	0	0	17	77	18	16	8	3	1	0	0	6	1	13	1	0	0	3	.000	0	0	4.24

Year Team	Lg Org	G	GS	CG	GF	IP	BFP	H	R	ER	HR	SH	SF	HB	TBB	IBB	SO	WP	Bk	W	L	Pct.	ShO	Sv	ERA
Macon	A Atl	31	0	0	20	54.2	230	39	22	20	1	3	4	4	32	1	55	7	2	3	1	.750	0	5	3.29
1996 Daytona	A+ ChN	35	0	0	11	52.2	221	42	20	16	3	7	2	3	20	4	43	2	0	4	4	.500	0	4	2.73
1997 Orlando	AA ChN	18	0	0	5	30	134	28	15	14	1	0	0	1	18	1	24	1	0	0	0	.000	0	0	4.20
Daytona	A+ ChN	29	1	0	6	38.2	166	33	16	12	3	0	1	2	20	1	32	3	2	2	3	.400	0	1	2.79
5 Min. YEARS		141	19	0	45	283	1223	242	132	102	15	11	9	16	149	10	244	20	6	14	18	.438	0	10	3.24

Jarvis Brown

Bats: Right **Throws:** Right **Pos:** OF **Ht:** 5'7" **Wt:** 170 **Born:** 9/26/67 **Age:** 30

Year Team	Lg Org	G	AB	H	2B	3B	HR	TB	R	RBI	TBB	IBB	SO	HBP	SH	SF	SB	CS	SB%	GDP	Avg	OBP	SLG
1986 Elizabethtn	R+ Min	49	180	41	4	0	3	54	28	23	18	0	41	4	5	1	15	3	.83	3	.228	.310	.300
1987 Elizabethtn	R+ Min	67	258	63	9	1	1	77	52	15	48	1	50	5	3	0	30	2	.94	3	.244	.373	.298
Kenosha	A Min	43	117	22	4	1	3	37	17	16	19	0	24	2	1	2	6	2	.75	2	.188	.307	.316
1988 Kenosha	A Min	138	531	156	25	7	7	216	108	45	71	0	89	10	7	5	72	15	.83	10	.294	.384	.407
1989 Visalia	A+ Min	141	545	131	21	6	4	176	95	46	73	0	112	13	4	4	49	13	.79	12	.240	.342	.323
1990 Orlando	AA Min	135	527	137	22	7	14	215	104	57	80	1	79	9	5	2	33	19	.63	13	.260	.366	.408
1991 Portland	AAA Min	108	436	126	5	8	3	156	62	37	36	1	66	6	3	1	26	12	.68	6	.289	.351	.358
1992 Portland	AAA Min	62	224	56	8	2	2	74	25	16	20	0	37	5	1	1	17	1	.94	2	.250	.324	.330
1993 Las Vegas	AAA SD	100	402	124	27	9	3	178	74	47	41	1	55	5	5	2	22	5	.81	10	.308	.378	.443
1994 Richmond	AAA Atl	71	270	72	11	5	4	105	41	30	36	1	35	4	2	3	8	3	.73	4	.267	.358	.389
1995 Norfolk	AAA NYN	45	148	42	12	3	0	60	29	17	18	0	29	1	2	0	6	3	.67	3	.284	.365	.405
Bowie	AA Bal	58	219	61	12	1	6	93	50	23	33	0	49	4	2	1	12	3	.80	5	.279	.381	.425
Rochester	AAA Bal	17	70	22	4	2	0	30	12	4	10	0	20	2	1	0	1	1	.50	2	.314	.400	.429
1996 Rochester	AAA Bal	57	204	43	6	6	4	73	28	19	19	0	36	2	0	3	9	1	.90	5	.211	.281	.358
Thunder Bay	IND —	43	160	48	7	1	4	69	27	20	19	0	20	2	0	2	9	3	.75	4	.300	.377	.431
1997 Tucson	AAA Mil	112	385	102	21	3	6	147	65	35	52	0	84	2	3	6	14	6	.70	15	.265	.351	.382
1991 Minnesota	AL	38	37	8	0	0	0	8	10	0	2	0	8	0	1	0	7	1	.88	0	.216	.256	.216
1992 Minnesota	AL	35	15	1	0	0	0	1	8	0	2	0	4	1	0	0	2	2	.50	0	.067	.222	.067
1993 San Diego	NL	47	133	31	9	2	0	44	21	8	15	0	26	6	2	1	3	3	.50	4	.233	.335	.331
1994 Atlanta	NL	17	15	2	1	0	1	6	3	1	0	0	2	0	1	0	0	0	.00	1	.133	.133	.400
1995 Baltimore	AL	18	27	4	1	0	0	5	2	1	7	0	9	0	1	0	1	1	.50	0	.148	.324	.185
12 Min. YEARS		1246	4676	1246	198	62	64	1760	817	450	593	5	826	74	45	33	329	92	.78	99	.266	.356	.376
5 Maj. YEARS		155	227	46	11	2	1	64	44	10	26	0	49	7	7	1	13	7	.65	5	.203	.303	.282

Michael Brown

Bats: Left **Throws:** Left **Pos:** P **Ht:** 6'7" **Wt:** 235 **Born:** 11/4/71 **Age:** 26

Year Team	Lg Org	G	GS	CG	GF	IP	BFP	H	R	ER	HR	SH	SF	HB	TBB	IBB	SO	WP	Bk	W	L	Pct.	ShO	Sv	ERA
1996 Lynchburg	A+ Pit	34	11	0	6	69.1	356	91	66	54	6	2	4	8	52	1	62	8	2	1	5	.167	0	0	7.01
1997 Pirates	R Pit	2	0	0	0	4.1	18	3	2	1	0	1	0	0	3	0	6	0	0	0	0	.000	0	0	4.15
Carolina	AA Pit	1	0	0	0	2	13	5	5	4	0	0	0	0	1	0	2	1	0	0	0	.000	0	0	18.00
2 Min. YEARS		37	11	0	6	75.2	387	99	73	60	7	2	5	8	56	1	70	9	2	1	5	.167	0	0	7.14

Randy Brown

Bats: Right **Throws:** Right **Pos:** SS **Ht:** 5'11" **Wt:** 160 **Born:** 5/1/70 **Age:** 28

Year Team	Lg Org	G	AB	H	2B	3B	HR	TB	R	RBI	TBB	IBB	SO	HBP	SH	SF	SB	CS	SB%	GDP	Avg	OBP	SLG
1990 Elmira	A- Bos	74	212	50	4	0	1	57	27	8	17	0	47	4	9	0	17	4	.81	1	.236	.305	.269
1991 Red Sox	R Bos	44	143	27	7	0	0	34	25	10	23	0	31	2	3	1	19	0	1.00	1	.189	.308	.238
Winter Havn	A+ Bos	63	135	21	3	0	0	24	14	5	16	0	42	1	4	0	10	3	.77	2	.156	.250	.178
1992 Winter Havn	A+ Bos	121	430	101	18	2	2	129	39	24	28	0	115	6	8	4	8	9	.47	1	.235	.288	.300
1993 Lynchburg	A+ Bos	128	483	114	25	7	2	159	57	45	25	0	127	13	2	4	10	8	.56	6	.236	.290	.329
1994 New Britain	AA Bos	114	389	87	14	2	8	129	51	30	30	0	102	5	7	4	5	5	.64	1	.224	.285	.332
1995 Pawtucket	AAA Bos	74	212	53	6	1	2	67	27	12	10	0	53	4	4	2	5	1	.83	4	.250	.294	.316
1996 Pawtucket	AAA Bos	3	6	1	0	0	0	1	0	1	1	0	1	0	0	0	0	0	.00	1	.167	.286	.167
Trenton	AA Bos	72	245	73	15	2	11	125	46	38	27	2	56	5	1	0	9	4	.69	3	.298	.379	.510
1997 Trenton	AA Bos	97	336	86	11	4	8	129	51	49	38	3	102	4	3	4	9	7	.56	6	.256	.335	.384
Norwich	AA NYA	19	60	13	2	0	3	24	10	8	9	0	22	2	0	0	2	1	.67	1	.217	.338	.400
8 Min. YEARS		809	2651	626	105	18	37	878	347	230	224	5	698	46	41	19	98	42	.70	30	.236	.305	.331

Ray Brown

Bats: Left **Throws:** Right **Pos:** 1B-OF **Ht:** 6'2" **Wt:** 205 **Born:** 7/30/72 **Age:** 25

Year Team	Lg Org	G	AB	H	2B	3B	HR	TB	R	RBI	TBB	IBB	SO	HBP	SH	SF	SB	CS	SB%	GDP	Avg	OBP	SLG
1994 Billings	R+ Cin	60	218	80	19	3	9	132	50	49	27	1	32	10	0	5	3	5	.38	5	.367	.450	.606
1995 Winston-Sal	A+ Cin	122	445	118	26	0	19	201	63	77	52	12	85	11	0	4	3	2	.60	8	.265	.354	.452
Chston-WV	A Cin	6	17	2	1	0	0	3	3	0	4	0	3	0	0	0	0	0	.00	0	.118	.286	.176
1996 Chattanooga	AA Cin	115	364	119	26	5	13	194	68	52	52	7	62	3	0	3	2	1	.67	11	.327	.412	.533
1997 Las Vegas	AAA SD	41	140	36	13	0	2	55	12	15	11	1	28	1	1	0	1	0	1.00	11	.257	.316	.393
Mobile	AA SD	57	179	63	16	0	4	91	28	30	33	1	33	1	0	1	1	0	1.00	6	.352	.453	.508
4 Min. YEARS		401	1363	418	101	8	47	676	224	223	179	22	243	26	1	13	10	8	.56	41	.307	.394	.496

35

Ron Brown

Bats: Right Throws: Right Pos: OF Ht: 6'3" Wt: 185 Born: 1/17/70 Age: 28

Year Team	Lg Org	G	AB	H	2B	3B	HR	TB	R	RBI	TBB	IBB	SO	HBP	SH	SF	SB	CS	SB%	GDP	Avg	OBP	SLG
1993 Elmira	A- Fla	75	285	82	22	1	9	133	53	55	37	2	59	2	1	3	4	2	.67	2	.288	.370	.467
1994 Kane County	A Fla	109	411	109	22	3	9	164	51	75	26	1	75	4	0	5	4	2	.67	14	.265	.312	.399
1995 Brevard Cty	A+ Fla	121	404	105	22	2	3	140	48	51	31	0	79	3	1	9	6	12	.33	14	.260	.311	.347
1996 Portland	AA Fla	4	10	1	0	1	0	3	3	1	1	0	1	0	0	0	0	0	.00	0	.100	.182	.300
Duluth-Sup.	IND —	61	231	61	16	0	7	98	36	35	22	1	38	1	1	4	4	2	.67	4	.264	.326	.424
1997 Columbus	AAA NYA	10	33	6	0	1	0	8	4	1	2	0	3	0	1	0	1	0	1.00	0	.182	.229	.242
Tampa	A+ NYA	5	17	1	0	0	0	3	1	3	2	0	4	0	0	0	1	1	.50	0	.059	.158	.176
Norwich	AA NYA	100	362	104	17	3	5	142	47	50	35	1	59	1	1	3	5	7	.42	11	.287	.350	.392
5 Min. YEARS		485	1753	469	99	12	33	691	241	271	156	5	318	11	7	23	25	26	.49	45	.268	.327	.394

Byron Browne

Pitches: Right Bats: Right Pos: P Ht: 6'7" Wt: 200 Born: 8/8/70 Age: 27

Year Team	Lg Org	G	GS	CG	GF	IP	BFP	H	R	ER	HR	SH	SF	HB	TBB	IBB	SO	WP	Bk	W	L	Pct.	ShO	Sv	ERA
1991 Brewers	R Mil	13	11	0	0	58	312	68	65	52	2	0	4	5	67	1	68	14	2	1	6	.143	0	0	8.07
1992 Beloit	A Mil	25	25	2	0	134.2	621	109	84	76	8	8	4	11	114	0	111	24	6	9	8	.529	0	0	5.08
1993 Stockton	A+ Mil	27	27	0	0	143.2	661	117	73	65	9	7	6	11	117	1	110	13	0	10	5	.667	0	0	4.07
1994 Stockton	A+ Mil	11	11	1	0	62	260	46	30	19	4	4	1	3	30	0	67	3	0	2	6	.250	0	0	2.76
El Paso	AA Mil	5	5	0	0	29	124	26	11	8	3	0	1	0	13	0	33	1	0	2	1	.667	0	0	2.48
1995 El Paso	AA Mil	25	20	2	3	126	541	106	55	48	7	3	9	6	78	2	110	7	0	10	4	.714	1	0	3.43
1996 New Orleans	AAA Mil	23	21	1	0	107.1	489	104	79	74	18	3	5	7	73	1	80	7	1	3	9	.250	0	0	6.20
1997 Stockton	A+ Mil	8	7	0	1	27.2	120	22	12	11	0	0	0	3	22	0	24	4	0	1	3	.250	0	0	3.58
El Paso	AA Mil	1	1	0	0	6	27	8	5	5	1	0	0	0	3	0	3	1	0	0	1	.000	0	0	7.50
Tucson	AAA Mil	3	3	0	0	10.1	52	13	9	6	0	0	0	0	8	0	7	1	1	0	1	.000	0	0	5.23
7 Min. YEARS		141	131	6	4	704.2	3207	619	423	364	52	25	30	46	525	5	613	75	10	38	44	.463	1	0	4.65

Mark Brownson

Pitches: Right Bats: Left Pos: P Ht: 6'2" Wt: 175 Born: 6/17/75 Age: 23

Year Team	Lg Org	G	GS	CG	GF	IP	BFP	H	R	ER	HR	SH	SF	HB	TBB	IBB	SO	WP	Bk	W	L	Pct.	ShO	Sv	ERA
1994 Rockies	R Col	19	4	0	6	54.1	224	48	18	10	2	2	2	3	6	0	72	2	2	4	1	.800	0	1	1.66
1995 Asheville	A Col	23	12	0	4	98.2	422	106	52	44	12	2	2	4	29	0	94	4	2	6	7	.462	0	1	4.01
New Haven	AA Col	1	1	0	0	6	24	4	2	1	1	0	0	0	1	0	4	0	0	0	0	.000	0	0	1.50
Salem	A+ Col	9	1	0	5	15.2	71	16	8	7	0	0	0	1	10	4	9	4	0	2	1	.667	0	1	4.02
1996 New Haven	AA Col	37	19	1	10	144	619	141	73	56	10	6	3	6	43	5	155	7	2	8	13	.381	0	3	3.50
1997 New Haven	AA Col	29	29	2	0	184.2	779	172	101	86	24	8	5	14	55	1	170	5	2	10	9	.526	0	0	4.19
4 Min. YEARS		118	66	3	25	503.1	2139	487	254	204	49	18	12	28	144	10	504	22	8	30	31	.492	0	8	3.65

Julio Bruno

Bats: Right Throws: Right Pos: 3B Ht: 5'11" Wt: 190 Born: 10/15/72 Age: 25

Year Team	Lg Org	G	AB	H	2B	3B	HR	TB	R	RBI	TBB	IBB	SO	HBP	SH	SF	SB	CS	SB%	GDP	Avg	OBP	SLG
1990 Chston-SC	A SD	19	75	17	1	1	0	20	11	5	1	0	21	0	1	1	0	0	.00	0	.227	.234	.267
Spokane	A- SD	68	251	63	7	2	2	80	36	22	25	1	78	2	0	0	7	5	.58	10	.251	.324	.319
1991 Waterloo	A SD	86	277	64	10	3	1	83	34	25	29	0	78	4	4	1	11	6	.65	8	.231	.312	.300
1992 High Desert	A+ SD	118	418	116	22	5	3	157	57	62	33	4	92	1	5	3	2	3	.40	8	.278	.330	.376
1993 Rancho Cuca	A+ SD	54	201	62	11	2	3	86	37	16	19	2	56	1	1	2	15	6	.71	7	.308	.368	.428
Wichita	AA SD	70	246	70	17	1	3	98	34	24	11	3	46	2	1	1	3	5	.38	9	.285	.319	.398
1994 Rancho Cuca	A+ SD	6	25	14	2	1	2	24	11	7	4	0	4	1	0	0	2	0	1.00	0	.560	.633	.960
Las Vegas	AAA SD	123	450	117	25	4	6	168	48	52	24	3	83	4	5	5	4	5	.44	15	.260	.300	.373
1995 Las Vegas	AAA SD	38	139	34	6	1	0	42	13	6	8	0	24	0	1	1	1	3	.25	6	.245	.284	.302
Memphis	AA SD	59	196	53	6	3	2	71	16	25	8	0	35	2	3	2	3	2	.60	9	.270	.303	.362
1996 Memphis	AA SD	27	84	20	8	1	0	30	11	9	6	1	18	0	1	1	1	2	.33	2	.238	.286	.357
Las Vegas	AAA SD	80	297	81	16	1	2	105	36	30	17	3	33	2	1	1	6	5	.55	3	.273	.315	.354
1997 Jacksnville	AA Det	120	438	116	22	3	6	162	51	57	38	1	70	3	0	1	6	3	.67	9	.265	.327	.370
8 Min. YEARS		868	3097	827	153	28	30	1126	395	340	223	18	638	22	26	19	61	45	.58	86	.267	.319	.364

William Brunson

Pitches: Left Bats: Left Pos: P Ht: 6'4" Wt: 185 Born: 3/20/70 Age: 28

Year Team	Lg Org	G	GS	CG	GF	IP	BFP	H	R	ER	HR	SH	SF	HB	TBB	IBB	SO	WP	Bk	W	L	Pct.	ShO	Sv	ERA
1992 Princeton	R+ Cin	13	13	0	0	72.2	313	68	34	29	6	4	2	3	28	0	48	2	0	5	5	.500	0	0	3.59
1993 Chston-WV	A Cin	37	15	0	4	123.2	545	119	68	54	10	4	4	11	50	1	103	7	2	5	6	.455	0	0	3.93
1994 Winston-Sal	A+ Cin	30	22	3	3	165	711	161	83	73	12	5	7	12	58	2	129	6	4	12	7	.632	0	0	3.98
1995 San Berndno	A+ LA	13	13	0	0	83.1	334	68	24	19	4	3	5	5	21	0	70	3	0	10	0	1.000	0	0	2.05
San Antonio	AA LA	14	14	0	0	80	356	105	46	44	4	3	1	4	22	0	44	5	1	4	5	.444	0	0	4.95
1996 San Antonio	AA LA	11	5	0	1	42	166	32	13	10	2	2	0	1	15	0	38	2	1	3	1	.750	0	0	2.14
Albuquerque	AAA LA	9	9	1	0	54.1	239	53	29	27	7	2	1	2	23	1	47	2	0	3	4	.429	0	0	4.47
1997 Albuquerque	AAA LA	27	0	0	9	26.1	125	39	19	19	3	1	1	1	10	1	25	0	0	1	1	.500	0	0	6.49
San Antonio	AA LA	17	11	2	4	72.2	299	68	30	28	8	3	1	6	13	0	71	2	0	5	5	.500	0	0	3.47
6 Min. YEARS		171	102	6	21	720	3088	713	346	303	66	27	22	45	240	5	575	29	8	48	34	.585	1	0	3.79

Adam Bryant

Pitches: Right Bats: Right Pos: P   Ht: 6'6" Wt: 225 Born: 12/27/71 Age: 26

				HOW MUCH HE PITCHED					WHAT HE GAVE UP											THE RESULTS					
Year Team	Lg Org	G	GS	CG	GF	IP	BFP	H	R	ER	HR	SH	SF	HB	TBB	IBB	SO	WP	Bk	W	L	Pct.	ShO	Sv	ERA
1994 Billings	R+ Cin	23	0	0	16	41.1	164	32	15	13	0	2	1	3	11	0	49	4	2	3	1	.750	0	4	2.83
1995 Billings	R+ Cin	29	0	0	26	37.1	157	39	13	13	3	0	1	2	5	1	30	4	4	4	2	.667	0	11	3.13
1996 Chston-WV	A Cin	22	0	0	20	29.2	114	22	7	7	2	0	1	2	2	0	25	1	0	1	1	.500	0	7	2.12
Winston-Sal	A+ Cin	28	0	0	23	34	149	39	13	9	1	0	3	2	10	0	16	0	1	4	3	.571	0	8	2.38
Chattanooga	AA Cin	1	0	0	0	1	3	0	0	0	0	0	0	0	0	0	1	0	0	0	0	.000	0	0	0.00
1997 Chattanooga	AA Cin	6	0	0	1	9	43	15	8	7	2	0	0	3	1	1	4	0	0	1	0	1.000	0	0	7.00
Chico	IND —	43	0	0	11	61.1	260	54	19	14	3	2	3	2	21	2	69	1	0	3	4	.429	0	2	2.05
4 Min. YEARS		152	0	0	97	213.2	890	201	75	63	11	4	9	14	50	4	194	10	7	16	11	.593	0	32	2.65

Pat Bryant

Bats: Right Throws: Right Pos: OF   Ht: 5'11" Wt: 182 Born: 10/27/72 Age: 25

							BATTING										BASERUNNING				PERCENTAGES		
Year Team	Lg Org	G	AB	H	2B	3B	HR	TB	R	RBI	TBB	IBB	SO	HBP	SH	SF	SB	CS	SB%	GDP	Avg	OBP	SLG
1990 Indians	R Cle	17	51	10	2	0	0	12	3	3	8	0	18	4	0	1	2	0	1.00	0	.196	.344	.235
Burlington	R+ Cle	17	50	5	0	0	1	8	3	2	7	0	23	0	0	0	7	1	.88	0	.100	.211	.160
1991 Columbus	A Cle	100	326	68	11	0	7	100	51	27	49	0	108	7	2	2	30	6	.83	2	.209	.323	.307
1992 Columbus	A Cle	49	151	33	14	2	2	57	36	19	30	2	52	7	2	0	10	2	.83	1	.219	.372	.377
Watertown	A- Cle	63	220	58	13	1	7	94	41	30	33	1	61	5	1	1	35	8	.81	0	.264	.371	.427
1993 Columbus	A Cle	121	483	127	26	2	16	205	82	61	43	1	117	13	0	2	43	11	.80	6	.263	.338	.424
1994 Canton-Akrn	AA Cle	124	377	89	14	2	12	143	61	53	48	0	87	5	5	3	23	14	.62	4	.236	.328	.379
1995 Canton-Akrn	AA Cle	127	421	109	22	3	17	188	60	59	52	0	116	4	4	5	16	8	.67	5	.259	.344	.447
1996 Canton-Akrn	AA Cle	34	109	21	2	1	3	34	13	17	17	1	24	4	1	2	8	2	.80	1	.193	.318	.312
Buffalo	AAA Cle	27	64	11	1	0	0	12	6	0	5	0	20	1	1	0	2	0	.00	2	.172	.243	.188
1997 Trenton	AA Bos	104	379	109	20	3	19	192	73	77	60	1	76	9	2	2	18	7	.72	3	.288	.396	.507
Pawtucket	AAA Bos	9	34	10	2	1	0	14	3	4	1	0	11	0	0	0	2	0	1.00	0	.294	.314	.412
8 Min. YEARS		792	2665	650	127	15	84	1059	432	352	353	6	713	59	19	16	194	61	.76	24	.244	.343	.397

Brian Buchanan

Bats: Right Throws: Right Pos: OF   Ht: 6'4" Wt: 220 Born: 7/21/73 Age: 24

							BATTING										BASERUNNING				PERCENTAGES		
Year Team	Lg Org	G	AB	H	2B	3B	HR	TB	R	RBI	TBB	IBB	SO	HBP	SH	SF	SB	CS	SB%	GDP	Avg	OBP	SLG
1994 Oneonta	A- NYA	50	177	40	9	2	4	65	28	26	24	2	53	6	0	2	5	3	.63	2	.226	.335	.367
1995 Greensboro	A NYA	23	96	29	3	0	3	41	19	12	9	1	17	1	0	0	7	1	.88	1	.302	.368	.427
1996 Tampa	A+ NYA	131	526	137	22	4	10	197	65	58	37	6	108	10	1	1	23	8	.74	14	.260	.321	.375
1997 Columbus	AAA NYA	18	61	17	1	0	4	30	8	7	4	0	11	3	1	1	2	1	.67	3	.279	.348	.492
Norwich	AA NYA	116	470	145	25	2	10	204	75	69	32	0	85	11	0	6	11	9	.55	11	.309	.362	.434
4 Min. YEARS		338	1330	368	60	8	31	537	195	172	106	9	274	31	2	10	48	22	.69	31	.277	.342	.404

Brandall Buckles

Pitches: Right Bats: Right Pos: P   Ht: 6'1" Wt: 190 Born: 6/19/73 Age: 25

				HOW MUCH HE PITCHED					WHAT HE GAVE UP											THE RESULTS					
Year Team	Lg Org	G	GS	CG	GF	IP	BFP	H	R	ER	HR	SH	SF	HB	TBB	IBB	SO	WP	Bk	W	L	Pct.	ShO	Sv	ERA
1994 Hudson Vall	A- Tex	27	0	0	24	45.2	173	31	10	7	0	0	2	2	8	0	51	1	0	3	1	.750	0	18	1.38
1995 Charlotte	A+ Tex	48	0	0	43	69	293	70	29	24	5	5	2	0	21	3	43	4	2	2	9	.182	0	16	3.13
1996 Charlotte	A+ Tex	21	3	0	5	55	228	55	25	22	3	5	1	2	13	1	43	2	1	1	4	.200	0	1	3.60
1997 Tulsa	AA Tex	34	0	0	19	45	204	59	38	35	5	0	2	1	20	0	29	2	0	2	2	.500	0	1	7.00
Okla City	AAA Tex	5	0	0	1	11.2	50	12	3	1	0	2	1	0	4	0	5	0	0	0	0	.000	0	0	0.77
4 Min. YEARS		135	3	0	92	226.1	948	227	105	89	13	12	8	5	66	4	171	9	3	8	16	.333	0	35	3.54

Travis Buckley

Pitches: Right Bats: Right Pos: P   Ht: 6'4" Wt: 208 Born: 6/15/70 Age: 28

				HOW MUCH HE PITCHED					WHAT HE GAVE UP											THE RESULTS					
Year Team	Lg Org	G	GS	CG	GF	IP	BFP	H	R	ER	HR	SH	SF	HB	TBB	IBB	SO	WP	Bk	W	L	Pct.	ShO	Sv	ERA
1989 Rangers	R Tex	16	4	0	2	50.1	211	41	28	19	1	1	2	0	24	1	34	3	5	3	3	.500	0	0	3.40
1990 Gastonia	A Tex	27	26	3	0	161.2	684	149	66	51	10	3	5	4	61	0	149	7	0	12	6	.667	0	0	2.84
1991 Charlotte	A+ Tex	28	21	3	3	128	553	115	58	46	7	8	5	6	67	4	131	8	1	8	9	.471	3	1	3.23
1992 Harrisburg	AA Mon	26	26	0	0	160	676	146	58	51	8	2	4	12	64	2	123	4	1	7	7	.500	0	0	2.87
1993 Colo Spmgs	AAA Col	6	1	0	1	9	48	12	13	6	0	1	1	3	7	0	5	2	0	1	2	.333	0	0	6.00
Chattanooga	AA Cin	2	2	0	0	8	37	7	6	3	1	0	1	1	4	0	6	2	0	1	0	1.000	0	0	3.38
Jacksnville	AA Sea	10	9	0	0	48.1	216	57	35	33	7	0	5	3	18	0	38	1	1	2	3	.400	0	0	6.14
1994 Jacksnville	AA Sea	14	11	0	2	71.1	308	70	41	38	3	2	6	3	30	2	31	8	0	2	6	.250	0	0	4.79
Chattanooga	AA Cin	27	24	2	2	156.1	659	145	73	64	9	4	9	7	56	3	96	14	0	9	8	.529	0	0	3.68
1995 Chattanooga	AA Cin	3	3	0	0	14.1	69	21	12	12	4	0	1	1	5	0	10	1	0	1	2	.333	0	0	7.53
Indianapols	AAA Cin	23	18	3	0	132	561	141	80	69	8	3	4	3	33	3	85	4	0	10	9	.526	2	0	4.70
1996 Chattanooga	AA Cin	8	8	2	0	53.2	234	57	40	29	6	3	2	2	13	1	41	3	0	4	3	.429	1	0	4.86
Indianapols	AAA Cin	22	20	1	0	122	518	126	68	61	23	2	3	4	32	0	58	2	0	11	7	.611	0	0	4.50
1997 Vancouver	AAA Ana	32	25	1	4	176	785	223	116	100	21	6	8	8	51	3	119	6	0	7	11	.389	0	1	5.11
9 Min. YEARS		244	198	15	14	1291	5559	1310	694	582	112	35	56	57	465	19	926	65	8	76	78	.494	6	2	4.06

Mike Buddie

Pitches: Right Bats: Right Pos: P   Ht: 6'3" Wt: 210 Born: 12/12/70 Age: 27

Year Team	Lg Org	G	GS	CG	GF	IP	BFP	H	R	ER	HR	SH	SF	HB	TBB	IBB	SO	WP	Bk	W	L	Pct.	ShO	Sv	ERA
1992 Oneonta	A- NYA	13	13	1	0	67.1	301	69	36	29	3	0	1	3	34	0	87	7	5	1	4	.200	0	0	3.88
1993 Greensboro	A NYA	27	26	0	0	155.1	686	138	104	84	19	2	4	8	89	0	143	22	2	13	10	.565	0	0	4.87
1994 Tampa	A+ NYA	25	24	2	0	150.1	643	143	75	67	7	5	8	5	66	2	113	9	4	12	5	.706	0	0	4.01
1995 Norwich	AA NYA	29	27	2	1	149.2	689	155	102	80	4	6	8	15	81	2	106	13	1	10	12	.455	0	1	4.81
1996 Norwich	AA NYA	29	26	4	0	159.2	708	176	101	79	10	8	5	8	71	5	103	16	0	7	12	.368	0	0	4.45
1997 Norwich	AA NYA	1	0	0	1	1	3	0	0	0	0	0	0	0	0	0	3	0	0	0	0	.000	0	0	0.00
Columbus	AAA NYA	53	0	0	13	75	319	85	24	22	4	4	3	2	25	0	67	5	0	6	6	.500	0	2	2.64
6 Min. YEARS		177	116	9	14	758.1	3349	766	442	361	47	25	29	41	366	9	622	72	12	49	49	.500	0	3	4.28

Jason Bullard

Pitches: Right Bats: Right Pos: P   Ht: 6'2" Wt: 185 Born: 10/23/68 Age: 29

Year Team	Lg Org	G	GS	CG	GF	IP	BFP	H	R	ER	HR	SH	SF	HB	TBB	IBB	SO	WP	Bk	W	L	Pct.	ShO	Sv	ERA
1991 Welland	A- Pit	6	0	0	6	7	28	4	0	0	0	0	0	0	4	0	8	0	0	0	0	.000	0	0	0.00
Augusta	A Pit	21	0	0	17	25.2	116	21	13	10	1	1	0	1	15	1	29	2	1	2	2	.500	0	4	3.51
1992 Carolina	AA Pit	19	0	0	10	24.1	121	37	25	20	3	2	2	2	11	1	23	3	0	0	2	.000	0	3	7.40
1993 Pirates	R Pit	4	0	0	1	7	33	11	3	3	0	1	0	1	2	0	8	1	0	0	1	.000	0	0	3.86
1994 St. Paul	IND —	33	4	0	23	59.1	248	53	31	25	2	5	2	4	25	1	47	10	0	6	5	.545	0	10	3.79
1995 Colo Spmgs	AAA Col	4	0	0	1	8.2	48	18	13	7	1	0	0	1	5	1	5	0	1	0	0	.000	0	0	7.27
St. Paul	IND —	17	17	0	0	88.1	406	113	58	51	9	0	5	7	33	1	47	8	0	3	3	.500	0	0	5.20
1996 Norfolk	AAA NYN	24	0	0	7	38.2	178	45	23	21	2	2	2	6	16	1	24	6	0	0	3	.000	0	0	4.89
Binghamton	AA NYN	5	0	0	3	10	46	11	4	3	0	1	0	0	5	2	10	0	0	0	0	.000	0	0	2.70
Canton-Akrn	AA Cle	9	0	0	5	11	45	7	3	3	1	2	0	1	6	1	12	0	0	1	1	.500	0	0	2.45
1997 Bowie	AA Bal	61	0	0	15	92.2	391	84	39	27	6	3	4	10	38	9	77	10	0	7	2	.778	0	3	2.62
7 Min. YEARS		206	21	0	88	372.2	1660	404	212	170	25	17	15	33	160	18	290	40	2	19	19	.500	0	27	4.11

Scott Bullett

Bats: Left Throws: Left Pos: OF   Ht: 6'2" Wt: 220 Born: 12/25/68 Age: 29

Year Team	Lg Org	G	AB	H	2B	3B	HR	TB	R	RBI	TBB	IBB	SO	HBP	SH	SF	SB	CS	SB%	GDP	Avg	OBP	SLG
1988 Pirates	R Pit	21	61	11	1	0	0	12	6	8	7	1	9	0	1	1	2	5	.29	0	.180	.261	.197
1989 Pirates	R Pit	46	165	42	7	3	1	58	24	16	12	2	31	5	1	0	15	5	.75	2	.255	.324	.352
1990 Welland	A- Pit	74	256	77	11	4	3	105	46	33	13	2	50	2	1	0	30	6	.83	7	.301	.339	.410
1991 Augusta	A Pit	95	384	109	21	6	1	145	61	36	27	2	79	2	1	0	48	17	.74	1	.284	.333	.378
Salem	A+ Pit	39	156	52	7	5	2	75	21	8	1		29	0	0	0	15	7	.68	0	.333	.366	.481
1992 Carolina	AA Pit	132	518	140	20	5	8	194	59	45	28	5	98	10	2	7	29	21	.58	0	.270	.316	.375
Buffalo	AAA Pit	3	10	4	0	2	0	8	1	0	0	0	2	0	0	0	0	0	.00	0	.400	.400	.800
1993 Buffalo	AAA Pit	110	408	117	13	6	1	145	62	30	39	0	67	1	8	0	28	17	.62	5	.287	.350	.355
1994 Iowa	AAA ChN	135	530	163	28	4	13	238	75	69	19	4	110	5	11	6	27	16	.63	5	.308	.334	.449
1996 Orlando	AA ChN	3	11	2	0	0	0	2	2	0	1	0	2	0	0	0	2	0	1.00	0	.182	.250	.182
1997 Rochester	AAA Bal	136	512	128	24	8	9	195	73	58	45	2	112	7	0	2	19	11	.63	17	.250	.318	.381
1991 Pittsburgh	NL	11	4	0	0	0	0	0	2	0	0	0	3	1	0	0	1	1	.50	0	.000	.200	.000
1993 Pittsburgh	NL	23	55	11	0	2	0	15	2	4	3	0	15	1	0	1	3	2	.60	1	.200	.237	.273
1995 Chicago	NL	104	150	41	5	7	3	69	19	22	12	2	30	1	1	0	8	3	.73	4	.273	.331	.460
1996 Chicago	NL	109	165	35	5	0	3	49	26	16	10	0	54	0	1	2	7	3	.70	2	.212	.256	.297
9 Min. YEARS		794	3011	845	132	43	38	1177	431	310	199	22	589	32	25	17	215	105	.67	44	.281	.330	.391
4 Maj. YEARS		247	374	87	10	9	6	133	49	42	25	2	102	2	2	2	19	9	.68	7	.233	.283	.356

Kirk Bullinger

Pitches: Right Bats: Right Pos: P   Ht: 6'2" Wt: 170 Born: 10/28/69 Age: 28

Year Team	Lg Org	G	GS	CG	GF	IP	BFP	H	R	ER	HR	SH	SF	HB	TBB	IBB	SO	WP	Bk	W	L	Pct.	ShO	Sv	ERA
1992 Hamilton	A- StL	35	0	0	7	48.2	191	24	7	6	0	1	1	2	15	4	61	3	1	2	2	.500	0	2	1.11
1993 Springfield	A StL	50	0	0	46	51.1	208	26	19	13	5	3	2	2	21	1	72	6	0	1	3	.250	0	33	2.28
1994 St. Pete	A+ StL	39	0	0	18	53.2	220	37	16	7	0	4	0	1	20	5	50	4	3	2	0	1.000	0	6	1.17
1995 Harrisburg	AA Mon	56	0	0	39	67	282	61	22	18	4	4	1	0	25	5	42	2	2	5	3	.625	0	7	2.42
1996 Ottawa	AAA Mon	10	0	0	4	15.1	62	10	6	6	3	0	0	0	9	1	9	1	0	2	1	.667	0	0	3.52
Harrisburg	AA Mon	47	0	0	40	45.2	193	46	16	10	5	3	1	1	18	3	29	3	0	3	4	.429	0	22	1.97
1997 Wst Plm Bch	A+ Mon	2	0	0	0	3.2	15	3	0	0	0	0	0	0	0	0	7	1	0	2	0	1.000	0	0	0.00
Harrisburg	AA Mon	21	0	0	12	27	106	22	9	8	4	1	0	1	6	0	21	0	0	3	0	1.000	0	6	2.67
Ottawa	AAA Mon	22	0	0	14	31.2	119	17	7	6	0	2	1	0	10	0	15	1	0	3	4	.429	0	5	1.71
6 Min. YEARS		282	0	0	180	344	1396	246	102	74	21	18	6	7	124	19	306	21	6	23	17	.575	0	81	1.94

Mel Bunch

Pitches: Right Bats: Right Pos: P   Ht: 6'1" Wt: 170 Born: 11/4/71 Age: 26

Year Team	Lg Org	G	GS	CG	GF	IP	BFP	H	R	ER	HR	SH	SF	HB	TBB	IBB	SO	WP	Bk	W	L	Pct.	ShO	Sv	ERA
1992 Royals	R KC	5	4	0	1	24	87	11	6	4	2	0	0	1	3	0	26	0	0	2	1	.667	0	0	1.50
Eugene	A- KC	10	10	0	0	64.2	265	62	23	20	5	2	2	1	13	0	69	2	1	5	3	.625	0	0	2.78
1993 Rockford	A KC	19	11	0	8	85	337	79	24	20	4	3	2	2	18	0	71	6	1	6	4	.600	0	4	2.12
Wilmington	A+ KC	10	10	1	0	65.2	256	52	22	17	3	1	2	0	14	0	54	2	0	6	2	.625	0	0	2.33
1994 Wilmington	A+ KC	15	12	0	0	61	252	52	30	23	8	1	1	0	15	0	62	2	0	5	3	.625	0	0	3.39
1995 Omaha	AAA KC	12	11	1	0	65	272	63	40	33	10	3	4	0	20	2	50	8	1	1	7	.125	0	0	4.57
1996 Omaha	AAA KC	33	27	0	2	146.2	663	181	106	99	32	4	4	7	59	1	94	8	1	8	9	.471	0	0	6.08

Year Team	Lg Org	G	GS	CG	GF	IP	BFP	H	R	ER	HR	SH	SF	HB	TBB	IBB	SO	WP	Bk	W	L	Pct	ShO	Sv	ERA
		HOW MUCH HE PITCHED						WHAT HE GAVE UP												THE RESULTS					
1997 Harrisburg	AA Mon	9	9	0	0	49.1	210	45	27	23	7	5	0	4	22	0	50	2	0	3	3	.500	0	0	4.20
Ottawa	AAA Mon	16	14	0	0	78	369	102	63	55	13	1	7	2	45	5	58	8	0	4	4	.500	0	0	6.35
1995 Kansas City	AL	13	5	0	3	40	175	42	25	25	11	0	0	0	14	1	19	6	0	1	3	.250	0	0	5.63
6 Min. YEARS		129	108	3	11	639.1	2711	647	338	294	84	21	23	18	209	8	534	38	4	39	37	.513	0	4	4.14

John Burgos

Pitches: Left **Bats:** Left **Pos:** P **Ht:** 5'11" **Wt:** 170 **Born:** 8/2/67 **Age:** 30

Year Team	Lg Org	G	GS	CG	GF	IP	BFP	H	R	ER	HR	SH	SF	HB	TBB	IBB	SO	WP	Bk	W	L	Pct	ShO	Sv	ERA
		HOW MUCH HE PITCHED						WHAT HE GAVE UP												THE RESULTS					
1986 Rangers	R Tex	12	12	0	0	63.2	256	55	18	11	1	0	1	0	22	1	53	2	2	3	3	.500	0	0	1.55
1987 Gastonia	A Tex	21	3	0	6	55	241	61	34	32	4	1	3	3	14	2	42	4	0	0	2	.000	0	0	5.24
Butte	R+ Tex	10	10	2	0	62.2	278	77	48	39	4	1	3	1	20	0	38	5	0	4	6	.400	0	0	5.60
1988 Gastonia	A Tex	28	2	0	11	58	252	54	28	19	4	3	8	1	28	2	52	3	2	4	1	.800	0	2	2.95
1989 Savannah	A StL	4	4	1	0	27.1	100	16	4	2	0	1	0	0	7	0	16	2	0	3	0	1.000	1	0	0.66
St. Pete	A+ StL	1	1	0	0	6	21	4	0	0	0	0	0	0	0	0	4	0	0	1	0	1.000	0	0	0.00
1990 St. Pete	A+ StL	19	14	0	1	92.2	382	77	37	32	5	3	2	1	36	1	67	3	3	7	4	.636	0	0	3.11
Arkansas	AA StL	6	6	1	0	39	160	37	13	12	1	1	2	3	10	1	15	0	1	2	3	.400	1	0	2.77
1991 Reading	AA Phi	15	0	0	8	23	105	27	13	12	2	1	2	0	13	3	10	0	0	2	0	1.000	0	0	4.70
Scranton-WB	AAA Phi	24	6	1	1	64	265	54	25	21	4	7	1	1	29	1	32	3	0	1	3	.250	0	0	2.95
1992 Quad City	A Ana	4	0	0	3	7.1	33	9	2	2	0	0	0	0	3	0	7	1	0	0	0	.000	0	0	2.45
1993 Chattanooga	AA Cin	31	1	0	14	48	189	33	21	19	2	2	4	2	14	4	35	4	0	2	2	.500	0	1	3.56
1994 Chston-WV	A Cin	8	4	0	4	35.1	135	31	5	5	2	1	1	1	2	0	26	1	0	3	0	1.000	0	0	1.27
Winston-Sal	A+ Cin	5	4	0	1	21.2	112	35	26	23	5	0	1	3	11	1	16	3	0	0	3	.000	0	0	9.55
Chattanooga	AA Cin	34	2	0	21	53.2	218	43	20	18	3	4	3	1	16	5	33	1	0	1	3	.250	0	3	3.02
1995 Chattanooga	AA Cin	44	3	0	9	100.1	424	95	42	31	7	5	3	4	19	4	82	2	1	3	5	.375	0	0	2.78
1996 St. Paul	IND —	3	3	0	0	17	74	15	5	4	0	2	0	1	5	1	18	1	0	2	0	1.000	0	0	2.12
1997 Okla City	AAA Tex	7	3	0	2	28	116	27	8	8	3	0	1	2	8	0	15	0	0	2	0	1.000	0	0	2.57
12 Min. YEARS		276	78	5	81	802.2	3361	750	349	290	49	31	36	23	257	26	561	35	9	40	35	.533	3	7	3.25

Travis Burgus

Pitches: Left **Bats:** Left **Pos:** P **Ht:** 6'2" **Wt:** 185 **Born:** 11/6/72 **Age:** 25

Year Team	Lg Org	G	GS	CG	GF	IP	BFP	H	R	ER	HR	SH	SF	HB	TBB	IBB	SO	WP	Bk	W	L	Pct	ShO	Sv	ERA
		HOW MUCH HE PITCHED						WHAT HE GAVE UP												THE RESULTS					
1995 Elmira	A- Fla	15	15	0	0	88	369	84	45	34	7	3	3	4	29	0	68	4	1	7	5	.583	0	0	3.48
1996 Kane County	A Fla	30	7	1	11	96.1	404	80	29	19	1	4	3	5	39	1	111	9	1	5	4	.556	0	4	1.78
1997 Portland	AA Fla	16	9	0	1	52	244	63	47	39	12	0	1	4	26	1	29	0	0	4	3	.571	0	0	6.75
3 Min. YEARS		61	31	1	12	236.1	1017	227	121	92	20	7	7	13	94	2	208	13	2	16	12	.571	0	4	3.50

Jamie Burke

Bats: Right **Throws:** Right **Pos:** 3B **Ht:** 6'0" **Wt:** 195 **Born:** 9/24/71 **Age:** 26

Year Team	Lg Org	G	AB	H	2B	3B	HR	TB	R	RBI	TBB	IBB	SO	HBP	SH	SF	SB	CS	SB%	GDP	Avg	OBP	SLG
		BATTING															BASERUNNING				PERCENTAGES		
1993 Boise	A- Ana	66	226	68	11	1	1	84	32	30	39	3	28	5	2	2	2	3	.40	4	.301	.412	.372
1994 Cedar Rapds	A Ana	127	469	124	24	1	1	153	57	47	40	3	64	12	4	8	6	8	.43	15	.264	.333	.326
1995 Lk Elsinore	A+ Ana	106	365	100	15	6	2	133	47	56	32	1	53	9	11	4	6	4	.60	12	.274	.344	.364
1996 Midland	AA Ana	45	144	46	8	2	2	64	24	16	20	1	22	2	1	0	1	1	.50	1	.319	.410	.444
Vancouver	AAA Ana	41	156	39	5	0	1	47	12	14	7	0	18	1	1	2	2	1	.67	5	.250	.283	.301
1997 Midland	AA Ana	116	428	141	44	3	6	209	77	72	40	0	46	8	0	3	2	3	.40	12	.329	.395	.488
Vancouver	AAA Ana	8	27	8	1	0	0	9	4	3	3	0	2	1	0	0	0	0	.00	1	.296	.387	.333
5 Min. YEARS		509	1815	526	108	13	13	699	253	238	181	8	233	38	19	19	19	20	.49	50	.290	.363	.385

Darren Burton

Bats: Both **Throws:** Right **Pos:** OF **Ht:** 6'1" **Wt:** 185 **Born:** 9/16/72 **Age:** 25

Year Team	Lg Org	G	AB	H	2B	3B	HR	TB	R	RBI	TBB	IBB	SO	HBP	SH	SF	SB	CS	SB%	GDP	Avg	OBP	SLG
		BATTING															BASERUNNING				PERCENTAGES		
1990 Royals	R KC	15	58	12	0	1	0	14	10	2	4	0	17	0	1	2	6	0	1.00	0	.207	.250	.241
1991 Appleton	A KC	134	532	143	32	6	2	193	78	51	45	4	122	1	3	6	37	12	.76	18	.269	.324	.363
1992 Baseball Cy	A+ KC	123	431	106	15	6	4	145	54	36	49	7	93	6	4	3	16	14	.53	7	.246	.329	.336
1993 Wilmington	A+ KC	134	549	152	23	5	10	215	82	45	48	1	111	1	13	4	30	10	.75	7	.277	.334	.392
1994 Memphis	AA KC	97	373	95	12	3	3	122	55	37	35	4	53	1	4	5	10	6	.63	5	.255	.316	.327
1995 Omaha	AAA KC	2	5	0	0	0	0	0	0	0	0	0	1	0	0	0	0	0	.00	0	.000	.000	.000
Wichita	AA KC	41	163	39	9	1	1	53	13	20	12	0	27	1	9	0	6	6	.50	2	.239	.295	.325
Orlando	AA ChN	62	222	68	16	2	4	100	40	21	27	2	42	0	0	4	7	4	.64	5	.306	.382	.450
1996 Omaha	AAA KC	129	463	125	28	5	15	208	75	67	59	6	82	6	9	4	7	7	.50	10	.270	.357	.449
1997 Scranton-WB	AAA Phi	70	253	63	16	3	8	109	34	39	19	1	40	3	1	4	3	0	1.00	6	.249	.305	.431
Reading	AA Phi	45	184	58	11	3	8	99	23	34	9	2	39	3	2	3	1	1	.50	1	.315	.352	.538
8 Min. YEARS		852	3233	861	162	35	55	1258	464	352	307	27	627	22	46	31	123	60	.67	61	.266	.331	.389

Essex Burton

Bats: Right **Throws:** Right **Pos:** OF **Ht:** 5'9" **Wt:** 155 **Born:** 5/16/69 **Age:** 29

Year Team	Lg Org	G	AB	H	2B	3B	HR	TB	R	RBI	TBB	IBB	SO	HBP	SH	SF	SB	CS	SB%	GDP	Avg	OBP	SLG
		BATTING															BASERUNNING				PERCENTAGES		
1991 White Sox	R ChA	50	194	54	5	2	0	63	37	17	26	0	27	1	3	0	21	7	.75	2	.278	.367	.325
Utica	A- ChA	15	58	16	0	0	0	16	11	4	8	0	12	1	2	0	6	2	.75	0	.276	.373	.276
1992 South Bend	A ChA	122	459	116	6	3	0	128	78	29	67	0	109	3	9	1	65	23	.74	1	.253	.351	.279

Year Team	Lg Org	G	AB	H	2B	3B	HR	TB	R	RBI	TBB	IBB	SO	HBP	SH	SF	SB	CS	SB%	GDP	Avg	OBP	SLG
																	BASERUNNING				PERCENTAGES		
1993 South Bend	A ChA	134	501	128	6	8	1	153	95	36	85	0	94	4	8	2	74	24	.76	3	.255	.367	.305
1994 Pr William	A+ ChA	131	503	143	22	10	3	194	94	50	67	1	88	5	6	6	66	19	.78	4	.284	.370	.386
1995 Birmingham	AA ChA	142	554	141	15	2	1	163	95	43	80	4	79	5	15	2	60	22	.73	9	.255	.353	.294
1996 Scranton-WB	AAA Phi	16	58	10	3	0	0	13	4	1	7	0	16	1	0	0	5	3	.63	1	.172	.273	.224
Reading	AA Phi	102	381	116	19	5	1	148	66	30	37	0	56	2	16	2	40	12	.77	4	.304	.367	.388
1997 Tulsa	AA Tex	17	63	13	2	1	0	17	8	2	3	0	7	1	0	0	3	2	.60	4	.206	.254	.270
Massachusts	IND —	37	150	52	8	2	1	67	34	18	19	1	26	3	3	0	8	3	.73	0	.347	.430	.447
7 Min. YEARS		766	2921	789	86	33	7	962	522	230	399	6	514	26	62	13	348	117	.75	30	.270	.361	.329

Mike Busch

Bats: Right **Throws:** Right **Pos:** DH **Ht:** 6' 5" **Wt:** 220 **Born:** 7/7/68 **Age:** 29

Year Team	Lg Org	G	AB	H	2B	3B	HR	TB	R	RBI	TBB	IBB	SO	HBP	SH	SF	SB	CS	SB%	GDP	Avg	OBP	SLG
																	BASERUNNING				PERCENTAGES		
1990 Great Falls	R+ LA	61	220	72	18	2	13	133	48	47	39	2	50	3	0	3	3	2	.60	8	.327	.430	.605
1991 Bakersfield	A+ LA	21	72	20	3	1	4	37	13	16	12	0	21	0	0	1	0	1	.00	1	.278	.376	.514
1992 San Antonio	AA LA	115	416	99	14	2	18	171	58	51	36	2	111	4	0	3	3	2	.60	7	.238	.303	.411
1993 Albuquerque	AAA LA	122	431	122	32	4	22	228	87	70	53	4	89	8	0	5	1	2	.33	12	.283	.368	.529
1994 Albuquerque	AAA LA	126	460	121	23	3	27	231	73	83	50	0	101	4	0	1	2	3	.40	8	.263	.340	.502
1995 Albuquerque	AAA LA	121	443	119	32	1	18	207	68	62	42	3	103	7	0	0	2	2	.50	12	.269	.341	.467
1996 Albuquerque	AAA LA	38	142	43	6	1	12	87	30	36	22	4	45	2	0	0	0	1	.00	1	.303	.404	.613
1997 Buffalo	AAA Cle	51	166	30	4	0	12	70	24	29	22	1	68	1	0	2	0	0	.00	6	.181	.277	.422
1995 Los Angeles	NL	13	17	4	0	0	3	13	3	6	0	0	7	0	0	0	0	0	.00	0	.235	.235	.765
1996 Los Angeles	NL	38	83	18	4	0	4	34	8	17	5	0	33	0	0	0	0	0	.00	2	.217	.261	.410
8 Min. YEARS		655	2350	626	132	14	126	1164	401	394	276	16	588	29	0	15	11	13	.46	55	.266	.349	.495
2 Maj. YEARS		51	100	22	4	0	7	47	11	23	5	0	40	0	0	0	2	0	.00	2	.220	.257	.470

Todd Bussa

Pitches: Right **Bats:** Right **Pos:** P **Ht:** 5'11" **Wt:** 170 **Born:** 12/13/72 **Age:** 25

Year Team	Lg Org	G	GS	CG	GF	IP	BFP	H	R	ER	HR	SH	SF	HB	TBB	IBB	SO	WP	Bk	W	L	Pct.	ShO	Sv	ERA
		HOW MUCH HE PITCHED						WHAT HE GAVE UP												THE RESULTS					
1991 Bristol	R+ Det	12	1	0	7	29.2	138	28	16	9	0	0	1	1	17	1	26	2	1	1	2	.333	0	1	2.73
1992 Fayettevlle	A Det	44	0	0	24	67.1	301	65	37	29	3	4	0	9	30	1	52	3	0	2	9	.182	0	4	3.88
1993 Fayettevlle	A Det	39	0	0	17	79	335	70	33	32	2	3	1	3	36	1	92	6	0	4	3	.571	0	7	3.65
1994 Fayettevlle	A Det	5	0	0	2	15	62	10	1	0	0	1	0	2	4	0	13	2	0	2	0	1.000	0	1	0.00
Lakeland	A+ Det	28	1	0	13	53	244	67	30	28	4	3	3	2	25	2	27	5	1	3	5	.375	0	1	4.75
1995 Kane County	A Fla	36	0	0	33	42	162	20	4	4	1	1	1	6	15	5	38	3	0	0	1	.000	0	14	0.86
1996 Rancho Cuca	A+ SD	16	0	0	5	16.2	93	27	20	18	3	1	0	1	16	1	19	0	0	0	1	.000	0	0	9.72
Clinton	A SD	32	0	0	31	34.2	140	22	7	5	0	1	0	3	7	0	50	1	0	1	0	1.000	0	18	1.30
1997 Modesto	A+ Oak	30	0	0	19	46.1	192	34	15	9	2	4	2	2	16	2	61	2	0	5	4	.556	0	8	1.75
Huntsville	AA Oak	19	0	0	13	21.1	99	20	13	10	2	0	0	4	12	0	27	3	1	2	1	.667	0	7	4.22
7 Min. YEARS		261	2	0	164	405	1766	363	176	144	17	18	8	33	178	13	405	27	3	20	26	.435	0	61	3.20

Shane Buteaux

Pitches: Right **Bats:** Right **Pos:** P **Ht:** 6'3" **Wt:** 202 **Born:** 12/28/71 **Age:** 26

Year Team	Lg Org	G	GS	CG	GF	IP	BFP	H	R	ER	HR	SH	SF	HB	TBB	IBB	SO	WP	Bk	W	L	Pct.	ShO	Sv	ERA
		HOW MUCH HE PITCHED						WHAT HE GAVE UP												THE RESULTS					
1994 White Sox	R ChA	12	10	0	0	55	236	60	33	26	0	2	4	5	15	0	28	4	5	1	5	.167	0	0	4.25
1995 Hickory	A ChA	13	13	0	0	66.2	316	90	63	54	10	4	5	3	32	2	30	2	1	2	7	.222	0	0	7.29
Bristol	R+ ChA	13	13	1	0	74	337	72	45	35	9	0	4	8	41	0	49	4	0	7	6	.538	0	0	4.26
1996 South Bend	A ChA	25	0	0	11	39	178	37	20	13	0	1	3	2	15	0	33	4	1	3	4	.429	0	2	3.00
Pr William	A+ ChA	23	0	0	17	40.1	171	34	18	15	3	7	1	3	22	1	29	2	0	2	3	.400	0	2	3.35
1997 Birmingham	AA ChA	44	0	0	16	73	328	74	41	34	4	1	6	7	34	1	34	5	1	2	2	.500	0	2	4.19
4 Min. YEARS		130	36	1	44	348	1566	367	220	177	26	15	23	28	159	4	203	26	12	17	27	.386	0	6	4.58

Adam Butler

Pitches: Left **Bats:** Left **Pos:** P **Ht:** 6'2" **Wt:** 225 **Born:** 8/17/73 **Age:** 24

Year Team	Lg Org	G	GS	CG	GF	IP	BFP	H	R	ER	HR	SH	SF	HB	TBB	IBB	SO	WP	Bk	W	L	Pct.	ShO	Sv	ERA
		HOW MUCH HE PITCHED						WHAT HE GAVE UP												THE RESULTS					
1995 Eugene	A- Atl	23	0	0	18	25.1	109	15	9	7	0	4	0	3	12	5	50	1	0	4	1	.800	0	8	2.49
1996 Macon	A Atl	12	0	0	12	14.2	53	5	3	2	1	0	0	1	3	0	23	1	0	0	1	.000	0	8	1.23
Durham	A+ Atl	9	0	0	9	11	41	2	0	0	0	0	0	1	7	0	14	0	0	0	0	.000	0	5	0.00
Greenville	AA Atl	38	0	0	31	35.1	161	36	22	20	6	5	3	2	16	3	31	3	0	1	4	.200	0	17	5.09
1997 Greenville	AA Atl	46	0	0	38	49	203	40	16	14	3	3	2	4	15	2	56	1	0	5	1	.833	0	22	2.57
3 Min. YEARS		128	0	0	108	135.1	567	98	50	43	10	9	5	11	53	10	174	6	0	10	7	.588	0	60	2.86

Danny Buxbaum

Bats: Right **Throws:** Right **Pos:** 1B **Ht:** 6'4" **Wt:** 217 **Born:** 1/17/73 **Age:** 25

Year Team	Lg Org	G	AB	H	2B	3B	HR	TB	R	RBI	TBB	IBB	SO	HBP	SH	SF	SB	CS	SB%	GDP	Avg	OBP	SLG
																	BASERUNNING				PERCENTAGES		
1995 Boise	A- Ana	68	231	76	15	0	8	115	46	51	49	5	31	4	0	5	1	0	1.00	3	.329	.446	.498
1996 Lk Elsinore	A+ Ana	74	298	87	17	2	14	150	53	60	31	2	41	2	0	2	1	0	1.00	8	.292	.360	.503
1997 Midland	AA Ana	130	514	148	42	2	10	224	78	70	51	3	91	2	0	3	1	1	.50	9	.288	.353	.436
3 Min. YEARS		272	1043	311	74	4	32	489	177	181	131	10	163	8	0	10	3	1	.75	20	.298	.378	.469

Jimmie Byington

Bats: Right **Throws:** Right **Pos:** OF **Ht:** 6'0" **Wt:** 170 **Born:** 8/22/73 **Age:** 24

								BATTING										BASERUNNING				PERCENTAGES		
Year Team	Lg Org	G	AB	H	2B	3B	HR	TB	R	RBI	TBB	IBB	SO	HBP	SH	SF	SB	CS	SB%	GDP	Avg	OBP	SLG
1993 Eugene	A- KC	53	170	44	5	0	8	73	23	32	14	0	45	3	1	1	9	1	.90	2	.259	.324	.429
1994 Rockford	A KC	105	328	82	14	3	1	105	44	48	26	0	64	5	0	5	14	7	.67	5	.250	.310	.320
1995 Wilmington	A+ KC	92	273	61	6	1	0	69	24	23	13	0	33	4	3	2	12	6	.67	3	.223	.267	.253
1996 Wilmington	A+ KC	105	297	88	20	2	1	115	46	32	19	0	44	5	6	5	12	8	.60	4	.296	.344	.387
1997 Wichita	AA KC	92	196	46	8	0	2	60	30	16	15	0	39	4	3	2	5	6	.45	3	.235	.300	.306
5 Min. YEARS		447	1264	321	53	6	12	422	167	151	87	0	225	21	13	15	52	28	.65	17	.254	.309	.334

Matt Byrd

Pitches: Right **Bats:** Both **Pos:** P **Ht:** 6'2" **Wt:** 200 **Born:** 5/17/71 **Age:** 27

		HOW MUCH HE PITCHED						WHAT HE GAVE UP												THE RESULTS					
Year Team	Lg Org	G	GS	CG	GF	IP	BFP	H	R	ER	HR	SH	SF	HB	TBB	IBB	SO	WP	Bk	W	L	Pct.	ShO	Sv	ERA
1993 Danville	R+ Atl	25	0	0	15	41.1	169	23	10	9	2	4	1	2	17	2	57	5	0	5	2	.714	0	7	1.96
1994 Durham	A+ Atl	29	0	0	28	37.1	156	22	20	19	7	0	0	2	19	2	39	5	0	2	4	.333	0	3	4.58
1995 Durham	A+ Atl	60	0	0	53	69.2	296	52	24	23	8	0	3	3	32	4	79	9	0	5	4	.556	0	27	2.97
1996 Greenville	AA Atl	51	4	0	29	90.1	421	108	77	70	12	8	5	2	40	4	66	11	0	4	9	.308	0	2	6.97
1997 Greenville	AA Atl	28	0	0	12	45	210	58	31	30	9	3	2	2	21	1	38	7	1	3	2	.600	0	0	6.00
New Haven	AA Col	10	3	0	1	23.1	105	22	15	13	3	1	0	0	12	1	17	1	0	1	3	.250	0	0	5.01
5 Min. YEARS		203	7	0	133	307	1357	285	177	164	41	16	11	11	141	14	296	38	1	20	24	.455	0	39	4.81

Earl Byrne

Pitches: Left **Bats:** Left **Pos:** P **Ht:** 6'1" **Wt:** 165 **Born:** 7/2/72 **Age:** 25

		HOW MUCH HE PITCHED						WHAT HE GAVE UP												THE RESULTS					
Year Team	Lg Org	G	GS	CG	GF	IP	BFP	H	R	ER	HR	SH	SF	HB	TBB	IBB	SO	WP	Bk	W	L	Pct.	ShO	Sv	ERA
1994 Cubs	R ChN	4	1	0	1	11	41	5	3	2	0	1	1	0	6	0	11	0	1	1	1	.500	0	0	1.64
1995 Rockford	A ChN	13	11	0	0	60	269	54	36	31	2	3	6	3	38	0	51	8	1	4	3	.571	0	0	4.65
1996 Orlando	AA ChN	11	6	1	2	37	170	36	28	23	5	1	0	0	26	1	30	1	2	1	2	.333	0	1	5.59
Daytona	A+ ChN	18	3	1	6	45.1	201	44	22	17	5	2	0	1	21	2	47	4	2	1	4	.200	0	1	3.38
1997 Orlando	AA ChN	32	20	0	2	130	554	102	62	57	16	5	5	2	73	1	128	6	7	5	5	.500	0	1	3.95
4 Min. YEARS		78	41	2	11	283.1	1235	241	151	130	28	12	10	6	164	4	267	19	13	12	15	.444	0	1	4.13

Jolbert Cabrera

Bats: Right **Throws:** Right **Pos:** 3B **Ht:** 6'0" **Wt:** 177 **Born:** 12/8/72 **Age:** 25

								BATTING										BASERUNNING				PERCENTAGES		
Year Team	Lg Org	G	AB	H	2B	3B	HR	TB	R	RBI	TBB	IBB	SO	HBP	SH	SF	SB	CS	SB%	GDP	Avg	OBP	SLG
1991 Sumter	A Mon	101	324	66	4	0	1	73	33	20	19	0	62	4	4	2	10	11	.48	5	.204	.255	.225
1992 Albany	A Mon	118	377	86	9	2	0	99	44	23	34	0	77	1	6	0	22	11	.67	8	.228	.294	.263
1993 Burlington	A Mon	128	507	129	24	2	0	157	62	38	39	0	93	7	11	4	31	11	.74	13	.254	.314	.310
1994 Wst Plm Bch	A+ Mon	83	266	54	4	0	0	58	32	13	14	0	48	8	4	0	7	10	.41	4	.203	.264	.218
San Berndno	A+ Mon	30	109	27	5	1	0	34	14	11	14	0	24	0	4	2	2	2	.50	1	.248	.328	.312
Harrisburg	AA Mon	3	2	0	0	0	0	0	0	0	0	0	1	0	0	0	0	0	.00	0	.000	.000	.000
1995 Wst Plm Bch	A+ Mon	103	357	102	23	2	1	132	62	25	38	0	61	8	6	4	19	12	.61	3	.286	.364	.370
Harrisburg	AA Mon	9	35	10	2	0	0	12	4	1	1	0	3	0	2	0	3	1	.75	1	.286	.306	.343
1996 Harrisburg	AA Mon	107	354	85	18	2	3	116	40	29	23	3	63	1	5	4	10	5	.67	9	.240	.285	.328
1997 Harrisburg	AA Mon	48	171	43	9	0	2	58	28	11	28	0	28	1	3	0	5	4	.56	4	.251	.360	.339
Ottawa	AAA Mon	68	191	54	10	4	0	72	28	12	11	0	31	0	4	1	15	5	.75	5	.283	.320	.377
7 Min. YEARS		798	2693	656	108	13	7	811	347	183	221	3	491	30	49	17	124	72	.63	53	.244	.306	.301

Edgar Caceres

Bats: Both **Throws:** Right **Pos:** 2B **Ht:** 6'1" **Wt:** 170 **Born:** 6/6/64 **Age:** 34

								BATTING										BASERUNNING				PERCENTAGES		
Year Team	Lg Org	G	AB	H	2B	3B	HR	TB	R	RBI	TBB	IBB	SO	HBP	SH	SF	SB	CS	SB%	GDP	Avg	OBP	SLG
1984 Dodgers	R LA	20	77	23	3	1	0	28	11	11	10	0	6	0	1	0	5	2	.71	0	.299	.379	.364
1985 Dodgers	R LA	53	176	53	6	0	0	59	37	22	18	1	11	2	2	0	5	2	.71	4	.301	.372	.335
1986 Wst Plm Bch	A+ Mon	111	382	106	9	5	0	125	52	37	24	2	28	2	4	4	25	6	.81	4	.277	.320	.327
1987 Jacksnville	AA Mon	18	62	8	0	1	0	10	7	3	3	0	7	0	0	0	2	0	1.00	2	.129	.169	.161
Wst Plm Bch	A+ Mon	105	390	105	14	1	2	127	55	37	27	0	30	5	7	1	30	5	.86	4	.269	.324	.326
1988 Rockford	A Mon	36	117	31	2	0	0	33	25	8	12	0	12	0	5	1	13	3	.81	2	.265	.331	.282
Tampa	A+ ChA	32	74	15	2	0	0	20	5	8	10	2	8	1	2	3	3	0	1.00	2	.203	.295	.270
1989 Sarasota	A+ ChA	106	373	110	16	4	0	134	45	50	24	4	38	2	9	2	8	3	.73	12	.295	.339	.359
1990 Birmingham	AA ChA	62	213	56	5	1	0	63	31	17	16	0	26	1	3	1	7	4	.64	7	.263	.316	.296
1992 El Paso	AA Mil	114	378	118	14	6	2	150	50	52	23	4	41	2	5	1	9	2	.82	8	.312	.354	.397
1993 New Orleans	AAA Mil	114	420	133	20	2	5	172	73	45	35	5	39	1	3	3	7	4	.64	14	.317	.368	.410
1994 Omaha	AAA KC	67	236	64	7	3	2	83	39	18	16	1	23	0	6	3	5	3	.63	7	.271	.314	.352
1995 Omaha	AAA KC	37	107	22	3	1	0	27	13	12	8	3	10	0	1	1	3	1	.75	2	.206	.259	.252
1996 New Orleans	AAA Mil	115	397	107	10	2	4	133	40	29	23	3	32	2	5	2	8	5	.62	9	.270	.311	.335
1997 Vancouver	AAA Ana	82	258	80	13	0	2	99	30	37	19	0	23	1	12	3	6	6	.50	8	.310	.356	.384
1995 Kansas City	AL	55	117	28	6	2	1	41	13	17	8	0	15	1	3	1	2	2	.50	3	.239	.291	.350
13 Min. YEARS		1072	3660	1031	124	27	18	1263	513	386	268	25	334	19	65	25	136	46	.75	85	.282	.332	.345

Rocco Cafaro

Pitches: Right Bats: Right Pos: P Ht: 6'0" Wt: 175 Born: 12/2/72 Age: 25

Year Team	Lg Org	G	GS	CG	GF	IP	BFP	H	R	ER	HR	SH	SF	HB	TBB	IBB	SO	WP	Bk	W	L	Pct.	ShO	Sv	ERA
1993 Orioles	R Bal	14	8	1	2	80.2	312	58	21	16	1	1	3	3	12	0	52	2	2	2	2	.500	0	1	1.79
1994 Albany	A Bal	30	1	0	15	68.1	304	73	41	37	3	3	4	8	27	4	53	7	4	3	5	.375	0	3	4.87
1995 High Desert	A+ Bal	44	1	0	39	66.2	290	69	42	33	10	2	4	2	25	0	52	6	1	4	5	.444	0	8	4.46
1996 Bowie	AA Bal	27	15	1	1	103.1	467	130	67	57	14	3	5	5	36	0	55	5	2	4	8	.333	0	0	4.96
Frederick	A+ Bal	8	0	0	7	20	85	19	10	10	2	0	0	1	6	0	16	0	0	1	3	.250	0	2	4.50
1997 Bowie	AA Bal	13	6	0	0	48.1	208	50	34	29	9	1	2	1	16	0	43	2	4	3	3	.500	0	0	5.40
St. Pete	A+ TB	19	2	0	8	40.2	163	35	10	9	0	2	1	0	5	1	28	1	1	2	2	.500	0	0	1.99
5 Min. YEARS		155	33	2	72	428	1829	434	225	191	39	12	19	20	127	5	304	23	14	19	28	.404	0	14	4.02

Tim Cain

Pitches: Right Bats: Both Pos: P Ht: 6'1" Wt: 180 Born: 10/9/69 Age: 28

Year Team	Lg Org	G	GS	CG	GF	IP	BFP	H	R	ER	HR	SH	SF	HB	TBB	IBB	SO	WP	Bk	W	L	Pct.	ShO	Sv	ERA
1990 Rangers	R Tex	16	1	0	4	36	146	27	22	15	1	0	0	5	6	0	38	2	2	0	3	.000	0	1	3.75
1991 Bend	A- Tex	17	6	0	4	58.1	267	65	49	37	2	0	1	4	25	0	59	8	0	1	3	.250	0	2	5.71
1993 Rochester	IND —	20	12	2	1	102.1	428	76	37	27	4	7	1	13	28	0	73	3	1	4	4	.500	1	1	2.37
1994 Winnipeg	IND —	6	6	1	0	43	167	30	11	11	2	1	0	1	6	0	50	1	0	5	1	.833	0	0	2.30
New Britain	AA Bos	10	10	0	0	50.2	226	65	39	32	8	2	0	3	18	0	37	1	1	2	4	.333	0	0	5.68
1995 Trenton	AA Bos	29	1	0	8	50.2	215	46	25	21	1	4	0	6	17	3	45	3	0	4	3	.571	0	4	3.73
Pawtucket	AAA Bos	14	0	0	5	27.2	111	24	7	7	0	1	1	1	8	1	19	1	0	4	0	1.000	0	4	2.28
1996 Pawtucket	AAA Bos	11	0	0	1	19.1	80	15	4	4	1	0	0	2	6	1	10	0	0	1	0	1.000	0	0	1.86
1997 Pawtucket	AAA Bos	17	0	0	4	30.1	138	34	22	20	6	2	1	4	12	0	13	0	0	3	3	.500	0	2	5.93
Syracuse	AAA Tor	13	1	0	6	22	107	26	13	13	4	0	4	3	14	0	14	1	0	0	2	.000	0	0	5.32
7 Min. YEARS		153	37	3	33	440.1	1885	408	229	187	29	17	8	42	140	5	358	20	4	24	23	.511	1	14	3.82

Enrique Calero

Pitches: Right Bats: Right Pos: P Ht: 6'2" Wt: 175 Born: 1/9/75 Age: 23

Year Team	Lg Org	G	GS	CG	GF	IP	BFP	H	R	ER	HR	SH	SF	HB	TBB	IBB	SO	WP	Bk	W	L	Pct.	ShO	Sv	ERA
1996 Spokane	A- KC	17	11	0	3	75	318	77	34	21	5	0	6	3	18	0	61	2	2	4	2	.667	0	1	2.52
1997 Wichita	AA KC	23	22	2	0	127.2	541	120	78	63	15	4	6	4	44	0	100	2	2	11	9	.550	0	0	4.44
2 Min. YEARS		40	33	2	3	202.2	859	197	112	84	20	4	12	7	62	0	161	4	4	15	11	.577	0	1	3.73

Lance Calmus

Pitches: Right Bats: Right Pos: P Ht: 6'5" Wt: 225 Born: 1/19/73 Age: 25

Year Team	Lg Org	G	GS	CG	GF	IP	BFP	H	R	ER	HR	SH	SF	HB	TBB	IBB	SO	WP	Bk	W	L	Pct.	ShO	Sv	ERA
1996 Watertown	A- Cle	11	11	0	0	46.1	212	53	40	33	8	2	0	0	18	1	51	2	0	1	3	.250	0	0	6.41
1997 Columbus	A Cle	23	15	0	2	88	400	94	64	57	12	0	7	4	41	0	78	8	0	1	5	.167	0	0	5.83
Akron	AA Cle	5	1	0	2	10.1	46	6	7	7	3	0	0	1	9	0	10	1	0	1	1	.500	0	0	6.10
2 Min. YEARS		39	27	0	4	144.2	658	153	111	97	23	2	7	5	68	1	139	11	0	3	9	.250	0	0	6.03

Jared Camp

Pitches: Right Bats: Right Pos: P Ht: 6'1" Wt: 195 Born: 5/4/75 Age: 23

Year Team	Lg Org	G	GS	CG	GF	IP	BFP	H	R	ER	HR	SH	SF	HB	TBB	IBB	SO	WP	Bk	W	L	Pct.	ShO	Sv	ERA
1995 Helena	R+ Mil	8	8	0	0	34.1	166	44	39	33	1	1	3	3	22	0	26	6	2	1	4	.200	0	0	8.65
1996 Beloit	A Mil	11	11	0	0	53	251	56	42	32	4	3	9	2	39	0	47	10	1	3	5	.375	0	0	5.43
Watertown	A- Cle	15	15	1	0	95.2	380	68	29	18	2	1	1	7	30	0	99	6	0	10	2	.833	1	0	1.69
1997 Akron	AA Cle	12	12	1	0	64	293	79	49	44	13	4	1	1	26	1	39	4	0	2	8	.200	0	0	6.19
Kinston	A+ Cle	13	12	0	0	73.2	297	57	36	31	11	5	1	2	20	0	64	1	1	5	4	.556	0	0	3.79
3 Min. YEARS		59	58	2	0	320.2	1387	304	195	158	31	14	15	15	135	1	275	27	4	21	23	.477	1	0	4.43

Jesus Campos

Bats: Right Throws: Right Pos: OF Ht: 5'9" Wt: 145 Born: 10/12/73 Age: 24

Year Team	Lg Org	G	AB	H	2B	3B	HR	TB	R	RBI	TBB	IBB	SO	HBP	SH	SF	SB	CS	SB%	GDP	Avg	OBP	SLG
1993 Expos	R Mon	2	8	1	0	0	0	1	1	1	2	0	1	0	0	0	0	0	.00	0	.125	.300	.125
Jamestown	A- Mon	70	285	69	6	6	1	90	43	22	18	0	39	2	0	0	9	9	.50	12	.242	.290	.316
1994 Burlington	A Mon	12	44	6	0	0	0	6	1	1	1	0	7	0	2	0	0	1	.00	2	.136	.156	.136
Expos	R Mon	3	11	4	0	0	0	4	0	3	1	0	1	0	0	1	0	0	.00	0	.364	.385	.364
Wst Plm Bch	A+ Mon	62	240	66	11	2	0	81	37	16	17	1	23	0	1	1	13	2	.87	5	.275	.322	.338
1995 Wst Plm Bch	A+ Mon	107	326	72	6	2	0	82	32	21	25	0	40	2	6	2	18	7	.72	5	.221	.279	.252
1996 Wst Plm Bch	A+ Mon	44	148	37	6	1	0	45	24	20	12	0	24	2	1	2	8	3	.73	1	.250	.311	.304
Harrisburg	AA Mon	73	208	54	4	0	0	58	15	17	9	2	17	2	1	0	5	9	.36	5	.260	.297	.279
1997 Wst Plm Bch	A+ Mon	28	84	16	3	1	0	21	11	7	1	0	9	0	0	1	0	1	.00	2	.190	.198	.250
Harrisburg	AA Mon	82	286	88	12	1	5	117	33	36	8	0	24	2	6	6	6	8	.43	9	.308	.325	.409
5 Min. YEARS		483	1640	413	48	13	6	505	197	144	94	3	184	10	15	15	59	40	.60	42	.252	.294	.308

Benjamin Candelaria

Bats: Left **Throws:** Right **Pos:** OF **Ht:** 5'11" **Wt:** 167 **Born:** 1/29/75 **Age:** 23

				BATTING														BASERUNNING				PERCENTAGES		
Year Team	Lg Org	G	AB	H	2B	3B	HR	TB	R	RBI	TBB	IBB	SO	HBP	SH	SF		SB	CS	SB%	GDP	Avg	OBP	SLG
1992 Blue Jays	R Tor	29	77	12	2	1	0	16	10	3	6	0	16	0	1	1		4	3	.57	0	.156	.214	.208
1993 Medicne Hat	R+ Tor	62	208	55	7	1	5	79	24	34	27	1	49	3	5	4		3	3	.50	3	.264	.351	.380
1994 Hagerstown	A Tor	3	13	3	0	0	1	6	2	3	0	0	4	0	0	0		0	0	.00	0	.231	.231	.462
St. Cathrns	A- Tor	71	250	66	15	1	2	89	36	37	35	1	55	1	3	1		8	4	.67	6	.264	.355	.356
1995 Dunedin	A+ Tor	125	471	122	21	5	5	168	66	49	53	1	98	0	3	5		11	4	.73	11	.259	.337	.357
1996 Knoxville	AA Tor	55	162	45	11	2	3	69	16	14	18	0	40	2	2	0		3	3	.50	7	.278	.357	.426
Dunedin	A+ Tor	39	125	25	5	0	1	33	13	6	12	0	25	0	1	0		4	3	.57	1	.200	.270	.264
1997 Knoxville	AA Tor	120	472	139	32	5	15	226	81	67	42	2	89	5	4	6		4	3	.57	9	.294	.354	.479
6 Min. YEARS		504	1778	467	93	15	32	686	248	213	193	5	376	11	19	17		34	24	.59	37	.263	.336	.386

Jay Canizaro

Bats: Right **Throws:** Right **Pos:** 2B **Ht:** 5'9" **Wt:** 170 **Born:** 7/4/73 **Age:** 24

				BATTING														BASERUNNING				PERCENTAGES		
Year Team	Lg Org	G	AB	H	2B	3B	HR	TB	R	RBI	TBB	IBB	SO	HBP	SH	SF		SB	CS	SB%	GDP	Avg	OBP	SLG
1993 Giants	R SF	49	180	47	10	6	3	78	34	41	22	1	40	0	0	3		12	3	.80	4	.261	.337	.433
1994 San Jose	A+ SF	126	464	117	16	2	15	182	77	69	46	1	98	5	0	3		12	6	.67	7	.252	.324	.392
1995 Shreveport	AA SF	126	440	129	25	7	12	204	83	60	58	4	98	6	4	5		16	9	.64	9	.293	.379	.464
1996 Phoenix	AAA SF	102	363	95	21	2	7	141	50	64	46	2	77	4	1	5		2	2	.50	7	.262	.347	.388
1997 Phoenix	AAA SF	23	81	16	7	0	2	29	12	12	9	0	24	0	1	0		2	2	.50	2	.198	.278	.358
Shreveport	AA SF	50	176	45	9	0	11	87	36	38	26	0	44	2	0	2		2	2	.50	4	.256	.354	.494
1996 San Francisco	NL	43	120	24	4	1	2	36	11	8	9	0	38	1	1	1		0	2	.00	5	.200	.260	.300
5 Min. YEARS		476	1704	449	88	17	50	721	292	284	207	8	381	17	6	18		58	26	.69	33	.263	.346	.423

Kevan Cannon

Pitches: Left **Bats:** Left **Pos:** P **Ht:** 6'3" **Wt:** 215 **Born:** 8/24/74 **Age:** 23

		HOW MUCH HE PITCHED						WHAT HE GAVE UP										THE RESULTS					
Year Team	Lg Org	G	GS	CG	GF	IP	BFP	H	R	ER	HR	SH	SF	HB	TBB	IBB	SO	WP	Bk	W	L	Pct.	ShO	Sv	ERA
1995 Red Sox	R Bos	5	3	1	0	26.2	107	14	6	2	1	0	0	0	9	0	38	0	1	2	1	.667	0	0	0.68
Utica	A- Bos	9	9	1	0	61	260	59	33	23	2	0	3	5	23	1	51	2	2	3	4	.429	0	0	3.39
1996 Michigan	A Bos	37	0	0	17	73	308	70	24	21	0	5	3	4	21	4	72	5	1	2	6	.250	0	5	2.59
Sarasota	A+ Bos	2	0	0	1	1	5	1	0	0	0	0	0	0	0	0	3	0	0	0	0	.000	0	0	0.00
1997 Sarasota	A+ Bos	32	0	0	20	43.1	195	41	27	20	1	2	1	3	26	0	35	5	0	5	0	1.000	0	5	4.15
Trenton	AA Bos	13	0	0	7	16	67	7	7	5	1	1	0	1	12	1	11	2	0	1	1	.500	0	1	2.81
3 Min. YEARS		98	12	2	45	221	942	192	97	71	5	8	7	14	91	6	210	14	4	13	12	.520	0	11	2.89

Carmine Cappuccio

Bats: Left **Throws:** Right **Pos:** OF **Ht:** 6'3" **Wt:** 185 **Born:** 2/1/70 **Age:** 28

				BATTING														BASERUNNING				PERCENTAGES		
Year Team	Lg Org	G	AB	H	2B	3B	HR	TB	R	RBI	TBB	IBB	SO	HBP	SH	SF		SB	CS	SB%	GDP	Avg	OBP	SLG
1992 Utica	A- ChA	22	87	24	4	2	0	32	15	13	6	0	10	1	0	1		5	0	1.00	3	.276	.326	.368
South Bend	A ChA	49	182	53	9	2	0	66	23	19	21	1	21	1	1	1		2	3	.40	4	.291	.366	.363
1993 Sarasota	A+ ChA	24	90	17	2	2	1	26	9	12	4	1	10	0	0	0		2	0	1.00	1	.189	.223	.289
South Bend	A ChA	101	383	117	26	5	4	165	59	52	42	6	56	6	0	1		2	6	.25	11	.305	.382	.431
1994 Pr William	A+ ChA	101	401	117	30	1	12	185	71	60	25	1	53	9	2	4		8	4	.67	7	.292	.344	.461
1995 Birmingham	AA ChA	65	248	69	13	3	4	100	34	38	22	4	21	2	3	2		2	2	.50	10	.278	.339	.403
Nashville	AAA ChA	66	216	59	14	0	5	88	30	24	29	4	26	1	1	1		1	0	1.00	9	.273	.360	.407
1996 Nashville	AAA ChA	120	407	111	22	3	10	169	55	61	25	7	48	6	3	2		1	3	.25	15	.273	.323	.415
1997 Nashville	AAA ChA	55	177	39	11	0	4	62	22	21	16	2	24	0	1	2		1	0	1.00	10	.220	.282	.350
6 Min. YEARS		603	2191	606	131	18	40	893	318	300	190	26	269	26	11	14		24	20	.55	67	.277	.340	.408

Ramon Caraballo

Bats: Both **Throws:** Right **Pos:** 2B **Ht:** 5'7" **Wt:** 150 **Born:** 5/23/69 **Age:** 29

				BATTING														BASERUNNING				PERCENTAGES		
Year Team	Lg Org	G	AB	H	2B	3B	HR	TB	R	RBI	TBB	IBB	SO	HBP	SH	SF		SB	CS	SB%	GDP	Avg	OBP	SLG
1989 Braves	R Atl	20	77	19	3	1	1	27	9	10	10	0	14	0	1	1		5	4	.56	0	.247	.330	.351
Sumter	A Atl	45	171	45	10	5	1	68	22	32	16	0	38	2	1	3		9	4	.69	5	.263	.328	.398
1990 Burlington	A Atl	102	390	113	18	14	7	180	84	54	49	2	69	7	2	2		41	20	.67	9	.290	.377	.462
1991 Durham	A+ Atl	120	444	111	13	8	6	158	73	52	38	1	91	3	3	2		53	23	.70	5	.250	.312	.356
1992 Greenville	AA Atl	24	93	29	4	4	1	44	15	8	14	0	13	0	0	1		10	6	.63	1	.312	.398	.473
Richmond	AAA Atl	101	405	114	20	3	2	146	42	40	22	1	60	3	7	1		20	14	.59	3	.281	.323	.360
1993 Richmond	AAA Atl	126	470	128	25	9	3	180	73	41	30	3	81	7	7	5		20	14	.59	3	.272	.323	.383
1994 Richmond	AAA Atl	22	75	10	1	0	0	11	5	0	7	0	12	1	0	0		4	4	.50	1	.133	.217	.147
Greenville	AA Atl	72	243	58	4	6	9	101	32	30	12	1	46	7	2	5		14	4	.78	5	.239	.288	.416
1995 Louisville	AAA StL	69	245	58	10	1	8	114	38	25	19	1	42	4	4	4		5	2	.71	5	.318	.371	.465
1997 Iowa	AAA ChN	49	133	28	8	0	4	48	16	21	18	1	25	6	0	1		5	2	.71	5	.211	.329	.361
1993 Atlanta	NL	6	0	0	0	0	0	0	0	0	0	0	0	0	0	0		0	0	.00	0	.000	.000	.000
1995 St. Louis	NL	34	99	20	4	1	2	32	10	3	6	0	33	3	2	0		3	2	.60	1	.202	.269	.323
8 Min. YEARS		750	2746	733	116	51	42	1077	409	313	235	10	491	40	27	25		184	104	.64	39	.267	.331	.392
2 Maj. YEARS		40	99	20	4	1	2	32	10	3	6	0	33	3	2	0		3	2	.60	1	.202	.269	.323

43

Todd Carey

Bats: Left Throws: Right Pos: 1B   Ht: 6'1" Wt: 180 Born: 8/14/71 Age: 26

Year Team	Lg Org	G	AB	H	2B	3B	HR	TB	R	RBI	TBB	IBB	SO	HBP	SH	SF	SB	CS	SB%	GDP	Avg	OBP	SLG
1992 Elmira	A- Bos	54	197	40	7	2	0	51	18	19	9	1	40	0	1	3	0	4	.00	2	.203	.234	.259
1993 Ft. Laud	A+ Bos	118	444	109	14	5	3	142	41	31	24	1	44	0	5	3	2	6	.25	10	.245	.282	.320
1994 Lynchburg	A+ Bos	105	363	85	14	2	13	142	42	42	49	0	77	3	1	2	1	4	.20	5	.234	.329	.391
1995 Sarasota	A+ Bos	25	85	26	6	0	4	44	15	19	9	0	17	0	0	0	2	1	.67	3	.306	.372	.518
Trenton	AA Bos	76	228	62	11	1	8	99	30	36	28	0	44	4	1	0	3	4	.43	3	.272	.359	.434
1996 Trenton	AA Bos	125	440	110	34	3	20	210	78	78	48	9	123	3	3	3	4	4	.50	3	.250	.326	.477
1997 Pawtucket	AAA Bos	113	380	82	16	0	12	134	35	58	34	1	114	2	4	4	1	2	.33	11	.216	.281	.353
6 Min. YEARS		616	2137	514	102	13	60	822	259	283	201	12	459	12	15	17	13	25	.34	36	.241	.307	.385

Ken Carlyle

Pitches: Right Bats: Right Pos: P   Ht: 6'1" Wt: 185 Born: 9/16/69 Age: 28

Year Team	Lg Org	G	GS	CG	GF	IP	BFP	H	R	ER	HR	SH	SF	HB	TBB	IBB	SO	WP	Bk	W	L	Pct	ShO	Sv	ERA
1992 Niagara Fal	A- Det	1	1	0	0	6	26	6	1	1	0	0	0	0	1	0	9	1	1	1	0	1.000	0	0	1.50
Fayettevlle	A Det	14	14	1	0	79.2	319	64	21	17	3	0	1	4	24	0	59	6	1	8	4	.667	1	0	1.92
1993 Toledo	AAA Det	15	14	1	0	75.2	339	88	59	54	13	2	2	1	36	1	43	4	2	2	10	.167	0	0	6.42
London	AA Det	12	12	1	0	78	341	72	40	32	8	1	3	5	35	1	50	0	2	4	6	.400	0	0	3.69
1994 Trenton	AA Det	19	19	5	0	116.1	519	125	75	53	6	4	3	3	47	3	69	5	2	3	9	.250	1	0	4.10
Toledo	AAA Det	12	1	0	3	24.1	104	23	13	11	2	1	2	2	8	0	12	1	0	1	0	1.000	1	0	4.07
1995 Toledo	AAA Det	32	20	0	0	124.2	541	139	65	60	10	2	5	4	44	2	63	7	0	8	8	.500	0	0	4.33
1996 Jacksnville	AA Det	27	26	1	0	155.2	671	167	92	70	8	7	6	9	51	2	89	6	0	8	5	.615	1	0	4.05
1997 Richmond	AAA Atl	16	11	1	1	69.2	284	69	26	22	4	0	1	1	19	0	48	0	0	4	1	.800	1	0	2.84
6 Min. YEARS		148	118	10	4	730	3144	753	392	320	54	17	23	29	265	9	442	30	8	39	43	.476	4	1	3.95

Bartt Carney

Bats: Both Throws: Right Pos: OF   Ht: 5'11" Wt: 170 Born: 12/16/73 Age: 24

Year Team	Lg Org	G	AB	H	2B	3B	HR	TB	R	RBI	TBB	IBB	SO	HBP	SH	SF	SB	CS	SB%	GDP	Avg	OBP	SLG
1996 Orioles	R Bal	6	12	3	0	0	0	3	4	1	5	0	1	0	0	0	1	0	1.00	0	.250	.471	.250
High Desert	A+ Bal	47	116	29	3	3	1	41	31	11	15	0	26	4	2	0	6	4	.60	1	.250	.356	.353
1997 Delmarva	A Bal	14	30	3	1	0	0	4	3	1	5	0	10	0	1	0	1	0	.80	0	.100	.229	.133
Frederick	A+ Bal	4	6	0	0	0	0	0	2	0	2	0	0	0	0	0	0	0	.00	0	.000	.250	.000
Bowie	AA Bal	66	156	42	5	0	0	47	27	8	31	1	31	3	4	1	8	5	.62	0	.269	.398	.301
Rochester	AAA Bal	4	6	0	0	0	0	0	1	0	3	0	2	0	0	0	0	0	.00	0	.000	.333	.000
2 Min. YEARS		141	326	77	9	3	1	95	68	21	61	1	70	7	7	1	19	10	.66	1	.236	.367	.291

Brian Carpenter

Pitches: Right Bats: Right Pos: P   Ht: 6'0" Wt: 225 Born: 3/3/71 Age: 27

Year Team	Lg Org	G	GS	CG	GF	IP	BFP	H	R	ER	HR	SH	SF	HB	TBB	IBB	SO	WP	Bk	W	L	Pct	ShO	Sv	ERA
1993 Savannah	A StL	28	28	0	0	154.1	629	145	55	49	8	2	5	2	41	0	147	2	1	10	8	.556	0	0	2.86
1994 St. Pete	A+ StL	26	20	0	3	131.2	572	152	76	70	16	2	5	7	38	1	76	2	1	12	7	.632	0	1	4.78
1995 St. Pete	A+ StL	16	7	0	2	59	226	40	17	14	4	1	1	0	11	0	51	4	0	5	3	.625	0	0	2.14
Arkansas	AA StL	17	4	0	1	52.2	232	57	32	29	6	6	2	3	21	1	35	1	1	2	1	.667	0	0	4.96
1996 Arkansas	AA StL	37	6	0	3	74	305	63	26	26	6	2	7	1	26	3	53	2	0	1	2	.333	0	0	3.16
1997 Louisville	AAA StL	4	0	0	2	8.1	42	11	4	4	1	1	2	1	5	0	9	2	0	0	0	.000	0	0	4.32
Binghamton	AA NYN	17	0	0	7	23	112	37	23	23	4	0	2	2	12	2	22	2	0	0	1	.000	0	1	9.00
5 Min. YEARS		145	65	0	18	503	2118	505	233	215	45	14	24	14	154	7	393	13	3	30	22	.577	0	2	3.85

Bubba Carpenter

Bats: Left Throws: Left Pos: OF   Ht: 6'1" Wt: 185 Born: 7/23/68 Age: 29

Year Team	Lg Org	G	AB	H	2B	3B	HR	TB	R	RBI	TBB	IBB	SO	HBP	SH	SF	SB	CS	SB%	GDP	Avg	OBP	SLG
1991 Pr William	A+ NYA	69	236	66	10	3	6	100	33	34	40	3	50	2	1	3	4	1	.80	7	.280	.384	.424
1992 Albany-Colo	AA NYA	60	221	51	11	5	4	84	24	31	25	0	41	2	0	1	2	3	.40	4	.231	.313	.380
Pr William	A+ NYA	68	240	76	15	2	5	110	41	41	35	2	44	1	1	6	4	4	.50	4	.317	.397	.458
1993 Albany-Colo	AA NYA	14	53	17	4	0	2	27	8	14	7	0	4	0	0	1	2	2	.50	2	.321	.393	.509
Columbus	AAA NYA	70	199	53	9	0	5	77	29	17	29	3	35	3	0	1	2	2	.50	4	.266	.366	.387
1994 Albany-Colo	AA NYA	116	378	109	14	1	13	164	47	51	58	5	65	3	3	3	9	5	.64	3	.288	.385	.434
Columbus	AAA NYA	7	15	4	0	0	0	4	0	2	0	0	2	0	0	0	0	0	.00	1	.267	.267	.267
1995 Louisville	AAA NYA	116	374	92	12	3	11	143	57	49	40	2	70	1	2	3	13	6	.68	2	.246	.318	.382
1996 Columbus	AAA NYA	132	466	114	23	3	7	164	55	48	48	1	80	0	2	1	10	7	.59	7	.245	.315	.352
1997 Columbus	AAA NYA	85	271	76	12	4	6	114	47	39	48	0	46	0	3	1	4	8	.33	3	.280	.388	.421
7 Min. YEARS		737	2453	658	110	21	59	987	341	326	330	16	442	12	12	20	50	38	.57	41	.268	.355	.402

Jeremy Carr

Bats: Right Throws: Right Pos: OF   Ht: 5'10" Wt: 170 Born: 3/30/71 Age: 27

Year Team	Lg Org	G	AB	H	2B	3B	HR	TB	R	RBI	TBB	IBB	SO	HBP	SH	SF	SB	CS	SB%	GDP	Avg	OBP	SLG
1993 Eugene	A- KC	42	136	31	2	5	0	43	33	12	20	1	18	6	2	2	30	3	.91	4	.228	.348	.316
1994 Rockford	A KC	121	437	112	9	5	1	134	85	32	60	1	59	16	2	4	52	22	.70	8	.256	.364	.307
1995 Wilmington	A+ KC	5	13	3	1	0	0	4	1	0	1	0	3	0	0	0	0	1	.00	0	.231	.286	.308
Bakersfield	A+ KC	128	499	128	22	2	1	157	92	38	79	0	73	11	6	0	52	21	.71	9	.257	.370	.315

Year Team	Lg Org	G	AB	H	2B	3B	HR	TB	R	RBI	TBB	IBB	SO	HBP	SH	SF	SB	CS	SB%	GDP	Avg	OBP	SLG
1996 Wichita	AA KC	129	453	118	23	2	6	163	68	40	47	1	64	12	3	3	41	9	.82	15	.260	.344	.360
1997 Wichita	AA KC	91	340	104	19	1	8	149	76	40	50	1	53	9	3	1	39	8	.83	4	.306	.408	.438
Omaha	AAA KC	35	120	32	3	2	2	45	17	9	15	0	17	3	1	0	12	3	.80	3	.267	.362	.375
5 Min. YEARS		551	1998	528	79	17	18	695	372	171	272	4	287	57	17	10	226	67	.77	43	.264	.367	.348

Troy Carrasco

Pitches: Left Bats: Both Pos: P   Ht: 5'11" Wt: 172 Born: 1/27/75 Age: 23

Year Team	Lg Org	G	GS	CG	GF	IP	BFP	H	R	ER	HR	SH	SF	HB	TBB	IBB	SO	WP	Bk	W	L	Pct.	ShO	Sv	ERA
1993 Elizabethtn	R+ Min	14	10	0	3	70.1	292	46	32	25	2	5	1	3	39	3	75	6	2	2	4	.333	0	2	3.20
1994 Ft. Wayne	A Min	28	28	2	0	160.2	685	159	84	73	14	5	1	4	60	0	146	9	0	10	10	.500	1	0	4.09
1995 Ft. Myers	A+ Min	25	25	2	0	138	596	131	62	48	6	4	7	8	63	0	96	11	2	12	4	.750	0	0	3.13
1996 Hardware City	AA Min	34	17	1	8	110	504	113	74	62	9	5	2	9	66	1	69	15	1	6	9	.400	1	0	5.07
1997 Ft. Myers	A+ Min	12	8	0	3	55.1	241	61	37	33	5	3	2	0	18	2	36	4	1	3	3	.500	0	0	5.37
New Britain	AA Min	31	3	0	16	65.1	305	69	53	36	11	4	2	2	44	4	46	4	1	4	4	.500	0	1	4.96
5 Min. YEARS		144	91	5	30	599.2	2623	579	346	277	47	26	15	26	290	10	468	49	7	37	34	.521	2	3	4.16

Cale Carter

Bats: Left Throws: Right Pos: OF   Ht: 5'10" Wt: 185 Born: 9/18/73 Age: 24

Year Team	Lg Org	G	AB	H	2B	3B	HR	TB	R	RBI	TBB	IBB	SO	HBP	SH	SF	SB	CS	SB%	GDP	Avg	OBP	SLG
1996 Lk Elsinore	A+ Ana	38	113	33	9	0	1	45	12	15	14	1	21	0	2	0	4	4	.50	3	.292	.370	.398
1997 Cedar Rapds	A Ana	30	86	19	3	0	0	22	18	8	8	0	16	4	1	1	2	1	.67	2	.221	.313	.256
Midland	AA Ana	7	24	4	0	0	0	4	3	2	3	0	7	0	0	0	1	0	1.00	0	.167	.259	.167
Lk Elsinore	A+ Ana	25	79	18	2	0	1	23	19	5	9	2	15	2	1	0	2	0	1.00	3	.228	.322	.291
2 Min. YEARS		100	302	74	14	0	2	94	52	30	34	3	59	6	4	1	9	5	.64	8	.245	.332	.311

John Carter

Pitches: Right Bats: Right Pos: P   Ht: 6'1" Wt: 195 Born: 2/16/72 Age: 26

Year Team	Lg Org	G	GS	CG	GF	IP	BFP	H	R	ER	HR	SH	SF	HB	TBB	IBB	SO	WP	Bk	W	L	Pct.	ShO	Sv	ERA
1991 Pirates	R Pit	10	9	0	0	41	179	42	20	15	0	0	0	5	13	0	28	5	2	5	4	.556	0	0	3.29
1992 Augusta	A Pit	1	1	0	0	5	19	3	0	0	0	1	0	1	1	0	4	0	1	0	0	.000	0	0	0.00
Welland	A- Pit	3	3	0	0	15.2	68	12	11	6	2	0	1	1	7	0	15	1	1	0	3	.000	0	0	3.45
Watertown	A- Cle	13	11	3	0	63	269	55	36	29	2	0	3	2	32	0	39	4	4	4	4	.500	0	0	4.14
1993 Columbus	A Cle	29	29	1	0	180.1	731	147	72	56	7	4	2	7	48	0	134	8	2	17	7	.708	0	0	2.79
1994 Canton-Akrn	AA Cle	22	22	3	0	131	564	134	68	63	15	4	2	6	53	1	73	7	1	9	6	.600	1	0	4.33
1995 Canton-Akrn	AA Cle	5	5	0	0	27.1	118	27	13	12	0	0	0	3	13	2	14	1	0	1	2	.333	0	0	3.95
1996 St. Lucie	A+ NYN	4	4	0	0	20	93	26	18	16	2	1	0	1	11	1	6	3	1	1	2	.333	0	0	7.20
Binghamton	AA NYN	19	19	3	0	110.2	485	120	60	52	10	6	3	6	54	1	48	6	0	9	3	.750	1	0	4.23
1997 Binghamton	AA NYN	9	0	0	4	13.2	66	19	15	10	4	1	1	1	4	0	14	0	0	0	0	.000	0	0	6.59
Calgary	AAA Pit	15	2	0	3	25.1	150	45	41	41	6	3	4	3	27	2	18	4	1	1	2	.333	0	0	14.57
Carolina	AA Pit	1	0	0	0	1	4	4	6	6	1	0	1	0	2	0	0	0	0	0	1	.000	0	0	54.00
Akron	AA Cle	10	0	0	1	25.1	129	32	30	29	7	3	0	2	22	1	10	5	0	1	2	.333	0	0	10.30
7 Min. YEARS		141	105	10	8	659.1	2880	666	390	335	52	20	19	43	287	8	403	44	12	48	35	.578	2	0	4.57

Mike Carter

Bats: Right Throws: Right Pos: OF   Ht: 5'9" Wt: 170 Born: 5/5/69 Age: 29

Year Team	Lg Org	G	AB	H	2B	3B	HR	TB	R	RBI	TBB	IBB	SO	HBP	SH	SF	SB	CS	SB%	GDP	Avg	OBP	SLG
1990 Helena	R+ Mil	61	241	74	11	3	0	91	45	30	16	0	20	6	2	5	22	7	.76	0	.307	.358	.378
1991 Beloit	A Mil	123	452	126	24	4	2	164	62	40	26	5	42	4	2	3	46	13	.78	5	.279	.322	.363
1992 Stockton	A+ Mil	67	252	66	9	1	3	86	38	26	17	1	26	2	3	5	31	8	.79	4	.262	.308	.341
El Paso	AA Mil	50	165	42	4	1	3	57	20	15	16	2	31	0	3	1	10	8	.56	3	.255	.319	.345
1993 El Paso	AA Mil	17	73	27	4	1	2	39	16	3	6	0	7	0	0	0	4	6	.60	1	.370	.395	.534
New Orleans	AAA Mil	104	369	102	18	5	3	139	49	31	17	0	52	4	11	4	20	11	.65	6	.276	.312	.377
1994 Iowa	AAA ChN	122	421	122	24	3	6	170	56	30	14	1	43	4	12	4	16	14	.53	7	.290	.316	.404
1995 Iowa	AAA ChN	107	421	137	16	3	8	183	57	40	14	3	46	6	3	3	12	12	.50	5	.325	.354	.435
1996 Iowa	AAA ChN	113	384	102	13	1	2	123	41	18	10	0	42	1	5	1	4	6	.40	5	.266	.285	.320
1997 Midland	AA Ana	15	65	18	3	1	0	23	9	2	2	0	8	0	1	0	5	2	.71	1	.277	.299	.354
8 Min. YEARS		779	2843	816	126	26	27	1075	393	248	135	12	317	27	42	26	172	85	.67	37	.287	.323	.378

Clay Caruthers

Pitches: Right Bats: Both Pos: P   Ht: 6'2" Wt: 200 Born: 11/20/72 Age: 25

Year Team	Lg Org	G	GS	CG	GF	IP	BFP	H	R	ER	HR	SH	SF	HB	TBB	IBB	SO	WP	Bk	W	L	Pct.	ShO	Sv	ERA
1994 Billings	R+ Cin	14	14	1	0	81	357	85	47	35	2	1	3	3	36	1	63	7	0	5	3	.625	0	0	3.89
1995 Chston-WV	A Cin	27	27	0	0	138.2	600	149	67	57	6	5	4	14	50	1	105	13	2	11	7	.611	0	0	3.70
1996 Winston-Sal	A+ Cin	28	28	2	0	169	745	179	93	82	20	3	7	13	60	1	105	11	2	10	10	.500	0	0	4.37
1997 Burlington	A Cin	17	13	0	3	74	353	103	63	48	6	4	0	5	26	0	44	0	1	3	7	.300	0	0	5.84
Chattanooga	AA Cin	9	6	0	1	34.2	175	63	36	35	4	1	0	1	17	1	30	2	1	2	4	.333	0	0	9.09
4 Min. YEARS		95	88	3	4	497.1	2230	579	306	257	38	14	19	36	189	4	347	33	6	31	31	.500	0	0	4.65

Jhonny Carvajal

Bats: Right **Throws:** Right **Pos:** 3B-SS   **Ht:** 5'10" **Wt:** 165 **Born:** 7/24/74 **Age:** 23

Year Team	Lg Org	G	AB	H	2B	3B	HR	TB	R	RBI	TBB	IBB	SO	HBP	SH	SF	SB	CS	SB%	GDP	Avg	OBP	SLG
1993 Princeton	R+ Cin	67	253	74	10	5	0	94	41	16	29	1	31	4	8	0	7	11	.39	3	.292	.374	.372
1994 Chston-WV	A Cin	67	198	45	6	0	0	51	27	13	19	0	25	2	2	3	12	3	.80	3	.227	.297	.258
Princeton	R+ Cin	53	218	59	10	4	2	83	35	29	14	2	38	5	5	3	31	11	.74	0	.271	.325	.381
1995 Chston-WV	A Cin	135	486	128	18	5	0	156	78	42	58	0	77	6	4	4	44	19	.70	4	.263	.347	.321
1996 Wst Plm Bch	A+ Mon	114	426	101	18	0	2	125	50	38	44	0	73	6	7	4	14	16	.47	9	.237	.315	.293
Harrisburg	AA Mon	16	60	18	3	2	0	25	7	4	5	0	10	1	1	0	1	1	.50	1	.300	.364	.417
1997 Harrisburg	AA Mon	116	378	98	12	1	1	115	36	31	27	3	66	4	4	3	10	7	.59	6	.259	.313	.304
5 Min. YEARS		568	2019	523	77	17	5	649	274	173	196	6	320	28	31	17	119	68	.64	28	.259	.331	.321

Jovino Carvajal

Bats: Both **Throws:** Right **Pos:** OF   **Ht:** 6'1" **Wt:** 160 **Born:** 9/2/68 **Age:** 29

Year Team	Lg Org	G	AB	H	2B	3B	HR	TB	R	RBI	TBB	IBB	SO	HBP	SH	SF	SB	CS	SB%	GDP	Avg	OBP	SLG
1990 Oneonta	A- NYA	52	171	49	3	1	0	54	19	18	7	0	37	0	3	0	15	11	.58	1	.287	.315	.316
1991 Ft. Laud	A+ NYA	117	416	96	6	9	1	123	49	29	28	5	84	0	3	1	33	17	.66	7	.231	.279	.296
1992 Ft. Laud	A+ NYA	113	435	100	7	1	1	112	53	29	30	0	63	1	3	4	40	14	.74	6	.230	.279	.257
1993 Pr William	A+ NYA	120	445	118	20	9	1	159	52	42	21	1	69	1	8	3	17	13	.57	8	.265	.298	.357
1994 Cedar Rapds	A Ana	121	503	147	23	8	6	204	82	54	40	3	76	1	3	1	68	25	.73	5	.292	.345	.406
1995 Midland	AA Ana	79	348	109	13	5	2	138	58	23	18	2	42	1	5	2	39	21	.65	3	.313	.347	.397
Vancouver	AAA Ana	41	163	53	3	3	1	65	25	10	3	0	18	1	1	0	10	7	.59	6	.325	.341	.399
1996 Vancouver	AAA Ana	77	272	65	6	2	4	87	29	31	14	2	38	1	6	3	17	7	.71	8	.239	.276	.320
Midland	AA Ana	41	160	43	5	2	2	58	20	22	10	1	24	0	1	0	7	7	.50	4	.269	.312	.363
1997 Vancouver	AAA Ana	131	480	137	20	20	2	203	80	51	21	3	85	4	4	1	28	9	.76	10	.285	.320	.423
8 Min. YEARS		892	3393	917	106	60	20	1203	467	309	192	17	536	10	37	15	274	131	.68	58	.270	.310	.355

Steve Carver

Bats: Left **Throws:** Right **Pos:** OF   **Ht:** 6'3" **Wt:** 215 **Born:** 9/27/72 **Age:** 25

Year Team	Lg Org	G	AB	H	2B	3B	HR	TB	R	RBI	TBB	IBB	SO	HBP	SH	SF	SB	CS	SB%	GDP	Avg	OBP	SLG
1995 Batavia	A- Phi	56	217	66	13	2	7	104	35	41	17	1	29	0	1	1	2	1	.67	3	.304	.353	.479
1996 Clearwater	A+ Phi	117	436	121	32	0	17	204	59	79	52	7	89	1	0	4	1	1	.50	12	.278	.353	.468
1997 Reading	AA Phi	79	282	74	11	3	15	136	41	43	36	9	69	3	0	1	2	2	.50	8	.262	.351	.482
3 Min. YEARS		252	935	261	56	5	39	444	135	163	105	17	187	4	1	6	5	4	.56	23	.279	.352	.475

Pedro Castellano

Bats: Right **Throws:** Right **Pos:** 3B   **Ht:** 6'1" **Wt:** 180 **Born:** 3/11/70 **Age:** 28

Year Team	Lg Org	G	AB	H	2B	3B	HR	TB	R	RBI	TBB	IBB	SO	HBP	SH	SF	SB	CS	SB%	GDP	Avg	OBP	SLG
1989 Wytheville	R+ ChN	66	244	76	17	4	9	128	55	42	46	2	44	3	1	3	5	2	.71	9	.311	.422	.525
1990 Peoria	A ChN	117	417	115	27	4	2	156	61	44	63	2	72	3	3	4	7	1	.88	9	.276	.372	.374
Winston-Sal	A+ ChN	19	66	13	0	0	1	16	6	8	10	0	11	2	2	0	1	0	1.00	3	.197	.321	.242
1991 Winston-Sal	A+ ChN	129	459	139	25	3	10	200	59	88	72	4	97	3	2	5	11	10	.52	13	.303	.397	.436
Charlotte	AA ChN	7	19	8	0	0	0	8	2	2	1	0	6	1	0	1	0	0	.00	1	.421	.455	.421
1992 Iowa	AAA ChN	74	238	59	14	4	2	87	25	20	32	0	42	1	8	1	2	2	.50	6	.248	.338	.366
Charlotte	AA ChN	45	147	33	3	0	1	39	16	15	19	0	21	4	3	2	1	0	1.00	2	.224	.326	.265
1993 Colo Sprngs	AAA Col	90	304	95	21	2	12	156	61	60	36	0	63	6	1	8	3	5	.38	2	.313	.387	.513
1994 Colo Sprngs	AAA Col	33	120	42	11	2	4	69	23	24	13	1	17	2	0	2	1	1	.50	3	.350	.416	.575
1995 Colo Sprngs	AAA Col	99	334	89	23	2	9	143	40	47	24	1	56	2	3	5	2	0	1.00	10	.266	.315	.428
1996 Colo Sprngs	AAA Min	94	362	122	30	3	13	197	56	59	40	4	46	4	0	8	0	2	.00	8	.337	.406	.544
1997 Salt Lake	AAA Min	43	165	59	9	1	7	91	29	36	20	1	31	2	0	2	0	1	.00	4	.358	.429	.552
1993 Colorado	NL	34	71	13	2	0	3	24	12	7	8	0	16	0	0	1	1	1	.50	1	.183	.266	.338
1995 Colorado	NL	4	5	0	0	0	0	0	0	0	2	0	3	0	0	0	0	0	.00	0	.000	.286	.000
1996 Colorado	NL	13	17	2	0	0	0	2	1	2	3	1	6	1	0	0	0	0	.00	0	.118	.286	.118
9 Min. YEARS		816	2875	850	180	25	70	1290	433	445	376	15	506	33	23	36	32	25	.56	76	.296	.379	.449
3 Maj. YEARS		51	93	15	2	0	3	26	13	9	13	1	25	1	0	0	1	1	.50	1	.161	.271	.280

Marino Castillo

Pitches: Right **Bats:** Right **Pos:** P   **Ht:** 6'0" **Wt:** 168 **Born:** 3/17/71 **Age:** 27

| | | HOW MUCH HE PITCHED | | | | | | WHAT HE GAVE UP | | | | | | | | | | THE RESULTS | | | | | |
Year Team	Lg Org	G	GS	CG	GF	IP	BFP	H	R	ER	HR	SH	SF	HB	TBB	IBB	SO	WP	Bk	W	L	Pct.	ShO	Sv	ERA
1992 San Jose	A+ SF	10	1	0	2	21	92	19	15	10	1	2	2	0	10	0	10	2	2	0	3	.000	0	0	4.29
Clinton	A SF	13	0	0	5	19.1	88	23	15	13	1	1	0	2	5	1	15	1	0	1	3	.250	0	1	6.05
1993 Clinton	A SF	40	0	0	19	69	291	64	31	26	3	4	6	1	19	1	59	1	0	4	2	.667	0	6	3.39
1994 San Jose	A+ SF	45	0	0	15	106.2	448	106	49	41	10	9	2	2	27	2	81	5	0	10	7	.588	0	5	3.46
1995 San Jose	A+ SF	21	0	0	8	56.2	226	49	14	10	1	2	0	2	13	0	51	1	0	4	4	.500	0	3	1.59
Shreveport	AA SF	22	0	0	4	37.1	161	38	17	13	4	4	0	1	13	3	31	0	0	3	1	.750	0	3	3.13
1996 Shreveport	AA SF	38	0	0	26	50.1	208	48	21	20	7	3	0	3	14	2	53	2	0	5	5	.500	0	3	3.58
San Jose	A+ SF	10	0	0	2	11.1	42	8	1	1	1	0	0	0	2	0	19	0	0	3	0	1.000	0	1	0.79
1997 Mobile	AA SD	8	0	0	5	8.1	43	14	4	4	0	1	0	0	5	1	10	1	0	0	1	.000	0	0	4.32
Las Vegas	AAA SD	30	19	0	0	126	567	146	88	72	18	2	4	2	43	2	102	3	2	6	5	.545	0	0	5.14
6 Min. YEARS		237	20	0	92	506	2166	515	255	210	46	28	14	12	149	12	431	16	4	36	31	.537	0	20	3.74

Kevin Castleberry

Bats: Left **Throws:** Right **Pos:** OF **Ht:** 5'10" **Wt:** 170 **Born:** 4/22/68 **Age:** 30

Year Team	Lg Org	G	AB	H	2B	3B	HR	TB	R	RBI	TBB	IBB	SO	HBP	SH	SF	SB	CS	SB%	GDP	Avg	OBP	SLG
1989 Burlington	A Atl	64	224	55	8	0	1	66	27	20	20	1	32	0	2	2	14	8	.64	5	.246	.305	.295
1990 Durham	A+ Atl	119	372	90	18	4	7	137	59	27	23	1	64	2	3	2	15	4	.79	3	.242	.288	.368
1991 Miami	A+ Atl	20	64	14	4	2	0	22	12	4	9	0	9	0	2	0	8	1	.89	1	.219	.315	.344
Birmingham	AA ChA	1	1	0	0	0	0	0	0	0	0	0	0	0	0	0	0	0	.00	0	.000	.000	.000
Sarasota	A+ ChA	94	346	94	14	3	4	126	70	39	54	3	54	4	6	7	23	9	.72	2	.272	.370	.364
1992 Sarasota	A+ ChA	24	98	28	4	0	0	32	16	10	14	0	12	1	1	1	8	3	.73	2	.286	.383	.327
Birmingham	AA ChA	104	382	98	9	5	2	123	57	26	48	1	59	3	0	1	13	10	.57	3	.257	.343	.322
1993 El Paso	AA Mil	98	327	98	9	5	2	123	46	49	26	3	38	2	0	3	13	3	.81	9	.300	.352	.376
1994 El Paso	AA Mil	74	251	69	6	8	1	94	44	35	26	1	50	3	2	0	12	7	.63	4	.275	.350	.375
1995 Ottawa	AAA Mon	118	428	126	18	4	7	173	65	56	52	3	59	0	5	4	9	7	.56	5	.294	.368	.404
1996 Ottawa	AAA Mon	66	193	54	8	3	3	77	27	22	21	4	27	0	6	2	9	5	.64	2	.280	.347	.399
1997 Okla City	AAA Tex	40	111	30	6	1	1	41	14	9	9	2	21	0	1	1	1	2	.33	1	.270	.322	.369
9 Min. YEARS		822	2797	756	104	35	28	1014	437	297	302	19	425	16	28	23	125	59	.68	37	.270	.342	.363

Jose Castro

Bats: Left **Throws:** Left **Pos:** OF **Ht:** 5'11" **Wt:** 192 **Born:** 12/19/75 **Age:** 22

Year Team	Lg Org	G	AB	H	2B	3B	HR	TB	R	RBI	TBB	IBB	SO	HBP	SH	SF	SB	CS	SB%	GDP	Avg	OBP	SLG
1996 Everett	A- Sea	1	4	1	0	0	0	1	0	0	0	0	1	0	0	0	0	0	.00	0	.250	.250	.250
Wisconsin	A Sea	37	111	24	3	0	0	27	12	10	9	0	22	1	2	1	2	5	.29	4	.216	.279	.243
1997 Tacoma	AAA Sea	2	1	0	0	0	0	0	0	0	0	0	0	0	0	0	0	0	.00	0	.000	.000	.000
Wisconsin	A Sea	64	248	60	12	1	1	77	29	19	13	0	50	1	1	0	3	4	.43	6	.242	.282	.310
2 Min. YEARS		104	364	85	15	1	1	105	41	29	22	0	73	2	3	1	5	9	.36	10	.234	.280	.288

Jose Castro

Bats: Both **Throws:** Right **Pos:** 2B **Ht:** 5'10" **Wt:** 165 **Born:** 10/15/74 **Age:** 23

Year Team	Lg Org	G	AB	H	2B	3B	HR	TB	R	RBI	TBB	IBB	SO	HBP	SH	SF	SB	CS	SB%	GDP	Avg	OBP	SLG
1994 Athletics	R Oak	42	150	42	5	3	1	56	27	11	22	0	34	4	0	0	17	7	.71	0	.280	.386	.373
1995 W Michigan	A Oak	113	409	98	20	2	2	128	76	40	76	2	94	11	13	0	51	20	.72	2	.240	.373	.313
1996 Modesto	A+ Oak	95	363	82	16	1	8	124	58	48	42	0	124	3	8	3	25	12	.68	4	.226	.309	.342
1997 Edmonton	AAA Oak	2	6	1	0	0	0	1	0	0	1	0	2	0	0	0	0	1	.00	0	.167	.286	.167
Modesto	A+ Oak	112	368	78	17	4	5	118	67	28	58	0	125	2	11	0	27	13	.68	2	.212	.322	.321
Huntsville	AA Oak	5	13	5	0	0	0	5	4	0	4	0	2	1	0	0	0	0	.00	0	.385	.556	.385
4 Min. YEARS		369	1309	306	58	10	16	432	232	127	203	2	381	21	32	3	120	53	.69	8	.234	.345	.330

Tony Castro

Pitches: Right **Bats:** Right **Pos:** P **Ht:** 6'2" **Wt:** 175 **Born:** 7/9/71 **Age:** 26

Year Team	Lg Org	G	GS	CG	GF	IP	BFP	H	R	ER	HR	SH	SF	HB	TBB	IBB	SO	WP	Bk	W	L	Pct.	ShO	Sv	ERA
1993 Cedar Rapds	A Ana	13	2	0	7	26	121	25	22	21	1	1	0	2	23	0	22	3	1	2	1	.667	0	0	7.27
1994 Angels	R Ana	11	1	0	9	18.2	81	22	6	6	0	0	0	6	6	0	16	2	0	1	0	1.000	0	4	2.89
Boise	A- Ana	2	0	0	2	9	2	2	1	1	0	0	0	1	1	0	4	0	0	0	0	.000	0	0	4.50
Cedar Rapds	A Ana	10	0	0	6	17	74	15	12	10	1	2	1	0	7	0	8	2	0	1	1	.500	0	1	5.29
1995 Lk Elsinore	A+ Ana	8	0	0	2	11.1	57	15	9	7	1	1	1	0	8	0	9	2	0	0	0	.000	0	0	5.56
Sioux City	IND —	3	0	0	2	4.1	22	8	2	0	0	0	0	0	1	0	5	0	0	0	0	.000	0	0	0.00
Duluth-Sup.	IND —	20	12	1	2	88	387	86	43	32	4	3	2	4	48	0	65	1	1	6	4	.600	0	0	3.27
1996 Kane County	A Fla	39	0	0	16	66.1	287	55	38	26	2	4	3	1	31	0	63	7	3	6	7	.462	0	7	3.53
1997 Brevard Cty	A+ Fla	14	0	0	6	25	111	29	18	16	3	1	2	2	7	0	16	2	1	1	0	1.000	0	1	5.76
Portland	AA Fla	27	0	0	6	39.1	176	47	21	20	5	4	1	3	17	1	21	4	0	1	2	.333	0	0	4.58
Charlotte	AAA Fla	2	0	0	1	3.2	14	2	2	2	1	0	0	0	2	0	1	0	0	0	0	.000	0	0	4.91
5 Min. YEARS		149	15	1	59	301.2	1339	306	174	141	18	16	10	19	151	1	230	23	7	18	15	.545	0	13	4.21

Brett Cederblad

Pitches: Right **Bats:** Both **Pos:** P **Ht:** 6'5" **Wt:** 195 **Born:** 3/6/73 **Age:** 25

Year Team	Lg Org	G	GS	CG	GF	IP	BFP	H	R	ER	HR	SH	SF	HB	TBB	IBB	SO	WP	Bk	W	L	Pct.	ShO	Sv	ERA
1995 Sarasota	A+ Bos	24	12	0	2	92.1	384	98	50	42	4	0	4	6	21	0	71	7	2	7	6	.538	0	0	4.09
Trenton	AA Bos	8	5	2	1	44.2	182	43	19	18	4	2	2	0	11	1	36	2	0	3	2	.600	1	0	3.63
1996 Trenton	AA Bos	27	3	0	9	58	245	59	27	24	8	1	3	3	16	3	49	5	1	1	3	.250	0	2	3.72
Pawtucket	AAA Bos	10	0	0	2	20	90	26	10	8	4	0	0	1	4	0	19	3	0	0	0	.000	0	0	3.60
1997 Red Sox	R Bos	1	0	0	0	2	7	0	0	0	0	0	0	0	1	0	1	0	0	0	0	.000	0	0	0.00
Trenton	AA Bos	6	0	0	2	9.1	42	12	10	9	1	0	0	0	2	0	7	1	0	0	0	.000	0	0	8.68
3 Min. YEARS		76	20	2	16	226.1	950	238	116	101	21	3	9	10	55	4	183	18	3	11	11	.500	1	2	4.02

Silvio Censale

Pitches: Left **Bats:** Left **Pos:** P **Ht:** 6'2" **Wt:** 195 **Born:** 11/21/71 **Age:** 26

Year Team	Lg Org	G	GS	CG	GF	IP	BFP	H	R	ER	HR	SH	SF	HB	TBB	IBB	SO	WP	Bk	W	L	Pct.	ShO	Sv	ERA
1993 Batavia	A- Phi	9	9	1	0	52	207	39	20	12	1	1	3	0	19	0	54	3	0	5	2	.714	0	0	2.08
1995 Piedmont	A Phi	22	21	0	0	120	507	96	54	42	6	5	4	5	54	0	123	10	3	10	6	.625	0	0	3.15
1996 Clearwater	A+ Phi	24	22	1	1	126.1	546	118	65	55	5	3	6	7	54	1	100	4	3	9	4	.471	1	0	3.92
1997 Reading	AA Phi	20	20	0	0	107.1	456	88	58	52	21	4	1	4	56	0	102	5	1	9	4	.692	0	0	4.36

		HOW MUCH HE PITCHED				WHAT HE GAVE UP										THE RESULTS					
Year Team	Lg Org	G	GS	CG	GF	IP	BFP	H	R	ER	HR	SH	SF	HB	TBB	IBB	SO	WP	Bk	W	L	Pct.	ShO	Sv	ERA
4 Min. YEARS		75	72	2	1	405.2	1716	341	197	161	33	13	14	16	183	1	379	22	7	32	21	.604	1	0	3.57

Wes Chamberlain

Bats: Right **Throws:** Right **Pos:** OF **Ht:** 6'2" **Wt:** 230 **Born:** 4/13/66 **Age:** 32

		BATTING														BASERUNNING				PERCENTAGES		
Year Team	Lg Org	G	AB	H	2B	3B	HR	TB	R	RBI	TBB	IBB	SO	HBP	SH	SF	SB	CS	SB%	GDP	Avg	OBP	SLG
1987 Watertown	A- Pit	66	258	67	13	4	5	103	50	35	25	2	48	1	0	3	22	7	.76	6	.260	.324	.399
1988 Augusta	A+ Pit	27	107	36	7	2	1	50	22	17	11	0	11	1	2	0	1	3	.25	4	.336	.403	.467
Salem	A+ Pit	92	365	100	15	1	11	150	66	50	38	2	59	0	0	2	14	4	.78	7	.274	.341	.411
1989 Harrisburg	AA Pit	129	471	144	26	3	21	239	65	87	32	4	82	2	0	7	11	10	.52	14	.306	.348	.507
1990 Buffalo	AAA Pit	123	416	104	24	2	6	150	43	52	34	0	58	8	2	5	14	19	.42	19	.250	.315	.361
1991 Scranton-WB	AAA Phi	39	144	37	7	2	2	54	12	20	8	1	13	0	0	4	7	4	.64	6	.257	.288	.375
1992 Scranton-WB	AAA Phi	34	127	42	6	2	4	64	16	26	11	0	13	2	1	2	6	2	.75	2	.331	.387	.504
1994 Clearwater	A+ Pit	6	25	9	1	0	3	19	5	6	1	1	1	1	0	0	0	1	.00	1	.360	.407	.760
1995 Pawtucket	AAA Bos	48	183	64	17	1	12	119	28	40	3	0	45	3	0	1	5	3	.63	3	.350	.368	.650
Omaha	AAA KC	16	64	14	3	0	1	20	2	6	2	0	15	2	0	1	0	0	.00	0	.219	.261	.313
1996 Syracuse	AAA Tor	37	131	45	5	0	10	80	20	37	19	2	19	0	0	1	2	1	.67	5	.344	.424	.611
1997 Calgary	AAA Pit	18	60	19	4	0	2	29	7	9	0	0	14	0	0	0	1	0	1.00	1	.317	.317	.483
Norfolk	AAA NYN	97	336	92	16	2	7	133	33	50	24	1	58	10	0	1	7	2	.78	13	.274	.340	.396
1990 Philadelphia	NL	18	46	13	3	0	2	22	9	4	1	0	9	0	0	0	4	0	1.00	0	.283	.298	.478
1991 Philadelphia	NL	101	383	92	16	3	13	153	51	50	31	0	73	2	1	0	9	4	.69	8	.240	.300	.399
1992 Philadelphia	NL	76	275	71	18	0	9	116	26	41	10	2	55	1	1	2	4	0	1.00	7	.258	.285	.422
1993 Philadelphia	NL	96	284	80	20	2	12	140	34	45	17	3	51	1	0	4	2	1	.67	4	.282	.320	.493
1994 Philadelphia	NL	24	69	19	5	0	2	30	7	6	3	0	12	0	0	0	0	0	.00	3	.275	.306	.435
Boston	AL	51	164	42	9	1	4	65	13	20	12	2	38	0	0	0	2	0	1.00	6	.256	.307	.396
1995 Boston	AL	19	42	5	1	0	1	9	4	1	3	0	11	0	0	0	1	0	1.00	2	.119	.178	.214
10 Min. YEARS		732	2687	773	144	19	85	1210	369	435	208	13	436	30	5	27	90	56	.62	84	.288	.342	.450
6 Maj. YEARS		385	1263	322	72	6	43	535	144	167	77	7	249	4	2	6	20	7	.74	34	.255	.299	.424

Frank Charles

Bats: Right **Throws:** Right **Pos:** C **Ht:** 6'4" **Wt:** 210 **Born:** 2/23/69 **Age:** 29

		BATTING														BASERUNNING				PERCENTAGES		
Year Team	Lg Org	G	AB	H	2B	3B	HR	TB	R	RBI	TBB	IBB	SO	HBP	SH	SF	SB	CS	SB%	GDP	Avg	OBP	SLG
1991 Everett	A- SF	62	239	76	17	1	9	122	31	49	21	0	55	1	0	1	1	2	.33	5	.318	.374	.510
1992 Clinton	A SF	2	5	0	0	0	0	0	1	0	0	0	3	0	0	0	0	0	.00	0	.000	.000	.000
San Jose	A+ SF	87	286	83	16	1	0	101	27	34	11	2	61	4	1	0	4	4	.50	12	.290	.326	.353
1993 St. Paul	IND —	58	216	59	13	0	2	78	27	27	11	0	33	3	5	1	5	3	.63	9	.273	.316	.361
1994 Charlotte	A+ Tex	79	254	67	17	1	2	92	23	33	16	1	52	3	3	2	2	3	.40	2	.264	.313	.362
1995 Tulsa	AA Tex	126	479	121	24	3	13	190	51	72	22	0	92	4	1	4	1	0	1.00	19	.253	.289	.397
1996 Okla City	AAA Tex	35	113	21	7	2	1	35	10	8	4	0	29	1	0	2	0	3	.00	1	.186	.217	.310
Tulsa	AA Tex	41	147	39	6	0	5	60	18	15	10	0	28	0	0	0	2	0	1.00	1	.265	.312	.408
1997 Tulsa	AA Tex	95	335	77	18	2	9	126	38	49	24	1	81	3	1	1	2	2	.50	9	.230	.287	.376
7 Min. YEARS		585	2074	543	118	10	41	804	226	297	119	4	434	19	13	11	17	17	.50	60	.262	.306	.388

David Chavarria

Pitches: Right **Bats:** Left **Pos:** P **Ht:** 6'7" **Wt:** 195 **Born:** 5/19/73 **Age:** 25

		HOW MUCH HE PITCHED						WHAT HE GAVE UP											THE RESULTS					
Year Team	Lg Org	G	GS	CG	GF	IP	BFP	H	R	ER	HR	SH	SF	HB	TBB	IBB	SO	WP	Bk	W	L	Pct.	ShO	Sv	ERA
1991 Rangers	R Tex	8	7	0	0	29.2	132	36	19	14	1	0	1	0	11	0	26	3	2	0	6	.000	0	0	4.25
1992 Butte	R+ Tex	13	12	0	0	47.1	229	54	44	33	0	2	3	2	30	0	33	6	3	2	7	.222	0	0	6.27
1994 Hudson Vall	A- Tex	14	0	0	6	17.1	82	17	11	5	0	0	2	2	17	0	14	3	1	1	0	1.000	0	0	2.60
1995 Chston-SC	A Tex	52	0	0	22	62	277	55	33	27	5	2	5	1	38	3	68	16	0	3	5	.375	0	6	3.92
1996 Charlotte	A+ Tex	38	4	0	22	81.2	364	76	46	28	4	3	8	0	43	0	76	14	1	1	6	.143	0	7	3.09
1997 Arkansas	AA StL	28	14	0	4	90	394	85	56	45	10	4	5	3	41	1	62	13	2	3	6	.333	0	2	4.50
6 Min. YEARS		153	37	0	54	328	1478	323	209	152	20	11	24	8	180	4	279	55	9	9	31	.225	0	15	4.17

Rafael Chaves

Pitches: Right **Bats:** Right **Pos:** P **Ht:** 6'0" **Wt:** 195 **Born:** 11/1/68 **Age:** 29

		HOW MUCH HE PITCHED						WHAT HE GAVE UP											THE RESULTS					
Year Team	Lg Org	G	GS	CG	GF	IP	BFP	H	R	ER	HR	SH	SF	HB	TBB	IBB	SO	WP	Bk	W	L	Pct.	ShO	Sv	ERA
1986 Charleston	A SD	39	2	0	8	81	354	77	46	30	6	2	2	2	37	2	43	1	3	5	3	.625	0	1	3.33
1987 Chston-SC	A SD	53	0	0	32	87.1	371	86	36	29	2	2	1	3	21	6	59	3	0	8	5	.615	0	11	2.99
1988 Riverside	A+ SD	46	0	0	34	64.2	273	58	20	17	1	1	3	2	28	1	49	2	4	2	3	.400	0	19	2.37
1989 Wichita	AA SD	37	2	0	12	76	338	84	51	45	4	4	2	2	32	9	43	9	3	1	5	.167	0	5	5.33
1990 Wichita	AA SD	46	1	0	36	84	354	85	46	39	4	3	4	3	16	1	46	8	1	6	5	.545	0	9	4.18
1991 Wichita	AA SD	38	0	0	11	71	338	80	54	41	6	3	2	6	41	3	39	4	0	3	0	1.000	0	3	5.20
1992 High Desert	A+ Bal	68	0	0	53	88.1	356	64	28	18	5	5	4	3	36	3	67	2	0	4	5	.444	0	34	1.83
1993 Bowie	AA Bal	45	0	0	40	48	210	56	23	21	4	1	1	1	16	2	39	4	0	2	5	.286	0	20	3.94
1994 Portland	AA Fla	12	0	0	6	16	82	17	14	12	0	0	3	1	13	1	10	3	1	0	0	.000	0	1	6.75
1995 Lynchburg	A+ Pit	42	0	0	41	47.1	191	35	17	14	3	4	0	1	13	3	45	5	1	1	3	.250	0	22	2.66
Augusta	A Pit	7	0	0	2	8.2	36	2	3	2	0	2	0	0	6	0	9	0	0	1	0	1.000	0	2	2.08
1996 Lynchburg	A+ Pit	30	0	0	28	32	139	35	18	9	3	3	0	3	8	6	20	1	1	1	3	.250	0	5	2.53
Carolina	AA Pit	19	0	0	9	26.1	107	21	5	4	1	1	0	0	8	3	15	2	0	1	2	.333	0	1	1.37
1997 Carolina	AA Pit	5	0	0	4	7.1	39	12	8	7	1	0	1	0	4	2	6	0	0	0	2	.000	0	0	8.59
12 Min. YEARS		487	5	0	316	738	3190	712	369	288	40	31	22	27	279	42	500	47	14	35	41	.461	0	130	3.51

Carlos Chavez

Pitches: Right **Bats:** Right **Pos:** P   **Ht:** 6'1" **Wt:** 200 **Born:** 8/25/72 **Age:** 25

Year Team	Lg Org	G	GS	CG	GF	IP	BFP	H	R	ER	HR	SH	SF	HB	TBB	IBB	SO	WP	Bk	W	L	Pct.	ShO	Sv	ERA
1992 Bluefield	R+ Bal	15	7	0	3	45.2	219	49	42	35	5	1	4	1	34	0	44	10	6	1	2	.333	0	1	6.90
1993 Albany	A Bal	20	0	0	13	34	155	33	20	20	3	3	0	3	18	0	28	6	2	1	3	.250	0	3	5.29
Bluefield	R+ Bal	14	13	0	0	82	356	80	43	34	15	1	2	3	37	1	71	14	1	6	3	.667	0	0	3.73
1994 Albany	A Bal	5	0	0	3	9.1	41	9	3	3	0	0	0	0	7	0	4	0	0	1	0	1.000	0	0	2.89
Bluefield	R+ Bal	13	13	2	0	85.2	346	58	38	28	11	2	5	6	32	0	92	12	1	7	5	.583	1	0	2.94
1995 Frederick	A+ Bal	43	1	0	16	81.1	342	62	38	23	4	1	0	2	40	2	107	16	1	5	5	.500	0	6	2.55
Rochester	AAA Bal	1	0	0	0	1.2	11	3	2	2	0	0	1	0	3	0	1	2	0	0	0	.000	0	0	10.80
Bowie	AA Bal	1	0	0	0	2	6	0	0	0	0	0	0	0	1	0	2	0	0	0	0	.000	0	0	0.00
1996 Bowie	AA Bal	56	1	0	27	83	369	69	44	40	8	1	3	6	52	0	80	19	0	4	6	.400	0	7	4.34
1997 Portland	AA Fla	30	0	0	13	39.1	169	35	23	23	4	1	1	3	16	1	32	9	0	2	1	.667	0	1	5.26
Sioux Falls	IND —	10	0	0	3	15	67	19	11	10	3	2	2	0	4	1	15	4	0	0	2	.000	0	0	6.00
Stockton	A+ Mil	4	0	0	1	3.1	15	5	2	2	1	0	0	0	0	0	5	0	0	0	0	.000	0	0	5.40
6 Min. YEARS		212	35	2	79	482.1	2096	422	266	220	54	12	18	24	244	5	481	92	11	27	27	.500	1	18	4.11

Eric Chavez

Bats: Right **Throws:** Right **Pos:** C   **Ht:** 5'11" **Wt:** 212 **Born:** 9/7/70 **Age:** 27

Year Team	Lg Org	G	AB	H	2B	3B	HR	TB	R	RBI	TBB	IBB	SO	HBP	SH	SF	SB	CS	SB%	GDP	Avg	OBP	SLG
1992 Bluefield	R+ Bal	56	192	57	14	1	9	100	35	32	34	0	48	4	1	1	2	2	.50	3	.297	.411	.521
1993 Albany	A Bal	139	476	119	38	2	18	215	74	74	79	6	124	5	2	4	3	3	.50	7	.250	.360	.452
1994 Frederick	A+ Bal	124	388	103	26	3	23	204	75	82	65	0	100	3	2	8	3	2	.60	5	.265	.369	.526
1995 Bowie	AA Bal	14	51	10	2	0	2	18	5	4	4	0	17	1	0	0	0	0	.00	1	.196	.268	.353
High Desert	A+ Bal	74	254	59	15	0	14	116	38	37	27	0	74	4	0	2	4	2	.67	4	.232	.314	.457
1996 Frederick	A+ Bal	122	416	116	29	1	18	201	60	64	72	5	101	3	2	5	5	3	.63	10	.279	.385	.483
1997 Bowie	AA Bal	1	0	0	0	0	0	0	0	0	0	0	0	0	0	0	0	0	.00	0	.000	.000	.000
Delmarva	A Bal	26	85	19	4	0	1	26	10	12	10	2	23	1	1	1	0	1	1.00	4	.224	.306	.306
Frederick	A+ Bal	82	272	51	16	0	11	100	29	34	22	0	69	4	0	4	1	3	.25	6	.188	.255	.368
6 Min. YEARS		638	2134	534	144	7	96	980	326	339	313	13	556	25	8	26	19	15	.56	40	.250	.349	.459

Dan Chergey

Pitches: Right **Bats:** Right **Pos:** P   **Ht:** 6'2" **Wt:** 195 **Born:** 1/29/71 **Age:** 27

Year Team	Lg Org	G	GS	CG	GF	IP	BFP	H	R	ER	HR	SH	SF	HB	TBB	IBB	SO	WP	Bk	W	L	Pct.	ShO	Sv	ERA
1993 Elmira	A- Fla	15	10	1	1	79.2	329	85	34	31	5	3	3	8	14	0	53	3	1	3	5	.375	0	0	3.50
1994 Edmonton	AAA Fla	13	0	0	6	19.2	88	22	13	13	2	0	1	2	5	0	17	0	0	2	1	.667	0	0	5.95
Brevard Cty	A+ Fla	32	0	0	21	42	160	29	12	8	1	1	0	1	11	1	41	0	0	1	3	.250	0	9	1.71
1995 Portland	AA Fla	55	0	0	27	80.1	331	62	35	31	7	7	2	3	26	6	75	2	0	6	7	.462	0	5	3.47
1996 Portland	AA Fla	13	0	0	8	18	80	18	9	8	1	1	0	0	6	2	16	0	0	0	2	.000	0	2	4.00
Charlotte	AAA Fla	45	1	0	11	75.1	333	86	55	52	16	0	6	1	28	0	43	2	0	0	1	.000	0	1	6.21
1997 Portland	AA Fla	32	0	0	18	39	154	30	14	14	5	1	0	0	7	0	44	1	1	2	0	1.000	0	7	3.23
Charlotte	AAA Fla	27	4	0	9	43	174	37	18	15	5	1	4	2	9	1	40	2	0	3	1	.750	0	6	3.14
5 Min. YEARS		232	15	1	101	397	1649	369	190	172	42	14	16	17	106	10	329	10	2	17	20	.459	0	30	3.90

Dan Cholowsky

Bats: Right **Throws:** Right **Pos:** C   **Ht:** 6'0" **Wt:** 195 **Born:** 10/30/70 **Age:** 27

Year Team	Lg Org	G	AB	H	2B	3B	HR	TB	R	RBI	TBB	IBB	SO	HBP	SH	SF	SB	CS	SB%	GDP	Avg	OBP	SLG
1991 Hamilton	A- StL	20	69	16	1	1	1	22	9	6	9	0	17	1	0	0	6	3	.67	0	.232	.329	.319
1992 Savannah	A StL	69	232	76	6	4	8	114	44	34	51	2	48	3	0	0	34	16	.68	1	.328	.451	.491
St. Pete	A+ StL	59	201	57	8	0	1	68	19	17	33	0	31	2	1	4	14	10	.58	8	.284	.383	.338
1993 St. Pete	A+ StL	54	208	60	12	0	2	78	30	22	20	2	54	2	0	0	6	8	.43	5	.288	.357	.375
Arkansas	AA StL	68	212	46	10	2	3	69	31	16	38	3	54	2	1	1	10	2	.83	7	.217	.340	.325
1994 Arkansas	AA StL	131	454	101	18	4	14	169	57	51	65	2	114	4	1	1	20	9	.69	9	.222	.324	.372
1995 Arkansas	AA StL	54	190	59	12	0	7	92	41	35	24	2	41	5	0	2	7	6	.54	2	.311	.398	.484
Louisville	AAA StL	76	238	52	9	1	7	84	27	25	36	0	64	5	0	6	10	4	.71	5	.218	.326	.353
1996 Louisville	AAA StL	17	56	10	2	0	1	15	3	6	4	0	16	1	0	0	1	2	.33	1	.179	.246	.268
Iowa	AAA ChN	26	52	9	5	0	2	20	10	5	11	0	18	0	1	0	0	0	.00	0	.173	.317	.385
Orlando	AA ChN	45	143	34	4	0	4	50	21	14	23	0	38	3	0	1	2	4	.33	3	.238	.353	.350
1997 Iowa	AAA ChN	36	65	12	2	0	1	17	12	4	9	0	17	0	0	0	2	1	.67	2	.185	.284	.262
Colo Spngs	AAA Col	26	84	28	6	0	5	49	17	19	15	1	21	1	0	0	1	1	.50	1	.333	.440	.583
7 Min. YEARS		681	2204	560	95	12	56	847	321	254	338	12	533	29	4	17	113	66	.63	44	.254	.358	.384

Bobby Chouinard

Pitches: Right **Bats:** Right **Pos:** P   **Ht:** 6'1" **Wt:** 172 **Born:** 5/1/72 **Age:** 26

Year Team	Lg Org	G	GS	CG	GF	IP	BFP	H	R	ER	HR	SH	SF	HB	TBB	IBB	SO	WP	Bk	W	L	Pct.	ShO	Sv	ERA
1990 Bluefield	R+ Bal	10	10	2	0	56	237	61	34	23	10	1	2	1	14	0	30	2	0	2	5	.286	1	0	3.70
1991 Kane County	A Bal	6	6	1	0	33	147	45	24	17	3	0	3	2	5	0	17	3	1	2	4	.333	0	0	4.64
Bluefield	R+ Bal	6	6	0	0	33.2	150	44	19	13	1	0	2	1	11	0	31	1	2	5	1	.833	0	0	3.48
1992 Kane County	A Bal	26	26	9	0	181.2	735	151	60	42	4	9	7	6	38	3	112	13	5	10	14	.417	2	0	2.08
1993 Modesto	A+ Oak	24	24	1	0	145.2	623	154	75	69	15	3	8	4	56	1	82	4	1	8	10	.444	0	0	4.26
1994 Modesto	A+ Oak	29	20	0	5	145.2	599	147	53	42	5	8	2	8	32	1	74	5	1	12	5	.706	0	3	2.59
1995 Huntsville	AA Oak	29	29	1	0	166.2	694	155	81	67	10	9	1	4	50	5	106	4	0	14	8	.636	1	0	3.62
1996 Edmonton	AAA Oak	15	15	0	0	84.1	344	70	32	26	7	1	2	1	24	2	45	1	0	10	2	.833	0	0	2.77

		HOW MUCH HE PITCHED						WHAT HE GAVE UP													THE RESULTS					
Year Team	Lg Org	G	GS	CG	GF	IP	BFP	H	R	ER	HR	SH	SF	HB	TBB	IBB	SO	WP	Bk	W	L	Pct.	ShO	Sv	ERA
1997 Edmonton	AAA Oak	25	21	1	1	100	446	129	80	67	19	1	1	0	26	0	58	6	0	6	6	.500	0	0	6.03
1996 Oakland	AL	13	11	0	0	59	278	75	41	40	10	3	3	3	32	3	32	0	0	4	2	.667	0	0	6.10
8 Min. YEARS		170	157	15	6	946.2	3975	956	458	366	74	32	26	28	256	12	555	39	12	69	55	.556	4	3	3.48

Ryan Christenson

Bats: Right Throws: Right Pos: OF   Ht: 5'11" Wt: 175 Born: 3/28/74 Age: 24

		BATTING														BASERUNNING				PERCENTAGES		
Year Team	Lg Org	G	AB	H	2B	3B	HR	TB	R	RBI	TBB	IBB	SO	HBP	SH	SF	SB	CS	SB%	GDP	Avg	OBP	SLG
1995 Sou. Oregon	A- Oak	49	158	30	4	1	1	39	14	16	22	0	33	0	1	2	5	5	.50	3	.190	.286	.247
1996 Sou. Oregon	A- Oak	36	136	39	11	0	5	65	31	21	19	1	21	1	1	1	8	6	.57	3	.287	.376	.478
W Michigan	A Oak	33	122	38	2	2	2	50	21	18	13	0	22	4	1	3	2	4	.33	2	.311	.387	.410
1997 Visalia	A+ Oak	83	308	90	18	8	13	163	69	54	70	1	72	2	3	1	20	11	.65	4	.292	.425	.529
Huntsville	AA Oak	29	120	44	9	3	2	65	39	18	24	0	23	0	0	1	5	4	.56	3	.367	.469	.542
Edmonton	AAA Oak	16	49	14	2	2	2	26	12	5	11	0	11	2	0	0	2	0	1.00	1	.286	.435	.531
3 Min. YEARS		246	893	255	46	16	25	408	186	132	159	2	182	9	6	8	42	30	.58	16	.286	.396	.457

Eddie Christian

Bats: Both Throws: Left Pos: OF-DH   Ht: 5'11" Wt: 180 Born: 8/26/71 Age: 26

		BATTING														BASERUNNING				PERCENTAGES		
Year Team	Lg Org	G	AB	H	2B	3B	HR	TB	R	RBI	TBB	IBB	SO	HBP	SH	SF	SB	CS	SB%	GDP	Avg	OBP	SLG
1992 Marlins	R Fla	59	219	61	10	3	0	77	33	29	31	2	35	1	0	3	14	5	.74	6	.279	.366	.352
1993 Kane County	A Fla	112	366	98	21	5	3	138	49	46	58	6	77	0	3	10	9	11	.45	7	.268	.359	.377
1994 Portland	AA Fla	65	228	53	11	0	1	67	27	21	19	0	52	1	3	2	1	4	.20	7	.232	.292	.294
Brevard Cty	A+ Fla	54	192	50	11	0	2	67	20	22	18	0	35	1	4	3	6	2	.60	5	.260	.322	.349
1995 Long Beach	IND —	83	333	113	27	2	1	147	66	50	48	1	39	0	9	1	27	11	.71	9	.339	.421	.441
1996 Lk Elsinore	A+ Ana	16	58	23	5	0	2	34	10	9	12	0	10	2	1	0	1	2	.33	0	.397	.514	.586
Midland	AA Ana	107	426	130	30	5	5	185	59	46	36	0	72	0	4	3	7	9	.44	8	.305	.357	.434
1997 Memphis	AA Sea	68	238	80	20	0	4	112	50	39	36	6	24	1	2	3	8	3	.73	11	.336	.421	.471
Tacoma	AAA Sea	35	135	43	5	1	1	53	16	9	14	0	24	0	3	0	3	2	.60	3	.319	.383	.393
6 Min. YEARS		599	2195	651	140	16	19	880	330	271	272	15	368	6	29	25	73	49	.60	56	.297	.372	.401

Scott Christman

Pitches: Left Bats: Left Pos: P   Ht: 6'3" Wt: 190 Born: 12/3/71 Age: 26

		HOW MUCH HE PITCHED						WHAT HE GAVE UP													THE RESULTS					
Year Team	Lg Org	G	GS	CG	GF	IP	BFP	H	R	ER	HR	SH	SF	HB	TBB	IBB	SO	WP	Bk	W	L	Pct.	ShO	Sv	ERA
1993 White Sox	R ChA	4	2	0	1	11.1	39	3	1	0	0	0	0	0	4	0	15	0	1	0	0	.000	0	1	0.00
Sarasota	A+ ChA	2	2	0	0	10.1	42	5	4	1	0	0	1	1	5	0	6	0	1	0	1	.000	0	0	0.87
1994 Pr William	A+ ChA	20	20	2	0	116	497	116	64	49	7	3	2	2	44	0	94	5	4	6	11	.353	0	0	3.80
1995 Birmingham	AA ChA	12	12	0	0	62	284	76	49	44	6	2	4	3	24	1	37	6	0	2	5	.286	0	0	6.39
Pr William	A+ ChA	13	13	1	0	85.1	346	83	38	34	7	1	6	2	19	2	56	3	0	4	4	.500	0	0	3.59
1996 White Sox	R ChA	4	4	0	0	12	57	13	8	5	0	0	1	2	4	0	13	1	0	1	1	.500	0	0	3.75
Pr William	A+ ChA	1	1	0	0	5	21	4	0	0	0	0	0	0	3	0	4	0	0	1	0	1.000	0	0	0.00
1997 Birmingham	AA ChA	15	14	0	0	63.2	325	100	74	64	8	1	1	5	38	0	39	5	0	2	7	.222	0	0	9.05
5 Min. YEARS		71	68	3	1	365.2	1611	400	238	197	28	7	15	15	141	3	264	20	6	16	29	.356	0	1	4.85

Eric Christopherson

Bats: Right Throws: Right Pos: C   Ht: 6'1" Wt: 190 Born: 4/25/69 Age: 29

		BATTING														BASERUNNING				PERCENTAGES		
Year Team	Lg Org	G	AB	H	2B	3B	HR	TB	R	RBI	TBB	IBB	SO	HBP	SH	SF	SB	CS	SB%	GDP	Avg	OBP	SLG
1990 San Jose	A+ SF	7	23	4	0	0	0	4	4	1	3	0	6	0	0	0	0	0	.00	0	.174	.269	.174
Everett	A- SF	48	162	43	8	1	1	56	20	22	31	1	28	0	1	2	7	2	.78	2	.265	.379	.346
1991 Clinton	A SF	110	345	93	18	0	5	126	45	58	68	1	54	1	1	6	10	7	.59	10	.270	.386	.365
1992 Shreveport	AA SF	80	270	68	10	1	6	98	36	34	37	0	44	1	0	2	1	6	.14	5	.252	.342	.363
1993 Giants	R SF	8	22	9	1	0	1	12	7	4	9	0	1	0	0	0	0	0	.00	0	.409	.581	.545
Shreveport	AA SF	15	46	7	2	0	0	9	5	2	9	0	10	0	0	0	1	1	.50	1	.152	.291	.196
1994 Shreveport	AA SF	88	267	67	22	0	6	107	30	39	42	4	55	0	1	2	5	1	.83	2	.251	.350	.401
1995 Phoenix	AAA SF	94	282	62	9	1	1	76	21	25	35	1	54	3	5	5	1	1	.50	12	.220	.308	.270
1996 Tucson	AAA Hou	67	223	64	15	3	6	103	31	36	21	2	47	1	1	4	2	0	1.00	1	.287	.345	.462
1997 New Orleans	AAA Hou	9	21	4	0	0	0	4	3	0	4	0	7	0	0	0	0	0	.00	0	.190	.320	.190
Tulsa	AA Tex	39	123	30	9	0	6	57	26	34	25	0	22	0	0	3	1	1	.50	4	.244	.364	.463
8 Min. YEARS		565	1784	451	94	7	31	652	228	255	284	9	328	6	9	24	28	19	.60	37	.253	.353	.365

Chris Clapinski

Bats: Both Throws: Right Pos: 2B   Ht: 6'0" Wt: 175 Born: 8/20/71 Age: 26

		BATTING														BASERUNNING				PERCENTAGES		
Year Team	Lg Org	G	AB	H	2B	3B	HR	TB	R	RBI	TBB	IBB	SO	HBP	SH	SF	SB	CS	SB%	GDP	Avg	OBP	SLG
1992 Marlins	R Fla	59	212	51	8	1	1	64	36	15	49	2	42	4	3	2	5	6	.45	4	.241	.390	.302
1993 Kane County	A Fla	82	214	45	12	1	0	59	22	27	31	0	55	1	8	4	3	8	.27	3	.210	.308	.276
1994 Brevard Cty	A+ Fla	65	157	45	12	3	1	66	33	13	23	2	28	3	7	1	3	2	.60	2	.287	.386	.420
1995 Portland	AA Fla	87	208	49	9	3	4	76	32	30	28	2	44	2	5	5	5	2	.71	4	.236	.325	.365
1996 Portland	AA Fla	23	73	19	7	0	3	35	15	11	13	1	13	2	1	1	3	1	.75	2	.260	.382	.479
Charlotte	AAA Fla	105	362	103	20	1	10	155	74	39	47	0	54	3	8	5	13	6	.68	7	.285	.367	.428
1997 Charlotte	AAA Fla	110	340	89	24	2	12	153	62	52	48	4	64	9	6	2	14	2	.88	9	.262	.366	.450
6 Min. YEARS		531	1566	401	92	11	31	608	274	187	239	11	300	24	38	20	46	27	.63	31	.256	.359	.388

Howie Clark

Bats: Left **Throws:** Right **Pos:** 3B   **Ht:** 5'10" **Wt:** 171 **Born:** 2/13/74 **Age:** 24

Year Team	Lg Org	G	AB	H	2B	3B	HR	TB	R	RBI	TBB	IBB	SO	HBP	SH	SF	SB	CS	SB%	GDP	Avg	OBP	SLG
1992 Orioles	R Bal	43	138	33	7	1	0	42	12	6	12	2	21	2	1	0	1	2	.33	2	.239	.309	.304
1993 Albany	A Bal	7	17	4	0	0	0	4	2	1	0	0	3	0	0	0	1	0	1.00	1	.235	.235	.235
Bluefield	R+ Bal	58	180	53	10	1	3	74	29	30	26	2	34	4	1	4	2	2	.50	4	.294	.388	.411
1994 Frederick	A+ Bal	2	7	1	1	0	0	2	1	0	0	0	2	0	0	0	0	0	.00	1	.143	.143	.286
Albany	A Bal	108	353	95	22	7	2	137	56	47	51	3	58	7	4	1	5	4	.56	7	.269	.371	.388
1995 High Desert	A+ Bal	100	329	85	20	2	5	124	50	40	32	0	51	4	3	3	12	6	.67	4	.258	.329	.377
1996 Bowie	AA Bal	127	449	122	29	3	4	169	55	52	59	1	54	2	10	7	2	8	.20	8	.272	.354	.376
1997 Bowie	AA Bal	105	314	90	16	0	9	133	39	37	32	2	38	1	1	3	2	2	.50	5	.287	.351	.424
6 Min. YEARS		550	1787	483	105	14	23	685	244	213	212	10	261	20	20	18	25	24	.51	32	.270	.351	.383

Patricio Claudio

Bats: Right **Throws:** Right **Pos:** OF   **Ht:** 6'0" **Wt:** 173 **Born:** 4/12/72 **Age:** 26

Year Team	Lg Org	G	AB	H	2B	3B	HR	TB	R	RBI	TBB	IBB	SO	HBP	SH	SF	SB	CS	SB%	GDP	Avg	OBP	SLG
1992 Burlington	R+ Cle	48	165	43	4	0	2	53	31	12	20	0	43	1	4	1	20	7	.74	1	.261	.342	.321
1993 Columbus	A Cle	98	312	80	8	6	0	100	48	26	23	0	67	2	1	0	40	12	.77	1	.256	.312	.321
1994 Kinston	A+ Cle	121	454	111	16	2	1	134	56	24	42	1	117	6	4	2	34	20	.63	6	.244	.315	.295
1995 Bakersfield	A+ Cle	32	128	36	9	3	1	54	19	9	13	0	26	2	2	0	5	7	.42	3	.281	.357	.422
Kinston	A+ Cle	89	298	79	7	4	5	109	37	27	26	2	73	0	5	1	27	11	.71	2	.265	.323	.366
1996 Kinston	A+ Cle	100	361	105	15	2	1	127	67	38	47	2	74	6	2	3	36	14	.72	2	.291	.379	.352
1997 Akron	AA Cle	17	33	7	1	0	0	8	6	6	3	0	14	1	0	0	2	2	.50	1	.212	.297	.242
Kinston	A+ Cle	24	89	27	5	0	1	35	14	9	2	0	16	0	3	0	1	2	.33	1	.303	.319	.393
6 Min. YEARS		529	1840	488	65	17	11	620	278	151	176	5	430	18	21	7	165	75	.69	17	.265	.334	.337

Craig Clayton

Pitches: Right **Bats:** Right **Pos:** P   **Ht:** 6'0" **Wt:** 185 **Born:** 11/29/70 **Age:** 27

Year Team	Lg Org	G	GS	CG	GF	IP	BFP	H	R	ER	HR	SH	SF	HB	TBB	IBB	SO	WP	Bk	W	L	Pct.	ShO	Sv	ERA
1991 Bellingham	A- Sea	1	0	0	1	0.2	3	1	0	0	0	0	0	0	1	0	0	0	0	0	0	.000	0	0	0.00
1993 Jacksnville	AA Sea	3	0	0	3	4	17	3	0	0	0	0	0	1	1	0	1	0	0	0	0	.000	0	0	0.00
1994 Jacksnville	AA Sea	10	0	0	6	12.1	52	8	6	5	1	0	0	1	6	0	13	3	4	0	0	.000	0	1	3.65
Riverside	A+ Sea	20	1	0	4	26.1	135	29	24	23	7	2	1	1	26	0	35	1	0	1	1	.500	0	0	7.86
1995 Riverside	A+ Sea	28	28	0	0	160.1	738	171	102	89	16	11	6	7	83	3	156	7	1	9	8	.529	0	0	5.00
1996 Rancho Cuca	A+ SD	11	3	0	2	28.1	127	34	18	15	4	0	0	2	8	0	29	5	0	2	3	.400	0	0	4.76
Memphis	AA SD	5	0	0	0	9.2	52	14	12	6	3	0	1	1	5	0	9	3	0	0	0	.000	0	0	5.59
Clinton	A SD	27	0	0	18	37.1	154	27	10	6	1	0	1	3	8	0	29	3	0	2	1	.667	0	9	1.45
1997 Rancho Cuca	A+ SD	10	0	0	6	12.1	57	14	10	9	1	2	0	0	5	1	15	3	0	2	1	.667	0	1	6.57
Mobile	AA SD	3	0	0	0	2.1	11	1	0	0	0	0	0	1	3	0	2	0	0	0	0	.000	0	0	0.00
Grand Forks	IND —	11	7	0	2	42.2	191	44	26	22	5	1	0	5	17	1	36	6	0	2	2	.500	0	0	4.64
6 Min. YEARS		129	39	0	42	336.1	1537	346	208	175	38	16	9	22	162	5	325	31	5	18	16	.529	0	11	4.68

Matt Clement

Pitches: Right **Bats:** Right **Pos:** P   **Ht:** 6'3" **Wt:** 190 **Born:** 8/12/74 **Age:** 23

Year Team	Lg Org	G	GS	CG	GF	IP	BFP	H	R	ER	HR	SH	SF	HB	TBB	IBB	SO	WP	Bk	W	L	Pct.	ShO	Sv	ERA
1994 Spokane	A- SD	2	2	0	0	7.1	39	8	7	5	0	0	0	1	11	0	4	1	1	1	1	.500	0	0	6.14
Padres	R SD	13	13	0	0	67	286	65	38	33	0	1	0	6	17	0	76	10	0	8	5	.615	0	0	4.43
1995 Rancho Cuca	A+ SD	12	12	0	0	57.1	267	61	37	27	1	2	4	5	49	0	33	12	0	3	4	.429	0	0	4.24
Idaho Falls	R+ SD	14	14	0	0	81	349	61	53	39	3	6	3	13	42	0	65	19	2	6	3	.667	0	0	4.33
1996 Clinton	A SD	16	16	1	0	96.1	410	66	31	30	3	1	3	9	52	0	109	15	0	8	3	.727	1	0	2.80
Rancho Cuca	A+ SD	11	11	0	0	56.1	261	61	40	35	8	5	3	9	26	0	75	5	1	4	5	.444	0	0	5.59
1997 Rancho Cuca	A+ SD	14	14	2	0	101	410	74	30	18	3	2	1	9	31	1	109	6	0	6	3	.667	1	0	1.60
Mobile	AA SD	13	13	1	0	88	382	83	37	25	4	4	1	12	32	0	92	12	0	6	5	.545	1	0	2.56
4 Min. YEARS		95	95	4	0	554.1	2404	479	273	212	22	21	15	64	260	1	563	80	4	42	29	.592	3	0	3.44

Pat Cline

Bats: Right **Throws:** Right **Pos:** C   **Ht:** 6'3" **Wt:** 220 **Born:** 10/9/74 **Age:** 23

Year Team	Lg Org	G	AB	H	2B	3B	HR	TB	R	RBI	TBB	IBB	SO	HBP	SH	SF	SB	CS	SB%	GDP	Avg	OBP	SLG
1993 Huntington	R+ ChN	33	96	18	5	0	2	29	17	13	17	0	28	1	1	3	0	0	.00	1	.188	.308	.302
1994 Cubs	R ChN	3	0	0	0	0	0	0	0	0	0	0	0	0	0	0	0	0	.00	0	.000	.000	.000
1995 Rockford	A ChN	112	390	106	27	0	13	172	65	77	58	3	93	11	0	5	6	1	.86	6	.272	.377	.441
1996 Daytona	A+ ChN	124	434	121	30	2	17	206	75	76	54	2	79	12	0	2	10	2	.83	6	.279	.373	.475
1997 Iowa	AAA ChN	27	95	21	2	0	3	32	6	10	10	1	24	0	0	1	0	1	.00	4	.221	.292	.337
Orlando	AA ChN	78	271	69	19	0	7	109	39	37	27	1	78	5	0	2	2	2	.50	7	.255	.331	.402
5 Min. YEARS		377	1286	335	83	2	42	548	202	213	166	7	302	29	1	13	18	6	.75	24	.260	.355	.426

Trevor Cobb

Pitches: Left **Bats:** Left **Pos:** P   **Ht:** 6'2" **Wt:** 185 **Born:** 7/13/73 **Age:** 24

Year Team	Lg Org	G	GS	CG	GF	IP	BFP	H	R	ER	HR	SH	SF	HB	TBB	IBB	SO	WP	Bk	W	L	Pct.	ShO	Sv	ERA
1992 Twins	R Min	11	11	1	0	59.2	252	54	34	24	1	1	0	0	17	0	40	5	1	3	3	.500	0	0	3.62
1993 Elizabethtn	R+ Min	13	13	1	0	82.2	356	71	48	36	7	4	4	5	40	0	53	7	1	5	4	.556	0	0	3.92

		HOW MUCH HE PITCHED						WHAT HE GAVE UP													THE RESULTS					
Year Team	Lg Org	G	GS	CG	GF	IP	BFP	H	R	ER	HR	SH	SF	HB	TBB	IBB	SO	WP	Bk	W	L	Pct.	ShO	Sv	ERA
1994 Elizabethtn	R+ Min	12	12	1	0	78.2	318	61	33	25	2	4	0	5	19	0	68	8	1	9	1	.900	1	0	2.86
1995 Twins	R Min	3	3	0	0	19	74	11	5	2	0	1	0	1	7	0	15	2	0	2	0	1.000	0	0	0.95
Ft. Wayne	A Min	11	10	0	0	53.1	226	51	26	23	1	3	0	3	18	0	46	6	0	4	4	.500	0	0	3.88
1996 Ft. Myers	A+ Min	31	14	1	5	126.1	520	101	44	37	1	4	6	5	43	0	98	12	1	7	3	.700	1	0	2.64
1997 Ft. Myers	A+ Min	15	7	1	0	60.2	246	49	29	20	2	3	1	2	16	0	48	2	0	7	0	1.000	1	0	2.97
New Britain	AA Min	19	13	3	1	94.1	386	77	41	36	6	4	3	4	39	0	68	12	0	6	4	.600	0	1	3.43
6 Min. YEARS		115	83	8	6	574.2	2378	475	260	203	22	23	14	25	199	0	436	54	4	43	19	.694	3	1	3.18

Craig Colbert

Bats: Right **Throws:** Right **Pos:** DH **Ht:** 6' 0" **Wt:** 214 **Born:** 2/13/65 **Age:** 33

		BATTING														BASERUNNING				PERCENTAGES		
Year Team	Lg Org	G	AB	H	2B	3B	HR	TB	R	RBI	TBB	IBB	SO	HBP	SH	SF	SB	CS	SB%	GDP	Avg	OBP	SLG
1986 Clinton	A SF	72	263	60	12	0	1	75	26	17	23	1	53	3	0	1	4	1	.80	7	.228	.297	.285
1987 Fresno	A+ SF	115	388	95	12	4	6	133	41	51	22	2	89	4	3	5	5	5	.50	11	.245	.289	.343
1988 Clinton	A SF	124	455	106	19	2	11	162	56	64	41	0	100	1	2	2	8	9	.47	4	.233	.297	.356
1989 Shreveport	AA SF	106	363	94	19	3	7	140	47	34	23	5	67	0	2	2	3	7	.30	11	.259	.302	.386
1990 Phoenix	AAA SF	111	400	112	22	2	8	162	41	47	31	3	80	3	1	2	4	5	.44	8	.280	.335	.405
1991 Phoenix	AAA SF	42	142	35	6	2	2	51	9	13	11	2	38	0	0	1	0	1	.00	7	.246	.299	.359
1992 Phoenix	AAA SF	36	140	45	8	1	1	58	16	12	3	0	16	1	2	2	0	1	.00	1	.321	.336	.414
1993 Phoenix	AAA SF	13	45	10	2	1	1	17	5	7	0	0	11	1	0	1	0	0	.00	1	.222	.234	.378
1994 Charlotte	AAA Cle	69	182	47	7	1	4	68	19	25	19	1	40	0	1	1	1	1	.50	9	.258	.327	.374
1995 Las Vegas	AAA SD	74	241	60	8	1	1	73	30	24	21	0	44	0	1	1	1	0	1.00	14	.249	.308	.303
1996 Las Vegas	AAA SD	65	200	50	8	0	5	73	18	19	8	0	48	0	0	4	3	1	.75	4	.250	.274	.365
1997 Las Vegas	AAA SD	2	2	2	1	0	0	3	0	0	0	0	0	0	0	0	0	0	.00	0	1.000	1.000	1.500
1992 San Francisco	NL	49	126	29	5	2	1	41	10	16	9	0	22	0	2	0	1	0	1.00	8	.230	.277	.325
1993 San Francisco	NL	23	37	6	2	0	1	11	2	5	3	1	13	0	0	0	0	0	.00	0	.162	.225	.297
12 Min. YEARS		829	2821	716	124	17	47	1015	308	313	202	14	586	13	12	22	29	31	.48	80	.254	.304	.360
2 Maj. YEARS		72	163	35	7	2	2	52	12	21	12	1	35	0	2	2	1	0	1.00	8	.215	.266	.319

Alex Cole

Bats: Left **Throws:** Left **Pos:** OF **Ht:** 6' 0" **Wt:** 184 **Born:** 8/17/65 **Age:** 32

		BATTING														BASERUNNING				PERCENTAGES		
Year Team	Lg Org	G	AB	H	2B	3B	HR	TB	R	RBI	TBB	IBB	SO	HBP	SH	SF	SB	CS	SB%	GDP	Avg	OBP	SLG
1985 Johnson Cty	R+ StL	66	232	61	5	1	1	71	60	13	30	0	27	1	0	1	46	8	.85	4	.263	.348	.306
1986 St. Pete	A+ StL	74	286	98	9	1	0	109	76	26	54	1	37	2	2	1	56	22	.72	2	.343	.449	.381
Louisville	AAA StL	63	200	50	2	4	1	63	25	16	17	0	30	1	0	1	24	13	.65	3	.250	.311	.315
1987 Arkansas	AA StL	125	477	122	12	4	2	148	68	27	44	5	55	0	5	3	68	29	.70	3	.256	.318	.310
1988 Louisville	AAA StL	120	392	91	7	8	0	114	44	24	42	1	59	1	6	1	40	15	.73	2	.232	.307	.291
1989 St. Pete	A+ StL	8	32	6	0	0	0	6	2	1	3	0	7	0	0	0	4	1	.80	1	.188	.257	.188
Louisville	AAA StL	127	455	128	5	5	2	149	75	29	71	1	76	1	4	1	47	19	.71	3	.281	.379	.327
1990 Las Vegas	AAA SD	90	341	99	7	4	0	114	58	28	47	1	62	1	8	1	32	15	.68	4	.290	.376	.334
Colo Sprngs	AAA Cle	14	49	21	2	0	0	23	13	3	8	0	7	0	0	0	6	4	.60	1	.429	.509	.469
1991 Colo Sprngs	AAA Cle	8	32	6	0	1	0	8	6	3	4	0	3	1	0	0	1	3	.25	0	.188	.297	.250
1996 Pawtucket	AAA Bos	82	304	90	14	8	4	132	57	39	50	0	47	2	4	3	11	7	.61	3	.296	.397	.434
1997 Charlotte	AAA Fla	39	105	22	5	0	2	33	20	7	18	0	20	1	2	0	4	1	.80	1	.210	.331	.314
Madison	IND —	27	112	38	6	1	2	52	20	21	16	0	19	8	2	0	6	2	.75	3	.339	.431	.464
1990 Cleveland	AL	63	227	68	5	4	0	81	43	13	28	0	38	1	0	0	40	9	.82	2	.300	.379	.357
1991 Cleveland	AL	122	387	114	17	3	0	137	58	21	58	2	47	1	4	2	27	17	.61	8	.295	.386	.354
1992 Cleveland	AL	41	97	20	1	0	0	21	11	5	10	0	21	1	0	1	9	2	.82	2	.206	.284	.216
Pittsburgh	NL	64	205	57	3	7	0	74	33	10	18	1	46	0	1	1	7	4	.64	2	.278	.335	.361
1993 Colorado	NL	126	348	89	9	4	0	106	50	24	43	3	58	2	4	2	30	13	.70	6	.256	.339	.305
1994 Minnesota	AL	105	345	102	15	5	4	139	68	23	44	2	60	1	6	2	29	8	.78	3	.296	.375	.403
1995 Minnesota	AL	28	79	27	3	2	1	37	10	14	8	0	15	1	2	0	1	3	.25	0	.342	.409	.468
1996 Boston	AL	24	72	16	5	1	0	23	13	7	8	0	11	0	2	1	5	3	.63	2	.222	.296	.319
9 Min. YEARS		843	3017	832	74	37	14	1022	524	237	404	9	438	13	31	10	345	139	.71	30	.276	.363	.339
7 Maj. YEARS		573	1760	493	58	26	5	618	286	117	217	8	296	7	19	9	148	59	.71	25	.280	.360	.351

Jason Cole

Pitches: Right **Bats:** Right **Pos:** P **Ht:** 6'3" **Wt:** 198 **Born:** 9/8/72 **Age:** 25

		HOW MUCH HE PITCHED						WHAT HE GAVE UP													THE RESULTS					
Year Team	Lg Org	G	GS	CG	GF	IP	BFP	H	R	ER	HR	SH	SF	HB	TBB	IBB	SO	WP	Bk	W	L	Pct.	ShO	Sv	ERA
1994 Vermont	A- Mon	14	0	0	8	13	61	11	4	2	0	2	2	3	5	0	7	2	1	1	0	1.000	0	3	1.38
1995 Albany	A Mon	32	4	0	11	57.2	257	67	33	28	3	2	2	4	22	2	51	2	1	3	3	.500	0	1	4.37
1996 Delmarva	A Mon	10	0	0	2	17.2	65	11	4	2	1	1	0	0	1	0	20	1	0	1	2	.333	0	1	1.02
Wst Plm Bch	A+ Mon	39	0	0	24	51.2	256	57	25	16	2	3	1	2	20	0	40	1	0	6	1	.857	0	3	2.31
1997 Wst Plm Bch	A+ Mon	11	0	0	5	19	80	21	7	5	1	0	0	1	4	0	8	2	0	2	1	.667	0	2	2.37
Harrisburg	AA Mon	37	0	0	16	58	254	52	31	23	5	3	1	3	19	2	31	1	0	2	3	.400	0	0	3.57
4 Min. YEARS		143	4	0	66	227.2	973	219	104	76	12	11	6	13	71	4	157	9	2	15	10	.600	0	10	3.00

Dan Collier

Bats: Right **Throws:** Right **Pos:** DH-OF **Ht:** 6'3" **Wt:** 200 **Born:** 8/13/70 **Age:** 27

		BATTING														BASERUNNING				PERCENTAGES		
Year Team	Lg Org	G	AB	H	2B	3B	HR	TB	R	RBI	TBB	IBB	SO	HBP	SH	SF	SB	CS	SB%	GDP	Avg	OBP	SLG
1991 Red Sox	R Bos	42	131	33	4	2	6	59	27	25	27	1	42	14	0	0	1	1	.50	1	.252	.430	.450
1992 Elmira	A- Bos	59	193	34	8	0	9	69	26	24	9	0	86	10	2	1	2	2	.50	0	.176	.249	.358
1993 Utica	A- Bos	67	226	49	11	1	15	107	39	48	29	1	95	7	0	2	4	0	1.00	5	.217	.322	.473
1994 Lynchburg	A+ Bos	84	299	67	16	0	11	116	39	40	16	1	134	8	1	1	5	2	.71	6	.224	.281	.388

Year Team	Lg Org	G	AB	H	2B	3B	HR	TB	R	RBI	TBB	IBB	SO	HBP	SH	SF	SB	CS	SB%	GDP	Avg	OBP	SLG
1995 Sarasota	A+ Bos	67	242	62	12	1	12	112	30	44	20	0	83	5	0	3	5	9	.36	3	.256	.322	.463
1996 Trenton	AA Bos	28	94	20	3	0	4	35	12	9	9	1	36	0	1	0	2	1	.67	4	.213	.282	.372
Bakersfield	A+ Bos	56	212	58	15	1	5	90	22	40	6	0	63	7	2	2	9	3	.75	2	.274	.313	.425
1997 Tulsa	AA Tex	115	389	100	20	0	26	198	60	79	44	1	134	14	1	3	1	2	.33	3	.257	.351	.509
7 Min. YEARS		518	1786	423	89	5	88	786	255	309	160	5	673	65	7	12	29	20	.59	24	.237	.320	.440

Dennis Colon

Bats: Left   Throws: Right   Pos: 1B   Ht: 5'10"   Wt: 165   Born: 8/4/73   Age: 24

Year Team	Lg Org	G	AB	H	2B	3B	HR	TB	R	RBI	TBB	IBB	SO	HBP	SH	SF	SB	CS	SB%	GDP	Avg	OBP	SLG
1991 Astros	R Hou	54	193	46	5	2	2	61	20	28	10	2	28	1	1	1	4	7	.36	4	.238	.278	.316
1992 Burlington	A Hou	123	458	116	27	7	6	175	54	63	32	1	50	2	2	6	4	7	.36	9	.253	.301	.382
1993 Osceola	A+ Hou	118	469	148	20	6	2	186	51	59	17	1	41	0	0	3	10	4	.71	12	.316	.337	.397
1994 Jackson	AA Hou	118	380	105	17	6	5	149	37	52	18	5	43	0	4	5	8	5	.62	12	.276	.305	.392
1995 Jackson	AA Hou	106	379	85	10	0	5	110	33	31	24	2	38	4	2	6	3	6	.33	8	.224	.274	.290
1996 Jackson	AA Hou	127	432	121	23	1	12	182	49	58	21	6	49	0	0	0	0	3	.00	19	.280	.313	.421
1997 New Orleans	AAA Hou	129	400	108	23	1	6	151	49	64	42	6	48	6	2	8	2	2	.50	10	.270	.342	.378
7 Min. YEARS		775	2711	729	125	23	38	1014	293	355	164	23	297	13	11	29	31	34	.48	74	.269	.311	.374

Jeff Conger

Bats: Left   Throws: Left   Pos: OF   Ht: 6'0"   Wt: 185   Born: 8/6/71   Age: 26

Year Team	Lg Org	G	AB	H	2B	3B	HR	TB	R	RBI	TBB	IBB	SO	HBP	SH	SF	SB	CS	SB%	GDP	Avg	OBP	SLG
1990 Pirates	R Pit	46	120	22	3	1	0	27	19	6	18	0	52	1	1	0	3	1	.75	0	.183	.295	.225
1991 Pirates	R Pit	15	37	12	0	0	0	12	5	4	4	0	8	0	0	0	7	2	.78	0	.324	.390	.324
Welland	A- Pit	32	81	22	2	2	1	31	15	7	7	0	31	1	0	0	5	2	.71	0	.272	.337	.383
1992 Augusta	A Pit	98	303	74	12	6	6	116	56	36	44	2	93	3	2	1	36	13	.73	1	.244	.345	.383
1993 Salem	A+ Pit	110	391	90	12	1	4	116	40	31	31	2	125	1	7	1	24	10	.71	7	.230	.288	.297
1994 Salem	A+ Pit	111	362	83	8	3	9	124	65	37	53	0	105	9	6	4	13	8	.62	5	.229	.339	.343
1995 Lynchburg	A+ Pit	90	318	84	13	5	3	116	44	23	35	1	74	6	7	3	26	16	.62	1	.264	.345	.365
Carolina	AA Pit	39	128	37	6	1	1	48	15	17	18	2	31	1	2	1	8	2	.80	0	.289	.378	.375
1996 Carolina	AA Pit	66	177	41	7	1	3	59	19	17	17	1	51	3	4	0	12	4	.75	3	.232	.310	.333
1997 Lynchburg	A+ Pit	24	61	13	3	2	1	23	12	5	6	0	18	3	1	0	2	1	.67	0	.213	.314	.377
Carolina	AA Pit	58	138	27	5	1	3	43	15	12	19	1	53	2	2	0	4	0	1.00	0	.196	.302	.312
8 Min. YEARS		689	2116	505	71	23	31	715	305	195	252	9	641	30	32	10	140	59	.70	17	.239	.327	.338

Steve Connelly

Pitches: Right   Bats: Right   Pos: P   Ht: 6'3"   Wt: 210   Born: 4/27/74   Age: 24

Year Team	Lg Org	G	GS	CG	GF	IP	BFP	H	R	ER	HR	SH	SF	HB	TBB	IBB	SO	WP	Bk	W	L	Pct.	ShO	Sv	ERA
1995 Sou. Oregon	A- Oak	17	0	0	10	28.1	133	29	17	12	1	3	2	4	14	4	19	6	0	2	4	.333	0	2	3.81
1996 Modesto	A+ Oak	52	0	0	42	64.2	283	58	33	27	5	1	1	5	32	1	65	5	2	4	7	.364	0	14	3.76
1997 Huntsville	AA Oak	43	0	0	22	69.2	297	74	33	29	3	2	1	4	20	2	49	5	0	3	3	.500	0	7	3.75
3 Min. YEARS		112	0	0	74	162.2	713	161	83	68	9	6	4	13	66	7	133	16	2	9	14	.391	0	23	3.76

Decomba Conner

Bats: Right   Throws: Right   Pos: OF   Ht: 5'10"   Wt: 184   Born: 7/17/73   Age: 24

Year Team	Lg Org	G	AB	H	2B	3B	HR	TB	R	RBI	TBB	IBB	SO	HBP	SH	SF	SB	CS	SB%	GDP	Avg	OBP	SLG
1994 Princeton	R+ Cin	46	158	53	7	5	7	91	45	19	24	3	39	0	1	2	30	4	.88	0	.335	.418	.576
1995 Princeton	R+ Cin	6	16	2	2	0	0	4	2	5	3	0	3	0	0	1	2	0	1.00	0	.125	.250	.250
Chston-WV	A Cin	91	308	81	10	7	5	120	55	40	39	1	77	3	4	6	22	5	.81	6	.263	.346	.390
1996 Winston-Sal	A+ Cin	129	512	144	18	5	20	232	77	64	43	1	117	2	5	4	33	11	.75	6	.281	.337	.453
1997 Jacksnville	AA Det	47	154	32	6	3	4	56	22	17	30	1	45	2	0	1	5	1	.83	4	.208	.342	.364
Lakeland	A+ Det	56	201	64	7	4	7	100	35	29	21	1	47	0	3	1	9	2	.82	1	.318	.381	.498
4 Min. YEARS		375	1349	376	50	24	43	603	236	174	160	7	328	7	13	15	101	23	.81	17	.279	.355	.447

Hayward Cook

Bats: Right   Throws: Right   Pos: OF   Ht: 5'10"   Wt: 195   Born: 6/24/72   Age: 26

Year Team	Lg Org	G	AB	H	2B	3B	HR	TB	R	RBI	TBB	IBB	SO	HBP	SH	SF	SB	CS	SB%	GDP	Avg	OBP	SLG
1994 Elmira	A- Fla	63	227	62	10	8	5	103	36	29	20	0	45	2	1	1	7	6	.54	1	.273	.336	.454
1995 Kane County	A Fla	78	261	73	5	1	8	104	50	23	12	0	61	1	2	1	23	4	.85	4	.280	.313	.398
1996 Brevard Cty	A+ Fla	80	284	83	11	9	7	133	45	47	29	1	87	6	1	1	14	7	.67	5	.292	.369	.468
Portland	AA Fla	14	46	14	3	0	0	17	7	2	4	0	11	0	0	0	2	1	.67	1	.304	.360	.370
1997 Portland	AA Fla	69	166	49	13	0	5	77	37	21	13	0	44	1	2	1	2	5	.29	3	.295	.348	.464
4 Min. YEARS		304	984	281	42	18	25	434	175	122	78	1	248	10	6	4	48	23	.68	14	.286	.343	.441

Jason Cook

Bats: Right   Throws: Right   Pos: 2B-3B   Ht: 6'0"   Wt: 180   Born: 12/9/71   Age: 26

Year Team	Lg Org	G	AB	H	2B	3B	HR	TB	R	RBI	TBB	IBB	SO	HBP	SH	SF	SB	CS	SB%	GDP	Avg	OBP	SLG
1993 Mariners	R Sea	45	160	51	10	4	2	75	31	24	16	0	20	3	2	3	9	1	.90	1	.319	.385	.469
1994 Appleton	A Sea	51	172	43	5	4	3	65	23	18	23	0	34	0	1	0	3	3	.50	7	.250	.338	.378

53

		BATTING															BASERUNNING				PERCENTAGES		
Year Team	Lg Org	G	AB	H	2B	3B	HR	TB	R	RBI	TBB	IBB	SO	HBP	SH	SF	SB	CS	SB%	GDP	Avg	OBP	SLG
1995 Riverside	A+ Sea	6	21	4	1	0	0	5	9	3	5	0	4	0	0	0	0	0	.00	0	.190	.346	.238
Wisconsin	A Sea	117	405	109	24	2	5	152	61	64	64	7	44	12	3	6	12	5	.71	8	.269	.380	.375
1996 Lancaster	A+ Sea	124	450	130	22	4	5	175	95	58	89	0	68	16	4	4	5	2	.71	6	.289	.420	.389
1997 Memphis	AA Sea	53	162	35	7	0	0	42	23	19	21	0	24	3	2	3	2	1	.67	9	.216	.312	.259
5 Min. YEARS		396	1370	372	69	14	15	514	242	186	218	7	194	34	12	16	31	12	.72	31	.272	.381	.375

O.J. Cook

Pitches: Right **Bats:** Right **Pos:** P **Ht:** 6'3" **Wt:** 195 **Born:** 12/13/76 **Age:** 21

		HOW MUCH HE PITCHED						WHAT HE GAVE UP												THE RESULTS					
Year Team	Lg Org	G	GS	CG	GF	IP	BFP	H	R	ER	HR	SH	SF	HB	TBB	IBB	SO	WP	Bk	W	L	Pct.	ShO	Sv	ERA
1995 Pirates	R Pit	12	7	0	4	34.2	154	33	24	14	1	0	1	1	22	0	25	4	0	0	4	.000	0	2	3.63
1996 Pirates	R Pit	11	6	0	1	50.2	211	43	23	20	4	1	1	2	19	0	36	4	1	5	2	.714	0	0	3.55
1997 Carolina	AA Pit	1	0	0	0	1.1	10	5	3	3	1	0	0	0	1	0	2	0	1	0	0	.000	0	0	20.25
Erie	A- Pit	34	0	0	26	39	168	37	14	9	2	0	0	0	20	0	43	7	0	5	2	.714	0	10	2.08
3 Min. YEARS		58	13	0	31	125.2	543	118	64	46	8	1	2	3	62	0	106	15	2	10	8	.556	0	12	3.29

Mike Coolbaugh

Bats: Right **Throws:** Right **Pos:** 3B **Ht:** 6'1" **Wt:** 190 **Born:** 6/5/72 **Age:** 26

		BATTING															BASERUNNING				PERCENTAGES		
Year Team	Lg Org	G	AB	H	2B	3B	HR	TB	R	RBI	TBB	IBB	SO	HBP	SH	SF	SB	CS	SB%	GDP	Avg	OBP	SLG
1990 Medicne Hat	R+ Tor	58	211	40	9	0	2	55	21	16	13	0	47	1	1	2	3	2	.60	8	.190	.238	.261
1991 St. Cathms	A- Tor	71	255	58	13	2	3	84	28	26	17	0	40	3	4	4	4	5	.44	1	.227	.280	.329
1992 St. Cathms	A- Tor	15	49	14	1	1	0	17	3	2	3	0	12	0	2	0	2	0	.00	1	.286	.327	.347
1993 Hagerstown	A Tor	112	389	94	23	1	16	167	58	62	32	5	94	3	4	4	4	3	.57	9	.242	.301	.429
1994 Dunedin	A+ Tor	122	456	120	33	3	16	207	53	66	28	3	94	7	3	4	3	4	.43	14	.263	.313	.454
1995 Knoxville	AA Tor	142	500	120	32	2	9	183	71	56	37	3	110	11	4	3	7	11	.39	13	.240	.305	.366
1996 Charlotte	A+ Tex	124	449	129	33	4	15	215	76	75	42	4	80	8	0	3	8	10	.44	10	.287	.357	.479
Tulsa	AA Tex	7	23	8	3	0	2	17	6	9	2	0	3	2	0	0	1	0	1.00	1	.348	.444	.739
1997 Huntsville	AA Oak	139	559	172	37	2	30	303	100	132	52	3	105	7	2	8	8	3	.73	17	.308	.369	.542
8 Min. YEARS		790	2891	755	184	15	93	1248	416	444	226	18	585	42	20	28	38	40	.49	73	.261	.321	.432

Scott Coolbaugh

Bats: Right **Throws:** Right **Pos:** 3B **Ht:** 5'11" **Wt:** 195 **Born:** 6/13/66 **Age:** 32

		BATTING															BASERUNNING				PERCENTAGES		
Year Team	Lg Org	G	AB	H	2B	3B	HR	TB	R	RBI	TBB	IBB	SO	HBP	SH	SF	SB	CS	SB%	GDP	Avg	OBP	SLG
1987 Charlotte	A+ Tex	66	233	64	21	0	2	91	27	20	24	1	56	0	1	2	0	1	.00	5	.275	.340	.391
1988 Tulsa	AA Tex	136	470	127	15	4	13	189	52	75	76	4	79	1	2	8	2	4	.33	14	.270	.368	.402
1989 Okla City	AAA Tex	144	527	137	28	0	18	219	66	74	57	5	93	2	2	3	1	2	.33	13	.260	.333	.416
1990 Okla City	AAA Tex	76	293	66	17	2	6	105	39	30	27	2	62	1	0	3	0	1	.00	6	.225	.290	.358
1991 Las Vegas	AAA SD	60	209	60	9	2	7	94	29	29	34	2	53	0	0	2	2	2	.50	9	.287	.384	.450
1992 Las Vegas	AAA SD	65	199	48	13	2	8	89	30	39	19	1	52	3	1	1	0	0	.00	8	.241	.315	.447
Nashville	AAA Cin	59	188	48	8	3	5	77	25	23	32	0	50	0	2	5	3	2	.60	5	.255	.356	.410
1993 Rochester	AAA Bal	118	421	103	26	4	18	191	52	67	27	2	110	2	1	2	0	0	.00	9	.245	.292	.454
1994 Louisville	AAA StL	94	333	101	25	6	19	195	60	75	39	10	69	10	0	4	3	5	.38	10	.303	.389	.586
1996 Ottawa	AAA Mon	58	173	36	12	1	3	59	20	22	23	1	37	0	1	4	2	2	.50	7	.208	.295	.341
1997 Birmingham	AA ChA	68	235	68	18	0	11	119	35	50	37	3	60	4	0	4	0	0	.00	8	.289	.389	.506
1989 Texas	AL	25	51	14	1	0	2	21	7	7	4	0	12	0	1	1	0	0	.00	2	.275	.321	.412
1990 Texas	AL	67	180	36	6	0	2	48	21	13	15	0	47	1	4	1	1	0	1.00	4	.200	.264	.267
1991 San Diego	NL	60	180	39	8	1	2	55	12	15	19	2	45	1	4	1	0	3	.00	8	.217	.294	.306
1994 St. Louis	NL	15	21	4	0	0	2	10	4	6	1	0	4	0	0	1	0	0	.00	1	.190	.217	.476
10 Min. YEARS		944	3281	858	192	24	110	1428	435	504	395	31	721	23	10	38	13	19	.41	89	.262	.341	.435
4 Maj. YEARS		167	432	93	15	1	8	134	44	41	39	2	108	2	9	4	1	3	.25	15	.215	.281	.310

Kyle Cooney

Bats: Right **Throws:** Right **Pos:** C **Ht:** 6'2" **Wt:** 200 **Born:** 3/31/73 **Age:** 25

		BATTING															BASERUNNING				PERCENTAGES		
Year Team	Lg Org	G	AB	H	2B	3B	HR	TB	R	RBI	TBB	IBB	SO	HBP	SH	SF	SB	CS	SB%	GDP	Avg	OBP	SLG
1994 Great Falls	R+ LA	44	163	49	10	2	2	69	28	15	5	1	22	6	0	2	1	3	.25	0	.301	.341	.423
1995 Vero Beach	A+ LA	105	356	99	11	2	6	132	44	54	17	1	50	23	1	2	4	3	.57	15	.278	.349	.371
1996 San Berndno	A+ LA	107	406	111	20	0	14	173	57	67	28	1	78	14	0	5	9	8	.53	8	.273	.338	.426
1997 San Antonio	AA LA	72	252	73	16	2	8	117	39	49	7	0	44	13	1	2	4	2	.67	5	.290	.339	.464
4 Min. YEARS		328	1177	332	57	6	30	491	168	185	57	3	194	56	2	11	18	16	.53	28	.282	.342	.417

Trace Coquillette

Bats: Right **Throws:** Right **Pos:** 2B **Ht:** 5'11" **Wt:** 165 **Born:** 6/4/74 **Age:** 24

		BATTING															BASERUNNING				PERCENTAGES		
Year Team	Lg Org	G	AB	H	2B	3B	HR	TB	R	RBI	TBB	IBB	SO	HBP	SH	SF	SB	CS	SB%	GDP	Avg	OBP	SLG
1993 Wst Plm Bch	A+ Mon	6	18	5	3	0	0	8	2	3	2	0	5	0	1	0	0	0	.00	0	.278	.350	.444
Expos	R Mon	44	159	40	4	3	2	56	27	11	37	0	28	7	1	3	16	3	.84	0	.252	.408	.352
1994 Burlington	A Mon	5	17	3	1	0	0	4	2	0	1	0	4	0	0	0	1	0	1.00	0	.176	.222	.235
Vermont	A- Mon	70	252	77	11	5	9	125	54	52	23	0	40	8	1	6	7	2	.78	5	.306	.374	.496
1995 Albany	A Mon	128	458	123	27	4	3	167	67	57	64	2	91	9	4	6	17	16	.52	5	.269	.365	.365
1996 Expos	R Mon	7	25	4	1	0	0	5	4	0	4	0	6	0	0	0	1	0	1.00	0	.160	.276	.200
Wst Plm Bch	A+ Mon	72	266	67	17	4	1	95	39	27	27	1	72	8	0	3	9	7	.56	5	.252	.336	.357
1997 Wst Plm Bch	A+ Mon	53	188	60	18	2	8	106	34	33	27	0	27	6	1	1	8	7	.53	1	.319	.419	.564

Year Team	Lg Org	G	AB	H	2B	3B	HR	TB	R	RBI	TBB	IBB	SO	HBP	SH	SF	SB	CS	SB%	GDP	Avg	OBP	SLG
Harrisburg	AA Mon	81	293	76	17	3	10	129	46	51	25	0	40	14	1	1	9	4	.69	5	.259	.345	.440
5 Min. YEARS		466	1676	455	99	21	33	695	275	234	210	3	313	52	9	20	68	39	.64	24	.271	.366	.415

Alex Cora

Bats: Left Throws: Right Pos: SS Ht: 6'0" Wt: 180 Born: 10/18/75 Age: 22

Year Team	Lg Org	G	AB	H	2B	3B	HR	TB	R	RBI	TBB	IBB	SO	HBP	SH	SF	SB	CS	SB%	GDP	Avg	OBP	SLG
1996 Vero Beach	A+ LA	61	214	55	5	4	0	68	26	26	12	0	36	3	4	0	5	5	.50	1	.257	.306	.318
1997 San Antonio	AA LA	127	448	105	20	4	3	142	52	48	25	4	60	3	7	1	12	9	.57	17	.234	.279	.317
2 Min. YEARS		188	662	160	25	8	3	210	78	74	37	4	96	6	11	1	17	14	.55	18	.242	.288	.317

Archie Corbin

Pitches: Right Bats: Right Pos: P Ht: 6'4" Wt: 190 Born: 12/30/67 Age: 30

Year Team	Lg Org	G	GS	CG	GF	IP	BFP	H	R	ER	HR	SH	SF	HB	TBB	IBB	SO	WP	Bk	W	L	Pct.	ShO	Sv	ERA
1986 Kingsport	R+ NYN	18	1	0	9	30.1	149	31	23	16	3	0	1	0	28	0	30	8	1	1	1	.500	0	0	4.75
1987 Kingsport	R+ NYN	6	6	0	0	25.2	128	24	21	18	3	0	0	2	26	0	17	6	0	2	3	.400	0	0	6.31
1988 Kingsport	R+ NYN	11	10	4	0	69.1	277	47	23	12	5	2	0	3	17	0	47	1	1	7	2	.778	1	0	1.56
1989 Columbia	A NYN	27	23	4	3	153.2	664	149	86	77	16	4	4	5	72	0	130	2	0	9	9	.500	2	1	4.51
1990 St. Lucie	A+ NYN	20	18	3	2	118	494	97	47	39	2	4	3	7	59	0	105	10	0	7	8	.467	0	0	2.97
1991 Memphis	AA KC	28	25	1	0	156.1	692	139	90	81	7	4	6	8	90	1	166	13	0	8	8	.500	0	0	4.66
1992 Memphis	AA KC	27	20	2	1	112.1	503	115	64	59	7	3	1	1	73	0	100	11	0	7	8	.467	0	0	4.73
Harrisburg	AA Mon	1	1	0	0	3	11	2	0	0	0	0	0	0	1	0	3	0	0	0	0	.000	0	0	0.00
1993 Harrisburg	AA Mon	42	2	0	21	73.1	314	43	31	30	0	1	5	2	59	1	91	5	1	5	3	.625	0	4	3.68
1994 Buffalo	AAA Pit	14	1	0	3	22.2	99	14	13	12	0	1	1	1	18	0	23	2	0	0	0	.000	0	0	4.76
1995 Calgary	AAA Pit	47	1	0	13	61	309	76	63	58	6	0	5	3	55	0	54	7	0	1	5	.167	0	1	8.56
1996 Rochester	AAA Bal	25	5	0	10	43.2	197	44	25	23	5	1	1	1	25	0	47	4	0	0	2	.000	0	1	4.74
1997 Rochester	AAA Bal	43	1	0	22	69.2	314	47	32	31	5	2	3	1	62	0	66	10	0	4	3	.571	0	5	4.00
1991 Kansas City	AL	2	0	0	2	2.1	12	3	1	1	0	0	0	0	2	0	1	0	1	0	0	.000	0	0	3.86
1996 Baltimore	AL	18	0	0	5	27.1	123	22	7	7	2	0	1	1	22	0	20	2	0	2	0	1.000	0	0	2.30
12 Min. YEARS		304	114	14	84	939	4151	828	518	456	59	22	30	34	585	2	879	79	3	51	52	.495	3	12	4.37
2 Maj. YEARS		20	0	0	7	29.2	135	25	8	8	2	0	1	1	24	0	21	2	1	2	0	1.000	0	0	2.43

Edward Cordero

Bats: Right Throws: Right Pos: SS Ht: 6'0" Wt: 155 Born: 6/6/75 Age: 23

Year Team	Lg Org	G	AB	H	2B	3B	HR	TB	R	RBI	TBB	IBB	SO	HBP	SH	SF	SB	CS	SB%	GDP	Avg	OBP	SLG
1993 Bristol	R+ Det	1	1	0	0	0	0	0	0	0	0	0	0	0	0	0	0	0	.00	0	.000	.000	.000
1995 Tigers	R Det	49	126	27	2	2	0	33	17	11	12	0	23	4	2	1	11	5	.69	2	.214	.301	.262
1996 Durham	A+ Atl	68	177	35	6	1	0	43	27	12	15	1	59	2	4	1	1	3	.25	1	.198	.267	.243
1997 Greenville	AA Atl	3	5	2	0	0	0	2	1	0	0	0	1	0	1	0	0	0	.00	0	.400	.400	.400
Durham	A+ Atl	57	165	37	6	0	2	49	19	15	15	1	45	4	2	3	7	4	.64	1	.224	.299	.297
4 Min. YEARS		178	474	101	14	3	2	127	64	38	42	2	128	10	9	5	19	12	.61	4	.213	.288	.268

Bryan Corey

Pitches: Right Bats: Right Pos: P Ht: 6'1" Wt: 170 Born: 10/21/73 Age: 24

Year Team	Lg Org	G	GS	CG	GF	IP	BFP	H	R	ER	HR	SH	SF	HB	TBB	IBB	SO	WP	Bk	W	L	Pct.	ShO	Sv	ERA
1995 Jamestown	A- Det	29	0	0	28	28	116	21	14	12	2	0	1	1	12	1	41	4	0	2	2	.500	0	10	3.86
1996 Fayetteville	A Det	60	0	0	53	82	315	50	19	11	2	4	6	2	17	3	101	6	2	6	4	.600	0	34	1.21
1997 Jacksnville	AA Det	52	0	0	36	68	298	74	42	36	8	5	3	1	21	3	37	4	0	3	8	.273	0	9	4.76
3 Min. YEARS		141	0	0	117	178	729	145	75	59	12	9	10	4	50	7	179	14	2	11	14	.440	0	53	2.98

Reid Cornelius

Pitches: Right Bats: Right Pos: P Ht: 6'0" Wt: 200 Born: 6/2/70 Age: 28

Year Team	Lg Org	G	GS	CG	GF	IP	BFP	H	R	ER	HR	SH	SF	HB	TBB	IBB	SO	WP	Bk	W	L	Pct.	ShO	Sv	ERA
1989 Rockford	A Mon	29	17	0	0	84.1	391	71	58	40	6	3	3	11	63	0	66	13	3	5	6	.455	0	0	4.27
1990 Wst Plm Bch	A+ Mon	11	11	0	0	56	245	54	25	21	1	0	4	5	25	0	47	3	3	2	3	.400	0	0	3.38
1991 Wst Plm Bch	A+ Mon	17	17	0	0	109.1	449	79	31	29	3	9	4	7	43	1	81	3	6	8	3	.727	0	0	2.39
Harrisburg	AA Mon	3	3	1	0	18.2	76	15	6	6	3	0	0	2	7	0	12	0	0	2	1	.667	1	0	2.89
1992 Harrisburg	AA Mon	4	4	0	0	23	92	11	8	8	0	2	0	6	8	0	17	1	0	1	0	1.000	0	0	3.13
1993 Harrisburg	AA Mon	27	27	1	0	157.2	698	146	95	73	10	3	5	13	82	1	119	8	0	10	7	.588	0	0	4.17
1994 Ottawa	AAA Mon	25	24	1	1	148	661	149	89	72	18	1	4	8	75	2	87	10	0	9	8	.529	0	0	4.38
1995 Ottawa	AAA Mon	4	3	0	0	10.2	54	16	12	8	1	0	1	2	5	0	7	2	0	1	1	.500	0	0	6.75
Norfolk	AAA NYN	10	10	1	0	70.1	287	57	10	7	2	4	2	6	19	0	43	1	0	7	0	1.000	0	0	0.90
1996 Buffalo	AAA Cle	20	18	0	2	90	422	101	64	56	6	4	2	5	49	1	62	3	0	5	7	.417	0	0	5.60
1997 Portland	AA Fla	6	6	0	0	33	146	32	11	10	1	0	0	1	17	0	24	1	0	5	0	1.000	0	0	2.73
Charlotte	AAA Fla	22	22	1	0	130.2	555	134	82	74	19	5	8	4	43	1	80	5	1	12	5	.706	0	0	5.10
1995 Montreal	NL	8	0	0	1	9	43	11	8	8	3	0	0	2	5	0	4	1	0	0	0	.000	0	0	8.00
New York	NL	10	10	0	0	57.2	258	64	36	33	8	4	3	1	25	5	35	1	1	3	7	.300	0	0	5.15
9 Min. YEARS		166	162	5	3	931.2	4076	865	491	404	70	30	32	70	436	6	645	50	13	67	41	.620	1	0	3.90

Edwin Corps

Pitches: Right **Bats:** Right **Pos:** P **Ht:** 5'11" **Wt:** 180 **Born:** 11/3/72 **Age:** 25

		HOW MUCH HE PITCHED				WHAT HE GAVE UP								THE RESULTS					
Year Team	Lg Org	G	GS	CG	GF	IP	BFP	H	R	ER	HR	SH	SF	HB	TBB	IBB	SO	WP	Bk	W	L	Pct.	ShO	Sv	ERA
1994 San Jose	A+ SF	29	29	0	0	168.1	731	180	95	74	6	5	6	20	43	1	91	4	1	10	6	.625	0	0	3.96
1995 Shreveport	AA SF	27	27	2	0	165.2	712	195	80	71	16	2	6	8	41	2	53	4	2	13	6	.684	0	0	3.86
1996 Shreveport	AA SF	38	3	0	6	70.1	305	74	46	35	6	1	1	3	26	2	39	2	0	2	3	.400	0	0	4.48
1997 Phoenix	AAA SF	7	2	0	1	19	88	26	14	12	0	0	2	0	8	1	8	0	0	2	1	.667	0	0	5.68
Shreveport	AA SF	43	1	0	20	72.1	306	66	38	35	6	5	4	0	35	2	24	4	0	5	3	.625	0	6	4.35
4 Min. YEARS		144	62	2	27	495.2	2142	541	273	227	34	13	19	31	153	8	215	14	3	32	19	.627	0	7	4.12

Miguel Correa

Bats: Both **Throws:** Right **Pos:** OF **Ht:** 6'2" **Wt:** 165 **Born:** 9/10/71 **Age:** 26

		BATTING															BASERUNNING				PERCENTAGES		
Year Team	Lg Org	G	AB	H	2B	3B	HR	TB	R	RBI	TBB	IBB	SO	HBP	SH	SF	SB	CS	SB%	GDP	Avg	OBP	SLG
1990 Braves	R Atl	33	109	26	6	0	0	32	19	10	6	1	20	0	3	2	10	4	.71	1	.239	.274	.294
1991 Braves	R+ Atl	47	171	43	8	2	0	55	21	6	7	0	29	1	2	0	10	6	.63	2	.251	.285	.322
1992 Idaho Falls	R+ Atl	66	266	79	7	5	3	105	43	28	14	0	49	4	0	0	14	10	.58	2	.297	.342	.395
1993 Macon	A Atl	131	495	131	26	8	10	203	58	61	30	5	84	4	2	5	18	17	.51	6	.265	.309	.410
1994 Greenville	AA Atl	38	124	25	2	0	0	27	11	6	6	2	22	1	6	0	4	4	.50	0	.202	.244	.218
Durham	A+ Atl	83	290	64	12	4	8	108	43	19	18	0	53	2	2	0	12	7	.63	3	.221	.271	.372
1995 Durham	A+ Atl	118	398	94	19	1	19	172	43	70	19	2	95	3	2	3	9	13	.41	6	.236	.274	.432
1996 Greenville	AA Atl	64	225	50	13	2	5	82	20	25	11	2	65	1	5	0	2	2	.50	3	.222	.262	.364
Durham	A+ Atl	65	248	64	17	2	7	106	39	27	14	2	46	2	2	1	15	6	.71	2	.258	.302	.427
1997 Lancaster	A+ Sea	51	213	70	21	4	15	144	46	47	17	4	43	0	0	2	3	7	.30	3	.329	.375	.676
Memphis	AA Sea	68	250	65	13	0	6	96	33	31	16	0	49	2	2	2	2	2	.50	5	.260	.307	.384
8 Min. YEARS		764	2789	711	144	28	73	1130	376	330	158	18	555	20	26	15	99	78	.56	33	.255	.298	.405

Rod Correia

Bats: Right **Throws:** Right **Pos:** 2B **Ht:** 5'11" **Wt:** 185 **Born:** 9/13/67 **Age:** 30

		BATTING															BASERUNNING				PERCENTAGES		
Year Team	Lg Org	G	AB	H	2B	3B	HR	TB	R	RBI	TBB	IBB	SO	HBP	SH	SF	SB	CS	SB%	GDP	Avg	OBP	SLG
1988 Sou. Oregon	A- Oak	56	207	52	7	3	1	68	23	19	18	0	42	3	1	1	6	1	.86	9	.251	.319	.329
1989 Modesto	A+ Oak	107	339	71	9	3	0	86	31	26	34	0	64	12	4	1	7	7	.50	10	.209	.303	.254
1990 Modesto	A+ Oak	87	246	60	6	3	0	72	27	16	22	0	41	4	5	1	4	6	.40	6	.244	.315	.293
1991 Modesto	A+ Oak	5	19	5	0	0	0	5	8	3	2	0	1	0	1	0	1	0	1.00	1	.263	.333	.263
Tacoma	AAA Oak	17	56	14	0	0	1	17	9	7	4	0	6	1	3	0	0	0	.00	1	.250	.311	.304
Huntsville	AA Oak	87	290	64	10	1	1	79	25	22	31	0	50	6	8	1	2	4	.33	11	.221	.308	.272
1992 Midland	AA Ana	123	482	140	23	1	6	183	73	56	28	2	72	8	5	6	20	11	.65	14	.290	.336	.380
1993 Vancouver	AAA Ana	60	207	56	10	4	4	86	43	28	15	1	25	1	3	5	11	4	.73	5	.271	.316	.415
1994 Vancouver	AAA Ana	106	376	103	12	3	6	139	54	49	25	0	54	6	8	7	8	7	.53	11	.274	.324	.370
1995 Vancouver	AAA Ana	73	264	80	6	5	1	99	42	39	26	3	33	0	4	4	8	4	.67	7	.303	.361	.375
1996 Louisville	AAA StL	35	113	18	3	0	2	27	7	8	3	0	22	0	1	0	1	2	.33	3	.159	.181	.239
Edmonton	AAA Oak	8	23	2	0	0	0	2	1	0	0	0	2	0	0	0	1	0	1.00	1	.087	.087	.087
Huntsville	AA Oak	66	241	61	9	1	2	78	38	30	28	1	24	7	3	4	11	1	.92	8	.253	.343	.324
1997 Pawtucket	AAA Bos	35	128	25	4	1	1	34	17	15	5	0	14	2	1	1	3	0	1.00	4	.195	.235	.266
Trenton	AA Bos	67	249	73	18	1	7	114	40	33	22	0	32	6	4	1	4	2	.67	7	.293	.363	.458
1993 California	AL	64	128	34	5	0	0	39	12	9	6	0	20	4	5	0	2	4	.33	1	.266	.319	.305
1994 California	AL	6	17	4	1	0	0	5	4	0	0	0	0	2	0	0	0	0	.00	0	.235	.316	.294
1995 California	AL	14	21	5	1	1	0	8	3	3	3	0	5	0	1	0	0	0	.00	0	.238	.238	.381
10 Min. YEARS		932	3240	824	117	26	32	1089	438	351	263	7	482	56	51	32	87	49	.64	98	.254	.318	.336
3 Maj. YEARS		84	166	43	7	1	0	52	19	12	6	0	25	6	6	0	2	4	.33	1	.259	.309	.313

David Cortes

Pitches: Right **Bats:** Right **Pos:** P **Ht:** 5'11" **Wt:** 195 **Born:** 10/15/73 **Age:** 24

		HOW MUCH HE PITCHED				WHAT HE GAVE UP								THE RESULTS					
Year Team	Lg Org	G	GS	CG	GF	IP	BFP	H	R	ER	HR	SH	SF	HB	TBB	IBB	SO	WP	Bk	W	L	Pct.	ShO	Sv	ERA
1996 Eugene	A- Atl	15	0	0	11	24.2	95	13	2	2	0	1	0	0	6	0	33	0	0	2	1	.667	0	4	0.73
1997 Macon	A Atl	27	0	0	24	31.1	114	16	3	2	0	2	1	2	4	0	32	0	0	3	0	1.000	0	15	0.57
Durham	A+ Atl	19	0	0	16	19.1	76	15	5	5	1	0	1	0	5	0	16	1	0	2	0	1.000	0	8	2.33
Greenville	AA Atl	3	0	0	1	5	20	4	1	1	1	0	0	0	1	0	7	0	0	1	0	1.000	0	0	1.80
2 Min. YEARS		64	0	0	52	80.1	305	48	11	10	2	3	2	2	16	0	88	1	0	8	1	.889	0	27	1.12

Tim Cossins

Bats: Right **Throws:** Right **Pos:** C **Ht:** 6'1" **Wt:** 192 **Born:** 3/31/70 **Age:** 28

		BATTING															BASERUNNING				PERCENTAGES		
Year Team	Lg Org	G	AB	H	2B	3B	HR	TB	R	RBI	TBB	IBB	SO	HBP	SH	SF	SB	CS	SB%	GDP	Avg	OBP	SLG
1993 Erie	A- Tex	4	10	4	1	0	0	5	1	3	2	0	0	0	0	0	0	1	.00	0	.400	.500	.500
Chston-SC	A Tex	27	89	13	2	0	0	15	8	10	7	0	21	3	0	1	0	1	.00	3	.146	.230	.169
1994 Hudson Vall	A- Tex	6	17	2	1	0	1	6	1	2	0	0	4	0	0	0	0	0	.00	0	.118	.118	.353
Charlotte	A+ Tex	10	28	3	0	0	0	3	2	2	4	0	6	0	1	0	1	0	1.00	1	.107	.219	.107
1995 Rangers	R Tex	2	4	0	0	0	0	0	0	0	0	0	1	0	0	0	0	0	.00	0	.000	.000	.000
Chston-SC	A Tex	22	59	12	5	0	1	20	8	8	9	0	13	1	0	0	2	0	1.00	0	.203	.319	.339
Charlotte	A+ Tex	7	17	1	0	0	0	1	1	0	4	1	5	0	0	0	0	1	.00	0	.059	.238	.059
1996 Tulsa	AA Tex	3	4	2	0	0	0	2	0	1	3	0	0	0	0	0	0	0	.00	0	.500	.714	.500
Charlotte	A+ Tex	67	233	56	16	0	3	81	34	32	13	0	44	2	3	2	1	1	.50	11	.240	.284	.348
1997 Tulsa	AA Tex	36	108	32	5	1	4	51	11	17	8	0	24	0	2	2	2	0	1.00	2	.296	.339	.472
5 Min. YEARS		184	569	125	30	1	9	184	66	75	50	1	118	6	6	5	6	4	.60	18	.220	.287	.323

Tony Costa

Pitches: Right **Bats:** Right **Pos:** P   **Ht:** 6'4" **Wt:** 210 **Born:** 12/19/70 **Age:** 27

Year Team	Lg Org	G	GS	CG	GF	IP	BFP	H	R	ER	HR	SH	SF	HB	TBB	IBB	SO	WP	Bk	W	L	Pct.	ShO	Sv	ERA
1992 Martinsvlle	R+ Phi	12	4	0	6	24.2	133	44	40	25	3	0	0	2	13	0	21	5	3	0	4	.000	0	1	9.12
1993 Batavia	A- Phi	10	9	0	0	51	228	56	32	28	1	3	3	2	19	0	37	5	0	3	4	.429	0	0	4.94
1994 Spartanburg	A Phi	17	17	2	0	116.1	487	109	60	46	11	5	0	13	31	0	106	4	2	6	9	.400	0	0	3.56
Clearwater	A+ Phi	8	8	1	0	47	204	44	25	22	3	0	1	0	31	0	27	1	0	3	5	.375	1	0	4.21
1995 Clearwater	A+ Phi	25	25	2	0	145	631	155	75	62	5	6	5	10	39	0	71	11	4	9	10	.474	1	0	3.85
1996 Reading	AA Phi	27	26	1	0	153.1	702	150	107	82	20	5	4	14	92	2	112	16	3	5	13	.278	0	0	4.81
1997 Reading	AA Phi	28	28	2	0	165	736	174	111	96	24	7	4	12	72	0	110	8	0	7	12	.368	0	0	5.24
6 Min. YEARS		127	117	8	6	702.1	3121	732	450	361	67	26	17	53	297	2	484	50	12	33	57	.367	2	1	4.63

Brian Costello

Bats: Right **Throws:** Right **Pos:** OF   **Ht:** 6'1" **Wt:** 195 **Born:** 10/4/74 **Age:** 23

Year Team	Lg Org	G	AB	H	2B	3B	HR	TB	R	RBI	TBB	IBB	SO	HBP	SH	SF	SB	CS	SB%	GDP	Avg	OBP	SLG
1993 Martinsvlle	R+ Phi	60	209	53	8	1	5	78	28	19	37	1	52	3	0	0	6	3	.67	3	.254	.373	.373
1994 Spartanburg	A Phi	126	456	107	17	2	6	146	58	65	40	2	122	5	2	4	13	10	.57	8	.235	.301	.320
1995 Clearwater	A+ Phi	112	406	101	19	2	9	151	52	56	37	0	88	2	0	0	14	9	.61	9	.249	.315	.372
1996 Clearwater	A+ Phi	81	282	58	13	2	2	81	28	31	17	0	84	4	4	4	6	4	.60	3	.206	.257	.287
1997 Clearwater	A+ Phi	87	282	68	11	2	10	113	37	43	15	0	73	5	0	3	8	3	.73	3	.241	.289	.401
Reading	AA Phi	16	36	7	2	1	1	14	6	5	2	0	12	2	1	0	0	1	.00	0	.194	.275	.389
5 Min. YEARS		482	1671	394	70	10	33	583	209	219	148	3	431	21	7	11	47	30	.61	26	.236	.304	.349

Tim Costo

Bats: Right **Throws:** Right **Pos:** 1B   **Ht:** 6'5" **Wt:** 230 **Born:** 2/16/69 **Age:** 29

Year Team	Lg Org	G	AB	H	2B	3B	HR	TB	R	RBI	TBB	IBB	SO	HBP	SH	SF	SB	CS	SB%	GDP	Avg	OBP	SLG
1990 Kinston	A+ Cle	56	206	65	13	1	4	92	34	42	23	0	47	6	0	8	4	0	1.00	4	.316	.387	.447
1991 Canton-Akrn	AA Cle	52	192	52	10	3	1	71	28	24	15	0	44	0	0	6	2	1	.67	10	.271	.315	.370
Chattanooga	AA Cin	85	293	82	19	3	5	122	31	29	20	0	65	4	0	2	11	4	.73	5	.280	.332	.416
1992 Chattanooga	AA Cin	121	424	102	18	2	28	208	63	71	48	1	128	11	1	2	4	5	.44	10	.241	.332	.491
1993 Indianapols	AAA Cin	106	362	118	30	2	11	185	49	57	22	1	60	5	1	1	3	2	.60	5	.326	.372	.511
1994 Indianapols	AAA Cin	19	36	7	3	0	0	10	6	5	6	0	4	1	1	0	0	0	.00	0	.194	.326	.278
1995 Buffalo	AAA Cle	105	324	80	11	2	11	128	41	60	27	0	65	8	3	7	2	0	1.00	7	.247	.314	.395
1996 Buffalo	AAA Cle	83	252	54	12	0	8	90	25	28	19	4	59	0	4	1	1	2	.33	7	.214	.268	.357
1997 Louisville	AAA StL	121	400	121	26	2	14	193	52	54	41	1	72	3	2	2	4	4	.50	4	.303	.370	.483
1992 Cincinnati	NL	12	36	8	2	0	0	10	3	2	5	0	6	0	0	1	0	0	.00	0	.222	.310	.278
1993 Cincinnati	NL	31	98	22	5	0	3	36	13	12	4	0	17	0	0	2	0	0	.00	5	.224	.250	.367
8 Min. YEARS		748	2489	681	142	15	82	1099	329	370	221	7	544	38	12	29	31	18	.63	51	.274	.338	.442
2 Maj. YEARS		43	134	30	7	0	3	46	16	14	9	0	23	0	0	3	0	0	.00	5	.224	.267	.343

John Cotton

Bats: Left **Throws:** Right **Pos:** OF   **Ht:** 6'0" **Wt:** 170 **Born:** 10/30/70 **Age:** 27

Year Team	Lg Org	G	AB	H	2B	3B	HR	TB	R	RBI	TBB	IBB	SO	HBP	SH	SF	SB	CS	SB%	GDP	Avg	OBP	SLG
1989 Burlington	R+ Cle	64	227	47	5	1	2	60	36	22	22	0	56	3	4	1	20	3	.87	5	.207	.285	.264
1990 Watertown	A- Cle	73	286	60	9	4	2	83	53	27	40	3	71	2	2	1	24	7	.77	4	.210	.310	.290
1991 Columbus	A Cle	122	405	92	11	9	13	160	88	42	93	1	135	3	3	3	56	15	.79	6	.227	.373	.395
1992 Kinston	A+ Cle	103	360	72	7	3	11	118	67	39	48	1	106	2	1	2	23	7	.77	4	.200	.296	.328
1993 Kinston	A+ Cle	127	454	120	16	3	13	181	81	51	59	1	130	11	5	2	28	24	.54	3	.264	.361	.399
1994 Springfield	A SD	24	82	19	5	3	1	33	14	8	12	0	19	0	0	0	7	1	.88	2	.232	.330	.402
Wichita	AA SD	34	85	16	4	0	3	29	9	14	13	3	20	1	0	2	2	0	1.00	1	.188	.297	.341
Rancho Cuca	A+ SD	48	157	33	6	1	2	54	35	19	22	0	48	2	0	0	9	3	.75	3	.205	.303	.316
1995 Memphis	AA SD	121	407	103	19	8	12	174	60	47	38	0	101	4	6	4	15	6	.71	2	.253	.320	.428
1996 Toledo	AAA Det	50	171	32	7	1	4	53	14	19	7	0	64	2	2	0	4	4	.50	1	.187	.228	.310
Jacksnville	AA Det	63	217	52	7	4	13	106	34	39	19	2	66	2	0	1	15	3	.83	2	.240	.305	.488
1997 Birmingham	AA ChA	33	124	36	10	2	7	71	23	26	9	0	33	2	0	1	1	2	.33	3	.290	.346	.573
Nashville	AAA ChA	94	323	87	14	3	14	161	45	50	24	1	94	0	1	2	8	2	.80	7	.269	.318	.433
9 Min. YEARS		956	3312	771	117	43	96	1262	559	403	406	12	943	34	24	19	212	77	.73	42	.233	.321	.381

Kevin Coughlin

Bats: Left **Throws:** Left **Pos:** OF   **Ht:** 6'0" **Wt:** 175 **Born:** 9/7/70 **Age:** 27

Year Team	Lg Org	G	AB	H	2B	3B	HR	TB	R	RBI	TBB	IBB	SO	HBP	SH	SF	SB	CS	SB%	GDP	Avg	OBP	SLG
1989 White Sox	R ChA	24	74	19	2	0	0	21	11	13	12	0	8	0	0	0	9	2	.82	1	.257	.360	.284
1990 Utica	A- ChA	68	215	59	6	3	0	71	37	16	27	2	41	0	3	2	17	8	.68	4	.274	.352	.330
1991 South Bend	A ChA	131	431	131	12	2	0	147	60	38	62	3	67	2	19	3	19	17	.53	6	.304	.392	.341
1992 White Sox	R ChA	4	15	5	0	0	0	5	1	2	2	0	1	0	0	0	0	0	.00	0	.333	.412	.333
Sarasota	A+ ChA	81	291	79	7	1	1	91	39	28	22	1	51	2	8	1	14	4	.78	3	.271	.326	.313
1993 Sarasota	A+ ChA	112	415	128	19	2	2	157	53	32	42	5	51	0	4	2	4	4	.50	9	.308	.370	.378
Nashville	AAA ChA	2	7	4	1	0	0	5	0	3	0	0	1	0	0	0	0	0	.00	0	.571	.571	.714
1994 Birmingham	AA ChA	112	369	95	10	0	0	105	51	26	40	3	42	3	4	0	5	8	.38	9	.257	.332	.285
1995 Nashville	AAA ChA	10	22	4	1	0	0	5	0	0	4	0	3	0	0	0	1	0	.00	1	.182	.308	.227
Birmingham	AA ChA	96	327	126	29	2	3	168	56	49	34	7	43	5	8	2	5	2	.71	3	.385	.448	.514
1996 Trenton	AA Bos	52	170	46	2	1	0	50	24	18	22	4	24	3	4	3	5	4	.56	2	.271	.359	.294
1997 Arkansas	AA StL	26	90	27	6	1	1	38	15	8	9	0	12	1	0	0	0	0	.00	2	.300	.366	.422

		BATTING															BASERUNNING				PERCENTAGES		
Year Team	Lg Org	G	AB	H	2B	3B	HR	TB	R	RBI	TBB	IBB	SO	HBP	SH	SF	SB	CS	SB%	GDP	Avg	OBP	SLG
Louisville AAA StL		12	35	9	1	0	0	10	2	2	1	0	7	0	0	0	0	1	.00	0	.257	.278	.286
Chattanooga AA Cin		54	168	49	7	0	3	65	22	15	15	1	20	1	1	1	0	2	.00	3	.292	.351	.387
9 Min. YEARS		784	2629	781	103	12	10	938	371	250	292	26	371	17	51	19	78	53	.60	43	.297	.369	.357

John Courtright

Pitches: Left Bats: Left Pos: P   Ht: 6' 2" Wt: 185 Born: 5/30/70 Age: 28

		HOW MUCH HE PITCHED						WHAT HE GAVE UP										THE RESULTS					
Year Team	Lg Org	G	GS	CG	GF	IP	BFP	H	R	ER	HR	SH	SF	HB	TBB	IBB	SO	WP	Bk	W	L	Pct.	ShO	Sv	ERA
1991 Billings	R+ Cin	1	1	0	0	6	21	2	0	0	0	0	0	0	1	0	4	0	1	1	0	1.000	0	0	0.00
1992 Chston-WV	A Cin	27	26	1	0	173	688	147	64	48	5	5	4	7	55	2	147	9	5	10	5	.667	1	0	2.50
1993 Chattanooga	AA Cin	27	27	1	0	175	752	179	81	68	5	8	11	8	70	6	96	5	2	5	11	.313	0	0	3.50
1994 Chattanooga	AA Cin	4	4	0	0	21.2	95	19	16	13	2	2	1	1	14	0	12	1	0	1	2	.333	0	0	5.40
Indianapols	AAA Cin	24	23	2	0	142	595	144	61	56	9	8	1	4	46	3	73	2	1	9	10	.474	2	0	3.55
1995 Indianapols	AAA Cin	13	2	0	1	33.2	147	29	18	16	2	2	1	2	15	1	13	4	1	2	1	.667	0	0	4.28
Salt Lake	AAA Min	18	17	1	0	84.2	384	108	70	64	6	5	7	0	36	7	42	4	2	3	7	.300	0	0	6.80
1996 Hardware City	AA Min	14	3	0	3	32.2	154	42	25	24	2	3	1	1	16	0	12	1	2	1	1	.500	0	0	6.61
Bowie	AA Bal	9	0	0	3	15.1	75	19	15	11	2	1	0	1	8	1	10	0	0	0	0	.000	0	0	6.46
Chattanooga	AA Cin	9	9	0	0	60.1	236	52	18	16	3	1	3	2	11	0	36	2	1	8	0	1.000	0	0	2.39
1997 Chattanooga	AA Cin	20	16	0	1	92.1	447	137	79	70	8	3	3	2	42	1	42	2	1	5	7	.417	0	0	6.82
1995 Cincinnati	NL	1	0	0	0	1	5	2	1	1	0	1	0	0	0	0	0	0	0	0	0	.000	0	0	9.00
7 Min. YEARS		166	128	5	8	836.2	3594	878	447	386	44	38	32	28	314	21	487	30	16	45	44	.506	3	0	4.15

Darron Cox

Bats: Right Throws: Right Pos: C   Ht: 6'1" Wt: 205 Born: 11/21/67 Age: 30

		BATTING															BASERUNNING				PERCENTAGES		
Year Team	Lg Org	G	AB	H	2B	3B	HR	TB	R	RBI	TBB	IBB	SO	HBP	SH	SF	SB	CS	SB%	GDP	Avg	OBP	SLG
1989 Billings	R+ Cin	49	157	43	6	0	0	49	20	18	21	0	34	5	2	0	11	3	.79	1	.274	.377	.312
1990 Chston-WV	A Cin	103	367	93	11	3	1	113	53	44	40	2	75	7	4	3	14	3	.82	12	.253	.336	.308
1991 Cedar Rapds	A Cin	21	60	16	4	0	0	20	12	4	8	0	11	4	1	0	7	1	.88	2	.267	.389	.333
Chattanooga	AA Cin	13	38	7	1	0	0	8	2	3	2	0	9	0	1	1	0	0	.00	1	.184	.220	.211
Chston-WV	A Cin	79	294	71	14	1	2	93	37	28	24	0	40	2	1	7	8	4	.67	7	.241	.297	.316
1992 Chattanooga	AA Cin	98	331	84	19	1	1	108	29	38	15	0	63	5	1	6	8	3	.73	7	.254	.291	.326
1993 Chattanooga	AA Cin	89	300	65	9	5	3	93	35	26	38	2	63	3	7	1	7	4	.64	7	.217	.310	.310
1994 Iowa	AAA ChN	99	301	80	15	1	3	106	35	26	28	4	47	4	3	0	5	2	.71	12	.266	.336	.352
1995 Orlando	AA ChN	33	102	29	5	0	4	46	8	15	8	0	16	1	2	2	3	3	.50	3	.284	.336	.451
Iowa	AAA ChN	33	94	22	6	0	1	31	7	14	8	0	21	2	2	4	0	0	.00	0	.234	.296	.330
1996 Richmond	AAA Atl	55	168	40	9	0	3	58	19	20	5	0	22	3	2	2	1	0	1.00	5	.238	.270	.345
1997 Orlando	AA ChN	3	9	2	1	0	1	6	2	4	1	0	1	0	0	0	0	0	.00	0	.222	.273	.667
9 Min. YEARS		675	2221	552	100	11	19	731	259	240	198	8	402	36	26	27	64	23	.74	58	.249	.317	.329

Steven Cox

Bats: Left Throws: Left Pos: 1B   Ht: 6'4" Wt: 225 Born: 10/31/74 Age: 23

		BATTING															BASERUNNING				PERCENTAGES		
Year Team	Lg Org	G	AB	H	2B	3B	HR	TB	R	RBI	TBB	IBB	SO	HBP	SH	SF	SB	CS	SB%	GDP	Avg	OBP	SLG
1992 Athletics	R Oak	52	184	43	4	1	1	52	30	35	27	1	51	3	0	2	2	1	.67	2	.234	.338	.283
1993 Sou. Oregon	A- Oak	15	57	18	4	1	2	30	10	16	5	0	15	0	0	2	0	0	.00	0	.316	.359	.526
1994 W Michigan	A Oak	99	311	75	19	2	6	116	37	32	41	3	95	4	1	3	2	6	.25	5	.241	.334	.373
1995 Modesto	A+ Oak	132	483	144	29	3	30	269	95	110	84	6	88	14	0	10	5	4	.56	12	.298	.409	.557
1996 Huntsville	AA Oak	104	381	107	21	1	12	166	59	61	51	6	65	6	2	3	2	2	.50	10	.281	.372	.436
1997 Edmonton	AAA Oak	131	467	128	34	1	15	209	84	93	88	4	90	2	2	9	1	3	.25	16	.274	.385	.448
6 Min. YEARS		533	1883	515	111	9	66	842	315	347	296	20	404	29	5	29	12	16	.43	45	.273	.376	.447

Rickey Cradle

Bats: Right Throws: Right Pos: OF   Ht: 6'2" Wt: 180 Born: 6/20/73 Age: 25

		BATTING															BASERUNNING				PERCENTAGES		
Year Team	Lg Org	G	AB	H	2B	3B	HR	TB	R	RBI	TBB	IBB	SO	HBP	SH	SF	SB	CS	SB%	GDP	Avg	OBP	SLG
1991 Blue Jays	R Tor	44	132	28	4	3	1	41	16	6	24	1	37	3	1	1	4	5	.44	1	.212	.344	.311
1992 Medcine Hat	R+ Tor	65	217	49	8	0	9	84	38	36	42	0	69	6	1	2	16	2	.89	5	.226	.363	.387
1993 Hagerstown	A Tor	129	441	112	26	4	13	185	72	62	68	2	125	11	1	4	19	14	.58	5	.254	.365	.420
1994 Dunedin	A+ Tor	114	344	88	14	3	10	138	65	39	59	0	87	9	0	1	20	10	.67	5	.256	.378	.401
1995 Knoxville	AA Tor	41	117	21	5	1	4	40	17	13	17	0	29	3	1	1	3	3	.50	3	.179	.297	.342
Dunedin	A+ Tor	50	178	49	10	3	7	86	33	27	28	0	49	2	1	2	6	2	.75	2	.275	.376	.483
1996 Knoxville	AA Tor	92	333	94	23	2	12	157	59	47	55	1	65	10	7	1	15	11	.58	7	.282	.393	.471
Syracuse	AAA Tor	40	130	26	5	3	8	61	22	22	14	1	39	1	0	2	1	0	1.00	5	.200	.279	.469
1997 Syracuse	AAA Tor	11	25	3	0	0	1	6	4	3	2	0	9	2	0	0	0	1	.00	0	.120	.241	.240
Knoxville	AA Tor	84	257	55	16	1	10	103	50	34	41	0	67	7	2	1	5	6	.45	5	.214	.337	.401
7 Min. YEARS		670	2174	525	111	20	75	901	376	289	350	5	576	54	14	21	89	54	.62	29	.241	.357	.414

Carlos Crawford

Pitches: Right Bats: Right Pos: P   Ht: 6' 1" Wt: 190 Born: 10/4/71 Age: 26

		HOW MUCH HE PITCHED						WHAT HE GAVE UP										THE RESULTS					
Year Team	Lg Org	G	GS	CG	GF	IP	BFP	H	R	ER	HR	SH	SF	HB	TBB	IBB	SO	WP	Bk	W	L	Pct.	ShO	Sv	ERA
1990 Indians	R Cle	10	9	0	0	53.2	257	68	43	26	0	0	2	8	25	0	39	6	4	2	3	.400	0	0	4.36
1991 Burlington	R+ Cle	13	13	2	0	80.1	325	62	28	22	3	2	2	9	14	0	80	6	3	6	3	.667	1	0	2.46
1992 Columbus	A Cle	28	28	6	0	188.1	805	167	78	61	7	5	4	12	85	4	127	3	2	10	11	.476	3	0	2.92

Year Team	Lg Org	G	GS	CG	GF	IP	BFP	H	R	ER	HR	SH	SF	HB	TBB	IBB	SO	WP	Bk	W	L	Pct.	ShO	Sv	ERA
						HOW MUCH HE PITCHED				**WHAT HE GAVE UP**												**THE RESULTS**			
1993 Kinston	A+ Cle	28	28	4	0	165	703	158	87	67	11	10	4	10	46	0	124	8	4	7	9	.438	1	0	3.65
1994 Canton-Akrn	AA Cle	26	25	3	0	175	734	164	83	67	15	3	7	6	59	2	99	8	2	12	6	.667	0	0	3.45
1995 Buffalo	AAA Cle	13	3	0	3	30.1	137	36	22	19	2	2	0	0	12	0	15	0	0	0	1	.000	0	1	5.64
Canton-Akrn	AA Cle	8	8	2	0	51.2	212	47	19	15	1	1	0	1	15	0	36	2	0	2	2	.500	0	0	2.61
1996 Scranton-WB	AAA Phi	28	25	3	3	158.2	695	169	87	80	15	5	5	4	63	5	89	3	2	9	10	.474	1	1	4.54
1997 Carolina	AA Pit	29	3	0	10	62.1	273	62	34	29	4	1	1	2	25	2	39	4	0	3	2	.600	0	4	4.19
Calgary	AAA Pit	9	9	0	0	50	228	60	43	33	8	1	1	3	19	3	26	3	0	1	5	.167	0	0	5.94
1996 Philadelphia	NL	1	1	0	0	3.2	22	7	10	2	1	1	0	1	2	0	4	0	0	0	1	.000	0	0	4.91
8 Min. YEARS		192	151	20	16	1015.1	4369	993	524	419	66	30	26	55	363	16	674	43	17	52	52	.500	6	6	3.71

Ryan Creek

Pitches: Right Bats: Right Pos: P Ht: 6'1" Wt: 180 Born: 9/24/72 Age: 25

Year Team	Lg Org	G	GS	CG	GF	IP	BFP	H	R	ER	HR	SH	SF	HB	TBB	IBB	SO	WP	Bk	W	L	Pct.	ShO	Sv	ERA
						HOW MUCH HE PITCHED				**WHAT HE GAVE UP**												**THE RESULTS**			
1993 Astros	R Hou	12	11	2	1	69.1	291	53	22	18	0	1	5	4	30	0	62	6	0	7	3	.700	1	1	2.34
1994 Quad City	A Hou	21	15	0	3	74	356	86	62	41	6	3	5	14	41	2	66	9	3	3	5	.375	0	0	4.99
1995 Jackson	AA Hou	26	24	1	1	143.2	622	137	74	58	11	6	8	6	64	0	120	12	2	9	7	.563	1	0	3.63
1996 Jackson	AA Hou	27	26	1	1	142	674	139	95	83	9	3	7	11	121	0	119	14	1	7	15	.318	0	0	5.26
1997 Jackson	AA Hou	19	19	0	0	105	471	95	57	48	10	5	1	3	74	1	88	14	0	10	5	.667	0	0	4.11
5 Min. YEARS		105	95	4	6	534	2414	510	310	248	36	18	26	38	330	3	455	55	6	36	35	.507	2	1	4.18

Andy Croghan

Pitches: Right Bats: Right Pos: P Ht: 6'5" Wt: 205 Born: 10/26/69 Age: 28

Year Team	Lg Org	G	GS	CG	GF	IP	BFP	H	R	ER	HR	SH	SF	HB	TBB	IBB	SO	WP	Bk	W	L	Pct.	ShO	Sv	ERA
						HOW MUCH HE PITCHED				**WHAT HE GAVE UP**												**THE RESULTS**			
1991 Oneonta	A- NYA	14	14	0	0	78.1	352	92	59	49	6	1	1	2	28	0	54	5	0	5	4	.556	0	0	5.63
1992 Greensboro	A NYA	33	19	1	3	122.1	544	128	78	61	11	2	9	3	57	0	98	9	0	10	8	.556	0	0	4.49
1993 Pr William	A+ NYA	39	14	1	19	105	455	117	66	56	9	4	4	3	27	0	80	6	0	5	11	.313	0	11	4.80
1994 Albany-Colo	AA NYA	36	0	0	33	36.2	153	33	7	7	1	2	1	0	14	0	38	1	0	0	1	.000	0	16	1.72
Columbus	AAA NYA	21	0	0	17	24	110	25	11	11	6	5	0	0	13	1	28	3	0	2	2	.500	0	8	4.13
1995 Columbus	AAA NYA	20	0	0	13	25	113	21	10	10	1	0	0	1	22	0	22	1	2	1	1	.500	0	4	3.60
1996 Columbus	AAA NYA	14	0	0	3	22.1	108	27	24	21	6	3	1	2	13	0	21	3	0	2	0	1.000	0	8	8.46
Norwich	AA NYA	35	0	0	19	41	181	41	23	14	4	2	0	1	16	3	49	5	0	9	5	.643	0	4	3.07
1997 Norwich	AA NYA	42	1	0	13	67.2	308	72	48	43	9	1	3	1	36	2	85	3	0	2	1	.667	0	4	5.72
7 Min. YEARS		254	48	2	120	522.1	2324	556	326	272	53	20	19	13	226	6	475	36	2	36	33	.522	0	47	4.69

Brandon Cromer

Bats: Left Throws: Right Pos: SS Ht: 6'2" Wt: 175 Born: 1/25/74 Age: 24

Year Team	Lg Org	G	AB	H	2B	3B	HR	TB	R	RBI	TBB	IBB	SO	HBP	SH	SF	SB	CS	SB%	GDP	Avg	OBP	SLG
							BATTING										**BASERUNNING**				**PERCENTAGES**		
1992 Blue Jays	R Tor	49	180	51	12	3	1	72	26	21	14	0	26	5	2	2	7	8	.47	2	.283	.348	.400
1993 St. Cathrns	A- Tor	75	278	64	9	2	5	92	29	20	21	2	64	1	3	1	2	4	.33	1	.230	.286	.331
1994 Hagerstown	A Tor	80	259	35	8	5	6	71	25	26	25	0	98	0	2	3	0	2	.00	4	.135	.209	.274
1995 Dunedin	A+ Tor	106	329	78	11	3	6	113	40	43	43	3	84	5	5	3	0	5	.00	6	.237	.332	.343
1996 Knoxville	AA Tor	98	318	88	15	8	7	140	56	32	60	3	84	2	2	3	3	6	.33	2	.277	.392	.440
1997 Carolina	AA Pit	55	193	44	12	4	4	76	23	14	29	0	50	0	4	2	1	5	.17	0	.228	.326	.394
Calgary	AAA Pit	68	228	53	15	2	8	96	30	36	19	2	46	0	1	3	3	1	.75	5	.232	.288	.421
6 Min. YEARS		531	1785	413	82	27	37	660	229	192	211	10	452	13	19	17	16	31	.34	20	.231	.314	.370

D.T. Cromer

Bats: Left Throws: Left Pos: 1B Ht: 6'2" Wt: 205 Born: 3/19/71 Age: 27

Year Team	Lg Org	G	AB	H	2B	3B	HR	TB	R	RBI	TBB	IBB	SO	HBP	SH	SF	SB	CS	SB%	GDP	Avg	OBP	SLG
							BATTING										**BASERUNNING**				**PERCENTAGES**		
1992 Sou. Oregon	A- Oak	50	168	35	7	0	4	54	17	26	13	1	34	1	1	2	4	3	.57	2	.208	.266	.321
1993 Madison	A Oak	98	321	84	20	4	4	124	37	41	22	0	72	1	1	2	8	6	.57	1	.262	.309	.386
1994 W Michigan	A Oak	102	349	89	20	5	10	149	50	58	33	1	76	4	3	2	11	10	.52	5	.255	.325	.427
1995 Modesto	A+ Oak	108	378	98	18	5	14	168	59	52	36	1	66	4	6	6	5	7	.42	10	.259	.325	.444
1996 Modesto	A+ Oak	124	505	166	40	10	30	316	100	130	32	4	67	6	3	4	20	7	.74	5	.329	.373	.626
1997 Huntsville	AA Oak	134	545	176	40	6	15	273	100	121	60	4	102	3	0	6	12	7	.63	8	.323	.389	.501
6 Min. YEARS		616	2266	648	145	30	77	1084	363	428	196	11	417	19	20	22	60	40	.60	31	.286	.345	.478

Rich Croushore

Pitches: Right Bats: Right Pos: P Ht: 6'4" Wt: 210 Born: 8/7/70 Age: 27

Year Team	Lg Org	G	GS	CG	GF	IP	BFP	H	R	ER	HR	SH	SF	HB	TBB	IBB	SO	WP	Bk	W	L	Pct.	ShO	Sv	ERA
						HOW MUCH HE PITCHED				**WHAT HE GAVE UP**												**THE RESULTS**			
1993 Glens Falls	A- StL	31	0	0	11	41.1	184	38	16	14	1	4	1	2	22	4	36	6	0	4	1	.800	0	1	3.05
1994 Madison	A StL	62	0	0	14	94.1	410	90	49	43	5	4	2	5	46	2	103	10	4	6	6	.500	0	0	4.10
1995 St. Pete	A+ StL	12	11	0	0	59	251	44	25	23	2	3	1	4	32	0	57	5	0	6	4	.600	0	0	3.51
1996 Arkansas	AA StL	34	17	2	11	108	486	113	75	59	18	4	1	2	51	1	85	7	0	5	10	.333	0	3	4.92
1997 Arkansas	AA StL	17	16	1	1	92.2	421	111	52	43	7	1	5	4	37	0	67	8	2	7	5	.583	0	0	4.18
Louisville	AAA StL	14	6	0	3	43.2	173	37	14	12	3	0	0	0	13	0	41	4	0	1	2	.333	0	1	2.47
5 Min. YEARS		170	50	3	40	439	1925	433	231	194	36	16	10	17	201	7	389	40	6	29	28	.509	0	5	3.98

Dean Crow

Pitches: Right **Bats:** Left **Pos:** P   **Ht:** 6' 4" **Wt:** 215 **Born:** 8/21/72 **Age:** 25

Year Team	Lg Org	G	GS	CG	GF	IP	BFP	H	R	ER	HR	SH	SF	HB	TBB	IBB	SO	WP	Bk	W	L	Pct.	ShO	Sv	ERA
1993 Bellingham	A- Sea	25	0	0	12	47.2	190	31	14	10	1	1	2	0	21	1	38	0	0	5	3	.625	0	4	1.89
1994 Appleton	A Sea	16	0	0	8	15.1	80	25	15	12	4	2	3	1	7	4	11	1	0	2	4	.333	0	2	7.04
1995 Riverside	A+ Sea	51	0	0	47	61.2	249	54	21	18	1	3	2	3	13	0	46	2	0	3	4	.429	0	22	2.63
1996 Port City	AA Sea	60	0	0	49	68	285	64	35	23	4	5	1	1	20	1	43	6	0	2	3	.400	0	26	3.04
1997 Tacoma	AAA Sea	33	0	0	23	43.1	200	56	25	23	3	2	3	1	19	1	36	3	0	4	2	.667	0	7	4.78
Toledo	AAA Det	18	0	0	10	18.1	90	26	16	16	1	2	1	2	10	1	10	0	0	3	0	1.000	0	2	7.85
5 Min. YEARS		203	0	0	149	254.1	1094	256	126	102	14	15	12	8	90	8	184	12	0	19	16	.543	0	63	3.61

Fausto Cruz

Bats: Right **Throws:** Right **Pos:** 2B   **Ht:** 5'10" **Wt:** 165 **Born:** 5/1/72 **Age:** 26

Year Team	Lg Org	G	AB	H	2B	3B	HR	TB	R	RBI	TBB	IBB	SO	HBP	SH	SF	SB	CS	SB%	GDP	Avg	OBP	SLG
1991 Modesto	A+ Oak	18	58	12	1	0	0	13	9	0	8	0	13	1	0	0	1	2	.33	1	.207	.313	.224
Athletics	R Oak	52	180	49	2	1	2	59	38	36	32	0	23	3	3	7	3	0	1.00	10	.272	.378	.328
1992 Reno	A+ Oak	127	489	156	22	11	9	227	86	90	70	1	66	7	3	7	8	7	.53	17	.319	.407	.464
1993 Modesto	A+ Oak	43	165	39	3	0	1	45	21	20	25	0	34	0	5	4	6	4	.60	2	.236	.330	.273
Huntsville	AA Oak	63	251	84	15	2	3	112	45	31	20	0	42	1	4	2	4	4	.33	8	.335	.383	.446
Tacoma	AAA Oak	21	74	18	2	1	0	22	13	6	5	0	16	0	2	0	3	3	.50	7	.243	.291	.297
1994 Tacoma	AAA Oak	65	218	70	19	0	1	92	27	17	17	0	32	3	4	1	2	2	.50	7	.321	.377	.422
1995 Edmonton	AAA Oak	114	448	126	23	2	11	186	72	67	34	2	67	5	4	7	7	5	.58	15	.281	.334	.415
1996 Toledo	AAA Det	107	384	96	18	2	12	154	49	59	33	0	81	1	2	2	11	10	.52	7	.250	.310	.401
1997 Vancouver	AAA Ana	118	413	119	28	1	11	182	52	67	18	0	81	5	4	4	5	8	.38	10	.288	.323	.441
1994 Oakland	AL	17	28	3	0	0	0	3	2	0	4	0	6	0	0	0	0	0	.00	1	.107	.219	.107
1995 Oakland	AL	8	23	5	0	0	0	5	3	0	5	0	5	0	2	2	1	1	.50	1	.217	.286	.217
1996 Detroit	AL	14	38	9	2	0	0	11	5	0	1	0	11	0	1	0	0	0	.00	0	.237	.256	.289
7 Min. YEARS		728	2680	769	133	20	50	1092	412	393	262	3	455	26	31	34	48	45	.52	84	.287	.352	.407
3 Maj. YEARS		39	89	17	2	0	0	19	7	5	8	0	22	0	3	2	1	1	.50	2	.191	.253	.213

Chris Cumberland

Pitches: Left **Bats:** Right **Pos:** P   **Ht:** 6'1" **Wt:** 185 **Born:** 1/15/73 **Age:** 25

Year Team	Lg Org	G	GS	CG	GF	IP	BFP	H	R	ER	HR	SH	SF	HB	TBB	IBB	SO	WP	Bk	W	L	Pct.	ShO	Sv	ERA
1993 Oneonta	A- NYA	15	15	0	0	89	393	109	43	33	2	1	5	0	28	0	62	6	2	4	4	.500	1	0	3.34
1994 Greensboro	A NYA	22	22	1	0	137.2	559	123	55	45	9	4	2	4	41	0	95	11	2	14	5	.737	1	0	2.94
1995 Yankees	R NYA	4	4	0	0	7	26	3	1	1	0	0	0	0	1	0	7	0	0	1	0	1.000	0	0	1.29
Tampa	A+ NYA	5	5	0	0	24.2	104	28	10	5	1	1	0	1	5	0	10	1	0	1	2	.333	0	0	1.82
1996 Columbus	AAA NYA	12	12	1	0	58	272	86	45	42	9	4	1	4	23	0	35	3	0	2	7	.222	0	0	6.52
Norwich	AA NYA	16	16	2	0	95.2	427	112	73	56	13	2	5	4	37	2	44	4	0	5	7	.417	1	0	5.27
1997 Norwich	AA NYA	25	25	3	0	154.2	686	188	100	69	12	5	3	5	59	1	81	10	4	11	10	.524	1	0	4.02
New Britain	AA Min	1	1	0	0	5.2	22	5	2	2	0	0	0	0	2	0	2	2	0	1	0	1.000	0	0	3.18
5 Min. YEARS		100	100	7	0	572.1	2489	654	329	253	46	17	16	18	196	3	336	37	8	38	36	.514	3	0	3.98

John Curl

Bats: Left **Throws:** Right **Pos:** DH   **Ht:** 6'3" **Wt:** 205 **Born:** 11/10/72 **Age:** 25

Year Team	Lg Org	G	AB	H	2B	3B	HR	TB	R	RBI	TBB	IBB	SO	HBP	SH	SF	SB	CS	SB%	GDP	Avg	OBP	SLG
1995 Medcne Hat	R+ Tor	69	270	86	26	1	7	135	47	63	31	8	61	0	0	3	5	1	.83	11	.319	.385	.500
1996 Dunedin	A+ Tor	125	447	110	20	2	18	188	52	62	44	1	133	1	2	5	7	4	.64	6	.246	.312	.421
1997 Knoxville	AA Tor	10	29	6	1	0	0	7	0	1	3	0	6	0	0	0	0	0	.00	0	.207	.281	.241
Dunedin	A+ Tor	74	231	59	14	0	15	118	36	48	24	4	53	0	0	1	3	2	.60	4	.255	.324	.511
3 Min. YEARS		278	977	261	61	3	40	448	135	174	102	13	253	1	2	9	15	7	.68	21	.267	.334	.459

Chris Curtis

Pitches: Right **Bats:** Right **Pos:** P   **Ht:** 6'2" **Wt:** 185 **Born:** 5/8/71 **Age:** 27

Year Team	Lg Org	G	GS	CG	GF	IP	BFP	H	R	ER	HR	SH	SF	HB	TBB	IBB	SO	WP	Bk	W	L	Pct.	ShO	Sv	ERA
1991 Butte	R+ Tex	6	3	0	2	12.2	69	27	23	14	1	0	0	1	4	0	7	0	3	0	2	.000	0	0	9.95
Rangers	R Tex	7	7	0	0	35	134	27	9	8	1	0	4	2	9	0	23	0	2	4	0	1.000	0	0	2.06
1992 Gastonia	A Tex	24	24	1	0	147	590	117	60	43	3	1	5	6	54	0	107	6	7	8	11	.421	1	0	2.63
1993 Charlotte	A+ Tex	27	26	1	0	151	637	159	76	67	6	4	2	8	51	0	55	4	5	8	8	.500	0	0	3.99
1994 Tulsa	AA Tex	25	23	3	1	142.2	639	173	102	85	17	4	7	7	57	5	62	9	7	13	13	.188	1	0	5.36
1995 Okla City	AAA Tex	51	0	0	22	77.1	358	81	53	43	5	6	3	5	39	3	40	2	0	3	5	.375	0	5	5.00
1996 Okla City	AAA Tex	41	2	0	13	75.2	344	91	50	43	6	4	2	3	34	3	38	10	1	2	5	.286	0	1	5.11
1997 Bowie	AA Bal	36	6	0	14	87	361	100	41	35	10	3	2	2	17	1	48	4	2	6	1	.857	0	2	3.62
7 Min. YEARS		217	91	5	52	728.1	3132	775	414	338	49	22	25	34	265	12	380	35	27	34	45	.430	2	8	4.18

Kevin Curtis

Bats: Right **Throws:** Right **Pos:** OF   **Ht:** 6'2" **Wt:** 210 **Born:** 8/19/72 **Age:** 25

Year Team	Lg Org	G	AB	H	2B	3B	HR	TB	R	RBI	TBB	IBB	SO	HBP	SH	SF	SB	CS	SB%	GDP	Avg	OBP	SLG
1993 Albany	A Bal	59	180	36	7	0	7	64	26	27	38	0	36	3	1	1	4	3	.57	6	.200	.347	.356
1994 Orioles	R Bal	12	38	15	5	0	1	23	3	4	6	0	4	0	0	0	1	0	1.00	1	.395	.477	.605
Albany	A Bal	20	67	15	3	0	1	21	5	7	8	0	14	2	0	0	0	2	.00	1	.224	.325	.313

Year Team	Lg Org	G	AB	H	2B	3B	HR	TB	R	RBI	TBB	IBB	SO	HBP	SH	SF	SB	CS	SB%	GDP	Avg	OBP	SLG
1995 High Desert	A+ Bal	112	399	117	26	1	21	208	70	70	54	1	83	12	0	5	8	6	.57	7	.293	.389	.521
1996 Bowie	AA Bal	129	460	113	21	2	18	192	69	58	54	4	95	3	0	1	2	1	.67	10	.246	.328	.417
1997 Bowie	AA Bal	22	67	18	6	0	1	27	7	13	7	0	22	0	1	1	1	1	.50	0	.269	.333	.403
New Haven	AA Col	105	362	99	24	0	17	174	58	69	34	0	82	6	0	6	0	2	.00	9	.273	.341	.481
5 Min. YEARS		459	1573	413	92	3	66	709	238	248	201	5	336	26	2	14	16	15	.52	34	.263	.353	.451

Randy Curtis

Bats: Left   Throws: Left   Pos: OF   Ht: 5'10"   Wt: 180   Born: 1/16/71   Age: 27

Year Team	Lg Org	G	AB	H	2B	3B	HR	TB	R	RBI	TBB	IBB	SO	HBP	SH	SF	SB	CS	SB%	GDP	Avg	OBP	SLG
1991 Pittsfield	A- NYN	75	299	86	12	1	2	106	72	33	60	1	63	2	2	2	25	9	.74	3	.288	.408	.355
1992 Columbia	A NYN	102	353	104	11	5	1	128	53	56	62	2	80	5	3	3	33	16	.67	1	.295	.404	.363
1993 St. Lucie	A+ NYN	126	467	149	30	12	2	209	91	38	93	2	72	5	4	4	52	17	.75	4	.319	.434	.448
1994 Las Vegas	AAA SD	30	77	16	1	0	2	23	8	6	11	0	27	0	1	0	3	1	.75	1	.208	.307	.299
Wichita	AA SD	59	200	54	9	3	4	81	30	21	24	0	56	4	1	2	12	9	.57	1	.270	.357	.405
1996 Rancho Cuca	A+ SD	104	359	96	14	5	5	135	63	52	76	2	94	4	4	8	22	6	.79	2	.267	.394	.376
1997 Akron	AA Cle	29	93	22	3	0	5	40	19	15	22	0	27	0	2	2	2	3	.40	1	.237	.376	.430
Buffalo	AAA Cle	41	111	30	7	0	5	52	14	15	14	1	22	3	0	0	1	1	.50	2	.270	.367	.468
6 Min. YEARS		566	1959	557	87	26	26	774	350	236	362	8	441	23	17	21	150	62	.71	15	.284	.398	.395

Scooter Cushman

Pitches: Right   Bats: Right   Pos: P   Ht: 6'0"   Wt: 175   Born: 11/27/71   Age: 26

Year Team	Lg Org	G	GS	CG	GF	IP	BFP	H	R	ER	HR	SH	SF	HB	TBB	IBB	SO	WP	Bk	W	L	Pct.	ShO	Sv	ERA
1995 Princeton	R+ Cin	26	0	0	21	35	159	33	21	12	1	0	1	1	15	2	40	2	0	2	3	.400	0	8	3.09
1996 Chston-WV	A Cin	55	0	0	39	73	308	70	29	17	2	4	2	6	13	3	57	0	1	3	5	.375	0	15	2.10
1997 Chattanooga	AA Cin	1	0	0	0	1.2	10	4	3	3	0	0	0	0	1	0	1	0	0	0	0	.000	0	0	16.20
Burlington	A Cin	47	0	0	39	50.2	229	45	22	17	2	5	0	5	25	4	54	3	0	1	4	.200	0	19	3.02
3 Min. YEARS		129	0	0	99	160.1	706	152	75	49	5	9	3	12	54	9	152	5	0	6	12	.333	0	42	2.75

Jim Czajkowski

Pitches: Right   Bats: Both   Pos: P   Ht: 6'4"   Wt: 215   Born: 12/18/63   Age: 34

Year Team	Lg Org	G	GS	CG	GF	IP	BFP	H	R	ER	HR	SH	SF	HB	TBB	IBB	SO	WP	Bk	W	L	Pct.	ShO	Sv	ERA
1986 Idaho Falls	R+ Atl	16	13	3	1	88.2	0	90	44	36	5	0	0	3	16	0	46	3	0	7	5	.583	0	0	3.65
1987 Sumter	A Atl	50	0	0	40	68.2	288	63	26	17	2	2	1	2	17	3	59	4	0	4	6	.400	0	20	2.23
1988 Durham	A+ Atl	48	0	0	39	58.1	263	65	26	22	4	5	3	0	24	5	26	5	2	8	5	.615	0	17	3.39
1989 Durham	A+ Atl	32	0	0	23	45.1	178	33	8	5	2	2	4	2	10	2	34	2	0	2	3	.400	0	14	0.99
Greenville	AA Atl	17	4	0	3	34	161	39	31	21	4	1	2	1	16	0	18	0	0	1	6	.143	0	0	5.56
1990 Harrisburg	A Pit	9	0	0	4	14.2	67	17	7	7	1	0	1	1	6	0	6	1	0	0	0	.000	0	0	4.30
Salem	A+ Pit	18	0	0	17	28	113	17	10	8	3	3	2	3	11	3	26	1	0	1	1	.500	0	6	2.57
Beloit	A Mil	21	0	0	21	27.1	110	16	7	5	1	1	2	3	8	4	37	0	0	2	0	1.000	0	11	1.65
Stockton	A+ Mil	2	0	0	1	2.2	10	1	0	0	0	1	0	0	2	0	2	0	0	0	0	.000	0	1	0.00
1991 El Paso	AA Mil	43	0	0	32	78.1	366	100	54	43	5	4	2	3	29	4	69	5	1	5	2	.714	0	11	4.94
1992 El Paso	AA Mil	57	2	0	28	79.1	351	92	44	43	8	4	1	7	26	4	62	1	0	5	7	.417	0	10	4.88
1993 Orlando	AA ChN	10	0	0	4	19	76	15	7	6	0	0	1	1	3	1	16	0	1	1	2	.333	0	1	2.84
Iowa	AAA ChN	42	0	0	18	70.1	304	64	31	30	3	4	3	3	32	2	43	4	0	7	5	.583	0	3	3.84
1994 Colo Sprngs	AAA Col	44	1	0	21	63	254	53	24	19	4	3	5	5	16	1	36	3	1	5	4	.556	0	8	2.71
1995 Colo Sprngs	AAA Col	60	0	0	44	83.2	382	90	54	47	8	6	8	2	52	7	56	4	0	3	10	.231	0	17	5.06
1996 Syracuse	AAA Tor	48	2	0	20	89.1	395	85	52	38	4	6	9	3	37	6	71	3	0	6	4	.600	0	1	3.83
1997 Syracuse	AAA Tor	16	0	0	6	22.2	101	21	11	8	2	1	0	0	14	1	13	0	0	0	2	.000	0	2	3.18
Knoxville	AA Tor	25	0	0	18	32	149	43	27	23	5	2	1	2	11	1	33	0	0	2	2	.500	0	5	6.47
1994 Colorado	NL	5	0	0	2	8.2	42	9	4	4	2	1	0	3	6	1	2	1	0	0	0	.000	0	0	4.15
12 Min. YEARS		558	22	3	340	905.1	3568	904	463	378	61	45	45	41	330	44	653	36	5	59	64	.480	0	122	3.76

Jeffrey D'Amico

Pitches: Right   Bats: Right   Pos: P   Ht: 6'3"   Wt: 200   Born: 11/9/74   Age: 23

Year Team	Lg Org	G	GS	CG	GF	IP	BFP	H	R	ER	HR	SH	SF	HB	TBB	IBB	SO	WP	Bk	W	L	Pct.	ShO	Sv	ERA
1996 Athletics	R Oak	8	0	0	2	19	72	14	3	3	0	0	0	3	2	0	15	0	1	3	0	1.000	0	0	1.42
Modesto	A+ Oak	1	0	0	1	1	7	3	3	2	0	0	0	1	0	0	0	0	0	0	0	.000	0	0	18.00
1997 Modesto	A+ Oak	20	13	0	5	97	442	115	51	41	5	1	4	7	34	1	89	9	1	7	3	.700	0	1	3.80
Edmonton	AAA Oak	10	7	0	1	30.2	141	42	29	28	7	1	2	2	6	0	19	3	0	1	2	.333	0	1	8.22
2 Min. YEARS		39	20	0	8	147.2	662	174	92	74	12	2	6	13	42	1	123	12	2	11	5	.688	0	2	4.51

Derek Dace

Pitches: Left   Bats: Left   Pos: P   Ht: 6'7"   Wt: 200   Born: 4/9/75   Age: 23

Year Team	Lg Org	G	GS	CG	GF	IP	BFP	H	R	ER	HR	SH	SF	HB	TBB	IBB	SO	WP	Bk	W	L	Pct.	ShO	Sv	ERA
1994 Astros	R Hou	11	11	1	0	59	245	55	26	22	2	5	2	1	21	0	52	2	3	2	3	.400	0	0	3.36
1995 Astros	R Hou	11	10	2	1	69.1	274	60	20	15	2	3	1	1	6	0	77	5	2	3	4	.429	1	0	1.95
Kissimmee	A+ Hou	1	1	0	0	2.2	17	4	5	5	0	0	1	0	5	0	1	0	0	0	0	1.000	0	0	16.88
1996 Kissimmee	A+ Hou	12	0	0	3	18.1	73	19	6	6	0	0	0	0	7	0	11	1	0	0	0	.000	0	1	2.95
Jackson	AA Hou	1	1	0	0	4	21	5	1	1	1	0	0	0	5	0	0	0	0	0	0	.000	0	0	2.25
Auburn	A- Hou	15	15	0	0	97	400	89	41	35	7	2	1	2	35	2	87	1	0	9	4	.692	0	0	3.25

		HOW MUCH HE PITCHED				WHAT HE GAVE UP				THE RESULTS		
Year Team	Lg Org	G GS CG GF	IP	BFP	H R ER HR SH SF HB	TBB IBB SO WP Bk	W L Pct. ShO Sv ERA
1997 Lakeland	A+ Det	2 0 0 1	2.1	9	2 1 1 1 0 0 0	1 0 0 0 0	0 0 .000 0 0 3.86
W Michigan	A Det	10 2 0 3	25	100	23 2 2 0 0 0 1	4 0 24 0 0	1 0 1.000 0 2 0.72
Toledo	AAA Det	5 0 0 3	10	48	13 8 4 0 1 0 1	6 0 6 1 0	0 0 .000 0 0 3.60
4 Min. YEARS		68 40 3 11	287.2	1187	270 110 91 13 11 5 6	90 2 258 10 5	15 12 .556 1 3 2.85

Craig Daedelow

Bats: Right **Throws:** Right **Pos:** SS   **Ht:** 5'11" **Wt:** 175 **Born:** 4/3/76 **Age:** 22

			BATTING												BASERUNNING				PERCENTAGES		
Year Team	Lg Org	G	AB	H	2B	3B	HR	TB	R	RBI	TBB	IBB	SO	HBP	SH	SF	SB	CS	SB%	GDP	Avg	OBP	SLG
1994 Orioles	R Bal	46	116	26	2	0	0	28	19	8	19	0	20	2	1	0	6	1	.86	0	.224	.343	.241
1995 Orioles	R Bal	49	170	44	9	0	1	56	35	11	24	0	19	3	1	0	7	2	.78	5	.259	.360	.329
Bluefield	R+ Bal	5	13	0	0	0	0	0	1	1	4	0	3	0	0	1	0	1	.00	0	.000	.222	.000
1996 Bakersfield	A+ Bal	86	298	70	17	1	1	92	37	28	31	0	60	4	4	2	10	4	.71	6	.235	.313	.309
Frederick	A+ Bal	26	72	15	4	0	0	19	13	8	6	1	9	1	2	0	2	0	1.00	0	.208	.278	.264
1997 Bowie	AA Bal	1	1	0	0	0	0	0	0	0	0	0	1	0	0	0	0	0	.00	0	.000	.000	.000
Delmarva	A Bal	101	277	74	17	1	1	96	37	35	24	1	46	0	5	4	11	5	.69	9	.267	.321	.347
4 Min. YEARS		314	947	229	49	2	3	291	142	91	108	2	158	10	13	7	36	13	.73	20	.242	.324	.307

Carl Dale

Pitches: Right **Bats:** Right **Pos:** P   **Ht:** 6'2" **Wt:** 215 **Born:** 12/7/72 **Age:** 25

		HOW MUCH HE PITCHED				WHAT HE GAVE UP				THE RESULTS		
Year Team	Lg Org	G GS CG GF	IP	BFP	H R ER HR SH SF HB	TBB IBB SO WP Bk	W L Pct. ShO Sv ERA
1994 New Jersey	A- StL	15 15 0 0	73	333	79 44 37 2 3 2 3	38 0 75 10 0	2 7 .222 0 0 4.56
1995 Peoria	A StL	24 24 2 0	143.2	613	124 66 47 8 3 2 1	62 0 104 4 1	9 9 .500 1 0 2.94
1996 Modesto	A+ Oak	26 24 0 0	128.1	565	124 79 61 11 2 5 5	72 0 102 12 0	8 2 .800 0 0 4.28
1997 Huntsville	AA Oak	20 16 0 2	85.1	389	95 61 51 10 1 3 8	43 0 57 4 0	6 4 .600 0 0 5.38
4 Min. YEARS		85 79 2 2	430.1	1900	422 250 196 31 9 12 17	215 0 338 30 1	25 22 .532 1 0 4.10

Mark Dalesandro

Bats: Right **Throws:** Right **Pos:** C   **Ht:** 6'0" **Wt:** 185 **Born:** 5/14/68 **Age:** 30

			BATTING												BASERUNNING				PERCENTAGES		
Year Team	Lg Org	G	AB	H	2B	3B	HR	TB	R	RBI	TBB	IBB	SO	HBP	SH	SF	SB	CS	SB%	GDP	Avg	OBP	SLG
1990 Boise	A- Ana	55	223	75	10	2	6	107	35	44	19	2	42	1	0	1	6	1	.86	6	.336	.389	.480
1991 Quad City	A Ana	125	487	133	17	8	5	181	63	69	34	1	58	6	0	4	1	2	.33	10	.273	.326	.372
1992 Palm Spring	A+ Ana	126	492	146	30	3	7	203	72	92	33	6	50	5	0	6	6	2	.75	20	.297	.343	.413
1993 Palm Spring	A+ Ana	46	176	43	5	3	1	57	22	25	15	1	20	0	0	0	3	2	.60	9	.244	.293	.324
Midland	AA Ana	57	235	69	9	0	2	84	33	36	8	2	30	4	0	5	1	1	.50	9	.294	.321	.357
Vancouver	AAA Ana	26	107	32	8	1	2	48	16	15	6	1	13	1	0	1	1	0	1.00	6	.299	.339	.449
1994 Vancouver	AAA Ana	51	199	63	9	1	1	77	29	31	7	0	19	1	0	2	1	0	1.00	6	.317	.340	.387
1995 Vancouver	AAA Ana	34	123	41	13	1	1	59	16	18	6	0	12	1	0	1	2	0	1.00	2	.333	.366	.480
1996 Columbus	AAA NYA	78	255	72	29	4	2	115	34	38	17	0	31	5	0	2	2	0	1.00	9	.282	.337	.451
1997 Iowa	AAA ChN	115	405	106	14	0	8	144	48	48	33	3	51	2	0	5	0	0	.00	15	.262	.317	.356
1994 California	AL	19	25	5	1	0	1	9	5	2	2	0	4	0	0	0	0	0	.00	2	.200	.259	.360
1995 California	AL	11	10	1	1	0	0	2	1	0	0	0	2	0	0	0	0	0	.00	0	.100	.100	.200
8 Min. YEARS		713	2702	780	144	23	35	1075	368	416	178	16	326	26	0	34	23	8	.74	90	.289	.335	.398
2 Maj. YEARS		30	35	6	2	0	1	11	6	2	2	0	6	0	0	0	0	0	.00	2	.171	.216	.314

Dee Dalton

Bats: Right **Throws:** Right **Pos:** 3B   **Ht:** 5'11" **Wt:** 170 **Born:** 6/17/72 **Age:** 26

			BATTING												BASERUNNING				PERCENTAGES		
Year Team	Lg Org	G	AB	H	2B	3B	HR	TB	R	RBI	TBB	IBB	SO	HBP	SH	SF	SB	CS	SB%	GDP	Avg	OBP	SLG
1993 Johnson Cty	R+ StL	68	240	65	13	2	11	115	36	46	30	0	56	2	4	4	5	3	.63	4	.271	.351	.479
1994 Madison	A StL	129	466	112	33	5	12	191	69	77	53	2	104	4	2	6	11	6	.65	11	.240	.319	.410
1995 St. Pete	A+ StL	118	385	79	16	1	2	103	36	30	45	0	81	3	2	3	10	4	.71	7	.205	.291	.268
1996 Arkansas	AA StL	113	345	82	17	2	6	121	38	42	38	2	61	2	6	5	4	4	.50	10	.238	.314	.351
1997 Arkansas	AA StL	116	360	82	16	0	4	110	52	43	38	0	66	3	2	5	2	5	.29	10	.228	.303	.306
5 Min. YEARS		544	1796	420	95	10	35	640	231	238	204	4	368	14	16	21	32	22	.59	42	.234	.314	.356

Jed Dalton

Bats: Right **Throws:** Right **Pos:** OF   **Ht:** 6'1" **Wt:** 190 **Born:** 4/3/73 **Age:** 25

			BATTING												BASERUNNING				PERCENTAGES		
Year Team	Lg Org	G	AB	H	2B	3B	HR	TB	R	RBI	TBB	IBB	SO	HBP	SH	SF	SB	CS	SB%	GDP	Avg	OBP	SLG
1995 Boise	A- Ana	48	126	33	8	1	0	43	10	10	8	1	20	0	1	0	1	1	.50	2	.262	.306	.341
1996 Cedar Rapds	A Ana	79	304	85	16	1	12	139	52	47	23	0	38	12	0	2	20	8	.71	10	.280	.352	.457
Lk Elsinore	A+ Ana	38	121	31	4	2	1	42	19	15	11	0	19	2	2	1	6	3	.67	3	.256	.326	.347
1997 Midland	AA Ana	94	360	81	18	2	11	136	63	48	35	0	58	5	4	1	7	12	.37	6	.225	.302	.378
3 Min. YEARS		259	911	230	46	6	24	360	144	120	77	1	135	19	7	4	34	24	.59	21	.252	.322	.395

Vic Darensbourg

Pitches: Left **Bats:** Left **Pos:** P   **Ht:** 5'10" **Wt:** 165 **Born:** 11/13/70 **Age:** 27

		HOW MUCH HE PITCHED				WHAT HE GAVE UP				THE RESULTS		
Year Team	Lg Org	G GS CG GF	IP	BFP	H R ER HR SH SF HB	TBB IBB SO WP Bk	W L Pct. ShO Sv ERA
1992 Marlins	R Fla	8 4 0 2	42	161	28 5 3 1 0 0 3	11 2 37 0 0	2 1 .667 0 2 0.64
1993 Kane County	A Fla	46 0 0 31	71.1	300	58 17 17 3 3 3 4	28 3 89 2 0	9 1 .900 0 16 2.14

		HOW MUCH HE PITCHED				WHAT HE GAVE UP								THE RESULTS					
Year Team	Lg Org	G	GS	CG	GF	IP	BFP	H	R	ER	HR	SH	SF	HB	TBB	IBB	SO	WP	Bk	W	L	Pct.	ShO	Sv	ERA
High Desert	A+ Fla	1	0	0	0	1	4	1	0	0	0	0	0	0	0	0	1	0	0	0	0	.000	0	0	0.00
1994 Portland	AA Fla	34	21	1	9	149	631	146	76	63	18	7	4	6	60	3	103	4	2	10	7	.588	1	4	3.81
1996 Brevard Cty	A+ Fla	2	0	0	1	3	10	1	0	0	0	0	0	0	1	0	5	0	0	0	0	.000	0	0	0.00
Charlotte	AAA Fla	47	0	0	25	63.1	280	61	30	26	7	3	2	2	32	3	66	3	1	1	5	.167	0	7	3.69
1997 Charlotte	AAA Fla	27	0	0	6	24.2	110	22	12	12	4	2	0	2	15	3	21	1	0	4	2	.667	0	2	4.38
5 Min. YEARS		165	25	1	74	354.1	1496	317	140	121	33	15	9	17	147	14	322	10	3	26	16	.619	1	31	3.07

Doug Dascenzo

Bats: Both **Throws:** Left **Pos:** OF **Ht:** 5'8" **Wt:** 160 **Born:** 6/30/64 **Age:** 34

		BATTING													BASERUNNING				PERCENTAGES		
Year Team	Lg Org	G	AB	H	2B	3B	HR	TB	R	RBI	TBB	IBB	SO	HBP	SH	SF	SB	CS	SB%	GDP	Avg	OBP	SLG
1985 Geneva	A- ChN	70	252	84	15	1	3	110	59	23	61	4	20	2	1	4	33	9	.79	1	.333	.461	.437
1986 Winston-Sal	A+ ChN	138	545	178	29	11	6	247	107	83	63	5	44	2	12	5	57	13	.81	9	.327	.395	.453
1987 Pittsfield	AA ChN	134	496	152	32	6	3	205	84	56	73	5	38	1	7	5	36	7	.84	5	.306	.393	.413
1988 Iowa	AAA ChN	132	505	149	22	5	6	199	73	49	37	4	41	2	7	5	30	14	.68	7	.295	.342	.394
1989 Iowa	AAA ChN	111	431	121	18	4	4	159	59	33	51	3	41	0	9	2	34	21	.62	7	.281	.355	.369
1993 Okla City	AAA Tex	38	157	39	8	2	1	54	21	13	16	0	16	0	2	1	6	5	.55	7	.248	.316	.344
1994 Norfolk	AAA NYN	68	246	68	13	1	4	95	30	27	22	3	23	0	4	1	5	7	.42	5	.276	.335	.386
1995 St. Paul	IND —	9	38	11	2	0	0	13	8	7	8	0	2	0	0	1	2	2	.50	0	.289	.404	.342
Charlotte	AAA Fla	75	265	69	9	0	4	90	51	26	25	0	30	0	1	4	14	9	.61	7	.260	.320	.340
1996 Las Vegas	AAA SD	86	320	91	17	3	0	114	48	20	32	2	38	2	10	2	15	13	.54	6	.284	.351	.356
1997 Las Vegas	AAA SD	109	433	120	23	4	9	178	61	45	45	4	42	1	6	1	16	8	.67	7	.277	.346	.411
1988 Chicago	NL	26	75	16	3	0	0	19	9	4	9	1	4	0	1	0	6	1	.86	2	.213	.298	.253
1989 Chicago	NL	47	139	23	1	0	1	27	20	12	13	0	13	0	3	2	6	3	.67	2	.165	.234	.194
1990 Chicago	NL	113	241	61	9	5	1	83	27	26	21	2	18	1	5	3	15	6	.71	3	.253	.312	.344
1991 Chicago	NL	118	239	61	11	0	1	75	40	18	24	2	26	2	6	1	14	7	.67	3	.255	.327	.314
1992 Chicago	NL	139	376	96	13	4	0	117	37	20	27	2	32	0	4	2	6	8	.43	3	.255	.304	.311
1993 Texas	AL	76	146	29	5	1	2	42	20	10	8	0	22	0	3	1	2	0	1.00	1	.199	.239	.288
1996 San Diego	NL	21	9	1	0	0	0	1	3	0	1	0	2	0	0	0	1	0	.00	0	.111	.200	.111
10 Min. YEARS		970	3688	1082	188	37	40	1464	601	382	433	30	335	10	59	31	248	108	.70	61	.293	.366	.397
7 Maj. YEARS		540	1225	287	42	10	5	364	156	90	103	7	117	3	22	9	49	26	.65	14	.234	.293	.297

Fernando DaSilva

Pitches: Right **Bats:** Right **Pos:** P **Ht:** 6'2" **Wt:** 194 **Born:** 9/6/71 **Age:** 26

		HOW MUCH HE PITCHED						WHAT HE GAVE UP										THE RESULTS					
Year Team	Lg Org	G	GS	CG	GF	IP	BFP	H	R	ER	HR	SH	SF	HB	TBB	IBB	SO	WP	Bk	W	L	Pct.	ShO	Sv	ERA
1992 Expos	R Mon	12	12	8	0	95	347	59	16	15	1	1	2	5	10	0	86	2	0	10	1	.909	4	0	1.42
Albany	A Mon	1	1	0	0	8	29	4	1	1	1	0	0	0	1	0	9	0	0	1	0	1.000	0	0	1.13
1993 Burlington	A Mon	11	10	0	0	60.2	264	66	38	32	10	0	4	3	18	2	50	1	1	0	4	.000	0	0	4.75
Jamestown	A- Mon	15	14	0	1	92.1	404	107	58	43	6	2	1	1	25	0	59	2	2	3	8	.273	0	0	4.19
1994 Burlington	A Mon	28	25	4	0	162.1	702	179	96	79	20	2	8	6	51	2	126	9	0	9	8	.529	2	0	4.38
1995 Wst Plm Bch	A+ Mon	27	20	2	1	124	530	136	61	51	3	2	9	11	31	1	54	5	1	7	10	.412	0	0	3.70
1996 Wst Plm Bch	A+ Mon	40	0	0	10	66.2	275	58	23	19	4	3	2	3	20	3	45	2	0	4	2	.667	0	0	2.57
1997 Harrisburg	AA Mon	12	0	0	0	13.2	75	21	23	21	6	1	1	1	10	0	11	0	0	0	3	.000	0	0	13.83
Wst Plm Bch	A+ Mon	30	4	0	11	59.2	259	73	38	35	4	2	1	1	12	1	59	3	1	8	5	.615	0	0	5.28
6 Min. YEARS		176	86	14	29	682.1	2885	703	354	296	55	13	28	31	178	9	499	24	5	42	41	.506	6	0	3.90

Jamie Daspit

Pitches: Right **Bats:** Right **Pos:** P **Ht:** 6'7" **Wt:** 210 **Born:** 8/10/69 **Age:** 28

		HOW MUCH HE PITCHED						WHAT HE GAVE UP										THE RESULTS					
Year Team	Lg Org	G	GS	CG	GF	IP	BFP	H	R	ER	HR	SH	SF	HB	TBB	IBB	SO	WP	Bk	W	L	Pct.	ShO	Sv	ERA
1990 Great Falls	R+ LA	14	9	0	1	51	222	45	26	23	0	3	2	5	30	0	40	1	0	5	2	.714	0	0	4.06
1991 Bakersfield	A+ LA	22	9	0	6	64.2	276	58	29	23	1	4	2	1	36	2	47	6	1	3	2	.600	0	2	3.20
1992 Vero Beach	A+ LA	26	25	0	0	149.1	625	135	67	57	10	6	3	7	57	1	109	7	1	6	12	.333	0	0	3.44
1993 Vero Beach	A+ LA	1	1	0	0	3	15	4	0	0	0	0	0	0	2	0	2	0	0	0	0	.000	0	0	0.00
San Antonio	AA LA	15	15	0	0	81.1	363	92	48	40	5	4	4	8	33	0	58	5	0	3	8	.273	0	0	4.43
1994 Jackson	AA Hou	28	10	1	7	71	274	48	22	18	1	2	0	2	23	0	74	3	0	5	1	.833	1	1	2.28
1995 Tucson	AAA Hou	36	0	0	11	63	272	63	30	25	3	2	5	2	22	1	49	5	0	5	1	.833	0	1	3.57
Edmonton	AAA Oak	2	0	0	0	5	22	6	6	6	2	0	0	0	2	0	5	2	0	0	1	.000	0	0	10.80
1996 Edmonton	AAA Oak	33	9	0	5	89.2	394	96	50	41	5	1	4	4	29	9	76	6	0	4	5	.444	0	0	4.12
1997 Las Vegas	AAA SD	10	2	0	0	20	88	22	17	16	5	1	0	0	7	2	12	4	0	1	0	1.000	0	0	7.20
Edmonton	AAA Oak	3	0	0	0	7.2	31	9	5	5	1	0	0	0	2	1	2	0	0	0	1	.000	0	0	5.87
8 Min. YEARS		190	80	1	30	605.2	2582	578	300	254	33	23	20	29	243	16	474	39	2	31	34	.477	1	4	3.77

Brian Daubach

Bats: Left **Throws:** Right **Pos:** 1B **Ht:** 6'1" **Wt:** 201 **Born:** 2/11/72 **Age:** 26

		BATTING													BASERUNNING				PERCENTAGES		
Year Team	Lg Org	G	AB	H	2B	3B	HR	TB	R	RBI	TBB	IBB	SO	HBP	SH	SF	SB	CS	SB%	GDP	Avg	OBP	SLG
1990 Mets	R NYN	45	152	41	8	4	1	60	26	19	22	0	41	2	0	3	2	1	.67	2	.270	.363	.395
1991 Kingsport	R+ NYN	65	217	52	9	1	7	84	30	42	33	5	64	6	1	2	1	3	.25	1	.240	.353	.387
1992 Pittsfield	A- NYN	72	260	63	15	2	2	88	26	40	30	2	61	3	1	4	4	0	1.00	5	.242	.323	.338
1993 Capital Cty	A NYN	102	379	106	19	3	7	152	50	72	52	5	84	5	1	7	6	1	.86	14	.280	.368	.401
1994 St. Lucie	A+ NYN	129	450	123	30	4	6	175	52	74	58	5	120	5	3	4	14	9	.61	9	.273	.360	.389
1995 Binghamton	AA NYN	135	469	115	25	2	10	174	61	72	51	5	104	7	1	7	6	2	.75	5	.245	.324	.371
Norfolk	AAA NYN	2	7	0	0	0	0	0	0	0	2	1	0	0	0	0	0	0	.00	0	.000	.222	.000
1996 Norfolk	AAA NYN	17	54	11	2	0	0	13	7	6	6	0	14	0	0	1	1	1	.50	1	.204	.279	.241
Binghamton	AA NYN	122	436	129	24	1	22	221	80	76	74	9	103	7	0	4	7	9	.44	8	.296	.403	.507

	BATTING																BASERUNNING				PERCENTAGES		
Year Team	Lg Org	G	AB	H	2B	3B	HR	TB	R	RBI	TBB	IBB	SO	HBP	SH	SF	SB	CS	SB%	GDP	Avg	OBP	SLG
1997 Charlotte	AAA Fla	136	461	128	40	2	21	235	66	93	65	4	126	6	1	10	4	8	.11	7	.278	.367	.510
8 Min. YEARS		825	2885	768	172	17	76	1202	398	494	393	36	717	41	8	42	42	34	.55	46	.266	.358	.417

David Davalillo

Bats: Right Throws: Right Pos: 3B-SS   Ht: 5'8" Wt: 170 Born: 8/17/74 Age: 23

	BATTING																BASERUNNING				PERCENTAGES		
Year Team	Lg Org	G	AB	H	2B	3B	HR	TB	R	RBI	TBB	IBB	SO	HBP	SH	SF	SB	CS	SB%	GDP	Avg	OBP	SLG
1994 Angels	R Ana	54	231	58	8	3	3	81	28	31	12	0	39	0	4	1	1	1	.50	4	.251	.287	.351
1995 Cedar Rapds	A Ana	44	141	38	7	1	0	47	17	16	7	0	32	0	4	1	1	0	1.00	3	.270	.302	.333
Boise	A- Ana	36	112	25	9	1	1	39	17	12	6	0	21	1	1	0	1	0	1.00	4	.223	.269	.348
1996 Cedar Rapds	A Ana	98	378	104	22	0	3	135	63	34	28	0	51	3	3	3	4	6	.40	4	.275	.328	.357
Midland	AA Ana	25	82	14	1	0	0	15	6	5	4	0	16	1	3	0	2	0	1.00	2	.171	.218	.183
1997 Lk Elsinore	A+ Ana	37	126	28	6	2	0	38	15	9	7	0	33	0	2	1	3	1	.75	1	.222	.261	.302
Midland	AA Ana	49	176	44	6	2	1	57	21	12	6	0	26	0	6	0	1	2	.33	4	.250	.275	.324
4 Min. YEARS		343	1246	311	59	9	8	412	167	119	70	0	218	5	23	6	13	10	.57	26	.250	.291	.331

Tom Davey

Pitches: Right Bats: Right Pos: P   Ht: 6'7" Wt: 215 Born: 9/11/73 Age: 24

	HOW MUCH HE PITCHED						WHAT HE GAVE UP												THE RESULTS					
Year Team	Lg Org	G	GS	CG	GF	IP	BFP	H	R	ER	HR	SH	SF	HB	TBB	IBB	SO	WP	Bk	W	L	Pct.	ShO	Sv	ERA
1994 Medcne Hat	R+ Tor	14	14	0	0	65	318	76	59	37	3	2	2	3	59	0	35	11	0	2	8	.200	0	0	5.12
1995 St. Cathms	A- Tor	7	7	0	0	38	160	27	19	14	2	0	2	3	21	0	29	3	1	4	3	.571	0	0	3.32
Hagerstown	A Tor	8	8	0	0	37.1	167	29	23	14	2	1	1	2	31	0	25	9	0	4	1	.800	0	0	3.38
1996 Hagerstown	A Tor	26	26	2	0	155.2	675	132	76	67	7	5	5	15	91	0	98	15	1	10	9	.526	1	0	3.87
1997 Dunedin	A+ Tor	7	6	0	0	39.2	172	44	21	19	4	0	0	2	15	0	36	5	1	1	3	.250	0	0	4.31
Knoxville	AA Tor	20	16	0	1	92.2	429	108	65	60	5	1	1	6	50	0	72	14	0	6	7	.462	0	0	5.83
4 Min. YEARS		82	77	2	1	428.1	1921	416	263	211	23	9	11	31	267	0	295	57	3	27	31	.466	1	0	4.43

Clint Davis

Pitches: Right Bats: Right Pos: P   Ht: 6'3" Wt: 205 Born: 9/26/69 Age: 28

	HOW MUCH HE PITCHED						WHAT HE GAVE UP												THE RESULTS					
Year Team	Lg Org	G	GS	CG	GF	IP	BFP	H	R	ER	HR	SH	SF	HB	TBB	IBB	SO	WP	Bk	W	L	Pct.	ShO	Sv	ERA
1991 Cardinals	R StL	21	0	0	9	26.2	130	35	23	17	0	2	3	3	12	0	25	1	2	3	3	.500	0	0	5.74
1992 Savannah	A StL	51	0	0	23	65	272	49	24	16	0	4	3	4	21	6	61	3	0	4	2	.667	0	1	2.22
1993 St. Pete	A+ StL	29	0	0	26	28	118	26	8	6	0	1	0	0	10	0	44	0	0	1	0	1.000	0	19	1.93
Arkansas	AA StL	28	0	0	10	37	143	22	10	8	1	2	1	3	10	3	37	0	0	2	0	1.000	0	1	1.95
1995 Louisville	AAA StL	4	0	0	0	3.2	19	6	5	5	1	0	0	0	2	1	4	0	1	0	0	.000	0	0	12.27
Rio Grande	IND —	38	0	0	36	40	162	29	17	12	4	2	0	1	9	2	59	0	1	3	2	.600	0	21	2.70
1996 Okla City	AAA Tex	8	0	0	1	13	60	14	5	5	1	1	0	3	6	0	16	0	0	0	0	.000	0	0	3.46
Tulsa	AA Tex	32	0	0	24	48	186	31	11	10	3	4	1	3	12	1	40	1	0	3	3	.500	0	10	1.88
1997 Okla City	AAA Tex	40	1	0	11	70.1	309	55	28	25	4	0	3	5	46	9	53	1	0	6	1	.857	0	0	3.20
6 Min. YEARS		251	1	0	140	331.2	1399	267	131	104	14	16	11	22	128	22	339	6	4	22	11	.667	0	52	2.82

Eddie Davis

Bats: Right Throws: Right Pos: OF   Ht: 6'0" Wt: 202 Born: 12/22/72 Age: 25

	BATTING																BASERUNNING				PERCENTAGES		
Year Team	Lg Org	G	AB	H	2B	3B	HR	TB	R	RBI	TBB	IBB	SO	HBP	SH	SF	SB	CS	SB%	GDP	Avg	OBP	SLG
1993 Great Falls	R+ LA	60	205	46	8	1	8	80	32	44	28	1	54	5	0	1	11	10	.52	4	.224	.331	.390
1994 Bakersfield	A+ LA	56	198	51	7	1	7	81	25	22	18	0	67	4	2	0	8	10	.44	3	.258	.332	.409
Vero Beach	A+ LA	61	192	33	5	0	3	47	20	16	10	0	65	2	2	1	5	4	.56	4	.172	.220	.245
1995 San Berndno	A+ LA	5	0	0	0	0	0	0	0	0	0	0	0	0	0	0	0	0	.00	0	.000	.000	.000
Yakima	A- LA	20	0	0	0	0	0	0	0	0	0	0	0	0	0	0	0	0	.00	0	.000	.000	.000
1996 San Berndno	A+ LA	136	546	140	34	2	29	265	107	89	62	1	150	8	3	4	31	23	.57	8	.256	.339	.485
1997 San Antonio	AA LA	74	206	43	8	2	11	88	30	34	15	0	69	3	5	1	2	3	.40	8	.209	.271	.427
5 Min. YEARS		412	1347	313	62	6	58	561	214	205	133	2	405	22	12	7	57	50	.53	27	.232	.310	.416

Jeff Davis

Pitches: Right Bats: Right Pos: P   Ht: 6'0" Wt: 170 Born: 9/20/72 Age: 25

	HOW MUCH HE PITCHED						WHAT HE GAVE UP												THE RESULTS					
Year Team	Lg Org	G	GS	CG	GF	IP	BFP	H	R	ER	HR	SH	SF	HB	TBB	IBB	SO	WP	Bk	W	L	Pct.	ShO	Sv	ERA
1993 Erie	A- Tex	27	0	0	24	37	155	32	18	15	3	2	2	4	10	2	41	2	0	0	5	.000	0	13	3.65
1994 Chston-SC	A Tex	45	0	0	43	49.2	214	53	25	22	3	0	1	2	11	0	72	2	1	2	3	.400	0	19	3.99
1995 Tulsa	AA Tex	1	1	0	0	7	24	2	0	0	0	0	0	0	1	0	4	1	0	1	0	1.000	0	0	0.00
Charlotte	A+ Tex	26	26	0	0	165.1	691	159	74	53	10	6	2	11	37	0	105	6	2	12	7	.632	0	0	2.89
1996 Tulsa	AA Tex	16	15	3	0	98	420	110	57	50	10	2	6	2	20	1	51	1	0	7	2	.778	0	4	4.59
1997 Tulsa	AA Tex	11	11	2	0	69	299	76	41	28	5	4	6	2	17	0	25	2	1	4	6	.400	1	0	3.65
5 Min. YEARS		126	53	5	67	426	1803	432	215	168	31	14	17	21	96	3	298	14	4	26	23	.531	1	32	3.55

Kane Davis

Pitches: Right Bats: Right Pos: P   Ht: 6'3" Wt: 180 Born: 6/25/75 Age: 23

	HOW MUCH HE PITCHED						WHAT HE GAVE UP												THE RESULTS					
Year Team	Lg Org	G	GS	CG	GF	IP	BFP	H	R	ER	HR	SH	SF	HB	TBB	IBB	SO	WP	Bk	W	L	Pct.	ShO	Sv	ERA
1993 Pirates	R Pit	11	4	0	5	28	140	34	30	22	0	3	2	0	19	1	24	2	0	0	4	.000	0	0	7.07
1994 Welland	A- Pit	15	15	2	0	98.1	400	90	36	29	4	2	2	3	32	1	74	7	1	5	5	.500	0	0	2.65

		HOW MUCH HE PITCHED				WHAT HE GAVE UP							THE RESULTS					

Year Team	Lg Org	G	GS	CG	GF	IP	BFP	H	R	ER	HR	SH	SF	HB	TBB	IBB	SO	WP	Bk	W	L	Pct.	ShO	Sv	ERA
1995 Augusta	A Pit	26	25	1	0	139.1	602	136	73	58	4	3	4	9	43	0	78	10	1	12	6	.667	0	0	3.75
1996 Lynchburg	A+ Pit	26	26	3	0	157.1	684	160	84	75	12	12	3	10	56	0	116	11	2	11	9	.550	1	0	4.29
1997 Carolina	AA Pit	6	6	0	0	28.2	128	22	17	12	2	2	1	3	16	1	23	2	0	0	3	.000	0	0	3.77
5 Min. YEARS		84	76	6	5	451.2	1954	442	240	196	22	22	12	25	166	3	315	32	4	28	27	.509	1	0	3.91

Tommy Davis

Bats: Right **Throws:** Right **Pos:** 1B   **Ht:** 6'1" **Wt:** 195 **Born:** 5/21/73 **Age:** 25

Year Team	Lg Org	G	AB	H	2B	3B	HR	TB	R	RBI	TBB	IBB	SO	HBP	SH	SF	SB	CS	SB%	GDP	Avg	OBP	SLG
1994 Albany	A Bal	61	216	59	10	1	5	86	35	35	18	0	52	2	0	3	2	4	.33	6	.273	.331	.398
1995 Frederick	A+ Bal	130	496	133	26	3	15	210	62	57	41	7	105	4	1	3	7	1	.88	14	.268	.327	.423
Bowie	AA Bal	9	32	10	3	0	3	22	5	10	1	0	9	1	0	0	0	0	.00	1	.313	.353	.688
1996 Bowie	AA Bal	137	524	137	32	2	14	215	75	54	41	4	113	10	3	3	5	8	.38	16	.261	.325	.410
1997 Rochester	AAA Bal	119	438	133	22	2	15	204	74	62	43	2	90	2	3	1	6	1	.86	16	.304	.368	.466
4 Min. YEARS		456	1706	472	93	8	52	737	251	218	144	13	369	19	7	10	20	14	.59	53	.277	.338	.432

Walt Dawkins

Bats: Right **Throws:** Right **Pos:** OF   **Ht:** 5'10" **Wt:** 190 **Born:** 8/6/72 **Age:** 25

Year Team	Lg Org	G	AB	H	2B	3B	HR	TB	R	RBI	TBB	IBB	SO	HBP	SH	SF	SB	CS	SB%	GDP	Avg	OBP	SLG
1995 Batavia	A- Phi	58	203	64	11	4	1	86	46	31	27	0	36	4	2	3	15	6	.71	6	.315	.401	.424
1996 Clearwater	A+ Phi	47	174	51	13	2	2	74	22	23	20	0	38	3	1	1	4	5	.44	3	.293	.374	.425
Reading	AA Phi	77	254	68	16	3	4	102	40	28	37	0	48	0	1	0	4	4	.50	3	.268	.361	.402
1997 Reading	AA Phi	106	331	79	13	1	8	118	48	40	35	0	90	2	6	3	4	5	.44	6	.239	.313	.356
3 Min. YEARS		288	962	262	53	10	15	380	156	122	119	0	212	9	10	7	27	20	.57	18	.272	.356	.395

Jason Dawsey

Pitches: Left **Bats:** Left **Pos:** P   **Ht:** 5'8" **Wt:** 165 **Born:** 5/27/74 **Age:** 24

Year Team	Lg Org	G	GS	CG	GF	IP	BFP	H	R	ER	HR	SH	SF	HB	TBB	IBB	SO	WP	Bk	W	L	Pct.	ShO	Sv	ERA
1995 Helena	R+ Mil	9	8	0	0	42.2	183	40	15	13	1	0	3	2	23	0	47	5	1	3	0	1.000	0	0	2.74
1996 Beloit	A Mil	31	14	1	4	101.1	411	71	21	17	4	4	0	1	42	0	119	2	1	6	4	.600	1	2	1.51
1997 El Paso	AA Mil	8	7	0	0	38.1	182	50	30	29	3	0	1	2	23	0	14	4	1	2	2	.500	0	0	6.81
3 Min. YEARS		48	29	1	4	182.1	776	161	66	59	8	4	4	5	88	0	180	11	3	11	6	.647	1	2	2.91

Fernando de la Cruz

Pitches: Right **Bats:** Right **Pos:** P   **Ht:** 6'0" **Wt:** 175 **Born:** 1/25/71 **Age:** 27

Year Team	Lg Org	G	GS	CG	GF	IP	BFP	H	R	ER	HR	SH	SF	HB	TBB	IBB	SO	WP	Bk	W	L	Pct.	ShO	Sv	ERA
1995 Boise	A- Ana	1	0	0	0	1.1	11	3	6	2	1	0	0	1	2	0	4	0	0	0	0	.000	0	0	13.50
1996 Lk Elsinore	A+ Ana	5	0	0	3	7.1	40	8	12	7	2	0	0	1	10	0	3	2	1	0	0	.000	0	0	8.59
Cedar Rapids	A Ana	6	6	0	0	27	139	35	25	24	1	1	3	7	21	0	18	4	3	0	5	.000	0	0	8.00
Boise	A- Ana	15	15	0	0	85.2	400	85	55	47	5	0	1	13	51	3	61	6	2	6	3	.667	0	0	4.94
1997 Cedar Rapds	A Ana	10	0	0	4	13.1	80	19	22	17	1	1	2	6	14	0	10	2	0	0	2	.000	0	1	11.48
Lk Elsinore	A+ Ana	8	6	0	1	37.2	165	36	22	19	3	1	2	2	17	0	26	1	2	2	2	.500	0	0	4.54
Midland	AA Ana	13	13	0	0	71.2	348	81	70	62	10	3	3	10	46	0	44	8	2	2	5	.286	0	0	7.79
3 Min. YEARS		58	40	0	8	244	1183	267	212	178	23	6	11	40	161	3	166	23	10	10	17	.370	0	1	6.57

Francisco de la Cruz

Pitches: Right **Bats:** Right **Pos:** P   **Ht:** 6'2" **Wt:** 175 **Born:** 7/9/73 **Age:** 24

Year Team	Lg Org	G	GS	CG	GF	IP	BFP	H	R	ER	HR	SH	SF	HB	TBB	IBB	SO	WP	Bk	W	L	Pct.	ShO	Sv	ERA
1997 Norwich	AA NYA	2	2	0	0	8.1	39	8	3	3	0	1	0	2	7	0	0	0	0	0	1	.000	0	0	3.24
Tampa	A+ NYA	8	8	0	0	36.2	174	39	30	28	5	3	2	1	29	1	22	2	0	0	2	.000	0	0	6.87
Greensboro	A NYA	13	13	1	0	84.2	359	71	41	31	6	2	2	4	36	1	75	3	2	5	4	.556	0	0	3.30
1 Min. YEARS		23	23	1	0	129.2	572	118	74	62	11	6	4	7	72	2	97	5	2	5	7	.417	0	0	4.30

Lorenzo de la Cruz

Bats: Right **Throws:** Right **Pos:** DH   **Ht:** 6'1" **Wt:** 199 **Born:** 9/5/71 **Age:** 26

Year Team	Lg Org	G	AB	H	2B	3B	HR	TB	R	RBI	TBB	IBB	SO	HBP	SH	SF	SB	CS	SB%	GDP	Avg	OBP	SLG
1993 Medicne Hat	R+ Tor	62	208	62	11	6	11	118	44	43	23	0	59	7	3	2	5	1	.83	5	.298	.383	.567
St. Cathms	A- Tor	6	16	0	0	0	0	0	2	0	3	0	5	0	1	0	0	0	.00	0	.000	.158	.000
1994 Hagerstown	A Tor	125	457	111	20	4	19	196	72	62	30	1	152	6	1	0	12	8	.60	13	.243	.298	.429
1995 Knoxville	AA Tor	140	508	139	20	12	8	207	63	61	36	3	129	15	1	0	11	11	.50	14	.274	.340	.407
1996 Knoxville	AA Tor	122	441	109	24	4	18	195	60	79	36	1	123	7	0	4	8	4	.67	11	.247	.311	.442
1997 Knoxville	AA Tor	39	146	49	7	2	7	81	32	26	14	1	38	5	0	1	2	2	.50	2	.336	.410	.555
Syracuse	AAA Tor	39	128	28	4	0	5	47	11	13	6	1	35	0	0	0	1	2	.33	0	.219	.254	.367
5 Min. YEARS		533	1904	498	86	28	68	844	284	284	148	7	541	40	6	7	39	28	.58	42	.262	.327	.443

Maximo de la Rosa

Pitches: Right **Bats:** Right **Pos:** P   **Ht:** 5'11" **Wt:** 170 **Born:** 7/12/71 **Age:** 26

		HOW MUCH HE PITCHED						WHAT HE GAVE UP										THE RESULTS					
Year Team	Lg Org	G	GS	CG	GF	IP	BFP	H	R	ER	HR	SH	SF	HB	TBB	IBB	SO	WP	Bk	W	L	Pct.	ShO	Sv	ERA
1993 Burlington	R+ Cle	14	14	2	0	76.1	319	53	38	32	3	3	2	5	37	2	69	3	2	7	2	.778	1	0	3.77
1994 Columbus	A Cle	14	14	0	0	75.1	310	49	33	28	2	1	1	10	38	0	71	5	2	4	2	.667	0	0	3.35
Kinston	A+ Cle	13	13	0	0	69.2	324	82	56	39	7	2	4	4	38	0	53	3	2	0	11	.000	0	0	5.04
1995 Canton-Akrn	AA Cle	1	0	0	0	0.1	3	1	2	2	1	0	0	0	1	0	0	0	0	0	0	.000	0	0	54.00
Kinston	A+ Cle	43	0	0	21	61.2	266	46	23	15	0	5	2	4	37	3	61	7	1	5	2	.714	0	8	2.19
1996 Canton-Akrn	AA Cle	40	15	0	17	119.2	530	104	60	52	7	2	4	3	81	3	109	12	2	11	5	.688	0	3	3.91
1997 Buffalo	AAA Cle	15	4	0	3	43	208	43	34	31	10	2	3	9	33	0	31	1	0	2	2	.500	0	0	6.49
Akron	AA Cle	17	13	5	2	97.1	435	112	63	48	11	8	4	5	32	3	70	2	4	4	9	.308	0	0	4.44
5 Min. YEARS		157	73	7	43	543.1	2395	490	309	247	41	23	20	40	297	11	464	33	13	33	33	.500	1	11	4.09

Luis de los Santos

Pitches: Right **Bats:** Right **Pos:** P   **Ht:** 6'2" **Wt:** 187 **Born:** 11/1/77 **Age:** 20

		HOW MUCH HE PITCHED						WHAT HE GAVE UP										THE RESULTS					
Year Team	Lg Org	G	GS	CG	GF	IP	BFP	H	R	ER	HR	SH	SF	HB	TBB	IBB	SO	WP	Bk	W	L	Pct.	ShO	Sv	ERA
1995 Yankees	R NYA	2	0	0	1	5	23	5	2	0	0	0	0	1	2	0	6	0	0	0	0	.000	0	0	0.00
1996 Greensboro	A NYA	7	6	0	0	31.2	141	39	17	17	4	0	1	0	11	0	21	0	0	4	1	.800	0	0	4.83
Oneonta	A- NYA	10	10	3	0	58	240	44	28	24	3	0	3	3	21	0	62	2	1	4	4	.500	2	0	3.72
1997 Greensboro	A NYA	14	14	1	0	88.2	377	91	45	30	3	3	6	7	13	0	62	4	0	5	6	.455	0	0	3.05
Tampa	A+ NYA	10	10	0	0	61.2	240	49	19	16	4	0	3	2	8	0	39	0	1	5	0	1.000	0	0	2.34
Norwich	AA NYA	4	4	0	0	25	104	23	9	7	4	1	1	0	7	0	15	0	1	1	1	.500	0	0	2.52
3 Min. YEARS		47	44	4	1	270	1125	251	120	94	18	4	14	13	62	0	205	6	3	19	12	.613	2	0	3.13

Valerio de los Santos

Pitches: Left **Bats:** Left **Pos:** P   **Ht:** 6'4" **Wt:** 185 **Born:** 10/6/75 **Age:** 22

		HOW MUCH HE PITCHED						WHAT HE GAVE UP										THE RESULTS					
Year Team	Lg Org	G	GS	CG	GF	IP	BFP	H	R	ER	HR	SH	SF	HB	TBB	IBB	SO	WP	Bk	W	L	Pct.	ShO	Sv	ERA
1995 Brewers	R Mil	14	12	0	1	82	341	81	34	20	3	5	4	6	12	2	57	6	2	4	6	.400	0	0	2.20
1996 Beloit	A Mil	33	23	5	10	164.2	715	164	83	65	11	8	5	3	59	4	137	8	3	10	8	.556	1	4	3.55
1997 El Paso	AA Mil	26	16	1	3	114.1	516	146	83	73	6	5	4	4	38	2	61	7	1	6	10	.375	0	2	5.75
3 Min. YEARS		73	51	6	14	361	1572	391	200	158	20	18	13	13	109	8	255	21	6	20	24	.455	1	6	3.94

Chris Dean

Bats: Both **Throws:** Right **Pos:** 2B   **Ht:** 5'10" **Wt:** 178 **Born:** 1/3/74 **Age:** 24

		BATTING														BASERUNNING				PERCENTAGES		
Year Team	Lg Org	G	AB	H	2B	3B	HR	TB	R	RBI	TBB	IBB	SO	HBP	SH	SF	SB	CS	SB%	GDP	Avg	OBP	SLG
1994 Bellingham	A- Sea	72	272	79	16	0	9	122	50	30	26	1	65	8	3	2	15	7	.68	6	.290	.367	.449
1995 Riverside	A+ Sea	116	407	102	16	8	6	152	56	45	49	1	98	16	3	7	13	10	.57	6	.251	.349	.373
1996 Wisconsin	A Sea	53	210	57	8	2	4	81	32	32	18	1	46	4	1	1	11	7	.61	5	.271	.339	.386
Lancaster	A+ Sea	48	174	48	10	1	5	75	30	22	16	0	31	3	1	1	7	1	.88	3	.276	.345	.431
1997 Lancaster	A+ Sea	68	263	88	23	5	8	145	59	38	41	1	51	8	3	2	15	10	.60	2	.335	.436	.551
Memphis	AA Sea	67	237	60	11	5	3	90	24	18	25	2	37	2	2	1	3	5	.38	6	.253	.328	.380
4 Min. YEARS		424	1563	434	84	21	35	665	251	185	175	6	328	41	13	14	64	40	.62	28	.278	.363	.425

Joe DeBerry

Bats: Left **Throws:** Left **Pos:** OF   **Ht:** 6'2" **Wt:** 195 **Born:** 6/30/70 **Age:** 28

		BATTING														BASERUNNING				PERCENTAGES		
Year Team	Lg Org	G	AB	H	2B	3B	HR	TB	R	RBI	TBB	IBB	SO	HBP	SH	SF	SB	CS	SB%	GDP	Avg	OBP	SLG
1991 Billings	R+ Cin	65	236	62	13	0	10	105	41	47	36	1	46	3	0	1	5	4	.56	4	.263	.366	.445
1992 Cedar Rapds	A Cin	127	455	109	22	4	15	184	58	68	43	1	102	2	0	3	3	3	.50	5	.240	.306	.404
1993 Albany-Colo	AA NYA	125	446	114	19	7	12	183	58	63	24	1	111	3	2	5	3	7	.30	6	.256	.295	.410
1994 Albany-Colo	AA NYA	15	53	15	4	1	0	21	3	3	5	0	11	0	0	0	0	1	.00	2	.283	.345	.396
1995 Columbus	AAA NYA	10	24	7	2	2	0	13	3	4	1	0	6	0	0	0	0	0	.00	0	.292	.320	.542
Norwich	AA NYA	2	4	0	0	0	0	0	0	0	0	0	2	0	0	0	0	0	.00	0	.000	.000	.000
Greensboro	A NYA	12	45	18	3	0	5	36	14	11	9	3	6	0	0	0	0	0	.00	0	.400	.500	.800
Tampa	A+ NYA	58	196	44	9	3	1	62	16	18	19	3	45	0	0	1	1	0	1.00	3	.224	.292	.316
1996 Norwich	AA NYA	9	26	4	0	0	0	4	1	6	0	0	7	0	0	0	0	0	.00	1	.154	.154	.154
Stockton	A+ Mil	54	190	51	7	2	7	83	33	25	23	0	55	1	0	3	3	0	1.00	6	.268	.346	.437
1997 Wichita	AA KC	30	82	20	5	0	1	28	9	5	10	3	20	1	0	0	3	0	1.00	0	.244	.333	.341
7 Min. YEARS		507	1757	444	84	19	51	719	236	250	170	12	411	10	2	13	18	15	.55	23	.253	.320	.409

Rob DeBoer

Bats: Right **Throws:** Right **Pos:** DH-C   **Ht:** 5'10" **Wt:** 205 **Born:** 2/4/71 **Age:** 27

		BATTING														BASERUNNING				PERCENTAGES		
Year Team	Lg Org	G	AB	H	2B	3B	HR	TB	R	RBI	TBB	IBB	SO	HBP	SH	SF	SB	CS	SB%	GDP	Avg	OBP	SLG
1994 Sou. Oregon	A- Oak	45	129	33	4	0	4	49	23	21	18	0	43	2	0	1	7	0	1.00	4	.256	.353	.380
1995 W Michigan	A Oak	104	339	82	25	2	6	129	57	50	58	1	110	4	1	4	11	6	.65	6	.242	.356	.381
1996 Modesto	A+ Oak	73	249	71	8	6	12	127	68	52	74	0	75	4	0	2	12	5	.71	5	.285	.453	.510
Huntsville	AA Oak	44	122	34	6	0	5	55	24	21	25	0	45	1	1	1	1	3	.25	3	.279	.403	.451
1997 Huntsville	AA Oak	91	288	70	16	1	18	142	55	48	60	3	111	7	3	1	8	5	.62	6	.243	.385	.493
4 Min. YEARS		357	1127	290	59	9	45	502	227	192	235	4	384	18	5	9	39	19	.67	24	.257	.391	.445

Steve Decker

Bats: Right **Throws:** Right **Pos:** C **Ht:** 6' 3" **Wt:** 220 **Born:** 10/25/65 **Age:** 32

Year Team	Lg Org	G	AB	H	2B	3B	HR	TB	R	RBI	TBB	IBB	SO	HBP	SH	SF	SB	CS	SB%	GDP	Avg	OBP	SLG
1988 Everett	A- SF	13	42	22	2	0	2	30	11	13	7	0	5	1	0	3	0	0	.00	1	.524	.566	.714
San Jose	A+ SF	47	175	56	9	0	4	77	31	34	21	1	21	1	1	0	0	0	.00	4	.320	.396	.440
1989 San Jose	A+ SF	64	225	65	12	0	3	86	27	46	44	3	36	0	0	5	8	5	.62	9	.289	.398	.382
Shreveport	AA SF	44	142	46	8	0	1	57	19	18	11	0	24	0	1	1	0	3	.00	5	.324	.370	.401
1990 Shreveport	AA SF	116	403	118	22	1	15	187	52	80	40	2	64	2	0	7	3	7	.30	11	.293	.354	.464
1991 Phoenix	AAA SF	31	111	28	5	1	6	53	20	14	13	0	29	1	0	0	0	0	.00	1	.252	.336	.477
1992 Phoenix	AAA SF	125	450	127	22	2	8	177	50	74	47	2	64	3	0	9	2	4	.33	19	.282	.348	.393
1994 Edmonton	AAA Fla	73	259	101	23	0	11	157	38	48	27	1	24	2	1	3	0	1	.00	7	.390	.447	.606
1996 Colo Spngs	AAA Col	7	25	10	1	0	0	11	4	3	4	1	3	1	0	0	0	0	.00	1	.400	.500	.440
1997 Tacoma	AAA Sea	99	350	104	25	1	10	161	44	52	22	0	37	1	0	5	0	0	.00	10	.297	.336	.460
1990 San Francisco	NL	15	54	16	2	0	3	27	5	8	1	0	10	0	1	0	0	0	.00	1	.296	.309	.500
1991 San Francisco	NL	79	233	48	7	1	5	72	11	24	16	1	44	3	2	4	0	1	.00	7	.206	.262	.309
1992 San Francisco	NL	15	43	7	1	0	0	8	3	1	6	0	7	1	0	0	0	0	.00	2	.163	.280	.186
1993 Florida	NL	8	15	0	0	0	0	0	0	1	3	0	3	0	0	1	0	0	.00	2	.000	.158	.000
1995 Florida	NL	51	133	30	2	1	3	43	12	13	19	1	22	0	0	2	1	0	1.00	1	.226	.318	.323
1996 San Francisco	NL	57	122	28	1	0	1	32	16	12	15	4	26	0	3	2	0	0	.00	3	.230	.309	.262
Colorado	NL	10	25	8	2	0	1	13	8	8	3	0	3	0	1	0	1	0	1.00	1	.320	.393	.520
8 Min. YEARS		619	2182	677	129	5	60	996	296	382	236	10	307	12	3	33	13	22	.37	68	.310	.376	.456
6 Maj. YEARS		235	625	137	15	2	13	195	55	67	63	6	115	4	7	9	2	1	.67	14	.219	.291	.312

Jon DeClue

Pitches: Left **Bats:** Right **Pos:** P **Ht:** 6'2" **Wt:** 198 **Born:** 9/17/70 **Age:** 27

Year Team	Lg Org	G	GS	CG	GF	IP	BFP	H	R	ER	HR	SH	SF	HB	TBB	IBB	SO	WP	Bk	W	L	Pct.	ShO	Sv	ERA
1994 Cedar Rapids	A Ana	22	3	0	9	62.1	271	67	28	26	4	1	1	4	13	2	56	6	2	6	1	.857	0	0	3.75
1995 Visalia	A+ Ana	21	14	0	3	103	421	95	48	40	11	3	2	3	27	0	91	3	1	6	5	.545	0	0	3.50
Lk Elsinore	A+ Ana	9	4	0	2	40.1	169	50	16	16	5	1	1	2	5	0	22	1	0	5	1	.833	0	0	3.57
1996 Midland	AA Ana	32	16	2	5	111.2	512	137	83	66	11	4	2	2	51	1	76	6	1	6	9	.400	0	0	5.32
1997 Jackson	AA Hou	9	0	0	5	8.1	48	13	13	12	2	1	0	1	11	2	7	2	0	0	2	.000	0	0	12.96
Kissimmee	A+ Hou	7	0	0	5	15	64	10	4	3	2	0	1	1	9	0	13	0	0	2	0	1.000	0	0	1.80
4 Min. YEARS		100	36	2	27	340.2	1485	372	192	163	35	10	7	13	116	5	264	18	4	25	18	.581	0	0	4.31

Jim Dedrick

Pitches: Right **Bats:** Both **Pos:** P **Ht:** 6' 0" **Wt:** 185 **Born:** 4/4/68 **Age:** 30

Year Team	Lg Org	G	GS	CG	GF	IP	BFP	H	R	ER	HR	SH	SF	HB	TBB	IBB	SO	WP	Bk	W	L	Pct.	ShO	Sv	ERA
1990 Wausau	A Bal	3	1	0	1	10	41	6	4	3	0	0	0	0	4	0	8	0	3	1	0	.000	0	0	2.70
1991 Kane County	A Bal	16	15	0	0	88.1	380	84	38	29	2	1	2	5	38	1	71	5	2	4	5	.444	0	0	2.95
1992 Frederick	A+ Bal	38	5	1	19	108.2	454	94	41	37	5	5	0	5	42	4	86	4	3	8	4	.667	0	3	3.06
1993 Bowie	AA Bal	38	6	1	14	106.1	426	84	36	30	4	5	0	3	32	1	78	1	0	8	3	.727	1	3	2.54
Rochester	AAA Bal	1	1	1	0	7	27	6	2	2	2	0	0	0	0	0	3	0	0	1	0	1.000	0	0	2.57
1994 Rochester	AAA Bal	44	1	0	18	99	421	98	56	42	7	3	1	3	35	7	70	4	1	3	6	.333	0	1	3.82
1995 Bowie	AA Bal	10	10	0	0	60.1	267	59	24	20	7	2	2	5	25	2	48	5	1	4	2	.667	0	0	2.98
Rochester	AAA Bal	24	2	0	4	45.2	190	45	9	9	0	2	4	1	14	1	31	4	0	4	0	1.000	0	1	1.77
1996 Rochester	AAA Bal	39	3	0	20	66.1	316	88	59	48	14	2	4	1	41	0	37	5	1	6	3	.667	0	4	6.51
Bowie	AA Bal	13	0	0	4	26.2	116	28	10	10	3	1	0	0	14	1	21	1	0	1	1	.500	0	0	3.38
1997 Harrisburg	AA Mon	15	0	0	7	19.1	78	18	8	6	1	1	0	0	8	0	17	0	1	2	1	.667	0	1	2.79
Ottawa	AAA Mon	8	0	0	2	14	68	15	12	11	2	1	0	0	13	0	14	0	0	0	1	.000	0	0	7.07
Tulsa	AA Tex	12	0	0	2	23	100	26	9	6	0	0	1	0	9	0	16	5	0	1	0	1.000	0	0	2.35
Okla City	AAA Tex	8	0	0	4	10.2	57	16	7	7	0	0	0	0	10	0	2	1	0	0	0	.000	0	3	5.91
1995 Baltimore	AL	6	0	0	1	7.2	35	8	2	2	1	0	2	1	6	0	3	0	0	0	0	.000	0	0	2.35
8 Min. YEARS		269	44	3	95	685.1	2941	667	315	260	47	23	14	23	285	17	502	35	12	42	27	.609	1	16	3.41

Alex Delgado

Bats: Right **Throws:** Right **Pos:** C **Ht:** 6' 0" **Wt:** 160 **Born:** 1/11/71 **Age:** 27

Year Team	Lg Org	G	AB	H	2B	3B	HR	TB	R	RBI	TBB	IBB	SO	HBP	SH	SF	SB	CS	SB%	GDP	Avg	OBP	SLG
1988 R.S./Marnrs	R Bos	34	111	39	10	0	0	49	11	22	6	0	5	1	3	2	2	4	.33	1	.351	.383	.441
1989 Winter Havn	A+ Bos	78	285	64	7	0	0	71	27	16	17	0	30	1	5	0	7	3	.70	9	.225	.271	.249
1990 New Britain	AA Bos	7	18	1	1	0	0	2	3	0	2	0	5	0	0	0	0	0	.00	1	.056	.150	.111
Winter Havn	A+ Bos	89	303	68	9	2	1	84	37	25	37	0	37	3	5	3	10	4	.71	7	.224	.312	.277
1991 Lynchburg	A+ Bos	61	179	38	8	0	0	46	21	17	16	0	19	2	1	1	2	1	.67	6	.212	.283	.257

Year Team	Lg Org	G	AB	H	2B	3B	HR	TB	R	RBI	TBB	IBB	SO	HBP	SH	SF	SB	CS	SB%	GDP	Avg	OBP	SLG
1992 Winter Havn	A+ Bos	56	167	35	2	0	2	43	11	12	16	0	11	1	4	1	1	1	.50	6	.210	.281	.257
1993 Ft. Laud	A+ Bos	63	225	57	9	0	2	72	26	25	9	1	21	5	7	1	2	2	.50	4	.253	.296	.320
New Britain	AA Bos	33	87	16	2	0	1	21	10	9	4	0	11	4	4	2	1	1	.50	5	.184	.247	.241
1994 Red Sox	R Bos	7	24	4	1	0	0	5	3	7	2	1	2	2	0	1	0	0	.00	0	.167	.276	.208
New Britain	AA Bos	40	140	36	3	0	2	45	16	12	4	0	21	2	1	1	1	1	.50	7	.257	.286	.321
1995 Pawtucket	AAA Bos	44	107	27	3	0	5	45	14	12	6	0	12	1	0	0	0	0	.00	4	.252	.298	.421
Trenton	AA Bos	23	72	24	1	0	3	34	13	14	9	0	8	3	1	1	0	0	.00	2	.333	.424	.472
1996 Trenton	AA Bos	21	81	18	4	0	3	31	7	14	9	1	8	1	1	1	1	0	1.00	1	.222	.304	.383
Pawtucket	AAA Bos	27	88	19	3	0	1	25	15	6	7	0	11	0	0	0	0	0	.00	5	.216	.274	.284
1997 Charlotte	AAA Fla	14	38	8	1	0	0	9	1	6	3	0	7	0	3	1	0	0	.00	1	.211	.262	.237
1996 Boston	AL	26	20	5	0	0	0	5	5	1	3	0	3	0	1	0	0	0	.00	0	.250	.348	.250
10 Min. YEARS		597	1925	454	64	2	20	582	215	197	147	3	208	26	35	15	27	17	.61	58	.236	.297	.302

Nick Delvecchio

Bats: Left **Throws:** Right **Pos:** DH **Ht:** 6'5" **Wt:** 203 **Born:** 1/23/70 **Age:** 28

Year Team	Lg Org	G	AB	H	2B	3B	HR	TB	R	RBI	TBB	IBB	SO	HBP	SH	SF	SB	CS	SB%	GDP	Avg	OBP	SLG
1992 Oneonta	A- NYA	68	241	66	12	1	12	116	43	35	35	3	76	8	1	0	0	1	.00	3	.274	.384	.481
1993 Greensboro	A NYA	137	485	131	30	3	21	230	90	80	80	9	156	23	0	2	4	3	.57	9	.270	.397	.474
1994 Yankees	R NYA	4	13	5	0	0	0	5	1	0	2	0	3	0	0	0	0	0	.00	0	.385	.467	.385
Tampa	A+ NYA	27	95	27	3	0	7	51	17	18	11	0	20	1	0	1	0	0	.00	0	.284	.361	.537
1995 Norwich	AA NYA	125	430	112	23	4	19	200	66	74	72	8	133	23	0	6	2	1	.67	6	.260	.390	.465
1996 Columbus	AAA NYA	2	1	1	0	0	0	1	0	0	3	0	0	0	0	0	0	0	.00	0	1.000	1.000	1.000
Yankees	R NYA	5	18	11	4	0	2	21	4	8	6	0	1	1	0	0	1	0	1.00	1	.611	.720	1.167
Tampa	A+ NYA	17	52	14	2	0	2	22	9	4	17	1	15	3	0	0	2	1	.67	2	.269	.472	.423
Norwich	AA NYA	12	36	10	3	0	2	19	7	7	6	0	9	5	0	0	1	0	1.00	2	.278	.447	.528
1997 Columbus	AAA NYA	31	95	17	1	1	4	32	16	10	17	0	39	1	0	0	1	0	1.00	3	.179	.310	.337
6 Min. YEARS		428	1466	394	78	9	69	697	253	236	249	21	452	65	1	9	11	6	.65	26	.269	.396	.475

Chris Demetral

Bats: Left **Throws:** Right **Pos:** 2B **Ht:** 5'11" **Wt:** 175 **Born:** 12/8/69 **Age:** 28

Year Team	Lg Org	G	AB	H	2B	3B	HR	TB	R	RBI	TBB	IBB	SO	HBP	SH	SF	SB	CS	SB%	GDP	Avg	OBP	SLG
1991 Yakima	A- LA	65	226	64	11	0	2	81	43	41	34	2	32	1	6	0	4	3	.57	2	.283	.379	.358
1992 Bakersfield	A+ LA	90	306	84	14	1	4	112	38	36	33	7	45	1	4	3	7	8	.47	3	.275	.344	.366
1993 Vero Beach	A+ LA	122	437	142	22	3	5	185	63	48	69	2	47	2	6	3	6	6	.50	9	.325	.417	.423
1994 San Antonio	AA LA	108	368	96	26	3	6	146	44	39	34	5	44	1	11	2	5	2	.71	8	.261	.323	.397
1995 Albuquerque	AAA LA	87	187	52	7	1	3	70	34	19	24	2	28	0	3	0	1	6	.14	7	.278	.360	.374
1996 San Berndno	A+ LA	11	32	9	3	0	1	15	5	4	6	1	5	0	0	0	0	3	.00	0	.281	.395	.469
Albuquerque	AAA LA	99	209	55	8	0	4	75	30	26	40	5	35	0	5	5	4	3	.57	6	.263	.374	.359
1997 Albuquerque	AAA LA	12	24	6	2	0	1	11	1	1	6	0	3	0	0	0	1	0	1.00	1	.250	.400	.458
Vero Beach	A+ LA	86	278	77	13	3	12	132	52	45	48	0	40	2	2	4	5	2	.71	6	.277	.383	.475
7 Min. YEARS		680	2067	585	106	11	38	827	310	259	294	24	279	7	37	17	32	34	.48	42	.283	.371	.400

Les Dennis

Bats: Right **Throws:** Right **Pos:** SS **Ht:** 6'0" **Wt:** 175 **Born:** 6/3/73 **Age:** 25

Year Team	Lg Org	G	AB	H	2B	3B	HR	TB	R	RBI	TBB	IBB	SO	HBP	SH	SF	SB	CS	SB%	GDP	Avg	OBP	SLG
1995 Oneonta	A- NYA	48	148	39	6	1	1	52	24	13	14	0	40	3	0	2	5	2	.71	4	.264	.335	.351
1996 Greensboro	A NYA	33	75	19	3	0	1	25	15	9	11	0	27	1	2	0	1	2	.33	2	.253	.356	.333
Oneonta	A- NYA	72	276	67	3	2	0	74	36	43	33	1	76	1	5	6	20	9	.69	2	.243	.320	.268
1997 Norwich	AA NYA	10	30	10	1	0	0	11	4	2	5	0	11	0	2	0	1	1	.50	0	.333	.429	.367
Tampa	A+ NYA	85	177	46	4	0	0	50	24	17	16	0	36	1	6	1	1	6	.14	6	.260	.323	.282
3 Min. YEARS		248	706	181	17	4	2	212	103	84	79	1	190	6	15	9	28	20	.58	14	.256	.333	.300

Joe DePastino

Bats: Right **Throws:** Right **Pos:** C **Ht:** 6'2" **Wt:** 210 **Born:** 9/4/73 **Age:** 24

Year Team	Lg Org	G	AB	H	2B	3B	HR	TB	R	RBI	TBB	IBB	SO	HBP	SH	SF	SB	CS	SB%	GDP	Avg	OBP	SLG
1992 Red Sox	R Bos	40	157	41	6	1	1	52	13	16	7	1	25	3	0	2	1	1	.50	7	.261	.302	.331
1993 Utica	A- Bos	62	221	56	9	1	2	73	28	32	16	0	51	4	1	5	3	2	.60	4	.253	.309	.330
1994 Utica	A- Bos	51	172	46	11	1	5	74	23	31	22	1	41	3	1	2	5	2	.71	1	.267	.357	.430
1995 Michigan	A Bos	98	325	90	20	4	10	148	47	53	30	1	70	8	0	5	3	3	.50	5	.277	.348	.455
1996 Sarasota	A+ Bos	97	344	90	16	2	6	128	35	44	29	1	71	3	0	4	2	3	.40	7	.262	.321	.372
1997 Trenton	AA Bos	79	276	70	14	1	17	137	51	55	32	0	63	7	0	1	1	2	.33	10	.254	.345	.496
6 Min. YEARS		427	1495	393	76	10	41	612	197	231	136	4	321	28	2	19	15	13	.54	34	.263	.332	.409

Tony DeRosso

Bats: Right **Throws:** Right **Pos:** 3B **Ht:** 6'3" **Wt:** 215 **Born:** 11/7/75 **Age:** 22

Year Team	Lg Org	G	AB	H	2B	3B	HR	TB	R	RBI	TBB	IBB	SO	HBP	SH	SF	SB	CS	SB%	GDP	Avg	OBP	SLG
1994 Red Sox	R Bos	46	168	42	6	0	4	60	23	22	12	0	33	5	0	3	1	0	1.00	2	.250	.314	.357
1995 Michigan	A Bos	106	382	89	20	1	13	150	57	50	38	2	93	11	1	2	9	1	.90	5	.233	.319	.393
1996 Sarasota	A+ Bos	116	416	107	19	5	14	178	64	60	31	2	84	8	2	5	15	2	.88	10	.257	.317	.428
1997 Trenton	AA Bos	102	357	77	18	1	14	139	50	40	26	0	94	2	3	2	13	1	.93	5	.216	.271	.389

		BATTING						BASERUNNING	PERCENTAGES
Year Team	Lg Org	G AB H	2B 3B HR TB	R RBI	TBB IBB SO	HBP SH SF	SB CS SB% GDP	Avg OBP SLG
4 Min. YEARS		370 1323 315	63 7 45 527	194 172	107 4 304	26 6 12	38 4 .90 22	.238 .305 .398

Kris Detmers

Pitches: Left Bats: Both Pos: P   **Ht: 6'5" Wt: 215 Born: 6/22/74 Age: 24**

		HOW MUCH HE PITCHED		WHAT HE GAVE UP		THE RESULTS
Year Team	Lg Org	G GS CG GF	IP BFP	H R ER HR SH SF HB	TBB IBB SO WP Bk	W L Pct. ShO Sv ERA
1994 Madison	A StL	16 16 0 0	90.1 380	88 45 34 4 1 1 4	31 0 74 0 1	5 7 .417 0 0 3.39
1995 St. Pete	A+ StL	25 25 1 0	146.2 606	120 64 53 12 3 7 2	57 0 150 3 2	10 9 .526 0 0 3.25
1996 Arkansas	AA StL	27 27 0 0	163.2 698	154 72 61 15 6 3 4	70 0 97 8 0	12 8 .600 0 0 3.35
1997 Louisville	AAA StL	10 5 0 0	35 164	43 28 28 3 0 2 2	17 0 22 1 0	3 3 .500 0 0 7.20
Arkansas	AA StL	15 15 0 0	78 346	99 54 50 11 3 2 2	27 0 44 1 0	5 7 .417 0 0 5.77
4 Min. YEARS		93 88 1 0	513.2 2194	504 263 226 45 13 15 14	202 0 387 13 3	35 34 .507 0 0 3.96

Cesar Devarez

Bats: Right Throws: Right Pos: C   **Ht: 5'10" Wt: 175 Born: 9/22/69 Age: 28**

		BATTING						BASERUNNING	PERCENTAGES
Year Team	Lg Org	G AB H	2B 3B HR TB	R RBI	TBB IBB SO	HBP SH SF	SB CS SB% GDP	Avg OBP SLG
1989 Bluefield	R+ Bal	12 42 9	4 0 0 13	3 7	1 0 5	0 0 0	0 0 .00 3	.214 .233 .310
1990 Wausau	A Bal	56 171 34	4 1 3 49	7 19	7 0 28	0 0 2	2 3 .40 3	.199 .230 .287
1991 Frederick	A+ Bal	74 235 59	13 2 3 85	25 29	14 0 28	4 2 1	2 2 .50 9	.251 .303 .362
1992 Hagerstown	AA Bal	110 319 72	8 1 2 88	20 32	17 0 49	6 2 2	2 5 .29 3	.226 .276 .276
1993 Frederick	A+ Bal	38 124 36	8 0 2 50	15 16	12 1 18	1 1 0	1 4 .20 2	.290 .358 .403
Bowie	AA Bal	57 174 39	7 1 0 48	14 15	5 0 21	2 2 0	5 1 .83 6	.224 .251 .276
1994 Bowie	AA Bal	73 249 78	13 4 6 117	43 48	8 1 25	1 3 4	7 2 .78 10	.313 .332 .470
1995 Rochester	AAA Bal	67 240 60	12 1 1 77	32 21	7 0 25	0 1 1	2 2 .50 8	.250 .270 .321
1996 Rochester	AAA Bal	67 223 64	9 1 4 87	24 27	9 0 26	1 2 4	5 1 .83 7	.287 .312 .390
1997 Devil Rays	R TB	4 6 0	0 0 0 0	0 0	4 0 2	0 0 0	0 0 .00 0	.000 .400 .000
Orlando	AA ChN	34 96 27	4 1 5 48	13 17	8 2 15	0 1 0	1 0 1.00 2	.281 .337 .500
1995 Baltimore	AL	6 4 0	0 0 0 0	0 0	0 0 1	0 0 0	0 0 .00 0	.000 .000 .000
1996 Baltimore	AL	10 18 2	1 0 1 4	3 0	1 0 3	0 0 0	0 0 .00 0	.111 .158 .222
9 Min. YEARS		592 1879 478	82 12 26 662	196 231	92 4 242	15 16 14	27 20 .57 53	.254 .293 .352
2 Maj. YEARS		16 22 2	1 0 1 4	3 0	1 0 3	0 1 0	0 0 .00 0	.091 .130 .182

Cesar Diaz

Bats: Right Throws: Right Pos: C   **Ht: 6'3" Wt: 185 Born: 7/12/74 Age: 23**

		BATTING						BASERUNNING	PERCENTAGES
Year Team	Lg Org	G AB H	2B 3B HR TB	R RBI	TBB IBB SO	HBP SH SF	SB CS SB% GDP	Avg OBP SLG
1991 Kingsport	R+ NYN	38 125 29	6 0 1 38	11 15	7 0 37	2 1 0	0 4 .00 1	.232 .284 .304
1992 Columbia	A NYN	16 62 12	0 1 0 14	4 6	2 0 21	0 0 0	2 0 1.00 0	.194 .219 .226
Pittsfield	A- NYN	66 226 47	9 4 5 79	32 25	27 2 86	4 0 4	4 1 .80 5	.208 .299 .350
1993 Kingsport	R+ NYN	55 211 69	12 1 11 116	36 37	15 2 41	6 0 1	1 0 1.00 2	.327 .386 .550
Pittsfield	A- NYN	14 48 9	1 0 0 10	6 8	3 0 11	0 0 2	4 0 1.00 2	.188 .226 .208
1994 Capital City	A NYN	66 225 55	13 1 7 91	26 27	21 0 46	5 0 2	3 2 .60 3	.244 .320 .404
1995 St. Lucie	A+ NYN	102 361 84	17 2 6 123	33 40	19 1 91	2 3 1	0 5 .00 13	.233 .274 .341
Norfolk	AAA NYN	3 11 2	0 0 0 2	2 0	0 0 2	0 0 0	0 0 .00 0	.182 .182 .182
Binghamton	AA NYN	13 47 8	2 0 0 10	5 5	6 0 20	0 0 0	1 0 1.00 0	.170 .264 .213
1996 St. Lucie	A+ NYN	74 247 59	15 1 7 97	29 34	18 1 72	3 0 3	9 2 .82 12	.239 .295 .393
1997 Knoxville	AA Tor	7 15 3	1 0 1 7	2 3	5 0 2	0 0 0	0 0 .00 0	.200 .400 .467
Dunedin	A+ Tor	108 379 110	23 1 12 171	50 56	36 2 108	0 5 3	4 7 .36 5	.290 .349 .451
7 Min. YEARS		562 1957 487	99 11 50 758	236 256	159 8 537	22 9 16	26 23 .53 48	.249 .310 .387

Edwin Diaz

Bats: Right Throws: Right Pos: 2B   **Ht: 5'11" Wt: 170 Born: 1/15/75 Age: 23**

		BATTING						BASERUNNING	PERCENTAGES
Year Team	Lg Org	G AB H	2B 3B HR TB	R RBI	TBB IBB SO	HBP SH SF	SB CS SB% GDP	Avg OBP SLG
1993 Rangers	R Tex	43 154 47	10 5 1 70	27 23	19 1 21	4 0 2	12 5 .71 4	.305 .391 .455
1994 Chston-SC	A Tex	122 413 109	22 7 11 178	52 60	22 0 107	8 8 9	11 14 .44 7	.264 .308 .431
1995 Charlotte	A+ Tex	115 450 128	26 5 8 188	46 55	33 0 94	7 3 2	8 13 .38 10	.284 .341 .418
1996 Tulsa	AA Tex	121 499 132	33 6 16 225	70 65	25 4 122	9 8 4	8 9 .47 9	.265 .309 .451
1997 Okla City	AAA Tex	20 73 8	3 1 1 16	6 4	2 0 27	2 1 0	1 1 .50 1	.110 .156 .219
Tulsa	AA Tex	105 440 121	31 1 15 199	65 46	33 0 102	8 2 2	6 9 .40 6	.275 .335 .452
5 Min. YEARS		526 2029 545	125 25 52 876	268 254	134 5 473	38 22 19	46 51 .47 37	.269 .323 .432

Freddie Diaz

Bats: Both Throws: Right Pos: SS   **Ht: 5'11" Wt: 175 Born: 9/10/72 Age: 25**

		BATTING						BASERUNNING	PERCENTAGES
Year Team	Lg Org	G AB H	2B 3B HR TB	R RBI	TBB IBB SO	HBP SH SF	SB CS SB% GDP	Avg OBP SLG
1992 Angels	R Ana	14 37 10	3 0 0 13	6 4	5 0 7	0 2 1	3 1 .75 0	.270 .349 .351
1993 Boise	A- Ana	26 75 22	4 1 2 34	13 14	9 0 11	0 3 0	1 3 .25 0	.293 .369 .453
1994 Lk Elsinore	A+ Ana	110 350 100	29 1 5 146	48 64	35 0 71	4 7 6	4 4 .50 5	.286 .352 .417
1995 Midland	AA Ana	8 25 6	3 0 0 9	3 4	0 0 12	0 2 1	0 0 .00 1	.240 .240 .360
Lk Elsinore	A+ Ana	49 149 35	12 2 1 54	25 25	11 0 54	0 3 6	1 1 .50 3	.235 .277 .362
1996 Midland	AA Ana	54 156 31	7 2 3 51	23 18	13 1 43	0 4 3	1 1 .50 2	.199 .256 .327
Vancouver	AAA Ana	34 123 32	9 2 3 54	19 23	14 0 25	0 3 3	0 0 .00 1	.260 .329 .439
1997 Midland	AA Ana	43 135 36	9 0 2 51	21 18	18 0 30	1 2 2	0 0 .00 3	.267 .353 .378

			BATTING														BASERUNNING				PERCENTAGES		
Year Team	Lg Org	G	AB	H	2B	3B	HR	TB	R	RBI	TBB	IBB	SO	HBP	SH	SF	SB	CS	SB%	GDP	Avg	OBP	SLG
6 Min. YEARS		338	1050	272	76	8	16	412	158	170	105	1	253	5	26	21	10	10	.50	19	.259	.323	.392

Lino Diaz

Bats: Right **Throws:** Right **Pos:** 3B   **Ht:** 5'11" **Wt:** 182 **Born:** 7/22/70 **Age:** 27

			BATTING														BASERUNNING				PERCENTAGES		
Year Team	Lg Org	G	AB	H	2B	3B	HR	TB	R	RBI	TBB	IBB	SO	HBP	SH	SF	SB	CS	SB%	GDP	Avg	OBP	SLG
1993 Eugene	A- KC	53	183	46	7	1	1	58	19	23	13	0	25	3	2	4	6	2	.75	2	.251	.305	.317
1994 Rockford	A KC	127	414	131	23	1	4	168	57	44	32	4	33	14	2	5	11	6	.65	14	.316	.381	.406
1995 Wilmington	A+ KC	51	173	52	6	2	2	68	20	23	11	0	9	4	2	0	0	5	.00	2	.301	.356	.393
Wichita	AA KC	62	226	79	15	3	6	118	40	43	14	0	21	6	0	1	0	3	.00	1	.350	.401	.522
1996 Omaha	AAA KC	75	266	72	13	2	3	98	32	28	17	0	29	6	1	1	0	3	.00	9	.271	.328	.368
Wichita	AA KC	44	159	40	8	1	3	59	18	19	9	0	11	2	0	0	2	1	.67	1	.252	.300	.371
1997 Wichita	AA KC	92	289	82	26	3	2	120	36	51	23	0	27	7	3	3	3	6	.33	7	.284	.348	.415
5 Min. YEARS		504	1710	502	98	13	21	689	222	231	119	4	155	42	10	14	22	26	.46	46	.294	.352	.403

John Dillinger

Pitches: Right **Bats:** Right **Pos:** P   **Ht:** 6'6" **Wt:** 230 **Born:** 8/28/73 **Age:** 24

		HOW MUCH HE PITCHED						WHAT HE GAVE UP										THE RESULTS					
Year Team	Lg Org	G	GS	CG	GF	IP	BFP	H	R	ER	HR	SH	SF	HB	TBB	IBB	SO	WP	Bk	W	L	Pct.	ShO	Sv	ERA
1992 Pirates	R Pit	13	10	0	1	52.1	250	43	37	20	1	0	5	6	42	0	45	6	2	3	3	.500	0	1	3.44
1993 Lethbridge	R+ Pit	15	15	3	0	80.1	367	65	55	35	2	3	5	5	60	1	94	9	3	3	10	.231	0	0	3.92
1994 Augusta	A Pit	23	22	1	1	119.2	524	107	77	57	5	6	2	3	54	1	118	8	5	5	9	.357	0	0	4.29
1995 Lynchburg	A+ Pit	27	22	0	1	123	540	111	62	55	10	5	5	7	67	4	97	9	7	6	6	.500	0	0	4.02
1996 Lynchburg	A+ Pit	33	15	2	0	132.1	554	101	65	55	11	3	3	4	58	0	113	11	1	10	5	.667	0	0	3.74
1997 Carolina	AA Pit	23	11	0	3	81	382	88	66	54	8	3	4	5	52	0	64	7	1	6	4	.600	0	1	6.00
6 Min. YEARS		134	95	6	6	588.2	2617	515	358	276	37	20	24	30	333	6	531	50	19	33	37	.471	0	1	4.22

Mike Diorio

Pitches: Right **Bats:** Right **Pos:** P   **Ht:** 6'1" **Wt:** 170 **Born:** 3/1/73 **Age:** 25

		HOW MUCH HE PITCHED						WHAT HE GAVE UP										THE RESULTS					
Year Team	Lg Org	G	GS	CG	GF	IP	BFP	H	R	ER	HR	SH	SF	HB	TBB	IBB	SO	WP	Bk	W	L	Pct.	ShO	Sv	ERA
1993 Auburn	A- Hou	15	15	0	0	79	356	98	57	45	6	2	2	3	27	0	57	6	0	3	7	.300	0	0	5.13
1994 Astros	R Hou	2	0	0	0	2.1	15	5	6	6	1	0	0	0	3	0	2	0	0	0	1	.000	0	0	23.14
Osceola	A+ Hou	13	7	0	0	44	191	48	24	14	4	1	2	0	11	0	27	2	0	3	2	.600	0	0	2.86
1995 Quad City	A Hou	33	11	0	4	91.2	391	82	39	33	6	4	0	4	36	1	81	13	2	6	4	.600	0	1	3.24
1997 Jackson	AA Hou	8	0	0	2	11.1	63	18	17	12	1	1	0	2	6	1	9	1	2	1	3	.250	0	1	9.53
Kissimmee	A+ Hou	36	0	0	30	39.1	161	33	15	13	1	1	0	1	10	1	30	1	1	3	2	.600	0	19	2.97
4 Min. YEARS		107	33	0	36	267.2	1177	284	158	123	19	9	4	10	93	3	206	23	5	16	19	.457	0	21	4.14

Jamie Dismuke

Bats: Left **Throws:** Right **Pos:** 1B   **Ht:** 6'1" **Wt:** 210 **Born:** 10/17/69 **Age:** 28

			BATTING														BASERUNNING				PERCENTAGES		
Year Team	Lg Org	G	AB	H	2B	3B	HR	TB	R	RBI	TBB	IBB	SO	HBP	SH	SF	SB	CS	SB%	GDP	Avg	OBP	SLG
1989 Reds	R Cin	34	98	18	1	0	1	22	6	5	8	2	19	3	0	0	0	1	.00	4	.184	.266	.224
1990 Reds	R Cin	39	124	44	8	4	7	81	22	28	28	5	8	5	0	2	3	3	.50	4	.355	.484	.653
1991 Cedar Rapds	A Cin	133	492	125	35	1	8	186	56	72	50	3	80	4	2	9	4	2	.67	10	.254	.323	.378
1992 Chston-WV	A Cin	134	475	135	22	0	17	208	77	71	67	5	71	15	3	5	3	4	.43	15	.284	.386	.438
1993 Chattanooga	AA Cin	136	497	152	22	1	20	236	69	91	48	6	60	14	0	4	2	6	.25	11	.306	.380	.475
1994 Indianapols	AAA Cin	121	391	104	22	0	13	165	51	49	47	6	52	7	2	2	1	0	1.00	13	.266	.353	.422
1995 Indianapols	AAA Cin	13	36	9	1	0	0	10	6	2	3	1	3	0	0	0	0	0	.00	1	.250	.308	.278
Chattanooga	AA Cin	99	347	99	11	0	20	170	56	69	44	10	45	10	0	1	0	0	.00	11	.285	.381	.490
1996 Syracuse	AAA Tor	19	42	7	1	0	0	8	3	5	5	0	5	0	0	1	0	1	1.00	1	.167	.250	.190
Jacksnville	AA Det	29	79	21	4	1	4	39	7	12	14	2	14	2	0	0	0	0	.00	3	.266	.389	.494
1997 Chattanooga	AA Cin	36	98	28	5	0	4	45	21	25	18	0	10	2	0	1	0	1	.00	0	.286	.407	.459
9 Min. YEARS		793	2679	742	132	7	94	1170	374	429	332	40	367	62	7	24	16	13	.55	68	.277	.367	.437

Bubba Dixon

Pitches: Left **Bats:** Right **Pos:** P   **Ht:** 5'10" **Wt:** 165 **Born:** 1/7/72 **Age:** 26

		HOW MUCH HE PITCHED						WHAT HE GAVE UP										THE RESULTS					
Year Team	Lg Org	G	GS	CG	GF	IP	BFP	H	R	ER	HR	SH	SF	HB	TBB	IBB	SO	WP	Bk	W	L	Pct.	ShO	Sv	ERA
1994 Spokane	A- SD	32	0	0	26	45.1	189	31	8	6	0	1	3	1	24	5	81	2	0	2	1	.667	0	11	1.19
1995 Rancho Cuca	A+ SD	47	12	2	15	141.2	572	118	61	51	14	5	1	8	46	0	133	6	2	10	7	.588	0	5	3.24
1996 Memphis	AA SD	42	0	0	12	63.1	267	53	32	29	6	2	1	2	28	2	77	4	1	2	3	.400	0	4	4.12
Rancho Cuca	A+ SD	11	0	0	3	16.1	73	20	16	13	3	0	1	0	4	0	20	1	0	0	0	.000	0	0	7.16
1997 Mobile	AA SD	56	0	0	25	75.2	329	67	31	29	4	6	3	1	37	3	88	11	1	7	2	.778	0	1	3.45
4 Min. YEARS		188	12	2	81	342.1	1430	289	148	128	27	14	9	12	139	10	399	24	4	21	16	.568	0	20	3.37

Tim Dixon

Pitches: Left **Bats:** Left **Pos:** P   **Ht:** 6'2" **Wt:** 215 **Born:** 2/26/72 **Age:** 26

		HOW MUCH HE PITCHED						WHAT HE GAVE UP										THE RESULTS					
Year Team	Lg Org	G	GS	CG	GF	IP	BFP	H	R	ER	HR	SH	SF	HB	TBB	IBB	SO	WP	Bk	W	L	Pct.	ShO	Sv	ERA
1995 Vermont	A- Mon	18	9	0	4	69	287	58	20	14	0	3	0	8	16	0	58	5	7	7	2	.778	0	1	1.83
1996 Wst Plm Bch	A+ Mon	37	16	0	8	124	528	126	55	40	10	8	5	6	35	3	87	7	0	5	11	.313	0	2	2.90
1997 Ottawa	AAA Mon	5	0	0	1	9.1	45	12	10	10	2	1	1	0	5	1	8	2	0	1	1	.500	0	0	9.64

		HOW MUCH HE PITCHED		WHAT HE GAVE UP			THE RESULTS		
Year Team	Lg Org	G GS CG GF	IP BFP	H R ER	HR SH SF HB	TBB IBB	SO	WP Bk	W L	Pct.	ShO Sv	ERA
Harrisburg	AA Mon	37 2 0 6	69.1 296	66 34 26	6 4 3 4	24 2	75	4 0	5 2	.714	0 0	3.38
3 Min. YEARS		97 27 0 17	271.2 1156	262 119 90	18 16 9 18	80 6	228	18 7	18 16	.529	0 3	2.98

Bill Dobrolsky

Bats: Right **Throws:** Right **Pos:** C   **Ht:** 6'2" **Wt:** 205 **Born:** 3/16/70 **Age:** 28

		BATTING													BASERUNNING				PERCENTAGES		
Year Team	Lg Org	G	AB	H	2B	3B	HR	TB	R	RBI	TBB	IBB	SO	HBP	SH	SF	SB	CS	SB%	GDP	Avg	OBP	SLG
1991 Brewers	R Mil	5	23	7	4	0	0	11	3	5	0	0	3	1	0	0	0	0	.00	0	.304	.333	.478
Helena	R+ Mil	9	31	5	2	0	0	7	2	2	3	0	7	0	0	0	0	0	.00	0	.161	.235	.226
1992 Denver	AAA Mil	1	1	0	0	0	0	0	0	0	0	0	0	0	0	0	0	0	.00	0	.000	.000	.000
Helena	R+ Mil	11	29	7	3	0	0	10	4	4	5	0	8	0	0	0	0	1	.00	1	.241	.353	.345
Beloit	A Mil	48	133	38	5	0	3	52	13	19	14	0	28	1	1	1	3	2	.60	4	.286	.356	.391
1993 Stockton	A+ Mil	67	190	40	2	0	1	45	18	21	16	0	43	5	2	1	2	1	.67	4	.211	.288	.237
1994 Beloit	A Mil	72	197	52	12	0	3	73	29	25	35	0	55	3	5	0	1	1	.50	4	.264	.383	.371
1995 Stockton	A+ Mil	88	252	68	14	3	2	94	28	30	25	0	37	6	2	5	3	4	.43	4	.270	.344	.373
1996 El Paso	AA Mil	68	202	57	11	1	2	76	26	21	17	0	37	5	3	3	1	4	.20	5	.282	.348	.376
1997 El Paso	AA Mil	102	303	80	23	0	5	118	44	45	38	0	63	8	6	2	1	3	.25	7	.264	.359	.389
7 Min. YEARS		471	1361	354	76	4	16	486	167	172	153	0	281	29	19	12	11	16	.41	29	.260	.345	.357

Robert Dodd

Pitches: Left **Bats:** Left **Pos:** P   **Ht:** 6'3" **Wt:** 195 **Born:** 3/14/73 **Age:** 25

		HOW MUCH HE PITCHED				WHAT HE GAVE UP									THE RESULTS				
Year Team	Lg Org	G	GS	CG	GF	IP	BFP	H	R	ER	HR	SH	SF	HB	TBB	IBB	SO	WP	Bk	W	L	Pct.	ShO	Sv	ERA
1994 Batavia	A- Phi	14	7	0	2	52	209	42	16	13	0	2	1	2	14	1	44	4	0	2	4	.333	0	1	2.25
1995 Clearwater	A+ Phi	26	26	0	0	151	636	144	64	53	4	3	6	1	58	0	110	3	7	8	7	.533	0	0	3.16
Reading	AA Phi	1	0	0	0	1.1	5	0	0	0	0	0	0	0	2	0	0	0	0	0	0	.000	0	0	0.00
1996 Reading	AA Phi	18	5	0	4	43	185	41	21	17	4	4	3	3	24	2	35	0	1	2	3	.400	0	0	3.56
Scranton-WB	AAA Phi	8	2	0	2	20	101	32	21	18	4	0	1	0	9	0	12	1	0	0	0	.000	0	0	8.10
1997 Reading	AA Phi	63	0	0	23	80.1	314	61	29	29	8	6	0	1	21	1	94	1	0	9	4	.692	0	8	3.25
4 Min. YEARS		130	40	0	31	347.2	1450	320	151	130	20	15	10	7	128	4	295	9	8	21	18	.538	0	9	3.37

Bo Dodson

Bats: Left **Throws:** Left **Pos:** 1B   **Ht:** 6'2" **Wt:** 195 **Born:** 12/7/70 **Age:** 27

		BATTING													BASERUNNING				PERCENTAGES		
Year Team	Lg Org	G	AB	H	2B	3B	HR	TB	R	RBI	TBB	IBB	SO	HBP	SH	SF	SB	CS	SB%	GDP	Avg	OBP	SLG
1989 Helena	R+ Mil	65	216	67	13	1	6	100	38	42	52	2	52	4	1	3	5	1	.83	4	.310	.447	.463
1990 Stockton	A+ Mil	120	363	99	16	4	6	141	70	46	73	2	103	3	1	1	1	1	.50	3	.273	.398	.388
1991 Stockton	A+ Mil	88	298	78	13	3	9	124	51	42	66	7	63	4	0	2	4	2	.67	7	.262	.400	.416
1992 El Paso	AA Mil	109	335	83	19	6	4	126	47	46	72	6	81	0	0	1	3	7	.30	7	.248	.380	.376
1993 El Paso	AA Mil	101	330	103	27	4	9	165	58	59	42	4	69	6	0	2	1	6	.14	3	.312	.397	.500
1994 El Paso	AA Mil	26	68	10	3	0	0	13	6	7	12	0	18	1	0	0	1	0	.00	2	.147	.284	.191
New Orleans	AAA Mil	79	257	67	13	0	2	86	41	29	42	2	44	2	3	1	2	3	.40	8	.261	.368	.335
1995 El Paso	AA Mil	63	223	80	20	4	7	129	46	43	37	2	42	7	0	0	1	1	.50	6	.359	.464	.578
New Orleans	AAA Mil	62	203	57	5	1	9	91	29	34	36	6	27	0	0	5	0	0	.00	4	.281	.381	.448
1996 Pawtucket	AAA Bos	82	276	95	20	0	11	148	37	43	32	1	50	1	1	3	4	0	1.00	7	.344	.410	.536
1997 Red Sox	R Bos	12	36	15	5	0	1	23	6	9	4	0	5	0	0	1	0	0	.00	1	.417	.463	.639
Pawtucket	AAA Bos	17	61	18	6	0	0	24	8	6	5	0	11	1	0	0	0	0	.00	0	.295	.358	.393
9 Min. YEARS		824	2666	772	160	23	64	1170	437	406	473	32	565	29	6	19	21	22	.49	46	.290	.400	.439

Roger Doman

Pitches: Right **Bats:** Right **Pos:** P   **Ht:** 6'5" **Wt:** 185 **Born:** 1/26/73 **Age:** 25

		HOW MUCH HE PITCHED						WHAT HE GAVE UP									THE RESULTS				
Year Team	Lg Org	G	GS	CG	GF	IP	BFP	H	R	ER	HR	SH	SF	HB	TBB	IBB	SO	WP	Bk	W	L	Pct.	ShO	Sv	ERA
1991 Blue Jays	R Tor	13	10	0	0	50.1	214	54	29	27	2	0	1	2	17	0	28	9	1	2	2	.500	0	0	4.83
1992 St. Cathrns	A- Tor	15	14	0	1	68.2	316	70	47	35	3	3	2	2	47	0	53	12	1	2	7	.222	0	0	4.59
1993 Hagerstown	A Tor	26	26	0	0	146.2	650	153	78	67	11	3	4	6	73	0	102	15	2	8	6	.571	0	0	4.11
1994 Dunedin	A+ Tor	32	12	0	11	103.1	460	119	72	60	10	2	7	3	40	0	64	12	0	3	9	.250	0	2	5.23
1995 Knoxville	AA Tor	14	0	0	6	30.2	142	42	25	20	2	1	1	1	11	0	16	3	0	0	0	.000	0	0	5.87
Hagerstown	A Tor	14	6	0	3	51	233	65	32	25	0	0	1	3	13	0	24	4	0	2	2	.500	0	1	4.41
1996 Dunedin	A+ Tor	18	0	0	9	30	148	36	22	11	2	1	2	1	14	2	19	0	0	1	0	.000	0	0	3.30
Hagerstown	A Tor	2	1	0	0	4	19	4	3	3	0	0	0	1	4	0	4	3	0	0	0	.000	0	0	6.75
Knoxville	AA Tor	17	1	0	6	39.1	177	51	30	24	2	0	0	0	14	0	30	5	1	1	1	.500	0	0	5.49
1997 Syracuse	AAA Tor	8	0	0	1	10.2	50	11	9	9	3	1	0	0	6	0	8	1	0	1	2	.333	0	0	7.59
Knoxville	AA Tor	48	1	0	13	100.2	425	99	46	41	5	4	2	8	29	6	71	9	1	7	3	.700	0	4	3.67
7 Min. YEARS		207	71	0	50	635.1	2832	704	393	322	40	15	20	27	268	8	419	73	6	26	36	.419	0	7	4.56

Dan Donato

Bats: Left **Throws:** Right **Pos:** 3B   **Ht:** 6'1" **Wt:** 205 **Born:** 11/15/72 **Age:** 25

		BATTING													BASERUNNING				PERCENTAGES		
Year Team	Lg Org	G	AB	H	2B	3B	HR	TB	R	RBI	TBB	IBB	SO	HBP	SH	SF	SB	CS	SB%	GDP	Avg	OBP	SLG
1995 Greensboro	A NYA	108	387	123	30	1	7	176	55	69	37	5	46	4	0	3	7	6	.54	12	.318	.381	.455
Tampa	A+ NYA	3	8	2	0	0	0	2	1	1	0	0	2	1	0	0	0	0	.00	0	.250	.333	.625
1996 Norwich	AA NYA	134	459	131	27	1	2	166	47	48	34	2	51	7	5	1	5	6	.45	19	.285	.343	.362
1997 Norwich	AA NYA	96	349	96	16	1	5	129	44	43	26	2	44	9	0	1	7	4	.64	13	.275	.340	.370
3 Min. YEARS		341	1203	352	73	3	15	476	147	161	97	9	143	21	5	5	19	16	.54	44	.293	.354	.396

Brendan Donnelly

Pitches: Right Bats: Right Pos: P   Ht: 6'3" Wt: 200 Born: 7/4/71 Age: 26

		HOW MUCH HE PITCHED						WHAT HE GAVE UP									THE RESULTS					
Year Team	Lg Org	G	GS	CG	GF	IP	BFP	H	R	ER	HR	SH	SF	HB	TBB	IBB	SO	WP	Bk	W	L	Pct.	ShO	Sv	ERA
1992 White Sox	R ChA	9	7	0	1	41.2	191	41	25	17	0	0	2	8	21	0	31	6	0	0	3	.000	0	1	3.67
1993 Geneva	A- ChN	21	3	0	7	43	198	39	34	30	4	1	1	6	29	0	29	7	3	4	0	1.000	0	1	6.28
1994 Ohio Valley	IND —	10	0	0	1	13.2	59	13	5	4	1	0	0	3	4	0	20	1	0	1	1	.500	0	0	2.63
1995 Chston-WV	A Cin	24	0	0	22	30.1	112	14	4	4	0	1	2	1	7	1	33	1	0	1	1	.500	0	12	1.19
Winston-Sal	A+ Cin	23	0	0	14	35.1	138	20	6	4	1	2	0	2	14	2	32	0	1	1	2	.333	0	2	1.02
Indianapolis	AAA Cin	3	0	0	0	2.2	18	7	8	7	2	0	1	1	2	0	1	2	0	1	1	.500	0	0	23.63
1996 Chattanooga	AA Cin	22	0	0	10	29.1	133	27	21	18	4	0	1	1	17	2	22	1	0	1	2	.333	0	0	5.52
1997 Chattanooga	AA Cin	62	0	0	21	82.2	359	71	43	30	6	4	3	4	37	4	64	9	0	6	4	.600	0	6	3.27
6 Min. YEARS		174	10	0	76	278.2	1208	232	146	114	18	8	10	26	131	9	232	27	4	15	14	.517	0	22	3.68

David Doster

Bats: Right Throws: Right Pos: 2B   Ht: 5'10" Wt: 185 Born: 10/8/70 Age: 27

		BATTING														BASERUNNING				PERCENTAGES		
Year Team	Lg Org	G	AB	H	2B	3B	HR	TB	R	RBI	TBB	IBB	SO	HBP	SH	SF	SB	CS	SB%	GDP	Avg	OBP	SLG
1993 Spartanburg	A Phi	60	223	61	15	0	3	85	34	20	25	1	36	3	6	1	1	0	1.00	5	.274	.353	.381
Clearwater	A+ Phi	9	28	10	3	1	0	15	4	2	2	0	2	0	0	0	0	0	.00	1	.357	.400	.536
1994 Clearwater	A+ Phi	131	480	135	42	4	13	224	76	74	54	3	71	11	3	8	12	7	.63	12	.281	.362	.467
1995 Reading	AA Phi	139	551	146	39	3	21	254	84	79	51	2	61	7	8	4	11	7	.61	11	.265	.333	.461
1996 Scranton-WB	AAA Phi	88	322	83	20	0	7	124	37	48	26	1	54	2	3	5	7	3	.70	8	.258	.313	.385
1997 Scranton-WB	AAA Phi	108	410	129	32	2	16	213	70	79	30	1	60	8	2	3	5	5	.50	9	.315	.370	.520
1996 Philadelphia	NL	39	105	28	8	0	1	39	14	8	7	0	21	0	1	0	0	0	.00	1	.267	.313	.371
5 Min. YEARS		535	2014	564	151	10	60	915	305	302	188	8	284	31	22	21	36	22	.62	46	.280	.347	.454

Octavio Dotel

Pitches: Right Bats: Right Pos: P   Ht: 6'5" Wt: 160 Born: 11/25/73 Age: 24

		HOW MUCH HE PITCHED						WHAT HE GAVE UP									THE RESULTS					
Year Team	Lg Org	G	GS	CG	GF	IP	BFP	H	R	ER	HR	SH	SF	HB	TBB	IBB	SO	WP	Bk	W	L	Pct.	ShO	Sv	ERA
1995 Mets	R NYN	13	12	2	1	74.1	293	48	23	18	0	1	0	5	17	1	86	9	0	7	4	.636	0	0	2.18
St. Lucie	A+ NYN	3	0	0	2	8	38	10	5	5	1	1	2	0	4	0	9	2	0	1	0	1.000	0	0	5.63
1996 Capital City	A NYN	22	19	0	3	115.1	480	89	49	46	7	1	4	7	49	0	142	12	4	11	3	.786	0	0	3.59
1997 Mets	R NYN	3	2	0	1	9.1	39	9	1	1	0	0	0	1	2	0	7	0	0	0	0	.000	0	1	0.96
St. Lucie	A+ NYN	9	8	1	1	50	212	44	18	14	2	0	1	1	23	0	39	5	1	5	2	.714	1	0	2.52
Binghamton	AA NYN	12	12	0	0	55.2	266	66	50	37	5	1	0	0	38	1	40	2	1	3	4	.429	0	0	5.98
3 Min. YEARS		62	53	3	8	312.2	1328	266	146	121	15	4	7	14	133	2	323	30	6	27	13	.675	1	1	3.48

Anthony Dougherty

Pitches: Right Bats: Right Pos: P   Ht: 6'2" Wt: 205 Born: 4/12/73 Age: 25

		HOW MUCH HE PITCHED						WHAT HE GAVE UP									THE RESULTS					
Year Team	Lg Org	G	GS	CG	GF	IP	BFP	H	R	ER	HR	SH	SF	HB	TBB	IBB	SO	WP	Bk	W	L	Pct.	ShO	Sv	ERA
1994 Watertown	A- Cle	26	0	0	13	40.2	178	33	20	13	0	3	0	4	19	2	37	3	2	6	1	.857	0	2	2.88
1995 Columbus	A Cle	27	10	0	3	87.2	405	85	61	46	5	2	4	8	50	4	78	4	1	4	4	.500	0	0	4.72
1996 Columbus	A Cle	19	1	0	8	49	202	30	16	16	3	2	2	4	22	0	44	4	1	3	1	.750	0	2	2.94
Kinston	A+ Cle	3	0	0	0	5	26	3	5	5	1	0	0	0	8	1	6	0	0	0	0	.000	0	0	9.00
1997 Akron	AA Cle	18	0	0	15	33.1	135	29	6	6	2	3	0	1	11	2	32	3	1	3	1	.750	0	8	1.62
Akron	AA Cle	28	0	0	26	39	163	31	11	11	2	1	2	1	19	1	31	0	0	0	2	.000	0	8	2.54
Buffalo	AAA Cle	18	0	0	7	28.2	128	31	17	12	2	1	0	0	18	0	21	5	0	2	0	1.000	0	2	3.77
4 Min. YEARS		139	11	0	72	283.1	1237	242	136	109	15	12	8	18	147	10	249	19	5	18	9	.667	0	22	3.46

Jim Dougherty

Pitches: Right Bats: Right Pos: P   Ht: 6'0" Wt: 210 Born: 3/8/68 Age: 30

		HOW MUCH HE PITCHED						WHAT HE GAVE UP									THE RESULTS					
Year Team	Lg Org	G	GS	CG	GF	IP	BFP	H	R	ER	HR	SH	SF	HB	TBB	IBB	SO	WP	Bk	W	L	Pct.	ShO	Sv	ERA
1991 Asheville	A Hou	61	0	0	48	82	324	63	17	14	0	7	0	3	24	6	76	0	2	3	1	.750	0	27	1.54
1992 Osceola	A+ Hou	57	0	0	52	81	325	66	21	14	1	4	2	2	22	4	77	0	1	5	2	.714	0	31	1.56
1993 Jackson	AA Hou	52	0	0	50	53	207	39	15	11	3	0	0	1	21	0	55	0	0	2	2	.500	0	36	1.87
1994 Tucson	AAA Hou	55	0	0	48	59	276	70	32	27	9	1	1	2	30	6	49	4	0	5	4	.556	0	21	4.12
1995 Tucson	AAA Hou	8	0	0	3	11	46	11	4	4	1	0	0	0	5	0	12	0	1	1	0	1.000	0	1	3.27
1996 Tucson	AAA Hou	46	0	0	23	61.2	269	65	35	24	4	0	1	2	27	3	53	2	1	4	3	.571	0	1	3.50
1997 Norfolk	AAA NYN	49	0	0	24	62	259	45	11	10	3	4	2	2	43	3	59	4	0	10	1	.909	0	4	1.45
1995 Houston	NL	56	0	0	11	67.2	294	76	37	37	7	3	3	3	25	1	49	1	0	8	4	.667	0	0	4.92
1996 Houston	NL	12	0	0	2	13	64	14	14	13	2	1	1	1	11	1	6	0	0	0	2	.000	0	0	9.00
7 Min. YEARS		328	0	0	248	409.2	1706	359	135	104	17	17	6	12	172	22	381	10	5	30	13	.698	0	121	2.28
2 Maj. YEARS		68	0	0	13	80.2	358	90	51	50	9	4	4	4	36	2	55	1	0	8	6	.571	0	0	5.58

Dee Dowler

Bats: Right Throws: Right Pos: OF   Ht: 5'9" Wt: 175 Born: 7/23/71 Age: 26

		BATTING														BASERUNNING				PERCENTAGES		
Year Team	Lg Org	G	AB	H	2B	3B	HR	TB	R	RBI	TBB	IBB	SO	HBP	SH	SF	SB	CS	SB%	GDP	Avg	OBP	SLG
1993 Geneva	A- ChN	75	291	79	26	2	5	124	49	38	24	0	54	8	2	2	21	11	.66	3	.271	.342	.426
1994 Daytona	A+ ChN	126	481	136	17	3	9	186	80	62	36	2	83	6	10	3	15	7	.68	6	.283	.338	.387
1995 Orlando	AA ChN	9	31	7	2	0	0	9	6	1	2	0	5	0	0	0	1	0	1.00	1	.226	.273	.290
Daytona	A+ ChN	112	415	104	12	2	3	129	70	59	45	0	51	8	7	4	26	15	.63	11	.251	.333	.311
1996 Daytona	A+ ChN	12	47	19	3	0	0	22	5	8	5	0	5	1	2	1	4	1	.80	1	.404	.463	.468

		BATTING															BASERUNNING				PERCENTAGES		
Year Team	Lg Org	G	AB	H	2B	3B	HR	TB	R	RBI	TBB	IBB	SO	HBP	SH	SF	SB	CS	SB%	GDP	Avg	OBP	SLG
Orlando	AA ChN	113	352	98	15	6	6	143	59	47	47	2	42	3	6	2	25	5	.83	10	.278	.366	.406
1997 Iowa	AAA ChN	42	100	23	2	0	2	31	14	12	10	0	16	2	1	1	6	1	.86	2	.230	.310	.310
Orlando	AA ChN	52	178	45	7	0	3	61	32	19	21	2	23	5	4	1	8	4	.67	10	.253	.346	.343
5 Min. YEARS		541	1895	511	84	13	28	705	315	246	190	6	279	33	32	14	106	44	.71	43	.270	.344	.372

Brian Downs

Bats: Right **Throws:** Right **Pos:** C   **Ht:** 6'2" **Wt:** 210 **Born:** 4/10/75 **Age:** 23

		BATTING															BASERUNNING				PERCENTAGES		
Year Team	Lg Org	G	AB	H	2B	3B	HR	TB	R	RBI	TBB	IBB	SO	HBP	SH	SF	SB	CS	SB%	GDP	Avg	OBP	SLG
1995 White Sox	R ChA	37	130	37	8	0	2	51	22	18	7	0	27	2	0	0	0	1	.00	2	.285	.331	.392
1996 Hickory	A ChA	84	279	58	10	0	3	77	23	28	15	0	78	4	3	2	0	1	.00	6	.208	.257	.276
1997 Hickory	A ChA	25	82	19	4	0	4	35	8	7	3	0	22	0	0	0	0	0	.00	0	.232	.259	.427
Nashville	AAA ChA	7	18	4	0	0	0	4	1	1	0	0	5	0	0	0	0	1	.00	0	.222	.222	.222
Winston-Sal	A+ ChA	33	100	26	7	1	3	44	13	12	8	1	22	2	1	1	0	0	.00	3	.260	.324	.440
3 Min. YEARS		186	609	144	29	1	12	211	67	66	33	1	154	8	4	3	0	3	.00	11	.236	.283	.346

Tom Doyle

Pitches: Left **Bats:** Left **Pos:** P   **Ht:** 6'3" **Wt:** 205 **Born:** 1/20/70 **Age:** 28

		HOW MUCH HE PITCHED						WHAT HE GAVE UP										THE RESULTS					
Year Team	Lg Org	G	GS	CG	GF	IP	BFP	H	R	ER	HR	SH	SF	HB	TBB	IBB	SO	WP	Bk	W	L	Pct.	ShO	Sv	ERA
1993 Spokane	A- SD	6	0	0	2	6	37	12	9	9	0	1	0	3	6	0	5	2	0	0	0	.000	0	0	13.50
Waterloo	A SD	4	0	0	1	6.2	34	7	6	5	2	0	1	2	6	0	7	2	0	0	0	.000	0	0	6.75
1994 Riverside	A+ Sea	9	0	0	5	11	68	21	20	19	0	0	0	3	11	0	12	1	2	0	0	.000	0	0	15.55
Regina	IND —	19	10	1	5	74	343	74	57	43	6	2	0	7	49	0	76	8	2	3	7	.300	0	1	5.23
1995 Chston-WV	A Cin	14	12	1	0	62	272	57	34	30	3	2	1	7	30	3	66	9	0	6	4	.600	0	0	4.35
Winston-Sal	A+ Cin	21	3	0	3	31.1	140	32	18	12	2	1	0	3	12	0	22	5	0	3	1	.750	0	1	3.45
1996 Chattanooga	AA Cin	53	0	0	14	54.1	246	54	34	29	1	2	4	3	39	3	32	8	2	4	2	.667	0	0	4.80
Indianapols	AAA Cin	1	0	0	1	2.1	10	2	1	1	0	1	0	0	1	1	1	0	0	0	1	.000	0	0	3.86
1997 Chattanooga	AA Cin	65	0	0	21	66.2	298	62	32	26	5	4	0	11	38	5	46	6	1	7	3	.700	0	0	3.51
5 Min. YEARS		192	25	2	52	314.1	1448	321	211	174	19	13	6	39	192	12	267	41	7	23	18	.561	0	2	4.98

Brian Drahman

Pitches: Right **Bats:** Right **Pos:** P   **Ht:** 6'3" **Wt:** 231 **Born:** 11/7/66 **Age:** 31

		HOW MUCH HE PITCHED						WHAT HE GAVE UP										THE RESULTS					
Year Team	Lg Org	G	GS	CG	GF	IP	BFP	H	R	ER	HR	SH	SF	HB	TBB	IBB	SO	WP	Bk	W	L	Pct.	ShO	Sv	ERA
1986 Helena	R+ Mil	18	10	0	5	65.1	0	79	49	43	4	0	0	0	33	1	40	4	0	4	6	.400	0	2	5.92
1987 Beloit	A Mil	46	0	0	41	79	318	63	28	19	2	4	2	3	22	3	60	5	1	6	5	.545	0	18	2.16
1988 Stockton	A+ Mil	44	0	0	40	62.1	266	57	17	14	2	1	0	1	27	3	50	3	0	4	5	.444	0	14	2.02
1989 El Paso	AA Mil	19	0	0	8	31	151	52	31	25	3	3	0	1	11	1	23	3	0	4	3	.429	0	2	7.26
Stockton	A+ Mil	12	0	0	10	27.2	112	22	11	10	0	1	0	2	9	0	30	2	0	3	2	.600	0	4	3.25
Sarasota	A+ ChA	7	2	0	3	16.2	73	18	9	6	1	1	0	1	5	1	9	1	0	0	1	.000	0	1	3.24
1990 Birmingham	AA ChA	50	1	0	31	90.1	383	90	50	41	6	9	4	3	24	2	72	12	1	6	4	.600	0	17	4.08
1991 Vancouver	AAA ChA	22	0	0	21	24.1	106	21	12	12	2	4	0	0	13	1	17	1	1	2	3	.400	0	12	4.44
1992 Vancouver	AAA ChA	48	0	0	44	58.1	242	44	16	13	5	3	2	0	31	1	34	2	0	2	4	.333	0	30	2.01
1993 Nashville	AAA ChA	54	0	0	50	55.2	249	59	29	18	3	3	4	2	19	8	49	6	0	9	4	.692	0	20	2.91
1994 Edmonton	AAA Fla	45	0	0	35	60.1	261	60	38	32	9	2	2	1	25	0	62	4	0	3	2	.600	0	13	4.77
1995 Charlotte	AAA Fla	21	0	0	15	20	99	28	14	14	1	2	1	0	11	1	17	3	0	2	1	.667	0	4	6.30
Okla City	AAA Tex	22	0	0	15	32	145	36	11	11	3	1	1	2	14	3	19	0	0	2	2	.500	0	4	3.09
Indianapols	AAA Cin	2	0	0	0	3	12	3	0	0	0	0	0	0	1	0	3	0	0	0	0	.000	0	0	0.00
1996 Indianapols	AAA Cin	3	0	0	0	5	27	7	6	4	0	0	0	0	4	0	1	1	0	0	0	.000	0	0	7.20
Las Vegas	AAA SD	9	0	0	4	9	33	4	1	1	0	1	0	0	4	0	10	0	0	1	0	1.000	0	1	1.00
1997 Las Vegas	AAA SD	33	0	0	6	42.2	205	51	32	30	5	2	3	2	28	4	39	2	0	2	1	.667	0	1	6.33
1991 Chicago	AL	28	0	0	8	30.2	125	21	12	11	4	2	1	0	13	1	18	0	0	3	2	.600	0	0	3.23
1992 Chicago	AL	5	0	0	2	7	29	6	3	2	0	0	0	0	2	0	1	1	0	0	0	.000	0	0	2.57
1993 Chicago	AL	5	0	0	4	5.1	24	7	0	0	0	0	0	0	2	0	3	0	0	0	0	.000	0	1	0.00
1994 Florida	NL	3	0	0	3	13	59	15	9	9	2	1	2	0	6	1	7	2	0	0	0	.000	0	0	6.23
12 Min. YEARS		455	13	0	328	682.2	2682	694	354	293	46	37	19	18	281	29	535	49	3	49	44	.527	0	142	3.86
4 Maj. YEARS		47	0	0	17	56	236	49	24	22	6	3	3	0	23	2	29	3	0	3	2	.600	0	1	3.54

Kirk Dressendorfer

Pitches: Right **Bats:** Right **Pos:** P   **Ht:** 5'11" **Wt:** 190 **Born:** 4/8/69 **Age:** 29

		HOW MUCH HE PITCHED						WHAT HE GAVE UP										THE RESULTS					
Year Team	Lg Org	G	GS	CG	GF	IP	BFP	H	R	ER	HR	SH	SF	HB	TBB	IBB	SO	WP	Bk	W	L	Pct.	ShO	Sv	ERA
1990 Sou. Oregon	A- Oak	7	4	0	0	19.1	78	18	7	5	0	1	1	1	2	0	22	1	0	0	1	.000	0	0	2.33
1991 Tacoma	AAA Oak	8	7	0	0	24	120	31	29	29	4	1	2	1	20	0	19	2	0	1	3	.250	0	0	10.88
1992 Modesto	A+ Oak	3	3	0	0	13	56	8	7	7	1	0	0	1	6	0	18	1	0	2	0	.000	0	0	4.85
1993 Modesto	A+ Oak	5	5	0	0	11.1	51	14	5	5	2	0	0	0	5	0	15	0	0	0	0	.000	0	0	3.97
1994 Athletics	R Oak	6	6	0	0	12.1	45	3	1	0	0	0	0	1	4	0	17	0	0	0	0	.000	0	0	0.00
1995 Modesto	A+ Oak	27	16	0	2	37	171	39	24	19	5	2	2	2	18	0	50	6	0	0	6	.000	0	0	4.62
Huntsville	AA Oak	9	4	0	1	20	79	13	7	7	1	0	2	0	5	0	18	1	0	0	1	.000	0	0	3.15
1996 Edmonton	AAA Oak	10	0	0	2	13	66	23	11	8	1	0	0	0	3	1	10	0	0	0	0	.000	0	0	5.54
Huntsville	AA Oak	30	1	0	14	52.1	233	54	38	29	3	1	1	4	21	1	43	6	0	4	4	.500	0	2	4.99
1997 Albuquerque	AAA LA	7	7	0	0	30	141	43	18	15	5	1	1	3	10	0	14	1	0	2	2	.500	0	0	4.50
1991 Oakland	AL	7	7	0	0	34.2	159	33	28	21	5	2	1	0	21	0	17	3	0	3	3	.500	0	0	5.45
8 Min. YEARS		112	53	0	19	232.1	1040	246	147	124	22	6	9	13	94	2	226	21	0	5	21	.192	0	2	4.80

Matt Drews

Pitches: Right Bats: Right Pos: P Ht: 6'8" Wt: 205 Born: 8/29/74 Age: 23

Year Team	Lg Org	G	GS	CG	GF	IP	BFP	H	R	ER	HR	SH	SF	HB	TBB	IBB	SO	WP	Bk	W	L	Pct.	ShO	Sv	ERA
1994 Oneonta	A- NYA	14	14	1	0	90	369	76	31	21	1	1	2	8	19	0	69	3	0	7	6	.538	1	0	2.10
1995 Tampa	A+ NYA	28	28	3	0	182	748	142	73	46	5	5	5	17	58	0	140	8	2	15	7	.682	0	0	2.27
1996 Columbus	AAA NYA	7	7	0	0	20.1	113	28	27	19	4	1	5	7	27	0	7	8	0	0	4	.000	0	0	8.41
Tampa	A+ NYA	4	4	0	0	17.2	93	26	20	14	2	1	2	3	12	2	12	1	0	0	3	.000	0	0	7.13
Norwich	AA NYA	9	9	0	0	46	210	40	26	23	4	1	0	5	33	1	37	1	0	1	3	.250	0	0	4.50
Jacksnville	AA Det	6	6	1	0	31	138	26	18	15	3	0	0	4	19	0	40	2	1	0	4	.000	0	0	4.35
1997 Jacksnville	AA Det	24	24	4	0	144.1	652	160	109	88	23	1	6	16	50	0	85	3	0	8	11	.421	1	0	5.49
Toledo	AAA Det	3	3	0	0	15	72	14	11	11	2	2	0	0	14	1	7	2	0	0	2	.000	0	0	6.60
4 Min. YEARS		95	95	9	0	546.1	2395	502	315	237	42	13	19	60	232	4	397	28	3	31	40	.437	2	0	3.90

Steve Dreyer

Pitches: Right Bats: Right Pos: P Ht: 6'3" Wt: 188 Born: 11/19/69 Age: 28

Year Team	Lg Org	G	GS	CG	GF	IP	BFP	H	R	ER	HR	SH	SF	HB	TBB	IBB	SO	WP	Bk	W	L	Pct.	ShO	Sv	ERA
1990 Butte	R+ Tex	8	8	0	0	35.2	146	32	21	18	2	0	0	0	10	0	29	1	0	1	1	.500	0	0	4.54
1991 Gastonia	A Tex	25	25	3	0	162	661	137	51	43	5	5	4	5	62	1	122	4	0	7	10	.412	1	0	2.39
1992 Charlotte	A+ Tex	26	26	4	0	168.2	675	164	54	45	8	10	0	6	37	2	111	4	0	11	7	.611	3	0	2.40
1993 Tulsa	AA Tex	5	5	1	0	31.1	128	26	13	13	4	0	1	0	8	1	27	0	0	2	2	.500	1	0	3.73
Okla City	AAA Tex	16	16	1	0	107	445	108	39	36	5	4	3	2	31	1	59	1	0	4	6	.400	0	0	3.03
1994 Okla City	AAA Tex	4	4	0	0	23	103	26	14	9	2	0	0	0	9	0	16	1	0	0	1	.000	0	0	3.52
1995 Rangers	R Tex	2	2	0	0	9	34	6	1	1	0	1	0	0	2	0	7	0	0	0	1	.000	0	0	1.00
Tulsa	AA Tex	10	10	1	0	62.1	252	56	22	20	6	2	1	2	19	1	48	4	0	2	4	.333	0	0	2.89
1996 Okla City	AAA Tex	29	14	0	0	118	500	130	55	51	6	1	3	4	31	1	79	2	0	6	8	.429	0	0	3.89
1997 Salt Lake	AAA Min	27	0	0	12	44	202	65	38	36	4	2	3	4	10	2	34	1	0	1	0	1.000	0	0	7.36
1993 Texas	AL	10	6	0	1	41	186	48	26	26	7	0	1	0	20	1	23	0	0	3	3	.500	0	0	5.71
1994 Texas	AL	5	3	0	0	17.1	80	19	15	11	1	0	1	1	8	0	11	1	0	1	1	.500	0	0	5.71
8 Min. YEARS		152	110	10	21	761	3146	750	308	272	42	24	16	20	219	9	532	21	0	34	40	.459	5	4	3.22
2 Maj. YEARS		15	9	0	1	58.1	266	67	41	37	8	0	1	2	28	1	34	1	0	4	4	.500	0	0	5.71

Travis Driskill

Pitches: Right Bats: Right Pos: P Ht: 6'0" Wt: 185 Born: 8/1/71 Age: 26

Year Team	Lg Org	G	GS	CG	GF	IP	BFP	H	R	ER	HR	SH	SF	HB	TBB	IBB	SO	WP	Bk	W	L	Pct.	ShO	Sv	ERA
1993 Watertown	A- Cle	21	8	0	7	63	276	62	38	29	4	3	6	5	21	0	53	6	0	5	4	.556	0	3	4.14
1994 Columbus	A Cle	62	0	0	59	64.1	267	51	25	18	2	5	2	1	30	4	88	6	0	5	5	.500	0	35	2.52
1995 Canton-Akrn	AA Cle	33	0	0	22	46.1	200	46	24	24	3	1	1	1	19	1	39	0	1	3	4	.429	0	4	4.66
Kinston	A+ Cle	15	0	0	9	23	90	17	7	7	2	0	3	1	5	1	24	1	0	0	2	.000	0	0	2.74
1996 Canton-Akrn	AA Cle	29	24	4	0	172	732	169	89	69	8	6	6	3	63	0	148	10	2	13	7	.650	2	0	3.61
1997 Buffalo	AAA Cle	29	24	1	1	147	645	159	86	76	22	2	6	3	60	0	102	15	1	8	7	.533	0	0	4.65
5 Min. YEARS		189	56	5	98	515.2	2210	504	269	223	41	17	24	14	198	6	454	38	4	34	29	.540	2	42	3.89

Mike Drumright

Pitches: Right Bats: Left Pos: P Ht: 6'4" Wt: 210 Born: 4/19/74 Age: 24

Year Team	Lg Org	G	GS	CG	GF	IP	BFP	H	R	ER	HR	SH	SF	HB	TBB	IBB	SO	WP	Bk	W	L	Pct.	ShO	Sv	ERA
1995 Lakeland	A+ Det	5	5	0	0	21	87	19	11	10	2	1	0	0	9	0	19	1	2	1	1	.500	0	0	4.29
Jacksnville	AA Det	5	5	0	0	31.2	137	30	13	13	4	0	0	2	15	1	34	1	5	0	1	.000	0	0	3.69
1996 Jacksnville	AA Det	18	18	1	0	99.2	418	80	51	44	11	1	3	3	48	1	109	10	6	6	4	.600	1	0	3.97
1997 Jacksnville	AA Det	5	5	0	0	28.2	112	16	7	5	0	1	1	3	13	0	24	2	0	1	1	.500	0	0	1.57
Toledo	AAA Det	23	23	0	0	133.1	612	134	78	75	22	8	8	4	91	1	115	5	4	5	10	.333	0	0	5.06
3 Min. YEARS		56	56	1	0	314.1	1366	279	160	147	39	11	12	12	176	2	301	19	17	13	17	.433	1	0	4.21

Derek Dukart

Bats: Left Throws: Right Pos: 3B Ht: 6'4" Wt: 205 Born: 8/17/71 Age: 26

Year Team	Lg Org	G	AB	H	2B	3B	HR	TB	R	RBI	TBB	IBB	SO	HBP	SH	SF	SB	CS	SB%	GDP	Avg	OBP	SLG
1994 Oneonta	A- NYA	63	234	69	8	0	0	77	25	33	19	0	36	2	1	2	0	2	.00	3	.295	.350	.329
1995 Greensboro	A NYA	86	305	78	21	2	6	121	35	40	28	4	59	2	2	4	2	3	.40	11	.256	.319	.397
1996 Tampa	A+ NYA	59	194	61	17	0	2	84	19	27	8	0	28	2	5	3	1	2	.33	9	.314	.343	.433
1997 Norwich	AA NYA	9	32	11	2	0	0	13	4	5	3	0	4	3	0	0	0	0	.00	1	.344	.447	.406
Tampa	A+ NYA	37	110	30	2	0	1	35	10	10	8	0	9	1	1	2	1	1	.50	3	.273	.322	.318
4 Min. YEARS		254	875	249	50	2	9	330	93	115	66	4	136	10	9	11	4	8	.33	27	.285	.338	.377

Matt Dunbar

Pitches: Left Bats: Left Pos: P Ht: 6'0" Wt: 160 Born: 10/15/68 Age: 29

Year Team	Lg Org	G	GS	CG	GF	IP	BFP	H	R	ER	HR	SH	SF	HB	TBB	IBB	SO	WP	Bk	W	L	Pct.	ShO	Sv	ERA
1990 Yankees	R NYA	3	0	0	2	6	24	4	2	2	0	1	0	2	3	0	7	0	1	0	0	.000	0	1	3.00
Oneonta	A- NYA	19	2	0	8	30.1	145	32	23	14	1	2	2	1	24	2	24	5	1	1	4	.200	0	0	4.15
1991 Greensboro	A NYA	24	2	1	14	44.2	184	36	14	11	1	0	1	3	15	0	40	2	0	2	2	.500	0	1	2.22
1992 Pr William	A+ NYA	44	0	0	21	81.2	350	68	34	26	5	7	4	6	33	2	68	7	1	5	4	.556	0	2	2.87
1993 Pr William	A+ NYA	49	0	0	20	73	292	50	21	14	0	6	0	3	30	1	66	6	0	3	1	.750	0	4	1.73
Albany-Colo	AA NYA	15	0	0	6	23.2	91	23	8	7	0	0	0	0	6	0	18	0	0	1	0	1.000	0	0	2.66

Year Team	Lg Org	G	GS	CG	GF	IP	BFP	H	R	ER	HR	SH	SF	HB	TBB	IBB	SO	WP	Bk	W	L	Pct.	ShO	Sv	ERA
1994 Albany-Colo	AA NYA	34	0	0	12	39.2	163	30	10	9	1	2	2	4	14	0	41	1	0	2	1	.667	0	4	2.04
Columbus	AAA NYA	19	0	0	6	26	104	20	5	5	1	0	1	1	10	1	21	2	1	0	1	.000	0	2	1.73
1995 Columbus	AAA NYA	36	0	0	9	44.1	201	50	22	20	1	0	1	3	19	2	33	5	1	2	3	.400	0	0	4.06
1996 Greensboro	A NYA	2	2	0	0	14	56	6	3	3	1	0	0	1	4	0	19	1	0	1	1	.500	0	0	1.93
Norwich	AA NYA	33	6	0	11	70.2	306	59	33	14	3	6	4	5	28	3	59	2	0	4	2	.667	0	1	1.78
Columbus	AAA NYA	14	0	0	1	20.2	84	12	6	4	0	0	1	2	13	0	16	0	0	2	0	1.000	0	0	1.74
1997 Huntsville	AA Oak	5	0	0	2	5	23	8	3	3	0	0	0	0	1	0	7	0	0	1	0	1.000	0	0	5.40
Edmonton	AAA Oak	12	1	0	3	21.2	98	29	12	12	2	1	3	1	8	1	18	0	0	1	0	1.000	0	0	4.98
Vancouver	AAA Ana	2	0	0	1	2	14	3	6	6	2	0	0	0	6	0	2	2	0	0	0	.000	0	0	27.00
1995 Florida	NL	8	0	1	0	7	45	12	9	9	0	2	2	1	11	3	5	1	0	0	1	.000	0	0	11.57
8 Min. YEARS		311	13	1	116	503.1	2135	430	205	150	18	25	19	32	214	12	439	33	5	28	20	.583	0	15	2.68

Chip Duncan

Pitches: Right Bats: Right Pos: P   Ht: 5'11" Wt: 185 Born: 6/27/65 Age: 33

Year Team	Lg Org	G	GS	CG	GF	IP	BFP	H	R	ER	HR	SH	SF	HB	TBB	IBB	SO	WP	Bk	W	L	Pct.	ShO	Sv	ERA
1987 Watertown	A- Pit	24	0	0	16	49.2	222	45	20	13	1	5	2	3	22	3	57	4	0	4	2	.667	0	4	2.36
1988 Salem	A+ Pit	28	28	0	0	156.2	713	168	103	79	18	5	4	5	70	2	102	17	8	8	10	.444	0	0	4.54
1989 Salem	A+ Pit	26	4	0	10	68.2	305	64	49	39	4	3	8	6	33	1	55	5	4	2	4	.333	0	2	5.11
1990 Salem	A+ Pit	37	3	2	17	84.2	406	105	61	49	5	4	3	4	48	3	95	9	1	6	4	.600	0	1	5.21
1991 Carolina	AA Pit	6	0	0	6	8	45	17	8	7	1	0	0	1	4	0	9	1	0	0	0	.000	0	1	7.88
Memphis	AA KC	22	9	2	5	80.1	342	82	42	40	11	2	1	3	28	0	58	5	1	6	3	.667	1	0	4.48
1992 Memphis	AA KC	33	2	1	12	73.1	316	72	49	38	7	6	4	2	24	1	51	3	1	0	3	.000	0	3	4.66
1994 Reading	AA Phi	17	11	0	2	77.2	339	79	40	36	9	1	3	4	34	2	62	3	4	4	2	.667	0	0	4.17
1995 Okla City	AAA Tex	3	0	0	1	5.1	22	6	2	2	0	1	1	0	1	0	3	0	0	0	0	.000	0	0	3.38
Tulsa	AA Tex	17	1	0	11	36	153	34	12	12	2	1	0	1	17	6	31	4	0	2	1	.667	0	1	3.00
New Orleans	AAA Mil	14	5	0	5	34.1	161	44	26	24	7	1	2	2	18	2	23	5	1	1	4	.200	0	0	6.29
1996 Greenville	AA Atl	8	1	0	2	13.1	69	23	17	17	2	1	1	0	11	1	10	0	0	0	2	.000	0	0	11.48
1997 Salt Lake	AAA Min	5	1	0	1	11.1	55	17	13	10	1	0	1	0	3	0	16	6	1	0	0	.000	0	0	7.94
10 Min. YEARS		240	65	5	88	699.1	3148	756	442	366	68	30	30	31	313	21	572	62	21	33	35	.485	1	12	4.71

Courtney Duncan

Pitches: Right Bats: Left Pos: P   Ht: 5'11" Wt: 175 Born: 10/9/74 Age: 23

Year Team	Lg Org	G	GS	CG	GF	IP	BFP	H	R	ER	HR	SH	SF	HB	TBB	IBB	SO	WP	Bk	W	L	Pct.	ShO	Sv	ERA
1996 Williamsprt	A- ChN	15	15	1	0	90.1	360	58	28	22	6	3	0	5	34	0	91	8	0	11	1	.917	0	0	2.19
1997 Daytona	A+ ChN	19	19	1	0	121.2	489	90	35	22	3	6	1	8	35	0	120	8	1	8	4	.667	0	0	1.63
Orlando	AA ChN	8	8	0	0	45	196	37	28	17	2	1	2	1	29	5	45	4	0	2	2	.500	0	0	3.40
2 Min. YEARS		42	42	2	0	257	1045	185	91	61	11	10	3	14	98	5	256	20	1	21	7	.750	0	0	2.14

Mike Durant

Bats: Right Throws: Right Pos: C   Ht: 6' 2" Wt: 200 Born: 9/14/69 Age: 28

Year Team	Lg Org	G	AB	H	2B	3B	HR	TB	R	RBI	TBB	IBB	SO	HBP	SH	SF	SB	CS	SB%	GDP	Avg	OBP	SLG
1991 Kenosha	A Min	66	217	44	10	0	2	60	27	20	25	0	35	3	2	1	20	5	.80	4	.203	.286	.276
1992 Visalia	A+ Min	119	418	119	18	2	6	159	61	57	55	0	35	5	5	3	19	15	.56	10	.285	.368	.380
1993 Nashville	AA Min	123	437	106	23	1	8	155	58	57	44	1	68	6	4	3	16	4	.80	2	.243	.318	.355
1994 Salt Lake	AAA Min	103	343	102	24	4	4	146	67	51	35	0	47	4	5	0	9	3	.75	7	.297	.369	.426
1995 Salt Lake	AAA Min	85	295	74	15	3	2	101	40	23	20	0	31	2	3	2	11	7	.61	13	.251	.301	.342
1996 Salt Lake	AAA Min	31	101	29	7	0	1	39	21	12	11	1	21	4	1	0	7	2	.78	3	.287	.379	.386
1997 Salt Lake	AAA Min	66	223	46	13	1	8	85	33	36	21	0	42	6	0	0	4	1	.80	6	.206	.292	.381
1996 Minnesota	AL	40	81	17	3	0	0	20	15	5	10	0	15	0	0	4	3	0	1.00	2	.210	.293	.247
7 Min. YEARS		593	2034	520	110	11	31	745	307	256	211	2	279	30	18	14	86	37	.70	47	.256	.332	.366

Chris Durkin

Bats: Left Throws: Left Pos: OF   Ht: 6'6" Wt: 247 Born: 8/12/70 Age: 27

Year Team	Lg Org	G	AB	H	2B	3B	HR	TB	R	RBI	TBB	IBB	SO	HBP	SH	SF	SB	CS	SB%	GDP	Avg	OBP	SLG
1991 Auburn	A- Hou	69	246	63	10	3	5	94	31	35	30	1	64	2	0	2	20	7	.74	3	.256	.339	.382
1992 Asheville	A Hou	100	314	80	21	2	8	129	59	55	67	5	89	3	0	2	27	17	.61	6	.255	.389	.411
1993 Quad City	A Hou	25	77	21	6	1	1	32	14	6	15	3	13	0	0	0	6	4	.60	0	.273	.391	.416
1994 Osceola	A+ Hou	103	329	77	21	1	4	112	46	31	53	3	86	3	0	5	20	9	.69	5	.234	.341	.340
1995 San Berndno	A+ LA	57	164	44	10	1	8	80	24	31	28	0	48	1	1	3	9	6	.60	3	.268	.372	.488
1996 Vero Beach	A+ LA	56	202	54	11	0	16	113	49	34	28	3	54	1	0	1	4	0	1.00	3	.267	.358	.559
San Antonio	AA LA	8	30	9	2	0	1	14	6	3	4	0	9	0	0	0	0	0	.00	0	.300	.382	.467
1997 San Antonio	AA LA	38	125	34	11	0	4	57	18	18	13	0	33	1	1	1	8	2	.80	1	.272	.343	.456
San Berndno	A+ LA	3	12	2	0	0	0	2	1	0	1	0	4	0	0	0	0	0	.00	0	.167	.167	.167
7 Min. YEARS		459	1499	384	92	8	47	633	248	213	238	15	400	11	2	14	94	45	.68	21	.256	.359	.422

Mike Duvall

Pitches: Left Bats: Right Pos: P   Ht: 6'0" Wt: 185 Born: 10/11/74 Age: 23

Year Team	Lg Org	G	GS	CG	GF	IP	BFP	H	R	ER	HR	SH	SF	HB	TBB	IBB	SO	WP	Bk	W	L	Pct.	ShO	Sv	ERA
1995 Marlins	R Fla	16	1	0	10	28.1	120	15	8	7	1	0	0	2	12	1	34	4	2	5	0	1.000	0	1	2.22
1996 Kane County	A Fla	41	0	0	28	48	210	43	20	11	0	2	0	0	21	2	46	3	0	4	1	.800	0	8	2.06

		HOW MUCH HE PITCHED				WHAT HE GAVE UP									THE RESULTS					
Year Team	Lg Org	G GS CG GF	IP	BFP	H	R	ER	HR SH SF HB	TBB	IBB	SO	WP	Bk	W	L	Pct.	ShO	Sv	ERA
1997 Brevard Cty	A+ Fla	11 0 0 11	12.1	45	7	1	1	0 0 0 0	3	1	9	0	0	1	0	1.000	0	6	0.73
Portland	AA Fla	45 0 0 25	68.1	291	63	20	14	4 9 1 2	20	2	49	2	0	4	6	.400	0	18	1.84
3 Min. YEARS		113 1 0 74	157	666	128	49	33	5 11 1 4	56	6	138	9	2	14	7	.667	0	33	1.89

Mike Dyer

Pitches: Right **Bats:** Right **Pos:** P   **Ht:** 6'3" **Wt:** 200 **Born:** 9/8/66 **Age:** 31

		HOW MUCH HE PITCHED				WHAT HE GAVE UP									THE RESULTS					
Year Team	Lg Org	G GS CG GF	IP	BFP	H	R	ER	HR SH SF HB	TBB	IBB	SO	WP	Bk	W	L	Pct.	ShO	Sv	ERA
1986 Elizabethtn	R+ Min	14 14 3 0	72.1	332	70	50	28	6 1 1 3	42	1	62	5	1	5	7	.417	1	0	3.48
1987 Kenosha	A Min	27 27 2 0	167	704	124	72	57	9 2 6 8	84	1	163	7	2	16	5	.762	0	0	3.07
1988 Orlando	AA Min	27 27 3 0	162.1	698	155	84	72	6 2 6 5	86	1	125	6	7	11	13	.458	0	0	3.99
1989 Portland	AAA Min	15 15 2 0	89.1	386	80	56	44	8 3 4 2	51	0	63	3	4	3	6	.333	0	0	4.43
1990 Portland	AAA Min	2 2 0 0	2.1	21	6	10	9	1 0 1 0	9	0	0	0	0	0	1	.000	0	0	34.71
1992 Portland	AAA Min	27 16 0 4	105	480	119	62	59	7 2 1 7	56	2	85	14	1	7	6	.538	0	1	5.06
1993 Iowa	AAA ChN	14 0 0 3	24.1	110	18	14	13	4 0 1 0	20	0	18	2	2	1	0	1.000	0	0	4.81
Canton-Akrn	AA Cle	17 17 0 0	94	415	90	64	58	8 2 5 4	55	0	75	13	0	7	4	.636	0	0	5.55
1994 Buffalo	AAA Pit	29 0 0 24	34.2	152	33	11	9	2 3 2 2	16	1	26	2	0	3	3	.500	0	12	2.34
1997 Richmond	AAA Atl	29 0 0 8	40.2	183	42	25	22	5 3 1 0	24	1	23	2	0	2	1	.667	0	1	4.87
1989 Minnesota	AL	16 12 1 0	71	317	74	43	38	2 5 2 2	37	0	37	1	1	4	7	.364	0	0	4.82
1994 Pittsburgh	NL	14 0 0 7	15.1	74	15	12	10	1 1 2 3	12	4	13	0	1	1	1	.500	0	4	5.87
1995 Pittsburgh	NL	55 0 0 15	74.2	327	81	40	36	9 3 1 5	30	3	53	4	1	4	5	.444	0	0	4.34
1996 Montreal	NL	70 1 0 20	75.2	334	79	40	37	7 6 4 5	34	4	51	4	0	5	5	.500	0	2	4.40
9 Min. YEARS		201 118 10 39	792	3481	737	448	371	56 18 28 31	443	7	640	54	17	55	46	.545	1	14	4.22
4 Maj. YEARS		155 13 1 42	236.2	1052	249	135	121	19 15 9 15	113	11	154	9	3	14	18	.438	0	6	4.60

Radhames Dykhoff

Pitches: Left **Bats:** Left **Pos:** P   **Ht:** 6'0" **Wt:** 205 **Born:** 9/27/74 **Age:** 23

		HOW MUCH HE PITCHED				WHAT HE GAVE UP									THE RESULTS					
Year Team	Lg Org	G GS CG GF	IP	BFP	H	R	ER	HR SH SF HB	TBB	IBB	SO	WP	Bk	W	L	Pct.	ShO	Sv	ERA
1993 Orioles	R Bal	14 3 0 1	45	184	37	22	17	2 3 3 2	11	0	29	3	0	1	2	.333	0	1	3.40
1994 Orioles	R Bal	12 11 1 0	73	307	69	34	27	2 0 5 0	17	0	67	4	1	3	6	.333	0	0	3.33
1995 High Desert	A+ Bal	34 2 0 10	80.2	389	95	68	45	8 7 7 0	44	2	88	0	2	1	5	.167	0	3	5.02
1996 Frederick	A+ Bal	33 0 0 15	62	290	77	45	39	7 4 4 1	22	2	75	0	0	2	6	.250	0	3	5.66
1997 Bowie	AA Bal	7 0 0 4	8.2	43	10	9	8	2 0 0 0	7	0	7	0	0	0	0	.000	0	0	8.31
Delmarva	A Bal	1 0 0 1	3	12	3	0	0	0 0 0 0	0	0	0	0	0	0	0	.000	0	1	0.00
Frederick	A+ Bal	31 0 0 18	67	282	48	19	18	4 6 1 0	38	3	98	0	1	3	3	.500	0	5	2.42
5 Min. YEARS		132 17 1 49	339.1	1507	339	197	154	25 20 20 3	139	7	367	7	4	10	22	.313	0	13	4.08

Mike Eaglin

Bats: Right **Throws:** Right **Pos:** 2B   **Ht:** 5'10" **Wt:** 170 **Born:** 4/25/73 **Age:** 25

		BATTING													BASERUNNING				PERCENTAGES		
Year Team	Lg Org	G	AB	H	2B	3B	HR	TB	R	RBI	TBB	IBB	SO	HBP	SH	SF	SB	CS	SB%	GDP	Avg	OBP	SLG
1992 Braves	R Atl	14	45	11	1	0	0	12	4	3	4	0	8	0	2	1	3	1	.75	0	.244	.300	.267
1993 Idaho Falls	R+ Atl	66	236	77	5	4	2	96	50	35	29	0	48	1	2	2	28	11	.72	1	.326	.399	.407
1994 Macon	A Atl	26	77	18	0	0	0	18	8	5	9	0	18	2	2	0	7	2	.78	1	.234	.330	.234
1995 Macon	A Atl	129	530	141	15	4	2	170	82	30	64	0	94	7	5	1	41	13	.76	8	.266	.352	.321
1996 Durham	A+ Atl	131	466	118	25	2	11	180	84	54	50	0	88	18	4	4	23	12	.66	1	.253	.346	.386
1997 Greenville	AA Atl	126	396	114	15	3	5	150	62	47	41	4	66	9	13	3	15	10	.60	5	.288	.365	.379
6 Min. YEARS		492	1750	479	61	13	20	626	290	174	197	4	322	37	28	11	117	49	.70	16	.274	.357	.358

Derrin Ebert

Pitches: Left **Bats:** Right **Pos:** P   **Ht:** 6'3" **Wt:** 175 **Born:** 8/21/76 **Age:** 21

		HOW MUCH HE PITCHED				WHAT HE GAVE UP									THE RESULTS					
Year Team	Lg Org	G GS CG GF	IP	BFP	H	R	ER	HR SH SF HB	TBB	IBB	SO	WP	Bk	W	L	Pct.	ShO	Sv	ERA
1994 Braves	R Atl	10 7 1 2	43	176	40	18	14	4 0 0 1	8	0	25	1	3	1	3	.250	1	0	2.93
1995 Macon	A Atl	28 28 0 0	182	766	184	87	67	12 5 4 7	46	0	124	3	2	14	5	.737	0	0	3.31
1996 Durham	A+ Atl	27 27 2 0	166.1	711	189	102	74	13 8 9 4	37	1	99	5	0	12	9	.571	0	0	4.00
1997 Greenville	AA Atl	27 25 0 0	175.2	743	191	95	80	24 9 6 4	48	1	101	10	0	11	8	.579	0	0	4.10
4 Min. YEARS		92 87 3 2	567	2396	604	302	235	53 22 19 16	139	2	349	19	5	38	25	.603	1	0	3.73

Steve Eddie

Bats: Right **Throws:** Right **Pos:** 3B   **Ht:** 6'1" **Wt:** 185 **Born:** 1/6/71 **Age:** 27

		BATTING													BASERUNNING				PERCENTAGES		
Year Team	Lg Org	G	AB	H	2B	3B	HR	TB	R	RBI	TBB	IBB	SO	HBP	SH	SF	SB	CS	SB%	GDP	Avg	OBP	SLG
1993 Billings	R+ Cin	67	231	66	8	3	3	85	31	38	23	0	33	2	3	0	5	9	.36	4	.286	.355	.368
1994 Chston-WV	A Cin	132	470	116	28	1	1	149	40	57	24	0	82	4	4	6	1	5	.17	11	.247	.286	.317
1995 Chston-WV	A Cin	115	331	91	16	3	6	131	45	47	24	0	46	7	3	6	10	3	.77	9	.275	.332	.396
1996 Winston-Sal	A+ Cin	137	497	135	23	2	9	189	56	64	45	3	78	4	6	4	14	9	.61	14	.272	.335	.380
1997 Chattanooga	AA Cin	118	394	113	25	4	8	170	57	49	21	4	64	1	3	7	3	2	.60	10	.287	.319	.431
5 Min. YEARS		569	1923	521	100	11	27	724	229	255	137	7	303	18	19	23	33	28	.54	48	.271	.322	.376

Chris Eddy

Pitches: Left Bats: Left Pos: P

Ht: 6' 3" Wt: 200 Born: 11/27/69 Age: 28

		HOW MUCH HE PITCHED						WHAT HE GAVE UP										THE RESULTS					
Year Team	Lg Org	G	GS	CG	GF	IP	BFP	H	R	ER	HR	SH	SF	HB	TBB	IBB	SO	WP	Bk	W	L	Pct.	ShO	Sv	ERA
1992 Eugene	A- KC	23	0	0	11	45.1	191	25	13	8	1	2	2	6	23	1	63	3	3	4	2	.667	0	5	1.59
1993 Wilmington	A+ KC	55	0	0	38	54	237	39	23	18	4	4	6	3	37	1	67	8	1	2	2	.500	0	14	3.00
1994 Memphis	AA KC	43	0	0	19	78.1	336	74	37	34	3	4	2	1	32	3	86	5	0	9	2	.818	0	1	3.91
1995 Omaha	AAA KC	14	0	0	6	17.1	84	20	15	14	1	1	2	2	12	2	12	0	0	1	1	.500	0	0	7.27
Wichita	AA KC	9	0	0	5	9	38	8	4	4	1	0	0	1	3	0	10	0	0	1	0	1.000	0	1	4.00
1996 Wichita	AA KC	30	0	0	16	30.1	138	33	16	10	6	1	0	1	18	1	22	3	0	0	0	.000	0	0	2.97
New Orleans	AAA Mil	12	0	0	4	8.1	49	13	9	9	3	0	0	0	11	0	11	1	0	0	0	.000	0	0	9.72
1997 Tulsa	AA Tex	41	0	0	24	51	222	48	24	18	1	1	4	1	24	0	45	2	0	4	0	1.000	0	5	3.18
1995 Oakland	AL	6	0	0	0	3.2	22	7	3	3	0	2	0	2	2	0	2	1	0	0	0	.000	0	0	7.36
6 Min. YEARS		227	0	0	123	293.2	1295	260	141	115	20	13	16	15	160	8	316	22	4	21	7	.750	0	26	3.52

Ken Edenfield

Pitches: Right Bats: Right Pos: P

Ht: 6' 1" Wt: 165 Born: 3/18/67 Age: 31

		HOW MUCH HE PITCHED						WHAT HE GAVE UP										THE RESULTS					
Year Team	Lg Org	G	GS	CG	GF	IP	BFP	H	R	ER	HR	SH	SF	HB	TBB	IBB	SO	WP	Bk	W	L	Pct.	ShO	Sv	ERA
1990 Boise	A- Ana	31	0	0	24	54.1	225	38	15	10	1	5	1	4	20	3	57	2	0	8	4	.667	0	9	1.66
1991 Quad City	A Ana	47	0	0	40	87	356	69	30	25	3	5	3	4	30	2	106	5	1	8	5	.615	0	15	2.59
1992 Palm Spring	A+ Ana	13	0	0	13	18.1	70	12	1	1	0	0	0	0	7	0	20	0	0	0	0	.000	0	7	0.49
Midland	AA Ana	31	0	0	17	49.2	225	60	35	33	5	3	2	4	24	3	43	4	0	1	5	.167	0	2	5.98
1993 Midland	AA Ana	48	3	1	19	93.2	404	93	56	48	10	2	5	8	35	5	84	14	2	5	8	.385	0	4	4.61
Vancouver	AAA Ana	2	0	0	2	3.2	13	1	0	0	0	0	0	1	1	0	5	0	0	0	0	.000	0	0	0.00
1994 Vancouver	AAA Ana	51	0	0	28	87.2	368	69	38	33	7	3	4	9	36	3	84	12	0	9	4	.692	0	4	3.39
1995 Vancouver	AAA Ana	33	0	0	4	60	259	56	24	23	2	3	3	5	25	2	44	5	0	7	2	.778	0	0	3.45
1996 Vancouver	AAA Ana	19	0	0	7	32	139	26	13	10	1	3	2	1	20	5	18	2	1	2	4	.333	0	0	2.81
Columbus	AAA NYA	33	0	0	13	42.1	172	32	12	11	1	4	0	4	15	1	28	2	0	4	1	.800	0	3	2.34
1997 Columbus	AAA NYA	9	0	0	3	13	74	23	19	11	2	0	1	0	8	0	11	3	0	1	0	1.000	0	0	6.92
1995 California	AL	7	0	0	3	12.2	56	15	7	6	1	0	1	0	5	0	6	3	0	0	0	.000	0	0	4.26
1996 California	AL	2	0	0	0	4.1	26	10	5	5	2	0	0	1	2	0	4	0	0	0	0	.000	0	0	10.38
8 Min. YEARS		317	3	1	170	541.2	2305	479	243	204	32	28	21	41	221	24	500	49	4	45	33	.577	0	44	3.39
2 Maj. YEARS		9	0	0	3	17	82	25	12	11	3	0	1	1	7	0	10	3	0	0	0	.000	0	0	5.82

Tim Edge

Bats: Right Throws: Right Pos: C

Ht: 6'0" Wt: 210 Born: 10/26/68 Age: 29

		BATTING															BASERUNNING				PERCENTAGES		
Year Team	Lg Org	G	AB	H	2B	3B	HR	TB	R	RBI	TBB	IBB	SO	HBP	SH	SF	SB	CS	SB%	GDP	Avg	OBP	SLG
1990 Welland	A- Pit	63	149	32	5	0	1	40	6	12	19	1	27	2	0	1	4	3	.57	1	.215	.310	.268
1991 Salem	A+ Pit	96	298	67	16	2	6	105	36	30	44	1	67	5	5	0	4	2	.67	7	.225	.334	.352
1992 Carolina	AA Pit	4	9	1	0	0	0	1	1	0	2	1	5	0	0	0	0	0	.00	0	.111	.273	.111
Salem	A+ Pit	68	216	39	5	1	6	64	18	26	21	0	55	5	0	1	3	2	.60	3	.181	.267	.296
1993 Buffalo	AAA Pit	1	2	0	0	0	0	0	0	0	0	0	0	0	0	0	0	0	.00	0	.000	.000	.000
Carolina	AA Pit	46	160	35	8	0	3	52	12	16	11	0	41	1	2	0	1	2	.33	5	.219	.273	.325
1994 Augusta	A Pit	11	29	9	3	0	0	12	2	4	3	0	5	0	0	0	0	0	.00	0	.310	.375	.414
Carolina	AA Pit	6	20	3	1	0	0	4	1	2	1	0	9	0	0	0	0	0	.00	0	.150	.190	.200
Buffalo	AAA Pit	8	18	4	2	0	0	6	0	0	1	0	4	0	0	0	0	0	.00	4	.222	.263	.333
1995 Calgary	AAA Pit	45	126	27	5	0	4	44	15	19	10	0	33	0	1	0	0	0	.00	2	.214	.270	.349
1996 Calgary	AAA Pit	12	36	12	3	0	2	21	6	11	2	0	9	0	1	0	0	0	.00	2	.333	.368	.583
Carolina	AA Pit	53	153	37	10	0	4	59	18	21	16	1	44	2	2	1	1	0	1.00	4	.242	.320	.386
1997 Calgary	AAA Pit	62	187	44	13	2	3	70	23	22	13	2	50	5	3	0	0	2	.00	4	.235	.302	.374
8 Min. YEARS		475	1403	310	71	5	29	478	138	163	143	6	349	20	12	4	13	11	.54	28	.221	.301	.341

Brian Edmondson

Pitches: Right Bats: Right Pos: P

Ht: 6'2" Wt: 165 Born: 1/29/73 Age: 25

		HOW MUCH HE PITCHED						WHAT HE GAVE UP										THE RESULTS					
Year Team	Lg Org	G	GS	CG	GF	IP	BFP	H	R	ER	HR	SH	SF	HB	TBB	IBB	SO	WP	Bk	W	L	Pct.	ShO	Sv	ERA
1991 Bristol	R+ Det	12	12	1	0	69	289	72	38	35	7	1	2	3	23	1	42	5	2	4	4	.500	0	0	4.57
1992 Fayetteville	A Det	28	27	3	0	155.1	665	145	69	58	10	5	3	6	67	0	125	6	2	10	6	.625	1	0	3.36
1993 Lakeland	A+ Det	19	19	1	0	114.1	483	115	44	38	6	1	0	3	43	0	64	7	0	8	5	.615	0	0	2.99
London	AA Det	5	5	1	0	23	109	30	23	16	2	1	0	2	13	0	17	1	0	0	4	.000	0	0	6.26
1994 Trenton	AA Det	26	26	2	0	162	703	171	89	82	12	2	6	6	61	1	90	11	2	11	9	.550	0	0	4.56
1995 Binghamton	AA NYN	23	22	0	0	134.1	601	150	82	71	17	5	5	6	59	2	69	7	0	7	11	.389	1	0	4.76
1996 Binghamton	AA NYN	39	13	1	9	114.1	502	130	69	54	16	7	7	4	38	5	83	3	1	6	6	.500	0	3	4.25
1997 Binghamton	AA NYN	14	0	0	7	22	95	17	4	3	2	1	0	0	7	0	18	1	0	2	0	1.000	0	0	1.23
Norfolk	AAA NYN	31	4	0	8	68.1	296	62	27	22	5	3	3	4	37	2	65	4	1	4	3	.571	0	1	2.90
7 Min. YEARS		197	128	11	24	862.2	3733	892	445	379	75	27	26	32	348	11	573	45	8	52	48	.520	2	4	3.95

Geoff Edsell

Pitches: Right Bats: Right Pos: P

Ht: 6'2" Wt: 200 Born: 12/10/71 Age: 26

		HOW MUCH HE PITCHED						WHAT HE GAVE UP										THE RESULTS					
Year Team	Lg Org	G	GS	CG	GF	IP	BFP	H	R	ER	HR	SH	SF	HB	TBB	IBB	SO	WP	Bk	W	L	Pct.	ShO	Sv	ERA
1993 Boise	A- Ana	13	13	1	0	64	296	64	52	49	10	1	5	3	40	0	63	6	3	4	3	.571	0	0	6.89
1994 Cedar Rapds	A Ana	17	17	4	0	125.1	538	109	54	42	10	5	0	6	65	1	84	10	4	11	5	.688	1	0	3.02
Lk Elsinore	A+ Ana	9	7	0	1	40	174	38	21	18	3	0	0	2	24	1	26	3	2	2	2	.500	0	0	4.05
1995 Lk Elsinore	A+ Ana	23	22	1	0	139.2	600	127	81	57	11	7	3	7	67	0	134	6	1	8	12	.400	1	0	3.67
Midland	AA Ana	5	5	1	0	32	140	39	26	21	4	1	2	0	16	0	19	5	0	2	3	.400	0	0	5.91

Year Team	Lg Org	G	GS	CG	GF	IP	BFP	H	R	ER	HR	SH	SF	HB	TBB	IBB	SO	WP	Bk	W	L	Pct	ShO	Sv	ERA
1996 Midland	AA Ana	14	14	0	0	88	382	84	53	46	10	3	5	6	47	0	60	5	1	5	5	.500	0	0	4.70
Vancouver	AAA Ana	15	15	3	0	105	437	93	45	40	7	5	4	3	45	1	48	2	2	4	6	.400	2	0	3.43
1997 Vancouver	AAA Ana	30	29	6	1	183.1	826	196	121	105	11	5	6	12	96		95	8	0	14	11	.560	1	0	5.15
5 Min. YEARS		126	122	16	2	777.1	3393	750	453	378	67	27	25	39	400	4	529	45	13	50	47	.515	5	0	4.38

Dave Eiland

Pitches: Right Bats: Right Pos: P Ht: 6'3" Wt: 210 Born: 7/5/66 Age: 31

Year Team	Lg Org	G	GS	CG	GF	IP	BFP	H	R	ER	HR	SH	SF	HB	TBB	IBB	SO	WP	Bk	W	L	Pct	ShO	Sv	ERA
1987 Oneonta	A- NYA	5	5	0	0	29.1	109	20	6	6	1	0	0	0	3	0	16	2	0	4	0	1.000	0	0	1.84
Ft. Laud	A+ NYA	8	8	4	0	62.1	248	57	17	13	0	2	0	0	8	0	28	1	1	5	3	.625	1	0	1.88
1988 Albany-Colo	AA NYA	18	18	7	0	119.1	472	95	39	34	8	4	5	1	22	3	66	2	0	9	5	.643	2	0	2.56
Columbus	AAA NYA	4	4	0	0	24.1	106	25	8	7	4	0	1	1	6	0	13	1	0	1	1	.500	0	0	2.59
1989 Columbus	AAA NYA	18	18	2	0	103	427	107	47	43	10	1	3	1	21	0	45	1	1	9	4	.692	0	0	3.76
1990 Columbus	AAA NYA	27	26	11	0	175.1	707	155	63	56	8	3	1	1	32	0	96	2	2	16	5	.762	3	0	2.87
1991 Columbus	AAA NYA	9	9	2	0	60	244	54	22	16	5	1	1	2	7	0	18	1	0	6	1	.857	0	0	2.40
1992 Las Vegas	AAA SD	14	14	0	0	63.2	276	78	43	37	4	7	6	0	11	2	31	0	0	4	5	.444	0	0	5.23
1993 Charlotte	AAA Cle	8	8	0	0	35.2	154	42	22	21	8	1	0	0	12	0	13	0	0	1	3	.250	0	0	5.30
Okla City	AAA Tex	7	7	1	0	35.2	155	39	18	17	1	1	1	0	9	0	15	0	0	3	1	.750	0	0	4.29
1994 Columbus	AAA NYA	26	26	0	0	140.2	597	141	72	56	12	6	7	1	33	0	84	2	0	9	6	.600	0	0	3.58
1995 Columbus	AAA NYA	19	18	1	0	109	444	109	44	38	0	2	1	3	22	2	62	1	0	8	7	.533	1	0	3.14
1996 Louisville	AAA StL	8	6	0	0	24.1	110	27	17	15	2	2	1	2	8	0	17	0	0	1	1	.500	0	0	5.55
Columbus	AAA NYA	15	15	3	0	92.1	360	77	37	30	9	3	3	2	13	0	76	2	0	8	4	.667	0	0	2.92
1997 Yankees	R NYA	2	1	0	0	7	34	12	8	7	0	0	0	0	0	0	5	0	0	1	0	.000	0	0	9.00
Tampa	A+ NYA	3	3	0	0	12	48	11	5	5	0	0	1	0	0	0	11	0	0	1	0	1.000	0	0	3.75
Columbus	AAA NYA	13	11	0	2	62.1	277	80	47	46	8	0	0	0	14	0	43	0	0	4	2	.667	0	0	6.64
1988 New York	AL	3	3	0	0	12.2	57	15	9	9	6	0	0	2	4	0	7	0	0	0	0	.000	0	0	6.39
1989 New York	AL	6	6	0	0	34.1	152	44	25	22	5	1	2	2	13	3	11	0	0	1	3	.250	0	0	5.77
1990 New York	AL	5	5	0	0	30.1	127	31	14	12	2	0	0	0	5	0	16	0	0	2	1	.667	0	0	3.56
1991 New York	AL	18	13	0	0	72.2	317	87	51	43	10	0	3	3	23	1	18	0	0	2	5	.286	0	0	5.33
1992 San Diego	NL	7	7	0	0	27	120	33	21	17	1	0	0	0	5	0	10	0	0	0	2	.000	0	0	5.67
1993 San Diego	NL	10	9	0	0	48.1	217	58	33	28	5	2	2	1	17	1	14	1	0	0	3	.000	0	0	5.21
1995 New York	AL	4	1	0	1	10	51	16	10	7	1	0	1	0	3	1	6	1	0	1	1	.500	0	0	6.30
11 Min. YEARS		204	197	31	2	1156.1	4768	1129	515	447	80	33	31	16	221	7	639	15	4	88	49	.642	7	0	3.48
7 Maj. YEARS		53	44	0	5	235.1	1041	284	163	138	30	3	8	9	70	6	82	2	1	6	15	.286	0	0	5.28

Scott Elarton

Pitches: Right Bats: Right Pos: P Ht: 6'8" Wt: 225 Born: 2/23/76 Age: 22

Year Team	Lg Org	G	GS	CG	GF	IP	BFP	H	R	ER	HR	SH	SF	HB	TBB	IBB	SO	WP	Bk	W	L	Pct	ShO	Sv	ERA
1994 Astros	R Hou	5	5	0	0	28	92	9	0	0	0	0	0	0	5	0	28	1	0	4	0	1.000	0	0	0.00
Quad City	A Hou	9	9	0	0	54.2	220	42	23	20	4	2	2	1	18	0	42	3	1	4	1	.800	0	0	3.29
1995 Quad City	A Hou	26	26	0	0	149.2	668	149	86	74	12	8	4	8	71	2	112	12	0	13	7	.650	0	0	4.45
1996 Kissimmee	A+ Hou	27	27	3	0	172.1	715	154	67	56	13	7	6	8	54	0	130	5	0	12	7	.632	1	0	2.92
1997 Jackson	AA Hou	20	20	2	0	133.1	544	103	57	48	6	3	1	2	47	3	141	5	0	7	4	.636	0	0	3.24
New Orleans	AAA Hou	9	9	0	0	54	228	51	36	32	5	3	1	1	17	1	50	4	0	4	4	.500	0	0	5.33
4 Min. YEARS		96	96	5	0	592	2467	508	269	230	40	23	14	20	212	6	503	30	1	44	23	.657	1	0	3.50

Kevin Ellis

Bats: Right Throws: Right Pos: OF Ht: 6'0" Wt: 210 Born: 11/21/71 Age: 26

Year Team	Lg Org	G	AB	H	2B	3B	HR	TB	R	RBI	TBB	IBB	SO	HBP	SH	SF	SB	CS	SB%	GDP	Avg	OBP	SLG
1993 Huntington	R+ ChN	59	225	60	11	2	13	114	44	48	25	3	43	0	0	2	6	5	.55	2	.267	.337	.507
1994 Peoria	A ChN	105	386	109	18	4	14	177	65	67	42	3	93	7	0	2	3	1	.75	8	.282	.362	.459
1995 Daytona	A+ ChN	120	430	116	17	6	6	163	57	66	26	1	73	10	0	4	6	3	.67	11	.270	.323	.379
1996 Daytona	A+ ChN	128	481	131	23	2	16	206	69	89	25	1	64	7	0	5	5	4	.56	15	.272	.315	.428
1997 Orlando	AA ChN	104	330	84	15	4	8	131	41	41	25	1	66	5	1	2	6	1	.86	7	.255	.315	.397
5 Min. YEARS		516	1852	500	84	18	57	791	276	311	143	9	339	29	1	15	26	14	.65	43	.270	.330	.427

Robert Ellis

Pitches: Right Bats: Right Pos: P Ht: 6'5" Wt: 220 Born: 12/15/70 Age: 27

Year Team	Lg Org	G	GS	CG	GF	IP	BFP	H	R	ER	HR	SH	SF	HB	TBB	IBB	SO	WP	Bk	W	L	Pct	ShO	Sv	ERA
1991 Utica	A- ChA	15	15	1	0	87.2	407	87	66	45	4	6	5	6	61	0	66	13	0	3	9	.250	1	0	4.62
1992 White Sox	R ChA	1	1	0	0	5	24	10	6	6	0	0	0	0	1	0	4	0	0	1	0	1.000	0	0	10.80
South Bend	A ChA	18	18	1	0	123	481	90	46	32	3	4	2	4	35	0	97	7	2	6	5	.545	1	0	2.34
1993 Sarasota	A+ ChA	15	15	8	0	104	414	81	37	29	3	4	3	3	31	1	79	6	1	7	8	.467	2	0	2.51
Birmingham	AA ChA	12	12	2	0	81.1	336	68	33	28	2	1	1	4	21	0	77	6	0	6	3	.667	1	0	3.10
1994 Nashville	AAA ChA	19	19	1	0	105	483	126	77	71	19	5	6	2	55	1	76	1	4	4	10	.286	0	0	6.09
1995 Nashville	AAA ChA	4	4	0	0	20.2	85	16	7	5	2	0	1	1	10	0	9	1	0	1	1	.500	0	0	2.18
1996 Nashville	AAA ChA	19	13	1	2	70.1	327	78	49	47	6	5	3	7	45	3	35	8	0	3	8	.273	0	0	6.01
Birmingham	AA ChA	2	2	0	0	7.1	35	6	9	9	1	0	1	1	8	0	8	1	0	0	1	.000	0	0	11.05
Vancouver	AAA Ana	7	7	1	0	44.1	186	30	19	16	2	2	2	0	28	0	29	5	0	2	3	.400	0	0	3.25
1997 Vancouver	AAA Ana	29	23	3	1	149	698	185	108	98	15	6	6	7	83	1	70	15	1	9	10	.474	0	0	5.92
1996 California	AL	3	0	0	3	5	19	0	0	0	0	0	0	0	4	0	5	1	0	0	0	.000	0	0	0.00
7 Min. YEARS		141	129	18	3	797.2	3476	777	457	386	57	33	30	35	378	6	550	63	8	42	58	.420	5	0	4.36

Narciso Elvira

Pitches: Left Bats: Left Pos: P Ht: 5'10" Wt: 160 Born: 10/29/67 Age: 30

Year Team	Lg Org	G	GS	CG	GF	IP	BFP	H	R	ER	HR	SH	SF	HB	TBB	IBB	SO	WP	Bk	W	L	Pct.	ShO	Sv	ERA
1987 Beloit	A Mil	4	4	1	0	27	102	15	5	4	1	1	0	0	12	0	29	3	0	3	0	1.000	1	0	1.33
1988 Stockton	A+ Mil	25	23	0	1	135.1	563	87	49	44	6	6	7	7	79	1	161	10	4	7	6	.538	0	0	2.93
1989 El Paso	AA Mil	7	7	0	0	33	157	48	34	28	4	0	1	1	23	0	18	4	3	2	2	.500	0	0	7.64
Stockton	A+ Mil	17	17	6	0	115.1	470	92	45	39	5	3	1	5	43	0	135	11	1	8	5	.615	2	0	3.04
1990 Beloit	A Mil	8	7	0	1	38.1	160	37	16	10	1	1	2	0	9	0	45	2	0	3	2	.600	0	1	2.35
El Paso	AA Mil	4	4	0	0	18	77	17	11	9	4	0	0	0	6	0	12	0	0	0	2	.000	0	0	4.50
1991 Denver	AAA Mil	18	13	1	1	80	374	100	62	53	8	6	3	4	40	1	52	3	1	0	4	.000	0	0	5.96
1992 Okla City	AAA Tex	19	16	0	2	88.2	370	87	54	49	9	5	3	3	28	0	45	2	1	4	5	.444	0	0	4.97
1996 Albuquerque	AAA LA	3	3	0	0	17	76	19	12	9	1	0	1	0	9	0	14	0	1	1	1	.500	0	0	4.76
1997 Albuquerque	AAA LA	4	0	0	0	2.2	17	5	6	5	2	0	0	0	3	0	1	0	0	0	0	.000	0	0	16.88
1990 Milwaukee	AL	4	0	0	2	5	25	6	3	3	0	0	0	0	5	0	6	0	0	0	0	.000	0	0	5.40
8 Min. YEARS		109	94	8	5	555.1	2366	507	294	250	41	22	18	20	252	2	515	36	10	28	27	.509	3	1	4.05

Chad Epperson

Bats: Both Throws: Right Pos: C Ht: 6'3" Wt: 221 Born: 3/26/72 Age: 26

Year Team	Lg Org	G	AB	H	2B	3B	HR	TB	R	RBI	TBB	IBB	SO	HBP	SH	SF	SB	CS	SB%	GDP	Avg	OBP	SLG
1992 Mets	R NYN	37	97	16	2	0	1	21	7	12	12	0	20	3	0	3	1	1	.50	2	.165	.270	.216
1993 Kingsport	R+ NYN	38	117	40	7	0	6	65	15	26	18	0	24	1	1	0	3	1	.75	4	.342	.434	.556
1994 St. Lucie	A+ NYN	50	148	32	7	0	2	45	15	10	16	2	42	0	1	2	1	2	.33	2	.216	.289	.304
1995 Binghamton	AA NYN	7	17	1	0	0	0	3	0	0	1	1	8	0	0	0	1	0	1.00	0	.059	.111	.176
St. Lucie	A+ NYN	42	121	23	7	1	1	35	7	14	17	2	32	0	1	2	1	0	1.00	7	.190	.286	.289
1996 Lafayette	IND —	56	217	73	15	4	10	126	46	49	29	1	44	0	1	3	9	3	.75	4	.336	.410	.581
1997 Sarasota	A+ Bos	107	367	100	25	1	8	151	45	48	32	3	95	1	1	1	13	8	.62	8	.272	.332	.411
Trenton	AA Bos	3	9	3	1	0	0	4	2	1	0	0	2	0	0	0	1	0	1.00	0	.333	.333	.444
6 Min. YEARS		340	1093	288	64	7	28	450	137	160	125	9	267	5	5	11	30	15	.67	27	.263	.339	.412

Ramon Espinosa

Bats: Right Throws: Right Pos: OF Ht: 6'0" Wt: 175 Born: 2/7/72 Age: 26

Year Team	Lg Org	G	AB	H	2B	3B	HR	TB	R	RBI	TBB	IBB	SO	HBP	SH	SF	SB	CS	SB%	GDP	Avg	OBP	SLG
1991 Pirates	R Pit	19	63	15	2	0	0	17	7	5	2	0	7	0	0	0	3	0	1.00	3	.238	.262	.270
1992 Welland	A- Pit	60	208	56	12	5	4	90	27	22	9	0	23	0	0	0	10	5	.67	9	.269	.297	.433
1993 Augusta	A Pit	70	266	79	9	3	2	100	32	27	12	2	51	2	1	3	17	5	.77	12	.297	.329	.376
Salem	A+ Pit	54	208	56	8	2	8	92	30	25	6	0	36	1	2	0	11	6	.65	6	.269	.293	.442
1994 Carolina	AA Pit	82	291	78	16	3	2	106	44	40	11	1	38	1	2	4	12	10	.55	4	.268	.293	.364
1995 Carolina	AA Pit	134	489	140	28	2	3	181	69	48	17	3	64	5	8	1	14	6	.70	15	.286	.316	.370
1996 Calgary	AAA Pit	78	245	69	8	8	0	93	37	25	6	3	28	2	3	0	2	3	.40	7	.282	.304	.380
1997 Carolina	AA Pit	19	72	20	2	1	1	27	10	10	3	0	15	0	0	0	0	2	.00	3	.278	.307	.375
Binghamton	AA NYN	67	255	69	7	1	11	111	32	37	13	1	39	4	2	2	10	1	.91	6	.271	.314	.435
Norfolk	AAA NYN	27	77	26	3	1	0	31	7	8	2	1	10	1	0	0	2	1	.67	1	.338	.363	.403
7 Min. YEARS		610	2174	608	95	26	31	848	295	247	81	11	311	16	18	12	81	39	.68	68	.280	.309	.390

Horacio Estrada

Pitches: Left Bats: Left Pos: P Ht: 6'1" Wt: 185 Born: 10/19/75 Age: 22

Year Team	Lg Org	G	GS	CG	GF	IP	BFP	H	R	ER	HR	SH	SF	HB	TBB	IBB	SO	WP	Bk	W	L	Pct.	ShO	Sv	ERA
1992 Brewers	R Mil	12	6	1	3	31	158	40	37	34	2	3	1	7	19	1	16	3	0	0	4	.000	0	0	9.87
1995 Brewers	R Mil	8	1	0	3	17	73	13	9	7	1	1	1	0	8	0	21	4	2	0	1	.000	0	2	3.71
Helena	R+ Mil	13	0	0	1	30	144	27	21	18	3	5	0	3	24	0	30	2	0	1	2	.333	0	0	5.40
1996 Beloit	A Mil	17	0	0	9	29.1	113	21	8	4	2	2	0	0	11	1	34	5	1	2	1	.667	0	1	1.23
Stockton	A+ Mil	29	0	0	11	51	214	43	29	26	7	1	1	2	21	2	63	3	0	1	3	.250	0	3	4.59
1997 El Paso	AA Mil	29	23	0	2	153.2	694	174	93	81	11	4	4	4	70	0	127	8	3	8	10	.444	0	1	4.74
4 Min. YEARS		108	28	1	29	312	1396	318	197	170	26	16	7	16	153	4	290	25	6	12	21	.364	0	7	4.90

Osmani Estrada

Bats: Right Throws: Right Pos: 2B Ht: 5'8" Wt: 180 Born: 1/23/69 Age: 29

Year Team	Lg Org	G	AB	H	2B	3B	HR	TB	R	RBI	TBB	IBB	SO	HBP	SH	SF	SB	CS	SB%	GDP	Avg	OBP	SLG
1993 Erie	A- Tex	60	225	60	11	0	4	83	24	22	17	1	26	6	1	2	1	7	.13	4	.267	.332	.369
1994 Charlotte	A+ Tex	131	501	128	29	4	4	177	64	30	57	0	60	11	7	5	8	10	.44	10	.255	.341	.353
1995 Tulsa	AA Tex	120	410	109	23	3	3	147	44	43	35	2	49	9	5	4	2	2	.00	9	.266	.334	.359
1996 Tulsa	AA Tex	27	85	22	4	0	2	32	12	16	9	0	13	1	0	1	1	1	.50	2	.259	.333	.376
Okla City	AAA Tex	50	130	34	6	1	1	45	15	13	14	0	26	1	1	1	3	1	.75	3	.262	.336	.346
1997 Okla City	AAA Tex	91	288	65	9	0	1	77	22	20	20	0	37	2	3	4	7	2	.78	8	.226	.277	.267
5 Min. YEARS		479	1639	418	82	8	15	561	181	144	152	3	211	30	17	17	20	23	.47	36	.255	.326	.342

Todd Etler

Pitches: Right Bats: Right Pos: P Ht: 6'0" Wt: 205 Born: 4/18/74 Age: 24

Year Team	Lg Org	G	GS	CG	GF	IP	BFP	H	R	ER	HR	SH	SF	HB	TBB	IBB	SO	WP	Bk	W	L	Pct.	ShO	Sv	ERA
1992 Princeton	R+ Cin	12	0	0	0	52	241	62	40	28	3	2	2	4	21	0	29	5	0	4	4	.500	0	0	4.85
1993 Billings	R+ Cin	15	15	1	0	89.2	359	75	33	27	4	2	4	7	30	0	55	4	0	8	1	.889	1	0	2.71

Year Team	Lg Org	G	GS	CG	GF	IP	BFP	H	R	ER	HR	SH	SF	HB	TBB	IBB	SO	WP	Bk	W	L	Pct.	ShO	Sv	ERA
1994 Chston-WV	A Cin	7	7	1	0	47.2	190	48	17	14	4	1	0	2	3	1	31	0	0	4	2	.667	1	0	2.64
Winston-Sal	A+ Cin	19	19	1	0	106	479	141	84	76	25	1	5	3	31	0	61	5	1	5	11	.313	1	0	6.45
1995 Winston-Sal	A+ Cin	24	23	3	0	153.2	628	148	71	63	13	4	5	2	49	2	78	3	2	6	12	.333	0	0	3.69
1996 Winston-Sal	A+ Cin	33	1	0	16	77.1	321	72	30	30	7	3	2	5	17	0	59	2	0	4	5	.444	0	2	3.49
1997 Burlington	A Cin	25	0	0	12	43	175	34	13	10	2	2	0	2	14	2	40	2	0	2	3	.400	0	3	2.09
Chattanooga	AA Cin	23	0	0	6	37	172	38	29	27	6	1	1	1	24	4	29	5	0	0	3	.000	0	0	6.57
6 Min. YEARS		158	75	6	34	606.1	2565	618	317	275	64	16	19	26	189	9	382	26	3	33	41	.446	3	5	4.08

Bart Evans

Pitches: Right **Bats:** Right **Pos:** P   **Ht:** 6'1" **Wt:** 190 **Born:** 12/30/70 **Age:** 27

Year Team	Lg Org	G	GS	CG	GF	IP	BFP	H	R	ER	HR	SH	SF	HB	TBB	IBB	SO	WP	Bk	W	L	Pct.	ShO	Sv	ERA
1992 Eugene	A- KC	13	1	0	4	26	126	17	20	18	1	1	2	4	31	0	39	14	0	1	1	.500	0	0	6.23
1993 Rockford	A KC	27	16	0	4	99	439	95	52	48	5	1	2	4	60	0	120	10	1	10	4	.714	0	0	4.36
1994 Wilmington	A+ KC	26	26	0	0	145	587	107	53	48	7	1	0	4	61	0	145	10	0	10	3	.769	0	0	2.98
1995 Wichita	AA KC	7	7	0	0	22.1	123	22	28	26	3	1	0	1	45	0	13	7	1	0	4	.000	0	0	10.48
Wilmington	A+ KC	16	6	0	4	46.2	215	30	21	15	0	0	1	5	44	0	47	7	0	4	1	.800	0	2	2.89
1996 Wichita	AA KC	9	7	0	0	24.1	146	31	38	32	7	3	2	6	36	0	16	12	0	1	2	.333	0	0	11.84
1997 Wilmington	A+ KC	16	2	0	8	20.2	101	22	18	15	1	0	2	3	15	0	22	3	0	1	0	.000	0	0	6.53
Wichita	AA KC	32	0	0	22	33.1	148	45	20	17	4	2	1	0	8	2	28	1	0	1	2	.333	0	6	4.59
6 Min. YEARS		146	65	0	42	417.1	1885	369	250	219	28	9	10	27	300	2	430	64	2	27	18	.600	0	8	4.72

Jason Evans

Bats: Both **Throws:** Right **Pos:** OF   **Ht:** 5'11" **Wt:** 187 **Born:** 2/11/71 **Age:** 27

Year Team	Lg Org	G	AB	H	2B	3B	HR	TB	R	RBI	TBB	IBB	SO	HBP	SH	SF	SB	CS	SB%	GDP	Avg	OBP	SLG
1992 Utica	A- ChA	32	120	32	5	1	1	42	15	22	13	2	17	2	0	1	4	1	.80	2	.267	.346	.350
1993 Hickory	A ChA	82	274	58	6	1	1	69	26	29	31	2	56	2	3	3	11	4	.73	2	.212	.294	.252
1994 South Bend	A ChA	97	355	94	15	3	6	133	53	48	47	3	70	2	8	5	8	8	.50	3	.265	.350	.375
1995 South Bend	A ChA	101	336	94	17	4	6	137	70	36	79	1	74	6	6	3	11	4	.73	2	.280	.422	.408
1996 Pr William	A+ ChA	95	329	87	24	2	4	127	41	41	58	1	80	2	2	3	4	3	.57	7	.264	.375	.386
1997 Birmingham	AA ChA	63	223	68	16	1	5	101	33	25	28	4	51	0	3	1	2	2	.50	2	.305	.381	.453
Nashville	AAA ChA	65	194	55	10	1	1	70	38	27	49	1	45	4	2	0	6	3	.67	1	.284	.437	.361
6 Min. YEARS		535	1831	488	93	13	24	679	276	228	305	14	393	18	26	16	46	25	.65	20	.267	.374	.371

Ethan Faggett

Bats: Left **Throws:** Left **Pos:** OF   **Ht:** 6'0" **Wt:** 190 **Born:** 8/21/74 **Age:** 23

Year Team	Lg Org	G	AB	H	2B	3B	HR	TB	R	RBI	TBB	IBB	SO	HBP	SH	SF	SB	CS	SB%	GDP	Avg	OBP	SLG
1992 Red Sox	R Bos	34	103	18	1	1	1	24	9	9	10	0	37	2	0	0	1	2	.33	1	.175	.261	.233
1993 Red Sox	R Bos	23	58	10	2	1	0	14	4	2	10	0	15	1	0	1	5	1	.83	0	.172	.300	.241
1994 Red Sox	R Bos	41	117	34	2	2	1	43	14	17	12	0	33	2	0	0	10	7	.59	0	.291	.366	.368
1995 Michigan	A Bos	115	399	97	11	7	8	146	56	47	37	3	112	4	3	2	23	7	.77	9	.243	.312	.366
1996 Sarasota	A+ Bos	110	408	112	12	8	4	152	48	35	35	0	118	6	7	1	24	10	.71	9	.275	.340	.373
1997 Sarasota	A+ Bos	114	410	120	19	9	3	166	56	46	43	4	87	7	4	4	23	12	.66	4	.293	.366	.405
Trenton	AA Bos	17	56	16	2	0	2	24	10	8	8	0	17	1	2	1	2	0	1.00	0	.286	.379	.429
6 Min. YEARS		454	1551	407	49	28	19	569	197	164	155	7	419	23	16	9	88	39	.69	25	.262	.337	.367

Dan Fagley

Bats: Right **Throws:** Right **Pos:** C   **Ht:** 5'10" **Wt:** 185 **Born:** 12/18/74 **Age:** 23

Year Team	Lg Org	G	AB	H	2B	3B	HR	TB	R	RBI	TBB	IBB	SO	HBP	SH	SF	SB	CS	SB%	GDP	Avg	OBP	SLG
1994 Marlins	R Fla	14	41	6	1	0	0	7	4	2	7	0	15	1	0	0	0	1	.00	1	.146	.286	.171
1995 Marlins	R Fla	16	33	6	0	0	0	6	4	4	4	0	8	1	0	0	0	0	.00	0	.182	.289	.182
1996 Utica	A- Fla	1	3	0	0	0	0	0	0	0	1	0	2	0	0	0	0	0	.00	0	.000	.250	.000
Brevard Cty	A+ Fla	20	53	5	2	0	0	7	1	2	5	0	19	2	1	0	0	0	.00	0	.094	.200	.132
Charlotte	AAA Fla	2	1	0	0	0	0	0	1	0	0	0	0	0	0	0	0	0	.00	3	.000	.000	.000
1997 Brevard Cty	A+ Fla	6	14	3	1	0	0	4	3	1	1	0	6	2	0	0	0	0	.00	0	.214	.353	.286
Birmingham	AA ChA	20	19	7	1	0	0	8	1	0	1	0	5	1	0	0	0	0	.00	1	.368	.400	.421
Hickory	A ChA	9	20	4	2	0	0	6	4	2	4	0	9	0	1	0	0	0	.00	0	.200	.333	.300
4 Min. YEARS		88	184	31	7	0	0	38	18	11	22	0	64	7	2	0	0	1	.00	5	.168	.282	.207

Brian Falkenborg

Pitches: Right **Bats:** Right **Pos:** P   **Ht:** 6'6" **Wt:** 187 **Born:** 1/18/78 **Age:** 20

Year Team	Lg Org	G	GS	CG	GF	IP	BFP	H	R	ER	HR	SH	SF	HB	TBB	IBB	SO	WP	Bk	W	L	Pct.	ShO	Sv	ERA
1996 Orioles	R Bal	8	6	0	1	28	116	21	13	8	1	0	0	1	8	0	36	2	1	0	3	.000	0	0	2.57
High Desert	A+ Bal	1	0	0	0	1	3	1	0	0	0	0	0	0	0	0	1	0	0	0	0	.000	0	0	0.00
1997 Bowie	AA Bal	1	1	0	0	1.2	11	3	3	3	0	0	0	0	3	0	0	0	0	0	1	.000	0	0	16.20
Delmarva	A Bal	25	25	0	0	127	547	122	73	63	6	3	2	13	46	2	107	17	0	7	9	.438	0	0	4.46
2 Min. YEARS		35	32	0	1	157.2	677	147	89	74	7	3	2	14	57	2	144	19	1	7	13	.350	0	0	4.22

Mike Farmer

Pitches: Left Bats: Right Pos: P Ht: 6'1" Wt: 193 Born: 7/3/68 Age: 29

Year Team	Lg Org	G	GS	CG	GF	IP	BFP	H	R	ER	HR	SH	SF	HB	TBB	IBB	SO	WP	Bk	W	L	Pct.	ShO	Sv	ERA
1992 Clearwater	A+ Phi	11	9	1	2	53	209	33	16	11	1	1	1	1	13	1	41	2	5	3	3	.500	1	0	1.87
1993 Reading	AA Phi	22	18	0	1	102	455	125	62	57	18	5	5	1	34	2	64	8	4	5	10	.333	0	0	5.03
1994 Central Val	A+ Col	14	3	0	4	28.2	125	28	17	15	4	1	1	3	11	1	28	4	1	1	4	.200	0	1	4.71
New Haven	AA Col	10	0	0	4	14	54	7	2	2	1	1	1	0	5	0	13	0	0	0	0				1.29
1995 New Haven	AA Col	40	12	0	7	110.1	475	117	63	60	8	6	2	5	35	4	77	5	3	10	5	.667	0	0	4.89
1996 Colo Spngs	AAA Col	9	9	2	0	57.1	245	51	27	21	4	2	3	2	25	2	28	2	0	3	3	.500	1	0	3.30
1997 Colo Spngs	AAA Col	18	8	0	3	54.2	243	70	42	41	14	3	1	5	18	0	29	4	1	5	5	.500	0	0	6.75
1996 Colorado	NL	7	4	0	1	28	127	32	25	24	8	2	0	0	13	0	16	1	0	0	1	.000	0	0	7.71
6 Min. YEARS		124	59	3	23	420	1806	431	229	207	50	19	14	17	141	10	280	25	14	27	30	.474	2	3	4.44

Terry Farrar

Pitches: Left Bats: Both Pos: P Ht: 6'1" Wt: 180 Born: 9/10/69 Age: 28

Year Team	Lg Org	G	GS	CG	GF	IP	BFP	H	R	ER	HR	SH	SF	HB	TBB	IBB	SO	WP	Bk	W	L	Pct.	ShO	Sv	ERA
1991 Bluefield	R+ Bal	3	3	0	0	13	57	11	9	6	1	0	0	2	6	0	17	1	3	1	1	.500	0	0	4.15
Kane County	A Bal	12	11	0	1	65.2	292	73	33	27	4	3	1	6	28	1	35	6	6	6	3	.667	0	0	3.70
1992 Frederick	A+ Bal	28	28	5	0	182.1	762	160	88	71	14	6	5	5	65	0	122	11	3	11	10	.524	1	0	3.50
1993 Bowie	AA Bal	24	21	2	0	116	497	114	51	45	10	5	2	4	40	0	85	5	2	7	7	.500	0	0	3.49
1994 Carolina	AA Pit	3	1	0	1	6	34	7	7	4	0	1	0	0	9	0	5	1	0	1	0	1.000	0	0	6.00
Salem	A+ Pit	30	3	0	7	50	236	68	39	36	9	2	2	3	22	3	41	4	0	0	2	.000	0	0	6.48
1995 Adirondack	IND —	14	14	2	0	86.2	367	87	49	39	2	3	3	8	30	1	79	10	0	8	5	.615	0	0	4.05
1996 Adirondack	IND —	4	3	0	0	12	67	21	20	10	4	1	0	2	7	0	11	2	0	0	1	.000	0	0	7.50
Albany	IND —	10	10	0	0	66.1	289	56	37	25	6	4	3	6	26	2	62	4	2	5	3	.625	0	0	3.39
1997 Tulsa	AA Tex	6	3	0	1	20	92	18	12	11	1	1	0	2	15	0	16	0	0	1	2	.333	0	1	4.95
7 Min. YEARS		134	97	9	10	618	2693	615	345	274	51	26	16	38	248	7	473	44	16	40	34	.541	1	1	3.99

Jim Farrell

Pitches: Right Bats: Right Pos: P Ht: 6'1" Wt: 180 Born: 11/1/73 Age: 24

Year Team	Lg Org	G	GS	CG	GF	IP	BFP	H	R	ER	HR	SH	SF	HB	TBB	IBB	SO	WP	Bk	W	L	Pct.	ShO	Sv	ERA
1995 Red Sox	R Bos	1	1	0	0	6	20	2	1	1	1	0	0	0	1	0	3	0	0	1	0	1.000	0	0	1.50
Michigan	A Bos	13	13	1	0	69	291	62	34	28	10	1	1	5	23	0	70	3	1	3	2	.600	0	0	3.65
1996 Michigan	A Bos	7	7	2	0	44	185	39	15	12	2	1	0	1	17	1	32	1	0	6	1	.857	0	0	2.45
Sarasota	A+ Bos	21	21	3	0	133.1	539	116	58	52	11	4	5	4	34	0	92	9	0	9	8	.529	1	0	3.51
1997 Trenton	AA Bos	26	26	0	0	162.2	706	173	93	79	24	1	5	7	57	0	110	11	0	12	7	.632	0	0	4.37
Pawtucket	AAA Bos	1	1	0	0	5	21	4	0	0	0	0	0	0	2	0	6	1	0	0	0	.000	0	0	0.00
3 Min. YEARS		69	69	6	0	420	1762	396	201	172	48	8	11	17	134	1	313	25	1	31	18	.633	1	0	3.69

Lauro Felix

Bats: Right Throws: Right Pos: 2B Ht: 5'9" Wt: 160 Born: 6/24/70 Age: 28

Year Team	Lg Org	G	AB	H	2B	3B	HR	TB	R	RBI	TBB	IBB	SO	HBP	SH	SF	SB	CS	SB%	GDP	Avg	OBP	SLG
1992 Sou. Oregon	A- Oak	11	24	10	1	0	1	14	5	3	8	0	5	0	0	1	2	1	.67	0	.417	.545	.583
Madison	A Oak	53	199	42	4	0	0	46	29	13	29	0	41	3	8	0	7	6	.54	2	.211	.320	.231
1993 Modesto	A+ Oak	102	302	62	6	2	2	78	55	35	69	0	70	1	8	2	7	4	.64	10	.205	.353	.258
1994 Modesto	A+ Oak	49	141	34	12	1	3	57	17	16	15	0	40	3	3	0	4	1	.80	0	.241	.327	.404
Tacoma	AAA Oak	43	131	23	5	0	0	28	13	5	17	0	34	2	4	1	0	4	.00	5	.176	.278	.214
1995 Huntsville	AA Oak	10	27	3	0	0	0	6	3	1	2	0	8	0	0	0	0	0	.00	1	.111	.172	.222
El Paso	AA Mil	83	220	61	13	1	3	85	51	25	45	0	44	4	5	2	6	1	.86	4	.277	.406	.386
1996 New Orleans	AAA Mil	2	4	0	0	0	0	0	0	0	0	0	2	0	0	0	0	0	.00	0	.000	.000	.000
Stockton	A+ Mil	12	33	6	0	0	2	12	5	5	18	0	9	1	1	0	1	2	.33	0	.182	.481	.364
El Paso	AA Mil	101	301	81	15	2	10	130	71	59	74	1	69	6	12	6	11	5	.69	4	.269	.416	.432
1997 Tucson	AAA Mil	19	47	15	5	0	1	23	7	5	5	0	15	0	2	0	0	0	.00	0	.319	.385	.489
El Paso	AA Mil	49	128	33	9	2	1	49	27	17	20	0	24	4	2	3	1	2	.33	6	.258	.368	.383
6 Min. YEARS		534	1557	370	70	8	24	528	283	184	302	1	361	24	45	15	39	26	.60	32	.238	.367	.339

Jeff Ferguson

Bats: Right Throws: Right Pos: 2B Ht: 5'10" Wt: 175 Born: 6/18/73 Age: 25

Year Team	Lg Org	G	AB	H	2B	3B	HR	TB	R	RBI	TBB	IBB	SO	HBP	SH	SF	SB	CS	SB%	GDP	Avg	OBP	SLG
1994 Ft. Wayne	A Min	22	89	23	7	1	1	35	15	6	11	0	18	1	0	0	4	1	.80	1	.258	.347	.393
1996 Hardware City	AA Min	89	284	81	16	2	5	116	46	20	37	2	67	3	0	1	5	4	.56	2	.285	.372	.408
1997 New Britain	AA Min	36	135	33	4	0	1	40	19	21	12	0	31	1	1	1	1	1	.50	2	.244	.309	.296
Salt Lake	AAA Min	65	241	68	19	2	8	115	51	35	24	0	48	6	1	1	4	2	.67	5	.282	.360	.477
3 Min. YEARS		212	749	205	46	5	15	306	131	82	84	2	164	11	2	3	14	8	.64	10	.274	.354	.409

Ramon Fermin

Pitches: Right Bats: Right Pos: P Ht: 6'3" Wt: 180 Born: 11/25/72 Age: 25

Year Team	Lg Org	G	GS	CG	GF	IP	BFP	H	R	ER	HR	SH	SF	HB	TBB	IBB	SO	WP	Bk	W	L	Pct.	ShO	Sv	ERA
1991 Athletics	R Oak	7	3	1	1	25.1	102	20	6	6	2	1	0	4	4	0	11	0	1	3	0	1.000	0	0	2.13
Modesto	A+ Oak	3	2	0	0	12.1	52	16	7	6	1	1	0	1	3	0	5	0	0	1	0				4.38
1992 Madison	A Oak	14	14	1	0	77.2	330	66	33	21	2	2	4	1	35	0	37	6	2	5	5	.500	0	0	2.43

		HOW MUCH HE PITCHED					WHAT HE GAVE UP					THE RESULTS		
Year Team	Lg Org	G GS CG GF	IP	BFP	H R ER	HR SH SF HB	TBB IBB SO	WP Bk	W L	Pct. ShO Sv	ERA
Modesto	A+ Oak	14 5 0 4	42.2	196	50 31 27	5 1 0 2	19 1 18	3 1	2 3	.400 0 1	5.70
1993 Modesto	A+ Oak	31 5 0 8	67.1	321	78 56 46	7 3 2 5	37 5 47	10 0	4 6	.400 0 1	6.15
1994 Modesto	A+ Oak	29 18 0 8	133	565	129 71 53	12 3 3 9	42 1 120	16 1	9 6	.600 0 5	3.59
1995 Huntsville	AA Oak	32 13 0 16	100.1	435	105 53 43	5 6 1 6	45 5 58	6 1	6 7	.462 0 7	3.86
1996 Jacksnville	AA Det	46 6 0 13	84	378	82 56 42	5 2 3 5	46 2 48	11 0	6 6	.500 0 3	4.50
1997 Toledo	AAA Det	41 8 0 12	80.1	376	103 53 44	10 5 5 4	33 3 46	4 0	4 2	.667 0 3	4.93
1995 Oakland	AL	1 0 0 1	1.1	9	4 2 2	0 0 0 0	1 0 1	0 1	0 0	.000 0 0	13.50
7 Min. YEARS		217 74 2 62	623	2755	649 366 288	49 24 18 37	264 17 390	56 6	40 35	.533 0 17	4.16

Jared Fernandez

Pitches: Right Bats: Right Pos: P   Ht: 6'2" Wt: 225 Born: 2/2/72 Age: 26

		HOW MUCH HE PITCHED					WHAT HE GAVE UP					THE RESULTS		
Year Team	Lg Org	G GS CG GF	IP	BFP	H R ER	HR SH SF HB	TBB IBB SO	WP Bk	W L	Pct. ShO Sv	ERA
1994 Utica	A- Bos	21 1 0 15	30	144	43 18 12	4 0 0 0	8 2 24	0 1	1 1	.500 0 4	3.60
1995 Utica	A- Bos	5 5 1 0	38	148	30 11 8	2 0 1 1	9 1 23	1 0	3 2	.600 0 0	1.89
Trenton	AA Bos	11 10 1 0	67	290	64 32 29	4 3 1 5	28 1 40	2 0	5 4	.556 0 0	3.90
1996 Trenton	AA Bos	30 29 3 0	179	798	185 115 101	19 5 9 10	83 5 94	10 0	9 9	.500 0 0	5.08
1997 Pawtucket	AAA Bos	11 11 0 0	60.2	281	76 45 39	7 2 2 5	28 1 33	4 0	0 3	.000 0 0	5.79
Trenton	AA Bos	21 16 1 4	121.1	560	138 90 73	12 2 2 0	66 0 73	14 0	4 6	.400 0 0	5.41
4 Min. YEARS		99 72 6 19	496	2221	536 311 262	48 12 15 21	222 10 287	31 1	22 25	.468 0 4	4.75

Jose Fernandez

Bats: Right Throws: Right Pos: 3B   Ht: 6'2" Wt: 210 Born: 11/2/74 Age: 23

		BATTING													BASERUNNING				PERCENTAGES		
Year Team	Lg Org	G AB H	2B	3B	HR	TB	R	RBI	TBB	IBB	SO	HBP	SH	SF	SB	CS	SB%	GDP	Avg	OBP	SLG
1994 Expos	R Mon	44 168 39	8	0	5	62	27	23	13	0	33	2	0	1	11	1	.92	2	.232	.293	.369
1995 Vermont	A- Mon	66 270 74	6	7	4	106	38	41	13	2	51	1	1	2	29	4	.88	2	.274	.308	.393
1996 Delmarva	A- Mon	126 421 115	23	6	12	186	72	70	50	5	76	7	0	3	23	13	.64	5	.273	.358	.442
1997 Wst Plm Bch	A+ Mon	97 350 108	21	3	9	162	49	58	37	3	76	7	0	0	22	14	.61	8	.309	.386	.463
Harrisburg	AA Mon	29 96 22	3	1	4	39	10	11	11	0	28	1	0	0	2	0	1.00	4	.229	.315	.406
4 Min. YEARS		362 1305 358	61	17	34	555	196	203	124	10	264	18	1	6	87	32	.73	21	.274	.344	.425

Osvaldo Fernandez

Pitches: Left Bats: Left Pos: P   Ht: 6'2" Wt: 193 Born: 4/15/70 Age: 28

		HOW MUCH HE PITCHED					WHAT HE GAVE UP					THE RESULTS		
Year Team	Lg Org	G GS CG GF	IP	BFP	H R ER	HR SH SF HB	TBB IBB SO	WP Bk	W L	Pct. ShO Sv	ERA
1994 Riverside	A+ Sea	14 13 1 0	84.2	353	67 33 27	8 1 2 3	37 0 80	3 4	8 2	.800 1 0	2.87
1995 Port City	AA Sea	27 26 0 0	156.1	654	139 86 62	6 4 1 5	60 1 160	12 1	12 7	.632 0 0	3.57
1996 Tacoma	AAA Sea	1 1 0 0	3.1	15	4 2 2	0 0 0 0	0 0 6	0 0	0 0	.000 0 0	5.40
1997 Memphis	AA Sea	1 1 0 0	4.1	18	2 1 1	0 0 0 0	4 0 4	1 1	0 0	.000 0 0	2.08
4 Min. YEARS		43 41 1 0	248.2	1040	212 114 92	14 5 3 8	101 1 248	16 6	20 9	.690 1 0	3.33

Sean Fesh

Pitches: Left Bats: Left Pos: P   Ht: 6'2" Wt: 165 Born: 11/3/72 Age: 25

		HOW MUCH HE PITCHED					WHAT HE GAVE UP					THE RESULTS		
Year Team	Lg Org	G GS CG GF	IP	BFP	H R ER	HR SH SF HB	TBB IBB SO	WP Bk	W L	Pct. ShO Sv	ERA
1991 Astros	R Hou	6 0 0 2	12.1	53	5 4 3	0 0 0 0	11 0 7	4 0	0 0	.000 0 0	2.19
1992 Osceola	A+ Hou	3 0 0 2	5.1	24	5 3 1	0 0 0 0	1 0 5	3 0	0 1	.000 0 0	1.69
Astros	R Hou	18 0 0 12	36.1	142	25 7 7	0 3 0 4	8 0 35	4 0	1 0	1.000 0 6	1.73
1993 Asheville	A Hou	65 0 0 58	82.1	353	75 39 33	4 11 6 5	37 8 49	4 1	10 6	.625 0 20	3.61
1994 Osceola	A+ Hou	43 0 0 29	49.2	222	50 27 14	2 5 0 6	24 6 32	2 0	2 4	.333 0 11	2.54
Jackson	AA Hou	20 1 0 5	25.2	122	34 17 12	2 2 1 0	11 0 19	2 0	1 2	.333 0 0	4.21
1995 Tucson	AAA Hou	10 0 0 1	13.1	52	11 2 2	0 0 0 0	3 0 7	0 0	1 0	1.000 0 0	1.35
Las Vegas	AAA SD	30 0 0 11	38	185	53 21 14	2 4 0 3	16 5 18	1 1	2 1	.667 0 1	3.32
1996 Memphis	AA SD	7 0 0 2	8	36	7 5 5	2 0 0 0	7 1 5	0 0	1 1	.500 0 0	5.63
1997 Rancho Cuca	A+ SD	4 0 0 1	4.2	28	10 7 6	2 1 0 1	3 0 5	0 0	0 1	.000 0 0	11.57
Binghamton	AA NYN	45 0 0 13	55.1	255	60 26 20	3 0 1 2	24 0 37	2 3	3 1	.750 0 4	3.25
7 Min. YEARS		251 1 0 136	331	1472	335 158 117	17 26 8 21	145 20 219	22 5	21 17	.553 0 42	3.18

Dave Feuerstein

Bats: Right Throws: Right Pos: OF   Ht: 6'2" Wt: 200 Born: 7/19/73 Age: 24

		BATTING													BASERUNNING				PERCENTAGES		
Year Team	Lg Org	G AB H	2B	3B	HR	TB	R	RBI	TBB	IBB	SO	HBP	SH	SF	SB	CS	SB%	GDP	Avg	OBP	SLG
1995 Portland	A- Col	70 269 72	10	3	5	103	40	44	23	2	41	2	3	3	20	8	.71	9	.268	.327	.383
1996 Asheville	A Col	130 514 147	27	7	1	191	69	69	42	0	68	5	5	5	21	10	.68	7	.286	.343	.372
1997 Salem	A+ Col	94 327 76	13	3	1	98	47	34	21	3	45	4	7	2	20	6	.77	8	.232	.285	.300
New Haven	AA Col	26 104 27	4	3	0	37	8	10	7	0	20	0	0	0	2	1	.67	4	.260	.306	.356
3 Min. YEARS		320 1214 322	54	16	7	429	164	157	93	5	174	11	15	10	63	25	.72	28	.265	.321	.353

Chris Fick

Bats: Left Throws: Right Pos: DH   Ht: 6'2" Wt: 190 Born: 10/4/69 Age: 28

		BATTING													BASERUNNING				PERCENTAGES		
Year Team	Lg Org	G AB H	2B	3B	HR	TB	R	RBI	TBB	IBB	SO	HBP	SH	SF	SB	CS	SB%	GDP	Avg	OBP	SLG
1994 San Berndno	A+ —	44 144 32	10	1	7	65	20	28	15	0	47	3	1	0	2	3	.40	2	.222	.309	.451

	BATTING																BASERUNNING				PERCENTAGES		
Year Team	Lg Org	G	AB	H	2B	3B	HR	TB	R	RBI	TBB	IBB	SO	HBP	SH	SF	SB	CS	SB%	GDP	Avg	OBP	SLG
1995 St. Pete	A+ StL	113	348	102	25	3	13	172	56	52	38	2	79	10	0	3	1	2	.33	9	.293	.376	.494
1996 Arkansas	AA StL	134	448	115	25	2	19	201	64	74	67	8	93	4	0	5	2	5	.29	16	.257	.355	.449
1997 Shreveport	AA SF	4	5	0	0	0	0	0	1	0	1	1	4	0	0	0	0	0	.00	0	.000	.167	.000
High Desert	A+ Ari	17	54	13	3	0	2	22	12	10	11	1	12	2	0	2	1	0	1.00	1	.241	.377	.407
4 Min. YEARS		312	999	262	63	6	41	460	153	164	132	12	235	19	1	10	6	10	.38	28	.262	.356	.460

Mick Fieldbinder

Pitches: Right Bats: Right Pos: P **Ht: 6'4" Wt: 200 Born: 10/2/73 Age: 24**

	HOW MUCH HE PITCHED						WHAT HE GAVE UP										THE RESULTS					
Year Team	Lg Org	G	GS	CG	GF	IP	BFP	H	R	ER	HR	SH	SF	HB	TBB	IBB	SO	WP	Bk	W	L	Pct.	ShO	Sv	ERA
1996 Helena	R+ Mil	2	2	0	0	10	40	8	4	4	1	0	0	1	0	12	1	0	2	0	1.000	0	0	3.60
Beloit	A Mil	12	12	1	0	77	312	74	33	29	2	1	2	1	18	2	66	5	1	9	2	.818	0	0	3.39
1997 Stockton	A+ Mil	21	21	4	0	143.1	594	141	58	45	9	4	3	3	38	2	68	10	0	11	6	.647	1	0	2.83
El Paso	AA Mil	6	6	0	0	37.2	176	55	32	24	3	3	1	0	12	0	20	4	0	2	3	.400	0	0	5.73
2 Min. YEARS		41	41	5	0	268	1122	278	127	102	15	8	6	5	69	4	166	20	1	24	11	.686	1	0	3.43

Nelson Figueroa

Pitches: Right Bats: Both Pos: P **Ht: 6'1" Wt: 165 Born: 5/18/74 Age: 24**

	HOW MUCH HE PITCHED						WHAT HE GAVE UP										THE RESULTS					
Year Team	Lg Org	G	GS	CG	GF	IP	BFP	H	R	ER	HR	SH	SF	HB	TBB	IBB	SO	WP	Bk	W	L	Pct.	ShO	Sv	ERA
1995 Kingsport	R+ NYN	12	12	1	0	76.1	304	57	31	26	3	2	5	2	22	1	79	5	0	7	3	.700	2	0	3.07
1996 Capital City	A NYN	26	25	8	1	185.1	723	119	55	42	10	3	2	2	58	1	200	9	2	14	7	.667	4	0	2.04
1997 Binghamton	AA NYN	33	22	0	3	143	617	137	76	69	14	7	2	6	68	1	116	7	0	5	11	.313	0	0	4.34
3 Min. YEARS		71	59	10	4	404.2	1644	313	162	137	27	13	6	13	148	3	395	21	2	26	21	.553	6	0	3.05

John Finn

Bats: Right Throws: Right Pos: 3B **Ht: 5'8" Wt: 168 Born: 10/18/67 Age: 30**

	BATTING																BASERUNNING				PERCENTAGES		
Year Team	Lg Org	G	AB	H	2B	3B	HR	TB	R	RBI	TBB	IBB	SO	HBP	SH	SF	SB	CS	SB%	GDP	Avg	OBP	SLG
1989 Beloit	A Mil	73	274	82	8	7	1	107	49	20	38	0	27	4	5	2	29	11	.73	3	.299	.390	.391
1990 Stockton	A+ Mil	95	290	60	4	0	1	67	48	23	52	0	50	1	6	6	29	15	.66	1	.207	.324	.231
1991 Stockton	A+ Mil	65	223	57	12	1	0	71	45	25	44	1	28	9	6	3	19	9	.68	5	.256	.394	.318
El Paso	AA Mil	63	230	69	12	2	2	91	48	24	16	0	27	2	5	2	4	2	.67	0	.300	.348	.396
1992 El Paso	AA Mil	124	439	121	12	6	1	148	83	47	71	3	44	11	9	7	30	12	.71	7	.276	.384	.337
1993 New Orleans	AAA Mil	117	335	94	13	2	1	114	47	37	33	1	36	6	9	0	27	9	.75	8	.281	.356	.340
1994 New Orleans	AAA Mil	76	229	66	12	0	2	84	36	24	35	1	21	7	6	4	15	10	.60	3	.288	.393	.367
1995 New Orleans	AAA Mil	35	117	38	4	1	3	53	20	19	13	2	7	2	4	0	9	2	.82	1	.325	.402	.453
1996 Calgary	AAA Pit	69	193	49	13	1	0	64	24	32	25	4	28	3	2	5	2	5	.29	4	.254	.341	.332
Iowa	AAA ChN	17	55	15	1	0	1	19	10	5	4	0	7	2	2	1	1	1	.50	2	.273	.339	.345
1997 Birmingham	AA ChA	73	246	68	15	0	0	83	49	27	39	0	28	8	4	1	13	2	.87	5	.276	.391	.337
9 Min. YEARS		807	2631	719	106	20	12	901	459	283	370	12	303	55	58	31	182	80	.69	39	.273	.371	.342

Tony Fiore

Pitches: Right Bats: Right Pos: P **Ht: 6'4" Wt: 200 Born: 10/12/71 Age: 26**

	HOW MUCH HE PITCHED						WHAT HE GAVE UP										THE RESULTS					
Year Team	Lg Org	G	GS	CG	GF	IP	BFP	H	R	ER	HR	SH	SF	HB	TBB	IBB	SO	WP	Bk	W	L	Pct.	ShO	Sv	ERA
1992 Martinsville	R+ Phi	17	2	0	9	32.1	161	32	20	15	0	2	1	3	31	1	30	11	0	2	3	.400	0	0	4.18
1993 Batavia	A- Phi	16	16	1	0	97.1	411	82	51	33	1	3	4	4	40	0	55	15	0	2	8	.200	0	0	3.05
1994 Spartanburg	A Phi	28	28	9	0	166.2	719	162	94	76	10	2	5	4	77	1	113	19	1	12	13	.480	1	0	4.10
1995 Clearwater	A+ Phi	24	10	0	3	70.1	323	70	41	29	4	3	5	2	44	2	45	9	3	6	2	.750	0	0	3.71
1996 Clearwater	A+ Phi	22	22	3	0	128	533	102	61	45	4	1	1	5	56	1	80	13	1	8	4	.667	1	0	3.16
Reading	AA Phi	5	5	0	0	31	146	32	21	15	2	0	1	1	18	0	19	6	0	1	2	.333	0	0	4.35
1997 Reading	AA Phi	17	16	0	0	104.2	434	89	47	35	8	4	5	0	40	0	64	10	1	8	3	.727	0	0	3.01
Scranton-WB	AAA Phi	9	9	1	0	60.2	268	60	34	26	3	3	1	0	26	1	56	6	1	3	5	.375	0	0	3.86
6 Min. YEARS		138	108	14	12	691	2995	629	369	274	30	22	22	24	332	6	462	89	7	42	40	.512	2	0	3.57

Grant Fithian

Bats: Right Throws: Right Pos: C **Ht: 6'0" Wt: 192 Born: 11/20/71 Age: 26**

	BATTING																BASERUNNING				PERCENTAGES		
Year Team	Lg Org	G	AB	H	2B	3B	HR	TB	R	RBI	TBB	IBB	SO	HBP	SH	SF	SB	CS	SB%	GDP	Avg	OBP	SLG
1994 Tampa	A+ NYA	5	11	2	1	0	0	3	1	0	1	0	3	0	0	0	0	0	.00	1	.182	.250	.273
1995 Tampa	A+ NYA	3	4	1	0	0	0	1	0	1	0	0	2	0	0	0	0	0	.00	0	.250	.250	.250
Greensboro	A NYA	51	151	34	8	1	2	50	16	12	19	0	45	1	3	3	5	4	.56	5	.225	.310	.331
1996 Norwich	AA NYA	63	178	35	7	1	5	59	19	26	11	1	46	1	4	1	1	0	1.00	4	.197	.246	.331
1997 Norwich	AA NYA	79	253	71	16	1	8	113	38	51	41	0	52	0	0	1	1	1	.50	3	.281	.380	.447
4 Min. YEARS		201	597	143	32	3	15	226	74	90	72	1	148	2	7	5	7	5	.58	13	.240	.321	.379

Ben Fleetham

Pitches: Right Bats: Right Pos: P **Ht: 6'1" Wt: 205 Born: 8/3/72 Age: 25**

	HOW MUCH HE PITCHED						WHAT HE GAVE UP										THE RESULTS					
Year Team	Lg Org	G	GS	CG	GF	IP	BFP	H	R	ER	HR	SH	SF	HB	TBB	IBB	SO	WP	Bk	W	L	Pct.	ShO	Sv	ERA
1994 Vermont	A- Mon	17	0	0	2	28.2	125	23	13	8	0	2	2	1	16	1	29	0	2	0	0	.000	0	2	2.51
Burlington	A Mon	6	0	0	2	13.1	51	5	4	3	1	0	1	0	4	0	27	2	3	1	0	1.000	0	0	2.03
Harrisburg	AA Mon	2	0	0	2	3	14	2	0	0	0	0	0	0	2	0	1	1	0	0	0	.000	0	0	0.00

Year Team	Lg Org	G	GS	CG	GF	IP	BFP	H	R	ER	HR	SH	SF	HB	TBB	IBB	SO	WP	Bk	W	L	Pct.	ShO	Sv	ERA
		HOW MUCH HE PITCHED						**WHAT HE GAVE UP**												**THE RESULTS**					
1995 Pueblo	IND —	2	0	0	2	2	8	1	0	0	0	0	0	0	0	0	2	0	0	0	0	.000	0	1	0.00
1996 Delmarva	A Mon	16	0	0	15	19.2	74	9	4	3	2	2	0	0	7	0	34	3	0	1	0	1.000	0	13	1.37
Wst Plm Bch	A+ Mon	31	0	0	29	30.2	122	15	8	7	0	0	1	0	15	0	48	9	2	0	1	.000	0	17	2.05
Harrisburg	AA Mon	4	0	0	3	6	23	2	0	0	0	0	0	0	5	0	6	1	0	0	0	.000	0	1	0.00
1997 Ottawa	AAA Mon	9	0	0	6	9	40	2	3	2	1	0	0	1	10	0	14	2	0	1	2	.333	0	1	2.00
Harrisburg	AA Mon	49	0	0	46	50.1	216	28	21	17	4	3	2	2	33	2	69	4	0	2	1	.667	0	30	3.04
4 Min. YEARS		136	0	0	107	162.2	673	87	53	40	8	7	5	5	92	3	229	23	8	5	4	.556	0	65	2.21

Paul Fletcher

Pitches: Right **Bats:** Right **Pos:** P   **Ht:** 6' 1" **Wt:** 193 **Born:** 1/14/67 **Age:** 31

Year Team	Lg Org	G	GS	CG	GF	IP	BFP	H	R	ER	HR	SH	SF	HB	TBB	IBB	SO	WP	Bk	W	L	Pct.	ShO	Sv	ERA
		HOW MUCH HE PITCHED						**WHAT HE GAVE UP**												**THE RESULTS**					
1988 Martinsvlle	R+ Phi	15	14	1	1	69.1	320	81	44	36	4	1	3	4	33	0	61	3	1	1	3	.250	0	1	4.67
1989 Batavia	A- Phi	14	14	3	0	82.1	339	77	41	30	13	2	2	3	28	0	73	3	1	7	5	.583	0	0	3.28
1990 Spartanburg	A Phi	9	9	1	0	49.1	207	46	24	18	3	1	1	2	18	0	53	7	1	2	4	.333	0	0	3.28
Clearwater	A+ Phi	20	18	2	1	117.1	498	104	56	44	3	6	6	13	49	0	106	7	2	5	8	.385	0	1	3.38
1991 Clearwater	A+ Phi	14	4	0	5	29.1	119	22	6	4	1	1	2	0	8	1	27	2	0	0	1	.000	0	1	1.23
Reading	AA Phi	21	19	3	1	120.2	517	111	56	47	12	3	2	1	56	3	90	6	1	7	9	.438	1	0	3.51
1992 Reading	AA Phi	22	20	2	0	127	521	103	45	40	10	1	1	5	47	2	103	7	0	9	4	.692	1	0	2.83
Scranton-WB	AAA Phi	4	4	0	0	22.2	85	17	8	7	1	0	0	1	2	0	26	2	0	3	0	1.000	1	0	2.78
1993 Scranton-WB	AAA Phi	34	19	2	5	140	625	146	99	88	21	4	4	9	60	3	116	21	0	4	12	.250	1	0	5.66
1994 Scranton-WB	AAA Phi	42	13	3	8	138.1	604	144	78	72	12	4	1	6	54	0	92	6	0	4	9	.308	1	3	4.68
1995 Scranton-WB	AAA Phi	52	0	0	7	61	257	45	33	21	7	7	3	1	28	4	48	8	0	4	1	.800	0	2	3.10
1996 Edmonton	AAA Oak	38	0	0	5	83.1	349	66	28	25	8	2	1	2	41	6	76	3	0	4	6	.400	0	1	2.70
1997 Iowa	AAA ChN	54	0	0	14	78.1	330	63	32	31	11	4	1	1	39	1	67	15	0	10	6	.625	0	0	3.56
1993 Philadelphia	NL	1	0	0	0	0.1	1	0	0	0	0	0	0	0	0	0	0	1	0	0	0	.000	0	0	0.00
1995 Philadelphia	NL	10	0	0	1	13.1	64	15	8	8	2	1	1	1	9	2	10	2	0	1	0	1.000	0	0	5.40
1996 Oakland	AL	1	0	0	0	1.1	10	6	3	3	0	0	0	0	1	0	0	0	0	0	0	.000	0	0	20.25
10 Min. YEARS		339	134	17	47	1119	4771	1025	550	463	106	36	27	48	463	20	923	90	6	60	68	.469	4	9	3.72
3 Maj. YEARS		12	0	0	1	15	75	21	11	11	2	1	1	1	10	2	10	3	0	1	0	1.000	0	0	6.60

Kevin Flora

Bats: Right **Throws:** Right **Pos:** OF   **Ht:** 6' 0" **Wt:** 185 **Born:** 6/10/69 **Age:** 29

Year Team	Lg Org	G	AB	H	2B	3B	HR	TB	R	RBI	TBB	IBB	SO	HBP	SH	SF	SB	CS	SB%	GDP	Avg	OBP	SLG
		BATTING															**BASERUNNING**				**PERCENTAGES**		
1987 Salem	A- Ana	35	88	24	5	1	0	31	17	12	21	0	14	0	3	0	8	4	.67	2	.273	.413	.352
1988 Quad City	A Ana	48	152	33	3	4	0	44	19	15	18	4	33	0	1	0	5	3	.63	4	.217	.300	.289
1989 Quad City	A Ana	120	372	81	8	4	1	100	46	21	57	2	107	6	5	3	30	10	.75	3	.218	.329	.269
1990 Midland	AA Ana	71	232	53	16	5	5	94	35	32	23	0	53	0	3	1	11	5	.69	6	.228	.297	.405
1991 Midland	AA Ana	124	484	138	14	15	12	218	97	67	37	0	92	3	3	3	40	8	.83	2	.285	.338	.450
1992 Edmonton	AAA Ana	52	170	55	8	4	3	80	35	19	29	0	25	1	4	2	9	8	.53	6	.324	.421	.471
1993 Vancouver	AAA Ana	30	94	31	2	0	1	36	17	12	10	0	20	1	2	1	6	2	.75	2	.330	.396	.383
1994 Vancouver	AAA Ana	6	12	2	1	0	0	3	5	1	4	0	4	0	1	0	1	0	1.00	1	.167	.375	.250
Lk Elsinore	A+ Ana	19	72	13	3	2	0	20	13	6	12	0	17	0	1	1	7	1	.88	1	.181	.294	.278
1995 Vancouver	AAA Ana	38	124	37	7	0	3	53	22	14	16	0	33	0	1	1	7	4	.64	2	.298	.376	.427
1996 St. Lucie	A+ NYN	11	39	6	0	2	0	10	8	3	9	1	14	0	0	0	2	0	1.00	0	.154	.313	.256
Norfolk	AAA NYN	46	135	30	8	1	3	49	20	15	11	2	40	4	0	0	9	2	.82	5	.222	.300	.363
1997 New Orleans	AAA Hou	31	109	28	1	3	2	41	14	14	16	1	25	0	1	0	8	2	.80	3	.257	.352	.376
Astros	R Hou	3	10	2	0	0	0	2	1	0	0	0	1	0	0	0	0	0	.00	0	.200	.200	.200
Jackson	AA Hou	1	5	0	0	0	0	0	0	0	0	0	3	0	0	0	0	0	.00	0	.000	.000	.000
1991 California	AL	3	8	1	0	0	0	1	1	0	1	0	5	0	1	0	1	0	1.00	1	.125	.222	.125
1995 California	AL	2	1	0	0	0	0	0	1	0	0	0	1	0	0	0	0	0	.00	0	.000	.000	.000
Philadelphia	NL	24	75	16	3	0	2	25	12	7	4	0	22	0	2	0	1	0	1.00	0	.213	.253	.333
11 Min. YEARS		635	2098	533	76	41	30	781	349	231	263	10	481	15	25	12	143	49	.74	38	.254	.340	.372
2 Maj. YEARS		29	84	17	3	0	2	26	14	7	5	0	28	0	3	0	2	0	1.00	1	.202	.247	.310

Ignacio Flores

Pitches: Right **Bats:** Right **Pos:** P   **Ht:** 6'2" **Wt:** 188 **Born:** 5/8/75 **Age:** 23

Year Team	Lg Org	G	GS	CG	GF	IP	BFP	H	R	ER	HR	SH	SF	HB	TBB	IBB	SO	WP	Bk	W	L	Pct.	ShO	Sv	ERA
		HOW MUCH HE PITCHED						**WHAT HE GAVE UP**												**THE RESULTS**					
1995 Great Falls	R+ LA	16	12	0	1	68.2	301	66	42	36	3	0	1	4	38	0	76	4	2	6	4	.600	0	0	4.72
1997 San Antonio	AA LA	27	18	0	3	133	547	125	59	48	5	3	2	3	39	0	102	14	2	10	7	.588	0	1	3.25
2 Min. YEARS		43	30	0	4	201.2	848	191	101	84	8	3	3	7	77	0	178	18	4	16	11	.593	0	1	3.75

Jose Flores

Bats: Right **Throws:** Right **Pos:** 2B-3B   **Ht:** 5'11" **Wt:** 160 **Born:** 6/26/73 **Age:** 25

Year Team	Lg Org	G	AB	H	2B	3B	HR	TB	R	RBI	TBB	IBB	SO	HBP	SH	SF	SB	CS	SB%	GDP	Avg	OBP	SLG
		BATTING															**BASERUNNING**				**PERCENTAGES**		
1994 Batavia	A- Phi	68	229	58	7	3	0	71	41	16	41	0	31	6	2	2	23	8	.74	3	.253	.378	.310
1995 Clearwater	A+ Phi	49	185	41	4	3	1	54	25	19	15	0	27	4	7	1	12	5	.71	4	.222	.293	.292
Piedmont	A Phi	61	186	49	7	0	0	56	22	19	24	0	29	3	5	4	11	8	.58	6	.263	.350	.301
1996 Scranton-WB	AAA Phi	26	70	18	1	0	0	19	10	3	12	0	10	2	1	1	0	1	.00	2	.257	.376	.271
Clearwater	A+ Phi	84	281	64	6	5	1	83	39	39	34	0	42	3	5	1	15	2	.88	6	.228	.317	.295
1997 Scranton-WB	AAA Phi	71	204	51	14	1	1	70	32	18	28	1	51	2	5	2	3	1	.75	2	.250	.343	.343
4 Min. YEARS		359	1155	281	39	12	3	353	169	114	154	1	190	20	25	11	64	25	.72	23	.243	.340	.306

Tim Florez

Bats: Right **Throws:** Right **Pos:** 2B **Ht:** 5'10" **Wt:** 170 **Born:** 7/23/69 **Age:** 28

Year Team	Lg Org	G	AB	H	2B	3B	HR	TB	R	RBI	TBB	IBB	SO	HBP	SH	SF	SB	CS	SB%	GDP	Avg	OBP	SLG
1991 Everett	A- SF	59	193	48	8	4	0	64	33	25	12	1	33	1	2	1	7	1	.88	4	.249	.295	.332
1992 Clinton	A SF	81	292	68	12	2	2	90	39	25	30	2	53	3	0	2	20	5	.80	6	.233	.309	.308
San Jose	A+ SF	38	131	32	6	1	1	43	15	17	4	0	21	0	4	4	3	3	.50	2	.244	.259	.328
1993 Shreveport	AA SF	106	318	81	17	2	1	105	33	26	16	4	43	2	3	2	3	5	.38	9	.255	.293	.330
1994 Phoenix	AAA SF	13	24	6	1	0	1	10	5	2	1	0	4	0	0	0	0	0	.00	1	.250	.280	.417
Shreveport	AA SF	61	158	34	10	0	1	47	21	13	21	3	34	1	2	1	0	3	.00	4	.215	.309	.297
1995 Shreveport	AA SF	100	295	79	11	2	9	121	37	46	26	1	49	4	3	3	4	3	.57	7	.268	.332	.410
1996 Shreveport	AA SF	18	66	18	1	0	2	25	9	8	7	1	11	1	0	0	2	0	1.00	0	.273	.351	.379
Phoenix	AAA SF	113	366	106	31	3	4	155	42	39	34	4	56	10	0	3	0	5	.00	12	.290	.363	.423
1997 Phoenix	AAA SF	114	402	121	24	4	7	174	57	61	32	2	68	8	5	1	6	3	.67	5	.301	.363	.433
7 Min. YEARS		703	2245	593	121	18	28	834	291	262	183	18	372	30	19	17	45	28	.62	50	.264	.326	.371

Pat Flury

Pitches: Right **Bats:** Right **Pos:** P **Ht:** 6'2" **Wt:** 205 **Born:** 3/14/73 **Age:** 25

Year Team	Lg Org	G	GS	CG	GF	IP	BFP	H	R	ER	HR	SH	SF	HB	TBB	IBB	SO	WP	Bk	W	L	Pct.	ShO	Sv	ERA
1993 Eugene	A- KC	27	0	0	18	33	144	25	15	12	0	2	0	1	22	1	34	4	0	2	2	.500	0	7	3.27
1994 Rockford	A KC	34	0	0	18	55	254	61	27	24	3	2	2	5	33	2	41	3	2	1	3	.250	0	2	3.93
1995 Wilmington	A+ KC	15	0	0	6	22	89	18	6	6	2	0	1	1	9	1	14	1	1	1	0	1.000	0	1	2.45
Springfield	A KC	34	0	0	19	54.1	246	65	32	26	5	4	1	1	24	0	35	2	0	2	6	.250	0	1	4.31
1996 Wilmington	A+ KC	45	0	0	19	84.1	339	66	22	18	2	2	1	0	29	4	67	9	0	7	2	.778	0	5	1.92
1997 Wichita	AA KC	42	0	0	19	48	215	47	26	19	4	2	3	4	18	3	47	1	0	8	3	.727	0	5	3.56
Omaha	AAA KC	18	0	0	7	26.2	124	29	18	18	5	2	0	2	16	2	24	1	0	1	0	1.000	0	0	6.08
5 Min. YEARS		215	0	0	107	323.1	1411	311	146	123	21	14	8	14	151	13	262	21	3	22	16	.579	0	21	3.42

Kenneth Folkers

Pitches: Right **Bats:** Right **Pos:** P **Ht:** 6'3" **Wt:** 205 **Born:** 10/11/74 **Age:** 23

Year Team	Lg Org	G	GS	CG	GF	IP	BFP	H	R	ER	HR	SH	SF	HB	TBB	IBB	SO	WP	Bk	W	L	Pct.	ShO	Sv	ERA
1997 St. Cathms	A- Tor	14	0	0	5	29.2	124	27	16	10	3	2	2	1	7	0	28	3	0	1	0	1.000	0	0	3.03
Knoxville	AA Tor	1	0	0	1	4.1	15	1	0	0	0	0	0	0	0	0	4	0	0	1	0	1.000	0	0	0.00
Hagerstown	A Tor	5	0	0	2	6.1	22	3	0	0	0	0	0	0	2	0	4	1	0	0	0	.000	0	0	0.00
1 Min. YEARS		20	0	0	8	40.1	161	31	16	10	3	2	2	1	9	0	36	4	0	2	0	1.000	0	0	2.23

Franklin Font

Bats: Right **Throws:** Right **Pos:** SS-2B **Ht:** 5'10" **Wt:** 175 **Born:** 11/4/77 **Age:** 20

Year Team	Lg Org	G	AB	H	2B	3B	HR	TB	R	RBI	TBB	IBB	SO	HBP	SH	SF	SB	CS	SB%	GDP	Avg	OBP	SLG
1996 Cubs	R ChN	59	239	72	5	4	0	85	43	18	17	0	36	4	2	2	31	9	.78	0	.301	.355	.356
1997 Williamsprt	A- ChN	33	135	42	6	2	0	52	13	12	7	0	20	2	1	2	10	4	.71	2	.311	.349	.385
Orlando	AA ChN	10	20	6	0	0	0	6	3	2	2	0	1	0	0	0	0	1	.00	1	.300	.364	.300
Daytona	A+ ChN	19	59	13	2	1	0	17	8	2	4	0	13	0	1	0	2	1	.67	0	.220	.270	.288
2 Min. YEARS		121	453	133	13	7	0	160	67	34	30	0	70	6	4	4	43	15	.74	3	.294	.343	.353

Joe Fontenot

Pitches: Right **Bats:** Right **Pos:** P **Ht:** 6'2" **Wt:** 185 **Born:** 3/20/77 **Age:** 21

Year Team	Lg Org	G	GS	CG	GF	IP	BFP	H	R	ER	HR	SH	SF	HB	TBB	IBB	SO	WP	Bk	W	L	Pct.	ShO	Sv	ERA
1995 Bellingham	A- SF	6	6	0	0	18.2	77	14	5	4	0	0	0	0	10	0	14	0	2	0	3	.000	0	0	1.93
1996 San Jose	A+ SF	26	23	0	1	144	642	137	87	71	7	10	6	11	74	0	124	13	1	9	4	.692	0	0	4.44
1997 Shreveport	AA SF	26	26	1	0	151.1	688	171	105	93	12	8	1	12	65	0	103	10	0	10	11	.476	0	0	5.53
3 Min. YEARS		58	55	1	1	314	1407	322	197	168	19	18	7	23	149	0	241	23	3	19	18	.514	0	0	4.82

P.J. Forbes

Bats: Right **Throws:** Right **Pos:** 2B-3B **Ht:** 5'10" **Wt:** 160 **Born:** 9/22/67 **Age:** 30

Year Team	Lg Org	G	AB	H	2B	3B	HR	TB	R	RBI	TBB	IBB	SO	HBP	SH	SF	SB	CS	SB%	GDP	Avg	OBP	SLG
1990 Boise	A- Ana	43	170	42	9	1	0	53	29	19	23	1	21	0	7	1	11	4	.73	5	.247	.335	.312
1991 Palm Spring	A+ Ana	94	349	93	14	2	2	117	45	26	36	1	44	4	12	0	18	8	.69	7	.266	.342	.335
1992 Quad City	A Ana	105	376	106	16	5	2	138	53	46	44	1	51	2	24	5	15	6	.71	4	.282	.356	.367
1993 Midland	AA Ana	126	498	159	23	2	15	231	90	64	26	1	50	4	14	2	6	8	.43	13	.319	.357	.464
Vancouver	AAA Ana	5	16	4	2	0	0	6	1	3	0	0	3	0	1	0	0	0	.00	1	.250	.250	.375
1994 Angels	R Ana	2	6	0	0	0	0	0	1	0	0	0	1	0	0	0	0	0	.00	0	.000	.000	.000
Vancouver	AAA Ana	90	318	91	21	2	1	119	39	40	22	0	42	2	7	5	4	2	.67	6	.286	.331	.374
1995 Vancouver	AAA Ana	109	369	101	22	3	1	132	47	52	21	0	46	2	7	10	4	6	.40	4	.274	.308	.358
1996 Vancouver	AAA Ana	117	409	112	24	2	0	140	58	46	42	3	44	5	10	4	4	3	.57	13	.274	.346	.342
1997 Rochester	AAA Bal	116	434	118	22	2	8	168	67	54	35	0	42	6	8	3	15	4	.79	11	.272	.333	.387
8 Min. YEARS		807	2945	826	153	19	29	1104	430	350	249	7	344	25	90	30	77	41	.65	64	.280	.339	.375

Ben Ford

Pitches: Right **Bats:** Right **Pos:** P   **Ht:** 6'7" **Wt:** 200 **Born:** 8/15/75 **Age:** 22

Year Team	Lg Org	G	GS	CG	GF	IP	BFP	H	R	ER	HR	SH	SF	HB	TBB	IBB	SO	WP	Bk	W	L	Pct.	ShO	Sv	ERA
1994 Yankees	R NYA	18	0	0	11	34	143	27	13	9	0	0	0	6	8	0	31	3	0	2	2	.500	0	3	2.38
1995 Greensboro	A NYA	7	0	0	2	7	31	4	4	4	1	1	0	0	5	1	8	2	0	0	0	.000	0	0	5.14
Oneonta	A- NYA	29	0	0	10	52	224	39	23	5	1	0	2	5	16	0	50	8	0	5	0	1.000	0	0	0.87
1996 Greensboro	A NYA	43	0	0	16	82.1	359	75	48	39	3	4	1	11	33	6	84	9	0	2	6	.250	0	2	4.26
1997 Tampa	A+ NYA	32	0	0	30	37.1	155	27	8	8	1	2	0	6	14	1	37	4	0	4	0	1.000	0	18	1.93
Norwich	AA NYA	28	0	0	14	42.2	183	35	28	20	1	1	2	3	19	1	38	4	0	4	3	.571	0	1	4.22
4 Min. YEARS		157	0	0	83	255.1	1095	207	124	85	7	8	5	31	95	9	248	30	0	17	11	.607	0	24	3.00

Troy Forkerway

Bats: Right **Throws:** Right **Pos:** 2B   **Ht:** 5'11" **Wt:** 175 **Born:** 5/17/71 **Age:** 27

Year Team	Lg Org	G	AB	H	2B	3B	HR	TB	R	RBI	TBB	IBB	SO	HBP	SH	SF	SB	CS	SB%	GDP	Avg	OBP	SLG
1994 Thunder Bay	IND —	78	269	72	9	0	1	84	35	28	31	0	29	3	9	3	10	7	.59	5	.268	.346	.312
1995 Daytona	A+ ChN	75	188	38	4	0	1	45	22	11	20	0	29	1	4	1	10	1	.91	5	.202	.281	.239
1996 Daytona	A+ ChN	49	143	40	6	1	0	48	27	13	17	0	17	1	1	1	7	6	.54	0	.280	.366	.336
Orlando	AA ChN	59	161	39	9	1	3	59	22	20	11	0	24	4	1	3	0	2	.00	8	.242	.302	.366
1997 Orlando	AA ChN	75	166	33	6	0	1	42	19	10	25	3	30	2	2	3	4	4	.50	6	.199	.306	.253
4 Min. YEARS		336	927	222	34	2	6	278	125	82	104	3	129	13	17	11	31	20	.61	24	.239	.321	.300

Tim Forkner

Bats: Left **Throws:** Right **Pos:** 3B   **Ht:** 5'11" **Wt:** 180 **Born:** 3/28/73 **Age:** 25

Year Team	Lg Org	G	AB	H	2B	3B	HR	TB	R	RBI	TBB	IBB	SO	HBP	SH	SF	SB	CS	SB%	GDP	Avg	OBP	SLG
1993 Auburn	A- Hou	72	267	76	14	9	0	108	32	39	38	0	29	3	1	1	3	3	.50	8	.285	.379	.404
1994 Quad City	A Hou	124	429	128	23	4	6	177	57	57	57	3	72	7	10	8	6	8	.43	10	.298	.383	.413
1995 Kissimmee	A+ Hou	89	296	84	20	1	3	115	42	34	60	2	40	5	2	4	4	2	.67	11	.284	.408	.389
Jackson	AA Hou	35	119	32	11	0	3	52	19	23	19	0	14	2	0	0	1	3	.25	3	.269	.379	.437
1996 Jackson	AA Hou	114	379	111	20	3	7	158	55	46	55	1	47	4	4	2	0	4	.00	10	.293	.386	.417
1997 Jackson	AA Hou	116	398	104	23	1	7	150	52	46	60	1	68	2	1	5	4	0	1.00	12	.261	.357	.377
5 Min. YEARS		550	1888	535	111	21	24	760	257	245	289	7	270	23	18	20	18	20	.47	54	.283	.382	.403

Scott Forster

Pitches: Left **Bats:** Right **Pos:** P   **Ht:** 6'1" **Wt:** 194 **Born:** 10/27/71 **Age:** 26

Year Team	Lg Org	G	GS	CG	GF	IP	BFP	H	R	ER	HR	SH	SF	HB	TBB	IBB	SO	WP	Bk	W	L	Pct.	ShO	Sv	ERA
1994 Auburn	A- Mon	12	9	0	0	52.2	236	38	32	19	0	0	1	4	34	0	39	6	2	1	6	.143	0	0	3.25
1995 Wst Plm Bch	A+ Mon	26	26	1	0	146.2	643	129	78	66	6	5	4	7	80	1	92	16	0	6	11	.353	0	0	4.05
1996 Harrisburg	AA Mon	28	28	0	0	176.1	755	164	92	74	15	3	4	7	67	2	97	5	0	10	7	.588	0	0	3.78
1997 Harrisburg	AA Mon	17	15	0	2	79.1	365	77	45	20	7	7	6	6	48	0	71	4	0	3	6	.333	0	0	2.27
4 Min. YEARS		83	78	1	2	455	1999	408	247	179	28	15	15	24	229	3	299	31	2	20	30	.400	0	0	3.54

Troy Fortin

Bats: Right **Throws:** Right **Pos:** 1B   **Ht:** 5'11" **Wt:** 200 **Born:** 2/24/75 **Age:** 23

Year Team	Lg Org	G	AB	H	2B	3B	HR	TB	R	RBI	TBB	IBB	SO	HBP	SH	SF	SB	CS	SB%	GDP	Avg	OBP	SLG
1993 Twins	R Min	30	101	26	3	0	2	35	6	15	8	0	11	1	0	1	3	0	1.00	2	.257	.315	.347
1994 Ft. Wayne	A Min	1	4	0	0	0	0	0	0	1	0	0	1	0	0	0	0	0	.00	0	.000	.200	.000
Elizabethtn	R+ Min	63	221	68	17	1	8	111	48	40	41	3	28	7	0	0	1	2	.33	8	.308	.431	.502
1995 Ft. Wayne	A Min	112	407	105	21	1	7	149	49	48	38	1	69	8	0	3	4	5	.44	7	.258	.331	.366
1996 Ft. Myers	A+ Min	104	358	89	11	2	7	125	40	52	29	0	29	4	6	4	1	1	.50	10	.249	.309	.349
1997 New Britain	AA Min	12	47	11	2	0	0	13	11	4	3	0	7	4	1	0	0	0	.00	1	.234	.333	.277
Ft. Myers	A+ Min	111	383	113	20	0	13	172	58	59	34	1	37	10	3	4	1	2	.33	11	.295	.364	.449
5 Min. YEARS		433	1521	412	74	4	37	605	212	219	153	5	181	35	10	12	10	10	.50	39	.271	.349	.398

Tim Fortugno

Pitches: Left **Bats:** Left **Pos:** P   **Ht:** 6'0" **Wt:** 185 **Born:** 4/11/62 **Age:** 36

Year Team	Lg Org	G	GS	CG	GF	IP	BFP	H	R	ER	HR	SH	SF	HB	TBB	IBB	SO	WP	Bk	W	L	Pct.	ShO	Sv	ERA
1986 Bellingham	A- Sea	6	0	0	4	8	0	2	2	1	0	0	0	1	12	1	11	1	0	0	0	.000	0	1	1.13
Wausau	A Sea	19	0	0	13	31	139	18	17	9	0	2	2	0	26	0	38	6	1	1	1	.500	0	3	2.61
1987 Salinas	A+ Sea	46	4	1	17	93.1	409	43	36	29	1	3	3	3	84	1	141	19	3	8	2	.800	1	6	2.80
1988 Reading	AA Phi	29	4	0	11	50.2	229	42	29	25	5	1	4	1	36	0	48	5	6	1	5	.167	0	0	4.44
Clearwater	A+ Phi	9	3	0	2	26	109	17	10	7	1	1	1	0	15	0	28	2	3	1	3	.250	0	0	2.42
1989 Reno	A+ —	5	5	1	0	35.2	161	28	20	10	2	2	0	3	20	2	38	2	2	2	3	.400	0	0	2.52
El Paso	AA Mil	10	4	0	2	26	126	29	24	23	3	1	1	1	21	2	22	4	0	0	3	.000	0	0	7.96
Stockton	A+ Mil	13	2	0	3	33	134	9	6	5	0	1	0	4	20	1	52	2	1	2	1	.667	0	1	1.36
1990 Beloit	A Mil	31	0	0	29	63.1	263	38	16	11	1	3	0	0	38	3	106	4	0	8	4	.667	0	7	1.56
El Paso	AA Mil	12	2	0	4	28.2	133	23	12	10	0	2	3	1	22	2	24	4	0	2	3	.400	0	2	3.14
1991 El Paso	AA Mil	20	3	0	13	54.1	227	40	15	12	1	0	2	0	25	1	73	3	1	5	1	.833	0	1	1.99
Denver	AAA Mil	26	0	0	10	35.1	152	30	15	14	1	3	2	3	20	2	39	4	0	1	0	1.000	0	2	3.57
1992 Edmonton	AAA Ana	26	7	0	4	73.1	318	69	36	29	5	0	1	2	33	0	82	3	1	6	4	.600	0	1	3.56
1993 Ottawa	AAA Mon	28	4	0	7	40	175	28	17	16	4	0	1	4	31	4	42	7	1	2	1	.667	0	1	3.60
1994 Chattanooga	AA Cin	22	0	0	17	26.2	115	19	15	8	0	2	1	1	16	1	36	4	1	0	1	.000	0	8	2.70

Year Team	Lg Org	G	GS	CG	GF	IP	BFP	H	R	ER	HR	SH	SF	HB	TBB	IBB	SO	WP	Bk	W	L	Pct.	ShO	Sv	ERA
1995 Vancouver	AAA Ana	10	0	0	7	11.2	45	8	2	2	1	0	0	0	4	1	7	0	0	1	1	.500	0	1	1.54
1996 Chattanooga	AA Cin	11	0	0	9	11.1	38	4	0	0	0	0	0	0	4	0	10	0	0	2	0	1.000	0	6	0.00
Indianapolis	AAA Cin	41	5	0	19	58	253	55	27	22	6	7	3	2	25	3	46	3	1	5	5	.500	0	2	3.41
1997 Scranton-WB	AAA Phi	19	0	0	12	17.2	82	21	13	13	4	0	1	0	8	1	15	6	2	0	1	.000	0	3	6.62
Vancouver	AAA Ana	34	0	0	11	31	137	29	21	18	2	2	0	2	17	0	36	3	0	4	2	.667	0	0	5.23
1992 California	AL	14	5	1	5	41.2	177	37	24	24	5	0	1	0	19	0	31	2	1	1	1	.500	1	1	5.18
1994 Cincinnati	NL	25	0	0	9	30	132	32	14	14	2	3	1	3	14	0	29	4	2	1	0	1.000	0	0	4.20
1995 Chicago	AL	37	0	0	11	38.2	163	30	24	24	7	1	2	0	19	2	24	5	3	1	3	.250	0	0	5.59
12 Min. YEARS		417	43	2	194	755	3245	552	333	264	37	31	25	28	477	25	894	82	23	50	42	.543	1	45	3.15
3 Maj. YEARS		76	5	1	25	110.1	472	99	62	62	14	4	4	3	52	2	84	11	6	3	4	.429	1	1	5.06

Jim Foster

Bats: Right **Throws:** Right **Pos:** C **Ht:** 6'4" **Wt:** 220 **Born:** 8/18/71 **Age:** 26

Year Team	Lg Org	G	AB	H	2B	3B	HR	TB	R	RBI	TBB	IBB	SO	HBP	SH	SF	SB	CS	SB%	GDP	Avg	OBP	SLG
1993 Bluefield	R+ Bal	61	218	71	21	1	10	124	59	45	42	1	34	3	0	3	3	1	.75	4	.326	.436	.569
1994 Albany	A Bal	121	421	112	29	3	8	171	61	56	54	0	59	11	0	6	5	3	.63	13	.266	.360	.406
1995 Frederick	A+ Bal	128	429	112	27	3	6	163	44	56	51	5	63	8	0	5	2	3	.40	10	.261	.347	.380
1996 Frederick	A+ Bal	82	278	70	20	2	7	115	35	42	39	1	32	4	0	3	6	3	.67	7	.252	.349	.414
Bowie	AA Bal	9	33	10	0	1	2	18	7	9	7	0	6	0	0	1	0	0	.00	0	.303	.415	.545
1997 Rochester	AAA Bal	3	9	5	2	0	0	7	4	4	3	0	0	0	0	0	1	1	.00	0	.556	.667	.778
Frederick	A+ Bal	61	200	70	12	1	16	132	48	65	45	7	28	7	0	3	8	0	1.00	5	.350	.478	.660
Bowie	AA Bal	63	211	58	12	0	7	91	36	41	36	0	31	1	1	2	1	1	.50	6	.275	.380	.431
5 Min. YEARS		528	1799	508	123	11	56	821	294	318	277	14	253	34	1	23	25	12	.68	45	.282	.384	.456

Mark Foster

Pitches: Left **Bats:** Left **Pos:** P **Ht:** 6'1" **Wt:** 200 **Born:** 12/24/71 **Age:** 26

Year Team	Lg Org	G	GS	CG	GF	IP	BFP	H	R	ER	HR	SH	SF	HB	TBB	IBB	SO	WP	Bk	W	L	Pct.	ShO	Sv	ERA
1993 Martinsville	R+ Phi	13	13	0	0	69.1	330	77	55	38	3	1	4	6	42	1	50	6	4	1	9	.100	0	0	4.93
1994 Spartanburg	A Phi	32	0	0	25	42.1	192	41	23	21	0	5	1	4	24	0	40	10	3	4	2	.667	0	11	4.46
Clearwater	A+ Phi	16	1	0	5	26.2	118	28	13	10	0	0	0	0	14	0	22	0	1	2	2	.500	0	1	3.38
1995 Reading	AA Phi	25	0	0	4	20.2	106	25	15	13	1	2	1	1	17	3	15	2	4	1	1	.500	0	1	5.66
Clearwater	A+ Phi	24	0	0	6	23.1	108	30	17	14	1	1	0	0	10	0	13	1	1	0	1	.000	0	1	5.40
1996 Reading	AA Phi	50	8	0	12	76	349	84	54	49	6	4	4	4	45	6	56	4	1	4	5	.444	0	0	5.80
1997 Reading	AA Phi	9	0	0	6	17	80	20	16	12	4	0	1	0	8	2	9	0	0	2	2	.500	0	1	6.35
5 Min. YEARS		169	22	0	58	275.1	1283	305	193	157	15	13	11	19	160	12	205	23	14	14	22	.389	0	15	5.13

Eric Fox

Bats: Both **Throws:** Left **Pos:** OF **Ht:** 5'10" **Wt:** 180 **Born:** 8/15/63 **Age:** 34

Year Team	Lg Org	G	AB	H	2B	3B	HR	TB	R	RBI	TBB	IBB	SO	HBP	SH	SF	SB	CS	SB%	GDP	Avg	OBP	SLG
1986 Salinas	A+ Sea	133	526	137	17	3	5	175	80	42	69	7	78	1	9	4	41	27	.60	1	.260	.345	.333
1987 Chattanooga	AA Sea	134	523	139	28	10	8	211	76	54	40	5	93	2	4	5	22	10	.69	2	.266	.318	.403
1988 Vermont	AA Sea	129	478	120	20	6	3	161	55	39	39	3	69	2	7	4	33	12	.73	1	.251	.306	.337
1989 Huntsville	AA Oak	139	498	125	10	5	15	190	84	51	72	1	85	0	11	4	49	15	.77	3	.251	.344	.382
1990 Tacoma	AAA Oak	62	221	61	9	2	4	86	37	34	20	0	34	0	5	2	8	8	.50	2	.276	.333	.389
1991 Tacoma	AAA Oak	127	522	141	24	4	8	193	85	52	57	4	82	2	9	4	17	11	.61	6	.270	.342	.370
1992 Huntsville	AA Oak	59	240	65	16	2	5	100	42	14	27	4	43	0	0	3	16	5	.76	2	.271	.341	.417
Tacoma	AAA Oak	37	121	24	3	1	1	32	16	7	16	1	25	0	2	2	5	0	1.00	2	.198	.286	.264
1993 Tacoma	AAA Oak	92	317	99	14	5	11	156	49	52	41	3	48	1	7	3	18	8	.69	4	.312	.390	.492
1994 Tacoma	AAA Oak	52	191	60	15	2	3	88	30	19	20	2	28	2	4	1	7	2	.78	4	.314	.383	.461
1995 Okla City	AAA Tex	92	349	97	22	5	6	147	52	50	30	7	68	2	4	7	5	5	.50	7	.278	.336	.421
1996 Albuquerque	AAA LA	30	91	30	6	1	0	38	8	2	4	1	20	0	0	0	1	2	.33	2	.330	.358	.418
1997 Rochester	AAA Bal	5	18	4	1	0	0	5	2	0	2	0	2	0	0	0	0	0	.00	0	.222	.300	.278
Scranton-WB	AAA Phi	87	246	70	16	3	3	101	39	26	19	1	48	0	0	3	2	3	.40	10	.285	.332	.411
1992 Oakland	AL	51	143	34	5	2	3	52	24	13	13	0	29	0	6	1	3	4	.43	1	.238	.299	.364
1993 Oakland	AL	29	56	8	1	0	1	12	5	5	2	0	3	0	0	0	0	3	.00	0	.143	.172	.214
1994 Oakland	AL	26	44	9	2	0	1	14	7	1	3	0	8	0	0	0	2	0	1.00	0	.205	.255	.318
1995 Texas	AL	10	15	0	0	0	0	0	2	0	3	0	4	0	0	0	0	0	.00	0	.000	.167	.000
12 Min. YEARS		1178	4341	1172	201	53	68	1683	655	442	456	39	723	12	62	36	224	108	.67	46	.270	.338	.388
4 Maj. YEARS		116	258	51	8	2	5	78	38	19	21	0	48	0	10	1	5	6	.45	1	.198	.257	.302

Ryan Franklin

Pitches: Right **Bats:** Right **Pos:** P **Ht:** 6'3" **Wt:** 160 **Born:** 3/5/73 **Age:** 25

Year Team	Lg Org	G	GS	CG	GF	IP	BFP	H	R	ER	HR	SH	SF	HB	TBB	IBB	SO	WP	Bk	W	L	Pct.	ShO	Sv	ERA
1993 Bellingham	A- Sea	15	14	1	0	74	321	72	38	24	2	2	1	3	27	0	55	7	3	5	3	.625	1	0	2.92
1994 Appleton	A Sea	18	18	5	0	118	493	105	60	41	6	3	1	17	23	0	102	6	3	9	6	.600	1	0	3.13
Calgary	AAA Sea	1	1	0	0	5.2	28	9	6	5	2	0	0	0	1	0	2	0	0	0	0	.000	0	0	7.94
Riverside	A+ Sea	8	8	1	0	61.2	261	61	26	21	5	1	3	4	14	0	35	0	1	4	2	.667	1	0	3.06
1995 Port City	AA Sea	31	20	1	2	146	627	153	84	70	13	11	3	12	43	4	102	6	2	6	10	.375	1	0	4.32
1996 Port City	AA Sea	28	27	2	0	182	764	186	99	81	23	6	3	16	37	0	127	4	2	6	12	.333	0	0	4.01
1997 Memphis	AA Sea	11	8	2	2	59.1	234	45	24	20	4	0	3	1	14	1	49	1	0	4	2	.667	2	0	3.03
Tacoma	AAA Sea	14	14	0	0	90.1	386	97	48	42	11	7	2	8	24	1	59	1	1	5	5	.500	0	0	4.18
5 Min. YEARS		126	110	12	4	737	3114	728	383	304	66	30	16	61	177	6	531	25	12	39	40	.494	6	0	3.71

Joe Fraser

Bats: Right **Throws:** Right **Pos:** OF　　　**Ht:** 6'1" **Wt:** 200 **Born:** 8/23/74 **Age:** 23

					BATTING												BASERUNNING				PERCENTAGES		
Year Team	Lg Org	G	AB	H	2B	3B	HR	TB	R	RBI	TBB	IBB	SO	HBP	SH	SF	SB	CS	SB%	GDP	Avg	OBP	SLG
1995 Elizabethtn	R+ Min	46	184	48	4	0	4	64	29	21	20	0	22	2	2	2	5	4	.56	5	.261	.337	.348
Ft. Wayne	A Min	5	15	3	0	0	0	3	0	2	0	0	5	0	0	1	1	0	1.00	6	.200	.188	.200
1996 Ft. Wayne	A Min	101	331	74	17	1	6	111	42	43	26	2	60	8	8	2	7	2	.78	7	.224	.294	.335
1997 New Britain	AA Min	79	238	57	11	1	1	73	33	16	29	0	50	1	8	2	11	6	.65	3	.239	.322	.307
3 Min. YEARS		231	768	182	32	2	11	251	104	82	75	2	137	11	18	7	24	12	.67	15	.237	.311	.327

Lou Frazier

Bats: Both **Throws:** Right **Pos:** OF　　　**Ht:** 6'2" **Wt:** 175 **Born:** 1/26/65 **Age:** 33

					BATTING												BASERUNNING				PERCENTAGES		
Year Team	Lg Org	G	AB	H	2B	3B	HR	TB	R	RBI	TBB	IBB	SO	HBP	SH	SF	SB	CS	SB%	GDP	Avg	OBP	SLG
1986 Astros	R Hou	51	178	51	7	2	1	65	39	23	32	0	25	1	3	1	17	8	.68	3	.287	.396	.365
1987 Asheville	A Hou	108	399	103	9	2	1	119	83	33	68	1	89	2	4	3	75	24	.76	3	.258	.367	.298
1988 Osceola	A+ Hou	130	468	110	11	3	0	127	79	34	90	5	104	4	5	1	87	16	.84	5	.235	.362	.271
1989 Columbus	AA Hou	135	460	106	10	1	4	130	65	31	76	2	101	1	2	2	43	14	.75	7	.230	.340	.283
1990 London	AA Det	81	242	53	4	1	0	59	29	15	27	0	52	0	1	1	20	3	.87	5	.219	.296	.244
1991 London	AA Det	122	439	105	9	4	3	131	69	40	77	5	86	1	3	1	42	17	.71	8	.239	.353	.298
1992 London	AA Det	129	477	120	16	3	0	142	85	34	95	1	107	0	2	2	58	23	.72	3	.252	.375	.298
1995 Ottawa	AAA Mon	31	110	24	3	0	1	30	11	10	13	0	20	1	1	1	10	1	.91	2	.218	.304	.273
1996 Okla City	AAA Tex	58	208	51	8	3	3	74	28	16	14	2	42	1	3	1	13	4	.76	3	.245	.295	.356
1997 Bowie	AA Bal	25	103	24	4	2	0	32	20	8	21	0	20	0	3	0	13	1	.93	1	.233	.363	.311
Rochester	AAA Bal	84	302	75	12	4	2	101	40	39	36	1	68	1	3	3	24	6	.80	9	.248	.327	.334
1993 Montreal	NL	112	189	54	7	1	1	66	27	16	16	0	24	0	5	1	17	2	.89	3	.286	.340	.349
1994 Montreal	NL	76	140	38	3	1	0	43	25	14	18	0	23	1	1	0	20	4	.83	1	.271	.358	.307
1995 Montreal	NL	35	63	12	2	0	0	14	6	3	8	0	12	2	0	1	4	0	1.00	1	.190	.297	.222
Texas	AL	49	99	21	2	0	0	23	19	8	7	0	20	2	3	0	9	1	.90	2	.212	.278	.232
1996 Texas	AL	30	50	13	2	1	0	17	5	5	8	0	10	1	1	0	4	2	.67	2	.260	.373	.340
10 Min. YEARS		954	3386	822	93	25	15	1010	548	283	549	17	714	12	30	16	402	117	.77	54	.243	.349	.298
4 Maj. YEARS		302	541	138	16	3	1	163	82	46	57	0	89	6	10	2	54	9	.86	9	.255	.332	.301

Scott Fredrickson

Pitches: Right **Bats:** Right **Pos:** P　　　**Ht:** 6'3" **Wt:** 215 **Born:** 8/19/67 **Age:** 30

		HOW MUCH HE PITCHED					WHAT HE GAVE UP											THE RESULTS					
Year Team	Lg Org	G	GS	CG	GF	IP	BFP	H	R	ER	HR	SH	SF	HB	TBB	IBB	SO	WP	Bk	W	L	Pct.	ShO	Sv	ERA
1990 Spokane	A- SD	26	1	0	15	46.2	197	35	22	17	3	4	1	2	17	1	61	6	4	3	3	.500	0	8	3.28
1991 Waterloo	A SD	26	0	0	22	38.1	153	24	9	5	1	1	2	1	15	3	40	3	2	3	5	.375	0	6	1.17
High Desert	A+ SD	23	0	0	19	35	154	31	15	9	2	2	1	1	18	2	26	6	0	4	1	.800	0	7	2.31
1992 Wichita	AA SD	56	0	0	22	73.1	303	50	29	26	9	2	5	2	38	3	66	11	0	4	7	.364	0	5	3.19
1993 Colo Sprngs	AAA Col	23	0	0	18	26.1	119	25	16	16	3	2	1	0	19	3	20	2	0	1	3	.250	0	7	5.47
1995 Colo Sprngs	AAA Col	58	1	0	20	75.2	348	70	40	29	2	8	3	5	47	5	70	15	2	11	3	.786	0	4	3.45
1996 Colo Sprngs	AAA Col	55	0	0	17	63.2	303	71	56	47	9	3	6	3	40	6	66	8	0	2	2	.500	0	2	6.64
1997 Carolina	AA Pit	19	0	0	8	23.2	117	22	21	16	3	1	1	3	19	1	17	0	0	0	3	.000	0	1	6.08
1993 Colorado	NL	25	0	0	4	29	137	33	25	20	3	2	2	1	17	2	20	4	1	0	1	.000	0	0	6.21
7 Min. YEARS		286	2	0	141	382.2	1694	328	208	165	32	23	20	17	213	24	366	51	8	28	27	.509	0	40	3.88

Mike Freehill

Pitches: Right **Bats:** Right **Pos:** P　　　**Ht:** 6'3" **Wt:** 177 **Born:** 6/2/71 **Age:** 27

		HOW MUCH HE PITCHED					WHAT HE GAVE UP											THE RESULTS					
Year Team	Lg Org	G	GS	CG	GF	IP	BFP	H	R	ER	HR	SH	SF	HB	TBB	IBB	SO	WP	Bk	W	L	Pct.	ShO	Sv	ERA
1994 Boise	A- Ana	28	0	0	19	45	179	37	20	16	2	4	0	1	10	5	38	2	1	3	6	.333	0	8	3.20
1995 Cedar Rapids	A Ana	54	0	0	49	55	234	54	25	16	4	3	0	7	12	5	47	10	1	4	5	.444	0	28	2.62
1996 Vancouver	AAA Ana	7	0	0	3	10	53	16	11	11	1	0	1	1	8	1	5	4	0	1	1	.500	0	0	9.90
Midland	AA Ana	47	0	0	45	50	224	49	25	19	4	3	1	1	21	1	48	10	2	7	6	.538	0	17	3.42
1997 Midland	AA Ana	35	0	0	28	37	177	* 46	33	29	4	3	4	3	20	0	32	8	2	0	7	.000	0	10	7.05
Lk Elsinore	A+ Ana	21	0	0	18	22.2	89	18	7	5	1	0	0	0	8	0	20	1	0	0	1	.000	0	8	1.99
4 Min. YEARS		192	0	0	162	219.2	956	220	121	96	16	13	6	13	79	12	190	35	6	15	26	.366	0	71	3.93

Ryan Freel

Bats: Right **Throws:** Right **Pos:** SS　　　**Ht:** 5'10" **Wt:** 175 **Born:** 3/8/76 **Age:** 22

					BATTING												BASERUNNING				PERCENTAGES		
Year Team	Lg Org	G	AB	H	2B	3B	HR	TB	R	RBI	TBB	IBB	SO	HBP	SH	SF	SB	CS	SB%	GDP	Avg	OBP	SLG
1995 St. Cathms	A- Tor	65	243	68	10	5	3	97	30	29	22	0	49	7	7	5	12	7	.63	3	.280	.350	.399
1996 Dunedin	A+ Tor	104	381	97	23	5	4	138	64	41	33	0	76	5	14	2	19	15	.56	4	.255	.321	.362
1997 Knoxville	AA Tor	33	94	19	1	1	0	22	18	4	19	0	13	2	1	0	5	3	.63	3	.202	.348	.234
Dunedin	A+ Tor	61	181	51	8	2	3	72	42	17	46	2	28	9	6	1	24	5	.83	3	.282	.447	.398
3 Min. YEARS		263	899	235	42	11	10	329	154	91	120	2	166	23	28	8	60	30	.67	13	.261	.360	.366

Chris Freeman

Pitches: Right **Bats:** Right **Pos:** P　　　**Ht:** 6'4" **Wt:** 205 **Born:** 8/27/72 **Age:** 25

		HOW MUCH HE PITCHED					WHAT HE GAVE UP											THE RESULTS					
Year Team	Lg Org	G	GS	CG	GF	IP	BFP	H	R	ER	HR	SH	SF	HB	TBB	IBB	SO	WP	Bk	W	L	Pct.	ShO	Sv	ERA
1994 Dunedin	A+ Tor	17	3	0	5	50.2	205	44	16	14	1	2	2	0	21	1	45	5	2	3	2	.600	0	1	2.49
1995 Knoxville	AA Tor	39	5	0	16	81.1	354	78	53	49	12	5	5	1	38	0	80	1	0	2	3	.400	0	8	5.42
1996 Knoxville	AA Tor	26	0	0	8	45.2	200	45	23	17	3	0	3	1	23	3	54	1	0	6	1	.857	0	0	3.35
1997 Knoxville	AA Tor	47	2	0	21	83.1	362	71	32	23	8	6	2	3	36	7	86	4	0	3	3	.500	0	8	2.48

		HOW MUCH HE PITCHED				WHAT HE GAVE UP								THE RESULTS					
Year Team	Lg Org	G	GS	CG	GF	IP	BFP	H	R	ER	HR	SH	SF	HB	TBB	IBB	SO	WP	Bk	W	L	Pct. ShO Sv ERA
4 Min. YEARS		129	10	0	50	261	1121	238	124	103	24	13	12	5	118	11	265	11	2	14	9	.609 0 17 3.55

Marvin Freeman

Pitches: Right **Bats:** Right **Pos:** P **Ht:** 6' 7" **Wt:** 222 **Born:** 4/10/63 **Age:** 35

		HOW MUCH HE PITCHED						WHAT HE GAVE UP												THE RESULTS					
Year Team	Lg Org	G	GS	CG	GF	IP	BFP	H	R	ER	HR	SH	SF	HB	TBB	IBB	SO	WP	Bk	W	L	Pct.	ShO	Sv	ERA
1984 Bend	A- Phi	15	15	2	0	89.2	0	64	41	26	1	0	0	1	52	0	79	7	0	8	5	.615	1	0	2.61
1985 Reading	AA Phi	11	11	2	0	65.1	293	51	41	39	11	5	5	1	52	1	35	3	0	1	7	.125	0	0	5.37
Clearwater	A+ Phi	14	13	3	1	88.1	366	72	32	30	0	1	4	1	36	1	55	7	1	6	5	.545	3	0	3.06
1986 Reading	AA Phi	27	27	4	0	163	720	130	89	73	12	5	8	1	111	3	113	11	1	13	6	.684	2	0	4.03
1987 Maine	AAA Phi	10	10	2	0	46	223	56	38	32	8	1	0	0	30	2	29	6	0	0	7	.000	0	0	6.26
Reading	AA Phi	9	9	0	0	49.2	222	45	30	28	7	0	0	0	32	1	40	6	1	3	3	.500	0	0	5.07
1988 Maine	AAA Phi	18	14	2	0	74	325	62	43	38	8	3	1	0	46	3	37	11	0	5	5	.500	1	0	4.62
1989 Scranton-WB	AAA Phi	5	5	0	0	14	57	11	8	7	0	0	0	0	5	0	8	5	0	1	1	.500	0	0	4.50
1990 Scranton-WB	AAA Phi	7	7	0	0	35.1	163	39	23	20	5	3	0	1	19	0	33	3	1	2	4	.333	0	0	5.09
Richmond	AAA Atl	7	7	1	0	39	159	33	20	20	3	2	1	0	22	0	23	1	1	2	3	.400	1	0	4.62
1993 Richmond	AAA Atl	2	2	0	0	4	18	4	1	1	0	0	0	1	1	0	5	0	0	0	0	.000	0	0	2.25
1997 Syracuse	AAA Tor	1	0	0	0	1	4	1	1	1	0	1	0	0	1	0	0	0	0	0	0	.000	0	0	9.00
1986 Philadelphia	NL	3	3	0	0	16	61	6	4	4	0	0	1	0	10	0	8	1	0	2	0	1.000	0	0	2.25
1988 Philadelphia	NL	11	11	0	0	51.2	249	55	36	35	2	5	1	1	43	2	37	3	1	2	3	.400	0	0	6.10
1989 Philadelphia	NL	1	1	0	0	3	16	2	2	2	0	0	0	0	5	0	0	1	0	0	0	.000	0	0	6.00
1990 Philadelphia	NL	16	3	0	4	32.1	147	34	21	20	5	1	0	3	14	2	26	4	0	0	2	.000	0	1	5.57
Atlanta	NL	9	0	0	1	15.2	60	7	3	3	0	1	0	2	3	0	12	0	0	1	0	1.000	0	0	1.72
1991 Atlanta	NL	34	0	0	6	48	190	37	19	16	2	1	1	2	13	1	34	4	0	1	0	1.000	0	1	3.00
1992 Atlanta	NL	58	0	0	15	64.1	276	61	26	23	7	2	1	1	29	7	41	4	0	7	5	.583	0	3	3.22
1993 Atlanta	NL	21	0	0	5	23.2	103	24	16	16	1	0	0	1	10	2	25	3	0	2	0	1.000	0	0	6.08
1994 Colorado	NL	19	18	0	0	112.2	465	113	39	35	10	4	1	5	23	2	67	4	0	10	2	.833	0	0	2.80
1995 Colorado	NL	22	18	0	0	94.2	437	122	64	62	15	7	3	2	41	1	61	5	1	3	7	.300	0	0	5.89
1996 Colorado	NL	26	23	0	1	129.2	588	151	100	87	21	9	3	6	57	1	71	13	1	7	9	.438	0	0	6.04
Chicago	AL	1	1	0	0	2	12	4	3	3	0	0	0	0	1	0	1	0	0	0	0	.000	0	0	13.50
9 Min. YEARS		126	120	16	1	669.1	2550	568	367	315	55	21	20	6	407	11	457	60	5	41	46	.471	8	0	4.24
10 Maj. YEARS		221	78	0	32	593.2	2604	616	333	306	63	30	11	23	249	18	383	41	4	35	28	.556	0	5	4.64

Ricky Freeman

Bats: Right **Throws:** Right **Pos:** 1B **Ht:** 6'4" **Wt:** 205 **Born:** 2/3/72 **Age:** 26

		BATTING													BASERUNNING				PERCENTAGES		
Year Team	Lg Org	G	AB	H	2B	3B	HR	TB	R	RBI	TBB	IBB	SO	HBP	SH	SF	SB	CS	SB%	GDP	Avg	OBP	SLG
1994 Huntington	R+ ChN	64	218	49	10	3	0	65	23	30	35	0	22	3	0	7	12	6	.67	6	.225	.331	.298
1995 Rockford	A ChN	131	466	127	33	5	11	203	89	67	61	3	57	7	0	1	8	3	.73	11	.273	.364	.436
1996 Daytona	A+ ChN	127	477	145	36	6	13	232	70	64	36	2	72	10	0	2	10	8	.56	9	.304	.364	.486
1997 Iowa	AAA ChN	31	77	13	0	0	1	16	7	4	8	0	20	3	0	0	1	0	1.00	4	.169	.273	.208
Orlando	AA ChN	81	308	96	19	2	16	167	58	73	29	6	51	5	0	2	8	5	.62	3	.312	.378	.542
4 Min. YEARS		434	1546	430	98	16	41	683	247	238	169	11	222	28	0	12	39	22	.64	33	.278	.357	.442

Mike Freitas

Pitches: Right **Bats:** Right **Pos:** P **Ht:** 6'1" **Wt:** 160 **Born:** 9/22/69 **Age:** 28

		HOW MUCH HE PITCHED						WHAT HE GAVE UP												THE RESULTS					
Year Team	Lg Org	G	GS	CG	GF	IP	BFP	H	R	ER	HR	SH	SF	HB	TBB	IBB	SO	WP	Bk	W	L	Pct.	ShO	Sv	ERA
1989 Pittsfield	A- NYN	13	2	0	8	33.1	137	37	19	15	2	4	1	0	5	1	16	2	4	3	0	1.000	0	0	4.05
1990 Pittsfield	A- NYN	5	0	0	1	9.1	37	7	4	4	0	1	1	0	4	0	8	0	2	1	0	1.000	0	0	3.86
Columbia	A NYN	13	9	0	2	70	285	60	27	19	5	1	1	2	14	0	47	5	0	5	2	.714	0	0	2.44
1991 Columbia	A NYN	25	12	4	11	114.1	475	115	48	42	4	2	3	6	31	0	111	4	1	5	8	.385	2	2	3.31
St. Lucie	A+ NYN	5	0	0	4	10.2	45	11	4	3	1	2	0	1	1	0	6	0	0	1	0	.000	0	0	2.53
1992 St. Lucie	A+ NYN	45	0	0	39	57.2	231	51	17	8	2	1	6	4	9	1	30	0	2	6	3	.667	0	24	1.25
1993 Wichita	AA SD	8	0	0	7	7.2	43	13	14	9	1	0	1	0	2	0	4	2	0	2	0	.000	0	0	10.57
1994 Padres	R SD	4	0	0	2	6	23	2	1	1	0	0	0	0	3	0	7	1	0	1	0	1.000	0	1	1.50
1995 Memphis	AA SD	54	0	0	16	59	246	55	26	24	3	2	3	2	26	8	36	3	1	0	6	.000	0	2	3.66
1996 Las Vegas	AAA SD	3	0	0	2	5.2	25	8	2	2	1	0	0	0	1	1	1	0	0	0	0	.000	0	0	3.18
Memphis	AA SD	44	0	0	6	68.2	307	78	41	39	8	3	0	3	26	2	36	6	0	3	0	1.000	0	0	5.11
1997 Carolina	AA Pit	6	0	0	4	5.1	30	8	8	8	1	1	0	2	4	1	2	0	0	1	0	1.000	0	0	13.50
9 Min. YEARS		225	23	4	102	447.2	1884	445	211	174	28	17	16	20	126	14	304	23	10	25	23	.521	2	30	3.50

Anton French

Bats: Both **Throws:** Right **Pos:** OF **Ht:** 5'10" **Wt:** 175 **Born:** 7/25/75 **Age:** 22

		BATTING													BASERUNNING				PERCENTAGES		
Year Team	Lg Org	G	AB	H	2B	3B	HR	TB	R	RBI	TBB	IBB	SO	HBP	SH	SF	SB	CS	SB%	GDP	Avg	OBP	SLG
1993 Cardinals	R StL	34	106	29	3	2	1	39	19	17	10	0	22	0	1	1	15	5	.75	0	.274	.333	.368
1994 Cardinals	R StL	52	204	45	8	8	2	75	30	29	16	1	53	0	0	2	11	3	.79	6	.221	.275	.368
1995 Peoria	A StL	116	417	114	19	5	10	173	71	37	37	2	98	6	7	0	57	16	.78	6	.273	.341	.415
Durham	A+ Atl	7	26	7	1	0	0	8	3	2	3	0	2	1	0	0	4	1	.80	0	.269	.367	.308
1996 Durham	A+ Atl	52	210	52	10	2	5	81	25	22	13	0	42	0	2	0	23	3	.88	0	.248	.291	.386
Lakeland	A+ Det	61	253	70	10	6	0	92	36	14	12	0	38	2	0	1	24	10	.71	2	.277	.313	.364
1997 Knoxville	AA Tor	2	6	2	0	1	0	4	2	1	0	0	2	0	0	0	0	0	.00	0	.333	.333	.667
Dunedin	A+ Tor	78	261	58	5	3	3	78	34	17	25	1	51	2	5	2	35	15	.70	4	.222	.293	.299
5 Min. YEARS		402	1483	377	56	27	21	550	220	139	116	4	308	11	15	6	169	53	.76	12	.254	.312	.371

Pitches: Left **Bats:** Left **Pos:** P

Steve Frey

Ht: 5' 9" **Wt:** 170 **Born:** 7/29/63 **Age:** 34

		HOW MUCH HE PITCHED						WHAT HE GAVE UP												THE RESULTS					
Year Team	Lg Org	G	GS	CG	GF	IP	BFP	H	R	ER	HR	SH	SF	HB	TBB	IBB	SO	WP	Bk	W	L	Pct.	ShO	Sv	ERA
1983 Oneonta	A- NYA	28	1	0	24	72.1	—	47	27	22	2	—	—	0	35	1	86	5	0	4	6	.400	0	9	2.74
1984 Ft. Laud	A+ NYA	47	0	0	25	64.2	281	46	26	15	2	1	3	0	34	2	66	4	0	4	2	.667	0	4	2.09
1985 Ft. Laud	A+ NYA	19	0	0	13	22.1	89	11	4	3	0	1	0	1	12	0	15	0	0	1	1	.500	0	7	1.21
Albany-Colo	AA NYA	40	0	0	14	61.1	261	53	30	26	4	2	0	3	25	5	54	0	0	4	7	.364	0	3	3.82
1986 Columbus	AAA NYA	11	0	0	2	19	93	29	17	17	3	0	2	0	10	1	11	0	0	0	2	.000	0	0	8.05
Albany-Colo	AA NYA	40	0	0	26	73	287	50	25	17	5	2	4	2	18	1	62	2	0	3	4	.429	0	4	2.10
1987 Albany-Colo	AA NYA	14	0	0	10	28	111	20	6	6	0	1	0	0	7	1	19	1	0	0	2	.000	0	1	1.93
Columbus	AAA NYA	23	0	0	11	47.1	196	45	19	16	2	1	3	0	10	0	35	4	0	2	1	.667	0	6	3.04
1988 Tidewater	AAA NYN	58	1	0	22	54.2	230	38	23	19	3	4	2	3	25	6	58	1	3	6	3	.667	0	6	3.13
1989 Indianapols	AAA Mon	21	0	0	8	25.1	97	18	7	5	1	2	0	0	6	1	23	0	0	2	1	.667	0	3	1.78
1990 Indianapols	AAA Mon	2	0	0	1	3	10	0	0	0	0	0	0	0	1	0	3	0	0	0	0	.000	0	1	0.00
1991 Indianapols	AAA Mon	30	0	0	15	35.2	145	25	6	6	1	1	0	1	15	2	45	1	1	3	1	.750	0	3	1.51
1995 Scranton-WB	AAA Phi	4	0	0	2	5	21	3	1	1	0	1	0	0	2	1	3	1	0	0	0	.000	0	1	1.80
1996 Scranton-WB	AAA Phi	10	0	0	2	13.1	57	11	8	8	1	1	0	0	8	0	9	0	0	2	2	.500	0	0	5.40
1997 Vancouver	AAA Ana	31	1	0	10	41.1	183	45	23	23	6	3	0	1	21	1	28	0	0	3	3	.500	0	4	5.01
1989 Montreal	NL	20	0	0	11	21.1	103	29	15	13	4	0	2	1	11	1	15	1	1	3	2	.600	0	0	5.48
1990 Montreal	NL	51	0	0	21	55.2	236	44	15	13	4	3	2	1	29	6	29	0	0	8	2	.800	0	9	2.10
1991 Montreal	NL	31	0	0	5	39.2	182	43	31	22	3	3	2	1	23	4	21	3	1	0	1	.000	0	1	4.99
1992 California	AL	51	0	0	20	45.1	193	39	18	18	6	2	3	2	22	3	24	1	0	4	2	.667	0	4	3.57
1993 California	AL	55	0	0	28	48.1	212	41	20	16	1	4	1	3	26	1	22	3	0	2	3	.400	0	13	2.98
1994 San Francisco	NL	44	0	0	12	31	137	37	17	17	6	1	4	2	15	3	20	1	0	1	0	1.000	0	0	4.94
1995 San Francisco	NL	9	0	0	1	6.1	29	7	6	3	1	1	1	0	2	0	5	0	0	0	1	.000	0	0	4.26
Seattle	AL	13	0	0	3	11.1	56	16	7	6	0	3	1	1	6	1	7	0	0	0	3	.000	0	0	4.76
Philadelphia	NL	9	0	0	3	10.2	36	3	1	1	1	1	0	0	2	1	2	0	0	0	0	.000	0	1	0.84
1996 Philadelphia	NL	31	0	0	12	34.1	151	38	19	18	4	2	0	0	18	3	12	0	0	0	1	.000	0	0	4.72
12 Min. YEARS		378	3	0	185	566.1	2061	441	222	184	30	20	14	12	229	22	517	19	4	34	35	.493	0	51	2.92
8 Maj. YEARS		314	0	0	116	304	1335	297	149	127	30	20	18	11	154	23	157	9	2	18	15	.545	0	28	3.76

Pitches: Right **Bats:** Right **Pos:** P

Chad Frontera

Ht: 6'2" **Wt:** 195 **Born:** 11/22/72 **Age:** 25

		HOW MUCH HE PITCHED						WHAT HE GAVE UP												THE RESULTS					
Year Team	Lg Org	G	GS	CG	GF	IP	BFP	H	R	ER	HR	SH	SF	HB	TBB	IBB	SO	WP	Bk	W	L	Pct.	ShO	Sv	ERA
1994 Everett	A- SF	13	12	0	0	59.2	273	60	35	23	3	1	2	7	27	2	50	6	0	4	4	.500	0	0	3.47
1995 Shreveport	AA SF	20	13	0	2	82	368	88	45	38	9	2	3	6	39	0	52	2	0	3	5	.375	0	1	4.17
1997 Shreveport	AA SF	15	15	0	0	70.2	312	78	48	46	15	4	2	4	31	1	42	2	1	4	4	.500	0	0	5.86
Phoenix	AAA SF	5	5	0	0	24.2	114	32	19	17	2	0	2	2	9	0	13	3	1	2	0	1.000	0	0	6.20
3 Min. YEARS		53	45	0	2	237	1067	258	147	124	29	7	9	19	106	3	157	13	2	13	13	.500	0	1	4.71

Bats: Both **Throws:** Right **Pos:** OF

Aaron Fuller

Ht: 5'10" **Wt:** 170 **Born:** 9/7/71 **Age:** 26

		BATTING															BASERUNNING				PERCENTAGES		
Year Team	Lg Org	G	AB	H	2B	3B	HR	TB	R	RBI	TBB	IBB	SO	HBP	SH	SF	SB	CS	SB%	GDP	Avg	OBP	SLG
1993 Red Sox	R Bos	6	11	6	0	1	0	8	5	2	3	0	0	0	0	0	3	0	1.00	1	.545	.643	.727
Utica	A- Bos	53	176	44	3	0	1	50	31	17	20	0	26	4	5	3	24	4	.86	0	.250	.335	.284
1994 Sarasota	A+ Bos	118	414	108	17	2	2	135	89	28	82	1	90	5	14	2	45	13	.78	7	.261	.388	.326
1995 Trenton	AA Bos	58	204	40	7	4	0	55	27	10	15	0	45	2	3	1	16	4	.80	2	.196	.257	.270
Visalia	A+ Bos	49	186	47	7	3	1	63	27	19	19	0	32	1	3	2	11	10	.52	0	.253	.322	.339
1996 Sarasota	A+ Bos	115	434	130	20	5	5	175	74	49	63	0	60	4	4	5	33	12	.73	4	.300	.389	.403
Pawtucket	AAA Bos	1	2	1	0	0	0	1	0	0	0	0	0	0	0	0	0	0	.00	0	.500	.500	.500
1997 Trenton	AA Bos	128	481	125	17	6	6	172	87	46	95	4	84	4	5	4	40	15	.73	8	.260	.384	.358
5 Min. YEARS		528	1908	501	71	21	15	659	340	171	297	5	337	20	34	17	172	58	.75	22	.263	.365	.345

Pitches: Left **Bats:** Left **Pos:** P

Aaron Fultz

Ht: 6'0" **Wt:** 196 **Born:** 9/4/73 **Age:** 24

		HOW MUCH HE PITCHED						WHAT HE GAVE UP												THE RESULTS					
Year Team	Lg Org	G	GS	CG	GF	IP	BFP	H	R	ER	HR	SH	SF	HB	TBB	IBB	SO	WP	Bk	W	L	Pct.	ShO	Sv	ERA
1992 Giants	R SF	14	14	0	0	67.2	282	51	24	16	0	4	1	4	33	0	72	7	0	3	2	.600	0	0	2.13
1993 Clinton	A SF	26	25	2	0	148	641	132	63	56	8	12	2	11	64	2	144	10	2	14	8	.636	1	0	3.41
Ft. Wayne	A Min	1	1	0	0	4	21	10	4	4	0	0	0	0	0	0	3	0	0	0	0	.000	0	0	9.00
1994 Ft. Myers	A+ Min	28	28	3	0	168.1	745	193	95	81	9	6	4	7	60	5	132	9	2	9	10	.474	0	0	4.33
1995 Hardware City	AA Min	3	3	0	0	15	64	11	12	11	1	0	2	0	9	0	12	0	0	0	2	.000	0	0	6.60
Ft. Myers	A+ Min	21	21	2	0	122	516	115	52	44	10	4	3	8	41	1	127	7	1	6	3	.333	2	0	3.25
1996 San Jose	A+ SF	36	12	0	11	104.2	460	101	52	46	7	9	3	8	54	2	103	13	0	9	5	.643	0	0	3.96
1997 Shreveport	AA SF	49	0	0	20	70	293	65	30	22	6	4	5	2	19	0	60	4	1	6	3	.667	0	1	2.83
6 Min. YEARS		178	104	7	31	699.2	3022	678	332	280	41	39	20	40	280	10	653	50	6	44	36	.550	3	2	3.60

Pitches: Right **Bats:** Right **Pos:** P

Chris Fussell

Ht: 6'2" **Wt:** 185 **Born:** 5/19/76 **Age:** 22

		HOW MUCH HE PITCHED						WHAT HE GAVE UP												THE RESULTS					
Year Team	Lg Org	G	GS	CG	GF	IP	BFP	H	R	ER	HR	SH	SF	HB	TBB	IBB	SO	WP	Bk	W	L	Pct.	ShO	Sv	ERA
1994 Orioles	R Bal	14	8	0	2	56.1	245	53	30	26	2	1	4	4	24	0	65	6	1	3	2	.400	0	0	4.15
1995 Bluefield	R+ Bal	12	12	1	0	65.2	265	37	18	16	4	1	1	7	32	0	98	3	1	9	1	.900	1	0	2.19
1996 Frederick	A+ Bal	15	14	1	0	86.1	369	71	36	27	8	1	1	5	44	0	94	5	0	5	2	.714	1	0	2.81
1997 Bowie	AA Bal	19	18	0	0	82.1	398	102	71	65	12	1	5	10	58	3	71	7	0	1	8	.111	0	0	7.11
Frederick	A+ Bal	9	9	1	0	50	218	42	23	22	5	2	3	3	31	2	54	3	0	3	3	.500	1	0	3.96
4 Min. YEARS		69	61	3	2	340.2	1495	305	178	156	31	6	14	29	189	5	382	24	2	20	17	.541	3	0	4.12

Steve Gajkowski

Pitches: Right Bats: Right Pos: P Ht: 6'2" Wt: 200 Born: 12/30/69 Age: 28

Year Team	Lg Org	G	GS	CG	GF	IP	BFP	H	R	ER	HR	SH	SF	HB	TBB	IBB	SO	WP	Bk	W	L	Pct.	ShO	Sv	ERA
1990 Burlington	R+ Cle	14	10	1	1	63.2	287	74	34	29	0	0	3	3	23	0	44	0	1	2	6	.250	0	0	4.10
1991 Columbus	A Cle	3	0	0	2	6	24	3	2	2	0	0	0	0	5	0	5	0	0	0	0	.000	0	0	3.00
Watertown	A- Cle	20	4	0	7	48	221	41	36	28	0	1	2	6	32	1	34	7	2	3	3	.500	0	0	5.25
1992 Utica	A- ChA	29	0	0	26	47	184	33	14	7	1	0	2	1	10	1	38	6	0	3	2	.600	0	14	1.34
1993 Sarasota	A+ ChA	43	0	0	38	69.2	273	52	21	16	1	3	3	4	17	5	45	5	1	3	3	.500	0	15	2.07
Birmingham	AA ChA	1	0	0	0	2.1	8	0	0	0	0	0	0	0	0	0	2	0	0	0	0	.000	0	0	0.00
1994 Birmingham	AA ChA	58	0	0	32	82.1	355	78	35	28	6	6	3	5	26	1	44	2	0	11	5	.688	0	8	3.06
1995 Nashville	AAA ChA	15	0	0	5	24.2	103	26	15	7	2	0	1	1	8	1	12	1	0	0	1	.000	0	2	2.55
Birmingham	AA ChA	35	0	0	14	51.2	230	64	27	24	4	2	0	2	16	1	29	1	0	4	4	.500	0	2	4.18
1996 Nashville	AAA ChA	49	8	0	17	107.1	472	113	61	47	11	4	5	5	41	5	47	6	0	5	6	.455	0	2	3.94
1997 Tacoma	AAA Sea	44	3	0	10	93	394	100	43	40	11	2	1	5	24	0	48	3	1	5	3	.625	0	2	3.87
8 Min. YEARS		311	25	1	152	595.2	2551	584	288	228	36	18	20	32	202	15	348	31	6	36	33	.522	0	43	3.44

Kevin Gallaher

Pitches: Right Bats: Left Pos: P Ht: 6'3" Wt: 190 Born: 8/1/68 Age: 29

Year Team	Lg Org	G	GS	CG	GF	IP	BFP	H	R	ER	HR	SH	SF	HB	TBB	IBB	SO	WP	Bk	W	L	Pct.	ShO	Sv	ERA
1991 Auburn	A- Hou	16	8	0	3	48	243	59	48	37	2	3	9	9	37	0	25	6	1	2	5	.286	0	0	6.94
1992 Osceola	A+ Hou	1	1	0	0	6.1	26	2	2	2	1	0	0	0	3	0	5	1	0	0	1	.000	0	0	2.84
Burlington	A Hou	20	20	1	0	117	529	108	70	50	5	7	4	9	80	0	89	9	1	6	10	.375	0	0	3.85
1993 Osceola	A+ Hou	21	21	1	0	135	586	132	68	57	7	3	3	4	57	1	93	8	3	7	7	.500	1	0	3.80
Jackson	AA Hou	4	4	0	0	24	95	14	7	7	3	1	2	2	10	0	30	6	0	0	2	.000	0	0	2.63
1994 Jackson	AA Hou	18	18	0	0	106	468	88	57	46	5	1	2	8	67	1	112	13	0	6	6	.500	0	0	3.91
Tucson	AAA Hou	9	9	2	0	53.2	240	55	35	32	5	3	2	3	25	0	58	3	0	3	4	.429	0	0	5.37
1995 Kissimmee	A+ Hou	7	7	0	0	17.1	86	8	11	11	0	0	0	3	24	0	21	2	0	1	1	.500	0	0	5.71
Jackson	AA Hou	6	6	1	0	42.1	179	31	18	16	1	3	1	0	23	1	28	4	0	2	2	.500	0	0	3.40
Tucson	AAA Hou	3	3	0	0	14	70	19	11	10	1	0	2	2	9	0	11	2	0	1	1	.500	0	0	6.43
1996 Tucson	AAA Hou	35	3	0	6	87	392	88	50	45	5	5	6	3	45	3	81	11	1	4	2	.667	0	1	4.66
Toledo	AAA Det	2	0	0	0	3	22	9	7	7	0	0	0	0	4	1	4	1	0	0	0	.000	0	0	21.00
1997 Toledo	AAA Det	9	0	0	2	19	88	16	12	10	1	1	0	2	17	0	13	2	1	1	1	.500	0	0	4.74
Jacksnville	AA Det	10	10	2	0	57	271	70	45	41	10	1	3	6	32	0	33	5	0	4	3	.571	0	0	6.47
Bowie	AA Bal	26	1	0	20	42.1	187	50	27	21	2	1	2	5	15	1	36	6	0	1	5	.167	0	8	4.46
7 Min. YEARS		187	111	7	31	772	3482	749	468	392	48	29	36	56	448	8	639	79	7	38	50	.432	1	9	4.57

Rick Gama

Bats: Right Throws: Right Pos: 2B Ht: 5'10" Wt: 180 Born: 4/27/73 Age: 25

Year Team	Lg Org	G	AB	H	2B	3B	HR	TB	R	RBI	TBB	IBB	SO	HBP	SH	SF	SB	CS	SB%	GDP	Avg	OBP	SLG
1995 Idaho Falls	R+ SD	70	266	85	16	2	8	129	71	58	55	1	29	2	3	10	17	4	.81	2	.320	.426	.485
1996 Rancho Cuca	A+ SD	108	417	113	28	2	7	166	59	50	37	1	57	4	5	4	13	5	.72	10	.271	.333	.398
1997 Rancho Cuca	A+ SD	25	115	29	9	0	2	44	17	12	6	0	12	0	2	0	4	2	.67	3	.252	.289	.383
Mobile	AA SD	88	295	85	16	2	6	123	56	43	51	0	41	2	1	6	9	3	.75	3	.288	.390	.417
3 Min. YEARS		291	1093	312	69	6	23	462	203	163	149	2	139	8	11	20	43	14	.75	18	.285	.369	.423

Javier Gamboa

Pitches: Right Bats: Right Pos: P Ht: 6'1" Wt: 185 Born: 3/17/74 Age: 24

Year Team	Lg Org	G	GS	CG	GF	IP	BFP	H	R	ER	HR	SH	SF	HB	TBB	IBB	SO	WP	Bk	W	L	Pct.	ShO	Sv	ERA
1994 Eugene	A- KC	16	14	0	1	62	277	58	45	40	8	1	2	7	29	0	62	6	2	0	5	.000	0	0	5.81
1995 Springfield	A KC	19	19	1	0	105.2	429	83	45	37	10	3	2	0	32	0	66	4	0	6	6	.500	0	0	3.15
Wilmington	A+ KC	8	8	0	0	49	202	42	23	22	6	3	0	1	13	0	33	2	0	3	4	.429	0	0	4.04
1996 Wilmington	A+ KC	6	6	0	0	34.1	138	36	12	12	3	1	0	1	2	0	24	1	0	3	1	.750	0	0	3.15
Wichita	AA KC	15	15	0	0	91	414	118	68	60	19	3	5	2	33	0	39	2	0	5	5	.500	0	0	5.93
1997 Royals	R KC	2	2	0	0	8	26	4	1	1	0	0	0	1	1	0	7	0	1	0	0	.000	0	0	1.13
Wichita	AA KC	6	6	0	0	29	139	49	30	28	3	1	1	2	8	0	16	1	0	0	3	.000	0	0	8.69
4 Min. YEARS		72	70	1	1	379	1625	390	224	200	49	12	10	14	118	0	247	16	3	17	24	.415	0	0	4.75

Bob Gamez

Pitches: Left Bats: Left Pos: P Ht: 6'5" Wt: 185 Born: 11/18/68 Age: 29

Year Team	Lg Org	G	GS	CG	GF	IP	BFP	H	R	ER	HR	SH	SF	HB	TBB	IBB	SO	WP	Bk	W	L	Pct.	ShO	Sv	ERA
1988 Rangers	R Tex	2	0	0	0	2.2	10	0	0	0	0	0	0	0	4	0	1	0	0	0	0	.000	0	0	0.00
1989 Rangers	R Tex	23	1	0	5	40.2	172	35	17	17	0	0	0	0	18	0	44	3	0	2	1	.667	0	0	3.76
1990 Boise	A- Ana	14	7	0	0	46.1	196	42	19	15	3	0	0	2	15	2	38	5	0	3	0	1.000	0	0	2.91
1991 Quad City	A Ana	41	5	0	11	76.2	341	75	38	31	6	5	6	3	38	4	83	10	0	4	3	.571	0	0	3.64
1992 Palm Spring	A+ Ana	38	13	0	8	98.1	431	106	63	54	4	7	6	2	44	5	70	10	1	8	8	.500	0	3	4.94
1993 Midland	AA Ana	44	0	0	13	60.2	260	68	27	22	7	1	0	2	18	0	50	5	0	5	2	.714	0	3	3.26
Vancouver	AAA Ana	9	0	0	3	13.1	60	11	9	7	1	1	0	1	9	0	15	2	0	1	0	1.000	0	0	4.73
1994 Phoenix	AAA SF	39	14	0	13	98	459	130	73	66	11	4	4	7	51	2	60	9	0	5	10	.333	0	3	6.06
1995 Phoenix	AAA SF	36	9	0	8	66	292	76	46	41	8	4	1	0	27	4	41	7	0	3	5	.375	0	1	5.59
1997 Midland	AA Ana	51	0	0	14	47.2	221	62	37	27	4	0	1	3	20	1	46	4	1	7	2	.778	0	1	5.10
9 Min. YEARS		297	49	0	72	550.1	2442	605	329	280	41	22	19	14	244	18	448	55	2	38	31	.551	0	11	4.58

Gus Gandarillas

Pitches: Right **Bats:** Right **Pos:** P **Ht:** 6'0" **Wt:** 180 **Born:** 7/19/71 **Age:** 26

Year Team	Lg Org	G	GS	CG	GF	IP	BFP	H	R	ER	HR	SH	SF	HB	TBB	IBB	SO	WP	Bk	W	L	Pct.	ShO	Sv	ERA
1992 Elizabethtn	R+ Min	29	0	0	29	36	148	24	14	12	1	0	0	3	10	2	34	4	1	1	2	.333	0	13	3.00
1993 Ft. Wayne	A Min	52	0	0	48	66.1	295	66	37	24	8	5	5	1	22	2	59	4	0	5	5	.500	0	25	3.26
1994 Ft. Myers	A+ Min	37	0	0	34	46.2	190	37	7	4	0	3	2	2	13	4	39	5	0	4	1	.800	0	20	0.77
Nashville	AA Min	28	0	0	20	37	156	34	13	13	1	2	1	4	10	0	29	6	0	2	2	.500	0	8	3.16
1995 Salt Lake	AAA Min	22	0	0	13	29.1	135	34	23	21	5	3	1	1	19	4	17	5	0	2	3	.400	0	2	6.44
Hardware City	AA Min	25	0	0	18	32.1	152	38	26	22	1	2	0	3	16	0	25	3	0	2	4	.333	0	7	6.12
1996 Twins	R Min	3	1	0	2	9	43	10	3	1	1	1	0	0	3	0	14	1	0	0	0	.000	0	1	1.00
Ft. Myers	A+ Min	4	0	0	3	6	35	9	7	6	0	0	0	1	8	0	3	1	0	0	0	.000	0	1	9.00
1997 New Britain	AA Min	17	7	1	2	61.1	253	67	34	32	6	0	2	3	15	0	29	5	0	2	4	.333	0	0	4.70
Salt Lake	AAA Min	11	2	0	2	22.2	93	22	8	8	1	0	0	0	6	1	13	1	0	1	0	1.000	0	2	3.18
6 Min. YEARS		228	10	1	171	346.2	1500	341	172	143	24	16	11	19	122	13	262	35	1	19	21	.475	0	80	3.71

Al Garcia

Pitches: Right **Bats:** Right **Pos:** P **Ht:** 6'2" **Wt:** 175 **Born:** 6/11/74 **Age:** 24

Year Team	Lg Org	G	GS	CG	GF	IP	BFP	H	R	ER	HR	SH	SF	HB	TBB	IBB	SO	WP	Bk	W	L	Pct.	ShO	Sv	ERA
1993 Cubs	R ChN	9	7	0	2	49.2	210	47	26	18	0	5	3	4	7	0	33	3	5	2	5	.286	0	0	3.26
Huntington	R+ ChN	3	3	0	0	20	86	23	11	11	2	0	2	2	1	0	11	0	0	1	2	.333	0	0	4.95
1994 Huntington	R+ ChN	8	4	0	3	30	129	35	23	15	3	0	0	1	6	0	28	0	0	1	4	.200	0	1	4.50
Williamsprt	A- ChN	8	7	3	1	45.1	190	41	16	15	1	1	3	1	17	1	39	4	1	3	3	.500	1	1	2.98
1995 Rockford	A ChN	27	27	1	0	177	755	176	94	74	13	4	4	15	43	0	120	10	0	14	9	.609	1	0	3.76
1996 Daytona	A+ ChN	7	7	0	0	47	187	48	20	15	1	3	1	2	5	0	28	2	0	4	1	.800	0	0	2.87
Orlando	AA ChN	23	16	1	3	118.2	528	149	71	64	17	6	5	7	32	1	66	4	0	6	7	.462	0	0	4.85
1997 Orlando	AA ChN	12	12	0	0	72.1	315	87	39	28	6	2	2	4	23	1	27	1	1	4	4	.500	0	0	3.48
5 Min. YEARS		97	83	5	9	560	2400	606	300	240	43	21	20	36	134	3	352	24	7	35	35	.500	2	2	3.86

Frank Garcia

Pitches: Right **Bats:** Right **Pos:** P **Ht:** 5'11" **Wt:** 170 **Born:** 3/5/74 **Age:** 24

Year Team	Lg Org	G	GS	CG	GF	IP	BFP	H	R	ER	HR	SH	SF	HB	TBB	IBB	SO	WP	Bk	W	L	Pct.	ShO	Sv	ERA
1994 Cardinals	R StL	27	0	0	25	29.2	116	16	7	4	0	1	0	3	7	0	39	0	0	1	1	.500	0	18	1.21
1995 Savannah	A StL	34	0	0	32	37	156	26	17	13	3	0	1	2	15	0	41	8	0	0	3	.000	0	24	3.16
St. Pete	A+ StL	16	0	0	8	16.2	98	27	22	19	1	0	1	1	18	0	8	3	0	0	1	.000	0	0	10.26
1996 St. Pete	A+ StL	28	0	0	5	32	147	35	11	9	1	1	0	1	18	2	24	2	0	2	0	1.000	0	0	2.53
Arkansas	AA StL	11	0	0	2	19.1	84	20	11	8	1	1	1	1	7	0	12	1	0	0	0	.000	0	0	3.72
1997 Pr William	A+ StL	18	0	0	5	24	122	36	30	24	2	0	2	1	12	0	14	5	0	2	2	.500	0	0	9.00
Arkansas	AA StL	28	0	0	3	38	183	43	38	28	6	0	2	2	24	0	25	0	1	1	3	.250	0	0	6.63
4 Min. YEARS		162	0	0	80	196.2	906	203	136	105	14	3	7	11	101	2	163	19	1	6	10	.375	0	43	4.81

Guillermo Garcia

Bats: Right **Throws:** Right **Pos:** C **Ht:** 6'3" **Wt:** 190 **Born:** 4/4/72 **Age:** 26

Year Team	Lg Org	G	AB	H	2B	3B	HR	TB	R	RBI	TBB	IBB	SO	HBP	SH	SF	SB	CS	SB%	GDP	Avg	OBP	SLG
1990 Mets	R NYN	42	136	25	1	2	0	30	9	6	7	1	34	1	2	1	1	1	.50	2	.184	.228	.221
1991 Kingsport	R+ NYN	15	33	8	1	1	0	11	9	2	4	0	4	0	0	0	0	0	.00	1	.242	.324	.333
Pittsfield	A- NYN	45	157	43	13	2	0	60	22	24	15	0	38	1	3	3	4	1	.80	5	.274	.335	.382
1992 Pittsfield	A- NYN	73	272	54	11	1	2	73	36	26	20	0	52	2	0	3	3	4	.43	5	.199	.256	.268
1993 Capital Cty	A NYN	119	429	124	28	2	3	165	64	72	49	1	60	10	1	3	10	8	.56	11	.289	.373	.385
1994 St. Lucie	A+ NYN	55	203	48	9	1	1	62	22	23	13	1	24	3	2	0	0	2	.00	6	.236	.292	.305
1995 Winston-Sal	A+ Cin	78	245	58	10	2	3	81	26	29	28	0	32	1	2	2	2	2	.50	7	.237	.315	.331
1996 Indianapols	AAA Cin	16	47	12	2	0	0	14	4	0	2	2	6	0	0	0	0	0	.00	5	.255	.286	.298
Chattanooga	AA Cin	60	203	64	12	0	6	94	25	36	12	2	32	1	2	1	3	3	.50	3	.315	.355	.463
1997 Chattanooga	AA Cin	20	74	21	1	1	4	36	11	19	8	0	13	0	0	1	0	0	.00	1	.284	.349	.486
Indianapols	AAA Cin	55	151	36	2	0	10	68	16	20	9	0	46	1	0	2	0	2	.00	4	.238	.282	.450
8 Min. YEARS		578	1950	493	90	12	29	694	244	257	167	7	341	20	12	16	23	23	.50	50	.253	.316	.356

Jesse Garcia

Bats: Right **Throws:** Right **Pos:** 2B **Ht:** 5'9" **Wt:** 165 **Born:** 9/24/73 **Age:** 24

Year Team	Lg Org	G	AB	H	2B	3B	HR	TB	R	RBI	TBB	IBB	SO	HBP	SH	SF	SB	CS	SB%	GDP	Avg	OBP	SLG
1993 Orioles	R Bal	48	156	37	4	0	0	41	20	16	21	1	32	1	8	3	14	6	.70	1	.237	.326	.263
1995 Frederick	A+ Bal	124	365	82	11	3	3	108	52	27	49	0	75	9	7	2	5	10	.33	5	.225	.329	.296
1996 High Desert	A+ Bal	137	459	122	21	5	10	183	94	66	57	0	81	8	20	4	25	7	.78	5	.266	.354	.399
1997 Bowie	AA Bal	141	437	103	18	1	5	138	52	42	38	0	71	6	24	2	7	7	.50	9	.236	.304	.316
4 Min. YEARS		450	1417	344	54	9	18	470	218	151	165	1	259	24	59	11	51	30	.63	22	.243	.330	.332

Jose Garcia

Pitches: Right **Bats:** Right **Pos:** P **Ht:** 6'3" **Wt:** 146 **Born:** 6/12/72 **Age:** 26

Year Team	Lg Org	G	GS	CG	GF	IP	BFP	H	R	ER	HR	SH	SF	HB	TBB	IBB	SO	WP	Bk	W	L	Pct.	ShO	Sv	ERA
1993 Bakersfield	A+ LA	27	0	0	22	29	142	47	23	22	6	1	4	0	12	1	25	3	2	0	3	.000	0	4	6.83
Yakima	A- LA	36	0	0	30	44.2	188	40	14	12	1	0	2	3	19	2	19	2	0	2	2	.500	0	5	2.42
1994 Vero Beach	A+ LA	20	0	0	13	32.2	129	32	7	5	0	1	0	0	2	0	24	2	1	3	1	.750	0	4	1.38

Year Team	Lg Org	G	GS	CG	GF	IP	BFP	H	R	ER	HR	SH	SF	HB	TBB	IBB	SO	WP	Bk	W	L	Pct.	ShO	Sv	ERA
San Antonio	AA LA	7	0	0	7	11	40	7	2	2	0	1	1	0	6	2	8	0	1	2	0	1.000	0	3	1.64
Albuquerque	AAA LA	37	0	0	7	57.2	258	66	39	33	6	2	3	3	26	5	38	2	0	4	1	.800	0	0	5.15
1995 Albuquerque	AAA LA	11	0	0	4	15.2	73	19	11	11	3	2	4	0	7	1	10	0	0	1	3	.250	0	0	6.32
San Antonio	AA LA	38	0	0	15	58	242	50	32	26	4	4	4	6	24	0	36	6	2	2	6	.250	0	2	4.03
1996 San Antonio	AA LA	8	0	0	5	11.1	38	4	0	0	0	1	0	0	0	0	8	1	0	2	0	1.000	0	2	0.00
Albuquerque	AAA LA	44	0	0	10	78.1	361	97	49	41	10	4	1	2	40	10	34	2	0	6	1	.857	0	0	4.71
1997 Albuquerque	AAA LA	33	0	0	13	45.2	203	57	27	26	5	3	1	3	14	2	44	6	0	3	3	.500	0	0	5.12
San Antonio	AA LA	10	0	0	5	20	82	19	8	7	1	2	1	3	4	1	14	1	0	3	1	.750	0	1	3.15
5 Min. YEARS		271	0	0	131	404	1756	438	212	185	36	21	21	20	154	24	260	25	6	28	21	.571	0	21	4.12

Luis Garcia

Bats: Right Throws: Right Pos: SS   Ht: 6'0" Wt: 174 Born: 5/20/75 Age: 23

Year Team	Lg Org	G	AB	H	2B	3B	HR	TB	R	RBI	TBB	IBB	SO	HBP	SH	SF	SB	CS	SB%	GDP	Avg	OBP	SLG
1993 Bristol	R+ Det	24	57	12	1	0	1	16	7	7	3	0	11	0	1	0	3	1	.75	1	.211	.250	.281
1994 Jamestown	A- Det	67	239	47	8	2	1	62	21	19	8	0	48	1	6	3	6	9	.40	4	.197	.223	.259
1995 Lakeland	A+ Det	102	361	101	10	4	2	125	39	35	8	0	42	1	4	4	9	10	.47	6	.280	.294	.346
Jacksnville	AA Det	17	47	13	0	0	0	13	6	5	1	0	8	1	0	0	2	1	.67	0	.277	.306	.277
1996 Jacksnville	AA Det	131	522	128	22	4	9	185	68	46	12	1	90	2	7	2	15	12	.56	9	.245	.264	.354
1997 Jacksnville	AA Det	126	456	122	19	1	5	158	55	48	10	0	59	3	6	6	3	2	.60	15	.268	.284	.346
5 Min. YEARS		467	1682	423	60	11	18	559	196	160	42	1	258	8	24	15	38	35	.52	35	.251	.271	.332

Vicente Garcia

Bats: Right Throws: Right Pos: 2B   Ht: 6'0" Wt: 170 Born: 2/14/75 Age: 23

Year Team	Lg Org	G	AB	H	2B	3B	HR	TB	R	RBI	TBB	IBB	SO	HBP	SH	SF	SB	CS	SB%	GDP	Avg	OBP	SLG
1993 Rockies	R Col	38	137	41	10	0	0	51	13	13	18	0	27	1	0	0	12	2	.86	2	.299	.385	.372
1994 Asheville	A Col	123	397	87	22	1	4	123	41	44	35	0	56	5	6	3	5	10	.33	9	.219	.289	.310
1995 Salem	A+ Col	119	457	111	26	1	10	169	62	41	53	1	73	1	5	2	5	0	1.00	10	.243	.322	.370
1996 New Haven	AA Col	87	295	63	10	1	3	84	32	18	28	1	43	5	6	2	1	2	.33	7	.214	.291	.285
1997 New Haven	AA Col	22	58	9	2	0	2	17	9	11	12	0	19	0	1	2	0	1	.00	1	.155	.292	.293
Salem	A+ Col	98	319	82	22	1	4	118	49	37	44	2	51	6	5	2	11	5	.69	8	.257	.356	.370
5 Min. YEARS		487	1663	393	92	4	23	562	206	164	190	6	269	18	23	11	34	20	.63	37	.236	.319	.338

Mike Gardiner

Pitches: Right Bats: Both Pos: P   Ht: 6'0" Wt: 200 Born: 10/19/65 Age: 32

Year Team	Lg Org	G	GS	CG	GF	IP	BFP	H	R	ER	HR	SH	SF	HB	TBB	IBB	SO	WP	Bk	W	L	Pct.	ShO	Sv	ERA
1987 Bellingham	A- Sea	2	1	0	0	10	35	6	0	0	0	0	0	0	1	0	11	0	0	2	0	1.000	0	0	0.00
Wausau	A Sea	13	13	2	0	81	368	91	54	47	9	2	5	3	33	2	80	3	1	3	5	.375	1	0	5.22
1988 Wausau	A Sea	11	6	0	0	31.1	132	31	16	11	1	0	0	1	13	0	24	1	0	2	1	.667	0	1	3.16
1989 Wausau	A Sea	15	1	0	11	30.1	120	21	5	2	0	2	0	1	11	0	48	0	0	4	0	1.000	0	7	0.59
Williamsprt	AA Sea	30	3	1	14	63.1	274	54	25	20	6	1	3	1	32	6	60	4	1	4	6	.400	1	2	2.84
1990 Williamsprt	AA Sea	26	26	5	0	179.2	697	136	47	38	8	4	3	1	29	1	149	4	1	12	8	.600	1	0	1.90
1991 Pawtucket	AAA Bos	8	8	2	0	57.2	220	39	16	15	2	3	2	1	11	0	42	0	0	7	1	.875	1	0	2.34
1992 Pawtucket	AAA Bos	5	5	2	0	32.2	138	32	14	12	3	0	0	0	9	0	37	0	0	1	3	.250	0	0	3.31
1993 Ottawa	AAA Mon	5	5	0	0	25	101	17	8	6	2	1	2	0	9	0	25	1	0	1	1	.500	0	0	2.16
Toledo	AAA Det	4	0	0	2	5	22	6	3	3	0	0	0	0	2	0	10	2	0	0	0	.000	0	1	5.40
1995 Toledo	AAA Det	11	1	0	4	16.1	77	19	8	8	2	1	1	0	13	0	10	1	0	0	1	.000	0	0	4.41
1996 Norfolk	AAA NYN	24	24	2	0	146	590	125	58	52	18	3	5	2	38	3	125	3	0	13	3	.813	2	0	3.21
1997 New Orleans	AAA Hou	11	4	0	3	31	147	43	32	28	3	1	2	1	14	0	24	0	0	2	1	.667	0	0	8.13
Columbus	AAA NYA	14	13	1	0	85	348	83	40	37	10	5	2	3	24	0	65	3	0	5	4	.556	0	0	3.92
1990 Seattle	AL	5	3	0	1	12.2	66	22	17	15	1	0	1	2	5	0	6	0	0	0	2	.000	0	0	10.66
1991 Boston	AL	22	22	0	0	130	562	140	79	70	18	1	3	0	47	2	91	1	0	9	10	.474	0	0	4.85
1992 Boston	AL	28	18	0	3	130.2	566	126	78	69	12	3	5	2	58	2	79	8	0	4	10	.286	0	0	4.75
1993 Montreal	NL	24	2	0	3	38	173	40	28	22	3	1	3	1	19	2	21	0	0	2	3	.400	0	0	5.21
Detroit	AL	10	0	0	1	11.1	51	12	5	5	0	1	0	0	7	1	4	2	0	0	0	.000	0	0	3.97
1994 Detroit	AL	38	1	0	14	58.2	254	53	35	27	10	2	2	0	23	5	31	1	0	2	2	.500	0	5	4.14
1995 Detroit	AL	9	0	0	1	12.1	66	27	20	20	5	3	2	0	2	1	7	1	0	0	0	.000	0	0	14.59
10 Min. YEARS		179	110	15	38	794.1	3269	703	326	279	64	23	25	14	239	12	710	22	4	56	35	.615	5	11	3.16
6 Maj. YEARS		136	46	0	23	393.2	1738	420	262	228	49	11	16	5	161	13	239	13	0	17	27	.386	0	5	5.21

Scott Gardner

Pitches: Right Bats: Both Pos: P   Ht: 6'5" Wt: 225 Born: 9/30/71 Age: 26

Year Team	Lg Org	G	GS	CG	GF	IP	BFP	H	R	ER	HR	SH	SF	HB	TBB	IBB	SO	WP	Bk	W	L	Pct.	ShO	Sv	ERA
1990 Huntington	R+ ChN	13	4	0	5	43.1	191	36	16	10	1	3	1	2	20	0	52	5	1	3	2	.600	0	2	2.08
1991 Peoria	A ChN	3	3	1	0	12	56	16	9	7	0	0	0	2	7	0	6	1	0	1	2	.333	0	0	5.25
Huntington	R+ ChN	7	7	0	0	39.1	164	38	16	14	3	2	2	2	16	0	25	4	1	2	3	.400	0	0	3.20
1992 Geneva	A- ChN	10	2	0	1	20	90	19	11	6	0	1	1	1	6	0	20	1	0	2	1	.667	0	0	2.70
1993 Peoria	A ChN	39	9	1	12	88.1	379	81	60	53	7	3	3	7	36	1	99	7	1	5	6	.455	0	3	5.40
1995 Lakeland	A+ Det	5	0	0	2	13	54	10	6	4	1	0	0	0	7	0	14	0	0	0	0	.000	0	0	2.77
Fayettevlle	A Det	49	1	0	22	87.1	351	62	26	20	5	1	0	2	24	1	112	8	2	6	3	.667	0	4	2.06
1996 Stockton	A+ Mil	27	21	3	0	144	608	127	77	66	11	4	0	7	52	0	148	19	2	10	8	.556	1	0	4.13
1997 El Paso	AA Mil	29	22	1	4	139.1	625	166	93	79	8	7	8	8	56	1	89	17	1	7	8	.467	0	0	5.10
Tucson	AAA Mil	1	1	0	0	6	26	6	2	2	0	0	1	0	3	0	6	0	0	1	0	1.000	0	0	3.00
7 Min. YEARS		183	70	6	46	592.2	2544	561	316	261	36	21	16	31	227	3	571	62	8	37	33	.529	1	9	3.96

Hal Garrett

Pitches: Right **Bats:** Right **Pos:** P **Ht:** 6'1" **Wt:** 160 **Born:** 4/27/75 **Age:** 23

Year Team	Lg Org	G	GS	CG	GF	IP	BFP	H	R	ER	HR	SH	SF	HB	TBB	IBB	SO	WP	Bk	W	L	Pct.	ShO	Sv	ERA
1993 Padres	R SD	14	14	0	0	72.1	317	64	40	26	3	0	1	5	31	2	83	6	0	6	5	.545	0	0	3.24
1994 Springfield	A SD	21	20	0	0	102.1	454	93	67	54	8	2	5	6	54	2	79	9	2	7	4	.636	0	0	4.75
1995 Clinton	A SD	11	11	1	0	58	268	58	43	36	4	5	2	4	34	3	41	5	0	3	8	.273	0	0	5.59
Rancho Cuca	A+ SD	23	1	0	5	42	196	40	21	13	2	2	5	2	25	0	43	7	1	0	4	.000	0	0	2.79
1996 Clinton	A SD	25	3	0	11	49.2	229	45	28	25	4	2	2	5	31	2	60	3	0	2	3	.400	0	1	4.53
Rancho Cuca	A+ SD	24	1	0	3	51	214	41	12	11	3	1	2	3	20	0	56	6	0	4	1	.800	0	0	1.94
1997 Carolina	AA Pit	6	0	0	2	13.1	64	19	14	13	6	1	0	0	6	1	7	2	0	1	2	.333	0	0	8.78
Lynchburg	A+ Pit	29	5	0	11	56	250	56	36	30	5	4	3	4	22	3	45	5	0	2	5	.286	0	5	4.82
Savannah	A LA	8	1	0	4	16	78	21	15	15	0	1	0	2	7	0	13	4	0	0	3	.000	0	0	8.44
5 Min. YEARS		161	56	1	36	460.2	2070	437	276	223	35	18	20	31	230	13	427	47	3	25	35	.417	0	6	4.36

Webster Garrison

Bats: Right **Throws:** Right **Pos:** 2B **Ht:** 5'11" **Wt:** 193 **Born:** 8/24/65 **Age:** 32

Year Team	Lg Org	G	AB	H	2B	3B	HR	TB	R	RBI	TBB	IBB	SO	HBP	SH	SF	SB	CS	SB%	GDP	Avg	OBP	SLG
1984 Florence	A Tor	129	502	120	14	0	0	134	80	33	57	0	44	1	2	2	16	7	.70	9	.239	.317	.267
1985 Kinston	A+ Tor	129	449	91	14	1	1	110	40	30	42	0	76	3	2	5	22	5	.81	6	.203	.273	.245
1986 Florence	A Tor	105	354	85	10	0	3	104	47	40	56	3	53	2	0	3	4	7	.36	7	.240	.345	.294
Knoxville	AA Tor	5	6	0	0	0	0	0	0	0	0	0	2	0	0	0	1	0	1.00	0	.000	.000	.000
1987 Dunedin	A+ Tor	128	477	135	14	4	0	157	70	44	57	0	53	0	0	5	27	9	.75	12	.283	.356	.329
1988 Knoxville	AA Tor	138	534	136	24	5	0	170	61	40	53	0	74	1	2	4	42	15	.74	7	.255	.321	.318
1989 Knoxville	AA Tor	54	203	55	6	2	4	77	38	14	33	0	38	0	4	1	18	6	.75	5	.271	.371	.379
Syracuse	AAA Tor	50	151	43	7	1	0	52	18	9	18	1	25	2	4	0	3	2	.60	5	.285	.368	.344
1990 Syracuse	AAA Tor	37	101	20	5	1	0	27	12	10	14	0	20	0	3	1	0	3	.00	3	.198	.293	.267
1991 Tacoma	AAA Oak	75	237	51	11	2	2	72	28	28	26	0	34	2	7	2	4	0	1.00	6	.215	.296	.304
Huntsville	AA Oak	31	110	29	9	0	2	44	18	10	16	0	21	1	0	1	5	2	.71	1	.264	.359	.400
1992 Tacoma	AAA Oak	33	116	28	5	1	2	41	15	17	2	0	12	0	1	2	1	1	.50	5	.241	.250	.353
Huntsville	AA Oak	91	348	96	25	4	8	153	50	61	30	0	59	0	3	5	8	6	.57	12	.276	.329	.440
1993 Tacoma	AAA Oak	138	544	165	29	5	7	225	91	73	58	2	64	2	2	5	17	9	.65	17	.303	.369	.414
1994 Colo Sprngs	AAA Col	128	514	155	32	5	13	236	94	68	46	2	65	0	1	4	18	5	.78	11	.302	.356	.459
1995 Colo Sprngs	AAA Col	126	460	135	32	6	12	215	83	77	46	2	74	3	3	6	12	4	.75	9	.293	.357	.467
1996 Huntsville	AA Oak	47	178	50	12	2	7	87	28	31	22	0	33	1	0	1	1	1	.50	4	.281	.361	.489
Edmonton	AAA Oak	80	294	89	18	0	10	137	56	49	41	2	47	0	1	2	2	1	.67	11	.303	.386	.466
1997 Edmonton	AAA Oak	125	429	124	24	2	15	197	70	80	57	5	91	2	2	4	5	3	.63	6	.289	.372	.459
1996 Oakland	AL	5	9	0	0	0	0	0	0	0	1	0	0	0	0	0	0	0	.00	0	.000	.100	.000
14 Min. YEARS		1649	6007	1607	291	41	86	2238	899	714	674	17	885	20	37	53	206	86	.71	136	.268	.341	.373

Marty Gazarek

Bats: Right **Throws:** Right **Pos:** OF **Ht:** 6'2" **Wt:** 190 **Born:** 6/1/73 **Age:** 25

Year Team	Lg Org	G	AB	H	2B	3B	HR	TB	R	RBI	TBB	IBB	SO	HBP	SH	SF	SB	CS	SB%	GDP	Avg	OBP	SLG
1994 Williamsprt	A- ChN	45	181	68	13	0	2	87	22	18	6	0	17	2	3	0	14	7	.67	2	.376	.402	.481
Peoria	A ChN	23	89	29	6	0	1	38	18	12	2	0	14	3	0	2	2	3	.40	4	.326	.354	.427
1995 Rockford	A ChN	107	399	104	24	1	3	139	57	53	27	1	58	8	2	3	7	5	.58	8	.261	.318	.348
1996 Daytona	A+ ChN	129	472	131	31	4	11	203	68	77	28	0	52	12	0	5	15	13	.54	10	.278	.331	.430
1997 Orlando	AA ChN	76	290	96	23	0	10	149	55	52	20	2	31	5	0	2	10	3	.77	3	.331	.382	.514
4 Min. YEARS		380	1431	428	97	5	27	616	220	212	83	3	172	30	5	12	48	31	.61	27	.299	.348	.430

Phil Geisler

Bats: Left **Throws:** Left **Pos:** OF **Ht:** 6'3" **Wt:** 200 **Born:** 10/23/69 **Age:** 28

Year Team	Lg Org	G	AB	H	2B	3B	HR	TB	R	RBI	TBB	IBB	SO	HBP	SH	SF	SB	CS	SB%	GDP	Avg	OBP	SLG
1991 Martinsvlle	R+ Phi	32	114	37	5	0	1	45	22	18	23	1	25	1	0	0	1	0	1.00	1	.325	.442	.395
Spartanburg	A Phi	36	129	21	3	0	1	27	19	8	14	0	36	0	1	0	0	0	.00	2	.163	.245	.209
1992 Clearwater	A+ Phi	120	400	87	10	3	6	121	39	33	41	1	88	4	1	2	4	9	.31	8	.218	.295	.303
1993 Clearwater	A+ Phi	87	344	105	23	4	15	181	72	62	29	3	70	6	2	1	4	5	.44	5	.305	.368	.526
Reading	AA Phi	48	178	48	14	1	3	73	25	14	17	2	50	3	1	0	4	2	.67	3	.270	.343	.410
1994 Scranton-WB	AAA Phi	54	183	36	5	1	0	43	14	11	18	3	48	1	1	1	2	2	.50	3	.197	.270	.235
Reading	AA Phi	74	254	70	12	1	7	105	32	40	24	5	55	2	0	2	4	7	.36	5	.276	.340	.413
1995 Reading	AA Phi	76	272	63	10	3	2	85	27	35	21	3	65	4	0	2	4	2	.67	5	.232	.294	.313
Scranton-WB	AAA Phi	20	43	8	5	0	1	16	2	7	2	0	13	0	1	0	0	0	.00	2	.186	.222	.372
1996 Binghamton	AA NYN	107	355	89	17	2	11	143	47	59	33	6	96	3	1	5	5	4	.56	7	.251	.316	.403
1997 Norfolk	AAA NYN	109	336	86	24	0	9	137	28	57	24	4	90	1	0	6	2	5	.29	8	.256	.302	.408
7 Min. YEARS		763	2608	650	128	15	56	976	327	344	246	28	636	25	8	20	30	36	.45	49	.249	.318	.374

Scott Gentile

Pitches: Right **Bats:** Right **Pos:** P **Ht:** 5'11" **Wt:** 210 **Born:** 12/21/70 **Age:** 27

Year Team	Lg Org	G	GS	CG	GF	IP	BFP	H	R	ER	HR	SH	SF	HB	TBB	IBB	SO	WP	Bk	W	L	Pct.	ShO	Sv	ERA
1992 Jamestown	A- Mon	13	13	0	0	62.2	282	59	32	27	3	0	0	6	34	0	44	5	0	4	4	.500	0	0	3.88
1993 Wst Plm Bch	A+ Mon	25	25	0	0	138.1	592	132	72	62	8	4	5	7	54	0	108	6	0	8	9	.471	0	0	4.03
1994 Harrisburg	AA Mon	6	2	0	1	10.1	72	16	21	20	1	1	0	0	25	0	14	6	0	0	1	.000	0	0	17.42
Wst Plm Bch	A+ Mon	53	1	0	40	65.1	255	44	16	14	0	3	0	1	19	0	90	4	2	5	2	.714	0	26	1.93
1995 Harrisburg	AA Mon	37	0	0	26	49.2	202	36	19	19	3	2	1	4	15	2	48	1	0	2	2	.500	0	11	3.44

		HOW MUCH HE PITCHED					WHAT HE GAVE UP					THE RESULTS					
Year Team	Lg Org	G	GS	CG	GF	IP	BFP	H	R	ER	HR	SH	SF	HB	TBB	IBB	SO	WP	Bk	W	L	Pct.	ShO	Sv	ERA
1996 Expos	R Mon	5	1	0	2	7.1	30	5	4	4	0	0	0	0	4	0	5	0	1	1	1	.500	0	1	4.91
Wst Plm Bch	A+ Mon	7	0	0	5	10	39	8	0	0	0	1	0	0	2	0	5	1	0	0	0	.000	0	1	0.00
Harrisburg	AA Mon	15	0	0	6	24	100	14	8	7	2	2	0	3	14	1	23	0	0	2	2	.500	0	1	2.63
1997 Jacksnville	AA Det	43	0	0	27	63.2	273	69	41	37	8	3	3	0	21	0	52	2	0	1	5	.167	0	2	5.23
6 Min. YEARS		204	42	0	107	431.1	1845	383	213	190	25	16	9	21	188	3	389	25	3	23	26	.469	0	42	3.96

Jeremy Giambi

Bats: Left   Throws: Left   Pos: OF   **Ht: 6'0"   Wt: 185   Born: 9/30/74   Age: 23**

		BATTING														BASERUNNING				PERCENTAGES		
Year Team	Lg Org	G	AB	H	2B	3B	HR	TB	R	RBI	TBB	IBB	SO	HBP	SH	SF	SB	CS	SB%	GDP	Avg	OBP	SLG
1996 Spokane	A- KC	67	231	63	17	0	6	98	58	39	61	2	32	8	0	0	22	5	.81	5	.273	.440	.424
1997 Lansing	A KC	31	116	39	11	1	5	67	33	21	23	2	16	2	0	1	5	1	.83	1	.336	.451	.578
Wichita	AA KC	74	268	86	15	1	11	136	50	52	44	3	47	6	0	4	4	4	.50	7	.321	.422	.507
2 Min. YEARS		172	615	188	43	2	22	301	141	112	128	7	95	16	0	5	31	10	.76	13	.306	.435	.489

Ray Giannelli

Bats: Left   Throws: Right   Pos: DH   **Ht: 6'0"   Wt: 195   Born: 2/5/66   Age: 32**

		BATTING														BASERUNNING				PERCENTAGES		
Year Team	Lg Org	G	AB	H	2B	3B	HR	TB	R	RBI	TBB	IBB	SO	HBP	SH	SF	SB	CS	SB%	GDP	Avg	OBP	SLG
1988 Medicine Hat	R+ Tor	47	123	30	8	3	4	56	17	28	19	2	22	0	1	3	0	0	.00	6	.244	.338	.455
1989 Myrtle Bch	A Tor	127	458	138	17	1	18	211	76	84	78	4	53	5	1	8	2	6	.25	10	.301	.403	.461
1990 Dunedin	A+ Tor	118	416	120	18	1	18	194	64	57	66	7	56	1	1	3	4	8	.33	12	.288	.385	.466
1991 Knoxville	AA Tor	112	362	100	14	3	7	141	53	37	64	6	66	2	5	2	8	5	.62	6	.276	.386	.390
1992 Syracuse	AAA Tor	84	249	57	9	2	5	85	23	22	48	2	44	0	0	2	2	2	.50	4	.229	.351	.341
1993 Syracuse	AAA Tor	127	411	104	18	4	11	163	51	42	38	1	79	2	2	5	1	6	.14	8	.253	.316	.397
1994 Syracuse	AAA Tor	114	327	94	19	1	10	145	43	51	48	2	77	2	0	5	0	1	.00	5	.287	.379	.443
1995 Louisville	AAA StL	119	390	115	19	1	16	184	56	70	44	5	85	3	0	4	3	7	.30	6	.295	.367	.472
1996 Salt Lake	AAA Min	10	31	8	1	0	0	9	2	4	2	0	8	1	0	1	0	0	.00	0	.258	.314	.290
Colo Sprngs	AAA Col	44	117	26	8	0	2	40	14	13	23	1	19	1	0	0	1	2	.33	3	.222	.355	.342
1997 Louisville	AAA StL	39	95	21	4	0	3	34	12	12	17	0	18	0	0	0	0	0	.00	3	.221	.339	.358
Syracuse	AAA Tor	38	80	14	4	0	0	18	9	8	18	1	20	1	2	2	1	1	.50	3	.175	.327	.225
1991 Toronto	AL	9	24	4	1	0	0	5	2	0	5	0	9	0	0	0	0	1	1.00	0	.167	.310	.208
1995 St. Louis	NL	9	11	1	0	0	0	1	0	0	3	0	4	0	0	0	0	0	.00	0	.091	.286	.091
10 Min. YEARS		979	3059	827	139	16	94	1280	420	428	465	31	547	18	12	33	22	38	.37	66	.270	.366	.418
2 Maj. YEARS		18	35	5	1	0	0	6	2	0	8	0	13	0	0	0	1	0	1.00	0	.143	.302	.171

Ken Giard

Pitches: Right   Bats: Right   Pos: P   **Ht: 6'3"   Wt: 210   Born: 4/2/73   Age: 25**

		HOW MUCH HE PITCHED						WHAT HE GAVE UP											THE RESULTS					
Year Team	Lg Org	G	GS	CG	GF	IP	BFP	H	R	ER	HR	SH	SF	HB	TBB	IBB	SO	WP	Bk	W	L	Pct.	ShO	Sv	ERA
1991 Braves	R Atl	11	10	0	0	38	167	42	21	16	3	0	0	0	13	0	24	2	1	0	2	.000	0	0	3.79
1992 Idaho Falls	R+ Atl	11	10	0	0	51	228	49	29	22	1	1	3	2	35	0	36	0	1	0	3	.000	0	0	3.88
1993 Macon	A Atl	41	1	0	16	68	287	59	37	29	2	5	3	1	27	0	58	5	0	1	7	.125	0	2	3.84
1994 Durham	A+ Atl	20	0	0	4	30.1	146	31	23	23	4	1	1	0	27	1	39	3	0	1	2	.333	0	0	6.82
1995 Eugene	A- Atl	25	0	0	7	34	137	31	9	9	3	2	0	1	5	1	44	3	0	3	0	1.000	0	2	2.38
Macon	A Atl	5	0	0	3	13.1	51	7	1	1	0	1	0	0	5	0	19	2	0	1	0	1.000	0	1	0.68
1996 Macon	A Atl	5	0	0	4	5.2	20	3	1	1	0	0	0	0	1	0	9	0	0	1	0	1.000	0	1	1.59
Durham	A+ Atl	42	0	0	15	68	310	69	44	39	9	4	2	1	43	3	93	6	0	3	5	.375	0	1	5.16
1997 Durham	A+ Atl	30	0	0	28	38.2	175	28	14	10	2	2	2	2	35	2	47	5	0	2	2	.500	0	12	2.33
Greenville	AA Atl	25	0	0	9	36.2	152	30	9	8	1	0	1	0	11	1	39	2	0	3	0	1.000	0	6	1.96
7 Min. YEARS		215	21	0	86	383.2	1673	349	188	158	25	16	12	7	202	8	408	27	2	15	21	.417	0	24	3.71

Kevin Gibbs

Bats: Both   Throws: Right   Pos: OF   **Ht: 6'2"   Wt: 182   Born: 4/3/74   Age: 24**

		BATTING														BASERUNNING				PERCENTAGES		
Year Team	Lg Org	G	AB	H	2B	3B	HR	TB	R	RBI	TBB	IBB	SO	HBP	SH	SF	SB	CS	SB%	GDP	Avg	OBP	SLG
1995 Yakima	A- LA	52	182	57	6	4	1	74	36	16	36	1	46	5	2	3	38	6	.88	3	.313	.434	.407
Vero Beach	A+ LA	7	20	5	1	0	0	6	1	2	0	0	6	0	0	0	1	0	1.00	0	.250	.250	.300
San Berndno	A+ LA	5	13	3	1	0	0	4	1	0	0	0	22	0	0	0	1	0	1.00	0	.231	.231	.308
1996 Vero Beach	A+ LA	118	423	114	9	11	0	145	69	33	65	0	80	4	6	4	60	19	.76	6	.270	.369	.343
1997 San Antonio	AA LA	101	358	120	21	6	2	159	89	34	72	3	48	6	6	3	49	19	.72	2	.335	.451	.444
3 Min. YEARS		283	996	299	38	21	3	388	196	87	173	4	176	15	14	10	149	43	.78	11	.300	.408	.390

David Gibralter

Bats: Right   Throws: Right   Pos: 1B   **Ht: 6'3"   Wt: 215   Born: 6/19/75   Age: 23**

		BATTING														BASERUNNING				PERCENTAGES		
Year Team	Lg Org	G	AB	H	2B	3B	HR	TB	R	RBI	TBB	IBB	SO	HBP	SH	SF	SB	CS	SB%	GDP	Avg	OBP	SLG
1993 Red Sox	R Bos	48	177	48	14	0	3	71	23	27	11	1	34	6	1	2	1	1	.50	3	.271	.332	.401
1994 Sarasota	A+ Bos	51	184	35	5	1	4	54	20	18	6	1	41	1	0	0	1	2	.33	2	.190	.220	.293
Utica	A- Bos	62	222	57	11	0	5	83	31	32	14	2	40	5	1	2	3	1	.75	5	.257	.313	.374
1995 Michigan	A Bos	121	456	115	34	1	16	199	48	82	20	2	79	8	3	4	3	4	.43	7	.252	.290	.436
1996 Sarasota	A+ Bos	120	452	129	34	3	12	205	47	70	30	3	101	9	0	4	8	7	.53	9	.285	.339	.454
1997 Trenton	AA Bos	123	478	131	25	1	14	200	70	86	44	3	103	9	1	4	3	5	.38	10	.274	.344	.418
5 Min. YEARS		525	1969	515	123	6	54	812	239	315	125	12	398	38	6	16	19	20	.49	36	.262	.316	.412

Steve Gibralter

Bats: Right **Throws:** Right **Pos:** OF   **Ht:** 6' 0" **Wt:** 190 **Born:** 10/9/72 **Age:** 25

Year Team	Lg Org	G	AB	H	2B	3B	HR	TB	R	RBI	TBB	IBB	SO	HBP	SH	SF	SB	CS	SB%	GDP	Avg	OBP	SLG
1990 Reds	R Cin	52	174	45	11	3	4	74	26	27	23	1	30	3	3	1	8	2	.80	5	.259	.353	.425
1991 Chston-WV	A Cin	140	544	145	36	7	6	213	72	71	31	2	117	5	2	6	11	13	.46	14	.267	.309	.392
1992 Cedar Rapds	A Cin	137	529	162	32	3	19	257	92	99	51	4	99	12	1	3	12	9	.57	8	.306	.378	.486
1993 Chattanooga	AA Cin	132	477	113	25	3	11	177	65	47	20	2	108	7	3	4	7	12	.37	6	.237	.276	.371
1994 Chattanooga	AA Cin	133	460	124	28	3	14	200	71	63	47	0	114	9	4	5	10	8	.56	5	.270	.345	.435
1995 Indianapols	AAA Cin	79	263	83	19	3	18	162	49	63	25	3	70	4	1	2	2	0	.00	6	.316	.381	.616
1996 Indianapols	AAA Cin	126	447	114	29	2	11	180	58	54	26	6	114	2	1	3	2	3	.40	10	.255	.297	.403
1997 Chattanooga	AA Cin	30	97	25	9	0	2	40	20	12	13	1	22	2	1	3	0	0	.00	0	.258	.348	.412
1995 Cincinnati	NL	4	3	1	0	0	0	1	0	0	0	0	0	0	0	0	0	0	.00	0	.333	.333	.333
1996 Cincinnati	NL	2	2	0	0	0	0	0	0	0	0	0	2	0	0	0	0	0	.00	0	.000	.000	.000
8 Min. YEARS		829	2991	811	189	24	85	1303	453	436	236	19	674	44	16	27	50	49	.51	54	.271	.331	.436
2 Maj. YEARS		6	5	1	0	0	0	1	0	0	0	0	2	0	0	0	0	0	.00	0	.200	.200	.200

Derrick Gibson

Bats: Right **Throws:** Right **Pos:** OF   **Ht:** 6'2" **Wt:** 238 **Born:** 2/5/75 **Age:** 23

Year Team	Lg Org	G	AB	H	2B	3B	HR	TB	R	RBI	TBB	IBB	SO	HBP	SH	SF	SB	CS	SB%	GDP	Avg	OBP	SLG
1993 Rockies	R Col	34	119	18	2	2	0	24	13	10	5	0	55	3	0	1	3	0	1.00	1	.151	.203	.202
1994 Bend	A- Col	73	284	75	19	5	12	140	47	57	29	5	102	9	0	1	14	4	.78	4	.264	.350	.493
1995 Asheville	A Col	135	506	148	16	10	32	280	91	115	29	5	136	19	1	6	31	13	.70	10	.292	.350	.553
1996 New Haven	AA Col	122	449	115	21	4	15	189	58	62	31	1	125	8	1	4	3	12	.20	15	.256	.313	.421
1997 New Haven	AA Col	119	461	146	24	2	23	243	91	75	36	7	100	10	0	2	20	13	.61	8	.317	.377	.527
Colo Spmgs	AAA Col	21	78	33	7	0	3	49	14	12	5	1	9	0	0	2	0	2	.00	1	.423	.458	.628
5 Min. YEARS		504	1897	535	89	23	85	925	314	331	135	19	527	49	2	14	71	44	.62	39	.282	.343	.488

Charles Gipson

Bats: Right **Throws:** Right **Pos:** 3B   **Ht:** 6'0" **Wt:** 188 **Born:** 12/16/72 **Age:** 25

Year Team	Lg Org	G	AB	H	2B	3B	HR	TB	R	RBI	TBB	IBB	SO	HBP	SH	SF	SB	CS	SB%	GDP	Avg	OBP	SLG
1992 Mariners	R Sea	39	124	39	2	0	0	41	30	14	13	1	19	6	2	1	11	5	.69	0	.315	.403	.331
1993 Appleton	A Sea	109	348	89	13	1	0	104	63	20	61	0	76	27	9	1	21	15	.58	3	.256	.405	.299
1994 Riverside	A+ Sea	128	481	141	12	3	1	162	102	41	76	4	67	12	7	2	34	15	.69	8	.293	.401	.337
1995 Port City	AA Sea	112	391	87	11	2	0	102	36	29	30	0	66	8	7	1	10	12	.45	13	.223	.291	.261
1996 Port City	AA Sea	119	407	109	12	3	1	130	54	30	41	1	62	7	6	0	26	15	.63	9	.268	.345	.319
1997 Tacoma	AAA Sea	11	35	11	2	0	0	13	5	5	4	0	3	1	0	0	0	1	.00	0	.314	.400	.371
Memphis	AA Sea	88	320	79	9	4	1	99	56	28	34	2	71	13	2	1	31	6	.84	4	.247	.342	.309
6 Min. YEARS		606	2106	555	61	13	3	651	346	167	259	8	364	74	33	6	133	69	.66	37	.264	.363	.309

John Giudice

Bats: Right **Throws:** Right **Pos:** OF   **Ht:** 6'1" **Wt:** 205 **Born:** 6/19/71 **Age:** 27

Year Team	Lg Org	G	AB	H	2B	3B	HR	TB	R	RBI	TBB	IBB	SO	HBP	SH	SF	SB	CS	SB%	GDP	Avg	OBP	SLG
1993 Bend	A- Col	57	184	43	8	0	5	66	28	17	36	0	57	6	2	0	5	2	.71	5	.234	.376	.359
1994 Asheville	A Col	66	252	73	12	1	9	114	36	22	17	1	56	5	0	0	6	5	.55	2	.290	.347	.452
Central Val	A+ Col	53	195	55	13	2	4	84	30	33	18	1	55	6	2	2	6	2	.75	3	.282	.357	.431
1995 Salem	A+ Col	99	356	92	21	4	7	142	49	48	24	2	81	4	0	3	7	4	.64	7	.258	.310	.399
1996 Salem	A+ Col	101	373	109	30	1	16	189	58	67	45	6	66	7	3	3	11	8	.58	11	.292	.376	.507
New Haven	AA Col	32	118	30	4	1	4	48	13	13	10	2	25	0	0	1	2	4	.33	2	.254	.308	.407
1997 New Haven	AA Col	63	216	54	8	2	5	81	26	30	16	1	49	3	0	1	5	1	.83	6	.250	.309	.375
5 Min. YEARS		471	1694	456	96	11	50	724	240	230	166	13	389	31	7	11	42	26	.62	36	.269	.343	.427

Chip Glass

Bats: Left **Throws:** Left **Pos:** OF   **Ht:** 5'11" **Wt:** 180 **Born:** 6/24/71 **Age:** 27

Year Team	Lg Org	G	AB	H	2B	3B	HR	TB	R	RBI	TBB	IBB	SO	HBP	SH	SF	SB	CS	SB%	GDP	Avg	OBP	SLG
1994 Watertown	A- Cle	60	237	73	8	6	2	99	51	22	26	1	34	0	1	1	12	10	.55	1	.308	.375	.418
1995 Columbus	A Cle	115	402	116	17	5	5	158	70	45	37	1	47	5	5	0	37	8	.82	4	.289	.356	.393
1996 Kinston	A+ Cle	134	479	128	18	9	5	179	64	52	40	2	67	4	5	1	11	6	.65	8	.267	.328	.374
1997 Akron	AA Cle	113	394	102	17	4	5	142	74	37	56	1	61	7	3	1	16	10	.62	11	.259	.360	.360
4 Min. YEARS		422	1512	419	60	24	17	578	259	156	159	5	209	16	14	3	76	34	.69	24	.277	.351	.382

Keith Glauber

Pitches: Right **Bats:** Right **Pos:** P   **Ht:** 6'2" **Wt:** 190 **Born:** 1/18/72 **Age:** 26

Year Team	Lg Org	G	GS	CG	GF	IP	BFP	H	R	ER	HR	SH	SF	HB	TBB	IBB	SO	WP	Bk	W	L	Pct.	ShO	Sv	ERA
1994 New Jersey	A- StL	17	10	0	3	68.2	289	67	36	32	3	4	2	2	26	1	51	8	0	4	6	.400	0	0	4.19
1995 Savannah	A StL	40	0	0	3	62.2	277	50	29	26	2	2	3	5	36	3	62	9	1	2	1	.667	0	0	3.73
1996 Peoria	A StL	54	0	0	36	64	276	54	31	22	2	2	5	1	26	2	80	2	1	3	3	.500	0	14	3.09
1997 Arkansas	AA StL	50	0	0	22	59	245	48	22	18	3	2	4	2	25	2	53	5	0	5	7	.417	0	3	2.75
Louisville	AAA StL	15	0	0	12	15.2	71	18	14	9	2	1	0	1	4	0	14	0	0	1	3	.250	0	5	5.17
4 Min. YEARS		176	10	0	76	270	1158	237	132	107	12	11	14	11	117	8	260	24	2	15	20	.429	0	22	3.57

Ryan Glynn

Pitches: Right **Bats:** Right **Pos:** P — **Ht:** 6'3" **Wt:** 200 **Born:** 11/1/74 **Age:** 23

Year Team	Lg Org	G	GS	CG	GF	IP	BFP	H	R	ER	HR	SH	SF	HB	TBB	IBB	SO	WP	Bk	W	L	Pct.	ShO	Sv	ERA
1995 Hudson Vall	A- Tex	9	8	0	0	44	192	56	27	23	0	0	1	3	16	1	21	10	3	3	3	.500	0	0	4.70
1996 Chston-SC	A Tex	19	19	2	0	121	526	118	70	61	10	6	6	8	59	2	72	12	0	8	7	.533	1	0	4.54
1997 Charlotte	A+ Tex	23	22	5	1	134	579	148	81	74	13	2	7	4	44	0	96	9	1	8	7	.533	1	1	4.97
Tulsa	AA Tex	3	3	0	0	21.1	94	21	9	8	1	1	2	2	10	0	18	2	0	1	1	.500	0	0	3.38
3 Min. YEARS		54	52	7	1	320.1	1391	343	187	166	24	9	16	17	129	3	207	33	4	20	18	.526	2	1	4.66

Greg Gohr

Pitches: Right **Bats:** Right **Pos:** P — **Ht:** 6'3" **Wt:** 205 **Born:** 10/29/67 **Age:** 30

Year Team	Lg Org	G	GS	CG	GF	IP	BFP	H	R	ER	HR	SH	SF	HB	TBB	IBB	SO	WP	Bk	W	L	Pct.	ShO	Sv	ERA
1989 Fayettevlle	A Det	4	4	0	0	11.1	50	11	9	9	3	0	1	0	6	0	10	0	0	0	2	.000	0	0	7.15
1990 Lakeland	A+ Det	25	25	0	0	137.2	577	125	52	40	0	2	1	5	50	0	90	11	6	13	5	.722	0	0	2.62
1991 London	AA Det	2	2	0	0	11	42	9	0	0	0	0	0	0	2	0	10	0	0	0	0	.000	0	0	0.00
Toledo	AAA Det	26	26	2	0	148.1	627	125	86	76	11	9	5	3	66	0	96	14	3	10	8	.556	1	0	4.61
1992 Toledo	AAA Det	22	20	2	0	130.2	551	124	65	58	9	3	3	3	46	1	94	5	1	8	10	.444	0	0	3.99
1993 Toledo	AAA Det	18	17	2	1	107	484	127	74	69	16	1	8	5	38	2	77	5	0	3	10	.231	0	0	5.80
1994 Toledo	AAA Det	12	12	0	0	73.1	310	75	34	29	7	1	2	2	18	1	56	0	0	6	4	.600	0	0	3.56
1995 Toledo	AAA Det	6	4	0	1	15.2	68	16	9	5	1	0	0	0	8	0	15	1	0	0	2	.000	0	0	2.87
1996 Toledo	AAA Det	2	2	0	0	12	57	17	10	10	1	0	1	0	5	0	15	2	0	0	0	.000	0	0	7.50
1997 Vancouver	AAA Ana	8	7	0	0	47.1	202	51	23	20	3	0	3	1	14	0	27	3	0	5	1	.833	0	0	3.80
1993 Detroit	AL	16	0	0	9	22.2	108	26	15	15	1	1	1	2	14	2	23	1	0	0	0	.000	0	0	5.96
1994 Detroit	AL	8	6	0	1	34	159	36	19	17	3	0	1	0	21	1	21	2	1	2	2	.500	0	0	4.50
1995 Detroit	AL	10	0	0	1	10.1	41	9	1	1	0	1	0	0	3	0	12	1	0	1	0	1.000	0	0	0.87
1996 Detroit	AL	17	16	0	0	91.2	434	129	76	73	24	1	3	3	34	2	60	6	0	4	8	.333	0	0	7.17
California	AL	15	0	0	7	24	112	34	20	20	7	0	1	0	10	0	15	0	0	1	1	.500	0	1	7.50
9 Min. YEARS		125	119	6	2	694.1	2968	680	362	316	51	16	24	19	253	4	490	41	10	45	42	.517	1	0	4.10
4 Maj. YEARS		66	22	0	18	182.2	854	234	131	126	35	3	6	5	82	5	131	10	1	8	11	.421	0	1	6.21

Gary Goldsmith

Pitches: Right **Bats:** Right **Pos:** P — **Ht:** 6'2" **Wt:** 205 **Born:** 7/4/71 **Age:** 26

Year Team	Lg Org	G	GS	CG	GF	IP	BFP	H	R	ER	HR	SH	SF	HB	TBB	IBB	SO	WP	Bk	W	L	Pct.	ShO	Sv	ERA
1993 Niagara Fal	A- Det	21	5	0	12	54.2	231	43	21	14	3	2	0	4	20	3	64	4	0	4	2	.667	0	0	2.30
1994 Lakeland	A+ Det	23	19	1	3	120.2	499	105	50	44	4	4	4	7	51	2	81	7	2	7	7	.500	0	0	3.28
Trenton	AA Det	4	4	2	0	25.2	103	23	12	11	3	1	0	0	9	1	27	3	0	0	4	.000	0	0	3.86
1995 Jacksnville	AA Det	15	15	0	0	82	347	78	52	42	14	1	4	2	31	1	42	5	0	4	7	.364	0	0	4.61
1996 Visalia	A+ Det	28	27	0	0	170	752	188	108	94	23	4	10	7	76	1	120	2	1	10	11	.476	0	0	4.98
1997 Toledo	AAA Det	1	0	0	1	2	8	2	1	1	1	0	0	0	0	0	0	0	0	0	0	.000	0	0	4.50
Jacksnville	AA Det	31	8	1	5	97.1	415	97	48	44	16	2	4	5	30	0	45	1	0	4	5	.444	1	1	4.07
5 Min. YEARS		123	78	4	21	552.1	2355	536	292	250	64	14	22	25	217	8	380	22	3	29	36	.446	1	1	4.07

Rudy Gomez

Bats: Right **Throws:** Right **Pos:** 2B — **Ht:** 5'11" **Wt:** 180 **Born:** 9/14/74 **Age:** 23

Year Team	Lg Org	G	AB	H	2B	3B	HR	TB	R	RBI	TBB	IBB	SO	HBP	SH	SF	SB	CS	SB%	GDP	Avg	OBP	SLG
1996 Yankees	R NYA	16	58	16	6	0	0	22	12	10	9	2	7	4	0	1	0	1	.00	1	.276	.403	.379
Tampa	A+ NYA	40	130	38	9	1	1	52	15	24	26	0	12	0	4	3	4	1	.80	8	.292	.403	.400
1997 Norwich	AA NYA	102	393	118	18	7	5	165	65	52	61	0	64	10	1	3	11	7	.61	8	.300	.405	.420
2 Min. YEARS		158	581	172	33	8	6	239	92	86	96	2	83	14	5	7	15	9	.63	17	.296	.404	.411

Frank Gonzales

Pitches: Left **Bats:** Right **Pos:** P — **Ht:** 6'0" **Wt:** 185 **Born:** 3/12/68 **Age:** 30

Year Team	Lg Org	G	GS	CG	GF	IP	BFP	H	R	ER	HR	SH	SF	HB	TBB	IBB	SO	WP	Bk	W	L	Pct.	ShO	Sv	ERA
1989 Niagara Fal	A- Det	10	5	1	3	38	160	36	20	16	2	1	2	0	16	1	35	0	3	3	3	.500	1	0	3.79
1990 Fayetteville	A Det	25	25	0	0	143	606	123	54	48	2	1	7	4	66	0	101	9	1	10	6	.625	0	0	3.02
1991 Lakeland	A+ Det	25	25	1	0	146	603	130	62	55	3	5	9	3	55	0	99	3	1	11	5	.688	0	0	3.39
1992 London	AA Det	10	10	0	0	65.2	269	64	25	22	5	0	0	1	10	0	37	2	0	5	4	.556	0	0	3.02
Toledo	AAA Det	18	17	2	0	98.1	421	100	48	47	7	3	2	3	36	0	65	5	0	4	6	.400	1	0	4.30
1993 Toledo	AAA Det	29	15	2	3	109.1	464	116	56	48	12	2	2	3	37	1	71	4	0	6	3	.667	0	0	3.95
1994 Toledo	AAA Det	34	17	0	1	117	535	142	79	62	11	1	8	3	58	3	86	7	1	6	11	.353	0	0	4.77
1995 Toledo	AAA Det	49	0	0	6	51.2	217	43	23	19	4	2	0	3	17	1	54	2	0	3	2	.600	0	0	3.31
1997 Trenton	AA Bos	14	0	0	8	26	122	29	18	17	3	2	0	2	16	2	14	1	0	3	1	.750	0	2	5.88
Calgary	AAA Pit	25	0	0	11	31	143	43	25	25	5	1	4	1	9	2	24	0	1	1	0	1.000	0	1	7.26
Elmira	IND —	5	4	0	0	19.2	79	14	4	4	0	0	0	1	4	0	23	2	0	1	1	.500	0	0	1.83
8 Min. YEARS		244	118	6	32	845.2	3619	840	414	363	54	18	34	24	324	10	609	35	7	53	42	.558	2	3	3.86

Alex Gonzalez

Bats: Right **Throws:** Right **Pos:** SS — **Ht:** 6'0" **Wt:** 150 **Born:** 2/15/77 **Age:** 21

Year Team	Lg Org	G	AB	H	2B	3B	HR	TB	R	RBI	TBB	IBB	SO	HBP	SH	SF	SB	CS	SB%	GDP	Avg	OBP	SLG
1995 Brevard Cty	A+ Fla	17	59	12	2	1	0	16	6	8	1	0	14	1	0	0	1	1	.50	2	.203	.230	.271
Marlins	R Fla	53	187	55	7	4	2	76	30	30	19	0	27	2	1	4	11	2	.85	2	.294	.358	.406

Year Team	Lg Org	G	AB	H	2B	3B	HR	TB	R	RBI	TBB	IBB	SO	HBP	SH	SF	SB	CS	SB%	GDP	Avg	OBP	SLG
1996 Marlins	R Fla	10	41	16	3	0	0	19	6	6	2	0	4	0	0	0	1	0	1.00	1	.390	.419	.463
Kane County	A Fla	4	10	2	0	0	0	2	2	0	2	0	4	1	1	0	0	0	.00	1	.200	.385	.200
Portland	AA Fla	11	34	8	0	1	0	10	4	1	2	2	10	1	0	0	0	0	.00	2	.235	.297	.294
1997 Portland	AA Fla	133	449	114	16	4	19	195	69	65	27	5	83	7	3	3	4	7	.36	7	.254	.305	.434
3 Min. YEARS		228	780	207	28	10	21	318	117	110	53	7	142	12	5	7	17	10	.63	15	.265	.319	.408

Gabe Gonzalez

Pitches: Left **Bats:** Both **Pos:** P **Ht:** 6'1" **Wt:** 160 **Born:** 5/24/72 **Age:** 26

		HOW MUCH HE PITCHED						WHAT HE GAVE UP										THE RESULTS					
Year Team	Lg Org	G	GS	CG	GF	IP	BFP	H	R	ER	HR	SH	SF	HB	TBB	IBB	SO	WP	Bk	W	L	Pct.	ShO	Sv	ERA
1995 Kane County	A Fla	32	0	0	10	43.1	181	32	18	11	0	2	1	2	14	2	41	1	0	4	4	.500	0	1	2.28
1996 Charlotte	AAA Fla	2	0	0	1	3	15	4	1	1	0	0	0	0	2	0	3	0	0	0	0	.000	0	0	3.00
Brevard Cty	A+ Fla	47	0	0	32	76.1	308	56	20	15	2	9	1	3	23	7	62	2	0	2	7	.222	0	9	1.77
1997 Portland	AA Fla	29	0	0	10	42.2	171	43	12	10	1	3	3	0	5	1	28	1	0	3	2	.600	0	3	2.11
Charlotte	AAA Fla	37	1	0	11	42.2	176	38	15	13	3	1	2	2	14	1	24	0	0	2	2	.500	0	3	2.74
3 Min. YEARS		147	1	0	64	208	851	173	66	50	6	15	7	7	58	11	158	4	0	11	15	.423	0	16	2.16

Jimmy Gonzalez

Bats: Right **Throws:** Right **Pos:** C **Ht:** 6'3" **Wt:** 210 **Born:** 3/8/73 **Age:** 25

		BATTING															BASERUNNING				PERCENTAGES		
Year Team	Lg Org	G	AB	H	2B	3B	HR	TB	R	RBI	TBB	IBB	SO	HBP	SH	SF	SB	CS	SB%	GDP	Avg	OBP	SLG
1991 Astros	R Hou	34	103	21	3	0	0	24	7	3	7	0	33	0	1	0	3	5	.38	1	.204	.255	.233
1992 Burlington	A Hou	91	301	53	13	0	4	78	32	21	34	0	119	1	0	0	0	3	.00	6	.176	.262	.259
1993 Quad City	A Hou	47	154	35	9	1	0	46	20	15	14	1	36	4	1	1	2	2	.50	4	.227	.306	.299
Asheville	A Hou	43	149	33	5	0	4	50	16	15	7	0	37	0	2	1	3	1	.75	3	.221	.255	.336
1994 Jackson	AA Hou	4	6	0	0	0	0	0	0	0	0	0	0	0	0	0	0	0	.00	0	.000	.000	.000
Osceola	A+ Hou	99	321	74	18	0	5	107	33	38	20	0	80	4	2	2	2	0	1.00	10	.231	.282	.333
1995 Quad City	A Hou	35	78	19	3	1	1	27	4	14	8	0	13	1	0	1	1	2	.33	1	.244	.318	.346
1996 Jackson	AA Hou	2	5	1	0	0	0	1	1	0	1	0	1	0	0	0	0	0	.00	0	.200	.333	.200
Kissimmee	A+ Hou	73	208	35	4	1	6	59	19	17	25	0	59	3	2	3	1	0	1.00	8	.168	.264	.284
1997 Kissimmee	A+ Hou	12	44	15	6	2	2	31	7	6	1	0	9	3	0	1	0	0	.00	1	.341	.388	.705
Jackson	AA Hou	97	342	87	18	0	14	147	49	58	37	1	91	8	0	3	2	1	.67	7	.254	.338	.430
7 Min. YEARS		537	1711	373	79	5	36	570	188	187	154	2	478	24	8	12	14	14	.50	42	.218	.290	.333

Juan Gonzalez

Pitches: Right **Bats:** Right **Pos:** P **Ht:** 6'1" **Wt:** 188 **Born:** 1/28/75 **Age:** 23

		HOW MUCH HE PITCHED						WHAT HE GAVE UP										THE RESULTS					
Year Team	Lg Org	G	GS	CG	GF	IP	BFP	H	R	ER	HR	SH	SF	HB	TBB	IBB	SO	WP	Bk	W	L	Pct.	ShO	Sv	ERA
1994 Helena	R+ Mil	2	0	0	1	5.1	26	9	1	1	0	0	1	1	1	0	0	0	1	1	0	1.000	0	0	1.69
Brewers	R Mil	14	14	0	0	86.2	370	96	47	32	1	0	5	6	23	0	68	16	1	5	3	.625	0	0	3.32
1995 Beloit	A Mil	42	6	0	17	88.2	386	86	50	41	4	3	4	6	37	1	53	16	0	11	5	.688	0	6	4.16
1996 Brevard Cty	A+ Fla	23	17	0	2	86.1	385	102	57	51	6	5	3	7	27	0	48	12	1	1	9	.100	0	0	5.32
1997 Brevard Cty	A+ Fla	26	0	0	20	37.2	155	32	13	10	3	2	0	3	7	0	28	2	0	3	2	.600	0	6	2.39
Portland	AA Fla	17	0	0	7	29.1	131	32	25	22	10	1	2	2	10	0	21	2	0	0	1	.000	0	0	6.75
4 Min. YEARS		124	37	0	47	334	1453	357	193	157	24	11	15	25	105	1	218	48	3	21	20	.512	0	12	4.23

Raul Gonzalez

Bats: Right **Throws:** Right **Pos:** OF **Ht:** 5'8" **Wt:** 175 **Born:** 12/27/73 **Age:** 24

		BATTING															BASERUNNING				PERCENTAGES		
Year Team	Lg Org	G	AB	H	2B	3B	HR	TB	R	RBI	TBB	IBB	SO	HBP	SH	SF	SB	CS	SB%	GDP	Avg	OBP	SLG
1991 Royals	R KC	47	160	47	5	3	0	58	24	17	19	0	21	0	1	2	3	4	.43	4	.294	.365	.363
1992 Appleton	A KC	119	449	115	32	1	9	176	82	51	57	1	58	2	4	6	13	5	.72	4	.256	.339	.392
1993 Wilmington	A+ KC	127	461	124	30	3	11	193	59	55	54	1	58	4	1	4	13	5	.72	8	.269	.348	.419
1994 Wilmington	A+ KC	115	414	108	19	8	9	170	60	51	45	2	50	2	2	4	0	4	.00	8	.261	.333	.411
1995 Wichita	AA KC	22	79	23	3	2	2	36	14	11	8	0	13	0	0	0	4	0	1.00	1	.291	.356	.456
Wilmington	A+ KC	86	308	90	19	3	11	148	36	49	14	3	34	2	3	7	6	4	.60	3	.292	.320	.481
1996 Wichita	AA KC	23	84	24	5	1	1	34	17	9	5	0	12	1	0	1	1	2	.33	1	.286	.333	.405
1997 Wichita	AA KC	129	452	129	30	4	13	206	66	74	36	0	52	2	3	8	12	8	.60	12	.285	.335	.456
7 Min. YEARS		668	2407	660	143	25	56	1021	358	317	238	7	298	13	14	31	52	32	.62	43	.274	.339	.424

Wikleman Gonzalez

Bats: Right **Throws:** Right **Pos:** C **Ht:** 5'11" **Wt:** 175 **Born:** 5/17/74 **Age:** 24

		BATTING															BASERUNNING				PERCENTAGES		
Year Team	Lg Org	G	AB	H	2B	3B	HR	TB	R	RBI	TBB	IBB	SO	HBP	SH	SF	SB	CS	SB%	GDP	Avg	OBP	SLG
1994 Pirates	R Pit	41	143	48	8	2	4	72	25	26	13	1	13	3	1	1	2	4	.33	3	.336	.400	.503
1995 Augusta	A Pit	84	278	67	17	0	3	93	41	36	26	0	32	2	2	5	5	4	.56	7	.241	.305	.335
1996 Augusta	A Pit	118	419	106	21	3	4	145	52	62	58	1	41	7	2	5	4	6	.40	14	.253	.350	.346
1997 Rancho Cuca	A+ SD	33	110	33	9	1	5	59	18	26	7	1	25	0	1	1	1	1	.50	1	.300	.339	.536
Mobile	AA SD	47	143	39	7	1	4	60	15	25	10	0	12	2	0	1	1	1	.50	5	.273	.327	.420
4 Min. YEARS		323	1093	293	62	7	20	429	151	175	114	3	123	14	6	13	13	16	.45	30	.268	.341	.392

Arnie Gooch

Pitches: Right **Bats:** Right **Pos:** P Ht: 6'2" **Wt:** 195 **Born:** 11/12/76 **Age:** 21

Year Team	Lg Org	G	GS	CG	GF	IP	BFP	H	R	ER	HR	SH	SF	HB	TBB	IBB	SO	WP	Bk	W	L	Pct.	ShO	Sv	ERA
1994 Rockies	R Col	15	9	0	1	58	238	45	28	17	2	0	2	2	16	0	66	12	1	2	4	.333	0	0	2.64
1995 Asheville	A Col	21	21	1	0	128.2	541	111	51	42	8	3	3	4	57	0	117	13	0	5	8	.385	1	0	2.94
Capital City	A NYN	6	6	0	0	38.1	169	39	25	19	3	0	1	2	15	0	34	5	0	2	3	.400	0	0	4.46
1996 St. Lucie	A+ NYN	26	26	2	0	167.2	680	131	74	48	7	6	4	4	51	3	141	11	0	12	12	.500	0	0	2.58
1997 Binghamton	AA NYN	27	27	4	0	161	727	179	106	91	12	4	7	5	76	3	98	12	0	10	12	.455	1	0	5.09
4 Min. YEARS		95	89	7	1	553.2	2355	505	284	217	32	13	17	17	215	6	456	53	1	31	39	.443	2	0	3.53

Keith Gordon

Bats: Right **Throws:** Right **Pos:** OF Ht: 6'2" **Wt:** 200 **Born:** 1/22/69 **Age:** 29

Year Team	Lg Org	G	AB	H	2B	3B	HR	TB	R	RBI	TBB	IBB	SO	HBP	SH	SF	SB	CS	SB%	GDP	Avg	OBP	SLG
1990 Billings	R+ Cin	49	154	36	5	1	1	46	21	14	24	1	49	3	2	1	6	4	.60	2	.234	.346	.299
1991 Chston-WV	A Cin	123	388	104	14	10	8	162	63	46	50	2	134	5	7	1	25	9	.74	5	.268	.358	.418
1992 Cedar Rapds	A Cin	114	375	94	19	3	12	155	59	63	43	2	135	3	1	4	21	10	.68	5	.251	.329	.413
1993 Chattanooga	AA Cin	116	419	122	26	3	14	196	69	59	19	0	132	4	0	2	13	15	.43	15	.291	.327	.468
Chattanooga	AA Cin	18	58	12	1	0	1	16	3	4	4	0	25	0	1	0	0	0	.00	1	.207	.258	.276
1994 Indianapols	AAA Cin	82	254	71	16	2	8	115	46	38	21	0	74	1	0	2	11	7	.61	6	.280	.335	.453
1995 Indianapols	AAA Cin	89	265	70	14	1	6	104	36	38	15	0	94	0	1	0	3	4	.43	3	.264	.304	.392
1996 Rochester	AAA Bal	33	104	26	4	1	5	47	15	19	9	0	27	0	0	0	0	3	.00	3	.250	.310	.452
Bowie	AA Bal	82	306	80	13	2	5	112	38	28	22	0	80	1	1	0	13	11	.54	5	.261	.313	.366
1997 Chattanooga	AA Cin	4	12	2	0	0	1	5	2	2	3	0	7	0	0	0	1	1	.50	0	.167	.333	.417
1993 Cincinnati	NL	3	6	1	0	0	0	1	0	0	0	0	2	0	0	0	0	0	.00	0	.167	.167	.167
8 Min. YEARS		710	2335	617	112	23	61	958	352	311	210	5	757	17	13	10	93	66	.58	45	.264	.328	.410

Mike Gordon

Pitches: Right **Bats:** Left **Pos:** P Ht: 6'2" **Wt:** 195 **Born:** 11/30/72 **Age:** 25

Year Team	Lg Org	G	GS	CG	GF	IP	BFP	H	R	ER	HR	SH	SF	HB	TBB	IBB	SO	WP	Bk	W	L	Pct.	ShO	Sv	ERA
1992 Yankees	R NYA	11	10	0	1	53.1	223	33	21	18	1	2	3	5	33	0	55	5	4	3	4	.429	0	0	3.04
1993 Yankees	R NYA	11	9	0	1	64.2	266	43	23	12	0	2	1	0	27	0	61	6	1	4	2	.667	0	0	1.67
Oneonta	A- NYA	3	3	1	0	14.1	68	13	12	11	0	0	2	2	11	0	15	3	0	0	3	.000	0	0	6.91
1994 Greensboro	A NYA	23	22	0	0	107.1	501	128	88	77	15	1	3	8	54	0	116	11	1	2	10	.167	0	0	6.46
1995 Tampa	A+ NYA	21	21	1	0	124.1	521	111	54	42	6	3	1	4	49	0	96	9	2	4	6	.400	0	0	3.04
Dunedin	A+ Tor	7	6	0	0	36.2	179	44	32	24	6	2	2	5	24	0	36	2	0	1	2	.333	0	0	5.89
1996 Dunedin	A+ Tor	24	24	0	0	133.1	588	127	70	51	7	2	5	7	64	1	102	15	1	3	12	.200	0	0	3.44
1997 Akron	AA Cle	6	6	0	0	30.1	147	37	28	14	3	1	0	2	14	0	16	2	0	2	3	.400	0	0	4.15
Knoxville	AA Tor	33	6	0	7	72.2	341	91	46	43	5	3	2	1	40	3	64	6	0	3	2	.400	0	2	5.33
6 Min. YEARS		139	107	2	9	637	2834	627	374	292	43	16	17	32	316	4	561	59	9	20	44	.313	0	2	4.13

Tom Gourdin

Pitches: Right **Bats:** Right **Pos:** P Ht: 6'3" **Wt:** 205 **Born:** 5/24/73 **Age:** 25

Year Team	Lg Org	G	GS	CG	GF	IP	BFP	H	R	ER	HR	SH	SF	HB	TBB	IBB	SO	WP	Bk	W	L	Pct.	ShO	Sv	ERA
1992 Twins	R Min	13	0	0	4	22.1	108	26	22	15	0	0	1	4	9	0	3	3	0	3	1	.750	0	6	6.04
1993 Twins	R Min	24	4	0	8	51	228	53	34	26	1	0	3	3	17	0	33	5	1	1	2	.333	0	3	4.59
1994 Ft. Wayne	A Min	29	1	0	11	52.2	251	75	50	42	2	2	0	5	24	0	32	11	2	3	4	.400	0	1	7.18
1995 Ft. Wayne	A Min	41	0	0	19	89.2	384	90	49	44	10	3	3	9	32	0	74	11	2	6	6	.500	0	4	4.42
1996 Ft. Myers	A+ Min	52	1	0	32	63.1	277	64	37	30	6	6	1	3	29	3	44	7	1	4	4	.500	0	16	4.26
1997 New Britain	AA Min	49	0	0	40	61	271	62	36	36	8	1	3	3	29	0	32	16	0	2	2	.500	0	15	5.31
6 Min. YEARS		208	6	0	114	340	1519	370	228	193	27	12	11	27	140	3	218	53	6	18	20	.474	0	41	5.11

Timothy Gower

Pitches: Right **Bats:** Right **Pos:** P Ht: 6'1" **Wt:** 185 **Born:** 9/16/71 **Age:** 26

Year Team	Lg Org	G	GS	CG	GF	IP	BFP	H	R	ER	HR	SH	SF	HB	TBB	IBB	SO	WP	Bk	W	L	Pct.	ShO	Sv	ERA
1996 Salinas	IND —	52	0	0	50	64.2	243	45	14	11	5	3	3	2	6	3	68	0	0	4	3	.571	0	24	1.53
1997 Chston-WV	A Cin	35	0	0	32	37	154	31	13	11	1	4	1	2	9	2	30	3	0	4	2	.667	0	13	2.68
Chattanooga	AA Cin	24	0	0	11	45.1	194	52	24	23	6	3	2	3	12	4	28	0	1	2	0	1.000	0	0	4.57
2 Min. YEARS		111	0	0	93	147	591	128	51	45	12	10	6	7	27	9	126	3	1	10	5	.667	0	37	2.76

Gregory Grall

Bats: Right **Throws:** Right **Pos:** DH Ht: NA **Wt:** NA **Born:** 1/25/65 **Age:** 33

Year Team	Lg Org	G	AB	H	2B	3B	HR	TB	R	RBI	TBB	IBB	SO	HBP	SH	SF	SB	CS	SB%	GDP	Avg	OBP	SLG
1997 Chattanooga	AA Cin	2	4	1	0	0	0	1	0	0	0	0	2	0	0	0	0	0	.00	1	.250	.250	.250

Chris Granata

Pitches: Right **Bats:** Right **Pos:** P Ht: 6'0" **Wt:** 205 **Born:** 2/26/72 **Age:** 26

Year Team	Lg Org	G	GS	CG	GF	IP	BFP	H	R	ER	HR	SH	SF	HB	TBB	IBB	SO	WP	Bk	W	L	Pct.	ShO	Sv	ERA
1994 Watertown	A- Cle	22	1	0	7	49.2	203	44	23	19	3	2	0	1	17	1	39	1	0	1	2	.333	0	2	3.44
1995 Columbus	A Cle	33	12	0	6	113	477	94	43	31	2	6	3	4	53	7	93	8	1	11	5	.688	0	0	2.47

		HOW MUCH HE PITCHED			WHAT HE GAVE UP								THE RESULTS					
Year Team	Lg Org	G GS CG GF	IP	BFP	H R ER HR SH SF HB							TBB IBB SO WP Bk	W	L	Pct.	ShO	Sv	ERA
1996 Kinston	A+ Cle	35 6 1 6	95.1	417	105 51 46 5 2 4 6	43 4 57 9 0	7	6	.538	1	0	4.34
1997 Akron	AA Cle	4 0 0 1	5	27	8 5 4 0 0 0 0	4 0 3 1 0	0	0	1.000	0	0	7.20
Kinston	A+ Cle	9 1 0 5	20.2	95	30 23 23 5 0 0 0	7 0 11 1 0	0	0	.000	0	1	10.02
4 Min. YEARS		103 20 1 25	283.2	1219	281 145 123 15 10 7 11	124 12 203 20 1	20	14	.588	1	3	3.90

Beiker Graterol

Pitches: Right **Bats:** Right **Pos:** P — **Ht:** 6'2" **Wt:** 164 **Born:** 11/9/74 **Age:** 23

Year Team	Lg Org	G GS CG GF	IP	BFP	H R ER HR SH SF HB	TBB IBB SO WP Bk	W	L	Pct.	ShO	Sv	ERA
1996 St. Cathrns	A- Tor	14 13 1 0	84	330	59 24 14 6 3 3 4	21 0 66 2 1	9	1	.900	1	0	1.50
1997 Hagerstown	A Tor	4 0 0 4	11	45	7 1 0 0 0 0 1	3 0 12 1 0	1	0	1.000	0	2	0.00
Dunedin	A+ Tor	17 10 1 1	81	352	86 46 38 9 5 2 5	26 1 54 0 1	4	7	.364	0	0	4.22
Knoxville	AA Tor	3 3 0 0	16.2	81	24 12 10 1 0 0 1	9 0 11 0 0	2	1	.667	0	0	5.40
2 Min. YEARS		38 26 2 5	192.2	808	176 83 62 16 8 5 11	59 1 143 3 2	16	9	.640	1	3	2.90

Dennis Gray

Pitches: Left **Bats:** Left **Pos:** P — **Ht:** 6'6" **Wt:** 225 **Born:** 12/24/69 **Age:** 28

Year Team	Lg Org	G GS CG GF	IP	BFP	H R ER HR SH SF HB	TBB IBB SO WP Bk	W	L	Pct.	ShO	Sv	ERA
1991 St. Cathrns	A- Tor	15 14 0 0	77	341	63 42 32 1 3 1 1	54 0 78 4 4	4	4	.500	0	0	3.74
1992 Myrtle Bch	A Tor	28 28 0 0	155.1	659	122 82 66 8 2 5 6	93 0 141 13 4	11	12	.478	0	0	3.82
1993 Dunedin	A+ Tor	26 26 0 0	141.1	607	115 71 56 7 7 6 7	97 1 108 6 0	8	10	.444	0	0	3.57
1994 Knoxville	AA Tor	30 16 0 6	100.2	488	118 83 59 5 12 8 11	65 0 77 13 1	5	11	.313	0	0	5.27
1995 Syracuse	AAA Tor	15 0 0 3	24.1	106	27 16 12 3 0 0 2	10 0 15 3 0	2	2	.500	0	0	4.44
Knoxville	AA Tor	24 0 0 10	32.2	143	29 25 23 2 2 0 1	20 0 22 5 0	0	3	.000	0	0	6.34
1996 Harrisburg	AA Mon	9 0 0 1	10.2	54	12 9 9 1 0 0 0	14 0 10 0 1	0	0	.000	0	0	7.59
Ottawa	AAA Mon	3 0 0 2	5.1	32	9 4 4 1 0 0 2	5 0 3 1 0	0	1	.000	0	0	6.75
Port City	AA Sea	21 1 0 6	33.1	168	34 32 29 1 3 1 1	42 2 24 4 0	2	0	1.000	0	0	7.83
Greenville	AA Atl	7 0 0 3	13	58	11 8 7 1 1 0 0	9 2 13 1 0	1	2	.333	0	0	4.85
1997 Akron	AA Cle	10 0 0 3	7.1	42	13 10 10 2 1 0 0	9 0 5 1 0	0	2	.000	0	0	12.27
7 Min. YEARS		188 85 0 34	601	2698	553 382 307 32 31 21 31	418 5 496 51 10	33	47	.413	0	0	4.60

Brian Grebeck

Bats: Right **Throws:** Right **Pos:** SS — **Ht:** 5'7" **Wt:** 160 **Born:** 8/31/67 **Age:** 30

		BATTING														BASERUNNING				PERCENTAGES		
Year Team	Lg Org	G	AB	H	2B	3B	HR	TB	R	RBI	TBB	IBB	SO	HBP	SH	SF	SB	CS	SB%	GDP	Avg	OBP	SLG
1990 Boise	A- Ana	58	202	57	10	2	1	74	45	33	64	1	57	1	5	2	1	3	.25	3	.282	.454	.366
1991 Quad City	A Ana	121	408	100	20	3	0	126	80	34	103	0	76	10	15	4	19	10	.66	8	.245	.406	.309
1992 Palm Spring	A+ Ana	91	289	97	14	2	0	115	71	39	83	2	55	0	8	3	6	5	.55	10	.336	.480	.398
1993 Midland	AA Ana	118	405	119	20	4	5	162	65	54	64	1	81	8	6	7	6	1	.86	8	.294	.395	.400
1994 Midland	AA Ana	55	184	58	18	2	1	83	27	17	27	1	33	5	1	1	1	1	.50	7	.315	.415	.451
Vancouver	AAA Ana	38	127	38	7	0	2	51	23	18	16	0	14	3	2	3	1	2	.33	5	.299	.383	.402
1995 Vancouver	AAA Ana	81	241	59	11	2	5	89	41	30	38	1	38	5	5	3	4	0	1.00	6	.245	.355	.369
1996 Vancouver	AAA Ana	78	237	55	10	3	1	74	25	27	34	0	27	1	4	4	1	1	.50	2	.232	.326	.312
1997 New Orleans	AAA Hou	68	103	13	1	0	0	14	15	8	21	0	17	0	4	2	1	0	1.00	5	.126	.270	.136
8 Min. YEARS		708	2196	596	111	18	15	788	392	260	450	6	398	33	50	29	40	23	.63	54	.271	.398	.359

Rick Greene

Pitches: Right **Bats:** Right **Pos:** P — **Ht:** 6'5" **Wt:** 200 **Born:** 1/2/71 **Age:** 27

Year Team	Lg Org	G GS CG GF	IP	BFP	H R ER HR SH SF HB	TBB IBB SO WP Bk	W	L	Pct.	ShO	Sv	ERA
1993 Lakeland	A+ Det	26 0 0 11	40.2	184	57 28 28 1 6 0 1	16 1 32 5 2	2	3	.400	0	2	6.20
London	AA Det	23 0 0 11	29	135	31 22 21 1 3 3 1	20 3 19 3 2	2	2	.500	0	2	6.52
1994 Trenton	AA Det	20 0 0 14	19.1	92	17 17 17 0 3 2 0	21 2 15 2 0	1	1	.500	0	3	7.91
Lakeland	A+ Det	19 2 0 11	33.1	158	50 23 16 0 1 1 0	10 1 28 6 0	0	4	.000	0	4	4.32
1995 Jacksnville	AA Det	32 0 0 6	38.2	177	45 19 15 3 1 0 3	15 2 29 0 0	6	2	.750	0	0	3.49
1996 Jacksnville	AA Det	57 0 0 48	56	275	67 44 31 8 6 0 2	39 4 42 2 0	2	7	.222	0	30	4.98
1997 Toledo	AAA Det	57 0 0 14	70	289	49 29 22 4 7 2 5	32 3 51 8 0	6	8	.429	0	1	2.83
5 Min. YEARS		234 2 0 115	287	1310	316 182 150 17 27 8 12	153 16 206 26 4	19	27	.413	0	40	4.70

Kenny Greer

Pitches: Right **Bats:** Right **Pos:** P — **Ht:** 6'2" **Wt:** 215 **Born:** 5/12/67 **Age:** 31

Year Team	Lg Org	G GS CG GF	IP	BFP	H R ER HR SH SF HB	TBB IBB SO WP Bk	W	L	Pct.	ShO	Sv	ERA
1988 Oneonta	A- NYA	15 15 4 0	112.1	470	109 46 30 0 5 4 7	18 2 60 6 6	5	5	.500	0	0	2.40
1989 Pr William	A+ NYA	29 13 3 7	111.2	461	101 56 52 3 2 2 7	22 0 44 4 1	7	3	.700	1	2	4.19
1990 Ft. Laud	A+ NYA	38 5 0 11	89.1	417	115 64 54 5 5 5 7	33 2 55 3 3	4	9	.308	0	1	5.44
Pr William	A+ NYA	1 1 0 0	7.2	32	7 2 2 0 1 0 0	2 0 7 0 0	1	0	1.000	0	0	2.35
1991 Ft. Laud	A+ NYA	31 1 0 12	57.1	245	49 31 27 3 1 1 7	22 2 46 5 0	4	3	.571	0	4	4.24
1992 Pr William	A+ NYA	13 0 0 6	27	112	25 11 11 1 0 1 2	9 0 30 1 0	1	2	.333	0	1	3.67
Albany-Colo	AA NYA	40 1 0 18	68.2	280	48 19 14 1 2 1 0	30 4 53 6 0	4	1	.800	0	4	1.83
Columbus	AAA NYA	1 0 0 1	1	7	3 2 1 0 0 0 0	1 0 1 0 0	0	0	.000	0	0	9.00
1993 Columbus	AAA NYA	46 0 0 21	79.1	347	78 41 39 5 4 4 2	36 6 50 2 0	9	4	.692	0	6	4.42
1994 Mets	R NYN	4 2 0 0	6	24	7 2 2 0 0 0 0	0 0 3 1 0	0	0	.000	0	0	3.00
Norfolk	AAA NYN	25 0 0 12	31	138	35 14 13 2 1 3 1	11 2 8 3 0	1	1	.500	0	3	3.77

Year Team	Lg Org	G	GS	CG	GF	IP	BFP	H	R	ER	HR	SH	SF	HB	TBB	IBB	SO	WP	Bk	W	L	Pct.	ShO	Sv	ERA
1995 Phoenix	AAA SF	38	0	0	13	63.1	270	65	29	28	1	3	2	2	19	1	41	5	0	5	2	.714	0	1	3.98
1996 Calgary	AAA Pit	46	1	0	19	68	294	74	34	30	9	5	2	3	17	5	36	2	0	5	4	.556	0	3	3.97
1997 Calgary	AAA Pit	15	0	0	4	22.1	107	33	22	21	7	2	2	1	7	1	16	1	0	0	3	.000	0	0	8.46
Rochester	AAA Bal	15	0	0	7	23.1	105	30	15	15	4	1	1	2	5	0	14	0	0	0	2	.000	0	1	5.79
Bowie	AA Bal	11	0	0	4	17.2	71	17	9	8	1	0	1	1	3	1	12	0	0	1	1	.500	0	0	4.08
1993 New York	NL	1	0	0	1	1	3	0	0	0	0	0	0	0	0	0	2	0	0	1	0	1.000	0	0	0.00
1995 San Francisco	NL	8	0	0	1	12	61	15	11	7	3	2	1	1	5	2	7	0	0	0	2	.000	0	0	5.25
10 Min. YEARS		368	39	7	135	786	3380	796	397	347	42	34	27	43	235	26	476	39	10	47	40	.540	1	20	3.97
2 Maj. YEARS		9	0	0	2	13	64	15	12	7	3	2	1	1	5	2	9	0	0	1	2	.333	0	0	4.85

Seth Greisinger

Pitches: Right **Bats:** Right **Pos:** P — **Ht:** 6'4" **Wt:** 190 **Born:** 7/29/75 **Age:** 22

Year Team	Lg Org	G	GS	CG	GF	IP	BFP	H	R	ER	HR	SH	SF	HB	TBB	IBB	SO	WP	Bk	W	L	Pct.	ShO	Sv	ERA
1997 Jacksnville	AA Det	28	28	1	0	159.1	710	194	103	92	29	3	6	3	53	0	105	12	2	10	6	.625	0	0	5.20

Kris Gresham

Bats: Right **Throws:** Right **Pos:** C — **Ht:** 6'2" **Wt:** 206 **Born:** 8/30/70 **Age:** 27

Year Team	Lg Org	G	AB	H	2B	3B	HR	TB	R	RBI	TBB	IBB	SO	HBP	SH	SF	SB	CS	SB%	GDP	Avg	OBP	SLG
1991 Bluefield	R+ Bal	34	116	28	5	2	0	37	16	16	6	0	19	4	1	3	6	3	.67	6	.241	.295	.319
1992 Kane County	A Bal	38	113	22	4	0	2	32	10	17	4	0	21	0	2	0	0	0	.00	1	.195	.222	.283
1993 Frederick	A+ Bal	66	188	41	13	1	4	68	22	17	13	0	41	7	3	0	1	0	1.00	2	.218	.293	.362
1994 Bowie	AA Bal	69	204	40	8	2	3	61	27	20	10	0	57	6	1	3	1	0	1.00	6	.196	.251	.299
1995 Bowie	AA Bal	5	13	1	0	0	0	1	1	0	3	0	5	0	0	1	1	0	1.00	0	.077	.250	.077
Rochester	AAA Bal	21	64	16	2	1	0	20	5	4	4	0	15	2	0	0	0	0	.00	2	.250	.314	.313
High Desert	A+ Bal	47	140	36	8	0	5	59	25	15	12	1	31	4	2	2	1	3	.25	6	.257	.329	.421
1996 Bowie	AA Bal	42	129	26	7	0	0	33	12	6	10	1	28	5	1	1	1	2	.33	2	.202	.283	.256
High Desert	A+ Bal	2	8	3	0	0	2	9	2	4	0	0	1	0	0	0	0	0	.00	0	.375	.375	1.125
1997 Rochester	AAA Bal	13	28	3	1	0	0	4	1	0	2	0	8	0	0	1	0	0	.00	1	.107	.167	.143
Frederick	A+ Bal	43	131	31	7	0	3	47	17	19	15	0	30	6	5	0	3	2	.60	2	.237	.342	.359
7 Min. YEARS		380	1134	247	55	6	19	371	138	118	79	2	256	34	15	9	14	10	.58	28	.218	.287	.327

Tim Grieve

Pitches: Right **Bats:** Right **Pos:** P — **Ht:** 6'0" **Wt:** 180 **Born:** 8/17/71 **Age:** 26

Year Team	Lg Org	G	GS	CG	GF	IP	BFP	H	R	ER	HR	SH	SF	HB	TBB	IBB	SO	WP	Bk	W	L	Pct.	ShO	Sv	ERA
1994 Eugene	A- KC	25	0	0	6	58	227	28	12	10	1	3	1	3	26	0	84	1	1	7	1	.875	0	1	1.55
1996 Royals	R KC	2	0	0	0	3	11	1	1	0	0	0	0	0	1	0	2	0	0	0	0	.000	0	0	0.00
Lansing	A KC	3	0	0	3	3	15	0	1	1	0	1	0	0	6	1	5	1	0	0	1	.000	0	0	3.00
Wilmington	A+ KC	22	0	0	13	34.1	143	28	9	5	1	2	1	0	13	3	30	1	0	4	1	.800	0	4	1.31
1997 Wilmington	A+ KC	26	0	0	19	38.1	154	24	11	8	3	4	1	0	20	4	34	1	0	4	1	.800	0	7	1.88
Wichita	AA KC	17	0	0	4	37.1	160	30	15	14	3	1	0	3	21	0	36	4	0	3	1	.750	0	1	3.38
3 Min. YEARS		95	0	0	45	174	710	111	49	38	8	11	3	6	87	8	191	8	1	18	6	.750	0	13	1.97

Craig Griffey

Bats: Right **Throws:** Right **Pos:** OF — **Ht:** 5'11" **Wt:** 175 **Born:** 6/3/71 **Age:** 27

Year Team	Lg Org	G	AB	H	2B	3B	HR	TB	R	RBI	TBB	IBB	SO	HBP	SH	SF	SB	CS	SB%	GDP	Avg	OBP	SLG
1991 Mariners	R Sea	45	150	38	1	1	0	41	36	20	28	0	35	1	2	2	11	6	.65	0	.253	.370	.273
1992 Bellingham	A- Sea	63	220	55	6	1	1	66	30	21	22	0	35	3	2	2	15	8	.65	1	.250	.324	.300
1993 Appleton	A Sea	37	102	26	7	0	2	39	14	20	12	0	18	1	1	3	9	3	.75	1	.255	.331	.382
Riverside	A+ Sea	58	191	46	4	4	3	67	30	25	17	3	25	2	3	7	10	2	.83	3	.241	.300	.351
1994 Jacksnville	AA Sea	106	327	72	13	1	3	96	37	29	33	0	68	3	10	5	20	10	.67	3	.220	.293	.294
1995 Port City	AA Sea	96	299	53	11	1	0	66	43	24	46	0	77	9	3	3	13	3	.81	5	.177	.303	.221
1996 Port City	AA Sea	120	396	88	14	7	2	122	43	35	46	0	88	6	2	6	20	7	.74	6	.222	.308	.308
1997 Tacoma	AAA Sea	3	3	1	0	1	0	3	1	0	0	0	0	0	0	0	0	1	.00	0	.333	.333	1.000
Memphis	AA Sea	35	120	26	3	1	0	31	20	5	13	0	22	0	2	2	6	1	.86	5	.217	.289	.258
Chattanooga	AA Cin	55	180	41	5	1	0	48	28	15	24	2	41	0	3	0	8	7	.53	4	.228	.319	.267
7 Min. YEARS		618	1988	446	64	18	11	579	282	194	241	5	409	25	28	30	112	48	.70	28	.224	.312	.291

Pedro Grifol

Bats: Right **Throws:** Right **Pos:** C — **Ht:** 6'1" **Wt:** 205 **Born:** 11/28/69 **Age:** 28

Year Team	Lg Org	G	AB	H	2B	3B	HR	TB	R	RBI	TBB	IBB	SO	HBP	SH	SF	SB	CS	SB%	GDP	Avg	OBP	SLG
1991 Elizabethtn	R+ Min	55	202	53	12	0	7	86	24	36	16	0	33	2	0	4	0	0	.00	6	.262	.317	.426
Orlando	AA Min	6	20	3	0	0	0	3	0	2	0	0	6	0	0	0	0	0	.00	0	.150	.150	.150
1992 Miracle	A+ Min	94	333	76	13	1	4	103	24	32	17	1	38	2	3	1	0	1	1.00	19	.228	.269	.309
Orlando	AA Min	14	40	11	2	0	0	13	2	5	2	0	9	0	0	1	0	0	.00	2	.275	.302	.325
1993 Nashville	AA Min	58	197	40	13	0	5	68	22	29	11	0	38	2	5	3	0	1	.00	6	.203	.249	.345
Portland	AAA Min	28	94	31	4	2	2	45	14	17	4	0	14	0	2	2	0	0	.00	5	.330	.350	.479
1994 Nashville	AA Min	20	55	7	0	0	1	10	4	4	10	0	7	1	0	1	0	0	.00	8	.127	.269	.182
1995 Hardware City	AA Min	77	226	40	9	0	3	58	23	21	23	1	33	1	1	1	0	1	1.00	8	.177	.255	.257
1996 Binghamton	AA NYN	64	202	48	3	0	7	72	22	28	13	2	29	0	8	0	0	0	.00	6	.238	.284	.356
1997 Binghamton	AA NYN	61	200	40	6	0	3	55	15	15	9	0	29	3	3	3	1	1	.50	9	.200	.242	.275

Year Team	Lg Org	G	AB	H	2B	3B	HR	TB	R	RBI	TBB	IBB	SO	HBP	SH	SF	SB	CS	SB%	GDP	Avg	OBP	SLG
7 Min. YEARS		477	1569	349	62	3	32	513	150	189	105	4	236	11	22	16	3	3	.50	62	.222	.273	.327

Kevin Grijak

Bats: Left **Throws:** Right **Pos:** 1B   **Ht:** 6'2" **Wt:** 195 **Born:** 8/6/70 **Age:** 27

Year Team	Lg Org	G	AB	H	2B	3B	HR	TB	R	RBI	TBB	IBB	SO	HBP	SH	SF	SB	CS	SB%	GDP	Avg	OBP	SLG
1991 Idaho Falls	R+ Atl	52	202	68	9	1	10	109	33	58	16	1	15	1	2	4	4	1	.80	5	.337	.381	.540
1992 Pulaski	R+ Atl	10	31	11	3	0	0	14	1	6	6	0	0	0	0	0	2	2	.50	1	.355	.459	.452
Macon	A Atl	47	157	41	13	0	5	69	20	21	15	2	16	3	0	2	3	0	1.00	3	.261	.333	.439
1993 Macon	A Atl	120	389	115	26	5	7	172	50	58	37	4	37	6	2	12	9	5	.64	9	.296	.356	.442
1994 Durham	A+ Atl	22	68	25	3	0	11	61	18	22	12	4	6	3	0	1	1	1	.50	1	.368	.476	.897
Greenville	AA Atl	100	348	94	19	1	11	148	40	58	20	1	40	6	0	7	2	3	.40	11	.270	.315	.425
1995 Greenville	AA Atl	21	74	32	5	0	2	43	14	11	7	0	9	2	0	2	1	0	.00	0	.432	.482	.581
Richmond	AAA Atl	106	309	92	16	5	12	154	35	56	25	4	47	4	0	4	1	3	.25	10	.298	.354	.498
1996 Richmond	AAA Atl	13	30	11	3	0	1	17	3	8	5	0	7	1	0	0	0	1	.00	1	.367	.472	.567
1997 Greenville	AA Atl	72	240	60	12	1	13	113	35	48	18	2	35	5	1	3	0	1	.00	8	.250	.312	.471
7 Min. YEARS		563	1848	549	109	13	72	900	249	346	161	18	212	31	5	35	22	18	.55	49	.297	.357	.487

Jason Grimsley

Pitches: Right **Bats:** Right **Pos:** P   **Ht:** 6'3" **Wt:** 180 **Born:** 8/7/67 **Age:** 30

Year Team	Lg Org	G	GS	CG	GF	IP	BFP	H	R	ER	HR	SH	SF	HB	TBB	IBB	SO	WP	Bk	W	L	Pct.	ShO	Sv	ERA
1985 Bend	A- Phi	6	1	0	2	11.1	0	12	21	17	0	0	0	1	25	0	10	3	0	0	1	.000	0	0	13.50
1986 Utica	A- Phi	14	14	3	0	64.2	342	63	61	46	3	1	2	11	77	0	46	18	0	1	10	.091	0	0	6.40
1987 Spartanburg	A Phi	23	9	3	7	88.1	380	59	48	31	4	2	5	6	54	2	98	12	0	7	4	.636	0	0	3.16
1988 Clearwater	A+ Phi	16	15	2	1	101.1	422	80	48	42	2	4	4	9	37	1	90	12	2	4	7	.364	0	0	3.73
Reading	AA Phi	5	4	0	1	21.1	98	20	19	17	1	1	1	1	13	1	14	1	0	1	3	.250	0	0	7.17
1989 Reading	AA Phi	26	26	8	0	172	727	121	65	57	13	6	3	10	109	4	134	12	0	11	8	.579	2	0	2.98
1990 Scranton-WB	AAA Phi	22	22	0	0	128.1	563	111	68	56	7	4	6	4	78	1	99	18	3	8	5	.615	0	0	3.93
1991 Scranton-WB	AAA Phi	9	9	0	0	51.2	231	48	28	25	3	3	0	2	37	2	43	2	2	2	3	.400	0	0	4.35
1992 Tucson	AAA Hou	26	20	0	1	124.2	565	152	79	70	4	2	5	9	55	0	90	14	0	8	7	.533	0	0	5.05
1993 Charlotte	AAA Cle	28	19	3	5	135.1	579	138	64	51	10	3	1	1	49	1	102	18	0	6	6	.500	1	0	3.39
1994 Charlotte	AAA Cle	10	10	2	0	71	291	58	36	27	10	2	3	3	17	0	60	9	1	7	0	1.000	0	0	3.42
1995 Buffalo	AAA Cle	10	10	2	0	68	285	61	26	22	4	2	3	3	19	0	40	4	0	5	3	.625	0	0	2.91
1996 Vancouver	AAA Ana	2	2	1	0	15	55	8	2	2	0	1	1	1	3	0	11	0	1	2	0	1.000	0	0	1.20
1997 Tucson	AAA Mil	36	10	0	18	85.1	397	96	70	54	6	2	3	4	43	2	65	20	0	5	10	.333	0	4	5.70
Omaha	AAA KC	7	6	0	0	31	156	36	26	23	3	0	1	3	29	0	22	3	0	1	5	.167	0	0	6.68
1989 Philadelphia	NL	4	4	0	0	18.1	91	19	13	12	2	1	0	0	19	1	7	2	0	1	3	.250	0	0	5.89
1990 Philadelphia	NL	11	11	0	0	57.1	255	47	21	21	1	2	1	2	43	0	41	6	1	3	2	.600	0	0	3.30
1991 Philadelphia	NL	12	12	0	0	61	272	54	34	33	4	3	2	3	41	3	42	14	0	1	7	.125	0	0	4.87
1993 Cleveland	AL	10	6	0	1	42.1	194	52	26	25	3	1	0	1	20	1	27	2	0	3	4	.429	0	0	5.31
1994 Cleveland	AL	14	13	1	0	82.2	368	91	47	42	7	4	2	6	34	1	59	6	1	5	2	.714	0	0	4.57
1995 Cleveland	AL	15	2	0	2	34	165	37	24	23	4	1	2	2	32	1	25	7	0	0	0	.000	0	1	6.09
1996 California	AL	35	20	2	4	130.1	620	150	110	99	14	4	5	13	74	5	82	11	0	5	7	.417	1	0	6.84
13 Min. YEARS		240	177	24	35	1169.1	5091	1063	661	540	70	33	38	68	645	14	924	146	9	68	72	.486	3	4	4.16
7 Maj. YEARS		101	68	3	7	426	1965	450	275	255	35	16	12	27	263	12	283	48	2	18	25	.419	1	1	5.39

Mike Groppuso

Bats: Right **Throws:** Right **Pos:** 3B   **Ht:** 6'3" **Wt:** 195 **Born:** 3/9/70 **Age:** 28

Year Team	Lg Org	G	AB	H	2B	3B	HR	TB	R	RBI	TBB	IBB	SO	HBP	SH	SF	SB	CS	SB%	GDP	Avg	OBP	SLG
1991 Asheville	A Hou	63	197	36	12	1	4	62	31	25	34	2	60	3	0	0	3	1	.75	3	.183	.312	.315
1992 Osceola	A+ Hou	115	369	80	19	1	4	113	53	37	43	2	98	9	3	3	6	3	.67	4	.217	.311	.306
1993 Jackson	AA Hou	114	370	89	18	0	10	137	41	49	35	4	121	5	0	1	3	3	.50	8	.241	.314	.370
1994 Jackson	AA Hou	118	352	93	16	2	12	149	49	47	35	2	97	5	1	4	6	7	.46	10	.264	.336	.423
1995 Jackson	AA Hou	24	79	17	3	1	1	25	5	5	16	3	17	1	0	1	2	1	.67	1	.215	.351	.316
1996 Tucson	AAA Hou	50	145	37	3	1	5	57	15	18	8	0	45	2	0	2	2	0	1.00	3	.255	.299	.393
Jackson	AA Hou	33	111	28	0	2	3	41	17	12	11	1	35	3	0	0	1	1	.50	6	.252	.336	.369
1997 Rio Grande	IND —	40	134	45	7	0	10	82	36	30	35	4	24	3	0	1	6	0	1.00	4	.336	.480	.612
El Paso	AA Mil	29	87	30	6	2	8	64	15	23	10	1	19	0	0	2	1	1	.50	4	.345	.404	.736
7 Min. YEARS		586	1844	455	84	10	57	730	262	246	227	19	516	31	4	14	30	17	.64	41	.247	.337	.396

Rafael Gross

Bats: Right **Throws:** Right **Pos:** OF   **Ht:** 5'11" **Wt:** 185 **Born:** 8/15/74 **Age:** 23

Year Team	Lg Org	G	AB	H	2B	3B	HR	TB	R	RBI	TBB	IBB	SO	HBP	SH	SF	SB	CS	SB%	GDP	Avg	OBP	SLG
1994 Great Falls	R+ LA	65	258	60	11	9	4	101	39	35	26	1	48	9	3	3	9	4	.69	6	.233	.321	.391
1995 Yakima	A- LA	40	142	36	4	1	3	51	17	15	13	1	17	1	1	1	12	2	.86	3	.254	.318	.359
Vero Beach	A+ LA	35	115	29	4	1	0	35	18	8	3	0	15	3	1	2	5	4	.56	1	.252	.285	.304
1996 San Berndno	A+ LA	112	362	85	18	2	6	125	58	43	18	0	68	2	5	2	31	14	.69	5	.235	.273	.345
1997 Akron	AA Cle	49	49	14	4	0	0	18	7	2	2	0	13	0	0	0	3	3	.50	3	.286	.314	.367
Kinston	A+ Cle	73	266	71	20	0	9	118	53	36	30	0	68	4	0	2	17	10	.63	7	.267	.348	.444
4 Min. YEARS		344	1192	295	61	13	22	448	192	139	92	2	229	19	10	10	77	37	.68	25	.247	.309	.376

Matt Grott

Pitches: Left Bats: Left Pos: P   Ht: 6'1" Wt: 205 Born: 12/5/67 Age: 30

Year Team	Lg Org	G	GS	CG	GF	IP	BFP	H	R	ER	HR	SH	SF	HB	TBB	IBB	SO	WP	Bk	W	L	Pct.	ShO	Sv	ERA
1989 Athletics	R Oak	9	5	0	0	35	139	29	10	9	0	0	0	2	9	0	44	1	2	3	1	.750	0	0	2.31
1990 Madison	A Oak	22	0	0	19	25	102	15	5	1	0	0	0	0	14	1	36	1	1	2	0	1.000	0	12	0.36
Modesto	A+ Oak	12	0	0	8	17.2	78	10	7	4	0	1	0	0	14	1	28	4	0	2	0	1.000	0	4	2.04
Huntsville	AA Oak	10	0	0	6	15.2	62	8	5	5	1	1	3	0	10	0	12	0	0	0	0	.000	0	1	2.87
1991 Huntsville	AA Oak	42	0	0	23	57.2	276	65	40	33	6	8	3	0	37	7	65	6	0	2	9	.182	0	3	5.15
Harrisburg	AA Mon	10	1	0	2	15.1	69	14	8	8	4	0	0	0	8	0	16	0	0	2	1	.667	0	1	4.70
1992 Chattanooga	AA Cin	32	0	0	20	40.1	180	39	16	12	4	4	1	0	25	4	44	5	2	1	2	.333	0	6	2.68
1993 Indianapolis	AAA Cin	33	9	0	10	100.1	423	88	45	40	8	3	4	1	40	2	73	7	1	7	5	.583	0	1	3.59
1994 Indianapolis	AAA Cin	26	16	2	2	116.1	468	106	44	33	10	5	1	0	32	0	64	7	1	10	3	.769	1	1	2.55
1995 Indianapolis	AAA Cin	25	18	2	2	114.2	468	99	61	54	10	2	5	3	24	2	74	11	0	7	3	.700	1	2	4.24
1996 Scranton-WB	AAA Phi	27	12	0	4	86.2	365	92	48	47	18	2	4	1	22	2	63	4	1	1	3	.250	0	0	4.88
Rochester	AAA Bal	5	1	0	1	9.1	46	13	10	4	3	2	0	0	7	0	5	0	0	0	0	.000	0	0	3.86
Bowie	AA Bal	9	0	0	3	21.2	93	26	15	12	3	0	2	0	5	0	15	2	0	2	1	.667	0	0	4.98
1997 Tucson	AAA Mil	55	0	0	18	88.1	395	94	57	47	11	4	2	2	33	6	58	10	0	3	1	.750	0	4	4.79
1995 Cincinnati	NL	2	0	0	0	1.2	11	6	4	4	1	0	0	0	3	0	2	0	0	0	0	.000	0	0	21.60
9 Min. YEARS		317	62	4	118	744	3164	698	371	309	78	32	25	9	280	25	597	58	8	42	29	.592	2	35	3.74

Kelly Gruber

Bats: Right Throws: Right Pos: 2B   Ht: 6'0" Wt: 185 Born: 2/26/62 Age: 36

Year Team	Lg Org	G	AB	H	2B	3B	HR	TB	R	RBI	TBB	IBB	SO	HBP	SH	SF	SB	CS	SB%	GDP	Avg	OBP	SLG
1980 Batavia	A- Cle	61	212	46	3	2	2	59	27	19	15	-	46	-	-	-	6	3	.67	-	.217	-	.278
1981 Waterloo	A Cle	127	458	133	25	4	14	208	64	59	24	-	85	-	-	-	15	7	.68	-	.290	-	.454
1982 Chattanooga	AA Cle	128	441	107	18	4	13	172	53	54	21	-	89	-	-	-	11	6	.65	-	.243	-	.390
1983 Buffalo	AAA Cle	111	403	106	20	4	15	179	60	54	23	-	44	-	-	-	15	7	.68	-	.263	-	.444
1984 Syracuse	AAA Tor	97	342	92	12	2	21	171	53	55	23	0	67	7	0	1	12	2	.86	6	.269	.327	.500
1985 Syracuse	AAA Tor	121	473	118	16	5	21	207	71	69	28	2	92	7	1	5	20	8	.71	17	.249	.298	.438
1993 Palm Spring	A+ Ana	5	9	2	0	0	0	2	0	1	1	0	2	0	0	0	0	0	.00	0	.222	.300	.222
Vancouver	AAA Ana	8	24	11	1	0	1	15	4	5	1	0	2	0	0	1	0	0	.00	1	.458	.462	.625
1997 Rochester	AAA Bal	38	144	36	9	2	2	55	26	23	15	0	14	2	1	1	1	1	.50	1	.250	.327	.382
1984 Toronto	AL	15	16	1	0	0	1	4	1	2	0	0	5	0	0	0	0	0	.00	0	.063	.063	.250
1985 Toronto	AL	5	13	3	0	0	0	3	0	1	0	0	3	0	0	0	0	0	.00	0	.231	.231	.231
1986 Toronto	AL	87	143	28	4	1	5	49	20	15	5	0	27	0	2	2	2	5	.29	4	.196	.220	.343
1987 Toronto	AL	138	341	80	14	3	12	136	50	36	17	2	70	7	1	2	12	2	.86	11	.235	.283	.399
1988 Toronto	AL	158	569	158	33	5	16	249	75	81	38	1	92	7	5	4	23	5	.82	20	.278	.328	.438
1989 Toronto	AL	135	545	158	24	4	18	244	83	73	30	0	60	3	0	5	10	5	.67	13	.290	.328	.448
1990 Toronto	AL	150	592	162	36	6	31	303	92	118	48	2	94	8	1	13	14	2	.88	14	.274	.330	.512
1991 Toronto	AL	113	429	108	18	2	20	190	58	65	31	5	70	6	3	5	12	7	.63	7	.252	.308	.443
1992 Toronto	AL	120	446	102	16	3	11	157	42	43	26	3	72	4	1	4	7	7	.50	14	.229	.275	.352
1993 California	AL	18	65	18	3	0	3	30	10	9	2	0	11	1	2	0	0	0	.00	0	.277	.309	.462
8 Min. YEARS		696	2506	651	104	23	89	1068	358	339	151	2	441	16	- 2	8	80	34	.70	29	.260	.305	.426
10 Maj. YEARS		939	3159	818	148	24	117	1365	431	443	197	13	504	36	15	35	80	33	.71	86	.259	.307	.432

Phillip Grundy

Pitches: Right Bats: Right Pos: P   Ht: 6'2" Wt: 195 Born: 9/8/72 Age: 25

Year Team	Lg Org	G	GS	CG	GF	IP	BFP	H	R	ER	HR	SH	SF	HB	TBB	IBB	SO	WP	Bk	W	L	Pct.	ShO	Sv	ERA
1993 Eugene	A- KC	15	13	0	0	69	301	68	31	25	7	2	1	5	37	1	61	5	1	3	5	.375	0	0	3.26
1994 Rockford	A KC	27	26	2	0	151.1	622	135	65	54	6	1	4	1	51	3	116	14	0	15	8	.652	0	0	3.21
1995 Wichita	AA KC	6	2	0	1	17.1	75	16	17	16	6	1	1	1	7	0	11	3	0	1	1	.500	0	0	8.31
Wilmington	A+ KC	20	16	0	3	106	445	106	46	39	7	4	1	5	32	2	90	7	0	6	6	.500	0	1	3.31
1996 Wichita	AA KC	1	1	0	0	7	26	4	1	1	0	0	0	0	2	0	1	0	1	1	0	1.000	0	0	1.29
Wilmington	A+ KC	27	26	3	0	164.2	679	155	87	65	17	8	4	6	49	3	117	5	2	7	11	.389	0	1	3.55
1997 Wichita	AA KC	28	24	2	1	156.1	712	194	108	99	17	6	5	6	53	3	117	12	1	9	11	.450	0	0	5.70
5 Min. YEARS		124	108	7	5	671.2	2860	678	355	299	60	22	16	24	231	12	512	47	4	42	42	.500	2	1	4.01

Keith Grunewald

Bats: Both Throws: Right Pos: 2B   Ht: 6'1" Wt: 185 Born: 10/15/71 Age: 26

Year Team	Lg Org	G	AB	H	2B	3B	HR	TB	R	RBI	TBB	IBB	SO	HBP	SH	SF	SB	CS	SB%	GDP	Avg	OBP	SLG
1993 Bend	A- Col	56	183	50	4	2	3	67	29	21	30	1	44	0	1	0	7	2	.78	2	.273	.376	.366
1994 New Haven	AA Col	8	18	8	0	0	0	8	2	0	0	0	5	0	0	0	0	0	.00	1	.444	.444	.444
Asheville	A Col	111	406	109	11	0	10	150	47	37	36	2	98	0	4	1	4	5	.44	5	.268	.327	.369
1995 Salem	A+ Col	118	412	109	22	1	6	151	48	45	46	8	84	10	2	3	8	4	.67	8	.265	.350	.367
1996 Salem	A+ Col	10	37	9	1	0	0	10	1	4	2	0	12	1	1	1	0	3	.00	0	.243	.293	.270
New Haven	AA Col	111	352	80	13	2	3	106	27	28	25	3	98	5	7	3	2	1	.67	3	.227	.286	.301
1997 New Haven	AA Col	103	310	75	11	1	0	88	41	24	25	1	78	1	6	5	7	3	.70	8	.242	.296	.284
5 Min. YEARS		517	1718	440	62	6	22	580	195	159	164	15	419	17	21	13	28	18	.61	27	.256	.325	.338

Mike Grzanich

Pitches: Right Bats: Right Pos: P   Ht: 6'1" Wt: 180 Born: 8/24/72 Age: 25

Year Team	Lg Org	G	GS	CG	GF	IP	BFP	H	R	ER	HR	SH	SF	HB	TBB	IBB	SO	WP	Bk	W	L	Pct.	ShO	Sv	ERA
1992 Astros	R Hou	17	3	0	9	33.2	159	38	21	17	0	2	3	6	14	0	29	1	0	2	5	.286	0	3	4.54

Year Team	Lg Org	G	GS	CG	GF	IP	BFP	H	R	ER	HR	SH	SF	HB	TBB	IBB	SO	WP	Bk	W	L	Pct.	ShO	Sv	ERA
		HOW MUCH HE PITCHED						WHAT HE GAVE UP												THE RESULTS					
1993 Auburn	A- Hou	16	14	4	1	93.1	409	106	63	50	11	3	3	3	27	0	71	7	1	5	8	.385	1	0	4.82
1994 Quad City	A Hou	23	22	3	1	142.2	598	145	55	49	5	2	1	11	43	2	101	5	0	11	7	.611	0	0	3.09
1995 Jackson	AA Hou	50	0	0	23	65.2	276	55	22	20	0	5	3	6	38	5	44	4	0	5	3	.625	0	8	2.74
1996 Jackson	AA Hou	57	0	0	19	72.1	316	60	47	32	10	4	2	8	43	2	80	6	0	5	4	.556	0	6	3.98
1997 Jackson	AA Hou	38	13	0	21	101.2	472	114	68	56	10	4	5	8	46	2	73	2	0	7	6	.538	0	12	4.96
6 Min. YEARS		201	52	7	74	509.1	2230	518	276	224	36	20	17	42	211	11	398	25	1	35	33	.515	1	29	3.96

Creighton Gubanich

Bats: Right **Throws:** Right **Pos:** C   **Ht:** 6'4" **Wt:** 220 **Born:** 3/27/72 **Age:** 26

Year Team	Lg Org	G	AB	H	2B	3B	HR	TB	R	RBI	TBB	IBB	SO	HBP	SH	SF	SB	CS	SB%	GDP	Avg	OBP	SLG
		BATTING															BASERUNNING				PERCENTAGES		
1991 Sou. Oregon	A- Oak	43	132	30	7	2	4	53	23	18	19	0	35	6	0	0	4	4	.00	2	.227	.350	.402
1992 Madison	A Oak	121	404	100	19	3	9	152	46	55	41	1	102	16	8	1	0	7	.00	8	.248	.340	.376
1993 Madison	A Oak	119	373	100	19	2	19	180	65	78	63	2	105	11	2	12	3	3	.50	7	.268	.379	.483
1994 Modesto	A+ Oak	108	375	88	20	3	15	159	53	55	54	0	102	7	5	2	5	4	.56	9	.235	.340	.424
1995 Huntsville	AA Oak	94	274	60	7	1	13	108	37	43	48	0	82	7	2	5	1	0	1.00	2	.219	.344	.394
1996 Huntsville	AA Oak	62	217	60	19	0	9	106	40	43	31	1	71	4	3	2	1	0	1.00	5	.276	.374	.488
Edmonton	AAA Oak	34	117	29	7	1	4	50	14	19	6	0	33	1	0	1	3	0	1.00	5	.248	.288	.427
1997 Edmonton	AAA Oak	43	145	48	13	0	7	82	23	34	14	0	42	2	1	1	0	2	.00	4	.331	.395	.566
Tucson	AAA Mil	24	85	29	5	0	5	49	13	17	1	0	19	1	0	1	1	0	1.00	1	.341	.356	.576
Colo Sprngs	AAA Col	14	47	9	1	0	3	19	4	6	4	0	18	0	0	0	0	0	.00	4	.191	.255	.404
7 Min. YEARS		662	2169	553	117	12	88	958	318	368	281	4	609	55	21	24	14	20	.41	48	.255	.352	.442

Mark Guerra

Pitches: Right **Bats:** Right **Pos:** P   **Ht:** 6'2" **Wt:** 185 **Born:** 11/4/71 **Age:** 26

Year Team	Lg Org	G	GS	CG	GF	IP	BFP	H	R	ER	HR	SH	SF	HB	TBB	IBB	SO	WP	Bk	W	L	Pct.	ShO	Sv	ERA
		HOW MUCH HE PITCHED						WHAT HE GAVE UP												THE RESULTS					
1994 Pittsfield	A- NYN	14	14	2	0	94	392	105	47	36	4	4	5	4	21	1	62	2	2	7	6	.538	0	0	3.45
1995 St. Lucie	A+ NYN	23	23	4	0	160	644	148	55	47	5	4	4	4	33	1	110	2	3	9	9	.500	3	0	2.64
Binghamton	AA NYN	6	5	1	0	32.2	139	35	24	21	6	1	0	0	9	1	24	0	0	2	1	.667	0	0	5.79
1996 Binghamton	AA NYN	27	20	1	3	140.1	577	143	60	55	23	5	2	2	34	3	84	1	1	7	6	.538	0	0	3.53
1997 Binghamton	AA NYN	48	7	1	17	94.2	403	96	46	34	10	3	2	1	30	1	74	2	0	4	8	.333	0	7	3.23
4 Min. YEARS		118	69	9	20	521.2	2155	527	232	193	48	17	13	11	127	7	354	7	6	29	30	.492	3	7	3.33

Aaron Guiel

Bats: Left **Throws:** Right **Pos:** OF   **Ht:** 5'10" **Wt:** 190 **Born:** 10/5/72 **Age:** 25

Year Team	Lg Org	G	AB	H	2B	3B	HR	TB	R	RBI	TBB	IBB	SO	HBP	SH	SF	SB	CS	SB%	GDP	Avg	OBP	SLG
		BATTING															BASERUNNING				PERCENTAGES		
1993 Boise	A- Ana	35	104	31	6	4	2	51	24	12	26	1	21	4	2	0	3	0	1.00	1	.298	.455	.490
1994 Cedar Rapds	A Ana	127	454	122	30	1	18	208	84	82	64	2	93	6	5	3	21	7	.75	7	.269	.364	.458
1995 Lk Elsinore	A+ Ana	113	409	110	25	7	7	170	73	58	69	0	96	7	4	4	7	6	.54	7	.269	.380	.416
1996 Midland	AA Ana	129	439	118	29	7	10	191	72	48	56	0	71	10	2	1	11	7	.61	6	.269	.364	.435
1997 Midland	AA Ana	116	419	138	37	7	22	255	91	85	59	3	94	18	2	3	14	10	.58	9	.329	.431	.609
Mobile	AA SD	8	26	10	2	0	1	15	9	9	5	0	4	1	0	0	1	0	1.00	0	.385	.500	.577
5 Min. YEARS		528	1851	529	129	26	60	890	353	294	279	6	379	46	15	11	57	30	.66	30	.286	.390	.481

Matt Guiliano

Bats: Right **Throws:** Right **Pos:** SS   **Ht:** 5'7" **Wt:** 175 **Born:** 6/7/72 **Age:** 26

Year Team	Lg Org	G	AB	H	2B	3B	HR	TB	R	RBI	TBB	IBB	SO	HBP	SH	SF	SB	CS	SB%	GDP	Avg	OBP	SLG
		BATTING															BASERUNNING				PERCENTAGES		
1994 Martinsvlle	R+ Phi	58	190	42	5	0	5	62	33	16	24	0	57	7	3	2	16	3	.84	4	.221	.327	.326
1995 Piedmont	A Phi	129	451	102	22	12	4	160	67	59	51	1	114	7	9	6	6	8	.43	7	.226	.311	.355
1996 Reading	AA Phi	74	220	44	9	3	0	59	19	19	25	1	59	3	3	1	0	0	.00	4	.200	.268	.268
Clearwater	A+ Phi	55	166	37	8	2	1	52	12	14	6	0	46	6	6	3	2	3	.40	3	.223	.271	.313
1997 Reading	AA Phi	119	367	83	15	3	7	125	38	37	34	4	99	5	8	2	7	6	.54	8	.226	.299	.341
4 Min. YEARS		435	1394	308	59	20	17	458	169	145	140	6	375	28	29	14	31	20	.61	26	.221	.302	.329

Carlos Guillen

Bats: Both **Throws:** Right **Pos:** SS   **Ht:** 6'0" **Wt:** 150 **Born:** 9/30/75 **Age:** 22

Year Team	Lg Org	G	AB	H	2B	3B	HR	TB	R	RBI	TBB	IBB	SO	HBP	SH	SF	SB	CS	SB%	GDP	Avg	OBP	SLG
		BATTING															BASERUNNING				PERCENTAGES		
1995 Astros	R Hou	30	105	31	4	2	2	45	17	15	9	1	17	1	1	2	17	1	.94	0	.295	.350	.429
1996 Quad City	A Hou	29	112	37	7	1	3	55	23	17	16	2	25	0	0	3	13	6	.68	1	.330	.405	.491
1997 Jackson	AA Hou	115	390	99	16	1	10	147	47	39	38	1	78	2	4	2	6	5	.55	9	.254	.322	.377
New Orleans	AAA Hou	3	13	4	1	0	0	5	3	0	0	0	4	0	0	0	0	0	.00	0	.308	.308	.385
3 Min. YEARS		177	620	171	28	4	15	252	90	71	63	4	124	3	5	7	36	12	.75	10	.276	.342	.406

Shane Gunderson

Bats: Right **Throws:** Right **Pos:** OF   **Ht:** 6'0" **Wt:** 205 **Born:** 10/16/73 **Age:** 24

Year Team	Lg Org	G	AB	H	2B	3B	HR	TB	R	RBI	TBB	IBB	SO	HBP	SH	SF	SB	CS	SB%	GDP	Avg	OBP	SLG
		BATTING															BASERUNNING				PERCENTAGES		
1995 Elizabethtn	R+ Min	37	139	43	11	2	7	79	30	20	24	0	24	2	0	1	4	0	1.00	1	.309	.401	.568
Ft. Wayne	A Min	26	87	22	7	0	2	35	17	12	10	1	17	2	4	0	2	1	.67	0	.253	.343	.402
1996 Ft. Myers	A+ Min	117	410	103	20	5	5	148	61	50	63	2	85	14	6	2	12	8	.60	5	.251	.368	.361

Year Team	Lg Org	G	AB	H	2B	3B	HR	TB	R	RBI	TBB	IBB	SO	HBP	SH	SF	SB	CS	SB%	GDP	Avg	OBP	SLG
1997 New Britain	AA Min	33	117	30	7	3	2	49	17	10	19	0	31	1	4	0	7	2	.78	1	.256	.365	.419
Ft. Wayne	A Min	13	45	12	1	0	0	13	3	7	3	0	3	0	1	1	1	1	.50	2	.267	.306	.289
Ft. Myers	A+ Min	14	50	14	4	0	0	18	5	5	7	0	8	1	0	0	3	1	.75	2	.280	.379	.360
3 Min. YEARS		240	848	224	50	10	16	342	135	114	122	3	168	20	15	4	29	13	.69	13	.264	.368	.403

Jim Gutierrez

Pitches: Right **Bats:** Right **Pos:** P **Ht:** 6'2" **Wt:** 190 **Born:** 11/28/70 **Age:** 27

		HOW MUCH HE PITCHED						WHAT HE GAVE UP										THE RESULTS					
Year Team	Lg Org	G	GS	CG	GF	IP	BFP	H	R	ER	HR	SH	SF	HB	TBB	IBB	SO	WP	Bk	W	L	Pct.	ShO	Sv	ERA
1989 Bellingham	A- Sea	13	11	0	1	57.2	268	68	44	25	4	0	1	1	24	0	33	1	0	1	5	.167	0	0	3.90
1990 Peninsula	A+ Sea	28	28	4	0	186	758	171	82	71	9	6	11	6	41	0	95	6	1	11	13	.458	2	0	3.44
1991 San Berndno	A+ Sea	17	14	1	0	82.2	377	100	65	60	11	0	3	2	37	0	66	4	0	4	4	.500	0	0	6.53
1992 Jacksnville	AA Sea	15	11	0	1	54	234	58	34	30	7	1	2	3	17	0	44	0	0	1	5	.167	0	0	5.00
1993 Riverside	A+ Sea	27	27	2	0	171.1	742	182	95	72	15	11	6	4	53	2	84	5	1	12	9	.571	0	0	3.78
1994 Jacksnville	AA Sea	28	21	6	4	151.2	655	175	76	72	16	4	3	4	42	4	89	1	0	8	11	.421	1	0	4.27
1995 Jacksnville	AA Det	45	1	0	14	58.2	243	60	22	18	2	3	2	0	25	4	36	3	0	8	4	.667	0	4	2.76
1996 Jacksnville	AA Det	51	10	0	10	105.1	452	98	55	44	6	3	5	1	54	5	71	6	0	8	6	.571	0	1	3.76
1997 New Orleans	AAA Hou	7	0	0	5	11	46	11	4	4	1	0	1	0	2	0	8	2	0	1	0	1.000	0	0	3.27
Jackson	AA Hou	52	3	0	26	89	376	96	33	29	4	1	1	6	23	5	51	4	0	4	4	.500	0	5	2.93
9 Min. YEARS		283	126	13	61	967.1	4151	1019	510	425	75	29	35	27	318	20	577	32	2	57	62	.479	3	10	3.95

Edwards Guzman

Bats: Left **Throws:** Right **Pos:** 3B **Ht:** 5'11" **Wt:** 192 **Born:** 9/11/76 **Age:** 21

		BATTING															BASERUNNING				PERCENTAGES		
Year Team	Lg Org	G	AB	H	2B	3B	HR	TB	R	RBI	TBB	IBB	SO	HBP	SH	SF	SB	CS	SB%	GDP	Avg	OBP	SLG
1996 San Jose	A+ SF	106	367	99	19	5	1	131	41	40	39	4	60	5	6	5	3	5	.38	6	.270	.344	.357
1997 Shreveport	AA SF	118	380	108	15	4	3	140	52	42	33	4	57	1	5	3	3	1	.75	6	.284	.341	.368
2 Min. YEARS		224	747	207	34	9	4	271	93	82	72	8	117	6	11	8	6	6	.50	12	.277	.342	.363

Dave Haas

Pitches: Right **Bats:** Right **Pos:** P **Ht:** 6'1" **Wt:** 200 **Born:** 10/19/65 **Age:** 32

		HOW MUCH HE PITCHED						WHAT HE GAVE UP										THE RESULTS					
Year Team	Lg Org	G	GS	CG	GF	IP	BFP	H	R	ER	HR	SH	SF	HB	TBB	IBB	SO	WP	Bk	W	L	Pct.	ShO	Sv	ERA
1988 Fayettevlle	A Det	11	11	0	0	54.2	243	59	20	11	0	1	1	6	19	1	46	2	4	4	3	.571	0	0	1.81
1989 Lakeland	A+ Det	10	10	1	0	62	247	50	16	14	1	0	1	6	16	0	46	1	4	4	1	.800	1	0	2.03
London	AA Det	18	18	2	0	103.2	460	107	69	65	13	5	2	11	51	1	75	5	1	3	11	.214	1	0	5.64
1990 London	AA Det	27	27	3	0	177.2	740	151	64	59	10	4	3	10	74	1	116	14	1	13	8	.619	1	0	2.99
1991 Toledo	AAA Det	28	28	1	0	158.1	718	187	103	92	11	8	3	8	77	3	133	8	1	8	10	.444	0	0	5.23
1992 Toledo	AAA Det	22	22	2	0	148.2	636	149	72	69	11	5	5	9	53	1	112	5	0	9	8	.529	0	0	4.18
1993 Toledo	AAA Det	2	2	0	0	4.1	27	8	9	9	0	0	0	0	6	0	2	1	0	0	0	.000	0	0	18.69
1994 Lakeland	A+ Det	5	3	0	0	20	90	23	9	8	0	2	3	3	8	0	4	0	0	1	0	1.000	0	0	3.60
1995 Orlando	AA ChN	3	3	0	0	12.2	69	18	10	7	1	0	0	3	10	0	4	1	0	0	3	.000	0	0	4.97
Salinas	IND —	18	16	0	0	99.2	424	103	63	51	12	1	6	9	24	1	63	3	0	7	5	.583	3	0	4.61
1996 Abilene	IND —	21	20	5	0	148	619	139	52	40	6	6	2	13	36	1	102	2	0	13	4	.765	3	0	2.43
1997 Jackson	AA Hou	13	0	0	4	19.2	89	23	14	11	0	3	1	1	4	2	5	0	0	1	1	.500	0	0	5.03
1991 Detroit	AL	11	0	0	0	10.2	50	8	8	8	1	2	2	1	12	3	6	1	0	1	0	1.000	0	0	6.75
1992 Detroit	AL	12	11	1	1	61.2	264	68	30	27	8	1	0	1	16	1	29	2	0	5	3	.625	1	0	3.94
1993 Detroit	AL	20	0	0	5	28	131	45	20	19	9	2	1	0	8	5	17	0	0	1	2	.333	0	0	6.11
10 Min. YEARS		178	160	14	4	1009.1	4362	1017	501	436	65	35	27	80	378	11	708	42	8	63	54	.538	6	0	3.89
3 Maj. YEARS		43	11	1	6	100.1	445	121	58	54	18	5	3	2	36	9	52	3	0	7	5	.583	1	0	4.84

Matt Haas

Bats: Left **Throws:** Right **Pos:** OF **Ht:** 6'1" **Wt:** 175 **Born:** 2/1/72 **Age:** 26

		BATTING															BASERUNNING				PERCENTAGES		
Year Team	Lg Org	G	AB	H	2B	3B	HR	TB	R	RBI	TBB	IBB	SO	HBP	SH	SF	SB	CS	SB%	GDP	Avg	OBP	SLG
1994 Vermont	A- Mon	49	173	47	5	0	1	55	27	20	18	0	27	3	1	3	3	1	.75	2	.272	.345	.318
1995 Albany	A Mon	52	166	39	7	0	0	46	18	15	18	1	30	2	3	1	1	5	.17	1	.235	.316	.277
1996 Wst Plm Bch	A+ Mon	77	207	55	7	1	1	67	22	26	22	1	27	3	0	3	4	2	.67	4	.266	.340	.324
1997 Harrisburg	AA Mon	8	19	4	1	0	1	8	2	4	4	0	2	0	0	1	1	0	1.00	0	.211	.333	.421
Wst Plm Bch	A+ Mon	72	201	47	5	1	1	57	17	16	24	2	34	1	4	1	7	3	.70	1	.234	.317	.284
4 Min. YEARS		258	766	192	25	2	4	233	86	81	86	4	120	9	8	9	16	11	.59	7	.251	.330	.304

Luther Hackman

Pitches: Right **Bats:** Right **Pos:** P **Ht:** 6'4" **Wt:** 195 **Born:** 10/10/74 **Age:** 23

		HOW MUCH HE PITCHED						WHAT HE GAVE UP										THE RESULTS					
Year Team	Lg Org	G	GS	CG	GF	IP	BFP	H	R	ER	HR	SH	SF	HB	TBB	IBB	SO	WP	Bk	W	L	Pct.	ShO	Sv	ERA
1994 Rockies	R Col	12	12	0	0	55.2	234	50	21	13	1	0	0	1	16	0	63	5	1	1	3	.250	0	0	2.10
1995 Asheville	A Col	28	28	2	0	165	710	162	95	85	11	3	3	14	65	0	108	9	7	11	11	.500	0	0	4.64
1996 Salem	A+ Col	21	21	1	0	110.1	484	93	60	52	2	4	7	5	69	1	83	6	2	5	7	.417	0	0	4.24
1997 New Haven	AA Col	10	10	0	0	50.2	241	58	49	44	11	5	2	5	34	1	34	4	3	0	6	.000	0	0	7.82
Salem	A+ Col	15	15	2	0	80.2	384	99	60	52	14	4	5	9	37	0	59	8	0	1	4	.200	0	0	5.80
4 Min. YEARS		86	86	5	0	462.1	2053	462	285	246	39	16	17	34	221	2	347	32	13	18	31	.367	0	0	4.79

Dave Hajek

Bats: Right **Throws:** Right **Pos:** 3B-2B **Ht:** 5'10" **Wt:** 165 **Born:** 10/14/67 **Age:** 30

Year Team	Lg Org	G	AB	H	2B	3B	HR	TB	R	RBI	TBB	IBB	SO	HBP	SH	SF	SB	CS	SB%	GDP	Avg	OBP	SLG
1990 Asheville	A Hou	135	498	155	28	0	6	201	86	60	61	1	50	2	6	10	43	24	.64	16	.311	.382	.404
1991 Osceola	A+ Hou	63	232	61	9	4	0	78	35	20	23	0	30	1	4	1	8	5	.62	5	.263	.331	.336
Jackson	AA Hou	37	94	18	6	0	0	24	10	9	7	2	12	0	0	1	2	0	1.00	1	.191	.245	.255
1992 Osceola	A+ Hou	5	18	2	1	0	0	3	3	1	1	0	1	0	0	0	1	0	1.00	0	.111	.158	.167
Jackson	AA Hou	103	326	88	12	3	1	109	36	18	31	2	25	0	10	3	8	3	.73	5	.270	.331	.334
1993 Jackson	AA Hou	110	332	97	20	2	5	136	50	27	17	2	14	2	1	3	6	5	.55	10	.292	.328	.410
1994 Tucson	AAA Hou	129	484	157	29	5	7	217	71	70	29	5	23	2	5	5	12	7	.63	10	.324	.362	.448
1995 Tucson	AAA Hou	131	502	164	37	4	4	221	99	79	39	7	27	2	5	6	12	7	.63	11	.327	.373	.440
1996 Tucson	AAA Hou	121	508	161	31	5	4	214	81	64	25	5	36	1	1	4	9	6	.60	17	.317	.348	.421
1997 Toledo	AAA Det	72	253	55	14	2	4	85	27	32	21	0	18	0	2	2	0	2	.00	7	.217	.275	.336
Las Vegas	AAA SD	41	156	53	14	1	0	69	25	25	14	1	6	0	0	1	7	2	.78	7	.340	.392	.442
1995 Houston	NL	5	2	0	0	0	0	0	0	0	1	0	1	0	2	0	1	0	1.00	0	.000	.333	.000
1996 Houston	NL	8	10	3	1	0	0	4	3	0	2	0	0	0	0	3	0	0	.00	3	.300	.417	.400
8 Min. YEARS		947	3403	1011	201	26	31	1357	523	405	268	25	242	10	34	36	108	61	.64	89	.297	.347	.399
2 Maj. YEARS		13	12	3	1	0	0	4	3	0	3	0	1	0	2	0	1	0	1.00	3	.250	.400	.333

John Halama

Pitches: Left **Bats:** Left **Pos:** P **Ht:** 6'5" **Wt:** 195 **Born:** 2/22/72 **Age:** 26

Year Team	Lg Org	G	GS	CG	GF	IP	BFP	H	R	ER	HR	SH	SF	HB	TBB	IBB	SO	WP	Bk	W	L	Pct.	ShO	Sv	ERA
1994 Auburn	A- Hou	6	3	0	3	28	107	18	5	4	1	2	0	0	5	0	27	1	1	4	1	.800	0	1	1.29
Quad City	A Hou	9	9	1	0	51.1	222	63	31	26	2	3	0	1	18	1	37	3	0	3	4	.429	1	0	4.56
1995 Quad City	A Hou	55	0	0	26	62.1	241	48	16	14	7	2	1	3	22	1	56	1	0	1	2	.333	0	2	2.02
1996 Jackson	AA Hou	27	27	0	0	162.2	691	151	77	58	10	7	7	8	59	0	110	7	0	9	10	.474	0	0	3.21
1997 New Orleans	AAA Hou	26	24	1	2	171	673	150	57	49	9	4	7	1	32	1	126	2	2	13	3	.813	0	0	2.58
4 Min. YEARS		123	63	2	31	475.1	1934	430	186	151	29	18	15	14	136	3	356	14	3	30	20	.600	1	3	2.86

Chad Hale

Pitches: Left **Bats:** Right **Pos:** P **Ht:** 6'6" **Wt:** 245 **Born:** 8/3/71 **Age:** 26

Year Team	Lg Org	G	GS	CG	GF	IP	BFP	H	R	ER	HR	SH	SF	HB	TBB	IBB	SO	WP	Bk	W	L	Pct.	ShO	Sv	ERA
1994 Lynchburg	A+ Bos	20	0	0	13	24.1	102	28	12	10	2	2	0	0	9	1	15	2	1	0	3	.000	0	1	3.70
1995 Michigan	A Bos	42	0	0	14	69	280	68	27	19	4	2	5	2	13	1	49	3	0	6	3	.667	0	2	2.48
1996 Sarasota	A+ Bos	42	0	0	19	60.2	260	56	33	21	2	2	5	1	17	1	37	2	3	3	0	1.000	0	7	3.12
1997 Trenton	AA Bos	3	0	0	1	4.1	22	5	5	4	1	0	0	0	5	0	2	0	0	0	0	.000	0	0	8.31
Kissimmee	A+ Hou	46	0	0	18	52.1	225	56	30	28	2	4	3	1	11	4	46	3	1	2	4	.333	0	7	4.82
4 Min. YEARS		153	0	0	65	210.2	889	213	107	82	11	10	13	4	55	7	149	10	5	11	10	.524	0	17	3.50

Billy Hall

Bats: Both **Throws:** Right **Pos:** 2B **Ht:** 5'9" **Wt:** 180 **Born:** 6/17/69 **Age:** 29

Year Team	Lg Org	G	AB	H	2B	3B	HR	TB	R	RBI	TBB	IBB	SO	HBP	SH	SF	SB	CS	SB%	GDP	Avg	OBP	SLG
1991 Chston-SC	A SD	72	279	84	6	5	2	106	41	24	34	1	54	0	0	2	25	9	.74	2	.301	.375	.380
1992 High Desert	A+ SD	119	495	176	22	5	2	214	92	39	54	2	77	1	1	3	49	27	.64	2	.356	.418	.432
1993 Wichita	AA SD	124	486	131	27	7	4	184	80	46	37	1	88	3	4	4	29	19	.60	6	.270	.323	.379
1994 Wichita	AA SD	29	111	40	5	1	1	50	14	12	11	1	19	1	0	0	10	5	.67	5	.360	.423	.450
Las Vegas	AAA SD	70	280	74	11	3	3	100	43	21	32	0	61	1	5	1	24	6	.80	2	.264	.341	.357
1995 Las Vegas	AAA SD	86	249	56	3	1	1	64	42	22	20	1	47	1	1	3	22	5	.81	3	.225	.282	.257
1996 Chattanooga	AA Cin	117	461	136	24	3	2	172	80	43	57	5	72	0	4	2	34	11	.76	9	.295	.371	.373
1997 Indianapolis	AAA Cin	10	20	4	0	0	0	4	3	3	3	0	6	0	1	0	0	0	.00	0	.200	.238	.200
Chattanooga	AA Cin	58	215	55	4	2	3	72	31	19	24	0	35	1	1	0	13	8	.62	9	.256	.335	.335
Colo Sprngs	AAA Col	13	51	13	0	2	0	17	6	6	3	0	11	0	0	0	3	1	.75	2	.255	.296	.333
New Haven	AA Col	17	59	13	2	1	1	20	8	7	7	0	10	0	0	0	7	1	.88	1	.220	.303	.339
7 Min. YEARS		715	2706	782	104	30	19	1003	440	246	280	11	480	8	17	15	216	92	.70	41	.289	.356	.371

Roy Halladay

Pitches: Right **Bats:** Right **Pos:** P **Ht:** 6'6" **Wt:** 200 **Born:** 5/14/77 **Age:** 21

Year Team	Lg Org	G	GS	CG	GF	IP	BFP	H	R	ER	HR	SH	SF	HB	TBB	IBB	SO	WP	Bk	W	L	Pct.	ShO	Sv	ERA
1995 Blue Jays	R Tor	10	8	0	1	50.1	203	35	25	19	4	2	0	1	16	0	48	9	2	3	5	.375	0	0	3.40
1996 Dunedin	A+ Tor	27	27	0	0	164.2	688	158	75	50	7	5	1	6	46	0	109	1	2	15	7	.682	2	0	2.73
1997 Knoxville	AA Tor	7	7	0	0	36.2	165	46	26	22	4	1	0	0	11	0	30	4	0	2	3	.400	0	0	5.40
Syracuse	AAA Tor	22	22	2	0	125.2	537	132	74	64	13	4	1	1	53	1	64	8	3	7	10	.412	2	0	4.58
3 Min. YEARS		66	64	4	1	377.1	1593	371	200	155	28	12	2	8	126	1	251	22	7	27	25	.519	4	0	3.70

Mike Halperin

Pitches: Left **Bats:** Left **Pos:** P **Ht:** 5'10" **Wt:** 170 **Born:** 9/8/73 **Age:** 24

Year Team	Lg Org	G	GS	CG	GF	IP	BFP	H	R	ER	HR	SH	SF	HB	TBB	IBB	SO	WP	Bk	W	L	Pct.	ShO	Sv	ERA
1994 St. Cathrns	A- Tor	9	1	0	5	24	86	11	5	3	0	0	1	0	5	0	19	2	0	2	1	.667	0	1	1.13
Hagerstown	A Tor	6	6	0	0	30	116	25	4	4	1	1	0	0	7	0	27	3	1	1	2	.667	0	0	1.20
1995 Dunedin	A+ Tor	14	12	0	0	69.2	298	70	36	28	4	1	0	3	29	1	63	2	0	3	5	.375	0	0	3.62
1996 Knoxville	AA Tor	28	28	0	0	155	658	156	67	60	6	8	2	6	71	3	112	11	4	13	7	.650	0	0	3.48

Year Team	Lg Org	G	GS	CG	GF	IP	BFP	H	R	ER	HR	SH	SF	HB	TBB	IBB	SO	WP	Bk	W	L	Pct.	ShO	Sv	ERA
		HOW MUCH HE PITCHED						WHAT HE GAVE UP												THE RESULTS					
1997 Calgary	AAA Pit	15	4	0	3	28	148	44	24	20	3	3	1	1	24	0	18	0	2	1	0	1.000	0	0	6.43
Carolina	AA Pit	17	17	0	0	93	419	102	54	40	8	1	1	.8	40	0	66	8	0	6	7	.462	0	0	3.87
4 Min. YEARS		89	68	0	8	399.2	1725	408	190	155	22	14	5	18	176	4	305	26	7	27	21	.563	0	1	3.49

Brandon Hammack   Ht: 6'5" Wt: 240 Born: 3/5/73 Age: 25

Pitches: Right Bats: Right Pos: P

Year Team	Lg Org	G	GS	CG	GF	IP	BFP	H	R	ER	HR	SH	SF	HB	TBB	IBB	SO	WP	Bk	W	L	Pct.	ShO	Sv	ERA
		HOW MUCH HE PITCHED						WHAT HE GAVE UP												THE RESULTS					
1995 Williamsprt	A- ChN	27	0	0	17	32.1	151	32	20	15	3	2	1	2	14	1	40	2	2	1	5	.167	0	6	4.18
1996 Rockford	A ChN	30	0	0	28	31.2	140	22	13	8	0	2	0	1	19	1	45	1	0	2	3	.400	0	13	2.27
Daytona	A+ ChN	27	0	0	25	31.1	132	27	10	8	1	4	2	0	10	0	36	0	0	2	1	.667	0	16	2.30
1997 Orlando	AA ChN	39	0	0	28	42	212	58	43	34	5	1	2	1	28	3	36	7	0	0	6	.000	0	8	7.29
Daytona	A+ ChN	16	0	0	7	19	89	25	11	5	0	2	1	0	7	0	20	2	1	2	3	.400	0	2	2.37
3 Min. YEARS		139	0	0	105	156.1	724	164	97	70	9	11	6	4	78	5	177	12	3	7	18	.280	0	44	4.03

Lee Hancock   Ht: 6'4" Wt: 220 Born: 6/27/67 Age: 31

Pitches: Left Bats: Left Pos: P

Year Team	Lg Org	G	GS	CG	GF	IP	BFP	H	R	ER	HR	SH	SF	HB	TBB	IBB	SO	WP	Bk	W	L	Pct.	ShO	Sv	ERA
		HOW MUCH HE PITCHED						WHAT HE GAVE UP												THE RESULTS					
1988 Bellingham	A- Sea	16	16	2	0	100.1	411	83	37	29	3	2	3	2	31	0	102	5	2	6	5	.545	0	0	2.60
1989 San Berndno	A+ Sea	26	26	5	0	173	720	131	69	50	5	5	3	5	82	2	119	11	2	12	7	.632	0	0	2.60
1990 Williamsprt	AA Sea	7	7	0	0	47	193	39	20	14	2	0	1	0	20	1	27	1	0	3	2	.600	0	0	2.68
Harrisburg	AA Pit	20	19	3	0	117.2	513	106	51	45	4	5	0	1	57	1	65	8	4	6	7	.462	1	0	3.44
Buffalo	AAA Pit	1	0	0	0	0	1	0	0	0	0	0	0	0	1	0	0	0	0	0	0	.000	0	0	0.00
1991 Carolina	AA Pit	37	11	0	10	98	420	93	48	41	3	5	3	2	42	4	66	8	0	4	7	.364	0	4	3.77
1992 Buffalo	AAA Pit	10	0	0	7	9	38	9	2	2	0	1	0	0	3	1	5	2	1	0	2	.000	0	0	2.00
Carolina	AA Pit	23	1	0	6	40.1	166	32	13	10	2	0	0	0	12	4	40	6	0	1	1	.500	0	0	2.23
1993 Carolina	AA Pit	25	11	0	3	99.2	409	87	42	28	3	2	1	4	32	2	85	5	0	7	3	.700	0	0	2.53
Buffalo	AAA Pit	11	11	0	0	66	278	73	38	36	4	4	3	0	14	0	30	2	0	2	6	.250	0	0	4.91
1994 Buffalo	AAA Pit	37	7	0	8	86.2	371	103	35	33	8	0	3	1	22	3	39	1	0	4	5	.444	0	1	3.43
1995 Calgary	AAA Pit	34	17	1	5	113.2	510	146	78	64	9	5	0	4	27	2	49	4	1	6	10	.375	0	0	5.07
1996 Calgary	AAA Pit	9	1	0	3	15	58	9	3	3	0	0	0	0	5	2	9	1	0	0	0	.000	0	0	1.80
Phoenix	AAA SF	17	3	0	6	35.1	159	42	19	17	0	4	1	0	12	0	19	4	0	0	2	.000	0	0	4.33
1997 Phoenix	AAA SF	7	0	0	1	10.1	53	23	7	7	0	0	0	0	4	0	9	0	0	0	1	.000	0	0	6.10
Orlando	AA ChN	3	2	0	0	4.1	32	12	13	8	3	1	1	0	4	0	2	2	0	0	2	.000	0	0	16.62
1995 Pittsburgh	NL	11	0	0	3	14	54	10	3	3	0	0	0	0	2	0	6	0	0	0	0	.000	0	0	1.93
1996 Pittsburgh	NL	13	0	0	3	18.1	89	21	18	13	5	1	0	2	10	3	13	1	0	0	0	.000	0	0	6.38
10 Min. YEARS		283	132	11	49	1016.1	4332	988	475	387	46	34	19	19	368	22	666	60	10	51	60	.459	1	5	3.43
2 Maj. YEARS		24	0	0	6	32.1	143	31	21	16	5	1	0	2	12	3	19	3	0	0	0	.000	0	0	4.45

Ryan Hancock   Ht: 6'2" Wt: 220 Born: 11/11/71 Age: 26

Pitches: Right Bats: Right Pos: P

Year Team	Lg Org	G	GS	CG	GF	IP	BFP	H	R	ER	HR	SH	SF	HB	TBB	IBB	SO	WP	Bk	W	L	Pct.	ShO	Sv	ERA
		HOW MUCH HE PITCHED						WHAT HE GAVE UP												THE RESULTS					
1993 Boise	A- Ana	3	3	0	0	16.1	69	14	9	6	1	0	0	0	8	1	18	0	0	1	0	1.000	0	0	3.31
1994 Lk Elsinore	A+ Ana	18	18	3	0	116.1	494	113	62	49	10	1	5	5	36	1	95	2	5	9	6	.600	1	0	3.79
Midland	AA Ana	8	8	0	0	48	219	63	34	31	1	1	1	6	11	0	35	0	2	3	4	.429	0	0	5.81
1995 Midland	AA Ana	28	28	5	0	175.2	764	222	107	89	17	5	4	8	45	1	79	7	3	12	9	.571	1	0	4.56
1996 Vancouver	AAA Ana	19	11	1	1	80.1	347	69	38	33	7	7	0	5	38	0	65	1	1	4	6	.400	0	0	3.70
1997 Vancouver	AAA Ana	39	2	0	18	74.1	330	72	37	30	4	2	1	3	36	1	60	1	1	3	3	.500	0	2	3.63
Las Vegas	AAA SD	4	0	0	1	5	25	9	7	7	1	0	1	0	4	0	3	0	0	0	0	.000	0	0	12.60
1996 California	AL	11	4	0	4	27.2	130	34	23	23	2	0	0	2	17	1	19	2	0	4	1	.800	0	0	7.48
5 Min. YEARS		119	70	9	20	516	2248	562	294	245	41	17	12	27	178	4	355	11	12	32	28	.533	2	2	4.27

Marcus Hanel   Ht: 6'4" Wt: 205 Born: 10/19/71 Age: 26

Bats: Right Throws: Right Pos: C

Year Team	Lg Org	G	AB	H	2B	3B	HR	TB	R	RBI	TBB	IBB	SO	HBP	SH	SF	SB	CS	SB%	GDP	Avg	OBP	SLG
		BATTING															BASERUNNING				PERCENTAGES		
1989 Pirates	R Pit	28	78	18	3	1	0	23	11	8	6	0	18	0	4	0	2	1	.67	2	.231	.286	.295
1990 Welland	A- Pit	40	98	15	2	0	0	17	5	8	5	2	26	1	0	0	1	2	.33	2	.153	.202	.173
1991 Augusta	A Pit	104	364	60	10	1	1	75	33	29	17	1	88	9	2	5	9	3	.75	8	.165	.218	.206
1992 Salem	A+ Pit	75	231	43	8	0	3	60	12	17	11	0	53	2	6	1	4	0	1.00	6	.186	.229	.260
1993 Salem	A+ Pit	69	195	36	6	2	2	52	18	16	18	2	65	4	9	2	5	3	.63	2	.185	.265	.267
1994 Salem	A+ Pit	87	286	70	9	1	5	96	36	27	14	0	54	6	5	3	3	2	.60	5	.245	.291	.336
1995 Salem	AA Pit	21	60	11	1	0	0	12	1	3	4	0	18	1	1	1	0	1	.00	1	.183	.242	.200
Lynchburg	A+ Pit	40	135	25	4	1	3	40	14	8	4	0	33	1	2	0	0	1	.00	1	.185	.214	.296
Calgary	AAA Pit	2	8	1	0	0	0	1	0	1	0	0	1	0	0	0	0	0	.00	0	.125	.125	.125
1996 Carolina	AA Pit	101	332	59	19	1	5	95	22	36	16	4	57	7	3	4	2	2	.50	9	.178	.228	.286
1997 Carolina	AA Pit	56	173	41	5	0	2	52	15	12	9	3	39	2	3	0	0	0	.00	5	.237	.283	.301
9 Min. YEARS		623	1960	379	67	7	21	523	168	164	104	12	452	33	35	16	26	15	.63	42	.193	.244	.267

Todd Haney

Bats: Right **Throws:** Right **Pos:** 2B **Ht:** 5' 9" **Wt:** 165 **Born:** 7/30/65 **Age:** 32

						BATTING												BASERUNNING				PERCENTAGES		
Year Team	Lg Org	G	AB	H	2B	3B	HR	TB	R	RBI	TBB	IBB	SO	HBP	SH	SF	SB	CS	SB%	GDP	Avg	OBP	SLG
1987 Bellingham	A- Sea	66	252	64	11	2	5	94	57	27	44	0	33	2	1	2	18	10	.64	1	.254	.367	.373
1988 Wausau	A Sea	132	452	127	23	2	7	175	66	52	56	0	54	7	8	2	35	10	.78	7	.281	.368	.387
1989 San Berndno	A+ Sea	25	107	27	5	0	0	32	10	7	7	0	14	0	0	1	2	3	.40	2	.252	.296	.299
Williamsprt	AA Sea	115	401	108	20	4	2	142	59	31	49	2	43	5	7	3	13	8	.62	7	.269	.354	.354
1990 Williamsprt	AA Sea	1	2	1	1	0	0	2	0	0	1	0	0	0	0	0	0	0	.00	1	.500	.667	1.000
Calgary	AAA Sea	108	419	142	15	6	1	172	81	36	37	1	38	4	6	0	16	11	.59	11	.339	.398	.411
1991 Indianaplos	AAA Mon	132	510	159	32	3	2	203	68	39	47	3	49	9	7	4	11	10	.52	7	.312	.377	.398
1992 Indianaplos	AAA Mon	57	200	53	14	0	6	85	30	33	37	0	34	1	3	2	1	0	1.00	7	.265	.379	.425
1993 Ottawa	AAA Mon	136	506	147	30	4	3	194	69	46	36	1	56	3	5	2	11	8	.58	15	.291	.340	.383
1994 Iowa	AAA ChN	83	305	89	22	1	3	122	48	35	28	0	29	8	3	2	9	6	.60	8	.292	.364	.400
1995 Iowa	AAA ChN	90	326	102	20	2	4	138	38	30	28	0	21	6	4	2	2	2	.50	17	.313	.376	.423
1996 Iowa	AAA ChN	66	240	59	13	0	2	78	20	19	19	0	24	0	6	2	3	1	.75	6	.246	.299	.325
1997 Tacoma	AAA Sea	4	17	6	4	0	0	10	3	2	2	0	2	0	0	0	0	0	.00	0	.353	.421	.588
New Orleans	AAA Hou	115	454	128	25	0	2	159	63	63	43	0	50	3	10	7	5	2	.71	10	.282	.343	.350
1992 Montreal	NL	7	10	3	1	0	0	4	0	1	0	0	1	0	0	0	0	0	.00	1	.300	.300	.400
1994 Chicago	NL	17	37	6	0	0	1	9	6	2	3	0	3	1	1	1	2	1	.67	0	.162	.238	.243
1995 Chicago	NL	25	73	30	8	0	2	44	11	6	7	0	11	0	1	0	0	0	.00	0	.411	.463	.603
1996 Chicago	NL	49	82	11	1	0	0	12	11	3	7	0	15	0	2	1	0	1	.00	1	.134	.200	.146
11 Min. YEARS		1130	4191	1212	235	24	37	1606	612	420	434	7	447	48	60	29	126	71	.64	94	.289	.360	.383
4 Maj. YEARS		98	202	50	10	0	3	69	28	12	17	0	29	1	5	2	3	1	.75	2	.248	.306	.342

Shawn Hare

Bats: Left **Throws:** Left **Pos:** OF **Ht:** 6' 1" **Wt:** 200 **Born:** 3/26/67 **Age:** 31

						BATTING												BASERUNNING				PERCENTAGES		
Year Team	Lg Org	G	AB	H	2B	3B	HR	TB	R	RBI	TBB	IBB	SO	HBP	SH	SF	SB	CS	SB%	GDP	Avg	OBP	SLG
1989 Lakeland	A+ Det	93	290	94	16	4	2	124	32	36	41	4	32	2	2	1	11	5	.69	7	.324	.410	.428
1990 Toledo	AAA Det	127	429	109	25	4	9	169	53	55	49	9	77	4	0	3	9	6	.60	10	.254	.334	.394
1991 London	AA Det	31	125	34	12	0	4	58	20	28	12	1	23	1	0	0	2	2	.50	5	.272	.341	.464
Toledo	AAA Det	80	252	78	18	2	9	127	44	42	30	1	53	2	1	5	1	2	.33	6	.310	.381	.504
1992 Toledo	AAA Det	57	203	67	12	2	5	98	31	34	31	2	28	0	0	4	6	1	.86	8	.330	.412	.483
1993 Toledo	AAA Det	130	470	124	29	3	20	219	81	76	34	5	90	2	0	5	8	4	.67	7	.264	.313	.466
1994 Toledo	AAA Det	29	99	30	6	0	5	51	19	9	17	0	28	2	0	0	5	2	.71	0	.303	.415	.515
Norfolk	AAA NYN	64	209	58	15	1	6	93	26	28	33	5	42	1	0	3	4	4	.50	2	.278	.374	.445
1995 Okla City	AAA Tex	68	238	63	13	3	4	94	27	30	23	2	47	4	1	1	3	1	.75	9	.265	.338	.395
1996 Louisville	AAA StL	15	49	8	1	0	1	12	3	1	3	0	11	0	0	0	1	0	1.00	2	.163	.212	.245
1997 Toledo	AAA Det	23	61	11	4	0	1	18	9	6	18	2	25	0	0	0	0	0	.00	0	.180	.367	.295
Columbus	AAA NYA	11	24	5	1	0	0	6	3	2	4	0	9	0	0	0	0	0	.00	0	.208	.321	.250
1991 Detroit	AL	9	19	1	1	0	0	2	0	0	2	0	1	0	0	0	0	0	.00	3	.053	.143	.105
1992 Detroit	AL	15	26	3	1	0	0	4	0	5	2	0	4	0	0	1	0	0	.00	0	.115	.172	.154
1994 New York	NL	22	40	9	1	1	0	12	7	2	4	0	11	0	0	0	0	0	.00	0	.225	.295	.300
1995 Texas	AL	18	24	6	1	0	0	7	2	2	4	0	6	0	0	0	0	0	.00	4	.250	.357	.292
9 Min. YEARS		728	2449	681	152	19	66	1069	348	347	295	31	465	18	4	22	50	27	.65	57	.278	.357	.437
4 Maj. YEARS		64	109	19	4	1	0	25	9	9	12	0	22	0	0	1	0	0	.00	8	.174	.254	.229

Tim Harikkala

Pitches: Right **Bats:** Right **Pos:** P **Ht:** 6' 2" **Wt:** 185 **Born:** 7/15/71 **Age:** 26

		HOW MUCH HE PITCHED						WHAT HE GAVE UP												THE RESULTS					
Year Team	Lg Org	G	GS	CG	GF	IP	BFP	H	R	ER	HR	SH	SF	HB	TBB	IBB	SO	WP	Bk	W	L	Pct.	ShO	Sv	ERA
1992 Bellingham	A- Sea	15	2	0	2	33.1	145	37	15	10	2	3	2	0	16	0	18	1	2	2	0	1.000	0	1	2.70
1993 Bellingham	A- Sea	4	0	0	0	8	30	3	1	1	0	0	0	1	2	0	12	0	0	1	0	1.000	0	0	1.13
Appleton	A Sea	15	4	0	5	38.2	175	50	30	28	3	2	1	2	12	2	33	4	3	3	3	.500	0	0	6.52
1994 Appleton	A Sea	13	13	3	0	93.2	373	69	31	20	6	2	3	5	24	0	63	5	0	8	3	.727	0	0	1.92
Riverside	A+ Sea	4	4	0	0	29	108	16	6	2	1	0	1	0	10	0	30	1	0	4	0	1.000	0	0	0.62
Jacksnville	AA Sea	9	9	0	0	54.1	245	70	30	24	4	1	3	1	19	0	22	4	0	4	1	.800	0	0	3.98
1995 Tacoma	AAA Sea	25	24	4	0	146.1	638	151	78	69	13	3	4	2	55	3	73	7	0	5	12	.294	1	0	4.24
1996 Tacoma	AAA Sea	27	27	1	0	158.1	715	204	98	85	12	3	6	5	48	2	115	5	1	8	12	.400	1	0	4.83
1997 Tacoma	AAA Sea	21	21	0	0	113.1	538	160	93	81	11	3	5	4	50	2	86	7	0	6	8	.429	0	0	6.43
Memphis	AA Sea	5	5	1	0	33.2	146	39	18	14	3	0	1	3	4	0	26	1	0	3	1	.750	0	0	3.74
1995 Seattle	AL	1	0	0	1	3.1	18	7	6	6	1	0	0	0	1	0	1	0	0	0	0	.000	0	0	16.20
1996 Seattle	AL	1	1	0	0	4.1	20	4	6	6	1	1	0	1	2	0	1	0	0	0	1	.000	0	0	12.46
6 Min. YEARS		138	109	9	7	708.2	3113	799	400	334	55	17	26	23	240	9	478	35	6	44	40	.524	2	1	4.24
2 Maj. YEARS		2	1	0	1	7.2	38	11	12	12	2	1	0	1	3	0	2	0	0	0	1	.000	0	0	14.09

Tim Harkrider

Bats: Both **Throws:** Right **Pos:** SS **Ht:** 6'0" **Wt:** 180 **Born:** 9/5/71 **Age:** 26

						BATTING												BASERUNNING				PERCENTAGES		
Year Team	Lg Org	G	AB	H	2B	3B	HR	TB	R	RBI	TBB	IBB	SO	HBP	SH	SF	SB	CS	SB%	GDP	Avg	OBP	SLG
1993 Boise	A- Ana	3	10	4	2	0	0	6	4	1	5	0	0	0	0	0	0	0	.00	0	.400	.600	.600
Cedar Rapds	A Ana	54	190	48	11	0	0	59	29	14	22	0	28	1	8	0	7	4	.64	5	.253	.333	.311
1994 Midland	AA Ana	112	409	111	20	1	1	136	69	49	64	2	51	5	17	5	13	12	.52	10	.271	.373	.333
1995 Midland	AA Ana	124	460	134	22	4	2	170	66	39	48	3	36	2	14	4	3	5	.38	7	.291	.358	.370
1997 Midland	AA Ana	69	251	72	12	3	1	93	39	24	22	0	17	0	7	4	1	2	.33	7	.287	.339	.371
4 Min. YEARS		362	1320	369	67	8	4	464	207	127	161	5	132	8	46	13	24	23	.51	29	.280	.358	.352

Denny Harriger

Pitches: Right **Bats:** Right **Pos:** P   **Ht:** 5'11" **Wt:** 185 **Born:** 7/21/69 **Age:** 28

Year Team	Lg Org	G	GS	CG	GF	IP	BFP	H	R	ER	HR	SH	SF	HB	TBB	IBB	SO	WP	Bk	W	L	Pct.	ShO	Sv	ERA
1987 Kingsport	R+ NYN	12	7	0	2	43.2	198	43	31	21	3	4	1	4	22	0	24	1	0	2	5	.286	0	0	4.33
1988 Kingsport	R+ NYN	13	13	2	0	92.1	375	83	35	22	3	1	1	0	24	1	59	2	1	7	2	.778	1	0	2.14
1989 Pittsfield	A- NYN	3	3	1	0	21	84	20	4	4	0	2	0	1	0	0	17	0	0	2	0	1.000	1	0	1.71
St. Lucie	A+ NYN	11	11	0	0	67.2	284	72	33	24	6	0	0	2	17	0	17	1	0	5	3	.625	0	0	3.19
1990 St. Lucie	A+ NYN	27	7	1	9	71.2	293	73	36	28	0	0	0	1	20	0	47	2	1	5	3	.625	0	2	3.52
1991 Columbia	A NYN	2	2	1	0	11	37	5	0	0	0	1	0	0	2	0	13	0	0	2	0	1.000	1	0	0.00
St. Lucie	A+ NYN	14	11	2	1	71.1	286	67	20	18	2	4	2	1	12	0	37	1	0	6	1	.857	2	0	2.27
1992 Binghamton	AA NYN	11	0	0	5	21.1	88	22	11	9	2	2	0	1	7	0	8	0	0	2	2	.500	0	0	3.80
St. Lucie	A+ NYN	27	10	0	9	88.1	372	89	30	22	1	6	0	3	14	1	65	5	1	7	3	.700	0	3	2.24
1993 Binghamton	AA NYN	35	24	4	4	170.2	716	174	69	56	8	6	2	7	40	0	89	9	1	13	10	.565	3	1	2.95
1994 Las Vegas	AAA SD	30	25	3	0	157.1	720	216	122	104	16	6	5	4	44	0	87	3	1	6	11	.353	0	0	5.95
1995 Las Vegas	AAA SD	29	28	7	0	177	776	187	94	80	12	6	5	4	60	2	97	4	1	9	9	.500	2	0	4.07
1996 Las Vegas	AAA SD	26	25	1	0	164.1	711	183	91	77	12	3	8	7	51	1	102	4	1	10	7	.588	0	0	4.22
1997 Toledo	AAA Det	27	27	2	0	167	717	159	87	74	19	5	1	5	63	2	109	3	0	11	8	.579	1	0	3.99
11 Min. YEARS		267	193	24	30	1324.2	5657	1393	663	539	84	46	25	40	376	7	771	35	7	87	64	.576	11	6	3.66

Bryan Harris

Pitches: Left **Bats:** Left **Pos:** P   **Ht:** 6'2" **Wt:** 205 **Born:** 9/11/71 **Age:** 26

Year Team	Lg Org	G	GS	CG	GF	IP	BFP	H	R	ER	HR	SH	SF	HB	TBB	IBB	SO	WP	Bk	W	L	Pct.	ShO	Sv	ERA
1993 Boise	A- Ana	16	16	1	0	105	419	80	29	22	4	1	0	8	29	1	96	5	3	8	3	.727	1	0	1.89
1994 Lk Elsinore	A+ Ana	26	26	5	0	168.1	719	157	94	71	12	5	6	8	62	1	149	14	2	10	10	.500	1	0	3.80
1995 Midland	AA Ana	39	4	0	10	78.1	359	105	50	43	9	4	3	4	32	1	60	9	2	6	5	.545	0	0	4.94
1996 Lk Elsinore	A+ Ana	20	2	0	7	37	164	29	20	18	3	3	3	2	26	1	31	5	4	0	7	.000	0	0	4.38
1997 Midland	AA Ana	10	1	0	4	18.1	98	28	26	23	3	0	1	4	15	0	15	1	2	0	2	.000	0	1	11.29
Lk Elsinore	A+ Ana	31	0	0	12	43	184	35	23	19	4	2	0	2	23	3	39	2	0	5	5	.500	0	0	3.98
5 Min. YEARS		142	49	6	33	450	1943	434	242	196	35	15	13	28	187	7	390	36	13	29	32	.475	1	1	3.92

D.J. Harris

Pitches: Right **Bats:** Right **Pos:** P   **Ht:** 5'10" **Wt:** 190 **Born:** 4/11/71 **Age:** 27

Year Team	Lg Org	G	GS	CG	GF	IP	BFP	H	R	ER	HR	SH	SF	HB	TBB	IBB	SO	WP	Bk	W	L	Pct.	ShO	Sv	ERA
1993 Pocatello	R+ —	5	0	0	4	7	40	14	10	5	0	0	0	0	3	0	10	7	0	0	0	.000	0	1	6.43
1994 Winnipeg	IND —	9	0	0	4	16.1	81	22	15	14	1	0	3	2	11	0	10	2	1	0	0	.000	0	1	7.71
1995 Dunedin	A+ Tor	42	0	0	16	67	294	54	29	24	6	3	3	6	41	1	56	2	0	3	3	.500	0	2	3.22
1996 Dunedin	A+ Tor	35	0	0	19	43.1	203	49	30	25	3	3	3	4	19	1	31	3	0	4	3	.571	0	6	5.19
1997 Dunedin	A+ Tor	42	3	0	24	78.1	344	64	41	28	5	1	2	4	45	4	66	7	4	8	4	.667	0	5	3.22
Knoxville	AA Tor	2	2	0	0	11	43	6	2	2	1	0	0	0	6	0	8	1	0	1	1	.500	0	0	1.64
5 Min. YEARS		135	5	0	67	223	1005	209	127	98	16	7	11	16	125	6	181	22	5	16	11	.593	0	15	3.96

Jeff Harris

Pitches: Right **Bats:** Right **Pos:** P   **Ht:** 6'1" **Wt:** 190 **Born:** 7/4/74 **Age:** 23

Year Team	Lg Org	G	GS	CG	GF	IP	BFP	H	R	ER	HR	SH	SF	HB	TBB	IBB	SO	WP	Bk	W	L	Pct.	ShO	Sv	ERA
1995 Elizabethtn	R+ Min	21	0	0	10	33	154	42	15	14	2	1	0	4	13	1	27	6	1	1	3	.250	0	0	3.82
1996 Ft. Wayne	A Min	42	0	0	15	89.2	387	90	35	31	4	3	8	4	33	1	85	10	1	8	3	.727	0	3	3.11
1997 Ft. Myers	A+ Min	24	0	0	6	42	164	30	11	10	4	3	1	0	15	2	32	1	0	2	4	.333	0	1	2.14
New Britain	AA Min	28	0	0	14	42.1	175	30	15	11	2	3	2	3	16	0	44	3	0	2	1	.667	0	3	2.34
3 Min. YEARS		115	0	0	45	207	880	192	76	66	12	10	11	11	77	4	188	20	2	13	11	.542	0	7	2.87

Brian Harrison

Pitches: Right **Bats:** Right **Pos:** P   **Ht:** 6'1" **Wt:** 175 **Born:** 12/18/68 **Age:** 29

Year Team	Lg Org	G	GS	CG	GF	IP	BFP	H	R	ER	HR	SH	SF	HB	TBB	IBB	SO	WP	Bk	W	L	Pct.	ShO	Sv	ERA
1992 Appleton	A KC	16	15	1	0	98.2	419	114	47	40	5	1	5	1	16	0	54	2	1	5	6	.455	0	0	3.65
1993 Wilmington	A+ KC	26	26	1	0	173	707	168	76	63	16	7	6	2	38	0	98	6	1	13	6	.684	1	0	3.28
1994 Memphis	AA KC	28	28	1	0	172	717	180	87	69	11	5	9	5	31	0	94	2	0	9	10	.474	0	0	3.61
1995 Omaha	AAA KC	16	8	1	1	54.1	248	76	39	37	7	3	3	1	10	0	12	1	0	4	2	.667	0	0	6.13
Wichita	AA KC	15	0	0	5	26.2	120	35	18	14	1	1	1	1	7	1	11	0	0	1	1	.500	0	2	4.73
1996 Wichita	AA KC	49	7	0	17	118	472	118	54	48	11	1	5	2	14	3	80	0	0	9	2	.818	0	6	3.66
1997 Omaha	AAA KC	30	29	4	0	178.1	783	208	114	100	20	0	9	10	55	0	83	6	0	10	12	.455	0	0	5.05
6 Min. YEARS		180	113	8	23	821	3466	899	435	371	71	18	38	22	171	4	432	17	2	51	39	.567	1	8	4.07

Tommy Harrison

Pitches: Right **Bats:** Right **Pos:** P   **Ht:** 6'2" **Wt:** 180 **Born:** 9/30/71 **Age:** 26

Year Team	Lg Org	G	GS	CG	GF	IP	BFP	H	R	ER	HR	SH	SF	HB	TBB	IBB	SO	WP	Bk	W	L	Pct.	ShO	Sv	ERA
1995 Durham	A+ Atl	7	6	0	0	37.2	145	22	5	4	1	0	0	1	13	1	25	0	0	3	1	.750	0	0	0.96
Greenville	AA Atl	14	14	1	0	88.1	370	87	50	43	9	7	1	2	27	3	57	5	0	6	4	.600	0	0	4.38
Richmond	AAA Atl	9	6	0	1	42	182	34	17	15	2	4	3	2	20	1	16	0	1	2	1	.667	0	0	3.21
1996 Richmond	AAA Atl	10	0	0	3	19	87	16	12	11	5	0	2	2	12	0	12	3	0	0	0	.000	0	0	5.21
Greenville	AA Atl	20	16	0	3	99.1	421	88	55	52	11	2	6	3	34	0	82	7	1	8	4	.667	0	0	4.71
1997 Richmond	AAA Atl	22	22	1	0	122	519	118	64	57	21	2	4	5	40	2	92	3	0	9	7	.563	0	0	4.20

		HOW MUCH HE PITCHED					WHAT HE GAVE UP												THE RESULTS					
Year Team	Lg Org	G	GS	CG	GF	IP	BFP	H	R	ER	HR	SH	SF	HB	TBB	IBB	SO	WP	Bk	W	L	Pct.	ShO	Sv	ERA
3 Min. YEARS		82	64	2	7	408.1	1724	365	203	182	49	15	16	15	146	7	284	18	2	28	17	.622	0	1	4.01

Robin Harriss

Bats: Right Throws: Right Pos: C   Ht: 6'1" Wt: 205 Born: 8/7/71 Age: 26

		BATTING															BASERUNNING				PERCENTAGES		
Year Team	Lg Org	G	AB	H	2B	3B	HR	TB	R	RBI	TBB	IBB	SO	HBP	SH	SF	SB	CS	SB%	GDP	Avg	OBP	SLG
1994 Watertown	A- Cle	49	168	41	5	0	4	58	19	25	16	0	16	1	3	4	1	0	1.00	5	.244	.307	.345
1995 Kinston	A+ Cle	15	49	12	3	1	2	23	8	6	3	0	8	0	1	1	0	0	.00	1	.245	.283	.469
Columbus	A Cle	51	179	40	6	0	2	52	18	18	11	0	30	3	3	0	0	3	.00	8	.223	.280	.291
1996 Kinston	A+ Cle	89	262	57	7	1	5	81	25	32	16	1	57	5	12	3	1	2	.33	8	.218	.273	.309
1997 Akron	AA Cle	49	146	39	8	0	1	50	24	17	20	0	36	0	7	2	0	1	.00	8	.267	.351	.342
4 Min. YEARS		253	804	189	29	2	14	264	94	98	66	1	147	9	26	10	2	6	.25	30	.235	.297	.328

Jason Hart

Pitches: Right Bats: Right Pos: P   Ht: 6'0" Wt: 195 Born: 11/14/71 Age: 26

		HOW MUCH HE PITCHED						WHAT HE GAVE UP												THE RESULTS					
Year Team	Lg Org	G	GS	CG	GF	IP	BFP	H	R	ER	HR	SH	SF	HB	TBB	IBB	SO	WP	Bk	W	L	Pct.	ShO	Sv	ERA
1994 Peoria	A ChN	20	0	0	10	37.1	149	29	17	15	4	1	1	0	7	0	33	3	0	4	2	.667	0	3	3.62
Daytona	A+ ChN	26	0	0	23	37.1	150	26	11	7	1	0	2	2	6	0	39	3	0	3	3	.500	0	12	1.69
1995 Daytona	A+ ChN	37	0	0	34	40.2	172	29	15	10	2	2	0	1	18	2	50	0	0	0	3	.000	0	24	2.21
Orlando	AA ChN	14	0	0	10	17	69	14	5	4	0	1	3	1	4	0	20	1	0	0	1	.000	0	3	2.12
1996 Orlando	AA ChN	51	0	0	22	73	300	59	29	26	11	2	0	1	28	4	78	5	0	3	5	.375	0	4	3.21
1997 Iowa	AAA ChN	1	0	0	0	1	6	1	2	2	0	0	0	0	2	0	3	0	0	0	1	.000	0	0	18.00
Orlando	AA ChN	14	0	0	7	17.2	75	20	13	13	3	0	2	0	2	1	21	2	0	0	1	.000	0	0	6.62
Thunder Bay	IND —	36	0	0	35	41.1	186	40	24	20	4	1	1	1	23	1	58	4	0	4	4	.500	0	16	4.35
4 Min. YEARS		199	0	0	141	265.1	1107	218	116	97	25	7	9	6	90	8	302	18	0	14	20	.412	0	62	3.29

Dean Hartgraves

Pitches: Left Bats: Right Pos: P   Ht: 6'0" Wt: 185 Born: 8/12/66 Age: 31

		HOW MUCH HE PITCHED						WHAT HE GAVE UP												THE RESULTS					
Year Team	Lg Org	G	GS	CG	GF	IP	BFP	H	R	ER	HR	SH	SF	HB	TBB	IBB	SO	WP	Bk	W	L	Pct.	ShO	Sv	ERA
1987 Auburn	A- Hou	23	0	0	12	31.2	157	31	24	14	1	3	0	1	27	4	42	1	0	0	5	.000	0	2	3.98
1988 Asheville	A Hou	34	13	2	7	118.1	523	131	70	59	9	2	8	5	47	2	83	8	5	5	9	.357	1	0	4.49
1989 Asheville	A Hou	19	19	4	0	120.1	542	140	66	55	6	5	3	4	49	2	87	5	3	5	8	.385	0	0	4.11
Osceola	A+ Hou	7	6	1	0	39.2	165	36	20	13	0	2	2	2	12	0	21	4	0	3	3	.500	1	0	2.95
1990 Columbus	AA Hou	33	14	0	6	99.2	454	108	66	52	8	7	4	3	48	1	64	6	0	8	8	.500	0	0	4.70
1991 Jackson	AA Hou	19	9	3	5	74	302	60	25	22	3	6	4	2	25	3	44	4	0	6	5	.545	0	0	2.68
Tucson	AAA Hou	16	3	1	4	43.2	189	47	17	15	2	2	3	0	20	1	18	2	0	3	0	1.000	1	0	3.09
1992 Tucson	AAA Hou	5	1	0	0	8	61	26	24	22	1	0	0	0	9	0	6	4	0	0	1	.000	0	0	24.75
Jackson	AA Hou	22	22	3	0	146.2	585	127	54	45	7	4	1	3	40	1	92	9	1	9	6	.600	2	0	2.76
1993 Tucson	AAA Hou	23	10	0	2	77.2	369	90	65	55	7	2	6	4	40	0	42	5	0	1	6	.143	0	0	6.37
1994 Tucson	AAA Hou	47	4	0	16	97.2	429	106	64	55	11	3	4	1	36	2	54	4	0	7	2	.778	0	3	5.07
1995 Tucson	AAA Hou	14	0	0	9	21.1	91	21	6	5	0	0	1	0	5	2	15	0	0	3	2	.600	0	5	2.11
1996 Tucson	AAA Hou	18	0	0	9	19	79	17	6	4	1	0	1	0	8	1	13	1	0	2	1	.667	0	4	1.89
Richmond	AAA Atl	4	0	0	1	8.2	32	4	2	2	1	0	0	1	2	0	8	0	0	0	0	.000	0	0	2.08
1997 Richmond	AAA Atl	50	0	0	16	72.1	324	76	38	36	6	9	4	1	39	3	56	0	0	7	4	.636	0	3	4.48
1995 Houston	NL	40	0	0	11	36.1	150	30	14	13	2	1	1	0	16	2	24	1	0	2	0	1.000	0	0	3.22
1996 Houston	NL	19	0	0	5	19	89	18	11	11	1	1	1	1	16	3	16	2	0	0	0	.000	0	0	5.21
Atlanta	NL	20	0	0	4	18.2	78	16	10	9	3	0	1	1	7	0	14	0	0	1	0	1.000	0	0	4.34
11 Min. YEARS		334	101	14	87	978.2	4302	1020	547	454	63	45	41	28	407	22	645	53	9	59	60	.496	5	17	4.18
2 Maj. YEARS		79	0	0	20	74	317	64	35	33	6	2	3	2	39	5	54	3	0	3	0	1.000	0	0	4.01

Chad Hartvigson

Pitches: Left Bats: Left Pos: P   Ht: 6'2" Wt: 195 Born: 12/15/70 Age: 27

		HOW MUCH HE PITCHED						WHAT HE GAVE UP												THE RESULTS					
Year Team	Lg Org	G	GS	CG	GF	IP	BFP	H	R	ER	HR	SH	SF	HB	TBB	IBB	SO	WP	Bk	W	L	Pct.	ShO	Sv	ERA
1994 Everett	A- SF	12	1	0	1	40.2	168	34	16	15	5	1	0	0	14	3	51	4	2	2	2	.500	0	0	3.32
1995 San Jose	A+ SF	32	7	0	8	84	357	85	38	33	4	6	3	0	24	1	63	3	1	4	4	.500	0	4	3.54
1996 San Jose	A+ SF	36	10	0	7	103	427	94	46	37	10	1	4	1	30	0	114	4	0	4	7	.364	0	2	3.23
1997 Bakersfield	A+ SF	5	4	0	0	27	103	22	9	9	2	1	1	1	5	0	22	1	0	1	1	.500	0	0	3.00
Shreveport	AA SF	4	1	1	1	12.2	53	11	8	5	3	0	0	0	5	0	9	2	0	1	0	1.000	0	0	3.55
Phoenix	AAA SF	17	4	0	4	53.2	238	63	34	32	4	1	1	2	17	0	52	2	1	2	2	.500	0	0	5.37
Okla City	AAA Tex	14	1	0	6	25.2	121	35	21	19	5	1	1	0	9	0	22	0	0	2	2	.500	0	2	6.66
4 Min. YEARS		120	28	1	27	346.2	1467	344	172	150	33	11	10	4	104	4	333	16	4	16	18	.471	0	8	3.89

Bryan Harvey

Pitches: Right Bats: Right Pos: P   Ht: 6'2" Wt: 212 Born: 6/2/63 Age: 35

		HOW MUCH HE PITCHED						WHAT HE GAVE UP												THE RESULTS					
Year Team	Lg Org	G	GS	CG	GF	IP	BFP	H	R	ER	HR	SH	SF	HB	TBB	IBB	SO	WP	Bk	W	L	Pct.	ShO	Sv	ERA
1985 Quad City	A Ana	30	0	0	17	81.2	345	66	37	32	5	5	2	2	37	0	111	4	0	5	6	.455	0	4	3.53
1986 Palm Spring	A+ Ana	43	0	0	29	57	244	38	24	17	1	4	5	3	38	6	68	2	0	3	4	.429	0	15	2.68
1987 Midland	AA Ana	43	0	0	36	53	225	40	14	12	1	0	4	0	28	5	78	10	0	2	2	.500	0	20	2.04
1988 Edmonton	AAA Ana	5	0	0	5	5.2	30	7	2	2	0	0	0	0	4	0	10	3	0	0	0	.000	0	2	3.18
1994 Brevard Cty	A+ Fla	7	1	0	2	6	22	2	1	1	0	0	0	0	2	0	6	3	0	0	0	.000	0	2	1.50
1997 Greenville	AA Atl	22	8	0	5	24.1	110	23	15	14	5	0	0	0	16	0	18	3	1	1	1	.500	0	0	5.18

Year Team	Lg Org	G	GS	CG	GF	IP	BFP	H	R	ER	HR	SH	SF	HB	TBB	IBB	SO	WP	Bk	W	L	Pct.	ShO	Sv	ERA
Brevard Cty	A+ Fla	4	4	0	0	11	48	11	9	6	2	0	0	2	1	0	11	2	1	0	1	.000	0	0	4.91
Charlotte	AAA Fla	2	0	0	0	1.1	4	0	0	0	0	0	0	0	0	0	0	0	0	0	0	.000	0	0	0.00
1987 California	AL	3	0	0	2	5	22	6	0	0	0	0	0	0	2	0	3	3	0	0	0	.000	0	0	0.00
1988 California	AL	50	0	0	38	76	303	59	22	18	4	3	3	1	20	6	67	4	1	7	5	.583	0	17	2.13
1989 California	AL	51	0	0	42	55	245	36	21	21	6	5	2	0	41	1	78	5	0	3	3	.500	0	25	3.44
1990 California	AL	54	0	0	47	64.1	267	45	24	23	4	4	4	0	35	6	82	7	1	4	4	.500	0	25	3.22
1991 California	AL	67	0	0	63	78.2	309	51	20	14	6	3	2	1	17	3	101	2	2	2	4	.333	0	46	1.60
1992 California	AL	25	0	0	22	28.2	122	22	12	9	4	2	3	0	11	1	34	4	0	0	4	.000	0	13	2.83
1993 Florida	NL	59	0	0	54	69	264	45	14	13	4	3	6	0	13	2	73	0	1	1	5	.167	0	45	1.70
1994 Florida	NL	12	0	0	10	10.1	47	12	6	6	1	0	0	0	4	0	10	0	0	0	0	.000	0	6	5.23
1995 Florida	NL	1	0	0	0	0	3	2	3	3	1	0	0	0	0	0	0	0	0	0	0	.000	0	0	0.00
6 Min. YEARS		156	20	0	94	240	1028	187	102	84	14	9	11	7	126	11	302	24	4	11	14	.440	0	41	3.15
9 Maj. YEARS		322	0	0	278	387	1582	278	122	107	30	20	20	2	144	19	448	25	5	17	25	.405	0	177	2.49

Derek Hasselhoff

Pitches: Right **Bats:** Right **Pos:** P   **Ht:** 6'2" **Wt:** 185 **Born:** 10/10/73 **Age:** 24

Year Team	Lg Org	G	GS	CG	GF	IP	BFP	H	R	ER	HR	SH	SF	HB	TBB	IBB	SO	WP	Bk	W	L	Pct.	ShO	Sv	ERA
1995 Elmira	R+ ChA	12	11	0	1	66.1	281	66	32	27	4	1	1	2	14	0	46	2	2	7	3	.700	0	0	3.66
1996 South Bend	A ChA	35	0	0	29	47.2	205	46	19	17	4	4	1	2	17	0	39	5	0	6	3	.667	0	10	3.21
Pr William	A+ ChA	5	0	0	4	10.1	49	14	7	6	1	0	0	0	6	2	9	0	0	0	1	.000	0	1	5.23
1997 Winston-Sal	A+ ChA	20	0	0	11	34.2	138	22	10	6	1	2	1	0	15	3	41	4	0	3	2	.600	0	3	1.56
Birmingham	AA ChA	18	0	0	10	33.2	141	35	10	9	3	0	1	1	11	0	22	1	0	5	2	.714	0	3	2.41
Nashville	AAA ChA	6	0	0	1	7.1	37	9	8	8	2	0	0	0	7	0	2	0	0	1	1	.500	0	0	9.82
3 Min. YEARS		96	11	0	56	200	851	192	86	73	15	7	4	5	70	5	159	12	2	22	12	.647	0	17	3.29

Lionel Hastings

Bats: Right **Throws:** Right **Pos:** 2B   **Ht:** 5'9" **Wt:** 175 **Born:** 1/26/73 **Age:** 25

Year Team	Lg Org	G	AB	H	2B	3B	HR	TB	R	RBI	TBB	IBB	SO	HBP	SH	SF	SB	CS	SB%	GDP	Avg	OBP	SLG
1994 Elmira	A- Fla	73	282	77	10	0	5	109	39	43	28	0	48	4	3	4	4	5	.44	3	.273	.343	.387
1995 Brevard Cty	A+ Fla	120	469	128	20	0	7	169	60	45	44	0	64	3	5	2	3	3	.50	14	.273	.338	.360
1996 Portland	AA Fla	97	293	68	12	1	6	100	30	44	15	2	50	8	10	1	5	2	.71	8	.232	.287	.341
1997 Portland	AA Fla	93	279	96	21	0	10	147	55	35	39	1	53	3	3	3	6	3	.67	6	.344	.426	.527
4 Min. YEARS		383	1323	369	70	1	28	525	184	167	126	3	215	18	21	10	18	13	.58	31	.279	.347	.397

Chris Hatcher

Bats: Right **Throws:** Right **Pos:** OF-DH   **Ht:** 6'3" **Wt:** 220 **Born:** 1/7/69 **Age:** 29

Year Team	Lg Org	G	AB	H	2B	3B	HR	TB	R	RBI	TBB	IBB	SO	HBP	SH	SF	SB	CS	SB%	GDP	Avg	OBP	SLG
1990 Auburn	A- Hou	72	254	64	10	0	9	101	37	45	27	3	86	5	0	5	8	2	.80	4	.247	.324	.390
1991 Burlington	A Hou	129	497	117	23	6	13	191	69	65	46	4	180	9	0	4	10	5	.67	6	.235	.309	.384
1992 Osceola	A+ Hou	97	367	103	19	6	17	185	49	68	20	1	97	5	0	5	11	0	1.00	5	.281	.322	.504
1993 Jackson	AA Hou	101	367	95	15	3	15	161	45	64	11	0	104	11	0	3	5	8	.38	6	.259	.298	.439
1994 Tucson	AAA Hou	108	349	104	28	4	12	176	55	73	19	0	90	4	0	6	5	1	.83	6	.298	.336	.504
1995 Jackson	AA Hou	11	39	12	1	0	1	16	5	3	4	0	6	1	0	1	2	0	.00	1	.308	.378	.410
Tucson	AAA Hou	94	290	83	19	2	14	148	59	50	42	2	107	4	1	2	7	3	.70	9	.286	.382	.510
1996 Jackson	AA Hou	41	156	48	9	1	13	98	29	36	9	2	39	4	0	1	2	1	.67	5	.308	.359	.628
Tucson	AAA Hou	95	348	105	21	4	18	188	53	61	14	1	87	5	0	5	10	8	.56	9	.302	.333	.540
1997 Wichita	AA KC	11	42	11	0	0	5	26	7	7	4	0	16	1	0	0	1	0	1.00	0	.262	.340	.619
Omaha	AAA KC	68	222	51	9	0	11	93	34	24	17	2	68	6	0	3	0	1	.00	4	.230	.298	.419
8 Min. YEARS		827	2936	793	154	26	128	1383	442	496	213	15	880	55	1	35	59	31	.66	57	.270	.328	.471

Ryan Hawblitzel

Pitches: Right **Bats:** Right **Pos:** P   **Ht:** 6'2" **Wt:** 185 **Born:** 4/30/71 **Age:** 27

Year Team	Lg Org	G	GS	CG	GF	IP	BFP	H	R	ER	HR	SH	SF	HB	TBB	IBB	SO	WP	Bk	W	L	Pct.	ShO	Sv	ERA
1990 Huntington	R+ ChN	14	14	2	0	75.2	322	72	38	33	8	0	6	4	25	0	71	2	0	6	5	.545	1	0	3.93
1991 Winston-Sal	A+ ChN	20	20	5	0	134	552	110	40	34	7	5	7	7	47	0	103	8	1	15	2	.882	2	0	2.28
Charlotte	AA ChN	5	5	1	0	33.2	141	31	14	12	2	5	2	3	12	3	25	0	0	1	2	.333	1	0	3.21
1992 Charlotte	AA ChN	28	28	3	0	174.2	727	180	84	73	18	5	5	4	38	3	119	8	0	12	8	.600	1	0	3.76
1993 Colo Sprngs	AAA Col	29	28	2	0	165.1	764	221	129	113	16	10	9	4	49	0	90	3	0	8	13	.381	0	0	6.15
1994 Colo Sprngs	AAA Col	28	28	3	0	163	732	200	119	111	21	6	2	10	53	2	103	5	0	10	10	.500	1	0	6.13
1995 Colo Sprngs	AAA Col	21	14	0	1	83	352	88	47	42	7	3	5	3	17	1	40	2	0	5	3	.625	0	0	4.55
1996 Colo Sprngs	AAA Col	26	18	0	5	117	501	131	76	65	17	4	4	5	27	2	75	2	0	7	6	.538	0	1	5.00
1997 Scranton-WB	AAA Phi	34	15	1	9	115.1	498	132	65	64	16	3	4	4	33	3	80	1	0	6	9	.400	1	2	4.99
1996 Colorado	NL	8	0	0	3	15	69	18	12	10	2	0	1	0	6	0	7	1	0	0	1	.000	0	0	6.00
8 Min. YEARS		205	170	17	15	1061.2	4589	1165	612	547	112	41	38	46	301	14	706	31	1	70	58	.547	7	3	4.64

Kraig Hawkins

Bats: Right **Throws:** Right **Pos:** OF   **Ht:** 6'2" **Wt:** 170 **Born:** 12/4/71 **Age:** 26

Year Team	Lg Org	G	AB	H	2B	3B	HR	TB	R	RBI	TBB	IBB	SO	HBP	SH	SF	SB	CS	SB%	GDP	Avg	OBP	SLG
1992 Oneonta	A- NYA	70	227	50	1	0	0	51	24	18	26	0	67	1	7	0	14	5	.74	1	.220	.303	.225
1993 Greensboro	A NYA	131	418	106	13	1	0	121	66	45	67	1	112	1	9	3	67	18	.79	8	.254	.356	.289

		BATTING																BASERUNNING				PERCENTAGES		
Year Team	Lg Org	G	AB	H	2B	3B	HR	TB	R	RBI	TBB	IBB	SO	HBP	SH	SF	SB	CS	SB%	GDP	Avg	OBP	SLG
1994 Tampa	A+ NYA	108	437	104	7	1	0	113	72	29	61	0	105	2	3	0	37	19	.66	6	.238	.334	.259
1995 Norwich	AA NYA	12	45	10	0	0	0	10	5	3	7	0	11	0	2	0	7	2	.78	0	.222	.327	.222
Tampa	A+ NYA	111	432	105	9	3	1	123	56	19	66	0	95	2	11	1	28	14	.67	6	.243	.345	.285
1996 Tampa	A+ NYA	75	268	80	2	5	1	95	41	21	35	0	41	2	9	1	13	6	.68	2	.299	.382	.354
1997 Norwich	AA NYA	51	188	49	6	1	0	57	36	16	26	0	37	1	3	2	12	2	.86	1	.261	.350	.303
Tampa	A+ NYA	9	30	9	1	0	0	10	2	4	8	0	2	0	0	0	3	2	.60	1	.300	.447	.333
6 Min. YEARS		567	2045	513	39	11	2	580	302	155	296	1	470	9	44	7	181	68	.73	25	.251	.347	.284

Heath Haynes

Pitches: Right Bats: Right Pos: P Ht: 6'0" Wt: 175 Born: 11/30/68 Age: 29

		HOW MUCH HE PITCHED						WHAT HE GAVE UP												THE RESULTS					
Year Team	Lg Org	G	GS	CG	GF	IP	BFP	H	R	ER	HR	SH	SF	HB	TBB	IBB	SO	WP	Bk	W	L	Pct.	ShO	Sv	ERA
1991 Jamestown	A- Mon	29	0	0	23	56.1	221	31	15	13	3	5	1	4	18	4	93	4	3	10	1	.909	0	11	2.08
1992 Rockford	A Mon	45	0	0	36	57	239	49	19	12	0	4	1	4	15	3	78	1	3	3	1	.750	0	15	1.89
Harrisburg	AA Mon	3	0	0	1	4.2	17	2	1	1	1	0	0	0	1	0	6	0	0	2	0	1.000	0	0	1.93
1993 Harrisburg	AA Mon	57	0	0	22	66	270	46	27	19	2	5	3	2	19	4	78	4	2	8	0	1.000	0	5	2.59
1994 Ottawa	AA Mon	56	0	0	25	87	350	72	32	23	7	7	2	1	15	7	75	3	0	6	7	.462	0	4	2.38
1995 Edmonton	AAA Oak	12	0	0	1	18.2	87	21	14	13	1	0	3	0	11	3	13	2	0	2	0	1.000	0	0	6.27
1996 Lk Elsinore	A+ Ana	31	0	0	11	38.1	142	29	9	7	1	1	0	3	2	0	44	1	1	5	1	.833	0	2	1.64
1997 Trenton	AA Bos	14	0	0	3	26.2	116	26	8	7	2	1	0	2	8	3	26	0	1	1	1	.500	0	2	2.36
New Haven	AA Col	5	0	0	1	8	31	7	1	1	0	0	0	0	1	0	5	0	0	0	0	.000	0	1	1.13
Portland	AA Fla	28	0	0	11	38	163	36	16	16	4	3	2	3	7	4	39	0	1	4	0	1.000	0	1	3.79
1994 Montreal	NL	4	0	0	2	3.2	17	3	1	0	0	0	0	1	3	0	1	0	0	0	0	.000	0	0	0.00
7 Min. YEARS		280	0	0	134	400.2	1632	319	142	112	21	26	12	19	97	28	460	15	11	41	11	.788	0	40	2.52

Steve Hazlett

Bats: Right Throws: Right Pos: OF Ht: 5'11" Wt: 190 Born: 3/30/70 Age: 28

		BATTING																BASERUNNING				PERCENTAGES		
Year Team	Lg Org	G	AB	H	2B	3B	HR	TB	R	RBI	TBB	IBB	SO	HBP	SH	SF	SB	CS	SB%	GDP	Avg	OBP	SLG
1991 Elizabethtn	R+ Min	64	210	42	11	0	4	65	50	24	63	0	53	6	1	1	13	7	.65	0	.200	.396	.310
1992 Kenosha	A Min	107	362	96	23	4	6	145	68	32	52	0	77	7	2	4	20	9	.69	5	.265	.365	.401
1993 Ft. Myers	A+ Min	29	115	39	5	2	0	48	19	6	15	1	21	1	2	0	12	5	.71	0	.339	.420	.417
1994 Nashville	AA Min	123	457	134	31	1	14	209	63	54	37	1	99	8	6	3	9	3	.75	3	.293	.354	.457
1995 Salt Lake	AAA Min	127	427	128	25	6	4	177	71	49	41	1	65	4	2	3	8	10	.44	9	.300	.364	.415
1996 Salt Lake	AAA Min	101	301	61	14	4	10	113	44	41	33	1	85	5	2	5	7	2	.78	5	.203	.288	.375
1997 Carolina	AA Pit	45	153	36	7	3	2	55	22	17	14	0	31	4	0	1	1	6	.14	2	.235	.316	.359
Calgary	AAA Pit	37	94	28	12	2	3	53	18	15	12	2	19	2	1	1	0	1	1.00	1	.298	.385	.564
7 Min. YEARS		633	2119	564	128	22	43	865	355	238	267	6	450	37	16	17	71	42	.63	26	.266	.356	.408

Mike Heathcott

Pitches: Right Bats: Right Pos: P Ht: 6'3" Wt: 180 Born: 5/16/69 Age: 29

		HOW MUCH HE PITCHED						WHAT HE GAVE UP												THE RESULTS					
Year Team	Lg Org	G	GS	CG	GF	IP	BFP	H	R	ER	HR	SH	SF	HB	TBB	IBB	SO	WP	Bk	W	L	Pct.	ShO	Sv	ERA
1991 Utica	A- ChA	6	6	0	0	33	138	26	19	14	4	1	1	4	14	0	14	1	0	3	1	.750	0	0	3.55
1992 South Bend	A ChA	15	14	0	1	82	340	67	28	14	3	5	2	0	32	0	49	8	0	9	5	.643	0	0	1.54
1993 Sarasota	A+ ChA	26	26	6	0	179.1	739	174	90	72	5	12	10	4	62	7	83	16	1	11	10	.524	1	0	3.61
1994 Birmingham	AA ChA	17	17	0	0	98	449	126	71	63	11	1	6	2	44	4	44	9	0	3	7	.300	0	0	5.79
Pr William	A+ ChA	9	8	1	1	43	193	51	28	19	7	1	0	1	23	0	27	6	0	1	2	.333	0	0	3.98
1995 Pr William	A+ ChA	27	14	1	0	88.2	387	96	56	46	8	2	7	2	36	3	68	18	0	4	9	.308	0	3	4.67
1996 Birmingham	AA ChA	23	23	1	0	147.2	625	138	72	66	9	5	5	4	55	3	108	5	0	11	8	.579	0	0	4.02
1997 Nashville	AAA ChA	17	0	0	7	27	129	39	23	22	5	1	0	0	12	0	23	6	0	2	3	.400	0	0	7.33
Birmingham	AA ChA	30	1	0	12	59	247	50	20	12	2	3	0	1	25	0	47	3	0	3	1	.750	0	7	1.83
7 Min. YEARS		170	109	9	25	757.2	3247	767	407	327	54	31	31	15	303	17	463	72	1	47	46	.505	1	10	3.88

Doug Hecker

Pitches: Right Bats: Right Pos: P Ht: 6'4" Wt: 210 Born: 1/21/71 Age: 27

		HOW MUCH HE PITCHED						WHAT HE GAVE UP												THE RESULTS					
Year Team	Lg Org	G	GS	CG	GF	IP	BFP	H	R	ER	HR	SH	SF	HB	TBB	IBB	SO	WP	Bk	W	L	Pct.	ShO	Sv	ERA
1995 Visalia	A+ Bos	2	0	0	2	2	9	1	1	0	1	0	1	1	1	0	2	1	0	0	0	.000	0	0	0.00
Red Sox	R Bos	2	0	0	1	1.2	11	4	2	1	0	0	0	0	0	4	4	0	0	0	0	.000	0	0	5.40
Sarasota	A+ Bos	10	1	0	2	21	96	24	9	8	0	1	1	1	7	0	16	4	1	1	2	.333	0	1	3.43
1996 Sarasota	A+ Bos	26	3	0	15	41.2	180	46	25	23	0	3	1	1	12	0	39	3	3	2	2	.500	0	6	4.97
Trenton	AA Bos	13	0	0	7	20	82	18	5	5	1	2	2	1	5	2	12	2	0	0	1	.000	0	2	2.25
1997 Red Sox	R Bos	1	0	0	0	1	4	0	0	0	0	0	0	0	1	0	1	0	0	0	0	.000	0	0	0.00
Trenton	AA Bos	4	0	0	1	7	34	5	2	2	0	0	0	0	9	1	7	0	0	1	0	1.000	0	0	2.57
Stockton	A+ Mil	12	0	0	3	17	70	12	9	8	1	3	0	0	8	0	11	0	2	1	0	.000	0	0	4.24
3 Min. YEARS		70	4	0	31	111.1	486	110	53	47	2	9	5	4	43	3	92	10	6	4	6	.400	0	9	3.80

Bronson Heflin

Pitches: Right Bats: Right Pos: P Ht: 6'3" Wt: 200 Born: 8/29/71 Age: 26

		HOW MUCH HE PITCHED						WHAT HE GAVE UP												THE RESULTS					
Year Team	Lg Org	G	GS	CG	GF	IP	BFP	H	R	ER	HR	SH	SF	HB	TBB	IBB	SO	WP	Bk	W	L	Pct.	ShO	Sv	ERA
1994 Batavia	A- Phi	14	13	1	0	83	353	85	38	33	5	5	0	6	20	0	71	11	2	6	5	.545	0	0	3.58
1995 Clearwater	A+ Phi	57	0	0	44	61	256	52	25	20	3	6	1	0	21	5	84	4	0	2	3	.400	0	21	2.95
Reading	AA Phi	1	0	0	1	1	4	0	0	0	0	0	0	0	1	0	2	0	0	0	0	.000	0	0	0.00

Year Team	Lg Org	G	GS	CG	GF	IP	BFP	H	R	ER	HR	SH	SF	HB	TBB	IBB	SO	WP	Bk	W	L	Pct.	ShO	Sv	ERA
1996 Reading	AA Phi	25	0	0	12	29.1	139	37	20	17	3	2	0	2	15	2	27	2	0	2	2	.500	0	1	5.22
Scranton-WB	AAA Phi	30	0	0	27	38	140	25	11	11	4	0	3	-1	3	1	23	1	0	4	0	1.000	0	12	2.61
1997 Scranton-WB	AAA Phi	35	0	0	27	43.1	185	29	17	11	3	2	1	0	25	2	36	2	0	1	1	.500	0	13	2.28
1996 Philadelphia	NL	3	0	0	2	6.2	34	11	7	5	1	0	1	0	3	0	4	0	0	0	0	.000	0	0	6.75
4 Min. YEARS		162	13	1	111	255.2	1077	228	111	92	18	15	5	9	85	10	243	20	2	15	11	.577	0	47	3.24

Rick Heiserman

Pitches: Right **Bats:** Right **Pos:** P   **Ht:** 6'7" **Wt:** 220 **Born:** 2/22/73 **Age:** 25

Year Team	Lg Org	G	GS	CG	GF	IP	BFP	H	R	ER	HR	SH	SF	HB	TBB	IBB	SO	WP	Bk	W	L	Pct.	ShO	Sv	ERA
1994 Watertown	A- Cle	7	0	0	2	11.2	48	6	3	3	0	1	1	1	5	0	6	2	2	1	0	1.000	0	0	2.31
1995 Kinston	A+ Cle	19	19	1	0	113	470	97	55	47	13	3	4	9	42	1	86	6	1	9	3	.750	0	0	3.74
St. Pete	A+ StL	6	5	0	1	28	118	28	18	17	2	0	2	1	11	0	18	4	0	2	3	.400	0	0	5.46
1996 St. Pete	A+ StL	26	26	1	0	155.1	663	168	68	56	8	6	3	9	41	0	104	4	0	10	8	.556	1	0	3.24
1997 Arkansas	AA StL	34	20	1	9	131.2	569	151	73	61	19	6	2	8	36	2	90	8	0	5	8	.385	1	4	4.17
Louisville	AAA StL	1	0	0	1	2	10	2	1	1	1	0	0	0	1	0	0	0	0	0	0	.000	0	0	4.50
4 Min. YEARS		93	70	3	13	441.2	1878	452	218	185	43	15	12	28	136	3	304	24	3	27	22	.551	2	4	3.77

Dan Held

Bats: Right **Throws:** Right **Pos:** 1B   **Ht:** 6'0" **Wt:** 200 **Born:** 10/7/70 **Age:** 27

Year Team	Lg Org	G	AB	H	2B	3B	HR	TB	R	RBI	TBB	IBB	SO	HBP	SH	SF	SB	CS	SB%	GDP	Avg	OBP	SLG
1993 Batavia	A- Phi	45	151	31	8	1	3	50	18	16	16	0	40	6	1	1	2	3	.40	3	.205	.303	.331
1994 Spartanburg	A Phi	130	484	123	32	1	18	211	69	69	52	2	119	9	1	11	2	0	1.00	11	.254	.331	.436
1995 Clearwater	A+ Phi	134	489	133	35	1	21	233	82	82	56	1	127	19	1	4	2	1	.67	13	.272	.366	.476
Reading	AA Phi	2	4	2	1	0	1	6	2	3	2	0	1	0	0	0	1	0	1.00	0	.500	.667	1.500
1996 Reading	AA Phi	136	497	121	17	5	26	226	77	92	60	4	141	22	0	6	3	8	.27	10	.243	.347	.455
Scranton-WB	AAA Phi	4	14	0	0	0	0	0	1	0	1	0	6	1	0	0	0	0	.00	0	.000	.125	.000
1997 Reading	AA Phi	138	525	143	31	4	26	260	80	86	42	1	116	18	0	4	1	3	.25	14	.272	.345	.495
5 Min. YEARS		589	2164	553	124	12	95	986	329	348	229	8	550	75	3	27	11	15	.42	51	.256	.343	.456

Eric Helfand

Bats: Left **Throws:** Right **Pos:** C   **Ht:** 6'0" **Wt:** 195 **Born:** 3/25/69 **Age:** 29

Year Team	Lg Org	G	AB	H	2B	3B	HR	TB	R	RBI	TBB	IBB	SO	HBP	SH	SF	SB	CS	SB%	GDP	Avg	OBP	SLG
1990 Sou. Oregon	A- Oak	57	207	59	12	0	2	77	29	39	20	1	49	7	0	1	4	0	1.00	3	.285	.366	.372
1991 Modesto	A+ Oak	67	242	62	15	1	7	100	35	38	37	2	56	2	2	2	0	1	.00	6	.256	.357	.413
1992 Modesto	A+ Oak	72	249	72	15	0	10	117	40	44	47	4	46	6	1	3	0	0	.00	5	.289	.410	.470
Huntsville	AA Oak	37	114	26	7	0	2	39	13	9	5	0	32	1	0	0	0	0	.00	4	.228	.267	.342
1993 Huntsville	AA Oak	100	302	69	15	2	10	118	38	48	43	2	78	8	3	1	1	1	.50	5	.228	.333	.391
1994 Tacoma	AAA Oak	57	178	36	10	0	2	52	22	25	23	2	37	2	1	3	0	0	.00	3	.202	.296	.292
1995 Edmonton	AAA Oak	19	56	12	4	2	1	23	5	12	9	1	10	0	5	1	0	1	.00	0	.214	.318	.411
1996 Buffalo	AAA Cle	90	258	54	10	0	5	79	31	22	46	8	51	11	3	2	0	3	.00	4	.209	.350	.306
1997 Las Vegas	AAA SD	80	238	75	21	1	6	116	31	33	28	1	47	6	2	1	1	1	.50	9	.315	.401	.487
1993 Oakland	AL	8	13	3	0	0	0	3	1	1	0	0	3	0	0	0	0	0	.00	0	.231	.231	.231
1994 Oakland	AL	7	6	1	0	0	0	1	1	1	0	0	1	0	0	0	0	0	.00	0	.167	.167	.167
1995 Oakland	AL	38	86	14	2	1	1	18	9	7	11	0	25	1	4	3	0	0	.00	2	.163	.265	.209
8 Min. YEARS		579	1844	465	109	6	45	721	244	270	258	21	406	43	17	19	6	8	.43	40	.252	.354	.391
3 Maj. YEARS		53	105	18	2	1	1	22	11	9	11	0	27	1	3	0	0	0	.00	2	.171	.256	.210

Wes Helms

Bats: Right **Throws:** Right **Pos:** 3B   **Ht:** 6'4" **Wt:** 210 **Born:** 5/12/76 **Age:** 22

Year Team	Lg Org	G	AB	H	2B	3B	HR	TB	R	RBI	TBB	IBB	SO	HBP	SH	SF	SB	CS	SB%	GDP	Avg	OBP	SLG
1994 Braves	R Atl	56	184	49	15	1	4	78	22	29	22	0	36	4	0	1	6	1	.86	3	.266	.355	.424
1995 Macon	A Atl	136	539	149	32	1	11	216	89	85	50	0	107	10	0	3	2	2	.50	8	.276	.347	.401
1996 Durham	A+ Atl	67	258	83	19	2	13	145	40	54	12	0	51	7	0	1	1	1	.50	7	.322	.367	.562
Greenville	AA Atl	64	231	59	13	2	4	88	24	22	13	2	48	4	1	0	2	1	.67	6	.255	.306	.381
1997 Richmond	AAA Atl	32	110	21	4	0	3	34	11	15	10	1	34	5	0	1	1	1	.50	4	.191	.286	.309
Greenville	AA Atl	86	314	93	14	1	11	142	50	44	33	2	50	6	0	3	3	4	.43	14	.296	.371	.452
4 Min. YEARS		441	1636	454	97	7	46	703	236	249	140	5	326	36	1	9	15	10	.60	42	.278	.346	.430

Bret Hemphill

Bats: Both **Throws:** Right **Pos:** C   **Ht:** 6'3" **Wt:** 210 **Born:** 12/17/71 **Age:** 26

Year Team	Lg Org	G	AB	H	2B	3B	HR	TB	R	RBI	TBB	IBB	SO	HBP	SH	SF	SB	CS	SB%	GDP	Avg	OBP	SLG
1994 Boise	A- Ana	71	252	74	16	1	3	101	44	36	40	2	53	1	1	6	1	1	.50	6	.294	.385	.401
1995 Lk Elsinore	A+ Ana	45	146	29	7	0	1	39	12	17	18	0	36	3	0	3	2	1	.67	4	.199	.294	.267
Cedar Rapds	A Ana	72	234	59	11	1	8	96	36	28	21	0	54	4	1	4	0	2	.00	7	.252	.319	.410
1996 Lk Elsinore	A+ Ana	108	399	105	21	3	17	183	64	64	52	1	93	4	6	1	4	3	.57	7	.263	.353	.459
1997 Midland	AA Ana	78	266	82	15	2	10	131	46	63	47	2	56	6	1	5	0	2	.00	6	.308	.417	.492
4 Min. YEARS		374	1297	349	70	7	39	550	202	208	178	5	292	18	9	19	7	9	.44	30	.269	.360	.424

Rod Henderson

Pitches: Right Bats: Right Pos: P   Ht: 6'4" Wt: 193 Born: 3/11/71 Age: 27

Year Team	Lg Org	G	GS	CG	GF	IP	BFP	H	R	ER	HR	SH	SF	HB	TBB	IBB	SO	WP	Bk	W	L	Pct.	ShO	Sv	ERA
1992 Jamestown	A- Mon	1	1	0	0	3	13	2	3	2	0	0	0	0	5	0	2	0	0	0	0	.000	0	0	6.00
1993 Wst Plm Bch	A+ Mon	22	22	1	0	143	580	110	50	46	3	4	5	6	44	0	127	8	6	12	7	.632	1	0	2.90
Harrisburg	AA Mon	5	5	0	0	29.2	125	20	10	6	0	1	0	0	15	0	25	2	1	5	0	1.000	0	0	1.82
1994 Harrisburg	AA Mon	2	2	0	0	12	44	5	2	2	1	0	0	0	4	0	16	0	0	2	0	1.000	0	0	1.50
Ottawa	AAA Mon	23	21	0	1	122.2	545	123	67	63	16	2	5	2	67	3	100	1	0	6	9	.400	0	0	4.62
1995 Harrisburg	AA Mon	12	12	0	0	56.1	240	51	28	27	4	0	1	5	18	0	53	1	0	3	6	.333	0	0	4.31
1996 Ottawa	AAA Mon	25	23	3	0	121.1	528	117	75	70	12	1	4	4	52	1	83	2	0	4	11	.267	0	0	5.19
1997 Ottawa	AAA Mon	26	20	3	2	123.2	542	136	72	68	18	4	2	6	49	3	103	6	0	5	9	.357	1	1	4.95
1994 Montreal	NL	3	2	0	0	6.2	37	9	9	7	1	3	0	0	7	0	3	0	0	0	1	.000	0	0	9.45
6 Min. YEARS		116	106	6	4	611.2	2617	564	307	284	54	12	17	23	254	7	509	20	7	37	42	.468	3	2	4.18

Ryan Henderson

Pitches: Right Bats: Right Pos: P   Ht: 6'1" Wt: 190 Born: 9/30/69 Age: 28

Year Team	Lg Org	G	GS	CG	GF	IP	BFP	H	R	ER	HR	SH	SF	HB	TBB	IBB	SO	WP	Bk	W	L	Pct.	ShO	Sv	ERA
1992 Great Falls	R+ LA	11	11	1	0	55	228	37	22	13	0	3	0	2	25	0	54	5	6	5	1	.833	1	0	2.13
Bakersfield	A+ LA	3	3	0	0	16	72	17	10	9	1	0	0	0	9	1	15	0	3	0	2	.000	0	0	5.06
1993 Vero Beach	A+ LA	30	0	0	25	34	158	29	24	15	2	4	1	0	28	4	34	4	1	0	3	.000	0	10	3.97
San Antonio	AA LA	23	0	0	20	25	110	19	10	7	0	3	1	0	16	2	22	1	1	0	0	.000	0	5	2.52
1994 Bakersfield	A+ LA	29	0	0	27	31.1	145	26	14	10	1	2	0	1	26	0	38	8	1	0	1	.000	0	14	2.87
San Antonio	AA LA	11	1	0	0	21.2	105	25	18	17	2	0	1	1	18	1	15	3	1	1	2	.333	0	0	7.06
1995 San Antonio	A+ LA	39	6	0	10	104.1	453	98	53	45	1	6	1	5	58	3	86	9	2	11	5	.688	0	2	3.88
1996 Albuquerque	AAA LA	3	0	0	1	5.2	31	5	9	5	0	0	1	0	6	0	7	1	2	0	0	.000	0	0	7.94
San Antonio	AA LA	39	0	0	19	63.2	275	59	29	27	2	2	4	5	29	0	46	4	0	3	3	.500	0	6	3.82
1997 Albuquerque	AAA LA	13	0	0	0	17.1	87	20	14	12	0	3	0	1	14	3	17	1	0	1	3	.250	0	0	6.23
Colo Spmgs	AAA Col	6	1	0	2	13	67	20	18	18	3	0	0	1	9	1	12	0	0	1	1	.500	0	0	12.46
New Haven	AA Col	24	4	0	7	50.2	228	54	29	27	2	2	2	3	27	2	46	6	0	2	5	.286	0	0	4.80
6 Min. YEARS		231	26	1	115	437.2	1959	409	250	205	14	25	11	19	265	17	392	42	17	24	26	.480	1	37	4.22

Bob Henley

Bats: Right Throws: Right Pos: C   Ht: 6'2" Wt: 190 Born: 1/30/73 Age: 25

Year Team	Lg Org	G	AB	H	2B	3B	HR	TB	R	RBI	TBB	IBB	SO	HBP	SH	SF	SB	CS	SB%	GDP	Avg	OBP	SLG
1993 Jamestown	A- Mon	60	206	53	10	4	9	92	25	29	20	1	60	1	1	1	0	1	.00	5	.257	.325	.447
1994 Burlington	A Mon	98	346	104	20	1	20	186	72	67	49	1	91	10	1	3	1	2	.33	8	.301	.400	.538
1995 Albany	A Mon	102	335	94	20	1	3	125	45	46	83	3	57	11	1	2	1	2	.33	11	.281	.436	.373
1996 Harrisburg	AA Mon	103	289	66	12	1	3	89	33	27	70	1	78	3	9	2	1	2	.33	14	.228	.382	.308
1997 Harrisburg	AA Mon	79	280	85	19	0	12	140	41	49	32	2	40	5	0	4	5	1	.83	7	.304	.380	.500
5 Min. YEARS		442	1456	402	81	7	45	632	216	218	254	8	326	30	12	12	8	8	.50	45	.276	.392	.434

Santiago Henry

Bats: Right Throws: Right Pos: SS-2B   Ht: 5'11" Wt: 156 Born: 7/27/72 Age: 25

Year Team	Lg Org	G	AB	H	2B	3B	HR	TB	R	RBI	TBB	IBB	SO	HBP	SH	SF	SB	CS	SB%	GDP	Avg	OBP	SLG
1991 Blue Jays	R Tor	59	220	44	10	3	0	60	23	14	11	0	44	0	1	2	7	5	.58	2	.200	.236	.273
1992 St. Cathms	A- Tor	70	232	44	4	3	0	54	23	12	7	0	54	2	7	1	7	4	.64	1	.190	.219	.233
1993 Hagerstown	A Tor	115	404	111	30	12	8	189	65	54	20	0	110	2	3	1	13	4	.76	7	.275	.311	.468
1994 Dunedin	A+ Tor	109	408	103	22	6	6	155	56	46	19	2	99	7	2	4	9	4	.69	7	.252	.295	.380
1995 Knoxville	AA Tor	138	453	100	25	4	2	139	47	30	10	0	91	5	7	5	16	6	.73	7	.220	.243	.306
1996 Knoxville	AA Tor	110	371	100	15	7	3	138	37	32	19	1	66	3	4	2	11	7	.61	5	.270	.309	.372
1997 Syracuse	AAA Tor	44	116	28	5	1	2	41	15	16	2	0	21	1	1	1	5	1	.83	3	.241	.258	.353
Knoxville	AA Tor	52	196	57	10	1	5	84	25	26	4	1	35	1	0	3	3	2	.60	3	.291	.304	.429
7 Min. YEARS		697	2401	587	121	37	26	860	291	230	92	4	520	21	25	19	71	33	.68	35	.244	.276	.358

Kevin Henthorne

Pitches: Right Bats: Both Pos: P   Ht: 6'2" Wt: 182 Born: 12/9/69 Age: 28

Year Team	Lg Org	G	GS	CG	GF	IP	BFP	H	R	ER	HR	SH	SF	HB	TBB	IBB	SO	WP	Bk	W	L	Pct.	ShO	Sv	ERA
1994 Winnipeg	IND —	7	0	0	4	5.1	26	7	3	1	1	1	0	0	3	0	5	0	1	0	0	.000	0	0	1.69
1995 Laredo	IND —	11	10	2	1	74.2	306	65	29	24	5	1	1	1	27	0	51	3	1	5	2	.714	1	0	2.89
Corp.Chrsti	IND —	12	10	1	0	68	270	58	25	23	8	2	0	2	7	0	64	0	0	7	2	.778	0	0	3.04
1996 Norwich	AA NYA	12	8	0	2	59.2	252	50	25	15	3	1	2	2	22	2	47	3	1	5	3	.625	0	0	2.26
Tampa	A+ NYA	19	13	0	0	93.1	360	88	31	27	4	3	2	2	12	0	82	1	2	7	4	.636	0	0	2.60
1997 Norwich	AA NYA	33	6	0	12	73.1	313	72	32	27	8	0	4	4	14	0	64	2	0	2	1	.667	0	0	3.31
4 Min. YEARS		94	47	3	19	374.1	1527	340	145	117	29	8	9	11	85	2	313	9	5	26	12	.684	1	2	2.81

Russ Herbert

Pitches: Right Bats: Right Pos: P   Ht: 6'4" Wt: 200 Born: 4/21/72 Age: 26

Year Team	Lg Org	G	GS	CG	GF	IP	BFP	H	R	ER	HR	SH	SF	HB	TBB	IBB	SO	WP	Bk	W	L	Pct.	ShO	Sv	ERA
1994 White Sox	R ChA	4	2	0	0	13	46	6	3	3	0	0	0	0	2	0	19	0	0	0	1	.000	0	0	2.08
Hickory	A ChA	8	7	0	1	36.2	154	33	14	14	3	1	0	2	15	0	34	1	2	2	1	.667	0	0	3.44
1995 Hickory	A ChA	18	18	1	0	114.2	474	83	48	34	9	3	3	8	46	0	115	5	2	3	8	.273	1	0	2.67

Year Team	Lg Org	G	GS	CG	GF	IP	BFP	H	R	ER	HR	SH	SF	HB	TBB	IBB	SO	WP	Bk	W	L	Pct.	ShO	Sv	ERA
South Bend	A ChA	9	9	0	0	53.2	224	46	25	21	3	1	0	3	27	0	48	1	2	2	4	.333	0	0	3.52
1996 Pr William	A+ ChA	25	25	1	0	144	609	129	73	54	12	8	11	6	62	3	148	3	2	6	10	.375	0	0	3.38
1997 Birmingham	AA ChA	27	26	3	0	158.2	681	136	72	64	14	3	6	14	80	0	126	7	0	13	5	.722	1	0	3.63
4 Min. YEARS		91	87	5	2	520.2	2188	433	235	190	41	16	20	34	232	3	490	17	8	26	29	.473	2	0	3.28

Gil Heredia

Pitches: Right **Bats:** Right **Pos:** P   **Ht:** 6' 1" **Wt:** 210 **Born:** 10/26/65 **Age:** 32

Year Team	Lg Org	G	GS	CG	GF	IP	BFP	H	R	ER	HR	SH	SF	HB	TBB	IBB	SO	WP	Bk	W	L	Pct.	ShO	Sv	ERA
1987 Everett	A- SF	3	3	1	0	20	80	24	8	8	2	0	0	0	1	0	14	1	0	2	0	1.000	0	0	3.60
Fresno	A+ SF	11	11	5	0	80.2	321	62	28	26	8	2	5	0	23	1	60	2	2	5	3	.625	2	0	2.90
1988 San Jose	A+ SF	27	27	9	0	206.1	863	216	107	80	9	9	7	4	46	0	121	9	0	13	12	.520	0	0	3.49
1989 Shreveport	AA SF	7	2	1	1	24.2	104	28	10	7	1	1	0	1	4	0	8	2	0	1	0	1.000	0	0	2.55
1990 Phoenix	AAA SF	29	19	0	2	147	626	159	81	67	7	6	6	3	37	0	75	4	1	9	7	.563	0	1	4.10
1991 Phoenix	AAA SF	33	15	5	7	140.1	592	155	60	44	3	9	2	2	28	5	75	4	0	9	11	.450	1	1	2.82
1992 Phoenix	AAA SF	22	7	1	7	80.2	325	83	30	18	3	2	1	1	13	1	37	3	0	5	5	.500	1	1	2.01
Indianapolis	AAA Mon	3	3	0	0	17.2	72	18	2	2	1	0	0	1	3	0	10	0	1	2	0	1.000	0	0	1.02
1993 Ottawa	AAA Mon	16	16	1	0	102.2	429	97	46	34	7	4	0	3	26	2	66	6	0	8	4	.667	0	0	2.98
1996 Okla City	AAA Tex	6	0	0	3	9.2	38	11	3	2	0	0	0	0	0	0	4	0	0	0	0	.000	0	0	1.86
1997 Ottawa	AAA Mon	28	0	0	9	44	189	50	29	23	5	2	1	0	9	2	41	1	0	4	0	1.000	0	0	4.70
Iowa	AAA ChN	31	1	0	14	46.2	197	54	22	20	6	2	1	0	9	0	30	3	0	4	2	.667	0	1	3.86
1991 San Francisco	NL	7	4	0	1	33	126	27	14	14	4	2	1	0	7	2	13	1	0	2	0	.000	0	0	3.82
1992 San Francisco	NL	13	4	0	3	30	132	32	20	18	3	0	0	1	16	1	15	1	0	2	3	.400	0	0	5.40
Montreal	NL	7	1	0	1	14.2	55	12	3	3	1	2	1	0	4	0	7	0	0	0	0	.000	0	0	1.84
1993 Montreal	NL	20	9	1	2	57.1	246	66	28	25	4	4	1	2	14	2	40	0	0	4	2	.667	0	2	3.92
1994 Montreal	NL	39	3	0	8	75.1	325	85	34	29	7	3	4	2	13	3	62	4	1	6	3	.667	0	0	3.46
1995 Montreal	NL	40	18	0	5	119	509	137	60	57	7	9	4	5	21	1	74	1	0	5	6	.455	0	1	4.31
1996 Texas	AL	44	0	0	21	73.1	320	91	50	48	12	1	2	1	14	2	43	2	0	2	5	.286	0	1	5.89
9 Min. YEARS		216	104	23	43	920.1	3836	957	426	331	52	37	23	15	199	11	541	35	4	58	48	.547	4	4	3.24
6 Maj. YEARS		170	39	1	41	402.2	1713	450	209	194	38	21	13	11	89	11	254	9	1	19	21	.475	0	4	4.34

Matt Herges

Pitches: Right **Bats:** Left **Pos:** P   **Ht:** 6'0" **Wt:** 200 **Born:** 4/1/70 **Age:** 28

Year Team	Lg Org	G	GS	CG	GF	IP	BFP	H	R	ER	HR	SH	SF	HB	TBB	IBB	SO	WP	Bk	W	L	Pct.	ShO	Sv	ERA
1992 Yakima	A- LA	27	0	0	23	44.2	194	33	21	16	2	1	0	3	24	1	57	2	3	2	3	.400	0	9	3.22
1993 Bakersfield	A+ LA	51	0	0	17	90.1	403	70	49	37	6	6	4	10	56	6	84	4	3	2	6	.250	0	2	3.69
1994 Vero Beach	A+ LA	48	3	1	12	111	476	115	45	41	8	8	2	4	33	3	61	3	3	8	9	.471	0	3	3.32
1995 San Antonio	AA LA	19	0	0	13	27.2	130	34	16	15	2	3	0	0	16	1	18	3	0	0	3	.000	0	4	4.88
San Berndo	A+ LA	22	2	0	4	51.2	231	58	29	21	3	2	1	2	15	0	35	0	0	5	2	.714	0	1	3.66
1996 San Antonio	AA LA	30	6	0	10	83	355	83	38	25	3	2	5	2	28	0	45	5	1	3	2	.600	0	3	2.71
Albuquerque	AAA LA	10	4	2	1	34.2	140	33	11	10	2	2	2	0	14	0	15	1	0	4	1	.800	1	0	2.60
1997 Albuquerque	AAA LA	31	12	0	5	85	417	120	92	84	13	5	4	9	46	1	61	5	0	0	8	.000	0	0	8.89
San Antonio	AA LA	4	3	0	0	15.1	74	22	15	15	2	0	0	2	10	0	12	3	0	0	1	.000	0	0	8.80
6 Min. YEARS		242	30	3	85	543.1	2420	568	316	264	41	29	18	32	242	12	388	26	10	24	35	.407	1	26	4.37

Chad Hermansen

Bats: Right **Throws:** Right **Pos:** OF   **Ht:** 6'2" **Wt:** 185 **Born:** 9/10/77 **Age:** 20

Year Team	Lg Org	G	AB	H	2B	3B	HR	TB	R	RBI	TBB	IBB	SO	HBP	SH	SF	SB	CS	SB%	GDP	Avg	OBP	SLG
1995 Pirates	R Pit	24	92	28	10	1	3	49	14	17	9	1	19	0	0	1	0	0	.00	2	.304	.363	.533
Erie	A- Pit	44	165	45	8	3	6	77	30	25	18	0	39	4	0	1	4	2	.67	6	.273	.354	.467
1996 Augusta	A Pit	62	226	57	11	3	14	116	41	41	38	5	65	8	0	1	11	3	.79	1	.252	.377	.513
Lynchburg	A+ Pit	66	251	69	11	3	10	116	40	46	29	1	56	3	0	4	5	1	.83	8	.275	.352	.462
1997 Carolina	AA Pit	129	487	134	31	4	20	233	87	70	69	5	136	10	0	5	18	6	.75	3	.275	.373	.478
3 Min. YEARS		325	1221	333	71	14	53	591	212	199	163	12	315	25	0	13	38	12	.76	20	.273	.366	.484

Carlos Hernandez

Bats: Right **Throws:** Right **Pos:** 2B   **Ht:** 5'9" **Wt:** 160 **Born:** 12/12/75 **Age:** 22

Year Team	Lg Org	G	AB	H	2B	3B	HR	TB	R	RBI	TBB	IBB	SO	HBP	SH	SF	SB	CS	SB%	GDP	Avg	OBP	SLG
1994 Astros	R Hou	51	192	62	10	1	0	74	45	23	19	0	22	4	2	1	25	7	.78	1	.323	.394	.385
1995 Quad City	A Hou	126	470	122	19	6	4	165	74	40	39	1	68	11	9	1	58	21	.73	4	.260	.330	.351
1996 Quad City	A Hou	112	456	123	15	7	5	167	67	49	27	0	71	4	9	5	41	14	.75	6	.270	.313	.366
1997 Jackson	AA Hou	92	363	106	12	1	4	132	62	33	33	2	59	4	6	3	17	8	.68	7	.292	.355	.364
4 Min. YEARS		381	1481	413	56	15	13	538	248	145	118	3	220	23	26	10	141	50	.74	18	.279	.339	.363

Elvin Hernandez

Pitches: Right **Bats:** Right **Pos:** P   **Ht:** 6'1" **Wt:** 165 **Born:** 8/20/77 **Age:** 20

Year Team	Lg Org	G	GS	CG	GF	IP	BFP	H	R	ER	HR	SH	SF	HB	TBB	IBB	SO	WP	Bk	W	L	Pct.	ShO	Sv	ERA
1995 Erie	A- Pit	14	14	2	0	90.1	377	82	40	29	8	5	3	4	22	0	54	2	1	6	1	.857	1	0	2.89
1996 Augusta	A Pit	27	27	2	0	157.2	624	140	60	55	13	0	2	5	16	2	171	7	0	17	5	.773	1	0	3.14
1997 Carolina	AA Pit	17	17	0	0	92.2	409	104	67	59	11	2	2	3	26	2	66	4	0	2	7	.222	0	0	5.73
Lynchburg	A+ Pit	3	0	0	2	5	20	4	1	1	0	0	0	0	1	0	5	0	0	0	0	.000	0	1	1.80

Year Team	Lg Org	G	GS	CG	GF	IP	BFP	H	R	ER	HR	SH	SF	HB	TBB	IBB	SO	WP	Bk	W	L	Pct	ShO	Sv	ERA
3 Min. YEARS		61	58	4	2	345.2	1430	330	168	144	32	7	7	12	65	4	296	13	1	25	13	.658	2	1	3.75

Francis Hernandez

Pitches: Right **Bats:** Right **Pos:** P   **Ht:** 6'0" **Wt:** 160 **Born:** 12/17/76 **Age:** 21

		HOW MUCH HE PITCHED						WHAT HE GAVE UP												THE RESULTS					
Year Team	Lg Org	G	GS	CG	GF	IP	BFP	H	R	ER	HR	SH	SF	HB	TBB	IBB	SO	WP	Bk	W	L	Pct	ShO	Sv	ERA
1995 Orioles	R Bal	24	0	0	20	27.1	105	18	4	4	1	0	1	1	6	0	23	2	1	2	2	.500	0	11	1.32
Frederick	A+ Bal	3	0	0	3	3	15	3	2	2	1	0	1	0	3	0	3	0	0	0	1	.000	0	1	6.00
1996 Frederick	A+ Bal	37	0	0	30	45.1	197	44	26	23	6	5	1	1	21	7	39	2	0	4	3	.571	0	12	4.57
1997 Frederick	A+ Bal	49	0	0	46	58.1	244	51	23	15	8	3	3	1	21	1	51	1	0	4	4	.500	0	24	2.31
Bowie	AA Bal	6	0	0	2	5.2	26	7	1	1	0	0	0	0	4	1	2	0	0	0	0	.000	0	0	1.59
3 Min. YEARS		119	0	0	101	139.2	587	123	56	45	16	8	6	3	55	9	118	5	1	10	10	.500	0	48	2.90

Ramon Hernandez

Bats: Right **Throws:** Right **Pos:** C   **Ht:** 6'0" **Wt:** 170 **Born:** 5/20/76 **Age:** 22

		BATTING															BASERUNNING				PERCENTAGES		
Year Team	Lg Org	G	AB	H	2B	3B	HR	TB	R	RBI	TBB	IBB	SO	HBP	SH	SF	SB	CS	SB%	GDP	Avg	OBP	SLG
1995 Athletics	R Oak	48	143	52	9	6	4	85	37	37	39	1	16	8	0	4	6	2	.75	3	.364	.510	.594
1996 W Michigan	A Oak	123	447	114	26	2	12	180	62	68	69	1	62	4	1	7	2	3	.40	22	.255	.355	.403
1997 Visalia	A+ Oak	86	332	120	21	2	15	190	57	85	35	1	47	9	0	8	2	4	.33	5	.361	.427	.572
Huntsville	AA Oak	44	161	31	3	0	4	46	27	24	18	0	23	3	0	3	0	0	.00	8	.193	.281	.286
3 Min. YEARS		301	1083	317	59	10	35	501	183	214	161	3	148	24	1	22	10	9	.53	38	.293	.389	.463

Santos Hernandez

Pitches: Right **Bats:** Right **Pos:** P   **Ht:** 6'1" **Wt:** 172 **Born:** 11/3/72 **Age:** 25

		HOW MUCH HE PITCHED						WHAT HE GAVE UP												THE RESULTS					
Year Team	Lg Org	G	GS	CG	GF	IP	BFP	H	R	ER	HR	SH	SF	HB	TBB	IBB	SO	WP	Bk	W	L	Pct	ShO	Sv	ERA
1994 Clinton	A SF	32	0	0	11	48	201	47	23	20	5	6	2	4	10	1	48	4	4	5	7	.417	0	4	3.75
1995 Burlington	A SF	44	0	0	28	64.1	274	54	27	19	3	4	2	2	20	2	85	1	0	5	8	.385	0	9	2.66
1996 Burlington	A SF	61	0	0	58	66.2	249	39	15	14	4	3	1	2	13	0	79	7	1	3	3	.500	0	35	1.89
1997 San Jose	A+ SF	47	0	0	39	57	237	51	26	22	7	4	0	1	14	2	87	4	0	2	6	.250	0	15	3.47
Shreveport	AA SF	11	0	0	11	15.2	62	13	4	4	1	0	0	1	3	0	14	3	0	1	1	.500	0	6	2.30
4 Min. YEARS		195	0	0	147	251.2	1023	204	95	79	20	17	7	10	60	5	313	19	5	16	25	.390	0	69	2.83

Jose Herrera

Bats: Left **Throws:** Left **Pos:** OF   **Ht:** 6'0" **Wt:** 165 **Born:** 8/30/72 **Age:** 25

		BATTING															BASERUNNING				PERCENTAGES		
Year Team	Lg Org	G	AB	H	2B	3B	HR	TB	R	RBI	TBB	IBB	SO	HBP	SH	SF	SB	CS	SB%	GDP	Avg	OBP	SLG
1991 Medicne Hat	R+ Tor	40	143	35	5	1	1	45	21	11	6	1	38	3	1	0	6	7	.46	0	.245	.289	.315
St. Cathrns	A- Tor	3	9	3	1	0	0	4	3	2	1	0	2	1	0	0	0	1	.00	0	.333	.455	.444
1992 Medicne Hat	R+ Tor	72	265	72	9	2	0	85	45	21	32	1	62	6	7	0	32	8	.80	4	.272	.363	.321
1993 Hagerstown	A Tor	95	388	123	22	5	5	170	60	42	26	1	63	7	5	4	36	20	.64	3	.317	.367	.438
Madison	A Oak	4	14	3	0	0	0	3	1	0	0	0	6	0	1	0	1	1	.50	0	.214	.214	.214
1994 Modesto	A+ Oak	103	370	106	20	3	11	165	59	56	38	3	76	10	5	6	21	12	.64	5	.286	.363	.446
1995 Huntsville	AA Oak	92	358	101	11	4	6	138	37	45	27	2	58	2	0	2	9	8	.53	8	.282	.334	.385
1996 Huntsville	AA Oak	23	84	24	4	0	1	31	18	7	14	1	15	0	0	2	3	2	.60	2	.286	.380	.369
1997 Edmonton	AAA Oak	122	421	125	21	2	4	162	64	41	42	2	64	1	7	2	7	5	.58	12	.297	.361	.385
1995 Oakland	AL	33	70	17	1	2	0	22	9	2	6	0	11	0	0	1	1	3	.25	1	.243	.299	.314
1996 Oakland	AL	108	320	86	15	1	6	121	44	30	20	1	59	3	3	0	8	2	.80	5	.269	.318	.378
7 Min. YEARS		554	2052	592	93	17	28	803	308	225	186	11	384	30	26	16	115	64	.64	34	.288	.354	.391
2 Maj. YEARS		141	390	103	16	3	6	143	53	32	26	1	70	3	3	1	9	5	.64	6	.264	.314	.367

Jason Herrick

Bats: Left **Throws:** Left **Pos:** OF   **Ht:** 6'0" **Wt:** 175 **Born:** 7/29/73 **Age:** 24

		BATTING															BASERUNNING				PERCENTAGES		
Year Team	Lg Org	G	AB	H	2B	3B	HR	TB	R	RBI	TBB	IBB	SO	HBP	SH	SF	SB	CS	SB%	GDP	Avg	OBP	SLG
1992 Angels	R Ana	8	30	12	3	0	0	15	7	6	5	0	4	1	0	0	2	1	.67	0	.400	.500	.500
1993 Angels	R Ana	56	196	59	9	4	3	85	34	36	41	2	51	3	1	2	5	4	.56	6	.301	.423	.434
1994 Cedar Rapds	A Ana	109	339	85	18	5	7	134	62	51	42	2	92	3	2	6	10	3	.77	8	.251	.333	.395
1995 Cedar Rapds	A Ana	104	358	102	21	4	11	164	54	57	38	2	84	2	3	3	19	3	.86	7	.285	.354	.458
1996 Lk Elsinore	A+ Ana	58	210	67	13	2	6	102	35	30	25	2	52	0	2	2	4	4	.56	5	.319	.388	.486
1997 Midland	AA Ana	118	416	105	27	4	20	200	60	67	34	3	141	2	6	2	9	6	.60	7	.252	.311	.481
6 Min. YEARS		453	1549	430	91	19	47	700	252	247	185	11	424	10	14	15	50	21	.70	33	.278	.355	.452

Jamie Hicks

Bats: Right **Throws:** Right **Pos:** C   **Ht:** 6'2" **Wt:** 200 **Born:** 11/15/71 **Age:** 26

		BATTING															BASERUNNING				PERCENTAGES		
Year Team	Lg Org	G	AB	H	2B	3B	HR	TB	R	RBI	TBB	IBB	SO	HBP	SH	SF	SB	CS	SB%	GDP	Avg	OBP	SLG
1994 Idaho Falls	R+ Atl	5	21	8	1	0	0	9	0	4	0	0	1	0	0	0	0	0	.00	0	.381	.381	.429
Macon	A Atl	31	95	23	4	1	0	29	8	7	3	0	15	2	1	1	0	0	.00	2	.242	.277	.305
1995 Durham	A+ Atl	41	105	23	6	0	0	29	9	14	5	2	18	0	0	1	0	2	.00	0	.219	.252	.276
1996 Greenville	AA Atl	3	6	1	0	0	0	1	0	0	0	0	0	0	0	0	0	0	.00	0	.167	.167	.167
Macon	A Atl	68	186	41	7	0	3	57	17	17	9	1	33	1	0	2	3	1	.75	4	.220	.258	.306
1997 Greenville	AA Atl	8	17	5	0	0	1	8	3	1	2	0	3	0	0	0	1	0	1.00	0	.294	.368	.471

Year Team	Lg Org	G	AB	H	2B	3B	HR	TB	R	RBI	TBB	IBB	SO	HBP	SH	SF	SB	CS	SB%	GDP	Avg	OBP	SLG
4 Min. YEARS		156	430	101	18	1	4	133	37	43	19	3	70	3	1	4	4	3	.57	11	.235	.270	.309

Vee Hightower

Bats: Both Throws: Right Pos: OF   Ht: 6'5" Wt: 205 Born: 4/26/72 Age: 26

Year Team	Lg Org	G	AB	H	2B	3B	HR	TB	R	RBI	TBB	IBB	SO	HBP	SH	SF	SB	CS	SB%	GDP	Avg	OBP	SLG
1993 Peoria	A ChN	2	10	2	0	0	0	2	0	0	0	0	1	0	0	0	1	0	1.00	1	.200	.200	.200
1994 Peoria	A ChN	46	147	35	6	4	1	52	28	10	28	1	30	2	1	1	6	3	.67	5	.238	.365	.354
1995 Rockford	A ChN	64	238	63	11	1	7	97	51	36	39	1	52	6	0	1	23	6	.79	6	.265	.380	.408
1996 Orlando	AA ChN	19	75	5	0	0	0	5	2	4	4	0	24	0	0	0	3	0	1.00	1	.067	.114	.067
Daytona	A+ ChN	87	293	95	13	5	6	136	59	27	52	1	44	8	0	1	25	7	.78	3	.324	.438	.464
1997 Orlando	AA ChN	87	283	66	8	2	6	96	35	29	43	0	66	4	0	2	16	11	.59	10	.233	.340	.339
5 Min. YEARS		305	1046	266	38	12	20	388	175	106	166	3	217	20	1	5	74	27	.73	26	.254	.365	.371

Rich Hills

Bats: Right Throws: Right Pos: 3B   Ht: 6'0" Wt: 195 Born: 7/28/73 Age: 24

Year Team	Lg Org	G	AB	H	2B	3B	HR	TB	R	RBI	TBB	IBB	SO	HBP	SH	SF	SB	CS	SB%	GDP	Avg	OBP	SLG
1995 Idaho Falls	R+ SD	61	224	69	14	1	7	106	49	48	31	0	27	11	0	5	4	1	.80	5	.308	.410	.473
1996 Clinton	A SD	124	433	108	34	0	7	163	42	58	50	2	69	12	0	3	4	4	.50	11	.249	.341	.376
1997 Rancho Cuca	A+ SD	40	128	35	8	1	0	45	19	15	18	0	31	2	1	1	1	1	.50	2	.273	.369	.352
Mobile	AA SD	71	216	54	12	1	5	83	37	30	25	1	34	3	0	3	2	0	1.00	8	.250	.332	.384
3 Min. YEARS		296	1001	266	68	3	19	397	147	151	124	3	161	28	1	12	11	6	.65	26	.266	.359	.397

A.J. Hinch

Bats: Right Throws: Right Pos: C   Ht: 6'1" Wt: 195 Born: 5/15/74 Age: 24

Year Team	Lg Org	G	AB	H	2B	3B	HR	TB	R	RBI	TBB	IBB	SO	HBP	SH	SF	SB	CS	SB%	GDP	Avg	OBP	SLG
1997 Modesto	A+ Oak	95	333	103	25	3	20	194	70	73	42	3	68	11	4	4	8	3	.73	9	.309	.400	.583
Edmonton	AAA Oak	39	125	47	7	0	4	66	23	24	20	1	13	3	0	0	2	0	1.00	7	.376	.473	.528
1 Min. YEARS		134	458	150	32	3	24	260	93	97	62	4	81	14	4	4	10	3	.77	16	.328	.420	.568

Brett Hinchliffe

Pitches: Right Bats: Right Pos: P   Ht: 6'4" Wt: 205 Born: 7/21/74 Age: 23

		HOW MUCH HE PITCHED						WHAT HE GAVE UP										THE RESULTS					
Year Team	Lg Org	G	GS	CG	GF	IP	BFP	H	R	ER	HR	SH	SF	HB	TBB	IBB	SO	WP	Bk	W	L	Pct.	ShO	Sv	ERA
1992 Mariners	R Sea	24	0	0	20	35	161	42	17	9	0	3	0	3	9	0	26	1	1	5	4	.556	0	3	2.31
1993 Mariners	R Sea	10	9	0	0	44.1	190	55	32	25	4	1	3	3	5	0	29	4	1	0	4	.000	0	0	5.08
1994 Appleton	A Sea	27	27	3	0	173.2	721	140	79	62	16	7	4	10	50	4	160	5	2	11	7	.611	1	0	3.21
1995 Riverside	A+ Sea	15	15	0	0	77.2	373	110	69	57	10	5	3	8	35	3	68	4	0	3	8	.273	0	0	6.61
1996 Lancaster	A+ Sea	27	26	0	0	163.1	731	179	105	77	19	6	5	9	64	1	146	10	1	11	10	.524	0	0	4.24
1997 Memphis	AA Sea	24	24	5	0	145.2	627	159	81	72	20	3	4	9	45	2	107	2	1	10	10	.500	1	0	4.45
6 Min. YEARS		127	101	8	20	639.2	2803	685	383	302	69	25	19	42	208	10	536	26	6	40	43	.482	2	3	4.25

Rob Hinds

Bats: Right Throws: Right Pos: 2B   Ht: 6'1" Wt: 180 Born: 4/26/71 Age: 27

Year Team	Lg Org	G	AB	H	2B	3B	HR	TB	R	RBI	TBB	IBB	SO	HBP	SH	SF	SB	CS	SB%	GDP	Avg	OBP	SLG
1992 Oneonta	A- NYA	69	264	76	8	2	0	88	40	11	34	0	51	7	0	0	21	9	.70	3	.288	.384	.333
1993 Greensboro	A NYA	126	503	114	14	3	0	134	80	50	72	0	101	13	1	2	51	22	.70	12	.227	.337	.266
1994 Tampa	A+ NYA	110	405	118	10	3	1	137	63	32	31	0	76	4	7	3	24	11	.69	8	.291	.344	.338
1995 Norwich	AA NYA	132	445	112	8	1	1	125	71	37	50	0	102	12	6	3	27	10	.73	4	.252	.341	.281
1996 Columbus	AAA NYA	11	23	2	0	0	0	2	4	1	4	0	3	1	3	1	1	0	1.00	0	.087	.241	.087
Norwich	AA NYA	85	180	41	3	1	2	52	25	15	20	0	48	0	10	2	9	5	.64	1	.228	.302	.289
1997 Norwich	AA NYA	51	119	29	4	1	0	35	15	12	12	0	31	2	3	2	1	1	.50	5	.244	.319	.294
6 Min. YEARS		584	1939	492	47	11	4	573	298	158	223	0	412	39	30	13	134	58	.70	33	.254	.341	.296

Rich Hines

Pitches: Left Bats: Left Pos: P   Ht: 6'1" Wt: 185 Born: 5/20/69 Age: 29

		HOW MUCH HE PITCHED						WHAT HE GAVE UP										THE RESULTS					
Year Team	Lg Org	G	GS	CG	GF	IP	BFP	H	R	ER	HR	SH	SF	HB	TBB	IBB	SO	WP	Bk	W	L	Pct.	ShO	Sv	ERA
1990 Yankees	R NYA	11	9	0	0	61	242	44	18	12	0	0	3	2	19	0	73	9	1	5	2	.714	0	0	1.77
1991 Greensboro	A NYA	26	26	6	0	155.1	667	147	76	55	8	5	2	2	68	1	126	7	3	8	9	.471	2	0	3.19
1992 Pr William	A+ NYA	25	24	0	1	140	610	131	75	56	12	3	3	7	61	3	84	10	0	11	7	.611	0	0	3.60
1993 Albany-Colo	AA NYA	14	0	0	3	26	102	17	9	6	1	1	1	0	11	2	27	0	0	0	1	.000	0	0	2.08
Columbus	AAA NYA	43	0	0	17	56	248	50	28	25	3	1	1	1	34	6	40	2	1	2	5	.286	0	4	4.02
1994 Columbus	AAA NYA	49	2	0	12	84.1	367	87	48	43	11	1	2	0	41	4	54	6	0	3	2	.600	0	2	4.59
1995 Norwich	AA NYA	54	0	0	28	62	283	58	38	25	2	1	4	5	34	7	50	7	2	3	5	.375	0	7	3.63
1996 Columbus	AAA NYA	32	5	0	7	66.1	303	70	42	38	7	4	0	5	37	0	48	8	2	6	3	.667	0	0	5.16
1997 Greenville	AA Atl	41	0	0	13	67	308	85	56	49	10	4	5	1	22	1	49	4	0	4	0	1.000	0	1	6.58
8 Min. YEARS		295	66	6	81	718	3130	689	390	309	54	20	21	23	327	24	551	53	9	42	34	.553	2	14	3.87

117

Aaron Holbert

Bats: Right **Throws:** Right **Pos:** SS **Ht:** 6' 0" **Wt:** 160 **Born:** 1/9/73 **Age:** 25

Year Team	Lg Org	G	AB	H	2B	3B	HR	TB	R	RBI	TBB	IBB	SO	HBP	SH	SF	SB	CS	SB%	GDP	Avg	OBP	SLG
1990 Johnson Cty	R+ StL	54	176	30	4	1	1	39	27	18	24	1	33	3	1	1	3	5	.38	2	.170	.279	.222
1991 Springfield	A StL	59	215	48	5	1	1	58	22	24	15	0	26	6	1	2	5	8	.38	3	.223	.290	.270
1992 Savannah	A StL	119	438	117	17	4	1	145	53	34	40	0	57	8	6	3	62	25	.71	4	.267	.337	.331
1993 St. Pete	A+ StL	121	457	121	18	3	2	151	60	31	28	2	61	4	15	1	45	22	.67	6	.265	.312	.330
1994 Cardinals	R StL	5	12	2	0	0	0	2	3	0	2	0	2	0	0	0	2	0	1.00	0	.167	.286	.167
Arkansas	AA StL	59	233	69	10	6	2	97	41	19	14	0	25	2	4	1	9	7	.56	5	.296	.340	.416
1995 Louisville	AAA StL	112	401	103	16	4	9	154	57	40	20	1	60	5	3	5	14	6	.70	10	.257	.297	.384
1996 Louisville	AAA StL	112	436	115	16	6	4	155	54	32	21	0	61	2	5	4	20	14	.59	8	.264	.298	.356
1997 Louisville	AAA StL	93	314	80	14	3	4	112	32	32	15	1	56	2	3	4	9	5	.64	9	.255	.290	.357
1996 St. Louis	NL	1	3	0	0	0	0	0	0	0	0	0	0	0	0	0	0	0	.00	0	.000	.000	.000
8 Min. YEARS		734	2682	685	100	28	24	913	349	230	179	5	381	32	38	21	169	92	.65	47	.255	.307	.340

Ray Holbert

Bats: Right **Throws:** Right **Pos:** SS **Ht:** 6' 0" **Wt:** 175 **Born:** 9/25/70 **Age:** 27

Year Team	Lg Org	G	AB	H	2B	3B	HR	TB	R	RBI	TBB	IBB	SO	HBP	SH	SF	SB	CS	SB%	GDP	Avg	OBP	SLG
1988 Spokane	R SD	49	170	44	1	0	3	54	38	19	37	0	32	2	1	0	20	7	.74	4	.259	.397	.318
1989 Waterloo	A SD	117	354	55	7	1	0	64	37	20	41	0	99	2	7	1	13	13	.50	9	.155	.246	.181
1990 Waterloo	A SD	133	411	84	10	1	3	105	51	37	51	0	117	4	9	1	16	16	.50	10	.204	.298	.255
1991 High Desert	A+ SD	122	386	102	14	2	4	132	76	51	56	1	83	6	9	3	19	6	.76	10	.264	.364	.342
1992 Wichita	AA SD	95	304	86	7	3	2	105	46	23	42	2	68	1	3	1	26	8	.76	7	.283	.371	.345
1993 Wichita	AA SD	112	388	101	13	5	5	139	56	48	54	0	87	2	3	9	30	17	.64	6	.260	.347	.358
1994 Las Vegas	AAA SD	118	426	128	21	5	8	183	68	52	50	2	99	2	10	4	27	11	.71	8	.300	.373	.430
1995 Las Vegas	AAA SD	9	26	3	1	0	0	4	3	3	5	0	10	0	0	0	1	1	.50	1	.115	.258	.154
1996 Tucson	AAA Hou	28	97	24	3	2	0	31	13	10	7	0	19	2	0	1	4	1	.80	3	.247	.308	.320
1997 Toledo	AAA Det	109	372	90	18	7	7	143	43	37	32	0	109	4	7	2	16	7	.70	7	.242	.307	.384
1994 San Diego	NL	5	5	1	0	0	0	1	1	0	0	0	4	0	0	0	0	0	.00	0	.200	.200	.200
1995 San Diego	NL	63	73	13	2	1	2	23	11	5	8	1	20	2	3	0	4	0	1.00	3	.178	.277	.315
10 Min. YEARS		892	2934	717	95	26	32	960	431	300	375	5	723	25	49	22	172	87	.66	65	.244	.333	.327
2 Maj. YEARS		68	78	14	2	1	2	24	12	5	8	1	24	2	3	0	4	0	1.00	3	.179	.273	.308

Nate Holdren

Bats: Right **Throws:** Right **Pos:** 1B **Ht:** 6'4" **Wt:** 240 **Born:** 12/8/71 **Age:** 26

Year Team	Lg Org	G	AB	H	2B	3B	HR	TB	R	RBI	TBB	IBB	SO	HBP	SH	SF	SB	CS	SB%	GDP	Avg	OBP	SLG
1993 Bend	A- Col	62	203	46	10	2	12	96	30	43	24	5	78	4	0	1	8	0	1.00	4	.227	.319	.473
1994 Asheville	A Col	111	377	89	14	0	28	192	56	74	28	1	129	10	0	0	3	4	.43	5	.236	.306	.509
1995 Salem	A+ Col	119	420	103	16	2	15	168	48	69	34	0	126	6	2	2	6	3	.67	7	.245	.310	.400
1996 Salem	A+ Col	114	426	118	24	0	16	190	53	64	29	3	109	5	1	5	15	5	.75	6	.277	.327	.446
New Haven	AA Col	10	36	6	1	0	1	10	3	6	2	0	11	0	0	0	1	1	.50	0	.167	.211	.278
1997 New Haven	AA Col	25	82	15	2	0	4	29	9	9	3	0	28	1	0	0	0	2	.00	2	.183	.221	.354
5 Min. YEARS		441	1544	377	72	4	76	685	199	265	120	9	481	26	3	8	33	15	.69	24	.244	.308	.444

David Holdridge

Pitches: Right **Bats:** Right **Pos:** P **Ht:** 6'3" **Wt:** 195 **Born:** 2/5/69 **Age:** 29

Year Team	Lg Org	G	GS	CG	GF	IP	BFP	H	R	ER	HR	SH	SF	HB	TBB	IBB	SO	WP	Bk	W	L	Pct.	ShO	Sv	ERA
1988 Quad City	A Ana	28	28	0	0	153.2	686	151	92	66	4	5	4	13	79	1	110	8	4	6	12	.333	0	0	3.87
1989 Clearwater	A+ Phi	24	24	3	0	132.1	610	147	100	84	11	2	6	8	77	0	77	16	1	7	10	.412	0	0	5.71
1990 Reading	AA Phi	24	24	1	0	127.2	571	114	74	64	13	3	5	6	79	0	78	8	0	8	12	.400	0	0	4.51
1991 Reading	AA Phi	7	7	0	0	26.1	135	26	24	16	3	2	3	1	34	0	19	3	0	0	2	.000	0	0	5.47
Clearwater	A+ Phi	15	0	0	4	25	126	34	23	21	2	0	2	1	21	0	23	4	0	0	0	.000	0	1	7.56
1992 Palm Spring	A+ Ana	28	27	3	0	159	726	169	99	75	5	5	3	5	87	4	135	21	0	12	12	.500	2	0	4.25
1993 Midland	AA Ana	27	27	1	0	151	700	202	117	102	13	4	2	11	55	0	123	13	1	8	10	.444	1	0	6.08
1994 Vancouver	AAA Ana	4	0	0	1	7	36	12	7	4	1	0	1	1	4	0	4	0	0	0	0	.000	0	0	5.14
Midland	AA Ana	38	2	0	17	66.1	286	66	33	29	4	1	3	5	23	0	59	2	0	7	4	.636	0	2	3.93
1995 Lk Elsinore	A+ Ana	12	0	0	8	18.1	74	13	3	2	0	1	1	2	5	1	24	3	0	3	0	1.000	0	1	0.98
Midland	AA Ana	14	0	0	11	25.1	100	20	8	5	1	1	0	1	8	0	23	2	0	1	0	1.000	0	1	1.78
Vancouver	AAA Ana	11	0	0	6	13.2	68	18	10	7	0	2	0	1	7	1	13	3	0	0	2	.000	0	1	4.61
1996 Vancouver	AAA Ana	29	0	0	17	35	163	39	19	18	4	0	2	2	23	2	26	3	0	2	1	.667	0	1	4.63
Lk Elsinore	A+ Ana	12	0	0	12	13	53	11	3	3	1	0	0	1	2	0	21	0	0	0	0	.000	0	6	2.08
1997 Memphis	AA Sea	30	0	0	27	35	149	31	14	13	2	1	1	2	11	1	37	2	0	0	3	.000	0	17	3.34
Tacoma	AAA Sea	15	0	0	8	24.1	105	21	9	8	0	1	1	1	13	0	24	0	0	1	1	.500	0	1	2.96
10 Min. YEARS		318	139	8	111	1013	4588	1074	635	517	64	28	34	61	534	10	796	88	6	55	69	.444	3	30	4.59

Rick Holifield

Bats: Left **Throws:** Left **Pos:** OF **Ht:** 6'2" **Wt:** 165 **Born:** 3/25/70 **Age:** 28

Year Team	Lg Org	G	AB	H	2B	3B	HR	TB	R	RBI	TBB	IBB	SO	HBP	SH	SF	SB	CS	SB%	GDP	Avg	OBP	SLG
1988 Medcne Hat	R+ Tor	31	96	26	4	1	1	35	16	6	9	0	27	4	0	0	6	0	1.00	2	.271	.358	.365
1989 St. Cathrns	A- Tor	60	209	46	7	1	4	67	22	21	15	1	74	1	0	2	4	7	.36	2	.220	.273	.321
1990 Myrtle Bch	A Tor	99	279	56	9	2	3	78	37	18	28	0	88	6	1	0	13	8	.62	7	.201	.288	.280
1991 Myrtle Bch	A Tor	114	324	71	15	5	1	99	37	25	34	1	94	7	1	1	14	15	.48	0	.219	.306	.306
1992 Myrtle Bch	A Tor	93	281	56	15	2	8	99	32	27	23	1	81	5	3	3	6	5	.55	2	.199	.269	.352

Year Team	Lg Org	G	AB	H	2B	3B	HR	TB	R	RBI	TBB	IBB	SO	HBP	SH	SF	SB	CS	SB%	GDP	Avg	OBP	SLG
1993 Dunedin	A+ Tor	127	407	112	18	12	20	214	84	68	56	6	129	16	6	4	30	13	.70	2	.275	.381	.526
1994 Knoxville	AA Tor	71	238	59	10	9	4	99	31	31	24	2	64	3	1	1	23	5	.82	2	.248	.323	.416
Scranton-WB	AAA Phi	18	55	7	1	0	0	8	5	0	3	0	19	2	0	0	0	1	.00	0	.127	.200	.145
Reading	AA Phi	42	155	44	8	3	7	79	29	19	18	0	34	3	1	0	21	7	.75	1	.284	.369	.510
1995 Scranton-WB	AAA Phi	76	223	46	6	3	3	67	32	24	24	0	52	6	1	3	21	5	.81	0	.206	.297	.300
Reading	AA Phi	30	93	23	3	1	1	31	18	5	22	3	18	1	2	0	5	2	.71	0	.247	.397	.333
1996 Pawtucket	AAA Bos	9	29	2	1	0	0	3	1	1	1	0	12	0	0	0	1	1	.50	0	.069	.100	.103
Trenton	AA Bos	109	375	100	20	4	10	158	73	38	53	3	98	9	9	3	35	18	.66	2	.267	.368	.421
1997 Pirates	R Pit	4	15	5	1	0	1	9	2	3	2	0	3	0	0	0	1	0	1.00	1	.333	.412	.600
Carolina	AA Pit	51	185	40	12	5	5	77	27	23	14	1	59	1	1	1	8	3	.73	2	.216	.274	.416
10 Min. YEARS		934	2964	693	130	48	68	1123	446	309	326	18	852	64	26	18	188	90	.68	24	.234	.321	.379

Damon Hollins

Bats: Right Throws: Left Pos: OF Ht: 5'11" Wt: 180 Born: 6/12/74 Age: 24

Year Team	Lg Org	G	AB	H	2B	3B	HR	TB	R	RBI	TBB	IBB	SO	HBP	SH	SF	SB	CS	SB%	GDP	Avg	OBP	SLG
1992 Braves	R Atl	49	179	41	12	1	1	58	35	15	30	0	22	2	2	0	15	2	.88	3	.229	.346	.324
1993 Danville	R+ Atl	62	240	77	15	2	7	117	37	51	19	0	30	1	0	3	10	2	.83	5	.321	.369	.488
1994 Durham	A+ Atl	131	485	131	28	0	23	228	76	88	45	0	115	4	2	3	12	7	.63	9	.270	.335	.470
1995 Greenville	AA Atl	129	466	115	26	2	18	199	64	77	44	6	120	4	0	6	6	6	.50	7	.247	.313	.427
1996 Richmond	AAA Atl	42	146	29	9	0	0	38	16	8	16	1	37	0	1	0	2	3	.40	2	.199	.278	.260
1997 Richmond	AAA Atl	134	498	132	31	3	20	229	73	63	45	4	84	3	6	1	7	2	.78	18	.265	.329	.460
6 Min. YEARS		547	2014	525	121	8	69	869	301	302	199	11	408	14	11	13	52	22	.70	44	.261	.329	.431

Stacy Hollins

Pitches: Right Bats: Right Pos: P Ht: 6'3" Wt: 195 Born: 7/31/72 Age: 25

Year Team	Lg Org	G	GS	CG	GF	IP	BFP	H	R	ER	HR	SH	SF	HB	TBB	IBB	SO	WP	Bk	W	L	Pct.	ShO	Sv	ERA
1992 Athletics	R Oak	15	14	3	0	93	392	89	47	35	0	2	4	4	19	0	93	5	3	6	3	.667	2	0	3.39
1993 Madison	A Oak	26	26	2	0	150.2	653	145	100	86	21	4	4	8	52	6	105	4	1	10	11	.476	1	0	5.14
1994 Modesto	A+ Oak	29	22	0	3	143.1	610	133	57	54	10	4	2	8	55	1	131	7	1	13	6	.684	0	0	3.39
1995 Huntsville	AA Oak	15	15	0	0	82.2	364	80	52	49	10	4	2	4	42	6	62	8	2	3	8	.273	0	0	5.33
Edmonton	AAA Oak	7	7	0	0	29.2	156	47	43	34	4	0	1	1	21	3	25	6	0	0	7	.000	0	0	10.31
1996 Huntsville	AA Oak	28	26	3	0	141	623	149	100	80	18	3	2	6	56	6	102	13	1	9	9	.500	2	0	5.11
1997 Edmonton	AAA Oak	1	1	0	0	2.2	17	5	4	3	0	0	0	0	3	0	2	0	0	0	0	.000	0	0	10.13
Huntsville	AA Oak	32	17	0	4	114	514	110	77	68	11	3	3	5	72	4	68	15	0	5	4	.556	0	2	5.37
6 Min. YEARS		153	128	8	7	757	3329	758	480	409	74	20	16	36	320	26	588	58	8	46	48	.489	5	2	4.86

Craig Holman

Pitches: Right Bats: Both Pos: P Ht: 6'2" Wt: 200 Born: 3/13/69 Age: 29

Year Team	Lg Org	G	GS	CG	GF	IP	BFP	H	R	ER	HR	SH	SF	HB	TBB	IBB	SO	WP	Bk	W	L	Pct.	ShO	Sv	ERA
1991 Batavia	A- Phi	15	12	0	1	79.1	327	67	27	17	2	2	1	2	22	1	53	7	1	6	2	.750	0	0	1.93
1992 Spartanburg	A Phi	25	24	3	1	143.1	611	153	72	59	9	4	4	4	39	0	129	10	2	9	6	.600	1	0	3.70
1993 Clearwater	A+ Phi	7	1	0	2	18	71	17	7	5	1	0	0	0	1	0	7	1	0	0	0	.000	0	0	2.50
Reading	AA Phi	24	24	4	0	139	586	134	73	64	5	3	2	12	43	1	86	6	1	8	13	.381	1	0	4.14
1994 Reading	AA Phi	7	4	0	1	27.2	126	33	22	19	3	0	0	1	13	1	18	1	0	2	5	.286	0	0	6.18
1995 Reading	AA Phi	32	1	0	13	56.2	235	55	27	22	10	2	2	2	16	2	40	2	1	1	1	.500	0	1	3.49
1996 Scranton-WB	AAA Phi	36	3	0	9	62.2	291	77	44	41	10	6	5	4	34	5	36	6	1	3	2	.600	0	0	5.89
Reading	AA Phi	8	8	0	0	46.1	186	42	21	18	6	4	0	2	13	0	34	3	0	1	6	.857	0	0	3.50
1997 Scranton-WB	AAA Phi	48	0	0	18	75.2	346	100	44	39	7	3	1	4	27	4	75	6	0	3	1	.750	0	0	4.64
7 Min. YEARS		202	77	7	45	648.2	2779	678	337	284	53	24	15	31	208	14	478	42	6	38	31	.551	2	4	3.94

Chris Hook

Pitches: Right Bats: Right Pos: P Ht: 6'5" Wt: 230 Born: 8/4/68 Age: 29

Year Team	Lg Org	G	GS	CG	GF	IP	BFP	H	R	ER	HR	SH	SF	HB	TBB	IBB	SO	WP	Bk	W	L	Pct.	ShO	Sv	ERA
1989 Reds	R Cin	14	9	0	1	51	209	43	19	18	1	1	5	4	17	0	39	4	2	4	1	.800	0	0	3.18
1990 Chston-WV	A Cin	30	16	0	3	119.1	537	117	65	54	3	4	3	8	62	4	87	19	1	6	5	.545	0	0	4.07
1991 Chston-WV	A Cin	45	0	0	19	71	306	52	26	19	1	4	1	11	40	1	79	8	0	8	2	.800	0	0	2.41
1992 Cedar Rapds	A Cin	26	25	1	1	159	664	138	59	48	2	7	5	10	53	0	144	5	6	14	8	.636	0	0	2.72
1993 Chattanooga	AA Cin	28	28	1	0	166.2	723	163	85	67	7	11	7	12	66	2	122	9	1	12	8	.600	0	0	3.62
1994 Phoenix	AAA SF	27	11	0	8	90	401	109	48	46	6	3	4	5	29	0	57	4	1	7	2	.778	0	0	4.60
1995 Phoenix	AAA SF	4	0	0	0	6	22	2	1	1	0	0	0	0	3	0	5	0	1	0	0	.000	0	0	1.50
1996 Phoenix	AAA SF	32	20	0	3	128	560	139	75	68	18	7	3	6	51	1	70	9	1	7	10	.412	0	0	4.78
1997 Las Vegas	AAA SD	19	8	0	7	56.1	294	80	64	55	9	3	2	5	49	2	35	11	0	0	7	.000	0	0	8.79
Midland	AA Ana	22	2	0	7	35.2	169	41	34	28	6	3	2	2	19	1	24	3	0	1	4	.200	0	2	7.07
1995 San Francisco	NL	45	0	0	14	52.1	239	55	33	32	7	3	3	3	29	3	40	2	0	5	1	.833	0	0	5.50
1996 San Francisco	NL	10	0	0	3	13.1	72	16	13	11	3	2	1	2	14	2	4	1	0	0	1	.000	0	0	7.43
9 Min. YEARS		247	119	2	49	883	3885	884	476	404	53	42	29	63	389	11	662	72	13	59	47	.557	0	6	4.12
2 Maj. YEARS		55	0	0	17	65.2	310	71	46	43	10	5	4	5	43	5	44	3	0	5	2	.714	0	0	5.89

John Hope

Pitches: Right Bats: Right Pos: P Ht: 6'3" Wt: 206 Born: 12/21/70 Age: 27

Year Team	Lg Org	G	GS	CG	GF	IP	BFP	H	R	ER	HR	SH	SF	HB	TBB	IBB	SO	WP	Bk	W	L	Pct.	ShO	Sv	ERA
1989 Pirates	R Pit	4	3	0	0	15	68	15	12	8	0	1	3	1	6	0	14	0	1	0	1	.000	0	0	4.80
1991 Welland	A- Pit	3	3	0	0	17	67	12	1	1	0	0	0	2	3	0	15	0	0	2	0	1.000	0	0	0.53
Augusta	A Pit	7	7	0	0	46.1	188	29	20	18	1	0	1	4	19	0	37	2	1	4	2	.667	0	0	3.50
Salem	A+ Pit	6	5	0	1	27.2	122	38	20	19	5	0	1	0	4	0	18	0	0	2	2	.500	0	0	6.18
1992 Salem	A+ Pit	27	27	4	0	176.1	726	169	75	68	13	2	4	10	46	0	106	10	3	11	8	.579	0	0	3.47
1993 Carolina	AA Pit	21	20	0	0	111.1	478	123	69	54	7	2	6	8	29	4	66	10	2	9	4	.692	0	0	4.37
Buffalo	AAA Pit	4	4	0	0	21.1	92	30	16	15	4	0	0	1	2	0	6	2	0	2	1	.667	0	0	6.33
1994 Buffalo	AAA Pit	18	17	0	0	100	423	98	56	43	8	4	3	5	23	1	54	1	2	4	9	.308	0	0	3.87
1995 Calgary	AAA Pit	13	13	3	0	80.2	322	76	29	25	3	3	1	3	11	0	41	1	0	7	1	.875	1	0	2.79
1996 Calgary	AAA Pit	23	21	0	0	125	561	147	74	67	11	6	11	7	49	3	71	6	0	4	7	.364	0	0	4.82
1997 Colo Spngs	AAA Col	43	9	0	5	99.2	473	115	85	80	15	2	1	11	65	1	67	12	0	4	3	.571	0	0	7.22
1993 Pittsburgh	NL	7	7	0	0	38	166	47	19	17	2	5	1	2	8	3	8	1	0	0	2	.000	0	0	4.03
1994 Pittsburgh	NL	9	0	0	1	14	64	18	12	9	1	0	0	2	4	0	6	1	0	0	0	.000	0	0	5.79
1995 Pittsburgh	NL	3	0	0	0	2.1	21	8	8	8	0	0	1	3	4	0	2	0	0	0	0	.000	0	0	30.86
1996 Pittsburgh	NL	5	4	0	0	19.1	86	17	18	15	5	2	1	2	11	1	13	2	0	1	3	.250	0	0	6.98
8 Min. YEARS		169	129	7	6	820.1	3520	852	457	398	67	20	31	52	257	9	495	44	9	49	38	.563	1	0	4.37
4 Maj. YEARS		24	11	0	1	73.2	337	90	57	49	8	7	3	9	27	4	29	4	0	1	5	.167	0	0	5.99

Jeff Horn

Bats: Right Throws: Right Pos: C Ht: 6'1" Wt: 197 Born: 8/23/70 Age: 27

Year Team	Lg Org	G	AB	H	2B	3B	HR	TB	R	RBI	TBB	IBB	SO	HBP	SH	SF	SB	CS	SB%	GDP	Avg	OBP	SLG
1992 Elizabethtn	R+ Min	41	144	35	6	0	1	44	20	26	25	1	25	4	0	2	2	0	1.00	5	.243	.366	.306
1993 Ft. Wayne	A Min	66	200	39	7	0	5	61	19	23	18	0	51	4	1	4	1	2	.33	3	.195	.270	.305
1994 Ft. Myers	A+ Min	34	100	28	3	0	0	31	10	9	8	1	11	3	0	1	0	2	.00	6	.280	.348	.310
1995 Salt Lake	AAA Min	3	10	5	1	0	0	6	0	2	0	0	1	0	0	0	0	0	.00	0	.500	.500	.600
Ft. Myers	A+ Min	66	199	53	5	1	0	60	25	20	38	1	30	4	1	3	2	3	.40	4	.266	.389	.302
1996 Salt Lake	AAA Min	25	83	28	5	0	3	42	14	13	12	1	5	2	2	2	0	1	.00	4	.337	.424	.506
Hardware City	AA Min	12	45	12	2	0	0	14	4	3	6	1	7	0	0	0	0	1	.00	0	.267	.353	.311
1997 New Britain	AA Min	56	184	47	10	0	4	69	17	26	19	0	24	7	2	2	2	4	.33	7	.255	.344	.375
Salt Lake	AAA Min	23	78	26	6	0	1	35	16	13	11	0	22	1	0	0	0	0	.00	0	.333	.422	.449
6 Min. YEARS		326	1043	273	45	1	14	362	125	135	137	5	176	25	6	14	7	13	.35	29	.262	.357	.347

Mike Hostetler

Pitches: Right Bats: Right Pos: P Ht: 6'2" Wt: 195 Born: 6/5/70 Age: 28

Year Team	Lg Org	G	GS	CG	GF	IP	BFP	H	R	ER	HR	SH	SF	HB	TBB	IBB	SO	WP	Bk	W	L	Pct.	ShO	Sv	ERA
1991 Pulaski	R+ Atl	9	9	0	0	47	184	35	12	10	4	1	1	2	9	2	61	4	1	3	2	.600	0	0	1.91
1992 Durham	A+ Atl	13	13	3	0	88	354	75	25	21	2	0	1	2	19	3	88	2	3	9	3	.750	2	0	2.15
Greenville	AA Atl	16	13	1	0	80.2	339	78	37	35	11	3	2	4	23	1	57	3	0	6	2	.750	0	0	3.90
1993 Richmond	AAA Atl	9	9	0	0	48	212	50	29	27	5	1	0	4	18	2	36	0	0	1	3	.250	0	0	5.06
Greenville	AA Atl	19	19	2	0	135.2	559	122	48	41	9	4	2	7	36	3	105	6	0	8	5	.615	0	0	2.72
1994 Richmond	AAA Atl	6	6	0	0	23.1	105	27	16	16	3	0	1	1	10	1	13	0	2	0	2	.000	0	0	6.17
1995 Greenville	AA Atl	28	28	0	0	162.2	711	182	102	95	24	8	4	6	46	4	93	6	1	10	10	.500	0	0	5.26
1996 Richmond	AAA Atl	27	24	2	1	148	632	168	80	72	8	7	9	5	41	1	81	8	0	11	9	.550	0	0	4.38
1997 Richmond	AAA Atl	5	5	0	0	21	101	33	23	22	7	1	0	1	9	0	14	1	0	1	2	.333	0	0	9.43
7 Min. YEARS		132	126	8	1	754.1	3197	770	372	339	73	27	20	32	211	17	548	30	7	49	38	.563	2	0	4.04

Chris Howard

Pitches: Left Bats: Right Pos: P Ht: 6'0" Wt: 185 Born: 11/18/65 Age: 32

Year Team	Lg Org	G	GS	CG	GF	IP	BFP	H	R	ER	HR	SH	SF	HB	TBB	IBB	SO	WP	Bk	W	L	Pct.	ShO	Sv	ERA
1990 Albany-Colo	AA NYA	2	0	0	1	5	30	9	8	8	0	0	1	0	7	0	2	0	0	0	0	.000	0	0	14.40
Kinston	A+ Cle	8	0	0	3	14.2	73	21	5	4	0	0	0	2	6	0	16	0	2	1	1	.500	0	0	2.45
1991 Birmingham	AA ChA	38	0	0	24	53	219	43	14	12	2	6	2	3	16	1	52	2	1	6	1	.857	0	9	2.04
1992 White Sox	R ChA	1	0	0	0	2	9	3	1	1	0	0	0	0	0	0	3	0	0	0	0	.000	0	0	4.50
Vancouver	AAA ChA	20	0	0	5	24.2	111	18	9	8	3	6	2	0	22	3	23	0	1	3	1	.750	0	0	2.92
1993 Nashville	AAA ChA	43	0	0	17	66.2	271	55	32	25	9	3	5	0	16	4	53	7	2	4	3	.571	0	3	3.38
1994 Pawtucket	AAA Bos	13	0	0	1	24.1	95	14	6	6	2	1	0	0	10	0	21	1	0	3	0	1.000	0	0	2.22
1995 Sarasota	A+ Bos	6	5	0	0	10.1	45	10	6	6	1	1	2	0	4	0	7	1	3	0	2	.000	0	0	5.23
Pawtucket	AAA Bos	17	0	0	2	20.2	91	25	11	9	6	0	2	0	4	1	19	0	0	3	1	.750	0	0	3.92
1997 Mets	R NYN	4	2	0	0	7	29	7	4	4	0	0	0	0	2	0	11	0	0	1	0	1.000	0	0	5.14
St. Lucie	A+ NYN	10	0	0	2	11.1	52	12	9	9	1	0	0	2	6	0	10	0	0	1	1	.500	0	1	7.15
Binghamton	AA NYN	13	0	0	2	15.2	55	6	2	2	1	1	0	0	7	0	16	0	0	0	0	.000	0	1	1.15
1993 Chicago	AL	3	0	0	0	2.1	10	2	0	0	0	0	0	0	3	1	1	0	0	1	0	1.000	0	0	0.00
1994 Boston	AL	37	0	0	5	39.2	166	35	17	16	5	2	2	0	12	4	22	1	0	1	0	1.000	0	1	3.63
1995 Texas	AL	4	0	0	1	4	15	3	0	0	0	0	0	0	0	0	2	1	0	0	0	.000	0	0	0.00
7 Min. YEARS		175	7	0	57	255.1	1080	223	107	94	25	18	14	7	100	9	233	11	10	21	11	.656	0	14	3.31
3 Maj. YEARS		44	0	0	6	46	191	40	17	16	5	2	3	0	16	5	25	2	0	2	0	1.000	0	1	3.13

Matt Howard

Bats: Right **Throws:** Right **Pos:** SS **Ht:** 5'10" **Wt:** 170 **Born:** 9/22/67 **Age:** 30

Year Team	Lg Org	G	AB	H	2B	3B	HR	TB	R	RBI	TBB	IBB	SO	HBP	SH	SF	SB	CS	SB%	GDP	Avg	OBP	SLG
1989 Great Falls	R+ LA	59	186	62	8	2	3	83	39	34	21	0	14	9	5	2	23	8	.74	3	.333	.422	.446
1990 Bakersfield	A+ LA	137	551	144	22	3	1	175	75	54	37	1	39	13	4	6	47	10	.82	8	.261	.320	.318
1991 Vero Beach	A+ LA	128	441	115	21	3	3	151	79	39	56	2	49	10	14	6	50	18	.74	6	.261	.353	.342
1992 San Antonio	AA LA	95	345	93	12	5	2	121	40	34	28	1	38	4	16	1	18	15	.55	12	.270	.331	.351
Albuquerque	AAA LA	36	116	34	3	0	0	37	14	8	9	0	7	0	2	0	1	2	.33	2	.293	.344	.319
1993 Albuquerque	AAA LA	18	26	4	0	1	0	6	3	4	3	0	2	0	1	1	1	1	.50	1	.154	.233	.231
San Antonio	AA LA	41	122	35	5	1	0	42	12	5	16	1	14	3	2	0	4	5	.44	4	.287	.383	.344
1994 Albuquerque	AAA LA	88	267	79	12	6	1	106	44	33	14	0	13	6	4	1	15	8	.65	12	.296	.344	.397
1995 Bowie	AA Bal	70	251	76	8	2	1	91	42	15	29	1	27	5	3	1	22	4	.85	6	.303	.385	.363
1996 Columbus	AAA NYA	51	202	70	12	2	2	92	36	16	18	0	9	1	3	1	9	3	.75	5	.347	.401	.455
1997 Columbus	AAA NYA	122	478	149	28	7	6	209	90	67	54	1	33	10	3	3	22	7	.76	12	.312	.391	.437
1996 New York	AL	35	54	11	1	0	1	15	9	9	2	0	8	0	2	1	1	0	1.00	1	.204	.228	.278
9 Min. YEARS		845	2985	861	131	32	19	1113	474	309	285	7	245	61	57	22	212	81	.72	71	.288	.360	.373

Dann Howitt

Bats: Left **Throws:** Right **Pos:** DH **Ht:** 6'5" **Wt:** 205 **Born:** 2/13/64 **Age:** 34

Year Team	Lg Org	G	AB	H	2B	3B	HR	TB	R	RBI	TBB	IBB	SO	HBP	SH	SF	SB	CS	SB%	GDP	Avg	OBP	SLG
1986 Medford	A- Oak	66	208	66	9	2	6	97	36	37	49	3	37	1	1	1	5	1	.83	7	.317	.448	.466
1987 Modesto	A+ Oak	109	336	70	11	2	8	109	44	42	59	1	110	4	3	3	7	9	.44	8	.208	.331	.324
1988 Modesto	A+ Oak	132	480	121	20	2	18	199	75	86	81	3	106	2	0	2	11	5	.69	9	.252	.361	.415
Tacoma	AAA Oak	4	15	2	1	0	0	3	1	0	0	0	4	0	0	0	0	0	.00	0	.133	.133	.200
1989 Huntsville	AA Oak	138	509	143	28	2	26	253	78	111	68	7	107	3	2	6	2	1	.67	6	.281	.365	.497
1990 Tacoma	AAA Oak	118	437	116	30	1	11	181	58	69	38	3	95	2	0	4	4	4	.50	16	.265	.324	.414
1991 Tacoma	AAA Oak	122	449	120	28	6	14	202	58	73	49	2	92	2	1	5	5	2	.71	14	.267	.339	.450
1992 Tacoma	AAA Oak	43	140	41	13	1	1	59	25	27	23	0	20	2	0	5	5	3	.63	3	.293	.388	.421
Calgary	AAA Sea	50	178	54	9	5	6	91	29	33	12	1	38	1	2	1	4	0	1.00	1	.303	.349	.511
1993 Calgary	AAA Sea	95	333	93	20	1	21	178	57	77	39	2	67	1	1	7	7	5	.58	4	.279	.350	.535
1994 Nashville	AAA ChA	66	231	59	15	1	8	100	30	36	19	1	48	2	0	1	4	0	1.00	4	.255	.316	.433
1995 Nashville	AAA ChA	45	133	30	6	1	3	47	16	15	16	4	32	0	0	2	0	3	.00	2	.226	.305	.353
Buffalo	AAA Cle	41	119	36	8	3	4	62	19	18	14	2	30	0	0	0	0	0	.00	2	.303	.376	.521
1996 Louisville	AAA StL	46	141	36	6	1	4	56	19	18	16	2	31	1	2	1	4	1	.80	2	.255	.333	.397
Indianapolis	AAA Cin	50	156	43	6	1	4	63	19	22	14	2	35	1	0	1	0	3	.00	4	.276	.337	.404
1997 Colo Spngs	AAA Col	102	316	105	29	2	14	176	57	62	32	4	71	0	0	1	2	2	.50	7	.332	.393	.557
1989 Oakland	AL	3	3	0	0	0	0	0	0	0	0	0	2	0	0	0	0	0	.00	0	.000	.000	.000
1990 Oakland	AL	14	22	3	0	1	0	5	3	1	3	0	12	0	0	0	0	0	.00	0	.136	.240	.227
1991 Oakland	AL	21	42	7	1	0	1	11	5	3	1	0	12	0	0	1	0	0	.00	1	.167	.182	.262
1992 Oakland	AL	22	48	6	0	0	1	9	1	2	5	1	4	0	1	0	0	0	.00	4	.125	.208	.188
Seattle	AL	13	37	10	4	1	1	19	6	8	3	0	5	0	0	3	1	1	.50	2	.270	.302	.514
1993 Seattle	AL	32	76	16	3	1	2	27	6	8	4	0	18	0	0	0	0	0	.00	4	.211	.250	.355
1994 Chicago	AL	10	14	5	3	0	0	8	4	0	1	0	7	0	0	0	0	0	.00	0	.357	.400	.571
12 Min. YEARS		1227	4181	1135	239	29	148	1876	621	726	529	37	923	22	12	40	60	39	.61	98	.271	.353	.449
6 Maj. YEARS		115	242	47	11	3	5	79	25	22	17	1	60	0	1	4	1	1	.50	8	.194	.243	.326

Bob Howry

Pitches: Right **Bats:** Left **Pos:** P **Ht:** 6'5" **Wt:** 215 **Born:** 8/4/73 **Age:** 24

Year Team	Lg Org	G	GS	CG	GF	IP	BFP	H	R	ER	HR	SH	SF	HB	TBB	IBB	SO	WP	Bk	W	L	Pct.	ShO	Sv	ERA
1994 Everett	A- SF	5	5	0	0	19	97	29	19	15	3	0	1	1	10	2	16	5	0	0	4	.000	0	0	7.11
Clinton	A SF	9	8	0	0	49.1	219	61	29	23	1	3	4	3	16	0	22	4	2	1	3	.250	0	0	4.20
1995 San Jose	A+ SF	27	25	1	1	165.1	695	171	79	65	6	12	4	8	54	0	107	7	3	12	10	.545	0	0	3.54
1996 Shreveport	AA SF	27	27	0	0	156.2	682	163	90	81	17	6	4	9	56	3	57	3	1	10	8	.556	0	0	4.65
1997 Shreveport	AA SF	48	0	0	39	55	240	58	35	30	6	1	3	0	21	0	43	3	1	6	3	.667	0	22	4.91
Birmingham	AA ChA	12	0	0	6	12.2	54	16	4	4	1	0	0	0	3	0	3	0	0	0	0	.000	0	2	2.84
4 Min. YEARS		128	65	1	46	458	1987	498	256	218	34	22	16	21	160	5	248	22	7	29	28	.509	0	24	4.28

Mark Hubbard

Pitches: Left **Bats:** Left **Pos:** P **Ht:** 6'2" **Wt:** 190 **Born:** 2/2/70 **Age:** 28

Year Team	Lg Org	G	GS	CG	GF	IP	BFP	H	R	ER	HR	SH	SF	HB	TBB	IBB	SO	WP	Bk	W	L	Pct.	ShO	Sv	ERA
1994 Greensboro	A NYA	26	26	2	0	149.1	642	162	69	59	11	1	5	7	46	0	139	4	3	13	7	.650	1	0	3.56
Tampa	A+ NYA	2	1	0	1	6.2	33	9	6	3	2	0	0	1	2	0	5	0	0	0	1	.000	0	0	4.05
1995 Tampa	A+ NYA	13	11	0	0	68.1	269	52	22	14	2	1	2	4	21	0	40	2	0	4	3	.571	0	0	1.84
Norwich	AA NYA	13	12	0	1	72.2	310	81	38	34	2	2	2	6	25	1	39	1	1	4	4	.500	0	1	4.21
1996 Tampa	A+ NYA	4	4	0	0	22	96	27	17	14	1	0	0	3	6	0	12	0	0	1	2	.333	0	0	5.73
Norwich	AA NYA	4	4	0	0	19.2	89	19	13	12	2	1	0	1	10	1	14	0	0	2	0	1.000	0	0	5.49
1997 Norwich	AA NYA	2	0	0	2	2.1	13	6	4	4	1	0	0	0	1	0	0	0	0	0	0	.000	0	0	15.43
4 Min. YEARS		64	58	3	4	341	1452	356	169	140	21	5	9	22	111	2	249	7	4	24	17	.585	1	1	3.70

Dan Hubbs

Pitches: Right **Bats:** Right **Pos:** P **Ht:** 6'2" **Wt:** 200 **Born:** 1/23/71 **Age:** 27

Year Team	Lg Org	G	GS	CG	GF	IP	BFP	H	R	ER	HR	SH	SF	HB	TBB	IBB	SO	WP	Bk	W	L	Pct.	ShO	Sv	ERA
1993 Great Falls	R+ LA	3	0	0	1	7.2	29	3	1	1	0	0	0	2	2	0	12	0	1	1	1	.500	0	0	1.17

Year Team	Lg Org	G	GS	CG	GF	IP	BFP	H	R	ER	HR	SH	SF	HB	TBB	IBB	SO	WP	Bk	W	L	Pct.	ShO	Sv	ERA
Bakersfield	A+ LA	19	1	0	8	44.2	181	36	12	9	4	1	2	0	15	1	44	3	1	2	1	.667	0	1	1.81
1994 Bakersfield	A+ LA	13	0	0	6	35.1	145	29	17	15	3	3	0	1	10	0	51	0	0	3	1	.750	0	2	3.82
San Antonio	AA LA	38	1	0	13	80	340	82	34	28	3	1	6	4	27	7	75	5	0	5	5	.500	0	1	3.15
1995 San Antonio	AA LA	31	0	0	6	61	248	58	25	24	3	3	1	1	16	0	52	0	1	2	1	.667	0	0	3.54
1996 Albuquerque	AAA LA	49	0	0	15	75.2	356	89	51	40	4	0	3	3	47	12	82	2	0	7	1	.875	0	2	4.76
1997 Albuquerque	AAA LA	62	3	0	19	94.2	411	103	45	41	11	4	5	4	38	2	87	2	0	6	4	.600	0	3	3.90
5 Min. YEARS		215	5	0	68	399	1710	400	185	158	28	12	17	15	155	22	403	12	3	26	14	.650	0	9	3.56

Jeff Huber

Pitches: Left Bats: Right Pos: P   Ht: 6'4" Wt: 220 Born: 12/17/70 Age: 27

Year Team	Lg Org	G	GS	CG	GF	IP	BFP	H	R	ER	HR	SH	SF	HB	TBB	IBB	SO	WP	Bk	W	L	Pct.	ShO	Sv	ERA
1990 Padres	R SD	9	7	0	1	35.2	153	32	20	12	0	0	2	0	15	0	20	2	2	1	4	.200	0	1	3.03
1992 Chston-SC	A SD	46	0	0	30	77.1	309	66	31	25	3	2	0	4	21	2	59	6	5	8	3	.727	0	9	2.91
Waterloo	A SD	9	0	0	6	15	58	15	4	4	0	1	1	0	1	0	13	0	0	1	2	.333	0	1	2.40
1993 Rancho Cuca	A+ SD	42	0	0	41	48.2	199	43	22	17	4	2	0	0	18	0	43	4	0	4	1	.800	0	18	3.14
Wichita	AA SD	15	0	0	8	19.1	82	16	9	7	1	0	0	3	9	0	18	1	1	3	1	.750	0	3	3.26
1994 Wichita	AA SD	38	0	0	29	39.2	193	56	37	31	7	4	3	0	17	2	32	3	0	3	2	.600	0	12	7.03
1995 Memphis	AA SD	5	0	0	0	4.2	22	7	6	6	2	0	0	1	0	0	6	0	0	0	0	.000	0	0	11.57
Frederick	A+ Bal	21	0	0	4	19	92	29	16	11	5	1	2	0	5	1	11	2	0	2	0	1.000	0	1	5.21
Lubbock	IND —	12	0	0	4	19	79	21	9	8	2	0	0	0	7	0	10	1	0	1	2	.333	0	1	3.79
1996 Lubbock	IND —	17	0	0	16	18.1	69	9	2	1	0	0	0	0	6	0	19	0	0	0	0	.000	0	11	0.49
Stockton	A+ Mil	18	0	0	13	19.2	84	24	9	4	0	0	2	1	3	0	12	0	0	1	1	.500	0	6	1.83
1997 El Paso	AA Mil	19	0	0	7	26	121	35	14	10	2	2	0	1	11	2	20	2	1	3	1	.750	0	1	3.46
Tucson	AAA Mil	40	2	0	15	62.2	274	67	36	33	11	6	2	1	22	1	37	3	0	3	7	.300	0	5	4.74
7 Min. YEARS		291	9	0	174	405	1735	420	215	169	38	19	12	11	135	8	300	24	9	30	24	.556	0	68	3.76

Ken Huckaby

Bats: Right Throws: Right Pos: C   Ht: 6'1" Wt: 205 Born: 1/27/71 Age: 27

Year Team	Lg Org	G	AB	H	2B	3B	HR	TB	R	RBI	TBB	IBB	SO	HBP	SH	SF	SB	CS	SB%	GDP	Avg	OBP	SLG
1991 Great Falls	R+ LA	57	213	55	16	0	3	80	39	37	17	0	38	4	1	3	3	2	.60	4	.258	.321	.376
1992 Vero Beach	A+ LA	73	261	63	9	0	0	72	14	21	7	0	42	1	2	2	1	1	.50	5	.241	.262	.276
1993 Vero Beach	A+ LA	79	281	75	14	1	4	103	22	41	11	1	35	2	3	2	2	1	.67	3	.267	.297	.367
San Antonio	AA LA	28	82	18	1	0	0	19	4	5	2	1	7	2	0	1	0	0	.00	0	.220	.253	.232
1994 San Antonio	AA LA	11	41	11	1	0	1	15	3	9	1	1	1	0	0	0	1	0	1.00	1	.268	.286	.366
Bakersfield	A+ LA	77	270	81	18	1	2	107	29	30	10	0	37	2	0	1	2	3	.40	7	.300	.329	.396
1995 Albuquerque	AAA LA	89	278	90	16	2	1	113	30	40	12	1	26	4	3	1	3	1	.75	16	.324	.359	.406
1996 Albuquerque	AAA LA	103	286	79	16	2	3	108	37	41	17	1	35	2	3	1	0	0	.00	10	.276	.320	.378
1997 Albuquerque	AAA LA	69	201	40	5	1	0	47	14	18	9	1	36	0	3	2	1	0	1.00	5	.199	.231	.234
7 Min. YEARS		586	1913	512	96	7	14	664	192	242	86	6	257	17	15	13	13	8	.62	51	.268	.303	.347

Larry Huff

Bats: Right Throws: Right Pos: 3B   Ht: 6'0" Wt: 175 Born: 1/24/72 Age: 26

Year Team	Lg Org	G	AB	H	2B	3B	HR	TB	R	RBI	TBB	IBB	SO	HBP	SH	SF	SB	CS	SB%	GDP	Avg	OBP	SLG
1994 Martinsville	R+ Phi	39	143	36	2	1	1	43	24	7	29	0	20	6	1	0	17	4	.81	3	.252	.399	.301
Batavia	A- Phi	20	67	15	1	0	0	16	13	2	12	1	10	0	2	0	5	0	1.00	1	.224	.342	.239
1995 Piedmont	A Phi	130	481	131	26	4	1	168	86	51	74	5	64	10	7	4	26	8	.76	9	.272	.378	.349
1996 Clearwater	A+ Phi	128	483	132	17	5	0	159	73	37	60	1	65	6	10	4	37	11	.77	4	.273	.358	.329
1997 Reading	AA Phi	124	425	112	21	3	5	154	58	41	36	3	57	6	6	0	24	7	.77	10	.264	.330	.362
4 Min. YEARS		441	1599	426	67	13	7	540	254	138	211	10	216	28	26	8	109	30	.78	27	.266	.360	.338

Bobby Hughes

Bats: Right Throws: Right Pos: C   Ht: 6'4" Wt: 220 Born: 3/10/71 Age: 27

Year Team	Lg Org	G	AB	H	2B	3B	HR	TB	R	RBI	TBB	IBB	SO	HBP	SH	SF	SB	CS	SB%	GDP	Avg	OBP	SLG
1992 Helena	R+ Mil	11	40	7	1	1	0	10	5	6	4	0	14	2	0	0	0	0	.00	0	.175	.283	.250
1993 Beloit	A Mil	98	321	89	11	3	17	157	42	56	23	0	77	6	5	0	1	3	.25	2	.277	.337	.489
1994 El Paso	AA Mil	12	36	10	4	1	0	16	3	12	5	0	7	1	0	2	0	1	.00	1	.278	.364	.444
Stockton	A+ Mil	95	322	81	24	3	11	144	54	53	33	0	83	9	1	2	2	1	.67	6	.252	.336	.447
1995 Stockton	A+ Mil	52	179	42	9	2	8	79	22	31	17	1	41	1	0	3	2	2	.50	10	.235	.300	.441
El Paso	AA Mil	51	173	46	12	0	7	79	11	27	12	1	30	2	0	2	0	2	.00	4	.266	.317	.457
1996 New Orleans	AAA Mil	37	125	25	5	0	4	42	11	15	4	0	31	3	0	0	1	1	.50	2	.200	.242	.336
El Paso	AA Mil	67	237	72	18	1	15	137	43	39	30	1	40	2	0	3	3	3	.50	5	.304	.382	.578
1997 Tucson	AAA Mil	89	290	90	29	2	7	144	43	51	24	1	46	9	0	4	0	0	.00	5	.310	.376	.497
6 Min. YEARS		512	1723	462	113	13	69	808	234	290	152	4	369	35	6	16	9	13	.41	41	.268	.337	.469

Troy Hughes

Bats: Right Throws: Right Pos: OF   Ht: 6'4" Wt: 212 Born: 1/3/71 Age: 27

Year Team	Lg Org	G	AB	H	2B	3B	HR	TB	R	RBI	TBB	IBB	SO	HBP	SH	SF	SB	CS	SB%	GDP	Avg	OBP	SLG
1989 Braves	R Atl	36	110	24	5	0	0	29	17	10	11	0	29	1	1	1	8	4	.67	0	.218	.293	.264
1990 Pulaski	R+ Atl	46	145	39	7	1	1	51	22	17	16	0	39	0	2	1	5	1	.83	3	.269	.340	.352
1991 Macon	A Atl	112	404	121	33	2	9	185	69	80	36	1	76	3	1	5	22	13	.63	6	.300	.357	.458

		BATTING															BASERUNNING				PERCENTAGES		
Year Team	Lg Org	G	AB	H	2B	3B	HR	TB	R	RBI	TBB	IBB	SO	HBP	SH	SF	SB	CS	SB%	GDP	Avg	OBP	SLG
1992 Durham	A+ Atl	128	449	110	21	4	16	187	64	53	49	3	97	1	2	6	12	7	.63	7	.245	.317	.416
1993 Greenville	AA Atl	109	383	102	20	4	14	172	49	58	44	1	67	5	0	3	7	3	.70	10	.266	.347	.449
1994 Richmond	AAA Atl	81	228	49	9	1	1	63	24	18	29	3	48	5	0	6	6	2	.75	7	.215	.310	.276
Greenville	AA Atl	27	89	27	7	0	3	43	14	12	11	0	11	0	0	1	4	0	1.00	1	.303	.376	.483
1995 Greenville	AA Atl	73	200	51	7	1	6	78	24	25	17	0	52	2	0	2	3	6	.33	1	.255	.317	.390
Norwich	AA NYA	15	55	18	2	1	1	25	7	8	4	0	11	1	0	1	0	2	.00	3	.327	.377	.455
1996 Orlando	AA ChN	123	450	123	26	3	18	209	75	93	50	4	86	1	0	2	3	4	.43	8	.273	.346	.464
1997 Huntsville	AA Oak	72	258	54	12	0	5	81	37	33	23	0	50	1	0	3	2	1	.67	8	.209	.274	.314
9 Min. YEARS		822	2771	718	149	17	74	1123	402	407	290	12	566	20	6	31	72	43	.63	55	.259	.330	.405

Rick Huisman

Pitches: Right Bats: Right Pos: P Ht: 6' 3" Wt: 210 Born: 5/17/69 Age: 29

		HOW MUCH HE PITCHED						WHAT HE GAVE UP												THE RESULTS					
Year Team	Lg Org	G	GS	CG	GF	IP	BFP	H	R	ER	HR	SH	SF	HB	TBB	IBB	SO	WP	Bk	W	L	Pct.	ShO	Sv	ERA
1990 Everett	A- SF	1	0	0	0	2	10	3	1	1	0	0	0	0	2	0	2	1	0	0	0	.000	0	0	4.50
Clinton	A SF	14	13	0	0	79	315	57	19	18	2	1	2	0	33	0	103	5	4	6	5	.545	0	0	2.05
1991 San Jose	A+ SF	26	26	7	0	182.1	720	126	45	37	5	11	3	3	73	1	216	13	3	16	4	.800	4	0	1.83
1992 Shreveport	AA SF	17	16	1	0	103.1	403	79	33	27	3	2	0	5	31	1	100	3	1	7	4	.636	1	0	2.35
Phoenix	AAA SF	9	8	0	0	56	230	45	16	15	3	1	1	1	24	0	44	1	0	3	2	.600	0	0	2.41
1993 San Jose	A+ SF	4	4	1	0	23.1	97	19	6	6	0	2	1	2	12	0	15	1	0	2	1	.667	0	0	2.31
Phoenix	AAA SF	14	14	0	0	72.1	333	78	54	48	5	1	1	1	45	0	59	8	4	3	4	.429	0	0	5.97
Tucson	AAA Hou	2	0	0	0	3.2	18	6	5	3	0	0	0	0	1	0	4	5	0	1	0	1.000	0	0	7.36
1994 Jackson	AA Hou	49	0	0	46	50.1	204	32	10	9	1	1	1	2	24	2	63	1	0	3	0	1.000	0	31	1.61
1995 Tucson	AAA Hou	42	0	0	28	54.2	246	58	33	27	1	0	3	1	28	3	47	3	1	6	1	.857	0	6	4.45
Omaha	AAA KC	5	0	0	3	5	19	3	1	1	0	0	1	0	1	0	13	0	0	0	0	.000	0	1	1.80
1996 Omaha	AAA KC	27	4	0	0	57.1	243	54	32	31	9	0	1	2	24	0	50	0	1	2	4	.333	0	0	4.87
1997 Omaha	AAA KC	37	1	0	8	59.2	268	59	29	24	7	1	3	3	35	1	57	7	0	1	5	.167	0	2	3.62
1995 Kansas City	AL	7	0	0	2	9.2	44	14	8	8	2	1	0	0	1	0	12	0	0	0	0	.000	0	0	7.45
1996 Kansas City	AL	22	0	0	5	29.1	130	25	15	15	4	2	2	0	18	2	23	0	0	2	1	.667	0	0	4.60
8 Min. YEARS		247	86	9	91	749	3106	619	284	247	37	20	16	20	333	8	773	48	14	50	30	.625	5	40	2.97
2 Maj. YEARS		29	0	0	7	39	174	39	23	23	6	3	2	0	19	2	35	0	0	2	1	.667	0	0	5.31

Rich Humphrey

Pitches: Right Bats: Right Pos: P Ht: 6'1" Wt: 185 Born: 6/24/71 Age: 27

		HOW MUCH HE PITCHED						WHAT HE GAVE UP												THE RESULTS					
Year Team	Lg Org	G	GS	CG	GF	IP	BFP	H	R	ER	HR	SH	SF	HB	TBB	IBB	SO	WP	Bk	W	L	Pct.	ShO	Sv	ERA
1993 Auburn	A- Hou	29	0	0	26	39.2	168	34	18	11	2	1	1	3	10	2	49	2	1	4	3	.571	0	9	2.50
1994 Astros	R Hou	4	0	0	0	7	30	7	3	1	0	1	0	1	1	1	8	0	0	1	0	1.000	0	0	1.29
Osceola	A+ Hou	3	0	0	0	6	32	8	8	7	0	1	0	2	3	0	5	0	0	0	0	.000	0	0	10.50
1995 Kissimmee	A+ Hou	46	0	0	39	55	233	45	16	12	1	5	2	3	20	0	33	2	1	3	1	.750	0	14	1.96
Jackson	AA Hou	9	0	0	1	16	66	11	5	3	0	2	0	1	9	2	9	1	0	1	1	.500	0	1	1.69
1996 Tucson	AAA Hou	10	0	0	7	13.1	71	23	20	16	3	0	2	1	7	0	8	4	0	1	1	.500	0	0	10.80
Kissimmee	A+ Hou	5	0	0	5	8.2	34	6	3	2	0	2	0	1	1	0	5	0	0	0	0	.000	0	2	2.08
Jackson	AA Hou	43	0	0	22	64.2	257	53	21	18	6	3	1	3	15	0	37	2	0	4	2	.667	0	1	2.51
1997 Jackson	AA Hou	3	0	0	1	1.2	16	7	9	6	2	0	2	0	1	3	0	0	0	0	1	.000	0	0	32.40
5 Min. YEARS		152	0	0	101	212	907	194	103	76	12	17	7	16	69	5	154	12	2	14	10	.583	0	26	3.23

Brian Hunter

Bats: Right Throws: Left Pos: 1B-OF Ht: 6' 0" Wt: 225 Born: 3/4/68 Age: 30

		BATTING															BASERUNNING				PERCENTAGES		
Year Team	Lg Org	G	AB	H	2B	3B	HR	TB	R	RBI	TBB	IBB	SO	HBP	SH	SF	SB	CS	SB%	GDP	Avg	OBP	SLG
1987 Pulaski	R+ Atl	65	251	58	10	2	8	96	38	30	18	0	47	5	0	1	3	2	.60	7	.231	.295	.382
1988 Burlington	A Atl	117	417	108	17	0	22	191	58	71	45	2	90	8	1	7	7	2	.78	7	.259	.338	.458
Durham	A+ Atl	13	49	17	3	0	3	29	13	9	7	0	8	0	0	0	2	0	1.00	0	.347	.429	.592
1989 Greenville	AA Atl	124	451	114	19	2	19	194	57	82	33	2	61	7	1	9	5	4	.56	4	.253	.308	.430
1990 Richmond	AAA Atl	43	137	27	4	0	5	46	13	16	18	0	37	0	1	1	2	1	.67	0	.197	.288	.336
Greenville	AA Atl	88	320	77	13	1	14	134	45	55	43	1	62	3	0	4	3	4	.43	6	.241	.332	.419
1991 Richmond	AAA Atl	48	181	47	7	0	10	84	28	30	11	1	24	1	2	3	3	2	.60	6	.260	.301	.464
1993 Richmond	AAA Atl	30	99	24	7	0	6	49	16	26	10	0	21	3	0	0	4	2	.67	2	.242	.330	.495
1995 Indianapolis	AAA Cin	9	36	13	5	0	4	30	7	11	6	1	11	0	0	0	0	1	.00	0	.361	.452	.833
1996 Tacoma	AAA Sea	25	92	32	6	1	7	61	19	24	9	0	11	0	0	3	1	0	1.00	3	.348	.394	.663
1997 Indianapolis	AAA Cin	139	506	142	36	4	21	249	74	85	42	2	76	4	2	8	9	6	.60	9	.281	.336	.492
1991 Atlanta	NL	97	271	68	16	1	12	122	32	50	17	0	48	1	0	2	0	2	.00	6	.251	.296	.450
1992 Atlanta	NL	102	238	57	13	2	14	116	34	41	21	3	50	0	1	8	1	2	.33	2	.239	.292	.487
1993 Atlanta	NL	37	80	11	3	1	0	16	4	8	2	1	15	0	0	3	0	0	.00	1	.138	.153	.200
1994 Pittsburgh	NL	76	233	53	15	1	11	103	28	47	15	2	55	0	0	4	0	0	.00	4	.227	.270	.442
Cincinnati	NL	9	23	7	1	0	4	20	6	10	2	0	1	0	0	0	0	0	.00	0	.304	.346	.870
1995 Cincinnati	NL	40	79	17	6	0	1	26	9	9	11	1	21	1	0	2	1		.67	2	.215	.312	.329
1996 Seattle	AL	75	198	53	10	0	7	84	21	28	15	2	43	4	1	3	0	0	.00	6	.268	.327	.424
9 Min. YEARS		701	2539	659	127	10	119	1163	368	439	242	9	448	31	7	36	39	24	.62	44	.260	.327	.458
6 Maj. YEARS		436	1122	266	64	6	49	487	134	193	83	9	233	6	2	20	3	6	.33	20	.237	.288	.434

Rich Hunter

Pitches: Right Bats: Right Pos: P Ht: 6' 1" Wt: 185 Born: 9/25/74 Age: 23

		HOW MUCH HE PITCHED						WHAT HE GAVE UP												THE RESULTS					
Year Team	Lg Org	G	GS	CG	GF	IP	BFP	H	R	ER	HR	SH	SF	HB	TBB	IBB	SO	WP	Bk	W	L	Pct.	ShO	Sv	ERA
1993 Martinsville	R+ Phi	13	9	0	1	49	254	82	61	52	9	1	6	4	27	0	36	4	1	0	6	.000	0	0	9.55

(pitching, continued)

Year Team	Lg Org	HOW MUCH HE PITCHED					WHAT HE GAVE UP										THE RESULTS				
		G	GS	CG	GF	IP	BFP	H	R	ER	HR	SH	SF	HB	TBB	IBB	SO	WP	Bk	W	L	Pct.	ShO	Sv	ERA
1994 Martinsvlle	R+ Phi	18	0	0	8	38	153	31	19	19	3	1	2	3	9	1	39	1	0	3	2	.600	0	5	4.50
1995 Piedmont	A Phi	15	15	3	0	104	404	79	37	32	9	1	1	2	19	0	80	0	0	10	2	.833	2	0	2.77
Clearwater	A+ Phi	9	9	0	0	58.1	242	62	23	19	3	3	2	5	7	0	46	3	3	6	0	1.000	0	0	2.93
Reading	AA Phi	3	3	0	0	22	86	14	6	5	1	0	1	0	6	0	17	2	0	3	0	1.000	0	0	2.05
1996 Scranton-WB	AAA Phi	8	7	1	0	40.1	182	39	31	30	5	4	1	3	22	0	22	3	0	2	4	.333	0	0	6.69
Reading	AA Phi	10	10	2	0	71	290	69	26	25	7	1	1	7	12	0	40	3	1	4	3	.571	0	0	3.17
1997 Reading	AA Phi	29	28	1	0	163	730	191	100	85	20	4	6	13	60	4	104	2	0	6	11	.353	1	0	4.69
1996 Philadelphia	NL	14	14	0	0	69.1	322	84	54	50	10	3	4	5	33	2	32	4	0	3	7	.300	0	0	6.49
5 Min. YEARS		105	81	7	9	545.2	2341	567	303	267	57	15	20	34	162	5	384	18	5	34	28	.548	3	5	4.40

Scott Hunter

Bats: Right Throws: Right Pos: OF   Ht: 6'1" Wt: 195 Born: 12/17/75 Age: 22

Year Team	Lg Org	BATTING														BASERUNNING				PERCENTAGES		
		G	AB	H	2B	3B	HR	TB	R	RBI	TBB	IBB	SO	HBP	SH	SF	SB	CS	SB%	GDP	Avg	OBP	SLG
1994 Great Falls	R+ LA	64	237	75	12	4	2	101	45	28	25	1	40	5	4	3	17	5	.77	1	.316	.389	.426
1995 San Berndno	A+ LA	113	379	108	19	3	11	166	68	59	36	1	83	6	4	1	27	8	.77	0	.285	.355	.438
Capital City	A NYN	12	40	10	0	0	1	10	2	1	2	0	13	1	1	1	2	1	.67	2	.250	.295	.250
1996 St. Lucie	A+ NYN	127	475	122	19	1	2	149	71	38	38	4	68	8	3	3	49	12	.80	6	.257	.321	.314
1997 Binghamton	AA NYN	80	289	74	12	2	10	120	45	31	25	1	52	4	1	4	24	9	.73	6	.256	.320	.415
4 Min. YEARS		396	1420	389	62	10	25	546	231	157	126	7	256	24	13	12	119	35	.77	15	.274	.341	.385

Scott Huntsman

Pitches: Right Bats: Right Pos: P   Ht: 6'2" Wt: 230 Born: 10/28/72 Age: 25

Year Team	Lg Org	HOW MUCH HE PITCHED						WHAT HE GAVE UP									THE RESULTS				
		G	GS	CG	GF	IP	BFP	H	R	ER	HR	SH	SF	HB	TBB	IBB	SO	WP	Bk	W	L	Pct.	ShO	Sv	ERA
1994 Brewers	R Mil	4	0	0	4	3.2	12	1	0	0	0	0	0	0	0	0	3	0	0	0	0	.000	0	1	0.00
Helena	R+ Mil	17	0	0	11	20	99	28	19	15	2	3	1	1	11	1	22	1	0	1	0	1.000	0	5	6.75
1995 Beloit	A Mil	43	0	0	14	49.2	229	42	17	15	3	2	1	5	34	2	49	5	0	4	3	.571	0	2	2.72
1996 Stockton	A+ Mil	43	0	0	29	48.1	213	37	21	15	3	0	3	2	27	0	56	2	0	4	3	.571	0	12	2.79
1997 El Paso	AA Mil	42	0	0	13	55	272	76	56	44	5	0	5	4	21	2	37	4	2	4	4	.500	0	3	7.20
4 Min. YEARS		149	0	0	71	176.2	825	184	113	89	13	5	10	12	93	5	167	12	2	13	10	.565	0	22	4.53

Bill Hurst

Pitches: Right Bats: Right Pos: P   Ht: 6'7" Wt: 215 Born: 4/28/70 Age: 28

Year Team	Lg Org	HOW MUCH HE PITCHED						WHAT HE GAVE UP									THE RESULTS				
		G	GS	CG	GF	IP	BFP	H	R	ER	HR	SH	SF	HB	TBB	IBB	SO	WP	Bk	W	L	Pct.	ShO	Sv	ERA
1990 Johnson Cty	R+ StL	2	2	0	0	10.2	41	5	2	2	0	0	0	0	5	0	12	0	0	0	0	.000	0	0	1.69
Savannah	A StL	7	7	0	0	31.2	141	22	17	12	0	0	1	1	27	1	14	8	2	2	1	.667	0	0	3.41
1991 Johnson Cty	R+ StL	2	0	0	0	1.2	8	0	2	2	0	0	0	1	2	0	2	0	0	0	0	.000	0	0	10.80
1992 Hamilton	A- StL	3	3	0	0	14.2	64	11	7	6	1	0	0	3	4	0	9	3	1	0	1	.000	0	0	3.68
1995 Brevard Cty	A+ Fla	39	4	0	29	50.2	228	33	20	17	1	3	1	8	41	4	35	4	0	1	4	.200	0	12	3.02
1996 Portland	AA Fla	45	0	0	42	49	218	45	22	12	3	1	2	1	31	0	46	6	0	2	3	.400	0	30	2.20
1997 Charlotte	AAA Fla	27	0	0	14	29	147	39	27	25	3	0	4	1	22	2	15	5	0	1	2	.333	0	3	7.76
Portland	AA Fla	2	0	0	1	2	7	1	0	0	0	0	0	0	0	0	0	2	0	0	0	.000	0	0	0.00
1996 Florida	NL	2	0	0	2	2	10	3	0	0	0	0	0	0	1	0	1	1	0	0	0	.000	0	0	0.00
6 Min. YEARS		127	16	0	86	189.1	854	156	97	76	8	4	8	16	132	7	135	26	3	6	11	.353	0	45	3.61

Tim Hyers

Bats: Left Throws: Left Pos: 1B   Ht: 6'1" Wt: 195 Born: 10/3/71 Age: 26

Year Team	Lg Org	BATTING														BASERUNNING				PERCENTAGES		
		G	AB	H	2B	3B	HR	TB	R	RBI	TBB	IBB	SO	HBP	SH	SF	SB	CS	SB%	GDP	Avg	OBP	SLG
1990 Medcne Hat	R+ Tor	61	224	49	7	2	2	66	29	19	29	1	22	1	0	2	4	1	.80	5	.219	.309	.295
1991 Myrtle Bch	A Tor	132	398	80	8	0	3	97	31	37	27	0	52	2	4	3	4	4	.50	10	.201	.253	.244
1992 Dunedin	A+ Tor	124	464	114	24	3	8	168	54	59	41	4	54	3	2	5	2	1	.67	9	.246	.308	.362
1993 Knoxville	AA Tor	140	487	149	26	3	3	190	72	61	53	5	51	2	5	2	12	3	.80	7	.306	.375	.390
1994 Las Vegas	AAA SD	14	47	12	1	0	1	16	4	5	4	0	4	0	0	0	0	0	.00	2	.255	.314	.340
1995 Las Vegas	AAA SD	82	259	75	12	1	1	92	46	23	24	3	33	1	2	1	0	3	.00	7	.290	.351	.355
1996 Toledo	AAA Det	117	437	113	17	6	7	163	55	59	40	2	57	3	1	1	7	1	.88	8	.259	.322	.373
1997 Toledo	AAA Det	121	424	116	22	3	12	180	61	55	41	3	65	1	4	3	1	2	.33	7	.274	.337	.425
1994 San Diego	NL	52	118	30	3	0	0	33	13	7	9	0	15	0	2	0	3	0	1.00	1	.254	.307	.280
1995 San Diego	NL	6	5	0	0	0	0	0	0	0	0	0	1	0	0	0	0	0	.00	1	.000	.000	.000
1996 Detroit	AL	17	26	2	1	0	0	3	1	0	4	2	5	0	0	1	0	0	.00	1	.077	.200	.115
8 Min. YEARS		791	2740	708	117	18	37	972	352	318	259	18	338	13	18	21	30	15	.67	56	.258	.323	.355
3 Maj. YEARS		75	149	32	4	0	0	36	14	7	13	2	21	0	2	0	3	0	1.00	3	.215	.278	.242

Adam Hyzdu

Bats: Right Throws: Right Pos: OF   Ht: 6'2" Wt: 210 Born: 12/6/71 Age: 26

Year Team	Lg Org	BATTING														BASERUNNING				PERCENTAGES		
		G	AB	H	2B	3B	HR	TB	R	RBI	TBB	IBB	SO	HBP	SH	SF	SB	CS	SB%	GDP	Avg	OBP	SLG
1990 Everett	A- SF	69	253	62	16	1	6	98	31	34	28	1	78	2	0	5	2	4	.33	4	.245	.319	.387
1991 Clinton	A SF	124	410	96	14	5	5	135	47	50	64	1	131	3	7	2	4	5	.44	10	.234	.340	.329
1992 San Jose	A+ SF	128	457	127	25	5	9	189	60	60	55	4	134	1	1	8	10	5	.67	6	.278	.351	.414
1993 San Jose	A+ SF	44	165	48	11	3	13	104	35	38	29	0	53	0	1	2	1	1	.50	3	.291	.393	.630
Shreveport	AA SF	86	302	61	17	0	6	96	30	25	20	2	82	1	1	1	5	5	.00	5	.202	.253	.318
1994 Winston-Sal	A+ Cin	55	210	58	11	1	15	116	30	39	18	0	33	2	0	2	1	5	.17	3	.276	.336	.552

Year Team	Lg Org	G	AB	H	2B	3B	HR	TB	R	RBI	TBB	IBB	SO	HBP	SH	SF	SB	CS	SB%	GDP	Avg	OBP	SLG
Chattanooga	AA Cin	38	133	35	10	0	3	54	17	9	8	0	21	1	1	0	0	2	.00	1	.263	.310	.406
Indianapols	AAA Cin	12	25	3	2	0	0	5	3	3	1	0	5	0	0	2	0	0	.00	0	.120	.143	.200
1995 Chattanooga	AA Cin	102	312	82	14	1	13	137	55	48	45	2	56	4	2	1	3	2	.60	4	.263	.362	.439
1996 Trenton	AA Bos	109	374	126	24	3	25	231	71	80	56	6	75	2	0	2	1	8	.11	7	.337	.424	.618
1997 Pawtucket	AAA Bos	119	413	114	21	1	23	206	77	84	72	0	113	4	1	2	10	6	.63	6	.276	.387	.499
8 Min. YEARS		886	3054	812	165	20	118	1371	456	470	396	16	781	20	14	27	32	43	.43	49	.266	.351	.449

Anthony Iapoce

Bats: Both **Throws:** Left **Pos:** OF **Ht:** 5'10" **Wt:** 178 **Born:** 8/23/73 **Age:** 24

Year Team	Lg Org	G	AB	H	2B	3B	HR	TB	R	RBI	TBB	IBB	SO	HBP	SH	SF	SB	CS	SB%	GDP	Avg	OBP	SLG
1994 Brewers	R Mil	55	222	55	7	2	0	66	37	25	15	0	43	5	3	1	16	3	.84	1	.248	.309	.297
1995 Brewers	R Mil	3	3	1	0	0	0	1	2	0	1	0	1	0	0	0	1	0	1.00	0	.333	.500	.333
Helena	R+ Mil	39	146	44	7	0	0	51	43	13	28	0	24	2	2	0	19	3	.86	2	.301	.416	.349
1996 Beloit	A Mil	77	266	78	6	3	1	93	62	11	43	0	53	7	3	0	23	13	.64	4	.293	.405	.350
1997 Tucson	AAA Mil	7	21	7	4	0	0	11	5	3	1	0	4	0	0	0	0	1	.333	.364	.524
Stockton	A+ Mil	99	387	103	13	4	1	127	48	27	30	0	71	6	9	2	22	12	.65	3	.266	.327	.328
4 Min. YEARS		280	1045	288	37	9	2	349	197	79	118	0	196	20	17	5	81	31	.72	11	.276	.359	.334

Jesse Ibarra

Bats: Both **Throws:** Right **Pos:** 1B **Ht:** 6'3" **Wt:** 195 **Born:** 7/12/72 **Age:** 25

Year Team	Lg Org	G	AB	H	2B	3B	HR	TB	R	RBI	TBB	IBB	SO	HBP	SH	SF	SB	CS	SB%	GDP	Avg	OBP	SLG
1994 Everett	A- SF	67	252	57	15	1	10	104	32	37	34	0	82	1	0	0	0	0	.00	5	.226	.321	.413
1995 Burlington	A SF	129	437	144	30	1	34	278	72	96	77	6	94	4	0	1	1	2	.33	8	.330	.434	.636
San Jose	A+ SF	3	9	3	2	0	0	5	1	4	1	0	1	0	0	0	0	0	.00	2	.333	.400	.556
1996 San Jose	A+ SF	126	498	141	38	0	17	230	74	95	63	3	108	3	0	2	5	1	.83	12	.283	.366	.462
1997 Jacksnville	AA Det	115	441	125	24	1	25	226	73	91	55	4	85	3	0	5	3	2	.60	9	.283	.363	.512
4 Min. YEARS		440	1637	470	109	3	86	843	252	323	230	13	370	11	0	8	9	5	.64	36	.287	.377	.515

Mike Iglesias

Pitches: Right **Bats:** Right **Pos:** P **Ht:** 6'5" **Wt:** 215 **Born:** 11/9/72 **Age:** 25

Year Team	Lg Org	G	GS	CG	GF	IP	BFP	H	R	ER	HR	SH	SF	HB	TBB	IBB	SO	WP	Bk	W	L	Pct.	ShO	Sv	ERA
1991 Dodgers	R LA	8	6	0	1	23	109	26	13	12	1	1	1	0	17	0	17	2	3	1	1	.500	0	0	4.70
1992 Great Falls	R+ LA	12	12	0	0	56	272	69	56	38	4	0	1	4	26	0	37	10	1	3	6	.333	0	0	6.11
1993 Bakersfield	A+ LA	6	3	0	0	19.1	93	26	16	12	2	1	0	1	12	0	10	3	1	1	2	.333	0	0	5.59
Yakima	A- LA	10	5	0	0	30.2	150	42	29	26	1	0	5	2	21	1	24	5	1	0	3	.000	0	0	7.63
1994 Vero Beach	A+ LA	19	14	1	3	89.2	376	87	46	42	9	2	4	1	29	2	50	4	1	3	6	.333	0	0	4.22
1995 Bakersfield	A+ LA	24	23	2	0	143.2	586	124	65	52	11	5	3	11	38	0	108	7	0	7	10	.412	1	0	3.26
San Berndno	A+ LA	4	3	0	0	15	74	26	14	11	1	0	0	2	2	0	12	3	0	1	2	.333	0	0	6.60
1996 Vero Beach	A+ LA	31	16	0	14	104	463	112	68	59	9	1	4	5	37	1	101	6	1	5	8	.385	0	7	5.11
1997 San Antonio	AA LA	42	0	0	20	59.1	247	51	25	24	7	2	1	0	26	1	55	5	1	6	2	.750	0	8	3.64
7 Min. YEARS		156	82	3	38	540.2	2370	563	332	276	45	12	19	26	208	5	414	45	9	27	40	.403	1	15	4.59

Blaise Ilsley

Pitches: Left **Bats:** Left **Pos:** P **Ht:** 6'1" **Wt:** 195 **Born:** 4/9/64 **Age:** 34

Year Team	Lg Org	G	GS	CG	GF	IP	BFP	H	R	ER	HR	SH	SF	HB	TBB	IBB	SO	WP	Bk	W	L	Pct.	ShO	Sv	ERA
1985 Auburn	A- Hou	13	12	1	0	90	354	55	18	14	1	5	0	3	32	0	116	0	0	9	1	.900	0	0	1.40
1986 Asheville	A Hou	15	15	9	0	120	453	74	27	26	11	2	2	2	23	0	146	2	2	12	2	.857	3	0	1.95
Osceola	A+ Hou	14	13	6	1	86.2	337	67	24	17	1	3	4	0	19	0	74	6	1	8	4	.667	2	0	1.77
1987 Columbus	AA Hou	26	26	3	0	167.2	712	162	84	72	13	8	7	4	63	1	130	6	2	10	11	.476	0	0	3.86
1988 Columbus	AA Hou	8	8	0	0	39.1	187	49	28	26	4	0	0	0	21	0	38	2	0	3	1	.750	0	0	5.95
1989 Osceola	A+ Hou	2	2	0	0	7	28	8	5	5	2	0	0	0	0	0	6	0	0	0	0	.000	0	0	6.43
Columbus	AA Hou	4	4	0	0	20.2	87	19	10	3	2	1	0	0	5	0	11	2	1	1	1	.500	0	0	1.31
Tucson	AAA Hou	20	17	1	0	103	443	120	68	67	12	2	3	6	23	2	49	2	0	4	9	.308	0	0	5.85
1990 Columbus	AA Hou	12	12	3	0	83.2	324	70	26	18	5	4	0	3	13	1	70	1	0	6	4	.600	3	0	1.94
Tucson	AAA Hou	20	6	1	4	62.2	295	87	50	45	4	1	2	3	24	0	39	8	0	2	1	.667	0	2	6.46
1991 Tucson	AAA Hou	46	4	0	17	86.1	383	105	51	41	7	9	6	3	27	1	52	2	0	8	6	.571	0	4	4.27
1992 Louisville	AAA StL	33	10	1	10	98.1	429	114	56	47	15	7	4	4	23	2	56	3	0	5	4	.556	0	1	4.30
1993 Iowa	AAA ChN	48	16	0	13	134.2	565	147	61	59	10	5	3	4	32	2	78	7	0	12	7	.632	0	4	3.94
1994 Iowa	AAA ChN	22	16	2	0	116	487	120	68	57	11	1	7	3	21	0	51	2	1	10	4	.714	0	0	4.42
1995 Scranton-WB	AAA Phi	29	29	2	0	185.1	786	210	96	80	17	8	4	5	34	2	102	6	0	8	10	.444	1	0	3.88
1996 Ottawa	AAA Mon	20	4	0	1	45.1	198	49	27	26	9	2	1	1	15	0	22	2	0	5	2	.714	0	0	5.16
Scranton-WB	AAA Phi	5	3	0	1	16	75	24	12	11	2	0	0	4	0	9	1	0	1	2	.333	0	0	6.19
1997 Buffalo	AAA Cle	9	0	0	4	12.1	49	12	3	3	1	0	0	0	1	0	7	0	0	0	0	.000	0	2	2.19
1994 Chicago	NL	10	0	0	1	15	74	25	13	13	2	0	0	0	9	2	9	1	0	0	0	.000	0	0	7.80
13 Min. YEARS		346	197	30	52	1475	6192	1492	714	617	127	58	43	41	380	11	1056	52	7	104	69	.601	9	7	3.76

Johnny Isom

Bats: Right **Throws:** Right **Pos:** OF **Ht:** 5'11" **Wt:** 210 **Born:** 8/9/73 **Age:** 24

Year Team	Lg Org	G	AB	H	2B	3B	HR	TB	R	RBI	TBB	IBB	SO	HBP	SH	SF	SB	CS	SB%	GDP	Avg	OBP	SLG
1995 Bluefield	R+ Bal	59	212	73	14	4	6	113	47	56	25	0	27	1	2	7	9	2	.82	5	.344	.404	.533

		BATTING															BASERUNNING				PERCENTAGES		
Year Team	Lg Org	G	AB	H	2B	3B	HR	TB	R	RBI	TBB	IBB	SO	HBP	SH	SF	SB	CS	SB%	GDP	Avg	OBP	SLG
1996 Frederick	A+ Bal	124	486	141	27	3	18	228	69	104	40	4	87	7	0	6	8	6	.57	15	.290	.349	.469
1997 Bowie	AA Bal	135	518	142	28	4	20	238	70	94	44	4	121	11	2	4	1	5	.17	12	.274	.341	.459
3 Min. YEARS		318	1216	356	69	11	44	579	186	251	109	8	235	19	4	17	18	13	.58	32	.293	.356	.476

Gavin Jackson

Bats: Right **Throws:** Right **Pos:** SS **Ht:** 5'10" **Wt:** 170 **Born:** 7/19/73 **Age:** 24

		BATTING															BASERUNNING				PERCENTAGES		
Year Team	Lg Org	G	AB	H	2B	3B	HR	TB	R	RBI	TBB	IBB	SO	HBP	SH	SF	SB	CS	SB%	GDP	Avg	OBP	SLG
1993 Red Sox	R Bos	42	160	50	7	2	0	61	29	11	14	0	18	11	2	0	11	5	.69	2	.313	.405	.381
1994 Sarasota	A+ Bos	108	321	77	6	1	0	85	46	27	33	0	40	7	12	0	9	10	.47	1	.240	.324	.265
1995 Sarasota	A+ Bos	100	342	91	19	1	0	112	61	36	40	3	43	6	8	4	11	12	.48	8	.266	.349	.327
1996 Trenton	AA Bos	6	20	5	2	0	0	7	2	3	2	0	3	0	0	0	0	1	.00	0	.250	.318	.350
Pawtucket	AAA Bos	15	44	11	2	0	0	13	5	1	3	0	8	0	1	0	1	0	.00	0	.250	.298	.295
Sarasota	A+ Bos	87	276	66	13	2	0	83	26	24	33	0	47	7	8	3	4	6	.40	6	.239	.332	.301
1997 Trenton	AA Bos	100	301	82	12	0	1	97	46	46	48	0	36	6	12	2	2	6	.25	11	.272	.381	.322
5 Min. YEARS		458	1464	382	61	6	1	458	215	148	173	3	195	37	43	9	37	41	.47	28	.261	.352	.313

Ryan Jackson

Bats: Left **Throws:** Left **Pos:** OF **Ht:** 6'2" **Wt:** 195 **Born:** 11/15/71 **Age:** 26

		BATTING															BASERUNNING				PERCENTAGES		
Year Team	Lg Org	G	AB	H	2B	3B	HR	TB	R	RBI	TBB	IBB	SO	HBP	SH	SF	SB	CS	SB%	GDP	Avg	OBP	SLG
1994 Elmira	A- Fla	72	276	80	18	1	6	118	46	41	22	1	40	1	0	6	4	3	.57	2	.290	.338	.428
1995 Kane County	A Fla	132	471	138	39	6	10	219	78	82	67	7	74	4	0	5	13	8	.62	9	.293	.382	.465
1996 Marlins	R Fla	7	25	9	0	0	0	9	5	5	1	0	3	1	0	0	2	0	1.00	0	.360	.407	.360
Brevard Cty	A+ Fla	6	26	8	2	0	1	13	4	4	1	0	7	0	0	0	1	0	1.00	0	.308	.333	.500
1997 Portland	AA Fla	134	491	153	28	4	26	267	87	98	51	2	85	3	1	0	2	5	.29	6	.312	.380	.544
4 Min. YEARS		351	1289	388	87	11	43	626	220	230	142	10	209	9	1	11	22	16	.58	17	.301	.371	.486

Ryan Jacobs

Pitches: Left **Bats:** Right **Pos:** P **Ht:** 6'2" **Wt:** 175 **Born:** 2/3/74 **Age:** 24

		HOW MUCH HE PITCHED						WHAT HE GAVE UP										THE RESULTS					
Year Team	Lg Org	G	GS	CG	GF	IP	BFP	H	R	ER	HR	SH	SF	HB	TBB	IBB	SO	WP	Bk	W	L	Pct.	ShO	Sv	ERA
1992 Braves	R Atl	12	2	0	6	35	148	30	18	10	1	3	2	1	8	2	40	2	0	1	3	.250	0	1	2.57
1993 Danville	R+ Atl	10	10	0	0	42.2	188	35	24	19	5	1	2	1	25	0	32	6	0	4	3	.571	0	0	4.01
1994 Macon	A Atl	27	18	1	2	121.2	532	105	54	39	9	4	2	3	62	2	81	6	1	8	7	.533	1	1	2.88
1995 Durham	A+ Atl	29	25	1	3	148.2	640	145	72	58	12	6	5	3	57	3	99	10	0	11	6	.647	0	0	3.51
1996 Greenville	AA Atl	21	21	0	0	99.2	468	127	83	74	19	3	4	4	57	1	64	8	0	3	9	.250	0	0	6.68
1997 Greenville	AA Atl	28	6	0	3	68.2	328	84	61	55	8	1	5	2	43	1	52	6	0	1	8	.111	0	1	7.21
6 Min. YEARS		127	82	2	14	516.1	2304	526	312	255	54	18	20	14	252	9	368	38	1	28	36	.438	1	3	4.44

Joe Jacobsen

Pitches: Right **Bats:** Right **Pos:** P **Ht:** 6'3" **Wt:** 225 **Born:** 12/26/71 **Age:** 26

		HOW MUCH HE PITCHED						WHAT HE GAVE UP										THE RESULTS					
Year Team	Lg Org	G	GS	CG	GF	IP	BFP	H	R	ER	HR	SH	SF	HB	TBB	IBB	SO	WP	Bk	W	L	Pct.	ShO	Sv	ERA
1992 Dodgers	R LA	6	3	0	2	26	100	17	7	5	0	0	0	0	6	0	25	2	2	1	1	.500	0	0	1.73
Great Falls	R+ LA	6	6	1	0	32.1	143	37	22	19	2	0	1	1	9	0	24	3	0	2	2	.500	0	0	5.29
1993 Yakima	A- LA	25	0	0	7	37.2	174	27	16	10	0	2	3	1	28	2	55	1	0	1	0	1.000	0	3	2.39
Bakersfield	A+ LA	6	0	0	3	19.2	88	22	16	10	1	1	0	0	8	0	23	3	0	1	0	1.000	0	2	4.58
1994 Bakersfield	A+ LA	3	0	0	1	7.1	26	2	1	1	1	0	0	0	1	0	5	0	0	1	0	1.000	0	0	1.23
San Antonio	AA LA	18	0	0	12	25	108	21	9	7	0	2	2	2	12	2	15	2	1	2	1	.667	0	1	2.52
Vero Beach	A+ LA	37	0	0	34	43	193	40	15	13	1	3	0	2	23	2	44	3	0	0	5	.000	0	15	2.72
1995 Vero Beach	A+ LA	47	0	0	44	49	215	42	22	20	2	5	2	2	23	2	54	10	1	1	3	.250	0	32	3.67
San Berndno	A+ LA	4	0	0	3	3.2	17	4	2	0	0	0	0	0	2	0	5	1	0	0	0	.000	0	0	0.00
1996 San Antonio	AA LA	38	0	0	23	58	256	62	33	27	4	4	3	1	24	2	39	7	0	1	4	.200	0	5	4.19
1997 Portland	AA Fla	47	1	0	29	58.1	270	76	44	33	7	1	2	2	23	4	48	5	0	5	5	.500	0	11	5.09
6 Min. YEARS		237	10	1	158	360	1590	350	187	145	18	19	13	11	159	14	337	37	4	15	21	.417	0	71	3.63

Angel Jaime

Bats: Right **Throws:** Right **Pos:** OF **Ht:** 6'0" **Wt:** 160 **Born:** 3/6/73 **Age:** 25

		BATTING															BASERUNNING				PERCENTAGES		
Year Team	Lg Org	G	AB	H	2B	3B	HR	TB	R	RBI	TBB	IBB	SO	HBP	SH	SF	SB	CS	SB%	GDP	Avg	OBP	SLG
1992 Great Falls	R+ LA	62	236	64	8	2	1	79	38	34	32	0	58	1	4	1	21	7	.75	6	.271	.359	.335
1993 Bakersfield	A+ LA	46	152	35	5	0	0	40	21	8	18	0	34	4	4	0	14	6	.70	3	.230	.328	.263
Yakima	A- LA	50	168	44	8	3	2	64	29	25	18	0	27	1	2	2	9	4	.69	6	.262	.333	.381
1994 Vero Beach	A+ LA	127	482	136	15	9	6	187	85	38	38	1	64	4	10	6	16	10	.62	8	.282	.336	.388
1995 San Antonio	AA LA	9	22	8	0	0	1	11	5	2	2	0	3	0	0	0	2	1	.67	1	.364	.417	.500
1996 St. Lucie	A+ NYN	98	288	74	10	1	3	95	38	21	34	0	47	6	6	3	12	6	.67	5	.257	.344	.330
1997 Norfolk	AAA NYN	16	26	5	1	0	0	6	3	5	0	0	7	0	3	0	0	1	.00	0	.192	.192	.231
St. Lucie	A+ NYN	80	258	62	9	0	3	80	25	27	29	0	43	1	1	0	15	4	.79	2	.240	.319	.310
6 Min. YEARS		488	1632	428	56	15	16	562	244	160	171	1	283	17	30	12	89	39	.70	31	.262	.336	.344

Pete Janicki

Pitches: Right Bats: Right Pos: P Ht: 6'4" Wt: 190 Born: 1/26/71 Age: 27

Year Team	Lg Org	G	GS	CG	GF	IP	BFP	H	R	ER	HR	SH	SF	HB	TBB	IBB	SO	WP	Bk	W	L	Pct.	ShO	Sv	ERA
1993 Palm Spring	A+ Ana	1	1	0	0	1.2	10	3	2	2	0	0	0	0	2	0	2	0	1	0	0	.000	0	0	10.80
1994 Midland	AA Ana	14	14	1	0	70	327	86	68	54	4	3	1	6	33	1	54	15	3	2	6	.250	0	0	6.94
Lk Elsinore	A+ Ana	3	3	0	0	12	61	17	12	9	2	1	1	4	4	0	12	0	0	1	2	.333	0	0	6.75
1995 Lk Elsinore	A+ Ana	20	20	0	0	123.1	532	130	66	42	7	3	6	5	28	0	106	6	1	9	4	.692	0	0	3.06
Vancouver	AAA Ana	9	9	0	0	48.2	227	64	38	38	8	1	4	1	23	0	34	0	0	1	4	.200	0	0	7.03
1996 Midland	AA Ana	5	5	0	0	31	136	37	28	22	4	0	0	2	10	0	17	4	0	1	3	.250	0	0	6.39
Vancouver	AAA Ana	31	14	0	10	104	485	135	82	78	15	5	4	13	37	1	86	4	0	2	9	.182	0	1	6.75
1997 Vancouver	AAA Ana	42	0	0	19	47.1	232	48	43	41	9	2	3	1	44	4	43	6	0	1	4	.200	0	1	7.80
Midland	AA Ana	2	0	0	1	1.2	10	3	3	0	0	0	0	0	2	0	2	1	0	0	0	.000	0	0	0.00
5 Min. YEARS		127	66	1	30	439.2	2020	523	342	286	49	15	19	32	183	6	356	36	5	17	32	.347	0	2	5.85

Link Jarrett

Bats: Both Throws: Right Pos: SS Ht: 5'10" Wt: 165 Born: 1/26/72 Age: 26

Year Team	Lg Org	G	AB	H	2B	3B	HR	TB	R	RBI	TBB	IBB	SO	HBP	SH	SF	SB	CS	SB%	GDP	Avg	OBP	SLG
1994 Bend	A- Col	74	279	67	13	0	0	80	31	15	24	0	45	2	4	2	4	4	.50	6	.240	.303	.287
1995 Asheville	A Col	116	404	95	11	0	0	106	46	20	62	1	60	2	10	2	12	10	.55	5	.235	.338	.262
1996 New Haven	AA Col	56	164	32	6	0	1	41	18	9	14	0	23	0	3	1	1	1	.50	5	.195	.257	.250
Salem	A+ Col	38	98	22	3	1	0	27	9	8	8	0	14	1	3	0	1	2	.33	3	.224	.290	.276
1997 Salem	A+ Col	9	25	4	0	0	0	4	1	1	1	0	5	0	1	0	0	0	.00	1	.160	.192	.160
New Haven	AA Col	88	261	79	9	1	1	93	19	27	18	3	30	1	11	1	2	2	.50	3	.303	.349	.356
4 Min. YEARS		381	1231	299	42	2	2	351	124	80	127	4	177	6	32	6	20	19	.51	23	.243	.315	.285

Jason Jarvis

Pitches: Right Bats: Right Pos: P Ht: 6'1" Wt: 170 Born: 10/27/73 Age: 24

Year Team	Lg Org	G	GS	CG	GF	IP	BFP	H	R	ER	HR	SH	SF	HB	TBB	IBB	SO	WP	Bk	W	L	Pct.	ShO	Sv	ERA
1994 Oneonta	A- NYA	19	7	0	6	65.1	259	40	20	17	0	1	1	3	18	1	78	2	2	4	2	.667	0	2	2.34
Greensboro	A NYA	2	0	0	2	6.2	32	8	3	3	0	0	0	0	5	0	7	0	0	1	0	1.000	0	0	4.05
1995 Greensboro	A NYA	22	16	0	2	110.2	468	103	47	37	5	4	5	1	38	3	82	13	1	8	7	.533	0	0	3.01
Hagerstown	A Tor	8	8	0	0	50	210	49	27	20	3	2	4	3	13	1	42	7	1	4	3	.571	0	0	3.60
1996 Dunedin	A+ Tor	36	13	2	8	112.1	485	117	66	61	5	4	3	10	40	1	65	6	0	7	3	.700	1	1	4.89
1997 Knoxville	AA Tor	4	4	1	0	19.1	95	28	24	21	7	1	2	0	9	0	11	1	0	0	2	.000	0	0	9.78
Dunedin	A+ Tor	35	7	0	19	85	400	92	64	49	3	4	3	4	47	5	70	16	1	6	11	.353	0	1	5.19
4 Min. YEARS		126	55	3	37	449.1	1949	437	251	208	23	16	18	21	170	11	355	45	5	30	28	.517	1	4	4.17

Matt Jarvis

Pitches: Left Bats: Right Pos: P Ht: 6'4" Wt: 185 Born: 2/22/72 Age: 26

Year Team	Lg Org	G	GS	CG	GF	IP	BFP	H	R	ER	HR	SH	SF	HB	TBB	IBB	SO	WP	Bk	W	L	Pct.	ShO	Sv	ERA
1991 Orioles	R Bal	11	5	0	2	37.1	163	44	22	18	2	1	2	0	17	0	30	2	1	3	1	.750	0	1	4.34
1992 Kane County	A Bal	34	7	0	8	71.1	327	84	53	36	3	2	1	1	35	2	43	7	3	4	4	.500	0	0	4.54
1993 Albany	A Bal	29	29	8	0	185.1	797	173	82	63	7	5	2	5	82	4	118	10	1	11	13	.458	1	0	3.06
1994 Frederick	A+ Bal	31	14	0	3	103.2	459	92	58	48	7	5	2	9	48	0	67	3	0	10	4	.714	0	1	4.17
1995 Bowie	AA Bal	26	21	0	1	118	531	154	71	67	11	4	4	4	42	1	60	5	3	9	8	.529	0	0	5.11
1996 Bowie	AA Bal	6	4	0	0	19.1	91	31	17	16	2	0	2	1	7	0	13	4	1	1	3	.250	0	0	7.45
Winnipeg	IND —	17	15	2	1	103	454	99	46	41	11	3	2	6	55	1	63	3	3	11	3	.786	0	0	3.58
1997 Arkansas	AA StL	50	4	0	16	80	344	70	24	17	0	9	1	3	45	4	52	4	0	8	5	.615	0	2	1.91
7 Min. YEARS		204	99	10	31	718	3166	747	373	306	43	29	16	29	331	12	446	38	12	57	41	.582	1	4	3.84

Domingo Jean

Pitches: Right Bats: Right Pos: P Ht: 6'2" Wt: 175 Born: 1/9/69 Age: 29

Year Team	Lg Org	G	GS	CG	GF	IP	BFP	H	R	ER	HR	SH	SF	HB	TBB	IBB	SO	WP	Bk	W	L	Pct.	ShO	Sv	ERA
1990 White Sox	R ChA	13	13	1	0	78.2	312	55	32	20	1	0	1	6	16	0	65	10	2	2	5	.286	0	0	2.29
1991 South Bend	A ChA	25	25	2	0	158	680	121	75	58	7	3	7	10	65	0	141	17	5	12	8	.600	0	0	3.30
1992 Ft. Laud	A+ NYA	23	23	5	0	158.2	637	118	57	46	3	7	6	6	49	1	172	4	1	6	11	.353	1	0	2.61
Albany-Colo	AA NYA	1	1	0	0	4	17	3	2	1	0	0	0	0	0	0	4	1	0	0	0	.000	0	0	2.25
1993 Albany-Colo	AA NYA	11	11	1	0	61	257	42	24	17	1	1	1	5	33	0	41	4	0	5	3	.625	0	0	2.51
Columbus	AAA NYA	7	7	1	0	44.2	180	40	15	14	2	0	2	2	13	1	39	3	0	2	2	.500	0	0	2.82
Pr William	A+ NYA	1	0	0	0	1.2	6	1	0	0	0	0	0	0	0	0	1	0	0	0	0	.000	0	0	0.00
1994 Tucson	AAA Hou	6	3	0	1	19	88	20	13	12	3	0	1	2	11	1	16	0	0	0	0	.000	0	0	5.68
1995 Tucson	AAA Hou	3	3	0	0	13.2	62	15	10	10	1	0	0	0	7	0	14	3	0	2	1	.667	0	0	6.59
Okla City	AAA Tex	24	13	1	9	88	418	102	70	60	12	4	2	1	61	0	72	14	3	3	8	.273	0	1	6.14
Indianapols	AAA Cin	2	0	0	0	2	7	1	0	0	0	1	0	0	0	0	1	0	0	1	0	1.000	0	0	0.00
1996 Indianapols	AAA Cin	7	0	0	2	9.1	49	13	11	9	2	0	0	0	8	1	5	0	0	1	1	.500	0	0	8.68
Chattanooga	AA Cin	39	0	0	37	39.2	169	34	19	18	1	3	0	0	17	2	33	5	0	2	3	.400	0	31	4.08
1997 Chattanooga	AA Cin	10	0	0	4	12	69	17	20	13	2	0	2	1	15	1	9	1	0	1	1	.500	0	1	9.75
1993 New York	AL	10	6	0	1	40.1	176	37	20	20	7	1	0	1	19	1	20	1	0	1	1	.500	0	0	4.46
8 Min. YEARS		172	99	11	53	690.1	2951	582	348	278	35	19	22	33	298	8	615	62	11	37	43	.463	1	33	3.62

Geoff Jenkins

Bats: Left **Throws:** Right **Pos:** OF **Ht:** 6'1" **Wt:** 205 **Born:** 7/21/74 **Age:** 23

Year Team	Lg Org	G	AB	H	2B	3B	HR	TB	R	RBI	TBB	IBB	SO	HBP	SH	SF	SB	CS	SB%	GDP	Avg	OBP	SLG
1995 Helena	R+ Mil	7	28	9	0	1	0	11	2	9	3	0	11	0	0	1	0	2	.00	0	.321	.375	.393
Stockton	A+ Mil	13	47	12	2	0	3	23	13	12	10	0	12	0	0	2	2	0	1.00	0	.255	.373	.489
El Paso	AA Mil	22	79	22	4	2	1	33	12	13	8	0	23	0	0	1	3	1	.75	1	.278	.341	.418
1996 El Paso	AA Mil	22	77	22	5	4	1	38	17	11	12	1	21	2	0	1	1	2	.33	2	.286	.391	.494
Stockton	A+ Mil	37	138	48	8	4	3	73	27	25	20	1	32	3	1	3	3	3	.50	3	.348	.433	.529
1997 Tucson	AAA Mil	93	347	82	24	3	10	142	44	56	33	1	87	3	0	0	0	2	.00	7	.236	.308	.409
3 Min. YEARS		194	716	195	43	14	18	320	115	126	86	3	186	8	1	8	9	10	.47	13	.272	.353	.447

Mike Jerzembeck

Pitches: Right **Bats:** Right **Pos:** P **Ht:** 6'1" **Wt:** 185 **Born:** 5/18/72 **Age:** 26

Year Team	Lg Org	G	GS	CG	GF	IP	BFP	H	R	ER	HR	SH	SF	HB	TBB	IBB	SO	WP	Bk	W	L	Pct.	ShO	Sv	ERA
1993 Oneonta	A- NYA	14	14	0	0	77.1	327	70	25	23	1	3	1	3	26	0	76	2	2	8	4	.667	0	0	2.68
1994 Tampa	A+ NYA	16	16	0	0	68.2	274	59	27	24	6	1	2	2	22	0	45	2	1	4	3	.571	0	0	3.15
1995 Tampa	A+ NYA	2	0	0	0	3	17	5	4	3	1	0	0	0	2	0	1	1	0	0	1	.000	0	0	9.00
1996 Columbus	AAA NYA	1	0	0	0	1.2	7	1	1	1	0	0	0	0	1	0	0	0	0	0	0	.000	0	0	5.40
Norwich	AA NYA	14	13	1	0	69.2	303	74	38	35	9	4	2	3	26	0	65	2	4	3	6	.333	1	0	4.52
Tampa	A+ NYA	12	12	0	0	73.1	297	67	26	24	4	1	1	0	13	0	60	3	0	4	2	.667	0	0	2.95
1997 Norwich	AA NYA	8	8	0	0	42	164	21	10	8	1	2	0	0	16	0	42	2	1	2	1	.667	0	0	1.71
Columbus	AAA NYA	20	20	2	0	130.1	540	125	55	52	14	4	5	2	37	0	118	4	0	7	5	.583	0	0	3.59
5 Min. YEARS		87	83	3	0	466	1929	422	186	170	36	15	11	10	143	0	407	16	8	28	22	.560	1	0	3.28

D'Angelo Jimenez

Bats: Both **Throws:** Right **Pos:** SS **Ht:** 6'0" **Wt:** 160 **Born:** 12/21/77 **Age:** 20

Year Team	Lg Org	G	AB	H	2B	3B	HR	TB	R	RBI	TBB	IBB	SO	HBP	SH	SF	SB	CS	SB%	GDP	Avg	OBP	SLG
1995 Yankees	R NYA	57	214	60	14	8	2	96	41	28	23	1	31	1	3	4	6	3	.67	2	.280	.347	.449
1996 Greensboro	A NYA	138	537	131	25	5	6	184	68	48	56	2	113	3	4	3	15	17	.47	7	.244	.317	.343
1997 Columbus	AAA NYA	2	7	1	0	0	0	1	1	1	0	0	1	0	0	0	0	0	.00	1	.143	.125	.143
Tampa	A+ NYA	94	352	99	14	6	6	143	52	48	50	4	50	2	3	6	8	14	.36	3	.281	.368	.406
3 Min. YEARS		291	1110	291	53	19	14	424	162	125	129	7	195	6	10	14	29	34	.46	15	.262	.338	.382

Manny Jimenez

Bats: Right **Throws:** Right **Pos:** SS **Ht:** 5'11" **Wt:** 160 **Born:** 7/4/71 **Age:** 26

Year Team	Lg Org	G	AB	H	2B	3B	HR	TB	R	RBI	TBB	IBB	SO	HBP	SH	SF	SB	CS	SB%	GDP	Avg	OBP	SLG
1991 Pulaski	R+ Atl	57	234	66	10	7	1	93	37	29	12	2	48	1	2	0	19	8	.70	4	.282	.320	.397
1992 Macon	A Atl	117	401	88	9	3	1	106	25	32	16	1	106	8	4	2	13	15	.46	7	.219	.262	.264
1993 Durham	A+ Atl	127	427	96	16	4	6	138	55	29	21	0	93	7	10	1	7	9	.44	12	.225	.272	.323
1994 Greenville	AA Atl	64	195	39	6	1	1	50	13	14	5	0	38	1	1	1	3	4	.43	6	.200	.223	.256
Durham	A+ Atl	31	104	20	6	0	0	26	6	9	2	0	18	2	0	0	1	1	.50	2	.192	.222	.250
1995 Durham	A+ Atl	121	375	92	16	2	2	118	40	23	17	1	71	5	3	0	8	6	.57	11	.245	.287	.315
1996 Greenville	AA Atl	131	474	130	21	2	3	164	68	57	28	3	67	6	4	3	12	7	.63	18	.274	.321	.346
1997 Greenville	AA Atl	115	430	125	24	2	5	168	59	45	22	0	70	6	5	2	3	10	.23	20	.291	.333	.391
7 Min. YEARS		763	2640	656	108	21	19	863	303	238	123	7	511	36	29	9	66	60	.52	80	.248	.290	.327

Miguel Jimenez

Pitches: Right **Bats:** Right **Pos:** P **Ht:** 6'2" **Wt:** 205 **Born:** 8/19/69 **Age:** 28

Year Team	Lg Org	G	GS	CG	GF	IP	BFP	H	R	ER	HR	SH	SF	HB	TBB	IBB	SO	WP	Bk	W	L	Pct.	ShO	Sv	ERA
1991 Sou. Oregon	A- Oak	10	9	0	0	34.2	159	22	21	12	0	0	0	2	34	0	39	6	6	0	2	.000	0	0	3.12
1992 Madison	A Oak	26	19	2	0	120.1	514	78	48	39	3	2	2	8	78	1	135	12	14	7	7	.500	1	0	2.92
Huntsville	AA Oak	1	1	0	0	5	19	3	1	1	1	0	0	0	3	0	8	0	0	1	0	1.000	0	0	1.80
1993 Huntsville	AA Oak	20	19	0	0	107	476	92	49	35	10	2	1	4	64	0	105	6	2	10	6	.625	0	0	2.94
Tacoma	AAA Oak	8	8	0	0	37.2	164	32	23	20	4	2	1	0	24	0	34	3	0	2	3	.400	0	0	4.78
1994 Tacoma	AAA Oak	23	15	0	2	74	372	82	83	75	9	1	4	4	79	0	64	12	2	3	9	.250	0	0	9.12
1995 Edmonton	AAA Oak	6	3	0	2	7.1	43	12	10	10	0	0	1	0	10	0	4	0	0	0	0	.000	0	0	12.27
Modesto	A+ Oak	4	4	0	0	18	83	14	13	12	5	0	1	2	14	0	11	4	0	1	2	.333	0	0	6.00
Huntsville	AA Oak	6	6	0	0	30	124	25	16	12	3	1	0	0	11	0	28	1	0	3	2	.600	0	0	3.60
1996 Huntsville	AA Oak	19	2	0	5	37.2	180	43	37	37	7	0	4	2	27	2	28	5	0	0	4	.000	0	0	8.84
Modesto	A+ Oak	13	12	0	0	70.2	320	87	40	36	6	0	2	1	28	0	75	10	0	7	1	.875	0	0	4.58
1997 Huntsville	AA Oak	24	18	1	2	101.1	475	127	83	66	15	0	3	2	50	1	64	4	1	7	6	.538	0	0	5.86
Edmonton	AAA Oak	7	2	0	4	15.1	85	29	19	19	6	0	1	0	11	0	11	0	0	0	2	.000	0	0	11.15
1993 Oakland	AL	5	4	0	0	27	120	27	12	12	5	0	0	1	16	0	13	0	0	1	0	1.000	0	0	4.00
1994 Oakland	AL	8	7	0	0	34	173	38	33	28	9	1	1	1	32	2	22	3	3	1	4	.200	0	0	7.41
7 Min. YEARS		167	118	3	15	659	3014	646	439	374	69	8	20	25	433	4	606	63	25	41	44	.482	1	0	5.11
2 Maj. YEARS		13	11	0	0	61	293	65	45	40	14	1	1	2	48	2	35	3	3	2	4	.333	0	0	5.90

Doug Johns

Pitches: Left **Bats:** Right **Pos:** P **Ht:** 6'2" **Wt:** 185 **Born:** 12/19/67 **Age:** 30

Year Team	Lg Org	G	GS	CG	GF	IP	BFP	H	R	ER	HR	SH	SF	HB	TBB	IBB	SO	WP	Bk	W	L	Pct.	ShO	Sv	ERA
1990 Sou. Oregon	A- Oak	6	2	0	4	11	57	13	9	7	0	0	0	0	11	1	9	2	2	0	2	.000	0	1	5.73

128

Year Team	Lg Org	G	GS	CG	GF	IP	BFP	H	R	ER	HR	SH	SF	HB	TBB	IBB	SO	WP	Bk	W	L	Pct.	ShO	Sv	ERA
						HOW MUCH HE PITCHED		WHAT HE GAVE UP												THE RESULTS					
Athletics	R Oak	8	7	1	1	44	172	36	17	9	1	0	0	0	9	1	37	2	0	3	1	.750	0	0	1.84
1991 Madison	A Oak	38	14	1	9	128.1	549	108	59	46	5	6	2	8	54	1	104	13	0	12	6	.667	1	2	3.23
1992 Reno	A+ Oak	27	26	4	1	179.1	776	194	98	65	11	7	4	1	64	3	101	5	2	13	10	.565	1	0	3.26
Huntsville	AA Oak	3	1	0	1	16	74	21	11	7	0	1	0	0	5	0	4	1	0	0	0	.000	0	0	3.94
1993 Huntsville	AA Oak	40	6	0	11	91	379	82	41	30	3	7	2	2	31	4	56	2	1	7	5	.583	0	1	2.97
1994 Huntsville	AA Oak	9	0	0	2	15	70	16	2	2	1	2	0	1	12	5	9	1	3	3	0	1.000	0	0	1.20
Tacoma	AAA Oak	22	19	2	2	134	549	114	55	43	10	4	3	7	48	0	65	2	2	9	8	.529	1	0	2.89
1995 Edmonton	AAA Oak	23	21	0	1	132	567	148	55	50	8	3	1	3	43	3	70	6	3	9	5	.643	0	0	3.41
1997 Omaha	AAA KC	9	6	1	1	41.2	189	58	36	35	7	1	2	1	11	0	24	1	1	1	5	.167	0	0	7.56
Rochester	AAA Bal	9	8	2	0	55.1	233	57	25	23	5	1	2	1	13	1	42	1	1	3	1	.750	1	0	3.74
1995 Oakland	AL	11	9	1	1	54.2	229	44	32	28	5	2	1	5	26	1	25	5	1	5	3	.625	1	0	4.61
1996 Oakland	AL	40	23	1	4	158	710	187	112	105	21	2	3	6	69	5	71	9	0	6	12	.333	0	1	5.98
7 Min. YEARS		194	110	11	33	847.2	3615	847	408	317	51	32	16	24	301	19	521	36	16	60	43	.583	4	4	3.37
2 Maj. YEARS		51	32	2	5	212.2	939	231	144	133	26	4	4	11	95	6	96	14	1	11	15	.423	1	1	5.63

Keith Johns

Bats: Right **Throws:** Right **Pos:** SS   **Ht:** 6'1" **Wt:** 175 **Born:** 7/19/71 **Age:** 26

Year Team	Lg Org	G	AB	H	2B	3B	HR	TB	R	RBI	TBB	IBB	SO	HBP	SH	SF	SB	CS	SB%	GDP	Avg	OBP	SLG
						BATTING											BASERUNNING				PERCENTAGES		
1992 Hamilton	A- StL	70	275	78	11	1	1	94	36	28	27	0	42	1	1	3	15	10	.60	5	.284	.346	.342
1993 Springfield	A StL	132	467	121	24	1	2	153	74	40	70	0	68	4	9	5	40	20	.67	8	.259	.357	.328
1994 St. Pete	A+ StL	122	464	106	20	0	3	135	52	47	37	1	49	2	12	4	18	9	.67	7	.228	.286	.291
1995 Arkansas	AA StL	111	396	111	13	2	2	134	69	28	55	0	53	2	11	2	14	7	.67	11	.280	.369	.338
Louisville	AAA StL	5	10	0	0	0	0	0	0	0	0	0	2	0	0	0	0	0	.00	0	.000	.000	.000
1996 Arkansas	AA StL	127	447	110	17	1	1	132	52	40	47	0	61	4	7	1	8	9	.47	17	.246	.323	.295
1997 Tucson	AAA Mil	112	333	88	21	3	5	130	45	36	43	0	61	2	6	2	4	2	.67	7	.264	.350	.390
Rochester	AAA Bal	1	1	0	0	0	0	0	0	0	0	0	0	1	0	0	0	0	.00	0	.000	.500	.000
6 Min. YEARS		680	2393	614	106	8	14	778	328	219	279	1	336	16	46	17	99	57	.63	55	.257	.336	.325

Barry Johnson

Pitches: Right **Bats:** Right **Pos:** P   **Ht:** 6'4" **Wt:** 200 **Born:** 8/21/69 **Age:** 28

Year Team	Lg Org	G	GS	CG	GF	IP	BFP	H	R	ER	HR	SH	SF	HB	TBB	IBB	SO	WP	Bk	W	L	Pct.	ShO	Sv	ERA
						HOW MUCH HE PITCHED		WHAT HE GAVE UP												THE RESULTS					
1991 Expos	R Mon	7	1	0	3	12.2	55	10	9	5	0	0	0	4	6	0	10	2	0	0	2	.000	0	0	3.55
1992 South Bend	A ChA	16	16	5	0	109.1	463	111	56	46	5	1	5	6	23	0	74	8	1	7	5	.583	1	0	3.79
1993 Sarasota	A+ ChA	18	1	0	7	54.1	205	33	5	4	1	5	2	2	8	0	40	1	1	5	0	1.000	0	1	0.66
Birmingham	AA ChA	13	1	0	8	21.2	97	27	11	8	2	1	1	0	6	0	16	2	1	2	0	1.000	0	1	3.32
1994 Birmingham	AA ChA	51	4	0	12	97.2	427	100	51	35	7	8	3	2	30	3	67	2	0	6	2	.750	0	1	3.23
1995 Birmingham	AA ChA	47	0	0	10	78	308	64	21	16	1	2	1	2	15	1	53	2	1	7	4	.636	0	1	1.85
1996 Birmingham	AA ChA	9	0	0	7	10.2	35	2	0	0	0	1	0	0	1	0	15	0	0	0	0	.000	0	4	0.00
Nashville	AAA ChA	38	8	0	8	103	430	93	38	32	11	2	3	1	39	3	68	4	0	7	2	.778	0	0	2.80
1997 Nashville	AAA ChA	14	0	0	5	25.1	108	24	10	10	1	1	1	0	11	1	10	3	0	4	1	.800	0	2	3.55
Calgary	AAA Pit	34	1	0	12	56.2	247	55	30	26	7	1	3	1	23	2	51	3	0	5	2	.714	0	1	4.13
7 Min. YEARS		247	32	5	72	569.1	2375	519	231	182	35	22	19	18	162	10	404	27	4	43	18	.705	1	10	2.88

Earl Johnson

Bats: Right **Throws:** Right **Pos:** OF   **Ht:** 5'9" **Wt:** 163 **Born:** 10/3/71 **Age:** 26

Year Team	Lg Org	G	AB	H	2B	3B	HR	TB	R	RBI	TBB	IBB	SO	HBP	SH	SF	SB	CS	SB%	GDP	Avg	OBP	SLG
						BATTING											BASERUNNING				PERCENTAGES		
1992 Padres	R SD	35	101	17	1	0	0	19	18	20	1	0	28	1	0	0	19	5	.79	0	.168	.250	.178
1993 Spokane	A- SD	63	199	49	3	1	0	54	33	14	16	0	49	1	5	1	19	3	.86	2	.246	.304	.271
1994 Springfield	A SD	136	533	149	11	3	1	169	80	43	37	0	94	3	13	4	80	25	.76	2	.280	.328	.317
1995 Rancho Cuca	A+ SD	81	341	100	11	3	0	117	51	25	25	0	51	1	5	0	34	12	.74	5	.293	.343	.343
Memphis	AA SD	2	10	2	0	0	0	2	0	0	1	0	0	0	0	0	0	1	.00	0	.200	.273	.200
1996 Memphis	AA SD	82	337	85	10	6	2	113	50	33	18	1	59	1	5	3	15	13	.54	5	.252	.290	.335
1997 Mobile	AA SD	78	307	78	11	3	1	98	52	22	21	0	56	0	6	2	35	13	.73	2	.254	.300	.319
Jacksnville	AA Det	36	146	33	3	1	2	44	24	13	9	0	19	1	3	2	7	1	.88	3	.226	.272	.301
6 Min. YEARS		513	1974	513	50	17	6	615	310	151	137	1	356	8	37	12	209	73	.74	20	.260	.309	.312

J.J. Johnson

Bats: Right **Throws:** Right **Pos:** OF   **Ht:** 6'0" **Wt:** 195 **Born:** 8/31/73 **Age:** 24

Year Team	Lg Org	G	AB	H	2B	3B	HR	TB	R	RBI	TBB	IBB	SO	HBP	SH	SF	SB	CS	SB%	GDP	Avg	OBP	SLG
						BATTING											BASERUNNING				PERCENTAGES		
1991 Red Sox	R Bos	31	110	19	1	0	0	20	14	9	10	0	15	2	0	2	3	1	.75	2	.173	.250	.182
1992 Elmira	A- Bos	30	114	26	3	1	1	34	8	12	4	0	32	1	4	1	8	0	1.00	1	.228	.258	.298
1993 Utica	A- Bos	43	170	49	17	4	2	80	33	27	9	1	34	7	2	3	5	3	.63	2	.288	.344	.471
Lynchburg	A+ Bos	25	94	24	3	0	4	39	10	17	7	0	20	2	2	2	1	2	.33	3	.255	.314	.415
1994 Lynchburg	A+ Bos	131	515	120	28	4	14	198	66	51	36	3	132	4	1	1	4	7	.36	9	.233	.288	.384
1995 Sarasota	A+ Bos	107	391	108	16	4	10	162	49	43	26	0	74	6	2	2	7	8	.47	9	.276	.329	.414
Trenton	AA Bos	2	6	3	0	0	0	3	1	1	0	0	0	0	0	0	0	0	.00	0	.500	.500	.500
1996 Hardware City	AA Min	119	440	120	23	3	16	197	62	59	40	3	90	7	2	3	10	11	.48	4	.273	.341	.448
Salt Lake	AAA Min	13	56	19	3	1	1	27	8	13	1	0	11	1	1	0	0	1	.00	1	.339	.362	.482
1997 Salt Lake	AAA Min	26	82	12	1	1	0	15	6	5	4	0	24	1	1	0	2	2	.50	2	.146	.195	.183
New Britain	AA Min	103	356	84	11	3	3	110	60	42	38	1	94	4	3	6	13	1	.93	6	.236	.312	.309
7 Min. YEARS		630	2334	584	106	21	51	885	317	279	175	8	526	35	18	20	53	36	.60	40	.250	.310	.379

Jack Johnson

Bats: Right **Throws:** Right **Pos:** C **Ht:** 6'3" **Wt:** 205 **Born:** 3/24/70 **Age:** 28

Year Team	Lg Org	G	AB	H	2B	3B	HR	TB	R	RBI	TBB	IBB	SO	HBP	SH	SF	SB	CS	SB%	GDP	Avg	OBP	SLG
1991 Yakima	A- LA	36	105	27	6	0	4	45	15	11	14	0	22	3	2	0	1	1	.50	2	.257	.361	.429
1992 Bakersfield	A+ LA	49	153	35	10	0	3	54	15	21	9	2	32	3	3	0	0	2	.00	2	.229	.285	.353
1993 Orlando	AA ChN	33	82	19	6	0	0	25	9	5	12	0	22	1	3	1	0	1	.00	1	.232	.333	.305
Daytona	A+ ChN	3	9	1	0	0	0	1	0	0	0	0	3	0	0	0	0	0	.00	0	.111	.111	.111
Peoria	A ChN	39	96	18	7	0	0	25	10	10	23	0	33	1	4	2	3	0	1.00	4	.188	.344	.260
1994 Pr William	A+ ChA	22	57	9	2	0	1	14	6	5	1	0	17	0	1	1	0	0	.00	0	.158	.169	.246
1995 Rockford	A ChN	24	70	15	2	0	2	23	5	14	8	2	17	0	0	1	0	0	.00	1	.214	.291	.329
Daytona	A+ ChN	4	8	3	0	0	1	6	1	2	1	0	4	0	0	0	0	0	.00	0	.375	.444	.750
Pueblo	IND —	11	32	7	4	0	0	11	5	5	4	0	9	0	0	0	0	0	.00	0	.219	.306	.344
Orlando	AA ChN	25	68	15	0	0	0	15	3	4	7	0	11	1	0	1	1	3	.25	1	.221	.299	.221
1996 Abilene	IND —	91	285	75	20	0	7	116	47	46	39	1	72	7	1	4	4	1	.80	5	.263	.361	.407
1997 Midland	AA Ana	5	15	3	2	0	1	8	2	3	1	0	4	0	0	0	0	0	.00	0	.200	.250	.533
Tyler	IND —	74	250	68	18	0	4	98	35	37	33	0	59	6	2	6	5	2	.71	3	.272	.363	.392
7 Min. YEARS		416	1230	295	77	0	23	441	153	163	152	5	305	22	16	16	14	10	.58	19	.240	.330	.359

Jonathan Johnson

Pitches: Right **Bats:** Right **Pos:** P **Ht:** 6'0" **Wt:** 180 **Born:** 7/16/74 **Age:** 23

Year Team	Lg Org	G	GS	CG	GF	IP	BFP	H	R	ER	HR	SH	SF	HB	TBB	IBB	SO	WP	Bk	W	L	Pct.	ShO	Sv	ERA
1995 Charlotte	A+ Tex	8	7	1	1	43.1	178	34	14	13	2	2	0	1	16	0	25	3	3	1	5	.167	0	0	2.70
1996 Okla City	AAA Tex	1	1	1	0	9	29	2	0	0	0	0	0	0	1	0	6	0	0	1	0	1.000	1	0	0.00
Tulsa	AA Tex	26	25	6	1	174.1	728	176	86	69	15	3	5	6	41	1	97	2	3	13	10	.565	0	0	3.56
1997 Okla City	AAA Tex	13	12	1	0	58	276	83	54	47	6	1	3	1	29	3	33	2	1	1	8	.111	0	1	7.29
Tulsa	AA Tex	10	10	4	0	71.2	297	70	35	28	3	1	3	2	15	0	47	4	0	5	4	.556	0	0	3.52
3 Min. YEARS		58	55	13	3	356.1	1508	365	189	157	26	7	11	10	102	4	208	11	7	21	27	.438	1	1	3.97

Keith Johnson

Bats: Right **Throws:** Right **Pos:** 2B **Ht:** 5'11" **Wt:** 190 **Born:** 4/17/71 **Age:** 27

Year Team	Lg Org	G	AB	H	2B	3B	HR	TB	R	RBI	TBB	IBB	SO	HBP	SH	SF	SB	CS	SB%	GDP	Avg	OBP	SLG
1992 Yakima	A- LA	57	197	40	6	0	1	49	27	17	16	0	37	10	1	1	5	1	.83	4	.203	.295	.249
1993 Vero Beach	A+ LA	111	404	96	22	0	4	130	37	48	18	0	71	4	6	5	13	13	.50	4	.238	.274	.322
1994 Bakersfield	A+ LA	64	210	42	12	1	2	62	19	19	16	0	49	5	3	2	13	7	.65	3	.200	.270	.295
1995 San Berndno	A+ LA	111	417	101	26	1	17	180	64	68	17	0	83	4	11	2	20	12	.63	4	.242	.277	.432
1996 San Antonio	AA LA	127	521	143	28	6	10	213	74	57	17	1	82	4	9	3	15	8	.65	15	.274	.301	.409
Albuquerque	AAA LA	4	16	4	1	0	0	5	2	2	1	0	1	0	0	0	0	0	.00	0	.250	.294	.313
1997 San Antonio	AA LA	96	298	80	9	3	9	122	43	52	17	0	48	4	8	3	7	6	.54	4	.268	.314	.409
6 Min. YEARS		570	2063	506	104	11	43	761	266	263	102	1	371	31	38	16	73	47	.61	38	.245	.289	.369

Dax Jones

Bats: Right **Throws:** Right **Pos:** OF **Ht:** 6'0" **Wt:** 170 **Born:** 8/4/70 **Age:** 27

Year Team	Lg Org	G	AB	H	2B	3B	HR	TB	R	RBI	TBB	IBB	SO	HBP	SH	SF	SB	CS	SB%	GDP	Avg	OBP	SLG
1991 Everett	A- SF	53	180	55	5	6	5	87	42	29	27	0	26	1	1	3	15	8	.65	4	.306	.393	.483
1992 Clinton	A SF	79	295	88	12	4	1	111	45	42	21	0	32	1	1	1	18	5	.78	6	.298	.346	.376
Shreveport	AA SF	19	66	20	0	2	1	27	10	7	4	0	6	1	1	2	2	0	1.00	1	.303	.342	.409
1993 Shreveport	AA SF	118	436	124	19	4	4	165	59	36	26	6	53	4	3	2	13	8	.62	5	.284	.329	.378
1994 Phoenix	AAA SF	111	399	111	25	5	4	158	55	52	21	1	42	3	3	4	16	8	.67	14	.278	.316	.396
1995 Phoenix	AAA SF	112	404	108	21	3	2	141	47	45	31	3	52	2	2	5	11	10	.52	8	.267	.319	.349
1996 Phoenix	AAA SF	74	298	92	20	6	6	142	52	41	19	1	21	1	1	0	13	8	.62	7	.309	.352	.477
1997 Phoenix	AAA SF	93	271	69	7	5	3	95	48	28	39	0	39	1	3	4	9	10	.47	6	.255	.346	.351
1996 San Francisco	NL	34	58	10	0	2	1	17	7	7	8	0	12	0	0	1	2	2	.50	0	.172	.269	.293
7 Min. YEARS		659	2349	667	109	36	26	926	358	280	188	11	271	14	15	21	97	57	.63	51	.284	.338	.394

Ryan Jones

Bats: Right **Throws:** Right **Pos:** 1B **Ht:** 6'3" **Wt:** 220 **Born:** 11/5/74 **Age:** 23

Year Team	Lg Org	G	AB	H	2B	3B	HR	TB	R	RBI	TBB	IBB	SO	HBP	SH	SF	SB	CS	SB%	GDP	Avg	OBP	SLG
1993 Medicne Hat	R+ Tor	47	171	42	5	0	3	56	20	27	12	0	46	3	0	1	1	1	.50	9	.246	.305	.327
1994 Hagerstown	A Tor	115	402	96	29	0	18	179	60	72	45	0	124	6	0	5	1	0	1.00	6	.239	.321	.445
1995 Dunedin	A+ Tor	127	478	119	28	0	18	201	65	78	41	3	92	7	0	5	1	1	.50	7	.249	.315	.421
1996 Knoxville	AA Tor	134	506	137	26	3	20	229	70	97	60	6	88	6	0	6	2	2	.50	6	.271	.351	.453
1997 Syracuse	AAA Tor	41	123	17	5	1	3	33	8	16	15	0	28	3	0	4	0	2	.00	2	.138	.241	.268
Knoxville	AA Tor	86	328	84	19	3	12	145	41	51	27	1	63	0	0	4	0	1	.00	5	.256	.315	.442
5 Min. YEARS		550	2008	495	112	7	74	843	264	341	200	10	441	28	0	25	5	7	.42	35	.247	.320	.420

Stacy Jones

Pitches: Right **Bats:** Right **Pos:** P **Ht:** 6'6" **Wt:** 225 **Born:** 5/26/67 **Age:** 31

Year Team	Lg Org	G	GS	CG	GF	IP	BFP	H	R	ER	HR	SH	SF	HB	TBB	IBB	SO	WP	Bk	W	L	Pct.	ShO	Sv	ERA
1988 Erie	A- Bal	7	7	3	0	54.1	218	51	12	8	1	1	0	1	15	2	40	2	0	3	3	.500	2	0	1.33
Hagerstown	A+ Bal	6	6	3	0	37.2	156	35	14	12	2	1	4	1	12	0	23	2	0	3	1	.750	2	0	2.87
1989 Frederick	A+ Bal	15	15	3	0	82.2	374	93	57	45	11	1	3	2	35	0	58	3	4	5	6	.455	1	0	4.90

		HOW MUCH HE PITCHED						WHAT HE GAVE UP												THE RESULTS					
Year Team	Lg Org	G	GS	CG	GF	IP	BFP	H	R	ER	HR	SH	SF	HB	TBB	IBB	SO	WP	Bk	W	L	Pct.	ShO	Sv	ERA
1990 Frederick	A+ Bal	15	0	0	11	26.2	119	31	13	10	0	0	1	1	7	1	24	1	1	1	2	.333	0	2	3.38
Hagerstown	AA Bal	19	0	0	11	40.1	176	46	27	23	1	4	1	1	11	1	41	2	0	1	6	.143	0	2	5.13
1991 Hagerstown	AA Bal	12	0	0	4	30.1	130	24	6	6	1	2	0	1	15	1	26	1	0	0	1	.000	0	1	1.78
Rochester	AAA Bal	33	1	0	21	50.2	221	53	22	19	4	7	2	0	20	2	47	2	1	4	4	.500	0	8	3.38
1992 Frederick	A+ Bal	7	6	0	0	33.2	134	32	15	12	3	0	0	1	4	0	30	0	0	2	1	.667	0	0	3.21
Hagerstown	AA Bal	11	9	0	0	69.2	290	62	30	27	1	1	3	1	25	0	45	0	2	2	5	.286	0	0	3.49
Rochester	AAA Bal	2	0	0	1	2.2	11	2	2	2	1	0	0	0	1	0	1	0	0	0	0	.000	0	1	6.75
1993 Frederick	A+ Bal	4	2	0	0	12.2	60	24	17	14	4	1	0	0	1	0	7	0	1	0	2	.000	0	0	9.95
Shreveport	AA SF	24	2	0	9	50.1	210	53	21	20	2	1	2	1	19	1	28	0	0	4	1	.800	0	1	3.58
1994 Shreveport	AA SF	56	0	0	53	64	270	73	21	17	2	5	0	2	12	2	64	1	1	3	6	.333	0	34	2.39
1995 Phoenix	AAA SF	4	0	0	0	6.1	35	8	9	6	0	0	2	0	6	1	4	0	0	0	1	.000	0	0	8.53
El Paso	AA Mil	8	0	0	5	13.1	58	12	7	3	0	1	0	0	4	0	14	1	0	1	1	.500	0	3	2.03
New Orleans	AAA Mil	34	0	0	25	47.2	197	51	16	16	3	1	1	2	12	2	39	3	0	3	2	.600	0	6	3.02
1996 New Orleans	AAA Mil	9	0	0	2	12.2	64	18	10	10	2	1	1	2	7	1	10	1	0	1	1	.000	0	0	7.11
Birmingham	AA ChA	27	0	0	24	28	115	25	11	8	0	2	0	2	6	1	31	0	0	1	1	.500	0	14	2.57
Nashville	AAA ChA	19	0	0	18	21.2	81	17	3	2	0	0	1	0	6	2	18	0	0	3	0	1.000	0	12	0.83
1997 White Sox	R ChA	2	1	0	1	3	10	2	0	0	0	0	0	0	0	0	4	0	0	0	0	.000	0	1	0.00
Nashville	AAA ChA	1	0	0	0	0.1	6	4	3	2	0	0	0	0	0	0	0	0	0	0	0	.000	0	0	54.00
1991 Baltimore	AL	4	1	0	0	11	49	11	6	5	1	0	1	0	5	0	10	0	0	0	0	.000	0	0	4.09
1996 Chicago	AL	2	0	0	1	2	7	0	0	0	0	0	0	0	1	0	1	0	0	0	0	.000	0	0	0.00
10 Min. YEARS		315	49	9	185	688.2	2935	716	316	262	38	29	21	17	218	17	554	19	10	36	44	.450	5	85	3.42
2 Maj. YEARS		6	1	0	1	13	56	11	6	5	1	0	1	0	6	0	11	0	0	0	0	.000	0	0	3.46

Terry Jones

Bats: Both **Throws:** Right **Pos:** OF **Ht:** 5'10" **Wt:** 165 **Born:** 2/15/71 **Age:** 27

		BATTING															BASERUNNING				PERCENTAGES		
Year Team	Lg Org	G	AB	H	2B	3B	HR	TB	R	RBI	TBB	IBB	SO	HBP	SH	SF	SB	CS	SB%	GDP	Avg	OBP	SLG
1993 Bend	A- Col	33	138	40	5	4	0	53	21	18	12	1	19	0	2	0	16	6	.73	0	.290	.347	.384
Central Val	A+ Col	21	73	21	1	0	0	22	16	7	10	0	15	1	1	0	5	0	1.00	2	.288	.381	.301
1994 Central Val	A+ Col	129	536	157	20	1	2	185	94	34	42	1	85	1	10	1	44	12	.79	12	.293	.345	.345
1995 New Haven	AA Col	124	472	127	12	1	1	144	78	26	39	0	104	3	3	3	51	19	.73	6	.269	.327	.305
1996 Colo Sprngs	AAA Col	128	497	143	7	4	0	158	75	33	37	3	80	1	4	2	26	14	.65	5	.288	.337	.318
1997 Colo Sprngs	AAA Col	92	363	98	14	4	1	123	70	25	25	0	49	0	6	2	36	6	.86	3	.270	.315	.339
1996 Colorado	NL	12	10	3	0	0	0	3	6	1	0	0	3	0	0	1	0	0	.00	0	.300	.273	.300
5 Min. YEARS		527	2079	586	59	14	4	685	354	143	165	5	352	6	26	8	178	57	.76	28	.282	.335	.329

Ricky Jordan

Bats: Right **Throws:** Right **Pos:** DH-1B **Ht:** 6'3" **Wt:** 205 **Born:** 5/26/65 **Age:** 33

		BATTING															BASERUNNING				PERCENTAGES		
Year Team	Lg Org	G	AB	H	2B	3B	HR	TB	R	RBI	TBB	IBB	SO	HBP	SH	SF	SB	CS	SB%	GDP	Avg	OBP	SLG
1983 Helena	R+ Phi	60	247	71	7	1	5	97	32	33	12	0	35	0	0	1	3	0	1.00	-	.296	.327	.393
1984 Spartanburg	A Phi	128	490	143	23	4	10	204	72	76	32	2	63	4	0	5	8	2	.80	14	.292	.337	.416
1985 Clearwater	A+ Phi	139	528	146	22	8	7	205	60	62	25	3	59	1	2	4	26	8	.76	10	.274	.308	.388
1986 Reading	AA Phi	133	478	131	19	3	2	162	44	60	21	3	44	3	1	4	17	7	.71	5	.274	.306	.339
1987 Reading	AA Phi	132	475	151	28	3	16	233	78	95	28	4	22	3	0	9	15	9	.63	18	.318	.353	.491
1988 Maine	AAA Phi	87	338	104	23	1	7	150	42	36	6	0	30	0	0	1	10	0	1.00	15	.308	.319	.444
1990 Scranton-WB	AAA Phi	27	104	29	1	0	2	36	8	11	5	0	18	1	0	1	0	0	.00	6	.279	.315	.346
1992 Scranton-WB	AAA Phi	4	19	5	0	0	0	5	1	2	1	0	2	0	0	0	0	0	.00	0	.263	.300	.263
1995 Vancouver	AAA Ana	19	63	14	2	0	2	22	5	9	3	0	7	1	0	0	0	0	.00	2	.222	.269	.349
1996 Lancaster	A+ Sea	7	31	10	1	0	1	14	7	4	2	0	5	0	0	0	0	0	.00	2	.323	.364	.452
Everett	A- Sea	3	14	5	1	0	0	6	2	5	1	0	4	0	0	0	0	0	.00	0	.357	.400	.429
Tacoma	AAA Sea	13	50	10	0	0	2	16	3	7	5	1	6	0	0	1	0	0	.00	2	.200	.268	.320
1997 Carolina	AA Pit	52	188	59	9	2	7	93	25	33	8	0	25	2	0	3	1	1	.50	2	.314	.343	.495
1988 Philadelphia	NL	69	273	84	15	1	11	134	41	43	7	2	39	0	0	1	1	0	1.00	8	.308	.324	.491
1989 Philadelphia	NL	144	523	149	22	3	12	213	63	75	23	5	62	5	0	8	4	3	.57	19	.285	.317	.407
1990 Philadelphia	NL	92	324	78	21	0	5	114	32	44	13	6	39	5	0	4	2	0	1.00	9	.241	.277	.352
1991 Philadelphia	NL	101	301	82	21	3	9	136	38	49	14	2	49	2	0	5	3	0	1.00	8	.272	.304	.452
1992 Philadelphia	NL	94	276	84	19	0	4	115	33	34	5	0	44	0	0	3	0	0	.00	7	.304	.313	.417
1993 Philadelphia	NL	90	159	46	4	1	5	67	21	18	8	1	32	1	0	2	0	0	.00	4	.289	.324	.421
1994 Philadelphia	NL	72	220	62	14	2	8	104	29	37	6	1	32	1	0	1	0	0	.00	7	.282	.303	.473
1996 Seattle	AL	15	28	7	0	0	1	10	4	4	1	0	6	1	0	1	0	0	.00	2	.250	.290	.357
11 Min. YEARS		804	3025	880	136	22	61	1243	379	433	149	13	320	15	3	29	79	26	.75	73	.291	.325	.411
8 Maj. YEARS		677	2104	592	116	10	55	893	261	304	77	17	303	15	0	25	10	6	.63	61	.281	.308	.424

Randy Jorgensen

Bats: Left **Throws:** Left **Pos:** 1B **Ht:** 6'2" **Wt:** 200 **Born:** 4/3/72 **Age:** 26

		BATTING															BASERUNNING				PERCENTAGES		
Year Team	Lg Org	G	AB	H	2B	3B	HR	TB	R	RBI	TBB	IBB	SO	HBP	SH	SF	SB	CS	SB%	GDP	Avg	OBP	SLG
1993 Bellingham	A- Sea	67	228	60	13	0	5	88	42	22	37	2	33	3	2	4	7	4	.64	6	.263	.368	.386
1994 Riverside	A+ Sea	110	368	97	13	1	3	121	45	42	39	2	63	5	5	2	1	2	.33	19	.264	.341	.329
1995 Riverside	A+ Sea	133	495	148	32	1	12	220	78	97	46	1	74	10	0	8	4	7	.67	13	.299	.371	.444
1996 Port City	AA Sea	137	460	129	32	1	8	187	61	81	58	10	75	7	5	5	2	1	.67	15	.280	.366	.407
1997 Memphis	AA Sea	129	477	139	28	3	11	206	66	70	38	2	58	8	0	7	1	2	.33	10	.291	.349	.432
5 Min. YEARS		576	2028	573	118	7	39	822	292	312	218	17	303	38	12	26	15	11	.58	63	.283	.359	.405

Terry Joseph

Bats: Right Throws: Right Pos: OF   Ht: 5'9" Wt: 185 Born: 11/20/73 Age: 24

Year Team	Lg Org	G	AB	H	2B	3B	HR	TB	R	RBI	TBB	IBB	SO	HBP	SH	SF	SB	CS	SB%	GDP	Avg	OBP	SLG
1995 Williamsprt	A- ChN	70	260	76	8	1	0	107	49	34	30	1	33	7	1	0	18	6	.75	5	.292	.380	.412
1996 Rockford	A ChN	128	449	137	23	6	9	199	98	94	69	0	88	25	2	9	28	15	.65	7	.305	.418	.443
1997 Orlando	AA ChN	134	452	125	22	11	11	202	80	68	59	1	87	14	1	4	17	16	.52	11	.277	.374	.447
3 Min. YEARS		332	1161	338	53	27	21	508	227	196	158	2	208	46	4	13	63	37	.63	23	.291	.393	.438

Jarod Juelsgaard

Pitches: Right Bats: Right Pos: P   Ht: 6'3" Wt: 190 Born: 6/27/68 Age: 30

Year Team	Lg Org	G	GS	CG	GF	IP	BFP	H	R	ER	HR	SH	SF	HB	TBB	IBB	SO	WP	Bk	W	L	Pct.	ShO	Sv	ERA
1991 Everett	A- SF	20	6	0	8	62	270	62	36	30	3	1	1	2	27	2	46	16	4	3	5	.375	0	3	4.35
1992 Clinton	A SF	35	9	1	11	76.2	368	86	58	45	2	4	4	3	52	6	60	12	1	6	9	.400	0	2	5.28
1993 Kane County	A Fla	11	2	1	3	26	101	21	11	11	0	0	0	1	7	0	18	2	2	3	0	1.000	0	0	3.81
High Desert	A+ Fla	17	16	0	1	79.1	359	81	57	49	8	1	1	1	58	0	58	4	1	6	5	.545	0	0	5.56
1994 Portland	AA Fla	36	12	0	13	92.2	443	115	74	68	9	4	5	4	55	4	55	7	2	4	9	.308	0	0	6.60
1995 Portland	AA Fla	48	0	0	13	71.2	313	65	35	31	3	1	2	2	44	2	44	5	0	3	1	.750	0	2	3.89
1996 Charlotte	AAA Fla	26	5	0	9	44	192	43	23	17	1	1	2	0	21	0	29	3	0	4	2	.667	0	1	3.48
1997 Charlotte	AAA Fla	21	6	0	3	50.2	251	65	41	34	5	2	1	2	39	3	31	3	0	1	3	.250	0	0	6.04
7 Min. YEARS		214	56	2	61	503	2297	538	335	285	31	14	16	15	303	17	341	52	10	30	34	.469	0	8	5.10

James Kammerer

Pitches: Left Bats: Left Pos: P   Ht: 6'3" Wt: 205 Born: 7/21/73 Age: 24

Year Team	Lg Org	G	GS	CG	GF	IP	BFP	H	R	ER	HR	SH	SF	HB	TBB	IBB	SO	WP	Bk	W	L	Pct.	ShO	Sv	ERA
1995 Rockies	R Col	6	0	0	5	9.1	43	11	5	1	0	0	0	0	3	0	14	1	0	1	0	1.000	0	0	0.96
Portland	A- Col	11	5	0	0	35.1	135	24	8	6	0	1	1	0	11	0	17	1	0	2	1	.667	0	0	1.53
1996 Asheville	A Col	9	8	0	1	43	181	36	18	15	0	0	0	3	18	1	44	1	0	4	2	.667	0	0	3.14
1997 Asheville	A Col	12	3	1	2	38.1	162	37	15	12	1	0	1	1	20	0	27	1	0	0	2	.000	0	0	2.82
Salem	A+ Col	6	1	0	2	15.2	57	10	5	5	0	0	0	0	3	0	12	0	0	0	0	.000	0	0	2.87
New Haven	AA Col	1	1	0	0	5	21	3	2	2	1	1	0	0	3	0	1	0	0	0	0	.000	0	0	3.60
3 Min. YEARS		45	18	1	10	146.2	599	121	53	41	2	2	2	2	58	1	115	4	0	7	5	.583	0	0	2.52

Brad Kaufman

Pitches: Right Bats: Right Pos: P   Ht: 6'2" Wt: 210 Born: 4/26/72 Age: 26

Year Team	Lg Org	G	GS	CG	GF	IP	BFP	H	R	ER	HR	SH	SF	HB	TBB	IBB	SO	WP	Bk	W	L	Pct.	ShO	Sv	ERA
1993 Spokane	A- SD	25	8	1	11	53.2	264	56	56	41	8	0	3	3	41	2	48	4	2	5	4	.556	0	4	6.88
1994 Springfield	A SD	31	20	3	4	145.1	602	124	62	54	9	5	3	4	63	6	122	14	1	10	9	.526	0	0	3.34
1995 Memphis	AA SD	27	27	0	0	148.1	676	142	112	95	17	6	5	14	90	4	119	10	0	11	10	.524	0	0	5.76
1996 Memphis	AA SD	29	29	3	0	178.1	768	161	84	72	18	8	4	4	83	4	163	8	0	12	10	.545	1	0	3.63
1997 Las Vegas	AAA SD	6	6	0	0	32.1	151	40	37	29	9	0	1	1	15	0	19	1	0	0	5	.000	0	0	8.07
Mobile	AA SD	22	22	1	0	125.1	585	138	97	86	10	9	11	5	66	0	103	3	0	5	13	.278	0	0	6.18
5 Min. YEARS		140	112	8	15	683.1	3046	661	448	377	71	28	27	31	358	16	574	40	3	43	51	.457	1	4	4.97

Jamie Keefe

Bats: Right Throws: Right Pos: OF   Ht: 5'11" Wt: 180 Born: 8/29/73 Age: 24

Year Team	Lg Org	G	AB	H	2B	3B	HR	TB	R	RBI	TBB	IBB	SO	HBP	SH	SF	SB	CS	SB%	GDP	Avg	OBP	SLG
1992 Pirates	R Pit	33	100	19	0	1	0	21	12	8	11	0	23	1	0	0	5	3	.63	2	.190	.277	.210
1993 Pirates	R Pit	5	14	7	0	0	0	7	3	2	2	0	2	0	1	0	3	1	.75	0	.500	.563	.500
Lethbridge	R+ Pit	46	137	28	2	1	0	32	27	9	26	1	27	1	4	2	11	5	.69	3	.204	.331	.234
1994 Augusta	A Pit	50	124	33	3	0	0	36	16	7	13	1	27	3	5	0	11	7	.61	5	.266	.350	.290
Welland	A- Pit	27	87	20	4	0	0	24	6	9	4	0	17	0	3	0	2	5	.29	0	.230	.264	.276
1995 Clinton	A SD	67	175	42	3	1	1	50	28	10	23	0	42	2	3	0	12	3	.80	5	.240	.335	.286
1996 Clinton	A SD	32	106	32	5	0	3	46	25	15	34	0	18	1	0	0	8	1	.89	1	.302	.475	.434
Memphis	AA SD	12	17	3	0	0	0	3	2	0	3	0	5	1	1	0	0	0			.176	.333	.176
Rancho Cuca	A+ SD	24	64	15	5	1	2	28	12	10	11	0	26	2	0	2	1	0	1.00	3	.234	.354	.438
1997 Las Vegas	AAA SD	42	58	11	2	2	1	20	10	6	10	0	24	3	1	0	0	1	.00	0	.190	.338	.345
Mobile	AA SD	16	41	11	2	1	0	15	4	3	5	0	12	1	2	0	2	1	.67	0	.268	.362	.366
6 Min. YEARS		354	923	221	26	7	7	282	145	79	142	2	223	15	20	4	55	27	.67	16	.239	.349	.306

Rob Kell

Pitches: Left Bats: Right Pos: P   Ht: 6'2" Wt: 200 Born: 9/21/70 Age: 27

Year Team	Lg Org	G	GS	CG	GF	IP	BFP	H	R	ER	HR	SH	SF	HB	TBB	IBB	SO	WP	Bk	W	L	Pct.	ShO	Sv	ERA
1993 Erie	A- Tex	18	1	0	10	33.2	135	16	8	7	2	1	0	3	18	0	44	1	0	2	0	1.000	0	1	1.87
1994 Chston-SC	A Tex	38	0	0	17	54.2	228	43	27	24	6	4	2	3	21	0	57	7	0	0	2	.000	0	1	3.95
1995 Chston-SC	A Tex	7	7	0	0	44	184	38	20	17	2	3	1	2	9	0	47	3	0	1	4	.200	0	0	3.48
Charlotte	A+ Tex	11	0	0	5	20.2	93	16	9	7	1	0	0	2	15	0	21	2	0	1	0	1.000	0	1	3.05
1996 Bakersfield	A+ Tex	13	13	1	0	88	376	94	43	37	6	2	0	3	22	0	103	3	1	5	3	.625	1	0	3.78
Charlotte	A+ Tex	11	11	3	0	78	317	71	39	33	4	2	5	3	17	0	61	3	2	6	4	.600	2	0	3.81
Tulsa	AA Tex	2	0	0	1	0.2	3	1	0	0	0	0	1	0	0	0	0	0	0	0	0	.000	0	0	0.00
1997 Tulsa	AA Tex	28	2	0	8	41.1	197	60	32	27	7	1	2	1	14	2	35	4	0	0	2	.000	0	0	5.88
Okla City	AAA Tex	11	2	0	5	21.1	115	30	24	21	3	0	0	4	16	1	20	3	1	1	0	1.000	0	0	8.86

Frank Kellner

Bats: Both Throws: Right Pos: SS Ht: 5'11" Wt: 175 Born: 1/5/67 Age: 31

		HOW MUCH HE PITCHED				WHAT HE GAVE UP								THE RESULTS				
Year Team	Lg Org	G	GS	CG	GF	IP	BFP	H	R	ER	HR	SH	SF	HB	TBB	IBB	SO	WP	Bk
5 Min. YEARS		139	36	4	46	382.1	1648	369	202	173	31	13	11	21	132	3	388	26	4

(results: W 16 L 15 Pct. .516 ShO 3 Sv 4 ERA 4.07)

Year Team	Lg Org	G	AB	H	2B	3B	HR	TB	R	RBI	TBB	IBB	SO	HBP	SH	SF	SB	CS	SB%	GDP	Avg	OBP	SLG
1990 Osceola	A+ Hou	109	369	91	9	7	0	114	43	34	65	2	65	1	9	3	14	7	.67	11	.247	.358	.309
Tucson	AAA Hou	19	60	18	1	0	0	19	13	7	15	0	6	0	2	0	1	0	1.00	0	.300	.440	.317
1991 Osceola	A+ Hou	53	204	44	8	1	1	57	27	15	20	2	24	0	4	0	8	1	.89	6	.216	.286	.279
Jackson	AA Hou	83	311	84	7	4	2	105	47	25	29	2	37	0	2	2	6	5	.55	8	.270	.330	.338
1992 Jackson	AA Hou	125	474	113	18	5	3	150	45	48	42	5	89	3	4	2	8	7	.53	9	.238	.303	.316
1993 Jackson	AA Hou	121	355	107	27	2	4	150	51	36	38	5	51	2	2	6	11	12	.48	10	.301	.367	.423
1994 Tucson	AAA Hou	106	296	88	13	5	1	114	32	35	46	3	40	0	3	2	5	4	.56	4	.297	.390	.385
1995 Jackson	AA Hou	75	269	85	15	1	0	102	31	29	35	2	52	2	4	5	1	7	.13	2	.316	.392	.379
Tucson	AAA Hou	28	89	16	3	1	0	21	11	7	15	0	12	0	1	1	1	0	1.00	3	.180	.295	.236
1996 Tucson	AAA Hou	96	254	69	12	5	1	94	37	31	22	1	43	0	7	6	3	6	.33	7	.272	.323	.370
1997 Rio Grande	IND —	12	45	12	4	2	2	26	13	8	7	0	4	1	0	1	1	0	1.00	1	.267	.370	.578
Tucson	AAA Mil	67	230	66	14	4	0	88	31	25	16	0	38	1	5	2	2	1	.67	6	.287	.333	.383
8 Min. YEARS		894	2956	793	131	37	14	1040	381	300	350	22	461	10	43	30	61	50	.55	66	.268	.345	.352

Jeff Kelly

Pitches: Left Bats: Left Pos: P Ht: 6'6" Wt: 215 Born: 1/11/75 Age: 23

		HOW MUCH HE PITCHED						WHAT HE GAVE UP								THE RESULTS					
Year Team	Lg Org	G	GS	CG	GF	IP	BFP	H	R	ER	HR	SH	SF	HB	TBB	IBB	SO	WP	Bk	W	L	Pct.	ShO	Sv	ERA
1994 Pirates	R Pit	11	7	0	1	46.1	207	54	26	21	4	0	2	1	12	0	24	0	3	0	5	.000	0	0	4.08
1995 Augusta	A Pit	26	26	0	0	142.2	608	134	68	55	6	5	5	4	51	0	114	12	0	6	11	.353	0	0	3.47
1996 Augusta	A Pit	14	14	0	0	84	360	76	39	31	4	0	3	15	27	0	68	4	0	6	3	.667	0	0	3.32
Lynchburg	A+ Pit	13	13	0	0	75	335	77	45	30	7	0	0	10	24	0	57	6	1	4	5	.444	0	0	3.60
1997 Carolina	AA Pit	31	19	0	3	127.2	593	134	79	66	7	9	9	12	85	5	83	7	2	6	11	.353	0	0	4.65
4 Min. YEARS		95	79	0	4	475.2	2103	475	257	203	28	14	19	42	199	5	346	29	6	22	35	.386	0	0	3.84

Darryl Kennedy

Bats: Right Throws: Right Pos: C Ht: 5'10" Wt: 170 Born: 1/23/69 Age: 29

Year Team	Lg Org	G	AB	H	2B	3B	HR	TB	R	RBI	TBB	IBB	SO	HBP	SH	SF	SB	CS	SB%	GDP	Avg	OBP	SLG
1991 Rangers	R Tex	5	18	2	1	0	0	3	4	1	1	0	1	0	1	0	0	0	.00	0	.111	.158	.167
Charlotte	A+ Tex	23	68	7	3	0	0	10	5	4	5	0	11	2	1	2	0	0	.00	2	.103	.182	.147
1992 Gastonia	A Tex	13	33	3	1	0	0	4	2	2	6	1	6	1	0	1	0	2	.00	1	.091	.244	.121
Charlotte	A+ Tex	13	28	13	4	0	0	17	3	6	3	0	3	0	0	0	0	1	.00	0	.464	.516	.607
Tulsa	AA Tex	30	98	22	2	0	0	24	6	9	8	0	18	2	2	1	0	0	.00	4	.224	.294	.245
1993 Okla City	AAA Tex	16	16	1	0	0	0	1	2	0	3	0	4	0	1	0	0	0	.00	0	.063	.211	.063
Charlotte	A+ Tex	106	347	97	23	0	1	123	47	30	47	0	38	1	5	2	5	7	.42	7	.280	.365	.354
1994 Charlotte	A+ Tex	53	177	47	5	2	1	59	24	22	25	1	20	1	2	0	1	2	.33	7	.266	.360	.333
Tulsa	AA Tex	23	70	16	3	0	1	22	5	5	8	0	10	0	2	2	1	1	.50	1	.229	.308	.314
1995 Tulsa	AA Tex	61	195	49	8	1	3	69	26	26	17	0	22	3	3	4	0	0	.00	5	.251	.315	.354
Okla City	AAA Tex	3	11	2	0	0	1	5	1	3	0	0	2	0	0	0	0	0	.00	0	.182	.182	.455
1996 Okla City	AAA Tex	2	7	2	0	0	0	2	0	0	0	0	2	0	0	0	0	0	.00	0	.286	.286	.286
Tulsa	AA Tex	15	43	13	1	0	1	21	11	10	4	0	5	1	1	0	0	1	.00	2	.302	.375	.488
Phoenix	AAA SF	64	192	59	11	3	2	82	27	24	12	3	25	3	4	4	2	2	.50	5	.307	.351	.427
1997 Shreveport	AA SF	22	71	19	4	0	2	29	11	10	6	1	8	0	0	0	0	0	.00	2	.268	.325	.408
Phoenix	AAA SF	32	98	17	4	0	0	21	10	8	6	1	13	1	1	1	1	1	.50	2	.173	.224	.214
7 Min. YEARS		471	1472	369	73	7	12	492	184	160	151	7	188	15	22	16	10	17	.37	38	.251	.323	.334

Tim Kester

Pitches: Right Bats: Right Pos: P Ht: 6'4" Wt: 185 Born: 12/1/71 Age: 26

		HOW MUCH HE PITCHED						WHAT HE GAVE UP								THE RESULTS					
Year Team	Lg Org	G	GS	CG	GF	IP	BFP	H	R	ER	HR	SH	SF	HB	TBB	IBB	SO	WP	Bk	W	L	Pct.	ShO	Sv	ERA
1993 Auburn	A- Hou	15	13	2	0	96.1	398	78	40	22	2	2	0	10	19	1	83	5	2	4	6	.400	1	0	2.06
1994 Osceola	A+ Hou	24	22	2	0	134	580	159	85	73	7	8	5	8	30	5	71	3	0	5	12	.294	0	0	4.90
1995 Quad City	A Hou	28	23	2	3	160.2	665	158	80	53	8	5	6	10	20	1	111	4	0	12	5	.706	0	0	2.97
1996 Tucson	AAA Hou	1	1	0	0	1.2	15	8	8	8	1	1	1	0	1	0	1	0	0	0	1	.000	0	0	43.20
Jackson	AA Hou	48	4	0	7	103.2	435	105	52	43	8	4	4	6	16	0	55	8	0	2	4	.333	0	1	3.73
1997 Jackson	AA Hou	47	4	0	18	82.2	375	107	53	48	9	2	4	8	26	3	50	2	0	4	6	.400	0	2	5.23
5 Min. YEARS		163	67	8	29	579	2468	615	318	247	35	22	20	42	112	10	371	22	2	27	34	.443	1	3	3.84

Brian Keyser

Pitches: Right Bats: Right Pos: P Ht: 6'1" Wt: 180 Born: 10/31/66 Age: 31

		HOW MUCH HE PITCHED						WHAT HE GAVE UP								THE RESULTS					
Year Team	Lg Org	G	GS	CG	GF	IP	BFP	H	R	ER	HR	SH	SF	HB	TBB	IBB	SO	WP	Bk	W	L	Pct.	ShO	Sv	ERA
1989 Utica	A- ChA	14	13	4	1	93.2	374	79	37	31	6	2	2	2	22	0	70	5	3	4	4	.500	2	0	2.98
1990 Sarasota	A+ ChA	38	10	2	13	115.2	475	107	54	47	5	3	6	1	40	1	83	6	3	6	7	.462	1	2	3.66
1991 Sarasota	A+ ChA	27	14	2	9	129	527	110	40	33	5	8	3	6	45	8	94	3	3	6	7	.462	1	2	2.30
Birmingham	AA ChA	3	3	0	0	18	78	19	10	10	2	0	1	0	9	0	9	0	1	0	1	.000	0	0	5.00
1992 Birmingham	AA ChA	28	27	7	1	183.1	754	173	86	76	12	1	7	4	60	1	99	9	0	9	10	.474	3	0	3.73
1993 Birmingham	AA ChA	2	2	1	0	11	50	15	9	7	0	1	1	0	5	0	5	0	0	0	2	.000	0	0	5.73

Year Team	Lg Org	G	GS	CG	GF	IP	BFP	H	R	ER	HR	SH	SF	HB	TBB	IBB	SO	WP	Bk	W	L	Pct.	ShO	Sv	ERA
Nashville	AAA ChA	30	18	2	4	121.2	511	142	70	63	8	2	4	1	27	4	44	4	1	9	5	.643	0	1	4.66
1994 Birmingham	AA ChA	1	1	0	0	6	23	4	1	1	1	0	0	1	1	0	5	0	0	0	0	.000	0	0	1.50
Nashville	AAA ChA	37	10	2	15	135.2	556	123	49	42	9	7	5	3	36	4	76	9	0	9	5	.643	1	2	2.79
1995 Nashville	AAA ChA	10	10	2	0	72.1	273	49	23	19	4	3	3	1	9	0	40	1	0	2	4	.333	1	0	2.36
1996 Nashville	AAA ChA	6	6	2	0	44.2	178	38	11	10	2	2	3	0	13	1	22	0	0	3	3	.500	1	0	2.01
1997 Nashville	AAA ChA	44	9	3	7	119	500	114	44	38	10	4	6	1	45	1	68	7	0	7	5	.583	0	1	2.87
1995 Chicago	AL	23	10	0	0	92.1	404	114	53	51	10	0	2	2	27	1	48	1	1	5	6	.455	0	0	4.97
1996 Chicago	AL	28	0	0	10	59.2	275	78	35	33	3	6	3	0	28	8	19	2	0	1	2	.333	0	0	4.98
9 Min. YEARS		240	123	25	49	1050	4299	973	434	377	64	33	41	22	312	20	618	44	11	55	53	.509	8	8	3.23
2 Maj. YEARS		51	10	0	10	152	679	192	88	84	13	6	5	2	55	9	67	3	1	6	8	.429	0	1	4.97

Tim Killeen

Bats: Left Throws: Right Pos: C   Ht: 6'0" Wt: 195 Born: 7/26/70 Age: 27

Year Team	Lg Org	G	AB	H	2B	3B	HR	TB	R	RBI	TBB	IBB	SO	HBP	SH	SF	SB	CS	SB%	GDP	Avg	OBP	SLG
1992 Sou. Oregon	A- Oak	39	119	28	7	0	3	44	20	12	17	1	30	2	0	0	5	3	.63	2	.235	.341	.370
1993 Madison	A Oak	76	243	49	15	0	10	94	33	36	39	1	70	3	0	1	0	0	.00	1	.202	.318	.387
Tacoma	AAA Oak	3	9	4	0	0	0	4	4	0	1	0	4	0	0	0	0	1	.00	0	.444	.500	.444
1994 Modesto	A+ Oak	101	365	87	18	3	16	159	53	75	49	2	107	2	2	5	5	2	.71	5	.238	.328	.436
1995 Memphis	AA SD	77	230	54	14	0	9	95	27	40	27	6	71	0	0	1	2	0	1.00	5	.235	.314	.413
1996 Memphis	AA SD	83	224	58	10	6	11	113	44	51	27	1	57	1	1	6	0	2	.00	4	.259	.333	.504
1997 Mobile	AA SD	66	168	34	8	1	5	59	23	21	53	3	60	1	1	1	0	1	.00	2	.202	.395	.351
6 Min. YEARS		445	1358	314	72	10	54	568	204	235	213	14	399	9	4	14	12	9	.57	29	.231	.336	.418

Bill King

Pitches: Right Bats: Right Pos: P   Ht: 6'5" Wt: 225 Born: 2/18/73 Age: 25

Year Team	Lg Org	G	GS	CG	GF	IP	BFP	H	R	ER	HR	SH	SF	HB	TBB	IBB	SO	WP	Bk	W	L	Pct.	ShO	Sv	ERA
1994 Sou. Oregon	A- Oak	1	1	0	0	3	10	1	0	0	0	0	0	0	1	0	2	0	0	0	0	.000	0	0	0.00
W Michigan	A Oak	17	1	0	8	44.2	183	35	11	9	2	2	0	1	19	1	25	0	1	2	1	.667	0	4	1.81
1995 W Michigan	A Oak	30	18	0	3	148.1	633	152	75	55	6	5	1	5	41	0	95	6	5	9	7	.563	0	2	3.34
1996 Modesto	A+ Oak	29	27	0	1	163	716	193	102	86	11	3	8	8	40	0	100	8	2	16	4	.800	0	1	4.75
1997 Huntsville	AA Oak	28	27	1	0	176	762	216	99	82	18	8	3	10	28	0	103	7	0	9	7	.563	0	0	4.19
4 Min. YEARS		105	74	1	12	535	2304	597	287	232	37	18	12	24	129	1	325	21	8	36	19	.655	0	7	3.90

Brett King

Bats: Right Throws: Right Pos: 3B   Ht: 6'1" Wt: 190 Born: 7/20/72 Age: 25

Year Team	Lg Org	G	AB	H	2B	3B	HR	TB	R	RBI	TBB	IBB	SO	HBP	SH	SF	SB	CS	SB%	GDP	Avg	OBP	SLG
1993 Everett	A- SF	69	243	55	10	0	2	71	43	24	40	2	63	5	9	0	26	11	.70	2	.226	.347	.292
1994 San Jose	A+ SF	48	188	47	8	2	1	62	24	11	19	1	62	4	1	0	6	8	.43	0	.250	.332	.330
Clinton	A SF	68	261	57	13	2	5	89	45	30	23	1	86	2	3	2	12	3	.80	2	.218	.285	.341
1995 San Jose	A+ SF	107	394	108	29	4	3	154	61	41	41	1	86	5	5	6	28	8	.78	8	.274	.345	.391
1996 Shreveport	AA SF	127	459	107	23	4	7	159	61	48	49	6	116	6	17	3	19	9	.68	5	.233	.315	.346
1997 Shreveport	AA SF	79	193	42	6	1	6	68	28	20	30	1	55	1	1	1	4	5	.44	3	.218	.324	.352
5 Min. YEARS		498	1738	416	89	13	24	603	262	174	202	6	468	23	36	10	95	44	.68	20	.239	.325	.347

Cesar King

Bats: Right Throws: Right Pos: C   Ht: 6'0" Wt: 175 Born: 2/28/78 Age: 20

Year Team	Lg Org	G	AB	H	2B	3B	HR	TB	R	RBI	TBB	IBB	SO	HBP	SH	SF	SB	CS	SB%	GDP	Avg	OBP	SLG
1996 Chston-SC	A Tex	84	276	69	10	1	7	102	35	28	21	0	58	1	0	2	8	5	.62	5	.250	.303	.370
1997 Charlotte	A+ Tex	91	307	91	14	4	6	131	51	37	35	0	58	1	3	4	8	6	.57	5	.296	.366	.427
Tulsa	AA Tex	14	45	16	1	0	1	20	6	8	5	0	3	0	0	0	0	1	.00	2	.356	.420	.444
2 Min. YEARS		189	628	176	25	5	14	253	92	73	61	0	119	2	3	6	16	12	.57	12	.280	.343	.403

Raymond King

Pitches: Left Bats: Left Pos: P   Ht: 6'1" Wt: 221 Born: 1/15/74 Age: 24

Year Team	Lg Org	G	GS	CG	GF	IP	BFP	H	R	ER	HR	SH	SF	HB	TBB	IBB	SO	WP	Bk	W	L	Pct.	ShO	Sv	ERA
1995 Billings	R+ Cin	28	0	0	15	43	169	31	11	8	1	2	0	0	15	3	43	1	1	3	0	1.000	0	5	1.67
1996 Macon	A Atl	18	0	0	2	70.2	286	63	34	22	4	0	0	0	20	0	63	2	1	3	5	.375	0	0	2.80
Durham	A+ Atl	14	14	2	0	82.2	364	104	54	41	3	4	4	3	15	2	52	0	1	4	6	.333	0	0	4.46
1997 Greenville	AA Atl	12	9	0	0	65.2	305	85	53	50	9	0	0	1	24	2	42	4	0	5	5	.500	0	0	6.85
Durham	A+ Atl	24	6	0	6	71.2	335	89	54	43	6	7	1	4	26	4	60	4	0	6	9	.400	0	3	5.40
3 Min. YEARS		96	39	3	23	333.2	1459	372	206	164	23	13	5	8	100	11	260	13	3	20	25	.444	0	8	4.42

Eugene Kingsale

Bats: Both Throws: Right Pos: OF   Ht: 6'3" Wt: 170 Born: 8/20/76 Age: 21

Year Team	Lg Org	G	AB	H	2B	3B	HR	TB	R	RBI	TBB	IBB	SO	HBP	SH	SF	SB	CS	SB%	GDP	Avg	OBP	SLG
1994 Orioles	R Bal	50	168	52	2	3	0	60	26	9	18	0	24	1	1	5	15	6	.71		.310	.381	.357
1995 Bluefield	R+ Bal	47	171	54	11	2	2	69	45	16	27	0	31	5	4	2	20	8	.71	0	.316	.420	.404
1996 Frederick	A+ Bal	49	166	45	6	4	0	59	26	9	19	1	32	6	3	2	23	4	.85	1	.271	.363	.355

Year Team	Lg Org	G	AB	H	2B	3B	HR	TB	R	RBI	TBB	IBB	SO	HBP	SH	SF	SB	CS	SB%	GDP	Avg	OBP	SLG
1997 Orioles	R Bal	6	17	5	0	0	0	5	2	0	2	0	2	1	0	0	1	0	1.00	0	.294	.400	.294
Bowie	AA Bal	13	46	19	6	0	0	25	8	4	5	0	4	1	1	0	5	1	.83	2	.413	.481	.543
1996 Baltimore	AL	3	0	0	0	0	0	0	0	0	0	0	0	0	0	0	0	0	.00	0	.000	.000	.000
4 Min. YEARS		165	568	175	25	9	0	218	107	38	71	1	93	15	9	5	64	21	.75	4	.308	.396	.384

Mike Kinkade

Bats: Right Throws: Right Pos: 3B Ht: 6'1" Wt: 210 Born: 5/6/73 Age: 25

Year Team	Lg Org	G	AB	H	2B	3B	HR	TB	R	RBI	TBB	IBB	SO	HBP	SH	SF	SB	CS	SB%	GDP	Avg	OBP	SLG
1995 Helena	R+ Mil	69	266	94	19	1	4	127	76	39	43	2	38	10	0	6	26	9	.74	6	.353	.452	.477
1996 Beloit	A Mil	135	499	151	33	4	15	237	105	109	47	7	69	32	3	6	23	12	.66	10	.303	.394	.475
1997 El Paso	AA Mil	125	468	180	35	12	12	275	112	109	52	0	66	13	1	6	17	4	.81	13	.385	.455	.588
3 Min. YEARS		329	1233	425	87	17	31	639	293	248	142	9	173	55	4	18	66	25	.73	29	.345	.430	.518

Chris Kirgan

Bats: Right Throws: Right Pos: 1B Ht: 6'4" Wt: 235 Born: 6/29/73 Age: 25

Year Team	Lg Org	G	AB	H	2B	3B	HR	TB	R	RBI	TBB	IBB	SO	HBP	SH	SF	SB	CS	SB%	GDP	Avg	OBP	SLG
1994 Bluefield	R+ Bal	58	209	58	8	3	7	93	34	29	27	1	53	0	0	4	4	0	1.00	4	.278	.354	.445
1995 Frederick	A+ Bal	124	378	76	18	2	11	131	25	47	25	3	107	3	1	3	3	2	.60	7	.201	.254	.347
1996 High Desert	A+ Bal	136	529	157	23	1	35	287	96	131	54	3	162	5	1	2	2	3	.40	9	.297	.366	.543
1997 Bowie	AA Bal	139	504	116	25	0	19	198	72	71	60	1	141	2	0	3	0	0	.00	13	.230	.313	.393
4 Min. YEARS		457	1620	407	74	6	72	709	227	278	166	8	463	10	2	12	9	5	.64	33	.251	.322	.438

Jay Kirkpatrick

Bats: Left Throws: Right Pos: 1B-DH Ht: 6'4" Wt: 220 Born: 7/10/69 Age: 28

Year Team	Lg Org	G	AB	H	2B	3B	HR	TB	R	RBI	TBB	IBB	SO	HBP	SH	SF	SB	CS	SB%	GDP	Avg	OBP	SLG
1991 Great Falls	R+ LA	50	168	54	11	1	2	73	25	26	13	0	23	3	0	0	1	2	.33	3	.321	.380	.435
1992 Vero Beach	A+ LA	114	385	108	22	2	6	152	32	50	31	4	82	4	1	6	2	2	.50	9	.281	.336	.395
1993 Bakersfield	A+ LA	103	375	108	21	0	8	153	42	63	35	2	78	4	1	3	1	4	.20	7	.288	.353	.408
San Antonio	AA LA	27	97	31	6	1	6	57	17	17	14	4	15	0	0	0	0	1	.00	4	.320	.405	.588
1994 San Antonio	AA LA	123	449	133	40	1	18	229	61	75	45	7	91	3	0	6	2	2	.50	12	.296	.360	.510
Albuquerque	AAA LA	3	5	1	1	0	0	2	0	1	1	0	1	0	0	0	0	0	.00	0	.200	.333	.400
1995 Albuquerque	AAA LA	13	40	10	1	1	1	16	4	6	2	1	6	0	0	0	0	0	.00	0	.250	.286	.400
San Berndno	A+ LA	71	267	72	19	0	15	136	38	50	40	3	75	0	0	2	3	0	1.00	3	.270	.362	.509
1996 San Antonio	AA LA	30	91	22	4	0	3	35	6	10	11	3	26	0	0	1	1	0	1.00	5	.242	.324	.385
Albuquerque	AAA LA	51	107	26	5	0	3	31	12	9	10	2	35	0	0	2	0	0	.00	4	.243	.303	.290
1997 San Antonio	AA LA	62	215	56	9	0	8	89	22	42	8	0	53	0	0	0	0	1	.00	4	.260	.287	.414
7 Min. YEARS		647	2199	621	139	6	67	973	259	349	210	26	485	14	2	19	10	12	.45	51	.282	.346	.442

Daron Kirkreit

Pitches: Right Bats: Right Pos: P Ht: 6'6" Wt: 225 Born: 8/7/72 Age: 25

		HOW MUCH HE PITCHED						WHAT HE GAVE UP										THE RESULTS					
Year Team	Lg Org	G	GS	CG	GF	IP	BFP	H	R	ER	HR	SH	SF	HB	TBB	IBB	SO	WP	Bk	W	L	Pct.	ShO	Sv	ERA
1993 Watertown	A- Cle	7	7	1	0	36.1	156	33	14	9	1	1	0	0	11	0	44	1	1	4	1	.800	0	0	2.23
1994 Kinston	A+ Cle	20	19	4	1	127.2	510	92	48	38	9	3	1	7	40	0	116	6	0	8	7	.533	0	0	2.68
Canton-Akrn	AA Cle	9	9	0	0	46.1	217	53	35	32	5	2	1	0	25	2	54	4	0	3	5	.375	0	0	6.22
1995 Canton-Akrn	AA Cle	14	14	1	0	80.2	360	74	54	51	13	5	5	6	46	1	67	2	0	2	9	.182	0	0	5.69
Kinston	A+ Cle	3	3	0	0	13.2	63	14	9	9	1	1	1	2	6	0	14	1	0	1	1	.000	0	0	5.93
1996 Kinston	A+ Cle	6	6	0	0	32.2	125	23	7	7	3	0	1	2	10	0	19	3	0	2	0	1.000	0	0	1.93
1997 Buffalo	AAA Cle	1	1	1	0	7	23	3	0	0	0	0	0	0	1	0	2	0	0	1	0	1.000	1	0	0.00
Akron	AA Cle	26	20	1	3	117.2	562	131	96	68	15	9	4	13	69	3	83	10	1	8	9	.471	0	0	5.20
5 Min. YEARS		86	79	8	4	462	2016	423	263	214	47	21	13	30	208	6	399	27	2	28	32	.467	1	0	4.17

Ryan Kjos

Pitches: Right Bats: Right Pos: P Ht: 6'5" Wt: 230 Born: 3/4/73 Age: 25

		HOW MUCH HE PITCHED						WHAT HE GAVE UP										THE RESULTS					
Year Team	Lg Org	G	GS	CG	GF	IP	BFP	H	R	ER	HR	SH	SF	HB	TBB	IBB	SO	WP	Bk	W	L	Pct.	ShO	Sv	ERA
1995 Athletics	R Oak	3	0	0	0	3.2	23	9	10	8	1	0	0	1	1	0	5	2	0	0	0	.000	0	0	19.64
Sou. Oregon	A- Oak	9	0	0	4	11	47	9	4	3	2	0	0	1	5	0	16	2	0	2	0	1.000	0	2	2.45
1996 Sou. Oregon	A- Oak	24	1	0	6	48.1	217	41	33	20	6	1	3	3	26	3	64	5	0	0	3	.000	0	0	3.72
1997 Edmonton	AAA Oak	1	0	0	1	2	15	6	8	8	2	0	0	3	0	2	1	0	0	1	.000	0	0	36.00
Modesto	A+ Oak	34	0	0	16	61.1	272	57	38	26	6	2	5	3	30	1	73	7	0	2	2	.500	0	2	3.82
3 Min. YEARS		71	1	0	27	126.1	574	122	93	65	17	3	8	7	65	4	160	17	0	4	6	.400	0	2	4.63

Danny Klassen

Bats: Right Throws: Right Pos: SS Ht: 6'0" Wt: 175 Born: 9/22/75 Age: 22

Year Team	Lg Org	G	AB	H	2B	3B	HR	TB	R	RBI	TBB	IBB	SO	HBP	SH	SF	SB	CS	SB%	GDP	Avg	OBP	SLG
1993 Brewers	R Mil	38	117	26	5	0	2	37	26	20	24	3	28	8	1	4	14	3	.82	2	.222	.359	.316
Helena	R+ Mil	18	45	9	1	0	0	10	8	3	7	0	11	2	1	0	2	1	.67	2	.200	.333	.222
1994 Beloit	A Mil	133	458	119	20	3	6	163	61	54	58	0	123	12	17	3	28	14	.67	3	.260	.356	.356
1995 Beloit	A Mil	59	218	60	15	2	2	85	27	25	16	0	43	4	0	3	12	4	.75	4	.275	.332	.390

Year Team	Lg Org	G	AB	H	2B	3B	HR	TB	R	RBI	TBB	IBB	SO	HBP	SH	SF	SB	CS	SB%	GDP	Avg	OBP	SLG
								BATTING									BASERUNNING				PERCENTAGES		
1996 Stockton	A+ Mil	118	432	116	22	4	2	152	58	46	34	0	77	10	5	2	14	8	.64	12	.269	.335	.352
1997 El Paso	AA Mil	135	519	172	30	6	14	256	112	81	48	1	104	10	4	4	16	9	.64	13	.331	.396	.493
5 Min. YEARS		501	1789	502	93	15	26	703	292	229	187	4	386	46	28	16	86	39	.69	36	.281	.361	.393

Stacy Kleiner

Bats: Right **Throws:** Right **Pos:** 2B **Ht:** 6'0" **Wt:** 185 **Born:** 1/12/75 **Age:** 23

Year Team	Lg Org	G	AB	H	2B	3B	HR	TB	R	RBI	TBB	IBB	SO	HBP	SH	SF	SB	CS	SB%	GDP	Avg	OBP	SLG
								BATTING									BASERUNNING				PERCENTAGES		
1996 New Jersey	A- StL	56	177	52	10	2	2	72	24	23	9	0	32	1	2	0	2	1	.67	5	.294	.332	.407
1997 Pr William	A+ StL	91	310	97	22	4	4	139	37	32	28	2	69	4	1	1	1	1	.50	11	.313	.376	.448
Arkansas	AA StL	16	55	14	4	2	1	25	7	10	2	0	14	0	0	0	0	1	.00	2	.255	.281	.455
2 Min. YEARS		163	542	163	36	8	7	236	68	65	39	2	115	5	3	1	3	2	.60	18	.301	.353	.435

Scott Klingenbeck

Pitches: Right **Bats:** Right **Pos:** P **Ht:** 6'2" **Wt:** 205 **Born:** 2/3/71 **Age:** 27

Year Team	Lg Org	G	GS	CG	GF	IP	BFP	H	R	ER	HR	SH	SF	HB	TBB	IBB	SO	WP	Bk	W	L	Pct.	ShO	Sv	ERA
				HOW MUCH HE PITCHED				WHAT HE GAVE UP												THE RESULTS					
1992 Kane County	A Bal	11	11	0	0	68.1	283	50	31	20	3	2	0	1	28	1	64	4	8	3	4	.429	0	0	2.63
1993 Frederick	A+ Bal	23	23	0	0	139	593	151	62	46	7	2	2	2	35	1	146	5	2	13	4	.765	0	0	2.98
1994 Bowie	AA Bal	25	25	3	0	143.2	613	151	76	58	15	2	4	5	37	2	120	6	3	7	5	.583	0	0	3.63
1995 Rochester	AAA Bal	8	7	0	0	43	177	46	14	13	2	3	2	1	10	0	29	2	0	3	1	.750	0	0	2.72
1996 Salt Lake	AAA Min	22	22	5	0	150.2	635	159	64	52	8	4	6	3	41	2	100	9	1	9	3	.750	2	0	3.11
1997 Salt Lake	AAA Min	1	1	0	0	7	26	6	1	1	1	0	0	0	6	0	0	0	0	0	0	.000	0	0	1.29
Indianapols	AAA Cin	27	27	2	0	170.2	727	180	85	75	23	5	6	5	41	0	119	2	2	12	8	.600	0	0	3.96
1994 Baltimore	AL	1	1	0	0	7	31	6	4	3	1	0	1	1	4	1	5	0	0	1	0	1.000	0	0	3.86
1995 Baltimore	AL	6	5	0	0	31.1	137	32	17	17	6	0	0	0	18	0	15	2	0	2	2	.500	0	0	4.88
Minnesota	AL	18	4	0	4	48.1	236	69	48	46	16	3	1	4	24	0	27	5	0	0	2	.000	0	0	8.57
1996 Minnesota	AL	10	3	0	2	28.2	137	42	28	25	5	1	1	1	10	0	15	1	0	1	1	.500	0	0	7.85
6 Min. YEARS		117	116	10	0	722.1	3054	743	333	265	59	18	20	17	192	6	584	28	16	47	25	.653	2	0	3.30
3 Maj. YEARS		35	13	0	6	115.1	541	149	97	91	28	4	3	6	56	1	62	8	0	4	5	.444	0	0	7.10

Joe Kmak

Bats: Right **Throws:** Right **Pos:** C **Ht:** 6'0" **Wt:** 185 **Born:** 5/3/63 **Age:** 35

Year Team	Lg Org	G	AB	H	2B	3B	HR	TB	R	RBI	TBB	IBB	SO	HBP	SH	SF	SB	CS	SB%	GDP	Avg	OBP	SLG
								BATTING									BASERUNNING				PERCENTAGES		
1985 Everett	A- SF	40	129	40	10	1	1	55	21	14	20	0	23	3	0	1	0	1	.00	3	.310	.409	.426
1986 Fresno	A+ SF	60	163	44	5	0	1	52	23	9	15	0	38	3	0	1	3	2	.60	6	.270	.341	.319
1987 Fresno	A+ SF	48	154	34	8	0	0	42	18	12	15	0	32	3	3	0	1	2	.33	3	.221	.302	.273
Shreveport	AA SF	15	41	8	0	1	0	10	5	3	3	0	4	1	0	0	0	0	.00	1	.195	.267	.244
1988 Shreveport	AA SF	71	178	40	5	2	1	52	16	14	11	2	19	4	1	1	0	0	.00	3	.225	.284	.292
1989 Reno	A+ —	78	248	68	10	5	4	100	39	34	40	1	41	5	0	1	8	4	.67	9	.274	.384	.403
1990 El Paso	AA Mil	35	109	31	3	2	2	44	8	11	7	0	22	2	3	2	0	0	.00	2	.284	.333	.404
Denver	AAA Mil	28	95	22	3	0	1	28	12	10	4	0	16	3	5	0	1	1	.50	3	.232	.284	.295
1991 Denver	AAA Mil	100	294	70	17	2	1	94	34	33	28	0	44	5	8	1	7	3	.70	5	.238	.314	.320
1992 Denver	AAA Mil	67	225	70	11	4	3	98	27	31	19	0	39	3	5	2	6	3	.67	5	.311	.369	.436
1993 New Orleans	AAA Mil	24	76	23	3	2	1	33	9	13	8	0	14	0	0	0	1	0	1.00	1	.303	.369	.434
1994 Norfolk	AAA NYN	86	264	66	5	0	5	86	28	31	31	1	51	5	1	1	2	3	.40	6	.250	.339	.326
1995 Iowa	AAA ChN	34	98	17	3	0	2	26	6	7	6	0	24	0	3	2	0	0	.00	4	.173	.217	.265
1996 Indianapols	AAA Cin	48	143	40	3	0	2	49	20	19	26	1	35	1	1	0	3	0	1.00	3	.280	.394	.343
1997 Indianapols	AAA Cin	16	38	6	0	0	1	9	6	2	5	0	6	0	0	1	0	0	.00	2	.158	.250	.237
Charlotte	AAA Fla	36	93	22	6	1	0	30	7	12	11	1	28	0	2	1	1	0	1.00	3	.237	.314	.323
1993 Milwaukee	AL	51	110	24	5	0	0	29	9	7	14	0	13	2	1	0	6	2	.75	3	.218	.317	.264
1995 Chicago	NL	19	53	13	3	0	1	19	7	6	6	0	12	1	0	1	0	0	.00	2	.245	.328	.358
13 Min. YEARS		786	2348	601	92	20	25	808	279	255	249	6	436	38	32	15	33	19	.63	60	.256	.335	.344
2 Maj. YEARS		70	163	37	8	0	1	48	16	13	20	0	25	3	1	1	6	2	.75	4	.227	.321	.294

Brandon Knight

Pitches: Right **Bats:** Left **Pos:** P **Ht:** 6'0" **Wt:** 170 **Born:** 10/1/75 **Age:** 22

Year Team	Lg Org	G	GS	CG	GF	IP	BFP	H	R	ER	HR	SH	SF	HB	TBB	IBB	SO	WP	Bk	W	L	Pct.	ShO	Sv	ERA
				HOW MUCH HE PITCHED				WHAT HE GAVE UP												THE RESULTS					
1995 Rangers	R Tex	3	2	0	0	12	54	12	7	7	0	0	1	0	6	0	11	2	0	2	1	.667	0	0	5.25
Chston-SC	A Tex	9	9	0	0	54.2	218	37	22	19	5	0	4	0	21	0	52	4	1	4	2	.667	0	0	3.13
1996 Hudson Vall	A- Tex	9	9	0	0	53	236	59	29	26	1	2	1	1	21	0	52	2	1	2	2	.500	0	0	4.42
Charlotte	A+ Tex	19	17	2	0	102	463	118	65	58	9	4	7	2	45	0	74	6	0	4	10	.286	0	0	5.12
1997 Charlotte	A+ Tex	14	12	3	1	92.2	380	82	33	23	9	3	2	1	22	0	91	0	2	7	4	.636	1	0	2.23
Tulsa	AA Tex	14	14	0	0	90	383	83	52	45	12	0	4	2	35	0	84	9	4	6	4	.600	1	0	4.50
3 Min. YEARS		68	63	7	1	404.1	1734	391	208	178	36	9	19	6	150	0	364	23	8	25	23	.521	2	0	3.96

Eric Knowles

Bats: Right **Throws:** Right **Pos:** 3B-SS **Ht:** 6'0" **Wt:** 190 **Born:** 10/21/73 **Age:** 24

Year Team	Lg Org	G	AB	H	2B	3B	HR	TB	R	RBI	TBB	IBB	SO	HBP	SH	SF	SB	CS	SB%	GDP	Avg	OBP	SLG
								BATTING									BASERUNNING				PERCENTAGES		
1991 Yankees	R NYA	49	186	36	1	0	0	37	26	10	20	0	54	2	0	0	11	1	.92	1	.194	.279	.199
1992 Oneonta	A- NYA	58	196	35	6	2	1	48	22	22	29	0	66	2	3	6	2	1	.67	4	.179	.283	.245
1993 Pr William	A+ NYA	105	353	68	16	0	4	96	33	37	30	0	96	4	2	2	2	5	.29	7	.193	.262	.272

BATTING / BASERUNNING / PERCENTAGES

Year Team	Lg Org	G	AB	H	2B	3B	HR	TB	R	RBI	TBB	IBB	SO	HBP	SH	SF	SB	CS	SB%	GDP	Avg	OBP	SLG
1994 Greensboro	A NYA	125	439	114	31	3	2	157	68	42	62	1	104	3	4	7	11	5	.69	10	.260	.350	.358
1995 Tampa	A+ NYA	115	391	106	24	4	1	141	45	33	45	0	58	3	3	2	7	3	.70	8	.271	.349	.361
1996 Norwich	AA NYA	126	396	97	23	1	7	143	56	42	32	1	92	4	8	5	9	6	.60	8	.245	.304	.361
1997 St. Lucie	A+ NYN	24	84	14	5	0	1	22	8	10	7	0	16	0	0	1	3	1	.75	3	.167	.228	.262
Binghamton	AA NYN	51	157	37	10	0	3	56	16	22	16	1	34	1	0	2	7	0	1.00	5	.236	.307	.357
7 Min. YEARS		653	2202	507	116	10	19	700	274	218	241	3	520	19	20	25	52	22	.70	43	.230	.308	.318

Kurt Knudsen

Pitches: Right Bats: Right Pos: P   Ht: 6' 3" Wt: 210 Born: 2/20/67 Age: 31

HOW MUCH HE PITCHED / WHAT HE GAVE UP / THE RESULTS

Year Team	Lg Org	G	GS	CG	GF	IP	BFP	H	R	ER	HR	SH	SF	HB	TBB	IBB	SO	WP	Bk	W	L	Pct.	ShO	Sv	ERA
1988 Bristol	R+ Det	2	0	0	2	2.1	14	4	3	0	0	0	0	0	1	0	0	0	0	0	0	.000	0	0	0.00
Fayetteville	A Det	12	0	0	5	20	77	8	4	3	1	2	1	1	9	1	22	1	1	3	1	.750	0	1	1.35
Lakeland	A+ Det	7	0	0	4	9.1	39	7	2	1	0	0	0	0	7	0	6	2	0	0	0	.000	0	0	0.96
1989 Lakeland	A+ Det	45	0	0	26	54.1	225	43	16	13	1	5	2	1	22	7	68	2	3	3	2	.600	0	10	2.15
1990 Lakeland	A+ Det	14	8	0	5	67	253	42	18	17	2	2	1	0	22	0	70	5	2	5	0	1.000	0	3	2.28
London	AA Det	15	0	0	8	26	102	15	6	6	1	0	1	2	11	0	26	2	1	2	1	.667	0	1	2.08
1991 London	AA Det	34	0	0	18	51.2	226	42	29	20	1	4	5	1	30	2	56	4	1	2	3	.400	0	6	3.48
Toledo	AAA Det	12	0	0	3	18.1	79	13	11	3	1	0	0	0	10	1	28	2	0	1	2	.333	0	1	1.47
1992 Toledo	AAA Det	12	0	0	8	21.2	82	11	5	5	1	1	1	1	6	0	19	1	0	3	1	.750	0	1	2.08
1993 Toledo	AAA Det	23	0	0	15	33.1	136	24	15	14	3	1	0	1	11	1	39	2	0	2	2	.500	0	6	3.78
1994 Toledo	AAA Det	37	7	0	22	67.1	299	56	38	30	8	1	4	3	42	1	64	0	1	2	5	.286	0	4	4.01
1995 Phoenix	AAA SF	11	1	0	4	19.2	86	18	13	11	2	0	2	0	11	0	20	0	0	0	1	.000	0	1	5.03
1996 Sonoma Cty	IND —	19	18	0	1	104	461	112	59	48	6	3	2	4	37	0	98	2	0	5	4	.556	0	0	4.15
1997 Lk Elsinore	A+ Ana	7	0	0	7	10.1	46	13	9	8	1	0	0	0	4	0	10	1	0	1	2	.333	0	3	6.97
Midland	AA Ana	35	4	0	8	57	284	88	63	55	9	3	5	7	25	1	35	15	0	0	4	.000	0	0	8.68
1992 Detroit	AL	48	1	0	14	70.2	313	70	39	36	9	4	2	1	41	9	51	5	0	2	3	.400	0	5	4.58
1993 Detroit	AL	30	0	0	7	37.2	171	41	22	20	9	2	3	4	16	2	29	2	0	3	2	.600	0	2	4.78
1994 Detroit	AL	4	0	0	0	5.1	34	7	8	8	2	0	0	0	11	1	1	0	0	1	0	1.000	0	0	13.50
10 Min. YEARS		285	38	0	136	562.1	2409	496	291	234	37	22	24	21	248	14	561	39	9	29	28	.509	0	36	3.75
3 Maj. YEARS		82	1	0	21	113.2	518	118	69	64	20	6	5	5	68	12	81	7	0	6	5	.545	0	7	5.07

Brian Koelling

Bats: Right Throws: Right Pos: 2B   Ht: 6' 1" Wt: 185 Born: 6/11/69 Age: 29

BATTING / BASERUNNING / PERCENTAGES

Year Team	Lg Org	G	AB	H	2B	3B	HR	TB	R	RBI	TBB	IBB	SO	HBP	SH	SF	SB	CS	SB%	GDP	Avg	OBP	SLG
1991 Billings	R+ Cin	22	85	30	7	1	2	45	17	12	14	0	23	1	0	0	6	2	.75	0	.353	.450	.529
Cedar Rapds	A Cin	35	147	38	6	0	1	47	27	12	14	0	39	3	0	1	22	6	.79	0	.259	.333	.320
1992 Cedar Rapds	A Cin	129	460	121	18	7	5	168	81	43	49	0	137	1	9	2	47	16	.75	3	.263	.334	.365
1993 Chattanooga	AA Cin	110	430	119	17	6	4	160	64	47	32	1	105	2	4	3	34	13	.72	2	.277	.328	.372
Indianapols	AAA Cin	2	9	2	0	0	0	2	1	0	0	0	1	1	0	0	0	1	.00	0	.222	.300	.222
1994 Indianapols	AAA Cin	19	53	8	0	0	0	8	6	0	2	0	14	1	1	0	4	2	.67	0	.151	.196	.151
Chattanooga	AA Cin	92	343	96	11	5	3	126	54	31	24	1	64	4	7	1	27	18	.60	6	.280	.333	.367
1995 Chattanooga	AA Cin	107	432	128	21	7	3	172	71	44	40	1	63	3	8	3	30	12	.71	9	.296	.358	.398
Scranton-WB	AAA Phi	16	53	14	1	0	0	15	5	3	1	0	14	0	0	1	3	1	.75	1	.264	.273	.283
1997 Chattanooga	AA Cin	73	279	78	9	3	3	102	50	22	28	2	49	2	2	1	18	9	.67	5	.280	.348	.365
1993 Cincinnati	NL	7	15	1	0	0	0	1	2	0	0	0	2	1	0	0	0	0	.00	0	.067	.125	.067
6 Min. YEARS		605	2291	634	90	29	21	845	376	214	204	5	509	18	31	12	191	80	.70	26	.277	.339	.369

Ramsey Koeyers

Bats: Right Throws: Right Pos: C   Ht: 6'1" Wt: 187 Born: 8/7/74 Age: 23

BATTING / BASERUNNING / PERCENTAGES

Year Team	Lg Org	G	AB	H	2B	3B	HR	TB	R	RBI	TBB	IBB	SO	HBP	SH	SF	SB	CS	SB%	GDP	Avg	OBP	SLG
1992 Expos	R Mon	42	125	21	2	0	0	23	7	16	8	1	28	0	0	6	0	1	1.00	0	.168	.209	.184
1993 Wst Plm Bch	A+ Mon	4	12	2	0	0	0	2	0	3	0	0	3	0	1	0	0	0	.00	0	.167	.167	.167
Jamestown	A- Mon	65	233	52	9	2	4	77	25	29	10	0	69	2	0	2	1	1	.50	5	.223	.259	.330
1994 Wst Plm Bch	A+ Mon	79	241	62	11	1	3	84	27	31	21	0	61	1	3	0	3	3	.50	7	.257	.319	.349
1995 Wst Plm Bch	A+ Mon	77	244	46	6	1	0	54	19	18	9	0	64	0	5	3	2	1	.67	10	.189	.215	.221
1996 Harrisburg	AA Mon	25	77	16	3	0	1	22	6	9	2	0	27	1	3	0	0	0	.00	1	.208	.235	.286
Expos	R Mon	7	19	3	1	0	0	4	2	0	3	0	6	0	0	0	0	0	.00	0	.158	.273	.211
Wst Plm Bch	A+ Mon	10	33	4	0	0	0	6	2	2	0	0	8	0	0	0	0	0	.00	0	.121	.121	.182
1997 Portland	AA Fla	83	286	74	14	1	12	126	37	50	15	2	67	2	1	1	0	3	.00	5	.259	.299	.441
6 Min. YEARS		392	1270	280	48	5	20	398	125	158	68	3	333	6	13	13	7	9	.44	35	.220	.261	.313

Ryan Kohlmeier

Pitches: Right Bats: Right Pos: P   Ht: 6'2" Wt: 195 Born: 6/25/77 Age: 21

HOW MUCH HE PITCHED / WHAT HE GAVE UP / THE RESULTS

Year Team	Lg Org	G	GS	CG	GF	IP	BFP	H	R	ER	HR	SH	SF	HB	TBB	IBB	SO	WP	Bk	W	L	Pct.	ShO	Sv	ERA
1997 Bowie	AA Bal	2	0	0	1	2.2	9	0	0	0	0	0	0	0	2	0	5	0	1	0	0	.000	0	1	0.00
Delmarva	A Bal	50	0	0	41	74.2	276	48	22	22	8	2	2	1	17	1	99	2	1	2	2	.500	0	24	2.65
1 Min. YEARS		52	0	0	42	77.1	285	48	22	22	8	2	2	1	19	1	104	2	2	2	2	.500	0	25	2.56

Keiichi Kojima

Pitches: Left Bats: Left Pos: P Ht: 6'0" Wt: 185 Born: 7/1/68 Age: 29

Year Team	Lg Org	G	GS	CG	GF	IP	BFP	H	R	ER	HR	SH	SF	HB	TBB	IBB	SO	WP	Bk	W	L	Pct.	ShO	Sv	ERA
1997 Tulsa	AA Tex	13	10	0	1	53	258	83	55	52	6	3	1	0	18	0	40	1	1	1	8	.111	0	0	8.83
Charlotte	A+ Tex	11	0	0	11	26	104	24	5	5	1	1	1	0	5	0	25	0	0	0	1	.000	0	4	1.73
1 Min. YEARS		24	10	0	12	79	362	107	60	57	7	4	2	0	23	0	65	1	1	1	9	.100	0	4	6.49

Danny Kolb

Pitches: Right Bats: Right Pos: P Ht: 6'4" Wt: 190 Born: 3/29/75 Age: 23

Year Team	Lg Org	G	GS	CG	GF	IP	BFP	H	R	ER	HR	SH	SF	HB	TBB	IBB	SO	WP	Bk	W	L	Pct.	ShO	Sv	ERA
1995 Rangers	R Tex	12	11	0	0	53	219	38	22	13	0	0	2	3	28	0	46	8	2	1	7	.125	0	0	2.21
1996 Chston-SC	A Tex	20	20	4	0	126	514	80	50	36	5	6	0	6	60	2	127	22	4	8	6	.571	2	0	2.57
Charlotte	A+ Tex	6	6	0	0	38	162	38	18	18	1	1	0	1	14	0	28	2	0	2	2	.500	0	0	4.26
Tulsa	AA Tex	2	2	0	0	11.2	45	5	1	1	0	0	0	1	8	0	7	0	0	1	0	1.000	0	0	0.77
1997 Tulsa	AA Tex	2	2	0	0	11.1	50	7	7	6	1	0	0	0	11	0	6	4	0	0	2	.000	0	0	4.76
Charlotte	A+ Tex	24	23	3	0	133	600	146	91	72	10	8	5	8	62	1	83	12	0	4	10	.286	0	0	4.87
3 Min. YEARS		66	64	7	0	373	1590	314	189	146	17	15	7	19	183	3	297	48	6	16	27	.372	2	0	3.52

Brad Komminsk

Bats: Right Throws: Right Pos: DH Ht: 6'2" Wt: 205 Born: 4/4/61 Age: 37

Year Team	Lg Org	G	AB	H	2B	3B	HR	TB	R	RBI	TBB	IBB	SO	HBP	SH	SF	SB	CS	SB%	GDP	Avg	OBP	SLG
1979 Kingsport	R+ Atl	59	185	41	9	1	7	73	37	34	48	—	74	3	1	1	20	2	.91	—	.222	.388	.395
1980 Anderson	A Atl	121	425	111	17	5	20	198	86	67	74	—	102	7	3	5	27	9	.75	—	.261	.376	.466
1981 Durham	A+ Atl	132	459	148	27	2	33	278	108	104	110	8	101	8	0	4	35	12	.74	—	.322	.458	.606
1982 Savannah	AA Atl	133	454	124	18	7	26	234	88	78	72	3	114	4	1	1	14	3	.82	—	.273	.377	.515
Richmond	AAA Atl	5	17	6	1	0	2	13	4	5	2	0	5	0	0	0	0	1	.00	—	.353	.421	.765
1983 Richmond	AAA Atl	117	413	138	24	6	24	246	94	103	78	3	70	0	2	8	26	5	.84	—	.334	.433	.596
1984 Richmond	AAA Atl	42	144	37	11	3	5	69	23	28	31	1	20	0	0	2	8	2	.80	3	.257	.384	.479
1986 Richmond	AAA Atl	133	465	109	22	4	13	178	67	65	69	1	124	2	1	5	29	3	.91	12	.234	.333	.383
1987 Denver	AAA Mil	135	494	147	31	4	32	282	110	95	66	2	127	4	0	5	18	9	.67	6	.298	.381	.571
1988 Denver	AAA Mil	105	348	83	18	3	16	155	55	57	49	1	96	5	1	3	7	1	.88	8	.239	.338	.445
1989 Colo Sprngs	AAA Cle	54	190	55	17	0	9	99	30	34	18	0	40	2	0	4	7	1	.88	2	.289	.350	.521
1990 Rochester	AAA Bal	28	79	23	2	0	1	28	7	8	10	2	16	1	1	2	0	3	.00	1	.291	.370	.354
1991 Tacoma	AAA Oak	74	270	79	15	4	5	117	38	43	29	0	49	3	1	1	11	1	.92	8	.293	.366	.433
1992 Vancouver	AAA ChA	120	415	114	24	7	10	182	72	68	65	1	79	1	2	3	9	8	.53	13	.275	.372	.439
1993 Nashville	AAA ChA	118	383	102	18	2	11	157	55	49	52	3	92	1	2	3	7	8	.47	11	.266	.353	.410
1996 Winnipeg	IND —	77	277	77	16	1	16	143	47	66	45	0	67	1	0	9	1	1	.50	9	.278	.370	.516
1997 Toledo	AAA Det	1	3	2	1	0	0	3	0	0	0	0	0	0	0	0	0	0	.00	0	.667	.667	1.000
1983 Atlanta	NL	19	36	8	2	0	0	10	2	4	5	0	7	0	0	0	0	0	.00	1	.222	.317	.278
1984 Atlanta	NL	90	301	61	10	0	8	95	37	36	29	0	77	1	4	1	18	8	.69	5	.203	.276	.316
1985 Atlanta	NL	106	300	68	12	3	4	98	52	21	38	1	71	1	2	2	10	8	.56	4	.227	.314	.327
1986 Atlanta	NL	5	5	2	0	0	0	2	1	1	0	0	1	0	0	0	0	1	.00	0	.400	.400	.400
1987 Milwaukee	AL	7	15	1	0	0	0	1	0	0	1	0	7	0	0	0	1	0	1.00	0	.067	.125	.067
1989 Cleveland	AL	71	198	47	8	2	8	83	27	33	24	0	55	1	1	3	8	2	.80	4	.237	.319	.419
1990 San Francisco	NL	8	5	1	0	0	0	1	0	1	0	0	2	0	0	0	0	0	.00	0	.200	.333	.200
Baltimore	AL	46	101	24	4	0	3	37	18	8	14	1	29	2	2	0	1	1	.50	2	.238	.342	.366
1991 Oakland	AL	24	25	3	1	0	0	4	1	2	2	0	9	0	0	0	1	0	1.00	0	.120	.185	.160
16 Min. YEARS		1454	5021	1396	271	49	230	2455	921	904	818	25	1176	42	15	56	219	69	.76	73	.278	.380	.489
8 Maj. YEARS		376	986	215	37	5	23	331	140	105	114	2	258	6	7	6	39	20	.66	16	.218	.301	.336

Dennis Konuszewski

Pitches: Right Bats: Right Pos: P Ht: 6'3" Wt: 210 Born: 2/4/71 Age: 27

Year Team	Lg Org	G	GS	CG	GF	IP	BFP	H	R	ER	HR	SH	SF	HB	TBB	IBB	SO	WP	Bk	W	L	Pct.	ShO	Sv	ERA
1992 Welland	A- Pit	2	2	0	0	7	30	6	1	1	0	0	0	0	4	0	4	1	1	0	0	.000	0	0	1.29
Augusta	A Pit	17	0	0	4	62.1	258	50	19	16	1	4	0	5	19	0	45	2	1	3	3	.500	0	1	2.31
1993 Salem	A+ Pit	39	13	0	7	103	463	121	66	53	14	3	7	5	43	3	81	6	4	4	10	.286	0	1	4.63
1994 Carolina	AA Pit	51	0	0	19	77.2	366	81	39	31	5	2	2	2	31	5	53	6	1	6	5	.545	0	1	3.59
1995 Carolina	AA Pit	48	0	0	18	61.2	278	63	33	25	3	3	1	1	26	5	48	5	1	7	7	.500	0	2	3.65
1996 Carolina	AA Pit	32	10	0	8	80	362	103	61	56	12	3	4	6	36	0	59	3	0	2	8	.200	0	0	6.30
Calgary	AAA Pit	3	0	0	2	3.1	28	13	11	9	0	0	0	0	5	0	0	0	0	0	0	.000	0	0	24.30
1997 Carolina	AA Pit	15	0	0	5	22.1	103	20	12	11	3	0	1	1	15	2	21	2	0	1	0	1.000	0	0	4.43
1995 Pittsburgh	NL	1	0	0	0	0.1	5	3	2	2	0	1	0	0	1	0	0	0	0	0	0	.000	0	0	54.00
6 Min. YEARS		207	33	0	63	417.1	1868	457	242	202	38	16	15	20	179	15	311	25	14	23	33	.411	0	5	4.36

Clint Koppe

Pitches: Right Bats: Right Pos: P Ht: 6'4" Wt: 220 Born: 8/14/73 Age: 24

Year Team	Lg Org	G	GS	CG	GF	IP	BFP	H	R	ER	HR	SH	SF	HB	TBB	IBB	SO	WP	Bk	W	L	Pct.	ShO	Sv	ERA
1994 Billings	R+ Cin	14	14	1	0	89.1	360	85	48	42	4	3	2	2	23	3	61	4	2	9	2	.818	0	0	4.23
1995 Chston-WV	A Cin	30	22	2	1	157.2	653	144	66	59	10	4	5	4	47	5	119	8	1	7	13	.350	0	0	3.37
1996 Winston-Sal	A+ Cin	16	15	3	0	95.1	388	87	41	35	10	3	3	4	25	0	46	7	1	8	2	.800	1	0	3.30
Chattanooga	AA Cin	10	9	1	1	56.2	232	54	27	22	3	1	3	0	18	0	30	4	1	4	2	.667	0	1	3.49
1997 Chattanooga	AA Cin	13	13	0	0	68.1	331	82	58	56	12	1	3	2	44	2	33	4	0	2	5	.286	0	0	7.38
Chston-WV	A Cin	23	1	0	16	27.1	129	38	23	23	4	0	1	0	10	0	23	2	0	0	1	.000	0	4	7.57

Year Team	Lg Org	G	GS	CG	GF	IP	BFP	H	R	ER	HR	SH	SF	HB	TBB	IBB	SO	WP	Bk	W	L	Pct	ShO	Sv	ERA
4 Min. YEARS		106	74	7	18	494.2	2093	490	263	237	43	12	18	14	167	10	312	29	5	30	25	.545	1	5	4.31

Corey Koskie

Bats: Left **Throws:** Right **Pos:** 3B   **Ht:** 6'3" **Wt:** 215 **Born:** 6/28/73 **Age:** 25

Year Team	Lg Org	G	AB	H	2B	3B	HR	TB	R	RBI	TBB	IBB	SO	HBP	SH	SF	SB	CS	SB%	GDP	Avg	OBP	SLG
1994 Elizabethtn	R+ Min	34	107	25	2	1	3	38	13	10	18	0	27	2	0	0	0	0	.00	3	.234	.354	.355
1995 Ft. Wayne	A Min	123	462	143	37	5	16	238	64	78	38	3	79	9	1	5	2	4	.33	10	.310	.370	.515
1996 Ft. Myers	A+ Min	95	338	88	19	4	9	142	43	55	40	0	76	1	1	3	1	1	.50	4	.260	.338	.420
1997 New Britain	AA Min	131	437	125	26	6	23	232	88	79	90	10	106	7	0	2	9	5	.64	13	.286	.414	.531
4 Min. YEARS		383	1344	381	84	16	51	650	208	222	186	13	288	19	2	10	12	10	.55	30	.283	.376	.484

Kevin Koslofski

Bats: Left **Throws:** Right **Pos:** OF   **Ht:** 5'8" **Wt:** 175 **Born:** 9/24/66 **Age:** 31

Year Team	Lg Org	G	AB	H	2B	3B	HR	TB	R	RBI	TBB	IBB	SO	HBP	SH	SF	SB	CS	SB%	GDP	Avg	OBP	SLG
1984 Eugene	A- KC	53	155	29	2	2	1	38	23	10	25	0	37	0	1	1	10	2	.83	3	.187	.298	.245
1985 Royals	R KC	33	108	27	4	2	0	35	17	11	12	0	19	3	2	0	7	2	.78	1	.250	.341	.324
1986 Ft. Myers	A+ KC	103	331	84	13	5	0	107	44	29	47	2	59	2	7	4	12	6	.67	6	.254	.346	.323
1987 Ft. Myers	A+ KC	109	330	80	12	3	0	98	46	25	46	3	64	7	3	2	25	9	.74	4	.242	.345	.297
1988 Baseball Cy	A+ KC	108	368	97	7	8	3	129	52	30	44	5	71	4	4	2	32	11	.74	4	.264	.347	.351
1989 Baseball Cy	A+ KC	116	343	89	10	3	4	117	65	33	51	2	57	5	5	3	41	14	.75	9	.259	.361	.341
1990 Memphis	AA KC	118	367	78	11	5	3	108	52	32	54	1	89	2	7	3	12	7	.63	4	.213	.315	.294
1991 Memphis	AA KC	81	287	93	15	3	7	135	41	39	33	3	56	4	4	4	10	13	.43	2	.324	.396	.470
Omaha	AAA KC	25	94	28	3	2	2	41	13	19	15	0	19	1	2	1	4	3	.57	1	.298	.396	.436
1992 Omaha	AAA KC	78	280	87	12	5	4	121	29	32	21	3	47	2	7	1	8	3	.73	2	.311	.362	.432
1993 Omaha	AAA KC	111	395	109	22	5	7	162	58	45	43	3	73	2	3	2	15	7	.68	9	.276	.348	.410
1994 Omaha	AAA KC	93	307	66	8	3	6	98	43	39	37	4	90	1	4	3	10	4	.71	1	.215	.299	.319
1995 New Orleans	AAA Mil	105	321	68	18	4	7	115	41	35	34	2	100	2	3	3	4	2	.67	1	.212	.289	.358
1996 New Orleans	AAA Mil	75	238	55	8	3	4	81	39	25	31	1	64	2	2	2	5	2	.71	5	.231	.322	.340
1997 Louisville	AAA StL	106	285	60	14	3	9	107	37	27	43	2	78	2	5	2	1	9	.10	6	.211	.316	.375
1992 Kansas City	AL	55	133	33	0	2	3	46	20	13	12	0	23	1	3	1	2	1	.67	2	.248	.313	.346
1993 Kansas City	AL	15	26	7	0	0	1	10	4	2	4	0	5	1	1	0	0	1	.00	1	.269	.387	.385
1994 Kansas City	AL	2	4	1	0	0	0	1	2	0	2	1	1	0	0	0	0	0	.00	0	.250	.500	.250
1996 Milwaukee	AL	25	42	9	3	2	0	16	5	6	4	1	12	1	0	0	0	0	.00	1	.214	.298	.381
14 Min. YEARS		1314	4209	1050	159	56	57	1492	600	431	536	31	923	39	59	33	196	94	.68	58	.249	.337	.354
4 Maj. YEARS		97	205	50	3	4	4	73	31	21	22	2	41	3	4	1	2	2	.50	4	.244	.325	.356

Tom Kramer

Pitches: Right **Bats:** Both **Pos:** P   **Ht:** 6'0" **Wt:** 220 **Born:** 1/9/68 **Age:** 30

Year Team	Lg Org	G	GS	CG	GF	IP	BFP	H	R	ER	HR	SH	SF	HB	TBB	IBB	SO	WP	Bk	W	L	Pct	ShO	Sv	ERA
1987 Burlington	R+ Cle	12	11	2	1	71.2	292	57	31	24	2	0	1	1	26	0	71	0	0	7	3	.700	1	1	3.01
1988 Waterloo	A Cle	27	27	10	0	198.2	814	173	70	56	9	10	3	3	60	3	152	5	3	14	7	.667	2	0	2.54
1989 Kinston	A+ Cle	18	17	5	1	131.2	527	97	44	38	7	5	3	4	42	3	89	4	1	9	5	.643	1	0	2.60
Canton-Akrn	AA Cle	10	8	1	0	43.1	202	58	34	30	6	3	4	0	20	0	26	0	0	1	6	.143	0	0	6.23
1990 Kinston	A+ Cle	16	16	2	0	98	402	82	34	31	5	1	2	2	29	0	96	2	1	7	4	.636	1	0	2.85
Canton-Akrn	AA Cle	12	10	2	0	72	287	67	25	24	3	2	1	0	14	1	46	1	0	6	3	.667	0	0	3.00
1991 Canton-Akrn	AA Cle	35	5	0	13	79.1	320	61	23	21	5	6	1	1	34	3	61	3	0	7	3	.700	0	6	2.38
Colo Sprngs	AAA Cle	10	1	0	6	11.1	43	5	1	1	1	0	0	0	5	0	18	1	0	1	0	1.000	0	4	0.79
1992 Colo Sprngs	AAA Cle	38	3	0	11	75.2	344	88	43	41	2	4	3	1	43	2	72	0	0	8	3	.727	0	3	4.88
1994 Charlotte	AAA Cle	13	0	0	6	19	85	15	11	10	2	2	1	0	11	1	20	2	0	1	3	.250	0	0	4.74
Indianapolis	AAA Cin	23	13	0	3	102.2	431	109	55	51	12	5	3	2	32	2	54	6	0	5	4	.556	0	0	4.47
1995 Toledo	AAA Det	6	5	0	0	27.1	116	23	15	14	6	0	2	0	16	0	15	0	0	3	1	.750	0	0	4.61
Chattanooga	AA Cin	21	18	2	1	127	513	117	54	47	8	5	5	2	28	4	126	4	0	12	1	.923	0	0	3.33
1996 Colo Sprngs	AAA Col	41	10	0	17	112.1	512	129	74	67	16	5	5	0	47	3	79	4	2	8	4	.667	0	4	5.37
1997 Colo Sprngs	AAA Col	51	0	0	34	62	279	57	42	36	10	2	5	2	40	1	56	0	1	3	2	.600	0	11	5.23
1991 Cleveland	AL	4	0	0	1	4.2	30	10	9	9	1	0	3	0	6	0	4	0	0	0	0	.000	0	0	17.36
1993 Cleveland	AL	39	16	1	6	121	535	126	60	54	19	3	2	2	59	7	71	1	0	7	3	.700	0	0	4.02
10 Min. YEARS		333	144	24	93	1232	5167	1138	556	491	94	50	39	18	447	23	981	39	8	92	49	.652	5	29	3.59
2 Maj. YEARS		43	16	1	7	125.2	565	136	69	63	20	3	5	2	65	7	75	1	0	7	3	.700	0	0	4.51

Scott Krause

Bats: Right **Throws:** Right **Pos:** OF   **Ht:** 6'1" **Wt:** 195 **Born:** 8/16/73 **Age:** 24

Year Team	Lg Org	G	AB	H	2B	3B	HR	TB	R	RBI	TBB	IBB	SO	HBP	SH	SF	SB	CS	SB%	GDP	Avg	OBP	SLG
1994 Helena	R+ Mil	63	252	90	18	3	4	126	51	52	18	2	49	9	1	2	13	6	.68	2	.357	.416	.500
1995 Beloit	A Mil	134	481	119	30	4	13	196	83	76	50	5	126	12	3	7	24	10	.71	7	.247	.329	.407
1996 El Paso	AA Mil	24	85	27	5	2	3	45	16	11	2	0	19	1	1	0	2	0	1.00	1	.318	.341	.529
Stockton	A+ Mil	108	427	128	22	4	19	215	82	83	32	0	101	16	1	3	25	6	.81	9	.300	.368	.504
1997 El Paso	AA Mil	125	474	171	33	11	16	274	97	88	20	3	108	7	4	7	13	4	.76	7	.361	.390	.578
4 Min. YEARS		454	1719	535	108	24	55	856	329	310	122	10	403	45	10	19	77	26	.75	26	.311	.369	.498

Jeff Kubenka

Pitches: Left Bats: Right Pos: P Ht: 6'0" Wt: 195 Born: 8/24/74 Age: 23

Year Team	Lg Org	G	GS	CG	GF	IP	BFP	H	R	ER	HR	SH	SF	HB	TBB	IBB	SO	WP	Bk	W	L	Pct.	ShO	Sv	ERA
1996 Yakima	A- LA	28	0	0	24	32.1	127	20	11	9	2	0	0	0	10	1	61	4	1	5	1	.833	0	14	2.51
1997 San Berndno	A+ LA	34	0	0	32	39	152	24	4	4	1	4	2	1	11	1	62	3	0	5	1	.833	0	19	0.92
Albuquerque	AAA LA	8	0	0	6	7.1	37	11	9	7	2	0	0	0	2	0	10	3	0	0	2	.000	0	2	8.59
San Antonio	AA LA	19	0	0	17	25.2	93	10	2	2	1	0	1	0	6	0	38	1	0	3	0	1.000	0	4	0.70
2 Min. YEARS		89	0	0	79	104.1	409	65	26	22	6	4	3	1	29	2	171	11	1	13	4	.765	0	39	1.90

Robles Kuilan

Bats: Right Throws: Right Pos: C Ht: 5'11" Wt: 190 Born: 4/3/76 Age: 22

Year Team	Lg Org	G	AB	H	2B	3B	HR	TB	R	RBI	TBB	IBB	SO	HBP	SH	SF	SB	CS	SB%	GDP	Avg	OBP	SLG
1994 Marlins	R Fla	40	141	22	7	0	0	29	11	17	6	0	15	0	2	2	0	1	.00	4	.156	.188	.206
1995 Marlins	R Fla	48	153	38	8	0	0	46	14	27	17	1	20	1	2	2	4	1	.80	4	.248	.324	.301
Kane County	A Fla	2	7	0	0	0	0	0	0	0	0	0	1	0	0	0	0	0	.00	0	.000	.000	.000
1996 Kane County	A Fla	94	308	62	12	1	6	94	28	30	22	0	52	3	3	2	1	3	.25	7	.201	.260	.305
1997 Brevard Cty	A+ Fla	77	265	60	16	0	0	76	18	25	7	0	41	4	3	3	0	1	.00	12	.226	.254	.287
Charlotte	AAA Fla	14	39	4	0	0	0	4	3	3	2	0	8	0	0	0	0	0	.00	2	.103	.146	.103
4 Min. YEARS		275	913	186	43	1	6	249	74	102	54	1	137	8	10	9	5	6	.45	29	.204	.252	.273

Mike Kusiewicz

Pitches: Left Bats: Right Pos: P Ht: 6'2" Wt: 185 Born: 11/1/76 Age: 21

Year Team	Lg Org	G	GS	CG	GF	IP	BFP	H	R	ER	HR	SH	SF	HB	TBB	IBB	SO	WP	Bk	W	L	Pct.	ShO	Sv	ERA
1995 Salem	A+ Col	1	1	0	0	6	26	7	1	1	0	0	0	0	0	0	7	0	1	0	0	.000	0	0	1.50
Asheville	A Col	21	21	0	0	122.1	484	92	40	28	6	2	0	6	34	0	103	9	1	8	4	.667	0	0	2.06
1996 Salem	A+ Col	5	3	0	2	23	100	19	15	13	2	1	1	1	12	0	18	2	0	1	0	1.000	0	1	5.09
New Haven	AA Col	14	14	0	0	76.1	326	83	38	28	4	2	3	2	27	2	64	0	1	2	4	.333	0	0	3.30
1997 New Haven	AA Col	10	4	0	0	28.1	138	41	28	20	2	2	2	6	10	1	11	1	0	2	4	.333	0	0	6.35
Salem	A+ Col	19	18	1	0	117.2	480	99	44	33	5	4	5	9	32	0	107	7	1	8	6	.571	1	0	2.52
3 Min. YEARS		70	61	1	2	373.2	1554	341	166	123	19	11	11	26	115	3	310	19	4	20	19	.513	1	1	2.96

Steve Lackey

Bats: Right Throws: Right Pos: SS Ht: 5'11" Wt: 165 Born: 9/25/74 Age: 23

Year Team	Lg Org	G	AB	H	2B	3B	HR	TB	R	RBI	TBB	IBB	SO	HBP	SH	SF	SB	CS	SB%	GDP	Avg	OBP	SLG
1992 Mets	R NYN	12	47	9	1	0	0	10	6	3	3	0	7	1	1	0	0	1	.00	0	.191	.255	.213
Kingsport	R+ NYN	38	148	26	2	0	0	28	16	10	17	0	22	3	0	0	3	4	.43	5	.176	.274	.189
1993 Kingsport	R+ NYN	53	172	25	4	0	0	29	14	9	14	0	30	0	1	1	3	4	.43	4	.145	.209	.169
1994 Pittsfield	A- NYN	3	4	1	0	0	0	1	1	0	2	0	0	0	2	0	0	0	.00	0	.250	.500	.250
Kingsport	R+ NYN	56	187	37	6	1	0	45	22	7	24	1	31	3	3	0	2	2	.50	2	.198	.299	.241
1995 Pittsfield	A- NYN	21	75	18	5	0	0	23	7	6	2	0	16	1	1	1	1	0	1.00	1	.240	.266	.307
Capital City	A NYN	67	178	34	8	0	1	45	21	21	11	1	42	2	5	3	9	2	.82	1	.191	.242	.253
1996 Fayettevlle	A Det	82	310	67	13	0	4	92	38	43	28	0	58	3	5	5	24	6	.80	4	.216	.283	.297
Visalia	A+ Det	46	184	49	11	1	0	74	27	29	16	0	44	1	2	2	7	1	.88	7	.266	.325	.402
1997 Jacksnville	AA Det	5	13	1	0	0	0	1	1	0	0	0	0	1	0		1	0	1.00	0	.077	.077	.077
Lakeland	A+ Det	71	247	55	14	0	0	69	24	22	10	0	58	1	6	2	5	4	.56	3	.223	.254	.279
6 Min. YEARS		454	1565	322	64	2	9	417	177	150	127	2	309	15	27	14	55	24	.70	30	.206	.270	.266

Cleveland Ladell

Bats: Right Throws: Right Pos: OF Ht: 5'11" Wt: 170 Born: 9/19/70 Age: 27

Year Team	Lg Org	G	AB	H	2B	3B	HR	TB	R	RBI	TBB	IBB	SO	HBP	SH	SF	SB	CS	SB%	GDP	Avg	OBP	SLG
1992 Princeton	R+ Cin	64	241	64	6	4	4	90	37	32	13	0	45	1	2	2	24	3	.89	1	.266	.304	.373
Chston-WV	A Cin	8	30	6	0	0	0	6	3	0	3	0	14	0	0	0	3	1	.75	0	.200	.273	.200
1993 Winston-Sal	A+ Cin	132	531	151	15	7	20	240	90	66	16	0	95	3	4	5	24	7	.77	13	.284	.306	.452
1994 Chattanooga	AA Cin	33	99	16	4	1	1	25	9	9	4	0	26	0	0	1	4	1	.80	2	.162	.192	.253
Winston-Sal	A+ Cin	75	283	71	11	3	12	124	46	40	26	0	63	2	2	3	17	7	.71	3	.251	.315	.438
1995 Chattanooga	AA Cin	135	517	151	28	7	5	208	76	43	39	1	88	2	4	2	28	15	.65	12	.292	.343	.402
1996 Indianapolis	AAA Cin	8	7	0	0	0	0	0	0	0	1	0	1	0	0	0	0	0	.00	1	.000	.125	.000
Chattanooga	AA Cin	121	405	102	15	7	4	143	59	41	31	5	88	5	4	1	31	14	.69	11	.252	.312	.353
1997 Chattanooga	AA Cin	14	32	11	1	0	0	12	3	4	0	0	3	2	0	1	1	1	.50	0	.344	.371	.375
6 Min. YEARS		590	2145	572	80	29	46	848	323	235	133	6	423	15	16	15	132	49	.73	43	.267	.312	.395

Joe Lagarde

Pitches: Right Bats: Right Pos: P Ht: 5'9" Wt: 180 Born: 1/17/75 Age: 23

Year Team	Lg Org	G	GS	CG	GF	IP	BFP	H	R	ER	HR	SH	SF	HB	TBB	IBB	SO	WP	Bk	W	L	Pct.	ShO	Sv	ERA
1993 Yakima	A- LA	15	12	0	2	70.2	303	69	28	26	4	2	1	0	28	0	45	7	1	5	4	.556	0	2	3.31
1994 Vero Beach	A+ LA	25	15	0	3	105.2	446	101	57	49	5	2	3	7	41	0	66	8	1	6	8	.429	0	0	4.17
1995 San Berndno	A+ LA	24	24	0	0	123.1	557	135	83	63	9	4	7	9	68	0	102	10	1	5	10	.333	0	1	4.60
Bakersfield	A+ LA	4	4	0	0	21.2	98	19	8	7	1	0	0	0	13	0	25	5	0	1	1	.500	0	0	2.91
1996 Vero Beach	A+ LA	14	4	0	5	44.1	194	41	17	12	0	2	1	4	22	1	46	1	0	4	3	.571	0	0	2.44
San Antonio	AA LA	24	0	0	21	31	129	28	7	6	0	1	0	0	10	0	22	4	0	3	1	.750	0	9	1.74
Albuquerque	AAA LA	10	0	0	4	12	59	14	7	7	2	1	0	2	9	2	11	4	0	0	0	.000	0	0	5.25

			HOW MUCH HE PITCHED						WHAT HE GAVE UP										THE RESULTS					
Year Team	Lg Org	G	GS	CG	GF	IP	BFP	H	R	ER	HR	SH	SF	HB	TBB	IBB	SO	WP	Bk	W	L	Pct.	ShO	Sv	ERA
1997 San Antonio	AA LA	53	0	0	36	69.1	301	68	34	29	6	4	3	1	31	0	65	5	0	4	4	.500	0	17	3.76
5 Min. YEARS		169	59	0	71	478	2087	475	241	199	27	16	15	23	222	3	382	44	4	28	31	.475	0	29	3.75

David Lamb

Bats: Both **Throws:** Right **Pos:** 2B-SS **Ht:** 6'3" **Wt:** 175 **Born:** 6/6/75 **Age:** 23

					BATTING											BASERUNNING				PERCENTAGES		
Year Team	Lg Org	G	AB	H	2B	3B	HR	TB	R	RBI	TBB	IBB	SO	HBP	SH	SF	SB	CS	SB%	GDP	Avg	OBP	SLG
1993 Orioles	R Bal	16	56	10	1	0	0	11	4	6	10	0	8	0	0	0	2	0	1.00	1	.179	.303	.196
1994 Albany	A Bal	92	308	74	9	2	0	87	37	29	32	0	40	2	6	0	4	1	.80	4	.240	.316	.282
1995 Bowie	AA Bal	1	4	1	0	0	0	1	0	1	0	0	1	0	0	0	0	0	.00	0	.250	.250	.250
Frederick	A+ Bal	124	436	97	14	2	2	121	39	34	38	5	81	10	8	5	6	7	.46	10	.222	.297	.278
1996 High Desert	A+ Bal	116	460	118	24	3	3	157	63	55	50	1	68	10	5	2	5	6	.45	19	.257	.341	.341
1997 Frederick	A+ Bal	70	249	65	21	1	2	94	30	39	25	2	32	6	3	3	3	1	.75	10	.261	.339	.378
Bowie	AA Bal	73	269	89	20	2	4	125	46	38	34	0	35	4	4	4	0	0	.00	3	.331	.408	.465
5 Min. YEARS		492	1782	454	89	10	11	596	219	202	189	8	265	32	26	14	20	15	.57	47	.255	.335	.334

Todd Landry

Bats: Right **Throws:** Left **Pos:** 1B **Ht:** 6'4" **Wt:** 215 **Born:** 8/21/72 **Age:** 25

					BATTING											BASERUNNING				PERCENTAGES		
Year Team	Lg Org	G	AB	H	2B	3B	HR	TB	R	RBI	TBB	IBB	SO	HBP	SH	SF	SB	CS	SB%	GDP	Avg	OBP	SLG
1993 Helena	R+ Mil	29	124	39	10	1	5	66	27	24	8	1	20	2	0	1	5	0	1.00	1	.315	.363	.532
Beloit	A Mil	38	149	45	6	0	4	63	26	24	4	0	36	0	0	2	4	4	.50	6	.302	.316	.423
1994 Stockton	A+ Mil	105	356	95	12	6	8	143	55	49	28	0	53	5	4	4	1	1	.80	10	.267	.326	.402
1995 El Paso	AA Mil	132	511	149	33	4	16	238	76	79	33	1	99	7	2	4	9	7	.56	20	.292	.341	.466
1996 New Orleans	AAA Mil	113	391	94	19	2	5	132	41	44	32	0	61	3	2	3	14	4	.78	15	.240	.301	.338
1997 El Paso	AA Mil	106	346	109	24	3	7	160	43	69	15	1	52	6	2	8	5	5	.50	16	.315	.347	.462
5 Min. YEARS		523	1877	531	104	16	45	802	268	289	120	3	321	23	10	22	41	21	.66	69	.283	.330	.427

Aaron Lane

Pitches: Left **Bats:** Left **Pos:** P **Ht:** 6'1" **Wt:** 180 **Born:** 6/2/71 **Age:** 27

			HOW MUCH HE PITCHED						WHAT HE GAVE UP										THE RESULTS					
Year Team	Lg Org	G	GS	CG	GF	IP	BFP	H	R	ER	HR	SH	SF	HB	TBB	IBB	SO	WP	Bk	W	L	Pct.	ShO	Sv	ERA
1992 Bluefield	R+ Bal	14	7	0	1	45	195	36	24	15	7	.2	0	0	24	0	39	3	1	5	1	.833	0	0	3.00
1993 Albany	A Bal	29	11	0	8	76	359	92	62	42	6	6	1	6	42	2	48	6	3	2	10	.167	0	0	4.97
1994 Albany	A Bal	35	0	0	30	54.2	232	42	20	14	0	1	3	2	24	0	56	4	3	3	2	.600	0	11	2.30
Frederick	A+ Bal	5	0	0	5	7.1	32	10	3	3	1	0	0	0	3	0	6	1	0	1	1	.500	0	2	3.68
Bowie	AA Bal	40	0	0	18	45.1	200	45	23	21	2	5	0	1	21	3	31	3	1	5	3	.625	0	2	4.17
1995 Rochester	AAA Bal	9	0	0	2	10	47	11	11	7	2	0	0	2	5	0	9	2	0	0	0	.000	0	0	6.30
1996 Rochester	AAA Bal	9	0	0	2	22.1	104	31	16	14	0	0	1	2	8	0	13	1	0	1	0	1.000	0	1	5.64
Bowie	AA Bal	13	8	1	2	51	224	44	37	26	7	6	3	0	24	4	35	1	0	3	5	.375	1	2	4.59
1997 Bowie	AA Bal	7	0	0	2	5.2	31	6	5	5	2	0	0	2	7	0	4	0	0	0	1	.000	0	0	7.94
6 Min. YEARS		161	26	1	70	317.1	1424	317	201	147	27	20	8	15	158	9	241	21	10	20	23	.465	1	18	4.17

Ryan Lane

Bats: Right **Throws:** Right **Pos:** 2B **Ht:** 6'1" **Wt:** 185 **Born:** 7/6/74 **Age:** 23

					BATTING											BASERUNNING				PERCENTAGES		
Year Team	Lg Org	G	AB	H	2B	3B	HR	TB	R	RBI	TBB	IBB	SO	HBP	SH	SF	SB	CS	SB%	GDP	Avg	OBP	SLG
1993 Twins	R Min	43	138	20	3	2	0	27	15	5	15	0	38	2	3	1	3	1	.75	2	.145	.237	.196
1994 Elizabethtn	R+ Min	59	202	48	13	0	3	70	32	18	26	0	47	2	3	2	4	3	.57	4	.238	.328	.347
1995 Ft. Wayne	A Min	115	432	115	37	1	6	172	69	56	65	0	92	7	6	4	17	9	.65	9	.266	.368	.398
1996 Ft. Myers	A+ Min	106	404	110	20	7	9	171	74	62	60	0	96	6	6	9	21	9	.70	12	.272	.367	.423
Hardware City	AA Min	33	117	26	5	1	2	39	13	12	8	0	29	0	2	1	3	4	.43	1	.222	.270	.333
1997 New Britain	AA Min	128	444	115	26	2	5	160	63	56	43	0	79	1	8	7	18	7	.72	5	.259	.321	.360
5 Min. YEARS		484	1737	434	104	13	25	639	266	209	217	0	381	18	28	24	66	33	.67	23	.250	.335	.368

Frank Lankford

Pitches: Right **Bats:** Right **Pos:** P **Ht:** 6'2" **Wt:** 190 **Born:** 3/26/71 **Age:** 27

			HOW MUCH HE PITCHED						WHAT HE GAVE UP										THE RESULTS					
Year Team	Lg Org	G	GS	CG	GF	IP	BFP	H	R	ER	HR	SH	SF	HB	TBB	IBB	SO	WP	Bk	W	L	Pct.	ShO	Sv	ERA
1993 Oneonta	A- NYA	16	7	0	1	64.2	276	60	41	24	3	3	2	1	22	0	61	5	0	4	5	.444	0	0	3.34
1994 Greensboro	A NYA	54	0	0	27	82.1	352	79	37	27	3	6	1	1	18	3	74	7	1	7	6	.538	0	7	2.95
1995 Tampa	A+ NYA	55	0	0	36	73	305	64	29	21	0	7	0	2	22	6	58	1	0	4	6	.400	0	15	2.59
1996 Norwich	AA NYA	61	0	0	25	88	392	82	42	26	4	9	1	2	40	6	61	3	0	7	8	.467	0	4	2.66
1997 Norwich	AA NYA	11	11	2	0	68.1	277	58	28	22	3	1	1	2	15	1	39	1	1	4	2	.667	1	0	2.90
Columbus	AAA NYA	15	13	1	2	93.2	374	84	33	28	2	3	1	2	22	1	40	1	0	7	4	.636	1	0	2.69
5 Min. YEARS		212	31	3	91	470	1976	427	210	148	15	29	6	10	139	17	333	18	2	33	31	.516	1	26	2.83

Mike Lanza

Bats: Right **Throws:** Right **Pos:** SS **Ht:** 6'1" **Wt:** 170 **Born:** 10/22/73 **Age:** 24

					BATTING											BASERUNNING				PERCENTAGES		
Year Team	Lg Org	G	AB	H	2B	3B	HR	TB	R	RBI	TBB	IBB	SO	HBP	SH	SF	SB	CS	SB%	GDP	Avg	OBP	SLG
1994 Bellingham	A- Sea	61	186	51	7	0	1	61	26	18	19	1	35	2	4	2	7	5	.58	3	.274	.344	.328
1995 Wisconsin	A Sea	101	333	68	13	1	2	89	28	29	22	0	67	2	6	2	10	5	.67	7	.204	.256	.267
1996 Lancaster	A+ Sea	109	380	100	12	6	3	133	53	42	18	0	73	3	4	4	3	4	.43	7	.263	.299	.350

(continued)

Year Team	Lg Org	G	AB	H	2B	3B	HR	TB	R	RBI	TBB	IBB	SO	HBP	SH	SF	SB	CS	SB%	GDP	Avg	OBP	SLG
1997 Frederick	A+ Bal	23	67	15	4	0	0	19	4	5	3	0	13	1	0	1	1	2	.33	2	.224	.264	.284
Memphis	AA Sea	21	56	14	2	0	0	16	8	6	4	0	13	1	0	0	2	0	1.00	0	.250	.311	.286
4 Min. YEARS		315	1022	248	38	7	6	318	119	100	66	1	201	9	14	9	23	16	.59	19	.243	.292	.311

Jason LaRiviere

Bats: Right **Throws:** Right **Pos:** OF **Ht:** 5'10" **Wt:** 180 **Born:** 9/30/73 **Age:** 24

Year Team	Lg Org	G	AB	H	2B	3B	HR	TB	R	RBI	TBB	IBB	SO	HBP	SH	SF	SB	CS	SB%	GDP	Avg	OBP	SLG
1995 New Jersey	A- StL	33	100	28	3	1	0	33	13	9	14	0	10	0	2	0	8	2	.80	2	.280	.368	.330
1996 Peoria	A StL	64	225	56	13	1	1	74	33	36	25	0	31	0	0	3	6	5	.55	5	.249	.320	.329
St. Pete	A+ StL	41	140	42	6	0	3	57	27	18	18	1	19	0	4	1	1	1	.50	1	.300	.377	.407
1997 Arkansas	AA StL	118	372	102	24	5	6	154	50	60	33	1	69	0	3	4	4	3	.57	16	.274	.330	.414
3 Min. YEARS		256	837	228	46	7	10	318	123	123	90	2	129	0	11	8	19	11	.63	24	.272	.340	.380

Andy Larkin

Pitches: Right **Bats:** Right **Pos:** P **Ht:** 6'4" **Wt:** 175 **Born:** 6/27/74 **Age:** 24

Year Team	Lg Org	G	GS	CG	GF	IP	BFP	H	R	ER	HR	SH	SF	HB	TBB	IBB	SO	WP	Bk	W	L	Pct.	ShO	Sv	ERA
1992 Marlins	R Fla	14	4	0	2	41.1	187	41	26	24	0	1	1	7	19	0	20	4	0	1	2	.333	0	2	5.23
1993 Elmira	A- Fla	14	14	4	0	88	368	74	43	29	1	1	3	12	23	0	89	9	1	5	7	.417	1	0	2.97
1994 Kane County	A Fla	21	21	3	0	140	577	125	53	44	6	3	3	19	27	0	125	4	0	9	7	.563	1	0	2.83
1995 Portland	AA Fla	9	9	0	0	40	160	29	16	15	5	4	0	6	11	2	23	1	0	1	2	.333	0	0	3.38
1996 Brevard Cty	A+ Fla	6	6	0	0	27.2	126	34	20	13	0	0	1	7	7	0	18	3	0	0	4	.000	0	0	4.23
Portland	AA Fla	8	8	0	0	49.1	195	45	18	17	6	2	0	2	10	0	40	3	0	4	1	.800	0	0	3.10
1997 Charlotte	AAA Fla	28	27	3	0	144.1	669	166	109	97	23	3	3	15	76	2	103	4	1	6	11	.353	0	0	6.05
1996 Florida	NL	1	1	0	0	5	22	3	1	1	0	0	0	1	4	0	2	0	0	0	0	.000	0	0	1.80
6 Min. YEARS		100	89	10	2	530.2	2282	514	285	239	41	14	11	68	173	4	418	28	2	26	34	.433	2	2	4.05

Greg LaRocca

Bats: Right **Throws:** Right **Pos:** 2B **Ht:** 5'11" **Wt:** 185 **Born:** 11/10/72 **Age:** 25

Year Team	Lg Org	G	AB	H	2B	3B	HR	TB	R	RBI	TBB	IBB	SO	HBP	SH	SF	SB	CS	SB%	GDP	Avg	OBP	SLG
1994 Spokane	A- SD	42	158	46	9	2	0	59	20	14	14	0	18	2	2	0	7	2	.78	4	.291	.356	.373
Rancho Cuca	A+ SD	28	85	14	5	1	0	24	7	8	7	0	11	2	1	0	3	1	.75	2	.165	.242	.282
1995 Rancho Cuca	A+ SD	125	466	150	36	5	8	220	77	74	44	0	77	12	0	2	15	4	.79	13	.322	.393	.472
Memphis	AA SD	2	7	1	0	0	0	1	0	0	0	0	1	0	0	0	0	1	1.00	1	.143	.143	.143
1996 Memphis	AA SD	128	445	122	22	5	6	172	66	42	51	4	58	10	5	5	5	9	.36	9	.274	.358	.387
1997 Mobile	AA SD	76	300	80	16	2	3	109	44	31	26	0	46	8	0	5	8	3	.73	4	.267	.336	.363
4 Min. YEARS		401	1461	413	88	15	18	585	214	169	142	4	211	34	8	13	38	20	.66	33	.283	.357	.400

Brandon Larson

Bats: Right **Throws:** Right **Pos:** SS **Ht:** 5'11" **Wt:** 190 **Born:** 5/24/76 **Age:** 22

Year Team	Lg Org	G	AB	H	2B	3B	HR	TB	R	RBI	TBB	IBB	SO	HBP	SH	SF	SB	CS	SB%	GDP	Avg	OBP	SLG
1997 Chattanooga	AA Cin	11	41	11	5	1	0	18	4	6	1	0	10	0	0	1	0	0	.00	1	.268	.279	.439

Chris Lasater

Bats: Right **Throws:** Right **Pos:** C **Ht:** 5'11" **Wt:** 200 **Born:** 11/6/72 **Age:** 25

Year Team	Lg Org	G	AB	H	2B	3B	HR	TB	R	RBI	TBB	IBB	SO	HBP	SH	SF	SB	CS	SB%	GDP	Avg	OBP	SLG
1997 Bowie	AA Bal	3	4	1	0	0	0	1	0	0	0	0	1	0	0	0	0	0	.00	0	.250	.250	.250
Bluefield	R+ Bal	11	35	9	4	0	2	19	8	9	3	1	6	1	0	0	0	1	.00	1	.257	.333	.543
Delmarva	A Bal	25	72	13	5	0	2	24	6	11	7	0	16	1	0	0	0	0	.00	1	.181	.263	.333
1 Min. YEARS		39	111	23	9	0	4	44	14	20	10	1	23	2	0	0	0	1	.00	1	.207	.285	.396

Chip Lawrence

Bats: Right **Throws:** Right **Pos:** SS **Ht:** 6'2" **Wt:** 182 **Born:** 11/14/74 **Age:** 23

Year Team	Lg Org	G	AB	H	2B	3B	HR	TB	R	RBI	TBB	IBB	SO	HBP	SH	SF	SB	CS	SB%	GDP	Avg	OBP	SLG
1996 Bluefield	R+ Bal	15	34	7	0	0	1	10	6	4	4	0	4	2	0	0	0	0	.00	1	.206	.325	.294
Frederick	A+ Bal	43	132	31	1	1	0	34	9	14	8	0	13	1	4	0	6	3	.67	3	.235	.284	.258
1997 Rochester	AAA Bal	17	43	10	0	1	0	12	9	7	3	0	8	0	2	0	1	1	.50	1	.233	.283	.279
Frederick	A+ Bal	57	164	44	5	0	2	55	18	14	13	0	19	3	6	0	2	4	.33	1	.268	.333	.335
Bowie	AA Bal	7	13	3	0	0	0	3	1	0	1	0	3	0	0	0	0	0	.00	0	.231	.286	.231
2 Min. YEARS		139	386	95	6	2	3	114	43	39	29	0	47	6	12	0	9	8	.53	6	.246	.309	.295

Sean Lawrence

Pitches: Left **Bats:** Left **Pos:** P **Ht:** 6'4" **Wt:** 215 **Born:** 9/2/70 **Age:** 27

Year Team	Lg Org	G	GS	CG	GF	IP	BFP	H	R	ER	HR	SH	SF	HB	TBB	IBB	SO	WP	Bk	W	L	Pct.	ShO	Sv	ERA
1992 Welland	A- Pit	15	15	0	0	74	330	75	54	43	10	2	2	2	34	1	71	6	3	3	6	.333	0	0	5.23
1993 Augusta	A Pit	22	22	0	0	121	516	108	59	42	9	7	4	4	50	1	96	6	0	6	8	.429	0	0	3.12
Salem	A+ Pit	4	4	0	0	15	77	25	19	17	1	2	1	0	9	0	14	2	0	1	3	.250	0	0	10.20

Year Team	Lg Org	G	GS	CG	GF	IP	BFP	H	R	ER	HR	SH	SF	HB	TBB	IBB	SO	WP	Bk	W	L	Pct.	ShO	Sv	ERA
						HOW MUCH HE PITCHED				WHAT HE GAVE UP										THE RESULTS					
1994 Salem	A+ Pit	12	12	0	0	72	312	76	38	21	8	1	2	3	18	0	66	2	0	4	2	.667	0	0	2.63
1995 Carolina	AA Pit	12	3	0	3	21.1	96	27	13	13	2	0	0	1	8	1	19	0	0	0	2	.000	0	0	5.48
Lynchburg	A+ Pit	20	19	0	0	111	465	115	56	52	16	3	3	1	25	0	82	3	0	5	8	.385	0	0	4.22
1996 Carolina	AA Pit	37	9	0	13	82	362	80	40	36	11	2	1	3	36	1	81	0	1	3	5	.375	0	2	3.95
1997 Calgary	AAA Pit	26	26	2	0	143.1	641	154	83	67	17	9	6	3	57	3	116	6	0	8	9	.471	0	0	4.21
6 Min. YEARS		148	110	2	16	639.2	2799	660	363	291	74	26	19	17	237	7	545	25	4	30	43	.411	0	2	4.09

Jalal Leach

Bats: Left **Throws:** Left **Pos:** OF **Ht:** 6'2" **Wt:** 200 **Born:** 3/14/69 **Age:** 29

Year Team	Lg Org	G	AB	H	2B	3B	HR	TB	R	RBI	TBB	IBB	SO	HBP	SH	SF	SB	CS	SB%	GDP	Avg	OBP	SLG
					BATTING												BASERUNNING				PERCENTAGES		
1990 Oneonta	A- NYA	69	257	74	7	1	2	89	41	18	37	3	52	0	4	0	33	13	.72	1	.288	.378	.346
1991 Ft. Laud	A+ NYA	122	468	119	13	9	2	156	48	42	44	3	122	0	3	3	28	12	.70	5	.254	.317	.333
1992 Pr William	A+ NYA	128	462	122	22	7	5	173	61	65	47	2	114	0	3	5	18	9	.67	8	.264	.329	.374
1993 Albany-Colo	AA NYA	125	457	129	19	9	14	208	64	79	47	3	113	1	0	4	16	12	.57	5	.282	.348	.455
1994 Columbus	AAA NYA	132	444	116	18	9	6	170	56	56	39	3	106	1	3	4	14	12	.54	8	.261	.320	.383
1995 Columbus	AAA NYA	88	272	66	12	5	6	106	37	31	22	1	60	2	1	4	11	4	.73	5	.243	.300	.390
1996 Harrisburg	AA Mon	83	268	88	22	3	6	134	38	48	21	4	55	0	2	4	3	7	.30	6	.328	.372	.500
Ottawa	AAA Mon	37	101	32	4	0	3	45	12	9	8	1	17	0	0	0	0	0	.00	1	.317	.367	.446
1997 Tacoma	AAA Sea	115	415	128	26	3	9	187	56	55	32	2	74	1	2	3	6	6	.50	11	.308	.357	.451
8 Min. YEARS		899	3144	874	143	46	53	1268	413	403	297	22	713	5	18	27	129	75	.63	50	.278	.339	.403

Eric LeBlanc

Pitches: Right **Bats:** Left **Pos:** P **Ht:** 6'1" **Wt:** 195 **Born:** 7/6/73 **Age:** 24

Year Team	Lg Org	G	GS	CG	GF	IP	BFP	H	R	ER	HR	SH	SF	HB	TBB	IBB	SO	WP	Bk	W	L	Pct.	ShO	Sv	ERA
						HOW MUCH HE PITCHED				WHAT HE GAVE UP										THE RESULTS					
1996 Princeton	R+ Cin	9	6	0	3	45.2	198	39	29	23	0	0	1	2	16	0	51	2	1	4	1	.800	0	1	4.53
Chston-WV	A Cin	6	5	0	0	29	129	33	18	16	2	0	2	0	13	0	28	0	0	1	2	.333	0	0	4.97
1997 Chston-WV	A Cin	24	13	2	2	107	440	98	51	40	7	0	5	6	29	1	77	7	2	10	7	.588	0	1	3.36
Chattanooga	AA Cin	8	8	0	0	50	216	53	35	31	3	2	3	1	21	0	25	2	2	2	4	.333	0	0	5.58
2 Min. YEARS		47	32	2	5	231.2	983	223	133	110	12	2	11	9	79	1	181	11	5	17	14	.548	0	2	4.27

Jason LeCronier

Bats: Left **Throws:** Right **Pos:** OF **Ht:** 5'11" **Wt:** 200 **Born:** 3/30/73 **Age:** 25

Year Team	Lg Org	G	AB	H	2B	3B	HR	TB	R	RBI	TBB	IBB	SO	HBP	SH	SF	SB	CS	SB%	GDP	Avg	OBP	SLG
					BATTING												BASERUNNING				PERCENTAGES		
1995 Bluefield	R+ Bal	21	69	17	4	1	2	29	11	10	11	1	17	0	0	1	1	1	.50	1	.246	.346	.420
Frederick	A+ Bal	40	131	37	8	1	6	65	17	19	12	2	40	0	0	0	1	0	1.00	3	.282	.343	.496
1996 High Desert	A+ Bal	52	135	32	3	1	4	49	20	25	6	0	37	1	2	2	1	0	1.00	5	.237	.271	.363
Frederick	A+ Bal	29	92	21	3	0	4	36	13	12	10	4	29	1	1	2	0	0	.00	0	.228	.311	.391
1997 Bowie	AA Bal	6	10	3	0	0	0	3	0	2	0	0	4	0	0	1	0	0	.00	0	.300	.273	.300
Frederick	A+ Bal	117	421	115	25	2	19	201	68	59	31	1	112	2	5	1	6	0	1.00	13	.273	.325	.477
3 Min. YEARS		265	858	225	43	5	35	383	129	127	70	8	239	4	9	5	9	1	.90	22	.262	.319	.446

Ricky Ledee

Bats: Left **Throws:** Left **Pos:** OF **Ht:** 6'1" **Wt:** 160 **Born:** 11/22/73 **Age:** 24

Year Team	Lg Org	G	AB	H	2B	3B	HR	TB	R	RBI	TBB	IBB	SO	HBP	SH	SF	SB	CS	SB%	GDP	Avg	OBP	SLG
					BATTING												BASERUNNING				PERCENTAGES		
1990 Yankees	R NYA	19	37	4	2	0	0	6	5	1	6	0	18	0	0	0	2	0	1.00	1	.108	.233	.162
1991 Yankees	R NYA	47	165	44	6	2	0	54	22	18	22	0	41	0	0	1	3	1	.75	3	.267	.351	.327
1992 Yankees	R NYA	52	179	41	9	2	2	60	25	23	24	1	47	1	0	1	1	4	.20	2	.229	.322	.335
1993 Oneonta	A- NYA	52	192	49	7	6	8	92	32	20	25	0	46	2	1	0	7	5	.58	2	.255	.347	.479
1994 Greensboro	A NYA	134	484	121	23	9	22	228	87	71	91	4	126	4	3	6	10	11	.48	7	.250	.369	.471
1995 Greensboro	A NYA	89	335	90	16	6	14	160	65	49	51	6	66	2	0	1	10	4	.71	3	.269	.368	.478
1996 Norwich	AA NYA	39	137	50	11	1	8	87	27	37	16	0	25	1	1	5	2	2	.50	4	.365	.421	.635
Columbus	AAA NYA	96	358	101	22	6	21	198	79	64	44	2	95	1	0	2	6	3	.67	4	.282	.360	.553
1997 Yankees	R NYA	7	21	7	1	0	0	8	3	2	2	1	4	1	0	0	0	0	.00	1	.333	.417	.381
Columbus	AAA NYA	43	170	52	12	1	10	96	38	39	21	0	49	1	0	0	4	0	1.00	5	.306	.385	.565
8 Min. YEARS		578	2078	559	109	33	85	989	383	324	302	14	517	13	5	16	45	30	.60	32	.269	.363	.476

Derek Lee

Bats: Left **Throws:** Right **Pos:** OF **Ht:** 6'1" **Wt:** 200 **Born:** 7/28/66 **Age:** 31

Year Team	Lg Org	G	AB	H	2B	3B	HR	TB	R	RBI	TBB	IBB	SO	HBP	SH	SF	SB	CS	SB%	GDP	Avg	OBP	SLG
					BATTING												BASERUNNING				PERCENTAGES		
1988 Utica	A- ChA	76	252	86	7	5	2	109	51	47	50	5	48	3	3	4	54	15	.78	2	.341	.450	.433
1989 South Bend	A ChA	125	448	128	24	7	11	199	89	48	87	4	83	9	4	2	45	26	.63	5	.286	.410	.444
1990 Birmingham	AA ChA	126	411	105	21	3	7	153	68	75	71	5	93	6	3	5	14	10	.58	8	.255	.369	.372
1991 Birmingham	AA ChA	45	154	50	10	2	5	79	36	16	46	5	23	6	0	1	9	7	.56	1	.325	.493	.513
Vancouver	AAA ChA	87	319	94	28	5	6	150	54	44	35	2	62	2	3	1	4	2	.67	11	.295	.367	.470
1992 Vancouver	AAA ChA	115	381	104	20	6	7	157	58	50	56	7	65	6	4	2	17	7	.71	11	.273	.373	.412
1993 Portland	AAA Min	106	381	120	30	7	10	194	79	80	60	2	51	4	4	4	16	5	.76	10	.315	.410	.509
1994 Ottawa	AAA Mon	131	463	139	35	9	13	231	62	75	66	9	81	2	0	6	12	6	.67	7	.300	.385	.499
1995 Norfolk	AAA NYN	112	415	89	17	0	18	160	56	60	48	4	62	2	2	5	11	6	.65	11	.214	.350	.456
1996 Edmonton	AAA Oak	9	25	5	1	0	0	6	3	1	6	1	2	0	0	0	1	1	.00	2	.200	.355	.240
Okla City	AAA Tex	120	409	123	32	2	13	198	59	62	50	7	69	2	0	6	6	9	.40	13	.301	.375	.484

	BATTING						BASERUNNING		PERCENTAGES	
Year Team	Lg Org	G AB H	2B 3B HR TB	R RBI	TBB IBB SO	HBP SH SF	SB CS SB% GDP	Avg OBP SLG
1997 Las Vegas	AAA SD	75 231 68	16 1 5 101	22 35	32 4 35	0 0 2	4 1 .80 6	.294 .377 .437
1993 Minnesota	AL	15 33 5	1 0 0 6	3 4	1 0 4	0 0 0	0 0 .00 0	.152 .176 .182
10 Min. YEARS		1127 3825 1111	241 47 97 1737	637 593	607 55 674	47 23 38	192 95 .67 77	.290 .391 .454

Mark Lee

Pitches: Left **Bats:** Left **Pos:** P   **Ht:** 6' 3" **Wt:** 200 **Born:** 7/20/64 **Age:** 33

Year Team	Lg Org	G	GS	CG	GF	IP	BFP	H	R	ER	HR	SH	SF	HB	TBB	IBB	SO	WP	Bk	W	L	Pct.	ShO	Sv	ERA
1985 Bristol	R+ Det	15	1	0	11	33	127	18	5	4	1	1	0	0	12	0	40	2	0	3	0	1.000	0	5	1.09
1986 Lakeland	A+ Det	41	0	0	31	62.2	281	73	44	36	4	4	1	2	21	8	39	5	0	2	5	.286	0	10	5.17
1987 Glens Falls	AA Det	7	0	0	4	8.1	38	13	9	8	1	1	1	0	1	0	3	0	0	0	0	.000	0	0	8.64
Lakeland	A+ Det	30	0	0	15	53	223	48	17	15	1	0	1	1	18	3	42	1	0	3	2	.600	0	4	2.55
1988 Lakeland	A+ Det	10	0	0	2	19	73	16	7	3	0	2	3	0	4	1	15	0	1	1	0	1.000	0	1	1.42
Glens Falls	AA Det	14	0	0	6	26	106	27	10	7	0	2	1	0	4	2	25	0	0	3	0	1.000	0	1	2.42
Toledo	AAA Det	22	0	0	6	19.1	79	18	7	6	0	0	2	0	7	2	13	0	0	0	1	.000	0	0	2.79
1989 Memphis	AA KC	25	24	0	1	122.2	558	149	84	71	13	4	4	3	44	2	79	6	8	5	11	.313	0	0	5.21
1990 Stockton	A+ Mil	5	0	0	2	7.2	32	5	2	2	0	1	0	0	3	0	7	0	0	1	0	1.000	0	1	2.35
Denver	AAA Mil	20	0	0	6	28	110	25	7	7	2	1	0	0	6	1	35	1	1	3	1	.750	0	4	2.25
1992 Denver	AAA Mil	48	0	0	14	68.2	309	78	45	32	5	3	0	0	26	4	57	1	1	2	4	.333	0	1	4.19
1993 Okla City	AAA Tex	52	1	0	21	101.2	454	112	61	49	4	3	7	0	43	5	65	4	1	5	3	.625	0	4	4.34
1994 Iowa	AAA ChN	54	0	0	29	61.1	265	69	27	23	3	0	2	1	21	8	42	4	0	1	3	.250	0	10	3.38
1995 Rochester	AAA Bal	25	0	0	8	28.2	108	18	6	5	0	1	0	0	5	0	35	1	0	4	2	.667	0	3	1.57
1996 Norfolk	AAA NYN	33	0	0	9	32	136	39	11	9	3	3	2	1	6	1	35	2	0	2	1	.667	0	1	2.53
Richmond	AAA Atl	20	0	0	9	35	141	30	12	11	3	0	1	1	11	1	36	0	0	2	4	.333	0	2	2.83
1997 Colo Sprngs	AAA Col	48	0	0	16	67.1	309	93	49	47	15	1	3	2	21	2	63	0	0	1	2	.333	0	3	6.28
1988 Kansas City	AL	4	0	0	4	5	21	6	2	2	0	0	0	0	1	0	0	0	0	0	0	.000	0	0	3.60
1990 Milwaukee	AL	11	0	0	1	21.1	85	20	5	5	1	1	2	0	4	0	14	0	0	1	0	1.000	0	0	2.11
1991 Milwaukee	AL	62	0	0	9	67.2	291	72	33	29	10	4	1	1	31	7	43	0	0	2	5	.286	0	1	3.86
1995 Baltimore	AL	39	0	0	7	33.1	148	31	18	18	5	1	2	1	18	3	27	0	0	2	0	1.000	0	1	4.86
12 Min. YEARS		469	26	0	190	774.1	3349	831	403	335	55	27	28	11	253	40	631	27	12	38	39	.494	0	48	3.89
4 Maj. YEARS		116	0	0	21	127.1	545	129	58	54	16	6	5	2	54	10	84	0	0	5	5	.500	0	2	3.82

Travis Lee

Bats: Left **Throws:** Left **Pos:** 1B   **Ht:** 6'3" **Wt:** 205 **Born:** 5/26/75 **Age:** 23

	BATTING						BASERUNNING		PERCENTAGES	
Year Team	Lg Org	G AB H	2B 3B HR TB	R RBI	TBB IBB SO	HBP SH SF	SB CS SB% GDP	Avg OBP SLG
1997 High Desert	A+ Ari	61 226 82	18 1 18 156	63 63	47 6 36	3 0 3	5 1 .83 8	.363 .473 .690
Tucson	AAA Ari	59 227 68	16 2 14 130	42 46	31 2 46	2 0 1	2 0 1.00 10	.300 .387 .573
1 Min. YEARS		120 453 150	34 3 32 286	105 109	78 8 82	5 0 4	7 1 .88 18	.331 .431 .631

Kevin Legault

Pitches: Right **Bats:** Right **Pos:** P   **Ht:** 6'1" **Wt:** 185 **Born:** 3/5/71 **Age:** 27

Year Team	Lg Org	G	GS	CG	GF	IP	BFP	H	R	ER	HR	SH	SF	HB	TBB	IBB	SO	WP	Bk	W	L	Pct.	ShO	Sv	ERA
1992 Elizabethtn	R+ Min	17	2	0	6	55.2	221	38	20	13	0	4	2	2	11	0	53	1	0	7	0	1.000	0	2	2.10
1993 Ft. Wayne	A Min	12	0	0	3	26.2	120	28	13	10	1	0	0	2	12	1	28	4	3	1	1	.500	0	2	3.38
Ft. Myers	A+ Min	18	18	3	0	110.1	493	142	80	70	4	1	4	4	32	1	60	4	0	3	9	.250	0	0	5.71
1994 Ft. Myers	A+ Min	26	26	1	0	154.2	693	196	87	73	8	6	4	5	52	5	68	9	0	7	11	.389	1	0	4.25
1995 Hardware City	AA Min	47	1	0	17	87	367	79	31	31	3	6	5	4	28	4	52	5	0	6	1	.857	0	3	3.21
1996 Salt Lake	AAA Min	50	0	0	13	80.2	353	100	51	48	10	3	3	0	24	2	57	4	1	5	4	.556	0	0	5.36
1997 New Britain	AA Min	40	1	0	13	70	305	74	37	35	6	4	3	3	26	3	40	4	0	5	1	.833	0	3	4.50
Salt Lake	AAA Min	16	0	0	5	26.1	120	39	24	22	2	1	0	0	7	3	18	0	0	1	3	.250	0	0	7.52
6 Min. YEARS		226	48	4	57	611.1	2672	696	343	302	34	25	21	20	192	19	376	31	4	35	30	.538	0	10	4.45

Keith Legree

Bats: Left **Throws:** Right **Pos:** OF   **Ht:** 6'2" **Wt:** 195 **Born:** 12/26/71 **Age:** 26

	BATTING						BASERUNNING		PERCENTAGES	
Year Team	Lg Org	G AB H	2B 3B HR TB	R RBI	TBB IBB SO	HBP SH SF	SB CS SB% GDP	Avg OBP SLG
1991 Twins	R Min	45 165 49	5 5 1 67	33 17	21 0 38	2 0 2	15 3 .83 2	.297 .379 .406
1992 Elizabethtn	R+ Min	44 173 45	10 3 6 79	34 43	22 0 42	1 1 5	1 3 .25 1	.260 .338 .457
1993 Ft. Wayne	A Min	49 178 43	6 2 3 62	28 14	21 2 51	3 0 0	1 2 .33 5	.242 .332 .348
1994 Ft. Myers	A+ Min	55 186 45	8 1 4 67	16 15	23 1 52	1 0 2	8 3 .73 6	.242 .325 .360
1995 Hardware City	AA Min	43 110 22	2 0 0 24	10 6	21 0 33	0 0 0	3 1 .75 3	.200 .328 .218
1996 Ft. Myers	A+ Min	58 198 54	8 2 5 81	39 37	42 2 52	5 0 2	2 2 .50 2	.273 .409 .409
1997 New Britain	AA Min	113 343 83	19 2 9 133	46 58	56 5 70	3 1 4	10 4 .71 15	.242 .350 .388
7 Min. YEARS		407 1353 341	58 15 28 513	206 190	206 10 338	15 2 15	40 18 .69 34	.252 .354 .379

Scott Leius

Bats: Right **Throws:** Right **Pos:** 3B-DH   **Ht:** 6' 3" **Wt:** 200 **Born:** 9/24/65 **Age:** 32

	BATTING						BASERUNNING		PERCENTAGES	
Year Team	Lg Org	G AB H	2B 3B HR TB	R RBI	TBB IBB SO	HBP SH SF	SB CS SB% GDP	Avg OBP SLG
1986 Elizabethtn	R+ Min	61 237 66	14 1 4 94	37 23	26 0 45	3 2 1	5 0 1.00 6	.278 .358 .397
1987 Kenosha	A Min	126 414 99	16 4 8 147	65 51	50 0 88	3 5 4	6 4 .60 2	.239 .323 .355
1988 Visalia	A+ Min	93 308 73	14 4 3 104	44 46	42 0 50	3 8 1	3 1 .75 11	.237 .333 .338
1989 Orlando	AA Min	99 346 105	22 2 4 143	49 45	38 0 74	0 3 2	3 2 .60 4	.303 .370 .413

144

Year Team	Lg Org	G	AB	H	2B	3B	HR	TB	R	RBI	TBB	IBB	SO	HBP	SH	SF	SB	CS	SB%	GDP	Avg	OBP	SLG
1990 Portland	AAA Min	103	353	81	13	5	2	110	34	23	35	0	66	0	4	0	5	3	.63	8	.229	.299	.312
1996 Buffalo	AAA Cle	35	123	33	3	1	4	50	22	17	12	1	·16	2	0	1	0	0	.00	4	.268	.341	.407
1997 Nashville	AAA ChA	30	104	25	2	0	7	48	15	17	11	0	6	0	1	0	0	0	.00	1	.240	.313	.462
1990 Minnesota	AL	14	25	6	1	0	1	10	4	4	2	0	2	0	1	0	0	0	.00	2	.240	.296	.400
1991 Minnesota	AL	109	199	57	7	2	5	83	35	20	30	1	35	0	5	1	5	5	.50	4	.286	.378	.417
1992 Minnesota	AL	129	409	102	18	2	2	130	50	35	34	0	61	1	5	0	6	5	.55	10	.249	.309	.318
1993 Minnesota	AL	10	18	3	0	0	0	3	4	2	2	0	4	0	0	2	0	0	.00	1	.167	.227	.167
1994 Minnesota	AL	97	350	86	16	1	14	146	57	49	37	0	58	1	1	2	2	4	.33	9	.246	.318	.417
1995 Minnesota	AL	117	372	92	16	5	4	130	51	45	49	3	54	2	0	4	2	1	.67	14	.247	.335	.349
1996 Cleveland	AL	27	43	6	4	0	1	13	3	3	2	0	8	0	1	0	0	0	.00	1	.140	.178	.302
7 Min. YEARS		547	1885	482	84	17	32	696	266	222	214	1	345	11	23	9	22	10	.69	36	.256	.334	.369
7 Maj. YEARS		503	1416	352	62	10	27	515	204	158	156	4	222	4	13	9	15	15	.50	41	.249	.323	.364

Anthony Lewis

Bats: Left **Throws:** Left **Pos:** OF   **Ht:** 5'11" **Wt:** 205 **Born:** 2/2/71 **Age:** 27

Year Team	Lg Org	G	AB	H	2B	3B	HR	TB	R	RBI	TBB	IBB	SO	HBP	SH	SF	SB	CS	SB%	GDP	Avg	OBP	SLG
1989 Cardinals	R StL	51	187	46	10	0	2	62	32	27	11	1	45	0	0	4	11	3	.79	1	.246	.282	.332
1990 Savannah	A StL	128	465	118	22	4	8	172	55	49	24	6	79	1	2	1	10	13	.43	13	.254	.291	.370
1991 St. Pete	A+ StL	124	435	100	17	7	6	149	40	43	50	7	100	2	0	2	5	5	.50	7	.230	.311	.343
1992 St. Pete	A+ StL	128	454	101	18	2	15	168	50	55	46	6	105	5	1	4	2	4	.33	7	.222	.299	.370
1993 Arkansas	AA StL	112	326	86	28	2	13	157	48	50	25	3	98	0	1	3	3	4	.43	5	.264	.314	.482
1994 Arkansas	AA StL	88	335	85	18	1	17	156	58	50	27	0	69	0	0	2	2	1	.67	9	.254	.308	.466
Louisville	AAA StL	21	74	9	0	1	0	11	3	6	0	0	27	0	0	0	0	0	.00	1	.122	.122	.149
1995 Arkansas	AA StL	115	407	102	21	3	24	201	55	85	44	5	117	2	0	1	0	2	.00	9	.251	.326	.494
1996 Hardware City	AA Min	134	458	116	15	2	24	207	58	95	47	4	99	1	0	6	6	9	.40	9	.253	.320	.452
1997 New Haven	AA Col	51	167	38	9	0	12	83	32	36	13	0	39	0	0	3	1	1	.50	1	.228	.279	.497
9 Min. YEARS		952	3308	801	158	22	121	1366	431	496	287	32	778	11	4	26	40	42	.49	60	.242	.303	.413

Marc Lewis

Bats: Right **Throws:** Right **Pos:** OF   **Ht:** 6'2" **Wt:** 175 **Born:** 5/20/75 **Age:** 23

Year Team	Lg Org	G	AB	H	2B	3B	HR	TB	R	RBI	TBB	IBB	SO	HBP	SH	SF	SB	CS	SB%	GDP	Avg	OBP	SLG
1994 Red Sox	R Bos	50	197	64	13	2	3	90	32	32	10	0	19	1	2	4	16	3	.84	4	.325	.354	.457
Lynchburg	A+ Bos	8	32	6	1	0	1	10	3	5	3	0	4	0	0	0	0	2	.00	1	.188	.257	.313
1995 Michigan	A Bos	36	92	14	2	1	1	21	14	5	9	0	16	0	2	0	10	3	.77	1	.152	.228	.228
Utica	A- Bos	69	272	82	15	5	5	122	47	39	17	0	32	0	2	3	24	9	.73	6	.301	.339	.449
1996 Macon	A Atl	66	241	76	14	3	5	111	36	28	21	1	31	1	1	6	25	8	.76	6	.315	.364	.461
Durham	A+ Atl	68	262	78	12	2	6	112	43	26	24	2	37	2	3	1	25	9	.74	5	.298	.360	.427
1997 Greenville	AA Atl	135	512	140	17	3	17	214	64	67	25	3	84	8	4	2	21	14	.60	8	.273	.316	.418
4 Min. YEARS		432	1608	460	74	16	38	680	239	202	109	6	223	12	14	16	121	48	.72	31	.286	.333	.423

T.R. Lewis

Bats: Right **Throws:** Right **Pos:** OF   **Ht:** 6'0" **Wt:** 180 **Born:** 4/17/71 **Age:** 27

Year Team	Lg Org	G	AB	H	2B	3B	HR	TB	R	RBI	TBB	IBB	SO	HBP	SH	SF	SB	CS	SB%	GDP	Avg	OBP	SLG
1989 Bluefield	R+ Bal	40	151	50	11	1	10	93	31	32	9	0	21	0	0	2	0	2	.00	2	.331	.364	.616
1990 Wausau	A Bal	115	404	115	24	2	8	167	60	45	46	0	64	5	1	1	10	5	.67	14	.285	.364	.413
Frederick	A+ Bal	22	80	26	4	3	1	39	12	11	11	1	11	2	0	0	5	0	1.00	1	.325	.419	.488
1991 Frederick	A+ Bal	49	159	33	7	2	0	44	18	7	19	2	25	1	2	1	1	1	.50	4	.208	.294	.277
1992 Kane County	A Bal	45	134	40	10	0	2	56	26	22	13	0	22	3	1	4	5	4	.56	3	.299	.364	.418
Frederick	A+ Bal	84	313	96	27	6	7	156	58	54	36	0	46	2	0	5	5	2	.71	5	.307	.376	.498
1993 Bowie	AA Bal	127	480	146	26	2	5	191	73	64	36	4	80	3	0	7	22	8	.73	12	.304	.352	.398
1994 Orioles	R Bal	5	20	6	1	0	1	10	2	5	2	0	3	0	0	0	1	1	.50	0	.300	.364	.500
Bowie	AA Bal	17	72	18	5	0	3	32	13	8	6	0	15	0	0	1	1	0	1.00	1	.250	.304	.444
Rochester	AAA Bal	55	174	53	10	0	6	81	25	31	16	2	33	3	0	2	6	1	.86	1	.305	.369	.466
1995 Bowie	AA Bal	86	309	91	19	1	5	127	57	44	40	2	43	1	1	6	12	3	.80	8	.294	.371	.411
Rochester	AAA Bal	22	78	23	7	0	4	42	12	19	7	0	14	1	0	1	1	1	.50	2	.295	.356	.538
1996 Pawtucket	AAA Bos	79	274	86	23	1	14	153	55	52	34	1	50	2	1	2	2	2	.50	8	.314	.391	.558
1997 Richmond	AAA Atl	117	363	107	20	5	7	158	65	58	37	2	71	5	1	7	8	3	.73	9	.295	.362	.435
9 Min. YEARS		863	3011	890	194	23	73	1349	507	452	312	14	498	28	7	39	79	33	.71	70	.296	.363	.448

Kevin Lidle

Bats: Right **Throws:** Right **Pos:** C   **Ht:** 5'11" **Wt:** 170 **Born:** 3/22/72 **Age:** 26

Year Team	Lg Org	G	AB	H	2B	3B	HR	TB	R	RBI	TBB	IBB	SO	HBP	SH	SF	SB	CS	SB%	GDP	Avg	OBP	SLG
1992 Niagara Fal	A- Det	58	140	34	6	2	1	47	21	18	8	0	42	1	6	3	3	2	.60	1	.243	.283	.336
1993 Fayetteville	A Det	58	197	42	14	1	5	73	29	25	34	0	42	1	0	1	2	0	1.00	0	.213	.330	.371
1994 Lakeland	A+ Det	56	187	49	13	2	6	84	26	30	19	0	46	4	1	1	1	1	.50	2	.262	.341	.449
1995 Jacksnville	AA Det	36	80	13	7	0	1	23	12	5	1	0	31	0	1	0	1	0	1.00	1	.163	.173	.288
Fayetteville	A Det	36	113	16	4	1	4	34	15	13	16	0	44	1	3	2	0	1	.00	0	.142	.250	.301
1996 Lakeland	A+ Det	97	320	69	18	1	8	113	37	41	30	0	90	3	0	1	1	1	.50	0	.216	.288	.353
Jacksnville	AA Det	4	8	2	0	0	1	5	2	2	1	0	2	0	0	0	1	0	1.00	0	.250	.333	.625
1997 Jacksnville	AA Det	59	186	28	7	0	1	38	18	16	17	0	77	2	3	2	0	0	.00	0	.151	.227	.204
6 Min. YEARS		404	1231	253	69	7	27	417	160	150	126	0	374	12	14	10	9	5	.64	13	.206	.284	.339

Jeff Liefer

Bats: Left **Throws:** Right **Pos:** OF **Ht:** 6'3" **Wt:** 195 **Born:** 8/17/74 **Age:** 23

Year Team	Lg Org	G	AB	H	2B	3B	HR	TB	R	RBI	TBB	IBB	SO	HBP	SH	SF	SB	CS	SB%	GDP	Avg	OBP	SLG
1996 South Bend	A ChA	74	277	90	14	0	15	149	60	58	30	3	62	5	0	4	6	5	.55	3	.325	.396	.538
Pr William	A+ ChA	37	147	33	6	0	1	42	17	13	11	2	27	0	0	1	0	0	.00	6	.224	.277	.286
1997 Birmingham	AA ChA	119	474	113	24	9	15	200	67	71	38	3	115	7	1	4	2	0	1.00	10	.238	.302	.422
2 Min. YEARS		230	898	236	44	9	31	391	144	142	79	8	204	12	1	9	8	5	.62	19	.263	.328	.435

Tal Light

Bats: Right **Throws:** Right **Pos:** 3B **Ht:** 6'3" **Wt:** 205 **Born:** 11/28/73 **Age:** 24

Year Team	Lg Org	G	AB	H	2B	3B	HR	TB	R	RBI	TBB	IBB	SO	HBP	SH	SF	SB	CS	SB%	GDP	Avg	OBP	SLG
1995 Asheville	A Col	23	63	17	4	0	4	33	13	13	18	0	17	0	0	3	0	0	.00	0	.270	.417	.524
1996 Asheville	A Col	52	205	67	15	0	12	118	34	51	21	0	58	1	0	2	8	4	.67	3	.327	.389	.576
Salem	A+ Col	64	234	55	10	0	13	104	29	36	19	0	59	5	0	1	3	1	.75	6	.235	.305	.444
1997 New Haven	AA Col	25	83	20	6	0	5	41	10	11	5	0	36	0	1	0	0	1	.00	1	.241	.284	.494
Salem	A+ Col	104	373	99	19	2	15	167	57	65	59	2	144	4	0	4	0	1	.00	6	.265	.368	.448
3 Min. YEARS		268	958	258	54	2	49	463	143	176	122	2	314	10	1	10	11	7	.61	16	.269	.355	.483

Rich Linares

Pitches: Right **Bats:** Right **Pos:** P **Ht:** 5'11" **Wt:** 200 **Born:** 8/31/72 **Age:** 25

Year Team	Lg Org	G	GS	CG	GF	IP	BFP	H	R	ER	HR	SH	SF	HB	TBB	IBB	SO	WP	Bk	W	L	Pct.	ShO	Sv	ERA
1992 Dodgers	R LA	7	0	0	6	11.2	46	8	2	1	0	0	0	1	3	1	14	0	1	1	2	.333	0	1	0.77
Great Falls	R+ LA	19	0	0	6	47.2	198	32	22	13	4	3	2	6	11	0	53	2	1	3	1	.750	0	3	2.45
1993 Vero Beach	A+ LA	45	7	0	29	109.1	440	97	36	22	4	4	2	2	28	5	80	1	3	4	4	.500	0	13	1.81
1994 San Antonio	AA LA	5	0	0	2	6	28	4	7	6	0	1	0	0	7	1	2	1	0	0	2	.000	0	0	9.00
Bakersfield	A+ LA	41	3	1	14	107.1	434	95	45	41	13	5	5	8	20	2	65	4	0	5	3	.625	1	6	3.44
1995 Bakersfield	A+ LA	55	0	0	52	67.1	272	64	18	17	2	4	1	3	17	2	57	3	0	4	4	.500	0	20	2.27
1996 San Berndno	A+ LA	60	0	0	52	61.2	266	59	30	23	2	2	1	6	19	0	59	2	1	4	3	.571	0	33	3.36
1997 San Antonio	AA LA	18	0	0	8	23.2	112	37	21	19	3	1	0	0	6	1	11	1	0	2	1	.667	0	0	7.23
San Berndno	A+ LA	26	0	0	23	29	130	36	11	11	3	0	1	1	7	0	33	1	0	1	0	1.000	0	10	3.41
6 Min. YEARS		276	10	1	192	463.2	1926	432	192	153	31	20	12	27	118	12	374	15	6	24	20	.545	1	86	2.97

Keith Linebarger

Pitches: Right **Bats:** Right **Pos:** P **Ht:** 6'6" **Wt:** 220 **Born:** 5/11/71 **Age:** 27

Year Team	Lg Org	G	GS	CG	GF	IP	BFP	H	R	ER	HR	SH	SF	HB	TBB	IBB	SO	WP	Bk	W	L	Pct.	ShO	Sv	ERA
1992 Elizabethtn	R+ Min	11	8	1	0	52.1	227	47	25	17	3	1	1	4	26	0	41	6	0	4	2	.667	0	0	2.92
1993 Ft. Wayne	A Min	35	11	1	12	97.1	445	113	60	46	3	8	2	5	43	2	76	6	2	5	7	.417	1	0	4.25
1994 Ft. Wayne	A Min	23	0	0	10	45.1	177	24	11	10	1	2	0	2	21	0	41	4	0	3	0	1.000	0	4	1.99
Ft. Myers	A+ Min	16	0	0	10	27	138	39	22	18	0	1	2	1	14	0	21	2	0	2	2	.500	0	1	6.00
1995 Ft. Myers	A+ Min	29	10	1	12	103	418	74	30	24	6	3	2	9	35	1	73	4	0	7	4	.636	0	2	2.10
1996 Hardware City	AA Min	42	4	1	19	99	428	98	53	36	9	7	4	7	32	6	69	2	0	7	5	.583	0	4	3.27
1997 New Britain	AA Min	5	0	0	0	5	24	5	4	4	0	1	0	0	3	0	1	0	0	1	0	1.000	0	0	7.20
Salt Lake	AAA Min	41	7	0	17	97.2	468	135	79	72	10	4	2	4	42	4	59	5	0	4	6	.400	0	5	6.63
6 Min. YEARS		198	41	4	80	526.2	2325	535	284	227	32	27	13	32	216	13	381	29	2	32	27	.542	2	18	3.88

Cole Liniak

Bats: Right **Throws:** Right **Pos:** 3B **Ht:** 6'1" **Wt:** 181 **Born:** 8/23/76 **Age:** 21

Year Team	Lg Org	G	AB	H	2B	3B	HR	TB	R	RBI	TBB	IBB	SO	HBP	SH	SF	SB	CS	SB%	GDP	Avg	OBP	SLG
1995 Red Sox	R Bos	23	79	21	7	0	1	31	9	8	4	0	8	1	2	0	2	0	1.00	2	.266	.310	.392
1996 Michigan	A Bos	121	437	115	26	2	3	154	65	46	59	1	59	10	3	8	7	6	.54	12	.263	.358	.352
1997 Sarasota	A+ Bos	64	217	73	16	0	6	107	32	42	22	1	31	3	3	2	1	2	.33	2	.336	.402	.493
Trenton	AA Bos	53	200	56	11	0	2	73	20	18	17	0	29	1	3	1	0	1	.00	6	.280	.338	.365
3 Min. YEARS		261	933	265	60	2	12	365	126	114	102	2	127	15	11	11	10	9	.53	22	.284	.360	.391

Bob Lisanti

Bats: Right **Throws:** Right **Pos:** C **Ht:** 5'10" **Wt:** 180 **Born:** 5/28/73 **Age:** 25

Year Team	Lg Org	G	AB	H	2B	3B	HR	TB	R	RBI	TBB	IBB	SO	HBP	SH	SF	SB	CS	SB%	GDP	Avg	OBP	SLG
1996 Williamsprt	A- ChN	43	119	23	7	0	0	30	10	15	13	0	27	1	3	0	0	3	.00	2	.193	.278	.252
1997 Rockford	A ChN	66	182	43	8	0	0	51	18	21	15	0	42	5	1	4	1	3	.25	0	.236	.306	.280
Iowa	AAA ChN	4	11	4	0	0	0	4	2	1	2	0	5	0	0	0	0	0	.00	0	.364	.462	.364
2 Min. YEARS		113	312	70	15	0	0	85	30	37	30	0	74	6	4	4	1	6	.14	2	.224	.301	.272

Mark Little

Bats: Right **Throws:** Right **Pos:** OF **Ht:** 6'0" **Wt:** 200 **Born:** 7/11/72 **Age:** 25

Year Team	Lg Org	G	AB	H	2B	3B	HR	TB	R	RBI	TBB	IBB	SO	HBP	SH	SF	SB	CS	SB%	GDP	Avg	OBP	SLG
1994 Hudson Vall	A- Tex	54	208	61	15	5	3	95	33	27	22	1	38	1	0	4	14	5	.74	4	.293	.357	.457
1995 Charlotte	A+ Tex	115	438	112	31	8	9	186	75	50	51	1	108	14	2	2	20	14	.59	4	.256	.350	.425
1996 Tulsa	AA Tex	101	409	119	24	2	13	186	69	50	48	0	88	10	5	3	22	10	.69	4	.291	.377	.455
1997 Okla City	AAA Tex	121	415	109	23	4	15	185	72	45	39	1	100	8	8	0	21	9	.70	8	.263	.338	.446

		BATTING												BASERUNNING				PERCENTAGES		
Year Team	Lg Org	G	AB	H	2B	3B	HR	TB	R	RBI	TBB	IBB	SO	HBP	SH	SF	SB	CS	SB%	GDP	Avg	OBP	SLG
4 Min. YEARS		391	1470	401	93	19	40	652	249	172	160	3	334	33	15	9	77	38	.67	21	.273	.355	.444

Shane Livsey

Bats: Both **Throws:** Right **Pos:** 2B   Ht: 5'11" **Wt:** 180 **Born:** 7/21/73 **Age:** 24

Year Team	Lg Org	G	AB	H	2B	3B	HR	TB	R	RBI	TBB	IBB	SO	HBP	SH	SF	SB	CS	SB%	GDP	Avg	OBP	SLG
1991 Astros	R Hou	46	151	37	2	2	0	43	20	14	20	0	23	2	1	0	13	9	.59	2	.245	.341	.285
1992 Astros	R Hou	38	117	32	3	2	1	42	20	14	29	0	12	4	0	3	10	5	.67	2	.274	.425	.359
1993 Asheville	A Hou	124	453	119	26	1	2	153	50	60	62	0	92	9	1	6	26	15	.63	7	.263	.358	.338
1994 Osceola	A+ Hou	108	373	84	15	3	1	108	36	43	34	2	46	2	0	4	10	5	.67	7	.225	.291	.290
1995 Rockford	A ChN	57	226	64	10	1	2	82	39	27	22	3	30	2	0	0	21	7	.75	0	.283	.352	.363
1996 Daytona	A+ ChN	50	194	63	14	3	2	89	39	28	24	2	32	2	1	3	17	6	.74	1	.325	.399	.459
Orlando	AA ChN	75	257	66	15	2	2	91	36	33	27	0	39	5	3	5	13	8	.62	9	.257	.333	.354
1997 Orlando	AA ChN	13	30	8	2	0	1	13	6	2	7	1	4	0	0	0	2	0	1.00	0	.267	.405	.433
7 Min. YEARS		511	1801	473	87	14	11	621	246	221	225	8	278	26	6	21	112	55	.67	28	.263	.349	.345

Jose Lobaton

Bats: Right **Throws:** Right **Pos:** SS   Ht: 5'11" **Wt:** 154 **Born:** 3/29/74 **Age:** 24

Year Team	Lg Org	G	AB	H	2B	3B	HR	TB	R	RBI	TBB	IBB	SO	HBP	SH	SF	SB	CS	SB%	GDP	Avg	OBP	SLG
1993 Yankees	R NYA	44	165	57	8	6	1	80	30	16	19	0	28	2	1	2	24	2	.92	2	.345	.415	.485
1994 Oneonta	A- NYA	66	239	54	9	2	0	67	34	15	22	0	55	3	3	2	14	7	.67	7	.226	.297	.280
1995 Greensboro	A NYA	60	185	45	6	5	0	61	26	23	22	0	58	2	11	2	11	6	.65	3	.243	.327	.330
Oneonta	A- NYA	41	145	32	11	3	1	52	23	11	13	0	30	2	1	0	4	1	.80	2	.221	.294	.359
1996 Tampa	A+ NYA	113	375	87	16	5	5	128	39	37	34	1	74	8	11	4	11	7	.61	6	.232	.306	.341
1997 Tampa	A+ NYA	7	23	3	0	0	0	3	0	5	2	0	6	0	1	1	0	0	.00	2	.130	.192	.130
Norwich	AA NYA	68	197	38	6	0	1	47	16	15	12	0	60	2	5	2	2	3	.40	4	.193	.244	.239
5 Min. YEARS		399	1329	316	56	21	8	438	168	122	124	1	311	19	33	13	66	26	.72	26	.238	.309	.330

Dan Lock

Pitches: Left **Bats:** Right **Pos:** P   Ht: 6'5" **Wt:** 210 **Born:** 3/27/73 **Age:** 25

		HOW MUCH HE PITCHED					WHAT HE GAVE UP										THE RESULTS					
Year Team	Lg Org	G	GS	CG	GF	IP	BFP	H	R	ER	HR	SH	SF	HB	TBB	IBB	SO	WP	Bk	W	L	Pct.	ShO	Sv	ERA
1994 Auburn	A- Hou	11	11	0	0	59	246	46	21	15	3	2	2	4	20	0	47	3	0	3	1	.750	0	0	2.29
1995 Quad City	A Hou	27	27	1	0	143	642	152	94	66	13	8	4	10	58	0	90	5	0	8	15	.348	0	0	4.15
1996 Kissimmee	A+ Hou	27	27	1	0	147.2	672	166	109	78	3	9	8	7	62	0	72	8	1	5	18	.217	0	0	4.75
1997 Kissimmee	A+ Hou	17	0	0	6	27	123	28	17	8	0	1	1	1	11	1	23	0	1	0	2	.000	0	1	2.67
Jackson	AA Hou	35	0	0	8	33.2	159	43	29	23	1	3	2	0	17	0	20	5	0	2	2	.500	0	0	6.15
4 Min. YEARS		117	65	2	14	410.1	1842	435	270	190	20	23	17	22	168	1	252	21	2	18	38	.321	0	1	4.17

Paul LoDuca

Bats: Right **Throws:** Right **Pos:** C   Ht: 5'10" **Wt:** 193 **Born:** 4/12/72 **Age:** 26

Year Team	Lg Org	G	AB	H	2B	3B	HR	TB	R	RBI	TBB	IBB	SO	HBP	SH	SF	SB	CS	SB%	GDP	Avg	OBP	SLG
1993 Vero Beach	A+ LA	39	134	42	6	0	0	48	17	13	13	0	22	2	0	1	0	0	.00	2	.313	.380	.358
1994 Bakersfield	A+ LA	123	455	141	32	1	6	193	65	68	52	2	49	3	0	4	16	9	.64	5	.310	.381	.424
1995 San Antonio	AA LA	61	199	49	8	0	1	60	27	8	26	0	25	2	0	0	5	5	.50	12	.246	.339	.302
1996 Vero Beach	A+ LA	124	439	134	22	0	3	165	54	66	70	2	38	2	0	4	8	2	.80	14	.305	.400	.376
1997 San Antonio	AA LA	105	385	126	28	2	7	179	63	69	46	3	27	3	4	5	16	8	.67	17	.327	.399	.465
5 Min. YEARS		452	1612	492	96	3	17	645	226	224	207	7	161	12	4	14	45	24	.65	50	.305	.385	.400

Carlton Loewer

Pitches: Right **Bats:** Both **Pos:** P   Ht: 6'6" **Wt:** 220 **Born:** 9/24/73 **Age:** 24

		HOW MUCH HE PITCHED					WHAT HE GAVE UP										THE RESULTS					
Year Team	Lg Org	G	GS	CG	GF	IP	BFP	H	R	ER	HR	SH	SF	HB	TBB	IBB	SO	WP	Bk	W	L	Pct.	ShO	Sv	ERA
1995 Clearwater	A+ Phi	20	20	1	0	114.2	502	124	59	42	6	3	5	5	36	0	83	7	3	7	5	.583	0	0	3.30
Reading	AA Phi	8	8	0	0	50	212	42	17	12	3	1	4	1	31	0	35	4	0	4	1	.800	0	0	2.16
1996 Reading	AA Phi	27	27	3	0	171	753	191	115	100	24	7	3	8	57	3	119	9	1	7	10	.412	1	0	5.26
1997 Scranton-WB	AAA Phi	29	29	4	0	184	797	198	120	94	20	8	4	7	50	6	152	3	0	5	13	.278	0	0	4.60
3 Min. YEARS		84	84	8	0	519.2	2264	555	311	248	53	19	12	21	174	9	389	23	4	23	29	.442	1	0	4.30

Marcus Logan

Pitches: Right **Bats:** Right **Pos:** P   Ht: 6'0" **Wt:** 170 **Born:** 5/8/72 **Age:** 26

		HOW MUCH HE PITCHED					WHAT HE GAVE UP										THE RESULTS					
Year Team	Lg Org	G	GS	CG	GF	IP	BFP	H	R	ER	HR	SH	SF	HB	TBB	IBB	SO	WP	Bk	W	L	Pct.	ShO	Sv	ERA
1994 New Jersey	A- StL	13	13	2	0	64	274	53	32	28	3	2	4	4	27	0	53	10	1	5	4	.556	1	0	3.94
1995 Savannah	A StL	34	7	0	2	86.2	373	73	42	32	3	1	5	2	38	0	83	11	1	3	6	.333	0	0	3.32
1996 St. Pete	A+ StL	30	19	0	2	133	556	125	49	43	9	4	3	6	49	1	99	7	2	7	7	.500	0	0	2.91
1997 Arkansas	AA StL	27	25	1	1	153	663	152	75	70	15	9	2	7	64	1	101	4	2	11	7	.611	1	0	4.12
4 Min. YEARS		104	64	3	5	436.2	1866	403	198	173	30	16	12	19	178	2	336	32	6	26	24	.520	2	0	3.57

Kevin Lomon

Pitches: Right **Bats:** Right **Pos:** P   **Ht:** 6'1" **Wt:** 195 **Born:** 11/20/71 **Age:** 26

Year Team	Lg Org	G	GS	CG	GF	IP	BFP	H	R	ER	HR	SH	SF	HB	TBB	IBB	SO	WP	Bk	W	L	Pct.	ShO	Sv	ERA
1991 Pulaski	R+ Atl	10	5	1	1	44	168	17	9	3	0	0	0	4	13	0	70	4	6	6	0	1.000	1	1	0.61
Macon	A Atl	1	0	0	1	5	17	2	1	1	0	0	0	0	1	0	2	0	0	1	0	1.000	0	0	1.80
1992 Durham	A+ Atl	27	27	0	0	135	609	147	83	74	13	5	3	11	63	1	113	16	3	8	9	.471	0	0	4.93
1993 Durham	A+ Atl	14	14	1	0	85	358	80	36	35	6	0	1	2	30	1	68	5	3	4	2	.667	0	0	3.71
Greenville	AA Atl	13	13	1	0	79.1	338	76	41	34	4	3	3	4	31	2	68	4	0	3	4	.429	1	0	3.86
1994 Richmond	AAA Atl	28	26	0	0	147	628	159	69	63	12	1	2	3	53	2	97	9	0	10	8	.556	0	0	3.86
1995 Richmond	AAA Atl	32	3	0	8	60	261	62	23	20	2	4	4	0	32	4	52	4	0	1	2	.333	0	1	3.00
1996 Richmond	AAA Atl	26	26	2	0	141.1	607	151	82	68	11	5	4	4	44	2	102	6	1	9	8	.529	0	0	4.33
1997 Columbus	AAA NYA	3	3	0	0	14.1	71	21	12	10	2	1	1	2	7	0	14	1	0	1	1	.500	0	0	6.28
Norwich	AA NYA	18	18	2	0	115	487	104	51	41	5	1	5	6	50	0	117	5	1	9	7	.563	1	0	3.21
1995 New York	NL	6	0	0	1	9.1	47	17	8	7	0	0	0	0	5	1	6	0	0	0	1	.000	0	0	6.75
1996 Atlanta	NL	6	0	0	1	7.1	31	7	4	4	0	0	0	1	3	0	1	0	0	0	0	.000	0	0	4.91
7 Min. YEARS		172	135	7	10	826	3544	819	407	349	55	20	24	36	324	12	703	54	14	52	41	.559	3	2	3.80
2 Maj. YEARS		12	0	0	2	16.2	78	24	12	11	0	0	0	1	8	1	7	0	1	0	1	.000	0	0	5.94

R.D. Long

Bats: Both **Throws:** Right **Pos:** SS   **Ht:** 6'1" **Wt:** 183 **Born:** 4/2/71 **Age:** 27

Year Team	Lg Org	G	AB	H	2B	3B	HR	TB	R	RBI	TBB	IBB	SO	HBP	SH	SF	SB	CS	SB%	GDP	Avg	OBP	SLG
1992 Oneonta	A- NYA	42	153	39	9	1	0	50	26	15	24	0	31	0	2	2	13	3	.81	2	.255	.352	.327
1993 Greensboro	A NYA	58	170	41	4	4	3	62	21	20	33	0	45	0	4	1	6	4	.60	1	.241	.363	.365
1994 Tampa	A+ NYA	94	257	61	9	2	6	92	44	33	43	1	66	2	0	2	37	9	.80	3	.237	.349	.358
1995 Norwich	AA NYA	9	33	7	3	0	0	10	4	5	7	0	11	0	0	0	2	1	.67	1	.212	.350	.303
Tampa	A+ NYA	110	384	96	15	10	4	143	70	36	72	1	100	2	9	2	28	13	.68	4	.250	.370	.372
1996 Norwich	AA NYA	6	10	3	0	0	0	3	4	3	4	0	2	0	0	0	0	0	.00	0	.300	.500	.300
Columbus	AAA NYA	61	124	28	3	2	0	35	18	9	15	0	36	1	1	0	5	2	.71	4	.226	.314	.282
1997 Norwich	AA NYA	34	89	25	5	1	2	38	18	17	13	0	21	1	2	1	5	3	.63	2	.281	.375	.427
Columbus	AAA NYA	19	49	9	2	0	2	17	6	6	2	0	18	0	0	1	2	0	1.00	1	.184	.212	.347
6 Min. YEARS		433	1269	309	50	20	17	450	211	144	213	2	330	6	18	9	98	35	.74	17	.243	.353	.355

Brian Looney

Pitches: Left **Bats:** Left **Pos:** P   **Ht:** 5'10" **Wt:** 185 **Born:** 9/26/69 **Age:** 28

Year Team	Lg Org	G	GS	CG	GF	IP	BFP	H	R	ER	HR	SH	SF	HB	TBB	IBB	SO	WP	Bk	W	L	Pct.	ShO	Sv	ERA
1991 Jamestown	A- Mon	11	11	2	0	62.1	246	42	12	8	0	2	2	0	28	0	64	6	0	7	1	.875	1	0	1.16
1992 Rockford	A Mon	17	0	0	5	31.1	141	28	13	11	0	2	0	1	23	0	34	1	0	3	1	.750	0	0	3.16
Albany	A Mon	11	11	1	0	67.1	265	51	22	16	1	1	3	0	30	0	56	4	0	3	2	.600	1	0	2.14
1993 Wst Plm Bch	A+ Mon	18	16	0	1	106	451	108	48	37	2	7	3	5	29	0	109	2	1	4	6	.400	0	0	3.14
Harrisburg	AA Mon	8	8	1	0	56.2	221	36	15	15	2	1	1	1	17	1	76	0	0	3	2	.600	1	0	2.38
1994 Ottawa	AAA Mon	27	16	0	2	124.2	565	134	71	60	10	3	6	3	67	4	90	2	0	7	7	.500	0	0	4.33
1995 Pawtucket	AAA Bos	18	18	1	0	100.2	438	106	44	39	9	2	0	3	33	0	78	7	2	4	7	.364	0	0	3.49
1996 Pawtucket	AAA Bos	27	9	1	7	82.1	357	78	55	44	14	0	2	4	27	2	78	3	0	5	6	.455	1	1	4.81
1997 Salt Lake	AAA Min	17	0	0	6	24.2	103	20	7	6	4	1	0	0	10	2	21	2	0	2	0	.000	0	0	2.19
1993 Montreal	NL	3	1	0	1	6	28	8	2	2	0	0	0	0	2	0	7	0	1	0	0	.000	0	0	3.00
1994 Montreal	NL	1	0	0	0	2	11	4	5	5	1	0	0	1	0	0	2	0	0	0	0	.000	0	0	22.50
1995 Boston	AL	3	1	0	0	4.2	29	12	9	9	1	1	2	0	4	1	2	0	0	0	1	.000	0	0	17.36
7 Min. YEARS		154	89	6	21	656	2787	603	287	236	42	19	17	17	264	9	606	27	3	36	34	.514	4	2	3.24
3 Maj. YEARS		7	2	0	1	12.2	68	24	16	16	2	1	2	1	6	1	11	0	1	0	1	.000	0	0	11.37

Braden Looper

Pitches: Right **Bats:** Right **Pos:** P   **Ht:** 6'5" **Wt:** 225 **Born:** 10/28/74 **Age:** 23

Year Team	Lg Org	G	GS	CG	GF	IP	BFP	H	R	ER	HR	SH	SF	HB	TBB	IBB	SO	WP	Bk	W	L	Pct.	ShO	Sv	ERA
1997 Pr William	A+ StL	12	12	0	0	64.1	287	71	38	32	6	1	1	3	25	0	58	1	2	3	6	.333	0	0	4.48
Arkansas	AA StL	19	0	0	14	21.1	94	24	14	14	2	1	1	1	7	2	20	1	2	1	4	.200	0	5	5.91
1 Min. YEARS		31	12	0	14	85.2	381	95	52	46	8	2	2	4	32	2	78	2	4	4	10	.286	0	5	4.83

Johann Lopez

Pitches: Right **Bats:** Right **Pos:** P   **Ht:** 6'2" **Wt:** 170 **Born:** 4/4/75 **Age:** 23

Year Team	Lg Org	G	GS	CG	GF	IP	BFP	H	R	ER	HR	SH	SF	HB	TBB	IBB	SO	WP	Bk	W	L	Pct.	ShO	Sv	ERA
1992 Astros	R Hou	17	0	0	4	34	160	42	28	17	1	1	0	3	13	0	19	7	4	1	1	.500	0	0	4.50
1994 Auburn	A- Hou	14	14	2	0	76.2	339	86	49	41	4	2	4	4	24	0	74	7	3	7	5	.583	1	0	4.81
1995 Kissimmee	A+ Hou	18	12	0	3	69	283	55	30	20	3	1	2	3	25	0	67	5	3	5	5	.500	0	1	2.61
1996 Kissimmee	A+ Hou	19	19	2	0	98.1	434	114	50	41	5	0	5	1	35	1	70	9	3	3	10	.231	1	0	3.75
1997 Jackson	AA Hou	35	19	0	6	133.2	586	131	79	65	18	7	2	6	57	3	109	11	4	6	8	.429	0	1	4.38
5 Min. YEARS		103	64	4	12	411.2	1802	428	236	184	31	11	13	17	154	4	339	39	17	22	29	.431	2	2	4.02

Jose Lopez

Bats: Right **Throws:** Right **Pos:** DH-3B   **Ht:** 6'1" **Wt:** 175 **Born:** 8/4/75 **Age:** 22

Year Team	Lg Org	G	AB	H	2B	3B	HR	TB	R	RBI	TBB	IBB	SO	HBP	SH	SF	SB	CS	SB%	GDP	Avg	OBP	SLG
1994 Mets	R NYN	45	164	53	10	1	2	71	34	31	13	0	30	2	1	8	2	1	.67	1	.323	.364	.433

Year Team	Lg Org	G	AB	H	2B	3B	HR	TB	R	RBI	TBB	IBB	SO	HBP	SH	SF	SB	CS	SB%	GDP	Avg	OBP	SLG
Kingsport	R+ NYN	4	15	4	3	0	1	10	1	1	0	0	0	0	0	0	0	0	.00	1	.267	.267	.667
1995 Capital City	A NYN	82	280	65	17	4	5	105	37	38	35	3	76	4	2	7	7	2	.78	7	.232	.319	.375
St. Lucie	A+ NYN	1	2	2	0	0	0	2	0	1	2	0	0	0	0	0	0	0	.00	0	1.000	1.000	1.000
1996 St. Lucie	A+ NYN	121	419	122	17	5	11	182	63	60	39	2	103	9	1	2	18	10	.64	7	.291	.362	.434
1997 Norfolk	AAA NYN	2	6	2	0	0	0	2	1	0	0	0	2	0	0	0	0	0	.00	0	.333	.333	.333
St. Lucie	A+ NYN	23	87	17	3	1	4	34	14	13	3	0	25	1	0	0	2	0	1.00	1	.195	.231	.391
Binghamton	AA NYN	66	207	51	10	1	11	96	31	26	13	1	63	0	0	1	4	2	.67	4	.246	.290	.464
4 Min. YEARS		344	1180	316	60	12	34	502	181	170	105	6	299	16	4	18	33	15	.69	21	.268	.331	.425

Mendy Lopez

Bats: **Right** Throws: **Right** Pos: **SS** Ht: **6'2"** Wt: **165** Born: **10/15/74** Age: **23**

Year Team	Lg Org	G	AB	H	2B	3B	HR	TB	R	RBI	TBB	IBB	SO	HBP	SH	SF	SB	CS	SB%	GDP	Avg	OBP	SLG
1994 Royals	R KC	59	235	85	19	3	5	125	56	50	22	0	27	3	2	5	19	2	.90	5	.362	.415	.532
1995 Wilmington	A+ KC	130	428	116	29	3	2	157	42	36	28	0	73	5	7	2	18	10	.64	12	.271	.322	.367
1996 Wichita	AA KC	93	327	92	20	5	6	140	47	32	26	1	67	4	2	1	14	4	.78	6	.281	.341	.428
1997 Omaha	AAA KC	17	52	12	2	0	1	17	6	6	8	0	21	0	1	0	0	0	.00	6	.231	.333	.327
Wichita	AA KC	101	357	83	16	3	5	120	56	42	36	0	70	3	5	5	7	5	.58	8	.232	.304	.336
4 Min. YEARS		400	1399	388	86	14	19	559	207	166	120	1	258	15	17	13	58	21	.73	31	.277	.338	.400

Mickey Lopez

Bats: **Both** Throws: **Right** Pos: **2B** Ht: **5'9"** Wt: **165** Born: **11/17/73** Age: **24**

Year Team	Lg Org	G	AB	H	2B	3B	HR	TB	R	RBI	TBB	IBB	SO	HBP	SH	SF	SB	CS	SB%	GDP	Avg	OBP	SLG
1995 Helena	R+ Mil	57	235	76	19	2	1	99	66	41	38	3	20	5	2	4	12	8	.60	1	.324	.426	.440
1996 Beloit	A Mil	61	236	64	10	2	0	78	35	14	28	0	36	1	10	0	12	8	.60	2	.271	.351	.331
Stockton	A+ Mil	64	217	61	10	1	0	73	30	25	23	0	36	4	9	1	6	4	.60	0	.281	.359	.336
1997 El Paso	AA Mil	134	483	145	21	10	3	195	79	58	48	2	60	5	9	5	20	10	.67	10	.300	.366	.404
3 Min. YEARS		316	1161	343	60	15	4	445	210	138	137	5	152	15	30	10	50	30	.63	19	.295	.374	.383

Pedro Lopez

Bats: **Right** Throws: **Right** Pos: **C** Ht: **6'0"** Wt: **160** Born: **3/29/69** Age: **29**

Year Team	Lg Org	G	AB	H	2B	3B	HR	TB	R	RBI	TBB	IBB	SO	HBP	SH	SF	SB	CS	SB%	GDP	Avg	OBP	SLG
1988 Padres	R SD	42	156	44	4	6	1	63	18	22	10	0	24	0	0	0	9	4	.69	2	.282	.325	.404
1989 Waterloo	A SD	97	319	61	13	1	2	82	32	26	25	1	61	4	6	1	4	4	.50	12	.191	.258	.257
1990 Chston-SC	A SD	32	101	20	2	0	0	22	9	5	7	0	18	4	0	2	0	1	.00	2	.198	.272	.218
1991 Waterloo	A SD	102	342	97	13	1	8	136	49	57	47	5	66	2	2	4	3	3	.50	4	.284	.370	.398
1992 Wichita	AA SD	96	319	78	8	4	6	112	35	48	13	0	68	7	2	6	4	3	.57	7	.245	.284	.351
1993 Rancho Cuca	A+ SD	37	103	26	10	0	1	39	25	9	24	1	19	2	0	0	1	0	.00	3	.252	.403	.379
Wichita	AA SD	50	142	29	7	0	4	48	12	14	22	2	24	1	1	0	3	0	1.00	2	.204	.315	.338
1994 Wichita	AA SD	42	131	33	7	0	1	43	15	12	15	0	16	3	1	2	0	2	.00	2	.252	.338	.328
Rancho Cuca	A+ SD	7	20	5	2	0	0	7	1	1	1	0	2	0	0	0	0	0	.00	0	.250	.286	.350
Las Vegas	AAA SD	17	47	10	2	0	1	15	3	4	1	0	7	0	1	1	0	0	.00	1	.213	.224	.319
1995 El Paso	AA Mil	84	218	68	15	2	4	99	32	28	18	1	45	4	3	0	0	3	.00	8	.312	.375	.454
New Orleans	AAA Mil	3	8	0	0	0	0	0	0	0	0	0	3	0	0	0	0	0	.00	0	.000	.000	.000
1996 El Paso	AA Mil	46	144	44	10	1	2	62	22	20	17	1	24	0	3	2	2	2	.50	2	.306	.374	.431
New Orleans	AAA Mil	34	87	19	4	0	0	23	7	3	13	1	22	0	0	0	0	0	.00	4	.218	.320	.264
1997 Kissimmee	A+ Hou	25	69	14	4	1	0	20	7	8	4	0	11	0	0	1	0	1	.00	2	.203	.243	.290
Jackson	AA Hou	27	88	26	5	0	2	37	9	13	4	0	16	1	0	0	0	1	.00	4	.295	.333	.420
10 Min. YEARS		741	2294	574	106	16	32	808	276	270	221	12	426	28	19	19	25	25	.50	57	.250	.321	.352

Billy Lott

Bats: **Right** Throws: **Right** Pos: **OF** Ht: **6'4"** Wt: **210** Born: **8/16/70** Age: **27**

Year Team	Lg Org	G	AB	H	2B	3B	HR	TB	R	RBI	TBB	IBB	SO	HBP	SH	SF	SB	CS	SB%	GDP	Avg	OBP	SLG
1989 Dodgers	R LA	46	150	39	2	4	0	39	18	9	10	0	48	1	1	0	5	1	.83	6	.193	.248	.260
1990 Bakersfield	A+ LA	38	133	27	1	1	2	36	11	14	6	0	46	1	1	1	3	2	.60	3	.203	.241	.271
Yakima	A- LA	65	240	66	13	2	4	95	37	38	10	0	62	3	0	4	4	0	1.00	1	.275	.307	.396
1991 Bakersfield	A+ LA	92	314	70	10	1	5	97	40	35	25	0	90	3	3	6	11	4	.73	6	.223	.282	.309
1992 Vero Beach	A+ LA	126	435	107	17	4	3	141	42	35	22	3	107	3	2	5	11	5	.69	18	.246	.284	.324
1993 San Antonio	AA LA	114	418	106	17	2	15	172	49	49	23	3	111	1	1	2	5	11	.31	8	.254	.293	.411
1994 San Antonio	AA LA	122	448	131	25	4	12	200	61	62	31	2	100	4	2	3	20	10	.67	7	.292	.342	.446
1995 Albuquerque	AAA LA	41	146	46	7	2	5	72	23	26	13	2	48	0	1	0	1	2	.33	5	.315	.371	.493
1996 Albuquerque	AAA LA	114	418	111	20	1	19	190	67	66	46	1	124	5	0	0	6	7	.46	6	.266	.345	.455
1997 Ottawa	AAA Mon	32	108	24	5	0	2	35	12	18	8	1	22	0	1	2	1	1	.50	5	.222	.271	.324
Calgary	AAA Pit	71	239	75	18	0	15	138	45	55	35	6	56	3	1	2	6	0	1.00	9	.314	.405	.577
9 Min. YEARS		861	3049	792	135	21	82	1215	405	407	229	18	814	24	13	25	73	43	.63	70	.260	.314	.398

Brian Lott

Pitches: **Right** Bats: **Right** Pos: **P** Ht: **6'0"** Wt: **200** Born: **5/15/72** Age: **26**

Year Team	Lg Org	G	GS	CG	GF	IP	BFP	H	R	ER	HR	SH	SF	HB	TBB	IBB	SO	WP	Bk	W	L	Pct.	ShO	Sv	ERA
1994 Princeton	R+ Cin	14	14	2	0	94	391	97	39	33	5	4	1	4	20	0	61	9	3	6	4	.600	2	0	3.16
1995 Chston-WV	A Cin	28	20	0	3	138	586	155	56	53	9	4	1	6	33	3	96	3	3	8	7	.533	0	1	3.46

Year Team	Lg Org	G	GS	CG	GF	IP	BFP	H	R	ER	HR	SH	SF	HB	TBB	IBB	SO	WP	Bk	W	L	Pct.	ShO	Sv	ERA
						HOW MUCH HE PITCHED					**WHAT HE GAVE UP**											**THE RESULTS**			
1996 Winston-Sal	A+ Cin	26	26	2	0	147.1	659	169	99	71	19	1	5	3	49	0	85	8	1	8	11	.421	0	0	4.34
1997 Chattanooga	AA Cin	25	14	0	2	91.2	429	108	76	69	21	2	8	2	50	0	62	5	0	6	7	.462	0	0	6.77
4 Min. YEARS		93	74	4	5	471	2065	529	270	226	54	11	15	15	152	3	304	25	7	28	29	.491	2	1	4.32

Kevin Lovingier

Pitches: Left Bats: Left Pos: P   Ht: 6'1" Wt: 190 Born: 8/29/71 Age: 26

Year Team	Lg Org	G	GS	CG	GF	IP	BFP	H	R	ER	HR	SH	SF	HB	TBB	IBB	SO	WP	Bk	W	L	Pct.	ShO	Sv	ERA
						HOW MUCH HE PITCHED					**WHAT HE GAVE UP**											**THE RESULTS**			
1994 New Jersey	A- StL	35	0	0	5	52.1	211	36	13	9	3	3	0	2	19	1	71	3	0	1	0	1.000	0	1	1.55
1995 Savannah	A StL	38	0	0	18	47	195	35	14	7	1	3	1	1	21	5	54	3	0	6	3	.667	0	1	1.34
St. Pete	A+ StL	22	0	0	6	21.2	82	9	4	4	0	1	1	2	10	1	14	1	0	1	0	1.000	0	0	1.66
1996 Arkansas	AA StL	60	0	0	19	63.2	295	60	30	29	4	6	2	1	48	6	73	3	0	2	3	.400	0	1	4.10
1997 Arkansas	AA StL	59	0	0	22	74.1	314	68	27	21	4	3	0	1	26	2	82	5	1	4	3	.571	0	3	2.54
4 Min. YEARS		214	0	0	70	259	1097	208	88	70	12	16	4	7	124	15	294	15	1	14	9	.609	0	6	2.43

Torey Lovullo

Bats: Both Throws: Right Pos: 3B   Ht: 6'0" Wt: 185 Born: 7/25/65 Age: 32

Year Team	Lg Org	G	AB	H	2B	3B	HR	TB	R	RBI	TBB	IBB	SO	HBP	SH	SF	SB	CS	SB%	GDP	Avg	OBP	SLG
				BATTING													**BASERUNNING**				**PERCENTAGES**		
1987 Fayetteville	A Det	55	191	49	13	0	8	86	34	32	37	4	30	2	2	1	6	0	1.00	3	.257	.381	.450
Lakeland	A+ Det	18	60	16	3	0	1	22	11	16	10	0	8	0	0	3	0	0	.00	0	.267	.356	.367
1988 Glens Falls	AA Det	78	270	74	17	1	9	120	37	50	36	3	44	1	0	6	2	0	1.00	5	.274	.355	.444
Toledo	AAA Det	57	177	41	8	1	5	66	18	20	9	0	24	0	7	1	2	1	.67	1	.232	.267	.373
1989 Toledo	AAA Det	112	409	94	23	2	10	151	48	52	44	10	57	1	7	4	2	1	.67	10	.230	.303	.369
1990 Toledo	AAA Det	141	486	131	38	1	14	213	71	58	61	6	74	4	2	4	4	1	.80	12	.270	.353	.438
1991 Columbus	AAA NYA	106	395	107	24	5	10	171	74	75	59	4	56	0	2	6	4	4	.50	10	.271	.361	.433
1992 Columbus	AAA NYA	131	468	138	33	5	19	238	69	89	64	4	65	3	2	6	9	4	.69	8	.295	.379	.509
1994 Calgary	AAA Sea	54	211	62	18	1	11	115	43	47	34	1	28	1	2	2	2	1	.67	3	.294	.391	.545
1995 Buffalo	AAA Cle	132	474	121	20	5	16	199	84	61	70	7	62	2	1	5	3	1	.75	12	.255	.350	.420
1996 Edmonton	AAA Oak	26	93	26	4	0	4	42	18	19	18	1	12	1	1	1	0	0	.00	3	.280	.398	.452
1997 Ottawa	AAA Mon	28	64	9	3	0	0	12	6	6	6	0	13	1	0	1	0	0	.00	1	.141	.222	.188
Buffalo	AAA Cle	97	321	73	18	0	12	127	40	40	51	5	64	2	1	5	0	0	.00	6	.227	.332	.396
1988 Detroit	AL	12	21	8	1	1	1	14	2	2	1	0	2	0	1	0	0	0	.00	1	.381	.409	.667
1989 Detroit	AL	29	87	10	2	0	1	15	8	4	14	0	20	0	1	2	0	0	.00	3	.115	.233	.172
1991 New York	AL	22	51	9	2	0	0	11	0	2	5	1	7	0	3	0	0	0	.00	0	.176	.250	.216
1993 California	AL	116	367	92	20	0	6	130	42	30	36	1	49	1	3	2	7	6	.54	8	.251	.318	.354
1994 Seattle	AL	36	72	16	5	0	2	27	9	7	9	1	13	0	0	0	1	0	1.00	2	.222	.309	.375
1996 Oakland	AL	65	82	18	4	0	3	31	15	9	11	0	17	2	3	1	1	2	.33	0	.220	.323	.378
10 Min. YEARS		1035	3619	941	222	21	119	1562	553	565	499	45	537	18	27	45	34	18	.65	76	.260	.349	.432
6 Maj. YEARS		280	680	153	34	1	13	228	76	54	76	3	108	3	11	5	9	8	.53	14	.225	.304	.335

Benny Lowe

Pitches: Left Bats: Left Pos: P   Ht: 5'10" Wt: 185 Born: 6/13/74 Age: 24

Year Team	Lg Org	G	GS	CG	GF	IP	BFP	H	R	ER	HR	SH	SF	HB	TBB	IBB	SO	WP	Bk	W	L	Pct.	ShO	Sv	ERA
						HOW MUCH HE PITCHED					**WHAT HE GAVE UP**											**THE RESULTS**			
1994 Blue Jays	R Tor	22	1	0	5	22.1	104	20	16	11	0	4	0	2	14	1	27	1	1	2	1	.667	0	1	4.43
1995 St. Cathrns	A- Tor	15	15	0	0	78.2	358	89	43	38	3	3	3	9	40	0	61	10	1	4	5	.444	0	0	4.35
1996 Hagerstown	A Tor	46	1	0	34	65.2	289	40	24	17	2	2	1	7	52	0	89	2	0	2	3	.400	0	9	2.33
1997 Knoxville	AA Tor	18	0	0	8	26	124	33	21	16	6	1	1	2	14	1	29	2	2	3	1	.750	0	0	5.54
Dunedin	A+ Tor	13	0	0	13	14.2	57	7	3	3	0	0	1	1	3	0	19	1	0	2	1	.667	0	5	1.84
Hagerstown	A Tor	2	0	0	2	2	10	3	3	3	0	0	0	0	0	0	4	0	0	0	0	.000	0	0	0.00
4 Min. YEARS		116	17	0	62	209.1	942	192	110	85	11	10	6	21	123	2	229	16	4	13	11	.542	0	15	3.65

Mike Lowell

Bats: Right Throws: Right Pos: 3B   Ht: 6'4" Wt: 195 Born: 2/24/74 Age: 24

Year Team	Lg Org	G	AB	H	2B	3B	HR	TB	R	RBI	TBB	IBB	SO	HBP	SH	SF	SB	CS	SB%	GDP	Avg	OBP	SLG
				BATTING													**BASERUNNING**				**PERCENTAGES**		
1995 Oneonta	A- NYA	72	281	73	18	0	1	94	36	27	23	0	34	3	0	6	3	1	.75	5	.260	.316	.335
1996 Greensboro	A NYA	113	433	122	33	0	8	179	58	64	46	0	43	4	2	2	10	3	.77	7	.282	.355	.413
Tampa	A+ NYA	24	78	22	5	0	0	27	8	11	3	0	13	0	1	3	1	1	.50	2	.282	.298	.346
1997 Norwich	AA NYA	78	285	98	17	0	15	160	60	47	48	1	30	4	1	5	2	1	.67	11	.344	.439	.561
Columbus	AAA NYA	57	210	58	13	1	15	118	36	45	23	0	34	3	1	6	2	4	.33	6	.276	.347	.562
3 Min. YEARS		344	1287	373	86	1	39	578	198	194	143	1	154	14	5	22	18	10	.64	31	.290	.362	.449

Lou Lucca

Bats: Right Throws: Right Pos: 3B   Ht: 5'11" Wt: 210 Born: 10/13/70 Age: 27

Year Team	Lg Org	G	AB	H	2B	3B	HR	TB	R	RBI	TBB	IBB	SO	HBP	SH	SF	SB	CS	SB%	GDP	Avg	OBP	SLG
				BATTING													**BASERUNNING**				**PERCENTAGES**		
1992 Erie	A- Fla	76	263	74	16	1	13	131	51	44	33	0	40	5	0	2	6	3	.67	8	.281	.370	.498
1993 Kane County	A Fla	127	419	116	25	2	6	163	52	53	60	0	58	9	2	7	4	10	.29	9	.277	.374	.389
1994 Brevard Cty	A+ Fla	130	441	125	29	1	8	180	62	76	72	2	73	4	0	6	3	7	.30	18	.283	.384	.408
1995 Portland	AA Fla	112	388	107	28	1	9	164	57	64	59	5	77	5	0	2	4	4	.50	18	.276	.377	.423
1996 Charlotte	AAA Fla	87	273	71	14	1	7	108	26	35	11	0	62	4	0	3	0	3	.00	11	.260	.296	.396
1997 Charlotte	AAA Fla	96	292	83	22	1	18	161	40	51	22	4	56	2	0	3	5	4	.56	7	.284	.335	.551
6 Min. YEARS		628	2076	576	134	7	61	907	288	323	257	11	366	29	2	23	22	31	.42	71	.277	.361	.437

Robert Luce

Pitches: Right Bats: Both Pos: P   Ht: 6'0" Wt: 168 Born: 7/19/74 Age: 23

Year Team	Lg Org	G	GS	CG	GF	IP	BFP	H	R	ER	HR	SH	SF	HB	TBB	IBB	SO	WP	Bk	W	L	Pct.	ShO	Sv	ERA
1996 Everett	A- Sea	23	0	0	16	41	187	45	26	20	6	3	1	1	16	1	47	6	1	3	4	.429	0	7	4.39
1997 Lancaster	A+ Sea	14	14	0	0	86.1	372	100	43	27	8	0	2	5	24	0	57	4	0	10	1	.909	0	0	2.81
Memphis	AA Sea	13	13	1	0	75.2	315	90	40	33	5	2	0	1	14	0	41	3	0	5	2	.714	0	0	3.93
2 Min. YEARS		50	27	1	16	203	874	235	109	80	19	5	3	7	54	1	145	13	1	18	7	.720	0	7	3.55

Larry Luebbers

Pitches: Right Bats: Right Pos: P   Ht: 6'6" Wt: 205 Born: 10/11/69 Age: 28

Year Team	Lg Org	G	GS	CG	GF	IP	BFP	H	R	ER	HR	SH	SF	HB	TBB	IBB	SO	WP	Bk	W	L	Pct.	ShO	Sv	ERA
1990 Billings	R+ Cin	13	13	1	0	72.1	319	74	46	36	3	2	3	6	31	0	48	7	1	5	4	.556	1	0	4.48
1991 Cedar Rapds	A Cin	28	28	3	0	184.2	781	177	85	64	8	12	6	10	64	5	98	11	4	8	10	.444	0	0	3.12
1992 Cedar Rapds	A Cin	14	14	1	0	82.1	355	71	33	24	2	4	3	8	33	0	56	1	1	7	0	1.000	0	0	2.62
Chattanooga	AA Cin	14	14	1	0	87.1	368	86	34	22	5	2	1	4	34	1	56	5	2	6	5	.545	0	0	2.27
1993 Indianapolis	AAA Cin	15	15	0	0	84.1	380	81	45	39	7	6	2	6	47	5	51	1	0	4	7	.364	0	0	4.16
1994 Iowa	AAA ChN	27	26	0	0	138.2	630	149	100	93	22	4	7	5	87	3	90	7	4	10	12	.455	0	0	6.04
1995 Chattanooga	AA Cin	28	21	0	4	118	514	112	71	61	7	6	6	7	59	1	87	1	0	10	6	.625	0	0	4.65
1996 Chattanooga	AA Cin	11	11	0	0	69.1	292	64	32	28	6	3	1	3	26	0	38	5	0	3	5	.375	0	0	3.63
Indianapolis	AAA Cin	14	11	0	0	71.1	301	76	44	31	8	1	2	1	23	2	35	1	0	5	4	.556	0	0	3.91
1997 Richmond	AAA Atl	27	26	2	1	144	634	180	101	86	20	2	6	3	44	2	91	6	0	3	14	.176	0	0	5.38
1993 Cincinnati	NL	14	14	0	0	77.1	332	74	49	39	7	4	5	1	38	3	38	4	0	2	5	.286	0	0	4.54
8 Min. YEARS		191	179	8	5	1052.1	4574	1070	591	484	88	42	37	53	448	19	650	45	12	61	67	.477	1	0	4.14

Rob Lukachyk

Bats: Left Throws: Right Pos: OF   Ht: 6'0" Wt: 175 Born: 7/24/68 Age: 29

Year Team	Lg Org	G	AB	H	2B	3B	HR	TB	R	RBI	TBB	IBB	SO	HBP	SH	SF	SB	CS	SB%	GDP	Avg	OBP	SLG
1987 White Sox	R ChA	17	54	12	1	1	0	15	6	7	9	2	13	0	0	0	5	1	.83	1	.222	.333	.278
1988 Utica	A- ChA	71	227	64	10	8	7	111	42	48	31	1	48	3	2	1	9	6	.60	2	.282	.374	.489
1989 South Bend	A ChA	122	430	125	16	4	3	158	60	63	35	7	78	2	5	6	18	15	.55	5	.291	.342	.367
1990 Sarasota	A+ ChA	118	428	104	23	9	4	157	56	36	31	4	88	2	4	4	17	8	.68	6	.243	.295	.367
1991 Sarasota	A+ ChA	125	399	108	27	2	9	166	63	49	63	4	100	15	9	2	22	8	.73	2	.271	.388	.416
1992 Stockton	A+ Mil	105	359	99	21	14	15	193	77	81	53	3	86	9	0	5	44	15	.75	0	.276	.378	.538
1993 New Orleans	AAA Mil	8	24	4	1	0	2	11	5	6	3	0	6	0	2	0	0	0	.00	0	.167	.259	.458
El Paso	AA Mil	113	362	96	24	7	9	161	58	63	52	3	75	7	2	5	8	10	.44	10	.265	.364	.445
1994 Bowie	AA Bal	108	371	107	19	6	10	168	68	54	47	9	60	5	1	5	33	6	.85	5	.288	.371	.453
1995 Toledo	AAA Det	104	346	88	24	7	7	147	43	26	33	0	75	2	3	3	8	5	.62	5	.254	.320	.425
1996 Harrisburg	AA Mon	27	92	30	6	0	5	51	22	24	12	0	18	0	1	4	4	1	.80	0	.326	.400	.554
Ottawa	AAA Mon	70	246	65	15	4	9	115	38	39	13	1	54	0	3	2	10	2	.83	4	.264	.307	.467
1997 Harrisburg	AA Mon	42	153	42	6	3	7	75	26	26	11	0	26	3	1	1	5	3	.63	2	.275	.333	.490
Ottawa	AAA Mon	82	286	71	16	1	12	125	39	39	32	3	69	3	1	1	18	5	.78	10	.248	.329	.437
1996 Montreal	NL	2	2	0	0	0	0	0	0	0	0	0	1	0	0	0	0	0	.00	0	.000	.000	.000
11 Min. YEARS		1112	3777	1015	209	66	99	1653	603	561	425	37	796	54	33	36	201	85	.70	52	.269	.348	.438

Mark Lukasiewicz

Pitches: Left Bats: Left Pos: P   Ht: 6'5" Wt: 230 Born: 3/8/73 Age: 25

Year Team	Lg Org	G	GS	CG	GF	IP	BFP	H	R	ER	HR	SH	SF	HB	TBB	IBB	SO	WP	Bk	W	L	Pct.	ShO	Sv	ERA
1994 Hagerstown	A Tor	29	17	0	5	98	449	108	70	52	8	6	4	7	51	0	84	8	0	3	6	.333	0	0	4.78
1995 Dunedin	A+ Tor	31	13	0	11	88.1	383	80	62	55	13	1	2	7	42	0	71	7	0	3	6	.333	0	1	5.60
1996 Dunedin	A+ Tor	23	0	0	5	31.1	144	28	20	16	1	1	1	4	22	1	31	1	0	2	1	.667	0	1	4.60
Bakersfield	A+ Tor	7	0	0	3	12.2	66	17	14	13	2	1	0	1	11	0	9	1	0	0	2	.000	0	0	9.24
Hagerstown	A Tor	9	1	0	4	15.2	63	8	5	4	0	0	0	1	7	0	20	1	0	2	0	1.000	0	0	2.30
1997 Knoxville	AA Tor	27	0	0	8	37	149	26	17	15	2	1	1	1	14	1	43	4	0	2	0	1.000	0	7	3.65
Syracuse	AAA Tor	30	0	0	9	31.1	146	37	22	18	7	1	2	2	13	1	31	1	0	2	3	.400	0	0	5.17
4 Min. YEARS		156	31	0	45	314.1	1400	304	210	173	33	11	10	23	160	3	289	23	0	14	18	.438	0	9	4.95

Matt Luke

Bats: Left Throws: Left Pos: OF   Ht: 6'5" Wt: 220 Born: 2/26/71 Age: 27

Year Team	Lg Org	G	AB	H	2B	3B	HR	TB	R	RBI	TBB	IBB	SO	HBP	SH	SF	SB	CS	SB%	GDP	Avg	OBP	SLG
1992 Oneonta	A- NYA	69	271	67	11	7	2	98	30	34	19	3	32	2	0	3	4	1	.80	9	.247	.298	.362
1993 Greensboro	A NYA	135	549	157	37	5	21	267	83	91	47	4	79	7	0	6	11	3	.79	9	.286	.346	.486
1994 Albany-Colo	AA NYA	63	236	67	11	2	8	106	34	40	28	0	50	2	3	1	6	4	.60	6	.284	.363	.449
Tampa	A+ NYA	57	222	68	11	2	16	131	52	42	28	2	27	1	0	1	4	1	.80	7	.306	.385	.590
1995 Norwich	AA NYA	93	365	95	17	5	8	146	48	53	20	2	68	2	3	4	5	4	.56	6	.260	.299	.400
Columbus	AAA NYA	23	77	23	4	1	3	38	11	12	2	0	12	1	1	0	1	1	.50	3	.299	.325	.494
1996 Tampa	A+ NYA	2	7	2	0	0	0	2	1	1	1	0	1	0	0	0	0	0	.00	0	.286	.375	.286
Columbus	AAA NYA	74	264	74	14	2	19	149	46	70	17	0	52	6	1	5	1	1	.50	9	.280	.332	.564
1997 Columbus	AAA NYA	87	337	77	19	3	8	126	42	45	29	1	64	4	0	3	0	0	.00	9	.228	.296	.374
1996 New York	AL	1	0	0	0	0	0	0	0	0	0	0	0	0	0	0	0	0	.00	0	.000	.000	.000
6 Min. YEARS			603	2328	630	124	27	85	1063	347	388	191	12	385	25	8	21	32	18	.64	58	.271	.330	.457

David Lundquist

Pitches: Right Bats: Right Pos: P Ht: 6'2" Wt: 200 Born: 6/4/73 Age: 25

Year Team	Lg Org	HOW MUCH HE PITCHED						WHAT HE GAVE UP												THE RESULTS					
		G	GS	CG	GF	IP	BFP	H	R	ER	HR	SH	SF	HB	TBB	IBB	SO	WP	Bk	W	L	Pct.	ShO	Sv	ERA
1993 White Sox	R ChA	11	10	0	0	63	267	70	26	22	0	1	1	4	15	0	40	2	2	5	3	.625	0	0	3.14
1994 Hickory	A ChA	27	27	3	0	178.2	759	170	88	69	15	4	3	12	43	0	133	8	2	13	10	.565	2	0	3.48
1995 South Bend	A ChA	18	18	5	0	118	492	107	54	47	4	7	3	5	38	0	60	3	0	8	4	.667	1	0	3.58
1996 White Sox	R ChA	3	3	0	0	13.2	49	8	4	4	1	0	0	0	2	0	16	0	0	1	1	.500	0	0	2.63
Pr William	A+ ChA	5	5	0	0	27	125	31	17	17	2	1	1	0	14	1	23	2	1	0	2	.000	0	0	5.67
1997 Winston-Sal	A+ ChA	20	6	0	6	48	228	65	41	36	7	1	2	3	23	3	39	2	2	3	1	.750	0	0	6.75
Birmingham	AA ChA	7	0	0	5	13.1	73	26	20	13	3	0	1	0	5	0	15	0	0	0	0	.000	0	0	8.78
5 Min. YEARS		91	69	8	11	461.2	1993	477	250	208	32	14	10	25	140	4	326	17	7	30	21	.588	3	0	4.05

Keith Luuloa

Bats: Right Throws: Right Pos: 2B Ht: 6'1" Wt: 175 Born: 12/24/74 Age: 23

Year Team	Lg Org	BATTING																BASERUNNING				PERCENTAGES		
		G	AB	H	2B	3B	HR	TB	R	RBI	TBB	IBB	SO	HBP	SH	SF		SB	CS	SB%	GDP	Avg	OBP	SLG
1994 Angels	R Ana	28	97	29	4	1	1	38	14	10	8	0	14	4	1	3		3	4	.43	0	.299	.366	.392
1995 Lk Elsinore	A+ Ana	102	380	100	22	7	5	151	50	53	24	0	47	6	7	1		1	5	.17	9	.263	.316	.397
1996 Midland	AA Ana	134	531	138	24	2	7	187	80	44	47	0	54	6	8	3		4	6	.40	14	.260	.325	.352
1997 Midland	AA Ana	120	421	115	29	5	9	181	67	59	36	0	59	5	10	6		7	4	.64	18	.273	.333	.430
4 Min. YEARS		384	1429	382	79	15	22	557	211	166	115	0	174	21	26	13		15	19	.44	41	.267	.328	.390

Ryan Luzinski

Bats: Right Throws: Right Pos: C Ht: 6'1" Wt: 215 Born: 8/22/73 Age: 24

Year Team	Lg Org	BATTING																BASERUNNING				PERCENTAGES		
		G	AB	H	2B	3B	HR	TB	R	RBI	TBB	IBB	SO	HBP	SH	SF		SB	CS	SB%	GDP	Avg	OBP	SLG
1992 Great Falls	R+ LA	61	227	57	14	4	4	91	26	29	22	2	47	2	0	1		2	1	.67	1	.251	.321	.401
1993 Bakersfield	A+ LA	48	147	41	10	1	3	62	18	9	13	0	24	5	0	0		2	2	.50	3	.279	.358	.422
Yakima	A- LA	69	237	61	10	3	4	89	32	46	41	4	44	4	3	3		6	1	.86	2	.257	.372	.376
1994 Vero Beach	A+ LA	112	379	99	18	3	11	156	48	61	33	1	91	5	1	5		2	1	.67	11	.261	.325	.412
1995 San Antonio	AA LA	44	144	33	5	0	1	41	18	9	13	1	32	3	2	1		1	1	.50	6	.229	.304	.285
Vero Beach	A+ LA	38	134	45	12	0	5	72	15	23	9	3	21	0	0	1		1	0	1.00	4	.336	.375	.537
1996 Albuquerque	AAA LA	9	14	2	0	0	0	2	0	1	0	0	6	0	0	0		0	0	.00	1	.143	.143	.143
San Antonio	AA LA	32	103	30	6	0	0	36	12	10	11	0	19	1	1	0		2	1	1.00	6	.291	.365	.350
San Berndno	A+ LA	30	118	41	10	0	5	66	24	21	11	0	33	0	2	1		6	1	.86	2	.347	.400	.559
1997 Frederick	A+ Bal	1	3	2	0	0	0	2	1	0	1	0	0	0	0	0		0	0	.00	0	.667	.750	.667
Bowie	AA Bal	30	81	23	4	0	5	42	12	15	10	1	17	0	0	0		3	0	1.00	1	.284	.363	.519
Rochester	AAA Bal	42	125	26	7	1	2	41	12	16	19	0	49	3	1	1		0	1	.00	5	.208	.324	.328
6 Min. YEARS		516	1712	460	96	12	40	700	218	240	183	12	383	23	10	13		25	8	.76	41	.269	.345	.409

Curt Lyons

Pitches: Right Bats: Right Pos: P Ht: 6'5" Wt: 240 Born: 10/17/74 Age: 23

Year Team	Lg Org	HOW MUCH HE PITCHED						WHAT HE GAVE UP												THE RESULTS					
		G	GS	CG	GF	IP	BFP	H	R	ER	HR	SH	SF	HB	TBB	IBB	SO	WP	Bk	W	L	Pct.	ShO	Sv	ERA
1992 Princeton	R+ Cin	11	11	0	0	55.1	240	61	36	17	4	1	2	4	17	0	33	6	1	5	3	.625	0	0	2.77
1993 Billings	R+ Cin	15	12	2	0	84	353	89	36	28	3	2	2	3	20	0	64	10	0	7	3	.700	0	0	3.00
1994 Chston-WV	A Cin	12	11	0	0	65.1	276	64	30	28	2	1	1	8	22	0	55	12	0	3	6	.333	0	0	3.86
Princeton	R+ Cin	4	4	0	0	27.1	104	16	9	6	0	1	0	2	2	0	28	2	0	1	1	.500	0	0	1.98
1995 Winston-Sal	A+ Cin	26	26	0	0	160.1	672	139	66	53	10	6	2	15	67	3	122	9	3	9	9	.500	0	0	2.98
1996 Chattanooga	AA Cin	24	24	1	0	141.2	577	113	48	38	8	1	1	10	52	0	176	6	0	13	4	.765	0	0	2.41
1997 Iowa	AAA ChN	8	8	0	0	29.2	145	35	23	21	8	0	0	4	21	0	26	2	0	0	2	.000	0	0	6.37
Orlando	AA ChN	2	2	0	0	6	26	6	5	5	0	0	1	1	2	0	8	1	0	0	0	.000	0	0	7.50
1996 Cincinnati	NL	3	3	0	0	16	70	17	8	8	1	0	0	1	7	0	14	0	0	2	0	1.000	0	0	4.50
6 Min. YEARS		102	98	3	0	569.2	2393	523	252	196	35	12	9	47	203	3	512	48	4	38	28	.576	0	0	3.10

Kevin Maas

Bats: Left Throws: Left Pos: DH Ht: 6'3" Wt: 209 Born: 1/20/65 Age: 33

Year Team	Lg Org	BATTING																BASERUNNING				PERCENTAGES		
		G	AB	H	2B	3B	HR	TB	R	RBI	TBB	IBB	SO	HBP	SH	SF		SB	CS	SB%	GDP	Avg	OBP	SLG
1986 Oneonta	A- NYA	28	101	36	10	0	0	46	14	18	7	1	9	0	0	1		5	1	.83	1	.356	.394	.455
1987 Ft. Laud	A+ NYA	116	439	122	28	4	11	191	77	73	53	4	108	2	0	8		14	4	.78	5	.278	.353	.435
1988 Pr William	A+ NYA	29	108	32	7	0	12	75	24	35	17	1	28	4	0	4		3	1	.75	0	.296	.398	.694
Albany-Colo	AA NYA	109	392	98	14	3	16	166	66	55	64	4	103	4	3	2		5	1	.83	5	.263	.376	.446
1989 Columbus	AAA NYA	83	291	93	23	2	6	138	42	45	40	0	73	1	0	4		2	3	.40	5	.320	.399	.474
1990 Columbus	AAA NYA	57	194	55	15	2	13	113	37	38	34	1	45	0	0	4		2	2	.50	5	.284	.390	.582
1993 Columbus	AAA NYA	28	104	29	6	0	4	47	14	18	19	2	22	1	0	1		0	1	.00	1	.279	.392	.452
1994 Wichita	AA SD	4	15	8	3	0	3	20	4	8	3	0	0	0	0	0		0	0	.00	1	.533	.611	1.333
Las Vegas	AAA SD	29	90	22	6	2	4	44	15	12	9	0	25	1	0	1		0	1	1.00	1	.244	.317	.489
Indianapols	AAA Cin	78	283	82	18	2	19	161	55	45	29	0	49	2	1	3		2	3	.40	4	.290	.356	.569
1995 Yankees	R NYA	2	9	4	0	0	1	7	1	3	0	0	0	0	0	0		0	0	.00	1	.444	.444	.778
Columbus	AAA NYA	44	161	45	7	2	9	83	28	33	23	0	40	2	0	2		0	0	.00	2	.280	.372	.516
1996 New Orleans	AAA Mil	36	117	30	8	0	8	62	18	22	14	2	18	1	0	1		0	0	.00	2	.256	.338	.530
1997 Indianapols	AAA Cin	31	67	15	4	0	2	25	14	7	25	2	15	2	0	1		0	0	.00	0	.224	.442	.373
New Orleans	AAA Hou	55	193	42	19	1	5	78	24	27	23	2	41	1	0	3		0	0	.00	3	.218	.303	.404
1990 New York	AL	79	254	64	9	0	21	136	42	41	43	10	76	3	0	0		1	2	.33	4	.252	.367	.535
1991 New York	AL	148	500	110	14	1	23	195	69	63	83	3	128	4	0	5		5	1	.83	4	.220	.333	.390
1992 New York	AL	98	286	71	12	0	11	116	35	35	25	4	63	0	0	4		3	1	.75	1	.248	.305	.406

(continued)

Year Team	Lg Org	G	AB	H	2B	3B	HR	TB	R	RBI	TBB	IBB	SO	HBP	SH	SF	SB	CS	SB%	GDP	Avg	OBP	SLG
1993 New York	AL	59	151	31	4	0	9	62	20	25	24	2	32	1	0	1	1	1	.50	2	.205	.316	.411
1995 Minnesota	AL	22	57	11	4	0	1	18	5	7	2	2	11	0	0	0	0	0	.00	4	.193	.281	.316
10 Min. YEARS		729	2544	713	168	18	113	1256	433	439	360	19	576	21	4	29	34	16	.68	31	.280	.370	.494
5 Maj. YEARS		406	1248	287	43	1	65	527	171	169	182	21	310	8	0	10	10	5	.67	13	.230	.329	.422

Chris Macca

Pitches: Right **Bats:** Right **Pos:** P **Ht:** 6'2" **Wt:** 185 **Born:** 11/14/74 **Age:** 23

Year Team	Lg Org	G	GS	CG	GF	IP	BFP	H	R	ER	HR	SH	SF	HB	TBB	IBB	SO	WP	Bk	W	L	Pct.	ShO	Sv	ERA
1995 Portland	A- Col	24	0	0	16	35.2	152	25	15	13	1	2	2	6	17	1	41	6	0	3	2	.600	0	5	3.28
1996 Asheville	A Col	26	0	0	25	33.2	132	18	5	4	2	1	0	3	11	1	46	2	1	1	1	.500	0	15	1.07
New Haven	AA Col	28	0	0	28	33.2	135	18	6	5	0	2	1	2	18	2	33	2	0	3	1	.750	0	15	1.34
1997 New Haven	AA Col	46	0	0	32	44	172	47	40	38	3	1	3	7	55	1	29	8	0	0	4	.000	0	9	7.77
3 Min. YEARS		124	0	0	101	147	656	108	66	60	6	6	6	18	101	5	149	18	1	7	8	.467	0	44	3.67

Fausto Macey

Pitches: Right **Bats:** Right **Pos:** P **Ht:** 6'4" **Wt:** 185 **Born:** 10/9/75 **Age:** 22

Year Team	Lg Org	G	GS	CG	GF	IP	BFP	H	R	ER	HR	SH	SF	HB	TBB	IBB	SO	WP	Bk	W	L	Pct.	ShO	Sv	ERA
1994 Zanesville	R SF	9	9	0	0	50	194	37	14	12	0	2	2	0	8	0	26	1	0	2	2	.500	0	0	2.16
Everett	A- SF	5	5	0	0	27.2	120	30	12	11	1	1	0	0	8	0	22	1	2	2	2	.667	0	0	3.58
1995 San Jose	A+ SF	28	25	1	0	171	709	167	84	74	17	7	5	6	50	1	94	6	4	8	9	.471	0	0	3.89
1996 Shreveport	AA SF	27	26	1	0	157	673	165	86	75	22	4	5	8	47	0	62	7	2	10	7	.588	0	0	4.30
1997 Vancouver	AAA Ana	9	8	0	0	40	197	47	39	36	9	1	2	3	32	1	23	4	1	1	3	.250	0	0	8.10
Midland	AA Ana	17	17	1	0	96.1	464	141	93	86	15	3	7	7	46	1	38	5	2	6	9	.400	0	0	8.03
4 Min. YEARS		95	90	3	0	542	2357	587	328	294	64	18	21	24	191	3	265	24	11	29	31	.483	0	0	4.88

Chris Madonna

Bats: Left **Throws:** Right **Pos:** C **Ht:** 5'11" **Wt:** 190 **Born:** 3/13/73 **Age:** 25

Year Team	Lg Org	G	AB	H	2B	3B	HR	TB	R	RBI	TBB	IBB	SO	HBP	SH	SF	SB	CS	SB%	GDP	Avg	OBP	SLG
1994 Zanesville	IND —	49	139	29	5	0	1	37	20	22	33	1	26	1	0	1	12	5	.71	3	.209	.362	.266
1995 St. Lucie	A+ NYN	3	5	0	0	0	0	0	0	0	0	0	1	0	0	0	0	0	.00	0	.000	.000	.000
1996 Tri-City	IND —	63	150	41	11	3	4	70	21	22	17	1	36	0	2	2	1	1	.50	2	.273	.343	.467
1997 Trenton	AA Bos	14	41	14	3	0	0	17	7	6	6	0	11	0	0	0	2	2	.50	1	.341	.426	.415
Michigan	A Bos	16	34	5	2	0	0	7	4	1	6	0	9	1	0	1	1	0	1.00	0	.147	.286	.206
4 Min. YEARS		145	369	89	21	3	5	131	52	51	62	2	83	2	2	4	16	8	.67	6	.241	.350	.355

Katsuhiro Maeda

Pitches: Right **Bats:** Right **Pos:** P **Ht:** 6'2" **Wt:** 215 **Born:** 6/23/71 **Age:** 27

Year Team	Lg Org	G	GS	CG	GF	IP	BFP	H	R	ER	HR	SH	SF	HB	TBB	IBB	SO	WP	Bk	W	L	Pct.	ShO	Sv	ERA
1996 Yankees	R NYA	2	2	1	0	9	35	4	3	3	1	0	1	1	2	0	7	0	0	1	1	.500	1	0	3.00
Tampa	A+ NYA	2	2	0	0	10.2	50	5	5	0	1	0	2	6	0	8	0	0	0	0	0	.000	0	0	4.22
Norwich	AA NYA	9	9	1	0	53.1	221	49	25	24	4	1	2	8	21	0	30	4	0	3	2	.600	1	0	4.05
1997 Norwich	AA NYA	25	21	1	2	124.1	545	117	75	63	14	4	2	8	62	1	76	11	2	8	10	.444	1	0	4.56
2 Min. YEARS		38	34	3	2	197.1	851	181	108	95	19	6	5	12	91	1	121	15	2	12	13	.480	3	0	4.33

Ricky Magdaleno

Bats: Right **Throws:** Right **Pos:** SS **Ht:** 6'1" **Wt:** 170 **Born:** 7/6/74 **Age:** 23

Year Team	Lg Org	G	AB	H	2B	3B	HR	TB	R	RBI	TBB	IBB	SO	HBP	SH	SF	SB	CS	SB%	GDP	Avg	OBP	SLG
1993 Chston-WV	A Cin	131	447	107	15	4	3	139	49	25	37	0	103	1	6	1	8	8	.50	15	.239	.298	.311
1994 Winston-Sal	A+ Cin	127	437	114	22	2	13	179	52	49	49	1	80	0	2	4	7	9	.44	9	.261	.333	.410
1995 Chattanooga	AA Cin	11	40	7	2	0	1	12	2	2	4	0	13	0	0	0	0	0	.00	1	.175	.250	.300
Winston-Sal	A+ Cin	91	309	69	13	1	7	105	30	40	15	0	69	2	3	3	3	1	.75	4	.223	.261	.340
Indianapls	AAA Cin	4	8	1	0	0	0	1	1	1	0	0	3	0	1	0	0	0	.00	0	.125	.125	.500
1996 Chattanooga	AA Cin	132	424	94	21	1	17	168	60	63	64	4	135	1	5	4	2	7	.22	8	.222	.323	.396
1997 Chattanooga	AA Cin	61	187	49	13	1	8	88	33	34	42	1	51	1	1	1	1	1	.50	11	.262	.398	.471
Indianapls	AAA Cin	56	155	32	11	0	4	55	20	14	16	0	48	0	1	2	0	1	.00	4	.206	.277	.355
5 Min. YEARS		613	2007	473	97	9	54	750	247	228	227	6	502	5	19	15	21	27	.44	54	.236	.313	.374

Danny Magee

Bats: Right **Throws:** Right **Pos:** 3B **Ht:** 6'2" **Wt:** 175 **Born:** 11/25/74 **Age:** 23

Year Team	Lg Org	G	AB	H	2B	3B	HR	TB	R	RBI	TBB	IBB	SO	HBP	SH	SF	SB	CS	SB%	GDP	Avg	OBP	SLG
1993 Braves	R Atl	16	60	17	4	1	1	26	14	8	5	0	12	8	0	0	4	0	1.00	0	.283	.411	.433
Danville	R+ Atl	10	37	9	1	0	0	10	4	1	0	0	10	1	0	0	3	0	1.00	1	.243	.263	.270
1994 Macon	A Atl	111	357	97	17	2	1	121	29	34	18	0	71	8	1	4	12	8	.60	5	.272	.318	.339
1995 Durham	A+ Atl	76	266	68	11	1	4	93	38	29	11	0	46	12	1	0	7	5	.58	5	.256	.315	.350
1996 Durham	A+ Atl	95	344	103	19	3	12	164	59	40	20	0	70	14	4	1	17	5	.77	6	.299	.361	.477
1997 Greenville	AA Atl	7	22	6	0	0	1	9	1	3	1	0	6	1	0	0	0	1	.00	1	.273	.333	.409
5 Min. YEARS		315	1086	300	52	7	19	423	145	115	55	0	215	44	6	5	43	19	.69	18	.276	.335	.390

153

Alan Mahaffey

Pitches: Left Bats: Left Pos: P
Ht: 6'3" Wt: 200 Born: 2/2/74 Age: 24

Year Team	Lg Org	G	GS	CG	GF	IP	BFP	H	R	ER	HR	SH	SF	HB	TBB	IBB	SO	WP	Bk	W	L	Pct.	ShO	Sv	ERA
1995 Elizabethtn	R+ Min	13	12	1	0	70	308	66	42	27	4	6	2	3	21	0	73	4	8	5	6	.455	0	0	3.47
1996 Ft. Wayne	A Min	30	19	2	1	126.1	545	139	84	68	13	8	6	3	35	1	75	4	7	7	10	.412	0	0	4.84
1997 Ft. Myers	A+ Min	38	0	0	11	48.1	200	46	27	22	2	3	2	1	8	0	55	1	0	1	2	.333	0	1	4.10
New Britain	AA Min	13	1	0	5	22.2	98	19	11	9	2	1	3	0	10	0	29	4	0	1	2	.333	0	1	3.57
3 Min. YEARS		94	32	3	17	267.1	1151	270	164	126	21	18	13	7	74	1	232	13	15	14	20	.412	0	2	4.24

John Mahalik

Bats: Right Throws: Right Pos: 2B
Ht: 6'2" Wt: 190 Born: 7/28/71 Age: 26

Year Team	Lg Org	G	AB	H	2B	3B	HR	TB	R	RBI	TBB	IBB	SO	HBP	SH	SF	SB	CS	SB%	GDP	Avg	OBP	SLG
1993 Butte	R+ —	74	258	70	15	0	1	88	25	27	21	0	51	0	1	1	8	0	1.00	8	.271	.325	.341
1994 Burlington	A Mon	9	30	5	0	0	0	5	1	3	1	0	5	0	1	0	0	1	.00	0	.167	.194	.167
Wst Plm Bch	A+ Mon	63	161	43	9	2	0	56	30	12	29	0	20	4	4	2	4	4	.50	4	.267	.388	.348
1995 Binghamton	AA NYN	67	187	42	6	1	5	65	19	19	19	1	34	1	5	1	1	1	.50	6	.225	.298	.348
1996 Norfolk	AAA NYN	8	17	4	0	0	0	4	1	0	0	0	1	0	1	0	0	0	.00	0	.235	.235	.235
Binghamton	AA NYN	78	216	52	11	2	3	76	37	22	27	0	35	2	6	3	6	2	.75	3	.241	.327	.352
1997 Binghamton	AA NYN	74	189	41	12	0	1	56	19	18	11	1	39	4	2	2	2	3	.40	6	.217	.272	.296
5 Min. YEARS		373	1058	257	53	5	10	350	132	101	108	2	185	11	20	9	21	11	.66	27	.243	.317	.331

Mike Mahoney

Bats: Right Throws: Right Pos: C
Ht: 6'0" Wt: 185 Born: 12/5/72 Age: 25

Year Team	Lg Org	G	AB	H	2B	3B	HR	TB	R	RBI	TBB	IBB	SO	HBP	SH	SF	SB	CS	SB%	GDP	Avg	OBP	SLG
1995 Eugene	A- Atl	43	112	27	6	0	1	36	14	15	15	1	17	3	1	1	6	2	.75	5	.241	.344	.321
1996 Durham	A+ Atl	101	363	94	24	2	9	149	52	46	23	0	64	7	4	4	4	3	.57	6	.259	.312	.410
1997 Greenville	AA Atl	87	298	68	17	0	8	109	46	46	28	1	75	3	5	2	1	0	1.00	10	.228	.299	.366
3 Min. YEARS		231	773	189	47	2	18	294	112	107	66	2	156	13	10	7	11	5	.69	23	.245	.312	.380

Dalton Maine

Pitches: Right Bats: Right Pos: P
Ht: 6'3" Wt: 185 Born: 3/22/72 Age: 26

Year Team	Lg Org	G	GS	CG	GF	IP	BFP	H	R	ER	HR	SH	SF	HB	TBB	IBB	SO	WP	Bk	W	L	Pct.	ShO	Sv	ERA
1995 Frederick	A+ Bal	19	0	0	10	22	98	20	10	9	2	0	1	2	11	0	21	5	0	1	1	.500	0	0	3.68
Bluefield	R+ Bal	1	0	0	1	4	18	7	5	5	2	0	0	1	0	0	2	0	0	0	1	.000	0	0	11.25
Orioles	R Bal	18	0	0	6	30.1	122	24	7	7	0	0	1	0	9	1	32	1	0	1	0	1.000	0	2	2.08
1996 Bakersfield	A+ Bal	23	2	0	18	47.1	204	42	25	17	4	2	0	1	14	0	58	5	2	2	3	.400	0	6	3.23
Bowie	AA Bal	11	0	0	5	21.1	98	24	14	12	3	2	0	2	11	0	18	0	2	0	1	.000	0	0	5.06
High Desert	A+ Bal	10	0	0	6	12	45	8	2	2	1	0	2	0	2	0	9	1	0	1	0	1.000	0	2	1.50
1997 Orioles	R Bal	2	0	0	1	3	9	1	0	0	0	0	0	0	0	0	4	0	0	0	0	.000	0	1	0.00
Bowie	AA Bal	9	0	0	5	12.2	45	4	0	0	0	0	0	1	6	1	11	2	0	0	0	.000	0	0	0.00
3 Min. YEARS		93	2	0	52	152.2	639	130	63	52	12	4	4	7	53	2	155	14	4	5	6	.455	0	11	3.07

Scott Makarewicz

Bats: Right Throws: Right Pos: C
Ht: 6'0" Wt: 200 Born: 3/1/67 Age: 31

Year Team	Lg Org	G	AB	H	2B	3B	HR	TB	R	RBI	TBB	IBB	SO	HBP	SH	SF	SB	CS	SB%	GDP	Avg	OBP	SLG
1989 Auburn	A- Hou	61	216	52	17	0	4	81	22	24	14	0	43	4	5	1	2	0	1.00	1	.241	.298	.375
1990 Osceola	A+ Hou	94	343	95	12	2	4	123	35	49	21	0	63	4	8	3	0	1	.00	11	.277	.323	.359
Columbus	AA Hou	28	85	20	1	0	2	27	5	11	10	2	14	1	0	2	0	1	.00	3	.235	.316	.318
1991 Jackson	AA Hou	76	229	53	9	0	2	68	23	30	18	5	36	8	0	3	1	4	.20	7	.231	.306	.297
1992 Jackson	AA Hou	105	345	99	15	0	7	135	39	39	23	3	62	6	3	5	2	2	.50	4	.287	.338	.391
1993 Jackson	AA Hou	92	285	70	14	1	7	107	31	35	17	2	51	8	1	3	1	1	.50	7	.246	.304	.375
1994 Tucson	AAA Hou	63	171	49	10	1	3	70	24	32	13	0	28	4	6	1	0	0	.00	5	.287	.349	.409
1995 Tucson	AAA Hou	62	192	51	9	0	5	75	21	31	10	3	23	2	2	2	1	0	1.00	9	.266	.306	.391
1996 Jacksnville	AA Det	83	258	81	16	1	14	141	42	49	18	2	46	7	3	3	4	3	.57	9	.314	.371	.547
1997 Toledo	AAA Det	100	340	80	15	1	7	118	34	38	14	0	68	6	3	3	0	5	.00	13	.235	.275	.347
9 Min. YEARS		764	2464	650	118	6	55	945	276	338	158	17	434	50	31	26	11	17	.39	71	.264	.318	.384

Marty Malloy

Bats: Left Throws: Right Pos: 2B
Ht: 5'10" Wt: 160 Born: 7/6/72 Age: 25

Year Team	Lg Org	G	AB	H	2B	3B	HR	TB	R	RBI	TBB	IBB	SO	HBP	SH	SF	SB	CS	SB%	GDP	Avg	OBP	SLG
1992 Idaho Falls	R+ Atl	62	251	79	18	1	2	105	45	28	11	0	43	2	0	1	8	4	.67	2	.315	.347	.418
1993 Macon	A Atl	109	376	110	19	3	2	141	55	36	39	3	70	2	3	3	24	8	.75	4	.293	.360	.375
1994 Durham	A+ Atl	118	428	113	22	1	6	155	53	35	52	2	69	2	2	3	18	12	.60	9	.264	.344	.362
1995 Greenville	AA Atl	124	461	128	20	3	10	184	73	59	39	1	58	0	7	8	11	12	.48	6	.278	.329	.399
1996 Richmond	AAA Atl	18	64	13	2	1	0	17	7	8	5	1	7	2	0	1	3	0	1.00	1	.203	.257	.266
Greenville	AA Atl	111	429	134	27	2	4	177	82	36	54	6	50	4	6	2	11	10	.52	11	.312	.393	.413
1997 Richmond	AAA Atl	108	414	118	19	5	2	153	66	25	41	1	61	1	5	0	17	7	.71	6	.285	.351	.370
6 Min. YEARS		650	2423	695	127	16	26	932	381	227	241	14	358	11	25	18	92	53	.63	39	.287	.352	.385

Dwight Maness

Bats: Right **Throws:** Right **Pos:** OF   **Ht:** 6'3" **Wt:** 180 **Born:** 4/3/74 **Age:** 24

									BATTING									BASERUNNING				PERCENTAGES		
Year Team	Lg Org	G	AB	H	2B	3B	HR	TB	R	RBI	TBB	IBB	SO	HBP	SH	SF	SB	CS	SB%	GDP	Avg	OBP	SLG
1992 Dodgers	R LA	44	139	35	6	3	0	47	24	12	14	0	36	8	3	3	18	9	.67	1	.252	.348	.338
1993 Vero Beach	A+ LA	118	409	106	21	4	6	153	57	42	32	0	105	15	8	7	22	13	.63	3	.259	.330	.374
1994 San Antonio	AA LA	57	215	47	5	5	5	77	32	20	25	0	54	6	2	0	15	16	.48	1	.219	.317	.358
Bakersfield	A+ LA	74	248	62	13	1	3	86	38	26	29	3	67	11	5	5	21	9	.70	1	.250	.348	.347
1995 San Antonio	AA LA	57	179	40	2	3	5	63	29	24	20	0	44	5	5	2	4	6	.40	3	.223	.316	.352
Vero Beach	A+ LA	43	143	33	3	0	3	45	16	23	11	0	29	6	2	5	13	5	.72	2	.231	.303	.315
St. Lucie	A+ NYN	14	44	9	4	0	0	13	4	5	7	0	6	0	1	0	1	2	.33	0	.205	.314	.295
1996 Binghamton	AA NYN	130	399	97	14	7	6	143	65	47	52	2	80	8	7	5	25	8	.76	2	.243	.338	.358
1997 St. Lucie	A+ NYN	45	179	53	9	2	3	75	29	19	12	0	29	3	0	0	12	6	.67	1	.296	.351	.419
Binghamton	AA NYN	74	259	49	13	3	5	83	33	31	24	1	73	5	4	2	4	4	.50	2	.189	.269	.320
6 Min. YEARS		656	2214	531	90	28	36	785	327	249	226	6	523	67	37	29	135	78	.63	16	.240	.325	.355

David Manning

Pitches: Right **Bats:** Right **Pos:** P   **Ht:** 6'3" **Wt:** 205 **Born:** 8/14/71 **Age:** 26

		HOW MUCH HE PITCHED						WHAT HE GAVE UP										THE RESULTS					
Year Team	Lg Org	G	GS	CG	GF	IP	BFP	H	R	ER	HR	SH	SF	HB	TBB	IBB	SO	WP	Bk	W	L	Pct.	ShO	Sv	ERA
1992 Butte	R+ Tex	8	7	0	0	25.1	143	50	41	31	4	1	0	3	15	0	13	6	5	0	4	.000	0	0	11.01
Rangers	R Tex	5	3	0	0	16.1	75	22	13	11	0	1	0	1	4	0	9	1	0	1	1	.500	0	0	6.06
1993 Chston-SC	A Tex	37	10	0	8	116	495	119	69	60	5	4	3	6	39	4	83	11	3	6	7	.462	0	2	3.03
1994 Charlotte	A+ Tex	20	20	0	0	97	438	119	69	60	5	4	3	6	39	0	46	8	3	4	11	.267	0	0	5.57
1995 Charlotte	A+ Tex	26	20	0	2	128.2	545	127	56	50	7	3	3	3	46	0	66	0	5	9	5	.643	0	0	3.50
1996 Okla City	AAA Tex	1	1	0	0	5	21	6	3	3	0	0	1	0	2	0	1	0	0	0	0	.000	0	0	5.40
Tulsa	AA Tex	39	5	0	13	91	394	89	36	33	5	3	5	2	45	6	48	5	0	6	5	.545	0	3	3.26
1997 Tulsa	AA Tex	13	12	1	1	75.2	324	77	46	41	8	2	3	0	27	0	55	5	0	4	7	.364	0	0	4.88
Okla City	AAA Tex	5	5	1	0	28.2	130	33	17	14	6	0	0	2	9	0	15	1	0	1	3	.250	0	0	4.40
Charlotte	A+ Tex	1	1	0	0	6	26	4	1	1	1	0	0	0	4	0	4	0	0	0	0	.000	0	0	1.50
6 Min. YEARS		155	84	2	24	589.2	2591	639	336	283	39	19	20	24	230	10	340	37	16	31	43	.419	0	5	4.32

Derek Manning

Pitches: Left **Bats:** Left **Pos:** P   **Ht:** 6'4" **Wt:** 220 **Born:** 7/21/70 **Age:** 27

		HOW MUCH HE PITCHED						WHAT HE GAVE UP										THE RESULTS					
Year Team	Lg Org	G	GS	CG	GF	IP	BFP	H	R	ER	HR	SH	SF	HB	TBB	IBB	SO	WP	Bk	W	L	Pct.	ShO	Sv	ERA
1993 Sou. Oregon	A- Oak	15	13	2	0	79.1	322	71	35	32	5	2	3	3	21	2	63	3	4	5	4	.556	2	0	3.63
1994 W Michigan	A Oak	29	23	2	4	154	617	120	52	39	4	7	1	3	42	0	118	3	3	11	7	.611	1	2	2.28
1995 Huntsville	AA Oak	5	5	0	0	28	114	26	14	14	4	1	0	0	7	0	22	0	0	1	2	.333	0	0	4.50
Modesto	A+ Oak	25	12	0	4	111	467	112	43	30	7	6	4	1	25	0	102	3	1	10	1	.909	0	3	2.43
1996 Huntsville	AA Oak	18	12	0	1	72	324	96	59	54	10	2	3	1	22	1	51	2	4	0	4	.000	0	1	6.75
1997 Huntsville	AA Oak	21	0	0	8	44	195	57	31	29	7	1	3	1	12	0	27	2	0	1	2	.333	0	2	5.93
5 Min. YEARS		113	65	4	17	488.1	2039	482	234	198	37	19	14	9	129	3	383	13	12	28	20	.583	3	8	3.65

Len Manning

Pitches: Left **Bats:** Left **Pos:** P   **Ht:** 6'2" **Wt:** 195 **Born:** 12/30/71 **Age:** 26

		HOW MUCH HE PITCHED						WHAT HE GAVE UP										THE RESULTS					
Year Team	Lg Org	G	GS	CG	GF	IP	BFP	H	R	ER	HR	SH	SF	HB	TBB	IBB	SO	WP	Bk	W	L	Pct.	ShO	Sv	ERA
1994 Martinsvle	R+ Phi	15	4	1	1	45	208	40	26	18	3	0	4	3	32	2	57	10	2	2	4	.333	0	0	3.60
1995 Piedmont	A Phi	27	26	1	0	160	658	130	68	47	10	7	5	7	58	0	154	4	2	10	10	.500	0	0	2.64
1996 Clearwater	A+ Phi	20	18	1	1	102.1	448	94	51	42	6	5	1	4	63	1	77	10	1	3	7	.300	0	0	3.69
1997 Clearwater	A+ Phi	5	0	0	2	6	22	2	0	0	0	0	0	0	0	0	7	1	0	0	0	.000	0	0	0.00
Reading	AA Phi	28	7	0	8	62.1	295	66	40	37	4	2	2	7	46	0	41	3	1	3	1	.750	0	0	5.34
4 Min. YEARS		95	55	3	12	375.2	1631	332	185	144	23	14	12	21	199	3	336	28	6	18	22	.450	0	0	3.45

Matt Mantei

Pitches: Right **Bats:** Right **Pos:** P   **Ht:** 6'1" **Wt:** 181 **Born:** 7/7/73 **Age:** 24

		HOW MUCH HE PITCHED						WHAT HE GAVE UP										THE RESULTS					
Year Team	Lg Org	G	GS	CG	GF	IP	BFP	H	R	ER	HR	SH	SF	HB	TBB	IBB	SO	WP	Bk	W	L	Pct.	ShO	Sv	ERA
1991 Mariners	R Sea	17	5	0	4	40.1	202	54	40	30	0	2	3	1	28	2	28	7	8	1	5	.167	0	0	6.69
1992 Mariners	R Sea	3	3	0	0	16	68	18	10	10	1	0	0	0	5	0	19	0	0	1	1	.500	0	0	5.63
1993 Bellingham	A- Sea	26	0	0	21	25.2	120	26	19	17	2	4	0	1	15	0	34	4	0	1	1	.500	0	12	5.96
1994 Appleton	A Sea	48	0	0	43	48	201	42	14	11	2	2	2	1	21	3	70	6	0	5	1	.833	0	26	2.06
1995 Portland	AA Fla	8	0	0	4	11.1	48	10	3	3	0	1	0	1	5	0	15	0	0	1	0	1.000	0	1	2.38
Charlotte	AAA Fla	6	0	0	1	7	27	1	3	2	1	0	1	0	5	0	10	0	0	0	0	.000	0	2	2.57
1996 Charlotte	AAA Fla	7	0	0	6	7.2	36	6	4	4	1	0	1	0	7	0	8	3	0	0	2	.000	0	2	4.70
1997 Brevard Cty	A+ Tor	4	0	0	0	6	27	4	4	4	1	0	0	0	6	0	11	1	0	0	0	.000	0	0	6.00
Portland	AA Fla	5	0	0	1	4	21	1	3	3	0	1	0	0	8	0	7	0	0	1	0	1.000	0	0	6.75
1995 Florida	NL	12	0	0	3	13.1	64	12	8	7	1	1	1	0	13	0	15	1	0	0	1	.000	0	0	4.73
1996 Florida	NL	14	0	0	1	18.1	89	13	13	13	2	1	0	1	21	1	25	2	0	1	0	1.000	0	0	6.38
7 Min. YEARS		124	8	0	80	166	750	162	100	84	8	10	7	5	100	5	202	21	8	10	11	.476	0	41	4.55
2 Maj. YEARS		26	0	0	4	31.2	153	25	21	20	3	2	1	1	34	1	40	3	0	1	1	.500	0	0	5.68

Ravelo Manzanillo

Pitches: Left **Bats:** Left **Pos:** P **Ht:** 5'10" **Wt:** 195 **Born:** 10/17/63 **Age:** 34

Year Team	Lg Org	G	GS	CG	GF	IP	BFP	H	R	ER	HR	SH	SF	HB	TBB	IBB	SO	WP	Bk	W	L	Pct.	ShO	Sv	ERA
1984 Nashua	AA Pit	14	13	2	0	74.1	333	56	40	35	6	3	2	1	62	1	50	6	1	4	4	.500	1	0	4.24
1985 Nashua	AA Pit	33	17	2	10	123.1	553	99	70	64	4	10	8	3	96	3	62	11	0	6	10	.375	0	5	4.67
1988 Tampa	A+ ChA	24	20	2	3	130.1	526	93	53	44	2	1	2	4	49	0	140	10	10	10	6	.625	2	0	3.04
1989 Birmingham	AA ChA	22	22	0	0	129.1	557	105	66	56	11	5	6	6	72	0	89	2	8	8	7	.533	0	0	3.90
1990 Vancouver	AAA ChA	38	6	0	18	92.1	394	74	41	37	2	4	2	3	60	1	64	3	3	7	3	.700	0	4	3.61
1991 Syracuse	AAA Tor	12	0	0	4	23.2	108	26	10	9	3	0	1	0	14	0	20	4	1	3	0	1.000	0	1	3.42
1995 Calgary	AAA Pit	8	1	0	0	12	65	23	18	17	4	0	1	1	10	0	2	1	3	0	2	.000	0	0	12.75
1997 Tacoma	AAA Sea	18	0	0	11	29	138	34	22	21	2	1	0	2	22	2	25	2	2	2	1	.667	0	1	6.52
1988 Chicago	AL	2	2	0	0	9.1	46	7	6	6	1	0	0	1	12	0	10	1	0	0	1	.000	0	0	5.79
1994 Pittsburgh	NL	46	0	0	11	50	236	45	30	23	4	2	5	3	42	5	39	2	5	4	2	.667	0	1	4.14
1995 Pittsburgh	NL	5	0	0	0	3.2	16	3	3	2	0	0	0	1	2	0	1	0	0	0	0	.000	0	0	4.91
8 Min. YEARS		169	79	8	46	614.1	2674	510	320	283	34	24	22	20	385	7	452	39	28	40	33	.548	3	11	4.15
3 Maj. YEARS		53	2	0	11	63	298	55	39	31	5	2	5	5	56	5	50	3	5	4	3	.571	0	1	4.43

Del Marine

Bats: Right **Throws:** Right **Pos:** C **Ht:** 6'0" **Wt:** 205 **Born:** 10/18/71 **Age:** 26

Year Team	Lg Org	G	AB	H	2B	3B	HR	TB	R	RBI	TBB	IBB	SO	HBP	SH	SF	SB	CS	SB%	GDP	Avg	OBP	SLG
1992 Bristol	R+ Det	50	163	41	8	0	2	55	18	23	26	0	42	3	0	2	2	0	1.00	7	.252	.361	.337
1993 Fayetteville	A Det	25	75	21	7	0	0	28	4	4	16	0	25	0	0	0	1	0	1.00	1	.280	.407	.373
Niagara Fal	A- Det	55	182	48	12	0	7	81	29	32	20	0	48	3	0	1	5	5	.50	2	.264	.345	.445
1994 Fayetteville	A Det	85	284	73	18	0	7	112	32	33	30	1	55	6	1	2	4	6	.40	7	.257	.339	.394
1995 Lakeland	A+ Det	77	257	62	14	0	4	88	27	25	13	0	63	5	0	3	5	1	.83	3	.241	.288	.342
1996 Visalia	A+ Det	105	378	97	20	1	16	167	58	69	47	1	121	10	0	7	8	2	.80	6	.257	.348	.442
1997 Jacksnville	AA Det	99	328	78	22	1	12	138	45	43	48	1	92	7	0	1	1	0	.00	11	.238	.346	.421
6 Min. YEARS		496	1667	420	101	2	48	669	213	229	200	3	446	34	1	16	25	15	.63	37	.252	.341	.401

Jesus Marquez

Bats: Left **Throws:** Left **Pos:** OF **Ht:** 6'0" **Wt:** 175 **Born:** 3/12/73 **Age:** 25

Year Team	Lg Org	G	AB	H	2B	3B	HR	TB	R	RBI	TBB	IBB	SO	HBP	SH	SF	SB	CS	SB%	GDP	Avg	OBP	SLG
1992 Mariners	R Sea	40	148	40	4	3	2	56	20	21	14	1	21	1	1	0	9	3	.75	1	.270	.337	.378
1993 Riverside	A+ Sea	12	39	12	2	0	0	14	3	6	6	0	9	0	1	0	2	2	.50	1	.308	.400	.359
Appleton	A Sea	61	216	59	7	1	4	80	23	27	13	2	47	2	1	2	5	3	.63	6	.273	.318	.370
Jacksnville	AA Sea	11	32	10	0	0	2	16	7	5	9	1	9	2	1	1	3	2	.60	0	.313	.477	.500
1994 Appleton	A Sea	76	276	80	9	3	3	104	37	34	22	1	44	1	1	4	9	9	.50	2	.290	.340	.377
1995 Riverside	A+ Sea	84	312	74	9	2	2	93	42	26	18	0	62	4	2	4	4	5	.44	5	.237	.284	.298
1996 Lancaster	A+ Sea	126	490	147	31	10	20	258	84	106	45	1	78	9	4	9	19	8	.70	5	.300	.363	.527
1997 Jacksnville	AA Det	114	465	124	24	4	12	192	56	74	22	2	77	3	3	5	9	5	.64	12	.267	.301	.413
6 Min. YEARS		524	1978	546	86	23	45	813	272	299	149	8	347	22	14	25	60	37	.62	32	.276	.330	.411

Kenny Marrero

Pitches: Right **Bats:** Right **Pos:** P **Ht:** 6'3" **Wt:** 208 **Born:** 5/13/70 **Age:** 28

Year Team	Lg Org	G	GS	CG	GF	IP	BFP	H	R	ER	HR	SH	SF	HB	TBB	IBB	SO	WP	Bk	W	L	Pct.	ShO	Sv	ERA
1994 Jamestown	A- Det	27	0	0	15	55.1	222	43	14	13	3	5	1	2	18	2	54	4	1	4	1	.800	0	8	2.11
1995 Lakeland	A+ Det	37	0	0	18	55.2	239	54	28	23	5	1	2	0	28	1	46	6	1	1	4	.200	0	5	3.72
1996 Lakeland	A+ Det	34	0	0	13	66.2	282	60	26	17	1	0	2	1	25	1	82	6	0	0	3	.000	0	0	2.30
1997 Jacksnville	AA Det	37	0	0	12	64.1	275	45	32	21	4	2	0	1	37	1	60	2	0	4	3	.571	0	0	2.94
4 Min. YEARS		135	0	0	58	242	1018	202	100	74	13	8	5	4	108	5	242	18	2	9	11	.450	0	13	2.75

Oreste Marrero

Bats: Left **Throws:** Left **Pos:** OF **Ht:** 6'0" **Wt:** 195 **Born:** 10/31/69 **Age:** 28

Year Team	Lg Org	G	AB	H	2B	3B	HR	TB	R	RBI	TBB	IBB	SO	HBP	SH	SF	SB	CS	SB%	GDP	Avg	OBP	SLG
1987 Helena	R+ Mil	51	154	50	8	2	7	83	30	34	18	3	31	1	1	0	2	1	.67	1	.325	.399	.539
1988 Beloit	A Mil	19	52	9	2	0	1	14	5	7	3	0	16	0	0	0	0	1	.00	0	.173	.218	.269
Helena	R+ Mil	67	240	85	15	0	16	148	52	44	42	2	48	0	1	1	3	4	.43	4	.354	.449	.617
1989 Beloit	A Mil	14	40	5	1	0	0	6	1	3	3	0	20	0	0	1	1	0	1.00	0	.125	.182	.150
Brewers	R Mil	10	44	18	0	1	3	29	13	16	2	0	5	0	0	1	2	2	.50	0	.409	.426	.659
Boise	A- Mil	54	203	56	8	1	11	99	38	43	30	3	60	0	0	4	1	2	.33	3	.276	.363	.488
1990 Beloit	A Mil	119	400	110	25	1	16	185	59	55	45	3	107	0	0	1	8	4	.67	12	.275	.348	.463
1991 Stockton	A+ Mil	123	438	110	15	2	13	168	63	61	57	8	98	0	1	7	4	5	.44	5	.251	.333	.384
Stockton	A+ Mil	18	54	10	2	1	0	17	8	8	4	0	13	0	0	1	1	0	1.00	0	.185	.237	.315
1992 El Paso	AA Mil	76	254	67	17	0	7	105	35	51	44	6	49	1	1	1	3	2	.60	0	.276	.388	.432
1993 Harrisburg	AA Mon	85	255	85	18	1	10	135	39	49	22	2	46	0	3	4	3	3	.50	2	.333	.381	.529
1994 Ottawa	AAA Mon	88	254	62	14	7	7	111	41	31	29	1	56	0	1	2	1	1	.50	5	.244	.319	.437
1995 San Antonio	AA LA	125	445	115	25	3	21	209	60	86	64	5	98	3	0	3	5	2	.71	4	.258	.353	.470
Albuquerque	AAA LA	7	23	8	2	0	2	16	5	6	1	0	5	0	0	0	0	0	.00	0	.348	.375	.696
1996 Albuquerque	AAA LA	121	441	125	29	1	13	195	50	76	36	1	119	1	0	4	2	6	.25	12	.283	.336	.442
1997 Albuquerque	AAA LA	96	263	69	20	0	9	116	38	42	24	2	70	0	0	1	1	1	.50	8	.262	.323	.441
1993 Montreal	NL	32	81	17	5	1	1	27	10	4	14	0	16	0	0	0	1	3	.25	0	.210	.326	.333
1996 Los Angeles	NL	10	8	3	1	0	0	4	2	1	1	0	3	0	0	0	0	0	.00	0	.375	.444	.500
11 Min. YEARS		1073	3549	984	201	20	137	1636	537	612	424	36	841	6	8	31	37	34	.52	56	.277	.353	.461

			BATTING														BASERUNNING				PERCENTAGES		
Year Team	Lg Org	G	AB	H	2B	3B	HR	TB	R	RBI	TBB	IBB	SO	HBP	SH	SF	SB	CS	SB%	GDP	Avg	OBP	SLG
2 Maj. YEARS		42	89	20	6	1	1	31	12	5	15	0	19	0	0	0	1	3	.25	0	.225	.337	.348

Jeff Martin

Pitches: Right **Bats:** Right **Pos:** P **Ht:** 6'2" **Wt:** 195 **Born:** 3/28/73 **Age:** 25

		HOW MUCH HE PITCHED						WHAT HE GAVE UP											THE RESULTS				
Year Team	Lg Org	G	GS	CG	GF	IP	BFP	H	R	ER	HR	SH	SF	HB	TBB	IBB	SO	WP	Bk	W	L	Pct.	ShO	Sv	ERA
1991 Giants	R SF	12	10	0	1	54	244	58	40	34	3	0	4	1	22	0	41	1	4	1	4	.200	0	1	5.67
1992 Giants	R SF	13	13	1	0	72	291	65	31	25	0	1	2	2	13	0	64	6	1	7	3	.700	1	0	3.13
Everett	A- SF	1	1	0	0	2.1	16	6	8	7	0	0	0	1	2	0	1	2	0	0	1	.000	0	0	27.00
1993 Everett	A- SF	25	0	0	13	54	224	38	22	18	4	6	2	4	20	2	44	3	0	5	5	.500	0	4	3.00
1994 Clinton	A SF	55	0	0	50	89	372	81	34	28	3	5	4	6	24	6	104	7	2	5	5	.500	0	20	2.83
San Jose	A+ SF	1	0	0	0	2	7	1	0	0	0	0	0	0	0	0	2	0	0	0	0	.000	0	0	0.00
1995 San Jose	A+ SF	36	0	0	28	71	305	60	34	26	5	5	2	3	25	3	63	1	0	5	6	.455	0	5	3.30
1996 San Jose	A+ SF	42	0	0	17	60.1	268	52	36	31	4	4	3	4	29	3	54	6	1	4	4	.333	0	3	4.62
1997 San Jose	A+ SF	20	0	0	14	26.2	125	36	18	16	2	2	1	3	11	3	25	1	0	0	4	.000	0	6	5.40
Shreveport	AA SF	26	0	0	10	38	160	33	20	18	3	1	2	2	15	2	24	3	0	0	2	.000	0	1	4.26
7 Min. YEARS		231	24	1	134	469.1	2012	430	243	203	24	24	20	26	161	19	422	30	8	25	34	.424	1	40	3.89

Jim Martin

Bats: Left **Throws:** Right **Pos:** OF **Ht:** 6'1" **Wt:** 210 **Born:** 12/10/70 **Age:** 27

			BATTING														BASERUNNING				PERCENTAGES		
Year Team	Lg Org	G	AB	H	2B	3B	HR	TB	R	RBI	TBB	IBB	SO	HBP	SH	SF	SB	CS	SB%	GDP	Avg	OBP	SLG
1992 Great Falls	R+ LA	56	204	63	5	7	5	97	37	30	28	2	52	7	0	3	8	2	.80	0	.309	.405	.475
1993 Bakersfield	A+ LA	118	441	114	17	3	12	173	60	50	45	2	131	13	0	4	27	12	.69	3	.259	.342	.392
1994 Bakersfield	A+ LA	93	360	96	15	8	12	163	50	58	36	3	90	7	0	2	37	16	.70	3	.267	.343	.453
San Antonio	AA LA	29	101	22	8	0	1	33	7	10	8	0	23	0	0	0	3	5	.38	1	.218	.275	.327
1995 San Antonio	AA LA	95	327	77	20	3	4	115	43	36	36	2	83	5	0	4	18	10	.64	4	.235	.317	.352
Albuquerque	AAA LA	25	75	19	3	1	1	27	8	7	8	0	20	0	0	0	3	3	.50	3	.253	.325	.360
1996 San Antonio	AA LA	38	114	24	6	1	1	35	9	8	9	1	42	3	0	2	2	2	.50	2	.211	.281	.307
San Berndno	AA LA	50	152	37	1	1	6	58	26	23	16	1	53	1	3	2	9	4	.69	1	.243	.316	.382
1997 Binghamton	AA NYN	36	90	21	2	0	8	47	17	14	16	0	37	2	0	0	6	4	.60	0	.233	.361	.522
Norfolk	AAA NYN	37	104	26	4	2	3	43	10	18	8	2	44	1	1	1	5	2	.71	0	.250	.307	.413
Jackson	AA Hou	39	117	32	4	1	7	59	15	22	16	0	42	5	0	1	8	4	.67	0	.274	.381	.504
6 Min. YEARS		616	2085	531	85	27	60	850	282	276	226	13	617	44	4	19	126	64	.66	17	.255	.337	.408

Lincoln Martin

Bats: Both **Throws:** Right **Pos:** OF **Ht:** 5'10" **Wt:** 170 **Born:** 10/20/71 **Age:** 26

			BATTING														BASERUNNING				PERCENTAGES		
Year Team	Lg Org	G	AB	H	2B	3B	HR	TB	R	RBI	TBB	IBB	SO	HBP	SH	SF	SB	CS	SB%	GDP	Avg	OBP	SLG
1993 Bluefield	R+ Bal	64	245	67	15	6	0	100	50	34	44	1	52	5	1	4	26	7	.79	5	.273	.389	.408
1994 Frederick	A+ Bal	102	341	83	15	6	2	116	64	37	52	1	62	6	12	2	15	5	.75	8	.243	.352	.340
1995 High Desert	A+ Bal	54	150	36	7	2	1	50	27	12	28	0	37	0	4	2	7	4	.64	2	.240	.356	.333
1996 Frederick	A+ Bal	114	421	112	17	7	2	149	77	31	50	2	66	8	7	2	22	7	.76	9	.266	.353	.354
1997 Bowie	AA Bal	12	24	7	2	0	0	9	3	3	3	0	2	0	0	0	0	1	.00	0	.292	.370	.375
Frederick	A+ Bal	79	253	49	6	5	2	71	42	23	33	0	52	1	9	2	11	2	.85	3	.194	.287	.281
5 Min. YEARS		425	1434	354	62	20	13	495	263	140	210	4	271	20	33	12	81	26	.76	27	.247	.348	.345

Eddy Martinez

Bats: Right **Throws:** Right **Pos:** SS **Ht:** 6'2" **Wt:** 150 **Born:** 10/23/77 **Age:** 20

			BATTING														BASERUNNING				PERCENTAGES		
Year Team	Lg Org	G	AB	H	2B	3B	HR	TB	R	RBI	TBB	IBB	SO	HBP	SH	SF	SB	CS	SB%	GDP	Avg	OBP	SLG
1995 Bluefield	R+ Bal	57	185	57	11	3	1	77	42	35	23	0	42	5	1	1	5	5	.50	1	.308	.397	.416
1996 Frederick	A+ Bal	74	244	54	4	0	2	64	21	25	21	0	48	2	1	1	13	8	.62	5	.221	.287	.262
Bluefield	R+ Bal	37	122	27	3	0	1	33	18	15	13	0	29	2	3	0	15	5	.75	1	.221	.307	.270
1997 Bowie	AA Bal	16	45	7	3	0	0	10	3	1	6	0	12	0	3	0	2	0	1.00	0	.156	.255	.222
Frederick	A+ Bal	54	174	42	6	0	1	51	14	14	19	0	43	2	3	2	6	7	.46	9	.241	.320	.293
Rochester	AAA Bal	12	27	2	1	0	0	3	0	3	1	0	8	0	1	0	0	0	.00	0	.074	.107	.111
3 Min. YEARS		250	797	189	28	3	5	238	98	93	83	0	182	11	12	4	41	25	.62	16	.237	.316	.299

Gabby Martinez

Bats: Right **Throws:** Right **Pos:** SS **Ht:** 6'2" **Wt:** 170 **Born:** 1/7/74 **Age:** 24

			BATTING														BASERUNNING				PERCENTAGES		
Year Team	Lg Org	G	AB	H	2B	3B	HR	TB	R	RBI	TBB	IBB	SO	HBP	SH	SF	SB	CS	SB%	GDP	Avg	OBP	SLG
1992 Brewers	R Mil	48	165	43	7	2	0	54	29	24	12	0	19	3	2	2	7	5	.58	3	.261	.319	.327
1993 Beloit	A Mil	94	285	69	14	5	0	93	40	24	14	0	52	1	15	4	22	10	.69	4	.242	.276	.326
1994 Stockton	A+ Mil	112	364	90	18	3	0	114	37	32	17	1	66	4	4	4	19	11	.63	8	.247	.285	.313
1995 Stockton	A+ Mil	64	213	55	13	3	1	77	25	20	10	0	25	2	9	3	13	6	.68	6	.258	.294	.362
El Paso	AA Mil	44	133	37	3	2	0	44	13	11	2	0	22	2	3	1	5	1	.83	2	.278	.297	.331
1997 Yankees	R NYA	2	5	2	0	0	1	5	3	2	1	0	0	0	0	0	2	0	1.00	0	.400	.500	1.000
Norwich	AA NYA	77	312	100	12	5	6	140	49	54	11	0	44	5	10	3	21	6	.78	5	.321	.350	.449
5 Min. YEARS		441	1477	396	67	20	8	527	196	167	67	1	228	17	43	17	89	39	.70	24	.268	.304	.357

Greg Martinez

Bats: Both **Throws:** Right **Pos:** OF　　　　**Ht:** 5'10" **Wt:** 168 **Born:** 1/27/72 **Age:** 26

Year Team	Lg Org	G	AB	H	2B	3B	HR	TB	R	RBI	TBB	IBB	SO	HBP	SH	SF	SB	CS	SB%	GDP	Avg	OBP	SLG
1993 Brewers	R Mil	5	19	12	0	0	0	12	6	3	4	0	0	1	0	0	7	1	.88	0	.632	.708	.632
Helena	R+ Mil	52	183	53	4	2	0	61	45	19	30	0	26	6	3	5	30	6	.83	0	.290	.397	.333
1994 Beloit	A Mil	81	224	62	8	1	0	72	39	20	25	1	32	3	6	1	27	11	.71	4	.277	.356	.321
1995 Stockton	A+ Mil	114	410	113	8	2	0	125	80	43	69	1	64	2	10	1	55	9	.86	7	.276	.382	.305
1996 Stockton	A+ Mil	73	286	82	5	1	0	89	51	26	29	0	34	0	8	2	30	9	.77	3	.287	.350	.311
El Paso	AA Mil	41	166	52	2	2	1	61	27	21	13	0	19	3	6	1	14	4	.78	1	.313	.372	.367
1997 El Paso	AA Mil	95	381	111	10	10	1	144	75	29	32	0	55	3	9	2	39	7	.85	5	.291	.349	.378
Tucson	AAA Mil	3	12	5	2	0	0	7	2	3	0	0	1	0	0	0	0	0	.00	0	.417	.417	.583
5 Min. YEARS		464	1681	490	39	18	2	571	325	164	202	2	231	18	42	12	202	47	.81	23	.291	.371	.340

Jesus Martinez

Pitches: Left **Bats:** Left **Pos:** P　　　　**Ht:** 6'2" **Wt:** 145 **Born:** 3/13/74 **Age:** 24

Year Team	Lg Org	G	GS	CG	GF	IP	BFP	H	R	ER	HR	SH	SF	HB	TBB	IBB	SO	WP	Bk	W	L	Pct.	ShO	Sv	ERA
1992 Great Falls	R+ LA	6	6	0	0	18.1	112	36	30	27	4	0	0	2	21	0	23	9	0	0	3	.000	0	0	13.25
Dodgers	R LA	7	7	1	0	41	174	38	19	15	1	2	0	1	11	0	39	5	0	1	4	.200	0	0	3.29
1993 Bakersfield	A+ LA	30	21	0	2	145.2	653	144	95	67	12	5	11	5	75	0	108	6	5	13	13	.235	0	0	4.14
1994 San Antonio	AA LA	1	1	0	0	4	14	3	2	2	0	0	0	0	2	0	3	0	0	0	1	.000	0	0	4.50
Vero Beach	A+ LA	18	18	1	0	87.2	386	91	65	61	7	2	3	6	43	0	69	3	0	7	9	.438	1	0	6.26
1995 San Antonio	AA LA	24	24	1	0	139.2	603	129	64	55	6	7	4	7	71	0	83	16	4	6	9	.400	0	0	3.54
Albuquerque	AAA LA	2	0	0	1	4	20	4	2	2	0	1	1	1	4	2	5	0	0	1	1	.500	0	0	4.50
1996 San Antonio	AA LA	27	27	0	0	161.2	706	157	90	79	7	5	7	5	92	0	124	20	0	10	13	.435	0	0	4.40
1997 Albuquerque	AAA LA	26	12	0	6	84	404	112	64	58	8	3	1	1	52	0	80	15	1	7	1	.875	0	0	6.21
6 Min. YEARS		141	116	3	9	686	3072	714	431	366	45	25	27	28	371	2	534	74	10	36	54	.400	1	0	4.80

Johnny Martinez

Pitches: Right **Bats:** Right **Pos:** P　　　　**Ht:** 6'3" **Wt:** 168 **Born:** 11/25/72 **Age:** 25

Year Team	Lg Org	G	GS	CG	GF	IP	BFP	H	R	ER	HR	SH	SF	HB	TBB	IBB	SO	WP	Bk	W	L	Pct.	ShO	Sv	ERA
1993 Burlington	R+ Cle	11	10	1	0	73	290	63	21	18	3	2	0	1	25	2	54	3	4	6	1	.857	0	0	2.22
1994 Burlington	R+ Cle	11	11	1	0	70	305	73	45	31	4	2	1	3	16	1	72	8	3	2	6	.250	0	0	3.99
Kinston	A+ Cle	2	2	0	0	8	34	10	7	7	1	0	1	1	4	0	3	0	0	0	2	.000	0	0	7.88
1995 Columbus	A Cle	16	2	0	2	54	210	37	15	11	0	2	1	4	14	0	43	3	0	6	1	.857	0	0	1.83
Kinston	A+ Cle	6	0	0	5	11	44	9	2	2	0	0	0	1	4	0	13	1	0	3	0	1.000	0	2	1.64
1996 Canton-Akrn	AA Cle	5	0	0	2	8.1	39	9	6	5	1	0	0	2	4	0	3	0	0	0	1	.000	0	0	5.40
1997 Kinston	A+ Cle	9	0	0	3	20.1	80	16	5	5	2	1	2	0	6	1	14	2	0	1	2	.333	0	1	2.21
Akron	AA Cle	32	0	0	18	49	244	63	32	27	9	3	2	4	26	4	31	5	0	1	8	.111	0	2	4.96
5 Min. YEARS		92	25	2	30	293.2	1246	280	133	106	20	10	7	16	99	8	233	22	7	19	21	.475	0	5	3.25

Manny Martinez

Bats: Right **Throws:** Right **Pos:** OF　　　　**Ht:** 6'2" **Wt:** 169 **Born:** 10/3/70 **Age:** 27

Year Team	Lg Org	G	AB	H	2B	3B	HR	TB	R	RBI	TBB	IBB	SO	HBP	SH	SF	SB	CS	SB%	GDP	Avg	OBP	SLG
1990 Sou. Oregon	A- Oak	66	244	60	5	0	2	71	35	17	16	0	59	5	1	0	6	4	.60	5	.246	.306	.291
1991 Modesto	A+ Oak	125	502	136	32	3	3	183	73	55	34	2	80	7	7	3	26	19	.58	7	.271	.324	.365
1992 Modesto	A+ Oak	121	495	125	23	1	9	177	70	45	39	3	75	4	12	5	17	13	.57	7	.253	.309	.358
1993 San Berndno	A+ Oak	109	459	148	26	3	11	213	88	52	41	2	60	5	6	4	28	21	.57	10	.322	.381	.464
Tacoma	AAA Oak	20	59	18	2	0	1	23	9	6	4	0	12	0	1	0	2	3	.40	2	.305	.349	.390
1994 Tacoma	AAA Oak	137	536	137	25	5	9	199	76	60	28	3	72	10	9	5	18	10	.64	14	.256	.302	.371
1995 Iowa	AAA ChN	122	397	115	17	8	8	172	63	49	20	0	64	3	7	2	11	8	.58	3	.290	.327	.433
1996 Tacoma	AAA Sea	66	277	87	15	1	4	116	54	24	23	1	41	2	3	3	14	10	.58	6	.314	.367	.419
Scranton-WB	AAA Phi	17	67	14	1	1	0	17	8	5	4	0	17	1	0	0	3	0	1.00	6	.209	.264	.254
1997 Calgary	AAA Pit	109	420	139	34	1	16	223	78	66	33	4	80	0	2	1	17	9	.65	3	.331	.379	.531
1996 Seattle	AL	9	17	4	2	1	0	8	3	3	3	0	5	0	0	0	2	0	1.00	1	.235	.350	.471
Philadelphia	NL	13	36	8	0	2	0	12	2	0	1	0	11	1	1	0	2	1	.67	1	.222	.263	.333
8 Min. YEARS		892	3456	979	180	23	63	1394	554	379	242	15	560	37	48	23	142	97	.59	57	.283	.335	.403

Pablo Martinez

Bats: Both **Throws:** Right **Pos:** 2B　　　　**Ht:** 5'10" **Wt:** 155 **Born:** 6/29/69 **Age:** 29

Year Team	Lg Org	G	AB	H	2B	3B	HR	TB	R	RBI	TBB	IBB	SO	HBP	SH	SF	SB	CS	SB%	GDP	Avg	OBP	SLG
1989 Spokane	A- SD	2	8	2	0	0	0	2	3	0	0	0	0	0	0	0	1	0	1.00	1	.250	.250	.250
Padres	R SD	45	178	42	3	1	0	47	31	12	22	1	25	2	0	0	29	4	.88	1	.236	.327	.264
Chston-SC	A SD	31	80	14	2	0	0	16	13	4	11	0	21	0	3	1	0	1	.00	2	.175	.272	.200
1990 Chston-SC	A SD	136	453	100	12	6	0	124	51	33	41	0	104	4	7	2	16	10	.62	6	.221	.290	.274
1991 Chston-SC	A SD	121	442	118	17	6	3	156	62	36	42	1	64	0	6	2	39	19	.67	8	.267	.329	.353
1992 High Desert	A+ SD	126	427	102	8	4	0	118	60	39	50	0	74	1	2	4	19	14	.58	16	.239	.317	.276
1993 Wichita	AA SD	45	130	36	5	1	2	49	19	14	11	1	24	1	1	1	8	5	.62	2	.277	.336	.377
Las Vegas	AAA SD	76	251	58	4	1	2	70	24	20	18	3	46	3	10	2	8	2	.80	5	.231	.288	.279
1994 Norfolk	AAA NYN	34	80	12	1	0	0	13	8	5	4	0	22	0	3	0	1	1	.50	0	.150	.190	.163
Binghamton	AA NYN	13	48	9	2	2	0	15	3	4	5	0	12	0	2	0	1	0	1.00	3	.188	.264	.313
St. Lucie	A+ NYN	49	177	42	5	0	1	50	19	10	13	0	29	0	3	1	7	7	.50	4	.237	.288	.282
1995 Greenville	AA Atl	120	462	118	22	4	5	163	70	29	37	0	89	2	8	1	12	12	.50	7	.255	.313	.353
Richmond	AAA Atl	14	48	11	0	2	0	15	5	4	0	0	7	0	0	0	1	1	.50	3	.229	.260	.313

Year Team	Lg Org	G	AB	H	2B	3B	HR	TB	R	RBI	TBB	IBB	SO	HBP	SH	SF	SB	CS	SB%	GDP	Avg	OBP	SLG
1996 Greenville	AA Atl	9	37	12	2	2	1	21	7	11	2	0	6	0	1	1	3	0	1.00	1	.324	.350	.568
Richmond	AAA Atl	77	263	71	12	3	1	92	29	18	12	0	58	1	11	1	14	7	.67	3	.270	.303	.350
1997 Richmond	AAA Atl	96	296	76	14	1	4	104	32	20	26	0	77	0	8	2	9	11	.45	3	.257	.315	.351
1996 Atlanta	NL	4	2	1	0	0	0	1	1	0	0	0	0	0	1	0	0	1	.00	0	.500	.500	.500
9 Min. YEARS		994	3380	823	109	33	19	1055	436	259	296	6	658	14	65	18	167	95	.64	65	.243	.306	.312

Ramiro Martinez

Pitches: Left Bats: Left Pos: P Ht: 6'2" Wt: 185 Born: 1/28/72 Age: 26

Year Team	Lg Org	G	GS	CG	GF	IP	BFP	H	R	ER	HR	SH	SF	HB	TBB	IBB	SO	WP	Bk	W	L	Pct.	ShO	Sv	ERA
1992 Rangers	R Tex	10	10	1	0	45.2	184	28	15	6	0	0	1	4	22	0	52	3	1	4	1	.800	1	0	1.18
1993 Chston-SC	A Tex	27	27	2	0	124.2	588	129	91	81	10	2	3	10	90	4	129	11	0	6	10	.375	2	0	5.85
1994 Tulsa	AA Tex	23	23	2	0	139.1	589	126	79	70	21	1	3	4	69	0	107	2	1	6	10	.375	0	0	4.52
1995 Tulsa	AA Tex	13	5	0	0	47	220	53	29	27	5	0	3	1	34	2	37	3	0	0	5	.000	0	0	5.17
Charlotte	A+ Tex	14	6	0	6	46.1	192	45	21	21	3	3	3	0	15	0	30	3	0	2	2	.500	0	2	4.08
1996 Tulsa	AA Tex	11	0	0	3	13.2	65	23	13	13	2	0	0	0	5	0	7	0	0	0	2	.000	0	0	8.56
Harrisburg	AA Mon	8	5	0	3	24	109	23	13	12	2	3	0	2	15	0	10	2	0	0	4	.000	0	0	4.50
Wst Plm Bch	A+ Mon	9	7	0	1	42.1	185	47	20	16	1	1	3	1	14	0	44	2	0	1	0	1.000	0	0	3.40
1997 Harrisburg	AA Mon	37	3	0	15	75.2	330	64	36	31	11	3	2	5	33	1	69	0	0	4	4	.500	0	1	3.69
6 Min. YEARS		152	86	5	28	558.2	2462	538	317	277	55	13	18	27	297	7	485	28	2	23	38	.377	3	3	4.46

Ramon Martinez

Bats: Right Throws: Right Pos: SS Ht: 6'1" Wt: 170 Born: 10/10/72 Age: 25

Year Team	Lg Org	G	AB	H	2B	3B	HR	TB	R	RBI	TBB	IBB	SO	HBP	SH	SF	SB	CS	SB%	GDP	Avg	OBP	SLG
1993 Royals	R KC	37	97	23	5	0	0	28	16	9	8	0	6	2	2	2	3	0	1.00	5	.237	.303	.289
Wilmington	A+ KC	24	75	19	4	0	0	23	8	6	11	0	9	1	3	1	1	4	.20	2	.253	.352	.307
1994 Rockford	A KC	6	18	5	0	0	0	5	3	3	4	0	2	0	1	0	1	0	1.00	1	.278	.409	.278
Wilmington	A+ KC	90	325	87	13	2	2	110	40	35	35	0	25	4	20	5	6	3	.67	14	.268	.341	.338
1995 Wichita	AA KC	103	393	108	20	2	3	141	58	51	42	1	50	4	18	9	11	8	.58	11	.275	.344	.359
1996 Omaha	AAA KC	85	320	81	12	3	6	117	35	41	21	1	34	3	13	0	3	2	.60	4	.253	.305	.366
Wichita	AA KC	26	93	32	4	1	1	41	16	8	7	0	8	0	7	0	4	1	.80	4	.344	.390	.441
1997 Phoenix	AAA SF	18	57	16	2	0	1	21	6	7	5	0	9	0	1	0	1	0	1.00	3	.281	.333	.368
Shreveport	AA SF	105	404	129	32	4	5	184	72	54	40	1	48	3	4	3	4	5	.44	6	.319	.382	.455
5 Min. YEARS		494	1782	500	92	12	18	670	254	214	173	3	191	17	69	21	34	23	.60	50	.281	.346	.376

Eric Martins

Bats: Right Throws: Right Pos: 2B Ht: 5'10" Wt: 175 Born: 11/19/72 Age: 25

Year Team	Lg Org	G	AB	H	2B	3B	HR	TB	R	RBI	TBB	IBB	SO	HBP	SH	SF	SB	CS	SB%	GDP	Avg	OBP	SLG
1994 Sou. Oregon	A- Oak	56	236	78	16	3	4	112	47	34	23	1	36	5	2	0	17	10	.63	4	.331	.402	.475
W Michigan	A Oak	18	71	22	4	1	0	28	11	7	5	0	12	0	1	2	1	2	.33	2	.310	.346	.394
1995 Modesto	A+ Oak	106	407	118	17	5	1	148	71	54	62	0	74	4	18	4	7	8	.47	8	.290	.386	.364
1996 Huntsville	AA Oak	111	388	99	23	2	1	129	61	34	47	0	77	5	8	1	7	7	.50	6	.255	.342	.332
1997 Huntsville	AA Oak	61	205	53	10	3	3	78	33	31	23	0	31	2	3	2	2	1	.67	5	.259	.336	.380
Edmonton	AAA Oak	27	82	23	7	1	1	35	17	8	11	0	19	1	2	0	0	0	.00	3	.280	.372	.427
4 Min. YEARS		379	1389	393	77	15	10	530	240	168	171	1	249	17	34	9	34	28	.55	32	.283	.366	.382

Tim Marx

Bats: Right Throws: Right Pos: C Ht: 6'2" Wt: 190 Born: 11/27/68 Age: 29

Year Team	Lg Org	G	AB	H	2B	3B	HR	TB	R	RBI	TBB	IBB	SO	HBP	SH	SF	SB	CS	SB%	GDP	Avg	OBP	SLG
1992 Augusta	A Pit	44	138	30	7	0	0	37	20	9	23	0	16	1	3	0	0	1	.00	4	.217	.333	.268
1993 Salem	A+ Pit	13	43	10	0	0	0	10	2	5	7	0	9	0	1	1	1	1	.50	2	.233	.333	.233
Augusta	A Pit	53	162	45	8	0	3	62	28	21	34	0	18	2	2	2	3	4	.43	3	.278	.405	.383
Buffalo	AAA Pit	4	14	2	1	0	0	3	0	0	2	0	4	0	0	0	0	0	.00	1	.143	.250	.214
1994 Carolina	AA Pit	77	239	71	11	2	7	107	32	42	20	1	29	1	2	5	1	3	.25	6	.297	.347	.448
1995 Calgary	AAA Pit	61	185	55	11	1	1	71	27	12	19	2	16	0	1	3	2	3	.40	6	.297	.357	.384
1996 Calgary	AAA Pit	95	296	96	20	1	1	121	50	37	29	1	50	2	3	6	6	2	.75	16	.324	.388	.409
1997 Calgary	AAA Pit	90	300	75	18	2	3	106	42	40	23	1	42	5	1	1	9	1	.90	16	.250	.313	.353
6 Min. YEARS		437	1377	384	76	6	15	517	201	166	157	5	184	11	13	18	22	15	.59	44	.279	.353	.375

Justin Mashore

Bats: Right Throws: Right Pos: OF Ht: 5'9" Wt: 190 Born: 2/14/72 Age: 26

Year Team	Lg Org	G	AB	H	2B	3B	HR	TB	R	RBI	TBB	IBB	SO	HBP	SH	SF	SB	CS	SB%	GDP	Avg	OBP	SLG
1991 Bristol	R+ Det	58	177	36	3	0	3	48	29	11	28	1	65	0	2	0	17	6	.74	3	.203	.312	.271
1992 Fayetteville	A Det	120	401	96	18	3	4	132	54	43	36	2	117	3	9	1	31	8	.79	3	.239	.306	.329
1993 Lakeland	A+ Det	118	442	113	11	4	3	141	64	30	37	4	92	6	16	5	26	13	.67	9	.256	.318	.319
1994 Trenton	AA Det	131	450	100	13	5	7	144	63	45	36	0	120	3	8	3	31	7	.82	9	.222	.283	.320
1995 Toledo	AAA Det	72	223	49	4	3	4	71	32	21	14	1	62	3	9	2	12	9	.57	1	.220	.273	.318
Jacksnville	AA Det	40	148	36	8	2	4	60	26	15	6	0	41	3	3	0	5	1	.83	2	.243	.287	.405
1996 Jacksnville	AA Det	120	453	129	27	8	7	193	67	50	33	1	97	4	7	2	17	13	.57	10	.285	.337	.426
1997 Mobile	AA SD	90	281	67	10	5	11	120	53	41	32	2	70	5	3	3	11	8	.58	8	.238	.324	.427
7 Min. YEARS		749	2575	626	94	30	43	909	388	256	222	11	664	27	57	16	150	65	.70	43	.243	.308	.353

Joe Maskivish

Pitches: Right **Bats:** Right **Pos:** P **Ht:** 6'4" **Wt:** 180 **Born:** 8/14/71 **Age:** 26

Year Team	Lg Org	G	GS	CG	GF	IP	BFP	H	R	ER	HR	SH	SF	HB	TBB	IBB	SO	WP	Bk	W	L	Pct.	ShO	Sv	ERA
1994 Welland	A- Pit	28	0	0	21	28	115	19	8	6	0	1	1	2	10	0	27	2	0	2	0	1.000	0	14	1.93
1995 Augusta	A Pit	26	0	0	26	29.2	122	23	9	7	0	1	0	3	9	4	33	2	0	2	1	.667	0	20	2.12
1996 Lynchburg	A+ Pit	12	0	0	10	10.2	56	17	9	8	1	1	0	2	5	0	10	2	1	1	2	.333	0	4	6.75
Augusta	A Pit	50	0	0	40	50	217	46	18	12	0	0	1	4	14	0	58	4	0	1	4	.200	0	18	2.16
1997 Lynchburg	A+ Pit	32	0	0	27	33.1	141	31	12	11	1	1	2	4	13	2	24	4	1	2	0	1.000	0	17	2.97
Carolina	AA Pit	15	0	0	9	16	73	20	11	11	2	2	2	1	4	1	7	0	0	0	1	.000	0	0	6.19
4 Min. YEARS		163	0	0	133	167.2	724	156	67	55	4	6	6	16	55	7	159	14	2	8	8	.500	0	73	2.95

Del Mathews

Pitches: Left **Bats:** Left **Pos:** P **Ht:** 6'3" **Wt:** 200 **Born:** 10/31/74 **Age:** 23

Year Team	Lg Org	G	GS	CG	GF	IP	BFP	H	R	ER	HR	SH	SF	HB	TBB	IBB	SO	WP	Bk	W	L	Pct.	ShO	Sv	ERA
1993 Braves	R Atl	14	12	0	0	62	282	65	42	31	4	3	1	8	26	0	59	4	2	2	4	.333	0	0	4.50
1994 Macon	A Atl	26	18	0	2	117.2	540	133	73	59	9	2	7	8	50	2	92	6	0	10	7	.588	0	0	4.51
1995 Durham	A+ Atl	33	16	1	8	112	478	117	53	44	6	4	1	10	38	2	77	6	0	7	8	.467	0	1	3.54
1996 Durham	A+ Atl	42	2	0	26	65	292	74	39	32	9	1	3	6	26	0	46	6	0	4	3	.571	0	5	4.43
1997 Lynchburg	A+ Pit	18	5	0	6	48.2	209	48	25	19	3	4	1	3	13	3	48	3	0	2	5	.286	0	1	3.51
Carolina	AA Pit	21	1	0	5	50.1	225	53	25	17	5	4	2	1	20	1	51	2	1	5	2	.714	0	1	3.04
5 Min. YEARS		154	54	1	47	455.2	2026	490	257	202	36	18	15	36	173	8	373	27	3	30	29	.508	0	8	3.99

Francisco Matos

Bats: Right **Throws:** Right **Pos:** 2B **Ht:** 6'1" **Wt:** 160 **Born:** 7/23/69 **Age:** 28

Year Team	Lg Org	G	AB	H	2B	3B	HR	TB	R	RBI	TBB	IBB	SO	HBP	SH	SF	SB	CS	SB%	GDP	Avg	OBP	SLG
1989 Modesto	A+ Oak	65	200	41	5	1	1	51	14	23	12	0	41	0	0	1	6	5	.55	5	.205	.249	.255
1990 Modesto	A+ Oak	83	321	88	12	1	1	105	46	20	15	0	65	5	7	2	26	5	.84	2	.274	.315	.327
Huntsville	AA Oak	45	180	41	3	3	0	50	18	12	9	1	18	1	2	1	7	4	.64	3	.228	.267	.278
1991 Huntsville	AA Oak	55	191	37	1	2	0	42	18	19	17	1	28	2	5	0	12	2	.86	6	.194	.267	.220
Modesto	A+ Oak	50	189	53	4	0	1	60	32	22	30	1	24	1	4	1	19	8	.70	5	.280	.380	.317
1992 Huntsville	AA Oak	44	150	33	5	1	1	43	11	14	11	0	27	2	1	1	4	4	.50	4	.220	.280	.287
1993 Huntsville	AA Oak	123	461	127	12	3	1	148	69	32	22	1	54	4	4	3	16	6	.73	6	.275	.312	.321
1994 Tacoma	AAA Oak	86	336	103	10	1	0	115	40	30	14	0	32	0	4	3	16	9	.64	13	.307	.331	.342
1995 Calgary	AAA Pit	100	341	110	11	6	3	142	36	40	5	0	25	2	3	1	9	2	.82	11	.323	.335	.416
1996 Ottawa	AAA Mon	100	307	73	15	3	2	100	30	23	16	0	35	3	3	2	4	5	.44	14	.238	.280	.326
1997 Rochester	AAA Bal	101	389	126	17	4	4	163	51	51	9	0	42	4	9	3	8	2	.80	15	.324	.343	.419
1994 Oakland	AL	14	28	7	1	0	0	8	1	2	1	0	2	0	0	0	1	0	1.00	1	.250	.267	.286
9 Min. YEARS		852	3065	832	95	25	14	1019	365	286	160	4	391	24	42	18	127	52	.71	86	.271	.311	.332

Jeff Matranga

Pitches: Right **Bats:** Right **Pos:** P **Ht:** 6'2" **Wt:** 170 **Born:** 12/14/70 **Age:** 27

Year Team	Lg Org	G	GS	CG	GF	IP	BFP	H	R	ER	HR	SH	SF	HB	TBB	IBB	SO	WP	Bk	W	L	Pct.	ShO	Sv	ERA
1992 Johnson Cty	R+ StL	19	1	0	12	36.1	158	34	17	12	1	0	1	3	13	1	47	3	0	3	0	1.000	0	2	2.97
1993 St. Pete	A+ StL	5	3	0	1	28.1	113	23	10	7	1	0	0	0	6	0	21	3	0	2	0	1.000	0	0	2.22
Savannah	A StL	15	15	3	0	103	387	74	24	17	8	1	0	4	30	1	90	4	0	11	3	.786	2	0	1.49
1994 St. Pete	A+ StL	63	0	0	26	87.1	367	76	30	23	4	5	2	3	30	7	76	1	1	8	5	.615	0	3	2.37
1995 St. Pete	A+ StL	53	0	0	17	65.2	272	49	27	20	2	3	3	9	20	3	71	2	0	3	4	.429	0	2	2.74
Arkansas	AA StL	7	0	0	4	8	27	1	0	0	0	0	0	0	3	0	4	0	0	0	0	.000	0	0	0.00
1996 Arkansas	AA StL	62	0	0	31	79.2	327	56	22	19	6	5	2	8	30	3	82	0	0	6	5	.545	0	4	2.15
1997 Louisville	AAA StL	37	0	0	8	53.1	252	75	34	33	5	2	3	5	13	1	30	1	0	3	3	.500	0	0	5.57
6 Min. YEARS		261	19	3	99	461.2	1903	388	164	131	27	16	11	32	128	15	421	14	1	36	20	.643	2	12	2.55

Gary Matthews

Bats: Both **Throws:** Right **Pos:** OF **Ht:** 6'3" **Wt:** 185 **Born:** 8/25/74 **Age:** 23

Year Team	Lg Org	G	AB	H	2B	3B	HR	TB	R	RBI	TBB	IBB	SO	HBP	SH	SF	SB	CS	SB%	GDP	Avg	OBP	SLG
1994 Spokane	A- SD	52	191	40	6	1	0	48	23	18	19	1	58	2	0	1	3	5	.38	4	.209	.286	.251
1995 Clinton	A SD	128	421	100	18	4	2	132	57	40	68	1	109	6	3	3	28	8	.78	8	.238	.349	.314
1996 Rancho Cuca	A+ SD	123	435	118	21	11	7	182	65	54	60	1	102	6	4	2	7	8	.47	11	.271	.366	.418
1997 Rancho Cuca	A+ SD	69	268	81	15	4	8	128	66	40	49	2	57	3	0	0	10	4	.71	4	.302	.416	.478
Mobile	AA SD	28	90	22	4	1	2	34	14	12	15	1	29	1	0	2	3	1	.75	1	.244	.352	.378
4 Min. YEARS		400	1405	361	64	21	19	524	225	164	211	6	355	18	7	8	51	26	.66	28	.257	.359	.373

Mike Matthews

Pitches: Left **Bats:** Left **Pos:** P **Ht:** 6'2" **Wt:** 175 **Born:** 10/24/73 **Age:** 24

Year Team	Lg Org	G	GS	CG	GF	IP	BFP	H	R	ER	HR	SH	SF	HB	TBB	IBB	SO	WP	Bk	W	L	Pct.	ShO	Sv	ERA
1992 Burlington	R+ Cle	10	10	0	0	62.1	245	33	13	7	1	2	1	3	27	0	55	3	1	7	0	1.000	0	0	1.01
Watertown	A- Cle	2	2	0	0	11	47	10	4	4	0	0	1	0	8	0	5	1	0	1	0	1.000	0	0	3.27
1994 Columbus	A Cle	23	23	0	0	119.2	502	120	53	41	8	3	3	7	44	1	99	7	3	6	8	.429	0	0	3.08
1995 Canton-Akrn	AA Cle	15	15	1	0	74.1	345	82	62	49	6	2	8	2	43	1	37	6	1	5	8	.385	0	0	5.93
1996 Canton-Akrn	AA Cle	27	27	3	0	162.1	713	178	96	84	13	6	7	5	74	3	112	6	1	9	11	.450	0	0	4.66
1997 Buffalo	AAA Cle	5	5	0	0	21	106	32	19	18	7	2	0	0	10	0	17	1	0	0	2	.000	0	0	7.71

160

		HOW MUCH HE PITCHED						WHAT HE GAVE UP										THE RESULTS					
Year Team	Lg Org	G	GS	CG	GF	IP	BFP	H	R	ER	HR	SH	SF	HB	TBB	IBB	SO	WP	Bk	W	L	Pct.	ShO	Sv	ERA
Akron	AA Cle	19	19	3	0	113	492	116	62	48	13	3	0	7	57	0	69	5	4	6	8	.429	1	0	3.82
5 Min. YEARS		101	101	7	0	563.2	2450	571	309	251	48	16	22	24	263	5	394	31	10	34	37	.479	1	0	4.01

Mike Matvey

Bats: Right **Throws:** Right **Pos:** 3B   **Ht:** 6'0" **Wt:** 180 **Born:** 10/10/71 **Age:** 26

		BATTING														BASERUNNING				PERCENTAGES		
Year Team	Lg Org	G	AB	H	2B	3B	HR	TB	R	RBI	TBB	IBB	SO	HBP	SH	SF	SB	CS	SB%	GDP	Avg	OBP	SLG
1993 Glens Falls	A- StL	70	239	69	11	5	3	99	37	42	29	1	43	4	6	1	7	4	.64	4	.289	.374	.414
1994 Savannah	A StL	122	444	112	26	3	3	153	61	65	44	1	99	9	9	3	4	9	.31	16	.252	.330	.345
1995 St. Pete	A+ StL	87	304	83	15	4	0	106	32	20	40	1	67	3	2	1	1	5	.17	2	.273	.362	.349
1996 St. Pete	A+ StL	127	407	104	10	3	1	123	51	40	47	2	90	4	2	5	3	6	.33	8	.256	.335	.302
1997 Pr William	A+ StL	32	123	28	12	0	3	49	22	22	15	1	28	0	0	1	1	0	1.00	3	.228	.303	.398
Arkansas	AA StL	57	136	30	4	0	1	37	16	9	21	0	33	0	3	1	1	1	.50	3	.221	.323	.272
5 Min. YEARS		495	1653	426	78	15	11	567	219	198	196	6	360	20	22	15	17	25	.40	36	.258	.341	.343

Mike Maurer

Pitches: Right **Bats:** Right **Pos:** P   **Ht:** 6'2" **Wt:** 195 **Born:** 7/4/72 **Age:** 25

		HOW MUCH HE PITCHED						WHAT HE GAVE UP										THE RESULTS					
Year Team	Lg Org	G	GS	CG	GF	IP	BFP	H	R	ER	HR	SH	SF	HB	TBB	IBB	SO	WP	Bk	W	L	Pct.	ShO	Sv	ERA
1994 Sou. Oregon	A- Oak	17	8	0	5	49.1	285	68	42	25	2	4	4	5	20	1	67	7	3	2	6	.250	0	3	3.55
1995 Huntsville	AA Oak	17	0	0	14	20.2	100	34	18	15	0	2	1	0	5	2	19	2	0	0	2	.000	0	6	6.53
Modesto	A+ Oak	39	0	0	37	40.1	157	27	9	8	3	2	2	2	9	0	44	2	0	2	2	.500	0	18	1.79
1996 Huntsville	AA Oak	52	0	0	41	64.2	298	67	31	27	3	3	2	3	35	9	46	5	0	4	6	.400	0	3	3.76
1997 Huntsville	AA Oak	52	5	0	24	84.2	371	86	48	36	10	5	4	2	31	3	61	5	1	8	7	.533	0	2	3.83
4 Min. YEARS		177	13	0	121	273.2	1211	282	148	111	18	16	13	12	100	15	237	21	4	16	23	.410	0	37	3.65

Ron Maurer

Bats: Right **Throws:** Right **Pos:** SS   **Ht:** 6'1" **Wt:** 185 **Born:** 6/10/68 **Age:** 30

		BATTING														BASERUNNING				PERCENTAGES		
Year Team	Lg Org	G	AB	H	2B	3B	HR	TB	R	RBI	TBB	IBB	SO	HBP	SH	SF	SB	CS	SB%	GDP	Avg	OBP	SLG
1990 Great Falls	R+ LA	62	238	64	8	0	6	90	43	43	27	0	38	6	5	4	5	2	.71	4	.269	.353	.378
1991 Bakersfield	A+ LA	129	442	128	21	5	7	180	59	53	63	3	68	7	13	3	8	8	.50	15	.290	.384	.407
1992 San Antonio	AA LA	82	224	61	13	0	0	74	29	14	15	3	32	5	4	0	4	3	.57	6	.272	.332	.330
1993 San Antonio	AA LA	11	37	7	1	0	1	11	6	4	7	0	12	0	1	0	1	0	1.00	0	.189	.318	.297
Albuquerque	AAA LA	58	116	34	7	0	3	50	19	14	11	1	17	0	4	0	1	1	.50	6	.293	.354	.431
1994 Albuquerque	AAA LA	55	125	35	8	1	2	51	20	16	4	0	15	3	1	1	1	0	1.00	4	.280	.316	.408
1995 Albuquerque	AAA LA	84	185	48	14	2	5	81	29	25	19	2	34	3	1	1	1	2	.33	1	.259	.337	.438
1996 San Antonio	AA LA	6	19	5	0	0	0	5	3	0	3	0	7	0	0	0	0	0	.00	0	.263	.364	.263
Albuquerque	AAA LA	80	222	61	14	1	5	92	32	30	30	2	50	3	4	3	2	4	.33	5	.275	.364	.414
1997 Albuquerque	AAA LA	114	349	96	21	4	8	149	61	50	39	0	59	7	2	5	1	3	.50	10	.275	.355	.427
8 Min. YEARS		681	1957	539	107	13	37	783	301	249	218	11	332	34	35	17	25	24	.51	51	.275	.355	.400

Brian Maxcy

Pitches: Right **Bats:** Right **Pos:** P   **Ht:** 6'1" **Wt:** 170 **Born:** 5/4/71 **Age:** 27

		HOW MUCH HE PITCHED						WHAT HE GAVE UP										THE RESULTS					
Year Team	Lg Org	G	GS	CG	GF	IP	BFP	H	R	ER	HR	SH	SF	HB	TBB	IBB	SO	WP	Bk	W	L	Pct.	ShO	Sv	ERA
1992 Bristol	R+ Det	14	7	2	7	49.1	204	41	24	19	4	0	2	0	17	1	43	3	1	4	2	.667	2	3	3.47
1993 Fayettevlle	A Det	39	12	1	20	113.2	501	111	51	37	2	5	3	13	42	3	101	5	0	12	4	.750	1	9	2.93
1994 Trenton	AA Det	5	0	0	2	10.2	45	6	1	0	0	0	0	1	4	0	5	0	0	0	0	.000	0	1	0.00
Toledo	AAA Det	24	1	0	6	44.1	182	31	12	8	1	2	1	2	18	1	43	1	0	2	3	.400	0	3	1.62
1995 Toledo	AAA Det	20	0	0	9	25.2	120	32	20	15	3	4	0	1	11	1	11	3	0	1	3	.250	0	2	5.26
1996 Toledo	AAA Det	15	0	0	6	22.2	97	24	11	10	2	3	2	0	9	2	8	2	0	3	1	.750	0	3	3.97
Louisville	AAA StL	36	3	0	8	62	274	63	34	33	5	2	3	4	32	6	52	5	0	4	2	.667	0	1	4.79
1997 Louisville	AAA StL	15	0	0	20	38.1	176	36	18	16	4	3	2	4	24	3	22	2	0	2	2	.500	0	9	3.76
1995 Detroit	AL	41	0	0	14	52.1	247	61	48	40	6	3	3	2	31	7	20	6	2	4	5	.444	0	0	6.88
1996 Detroit	AL	2	0	0	0	3.1	19	8	5	5	2	0	0	0	2	0	1	0	0	0	0	.000	0	0	13.50
6 Min. YEARS		183	23	3	78	366.2	1599	344	171	138	21	19	13	25	157	17	285	21	1	28	17	.622	3	28	3.39
2 Maj. YEARS		43	0	0	14	55.2	266	69	53	45	8	3	3	2	33	7	21	6	2	4	5	.444	0	0	7.28

Jason Maxwell

Bats: Right **Throws:** Right **Pos:** SS   **Ht:** 6'0" **Wt:** 175 **Born:** 3/21/72 **Age:** 26

		BATTING														BASERUNNING				PERCENTAGES		
Year Team	Lg Org	G	AB	H	2B	3B	HR	TB	R	RBI	TBB	IBB	SO	HBP	SH	SF	SB	CS	SB%	GDP	Avg	OBP	SLG
1993 Huntington	R+ ChN	61	179	52	7	2	7	84	50	38	35	0	39	4	2	1	6	5	.55	0	.291	.416	.469
1994 Daytona	A+ ChN	116	368	85	18	2	10	137	71	32	55	0	96	8	6	2	7	7	.50	6	.231	.342	.372
1995 Daytona	A+ ChN	117	388	102	13	3	10	151	66	58	63	1	68	6	1	8	12	7	.63	6	.263	.368	.389
1996 Orlando	AA ChN	126	433	115	20	1	9	164	64	45	56	3	77	6	4	3	19	4	.83	5	.266	.355	.379
1997 Orlando	AA ChN	122	409	114	22	6	14	190	87	58	82	1	72	4	5	9	12	9	.57	6	.279	.397	.465
5 Min. YEARS		542	1777	468	80	14	50	726	338	231	291	5	352	28	18	23	56	32	.64	23	.263	.371	.409

161

Craig Mayes

Bats: Left **Throws:** Right **Pos:** C **Ht:** 5'10" **Wt:** 195 **Born:** 5/8/70 **Age:** 28

Year Team	Lg Org	G	AB	H	2B	3B	HR	TB	R	RBI	TBB	IBB	SO	HBP	SH	SF	SB	CS	SB%	GDP	Avg	OBP	SLG
1992 Everett	A- SF	38	110	38	3	0	0	41	17	10	10	1	13	0	0	0	3	3	.50	5	.345	.400	.373
1993 Clinton	A SF	75	226	67	12	1	3	90	25	37	10	0	52	0	3	3	1	0	1.00	8	.296	.322	.398
1994 Clinton	A SF	49	155	32	5	1	1	42	13	14	11	1	33	0	2	1	0	2	.00	4	.206	.257	.271
San Berndno	A+ SF	50	191	48	5	0	2	59	20	21	17	1	35	1	0	0	2	2	.50	3	.251	.316	.309
1995 Shreveport	AA SF	3	9	2	1	0	0	3	0	3	0	0	2	0	0	0	0	0	.00	0	.222	.222	.333
San Jose	A+ SF	90	318	80	17	4	0	105	34	39	27	1	50	0	1	2	3	1	.75	7	.252	.308	.330
1996 Shreveport	AA SF	10	40	16	2	0	0	18	5	3	5	1	2	0	0	0	0	0	.00	0	.400	.467	.450
Ohio Valley	IND —	4	6	1	0	0	0	1	0	0	1	0	0	0	0	0	1	0	1.00	0	.167	.286	.167
San Jose	A+ SF	114	472	155	26	4	3	198	56	68	29	2	43	0	2	4	6	8	.43	5	.328	.364	.419
1997 Shreveport	AA SF	86	293	80	8	5	2	104	27	38	14	1	29	1	0	3	1	0	1.00	17	.273	.305	.355
Phoenix	AAA SF	7	21	2	1	0	0	3	2	0	1	0	5	0	0	0	0	0	.00	2	.095	.136	.143
6 Min. YEARS		526	1841	521	80	15	11	664	199	233	125	8	264	2	8	13	17	17	.50	51	.283	.327	.361

Scott Maynard

Bats: Right **Throws:** Right **Pos:** C **Ht:** 6'1" **Wt:** 215 **Born:** 8/28/77 **Age:** 20

Year Team	Lg Org	G	AB	H	2B	3B	HR	TB	R	RBI	TBB	IBB	SO	HBP	SH	SF	SB	CS	SB%	GDP	Avg	OBP	SLG
1995 Tacoma	AAA Sea	1	1	0	0	0	0	0	0	0	0	0	0	0	0	0	0	0	.00	1	.000	.000	.000
Mariners	R Sea	21	72	17	2	0	1	22	6	12	9	0	21	0	1	2	0	0	.00	0	.236	.313	.306
1996 Mariners	R Sea	47	164	46	7	1	1	58	20	17	15	0	53	1	1	0	1	3	.25	3	.280	.344	.354
1997 Everett	A- Sea	24	86	19	3	0	2	28	11	13	5	0	30	0	2	0	3	0	1.00	0	.221	.264	.326
Memphis	AA Sea	14	38	6	0	0	0	6	3	3	1	0	12	1	0	0	0	0	.00	0	.158	.200	.158
3 Min. YEARS		107	361	88	12	1	4	114	40	45	30	0	116	2	4	2	4	3	.57	4	.244	.304	.316

Charles McBride

Bats: Right **Throws:** Right **Pos:** OF **Ht:** 5'10" **Wt:** 170 **Born:** 8/12/73 **Age:** 24

Year Team	Lg Org	G	AB	H	2B	3B	HR	TB	R	RBI	TBB	IBB	SO	HBP	SH	SF	SB	CS	SB%	GDP	Avg	OBP	SLG
1993 Idaho Falls	R+ Atl	49	142	41	6	4	2	61	25	20	13	0	27	3	0	1	8	3	.73	4	.289	.358	.430
1994 Macon	A Atl	81	296	100	21	6	13	172	60	54	29	0	80	0	4	3	17	4	.81	5	.338	.393	.581
1995 Durham	A+ Atl	102	360	85	15	1	13	141	60	59	54	1	109	5	1	2	11	4	.73	5	.236	.342	.392
1996 Durham	A+ Atl	14	49	12	4	0	2	22	7	6	5	0	14	0	0	0	1	0	1.00	3	.245	.315	.449
Greenville	AA Atl	85	291	78	17	5	4	117	38	50	27	1	75	3	0	3	4	3	.57	3	.268	.333	.402
1997 Durham	A+ Atl	5	18	2	1	0	0	3	1	1	2	0	4	0	0	0	1	0	1.00	0	.111	.200	.167
Greenville	AA Atl	45	127	31	5	0	5	51	24	15	11	1	20	2	1	2	0	1	.00	3	.244	.310	.402
5 Min. YEARS		381	1283	349	69	16	39	567	215	205	141	3	329	13	6	11	42	15	.74	23	.272	.347	.442

Chris McBride

Pitches: Right **Bats:** Left **Pos:** P **Ht:** 6'5" **Wt:** 210 **Born:** 10/13/73 **Age:** 24

		HOW MUCH HE PITCHED						WHAT HE GAVE UP										THE RESULTS					
Year Team	Lg Org	G	GS	CG	GF	IP	BFP	H	R	ER	HR	SH	SF	HB	TBB	IBB	SO	WP	Bk	W	L	Pct.	ShO	Sv	ERA
1994 St. Cathrns	A- Tor	13	13	1	0	69.2	302	81	39	33	4	1	1	4	12	0	30	5	0	4	4	.500	0	0	4.26
1995 Hagerstown	A Tor	19	19	2	0	107	461	121	61	51	4	5	3	5	27	1	52	3	1	5	10	.333	0	0	4.29
1996 St. Cathrns	A- Tor	6	6	1	0	43	169	37	14	12	2	0	0	4	7	0	28	2	0	3	1	.750	0	0	2.51
Hagerstown	A Tor	8	8	3	0	58.2	222	42	13	11	4	0	2	4	9	0	34	0	0	5	2	.714	2	0	1.69
1997 Dunedin	A+ Tor	10	4	0	1	31	153	44	25	21	4	0	3	3	17	0	25	5	0	3	0	1.000	0	0	6.10
Knoxville	AA Tor	10	10	0	0	60.2	256	61	30	25	5	2	1	3	14	0	33	3	1	4	4	.500	0	0	3.71
4 Min. YEARS		66	60	7	1	370	1563	386	182	153	23	8	7	23	86	1	202	18	2	24	21	.533	2	0	3.72

Rod McCall

Bats: Left **Throws:** Left **Pos:** 1B-DH **Ht:** 6'7" **Wt:** 235 **Born:** 11/4/71 **Age:** 26

Year Team	Lg Org	G	AB	H	2B	3B	HR	TB	R	RBI	TBB	IBB	SO	HBP	SH	SF	SB	CS	SB%	GDP	Avg	OBP	SLG
1990 Indians	R Cle	10	36	10	2	0	0	12	5	6	5	1	10	0	0	0	0	0	.00	0	.278	.366	.333
Burlington	R+ Cle	31	92	15	5	0	1	23	8	11	10	0	43	2	0	2	0	1	.00	1	.163	.255	.250
1991 Columbus	A Cle	103	323	70	14	1	5	101	34	35	61	3	128	3	0	1	2	2	.50	5	.217	.345	.313
1992 Columbus	A Cle	116	404	97	15	0	20	172	55	80	68	4	121	4	0	6	1	1	.50	9	.240	.351	.426
1993 Kinston	A+ Cle	71	245	51	13	0	9	91	32	33	32	2	85	3	0	4	3	1	.75	3	.208	.303	.371
1994 Kinston	A+ Cle	58	205	44	14	0	11	91	32	27	26	1	75	7	1	1	1	1	.50	2	.215	.324	.444
High Desert	A+ Cle	48	183	51	14	0	17	116	40	43	20	0	63	5	0	1	2	1	.67	4	.279	.364	.634
Canton-Akrn	AA Cle	20	66	13	4	0	3	26	8	9	2	0	27	2	1	1	0	0	.00	1	.197	.239	.394
1995 Bakersfield	A+ Cle	96	345	114	19	1	20	195	61	70	40	7	90	8	2	4	2	5	.29	4	.330	.408	.565
Canton-Akrn	AA Cle	26	95	26	5	0	9	58	16	18	12	3	21	1	0	0	1	1	.50	3	.274	.361	.611
1996 Canton-Akrn	AA Cle	120	440	132	29	2	27	246	80	85	52	4	118	6	0	0	2	0	1.00	4	.300	.382	.559
1997 Buffalo	AAA Cle	36	107	25	5	0	6	48	12	20	9	1	37	2	0	2	0	0	.00	3	.234	.300	.449
Orlando	AA ChN	19	70	21	2	0	6	41	11	20	10	0	24	2	0	1	0	0	.00	1	.300	.398	.586
Iowa	AAA ChN	49	148	42	5	0	14	89	26	35	22	2	53	2	0	0	0	0	.00	1	.284	.382	.601
8 Min. YEARS		803	2759	711	146	4	148	1309	420	492	369	28	895	47	4	23	14	13	.52	42	.258	.352	.474

Dave McCarty

Bats: Right **Throws:** Left **Pos:** 1B   **Ht:** 6'5" **Wt:** 213 **Born:** 11/23/69 **Age:** 28

Year Team	Lg Org	G	AB	H	2B	3B	HR	TB	R	RBI	TBB	IBB	SO	HBP	SH	SF	SB	CS	SB%	GDP	Avg	OBP	SLG
1991 Visalia	A+ Min	15	50	19	3	0	3	31	16	8	13	0	7	3	0	0	3	1	.75	0	.380	.530	.620
Orlando	AA Min	28	88	23	4	0	3	36	18	11	10	0	20	2	0	0	0	1	.00	1	.261	.350	.409
1992 Orlando	AA Min	129	456	124	16	2	18	198	75	79	55	5	89	8	1	6	6	6	.50	8	.272	.356	.434
Portland	AAA Min	7	26	13	2	0	1	18	7	8	5	0	3	1	1	0	1	0	1.00	1	.500	.594	.692
1993 Portland	AAA Min	40	143	55	11	0	8	90	42	31	27	2	25	1	0	3	5	2	.71	3	.385	.477	.629
1994 Salt Lake	AAA Min	55	186	47	9	3	3	71	32	19	35	0	34	4	1	2	1	3	.25	9	.253	.379	.382
1995 Indianapolis	AAA Cin	37	140	47	10	1	8	83	31	32	15	0	30	1	1	1	0	0	.00	5	.336	.401	.593
Phoenix	AAA SF	37	151	53	19	2	4	88	31	19	17	1	27	6	0	1	1	1	.50	6	.351	.434	.583
1996 Phoenix	AAA SF	6	25	10	1	1	1	16	4	7	2	0	4	0	0	1	0	0	.00	0	.400	.429	.640
1997 Phoenix	AAA SF	121	434	153	27	5	22	256	85	92	49	5	75	2	1	2	9	4	.69	18	.353	.419	.590
1993 Minnesota	AL	98	350	75	15	2	2	100	36	21	19	0	80	1	1	0	2	6	.25	13	.214	.257	.286
1994 Minnesota	AL	44	131	34	8	2	1	49	21	12	7	1	32	5	0	0	2	1	.67	3	.260	.322	.374
1995 Minnesota	AL	25	55	12	3	1	0	17	10	4	4	0	18	1	0	1	1	0	1.00	0	.218	.279	.309
San Francisco	NL	12	20	5	1	0	0	6	1	2	2	0	4	0	0	0	1	0	1.00	0	.250	.318	.300
1996 San Francisco	NL	91	175	38	3	0	6	59	16	24	18	0	43	2	0	2	2	1	.67	5	.217	.294	.337
7 Min. YEARS		475	1699	544	102	14	71	887	341	306	228	13	314	28	5	16	26	18	.59	51	.320	.406	.522
4 Maj. YEARS		270	731	164	30	5	9	231	84	63	50	1	177	9	1	3	7	9	.44	22	.224	.281	.316

Scott McClain

Bats: Right **Throws:** Right **Pos:** 3B   **Ht:** 6'4" **Wt:** 215 **Born:** 5/19/72 **Age:** 26

Year Team	Lg Org	G	AB	H	2B	3B	HR	TB	R	RBI	TBB	IBB	SO	HBP	SH	SF	SB	CS	SB%	GDP	Avg	OBP	SLG
1990 Bluefield	R+ Bal	40	107	21	2	0	4	35	20	15	22	0	35	2	0	4	2	3	.40	1	.196	.333	.327
1991 Kane County	A Bal	25	81	18	0	0	0	18	9	4	17	0	25	0	1	0	1	1	.50	4	.222	.357	.222
Bluefield	R+ Bal	41	149	39	5	0	0	44	16	24	14	0	39	3	0	1	5	3	.63	3	.262	.335	.295
1992 Kane County	A Bal	96	316	84	12	2	3	109	43	30	48	1	62	6	6	1	7	4	.64	5	.266	.372	.345
1993 Frederick	A+ Bal	133	427	111	22	2	9	164	65	54	70	0	88	6	3	2	10	6	.63	8	.260	.370	.384
1994 Bowie	AA Bal	133	427	103	29	1	11	167	71	58	72	2	89	1	2	7	6	3	.67	14	.241	.347	.391
1995 Rochester	AAA Bal	61	199	50	9	1	8	85	32	22	23	0	34	1	1	2	0	1	.00	5	.251	.329	.427
Bowie	AA Bal	70	259	72	14	1	13	127	41	61	25	1	44	3	0	4	2	1	.67	13	.278	.344	.490
1996 Rochester	AAA Bal	131	463	130	23	4	17	212	76	69	61	1	109	1	0	7	8	6	.57	6	.281	.361	.458
1997 Norfolk	AAA NYN	127	429	120	29	2	21	216	71	64	64	5	93	2	1	8	1	3	.25	8	.280	.370	.503
8 Min. YEARS		857	2857	748	145	13	86	1177	444	401	416	10	618	25	14	36	42	31	.58	67	.262	.357	.412

Jason McCommon

Pitches: Right **Bats:** Right **Pos:** P   **Ht:** 6'0" **Wt:** 190 **Born:** 8/9/71 **Age:** 26

Year Team	Lg Org	G	GS	CG	GF	IP	BFP	H	R	ER	HR	SH	SF	HB	TBB	IBB	SO	WP	Bk	W	L	Pct.	ShO	Sv	ERA
1994 Vermont	A- Mon	24	3	0	13	48	196	47	20	19	0	1	3	0	15	2	47	7	1	3	4	.429	0	4	3.56
1995 Wst Plm Bch	A+ Mon	26	26	3	0	156	650	153	75	65	13	7	6	10	38	0	94	6	7	7	11	.389	1	0	3.75
1996 Harrisburg	AA Mon	30	24	1	2	153	663	169	88	67	13	2	8	7	44	1	92	5	0	10	10	.500	1	1	3.94
1997 Harrisburg	AA Mon	29	8	0	7	82.2	358	81	50	46	13	0	0	3	39	0	58	4	1	6	3	.667	0	0	5.01
4 Min. YEARS		109	61	4	22	439.2	1867	450	233	197	39	10	17	20	136	3	291	22	9	26	28	.481	1	5	4.03

Keith McDonald

Bats: Right **Throws:** Right **Pos:** C   **Ht:** 6'2" **Wt:** 215 **Born:** 2/8/73 **Age:** 25

Year Team	Lg Org	G	AB	H	2B	3B	HR	TB	R	RBI	TBB	IBB	SO	HBP	SH	SF	SB	CS	SB%	GDP	Avg	OBP	SLG
1994 Johnson Cty	R+ StL	59	199	49	12	0	6	79	32	31	27	3	36	5	2	3	3	1	.75	9	.246	.346	.397
1995 Peoria	A StL	65	179	48	6	0	1	57	22	20	22	0	38	6	4	0	1	0	1.00	1	.268	.367	.318
1996 St. Pete	A+ StL	114	410	111	25	0	2	142	30	52	34	1	65	5	1	5	1	3	.25	18	.271	.330	.346
1997 Arkansas	AA StL	79	233	56	16	0	5	87	32	30	31	0	56	1	0	4	4	6	.40	4	.240	.337	.373
4 Min. YEARS		317	1021	264	59	0	14	365	116	133	114	4	195	19	8	8	4	6	.40	33	.259	.342	.357

Joe McEwing

Bats: Right **Throws:** Right **Pos:** OF   **Ht:** 5'10" **Wt:** 170 **Born:** 10/19/72 **Age:** 25

Year Team	Lg Org	G	AB	H	2B	3B	HR	TB	R	RBI	TBB	IBB	SO	HBP	SH	SF	SB	CS	SB%	GDP	Avg	OBP	SLG
1992 Cardinals	R StL	55	211	71	4	2	0	79	55	13	24	0	18	5	1	1	23	7	.77	1	.336	.415	.374
1993 Savannah	A StL	138	511	127	35	1	0	164	94	43	89	0	73	4	15	4	22	9	.71	7	.249	.362	.321
1994 Madison	A StL	90	346	112	24	2	4	152	58	47	32	4	53	1	5	3	18	15	.55	5	.324	.380	.439
St. Pete	A+ StL	50	197	49	7	0	1	59	22	20	19	0	32	1	4	3	8	4	.67	4	.249	.314	.299
1995 St. Pete	A+ StL	75	281	64	13	0	1	80	33	23	25	3	49	1	6	4	2	3	.40	5	.228	.289	.285
Arkansas	AA StL	42	121	30	4	0	2	40	16	12	9	2	13	1	6	0	3	2	.60	4	.248	.305	.331
1996 Arkansas	AA StL	106	216	45	7	3	2	64	27	14	13	0	32	0	5	1	2	4	.33	8	.208	.252	.296
1997 Arkansas	AA StL	103	263	68	6	3	4	92	33	35	19	4	39	1	3	2	2	4	.33	6	.259	.309	.350
6 Min. YEARS		659	2146	566	100	11	14	730	338	207	230	13	309	14	45	18	80	48	.63	40	.264	.336	.340

Tim McIntosh

Bats: Right **Throws:** Right **Pos:** C   **Ht:** 5'11" **Wt:** 195 **Born:** 3/21/65 **Age:** 33

Year Team	Lg Org	G	AB	H	2B	3B	HR	TB	R	RBI	TBB	IBB	SO	HBP	SH	SF	SB	CS	SB%	GDP	Avg	OBP	SLG
1986 Beloit	A Mil	49	173	45	3	2	4	64	26	21	18	0	33	2	0	3	0	0	.00	3	.260	.332	.370

		BATTING															BASERUNNING				PERCENTAGES		
Year Team	Lg Org	G	AB	H	2B	3B	HR	TB	R	RBI	TBB	IBB	SO	HBP	SH	SF	SB	CS	SB%	GDP	Avg	OBP	SLG
1987 Beloit	A Mil	130	461	139	30	3	20	235	83	85	49	2	96	7	1	3	7	4	.64	4	.302	.375	.510
1988 Stockton	A+ Mil	138	519	147	32	6	15	236	81	92	57	1	96	11	6	5	10	5	.67	6	.283	.363	.455
1989 El Paso	AA Mil	120	463	139	30	3	17	226	72	93	29	3	72	8	2	9	5	4	.56	8	.300	.346	.488
1990 Denver	AAA Mil	116	416	120	20	3	18	200	72	74	26	0	58	14	3	7	6	2	.75	9	.288	.346	.481
1991 Denver	AAA Mil	122	462	135	19	9	18	226	69	91	37	4	59	11	0	7	2	5	.29	13	.292	.354	.489
1993 Ottawa	AAA Mon	27	106	31	7	1	6	58	15	21	10	2	22	0	0	1	1	0	1.00	3	.292	.347	.547
1994 Salt Lake	AAA Min	118	464	157	34	0	18	245	87	96	26	0	48	14	2	6	1	0	1.00	10	.338	.386	.528
1996 Columbus	AAA NYA	67	206	57	11	1	10	100	30	28	11	1	40	6	2	2	0	0	.00	6	.277	.329	.485
1997 Iowa	AAA ChN	17	54	14	3	0	2	23	9	8	3	0	14	2	0	0	0	0	.00	0	.259	.322	.426
1990 Milwaukee	AL	5	5	1	0	0	1	4	1	1	0	0	2	0	0	0	0	0	.00	0	.200	.200	.800
1991 Milwaukee	AL	7	11	4	1	0	1	8	2	1	0	0	4	0	0	0	0	0	.00	0	.364	.364	.727
1992 Milwaukee	AL	35	77	14	3	0	0	17	7	6	3	0	9	2	1	1	1	3	.25	1	.182	.229	.221
1993 Milwaukee	AL	1	0	0	0	0	0	0	0	0	0	0	0	0	0	0	0	0	.00	0	.000	.000	.000
Montreal	NL	20	21	2	1	0	0	3	2	2	0	0	7	0	0	0	0	0	.00	0	.095	.095	.143
1996 New York	AL	3	3	0	0	0	0	0	0	0	0	0	0	0	0	0	0	0	.00	0	.000	.000	.000
10 Min. YEARS		904	3324	984	189	28	128	1613	544	609	266	13	538	75	16	44	32	20	.62	62	.296	.357	.485
5 Maj. YEARS		71	117	21	5	0	2	32	12	10	3	0	22	2	1	1	1	3	.25	1	.179	.211	.274

Scott McKenzie

Pitches: Right **Bats:** Right **Pos:** P   **Ht:** 6'0" **Wt:** 185 **Born:** 9/30/70 **Age:** 27

		HOW MUCH HE PITCHED						WHAT HE GAVE UP												THE RESULTS				
Year Team	Lg Org	G	GS	CG	GF	IP	BFP	H	R	ER	HR	SH	SF	HB	TBB	IBB	SO	WP	Bk	W	L	Pct.	ShO	Sv	ERA
1993 Billings	R+ Cin	14	1	0	5	30	130	27	16	12	2	2	3	1	14	0	37	6	4	1	2	.333	0	0	3.60
1994 Chston-WV	A Cin	17	17	5	0	105.2	434	105	50	43	6	3	4	5	20	0	65	2	0	8	5	.615	1	0	3.66
1995 Winston-Sal	A+ Cin	49	0	0	41	72	294	42	27	22	7	5	0	5	30	2	55	7	0	3	4	.429	0	20	2.75
1996 Chattanooga	AA Cin	27	0	0	7	47.2	214	51	25	18	7	0	2	0	23	3	28	4	0	2	4	.333	0	0	3.40
1997 Chattanooga	AA Cin	30	0	0	9	53	251	74	37	34	8	1	5	4	19	2	30	2	0	2	0	1.000	0	0	5.77
5 Min. YEARS		137	18	5	62	308.1	1323	299	155	129	30	11	14	15	106	7	215	21	4	16	15	.516	1	20	3.77

Sandy McKinnon

Bats: Right **Throws:** Right **Pos:** OF   **Ht:** 5'8" **Wt:** 175 **Born:** 9/20/73 **Age:** 24

		BATTING															BASERUNNING				PERCENTAGES		
Year Team	Lg Org	G	AB	H	2B	3B	HR	TB	R	RBI	TBB	IBB	SO	HBP	SH	SF	SB	CS	SB%	GDP	Avg	OBP	SLG
1993 White Sox	R ChA	6	11	2	0	0	0	2	2	0	3	0	2	2	1	0	4	0	1.00	0	.182	.438	.182
Hickory	A ChA	64	263	66	10	3	0	82	29	21	21	0	47	1	1	2	17	12	.59	1	.251	.307	.312
1994 South Bend	A ChA	117	462	111	9	4	3	137	64	28	32	0	83	4	7	3	36	14	.72	7	.240	.293	.297
1995 Pr William	A+ ChA	125	494	125	19	5	2	160	64	23	39	0	93	3	3	1	35	17	.67	6	.253	.311	.324
1996 Pr William	A+ ChA	113	410	108	28	5	8	170	56	60	23	0	68	2	9	2	20	10	.67	4	.263	.304	.415
1997 Birmingham	AA ChA	96	332	90	20	1	4	124	58	31	31	1	68	2	5	3	13	6	.68	3	.271	.334	.373
5 Min. YEARS		521	1972	502	86	18	17	675	273	163	149	1	361	14	26	11	125	59	.68	21	.255	.310	.342

Buck McNabb

Bats: Left **Throws:** Right **Pos:** OF   **Ht:** 6'0" **Wt:** 180 **Born:** 1/17/73 **Age:** 25

		BATTING															BASERUNNING				PERCENTAGES		
Year Team	Lg Org	G	AB	H	2B	3B	HR	TB	R	RBI	TBB	IBB	SO	HBP	SH	SF	SB	CS	SB%	GDP	Avg	OBP	SLG
1991 Astros	R Hou	48	174	51	3	3	0	60	34	9	12	0	33	4	3	2	23	8	.74	0	.293	.349	.345
1992 Burlington	A Hou	123	456	118	12	3	1	139	82	34	60	0	80	10	3	2	56	19	.75	4	.259	.356	.305
1993 Osceola	A+ Hou	125	487	139	15	7	1	171	69	35	52	2	66	6	4	1	28	15	.65	8	.285	.361	.351
1994 Jackson	AA Hou	125	454	124	25	7	0	163	67	27	26	0	63	1	4	2	15	17	.47	10	.273	.313	.359
1995 Jackson	AA Hou	15	50	13	1	0	0	14	4	3	5	0	11	0	0	0	1	0	1.00	0	.260	.327	.280
Canton-Akrn	AA Cle	19	48	8	0	0	0	8	3	1	6	0	14	1	2	0	0	1	.00	1	.167	.273	.167
Bakersfield	A+ Cle	63	237	71	8	1	0	81	34	27	38	1	38	0	0	5	11	1	.92	5	.300	.394	.342
1996 Kissimmee	A+ Hou	7	26	9	1	0	0	10	4	3	3	1	5	0	0	0	3	0	1.00	0	.346	.414	.385
Jackson	AA Hou	88	279	84	15	5	0	109	38	26	41	1	37	2	1	2	10	6	.63	3	.301	.392	.391
1997 New Orleans	AAA Hou	11	19	3	0	1	0	5	2	0	1	0	6	0	0	0	0	0	.00	0	.158	.200	.263
Jackson	AA Hou	112	395	102	16	2	1	125	65	30	42	0	58	4	7	0	10	9	.53	9	.258	.336	.316
7 Min. YEARS		736	2625	722	96	29	3	885	402	195	286	5	411	28	28	11	157	76	.67	40	.275	.351	.337

Sean McNally

Bats: Right **Throws:** Right **Pos:** 3B   **Ht:** 6'4" **Wt:** 205 **Born:** 12/14/72 **Age:** 25

		BATTING															BASERUNNING				PERCENTAGES		
Year Team	Lg Org	G	AB	H	2B	3B	HR	TB	R	RBI	TBB	IBB	SO	HBP	SH	SF	SB	CS	SB%	GDP	Avg	OBP	SLG
1994 Eugene	A- KC	74	278	69	16	2	3	98	44	30	24	1	66	4	2	2	4	7	.36	5	.248	.315	.353
1995 Springfield	A KC	132	479	130	28	8	12	210	60	79	35	6	119	8	0	6	6	3	.67	10	.271	.328	.438
1996 Wilmington	A+ KC	126	428	118	27	1	8	171	49	63	57	2	83	5	1	8	3	5	.50	8	.276	.361	.400
1997 Wichita	AA KC	18	53	13	4	0	0	17	9	2	11	0	12	0	0	1	2	2	.33	2	.245	.375	.321
Wilmington	A+ KC	95	323	86	22	2	17	163	51	68	40	4	98	2	3	1	2	1	.67	6	.266	.350	.505
4 Min. YEARS		445	1561	416	97	13	40	659	213	242	167	13	378	19	6	17	16	16	.50	31	.266	.341	.422

Brian McNichol

Pitches: Left **Bats:** Left **Pos:** P   **Ht:** 6'6" **Wt:** 210 **Born:** 5/20/74 **Age:** 24

		HOW MUCH HE PITCHED						WHAT HE GAVE UP												THE RESULTS				
Year Team	Lg Org	G	GS	CG	GF	IP	BFP	H	R	ER	HR	SH	SF	HB	TBB	IBB	SO	WP	Bk	W	L	Pct.	ShO	Sv	ERA
1995 Williamsprt	A- ChN	9	9	0	0	49.2	215	57	28	17	1	1	1	2	8	0	35	1	1	3	1	.750	0	0	3.08
1996 Daytona	A+ ChN	8	7	0	0	34.2	162	39	24	18	4	0	1	0	14	0	22	1	0	1	2	.333	0	0	4.67

	HOW MUCH HE PITCHED							WHAT HE GAVE UP												THE RESULTS					
Year Team	Lg Org	G	GS	CG	GF	IP	BFP	H	R	ER	HR	SH	SF	HB	TBB	IBB	SO	WP	Bk	W	L	Pct.	ShO	Sv	ERA
Cubs	R ChN	1	1	0	0	3.1	16	4	2	0	0	0	0	0	0	0	2	0	0	0	0	.000	0	0	0.00
1997 Daytona	A+ ChN	6	6	0	0	39	161	32	14	10	1	1	2	3	10	1	40	1	0	2	2	.500	0	0	2.31
Orlando	AA ChN	22	22	0	0	119.1	544	153	89	77	18	3	7	2	42	6	97	9	0	7	10	.412	0	0	5.81
3 Min. YEARS		46	45	0	0	246	1098	285	157	122	24	5	11	7	74	7	196	12	1	13	15	.464	0	0	4.46

Rusty Meacham

Pitches: Right Bats: Right Pos: P Ht: 6'3" Wt: 180 Born: 1/27/68 Age: 30

	HOW MUCH HE PITCHED							WHAT HE GAVE UP												THE RESULTS					
Year Team	Lg Org	G	GS	CG	GF	IP	BFP	H	R	ER	HR	SH	SF	HB	TBB	IBB	SO	WP	Bk	W	L	Pct.	ShO	Sv	ERA
1988 Fayetteville	A Det	6	5	0	0	24.2	117	37	19	17	3	0	1	2	6	1	16	2	5	0	3	.000	0	0	6.20
Bristol	R+ Det	13	9	2	1	75.1	303	55	14	12	2	1	1	7	22	0	85	5	1	9	1	.900	2	0	1.43
1989 Fayetteville	A Det	16	15	2	1	102	413	103	33	26	4	1	4	1	23	0	74	2	3	10	3	.769	2	0	2.29
Lakeland	A+ Det	11	9	4	1	64.2	259	59	15	14	3	3	0	2	12	2	39	0	0	5	4	.556	2	0	1.95
1990 London	AA Det	26	26	9	0	178	722	160	70	62	11	3	7	4	36	0	123	5	1	15	9	.625	3	0	3.13
1991 Toledo	AAA Det	26	17	3	4	125.1	517	117	53	43	8	2	5	1	40	3	70	6	0	9	7	.563	1	2	3.09
1993 Omaha	AAA KC	7	0	0	2	9.1	37	10	5	5	1	0	0	0	1	0	10	0	0	0	0	.000	0	0	4.82
1994 Omaha	AAA KC	8	0	0	5	9	40	9	7	7	0	0	1	0	3	0	16	1	1	1	1	.500	0	1	7.00
1996 Omaha	AAA KC	23	4	0	8	52.1	233	56	30	28	6	4	2	1	18	0	39	2	1	3	3	.500	0	2	4.82
Tacoma	AAA Sea	7	2	0	2	19.2	78	13	7	5	0	0	0	1	5	0	20	1	0	2	1	.667	0	2	2.29
1997 Pawtucket	AAA Bos	28	2	0	0	43.1	196	54	23	23	6	2	2	2	15	2	42	5	0	3	3	.500	0	1	4.78
1991 Detroit	AL	10	4	0	1	27.2	126	35	17	16	4	1	3	0	11	0	14	0	1	2	1	.667	0	0	5.20
1992 Kansas City	AL	64	0	0	20	101.2	412	88	39	31	5	3	9	1	21	5	64	4	0	10	4	.714	0	2	2.74
1993 Kansas City	AL	15	0	0	10	21	104	31	15	13	2	0	1	3	5	1	13	0	0	2	2	.500	0	0	5.57
1994 Kansas City	AL	36	0	0	15	50.2	213	51	23	21	7	1	4	2	12	1	36	4	0	3	3	.500	0	4	3.73
1995 Kansas City	AL	49	0	0	26	59.2	262	72	36	33	6	1	4	1	19	5	30	0	0	4	3	.571	0	2	4.98
1996 Seattle	AL	15	5	0	3	42.1	192	57	28	27	9	0	1	4	13	1	25	1	0	1	1	.500	0	1	5.74
8 Min. YEARS		171	89	20	33	703.2	2915	673	276	242	44	16	23	21	181	8	534	29	12	57	35	.620	8	8	3.10
6 Maj. YEARS		189	9	0	76	303	1309	334	158	141	33	6	22	11	81	13	182	9	1	22	14	.611	0	9	4.19

Brian Meadows

Pitches: Right Bats: Right Pos: P Ht: 6'4" Wt: 210 Born: 11/21/75 Age: 22

	HOW MUCH HE PITCHED							WHAT HE GAVE UP												THE RESULTS					
Year Team	Lg Org	G	GS	CG	GF	IP	BFP	H	R	ER	HR	SH	SF	HB	TBB	IBB	SO	WP	Bk	W	L	Pct.	ShO	Sv	ERA
1994 Marlins	R Fla	8	7	0	0	37	151	34	9	8	1	0	0	1	6	0	33	0	0	3	0	1.000	0	0	1.95
1995 Kane County	A Fla	26	26	1	0	147	646	163	90	69	11	8	4	12	41	0	103	3	2	9	9	.500	1	0	4.22
1996 Brevard Cty	A+ Fla	24	23	3	1	146	600	129	73	58	13	3	4	10	25	1	69	4	1	8	7	.533	1	0	3.58
Portland	AA Fla	4	4	1	0	27	108	26	15	13	1	3	1	1	4	0	13	0	0	0	1	.000	0	0	4.33
1997 Portland	AA Fla	29	29	4	0	175.2	763	204	99	90	23	9	2	4	48	4	115	7	1	9	7	.563	0	0	4.61
4 Min. YEARS		91	89	9	1	532.2	2268	556	286	238	49	23	11	28	124	5	333	14	4	29	24	.547	2	0	4.02

Rafael Medina

Pitches: Right Bats: Right Pos: P Ht: 6'3" Wt: 194 Born: 2/15/75 Age: 23

	HOW MUCH HE PITCHED							WHAT HE GAVE UP												THE RESULTS					
Year Team	Lg Org	G	GS	CG	GF	IP	BFP	H	R	ER	HR	SH	SF	HB	TBB	IBB	SO	WP	Bk	W	L	Pct.	ShO	Sv	ERA
1993 Yankees	R NYA	5	5	0	0	27.1	107	16	6	2	0	1	1		12	0	21	1	1	3	0	1.000	0	0	0.66
1994 Oneonta	A- NYA	14	14	1	0	73.1	319	67	54	38	7	2	5	1	35	0	59	7	3	3	7	.300	0	0	4.66
1995 Greensboro	A NYA	19	19	1	0	98.2	418	86	48	44	8	0	5	6	38	0	108	6	3	4	4	.500	0	0	4.01
Tampa	A+ NYA	6	6	0	0	30.1	131	29	12	8	0	0	0	1	12	0	25	2	0	2	2	.500	0	0	2.37
1996 Norwich	AA NYA	19	19	1	0	103	446	78	48	35	7	5	1	6	55	2	112	11	4	5	8	.385	0	0	3.06
1997 Rancho Cuca	A+ SD	3	3	0	0	18	86	13	4	4	1	1	0	0	5	0	14	1	0	2	0	1.000	0	0	2.00
Las Vegas	AAA SD	13	13	0	0	66.2	321	90	60	56	12	1	1	2	39	1	50	8	2	4	5	.444	0	0	7.56
5 Min. YEARS		79	79	3	0	417.1	1810	379	232	187	35	10	13	17	196	3	389	34	15	22	26	.458	0	0	4.03

Tony Medrano

Bats: Right Throws: Right Pos: 2B Ht: 5'11" Wt: 155 Born: 12/8/74 Age: 23

	BATTING																BASERUNNING				PERCENTAGES		
Year Team	Lg Org	G	AB	H	2B	3B	HR	TB	R	RBI	TBB	IBB	SO	HBP	SH	SF	SB	CS	SB%	GDP	Avg	OBP	SLG
1993 Blue Jays	R Tor	39	158	42	9	0	0	51	20	9	10	0	9	3	0	0	6	2	.75	1	.266	.322	.323
1994 Blue Jays	R Tor	6	22	8	4	0	1	15	2	5	1	0	0	0	0	0	0	0	.00	2	.364	.391	.682
Dunedin	A+ Tor	60	199	47	6	4	4	73	20	21	12	0	26	3	3	1	3	3	.50	4	.236	.288	.367
1995 Wichita	AA KC	1	5	0	0	0	0	0	0	0	0	0	3	0	0	0	0	0	.00	0	.000	.000	.000
Wilmington	A+ KC	123	460	131	20	6	3	172	69	43	34	2	42	5	15	4	11	6	.65	10	.285	.338	.374
1996 Wichita	AA KC	125	474	130	26	1	8	182	59	55	18	0	36	2	7	2	10	8	.56	8	.274	.302	.384
1997 Wichita	AA KC	108	349	86	9	1	4	109	45	42	26	1	32	1	9	4	8	2	.80	10	.246	.297	.312
Omaha	AAA KC	17	59	12	0	0	4	24	10	9	4	1	5	0	0	3	1		.00	1	.203	.242	.407
5 Min. YEARS		479	1726	456	74	12	24	626	225	184	105	4	153	14	34	14	38	22	.63	36	.264	.309	.363

Doug Meiners

Pitches: Right Bats: Right Pos: P Ht: 6'8" Wt: 190 Born: 5/16/74 Age: 24

	HOW MUCH HE PITCHED							WHAT HE GAVE UP												THE RESULTS					
Year Team	Lg Org	G	GS	CG	GF	IP	BFP	H	R	ER	HR	SH	SF	HB	TBB	IBB	SO	WP	Bk	W	L	Pct.	ShO	Sv	ERA
1992 Blue Jays	R Tor	7	7	0	0	28	112	20	10	7	0	0	0	1	9	0	17	2	1	1	2	.333	0	0	2.25
1993 St. Cathms	A- Tor	15	15	1	0	91	381	89	52	40	8	1	3	1	32	0	56	3	0	5	6	.455	1	0	3.96
1994 Hagerstown	A Tor	26	26	4	0	153	655	170	82	57	7	1	5	5	40	0	104	8	0	8	10	.444	2	0	3.35
1995 Hagerstown	A Tor	18	18	3	0	117.1	477	121	52	39	5	2	2	3	14	0	73	4	1	8	4	.667	0	0	2.99

Year Team	Lg Org	HOW MUCH HE PITCHED						WHAT HE GAVE UP												THE RESULTS					
		G	GS	CG	GF	IP	BFP	H	R	ER	HR	SH	SF	HB	TBB	IBB	SO	WP	Bk	W	L	Pct.	ShO	Sv	ERA
1996 Dunedin	A+ Tor	17	3	0	6	38.2	165	37	21	14	2	0	2	4	8	1	16	0	0	1	1	.500	0	0	3.26
1997 Knoxville	AA Tor	23	23	3	0	122.2	554	161	85	74	13	4	3	8	31	0	81	4	0	9	5	.643	0	0	5.43
6 Min. YEARS		106	92	11	6	550.2	2344	598	302	231	35	8	15	22	134	1	347	21	2	32	28	.533	3	0	3.78

Adam Meinershagen

Pitches: Right Bats: Right Pos: P   Ht: 6'4" Wt: 190 Born: 7/25/73 Age: 24

Year Team	Lg Org	HOW MUCH HE PITCHED						WHAT HE GAVE UP												THE RESULTS					
		G	GS	CG	GF	IP	BFP	H	R	ER	HR	SH	SF	HB	TBB	IBB	SO	WP	Bk	W	L	Pct.	ShO	Sv	ERA
1991 Blue Jays	R Tor	11	8	0	3	41	178	39	28	16	1	0	1	2	19	0	21	9	3	3	2	.600	0	0	3.51
1992 St. Cathms	A- Tor	11	8	0	1	44.1	199	44	24	22	6	1	3	3	20	0	36	8	6	1	7	.125	0	1	4.47
1993 Hagerstown	A Tor	5	5	0	0	25.2	119	37	22	21	3	1	1	0	11	0	16	3	0	0	3	.000	0	0	7.36
St. Cathms	A- Tor	13	13	1	0	86	329	53	19	18	2	2	1	3	26	0	87	1	0	8	1	.889	1	0	1.88
1994 Dunedin	A+ Tor	19	16	1	0	101.2	453	115	62	54	10	3	5	5	42	0	52	8	1	6	6	.500	0	0	4.78
1995 Knoxville	AA Tor	3	3	0	0	11.2	55	17	14	14	2	1	0	1	2	0	4	0	0	1	1	.500	0	0	10.80
Dunedin	A+ Tor	21	13	1	2	98.1	430	115	59	41	13	3	8	6	23	1	53	3	0	5	9	.357	0	0	3.75
1997 Knoxville	AA Tor	7	7	0	0	17	72	16	8	7	0	0	1	0	6	0	7	0	0	0	0	.000	0	0	3.71
Dunedin	A+ Tor	3	2	0	0	9	41	12	5	5	0	1	1	1	1	0	4	0	0	0	1	.000	0	0	5.00
6 Min. YEARS		93	75	3	6	434.2	1876	448	241	198	37	12	21	21	150	1	280	32	10	24	30	.444	1	1	4.10

Dan Melendez

Bats: Left Throws: Left Pos: 1B   Ht: 6'4" Wt: 195 Born: 1/4/71 Age: 27

Year Team	Lg Org	BATTING															BASERUNNING				PERCENTAGES		
		G	AB	H	2B	3B	HR	TB	R	RBI	TBB	IBB	SO	HBP	SH	SF	SB	CS	SB%	GDP	Avg	OBP	SLG
1992 Bakersfield	A+ LA	39	146	39	11	2	0	54	18	11	22	5	18	0	0	1	1	0	1.00	1	.267	.361	.370
1993 San Antonio	AA LA	47	158	38	11	0	7	70	25	30	11	0	29	1	0	5	0	0	.00	2	.241	.286	.443
1995 San Antonio	AA LA	128	464	121	28	1	7	172	46	59	51	5	66	1	0	6	0	3	.00	11	.261	.331	.371
1996 Albuquerque	AAA LA	31	46	7	2	0	0	9	5	2	8	0	14	0	0	1	0	0	.00	0	.152	.273	.196
San Antonio	AA LA	67	189	45	10	0	1	58	19	29	20	4	31	1	0	3	0	0	.00	3	.238	.316	.307
1997 San Antonio	AA LA	87	258	66	19	1	2	93	40	24	44	2	42	1	4	3	4	2	.67	3	.256	.363	.360
5 Min. YEARS		399	1261	316	81	4	17	456	153	155	156	16	200	6	4	19	5	5	.50	20	.251	.331	.362

David Melendez

Pitches: Right Bats: Both Pos: P   Ht: 6'0" Wt: 168 Born: 6/25/76 Age: 22

Year Team	Lg Org	HOW MUCH HE PITCHED						WHAT HE GAVE UP												THE RESULTS					
		G	GS	CG	GF	IP	BFP	H	R	ER	HR	SH	SF	HB	TBB	IBB	SO	WP	Bk	W	L	Pct.	ShO	Sv	ERA
1996 Fayetteville	A Det	27	21	1	2	130.2	549	114	56	38	7	4	2	16	40	1	121	8	8	11	4	.733	0	0	2.62
1997 Lakeland	A+ Det	15	15	2	0	102.1	409	70	28	20	5	0	3	7	32	0	79	3	3	8	4	.667	1	0	1.76
Jacksnville	AA Det	12	11	2	0	72.2	314	77	47	43	10	0	2	5	24	0	55	0	0	6	4	.600	0	0	5.33
2 Min. YEARS		54	47	5	2	305.2	1272	261	131	101	22	4	7	28	96	1	255	11	11	25	12	.676	1	0	2.97

Adam Melhuse

Bats: Both Throws: Right Pos: C   Ht: 6'2" Wt: 185 Born: 3/27/72 Age: 26

Year Team	Lg Org	BATTING															BASERUNNING				PERCENTAGES		
		G	AB	H	2B	3B	HR	TB	R	RBI	TBB	IBB	SO	HBP	SH	SF	SB	CS	SB%	GDP	Avg	OBP	SLG
1993 St. Cathms	A- Tor	73	266	68	14	2	5	101	40	32	45	4	61	0	2	3	4	0	1.00	4	.256	.360	.380
1994 Hagerstown	A Tor	118	422	109	16	3	11	164	61	58	53	3	77	1	1	6	6	8	.43	13	.258	.338	.389
1995 Dunedin	A+ Tor	123	428	92	20	0	4	124	43	41	61	1	87	1	1	4	6	1	.86	7	.215	.312	.290
1996 Dunedin	A+ Tor	97	315	78	23	2	13	144	50	51	69	2	68	3	0	4	3	1	.75	5	.248	.384	.457
Knoxville	AA Tor	32	94	20	3	0	1	26	13	6	14	1	29	0	1	1	0	1	.00	3	.213	.312	.277
1997 Knoxville	AA Tor	31	87	20	3	0	3	32	14	10	19	1	19	0	1	1	0	0	.00	1	.230	.364	.368
Syracuse	AAA Tor	38	118	28	5	1	2	41	7	9	12	0	18	1	0	1	1	1	.50	2	.237	.311	.347
5 Min. YEARS		512	1730	415	84	8	39	632	228	207	273	12	359	6	6	20	20	12	.63	35	.240	.342	.365

Juan Melo

Bats: Both Throws: Right Pos: SS   Ht: 6'3" Wt: 185 Born: 11/5/76 Age: 21

Year Team	Lg Org	BATTING															BASERUNNING				PERCENTAGES		
		G	AB	H	2B	3B	HR	TB	R	RBI	TBB	IBB	SO	HBP	SH	SF	SB	CS	SB%	GDP	Avg	OBP	SLG
1994 Spokane	A- SD	3	11	4	1	0	1	8	4	2	1	0	3	0	0	0	0	0	.00	1	.364	.417	.727
Las Vegas	AAA SD	0	0	0	0	0	0	0	0	0	0	0	0	0	0	0	0	0	.00	0	.000	.000	.000
Padres	R SD	37	145	41	3	3	0	50	20	15	10	0	36	6	0	1	3	2	.60	0	.283	.352	.345
1995 Clinton	A SD	134	479	135	32	1	5	184	65	46	33	0	88	5	5	2	12	10	.55	11	.282	.333	.384
1996 Rancho Cuca	A+ SD	128	503	153	27	6	8	216	75	75	22	0	102	10	0	1	6	8	.43	10	.304	.345	.429
1997 Las Vegas	AAA SD	12	48	13	4	0	1	20	6	6	1	0	10	1	0	1	0	0	.00	0	.271	.294	.417
Mobile	AA SD	113	456	131	22	2	7	178	52	67	29	4	90	0	0	2	7	9	.44	16	.287	.329	.390
4 Min. YEARS		428	1642	477	89	12	22	656	222	211	96	4	329	22	5	7	28	29	.49	43	.290	.337	.400

Mitch Meluskey

Bats: Both Throws: Right Pos: C   Ht: 5'11" Wt: 185 Born: 9/18/73 Age: 24

Year Team	Lg Org	BATTING															BASERUNNING				PERCENTAGES		
		G	AB	H	2B	3B	HR	TB	R	RBI	TBB	IBB	SO	HBP	SH	SF	SB	CS	SB%	GDP	Avg	OBP	SLG
1992 Burlington	R+ Cle	43	126	29	7	0	3	45	23	16	29	0	36	0	0	2	3	0	1.00	0	.230	.369	.357
1993 Columbus	A Cle	101	342	84	18	3	3	117	36	47	35	4	69	4	4	7	1	1	.50	5	.246	.317	.342
1994 Kinston	A+ Cle	100	319	77	16	1	3	104	36	41	49	0	62	2	2	4	3	4	.43	4	.241	.342	.326
1995 Kinston	A+ Cle	8	29	7	5	0	0	12	5	2	2	0	9	0	0	0	0	0	.00	1	.241	.290	.414

Year Team	Lg Org	G	AB	H	2B	3B	HR	TB	R	RBI	TBB	IBB	SO	HBP	SH	SF	SB	CS	SB%	GDP	Avg	OBP	SLG
Kissimmee	A+ Hou	78	261	56	18	1	3	85	23	31	27	2	33	1	2	4	3	0	1.00	12	.215	.287	.326
1996 Kissimmee	A+ Hou	74	231	77	19	0	1	99	29	31	29	5	26	1	1	5	1	1	.50	9	.333	.402	.429
Jackson	AA Hou	38	134	42	11	0	0	53	18	21	18	0	24	1	1	1	0	0	.00	6	.313	.396	.396
1997 Jackson	AA Hou	73	241	82	18	0	14	142	49	46	31	4	39	3	0	3	1	3	.25	7	.340	.417	.589
New Orleans	AAA Hou	51	172	43	7	0	3	59	22	21	25	1	38	1	0	1	0	0	.00	6	.250	.347	.343
6 Min. YEARS		566	1855	497	119	5	30	716	241	256	245	16	336	13	10	27	12	9	.57	50	.268	.353	.386

Carlos Mendez

Bats: Right Throws: Right Pos: 1B Ht: 6'1" Wt: 195 Born: 6/18/74 Age: 24

Year Team	Lg Org	G	AB	H	2B	3B	HR	TB	R	RBI	TBB	IBB	SO	HBP	SH	SF	SB	CS	SB%	GDP	Avg	OBP	SLG
1992 Royals	R KC	49	200	61	16	1	3	88	34	33	8	2	13	2	0	3	2	1	.67	2	.305	.333	.440
1993 Royals	R KC	50	163	51	10	0	4	73	18	27	4	1	15	2	0	4	6	1	.86	2	.313	.329	.448
1994 Rockford	A KC	104	363	120	26	2	5	174	45	51	13	2	50	5	4	4	0	2	.00	11	.273	.301	.384
1995 Wilmington	A+ KC	107	396	108	19	2	7	152	46	61	18	1	36	0	1	5	3	1	.75	6	.293	.329	.399
1996 Wilmington	A+ KC	109	406	119	25	3	4	162	40	59	22	4	39	3	3	7	4	7	.36	19	.293	.329	.399
1997 Wichita	AA KC	129	507	165	32	1	12	235	72	90	19	2	43	1	0	8	4	7	.36	19	.325	.346	.464
6 Min. YEARS		548	2035	633	128	9	35	884	255	321	84	12	196	13	8	31	15	16	.48	57	.311	.337	.434

Sergio Mendez

Bats: Right Throws: Right Pos: 1B Ht: 6'2" Wt: 180 Born: 10/12/73 Age: 24

Year Team	Lg Org	G	AB	H	2B	3B	HR	TB	R	RBI	TBB	IBB	SO	HBP	SH	SF	SB	CS	SB%	GDP	Avg	OBP	SLG
1992 Pirates	R Pit	36	52	14	1	0	0	15	6	5	1	0	8	0	0	1	3	0	1.00	1	.269	.278	.288
1993 Welland	A- Pit	32	121	30	4	1	0	36	12	10	0	0	28	4	0	1	0	1	.00	4	.248	.272	.298
1994 Augusta	A Pit	88	331	91	15	2	7	131	36	38	10	1	70	4	0	1	7	4	.64	4	.275	.303	.396
1995 Lynchburg	A+ Pit	65	236	58	13	0	8	95	30	35	9	1	49	3	2	2	9	4	.69	9	.246	.280	.403
1996 Augusta	A Pit	46	172	40	9	0	7	70	23	26	9	2	31	5	0	0	3	3	.50	4	.233	.290	.407
Lynchburg	A+ Pit	39	137	38	9	1	4	61	19	17	6	0	24	1	0	1	0	1	.00	2	.277	.310	.445
1997 Lynchburg	A+ Pit	17	64	9	2	0	2	17	5	6	1	0	18	2	0	0	1	1	.50	2	.141	.179	.266
Carolina	AA Pit	49	146	34	10	1	2	52	17	12	6	1	33	4	0	2	1	1	.50	10	.233	.278	.356
6 Min. YEARS		351	1259	314	63	5	30	477	148	149	42	5	261	23	2	7	23	15	.61	36	.249	.285	.379

Reynol Mendoza

Pitches: Right Bats: Right Pos: P Ht: 6'0" Wt: 215 Born: 10/27/70 Age: 27

Year Team	Lg Org	G	GS	CG	GF	IP	BFP	H	R	ER	HR	SH	SF	HB	TBB	IBB	SO	WP	Bk	W	L	Pct.	ShO	Sv	ERA
1992 Erie	A- Fla	15	15	1	0	69.2	310	70	46	36	5	2	3	8	25	0	59	6	1	3	6	.333	1	0	4.65
1993 Kane County	A Fla	26	23	3	3	163.2	647	129	59	52	5	6	0	9	45	3	153	13	3	12	5	.706	0	2	2.86
1994 Marlins	R Fla	2	1	0	0	4.1	16	1	0	0	0	0	0	0	2	0	6	0	0	0	0	.000	0	0	0.00
Brevard Cty	A+ Fla	10	9	1	0	37	183	47	33	26	2	3	1	2	26	0	26	4	2	1	3	.250	0	0	6.32
1995 Portland	AA Fla	27	27	1	0	168	715	163	73	64	6	10	4	9	69	3	120	15	0	9	10	.474	1	0	3.43
1996 Portland	AA Fla	10	10	2	0	63	255	60	27	24	7	0	0	3	14	0	41	5	0	4	2	.667	2	0	3.43
Charlotte	AAA Fla	15	14	2	1	91	413	112	67	57	18	6	2	4	33	0	41	8	0	7	4	.636	0	0	5.64
1997 Charlotte	AAA Fla	46	17	0	15	114.2	526	134	79	70	14	4	3	2	57	4	93	15	1	7	8	.467	0	9	5.49
6 Min. YEARS		151	116	10	19	711.1	3065	716	384	329	57	31	13	37	271	10	539	66	7	43	38	.531	4	11	4.16

Frankie Menechino

Bats: Right Throws: Right Pos: 2B Ht: 5'9" Wt: 175 Born: 1/7/71 Age: 27

Year Team	Lg Org	G	AB	H	2B	3B	HR	TB	R	RBI	TBB	IBB	SO	HBP	SH	SF	SB	CS	SB%	GDP	Avg	OBP	SLG
1993 White Sox	R ChA	17	45	11	4	1	1	20	10	9	12	0	4	4	0	0	3	1	.75	1	.244	.443	.444
Hickory	A ChA	50	178	50	6	3	4	74	35	19	33	0	28	4	1	1	11	2	.85	4	.281	.403	.416
1994 South Bend	A ChA	106	379	113	21	5	5	159	77	48	78	1	70	9	3	2	15	8	.65	8	.298	.427	.420
1995 Pr William	A+ ChA	137	476	124	31	3	6	179	65	58	96	2	75	11	3	8	6	2	.75	17	.261	.391	.376
1996 Birmingham	AA ChA	125	415	121	25	3	12	188	77	62	64	0	84	8	3	6	7	9	.44	5	.292	.391	.453
1997 Nashville	AAA ChA	37	113	26	4	0	4	42	20	11	26	1	31	6	0	1	3	2	.60	2	.230	.372	.372
Birmingham	AA ChA	90	318	95	28	4	12	167	78	60	79	0	77	11	1	6	7	3	.70	7	.299	.447	.525
5 Min. YEARS		562	1924	540	119	19	44	829	362	267	388	4	369	53	11	24	52	27	.66	44	.281	.411	.431

Hector Mercado

Pitches: Left Bats: Left Pos: P Ht: 6'3" Wt: 205 Born: 4/29/74 Age: 24

Year Team	Lg Org	G	GS	CG	GF	IP	BFP	H	R	ER	HR	SH	SF	HB	TBB	IBB	SO	WP	Bk	W	L	Pct.	ShO	Sv	ERA
1992 Astros	R Hou	13	3	0	4	30	140	22	17	14	0	1	0	3	25	0	36	7	6	1	2	.333	0	0	4.20
1993 Osceola	A+ Hou	2	2	0	0	8.2	39	9	7	5	0	0	0	0	6	1	5	0	0	1	1	.500	0	0	5.19
Astros	R Hou	11	11	1	0	67	278	49	26	18	1	0	3	1	29	0	59	10	2	5	4	.556	1	0	2.42
1994 Osceola	A+ Hou	25	25	1	0	136.2	601	123	75	60	5	11	4	1	79	4	88	9	3	6	13	.316	1	0	3.95
Jackson	AA Hou	8	7	0	0	30	157	36	33	26	5	2	1	2	32	1	20	4	0	1	4	.200	0	0	7.80
1995 Kissimmee	A+ Hou	19	17	2	0	104	433	96	50	40	2	2	3	3	37	0	75	4	1	6	8	.429	0	0	3.46
1996 Kissimmee	A+ Hou	56	0	0	18	80	353	78	43	37	4	3	1	4	48	1	68	6	0	3	5	.375	0	3	4.16
1997 Charlotte	AAA Fla	1	1	0	0	5	25	5	5	5	2	0	0	0	5	0	1	1	0	1	0	1.000	0	0	9.00
Portland	AA Fla	31	17	1	6	129.2	565	129	66	57	10	6	1	3	54	5	125	16	2	11	3	.786	1	0	3.96
6 Min. YEARS		166	83	5	28	591	2591	547	322	262	29	25	13	17	315	12	477	57	14	34	41	.453	3	3	3.99

Guillermo Mercedes

Bats: Both **Throws:** Right **Pos:** SS **Ht:** 5'11" **Wt:** 155 **Born:** 1/17/74 **Age:** 24

Year Team	Lg Org	G	AB	H	2B	3B	HR	TB	R	RBI	TBB	IBB	SO	HBP	SH	SF	SB	CS	SB%	GDP	Avg	OBP	SLG
1992 Rangers	R Tex	49	176	38	4	0	0	42	30	7	18	0	26	4	0	0	18	6	.75	1	.216	.303	.239
1993 Chston-SC	A Tex	127	457	109	12	2	0	125	55	30	47	0	60	2	8	3	41	17	.71	9	.239	.310	.274
1994 Charlotte	A+ Tex	132	443	98	7	1	0	107	44	37	47	0	67	5	11	4	14	13	.52	9	.221	.301	.242
1995 Tulsa	AA Tex	15	42	5	1	0	0	6	4	1	4	0	6	0	1	0	0	0	.00	2	.119	.196	.143
Charlotte	A+ Tex	33	110	24	2	0	0	26	10	5	7	0	12	1	2	1	1	2	.33	1	.218	.269	.236
Columbus	A Cle	55	183	35	5	1	2	48	23	8	18	0	19	3	1	0	6	3	.67	5	.191	.275	.262
1996 Kinston	A+ Cle	117	382	94	12	1	0	108	45	27	30	1	41	5	14	1	3	3	.50	13	.246	.309	.283
1997 Akron	AA Cle	97	288	60	7	1	0	69	37	27	28	0	38	5	10	5	2	3	.40	9	.208	.285	.240
6 Min. YEARS		625	2081	463	50	6	2	531	248	142	199	1	269	25	47	14	85	47	.64	49	.222	.296	.255

Mark Merchant

Bats: Both **Throws:** Right **Pos:** DH **Ht:** 6'2" **Wt:** 185 **Born:** 1/23/69 **Age:** 29

Year Team	Lg Org	G	AB	H	2B	3B	HR	TB	R	RBI	TBB	IBB	SO	HBP	SH	SF	SB	CS	SB%	GDP	Avg	OBP	SLG
1987 Pirates	R Pit	50	185	49	5	1	3	65	32	17	30	4	29	1	0	0	33	13	.72	0	.265	.370	.351
1988 Augusta	A Pit	60	211	51	6	0	2	63	36	19	41	2	38	2	0	2	14	3	.82	5	.242	.367	.299
1989 Augusta	A Pit	15	59	19	6	1	0	27	11	8	7	1	13	0	0	1	3	1	.75	1	.322	.388	.458
San Berndno	A+ Sea	119	429	90	15	2	11	142	65	46	61	1	101	2	0	4	17	6	.74	12	.210	.308	.331
1990 Williamsprt	AA Sea	44	156	28	5	0	0	33	16	10	14	2	36	1	0	0	7	2	.78	8	.179	.249	.212
San Berndno	A+ Sea	29	102	32	3	0	4	47	22	19	20	0	34	0	0	0	8	2	.80	1	.314	.426	.461
1991 Peninsula	A+ Sea	78	270	68	8	1	6	96	31	34	51	6	70	0	0	0	11	4	.73	7	.252	.371	.356
Jacksnville	AA Sea	51	156	44	10	0	5	69	22	17	21	4	37	1	0	1	3	4	.43	2	.282	.369	.442
1992 Jacksnville	AA Sea	109	381	93	9	1	13	143	42	47	37	2	91	2	1	6	3	2	.60	11	.244	.310	.375
1993 Indianapols	AAA Cin	3	6	1	1	0	0	2	2	0	2	0	3	0	1	0	0	0	.00	0	.167	.375	.333
Chattanooga	AA Cin	109	336	101	16	0	17	168	56	61	50	2	79	3	0	3	3	5	.38	9	.301	.393	.500
1994 Chattanooga	AA Cin	106	329	102	14	2	5	135	31	56	39	8	46	0	1	5	1	2	.33	10	.310	.378	.410
1995 Chattanooga	AA Cin	25	53	11	0	0	1	14	4	6	7	1	15	0	0	5	0	0	.00	4	.208	.300	.264
Sioux City	IND —	61	217	69	14	0	11	116	41	41	36	2	40	1	0	1	1	1	.50	2	.318	.416	.535
1996 Nashville	AAA ChA	42	131	28	6	0	4	46	21	15	17	1	29	2	1	1	1	1	.50	6	.214	.311	.351
Omaha	AAA KC	38	118	33	7	0	4	52	18	21	22	0	26	0	1	0	1	0	1.00	6	.280	.393	.441
1997 Omaha	AAA KC	2	5	0	0	0	0	0	0	0	0	0	4	0	0	0	0	0	.00	0	.000	.000	.000
Wichita	AA KC	49	147	50	9	0	9	86	27	38	23	0	35	1	2	0	0	1	.00	3	.340	.431	.585
11 Min. YEARS		990	3291	869	134	8	95	1304	477	455	478	36	726	17	5	28	106	47	.69	87	.264	.358	.396

Lou Merloni

Bats: Right **Throws:** Right **Pos:** 3B-2B **Ht:** 5'10" **Wt:** 188 **Born:** 4/6/71 **Age:** 27

Year Team	Lg Org	G	AB	H	2B	3B	HR	TB	R	RBI	TBB	IBB	SO	HBP	SH	SF	SB	CS	SB%	GDP	Avg	OBP	SLG
1993 Red Sox	R Bos	4	14	5	1	0	0	6	4	1	1	0	1	1	0	0	1	1	.50	0	.357	.438	.429
Ft. Laud	A+ Bos	44	156	38	1	1	2	47	14	21	13	1	26	1	0	4	1	1	.50	6	.244	.299	.301
1994 Sarasota	A+ Bos	113	419	120	16	2	1	143	59	63	36	4	57	7	7	10	5	2	.71	11	.286	.345	.341
1995 Trenton	AA Bos	93	318	88	16	1	1	109	42	30	39	3	50	11	11	2	7	7	.50	1	.277	.373	.343
1996 Trenton	AA Bos	28	95	22	6	1	3	39	11	16	9	1	18	5	1	0	0	2	.00	2	.232	.330	.411
Red Sox	R Bos	1	4	1	0	0	0	1	1	1	0	0	0	0	0	1	0	0	.00	0	.250	.200	.250
Pawtucket	AAA Bos	38	115	29	6	0	1	38	19	12	10	0	20	3	4	0	0	1	.00	1	.252	.328	.330
1997 Trenton	AA Bos	69	255	79	17	4	5	119	49	37	30	1	43	12	1	4	3	2	.60	2	.310	.402	.467
Pawtucket	AAA Bos	49	165	49	10	0	5	74	24	24	15	2	20	4	1	1	0	2	.00	4	.297	.368	.448
5 Min. YEARS		439	1541	431	73	9	18	576	223	205	153	12	235	44	25	22	17	18	.49	27	.280	.357	.374

Rafael Mesa

Pitches: Right **Bats:** Right **Pos:** P **Ht:** 6'4" **Wt:** 175 **Born:** 10/9/73 **Age:** 24

Year Team	Lg Org	G	GS	CG	GF	IP	BFP	H	R	ER	HR	SH	SF	HB	TBB	IBB	SO	WP	Bk	W	L	Pct.	ShO	Sv	ERA
1994 Burlington	R+ Cle	29	0	0	27	60	126	19	15	11	1	1	1	4	14	2	33	4	0	1	0	1.000	0	13	3.30
Kinston	A+ Cle	3	0	0	2	2.1	9	0	0	0	0	0	0	0	2	0	6	0	0	0	0	.000	0	0	0.00
1995 Kinston	A+ Cle	35	1	0	24	52	206	34	19	17	5	4	3	4	20	2	29	4	0	4	3	.571	0	0	2.94
1996 Kinston	A+ Cle	45	1	0	34	81.1	330	58	26	21	4	5	1	8	28	3	56	1	1	8	3	.727	0	15	2.32
1997 Akron	AA Cle	14	0	0	4	25.2	114	36	13	12	1	1	0	3	9	0	7	1	0	0	1	.000	0	0	4.21
4 Min. YEARS		126	2	0	91	191.1	785	147	73	61	11	11	5	19	73	7	131	10	1	13	7	.650	0	28	2.87

Mike Micucci

Bats: Left **Throws:** Right **Pos:** C **Ht:** 5'11" **Wt:** 185 **Born:** 12/15/72 **Age:** 25

Year Team	Lg Org	G	AB	H	2B	3B	HR	TB	R	RBI	TBB	IBB	SO	HBP	SH	SF	SB	CS	SB%	GDP	Avg	OBP	SLG
1994 Williamsprt	A- ChN	43	105	20	2	0	0	22	16	8	8	0	16	4	5	3	3	2	.60	1	.190	.267	.210
1995 Daytona	A+ ChN	23	41	8	2	0	0	10	4	3	4	0	9	0	2	0	0	0	.00	0	.195	.267	.244
1996 Daytona	A+ ChN	39	82	15	0	0	0	15	6	3	5	0	16	1	1	0	0	3	.00	3	.183	.239	.183
1997 Orlando	AA ChN	4	6	0	0	0	0	0	0	0	0	0	1	0	0	0	0	0	.00	0	.000	.000	.000
Daytona	A+ ChN	54	140	35	5	0	1	43	15	24	12	1	27	1	1	0	1	4	.20	3	.250	.314	.307
4 Min. YEARS		163	374	78	9	0	1	90	41	38	29	1	69	6	9	3	4	9	.31	7	.209	.274	.241

Doug Mientkiewicz

Bats: Left **Throws:** Right **Pos:** 1B **Ht:** 6'2" **Wt:** 190 **Born:** 6/19/74 **Age:** 24

Year Team	Lg Org	G	AB	H	2B	3B	HR	TB	R	RBI	TBB	IBB	SO	HBP	SH	SF	SB	CS	SB%	GDP	Avg	OBP	SLG
1995 Ft. Myers	A+ Min	38	110	27	6	1	1	38	9	15	18	1	19	1	2	0	2	2	.50	1	.245	.357	.345
1996 Ft. Myers	A+ Min	133	492	143	36	4	5	202	69	79	66	3	47	3	1	6	12	2	.86	10	.291	.374	.411
1997 New Britain	AA Min	132	467	119	28	2	15	196	87	61	98	2	67	7	5	2	21	8	.72	8	.255	.390	.420
3 Min. YEARS		303	1069	289	70	7	21	436	165	155	182	6	133	11	8	8	35	12	.74	19	.270	.380	.408

Adam Millan

Bats: Right **Throws:** Right **Pos:** C **Ht:** 6'0" **Wt:** 195 **Born:** 3/26/72 **Age:** 26

Year Team	Lg Org	G	AB	H	2B	3B	HR	TB	R	RBI	TBB	IBB	SO	HBP	SH	SF	SB	CS	SB%	GDP	Avg	OBP	SLG
1994 Batavia	A- Phi	17	53	17	4	0	0	21	10	11	10	0	6	1	0	1	0	0	.00	1	.321	.431	.396
Spartanburg	A Phi	48	153	41	12	0	4	65	20	29	33	1	21	1	0	1	1	1	.50	6	.268	.399	.425
1995 Reading	AA Phi	10	20	7	3	0	1	13	3	7	4	0	3	1	0	1	0	0	.00	1	.350	.462	.650
Piedmont	A Phi	107	394	116	25	2	10	175	69	64	44	3	45	7	1	3	1	4	.20	15	.294	.373	.444
1996 Clearwater	A+ Phi	101	348	94	21	1	11	150	55	55	52	2	52	3	0	6	1	2	.33	15	.270	.364	.431
1997 Clearwater	A+ Phi	13	55	16	3	1	1	24	7	8	5	0	8	0	0	1	1	0	1.00	1	.291	.344	.436
Scranton-WB	AAA Phi	1	2	1	0	0	0	1	0	1	1	1	0	0	0	0	0	0	.00	0	.500	.667	.500
Reading	AA Phi	95	266	65	10	0	9	102	43	43	44	0	52	2	2	4	0	0	.00	5	.244	.351	.383
4 Min. YEARS		392	1291	357	78	4	36	551	207	218	193	7	187	15	3	17	4	7	.36	44	.277	.373	.427

Kevin Millar

Bats: Right **Throws:** Right **Pos:** 1B **Ht:** 6'1" **Wt:** 195 **Born:** 9/24/71 **Age:** 26

Year Team	Lg Org	G	AB	H	2B	3B	HR	TB	R	RBI	TBB	IBB	SO	HBP	SH	SF	SB	CS	SB%	GDP	Avg	OBP	SLG
1994 Kane County	A Fla	135	477	144	35	2	19	240	75	93	74	2	88	13	0	6	3	3	.50	12	.302	.405	.503
1995 Brevard Cty	A+ Fla	129	459	132	32	2	13	207	53	68	70	2	66	12	0	10	4	4	.50	8	.288	.388	.451
1996 Portland	AA Fla	130	472	150	32	0	18	236	69	86	37	4	53	9	0	5	6	5	.55	13	.318	.375	.500
1997 Portland	AA Fla	135	511	175	34	2	32	309	94	131	66	9	53	10	0	7	2	3	.40	11	.342	.423	.605
4 Min. YEARS		529	1919	601	133	6	82	992	291	378	247	17	260	44	0	28	15	15	.50	44	.313	.399	.517

David Miller

Bats: Left **Throws:** Left **Pos:** OF **Ht:** 6'4" **Wt:** 200 **Born:** 12/9/73 **Age:** 24

Year Team	Lg Org	G	AB	H	2B	3B	HR	TB	R	RBI	TBB	IBB	SO	HBP	SH	SF	SB	CS	SB%	GDP	Avg	OBP	SLG
1996 Kinston	A+ Cle	129	488	124	23	1	7	170	71	54	38	4	94	0	2	5	14	7	.67	7	.254	.305	.348
1997 Akron	AA Cle	134	509	153	27	9	4	210	84	61	48	2	77	2	6	4	22	11	.67	5	.301	.361	.413
2 Min. YEARS		263	997	277	50	10	11	380	155	115	86	6	171	2	8	9	36	18	.67	12	.278	.334	.381

Ryan Miller

Bats: Right **Throws:** Right **Pos:** 2B **Ht:** 6'0" **Wt:** 175 **Born:** 10/22/72 **Age:** 25

Year Team	Lg Org	G	AB	H	2B	3B	HR	TB	R	RBI	TBB	IBB	SO	HBP	SH	SF	SB	CS	SB%	GDP	Avg	OBP	SLG
1994 Pittsfield	A- NYN	68	277	71	11	1	1	87	37	23	16	1	37	4	3	2	3	3	.50	0	.256	.304	.314
1995 St. Lucie	A+ NYN	89	279	68	10	3	2	90	32	23	13	0	42	7	8	2	5	3	.63	7	.244	.292	.323
Binghamton	AA NYN	9	19	1	0	0	0	1	3	0	2	0	4	0	1	0	1	0	1.00	1	.053	.143	.053
1996 St. Lucie	A+ NYN	86	310	79	8	3	2	99	32	23	22	1	51	3	13	1	8	5	.62	5	.255	.310	.319
1997 St. Lucie	A+ NYN	61	193	49	12	1	2	69	27	28	11	0	38	1	2	2	5	5	.50	3	.254	.295	.358
Kissimmee	A+ Hou	13	34	9	0	0	0	9	5	1	5	0	3	0	2	0	1	0	1.00	0	.265	.359	.265
Jackson	AA Hou	20	55	11	0	2	1	18	6	8	5	0	10	0	1	1	1	0	1.00	1	.200	.262	.327
4 Min. YEARS		346	1167	288	41	10	8	373	142	106	74	2	185	15	30	8	24	16	.60	16	.247	.298	.320

Trever Miller

Pitches: Left **Bats:** Right **Pos:** P **Ht:** 6'4" **Wt:** 195 **Born:** 5/29/73 **Age:** 25

Year Team	Lg Org	G	GS	CG	GF	IP	BFP	H	R	ER	HR	SH	SF	HB	TBB	IBB	SO	WP	Bk	W	L	Pct.	ShO	Sv	ERA
1991 Bristol	R+ Det	13	13	0	0	54	253	60	44	34	7	3	3	2	29	0	46	9	1	2	7	.222	0	0	5.67
1992 Bristol	R+ Det	12	12	1	0	69.1	311	75	45	38	4	3	3	1	27	0	64	4	1	3	8	.273	0	0	4.93
1993 Fayetteville	A Det	28	28	2	0	161	699	151	99	75	7	2	8	5	67	0	116	10	0	8	13	.381	0	0	4.19
1994 Trenton	AA Det	26	26	6	0	174.1	754	198	95	85	9	10	8	3	51	0	73	3	1	7	16	.304	0	0	4.39
1995 Jacksonville	AA Det	31	16	3	4	122.1	512	122	46	37	5	4	2	5	34	0	77	1	0	8	2	.800	2	0	2.72
1996 Toledo	AAA Det	27	27	0	0	165.1	722	167	98	90	19	4	1	9	65	1	115	3	2	13	6	.684	0	0	4.90
1997 New Orleans	AAA Hou	29	27	2	0	163.2	694	177	71	60	15	8	4	3	54	1	99	6	0	6	7	.462	0	0	3.30
1996 Detroit	AL	5	4	0	0	16.2	88	28	17	17	3	2	2	2	9	0	8	0	0	0	4	.000	0	0	9.18
7 Min. YEARS		166	149	14	4	910	3945	950	498	419	66	34	29	28	327	2	590	36	5	47	59	.443	2	0	4.14

Joe Millette

Bats: Right **Throws:** Right **Pos:** SS **Ht:** 6'1" **Wt:** 175 **Born:** 8/12/66 **Age:** 31

Year Team	Lg Org	G	AB	H	2B	3B	HR	TB	R	RBI	TBB	IBB	SO	HBP	SH	SF	SB	CS	SB%	GDP	Avg	OBP	SLG
1989 Batavia	A- Phi	11	42	10	3	0	0	13	4	4	4	0	6	0	0	0	3	0	1.00	0	.238	.304	.310
Spartanburg	A Phi	60	209	50	4	3	0	60	27	18	28	0	36	7	3	3	4	2	.67	5	.239	.344	.287
1990 Clearwater	A+ Phi	108	295	54	5	0	0	59	31	18	29	0	53	7	7	6	4	4	.50	5	.183	.267	.200
1991 Clearwater	A+ Phi	18	55	14	2	0	0	16	6	6	7	0	6	1	2	0	1	2	.33	1	.255	.338	.291

Year Team	Lg Org	G	AB	H	2B	3B	HR	TB	R	RBI	TBB	IBB	SO	HBP	SH	SF	SB	CS	SB%	GDP	Avg	OBP	SLG
Reading	AA Phi	115	353	87	9	4	3	113	52	28	36	2	54	7	10	3	6	6	.50	5	.246	.326	.320
1992 Scranton-WB	AAA Phi	78	256	68	11	1	1	84	24	23	15	0	30	6	7	0	3	2	.60	8	.266	.321	.328
1993 Scranton-WB	AAA Phi	107	343	77	15	2	1	99	27	24	19	2	56	5	7	1	5	4	.56	9	.224	.274	.289
1994 Edmonton	AAA Fla	118	406	107	22	3	4	147	41	38	13	3	73	6	6	2	5	5	.50	15	.264	.295	.362
1995 Charlotte	AAA Fla	74	193	36	6	0	4	54	22	20	10	0	36	4	1	4	1	1	.50	4	.187	.237	.280
1996 Calgary	AAA Pit	53	108	23	8	0	0	31	7	7	9	0	19	2	1	0	0	2	.00	4	.213	.286	.287
1997 Memphis	AA Sea	57	191	58	11	1	3	80	36	22	14	0	35	8	0	0	2	5	.29	4	.304	.376	.419
Tacoma	AAA Sea	46	123	26	2	1	0	30	12	5	8	0	23	2	0	0	1	1	.50	1	.211	.271	.244
1992 Philadelphia	NL	33	78	16	0	0	0	16	5	2	5	2	10	2	2	0	1	0	1.00	8	.205	.271	.205
1993 Philadelphia	NL	10	10	2	0	0	0	2	3	2	1	0	2	0	3	0	0	0	.00	1	.200	.273	.200
9 Min. YEARS		845	2574	610	98	15	16	786	289	213	192	7	427	55	45	21	35	34	.51	65	.237	.302	.305
2 Maj. YEARS		43	88	18	0	0	0	18	8	4	6	2	12	2	5	0	1	0	1.00	9	.205	.271	.205

Doug Million

Pitches: Left   Bats: Left   Pos: P   Ht: 6'4"   Wt: 175   Born: 10/13/75   Died: 9/23/97

Year Team	Lg Org	G	GS	CG	GF	IP	BFP	H	R	ER	HR	SH	SF	HB	TBB	IBB	SO	WP	Bk	W	L	Pct.	ShO	Sv	ERA
1994 Rockies	R Col	3	3	0	0	12	46	8	3	2	0	0	0	0	3	0	19	2	0	1	0	1.000	0	0	1.50
Bend	A- Col	10	10	0	0	57.2	246	50	23	15	4	1	0	4	21	0	75	4	0	5	3	.625	0	0	2.34
1995 Salem	A+ Col	24	23	0	0	111	513	111	71	57	6	6	1	9	79	4	85	9	4	5	7	.417	0	0	4.62
1996 Salem	A+ Col	17	16	1	0	106.2	443	84	37	30	1	2	0	2	60	1	99	8	1	7	5	.583	1	0	2.53
New Haven	AA Col	10	10	0	0	54.1	247	54	23	19	2	1	1	1	40	1	40	8	2	3	3	.500	0	0	3.15
1997 New Haven	AA Col	10	10	0	0	40	213	64	46	41	7	6	0	3	36	0	19	4	2	0	5	.000	0	0	9.23
Salem	A+ Col	18	17	1	0	96.2	436	104	59	55	13	3	3	8	55	1	58	5	0	5	9	.357	0	0	5.12
4 Min. YEARS		92	89	2	0	478.1	2144	475	262	219	33	19	5	27	294	7	395	40	9	26	32	.448	1	0	4.12

Eric Milton

Pitches: Left   Bats: Left   Pos: P   Ht: 6'3"   Wt: 200   Born: 8/4/75   Age: 22

Year Team	Lg Org	G	GS	CG	GF	IP	BFP	H	R	ER	HR	SH	SF	HB	TBB	IBB	SO	WP	Bk	W	L	Pct.	ShO	Sv	ERA
1997 Tampa	A+ NYA	14	14	1	0	93.1	371	78	35	32	8	2	1	3	14	0	95	4	3	8	3	.727	0	0	3.09
Norwich	AA NYA	14	14	1	0	77.2	322	59	29	27	2	1	4	0	36	0	67	3	4	6	3	.667	0	0	3.13
1 Min. YEARS		28	28	2	0	171	693	137	64	59	10	3	5	3	50	0	162	7	7	14	6	.700	0	0	3.11

Mark Mimbs

Pitches: Left   Bats: Left   Pos: P   Ht: 6'2"   Wt: 180   Born: 2/13/69   Age: 29

Year Team	Lg Org	G	GS	CG	GF	IP	BFP	H	R	ER	HR	SH	SF	HB	TBB	IBB	SO	WP	Bk	W	L	Pct.	ShO	Sv	ERA
1990 Great Falls	R+ LA	14	14	0	0	78	325	69	32	28	3	0	0	1	29	0	94	4	3	7	4	.636	0	0	3.23
1991 Bakersfield	A+ LA	27	25	0	1	170	687	134	49	42	2	3	2	3	59	2	164	4	2	12	6	.667	0	0	2.22
1992 Albuquerque	AAA LA	12	7	0	0	48.2	217	58	34	33	4	1	1	0	19	1	32	4	0	0	4	.000	0	0	6.10
San Antonio	AA LA	13	13	0	0	82.1	340	78	43	33	3	5	2	2	22	4	55	3	0	1	5	.167	0	0	3.61
1993 Albuquerque	AAA LA	19	1	0	3	18.2	90	20	21	21	0	2	2	0	16	1	12	2	1	0	1	.000	0	0	10.13
San Antonio	AA LA	49	0	0	23	67.2	272	49	21	12	0	6	4	2	18	7	77	2	0	3	3	.500	0	10	1.60
1994 Bakersfield	A+ LA	1	0	0	0	1.2	7	3	0	0	0	0	0	0	0	0	0	0	0	0	0	.000	0	0	0.00
Albuquerque	AAA LA	6	0	0	3	6.2	28	8	3	3	1	0	0	0	0	0	9	1	0	1	0	1.000	0	0	4.05
1995 Albuquerque	AAA LA	23	16	1	2	106	433	105	40	35	7	3	3	1	22	0	96	7	1	6	5	.545	0	0	2.97
1996 Albuquerque	AAA LA	34	23	1	1	151	656	165	93	77	14	4	2	3	43	2	136	7	1	8	8	.500	1	0	4.59
1997 Pawtucket	AAA Bos	15	14	0	0	83.2	376	97	58	47	11	1	3	2	35	3	81	2	2	3	8	.273	0	0	5.06
New Orleans	AAA Hou	22	3	0	5	33	144	36	19	16	2	3	2	3	9	1	26	0	0	1	2	.333	0	1	4.36
8 Min. YEARS		235	116	2	38	847.1	3575	822	413	347	47	28	21	17	272	21	782	36	10	42	46	.477	1	12	3.69

Steve Mintz

Pitches: Right   Bats: Left   Pos: P   Ht: 5'11"   Wt: 195   Born: 11/28/68   Age: 29

Year Team	Lg Org	G	GS	CG	GF	IP	BFP	H	R	ER	HR	SH	SF	HB	TBB	IBB	SO	WP	Bk	W	L	Pct.	ShO	Sv	ERA
1990 Yakima	A- LA	20	0	0	12	26	113	21	9	7	1	3	1	1	16	1	38	2	1	2	3	.400	0	3	2.42
1991 Bakersfield	A+ LA	28	11	0	6	92	419	85	56	44	2	5	4	4	58	1	101	6	6	6	6	.500	0	3	4.30
1992 Vero Beach	A+ LA	43	2	0	21	77.2	323	66	29	27	7	5	3	3	30	2	66	7	3	2	4	.333	0	6	3.13
1993 New Britain	AA SF	43	1	0	20	69.1	287	52	22	16	3	5	1	2	30	5	51	7	0	2	4	.333	0	7	2.08
1994 Phoenix	AAA SF	24	0	0	13	36	161	40	24	22	8	1	1	2	13	1	27	3	0	0	1	.000	0	3	5.50
Shreveport	AA SF	30	0	0	12	65.1	261	45	29	16	5	2	1	2	22	1	42	8	0	10	2	.833	0	2	2.20
1995 Phoenix	AAA SF	31	0	0	19	49	205	42	16	13	4	3	0	2	21	4	36	4	0	5	2	.714	0	7	2.39
1996 Phoenix	AAA SF	59	0	0	45	57	256	63	39	34	6	1	3	2	25	3	35	5	2	3	5	.375	0	27	5.37
1997 Las Vegas	AAA SD	27	0	0	16	34.2	171	50	31	31	7	1	2	2	17	3	28	2	0	5	2	.714	0	5	8.05
1995 San Francisco	NL	14	0	0	3	19.1	96	26	16	16	4	2	1	2	12	3	7	0	0	1	2	.333	0	0	7.45
8 Min. YEARS		305	14	0	164	507	2196	464	255	210	43	26	18	19	232	23	424	47	7	36	31	.537	0	61	3.73

Donovan Mitchell

Bats: Left   Throws: Right   Pos: OF   Ht: 5'9"   Wt: 175   Born: 11/27/69   Age: 28

Year Team	Lg Org	G	AB	H	2B	3B	HR	TB	R	RBI	TBB	IBB	SO	HBP	SH	SF	SB	CS	SB%	GDP	Avg	OBP	SLG
1992 Auburn	A- Hou	70	292	85	8	3	1	102	44	18	10	3	32	1	1	3	25	8	.76	4	.291	.324	.349
1993 Asheville	A Hou	113	453	132	20	3	3	167	67	45	33	1	52	1	2	1	28	18	.61	5	.291	.340	.369
1994 Osceola	A+ Hou	119	455	109	14	4	0	131	47	36	34	1	56	2	5	3	20	13	.61	7	.240	.294	.288

Year Team	Lg Org	G	AB	H	2B	3B	HR	TB	R	RBI	TBB	IBB	SO	HBP	SH	SF	SB	CS	SB%	GDP	Avg	OBP	SLG
1995 Quad City	A Hou	111	383	126	23	1	4	163	72	42	29	0	38	2	5	3	21	15	.58	10	.329	.376	.426
1996 Jackson	AA Hou	120	408	103	22	2	3	138	57	32	33	2	51	3	4	2	11	4	.73	8	.252	.312	.338
1997 Jackson	AA Hou	128	477	122	17	6	5	166	64	44	61	4	48	3	12	0	22	11	.67	9	.256	.344	.348
6 Min. YEARS		661	2468	677	104	19	16	867	351	217	203	8	277	12	31	9	127	69	.65	43	.274	.331	.351

Keith Mitchell

Bats: Right **Throws:** Right **Pos:** OF   **Ht:** 5'10" **Wt:** 180 **Born:** 8/6/69 **Age:** 28

Year Team	Lg Org	G	AB	H	2B	3B	HR	TB	R	RBI	TBB	IBB	SO	HBP	SH	SF	SB	CS	SB%	GDP	Avg	OBP	SLG
1987 Braves	R Atl	57	208	50	12	1	2	70	24	21	29	0	50	2	0	2	7	2	.78	4	.240	.336	.337
1988 Sumter	A Atl	98	341	85	16	1	5	118	35	33	41	0	50	4	3	2	9	6	.60	8	.249	.335	.346
1989 Burlington	A Atl	127	448	117	23	0	10	170	64	49	70	1	65	5	0	4	12	7	.63	9	.261	.364	.379
1990 Durham	A+ Atl	129	456	134	24	3	6	182	81	48	92	2	48	4	1	7	18	17	.51	16	.294	.411	.399
1991 Greenville	AA Atl	60	214	70	15	3	10	121	46	47	29	0	29	1	3	5	12	8	.60	5	.327	.402	.565
Richmond	AAA Atl	25	95	31	6	1	2	45	16	17	9	0	13	1	2	3	0	2	.00	3	.326	.380	.474
1992 Richmond	AAA Atl	121	403	91	19	1	4	124	45	50	66	2	55	4	2	4	14	9	.61	6	.226	.338	.308
1993 Richmond	AAA Atl	110	353	82	23	1	4	119	59	44	44	0	48	2	3	3	9	5	.64	11	.232	.318	.337
1994 Calgary	AAA Sea	9	39	10	0	0	4	22	6	12	2	0	4	0	0	1	0	0	.00	0	.256	.286	.564
1995 Indianapolis	AAA Cin	70	213	52	11	2	11	100	40	36	40	3	40	1	1	4	4	4	.50	7	.244	.360	.469
1996 Indianapolis	AAA Cin	112	357	107	21	3	16	182	60	66	64	2	68	1	0	6	9	1	.90	7	.300	.402	.510
1997 Indianapolis	AAA Cin	124	407	108	24	1	15	179	72	60	72	1	65	1	1	6	10	4	.71	11	.265	.372	.440
1991 Atlanta	NL	48	66	21	0	0	2	27	11	5	8	0	12	0	0	0	3	1	.75	1	.318	.392	.409
1994 Seattle	AL	46	128	29	2	0	5	46	21	15	18	0	22	1	1	1	0	0	.00	2	.227	.324	.359
1996 Cincinnati	NL	11	15	4	1	0	1	8	2	3	1	0	3	0	0	0	0	0	.00	0	.267	.313	.533
11 Min. YEARS		1042	3534	937	194	17	89	1432	548	483	558	11	535	26	16	47	104	65	.62	87	.265	.365	.405
3 Maj. YEARS		105	209	54	3	0	8	81	34	23	27	0	37	1	1	1	3	1	.75	3	.258	.345	.388

Larry Mitchell

Pitches: Right **Bats:** Right **Pos:** P   **Ht:** 6'1" **Wt:** 219 **Born:** 10/16/71 **Age:** 26

Year Team	Lg Org	G	GS	CG	GF	IP	BFP	H	R	ER	HR	SH	SF	HB	TBB	IBB	SO	WP	Bk	W	L	Pct.	ShO	Sv	ERA
1992 Martinsvlle	R+ Phi	3	3	0	0	19	77	17	8	3	0	0	0	1	6	0	18	0	0	1	0	1.000	0	0	1.42
Batavia	A- Phi	10	10	3	0	65	267	63	25	19	6	2	2	1	11	0	58	4	1	7	2	.778	1	0	2.63
1993 Spartanburg	A Phi	19	19	4	0	116.1	505	113	55	53	3	2	7	3	54	0	114	14	0	6	6	.500	2	0	4.10
Clearwater	A+ Phi	9	9	1	0	57	234	50	23	19	0	5	2	0	21	1	45	4	1	4	4	.500	0	0	3.00
1994 Reading	AA Phi	30	30	2	0	165.1	737	143	91	73	5	13	8	2	103	1	128	15	0	10	13	.435	0	0	3.97
1995 Reading	AA Phi	25	24	1	1	128.1	584	136	85	79	13	2	4	4	72	4	107	7	1	6	11	.353	1	0	5.54
1996 Reading	AA Phi	34	2	0	7	57	267	55	39	33	2	4	2	1	44	2	71	3	0	3	6	.333	0	1	5.21
Scranton-WB	AAA Phi	11	0	0	2	24.2	99	19	8	7	2	1	2	0	10	0	24	1	1	1	1	.500	0	1	2.55
1997 Norwich	AA NYA	57	0	0	12	95.1	430	98	45	37	10	5	2	3	37	1	99	10	0	9	9	.500	0	0	3.49
1996 Philadelphia	NL	7	0	0	2	12	51	14	6	6	1	0	1	0	5	1	7	0	0	0	0		0	0	4.50
6 Min. YEARS		198	97	11	22	728	3200	694	379	323	41	34	27	15	358	9	664	58	4	47	52	.475	4	1	3.99

Scott Mitchell

Pitches: Right **Bats:** Right **Pos:** P   **Ht:** 5'11" **Wt:** 170 **Born:** 3/19/73 **Age:** 25

Year Team	Lg Org	G	GS	CG	GF	IP	BFP	H	R	ER	HR	SH	SF	HB	TBB	IBB	SO	WP	Bk	W	L	Pct.	ShO	Sv	ERA
1995 Vermont	A- Mon	18	1	0	5	40.1	171	35	18	10	1	2	2	4	15	0	30	2	4	3	1	.750	0	1	2.23
1996 Delmarva	A Mon	33	5	1	10	76.2	320	69	29	20	7	3	1	5	24	1	76	3	3	5	6	.455	0	1	2.35
1997 Wst Plm Bch	A+ Mon	39	3	0	15	73.2	291	61	21	21	4	3	1	3	18	0	56	4	0	5	3	.625	0	3	2.57
Harrisburg	AA Mon	4	3	0	0	17.1	67	11	7	7	3	1	0	1	3	0	13	1	0	1	0	1.000	0	0	3.63
3 Min. YEARS		94	12	1	30	208	849	176	75	58	15	9	4	13	60	1	175	10	7	14	10	.583	0	5	2.51

Tony Mitchell

Bats: Both **Throws:** Right **Pos:** OF   **Ht:** 6'4" **Wt:** 225 **Born:** 10/14/70 **Age:** 27

Year Team	Lg Org	G	AB	H	2B	3B	HR	TB	R	RBI	TBB	IBB	SO	HBP	SH	SF	SB	CS	SB%	GDP	Avg	OBP	SLG
1989 Pirates	R Pit	13	40	11	0	0	0	11	4	1	4	0	10	0	0	0	1	0	1.00	3	.275	.333	.275
1990 Pirates	R Pit	44	102	30	4	2	3	47	18	13	8	0	21	1	0	0	3	4	.43	3	.294	.351	.461
1991 Welland	A- Pit	59	211	57	9	0	10	96	30	38	17	0	62	1	1	1	7	2	.78	4	.270	.326	.455
1992 Augusta	A Pit	66	219	65	8	3	13	118	34	47	29	1	60	0	0	0	6	3	.67	3	.297	.378	.539
Columbus	A Cle	55	202	59	8	2	10	101	36	36	22	3	54	0	0	0	5	6	.45	5	.292	.362	.500
1993 Kinston	A+ Cle	96	318	78	16	2	8	122	43	44	33	2	88	3	2	5	4	1	.56	8	.245	.318	.384
1994 Canton-Akrn	AA Cle	130	494	130	24	0	25	229	70	89	41	0	114	5	0	5	6	1	.86	13	.263	.323	.464
1995 Jackson	AA Hou	96	331	88	17	2	19	166	45	61	35	1	83	1	0	3	1	2	.33	10	.266	.335	.502
1996 Jacksnville	AA Det	51	173	54	13	0	11	100	30	41	21	2	45	2	1	2	1	0	1.00	8	.312	.389	.578
Toledo	AAA Det	82	288	80	10	4	12	134	45	43	41	1	89	1	0	2	3	2	.60	8	.278	.367	.465
1997 Toledo	AAA Det	22	70	13	2	0	2	21	7	9	16	1	19	0	0	0	1	1	.50	3	.186	.337	.300
Carolina	AA Pit	4	11	1	0	0	0	1	0	1	1	0	4	0	0	0	0	0	.00	0	.091	.167	.091
9 Min. YEARS		718	2459	666	111	15	113	1146	362	423	268	11	649	14	4	20	35	25	.58	64	.271	.343	.466

Greg Mix

Pitches: Right Bats: Right Pos: P Ht: 6'4" Wt: 210 Born: 8/21/71 Age: 26

		HOW MUCH HE PITCHED						WHAT HE GAVE UP												THE RESULTS					
Year Team	Lg Org	G	GS	CG	GF	IP	BFP	H	R	ER	HR	SH	SF	HB	TBB	IBB	SO	WP	Bk	W	L	Pct.	ShO	Sv	ERA
1993 Elmira	A- Fla	17	1	0	8	45.1	205	51	26	21	4	0	1	4	17	0	38	4	0	3	3	.500	0	2	4.17
1994 Brevard Cty	A+ Fla	44	0	0	22	78	314	65	29	27	2	4	4	2	20	2	51	1	0	6	2	.750	0	4	3.12
1995 Brevard Cty	A+ Fla	5	4	1	0	29.2	119	27	13	13	1	0	0	3	10	0	17	1	1	3	1	.750	0	0	3.94
Portland	AA Fla	24	13	0	1	92.1	401	98	51	48	9	2	4	4	25	5	56	3	0	6	4	.600	0	0	4.68
1996 Charlotte	AAA Fla	4	4	0	0	18.1	87	27	15	14	4	2	0	2	7	1	9	1	0	1	3	.250	0	0	6.87
Portland	AA Fla	25	5	0	8	65.2	296	80	40	33	4	4	5	5	19	5	57	6	2	3	0	1.000	0	1	4.52
1997 Portland	AA Fla	30	13	0	4	102.2	461	121	70	54	16	7	5	8	32	0	74	5	0	7	7	.500	0	0	4.73
5 Min. YEARS		149	40	1	43	432	1883	469	244	210	44	19	19	28	130	13	302	21	3	29	20	.592	0	7	4.38

Chris Miyake

Bats: Right Throws: Right Pos: SS Ht: 6'2" Wt: 185 Born: 5/18/74 Age: 24

		BATTING														BASERUNNING				PERCENTAGES		
Year Team	Lg Org	G	AB	H	2B	3B	HR	TB	R	RBI	TBB	IBB	SO	HBP	SH	SF	SB	CS	SB%	GDP	Avg	OBP	SLG
1995 Erie	A- Pit	61	227	70	6	5	2	92	34	25	12	0	31	5	1	1	14	6	.70	3	.308	.355	.405
1996 Augusta	A Pit	101	367	88	12	0	2	106	40	33	22	0	55	2	6	2	10	10	.50	7	.240	.285	.289
1997 Carolina	AA Pit	5	9	0	0	0	0	0	0	1	0	0	4	0	1	0	0	0	.00	0	.000	.000	.000
Lynchburg	A+ Pit	79	288	72	14	1	2	94	40	20	28	1	57	1	5	0	3	2	.60	6	.250	.319	.326
3 Min. YEARS		246	891	230	32	6	6	292	115	78	62	1	147	8	13	3	27	18	.60	16	.258	.311	.328

Doug Mlicki

Pitches: Right Bats: Right Pos: P Ht: 6'3" Wt: 175 Born: 4/23/71 Age: 27

		HOW MUCH HE PITCHED						WHAT HE GAVE UP												THE RESULTS					
Year Team	Lg Org	G	GS	CG	GF	IP	BFP	H	R	ER	HR	SH	SF	HB	TBB	IBB	SO	WP	Bk	W	L	Pct.	ShO	Sv	ERA
1992 Auburn	A- Hou	14	13	0	0	81.1	330	50	35	27	4	1	3	6	30	0	83	9	2	1	6	.143	0	0	2.99
1993 Osceola	A+ Hou	26	23	0	0	158.2	668	158	81	69	16	6	5	2	65	1	111	9	0	11	10	.524	0	0	3.91
1994 Jackson	AA Hou	23	23	1	0	138.2	575	107	62	52	20	5	2	8	54	5	130	13	3	13	7	.650	0	0	3.38
1995 Jackson	AA Hou	16	16	2	0	96.2	390	73	41	30	6	1	2	4	33	0	72	5	0	8	3	.727	0	0	2.79
Tucson	AAA Hou	6	6	0	0	34	155	44	27	21	3	2	1	2	6	0	22	1	0	1	2	.333	0	0	5.56
1996 Tucson	AAA Hou	26	26	0	0	137.1	624	171	89	72	9	4	9	4	41	2	98	12	0	5	11	.313	0	0	4.72
1997 Kissimmee	A+ Hou	1	1	0	0	4	17	4	0	0	0	0	0	0	0	0	2	0	0	0	0	.000	0	0	0.00
Jackson	AA Hou	9	9	0	0	48.2	229	69	36	29	7	0	1	3	20	0	35	3	0	4	4	.500	0	0	5.36
New Orleans	AAA Hou	14	3	0	4	30	124	27	12	12	4	0	1	1	10	0	18	1	0	4	3	.571	0	0	3.60
6 Min. YEARS		135	120	3	4	729.1	3112	703	383	312	69	19	23	30	259	8	571	53	5	47	46	.505	0	0	3.85

Ben Molina

Bats: Right Throws: Right Pos: C Ht: 5'11" Wt: 190 Born: 7/20/74 Age: 23

		BATTING														BASERUNNING				PERCENTAGES		
Year Team	Lg Org	G	AB	H	2B	3B	HR	TB	R	RBI	TBB	IBB	SO	HBP	SH	SF	SB	CS	SB%	GDP	Avg	OBP	SLG
1993 Angels	R Ana	27	80	21	6	2	0	31	9	10	10	0	4	1	0	1	0	2	.00	1	.263	.348	.388
1994 Cedar Rapds	A Ana	48	171	48	8	0	3	65	14	16	8	0	12	3	1	0	1	2	.33	3	.281	.324	.380
1995 Vancouver	AAA Ana	1	2	0	0	0	0	0	0	0	0	0	0	1	0	0	0	0	.00	0	.000	.000	.000
Cedar Rapds	A Ana	39	133	39	9	0	4	60	15	17	15	0	11	1	1	1	1	1	.50	4	.293	.367	.451
Lk Elsinore	A+ Ana	27	96	37	7	2	2	54	21	12	8	1	7	4	3	1	0	0	.00	2	.385	.450	.563
1996 Midland	AA Ana	108	365	100	21	2	8	149	45	54	25	1	25	6	4	5	0	1	.00	16	.274	.327	.408
1997 Lk Elsinore	A+ Ana	36	149	42	10	2	4	68	18	33	7	2	9	0	0	3	0	1	.00	5	.282	.308	.456
Midland	AA Ana	29	106	35	8	0	6	61	18	30	10	0	7	0	0	0	0	0	.00	2	.330	.381	.575
5 Min. YEARS		315	1102	322	69	8	27	488	140	172	83	4	76	15	9	13	2	7	.22	33	.292	.346	.443

Jose Molina

Bats: Right Throws: Right Pos: C Ht: 6'1" Wt: 180 Born: 6/3/75 Age: 23

		BATTING														BASERUNNING				PERCENTAGES		
Year Team	Lg Org	G	AB	H	2B	3B	HR	TB	R	RBI	TBB	IBB	SO	HBP	SH	SF	SB	CS	SB%	GDP	Avg	OBP	SLG
1993 Cubs	R ChN	33	78	17	2	0	0	19	5	4	12	0	12	0	4	0	3	2	.60	2	.218	.322	.244
Daytona	A+ ChN	3	7	1	0	0	0	1	0	1	2	0	0	0	0	0	0	1	.00	0	.143	.333	.143
1994 Peoria	A ChN	78	253	58	13	1	1	76	31	33	24	1	61	4	5	4	4	3	.57	5	.229	.302	.300
1995 Daytona	A+ ChN	82	233	55	9	1	1	69	27	19	29	0	53	7	2	2	1	0	1.00	5	.236	.336	.296
1996 Rockford	A ChN	96	305	69	10	1	2	87	35	27	36	0	71	3	7	4	2	4	.33	8	.226	.310	.285
1997 Daytona	A+ ChN	55	179	45	9	1	0	56	17	23	14	0	25	1	5	2	4	0	1.00	5	.251	.306	.313
Orlando	AA ChN	37	99	17	3	0	1	23	10	15	12	5	28	2	1	3	1	1	.00	4	.172	.267	.232
5 Min. YEARS		385	1157	263	46	4	5	332	125	122	130	6	251	17	24	15	14	11	.56	32	.227	.311	.287

Shane Monahan

Bats: Left Throws: Right Pos: OF Ht: 6'1" Wt: 200 Born: 8/12/74 Age: 23

		BATTING														BASERUNNING				PERCENTAGES		
Year Team	Lg Org	G	AB	H	2B	3B	HR	TB	R	RBI	TBB	IBB	SO	HBP	SH	SF	SB	CS	SB%	GDP	Avg	OBP	SLG
1995 Wisconsin	A Sea	59	233	66	9	6	1	90	34	32	11	0	40	2	7	3	9	2	.82	4	.283	.317	.386
1996 Lancaster	A+ Sea	132	585	164	31	12	14	261	107	97	30	2	124	4	3	8	19	5	.79	8	.280	.316	.446
1997 Memphis	AA Sea	107	401	121	24	6	12	193	52	76	30	2	100	2	1	2	14	7	.67	4	.302	.352	.481
Tacoma	AAA Sea	21	85	25	4	0	2	35	15	12	5	0	21	1	2	0	5	1	.83	1	.294	.341	.412
3 Min. YEARS		319	1304	376	68	24	29	579	208	217	76	4	285	9	13	13	47	15	.76	17	.288	.329	.444

Wonderful Monds

Bats: Right Throws: Right Pos: OF Ht: 6'3" Wt: 190 Born: 1/11/73 Age: 25

Year Team	Lg Org	G	AB	H	2B	3B	HR	TB	R	RBI	TBB	IBB	SO	HBP	SH	SF	SB	CS	SB%	GDP	Avg	OBP	SLG
1993 Idaho Falls	R+ Atl	60	214	64	13	8	4	105	47	35	25	1	43	2	2	0	16	4	.80	4	.299	.378	.491
1994 Durham	A+ Atl	18	53	11	2	0	2	19	7	10	2	1	11	0	0	1	5	0	1.00	3	.208	.232	.358
Macon	A Atl	104	365	106	23	12	10	183	70	41	22	0	82	9	8	2	42	9	.82	6	.290	.344	.501
1995 Braves	R Atl	4	15	2	0	0	0	2	1	1	1	0	8	0	0	0	2	1	.67	0	.133	.188	.133
Durham	A+ Atl	81	297	83	17	0	6	118	44	33	17	1	63	1	1	1	28	7	.80	7	.270	.320	.397
1996 Braves	R Atl	3	5	2	0	0	2	8	3	3	2	0	1	0	0	1	0	0	.00	0	.400	.500	1.600
Greenville	AA Atl	32	110	33	9	1	2	50	17	14	9	0	17	0	0	1	7	3	.70	2	.300	.350	.455
1997 Greenville	AA Atl	27	89	28	5	0	8	57	21	15	20	0	23	0	1	1	6	3	.67	1	.315	.436	.640
Braves	R Atl	2	4	1	0	0	1	4	2	1	1	0	1	0	0	0	0	0	.00	0	.250	.400	1.000
5 Min. YEARS		331	1152	330	69	21	35	546	212	153	99	3	249	12	12	7	106	27	.80	23	.286	.347	.474

Ivan Montane

Pitches: Right Bats: Right Pos: P Ht: 6'2" Wt: 195 Born: 6/3/73 Age: 25

Year Team	Lg Org	G	GS	CG	GF	IP	BFP	H	R	ER	HR	SH	SF	HB	TBB	IBB	SO	WP	Bk	W	L	Pct	ShO	Sv	ERA
1992 Mariners	R Sea	13	11	0	1	46	224	44	39	29	0	0	0	3	41	0	48	18	4	1	3	.250	0	0	5.67
1993 Bellingham	A- Sea	15	15	1	0	73.1	305	55	36	32	7	2	1	3	37	0	53	9	3	5	4	.556	0	0	3.93
1994 Appleton	A Sea	29	26	1	0	159	680	132	79	68	13	4	6	12	82	0	155	19	2	8	9	.471	1	0	3.85
1995 Riverside	A+ Sea	24	16	0	6	92.2	442	101	67	58	3	3	6	10	71	0	79	19	0	5	5	.500	0	0	5.63
1996 Lancaster	A+ Sea	11	11	0	0	59.1	273	57	37	24	2	5	3	2	43	0	54	9	0	2	2	.500	0	0	3.64
Port City	AA Sea	18	18	0	0	100.1	461	96	67	57	6	1	2	9	75	0	81	16	2	3	8	.273	0	0	5.11
1997 Memphis	AA Sea	22	12	0	6	71.2	347	83	70	60	16	1	5	6	51	0	63	11	0	0	8	.000	0	0	7.53
Lancaster	A+ Sea	6	6	0	0	32.1	150	40	25	19	2	1	2	1	34	1	34	8	1	1	2	.333	0	0	5.29
6 Min. YEARS		138	115	2	13	634.2	2882	608	420	347	49	17	25	47	413	1	567	109	12	25	41	.379	1	0	4.92

Steve Montgomery

Pitches: Right Bats: Right Pos: P Ht: 6'7" Wt: 230 Born: 2/21/74 Age: 24

Year Team	Lg Org	G	GS	CG	GF	IP	BFP	H	R	ER	HR	SH	SF	HB	TBB	IBB	SO	WP	Bk	W	L	Pct	ShO	Sv	ERA
1994 Royals	R KC	12	0	0	6	17.1	68	12	6	3	0	0	0	0	5	0	12	1	0	1	1	.500	0	3	1.56
1995 Johnstown	IND —	33	0	0	30	38.2	148	18	1	0	0	0	2	1	16	1	52	1	1	2	0	1.000	0	9	0.00
1996 High Desert	A+ Bal	44	3	0	17	71.2	331	85	54	42	8	0	2	8	34	3	79	7	1	5	6	.455	0	2	5.27
1997 Bowie	AA Bal	24	23	2	0	136.1	569	116	56	47	15	2	3	5	52	3	127	5	1	10	5	.667	0	0	3.10
Rochester	AAA Bal	2	1	0	0	6.2	39	15	12	9	1	0	0	0	3	0	2	0	0	0	2	.000	0	0	12.15
4 Min. YEARS		115	27	2	53	270.2	1155	246	129	101	24	3	7	15	110	7	272	14	3	18	14	.563	0	14	3.36

Norm Montoya

Pitches: Left Bats: Left Pos: P Ht: 6'1" Wt: 190 Born: 9/24/70 Age: 27

Year Team	Lg Org	G	GS	CG	GF	IP	BFP	H	R	ER	HR	SH	SF	HB	TBB	IBB	SO	WP	Bk	W	L	Pct	ShO	Sv	ERA
1990 Angels	R Ana	10	6	1	2	47	199	49	20	11	1	1	0	1	7	0	28	0	0	3	3	.500	0	1	2.11
Quad City	A Ana	4	4	1	0	28.2	117	30	12	10	0	1	1	0	6	0	13	0	1	3	1	.750	0	0	3.14
1991 Quad City	A Ana	8	8	0	0	40.1	186	55	27	23	2	1	0	2	12	0	22	4	1	4	1	.800	0	0	5.13
Palm Spring	A+ Ana	17	17	1	0	105	455	117	64	48	10	3	2	2	26	4	45	3	1	4	7	.364	0	0	4.11
1992 Palm Spring	A+ Ana	14	6	2	6	43.2	194	42	21	18	3	4	2	1	19	1	46	2	1	2	3	.400	0	0	3.71
1993 Palm Spring	A+ Ana	28	4	0	8	63.2	286	83	38	34	0	3	4	3	21	5	35	6	0	1	3	.250	0	0	4.81
1994 Stockton	A+ Mil	11	0	0	3	16.1	65	12	6	4	1	2	0	1	3	0	15	0	0	0	1	.000	0	1	2.20
El Paso	AA Mil	9	0	0	4	12.1	48	10	5	4	1	0	0	0	4	2	8	0	0	1	1	.500	0	1	2.92
1995 El Paso	AA Mil	51	0	0	9	76.1	330	88	36	29	3	5	2	2	18	5	43	4	0	0	0	.000	0	2	3.42
1996 New Orleans	AAA Mil	11	0	0	6	12.2	63	23	16	12	3	0	0	0	5	1	8	0	0	0	0	.000	0	2	8.53
El Paso	AA Mil	24	17	1	4	125.1	545	153	74	65	6	3	2	2	28	2	73	4	1	9	8	.529	0	1	4.67
1997 Tucson	AAA Mil	27	24	0	2	131	589	175	100	91	16	5	4	4	38	0	75	6	2	6	10	.375	0	0	6.25
8 Min. YEARS		214	86	6	44	702.1	3077	837	419	349	45	29	18	16	187	20	411	29	7	35	43	.449	0	8	4.47

Wilmer Montoya

Pitches: Right Bats: Right Pos: P Ht: 5'10" Wt: 165 Born: 3/15/74 Age: 24

Year Team	Lg Org	G	GS	CG	GF	IP	BFP	H	R	ER	HR	SH	SF	HB	TBB	IBB	SO	WP	Bk	W	L	Pct	ShO	Sv	ERA
1994 Watertown	A- Cle	11	11	1	0	49	199	39	18	14	2	2	0	2	23	0	50	3	1	3	2	.600	0	0	2.57
1995 Kinston	A+ Cle	1	0	0	0	3.1	15	4	2	2	0	1	0	0	1	0	2	0	0	1	0	1.000	0	0	5.40
Columbus	A Cle	51	0	0	41	80.2	337	65	33	28	4	1	0	2	36	1	91	6	2	3	3	.500	0	31	3.12
1996 Kinston	A+ Cle	11	0	0	10	15	64	10	5	2	0	1	1	1	6	0	12	1	0	1	2	.333	0	2	1.20
Canton-Akrn	AA Cle	43	0	0	38	50.2	225	41	24	19	2	4	3	8	28	3	42	2	3	2	5	.286	0	23	3.38
1997 Akron	AA Cle	2	0	0	1	2.1	14	4	3	3	0	0	0	0	2	0	1	1	0	0	0	.000	0	0	11.57
4 Min. YEARS		119	11	1	90	201	854	163	85	68	8	9	4	13	96	4	199	13	6	10	12	.455	0	56	3.04

Jose Monzon

Bats: Right Throws: Right Pos: C Ht: 6'1" Wt: 178 Born: 11/8/68 Age: 29

Year Team	Lg Org	G	AB	H	2B	3B	HR	TB	R	RBI	TBB	IBB	SO	HBP	SH	SF	SB	CS	SB%	GDP	Avg	OBP	SLG
1987 Bristol	R+ Det	7	12	3	0	0	0	4	3	1	0	0	1	0	0	0	0	0	.00	1	.250	.250	.333
Lakeland	A+ Det	4	5	0	0	0	0	0	0	0	2	0	4	0	2	0	0	0	.00	0	.000	.000	.000
Fayetteville	A Det	11	19	1	0	0	0	1	1	0	2	0	5	0	0	0	0	0	.00	0	.053	.143	.053
1989 Dunedin	A+ Tor	16	48	12	2	1	0	16	4	7	5	0	11	0	0	0	0	0	.00	0	.250	.321	.333

Year Team	Lg Org	G	AB	H	2B	3B	HR	TB	R	RBI	TBB	IBB	SO	HBP	SH	SF	SB	CS	SB%	GDP	Avg	OBP	SLG
Myrtle Bch	A Tor	50	165	39	7	0	1	49	18	10	19	0	31	0	0	0	3	2	.60	7	.236	.315	.297
1990 Dunedin	A+ Tor	30	76	23	5	1	0	30	11	7	10	0	18	1	1	0	1	0	1.00	0	.303	.391	.395
Knoxville	AA Tor	1	3	1	0	0	0	1	1	0	0	0	0	0	0	0	0	0	.00	0	.333	.333	.333
1991 Dunedin	A+ Tor	46	144	31	6	0	3	46	14	17	17	0	31	0	0	6	2	0	1.00	4	.215	.294	.319
Knoxville	AA Tor	44	116	31	5	0	0	36	12	11	13	1	23	0	1	1	1	1	.50	5	.267	.338	.310
1992 Knoxville	AA Tor	65	178	41	9	1	0	52	17	10	12	0	42	2	3	1	3	2	.60	3	.230	.285	.292
Syracuse	AAA Tor	9	18	1	0	0	0	1	3	1	2	0	1	0	0	0	0	0	.00	1	.056	.150	.056
1993 Syracuse	AAA Tor	71	197	47	7	0	3	63	14	21	11	0	37	0	4	0	0	0	.00	9	.239	.279	.320
1994 Midland	AA Ana	83	283	71	18	3	4	107	41	35	24	0	52	2	3	0	1	1	.50	7	.251	.314	.378
1995 Vancouver	AAA Ana	13	23	5	1	0	1	9	5	5	3	0	2	0	0	0	0	0	.00	1	.217	.308	.391
Midland	AA Ana	57	180	52	11	1	1	68	29	19	22	0	36	2	3	2	0	0	.00	6	.289	.369	.378
1996 Midland	AA Ana	43	140	39	4	0	3	52	15	22	9	1	22	0	0	2	1	0	1.00	6	.279	.318	.371
1997 Cedar Rapds	A Ana	34	111	25	3	0	4	40	12	14	12	1	14	0	1	0	0	0	.00	8	.225	.301	.360
Vancouver	AAA Ana	17	47	11	2	0	0	13	2	6	4	0	8	0	1	1	1	0	1.00	2	.234	.288	.277
10 Min. YEARS		601	1765	433	81	7	20	588	202	186	165	3	338	7	25	9	13	7	.65	61	.245	.311	.333

Pitches: Left   Bats: Left   Pos: P

Ritchie Moody

Ht: 6'1"   Wt: 185   Born: 2/22/71   Age: 27

Year Team	Lg Org	G	GS	CG	GF	IP	BFP	H	R	ER	HR	SH	SF	HB	TBB	IBB	SO	WP	Bk	W	L	Pct.	ShO	Sv	ERA
1992 Gastonia	A Tex	21	0	0	15	26.1	107	9	7	1	0	1	1	0	16	0	29	4	1	0	2	.000	0	11	0.34
Tulsa	AA Tex	7	0	0	7	6.1	26	3	2	1	0	0	0	1	2	0	6	1	0	0	0	.000	0	2	1.42
1993 Tulsa	AA Tex	46	0	0	38	66	287	58	27	16	1	2	3	2	34	2	60	10	2	3	2	.600	0	16	2.18
1994 Okla City	AAA Tex	8	8	0	0	42	191	40	29	28	3	2	2	3	31	0	32	7	0	0	5	.000	0	0	6.00
1995 Rangers	R Tex	2	2	0	0	10	46	10	3	3	0	0	0	0	6	0	10	1	0	0	0	.000	0	0	2.70
Charlotte	A+ Tex	1	1	0	0	4.1	22	3	3	3	0	1	0	0	8	0	0	0	0	1	0	.000	0	0	6.23
Tulsa	AA Tex	11	0	0	5	20.2	94	24	18	16	2	1	1	1	18	1	9	2	0	0	1	.000	0	0	6.97
1996 Rangers	R Tex	3	0	0	1	6	19	2	1	0	0	0	0	0	0	0	9	1	0	0	0	.000	0	0	0.00
Charlotte	A+ Tex	18	1	0	11	33.1	156	34	17	15	1	1	2	2	22	0	25	3	0	1	1	.500	0	1	4.05
1997 Tulsa	AA Tex	30	0	0	13	49	243	52	41	32	2	4	4	4	41	1	38	8	0	2	4	.333	0	0	5.88
6 Min. YEARS		147	12	0	90	264	1191	235	148	115	9	12	13	13	178	4	218	37	3	6	16	.273	0	30	3.92

Pitches: Right   Bats: Right   Pos: P

Bobby Moore

Ht: 6'5"   Wt: 217   Born: 3/27/73   Age: 25

Year Team	Lg Org	G	GS	CG	GF	IP	BFP	H	R	ER	HR	SH	SF	HB	TBB	IBB	SO	WP	Bk	W	L	Pct.	ShO	Sv	ERA
1995 Hudson Vall	A- Tex	13	13	0	0	63	280	77	45	38	5	2	5	4	13	0	45	10	3	2	3	.400	0	0	5.43
1996 Chston-SC	A Tex	25	25	2	0	142	599	128	82	64	11	8	5	9	45	0	125	6	4	11	11	.500	1	0	4.06
1997 Tulsa	AA Tex	35	7	0	11	72.1	327	74	50	43	8	3	3	2	34	0	41	3	1	4	6	.400	0	2	5.35
3 Min. YEARS		73	45	2	11	277.1	1206	279	177	145	24	13	13	15	92	0	211	19	8	17	20	.459	1	2	4.71

Bats: Right   Throws: Right   Pos: SS

Brandon Moore

Ht: 5'11"   Wt: 175   Born: 8/23/72   Age: 25

Year Team	Lg Org	G	AB	H	2B	3B	HR	TB	R	RBI	TBB	IBB	SO	HBP	SH	SF	SB	CS	SB%	GDP	Avg	OBP	SLG
1994 White Sox	R ChA	4	10	1	0	0	0	1	1	0	1	0	1	0	0	0	0	0	.00	0	.100	.182	.100
Hickory	A ChA	60	230	57	5	2	1	69	43	26	33	1	28	1	7	3	10	6	.63	7	.248	.341	.300
1995 South Bend	A ChA	132	510	131	9	5	0	146	75	37	48	1	49	3	7	5	34	8	.81	15	.257	.322	.286
1996 Pr William	A+ ChA	125	439	106	13	2	1	126	56	41	82	1	70	3	2	3	9	11	.45	14	.241	.362	.287
1997 Birmingham	AA ChA	125	414	106	15	1	1	126	58	47	45	0	48	1	21	4	4	7	.36	11	.256	.328	.304
4 Min. YEARS		446	1603	401	42	8	3	468	233	151	209	3	196	8	37	15	57	32	.64	47	.250	.337	.292

Pitches: Right   Bats: Left   Pos: P

Joel Moore

Ht: 6'2"   Wt: 200   Born: 8/13/72   Age: 25

Year Team	Lg Org	G	GS	CG	GF	IP	BFP	H	R	ER	HR	SH	SF	HB	TBB	IBB	SO	WP	Bk	W	L	Pct.	ShO	Sv	ERA
1993 Bend	A- Col	15	15	0	0	89.2	365	75	35	32	1	2	1	2	31	1	79	5	0	4	7	.364	0	0	3.21
1994 Central Val	A+ Col	25	24	0	0	133	607	149	78	67	8	6	1	8	64	1	89	12	1	11	8	.579	0	0	4.53
1995 New Haven	AA Col	27	26	1	0	157.1	682	156	69	56	8	6	6	8	67	2	102	5	1	14	6	.700	1	0	3.20
1996 Rockies	R Col	4	4	0	0	18	70	13	2	2	0	1	0	1	0	0	19	0	1	1	0	1.000	0	0	1.00
New Haven	AA Col	6	6	0	0	31.1	135	35	18	16	4	2	1	3	5	0	15	1	0	0	5	.000	0	0	4.60
1997 Colo Spmgs	AAA Col	5	5	0	0	26.2	133	47	26	23	4	0	3	1	12	1	20	0	0	3	1	.750	0	0	7.76
New Haven	AA Col	19	12	1	3	77.1	331	77	38	33	12	0	3	3	35	3	47	7	0	6	4	.600	0	0	3.84
5 Min. YEARS		101	92	2	3	533.1	2322	552	266	229	38	16	16	26	214	8	371	30	3	39	31	.557	1	0	3.86

Pitches: Right   Bats: Both   Pos: P

Marcus Moore

Ht: 6'5"   Wt: 195   Born: 11/2/70   Age: 27

Year Team	Lg Org	G	GS	CG	GF	IP	BFP	H	R	ER	HR	SH	SF	HB	TBB	IBB	SO	WP	Bk	W	L	Pct.	ShO	Sv	ERA
1989 Bend	A- Ana	14	14	1	0	81.2	373	84	55	41	2	3	4	5	51	1	74	14	6	2	5	.286	0	0	4.52
1990 Quad City	A Ana	27	27	2	0	160.1	717	150	83	59	6	2	7	3	106	1	160	13	6	16	5	.762	1	0	3.31
1991 Dunedin	A+ Tor	27	25	2	1	160.2	694	149	78	66	3	9	5	4	99	3	115	12	9	6	13	.316	0	0	3.70
1992 Knoxville	AA Tor	36	14	1	18	106.1	493	110	82	66	10	3	7	5	79	0	85	17	5	5	10	.333	0	0	5.59
1993 Central Val	A+ Col	8	0	0	8	12	53	7	3	1	0	1	0	0	9	0	15	1	0	0	0	.000	0	2	0.75
Colo Spmgs	AAA Col	30	0	0	14	44.1	209	54	26	22	3	3	1	1	29	0	38	4	0	1	5	.167	0	4	4.47
1994 Colo Spmgs	AAA Col	19	8	0	0	54	283	67	59	48	1	1	1	1	61	0	54	2	0	3	4	.429	0	0	8.00
1995 Indianapls	AAA Cin	7	1	0	2	12.2	62	13	8	7	0	1	0	0	14	2	6	0	0	1	0	1.000	0	1	4.97

Year Team	Lg Org	G	GS	CG	GF	IP	BFP	H	R	ER	HR	SH	SF	HB	TBB	IBB	SO	WP	Bk	W	L	Pct.	ShO	Sv	ERA
		HOW MUCH HE PITCHED						WHAT HE GAVE UP												THE RESULTS					
Chattanooga	AA Cin	36	0	0	8	43.1	192	31	24	24	6	2	2	2	34	1	57	3	1	6	1	.857	0	2	4.98
1996 Indianapolis	AAA Cin	15	15	0	0	88.2	369	72	41	34	8	1	2	3	38	1	70	2	0	4	7	.364	0	0	3.45
1997 Akron	AA Cle	13	10	1	0	71	323	84	50	39	9	5	3	1	32	1	63	4	1	3	5	.375	0	0	4.94
Buffalo	AAA Cle	10	10	3	0	71	291	54	26	20	6	1	0	0	31	1	72	0	0	5	3	.625	1	0	2.54
1993 Colorado	NL	27	0	0	8	26.1	128	30	25	20	4	0	4	1	20	0	13	4	0	3	1	.750	0	0	6.84
1994 Colorado	NL	29	0	0	13	33.2	158	33	26	23	4	1	0	5	21	2	33	4	1	1	1	.500	0	0	6.15
1996 Cincinnati	NL	23	0	0	11	26.1	129	26	21	17	3	3	3	2	22	1	27	1	0	3	3	.500	0	1	5.81
9 Min. YEARS		242	124	10	56	906	4059	865	535	427	58	32	32	25	583	10	809	72	31	53	58	.477	2	9	4.24
3 Maj. YEARS		79	0	0	32	86.1	415	89	72	60	11	4	7	8	63	3	73	9	1	7	5	.583	0	2	6.25

Mike Moore

Bats: Right Throws: Right Pos: OF   Ht: 6'4" Wt: 200 Born: 3/7/71 Age: 27

Year Team	Lg Org	G	AB	H	2B	3B	HR	TB	R	RBI	TBB	IBB	SO	HBP	SH	SF	SB	CS	SB%	GDP	Avg	OBP	SLG
		BATTING															BASERUNNING				PERCENTAGES		
1992 Yakima	A- LA	18	58	12	1	0	2	19	12	6	9	1	25	0	0	0	3	2	.60	1	.207	.313	.328
1993 Bakersfield	A+ LA	100	403	116	25	1	13	182	61	58	29	0	103	3	0	4	23	10	.70	6	.288	.337	.452
1994 San Antonio	AA LA	72	254	57	12	1	5	86	32	32	22	0	75	6	0	1	11	7	.61	2	.224	.300	.339
Bakersfield	A+ LA	21	81	24	5	0	2	35	17	8	13	1	21	0	0	0	2	0	1.00	3	.296	.394	.432
1995 Vero Beach	A+ LA	7	22	6	1	0	0	7	3	1	6	0	8	0	0	0	0	1	.00	1	.273	.429	.318
1996 San Antonio	AA LA	64	200	48	10	4	2	72	21	21	17	0	64	2	0	1	8	4	.67	4	.240	.305	.360
1997 Binghamton	AA NYN	50	130	39	11	1	2	58	19	13	18	1	47	1	0	1	7	3	.70	2	.300	.387	.446
Norfolk	AAA NYN	34	83	20	4	0	2	30	10	6	9	0	33	0	0	0	1	0	1.00	3	.241	.315	.361
6 Min. YEARS		366	1231	322	69	7	28	489	175	145	123	3	376	12	0	7	55	27	.67	22	.262	.333	.397

Trey Moore

Pitches: Left Bats: Left Pos: P   Ht: 6'1" Wt: 200 Born: 10/2/72 Age: 25

Year Team	Lg Org	G	GS	CG	GF	IP	BFP	H	R	ER	HR	SH	SF	HB	TBB	IBB	SO	WP	Bk	W	L	Pct.	ShO	Sv	ERA
		HOW MUCH HE PITCHED						WHAT HE GAVE UP												THE RESULTS					
1994 Bellingham	A- Sea	11	10	1	0	61.2	247	48	18	18	4	0	2	2	24	0	73	4	0	5	2	.714	0	0	2.63
1995 Riverside	A+ Sea	24	24	0	0	148.1	605	122	65	51	6	2	5	2	58	1	134	6	1	14	6	.700	0	0	3.09
1996 Port City	AA Sea	11	11	0	0	53.2	265	73	54	46	6	2	5	0	33	0	42	4	1	1	6	.143	0	0	7.71
Lancaster	A+ Sea	15	15	2	0	94.1	413	106	57	43	10	2	0	7	31	0	77	7	0	7	5	.583	0	0	4.10
1997 Harrisburg	AA Mon	27	27	2	0	162.2	701	152	91	75	15	6	3	10	66	1	137	4	0	11	6	.647	2	0	4.15
4 Min. YEARS		88	87	5	0	520.2	2231	501	285	233	41	12	15	21	212	2	463	25	2	38	25	.603	2	0	4.03

Melvin Mora

Bats: Right Throws: Right Pos: OF   Ht: 5'10" Wt: 160 Born: 2/2/72 Age: 26

Year Team	Lg Org	G	AB	H	2B	3B	HR	TB	R	RBI	TBB	IBB	SO	HBP	SH	SF	SB	CS	SB%	GDP	Avg	OBP	SLG
		BATTING															BASERUNNING				PERCENTAGES		
1992 Astros	R Hou	49	144	32	3	0	0	35	28	8	18	0	16	5	0	1	16	3	.84	2	.222	.307	.243
1993 Asheville	A Hou	108	365	104	22	2	2	136	66	31	36	0	46	9	5	8	20	13	.61	7	.285	.356	.373
1994 Osceola	A+ Hou	118	425	120	29	4	8	181	57	46	37	1	60	10	3	3	24	16	.60	8	.282	.352	.426
1995 Jackson	AA Hou	123	467	139	32	0	3	180	63	45	32	1	57	9	7	7	22	11	.67	7	.298	.350	.385
Tucson	AAA Hou	2	5	3	0	1	0	5	3	1	2	1	0	0	0	0	1	0	1.00	0	.600	.714	1.000
1996 Tucson	AAA Hou	62	228	64	11	2	3	88	35	26	17	1	27	1	3	4	3	5	.38	7	.281	.328	.386
Jackson	AA Hou	70	255	73	6	1	5	96	36	23	14	1	23	6	1	2	4	7	.36	4	.286	.336	.376
1997 New Orleans	AAA Hou	119	370	95	15	3	2	122	55	38	47	0	52	11	9	2	7	7	.50	7	.257	.356	.330
6 Min. YEARS		651	2259	630	118	13	23	843	343	218	203	5	281	51	28	27	97	62	.61	46	.279	.348	.373

Francisco Morales

Bats: Right Throws: Right Pos: C   Ht: 6'3" Wt: 180 Born: 1/31/73 Age: 25

Year Team	Lg Org	G	AB	H	2B	3B	HR	TB	R	RBI	TBB	IBB	SO	HBP	SH	SF	SB	CS	SB%	GDP	Avg	OBP	SLG
		BATTING															BASERUNNING				PERCENTAGES		
1992 Huntington	R+ ChN	13	39	7	1	0	1	11	4	9	10	0	13	1	1	0	1	2	.33	1	.179	.360	.282
Geneva	A- ChN	19	49	11	2	0	0	13	3	0	7	1	21	0	0	0	0	0	.00	2	.224	.321	.265
1993 Peoria	A ChN	19	49	10	1	1	3	22	9	11	9	0	16	0	4	0	1	0	1.00	2	.204	.328	.449
Geneva	A- ChN	45	123	24	4	0	2	34	12	20	15	0	41	1	0	2	1	0	1.00	1	.195	.284	.276
1994 Orlando	AA ChN	22	58	12	0	0	2	18	3	10	7	0	21	0	0	0	1	0	1.00	2	.207	.292	.310
Daytona	A+ ChN	38	120	29	7	1	1	41	9	10	9	0	37	1	0	1	1	0	1.00	2	.242	.298	.342
1995 Orlando	AA ChN	2	6	1	0	0	1	4	0	0	1	0	2	0	0	0	0	0	.00	0	.167	.286	.667
Daytona	A+ ChN	36	101	26	6	0	6	50	17	23	16	0	28	3	0	2	1	1	.50	2	.257	.369	.495
Savannah	A StL	19	75	11	3	0	2	20	3	4	4	0	23	1	0	1	0	2	.00	3	.195	.293	.322
St. Pete	A+ StL	28	87	17	5	0	2	28	10	10	11	0	29	1	0	0	1	0	1.00	1	.195	.293	.322
1996 St. Pete	A+ StL	21	67	14	5	1	1	24	6	6	5	0	25	2	0	1	0	0	.00	1	.209	.280	.358
Wst Plm Bch	A+ Mon	75	259	71	20	2	3	104	32	42	19	0	79	5	3	1	3	1	.75	5	.274	.335	.402
1997 Ottawa	AAA Mon	7	18	2	0	1	1	7	2	4	1	0	6	0	0	0	0	2	.00	2	.111	.158	.389
Wst Plm Bch	A+ Mon	45	127	36	7	1	4	57	15	13	10	1	37	0	1	0	0	0	.00	2	.283	.336	.449
Harrisburg	AA Mon	16	49	10	1	0	2	17	5	4	3	1	22	1	0	1	0	0	.00	2	.204	.259	.347
6 Min. YEARS		405	1227	281	62	7	30	447	130	166	127	3	400	16	9	9	8	9	.47	25	.229	.307	.364

Willie Morales

Bats: Right **Throws:** Right **Pos:** C   **Ht:** 5'10" **Wt:** 182 **Born:** 9/7/72 **Age:** 25

Year Team	Lg Org	G	AB	H	2B	3B	HR	TB	R	RBI	TBB	IBB	SO	HBP	SH	SF	SB	CS	SB%	GDP	Avg	OBP	SLG
1993 Sou. Oregon	A- Oak	60	208	56	16	0	1	75	34	27	19	2	36	4	1	4	0	3	.00	2	.269	.336	.361
1994 W Michigan	A Oak	111	380	101	26	0	13	166	47	51	36	4	64	3	3	2	3	5	.38	12	.266	.333	.437
1995 Modesto	A+ Oak	109	419	116	32	0	4	160	49	60	28	1	75	7	2	4	1	4	.20	13	.277	.330	.382
1996 Huntsville	AA Oak	108	377	110	24	0	18	188	54	73	38	2	67	7	4	6	0	2	.00	11	.292	.362	.499
1997 Huntsville	AA Oak	36	136	37	11	0	3	57	19	24	17	0	24	0	0	3	1	0	1.00	2	.272	.346	.419
Edmonton	AAA Oak	56	179	52	12	0	5	79	23	35	11	0	27	0	3	3	0	2	.00	4	.291	.326	.441
5 Min. YEARS		480	1699	472	121	0	44	725	226	270	149	9	293	21	13	22	5	16	.24	44	.278	.340	.427

Julio Moreno

Pitches: Right **Bats:** Right **Pos:** P   **Ht:** 6'1" **Wt:** 145 **Born:** 10/23/75 **Age:** 22

		HOW MUCH HE PITCHED						WHAT HE GAVE UP										THE RESULTS					
Year Team	Lg Org	G	GS	CG	GF	IP	BFP	H	R	ER	HR	SH	SF	HB	TBB	IBB	SO	WP	Bk	W	L	Pct.	ShO	Sv	ERA
1994 Orioles	R Bal	4	2	0	1	8.1	41	14	14	11	2	0	2	0	1	0	6	0	0	0	2	.000	0	0	11.88
1995 Orioles	R Bal	5	5	1	0	34	131	17	9	6	0	1	2	1	7	0	29	1	1	3	2	.600	1	0	1.59
Bluefield	R+ Bal	9	8	0	1	49.1	214	61	31	23	3	1	3	0	12	0	36	3	1	4	3	.571	0	0	4.20
1996 Frederick	A+ Bal	28	26	0	1	162	682	167	80	63	14	8	0	9	38	0	147	9	3	9	10	.474	0	0	3.50
1997 Bowie	AA Bal	27	25	1	0	138.2	596	141	76	59	20	2	3	6	64	4	106	6	3	9	6	.600	0	0	3.83
4 Min. YEARS		73	66	2	2	392.1	1664	400	210	162	39	12	10	16	122	4	324	19	8	25	23	.521	1	0	3.72

Dave Morgan

Bats: Right **Throws:** Right **Pos:** C   **Ht:** 6'4" **Wt:** 215 **Born:** 11/19/71 **Age:** 26

Year Team	Lg Org	G	AB	H	2B	3B	HR	TB	R	RBI	TBB	IBB	SO	HBP	SH	SF	SB	CS	SB%	GDP	Avg	OBP	SLG
1993 Medicne Hat	R+ Tor	62	210	50	9	0	5	74	35	34	36	0	57	5	2	2	2	1	.67	1	.238	.360	.352
1994 Medicne Hat	R+ Tor	16	50	14	1	0	1	18	4	5	2	0	12	2	0	0	1	0	1.00	1	.280	.333	.360
1995 Hagerstown	A Tor	67	249	66	14	1	4	94	26	26	18	1	53	2	1	2	1	0	1.00	4	.265	.317	.378
1996 Dunedin	A+ Tor	39	88	23	3	1	4	40	13	15	18	0	24	3	0	0	1	0	.00	3	.261	.404	.455
1997 Dunedin	A+ Tor	20	53	11	1	0	2	18	8	7	6	0	11	1	1	0	2	2	.50	1	.208	.300	.340
Knoxville	AA Tor	21	44	12	2	0	0	14	6	4	10	0	14	1	0	0	0	0	.00	0	.273	.418	.318
5 Min. YEARS		225	694	176	30	2	16	258	92	91	90	1	171	14	4	4	5	5	.50	10	.254	.349	.372

Scott Morgan

Bats: Right **Throws:** Right **Pos:** OF   **Ht:** 6'7" **Wt:** 230 **Born:** 7/19/73 **Age:** 24

Year Team	Lg Org	G	AB	H	2B	3B	HR	TB	R	RBI	TBB	IBB	SO	HBP	SH	SF	SB	CS	SB%	GDP	Avg	OBP	SLG
1995 Watertown	A- Cle	66	244	64	18	0	2	88	42	33	26	0	63	8	0	4	6	5	.55	11	.262	.348	.361
1996 Columbus	A Cle	87	305	95	25	1	22	188	62	80	46	0	70	11	0	4	9	5	.64	5	.311	.415	.616
1997 Kinston	A+ Cle	95	368	116	32	3	23	223	86	67	47	3	87	5	0	4	4	2	.67	8	.315	.396	.606
Akron	AA Cle	21	69	12	3	0	2	21	11	6	8	0	20	1	0	1	1	0	1.00	0	.174	.266	.304
3 Min. YEARS		269	986	287	78	4	49	520	201	186	127	3	240	25	0	13	20	12	.63	24	.291	.381	.527

Mike Moriarty

Bats: Right **Throws:** Right **Pos:** SS   **Ht:** 6'0" **Wt:** 169 **Born:** 3/8/74 **Age:** 24

Year Team	Lg Org	G	AB	H	2B	3B	HR	TB	R	RBI	TBB	IBB	SO	HBP	SH	SF	SB	CS	SB%	GDP	Avg	OBP	SLG
1995 Ft. Wayne	A Min	62	185	50	6	3	4	70	26	26	27	1	44	2	2	3	8	0	1.00	1	.227	.319	.345
1996 Ft. Myers	A+ Min	133	428	107	18	2	3	138	76	39	59	0	67	8	5	4	14	15	.48	2	.250	.349	.322
1997 New Britain	AA Min	135	421	93	22	5	6	143	60	48	53	1	68	3	10	5	12	5	.71	10	.221	.309	.340
3 Min. YEARS		330	1052	246	46	10	13	351	162	113	139	2	179	13	17	12	34	20	.63	13	.234	.327	.334

Cesar Morillo

Bats: Both **Throws:** Right **Pos:** SS   **Ht:** 5'11" **Wt:** 180 **Born:** 7/21/73 **Age:** 24

Year Team	Lg Org	G	AB	H	2B	3B	HR	TB	R	RBI	TBB	IBB	SO	HBP	SH	SF	SB	CS	SB%	GDP	Avg	OBP	SLG
1990 Royals	R KC	55	185	50	6	2	1	63	21	17	22	0	45	2	3	0	7	4	.64	4	.270	.354	.341
1991 Baseball Cy	A+ KC	62	226	39	8	0	0	47	11	13	13	0	68	2	7	2	6	5	.55	4	.173	.222	.208
Appleton	A KC	63	236	59	9	3	1	77	35	17	38	0	54	1	1	1	9	8	.53	2	.250	.355	.326
1992 Baseball Cy	A+ KC	35	102	17	5	1	0	24	8	7	10	0	23	1	3	1	1	0	1.00	7	.167	.246	.235
Eugene	A- KC	51	180	44	9	1	1	58	28	17	21	0	40	1	3	0	6	4	.60	1	.244	.327	.322
1993 Rockford	A KC	101	327	85	13	3	3	113	47	36	30	3	65	3	5	2	4	1	.80	4	.260	.326	.346
1994 Wilmington	A+ KC	16	55	9	1	0	0	10	3	4	5	1	17	1	0	1	1	0	1.00	1	.164	.242	.182
Rockford	A KC	70	242	68	11	2	2	89	23	25	15	2	35	2	1	2	4	3	.57	6	.281	.326	.368
1995 Bakersfield	A+ KC	108	371	113	18	1	1	143	41	37	31	2	71	4	5	1	4	12	.25	6	.305	.364	.385
1996 Wichita	AA KC	45	119	28	3	1	2	39	8	7	7	0	18	0	5	0	3	0	1.00	3	.235	.278	.328
1997 Tulsa	AA Tex	84	288	76	18	1	1	99	38	23	28	2	53	0	4	1	0	4	.00	3	.264	.328	.344
8 Min. YEARS		690	2331	588	108	15	12	762	263	203	220	10	489	17	37	11	45	41	.52	41	.252	.320	.327

Bobby Morris

Bats: Left **Throws:** Right **Pos:** 2B   **Ht:** 6'0" **Wt:** 180 **Born:** 11/22/72 **Age:** 25

Year Team	Lg Org	G	AB	H	2B	3B	HR	TB	R	RBI	TBB	IBB	SO	HBP	SH	SF	SB	CS	SB%	GDP	Avg	OBP	SLG
1993 Huntington	R+ ChN	50	170	49	8	3	1	66	29	24	24	0	29	1	2	3	6	7	.46	2	.288	.374	.388

176

BATTING

Year Team	Lg Org	G	AB	H	2B	3B	HR	TB	R	RBI	TBB	IBB	SO	HBP	SH	SF	SB	CS	SB%	GDP	Avg	OBP	SLG
1994 Peoria	A ChN	101	362	128	33	1	7	184	61	64	53	4	63	7	10	2	7	7	.50	10	.354	.443	.508
1995 Daytona	A+ ChN	95	344	106	18	2	2	134	44	55	38	6	46	8	2	5	22	8	.73	5	.308	.385	.390
1996 Orlando	AA ChN	131	465	122	29	3	8	181	72	62	65	4	73	6	0	8	12	14	.46	12	.262	.355	.389
1997 Orlando	AA ChN	4	16	5	1	0	0	6	3	1	2	0	3	0	0	0	0	0	.00	0	.313	.389	.375
Kinston	A+ Cle	10	32	5	1	0	2	12	6	10	4	0	6	2	0	1	0	0	.00	2	.156	.282	.375
Akron	AA Cle	42	119	30	9	1	1	44	17	15	22	0	21	2	2	1	1	2	.33	3	.252	.375	.370
5 Min. YEARS		433	1508	445	99	10	21	627	232	231	208	14	241	26	16	20	48	38	.56	34	.295	.385	.416

Warren Morris
Bats: Left **Throws:** Right **Pos:** 2B   **Ht:** 5'10" **Wt:** 175 **Born:** 1/11/74 **Age:** 24

BATTING

Year Team	Lg Org	G	AB	H	2B	3B	HR	TB	R	RBI	TBB	IBB	SO	HBP	SH	SF	SB	CS	SB%	GDP	Avg	OBP	SLG
1997 Charlotte	A+ Tex	128	494	151	27	9	12	232	78	75	62	3	100	7	3	1	16	5	.76	6	.306	.390	.470
Okla City	AAA Tex	8	32	7	1	0	1	11	3	3	3	0	5	0	0	0	0	0	.00	0	.219	.286	.344
1 Min. YEARS		136	526	158	28	9	13	243	81	78	65	3	105	7	3	1	16	5	.76	6	.300	.384	.462

Paul Morse
Pitches: Right **Bats:** Right **Pos:** P   **Ht:** 6'2" **Wt:** 185 **Born:** 2/27/73 **Age:** 25

HOW MUCH HE PITCHED / WHAT HE GAVE UP / THE RESULTS

Year Team	Lg Org	G	GS	CG	GF	IP	BFP	H	R	ER	HR	SH	SF	HB	TBB	IBB	SO	WP	Bk	W	L	Pct.	ShO	Sv	ERA
1994 Elizabethtn	R+ Min	7	0	0	5	7.1	35	8	7	6	2	0	1	2	3	0	8	0	0	0	0	.000	0	0	7.36
Ft. Wayne	A Min	16	0	0	11	20.1	97	27	15	13	2	1	0	2	10	0	17	0	0	0	3	.000	0	3	5.75
1995 Ft. Myers	A+ Min	35	0	0	29	61.1	247	57	30	26	3	1	4	3	12	0	56	4	1	3	1	.750	0	15	3.82
1996 Ft. Myers	A+ Min	13	0	0	12	14	50	8	4	4	1	0	0	0	5	0	10	0	0	1	0	1.000	0	9	2.57
Hardware City	AA Min	35	1	0	23	55.2	249	55	36	33	5	4	4	1	26	2	48	4	1	6	4	.600	0	4	5.34
1997 New Britain	AA Min	37	17	0	9	111.1	508	124	91	74	16	4	2	6	70	2	75	11	0	3	11	.214	0	1	5.98
4 Min. YEARS		143	18	0	89	270	1186	279	183	156	29	10	11	14	126	4	214	19	2	13	19	.406	0	32	5.20

Joe Morvay
Pitches: Right **Bats:** Left **Pos:** P   **Ht:** 6'4" **Wt:** 210 **Born:** 2/8/71 **Age:** 27

HOW MUCH HE PITCHED / WHAT HE GAVE UP / THE RESULTS

Year Team	Lg Org	G	GS	CG	GF	IP	BFP	H	R	ER	HR	SH	SF	HB	TBB	IBB	SO	WP	Bk	W	L	Pct.	ShO	Sv	ERA
1993 Erie	A- Tex	18	2	0	8	38.1	160	32	18	12	0	1	2	2	14	1	42	1	0	2	3	.400	0	2	2.82
1994 Chston-SC	A Tex	37	1	0	11	71	303	50	27	22	4	4	1	9	30	1	85	4	0	2	4	.333	0	0	2.79
1995 Tulsa	AA Tex	37	0	0	28	65.2	305	82	45	38	4	6	1	4	28	6	30	4	0	5	8	.385	0	8	5.21
1996 Tulsa	AA Tex	24	1	0	11	46	213	55	32	32	3	5	2	4	20	2	27	2	0	2	2	.500	0	2	6.26
1997 Wichita	AA KC	9	2	0	1	26.1	118	39	32	32	9	0	0	1	7	0	13	1	0	1	2	.333	0	0	10.94
Elmira	IND —	25	0	0	21	27.1	114	21	6	5	2	2	1	2	10	0	25	5	0	1	0	1.000	0	13	1.65
5 Min. YEARS		150	6	0	80	274.2	1213	279	160	141	22	18	7	22	109	10	222	17	0	13	19	.406	0	25	4.62

Damian Moss
Pitches: Left **Bats:** Right **Pos:** P   **Ht:** 6'0" **Wt:** 187 **Born:** 11/24/76 **Age:** 21

HOW MUCH HE PITCHED / WHAT HE GAVE UP / THE RESULTS

Year Team	Lg Org	G	GS	CG	GF	IP	BFP	H	R	ER	HR	SH	SF	HB	TBB	IBB	SO	WP	Bk	W	L	Pct.	ShO	Sv	ERA
1994 Danville	R+ Atl	12	12	1	0	60.1	265	30	28	24	1	1	0	14	55	0	77	12	3	2	5	.286	1	0	3.58
1995 Macon	A Atl	27	27	0	0	149.1	653	134	73	59	13	0	2	12	70	0	177	14	5	9	10	.474	0	0	3.56
1996 Durham	A+ Atl	14	14	0	0	84	333	52	25	21	9	3	3	2	40	0	89	7	2	9	1	.900	0	0	2.25
Greenville	AA Atl	11	10	0	0	58	262	57	41	32	5	0	3	3	35	0	48	12	0	2	5	.286	0	0	4.97
1997 Greenville	AA Atl	21	19	1	0	112.2	498	111	73	67	13	1	8	9	58	0	116	14	2	6	8	.429	0	0	5.35
4 Min. YEARS		85	82	2	0	464.1	2011	384	240	203	41	5	16	40	258	0	507	59	12	28	29	.491	1	0	3.93

Scott Moten
Pitches: Right **Bats:** Right **Pos:** P   **Ht:** 6'1" **Wt:** 198 **Born:** 4/12/72 **Age:** 26

HOW MUCH HE PITCHED / WHAT HE GAVE UP / THE RESULTS

Year Team	Lg Org	G	GS	CG	GF	IP	BFP	H	R	ER	HR	SH	SF	HB	TBB	IBB	SO	WP	Bk	W	L	Pct.	ShO	Sv	ERA
1992 Elizabethtn	R+ Min	13	12	1	0	78.2	334	60	31	21	1	1	1	6	32	0	71	2	2	8	1	.889	1	0	2.40
1993 Ft. Wayne	A Min	30	22	0	4	140.2	627	152	99	79	8	6	3	11	63	2	141	7	2	7	11	.389	0	1	5.05
1994 Ft. Myers	A+ Min	44	1	0	17	96	404	87	32	23	1	4	0	2	38	3	68	2	0	8	4	.667	0	7	2.16
Nashville	AA Min	3	0	0	0	4.2	23	5	4	2	0	0	0	1	2	0	4	1	0	0	1	.000	0	0	3.86
1995 Hardware City	AA Min	40	1	0	18	75.1	323	65	40	33	8	6	3	0	36	2	43	5	0	8	5	.615	0	3	3.94
1996 Iowa	AAA ChN	21	0	0	9	42	199	55	47	43	9	4	4	4	18	1	18	8	0	1	2	.333	0	0	9.21
Orlando	AA ChN	18	7	1	5	54.1	252	59	40	34	8	2	5	2	31	3	35	3	0	2	6	.250	0	1	5.63
1997 Orlando	AA ChN	4	1	0	2	6.2	33	9	10	10	2	0	1	1	6	0	1	0	0	0	1	.000	0	0	13.50
6 Min. YEARS		173	45	2	55	498.1	2195	492	303	245	37	23	16	27	226	11	381	28	4	34	31	.523	1	12	4.42

Tom Mott
Pitches: Right **Bats:** Right **Pos:** P   **Ht:** 6'3" **Wt:** 222 **Born:** 10/9/73 **Age:** 24

HOW MUCH HE PITCHED / WHAT HE GAVE UP / THE RESULTS

Year Team	Lg Org	G	GS	CG	GF	IP	BFP	H	R	ER	HR	SH	SF	HB	TBB	IBB	SO	WP	Bk	W	L	Pct.	ShO	Sv	ERA
1994 Elizabethtn	R+ Min	8	6	1	1	37.2	161	31	17	12	2	2	1	4	15	0	15	1	1	4	3	.571	0	0	2.87
1995 Ft. Wayne	A Min	25	25	1	0	129.2	557	123	67	58	6	6	3	10	48	0	64	14	0	13	4	.765	0	0	4.03
1996 Ft. Myers	A+ Min	14	14	0	0	74.2	328	80	43	40	5	3	0	3	37	0	48	10	0	7	5	.583	0	0	4.82
1997 Ft. Myers	A+ Min	14	0	0	3	31	127	25	13	11	1	1	2	2	12	0	23	6	0	2	0	1.000	0	0	3.19
New Britain	AA Min	1	0	0	0	1.1	5	2	0	0	0	0	0	0	0	0	0	0	0	0	0	.000	0	0	0.00

		HOW MUCH HE PITCHED		WHAT HE GAVE UP		THE RESULTS	
Year Team	Lg Org	G GS CG GF	IP BFP	H R ER HR SH SF HB	TBB IBB SO WP Bk	W L Pct. ShO Sv	ERA
4 Min. YEARS		62 45 2 4	274.1 1178	261 140 121 14 12 6 19	112 0 150 31 1	26 12 .684 0 0	3.97

Chad Mottola

Bats: Right **Throws:** Right **Pos:** OF   **Ht:** 6'3" **Wt:** 220 **Born:** 10/15/71 **Age:** 26

		BATTING				BASERUNNING	PERCENTAGES
Year Team	Lg Org	G AB H 2B 3B HR TB R RBI	TBB IBB SO	HBP SH SF		SB CS SB% GDP	Avg OBP SLG
1992 Billings	R+ Cin	57 213 61 8 3 12 111 53 37	25 0 43	0 0 0		12 3 .80 4	.286 .361 .521
1993 Winston-Sal	A+ Cin	137 493 138 25 3 21 232 76 91	62 2 109	2 0 3		13 7 .65 9	.280 .361 .471
1994 Chattanooga	AA Cin	118 402 97 19 1 7 139 44 41	30 1 68	1 2 2		9 12 .43 12	.241 .294 .346
1995 Chattanooga	AA Cin	51 181 53 13 1 10 98 32 39	13 0 32	1 0 1		1 2 .33 2	.293 .342 .541
Indianapolis	AAA Cin	69 239 62 11 1 8 99 40 37	20 0 50	0 1 1		8 1 .89 6	.259 .315 .414
1996 Indianapols	AAA Cin	103 362 95 24 3 9 152 45 47	21 3 93	4 0 4		9 6 .60 10	.262 .307 .420
1997 Chattanooga	AA Cin	46 174 63 9 3 5 93 35 32	16 1 23	1 1 5		7 1 .88 3	.362 .408 .534
Indianapols	AAA Cin	83 284 82 10 6 7 125 33 45	16 2 43	4 0 2		12 4 .75 6	.289 .333 .440
1996 Cincinnati	NL	35 79 17 3 0 3 29 10 6	6 1 16	0 0 0		2 2 .50 0	.215 .271 .367
6 Min. YEARS		664 2348 651 119 21 79 1049 358 369	203 9 461	13 4 18		71 36 .66 52	.277 .336 .447

Tony Mounce

Pitches: Left **Bats:** Left **Pos:** P   **Ht:** 6'2" **Wt:** 185 **Born:** 2/8/75 **Age:** 23

		HOW MUCH HE PITCHED		WHAT HE GAVE UP		THE RESULTS	
Year Team	Lg Org	G GS CG GF	IP BFP	H R ER HR SH SF HB	TBB IBB SO WP Bk	W L Pct. ShO Sv	ERA
1994 Astros	R Hou	11 11 0 0	59.2 246	56 24 18 1 2 1 1	18 0 72 2 2	4 2 .667 0 0	2.72
1995 Quad City	A Hou	25 25 3 0	159 649	118 55 43 6 6 6 3	57 2 143 6 2	16 8 .667 1 0	2.43
1996 Kissimmee	A+ Hou	25 25 4 0	155.2 675	139 65 39 7 6 3 10	68 1 102 7 0	9 9 .500 2 0	2.25
1997 New Orleans	AAA Hou	1 1 0 0	4.2 21	2 1 1 1 0 0 0	6 0 6 0 0	0 0 .000 0 0	1.93
Jackson	AA Hou	25 25 1 0	145 645	165 91 81 18 6 5 2	66 3 116 7 0	8 9 .471 0 0	5.03
4 Min. YEARS		87 87 8 0	524 2236	480 236 182 33 20 15 16	215 6 439 22 4	37 28 .569 3 0	3.13

Mike Moyle

Bats: Right **Throws:** Right **Pos:** C   **Ht:** 6'2" **Wt:** 200 **Born:** 9/8/71 **Age:** 26

		BATTING				BASERUNNING	PERCENTAGES
Year Team	Lg Org	G AB H 2B 3B HR TB R RBI	TBB IBB SO	HBP SH SF		SB CS SB% GDP	Avg OBP SLG
1992 Burlington	R+ Cle	18 41 9 1 0 0 10 4 2	13 0 12	0 0 0		0 0 .00 0	.220 .407 .244
1993 Burlington	R+ Cle	4 8 2 0 0 0 2 1 0	1 0 1	0 0 0		0 0 .00 0	.250 .333 .250
1994 Butte	R+ Cle	49 189 68 18 3 5 107 43 52	27 0 36	2 0 2		4 1 .80 8	.360 .441 .566
1995 Columbus	A Cle	73 227 46 7 0 6 71 19 31	35 0 46	1 3 6		2 3 .40 3	.203 .305 .313
1996 Kinston	A+ Cle	60 197 53 12 1 7 88 37 34	30 1 32	4 1 1		3 2 .60 3	.269 .375 .447
1997 Akron	AA Cle	104 342 79 15 0 16 142 56 53	53 1 71	6 1 2		3 0 1.00 17	.231 .342 .415
6 Min. YEARS		308 1004 257 53 4 34 420 160 172	159 2 198	13 5 11		12 6 .67 31	.256 .361 .418

Blaine Mull

Pitches: Right **Bats:** Right **Pos:** P   **Ht:** 6'4" **Wt:** 186 **Born:** 8/14/76 **Age:** 21

		HOW MUCH HE PITCHED		WHAT HE GAVE UP		THE RESULTS	
Year Team	Lg Org	G GS CG GF	IP BFP	H R ER HR SH SF HB	TBB IBB SO WP Bk	W L Pct. ShO Sv	ERA
1994 Royals	R KC	3 3 0 0	15 56	8 1 0 0 0 0 2	2 0 9 0 0	2 0 1.000 0 0	0.00
1995 Springfield	A KC	25 25 0 0	125.1 564	142 79 68 12 9 7 6	50 1 71 14 0	4 10 .286 0 0	4.88
1996 Lansing	A KC	28 28 1 0	174.2 734	186 91 63 9 7 5 9	40 0 114 6 0	15 8 .652 0 0	3.25
1997 Wichita	AA KC	8 8 0 0	44.2 225	66 41 33 4 0 1 0	23 0 16 1 1	1 2 .333 0 0	6.65
Wilmington	A+ KC	19 19 0 0	111.1 485	126 55 44 6 9 5 4	33 3 64 5 0	8 6 .571 0 0	3.56
4 Min. YEARS		83 83 1 0	471 2064	528 267 208 31 25 18 21	148 4 274 26 1	30 26 .536 0 0	3.97

Sean Mulligan

Bats: Right **Throws:** Right **Pos:** C   **Ht:** 6'2" **Wt:** 210 **Born:** 4/25/70 **Age:** 28

		BATTING				BASERUNNING	PERCENTAGES
Year Team	Lg Org	G AB H 2B 3B HR TB R RBI	TBB IBB SO	HBP SH SF		SB CS SB% GDP	Avg OBP SLG
1991 Chston-SC	A SD	60 215 56 9 3 4 83 24 30	17 0 56	6 1 1		4 1 .80 5	.260 .331 .386
1992 High Desert	A+ SD	35 118 19 4 0 4 35 14 14	11 1 38	3 0 1		0 0 .00 3	.161 .248 .297
Waterloo	A SD	79 278 70 13 1 5 100 24 43	20 0 62	5 2 4		1 0 1.00 10	.252 .309 .360
1993 Rancho Cuca	A+ SD	79 268 75 10 3 6 109 29 36	34 0 33	3 0 4		1 3 .25 16	.280 .362 .407
1994 Rancho Cuca	A+ SD	66 243 74 18 1 9 121 45 49	24 1 39	5 1 8		1 0 1.00 4	.305 .368 .498
Wichita	AA SD	56 208 73 14 0 1 90 29 30	11 2 25	5 0 3		2 3 .40 9	.351 .392 .433
1995 Las Vegas	AAA SD	101 339 93 20 1 7 136 34 43	27 2 61	8 1 3		0 0 .00 7	.274 .340 .401
1996 Las Vegas	AAA SD	102 358 103 24 3 19 190 55 75	30 4 68	7 0 2		1 2 .33 8	.288 .353 .531
1997 Akron	AA Cle	2 7 3 1 0 0 4 1 1	1 0 0	0 0 0		0 0 .00 8	.429 .500 .571
1996 San Diego	NL	2 1 0 0 0 0 0 0 0	0 0 0	0 0 0		0 0 .00 0	.000 .000 .000
7 Min. YEARS		580 2034 566 113 12 55 868 255 321	175 10 382	42 5 26		10 9 .53 62	.278 .344 .427

Greg Mullins

Pitches: Left **Bats:** Left **Pos:** P   **Ht:** 6'0" **Wt:** 160 **Born:** 12/13/71 **Age:** 26

		HOW MUCH HE PITCHED		WHAT HE GAVE UP		THE RESULTS	
Year Team	Lg Org	G GS CG GF	IP BFP	H R ER HR SH SF HB	TBB IBB SO WP Bk	W L Pct. ShO Sv	ERA
1995 Helena	R+ Mil	4 4 0 0	23 98	22 7 7 0 0 0 2	6 0 14 0 2	4 0 1.000 0 0	2.74
Beloit	A Mil	15 4 0 6	36.1 151	26 16 16 2 0 1 5	14 0 48 2 3	3 1 .750 0 2	3.96
1996 El Paso	AA Mil	23 1 0 6	28 130	30 25 22 7 3 0 1	17 2 28 0 1	1 5 .167 0 2	7.07

			HOW MUCH HE PITCHED						WHAT HE GAVE UP										THE RESULTS					
Year Team	Lg Org	G	GS	CG	GF	IP	BFP	H	R	ER	HR	SH	SF	HB	TBB	IBB	SO	WP	Bk	W	L	Pct.	ShO	Sv	ERA
Stockton	A+ Mil	10	0	0	3	11.1	51	13	5	5	0	0	0	1	4	0	12	0	0	0	0	.000	0	1	3.97
1997 Stockton	A+ Mil	30	0	0	30	33	131	22	9	8	2	0	0	1	12	0	52	4	0	0	2	.000	0	19	2.18
El Paso	AA Mil	25	0	0	22	23.1	100	19	8	7	2	2	1	1	11	1	21	2	0	1	1	.500	0	13	2.70
3 Min. YEARS		107	9	0	67	155	661	132	70	65	13	5	2	11	64	3	175	8	6	9	9	.500	0	37	3.77

Rob Mummau

Bats: Right **Throws:** Right **Pos:** 2B   **Ht:** 5'11" **Wt:** 180 **Born:** 8/21/71 **Age:** 26

					BATTING												BASERUNNING				PERCENTAGES		
Year Team	Lg Org	G	AB	H	2B	3B	HR	TB	R	RBI	TBB	IBB	SO	HBP	SH	SF	SB	CS	SB%	GDP	Avg	OBP	SLG
1993 St. Cathrns	A- Tor	75	257	62	9	3	3	86	35	21	23	1	44	5	2	0	7	12	.37	3	.241	.316	.335
1994 Dunedin	A+ Tor	21	50	11	1	0	0	12	5	6	4	0	15	0	1	0	0	2	.00	0	.220	.278	.240
Hagerstown	A Tor	46	169	50	10	2	1	67	20	24	10	0	32	2	0	3	2	2	.50	4	.296	.337	.396
1995 Hagerstown	A Tor	107	366	94	17	3	5	132	63	42	42	1	74	14	6	3	6	1	.86	7	.257	.353	.361
1996 Dunedin	A+ Tor	36	106	22	3	0	0	25	10	10	12	0	22	0	7	0	2	4	.33	2	.208	.288	.236
Syracuse	AAA Tor	4	3	0	0	0	0	0	1	0	0	0	1	0	0	0	0	0	.00	0	.000	.000	.000
Knoxville	AA Tor	47	154	43	11	0	2	60	23	22	15	1	25	3	3	1	1	4	.20	6	.279	.351	.390
1997 Syracuse	AAA Tor	103	333	85	17	2	8	130	47	40	35	3	60	7	5	2	2	3	.40	3	.255	.337	.390
5 Min. YEARS		439	1438	367	68	10	19	512	204	165	141	6	273	31	24	10	20	28	.42	25	.255	.333	.356

Juan Munoz

Bats: Left **Throws:** Left **Pos:** OF   **Ht:** 5'9" **Wt:** 170 **Born:** 3/27/74 **Age:** 24

					BATTING												BASERUNNING				PERCENTAGES		
Year Team	Lg Org	G	AB	H	2B	3B	HR	TB	R	RBI	TBB	IBB	SO	HBP	SH	SF	SB	CS	SB%	GDP	Avg	OBP	SLG
1995 Johnson Cty	R+ StL	57	190	66	12	1	7	101	43	31	27	0	17	0	0	2	13	2	.87	1	.347	.425	.532
1996 Peoria	A StL	31	111	38	9	0	0	47	19	19	14	0	14	1	0	3	4	1	.80	2	.342	.411	.423
St. Pete	A+ StL	90	330	80	12	3	1	101	41	46	38	0	35	1	3	3	6	5	.55	8	.242	.320	.306
1997 Pr William	A+ StL	66	256	80	16	7	4	122	41	48	19	3	25	0	0	4	3	1	.75	5	.313	.355	.477
Arkansas	AA StL	58	215	60	9	2	6	91	28	31	16	0	26	1	2	1	6	10	.38	2	.279	.330	.423
3 Min. YEARS		302	1102	324	58	13	18	462	172	175	114	3	117	3	5	13	32	19	.63	18	.294	.358	.419

Peter Munro

Pitches: Right **Bats:** Right **Pos:** P   **Ht:** 6'2" **Wt:** 185 **Born:** 6/14/75 **Age:** 23

			HOW MUCH HE PITCHED						WHAT HE GAVE UP										THE RESULTS					
Year Team	Lg Org	G	GS	CG	GF	IP	BFP	H	R	ER	HR	SH	SF	HB	TBB	IBB	SO	WP	Bk	W	L	Pct.	ShO	Sv	ERA
1995 Utica	A- Bos	14	14	0	0	90	389	79	38	26	3	3	3	7	33	1	74	4	0	4	5	.556	0	0	2.60
1996 Sarasota	A+ Bos	27	25	2	1	155	667	153	76	62	4	3	2	7	62	1	115	7	1	11	6	.647	2	1	3.60
1997 Trenton	AA Bos	22	22	1	0	116.1	506	113	76	64	12	10	6	8	47	0	109	6	3	7	10	.412	0	0	4.95
3 Min. YEARS		63	61	3	1	361.1	1562	345	190	152	19	16	11	22	142	2	298	17	4	23	20	.535	2	1	3.79

Mike Murphy

Bats: Right **Throws:** Right **Pos:** OF   **Ht:** 6'2" **Wt:** 185 **Born:** 1/23/72 **Age:** 26

					BATTING												BASERUNNING				PERCENTAGES		
Year Team	Lg Org	G	AB	H	2B	3B	HR	TB	R	RBI	TBB	IBB	SO	HBP	SH	SF	SB	CS	SB%	GDP	Avg	OBP	SLG
1990 Martinsvlle	R+ Phi	9	31	3	0	0	0	3	4	1	7	0	17	0	0	0	1	2	.33	1	.097	.263	.097
1991 Martinsvlle	R+ Phi	44	156	34	3	0	0	37	15	7	11	1	40	1	2	0	9	2	.82	6	.218	.274	.237
1992 Batavia	A- Phi	63	228	58	6	2	2	74	32	27	21	0	48	4	3	0	15	8	.65	6	.254	.328	.325
1993 Spartanburg	A Phi	133	509	147	29	6	3	197	70	60	35	1	91	9	9	2	33	14	.70	15	.289	.344	.387
1994 Dunedin	A+ Tor	125	469	129	11	4	1	151	57	34	55	3	106	4	9	3	31	10	.76	9	.275	.360	.322
1995 Canton-Akrn	AA Cle	10	23	1	0	0	0	1	3	0	4	0	3	0	0	0	0	0	.00	0	.043	.185	.043
Kinston	A+ Cle	67	177	41	6	0	1	50	26	15	15	1	30	3	1	1	13	4	.76	2	.232	.301	.282
1996 Charlotte	A+ Tex	87	358	119	20	7	7	174	73	52	32	1	94	3	3	0	22	9	.71	5	.332	.392	.486
Tulsa	AA Tex	34	121	28	7	2	4	51	22	16	21	0	29	3	1	1	1	0	1.00	2	.231	.356	.421
1997 Tulsa	AA Tex	46	156	40	10	1	4	64	30	19	35	0	45	4	0	0	3	3	.67	3	.256	.405	.410
Okla City	AAA Tex	73	243	80	13	5	5	118	37	25	38	1	66	4	4	2	14	5	.74	5	.329	.425	.486
8 Min. YEARS		691	2471	680	105	27	27	920	369	256	274	8	569	40	27	9	145	58	.71	49	.275	.356	.372

Calvin Murray

Bats: Right **Throws:** Right **Pos:** OF   **Ht:** 5'11" **Wt:** 185 **Born:** 7/30/71 **Age:** 26

					BATTING												BASERUNNING				PERCENTAGES		
Year Team	Lg Org	G	AB	H	2B	3B	HR	TB	R	RBI	TBB	IBB	SO	HBP	SH	SF	SB	CS	SB%	GDP	Avg	OBP	SLG
1993 Shreveport	AA SF	37	138	26	6	0	0	32	15	6	14	0	29	2	3	1	12	6	.67	0	.188	.271	.232
San Jose	A+ SF	85	345	97	24	1	9	150	61	42	40	0	63	4	2	0	42	10	.81	4	.281	.362	.435
Phoenix	AAA SF	5	19	6	1	1	0	9	4	0	2	0	5	0	0	0	1	1	.50	0	.316	.381	.474
1994 Shreveport	AA SF	129	480	111	19	5	2	146	67	35	47	0	81	5	8	4	33	13	.72	4	.231	.304	.304
1995 Phoenix	AAA SF	13	50	9	1	0	4	22	8	10	4	0	6	0	1	1	2	2	.50	2	.180	.236	.440
Shreveport	AA SF	110	441	104	17	3	2	133	77	29	59	2	70	3	5	1	26	10	.72	5	.236	.329	.302
1996 Shreveport	AA SF	50	169	44	7	0	7	72	32	24	25	0	33	1	3	4	6	5	.55	5	.260	.352	.426
Phoenix	AAA SF	83	311	76	16	6	3	113	50	28	43	0	60	3	5	1	12	6	.67	1	.244	.341	.363
1997 Shreveport	AA SF	122	419	114	25	3	10	175	83	56	66	0	73	4	1	2	52	6	.90	7	.272	.375	.418
5 Min. YEARS		634	2372	587	116	19	37	852	397	230	300	2	420	22	28	14	186	59	.76	28	.247	.336	.359

Glenn Murray

Bats: Right **Throws:** Right **Pos:** OF **Ht:** 6' 2" **Wt:** 225 **Born:** 11/23/70 **Age:** 27

Year Team	Lg Org	G	AB	H	2B	3B	HR	TB	R	RBI	TBB	IBB	SO	HBP	SH	SF	SB	CS	SB%	GDP	Avg	OBP	SLG
																	BASERUNNING				**PERCENTAGES**		
1989 Expos	R Mon	27	87	15	6	2	0	25	10	7	6	0	30	2	0	1	8	1	.89	1	.172	.240	.287
Jamestown	A- Mon	3	10	3	1	0	0	4	1	1	1	0	1	0	0	0	0	0	.00	0	.300	.364	.400
1990 Jamestown	A- Mon	53	165	37	8	4	1	56	20	14	21	0	43	3	0	0	11	3	.79	3	.224	.323	.339
1991 Rockford	A Mon	124	479	113	16	14	5	172	73	60	77	3	137	2	0	8	22	19	.54	8	.236	.339	.359
1992 Wst Plm Bch	A+ Mon	119	414	96	14	5	13	159	79	41	75	3	150	4	2	1	26	11	.70	4	.232	.354	.384
1993 Harrisburg	AA Mon	127	475	120	21	4	26	227	82	96	56	1	111	8	0	2	16	7	.70	3	.253	.340	.478
1994 Pawtucket	AAA Bos	130	465	104	17	1	25	198	74	64	55	4	134	4	0	2	9	3	.75	10	.224	.310	.426
1995 Pawtucket	AAA Bos	104	336	82	15	0	25	172	66	66	34	1	109	11	1	5	5	6	.45	4	.244	.329	.512
1996 Scranton-WB	AAA Phi	41	142	52	10	2	7	87	31	22	22	0	29	1	0	1	7	0	1.00	1	.366	.452	.613
1997 Indianapols	AAA Cin	7	12	2	1	0	0	3	1	0	2	0	3	0	0	0	0	0	.00	1	.167	.286	.250
Chattanooga	AA Cin	94	329	93	16	2	26	191	66	73	56	2	91	4	0	6	7	5	.58	5	.283	.387	.581
1996 Philadelphia	NL	38	97	19	3	0	2	28	8	6	7	0	36	0	0	0	1	1	.50	0	.196	.250	.289
9 Min. YEARS		829	2914	717	125	34	128	1294	503	444	405	14	838	39	3	26	111	55	.67	40	.246	.343	.444

Jason Myers

Pitches: Left **Bats:** Left **Pos:** P **Ht:** 6'4" **Wt:** 200 **Born:** 9/19/73 **Age:** 24

Year Team	Lg Org	G	GS	CG	GF	IP	BFP	H	R	ER	HR	SH	SF	HB	TBB	IBB	SO	WP	Bk	W	L	Pct.	ShO	Sv	ERA
				HOW MUCH HE PITCHED						**WHAT HE GAVE UP**										**THE RESULTS**				
1993 Giants	R SF	13	13	0	0	74.2	92	50	19	14	0	1	0	2	16	0	105	3	0	8	1	.889	0	0	1.69
1994 Clinton	A SF	26	26	2	0	146.2	616	150	77	69	14	8	5	4	36	0	100	8	0	10	6	.625	1	0	4.23
1995 Burlington	A SF	16	16	1	0	95	413	109	64	53	14	3	5	2	26	0	85	4	0	2	9	.182	0	0	5.02
1996 San Jose	A+ SF	33	16	1	10	119.2	529	140	74	65	10	3	2	3	38	1	82	7	0	8	7	.533	1	1	4.89
1997 Bakersfield	A+ SF	10	9	0	0	47.2	221	64	43	34	7	1	2	1	14	0	32	3	0	4	3	.571	0	0	6.42
Shreveport	AA SF	7	0	0	2	12	50	14	7	1	1	0	1	0	0	0	12	0	0	1	0	1.000	0	0	0.75
5 Min. YEARS		105	80	4	12	495.2	2114	527	284	236	46	16	15	12	130	1	416	25	0	33	26	.559	2	1	4.29

Jimmy Myers

Pitches: Right **Bats:** Right **Pos:** P **Ht:** 6' 1" **Wt:** 190 **Born:** 4/28/69 **Age:** 29

Year Team	Lg Org	G	GS	CG	GF	IP	BFP	H	R	ER	HR	SH	SF	HB	TBB	IBB	SO	WP	Bk	W	L	Pct.	ShO	Sv	ERA
				HOW MUCH HE PITCHED						**WHAT HE GAVE UP**										**THE RESULTS**				
1987 Pocatello	R+ SF	10	2	0	4	19.2	92	29	21	19	1	1	1	1	16	1	12	5	2	0	0	.000	0	0	8.69
1988 Pocatello	R+ SF	12	12	0	0	58.1	283	72	50	35	3	2	1	1	32	1	39	7	1	4	5	.444	0	0	5.40
1989 Clinton	A SF	32	21	0	5	137.2	592	139	71	57	6	8	5	9	58	5	63	11	0	4	12	.250	0	0	3.73
1990 San Jose	A+ SF	60	0	0	50	84	361	80	44	30	2	3	3	2	34	6	51	3	1	5	8	.385	0	25	3.21
1991 Shreveport	AA SF	62	0	0	55	76.1	325	71	22	21	2	6	0	2	30	5	51	4	0	6	4	.600	0	24	2.48
1992 Phoenix	AAA SF	25	0	0	19	23.2	114	32	20	15	1	2	1	0	13	5	11	0	0	0	0	.000	0	10	5.70
Shreveport	AA SF	33	0	0	32	32	141	39	17	17	0	2	2	2	10	1	15	1	0	2	4	.333	0	18	4.78
1993 Shreveport	AA SF	29	0	0	14	49.1	210	50	14	11	1	2	0	2	19	3	23	4	0	2	2	.500	0	1	2.01
Phoenix	AAA SF	31	3	0	5	58.2	259	69	35	24	2	3	0	3	22	2	20	5	0	2	5	.286	0	4	3.68
1994 Memphis	AA KC	33	2	0	12	64.1	286	68	38	35	3	7	2	4	32	4	35	7	1	4	4	.500	0	3	4.90
Carolina	AA Pit	44	2	0	17	76	335	75	41	38	3	7	3	7	39	5	42	8	1	5	5	.500	0	7	4.50
1995 Rochester	AAA Bal	55	0	0	28	64.2	289	72	28	22	2	3	2	1	29	1	31	4	0	0	4	.000	0	6	3.06
1996 Rochester	AAA Bal	39	0	0	35	53	220	53	19	17	1	8	0	2	12	4	21	5	0	7	5	.583	0	12	2.89
1997 Norfolk	AAA NYN	45	0	0	14	69	288	57	23	14	1	2	1	4	33	5	31	4	2	4	4	.333	0	2	1.83
1996 Baltimore	AL	11	0	0	5	14	64	18	13	11	4	0	2	0	3	1	6	1	0	0	0	.000	0	0	7.07
11 Min. YEARS		510	42	0	290	866.2	3795	906	443	355	28	56	21	40	379	48	455	65	8	43	68	.387	0	108	3.69

Noe Najera

Pitches: Left **Bats:** Left **Pos:** P **Ht:** 6'2" **Wt:** 190 **Born:** 12/9/70 **Age:** 27

Year Team	Lg Org	G	GS	CG	GF	IP	BFP	H	R	ER	HR	SH	SF	HB	TBB	IBB	SO	WP	Bk	W	L	Pct.	ShO	Sv	ERA
				HOW MUCH HE PITCHED						**WHAT HE GAVE UP**										**THE RESULTS**				
1992 Watertown	A- Cle	15	8	0	2	55	256	46	33	26	1	2	1	7	41	0	48	5	0	2	4	.333	0	0	4.25
1994 Watertown	A- Cle	21	1	0	6	34	161	36	20	17	1	2	1	1	22	4	37	4	0	2	1	.667	0	2	4.50
1995 Columbus	A Cle	43	0	0	15	42.2	189	34	20	16	3	1	1	6	24	3	53	4	2	3	1	.750	0	1	3.38
Kinston	A+ Cle	8	3	0	2	20	78	10	6	5	0	1	0	2	9	1	14	0	0	0	1	.000	0	0	2.25
1996 Kinston	A+ Cle	24	24	1	0	140	576	124	52	42	12	0	3	3	62	1	131	9	0	12	2	.857	0	0	2.70
1997 Akron	AA Cle	25	14	1	4	84.2	383	96	63	57	3	3	1	3	40	1	50	2	1	4	8	.333	0	0	6.06
5 Min. YEARS		136	50	2	29	376.1	1643	346	194	163	20	10	7	19	198	10	333	24	3	23	17	.575	0	3	3.90

Lipso Nava

Bats: Right **Throws:** Right **Pos:** 3B **Ht:** 6' 2" **Wt:** 175 **Born:** 11/28/68 **Age:** 29

Year Team	Lg Org	G	AB	H	2B	3B	HR	TB	R	RBI	TBB	IBB	SO	HBP	SH	SF	SB	CS	SB%	GDP	Avg	OBP	SLG
																	BASERUNNING				**PERCENTAGES**		
1990 Bellingham	A- Sea	46	171	43	12	0	0	55	11	15	15	2	31	2	3	0	2	2	.50	5	.251	.319	.322
San Berndno	A+ Sea	7	23	4	1	0	0	5	1	1	0	0	9	2	1	0	0	0	.00	1	.174	.240	.217
1991 San Berndno	A+ Sea	86	258	70	5	0	2	81	19	33	20	0	44	6	3	2	5	4	.56	4	.271	.336	.314
1992 Peninsula	A+ Sea	102	346	78	16	2	3	107	32	35	18	1	56	8	4	1	7	3	.70	8	.225	.279	.309
1993 Jacksnville	AA Sea	114	396	101	20	0	7	142	52	41	31	1	43	13	12	3	5	6	.45	11	.255	.327	.359
1994 Riverside	A+ Sea	28	102	26	9	1	0	37	15	13	12	1	19	2	0	2	0	0	.00	5	.255	.339	.363
Jacksnville	AA Sea	41	131	25	6	1	3	42	13	10	7	0	20	2	6	0	2	2	.50	1	.191	.243	.321
1995 Trenton	AA Bos	20	51	11	3	0	1	17	7	7	1	0	5	3	1	1	1	0	1.00	1	.216	.268	.333
Sarasota	A+ Bos	21	62	16	4	0	2	26	11	10	7	0	7	4	0	1	1	0	1.00	3	.258	.370	.419
1996 Rio Grande	IND —	92	360	119	20	2	17	194	66	72	33	0	38	6	0	2	29	7	.81	3	.331	.394	.539
1997 Iowa	AAA ChN	109	319	85	17	1	9	131	37	36	22	0	53	7	0	2	2	3	.40	16	.266	.326	.411

		BATTING														BASERUNNING				PERCENTAGES		
Year Team	Lg Org	G	AB	H	2B	3B	HR	TB	R	RBI	TBB	IBB	SO	HBP	SH	SF	SB	CS	SB%	GDP	Avg	OBP	SLG
8 Min. YEARS		666	2219	578	113	7	44	837	264	273	166	5	325	55	30	13	54	27	.67	58	.260	.326	.377

Billy Neal

Pitches: Right **Bats:** Right **Pos:** P   **Ht:** 6'0" **Wt:** 201 **Born:** 9/20/71 **Age:** 26

		HOW MUCH HE PITCHED					WHAT HE GAVE UP								THE RESULTS						
Year Team	Lg Org	G	GS	CG	GF	IP	BFP	H	R	ER	HR	SH	SF	HB	TBB	IBB	SO	WP	Bk	W	L	Pct	ShO	Sv	ERA
1995 Great Falls	R+ LA	6	1	0	3	12.1	61	19	12	8	0	1	0	2	4	1	8	0	2	0	1	.000	0	0	5.84
Lethbridge	R+ LA	10	8	1	0	53	229	55	30	19	1	0	2	2	20	0	47	6	1	3	2	.600	0	0	3.23
1996 Vero Beach	A+ LA	51	0	0	12	110.2	455	94	37	28	4	4	3	5	39	4	75	6	2	16	6	.727	0	1	2.28
1997 San Antonio	AA LA	25	0	0	10	31	145	35	25	21	1	3	2	1	16	1	12	2	0	2	4	.333	0	0	6.10
San Berndno	A+ LA	24	0	0	9	46.2	207	50	30	22	4	3	0	1	17	0	31	2	0	0	5	.000	0	1	4.24
3 Min. YEARS		116	9	1	34	253.2	1097	253	134	98	10	11	7	11	96	6	173	16	5	21	18	.538	0	2	3.48

Mike Neal

Bats: Right **Throws:** Right **Pos:** 2B-SS   **Ht:** 6'1" **Wt:** 180 **Born:** 11/5/71 **Age:** 26

		BATTING															BASERUNNING				PERCENTAGES		
Year Team	Lg Org	G	AB	H	2B	3B	HR	TB	R	RBI	TBB	IBB	SO	HBP	SH	SF	SB	CS	SB%	GDP	Avg	OBP	SLG
1993 Watertown	A- Cle	67	234	68	15	3	4	101	47	43	55	4	45	6	1	3	7	1	.88	2	.291	.433	.432
1994 Kinston	A+ Cle	101	378	99	21	1	5	137	51	38	40	1	94	3	3	1	8	12	.40	6	.262	.336	.362
1995 Canton-Akrn	AA Cle	134	419	112	24	2	5	155	64	46	71	3	79	9	4	8	5	6	.45	7	.267	.379	.370
1996 Canton-Akrn	AA Cle	94	254	57	9	3	4	84	42	32	39	0	53	5	2	6	2	3	.40	3	.224	.332	.331
1997 Akron	AA Cle	126	457	129	24	2	17	208	77	69	55	0	103	12	5	3	8	7	.53	7	.282	.372	.455
5 Min. YEARS		522	1742	465	93	11	35	685	281	228	260	8	374	35	15	21	30	29	.51	25	.267	.369	.393

Mike Neill

Bats: Left **Throws:** Left **Pos:** OF   **Ht:** 6'2" **Wt:** 200 **Born:** 4/27/70 **Age:** 28

		BATTING															BASERUNNING				PERCENTAGES		
Year Team	Lg Org	G	AB	H	2B	3B	HR	TB	R	RBI	TBB	IBB	SO	HBP	SH	SF	SB	CS	SB%	GDP	Avg	OBP	SLG
1991 Sou. Oregon	A- Oak	63	240	84	14	0	5	113	42	42	35	3	54	0	4	1	9	3	.75	1	.350	.431	.471
1992 Reno	A+ Oak	130	473	159	26	7	5	214	101	76	81	2	96	5	6	2	23	11	.68	15	.336	.437	.452
Huntsville	AA Oak	5	16	5	0	0	0	5	4	2	2	0	7	0	1	1	1	0	1.00	0	.313	.368	.313
1993 Huntsville	AA Oak	54	179	44	8	0	1	55	30	15	34	0	45	1	0	1	3	4	.43	4	.246	.367	.307
Modesto	A+ Oak	17	62	12	3	0	0	15	4	4	12	0	12	0	1	0	0	1	.00	0	.194	.324	.242
1994 Tacoma	AAA Oak	7	22	5	1	0	0	6	1	2	3	0	7	0	0	0	0	0	.00	0	.227	.320	.273
Modesto	A+ Oak	47	165	48	4	1	2	60	22	18	26	1	50	1	2	1	1	1	.50	6	.291	.389	.364
1995 Modesto	A+ Oak	71	257	71	17	1	6	108	39	36	34	2	65	2	5	1	4	4	.50	6	.276	.364	.420
Huntsville	AA Oak	33	107	32	6	1	2	46	11	16	12	1	29	0	0	1	1	0	1.00	1	.299	.367	.430
1996 Edmonton	AAA Oak	6	20	3	1	0	1	7	4	4	2	0	3	0	1	0	0	0	.00	0	.150	.227	.350
Modesto	A+ Oak	114	442	150	20	6	19	239	101	78	68	4	123	4	2	2	28	7	.80	3	.339	.430	.541
1997 Edmonton	AAA Oak	7	21	4	0	0	0	4	3	3	7	0	7	0	2	0	1	1	.50	0	.190	.393	.190
Huntsville	AA Oak	122	486	165	30	2	14	241	129	80	72	0	113	4	3	3	16	7	.70	8	.340	.427	.496
7 Min. YEARS		676	2490	782	130	18	55	1113	491	376	388	13	611	17	27	13	87	39	.69	45	.314	.408	.447

Bry Nelson

Bats: Both **Throws:** Right **Pos:** 3B   **Ht:** 5'10" **Wt:** 170 **Born:** 1/27/74 **Age:** 24

		BATTING															BASERUNNING				PERCENTAGES		
Year Team	Lg Org	G	AB	H	2B	3B	HR	TB	R	RBI	TBB	IBB	SO	HBP	SH	SF	SB	CS	SB%	GDP	Avg	OBP	SLG
1994 Quad City	A Hou	45	156	38	6	0	1	47	20	6	11	0	15	0	0	0	3	5	.38	3	.244	.293	.301
Auburn	A- Hou	65	261	84	16	7	6	132	53	35	11	0	13	1	3	1	2	1	.67	9	.322	.350	.506
1995 Kissimmee	A+ Hou	105	395	129	34	5	3	182	47	52	20	0	37	1	1	6	0	0	.00	8	.327	.355	.461
Quad City	A Hou	6	26	1	1	0	0	2	1	2	0	0	3	0	0	0	0	0	.00	0	.038	.038	.077
1996 Kissimmee	A+ Hou	89	345	87	21	6	3	129	38	52	19	3	27	1	1	4	8	2	.80	13	.252	.290	.374
1997 Orlando	AA ChN	110	382	110	33	2	8	171	51	58	45	4	43	1	1	6	5	7	.42	15	.288	.359	.448
4 Min. YEARS		420	1565	449	111	20	21	663	210	205	106	7	138	4	6	17	32	25	.56	50	.287	.330	.424

Chris Nelson

Pitches: Right **Bats:** Both **Pos:** P   **Ht:** 6'3" **Wt:** 180 **Born:** 1/26/73 **Age:** 25

		HOW MUCH HE PITCHED					WHAT HE GAVE UP								THE RESULTS						
Year Team	Lg Org	G	GS	CG	GF	IP	BFP	H	R	ER	HR	SH	SF	HB	TBB	IBB	SO	WP	Bk	W	L	Pct	ShO	Sv	ERA
1995 Sou. Oregon	A- Oak	16	6	0	3	54.1	218	43	25	21	5	3	3	3	13	1	52	1	1	2	3	.400	0	1	3.48
Modesto	A+ Oak	2	2	0	0	10	37	4	1	1	0	0	0	0	4	0	8	1	0	2	0	1.000	0	0	0.90
1996 W Michigan	A Oak	16	9	0	3	70.2	275	53	19	19	3	3	1	1	20	0	79	4	8	3	1	.750	0	1	2.42
Modesto	A+ Oak	14	13	0	0	63.1	292	86	50	38	7	1	3	4	17	0	62	6	1	3	5	.375	0	0	5.40
1997 Modesto	A+ Oak	8	8	0	0	47	198	52	23	20	4	0	1	1	7	0	53	2	2	3	3	.500	0	0	3.83
Huntsville	AA Oak	20	15	1	0	99.2	430	116	60	55	10	3	3	1	25	1	71	4	2	9	3	.750	1	0	4.97
3 Min. YEARS		76	53	1	6	345	1450	357	178	154	29	10	11	10	86	2	325	18	14	22	15	.595	1	2	4.02

Erick Nelson

Pitches: Left **Bats:** Left **Pos:** P   **Ht:** 6'2" **Wt:** 185 **Born:** 5/22/72 **Age:** 26

		HOW MUCH HE PITCHED					WHAT HE GAVE UP								THE RESULTS						
Year Team	Lg Org	G	GS	CG	GF	IP	BFP	H	R	ER	HR	SH	SF	HB	TBB	IBB	SO	WP	Bk	W	L	Pct	ShO	Sv	ERA
1994 Minneapolis	IND —	26	2	0	8	39.1	176	43	26	21	7	2	0	2	18	0	16	3	0	4	2	.667	0	0	4.81
1997 Greenville	AA Atl	5	0	0	3	6	28	9	4	3	1	0	0	0	4	0	4	0	0	0	1	.000	0	0	4.50
Durham	A+ Atl	41	1	0	14	70	326	76	49	37	6	6	4	3	30	4	42	6	1	6	8	.429	0	1	4.76

		HOW MUCH HE PITCHED				WHAT HE GAVE UP											THE RESULTS					
Year Team	Lg Org	G	GS	CG	GF	IP	BFP	H	R	ER	HR	SH	SF	HB	TBB	IBB	SO	WP	Bk	W	L	Pct.	ShO	Sv	ERA
2 Min. YEARS		72	3	0	25	115.1	530	128	79	61	14	8	4	5	52	4	62	9	1	10	11	.476	0	1	4.76

Tom Nevers

Bats: Right **Throws:** Right **Pos:** SS **Ht:** 6'1" **Wt:** 175 **Born:** 9/13/71 **Age:** 26

		BATTING															BASERUNNING				PERCENTAGES		
Year Team	Lg Org	G	AB	H	2B	3B	HR	TB	R	RBI	TBB	IBB	SO	HBP	SH	SF	SB	CS	SB%	GDP	Avg	OBP	SLG
1990 Astros	R Hou	50	185	44	10	5	2	70	23	32	27	0	38	3	0	3	13	3	.81	3	.238	.339	.378
1991 Asheville	A Hou	129	441	111	26	2	16	189	59	71	53	0	124	3	2	5	10	12	.45	11	.252	.333	.429
1992 Osceola	A+ Hou	125	455	114	24	6	8	174	49	55	22	1	124	3	2	1	6	2	.75	10	.251	.289	.382
1993 Jackson	AA Hou	55	184	50	8	2	1	65	21	10	16	2	36	2	1	1	7	2	.78	5	.272	.335	.353
1994 Jackson	AA Hou	125	449	120	25	2	8	173	54	62	31	2	101	4	1	7	10	5	.67	8	.267	.316	.385
1995 Jackson	AA Hou	83	298	72	7	3	8	109	36	35	24	2	58	2	0	2	5	2	.71	10	.242	.301	.366
Stockton	A+ Mil	4	14	4	0	0	0	4	2	3	0	0	6	2	0	0	1	0	1.00	0	.286	.375	.286
El Paso	AA Mil	35	118	30	5	1	1	40	19	12	11	0	21	3	0	0	2	1	.67	6	.254	.333	.339
1996 Hardware City	AA Min	127	459	121	27	7	7	183	65	44	46	1	87	3	2	3	3	10	.23	18	.264	.333	.399
1997 Louisville	AAA StL	71	227	53	9	0	8	86	22	27	12	0	48	2	2	2	1	3	.25	12	.233	.276	.379
8 Min. YEARS		804	2830	719	141	28	59	1093	350	351	242	8	643	27	10	24	58	40	.59	83	.254	.316	.386

David Newhan

Bats: Left **Throws:** Right **Pos:** 2B **Ht:** 5'11" **Wt:** 180 **Born:** 9/7/73 **Age:** 24

		BATTING															BASERUNNING				PERCENTAGES		
Year Team	Lg Org	G	AB	H	2B	3B	HR	TB	R	RBI	TBB	IBB	SO	HBP	SH	SF	SB	CS	SB%	GDP	Avg	OBP	SLG
1995 Sou. Oregon	A- Oak	42	145	39	8	1	6	67	25	21	29	1	30	1	1	3	10	5	.67	2	.269	.388	.462
W Michigan	A Oak	25	96	21	5	0	3	35	9	8	13	1	26	1	1	1	3	2	.60	2	.219	.315	.365
1996 Modesto	A+ Oak	117	455	137	27	3	25	245	96	75	62	1	106	2	6	2	17	8	.68	8	.301	.386	.538
1997 Visalia	A+ Oak	67	241	67	15	2	7	107	52	48	44	2	58	3	2	5	9	3	.75	5	.278	.389	.444
Huntsville	AA Oak	57	212	67	13	2	5	99	40	35	28	2	59	2	1	2	5	5	.50	4	.316	.398	.467
3 Min. YEARS		308	1149	331	68	8	46	553	222	187	176	7	279	9	11	13	44	23	.66	21	.288	.383	.481

Alan Newman

Pitches: Left **Bats:** Left **Pos:** P **Ht:** 6'6" **Wt:** 225 **Born:** 10/2/69 **Age:** 28

		HOW MUCH HE PITCHED						WHAT HE GAVE UP												THE RESULTS					
Year Team	Lg Org	G	GS	CG	GF	IP	BFP	H	R	ER	HR	SH	SF	HB	TBB	IBB	SO	WP	Bk	W	L	Pct.	ShO	Sv	ERA
1988 Elizabethtn	R+ Min	13	12	2	0	55.1	279	57	62	50	3	2	2	2	56	0	51	17	3	2	8	.200	0	0	8.13
1989 Kenosha	A Min	18	18	1	0	88.2	398	65	41	28	2	5	0	4	74	0	82	3	9	3	9	.250	0	0	2.84
1990 Kenosha	A Min	22	22	5	0	154	614	94	41	28	2	4	0	6	78	2	158	10	2	10	4	.714	1	0	1.64
Visalia	A+ Min	5	5	0	0	36.1	155	29	15	9	0	3	2	1	22	0	42	1	0	3	1	.750	0	0	2.23
1991 Visalia	A+ Min	15	15	0	0	92.1	411	86	49	36	2	4	0	6	49	2	79	11	0	6	5	.545	0	0	3.51
Orlando	AA Min	11	11	2	0	67	275	53	28	20	0	2	1	1	30	1	53	8	0	5	4	.556	0	0	2.69
1992 Orlando	AA Min	18	18	2	0	102	454	94	54	47	3	4	3	4	67	0	86	9	3	4	8	.333	1	0	4.15
1993 Nashville	AA Min	14	11	1	1	65.2	304	75	52	44	4	4	2	1	40	0	35	6	0	1	6	.143	0	0	6.03
Indianapolis	AAA Cin	8	3	0	3	20	111	24	23	19	3	0	2	1	27	0	15	5	1	1	3	.250	0	0	8.55
1995 Alexandria	IND —	23	21	5	1	137	612	141	87	79	9	13	0	2	74	2	129	12	0	10	8	.556	2	0	5.19
1996 Alexandria	IND —	35	11	0	10	118.1	522	136	70	60	8	7	4	4	43	1	82	6	0	6	6	.500	0	2	4.56
1997 Birmingham	AA ChA	44	0	0	33	72.1	314	55	34	20	0	4	2	0	40	4	64	9	0	7	3	.700	0	10	2.49
9 Min. YEARS		226	147	18	48	1009	4449	909	556	440	36	52	18	32	600	12	876	96	18	58	65	.472	4	12	3.92

Doug Newstrom

Bats: Left **Throws:** Right **Pos:** C **Ht:** 6'1" **Wt:** 195 **Born:** 9/18/71 **Age:** 26

		BATTING															BASERUNNING				PERCENTAGES		
Year Team	Lg Org	G	AB	H	2B	3B	HR	TB	R	RBI	TBB	IBB	SO	HBP	SH	SF	SB	CS	SB%	GDP	Avg	OBP	SLG
1993 Yakima	A- LA	75	279	83	16	2	2	109	51	36	53	4	44	1	1	3	11	1	.92	7	.297	.408	.391
1994 Vero Beach	A+ LA	119	405	117	22	5	2	155	47	46	59	3	51	2	0	5	4	5	.44	5	.289	.378	.383
1995 San Berndno	A+ LA	97	316	92	22	1	6	134	53	58	40	0	58	2	6	3	19	9	.68	7	.291	.371	.424
1996 High Desert	A+ Bal	122	403	126	30	3	11	195	84	75	72	0	62	0	2	6	15	8	.65	9	.313	.442	.484
1997 New Haven	AA Col	95	244	65	10	1	1	80	29	43	39	1	32	1	2	4	9	5	.64	8	.266	.365	.328
5 Min. YEARS		508	1647	483	100	12	22	673	264	258	263	8	247	6	11	21	58	28	.67	36	.293	.388	.409

Darrell Nicholas

Bats: Right **Throws:** Right **Pos:** OF **Ht:** 6'0" **Wt:** 180 **Born:** 5/26/72 **Age:** 26

		BATTING															BASERUNNING				PERCENTAGES		
Year Team	Lg Org	G	AB	H	2B	3B	HR	TB	R	RBI	TBB	IBB	SO	HBP	SH	SF	SB	CS	SB%	GDP	Avg	OBP	SLG
1994 Helena	R+ Mil	15	61	23	3	2	0	30	18	13	10	0	10	1	0	0	11	3	.79	0	.377	.472	.492
Beloit	A Mil	59	221	63	8	3	1	80	33	35	22	1	54	1	2	4	17	4	.81	4	.285	.347	.362
1995 El Paso	AA Mil	15	39	8	0	1	0	10	4	2	0	0	11	0	1	0	4	0	1.00	6	.205	.205	.256
Stockton	A+ Mil	87	350	112	16	3	5	149	54	39	23	1	75	1	11	1	26	8	.76	6	.320	.363	.426
1996 El Paso	AA Mil	70	237	65	12	4	2	91	46	24	27	2	57	1	4	1	7	9	.44	6	.274	.350	.384
1997 El Paso	AA Mil	127	518	163	47	5	14	262	79	68	27	1	116	2	6	3	17	6	.74	14	.315	.349	.506
4 Min. YEARS		373	1426	434	86	18	22	622	234	181	109	5	323	6	24	9	82	30	.73	30	.304	.354	.436

Chris Nichting

Pitches: Right **Bats:** Right **Pos:** P   **Ht:** 6' 1" **Wt:** 205 **Born:** 5/13/66 **Age:** 32

Year Team	Lg Org	G	GS	CG	GF	IP	BFP	H	R	ER	HR	SH	SF	HB	TBB	IBB	SO	WP	Bk	W	L	Pct.	ShO	Sv	ERA
1988 Vero Beach	A+ LA	21	19	5	2	138	545	90	40	32	7	0	2	2	51	0	151	7	0	11	4	.733	1	1	2.09
1989 San Antonio	AA LA	26	26	2	0	154	698	160	96	86	13	9	6	6	101	6	136	14	4	4	14	.222	0	0	5.03
1992 Albuquerque	AAA LA	10	9	0	0	42	205	64	42	37	2	2	0	0	23	1	25	5	1	1	3	.250	0	0	7.93
San Antonio	AA LA	13	13	0	0	78.2	309	58	25	22	3	4	0	1	37	0	81	4	0	4	5	.444	0	0	2.52
1993 Vero Beach	A+ LA	4	4	0	0	17.1	75	18	9	8	2	0	0	0	6	0	18	1	0	0	1	.000	0	0	4.15
1994 Albuquerque	AAA LA	10	7	0	1	41.1	209	61	39	34	5	0	0	3	28	1	25	6	0	2	2	.500	0	0	7.40
San Antonio	AA LA	21	8	0	8	65.2	277	47	21	12	1	4	1	2	34	1	74	7	1	3	4	.429	0	1	1.64
1995 Okla City	AAA Tex	23	7	3	8	67.2	275	58	19	16	4	4	2	2	19	0	72	2	0	5	5	.500	2	1	2.13
1996 Okla City	AAA Tex	4	1	0	1	9	37	9	1	1	0	0	0	0	3	0	7	0	0	1	0	1.000	0	0	1.00
1997 Edmonton	AAA Oak	33	24	3	3	131	602	170	120	113	21	0	7	3	46	2	90	8	1	7	13	.350	0	1	7.76
1995 Texas	AL	13	0	0	3	24.1	122	36	19	19	1	1	2	1	13	1	6	3	0	0	0	.000	0	0	7.03
8 Min. YEARS		165	118	13	23	744.2	3232	735	412	361	58	23	18	19	348	11	679	54	7	38	51	.427	3	4	4.36

Brad Niedermaier

Pitches: Right **Bats:** Right **Pos:** P   **Ht:** 6'3" **Wt:** 205 **Born:** 2/9/73 **Age:** 25

Year Team	Lg Org	G	GS	CG	GF	IP	BFP	H	R	ER	HR	SH	SF	HB	TBB	IBB	SO	WP	Bk	W	L	Pct.	ShO	Sv	ERA
1995 Elizabethtn	R+ Min	7	7	0	0	40.2	171	33	14	10	1	0	1	0	17	0	47	9	0	2	0	1.000	0	0	2.21
1996 Ft. Wayne	A Min	32	3	0	14	69.1	295	64	39	25	3	3	4	0	29	2	72	11	0	6	4	.600	0	2	3.25
1997 Ft. Myers	A+ Min	32	0	0	29	36.2	154	27	15	6	2	2	4	0	12	2	47	4	0	2	3	.400	0	17	1.47
Salt Lake	AAA Min	16	0	0	5	26	118	29	22	17	7	2	0	0	13	2	20	1	0	2	1	.667	0	0	5.88
3 Min. YEARS		87	10	0	48	172.2	738	153	90	58	13	7	9	0	71	6	186	25	0	12	8	.600	0	19	3.02

C.J. Nitkowski

Pitches: Left **Bats:** Left **Pos:** P   **Ht:** 6' 3" **Wt:** 190 **Born:** 3/3/73 **Age:** 25

Year Team	Lg Org	G	GS	CG	GF	IP	BFP	H	R	ER	HR	SH	SF	HB	TBB	IBB	SO	WP	Bk	W	L	Pct.	ShO	Sv	ERA
1994 Chattanooga	AA Cin	14	14	0	0	74.2	318	61	30	29	4	5	0	4	40	0	60	2	5	6	3	.667	0	0	3.50
1995 Chattanooga	AA Cin	8	8	0	0	50.1	204	39	20	14	1	3	0	1	20	0	52	1	1	4	2	.667	0	0	2.50
Indianapols	AAA Cin	6	6	0	0	27.2	120	28	16	16	3	0	2	1	10	0	21	0	1	0	2	.000	0	0	5.20
1996 Toledo	AAA Det	19	19	1	0	111	471	104	60	55	13	4	1	3	53	1	103	6	1	4	6	.400	0	0	4.46
1997 New Orleans	AAA Hou	28	28	1	0	174.1	738	183	85	77	10	6	8	6	56	2	141	6	3	8	10	.444	0	0	3.98
1995 Cincinnati	NL	9	7	0	0	32.1	154	41	25	22	4	2	1	2	15	1	18	1	2	1	3	.250	0	0	6.12
Detroit	AL	11	11	0	0	39.1	184	53	32	31	7	0	3	3	20	2	13	1	0	1	4	.200	0	0	7.09
1996 Detroit	AL	11	8	0	0	45.2	234	62	44	41	7	0	2	7	38	1	36	2	0	2	3	.400	0	0	8.08
4 Min. YEARS		75	75	2	0	438	1851	415	208	191	31	18	11	15	179	3	377	15	11	22	23	.489	0	0	3.92
2 Maj. YEARS		31	26	0	0	117.1	572	156	101	94	18	2	6	12	73	4	67	4	2	4	10	.286	0	0	7.21

Jim Nix

Pitches: Right **Bats:** Right **Pos:** P   **Ht:** 5'11" **Wt:** 175 **Born:** 9/6/70 **Age:** 27

Year Team	Lg Org	G	GS	CG	GF	IP	BFP	H	R	ER	HR	SH	SF	HB	TBB	IBB	SO	WP	Bk	W	L	Pct.	ShO	Sv	ERA
1992 Princeton	R+ Cin	27	0	0	24	34.2	142	27	16	11	3	3	0	0	13	2	44	4	1	0	4	.000	0	13	2.86
Chston-WV	A Cin	2	0	0	2	3.1	15	3	0	0	0	0	0	0	1	1	5	0	0	0	0	.000	0	0	0.00
1993 Chston-WV	A Cin	26	5	1	18	60.2	237	28	19	15	1	2	1	5	24	3	75	5	1	7	2	.778	0	5	2.23
Winston-Sal	A+ Cin	11	4	0	3	35.1	153	37	24	14	8	0	1	0	15	0	33	2	0	3	3	.500	0	1	3.57
1994 Winston-Sal	A+ Cin	29	28	1	1	169	753	168	103	86	23	6	9	9	87	1	139	10	2	11	10	.524	0	0	4.58
1995 Chattanooga	AA Cin	40	5	0	14	84.1	360	84	43	30	8	6	4	2	30	1	71	7	1	3	5	.375	0	2	3.20
1996 Chattanooga	AA Cin	62	0	0	25	89	378	80	43	33	5	4	1	2	46	2	93	5	0	7	2	.778	0	11	3.34
1997 Chattanooga	AA Cin	28	0	0	6	37.1	160	31	15	13	7	0	1	0	20	2	32	4	0	6	1	.857	0	2	3.13
Indianapols	AAA Cin	12	0	0	1	16.1	80	18	16	16	0	0	2	0	16	0	13	1	0	3	0	1.000	0	0	8.82
6 Min. YEARS		237	42	2	93	530	2278	476	279	218	55	21	19	19	252	12	505	38	5	40	27	.597	0	31	3.70

Trot Nixon

Bats: Left **Throws:** Left **Pos:** OF   **Ht:** 6' 2" **Wt:** 196 **Born:** 4/11/74 **Age:** 24

Year Team	Lg Org	G	AB	H	2B	3B	HR	TB	R	RBI	TBB	IBB	SO	HBP	SH	SF	SB	CS	SB%	GDP	Avg	OBP	SLG
1994 Lynchburg	A+ Bos	71	264	65	12	0	12	113	33	43	44	1	53	3	1	3	10	3	.77	5	.246	.357	.428
1995 Sarasota	A+ Bos	73	264	80	11	4	5	114	43	39	45	3	46	1	0	2	7	5	.58	5	.303	.404	.432
Trenton	AA Bos	25	94	15	3	1	2	26	9	8	7	0	20	0	2	2	2	1	.67	0	.160	.214	.277
1996 Trenton	AA Bos	123	438	110	11	4	11	162	55	63	50	3	65	3	6	5	7	9	.44	6	.251	.329	.370
1997 Pawtucket	AAA Bos	130	475	116	18	3	20	200	80	61	63	2	86	1	9	4	11	4	.73	11	.244	.331	.421
1996 Boston	AL	2	4	2	1	0	0	3	2	0	0	0	1	0	0	0	1	0	1.00	0	.500	.500	.750
4 Min. YEARS		422	1535	386	55	12	50	615	220	214	209	9	270	8	18	16	37	22	.63	27	.251	.341	.401

Les Norman

Bats: Right **Throws:** Right **Pos:** OF   **Ht:** 6' 1" **Wt:** 185 **Born:** 2/25/69 **Age:** 29

Year Team	Lg Org	G	AB	H	2B	3B	HR	TB	R	RBI	TBB	IBB	SO	HBP	SH	SF	SB	CS	SB%	GDP	Avg	OBP	SLG
1991 Eugene	A- KC	30	102	25	4	1	2	37	14	18	9	0	18	1	2	1	2	1	.67	4	.245	.310	.363
1992 Appleton	A KC	59	218	82	17	1	4	113	38	47	22	0	18	1	2	3	8	6	.57	5	.376	.430	.518
Memphis	AA KC	72	271	74	14	5	3	107	32	20	22	0	37	2	1	1	4	4	.50	2	.273	.331	.395
1993 Memphis	AA KC	133	484	141	32	5	17	234	78	81	50	3	88	14	7	2	11	9	.55	8	.291	.373	.483
1994 Omaha	AAA KC	13	38	7	3	0	1	13	4	4	6	0	11	1	1	0	1	0	1.00	2	.184	.311	.342

BATTING

Year Team	Lg Org	G	AB	H	2B	3B	HR	TB	R	RBI	TBB	IBB	SO	HBP	SH	SF	SB	CS	SB%	GDP	Avg	OBP	SLG
Memphis	AA KC	106	383	101	19	4	13	167	53	55	36	1	44	7	3	2	7	7	.50	0	.264	.336	.436
1995 Omaha	AAA KC	83	313	89	19	3	9	141	46	33	18	2	48	4	3	2	5	3	.63	3	.284	.329	.450
1996 Omaha	AAA KC	24	77	20	6	0	1	29	8	13	6	0	8	1	0	1	0	1	.00	2	.260	.318	.377
1997 Buffalo	AAA Cle	118	428	111	20	1	17	184	71	56	43	2	80	8	6	4	7	6	.54	5	.259	.335	.430
1995 Kansas City	AL	24	40	9	0	1	0	11	6	4	6	0	6	0	1	0	0	1	.00	0	.225	.326	.275
1996 Kansas City	AL	54	49	6	0	0	0	6	9	0	6	0	14	1	0	0	1	1	.50	0	.122	.232	.122
7 Min. YEARS		638	2314	650	134	20	67	1025	344	327	212	8	352	39	25	16	44	38	.54	31	.281	.349	.443
2 Maj. YEARS		78	89	15	0	1	0	17	15	4	12	0	20	1	1	0	1	2	.33	0	.169	.275	.191

Scott Norman

Pitches: Right Bats: Right Pos: P   Ht: 6'0" Wt: 195 Born: 9/1/72 Age: 25

		HOW MUCH HE PITCHED						WHAT HE GAVE UP												THE RESULTS					
Year Team	Lg Org	G	GS	CG	GF	IP	BFP	H	R	ER	HR	SH	SF	HB	TBB	IBB	SO	WP	Bk	W	L	Pct.	ShO	Sv	ERA
1993 Bristol	R+ Det	13	13	1	0	77	355	100	54	45	7	1	1	6	18	0	43	9	5	3	6	.333	0	0	5.26
1994 Fayetteville	A Det	25	25	4	0	165	672	148	63	51	9	3	4	4	41	0	95	12	0	14	7	.667	2	0	2.78
Lakeland	A+ Det	3	3	1	0	18.1	77	19	7	6	2	0	1	1	5	0	9	2	0	0	2	.000	1	0	2.95
1995 Jacksnville	AA Det	4	4	2	0	29	122	31	12	8	4	1	0	1	6	0	9	1	0	1	3	.250	0	0	2.48
Lakeland	A+ Det	22	21	3	0	128.1	571	141	86	58	4	2	9	6	38	1	63	4	2	7	7	.500	0	0	4.07
1996 Jacksnville	AA Det	27	14	0	5	97	437	122	58	52	8	4	1	4	37	4	30	5	1	6	5	.545	0	0	4.82
1997 New Haven	AA Col	29	0	0	9	41.1	192	58	38	31	3	2	2	2	15	2	21	3	0	1	5	.167	0	1	6.75
Salem	A+ Col	18	0	0	11	25	109	29	12	11	4	0	0	0	8	1	13	0	0	1	0	.000	0	1	3.96
5 Min. YEARS		141	80	11	25	581	2535	648	330	262	41	13	18	24	168	8	283	36	8	32	36	.471	3	2	4.06

Dax Norris

Bats: Right Throws: Right Pos: DH-C   Ht: 5'10" Wt: 190 Born: 11/14/73 Age: 24

		BATTING															BASERUNNING				PERCENTAGES		
Year Team	Lg Org	G	AB	H	2B	3B	HR	TB	R	RBI	TBB	IBB	SO	HBP	SH	SF	SB	CS	SB%	GDP	Avg	OBP	SLG
1996 Eugene	A- Atl	60	232	67	17	0	7	105	31	37	18	0	32	3	3	1	2	0	1.00	4	.289	.346	.453
1997 Greenville	AA Atl	2	9	3	0	0	1	6	3	3	0	0	0	0	0	0	0	0	.00	0	.333	.333	.667
Durham	A+ Atl	95	338	80	19	0	7	120	29	45	32	1	49	4	0	3	2	5	.29	10	.237	.308	.355
2 Min. YEARS		157	579	150	36	0	15	231	63	85	50	1	82	7	3	4	4	5	.44	14	.259	.323	.399

Joe Norris

Pitches: Right Bats: Right Pos: P   Ht: 6'4" Wt: 215 Born: 11/29/70 Age: 27

		HOW MUCH HE PITCHED						WHAT HE GAVE UP												THE RESULTS					
Year Team	Lg Org	G	GS	CG	GF	IP	BFP	H	R	ER	HR	SH	SF	HB	TBB	IBB	SO	WP	Bk	W	L	Pct.	ShO	Sv	ERA
1990 Jamestown	A- Mon	13	13	1	0	62.1	290	63	48	36	2	1	2	4	43	0	72	9	5	3	7	.300	0	0	5.20
1991 Sumter	A Mon	8	8	0	0	35	161	41	25	20	2	0	1	3	17	0	42	6	2	1	3	.250	0	0	5.14
1992 Rockford	A Mon	27	27	1	0	163	723	160	88	68	5	11	5	10	79	2	143	21	3	5	15	.250	0	0	3.75
1993 Wst Plm Bch	A+ Mon	26	13	0	4	81	336	62	27	24	3	2	4	9	29	0	63	6	0	7	4	.636	0	0	2.67
1994 Nashville	AA Min	36	13	0	8	111	474	106	58	52	6	4	7	7	45	2	83	10	3	6	8	.429	0	1	4.22
1995 Harwick City	AA Min	46	0	0	20	82.2	364	79	42	33	4	11	3	2	36	5	81	4	0	5	6	.455	0	5	3.59
1996 Salt Lake	AAA Min	21	0	0	5	37.1	174	48	27	24	3	3	1	0	17	0	38	4	0	1	1	.500	0	2	5.79
1997 Portland	AAA Fla	9	0	0	1	12	53	11	9	9	2	0	1	1	5	0	14	0	0	2	0	1.000	0	0	6.75
Charlotte	AAA Fla	9	1	0	3	16	84	23	22	21	4	1	0	4	13	0	10	2	0	0	0	.000	0	0	11.81
Tyler	IND —	13	8	1	1	50.2	226	53	29	25	0	3	4	7	16	2	44	8	1	4	2	.667	0	0	4.44
8 Min. YEARS		208	83	3	42	651	2885	646	375	312	31	36	28	47	300	11	590	70	14	34	46	.425	0	8	4.31

Jamie Northeimer

Bats: Right Throws: Right Pos: C   Ht: 5'10" Wt: 174 Born: 7/5/72 Age: 25

		BATTING															BASERUNNING				PERCENTAGES		
Year Team	Lg Org	G	AB	H	2B	3B	HR	TB	R	RBI	TBB	IBB	SO	HBP	SH	SF	SB	CS	SB%	GDP	Avg	OBP	SLG
1994 Batavia	A- Phi	45	144	38	9	2	2	57	16	20	14	2	22	4	1	3	0	5	.00	3	.264	.339	.396
1995 Piedmont	A Phi	115	392	114	24	4	1	149	56	54	53	1	72	20	4	2	9	4	.69	13	.291	.400	.380
Clearwater	A+ Phi	6	19	6	1	0	0	7	1	5	3	0	4	2	0	0	0	0	.00	0	.316	.458	.368
1996 Clearwater	A+ Phi	101	327	83	21	0	10	134	52	42	60	1	69	16	4	4	0	2	.00	7	.254	.391	.410
1997 Clearwater	A+ Phi	20	71	18	6	0	3	33	13	8	9	0	13	2	1	0	0	0	.00	0	.254	.354	.465
Reading	AA Phi	44	100	20	6	0	1	29	14	16	25	1	22	5	2	0	0	0	.00	2	.200	.385	.290
Scranton-WB	AAA Phi	4	13	2	0	0	0	2	1	1	1	0	6	0	0	0	0	0	.00	0	.154	.214	.154
4 Min. YEARS		335	1066	281	67	6	17	411	153	146	165	5	208	49	12	9	9	11	.45	25	.264	.384	.386

Chris Norton

Bats: Right Throws: Right Pos: DH   Ht: 6'2" Wt: 215 Born: 9/21/70 Age: 27

		BATTING															BASERUNNING				PERCENTAGES		
Year Team	Lg Org	G	AB	H	2B	3B	HR	TB	R	RBI	TBB	IBB	SO	HBP	SH	SF	SB	CS	SB%	GDP	Avg	OBP	SLG
1992 Watertown	A- Cle	1	4	0	0	0	0	0	1	0	0	0	2	0	0	0	0	0	.00	0	.000	.000	.000
Burlington	R+ Cle	4	12	3	0	0	0	3	2	2	1	0	4	0	0	0	0	0	.00	0	.250	.286	.250
Jamestown	A- Mon	60	207	42	4	1	4	60	15	27	15	0	64	2	0	2	3	0	1.00	3	.203	.261	.290
1993 Cardinals	R StL	27	83	19	5	3	0	30	10	11	11	1	23	1	0	0	0	0	.00	2	.229	.326	.361
1994 Savannah	A StL	126	439	116	11	2	26	209	75	82	73	4	144	4	3	2	6	4	.60	11	.264	.373	.476
1995 Arkansas	AA StL	10	25	6	2	0	0	8	6	6	11	2	5	0	0	1	0	0	.00	0	.240	.459	.320
Lubbock	IND —	97	327	95	16	3	21	180	61	61	75	7	87	1	0	0	6	2	.75	5	.291	.422	.550
1996 Lubbock	IND —	51	187	71	13	1	15	131	39	54	27	3	27	4	0	2	6	0	1.00	7	.380	.464	.701
Norwich	AA NYA	47	172	48	12	1	7	83	24	28	15	0	43	1	0	0	3	2	.60	3	.279	.340	.483
1997 Lk Elsinore	A+ Ana	37	138	38	7	2	11	82	34	34	22	1	41	2	0	1	0	1	.00	2	.275	.380	.594

BATTING																	BASERUNNING				PERCENTAGES		
Year Team	Lg Org	G	AB	H	2B	3B	HR	TB	R	RBI	TBB	IBB	SO	HBP	SH	SF	SB	CS	SB%	GDP	Avg	OBP	SLG
Midland	AA Ana	58	200	53	8	1	16	111	40	47	35	0	57	0	0	2	2	1	.67	8	.265	.371	.555
Vancouver	AAA Ana	1	5	1	0	0	1	4	1	1	0	0	2	0	0	0	0	0	.00	0	.200	.200	.800
6 Min. YEARS		519	1799	492	78	14	101	901	308	354	285	18	499	15	3	13	26	10	.72	41	.273	.375	.501

Phillip Norton

Pitches: Left Bats: Right Pos: P   Ht: 6'1" Wt: 180 Born: 2/1/76 Age: 22

HOW MUCH HE PITCHED								WHAT HE GAVE UP										THE RESULTS						
Year Team	Lg Org	G	GS	CG	GF	IP	BFP	H	R	ER	HR	SH	SF	HB	TBB	IBB	SO	WP	Bk	W	L	Pct.	ShO	Sv	ERA
1996 Cubs	R ChN	1	0	0	1	3	10	1	0	0	0	0	0	0	0	0	6	0	1	0	0	.000	0	0	0.00
Williamsprt	A- ChN	15	13	2	1	85	364	68	33	24	1	3	2	3	33	2	77	7	3	7	4	.636	1	0	2.54
1997 Rockford	A ChN	18	18	3	0	109	460	92	51	39	4	3	1	1	44	1	114	12	1	9	3	.750	0	0	3.22
Daytona	A+ ChN	7	6	3	0	42.1	171	40	11	11	5	1	0	0	12	0	44	0	0	3	2	.600	0	0	2.34
Orlando	AA ChN	2	1	0	1	7	28	8	2	2	0	0	0	0	2	1	7	0	0	1	0	1.000	0	0	2.57
2 Min. YEARS		43	38	8	3	246.1	1033	209	97	76	10	7	5	4	91	4	248	19	5	20	9	.690	1	0	2.78

Maximo Nunez

Pitches: Right Bats: Right Pos: P   Ht: 6'5" Wt: 165 Born: 1/15/73 Age: 25

HOW MUCH HE PITCHED								WHAT HE GAVE UP										THE RESULTS						
Year Team	Lg Org	G	GS	CG	GF	IP	BFP	H	R	ER	HR	SH	SF	HB	TBB	IBB	SO	WP	Bk	W	L	Pct.	ShO	Sv	ERA
1994 Blue Jays	R Tor	20	0	0	15	24.2	119	32	23	11	0	1	1	1	10	0	17	2	2	1	5	.167	0	2	4.01
1995 Hagerstown	A Tor	22	0	0	11	37.1	172	40	29	23	4	3	2	3	20	0	21	8	0	1	1	.500	0	0	5.54
St. Cathrns	A- Tor	7	0	0	4	7.2	42	11	10	8	1	2	0	1	7	0	6	1	0	1	0	1.000	0	0	9.39
1996 Hickory	A ChA	31	24	3	3	152.1	660	173	93	79	12	3	9	7	45	0	105	5	3	5	16	.238	1	0	4.67
1997 Winston-Sal	A+ ChA	28	0	0	19	52	210	35	15	10	5	3	2	1	21	1	53	2	0	0	2	.000	0	8	1.73
Birmingham	AA ChA	14	0	0	3	17.2	85	19	18	15	1	0	1	1	13	0	14	3	2	0	0	.000	0	0	7.64
4 Min. YEARS		122	24	3	55	291.2	1288	310	188	146	23	12	15	14	116	1	216	21	7	8	24	.250	1	10	4.51

Ramon Nunez

Bats: Right Throws: Right Pos: 3B   Ht: 6'0" Wt: 150 Born: 9/22/72 Age: 25

BATTING																	BASERUNNING				PERCENTAGES		
Year Team	Lg Org	G	AB	H	2B	3B	HR	TB	R	RBI	TBB	IBB	SO	HBP	SH	SF	SB	CS	SB%	GDP	Avg	OBP	SLG
1992 Pulaski	R+ Atl	59	218	55	9	2	5	83	28	32	14	1	57	3	0	1	8	3	.73	7	.252	.305	.381
1993 Macon	A Atl	115	377	108	18	5	7	157	57	40	37	2	73	4	6	2	6	5	.55	6	.286	.355	.416
1994 Durham	A+ Atl	124	453	125	23	0	17	199	59	62	38	1	98	2	0	4	4	9	.31	9	.276	.332	.439
1995 Durham	A+ Atl	17	54	20	4	0	5	39	13	15	8	0	9	0	1	1	0	0	.00	4	.370	.444	.722
Greenville	AA Atl	81	241	63	15	2	9	109	34	34	15	0	63	3	0	3	1	1	.50	8	.261	.309	.452
1996 Greenville	AA Atl	58	169	34	6	0	4	52	15	26	9	1	43	1	1	2	1	2	.33	2	.201	.243	.308
Durham	A+ Atl	65	243	75	18	1	10	125	30	55	12	1	45	1	1	7	2	2	.50	6	.309	.335	.514
1997 Orlando	AA ChN	106	351	104	13	3	16	171	59	65	15	2	65	3	1	1	1	2	.33	5	.296	.330	.487
6 Min. YEARS		625	2106	584	106	13	73	935	295	329	148	8	453	17	10	21	23	24	.49	47	.277	.327	.444

Sergio Nunez

Bats: Right Throws: Right Pos: 2B   Ht: 5'11" Wt: 155 Born: 1/3/75 Age: 23

BATTING																	BASERUNNING				PERCENTAGES		
Year Team	Lg Org	G	AB	H	2B	3B	HR	TB	R	RBI	TBB	IBB	SO	HBP	SH	SF	SB	CS	SB%	GDP	Avg	OBP	SLG
1994 Royals	R KC	59	232	92	9	7	5	130	64	24	32	0	17	6	0	4	37	12	.76	2	.397	.474	.560
1995 Wilmington	A+ KC	124	460	109	10	2	4	135	63	25	51	4	66	3	13	1	33	19	.63	8	.237	.317	.293
1996 Wilmington	A+ KC	105	402	109	23	6	3	153	60	40	38	0	54	4	6	2	44	11	.80	6	.271	.339	.381
1997 Royals	R KC	5	14	4	1	1	0	7	3	0	0	0	4	1	0	0	2	0	1.00	1	.286	.333	.500
Wichita	AA KC	34	137	38	1	1	1	44	18	11	6	0	17	0	1	0	12	3	.80	3	.277	.308	.321
4 Min. YEARS		327	1245	352	44	17	13	469	208	100	127	4	158	14	20	7	128	45	.74	16	.283	.354	.377

Paul O'Malley

Pitches: Right Bats: Right Pos: P   Ht: 6'3" Wt: 180 Born: 12/20/72 Age: 25

HOW MUCH HE PITCHED								WHAT HE GAVE UP										THE RESULTS						
Year Team	Lg Org	G	GS	CG	GF	IP	BFP	H	R	ER	HR	SH	SF	HB	TBB	IBB	SO	WP	Bk	W	L	Pct.	ShO	Sv	ERA
1994 Auburn	A- Hou	9	9	1	0	44.2	205	51	30	27	3	1	1	5	18	0	38	7	2	3	4	.429	0	0	5.44
1995 Kissimmee	A+ Hou	27	27	0	0	147	661	148	86	59	7	3	3	18	62	0	80	13	2	8	10	.444	0	0	3.61
1996 Quad City	A Hou	26	26	1	0	178	753	173	80	66	10	7	9	11	51	0	111	15	2	11	9	.550	0	0	3.34
1997 Jackson	AA Hou	28	0	0	7	44.2	211	53	32	32	4	1	5	5	21	1	20	5	4	0	2	.000	0	0	6.45
Kissimmee	A+ Hou	24	0	0	13	35.1	145	24	12	11	3	1	2	1	19	3	20	1	0	2	2	.500	0	5	2.80
4 Min. YEARS		114	62	2	20	449.2	1975	449	240	195	27	13	20	40	171	4	274	40	6	24	27	.471	0	5	3.90

Troy O'Neal

Bats: Right Throws: Right Pos: C   Ht: 5'11" Wt: 190 Born: 4/24/72 Age: 26

BATTING																	BASERUNNING				PERCENTAGES		
Year Team	Lg Org	G	AB	H	2B	3B	HR	TB	R	RBI	TBB	IBB	SO	HBP	SH	SF	SB	CS	SB%	GDP	Avg	OBP	SLG
1995 Lethbridge	R+ —	43	135	31	2	1	0	35	17	15	21	1	21	9	0	4	3	3	.50	6	.230	.361	.259
Helena	R+ Mil	4	14	5	1	0	0	6	5	1	1	0	0	0	0	0	0	0	.00	0	.357	.400	.429
1996 Beloit	A Mil	74	206	50	4	0	0	54	18	20	16	0	28	6	4	2	1	2	.33	8	.243	.313	.262
1997 Stockton	A+ Mil	4	15	7	1	0	0	8	0	3	0	0	2	1	0	0	0	0	.00	0	.467	.529	.533
El Paso	AA Mil	40	122	35	1	0	1	39	18	11	4	0	29	4	1	1	0	0	.00	3	.287	.328	.320
3 Min. YEARS		165	492	128	9	1	1	142	58	50	42	1	79	21	6	7	4	5	.44	17	.260	.340	.289

Doug O'Neill

Bats: Right **Throws:** Right **Pos:** OF   **Ht:** 5'10" **Wt:** 200 **Born:** 6/29/70 **Age:** 28

Year Team	Lg Org	G	AB	H	2B	3B	HR	TB	R	RBI	TBB	IBB	SO	HBP	SH	SF	SB	CS	SB%	GDP	Avg	OBP	SLG
1991 Jamestown	A- Mon	33	119	28	4	0	2	38	19	11	14	0	29	2	0	0	17	4	.81	2	.235	.326	.319
1992 Expos	R Mon	3	10	2	0	0	0	2	0	0	2	0	3	0	0	0	1	1	.50	0	.200	.333	.200
Albany	A Mon	11	36	9	3	0	0	12	3	3	6	0	13	0	0	0	1	1	.50	1	.250	.357	.333
1993 Burlington	A Mon	67	203	43	6	3	3	64	26	20	33	1	69	2	2	1	3	1	.75	2	.212	.326	.315
1994 Ogden	R+ —	70	259	72	21	4	10	131	55	53	45	0	101	0	3	2	10	6	.63	2	.278	.382	.506
1995 St. Paul	IND —	84	356	111	20	2	17	186	75	58	38	0	68	2	4	5	24	9	.73	7	.312	.377	.522
1996 Portland	AA Fla	72	241	62	10	2	7	97	39	26	26	1	64	2	2	2	8	4	.67	3	.257	.332	.402
Tulsa	AA Tex	20	75	23	3	0	5	41	8	15	11	0	19	1	1	0	1	2	.33	2	.307	.402	.547
1997 Okla City	AAA Tex	11	31	6	3	0	0	9	2	1	3	0	10	0	0	0	1	1	.50	1	.194	.265	.290
Tulsa	AA Tex	118	412	114	21	0	20	195	69	64	49	2	122	4	1	4	12	4	.75	4	.277	.356	.473
7 Min. YEARS		489	1742	470	91	11	64	775	296	251	227	4	498	13	13	14	78	33	.70	24	.270	.356	.445

Jamie Ogden

Bats: Left **Throws:** Left **Pos:** OF   **Ht:** 6'5" **Wt:** 233 **Born:** 1/19/72 **Age:** 26

Year Team	Lg Org	G	AB	H	2B	3B	HR	TB	R	RBI	TBB	IBB	SO	HBP	SH	SF	SB	CS	SB%	GDP	Avg	OBP	SLG
1990 Twins	R Min	28	101	20	1	2	0	25	11	5	7	0	41	0	0	0	2	0	1.00	2	.198	.250	.248
1991 Twins	R Min	37	122	39	9	7	2	68	22	25	11	0	30	0	0	4	7	4	.64	0	.320	.365	.557
1992 Kenosha	A Min	108	372	91	14	3	3	120	36	51	52	1	108	2	0	4	9	2	.82	9	.245	.337	.323
1993 Ft. Myers	A+ Min	118	396	96	22	4	8	150	37	46	34	1	89	6	4	1	7	1	.88	11	.242	.311	.379
1994 Ft. Myers	A+ Min	69	251	66	12	0	7	99	32	22	16	0	52	2	1	1	12	8	.60	6	.263	.311	.394
1995 Hardware City	AA Min	117	384	109	22	1	13	172	54	61	48	5	90	1	0	5	6	5	.55	10	.284	.361	.448
1996 Salt Lake	AAA Min	123	448	118	22	2	18	198	80	74	45	6	105	2	2	2	17	2	.89	5	.263	.332	.442
1997 Salt Lake	AAA Min	97	367	105	18	5	14	175	67	53	35	2	99	2	0	0	14	3	.82	11	.286	.351	.477
8 Min. YEARS		697	2441	644	120	24	65	1007	339	337	248	15	614	15	7	17	74	25	.75	58	.264	.333	.413

Kevin Ohme

Pitches: Left **Bats:** Left **Pos:** P   **Ht:** 6'1" **Wt:** 175 **Born:** 4/13/71 **Age:** 27

Year Team	Lg Org	G	GS	CG	GF	IP	BFP	H	R	ER	HR	SH	SF	HB	TBB	IBB	SO	WP	Bk	W	L	Pct.	ShO	Sv	ERA
1993 Ft. Wayne	A Min	15	4	0	6	46.1	184	38	19	13	1	2	2	1	15	1	45	4	1	3	2	.600	0	0	2.53
1994 Ft. Wayne	A Min	2	2	0	0	7	29	7	2	2	0	0	0	1	0	0	8	0	0	0	1	.000	0	0	2.57
1995 Hardware City	AA Min	35	11	0	7	101.1	427	89	51	39	5	7	7	3	45	1	52	7	0	3	4	.429	0	0	3.46
1996 Hardware City	AA Min	51	0	0	22	81	363	83	49	39	7	6	4	6	33	5	42	5	2	5	6	.455	0	3	4.33
1997 Salt Lake	AAA Min	56	0	0	34	73.2	324	70	49	46	6	5	1	6	34	4	45	4	1	2	5	.286	0	11	5.62
5 Min. YEARS		159	17	0	69	309.1	1327	287	170	139	19	20	14	17	127	11	192	20	4	13	18	.419	0	14	4.04

Augie Ojeda

Bats: Both **Throws:** Right **Pos:** SS   **Ht:** 5'9" **Wt:** 171 **Born:** 12/20/74 **Age:** 23

Year Team	Lg Org	G	AB	H	2B	3B	HR	TB	R	RBI	TBB	IBB	SO	HBP	SH	SF	SB	CS	SB%	GDP	Avg	OBP	SLG
1997 Frederick	A+ Bal	34	128	44	11	1	1	60	25	20	18	1	18	1	4	0	2	5	.29	1	.344	.429	.469
Bowie	AA Bal	58	204	60	9	1	2	77	33	23	31	1	17	3	4	3	7	0	1.00	6	.294	.390	.377
Rochester	AAA Bal	15	47	11	3	1	0	16	5	6	8	0	4	0	3	0	1	2	.33	2	.234	.345	.340
1 Min. YEARS		107	379	115	23	3	3	153	63	49	57	2	39	4	11	3	10	7	.59	9	.303	.397	.404

Jose Olmeda

Bats: Both **Throws:** Right **Pos:** OF   **Ht:** 5'9" **Wt:** 155 **Born:** 6/20/68 **Age:** 30

Year Team	Lg Org	G	AB	H	2B	3B	HR	TB	R	RBI	TBB	IBB	SO	HBP	SH	SF	SB	CS	SB%	GDP	Avg	OBP	SLG
1989 Idaho Falls	R+ Atl	61	230	57	5	6	1	77	36	27	31	0	40	0	0	1	9	4	.69	7	.248	.336	.335
1990 Sumter	A Atl	103	367	93	14	6	7	140	60	40	55	2	49	2	4	4	17	9	.65	3	.253	.350	.381
Burlington	A Atl	27	112	29	3	0	0	32	6	7	8	0	17	0	0	1	1	1	.50	1	.259	.306	.286
Greenville	AA Atl	2	8	1	0	0	0	1	1	0	1	0	3	0	0	0	0	0	.00	1	.125	.222	.125
1991 Macon	A Atl	81	305	84	16	8	3	125	66	30	38	0	38	1	2	1	34	7	.83	3	.275	.357	.410
Greenville	AA Atl	50	173	35	10	1	3	56	18	16	15	0	36	2	5	2	9	2	.82	2	.202	.271	.324
1992 Durham	A+ Atl	24	89	23	6	1	2	37	17	9	14	0	14	0	1	0	7	4	.64	0	.258	.359	.416
Greenville	AA Atl	106	341	84	22	4	2	120	54	33	38	3	50	0	5	9	15	7	.68	4	.246	.317	.352
1993 Greenville	AA Atl	122	451	126	33	2	9	190	61	51	29	2	63	0	5	9	15	7	.68	4	.279	.317	.421
1994 Richmond	AAA Atl	109	387	89	19	6	4	132	49	39	30	6	74	1	8	1	17	4	.81	12	.230	.286	.341
1995 Richmond	AAA Atl	80	241	61	11	3	1	81	22	24	16	2	41	1	3	2	2	1	.67	5	.253	.300	.336
Greenville	AA Atl	31	108	27	5	1	4	46	16	10	7	0	18	0	1	0	1	0	1.00	5	.250	.296	.426
1996 Charlotte	AAA Fla	115	375	120	26	1	9	175	52	49	21	0	58	1	4	3	7	6	.54	7	.320	.355	.467
1997 Charlotte	AAA Fla	83	242	50	11	1	1	66	24	29	21	1	41	2	2	5	3	2	.60	7	.207	.270	.273
9 Min. YEARS		994	3429	879	181	40	46	1278	482	364	324	16	542	10	35	35	134	53	.72	63	.256	.319	.373

Jo Olsen

Pitches: Right **Bats:** Right **Pos:** P   **Ht:** 6'4" **Wt:** 210 **Born:** 3/16/75 **Age:** 23

Year Team	Lg Org	G	GS	CG	GF	IP	BFP	H	R	ER	HR	SH	SF	HB	TBB	IBB	SO	WP	Bk	W	L	Pct.	ShO	Sv	ERA
1996 South Bend	A ChA	9	9	0	0	56.2	220	39	16	11	3	2	1	2	13	0	55	3	0	4	1	.800	0	0	1.75
Hickory	A ChA	4	4	1	0	26.1	101	19	5	4	1	0	0	0	6	0	32	0	0	2	1	.667	0	0	1.37
Pr William	A+ ChA	12	12	0	0	79	343	74	39	34	5	0	2	5	31	1	55	3	0	6	4	.600	0	0	3.87

Year Team	Lg Org	G	GS	CG	GF	IP	BFP	H	R	ER	HR	SH	SF	HB	TBB	IBB	SO	WP	Bk	W	L	Pct.	ShO	Sv	ERA
1997 Birmingham	AA ChA	28	27	1	0	160.1	709	183	101	87	14	11	5	3	58	2	121	9	0	9	14	.391	1	0	4.88
2 Min. YEARS		53	52	2	0	322.1	1373	315	161	136	23	13	8	10	108	3	263	15	0	21	20	.512	1	0	3.80

Steve Olsen

Pitches: Right **Bats:** Right **Pos:** P — **Ht:** 6'4" **Wt:** 225 **Born:** 11/2/69 **Age:** 28

Year Team	Lg Org	G	GS	CG	GF	IP	BFP	H	R	ER	HR	SH	SF	HB	TBB	IBB	SO	WP	Bk	W	L	Pct.	ShO	Sv	ERA
1991 Utica	A- ChA	2	2	0	0	14	51	3	3	1	0	0	0	0	4	0	20	1	0	1	0	1.000	0	0	0.64
South Bend	A ChA	13	13	0	0	81.2	352	80	44	33	4	2	4	3	28	1	76	3	3	5	2	.714	0	0	3.64
1992 Sarasota	A+ ChA	13	13	3	0	88	363	68	22	19	4	2	1	3	32	0	85	3	2	11	1	.917	1	0	1.94
Birmingham	AA ChA	12	12	1	0	77.1	320	68	28	26	5	0	2	0	29	1	46	2	0	6	4	.600	0	0	3.03
1993 Birmingham	AA ChA	25	25	1	0	142	618	156	87	75	22	1	5	7	52	2	92	4	0	10	9	.526	1	0	4.75
1994 Birmingham	AA ChA	16	16	1	0	102.2	432	100	47	42	8	2	2	3	28	1	69	9	0	5	7	.417	0	0	3.68
Nashville	AAA ChA	11	11	2	0	71.1	289	69	30	26	4	2	1	0	18	0	58	0	1	7	2	.778	0	0	3.28
1995 Nashville	AAA ChA	14	14	0	0	77	329	85	44	41	10	3	5	0	16	0	45	4	0	1	7	.125	0	0	4.79
Birmingham	AA ChA	14	14	2	0	85.1	357	84	44	33	4	3	7	1	21	2	56	1	0	8	3	.727	1	0	3.48
1996 Wichita	AA KC	15	3	0	3	55.1	213	40	18	17	9	1	2	0	14	0	39	3	0	6	0	1.000	0	0	2.77
Omaha	AAA KC	24	4	1	6	65.2	283	70	39	37	7	2	1	4	23	4	41	6	0	7	4	.636	1	0	5.07
1997 Omaha	AAA KC	22	13	0	2	84.1	402	96	67	54	11	2	3	3	48	3	43	5	1	4	5	.444	0	0	5.76
Wichita	AA KC	3	2	0	0	14.2	56	11	1	0	0	1	0	0	2	0	7	0	0	2	0	1.000	0	0	0.00
7 Min. YEARS		184	142	11	11	959.1	4065	930	474	404	88	21	33	24	315	14	677	41	7	73	44	.624	4	1	3.79

Eric Olszewski

Pitches: Right **Bats:** Left **Pos:** P — **Ht:** 6'3" **Wt:** 205 **Born:** 11/4/74 **Age:** 23

Year Team	Lg Org	G	GS	CG	GF	IP	BFP	H	R	ER	HR	SH	SF	HB	TBB	IBB	SO	WP	Bk	W	L	Pct.	ShO	Sv	ERA
1993 Braves	R Atl	13	0	0	3	30.2	148	33	25	19	0	4	0	3	20	0	26	3	1	3	3	.500	0	0	5.58
1994 Idaho Falls	R+ Atl	15	13	0	1	67.1	345	91	67	55	8	2	2	3	57	1	51	13	0	3	7	.300	0	0	7.35
1995 Macon	A Atl	35	1	0	15	81.1	351	54	37	34	3	1	1	8	50	1	103	11	3	2	5	.286	0	5	3.76
1996 Durham	A+ Atl	32	0	0	15	52.2	212	34	12	11	3	2	2	4	21	0	69	5	0	2	2	.500	0	4	1.88
1997 Greenville	AA Atl	4	0	0	1	6	34	9	6	4	0	2	1	0	8	0	7	0	0	0	0	.000	0	0	6.00
5 Min. YEARS		99	14	0	35	238	1090	221	147	123	14	11	6	18	156	2	256	32	4	10	17	.370	0	9	4.65

Rafael Orellano

Pitches: Left **Bats:** Left **Pos:** P — **Ht:** 6'2" **Wt:** 160 **Born:** 4/28/73 **Age:** 25

Year Team	Lg Org	G	GS	CG	GF	IP	BFP	H	R	ER	HR	SH	SF	HB	TBB	IBB	SO	WP	Bk	W	L	Pct.	ShO	Sv	ERA
1993 Utica	A- Bos	11	0	0	7	18.2	84	22	15	12	4	2	1	1	7	0	13	1	0	1	2	.333	0	2	5.79
1994 Red Sox	R Bos	4	3	0	0	13.1	50	6	3	3	0	0	0	0	4	0	10	1	2	1	0	1.000	0	0	2.03
Sarasota	A+ Bos	16	16	2	0	97.1	375	68	28	26	5	1	0	4	25	0	103	2	3	11	3	.786	1	0	2.40
1995 Trenton	AA Bos	27	27	2	0	186.2	772	146	68	64	18	4	1	11	72	0	160	9	4	11	7	.611	0	0	3.09
1996 Pawtucket	AAA Bos	22	20	0	0	99.1	476	124	94	87	20	2	9	6	62	0	66	10	1	4	11	.267	0	0	7.88
1997 Pawtucket	AAA Bos	16	12	1	0	69.1	323	65	58	55	12	2	7	2	55	0	46	4	0	3	5	.375	0	0	7.14
Trenton	AA Bos	2	2	0	0	6.1	42	14	12	12	1	0	1	0	7	0	5	1	0	1	0	1.000	0	0	17.05
Red Sox	R Bos	2	1	0	0	7	23	2	1	1	0	0	0	0	1	0	9	0	0	0	1	1.000	0	0	1.29
5 Min. YEARS		100	81	5	7	498	2145	447	279	260	60	11	19	24	233	0	412	28	11	32	29	.525	1	2	4.70

Eddie Oropesa

Pitches: Left **Bats:** Left **Pos:** P — **Ht:** 6'2" **Wt:** 200 **Born:** 11/23/71 **Age:** 26

Year Team	Lg Org	G	GS	CG	GF	IP	BFP	H	R	ER	HR	SH	SF	HB	TBB	IBB	SO	WP	Bk	W	L	Pct.	ShO	Sv	ERA
1994 Vero Beach	A+ LA	19	10	1	3	72	285	54	24	17	2	3	2	4	25	2	67	2	0	4	3	.571	1	0	2.13
1995 San Antonio	AA LA	16	0	0	7	17.1	87	22	8	6	2	1	2	3	12	1	16	0	1	1	1	.500	0	1	3.12
Vero Beach	A+ LA	19	1	0	7	28.1	120	25	12	12	0	0	2	0	10	0	23	4	2	3	1	.750	0	1	3.81
San Berndno	A+ LA	1	0	0	1	1	3	0	0	0	0	0	0	0	0	0	0	0	0	0	0	.000	0	1	0.00
1996 San Berndno	A+ LA	33	19	0	2	156.1	669	133	74	58	8	1	3	6	77	1	133	8	4	11	6	.647	0	1	3.34
1997 Shreveport	AA SF	43	9	1	12	124	531	122	58	54	7	7	4	4	64	0	65	6	6	7	7	.500	0	0	3.92
4 Min. YEARS		131	39	2	32	399	1695	356	176	147	19	13	13	20	188	4	304	20	13	26	18	.591	1	4	3.32

Bo Ortiz

Bats: Right **Throws:** Right **Pos:** OF — **Ht:** 5'11" **Wt:** 170 **Born:** 4/4/70 **Age:** 28

Year Team	Lg Org	G	AB	H	2B	3B	HR	TB	R	RBI	TBB	IBB	SO	HBP	SH	SF	SB	CS	SB%	GDP	Avg	OBP	SLG
1991 Bluefield	R+ Bal	12	53	16	2	1	1	23	4	7	2	0	6	0	0	1	1	0	1.00	2	.302	.321	.434
Kane County	A Bal	57	215	58	8	1	0	68	34	27	17	1	38	2	4	2	2	2	.50	4	.270	.326	.316
1992 Frederick	A+ Bal	54	182	50	11	3	0	67	26	19	18	0	40	3	2	1	7	3	.70	4	.275	.348	.368
1993 Frederick	A+ Bal	104	351	99	18	7	10	161	72	60	44	0	65	7	6	1	12	11	.52	7	.282	.372	.459
Bowie	AA Bal	8	30	6	0	1	0	8	3	1	0	5	1	2	0	.00	0	.200	.250	.267
1994 Bowie	AA Bal	85	320	99	21	3	10	156	58	54	28	2	47	4	1	0	13	4	.76	10	.309	.372	.488
Midland	AA Ana	22	80	14	4	0	0	18	9	6	6	0	11	1	0	0	3	1	.75	2	.175	.241	.225
1995 Midland	AA Ana	96	360	99	10	3	8	139	48	56	17	2	40	2	4	5	12	11	.52	6	.275	.307	.386
1996 Midland	AA Ana	127	507	150	32	5	11	225	73	64	32	0	80	2	4	4	12	7	.63	9	.296	.338	.444
1997 Harrisburg	AA Mon	60	188	42	2	3	7	71	24	21	12	0	25	0	2	2	5	0	1.00	3	.223	.267	.378
7 Min. YEARS			625	2286	633	108	27	47	936	349	317	177	5	357	22	25	16	67	39	.63	47	.277	.333	.409

Hector Ortiz

Bats: Right **Throws:** Right **Pos:** C   **Ht:** 6'0" **Wt:** 178 **Born:** 10/14/69 **Age:** 28

Year Team	Lg Org	G	AB	H	2B	3B	HR	TB	R	RBI	TBB	IBB	SO	HBP	SH	SF	SB	CS	SB%	GDP	Avg	OBP	SLG
1988 Salem	A- LA	32	77	11	1	0	0	12	5	4	5	0	16	1	1	0	0	2	.00	5	.143	.205	.156
1989 Vero Beach	A+ LA	42	85	12	0	1	0	14	5	4	6	0	15	2	4	0	0	0	.00	1	.141	.215	.165
Salem	A- LA	44	140	32	3	1	0	37	13	12	4	0	24	1	2	0	2	1	.67	6	.229	.255	.264
1990 Yakima	A- LA	52	173	47	3	1	0	52	16	12	5	0	15	1	1	0	1	1	.50	6	.272	.296	.301
1991 Vero Beach	A+ LA	42	123	28	2	0	0	30	3	8	5	0	8	3	0	0	0	0	.00	2	.228	.275	.244
1992 Bakersfield	A+ LA	63	206	58	8	1	1	71	19	31	21	0	16	5	3	2	2	3	.40	8	.282	.359	.345
San Antonio	AA LA	26	59	12	1	0	0	13	1	5	11	0	13	1	1	0	0	0	.00	2	.203	.338	.220
1993 San Antonio	AA LA	49	131	28	5	0	1	36	6	6	9	2	17	0	3	0	0	2	.00	3	.214	.264	.275
Albuquerque	AAA LA	18	44	8	1	1	0	11	0	3	0	0	6	1	2	0	0	0	.00	1	.182	.200	.250
1994 Albuquerque	AAA LA	34	93	28	1	0	0	31	7	10	3	0	12	0	0	1	0	0	.00	7	.301	.320	.333
San Antonio	AA LA	24	75	9	0	0	0	9	4	4	2	0	7	1	0	2	0	0	.00	1	.120	.150	.120
1995 Orlando	AA ChN	96	299	70	12	0	0	82	13	18	20	0	39	1	1	4	0	5	.00	10	.234	.281	.274
1996 Orlando	AA ChN	78	216	47	8	0	0	55	16	15	26	2	23	0	1	3	1	2	.33	12	.218	.298	.255
Iowa	AAA ChN	27	79	19	2	0	0	21	6	3	3	1	16	0	0	1	0	0	.00	5	.241	.265	.266
1997 Omaha	AAA KC	21	63	12	3	0	0	15	7	3	13	0	15	0	0	0	0	0	.00	1	.190	.329	.238
Wichita	AA KC	59	180	45	3	0	1	51	20	25	21	0	15	2	4	2	1	2	.33	10	.250	.332	.283
10 Min. YEARS		707	2043	466	53	6	3	540	141	163	154	5	257	19	23	15	7	18	.28	83	.228	.286	.264

Luis Ortiz

Bats: Right **Throws:** Right **Pos:** DH-1B   **Ht:** 6'0" **Wt:** 195 **Born:** 5/25/70 **Age:** 28

Year Team	Lg Org	G	AB	H	2B	3B	HR	TB	R	RBI	TBB	IBB	SO	HBP	SH	SF	SB	CS	SB%	GDP	Avg	OBP	SLG
1991 Red Sox	R Bos	42	153	51	11	2	4	78	21	29	7	0	9	2	1	1	2	1	.67	1	.333	.368	.510
1992 Lynchburg	A+ Bos	94	355	103	27	1	10	162	43	61	22	3	55	2	0	5	4	2	.67	8	.290	.331	.456
1993 Pawtucket	AAA Bos	102	402	118	28	1	18	202	45	81	13	3	74	2	1	4	1	1	.50	10	.294	.316	.502
1994 Pawtucket	AAA Bos	81	317	99	15	3	6	138	47	36	29	5	29	0	0	0	1	4	.20	9	.312	.370	.435
1995 Okla City	AAA Tex	47	170	52	10	5	2	78	19	20	8	2	20	0	1	3	1	1	.50	7	.306	.331	.459
1996 Okla City	AAA Tex	124	501	159	25	0	14	226	70	73	22	2	36	4	0	6	0	5	.00	17	.317	.347	.451
1997 Okla City	AAA Tex	22	82	25	5	0	1	33	9	11	5	0	7	0	0	3	1	1	.50	2	.305	.333	.402
1993 Boston	AL	9	12	3	0	0	0	3	0	1	0	0	2	0	0	0	0	0	.00	0	.250	.250	.250
1994 Boston	AL	7	18	3	2	0	0	5	3	6	1	0	5	0	1	3	0	0	.00	0	.167	.182	.278
1995 Texas	AL	41	108	25	5	2	1	37	10	18	6	0	18	0	0	1	0	1	.00	7	.231	.270	.343
1996 Texas	AL	3	7	2	0	1	1	7	1	1	0	0	1	0	0	0	0	0	.00	0	.286	.286	1.000
7 Min. YEARS		512	1980	607	121	12	55	917	254	311	106	15	230	10	2	22	10	15	.40	54	.307	.341	.463
4 Maj. YEARS		60	145	33	7	3	2	52	14	26	7	0	26	0	1	4	0	1	.00	7	.228	.256	.359

Nicky Ortiz

Bats: Right **Throws:** Right **Pos:** 2B   **Ht:** 6'0" **Wt:** 165 **Born:** 7/9/73 **Age:** 24

Year Team	Lg Org	G	AB	H	2B	3B	HR	TB	R	RBI	TBB	IBB	SO	HBP	SH	SF	SB	CS	SB%	GDP	Avg	OBP	SLG
1991 Red Sox	R Bos	35	100	26	3	1	0	31	16	13	22	0	24	4	1	0	1	2	.33	1	.260	.413	.310
1992 Red Sox	R Bos	50	163	43	9	3	0	58	25	15	28	0	36	0	2	1	3	2	.60	4	.264	.370	.356
Elmira	A- Bos	9	28	5	3	0	0	8	2	1	5	0	13	0	0	0	0	0	.00	0	.179	.303	.286
1993 Ft. Laud	A+ Bos	36	112	23	9	1	1	37	9	14	9	0	39	0	4	0	2	1	.67	4	.205	.264	.330
Utica	A- Bos	63	197	53	14	1	2	75	31	26	19	0	56	6	1	2	4	1	.80	3	.269	.348	.381
1994 Sarasota	A+ Bos	81	283	76	18	3	2	106	34	40	21	1	57	3	6	3	7	2	.78	11	.269	.323	.375
1995 Sarasota	A+ Bos	91	304	75	20	1	5	112	38	38	27	0	68	4	1	1	6	4	.60	3	.247	.315	.368
1996 Michigan	A Bos	73	242	73	14	4	2	101	37	25	20	1	44	5	1	1	1	1	.50	4	.302	.366	.417
Trenton	AA Bos	38	130	29	4	0	3	42	20	13	13	2	28	0	1	0	2	2	.50	3	.223	.294	.323
1997 Trenton	AA Bos	87	288	81	17	2	8	126	47	53	27	1	55	5	6	5	3	2	.60	8	.281	.348	.438
7 Min. YEARS		563	1847	484	111	16	23	696	259	238	191	5	420	27	23	13	29	17	.63	41	.262	.338	.377

Russ Ortiz

Pitches: Right **Bats:** Right **Pos:** P   **Ht:** 6'1" **Wt:** 200 **Born:** 6/5/74 **Age:** 24

Year Team	Lg Org	G	GS	CG	GF	IP	BFP	H	R	ER	HR	SH	SF	HB	TBB	IBB	SO	WP	Bk	W	L	Pct.	ShO	Sv	ERA
1995 Bellingham	A- SF	25	0	0	20	34.1	131	19	4	2	1	0	1	0	13	0	55	2	1	2	0	1.000	0	11	0.52
San Jose	A+ SF	5	0	0	5	6	24	4	1	1	0	0	1	0	2	0	7	0	0	0	1	.000	0	0	1.50
1996 San Jose	A+ SF	34	0	0	31	36.2	145	16	2	1	0	0	0	2	20	0	63	0	0	0	0	.000	0	23	0.25
Shreveport	AA SF	26	0	0	20	26.2	123	22	14	12	0	0	0	2	21	3	29	1	0	1	2	.333	0	13	4.05
1997 Shreveport	AA SF	12	12	0	0	56.2	249	52	28	26	3	4	1	1	37	0	50	2	3	2	3	.400	0	0	4.13
Phoenix	AAA SF	14	14	0	0	85	376	96	57	52	11	2	3	2	34	0	70	3	1	4	3	.571	0	0	5.51
3 Min. YEARS		116	26	0	76	245.1	1048	209	106	94	15	6	6	7	127	3	274	8	3	9	9	.500	0	47	3.45

Mark Osborne

Bats: Left **Throws:** Right **Pos:** C   **Ht:** 6'4" **Wt:** 204 **Born:** 2/1/78 **Age:** 20

Year Team	Lg Org	G	AB	H	2B	3B	HR	TB	R	RBI	TBB	IBB	SO	HBP	SH	SF	SB	CS	SB%	GDP	Avg	OBP	SLG
1996 Diamondback	R Ari	31	105	28	6	3	1	43	15	16	9	0	24	3	0	1	0	0	.00	2	.267	.339	.410
1997 High Desert	A+ Ari	15	42	8	1	1	1	14	6	5	10	0	14	0	1	0	0	0	.00	1	.190	.346	.333
South Bend	A Ari	96	333	88	25	2	8	141	38	51	43	1	98	1	1	1	2	2	.50	6	.264	.349	.423
New Haven	AA Col	3	5	0	0	0	0	0	1	0	2	0	4	0	0	0	0	0	.00	0	.000	.286	.000
2 Min. YEARS		145	485	124	32	6	10	198	60	72	64	1	140	4	2	2	2	2	.50	9	.256	.346	.408

Gavin Osteen

Pitches: Left **Bats:** Right **Pos:** P   **Ht:** 6'0" **Wt:** 195 **Born:** 11/27/69 **Age:** 28

Year Team	Lg Org	G	GS	CG	GF	IP	BFP	H	R	ER	HR	SH	SF	HB	TBB	IBB	SO	WP	Bk	W	L	Pct.	ShO	Sv	ERA
1989 Sou. Oregon	A- Oak	16	6	0	3	46.1	211	44	24	18	3	4	1	3	29	0	42	9	0	2	2	.500	0	0	3.50
1990 Madison	A Oak	27	27	1	0	154	659	126	69	53	6	5	6	3	80	0	120	10	4	10	10	.500	1	0	3.10
1991 Huntsville	AA Oak	28	28	2	0	173	742	176	82	68	4	6	9	4	65	2	105	4	2	13	9	.591	1	0	3.54
1992 Tacoma	AAA Oak	4	4	0	0	14.1	77	21	18	16	4	2	3	2	13	0	7	1	1	0	2	.000	0	0	10.05
Huntsville	AA Oak	16	16	1	0	102.1	425	106	45	41	9	5	5	1	27	0	56	2	2	5	5	.500	0	0	3.61
1993 Huntsville	AA Oak	11	11	2	0	70.1	288	56	21	18	1	1	1	2	25	1	46	2	0	7	3	.700	0	0	2.30
Tacoma	AAA Oak	16	15	0	0	83.1	356	89	51	47	4	4	5	1	31	1	46	0	1	7	7	.500	0	0	5.08
1994 Tacoma	AAA Oak	24	24	2	0	138.1	618	169	95	81	17	3	12	4	39	0	71	0	0	8	9	.471	1	0	5.27
1995 Athletics	R Oak	1	1	0	0	2	7	1	0	0	0	0	0	0	0	0	1	0	0	0	0	.000	0	0	0.00
1997 Bowie	AA Bal	18	2	0	2	30.2	119	20	7	7	1	0	0	0	11	0	22	2	0	1	1	.500	0	0	2.05
8 Min. YEARS		161	134	8	5	814.2	3502	808	412	349	49	30	42	21	320	4	516	30	10	53	48	.525	3	0	3.86

Willis Otanez

Bats: Right **Throws:** Right **Pos:** 3B   **Ht:** 5'11" **Wt:** 150 **Born:** 4/19/73 **Age:** 25

Year Team	Lg Org	G	AB	H	2B	3B	HR	TB	R	RBI	TBB	IBB	SO	HBP	SH	SF	SB	CS	SB%	GDP	Avg	OBP	SLG
1991 Great Falls	R+ LA	58	222	64	9	2	6	95	38	39	19	0	34	2	1	4	3	3	.50	7	.288	.344	.428
1992 Vero Beach	A+ LA	117	390	86	18	0	3	113	27	27	24	0	60	4	5	3	2	4	.33	10	.221	.271	.290
1993 Bakersfield	A+ LA	95	325	85	11	2	10	130	34	39	29	1	63	2	4	2	1	4	.20	9	.262	.324	.400
1994 Vero Beach	A+ LA	131	476	132	27	1	19	218	77	72	53	2	98	4	0	7	4	2	.67	10	.277	.350	.458
1995 Vero Beach	A+ LA	92	354	92	24	0	10	146	39	53	28	3	59	2	0	5	1	1	.50	15	.260	.314	.412
San Antonio	AA LA	27	100	24	4	1	1	33	8	7	6	0	25	0	0	1	0	1	.00	3	.240	.278	.330
1996 Bowie	AA Bal	138	506	134	27	2	24	237	60	75	45	2	97	1	2	5	3	7	.30	17	.265	.323	.468
1997 Orioles	R Bal	8	25	8	2	0	2	16	5	3	2	0	4	1	0	0	0	0	.00	1	.320	.393	.640
Bowie	AA Bal	19	78	26	9	0	3	44	13	13	9	0	19	0	0	1	0	1	.00	3	.333	.398	.564
Rochester	AAA Bal	49	168	35	9	0	5	59	20	25	15	0	35	0	0	3	0	0	.00	8	.208	.269	.351
7 Min. YEARS		734	2644	686	140	8	83	1091	321	353	230	8	494	16	12	32	14	23	.38	83	.259	.319	.413

Jayhawk Owens

Bats: Right **Throws:** Right **Pos:** C   **Ht:** 6'1" **Wt:** 213 **Born:** 2/10/69 **Age:** 29

Year Team	Lg Org	G	AB	H	2B	3B	HR	TB	R	RBI	TBB	IBB	SO	HBP	SH	SF	SB	CS	SB%	GDP	Avg	OBP	SLG
1990 Kenosha	A Min	66	216	51	9	2	5	79	31	30	39	0	59	13	1	1	15	7	.68	8	.236	.383	.366
1991 Visalia	A+ Min	65	233	57	16	1	6	93	33	33	35	1	70	8	0	2	14	6	.70	4	.245	.360	.399
1992 Orlando	AA Min	102	330	88	24	0	4	124	50	30	36	0	67	11	0	5	10	2	.83	5	.267	.353	.376
1993 Colo Sprngs	AAA Col	55	174	54	11	3	6	89	24	43	21	0	56	5	0	3	5	3	.63	4	.310	.394	.511
1994 Colo Sprngs	AAA Col	77	257	69	11	7	6	112	43	44	32	2	66	6	3	3	3	3	.50	7	.268	.359	.436
1995 Colo Sprngs	AAA Col	70	221	65	13	5	12	124	47	48	20	2	61	7	1	2	2	1	.67	2	.294	.368	.561
1996 Colo Sprngs	AAA Col	6	22	5	3	0	0	8	6	6	3	0	6	0	1	0	0	0	.00	1	.227	.320	.364
1997 Colo Sprngs	AAA Col	95	289	75	17	0	10	122	57	34	55	4	98	11	1	2	4	1	.80	3	.260	.395	.422
1993 Colorado	NL	33	86	18	5	0	3	32	12	6	6	1	30	2	0	0	1	0	1.00	1	.209	.277	.372
1994 Colorado	NL	6	12	3	0	1	0	5	4	1	3	0	3	0	0	0	0	0	.00	1	.250	.400	.417
1995 Colorado	NL	18	45	11	2	0	4	25	7	12	2	0	15	1	0	1	0	0	.00	0	.244	.286	.556
1996 Colorado	NL	73	180	43	9	1	4	66	31	17	27	0	56	1	3	2	4	1	.80	1	.239	.338	.367
8 Min. YEARS		536	1742	464	104	18	49	751	291	268	241	9	483	61	7	18	53	23	.70	34	.266	.371	.431
4 Maj. YEARS		130	323	75	16	2	11	128	54	36	38	1	104	4	3	3	5	1	.83	3	.232	.318	.396

Yudith Ozorio

Bats: Both **Throws:** Right **Pos:** OF   **Ht:** 5'11" **Wt:** 155 **Born:** 1/1/75 **Age:** 23

Year Team	Lg Org	G	AB	H	2B	3B	HR	TB	R	RBI	TBB	IBB	SO	HBP	SH	SF	SB	CS	SB%	GDP	Avg	OBP	SLG
1993 Mets	R NYN	55	213	49	7	2	0	60	38	13	33	0	35	5	3	1	39	11	.78	3	.230	.345	.282
1994 Pittsfield	A- NYN	66	246	70	3	2	0	77	41	17	15	0	54	1	1	2	24	7	.77	1	.285	.326	.313
1995 Capital City	A NYN	123	456	99	12	2	2	121	59	33	34	3	113	3	9	2	40	15	.73	8	.217	.275	.265
1996 St. Pete	A+ StL	136	505	122	11	10	1	156	67	42	57	1	110	1	8	2	30	8	.79	5	.242	.319	.309
1997 Arkansas	AA StL	84	144	30	2	1	0	34	23	9	12	0	44	0	2	0	6	2	.75	0	.208	.269	.236
5 Min. YEARS		464	1564	370	35	17	3	448	228	114	151	4	356	10	23	7	139	43	.76	17	.237	.307	.286

Scotty Pace

Pitches: Left **Bats:** Left **Pos:** P   **Ht:** 6'4" **Wt:** 210 **Born:** 9/16/71 **Age:** 26

Year Team	Lg Org	G	GS	CG	GF	IP	BFP	H	R	ER	HR	SH	SF	HB	TBB	IBB	SO	WP	Bk	W	L	Pct.	ShO	Sv	ERA
1994 Elmira	A- Fla	13	12	2	0	70.2	307	73	35	32	3	0	1	1	27	2	50	7	0	3	7	.300	0	0	4.08
1995 Hagerstown	A Tor	11	6	2	2	57.2	211	32	8	7	2	1	0	2	12	0	57	4	0	4	2	.667	1	1	1.09
Knoxville	AA Tor	18	18	1	0	102.1	462	117	66	52	8	6	6	4	48	3	71	7	0	6	8	.429	1	0	4.57
1996 Dunedin	A+ Tor	19	0	0	12	30.1	123	24	7	6	0	2	0	3	13	1	20	3	0	0	0	.000	0	6	1.78
Syracuse	AAA Tor	20	5	1	11	51.2	227	53	37	29	4	0	1	2	27	0	35	4	0	3	3	.500	0	0	5.05
Knoxville	AA Tor	4	1	0	0	12	49	8	4	4	2	0	1	0	6	0	5	1	0	2	0	1.000	0	0	3.00
1997 Tucson	AAA Mil	2	0	0	1	5.2	25	6	2	1	0	0	0	0	4	0	2	1	0	0	0	.000	0	0	1.59
El Paso	AA Mil	41	2	0	18	65.1	305	86	52	43	12	2	3	3	31	0	38	5	0	0	5	.000	0	0	5.92
4 Min. YEARS		128	44	6	44	395.2	1709	399	211	174	31	14	11	15	168	6	278	32	0	18	25	.419	2	7	3.96

Alex Pacheco

Pitches: Right Bats: Right Pos: P Ht: 6'3" Wt: 200 Born: 7/19/73 Age: 24

Year Team	Lg Org	G	GS	CG	GF	IP	BFP	H	R	ER	HR	SH	SF	HB	TBB	IBB	SO	WP	Bk	W	L	Pct.	ShO	Sv	ERA
1990 Expos	R Mon	6	0	0	0	8.2	41	11	7	5	0	0	0	0	4	0	5	2	1	1	0	1.000	0	0	5.19
1991 Expos	R Mon	15	4	0	3	44.1	209	56	32	25	0	1	2	1	26	0	19	6	0	3	0	1.000	0	1	5.08
1992 Jamestown	A- Mon	16	5	0	4	50.1	229	53	36	31	5	2	2	3	29	1	32	2	1	3	3	.500	0	1	5.54
1993 Jamestown	A- Mon	6	1	0	1	14	60	11	7	5	0	0	1	0	4	0	15	4	0	0	1	.000	0	0	3.21
Burlington	A Mon	13	7	0	2	43	194	47	31	20	3	2	2	3	12	0	24	3	0	3	5	.375	0	1	4.19
1994 Burlington	A Mon	37	4	0	19	68.1	302	79	51	39	6	7	2	6	22	1	69	5	0	3	8	.273	0	5	5.14
Wst Plm Bch	A+ Mon	9	0	0	0	12	47	9	3	3	1	0	1	0	4	0	12	2	0	1	0	1.000	0	0	2.25
1995 Harrisburg	AA Mon	45	0	0	29	86.1	371	76	45	41	8	1	1	8	31	4	88	4	0	9	7	.563	0	4	4.27
Ottawa	AAA Mon	4	0	0	0	8.2	35	8	6	6	2	0	0	0	5	0	4	0	0	1	0	1.000	0	0	6.23
1996 Harrisburg	AA Mon	18	0	0	4	26.1	113	26	10	8	2	1	1	1	12	1	27	0	0	5	2	.714	0	0	2.73
Ottawa	AAA Mon	33	0	0	12	41.2	191	47	32	30	6	5	1	6	18	0	34	2	0	2	2	.500	0	6	6.48
1997 Tacoma	AAA Sea	15	2	0	4	27.2	143	45	27	27	4	0	0	3	15	1	21	1	0	0	2	.000	0	0	8.78
Memphis	AA Sea	9	0	0	6	12	50	7	5	5	0	0	0	0	9	0	13	2	0	1	1	.500	0	0	3.75
1996 Montreal	NL	5	0	0	2	5.2	26	8	7	7	2	0	0	0	1	0	7	0	0	0	0	.000	0	0	11.12
8 Min. YEARS		226	23	0	84	443.1	1985	475	292	245	37	19	13	31	191	8	363	33	2	32	31	.508	0	17	4.97

John Pachot

Bats: Right Throws: Right Pos: C Ht: 6'2" Wt: 168 Born: 11/11/74 Age: 23

Year Team	Lg Org	G	AB	H	2B	3B	HR	TB	R	RBI	TBB	IBB	SO	HBP	SH	SF	SB	CS	SB%	GDP	Avg	OBP	SLG
1993 Expos	R Mon	35	121	37	4	1	0	43	13	16	2	0	7	0	4	2	0	1	.00	0	.306	.312	.355
1994 Burlington	A Mon	100	351	89	17	0	1	109	37	26	13	1	46	3	5	4	1	2	.33	12	.254	.283	.311
1995 Wst Plm Bch	A+ Mon	67	227	57	10	0	0	67	17	23	12	0	38	2	3	1	1	2	.33	4	.251	.293	.295
1996 Expos	R Mon	8	30	9	1	1	0	12	3	3	1	0	0	1	1	0	0	0	.00	0	.300	.344	.400
Wst Plm Bch	A+ Mon	44	163	31	9	0	0	40	8	19	2	0	19	0	1	0	0	1	.00	1	.190	.200	.245
1997 Harrisburg	AA Mon	94	323	90	23	3	7	140	40	50	22	0	42	3	2	5	6	6	.50	10	.279	.326	.433
5 Min. YEARS		348	1215	313	64	5	8	411	118	137	52	1	152	9	16	12	8	12	.40	27	.258	.290	.338

Scott Pagano

Bats: Both Throws: Right Pos: OF Ht: 5'11" Wt: 175 Born: 4/26/71 Age: 27

Year Team	Lg Org	G	AB	H	2B	3B	HR	TB	R	RBI	TBB	IBB	SO	HBP	SH	SF	SB	CS	SB%	GDP	Avg	OBP	SLG
1992 Niagara Fal	A- Det	67	193	47	9	2	1	63	17	22	14	1	27	4	3	2	6	10	.38	7	.244	.305	.326
1993 Niagara Fal	A- Det	5	6	1	0	0	1	4	1	3	1	0	0	0	0	0	1	0	1.00	1	.167	.286	.667
1994 Ohio Valley	IND —	58	232	89	19	1	7	131	62	31	32	2	29	2	1	1	53	17	.76	4	.384	.461	.565
1995 Durham	A+ Atl	110	354	94	12	1	1	111	47	26	38	5	75	5	7	1	41	21	.66	8	.266	.344	.314
1996 Binghamton	AA NYN	126	464	120	15	3	1	144	63	46	43	3	55	7	9	2	26	16	.62	11	.259	.329	.310
1997 Reading	AA Phi	117	468	128	16	3	3	159	77	44	48	3	62	8	2	4	17	13	.57	11	.274	.348	.340
6 Min. YEARS		483	1717	479	71	10	14	612	267	172	176	14	248	26	22	10	144	77	.65	42	.279	.353	.356

Mike Parisi

Pitches: Right Bats: Right Pos: P Ht: 6'3" Wt: 195 Born: 6/18/73 Age: 25

Year Team	Lg Org	G	GS	CG	GF	IP	BFP	H	R	ER	HR	SH	SF	HB	TBB	IBB	SO	WP	Bk	W	L	Pct.	ShO	Sv	ERA
1994 Elmira	A- Fla	13	13	3	0	78.1	328	64	32	26	3	3	1	9	26	0	56	5	1	5	5	.500	1	0	2.99
1995 Kane County	A Fla	26	26	2	0	164.1	687	152	73	60	7	2	6	9	42	1	113	11	0	11	8	.579	1	0	3.29
1996 Brevard Cty	A+ Fla	21	19	1	0	119.1	515	117	59	55	9	2	4	10	39	1	65	1	0	6	8	.429	0	0	4.15
1997 Portland	AA Fla	9	9	0	0	40.2	193	56	36	32	8	4	1	5	14	3	27	1	0	1	3	.250	0	0	7.08
4 Min. YEARS		69	67	6	0	402.2	1723	389	200	173	27	11	12	33	121	5	261	18	1	23	24	.489	2	0	3.87

Rick Parker

Bats: Right Throws: Right Pos: OF Ht: 6'0" Wt: 185 Born: 3/20/63 Age: 35

Year Team	Lg Org	G	AB	H	2B	3B	HR	TB	R	RBI	TBB	IBB	SO	HBP	SH	SF	SB	CS	SB%	GDP	Avg	OBP	SLG
1985 Bend	A- Phi	55	205	51	9	1	2	68	45	20	40	0	42	4	0	3	14	7	.67	2	.249	.377	.332
1986 Spartanburg	A Phi	62	233	69	7	3	5	97	39	28	36	0	39	2	2	0	14	9	.61	7	.296	.395	.416
Clearwater	A+ Phi	63	218	51	10	2	0	65	24	15	21	1	29	2	3	2	8	9	.47	2	.234	.305	.298
1987 Clearwater	A+ Phi	101	330	83	13	3	3	111	56	34	31	3	36	3	2	3	6	4	.60	4	.252	.319	.336
1988 Reading	AA Phi	116	362	93	13	3	3	121	50	47	36	2	50	3	1	6	24	6	.80	6	.257	.324	.334
1989 Reading	AA Phi	103	388	92	7	9	3	126	59	32	42	0	62	5	2	3	17	13	.57	8	.237	.317	.325
Phoenix	AAA SF	18	68	18	2	2	0	24	5	11	2	0	14	1	1	0	1	2	.33	1	.265	.296	.353
1990 Phoenix	AAA SF	44	173	58	7	4	1	76	38	18	22	0	25	0	0	0	18	10	.64	1	.335	.410	.439
1991 Phoenix	AAA SF	85	297	89	10	9	6	135	41	41	26	1	35	2	0	6	16	3	.84	7	.300	.353	.455
1992 Tucson	AAA Hou	105	319	103	10	11	4	147	51	38	28	0	36	3	3	0	20	3	.87	7	.323	.383	.461
1993 Tucson	AAA Hou	29	120	37	9	3	2	58	28	12	14	1	20	0	0	0	6	2	.75	2	.308	.381	.483
1994 Norfolk	AAA NYN	73	228	61	9	4	0	76	29	16	29	1	39	6	4	1	9	5	.64	7	.268	.364	.333
1995 Albuquerque	AAA LA	58	175	49	7	2	1	63	33	14	27	4	17	3	1	1	1	6	.14	4	.280	.383	.360
1996 Albuquerque	AAA LA	50	175	53	7	3	0	66	26	23	23	1	27	3	4	2	7	6	.54	2	.303	.389	.377
1997 Albuquerque	AAA LA	49	151	41	7	3	6	72	33	21	10	0	26	5	0	0	6	0	1.00	4	.272	.337	.477
1990 San Francisco	NL	54	107	26	5	0	2	37	19	14	10	0	15	1	3	0	6	1	.86	1	.243	.314	.346
1991 San Francisco	NL	13	14	1	0	0	0	1	0	1	1	0	5	0	0	0	0	0	.00	0	.071	.133	.071
1993 Houston	NL	45	45	15	3	0	0	18	11	4	3	0	8	0	1	0	1	2	.33	2	.333	.375	.400
1994 New York	NL	8	16	1	0	0	0	1	1	0	0	0	2	0	2	0	0	0	.00	0	.063	.063	.063
1995 Los Angeles	NL	27	29	8	0	0	0	8	3	4	2	0	4	0	2	0	1	1	.50	1	.276	.323	.276

Year Team	Lg Org	G	AB	H	2B	3B	HR	TB	R	RBI	TBB	IBB	SO	HBP	SH	SF	SB	CS	SB%	GDP	Avg	OBP	SLG
BATTING																	**BASERUNNING**				**PERCENTAGES**		
1996 Los Angeles	NL	16	14	4	1	0	0	5	2	1	0	0	2	1	0	0	1	0	1.00	1	.286	.333	.357
13 Min. YEARS		1011	3442	948	127	58	38	1305	557	370	387	14	497	42	23	27	167	85	.66	64	.275	.353	.379
6 Maj. YEARS		163	225	55	9	0	2	70	36	24	16	0	36	2	8	0	9	4	.69	5	.244	.300	.311

Jim Parque

Pitches: Left **Bats:** Left **Pos:** P   **Ht:** 5'10" **Wt:** 166 **Born:** 2/8/76 **Age:** 22

Year Team	Lg Org	G	GS	CG	GF	IP	BFP	H	R	ER	HR	SH	SF	HB	TBB	IBB	SO	WP	Bk	W	L	Pct.	ShO	Sv	ERA
		HOW MUCH HE PITCHED						**WHAT HE GAVE UP**												**THE RESULTS**					
1997 Winston-Sal	A+ ChA	11	11	0	0	61.2	231	29	19	19	3	0	1	0	23	0	76	2	2	7	2	.778	0	0	2.77
Nashville	AAA ChA	2	2	0	0	10.2	49	9	5	5	0	0	1	0	9	0	5	1	0	1	0	1.000	0	0	4.22
1 Min. YEARS		13	13	0	0	72.1	280	38	24	24	3	0	2	0	32	0	81	3	2	8	2	.800	0	0	2.99

Franklin Parra

Bats: Both **Throws:** Right **Pos:** SS   **Ht:** 6'0" **Wt:** 165 **Born:** 7/8/71 **Age:** 26

Year Team	Lg Org	G	AB	H	2B	3B	HR	TB	R	RBI	TBB	IBB	SO	HBP	SH	SF	SB	CS	SB%	GDP	Avg	OBP	SLG
		BATTING															**BASERUNNING**				**PERCENTAGES**		
1990 Rangers	R Tex	37	116	30	2	1	0	34	11	9	4	0	28	1	0	1	8	3	.73	0	.259	.287	.293
1991 Butte	R+ Tex	61	221	56	10	2	4	82	28	29	7	0	61	0	0	2	9	8	.53	3	.253	.274	.371
1992 Gastonia	A Tex	45	157	33	7	1	1	45	15	7	9	0	40	3	3	1	13	6	.68	1	.210	.265	.287
Butte	R+ Tex	73	300	83	16	4	2	113	58	27	23	1	67	5	4	1	24	9	.73	6	.277	.337	.377
1993 Chston-SC	A Tex	125	446	95	13	6	5	135	52	25	37	0	99	3	3	3	18	13	.58	5	.213	.276	.303
1994 Charlotte	A+ Tex	106	431	115	19	8	6	168	61	35	16	1	68	2	3	3	10	7	.59	5	.267	.294	.390
1995 Okla City	AAA Tex	6	18	3	1	0	0	4	0	1	2	0	4	0	0	1	1	0	1.00	1	.167	.238	.222
Tulsa	AA Tex	71	261	64	9	2	2	83	27	26	12	0	51	0	5	5	7	9	.44	5	.245	.273	.318
1997 Elmira	IND —	21	96	34	9	0	1	46	13	9	1	0	7	0	0	0	9	3	.75	1	.354	.361	.479
Binghamton	AA NYN	5	15	3	1	0	0	4	2	1	0	0	5	0	1	0	0	0	.00	0	.200	.200	.267
St. Lucie	A+ NYN	56	199	52	10	3	2	74	23	25	22	0	33	3	0	2	11	5	.69	4	.261	.341	.372
7 Min. YEARS		606	2260	568	97	27	23	788	290	194	133	2	463	17	19	19	110	63	.64	31	.251	.296	.349

Jose Parra

Pitches: Right **Bats:** Right **Pos:** P   **Ht:** 5'11" **Wt:** 165 **Born:** 11/28/72 **Age:** 25

Year Team	Lg Org	G	GS	CG	GF	IP	BFP	H	R	ER	HR	SH	SF	HB	TBB	IBB	SO	WP	Bk	W	L	Pct.	ShO	Sv	ERA
		HOW MUCH HE PITCHED						**WHAT HE GAVE UP**												**THE RESULTS**					
1990 Dodgers	R LA	10	10	1	0	57.1	228	50	22	17	1	0	3	1	18	0	50	1	1	5	3	.625	0	0	2.67
1991 Great Falls	R+ LA	14	14	1	0	64.1	298	86	58	44	5	2	7	2	18	0	55	0	4	4	6	.400	1	0	6.16
1992 Bakersfield	A+ LA	24	23	3	0	143	618	151	73	57	5	4	4	4	47	4	107	5	1	7	8	.467	0	0	3.59
San Antonio	AA LA	3	3	0	0	14.2	72	22	12	10	0	2	1	1	7	0	7	0	1	2	0	1.000	0	0	6.14
1993 San Antonio	AA LA	17	17	0	0	111.1	452	103	46	39	10	9	3	6	12	2	87	1	0	1	8	.111	0	0	3.15
1994 Albuquerque	AAA LA	27	27	1	0	145	636	190	92	77	10	4	4	5	38	2	90	10	0	10	10	.500	0	0	4.78
1995 Albuquerque	AAA LA	12	10	1	1	52.2	232	62	33	30	7	4	2	1	17	3	33	2	0	3	2	.600	1	1	5.13
1996 Salt Lake	AAA Min	23	1	0	11	44	192	51	25	25	2	3	2	1	13	2	26	1	0	5	3	.625	0	8	5.11
1997 Salt Lake	AAA Min	50	4	0	31	94	441	126	73	63	8	3	5	9	30	7	61	9	0	2	8	.200	0	8	6.03
1995 Los Angeles	NL	8	0	0	0	10.1	47	10	8	5	2	0	1	0	6	1	7	0	1	0	0	.000	0	0	4.35
Minnesota	AL	12	12	0	0	61.2	292	83	59	52	11	0	3	2	22	0	29	3	0	1	5	.167	0	0	7.59
1996 Minnesota	AL	27	5	0	7	70	320	88	48	47	15	1	3	3	27	0	50	4	1	5	5	.500	0	0	6.04
8 Min. YEARS		180	109	7	43	726.1	3171	841	434	362	48	31	31	30	200	20	516	29	7	39	48	.448	2	17	4.49
2 Maj. YEARS		47	17	0	7	142	659	181	115	104	28	1	7	6	55	1	86	7	2	6	10	.375	0	0	6.59

Steve Parris

Pitches: Right **Bats:** Right **Pos:** P   **Ht:** 6'0" **Wt:** 190 **Born:** 12/17/67 **Age:** 30

Year Team	Lg Org	G	GS	CG	GF	IP	BFP	H	R	ER	HR	SH	SF	HB	TBB	IBB	SO	WP	Bk	W	L	Pct.	ShO	Sv	ERA
		HOW MUCH HE PITCHED						**WHAT HE GAVE UP**												**THE RESULTS**					
1989 Batavia	A- Phi	13	10	1	1	66.2	291	69	38	29	6	3	2	4	20	1	46	4	0	3	5	.375	0	0	3.92
1990 Batavia	A- Phi	14	14	0	0	81.2	333	70	34	24	1	3	4	3	22	2	50	7	3	7	1	.875	0	0	2.64
1991 Clearwater	A+ Phi	43	6	0	8	93	394	101	43	35	1	4	0	9	25	4	59	3	4	7	5	.583	0	0	3.39
1992 Reading	AA Phi	18	14	0	0	85.1	370	94	55	44	9	3	4	3	21	1	60	2	0	5	7	.417	0	0	4.64
Scranton-WB	AAA Phi	11	6	0	2	51.1	223	57	25	23	1	1	4	3	17	1	29	6	1	3	3	.500	0	1	4.03
1993 Scranton-WB	AAA Phi	3	0	0	0	5.2	30	9	9	8	3	0	0	1	3	0	4	1	0	0	1	.000	0	0	12.71
Jacksnville	AA Sea	7	1	0	0	13.2	64	15	9	9	3	0	1	2	6	0	5	0	0	0	1	.000	0	0	5.93
1994 Salem	A+ Pit	17	7	0	1	57	247	58	24	23	7	0	2	6	21	1	48	1	0	3	3	.500	0	0	3.63
1995 Carolina	AA Pit	14	14	2	0	89.2	344	61	25	25	2	3	1	4	16	1	86	3	0	9	1	.900	2	0	2.51
1996 Augusta	A Pit	1	1	0	0	5	16	1	0	0	0	0	0	0	0	0	6	0	0	0	0	.000	0	0	0.00
Carolina	AA Pit	5	5	0	0	26.2	108	24	11	9	1	0	0	0	6	0	22	2	0	2	0	1.000	0	0	3.04
1997 Chattanooga	AA Cin	14	14	0	0	80.2	345	78	44	37	9	1	1	1	29	0	68	2	0	6	2	.750	0	0	4.13
Indianapols	AAA Cin	5	5	1	0	35.1	143	26	15	14	4	1	1	0	11	1	27	0	0	2	3	.400	1	0	3.57
1995 Pittsburgh	NL	15	15	1	0	82	360	89	49	49	12	3	2	7	33	1	61	4	0	6	6	.500	1	0	5.38
1996 Pittsburgh	NL	8	4	0	3	26.1	123	35	22	21	4	1	1	1	11	0	27	2	0	0	3	.000	0	0	7.18
9 Min. YEARS		165	97	4	12	691.2	2908	663	332	280	47	19	17	39	198	12	510	31	8	47	31	.603	3	2	3.64
2 Maj. YEARS		23	19	1	3	108.1	483	124	71	70	16	4	3	8	44	1	88	6	0	6	9	.400	1	0	5.82

John Parrish

Pitches: Left **Bats:** Left **Pos:** P   **Ht:** 5'11" **Wt:** 165 **Born:** 11/26/77 **Age:** 20

Year Team	Lg Org	G	GS	CG	GF	IP	BFP	H	R	ER	HR	SH	SF	HB	TBB	IBB	SO	WP	Bk	W	L	Pct.	ShO	Sv	ERA
		HOW MUCH HE PITCHED						**WHAT HE GAVE UP**												**THE RESULTS**					
1996 Orioles	R Bal	11	0	0	6	19.1	83	13	5	4	0	0	0	0	11	0	33	2	0	2	0	1.000	0	2	1.86

191

	HOW MUCH HE PITCHED					WHAT HE GAVE UP							THE RESULTS								
Year Team	Lg Org	G	GS	CG	GF	IP	BFP	H	R	ER	HR	SH	SF	HB	TBB	IBB	SO	WP	Bk	W	L	Pct.	ShO	Sv	ERA
Bluefield	R+ Bal	8	0	0	5	13.1	60	11	6	4	0	1	2	0	9	1	18	2	0	2	1	.667	0	1	2.70
1997 Bowie	AA Bal	1	1	0	0	5	20	3	1	1	0	0	0	0	2	0	3	0	0	1	0	1.000	0	0	1.80
Frederick	A+ Bal	5	5	0	0	22.1	103	23	18	15	3	1	0	2	16	0	17	3	0	1	3	.250	0	0	6.04
Delmarva	A Bal	23	10	0	5	72.2	315	69	39	31	7	2	3	2	32	3	76	9	0	3	3	.500	0	1	3.84
2 Min. YEARS		48	16	0	16	132.2	581	119	69	55	10	4	5	4	70	4	147	16	0	9	7	.563	0	4	3.73

Bronswell Patrick

Pitches: Right Bats: Right Pos: P   Ht: 6'1" Wt: 205 Born: 9/16/70 Age: 27

	HOW MUCH HE PITCHED					WHAT HE GAVE UP							THE RESULTS								
Year Team	Lg Org	G	GS	CG	GF	IP	BFP	H	R	ER	HR	SH	SF	HB	TBB	IBB	SO	WP	Bk	W	L	Pct.	ShO	Sv	ERA
1988 Athletics	R Oak	14	13	2	0	96.1	390	99	37	32	7	1	2	2	16	1	64	1	2	8	3	.727	0	0	2.99
1989 Madison	A Oak	12	10	0	1	54.1	238	62	29	22	3	2	0	0	14	0	32	3	2	2	5	.286	0	0	3.64
1990 Modesto	A+ Oak	14	14	0	0	74.2	340	92	58	43	10	3	1	4	32	0	37	5	1	3	7	.300	0	0	5.18
Madison	A Oak	13	12	3	0	80	337	88	44	32	6	5	4	1	19	0	40	3	0	3	7	.300	0	0	3.60
1991 Modesto	A+ Oak	28	26	3	1	169.2	716	158	77	61	9	4	4	1	60	4	95	7	0	12	12	.500	1	0	3.24
1992 Huntsville	AA Oak	29	29	3	0	179.1	758	187	84	75	20	1	3	4	46	0	98	3	0	13	7	.650	0	0	3.76
1993 Tacoma	AAA Oak	35	13	1	12	104.2	496	156	87	82	12	3	12	4	42	3	56	3	0	3	8	.273	0	1	7.05
1994 Huntsville	AA Oak	7	3	0	1	27.2	120	31	11	9	2	1	0	2	10	0	16	1	1	2	0	1.000	0	1	2.93
Tacoma	AAA Oak	30	0	0	9	47.1	208	50	31	25	5	3	1	0	20	2	38	2	0	1	1	.500	0	2	4.75
1995 Tucson	AAA Hou	43	4	0	10	81.2	352	91	42	38	3	2	3	1	21	1	62	4	0	5	1	.833	0	1	4.19
1996 Tucson	AAA Hou	33	15	0	2	118	521	137	59	46	7	1	14	0	33	4	82	1	0	7	3	.700	0	0	3.51
1997 New Orleans	AAA Hou	30	12	1	10	100.2	426	108	45	36	10	6	2	0	30	4	88	5	0	6	5	.545	1	0	3.22
10 Min. YEARS		288	151	13	46	1134.1	4902	1259	604	501	94	32	46	19	343	19	708	38	6	65	59	.524	2	6	3.98

Ken Patterson

Pitches: Left Bats: Left Pos: P   Ht: 6'4" Wt: 222 Born: 7/8/64 Age: 33

	HOW MUCH HE PITCHED					WHAT HE GAVE UP							THE RESULTS								
Year Team	Lg Org	G	GS	CG	GF	IP	BFP	H	R	ER	HR	SH	SF	HB	TBB	IBB	SO	WP	Bk	W	L	Pct.	ShO	Sv	ERA
1985 Oneonta	A- NYA	6	6	0	0	22.1	103	23	14	12	0	1	0	2	14	0	21	1	0	2	2	.500	0	0	4.84
1986 Ft. Laud	A+ NYA	5	5	0	0	18.2	100	34	20	16	2	0	0	3	16	0	13	2	0	0	2	.000	0	0	7.71
Oneonta	A- NYA	15	15	5	0	100.1	399	67	25	15	2	1	1	4	45	0	102	7	1	9	3	.750	4	0	1.35
1987 Ft. Laud	A+ NYA	9	9	0	0	42.2	202	46	34	30	0	1	2	2	31	0	36	5	1	1	3	.250	0	0	6.33
Albany-Colo	AA NYA	24	8	1	14	63.2	272	59	31	28	2	3	3	2	31	1	47	4	0	3	6	.333	0	5	3.96
Hawaii	AAA ChA	3	0	0	3	3.1	14	1	0	0	0	0	0	0	3	0	5	0	0	0	0	.000	0	2	0.00
1988 Vancouver	AAA ChA	55	4	1	23	86.1	349	64	37	31	4	5	4	2	36	7	89	7	2	6	5	.545	0	13	3.23
1989 Vancouver	AAA ChA	2	2	0	0	9	35	6	2	1	0	1	1	1	1	0	17	2	0	0	1	.000	0	0	1.00
1992 Peoria	A ChN	2	0	0	1	3	16	5	4	4	0	0	0	0	2	0	5	0	0	0	0	.000	0	0	12.00
Iowa	AAA ChN	1	0	0	0	1.2	11	4	4	4	2	1	0	1	1	0	1	0	0	0	1	.000	0	0	21.60
1994 Vancouver	AAA Ana	3	0	0	1	5.2	30	5	7	6	0	0	1	0	6	0	5	0	0	0	0	.000	0	0	9.53
1995 Lk Elsinore	A+ Ana	6	0	0	2	9.2	35	7	0	0	0	0	0	0	1	0	9	1	0	0	0	.000	0	1	0.00
Angels	R Ana	1	1	0	0	3	10	0	0	0	0	0	0	0	1	0	3	0	0	0	0	.000	0	0	0.00
Vancouver	AAA Ana	8	0	0	3	11	46	12	1	1	0	0	0	0	4	1	4	1	0	0	0	.000	0	1	0.82
1996 Tyler	IND —	20	1	0	15	25.1	105	22	7	6	0	1	1	0	5	0	28	3	0	1	1	.500	0	6	2.13
Omaha	AAA KC	16	0	0	2	20	79	16	5	4	2	1	0	0	4	0	13	1	0	0	1	.000	0	1	1.80
1997 Omaha	AAA KC	22	0	0	13	30.2	132	34	17	14	5	0	0	0	10	0	28	2	0	2	2	.500	0	4	4.11
1988 Chicago	AL	9	2	0	3	20.2	92	25	11	11	2	0	0	0	7	0	8	1	1	0	2	.000	0	1	4.79
1989 Chicago	AL	50	1	0	18	65.2	284	64	37	33	11	1	4	2	28	3	43	3	1	6	1	.857	0	0	4.52
1990 Chicago	AL	43	0	0	16	66.1	283	58	27	25	6	2	5	2	34	1	40	2	0	2	1	.667	0	2	3.39
1991 Chicago	AL	43	0	0	13	63.2	265	48	22	20	5	3	2	1	35	1	32	2	0	3	0	1.000	0	1	2.83
1992 Chicago	NL	32	1	0	4	41.2	191	41	25	18	7	6	4	1	27	6	23	3	1	2	3	.400	0	0	3.89
1993 California	AL	46	0	0	19	59	255	54	30	30	7	2	1	0	35	5	36	2	0	1	1	.500	0	1	4.58
1994 California	AL	1	0	0	0	0.2	0	0	0	0	0	0	0	0	0	1	0	0	0	0	0	.000	0	0	0.00
10 Min. YEARS		198	51	7	77	456.1	1938	401	208	172	19	15	13	17	211	9	426	36	4	24	27	.471	4	33	3.39
7 Maj. YEARS		224	4	0	62	317.2	1372	290	152	137	38	14	16	6	166	16	183	13	3	14	8	.636	0	5	3.88

Jeff Patzke

Bats: Both Throws: Right Pos: 2B   Ht: 6'0" Wt: 170 Born: 11/19/73 Age: 24

	BATTING						BASERUNNING									PERCENTAGES		
Year Team	Lg Org	G	AB	H	2B	3B	HR	TB	R	RBI	TBB	IBB	SO	HBP	SH	SF	SB	CS	SB%	GDP	Avg	OBP	SLG
1992 Blue Jays	R Tor	6	21	2	0	0	0	2	3	1	3	0	2	0	0	0	0	1	.00	0	.095	.208	.095
Medicne Hat	R+ Tor	59	193	42	4	0	2	52	19	17	17	0	42	0	3	0	3	1	.75	4	.218	.281	.269
1993 Medicne Hat	R+ Tor	71	273	80	11	2	1	98	45	22	34	1	31	2	3	1	5	7	.42	5	.293	.354	.359
1994 Hagerstown	A Tor	80	271	55	10	1	4	79	43	22	36	1	57	3	2	3	7	3	.70	4	.203	.300	.292
1995 Dunedin	A+ Tor	129	470	124	32	6	11	201	68	75	85	8	81	2	1	2	5	3	.63	10	.264	.377	.428
1996 Knoxville	AA Tor	124	429	130	31	4	4	181	70	66	80	6	103	6	0	2	6	5	.55	2	.303	.418	.422
1997 Syracuse	AAA Tor	96	316	90	25	2	2	125	38	29	51	3	66	1	3	2	0	3	.00	4	.285	.384	.396
6 Min. YEARS		565	1973	523	113	15	24	738	286	232	306	19	382	14	12	10	26	23	.53	29	.265	.366	.374

Richard Paugh

Pitches: Left Bats: Left Pos: P   Ht: 6'1" Wt: 190 Born: 2/6/72 Age: 26

	HOW MUCH HE PITCHED					WHAT HE GAVE UP							THE RESULTS								
Year Team	Lg Org	G	GS	CG	GF	IP	BFP	H	R	ER	HR	SH	SF	HB	TBB	IBB	SO	WP	Bk	W	L	Pct.	ShO	Sv	ERA
1994 Welland	A- Pit	26	1	0	9	35.1	144	24	5	5	0	5	0	1	12	0	34	2	2	1	3	.250	0	3	1.27
1995 Augusta	A Pit	52	0	0	25	59	252	60	23	17	3	4	1	0	17	5	61	6	1	6	2	.750	0	2	2.59
1996 Lynchburg	A+ Pit	45	0	0	17	52	230	48	33	22	1	4	0	2	20	0	41	6	0	2	4	.200	0	4	3.81
1997 Carolina	AA Pit	5	0	0	2	8	31	8	5	5	2	1	0	0	1	0	3	0	0	0	0	.000	0	0	5.63
Lynchburg	A+ Pit	24	0	0	10	18.1	89	18	17	16	6	0	0	2	11	2	18	2	0	0	2	.000	0	5	7.85

		HOW MUCH HE PITCHED					WHAT HE GAVE UP						THE RESULTS					
Year Team	Lg Pit	G GS CG GF	IP	BFP	H	R	ER	HR	SH	SF	HB	TBB	IBB	SO	WP	Bk	W	L	Pct.	ShO	Sv	ERA
Augusta	A Pit	24 0 0 18	29.2	122	24	9	8	3	0	0		7	0	40	0	0	1	2	.333	0	8	2.43
4 Min. YEARS		176 1 0 81	202.1	868	182	92	73	15	15	1	5	68	7	197	16	3	9	13	.409	0	22	3.25

Josh Paul

Bats: Right Throws: Right Pos: C   Ht: 6'1" Wt: 185 Born: 5/19/75 Age: 23

		BATTING														BASERUNNING				PERCENTAGES		
Year Team	Lg Org	G	AB	H	2B	3B	HR	TB	R	RBI	TBB	IBB	SO	HBP	SH	SF	SB	CS	SB%	GDP	Avg	OBP	SLG
1996 White Sox	R ChA	1	0	0	0	0	0	0	0	0	1	0	0	0	0	0	0	0	.00	0	.000	1.000	.000
Hickory	A ChA	59	226	74	16	0	8	114	41	37	21	3	53	1	3	1	13	4	.76	2	.327	.386	.504
1997 White Sox	R ChA	5	14	6	0	1	0	8	3	0	1	0	3	0	1	0	1	0	1.00	1	.429	.467	.571
Birmingham	AA ChA	34	115	34	5	0	1	42	18	16	12	0	25	1	3	0	6	2	.75	4	.296	.367	.365
2 Min. YEARS		99	355	114	21	1	9	164	62	53	35	3	81	2	7	1	20	6	.77	7	.321	.384	.462

Carl Pavano

Pitches: Right Bats: Right Pos: P   Ht: 6'5" Wt: 230 Born: 1/8/76 Age: 22

		HOW MUCH HE PITCHED						WHAT HE GAVE UP							THE RESULTS					
Year Team	Lg Org	G GS CG GF	IP	BFP	H	R	ER	HR	SH	SF	HB	TBB	IBB	SO	WP	Bk	W	L	Pct.	ShO	Sv	ERA
1994 Red Sox	R Bos	9 7 0 0	44	176	31	14	9	1	0	1	1	7	0	47	4	1	4	3	.571	0	0	1.84
1995 Michigan	A Bos	22 22 1 0	141.1	591	118	63	54	7	6	7	6	52	0	138	9	0	6	6	.500	0	0	3.44
1996 Trenton	AA Bos	27 26 6 1	185	741	154	66	54	16	5	7	11	47	2	146	7	1	16	5	.762	2	0	2.63
1997 Pawtucket	AAA Bos	23 23 3 0	161.2	663	148	62	56	13	1	3	6	34	2	147	7	1	11	6	.647	0	0	3.12
4 Min. YEARS		81 78 10 1	532	2171	451	205	173	37	12	18	24	140	4	478	27	3	37	20	.649	2	0	2.93

Dave Pavlas

Pitches: Right Bats: Right Pos: P   Ht: 6'7" Wt: 205 Born: 8/12/62 Age: 35

		HOW MUCH HE PITCHED						WHAT HE GAVE UP							THE RESULTS					
Year Team	Lg Org	G GS CG GF	IP	BFP	H	R	ER	HR	SH	SF	HB	TBB	IBB	SO	WP	Bk	W	L	Pct.	ShO	Sv	ERA
1985 Peoria	A ChN	17 15 3 2	110	452	90	40	32	7	3	1	3	32	0	86	6	1	8	3	.727	1	1	2.62
1986 Winston-Sal	A+ ChN	28 26 5 0	173.1	739	172	91	74	8	6	4	6	57	2	143	11	1	14	6	.700	2	0	3.84
1987 Pittsfield	AA ChN	7 7 0 0	45	199	49	25	19	6	0	3	3	17	0	27	1	1	6	1	.857	0	0	3.80
Tulsa	AA Tex	13 12 0 1	59.2	280	79	51	51	9	1	0	3	27	0	46	7	0	1	6	.143	0	0	7.69
1988 Tulsa	AA Tex	26 5 1 9	77.1	299	52	26	17	3	6	2	5	18	1	69	4	6	5	2	.714	0	2	1.98
Okla City	AAA Tex	13 8 0 2	52.1	237	59	29	26	1	1	2	3	28	0	40	2	1	3	1	.750	0	0	4.47
1989 Okla City	AAA Tex	29 21 4 4	143.2	652	175	89	75	7	6	7	7	67	4	94	8	1	2	14	.125	0	0	4.70
1990 Iowa	AAA ChN	53 3 0 29	99.1	421	84	38	36	4	4	3	10	48	6	96	8	1	8	3	.727	0	8	3.26
1991 Iowa	AAA ChN	61 0 0 29	97.1	418	92	49	43	5	10	5	5	43	9	54	13	0	5	6	.455	0	7	3.98
1992 Iowa	AAA ChN	12 4 0 6	37.1	166	43	20	14	5	2	0	1	8	0	34	0	0	3	3	.500	0	0	3.38
1995 Columbus	AAA NYA	48 0 0 32	58.2	233	43	19	17	2	4	1	1	20	2	51	4	0	3	3	.500	0	18	2.61
1996 Columbus	AAA NYA	57 0 0 46	77	306	64	20	17	5	1	0	0	13	1	65	3	0	8	2	.800	0	26	1.99
1997 Columbus	AAA NYA	26 0 0 25	25.1	116	33	14	13	3	2	1	0	4	2	34	0	0	1	3	.250	0	12	4.62
1990 Chicago	NL	13 0 0 3	21.1	93	23	7	5	2	0	2	0	6	2	12	3	0	1	0	1.000	0	0	2.11
1991 Chicago	NL	1 0 0 1	1	5	3	2	2	1	1	0	0	0	0	0	0	0	0	0	.000	0	0	18.00
1995 New York	AL	4 0 0 1	5.2	24	8	2	2	0	0	0	0	0	0	3	0	0	0	0	.000	0	0	3.18
1996 New York	AL	16 0 0 8	23	97	23	7	6	0	2	0	1	7	2	18	3	0	1	0	.000	0	1	2.35
11 Min. YEARS		390 101 13 178	1056.1	4518	1035	511	434	65	46	29	47	382	27	839	67	12	67	53	.558	3	74	3.70
4 Maj. YEARS		34 0 0 13	51	219	57	18	15	3	3	2	1	13	4	33	6	0	2	0	1.000	0	1	2.65

Chris Paxton

Bats: Left Throws: Right Pos: DH-C   Ht: 6'2" Wt: 195 Born: 12/11/76 Age: 21

		BATTING														BASERUNNING				PERCENTAGES		
Year Team	Lg Org	G	AB	H	2B	3B	HR	TB	R	RBI	TBB	IBB	SO	HBP	SH	SF	SB	CS	SB%	GDP	Avg	OBP	SLG
1995 Orioles	R Bal	11	31	7	1	1	0	10	1	6	1	0	4	2	0	0	0	0	.00	0	.226	.294	.323
1996 Bakersfield	A+ Bal	85	270	67	14	0	11	114	30	39	35	0	90	3	2	2	0	0	.00	6	.248	.339	.422
1997 Bowie	AA Bal	12	22	3	1	0	0	4	1	1	1	0	7	0	0	0	0	0	.00	0	.136	.174	.182
Frederick	A+ Bal	4	15	4	0	0	1	7	1	1	0	0	5	0	0	0	0	0	.00	1	.267	.267	.467
Bluefield	R+ Bal	38	109	33	8	0	3	50	19	22	19	3	26	3	0	1	0	0	.00	3	.303	.417	.459
3 Min. YEARS		150	447	114	24	1	15	185	52	69	56	3	132	8	2	3	0	0	.00	10	.255	.346	.414

Eddie Pearson

Bats: Both Throws: Right Pos: 1B   Ht: 6'3" Wt: 225 Born: 1/31/74 Age: 24

		BATTING														BASERUNNING				PERCENTAGES		
Year Team	Lg Org	G	AB	H	2B	3B	HR	TB	R	RBI	TBB	IBB	SO	HBP	SH	SF	SB	CS	SB%	GDP	Avg	OBP	SLG
1992 White Sox	R ChA	28	102	24	5	0	0	29	10	12	9	1	17	2	0	1	1	3	.25	3	.235	.307	.284
1993 Hickory	A ChA	87	343	83	15	3	4	116	37	40	20	1	59	1	5	1	5	1	.83	8	.242	.285	.338
South Bend	A ChA	48	190	62	16	0	1	81	23	26	13	2	29	1	0	3	0	1	.00	1	.326	.367	.426
1994 Pr William	A+ ChA	130	502	139	28	3	12	209	58	80	45	1	80	3	0	3	0	0	.00	11	.277	.338	.416
1995 White Sox	R ChA	6	20	6	2	0	1	11	7	6	3	0	2	0	0	0	0	0	.00	0	.300	.391	.550
Birmingham	AA ChA	50	201	45	13	0	2	64	20	25	7	0	36	1	0	2	1	0	1.00	9	.224	.251	.318
1996 Birmingham	AA ChA	85	323	72	20	0	8	116	38	40	31	3	57	2	0	3	2	2	.50	3	.223	.292	.359
1997 Birmingham	AA ChA	95	382	125	33	1	5	175	59	59	23	1	50	2	0	3	1	1	.50	13	.327	.366	.458
Nashville	AAA ChA	41	148	33	4	0	4	49	17	16	6	1	23	0	0	1	1	1	.50	3	.223	.252	.331
6 Min. YEARS		570	2211	589	136	7	37	850	269	304	157	9	353	12	6	17	11	9	.55	54	.266	.316	.384

193

Aldo Pecorilli

Bats: Right **Throws:** Right **Pos:** 1B **Ht:** 5'11" **Wt:** 185 **Born:** 9/12/70 **Age:** 27

					BATTING												BASERUNNING				PERCENTAGES		
Year Team	Lg Org	G	AB	H	2B	3B	HR	TB	R	RBI	TBB	IBB	SO	HBP	SH	SF	SB	CS	SB%	GDP	Avg	OBP	SLG
1992 Johnson Cty	R+ StL	54	201	65	14	2	6	101	36	41	25	1	21	2	0	2	6	2	.75	4	.323	.400	.502
1993 Savannah	A StL	141	515	157	30	7	14	243	75	93	81	7	86	6	0	8	16	11	.59	5	.305	.400	.472
1994 St. Pete	A+ StL	135	508	141	26	3	18	227	76	78	56	4	69	4	1	3	13	9	.59	7	.278	.352	.447
1995 Greenville	AA Atl	70	265	102	17	2	7	144	51	42	22	2	39	6	1	4	2	8	.20	4	.385	.438	.543
Richmond	AAA Atl	49	127	33	3	0	6	54	16	17	19	2	20	2	2	0	0	0	.00	5	.260	.365	.425
1996 Richmond	AAA Atl	122	403	117	27	0	15	189	61	62	31	1	87	3	1	3	5	6	.45	8	.290	.343	.469
1997 Arkansas	AA StL	31	111	40	10	0	4	62	21	22	7	0	15	2	0	4	2	3	.40	2	.360	.395	.559
6 Min. YEARS		602	2130	655	127	14	70	1020	336	355	241	17	337	25	5	24	44	39	.53	35	.308	.381	.479

Lloyd Peever

Pitches: Right **Bats:** Right **Pos:** P **Ht:** 5'11" **Wt:** 185 **Born:** 9/15/71 **Age:** 26

			HOW MUCH HE PITCHED						WHAT HE GAVE UP								THE RESULTS					
Year Team	Lg Org	G	GS	CG	GF	IP	BFP	H	R	ER	HR	SH	SF	HB	TBB	IBB	SO	WP	Bk	W	L	Pct.	ShO	Sv	ERA
1992 Bristol	R+ Col	11	8	0	2	43.1	180	44	18	14	2	1	2	2	10	0	48	3	0	3	2	.600	0	1	2.91
1993 Central Val	A+ Col	16	7	1	6	66.2	278	65	31	31	6	0	2	1	17	0	69	5	0	2	4	.333	1	4	4.19
1994 New Haven	AA Col	23	21	3	1	131.1	536	109	59	50	8	6	5	3	37	1	126	3	2	9	8	.529	2	1	3.43
1995 Colo Spmgs	AAA Col	8	8	0	0	42	185	45	26	25	5	0	3	1	16	0	25	3	0	3	2	.600	0	0	5.36
1997 Salem	A+ Col	4	1	0	0	11	49	13	6	4	0	1	1	0	3	0	10	0	0	0	0	.000	0	0	3.27
New Haven	AA Col	20	10	0	2	73.2	310	70	49	45	14	4	1	5	24	2	46	2	0	5	5	.500	0	0	5.50
5 Min. YEARS		82	55	4	11	368	1538	346	189	169	35	12	14	12	107	3	324	16	2	22	21	.512	3	6	4.13

Steve Pegues

Bats: Right **Throws:** Right **Pos:** OF **Ht:** 6'2" **Wt:** 190 **Born:** 5/21/68 **Age:** 30

					BATTING												BASERUNNING				PERCENTAGES		
Year Team	Lg Org	G	AB	H	2B	3B	HR	TB	R	RBI	TBB	IBB	SO	HBP	SH	SF	SB	CS	SB%	GDP	Avg	OBP	SLG
1987 Bristol	R+ Det	59	236	67	6	5	2	89	36	23	16	0	43	0	0	2	22	7	.76	8	.284	.327	.377
1988 Fayetteville	A Det	118	437	112	17	5	6	157	50	46	21	3	90	3	2	4	21	11	.66	6	.256	.292	.359
1989 Fayetteville	A Det	70	269	83	11	6	1	109	35	38	15	2	52	2	1	3	16	10	.62	5	.309	.346	.405
Lakeland	A+ Det	55	193	49	7	2	0	60	24	15	7	0	19	2	0	1	12	4	.75	5	.254	.286	.311
1990 London	AA Det	126	483	131	22	5	8	187	48	63	12	1	58	3	3	4	17	8	.68	17	.271	.291	.387
1991 London	AA Det	56	216	65	3	2	6	90	24	26	8	0	24	6	0	2	4	7	.36	6	.301	.341	.417
Toledo	AAA Det	68	222	50	13	3	4	81	21	23	3	0	31	3	1	0	8	5	.62	7	.225	.246	.365
1992 Las Vegas	AAA SD	123	376	99	21	4	9	155	51	56	7	1	64	6	3	9	12	3	.80	8	.263	.281	.412
1993 Las Vegas	AAA SD	88	270	95	20	5	9	152	52	50	7	0	43	1	0	3	12	6	.67	8	.352	.367	.563
1994 Indianapols	AAA Cin	63	245	71	16	11	6	127	36	29	6	0	44	3	1	2	10	3	.77	9	.290	.313	.518
1996 Richmond	AAA Atl	52	167	57	10	1	7	90	31	30	6	0	43	4	0	1	0	0	.00	4	.341	.376	.539
1997 Ottawa	AAA Mon	66	190	57	12	1	3	80	19	28	9	1	29	1	0	3	4	4	.50	12	.300	.330	.421
Winnipeg	IND —	3	10	4	0	0	0	4	1	6	1	0	4	0	0	1	0	0	.00	0	.400	.417	.400
Iowa	AAA ChN	6	24	9	2	0	0	11	3	1	0	0	3	0	0	0	0	0	.00	0	.375	.375	.458
1994 Cincinnati	NL	11	10	3	0	0	0	3	1	0	1	0	3	0	0	0	0	0	.00	0	.300	.364	.300
Pittsburgh	NL	7	26	10	2	0	0	12	1	2	1	0	2	0	0	0	1	0	1.00	3	.385	.407	.462
1995 Pittsburgh	NL	82	171	42	8	0	6	68	17	16	4	0	36	1	0	3	1	2	.33	3	.246	.263	.398
10 Min. YEARS		933	3338	949	160	50	61	1392	431	434	118	8	547	34	11	35	138	68	.67	97	.284	.312	.417
2 Mai. YEARS		100	207	55	10	0	6	83	19	18	6	0	41	1	0	3	2	2	.50	6	.266	.286	.401

Kit Pellow

Bats: Right **Throws:** Right **Pos:** 3B **Ht:** 6'1" **Wt:** 200 **Born:** 8/28/73 **Age:** 24

					BATTING												BASERUNNING				PERCENTAGES		
Year Team	Lg Org	G	AB	H	2B	3B	HR	TB	R	RBI	TBB	IBB	SO	HBP	SH	SF	SB	CS	SB%	GDP	Avg	OBP	SLG
1996 Spokane	A- KC	71	279	80	18	2	18	156	48	66	20	0	52	8	1	7	8	3	.73	5	.287	.344	.559
1997 Lansing	A KC	65	256	76	17	2	11	130	39	52	24	1	74	6	0	4	2	0	1.00	5	.297	.366	.508
Wichita	AA KC	68	241	60	12	1	10	104	40	41	21	1	72	2	2	3	5	2	.71	5	.249	.311	.432
2 Min. YEARS		204	776	216	47	5	39	390	127	159	65	2	198	16	3	14	15	5	.75	15	.278	.341	.503

Juan Pena

Pitches: Right **Bats:** Right **Pos:** P **Ht:** 6'5" **Wt:** 210 **Born:** 6/27/77 **Age:** 21

			HOW MUCH HE PITCHED						WHAT HE GAVE UP								THE RESULTS					
Year Team	Lg Org	G	GS	CG	GF	IP	BFP	H	R	ER	HR	SH	SF	HB	TBB	IBB	SO	WP	Bk	W	L	Pct.	ShO	Sv	ERA
1995 Red Sox	R Bos	13	4	2	6	55.1	217	41	17	12	2	1	2	1	6	0	47	2	1	3	2	.600	1	1	1.95
Sarasota	A+ Bos	2	2	0	0	7.1	35	8	4	4	0	0	0	2	3	0	5	1	1	1	1	.500	0	0	4.91
1996 Michigan	A Bos	26	26	4	1	187.2	743	149	70	62	16	9	5	10	34	2	156	10	2	12	10	.545	0	0	2.97
1997 Sarasota	A+ Bos	13	13	3	0	91.1	359	67	39	30	8	1	2	2	23	1	88	1	0	4	6	.400	0	0	2.96
Trenton	AA Bos	16	14	0	2	97	418	98	56	51	13	6	3	2	31	0	79	5	1	5	6	.455	0	0	4.73
3 Min. YEARS		70	59	9	9	438.2	1772	363	186	159	39	17	12	17	97	3	375	19	5	25	25	.500	1	1	3.26

Brad Pennington

Pitches: Left **Bats:** Left **Pos:** P **Ht:** 6'6" **Wt:** 215 **Born:** 4/14/69 **Age:** 29

			HOW MUCH HE PITCHED						WHAT HE GAVE UP								THE RESULTS					
Year Team	Lg Org	G	GS	CG	GF	IP	BFP	H	R	ER	HR	SH	SF	HB	TBB	IBB	SO	WP	Bk	W	L	Pct.	ShO	Sv	ERA
1989 Bluefield	R+ Bal	15	14	0	0	64.1	319	50	58	47	2	1	3	6	74	0	81	14	8	2	7	.222	0	0	6.58
1990 Wausau	A Bal	32	18	1	7	106	523	81	89	61	12	6	4	4	121	1	142	10	1	4	9	.308	0	0	5.18
1991 Kane County	A Bal	23	0	0	19	23	112	16	17	15	1	0	0	0	25	0	43	6	0	0	2	.000	0	4	5.87
Frederick	A+ Bal	36	0	0	27	43.2	203	32	23	19	4	3	2	2	44	0	58	4	0	1	4	.200	0	13	3.92

		HOW MUCH HE PITCHED		WHAT HE GAVE UP		THE RESULTS	
Year Team	Lg Org	G GS CG GF	IP BFP	H R ER HR SH SF HB	TBB IBB SO WP Bk	W L Pct ShO Sv	ERA
1992 Frederick	A+ Bal	8 0 0 6	9 38	5 3 2 0 1 1 1	4 0 16 1 0	1 0 1.000 0 2	2.00
Hagerstown	AA Bal	19 0 0 16	28.1 121	20 9 8 0 4 3 3	17 0 33 4 0	1 2 .333 0 7	2.54
Rochester	AAA Bal	29 0 0 17	39 158	12 10 9 2 4 1 1	33 2 56 2 0	1 3 .250 0 5	2.08
1993 Rochester	AAA Bal	17 0 0 14	15.2 73	12 11 6 0 0 0 0	13 0 19 1 1	1 2 .333 0 8	3.45
1994 Rochester	AAA Bal	35 9 0 17	86.1 396	68 59 51 11 2 5 4	74 1 89 7 0	6 8 .429 0 3	5.32
1995 Indianapols	AAA Cin	11 2 0 1	14 79	17 19 16 3 0 1 0	21 1 11 2 0	0 0 .000 0 0	10.29
1996 Lk Elsinore	A+ Ana	2 2 0 0	3 11	0 0 0 0 0 0 0	2 0 5 0 0	0 0 .000 0 0	0.00
Vancouver	AAA Ana	11 2 0 1	27.2 124	20 20 13 2 0 1 0	22 0 43 1 0	3 0 1.000 0 1	4.23
1997 Wichita	AA KC	12 0 0 8	12 50	7 1 1 0 0 0 0	8 0 14 3 0	0 0 .000 0 3	0.75
Omaha	AAA KC	35 1 0 6	50 230	41 28 24 6 3 4 3	41 0 48 4 0	2 1 .667 0 4	4.32
1993 Baltimore	AL	34 0 0 16	33 158	34 25 24 7 2 1 2	25 0 39 3 0	3 2 .600 0 4	6.55
1994 Baltimore	AL	8 0 0 3	6 35	9 8 8 2 1 0 0	8 0 7 2 0	0 1 .000 0 0	12.00
1995 Baltimore	AL	8 0 0 2	6.2 33	3 7 6 1 0 0 0	11 1 10 1 0	0 1 .000 0 0	8.10
Cincinnati	NL	6 0 0 2	9.2 47	9 8 6 0 0 2 1	11 0 7 3 0	0 0 .000 0 0	5.59
1996 Boston	AL	14 0 0 6	13 59	6 5 4 1 0 1 0	15 1 13 1 0	0 0 .000 0 0	2.77
California	AL	8 0 0 2	7.1 43	5 10 10 1 0 0 0	16 0 7 1 0	0 0 .000 0 0	12.27
9 Min. YEARS		285 48 1 139	522 2437	381 347 272 43 24 25 24	499 5 658 59 10	22 38 .367 0 46	4.69
4 Maj. YEARS		78 0 0 31	75.2 375	66 63 58 12 3 4 3	86 2 83 11 0	3 6 .333 0 4	6.90

William Pennyfeather

Ht: 6'2" Wt: 215 Born: 5/25/68 Age: 30

Bats: Right Throws: Right Pos: OF

		BATTING									BASERUNNING	PERCENTAGES
Year Team	Lg Org	G AB H	2B 3B HR	TB	R RBI	TBB IBB SO HBP SH SF	SB CS SB% GDP	Avg OBP SLG
1988 Pirates	R Pit	17 74 18	2 1 1	25	6 7	2 0 18 0 0 1	3 3 .50 0	.243 .260 .338
Princeton	R+ Pit	16 57 19	2 0 1	24	11 5	6 0 15 0 0 0	7 2 .78 0	.333 .397 .421
1989 Welland	A- Pit	75 289 55	10 1 3	76	34 26	12 1 75 2 1 6	18 5 .78 6	.190 .223 .263
1990 Augusta	A Pit	122 465 122	14 4 4	156	69 48	23 0 85 3 3 3	21 10 .68 7	.262 .300 .335
1991 Salem	A+ Pit	81 319 85	17 3 8	132	35 46	8 0 52 1 1 2	11 8 .58 9	.266 .285 .414
Carolina	AA Pit	42 149 41	5 0 0	46	13 9	7 0 17 1 1 1	3 2 .60 8	.275 .310 .309
1992 Carolina	AA Pit	51 199 67	13 1 6	100	28 25	9 1 34 0 0 3	3 2 .60 4	.337 .360 .503
Buffalo	AAA Pit	55 160 38	6 2 1	51	19 12	2 0 24 3 2 0	3 2 .60 4	.238 .261 .319
1993 Buffalo	AAA Pit	112 457 114	18 3 14	180	54 41	18 2 92 0 1 1	10 12 .45 3	.249 .277 .394
1994 Buffalo	AAA Pit	10 36 9	2 0 0	11	2 3	3 0 9 0 1 0	0 0 .00 1	.250 .308 .306
Indianapols	AAA Cin	93 361 98	25 3 7	150	52 45	23 1 58 1 4 5	14 4 .78 5	.271 .313 .416
1995 Princeton	R+ Cin	1 3 0	0 0 0	0	0 0	0 0 1 0 0 0	0 0 .00 0	.000 .000 .000
1996 Vancouver	AAA Ana	108 413 117	36 3 5	174	56 63	19 0 71 1 5 2	19 10 .66 7	.283 .315 .421
1997 Albuquerque	AAA LA	115 402 102	21 4 17	182	59 54	26 1 73 1 2 2	11 11 .50 9	.254 .299 .453
1992 Pittsburgh	NL	15 9 2	0 0 0	2	2 0	0 0 0 0 1 0	0 0 .00 1	.222 .222 .222
1993 Pittsburgh	NL	21 34 7	1 0 0	8	4 2	0 0 6 0 0 0	0 0 .00 0	.206 .206 .235
1994 Pittsburgh	NL	4 3 0	0 0 0	0	0 0	0 0 0 0 0 0	0 0 .00 0	.000 .000 .000
10 Min. YEARS		898 3384 885	171 25 67	1307	438 384	158 6 624 13 28 26	127 75 .63 64	.262 .295 .386
3 Maj. YEARS		40 46 9	1 0 0	10	6 2	0 0 6 0 1 0	0 1 .00 2	.196 .196 .217

Billy Percibal

Ht: 6'1" Wt: 170 Born: 2/2/74 Age: 24

Pitches: Right Bats: Right Pos: P

		HOW MUCH HE PITCHED		WHAT HE GAVE UP		THE RESULTS	
Year Team	Lg Org	G GS CG GF	IP BFP	H R ER HR SH SF HB	TBB IBB SO WP Bk	W L Pct ShO Sv	ERA
1992 Orioles	R Bal	16 0 0 9	26.2 132	42 26 24 0 0 2 1	7 0 25 6 2	2 1 .667 0 0	8.10
1993 Bluefield	R+ Bal	13 13 2 0	82.2 355	71 48 35 7 0 5 1	33 0 81 8 1	6 0 1.000 0 0	3.81
1994 Albany	A Bal	28 28 3 0	169.1 744	160 80 67 9 1 3 1	90 0 132 13 4	13 9 .591 2 0	3.56
1995 High Desert	A+ Bal	21 20 2 0	128 547	123 63 46 10 2 2 3	55 0 105 7 4	7 6 .538 0 0	3.23
Bowie	AA Bal	2 2 0 0	14 52	7 0 0 0 0 0 0	7 0 7 0 1	1 0 1.000 0 0	0.00
1997 Orioles	R Bal	4 3 0 0	10 38	11 1 1 0 0 0 0	2 0 12 0 0	0 0 .000 0 0	0.90
Frederick	A+ Bal	7 6 0 0	26.2 118	28 18 17 1 1 1 0	18 0 28 1 2	1 3 .250 0 0	5.74
Bowie	AA Bal	1 1 1 0	6 22	5 2 2 0 0 1 0	1 0 5 0 0	1 0 1.000 0 0	3.00
5 Min. YEARS		92 73 8 9	463.1 2008	447 238 192 27 4 14 6	213 0 395 35 14	30 20 .600 2 0	3.73

David Perez

Ht: 5'11" Wt: 170 Born: 5/23/68 Age: 30

Pitches: Right Bats: Right Pos: P

		HOW MUCH HE PITCHED		WHAT HE GAVE UP		THE RESULTS	
Year Team	Lg Org	G GS CG GF	IP BFP	H R ER HR SH SF HB	TBB IBB SO WP Bk	W L Pct ShO Sv	ERA
1989 Butte	R+ Tex	17 4 1 3	54 242	57 30 15 2 1 2 2	19 0 45 0 0	3 2 .600 0 1	2.50
1990 Charlotte	A+ Tex	14 14 0 0	83.1 339	63 35 31 3 2 4 3	28 0 83 2 1	6 4 .600 0 0	3.35
1991 Tulsa	AA Tex	25 24 4 0	147 619	130 76 69 11 5 2 4	69 3 97 5 3	5 14 .263 2 0	4.22
1992 Charlotte	A+ Tex	13 7 1 5	59.1 227	44 14 14 3 1 0 1	15 2 31 2 0	5 2 .714 1 3	2.12
Tulsa	AA Tex	15 11 1 1	59.2 258	61 36 31 5 2 2 2	26 1 30 6 0	4 3 .571 0 0	4.68
1993 Tulsa	AA Tex	33 14 1 6	125.1 520	119 64 56 11 3 3 7	34 7 111 3 1	9 10 .474 0 2	4.02
Okla City	AAA Tex	2 1 0 0	7.1 34	8 10 10 1 0 1 0	4 0 3 2 0	1 0 1.000 0 0	12.27
1994 Okla City	AAA Tex	30 25 4 3	177 747	190 85 80 16 3 3 7	56 2 93 11 7	11 14 .440 1 0	4.07
1995 Tulsa	AA Tex	8 7 0 0	46.1 204	49 30 27 5 5 0 1	18 2 25 1 0	3 2 .600 0 0	5.24
Okla City	AAA Tex	20 20 1 0	103.1 461	120 71 64 16 0 0 13	34 1 74 5 0	5 12 .294 0 0	5.57
1997 New Britain	AA Min	1 1 0 0	4 17	5 3 3 0 0 1 0	3 0 3 0 0	0 1 .000 0 0	6.75
8 Min. YEARS		178 128 13 18	866.2 3668	846 454 400 73 22 18 40	304 18 595 37 13	52 64 .448 4 6	4.15

Jhonny Perez

Bats: Right Throws: Right Pos: DH   Ht: 5'10" Wt: 150 Born: 10/23/76 Age: 21

Year Team	Lg Org	G	AB	H	2B	3B	HR	TB	R	RBI	TBB	IBB	SO	HBP	SH	SF	SB	CS	SB%	GDP	Avg	OBP	SLG
1994 Astros	R Hou	36	144	46	12	2	1	65	37	27	15	1	16	1	1	1	18	3	.86	4	.319	.385	.451
1995 Kissimmee	A+ Hou	65	214	58	12	0	4	82	24	31	22	1	37	7	0	0	23	7	.77	5	.271	.358	.383
1996 Kissimmee	A+ Hou	90	322	87	20	2	12	147	54	49	26	1	70	2	3	0	16	16	.50	3	.270	.329	.457
1997 Kissimmee	A+ Hou	69	273	72	16	5	3	107	40	22	12	0	38	1	2	3	8	6	.57	5	.264	.294	.392
Jackson	AA Hou	48	154	39	7	0	3	55	16	17	12	0	26	1	1	0	4	3	.57	2	.253	.311	.357
4 Min. YEARS		308	1107	302	67	9	23	456	171	146	87	3	187	12	7	4	69	35	.66	19	.273	.331	.412

Julio Perez

Pitches: Right Bats: Right Pos: P   Ht: 6'1" Wt: 163 Born: 5/18/74 Age: 24

Year Team	Lg Org	G	GS	CG	GF	IP	BFP	H	R	ER	HR	SH	SF	HB	TBB	IBB	SO	WP	Bk	W	L	Pct.	ShO	Sv	ERA
1994 Burlington	R+ Cle	8	8	0	0	46.1	193	38	11	7	0	0	0	3	19	2	47	1	6	3	3	.500	0	0	1.36
Watertown	A- Cle	6	6	1	0	35	153	37	17	14	2	2	1	1	13	0	24	1	0	1	2	.333	0	0	3.60
1995 Columbus	A Cle	22	17	0	5	109.2	461	109	53	49	4	2	3	4	39	5	100	5	5	8	5	.615	0	1	4.02
1996 Kinston	A+ Cle	24	0	0	13	43.2	186	44	22	15	3	3	1	3	17	3	21	0	0	1	2	.333	0	3	3.09
1997 Kinston	A+ Cle	27	0	0	8	48.1	210	58	35	26	4	2	1	0	17	2	35	7	2	6	1	.857	0	0	4.84
Akron	AA Cle	9	0	0	4	24	115	27	16	15	3	0	1	2	13	0	23	1	1	1	0	1.000	0	1	5.63
4 Min. YEARS		96	31	1	30	307	1318	313	154	126	16	9	7	13	118	12	250	18	14	20	13	.606	0	5	3.69

Richard Perez

Bats: Right Throws: Right Pos: SS-3B   Ht: 6'2" Wt: 175 Born: 1/30/73 Age: 25

Year Team	Lg Org	G	AB	H	2B	3B	HR	TB	R	RBI	TBB	IBB	SO	HBP	SH	SF	SB	CS	SB%	GDP	Avg	OBP	SLG
1991 Huntington	R+ ChN	48	166	30	4	0	0	34	19	8	19	0	29	7	4	1	5	2	.71	5	.181	.290	.205
1992 Huntington	R+ ChN	51	190	55	7	3	0	68	33	22	17	0	25	4	4	3	5	3	.63	3	.289	.355	.358
1993 Peoria	A ChN	109	370	90	12	1	0	104	59	34	31	0	64	8	29	5	5	8	.38	3	.243	.312	.281
1994 Daytona	A+ ChN	99	325	77	9	1	0	88	45	21	22	0	54	5	10	0	8	5	.62	14	.237	.295	.271
1995 Daytona	A+ ChN	85	255	56	8	0	0	64	31	26	28	0	41	1	4	1	4	2	.67	5	.220	.298	.251
1996 Orlando	AA ChN	10	18	3	0	0	0	3	0	1	1	0	3	0	0	1	0	0	.00	1	.167	.200	.167
Rockford	A ChN	33	83	21	6	0	3	36	12	13	10	0	17	2	5	1	2	0	1.00	3	.253	.344	.434
Daytona	A+ ChN	52	184	42	7	1	0	51	20	8	12	0	24	3	3	0	4	3	.57	6	.228	.286	.277
1997 El Paso	AA Mil	14	30	9	2	1	0	13	5	4	5	0	1	0	0	0	0	0	.00	2	.300	.400	.433
Stockton	A+ Mil	35	102	27	5	0	0	32	3	13	8	0	18	3	1	3	0	6	.00	2	.265	.328	.314
7 Min. YEARS		536	1723	410	60	7	3	493	227	150	153	0	276	33	60	15	33	29	.53	44	.238	.310	.286

Dan Perkins

Pitches: Right Bats: Right Pos: P   Ht: 6'2" Wt: 184 Born: 3/15/75 Age: 23

Year Team	Lg Org	G	GS	CG	GF	IP	BFP	H	R	ER	HR	SH	SF	HB	TBB	IBB	SO	WP	Bk	W	L	Pct.	ShO	Sv	ERA
1993 Elizabethtn	R+ Min	10	10	0	0	45	210	46	33	25	3	1	1	5	25	0	30	5	1	3	3	.500	0	0	5.00
1994 Ft. Wayne	A Min	12	12	0	0	50.2	229	61	38	35	3	3	1	4	22	1	34	4	1	1	8	.111	0	0	6.22
Elizabethtn	R+ Min	10	9	1	0	54	223	51	31	22	2	2	1	7	14	0	34	9	1	0	2	.000	0	0	3.67
1995 Ft. Wayne	A Min	29	22	0	2	121.1	562	133	86	74	3	3	4	13	69	1	89	22	2	7	12	.368	0	0	5.49
1996 Ft. Myers	A+ Min	39	13	3	10	136.2	557	125	52	45	5	4	6	11	37	1	111	9	1	13	7	.650	1	2	2.96
1997 New Britain	AA Min	24	24	2	0	144.2	644	158	94	79	17	8	2	11	53	1	114	10	0	7	10	.412	0	0	4.91
5 Min. YEARS		124	90	6	12	552.1	2425	574	334	280	33	21	15	51	220	4	412	59	6	31	42	.425	1	2	4.56

Chan Perry

Bats: Right Throws: Right Pos: 1B-DH   Ht: 6'2" Wt: 200 Born: 9/13/72 Age: 25

Year Team	Lg Org	G	AB	H	2B	3B	HR	TB	R	RBI	TBB	IBB	SO	HBP	SH	SF	SB	CS	SB%	GDP	Avg	OBP	SLG
1994 Burlington	R+ Cle	52	185	58	16	1	5	91	28	32	18	0	28	1	0	4	6	0	1.00	9	.314	.370	.492
1995 Columbus	A Cle	113	411	117	30	4	9	182	64	50	53	1	49	2	2	4	7	2	.78	6	.285	.366	.443
1996 Kinston	A+ Cle	96	358	104	27	1	10	163	44	62	36	3	33	2	3	3	2	3	.40	4	.291	.356	.455
1997 Akron	AA Cle	119	476	150	34	2	20	248	74	96	28	0	61	5	1	6	3	3	.50	14	.315	.355	.521
4 Min. YEARS		380	1430	429	107	8	44	684	210	240	135	4	171	10	6	17	18	8	.69	38	.300	.361	.478

Chris Petersen

Bats: Both Throws: Right Pos: SS   Ht: 5'10" Wt: 160 Born: 11/6/70 Age: 27

Year Team	Lg Org	G	AB	H	2B	3B	HR	TB	R	RBI	TBB	IBB	SO	HBP	SH	SF	SB	CS	SB%	GDP	Avg	OBP	SLG
1992 Geneva	A- ChN	71	244	55	8	0	1	66	36	23	32	0	69	4	9	2	11	7	.61	4	.225	.323	.270
1993 Daytona	A+ ChN	130	473	101	10	0	0	111	66	28	58	0	105	9	17	1	19	11	.63	7	.214	.311	.235
1994 Orlando	AA ChN	117	376	85	12	3	1	106	34	26	37	0	89	2	16	1	8	11	.42	10	.226	.298	.282
1995 Orlando	AA ChN	125	382	81	10	3	4	109	48	36	45	3	97	4	5	3	7	3	.70	14	.212	.300	.285
1996 Orlando	AA ChN	47	152	45	3	4	2	62	21	12	18	0	31	5	0	1	3	5	.38	7	.296	.386	.408
Iowa	AAA ChN	63	194	48	6	3	2	66	12	23	12	1	46	1	2	1	1	2	.33	4	.247	.293	.340
1997 Iowa	AAA ChN	119	391	94	16	2	3	123	49	33	32	4	89	6	4	3	1	6	.14	15	.240	.306	.315
6 Min. YEARS		672	2212	509	65	15	13	643	266	181	234	8	526	31	53	12	50	45	.53	59	.230	.311	.291

Charles Peterson

Bats: Right **Throws:** Right **Pos:** OF **Ht:** 6'3" **Wt:** 200 **Born:** 5/8/74 **Age:** 24

Year Team	Lg Org	G	AB	H	2B	3B	HR	TB	R	RBI	TBB	IBB	SO	HBP	SH	SF	SB	CS	SB%	GDP	Avg	OBP	SLG
1993 Pirates	R Pit	49	188	57	11	3	1	77	28	23	22	0	22	0	0	1	8	6	.57	4	.303	.374	.410
1994 Augusta	A Pit	108	415	106	14	6	4	144	55	40	35	2	78	3	0	2	27	18	.60	7	.255	.316	.347
1995 Lynchburg	A+ Pit	107	391	107	9	4	7	145	61	51	43	1	73	2	6	5	31	17	.65	11	.274	.345	.371
Carolina	AA Pit	20	70	23	3	1	0	28	13	7	9	1	15	2	0	1	2	1	.67	1	.329	.415	.400
1996 Carolina	AA Pit	125	462	127	24	2	7	176	71	63	50	5	104	0	3	1	33	10	.77	18	.275	.345	.381
1997 Carolina	AA Pit	126	442	111	26	4	7	166	59	68	40	4	105	4	1	1	20	11	.65	11	.251	.318	.376
5 Min. YEARS		535	1968	531	87	20	26	736	287	252	199	13	397	11	10	11	121	63	.66	52	.270	.339	.374

Dean Peterson

Pitches: Right **Bats:** Right **Pos:** P **Ht:** 6'3" **Wt:** 200 **Born:** 8/3/72 **Age:** 25

Year Team	Lg Org	G	GS	CG	GF	IP	BFP	H	R	ER	HR	SH	SF	HB	TBB	IBB	SO	WP	Bk	W	L	Pct.	ShO	Sv	ERA
1993 Red Sox	R Bos	3	2	0	0	15	64	14	8	6	1	0	1	0	4	0	10	0	0	1	0	1.000	0	0	3.60
Utica	A- Bos	16	5	0	7	42	180	45	28	25	5	2	0	1	7	0	26	1	0	1	4	.200	0	2	5.36
1994 Sarasota	A+ Bos	21	20	6	0	141	572	141	65	57	9	7	8	2	26	0	94	4	0	9	7	.563	3	0	3.64
1995 Trenton	AA Bos	20	14	1	2	88.2	389	96	57	53	7	3	3	4	27	3	47	3	4	4	8	.333	0	0	5.38
Sarasota	A+ Bos	4	4	0	0	17.1	90	25	17	13	2	1	1	3	10	0	15	1	0	1	3	.250	0	0	6.75
1996 Red Sox	R Bos	2	2	0	0	6	25	4	0	0	0	0	0	0	0	0	7	0	0	0	0	.000	0	0	0.00
Sarasota	A+ Bos	26	3	0	11	62	252	45	30	21	5	3	1	2	21	1	58	0	2	7	2	.778	0	3	3.05
1997 Pawtucket	AAA Bos	2	0	0	2	3	13	2	1	1	0	0	0	0	1	0	2	0	1	0	0	.000	0	0	3.00
Red Sox	R Bos	2	0	0	1	2	8	1	0	0	0	0	1	0	1	0	1	0	0	0	0	.000	0	1	0.00
Trenton	AA Bos	33	1	0	19	58.2	268	67	30	30	4	4	2	4	30	3	48	5	1	1	3	.250	0	5	4.60
5 Min. YEARS		129	51	7	42	435.2	1861	440	236	206	34	20	16	17	127	7	308	14	8	24	28	.462	3	11	4.26

Mark Peterson

Pitches: Left **Bats:** Left **Pos:** P **Ht:** 5'11" **Wt:** 195 **Born:** 11/27/70 **Age:** 27

Year Team	Lg Org	G	GS	CG	GF	IP	BFP	H	R	ER	HR	SH	SF	HB	TBB	IBB	SO	WP	Bk	W	L	Pct.	ShO	Sv	ERA
1992 Everett	A- SF	20	5	0	7	53	226	58	23	19	5	2	0	1	17	1	47	0	4	3	2	.600	0	2	3.23
1993 San Jose	A+ SF	37	7	1	19	81.1	349	95	36	31	5	3	3	2	15	0	45	3	0	4	1	.800	1	0	3.43
1994 San Jose	A+ SF	9	4	0	2	36	139	36	16	16	4	2	2	0	6	1	27	1	0	3	3	.500	0	0	4.00
Shreveport	AA SF	28	3	1	11	55.2	223	56	24	21	1	2	2	1	6	1	31	0	0	3	2	.600	0	1	3.40
1995 Shreveport	AA SF	37	0	0	14	64	248	51	15	9	2	2	5	4	6	2	38	0	0	4	3	.571	0	2	1.27
1996 Shreveport	AA SF	41	0	0	16	56	235	58	23	20	5	1	2	4	8	2	32	0	0	5	3	.625	0	2	3.21
1997 Phoenix	AAA SF	3	0	0	1	3.2	15	6	4	3	0	0	0	1	1	0	2	0	0	0	0	.000	0	0	7.36
Jackson	AA Hou	6	0	0	3	5	23	7	3	3	3	0	0	0	2	1	6	0	0	0	1	.000	0	0	5.40
Sonoma Cty	IND —	2	2	0	0	10	50	15	9	9	1	0	0	0	3	0	8	0	0	0	0	.000	0	0	8.10
Orlando	AA ChN	9	0	0	2	13.2	68	26	15	15	1	2	1	0	4	1	8	1	0	0	2	.000	0	0	9.88
Grays Harbr	IND —	17	0	0	2	16.1	74	19	9	9	3	1	0	1	5	1	22	0	0	0	2	.000	0	0	4.96
6 Min. YEARS		209	21	2	74	394.2	1656	427	177	155	30	15	15	15	73	10	266	5	4	22	19	.537	1	8	3.53

Nate Peterson

Bats: Left **Throws:** Right **Pos:** OF **Ht:** 6'2" **Wt:** 185 **Born:** 7/12/71 **Age:** 26

Year Team	Lg Org	G	AB	H	2B	3B	HR	TB	R	RBI	TBB	IBB	SO	HBP	SH	SF	SB	CS	SB%	GDP	Avg	OBP	SLG
1993 Auburn	A- Hou	69	277	72	17	1	2	97	35	29	17	0	34	5	1	0	5	2	.71	14	.260	.314	.350
1994 Quad City	A Hou	68	215	59	11	2	4	86	27	21	14	3	29	2	0	1	1	3	.25	7	.274	.323	.400
1995 Kissimmee	A+ Hou	76	257	72	17	0	4	101	34	22	21	2	42	4	0	1	3	1	.75	5	.280	.343	.393
1996 Jackson	AA Hou	114	324	90	19	0	2	115	36	34	27	1	49	6	1	4	1	1	.50	5	.278	.341	.355
1997 Jackson	AA Hou	49	143	43	11	0	4	66	19	24	17	0	21	2	1	1	2	2	.50	2	.301	.380	.462
Harrisburg	AA Mon	52	140	34	4	2	4	54	17	18	17	5	27	1	1	0	1	0	1.00	5	.243	.329	.386
5 Min. YEARS		428	1356	370	79	5	20	519	168	148	113	11	202	20	4	7	13	9	.59	38	.273	.336	.383

Jose Pett

Pitches: Right **Bats:** Right **Pos:** P **Ht:** 6'6" **Wt:** 190 **Born:** 1/8/76 **Age:** 22

Year Team	Lg Org	G	GS	CG	GF	IP	BFP	H	R	ER	HR	SH	SF	HB	TBB	IBB	SO	WP	Bk	W	L	Pct.	ShO	Sv	ERA
1993 Blue Jays	R Tor	4	4	0	0	10	43	10	4	4	0	0	0	0	3	0	7	0	0	1	1	.500	0	0	3.60
1994 Dunedin	A+ Tor	15	15	1	0	90.2	389	103	47	38	1	5	5	3	20	0	49	3	3	4	8	.333	0	0	3.77
1995 Knoxville	AA Tor	26	25	1	0	141.2	602	132	87	67	16	4	4	4	48	0	89	8	0	8	9	.471	1	0	4.26
1996 Knoxville	AA Tor	7	7	1	0	44	169	37	20	20	4	1	0	0	10	0	38	1	1	4	2	.667	1	0	4.09
Syracuse	AAA Tor	20	18	1	0	109.2	503	134	81	71	10	4	4	10	42	1	50	6	1	2	9	.182	0	0	5.83
1997 Carolina	AA Pit	14	14	0	0	74.1	313	76	37	29	5	2	0	1	25	1	39	1	0	4	4	.500	0	0	3.51
Calgary	AAA Pit	3	3	0	0	14	74	25	15	15	4	0	0	0	8	0	8	0	0	0	3	.000	0	0	9.64
5 Min. YEARS		89	86	4	0	484.1	2093	517	291	244	40	16	13	18	156	2	280	19	5	23	36	.390	2	0	4.53

Tom Phelps

Pitches: Left **Bats:** Left **Pos:** P **Ht:** 6'3" **Wt:** 192 **Born:** 3/4/74 **Age:** 24

Year Team	Lg Org	G	GS	CG	GF	IP	BFP	H	R	ER	HR	SH	SF	HB	TBB	IBB	SO	WP	Bk	W	L	Pct.	ShO	Sv	ERA
1993 Burlington	A Mon	8	8	0	0	41	173	36	18	17	4	1	1	1	13	0	33	0	0	3	3	.333	0	0	3.73
Jamestown	A- Mon	16	15	1	0	92.1	416	102	62	47	4	4	3	5	37	1	74	7	1	3	8	.273	0	0	4.58
1994 Burlington	A Mon	23	23	1	0	118.1	534	143	91	73	9	7	7	5	48	1	82	7	0	8	8	.500	1	0	5.55

197

Year Team	Lg Org	G	GS	CG	GF	IP	BFP	H	R	ER	HR	SH	SF	HB	TBB	IBB	SO	WP	Bk	W	L	Pct.	ShO	Sv	ERA
1995 Wst Plm Bch	A+ Mon	2	2	0	0	5	33	10	10	9	0	0	0	0	11	0	5	2	0	0	2	.000	0	0	16.20
Albany	A Mon	24	24	1	0	135.1	597	142	76	50	6	0	4	5	45	0	119	5	1	10	9	.526	0	0	3.33
1996 Wst Plm Bch	A+ Mon	18	18	1	0	112	468	105	42	36	5	4	1	2	35	0	71	8	0	10	2	.833	1	0	2.89
Harrisburg	AA Mon	8	8	2	0	47.1	195	43	16	13	3	2	0	1	19	2	23	0	0	2	2	.500	2	0	2.47
1997 Harrisburg	AA Mon	18	18	0	0	101.1	462	115	68	53	14	8	5	5	39	1	86	3	1	10	6	.625	0	0	4.71
5 Min. YEARS		117	116	6	0	652.2	2878	696	383	298	45	26	21	24	247	5	493	34	3	45	41	.523	4	0	4.11

Jason Phillips

Pitches: Right Bats: Right Pos: P **Ht: 6'6" Wt: 215 Born: 3/22/74 Age: 24**

Year Team	Lg Org	G	GS	CG	GF	IP	BFP	H	R	ER	HR	SH	SF	HB	TBB	IBB	SO	WP	Bk	W	L	Pct.	ShO	Sv	ERA
1992 Pirates	R Pit	4	4	0	0	17	88	21	21	16	0	1	1	0	13	0	10	4	4	1	2	.333	0	0	8.47
1993 Welland	A- Pit	14	14	0	0	71.1	323	60	44	28	2	1	2	9	36	0	66	15	4	4	6	.400	0	0	3.53
1994 Augusta	A Pit	23	23	1	0	108.1	531	118	97	81	4	3	4	12	88	1	108	21	3	6	12	.333	0	0	6.73
1995 Augusta	A Pit	30	6	0	3	80	354	76	46	32	2	2	2	0	53	1	65	10	0	4	3	.571	0	0	3.60
1996 Augusta	A Pit	14	14	1	0	89.2	366	79	35	24	3	2	3	6	29	1	75	9	1	5	4	.556	1	0	2.41
Lynchburg	A+ Pit	13	13	1	0	73.2	343	82	47	37	3	2	2	5	35	0	63	6	1	5	6	.455	1	0	4.52
1997 Lynchburg	A+ Pit	23	23	2	0	138.2	577	129	66	58	10	4	2	6	35	0	140	9	1	11	6	.647	1	0	3.76
Carolina	AA Pit	4	4	2	0	31	127	21	8	8	1	1	2	4	9	0	22	2	0	1	2	.333	1	0	2.32
6 Min. YEARS		125	101	7	3	609.2	2709	586	364	284	25	16	18	42	298	3	549	76	14	37	41	.474	4	0	4.19

Randy Phillips

Pitches: Right Bats: Right Pos: P **Ht: 6'3" Wt: 210 Born: 3/18/71 Age: 27**

Year Team	Lg Org	G	GS	CG	GF	IP	BFP	H	R	ER	HR	SH	SF	HB	TBB	IBB	SO	WP	Bk	W	L	Pct.	ShO	Sv	ERA
1992 Medcine Hat	R+ Tor	15	13	1	0	91	390	88	48	34	9	1	2	9	25	0	69	4	3	2	4	.333	0	0	3.36
1993 Dunedin	A+ Tor	17	17	0	0	110.1	453	99	51	47	12	4	2	5	30	3	87	5	6	7	6	.538	0	0	3.83
Knoxville	AA Tor	5	5	0	0	25	120	32	20	17	3	2	0	2	12	0	12	3	2	2	2	.500	0	0	6.12
1994 Knoxville	AA Tor	8	8	0	0	48	192	37	16	13	4	1	2	1	12	0	31	2	2	3	2	.600	0	0	2.44
Syracuse	AAA Tor	22	19	0	1	108.2	493	126	81	73	16	1	4	7	45	1	81	4	2	6	9	.400	0	0	6.05
1995 Phoenix	AAA SF	25	24	2	0	132	574	155	83	75	11	4	6	4	40	2	66	8	2	4	13	.235	1	0	5.11
1996 Shreveport	AA SF	35	2	0	9	69.2	308	77	34	25	5	5	2	3	21	5	31	4	1	1	4	.200	0	4	3.23
1997 Shreveport	AA SF	11	0	0	3	20.1	78	17	6	6	1	0	1	0	3	0	8	1	0	2	0	1.000	0	1	2.66
Phoenix	AAA SF	21	3	0	4	47.1	198	44	20	16	5	2	0	2	18	2	27	2	0	5	4	.556	0	0	3.04
6 Min. YEARS		159	91	3	17	652.1	2806	675	359	306	66	20	19	33	206	13	412	33	18	32	44	.421	1	5	4.22

Tony Phillips

Pitches: Right Bats: Right Pos: P **Ht: 6'4" Wt: 195 Born: 6/9/69 Age: 29**

Year Team	Lg Org	G	GS	CG	GF	IP	BFP	H	R	ER	HR	SH	SF	HB	TBB	IBB	SO	WP	Bk	W	L	Pct.	ShO	Sv	ERA
1992 San Berndno	A+ Sea	37	0	0	29	51	227	44	23	18	1	4	4	2	28	2	40	3	3	4	3	.571	0	12	3.18
1993 Riverside	A+ Sea	25	0	0	23	30	118	22	8	6	1	2	2		4	1	19	1	1	3	1	.750	0	15	1.80
Jacksnville	AA Sea	26	0	0	21	30.1	125	34	6	6	1	1	0	0	5	1	23	1	1	1	3	.250	0	5	1.78
1994 Jacksnville	AA Sea	5	0	0	4	5.2	22	3	2	1	1	0	0	0	3	0	3	0	0	0	0	.000	0	1	1.59
Calgary	AAA Sea	55	1	0	29	98	438	132	66	61	11	2	5	2	23	5	51	2	4	6	3	.667	0	6	5.60
1995 Tacoma	AAA Sea	47	1	0	19	87.1	370	98	44	40	6	3	7	6	14	7	44	0	2	3	2	.600	0	1	4.12
1996 Tacoma	AAA Sea	21	3	0	9	52	233	70	40	37	10	1	4	3	9	1	24	0	1	1	3	.250	0	0	6.40
New Orleans	AAA Mil	20	6	0	4	52.1	214	51	25	17	6	0	3	4	7	0	32	2	0	2	1	.667	0	0	2.92
1997 Tucson	AAA Mil	29	1	0	10	58	258	67	43	36	9	4	2	3	21	5	32	1	1	3	2	.600	0	0	5.59
Edmonton	AAA Oak	11	1	0	5	23	100	28	13	13	2	0	0	4	6	0	14	0	1	1	0	1.000	0	0	5.09
6 Min. YEARS		276	13	0	153	487.2	2105	549	270	235	48	17	27	26	120	22	282	9	14	24	18	.571	0	41	4.34

Steve Phoenix

Pitches: Right Bats: Right Pos: P **Ht: 6'2" Wt: 185 Born: 1/31/68 Age: 30**

Year Team	Lg Org	G	GS	CG	GF	IP	BFP	H	R	ER	HR	SH	SF	HB	TBB	IBB	SO	WP	Bk	W	L	Pct.	ShO	Sv	ERA
1990 Athletics	R Oak	6	6	0	0	31	128	25	14	5	0	1	0	1	4	0	31	0	2	3	1	.750	0	0	1.45
Modesto	A+ Oak	6	6	0	0	37.1	164	43	21	19	2	0	1	2	10	0	23	3	0	4	1	.800	0	0	4.58
1991 Huntsville	AA Oak	2	0	0	1	3	18	7	3	2	1	0	0	0	1	0	3	0	0	0	0	.000	0	0	6.00
Madison	A Oak	7	2	0	3	21.1	96	26	8	7	0	2	0	0	10	0	19	0	0	3	0	1.000	0	0	2.95
Modesto	A+ Oak	27	3	1	10	84.1	372	87	44	35	13	3	1	5	33	4	65	3	0	5	2	.714	1	2	3.74
1992 Huntsville	AA Oak	32	24	0	1	174	722	179	68	54	8	4	5	7	36	1	124	5	1	11	5	.688	0	0	2.79
1993 Tacoma	AAA Oak	11	5	0	1	31	159	42	27	24	4	1	0	0	27	2	21	2	0	0	2	.000	0	0	6.97
Huntsville	AA Oak	11	0	0	7	19.1	73	13	5	3	0	1	0	1	5	2	15	0	0	2	2	.500	0	0	1.40
1994 Tacoma	AAA Oak	20	0	0	17	22	83	16	5	3	0	2	0	1	4	1	16	2	0	0	0	.000	0	1	1.23
Huntsville	AA Oak	38	0	0	33	48.2	202	42	9	7	1	3	2	1	16	4	40	0	0	6	2	.750	0	20	1.29
1995 Edmonton	AAA Oak	40	0	0	25	64	280	66	36	32	6	5	3	1	28	4	28	5	0	4	3	.571	0	5	4.50
1996 Calgary	AAA Pit	10	1	0	3	16	68	16	8	3	3	0	3	1	5	1	9	0	0	1	1	.500	0	0	1.69
Carolina	AA Pit	20	0	0	15	21.2	102	31	12	12	3	2	1	0	6	2	16	4	0	2	2	.500	0	5	4.98
1997 Huntsville	AA Oak	29	0	0	23	35.2	156	43	25	23	3	0	2	2	11	1	25	4	0	0	3	.000	0	9	5.80
1994 Oakland	AL	2	0	0	0	4.1	19	4	3	3	0	0	0	0	2	0	3	0	0	0	0	.000	0	0	6.23
1995 Oakland	AL	1	0	0	0	1.2	11	3	6	6	1	1	0	0	3	0	3	0	0	0	0	.000	0	0	32.40
8 Min. YEARS		259	47	1	139	609.1	2623	636	285	229	44	21	20	22	196	19	435	28	3	41	26	.612	1	53	3.38
2 Maj. YEARS		3	0	0	0	6	30	7	9	9	1	1	0	0	5	0	6	0	0	0	0	.000	0	0	13.50

Ricky Pickett

Pitches: Left **Bats:** Left **Pos:** P **Ht:** 6'0" **Wt:** 185 **Born:** 1/19/70 **Age:** 28

Year Team	Lg Org	G	GS	CG	GF	IP	BFP	H	R	ER	HR	SH	SF	HB	TBB	IBB	SO	WP	Bk	W	L	Pct.	ShO	Sv	ERA
1992 Billings	R+ Cin	20	4	0	4	53.2	225	35	21	14	2	1	2	5	28	0	41	3	1	1	2	.333	0	2	2.35
1993 Chston-WV	A Cin	44	1	0	5	43.2	227	42	40	33	1	1	1	5	48	0	65	6	3	1	2	.333	0	0	6.80
1994 Chston-WV	A Cin	28	0	0	19	27.1	121	14	8	6	1	0	1	2	20	0	48	4	0	1	1	.500	0	13	1.98
Winston-Sal	A+ Cin	21	0	0	17	24	112	16	11	10	0	1	1	2	23	1	33	2	0	2	1	.667	0	4	3.75
1995 Chattanooga	AA Cin	40	0	0	19	46.2	203	22	20	17	3	2	0	0	44	3	69	1	0	4	5	.444	0	9	3.28
Shreveport	AA SF	14	0	0	9	21	82	9	5	4	1	0	1	0	9	0	23	2	0	2	0	1.000	0	3	1.71
1996 Phoenix	AAA SF	8	0	0	2	8.1	43	12	8	8	1	0	0	1	5	0	7	1	0	0	3	.000	0	0	8.64
Shreveport	AA SF	29	0	0	12	48.2	214	35	21	15	4	3	2	3	35	3	51	2	0	4	1	.800	0	2	2.77
1997 Phoenix	AAA SF	61	0	0	29	67.2	302	52	27	24	2	4	1	4	49	3	85	4	0	3	3	.500	0	12	3.19
6 Min. YEARS		265	5	0	116	341	1529	237	161	131	15	12	9	22	261	10	422	25	4	18	18	.500	0	45	3.46

Kevin Pickford

Pitches: Left **Bats:** Left **Pos:** P **Ht:** 6'3" **Wt:** 200 **Born:** 3/12/75 **Age:** 23

Year Team	Lg Org	G	GS	CG	GF	IP	BFP	H	R	ER	HR	SH	SF	HB	TBB	IBB	SO	WP	Bk	W	L	Pct.	ShO	Sv	ERA
1993 Pirates	R Pit	15	0	0	1	34.1	151	24	14	13	1	1	2	3	20	0	28	0	2	0	4	.000	0	0	3.41
1994 Augusta	A Pit	2	2	0	0	8.2	37	9	6	4	1	0	0	0	5	0	7	1	0	0	1	.000	0	0	4.15
Welland	A- Pit	15	15	1	0	84.2	377	86	52	46	7	1	6	5	36	0	52	2	2	5	8	.385	1	0	4.89
1995 Lynchburg	A+ Pit	4	4	0	0	27.1	110	31	15	15	5	0	1	0	0	0	15	2	1	0	3	.000	0	0	4.94
Augusta	A Pit	16	16	0	0	85.2	354	85	28	19	5	2	1	5	16	1	59	2	0	7	3	.700	0	0	2.00
1996 Lynchburg	A+ Pit	28	28	4	0	172.1	749	195	99	78	15	7	6	11	25	0	100	4	1	11	11	.500	1	0	4.07
1997 Carolina	AA Pit	21	1	0	7	29.1	152	48	29	24	3	1	1	3	15	3	24	0	0	1	2	.333	0	1	7.36
Lynchburg	A+ Pit	14	10	0	1	73.1	296	72	31	29	3	4	1	2	11	0	50	2	0	3	4	.429	0	1	3.56
5 Min. YEARS		109	83	5	9	515.2	2226	550	279	228	40	16	18	29	128	4	335	13	6	27	36	.429	2	2	3.98

Jeff Pierce

Pitches: Right **Bats:** Right **Pos:** P **Ht:** 6'1" **Wt:** 185 **Born:** 6/7/69 **Age:** 29

Year Team	Lg Org	G	GS	CG	GF	IP	BFP	H	R	ER	HR	SH	SF	HB	TBB	IBB	SO	WP	Bk	W	L	Pct.	ShO	Sv	ERA
1992 South Bend	A ChA	52	0	0	46	69.2	281	46	22	16	1	5	4	6	18	0	88	8	0	3	5	.375	0	30	2.07
Sarasota	A+ ChA	1	0	0	1	0.2	3	0	0	0	0	0	0	0	0	0	1	0	0	0	0	.000	0	0	0.00
1993 Birmingham	AA ChA	33	0	0	26	48.2	188	34	16	14	3	4	2	3	7	0	45	1	1	3	4	.429	0	18	2.59
Chattanooga	AA Cin	13	0	0	8	20.2	87	17	6	6	1	0	1	0	9	1	22	2	0	0	0	.000	0	4	2.61
1994 New Britain	AA Bos	29	0	0	25	39.1	163	31	13	10	3	1	0	2	12	3	54	4	0	1	2	.333	0	10	2.29
Pawtucket	AAA Bos	32	0	0	14	60.1	249	53	27	23	4	2	2	0	21	1	57	2	1	6	1	.857	0	2	3.43
1995 Pawtucket	AAA Bos	23	3	0	8	41.1	172	34	21	19	5	2	2	2	16	1	43	2	1	4	2	.667	0	0	4.14
1996 Red Sox	R Bos	5	4	0	1	11.1	44	12	1	1	0	0	0	1	1	0	10	0	1	0	0	.000	0	0	0.79
Trenton	AA Bos	4	0	0	1	9	38	6	1	1	0	0	0	1	4	1	5	1	0	0	0	.000	0	0	1.00
Pawtucket	AAA Bos	12	3	0	2	31	136	37	18	17	6	2	1	0	8	0	22	2	0	2	1	.667	0	0	4.94
1997 Orlando	AA ChN	5	4	0	0	17.1	85	28	21	19	6	0	0	0	7	0	8	1	0	0	3	.000	0	0	9.87
1995 Boston	AL	12	0	0	2	15	72	16	12	11	0	1	1	0	14	4	12	0	0	0	3	.000	0	0	6.60
6 Min. YEARS		209	14	0	133	349.1	1446	298	146	126	29	15	10	16	103	7	355	23	4	19	15	.559	0	65	3.25

Jason Pierson

Pitches: Left **Bats:** Right **Pos:** P **Ht:** 6'0" **Wt:** 190 **Born:** 1/6/71 **Age:** 27

Year Team	Lg Org	G	GS	CG	GF	IP	BFP	H	R	ER	HR	SH	SF	HB	TBB	IBB	SO	WP	Bk	W	L	Pct.	ShO	Sv	ERA
1992 Utica	A- ChA	15	15	1	0	87	358	90	34	23	5	0	3	1	18	2	62	2	4	8	2	.800	1	0	2.38
1993 South Bend	A ChA	26	25	2	0	147.1	637	160	92	77	16	4	5	5	43	1	107	8	2	13	9	.591	0	0	4.70
1994 Pr William	A+ ChA	28	28	3	0	189.1	785	183	85	70	22	10	3	6	48	0	117	11	2	14	8	.636	1	0	3.33
1995 Birmingham	AA ChA	4	4	0	0	23.1	102	29	22	21	6	0	1	2	6	0	15	0	1	0	2	.000	0	0	8.10
Pr William	A+ ChA	21	12	0	5	91.2	382	91	48	45	9	1	4	2	22	0	69	1	0	5	4	.556	0	0	4.42
1996 Binghamton	AA NYN	34	5	0	12	53.1	227	56	21	20	6	2	1	0	15	2	42	0	0	5	3	.625	0	1	3.38
1997 Mets	R NYN	1	0	0	1	2	7	0	0	0	0	0	0	0	1	0	3	0	0	0	0	.000	0	0	0.00
Binghamton	AA NYN	13	0	0	4	16	88	33	22	14	3	3	2	1	7	0	7	0	0	2	2	.500	0	0	7.88
St. Lucie	A+ NYN	7	1	0	0	15.2	59	13	4	4	2	0	0	0	2	0	6	0	0	0	1	.000	0	0	2.30
6 Min. YEARS		149	90	6	22	625.2	2645	655	328	274	69	20	19	19	162	5	428	22	9	47	31	.603	2	1	3.94

Kinnis Pledger

Bats: Left **Throws:** Right **Pos:** OF **Ht:** 6'4" **Wt:** 215 **Born:** 7/17/68 **Age:** 29

Year Team	Lg Org	G	AB	H	2B	3B	HR	TB	R	RBI	TBB	IBB	SO	HBP	SH	SF	SB	CS	SB%	GDP	Avg	OBP	SLG
1987 White Sox	R ChA	37	127	32	6	3	1	47	18	13	13	3	46	0	0	1	20	0	1.00	1	.252	.319	.370
1988 South Bend	A ChA	107	371	75	13	4	3	105	42	34	39	2	106	0	4	3	18	10	.64	2	.202	.276	.283
1989 South Bend	A ChA	89	293	78	13	5	3	110	49	39	56	3	79	0	4	4	26	14	.65	0	.266	.380	.375
1990 Sarasota	A+ ChA	131	460	114	18	4	3	149	72	40	94	3	134	8	6	3	26	14	.65	10	.248	.382	.324
Vancouver	AAA ChA	1	1	0	0	0	0	0	0	0	0	0	0	0	0	0	0	0	.00	0	.000	.000	.000
1991 Birmingham	AA ChA	117	363	79	16	8	9	138	53	51	60	3	104	4	4	1	15	10	.60	2	.218	.334	.380
1992 Sarasota	A+ ChA	59	217	70	11	2	7	106	42	38	28	4	47	3	1	5	9	6	.59	6	.323	.406	.488
Birmingham	AA ChA	60	191	34	5	2	1	46	18	14	19	3	65	0	5	3	4	4	.33	5	.178	.249	.241
1993 Birmingham	AA ChA	125	393	95	10	6	14	159	70	56	74	0	120	3	5	4	19	6	.76	9	.242	.363	.405
1994 Daytona	A+ ChN	11	37	8	1	1	1	14	5	3	10	0	12	0	0	0	3	0	.00	2	.216	.383	.378
Orlando	AA ChN	23	70	19	3	1	2	30	4	8	7	1	17	1	0	0	3	1	.75	4	.271	.346	.429
Iowa	AAA ChN	69	230	65	17	3	8	112	47	34	24	1	54	1	0	3	2	5	.29	2	.283	.349	.487

Year Team	Lg Org	G	AB	H	2B	3B	HR	TB	R	RBI	TBB	IBB	SO	HBP	SH	SF	SB	CS	SB%	GDP	Avg	OBP	SLG
						BATTING												BASERUNNING				PERCENTAGES		
1995 Iowa	AAA ChN	9	24	2	0	0	0	2	1	0	2	0	12	0	0	0	0	0	.00	1	.083	.154	.083
Mobile	IND —	85	299	80	17	3	21	166	57	61	53	4	76	2	1	4	14	7	.67	2	.268	.377	.555
1996 Norwich	AA NYA	131	445	118	27	6	19	214	80	67	65	7	123	2	1	0	20	5	.80	4	.265	.361	.481
1997 Wichita	AA KC	12	37	3	1	1	0	6	3	0	5	0	14	0	0	0	0	0	.00	0	.081	.190	.162
New Haven	AA Col	61	201	51	10	2	10	95	35	26	30	2	53	1	2	1	2	2	.50	7	.254	.352	.473
11 Min. YEARS		1127	3759	923	168	51	102	1499	596	484	579	36	1062	25	38	28	180	87	.67	57	.246	.348	.399

Charles Poe

Bats: Right **Throws:** Right **Pos:** OF   **Ht:** 6'0" **Wt:** 185 **Born:** 11/9/71 **Age:** 26

Year Team	Lg Org	G	AB	H	2B	3B	HR	TB	R	RBI	TBB	IBB	SO	HBP	SH	SF	SB	CS	SB%	GDP	Avg	OBP	SLG
						BATTING												BASERUNNING				PERCENTAGES		
1990 White Sox	R ChA	46	147	26	3	2	0	33	13	16	16	0	38	4	0	4	10	5	.67	2	.177	.269	.224
1991 South Bend	A ChA	117	418	89	29	6	5	145	57	59	38	1	136	2	4	5	20	5	.80	5	.213	.279	.347
1992 South Bend	A ChA	67	228	41	9	3	3	65	26	26	23	0	64	2	2	3	4	1	.80	9	.180	.258	.285
Utica	A- ChA	47	164	49	8	1	5	74	27	29	18	0	39	2	0	2	10	2	.83	3	.299	.371	.451
1993 White Sox	R ChA	3	13	4	3	0	1	10	2	2	1	0	3	0	0	0	0	1	.00	0	.308	.357	.769
Sarasota	A+ ChA	95	313	78	16	6	11	139	45	47	33	0	91	4	2	0	5	8	.38	6	.249	.329	.444
1994 Pr William	A+ ChA	130	469	126	21	3	14	195	72	83	51	2	103	5	2	5	14	2	.88	5	.269	.345	.416
1995 Birmingham	AA ChA	120	427	121	28	2	13	192	75	60	51	4	79	10	7	5	19	4	.83	7	.283	.369	.450
1996 Huntsville	AA Oak	122	416	110	18	3	12	170	74	68	46	2	99	8	4	2	5	4	.56	14	.264	.347	.409
Edmonton	AAA Oak	3	15	3	0	0	0	3	2	0	1	1	5	0	1	0	0	0	.00	0	.200	.250	.200
1997 Mobile	AA SD	53	193	60	7	4	3	84	30	35	11	3	43	2	0	3	5	1	.83	2	.311	.349	.435
Las Vegas	AAA SD	54	180	47	9	3	8	86	28	34	22	4	32	2	1	4	1	2	.33	7	.261	.341	.478
8 Min. YEARS		857	2983	754	151	33	75	1196	451	459	311	17	732	41	23	30	93	35	.73	64	.253	.329	.401

Enohel Polanco

Bats: Right **Throws:** Right **Pos:** SS   **Ht:** 5'11" **Wt:** 140 **Born:** 8/11/75 **Age:** 22

Year Team	Lg Org	G	AB	H	2B	3B	HR	TB	R	RBI	TBB	IBB	SO	HBP	SH	SF	SB	CS	SB%	GDP	Avg	OBP	SLG
						BATTING												BASERUNNING				PERCENTAGES		
1995 Kingsport	R+ NYN	62	205	47	5	2	2	62	28	21	18	0	60	2	3	3	7	6	.54	5	.229	.294	.302
1996 Capital City	A NYN	92	299	65	12	1	1	82	34	24	18	0	78	5	9	1	6	3	.67	5	.217	.272	.274
1997 St. Lucie	A+ NYN	43	131	33	9	1	0	44	20	12	10	0	33	1	4	1	2	5	.29	4	.252	.308	.336
Binghamton	AA NYN	82	263	79	13	4	3	109	34	32	17	2	59	5	5	0	7	5	.58	3	.300	.354	.414
3 Min. YEARS		279	898	224	39	8	6	297	116	89	63	2	230	13	21	5	22	19	.54	17	.249	.306	.331

Placido Polanco

Bats: Right **Throws:** Right **Pos:** 2B   **Ht:** 5'10" **Wt:** 168 **Born:** 10/10/75 **Age:** 22

Year Team	Lg Org	G	AB	H	2B	3B	HR	TB	R	RBI	TBB	IBB	SO	HBP	SH	SF	SB	CS	SB%	GDP	Avg	OBP	SLG
						BATTING												BASERUNNING				PERCENTAGES		
1994 Cardinals	R StL	32	127	27	4	0	1	34	17	10	7	0	15	1	0	0	4	2	.67	2	.213	.259	.268
1995 Peoria	A StL	103	361	96	7	4	2	117	43	41	18	0	30	2	11	2	7	6	.54	8	.266	.303	.324
1996 St. Pete	A+ StL	137	540	157	29	5	0	196	65	51	24	1	34	5	6	3	4	4	.50	31	.291	.323	.363
1997 Arkansas	AA StL	129	508	148	16	3	2	176	71	51	29	1	51	3	6	3	19	5	.79	11	.291	.331	.346
4 Min. YEARS		401	1536	428	56	12	5	523	196	153	78	2	130	11	23	12	34	17	.67	52	.279	.316	.340

Wil Polidor

Bats: Both **Throws:** Right **Pos:** 2B   **Ht:** 6'1" **Wt:** 158 **Born:** 9/23/73 **Age:** 24

Year Team	Lg Org	G	AB	H	2B	3B	HR	TB	R	RBI	TBB	IBB	SO	HBP	SH	SF	SB	CS	SB%	GDP	Avg	OBP	SLG
						BATTING												BASERUNNING				PERCENTAGES		
1991 White Sox	R ChA	54	217	45	2	0	0	47	19	18	6	2	17	0	1	2	9	2	.82	6	.207	.227	.217
1992 White Sox	R ChA	27	78	22	2	0	0	24	3	4	2	0	8	0	0	0	1	3	.25	3	.282	.300	.308
Utica	A- ChA	16	42	14	1	0	0	15	5	5	1	0	6	0	2	0	2	1	.67	1	.333	.349	.357
1993 Hickory	A ChA	15	43	10	0	0	0	10	4	3	2	0	7	1	1	0	0	1	.00	0	.233	.283	.233
South Bend	A ChA	42	120	34	2	4	0	44	14	9	1	0	15	0	2	0	0	1	.00	6	.283	.289	.367
1994 South Bend	A ChA	97	355	101	14	2	3	128	43	36	10	0	40	3	4	5	1	2	.33	9	.285	.308	.361
1995 Pr William	A+ ChA	95	346	86	14	4	0	108	34	24	9	0	33	0	5	2	2	6	.25	18	.249	.266	.312
1996 Birmingham	AA ChA	25	81	19	3	0	0	22	7	6	2	0	13	0	1	0	0	0	.00	1	.235	.253	.272
Pr William	A+ ChA	72	276	64	7	3	2	83	26	26	15	0	34	0	5	4	2	4	.33	13	.232	.268	.301
1997 Birmingham	AA ChA	33	93	25	2	1	0	29	11	13	1	0	16	1	1	0	0	2	.00	1	.269	.284	.312
Nashville	AAA ChA	9	31	3	0	0	0	3	2	2	0	0	4	0	1	0	0	0	.00	1	.097	.097	.097
Winston-Sal	A+ ChA	41	149	37	7	0	0	44	14	11	2	0	16	1	1	0	6	1	.86	4	.248	.263	.295
7 Min. YEARS		526	1831	460	54	14	5	557	182	157	51	2	209	6	24	10	23	23	.50	63	.251	.272	.304

Cliff Politte

Pitches: Right **Bats:** Right **Pos:** P   **Ht:** 5'11" **Wt:** 185 **Born:** 2/27/74 **Age:** 24

Year Team	Lg Org	G	GS	CG	GF	IP	BFP	H	R	ER	HR	SH	SF	HB	TBB	IBB	SO	WP	Bk	W	L	Pct.	ShO	Sv	ERA
				HOW MUCH HE PITCHED						WHAT HE GAVE UP											THE RESULTS			
1996 Peoria	A StL	25	25	0	0	149.2	603	108	50	43	8	3	2	7	47	0	151	5	1	14	6	.700	0	0	2.59
1997 Pr William	A+ StL	19	19	0	0	120.1	475	89	37	30	11	0	3	2	31	0	118	2	2	11	1	.917	0	0	2.24
Arkansas	AA StL	6	6	0	0	37.2	152	35	15	9	3	6	1	0	9	1	26	0	0	4	1	.800	0	0	2.15
2 Min. YEARS		50	50	0	0	307.2	1230	232	102	82	22	9	6	9	87	1	295	7	3	29	8	.784	0	0	2.40

Dale Polley

Pitches: Left **Bats:** Right **Pos:** P
Ht: 6'0" **Wt:** 185 **Born:** 8/9/64 **Age:** 33

Year Team	Lg Org	G	GS	CG	GF	IP	BFP	H	R	ER	HR	SH	SF	HB	TBB	IBB	SO	WP	Bk	W	L	Pct.	ShO	Sv	ERA
1987 Pulaski	R+ Atl	13	1	0	8	25.2	103	18	7	5	1	0	1	0	9	0	37	1	0	0	2	.000	0	5	1.75
Sumter	A Atl	7	6	1	1	40.2	167	37	16	13	2	3	1	0	9	0	32	1	1	3	1	.750	1	0	2.88
1988 Greenville	AA Atl	36	16	0	10	128	531	102	56	45	18	5	3	1	49	0	67	4	2	9	6	.600	0	2	3.16
1989 Greenville	AA Atl	28	26	3	0	163.2	681	142	75	61	11	10	3	4	58	1	106	6	2	6	15	.286	2	0	3.35
1990 Richmond	AAA Atl	36	15	1	6	135	556	121	66	53	10	8	4	2	48	8	64	5	3	4	7	.364	1	0	3.53
1991 Richmond	AAA Atl	50	1	0	27	66.1	294	70	24	24	2	5	4	4	30	5	38	0	0	2	3	.400	0	4	3.26
1992 Richmond	AAA Atl	39	0	0	12	56.1	239	54	20	18	1	6	1	1	24	5	42	2	0	1	6	.143	0	2	2.88
1993 Greenville	AA Atl	42	0	0	18	59	238	44	28	27	8	3	0	3	21	2	66	2	1	8	1	.889	0	2	4.12
Richmond	AAA Atl	10	0	0	3	18.1	85	21	8	8	1	0	2	1	11	1	14	0	0	1	0	1.000	0	0	3.93
1995 Richmond	AAA Atl	47	0	0	22	63.1	261	51	15	11	2	2	3	2	20	5	60	2	0	3	2	.600	0	7	1.56
1996 Columbus	AAA NYA	31	0	0	6	31.2	130	29	11	11	1	0	0	0	9	0	29	2	0	2	2	.500	0	1	3.13
1997 Columbus	AAA NYA	62	0	0	13	68	202	47	20	20	2	1	3	3	20	1	49	2	0	2	2	.500	0	2	3.75
1996 New York	AL	32	0	0	9	21.2	103	23	20	19	5	1	1	3	11	1	14	0	0	1	3	.250	0	0	7.89
10 Min. YEARS		401	65	5	126	836	3487	736	347	296	59	43	25	21	308	28	604	27	9	41	47	.466	4	25	3.19

Sidney Ponson

Pitches: Right **Bats:** Right **Pos:** P
Ht: 6'1" **Wt:** 200 **Born:** 11/2/76 **Age:** 21

Year Team	Lg Org	G	GS	CG	GF	IP	BFP	H	R	ER	HR	SH	SF	HB	TBB	IBB	SO	WP	Bk	W	L	Pct.	ShO	Sv	ERA
1994 Orioles	R Bal	12	10	1	0	73	300	68	30	24	5	1	3	2	17	0	53	2	4	4	3	.571	0	0	2.96
1995 Bluefield	R+ Bal	13	13	0	0	77.2	324	79	44	36	7	1	2	1	16	0	56	4	3	6	3	.667	0	0	4.17
1996 Frederick	A+ Bal	18	16	3	2	107	443	98	56	41	6	3	4	5	28	0	110	6	3	7	6	.538	0	0	3.45
1997 Bowie	AA Bal	13	13	1	0	74.2	328	77	51	45	11	4	3	3	32	2	56	1	1	2	7	.222	1	0	5.42
Orioles	R Bal	1	0	0	0	2	6	0	0	0	0	0	0	0	0	0	0	0	0	1	0	1.000	0	0	0.00
4 Min. YEARS		57	52	5	2	334.1	1401	322	181	146	29	9	12	11	93	2	276	13	11	20	19	.513	1	0	3.93

Matt Pool

Pitches: Right **Bats:** Both **Pos:** P
Ht: 6'6" **Wt:** 190 **Born:** 7/8/73 **Age:** 24

Year Team	Lg Org	G	GS	CG	GF	IP	BFP	H	R	ER	HR	SH	SF	HB	TBB	IBB	SO	WP	Bk	W	L	Pct.	ShO	Sv	ERA
1994 Bend	A- Col	6	6	0	0	30.2	132	28	13	11	1	1	0	2	14	0	28	0	1	1	1	.500	0	0	3.23
Asheville	A Col	9	8	0	1	58	236	51	21	18	4	0	1	1	18	0	40	4	1	4	3	.571	0	1	2.79
1995 Salem	A+ Col	28	28	2	0	165	705	189	90	88	18	5	2	6	50	5	95	16	1	9	9	.500	0	0	4.80
1996 Salem	A+ Col	27	21	0	3	135.2	591	158	80	70	8	6	2	6	41	3	93	10	0	5	6	.455	0	0	4.64
New Haven	AA Col	4	0	0	3	6.2	30	9	2	2	1	0	2	1	7	1	0	0	1	.000		0	0	2.70
1997 New Haven	AA Col	29	1	0	0	48.1	217	57	36	23	9	2	1	1	16	3	23	2	0	3	5	.375	0	0	4.28
Orlando	AA ChN	9	8	1	0	47	207	47	28	24	6	4	3	1	21	1	38	6	0	4	2	.667	0	0	4.60
4 Min. YEARS		112	72	3	16	491.1	2118	541	270	236	46	19	9	19	161	12	324	39	3	26	27	.491	0	1	4.32

Bo Porter

Bats: Right **Throws:** Right **Pos:** OF
Ht: 6'1" **Wt:** 188 **Born:** 7/5/72 **Age:** 25

Year Team	Lg Org	G	AB	H	2B	3B	HR	TB	R	RBI	TBB	IBB	SO	HBP	SH	SF	SB	CS	SB%	GDP	Avg	OBP	SLG
1994 Peoria	A ChN	66	221	60	11	2	6	93	40	29	27	0	59	2	6	4	6	5	.55	5	.271	.350	.421
1995 Daytona	A+ ChN	113	336	73	12	2	3	98	54	19	32	0	104	2	4	3	22	10	.69	5	.217	.292	.292
1996 Daytona	A+ ChN	20	63	11	4	1	0	17	9	6	6	0	24	0	0	2	5	1	.83	0	.175	.239	.270
Rockford	A ChN	105	378	91	22	3	7	140	83	44	72	1	107	1	3	4	30	14	.68	7	.241	.360	.370
1997 Daytona	A+ ChN	122	440	135	20	6	17	218	87	65	61	1	115	3	1	3	23	13	.64	8	.307	.393	.495
Orlando	AA ChN	8	31	8	1	0	1	12	4	3	0	0	11	1	0	0	1	0	1.00	1	.258	.281	.387
4 Min. YEARS		434	1469	378	70	14	34	578	277	166	198	2	420	9	14	16	86	44	.66	26	.257	.346	.393

Dave Post

Bats: Right **Throws:** Right **Pos:** 2B
Ht: 5'11" **Wt:** 170 **Born:** 9/3/73 **Age:** 24

Year Team	Lg Org	G	AB	H	2B	3B	HR	TB	R	RBI	TBB	IBB	SO	HBP	SH	SF	SB	CS	SB%	GDP	Avg	OBP	SLG
1992 Great Falls	R+ LA	41	138	40	8	0	1	51	23	25	23	0	16	4	3	2	10	5	.67	4	.290	.401	.370
1993 Yakima	A- LA	60	210	53	8	1	1	66	34	22	35	1	27	4	3	3	7	4	.64	3	.252	.365	.314
1994 Bakersfield	A+ LA	31	106	25	5	1	0	32	16	9	13	0	9	3	0	0	6	4	.60	2	.236	.336	.302
Yakima	A- LA	70	263	77	14	1	1	96	46	27	56	3	42	5	1	5	18	5	.78	3	.293	.419	.365
1995 Vero Beach	A+ LA	52	114	27	2	1	0	31	16	11	23	0	11	2	3	1	3	0	1.00	5	.237	.371	.272
1996 Expos	R Mon	8	25	2	0	0	1	5	3	1	4	1	6	0	1	0	1	0	1.00	1	.080	.207	.200
Wst Plm Bch	A+ Mon	79	258	72	15	6	5	114	42	35	37	1	32	5	5	4	8	4	.67	6	.279	.375	.442
1997 Harrisburg	AA Mon	48	156	41	10	0	3	60	26	18	24	0	24	5	3	1	5	1	.83	1	.263	.376	.385
6 Min. YEARS		389	1270	337	62	10	12	455	206	148	215	6	167	28	19	16	58	23	.72	24	.265	.379	.358

Lou Pote

Pitches: Right **Bats:** Right **Pos:** P
Ht: 6'3" **Wt:** 190 **Born:** 8/27/71 **Age:** 26

Year Team	Lg Org	G	GS	CG	GF	IP	BFP	H	R	ER	HR	SH	SF	HB	TBB	IBB	SO	WP	Bk	W	L	Pct.	ShO	Sv	ERA
1991 Giants	R SF	8	8	0	0	42.1	184	38	23	12	0	0	1	0	18	0	41	5	0	2	3	.400	0	0	2.55
Everett	A- SF	5	4	0	0	28.2	117	24	8	8	2	0	1	2	7	0	26	2	0	2	0	1.000	0	0	2.51
1992 Shreveport	AA SF	20	3	0	9	37.2	146	20	7	4	1	3	1	1	15	2	26	3	0	4	2	.667	0	0	0.96
San Jose	A+ SF	4	3	0	1	9.2	46	11	5	5	0	1	1	0	7	0	8	3	0	0	1	.000	0	0	4.66

Year Team	Lg Org	G	GS	CG	GF	IP	BFP	H	R	ER	HR	SH	SF	HB	TBB	IBB	SO	WP	Bk	W	L	Pct.	ShO	Sv	ERA
1993 Shreveport	AA SF	19	19	0	0	108.1	458	111	53	49	10	1	3	0	45	1	81	3	1	8	7	.533	0	0	4.07
1994 Giants	R SF	4	4	0	0	19.2	73	9	0	0	0	1	0	0	6	0	30	0	0	1	0	1.000	0	0	0.00
Shreveport	AA SF	5	5	0	0	28.2	122	31	11	9	2	2	2	0	7	0	15	1	1	2	2	.500	0	0	2.83
1995 Shreveport	AA SF	28	0	0	11	50.2	226	53	41	30	8	4	1	0	26	1	30	4	0	2	2	.500	0	3	5.33
Harrisburg	AA Mon	9	4	0	2	28.1	123	32	17	17	3	0	2	1	7	0	24	1	0	0	1	.000	0	0	5.40
1996 Harrisburg	AA Mon	25	18	0	3	104.2	467	114	66	59	15	3	2	2	48	2	61	8	0	1	7	.125	0	1	5.07
1997 Arkansas	AA StL	7	3	0	1	23.1	94	15	10	4	1	1	2	0	8	0	21	2	0	0	0	.000	0	1	1.54
7 Min. YEARS		134	71	0	27	482	2056	458	241	197	42	16	14	6	194	6	363	32	2	22	25	.468	0	4	3.68

Chop Pough

Bats: Right Throws: Right Pos: 3B   Ht: 6'0" Wt: 173 Born: 12/25/69 Age: 28

Year Team	Lg Org	G	AB	H	2B	3B	HR	TB	R	RBI	TBB	IBB	SO	HBP	SH	SF	SB	CS	SB%	GDP	Avg	OBP	SLG
1988 Indians	R Cle	52	173	45	11	0	3	65	28	21	24	1	52	1	2	0	1	3	.25	3	.260	.354	.376
1989 Burlington	R+ Cle	67	225	58	15	1	8	99	39	37	36	0	64	3	0	2	9	5	.64	1	.258	.365	.440
1990 Reno	A+ Cle	16	53	8	0	1	0	10	1	2	6	1	18	0	0	0	0	1	.00	1	.151	.237	.189
Watertown	A- Cle	76	285	72	15	1	9	116	47	49	40	0	71	2	0	0	21	4	.84	7	.253	.344	.407
1991 Kinston	A+ Cle	11	30	5	1	0	0	6	2	2	1	0	9	1	0	0	1	0	1.00	1	.167	.219	.200
Columbus	A Cle	115	414	127	35	3	11	201	76	73	62	2	63	8	2	9	11	6	.65	6	.307	.400	.486
Colo Sprngs	AAA Cle	2	2	0	0	0	0	0	0	0	0	0	0	0	0	0	0	0	.00	0	.000	.000	.000
1992 Kinston	A+ Cle	114	411	93	23	1	11	151	59	58	50	1	98	6	4	5	12	3	.80	13	.226	.316	.367
1993 Kinston	A+ Cle	120	418	113	18	1	13	172	66	57	59	2	95	5	1	4	8	3	.73	8	.270	.364	.411
1994 Canton-Akrn	AA Cle	105	379	113	24	3	20	203	69	66	43	3	86	5	0	0	3	2	.60	9	.298	.372	.536
Charlotte	AAA Cle	16	42	9	4	0	0	13	1	4	6	0	13	0	0	1	0	0	.00	0	.214	.306	.310
1995 Trenton	AA Bos	97	363	101	23	5	21	197	68	69	50	8	101	7	0	4	11	5	.69	1	.278	.373	.543
Pawtucket	AAA Bos	30	99	23	8	1	5	48	12	23	7	1	27	1	0	1	0	0	.00	2	.232	.287	.485
1996 Pawtucket	AAA Bos	74	242	57	17	2	12	114	43	40	32	0	68	1	0	1	2	2	.50	7	.236	.326	.471
Jacksnville	AA Det	2	4	2	0	0	0	2	1	0	0	0	2	1	0	0	0	0	.00	0	.500	.600	.500
1997 Omaha	AAA KC	124	433	109	20	1	22	197	63	59	53	0	113	1	2	0	0	1	.00	15	.252	.335	.455
10 Min. YEARS		1021	3573	935	214	20	135	1594	575	560	469	19	880	42	11	37	79	35	.69	74	.262	.351	.446

John Powell

Pitches: Right Bats: Right Pos: P   Ht: 5'10" Wt: 180 Born: 4/7/71 Age: 27

Year Team	Lg Org	G	GS	CG	GF	IP	BFP	H	R	ER	HR	SH	SF	HB	TBB	IBB	SO	WP	Bk	W	L	Pct.	ShO	Sv	ERA
1994 Charlotte	A+ Tex	17	12	2	0	81.1	327	61	38	32	4	6	0	4	28	1	85	2	4	2	8	.200	0	0	3.54
1995 Tulsa	AA Tex	7	7	0	0	39.1	174	45	21	17	9	0	1	2	16	0	27	1	1	1	4	.200	0	0	3.89
Charlotte	A+ Tex	19	2	0	9	48	201	44	18	16	2	2	2	3	13	1	47	1	1	4	1	.800	0	2	3.00
1996 Tulsa	AA Tex	39	10	0	16	114	486	121	71	62	18	3	5	11	31	0	79	4	0	3	8	.273	0	4	4.89
1997 Okla City	AAA Tex	1	0	0	0	4	16	5	2	2	0	0	0	0	1	1	2	0	0	0	0	.000	0	0	4.50
Tulsa	AA Tex	43	0	0	34	63.1	265	54	22	18	8	2	4	2	23	2	56	2	1	4	3	.571	0	5	2.56
4 Min. YEARS		126	31	2	59	350	1469	330	172	147	41	13	12	22	112	5	296	10	7	14	24	.368	0	11	3.78

John Powers

Bats: Left Throws: Right Pos: 2B   Ht: 5'9" Wt: 165 Born: 6/2/74 Age: 24

Year Team	Lg Org	G	AB	H	2B	3B	HR	TB	R	RBI	TBB	IBB	SO	HBP	SH	SF	SB	CS	SB%	GDP	Avg	OBP	SLG
1996 Clinton	A SD	64	237	61	8	4	1	80	29	21	34	0	38	4	3	3	1	4	.20	5	.257	.356	.338
1997 Mobile	AA SD	14	48	12	0	0	1	15	8	8	8	0	9	2	0	2	2	0	1.00	1	.250	.367	.313
Rancho Cuca	A+ SD	107	402	102	28	5	10	170	77	44	63	0	90	11	5	3	7	8	.47	9	.254	.367	.423
2 Min. YEARS		185	687	175	36	9	12	265	114	73	105	0	137	17	8	8	10	12	.45	15	.255	.364	.386

Richard Pratt

Pitches: Left Bats: Left Pos: P   Ht: 6'3" Wt: 201 Born: 5/7/71 Age: 27

Year Team	Lg Org	G	GS	CG	GF	IP	BFP	H	R	ER	HR	SH	SF	HB	TBB	IBB	SO	WP	Bk	W	L	Pct.	ShO	Sv	ERA
1993 White Sox	R ChA	3	0	0	0	10	40	10	3	3	0	2	1	0	2	0	10	0	0	0	1	.000	0	0	2.70
Hickory	A ChA	13	4	0	6	44	193	36	23	18	3	1	1	7	24	1	29	1	1	1	4	.200	0	2	3.68
1994 Hickory	A ChA	29	23	3	0	165	661	138	51	37	9	5	4	3	24	0	153	1	1	11	6	.647	1	0	2.02
1995 Pr William	A+ ChA	25	25	2	0	152	619	139	66	53	12	2	5	4	42	0	120	10	2	5	11	.313	1	0	3.14
1996 Birmingham	AA ChA	27	27	5	0	177.1	732	180	87	76	24	3	7	6	40	2	122	5	1	13	9	.591	2	0	3.86
1997 Nashville	AAA ChA	29	24	2	1	149.1	649	165	89	76	22	3	5	8	50	1	71	6	7	9	8	.529	0	0	4.58
5 Min. YEARS		126	103	12	11	697.2	2894	668	319	263	70	16	23	28	187	4	505	23	12	39	39	.500	4	2	3.39

Gregg Press

Pitches: Right Bats: Right Pos: P   Ht: 6'3" Wt: 200 Born: 9/21/71 Age: 26

Year Team	Lg Org	G	GS	CG	GF	IP	BFP	H	R	ER	HR	SH	SF	HB	TBB	IBB	SO	WP	Bk	W	L	Pct.	ShO	Sv	ERA
1994 Elmira	A- Fla	14	12	0	0	64.2	293	77	30	26	3	4	4	2	17	1	56	7	2	3	4	.429	0	0	3.62
1995 Kane County	A Fla	29	21	0	1	132.1	571	127	72	53	8	5	3	5	37	1	82	10	0	10	8	.556	0	0	3.60
1996 Brevard Cty	A+ Fla	28	23	0	1	150.1	604	134	62	46	9	6	1	4	37	4	90	10	0	9	9	.500	0	0	2.75
1997 Charlotte	AAA Fla	1	1	0	0	6	25	5	3	3	1	0	0	0	4	0	2	0	0	0	0	.000	0	0	4.50
Portland	AA Fla	28	25	1	1	144.2	648	178	101	80	19	6	4	9	41	5	93	11	1	7	11	.389	0	0	4.98
4 Min. YEARS		100	82	1	3	498	2142	521	268	208	40	21	12	20	136	11	323	38	3	29	32	.475	0	0	3.76

Nick Presto

Bats: Right **Throws:** Right **Pos:** SS-2B   **Ht:** 5'10" **Wt:** 175 **Born:** 7/8/74 **Age:** 23

					BATTING											BASERUNNING				PERCENTAGES		
Year Team	Lg Org	G	AB	H	2B	3B	HR	TB	R	RBI	TBB	IBB	SO	HBP	SH	SF	SB	CS	SB%	GDP	Avg	OBP	SLG
1996 Princeton	R+ Cin	12	42	11	2	1	0	15	12	1	6	0	4	0	0	0	1	2	.33	1	.262	.354	.357
Billings	R+ Cin	4	16	2	0	0	0	2	2	1	2	0	6	0	0	1	0	1	.00	0	.125	.211	.125
1997 Chston-WV	A Cin	83	300	86	19	2	3	118	57	44	26	0	60	3	9	8	16	2	.89	0	.287	.341	.393
Chattanooga	AA Cin	9	31	7	1	0	0	8	2	6	2	0	7	1	0	1	1	0	1.00	1	.226	.286	.258
Burlington	A Cin	27	94	20	7	0	0	27	14	8	7	0	15	1	0	0	3	2	.60	1	.213	.275	.287
2 Min. YEARS		135	483	126	29	3	3	170	87	60	43	0	92	5	9	10	21	7	.75	3	.261	.322	.352

Corey Price

Bats: Both **Throws:** Right **Pos:** 2B   **Ht:** 6'0" **Wt:** 170 **Born:** 9/18/76 **Age:** 21

					BATTING											BASERUNNING				PERCENTAGES		
Year Team	Lg Org	G	AB	H	2B	3B	HR	TB	R	RBI	TBB	IBB	SO	HBP	SH	SF	SB	CS	SB%	GDP	Avg	OBP	SLG
1996 Billings	R+ Cin	49	131	25	3	0	0	28	18	16	24	0	32	0	3	2	2	2	.50	2	.191	.312	.214
1997 Chston-WV	A Cin	22	62	16	1	0	0	17	7	10	9	0	16	0	0	0	4	3	.57	2	.258	.352	.274
Chattanooga	AA Cin	1	3	1	0	0	0	1	0	1	0	0	1	0	0	0	0	0	.00	0	.333	.500	.333
Billings	R+ Cin	19	60	16	1	0	0	17	11	8	7	0	14	0	0	4	0	1	.00	1	.267	.324	.283
2 Min. YEARS		91	256	58	5	0	0	63	36	34	41	0	63	0	3	6	6	6	.50	5	.227	.327	.246

Jamey Price

Pitches: Right **Bats:** Left **Pos:** P   **Ht:** 6'7" **Wt:** 205 **Born:** 2/11/72 **Age:** 26

		HOW MUCH HE PITCHED					WHAT HE GAVE UP										THE RESULTS				
Year Team	Lg Org	G	GS	CG	GF	IP	BFP	H	R	ER	HR	SH	SF	HB	TBB	IBB	SO	WP	Bk	W	L	Pct.	ShO	Sv	ERA
1996 W Michigan	A Oak	20	16	0	1	89.1	360	80	22	17	1	0	2	1	19	1	88	2	1	6	1	.857	0	0	1.71
1997 Huntsville	AA Oak	20	20	0	0	110.1	502	153	71	65	16	1	0	3	38	0	80	2	0	9	3	.750	0	0	5.30
Edmonton	AAA Oak	2	1	0	1	11	44	9	3	2	0	1	0	0	1	0	10	0	0	2	0	1.000	0	0	1.64
2 Min. YEARS		42	37	0	2	210.2	906	242	96	84	17	2	2	4	58	1	178	4	1	17	4	.810	0	0	3.59

Tom Price

Pitches: Left **Bats:** Left **Pos:** P   **Ht:** 6'0" **Wt:** 190 **Born:** 3/19/72 **Age:** 26

		HOW MUCH HE PITCHED					WHAT HE GAVE UP										THE RESULTS				
Year Team	Lg Org	G	GS	CG	GF	IP	BFP	H	R	ER	HR	SH	SF	HB	TBB	IBB	SO	WP	Bk	W	L	Pct.	ShO	Sv	ERA
1994 Great Falls	R+ LA	19	0	0	10	38	164	40	20	13	3	2	5	2	9	2	22	5	0	3	4	.429	0	0	3.08
1995 San Berndno	A+ LA	42	13	2	9	151.2	605	145	49	37	5	5	1	3	14	4	82	5	0	10	5	.667	0	3	2.20
1996 San Antonio	AA LA	7	5	0	0	25	125	50	30	26	5	1	1	0	3	0	11	2	0	0	4	.000	0	0	9.36
San Berndno	A+ LA	15	11	1	1	82	344	94	42	35	8	5	1	3	5	0	60	1	0	5	3	.625	0	0	3.84
1997 New Haven	AA Col	48	1	0	18	57	246	55	25	20	6	5	3	3	21	2	48	1	0	1	3	.250	0	3	3.16
4 Min. YEARS		131	30	3	38	353.2	1484	384	166	131	27	18	11	11	52	8	223	14	0	19	19	.500	0	3	3.33

Eddie Priest

Pitches: Left **Bats:** Right **Pos:** P   **Ht:** 6'1" **Wt:** 200 **Born:** 4/8/74 **Age:** 24

		HOW MUCH HE PITCHED					WHAT HE GAVE UP										THE RESULTS				
Year Team	Lg Org	G	GS	CG	GF	IP	BFP	H	R	ER	HR	SH	SF	HB	TBB	IBB	SO	WP	Bk	W	L	Pct.	ShO	Sv	ERA
1994 Billings	R+ Cin	13	13	2	0	85	333	74	31	24	3	1	0	1	14	0	82	2	1	7	4	.636	0	0	2.54
1995 Winston-Sal	A+ Cin	12	12	1	0	67	275	60	32	27	7	2	2	0	22	0	60	2	0	5	5	.500	1	0	3.63
1996 Winston-Sal	A+ Cin	4	4	0	0	12.1	48	5	2	1	1	0	0	0	6	0	9	1	0	1	0	1.000	0	0	0.73
1997 Chston-WV	A Cin	14	14	0	0	77	321	79	38	31	6	2	3	2	10	0	70	5	0	5	3	.625	0	0	3.62
Chattanooga	AA Cin	14	14	1	0	91.2	379	101	39	35	7	2	2	0	17	1	63	3	1	4	6	.400	0	0	3.44
4 Min. YEARS		57	57	4	0	333	1356	319	142	118	24	7	7	3	69	1	284	13	2	22	18	.550	1	0	3.19

Chris Prieto

Bats: Left **Throws:** Left **Pos:** OF   **Ht:** 5'11" **Wt:** 180 **Born:** 8/24/72 **Age:** 25

					BATTING											BASERUNNING				PERCENTAGES		
Year Team	Lg Org	G	AB	H	2B	3B	HR	TB	R	RBI	TBB	IBB	SO	HBP	SH	SF	SB	CS	SB%	GDP	Avg	OBP	SLG
1993 Spokane	A- SD	73	280	81	17	5	1	111	64	28	47	0	30	5	0	3	36	3	.92	4	.289	.397	.396
1994 Rancho Cuca	A+ SD	102	354	87	10	3	1	106	64	29	52	1	49	5	6	4	29	11	.73	3	.246	.348	.300
1995 Rancho Cuca	A+ SD	114	366	100	12	6	2	130	80	35	64	2	55	5	8	5	39	14	.74	10	.273	.384	.355
1996 Rancho Cuca	A+ SD	55	217	52	11	2	2	73	36	23	39	1	36	0	1	0	23	8	.74	2	.240	.355	.336
Las Vegas	AAA SD	5	7	0	0	0	0	0	1	0	0	0	0	0	0	0	0	0	.00	0	.000	.000	.000
Memphis	AA SD	7	12	4	0	1	0	6	1	0	1	0	2	0	0	0	2	0	1.00	0	.333	.385	.500
1997 Rancho Cuca	A+ SD	22	82	23	4	0	4	39	21	12	19	1	16	0	3	0	4	3	.57	0	.280	.416	.476
Mobile	AA SD	109	388	124	22	9	2	170	80	58	59	0	55	10	1	5	26	6	.81	2	.320	.418	.438
5 Min. YEARS		487	1705	471	76	26	12	635	347	185	281	5	243	25	19	17	159	45	.78	21	.276	.383	.372

Steve Prihoda

Pitches: Left **Bats:** Right **Pos:** P   **Ht:** 6'6" **Wt:** 220 **Born:** 12/7/72 **Age:** 25

		HOW MUCH HE PITCHED					WHAT HE GAVE UP										THE RESULTS				
Year Team	Lg Org	G	GS	CG	GF	IP	BFP	H	R	ER	HR	SH	SF	HB	TBB	IBB	SO	WP	Bk	W	L	Pct.	ShO	Sv	ERA
1995 Spokane	A- KC	14	13	1	0	69.1	293	65	36	25	7	3	1	5	18	0	63	4	0	1	6	.143	0	0	3.25
1996 Wilmington	A+ KC	47	0	0	40	79.1	313	50	17	13	1	6	1	3	22	4	89	3	0	6	6	.500	0	25	1.47
1997 Wichita	AA KC	70	0	0	32	89	391	87	34	32	3	9	1	4	40	8	68	3	1	0	3	.000	0	10	3.24
3 Min. YEARS		131	13	1	72	237.2	997	202	87	70	11	18	3	12	80	12	220	10	1	7	15	.318	0	35	2.65

Chris Pritchett

Bats: Left Throws: Right Pos: 1B Ht: 6' 4" Wt: 185 Born: 1/31/70 Age: 28

Year Team	Lg Org	G	AB	H	2B	3B	HR	TB	R	RBI	TBB	IBB	SO	HBP	SH	SF	SB	CS	SB%	GDP	Avg	OBP	SLG
1991 Boise	A- Ana	70	255	68	10	3	9	111	41	50	47	3	41	2	0	3	1	0	1.00	7	.267	.381	.435
1992 Quad City	A Ana	128	448	130	19	1	13	190	79	72	71	6	88	5	2	5	9	4	.69	7	.290	.389	.424
1993 Midland	AA Ana	127	464	143	30	6	2	191	61	66	61	2	72	2	6	7	3	7	.30	17	.308	.386	.412
1994 Midland	AA Ana	127	460	142	25	4	6	193	86	91	92	9	87	2	3	7	5	3	.63	8	.309	.421	.420
1995 Vancouver	AAA Ana	123	434	120	27	4	8	179	66	53	56	6	79	5	2	1	2	3	.40	7	.276	.365	.412
1996 Vancouver	AAA Ana	130	485	143	39	1	16	232	78	73	71	11	96	6	0	6	5	4	.56	7	.295	.387	.478
1997 Vancouver	AAA Ana	109	383	107	30	3	7	164	60	47	42	6	72	5	5	2	5	3	.63	9	.279	.356	.428
1996 California	AL	5	13	2	0	0	0	2	1	1	0	0	3	0	0	0	0	0	.00	0	.154	.154	.154
7 Min. YEARS		814	2929	853	180	22	61	1260	471	452	440	43	535	27	18	31	30	24	.56	62	.291	.385	.430

Alan Probst

Bats: Right Throws: Right Pos: C Ht: 6'4" Wt: 205 Born: 10/24/70 Age: 27

Year Team	Lg Org	G	AB	H	2B	3B	HR	TB	R	RBI	TBB	IBB	SO	HBP	SH	SF	SB	CS	SB%	GDP	Avg	OBP	SLG
1992 Auburn	A- Hou	66	224	53	14	1	5	84	24	34	23	1	48	3	1	2	1	0	1.00	5	.237	.313	.375
1993 Asheville	A Hou	40	124	32	4	0	5	51	14	21	12	0	34	0	0	1	0	2	.00	5	.258	.321	.411
Quad City	A Hou	49	176	48	9	2	3	70	18	28	16	1	48	3	0	2	2	0	1.00	1	.273	.338	.398
1994 Quad City	A Hou	113	375	87	14	1	9	130	50	41	37	3	98	2	3	3	2	0	1.00	3	.232	.302	.347
1995 Quad City	A Hou	52	151	39	12	1	7	74	23	27	13	0	28	1	1	1	2	0	1.00	8	.258	.319	.490
Jackson	AA Hou	28	89	21	5	0	1	29	11	8	7	0	25	1	0	2	0	0	.00	3	.236	.293	.326
1996 Tucson	AAA Hou	2	7	2	1	0	0	3	0	1	1	0	3	0	0	0	0	0	.00	0	.286	.375	.429
Jackson	AA Hou	63	180	44	9	1	7	76	20	33	16	1	43	2	2	2	1	0	1.00	1	.244	.310	.422
1997 Jackson	AA Hou	8	24	8	2	0	1	13	2	7	3	0	7	0	0	0	0	0	.00	1	.333	.407	.542
New Orleans	AAA Hou	46	112	25	6	0	2	37	8	10	9	0	27	0	1	2	0	0	.00	4	.223	.276	.330
6 Min. YEARS		467	1462	359	76	6	40	567	170	210	137	6	361	12	8	16	8	7	.53	30	.246	.312	.388

Carlos Pulido

Pitches: Left Bats: Left Pos: P Ht: 6' 0" Wt: 200 Born: 8/5/71 Age: 26

Year Team	Lg Org	G	GS	CG	GF	IP	BFP	H	R	ER	HR	SH	SF	HB	TBB	IBB	SO	WP	Bk	W	L	Pct.	ShO	Sv	ERA
1989 Twins	R Min	22	0	0	11	36	143	22	9	9	0	0	2	3	14	0	46	6	3	3	0	1.000	0	2	2.25
1990 Kenosha	A Min	56	0	0	29	61.2	270	55	21	16	2	2	1	4	36	3	70	3	4	5	5	.500	0	6	2.34
1991 Visalia	A+ Min	57	0	0	32	80.2	334	77	34	18	2	5	2	0	23	2	102	3	1	1	5	.167	0	17	2.01
Portland	AAA Min	2	0	0	2	1.2	10	4	3	3	1	0	0	0	1	0	2	0	0	0	0	.000	0	0	16.20
1992 Orlando	AA Min	52	5	0	20	100.1	432	99	52	49	7	1	6	3	37	0	87	4	1	6	2	.750	0	1	4.40
1993 Portland	AAA Min	33	22	1	5	146	625	169	74	68	8	3	4	2	45	1	79	8	1	10	6	.625	0	0	4.19
1995 Salt Lake	AAA Min	43	3	0	9	71.1	321	87	42	37	10	1	0	2	20	4	38	0	1	8	1	.889	0	3	4.67
1996 Iowa	AAA ChN	28	17	0	3	101.2	461	133	64	60	17	6	3	3	36	3	48	5	1	2	8	.200	0	0	5.31
Orlando	AA ChN	6	0	0	1	9.2	50	17	9	8	0	0	0	0	3	0	12	3	0	2	2	.500	0	0	7.45
1997 Ottawa	AAA Mon	44	5	0	17	76.1	333	84	47	46	10	0	2	2	25	2	44	2	0	5	2	.714	0	0	5.42
1994 Minnesota	AL	19	14	0	1	84.1	366	87	57	56	17	2	4	1	40	1	32	3	2	3	7	.300	0	0	5.98
8 Min. YEARS		343	52	1	129	685.1	2979	747	355	314	57	18	20	19	240	15	528	34	12	42	31	.575	0	29	4.12

Bill Pulsipher

Pitches: Left Bats: Left Pos: P Ht: 6' 3" Wt: 208 Born: 10/9/73 Age: 24

Year Team	Lg Org	G	GS	CG	GF	IP	BFP	H	R	ER	HR	SH	SF	HB	TBB	IBB	SO	WP	Bk	W	L	Pct.	ShO	Sv	ERA
1992 Pittsfield	A- NYN	14	14	0	0	95	413	88	40	30	3	0	1	3	56	0	83	16	1	6	3	.667	0	0	2.84
1993 Capital Cty	A NYN	6	6	1	0	43.1	175	34	17	10	1	2	0	1	12	0	29	1	1	2	3	.400	0	0	2.08
St. Lucie	A+ NYN	13	13	6	0	96.1	374	63	27	24	2	3	1	0	39	0	102	3	1	7	3	.700	1	0	2.24
1994 Binghamton	AA NYN	28	28	5	0	201	849	179	90	72	18	7	1	3	89	2	171	9	5	14	9	.609	1	0	3.22
1995 Norfolk	AAA NYN	13	13	4	0	91.2	377	84	36	32	3	5	3	1	33	0	63	2	3	6	4	.600	2	0	3.14
1997 Norfolk	AAA NYN	8	5	0	1	27.2	142	23	29	24	1	3	0	1	38	0	18	5	1	0	5	.000	0	0	7.81
Mets	R NYN	2	2	0	0	5	18	3	1	1	0	0	0	0	1	0	4	0	0	0	0	.000	0	0	1.80
St. Lucie	A+ NYN	12	7	0	2	36.2	178	29	27	24	1	2	1	4	35	0	35	14	5	1	4	.200	0	0	5.89
Binghamton	AA NYN	10	0	0	1	12.2	55	11	3	2	0	2	0	0	7	1	12	0	0	0	0	.000	0	0	1.42
1995 New York	NL	17	17	2	0	126.2	530	122	58	56	11	2	1	4	45	0	81	2	1	5	7	.417	0	0	3.98
5 Min. YEARS		106	88	13	7	609.1	2581	514	270	219	29	24	7	13	310	3	517	50	17	36	31	.537	4	0	3.23

Shawn Purdy

Pitches: Right Bats: Right Pos: P Ht: 6'0" Wt: 205 Born: 7/30/68 Age: 29

Year Team	Lg Org	G	GS	CG	GF	IP	BFP	H	R	ER	HR	SH	SF	HB	TBB	IBB	SO	WP	Bk	W	L	Pct.	ShO	Sv	ERA
1991 Boise	A- Ana	15	15	1	0	95.2	394	87	37	32	3	3	2	4	27	2	78	6	0	8	4	.667	0	0	3.01
1992 Palm Spring	A+ Ana	26	26	7	0	168	740	203	90	77	7	2	7	5	51	3	113	5	3	13	8	.619	0	0	4.13
1993 Angels	R Ana	2	2	0	0	13	49	7	3	3	0	0	0	1	1	0	11	0	0	1	0	1.000	0	0	2.08
Boise	A- Ana	1	1	0	0	6	25	2	2	0	0	0	1	0	5	2	1	0	0	1	0	1.000	0	0	0.00
Palm Spring	A+ Ana	5	3	0	2	27	120	30	12	11	2	1	0	3	5	2	17	1	0	1	1	.500	0	1	3.67
Midland	AA Ana	5	5	1	0	32	136	38	19	18	2	1	2	1	9	0	18	2	0	2	2	.500	0	0	5.06
1994 Midland	AA Ana	10	5	0	1	36	170	48	39	35	2	2	2	2	15	1	19	6	1	0	0	.000	0	0	8.75
Lk Elsinore	A+ Ana	25	11	1	6	117.2	493	113	63	49	8	7	3	10	30	0	76	5	2	7	6	.143	0	0	3.75
1995 Shreveport	AA SF	52	1	0	40	62.1	260	61	31	26	7	1	3	1	18	2	33	3	0	6	3	.667	0	21	3.75
1996 Shreveport	AA SF	54	0	0	37	52.1	218	46	23	18	3	4	1	1	16	4	23	4	0	5	4	.556	0	16	3.10

		HOW MUCH HE PITCHED		WHAT HE GAVE UP		THE RESULTS	
Year Team	Lg Org	G GS CG GF	IP BFP	H R ER HR SH SF HB	TBB IBB SO WP Bk	W L Pct ShO Sv	ERA
1997 Phoenix	AAA SF	56 0 0 26	82.1 367	103 45 40 8 4 0 2	33 1 42 3 1	10 3 .769 0 2	4.37
7 Min. YEARS		251 69 10 112	692.1 2972	738 364 309 42 25 21 30	210 17 431 35 7	55 36 .604 0 40	4.02

Dave Pyc

Pitches: Left Bats: Left Pos: P   Ht: 6'3" Wt: 235 Born: 2/11/71 Age: 27

		HOW MUCH HE PITCHED		WHAT HE GAVE UP		THE RESULTS	
Year Team	Lg Org	G GS CG GF	IP BFP	H R ER HR SH SF HB	TBB IBB SO WP Bk	W L Pct ShO Sv	ERA
1992 Great Falls	R+ LA	25 0 0 19	34.2 155	32 15 11 0 3 1 1	16 5 34 1 0	2 3 .400 0 0	2.86
1993 Vero Beach	A+ LA	23 15 1 2	113.1 469	97 41 30 1 6 3 1	47 2 78 5 4	7 8 .467 0 0	2.38
1994 San Antonio	AA LA	25 25 0 0	154.2 656	165 77 64 2 9 4 3	47 5 120 3 0	4 11 .267 0 0	3.72
1995 San Antonio	AA LA	26 26 1 0	157 676	170 72 59 6 6 4 3	49 1 78 3 1	12 6 .667 0 0	3.38
Albuquerque	AAA LA	1 1 0 0	7 31	7 5 3 1 0 1 0	2 1 3 0 0	0 1 .000 0 0	3.86
1996 Albuquerque	AAA LA	13 4 0 2	35.1 179	53 39 36 4 1 1 5	19 3 27 2 0	2 3 .400 0 0	9.17
San Antonio	AA LA	14 14 1 0	96.2 415	106 45 32 5 10 1 2	24 0 62 4 0	7 5 .583 1 0	2.98
1997 Albuquerque	AAA LA	31 23 3 1	152 675	181 104 90 18 4 6 5	50 2 106 5 1	12 12 .500 2 1	5.33
6 Min. YEARS		158 108 6 24	750.2 3256	811 398 325 37 39 21 20	254 19 508 23 6	46 49 .484 3 10	3.90

Eddie Pye

Bats: Right Throws: Right Pos: DH   Ht: 5'10" Wt: 183 Born: 2/13/67 Age: 31

		BATTING														BASERUNNING				PERCENTAGES		
Year Team	Lg Org	G	AB	H	2B	3B	HR	TB	R	RBI	TBB	IBB	SO	HBP	SH	SF	SB	CS	SB%	GDP	Avg	OBP	SLG
1988 Great Falls	R+ LA	61	237	71	8	4	2	93	50	30	29	0	26	4	2	1	19	9	.68	6	.300	.384	.392
1989 Bakersfield	A+ LA	129	488	126	21	2	8	175	59	47	41	1	87	6	3	5	19	9	.68	6	.258	.323	.359
1990 San Antonio	AA LA	119	455	113	18	7	2	151	67	44	45	1	68	6	3	5	19	6	.76	7	.248	.321	.332
1991 Albuquerque	AAA LA	12	30	13	1	0	1	17	4	8	4	0	4	0	1	0	1	2	.33	0	.433	.500	.567
1992 Albuquerque	AAA LA	72	222	67	11	2	1	85	30	25	13	0	41	2	5	2	6	4	.60	4	.302	.343	.383
1993 Albuquerque	AAA LA	101	365	120	21	7	7	176	53	66	32	0	43	7	4	3	5	9	.36	13	.329	.391	.482
1994 Albuquerque	AAA LA	100	361	121	19	6	2	158	79	42	48	2	43	7	2	4	11	6	.65	5	.335	.419	.438
1995 Albuquerque	AAA LA	84	302	89	20	1	3	120	49	32	30	2	36	1	2	2	11	2	.85	7	.295	.358	.397
1996 Tucson	AAA Hou	92	275	71	15	6	2	104	39	25	29	2	41	1	2	3	5	3	.63	8	.258	.328	.378
1997 Norfolk	AAA NYN	3	12	1	0	0	0	1	3	0	4	0	2	0	0	0	0	0	.00	1	.083	.313	.083
1994 Los Angeles	NL	7	10	1	0	0	0	1	2	0	1	0	4	0	1	0	0	0	.00	0	.100	.182	.100
1995 Los Angeles	NL	7	8	0	0	0	0	0	0	0	0	0	4	0	0	0	0	0	.00	0	.000	.000	.000
10 Min. YEARS		773	2747	792	134	35	28	1080	433	319	275	8	391	34	24	20	96	50	.66	57	.288	.358	.393
2 Maj. YEARS		14	18	1	0	0	0	1	2	0	1	0	8	0	1	0	0	0	.00	0	.056	.105	.056

Tom Quinlan

Bats: Right Throws: Right Pos: 3B   Ht: 6'3" Wt: 214 Born: 3/27/68 Age: 30

		BATTING														BASERUNNING				PERCENTAGES		
Year Team	Lg Org	G	AB	H	2B	3B	HR	TB	R	RBI	TBB	IBB	SO	HBP	SH	SF	SB	CS	SB%	GDP	Avg	OBP	SLG
1987 Myrtle Bch	A Tor	132	435	97	20	3	5	138	42	51	34	0	130	6	3	6	0	2	.00	4	.223	.285	.317
1988 Knoxville	AA Tor	98	326	71	19	1	8	116	33	47	35	1	99	5	3	2	4	9	.31	5	.218	.302	.356
1989 Knoxville	AA Tor	139	452	95	21	3	16	170	62	57	41	0	118	9	3	4	6	4	.60	11	.210	.287	.376
1990 Knoxville	AA Tor	141	481	124	24	6	15	205	70	51	49	2	157	14	7	1	8	9	.47	5	.258	.343	.426
1991 Syracuse	AAA Tor	132	466	112	24	6	10	178	56	49	72	3	163	5	3	2	9	4	.69	7	.240	.347	.382
1992 Syracuse	AAA Tor	107	349	75	17	1	6	112	43	36	43	0	112	10	1	2	3	1	.25	11	.215	.317	.321
1993 Syracuse	AAA Tor	141	461	109	20	5	16	187	63	53	56	2	156	19	2	6	6	1	.86	9	.236	.339	.406
1994 Scranton-WB	AAA Phi	76	262	63	12	2	9	106	38	23	28	0	91	4	1	1	4	2	.67	7	.240	.322	.405
1995 Salt Lake	AAA Min	130	466	130	22	6	17	215	78	88	39	2	124	15	1	6	6	3	.67	12	.279	.350	.461
1996 Salt Lake	AAA Min	121	491	139	38	1	15	224	81	81	38	2	121	15	0	8	4	8	.33	8	.283	.348	.456
1997 Colo Spmgs	AAA Col	134	509	145	36	2	23	254	85	113	50	4	117	12	1	8	1	1	.50	15	.285	.358	.499
1990 Toronto	AL	1	2	1	0	0	0	1	0	0	0	0	1	1	0	0	0	0	.00	0	.500	.667	.500
1992 Toronto	AL	13	15	1	1	0	0	2	2	2	2	0	9	0	0	0	0	0	.00	0	.067	.176	.133
1994 Philadelphia	NL	24	35	7	2	0	1	12	6	3	3	1	13	0	1	0	0	0	.00	0	.200	.263	.343
1996 Minnesota	AL	4	6	0	0	0	0	0	0	0	0	0	3	0	0	0	0	0	.00	0	.000	.000	.000
11 Min. YEARS		1351	4698	1160	253	36	140	1905	651	649	485	16	1388	114	25	46	49	46	.52	92	.247	.329	.405
4 Maj. YEARS		42	58	9	3	0	1	15	8	5	5	1	26	1	1	0	0	0	.00	0	.155	.234	.259

Mark Quinn

Bats: Right Throws: Right Pos: OF   Ht: 6'1" Wt: 185 Born: 5/21/74 Age: 24

		BATTING														BASERUNNING				PERCENTAGES		
Year Team	Lg Org	G	AB	H	2B	3B	HR	TB	R	RBI	TBB	IBB	SO	HBP	SH	SF	SB	CS	SB%	GDP	Avg	OBP	SLG
1995 Spokane	A- KC	44	162	46	12	2	6	80	28	37	15	0	28	5	0	3	0	1	.00	5	.284	.357	.494
1996 Lansing	A KC	113	437	132	23	3	9	188	63	71	43	2	54	5	0	6	14	8	.64	12	.302	.367	.430
1997 Wilmington	A+ KC	87	299	92	22	3	16	168	51	71	42	4	47	8	0	6	3	2	.60	10	.308	.400	.562
Wichita	AA KC	26	96	36	13	0	2	55	26	19	15	0	19	3	0	0	1	1	.50	2	.375	.474	.573
3 Min. YEARS		270	994	306	70	8	33	491	168	198	115	6	148	21	0	15	18	12	.60	29	.308	.386	.494

Rafael Quirico

Pitches: Left Bats: Left Pos: P   Ht: 6'2" Wt: 212 Born: 9/7/69 Age: 28

Year Team	Lg Org	G	GS	CG	GF	IP	BFP	H	R	ER	HR	SH	SF	HB	TBB	IBB	SO	WP	Bk	W	L	Pct.	ShO	Sv	ERA
1989 Yankees	R NYA	17	7	0	1	63.2	268	61	32	27	2	1	3	3	20	0	55	0	8	2	2	.500	0	1	3.82
1990 Greensboro	A NYA	13	13	1	0	72	325	74	60	40	4	1	2	3	30	0	52	5	10	2	6	.250	0	0	5.00
Oneonta	A- NYA	14	14	1	0	87	359	69	38	31	2	2	4	4	39	0	69	9	9	6	3	.667	0	0	3.21
1991 Greensboro	A NYA	26	26	1	0	155.1	641	103	59	39	5	1	2	7	80	0	162	12	9	12	8	.600	1	0	2.26
1992 Pr William	A+ NYA	23	23	2	0	130.2	570	128	84	46	11	8	1	1	50	1	123	7	7	6	11	.353	0	0	3.17
Columbus	AAA NYA	1	1	0	0	6	27	6	3	2	0	0	0	0	4	0	1	1	0	1	0	1.000	0	0	3.00
1993 Albany-Colo	AA NYA	36	11	0	15	94.2	403	92	46	37	15	5	1	1	33	2	79	6	1	4	10	.286	0	7	3.52
Columbus	AAA NYA	5	2	0	0	11	53	12	10	9	3	0	0	0	7	0	16	1	0	2	0	1.000	0	0	7.36
1994 Columbus	AAA NYA	37	0	0	12	63.2	289	63	41	33	6	1	2	3	36	1	49	9	1	0	4	.000	0	1	4.66
1995 Columbus	AAA NYA	20	0	0	8	23	96	15	14	12	1	0	1	3	14	0	21	5	2	0	0	.000	0	0	4.70
1996 Clearwater	A+ Phi	2	2	0	0	10.1	45	13	9	9	2	0	0	1	1	0	12	0	4	1	0	1.000	0	0	7.84
Reading	AA Phi	5	5	0	0	30	124	22	6	6	2	0	2	2	11	1	23	0	1	1	0	1.000	0	0	1.80
Scranton-WB	AAA Phi	13	13	1	0	65	273	48	29	24	8	3	1	7	26	0	51	3	1	4	4	.500	0	0	3.32
Norwich	AA NYA	4	0	0	4	6.2	37	5	3	3	1	0	0	0	3	0	9	1	0	1	0	1.000	0	0	4.05
1997 Midland	AA Ana	20	5	0	4	54.2	255	73	47	42	8	2	1	4	22	0	37	2	3	3	3	.500	0	0	6.91
Lk Elsinore	A+ Ana	14	13	0	0	92.1	399	94	43	29	5	4	5	7	29	0	74	5	2	8	4	.667	0	0	2.83
1996 Philadelphia	NL	1	1	0	0	1.2	14	4	7	7	1	0	0	0	5	0	1	0	1	1	0	.000	0	0	37.80
9 Min. YEARS		250	135	6	44	966	4154	878	524	389	75	28	25	46	405	5	833	66	58	53	55	.491	1	9	3.62

Ryan Radmanovich

Bats: Left Throws: Right Pos: OF   Ht: 6'2" Wt: 185 Born: 8/9/71 Age: 26

Year Team	Lg Org	G	AB	H	2B	3B	HR	TB	R	RBI	TBB	IBB	SO	HBP	SH	SF	SB	CS	SB%	GDP	Avg	OBP	SLG
1993 Ft. Wayne	A Min	62	204	59	7	5	8	100	36	38	30	2	60	7	2	2	8	2	.80	4	.289	.395	.490
1994 Ft. Myers	A+ Min	26	85	16	4	0	2	26	11	9	7	0	19	2	0	0	3	1	.75	0	.188	.266	.306
Ft. Wayne	A Min	101	383	105	20	6	19	194	64	69	45	3	98	3	1	1	19	14	.58	7	.274	.354	.507
1995 Ft. Myers	A+ Min	12	41	13	2	0	0	15	3	5	2	0	8	1	0	0	0	0	.00	0	.317	.364	.366
1996 Hardware City	AA Min	125	453	127	31	2	25	237	77	86	49	6	122	3	3	2	4	11	.27	12	.280	.353	.523
1997 Salt Lake	AAA Min	133	485	128	25	4	28	245	92	78	67	7	138	4	1	5	11	4	.73	4	.264	.355	.505
5 Min. YEARS		459	1651	448	89	17	82	817	283	285	200	18	445	20	7	10	45	32	.58	27	.271	.355	.495

Steve Rain

Pitches: Right Bats: Right Pos: P   Ht: 6'6" Wt: 225 Born: 6/2/75 Age: 23

Year Team	Lg Org	G	GS	CG	GF	IP	BFP	H	R	ER	HR	SH	SF	HB	TBB	IBB	SO	WP	Bk	W	L	Pct.	ShO	Sv	ERA
1993 Cubs	R ChN	10	6	0	3	37	162	37	20	16	0	1	1	2	17	0	29	5	1	1	3	.250	0	0	3.89
1994 Huntington	R+ ChN	14	10	1	1	68	272	55	26	20	2	2	2	2	19	0	55	4	4	3	3	.500	1	0	2.65
1995 Rockford	A ChN	53	0	0	51	59.1	234	38	12	8	0	3	2	2	23	3	66	8	0	5	2	.714	0	23	1.21
1996 Orlando	AA ChN	35	0	0	29	38.2	163	32	15	11	4	0	3	1	12	1	48	2	1	1	0	1.000	0	10	2.56
Iowa	AAA ChN	26	0	0	26	26	103	17	9	9	3	3	3	0	8	3	23	1	0	2	1	.667	0	10	3.12
1997 Iowa	AAA ChN	40	0	0	17	44.1	217	51	30	29	8	2	1	0	34	4	50	4	1	7	1	.875	0	1	5.89
Orlando	AA ChN	14	0	0	12	14.2	69	16	7	5	2	0	0	1	8	0	11	0	0	1	2	.333	0	4	3.07
5 Min. YEARS		192	16	1	139	288	1220	246	119	98	19	11	9	10	121	11	282	24	7	20	12	.625	1	48	3.06

Jason Rajotte

Pitches: Left Bats: Left Pos: P   Ht: 6'0" Wt: 185 Born: 12/15/72 Age: 25

Year Team	Lg Org	G	GS	CG	GF	IP	BFP	H	R	ER	HR	SH	SF	HB	TBB	IBB	SO	WP	Bk	W	L	Pct.	ShO	Sv	ERA
1993 Sou. Oregon	A- Oak	9	0	0	1	14.1	71	15	15	10	0	2	1	9	2	14	2	0	0	1	.000	0	0	6.28
1994 W Michigan	A Oak	36	0	0	23	47.2	208	47	28	22	0	2	1	1	20	6	31	2	1	0	4	.000	0	7	4.15
1995 W Michigan	A Oak	44	0	0	37	52	242	51	27	18	1	3	1	3	38	3	52	3	0	2	2	.500	0	13	3.12
1996 Modesto	A+ Oak	47	0	0	29	75	295	50	24	21	4	1	0	2	28	2	57	1	0	3	6	.333	0	7	2.52
1997 Huntsville	AA Oak	55	0	0	21	57.1	264	67	35	28	5	3	8	1	29	4	35	3	0	2	6	.250	0	3	4.40
5 Min. YEARS		191	0	0	111	246.1	1080	230	129	99	12	9	12	8	124	17	189	11	1	7	19	.269	0	30	3.62

Jason Rakers

Pitches: Right Bats: Right Pos: P   Ht: 6'2" Wt: 197 Born: 6/29/73 Age: 25

Year Team	Lg Org	G	GS	CG	GF	IP	BFP	H	R	ER	HR	SH	SF	HB	TBB	IBB	SO	WP	Bk	W	L	Pct.	ShO	Sv	ERA
1995 Watertown	A- Cle	14	14	1	0	75	315	72	27	25	3	0	2	0	24	1	73	6	2	4	3	.571	1	0	3.00
1996 Columbus	A Cle	14	14	1	0	77.1	319	84	37	31	5	1	1	3	17	0	64	8	1	5	4	.556	1	0	3.61
1997 Kinston	A+ Cle	17	17	2	0	102.2	405	93	41	35	10	1	0	1	18	0	105	2	1	8	5	.615	2	0	3.07
Buffalo	AAA Cle	1	1	0	0	7	26	5	0	0	0	0	0	0	1	0	3	0	0	1	0	1.000	0	0	0.00
Akron	AA Cle	7	7	1	0	41	168	36	21	20	3	1	2	4	11	0	31	1	0	1	4	.200	1	0	4.39
3 Min. YEARS		53	53	5	0	303	1233	290	126	111	21	3	5	8	71	1	276	17	4	19	16	.543	5	0	3.30

Matt Raleigh

Bats: Right Throws: Right Pos: 3B-1B   Ht: 5'11" Wt: 205 Born: 7/18/70 Age: 27

Year Team	Lg Org	G	AB	H	2B	3B	HR	TB	R	RBI	TBB	IBB	SO	HBP	SH	SF	SB	CS	SB%	GDP	Avg	OBP	SLG
1992 Jamestown	A- Mon	77	261	57	14	2	11	108	41	44	45	2	101	0	0	2	14	2	.88	3	.218	.331	.414
1993 Jamestown	A- Mon	77	263	62	17	0	15	124	51	42	39	0	99	1	0	4	5	2	.71	3	.236	.332	.471
1994 Burlington	A Mon	114	398	109	18	2	34	233	78	83	75	3	138	5	0	3	6	2	.75	8	.274	.393	.585

BATTING / BASERUNNING / PERCENTAGES

Year Team	Lg Org	G	AB	H	2B	3B	HR	TB	R	RBI	TBB	IBB	SO	HBP	SH	SF	SB	CS	SB%	GDP	Avg	OBP	SLG
1995 Wst Plm Bch	A+ Mon	66	179	37	11	0	2	54	29	18	54	1	64	6	1	3	4	2	.67	4	.207	.401	.302
1996 Frederick	A+ Bal	21	57	13	0	1	1	18	8	8	12	0	22	2	0	2	3	0	1.00	6	.228	.370	.316
High Desert	A+ Bal	27	84	24	6	0	7	51	17	13	14	0	33	0	0	1	2	0	1.00	2	.286	.384	.607
Bowie	AA Bal	4	8	2	1	0	0	3	0	2	1	0	3	0	0	0	0	0	.00	0	.250	.333	.375
1997 Binghamton	AA NYN	122	398	78	15	0	37	204	71	74	79	6	169	1	0	1	0	2	.00	7	.196	.330	.513
6 Min. YEARS		508	1648	382	82	5	107	795	295	284	319	12	629	15	1	16	34	10	.77	27	.232	.358	.482

Alex Ramirez

Bats: Right **Throws:** Right **Pos:** OF   **Ht:** 5'11" **Wt:** 176 **Born:** 10/3/74 **Age:** 23

Year Team	Lg Org	G	AB	H	2B	3B	HR	TB	R	RBI	TBB	IBB	SO	HBP	SH	SF	SB	CS	SB%	GDP	Avg	OBP	SLG
1993 Burlington	R+ Cle	64	252	68	14	4	13	129	44	58	13	1	52	4	0	3	12	8	.60	4	.270	.313	.512
Kinston	A+ Cle	3	12	2	0	0	0	2	0	1	0	0	5	0	0	0	0	1	.00	0	.167	.167	.167
1994 Columbus	A Cle	125	458	115	23	3	18	198	64	57	26	0	100	4	0	4	7	5	.58	11	.251	.295	.432
1995 Bakersfield	A+ Cle	98	406	131	25	2	10	190	56	52	18	1	76	3	0	1	13	9	.59	9	.323	.355	.468
Canton-Akrn	AA Cle	33	133	33	3	4	1	47	15	11	5	1	24	0	1	1	3	5	.38	5	.248	.273	.353
1996 Canton-Akrn	AA Cle	131	513	169	28	12	14	263	79	85	16	1	74	3	1	1	18	10	.64	8	.329	.353	.513
1997 Buffalo	AAA Cle	119	416	119	19	8	11	187	59	44	24	0	95	4	6	3	10	5	.67	9	.286	.329	.450
5 Min. YEARS		573	2190	637	112	33	67	1016	317	308	102	4	426	18	8	13	63	43	.59	46	.291	.326	.464

Angel Ramirez

Bats: Right **Throws:** Right **Pos:** OF   **Ht:** 5'10" **Wt:** 166 **Born:** 1/24/73 **Age:** 25

Year Team	Lg Org	G	AB	H	2B	3B	HR	TB	R	RBI	TBB	IBB	SO	HBP	SH	SF	SB	CS	SB%	GDP	Avg	OBP	SLG
1993 Medicne Hat	R+ Tor	62	227	80	8	5	4	110	40	30	8	0	43	4	1	1	15	9	.63	3	.352	.383	.485
St. Cathrns	A- Tor	6	22	6	1	0	0	7	2	2	0	0	7	0	0	0	2	2	.00	1	.273	.273	.318
1994 Hagerstown	A Tor	117	454	127	17	14	9	199	71	51	21	2	103	7	4	3	21	14	.60	3	.280	.320	.438
1995 Dunedin	A+ Tor	131	541	149	19	5	8	202	78	52	21	0	99	5	0	2	17	12	.59	12	.275	.308	.373
1996 Knoxville	AA Tor	102	392	110	25	7	5	164	64	51	15	1	69	6	1	4	16	6	.73	9	.281	.314	.418
1997 Syracuse	AAA Tor	7	23	4	1	0	0	5	4	0	0	0	7	0	2	0	0	0	.00	1	.174	.174	.217
Knoxville	AA Tor	85	369	114	24	7	5	167	55	37	10	0	48	3	0	2	11	6	.65	4	.309	.331	.453
Norwich	AA NYA	2	1	0	0	0	0	0	0	0	0	0	0	0	0	0	0	0	.00	0	.000	.000	.000
5 Min. YEARS		512	2029	590	95	38	31	854	314	223	75	3	377	25	8	12	80	49	.62	33	.291	.322	.421

Felix Ramirez

Pitches: Left **Bats:** Left **Pos:** P   **Ht:** 5'11" **Wt:** 170 **Born:** 1/7/75 **Age:** 23

		HOW MUCH HE PITCHED						WHAT HE GAVE UP												THE RESULTS					
Year Team	Lg Org	G	GS	CG	GF	IP	BFP	H	R	ER	HR	SH	SF	HB	TBB	IBB	SO	WP	Bk	W	L	Pct.	ShO	Sv	ERA
1996 Red Sox	R Bos	1	0	0	1	1	6	1	2	1	0	0	0	0	2	0	1	0	0	0	0	.000	0	0	9.00
Sarasota	A+ Bos	5	0	0	3	11	49	10	8	4	0	0	0	1	8	0	7	1	0	1	0	1.000	0	0	3.27
1997 Trenton	AA Bos	18	3	0	6	41.1	186	43	28	25	7	2	3	1	21	1	29	1	0	4	2	.667	0	2	5.44
Sarasota	A+ Bos	19	0	0	9	35.1	153	39	10	6	3	4	1	0	12	1	31	1	0	2	1	.667	0	1	1.53
2 Min. YEARS		43	3	0	19	88.2	394	93	48	36	10	6	4	2	42	2	68	3	0	7	3	.700	0	3	3.65

Hector Ramirez

Pitches: Right **Bats:** Right **Pos:** P   **Ht:** 6'3" **Wt:** 218 **Born:** 12/15/71 **Age:** 26

		HOW MUCH HE PITCHED						WHAT HE GAVE UP												THE RESULTS					
Year Team	Lg Org	G	GS	CG	GF	IP	BFP	H	R	ER	HR	SH	SF	HB	TBB	IBB	SO	WP	Bk	W	L	Pct.	ShO	Sv	ERA
1989 Mets	R NYN	15	5	0	8	42	189	35	29	21	0	0	3	3	24	0	14	8	2	0	5	.000	0	0	4.50
1990 Mets	R NYN	11	8	1	1	50.2	226	54	34	23	2	1	4	4	21	1	43	2	2	3	5	.375	0	0	4.09
1991 Kingsport	R+ NYN	14	13	1	0	85	364	83	39	24	5	0	5	4	28	2	64	9	0	8	2	.800	0	0	2.54
1992 Columbia	A NYN	17	17	1	0	94.2	404	93	50	38	5	3	3	3	33	1	53	4	3	5	4	.556	0	0	3.61
1993 Mets	R NYN	1	1	0	0	7	26	5	1	0	0	0	0	0	1	0	6	0	0	1	0	1.000	0	0	0.00
Capital Cty	A NYN	14	14	0	0	64	294	86	51	38	2	3	4	2	23	0	42	7	0	4	6	.400	0	0	5.34
1994 St. Lucie	A+ NYN	27	27	6	0	194	802	202	86	74	10	10	6	5	50	2	110	6	8	11	12	.478	1	0	3.43
1995 Binghamton	AA NYN	20	20	2	0	123.1	534	127	69	63	12	2	2	3	48	2	63	3	5	4	12	.250	0	0	4.60
1996 Norfolk	AAA NYN	3	1	0	0	10.2	49	13	7	4	1	1	1	0	3	0	8	1	0	1	0	1.000	0	0	3.38
Binghamton	AA NYN	38	0	0	17	56	245	54	34	32	3	5	3	6	23	5	49	4	2	1	5	.167	0	6	5.14
1997 Rochester	AAA Bal	39	9	0	10	102.2	456	114	65	56	11	1	8	7	38	2	50	11	3	8	7	.533	0	2	4.91
9 Min. YEARS		199	115	11	37	830	3589	863	465	373	51	26	36	37	292	15	502	55	25	46	58	.442	1	9	4.04

Peto Ramirez

Bats: Right **Throws:** Right **Pos:** C   **Ht:** 6'2" **Wt:** 200 **Born:** 9/10/72 **Age:** 25

Year Team	Lg Org	G	AB	H	2B	3B	HR	TB	R	RBI	TBB	IBB	SO	HBP	SH	SF	SB	CS	SB%	GDP	Avg	OBP	SLG
1991 Giants	R SF	26	49	8	1	0	0	9	5	4	8	0	17	1	0	1	0	2	.00	1	.163	.293	.184
1992 Giants	R SF	42	143	39	4	3	3	58	23	21	16	1	36	1	0	0	2	0	1.00	4	.273	.350	.406
1993 Giants	R SF	54	201	59	14	1	3	84	31	34	26	3	40	1	2	2	3	2	.60	7	.294	.374	.418
1994 Clinton	A SF	55	180	58	12	0	7	91	30	23	18	1	47	2	1	0	0	1	.00	4	.322	.390	.506
1995 Sarasota	A+ Bos	40	140	26	2	0	2	34	13	12	3	0	29	0	2	1	3	2	.60	2	.186	.201	.243
1996 Burlington	A SF	101	327	80	17	0	11	130	42	55	52	1	94	3	2	3	2	1	.67	13	.245	.351	.398
Shreveport	AA SF	1	3	3	1	0	0	4	2	4	0	0	0	0	0	0	0	0	.00	0	1.000	1.000	1.333
1997 San Jose	A+ SF	43	135	36	7	0	7	64	17	26	15	1	31	1	2	1	0	0	.00	3	.267	.342	.474
Shreveport	AA SF	41	113	20	6	0	1	29	8	9	7	2	37	1	0	1	0	0	.00	4	.177	.230	.257
7 Min. YEARS		403	1291	329	64	4	34	503	171	188	145	9	331	10	9	8	10	8	.56	38	.255	.333	.390

Roberto Ramirez

Bats: Right **Throws:** Right **Pos:** OF   **Ht:** 6'2" **Wt:** 180 **Born:** 3/18/70 **Age:** 28

Year Team	Lg Org	G	AB	H	2B	3B	HR	TB	R	RBI	TBB	IBB	SO	HBP	SH	SF	SB	CS	SB%	GDP	Avg	OBP	SLG
1991 Clinton	A SF	17	55	10	0	1	0	12	4	5	2	0	18	0	0	2	0	1	.00	1	.182	.203	.218
Everett	A- SF	53	153	35	10	2	1	52	20	10	19	0	51	0	0	0	7	7	.50	5	.229	.314	.340
1992 Sou. Oregon	A- Oak	5	22	10	3	1	2	21	8	4	1	0	4	0	0	0	0	0	.00	0	.455	.478	.955
Reno	A+ Oak	55	190	65	13	3	7	105	31	29	15	2	45	2	2	2	3	5	.38	5	.342	.392	.553
1993 Madison	A Oak	14	55	17	4	0	1	24	9	7	3	0	10	1	0	1	2	2	.50	2	.309	.350	.436
Modesto	A+ Oak	41	140	36	8	0	3	53	17	14	17	0	36	1	0	2	2	5	.29	3	.257	.338	.379
1994 Riverside	A+ Sea	117	430	129	28	7	14	213	70	79	25	0	88	4	1	4	8	4	.67	5	.300	.341	.495
1995 Port City	AA Sea	129	490	136	24	6	17	223	67	82	35	4	98	6	3	6	11	10	.52	14	.278	.330	.455
1996 Port City	AA Sea	52	182	41	12	1	3	64	19	19	15	1	37	0	2	0	1	1	.50	6	.225	.284	.352
Lubbock	IND —	46	180	55	14	1	11	104	35	45	18	1	29	0	0	2	1	0	1.00	5	.306	.365	.578
1997 Visalia	A+ Oak	63	242	72	12	1	3	95	28	29	19	1	46	1	0	2	4	3	.57	5	.298	.348	.393
Huntsville	AA Oak	19	66	21	4	0	0	25	7	6	0	0	16	1	1	0	2	0	1.00	1	.318	.328	.379
7 Min. YEARS		611	2205	627	132	23	62	991	315	329	169	9	478	16	9	21	41	38	.52	52	.284	.337	.449

Fred Rath

Pitches: Right **Bats:** Right **Pos:** P   **Ht:** 6'3" **Wt:** 205 **Born:** 1/5/73 **Age:** 25

Year Team	Lg Org	G	GS	CG	GF	IP	BFP	H	R	ER	HR	SH	SF	HB	TBB	IBB	SO	WP	Bk	W	L	Pct.	ShO	Sv	ERA
1995 Elizabethtn	R+ Min	27	0	0	25	33.1	134	20	8	5	2	2	0	1	11	1	50	3	0	1	1	.500	0	12	1.35
1996 Ft. Wayne	A Min	32	0	0	29	41.2	163	26	12	7	1	0	2	0	10	0	63	3	0	1	2	.333	0	14	1.51
Ft. Myers	A+ Min	22	0	0	16	29	123	25	10	9	1	1	0	2	10	0	29	3	0	2	5	.286	0	4	2.79
1997 Ft. Myers	A+ Min	17	0	0	11	22	87	18	4	4	2	1	1	0	3	1	22	1	0	4	0	1.000	0	2	1.64
New Britain	AA Min	33	0	0	23	50.1	200	43	17	15	1	1	3	1	13	0	33	3	0	3	3	.500	0	12	2.68
Salt Lake	AAA Min	10	0	0	9	11	46	11	2	2	1	0	0	0	2	0	11	0	0	0	1	.000	0	3	1.64
3 Min. YEARS		141	0	0	113	187.1	753	143	53	42	8	5	6	4	49	2	208	13	0	11	12	.478	0	47	2.02

Gary Rath

Pitches: Left **Bats:** Left **Pos:** P   **Ht:** 6'2" **Wt:** 185 **Born:** 1/10/73 **Age:** 25

Year Team	Lg Org	G	GS	CG	GF	IP	BFP	H	R	ER	HR	SH	SF	HB	TBB	IBB	SO	WP	Bk	W	L	Pct.	ShO	Sv	ERA
1994 Vero Beach	A+ LA	13	11	0	0	62.2	261	55	26	19	3	3	3	2	23	0	50	4	0	5	6	.455	0	0	2.73
1995 San Antonio	AA LA	18	18	3	0	117	483	96	42	36	6	3	2	4	48	0	81	4	2	13	3	.813	1	0	2.77
Albuquerque	AAA LA	8	8	0	0	39	178	46	31	22	4	1	1	2	20	0	23	2	0	3	5	.375	0	0	5.08
1996 Albuquerque	AAA LA	30	30	1	0	180.1	784	177	97	84	13	9	4	3	89	8	125	8	0	10	11	.476	1	0	4.19
1997 Albuquerque	AAA LA	24	24	0	0	132.1	615	177	107	89	17	7	4	4	49	1	100	7	0	7	11	.389	0	0	6.05
4 Min. YEARS		93	91	4	0	531.1	2321	551	303	250	43	23	14	15	229	9	379	25	2	38	36	.514	2	0	4.23

Jon Ratliff

Pitches: Right **Bats:** Right **Pos:** P   **Ht:** 6'5" **Wt:** 200 **Born:** 12/22/71 **Age:** 26

Year Team	Lg Org	G	GS	CG	GF	IP	BFP	H	R	ER	HR	SH	SF	HB	TBB	IBB	SO	WP	Bk	W	L	Pct.	ShO	Sv	ERA
1993 Geneva	A- ChN	3	3	0	0	14	65	12	8	5	0	0	0	2	8	0	7	0	0	1	1	.500	0	0	3.21
Daytona	A+ ChN	8	8	0	0	41	194	50	29	18	0	2	3	5	23	0	15	3	1	2	4	.333	0	0	3.95
1994 Daytona	A+ ChN	8	8	1	0	54	227	64	23	21	5	2	1	4	5	0	17	4	0	3	2	.600	0	0	3.50
Iowa	AAA ChN	5	4	0	0	28.1	131	39	19	17	7	1	1	2	7	0	10	3	0	1	3	.250	0	0	5.40
Orlando	AA ChN	12	12	1	0	62.1	292	78	44	39	4	4	5	8	26	1	19	5	0	1	9	.100	0	0	5.63
1995 Orlando	AA ChN	26	25	1	1	140	599	143	67	54	9	2	8	10	42	1	94	13	0	10	5	.667	1	0	3.47
1996 Iowa	AAA ChN	32	13	0	5	93.2	419	107	63	55	10	3	6	6	31	2	59	3	0	4	8	.333	0	1	5.28
1997 Iowa	AAA ChN	9	4	0	1	32.1	134	30	20	20	6	1	0	2	7	0	25	2	0	1	3	.250	0	1	5.57
Orlando	AA ChN	18	15	0	1	101.1	443	112	59	49	10	5	2	1	32	3	68	12	1	6	4	.600	0	2	4.35
5 Min. YEARS		121	92	3	8	567	2504	635	332	278	51	20	26	40	181	7	314	45	2	29	39	.426	1	2	4.41

Luis Raven

Bats: Right **Throws:** Right **Pos:** DH   **Ht:** 6'4" **Wt:** 230 **Born:** 11/19/68 **Age:** 29

Year Team	Lg Org	G	AB	H	2B	3B	HR	TB	R	RBI	TBB	IBB	SO	HBP	SH	SF	SB	CS	SB%	GDP	Avg	OBP	SLG
1989 Angels	R Ana	43	145	30	6	2	1	43	15	20	8	0	43	1	0	3	3	0	1.00	3	.207	.248	.297
1991 Boise	A- Ana	38	84	23	2	0	2	31	13	13	9	0	19	1	0	1	1	1	.50	6	.274	.351	.369
1992 Palm Spring	A+ Ana	107	378	109	16	2	9	156	59	55	24	2	81	2	0	4	18	7	.72	5	.288	.331	.413
1993 Midland	AA Ana	43	167	43	12	1	2	63	21	30	5	1	45	1	1	0	4	2	.67	4	.257	.283	.377
Palm Spring	A+ Ana	85	343	95	20	2	7	140	38	52	22	0	84	3	1	2	15	11	.58	6	.277	.324	.408
1994 Midland	AA Ana	47	191	58	8	5	18	130	41	57	5	2	51	3	0	3	4	1	.80	9	.304	.327	.681
Vancouver	AAA Ana	85	328	100	13	4	13	160	66	59	22	1	88	2	0	8	7	0	1.00	6	.305	.344	.488
1995 Lk Elsinore	A+ Ana	6	24	10	2	1	2	20	5	6	5	0	7	1	0	0	1	0	1.00	1	.417	.533	.833
Vancouver	AAA Ana	37	135	33	11	1	5	61	18	26	15	0	35	0	1	1	3	1	.75	6	.244	.318	.452
Midland	AA Ana	21	86	23	2	1	5	42	9	15	4	0	30	1	0	1	1	1	.50	2	.267	.304	.488
1996 Canton-Akrn	AA Cle	74	268	81	17	0	21	161	57	64	38	6	73	1	0	2	0	0	.00	6	.302	.388	.601
1997 Birmingham	AA ChA	117	456	153	30	3	30	279	88	112	46	7	126	5	0	7	4	3	.57	5	.336	.397	.612
8 Min. YEARS		703	2605	758	139	22	115	1286	430	509	203	19	682	21	3	31	61	27	.69	58	.291	.343	.494

Kevin Rawitzer

Pitches: Left Bats: Left Pos: P   Ht: 5'10" Wt: 185 Born: 2/28/71 Age: 27

Year Team	Lg Org	G	GS	CG	GF	IP	BFP	H	R	ER	HR	SH	SF	HB	TBB	IBB	SO	WP	Bk	W	L	Pct.	ShO	Sv	ERA
1993 Eugene	A- KC	6	4	0	0	18	69	13	1	1	0	0	0	1	5	0	20	0	0	1	0	1.000	0	0	0.50
Rockford	A KC	5	5	0	0	30	126	23	7	5	0	0	0	1	11	0	34	0	0	3	0	1.000	0	0	1.50
1994 Rockford	A KC	15	15	0	0	76.1	329	80	27	21	5	0	4	3	27	1	75	6	1	5	2	.714	0	0	2.48
Wilmington	A+ KC	7	1	0	2	17.2	79	18	10	9	0	1	0	0	11	0	13	1	0	0	1	.000	0	1	4.58
1995 Wilmington	A+ KC	15	1	0	7	27	111	21	8	7	0	1	0	3	8	1	22	1	0	2	0	1.000	0	3	2.33
Wichita	AA KC	28	3	0	7	48	209	48	30	28	4	0	2	1	19	0	42	1	0	6	4	.600	0	1	5.25
1996 Wichita	AA KC	42	0	0	17	68.1	314	77	52	36	8	2	2	5	39	1	48	3	0	0	6	.000	0	3	4.74
1997 Wichita	AA KC	44	9	0	6	97	457	125	68	62	10	2	1	6	44	4	75	1	1	5	1	.833	0	0	5.75
5 Min. YEARS		162	38	0	39	382.1	1694	405	203	169	27	6	9	20	164	7	329	13	2	22	14	.611	0	8	3.98

Ken Ray

Pitches: Right Bats: Right Pos: P   Ht: 6'2" Wt: 160 Born: 11/27/74 Age: 23

Year Team	Lg Org	G	GS	CG	GF	IP	BFP	H	R	ER	HR	SH	SF	HB	TBB	IBB	SO	WP	Bk	W	L	Pct.	ShO	Sv	ERA
1993 Royals	R KC	13	7	0	3	47.1	204	44	21	12	1	1	3	0	17	0	45	6	0	2	3	.400	0	0	2.28
1994 Rockford	A KC	27	18	0	6	128.2	516	94	34	26	5	4	1	0	56	2	128	18	2	10	4	.714	0	3	1.82
1995 Wilmington	A+ KC	13	13	1	0	77	320	74	32	23	3	3	3	1	22	2	63	17	2	6	4	.600	0	0	2.69
Wichita	AA KC	14	14	0	0	75.1	342	83	55	50	7	1	0	1	46	0	53	8	1	4	5	.444	0	0	5.97
1996 Wichita	AA KC	22	22	1	0	120.2	553	151	94	82	17	5	6	1	57	1	79	15	1	4	12	.250	0	0	6.12
1997 Omaha	AAA KC	25	21	2	1	113	516	131	86	80	21	2	5	4	63	2	96	8	1	5	12	.294	0	0	6.37
5 Min. YEARS		114	95	4	10	562	2451	577	322	273	54	16	18	7	261	7	464	72	7	31	40	.437	0	3	4.37

Bobby Rector

Pitches: Right Bats: Right Pos: P   Ht: 6'1" Wt: 170 Born: 9/24/74 Age: 23

Year Team	Lg Org	G	GS	CG	GF	IP	BFP	H	R	ER	HR	SH	SF	HB	TBB	IBB	SO	WP	Bk	W	L	Pct.	ShO	Sv	ERA
1994 Giants	R SF	9	5	0	0	30.1	117	19	8	4	0	1	1	1	8	0	37	2	0	1	2	.333	0	0	1.19
1995 Burlington	A SF	27	24	0	0	135.2	589	135	78	62	7	4	5	6	59	3	102	9	2	9	11	.450	0	0	4.11
1996 San Jose	A+ SF	28	26	1	1	165.1	694	161	77	66	14	4	5	8	43	0	145	4	0	12	8	.600	0	0	3.59
1997 Bakersfield	A+ SF	8	8	0	0	48.1	199	52	27	22	8	1	1	1	12	1	32	1	1	2	4	.333	0	0	4.10
Kane County	A Fla	3	3	1	0	21	76	11	2	2	1	1	0	0	4	0	24	0	0	1	0	1.000	1	0	0.86
Portland	AA Fla	6	6	0	0	33.2	155	45	20	18	7	2	1	1	11	0	23	2	0	2	2	.500	0	0	4.81
4 Min. YEARS		81	72	2	1	434.1	1830	423	212	174	37	13	13	17	137	4	363	18	3	27	27	.500	1	0	3.61

Mark Redman

Pitches: Left Bats: Left Pos: P   Ht: 6'5" Wt: 220 Born: 1/5/74 Age: 24

Year Team	Lg Org	G	GS	CG	GF	IP	BFP	H	R	ER	HR	SH	SF	HB	TBB	IBB	SO	WP	Bk	W	L	Pct.	ShO	Sv	ERA
1995 Ft. Myers	A+ Min	8	5	0	0	32.2	134	28	13	10	4	1	2	1	13	0	26	2	0	2	1	.667	0	0	2.76
1996 Ft. Myers	A+ Min	13	13	1	0	82.2	335	63	24	17	1	6	3	5	34	0	75	4	1	3	4	.429	0	0	1.85
Hardware City	AA Min	16	16	3	0	106.1	467	101	51	45	5	1	6	8	50	1	96	4	1	7	7	.500	0	0	3.81
Salt Lake	AAA Min	1	1	0	0	4	21	7	4	4	1	0	0	1	2	0	4	0	0	0	0	.000	0	0	9.00
1997 Salt Lake	AAA Min	29	28	0	1	158.1	739	204	123	111	19	3	6	4	80	3	125	12	2	8	15	.348	0	1	6.31
3 Min. YEARS		67	63	4	1	384	1696	403	215	187	30	11	17	19	179	4	326	22	4	20	27	.426	0	1	4.38

Mike Redmond

Bats: Right Throws: Right Pos: DH-C   Ht: 6'0" Wt: 190 Born: 5/5/71 Age: 27

Year Team	Lg Org	G	AB	H	2B	3B	HR	TB	R	RBI	TBB	IBB	SO	HBP	SH	SF	SB	CS	SB%	GDP	Avg	OBP	SLG
1993 Kane County	A Fla	43	100	22	2	0	0	22	10	10	6	0	17	4	2	0	2	0	1.00	1	.200	.273	.220
1994 Kane County	A Fla	92	306	83	10	0	0	96	39	24	26	0	31	9	6	2	3	4	.43	10	.271	.344	.314
Brevard Cty	A+ Fla	12	42	11	4	0	0	15	4	2	3	0	4	1	0	0	0	0	.00	1	.262	.326	.357
1995 Portland	AA Fla	105	333	85	11	1	3	107	37	39	22	2	27	3	4	3	2	2	.50	9	.255	.305	.321
1996 Portland	AA Fla	120	394	113	22	0	4	147	43	44	26	2	45	5	5	5	3	4	.43	12	.287	.335	.373
1997 Charlotte	AAA Fla	22	61	13	5	1	1	23	8	2	1	1	10	3	2	0	1	1	.00	1	.213	.262	.377
Marlins	R Fla	16	55	19	3	0	0	22	7	5	9	0	5	3	0	0	2	0	1.00	0	.345	.463	.400
Brevard Cty	A+ Fla	5	17	0	0	0	0	0	2	0	2	0	2	0	0	0	0	0	.00	2	.000	.105	.000
5 Min. YEARS		415	1308	344	57	2	9	432	150	126	95	5	141	28	19	10	12	11	.52	37	.263	.324	.330

Brandon Reed

Pitches: Right Bats: Right Pos: P   Ht: 6'4" Wt: 185 Born: 12/18/74 Age: 23

Year Team	Lg Org	G	GS	CG	GF	IP	BFP	H	R	ER	HR	SH	SF	HB	TBB	IBB	SO	WP	Bk	W	L	Pct.	ShO	Sv	ERA
1994 Bristol	R+ Det	13	13	0	0	78	337	82	41	31	3	1	3	9	10	0	68	4	0	3	5	.375	0	0	3.58
1995 Fayettevlle	A Det	55	0	0	53	64.2	252	40	11	7	1	1	0	3	18	1	78	8	0	3	0	1.000	0	41	0.97
1996 Tigers	R Det	1	1	0	0	2	6	0	0	0	0	0	0	0	0	0	2	0	0	0	0	.000	0	0	0.00
Jacksnville	AA Det	7	3	0	1	26	94	18	6	6	1	0	1	1	3	0	18	0	0	1	0	1.000	0	0	2.08
1997 Jacksnville	AA Det	27	27	2	0	176	754	190	100	89	25	6	10	8	54	0	90	9	0	11	9	.550	0	0	4.55
4 Min. YEARS		103	44	2	54	346.2	1443	330	158	133	30	8	14	22	85	1	256	21	0	18	14	.563	0	42	3.45

Chris Reed

Pitches: Right **Bats:** Right **Pos:** P **Ht:** 6'3" **Wt:** 206 **Born:** 8/25/73 **Age:** 24

			HOW MUCH HE PITCHED						WHAT HE GAVE UP										THE RESULTS					
Year Team	Lg Org	G	GS	CG	GF	IP	BFP	H	R	ER	HR	SH	SF	HB	TBB	IBB	SO	WP	Bk	W	L	Pct.	ShO	Sv	ERA
1991 Princeton	R+ Cin	13	13	0	0	63	290	68	53	34	5	0	3	7	30	2	51	10	6	3	6	.333	0	0	4.86
1992 Billings	R+ Cin	10	10	0	0	48	221	46	30	27	2	2	4	3	32	0	39	5	1	6	3	.667	0	0	5.06
1993 Chston-WV	A Cin	21	21	0	0	112.1	498	99	63	51	1	8	6	10	58	0	84	6	3	7	9	.438	0	0	4.09
1994 Chston-WV	A Cin	26	25	1	1	145.2	650	156	90	78	12	3	3	11	72	2	99	9	1	11	7	.611	0	0	4.82
1995 Winston-Sal	A+ Cin	24	24	3	0	149	613	116	63	55	11	3	1	4	68	1	104	3	1	10	7	.588	1	0	3.32
1996 Chattanooga	AA Cin	28	27	2	1	176	752	157	89	80	15	5	9	9	91	1	135	17	0	13	10	.565	0	1	4.09
1997 Indianapols	AAA Cin	3	3	0	0	14	68	19	11	9	3	0	1	1	9	0	4	1	0	0	1	.000	0	0	5.79
Chattanooga	AA Cin	23	23	0	0	129.2	585	140	93	77	11	3	1	7	68	4	96	3	0	6	8	.429	0	0	5.34
7 Min. YEARS		148	146	6	2	837.2	3677	801	492	411	60	24	28	52	428	10	612	54	12	56	51	.523	1	1	4.42

Glenn Reeves

Bats: Right **Throws:** Right **Pos:** OF **Ht:** 6'0" **Wt:** 175 **Born:** 1/19/74 **Age:** 24

					BATTING												BASERUNNING				PERCENTAGES		
Year Team	Lg Org	G	AB	H	2B	3B	HR	TB	R	RBI	TBB	IBB	SO	HBP	SH	SF	SB	CS	SB%	GDP	Avg	OBP	SLG
1993 Marlins	R Fla	48	177	50	6	2	0	60	36	19	22	0	29	2	3	1	6	3	.67	1	.282	.366	.339
1994 Kane County	A Fla	102	370	95	15	3	3	125	65	34	66	0	76	2	5	0	5	4	.56	15	.257	.372	.338
1995 Brevard Cty	A+ Fla	117	415	112	22	2	1	141	68	33	78	0	78	6	2	3	6	7	.46	12	.270	.390	.340
1996 Brevard Cty	A+ Fla	123	478	143	29	4	6	198	72	41	63	0	82	5	4	4	8	5	.62	6	.299	.384	.414
1997 Portland	AA Fla	66	222	78	14	2	6	114	53	35	39	0	43	4	0	2	9	4	.69	3	.351	.453	.514
5 Min. YEARS		456	1662	478	86	13	16	638	294	162	268	0	308	19	14	10	34	23	.60	37	.288	.391	.384

Kevin Reimer

Bats: Left **Throws:** Right **Pos:** DH **Ht:** 6'2" **Wt:** 230 **Born:** 6/28/64 **Age:** 34

					BATTING												BASERUNNING				PERCENTAGES		
Year Team	Lg Org	G	AB	H	2B	3B	HR	TB	R	RBI	TBB	IBB	SO	HBP	SH	SF	SB	CS	SB%	GDP	Avg	OBP	SLG
1985 Burlington	A Tex	80	292	67	12	0	8	103	25	33	22	0	43	8	0	1	0	4	.00	10	.229	.300	.353
1986 Salem	A+ Tex	133	453	111	21	2	16	184	57	76	61	6	71	7	2	2	4	5	.44	15	.245	.342	.406
1987 Charlotte	A+ Tex	74	271	66	13	7	6	111	36	34	29	2	48	2	0	2	2	1	.67	6	.244	.319	.410
1988 Tulsa	AA Tex	133	486	147	30	11	21	262	74	76	38	9	95	5	0	5	4	4	.50	9	.302	.356	.539
1989 Okla City	AAA Tex	133	514	137	37	7	10	218	59	73	33	3	91	2	1	4	4	1	.80	13	.267	.311	.424
1990 Okla City	AAA Tex	51	198	56	18	2	4	90	24	33	18	3	25	0	1	1	2	0	1.00	7	.283	.341	.455
1996 Salt Lake	AAA Min	54	193	55	9	0	10	94	29	33	11	3	31	5	0	3	4	1	.80	4	.285	.335	.487
Tacoma	AAA Sea	24	93	26	3	0	3	38	9	11	3	0	12	3	0	1	0	0	.00	3	.280	.320	.409
1997 Tacoma	AAA Sea	46	168	58	18	0	3	85	21	21	12	0	22	2	0	3	0	3	.00	8	.345	.389	.506
1988 Texas	AL	12	25	3	0	0	1	6	2	2	0	0	6	0	0	1	0	0	.00	0	.120	.115	.240
1989 Texas	AL	3	5	0	0	0	0	0	0	0	0	0	1	0	0	0	0	0	.00	1	.000	.000	.000
1990 Texas	AL	64	100	26	9	1	2	43	5	15	10	0	22	1	0	0	0	1	.00	3	.260	.333	.430
1991 Texas	AL	136	394	106	22	0	20	188	46	69	33	6	93	7	0	6	0	3	.00	10	.269	.332	.477
1992 Texas	AL	148	494	132	32	2	16	216	56	58	42	5	103	10	0	1	2	4	.33	10	.267	.336	.437
1993 Milwaukee	AL	125	437	109	22	1	13	172	53	60	30	4	72	5	1	4	5	4	.56	12	.249	.303	.394
8 Min. YEARS		728	2668	723	161	29	81	1185	334	390	227	26	438	34	3	22	20	19	.51	75	.271	.333	.444
6 Maj. YEARS		488	1455	376	85	4	52	625	162	204	115	15	297	23	1	12	7	12	.37	36	.258	.320	.430

Mike Rennhack

Bats: Both **Throws:** Right **Pos:** OF **Ht:** 6'3" **Wt:** 190 **Born:** 8/25/74 **Age:** 23

					BATTING												BASERUNNING				PERCENTAGES		
Year Team	Lg Org	G	AB	H	2B	3B	HR	TB	R	RBI	TBB	IBB	SO	HBP	SH	SF	SB	CS	SB%	GDP	Avg	OBP	SLG
1992 Astros	R Hou	35	126	26	2	4	0	36	11	16	14	2	18	0	0	1	6	4	.60	8	.206	.284	.286
1993 Asheville	A Hou	118	441	120	30	3	10	186	57	52	37	0	90	3	2	3	16	10	.62	8	.272	.331	.422
1994 Quad City	A Hou	127	449	102	14	1	10	148	54	48	50	2	83	2	8	5	12	5	.71	14	.227	.304	.330
1995 Quad City	A Hou	100	299	81	14	1	1	100	46	47	39	1	37	1	4	8	5	4	.79	3	.271	.349	.334
1996 Stockton	A+ Mil	121	456	146	32	4	17	237	67	103	53	1	66	4	2	7	8	10	.44	11	.320	.390	.520
1997 El Paso	AA Mil	106	369	102	28	7	9	171	59	64	38	1	81	2	2	6	4	3	.57	5	.276	.342	.463
6 Min. YEARS		607	2140	577	120	20	47	878	294	330	231	7	375	12	18	30	61	36	.63	49	.270	.340	.410

Greg Resz

Pitches: Right **Bats:** Left **Pos:** P **Ht:** 6'5" **Wt:** 215 **Born:** 12/25/71 **Age:** 26

				HOW MUCH HE PITCHED						WHAT HE GAVE UP										THE RESULTS					
Year Team	Lg Org	G	GS	CG	GF	IP	BFP	H	R	ER	HR	SH	SF	HB	TBB	IBB	SO	WP	Bk	W	L	Pct.	ShO	Sv	ERA
1993 Oneonta	A- NYA	24	0	0	18	26.1	117	18	14	11	2	1	1	4	16	1	16	4	0	3	0	1.000	0	9	3.76
1994 Greensboro	A NYA	7	0	0	7	7.2	32	6	3	3	0	0	0	0	2	0	14	1	0	0	0	.000	0	2	3.52
Tampa	A+ NYA	18	0	0	18	18.2	79	21	8	3	0	0	1	1	4	0	20	0	0	0	2	.000	0	6	1.45
1995 Tampa	A+ NYA	12	0	0	3	13.1	61	10	9	5	0	0	0	1	9	2	16	3	0	0	1	.000	0	1	3.38
1996 Norwich	AA NYA	19	2	0	9	39	172	38	17	11	1	1	0	1	18	1	37	3	0	1	1	.500	0	2	2.54
Tampa	A+ NYA	20	0	0	9	25	108	20	11	7	0	1	2	0	12	1	31	2	0	0	1	.000	0	4	2.52
1997 Tampa	A+ NYA	1	1	0	0	5.2	23	5	2	2	1	0	0	0	2	0	5	0	0	1	0	1.000	0	0	3.18
Norwich	AA NYA	25	13	0	6	90	410	94	59	47	9	3	6	3	43	0	75	17	0	5	4	.556	0	0	4.70
5 Min. YEARS		126	16	0	70	225.2	1002	212	123	89	13	6	10	11	106	5	214	30	0	10	9	.526	0	24	3.55

Kendall Rhine

Ht: 6'7" Wt: 215 Born: 11/27/70 Age: 27

Pitches: Right Bats: Right Pos: P

		HOW MUCH HE PITCHED						WHAT HE GAVE UP												THE RESULTS				
Year Team	Lg Org	G	GS	CG	GF	IP	BFP	H	R	ER	HR	SH	SF	HB	TBB	IBB	SO	WP	Bk	W	L	Pct.	ShO	Sv	ERA
1992 Auburn	A- Hou	8	8	0	0	31	153	34	21	17	2	1	3	2	31	0	21	8	2	0	3	.000	0	0	4.94
1993 Auburn	A- Hou	16	10	0	2	47.2	257	61	62	52	2	1	3	10	48	1	36	21	0	0	2	.000	0	0	9.82
1994 Auburn	A- Hou	8	0	0	2	19.2	92	18	14	11	1	1	0	3	11	0	15	6	1	0	1	.000	0	0	5.03
1995 Hagerstown	A Tor	42	0	0	36	55.1	230	41	20	16	2	4	0	3	28	1	49	8	0	3	3	.500	0	13	2.60
1996 Dunedin	A+ Tor	20	0	0	11	23	104	20	11	10	1	0	0	3	11	2	25	2	0	1	0	1.000	0	3	3.91
Knoxville	AA Tor	11	0	0	6	12.1	62	12	8	8	1	0	1	3	11	1	9	3	0	0	0	.000	0	2	5.84
1997 Dunedin	A+ Tor	4	0	0	2	4.1	26	9	7	6	1	0	0	0	4	1	2	0	0	0	0	.000	0	0	12.46
Knoxville	AA Tor	8	0	0	2	11.1	61	13	13	13	1	2	2	2	15	1	6	1	0	0	0	.000	0	0	10.32
Syracuse	AAA Tor	1	0	0	1	2	12	2	2	2	0	0	1	1	3	0	0	0	0	0	0	.000	0	0	9.00
6 Min. YEARS		118	18	0	62	206.2	997	210	158	135	11	9	10	28	162	7	163	49	3	4	9	.308	0	18	5.88

Chuck Ricci

Ht: 6'2" Wt: 180 Born: 11/20/68 Age: 29

Pitches: Right Bats: Right Pos: P

		HOW MUCH HE PITCHED						WHAT HE GAVE UP												THE RESULTS				
Year Team	Lg Org	G	GS	CG	GF	IP	BFP	H	R	ER	HR	SH	SF	HB	TBB	IBB	SO	WP	Bk	W	L	Pct.	ShO	Sv	ERA
1987 Bluefield	R+ Bal	13	12	1	0	62.1	288	74	52	45	11	1	0	2	38	1	40	3	0	5	5	.500	0	0	6.50
1988 Bluefield	R+ Bal	14	14	1	0	73	355	92	61	54	7	1	3	2	48	0	73	6	0	4	6	.400	0	0	6.66
1989 Waterloo	A Bal	29	25	9	1	181.1	760	160	89	60	11	11	5	12	59	5	89	14	1	10	12	.455	0	0	2.98
1990 Frederick	A+ Bal	26	18	2	5	122.1	539	126	79	60	8	6	3	6	47	3	94	8	0	7	12	.368	1	0	4.41
1991 Frederick	A+ Bal	30	29	2	0	173.2	752	147	91	60	12	3	10	3	84	2	144	15	1	12	14	.462	0	0	3.11
1992 Frederick	A+ Bal	1	0	0	0	2.1	11	2	1	0	0	0	0	0	1	0	2	0	0	0	0	.000	0	0	0.00
Hagerstown	AA Bal	20	6	0	4	57.2	275	58	40	37	4	3	4	3	47	1	58	8	2	1	4	.200	0	0	5.77
1993 Rochester	AAA Bal	4	0	0	3	8	36	11	5	5	1	0	0	0	3	0	6	0	0	0	0	.000	0	0	5.63
Bowie	AA Bal	34	1	0	16	81.2	334	72	35	29	7	5	2	3	20	0	83	8	0	7	4	.636	0	5	3.20
1994 Reading	AA Phi	14	0	0	2	19	71	10	1	0	0	0	0	0	4	2	23	0	0	1	0	1.000	0	0	0.00
Scranton-WB	AAA Phi	44	1	0	17	64.2	274	60	30	29	7	2	3	5	22	5	72	4	0	4	3	.571	0	6	4.04
1995 Scranton-WB	AAA Phi	68	0	0	48	65	269	48	22	18	6	4	1	4	24	5	66	1	0	4	3	.571	0	25	2.49
1996 Pawtucket	AAA Bos	60	0	0	43	80.2	326	56	30	27	12	2	3	1	32	2	79	9	0	8	4	.667	0	13	3.01
1997 Edmonton	AAA Oak	5	0	0	3	5.1	33	10	10	10	3	1	1	1	6	0	5	4	0	0	0	.000	0	0	16.88
Ottawa	AAA Mon	22	0	0	9	27	125	22	16	14	1	3	1	1	25	3	27	6	0	2	2	.500	0	0	4.67
1995 Philadelphia	NL	7	0	0	3	10	40	9	2	2	0	1	2	1	3	0	9	0	0	1	0	1.000	0	0	1.80
11 Min. YEARS		383	106	15	151	1024	4448	948	562	448	90	42	36	45	460	29	861	86	4	65	69	.485	1	49	3.94

Chris Richard

Ht: 6'2" Wt: 185 Born: 6/7/74 Age: 24

Bats: Left Throws: Left Pos: 1B

		BATTING															BASERUNNING				PERCENTAGES		
Year Team	Lg Org	G	AB	H	2B	3B	HR	TB	R	RBI	TBB	IBB	SO	HBP	SH	SF	SB	CS	SB%	GDP	Avg	OBP	SLG
1995 New Jersey	A- StL	75	284	80	14	3	3	109	36	43	47	3	31	6	0	2	6	6	.50	3	.282	.392	.384
1996 St. Pete	A+ StL	129	460	130	28	6	14	212	65	82	57	6	50	9	0	5	7	3	.70	11	.283	.369	.461
1997 Arkansas	AA StL	113	390	105	24	3	11	168	62	58	60	1	59	5	0	3	6	4	.60	8	.269	.371	.431
3 Min. YEARS		317	1134	315	66	12	28	489	163	183	164	10	140	20	0	10	19	13	.59	22	.278	.376	.431

Rowan Richards

Ht: 6'0" Wt: 195 Born: 5/17/74 Age: 24

Bats: Right Throws: Right Pos: OF

		BATTING															BASERUNNING				PERCENTAGES		
Year Team	Lg Org	G	AB	H	2B	3B	HR	TB	R	RBI	TBB	IBB	SO	HBP	SH	SF	SB	CS	SB%	GDP	Avg	OBP	SLG
1996 Hudson Vall	A- Tex	30	113	31	6	0	5	52	18	18	16	0	33	5	0	2	4	1	.80	4	.274	.382	.460
Charlotte	A+ Tex	34	118	20	3	1	1	28	10	10	5	0	33	2	1	2	2	1	.67	1	.169	.213	.237
1997 Tulsa	AA Tex	11	35	10	1	0	0	11	5	5	5	0	9	0	0	0	0	0	.00	3	.286	.375	.314
Charlotte	A+ Tex	60	178	47	12	1	3	70	18	26	22	1	54	3	1	1	5	2	.71	4	.264	.353	.393
2 Min. YEARS		135	444	108	22	2	9	161	51	59	48	1	129	10	2	5	11	4	.73	12	.243	.327	.363

Brian Richardson

Ht: 6'2" Wt: 190 Born: 8/31/75 Age: 22

Bats: Right Throws: Right Pos: 3B

		BATTING															BASERUNNING				PERCENTAGES		
Year Team	Lg Org	G	AB	H	2B	3B	HR	TB	R	RBI	TBB	IBB	SO	HBP	SH	SF	SB	CS	SB%	GDP	Avg	OBP	SLG
1992 Dodgers	R LA	37	122	26	6	2	0	36	8	15	11	0	27	0	0	2	3	0	1.00	3	.213	.274	.295
1993 Great Falls	R+ LA	54	178	40	11	0	0	51	16	13	14	1	47	3	1	2	1	2	.33	7	.225	.289	.287
1994 Vero Beach	A+ LA	19	52	12	0	1	0	14	3	3	4	0	15	0	0	2	3	0	1.00	2	.231	.276	.269
Yakima	A- LA	70	266	62	15	0	5	92	35	44	35	1	82	1	0	0	12	4	.75	3	.233	.325	.346
1995 San Berndno	A+ LA	127	462	131	18	1	12	187	68	58	35	2	122	7	6	3	17	16	.52	11	.284	.341	.405
1996 San Antonio	AA LA	19	62	20	1	1	0	23	10	7	2	0	10	2	0	0	0	2	.00	0	.323	.364	.371
Albuquerque	AAA LA	105	355	87	17	2	9	135	52	43	32	6	89	3	4	4	4	1	.80	5	.245	.310	.380
1997 San Antonio	AA LA	133	484	144	23	13	13	232	73	90	42	0	97	8	2	5	3	6	.33	12	.298	.360	.479
6 Min. YEARS		564	1981	522	91	20	39	770	265	273	175	10	489	24	13	18	43	31	.58	42	.264	.328	.389

Scott Richardson

Ht: 6'1" Wt: 175 Born: 2/19/71 Age: 27

Bats: Right Throws: Right Pos: OF

		BATTING															BASERUNNING				PERCENTAGES		
Year Team	Lg Org	G	AB	H	2B	3B	HR	TB	R	RBI	TBB	IBB	SO	HBP	SH	SF	SB	CS	SB%	GDP	Avg	OBP	SLG
1992 Helena	R+ Mil	69	289	83	10	5	2	109	58	36	35	1	43	4	1	0	22	5	.81	5	.287	.372	.377
1993 Beloit	A Mil	125	475	131	26	7	3	180	76	64	42	0	85	1	6	5	50	12	.81	6	.276	.333	.379
1994 Stockton	A+ Mil	131	495	131	25	3	2	168	76	33	73	0	64	1	9	0	49	12	.80	10	.265	.360	.339

(continued)

Year Team	Lg Org	G	AB	H	2B	3B	HR	TB	R	RBI	TBB	IBB	SO	HBP	SH	SF	SB	CS	SB%	GDP	Avg	OBP	SLG
1995 El Paso	AA Mil	82	256	65	9	6	1	89	29	29	16	0	42	5	2	0	8	6	.57	13	.254	.310	.348
Stockton	A+ Mil	24	80	18	4	1	2	30	12	14	6	0	16	3	1	0	8	3	.73	3	.225	.303	.375
1996 San Berndno	A+ LA	128	458	140	30	0	13	209	80	69	46	0	71	4	4	4	31	14	.69	9	.306	.371	.456
1997 San Antonio	AA LA	92	304	86	15	1	7	124	49	38	46	4	54	2	1	3	6	5	.55	6	.283	.377	.408
6 Min. YEARS		651	2357	654	119	23	30	909	380	283	264	5	375	20	24	12	174	57	.75	52	.277	.354	.386

Ray Ricken

Pitches: Right **Bats:** Right **Pos:** P **Ht:** 6'5" **Wt:** 225 **Born:** 8/11/73 **Age:** 24

Year Team	Lg Org	G	GS	CG	GF	IP	BFP	H	R	ER	HR	SH	SF	HB	TBB	IBB	SO	WP	Bk	W	L	Pct.	ShO	Sv	ERA
1994 Oneonta	A- NYA	10	10	0	0	50.1	206	45	25	20	1	1	1	2	17	1	55	6	3	2	3	.400	0	0	3.58
Greensboro	A NYA	5	5	0	0	25	109	27	13	13	1	0	1	0	12	0	19	3	0	1	2	.333	0	0	4.68
1995 Greensboro	A NYA	10	10	0	0	64.2	245	42	20	16	2	1	1	0	16	1	77	3	0	3	2	.600	0	0	2.23
Tampa	A+ NYA	11	11	1	0	75.1	291	47	25	18	3	2	1	1	27	0	58	1	2	3	4	.429	0	0	2.15
Norwich	AA NYA	8	8	1	0	53	217	44	21	16	2	2	0	1	24	2	43	3	0	4	2	.667	1	0	2.72
1996 Norwich	AA NYA	8	8	1	0	46.1	201	42	26	23	7	1	3	1	20	0	42	5	0	5	2	.714	1	0	4.47
Columbus	AAA NYA	20	11	1	2	68	301	62	44	36	4	1	3	3	37	2	58	8	0	4	5	.444	0	1	4.76
1997 Norwich	AA NYA	2	2	0	0	10.2	48	12	8	8	0	2	0	0	5	0	13	0	0	0	2	.000	0	0	6.75
Columbus	AAA NYA	26	26	0	0	152.2	701	172	104	94	12	3	3	6	81	2	99	16	1	11	7	.611	0	0	5.54
4 Min. YEARS		100	91	4	2	546	2319	493	286	244	32	13	13	14	239	8	464	45	6	33	29	.532	2	1	4.02

Chad Ricketts

Pitches: Right **Bats:** Right **Pos:** P **Ht:** 6'5" **Wt:** 195 **Born:** 2/12/75 **Age:** 23

Year Team	Lg Org	G	GS	CG	GF	IP	BFP	H	R	ER	HR	SH	SF	HB	TBB	IBB	SO	WP	Bk	W	L	Pct.	ShO	Sv	ERA
1995 Cubs	R ChN	2	2	0	0	9	32	1	1	0	0	0	0	1	1	0	5	0	0	1	0	1.000	0	0	0.00
Williamsprt	A- ChN	12	12	0	0	68.2	312	89	46	32	4	0	3	1	16	0	37	1	3	4	5	.444	0	0	4.19
1996 Rockford	A ChN	37	9	0	17	87.2	389	89	60	49	8	5	2	7	29	2	70	5	1	3	8	.273	0	4	5.03
1997 Rockford	A ChN	16	0	0	10	29	116	19	9	8	1	1	1	1	11	2	32	1	0	4	0	1.000	0	3	2.48
Daytona	A+ ChN	20	0	0	17	20.1	82	13	4	1	0	0	0	1	6	0	18	1	0	3	1	.750	0	8	0.44
Orlando	AA ChN	2	0	0	2	2	15	7	4	4	0	0	0	0	2	0	3	0	0	0	0	.000	0	0	18.00
3 Min. YEARS		89	23	0	44	216.2	946	218	124	94	13	6	6	18	65	4	165	8	4	15	14	.517	0	15	3.90

Kevin Riggs

Bats: Left **Throws:** Right **Pos:** 2B **Ht:** 5'11" **Wt:** 190 **Born:** 2/3/69 **Age:** 29

Year Team	Lg Org	G	AB	H	2B	3B	HR	TB	R	RBI	TBB	IBB	SO	HBP	SH	SF	SB	CS	SB%	GDP	Avg	OBP	SLG
1990 Billings	R+ Cin	57	192	61	9	2	1	77	49	21	50	2	27	2	0	0	16	3	.84	5	.318	.463	.401
Chston-WV	A Cin	2	4	1	0	0	0	1	0	1	0	0	1	0	0	0	0	1	.00	0	.250	.250	.250
1991 Cedar Rapds	A Cin	118	406	109	21	2	2	140	72	43	91	2	50	3	2	6	23	8	.74	11	.268	.401	.345
Chston-WV	A Cin	1	2	1	0	0	0	1	0	0	1	0	0	0	0	0	0	0	.00	0	.500	.667	.500
1992 Cedar Rapds	A Cin	126	457	132	24	4	2	170	87	44	97	3	63	5	4	5	23	15	.61	10	.289	.415	.372
1993 Stockton	A+ Mil	108	377	131	18	3	3	164	84	45	101	3	46	1	1	4	12	15	.44	8	.347	.482	.435
1994 El Paso	AA Mil	66	230	68	10	2	1	85	38	22	46	1	39	1	0	0	3	7	.30	2	.296	.415	.370
1995 Norwich	AA NYA	57	179	59	16	1	4	89	38	36	51	3	28	4	0	4	5	5	.50	4	.330	.479	.497
1996 Norwich	AA NYA	118	403	117	24	1	2	149	75	37	81	4	66	6	2	5	9	9	.50	7	.290	.412	.370
1997 Akron	AA Cle	53	178	40	9	0	1	52	34	20	34	2	35	3	1	2	3	1	.75	5	.225	.355	.292
8 Min. YEARS		706	2428	719	131	15	16	928	477	269	552	20	355	25	10	26	94	64	.59	52	.296	.428	.382

Marquis Riley

Bats: Both **Throws:** Right **Pos:** OF **Ht:** 5'10" **Wt:** 170 **Born:** 12/27/70 **Age:** 27

Year Team	Lg Org	G	AB	H	2B	3B	HR	TB	R	RBI	TBB	IBB	SO	HBP	SH	SF	SB	CS	SB%	GDP	Avg	OBP	SLG
1992 Boise	A- Ana	52	201	48	12	1	0	62	47	12	37	0	29	2	2	0	7	4	.64	3	.239	.363	.308
1993 Palm Spring	A+ Ana	130	508	134	10	2	1	151	93	42	90	1	117	0	5	2	69	25	.73	3	.264	.373	.297
1994 Midland	AA Ana	93	374	107	12	4	1	130	68	29	35	3	57	6	7	4	32	5	.86	10	.286	.353	.348
Vancouver	AAA Ana	4	14	3	0	0	0	3	3	1	3	0	3	0	0	0	1	0	1.00	1	.214	.353	.214
1995 Vancouver	AAA Ana	120	477	125	6	6	0	143	70	43	49	3	69	1	2	4	29	10	.74	11	.262	.330	.300
1996 Vancouver	AAA Ana	12	47	11	2	0	0	13	8	0	3	0	12	0	0	0	3	0	1.00	2	.234	.280	.277
Charlotte	AAA Fla	92	300	68	10	0	0	78	43	13	26	1	31	1	4	2	16	5	.76	8	.227	.289	.260
1997 Vancouver	AAA Ana	65	242	64	6	0	0	70	33	8	36	0	27	1	6	2	27	7	.79	4	.264	.359	.289
6 Min. YEARS		568	2163	560	58	13	2	650	365	148	279	8	345	11	26	14	184	56	.77	42	.259	.345	.301

Armando Rios

Bats: Left **Throws:** Left **Pos:** OF **Ht:** 5'9" **Wt:** 178 **Born:** 9/13/71 **Age:** 26

Year Team	Lg Org	G	AB	H	2B	3B	HR	TB	R	RBI	TBB	IBB	SO	HBP	SH	SF	SB	CS	SB%	GDP	Avg	OBP	SLG
1994 Clinton	A SF	119	407	120	23	4	8	175	67	60	59	2	69	4	1	7	16	12	.57	3	.295	.384	.430
1995 San Jose	A+ SF	128	488	143	34	3	8	207	76	75	74	3	75	1	4	7	51	10	.84	8	.293	.382	.424
1996 Shreveport	AA SF	92	329	93	22	2	12	155	62	49	44	3	42	1	3	4	9	9	.50	2	.283	.365	.471
1997 Shreveport	AA SF	127	461	133	30	4	14	217	86	79	63	1	85	0	4	6	17	7	.71	11	.289	.370	.471
4 Min. YEARS		466	1685	489	109	15	42	754	291	263	240	9	271	6	12	24	93	38	.71	28	.290	.376	.447

Rafael Rivera

Pitches: Right Bats: Right Pos: P   Ht: 6'0" Wt: 190 Born: 12/13/75 Age: 22

Year Team	Lg Org	G	GS	CG	GF	IP	BFP	H	R	ER	HR	SH	SF	HB	TBB	IBB	SO	WP	Bk	W	L	Pct.	ShO	Sv	ERA
1996 Everett	A- Sea	24	0	0	3	49.1	203	47	19	12	1	1	0	0	10	0	61	2	0	4	1	.800	0	0	2.19
1997 Lancaster	A+ Sea	24	1	0	15	48.2	209	47	27	19	3	4	2	3	17	4	46	4	0	1	3	.250	0	3	3.51
Memphis	AA Sea	6	0	0	3	7	33	7	3	2	0	0	0	0	7	0	8	0	0	0	0	.000	0	0	2.57
2 Min. YEARS		54	1	0	21	105	445	101	49	33	4	5	2	3	34	4	115	6	0	5	4	.556	0	3	2.83

Scott Rivette

Pitches: Right Bats: Both Pos: P   Ht: 6'2" Wt: 200 Born: 2/8/74 Age: 24

Year Team	Lg Org	G	GS	CG	GF	IP	BFP	H	R	ER	HR	SH	SF	HB	TBB	IBB	SO	WP	Bk	W	L	Pct.	ShO	Sv	ERA
1995 Sou. Oregon	A- Oak	9	1	0	3	19	83	16	5	2	0	1	1	1	11	2	22	1	0	1	0	1.000	0	2	0.95
W Michigan	A Oak	8	0	0	4	15.1	65	12	5	5	0	0	2	0	7	0	15	1	0	1	0	1.000	0	2	2.93
1996 W Michigan	A Oak	32	29	0	1	153.1	667	145	80	60	7	3	2	12	51	0	142	9	2	8	9	.471	0	1	3.52
1997 Modesto	A+ Oak	20	20	3	0	126	533	147	65	50	12	3	2	1	31	1	96	8	1	9	9	.500	0	0	3.57
Huntsville	AA Oak	7	6	0	0	39	180	52	29	29	3	2	3	0	19	0	33	3	1	3	1	.750	0	0	6.69
3 Min. YEARS		76	56	3	8	352.2	1528	372	184	146	22	8	11	20	119	3	308	22	4	23	19	.548	0	5	3.73

Todd Rizzo

Pitches: Left Bats: Right Pos: P   Ht: 6'3" Wt: 220 Born: 5/24/71 Age: 27

Year Team	Lg Org	G	GS	CG	GF	IP	BFP	H	R	ER	HR	SH	SF	HB	TBB	IBB	SO	WP	Bk	W	L	Pct.	ShO	Sv	ERA
1992 Yakima	A- LA	15	0	1	8	26	121	21	13	13	3	0	1	2	24	0	26	6	0	2	0	1.000	0	0	4.50
Dodgers	R LA	3	1	0	1	7	31	4	4	3	0	0	0	1	8	0	7	0	0	0	1	.000	0	0	3.86
1995 Pr William	A+ ChA	36	0	0	10	68	307	68	30	21	2	2	1	3	39	8	59	13	0	3	5	.375	0	1	2.78
1996 Birmingham	AA ChA	46	0	0	19	68.2	300	61	28	21	0	3	2	1	40	7	48	7	0	4	4	.500	0	10	2.75
1997 Nashville	AAA ChA	54	0	0	23	70.2	318	63	39	28	6	3	1	3	33	3	60	9	0	4	5	.444	0	6	3.57
4 Min. YEARS		154	1	0	61	240.1	1077	217	114	86	11	8	5	10	144	18	200	35	0	13	15	.464	0	17	3.22

Petie Roach

Pitches: Left Bats: Left Pos: P   Ht: 6'2" Wt: 180 Born: 9/19/70 Age: 27

Year Team	Lg Org	G	GS	CG	GF	IP	BFP	H	R	ER	HR	SH	SF	HB	TBB	IBB	SO	WP	Bk	W	L	Pct.	ShO	Sv	ERA
1994 Yakima	A- LA	8	4	0	2	40	147	24	5	3	0	4	1	0	6	0	32	0	1	3	1	.750	0	0	0.68
Vero Beach	A+ LA	7	6	0	0	36.2	157	41	20	18	0	0	1	1	12	0	19	1	1	2	3	.400	0	0	4.42
1995 San Berndno	A+ LA	30	0	0	14	33	143	28	16	11	2	2	2	2	14	1	38	5	0	1	2	.333	0	8	3.00
1996 Vero Beach	A+ LA	17	10	0	2	69	273	56	30	28	6	1	1	1	17	1	52	3	2	3	4	.429	0	0	3.65
San Antonio	AA LA	13	13	1	0	75.1	336	81	41	32	5	3	3	5	34	0	40	5	4	6	3	.667	0	0	3.82
1997 San Antonio	AA LA	13	13	1	0	82	351	76	39	34	14	3	2	1	35	0	56	7	0	7	4	.636	0	0	3.73
Albuquerque	AAA LA	31	0	0	6	49.1	232	56	31	29	6	3	4	6	27	3	33	8	0	0	5	.000	0	1	5.29
4 Min. YEARS		119	46	2	24	385.1	1639	362	182	155	33	12	13	17	145	5	270	29	8	22	22	.500	0	9	3.62

J.P. Roberge

Bats: Right Throws: Right Pos: OF   Ht: 6'0" Wt: 180 Born: 9/12/72 Age: 25

Year Team	Lg Org	G	AB	H	2B	3B	HR	TB	R	RBI	TBB	IBB	SO	HBP	SH	SF	SB	CS	SB%	GDP	Avg	OBP	SLG
1994 Great Falls	R+ LA	63	256	82	17	1	1	104	55	42	20	0	22	5	2	5	24	4	.86	7	.320	.374	.406
Yakima	A- LA	4	8	3	1	0	0	4	1	0	0	0	3	1	0	0	0	1	.00	0	.375	.444	.500
1995 Vero Beach	A+ LA	3	9	0	0	0	0	0	1	0	0	0	2	0	0	0	0	0	.00	0	.000	.000	.000
San Berndno	A+ LA	116	450	129	22	1	17	204	92	59	34	0	62	8	2	3	31	8	.79	9	.287	.345	.453
1996 San Berndno	A+ LA	12	44	16	3	1	1	24	8	6	3	0	9	2	0	1	1	2	.33	0	.364	.420	.545
San Antonio	AA LA	62	232	68	14	2	6	104	28	27	14	1	39	2	2	2	9	3	.75	5	.293	.336	.448
Albuquerque	AAA LA	53	156	50	6	1	4	70	17	17	14	1	28	1	3	0	3	0	1.00	1	.321	.380	.449
1997 San Antonio	AA LA	134	516	166	26	4	17	251	94	105	39	3	70	7	2	5	18	9	.67	13	.322	.374	.486
4 Min. YEARS		447	1671	514	89	10	46	761	296	256	124	5	235	26	11	16	86	27	.76	35	.308	.361	.455

Kevin Roberson

Bats: Both Throws: Right Pos: OF   Ht: 6'4" Wt: 210 Born: 1/29/68 Age: 30

Year Team	Lg Org	G	AB	H	2B	3B	HR	TB	R	RBI	TBB	IBB	SO	HBP	SH	SF	SB	CS	SB%	GDP	Avg	OBP	SLG
1988 Wytheville	R+ ChN	63	225	47	12	2	3	72	39	29	40	0	86	3	0	2	3	2	.60	0	.209	.333	.320
1989 Chston-WV	A ChN	126	429	109	19	1	13	169	49	57	70	4	149	5	2	3	3	6	.33	7	.254	.363	.394
1990 Winston-Sal	A+ ChN	85	313	84	23	3	5	128	49	45	25	0	70	3	1	2	7	3	.70	6	.268	.327	.409
Charlotte	AA ChN	31	119	29	6	2	5	54	14	16	8	0	23	0	1	2	2	0	1.00	3	.244	.287	.454
1991 Charlotte	AA ChN	136	507	130	23	2	19	214	77	67	39	1	125	9	0	5	17	3	.85	10	.256	.318	.422
1992 Iowa	AAA ChN	51	197	60	15	4	6	101	25	34	5	1	46	2	1	1	0	0	.00	4	.305	.327	.513
1993 Iowa	AAA ChN	67	263	80	20	1	16	150	48	50	19	3	66	4	0	3	3	2	.60	4	.304	.356	.570
1994 Iowa	AAA ChN	19	67	21	8	0	3	38	9	17	4	1	19	3	0	0	1	0	1.00	0	.313	.364	.567
1995 Tacoma	AAA Sea	42	157	37	6	1	6	63	17	17	19	1	51	2	0	1	1	1	.50	4	.236	.322	.401
1996 Norfolk	AAA NYN	70	215	57	13	3	7	97	26	33	14	2	65	7	1	2	0	0	.00	4	.265	.328	.451
1997 Phoenix	AAA SF	109	349	100	19	5	14	171	60	67	37	2	98	11	0	2	9	5	.64	6	.287	.371	.490
1993 Chicago	NL	62	180	34	4	1	9	67	23	27	12	0	48	3	0	0	0	1	.00	2	.189	.251	.372
1994 Chicago	NL	44	55	12	4	0	4	28	8	9	2	0	14	2	0	0	0	0	.00	0	.218	.271	.509
1995 Chicago	NL	32	38	7	1	0	4	20	5	6	6	0	14	1	0	0	0	0	.00	1	.184	.311	.526
1996 New York	NL	27	36	8	1	0	3	18	8	9	7	0	17	1	0	0	0	0	.00	0	.222	.348	.500

213

Year Team	Lg Org	G	AB	H	2B	3B	HR	TB	R	RBI	TBB	IBB	SO	HBP	SH	SF	SB	CS	SB%	GDP	Avg	OBP	SLG
10 Min. YEARS		799	2841	754	164	24	97	1257	413	432	280	15	798	49	6	27	45	24	.65	48	.265	.339	.442
4 Maj. YEARS		165	309	61	10	1	20	133	44	51	27	0	93	7	0	2	0	2	.00	6	.197	.275	.430

Sid Roberson

Pitches: Left Bats: Left Pos: P   Ht: 5' 9" Wt: 170 Born: 9/7/71 Age: 26

Year Team	Lg Org	G	GS	CG	GF	IP	BFP	H	R	ER	HR	SH	SF	HB	TBB	IBB	SO	WP	Bk	W	L	Pct.	ShO	Sv	ERA
1992 Helena	R+ Mil	9	8	1	1	65	276	68	32	25	8	3	1	2	18	0	65	4	1	4	4	.500	0	0	3.46
1993 Stockton	A+ Mil	24	23	6	0	166	684	157	68	48	8	7	3	12	34	0	87	6	4	12	8	.600	1	0	2.60
1994 El Paso	AA Mil	25	25	8	0	181.1	771	190	70	57	7	5	7	17	48	3	119	4	1	15	8	.652	0	0	2.83
1995 New Orleans	AAA Mil	4	3	0	0	13	69	20	11	11	1	0	2	1	10	0	8	0	0	0	2	.000	0	0	7.62
1996 New Orleans	AAA Mil	2	2	0	0	11	48	10	6	6	2	0	1	0	9	0	3	1	0	0	1	.000	0	0	4.91
1997 Tucson	AAA Mil	10	4	0	4	22	129	47	29	28	5	0	2	4	14	3	8	1	0	0	2	.000	0	0	11.45
1995 Milwaukee	AL	26	13	0	8	84.1	379	102	55	54	16	0	2	8	37	3	40	3	0	6	4	.600	0	0	5.76
6 Min. YEARS		74	65	15	5	458.1	1977	492	216	175	31	15	16	36	133	6	290	16	6	31	25	.554	1	0	3.44

Brett Roberts

Pitches: Right Bats: Right Pos: P   Ht: 6'7" Wt: 225 Born: 3/24/70 Age: 28

Year Team	Lg Org	G	GS	CG	GF	IP	BFP	H	R	ER	HR	SH	SF	HB	TBB	IBB	SO	WP	Bk	W	L	Pct.	ShO	Sv	ERA
1991 Elizabethtn	R+ Min	6	6	1	0	28	112	21	8	7	0	0	0	0	10	0	27	2	4	3	0	1.000	0	0	2.25
1992 Kenosha	A Min	7	6	0	1	22.2	105	23	18	14	4	1	0	0	15	0	23	1	0	1	1	.500	0	0	5.56
1993 Ft. Myers	A+ Min	28	28	3	0	173.2	772	184	93	84	5	5	5	4	86	5	108	10	2	9	16	.360	0	0	4.35
1994 Ft. Myers	A+ Min	21	21	1	0	116.2	520	123	71	56	5	4	8	3	47	3	75	8	0	6	7	.462	0	0	4.32
Nashville	AA Min	5	5	0	0	20	102	30	18	15	1	0	1	1	12	1	11	0	0	2	1	.667	0	0	6.75
1995 Hardware City	AA Min	28	28	5	0	174	729	162	72	66	9	4	5	5	50	0	135	6	0	11	9	.550	1	0	3.41
1996 Salt Lake	AAA Min	31	30	2	1	168.1	772	211	115	101	28	2	5	9	71	0	86	7	0	9	7	.563	1	0	5.40
1997 Salt Lake	AAA Min	24	6	0	7	58.2	286	89	51	45	11	0	2	2	33	0	33	4	0	1	3	.250	0	1	6.90
Fargo-Mh	IND —	8	8	0	0	43.1	184	40	24	17	4	0	0	0	12	0	41	1	1	5	2	.714	0	0	3.53
7 Min. YEARS		158	138	12	9	805.1	3582	883	470	405	67	16	26	24	336	9	539	39	7	47	46	.505	2	1	4.53

Chris Roberts

Pitches: Left Bats: Right Pos: P   Ht: 5'10" Wt: 185 Born: 6/25/71 Age: 27

Year Team	Lg Org	G	GS	CG	GF	IP	BFP	H	R	ER	HR	SH	SF	HB	TBB	IBB	SO	WP	Bk	W	L	Pct.	ShO	Sv	ERA
1993 St. Lucie	A+ NYN	25	25	3	0	173.1	703	162	64	53	3	2	4	7	36	0	111	2	1	13	5	.722	2	0	2.75
1994 Binghamton	AA NYN	27	27	2	0	175.1	751	164	77	64	11	8	5	6	77	1	128	12	1	13	8	.619	2	0	3.29
1995 Norfolk	AAA NYN	25	25	2	0	150	676	197	99	92	24	6	4	8	58	0	88	5	0	7	13	.350	0	0	5.52
1996 Mets	R NYN	3	3	0	0	13	48	11	2	2	0	0	0	1	0	0	12	1	0	0	0	.000	0	0	1.38
St. Lucie	A+ NYN	1	1	0	0	6	21	1	0	0	0	0	0	0	3	0	2	0	0	1	0	1.000	0	0	0.00
Binghamton	AA NYN	9	9	1	0	46	225	55	40	37	6	6	2	1	37	0	30	1	0	2	7	.222	0	0	7.24
1997 Binghamton	AA NYN	19	19	1	0	105.1	448	103	69	58	18	6	2	8	33	0	66	1	1	5	8	.385	0	0	4.96
Norfolk	AAA NYN	7	6	0	1	37.1	164	38	17	12	2	2	1	2	17	0	21	0	0	0	4	.000	0	0	2.89
5 Min. YEARS		116	115	9	1	706.1	3036	731	368	318	64	30	18	33	261	1	458	22	4	41	45	.477	4	0	4.05

David Roberts

Bats: Left Throws: Left Pos: DH   Ht: 5'10" Wt: 172 Born: 5/31/72 Age: 26

Year Team	Lg Org	G	AB	H	2B	3B	HR	TB	R	RBI	TBB	IBB	SO	HBP	SH	SF	SB	CS	SB%	GDP	Avg	OBP	SLG
1994 Jamestown	A- Det	54	178	52	7	2	0	63	33	12	29	4	27	1	3	1	12	8	.60	0	.292	.392	.354
1995 Lakeland	A+ Det	92	357	108	10	5	3	137	67	30	39	2	43	1	2	2	30	8	.79	7	.303	.371	.384
1996 Visalia	A+ Det	126	482	131	24	7	5	184	112	37	98	0	105	1	3	7	65	21	.76	6	.272	.391	.382
Jacksnville	AA Det	3	9	2	0	0	0	2	0	0	1	0	0	0	0	0	0	1	.00	0	.222	.300	.222
1997 Jacksnville	AA Det	105	415	123	24	2	4	163	76	41	45	1	62	2	9	2	23	5	.82	5	.296	.366	.393
4 Min. YEARS		380	1441	416	65	16	12	549	288	120	212	7	237	5	17	12	130	43	.75	18	.289	.379	.381

Lonell Roberts

Bats: Both Throws: Right Pos: OF   Ht: 6'0" Wt: 172 Born: 6/7/71 Age: 27

Year Team	Lg Org	G	AB	H	2B	3B	HR	TB	R	RBI	TBB	IBB	SO	HBP	SH	SF	SB	CS	SB%	GDP	Avg	OBP	SLG
1989 Medicne Hat	R+ Tor	29	78	11	1	0	0	12	2	6	7	0	27	1	1	0	3	3	.50	1	.141	.221	.154
1990 Medicne Hat	R+ Tor	38	118	25	2	0	0	27	14	8	5	0	29	0	0	0	8	1	.89	3	.212	.244	.229
1991 Myrtle Bch	A Tor	110	388	86	7	2	2	103	39	27	27	1	84	2	10	2	35	14	.71	0	.222	.274	.265
1992 St. Cathrns	A- Tor	62	244	50	3	1	0	55	37	11	19	1	75	3	4	0	33	13	.72	0	.205	.271	.225
Knoxville	AA Tor	5	14	0	0	0	0	0	1	0	1	0	4	0	0	0	1	0	1.00	0	.000	.067	.000
1993 Hagerstown	A Tor	131	501	120	21	4	3	158	78	46	53	1	103	4	2	3	54	15	.78	8	.240	.316	.315
1994 Dunedin	A+ Tor	118	490	132	18	3	3	165	74	31	32	3	104	3	2	2	61	12	.84	4	.269	.316	.337
1995 Knoxville	AA Tor	116	454	107	12	3	1	128	66	29	27	1	97	3	4	4	57	18	.76	7	.236	.281	.282
1996 Knoxville	AA Tor	58	237	69	1	0	1	73	35	12	32	1	39	0	3	0	24	14	.63	1	.291	.375	.308
1997 Knoxville	AA Tor	7	21	4	0	1	0	6	5	0	2	0	3	2	2	0	0	2	.00	0	.190	.320	.286
Syracuse	AAA Tor	77	173	27	4	0	3	40	17	10	19	0	50	0	2	0	6	7	.46	1	.156	.240	.231
9 Min. YEARS		751	2718	631	69	14	13	767	368	180	224	8	615	18	30	13	282	99	.74	25	.232	.294	.282

Willis Roberts

Pitches: Right **Bats:** Right **Pos:** P   Ht: 6'3" Wt: 175 Born: 6/19/75 Age: 23

Year Team	Lg Org	G	GS	CG	GF	IP	BFP	H	R	ER	HR	SH	SF	HB	TBB	IBB	SO	WP	Bk	W	L	Pct.	ShO	Sv	ERA
1993 Bristol	R+ Det	10	2	0	2	26	116	24	16	4	0	2	0	1	11	0	23	2	0	2	3	.400	0	1	1.38
1994 Bristol	R+ Det	4	4	0	0	20.2	81	9	9	9	1	0	1	2	8	0	17	2	0	1	2	.333	0	0	3.92
1995 Fayettevlle	A Det	17	15	0	0	80	339	72	33	24	2	1	2	6	40	0	52	15	3	6	3	.667	0	0	2.70
1996 Lakeland	A+ Det	23	22	2	0	149.1	636	133	60	48	5	8	9	9	69	0	105	13	3	9	7	.563	0	0	2.89
1997 Jacksnville	AA Det	26	26	2	0	149	685	181	120	104	18	6	7	6	64	0	86	6	6	6	15	.286	0	0	6.28
5 Min. YEARS		80	69	4	2	425	1857	419	238	189	26	17	19	24	192	0	283	38	12	24	30	.444	0	1	4.00

Hassan Robinson

Bats: Right **Throws:** Right **Pos:** OF   Ht: 6'3" Wt: 180 Born: 9/22/72 Age: 25

Year Team	Lg Org	G	AB	H	2B	3B	HR	TB	R	RBI	TBB	IBB	SO	HBP	SH	SF	SB	CS	SB%	GDP	Avg	OBP	SLG
1994 Auburn	A- Hou	43	149	36	3	0	0	39	13	12	2	0	12	3	2	3	4	1	.80	5	.242	.261	.262
1995 Auburn	A- Hou	65	245	65	8	1	0	75	32	18	9	0	25	2	2	1	12	2	.86	9	.265	.296	.306
1996 Quad City	A Hou	106	373	100	11	2	1	119	53	38	14	2	35	3	5	3	15	6	.71	4	.271	.300	.319
1997 Jackson	AA Hou	9	23	4	1	0	0	5	3	1	0	0	2	0	0	1	0	0	.00	1	.174	.167	.217
Kissimmee	A+ Hou	35	115	29	4	0	0	33	12	12	3	0	14	1	1	1	3	3	.50	1	.252	.275	.287
4 Min. YEARS		258	905	235	27	3	1	271	113	81	28	2	88	9	10	9	34	12	.74	20	.260	.286	.299

Kerry Robinson

Bats: Left **Throws:** Left **Pos:** OF   Ht: 6'0" Wt: 175 Born: 10/3/73 Age: 24

Year Team	Lg Org	G	AB	H	2B	3B	HR	TB	R	RBI	TBB	IBB	SO	HBP	SH	SF	SB	CS	SB%	GDP	Avg	OBP	SLG
1995 Johnson Cty	R+ StL	60	250	74	12	8	1	105	44	26	16	1	30	0	3	2	14	10	.58	3	.296	.336	.420
1996 Peoria	A StL	123	440	158	17	14	2	209	98	47	51	5	51	3	4	8	50	26	.66	2	.359	.422	.475
1997 Arkansas	AA StL	136	523	168	16	3	2	196	80	62	54	1	64	2	5	2	40	23	.63	7	.321	.386	.375
Louisville	AAA StL	2	9	1	0	0	0	1	0	0	0	0	1	0	0	0	0	0	.00	0	.111	.111	.111
3 Min. YEARS		321	1222	401	45	25	5	511	222	135	121	7	146	5	12	12	104	59	.64	12	.328	.388	.418

Oscar Robles

Bats: Left **Throws:** Right **Pos:** 2B   Ht: 5'11" Wt: 155 Born: 4/9/76 Age: 22

Year Team	Lg Org	G	AB	H	2B	3B	HR	TB	R	RBI	TBB	IBB	SO	HBP	SH	SF	SB	CS	SB%	GDP	Avg	OBP	SLG
1994 Astros	R Hou	55	165	54	5	1	0	61	46	19	32	0	17	2	10	0	14	9	.61	5	.327	.442	.370
1995 Auburn	A- Hou	58	216	62	9	1	0	73	49	19	39	1	15	0	1	1	8	2	.80	5	.287	.395	.338
1996 Kissimmee	A+ Hou	125	427	115	13	2	0	132	57	29	74	3	37	6	8	2	10	8	.56	13	.269	.383	.309
1997 New Orleans	AAA Hou	2	3	1	0	0	0	1	0	0	1	0	1	0	0	0	0	0	.00	0	.333	.500	.333
Kissimmee	A+ Hou	66	236	53	4	0	0	57	39	21	43	0	28	1	8	2	0	1	.00	4	.225	.344	.242
4 Min. YEARS		306	1047	285	31	4	0	324	185	88	189	4	98	9	27	5	32	20	.62	27	.272	.386	.309

John Rocker

Pitches: Left **Bats:** Right **Pos:** P   Ht: 6'4" Wt: 205 Born: 10/17/74 Age: 23

Year Team	Lg Org	G	GS	CG	GF	IP	BFP	H	R	ER	HR	SH	SF	HB	TBB	IBB	SO	WP	Bk	W	L	Pct.	ShO	Sv	ERA
1994 Danville	R+ Atl	12	12	1	0	63.2	285	50	36	25	4	3	4	6	38	1	72	13	4	1	5	.167	0	0	3.53
1995 Macon	A Atl	16	16	0	0	86	375	86	50	43	5	1	1	4	52	0	61	5	1	4	4	.500	0	0	4.50
Eugene	A- Atl	12	12	0	0	59.1	260	45	40	34	4	1	1	2	36	0	74	7	2	1	5	.167	0	0	5.16
1996 Macon	A Atl	20	19	2	1	106.1	453	85	60	46	7	1	4	6	63	1	107	12	3	5	3	.625	2	0	3.89
Durham	A+ Atl	9	9	0	0	58.1	245	63	24	22	4	0	0	1	25	0	43	4	0	4	3	.571	0	0	3.39
1997 Durham	A+ Atl	11	1	0	3	35.1	157	33	21	17	3	2	1	2	22	0	39	5	1	1	1	.500	0	0	4.33
Greenville	AA Atl	22	18	0	1	113	507	119	69	61	12	3	1	0	61	0	96	17	2	5	6	.455	0	0	4.86
4 Min. YEARS		102	87	3	5	522	2282	481	300	248	39	11	12	21	297	2	492	63	13	21	27	.438	2	0	4.28

Raul Rodarte

Bats: Right **Throws:** Right **Pos:** OF   Ht: 5'11" Wt: 190 Born: 4/9/70 Age: 28

Year Team	Lg Org	G	AB	H	2B	3B	HR	TB	R	RBI	TBB	IBB	SO	HBP	SH	SF	SB	CS	SB%	GDP	Avg	OBP	SLG
1991 Peninsula	A+ Sea	65	216	48	4	1	0	54	19	14	32	0	56	0	1	2	5	1	.83	5	.222	.320	.250
1992 Peninsula	A+ Sea	94	290	72	8	6	2	98	37	22	35	2	37	1	3	2	15	10	.60	7	.248	.329	.338
1993 Riverside	A+ Sea	106	402	116	19	1	5	152	79	48	51	0	66	0	6	2	13	14	.48	7	.289	.367	.378
1994 Jacksnville	AA Sea	34	91	22	3	1	3	36	13	13	8	1	15	1	3	0	2	2	.50	2	.242	.310	.396
Riverside	A+ Sea	39	156	50	6	4	4	76	29	37	15	1	31	2	1	1	5	2	.71	3	.321	.385	.487
1995 Lynchburg	A+ Pit	104	346	99	18	2	12	157	57	48	35	2	49	4	2	1	19	13	.59	8	.286	.358	.454
Carolina	AA Pit	16	54	20	5	1	0	27	8	11	10	3	14	0	2	0	2	2	.50	2	.370	.469	.500
1996 Carolina	AA Pit	20	43	9	1	0	0	10	6	6	12	0	12	1	1	0	2	1	.67	1	.209	.393	.233
Greenville	AA Atl	48	176	58	11	0	6	87	33	28	16	2	23	0	1	3	0	3	.00	6	.330	.379	.494
Richmond	AAA Atl	61	219	74	12	2	9	117	30	46	19	1	43	1	0	4	4	2	.67	6	.338	.387	.534
1997 Greenville	AA Atl	55	172	38	8	1	7	69	29	22	26	0	30	2	1	0	10	6	.63	4	.242	.321	.401
Richmond	AAA Atl	41	95	23	4	0	0	27	13	10	10	0	22	1	0	0	2	2	.50	5	.242	.321	.284
7 Min. YEARS		683	2260	629	99	19	48	910	353	305	269	12	398	13	21	15	79	58	.58	56	.278	.356	.403

Adam Rodriguez

Bats: Right Throws: Right Pos: C Ht: 5'10" Wt: 195 Born: 3/16/71 Age: 27

Year Team	Lg Org	G	AB	H	2B	3B	HR	TB	R	RBI	TBB	IBB	SO	HBP	SH	SF	SB	CS	SB%	GDP	Avg	OBP	SLG
1993 Bristol	R+ Det	42	131	29	4	2	5	52	19	19	13	1	36	1	1	1	5	1	.83	1	.221	.295	.397
Lakeland	A+ Det	3	6	1	0	0	1	4	4	2	2	0	3	1	0	0	0	0	.00	0	.167	.444	.667
1994 Fayettevlle	A Det	46	164	42	14	1	5	73	25	23	15	2	28	1	0	0	2	2	.50	2	.256	.322	.445
1995 Fayettevlle	A Det	39	139	42	14	1	4	70	16	25	9	0	25	2	1	0	0	1	.00	5	.302	.353	.504
Lakeland	A+ Det	30	88	22	4	0	1	29	8	10	8	0	17	0	0	0	1	0	1.00	1	.250	.313	.330
1996 Lakeland	A+ Det	57	160	38	7	1	3	56	18	25	20	0	37	1	1	6	0	0	.00	7	.238	.316	.350
1997 Jacksnville	AA Det	2	5	1	0	0	0	1	0	0	2	0	0	0	0	0	0	0	.00	0	.200	.429	.200
Toledo	AAA Det	29	70	14	2	0	1	19	4	3	3	0	17	1	1	0	0	1	.00	3	.200	.243	.271
5 Min. YEARS		248	763	189	45	5	20	304	94	107	72	3	163	7	4	7	8	5	.62	19	.248	.316	.398

Frank Rodriguez

Pitches: Right Bats: Right Pos: P Ht: 5'9" Wt: 170 Born: 1/6/73 Age: 25

Year Team	Lg Org	G	GS	CG	GF	IP	BFP	H	R	ER	HR	SH	SF	HB	TBB	IBB	SO	WP	Bk	W	L	Pct.	ShO	Sv	ERA
1992 Brewers	R Mil	9	7	0	0	49	193	35	9	6	1	0	1	1	14	0	37	1	0	3	1	.750	0	0	1.10
Helena	R+ Mil	6	1	0	2	10.2	46	14	6	3	1	0	0	1	3	0	3	3	0	1	1	.500	0	0	2.53
1993 Helena	R+ Mil	18	1	0	9	41	176	31	19	11	0	2	0	1	17	3	63	8	1	2	1	.667	0	5	2.41
1994 Stockton	A+ Mil	26	24	3	0	151	627	139	67	57	6	6	9	13	52	1	124	6	1	10	9	.526	1	0	3.40
1995 El Paso	AA Mil	28	27	1	1	142.2	650	157	90	79	9	9	9	5	80	2	129	16	1	9	8	.529	0	0	4.98
1996 New Orleans	AAA Mil	13	1	0	7	18.2	87	24	15	14	1	1	1	0	11	3	16	0	0	0	2	.000	0	0	6.75
El Paso	AA Mil	16	7	0	3	34.1	169	45	32	26	1	0	2	2	24	0	39	1	0	3	4	.429	0	0	6.82
1997 El Paso	AA Mil	16	3	0	0	50.1	210	46	23	19	2	2	7	3	13	0	40	4	0	2	2	.500	0	4	3.40
Tucson	AAA Mil	12	6	1	0	47	204	53	25	23	1	2	1	2	19	1	41	1	0	3	1	.750	1	0	4.40
6 Min. YEARS		159	74	5	39	544.2	2362	544	286	238	22	22	30	28	233	10	492	40	2	33	29	.532	2	9	3.93

Luis Rodriguez

Bats: Right Throws: Right Pos: C Ht: 5'9" Wt: 160 Born: 1/3/74 Age: 24

Year Team	Lg Org	G	AB	H	2B	3B	HR	TB	R	RBI	TBB	IBB	SO	HBP	SH	SF	SB	CS	SB%	GDP	Avg	OBP	SLG
1995 St. Cathms	A- Tor	66	257	71	16	2	1	94	22	20	10	1	49	1	2	1	2	4	.33	7	.276	.305	.366
1996 Hagerstown	A Tor	79	256	53	8	1	1	66	19	25	24	0	58	1	5	1	6	4	.60	3	.207	.277	.258
1997 Syracuse	AAA Tor	3	2	0	0	0	0	0	0	0	0	0	2	0	0	0	0	0	.00	0	.000	.000	.000
Hagerstown	A Tor	27	94	25	6	0	2	37	13	14	2	0	20	1	3	2	3	0	1.00	2	.266	.283	.394
Knoxville	AA Tor	24	78	21	3	1	0	26	6	6	3	0	20	1	0	0	0	1	.00	1	.269	.305	.333
3 Min. YEARS		199	687	170	33	4	4	223	60	65	39	1	149	4	10	4	11	9	.55	13	.247	.290	.325

Maximo Rodriguez

Bats: Right Throws: Right Pos: C Ht: 6'0" Wt: 170 Born: 11/18/73 Age: 24

Year Team	Lg Org	G	AB	H	2B	3B	HR	TB	R	RBI	TBB	IBB	SO	HBP	SH	SF	SB	CS	SB%	GDP	Avg	OBP	SLG
1993 Marlins	R Fla	48	187	61	8	5	0	79	30	29	10	1	26	1	0	2	3	2	.60	5	.326	.360	.422
1994 Brevard Cty	A+ Fla	12	40	5	1	0	2	12	4	12	1	0	16	1	0	0	0	0	.00	5	.125	.167	.300
Marlins	R Fla	5	21	4	1	0	0	5	3	2	1	0	4	1	0	0	0	0	.00	1	.190	.261	.238
Elmira	A- Fla	51	170	40	9	1	2	57	20	19	8	0	42	1	1	0	3	1	.75	4	.235	.274	.335
1995 Kane County	A Fla	72	236	45	7	1	5	69	18	30	18	0	65	2	1	2	0	1	.00	7	.191	.252	.292
1996 Brevard Cty	A+ Fla	84	273	62	16	0	3	87	19	39	18	2	62	3	2	4	3	3	.50	17	.227	.279	.319
Portland	AA Fla	6	17	3	0	0	0	3	1	1	1	0	6	0	0	0	0	1	.00	1	.176	.222	.176
1997 Charlotte	AAA Fla	7	21	1	0	0	0	1	2	0	1	0	7	0	0	0	0	0	.00	0	.048	.091	.048
Brevard Cty	A+ Fla	42	118	24	4	2	2	38	14	10	10	0	30	1	2	0	0	1	.00	5	.203	.271	.322
5 Min. YEARS		327	1083	245	46	9	14	351	111	142	68	3	258	10	6	8	9	9	.50	42	.226	.276	.324

Noel Rodriguez

Bats: Right Throws: Right Pos: DH Ht: 6'3" Wt: 180 Born: 12/5/73 Age: 24

Year Team	Lg Org	G	AB	H	2B	3B	HR	TB	R	RBI	TBB	IBB	SO	HBP	SH	SF	SB	CS	SB%	GDP	Avg	OBP	SLG
1991 Astros	R Hou	22	55	9	1	0	0	10	4	6	1	0	11	0	0	0	2	0	1.00	3	.164	.179	.182
1992 Astros	R Hou	37	134	42	7	0	1	52	8	16	4	1	22	1	0	3	3	6	.33	2	.313	.331	.388
1993 Asheville	A Hou	38	133	35	8	0	1	46	23	12	9	0	31	2	1	0	3	0	1.00	6	.263	.319	.346
Auburn	A- Hou	69	273	82	12	4	6	120	41	54	12	0	52	3	0	7	0	2	.00	4	.300	.329	.440
1994 Quad City	A Hou	64	242	68	11	1	4	93	28	29	11	1	56	2	0	2	0	3	.00	4	.281	.315	.384
1995 Quad City	A Hou	109	386	120	26	5	8	180	48	71	28	1	49	4	0	4	4	5	.44	11	.311	.360	.466
1996 Quad City	A Hou	39	144	39	10	0	4	61	26	19	14	0	18	1	0	0	1	0	1.00	1	.271	.340	.424
Kissimmee	A+ Hou	82	291	73	16	1	5	106	24	38	26	1	31	3	2	1	0	1	.00	9	.251	.318	.364
1997 Jackson	AA Hou	33	85	20	3	0	4	35	12	17	11	1	18	2	0	4	0	2	.00	1	.235	.324	.412
Kissimmee	A+ Hou	65	228	72	15	1	4	101	26	36	23	0	24	3	1	1	1	5	.17	8	.316	.384	.443
7 Min. YEARS		558	1971	560	109	12	37	804	240	298	139	5	312	21	4	22	14	24	.37	49	.284	.334	.408

Steve Rodriguez

Bats: Right Throws: Right Pos: 3B Ht: 5'8" Wt: 170 Born: 11/29/70 Age: 27

Year Team	Lg Org	G	AB	H	2B	3B	HR	TB	R	RBI	TBB	IBB	SO	HBP	SH	SF	SB	CS	SB%	GDP	Avg	OBP	SLG
1992 Winter Havn	A+ Bos	26	87	15	0	0	1	18	13	5	9	0	17	2	3	0	4	1	.80	3	.172	.265	.207
1993 Lynchburg	A+ Bos	120	493	135	26	3	3	176	78	42	31	0	69	4	8	3	20	13	.61	15	.274	.320	.357

Year Team	Lg Org	G	AB	H	2B	3B	HR	TB	R	RBI	TBB	IBB	SO	HBP	SH	SF	SB	CS	SB%	GDP	Avg	OBP	SLG
					BATTING												**BASERUNNING**				**PERCENTAGES**		
1994 New Britain	AA Bos	38	159	45	5	2	0	54	25	14	9	0	14	1	3	1	8	4	.67	3	.283	.324	.340
Pawtucket	AAA Bos	62	233	70	11	0	1	84	28	21	14	0	30	1	3	2	11	3	.79	6	.300	.340	.361
1995 Pawtucket	AAA Bos	82	324	78	16	3	1	103	39	24	25	1	34	4	2	3	12	10	.55	7	.241	.301	.318
1996 Toledo	AAA Det	96	333	95	18	2	4	129	49	30	23	0	43	2	7	2	18	3	.86	8	.285	.333	.387
1997 Toledo	AAA Det	107	425	99	30	1	4	143	57	38	26	0	58	4	6	5	18	5	.78	6	.233	.280	.336
1995 Boston	AL	6	8	1	0	0	0	1	1	0	1	0	1	0	0	0	1	0	1.00	0	.125	.222	.125
Detroit	AL	12	31	6	1	0	0	7	4	0	5	0	9	0	0	0	1	2	.33	1	.194	.306	.226
6 Min. YEARS		531	2054	537	106	11	14	707	289	174	137	1	265	18	32	16	91	39	.70	48	.261	.311	.344

Tony Rodriguez

Bats: **Right** Throws: **Right** Pos: **SS** Ht: **5'11"** Wt: **178** Born: **8/15/70** Age: **27**

Year Team	Lg Org	G	AB	H	2B	3B	HR	TB	R	RBI	TBB	IBB	SO	HBP	SH	SF	SB	CS	SB%	GDP	Avg	OBP	SLG
					BATTING												**BASERUNNING**				**PERCENTAGES**		
1991 Elmira	A- Bos	77	272	70	10	2	1	87	48	23	32	0	45	3	2	4	29	4	.88	6	.257	.338	.320
1992 Lynchburg	A+ Bos	128	516	115	14	4	1	140	59	27	25	0	84	3	7	3	11	6	.65	11	.223	.261	.271
1993 New Britain	AA Bos	99	355	81	16	4	0	105	37	31	16	0	52	4	4	5	7	7	.50	8	.228	.266	.296
1994 Sarasota	A+ Bos	15	49	11	0	0	0	11	4	5	4	0	9	0	2	0	1	0	1.00	3	.224	.283	.224
New Britain	AA Bos	6	20	3	0	1	0	5	1	0	0	0	7	0	0	0	0	0	.00	1	.150	.150	.250
Pawtucket	AAA Bos	64	169	43	4	1	4	61	16	18	5	0	22	0	7	2	3	3	.50	7	.254	.273	.361
1995 Pawtucket	AAA Bos	96	317	85	15	2	0	104	37	21	15	0	39	6	11	4	11	5	.69	8	.268	.310	.328
1996 Sarasota	A+ Bos	8	21	6	0	0	0	6	0	0	1	0	2	0	0	0	2	0	.00	2	.286	.318	.286
Pawtucket	AAA Bos	72	265	65	14	1	3	90	37	28	15	1	32	3	10	0	3	1	.75	10	.245	.293	.340
1997 Pawtucket	AAA Bos	82	285	71	12	0	2	89	27	19	9	0	47	2	2	0	5	2	.71	12	.249	.277	.312
1996 Boston	AL	27	67	16	1	0	1	20	7	9	4	0	8	1	5	0	0	0	.00	3	.239	.292	.299
7 Min. YEARS		647	2269	550	85	15	11	698	266	172	122	1	339	21	45	18	70	28	.71	70	.242	.285	.308

Victor Rodriguez

Bats: **Right** Throws: **Right** Pos: **2B** Ht: **6'2"** Wt: **175** Born: **10/25/76** Age: **21**

Year Team	Lg Org	G	AB	H	2B	3B	HR	TB	R	RBI	TBB	IBB	SO	HBP	SH	SF	SB	CS	SB%	GDP	Avg	OBP	SLG
					BATTING												**BASERUNNING**				**PERCENTAGES**		
1994 Marlins	R Fla	24	96	31	2	0	0	33	13	17	7	0	7	0	0	3	2	0	1.00	3	.323	.358	.344
1995 Kane County	A Fla	127	472	122	9	1	0	122	65	43	40	0	47	2	16	4	18	6	.75	17	.235	.295	.258
1996 Brevard Cty	A+ Fla	114	438	120	14	4	0	142	54	26	32	0	42	2	8	3	20	7	.74	13	.274	.324	.324
1997 Portland	AA Fla	113	401	111	18	4	3	146	63	38	30	0	43	0	10	3	13	7	.65	15	.277	.325	.364
4 Min. YEARS		378	1407	373	43	9	3	443	195	124	109	0	139	4	34	13	53	20	.73	48	.265	.317	.315

Bryan Rogers

Pitches: **Right** Bats: **Right** Pos: **P** Ht: **5'11"** Wt: **170** Born: **10/30/67** Age: **30**

Year Team	Lg Org	G	GS	CG	GF	IP	BFP	H	R	ER	HR	SH	SF	HB	TBB	IBB	SO	WP	Bk	W	L	Pct.	ShO	Sv	ERA
						HOW MUCH HE PITCHED				**WHAT HE GAVE UP**												**THE RESULTS**			
1988 Kingsport	R+ NYN	15	2	0	5	31.1	135	30	23	22	1	0	0	1	14	1	35	1	4	2	3	.400	0	0	6.32
1989 Columbia	A NYN	14	4	0	6	43.1	181	36	16	15	1	5	0	2	14	0	36	0	1	3	2	.600	0	3	3.12
1990 St. Lucie	A+ NYN	29	19	5	6	148.2	599	127	66	51	3	2	8	4	26	0	96	7	1	9	8	.529	2	4	3.09
1991 Williamsprt	AA NYN	41	0	0	32	61	267	73	33	32	5	5	2	1	18	1	33	1	0	6	8	.429	0	15	4.72
1992 Binghamton	AA NYN	22	0	0	10	35.1	152	37	21	17	4	2	1	1	7	0	20	0	0	3	2	.600	0	1	4.33
St. Lucie	A+ NYN	17	0	0	6	30.2	123	24	12	10	1	3	1	2	7	2	17	1	0	2	4	.333	0	2	2.93
1993 Binghamton	AA NYN	62	0	0	40	84.2	347	80	29	22	4	5	4	0	25	2	42	4	0	5	4	.556	0	8	2.34
1994 Norfolk	AAA NYN	20	0	0	4	30	133	35	19	18	4	1	2	1	10	2	8	0	0	2	2	.500	0	0	5.40
Binghamton	AA NYN	41	0	0	21	60	236	49	17	11	1	3	0	1	14	5	46	2	0	5	1	.833	0	11	1.65
1995 Norfolk	AAA NYN	56	0	0	34	77.1	303	58	22	19	4	4	3	0	22	1	50	8	0	8	3	.727	0	10	2.21
1996 St. Lucie	A+ NYN	9	0	0	4	11.2	50	12	2	2	0	0	0	0	4	0	11	0	1	2	0	1.000	0	1	1.54
Norfolk	AAA NYN	20	0	0	9	24	103	20	11	9	2	2	0	0	11	2	23	2	0	0	2	.000	0	0	3.38
1997 Greenville	AA Atl	19	0	0	11	26.1	109	20	11	9	2	2	1	0	12	3	14	3	1	2	3	.400	0	1	3.08
Richmond	AAA Atl	21	0	0	9	38.1	178	45	26	22	4	0	1	0	16	2	25	2	0	1	1	.500	0	0	5.17
10 Min. YEARS		386	25	5	197	702.2	2916	646	308	259	36	34	23	13	200	21	456	31	8	50	43	.538	0	55	3.32

Kevin Rogers

Pitches: **Left** Bats: **Both** Pos: **P** Ht: **6'2"** Wt: **198** Born: **8/20/68** Age: **29**

Year Team	Lg Org	G	GS	CG	GF	IP	BFP	H	R	ER	HR	SH	SF	HB	TBB	IBB	SO	WP	Bk	W	L	Pct.	ShO	Sv	ERA
						HOW MUCH HE PITCHED				**WHAT HE GAVE UP**												**THE RESULTS**			
1988 Pocatello	R+ SF	13	13	1	0	69.2	314	73	54	48	4	0	3	2	35	0	71	5	4	2	8	.200	0	0	6.20
1989 Clinton	A SF	29	28	4	0	169.1	722	128	74	48	4	2	6	6	78	1	168	5	7	13	8	.619	0	0	2.55
1990 San Jose	A+ SF	28	26	1	1	172	731	143	86	69	9	6	8	11	68	1	186	19	3	14	5	.737	1	0	3.61
1991 Shreveport	AA SF	22	22	2	0	118	528	124	63	44	8	5	5	2	54	4	108	11	2	4	6	.400	0	0	3.36
1992 Shreveport	AA SF	16	16	2	0	101	413	87	34	29	3	2	1	4	29	0	110	7	0	8	5	.615	2	0	2.58
Phoenix	AAA SF	11	11	1	0	69.2	287	63	34	31	0	5	3	1	22	1	62	2	1	3	3	.500	1	0	4.00
1995 San Jose	A+ SF	4	4	0	0	10	38	10	2	2	0	0	0	0	1	0	5	0	0	0	0	.000	0	0	1.80
Phoenix	AAA SF	3	1	0	0	4.1	22	9	2	2	0	0	0	0	2	0	1	2	0	0	0	.000	0	0	4.15
1997 Richmond	AAA Atl	10	0	0	4	11	53	15	11	9	2	0	1	0	5	0	9	1	0	0	0	.000	0	0	7.36
San Jose	A+ SF	8	8	0	0	29.1	118	29	9	9	1	0	1	1	6	0	27	1	0	0	0	.000	0	0	2.76
1992 San Francisco	NL	6	6	0	0	34	148	37	17	16	4	2	0	1	13	1	26	2	0	0	2	.000	0	0	4.24
1993 San Francisco	NL	64	0	0	24	80.2	334	71	28	24	3	0	1	4	28	5	62	3	0	2	2	.500	0	0	2.68
1994 San Francisco	NL	9	0	0	2	10.1	46	10	4	4	1	0	0	0	6	0	7	0	0	0	0	.000	0	0	3.48
7 Min. YEARS		144	129	11	5	754.1	3226	681	366	291	31	20	28	27	300	7	747	53	17	44	39	.530	4	0	3.47
3 Maj. YEARS		79	6	0	26	125	528	118	49	44	8	2	1	5	47	6	95	5	0	2	4	.333	0	0	3.17

Francisco Rogue

Bats: Right **Throws:** Right **Pos:** C   **Ht:** 6'2" **Wt:** 170 **Born:** 11/22/75 **Age:** 22

						BATTING												BASERUNNING				PERCENTAGES		
Year Team	Lg Org	G	AB	H	2B	3B	HR	TB	R	RBI	TBB	IBB	SO	HBP	SH	SF	SB	CS	SB%	GDP	Avg	OBP	SLG
1994 Brewers	R Mil	38	112	23	3	3	0	32	11	15	4	1	21	0	0	3	1	2	.33	0	.205	.227	.286
1995 Brewers	R Mil	19	62	14	3	1	0	19	10	10	1	0	9	0	0	0	0	0	.00	2	.226	.238	.306
1996 Helena	R+ Mil	30	109	25	3	0	0	28	14	8	8	0	19	2	1	2	1	0	1.00	0	.229	.289	.257
1997 El Paso	AA Mil	13	24	3	1	0	0	4	3	1	1	0	5	0	0	0	0	0	.00	0	.125	.160	.167
Beloit	A Mil	17	53	9	2	0	0	11	1	7	4	0	7	0	0	0	0	0	.00	1	.170	.228	.208
4 Min. YEARS		117	360	74	12	4	0	94	39	41	18	1	61	2	1	5	2	2	.50	5	.206	.244	.261

Mike Romano

Pitches: Right **Bats:** Right **Pos:** P   **Ht:** 6'2" **Wt:** 195 **Born:** 3/3/72 **Age:** 26

		HOW MUCH HE PITCHED						WHAT HE GAVE UP										THE RESULTS				
Year Team	Lg Org	G	GS	CG	GF	IP	BFP	H	R	ER	HR	SH	SF	HB	TBB	IBB	SO	WP	Bk	W	L	Pct.	ShO	Sv	ERA
1993 Medicne Hat	R+ Tor	9	8	0	0	41	175	34	20	12	1	0	0	7	11	0	28	3	0	4	1	.800	0	0	2.63
1994 Hagerstown	A Tor	18	18	2	0	108.1	453	91	47	37	10	2	3	9	40	0	90	5	2	10	2	.833	0	0	3.07
1995 Dunedin	A+ Tor	28	26	1	1	150.1	654	141	79	69	15	4	3	11	75	0	102	5	3	11	7	.611	1	0	4.13
1996 Knoxville	AA Tor	34	21	0	5	130	600	148	98	72	17	5	8	5	72	1	92	5	1	9	9	.500	0	1	4.98
1997 Syracuse	AAA Tor	40	12	0	9	108	487	100	56	51	10	1	3	6	74	2	83	7	0	2	4	.333	0	0	4.25
5 Min. YEARS		129	85	3	15	537.2	2369	514	300	241	53	12	17	38	272	3	395	25	7	36	23	.610	1	1	4.03

Wilfredo Romero

Bats: Right **Throws:** Right **Pos:** OF   **Ht:** 5'11" **Wt:** 158 **Born:** 8/5/74 **Age:** 23

						BATTING												BASERUNNING				PERCENTAGES		
Year Team	Lg Org	G	AB	H	2B	3B	HR	TB	R	RBI	TBB	IBB	SO	HBP	SH	SF	SB	CS	SB%	GDP	Avg	OBP	SLG
1993 Great Falls	R+ LA	15	58	16	5	0	0	21	12	9	2	0	9	0	0	0	2	1	.67	2	.276	.300	.362
Yakima	A- LA	13	51	13	0	0	0	13	8	1	1	0	12	2	0	1	3	0	1.00	1	.255	.291	.255
Bakersfield	A+ LA	20	77	27	5	0	1	35	8	12	5	0	16	0	0	0	4	2	.67	2	.351	.390	.455
1994 Vero Beach	A+ LA	38	126	29	6	0	2	41	15	13	9	0	19	1	2	0	0	2	.00	2	.230	.287	.325
Bakersfield	A+ LA	70	260	71	19	1	7	113	36	36	19	0	53	3	1	0	15	5	.75	3	.273	.330	.435
1995 San Antonio	AA LA	105	376	100	20	1	7	143	46	44	40	1	69	5	0	6	10	12	.45	7	.266	.340	.380
1996 San Antonio	AA LA	122	444	131	36	6	6	197	66	48	34	2	52	3	2	8	21	15	.58	11	.295	.344	.444
Albuquerque	AAA LA	4	13	5	0	0	1	8	1	3	1	0	1	0	0	0	1	0	1.00	0	.385	.429	.615
1997 San Antonio	AA LA	30	108	35	8	1	1	48	22	16	15	0	11	2	2	5	7	4	.64	1	.324	.400	.444
5 Min. YEARS		417	1513	427	99	9	25	619	214	182	126	3	242	16	7	20	63	41	.61	29	.282	.340	.409

Marc Ronan

Bats: Left **Throws:** Right **Pos:** C   **Ht:** 6'2" **Wt:** 190 **Born:** 9/19/69 **Age:** 28

						BATTING												BASERUNNING				PERCENTAGES		
Year Team	Lg Org	G	AB	H	2B	3B	HR	TB	R	RBI	TBB	IBB	SO	HBP	SH	SF	SB	CS	SB%	GDP	Avg	OBP	SLG
1990 Hamilton	A- StL	56	167	38	6	0	1	47	14	15	15	0	37	1	0	3	1	2	.33	4	.228	.290	.281
1991 Savannah	A StL	108	343	81	10	1	0	93	41	45	37	1	54	4	3	1	11	2	.85	13	.236	.317	.271
1992 Springfield	A StL	110	376	81	19	2	6	122	45	48	23	2	58	1	0	4	4	5	.44	11	.215	.260	.324
1993 St. Pete	A+ StL	25	87	27	5	0	0	32	13	6	6	0	10	0	3	2	0	0	.00	1	.310	.347	.368
Arkansas	AA StL	96	281	60	16	1	7	99	33	34	26	2	47	2	3	3	1	3	.25	4	.214	.282	.352
1994 Louisville	AAA StL	84	269	64	11	2	2	85	32	21	12	2	43	2	2	2	3	1	.75	9	.238	.274	.316
1995 Louisville	AAA StL	78	225	48	8	0	0	56	15	8	14	2	42	0	2	0	4	3	.57	10	.213	.259	.249
1996 Charlotte	AAA Fla	79	220	67	10	0	4	89	23	20	16	2	37	2	0	2	3	4	.43	4	.305	.354	.405
1997 Columbus	AAA NYA	55	156	43	12	0	1	58	16	19	27	3	24	1	1	3	3	9	.25	9	.276	.386	.372
1993 St. Louis	NL	6	12	1	0	0	0	1	0	0	0	0	5	0	0	0	0	0	.00	0	.083	.083	.083
8 Min. YEARS		691	2124	509	97	6	21	681	232	216	176	14	352	13	13	17	28	23	.55	64	.240	.300	.321

Rafael Roque

Pitches: Left **Bats:** Left **Pos:** P   **Ht:** 6'4" **Wt:** 186 **Born:** 1/1/72 **Age:** 26

		HOW MUCH HE PITCHED						WHAT HE GAVE UP										THE RESULTS				
Year Team	Lg Org	G	GS	CG	GF	IP	BFP	H	R	ER	HR	SH	SF	HB	TBB	IBB	SO	WP	Bk	W	L	Pct.	ShO	Sv	ERA
1992 Mets	R NYN	20	0	0	18	33.2	149	28	13	8	0	4	0	1	16	2	33	3	1	3	1	.750	0	8	2.14
1993 Kingsport	R+ NYN	14	7	0	4	45.1	222	58	44	31	9	3	2	7	26	0	36	8	1	1	3	.250	0	0	6.15
1994 St. Lucie	A+ NYN	2	0	0	2	3	15	2	1	0	0	1	1	1	3	1	2	0	0	0	0	.000	0	0	0.00
Capital City	A NYN	15	15	1	0	86.1	353	73	26	23	6	1	3	4	30	1	74	7	1	6	3	.667	0	0	2.40
1995 St. Lucie	A+ NYN	24	24	1	0	136.2	582	114	65	54	7	2	4	4	72	1	81	11	4	6	9	.400	1	0	3.56
1996 Binghamton	AA NYN	13	13	0	0	60.2	291	71	57	49	8	2	1	2	39	0	46	4	0	0	4	.000	0	0	7.27
St. Lucie	A+ NYN	14	12	1	1	76.1	311	57	22	18	2	5	0	3	39	0	59	8	0	6	4	.600	0	0	2.12
1997 Binghamton	AA NYN	16	0	0	5	26.1	126	35	26	20	7	2	0	1	17	1	23	1	0	1	1	.500	0	0	6.84
St. Lucie	A+ NYN	17	13	1	1	77.2	325	81	42	37	8	3	4	1	25	0	54	2	1	2	10	.167	0	0	4.29
6 Min. YEARS		135	84	5	31	546	2374	519	296	240	47	23	15	24	267	6	408	44	8	25	35	.417	1	8	3.96

Brian Rose

Pitches: Right **Bats:** Right **Pos:** P   **Ht:** 6'1" **Wt:** 195 **Born:** 10/7/72 **Age:** 25

		HOW MUCH HE PITCHED						WHAT HE GAVE UP										THE RESULTS				
Year Team	Lg Org	G	GS	CG	GF	IP	BFP	H	R	ER	HR	SH	SF	HB	TBB	IBB	SO	WP	Bk	W	L	Pct.	ShO	Sv	ERA
1994 Bend	A- Col	24	4	0	8	60	263	49	28	24	1	1	2	9	26	1	75	4	1	2	3	.400	0	5	3.60
1995 Portland	A- Col	5	5	0	0	8.2	40	10	5	5	1	2	1	2	6	1	11	0	0	1	1	.500	0	0	5.19
Asheville	A Col	10	1	0	5	14.2	62	14	8	8	0	0	0	4	2	0	15	1	0	1	0	1.000	0	0	4.91
1996 Salem	A+ Col	5	0	0	3	7.1	32	10	7	5	0	0	0	0	2	0	2	1	1	0	0	.000	0	0	6.14
Asheville	A Col	38	1	0	14	68.1	273	53	30	27	4	6	5	3	16	2	73	4	1	4	5	.444	0	3	3.56

218

Year Team	Lg Org	G	GS	CG	GF	IP	BFP	H	R	ER	HR	SH	SF	HB	TBB	IBB	SO	WP	Bk	W	L	Pct.	ShO	Sv	ERA
1997 Michigan	A Bos	10	0	0	1	15.1	60	12	3	3	0	1	1	2	2	0	19	1	0	4	1	.800	0	0	1.76
Sarasota	A+ Bos	21	0	0	17	33	145	35	16	11	1	2	1	0	12	0	34	1	0	4	1	.800	0	7	3.00
Trenton	AA Bos	15	0	0	6	25.1	107	23	8	8	4	0	0	0	10	0	18	0	0	2	1	.667	0	0	2.84
4 Min. YEARS		128	6	0	55	232.2	982	206	105	91	11	12	10	20	76	4	247	12	3	18	12	.600	0	15	3.52

Scott Rose

Pitches: Right Bats: Right Pos: P   Ht: 6'3" Wt: 200 Born: 5/12/70 Age: 28

Year Team	Lg Org	G	GS	CG	GF	IP	BFP	H	R	ER	HR	SH	SF	HB	TBB	IBB	SO	WP	Bk	W	L	Pct.	ShO	Sv	ERA
1990 Athletics	R Oak	9	1	0	4	18.1	69	12	5	3	0	0	0	0	3	0	21	1	0	0	0	.000	0	2	1.47
Modesto	A+ Oak	6	0	0	3	14	61	14	5	2	0	0	0	0	6	1	10	2	0	0	0	.000	0	1	1.29
1991 Modesto	A+ Oak	13	13	0	0	67.2	306	66	45	33	7	3	3	2	38	1	31	7	1	3	3	.500	0	0	4.39
1992 Madison	A Oak	8	8	1	0	36	154	35	22	17	2	1	2	2	10	0	15	3	1	2	2	.500	0	0	4.25
Reno	A+ Oak	20	9	0	2	64	314	97	73	60	11	2	2	2	37	3	29	4	0	2	4	.333	0	0	8.44
1993 San Berndno	A+ Oak	28	25	1	0	173.1	765	184	110	82	16	6	8	10	63	6	73	10	0	9	10	.474	1	0	4.26
1994 Huntsville	AA Oak	41	0	0	25	73	328	87	44	38	2	9	4	2	24	8	43	9	0	6	10	.375	0	3	4.68
1995 Edmonton	AAA Oak	5	1	0	2	10	45	13	7	7	0	1	0	0	7	0	0	0	0	0	2	.000	0	0	6.30
Huntsville	AA Oak	38	5	0	23	80	316	70	24	23	2	5	3	2	23	5	35	6	0	4	6	.400	0	13	2.59
1996 Edmonton	AAA Oak	50	0	0	41	55.2	239	57	21	18	2	4	2	1	16	4	20	4	0	4	4	.500	0	10	2.91
1997 Columbus	AAA NYA	26	0	0	22	24.1	99	24	11	10	2	2	1	0	6	1	13	0	0	2	2	.500	0	11	3.70
Norwich	AA NYA	21	0	0	12	30.1	129	34	17	9	1	1	1	0	8	0	20	5	0	0	2	.000	0	4	2.67
8 Min. YEARS		265	62	2	134	646.2	2825	693	384	302	45	34	26	21	241	29	310	51	2	32	45	.416	1	44	4.20

John Rosengren

Pitches: Left Bats: Left Pos: P   Ht: 6'4" Wt: 190 Born: 8/10/72 Age: 25

Year Team	Lg Org	G	GS	CG	GF	IP	BFP	H	R	ER	HR	SH	SF	HB	TBB	IBB	SO	WP	Bk	W	L	Pct.	ShO	Sv	ERA
1992 Bristol	R+ Det	14	3	0	3	23	113	16	21	20	2	0	5	0	30	0	28	6	2	0	3	.000	0	0	7.83
1993 Niagara Fal	A- Det	15	15	0	0	82	333	52	32	22	3	1	4	6	38	0	91	6	1	7	3	.700	0	0	2.41
1994 Lakeland	A+ Det	22	22	4	0	135.2	569	113	51	38	4	2	4	7	56	0	101	3	2	9	6	.600	3	0	2.52
Trenton	AA Det	3	3	0	0	17.1	79	21	15	14	2	1	1	0	11	0	7	0	1	0	2	.000	0	0	7.27
1995 Jacksnville	AA Det	14	13	0	0	67.2	308	73	39	34	7	2	2	5	40	0	59	12	2	2	7	.222	0	0	4.52
Lakeland	A+ Det	13	8	0	1	56.1	253	46	33	25	6	2	2	7	36	0	35	2	0	3	3	.500	0	0	3.99
1996 Jacksnville	AA Det	60	0	0	15	55.1	249	48	36	28	9	2	1	3	37	3	47	4	0	5	1	.833	0	1	4.55
1997 Toledo	AAA Det	54	0	0	16	56.1	266	44	29	25	1	1	3	7	49	1	53	7	1	1	3	.250	0	2	3.99
6 Min. YEARS		195	64	4	35	493.2	2170	413	256	206	34	11	22	35	297	4	421	40	9	27	28	.491	3	3	3.76

John Roskos

Bats: Right Throws: Right Pos: C   Ht: 5'11" Wt: 198 Born: 11/19/74 Age: 23

Year Team	Lg Org	G	AB	H	2B	3B	HR	TB	R	RBI	TBB	IBB	SO	HBP	SH	SF	SB	CS	SB%	GDP	Avg	OBP	SLG
1993 Marlins	R Fla	11	44	7	1	0	1	11	6	3	5	0	11	1	0	0	1	1	.50	0	.175	.283	.275
1994 Elmira	A- Fla	39	136	38	7	0	4	57	11	23	27	0	37	0	0	2	0	1	.00	0	.279	.394	.419
1995 Kane County	A Fla	114	418	124	36	3	12	202	74	88	42	1	86	6	0	6	2	0	1.00	6	.297	.364	.483
1996 Portland	AA Fla	121	396	109	26	3	9	168	53	58	67	4	102	5	0	2	3	4	.43	5	.275	.385	.424
1997 Portland	AA Fla	123	451	139	31	1	24	244	66	84	50	2	81	0	2	6	4	6	.40	17	.308	.373	.541
5 Min. YEARS		408	1441	417	101	7	50	682	210	256	191	7	317	12	2	16	10	12	.45	28	.289	.373	.473

Mike Rossiter

Pitches: Right Bats: Right Pos: P   Ht: 6'6" Wt: 230 Born: 6/20/73 Age: 25

Year Team	Lg Org	G	GS	CG	GF	IP	BFP	H	R	ER	HR	SH	SF	HB	TBB	IBB	SO	WP	Bk	W	L	Pct.	ShO	Sv	ERA
1991 Athletics	R Oak	10	9	0	0	38.1	179	43	24	17	3	1	0	2	22	0	35	6	0	3	4	.429	0	0	3.99
1992 Madison	A Oak	27	27	2	0	154.2	651	135	83	68	17	2	5	4	68	1	135	4	3	8	14	.364	0	0	3.96
1993 Modesto	A+ Oak	20	17	2	0	112	491	120	62	54	14	4	1	1	45	0	96	5	0	8	6	.571	0	0	4.34
1994 Athletics	R Oak	2	0	0	0	3.2	20	8	6	2	0	1	0	0	0	0	3	1	0	0	1	.000	0	0	4.91
1995 Modesto	A+ Oak	18	7	0	3	68.2	290	68	33	32	5	2	2	2	19	0	70	1	1	7	2	.778	0	0	4.19
1996 Huntsville	AA Oak	27	25	2	1	145	636	167	92	78	15	2	10	7	44	4	116	5	0	8	9	.471	1	0	4.84
1997 Stockton	A+ Mil	34	8	0	9	86	368	83	31	26	6	2	2	15	27	0	79	3	0	8	1	.889	0	0	2.72
El Paso	AA Mil	8	0	0	4	20.2	87	22	6	6	0	1	1	1	8	0	11	1	0	0	0	1.000	0	0	2.61
7 Min. YEARS		146	93	6	17	629	2722	646	337	283	60	15	21	32	233	5	545	26	4	43	37	.538	1	0	4.05

Rico Rossy

Bats: Right Throws: Right Pos: SS   Ht: 5'10" Wt: 175 Born: 2/16/64 Age: 34

Year Team	Lg Org	G	AB	H	2B	3B	HR	TB	R	RBI	TBB	IBB	SO	HBP	SH	SF	SB	CS	SB%	GDP	Avg	OBP	SLG
1985 Newark	A- Bal	73	246	53	14	2	3	80	38	25	32	1	22	1	3		17	7	.71	13	.215	.307	.325
1986 Miami	A+ Bal	38	134	34	7	1	1	46	26	9	24	0	8	1	6	1	10	6	.63	4	.254	.369	.343
Charlotte	AA Bal	77	232	68	16	2	3	97	40	25	26	0	19	2	8	1	13	5	.72	2	.293	.368	.418
1987 Charlotte	AA Bal	127	471	135	22	3	4	175	69	50	43	0	38	3	3	1	20	9	.69	20	.287	.349	.372
1988 Charlotte	AAA Pit	68	187	46	4	0	1	53	12	20	13	0	17	0	0	1	1	5	.17	4	.246	.294	.283
1989 Harrisburg	AA Pit	78	238	60	16	1	2	84	20	25	27	0	19	3	0	2	2	4	.33	5	.252	.333	.353
Buffalo	AAA Pit	38	109	21	5	0	0	26	11	10	18	1	11	1	1	2	4	0	1.00	4	.193	.308	.239
1990 Buffalo	AAA Pit	8	17	3	0	1	0	5	3	2	4	0	2	0	1	1	1	0	1.00	0	.176	.318	.294
Greenville	AA Atl	5	21	4	1	0	0	5	4	0	1	0	2	0	0	0	2		.00	1	.190	.227	.238

219

Year Team	Lg Org	G	AB	H	2B	3B	HR	TB	R	RBI	TBB	IBB	SO	HBP	SH	SF	SB	CS	SB%	GDP	Avg	OBP	SLG
Richmond	AAA Atl	107	380	88	13	0	4	113	58	32	69	1	43	3	7	2	11	6	.65	12	.232	.352	.297
1991 Richmond	AAA Atl	139	482	124	25	1	2	157	58	48	67	1	46	5	13	3	4	8	.33	12	.257	.352	.326
1992 Omaha	AAA KC	48	174	55	10	1	4	79	29	17	34	0	14	0	2	3	5	3	.38	5	.316	.422	.454
1993 Omaha	AAA KC	37	131	39	10	1	5	66	25	21	20	1	19	3	0	1	3	2	.60	1	.298	.400	.504
1994 Omaha	AAA KC	120	412	97	23	0	11	153	49	63	61	1	60	5	5	4	9	10	.47	14	.235	.338	.371
1995 Las Vegas	AAA SD	98	316	95	11	2	1	113	44	45	55	2	36	2	2	6	3	7	.30	13	.301	.401	.358
1996 Las Vegas	AAA SD	130	413	104	21	2	4	141	56	35	70	7	63	6	9	5	6	6	.50	11	.252	.364	.341
1997 Ottawa	AAA Mon	117	375	94	23	0	10	147	56	52	37	2	64	4	8	4	5	0	1.00	14	.251	.321	.392
1991 Atlanta	NL	5	1	0	0	0	0	0	0	0	0	0	0	1	0	0	0	0	.00	0	.000	.000	.000
1992 Kansas City	AL	59	149	32	8	1	1	45	21	12	20	1	20	1	7	1	0	3	.00	6	.215	.310	.302
1993 Kansas City	AL	46	86	19	4	0	2	29	10	12	9	0	11	1	1	0	0	0	.00	0	.221	.302	.337
13 Min. YEARS		1308	4338	1120	221	17	55	1540	598	479	601	17	483	39	68	38	112	82	.58	135	.258	.351	.355
3 Maj. YEARS		110	236	51	12	1	3	74	31	24	29	1	32	2	8	1	0	3	.00	6	.216	.306	.314

Rich Rowland

Bats: Right **Throws:** Right **Pos:** C **Ht:** 6' 1" **Wt:** 215 **Born:** 2/25/64 **Age:** 34

Year Team	Lg Org	G	AB	H	2B	3B	HR	TB	R	RBI	TBB	IBB	SO	HBP	SH	SF	SB	CS	SB%	GDP	Avg	OBP	SLG
1988 Bristol	R+ Det	56	186	51	10	1	4	75	29	41	27	1	39	1	0	3	1	2	.33	2	.274	.364	.403
1989 Fayetteville	A Det	108	375	102	17	1	9	148	43	59	54	2	98	3	3	3	4	1	.80	8	.272	.366	.395
1990 London	AA Det	47	161	46	10	0	8	80	22	30	20	3	33	3	0	1	1	1	.50	7	.286	.373	.497
Toledo	AAA Det	62	192	50	12	0	7	83	28	22	15	0	33	1	3	2	2	3	.40	3	.260	.314	.432
1991 Toledo	AAA Det	109	383	104	25	0	13	168	56	68	60	3	77	3	0	1	4	2	.67	8	.272	.374	.439
1992 Toledo	AAA Det	136	473	111	19	1	25	207	75	82	56	6	112	3	0	4	9	3	.75	20	.235	.317	.438
1993 Toledo	AAA Det	96	325	87	24	2	21	178	58	59	51	3	72	3	0	3	1	6	.14	11	.268	.369	.548
1995 Pawtucket	AAA Bos	34	124	32	7	0	8	63	20	24	7	1	24	1	0	1	0	1	.00	2	.258	.301	.508
1996 Syracuse	AAA Tor	96	288	65	24	2	8	117	43	45	50	3	79	4	2	4	1	1	.50	9	.226	.344	.406
1997 Phoenix	AAA SF	19	59	14	5	0	2	25	10	13	7	0	13	0	0	0	0	0	.00	2	.237	.318	.424
1990 Detroit	AL	7	19	3	1	0	0	4	3	0	2	1	4	0	0	0	0	0	.00	1	.158	.238	.211
1991 Detroit	AL	4	4	1	0	0	0	1	0	1	1	0	2	0	0	0	0	0	.00	0	.250	.333	.250
1992 Detroit	AL	6	14	3	0	0	0	3	2	0	3	0	3	0	0	0	0	0	.00	0	.214	.353	.214
1993 Detroit	AL	21	46	10	3	0	0	13	2	4	5	0	16	0	1	0	0	0	.00	1	.217	.294	.283
1994 Boston	AL	46	118	27	3	0	9	57	14	20	11	0	35	0	0	0	0	0	.00	2	.229	.295	.483
1995 Boston	AL	14	29	5	1	0	0	6	1	1	0	0	11	0	0	0	0	0	.00	0	.172	.172	.207
9 Min. YEARS		763	2566	662	153	7	105	1144	384	443	347	22	580	22	8	22	23	20	.53	72	.258	.349	.446
6 Maj. YEARS		98	230	49	8	0	9	84	22	26	22	1	71	0	1	0	0	0	.00	5	.213	.281	.365

Aaron Royster

Bats: Right **Throws:** Right **Pos:** OF **Ht:** 6'1" **Wt:** 220 **Born:** 11/30/72 **Age:** 25

Year Team	Lg Org	G	AB	H	2B	3B	HR	TB	R	RBI	TBB	IBB	SO	HBP	SH	SF	SB	CS	SB%	GDP	Avg	OBP	SLG
1994 Martinsvlle	R+ Phi	54	168	46	11	2	7	82	31	39	28	1	47	2	0	1	7	4	.64	2	.274	.382	.488
1995 Piedmont	A Phi	126	489	129	23	3	8	182	73	58	39	1	106	7	0	4	22	9	.71	16	.264	.325	.372
1996 Clearwater	A+ Phi	72	289	81	10	2	11	128	35	60	23	1	56	3	3	2	4	3	.57	7	.280	.338	.443
Reading	AA Phi	65	230	59	11	0	4	82	42	20	30	2	56	5	3	1	4	5	.44	3	.257	.353	.357
1997 Reading	AA Phi	112	412	106	18	5	15	179	59	62	53	0	104	1	0	2	2	3	.40	12	.257	.342	.434
4 Min. YEARS		429	1588	421	73	12	45	653	240	239	173	5	369	18	6	10	39	24	.62	40	.265	.342	.411

Johnny Ruffin

Pitches: Right **Bats:** Right **Pos:** P **Ht:** 6' 3" **Wt:** 170 **Born:** 7/29/71 **Age:** 26

Year Team	Lg Org	G	GS	CG	GF	IP	BFP	H	R	ER	HR	SH	SF	HB	TBB	IBB	SO	WP	Bk	W	L	Pct.	ShO	Sv	ERA
1988 White Sox	R ChA	13	11	1	1	58.2	246	43	27	15	3	1	2	4	22	0	31	9	2	4	1	.667	0	0	2.30
1989 Utica	A- ChA	15	15	0	0	88.1	376	67	43	33	3	5	1	1	46	0	92	8	0	4	8	.333	0	0	3.36
1990 South Bend	A ChA	24	24	0	0	123	568	117	86	57	7	1	5	3	82	0	92	17	4	7	6	.538	0	0	4.17
1991 Sarasota	A+ ChA	26	26	6	0	158.2	655	126	68	57	9	3	5	5	62	0	117	10	2	11	4	.733	2	0	3.23
1992 Birmingham	AA ChA	10	10	0	0	47.2	228	51	48	32	3	1	5	1	34	0	44	9	0	0	7	.000	0	0	6.04
Sarasota	A+ ChA	23	8	0	0	62.2	290	56	46	41	5	2	1	4	41	0	61	10	2	3	7	.300	0	0	5.89
1993 Birmingham	AA ChA	11	0	0	10	22.1	92	16	9	7	2	2	1	0	9	1	23	0	0	0	4	.000	0	2	2.82
Nashville	AAA ChA	29	0	0	11	60	242	48	24	22	5	2	2	1	16	4	69	10	0	3	4	.429	0	1	3.30
Indianapols	AAA Cin	3	0	0	3	6.2	25	3	1	1	0	1	0	0	2	1	6	0	0	1	1	.500	0	1	1.35
1995 Indianapols	AAA Cin	36	1	0	4	49.2	213	27	19	16	3	2	1	0	37	2	58	7	0	3	1	.750	0	0	2.90
1997 Pawtucket	AAA Bos	6	0	0	2	14	60	7	7	7	0	0	0	0	16	0	16	4	0	0	1	.000	0	0	4.50
1993 Cincinnati	NL	21	0	0	5	37.2	159	36	16	15	4	1	0	1	11	1	30	2	0	2	1	.667	0	2	3.58
1994 Cincinnati	NL	51	0	0	13	70	287	57	26	24	7	2	2	0	27	3	44	5	1	7	2	.778	0	1	3.09
1995 Cincinnati	NL	10	0	0	6	13.1	54	4	3	2	0	0	0	0	11	0	11	3	0	0	0	.000	0	0	1.35
1996 Cincinnati	NL	49	0	0	13	62.1	289	71	42	38	10	4	3	2	37	5	69	8	0	1	3	.250	0	0	5.49
8 Min. YEARS		196	96	7	37	691.2	2995	559	378	288	40	20	23	19	367	8	609	84	10	36	45	.444	2	4	3.75
4 Maj. YEARS		131	0	0	37	183.1	789	168	87	79	21	7	5	3	86	9	154	18	1	10	6	.625	0	3	3.88

Tim Rumer

Pitches: Left **Bats:** Left **Pos:** P **Ht:** 6'3" **Wt:** 205 **Born:** 8/8/69 **Age:** 28

Year Team	Lg Org	G	GS	CG	GF	IP	BFP	H	R	ER	HR	SH	SF	HB	TBB	IBB	SO	WP	Bk	W	L	Pct.	ShO	Sv	ERA
1990 Yankees	R NYA	12	12	2	0	74	291	34	23	14	1	1	0	3	20	0	88	4	3	6	3	.667	0	0	1.70
1991 Ft. Laud	A+ NYA	24	23	3	0	149.1	623	125	59	48	9	3	5		49	2	112	7	1	10	7	.588	2	0	2.89
1992 Pr William	A+ NYA	23	23	1	0	128	538	122	61	51	8	6	5		34	2	105	0	1	10	7	.588	0	0	3.59

220

		HOW MUCH HE PITCHED						WHAT HE GAVE UP												THE RESULTS					
Year Team	Lg Org	G	GS	CG	GF	IP	BFP	H	R	ER	HR	SH	SF	HB	TBB	IBB	SO	WP	Bk	W	L	Pct.	ShO	Sv	ERA
Columbus	AAA NYA	1	1	0	0	1	3	0	0	0	0	0	0	0	0	0	1	0	0	0	0	.000	0	0	0.00
1994 Albany-Colo	AA NYA	25	25	2	0	150.2	639	127	61	52	10	2	4	9	75	0	130	7	0	8	10	.444	1	0	3.11
1995 Columbus	AAA NYA	28	25	0	1	141.1	654	156	98	82	13	7	5	16	76	1	110	5	1	10	8	.556	0	0	5.22
1996 Yankees	R NYA	2	1	0	0	8	29	1	0	0	0	0	0	0	2	0	15	0	0	0	0	.000	0	0	0.00
Norwich	AA NYA	8	7	0	0	40	165	32	12	10	3	2	0	0	18	0	44	1	0	3	1	.750	0	0	2.25
Columbus	AAA NYA	12	8	0	1	49.2	204	39	20	15	3	1	1	2	14	0	35	5	0	3	1	.750	0	0	2.72
1997 Columbus	AAA NYA	17	12	1	2	68.2	315	79	54	47	8	2	2	2	41	1	46	3	3	4	7	.364	0	0	6.16
Jackson	AA Hou	7	6	0	0	34.2	147	32	21	15	3	0	2	1	10	1	31	2	0	1	2	.333	0	0	3.89
7 Min. YEARS		159	143	9	4	845.1	3608	747	409	334	55	30	22	43	339	7	717	34	9	55	46	.545	3	0	3.56

Toby Rumfield

Bats: Right **Throws:** Right **Pos:** 1B **Ht:** 6'3" **Wt:** 190 **Born:** 9/4/72 **Age:** 25

		BATTING															BASERUNNING				PERCENTAGES		
Year Team	Lg Org	G	AB	H	2B	3B	HR	TB	R	RBI	TBB	IBB	SO	HBP	SH	SF	SB	CS	SB%	GDP	Avg	OBP	SLG
1991 Princeton	R+ Cin	59	226	62	13	3	3	90	22	30	9	0	43	5	2	3	1	7	.13	6	.274	.313	.398
1992 Billings	R+ Cin	66	253	68	15	3	4	101	34	50	7	0	34	4	0	4	5	2	.71	4	.269	.295	.399
1993 Chston-WV	A Cin	97	333	75	20	1	5	112	36	50	26	1	74	3	0	4	6	4	.60	7	.225	.284	.336
1994 Winston-Sal	A+ Cin	123	462	115	11	4	29	221	79	88	48	1	107	2	0	7	2	3	.40	9	.249	.318	.478
1995 Chattanooga	AA Cin	92	273	72	12	1	8	110	32	53	26	2	47	3	3	5	0	3	.00	14	.264	.329	.403
1996 Chattanooga	AA Cin	113	364	102	25	1	9	156	49	53	37	1	51	6	3	6	2	1	.67	12	.280	.351	.429
1997 Chattanooga	AA Cin	101	331	95	22	1	5	134	35	38	18	3	32	2	4	2	0	1	.00	12	.287	.326	.405
7 Min. YEARS		651	2242	589	118	14	63	924	287	362	171	8	388	25	12	31	16	21	.43	64	.263	.318	.412

Sean Runyan

Pitches: Left **Bats:** Left **Pos:** P **Ht:** 6'3" **Wt:** 200 **Born:** 6/21/74 **Age:** 24

		HOW MUCH HE PITCHED						WHAT HE GAVE UP												THE RESULTS					
Year Team	Lg Org	G	GS	CG	GF	IP	BFP	H	R	ER	HR	SH	SF	HB	TBB	IBB	SO	WP	Bk	W	L	Pct.	ShO	Sv	ERA
1992 Astros	R Hou	10	10	0	0	45	203	54	19	16	0	1	0	5	16	0	30	8	1	3	3	.500	0	0	3.20
1993 Astros	R Hou	12	12	0	0	66.1	302	66	35	22	2	1	3	2	24	0	52	4	0	4	3	.571	0	0	2.98
1994 Auburn	A- Hou	14	14	2	0	95.1	396	90	49	37	5	1	1	2	19	0	66	12	1	7	5	.583	1	0	3.49
1995 Quad City	A Hou	22	11	0	2	76.1	327	67	37	31	10	1	2	3	29	0	65	4	0	4	6	.400	0	0	3.66
1996 Quad City	A Hou	29	17	0	3	132.1	551	128	61	57	10	1	5	14	30	0	104	4	1	9	4	.692	0	0	3.88
1997 Mobile	AA SD	40	1	0	15	61.2	261	54	25	16	4	2	1	3	28	3	52	1	1	5	2	.714	0	1	2.34
6 Min. YEARS		127	65	2	20	477	2040	459	226	179	31	7	12	29	146	3	369	33	4	32	23	.582	1	1	3.38

Brian Rupp

Bats: Right **Throws:** Right **Pos:** 3B-1B **Ht:** 6'5" **Wt:** 185 **Born:** 9/20/71 **Age:** 26

		BATTING															BASERUNNING				PERCENTAGES		
Year Team	Lg Org	G	AB	H	2B	3B	HR	TB	R	RBI	TBB	IBB	SO	HBP	SH	SF	SB	CS	SB%	GDP	Avg	OBP	SLG
1992 Cardinals	R StL	56	207	80	20	1	0	102	34	40	21	5	16	1	0	7	10	7	.59	3	.386	.432	.493
1993 Savannah	A StL	122	472	151	31	7	4	208	80	81	48	2	70	3	1	5	3	2	.60	11	.320	.383	.441
1994 St. Pete	A+ StL	129	438	115	19	4	2	148	40	34	61	1	77	0	5	0	9	3	.75	20	.263	.353	.338
1995 St. Pete	A+ StL	90	325	90	12	2	0	106	30	23	27	1	43	1	4	0	0	0	.00	14	.277	.334	.326
Arkansas	AA StL	23	77	25	3	0	0	28	10	6	6	0	12	0	1	0	1	0	.00	3	.325	.373	.364
1996 Arkansas	AA StL	114	353	107	17	2	4	140	46	41	33	4	44	0	5	4	5	6	.45	14	.303	.359	.397
1997 Arkansas	AA StL	36	122	36	9	0	1	48	18	15	13	0	16	3	2	1	0	3	.00	2	.295	.374	.393
Louisville	AAA StL	59	189	52	7	2	0	63	17	16	19	1	36	0	1	1	1	1	.50	5	.275	.340	.333
6 Min. YEARS		629	2183	656	118	18	11	843	275	256	228	14	314	8	19	18	28	23	.55	72	.301	.366	.386

Chad Rupp

Bats: Right **Throws:** Right **Pos:** 1B-DH **Ht:** 6'2" **Wt:** 215 **Born:** 9/30/71 **Age:** 26

		BATTING															BASERUNNING				PERCENTAGES		
Year Team	Lg Org	G	AB	H	2B	3B	HR	TB	R	RBI	TBB	IBB	SO	HBP	SH	SF	SB	CS	SB%	GDP	Avg	OBP	SLG
1993 Elizabethtn	R+ Min	67	228	56	14	1	10	102	54	36	44	2	79	9	1	4	0	1	.00	2	.246	.382	.447
1994 Ft. Wayne	A Min	85	257	63	20	0	15	128	46	50	50	0	79	4	0	7	2	0	1.00	0	.245	.368	.498
1995 Ft. Myers	A+ Min	107	376	100	23	1	12	161	44	52	38	1	77	2	0	3	14	3	.82	10	.266	.334	.428
1996 Hardware City	AA Min	77	278	70	14	0	18	138	38	48	13	0	56	4	3	5	3	2	.60	8	.252	.290	.496
1997 Salt Lake	AAA Min	117	426	116	19	7	32	245	77	94	49	1	112	7	3	6	2	1	.67	10	.272	.352	.575
5 Min. YEARS		453	1565	405	90	9	87	774	259	280	194	4	403	26	7	25	21	7	.75	30	.259	.345	.495

Will Rushing

Pitches: Left **Bats:** Left **Pos:** P **Ht:** 6'3" **Wt:** 193 **Born:** 11/8/72 **Age:** 25

		HOW MUCH HE PITCHED						WHAT HE GAVE UP												THE RESULTS					
Year Team	Lg Org	G	GS	CG	GF	IP	BFP	H	R	ER	HR	SH	SF	HB	TBB	IBB	SO	WP	Bk	W	L	Pct.	ShO	Sv	ERA
1995 Ft. Wayne	A Min	13	0	0	5	25.1	100	15	11	5	0	0	0	0	10	0	25	4	0	1	1	.500	0	1	1.78
1996 Ft. Myers	A+ Min	28	25	2	1	165	699	157	72	64	10	8	3	9	74	0	111	5	2	13	6	.684	1	1	3.49
1997 Ft. Myers	A+ Min	12	7	0	0	38.1	191	54	41	32	4	1	5	0	22	0	34	1	0	1	5	.167	0	0	7.51
New Britain	AA Min	3	2	0	0	11.1	50	14	5	5	0	0	0	0	3	0	9	0	1	1	2	.333	0	0	3.97
3 Min. YEARS		56	34	2	6	240	1040	240	129	106	14	9	8	9	109	0	179	10	5	16	14	.533	1	2	3.98

LaGrande Russell

Pitches: Right **Bats:** Right **Pos:** P **Ht:** 6'2" **Wt:** 175 **Born:** 8/20/70 **Age:** 27

			HOW MUCH HE PITCHED						WHAT HE GAVE UP										THE RESULTS				
Year Team	Lg Org	G	GS	CG	GF	IP	BFP	H	R	ER	HR	SH	SF	HB	TBB	IBB	SO	WP	Bk	W	L	Pct.	ShO	Sv	ERA
1990 Mariners	R Sea	19	5	0	3	55	251	50	33	19	1	0	3	6	27	1	51	1	1	5	1	.833	0	0	3.11
1991 Bellingham	A- Sea	15	15	0	0	95.1	414	85	48	31	6	3	1	1	43	1	77	13	0	6	7	.462	0	0	2.93
1992 Peninsula	A+ Sea	27	26	2	1	157.1	665	132	76	55	4	6	3	8	59	4	130	5	1	7	10	.412	1	0	3.15
1993 Jacksnville	AA Sea	17	17	0	0	89.2	400	115	67	55	14	2	2	2	32	1	52	5	0	4	9	.308	0	0	5.52
1994 Jacksnville	AA Sea	36	3	0	19	71.2	314	82	44	36	8	3	2	0	25	5	39	5	0	1	9	.100	0	3	4.52
1995 Port City	AA Sea	39	0	0	13	72.1	329	68	32	26	7	4	3	1	43	3	54	9	0	4	3	.571	0	1	3.24
1996 Port City	AA Sea	42	9	1	12	118.1	526	127	70	57	8	8	4	2	50	1	89	3	0	7	7	.500	0	2	4.34
1997 Orlando	AA ChN	25	9	1	2	81	365	102	66	56	8	3	2	3	27	1	43	6	3	6	4	.600	0	0	6.22
Iowa	AAA ChN	7	3	0	1	18.2	93	36	26	26	5	0	1	0	8	0	3	1	0	0	3	.000	0	0	12.54
8 Min. YEARS		227	87	4	51	759.1	3357	797	462	361	61	29	21	23	314	17	538	48	5	40	53	.430	1	6	4.28

Paul Russo

Bats: Right **Throws:** Right **Pos:** DH **Ht:** 5'11" **Wt:** 215 **Born:** 8/26/69 **Age:** 28

				BATTING														BASERUNNING				PERCENTAGES		
Year Team	Lg Org	G	AB	H	2B	3B	HR	TB	R	RBI	TBB	IBB	SO	HBP	SH	SF	SB	CS	SB%	GDP	Avg	OBP	SLG
1990 Elizabethtn	R+ Min	62	221	74	9	3	22	155	58	67	38	5	56	1	0	2	4	1	.80	3	.335	.431	.701
1991 Kenosha	A Min	125	421	114	20	3	20	200	60	100	64	4	105	7	0	10	4	1	.80	5	.271	.369	.475
1992 Orlando	AA Min	126	420	107	13	2	22	190	63	74	48	0	122	1	2	5	0	0	.00	17	.255	.329	.452
1993 Portland	AAA Min	83	288	81	24	2	10	139	43	47	29	0	69	0	0	6	0	1	.00	10	.281	.341	.483
1994 Salt Lake	AAA Min	35	115	34	7	0	3	50	18	17	12	0	28	2	0	3	0	3	.00	4	.296	.364	.435
Nashville	AA Min	82	299	68	14	3	10	118	43	40	31	1	77	3	3	0	1	0	1.00	11	.227	.306	.395
1995 Memphis	AA SD	45	122	38	9	1	6	67	19	18	22	1	33	1	0	0	1	0	1.00	4	.311	.421	.549
Las Vegas	AAA SD	44	148	44	10	0	4	66	17	19	9	2	31	0	1	2	0	1	.00	4	.297	.333	.446
1996 Las Vegas	AAA SD	80	226	57	15	2	4	88	16	33	23	1	53	1	0	2	2	1	.67	7	.252	.321	.389
1997 Columbus	AAA NYA	9	22	3	0	0	2	9	3	4	5	0	0	0	0	0	0	0	.00	0	.136	.296	.409
8 Min. YEARS		691	2282	620	121	16	103	1082	340	419	281	14	580	16	6	30	12	8	.60	66	.272	.351	.474

Matt Ryan

Pitches: Right **Bats:** Right **Pos:** P **Ht:** 6'5" **Wt:** 190 **Born:** 3/20/72 **Age:** 26

				HOW MUCH HE PITCHED						WHAT HE GAVE UP									THE RESULTS				
Year Team	Lg Org	G	GS	CG	GF	IP	BFP	H	R	ER	HR	SH	SF	HB	TBB	IBB	SO	WP	Bk	W	L	Pct.	ShO	Sv	ERA
1993 Pirates	R Pit	9	0	0	5	19.1	81	17	8	5	0	1	0	1	9	0	20	0	0	1	1	.500	0	2	2.33
Welland	A- Pit	16	0	0	12	17.1	84	11	10	3	0	0	1	1	12	1	25	5	0	0	1	.000	0	5	1.56
1994 Augusta	A Pit	34	0	0	31	41	174	33	14	6	0	1	0	4	7	1	49	0	0	2	1	.667	0	13	1.32
Salem	A+ Pit	25	0	0	16	28.1	120	27	12	6	0	3	0	2	8	1	13	2	0	2	2	.500	0	7	1.91
1995 Calgary	AAA Pit	5	0	0	4	4.2	20	5	1	1	0	0	0	1	1	1	2	0	0	0	0	.000	0	1	1.93
Carolina	AA Pit	44	0	0	38	46	188	33	10	8	0	4	0	2	19	2	23	3	0	2	1	.667	0	26	1.57
1996 Calgary	AAA Pit	51	0	0	44	52.2	259	70	39	31	4	3	1	6	28	8	35	6	0	1	3	.250	0	20	5.30
1997 Carolina	AA Pit	48	0	0	39	52.2	229	32	18	13	2	4	1	12	21	4	43	9	0	4	3	.571	0	14	2.22
5 Min. YEARS		232	0	0	189	262	1155	228	112	73	6	16	3	29	105	18	210	25	0	13	15	.464	0	88	2.51

Derek Ryder

Bats: Right **Throws:** Right **Pos:** C **Ht:** 6'1" **Wt:** 190 **Born:** 3/30/73 **Age:** 25

				BATTING														BASERUNNING				PERCENTAGES		
Year Team	Lg Org	G	AB	H	2B	3B	HR	TB	R	RBI	TBB	IBB	SO	HBP	SH	SF	SB	CS	SB%	GDP	Avg	OBP	SLG
1995 Cedar Rapds	A Ana	17	21	2	0	0	0	2	1	2	5	0	7	0	3	0	0	1	.00	1	.095	.269	.095
1996 Cedar Rapds	A Ana	62	153	36	5	2	0	45	11	11	21	0	31	2	6	1	0	2	.00	5	.235	.333	.294
1997 Lk Elsinore	A+ Ana	36	91	21	5	2	1	33	12	13	8	0	17	0	3	1	1	2	.33	1	.231	.290	.363
Midland	AA Ana	25	78	18	2	0	0	20	4	6	2	0	6	0	1	1	1	0	1.00	2	.231	.247	.256
3 Min. YEARS		140	343	77	12	4	1	100	28	32	36	0	61	2	13	3	2	5	.29	9	.224	.299	.292

Brian Sackinsky

Pitches: Right **Bats:** Right **Pos:** P **Ht:** 6'4" **Wt:** 220 **Born:** 6/22/71 **Age:** 27

				HOW MUCH HE PITCHED						WHAT HE GAVE UP									THE RESULTS				
Year Team	Lg Org	G	GS	CG	GF	IP	BFP	H	R	ER	HR	SH	SF	HB	TBB	IBB	SO	WP	Bk	W	L	Pct.	ShO	Sv	ERA
1992 Frederick	A+ Bal	5	3	0	0	10.1	55	20	15	15	3	0	1	0	6	0	10	4	0	0	3	.000	0	0	13.06
Bluefield	R+ Bal	5	5	0	0	27.2	124	30	15	11	0	0	0	2	9	0	33	2	0	2	2	.500	0	0	3.58
1993 Albany	A Bal	9	8	0	0	50.2	217	50	29	18	2	0	4	0	16	0	41	5	0	3	4	.429	0	0	3.20
Frederick	A+ Bal	18	18	1	0	121	512	117	55	43	13	3	3	2	37	2	112	17	1	6	8	.429	0	0	3.20
1994 Bowie	AA Bal	28	26	4	0	177	721	165	73	66	24	5	9	0	39	0	145	6	0	11	7	.611	0	0	3.36
1995 Rochester	AAA Bal	14	11	0	0	62.2	260	70	33	32	6	1	4	1	10	0	42	4	0	3	3	.500	0	0	4.60
1996 Orioles	R Bal	3	1	0	0	8.2	37	11	6	5	0	0	0	0	1	0	3	1	0	1	0	1.000	0	0	5.19
Rochester	AAA Bal	14	13	1	1	67.2	276	75	28	26	12	4	3	0	15	0	38	1	0	7	3	.700	0	0	3.46
1997 Rochester	AAA Bal	2	2	0	0	12.1	49	12	7	7	3	0	0	0	3	0	6	0	0	1	0	1.000	0	0	5.11
1996 Baltimore	AL	3	0	0	2	4.2	22	6	2	2	1	0	0	0	3	0	2	0	1	0	0	.000	0	0	3.86
6 Min. YEARS		98	87	6	1	538	2251	550	261	223	63	13	24	5	136	2	430	40	0	34	30	.531	0	0	3.73

Al Sadler

Pitches: Right **Bats:** Right **Pos:** P **Ht:** 6'6" **Wt:** 192 **Born:** 2/10/72 **Age:** 26

				HOW MUCH HE PITCHED						WHAT HE GAVE UP									THE RESULTS				
Year Team	Lg Org	G	GS	CG	GF	IP	BFP	H	R	ER	HR	SH	SF	HB	TBB	IBB	SO	WP	Bk	W	L	Pct.	ShO	Sv	ERA
1992 Brewers	R Mil	7	5	0	0	30	127	32	12	7	0	1	0	0	6	0	33	3	1	2	2	.500	0	0	2.10
Helena	R+ Mil	4	3	0	1	23	96	19	10	7	1	0	2	3	7	0	19	3	0	1	1	.500	0	0	2.74

Year Team	Lg Org	G	GS	CG	GF	IP	BFP	H	R	ER	HR	SH	SF	HB	TBB	IBB	SO	WP	Bk	W	L	Pct.	ShO	Sv	ERA
1993 Beloit	A Mil	20	20	1	0	116	510	126	67	53	9	5	6	9	47	1	87	10	0	6	6	.500	0	0	4.11
1994 Beloit	A Mil	16	16	5	0	99	428	96	48	39	9	3	3	3	51	1	79	13	0	7	4	.636	1	0	3.55
1995 Stockton	A+ Mil	37	14	1	10	114	501	113	62	56	9	3	2	8	59	0	82	6	2	4	9	.308	1	2	4.42
1996 Stockton	A+ Mil	18	0	0	17	20	79	12	7	6	3	1	0	0	7	0	19	1	0	1	2	.333	0	7	2.70
El Paso	AA Mil	26	0	0	10	42	207	39	28	22	3	2	1	3	40	2	31	4	0	3	3	.500	0	1	4.71
1997 El Paso	AA Mil	35	9	0	21	66.2	327	102	59	49	5	2	2	3	28	0	58	10	2	6	6	.500	0	4	6.62
Tucson	AAA Mil	1	1	0	0	6	28	7	1	1	0	0	0	0	4	0	1	2	0	1	0	1.000	0	0	1.50
6 Min. YEARS		164	68	7	59	516.2	2303	546	294	240	39	17	16	29	249	4	409	52	5	31	33	.484	2	14	4.18

Donnie Sadler

Bats: Right Throws: Right Pos: 2B-SS   Ht: 5'6" Wt: 165 Born: 6/17/75 Age: 23

Year Team	Lg Org	G	AB	H	2B	3B	HR	TB	R	RBI	TBB	IBB	SO	HBP	SH	SF	SB	CS	SB%	GDP	Avg	OBP	SLG
1994 Red Sox	R Bos	53	206	56	8	6	1	79	52	16	23	0	27	3	1	3	32	8	.80	1	.272	.349	.383
1995 Michigan	A Bos	118	438	124	25	8	9	192	103	55	79	0	85	6	3	3	41	13	.76	5	.283	.397	.438
1996 Trenton	AA Bos	115	454	121	20	8	6	175	68	46	38	3	75	6	6	3	34	8	.81	6	.267	.329	.385
1997 Pawtucket	AAA Bos	125	481	102	18	2	11	157	74	36	57	0	121	2	3	6	20	14	.59	11	.212	.295	.326
4 Min. YEARS		411	1579	403	71	24	27	603	297	153	197	3	308	17	13	15	127	43	.75	23	.255	.341	.382

Jon Saffer

Bats: Left Throws: Right Pos: OF   Ht: 6'2" Wt: 200 Born: 7/6/73 Age: 24

Year Team	Lg Org	G	AB	H	2B	3B	HR	TB	R	RBI	TBB	IBB	SO	HBP	SH	SF	SB	CS	SB%	GDP	Avg	OBP	SLG
1992 Expos	R Mon	36	139	38	2	0	0	40	18	11	11	0	23	1	2	1	7	5	.58	2	.273	.329	.288
1993 Wst Plm Bch	A+ Mon	7	24	5	0	0	0	5	3	2	2	0	5	1	1	0	1	3	.25	0	.208	.296	.208
Jamestown	A- Mon	61	225	58	17	5	0	85	31	18	31	1	46	2	3	1	11	5	.69	4	.258	.351	.378
1994 Vermont	A- Mon	70	263	83	18	5	3	120	44	43	33	1	47	1	1	1	14	3	.82	9	.316	.393	.456
1995 Wst Plm Bch	A+ Mon	92	324	103	10	6	4	137	60	35	53	1	49	2	4	1	18	9	.67	7	.318	.416	.423
Harrisburg	AA Mon	20	76	18	4	0	0	22	9	4	6	0	14	0	0	0	2	1	.67	2	.237	.293	.289
1996 Harrisburg	AA Mon	134	487	146	26	4	10	210	96	52	78	1	77	6	5	3	8	16	.33	8	.300	.401	.431
1997 Ottawa	AAA Mon	134	483	129	20	9	15	212	81	60	76	1	74	8	0	3	13	6	.68	12	.267	.374	.439
6 Min. YEARS		554	2021	580	97	29	32	831	342	225	290	5	335	21	16	10	74	48	.61	44	.287	.380	.411

Matt Saier

Pitches: Right Bats: Right Pos: P   Ht: 6'2" Wt: 192 Born: 1/29/73 Age: 25

Year Team	Lg Org	G	GS	CG	GF	IP	BFP	H	R	ER	HR	SH	SF	HB	TBB	IBB	SO	WP	Bk	W	L	Pct.	ShO	Sv	ERA
1995 Spokane	A- KC	16	0	0	9	35.1	138	24	14	13	2	2	1	2	12	0	41	4	0	1	2	.333	0	4	3.31
1996 Wilmington	A+ KC	26	26	0	0	134	585	136	74	60	9	4	0	6	52	2	129	9	2	9	9	.500	0	0	4.03
1997 Wilmington	A+ KC	9	9	0	0	42.2	173	31	11	8	4	0	2	0	15	0	47	2	0	2	2	.500	0	0	1.69
Wichita	AA KC	17	17	0	0	101	452	112	66	55	6	5	4	7	48	4	53	7	0	7	5	.583	0	0	4.90
3 Min. YEARS		68	52	0	9	313	1348	303	165	136	21	11	7	15	127	6	270	22	2	19	18	.514	0	4	3.91

Mike Saipe

Pitches: Right Bats: Right Pos: P   Ht: 6'1" Wt: 190 Born: 9/10/73 Age: 24

Year Team	Lg Org	G	GS	CG	GF	IP	BFP	H	R	ER	HR	SH	SF	HB	TBB	IBB	SO	WP	Bk	W	L	Pct.	ShO	Sv	ERA
1994 Bend	A- Col	16	16	0	0	84.1	363	73	52	39	7	3	4	7	34	0	74	6	2	3	7	.300	0	0	4.16
1995 Salem	A+ Col	21	9	0	7	85.1	347	68	35	33	7	1	1	2	32	4	90	9	1	4	5	.444	0	3	3.48
1996 New Haven	AA Col	32	19	1	5	138	562	114	53	47	12	4	3	4	42	6	126	4	4	10	7	.588	1	3	3.07
1997 New Haven	AA Col	19	19	4	0	136.2	550	127	57	47	18	3	1	5	29	2	123	4	1	8	5	.615	2	0	3.10
Colo Spmgs	AAA Col	10	10	1	0	60.1	278	74	42	37	10	1	0	4	24	3	40	2	3	4	3	.571	0	0	5.52
4 Min. YEARS		98	73	6	12	504.2	2100	456	239	203	54	12	9	22	161	15	453	25	11	29	27	.518	3	6	3.62

Roger Salkeld

Pitches: Right Bats: Right Pos: P   Ht: 6'5" Wt: 215 Born: 3/6/71 Age: 27

Year Team	Lg Org	G	GS	CG	GF	IP	BFP	H	R	ER	HR	SH	SF	HB	TBB	IBB	SO	WP	Bk	W	L	Pct.	ShO	Sv	ERA
1989 Bellingham	A- Sea	8	6	0	1	42	168	27	17	6	0	0	1	4	10	0	55	3	3	2	2	.500	0	0	1.29
1990 San Berndno	A+ Sea	25	25	2	0	153.1	677	140	77	58	3	7	1	3	83	0	167	9	2	11	5	.688	0	0	3.40
1991 Jacksnville	AA Sea	23	23	5	0	153.2	634	131	56	52	9	5	5	10	55	1	159	12	2	8	8	.500	0	0	3.05
Calgary	AAA Sea	4	4	0	0	19.1	90	18	16	11	2	1	0	4	13	0	21	1	0	2	1	.667	0	0	5.12
1993 Jacksnville	AA Sea	14	14	0	0	77	334	71	39	28	8	3	5	5	29	1	56	2	1	4	3	.571	0	0	3.27
1994 Calgary	AAA Sea	13	13	0	0	67.1	315	74	54	46	11	0	5	4	39	2	54	5	0	3	7	.300	0	0	6.15
1995 Tacoma	AAA Sea	4	3	0	1	15	59	8	4	3	0	0	0	0	7	0	11	0	0	1	0	1.000	0	1	1.80
Indianapols	AAA Cin	20	20	1	0	119.1	497	96	60	56	13	3	4	2	57	1	86	3	0	12	2	.857	0	1	4.22
1997 Indianapols	AAA Cin	36	11	0	7	88	421	91	75	66	16	2	2	5	60	2	88	6	0	4	8	.333	0	1	6.75
1993 Seattle	AL	3	2	0	0	14.1	61	13	4	4	0	0	0	1	4	0	13	0	0	0	0	.000	0	0	2.51
1994 Seattle	AL	13	13	0	0	59	291	76	47	47	7	0	3	1	45	1	46	2	0	2	5	.286	0	0	7.17
1996 Cincinnati	NL	29	19	1	2	116	509	114	69	67	18	10	3	6	54	2	82	7	1	8	5	.615	1	0	5.20
7 Min. YEARS		147	119	8	9	735	3195	656	398	326	62	21	23	37	353	7	697	41	8	47	36	.566	0	2	3.99
3 Maj. YEARS		45	34	1	2	189.1	861	203	120	118	25	10	6	8	103	3	141	9	1	10	10	.500	1	0	5.61

Benj Sampson

Pitches: Left **Bats:** Right **Pos:** P | **Ht:** 6'0" **Wt:** 197 **Born:** 4/27/75 **Age:** 23

Year Team	Lg Org	G	GS	CG	GF	IP	BFP	H	R	ER	HR	SH	SF	HB	TBB	IBB	SO	WP	Bk	W	L	Pct.	ShO	Sv	ERA
1993 Elizabethtn	R+ Min	11	6	0	2	42.1	171	33	12	9	1	2	0	1	15	1	34	5	0	4	1	.800	0	1	1.91
1994 Ft. Wayne	A Min	25	25	0	0	139.2	617	149	72	59	10	7	5	5	60	0	111	5	4	6	9	.400	0	0	3.80
1995 Ft. Myers	A+ Min	28	27	3	1	160	664	148	71	62	11	8	8	4	52	0	95	5	0	11	9	.550	2	0	3.49
1996 Ft. Myers	A+ Min	11	11	2	0	70	282	55	28	27	5	1	2	1	26	0	65	1	0	7	1	.875	0	0	3.47
Hardware City	AA Min	16	16	1	0	75.1	353	108	54	48	8	0	2	2	25	0	51	2	1	5	7	.417	0	0	5.73
1997 New Britain	AA Min	25	20	0	1	118	498	112	56	55	12	2	5	1	49	1	92	4	2	10	6	.625	0	0	4.19
5 Min. YEARS		116	105	6	4	605.1	2585	605	293	260	47	20	22	14	227	2	448	22	7	43	33	.566	2	1	3.87

Scott Samuels

Bats: Left **Throws:** Right **Pos:** OF | **Ht:** 5'11" **Wt:** 190 **Born:** 5/19/71 **Age:** 27

Year Team	Lg Org	G	AB	H	2B	3B	HR	TB	R	RBI	TBB	IBB	SO	HBP	SH	SF	SB	CS	SB%	GDP	Avg	OBP	SLG
1992 Erie	A- Fla	43	128	26	7	1	0	35	17	14	19	0	39	2	0	0	7	3	.70	2	.203	.315	.273
1993 High Desert	A+ Fla	76	219	65	10	4	6	101	43	40	45	0	55	1	0	1	12	4	.75	7	.297	.417	.461
1994 Brevard Cty	A+ Fla	89	281	65	11	0	3	85	35	25	46	1	70	4	1	1	11	5	.69	7	.231	.346	.302
1995 Orlando	AA ChN	5	21	6	1	0	1	10	3	4	3	0	4	0	0	0	2	0	1.00	0	.286	.375	.476
Daytona	A+ ChN	112	388	127	29	12	2	186	92	42	69	7	63	8	3	4	38	14	.73	8	.327	.435	.479
1996 Orlando	AA ChN	106	342	89	19	5	2	124	62	33	62	2	81	0	3	1	21	10	.68	3	.260	.373	.363
1997 Orlando	AA ChN	34	127	36	7	3	3	58	30	17	18	0	34	1	1	0	5	4	.56	4	.283	.377	.457
Ottawa	AAA Mon	20	55	19	3	0	1	25	6	7	7	3	12	0	1	0	2	0	1.00	2	.345	.419	.455
Harrisburg	AA Mon	64	223	66	19	1	5	102	32	32	34	3	43	1	1	0	13	4	.76	0	.296	.391	.457
6 Min. YEARS		549	1784	499	106	26	23	726	320	214	303	16	401	17	10	7	111	44	.72	33	.280	.388	.407

Jesus Sanchez

Pitches: Left **Bats:** Left **Pos:** P | **Ht:** 5'10" **Wt:** 153 **Born:** 10/11/74 **Age:** 23

Year Team	Lg Org	G	GS	CG	GF	IP	BFP	H	R	ER	HR	SH	SF	HB	TBB	IBB	SO	WP	Bk	W	L	Pct.	ShO	Sv	ERA
1994 Kingsport	R+ NYN	13	12	3	0	87.1	346	61	27	19	2	1	4	2	24	0	71	7	1	7	4	.636	0	0	1.96
1995 Capital City	A NYN	27	27	4	0	169.2	705	154	76	59	9	2	5	7	58	0	177	10	4	9	7	.563	0	0	3.13
1996 St. Lucie	A+ NYN	16	16	2	0	92	344	53	22	20	6	3	1	1	24	0	81	4	2	9	3	.750	1	0	1.96
1997 Binghamton	AA NYN	26	26	3	0	165.1	693	146	87	79	25	4	6	5	61	2	176	4	3	13	10	.565	0	0	4.30
4 Min. YEARS		82	81	12	0	514.1	2088	414	212	177	42	10	13	17	167	2	505	25	10	38	24	.613	1	0	3.10

Victor Sanchez

Bats: Right **Throws:** Right **Pos:** OF | **Ht:** 5'11" **Wt:** 175 **Born:** 12/20/71 **Age:** 26

Year Team	Lg Org	G	AB	H	2B	3B	HR	TB	R	RBI	TBB	IBB	SO	HBP	SH	SF	SB	CS	SB%	GDP	Avg	OBP	SLG
1994 Auburn	A- Hou	58	219	63	15	0	3	87	33	35	13	1	40	4	0	1	0	1	.00	7	.288	.338	.397
1995 Quad City	A Hou	13	34	8	0	0	0	8	3	1	6	0	10	0	0	0	1	0	1.00	0	.235	.350	.235
Kissimmee	A+ Hou	78	272	73	11	0	7	105	34	38	23	1	69	8	1	4	6	3	.67	6	.268	.339	.386
1996 Jackson	AA Hou	86	210	46	9	0	13	94	30	34	15	0	58	4	0	0	4	1	.80	7	.219	.284	.448
1997 Jackson	AA Hou	69	175	37	4	0	8	65	22	35	23	1	42	1	1	1	1	2	.33	5	.211	.308	.371
4 Min. YEARS		304	910	227	39	0	31	359	122	143	80	3	219	18	2	6	12	7	.63	27	.249	.321	.395

Anthony Sanders

Bats: Right **Throws:** Right **Pos:** OF | **Ht:** 6'2" **Wt:** 180 **Born:** 3/2/74 **Age:** 24

Year Team	Lg Org	G	AB	H	2B	3B	HR	TB	R	RBI	TBB	IBB	SO	HBP	SH	SF	SB	CS	SB%	GDP	Avg	OBP	SLG
1993 Medicne Hat	R+ Tor	63	225	59	9	3	4	86	44	33	20	0	49	2	3	1	6	5	.55	2	.262	.327	.382
1994 St. Cathrns	A- Tor	74	258	66	17	3	6	107	36	45	27	0	53	1	4	2	8	7	.53	2	.256	.326	.415
1995 Hagerstown	A Tor	133	512	119	28	1	8	173	72	48	52	0	103	5	9	5	26	14	.65	8	.232	.307	.338
1996 Dunedin	A+ Tor	102	417	108	25	0	17	184	75	50	34	0	93	6	0	0	16	12	.57	5	.259	.324	.441
1997 Dunedin	A+ Tor	38	133	36	8	0	1	47	16	18	7	0	33	2	1	0	1	3	.25	0	.271	.317	.353
Knoxville	AA Tor	111	429	114	20	4	26	220	68	69	44	3	121	3	4	4	20	12	.63	9	.266	.335	.513
5 Min. YEARS		522	1979	503	108	11	62	819	311	264	185	3	453	19	21	12	77	53	.59	26	.254	.322	.414

Tracy Sanders

Bats: Left **Throws:** Right **Pos:** 1B | **Ht:** 6'0" **Wt:** 206 **Born:** 7/26/69 **Age:** 28

Year Team	Lg Org	G	AB	H	2B	3B	HR	TB	R	RBI	TBB	IBB	SO	HBP	SH	SF	SB	CS	SB%	GDP	Avg	OBP	SLG
1990 Burlington	R+ Cle	51	178	50	12	1	10	94	38	34	33	0	36	2	0	1	10	3	.77	2	.281	.397	.528
Kinston	A+ Cle	10	32	14	3	3	0	23	6	9	7	0	6	0	0	0	1	1	.50	0	.438	.538	.719
1991 Kinston	A+ Cle	118	421	112	20	8	18	202	80	63	83	4	95	6	2	2	8	5	.62	9	.266	.393	.480
1992 Canton-Akrn	AA Cle	114	381	92	11	3	21	172	66	87	77	3	113	3	4	3	3	6	.33	8	.241	.371	.451
1993 Canton-Akrn	AA Cle	42	136	29	6	2	5	54	20	20	31	1	30	1	0	1	4	1	.80	1	.213	.361	.397
Wichita	AA SD	77	266	86	13	4	13	146	44	47	34	1	67	2	0	1	6	5	.55	2	.323	.403	.549
1994 Binghamton	AA NYN	101	275	66	20	4	8	118	44	37	60	1	88	3	0	5	8	6	.57	1	.240	.376	.429
1995 Binghamton	AA NYN	9	32	9	3	0	2	18	6	8	5	0	11	0	0	0	1	0	1.00	0	.281	.378	.563
Norfolk	AAA NYN	64	110	25	6	0	4	43	21	14	34	0	34	4	0	0	3	1	.75	2	.227	.426	.391
1996 Tulsa	AA Tex	52	168	39	10	0	7	70	31	20	33	2	49	2	0	0	2	1	.67	3	.232	.365	.417
Tri-City	IND —	35	123	30	6	0	9	63	25	24	29	1	38	2	0	0	5	3	.63	0	.244	.396	.512
1997 Carolina	AA Pit	116	376	102	23	1	21	190	77	78	74	0	88	6	1	3	7	6	.54	2	.271	.397	.505

Year Team	Lg Org	BATTING																BASERUNNING				PERCENTAGES		
		G	AB	H	2B	3B	HR	TB	R	RBI	TBB	IBB	SO	HBP	SH	SF		SB	CS	SB%	GDP	Avg	OBP	SLG
8 Min. YEARS		790	2498	654	133	26	118	1193	458	441	500	13	655	31	7	16		58	38	.60	30	.262	.389	.478

Francisco Saneaux

Pitches: Right Bats: Right Pos: P   Ht: 6'4" Wt: 180 Born: 3/3/74 Age: 24

Year Team	Lg Org	HOW MUCH HE PITCHED						WHAT HE GAVE UP										THE RESULTS					
		G	GS	CG	GF	IP	BFP	H	R	ER	HR	SH	SF	HB	TBB	IBB	SO	WP	Bk	W	L	Pct	ShO	Sv	ERA
1991 Orioles	R Bal	12	6	0	4	41	198	42	31	18	1	4	2	3	22	0	27	4	1	1	4	.200	0	1	3.95
1992 Bluefield	R+ Bal	4	1	0	0	8	40	7	6	6	0	0	0	1	7	0	7	0	1	2	0	1.000	0	0	6.75
1993 Bluefield	R+ Bal	6	6	0	0	32.1	141	30	14	13	3	1	1	4	14	0	28	4	0	2	1	.667	0	0	3.62
1994 Albany	A Bal	26	21	1	4	106	501	97	93	77	8	2	5	12	91	0	100	15	3	4	12	.250	0	0	6.54
1995 High Desert	A+ Bal	23	11	0	4	52.2	296	56	77	62	8	0	6	11	72	1	64	10	4	0	8	.000	0	1	10.59
1996 Frederick	A+ Bal	2	1	0	0	2.2	23	9	11	11	3	0	0	1	6	0	3	0	0	0	0	.000	0	0	37.13
High Desert	A+ Bal	20	19	0	0	102	474	98	71	63	13	4	0	7	91	4	101	17	2	4	5	.444	0	0	5.56
1997 Bowie	AA Bal	8	0	0	1	13.2	81	8	14	13	1	1	1	5	32	0	13	7	0	0	0	.000	0	0	8.56
Frederick	A+ Bal	32	5	0	10	74	358	56	48	37	8	2	5	8	84	3	89	24	0	2	6	.250	0	0	4.50
7 Min. YEARS		133	70	1	23	432.1	2112	403	365	300	45	14	20	52	419	8	432	81	11	15	36	.294	0	2	6.25

Chance Sanford

Bats: Left Throws: Right Pos: 3B   Ht: 5'10" Wt: 165 Born: 6/2/72 Age: 26

Year Team	Lg Org	BATTING																BASERUNNING				PERCENTAGES		
		G	AB	H	2B	3B	HR	TB	R	RBI	TBB	IBB	SO	HBP	SH	SF		SB	CS	SB%	GDP	Avg	OBP	SLG
1992 Welland	A- Pit	59	214	61	11	3	5	93	36	21	35	4	39	0	0	3		13	4	.76	2	.285	.381	.435
Augusta	A Pit	14	46	5	1	0	0	6	3	2	3	0	10	1	0	0		0	2	.00	0	.109	.180	.130
1993 Salem	A+ Pit	115	428	109	21	5	10	170	54	37	33	0	80	1	3	2		11	10	.52	0	.255	.308	.397
1994 Salem	A+ Pit	127	474	130	32	6	19	231	81	78	56	0	95	2	1	4		12	6	.67	7	.274	.351	.487
1995 Carolina	AA Pit	16	36	10	3	1	3	24	6	10	5	1	7	1	0	0		3	1	.75	0	.278	.381	.667
Pirates	R Pit	6	19	4	0	0	1	7	2	1	2	0	2	0	0	0		0	0	.00	0	.211	.286	.368
Lynchburg	A+ Pit	16	66	22	4	0	3	35	8	14	7	0	13	0	0	1		1	0	1.00	1	.333	.392	.530
1996 Carolina	AA Pit	131	470	115	16	13	4	169	62	56	72	2	108	0	2	7		11	11	.50	9	.245	.341	.360
1997 Carolina	AA Pit	44	149	39	10	2	9	80	30	36	20	1	39	2	2	4		3	1	.75	1	.262	.349	.537
Calgary	AAA Pit	89	325	95	27	9	6	158	58	60	39	0	82	3	1	5		9	7	.56	5	.292	.368	.486
6 Min. YEARS		617	2227	590	125	39	60	973	340	315	272	8	475	10	9	26		63	42	.60	25	.265	.344	.437

Marino Santana

Pitches: Right Bats: Right Pos: P   Ht: 6'1" Wt: 188 Born: 5/10/72 Age: 26

Year Team	Lg Org	HOW MUCH HE PITCHED						WHAT HE GAVE UP										THE RESULTS					
		G	GS	CG	GF	IP	BFP	H	R	ER	HR	SH	SF	HB	TBB	IBB	SO	WP	Bk	W	L	Pct	ShO	Sv	ERA
1993 Bellingham	A- Sea	15	0	0	8	21.2	117	27	19	14	3	0	1	0	22	1	24	4	2	0	1	.000	0	0	5.82
1994 Bellingham	A- Sea	15	15	1	0	80	331	68	35	28	3	1	1	3	26	0	88	10	3	6	3	.667	0	0	3.15
1995 Wisconsin	A Sea	15	15	2	0	96.2	368	57	26	19	5	2	2	1	25	0	110	6	0	8	3	.727	1	0	1.77
Riverside	A+ Sea	9	9	0	0	48	214	44	47	33	10	3	4	2	25	0	57	2	3	3	5	.375	0	0	6.19
1996 Lancaster	A+ Sea	28	28	1	0	157.1	688	164	105	88	26	5	8	8	57	0	167	18	6	8	15	.348	0	0	5.03
1997 Jacksnville	AA Det	39	0	0	10	74	317	55	28	27	8	1	1	1	43	0	98	13	1	4	1	.800	0	1	3.28
5 Min. YEARS		121	67	4	18	477.2	2035	415	260	209	55	12	17	15	198	1	544	53	15	29	28	.509	1	1	3.94

Scott Sauerbeck

Pitches: Left Bats: Right Pos: P   Ht: 6'3" Wt: 190 Born: 11/9/71 Age: 26

Year Team	Lg Org	HOW MUCH HE PITCHED						WHAT HE GAVE UP										THE RESULTS					
		G	GS	CG	GF	IP	BFP	H	R	ER	HR	SH	SF	HB	TBB	IBB	SO	WP	Bk	W	L	Pct	ShO	Sv	ERA
1994 Pittsfield	A- NYN	21	0	0	9	48.1	200	39	16	11	0	3	1	1	19	2	39	4	0	3	1	.750	0	1	2.05
1995 St. Lucie	A+ NYN	20	1	0	4	26.2	116	26	10	6	0	0	2	0	14	1	25	2	2	0	1	.000	0	0	2.03
Capital City	A NYN	19	0	0	13	33	139	28	14	12	2	2	0	1	14	1	33	3	1	5	4	.556	0	2	3.27
1996 St. Lucie	A+ NYN	17	16	2	0	99.1	406	101	37	25	1	3	0	1	27	0	62	4	1	6	6	.500	2	0	2.27
Binghamton	AA NYN	8	2	0	0	46.2	191	48	24	18	4	1	2	1	12	0	30	0	0	3	3	.500	0	0	3.47
1997 Norfolk	AAA NYN	1	1	0	0	5	20	3	2	2	0	0	1	0	4	0	4	1	0	1	0	1.000	0	0	3.60
Binghamton	AA NYN	27	20	2	1	131.1	575	144	89	72	15	7	1	3	50	0	88	4	2	8	9	.471	0	0	4.93
4 Min. YEARS		113	46	6	27	390.1	1647	389	192	146	22	16	7	7	140	4	281	18	6	26	24	.520	2	3	3.37

Chris Saunders

Bats: Right Throws: Right Pos: 3B   Ht: 6'1" Wt: 203 Born: 7/19/70 Age: 27

Year Team	Lg Org	BATTING																BASERUNNING				PERCENTAGES		
		G	AB	H	2B	3B	HR	TB	R	RBI	TBB	IBB	SO	HBP	SH	SF		SB	CS	SB%	GDP	Avg	OBP	SLG
1992 Pittsfield	A- NYN	72	254	64	11	2	2	85	34	32	34	0	50	1	1	5		5	2	.71	5	.252	.337	.335
1993 St. Lucie	A+ NYN	123	456	115	14	4	4	149	45	64	40	4	89	1	1	4		6	7	.46	10	.252	.311	.327
1994 Binghamton	AA NYN	132	499	134	29	0	10	193	68	70	43	0	96	4	2	7		6	6	.50	12	.269	.327	.387
1995 Norfolk	AAA NYN	16	56	13	3	1	3	27	9	7	9	0	15	0	0	0		1	1	.50	1	.232	.338	.482
Binghamton	AA NYN	122	441	114	22	5	8	170	58	66	45	1	98	5	5	7		3	6	.33	7	.259	.329	.385
1996 Binghamton	AA NYN	141	510	152	27	3	17	236	82	105	73	3	88	8	2	11		5	4	.56	11	.298	.388	.463
1997 Binghamton	AA NYN	30	111	36	13	0	3	58	16	22	12	1	20	2	0	4		3	1	.75	2	.324	.388	.523
Norfolk	AAA NYN	68	173	43	9	0	0	52	24	24	37	2	37	2	1	1		2	2	.50	6	.249	.385	.301
6 Min. YEARS		704	2500	671	128	15	47	970	336	390	293	11	493	23	13	39		31	29	.52	54	.268	.346	.388

225

Doug Saunders

Bats: Right Throws: Right Pos: 3B Ht: 6' 0" Wt: 172 Born: 12/13/69 Age: 28

Year Team	Lg Org	G	AB	H	2B	3B	HR	TB	R	RBI	TBB	IBB	SO	HBP	SH	SF	SB	CS	SB%	GDP	Avg	OBP	SLG
1988 Mets	R NYN	16	64	16	4	1	0	22	8	10	9	0	14	0	2	0	2	3	.40	0	.250	.342	.344
Little Fall	A- NYN	29	100	30	6	1	0	38	10	11	6	0	15	0	1	0	1	4	.20	2	.300	.340	.380
1989 Columbia	A NYN	115	377	99	18	4	4	137	53	38	35	2	78	3	4	3	5	5	.50	5	.263	.328	.363
1990 St. Lucie	A+ NYN	115	408	92	8	4	1	111	52	43	43	0	96	2	7	2	24	10	.71	7	.225	.301	.272
1991 St. Lucie	A+ NYN	70	230	54	9	2	2	73	19	18	25	0	43	4	5	0	5	6	.45	6	.235	.320	.317
1992 Binghamton	AA NYN	130	435	108	16	2	5	143	45	38	52	0	68	1	5	4	8	12	.40	9	.248	.327	.329
1993 Norfolk	AAA NYN	105	356	88	12	6	2	118	37	24	44	1	63	3	7	1	6	5	.55	13	.247	.334	.331
1994 Binghamton	AA NYN	96	338	96	19	4	8	147	48	45	43	2	63	0	6	4	3	4	.43	6	.284	.361	.435
1995 Edmonton	AAA Oak	5	16	3	2	1	0	7	2	4	0	0	2	0	0	0	0	0	.00	0	.188	.188	.438
Tacoma	AAA Sea	50	135	38	5	2	5	62	19	24	7	0	30	1	1	2	0	0	.00	3	.281	.317	.459
Port City	AA Sea	28	114	30	9	1	4	53	13	16	10	1	28	2	0	2	2	0	1.00	4	.263	.328	.465
1996 Tacoma	AAA Sea	40	131	33	6	0	3	48	16	13	19	0	22	0	3	0	1	0	1.00	1	.252	.347	.366
1997 Memphis	AA Sea	73	232	60	15	0	2	81	33	28	46	2	44	0	2	3	0	3	.00	5	.259	.377	.349
1993 New York	NL	28	67	14	2	0	0	16	8	0	3	0	4	0	3	0	0	0	.00	2	.209	.243	.239
10 Min. YEARS		872	2936	747	129	28	36	1040	355	312	339	8	566	16	43	21	57	52	.52	61	.254	.333	.354

Rich Sauveur

Pitches: Left Bats: Left Pos: P Ht: 6' 4" Wt: 185 Born: 11/23/63 Age: 34

Year Team	Lg Org	G	GS	CG	GF	IP	BFP	H	R	ER	HR	SH	SF	HB	TBB	IBB	SO	WP	Bk	W	L	Pct.	ShO	Sv	ERA
1983 Watertown	A- Pit	16	12	1	0	93.2	—	80	41	24	6	—	—	1	31	0	73	2	4	7	5	.583	2	0	2.31
1984 Pr William	A+ Pit	10	10	0	0	54.2	240	43	22	19	5	2	1	1	31	0	54	3	0	3	3	.500	0	0	3.13
Nashua	AA Pit	10	10	2	0	70.2	291	54	27	23	4	4	1	3	34	1	48	2	4	5	3	.625	2	0	2.93
1985 Nashua	AA Pit	25	25	4	0	157.1	666	146	73	62	7	9	6	3	78	2	85	7	4	9	10	.474	2	0	3.55
1986 Nashua	AA Pit	5	5	2	0	38	141	21	5	5	1	1	0	1	11	0	28	1	1	3	1	.750	1	0	1.18
Hawaii	AAA Pit	14	14	0	0	92	391	73	40	31	3	2	0	6	45	1	68	4	8	7	6	.538	1	0	3.03
1987 Harrisburg	AA Mon	30	27	7	0	195	825	174	71	62	9	7	9	9	96	3	160	9	7	13	6	.684	1	0	2.86
1988 Jacksnville	AA Mon	8	0	0	4	6.2	32	7	5	3	0	0	0	0	5	0	8	0	0	0	2	.000	0	1	4.05
Indianapols	AAA Mon	43	3	0	18	81.1	318	60	26	22	8	5	1	1	28	5	58	3	3	7	4	.636	0	10	2.43
1989 Indianapols	AAA Mon	4	0	0	4	9.2	44	10	8	8	1	0	1	0	6	0	8	0	0	0	1	.000	0	1	7.45
1990 Miami	A+ —	11	6	1	2	40.2	178	41	16	15	2	2	0	4	17	0	34	0	3	0	4	.000	0	0	3.32
Indianapols	AAA Mon	14	7	0	0	56	232	45	14	12	1	2	2	3	25	0	24	1	3	2	2	.500	0	0	1.93
1991 Tidewater	AAA NYN	42	0	0	21	45.1	188	31	14	12	0	4	0	0	23	5	49	3	2	2	2	.500	0	6	2.38
1992 Omaha	AAA KC	34	13	1	7	117.1	467	93	54	42	8	3	5	2	39	1	88	4	4	7	6	.538	0	0	3.22
1993 Indianapols	AAA Cin	5	5	0	0	34.2	146	41	10	7	2	2	0	2	7	2	21	0	0	2	0	1.000	0	0	1.82
1994 Indianapols	AAA Cin	53	1	0	30	67	268	47	25	21	7	4	0	1	23	4	65	1	0	3	3	.500	0	12	2.82
1995 Indianapols	AAA Cin	52	0	0	43	57	228	43	17	13	3	1	1	2	18	3	47	3	0	5	2	.714	0	15	2.05
1996 Nashville	AAA ChA	61	3	0	20	73	311	63	34	30	8	2	3	3	28	4	69	3	0	4	3	.571	0	8	3.70
1997 Iowa	AAA ChN	39	1	0	19	45.1	198	46	19	17	4	2	1	3	21	5	37	0	0	1	3	.250	0	2	3.38
1986 Pittsburgh	NL	3	3	0	0	12	57	17	8	8	3	1	0	2	6	0	6	0	2	0	0	.000	0	0	6.00
1988 Montreal	NL	4	0	0	0	3	14	3	2	2	1	0	0	0	2	0	3	0	0	0	0	.000	0	0	6.00
1991 New York	NL	6	0	0	0	3.1	19	7	4	4	1	2	0	0	2	0	4	0	0	0	0	.000	0	0	10.80
1992 Kansas City	AL	8	0	0	2	14.1	65	15	7	7	1	0	0	2	8	1	7	0	1	0	1	.000	0	0	4.40
1996 Chicago	AL	3	0	0	0	3	15	3	5	5	1	0	0	0	5	0	1	0	0	0	0	.000	0	0	15.00
15 Min. YEARS		480	142	24	168	1335.1	5164	1118	521	428	79	52	31	45	566	36	1024	46	44	80	66	.548	7	55	2.88
5 Maj. YEARS		24	3	0	2	35.2	170	26	26	26	7	3	0	5	23	1	21	0	3	0	1	.000	0	0	6.56

Warren Sawkiw

Bats: Both Throws: Right Pos: 2B Ht: 5'11" Wt: 180 Born: 1/19/68 Age: 30

Year Team	Lg Org	G	AB	H	2B	3B	HR	TB	R	RBI	TBB	IBB	SO	HBP	SH	SF	SB	CS	SB%	GDP	Avg	OBP	SLG
1990 Niagara Fal	A- Det	7	20	8	1	1	0	11	7	4	15	2	3	0	0	0	2	0	1.00	0	.400	.657	.550
Fayetteville	A Det	59	210	54	6	0	1	63	31	18	30	1	35	1	2	4	4	1	.80	6	.257	.347	.300
1991 Lakeland	A+ Det	112	420	114	20	7	2	154	58	42	42	2	87	3	3	3	2	9	.18	8	.271	.340	.367
1992 Lakeland	A+ Det	118	423	103	18	4	2	135	56	47	39	1	62	3	0	7	6	7	.46	13	.243	.307	.319
1993 Rochester	IND —	70	272	89	21	2	9	141	42	45	31	2	53	1	0	2	14	2	.88	6	.327	.395	.518
1994 Winnipeg	IND —	20	76	19	3	0	1	25	7	10	9	0	13	0	0	2	3	1	.75	0	.250	.322	.329
Thunder Bay	IND —	48	183	63	11	0	3	83	25	27	22	1	32	0	0	3	2	6	.25	2	.344	.411	.454
1995 Syracuse	AAA Tor	11	42	8	1	0	0	9	3	0	5	0	8	0	0	0	2	0	1.00	1	.190	.277	.214
Knoxville	AA Tor	44	121	30	4	1	1	39	11	11	13	0	36	0	1	1	2	2	.50	2	.248	.319	.322
1996 Grand Forks	IND —	33	138	48	5	3	9	86	26	39	15	1	19	0	0	2	3	4	.43	1	.348	.406	.623
Birmingham	AA ChA	20	56	13	2	0	0	15	7	5	11	1	17	1	0	0	2	3	.40	0	.232	.368	.268
1997 Birmingham	AA ChA	4	7	2	0	0	1	5	1	3	0	0	1	0	0	0	0	0	.00	0	.286	.286	.714
Elmira	IND —	78	300	84	20	1	1	109	42	24	24	2	61	8	6	2	7	4	.64	2	.280	.347	.363
8 Min. YEARS		624	2268	635	112	19	30	875	316	275	256	13	427	17	17	25	49	39	.56	41	.280	.354	.386

Jamie Saylor

Bats: Left Throws: Right Pos: SS Ht: 5'11" Wt: 185 Born: 9/11/74 Age: 23

Year Team	Lg Org	G	AB	H	2B	3B	HR	TB	R	RBI	TBB	IBB	SO	HBP	SH	SF	SB	CS	SB%	GDP	Avg	OBP	SLG
1993 Astros	R Hou	51	162	38	5	2	0	47	29	14	23	0	28	0	1	0	5	3	.63	1	.235	.330	.290
1994 Quad City	A Hou	92	321	84	16	2	2	110	57	22	28	2	65	7	7	1	14	5	.74	0	.262	.333	.343
1995 Kissimmee	A+ Hou	89	289	66	4	1	2	78	38	19	22	1	58	6	0	2	13	6	.68	5	.228	.295	.270
1996 Kissimmee	A+ Hou	59	181	37	3	3	1	49	17	6	10	0	43	0	3	2	8	6	.57	3	.204	.244	.271
Quad City	A Hou	23	58	7	1	0	0	8	8	5	3	0	13	2	2	0	4	2	.67	1	.121	.185	.138
1997 Quad City	A Hou	20	61	15	5	0	0	20	10	2	11	1	16	0	2	0	3	2	.60	3	.246	.361	.328

Year Team	Lg Org	G	AB	H	2B	3B	HR	TB	R	RBI	TBB	IBB	SO	HBP	SH	SF	SB	CS	SB%	GDP	Avg	OBP	SLG
								BATTING										BASERUNNING			PERCENTAGES		
New Orleans	AAA Hou	2	0	0	0	0	0	0	0	0	0	0	0	0	0	0	0	0	.00	0	.000	.000	.000
Jackson	AA Hou	63	205	52	12	3	5	85	23	21	18	1	43	3	3	0	3	2	.60	1	.254	.323	.415
5 Min. YEARS		399	1277	299	46	11	10	397	182	89	115	5	266	18	18	7	50	26	.66	13	.234	.305	.311

Jon Sbrocco

Bats: Left Throws: Right Pos: 2B   Ht: 5'10" Wt: 165 Born: 1/5/71 Age: 27

Year Team	Lg Org	G	AB	H	2B	3B	HR	TB	R	RBI	TBB	IBB	SO	HBP	SH	SF	SB	CS	SB%	GDP	Avg	OBP	SLG
								BATTING										BASERUNNING			PERCENTAGES		
1993 Everett	A- SF	2	3	1	0	0	0	1	0	0	0	0	0	1	0	0	0	0	.00	0	.333	.500	.333
Clinton	A SF	56	179	48	6	2	0	58	28	17	29	0	31	4	5	0	8	6	.57	2	.268	.382	.324
1994 Clinton	A SF	64	214	53	8	0	0	61	48	22	42	1	27	6	7	1	6	3	.67	3	.248	.384	.285
1995 San Jose	A+ SF	120	425	128	14	5	2	158	66	46	55	3	43	10	17	1	12	10	.55	5	.301	.393	.372
1996 San Jose	A+ SF	95	358	111	12	5	2	139	76	48	67	1	36	8	8	3	29	11	.73	6	.310	.427	.388
Shreveport	AA SF	23	81	20	2	1	1	27	16	5	11	0	10	2	2	1	5	0	1.00	2	.247	.347	.333
1997 Shreveport	AA SF	97	271	71	15	3	2	98	32	27	40	0	21	3	7	2	7	8	.47	7	.262	.361	.362
5 Min. YEARS		457	1531	432	57	16	7	542	266	165	244	5	168	34	46	8	67	38	.64	25	.282	.391	.354

Bob Scanlan

Pitches: Right Bats: Right Pos: P   Ht: 6' 8" Wt: 215 Born: 8/9/66 Age: 31

Year Team	Lg Org	G	GS	CG	GF	IP	BFP	H	R	ER	HR	SH	SF	HB	TBB	IBB	SO	WP	Bk	W	L	Pct.	ShO	Sv	ERA
				HOW MUCH HE PITCHED						WHAT HE GAVE UP											THE RESULTS			
1984 Phillies	R Phi	13	6	0	2	33.1	173	43	31	24	2	3	2	0	30	0	17	4	1	0	2	.000	0	0	6.48
1985 Spartanburg	A Phi	26	25	4	0	152.1	669	160	95	70	7	3	6	4	53	0	108	8	0	8	12	.400	1	0	4.14
1986 Clearwater	A+ Phi	24	22	5	0	125.2	559	146	73	58	1	6	4	5	45	4	51	4	1	8	12	.400	0	0	4.15
1987 Reading	AA Phi	27	26	3	0	164	718	187	98	93	12	9	9	11	55	3	91	4	1	15	5	.750	1	0	5.10
1988 Maine	AAA Phi	28	27	4	0	161	713	181	110	100	10	13	7	8	50	7	79	17	8	5	18	.217	1	0	5.59
1989 Reading	AA Phi	31	17	4	8	118.1	531	124	88	76	9	3	5	5	58	1	63	12	1	6	10	.375	1	0	5.78
1990 Scranton-WB	AAA Phi	23	23	1	0	130	565	128	79	70	11	3	4	7	59	3	74	3	0	8	11	.421	0	0	4.85
1991 Iowa	AAA ChN	4	3	0	1	18.1	79	14	8	6	0	2	0	0	10	1	15	3	0	2	0	1.000	0	0	2.95
1995 New Orleans	AAA Mil	3	3	0	0	11.2	51	17	7	7	0	0	0	1	3	0	5	1	0	0	1	.000	0	0	5.40
1996 Lakeland	A+ Det	2	2	0	0	9	39	9	6	5	0	1	0	0	3	0	4	2	0	0	1	.000	0	0	5.00
Toledo	AAA Det	14	5	0	3	36	171	46	35	30	5	2	1	3	15	0	18	5	0	1	3	.250	0	0	7.50
Omaha	AAA KC	12	0	0	12	12.1	45	10	2	1	0	0	0	0	3	0	9	0	0	0	0	.000	0	5	0.73
1997 Las Vegas	AAA SD	36	1	0	11	51	218	51	24	20	4	1	0	6	17	1	20	1	0	3	1	.750	0	1	3.53
1991 Chicago	NL	40	13	0	16	111	482	114	60	48	5	8´	6	3	40	3	44	5	1	7	8	.467	0	1	3.89
1992 Chicago	NL	69	0	0	41	87.1	360	76	32	28	4	4	2	1	30	6	42	6	4	3	6	.333	0	14	2.89
1993 Chicago	NL	70	0	0	13	75.1	323	79	41	38	6	2	6	3	28	7	44	0	2	4	5	.444	0	0	4.54
1994 Milwaukee	AL	30	12	0	9	103	441	117	53	47	11	1	2	4	28	2	65	3	1	2	6	.250	0	2	4.11
1995 Milwaukee	AL	17	14	0	1	83.1	389	101	66	61	9	0	6	7	44	3	29	3	0	4	7	.364	0	0	6.59
1996 Detroit	AL	8	0	0	2	11	57	16	15	13	1	1	0	1	9	1	3	1	0	0	0	.000	0	0	10.64
Kansas City	AL	9	0	0	2	11.1	48	13	4	4	1	0	0	1	3	1	1	0	0	0	0	.000	0	0	3.18
11 Min. YEARS		243	160	21	37	1023	4531	1116	656	560	59	46	38	50	401	20	554	64	12	56	76	.424	4	6	4.93
6 Maj. YEARS		243	39	0	84	482.1	2100	516	271	239	37	16	22	20	182	23	230	18	8	20	33	.377	0	17	4.46

Jon Schaeffer

Bats: Right Throws: Right Pos: C   Ht: 6'1" Wt: 205 Born: 1/20/76 Age: 22

Year Team	Lg Org	G	AB	H	2B	3B	HR	TB	R	RBI	TBB	IBB	SO	HBP	SH	SF	SB	CS	SB%	GDP	Avg	OBP	SLG
								BATTING										BASERUNNING			PERCENTAGES		
1997 Elizabethtn	R+ Min	48	165	55	13	0	6	86	35	34	33	3	32	4	0	2	0	1	.00	5	.333	.451	.521
New Britain	AA Min	10	29	6	2	0	0	8	1	4	2	0	7	0	0	0	1	1	.50	1	.207	.258	.276
1 Min. YEARS		58	194	61	15	0	6	94	36	38	35	3	39	4	0	2	1	2	.33	6	.314	.426	.485

Gene Schall

Bats: Right Throws: Right Pos: DH   Ht: 6' 3" Wt: 201 Born: 6/5/70 Age: 28

Year Team	Lg Org	G	AB	H	2B	3B	HR	TB	R	RBI	TBB	IBB	SO	HBP	SH	SF	SB	CS	SB%	GDP	Avg	OBP	SLG
								BATTING										BASERUNNING			PERCENTAGES		
1991 Batavia	A- Phi	13	44	15	1	0	2	22	5	8	3	2	16	0	0	0	0	1	.00	1	.341	.383	.500
1992 Spartanburg	A Phi	77	276	74	13	1	8	113	44	41	29	0	52	3	2	2	3	2	.60	8	.268	.342	.409
Clearwater	A+ Phi	40	133	33	4	2	4	53	16	19	14	0	29	4	1	3	1	2	.33	2	.248	.331	.398
1993 Reading	AA Phi	82	285	93	12	4	15	158	51	60	24	0	56	10	0	3	2	1	.67	15	.326	.394	.554
Scranton-WB	AAA Phi	40	139	33	6	1	4	53	16	16	19	1	38	7	1	1	4	2	.67	4	.237	.355	.381
1994 Scranton-WB	AAA Phi	127	463	132	35	4	16	223	54	89	50	5	86	6	0	6	9	1	.90	11	.285	.358	.482
1995 Scranton-WB	AAA Phi	92	320	100	25	4	12	169	52	63	49	2	54	10	0	4	3	3	.50	14	.313	.415	.528
1996 Scranton-WB	AAA Phi	104	371	107	16	5	17	184	66	67	48	2	92	9	0	5	1	0	1.00	9	.288	.379	.496
1997 Nashville	AAA ChA	33	112	22	0	1	5	39	11	17	11	0	32	1	1	1	0	1	.50	1	.196	.274	.348
1995 Philadelphia	NL	24	65	15	2	0	0	17	2	5	6	1	16	1	0	0	0	0	.00	1	.231	.306	.262
1996 Philadelphia	NL	28	66	18	5	1	2	31	7	10	12	0	15	1	0	0	0	0	.00	2	.273	.392	.470
7 Min. YEARS		608	2143	609	112	22	83	1014	315	380	247	12	455	50	5	24	24	13	.65	63	.284	.368	.473
2 Maj. YEARS		52	131	33	7	1	2	48	9	15	18	1	31	2	0	0	0	0	.00	3	.252	.351	.366

Brett Schlomann

Pitches: Right Bats: Right Pos: P   Ht: 6'1" Wt: 185 Born: 7/31/74 Age: 23

Year Team	Lg Org	G	GS	CG	GF	IP	BFP	H	R	ER	HR	SH	SF	HB	TBB	IBB	SO	WP	Bk	W	L	Pct.	ShO	Sv	ERA
				HOW MUCH HE PITCHED						WHAT HE GAVE UP											THE RESULTS			
1994 Yankees	R NYA	10	10	1	0	54	230	56	22	18	1	4	1	0	16	0	51	2	0	6	3	.667	1	0	3.00

Year Team	Lg Org	G	GS	CG	GF	IP	BFP	H	R	ER	HR	SH	SF	HB	TBB	IBB	SO	WP	Bk	W	L	Pct.	ShO	Sv	ERA
Oneonta	A- NYA	1	1	0	0	5	24	4	4	3	1	0	1	0	4	0	6	0	0	0	0	.000	0	0	5.40
1995 Greensboro	A NYA	25	25	1	0	147.2	639	144	76	64	10	2	1	9	54	1	140	8	1	10	7	.588	0	0	3.90
Tampa	A+ NYA	2	2	0	0	11	44	10	6	2	2	0	0	0	0	0	5	0	0	2	0	1.000	0	0	1.64
1996 Tampa	A+ NYA	26	26	1	0	145.2	628	152	81	69	13	3	4	8	49	2	103	10	1	11	8	.579	1	0	4.26
1997 Norwich	AA NYA	10	10	0	0	47	224	66	43	41	6	0	3	3	17	0	36	1	0	1	4	.200	0	0	7.85
Tampa	A+ NYA	19	18	1	0	118.1	503	129	55	48	8	3	2	2	29	0	86	2	0	8	4	.667	1	0	3.65
4 Min. YEARS		93	92	4	0	528.2	2292	561	287	245	41	12	12	22	169	3	427	23	2	38	26	.594	3	0	4.17

Pitches: Right **Bats:** Right **Pos:** P

Curt Schmidt

Ht: 6' 5" **Wt:** 200 **Born:** 3/16/70 **Age:** 28

Year Team	Lg Org	G	GS	CG	GF	IP	BFP	H	R	ER	HR	SH	SF	HB	TBB	IBB	SO	WP	Bk	W	L	Pct.	ShO	Sv	ERA
1992 Jamestown	A- Mon	29	1	1	19	63.1	261	42	21	19	1	3	0	5	29	2	61	6	1	3	4	.429	1	2	2.70
Wst Plm Bch	A+ Mon	3	0	0	2	5	18	3	0	0	0	0	0	0	1	0	3	0	0	0	0	.000	0	0	0.00
1993 Expos	R Mon	1	1	0	0	5	16	1	0	0	0	0	0	0	0	0	7	0	0	1	0	1.000	0	0	0.00
Wst Plm Bch	A+ Mon	44	2	0	22	65.1	285	63	32	23	3	5	1	0	25	3	51	1	1	6	4	.600	0	5	3.17
1994 Harrisburg	AA Mon	53	0	0	26	71.2	291	51	19	15	4	6	4	0	29	1	75	4	0	6	2	.750	0	5	1.88
1995 Ottawa	AAA Mon	43	0	0	38	52.2	206	40	14	13	1	0	1	4	18	0	39	3	0	2	2	.500	0	22	2.22
1996 Ottawa	AAA Mon	54	0	0	31	70.1	283	60	27	19	2	5	6	1	22	3	45	1	0	5	0	1.000	0	15	2.43
1997 Ottawa	AAA Mon	31	0	0	23	31.1	157	44	24	23	2	5	0	2	22	5	18	1	0	1	5	.167	0	13	6.61
Calgary	AAA Pit	25	0	0	17	31.2	152	43	19	15	3	1	0	3	14	1	30	1	0	2	3	.400	0	7	4.26
1995 Montreal	NL	11	0	0	0	10.1	54	15	8	8	1	1	0	2	9	0	7	0	0	0	0	.000	0	0	6.97
6 Min. YEARS		283	4	1	178	396.1	1669	347	156	127	16	25	12	15	160	18	328	16	2	22	23	.489	1	52	2.88

Pitches: Right **Bats:** Right **Pos:** P

Jeff Schmidt

Ht: 6' 5" **Wt:** 205 **Born:** 2/21/71 **Age:** 27

Year Team	Lg Org	G	GS	CG	GF	IP	BFP	H	R	ER	HR	SH	SF	HB	TBB	IBB	SO	WP	Bk	W	L	Pct.	ShO	Sv	ERA
1992 Boise	A- Ana	11	11	0	0	52.1	236	57	41	26	4	1	0	4	18	1	41	3	4	1	6	.143	0	0	4.47
1993 Cedar Rapds	A Ana	26	25	3	0	152.1	696	166	105	83	16	9	6	16	58	3	107	11	4	3	14	.176	0	0	4.90
1994 Lk Elsinore	A+ Ana	39	11	0	14	92	395	94	54	42	8	7	0	4	28	2	70	4	6	1	5	.167	0	12	4.11
1995 Midland	AA Ana	20	20	0	0	100.1	466	127	75	65	12	2	4	5	48	1	46	18	1	4	12	.250	0	0	5.83
1996 Vancouver	AAA Ana	35	0	0	30	37.2	164	29	12	12	0	2	4	2	25	0	19	7	1	0	1	.000	0	19	2.87
1997 Vancouver	AAA Ana	27	0	0	16	22	104	22	14	13	2	0	1	0	20	2	14	6	0	1	2	.333	0	10	5.32
1996 California	AL	9	0	0	0	8	42	13	9	7	2	0	1	0	8	0	2	1	0	1	0	1.000	0	0	7.88
6 Min. YEARS		158	67	3	60	456.2	2061	493	301	241	42	21	15	31	197	9	297	49	16	10	40	.200	0	41	4.75

Bats: Right **Throws:** Right **Pos:** 3B

Tom Schmidt

Ht: 6'3" **Wt:** 200 **Born:** 2/12/73 **Age:** 25

Year Team	Lg Org	G	AB	H	2B	3B	HR	TB	R	RBI	TBB	IBB	SO	HBP	SH	SF	SB	CS	SB%	GDP	Avg	OBP	SLG
1992 Bend	A- Col	68	249	64	13	1	7	100	39	27	24	1	78	4	0	1	17	3	.85	5	.257	.331	.402
1993 Central Val	A+ Col	126	478	117	15	1	19	191	61	62	40	2	107	4	1	5	5	3	.63	15	.245	.306	.400
1994 Central Val	A+ Col	99	334	81	8	1	9	118	36	50	52	2	100	8	2	3	3	4	.43	3	.243	.356	.353
1995 New Haven	AA Col	115	423	92	25	3	6	141	55	49	24	2	99	5	1	5	2	1	.67	11	.217	.265	.333
1996 Jacksnville	AA Det	115	385	85	24	2	11	146	45	45	31	1	91	2	2	2	4	1	.80	12	.221	.281	.379
1997 Jacksnville	AA Det	82	291	75	17	1	9	121	37	44	29	0	81	2	0	1	2	0	1.00	9	.258	.328	.416
6 Min. YEARS		605	2160	514	102	9	61	817	273	277	200	8	556	25	6	16	33	12	.73	57	.238	.308	.378

Pitches: Right **Bats:** Right **Pos:** P

Todd Schmitt

Ht: 6'2" **Wt:** 170 **Born:** 2/12/70 **Age:** 28

Year Team	Lg Org	G	GS	CG	GF	IP	BFP	H	R	ER	HR	SH	SF	HB	TBB	IBB	SO	WP	Bk	W	L	Pct.	ShO	Sv	ERA
1992 Spokane	A- SD	29	0	0	29	38	162	23	7	5	4	2	2	1	23	5	48	3	0	6	1	.857	0	15	1.18
1993 Waterloo	A SD	51	0	0	47	58.2	254	41	15	13	0	1	1	6	33	5	76	5	2	1	4	.200	0	25	1.99
1994 Rancho Cuca	A+ SD	53	0	0	50	50.2	215	43	15	11	2	5	1	2	24	1	45	2	1	2	4	.333	0	29	1.95
1995 Memphis	AA SD	26	0	0	24	27.2	108	18	4	4	2	0	1	1	11	2	27	0	0	0	0	.000	0	18	1.30
Las Vegas	AAA SD	12	0	0	8	12.2	62	16	11	11	0	0	1	2	9	0	6	2	0	0	2	.000	0	2	7.82
1996 Rancho Cuca	A+ SD	7	0	0	7	6.2	33	6	6	5	1	1	1	4	3	0	8	1	0	0	1	.000	0	4	6.75
Las Vegas	AAA SD	4	0	0	1	4	22	2	2	2	1	0	1	1	6	0	6	0	0	0	0	.000	0	0	4.50
Memphis	AA SD	38	0	0	25	39.1	181	39	26	15	1	3	0	1	21	1	47	4	4	4	4	.500	0	11	3.43
1997 Las Vegas	AAA SD	48	0	0	27	53.2	254	55	34	30	7	4	2	6	38	4	59	2	1	5	2	.714	0	4	5.03
6 Min. YEARS		268	0	0	218	291.1	1290	243	120	96	15	17	8	25	168	18	322	19	10	18	18	.500	0	108	2.97

Pitches: Left **Bats:** Left **Pos:** P

Scott Schoeneweis

Ht: 6'0" **Wt:** 180 **Born:** 10/2/73 **Age:** 24

Year Team	Lg Org	G	GS	CG	GF	IP	BFP	H	R	ER	HR	SH	SF	HB	TBB	IBB	SO	WP	Bk	W	L	Pct.	ShO	Sv	ERA
1996 Lk Elsinore	A+ Ana	14	12	0	1	93.2	387	86	47	41	6	3	2	2	27	0	83	2	1	8	3	.727	0	0	3.94
1997 Midland	AA Ana	20	20	3	0	113.1	510	145	84	75	7	1	5	1	39	0	94	8	1	7	5	.583	0	0	5.96
2 Min. YEARS		34	32	3	1	207	897	231	131	116	13	4	7	3	66	0	177	10	2	15	8	.652	0	0	5.04

Carl Schramm

Pitches: Right **Bats:** Right **Pos:** P   **Ht:** 6'4" **Wt:** 200 **Born:** 6/10/70 **Age:** 28

Year Team	Lg Org	G	GS	CG	GF	IP	BFP	H	R	ER	HR	SH	SF	HB	TBB	IBB	SO	WP	Bk	W	L	Pct.	ShO	Sv	ERA
1991 Geneva	A- ChN	15	15	2	0	97.2	401	80	47	37	7	1	6	7	33	1	64	9	2	5	7	.417	1	0	3.41
1992 Peoria	A ChN	32	12	2	8	117.1	491	117	62	54	13	1	4	5	40	2	94	9	2	5	7	.417	1	1	4.14
1993 Daytona	A+ ChN	34	13	0	9	121	509	119	58	47	4	2	2	6	29	0	89	9	1	8	4	.667	0	2	3.50
1994 St. Paul	IND —	24	8	0	7	68.2	308	80	43	36	7	7	4	3	30	3	49	5	0	2	4	.333	0	2	4.72
1995 San Jose	A+ SF	37	0	0	19	71	297	57	23	20	4	8	2	2	24	3	68	5	0	6	4	.600	0	3	2.54
1996 San Jose	A+ SF	39	0	0	10	70.1	303	64	31	27	5	8	0	5	25	1	66	4	1	7	3	.700	0	1	3.45
1997 Shreveport	AA SF	3	1	0	0	7	30	10	6	5	1	0	0	0	0	0	5	0	0	1	0	1.000	0	0	6.43
San Jose	A+ SF	36	4	0	9	93	410	103	54	51	10	2	3	3	33	0	75	6	0	4	4	.500	0	0	4.94
7 Min. YEARS		220	53	4	62	646	2749	630	324	277	51	29	21	31	214	10	510	47	6	38	33	.535	2	9	3.86

Steve Schrenk

Pitches: Right **Bats:** Right **Pos:** P   **Ht:** 6'3" **Wt:** 185 **Born:** 11/20/68 **Age:** 29

Year Team	Lg Org	G	GS	CG	GF	IP	BFP	H	R	ER	HR	SH	SF	HB	TBB	IBB	SO	WP	Bk	W	L	Pct.	ShO	Sv	ERA
1987 White Sox	R ChA	8	6	1	0	28.1	115	23	10	3	0	3	0	2	12	0	19	2	1	1	2	.333	1	0	0.95
1988 South Bend	A ChA	21	18	1	1	90	417	95	63	50	4	0	3	13	37	0	58	7	2	3	7	.300	0	0	5.00
1989 South Bend	A ChA	16	16	1	0	79	353	71	44	38	6	2	0	8	44	1	49	9	0	5	2	.714	1	0	4.33
1990 South Bend	A ChA	20	14	2	2	103.2	419	79	44	34	7	3	3	11	25	0	92	7	1	7	6	.538	1	0	2.95
1991 White Sox	R ChA	11	7	0	2	37	144	30	20	12	0	1	0	5	6	0	39	1	0	1	3	.250	0	0	2.92
1992 Sarasota	A+ ChA	25	22	4	2	154	621	130	48	35	1	4	6	7	40	2	113	7	6	15	2	.882	2	1	2.05
Birmingham	AA ChA	2	2	0	0	12.1	59	13	5	5	0	0	1	1	11	0	9	1	0	1	1	.500	0	0	3.65
1993 Birmingham	AA ChA	8	8	2	0	61.2	224	31	11	8	2	1	1	1	7	0	51	3	0	5	1	.833	1	0	1.17
Nashville	AAA ChA	21	20	0	0	122.1	526	117	61	53	11	5	2	3	47	3	78	6	3	6	8	.429	0	0	3.90
1994 Nashville	AAA ChA	29	28	2	0	178.2	769	175	82	69	15	10	4	6	69	3	134	14	1	14	6	.700	1	0	3.48
1995 White Sox	R ChA	2	2	0	0	7	27	5	2	0	0	0	0	0	0	0	6	0	0	0	1	.000	0	0	0.00
1996 Nashville	AAA ChA	16	15	1	1	95.2	395	93	54	47	12	3	1	3	29	2	58	3	0	4	10	.286	0	0	4.42
1997 Rochester	AAA Bal	25	24	1	0	125.2	539	127	73	65	21	2	1	6	36	0	99	3	2	4	7	.364	0	0	4.66
11 Min. YEARS		204	182	15	8	1095.1	4608	989	517	419	79	34	22	66	363	11	805	63	16	66	56	.541	7	1	3.44

Chad Schroeder

Pitches: Right **Bats:** Right **Pos:** P   **Ht:** 6'3" **Wt:** 200 **Born:** 9/21/73 **Age:** 24

Year Team	Lg Org	G	GS	CG	GF	IP	BFP	H	R	ER	HR	SH	SF	HB	TBB	IBB	SO	WP	Bk	W	L	Pct.	ShO	Sv	ERA
1996 Jamestown	A- Det	31	0	0	26	38.2	153	29	15	6	1	1	3	0	6	0	41	0	0	5	0	1.000	0	6	1.40
1997 W Michigan	A Det	18	0	0	8	26.2	120	22	14	11	0	1	1	0	16	2	24	3	1	2	3	.400	0	0	3.71
Lakeland	A+ Det	12	1	0	5	22.2	98	25	14	12	1	1	2	0	8	1	8	1	0	0	3	.000	0	0	4.76
Jacksnville	AA Det	2	0	0	1	3.2	11	1	0	0	0	0	0	0	1	0	4	0	0	0	0	.000	0	0	0.00
2 Min. YEARS		63	1	0	40	91.2	382	77	43	29	2	3	6	0	31	3	77	4	1	7	6	.538	0	6	2.85

Rick Schu

Bats: Right **Throws:** Right **Pos:** 3B   **Ht:** 6'0" **Wt:** 190 **Born:** 1/26/62 **Age:** 36

Year Team	Lg Org	G	AB	H	2B	3B	HR	TB	R	RBI	TBB	IBB	SO	HBP	SH	SF	SB	CS	SB%	GDP	Avg	OBP	SLG
1981 Bend	A- Phi	68	258	69	10	0	2	85	41	42	35	0	53	1	1	5	15	5	.75	—	.267	.351	.329
1982 Spartanburg	A Phi	125	429	117	28	1	12	183	78	60	55	1	66	1	0	5	37	12	.76	—	.273	.353	.427
1983 Peninsula	A+ Phi	122	444	119	22	3	14	189	69	63	48	1	83	3	1	3	29	8	.78	—	.268	.341	.426
Portland	AAA Phi	9	29	11	2	1	1	18	7	3	3	0	1	1	0	0	0	1	1.00	—	.379	.455	.621
1984 Portland	AAA Phi	140	552	166	35	14	12	265	70	82	43	3	83	3	1	8	7	4	.64	9	.301	.350	.480
1985 Portland	AAA Phi	42	150	42	8	3	4	68	19	22	14	0	20	2	0	0	1	6	.14	4	.280	.349	.453
1989 Rochester	AAA Bal	28	94	21	6	1	1	32	11	10	16	1	21	1	0	2	3	2	.60	1	.223	.336	.340
1990 Edmonton	AAA Ana	18	60	18	7	0	1	28	8	8	6	0	3	1	0	2	0	0	.00	2	.300	.362	.467
1991 Scranton-WB	AAA Phi	106	355	114	30	5	14	196	69	57	50	2	38	4	0	4	7	1	.88	9	.321	.407	.552
1992 Scranton-WB	AAA Phi	111	400	124	18	3	10	178	56	49	45	5	62	4	0	1	3	1	.75	9	.310	.384	.445
1995 Okla City	AAA Tex	110	398	108	19	3	12	169	49	57	40	1	63	5	0	2	5	3	.63	8	.271	.344	.425
1996 Ottawa	AAA Mon	116	395	107	24	3	12	173	48	54	41	5	51	9	0	4	9	3	.75	5	.271	.350	.438
1997 Ottawa	AAA Mon	8	21	4	1	0	1	8	3	3	0	0	4	0	0	0	0	0	.00	1	.190	.190	.381
1984 Philadelphia	NL	17	29	8	2	1	2	18	12	5	6	0	6	0	0	0	0	0	.00	0	.276	.389	.621
1985 Philadelphia	NL	112	416	105	21	4	7	155	54	24	38	3	78	2	1	0	8	6	.57	7	.252	.318	.373
1986 Philadelphia	NL	92	208	57	10	1	8	93	32	25	18	1	44	2	3	2	2	2	.50	1	.274	.335	.447
1987 Philadelphia	NL	92	196	46	6	3	7	79	24	23	20	1	36	2	0	1	0	0	.00	1	.235	.311	.403
1988 Baltimore	AL	89	270	69	9	4	4	98	22	20	21	0	49	3	0	0	6	4	.60	7	.256	.316	.363
1989 Baltimore	AL	1	0	0	0	0	0	0	0	0	0	0	0	0	0	0	0	0	.00	0	.000	.000	.000
Detroit	AL	98	266	57	11	0	7	89	25	21	24	0	37	0	2	1	1	2	.33	6	.214	.278	.335
1990 California	AL	61	157	42	8	0	6	68	19	14	11	0	25	0	0	1	0	0	.00	4	.268	.314	.433
1991 Philadelphia	NL	17	22	2	0	0	0	2	1	2	1	0	7	0	0	1	0	0	.00	1	.091	.125	.091
1996 Montreal	NL	0	0	0	0	0	0	0	0	0	0	0	0	0	0	0	0	0	.00	0	.000	.000	.000
12 Min. YEARS		1003	3585	1020	210	37	96	1592	528	510	396	19	548	35	3	36	116	46	.72	46	.285	.358	.444
9 Maj. YEARS		580	1568	386	67	13	41	602	189	134	139	5	282	9	6	7	17	16	.52	27	.246	.310	.384

Carl Schutz

Pitches: Left **Bats:** Left **Pos:** P   **Ht:** 5'11" **Wt:** 200 **Born:** 8/22/71 **Age:** 26

Year Team	Lg Org	G	GS	CG	GF	IP	BFP	H	R	ER	HR	SH	SF	HB	TBB	IBB	SO	WP	Bk	W	L	Pct.	ShO	Sv	ERA
1993 Danville	R+ Atl	13	0	0	9	14.2	57	6	1	1	0	1	0	0	6	0	25	1	0	1	0	1.000	0	4	0.61

229

Year Team	Lg Org	G	GS	CG	GF	IP	BFP	H	R	ER	HR	SH	SF	HB	TBB	IBB	SO	WP	Bk	W	L	Pct.	ShO	Sv	ERA
Greenville	AA Atl	22	0	0	16	21.1	101	17	17	12	3	2	3	1	22	1	19	2	0	2	1	.667	0	3	5.06
1994 Durham	A+ Atl	53	0	0	47	53.1	240	35	30	29	6	4	1	2	46	1	81	10	0	3	3	.500	0	20	4.89
1995 Greenville	AA Atl	51	0	0	46	58.1	258	53	36	32	4	2	2	1	36	3	56	3	0	3	7	.300	0	26	4.94
1996 Richmond	AAA Atl	41	7	0	13	69.2	320	86	46	41	4	7	4	0	26	3	52	8	0	4	3	.571	0	5	5.30
1997 Richmond	AAA Atl	27	10	0	7	79.1	366	83	56	47	12	1	2	2	51	2	66	6	0	4	6	.400	0	3	5.33
1996 Atlanta	NL	3	0	0	1	3.1	13	3	1	1	0	0	0	0	2	1	5	0	0	0	0	.000	0	0	2.70
5 Min. YEARS		207	17	0	138	296.2	1342	280	186	162	29	17	12	6	187	10	299	30	0	17	20	.459	0	56	4.91

Matt Schwenke

Bats: Both **Throws:** Right **Pos:** 1B   **Ht:** 6'2" **Wt:** 210 **Born:** 8/12/72 **Age:** 25

Year Team	Lg Org	G	AB	H	2B	3B	HR	TB	R	RBI	TBB	IBB	SO	HBP	SH	SF	SB	CS	SB%	GDP	Avg	OBP	SLG
1993 Bakersfield	A+ LA	13	41	9	0	0	0	9	2	4	3	0	12	0	0	0	0	0	.00	0	.220	.273	.220
Great Falls	R+ LA	29	79	18	4	0	0	22	6	4	10	0	21	0	2	0	0	0	.00	2	.228	.315	.278
1994 Bakersfield	A+ LA	42	131	22	3	0	1	28	7	14	6	0	41	3	2	0	0	0	.00	3	.168	.221	.214
1995 Clinton	A SD	36	100	19	5	1	1	29	3	8	2	0	34	1	2	1	0	0	.00	0	.190	.212	.290
Rancho Cuca	A+ SD	22	56	10	2	0	0	12	7	7	2	0	20	0	1	1	0	0	.00	0	.179	.203	.214
Memphis	AA SD	23	62	15	0	0	0	15	8	7	4	3	0	16	1	1	1	0	0	.00	0	.242	.284	.290
1996 Clinton	A SD	28	86	13	3	0	0	16	4	2	6	0	28	3	0	0	0	1	.00	3	.151	.232	.186
Rancho Cuca	A+ SD	10	29	6	0	0	1	9	2	2	2	0	13	1	2	0	0	0	.00	1	.207	.281	.310
Las Vegas	AAA SD	11	16	4	0	0	0	4	0	2	0	0	7	1	0	0	0	0	.00	0	.250	.294	.250
1997 Mobile	AA SD	1	1	0	0	0	0	0	0	0	0	0	0	0	0	0	0	0	.00	0	.000	.000	.000
Rancho Cuca	A+ SD	69	242	49	9	2	4	74	27	30	19	2	67	4	0	1	4	0	1.00	4	.202	.271	.306
5 Min. YEARS		284	843	165	29	3	7	221	65	77	53	2	259	14	10	4	4	1	.80	16	.196	.254	.262

Darryl Scott

Pitches: Right **Bats:** Right **Pos:** P   **Ht:** 6'1" **Wt:** 185 **Born:** 8/6/68 **Age:** 29

Year Team	Lg Org	G	GS	CG	GF	IP	BFP	H	R	ER	HR	SH	SF	HB	TBB	IBB	SO	WP	Bk	W	L	Pct.	ShO	Sv	ERA
1990 Boise	A- Ana	27	0	0	11	53.2	221	40	11	8	3	0	1	0	19	1	57	5	0	2	1	.667	0	5	1.34
1991 Quad City	A Ana	47	0	0	36	75.1	285	35	18	13	2	2	0	1	26	4	123	9	1	4	3	.571	0	19	1.55
1992 Midland	AA Ana	27	0	0	22	29.2	126	20	9	6	0	2	2	2	14	1	35	4	0	1	1	.500	0	9	1.82
Edmonton	AAA Ana	31	0	0	17	36.1	164	41	21	21	1	0	3	0	21	1	48	4	2	0	2	.000	0	6	5.20
1993 Vancouver	AAA Ana	46	0	0	33	51.2	206	33	12	12	4	2	1	1	19	2	57	3	0	7	1	.875	0	15	2.09
1995 Colo Spmgs	AAA Col	59	1	0	27	95.2	429	113	63	50	7	4	7	3	41	7	77	7	0	4	10	.286	0	4	4.70
1996 Buffalo	AAA Cle	50	1	0	30	81	323	61	29	26	11	4	2	0	24	4	73	2	0	3	5	.375	0	9	2.89
1997 Buffalo	AAA Cle	48	0	0	35	65.2	272	52	24	21	10	4	1	0	28	2	29	4	0	5	6	.455	0	12	2.88
1993 California	AL	16	0	0	2	20	90	19	13	13	1	0	2	1	11	1	13	2	0	1	2	.333	0	0	5.85
7 Min. YEARS		335	2	0	211	489	2026	397	187	157	38	18	17	7	192	22	499	38	3	26	29	.473	0	79	2.89

Marcos Scutaro

Bats: Right **Throws:** Right **Pos:** 2B   **Ht:** 5'10" **Wt:** 170 **Born:** 10/30/75 **Age:** 22

Year Team	Lg Org	G	AB	H	2B	3B	HR	TB	R	RBI	TBB	IBB	SO	HBP	SH	SF	SB	CS	SB%	GDP	Avg	OBP	SLG
1996 Columbus	A Cle	85	315	79	12	3	10	127	66	45	38	0	86	4	4	4	6	3	.67	6	.251	.334	.403
1997 Buffalo	AAA Cle	21	57	15	3	0	1	21	8	6	6	0	8	0	1	1	0	1	.00	4	.263	.328	.368
Kinston	A+ Cle	97	378	103	17	6	10	162	58	59	35	0	72	9	2	3	23	7	.77	3	.272	.346	.429
2 Min. YEARS		203	750	197	32	9	21	310	132	110	79	0	166	13	7	9	29	11	.73	13	.263	.340	.413

Scot Sealy

Bats: Right **Throws:** Right **Pos:** C   **Ht:** 6'4" **Wt:** 225 **Born:** 2/10/71 **Age:** 27

Year Team	Lg Org	G	AB	H	2B	3B	HR	TB	R	RBI	TBB	IBB	SO	HBP	SH	SF	SB	CS	SB%	GDP	Avg	OBP	SLG
1992 Gastonia	A Tex	56	175	42	8	0	3	59	16	16	14	0	46	0	0	2	1	2	.33	4	.240	.293	.337
1993 Chston-SC	A Tex	2	7	1	0	0	0	1	0	0	0	0	4	0	0	0	0	0	.00	0	.143	.143	.143
1995 Tacoma	AAA Sea	4	10	3	0	0	0	3	1	0	0	0	0	0	0	0	0	0	.00	0	.300	.300	.300
Riverside	A+ Sea	58	206	50	5	0	2	61	23	30	16	0	36	1	1	1	2	2	.50	4	.243	.299	.296
1996 Lancaster	A+ Sea	75	254	69	22	3	9	124	47	49	41	2	63	8	2	1	3	2	.60	7	.272	.388	.488
Port City	AA Sea	18	59	5	1	0	0	6	2	1	8	0	24	0	1	1	0	2	.00	1	.085	.191	.102
1997 Memphis	AA Sea	45	143	34	9	0	6	61	17	20	15	0	33	4	1	0	1	2	.33	2	.238	.327	.427
Tacoma	AAA Sea	18	55	15	3	0	3	27	8	10	5	0	13	2	0	1	0	1	.00	2	.273	.349	.491
5 Min. YEARS		276	909	219	48	3	23	342	114	126	99	0	219	15	6	6	7	11	.39	20	.241	.324	.376

Rudy Seanez

Pitches: Right **Bats:** Right **Pos:** P   **Ht:** 5'10" **Wt:** 190 **Born:** 10/20/68 **Age:** 29

Year Team	Lg Org	G	GS	CG	GF	IP	BFP	H	R	ER	HR	SH	SF	HB	TBB	IBB	SO	WP	Bk	W	L	Pct.	ShO	Sv	ERA
1986 Burlington	R+ Cle	13	12	1	1	76	318	59	37	27	5	1	3	3	32	0	56	6	0	5	2	.714	1	0	3.20
1987 Waterloo	A Cle	10	10	0	0	34.2	159	35	29	26	6	0	1	1	23	0	23	2	2	0	4	.000	0	0	6.75
1988 Waterloo	A Cle	22	22	1	0	113.1	505	98	69	59	10	2	2	6	68	0	93	14	2	6	9	.500	1	0	4.69
1989 Kinston	A+ Cle	25	25	1	0	113	539	94	66	52	0	1	1	5	111	1	149	13	1	8	10	.444	0	0	4.14
Colo Spmgs	AAA Cle	1	0	0	1	1	4	1	0	0	0	0	0	0	0	0	0	0	0	0	0	.000	0	0	0.00
1990 Canton-Akrn	AA Cle	15	0	0	10	16.2	68	9	4	4	0	2	0	1	12	0	27	0	0	1	0	1.000	0	5	2.16
Colo Spmgs	AAA Cle	12	0	0	10	12	59	15	10	9	2	0	1	0	10	0	7	3	0	1	4	.200	0	1	6.75
1991 Canton-Akrn	AA Cle	25	0	0	18	38.1	161	17	12	11	2	0	1	1	30	1	73	1	0	4	2	.667	0	7	2.58

Year Team	Lg Org	G	GS	CG	GF	IP	BFP	H	R	ER	HR	SH	SF	HB	TBB	IBB	SO	WP	Bk	W	L	Pct.	ShO	Sv	ERA
Colo Spmgs	AAA Cle	16	0	0	11	17.1	86	17	14	14	0	0	1	1	22	0	19	5	0	0	0	.000	0	0	7.27
1993 Central Val	A+ Col	5	1	0	1	8.1	46	9	9	9	0	0	1	0	11	0	7	1	0	0	2	.000	0	0	9.72
Colo Spmgs	AAA Col	3	0	0	3	3	13	3	3	3	1	0	0	0	1	0	5	0	0	0	0	.000	0	0	9.00
Las Vegas	AAA SD	14	0	0	8	19.2	90	24	15	14	2	0	1	0	11	0	14	7	1	0	1	.000	0	0	6.41
1994 Albuquerque	AAA LA	20	0	0	16	22	105	28	14	13	3	0	1	0	13	1	26	8	0	2	1	.667	0	9	5.32
1995 San Berndno	A+ LA	4	0	0	2	6	23	2	0	0	0	0	0	0	3	0	5	0	0	2	0	1.000	0	1	0.00
1996 Albuquerque	AAA LA	21	0	0	13	19.1	98	27	18	14	0	1	2	1	11	1	20	3	0	0	2	.000	0	6	6.52
1997 Omaha	AAA KC	28	3	0	8	47	226	53	42	34	13	1	2	2	25	0	46	2	0	2	5	.286	0	0	6.51
Norfolk	AAA NYN	9	0	0		13.1	63	12	8	6	1	0	0	0	11	0	17	0	0	1	0	1.000	0	0	4.05
1989 Cleveland	AL	5	0	0	2	5	20	1	2	2	0	0	2	0	4	1	7	1	1	0	0	.000	0	0	3.60
1990 Cleveland	AL	24	0	0	12	27.1	127	22	17	17	2	0	1	1	25	1	24	5	0	2	1	.667	0	0	5.60
1991 Cleveland	AL	5	0	0	0	5	33	10	12	9	2	0	0	0	7	0	7	2	0	0	0	.000	0	0	16.20
1993 San Diego	NL	3	0	0	3	3.1	20	8	6	5	1	1	0	0	2	0	1	0	0	0	0	.000	0	0	13.50
1994 Los Angeles	NL	17	0	0	6	23.2	104	24	7	7	2	4	2	1	9	1	18	3	0	1	1	.500	0	1	2.66
1995 Los Angeles	NL	37	0	0	12	34.2	159	39	27	26	5	3	0	1	18	3	29	0	0	1	3	.250	0	3	6.75
11 Min. YEARS		243	73	3	103	561	2563	503	350	295	47	8	18	21	394	4	587	65	6	32	39	.451	2	29	4.73
6 Maj. YEARS		91	0	0	35	99	463	104	71	66	12	8	5	3	65	6	86	11	1	4	5	.444	0	3	6.00

Reed Secrist

Bats: Left Throws: Right Pos: 3B   Ht: 6'1" Wt: 205 Born: 5/7/70 Age: 28

Year Team	Lg Org	G	AB	H	2B	3B	HR	TB	R	RBI	TBB	IBB	SO	HBP	SH	SF	SB	CS	SB%	GDP	Avg	OBP	SLG
1992 Welland	A- Pit	42	117	25	6	0	1	34	16	13	19	0	36	2	2	1	4	3	.57	2	.214	.331	.291
1993 Augusta	A Pit	90	266	71	16	3	6	111	38	47	27	1	43	1	2	4	4	1	.80	10	.267	.332	.417
1994 Salem	A+ Pit	80	221	54	12	0	10	96	29	35	22	0	58	1	2	1	2	2	.50	4	.244	.314	.434
1995 Lynchburg	A+ Pit	112	380	107	18	3	19	188	60	75	54	7	88	3	1	4	3	4	.43	6	.282	.372	.495
1996 Calgary	AAA Pit	128	420	129	30	0	17	210	68	66	52	11	105	4	3	5	2	4	.33	8	.307	.385	.500
1997 Calgary	AAA Pit	40	121	32	7	3	5	60	19	18	14	0	32	0	1	0	0	1	.00	3	.264	.341	.496
6 Min. YEARS		492	1525	418	89	9	58	699	230	254	188	19	362	11	11	15	15	15	.50	33	.274	.355	.458

Tate Seefried

Bats: Left Throws: Right Pos: 1B   Ht: 6'4" Wt: 180 Born: 4/22/72 Age: 26

Year Team	Lg Org	G	AB	H	2B	3B	HR	TB	R	RBI	TBB	IBB	SO	HBP	SH	SF	SB	CS	SB%	GDP	Avg	OBP	SLG
1990 Yankees	R NYA	52	178	28	3	0	0	31	15	20	22	0	53	2	0	1	2	1	.67	6	.157	.256	.174
1991 Oneonta	A- NYA	73	264	65	19	0	7	105	40	51	32	0	66	2	0	7	12	3	.80	6	.246	.325	.398
1992 Greensboro	A NYA	141	532	129	23	5	20	222	73	90	51	0	166	2	1	3	8	8	.50	12	.242	.310	.417
1993 Pr William	A+ NYA	125	464	123	25	4	21	219	63	89	50	4	150	2	3	6	8	8	.50	8	.265	.335	.472
1994 Albany-Colo	AA NYA	118	444	100	14	2	27	199	63	83	48	4	149	5	1	2	1	5	.17	12	.225	.307	.448
1995 Columbus	AAA NYA	29	110	18	6	0	1	27	7	12	1	0	34	0	0	2	0	0	.00	2	.164	.168	.245
Norwich	AA NYA	77	274	62	18	1	5	97	34	33	31	4	86	4	1	4	0	1	.00	6	.226	.310	.354
1996 Norwich	AA NYA	115	361	75	17	0	14	134	52	47	47	3	128	1	2	1	2	3	.40	9	.208	.300	.371
1997 Binghamton	AA NYN	96	335	105	16	0	29	208	59	79	54	10	99	0	0	4	9	4	.69	5	.313	.405	.621
Norfolk	AAA NYN	33	96	22	6	1	3	39	11	13	13	0	31	0	0	0	2	0	1.00	3	.229	.321	.406
8 Min. YEARS		859	3058	727	147	13	127	1281	417	517	349	25	962	18	8	30	44	33	.57	66	.238	.317	.419

Chris Seelbach

Pitches: Right Bats: Right Pos: P   Ht: 6'4" Wt: 180 Born: 12/18/72 Age: 25

Year Team	Lg Org	G	GS	CG	GF	IP	BFP	H	R	ER	HR	SH	SF	HB	TBB	IBB	SO	WP	Bk	W	L	Pct.	ShO	Sv	ERA
1991 Braves	R Atl	4	4	0	0	15	65	13	7	7	3	1	0	0	6	0	19	3	1	0	1	.000	0	0	4.20
1992 Macon	A Atl	27	27	1	0	157.1	662	134	65	58	11	3	5	9	68	0	144	5	1	9	11	.450	0	0	3.32
1993 Durham	A+ Atl	25	25	0	0	131.1	590	133	85	72	15	4	4	7	74	1	112	10	0	9	9	.500	0	0	4.93
1994 Greenville	AA Atl	15	15	2	0	92.2	363	64	26	24	3	5	3	4	38	2	79	5	0	4	6	.400	0	0	2.33
Richmond	AAA Atl	12	11	0	0	61.1	273	68	37	33	6	2	3	0	36	2	35	3	0	3	5	.375	0	0	4.84
1995 Greenville	AA Atl	9	9	1	0	60.1	249	38	15	11	2	5	3	4	30	0	65	3	1	6	0	1.000	1	0	1.64
Richmond	AAA Atl	14	14	1	0	73.1	314	64	39	38	7	0	3	2	39	0	65	3	0	4	6	.400	0	0	4.66
1996 Charlotte	AAA Fla	25	25	1	0	138.1	650	167	123	113	26	2	5	5	76	3	98	9	1	6	13	.316	0	0	7.35
1997 Charlotte	AAA Fla	16	6	0	1	50.1	241	58	36	35	7	3	3	1	34	2	50	3	0	5	0	1.000	0	0	6.26
7 Min. YEARS		147	136	6	1	780	3407	739	433	391	80	25	29	32	401	10	667	44	4	46	51	.474	1	0	4.51

Brad Seitzer

Bats: Right Throws: Right Pos: 3B-1B   Ht: 6'2" Wt: 195 Born: 2/2/70 Age: 28

Year Team	Lg Org	G	AB	H	2B	3B	HR	TB	R	RBI	TBB	IBB	SO	HBP	SH	SF	SB	CS	SB%	GDP	Avg	OBP	SLG
1991 Bluefield	R+ Bal	12	45	13	2	0	3	24	5	5	5	0	10	0	0	0	1	1	.50	1	.289	.360	.533
Kane County	A Bal	58	197	55	11	1	2	74	34	28	36	3	36	1	1	1	1	0	1.00	3	.279	.391	.376
1992 Frederick	A+ Bal	129	459	114	21	3	14	183	59	61	38	2	111	7	4	3	2	4	.33	9	.248	.314	.399
1993 Frederick	A+ Bal	130	439	111	24	3	10	171	44	68	58	1	95	5	3	9	3	3	.50	9	.253	.341	.390
1994 Beloit	A Mil	102	343	86	13	0	11	132	45	53	58	1	78	3	6	4	2	2	.50	7	.251	.360	.385
1995 Stockton	A+ Mil	127	428	132	28	3	6	184	66	56	72	2	68	3	2	2	7	4	.64	10	.308	.410	.430
1996 El Paso	AA Mil	115	433	138	31	1	17	222	78	87	51	0	67	7	2	5	6	4	.60	9	.319	.395	.513
1997 Tucson	AAA Mil	62	234	74	13	3	9	120	50	42	22	0	33	3	0	4	1	2	.33	9	.316	.376	.513
Ottawa	AAA Mon	18	56	14	1	0	1	18	4	7	8	0	11	1	0	0	1	2	.33	1	.250	.354	.321
Omaha	AAA KC	21	63	12	3	0	0	15	4	4	5	0	10	0	0	1	0	0	.00	4	.190	.246	.238
Memphis	AA Sea	17	70	23	8	1	2	39	14	13	6	0	13	1	0	1	0	1	1.00	4	.329	.385	.557
7 Min. YEARS		791	2767	772	155	15	75	1182	403	424	359	9	532	31	18	30	24	21	.53	65	.279	.365	.427

Chris Sexton

Bats: Right **Throws:** Right **Pos:** SS **Ht:** 5'11" **Wt:** 180 **Born:** 8/3/71 **Age:** 26

Year Team	Lg Org	G	AB	H	2B	3B	HR	TB	R	RBI	TBB	IBB	SO	HBP	SH	SF	SB	CS	SB%	GDP	Avg	OBP	SLG
1993 Billings	R+ Cin	72	273	91	14	4	4	125	63	46	35	1	27	1	0	8	13	4	.76	6	.333	.401	.458
1994 Chston-WV	A Cin	133	467	140	21	4	5	184	82	59	91	3	67	2	6	6	18	11	.62	9	.300	.412	.394
1995 Winston-Sal	A+ Cin	4	15	6	0	0	1	9	3	5	4	0	0	0	0	0	0	0	.00	0	.400	.526	.600
Salem	A+ Col	123	461	123	16	6	4	163	81	32	93	2	55	1	12	1	14	11	.56	11	.267	.390	.354
New Haven	AA Col	1	3	0	0	0	0	0	0	0	0	0	0	0	0	0	0	0	.00	0	.000	.000	.000
1996 New Haven	AA Col	127	444	96	12	2	0	112	50	28	71	2	68	1	7	3	8	5	.62	10	.216	.324	.252
1997 New Haven	AA Col	98	360	107	22	4	1	140	65	38	62	0	37	2	11	4	8	16	.33	8	.297	.400	.389
Colo Spmgs	AAA Col	33	112	30	3	1	1	38	18	8	16	0	21	0	1	0	1	1	.50	4	.268	.359	.339
5 Min. YEARS		591	2135	593	88	21	16	771	362	216	372	8	275	7	37	22	62	48	.56	48	.278	.383	.361

Jeff Sexton

Pitches: Right **Bats:** Right **Pos:** P **Ht:** 6'2" **Wt:** 190 **Born:** 10/4/71 **Age:** 26

Year Team	Lg Org	G	GS	CG	GF	IP	BFP	H	R	ER	HR	SH	SF	HB	TBB	IBB	SO	WP	Bk	W	L	Pct.	ShO	Sv	ERA
1993 Watertown	A- Cle	17	1	1	9	33.2	145	35	15	10	1	1	0	1	10	3	30	3	0	1	1	.500	1	2	2.67
1994 Watertown	A- Cle	10	0	0	5	23	95	19	3	1	0	1	0	0	7	2	16	3	1	1	0	1.000	0	3	0.39
Columbus	A Cle	14	2	0	6	30	121	17	13	12	2	1	0	3	9	2	35	1	0	1	0	1.000	0	1	3.60
1995 Columbus	A Cle	14	13	2	0	82.1	318	66	27	20	2	1	1	3	16	0	71	1	0	6	2	.750	2	0	2.19
Kinston	A+ Cle	8	8	2	0	57	226	52	17	16	3	0	0	2	7	0	41	6	1	5	1	.833	1	0	2.53
1996 Canton-Akrn	AA Cle	9	9	0	0	49.1	210	45	29	28	6	2	0	2	23	1	34	1	0	2	4	.333	0	0	5.11
1997 Akron	AA Cle	16	3	0	5	47.1	215	55	27	25	4	4	4	5	15	1	38	1	2	2	0	1.000	0	1	4.75
Buffalo	AAA Cle	15	0	0	11	23.2	100	17	14	14	3	1	0	0	12	0	15	2	0	2	1	.667	0	0	5.32
5 Min. YEARS		103	36	5	36	346.1	1430	306	145	126	21	11	5	16	99	9	280	18	4	20	9	.690	4	7	3.27

Jon Shave

Bats: Right **Throws:** Right **Pos:** SS **Ht:** 6'0" **Wt:** 180 **Born:** 11/4/67 **Age:** 30

Year Team	Lg Org	G	AB	H	2B	3B	HR	TB	R	RBI	TBB	IBB	SO	HBP	SH	SF	SB	CS	SB%	GDP	Avg	OBP	SLG
1990 Butte	R+ Tex	64	250	88	9	3	2	109	41	42	25	0	27	3	2	4	21	7	.75	8	.352	.411	.436
1991 Gastonia	A Tex	55	213	62	11	0	2	79	29	24	20	0	26	1	3	0	11	9	.55	3	.291	.355	.371
Charlotte	A+ Tex	56	189	43	4	1	1	52	17	20	18	1	30	5	2	4	7	7	.50	3	.228	.306	.275
1992 Tulsa	AA Tex	118	453	130	23	5	2	169	57	36	37	1	59	4	7	5	6	7	.46	10	.287	.343	.373
1993 Okla City	AAA Tex	100	399	105	17	3	4	140	58	41	20	0	60	2	9	1	4	3	.57	12	.263	.301	.351
1994 Okla City	AAA Tex	95	332	73	15	2	1	95	29	31	14	1	61	5	12	5	6	2	.75	6	.220	.258	.286
1995 Okla City	AAA Tex	32	83	17	1	0	0	18	10	5	7	0	28	1	1	0	1	0	1.00	1	.205	.275	.217
1996 Okla City	AAA Tex	116	414	110	20	2	7	155	54	41	41	0	97	10	4	4	8	6	.57	7	.266	.343	.374
1997 Salt Lake	AAA Min	103	395	130	27	3	7	184	75	60	39	0	62	6	1	8	6	6	.50	9	.329	.391	.466
1993 Texas	AL	17	47	15	2	0	0	17	3	7	0	0	8	0	3	2	1	3	.25	0	.319	.306	.362
8 Min. YEARS		739	2728	758	127	19	26	1001	370	300	221	3	450	37	41	31	70	47	.60	59	.278	.337	.367

Curtis Shaw

Pitches: Left **Bats:** Left **Pos:** P **Ht:** 6'2" **Wt:** 205 **Born:** 8/16/69 **Age:** 28

Year Team	Lg Org	G	GS	CG	GF	IP	BFP	H	R	ER	HR	SH	SF	HB	TBB	IBB	SO	WP	Bk	W	L	Pct.	ShO	Sv	ERA
1990 Sou. Oregon	A- Oak	17	9	0	3	66.1	274	54	28	26	4	1	0	3	30	0	74	5	1	4	6	.400	0	0	3.53
1991 Madison	A Oak	20	20	1	0	100.1	457	82	45	29	1	1	1	6	79	1	87	11	0	7	5	.583	0	0	2.60
1992 Modesto	A+ Oak	27	27	2	0	177.1	749	146	71	60	5	7	7	6	98	0	154	12	1	13	4	.765	0	0	3.05
1993 Huntsville	AA Oak	28	28	2	0	151.2	676	141	98	83	8	2	3	14	89	2	132	19	4	6	16	.273	1	0	4.93
1994 Huntsville	AA Oak	7	7	0	0	42	181	39	22	21	1	4	1	1	20	0	33	3	0	2	1	.667	0	0	4.50
Tacoma	AAA Oak	32	8	0	7	82	396	98	69	63	10	5	6	7	61	0	46	11	2	2	6	.250	0	0	6.91
1995 Edmonton	AAA Oak	42	3	0	11	98.1	454	91	60	51	4	5	6	6	88	8	52	17	1	6	5	.545	0	2	4.67
1996 Edmonton	AAA Oak	1	1	0	0	3	17	6	6	6	1	0	1	0	2	0	1	2	1	0	0	.000	0	0	18.00
Modesto	A+ Oak	39	10	0	11	107.1	481	101	63	45	5	8	2	10	63	0	89	9	2	10	5	.667	0	1	3.77
1997 Calgary	AAA Pit	21	0	0	8	31	147	31	26	18	2	1		2	18	1	23	2	1	0	3	.000	0	2	5.23
Carolina	AA Pit	27	0	0	6	41.2	189	30	23	13	1	3	0	1	28	1	46	9	1	1	1	.500	0	0	2.81
8 Min. YEARS		261	113	5	46	901	4021	819	511	415	39	39	27	56	576	13	737	100	14	51	52	.495	1	5	4.15

Chris Sheff

Bats: Right **Throws:** Right **Pos:** OF **Ht:** 6'3" **Wt:** 210 **Born:** 2/4/71 **Age:** 27

Year Team	Lg Org	G	AB	H	2B	3B	HR	TB	R	RBI	TBB	IBB	SO	HBP	SH	SF	SB	CS	SB%	GDP	Avg	OBP	SLG
1992 Erie	A- Fla	57	193	46	8	2	3	67	29	16	32	1	47	1	1	1	15	2	.88	8	.238	.348	.347
1993 Kane County	A Fla	129	456	124	22	5	5	171	79	50	58	2	100	2	3	5	33	10	.77	11	.272	.353	.375
1994 Brevard Cty	A+ Fla	32	118	44	8	3	1	61	21	19	17	0	23	0	0	1	7	2	.78	2	.373	.449	.517
Portland	AA Fla	106	395	101	19	1	5	137	50	30	31	0	76	0	3	2	18	4	.82	13	.256	.308	.347
1995 Portland	AA Fla	131	471	130	25	7	12	205	85	91	72	6	84	5	1	8	23	6	.79	10	.276	.372	.435
1996 Portland	AA Fla	27	105	31	12	2	2	53	16	17	13	3	23	0	0	0	3	2	.60	3	.295	.373	.505
Charlotte	AAA Fla	92	284	75	15	1	12	128	41	49	21	1	55	0	0	1	7	1	.88	10	.264	.314	.451
1997 Charlotte	AAA Fla	120	322	82	23	1	11	140	54	43	43	1	76	1	2	3	16	4	.80	5	.255	.341	.435
6 Min. YEARS		694	2344	633	132	22	51	962	375	315	287	14	484	9	10	21	122	31	.80	62	.270	.349	.410

Al Shepherd

Pitches: Right **Bats:** Right **Pos:** P   **Ht:** 6'7" **Wt:** 245 **Born:** 5/12/74 **Age:** 24

Year Team	Lg Org	G	GS	CG	GF	IP	BFP	H	R	ER	HR	SH	SF	HB	TBB	IBB	SO	WP	Bk	W	L	Pct.	ShO	Sv	ERA
1996 Frederick	A+ Bal	41	6	0	19	96.2	445	112	67	60	13	3	4	2	47	2	104	5	0	6	5	.545	0	10	5.59
1997 Bowie	AA Bal	22	19	0	0	106.1	460	98	68	63	19	3	5	2	57	1	80	10	1	10	6	.625	0	0	5.33
2 Min. YEARS		63	25	0	19	203	905	210	135	123	32	6	9	4	104	3	184	15	1	16	11	.593	0	10	5.45

Keith Shepherd

Pitches: Right **Bats:** Right **Pos:** P   **Ht:** 6'2" **Wt:** 215 **Born:** 1/21/68 **Age:** 30

Year Team	Lg Org	G	GS	CG	GF	IP	BFP	H	R	ER	HR	SH	SF	HB	TBB	IBB	SO	WP	Bk	W	L	Pct.	ShO	Sv	ERA
1990 Reno	A+ Cle	5	5	0	0	25	120	22	25	15	1	3	1	2	18	0	16	6	1	1	4	.200	0	0	5.40
Watertown	A- Cle	24	0	0	19	54.1	235	41	22	15	1	4	0	4	29	1	55	9	1	3	3	.500	0	3	2.48
1991 South Bend	A ChA	31	0	0	21	35.1	140	17	4	2	0	3	0	1	19	2	38	5	1	1	2	.333	0	10	0.51
Sarasota	A+ ChA	18	0	0	8	39.2	166	33	16	12	0	3	1	2	20	0	24	1	0	1	1	.500	0	2	2.72
1992 Birmingham	AA ChA	40	0	0	30	71.1	282	50	19	17	1	4	1	1	20	2	64	7	1	3	3	.500	0	7	2.14
Reading	AA Phi	4	3	0	1	22.2	87	17	7	7	1	2	0	1	4	1	9	0	0	0	1	.000	0	0	2.78
1993 Colo Sprngs	AAA Col	37	1	0	20	67.2	339	90	61	51	2	2	4	4	44	2	57	15	0	3	6	.333	0	8	6.78
1994 Colo Sprngs	AAA Col	18	0	0	6	29.2	148	40	33	30	4	0	0	3	22	0	21	8	0	0	1	.000	0	1	9.10
Pawtucket	AAA Bos	6	4	0	2	20.2	101	37	22	21	3	0	0	0	9	0	8	5	0	0	3	.000	0	0	9.15
Sarasota	A+ Bos	20	0	0	16	21	87	12	7	7	1	2	1	1	12	0	21	0	1	0	0	.000	0	7	3.00
1995 Charlotte	AAA Fla	4	0	0	1	4.2	29	11	11	11	1	0	1	1	3	0	2	0	0	1	1	.500	0	0	21.21
1996 Rochester	AAA Bal	27	11	2	15	94.1	414	91	54	42	12	2	4	4	37	0	98	5	0	4	7	.364	0	9	4.01
1997 Calgary	AAA Pit	10	1	0	4	17.2	88	23	16	15	1	1	0	1	14	3	16	1	0	0	1	.000	0	0	7.64
Norfolk	AAA NYN	19	18	0	1	107	482	119	61	52	10	3	2	3	55	1	78	3	1	8	8	.500	0	0	4.37
1992 Philadelphia	NL	12	0	0	6	22	91	19	10	8	0	4	3	0	6	1	10	1	0	1	1	.500	0	2	3.27
1993 Colorado	NL	14	1	0	3	19.1	85	26	16	15	4	1	1	0	4	0	7	1	0	1	3	.250	0	1	6.98
1995 Boston	AL	2	0	0	0	1	9	4	4	4	0	0	0	0	2	0	0	0	0	0	0	.000	0	0	36.00
1996 Baltimore	AL	13	0	0	6	20.2	111	31	27	20	6	1	1	0	18	1	17	0	0	0	1	.000	0	0	8.71
8 Min. YEARS		263	43	2	144	611	2718	603	358	297	38	29	15	28	306	12	507	65	6	25	41	.379	0	47	4.37
4 Maj. YEARS		41	1	0	15	63	296	80	57	47	10	6	5	1	30	2	34	2	0	2	5	.286	0	3	6.71

Al Shirley

Bats: Right **Throws:** Right **Pos:** OF   **Ht:** 6'1" **Wt:** 209 **Born:** 10/18/73 **Age:** 24

Year Team	Lg Org	G	AB	H	2B	3B	HR	TB	R	RBI	TBB	IBB	SO	HBP	SH	SF	SB	CS	SB%	GDP	Avg	OBP	SLG
1991 Mets	R NYN	51	187	33	3	1	3	47	21	12	14	0	62	2	0	0	17	4	.81	2	.176	.241	.251
1992 Kingsport	R+ NYN	29	99	31	3	1	7	57	26	22	26	0	37	1	0	1	9	2	.82	2	.313	.457	.576
1993 Capital Cty	A NYN	72	240	35	9	4	4	64	32	22	50	1	121	2	0	0	12	2	.86	1	.146	.298	.267
Kingsport	R+ NYN	43	133	24	5	1	0	31	22	11	42	0	57	4	3	0	6	5	.55	4	.180	.391	.233
1994 Capital City	A NYN	127	437	93	14	5	23	186	67	56	50	2	208	6	2	3	23	6	.79	2	.213	.300	.426
1995 Mets	R NYN	4	15	5	2	0	0	7	4	0	3	0	4	0	0	0	3	1	.75	0	.333	.444	.467
St. Lucie	A+ NYN	59	183	34	6	3	5	61	27	18	23	1	94	5	0	1	8	4	.67	2	.186	.292	.333
1996 Wilmington	A+ KC	116	340	78	13	2	17	146	54	47	57	3	149	9	0	1	8	7	.53	1	.229	.354	.429
1997 Wichita	AA KC	81	240	65	10	1	4	89	31	25	21	1	92	2	2	2	9	7	.56	3	.271	.332	.371
7 Min. YEARS		582	1874	398	65	18	63	688	284	213	286	8	824	31	7	8	95	38	.71	17	.212	.325	.367

Stephen Shoemaker

Pitches: Right **Bats:** Left **Pos:** P   **Ht:** 6'1" **Wt:** 195 **Born:** 2/3/73 **Age:** 25

Year Team	Lg Org	G	GS	CG	GF	IP	BFP	H	R	ER	HR	SH	SF	HB	TBB	IBB	SO	WP	Bk	W	L	Pct.	ShO	Sv	ERA
1994 Oneonta	A- NYA	12	12	0	0	58.2	262	62	32	28	7	2	1	3	28	0	46	5	1	3	5	.375	0	0	4.30
1995 Greensboro	A NYA	17	17	0	0	81	347	62	33	28	5	2	2	4	52	0	82	4	0	4	4	.500	0	0	3.11
Tampa	A+ NYA	3	2	0	0	16.2	73	9	5	2	1	2	1	0	13	0	12	2	0	0	1	.000	0	0	1.08
1996 Salem	A+ Col	25	13	0	5	86.1	371	63	49	45	6	1	5	4	63	0	105	1	1	2	7	.222	0	1	4.69
1997 Salem	A+ Col	9	9	1	0	52	215	31	21	16	3	2	1	5	25	0	76	2	3	3	3	.500	0	0	2.77
New Haven	AA Col	14	14	1	0	95.1	389	64	36	32	6	5	2	3	53	3	111	5	1	6	4	.600	0	0	3.02
Colo Sprngs	AAA Col	5	4	0	0	20.1	101	23	19	19	5	0	1	3	17	0	27	1	0	1	1	.500	0	0	8.41
4 Min. YEARS		85	71	2	5	410.1	1758	314	195	170	33	14	13	22	251	3	459	20	6	19	25	.432	0	1	3.73

Barry Short

Pitches: Right **Bats:** Right **Pos:** P   **Ht:** 6'3" **Wt:** 182 **Born:** 12/15/73 **Age:** 24

Year Team	Lg Org	G	GS	CG	GF	IP	BFP	H	R	ER	HR	SH	SF	HB	TBB	IBB	SO	WP	Bk	W	L	Pct.	ShO	Sv	ERA
1994 Pittsfield	R NYN	10	1	0	1	62.1	252	49	21	17	3	1	0	1	19	0	49	9	0	5	2	.714	0	0	2.45
Kingsport	R+ NYN	1	1	0	0	5.1	22	5	0	0	0	0	0	0	3	0	3	0	0	1	0	1.000	0	0	0.00
1995 Pittsfield	A- NYN	2	0	0	1	2	10	4	1	1	0	0	0	0	0	0	3	1	0	0	0	.000	0	1	4.50
Capital City	A NYN	40	1	0	15	77.2	319	63	22	17	1	2	0	2	22	2	56	5	2	4	3	.571	0	4	1.97
1996 St. Lucie	A+ NYN	58	0	0	24	88.1	350	70	28	23	5	4	1	1	18	1	70	1	0	6	2	.750	0	10	2.34
1997 Binghamton	AA NYN	6	0	0	2	10.1	45	9	3	3	1	1	0	0	4	0	6	0	0	2	0	1.000	0	0	2.61
4 Min. YEARS		117	9	0	43	246	998	200	75	61	10	8	1	4	66	3	187	16	2	18	7	.720	0	15	2.23

Brian Shouse

Pitches: Left Bats: Left Pos: P Ht: 5'11" Wt: 175 Born: 9/26/68 Age: 29

Year Team	Lg Org	G	GS	CG	GF	IP	BFP	H	R	ER	HR	SH	SF	HB	TBB	IBB	SO	WP	Bk	W	L	Pct.	ShO	Sv	ERA
1990 Welland	A- Pit	17	1	0	7	39.2	177	50	27	23	2	3	2	3	7	0	39	1	2	4	3	.571	0	2	5.22
1991 Augusta	A Pit	26	0	0	25	31	124	22	13	11	1	1	1	3	9	1	32	5	0	2	3	.400	0	8	3.19
Salem	A+ Pit	17	0	0	9	33.2	147	35	12	11	2	2	0	0	15	2	25	1	0	2	1	.667	0	3	2.94
1992 Carolina	AA Pit	59	0	0	33	77.1	323	71	31	21	3	8	2	2	28	4	79	4	1	5	6	.455	0	2	2.44
1993 Buffalo	AAA Pit	48	0	0	14	51.2	218	54	24	22	7	0	3	2	17	2	25	1	0	1	0	1.000	0	2	3.83
1994 Buffalo	AAA Pit	43	0	0	20	52	212	44	22	21	6	4	2	1	15	4	31	0	0	3	4	.429	0	0	3.63
1995 Calgary	AAA Pit	8	8	1	0	39.1	185	62	35	27	2	1	1	1	7	0	17	3	0	4	4	.500	0	0	6.18
Carolina	AA Pit	21	20	0	0	114.2	480	126	64	57	14	5	3	4	19	2	76	1	1	7	6	.538	0	0	4.47
1996 Calgary	AAA Pit	12	1	0	2	12.2	65	22	15	15	4	0	1	0	4	1	12	1	0	1	0	1.000	0	0	10.66
Rochester	AAA Bal	32	0	0	10	50	217	53	27	25	6	2	2	1	16	1	45	5	0	1	2	.333	0	2	4.50
1997 Rochester	AAA Bal	54	0	0	29	71.1	282	48	21	18	6	5	1	3	21	4	81	2	0	6	2	.750	0	9	2.27
1993 Pittsburgh	NL	6	0	0	1	4	22	7	4	4	1	0	1	0	2	0	3	1	0	0	0	.000	0	0	9.00
8 Min. YEARS		337	30	1	149	573.1	2430	587	291	251	53	31	18	20	158	21	462	24	4	36	31	.537	0	30	3.94

Joe Siddall

Bats: Left Throws: Right Pos: C Ht: 6'1" Wt: 200 Born: 10/25/67 Age: 30

Year Team	Lg Org	G	AB	H	2B	3B	HR	TB	R	RBI	TBB	IBB	SO	HBP	SH	SF	SB	CS	SB%	GDP	Avg	OBP	SLG
1988 Jamestown	A- Mon	53	178	38	5	3	1	52	18	16	14	1	29	1	4	2	5	4	.56	3	.213	.272	.292
1989 Rockford	A Mon	98	313	74	15	2	4	105	36	38	26	2	56	6	5	4	8	5	.62	3	.236	.304	.335
1990 Wst Plm Bch	A+ Mon	106	348	78	12	1	0	92	29	32	20	0	55	1	10	2	6	7	.46	7	.224	.267	.264
1991 Harrisburg	AA Mon	76	235	54	6	1	1	65	28	23	23	2	53	1	2	3	8	3	.73	7	.230	.298	.277
1992 Harrisburg	AA Mon	95	288	68	12	0	2	86	26	27	29	1	55	3	1	3	4	4	.50	7	.236	.310	.299
1993 Ottawa	AAA Mon	48	136	29	6	0	1	38	14	16	19	5	33	0	3	2	2	2	.50	6	.213	.306	.279
1994 Ottawa	AAA Mon	38	110	19	2	1	3	32	9	13	10	2	21	2	7	2	1	1	.50	3	.173	.250	.291
1995 Ottawa	AAA Mon	83	248	53	14	2	1	74	26	23	23	0	42	4	2	0	3	3	.50	6	.214	.291	.298
1996 Charlotte	AAA Fla	65	189	53	13	1	3	77	22	20	11	1	36	3	2	0	1	2	.33	2	.280	.330	.407
1997 Ottawa	AAA Mon	57	164	45	12	1	1	62	18	16	21	3	42	1	0	0	1	2	.33	2	.274	.360	.378
1993 Montreal	NL	19	20	2	1	0	0	3	0	1	1	1	5	0	0	0	0	0	.00	0	.100	.143	.150
1995 Montreal	NL	7	10	3	0	0	0	3	4	1	3	0	3	1	0	0	0	0	.00	0	.300	.500	.300
1996 Florida	NL	18	47	7	1	0	0	8	0	3	2	0	8	0	0	0	0	0	.00	0	.149	.184	.170
10 Min. YEARS		719	2209	511	97	12	17	683	226	224	196	17	422	22	36	18	39	33	.54	46	.231	.298	.309
3 Maj. YEARS		44	77	12	2	0	0	14	4	5	6	1	16	1	0	0	0	0	.00	0	.156	.226	.182

Mark Sievert

Pitches: Right Bats: Left Pos: P Ht: 6'4" Wt: 180 Born: 2/16/73 Age: 25

Year Team	Lg Org	G	GS	CG	GF	IP	BFP	H	R	ER	HR	SH	SF	HB	TBB	IBB	SO	WP	Bk	W	L	Pct.	ShO	Sv	ERA
1993 Medicne Hat	R+ Tor	15	15	0	0	63	280	63	40	35	2	2	2	3	30	0	52	12	0	6	3	.667	0	0	5.00
1994 St. Cathrns	A- Tor	14	14	1	0	81.2	319	59	30	28	4	1	3	1	28	0	82	4	0	7	4	.636	1	0	3.09
1995 Hagerstown	A Tor	27	27	3	0	160.2	644	126	59	52	14	5	1	2	46	0	140	4	0	12	6	.667	0	0	2.91
1996 Knoxville	AA Tor	17	17	0	0	101.1	415	79	32	29	6	2	0	3	51	0	75	3	0	9	2	.818	0	0	2.58
Syracuse	AAA Tor	10	10	1	0	54.2	256	64	40	36	6	4	1	1	33	0	46	4	0	2	5	.286	0	0	5.93
1997 Syracuse	AAA Tor	1	1	0	0	5.1	23	5	3	2	0	0	0	0	2	0	5	0	0	0	0	.000	0	0	3.38
Dunedin	A+ Tor	3	2	0	0	11	44	10	5	4	0	0	0	1	5	0	7	2	1	1	0	1.000	0	0	3.27
5 Min. YEARS		87	86	5	0	477.2	1981	404	209	186	32	14	7	11	195	0	407	27	1	37	20	.649	1	0	3.50

Brian Sikorski

Pitches: Right Bats: Right Pos: P Ht: 6'1" Wt: 190 Born: 7/27/74 Age: 23

Year Team	Lg Org	G	GS	CG	GF	IP	BFP	H	R	ER	HR	SH	SF	HB	TBB	IBB	SO	WP	Bk	W	L	Pct.	ShO	Sv	ERA
1995 Auburn	A- Hou	23	0	0	19	34.1	137	22	8	8	1	0	1	0	14	2	35	1	0	1	2	.333	0	12	2.10
Quad City	A Hou	2	0	0	0	3	11	1	1	0	0	0	0	0	0	0	4	0	0	1	0	1.000	0	0	0.00
1996 Quad City	A Hou	26	25	1	0	166.2	704	140	79	58	12	4	7	10	70	0	150	7	9	11	8	.579	0	0	3.13
1997 Kissimmee	A+ Hou	11	11	0	0	67.2	279	64	29	23	2	0	1	6	16	0	46	0	3	8	2	.800	0	0	3.06
Jackson	AA Hou	17	17	0	0	93.1	402	91	55	48	8	5	2	4	31	2	74	0	2	5	5	.500	0	0	4.63
3 Min. YEARS		79	53	1	20	365	1533	318	172	137	23	9	11	20	131	6	309	8	14	26	17	.605	0	12	3.38

Ted Silva

Pitches: Right Bats: Right Pos: P Ht: 6'0" Wt: 170 Born: 8/4/74 Age: 23

Year Team	Lg Org	G	GS	CG	GF	IP	BFP	H	R	ER	HR	SH	SF	HB	TBB	IBB	SO	WP	Bk	W	L	Pct.	ShO	Sv	ERA
1995 Chston-SC	A Tex	11	11	0	0	66.2	276	59	26	25	4	1	3	7	12	2	66	5	2	5	4	.556	0	0	3.38
1996 Charlotte	A+ Tex	16	16	4	0	113.1	463	98	39	36	9	1	2	3	27	1	95	3	1	10	2	.833	0	0	2.86
Tulsa	AA Tex	11	11	2	0	75.1	314	72	27	25	5	4	2	2	16	0	27	0	0	7	2	.778	1	0	2.99
1997 Tulsa	AA Tex	26	25	4	1	171.2	728	178	88	78	21	9	7	3	42	1	121	7	1	13	10	.565	0	0	4.09
3 Min. YEARS		64	63	10	1	427	1781	407	180	164	39	15	14	15	97	4	309	15	4	35	18	.660	1	0	3.46

Juan Silvestre

Bats: Right Throws: Right Pos: OF Ht: 5'11" Wt: 180 Born: 1/10/78 Age: 20

Year Team	Lg Org	G	AB	H	2B	3B	HR	TB	R	RBI	TBB	IBB	SO	HBP	SH	SF	SB	CS	SB%	GDP	Avg	OBP	SLG
1997 Mariners	R Sea	34	135	46	11	3	7	84	32	36	15	1	31	2	0	3	4	2	.67	1	.341	.406	.622

		BATTING													BASERUNNING				PERCENTAGES		
Year Team	Lg Org	G	AB	H	2B	3B	HR	TB	R	RBI	TBB	IBB	SO	HBP	SH	SF	SB	CS	SB%	GDP	Avg	OBP	SLG
Tacoma	AAA Sea	8	28	7	3	0	0	10	5	0	2	0	9	0	0	0	0	0	.00	0	.250	.300	.357
Everett	A- Sea	14	54	17	3	1	3	31	9	9	4	0	19	2	0	1	1	0	1.00	0	.315	.377	.574
1 Min. YEARS		56	217	70	17	4	10	125	46	45	21	1	59	4	0	4	5	2	.71	1	.323	.386	.576

Brian Simmons

Bats: Both **Throws:** Right **Pos:** OF **Ht:** 6'2" **Wt:** 191 **Born:** 9/4/73 **Age:** 24

		BATTING													BASERUNNING				PERCENTAGES		
Year Team	Lg Org	G	AB	H	2B	3B	HR	TB	R	RBI	TBB	IBB	SO	HBP	SH	SF	SB	CS	SB%	GDP	Avg	OBP	SLG
1995 White Sox	R ChA	5	17	3	1	0	1	7	5	5	6	0	1	0	0	0	0	0	.00	1	.176	.391	.412
Hickory	A ChA	41	163	31	6	1	2	45	13	11	19	0	44	2	0	0	4	4	.50	2	.190	.283	.276
1996 South Bend	A ChA	92	356	106	29	6	17	198	73	58	48	2	69	2	1	4	14	9	.61	3	.298	.380	.556
Pr William	A+ ChA	33	131	26	4	3	4	48	17	14	9	1	39	0	1	0	2	0	1.00	3	.198	.250	.366
1997 Birmingham	AA ChA	138	546	143	28	12	15	240	108	72	88	5	124	2	2	3	15	12	.56	10	.262	.365	.440
3 Min. YEARS		309	1213	309	68	22	39	538	216	160	170	8	277	6	4	7	35	25	.58	19	.255	.347	.444

Scott Simmons

Pitches: Left **Bats:** Right **Pos:** P **Ht:** 6'2" **Wt:** 200 **Born:** 8/15/69 **Age:** 28

		HOW MUCH HE PITCHED					WHAT HE GAVE UP								THE RESULTS						
Year Team	Lg Org	G	GS	CG	GF	IP	BFP	H	R	ER	HR	SH	SF	HB	TBB	IBB	SO	WP	Bk	W	L	Pct.	ShO	Sv	ERA
1991 Hamilton	A- StL	15	14	0	0	90.1	376	82	34	26	4	0	2	1	25	0	78	1	2	6	4	.600	0	0	2.59
1992 Springfield	A StL	27	27	2	0	170.1	699	160	63	53	10	9	3	2	39	0	116	10	2	15	7	.682	1	0	2.80
1993 St. Pete	A+ StL	13	12	1	1	78.2	326	70	38	30	1	4	4	0	31	0	54	6	1	4	5	.444	0	0	3.43
Arkansas	AA StL	13	10	0	0	76.2	306	68	26	23	1	2	2	0	18	3	35	4	0	6	3	.667	0	0	2.70
1994 Arkansas	AA StL	26	26	2	0	162.1	663	148	63	49	4	10	4	3	39	1	115	4	1	7	11	.389	1	0	2.72
1995 Louisville	AAA StL	2	2	0	0	9	40	11	9	8	3	0	0	1	1	0	2	0	0	0	2	.000	0	0	8.00
Arkansas	AA StL	22	22	1	0	139	569	145	66	53	9	5	6	1	28	1	73	5	0	11	9	.550	1	0	3.43
1996 Louisville	AAA StL	30	8	0	10	99.2	416	98	51	46	17	1	1	0	35	5	58	4	1	5	6	.455	0	1	4.15
Port City	AA Sea	11	0	0	3	19	79	19	8	8	1	1	0	0	6	1	12	3	0	1	1	.500	0	1	3.79
1997 Memphis	AA Sea	40	7	0	6	90.2	380	77	40	33	10	3	1	4	40	3	85	5	2	8	4	.667	0	1	3.28
7 Min. YEARS		199	128	6	20	935.2	3854	878	398	329	60	35	23	12	262	14	628	42	9	63	52	.548	3	2	3.16

Mitch Simons

Bats: Right **Throws:** Right **Pos:** 2B **Ht:** 5'9" **Wt:** 170 **Born:** 12/13/68 **Age:** 29

		BATTING													BASERUNNING				PERCENTAGES		
Year Team	Lg Org	G	AB	H	2B	3B	HR	TB	R	RBI	TBB	IBB	SO	HBP	SH	SF	SB	CS	SB%	GDP	Avg	OBP	SLG
1991 Jamestown	A- Mon	41	153	47	12	0	1	62	38	16	39	1	20	0	2	2	23	5	.82	1	.307	.443	.405
Wst Plm Bch	A+ Mon	15	50	9	2	1	0	13	3	4	5	0	8	0	0	0	1	0	1.00	1	.180	.255	.260
1992 Albany	A Mon	130	481	136	26	5	1	175	57	61	60	0	47	7	2	10	34	12	.74	6	.283	.364	.364
1993 Wst Plm Bch	A+ Mon	45	156	40	4	1	1	49	24	13	19	0	9	3	1	2	14	8	.64	3	.256	.344	.314
Harrisburg	AA Mon	29	77	18	1	1	0	21	5	5	7	0	14	0	2	1	2	0	1.00	1	.234	.294	.273
1994 Nashville	AA Min	102	391	124	26	0	3	159	46	48	39	0	38	6	3	5	30	9	.77	6	.317	.383	.407
1995 Salt Lake	AAA Min	130	480	156	34	4	3	207	87	46	47	2	45	10	4	2	32	16	.67	9	.325	.395	.431
1996 Salt Lake	AAA Min	129	512	135	27	8	5	193	76	59	43	3	59	8	3	4	35	11	.76	7	.264	.328	.377
1997 Salt Lake	AAA Min	115	462	138	34	10	5	207	87	59	47	4	48	5	5	5	26	5	.84	7	.299	.366	.448
7 Min. YEARS		736	2762	803	166	30	19	1086	423	311	306	10	288	39	26	31	197	66	.75	40	.291	.366	.393

Benji Simonton

Bats: Right **Throws:** Right **Pos:** 1B **Ht:** 6'1" **Wt:** 225 **Born:** 5/12/72 **Age:** 26

		BATTING													BASERUNNING				PERCENTAGES		
Year Team	Lg Org	G	AB	H	2B	3B	HR	TB	R	RBI	TBB	IBB	SO	HBP	SH	SF	SB	CS	SB%	GDP	Avg	OBP	SLG
1992 Everett	A- SF	68	225	55	10	0	6	83	37	34	39	0	78	3	2	3	9	4	.69	1	.244	.359	.369
1993 Clinton	A SF	100	310	79	18	4	12	141	52	49	40	2	112	6	0	2	8	7	.53	3	.255	.349	.455
1994 Clinton	A SF	67	237	64	16	4	14	130	47	57	52	3	73	5	1	0	10	3	.77	1	.270	.412	.549
San Jose	A+ SF	68	259	77	20	4	14	139	41	51	32	0	86	5	1	1	0	2	.00	5	.297	.384	.537
1995 San Jose	A+ SF	61	225	65	9	6	8	110	38	37	40	2	78	10	0	4	7	0	1.00	5	.289	.412	.489
Shreveport	AA SF	38	108	33	9	3	4	60	18	30	11	0	32	2	1	1	3	1	.75	1	.306	.377	.556
1996 Shreveport	AA SF	137	469	117	25	1	23	213	86	76	101	4	144	6	1	0	6	4	.60	12	.249	.389	.454
Phoenix	AAA SF	4	4	3	0	0	1	6	1	2	1	0	0	0	0	0	0	0	.00	0	.750	.800	1.500
1997 Shreveport	AA SF	116	387	99	15	2	20	178	73	79	81	1	120	6	0	4	7	5	.58	14	.256	.388	.460
6 Min. YEARS		656	2224	592	122	20	102	1060	393	415	397	12	723	43	6	16	50	26	.66	48	.266	.385	.477

Steve Sinclair

Pitches: Left **Bats:** Left **Pos:** P **Ht:** 6'2" **Wt:** 172 **Born:** 8/2/71 **Age:** 26

		HOW MUCH HE PITCHED					WHAT HE GAVE UP								THE RESULTS						
Year Team	Lg Org	G	GS	CG	GF	IP	BFP	H	R	ER	HR	SH	SF	HB	TBB	IBB	SO	WP	Bk	W	L	Pct.	ShO	Sv	ERA
1991 Medcine Hat	R+ Tor	12	0	0	8	14.2	76	17	15	11	1	1	0	3	11	0	14	0	0	0	1	.000	0	0	6.75
1992 Blue Jays	R Tor	5	4	0	0	23	92	23	10	7	2	0	0	0	5	0	18	1	0	1	2	.333	0	0	2.74
Medcine Hat	R+ Tor	9	7	0	1	43	189	54	25	22	2	2	3	1	12	0	28	3	0	2	3	.400	0	0	4.60
1993 Medcne Hat	R+ Tor	15	12	0	0	78.1	335	87	41	29	5	2	2	1	16	0	45	5	1	5	2	.714	0	0	3.33
1994 Hagerstown	A Tor	38	1	0	16	105	458	127	53	44	9	4	5	2	25	0	75	3	0	9	2	.818	0	3	3.77
1995 Dunedin	A+ Tor	46	0	0	18	73	297	69	26	21	4	1	1	3	17	1	52	2	3	5	3	.625	0	2	2.59
1996 Dunedin	A+ Tor	3	0	0	1	2.2	12	4	2	1	1	0	0	0	0	0	1	0	0	1	0	1.000	0	0	3.38
1997 Dunedin	A+ Tor	43	0	0	20	68.1	296	63	36	22	4	4	1	2	26	3	66	4	1	2	5	.286	0	3	2.90
Syracuse	AAA Tor	6	0	0	1	9	40	11	6	6	0	0	0	0	3	0	9	0	0	0	1	.000	0	0	6.00
7 Min. YEARS		177	24	0	65	417	1795	455	214	163	28	14	12	12	115	4	308	18	5	24	19	.558	0	8	3.52

Chris Singleton

Bats: Left **Throws:** Left **Pos:** OF **Ht:** 6'2" **Wt:** 195 **Born:** 8/15/72 **Age:** 25

Year Team	Lg Org	G	AB	H	2B	3B	HR	TB	R	RBI	TBB	IBB	SO	HBP	SH	SF	SB	CS	SB%	GDP	Avg	OBP	SLG
1993 Everett	A- SF	58	219	58	14	4	3	89	39	18	18	0	46	1	5	1	14	3	.82	3	.265	.322	.406
1994 San Jose	A+ SF	113	425	106	17	5	2	139	51	49	27	0	62	3	5	3	19	6	.76	9	.249	.297	.327
1995 San Jose	A+ SF	94	405	112	13	5	2	141	55	31	17	1	49	5	5	1	33	13	.72	5	.277	.313	.348
1996 Shreveport	AA SF	129	500	149	31	9	5	213	68	72	24	2	58	6	3	8	27	12	.69	12	.298	.333	.426
Phoenix	AAA SF	9	32	4	0	0	0	4	3	0	1	0	2	0	1	0	0	0	.00	0	.125	.152	.125
1997 Shreveport	AA SF	126	464	147	26	10	9	220	85	61	22	4	50	1	2	9	27	11	.71	7	.317	.343	.474
5 Min. YEARS		529	2045	576	101	33	21	806	301	231	109	7	267	16	21	22	120	45	.73	36	.282	.320	.394

Duane Singleton

Bats: Left **Throws:** Right **Pos:** OF **Ht:** 6'1" **Wt:** 177 **Born:** 8/6/72 **Age:** 25

Year Team	Lg Org	G	AB	H	2B	3B	HR	TB	R	RBI	TBB	IBB	SO	HBP	SH	SF	SB	CS	SB%	GDP	Avg	OBP	SLG
1990 Brewers	R Mil	46	134	31	6	1	1	42	30	13	41	0	39	1	1	1	5	9	.36	1	.231	.412	.313
1991 Beloit	A Mil	101	388	112	13	7	3	148	57	44	40	7	57	3	5	2	42	17	.71	7	.289	.358	.381
1992 Salinas	A+ Mil	19	72	22	5	2	1	34	6	8	6	0	11	0	0	0	4	1	.80	0	.306	.359	.472
Stockton	A+ Mil	97	389	112	15	10	5	162	73	51	39	0	66	3	3	6	34	15	.69	7	.288	.352	.416
1993 El Paso	AA Mil	125	456	105	21	6	2	144	52	61	34	0	90	3	2	5	23	19	.55	4	.230	.285	.316
1994 Stockton	A+ Mil	38	134	39	6	0	4	57	31	13	18	0	23	0	0	0	15	6	.71	1	.291	.375	.425
El Paso	AA Mil	39	139	40	11	3	2	63	25	24	19	0	33	2	1	0	10	5	.67	6	.288	.381	.453
New Orleans	AAA Mil	41	133	37	4	5	0	51	26	14	18	0	26	0	5	1	6	4	.60	1	.278	.362	.383
1995 New Orleans	AAA Mil	106	355	95	10	4	4	125	48	29	39	2	63	3	3	1	31	15	.67	7	.268	.344	.352
1996 Toledo	AAA Det	88	294	65	15	6	8	116	42	30	36	4	84	1	1	3	17	7	.71	4	.221	.305	.395
1997 Midland	AA Ana	13	55	17	5	1	2	30	15	8	6	0	8	0	0	1	4	0	1.00	1	.309	.371	.545
Vancouver	AAA Ana	108	383	79	17	3	5	117	56	36	37	1	79	4	6	2	15	12	.56	15	.206	.282	.305
1994 Milwaukee	AL	2	0	0	0	0	0	0	0	0	0	0	0	0	0	0	0	0	.00	0	.000	.000	.000
1995 Milwaukee	AL	13	31	2	0	0	0	2	0	0	1	0	10	0	0	0	1	0	1.00	0	.065	.094	.065
1996 Detroit	AL	18	56	9	1	0	0	10	5	3	4	0	15	1	0	0	0	2	.00	2	.161	.230	.179
8 Min. YEARS		821	2932	754	128	48	37	1089	461	331	333	14	579	20	27	22	206	110	.65	53	.257	.335	.371
3 Maj. YEARS		33	87	11	1	0	0	12	5	3	5	0	25	1	0	0	1	2	.33	2	.126	.183	.138

Steve Sisco

Bats: Right **Throws:** Right **Pos:** 2B **Ht:** 5'9" **Wt:** 180 **Born:** 12/2/69 **Age:** 28

Year Team	Lg Org	G	AB	H	2B	3B	HR	TB	R	RBI	TBB	IBB	SO	HBP	SH	SF	SB	CS	SB%	GDP	Avg	OBP	SLG
1992 Eugene	A- KC	67	261	86	7	1	0	95	41	30	26	0	32	4	2	2	22	12	.65	7	.330	.396	.364
Appleton	A KC	1	4	1	0	0	0	1	1	0	0	0	1	0	0	0	0	0	.00	0	.250	.250	.250
1993 Rockford	A KC	124	460	132	22	4	2	168	62	57	42	2	65	2	4	5	25	10	.71	14	.287	.346	.365
1994 Wilmington	A+ KC	76	270	74	11	4	3	102	41	32	37	0	39	2	6	4	5	6	.45	2	.274	.361	.378
1995 Omaha	AAA KC	7	24	5	1	0	0	6	4	0	2	0	8	0	1	0	0	0	.00	0	.208	.269	.250
Wichita	AA KC	54	209	63	12	1	3	86	29	23	15	0	31	1	1	1	3	1	.75	5	.301	.350	.411
1996 Wichita	AA KC	122	462	137	24	1	13	202	80	74	40	0	69	3	5	5	4	2	.67	14	.297	.353	.437
1997 Wichita	AA KC	55	182	52	8	2	3	73	34	24	24	0	29	0	1	2	3	1	.75	5	.286	.365	.401
Omaha	AAA KC	54	188	49	8	0	3	66	23	12	8	0	34	0	3	1	2	1	.67	4	.261	.289	.351
6 Min. YEARS		560	2060	599	93	13	27	799	315	252	194	2	308	12	23	20	64	33	.66	51	.291	.352	.388

Will Skett

Bats: Right **Throws:** Right **Pos:** OF **Ht:** 5'11" **Wt:** 190 **Born:** 5/22/74 **Age:** 24

Year Team	Lg Org	G	AB	H	2B	3B	HR	TB	R	RBI	TBB	IBB	SO	HBP	SH	SF	SB	CS	SB%	GDP	Avg	OBP	SLG
1996 St. Cathrns	A- Tor	75	272	75	13	1	15	135	47	52	33	0	73	10	5	4	13	3	.81	2	.276	.370	.496
1997 Dunedin	A+ Tor	98	361	97	22	3	19	182	63	71	45	3	100	19	3	5	12	7	.63	7	.269	.374	.504
Knoxville	AA Tor	30	110	30	6	1	3	47	18	15	4	0	31	1	1	1	4	4	.50	2	.273	.302	.427
2 Min. YEARS		203	743	202	41	5	37	364	128	138	82	3	204	30	9	10	29	14	.67	11	.272	.363	.490

Matt Skrmetta

Pitches: Right **Bats:** Both **Pos:** P **Ht:** 6'3" **Wt:** 220 **Born:** 11/6/72 **Age:** 25

Year Team	Lg Org	G	GS	CG	GF	IP	BFP	H	R	ER	HR	SH	SF	HB	TBB	IBB	SO	WP	Bk	W	L	Pct.	ShO	Sv	ERA
1993 Bristol	R+ Det	8	5	0	1	35	158	30	23	19	1	0	3	3	22	1	29	6	3	2	3	.400	0	0	4.89
1994 Jamestown	A- Det	17	15	1	1	93.2	389	74	42	33	4	2	3	7	37	0	56	2	3	5	3	.625	0	0	3.17
1995 Fayettevlle	A Det	44	2	0	15	89.2	371	66	36	27	9	6	1	3	35	2	105	2	1	9	4	.692	0	2	2.71
1996 Jacksnville	AA Det	4	0	0	1	6	27	4	3	3	0	0	1	0	5	1	7	1	0	0	0	.000	0	0	4.50
Lakeland	A+ Det	40	0	0	20	52.2	223	44	23	21	5	2	0	2	19	1	52	2	1	5	5	.500	0	5	3.59
1997 Mobile	AA SD	21	0	0	7	32.2	154	32	21	19	4	0	1	2	21	3	30	3	0	2	3	.400	0	1	5.23
Rancho Cuca	A+ SD	17	0	0	8	28.1	122	27	7	5	2	1	0	1	10	0	36	4	0	0	1	.000	0	0	1.59
5 Min. YEARS		151	22	1	53	338	1444	277	155	127	25	11	9	18	149	8	315	20	7	23	19	.548	0	8	3.38

Nick Skuse

Pitches: Right **Bats:** Right **Pos:** P **Ht:** 6'7" **Wt:** 240 **Born:** 1/9/72 **Age:** 26

Year Team	Lg Org	G	GS	CG	GF	IP	BFP	H	R	ER	HR	SH	SF	HB	TBB	IBB	SO	WP	Bk	W	L	Pct.	ShO	Sv	ERA
1994 Boise	A- Ana	18	8	0	3	54.1	241	67	35	31	5	1	2	4	17	0	53	5	2	4	2	.667	0	0	5.13
1995 Cedar Rapds	A Ana	26	25	3	1	147	650	155	84	66	10	3	3	9	61	1	116	12	3	13	7	.650	1	0	4.04

Year Team	Lg Org	G	GS	CG	GF	IP	BFP	H	R	ER	HR	SH	SF	HB	TBB	IBB	SO	WP	Bk	W	L	Pct.	ShO	Sv	ERA
1996 Lk Elsinore	A+ Ana	6	6	0	0	32	155	36	27	23	1	5	3	0	22	0	18	7	2	0	3	.000	0	0	6.47
Cedar Rapds	A Ana	18	16	0	1	94.2	415	77	47	43	10	2	0	5	58	2	50	7	4	5	6	.455	0	0	4.09
1997 Lk Elsinore	A+ Ana	17	0	0	7	26.2	113	23	13	6	2	1	0	3	8	0	40	6	1	0	0	.000	0	0	2.03
Midland	AA Ana	30	0	0	27	33	148	31	26	23	4	0	1	4	15	0	30	5	0	0	0	.000	0	16	6.27
Vancouver	AAA Ana	1	0	0	1	1	3	0	0	0	0	0	0	0	0	0	2	0	0	0	0	.000	0	0	0.00
4 Min. YEARS		116	55	3	40	388.2	1725	389	232	192	32	12	9	25	181	3	309	42	12	22	18	.550	1	16	4.45

Mark Small

Pitches: Right Bats: Right Pos: P Ht: 6'3" Wt: 205 Born: 11/12/67 Age: 30

Year Team	Lg Org	G	GS	CG	GF	IP	BFP	H	R	ER	HR	SH	SF	HB	TBB	IBB	SO	WP	Bk	W	L	Pct.	ShO	Sv	ERA
1989 Auburn	A- Hou	10	3	0	4	19.2	87	17	13	11	3	0	1	1	11	0	23	3	0	0	1	.000	0	2	5.03
1990 Asheville	A Hou	34	0	0	16	52	252	54	36	24	2	4	3	4	37	5	34	9	0	3	4	.429	0	6	4.15
1991 Osceola	A+ Hou	26	0	0	10	44.2	172	30	10	8	2	1	0	1	19	1	44	2	0	3	0	1.000	0	2	1.61
1992 Osceola	A+ Hou	22	20	1	2	105	435	97	56	45	8	3	3	0	38	0	69	5	1	5	9	.357	0	0	3.86
1993 Jackson	AA Hou	51	0	0	18	84.2	361	71	34	30	8	8	3	3	41	6	64	8	2	7	2	.778	0	0	3.19
1994 Jackson	AA Hou	16	0	0	9	21	97	22	16	9	1	1	2	1	10	2	14	4	0	3	1	.750	0	3	3.86
Tucson	AAA Hou	41	0	0	12	70	321	88	48	41	9	3	3	2	34	2	30	13	0	8	5	.615	0	4	5.27
1995 Tucson	AAA Hou	51	0	0	40	66	285	74	32	30	5	1	2	1	19	2	51	8	0	3	3	.500	0	19	4.09
1996 Tucson	AAA Hou	32	0	0	20	39	166	32	17	9	3	3	0	0	18	4	36	4	1	3	3	.500	0	7	2.08
1997 New Orleans	AAA Hou	7	0	0	4	9.1	43	11	9	6	1	0	1	0	3	1	7	1	0	1	1	.500	0	0	5.79
Jackson	AA Hou	37	0	0	25	43	196	46	20	15	1	4	1	1	19	2	40	0	1	3	4	.429	0	9	3.14
1996 Houston	NL	16	0	0	4	24.1	122	33	23	16	1	1	0	1	13	3	16	1	1	0	1	.000	0	0	5.92
9 Min. YEARS		327	23	1	160	554.1	2415	542	291	228	43	28	19	14	249	25	412	57	5	39	33	.542	0	52	3.70

J.D. Smart

Pitches: Right Bats: Right Pos: P Ht: 6'2" Wt: 185 Born: 11/12/73 Age: 24

Year Team	Lg Org	G	GS	CG	GF	IP	BFP	H	R	ER	HR	SH	SF	HB	TBB	IBB	SO	WP	Bk	W	L	Pct.	ShO	Sv	ERA
1995 Expos	R Mon	2	2	0	0	10.2	43	10	2	2	0	0	1	2	1	0	6	0	0	2	0	1.000	0	0	1.69
Vermont	A- Mon	5	5	0	0	27.2	118	29	9	7	1	1	3	3	7	0	21	0	0	0	1	.000	0	0	2.28
1996 Delmarva	A Mon	25	25	3	0	156.2	655	155	75	59	14	2	7	10	31	0	109	8	0	9	8	.529	2	0	3.39
1997 Wst Plm Bch	A+ Mon	17	13	1	1	102	422	105	45	37	10	2	3	2	21	0	65	3	0	5	4	.556	0	1	3.26
Harrisburg	AA Mon	12	12	0	0	70.2	308	75	34	29	7	6	3	3	24	0	43	3	0	6	3	.667	0	0	3.69
3 Min. YEARS		61	57	4	1	367.2	1546	374	165	134	32	11	17	20	84	0	244	14	0	22	16	.579	2	1	3.28

Steve Smetana

Pitches: Left Bats: Left Pos: P Ht: 6'0" Wt: 205 Born: 4/14/73 Age: 25

Year Team	Lg Org	G	GS	CG	GF	IP	BFP	H	R	ER	HR	SH	SF	HB	TBB	IBB	SO	WP	Bk	W	L	Pct.	ShO	Sv	ERA
1996 Lowell	A- Bos	19	0	0	9	31	116	22	5	5	1	2	1	0	3	0	33	1	0	5	0	1.000	0	2	1.45
1997 Michigan	A Bos	18	0	0	6	30.2	132	23	16	8	1	1	3	1	12	0	29	2	0	2	1	.667	0	2	2.35
Trenton	AA Bos	18	0	0	10	21.1	97	25	9	7	2	2	1	2	7	1	16	1	0	1	2	.333	0	3	2.95
Sarasota	A+ Bos	10	1	0	3	21	90	25	12	11	1	0	1	0	7	0	20	2	0	0	1	.000	0	0	4.71
2 Min. YEARS		65	1	0	28	104	435	95	42	31	5	5	6	3	29	1	98	6	0	8	4	.667	0	7	2.68

Bobby Smith

Bats: Right Throws: Right Pos: SS Ht: 6'3" Wt: 190 Born: 4/10/74 Age: 24

Year Team	Lg Org	G	AB	H	2B	3B	HR	TB	R	RBI	TBB	IBB	SO	HBP	SH	SF	SB	CS	SB%	GDP	Avg	OBP	SLG
1992 Braves	R Atl	57	217	51	9	1	3	71	31	28	17	1	55	3	0	2	5	6	.45	5	.235	.297	.327
1993 Macon	A Atl	108	384	94	16	7	4	136	53	38	23	1	81	5	8	0	12	8	.60	1	.245	.296	.354
1994 Durham	A+ Atl	127	478	127	27	2	12	194	49	71	41	1	112	4	1	0	18	7	.72	19	.266	.329	.406
1995 Greenville	AA Atl	127	444	116	27	3	14	191	75	58	40	2	109	7	4	1	12	6	.67	12	.261	.331	.430
1996 Richmond	AAA Atl	124	445	114	27	0	8	165	49	58	32	0	114	4	2	3	15	9	.63	12	.256	.310	.371
1997 Richmond	AAA Atl	100	357	88	10	2	12	138	47	47	44	2	109	7	2	1	6	5	.55	4	.246	.340	.387
6 Min. YEARS		643	2325	590	116	15	53	895	304	300	197	7	580	30	17	7	68	41	.62	53	.254	.319	.385

Brian Smith

Pitches: Right Bats: Right Pos: P Ht: 5'11" Wt: 185 Born: 7/19/72 Age: 25

Year Team	Lg Org	G	GS	CG	GF	IP	BFP	H	R	ER	HR	SH	SF	HB	TBB	IBB	SO	WP	Bk	W	L	Pct.	ShO	Sv	ERA
1994 Medicne Hat	R+ Tor	20	5	0	11	64	268	58	36	24	3	2	4	5	20	0	53	6	3	5	4	.556	0	4	3.38
1995 Hagerstown	A Tor	47	0	0	36	104	402	77	18	10	1	5	0	5	16	1	101	2	2	9	1	.900	0	21	0.87
1996 Knoxville	AA Tor	54	0	0	43	75.2	333	76	42	32	7	6	3	4	31	6	58	4	0	3	5	.375	0	16	3.81
1997 Knoxville	AA Tor	1	0	0	0	1	4	0	0	0	0	0	0	0	1	0	1	0	0	0	0	.000	0	0	0.00
Syracuse	AAA Tor	31	21	0	2	137.1	619	169	89	82	12	2	6	8	51	1	73	4	3	7	11	.389	0	0	5.37
4 Min. YEARS		153	26	0	92	382	1626	380	185	148	23	15	13	22	119	8	286	16	8	24	21	.533	0	41	3.49

Bubba Smith

Bats: Right Throws: Right Pos: 1B-DH Ht: 6'2" Wt: 225 Born: 12/18/69 Age: 28

Year Team	Lg Org	G	AB	H	2B	3B	HR	TB	R	RBI	TBB	IBB	SO	HBP	SH	SF	SB	CS	SB%	GDP	Avg	OBP	SLG
1991 Bellingham	A- Sea	66	253	66	14	2	10	114	28	43	13	1	47	2	0	2	0	2	.00	9	.261	.300	.451

BATTING

Year Team	Lg Org	G	AB	H	2B	3B	HR	TB	R	RBI	TBB	IBB	SO	HBP	SH	SF	SB	CS	SB%	GDP	Avg	OBP	SLG
1992 Peninsula	A+ Sea	137	482	126	22	1	32	246	70	93	65	7	138	5	0	5	4	10	.29	13	.261	.352	.510
1993 Jacksnville	AA Sea	37	137	30	8	0	6	56	12	21	7	0	52	2	0	1	0	3	.00	1	.219	.265	.409
Riverside	A+ Cin	5	19	8	3	0	0	11	5	3	7	0	3	0	0	0	0	0	.00	1	.421	.577	.579
Winston-Sal	A+ Cin	92	342	103	16	0	27	200	55	81	35	1	109	7	0	4	2	0	1.00	8	.301	.374	.585
1994 Chattanooga	AA Cin	4	9	0	0	0	0	0	0	0	0	0	7	0	0	0	0	0	.00	0	.000	.000	.000
Chston-WV	A Cin	100	354	83	26	1	15	156	38	59	20	1	113	5	1	2	1	2	.33	9	.234	.283	.441
1995 Ft. Myers	A+ Min	60	176	58	15	0	13	112	27	51	16	4	38	0	0	3	1	2	.33	8	.330	.379	.636
Hardware City	AA Min	42	148	36	11	0	6	65	20	21	6	1	41	0	0	1	0	0	.00	5	.243	.271	.439
1996 Tulsa	AA Tex	134	513	150	28	0	32	274	82	94	48	5	121	5	0	3	0	1	.00	10	.292	.357	.534
1997 Okla City	AAA Tex	140	514	131	30	1	27	244	60	94	53	2	139	4	0	4	2	2	.50	16	.255	.327	.475
7 Min. YEARS		817	2947	791	173	5	168	1478	397	560	270	22	808	30	1	25	10	22	.31	80	.268	.333	.502

Cam Smith

Pitches: Right **Bats:** Right **Pos:** P **Ht:** 6'3" **Wt:** 190 **Born:** 9/20/73 **Age:** 24

HOW MUCH HE PITCHED — WHAT HE GAVE UP — THE RESULTS

Year Team	Lg Org	G	GS	CG	GF	IP	BFP	H	R	ER	HR	SH	SF	HB	TBB	IBB	SO	WP	Bk	W	L	Pct.	ShO	Sv	ERA
1993 Bristol	R+ Det	9	7	1	2	37.2	162	25	22	15	5	0	0	6	22	0	33	2	3	3	1	.750	0	0	3.58
Niagara Fal	A- Det	2	2	0	0	5	31	12	11	10	0	0	2	0	6	0	2	0	0	0	0	.000	0	0	18.00
1994 Fayettevlle	A Det	26	26	1	0	133.2	619	133	100	90	10	6	5	18	86	0	128	17	1	5	13	.278	0	0	6.06
1995 Fayettevlle	A Det	29	29	2	0	149	652	110	75	63	6	3	3	18	87	0	166	21	1	13	8	.619	2	0	3.81
1996 Lakeland	A+ Det	22	21	0	1	113.2	500	93	64	58	10	1	5	7	71	0	114	8	0	5	8	.385	0	0	4.59
1997 Mobile	AA SD	26	15	0	4	79.1	390	85	70	62	5	1	1	3	73	0	88	14	0	3	5	.375	0	1	7.03
5 Min. YEARS		114	100	4	5	518.1	2354	458	342	298	36	11	16	52	345	0	529	64	5	29	35	.453	2	1	5.17

Chuck Smith

Pitches: Right **Bats:** Right **Pos:** P **Ht:** 6'1" **Wt:** 175 **Born:** 10/21/69 **Age:** 28

HOW MUCH HE PITCHED — WHAT HE GAVE UP — THE RESULTS

Year Team	Lg Org	G	GS	CG	GF	IP	BFP	H	R	ER	HR	SH	SF	HB	TBB	IBB	SO	WP	Bk	W	L	Pct.	ShO	Sv	ERA
1991 Astros	R Hou	15	7	1	2	59.1	272	56	36	23	2	3	0	7	37	0	64	7	5	4	3	.571	0	0	3.49
1992 Asheville	A Hou	28	20	1	3	132	596	128	93	76	14	5	4	4	78	1	117	4	1	9	9	.500	0	0	5.18
1993 Quad City	A Hou	22	17	2	3	110.2	488	109	73	57	16	3	2	6	52	0	103	7	4	7	5	.583	0	0	4.64
1994 Jackson	AA Hou	2	0	0	0	6	30	6	6	3	0	2	0	0	5	0	7	0	1	0	0	.000	0	0	4.50
Osceola	A+ Hou	35	2	0	11	84.2	376	73	41	35	2	2	2	2	49	3	60	7	3	4	4	.500	0	0	3.72
1995 South Bend	A ChA	26	25	4	1	167	688	128	70	50	8	7	2	13	61	0	145	21	11	10	10	.500	2	0	2.69
1996 Pr William	A+ ChA	20	20	2	0	123.1	545	125	65	55	7	3	2	10	49	1	99	13	1	6	6	.500	1	0	4.01
Birmingham	AA ChA	7	3	0	2	30.2	124	25	11	9	1	0	0	1	15	2	30	0	1	2	1	.667	0	1	2.64
Nashville	AAA ChA	1	0	0	0	0.2	5	2	2	2	0	0	0	0	1	0	1	0	0	0	0	.000	0	0	27.00
1997 Birmingham	AA ChA	25	1	0	6	62.2	280	63	35	22	4	1	2	5	27	5	57	8	3	2	2	.500	0	0	3.16
Nashville	AAA ChA	20	1	0	12	31.2	156	39	33	31	8	2	3	2	23	2	29	8	2	0	3	.000	0	0	8.81
7 Min. YEARS		201	95	10	40	808.2	3560	754	465	363	62	28	17	50	397	14	712	75	38	44	43	.506	3	2	4.04

Danny Smith

Pitches: Left **Bats:** Left **Pos:** P **Ht:** 6'5" **Wt:** 205 **Born:** 4/20/69 **Age:** 29

HOW MUCH HE PITCHED — WHAT HE GAVE UP — THE RESULTS

Year Team	Lg Org	G	GS	CG	GF	IP	BFP	H	R	ER	HR	SH	SF	HB	TBB	IBB	SO	WP	Bk	W	L	Pct.	ShO	Sv	ERA
1990 Butte	R+ Tex	5	5	0	0	24.2	102	23	10	10	3	2	0	2	6	0	27	3	1	2	0	1.000	0	0	3.65
Tulsa	AA Tex	7	7	0	0	38.1	151	27	16	16	2	0	3	0	16	0	32	0	0	3	2	.600	0	0	3.76
1991 Okla City	AAA Tex	28	27	3	1	151.2	713	195	114	93	10	6	8	4	75	1	85	5	5	4	17	.190	0	0	5.52
1992 Tulsa	AA Tex	24	23	4	0	146.1	571	110	48	41	4	9	3	6	34	0	122	3	3	11	7	.611	3	0	2.52
1993 Charlotte	A+ Tex	1	1	0	0	7	24	3	0	0	0	0	0	0	0	0	5	1	0	1	0	1.000	0	0	0.00
Okla City	AAA Tex	3	3	0	0	15.1	66	16	11	8	2	1	1	1	5	0	12	0	0	1	2	.333	0	0	4.70
1994 Charlotte	A+ Tex	2	0	0	0	3.2	13	2	1	1	0	1	0	0	1	0	3	0	0	0	0	.000	0	0	0.00
Okla City	AAA Tex	10	2	0	3	25.1	110	27	9	8	2	0	2	2	9	0	15	0	0	2	1	.667	0	2	2.84
1996 Okla City	AAA Tex	5	5	0	0	15	78	27	19	15	4	0	1	1	7	0	12	1	0	0	2	.000	0	0	9.00
Charlotte	A+ Tex	5	5	0	0	23	92	21	7	7	1	0	0	0	8	0	16	1	1	0	1	.000	0	0	2.74
Tulsa	AA Tex	9	9	0	0	50.1	227	53	27	24	6	3	3	1	21	0	29	0	0	2	3	.400	0	0	4.29
1997 Tulsa	AA Tex	5	5	0	0	29.2	128	25	18	12	3	0	2	0	15	0	27	1	0	1	1	.500	0	0	3.64
Okla City	AAA Tex	23	23	3	0	129.1	574	154	88	81	11	2	5	5	42	0	67	3	1	3	14	.176	1	0	5.64
1992 Texas	AL	4	2	0	1	14.1	67	18	8	8	1	2	1	0	8	1	5	0	0	0	3	.000	0	0	5.02
1994 Texas	AL	13	0	0	2	14.2	76	18	11	7	2	0	0	0	12	0	9	2	0	1	2	.333	0	0	4.30
7 Min. YEARS		127	115	10	4	659.2	2849	683	367	315	48	24	29	22	240	1	452	18	11	30	50	.375	4	2	4.30
2 Maj. YEARS		17	2	0	3	29	143	36	19	15	3	2	1	0	20	1	14	2	0	1	5	.167	0	0	4.66

Demond Smith

Bats: Both **Throws:** Right **Pos:** OF **Ht:** 5'11" **Wt:** 170 **Born:** 11/6/72 **Age:** 25

BATTING

Year Team	Lg Org	G	AB	H	2B	3B	HR	TB	R	RBI	TBB	IBB	SO	HBP	SH	SF	SB	CS	SB%	GDP	Avg	OBP	SLG
1990 Mets	R NYN	46	153	40	9	2	1	56	19	7	20	0	34	0	1	2	16	10	.62	2	.261	.343	.366
1991 Kingsport	R+ NYN	35	116	29	3	4	1	43	28	12	12	0	25	6	0	1	16	7	.70	0	.250	.348	.371
1992 Pittsfield	A- NYN	66	233	58	10	4	1	79	39	24	23	0	42	7	1	3	21	15	.58	0	.249	.331	.339
1993 Capital Cty	A NYN	1	2	0	0	0	0	0	0	0	1	0	1	0	0	0	2	0	1.00	0	.000	.333	.000
1994 Lk Elsinore	A+ Ana	12	26	3	0	1	0	5	1	1	4	0	8	0	0	0	0	4	.00	1	.115	.233	.192
Boise	A- Ana	71	279	78	9	7	5	116	60	45	43	2	57	2	7	4	26	9	.74	0	.280	.375	.416
1995 Cedar Rapds	A Ana	79	317	108	25	7	2	168	64	41	32	2	61	6	5	1	37	12	.76	3	.341	.410	.530
Lk Elsinore	A+ Ana	34	148	52	8	2	7	85	32	26	11	0	36	2	0	1	14	3	.82	1	.351	.401	.574
W Michigan	A Oak	8	32	10	1	1	2	19	6	3	2	1	8	1	1	0	3	2	.60	0	.313	.371	.594
1996 Huntsville	AA Oak	123	447	116	17	14	9	188	75	62	55	1	89	11	8	5	30	15	.67	6	.260	.351	.421

Year Team	Lg Org	G	AB	H	2B	3B	HR	TB	R	RBI	TBB	IBB	SO	HBP	SH	SF	SB	CS	SB%	GDP	Avg	OBP	SLG
									BATTING									BASERUNNING			PERCENTAGES		
Edmonton	AAA Oak	2	3	1	0	0	0	1	0	0	0	0	2	0	0	0	0	0	.00	0	.333	.333	.333
1997 Edmonton	AAA Oak	42	151	33	3	4	5	59	22	22	23	0	31	3	1	4	10	3	.77	3	.219	.326	.391
Huntsville	AA Oak	87	323	90	20	6	8	146	79	39	65	0	76	4	3	2	31	9	.78	3	.279	.404	.452
8 Min. YEARS		606	2230	618	105	52	46	965	425	282	291	6	469	42	28	23	206	89	.70	19	.277	.368	.433

Hut Smith

Pitches: Right Bats: Both Pos: P   Ht: 6'3" Wt: 195 Born: 6/8/73 Age: 25

Year Team	Lg Org	G	GS	CG	GF	IP	BFP	H	R	ER	HR	SH	SF	HB	TBB	IBB	SO	WP	Bk	W	L	Pct.	ShO	Sv	ERA
		HOW MUCH HE PITCHED						WHAT HE GAVE UP												THE RESULTS					
1992 Orioles	R Bal	11	10	2	1	60	241	37	20	13	0	1	3	7	18	0	54	8	3	4	3	.571	2	0	1.95
1993 Orioles	R Bal	3	0	0	2	4	13	0	0	0	0	0	0	1	1	0	5	0	0	0	0	.000	0	1	0.00
1994 Albany	A Bal	29	12	2	10	121	516	127	67	51	13	2	1	11	32	0	96	7	1	3	2	.471	0	1	3.79
1995 Frederick	A+ Bal	20	2	0	7	32	162	39	23	23	4	2	1	4	31	1	28	7	1	3	2	.600	0	2	6.47
High Desert	A+ Bal	11	9	0	1	46.1	216	58	54	47	10	2	5	8	15	0	38	4	1	3	4	.429	0	0	9.13
1996 High Desert	A+ Bal	10	7	1	0	50.1	216	59	34	30	7	1	1	3	16	0	34	6	3	3	4	.429	0	0	5.36
1997 Frederick	A+ Bal	16	11	0	1	79	323	63	42	34	7	2	2	3	27	0	77	3	1	4	1	.800	0	1	3.87
Bowie	AA Bal	14	13	0	1	81	347	90	45	38	14	4	2	7	22	1	46	2	0	5	4	.556	0	0	4.22
6 Min. YEARS		114	64	5	23	473.2	2034	473	285	236	55	14	15	43	162	2	378	37	10	30	27	.526	2	5	4.48

Ira Smith

Bats: Right Throws: Right Pos: OF-DH   Ht: 5'11" Wt: 185 Born: 8/4/67 Age: 30

Year Team	Lg Org	G	AB	H	2B	3B	HR	TB	R	RBI	TBB	IBB	SO	HBP	SH	SF	SB	CS	SB%	GDP	Avg	OBP	SLG
									BATTING									BASERUNNING			PERCENTAGES		
1990 Great Falls	R+ LA	50	142	37	7	3	1	53	31	28	25	0	32	3	2	3	8	6	.57	3	.261	.376	.373
1991 Vero Beach	A+ LA	52	176	57	5	3	1	71	27	24	18	0	30	2	0	0	15	3	.83	7	.324	.393	.403
1992 Bakersfield	A+ LA	118	413	119	17	4	7	165	79	45	48	3	56	6	8	6	26	14	.65	12	.288	.366	.400
San Antonio	AA LA	6	11	4	0	1	0	6	3	1	1	0	2	0	0	0	0	0	.00	0	.364	.417	.545
1993 Rancho Cuca	A+ SD	92	347	120	30	6	7	183	71	47	55	1	41	5	2	3	32	16	.67	1	.346	.439	.527
Wichita	AA SD	13	39	9	0	1	0	11	7	4	4	0	9	0	1	0	0	2	.00	2	.231	.302	.282
1994 Wichita	AA SD	107	358	115	17	6	7	165	58	41	53	2	59	3	3	6	6	12	.33	5	.321	.407	.461
1995 Memphis	AA SD	64	238	72	13	3	5	106	40	36	23	0	32	2	0	3	11	4	.73	6	.303	.365	.445
Las Vegas	AAA SD	59	209	68	19	5	3	106	39	22	13	0	25	2	4	1	5	4	.56	3	.325	.369	.507
1996 Las Vegas	AAA SD	72	252	61	16	1	5	94	37	25	20	0	27	1	5	1	3	3	.50	5	.242	.299	.373
1997 Jacksnville	AA Det	53	172	53	14	2	5	86	29	20	35	0	30	1	0	0	1	1	.50	4	.308	.428	.500
Toledo	AAA Det	39	148	36	8	0	1	47	19	13	11	0	29	2	2	0	1	0	.00	1	.243	.304	.318
8 Min. YEARS		725	2505	751	146	35	42	1093	440	306	306	6	372	27	27	23	107	66	.62	61	.300	.379	.436

Jeff Smith

Bats: Left Throws: Right Pos: C   Ht: 6'3" Wt: 211 Born: 6/17/74 Age: 24

Year Team	Lg Org	G	AB	H	2B	3B	HR	TB	R	RBI	TBB	IBB	SO	HBP	SH	SF	SB	CS	SB%	GDP	Avg	OBP	SLG
									BATTING									BASERUNNING			PERCENTAGES		
1996 Ft. Wayne	A Min	63	208	49	6	0	2	61	20	26	22	0	32	0	1	2	2	1	.67	4	.236	.306	.293
1997 Ft. Myers	A+ Min	49	121	34	5	0	4	51	17	26	12	0	18	0	0	6	0	2	.00	4	.281	.331	.421
New Britain	AA Min	5	18	4	1	0	0	5	1	3	2	0	4	0	0	0	0	0	.00	0	.222	.300	.278
Salt Lake	AAA Min	7	12	3	2	0	0	5	2	2	1	0	3	0	0	0	0	0	.00	0	.250	.308	.417
2 Min. YEARS		124	359	90	14	0	6	122	40	57	37	0	57	0	1	8	2	3	.40	8	.251	.314	.340

Matt Smith

Bats: Left Throws: Left Pos: 1B   Ht: 6'4" Wt: 215 Born: 6/2/76 Age: 22

Year Team	Lg Org	G	AB	H	2B	3B	HR	TB	R	RBI	TBB	IBB	SO	HBP	SH	SF	SB	CS	SB%	GDP	Avg	OBP	SLG
									BATTING									BASERUNNING			PERCENTAGES		
1994 Royals	R KC	32	101	24	5	3	1	38	13	12	12	2	26	1	0	0	0	1	1.00	1	.238	.325	.376
1995 Springfield	A KC	117	412	93	18	1	6	131	49	46	24	4	96	1	1	1	8	5	.62	11	.226	.269	.318
1996 Wilmington	A+ KC	125	451	112	17	2	5	148	48	59	42	5	110	5	1	7	3	4	.43	6	.248	.315	.328
1997 Wichita	AA KC	52	176	40	7	1	1	52	19	15	13	2	37	1	1	1	0	1	1.00	1	.227	.283	.295
Lansing	A KC	62	227	63	4	3	4	85	33	33	21	1	45	0	0	2	4	2	.67	2	.278	.336	.374
4 Min. YEARS		388	1367	332	51	10	17	454	162	165	112	14	314	8	3	11	17	11	.61	21	.243	.302	.332

Roy Smith

Pitches: Right Bats: Right Pos: P   Ht: 6'7" Wt: 210 Born: 5/18/76 Age: 22

Year Team	Lg Org	G	GS	CG	GF	IP	BFP	H	R	ER	HR	SH	SF	HB	TBB	IBB	SO	WP	Bk	W	L	Pct.	ShO	Sv	ERA
		HOW MUCH HE PITCHED						WHAT HE GAVE UP												THE RESULTS					
1994 Mariners	R Sea	11	5	0	1	45	164	30	9	8	2	1	1	1	4	0	35	2	0	3	1	.750	0	0	1.60
1995 Wisconsin	A Sea	27	27	1	0	149	669	179	100	89	9	5	2	3	54	2	109	10	2	7	14	.333	0	0	5.38
1996 Wisconsin	A Sea	27	27	0	0	146	679	164	113	83	9	6	4	8	73	3	99	11	2	6	13	.316	0	0	5.12
1997 Memphis	AA Sea	4	0	0	3	4.1	20	6	5	5	0	1	0	1	0	0	6	1	0	0	0	.000	0	0	10.38
Wisconsin	A Sea	18	11	0	4	66	304	81	50	41	3	1	2	2	31	0	38	14	2	3	4	.429	0	0	5.59
4 Min. YEARS		87	70	1	8	410.1	1836	460	277	226	23	13	10	14	163	5	287	38	6	19	32	.373	0	0	4.96

Ryan Smith

Pitches: Right Bats: Right Pos: P   Ht: 6'3" Wt: 215 Born: 11/11/71 Age: 26

Year Team	Lg Org	G	GS	CG	GF	IP	BFP	H	R	ER	HR	SH	SF	HB	TBB	IBB	SO	WP	Bk	W	L	Pct.	ShO	Sv	ERA
		HOW MUCH HE PITCHED						WHAT HE GAVE UP												THE RESULTS					
1991 Mariners	R Sea	13	13	2	0	75	350	87	59	38	3	4	1	11	42	0	51	10	0	4	6	.400	0	0	4.56

Year Team	Lg Org	G	GS	CG	GF	IP	BFP	H	R	ER	HR	SH	SF	HB	TBB	IBB	SO	WP	Bk	W	L	Pct.	ShO	Sv	ERA
		HOW MUCH HE PITCHED						**WHAT HE GAVE UP**												**THE RESULTS**					
1992 Bellingham	A- Sea	9	9	0	0	49	215	48	26	18	2	0	3	5	19	0	34	5	0	4	3	.571	0	0	3.31
1994 Appleton	A Sea	21	21	5	0	144.1	589	129	54	45	10	4	5	12	28	0	82	7	0	10	6	.625	1	0	2.81
1995 Riverside	A+ Sea	23	23	2	0	141.2	609	142	68	49	7	7	5	10	50	1	108	5	3	10	7	.588	1	0	3.11
1996 Port City	AA Sea	50	0	0	22	97.2	420	92	42	34	5	10	4	9	37	5	65	6	3	6	9	.400	0	2	3.13
1997 Tacoma	AAA Sea	1	1	0	0	5	17	4	0	0	0	0	0	0	1	0	2	0	0	1	0	1.000	0	0	0.00
Memphis	AA Sea	41	4	0	9	80.1	356	97	53	50	6	3	5	4	22	1	50	7	0	6	6	.333	0	1	5.60
6 Min. YEARS		158	71	9	31	593	2556	599	302	234	33	28	23	51	199	7	392	40	6	38	37	.507	2	3	3.55

Scott Smith

Bats: Right **Throws:** Right **Pos:** OF   **Ht:** 6'3" **Wt:** 215 **Born:** 10/14/71 **Age:** 26

Year Team	Lg Org	G	AB	H	2B	3B	HR	TB	R	RBI	TBB	IBB	SO	HBP	SH	SF	SB	CS	SB%	GDP	Avg	OBP	SLG
		BATTING															**BASERUNNING**				**PERCENTAGES**		
1994 Appleton	A Sea	60	178	38	7	0	2	51	26	13	23	0	46	4	1	1	3	4	.43	2	.213	.316	.287
1995 Riverside	A+ Sea	56	179	42	6	0	2	54	28	20	21	1	60	0	0	0	2	1	.67	7	.235	.315	.302
Wisconsin	A Sea	34	107	35	12	1	3	58	13	17	11	0	21	2	1	1	0	1	.00	7	.327	.397	.542
1996 Lancaster	A+ Sea	61	252	75	19	0	10	124	52	52	16	0	74	5	0	3	9	2	.82	5	.298	.348	.492
Wisconsin	A Sea	67	241	80	11	4	10	129	43	49	24	1	74	8	2	2	11	7	.61	1	.332	.407	.535
1997 Memphis	AA Sea	123	453	113	19	2	14	178	58	67	44	1	132	5	0	4	4	7	.36	12	.249	.320	.393
4 Min. YEARS		401	1410	383	74	7	41	594	220	218	139	3	407	24	4	11	29	22	.57	34	.272	.345	.421

Sloan Smith

Bats: Both **Throws:** Right **Pos:** OF   **Ht:** 6'4" **Wt:** 215 **Born:** 11/29/72 **Age:** 25

Year Team	Lg Org	G	AB	H	2B	3B	HR	TB	R	RBI	TBB	IBB	SO	HBP	SH	SF	SB	CS	SB%	GDP	Avg	OBP	SLG
		BATTING															**BASERUNNING**				**PERCENTAGES**		
1993 Oneonta	A- NYA	34	116	23	5	1	1	33	14	10	15	0	33	6	3	1	3	2	.60	1	.198	.319	.284
1994 Oneonta	A- NYA	38	138	34	5	5	0	49	24	16	25	0	41	2	1	0	2	1	.67	1	.246	.370	.355
Greensboro	A NYA	79	269	51	4	3	5	76	35	26	42	2	98	2	3	3	13	5	.72	4	.190	.301	.283
Albany-Colo	AA NYA	7	23	4	2	1	0	8	4	5	3	0	6	0	0	0	0	0	.00	1	.174	.269	.348
1995 Tampa	A+ NYA	124	412	107	23	1	13	171	61	64	74	3	136	4	1	3	6	8	.43	8	.260	.375	.415
1996 Norwich	AA NYA	60	202	44	10	2	2	64	27	20	30	2	96	0	3	0	4	1	.80	0	.218	.319	.317
Tampa	A+ NYA	61	194	43	10	1	4	67	25	21	46	2	60	0	1	2	5	6	.45	6	.222	.368	.345
1997 Norwich	AA NYA	2	5	1	0	0	0	1	1	1	2	0	2	0	1	0	0	0	.00	0	.200	.429	.200
Tampa	A+ NYA	65	186	41	9	1	4	64	32	23	33	5	64	2	0	4	2	4	.33	2	.220	.338	.344
5 Min. YEARS		470	1545	348	68	15	29	533	223	186	270	14	536	16	13	13	35	27	.56	23	.225	.344	.345

Toby Smith

Pitches: Right **Bats:** Right **Pos:** P   **Ht:** 6'6" **Wt:** 225 **Born:** 11/16/71 **Age:** 26

Year Team	Lg Org	G	GS	CG	GF	IP	BFP	H	R	ER	HR	SH	SF	HB	TBB	IBB	SO	WP	Bk	W	L	Pct.	ShO	Sv	ERA
		HOW MUCH HE PITCHED						**WHAT HE GAVE UP**												**THE RESULTS**					
1993 Eugene	A- KC	14	0	0	8	23	90	14	8	6	1	2	0	1	7	0	31	0	1	1	1	.500	0	4	2.35
1994 Rockford	A KC	29	16	0	12	121	489	104	50	44	8	3	3	4	31	1	91	14	2	11	9	.550	0	4	3.27
1995 Wilmington	A+ KC	30	7	0	13	79	320	67	32	27	9	2	1	3	20	2	65	6	2	5	7	.417	0	4	3.08
1996 Wichita	AA KC	42	0	0	30	52.1	221	46	25	24	7	4	2	2	19	4	44	7	0	4	2	.667	0	8	4.13
1997 Omaha	AAA KC	17	0	0	12	20.2	96	24	19	18	6	1	1	2	15	2	11	3	1	1	3	.250	0	3	7.84
Wichita	AA KC	8	8	0	0	44	195	49	30	24	7	1	2	0	11	0	29	4	2	2	3	.400	0	0	4.91
5 Min. YEARS		140	31	0	75	340	1411	304	164	143	38	13	9	12	103	9	271	34	8	24	25	.490	0	23	3.79

Travis Smith

Pitches: Right **Bats:** Right **Pos:** P   **Ht:** 5'10" **Wt:** 170 **Born:** 11/7/72 **Age:** 25

Year Team	Lg Org	G	GS	CG	GF	IP	BFP	H	R	ER	HR	SH	SF	HB	TBB	IBB	SO	WP	Bk	W	L	Pct.	ShO	Sv	ERA
		HOW MUCH HE PITCHED						**WHAT HE GAVE UP**												**THE RESULTS**					
1995 Helena	R+ Mil	20	7	0	11	56	224	41	16	15	4	0	0	7	19	0	63	4	4	4	2	.667	0	5	2.41
1996 Stockton	A+ Mil	14	6	0	3	58.2	241	56	17	12	4	1	0	4	21	0	48	2	4	6	1	.857	0	1	1.84
El Paso	AA Mil	17	17	3	0	107.2	478	119	56	50	6	4	5	6	39	0	68	2	0	7	4	.636	1	0	4.18
1997 El Paso	AA Mil	28	28	5	0	184.1	805	210	106	85	12	7	5	7	58	2	107	7	3	16	3	.842	1	0	4.15
3 Min. YEARS		79	58	8	14	406.2	1748	426	195	162	26	12	10	24	137	2	286	15	9	33	10	.767	2	6	3.59

John Snyder

Pitches: Right **Bats:** Right **Pos:** P   **Ht:** 6'3" **Wt:** 185 **Born:** 8/16/74 **Age:** 23

Year Team	Lg Org	G	GS	CG	GF	IP	BFP	H	R	ER	HR	SH	SF	HB	TBB	IBB	SO	WP	Bk	W	L	Pct.	ShO	Sv	ERA
		HOW MUCH HE PITCHED						**WHAT HE GAVE UP**												**THE RESULTS**					
1992 Angels	R Ana	15	0	0	7	44	195	40	27	16	0	2	5	3	16	1	38	1	4	2	4	.333	0	3	3.27
1993 Cedar Rapds	A Ana	21	16	1	0	99	467	126	88	65	13	7	5	8	39	1	79	6	4	5	6	.455	1	0	5.91
1994 Lk Elsinore	A+ Ana	26	26	2	0	159	698	181	101	79	16	5	5	6	56	0	108	11	2	10	11	.476	0	0	4.47
1995 Midland	AA Ana	21	21	4	0	133.1	591	158	93	85	12	3	6	10	48	1	81	7	3	8	9	.471	0	0	5.74
Birmingham	AA ChA	5	4	0	0	20.1	87	24	16	15	6	0	1	2	6	0	13	1	0	1	0	1.000	0	0	6.64
1996 White Sox	R ChA	4	4	0	0	16.1	58	5	3	3	1	1	0	0	4	0	23	0	0	1	0	1.000	0	0	1.65
Birmingham	AA ChA	9	9	0	0	54	236	59	35	29	10	2	2	1	16	1	58	4	3	3	5	.375	0	0	4.83
1997 Birmingham	AA ChA	20	20	2	0	114.1	510	130	76	59	9	1	3	6	43	0	90	6	2	7	8	.467	1	0	4.64
6 Min. YEARS		121	100	9	7	640.1	2842	723	439	351	67	21	27	36	228	4	490	36	18	37	43	.463	2	3	4.93

Matt Snyder

Pitches: Right Bats: Right Pos: P Ht: 5'11" Wt: 190 Born: 7/7/74 Age: 23

Year Team	Lg Org	G	GS	CG	GF	IP	BFP	H	R	ER	HR	SH	SF	HB	TBB	IBB	SO	WP	Bk	W	L	Pct.	ShO	Sv	ERA
1995 Bluefield	R+ Bal	17	0	0	15	34.2	150	35	9	4	1	0	0	3	13	0	46	1	0	0	0	.000	0	8	1.04
1996 High Desert	A+ Bal	58	0	0	49	72	317	60	34	30	6	5	2	1	38	2	93	9	1	6	2	.750	0	20	3.75
1997 Bowie	AA Bal	67	0	0	45	80	366	89	48	37	11	8	4	4	42	5	68	10	0	7	5	.583	0	19	4.16
3 Min. YEARS		142	0	0	109	186.2	833	184	91	71	18	13	6	8	93	7	207	20	1	13	7	.650	0	47	3.42

Steve Soderstrom

Pitches: Right Bats: Right Pos: P Ht: 6' 3" Wt: 205 Born: 4/3/72 Age: 26

Year Team	Lg Org	G	GS	CG	GF	IP	BFP	H	R	ER	HR	SH	SF	HB	TBB	IBB	SO	WP	Bk	W	L	Pct.	ShO	Sv	ERA
1994 San Jose	A+ SF	8	8	0	0	40.2	179	34	20	19	2	2	1	4	26	0	40	4	1	2	3	.400	0	0	4.20
1995 Shreveport	AA SF	22	22	0	0	116	508	106	53	44	6	5	2	10	51	0	91	12	2	9	5	.643	0	0	3.41
1996 Phoenix	AAA SF	29	29	0	0	171.1	728	178	94	84	13	8	4	7	58	1	80	9	5	7	8	.467	0	0	4.41
1997 Phoenix	AAA SF	31	15	0	8	105.2	498	141	81	76	12	2	2	6	52	1	78	10	1	4	8	.333	0	1	6.47
1996 San Francisco	NL	3	3	0	0	13.2	63	16	11	8	1	0	2	2	6	0	9	0	0	2	0	1.000	0	0	5.27
4 Min. YEARS		90	74	0	8	433.2	1913	459	248	223	33	17	9	27	187	2	289	35	9	22	24	.478	0	1	4.63

Fausto Solano

Bats: Right Throws: Right Pos: SS Ht: 5'9" Wt: 144 Born: 6/19/74 Age: 24

Year Team	Lg Org	G	AB	H	2B	3B	HR	TB	R	RBI	TBB	IBB	SO	HBP	SH	SF	SB	CS	SB%	GDP	Avg	OBP	SLG
1994 St. Cathrns	A- Tor	73	288	77	11	3	2	100	49	19	32	0	47	1	6	1	19	10	.66	4	.267	.342	.347
1995 Dunedin	A+ Tor	41	144	30	5	2	1	42	19	10	17	0	30	1	5	0	3	2	.60	4	.208	.296	.292
Blue Jays	R Tor	11	44	13	5	0	2	24	12	7	3	0	6	2	3	1	2	1	.67	4	.295	.360	.545
St. Cathrns	A- Tor	57	207	59	17	1	2	84	28	24	30	1	28	3	4	1	14	4	.78	5	.285	.382	.406
1996 Hagerstown	A Tor	134	514	132	32	5	3	183	89	36	89	2	72	7	3	4	35	25	.58	8	.257	.371	.356
1997 Knoxville	AA Tor	115	378	100	24	4	10	162	52	56	37	2	47	1	4	4	8	14	.36	11	.265	.329	.429
4 Min. YEARS		431	1575	411	94	15	20	595	249	152	208	5	230	15	25	11	81	56	.59	33	.261	.350	.378

Steve Soliz

Bats: Right Throws: Right Pos: C Ht: 5'10" Wt: 180 Born: 1/27/71 Age: 27

Year Team	Lg Org	G	AB	H	2B	3B	HR	TB	R	RBI	TBB	IBB	SO	HBP	SH	SF	SB	CS	SB%	GDP	Avg	OBP	SLG
1993 Watertown	A- Cle	56	209	62	12	0	0	74	30	35	15	0	41	1	2	3	2	0	1.00	3	.297	.342	.354
1994 Kinston	A+ Cle	51	163	43	7	1	3	61	26	19	16	0	32	1	2	1	3	0	1.00	6	.264	.331	.374
Canton-Akrn	AA Cle	18	54	10	1	0	0	11	4	0	2	0	9	1	1	0	0	0	.00	4	.185	.228	.204
1995 Bakersfield	A+ LA	44	159	39	5	0	1	47	9	11	15	0	34	2	0	0	2	1	.67	6	.245	.318	.296
Canton-Akrn	AA Cle	32	81	14	3	0	2	23	9	7	13	0	16	0	1	1	0	0	.00	3	.173	.284	.284
1996 Canton-Akrn	AA Cle	46	143	37	4	2	2	51	18	15	11	0	28	2	0	2	1	2	.33	1	.259	.316	.357
1997 Buffalo	AAA Cle	62	151	29	5	0	1	37	12	13	10	0	40	-0	5	3	0	1	.00	2	.192	.238	.245
5 Min. YEARS		309	960	234	37	3	9	304	108	100	82	0	200	7	11	10	8	4	.67	19	.244	.305	.317

Fred Soriano

Bats: Both Throws: Right Pos: SS Ht: 5'9" Wt: 160 Born: 8/5/74 Age: 23

Year Team	Lg Org	G	AB	H	2B	3B	HR	TB	R	RBI	TBB	IBB	SO	HBP	SH	SF	SB	CS	SB%	GDP	Avg	OBP	SLG
1993 Tacoma	AAA Oak	2	6	1	1	0	0	2	3	3	2	0	3	0	0	0	0	0	.00	0	.167	.375	.333
Athletics	R Oak	41	131	34	5	4	5	62	34	19	21	0	41	1	2	1	7	2	.78	6	.260	.364	.473
Modesto	A+ Oak	11	40	10	2	1	0	14	6	5	1	0	12	1	1	0	1	0	1.00	0	.250	.286	.350
1994 Modesto	A+ Oak	22	53	3	0	0	0	3	8	1	7	0	21	3	1	0	2	1	.67	2	.057	.206	.057
W Michigan	A Oak	78	201	45	2	1	1	52	30	16	21	0	70	12	12	0	23	7	.77	3	.224	.333	.259
1995 W Michigan	A Oak	107	305	80	7	3	3	102	68	32	51	1	72	8	18	2	40	6	.87	0	.262	.380	.334
1996 Modesto	A+ Oak	33	126	33	3	0	2	42	21	19	14	0	33	0	4	4	14	3	.82	1	.262	.326	.333
1997 Knoxville	AA Tor	7	17	1	0	0	0	1	3	0	3	0	4	2	0	0	1	1	.50	0	.059	.273	.059
Dunedin	A+ Tor	26	78	24	5	1	2	37	18	12	8	0	17	4	3	1	3	0	1.00	1	.308	.396	.474
Hagerstown	A Tor	38	120	29	9	0	0	38	18	6	5	0	27	2	2	0	8	2	.80	5	.242	.283	.317
Syracuse	AAA Tor	17	44	5	1	1	0	8	3	4	1	0	7	1	2	0	2	0	1.00	0	.114	.152	.182
5 Min. YEARS		382	1121	265	35	11	13	361	212	117	134	1	307	34	45	8	101	22	.82	12	.236	.334	.322

Vernon Spearman

Bats: Left Throws: Left Pos: OF Ht: 5'10" Wt: 160 Born: 12/17/69 Age: 28

Year Team	Lg Org	G	AB	H	2B	3B	HR	TB	R	RBI	TBB	IBB	SO	HBP	SH	SF	SB	CS	SB%	GDP	Avg	OBP	SLG
1991 Yakima	A- LA	71	248	72	8	0	0	80	63	17	50	0	37	4	7	1	56	9	.86	1	.290	.416	.323
1992 Vero Beach	A+ LA	73	276	84	13	1	0	99	50	16	26	1	25	1	3	1	33	14	.70	5	.304	.365	.359
San Antonio	AA LA	48	185	52	3	3	0	61	24	11	15	0	16	1	6	1	18	9	.67	2	.281	.337	.330
1993 San Antonio	AA LA	56	162	42	4	2	0	50	22	13	11	0	21	1	5	0	13	4	.76	3	.259	.310	.309
Albuquerque	AAA LA	62	185	47	6	5	0	63	31	15	17	0	28	0	4	0	11	4	.73	4	.254	.317	.341
1994 San Antonio	AA LA	105	331	88	14	3	0	108	43	24	39	0	39	2	15	0	21	15	.58	2	.266	.347	.326
1995 Albuquerque	AAA LA	22	29	5	0	1	0	7	7	2	11	0	4	0	0	0	2	2	.50	2	.172	.400	.241
San Berndno	A+ LA	93	365	105	15	7	3	143	78	36	56	1	50	0	8	4	43	12	.78	5	.288	.379	.392
1996 San Antonio	AA LA	123	471	121	15	9	1	157	66	30	35	0	38	5	7	3	26	17	.60	10	.257	.313	.333
1997 Albuquerque	AAA LA	30	92	20	3	1	0	25	13	8	14	0	11	2	3	0	5	1	.83	1	.217	.333	.272
San Antonio	AA LA	41	136	38	3	3	1	50	31	7	19	0	25	1	4	2	9	3	.75	2	.279	.367	.368

241

	BATTING								BASERUNNING		PERCENTAGES	
Year Team	Lg Org	G AB H	2B 3B HR TB	R RBI	TBB IBB	SO	HBP SH SF	SB CS SB% GDP	Avg OBP SLG
7 Min. YEARS		724 2480 674	84 35 5 843	428 179	293 2	294	17 62 12	237 90 .72 37	.272 .351 .340

Justin Speier

Pitches: Right **Bats:** Right **Pos:** P   **Ht:** 6'4" **Wt:** 195 **Born:** 11/6/73 **Age:** 24

		HOW MUCH HE PITCHED			WHAT HE GAVE UP			THE RESULTS		
Year Team	Lg Org	G GS CG GF	IP	BFP	H R ER HR SH SF HB	TBB IBB	SO	WP Bk	W L Pct. ShO Sv	ERA
1995 Williamsprt	A- ChN	30 0 0 22	36.1	142	27 6 6 1 2 2 1	4 0	39	0 0	2 1 .667 0 12	1.49
1996 Daytona	A+ ChN	33 0 0 29	38.1	168	32 19 16 3 3 2 2	19 3	34	5 0	2 4 .333 0 13	3.76
Orlando	AA ChN	24 0 0 19	26.1	110	23 7 6 2 1 1 2	5 1	14	0 0	4 1 .800 0 6	2.05
1997 Orlando	AA ChN	50 0 0 20	78.1	328	77 46 39 8 4 2 3	23 0	63	2 2	6 5 .545 0 6	4.48
Iowa	AAA ChN	8 0 0 4	12.1	41	5 0 0 0 1 0 0	1 0	9	0 0	2 0 1.000 0 1	0.00
3 Min. YEARS		145 0 0 94	191.2	789	164 78 67 14 11 7 8	52 4	159	7 2	16 11 .593 0 38	3.15

Shane Spencer

Pitches: Right **Bats:** Right **Pos:** OF   **Ht:** 5'11" **Wt:** 210 **Born:** 2/20/72 **Age:** 26

		BATTING							BASERUNNING		PERCENTAGES	
Year Team	Lg Org	G AB H	2B 3B HR TB	R RBI	TBB IBB	SO	HBP SH SF	SB CS SB% GDP	Avg OBP SLG
1990 Yankees	R NYA	42 147 27	4 0 0 31	20 7	20 0	23	1 0 1	11 2 .85 3	.184 .284 .211
1991 Yankees	R NYA	41 160 49	7 0 0 56	25 30	14 0	19	2 0 4	8 2 .80 6	.306 .361 .350
Oneonta	A- NYA	18 53 13	2 1 0 17	10 3	10 0	9	1 3 0	2 2 .50 1	.245 .375 .321
1992 Greensboro	A NYA	83 258 74	10 2 3 97	43 27	33 0	37	3 1 2	8 2 .80 12	.287 .372 .376
1993 Greensboro	A NYA	122 431 116	35 2 12 191	89 80	52 0	62	3 0 8	14 2 .88 8	.269 .346 .443
1994 Tampa	A+ NYA	90 334 97	22 3 8 149	44 53	30 0	53	1 1 1	5 3 .63 8	.290 .350 .446
1995 Tampa	A+ NYA	134 500 150	31 3 16 235	87 88	61 2	60	7 2 3	14 8 .64 7	.300 .382 .470
1996 Norwich	AA NYA	126 450 114	19 0 29 220	70 89	68 2	99	4 1 5	4 2 .67 6	.253 .353 .489
Columbus	AAA NYA	9 31 11	4 0 3 24	7 6	5 0	5	1 0 0	0 1 .00 0	.355 .459 .774
1997 Columbus	AAA NYA	125 452 109	34 4 30 241	78 86	71 1	105	4 1 5	0 2 .00 2	.241 .346 .533
8 Min. YEARS		790 2816 760	168 15 101 1261	473 469	364 5	472	27 9 29	66 26 .72 59	.270 .356 .448

Stan Spencer

Pitches: Right **Bats:** Right **Pos:** P   **Ht:** 6'3" **Wt:** 195 **Born:** 8/2/68 **Age:** 29

		HOW MUCH HE PITCHED			WHAT HE GAVE UP			THE RESULTS		
Year Team	Lg Org	G GS CG GF	IP	BFP	H R ER HR SH SF HB	TBB IBB	SO	WP Bk	W L Pct. ShO Sv	ERA
1991 Harrisburg	AA Mon	17 17 1 0	92	389	90 52 45 6 4 2 4	30 0	66	2 3	6 1 .857 0 0	4.40
1993 High Desert	A+ Fla	13 13 0 0	61.2	265	67 33 28 4 0 2 3	18 0	38	1 0	4 4 .500 0 0	4.09
1994 Brevard Cty	A+ Fla	6 5 0 1	20	84	20 9 7 0 0 1 1	6 0	22	1 0	1 0 1.000 0 0	3.15
Portland	AA Fla	20 20 1 0	124	505	113 52 48 12 4 6 2	30 2	96	3 1	9 4 .692 0 0	3.48
1995 Charlotte	AAA Fla	9 9 0 0	41.1	198	61 37 36 9 0 0 3	24 1	19	0 0	1 4 .200 0 0	7.84
Portland	AA Fla	8 8 0 0	39	193	57 39 32 9 0 4 2	19 0	32	0 0	1 4 .200 0 0	7.38
1997 Rancho Cuca	A+ SD	7 7 0 0	40.1	164	37 18 15 6 0 1 2	5 0	46	1 0	3 1 .750 0 0	3.35
Las Vegas	AAA SD	8 8 0 0	48	208	48 23 20 5 1 0 1	18 2	47	1 0	3 2 .600 0 0	3.75
5 Min. YEARS		88 87 2 1	466.1	2006	493 263 231 51 9 16 18	150 5	366	9 4	28 20 .583 0 0	4.46

T.J. Staton

Bats: Left **Throws:** Left **Pos:** OF   **Ht:** 6'3" **Wt:** 200 **Born:** 2/17/75 **Age:** 23

		BATTING							BASERUNNING		PERCENTAGES	
Year Team	Lg Org	G AB H	2B 3B HR TB	R RBI	TBB IBB	SO	HBP SH SF	SB CS SB% GDP	Avg OBP SLG
1993 Pirates	R Pit	32 115 41	9 2 1 57	23 18	8 0	14	0 0 0	10 2 .83 0	.357 .398 .496
1994 Welland	A- Pit	12 45 8	3 0 0 11	4 4	0 0	7	0 0 0	5 0 1.00 1	.178 .178 .244
Pirates	R Pit	11 39 10	3 0 1 16	3 5	1 0	8	1 0 0	0 0 .00 0	.256 .293 .410
Augusta	A Pit	37 125 27	6 1 0 35	9 5	10 0	38	0 1 1	6 1 .86 5	.216 .272 .280
1995 Augusta	A Pit	112 391 114	21 5 5 160	43 53	27 5	97	2 0 1	27 13 .68 6	.292 .340 .409
1996 Carolina	AA Pit	112 386 119	24 3 15 194	72 57	58 1	99	6 0 4	17 7 .71 4	.308 .403 .503
1997 Calgary	AAA Pit	65 199 47	14 0 2 67	30 22	22 0	51	2 1 1	3 3 .50 6	.236 .317 .337
Carolina	AA Pit	58 207 60	11 2 6 93	33 33	12 1	60	5 3 2	8 4 .67 3	.290 .341 .449
5 Min. YEARS		439 1507 426	91 13 30 633	217 197	138 7	374	16 5 9	76 30 .72 25	.283 .347 .420

Dave Steed

Bats: Right **Throws:** Right **Pos:** C   **Ht:** 6'1" **Wt:** 205 **Born:** 2/25/73 **Age:** 25

		BATTING							BASERUNNING		PERCENTAGES	
Year Team	Lg Org	G AB H	2B 3B HR TB	R RBI	TBB IBB	SO	HBP SH SF	SB CS SB% GDP	Avg OBP SLG
1994 Yakima	A- LA	48 147 37	5 2 5 61	21 24	28 0	43	5 1 0	1 2 .33 4	.252 .389 .415
1995 Vero Beach	A+ LA	59 195 49	16 0 0 65	11 24	18 0	53	3 1 1	0 0 .00 5	.251 .323 .333
San Antonio	AA LA	40 123 31	10 1 3 52	13 16	11 0	32	1 0 2	0 1 .00 2	.252 .314 .423
1996 San Berndno	A+ LA	28 87 26	6 0 1 35	11 13	14 0	19	1 0 1	2 3 .40 1	.299 .398 .402
Vero Beach	A+ LA	23 73 21	3 0 1 27	6 10	6 0	15	0 1 0	1 0 1.00 1	.288 .342 .370
San Antonio	AA LA	7 17 2	1 0 0 3	0 2	1 0	6	0 0 0	0 0 .00 1	.118 .167 .176
1997 Albuquerque	AAA LA	25 47 10	4 0 1 17	8 4	4 1	19	0 0 0	0 0 .00 0	.213 .275 .362
4 Min. YEARS		230 689 176	45 3 11 260	70 93	82 1	187	10 3 4	4 6 .40 14	.255 .341 .377

Kennie Steenstra

Pitches: Right **Bats:** Right **Pos:** P **Ht:** 6'5" **Wt:** 220 **Born:** 10/13/70 **Age:** 27

Year Team	Lg Org	G	GS	CG	GF	IP	BFP	H	R	ER	HR	SH	SF	HB	TBB	IBB	SO	WP	Bk	W	L	Pct.	ShO	Sv	ERA
1992 Geneva	A- ChN	3	3	1	0	20	76	11	4	2	0	0	0	0	3	0	12	0	1	3	0	1.000	0	0	0.90
Peoria	A ChN	12	12	4	0	89.2	364	79	29	21	5	2	1	3	21	1	68	4	3	6	3	.667	2	0	2.11
1993 Daytona	A+ ChN	13	13	1	0	81.1	317	64	26	23	2	3	2	8	12	1	57	2	1	5	3	.625	1	0	2.55
Iowa	AAA ChN	1	1	0	0	6.2	32	9	5	5	2	0	0	0	4	0	6	0	0	1	0	1.000	0	0	6.75
Orlando	AA ChN	14	14	2	0	100.1	427	103	47	40	4	4	2	9	25	0	60	5	2	8	3	.727	1	0	3.59
1994 Iowa	AAA ChN	3	3	0	0	13	68	24	21	19	2	0	2	2	4	0	10	0	0	1	2	.333	0	0	13.15
Orlando	AA ChN	23	23	2	0	158.1	654	146	55	46	12	9	3	9	39	4	83	4	1	9	7	.563	1	0	2.61
1995 Iowa	AAA ChN	29	26	6	1	171.1	722	174	85	74	15	6	6	8	48	3	96	6	0	9	12	.429	2	0	3.89
1996 Iowa	AAA ChN	26	26	1	0	158	686	170	96	88	24	5	9	9	47	4	101	2	0	8	12	.400	0	0	5.01
1997 Iowa	AAA ChN	25	25	4	0	160.2	663	161	85	70	15	4	9	0	41	4	111	7	0	5	10	.333	0	0	3.92
6 Min. YEARS		149	146	21	1	959.1	4009	941	453	388	81	33	34	48	244	17	604	30	8	55	52	.514	8	0	3.64

Mike Stefanski

Bats: Right **Throws:** Right **Pos:** C **Ht:** 6'2" **Wt:** 202 **Born:** 9/12/69 **Age:** 28

Year Team	Lg Org	G	AB	H	2B	3B	HR	TB	R	RBI	TBB	IBB	SO	HBP	SH	SF	SB	CS	SB%	GDP	Avg	OBP	SLG
1991 Brewers	R Mil	56	206	76	5	5	0	91	43	43	22	0	22	5	0	6	3	2	.60	4	.369	.431	.442
1992 Beloit	A Mil	116	385	105	12	0	4	129	66	45	55	1	81	4	3	3	9	4	.69	11	.273	.367	.335
1993 Stockton	A+ Mil	97	345	111	22	2	10	167	58	57	49	2	45	5	1	2	6	1	.86	15	.322	.411	.484
1994 El Paso	AA Mil	95	312	82	7	6	8	125	59	56	32	0	80	0	2	5	4	3	.57	5	.263	.327	.401
1995 El Paso	AA Mil	6	27	11	3	0	1	17	5	6	0	0	3	0	0	1	0	0	1.00	0	.407	.407	.630
New Orleans	AAA Mil	78	228	56	10	2	2	76	30	24	14	0	28	1	5	5	2	0	1.00	8	.246	.286	.333
1996 Louisville	AAA StL	53	126	26	7	1	2	41	11	9	11	1	11	1	1	2	1	2	.33	4	.206	.271	.325
1997 Arkansas	AA StL	1	4	1	0	1	0	3	1	0	0	0	0	0	0	0	0	0	.00	1	.250	.250	.750
Louisville	AAA StL	57	197	60	10	0	6	88	26	22	12	0	20	1	2	1	0	1	.00	6	.305	.346	.447
7 Min. YEARS		559	1830	528	76	17	33	737	299	262	195	4	290	17	14	24	26	13	.67	54	.289	.358	.403

Blake Stein

Pitches: Right **Bats:** Right **Pos:** P **Ht:** 6'7" **Wt:** 210 **Born:** 8/3/73 **Age:** 24

Year Team	Lg Org	G	GS	CG	GF	IP	BFP	H	R	ER	HR	SH	SF	HB	TBB	IBB	SO	WP	Bk	W	L	Pct.	ShO	Sv	ERA
1994 Johnson Cty	R+ StL	13	13	1	0	59.2	242	44	21	19	4	4	2	1	24	0	69	3	0	4	1	.800	0	0	2.87
1995 Peoria	A StL	27	27	1	0	139.2	596	122	69	59	12	1	4	5	61	0	133	4	1	10	6	.625	0	0	3.80
1996 St. Pete	A+ StL	28	27	2	1	172	667	122	48	41	4	3	4	5	54	0	159	4	0	16	5	.762	1	1	2.15
1997 Arkansas	AA StL	22	22	1	0	133.2	557	128	67	63	17	5	1	1	49	2	114	5	0	8	7	.533	0	0	4.24
Huntsville	AA Oak	7	7	0	0	34.2	157	36	24	22	3	0	1	0	20	1	25	6	0	3	2	.600	0	0	5.71
4 Min. YEARS		97	96	5	1	539.2	2219	452	229	204	40	13	12	12	208	3	500	20	1	41	21	.661	1	1	3.40

Rod Steph

Pitches: Right **Bats:** Right **Pos:** P **Ht:** 5'11" **Wt:** 185 **Born:** 8/27/69 **Age:** 28

Year Team	Lg Org	G	GS	CG	GF	IP	BFP	H	R	ER	HR	SH	SF	HB	TBB	IBB	SO	WP	Bk	W	L	Pct.	ShO	Sv	ERA
1991 Princeton	R+ Cin	7	7	1	0	46.1	186	37	19	16	1	0	1	4	11	0	52	4	3	2	3	.400	1	0	3.11
Cedar Rapds	A Cin	8	7	3	0	56.2	229	46	19	16	5	2	0	4	15	1	46	3	4	4	3	.571	2	0	2.54
1992 Cedar Rapds	A Cin	27	27	1	0	154.1	668	157	86	74	18	3	4	6	54	0	136	11	2	12	9	.571	1	0	4.32
1993 Winston-Sal	A+ Cin	28	28	4	0	167.2	717	166	101	73	21	6	3	8	57	0	130	14	0	7	11	.389	2	0	3.92
1994 Thunder Bay	IND —	13	13	3	0	88.1	354	68	30	24	5	3	1	4	17	0	76	5	0	8	1	.889	2	0	2.45
Canton-Akrn	AA Cle	3	3	1	0	20	89	27	13	12	2	1	0	4	4	0	6	1	0	1	2	.333	0	0	5.40
1995 Canton-Akrn	AA Cle	32	20	1	5	137	595	150	74	58	6	7	2	9	33	1	82	5	0	8	10	.444	0	0	3.81
1996 Greenville	AA Atl	2	0	0	0	3.1	10	1	0	0	0	0	0	0	0	0	3	1	0	0	0	.000	0	0	0.00
Richmond	AAA Atl	38	0	0	16	79.2	324	75	34	34	6	0	2	3	17	2	41	5	0	2	3	.400	0	1	3.84
1997 Bowie	AA Bal	7	0	0	0	13.2	50	6	3	2	1	1	0	0	3	1	9	1	0	1	0	1.000	0	0	1.32
Rochester	AAA Bal	41	0	0	32	48.2	208	49	24	23	6	3	4	2	12	1	51	2	0	3	3	.500	0	14	4.25
7 Min. YEARS		206	105	14	53	815.2	3430	782	403	332	71	26	17	40	223	6	632	51	9	48	45	.516	8	15	3.66

Brian Stephenson

Pitches: Right **Bats:** Right **Pos:** P **Ht:** 6'3" **Wt:** 205 **Born:** 7/17/73 **Age:** 24

Year Team	Lg Org	G	GS	CG	GF	IP	BFP	H	R	ER	HR	SH	SF	HB	TBB	IBB	SO	WP	Bk	W	L	Pct.	ShO	Sv	ERA
1994 Williamsprt	A- ChN	5	5	0	0	19	80	17	9	9	2	0	2	4	4	0	13	1	1	0	2	.000	0	0	4.26
Peoria	A ChN	6	6	2	0	42.1	180	41	18	15	3	3	0	6	6	1	29	1	0	3	1	.750	0	0	3.19
1995 Daytona	A+ ChN	26	26	0	0	150	640	145	79	66	7	6	3	7	58	2	109	14	2	10	9	.526	0	0	3.96
1996 Orlando	AA ChN	32	20	0	3	128.2	574	130	82	67	13	4	9	5	61	3	106	10	1	5	13	.278	0	1	4.69
1997 Orlando	AA ChN	6	0	0	2	9.1	42	10	10	10	4	0	1	0	5	0	9	4	0	0	2	.000	0	0	9.64
4 Min. YEARS		75	57	2	5	349.1	1516	343	198	167	29	13	15	22	134	6	266	30	4	18	27	.400	0	1	4.30

Jason Stevenson

Pitches: Right **Bats:** Right **Pos:** P **Ht:** 6'3" **Wt:** 180 **Born:** 8/11/74 **Age:** 23

Year Team	Lg Org	G	GS	CG	GF	IP	BFP	H	R	ER	HR	SH	SF	HB	TBB	IBB	SO	WP	Bk	W	L	Pct.	ShO	Sv	ERA
1994 Huntington	R+ ChN	5	1	0	1	10.2	47	12	5	2	3	1	0	0	6	0	5	1	0	1	1	.500	0	1	4.22
Cubs	R ChN	5	5	0	0	25	112	31	12	7	1	3	1	0	4	0	19	3	0	1	1	.500	0	0	2.52
1995 Rockford	A ChN	33	5	0	9	77.1	333	85	50	48	9	1	4	1	31	0	54	5	5	4	3	.571	0	2	5.59

Year Team	Lg Org	G	GS	CG	GF	IP	BFP	H	R	ER	HR	SH	SF	HB	TBB	IBB	SO	WP	Bk	W	L	Pct.	ShO	Sv	ERA
Daytona	A+ ChN	8	0	0	3	18.1	71	11	6	6	0	1	0	1	6	0	15	1	0	2	0	1.000	0	1	2.95
1996 Daytona	A+ ChN	27	17	2	5	122	519	136	56	48	7	6	5	5	22	2	86	8	1	8	5	.615	1	0	3.54
1997 Knoxville	AA Tor	26	26	2	0	149.2	640	166	88	71	18	5	5	7	43	1	101	7	1	12	9	.571	2	0	4.27
4 Min. YEARS		104	54	4	18	403	1722	441	217	185	37	19	16	14	112	3	280	25	7	28	19	.596	3	4	4.13

Rodney Stevenson

Pitches: Right **Bats:** Right **Pos:** P **Ht:** 6'2" **Wt:** 210 **Born:** 3/21/74 **Age:** 24

Year Team	Lg Org	G	GS	CG	GF	IP	BFP	H	R	ER	HR	SH	SF	HB	TBB	IBB	SO	WP	Bk	W	L	Pct.	ShO	Sv	ERA
1996 Vermont	A- Mon	22	0	0	5	31.2	133	24	11	10	1	1	0	1	13	0	46	2	2	5	2	.714	0	1	2.84
1997 Cape Fear	A Mon	16	0	0	15	17	66	7	3	1	0	0	0	0	6	1	20	1	0	1	1	.500	0	5	0.53
Wst Plm Bch	A+ Mon	26	0	0	12	35.1	158	31	13	7	2	2	1	1	16	0	39	0	0	3	3	.500	0	2	1.78
Harrisburg	AA Mon	4	0	0	2	7	33	9	5	3	1	0	0	0	5	1	6	1	0	0	0	.000	0	0	3.86
2 Min. YEARS		68	0	0	34	91	390	71	32	21	4	3	1	2	40	2	111	4	2	9	6	.600	0	8	2.08

Chaad Stewart

Pitches: Left **Bats:** Left **Pos:** P **Ht:** 6'4" **Wt:** 212 **Born:** 10/8/74 **Age:** 23

Year Team	Lg Org	G	GS	CG	GF	IP	BFP	H	R	ER	HR	SH	SF	HB	TBB	IBB	SO	WP	Bk	W	L	Pct.	ShO	Sv	ERA
1994 Orioles	R Bal	1	1	0	0	3	15	6	5	5	0	0	1	0	0	0	3	0	2	0	0	.000	0	0	15.00
Bluefield	R+ Bal	14	3	0	7	43.1	171	34	11	8	0	2	1	2	10	0	43	4	3	3	1	.750	0	0	1.66
1995 Frederick	A+ Bal	26	26	1	0	150.2	635	126	71	61	8	5	1	10	66	1	140	12	4	8	8	.500	1	0	3.64
1996 Greenville	AA Atl	24	13	0	2	71.1	348	89	55	48	4	6	3	0	48	2	74	12	2	5	5	.375	0	0	6.06
1997 Durham	A+ Atl	8	5	0	0	31	137	26	12	10	3	0	0	2	15	0	19	1	1	1	0	1.000	0	0	2.90
Greenville	AA Atl	6	3	0	0	18	84	20	18	17	3	1	1	0	12	0	11	1	0	1	2	.333	0	0	8.50
4 Min. YEARS		79	51	1	9	317.1	1390	301	172	149	18	14	7	14	151	3	290	30	12	16	16	.500	1	2	4.23

Phil Stidham

Pitches: Right **Bats:** Right **Pos:** P **Ht:** 6'0" **Wt:** 180 **Born:** 11/18/68 **Age:** 29

Year Team	Lg Org	G	GS	CG	GF	IP	BFP	H	R	ER	HR	SH	SF	HB	TBB	IBB	SO	WP	Bk	W	L	Pct.	ShO	Sv	ERA
1991 Fayettevlle	A Det	28	0	0	26	33.2	139	25	10	6	0	1	2	0	16	0	20	3	3	0	1	.000	0	8	1.60
1992 Lakeland	A+ Det	45	0	0	27	53.2	252	61	28	22	3	2	1	3	28	2	47	4	1	2	7	.222	0	4	3.69
1993 Lakeland	A+ Det	25	0	0	23	29.2	119	22	6	5	2	2	0	2	9	1	24	0	0	2	1	.667	0	9	1.52
London	AA Det	33	0	0	8	34	164	40	18	9	3	1	0	2	19	3	39	1	0	2	2	.500	0	2	2.38
1994 Trenton	AA Det	6	0	0	6	6	22	4	0	0	0	0	0	0	0	0	6	2	0	0	0	.000	0	3	0.00
Toledo	AAA Det	49	0	0	16	69	278	48	25	24	3	4	2	1	31	3	57	1	0	3	3	.500	0	3	3.13
1995 Binghamton	AA NYN	7	0	0	4	9.2	47	9	6	5	0	1	0	0	9	0	7	1	0	0	0	.000	0	0	4.66
Norfolk	AAA NYN	34	6	0	12	70	305	56	33	25	4	2	6	5	36	1	56	5	0	6	2	.750	0	1	3.21
1996 Hardware City	AA Min	12	0	0	4	13.2	61	11	5	4	1	2	1	2	8	1	16	4	0	1	0	1.000	0	1	2.63
Salt Lake	AAA Min	33	7	0	8	78.1	366	100	63	59	8	3	2	4	40	1	54	10	1	10	5	.667	0	6	6.78
1997 Colo Sprngs	AAA Col	26	0	0	10	36.1	162	55	43	40	8	2	2	1	26	2	20	7	0	5	2	.714	0	0	9.91
New Haven	AA Col	8	0	0	4	9.2	47	10	4	4	1	1	1	0	8	1	7	0	0	0	0	.000	0	1	3.72
1994 Detroit	AL	5	0	0	0	4.1	26	12	12	12	3	0	1	0	4	1	4	0	0	0	0	.000	0	0	24.92
7 Min. YEARS		306	13	0	148	443.2	1982	441	241	203	33	17		20	230	15	353	37	5	31	23	.574	0	34	4.12

Ricky Stone

Pitches: Right **Bats:** Right **Pos:** P **Ht:** 6'2" **Wt:** 173 **Born:** 2/28/75 **Age:** 23

Year Team	Lg Org	G	GS	CG	GF	IP	BFP	H	R	ER	HR	SH	SF	HB	TBB	IBB	SO	WP	Bk	W	L	Pct.	ShO	Sv	ERA
1994 Great Falls	R+ LA	13	7	0	4	50.2	232	55	40	25	5	0	1	2	24	0	48	9	0	2	2	.500	0	2	4.44
1995 San Berndno	A+ LA	12	12	0	0	58	273	79	50	42	7	6	3	2	25	0	31	5	0	3	5	.375	0	0	6.52
Yakima	A- LA	16	6	0	7	48	213	54	31	28	5	2	2	2	20	0	28	4	1	4	4	.500	0	2	5.25
1996 Savannah	A LA	5	5	0	0	31.2	130	34	15	14	2	2	1	0	9	0	31	5	0	2	1	.667	0	0	3.98
Vero Beach	A+ LA	21	21	1	0	112.2	488	115	58	48	9	4	3	3	46	0	74	10	0	8	6	.571	0	0	3.83
1997 San Antonio	AA LA	25	5	0	10	52.2	245	63	33	32	4	4	1	3	30	0	46	3	0	0	3	.000	0	3	5.47
San Berndno	A+ LA	8	8	0	0	53.2	206	40	22	20	4	2	1	2	10	0	40	2	0	3	3	.500	0	0	3.35
4 Min. YEARS		100	64	1	21	407.1	1787	440	249	209	36	20	12	14	164	0	298	38	1	22	24	.478	0	7	4.62

Darond Stovall

Bats: Both **Throws:** Left **Pos:** OF **Ht:** 6'1" **Wt:** 185 **Born:** 1/3/73 **Age:** 25

Year Team	Lg Org	G	AB	H	2B	3B	HR	TB	R	RBI	TBB	IBB	SO	HBP	SH	SF	SB	CS	SB%	GDP	Avg	OBP	SLG
1991 Johnson Cty	R+ StL	48	134	19	2	2	0	25	16	5	23	1	63	0	0	0	8	3	.73	1	.142	.268	.187
1992 Savannah	A StL	135	450	92	13	7	7	140	51	40	63	0	138	0	1	1	20	14	.59	13	.204	.302	.311
1993 Springfield	A StL	135	460	118	19	4	20	205	73	81	53	2	143	0	2	1	18	12	.60	5	.257	.333	.446
1994 St. Pete	A+ StL	134	507	113	20	6	15	190	68	69	62	4	154	0	2	5	24	8	.75	10	.223	.305	.375
1995 Wst Plm Bch	A+ Mon	121	461	107	22	2	4	145	52	51	44	2	117	0	2	3	18	12	.60	4	.232	.297	.315
1996 Expos	R Mon	9	34	15	3	2	0	22	5	7	3	0	6	0	0	0	3	0	1.00	0	.441	.486	.647
Wst Plm Bch	A+ Mon	8	31	14	4	0	1	21	8	8	6	0	7	0	0	0	2	2	.50	1	.452	.541	.677
Harrisburg	AA Mon	74	272	60	7	1	10	99	38	36	32	1	86	2	4	0	10	5	.67	5	.221	.307	.364
1997 Harrisburg	AA Mon	45	169	48	4	1	9	81	29	39	23	1	30	0	0	3	4	0	1.00	0	.284	.364	.479
Ottawa	AAA Mon	98	342	83	23	2	4	122	40	48	31	3	114	2	3	4	10	13	.43	6	.243	.306	.357
7 Min. YEARS		807	2860	669	117	27	70	1050	380	384	340	14	858	4	14	17	117	69	.63	48	.234	.314	.367

Chris Stowers

Bats: Left **Throws:** Left **Pos:** OF **Ht:** 6'3" **Wt:** 195 **Born:** 8/18/74 **Age:** 23

Year Team	Lg Org	G	AB	H	2B	3B	HR	TB	R	RBI	TBB	IBB	SO	HBP	SH	SF	SB	CS	SB%	GDP	Avg	OBP	SLG
1996 Vermont	A- Mon	72	282	90	21	9	7	150	58	44	21	6	37	2	0	0	16	5	.76	4	.319	.370	.532
1997 Wst Plm Bch	A+ Mon	111	414	113	15	5	4	150	56	30	30	5	77	7	2	2	19	14	.58	7	.273	.331	.362
Harrisburg	AA Mon	19	59	17	4	2	0	25	9	5	5	2	11	0	1	0	3	1	.75	1	.288	.344	.424
2 Min. YEARS		202	755	220	40	16	11	325	123	79	56	13	125	9	3	2	38	20	.66	5	.291	.347	.430

Mike Strange

Bats: Right **Throws:** Right **Pos:** 2B **Ht:** 6'0" **Wt:** 172 **Born:** 4/21/74 **Age:** 24

Year Team	Lg Org	G	AB	H	2B	3B	HR	TB	R	RBI	TBB	IBB	SO	HBP	SH	SF	SB	CS	SB%	GDP	Avg	OBP	SLG
1994 Medicne Hat	R+ Tor	55	177	44	7	3	1	60	30	20	22	0	50	6	2	2	4	2	.67	3	.249	.348	.339
1995 Hagerstown	A Tor	96	290	68	9	2	1	84	51	27	61	0	92	4	2	0	13	3	.81	7	.234	.375	.290
1996 Dunedin	A+ Tor	51	154	49	4	2	0	57	25	13	26	0	42	0	5	0	5	5	.50	3	.318	.417	.370
1997 Knoxville	AA Tor	12	21	2	0	1	0	4	1	0	3	0	4	0	0	0	0	0	.00	0	.095	.208	.190
Dunedin	A+ Tor	48	106	28	5	1	0	35	15	7	14	0	39	1	3	0	1	1	.50	0	.264	.355	.330
4 Min. YEARS		262	748	191	25	9	2	240	122	67	126	0	227	11	12	2	23	11	.68	13	.255	.370	.321

Mark Strittmatter

Bats: Right **Throws:** Right **Pos:** C **Ht:** 6'1" **Wt:** 200 **Born:** 4/4/69 **Age:** 29

Year Team	Lg Org	G	AB	H	2B	3B	HR	TB	R	RBI	TBB	IBB	SO	HBP	SH	SF	SB	CS	SB%	GDP	Avg	OBP	SLG
1992 Bend	A- Col	35	101	26	6	0	2	38	17	13	12	0	28	3	0	0	0	4	.00	2	.257	.353	.376
1993 Central Val	A+ Col	59	179	47	8	0	2	61	21	15	31	0	29	2	2	3	3	0	1.00	8	.263	.372	.341
Colo Sprngs	AAA Col	5	10	2	1	0	0	3	1	2	0	0	2	1	0	0	0	0	.00	2	.200	.273	.300
1994 New Haven	AA Col	73	215	49	8	0	2	63	20	26	33	1	39	9	3	4	1	2	.33	7	.228	.349	.293
1995 New Haven	AA Col	5	17	5	2	0	0	7	1	3	0	0	3	0	0	0	0	0	.00	0	.294	.294	.412
New Haven	AA Col	90	288	70	12	1	7	105	44	42	47	1	51	6	1	2	1	0	1.00	5	.243	.359	.365
1996 Colo Sprngs	AAA Col	58	159	37	8	1	2	53	21	18	17	3	30	7	1	0	2	1	.67	5	.233	.333	.333
1997 Colo Sprngs	AAA Col	45	114	28	8	0	2	42	16	12	11	3	21	5	4	1	0	1	.00	4	.246	.336	.368
6 Min. YEARS		370	1083	264	53	2	17	372	141	131	151	8	203	33	11	10	7	8	.47	33	.244	.351	.343

Jack Sturdivant

Bats: Left **Throws:** Left **Pos:** OF **Ht:** 5'10" **Wt:** 150 **Born:** 10/29/73 **Age:** 24

Year Team	Lg Org	G	AB	H	2B	3B	HR	TB	R	RBI	TBB	IBB	SO	HBP	SH	SF	SB	CS	SB%	GDP	Avg	OBP	SLG
1992 Mariners	R Sea	42	141	44	6	1	0	52	27	14	12	3	14	1	0	3	7	5	.58	0	.312	.363	.369
1993 Bellingham	A- Sea	64	238	61	8	3	4	87	34	32	22	1	28	2	2	0	8	5	.62	4	.256	.324	.366
1994 Appleton	A Sea	113	413	104	12	7	2	136	50	36	33	1	43	4	4	0	20	17	.54	7	.252	.313	.329
1995 Riverside	A+ Sea	99	347	95	13	5	1	121	60	34	39	1	41	1	2	4	31	13	.70	3	.274	.345	.349
1996 Lancaster	A+ Sea	68	292	83	19	6	0	114	54	31	32	1	35	3	0	1	23	9	.72	3	.284	.360	.390
Port City	AA Sea	63	243	69	11	4	2	94	34	23	26	1	33	0	0	2	13	7	.65	2	.284	.351	.387
1997 Memphis	AA Sea	112	432	117	18	5	2	151	71	35	63	0	61	1	2	3	21	17	.55	9	.271	.363	.350
6 Min. YEARS		561	2106	573	87	31	11	755	330	205	227	8	255	12	10	13	123	73	.63	28	.272	.344	.358

Mac Suzuki

Pitches: Right **Bats:** Right **Pos:** P **Ht:** 6'3" **Wt:** 195 **Born:** 5/31/75 **Age:** 23

Year Team	Lg Org	G	GS	CG	GF	IP	BFP	H	R	ER	HR	SH	SF	HB	TBB	IBB	SO	WP	Bk	W	L	Pct.	ShO	Sv	ERA
1992 Salinas	A+ —	1	0	0	0	1	3	0	0	0	0	0	0	0	0	0	1	0	0	0	0	.000	0	0	0.00
1993 San Berndno	A+ —	48	1	0	35	80.2	351	59	37	33	5	3	2	2	56	4	87	12	2	4	4	.500	0	12	3.68
1994 Jacksnville	AA Sea	8	0	0	1	12.2	58	15	4	4	1	0	1	0	6	0	10	0	0	1	0	1.000	0	1	2.84
1995 Mariners	R Sea	4	3	0	0	4	19	5	4	3	1	0	0	1	0	0	3	0	0	1	0	1.000	0	0	6.75
Riverside	A+ Sea	6	0	0	1	7.2	39	10	4	4	0	0	1	0	6	0	6	2	0	1	0	1.000	0	0	4.70
1996 Port City	AA Sea	16	16	0	0	74.1	320	69	41	39	10	2	1	2	32	0	66	0	0	3	6	.333	0	0	4.72
Tacoma	AAA Sea	13	2	0	6	22.1	110	31	19	18	3	2	0	0	12	2	14	3	0	0	3	.000	0	0	7.25
1997 Tacoma	AAA Sea	32	10	0	7	83.1	384	79	60	55	13	2	1	0	64	1	63	6	1	4	9	.308	0	0	5.94
1996 Seattle	AL	1	0	0	0	1.1	8	2	3	3	0	0	0	0	2	1	1	0	0	0	0	.000	0	0	20.25
6 Min. YEARS		128	32	0	50	286	1284	268	169	156	33	9	6	5	176	7	250	23	3	13	23	.361	0	13	4.91

Pedro Swann

Bats: Left **Throws:** Right **Pos:** OF **Ht:** 6'0" **Wt:** 195 **Born:** 10/27/70 **Age:** 27

Year Team	Lg Org	G	AB	H	2B	3B	HR	TB	R	RBI	TBB	IBB	SO	HBP	SH	SF	SB	CS	SB%	GDP	Avg	OBP	SLG
1991 Idaho Falls	R+ Atl	55	174	48	6	1	3	65	35	28	33	0	45	2	1	2	8	5	.62	4	.276	.393	.374
1992 Pulaski	R+ Atl	59	203	61	18	1	5	96	36	34	32	3	33	7	0	1	13	6	.68	6	.300	.412	.473
1993 Durham	A+ Atl	61	182	63	8	2	6	93	27	27	19	0	38	1	1	0	6	12	.33	2	.346	.411	.511
Greenville	AA Atl	44	157	48	9	2	3	70	19	21	9	0	23	1	1	0	2	2	.50	5	.306	.347	.446
1994 Greenville	AA Atl	126	428	121	25	2	10	180	55	49	46	2	85	4	0	2	16	9	.64	14	.283	.356	.421
1995 Richmond	AAA Atl	15	38	8	1	0	0	9	2	3	1	0	2	1	0	0	0	2	.00	0	.211	.250	.237
Greenville	AA Atl	102	339	110	24	2	11	171	57	64	45	2	63	3	0	3	14	11	.56	8	.324	.405	.504
1996 Greenville	AA Atl	35	129	40	5	0	3	54	15	20	18	2	23	3	1	1	4	4	.50	7	.310	.404	.419
Richmond	AAA Atl	93	296	74	11	4	4	105	42	35	22	2	56	4	2	3	7	7	.50	5	.250	.308	.355
1997 Greenville	AA Atl	124	465	133	29	2	24	238	78	83	49	5	75	4	0	1	5	5	.50	14	.286	.358	.512
7 Min. YEARS		714	2411	706	136	16	69	1081	366	364	274	16	443	30	5	13	75	63	.54	61	.293	.370	.448

Jon Sweet

Bats: Left **Throws:** Right **Pos:** C **Ht:** 6'0" **Wt:** 183 **Born:** 11/10/71 **Age:** 26

Year Team	Lg Org	G	AB	H	2B	3B	HR	TB	R	RBI	TBB	IBB	SO	HBP	SH	SF	SB	CS	SB%	GDP	Avg	OBP	SLG
1994 Welland	A- Pit	51	154	39	8	0	0	47	17	17	17	1	20	5	1	1	0	3	.00	3	.253	.345	.305
1995 Augusta	A Pit	87	267	76	9	1	1	90	28	22	18	2	31	5	2	2	5	4	.56	6	.285	.339	.337
1996 Lynchburg	A+ Pit	72	212	58	10	0	0	68	16	35	17	1	26	2	5	3	2	4	.33	0	.274	.329	.321
Carolina	AA Pit	20	40	4	2	0	0	6	2	1	0	0	3	0	2	0	0	0	.00	5	.100	.100	.150
1997 Carolina	AA Pit	82	273	67	15	1	1	87	22	27	15	2	20	1	1	1	1	1	.50	8	.245	.286	.319
4 Min. YEARS		312	946	244	44	2	2	298	85	102	67	6	100	13	11	7	8	12	.40	22	.258	.314	.315

Jeff Tackett

Bats: Right **Throws:** Right **Pos:** C **Ht:** 6'2" **Wt:** 206 **Born:** 12/1/65 **Age:** 32

Year Team	Lg Org	G	AB	H	2B	3B	HR	TB	R	RBI	TBB	IBB	SO	HBP	SH	SF	SB	CS	SB%	GDP	Avg	OBP	SLG
1984 Bluefield	R+ Bal	34	98	16	2	0	0	18	9	12	23	0	28	0	0	2	1	1	.50	1	.163	.317	.184
1985 Daytona Bch	A+ Bal	40	103	20	5	2	0	29	8	10	13	0	16	1	0	1	1	3	.25	6	.194	.288	.282
Newark	A- Bal	62	187	39	6	0	0	45	21	22	22	0	33	2	3	1	2	2	.50	4	.209	.297	.241
1986 Hagerstown	A+ Bal	83	246	70	15	1	0	87	53	21	36	0	36	5	0	1	16	5	.76	2	.285	.385	.354
1987 Charlotte	AA Bal	61	205	46	6	1	0	54	18	13	12	0	34	2	1	1	5	5	.50	2	.224	.273	.263
1988 Charlotte	AA Bal	81	272	56	9	0	0	65	24	18	42	0	46	2	0	1	6	4	.60	7	.206	.315	.239
1989 Rochester	AAA Bal	67	199	36	3	1	2	47	13	17	19	0	45	1	2	2	3	1	.75	3	.181	.253	.236
1990 Rochester	AAA Bal	108	306	73	8	3	4	99	37	33	47	0	50	7	3	0	4	8	.33	3	.239	.353	.324
1991 Rochester	AAA Bal	126	433	102	18	2	6	142	64	50	54	0	60	2	4	3	3	3	.50	15	.236	.321	.328
1993 Rochester	AAA Bal	8	25	8	2	0	0	10	1	2	3	0	8	2	0	1	0	0	.00	0	.320	.419	.400
1995 Toledo	AAA Det	96	301	81	15	0	6	114	32	30	35	0	46	7	5	1	2	1	.67	6	.269	.358	.379
1996 Toledo	AAA Det	89	283	67	10	3	7	104	41	49	36	1	54	6	2	4	4	2	.67	7	.237	.331	.367
1997 Okla City	AAA Tex	64	209	57	15	0	5	87	23	19	26	0	49	1	0	0	4	1	.80	6	.273	.356	.416
1991 Baltimore	AL	6	8	1	0	0	0	1	1	0	2	0	2	0	1	0	0	0	.00	0	.125	.300	.125
1992 Baltimore	AL	65	179	43	8	1	5	68	21	24	17	1	28	2	6	4	0	0	.00	11	.240	.307	.380
1993 Baltimore	AL	39	87	15	3	0	0	18	8	9	13	0	28	0	2	1	0	0	.00	5	.172	.277	.207
1994 Baltimore	AL	26	53	12	3	1	2	23	5	9	5	0	13	2	0	0	0	0	.00	4	.226	.317	.434
12 Min. YEARS		919	2867	671	114	13	30	901	344	296	368	1	505	38	20	18	51	36	.59	62	.234	.327	.314
4 Maj. YEARS		136	327	71	14	2	7	110	35	42	37	1	71	4	9	5	0	0	.00	20	.217	.300	.336

Jeff Tam

Pitches: Right **Bats:** Right **Pos:** P **Ht:** 6'1" **Wt:** 185 **Born:** 8/19/70 **Age:** 27

Year Team	Lg Org	G	GS	CG	GF	IP	BFP	H	R	ER	HR	SH	SF	HB	TBB	IBB	SO	WP	Bk	W	L	Pct.	ShO	Sv	ERA
1993 Pittsfield	A- NYN	21	1	0	13	40.1	180	50	21	15	0	0	1	1	7	0	31	1	3	3	3	.500	0	0	3.35
1994 Capital City	A NYN	26	0	0	26	28	115	23	14	4	0	1	0	2	6	0	22	0	2	1	1	.500	0	18	1.29
St. Lucie	A+ NYN	24	0	0	22	26.2	99	13	0	0	0	0	0	3	6	1	15	1	2	0	0	.000	0	16	0.00
Binghamton	AA NYN	4	0	0	1	6.2	35	9	6	6	0	1	0	1	5	0	7	0	0	0	0	.000	0	0	8.10
1995 Mets	R NYN	2	1	0	0	3	13	2	1	1	0	1	0	1	1	0	2	0	0	0	0	.000	0	0	3.00
Binghamton	AA NYN	14	0	0	7	18	83	20	11	9	1	2	1	4	4	2	9	3	0	0	2	.000	0	3	4.50
1996 Binghamton	AA NYN	49	0	0	18	62.2	241	51	19	17	6	2	1	2	16	3	48	2	1	6	2	.750	0	2	2.44
1997 Norfolk	AAA NYN	40	11	0	15	111.2	480	137	72	58	9	6	4	7	14	4	67	5	0	7	5	.583	0	6	4.67
5 Min. YEARS		180	13	0	102	297	1246	305	144	110	16	13	7	21	59	10	201	13	11	17	13	.567	0	45	3.33

Jimmy Tatum

Bats: Right **Throws:** Right **Pos:** OF **Ht:** 6'2" **Wt:** 200 **Born:** 10/9/67 **Age:** 30

Year Team	Lg Org	G	AB	H	2B	3B	HR	TB	R	RBI	TBB	IBB	SO	HBP	SH	SF	SB	CS	SB%	GDP	Avg	OBP	SLG
1985 Spokane	A- SD	74	281	64	9	1	1	78	21	32	20	0	60	5	4	1	0	1	.00	7	.228	.290	.278
1986 Charleston	A SD	120	431	112	19	2	10	165	55	62	41	2	83	2	4	5	2	4	.33	11	.260	.324	.383
1987 Chston-SC	A SD	128	468	131	22	2	9	184	52	72	46	2	65	8	4	9	8	5	.62	16	.280	.348	.393
1988 Wichita	AA SD	118	402	105	26	1	8	157	38	54	30	2	73	5	6	3	2	3	.40	5	.261	.318	.391
1990 Canton-Akrn	AA Cle	30	106	19	6	0	2	31	6	11	6	1	19	1	0	2	1	0	1.00	0	.179	.226	.292
Stockton	A+ Mil	70	260	68	16	0	12	120	41	59	13	0	49	8	0	4	4	5	.44	7	.262	.312	.462
1991 El Paso	AA Mil	130	493	158	27	8	18	255	99	128	63	5	79	15	2	20	5	7	.42	21	.320	.399	.517
1992 Denver	AAA Mil	130	492	162	36	3	19	261	74	101	40	3	87	9	4	11	8	9	.47	11	.329	.382	.530
1993 Colo Sprngs	AAA Col	13	45	10	2	0	2	18	5	7	2	0	9	1	0	0	0	1	.00	3	.222	.271	.400
1994 Colo Sprngs	AAA Col	121	439	154	43	1	21	262	76	97	44	4	84	5	1	10	2	2	.50	6	.351	.408	.597
1995 Colo Sprngs	AAA Col	27	93	30	7	0	6	55	17	18	6	0	21	1	0	2	2	0	1.00	2	.323	.363	.591
1996 Pawtucket	AAA Bos	19	66	18	2	0	5	35	11	16	7	0	12	1	0	0	2	0	1.00	3	.273	.351	.530
Las Vegas	AAA SD	64	233	80	20	1	12	138	40	56	23	6	53	3	0	1	4	0	1.00	9	.343	.408	.592
1997 Las Vegas	AAA SD	44	161	51	12	1	9	92	21	25	8	0	39	1	0	2	1	2	.33	1	.317	.349	.571
1992 Milwaukee	AL	5	8	1	0	0	0	1	0	1	0	0	2	0	0	0	0	0	.00	0	.125	.222	.125
1993 Colorado	NL	92	98	20	5	0	1	28	7	12	5	0	27	1	0	2	0	0	.00	0	.204	.245	.286
1995 Colorado	NL	34	34	8	1	1	0	11	4	4	1	0	7	0	0	0	0	0	.00	1	.235	.257	.324
1996 Boston	AL	2	8	1	0	0	0	1	1	0	0	0	2	0	0	0	0	0	.00	0	.125	.125	.125
San Diego	NL	5	3	0	0	0	0	0	0	0	0	0	1	0	0	0	0	0	.00	0	.000	.000	.000
12 Min. YEARS		1088	3970	1162	247	20	134	1851	556	738	349	25	733	65	25	70	39	40	.49	104	.293	.354	.466
4 Maj. YEARS		138	151	30	6	1	1	41	12	16	7	0	39	1	0	2	0	0	.00	1	.199	.236	.272

Andy Taulbee

Pitches: Right Bats: Right Pos: P   Ht: 6'4" Wt: 210 Born: 10/5/72 Age: 25

Year Team	Lg Org	G	GS	CG	GF	IP	BFP	H	R	ER	HR	SH	SF	HB	TBB	IBB	SO	WP	Bk	W	L	Pct.	ShO	Sv	ERA
1994 San Jose	A+ SF	13	13	0	0	71	300	66	28	21	5	5	1	6	20	0	51	0	5	4	3	.571	0	0	2.66
1995 San Jose	A+ SF	10	9	1	0	62.2	251	50	27	21	7	4	0	4	22	0	33	2	0	3	2	.600	1	0	3.02
Shreveport	AA SF	14	14	1	0	86.2	388	107	47	38	5	6	3	3	27	2	38	3	1	4	5	.444	1	0	3.95
1996 Shreveport	AA SF	27	24	0	3	138.2	617	169	87	77	10	5	4	6	47	2	55	2	1	6	10	.375	0	1	5.00
1997 Phoenix	AAA SF	19	6	0	5	40.2	195	64	41	34	4	4	0	0	14	0	20	0	0	2	2	.500	0	0	7.52
Shreveport	AA SF	14	14	1	0	85.1	376	104	59	49	9	3	6	1	32	0	46	5	3	4	8	.333	0	0	5.17
4 Min. YEARS		97	80	3	8	485	2127	560	289	240	40	27	14	20	162	4	243	12	10	23	30	.434	2	1	4.45

Jamie Taylor

Bats: Left Throws: Right Pos: 3B   Ht: 6'2" Wt: 220 Born: 10/10/70 Age: 27

Year Team	Lg Org	G	AB	H	2B	3B	HR	TB	R	RBI	TBB	IBB	SO	HBP	SH	SF	SB	CS	SB%	GDP	Avg	OBP	SLG
1992 Watertown	A- Cle	60	208	61	13	1	1	79	25	35	30	1	36	1	0	3	4	0	1.00	2	.293	.380	.380
1993 Columbus	A Cle	111	402	91	21	0	8	136	46	46	36	2	115	0	2	4	4	2	.67	2	.226	.287	.338
1994 Kinston	A+ Cle	76	217	51	14	0	5	80	30	19	29	0	63	2	2	1	3	4	.43	1	.235	.329	.369
1995 Canton-Akrn	AA Cle	4	11	0	0	0	0	0	0	0	0	0	4	1	1	0	0	0	.00	0	.000	.000	.000
Duluth-Sup.	IND —	75	285	84	18	1	4	116	36	28	31	1	50	1	2	2	1	2	.33	9	.295	.364	.407
1996 New Haven	AA Col	124	362	88	20	1	8	134	46	37	45	6	74	3	3	5	1	2	.33	12	.243	.328	.370
1997 Salem	A+ Col	23	80	21	4	1	1	30	13	9	13	0	27	2	1	0	2	2	.50	2	.263	.379	.375
New Haven	AA Col	104	329	107	17	1	8	150	43	41	35	7	49	2	5	4	2	3	.40	5	.325	.389	.456
6 Min. YEARS		577	1894	503	107	5	35	725	239	215	219	17	418	12	16	19	17	15	.53	34	.266	.342	.383

Kerry Taylor

Pitches: Right Bats: Right Pos: P   Ht: 6'3" Wt: 200 Born: 1/25/71 Age: 27

Year Team	Lg Org	G	GS	CG	GF	IP	BFP	H	R	ER	HR	SH	SF	HB	TBB	IBB	SO	WP	Bk	W	L	Pct.	ShO	Sv	ERA
1989 Elizabethtn	R+ Min	9	8	0	0	36	157	26	11	6	1	3	1	2	22	0	24	1	0	3	0	1.000	1	0	1.50
1990 Twins	R Min	14	13	1	1	63	275	57	37	25	2	0	4	4	33	0	59	5	4	3	1	.750	1	0	3.57
1991 Kenosha	A Min	26	26	2	0	132	586	121	74	56	4	2	5	10	84	1	84	11	1	7	11	.389	1	0	3.82
1992 Kenosha	A Min	27	27	2	0	170.1	733	150	71	52	3	6	2	10	68	0	158	11	1	10	9	.526	1	0	2.75
1994 Las Vegas	AAA SD	27	27	1	0	156	719	175	105	96	15	2	7	10	81	2	142	14	0	9	9	.500	0	0	5.54
1995 Las Vegas	AAA SD	8	8	0	0	37	174	44	21	18	3	4	0	2	21	1	21	0	0	2	2	.500	0	0	4.38
1997 Mobile	AA SD	5	5	0	0	26	117	27	14	14	4	0	0	1	13	0	30	2	0	2	1	.667	0	0	4.85
Las Vegas	AAA SD	22	22	3	0	144	628	150	84	69	15	8	8	11	55	3	103	4	0	7	9	.438	0	0	4.31
1993 San Diego	NL	36	7	0	9	68.1	326	72	53	49	5	10	3	4	49	0	45	4	0	0	5	.000	0	0	6.45
1994 San Diego	NL	1	1	0	0	4.1	24	9	4	4	1	0	0	1	1	0	3	0	0	0	0	.000	0	0	8.31
7 Min. YEARS		138	136	9	1	764.1	3389	750	417	336	47	25	27	50	377	7	621	48	6	43	42	.506	3	0	3.96
2 Maj. YEARS		37	8	0	9	72.2	350	81	57	53	6	10	3	5	50	0	48	4	0	0	5	.000	0	0	6.56

Scott Taylor

Pitches: Right Bats: Right Pos: P   Ht: 6'3" Wt: 200 Born: 10/3/66 Age: 31

Year Team	Lg Org	G	GS	CG	GF	IP	BFP	H	R	ER	HR	SH	SF	HB	TBB	IBB	SO	WP	Bk	W	L	Pct.	ShO	Sv	ERA
1989 Wausau	A Sea	16	16	6	0	106.1	445	92	49	38	5	3	2	6	37	1	65	8	3	9	7	.563	2	0	3.22
Williamsprt	AA Sea	10	7	1	1	40.2	185	49	26	26	6	1	5	1	20	1	22	2	0	1	4	.200	0	0	5.75
1990 San Berndno	A+ Sea	34	21	1	3	126.1	596	148	100	76	17	0	3	7	69	0	86	10	1	8	8	.500	0	1	5.41
1991 Durham	A+ Atl	24	16	2	5	111.1	452	94	32	27	3	6	2	2	33	3	78	10	0	10	3	.769	0	3	2.18
Greenville	AA Atl	8	7	1	0	43	191	49	25	20	4	1	1	2	16	2	26	6	0	3	4	.429	1	0	4.19
1992 Greenville	AA Atl	22	4	0	6	39	172	44	31	29	6	0	3	3	18	0	20	3	0	1	1	.500	0	1	6.69
El Paso	AA Mil	11	9	0	0	54.1	224	45	21	21	5	3	1	0	19	1	37	2	1	4	2	.667	0	0	3.48
1993 El Paso	AA Mil	17	16	1	1	104.1	434	105	53	44	4	2	2	11	31	2	76	0	0	6	6	.500	0	0	3.80
New Orleans	AAA Mil	12	8	1	3	62.1	244	48	17	16	3	5	1	2	21	1	47	1	1	5	1	.833	0	0	2.31
1994 New Orleans	AAA Mil	28	27	4	0	165.2	720	177	88	79	12	4	5	12	59	2	106	3	0	14	9	.609	1	0	4.29
1995 New Orleans	AAA Mil	2	2	0	0	11.1	47	10	3	3	0	0	0	1	3	0	9	0	0	1	0	1.000	0	0	2.38
Okla City	AAA Tex	22	19	1	0	118	510	122	59	48	12	4	2	6	38	0	65	5	0	7	8	.467	1	0	3.66
1996 Carolina	AA Pit	29	25	0	1	158	692	170	94	81	16	4	5	6	62	4	100	10	1	11	7	.611	0	0	4.61
1997 Las Vegas	AAA SD	2	0	0	0	1	9	4	2	2	0	0	1	0	1	0	1	0	0	0	0	.000	0	0	18.00
Calgary	AAA Pit	40	0	0	13	75.1	302	65	27	20	6	2	0	2	18	4	52	2	1	4	4	.556	0	4	2.39
1995 Texas	AL	3	3	0	0	15.1	71	25	16	16	6	0	0	2	5	0	10	0	0	1	2	.333	0	0	9.39
9 Min. YEARS		277	177	18	33	1217	5223	1222	627	530	99	35	33	62	445	21	790	62	8	85	64	.570	5	9	3.92

Nate Tebbs

Bats: Both Throws: Right Pos: SS   Ht: 5'11" Wt: 175 Born: 12/14/72 Age: 25

Year Team	Lg Org	G	AB	H	2B	3B	HR	TB	R	RBI	TBB	IBB	SO	HBP	SH	SF	SB	CS	SB%	GDP	Avg	OBP	SLG
1993 Red Sox	R Bos	43	146	38	4	1	0	44	21	4	15	1	16	0	7	0	7	1	.88	1	.260	.329	.301
1994 Utica	A- Bos	70	219	44	5	0	0	49	18	23	11	0	34	1	4	1	9	4	.69	1	.201	.241	.224
1995 Sarasota	A+ Bos	118	440	128	15	4	2	157	58	52	39	0	80	3	4	1	25	15	.63	7	.291	.352	.357
1996 Sarasota	A+ Bos	116	420	105	11	2	1	123	44	34	24	1	68	3	10	1	17	4	.81	7	.250	.295	.293
1997 Sarasota	A+ Bos	111	375	98	14	3	5	133	52	39	27	3	65	0	2	3	15	9	.63	9	.261	.309	.355
Trenton	AA Bos	5	16	5	0	0	0	5	2	0	2	0	1	0	0	0	0	1	.00	0	.313	.389	.313
5 Min. YEARS		463	1616	418	49	10	8	511	195	152	118	5	264	7	27	6	73	34	.68	25	.259	.311	.316

Fausto Tejero

Bats: Right **Throws:** Right **Pos:** C   **Ht:** 6'2" **Wt:** 205 **Born:** 10/26/68 **Age:** 29

Year Team	Lg Org	G	AB	H	2B	3B	HR	TB	R	RBI	TBB	IBB	SO	HBP	SH	SF	SB	CS	SB%	GDP	Avg	OBP	SLG
1990 Boise	A- Ana	39	74	16	2	0	0	18	14	7	23	1	23	2	3	3	1	0	1.00	0	.216	.402	.243
1991 Quad City	A Ana	83	244	42	7	0	1	52	16	18	14	0	52	4	3	1	0	1	.00	5	.172	.228	.213
1992 Edmonton	AAA Ana	8	17	4	1	0	0	5	0	0	4	0	2	1	2	0	0	2	.00	0	.235	.409	.294
Midland	AA Ana	84	266	50	11	0	2	67	21	30	11	0	63	4	5	3	1	2	.33	6	.188	.229	.252
1993 Palm Spring	A+ Ana	7	20	6	2	0	0	8	2	1	2	0	1	1	0	1	0	1	.00	0	.300	.364	.400
Vancouver	AAA Ana	20	59	9	0	0	0	9	2	2	4	1	12	1	2	1	1	1	.50	0	.153	.215	.153
Midland	AA Ana	26	69	9	1	1	1	15	3	7	8	0	17	2	1	1	0	0	.00	3	.130	.238	.217
1994 Midland	AA Ana	50	150	32	3	0	5	50	17	24	15	0	31	1	1	2	2	2	.50	6	.213	.286	.333
Vancouver	AAA Ana	16	45	9	2	0	0	11	6	6	4	0	9	0	2	1	1	1	.50	1	.200	.260	.244
1995 Lk Elsinore	A+ Ana	8	21	5	1	0	0	6	5	3	5	0	6	0	0	1	1	0	1.00	1	.238	.370	.286
Vancouver	AAA Ana	37	96	25	3	0	0	28	10	8	10	1	22	0	1	0	2	0	1.00	0	.260	.330	.292
Midland	AA Ana	16	53	12	3	0	1	18	7	11	1	0	13	1	0	1	0	1	.00	1	.226	.250	.340
1996 Vancouver	AAA Ana	54	155	31	4	1	1	40	21	12	22	0	41	1	6	0	0	1	.00	6	.200	.303	.258
1997 Richmond	AAA Atl	76	225	52	11	0	6	81	31	28	23	2	41	4	2	2	0	1	.00	6	.231	.311	.360
8 Min. YEARS		524	1494	302	51	2	17	408	155	157	146	5	333	21	29	16	9	13	.41	35	.202	.280	.273

Jim Telgheder

Pitches: Right **Bats:** Right **Pos:** P   **Ht:** 6'3" **Wt:** 210 **Born:** 3/22/71 **Age:** 27

Year Team	Lg Org	G	GS	CG	GF	IP	BFP	H	R	ER	HR	SH	SF	HB	TBB	IBB	SO	WP	Bk	W	L	Pct.	ShO	Sv	ERA
1993 Red Sox	R Bos	7	1	0	3	18.2	77	16	11	7	2	1	1	1	2	0	17	2	1	1	2	.333	0	1	3.38
Utica	A- Bos	2	0	0	1	2	9	0	1	0	0	0	0	1	1	0	0	0	0	0	0	.000	0	0	0.00
1994 Sarasota	A+ Bos	33	10	0	9	84	345	85	52	46	7	7	3	2	17	1	43	1	2	5	5	.500	0	6	4.93
1995 Sarasota	A+ Bos	22	0	0	5	25	122	30	20	18	3	2	0	2	15	2	24	4	1	0	3	.000	0	6	6.48
Michigan	A Bos	22	1	0	18	35	142	29	8	7	0	2	2	1	8	2	39	3	0	5	1	.833	0	4	1.80
1996 Wilmington	A+ KC	31	2	0	9	74.1	294	60	24	20	8	3	1	2	14	2	50	5	0	8	3	.727	0	2	2.42
Wichita	AA KC	13	0	0	6	21	92	23	9	8	2	0	0	1	6	1	11	1	0	0	2	.000	0	0	3.43
1997 Wichita	AA KC	28	12	0	5	86	393	104	66	60	22	2	1	2	30	4	47	6	0	4	7	.364	0	0	6.28
5 Min. YEARS		158	26	0	56	346	1474	347	191	166	44	17	8	12	93	12	231	22	4	23	23	.500	0	13	4.32

Jay Tessmer

Pitches: Right **Bats:** Right **Pos:** P   **Ht:** 6'3" **Wt:** 190 **Born:** 12/26/72 **Age:** 25

Year Team	Lg Org	G	GS	CG	GF	IP	BFP	H	R	ER	HR	SH	SF	HB	TBB	IBB	SO	WP	Bk	W	L	Pct.	ShO	Sv	ERA
1995 Oneonta	A- NYA	34	0	0	33	38	156	27	8	4	0	0	0	3	12	2	52	3	2	2	0	1.000	0	20	0.95
1996 Tampa	A+ NYA	68	0	0	63	97.1	381	68	18	16	2	6	0	6	19	3	104	1	0	12	4	.750	0	35	1.48
1997 Norwich	AA NYA	55	0	0	49	62.2	289	78	41	37	7	3	2	2	24	2	51	4	0	3	6	.333	0	17	5.31
3 Min. YEARS		157	0	0	145	198	826	173	67	57	9	9	2	11	55	7	207	8	2	17	10	.630	0	72	2.59

Robert Theodile

Pitches: Right **Bats:** Right **Pos:** P   **Ht:** 6'3" **Wt:** 190 **Born:** 9/16/72 **Age:** 25

Year Team	Lg Org	G	GS	CG	GF	IP	BFP	H	R	ER	HR	SH	SF	HB	TBB	IBB	SO	WP	Bk	W	L	Pct.	ShO	Sv	ERA
1992 White Sox	R ChA	4	1	0	0	13	45	7	1	1	0	0	0	0	4	0	12	2	0	2	0	1.000	0	0	0.69
1993 White Sox	R ChA	10	8	1	1	66	265	45	24	19	2	1	0	6	23	0	42	2	2	5	2	.714	1	1	2.59
Hickory	A ChA	8	8	0	0	45.1	211	63	40	34	1	0	2	1	21	0	23	5	0	0	4	.000	0	0	6.75
1994 Hickory	A ChA	18	16	2	1	86.1	383	81	53	46	7	1	2	2	47	0	68	11	1	7	4	.636	0	0	4.80
1995 South Bend	A ChA	7	4	0	0	26	130	45	30	22	1	1	1	1	13	0	16	5	0	1	2	.333	0	0	7.62
Hickory	A ChA	20	17	1	1	107	470	103	61	45	8	3	5	5	53	2	77	13	4	6	9	.400	1	0	3.79
1996 Pr William	A+ ChA	25	22	1	1	132	571	133	73	63	5	6	5	7	56	3	91	8	1	7	9	.438	1	1	4.30
1997 Birmingham	AA ChA	19	9	0	3	57.1	272	72	43	35	2	0	5	2	35	0	41	5	0	2	0	1.000	0	0	5.49
Winston-Sal	A+ ChA	13	12	0	1	82.2	344	66	34	27	6	2	4	6	33	0	75	5	0	7	3	.700	0	0	2.94
6 Min. YEARS		124	97	5	8	615.2	2691	615	359	292	32	14	24	30	285	5	445	56	8	37	33	.529	3	3	4.27

Steve Thobe

Bats: Right **Throws:** Right **Pos:** 3B   **Ht:** 6'7" **Wt:** 230 **Born:** 5/26/72 **Age:** 26

Year Team	Lg Org	G	AB	H	2B	3B	HR	TB	R	RBI	TBB	IBB	SO	HBP	SH	SF	SB	CS	SB%	GDP	Avg	OBP	SLG
1994 Welland	A- Pit	46	151	29	11	0	1	43	14	10	12	0	33	2	0	0	1	0	1.00	3	.192	.261	.285
1995 Augusta	A Pit	84	291	87	12	2	6	121	43	38	29	6	71	5	0	0	1	3	.25	2	.299	.372	.416
1996 Lynchburg	A+ Pit	109	359	82	15	0	11	130	49	42	29	0	93	6	0	0	4	4	.50	13	.228	.297	.362
1997 Lynchburg	A+ Pit	12	27	4	1	0	0	5	1	2	1	0	10	1	1	1	1	0	1.00	0	.148	.200	.185
Calgary	AAA Pit	34	102	26	8	0	5	49	16	14	15	0	25	2	0	0	2	1	.67	1	.255	.361	.480
Carolina	AA Pit	53	181	53	10	0	7	84	21	32	13	0	52	4	1	1	4	1	.80	4	.293	.352	.464
4 Min. YEARS		338	1111	281	57	2	30	432	144	138	99	6	284	20	2	2	13	9	.59	23	.253	.325	.389

Tom Thobe

Pitches: Left **Bats:** Left **Pos:** P   **Ht:** 6'6" **Wt:** 195 **Born:** 9/3/69 **Age:** 28

Year Team	Lg Org	G	GS	CG	GF	IP	BFP	H	R	ER	HR	SH	SF	HB	TBB	IBB	SO	WP	Bk	W	L	Pct.	ShO	Sv	ERA
1993 Macon	A Atl	43	0	0	22	70.1	299	70	25	21	0	6	1	2	16	1	55	8	0	7	5	.583	0	5	2.69
1994 Greenville	AA Atl	51	0	0	27	63.2	263	56	21	18	3	5	2	0	26	2	52	6	2	7	6	.538	0	9	2.54
1995 Richmond	AAA Atl	48	2	1	15	88	350	65	27	18	2	3	1	1	26	5	57	5	0	7	0	1.000	1	5	1.84

		HOW MUCH HE PITCHED		WHAT HE GAVE UP		THE RESULTS	
Year Team	Lg Org	G GS CG GF	IP BFP	H R ER HR SH SF HB	TBB IBB SO WP Bk	W L Pct. ShO Sv	ERA
1996 Richmond	AAA Atl	31 6 1 9	72 345	89 60 49 6 1 5 2	37 2 40 4 0	1 8 .111 0 3	6.13
1997 Richmond	AAA Atl	19 10 0 1	71.2 297	70 37 33 9 3 3 0	22 1 36 3 0	5 2 .714 0 0	4.14
1995 Atlanta	NL	3 0 0 1	3.1 17	7 4 4 0 0 0 0	0 0 2 0 0	0 0 .000 0 0	10.80
1996 Atlanta	NL	4 0 0 3	6 24	5 2 1 1 0 1 0	0 0 1 0 0	0 1 .000 0 0	1.50
5 Min. YEARS		192 18 2 74	365.2 1554	350 170 139 20 18 12 5	127 11 240 26 2	27 21 .563 1 22	3.42
2 Maj. YEARS		7 0 0 4	9.1 41	12 6 5 1 0 1 0	0 0 3 0 0	0 1 .000 0 0	4.82

Evan Thomas

Pitches: Right Bats: Right Pos: P   Ht: 5'10" Wt: 175 Born: 6/14/74 Age: 24

		HOW MUCH HE PITCHED		WHAT HE GAVE UP		THE RESULTS	
Year Team	Lg Org	G GS CG GF	IP BFP	H R ER HR SH SF HB	TBB IBB SO WP Bk	W L Pct. ShO Sv	ERA
1996 Batavia	A- Phi	13 13 0 0	81 321	60 29 25 3 1 3 5	23 0 75 6 0	10 2 .833 0 0	2.78
1997 Clearwater	A+ Phi	13 12 2 0	84.2 340	68 30 23 7 1 1 3	23 0 89 3 2	5 5 .500 0 0	2.44
Reading	AA Phi	15 15 0 0	83 377	98 51 38 10 5 2 7	32 1 83 3 2	3 6 .333 0 0	4.12
2 Min. YEARS		41 40 2 0	248.2 1038	226 110 86 20 7 6 15	78 1 247 12 4	18 13 .581 0 0	3.11

Greg Thomas

Bats: Left Throws: Left Pos: 1B   Ht: 6'3" Wt: 200 Born: 7/19/72 Age: 25

		BATTING				BASERUNNING	PERCENTAGES
Year Team	Lg Org	G AB H	2B 3B HR TB	R RBI TBB IBB SO	HBP SH SF	SB CS SB% GDP	Avg OBP SLG
1993 Watertown	A- Cle	73 277 85	20 5 9 142	48 63 27 3 47	2 0 1	3 4 .43 3	.307 .371 .513
1994 Kinston	A+ Cle	103 351 67	14 2 15 130	46 42 26 3 97	5 2 2	5 2 .71 4	.191 .255 .370
1995 Kinston	A+ Cle	102 329 72	21 0 11 126	32 43 25 4 98	3 1 7	0 2 .00 2	.219 .275 .383
1996 Canton-Akrn	AA Cle	97 301 84	14 4 13 145	44 55 26 4 56	1 1 2	2 1 .67 8	.279 .336 .482
1997 Buffalo	AAA Cle	11 13 1	1 0 0 2	1 2 3 0 6	0 0 0	0 0 .00 0	.077 .250 .154
Akron	AA Cle	67 242 59	13 2 7 97	27 42 29 1 50	0 0 2	2 1 .67 4	.244 .322 .401
5 Min. YEARS		453 1513 368	83 13 55 642	198 247 136 15 354	11 4 14	12 10 .55 21	.243 .308 .424

Juan Thomas

Bats: Right Throws: Right Pos: 1B-DH   Ht: 6'5" Wt: 240 Born: 4/17/72 Age: 26

		BATTING				BASERUNNING	PERCENTAGES
Year Team	Lg Org	G AB H	2B 3B HR TB	R RBI TBB IBB SO	HBP SH SF	SB CS SB% GDP	Avg OBP SLG
1992 White Sox	R ChA	55 189 42	6 1 6 68	30 29 18 0 76	3 0 2	8 1 .89 4	.222 .297 .360
1993 White Sox	R ChA	20 59 18	3 2 1 28	12 9 12 0 12	1 0 0	5 4 .56 1	.305 .431 .475
Hickory	A ChA	90 328 75	14 6 12 137	51 46 35 1 124	7 1 3	4 .33 7	.229 .314 .418
1994 South Bend	A ChA	119 446 112	20 6 18 198	57 79 27 2 143	9 0 5	3 4 .43 13	.251 .304 .444
1995 Pr William	A+ ChA	132 464 109	20 4 26 215	64 69 40 4 156	8 1 2	4 5 .44 16	.235 .305 .463
1996 Pr William	A+ ChA	134 495 148	28 6 20 248	88 71 54 3 129	5 0 2	9 3 .75 15	.299 .372 .501
1997 Winston-Sal	A+ ChA	45 164 43	7 0 13 89	28 28 17 0 61	1 0 0	1 1 .50 5	.262 .335 .543
Birmingham	AA ChA	80 311 94	16 2 10 144	50 55 23 1 92	4 0 4	1 2 .33 4	.302 .354 .463
6 Min. YEARS		675 2456 641	114 27 106 1127	380 386 226 11 793	38 2 18	33 24 .58 65	.261 .331 .459

Andy Thompson

Bats: Right Throws: Right Pos: 3B   Ht: 6'3" Wt: 210 Born: 10/8/75 Age: 22

		BATTING				BASERUNNING	PERCENTAGES
Year Team	Lg Org	G AB H	2B 3B HR TB	R RBI TBB IBB SO	HBP SH SF	SB CS SB% GDP	Avg OBP SLG
1995 Hagerstown	A Tor	124 461 110	19 2 6 151	48 57 29 2 108	8 1 3	2 3 .40 15	.239 .293 .328
1996 Dunedin	A+ Tor	129 425 120	26 5 11 189	64 50 60 1 108	1 1 3	16 4 .80 5	.282 .370 .445
1997 Knoxville	AA Tor	124 448 128	25 3 15 204	75 71 63 3 76	6 1 4	0 5 .00 18	.286 .378 .455
3 Min. YEARS		377 1334 358	70 10 32 544	187 178 152 6 292	15 3 10	18 12 .60 38	.268 .347 .408

John Thompson

Pitches: Right Bats: Right Pos: P   Ht: 6'2" Wt: 200 Born: 1/18/73 Age: 25

		HOW MUCH HE PITCHED		WHAT HE GAVE UP		THE RESULTS	
Year Team	Lg Org	G GS CG GF	IP BFP	H R ER HR SH SF HB	TBB IBB SO WP Bk	W L Pct. ShO Sv	ERA
1992 Mariners	R Sea	14 11 1 1	70.2 301	54 35 29 1 1 1 2	32 1 65 13 4	6 3 .667 1 0	3.69
1993 Bellingham	A- Sea	17 1 0 8	34 165	31 23 16 3 0 0 1	33 2 28 9 0	0 2 .000 0 0	4.24
1994 Bellingham	A- Sea	15 15 1 0	82 354	63 40 33 6 0 4 3	44 0 78 19 3	4 5 .444 0 0	3.62
1995 Wisconsin	A Sea	38 7 0 29	69.2 314	65 41 32 8 2 2 2	43 2 69 13 1	2 8 .200 0 19	4.13
Tacoma	AAA Sea	1 0 0 0	2.2 12	3 2 0 1 0 0 0	0 0 0 0 0	0 1 .000 0 0	0.00
1996 Lancaster	A+ Sea	50 0 0 41	61.2 287	72 50 42 12 3 4 5	29 1 53 6 1	3 8 .273 0 14	6.13
1997 Lancaster	A+ Sea	3 0 0 3	4 19	4 1 1 1 0 0 0	2 0 3 0 0	1 0 1.000 0 0	2.25
Memphis	AA Sea	45 0 0 30	60.1 278	59 33 31 6 1 5 3	48 0 44 13 1	3 2 .600 0 4	4.62
6 Min. YEARS		183 34 2 112	385 1730	351 225 184 37 8 16 16	231 6 340 73 10	19 29 .396 1 37	4.30

Karl Thompson

Bats: Right Throws: Right Pos: C   Ht: 6'0" Wt: 180 Born: 12/30/73 Age: 24

		BATTING				BASERUNNING	PERCENTAGES
Year Team	Lg Org	G AB H	2B 3B HR TB	R RBI TBB IBB SO	HBP SH SF	SB CS SB% GDP	Avg OBP SLG
1995 Everett	A- Sea	54 187 46	13 1 5 76	29 26 16 0 39	4 2 2	4 0 1.00 9	.246 .316 .406
1996 Wisconsin	A Sea	119 439 128	36 1 9 193	76 66 35 1 79	6 6 5	2 3 .33 9	.292 .348 .440
1997 Memphis	AA Sea	42 148 34	10 0 4 56	18 21 11 0 25	4 4 2	2 1 1.00 5	.230 .297 .378
Lancaster	A+ Sea	6 22 6	2 0 0 8	5 1 3 1 5	0 1 0	0 0 .00 1	.273 .360 .364
3 Min. YEARS		221 796 214	61 2 18 333	128 114 65 2 148	14 13 9	7 2 .78 24	.269 .331 .418

Ryan Thompson

Bats: Right **Throws:** Right **Pos:** OF **Ht:** 6'3" **Wt:** 215 **Born:** 11/4/67 **Age:** 30

Year Team	Lg Org	G	AB	H	2B	3B	HR	TB	R	RBI	TBB	IBB	SO	HBP	SH	SF	SB	CS	SB%	GDP	Avg	OBP	SLG
1987 Medicne Hat	R+ Tor	40	110	27	3	1	1	35	13	9	6	0	34	0	0	0	1	2	.33	1	.245	.284	.318
1988 St. Cathrns	A- Tor	23	57	10	4	0	0	14	13	2	24	0	21	4	1	0	2	2	.50	0	.175	.447	.246
Dunedin	A+ Tor	17	29	4	0	0	1	7	2	2	2	0	12	1	0	0	0	0	.00	0	.138	.219	.241
1989 St. Cathrns	A- Tor	74	278	76	14	1	6	110	39	36	16	0	60	4	0	3	9	6	.60	8	.273	.319	.396
1990 Dunedin	A+ Tor	117	438	101	15	5	6	144	56	37	20	1	100	2	3	4	18	5	.78	5	.231	.265	.329
1991 Knoxville	AA Tor	114	403	97	14	3	8	141	48	40	26	2	88	4	5	3	17	10	.63	11	.241	.291	.350
1992 Syracuse	AAA Tor	112	429	121	20	7	14	197	74	46	43	1	114	3	2	1	10	4	.71	5	.282	.351	.459
1993 Norfolk	AAA NYN	60	224	58	11	2	12	109	39	34	24	2	81	5	0	2	6	3	.67	2	.259	.341	.487
1995 Norfolk	AAA NYN	15	53	18	3	0	2	27	7	11	4	0	15	0	0	4	4	1	.80	0	.340	.361	.509
Binghamton	AA NYN	2	8	4	0	0	1	7	2	4	1	0	2	0	0	0	0	0	.00	0	.500	.556	.875
1996 Buffalo	AAA Cle	138	540	140	26	4	21	237	79	83	21	1	119	7	2	4	12	5	.71	14	.259	.294	.439
1997 Buffalo	AAA Cle	24	66	16	0	0	1	19	10	6	5	1	16	0	0	0	2	0	1.00	1	.242	.296	.288
Syracuse	AAA Tor	83	330	95	23	1	16	168	37	58	21	1	59	3	0	3	4	3	.57	10	.288	.333	.509
1992 New York	NL	30	108	24	7	1	3	42	15	10	8	0	24	0	0	1	2	2	.50	2	.222	.274	.389
1993 New York	NL	80	288	72	19	2	11	128	34	26	19	4	81	3	5	1	2	7	.22	5	.250	.302	.444
1994 New York	NL	98	334	75	14	1	18	145	39	59	28	7	94	10	3	4	1	1	.50	8	.225	.301	.434
1995 New York	NL	75	267	67	13	0	7	101	39	31	19	1	77	4	0	3	3	1	.75	12	.251	.306	.378
1996 Cleveland	AL	8	22	7	0	0	1	10	2	5	1	0	6	0	0	0	0	0	.00	0	.318	.348	.455
10 Min. YEARS		819	2965	767	133	24	89	1215	419	368	213	9	721	33	13	24	85	41	.67	57	.259	.313	.410
5 Maj. YEARS		291	1019	245	53	4	40	426	129	131	75	12	282	17	8	10	8	11	.42	27	.240	.301	.418

Travis Thurmond

Pitches: Right **Bats:** Right **Pos:** P **Ht:** 6'3" **Wt:** 200 **Born:** 12/8/73 **Age:** 24

Year Team	Lg Org	G	GS	CG	GF	IP	BFP	H	R	ER	HR	SH	SF	HB	TBB	IBB	SO	WP	Bk	W	L	Pct.	ShO	Sv	ERA
1992 Angels	R Ana	8	5	0	2	26.1	128	28	18	14	0	2	0	1	21	2	18	6	3	0	2	.000	0	0	4.78
1993 Angels	R Ana	12	0	0	5	19	82	20	14	9	0	1	0	0	8	0	19	2	0	0	0	.000	0	0	4.26
1994 Boise	A- Ana	8	0	0	3	13	50	8	3	3	1	0	2	0	6	0	17	1	0	1	0	1.000	0	0	2.08
Angels	R Ana	6	5	0	1	31	132	25	15	9	1	1	1	2	11	0	39	8	0	1	3	.250	0	0	2.61
Cedar Rapds	A Ana	2	0	0	0	4.2	19	3	1	1	1	0	0	0	3	0	2	0	0	1	0	1.000	0	0	1.93
1995 Cedar Rapds	A Ana	14	2	0	4	39	172	36	25	23	4	2	0	1	20	4	55	3	0	2	5	.286	0	2	5.31
Boise	A- Ana	16	15	4	1	101.1	401	75	36	35	7	0	3	3	31	0	93	7	0	9	3	.750	1	0	3.11
1996 Cedar Rapds	A Ana	4	4	1	0	29	120	20	6	5	1	0	0	1	14	0	29	2	0	2	0	1.000	0	0	1.55
Lk Elsinore	A+ Ana	6	5	0	0	36.2	159	36	18	16	4	0	2	2	17	0	39	2	1	2	2	.500	0	0	3.93
1997 Lk Elsinore	A+ Ana	9	9	2	0	60.2	247	41	21	17	6	2	1	5	22	0	53	5	0	3	3	.500	1	0	2.52
San Jose	A+ SF	12	12	0	0	69.2	320	83	53	44	8	3	3	5	28	0	61	6	0	3	5	.375	0	0	5.68
Shreveport	AA SF	2	1	0	0	6	36	10	9	4	1	1	1	0	9	0	4	1	0	0	1	.000	0	0	6.00
6 Min. YEARS		99	58	7	16	436.1	1866	385	219	180	34	12	13	20	190	6	429	43	4	24	24	.500	2	2	3.71

Jerrey Thurston

Bats: Right **Throws:** Right **Pos:** C **Ht:** 6'4" **Wt:** 200 **Born:** 4/17/72 **Age:** 26

Year Team	Lg Org	G	AB	H	2B	3B	HR	TB	R	RBI	TBB	IBB	SO	HBP	SH	SF	SB	CS	SB%	GDP	Avg	OBP	SLG
1990 Padres	R SD	42	144	33	6	1	0	41	22	16	14	0	37	0	2	0	4	1	.80	1	.229	.297	.285
1991 Chston-SC	A SD	42	137	14	2	0	0	16	5	4	9	0	50	0	1	1	1	1	.50	3	.102	.156	.117
Spokane	A- SD	60	201	43	9	0	1	55	26	20	20	1	61	2	2	2	2	2	.50	2	.214	.289	.274
1992 Waterloo	A SD	96	263	37	7	0	0	44	20	14	12	0	73	2	6	2	1	0	1.00	3	.141	.183	.167
1993 Wichita	AA SD	78	197	48	10	0	2	64	22	22	14	0	62	6	3	0	2	0	1.00	3	.244	.313	.325
1994 Wichita	AA SD	77	238	51	10	2	4	77	30	28	19	1	73	8	2	1	1	4	.20	8	.214	.293	.324
1995 Las Vegas	AAA SD	5	20	4	1	0	0	5	2	0	0	0	5	1	0	0	0	0	.00	0	.200	.238	.250
Rancho Cuca	A+ SD	76	200	44	9	0	1	56	24	13	21	0	64	7	4	3	1	0	1.00	2	.220	.312	.280
1996 Orlando	AA ChN	67	177	37	6	1	3	54	16	23	14	0	57	0	3	0	0	0	.00	5	.209	.267	.305
1997 Lk Elsinore	A+ Ana	2	6	3	1	0	0	4	1	1	0	0	2	0	0	0	0	0	.00	0	.500	.500	.667
Vancouver	AAA Ana	65	195	46	3	1	4	63	17	19	8	0	59	4	8	2	3	2	.60	2	.236	.278	.323
8 Min. YEARS		610	1778	360	64	5	15	479	185	160	131	2	543	30	31	11	15	10	.60	30	.202	.267	.269

Kevin Tolar

Pitches: Left **Bats:** Right **Pos:** P **Ht:** 6'3" **Wt:** 225 **Born:** 1/28/71 **Age:** 27

Year Team	Lg Org	G	GS	CG	GF	IP	BFP	H	R	ER	HR	SH	SF	HB	TBB	IBB	SO	WP	Bk	W	L	Pct.	ShO	Sv	ERA
1989 White Sox	R ChA	13	12	1	0	60	256	29	16	11	0	1	1	1	54	0	58	10	0	6	2	.750	0	0	1.65
1990 Utica	A- ChA	15	15	1	0	90.1	407	80	44	33	2	1	3	4	61	1	69	9	1	4	6	.400	0	0	3.29
1991 South Bend	A ChA	30	19	0	6	114.2	510	87	54	35	3	5	5	8	85	0	87	6	0	8	5	.615	0	0	2.75
1992 Salinas	A+ ChA	14	8	3	3	53.1	255	55	43	36	4	1	7	5	46	0	24	6	0	1	8	.111	0	0	6.08
South Bend	A ChA	18	10	0	6	81.1	339	59	34	26	5	7	4	2	41	0	81	5	1	6	5	.545	0	0	2.88
1993 Sarasota	A+ ChA	23	11	0	8	77.1	358	75	55	46	1	5	7	6	51	1	60	8	0	2	6	.250	0	1	5.35
1995 Lynchburg	A+ Pit	18	0	0	4	19.1	77	13	7	6	1	0	1	1	6	0	19	3	0	2	0	1.000	0	0	2.79
Carolina	AA Pit	12	0	0	3	12.1	59	16	5	5	0	0	2	0	7	0	9	2	0	1	0	1.000	0	0	3.65
1996 Canton-Akrn	AA Cle	50	0	0	15	44.2	201	42	19	13	1	4	2	3	26	2	39	5	0	1	3	.250	0	0	2.62
1997 Binghamton	AA NYN	22	0	0	9	31.2	157	38	20	18	3	4	1	2	22	1	26	6	0	1	1	.500	0	1	5.12
St. Lucie	A+ NYN	9	0	0	3	13.1	54	9	3	3	0	0	0	0	6	0	8	1	0	0	0	.000	0	1	2.03
8 Min. YEARS		224	75	5	57	598.1	2673	503	300	232	20	28	33	32	405	5	480	61	2	32	36	.471	0	4	3.49

Jose Tolentino

Bats: Left Throws: Left Pos: 1B Ht: 6'1" Wt: 195 Born: 6/3/61 Age: 37

Year Team	Lg Org	G	AB	H	2B	3B	HR	TB	R	RBI	TBB	IBB	SO	HBP	SH	SF	SB	CS	SB%	GDP	Avg	OBP	SLG
1983 Medford	A- Oak	49	181	60	11	1	7	94	33	39	15	2	17	2	3	2	1	1	.50	—	.331	.387	.519
1984 Modesto	A+ Oak	66	251	71	17	1	14	132	40	54	29	7	34	5	2	0	4	4	.50	6	.283	.368	.526
Albany-Colo	AA Oak	71	257	73	13	1	5	103	32	43	16	0	35	0	2	3	2	1	.67	5	.284	.322	.401
1985 Tacoma	AAA Oak	106	339	87	24	1	6	131	38	41	38	5	53	3	1	4	1	3	.25	9	.257	.333	.386
1986 Huntsville	AA Oak	137	540	170	28	0	16	246	80	105	53	6	57	4	2	7	7	2	.78	10	.315	.376	.456
1987 Tacoma	AAA Oak	59	202	46	8	0	3	63	16	26	21	0	29	0	2	0	0	0	.00	9	.228	.300	.312
Huntsville	AA Oak	49	173	41	6	0	6	65	20	25	21	2	28	1	1	1	1	0	1.00	4	.237	.321	.376
1988 Okla City	AAA Tex	48	131	28	4	0	0	32	6	8	20	3	20	0	4	0	0	1	.00	5	.214	.318	.244
Columbus	AA Hou	72	259	79	10	3	9	122	33	53	36	6	32	6	0	5	1	3	.25	7	.305	.395	.471
1989 Tucson	AAA Hou	128	408	111	27	1	9	167	61	64	62	6	72	3	3	10	2	4	.33	11	.272	.364	.409
1990 Tucson	AAA Hou	116	377	116	32	3	21	217	69	78	48	2	44	5	2	4	0	1	.00	12	.308	.389	.576
1991 Tucson	AAA Hou	90	303	88	24	5	6	140	44	51	44	8	44	2	0	1	2	3	.40	10	.290	.383	.462
1992 Buffalo	AAA Pit	78	209	63	16	1	8	105	39	34	24	4	28	3	1	5	0	1	.00	9	.301	.373	.502
1997 Rochester	AAA Bal	20	57	12	2	0	1	17	6	9	14	1	11	1	0	1	0	0	.00	5	.211	.370	.298
Calgary	AAA Pit	88	305	94	24	0	16	166	52	69	31	3	49	2	0	6	2	5	.29	10	.308	.369	.544
1991 Houston	NL	44	54	14	4	0	1	21	6	6	4	0	9	0	0	1	0	0	.00	2	.259	.305	.389
11 Min. YEARS		1177	3992	1139	246	17	127	1800	569	699	472	55	553	37	23	49	23	29	.44	112	.285	.362	.451

Brian Tollberg

Pitches: Right Bats: Right Pos: P Ht: 6'3" Wt: 195 Born: 9/16/72 Age: 25

Year Team	Lg Org	G	GS	CG	GF	IP	BFP	H	R	ER	HR	SH	SF	HB	TBB	IBB	SO	WP	Bk	W	L	Pct.	ShO	Sv	ERA
1994 Chillicothe	IND —	13	13	4	0	94.2	402	90	34	30	5	2	8	27	2	69	8	0	7	4	.636	0	0	2.85
1995 Beloit	A Mil	22	22	1	0	132	529	119	59	50	10	2	5	6	27	0	110	5	4	13	4	.765	1	0	3.41
1996 El Paso	AA Mil	26	26	0	0	154.1	663	183	90	84	15	2	3	10	23	0	109	4	1	7	5	.583	0	0	4.90
1997 Mobile	AA SD	31	13	1	5	123.1	512	123	60	51	15	2	1	4	24	2	108	4	0	6	3	.667	0	0	3.72
4 Min. YEARS		92	74	6	5	504.1	2106	515	243	215	45	8	11	28	101	4	396	21	5	33	16	.673	1	0	3.84

Ryan Topham

Bats: Left Throws: Left Pos: OF Ht: 6'3" Wt: 200 Born: 12/17/73 Age: 24

Year Team	Lg Org	G	AB	H	2B	3B	HR	TB	R	RBI	TBB	IBB	SO	HBP	SH	SF	SB	CS	SB%	GDP	Avg	OBP	SLG
1995 South Bend	A ChA	14	48	12	3	0	0	15	4	2	4	0	12	0	1	0	0	0	.00	0	.250	.308	.313
1996 South Bend	A ChA	114	392	91	17	7	5	137	50	39	53	0	106	3	5	3	18	9	.67	4	.232	.326	.349
1997 Winston-Sal	A+ ChA	58	193	46	13	2	4	75	26	21	24	0	53	1	0	2	0	2	.00	1	.238	.323	.389
Birmingham	AA ChA	17	47	10	5	1	0	17	6	8	6	0	15	2	1	1	1	0	1.00	0	.213	.321	.362
3 Min. YEARS		203	680	159	38	10	9	244	86	70	87	0	186	6	7	6	19	11	.63	5	.234	.323	.359

Paul Torres

Bats: Right Throws: Right Pos: 3B Ht: 6'3" Wt: 210 Born: 10/19/70 Age: 27

Year Team	Lg Org	G	AB	H	2B	3B	HR	TB	R	RBI	TBB	IBB	SO	HBP	SH	SF	SB	CS	SB%	GDP	Avg	OBP	SLG
1989 Wytheville	R+ ChN	54	191	45	9	1	7	77	34	38	32	0	55	6	0	2	2	4	.33	3	.236	.359	.403
1990 Peoria	A ChN	36	123	30	4	1	5	51	18	18	13	0	33	2	1	0	1	1	.50	2	.244	.326	.415
Geneva	A- ChN	77	271	72	23	1	10	127	46	45	39	1	72	10	2	5	9	3	.75	3	.266	.372	.469
1991 Winston-Sal	A+ ChN	27	87	10	1	0	2	17	9	7	11	0	30	2	0	1	4	0	1.00	1	.115	.228	.195
Peoria	A ChN	99	352	75	24	2	13	142	60	50	48	2	91	9	3	0	6	2	.75	7	.213	.323	.403
1992 Winston-Sal	A+ ChN	134	458	109	15	6	14	178	55	78	60	2	114	5	2	7	4	4	.50	10	.238	.328	.389
1993 Daytona	A+ ChN	100	353	98	17	5	13	164	63	43	52	0	94	8	1	3	4	5	.56	5	.278	.380	.465
Orlando	AA ChN	19	55	14	4	0	3	27	10	10	7	0	18	0	0	0	3	0	1.00	1	.255	.339	.491
1994 Orlando	AA ChN	61	160	38	2	1	10	72	21	26	31	1	41	2	1	2	2	6	.25	5	.238	.364	.450
Daytona	A+ ChN	26	90	28	6	3	4	52	12	20	11	2	26	0	0	1	4	1	.80	1	.311	.382	.578
1995 Orlando	AA ChN	63	228	68	14	1	10	114	38	45	29	4	40	1	0	2	0	3	.00	1	.298	.377	.500
Arkansas	AA StL	66	231	52	11	0	10	93	24	33	21	0	56	5	1	0	2	1	.67	9	.225	.304	.403
1996 Louisville	AAA StL	1	2	1	0	0	0	1	0	0	0	0	1	0	0	0	0	0	.00	0	.500	.500	.500
Arkansas	AA StL	102	309	81	16	0	11	130	38	44	44	1	62	2	0	1	1	1	.50	3	.262	.357	.421
1997 Memphis	AA Sea	62	218	75	8	3	6	107	40	55	38	1	30	2	0	4	3	1	.75	6	.344	.439	.491
Tacoma	AAA Sea	59	209	63	19	0	5	97	24	22	14	1	31	3	3	5	1	0	1.00	4	.301	.346	.464
9 Min. YEARS		986	3337	859	173	24	123	1449	492	534	450	15	794	57	14	33	47	31	.60	63	.257	.352	.434

Tony Torres

Bats: Right Throws: Right Pos: 2B Ht: 5'9" Wt: 165 Born: 6/1/70 Age: 28

Year Team	Lg Org	G	AB	H	2B	3B	HR	TB	R	RBI	TBB	IBB	SO	HBP	SH	SF	SB	CS	SB%	GDP	Avg	OBP	SLG
1992 Erie	A- Fla	40	157	46	9	1	0	57	31	16	20	0	26	4	0	2	13	5	.72	1	.293	.383	.363
1993 High Desert	A+ Fla	89	287	66	9	3	1	84	45	25	24	0	69	2	5	3	14	8	.64	7	.230	.291	.293
1994 Brevard Cty	A+ Fla	98	368	93	14	7	4	133	58	39	39	1	67	2	3	3	17	6	.74	6	.253	.325	.361
1995 Portland	AA Fla	58	81	24	3	2	0	31	15	4	11	0	23	1	8	0	9	0	1.00	1	.296	.387	.383
1996 Portland	AA Fla	47	126	34	11	0	1	48	21	13	14	0	24	5	1	0	3	1	.75	2	.270	.366	.381
1997 Portland	AA Fla	29	50	13	2	1	2	23	12	4	8	0	15	2	1	0	2	3	.40	0	.260	.383	.460
Charlotte	AAA Fla	29	68	19	3	0	1	25	9	8	7	0	26	0	1	0	3	2	.60	0	.279	.347	.368
6 Min. YEARS		390	1137	295	51	14	9	401	191	109	123	1	250	16	19	8	61	25	.71	17	.259	.338	.353

Dave Toth

Bats: Right **Throws:** Right **Pos:** C   **Ht:** 6'1" **Wt:** 195 **Born:** 12/8/69 **Age:** 28

Year Team	Lg Org	G	AB	H	2B	3B	HR	TB	R	RBI	TBB	IBB	SO	HBP	SH	SF	SB	CS	SB%	GDP	Avg	OBP	SLG
1990 Pulaski	R+ Atl	26	82	22	0	0	0	22	9	10	11	0	12	1	1	2	2	0	1.00	0	.268	.354	.268
1991 Idaho Falls	R+ Atl	47	160	34	3	0	4	49	27	22	18	1	21	4	1	2	1	0	1.00	6	.213	.304	.306
1992 Macon	A Atl	87	310	80	15	2	3	108	32	41	21	0	44	4	0	2	3	3	.50	6	.258	.312	.348
1993 Macon	A Atl	104	353	87	22	0	4	121	38	40	28	1	53	7	5	3	6	5	.55	11	.246	.312	.343
1994 Durham	A+ Atl	72	165	40	11	0	2	57	23	20	19	0	28	1	1	1	1	0	1.00	4	.242	.323	.345
1995 Richmond	AAA Atl	7	13	3	0	0	0	3	1	1	1	0	2	0	0	0	0	1	.00	1	.231	.286	.231
Durham	A+ Atl	85	257	63	6	0	6	87	20	26	25	1	42	6	0	1	3	3	.50	6	.245	.325	.339
1996 Greenville	AA Atl	120	376	100	31	1	10	163	63	55	58	0	61	11	1	4	2	3	.40	4	.266	.376	.434
1997 Richmond	AAA Atl	14	46	9	3	0	0	12	6	5	4	0	8	0	0	0	0	0	.00	3	.196	.260	.261
Greenville	AA Atl	58	184	45	9	0	7	75	23	24	25	0	35	4	0	0	2	2	.50	7	.245	.347	.408
8 Min. YEARS		620	1946	483	100	3	36	697	242	244	210	3	306	38	9	15	20	17	.54	48	.248	.331	.358

Robert Toth

Pitches: Right **Bats:** Right **Pos:** P   **Ht:** 6'2" **Wt:** 180 **Born:** 7/30/72 **Age:** 25

Year Team	Lg Org	G	GS	CG	GF	IP	BFP	H	R	ER	HR	SH	SF	HB	TBB	IBB	SO	WP	Bk	W	L	Pct.	ShO	Sv	ERA
1990 Royals	R KC	7	7	0	0	38	148	34	8	7	1	0	0	2	4	0	22	3	0	2	2	.500	0	0	1.66
1991 Baseball Cy	A+ KC	13	10	0	0	63.2	263	53	24	20	1	5	1	2	23	2	42	0	0	2	3	.400	0	0	2.83
1992 Appleton	A KC	23	22	2	1	127.1	515	111	58	48	9	6	5	5	34	0	100	3	0	7	6	.538	0	0	3.39
1993 Wilmington	A+ KC	25	24	0	1	151.2	609	129	57	49	13	5	2	3	40	1	129	7	1	8	7	.533	0	0	2.91
1994 Wilmington	A+ KC	11	7	3	1	59.1	234	52	14	12	3	2	0	2	9	0	36	0	0	6	1	.857	2	0	1.82
Memphis	AA KC	20	12	0	4	88.2	372	89	46	41	13	3	1	7	24	0	61	14	0	5	8	.385	0	1	4.16
1995 Wichita	AA KC	21	9	1	2	103.2	427	95	30	25	6	3	3	4	27	1	77	6	1	8	4	.667	0	0	2.17
Omaha	AAA KC	8	8	1	0	47.1	205	53	25	19	7	3	2	2	8	0	31	0	0	1	2	.333	0	0	3.61
1996 Omaha	AAA KC	11	8	0	0	46	214	63	40	36	6	1	2	3	17	1	20	2	0	3	3	.500	0	0	7.04
Wichita	AA KC	19	13	2	5	104.2	433	100	48	44	5	5	5	2	24	0	51	3	0	4	6	.400	0	4	3.78
1997 Wichita	AA KC	20	9	1	5	68	303	82	47	44	9	5	2	2	26	2	47	3	0	4	8	.333	0	0	5.82
Omaha	AAA KC	15	7	0	1	52.1	225	50	18	16	6	0	1	1	19	0	30	0	0	5	2	.714	0	0	2.75
8 Min. YEARS		193	136	10	20	950.2	3948	911	415	361	79	38	24	35	255	7	646	41	2	55	52	.514	2	5	3.42

Justin Towle

Bats: Right **Throws:** Right **Pos:** C   **Ht:** 6'3" **Wt:** 210 **Born:** 2/21/74 **Age:** 24

Year Team	Lg Org	G	AB	H	2B	3B	HR	TB	R	RBI	TBB	IBB	SO	HBP	SH	SF	SB	CS	SB%	GDP	Avg	OBP	SLG
1992 Princeton	R+ Cin	19	42	3	1	1	0	6	5	2	9	0	16	2	0	0	1	0	1.00	1	.071	.264	.143
Billings	R+ Cin	7	11	4	1	0	0	5	1	1	3	0	4	1	0	0	0	0	.00	0	.364	.533	.455
1993 Billings	R+ Cin	47	137	36	6	0	7	63	29	23	27	1	37	1	1	1	4	4	.50	3	.263	.386	.460
1994 Chston-WV	A Cin	83	221	49	9	0	2	64	27	19	26	1	59	2	1	0	2	6	.25	8	.222	.309	.290
Winston-Sal	A+ Cin	2	7	1	0	0	0	1	1	0	0	0	2	0	0	0	0	0	.00	1	.143	.143	.143
1995 Chston-WV	A Cin	107	343	92	22	2	8	142	54	60	44	0	95	1	1	3	3	6	.33	6	.268	.350	.414
1996 Winston-Sal	A+ Cin	116	351	90	19	1	16	159	60	47	93	3	96	4	2	1	17	3	.85	12	.256	.416	.453
1997 Chattanooga	AA Cin	119	418	129	37	5	11	209	62	70	55	1	77	2	0	3	5	5	.50	7	.309	.389	.500
6 Min. YEARS		500	1530	404	95	9	44	649	239	222	257	6	386	13	5	8	32	24	.57	38	.264	.373	.424

Dave Townsend

Pitches: Right **Bats:** Right **Pos:** P   **Ht:** 6'3" **Wt:** 230 **Born:** 8/2/74 **Age:** 23

Year Team	Lg Org	G	GS	CG	GF	IP	BFP	H	R	ER	HR	SH	SF	HB	TBB	IBB	SO	WP	Bk	W	L	Pct.	ShO	Sv	ERA
1996 Utica	A- Fla	14	14	2	0	77.2	320	69	38	31	4	1	4	4	18	0	51	4	3	3	6	.333	0	0	3.59
1997 Kane County	A Fla	12	11	1	0	63.2	260	54	20	17	4	0	2	8	16	0	51	5	1	5	1	.833	0	0	2.40
Portland	AA Fla	15	13	1	0	77.2	350	86	49	42	9	1	4	11	36	1	30	2	0	3	7	.300	0	0	4.87
2 Min. YEARS		41	38	4	0	219	930	209	107	90	17	2	7	23	70	1	132	11	4	11	14	.440	0	0	3.70

Gary Trammell

Bats: Left **Throws:** Right **Pos:** OF   **Ht:** 6'0" **Wt:** 180 **Born:** 10/16/72 **Age:** 25

Year Team	Lg Org	G	AB	H	2B	3B	HR	TB	R	RBI	TBB	IBB	SO	HBP	SH	SF	SB	CS	SB%	GDP	Avg	OBP	SLG
1993 Astros	R Hou	59	215	62	5	5	0	77	25	19	14	0	38	3	1	2	11	3	.79	2	.288	.338	.358
1994 Auburn	A- Hou	70	272	82	10	4	3	109	44	47	22	0	23	0	2	6	15	7	.68	3	.301	.347	.401
1995 Quad City	A Hou	103	336	100	12	3	2	124	44	33	33	0	62	1	5	3	14	8	.64	4	.298	.359	.369
1996 Kissimmee	A+ Hou	118	402	116	16	8	0	148	48	39	20	0	52	0	3	4	11	3	.79	5	.289	.319	.368
Tucson	AAA Hou	3	10	4	0	0	1	7	3	2	2	0	2	0	0	0	0	0	.00	1	.400	.500	.700
1997 Jackson	AA Hou	110	314	83	10	1	2	101	38	28	24	0	53	1	6	4	0	4	.00	8	.264	.315	.322
5 Min. YEARS		463	1549	447	53	21	8	566	202	168	115	0	230	5	17	19	51	25	.67	23	.289	.336	.365

Jody Treadwell

Pitches: Right **Bats:** Right **Pos:** P   **Ht:** 6'0" **Wt:** 190 **Born:** 12/14/68 **Age:** 29

Year Team	Lg Org	G	GS	CG	GF	IP	BFP	H	R	ER	HR	SH	SF	HB	TBB	IBB	SO	WP	Bk	W	L	Pct.	ShO	Sv	ERA
1990 Vero Beach	A+ LA	16	8	2	5	80.1	316	59	17	16	2	3	1	1	22	6	80	2	3	9	1	.900	1	1	1.79
1991 San Antonio	AA LA	10	10	1	0	61	271	73	41	32	7	2	1	4	22	1	43	0	0	3	3	.500	0	0	4.72
Bakersfield	A+ LA	17	14	0	0	91.1	392	92	46	38	8	2	0	4	34	2	84	7	1	5	4	.556	0	0	3.74
1992 San Antonio	AA LA	29	4	2	4	76	331	74	40	35	2	3	3	4	40	4	68	6	2	3	5	.375	1	1	4.14

Year Team	Lg Org	G	GS	CG	GF	IP	BFP	H	R	ER	HR	SH	SF	HB	TBB	IBB	SO	WP	Bk	W	L	Pct.	ShO	Sv	ERA
		HOW MUCH HE PITCHED						**WHAT HE GAVE UP**												**THE RESULTS**					
1993 Albuquerque	AAA LA	39	10	0	6	105.1	481	119	58	55	7	3	2	7	52	7	102	11	2	5	4	.556	0	0	4.70
1994 Albuquerque	AAA LA	33	24	0	4	158.2	676	151	78	75	11	5	2	10	59	3	114	7	1	10	6	.625	0	2	4.25
1995 Albuquerque	AAA LA	30	15	1	4	125	510	121	61	55	15	2	5	2	32	4	79	9	1	7	5	.583	1	1	3.96
1996 Albuquerque	AAA LA	5	3	0	0	18.1	93	30	18	16	4	0	3	0	10	1	16	0	0	1	1	.500	0	0	7.85
1997 Albuquerque	AAA LA	27	21	2	2	128.1	575	143	80	73	16	4	2	4	54	2	108	3	0	10	5	.667	0	1	5.12
8 Min. YEARS		206	109	8	25	844.1	3645	862	439	395	73	23	19	36	325	30	694	45	12	53	34	.609	3	6	4.21

Chad Tredaway

Bats: Both   Throws: Right   Pos: 3B   Ht: 6'0"   Wt: 193   Born: 6/18/72   Age: 26

Year Team	Lg Org	G	AB	H	2B	3B	HR	TB	R	RBI	TBB	IBB	SO	HBP	SH	SF	SB	CS	SB%	GDP	Avg	OBP	SLG
		BATTING															**BASERUNNING**				**PERCENTAGES**		
1992 Geneva	A- ChN	73	270	81	19	2	5	119	39	31	24	1	24	3	3	5	6	4	.60	3	.300	.358	.441
1993 Daytona	A+ ChN	66	242	62	12	0	0	74	32	21	27	2	25	0	3	4	4	3	.57	1	.256	.326	.306
1994 Orlando	AA ChN	45	146	28	3	0	1	34	13	15	10	0	20	1	1	3	2	0	1.00	3	.192	.244	.233
Daytona	A+ ChN	77	284	69	14	3	5	104	26	28	23	0	39	1	4	1	1	5	.17	6	.243	.301	.366
1995 Memphis	AA ChN	10	30	8	1	0	0	9	5	4	3	1	5	0	0	0	1	0	1.00	0	.267	.333	.300
Rancho Cuca	A+ SD	109	408	113	17	2	6	152	53	57	29	3	43	3	1	8	4	2	.67	10	.277	.324	.373
1996 Rancho Cuca	A+ SD	21	84	21	3	0	2	30	13	13	7	0	7	0	0	3	1	0	1.00	1	.250	.298	.357
Las Vegas	AAA SD	76	196	44	10	2	5	73	26	19	17	2	25	1	5	1	4	1	.80	4	.224	.288	.372
1997 Mobile	AA SD	4	12	1	0	0	0	1	2	0	2	0	1	0	0	0	0	0	.00	0	.083	.214	.083
Las Vegas	AAA SD	116	409	105	23	1	7	151	58	50	34	2	63	0	3	6	6	4	.60	9	.257	.310	.369
6 Min. YEARS		597	2081	532	102	10	31	747	267	238	176	11	252	9	20	31	29	19	.60	37	.256	.312	.359

Chris Tremie

Bats: Right   Throws: Right   Pos: C   Ht: 6'0"   Wt: 200   Born: 10/17/69   Age: 28

Year Team	Lg Org	G	AB	H	2B	3B	HR	TB	R	RBI	TBB	IBB	SO	HBP	SH	SF	SB	CS	SB%	GDP	Avg	OBP	SLG
		BATTING															**BASERUNNING**				**PERCENTAGES**		
1992 Utica	A- ChA	6	16	1	0	0	0	1	1	0	0	0	5	0	0	0	0	0	.00	0	.063	.063	.063
1993 White Sox	R ChA	2	4	0	0	0	0	0	0	0	0	0	0	0	0	0	0	0	.00	0	.000	.000	.000
Sarasota	A+ ChA	14	37	6	1	0	0	7	2	5	2	0	4	3	0	0	0	0	.00	1	.162	.262	.189
Hickory	A ChA	49	155	29	6	1	1	40	7	17	9	0	26	4	1	0	0	0	.00	5	.187	.250	.258
1994 Birmingham	AA ChA	92	302	68	13	0	2	87	32	29	17	0	44	6	3	2	4	1	.80	3	.225	.278	.288
1995 Nashville	AAA ChA	67	190	38	4	0	2	48	13	16	13	0	37	2	4	0	0	0	.00	6	.200	.259	.253
1996 Nashville	AAA ChA	70	215	47	10	1	0	59	17	26	18	0	48	2	6	3	2	0	1.00	4	.219	.282	.274
1997 Reading	AA Phi	97	295	60	11	1	2	79	20	31	36	0	61	5	5	5	0	5	.00	7	.203	.296	.268
1995 Chicago	AL	10	24	4	0	0	0	4	0	0	1	0	2	0	1	0	0	0	.00	0	.167	.200	.167
6 Min. YEARS		397	1214	249	45	3	7	321	92	124	95	0	225	22	19	10	6	6	.50	26	.205	.273	.264

Hector Trinidad

Pitches: Right   Bats: Right   Pos: P   Ht: 6'2"   Wt: 190   Born: 9/8/73   Age: 24

Year Team	Lg Org	G	GS	CG	GF	IP	BFP	H	R	ER	HR	SH	SF	HB	TBB	IBB	SO	WP	Bk	W	L	Pct.	ShO	Sv	ERA
		HOW MUCH HE PITCHED						**WHAT HE GAVE UP**												**THE RESULTS**					
1991 Huntington	R+ ChN	12	10	2	0	69	286	64	28	22	4	0	1	3	11	0	61	3	0	6	3	.667	0	0	2.87
1992 Geneva	A- ChN	15	15	2	0	93.2	377	78	33	25	6	5	0	4	13	2	70	1	0	8	6	.571	0	0	2.40
1993 Peoria	A ChN	22	22	4	0	153	622	142	56	42	6	5	7	4	29	1	118	7	1	7	6	.538	0	2	2.47
Orlando	AA ChN	4	4	1	0	24.2	108	34	19	18	5	1	0	1	7	0	13	2	0	1	3	.250	0	0	6.57
1994 Daytona	A+ ChN	28	27	4	1	175.2	726	171	72	63	8	7	3	7	40	0	142	3	1	11	9	.550	1	0	3.23
1995 Hardware City	AA Min	23	22	0	1	121	516	137	67	62	6	1	10	7	22	0	92	6	2	4	11	.267	0	0	4.61
1996 Hardware City	AA Min	25	24	1	0	138.1	583	137	75	59	6	4	1	7	31	0	93	7	0	6	6	.500	1	0	3.84
1997 Ft. Myers	A+ Min	2	1	0	0	8	28	2	0	0	0	0	1	1	1	0	5	1	0	1	0	1.000	0	0	0.00
New Britain	AA Min	6	3	0	0	21.1	95	26	18	15	5	2	1	1	8	0	11	1	0	0	2	.000	0	0	6.33
7 Min. YEARS		137	128	14	3	804.2	3341	791	368	306	46	25	23	35	162	3	605	31	4	44	46	.489	2	0	3.42

Jason Troilo

Bats: Right   Throws: Right   Pos: C   Ht: 6'1"   Wt: 195   Born: 9/7/72   Age: 25

Year Team	Lg Org	G	AB	H	2B	3B	HR	TB	R	RBI	TBB	IBB	SO	HBP	SH	SF	SB	CS	SB%	GDP	Avg	OBP	SLG
		BATTING															**BASERUNNING**				**PERCENTAGES**		
1994 Oneonta	A- NYA	7	15	2	1	0	0	3	0	1	4	0	3	0	1	0	0	0	.00	0	.133	.316	.200
Greensboro	A NYA	22	58	11	3	0	0	14	5	6	5	0	16	1	0	0	0	0	.00	3	.190	.266	.241
1995 Tampa	A+ NYA	1	2	0	0	0	0	0	0	0	0	0	2	1	0	0	0	0	.00	0	.000	.333	.000
Greensboro	A NYA	19	59	17	4	0	3	30	6	9	3	0	19	0	3	1	0	1	.00	0	.288	.317	.508
1996 Tampa	A+ NYA	11	25	5	1	0	1	9	2	5	1	0	7	1	0	0	0	0	.00	1	.200	.259	.360
Greensboro	A NYA	67	199	38	10	0	3	57	19	17	9	0	62	4	5	1	2	1	.67	3	.191	.239	.286
Norwich	AA NYA	3	8	4	0	0	2	10	3	2	0	0	1	0	0	0	0	0	.00	0	.500	.500	1.250
1997 Columbus	AAA NYA	8	22	3	2	0	0	5	1	1	4	0	9	0	1	0	0	0	.00	0	.136	.269	.227
Tampa	A+ NYA	3	9	3	0	0	0	3	0	0	1	0	5	0	0	0	0	0	.00	0	.333	.400	.333
4 Min. YEARS		141	397	83	21	0	9	131	36	41	27	0	124	7	10	2	2	2	.50	7	.209	.270	.330

Keith Troutman

Pitches: Right   Bats: Right   Pos: P   Ht: 6'1"   Wt: 200   Born: 5/29/73   Age: 25

Year Team	Lg Org	G	GS	CG	GF	IP	BFP	H	R	ER	HR	SH	SF	HB	TBB	IBB	SO	WP	Bk	W	L	Pct.	ShO	Sv	ERA
		HOW MUCH HE PITCHED						**WHAT HE GAVE UP**												**THE RESULTS**					
1992 Yakima	A- LA	26	0	0	19	37.1	163	33	19	14	2	2	2	1	15	3	43	2	2	4	1	.800	0	3	3.38
1993 Great Falls	R+ LA	27	0	0	23	42	166	26	12	8	2	1	3	2	12	1	48	2	0	1	1	.500	0	16	1.71
1994 Vero Beach	A+ LA	43	0	0	10	78.1	328	69	39	34	6	3	2	1	35	5	66	5	1	3	2	.600	0	0	3.91

| | | HOW MUCH HE PITCHED | | | | | | WHAT HE GAVE UP | | | | | | | | | | THE RESULTS | | | | | |
Year Team	Lg Org	G	GS	CG	GF	IP	BFP	H	R	ER	HR	SH	SF	HB	TBB	IBB	SO	WP	Bk	W	L	Pct.	ShO	Sv	ERA
1995 San Antonio	AA LA	38	0	0	22	65.2	268	64	24	23	3	1	3	1	18	1	50	3	0	1	2	.333	0	2	3.15
1996 Scranton-WB	AAA Phi	8	0	0	4	14	65	19	9	8	1	1	0	1	5	1	9	1	0	1	1	.500	0	0	5.14
Reading	AA Phi	52	1	0	13	73.1	323	62	36	27	7	3	2	3	40	3	73	3	1	6	3	.667	0	1	3.31
1997 Reading	AA Phi	57	3	0	19	107.1	440	94	48	45	17	8	4	2	34	6	103	4	0	6	5	.545	0	7	3.77
6 Min. YEARS		251	4	0	110	418	1753	367	187	159	38	19	16	11	159	20	392	20	4	22	15	.595	0	29	3.42

Eric Tryon

Pitches: Left **Bats:** Right **Pos:** P   **Ht:** 6'0" **Wt:** 195 **Born:** 9/3/75 **Age:** 22

| | | HOW MUCH HE PITCHED | | | | | | WHAT HE GAVE UP | | | | | | | | | | THE RESULTS | | | | | |
Year Team	Lg Org	G	GS	CG	GF	IP	BFP	H	R	ER	HR	SH	SF	HB	TBB	IBB	SO	WP	Bk	W	L	Pct.	ShO	Sv	ERA
1997 Chattanooga	AA Cin	6	6	0	0	26	124	35	27	24	7	1	1	0	16	0	7	7	0	0	4	.000	0	0	8.31
Burlington	A Cin	7	7	0	0	35.2	163	37	15	14	1	0	3	2	19	0	25	1	0	2	0	1.000	0	0	3.53
1 Min. YEARS		13	13	0	0	61.2	287	72	42	38	8	1	4	2	35	0	32	8	0	2	4	.333	0	0	5.55

Rich Turrentine

Pitches: Right **Bats:** Right **Pos:** P   **Ht:** 6'0" **Wt:** 175 **Born:** 5/21/71 **Age:** 27

| | | HOW MUCH HE PITCHED | | | | | | WHAT HE GAVE UP | | | | | | | | | | THE RESULTS | | | | | |
Year Team	Lg Org	G	GS	CG	GF	IP	BFP	H	R	ER	HR	SH	SF	HB	TBB	IBB	SO	WP	Bk	W	L	Pct.	ShO	Sv	ERA
1992 Yankees	R NYA	2	0	0	2	2	6	0	0	0	0	0	0	0	0	0	6	0	0	0	0	.000	0	1	0.00
Oneonta	A- NYA	1	0	0	0	2	2	1	2	2	0	0	0	0	1	0	0	0	0	0	0	.000	0	0	0.00
1994 Yankees	R NYA	6	0	0	1	8.2	40	10	8	7	1	1	0	1	4	0	11	2	0	0	0	.000	0	0	7.27
Tampa	A+ NYA	10	0	0	2	14.2	70	14	10	10	0	0	1	2	13	0	10	3	0	1	0	1.000	0	0	6.14
1995 Capital City	A NYN	26	14	0	8	104	437	70	38	29	3	6	4	6	60	1	111	16	1	4	4	.500	0	2	2.51
St. Lucie	A+ NYN	4	4	0	0	19.1	92	17	14	13	3	1	0	2	17	0	14	3	0	0	3	.000	0	0	6.05
1996 St. Lucie	A+ NYN	45	0	0	40	51.1	232	31	18	13	0	4	1	2	45	1	63	9	0	4	4	.500	0	21	2.28
Binghamton	AA NYN	8	0	0	7	9.1	43	12	3	3	0	0	1	0	5	0	10	0	0	1	1	.500	0	3	2.89
1997 Binghamton	AA NYN	61	0	0	45	62	292	66	38	36	3	4	1	2	54	2	58	17	0	2	4	.333	0	13	5.23
5 Min. YEARS		163	18	0	105	271.1	1214	221	131	113	10	16	8	15	199	4	283	50	1	12	16	.429	0	40	3.75

Brad Tweedlie

Pitches: Right **Bats:** Right **Pos:** P   **Ht:** 6'2" **Wt:** 215 **Born:** 12/9/71 **Age:** 26

| | | HOW MUCH HE PITCHED | | | | | | WHAT HE GAVE UP | | | | | | | | | | THE RESULTS | | | | | |
Year Team	Lg Org	G	GS	CG	GF	IP	BFP	H	R	ER	HR	SH	SF	HB	TBB	IBB	SO	WP	Bk	W	L	Pct.	ShO	Sv	ERA
1993 Billings	R+ Cin	11	8	0	1	44	187	28	22	21	2	0	2	3	31	1	31	8	2	3	3	.500	0	1	4.30
1994 Winston-Sal	A+ Cin	10	5	0	1	29.1	161	48	47	40	7	1	3	3	19	0	18	4	0	1	4	.200	0	0	12.27
Chston-WV	A Cin	8	8	0	0	38	173	42	27	24	4	2	0	2	20	0	30	9	2	3	4	.429	0	0	5.68
1995 Chston-WV	A Cin	19	7	0	4	49.2	226	46	36	34	3	0	4	3	34	0	40	5	1	2	4	.333	0	0	6.16
1996 Winston-Sal	A Cin	33	0	0	30	29.2	144	35	23	22	6	1	2	1	22	0	22	6	0	1	5	.167	0	11	6.67
Sarasota	A+ Bos	11	0	0	11	11.1	45	6	1	1	0	0	0	1	3	1	9	0	0	2	0	1.000	0	7	0.79
1997 Trenton	AA Bos	41	0	0	26	57.2	275	62	41	37	10	1	2	6	44	3	30	1	0	4	6	.400	0	5	5.77
5 Min. YEARS		133	28	0	73	259.2	1211	267	197	179	32	5	13	19	173	5	180	33	5	16	26	.381	0	24	6.20

Greg Twiggs

Pitches: Left **Bats:** Left **Pos:** P   **Ht:** 5'10" **Wt:** 155 **Born:** 10/15/71 **Age:** 26

| | | HOW MUCH HE PITCHED | | | | | | WHAT HE GAVE UP | | | | | | | | | | THE RESULTS | | | | | |
Year Team	Lg Org	G	GS	CG	GF	IP	BFP	H	R	ER	HR	SH	SF	HB	TBB	IBB	SO	WP	Bk	W	L	Pct.	ShO	Sv	ERA
1993 Geneva	A- ChN	14	14	2	0	79.2	340	65	39	28	4	6	3	1	37	2	67	6	0	5	6	.455	1	0	3.16
1994 Daytona	A+ ChN	45	0	0	14	70.1	316	70	48	34	4	4	3	3	33	2	45	3	1	3	4	.429	0	2	4.35
1995 Daytona	A+ ChN	18	13	1	1	89.1	355	64	30	14	3	1	1	5	28	0	80	4	0	8	3	.727	0	1	1.41
1996 Orlando	AA ChN	44	0	0	15	54.2	243	53	27	24	2	3	4	0	33	5	40	2	0	4	2	.667	0	1	3.95
1997 Orlando	AA ChN	48	1	0	14	62.2	285	79	33	30	4	2	2	2	24	3	38	2	0	2	4	.333	0	1	4.31
5 Min. YEARS		169	28	3	44	356.2	1539	331	177	130	17	16	13	11	155	12	270	17	1	22	19	.537	1	4	3.28

Brad Tyler

Bats: Left **Throws:** Right **Pos:** OF   **Ht:** 6'2" **Wt:** 175 **Born:** 3/3/69 **Age:** 29

| | | BATTING | | | | | | | | | | | | | | | BASERUNNING | | | | PERCENTAGES | | |
Year Team	Lg Org	G	AB	H	2B	3B	HR	TB	R	RBI	TBB	IBB	SO	HBP	SH	SF	SB	CS	SB%	GDP	Avg	OBP	SLG
1990 Wausau	A Bal	56	187	44	4	3	2	60	31	24	44	2	45	2	1	2	11	4	.73	2	.235	.383	.321
1991 Kane County	A Bal	60	199	54	10	3	3	79	35	29	44	1	25	1	1	2	5	3	.63	0	.271	.402	.397
Frederick	A+ Bal	56	187	48	6	0	4	66	26	26	33	3	33	2	1	1	3	2	.60	0	.257	.372	.353
1992 Frederick	A+ Bal	54	185	47	11	2	3	71	34	22	43	2	34	1	1	4	9	3	.75	2	.254	.393	.384
Hagerstown	AA Bal	83	256	57	9	1	2	74	41	21	34	2	45	2	1	0	23	5	.82	5	.223	.318	.289
1993 Bowie	AA Bal	129	437	103	23	17	10	190	85	44	84	2	89	1	1	3	24	11	.69	2	.236	.358	.435
1994 Rochester	AAA Bal	101	314	82	15	8	7	134	38	43	38	2	69	2	1	0	7	4	.64	4	.261	.345	.427
1995 Rochester	AAA Bal	114	361	93	17	3	17	167	60	52	71	4	63	4	0	5	10	5	.67	3	.258	.381	.463
1996 Rochester	AAA Bal	118	382	103	18	10	13	180	68	52	67	2	95	5	1	3	19	7	.73	2	.270	.383	.471
1997 Richmond	AAA Atl	129	383	101	15	10	18	190	69	77	55	2	110	3	3	7	13	6	.68	4	.264	.355	.496
8 Min. YEARS		900	2891	732	128	57	79	1211	487	390	513	22	608	24	11	27	124	50	.71	24	.253	.367	.419

Josh Tyler

Bats: Right **Throws:** Right **Pos:** 2B   **Ht:** 6'1" **Wt:** 185 **Born:** 9/6/73 **Age:** 24

| | | BATTING | | | | | | | | | | | | | | | BASERUNNING | | | | PERCENTAGES | | |
Year Team	Lg Org	G	AB	H	2B	3B	HR	TB	R	RBI	TBB	IBB	SO	HBP	SH	SF	SB	CS	SB%	GDP	Avg	OBP	SLG
1994 Brewers	R Mil	54	193	52	4	3	0	62	35	24	30	0	34	6	0	4	8	4	.67	6	.269	.378	.321

BATTING																	BASERUNNING				PERCENTAGES		
Year Team	Lg Org	G	AB	H	2B	3B	HR	TB	R	RBI	TBB	IBB	SO	HBP	SH	SF	SB	CS	SB%	GDP	Avg	OBP	SLG
1995 Beloit	A Mil	77	186	44	5	0	2	55	24	27	36	0	40	2	7	3	3	6	.33	4	.237	.361	.296
1996 Stockton	A+ Mil	75	273	88	14	2	2	112	42	33	25	0	35	11	7	2	4	8	.33	6	.322	.399	.410
1997 Tucson	AAA Mil	1	0	0	0	0	0	0	0	0	0	0	0	0	0	0	0	0	.00	0	.000	.000	.000
Stockton	A+ Mil	114	416	129	28	4	4	177	63	46	20	0	54	10	5	3	21	7	.75	7	.310	.354	.425
4 Min. YEARS		321	1068	313	51	9	8	406	164	130	111	0	163	29	19	12	36	25	.59	23	.293	.371	.380

Chris Unrat

Bats: Left **Throws:** Right **Pos:** DH   **Ht:** 6'1" **Wt:** 205 **Born:** 3/28/71 **Age:** 27

BATTING																	BASERUNNING				PERCENTAGES		
Year Team	Lg Org	G	AB	H	2B	3B	HR	TB	R	RBI	TBB	IBB	SO	HBP	SH	SF	SB	CS	SB%	GDP	Avg	OBP	SLG
1993 Rangers	R Tex	12	31	8	2	0	0	10	3	5	4	1	4	1	0	2	1	0	1.00	2	.258	.342	.323
Erie	A- Tex	36	124	36	8	1	8	70	25	22	11	0	27	0	0	0	1	1	.50	3	.290	.348	.565
1994 Chston-SC	A Tex	64	192	41	10	0	7	72	28	24	29	1	73	3	0	1	1	3	.25	3	.214	.324	.375
1995 Charlotte	A+ Tex	66	172	43	8	1	1	56	22	17	23	1	38	0	4	2	1	2	.33	6	.250	.335	.326
1996 Charlotte	A+ Tex	41	135	37	8	0	2	51	18	11	27	1	28	0	0	1	2	3	.40	4	.274	.395	.378
Tulsa	AA Tex	20	55	10	2	0	1	15	6	7	16	0	13	0	0	0	0	0	.00	2	.182	.366	.273
1997 Tulsa	AA Tex	19	51	11	3	0	0	14	4	7	16	1	7	0	0	0	0	0	.00	1	.216	.403	.275
Phoenix	AAA SF	1	2	1	0	0	0	1	0	0	1	0	0	0	0	0	0	0	.00	0	.500	.667	.500
San Jose	A+ SF	59	160	39	9	0	3	57	18	19	30	4	38	1	0	1	0	1	.00	4	.244	.365	.356
Shreveport	AA SF	6	12	4	1	0	0	5	2	4	1	0	0	1	0	0	0	0	.00	0	.333	.429	.417
5 Min. YEARS		324	934	230	51	2	22	351	126	116	158	9	228	6	4	6	6	10	.38	25	.246	.357	.376

Tom Urbani

Pitches: Left **Bats:** Left **Pos:** P   **Ht:** 6'1" **Wt:** 190 **Born:** 1/21/68 **Age:** 30

HOW MUCH HE PITCHED							WHAT HE GAVE UP												THE RESULTS					
Year Team	Lg Org	G	GS	CG	GF	IP	BFP	H	R	ER	HR	SH	SF	HB	TBB	IBB	SO	WP	Bk	W	L	Pct.	ShO	Sv	ERA
1990 Johnson Cty	R+ StL	9	9	0	0	48.1	217	44	35	18	2	1	0	1	15	0	40	4	0	4	3	.571	0	0	3.35
Hamilton	A- StL	5	5	0	0	26.1	125	33	26	18	4	0	3	3	15	1	17	1	0	0	4	.000	0	0	6.15
1991 Springfield	A StL	8	8	0	0	47.2	195	45	20	11	2	2	2	2	6	0	42	1	1	3	2	.600	0	0	2.08
St. Pete	A+ StL	19	19	2	0	118.2	474	109	39	31	3	8	5	2	25	0	64	3	1	8	7	.533	1	0	2.35
1992 Arkansas	AA StL	10	10	2	0	65.1	263	49	23	14	3	3	0	2	15	1	41	1	0	4	6	.400	1	0	1.93
Louisville	AAA StL	16	16	0	0	88.2	384	91	50	46	9	3	4	7	37	1	46	5	1	4	5	.444	0	0	4.67
1993 Louisville	AAA StL	18	13	0	2	94.2	377	86	29	26	4	3	0	2	23	1	65	2	0	9	5	.643	0	1	2.47
1994 Louisville	AAA StL	7	7	0	0	43.2	196	51	31	28	6	3	2	4	11	0	42	4	0	4	2	.667	0	0	5.77
1995 Louisville	AAA StL	2	2	0	0	15.1	65	16	6	5	0	0	0	0	5	0	11	0	0	1	1	.500	0	0	2.93
1996 Louisville	AAA StL	7	7	0	0	44	180	40	19	16	5	1	1	2	12	0	26	2	0	2	2	.500	0	0	3.27
Toledo	AAA Det	4	3	0	0	14	64	18	15	10	2	0	1	0	7	0	10	1	0	0	3	.000	0	0	6.43
1997 Okla City	AAA Tex	21	3	0	4	43	187	53	21	20	7	0	3	0	13	1	21	0	0	3	2	.600	0	1	4.19
Ottawa	AAA Mon	30	1	0	7	41.1	166	37	13	12	2	2	0	0	12	0	25	1	0	3	1	.750	0	0	2.61
1993 St. Louis	NL	18	9	0	2	62	283	73	44	32	4	4	6	0	26	2	33	1	1	1	3	.250	0	0	4.65
1994 St. Louis	NL	20	10	0	2	80.1	354	98	48	46	12	3	2	3	21	0	43	4	1	3	7	.300	0	0	5.15
1995 St. Louis	NL	24	13	0	2	82.2	354	99	40	34	11	6	0	2	21	4	52	5	0	3	5	.375	0	0	3.70
1996 St. Louis	NL	3	2	0	0	11.2	53	15	10	10	3	1	1	0	4	0	1	0	0	1	0	1.000	0	0	7.71
Detroit	AL	16	2	0	3	23.2	117	31	22	22	8	0	1	2	14	0	20	3	0	2	2	.500	0	0	8.37
8 Min. YEARS		156	103	4	13	691	2893	672	327	255	49	26	21	25	196	5	450	25	3	45	43	.511	2	2	3.32
4 Maj. YEARS		81	36	0	9	260.1	1161	316	164	144	38	14	10	7	86	6	149	13	2	10	17	.370	0	0	4.98

Dan Urbina

Pitches: Right **Bats:** Right **Pos:** P   **Ht:** 6'0" **Wt:** 195 **Born:** 11/13/74 **Age:** 23

HOW MUCH HE PITCHED							WHAT HE GAVE UP												THE RESULTS					
Year Team	Lg Org	G	GS	CG	GF	IP	BFP	H	R	ER	HR	SH	SF	HB	TBB	IBB	SO	WP	Bk	W	L	Pct.	ShO	Sv	ERA
1995 Vero Beach	A+ LA	18	16	0	0	91.2	412	90	56	44	4	0	5	3	52	0	68	13	4	5	7	.417	0	0	4.32
1996 San Berndno	A+ LA	3	3	0	0	10.2	45	11	8	7	0	0	1	3	9	0	13	1	0	0	0	.000	0	0	5.91
1997 San Berndno	A+ LA	13	2	0	2	35	150	26	14	10	2	0	2	4	22	2	33	5	1	3	2	.600	0	0	2.57
San Antonio	AA LA	9	0	0	5	14	67	19	8	6	0	1	1	0	13	0	26	3	0	0	0	.000	0	0	3.86
Vero Beach	A+ LA	3	3	0	0	9.1	44	11	9	9	2	0	0	0	5	0	10	0	0	2	0	.000	0	0	8.68
3 Min. YEARS		46	24	0	7	160.2	728	157	95	76	8	1	9	10	101	2	130	22	5	8	11	.421	0	0	4.26

Sal Urso

Pitches: Left **Bats:** Right **Pos:** P   **Ht:** 5'11" **Wt:** 195 **Born:** 1/19/72 **Age:** 26

HOW MUCH HE PITCHED							WHAT HE GAVE UP												THE RESULTS					
Year Team	Lg Org	G	GS	CG	GF	IP	BFP	H	R	ER	HR	SH	SF	HB	TBB	IBB	SO	WP	Bk	W	L	Pct.	ShO	Sv	ERA
1990 Mariners	R Sea	20	0	0	6	50.2	219	38	25	13	3	2	6	5	23	1	63	5	0	3	2	.600	0	1	2.31
1991 Peninsula	A+ Sea	46	0	0	29	61.2	290	74	36	21	1	3	4	5	30	7	44	6	0	0	3	.000	0	8	3.06
1992 San Berndno	A+ Sea	37	0	0	21	51.1	239	66	34	29	2	2	5	1	32	0	40	4	1	0	1	.000	0	1	5.08
1993 Appleton	A Sea	36	1	0	18	53.2	226	57	24	20	2	4	2	1	24	1	50	7	1	4	4	.500	0	2	3.35
1994 Riverside	A+ Sea	30	1	0	12	34.2	156	44	27	23	4	1	2	3	14	0	26	3	0	1	2	.333	0	0	5.97
1995 Port City	AA Sea	51	0	0	8	45.2	185	41	13	11	0	0	0	0	21	0	44	7	1	2	0	1.000	0	1	2.17
1996 Tacoma	AAA Sea	46	0	0	19	72.2	302	69	22	19	5	4	1	1	32	1	45	2	6	6	2	.750	0	3	2.35
1997 Columbus	AAA NYA	24	2	0	9	45.2	211	59	29	24	4	3	1	3	19	0	44	5	4	0	3	.000	0	0	4.73
Norwich	AA NYA	7	2	0	3	14.1	59	14	2	2	0	0	0	0	5	0	13	1	1	1	1	.500	0	0	1.26
8 Min. YEARS		297	6	0	125	430.1	1887	462	212	162	21	19	21	19	200	10	369	40	14	17	18	.486	0	17	3.39

Pedro Valdes

Bats: Left **Throws:** Left **Pos:** OF **Ht:** 6'1" **Wt:** 180 **Born:** 6/29/73 **Age:** 25

Year Team	Lg Org	G	AB	H	2B	3B	HR	TB	R	RBI	TBB	IBB	SO	HBP	SH	SF	SB	CS	SB%	GDP	Avg	OBP	SLG
1991 Huntington	R+ ChN	50	157	45	11	1	0	58	18	16	17	3	31	2	1	5	5	1	.83	7	.287	.354	.369
1992 Peoria	A ChN	33	112	26	7	0	0	33	8	20	7	3	32	0	0	4	0	0	.00	1	.232	.268	.295
Geneva	A- ChN	66	254	69	10	0	5	94	27	24	3	1	33	3	2	2	4	5	.44	2	.272	.286	.370
1993 Peoria	A ChN	65	234	74	11	1	7	108	33	36	10	4	40	0	5	4	2	2	.50	3	.316	.339	.462
Daytona	A+ ChN	60	230	66	16	1	8	108	27	49	9	1	30	2	0	5	3	4	.43	8	.287	.313	.470
1994 Orlando	AA ChN	116	365	103	14	4	1	128	39	37	20	3	45	2	2	1	2	6	.25	10	.282	.322	.351
1995 Orlando	AA ChN	114	426	128	28	3	7	183	57	68	37	3	77	5	0	6	3	6	.33	7	.300	.359	.430
1996 Iowa	AAA ChN	103	397	117	23	0	15	185	61	60	31	1	57	1	1	5	2	0	1.00	12	.295	.343	.466
1997 Iowa	AAA ChN	125	464	132	30	1	14	206	65	60	48	5	67	2	1	6	9	2	.82	13	.284	.350	.444
1996 Chicago	NL	9	8	1	0	0	0	2	2	1	1	0	5	0	0	0	0	0	.00	0	.125	.222	.250
7 Min. YEARS		732	2639	760	150	11	57	1103	335	370	182	24	412	17	12	38	30	26	.54	63	.288	.333	.418

Carlos Valdez

Pitches: Right **Bats:** Right **Pos:** P **Ht:** 5'11" **Wt:** 175 **Born:** 12/26/71 **Age:** 26

Year Team	Lg Org	G	GS	CG	GF	IP	BFP	H	R	ER	HR	SH	SF	HB	TBB	IBB	SO	WP	Bk	W	L	Pct.	ShO	Sv	ERA
1991 Giants	R SF	13	10	0	1	63.1	288	75	48	40	3	1	4	0	32	0	48	6	1	2	3	.400	0	0	5.68
1992 Everett	A- SF	3	0	0	2	6.1	29	4	2	1	0	0	1	2	7	0	6	1	0	0	1	.000	0	0	1.42
Giants	R SF	6	0	0	3	14.2	56	7	2	0	0	1	0	0	5	0	14	1	0	3	1	.750	0	0	0.00
1993 Clinton	A SF	35	2	0	14	90.1	389	74	47	40	6	7	3	2	44	1	85	8	0	4	7	.364	0	3	3.99
1994 San Jose	A+ SF	36	17	0	10	123.2	536	109	70	62	7	3	6	12	61	0	116	6	0	8	6	.571	0	0	4.51
1995 Shreveport	AA SF	22	3	0	8	64	240	40	11	9	0	1	0	3	14	2	51	1	0	3	2	.600	0	5	1.27
Phoenix	AAA SF	18	0	0	12	29.1	131	29	10	9	2	2	0	0	13	2	30	3	0	1	0	1.000	0	2	2.76
1996 Phoenix	AAA SF	44	0	0	17	59.2	276	63	38	33	4	4	2	4	34	5	38	6	1	4	3	.571	0	5	4.98
1997 Pawtucket	AAA Bos	35	8	0	6	78.2	346	73	49	41	7	3	4	0	46	4	64	5	0	0	4	.000	0	1	4.69
1995 San Francisco	NL	11	0	0	3	14.2	69	19	10	10	1	0	1	1	8	1	7	1	1	0	1	.000	0	0	6.14
7 Min. YEARS		212	40	0	73	530	2291	474	277	235	29	22	20	23	256	14	452	37	2	25	27	.481	0	16	3.99

Trovin Valdez

Bats: Right **Throws:** Right **Pos:** OF **Ht:** 5'10" **Wt:** 163 **Born:** 11/18/73 **Age:** 24

Year Team	Lg Org	G	AB	H	2B	3B	HR	TB	R	RBI	TBB	IBB	SO	HBP	SH	SF	SB	CS	SB%	GDP	Avg	OBP	SLG
1993 Orioles	R Bal	39	151	32	2	2	0	38	16	6	9	0	23	0	2	0	21	5	.81	1	.212	.256	.252
1994 Albany	A Bal	20	65	17	0	2	0	21	10	4	1	0	17	2	0	1	9	1	.90	1	.262	.290	.323
Bluefield	R+ Bal	55	184	53	7	3	3	75	43	18	11	1	26	5	5	5	20	6	.77	1	.288	.337	.408
1995 Bowie	AA Bal	2	0	0	0	0	0	0	0	0	0	0	0	0	0	0	0	0	.00	0	.000	.000	.000
Frederick	A+ Bal	112	375	92	12	4	0	112	51	13	18	0	77	5	6	1	34	21	.62	2	.245	.288	.299
1996 Winston-Sal	A+ Cin	90	343	87	11	3	3	113	49	30	22	1	62	2	6	1	26	14	.65	3	.254	.302	.329
Indianapolis	AAA Cin	1	1	0	0	0	0	0	0	0	0	0	0	0	0	0	0	0	.00	0	.000	.000	.000
1997 Burlington	A Cin	33	119	30	3	1	0	35	22	11	16	0	28	0	4	1	14	4	.78	2	.252	.338	.294
Wst Plm Bch	A+ Mon	55	188	44	4	3	2	60	19	14	10	1	24	5	2	1	12	6	.67	0	.234	.289	.319
Harrisburg	AA Mon	13	42	13	2	0	0	15	8	4	4	0	9	0	1	0	2	1	.67	1	.310	.370	.357
5 Min. YEARS		420	1468	368	41	18	8	469	218	100	91	3	266	19	26	10	138	58	.70	11	.251	.301	.319

Dave Valle

Bats: Right **Throws:** Right **Pos:** C **Ht:** 6'2" **Wt:** 220 **Born:** 10/30/60 **Age:** 37

Year Team	Lg Org	G	AB	H	2B	3B	HR	TB	R	RBI	TBB	IBB	SO	HBP	SH	SF	SB	CS	SB%	GDP	Avg	OBP	SLG
1978 Bellingham	A- Sea	57	167	34	2	0	2	42	12	21	16	—	34	1	4	1	3	4	.43	—	.204	.276	.251
1979 Alexandria	A+ Sea	58	169	36	5	0	6	59	17	25	23	—	24	4	3	2	1	2	.33	—	.213	.318	.349
1980 San Jose	A+ Sea	119	430	126	14	0	12	176	81	70	50	—	54	11	5	2	6	7	.46	—	.293	.379	.409
1981 Lynn	AA Sea	93	318	82	16	0	11	131	38	54	36	2	48	8	0	2	3	5	.38	—	.258	.346	.412
1982 Salt Lake City	AAA Sea	75	234	49	11	1	4	74	28	28	26	0	26	1	1	2	0	2	.00	—	.209	.289	.316
1983 Chattanooga	AA Sea	53	176	42	11	0	3	62	20	22	24	0	28	3	0	1	0	1	.00	—	.239	.338	.352
1984 Salt Lake City	AAA Sea	86	284	79	13	1	12	130	54	54	45	2	36	3	0	3	0	1	.00	6	.278	.379	.458
1985 Calgary	AAA Sea	42	131	45	8	0	6	71	17	26	20	1	19	0	0	0	0	0	.00	6	.344	.430	.542
1986 Calgary	AAA Sea	105	353	110	21	2	21	198	71	72	41	0	43	7	1	2	5	1	.83	13	.312	.392	.561
1989 Calgary	AAA Sea	2	6	0	0	0	0	0	0	0	0	0	0	0	0	0	0	0	.00	0	.000	.143	.000
1997 Richmond	AAA Atl	12	38	8	0	0	0	8	2	2	1	0	7	0	0	1	0	0	.00	3	.211	.225	.211
1984 Seattle	AL	13	27	8	1	0	1	12	4	4	1	0	5	0	0	0	0	0	.00	0	.296	.321	.444
1985 Seattle	AL	31	70	11	1	0	0	12	2	4	1	0	17	1	1	0	0	0	.00	0	.157	.181	.171
1986 Seattle	AL	22	53	18	3	0	5	36	10	15	7	0	7	0	0	0	0	0	.00	2	.340	.417	.679
1987 Seattle	AL	95	324	83	16	3	12	141	40	53	15	2	46	3	0	4	2	0	1.00	13	.256	.292	.435
1988 Seattle	AL	93	290	67	15	2	10	116	29	50	18	0	38	9	3	2	0	1	.00	13	.231	.295	.400
1989 Seattle	AL	94	316	75	10	3	7	112	32	34	29	2	32	6	1	3	0	0	.00	13	.237	.311	.354
1990 Seattle	AL	107	308	66	15	0	7	102	37	33	45	0	48	7	4	0	1	2	.33	11	.214	.328	.331
1991 Seattle	AL	132	324	63	8	1	8	97	38	32	34	0	49	9	6	3	0	0	.00	19	.194	.286	.299
1992 Seattle	AL	124	367	88	16	1	9	133	39	30	27	1	58	8	7	1	0	0	.00	7	.240	.305	.362
1993 Seattle	AL	135	423	109	19	0	13	167	48	63	48	4	56	17	8	4	1	0	1.00	18	.258	.354	.395
1994 Boston	AL	30	76	12	2	1	1	19	6	5	9	1	18	1	2	0	1	0	.00	2	.158	.256	.250
Milwaukee	AL	16	36	14	6	0	1	23	8	5	9	1	4	1	0	0	0	0	.00	0	.389	.522	.639
1995 Texas	AL	36	75	18	3	0	0	21	7	5	6	0	18	1	1	0	1	0	1.00	2	.240	.305	.280
1996 Texas	AL	42	86	26	6	1	3	43	14	17	9	0	17	0	0	0	0	0	.00	3	.302	.368	.500
11 Min. YEARS		702	2306	611	101	4	77	951	340	374	282	5	319	39	14	16	18	23	.44	28	.265	.353	.412
13 Maj. YEARS		970	2775	658	121	12	77	1034	314	350	258	11	413	63	33	17	5	7	.42	105	.237	.314	.373

Kerry Valrie

Bats: Right **Throws:** Right **Pos:** OF   Ht: 5'10"   Wt: 195   Born: 10/31/68   Age: 29

													BATTING							BASERUNNING			PERCENTAGES		
Year Team	Lg Org	G	AB	H	2B	3B	HR	TB	R	RBI	TBB	IBB	SO	HBP	SH	SF		SB	CS	SB%	GDP	Avg	OBP	SLG
1990 Utica	A- ChA	42	149	28	4	1	0	34	14	10	8	1	46	1	1	0		12	6	.67	4	.188	.234	.228
1991 South Bend	A ChA	87	331	71	11	2	6	104	47	29	23	1	78	3	3	0		32	6	.84	3	.215	.272	.314
1992 South Bend	A ChA	79	314	81	12	2	5	112	34	37	16	0	53	1	0	4		22	15	.59	6	.258	.293	.357
Sarasota	A+ ChA	51	174	41	9	0	1	53	13	23	14	0	42	1	0	2		13	1	.93	2	.236	.293	.305
1993 Sarasota	A+ ChA	115	386	82	14	2	12	136	47	52	17	1	81	4	2	7		19	7	.73	3	.212	.249	.352
1994 Birmingham	AA ChA	119	423	121	27	3	3	163	59	58	34	4	75	4	2	4		29	10	.74	3	.286	.342	.385
1995 Nashville	AAA ChA	138	544	136	30	3	7	193	75	55	40	0	107	3	2	4		22	15	.59	15	.250	.303	.355
1996 Nashville	AAA ChA	138	498	136	32	5	13	217	59	66	28	0	94	3	1	6		10	9	.53	12	.273	.312	.436
1997 Ottawa	AAA Mon	34	113	25	6	3	1	46	12	20	4	0	22	0	0	1		3	4	.43	2	.221	.246	.407
8 Min. YEARS		803	2932	721	145	21	50	1058	360	350	184	7	598	20	11	28		162	73	.69	50	.246	.292	.361

Todd Van Poppel

Pitches: Right **Bats:** Right **Pos:** P   Ht: 6'5"   Wt: 210   Born: 12/9/71   Age: 26

		HOW MUCH HE PITCHED						WHAT HE GAVE UP											THE RESULTS				
Year Team	Lg Org	G	GS	CG	GF	IP	BFP	H	R	ER	HR	SH	SF	HB	TBB	IBB	SO	WP	Bk	W	L	Pct.	ShO	Sv	ERA
1990 Sou. Oregon	A- Oak	5	5	0	0	24	92	10	5	3	1	0	1	2	9	0	32	0	0	1	1	.500	0	0	1.13
Madison	A Oak	3	3	0	0	13.2	61	8	11	6	0	0	1	1	10	0	17	0	0	2	1	.667	0	0	3.95
1991 Huntsville	AA Oak	24	24	1	0	132.1	607	118	69	51	2	4	6	6	90	0	115	12	1	6	13	.316	1	0	3.47
1992 Tacoma	AAA Oak	9	9	0	0	45.1	202	44	22	20	1	3	4	1	35	0	29	1	1	4	2	.667	0	0	3.97
1993 Tacoma	AAA Oak	16	16	0	0	78.2	355	67	53	51	5	3	3	4	54	0	71	2	0	4	8	.333	0	0	5.83
1997 Omaha	AAA KC	11	6	0	1	37	188	50	36	33	10	2	3	3	24	0	27	2	0	1	5	.167	0	0	8.03
Charlotte	A+ Tex	6	6	2	0	35.2	152	36	19	16	3	2	2	1	10	0	33	2	0	0	4	.000	0	0	4.04
Tulsa	AA Tex	7	7	0	0	42.2	197	53	27	24	2	3	3	1	15	0	26	2	1	3	3	.500	0	0	5.06
1991 Oakland	AL	1	1	0	0	4.2	21	7	5	5	1	0	0	0	2	0	6	0	0	0	0	.000	0	0	9.64
1993 Oakland	AL	16	16	0	0	84	380	76	50	47	10	1	2	2	62	0	47	3	0	6	6	.500	0	0	5.04
1994 Oakland	AL	23	23	0	0	116.2	532	108	80	79	20	4	4	3	89	2	83	3	1	7	10	.412	0	0	6.09
1995 Oakland	AL	36	14	1	10	138.1	582	125	77	75	16	3	6	4	56	1	122	4	0	4	8	.333	0	0	4.88
1996 Oakland	AL	28	6	0	8	63	301	86	56	54	13	3	5	2	33	3	37	4	0	1	5	.167	0	1	7.71
Detroit	AL	9	9	1	0	36.1	190	53	51	46	11	1	2	1	29	0	16	3	0	2	4	.333	1	0	11.39
5 Min. YEARS		81	76	3	1	409.1	1854	386	242	204	24	17	23	19	247	0	350	21	3	21	37	.362	1	0	4.49
5 Maj. YEARS		113	69	2	18	443	2006	455	319	306	71	12	19	12	271	6	311	17	1	20	33	.377	1	1	6.22

Doug Vanderweele

Pitches: Right **Bats:** Right **Pos:** P   Ht: 6'3"   Wt: 200   Born: 3/18/70   Age: 28

		HOW MUCH HE PITCHED						WHAT HE GAVE UP											THE RESULTS				
Year Team	Lg Org	G	GS	CG	GF	IP	BFP	H	R	ER	HR	SH	SF	HB	TBB	IBB	SO	WP	Bk	W	L	Pct.	ShO	Sv	ERA
1991 Everett	A- SF	15	15	0	0	87	371	73	42	19	1	1	3	8	35	1	65	12	7	6	4	.600	0	0	1.97
1992 Clinton	A SF	9	9	0	0	51	228	61	33	28	5	2	2	2	24	1	39	7	3	3	3	.500	0	0	4.94
San Jose	A+ SF	16	15	1	0	87.1	387	77	49	36	7	3	2	8	50	1	51	4	2	6	4	.600	0	0	3.71
Phoenix	AAA SF	1	0	0	0	1.2	8	3	2	2	0	0	0	0	0	0	0	0	0	0	0	.000	0	0	10.80
1993 Shreveport	AA SF	1	0	0	0	2	7	0	0	0	0	0	0	0	3	0	0	0	0	0	0	.000	0	0	0.00
San Jose	A+ SF	25	24	3	1	171	728	188	78	74	17	12	5	3	55	3	106	8	2	10	6	.625	0	0	3.89
1994 San Jose	A+ SF	8	8	0	0	51.2	215	46	21	16	3	4	1	5	10	0	33	0	0	3	3	.500	0	0	2.79
Shreveport	AA SF	21	21	1	0	125.1	533	146	62	53	7	7	3	3	32	2	55	4	0	6	9	.400	0	0	3.81
1995 Phoenix	AAA SF	11	4	1	1	38.1	178	57	29	26	9	2	3	1	11	3	20	1	1	2	4	.333	0	0	6.10
Shreveport	AA SF	13	9	0	0	64.1	253	61	18	18	3	1	0	2	13	0	22	3	0	5	2	.714	0	0	2.52
1996 Phoenix	AAA SF	41	3	0	6	89	397	101	55	53	13	4	5	2	35	4	42	4	0	4	2	.667	0	0	5.36
1997 Phoenix	AAA SF	36	2	0	8	68.2	313	99	38	35	6	2	3	5	18	2	35	3	0	6	4	.600	0	1	4.59
7 Min. YEARS		197	110	6	16	837.1	3618	912	427	360	71	38	27	39	283	17	471	47	15	51	41	.554	0	1	3.87

Ryan VanDeWeg

Pitches: Right **Bats:** Right **Pos:** P   Ht: 6'0"   Wt: 180   Born: 2/24/74   Age: 24

		HOW MUCH HE PITCHED						WHAT HE GAVE UP											THE RESULTS				
Year Team	Lg Org	G	GS	CG	GF	IP	BFP	H	R	ER	HR	SH	SF	HB	TBB	IBB	SO	WP	Bk	W	L	Pct.	ShO	Sv	ERA
1995 Clinton	A SD	15	15	1	0	91	400	92	56	42	5	3	2	7	32	3	89	3	1	6	4	.600	0	0	4.15
1996 Rancho Cuca	A+ SD	26	26	0	0	146.1	636	164	78	66	15	1	2	10	52	1	129	8	0	9	6	.600	0	0	4.06
1997 Mobile	AA SD	27	27	2	0	159	708	198	105	96	20	5	6	5	55	1	81	7	2	9	8	.529	0	0	5.43
3 Min. YEARS		68	68	3	0	396.1	1744	454	239	204	40	9	10	22	139	5	299	18	3	24	18	.571	0	0	4.63

Tim VanEgmond

Pitches: Right **Bats:** Right **Pos:** P   Ht: 6'2"   Wt: 180   Born: 5/31/69   Age: 29

		HOW MUCH HE PITCHED						WHAT HE GAVE UP											THE RESULTS				
Year Team	Lg Org	G	GS	CG	GF	IP	BFP	H	R	ER	HR	SH	SF	HB	TBB	IBB	SO	WP	Bk	W	L	Pct.	ShO	Sv	ERA
1991 Red Sox	R Bos	3	2	0	1	15	54	6	1	1	0	0	0	1	1	0	20	2	2	2	0	1.000	0	1	0.60
Winter Havn	A+ Bos	13	10	4	2	68.1	292	69	32	23	2	1	0	2	23	1	47	2	1	4	5	.444	2	2	3.03
1992 Lynchburg	A+ Bos	28	27	2	0	173.2	727	161	73	66	12	4	1	8	52	0	140	18	1	12	4	.750	1	0	3.42
1993 New Britain	AA Bos	29	29	1	0	190.1	794	182	99	84	18	3	2	14	44	1	163	11	3	6	12	.333	1	0	3.97
1994 Pawtucket	AAA Bos	20	20	1	0	119.1	510	110	58	50	9	0	3	7	42	2	87	5	0	9	5	.643	0	0	3.77
1995 Pawtucket	AAA Bos	12	12	0	0	66.2	279	66	32	29	10	1	2	4	21	1	47	5	0	5	3	.625	0	0	3.92
1996 Pawtucket	AAA Bos	11	11	1	0	61.2	262	66	37	30	9	0	2	3	24	1	46	1	1	5	3	.625	0	0	4.38
New Orleans	AAA Mil	7	7	0	0	48	180	28	8	8	2	2	0	1	11	0	32	1	0	5	1	.833	0	1	1.50
1997 Tucson	AAA Mil	1	0	0	0	1	6	3	1	1	0	0	0	0	0	0	1	0	0	1	0	1.000	0	0	9.00
1994 Boston	AL	7	7	1	0	38.1	173	38	27	27	7	0	3	0	21	3	22	1	0	2	3	.400	0	0	6.34
1995 Boston	AL	4	1	0	1	6.2	35	9	7	7	2	0	0	0	6	0	5	1	0	0	1	.000	0	0	9.45
1996 Milwaukee	AL	12	9	0	1	54.2	242	58	35	32	6	3	1	1	23	2	33	1	0	3	5	.375	0	0	5.27

		HOW MUCH HE PITCHED						WHAT HE GAVE UP								THE RESULTS					
Year Team	Lg Org	G	GS	CG	GF	IP	BFP	H	R	ER	HR	SH	SF	HB	TBB	IBB	SO	WP	Bk	W	L	Pct	ShO	Sv	ERA
7 Min. YEARS		124	118	9	3	744	3104	691	341	292	62	11	10	40	218	6	582	45	8	49	33	.598	4	3	3.53
3 Maj. YEARS		23	17	1	2	99.2	450	105	69	66	15	3	6	1	50	5	60	2	1	5	9	.357	0	0	5.96

Ben VanRyn

Pitches: Left **Bats:** Left **Pos:** P **Ht:** 6'5" **Wt:** 195 **Born:** 8/9/71 **Age:** 26

		HOW MUCH HE PITCHED						WHAT HE GAVE UP								THE RESULTS					
Year Team	Lg Org	G	GS	CG	GF	IP	BFP	H	R	ER	HR	SH	SF	HB	TBB	IBB	SO	WP	Bk	W	L	Pct	ShO	Sv	ERA
1990 Expos	R Mon	10	9	0	0	51.2	205	44	13	10	0	0	0	2	15	0	56	0	0	5	3	.625	0	0	1.74
1991 Sumter	A Mon	20	20	0	0	109.1	506	122	96	79	14	3	7	6	61	0	77	10	4	2	13	.133	0	0	6.50
Jamestown	A- Mon	6	6	1	0	32.1	143	37	19	18	1	0	0	2	12	0	23	4	0	3	3	.500	0	0	5.01
1992 Vero Beach	A+ LA	26	25	1	0	137.2	583	125	58	49	4	5	8	2	54	1	108	4	5	10	7	.588	1	0	3.20
1993 San Antonio	AA LA	21	21	0	0	134.1	557	118	43	33	5	4	1	3	38	1	144	2	4	14	4	.778	0	0	2.21
Albuquerque	AAA LA	6	6	0	0	24.1	120	35	30	29	1	1	2	0	17	0	9	0	0	1	4	.200	0	0	10.73
1994 Albuquerque	AAA LA	12	9	0	1	50.2	251	75	42	36	6	3	1	0	24	1	44	0	1	4	1	.800	0	0	6.39
San Antonio	AA LA	17	17	0	0	102.1	418	93	42	34	5	3	1	0	35	0	72	2	0	8	3	.727	0	0	2.99
1995 Chattanooga	AA Cin	5	3	0	0	12.2	69	22	18	13	2	0	2	1	6	0	6	0	0	0	1	.000	0	0	9.24
Vancouver	AAA Ana	11	5	0	2	29.1	123	29	10	10	1	2	2	0	9	1	20	2	0	2	0	1.000	0	0	3.07
Midland	AA Ana	19	0	0	8	32.1	133	33	10	10	4	0	0	2	12	0	24	2	0	1	1	.500	0	1	2.78
1996 Vancouver	AAA Ana	18	1	0	4	34.2	154	35	17	15	2	3	1	1	13	1	28	3	0	3	3	.500	0	0	3.89
Louisville	AAA StL	19	10	0	4	66.1	288	69	43	36	9	2	3	0	27	0	42	2	0	4	6	.400	0	1	4.88
1997 Iowa	AAA ChN	51	5	0	12	80.1	343	88	43	41	10	5	3	1	25	2	64	5	0	2	2	.500	0	3	4.59
1996 California	AL	1	0	0	1	1	5	1	0	0	0	0	0	0	1	0	0	0	0	0	0	.000	0	0	0.00
8 Min. YEARS		241	137	3	31	898.1	3893	925	484	413	64	31	31	20	348	7	717	36	14	59	51	.536	1	5	4.14

Leoner Vasquez

Pitches: Left **Bats:** Left **Pos:** P **Ht:** 6'4" **Wt:** 190 **Born:** 7/1/73 **Age:** 24

		HOW MUCH HE PITCHED						WHAT HE GAVE UP								THE RESULTS					
Year Team	Lg Org	G	GS	CG	GF	IP	BFP	H	R	ER	HR	SH	SF	HB	TBB	IBB	SO	WP	Bk	W	L	Pct	ShO	Sv	ERA
1997 Binghamton	AA NYN	1	1	0	0	5.1	26	7	6	6	3	1	2	0	2	0	2	0	0	0	1	.000	0	0	10.13
Capital City	A NYN	22	8	0	8	56	250	63	37	32	4	1	2	3	22	1	49	7	1	4	5	.444	0	1	5.14
1 Min. YEARS		23	9	0	8	61.1	276	70	43	38	7	2	4	3	24	1	51	7	1	4	6	.400	0	1	5.58

Jay Vaught

Pitches: Right **Bats:** Left **Pos:** P **Ht:** 6'1" **Wt:** 185 **Born:** 12/21/71 **Age:** 26

		HOW MUCH HE PITCHED						WHAT HE GAVE UP								THE RESULTS					
Year Team	Lg Org	G	GS	CG	GF	IP	BFP	H	R	ER	HR	SH	SF	HB	TBB	IBB	SO	WP	Bk	W	L	Pct	ShO	Sv	ERA
1994 Watertown	A- Cle	14	13	2	0	82.1	340	73	38	30	5	3	5	3	16	1	50	3	6	7	4	.636	0	0	3.28
1995 Kinston	A+ Cle	27	26	4	0	171	717	184	80	64	19	8	5	15	28	3	82	6	1	8	12	.400	1	0	3.37
1996 Canton-Akrn	AA Cle	51	0	0	26	94.1	415	101	58	50	10	5	2	4	35	9	78	6	1	5	4	.556	0	3	4.77
1997 Akron	AA Cle	29	4	0	9	70.2	312	65	43	41	8	6	6	5	40	1	56	4	0	2	3	.400	0	1	5.22
4 Min. YEARS		121	43	6	35	418.1	1784	423	219	185	42	22	18	27	119	14	266	19	8	22	23	.489	1	4	3.98

Mike Vavrek

Pitches: Left **Bats:** Left **Pos:** P **Ht:** 6'2" **Wt:** 185 **Born:** 4/23/74 **Age:** 24

		HOW MUCH HE PITCHED						WHAT HE GAVE UP								THE RESULTS					
Year Team	Lg Org	G	GS	CG	GF	IP	BFP	H	R	ER	HR	SH	SF	HB	TBB	IBB	SO	WP	Bk	W	L	Pct	ShO	Sv	ERA
1995 Portland	A- Col	3	3	0	0	14	52	8	0	0	0	0	0	3	0	14	0	0	0	0	.000	0	0	0.00
Asheville	A Col	12	12	1	0	76.2	322	64	24	17	3	0	1	5	25	0	54	4	5	5	4	.556	0	0	2.00
1996 Salem	A+ Col	26	25	2	0	149.2	658	167	92	81	15	6	8	5	59	0	103	10	0	10	8	.556	1	0	4.87
1997 Salem	A+ Col	10	9	0	0	62.2	255	55	21	15	3	1	4	3	18	0	48	3	0	2	2	.500	0	0	2.15
New Haven	AA Col	17	17	2	0	122.2	491	94	38	35	7	8	4	1	34	0	101	4	0	12	3	.800	0	0	2.57
3 Min. YEARS		68	66	5	0	425.2	1778	388	175	148	28	15	17	14	139	0	320	21	5	29	17	.630	1	0	3.13

Javier Vazquez

Pitches: Right **Bats:** Right **Pos:** P **Ht:** 6'2" **Wt:** 175 **Born:** 6/25/76 **Age:** 22

		HOW MUCH HE PITCHED						WHAT HE GAVE UP								THE RESULTS					
Year Team	Lg Org	G	GS	CG	GF	IP	BFP	H	R	ER	HR	SH	SF	HB	TBB	IBB	SO	WP	Bk	W	L	Pct	ShO	Sv	ERA
1994 Expos	R Mon	15	11	0	0	67.2	260	37	25	19	0	1	2	3	15	0	56	9	2	5	2	.714	1	0	2.53
1995 Albany	A Mon	21	21	1	0	102.2	459	109	67	58	8	1	2	9	47	0	87	2	2	6	6	.500	0	0	5.08
1996 Delmarva	A Mon	27	27	1	0	164.1	668	138	64	49	12	1	1	7	57	0	173	12	2	14	3	.824	0	0	2.68
1997 Wst Plm Bch	A+ Mon	19	19	1	0	112.2	461	98	40	27	8	1	2	6	28	0	100	2	2	6	3	.667	0	0	2.16
Harrisburg	AA Mon	6	6	1	0	42	155	15	5	5	2	0	1	2	12	0	47	2	0	4	0	1.000	1	0	1.07
4 Min. YEARS		88	84	5	0	489.1	2003	397	201	158	30	4	8	27	159	0	463	27	8	35	14	.714	1	0	2.91

Edgard Velazquez

Bats: Right **Throws:** Right **Pos:** OF **Ht:** 6'0" **Wt:** 170 **Born:** 12/15/75 **Age:** 22

		BATTING														BASERUNNING				PERCENTAGES		
Year Team	Lg Org	G	AB	H	2B	3B	HR	TB	R	RBI	TBB	IBB	SO	HBP	SH	SF	SB	CS	SB%	GDP	Avg	OBP	SLG
1993 Rockies	R Col	39	147	36	4	2	2	50	20	20	16	0	35	0	2	2	7	5	.58	2	.245	.315	.340
1994 Asheville	A Col	119	447	106	22	3	11	167	50	39	23	0	120	3	3	2	9	9	.50	14	.237	.278	.374
1995 Salem	A+ Col	131	497	149	25	6	13	225	74	69	40	4	102	4	3	7	7	10	.41	17	.300	.352	.453
1996 New Haven	AA Col	132	486	141	29	4	19	235	72	62	53	5	114	4	0	0	6	2	.75	7	.290	.365	.484
1997 Colo Spngs	AAA Col	120	438	123	24	10	17	218	70	73	34	2	119	6	1	2	6	3	.67	8	.281	.340	.498
5 Min. YEARS		541	2015	555	104	25	62	895	286	263	166	11	490	17	9	13	35	29	.55	48	.275	.334	.444

Mike Venafro

Pitches: Left **Bats:** Left **Pos:** P **Ht:** 5'10" **Wt:** 170 **Born:** 8/2/73 **Age:** 24

Year Team	Lg Org	G	GS	CG	GF	IP	BFP	H	R	ER	HR	SH	SF	HB	TBB	IBB	SO	WP	Bk	W	L	Pct.	ShO	Sv	ERA
1995 Hudson Vall	A- Tex	32	0	0	12	50.2	200	37	13	12	0	2	1	5	21	2	32	1	3	9	1	.900	0	2	2.13
1996 Chston-SC	A Tex	50	0	0	42	59	258	57	27	23	0	4	2	3	21	3	62	13	0	1	3	.250	0	19	3.51
1997 Charlotte	A+ Tex	35	0	0	27	44.2	196	51	17	17	2	4	3	1	21	1	35	1	0	4	2	.667	0	10	3.43
Tulsa	AA Tex	11	0	0	9	15.2	75	13	12	6	1	0	2	2	12	0	13	1	0	0	1	.000	0	1	3.45
3 Min. YEARS		128	0	0	90	170	729	158	69	58	3	10	8	11	75	6	142	16	3	14	7	.667	0	32	3.07

Jay Veniard

Pitches: Left **Bats:** Left **Pos:** P **Ht:** 6'4" **Wt:** 215 **Born:** 8/16/74 **Age:** 23

Year Team	Lg Org	G	GS	CG	GF	IP	BFP	H	R	ER	HR	SH	SF	HB	TBB	IBB	SO	WP	Bk	W	L	Pct.	ShO	Sv	ERA
1995 Blue Jays	R Tor	3	1	0	2	11	39	4	2	1	0	0	0	1	2	0	18	2	0	2	0	1.000	0	0	0.82
Medicne Hat	R+ Tor	11	10	0	0	63	280	67	34	19	2	2	3	3	21	0	43	6	2	4	1	.800	0	0	2.71
1996 Hagerstown	A Tor	8	8	1	0	44.2	187	35	28	20	5	0	2	1	24	0	43	2	1	3	3	.500	0	0	4.03
Dunedin	A+ Tor	14	14	0	0	64.2	270	63	37	29	7	0	2	5	19	0	40	4	1	5	4	.444	0	0	4.04
1997 Knoxville	AA Tor	17	15	2	0	75.1	369	97	59	49	6	2	2	8	37	2	54	14	2	3	8	.273	0	0	5.85
Dunedin	A+ Tor	10	8	0	1	52.2	229	49	23	11	2	2	2	4	35	1	32	4	1	1	3	.250	0	0	1.88
3 Min. YEARS		63	56	3	3	311.1	1374	315	183	129	22	6	11	22	138	3	230	32	7	17	20	.459	0	0	3.73

Andrew Vessel

Bats: Right **Throws:** Right **Pos:** OF **Ht:** 6'3" **Wt:** 205 **Born:** 3/11/75 **Age:** 23

Year Team	Lg Org	G	AB	H	2B	3B	HR	TB	R	RBI	TBB	IBB	SO	HBP	SH	SF	SB	CS	SB%	GDP	Avg	OBP	SLG
1993 Rangers	R Tex	51	192	42	10	2	1	59	23	30	8	0	28	1	0	6	6	2	.75	11	.219	.246	.307
1994 Chston-SC	A Tex	114	411	99	23	2	8	150	40	55	29	0	102	10	1	4	7	10	.41	5	.241	.304	.365
1995 Charlotte	A+ Tex	129	498	132	26	2	9	189	67	78	32	2	75	15	1	7	3	17	.15	11	.265	.324	.380
1996 Charlotte	A+ Tex	126	484	111	25	6	3	157	63	67	45	0	94	7	2	11	1	6	.14	14	.229	.298	.324
1997 Tulsa	AA Tex	138	517	135	35	1	12	208	78	75	41	2	87	6	4	5	3	1	.75	8	.261	.320	.402
5 Min. YEARS		558	2102	519	119	13	33	763	271	305	155	4	386	39	8	33	20	36	.36	49	.247	.306	.363

Mike Villano

Pitches: Right **Bats:** Right **Pos:** P **Ht:** 6'1" **Wt:** 200 **Born:** 8/10/71 **Age:** 26

Year Team	Lg Org	G	GS	CG	GF	IP	BFP	H	R	ER	HR	SH	SF	HB	TBB	IBB	SO	WP	Bk	W	L	Pct.	ShO	Sv	ERA
1995 Burlington	A SF	16	0	0	7	25.1	120	20	12	8	1	2	1	4	21	0	29	5	0	3	1	.750	0	1	2.84
San Jose	A+ SF	21	0	0	16	32.2	137	27	7	6	2	0	1	3	11	0	42	3	0	0	1	.000	0	1	1.65
1996 San Jose	A+ SF	39	2	0	21	88	341	48	12	7	2	1	1	0	33	4	133	7	1	7	1	.875	0	8	0.72
Shreveport	AA SF	2	2	0	0	12	47	6	4	4	0	0	0	0	8	0	7	1	0	2	0	1.000	0	0	3.00
1997 Shreveport	AA SF	30	0	0	15	34.1	158	41	25	24	5	2	0	0	20	2	26	4	1	3	1	.750	0	2	6.29
Phoenix	AAA SF	13	11	0	1	71.1	309	75	36	33	7	3	2	2	27	1	41	2	0	5	3	.625	0	0	4.16
3 Min. YEARS		121	15	0	60	263.2	1112	217	96	82	17	8	5	9	120	7	278	21	2	20	7	.741	0	12	2.80

Julio Vinas

Bats: Right **Throws:** Right **Pos:** DH **Ht:** 6'0" **Wt:** 200 **Born:** 2/14/73 **Age:** 25

Year Team	Lg Org	G	AB	H	2B	3B	HR	TB	R	RBI	TBB	IBB	SO	HBP	SH	SF	SB	CS	SB%	GDP	Avg	OBP	SLG
1991 White Sox	R ChA	50	187	42	9	0	3	60	21	29	19	0	40	1	0	2	2	3	.40	5	.225	.300	.321
1992 South Bend	A ChA	33	94	16	3	0	0	19	7	10	9	0	17	1	0	2	1	3	.25	1	.170	.245	.202
Utica	A- ChA	47	151	37	6	4	0	51	22	24	11	0	29	2	1	5	1	2	.33	2	.245	.296	.338
1993 South Bend	A ChA	55	188	60	15	1	9	104	24	37	12	1	29	1	2	2	1	1	.50	2	.319	.360	.553
Sarasota	A+ ChA	18	65	16	2	1	1	23	5	7	5	0	13	0	0	0	0	0	.00	2	.246	.300	.354
1994 South Bend	A ChA	121	466	118	31	1	9	178	68	75	43	4	75	4	6	6	3	3	.50	6	.253	.318	.382
1995 Birmingham	AA ChA	102	372	100	16	2	6	138	47	61	37	1	80	5	0	7	3	3	.50	9	.269	.337	.371
1996 Nashville	AAA ChA	104	338	80	18	2	11	135	48	52	36	2	63	2	0	4	1	4	.20	8	.237	.311	.399
1997 Nashville	AAA ChA	91	314	73	12	2	11	122	39	41	25	2	72	3	3	5	4	4	.50	6	.232	.289	.389
7 Min. YEARS		621	2175	542	112	13	50	830	281	336	197	10	418	19	12	33	13	22	.37	41	.249	.313	.382

Derek Wachter

Bats: Right **Throws:** Right **Pos:** OF **Ht:** 6'2" **Wt:** 195 **Born:** 8/28/70 **Age:** 27

Year Team	Lg Org	G	AB	H	2B	3B	HR	TB	R	RBI	TBB	IBB	SO	HBP	SH	SF	SB	CS	SB%	GDP	Avg	OBP	SLG
1991 Brewers	R Mil	51	186	59	16	5	6	103	52	42	40	1	59	1	0	4	3	0	1.00	5	.317	.433	.554
1992 Beloit	A Mil	111	363	98	17	9	10	163	53	61	43	1	113	1	5	3	6	5	.55	9	.270	.346	.449
1993 Stockton	A+ Mil	115	420	123	20	4	22	217	75	108	64	2	93	6	3	11	3	3	.50	7	.293	.385	.517
1994 El Paso	AA Mil	30	117	45	9	5	0	64	14	24	13	0	24	2	0	3	3	0	1.00	3	.385	.444	.547
New Orleans	AAA Mil	65	221	63	15	1	5	95	33	39	24	1	57	3	4	3	3	0	1.00	6	.285	.359	.430
1995 New Orleans	AAA Mil	112	382	98	23	1	8	147	44	45	39	2	67	5	0	3	2	2	.50	11	.257	.331	.385
1997 El Paso	AA Mil	13	49	15	0	0	1	18	8	8	4	0	7	2	0	0	1	1	.00	2	.306	.382	.367
Stockton	A+ Mil	49	177	55	7	3	3	77	21	28	26	1	24	3	0	0	2	4	.33	11	.311	.408	.435
Tucson	AAA Mil	46	142	41	12	0	2	59	24	28	18	0	28	3	1	6	2	2	.50	5	.289	.367	.415
6 Min. YEARS		592	2057	597	119	28	57	943	324	383	271	8	472	26	13	33	24	17	.59	55	.290	.375	.458

Bret Wagner

Pitches: Left **Bats:** Left **Pos:** P **Ht:** 6'0" **Wt:** 190 **Born:** 4/17/73 **Age:** 25

Year Team	Lg Org	G	GS	CG	GF	IP	BFP	H	R	ER	HR	SH	SF	HB	TBB	IBB	SO	WP	Bk	W	L	Pct.	ShO	Sv	ERA
1994 New Jersey	A- StL	3	3	0	0	12.1	53	10	9	7	0	0	0	0	4	0	10	3	0	0	1	.000	0	0	5.11
Savannah	A StL	7	7	0	0	44	161	27	8	6	2	0	1	0	6	0	43	3	1	4	1	.800	0	0	1.23
1995 St. Pete	A+ StL	17	17	1	0	93.1	373	77	36	22	3	3	2	2	28	0	59	4	0	5	4	.556	0	0	2.12
Arkansas	AA StL	6	6	0	0	36.2	161	34	14	13	1	1	1	0	18	0	31	3	0	1	2	.333	0	0	3.19
1996 Huntsville	AA Oak	27	27	0	0	134	597	125	77	63	6	5	5	7	77	3	98	19	2	8	8	.500	0	0	4.23
1997 Huntsville	AA Oak	3	0	0	0	2.2	24	7	11	6	0	0	1	2	6	0	3	2	0	0	0	.000	0	0	20.25
4 Min. YEARS		63	60	1	0	323	1369	280	155	117	12	9	10	11	139	3	244	34	3	18	16	.529	0	0	3.26

Joe Wagner

Pitches: Right **Bats:** Right **Pos:** P **Ht:** 6'1" **Wt:** 195 **Born:** 12/8/71 **Age:** 26

Year Team	Lg Org	G	GS	CG	GF	IP	BFP	H	R	ER	HR	SH	SF	HB	TBB	IBB	SO	WP	Bk	W	L	Pct.	ShO	Sv	ERA
1993 Helena	R+ Mil	8	7	0	0	41.1	181	39	17	12	1	2	0	3	20	0	30	2	1	3	2	.600	0	0	2.61
1994 Beloit	A Mil	28	28	7	0	185.1	793	178	99	81	10	8	3	6	71	3	137	20	1	13	9	.591	1	0	3.93
1995 El Paso	AA Mil	5	5	0	0	19	109	32	31	21	7	0	0	2	22	0	8	4	0	0	4	.000	0	0	9.95
Stockton	A+ Mil	20	18	0	1	107.2	494	124	62	52	8	8	3	4	53	0	76	7	0	7	6	.538	0	0	4.35
1996 Stockton	A+ Mil	28	28	0	0	167.1	745	171	102	89	16	6	3	12	86	0	103	7	0	12	6	.667	0	0	4.79
1997 El Paso	AA Mil	19	17	0	11	28	153	32	35	29	6	1	1	4	32	0	19	3	0	1	2	.333	0	1	9.32
Stockton	A+ Mil	14	14	0	0	72.1	345	83	61	54	10	0	3	11	44	0	36	6	0	3	5	.375	0	0	6.72
5 Min. YEARS		122	101	7	12	621	2820	659	407	338	58	25	13	42	328	3	409	49	2	39	34	.534	1	1	4.90

Mark Wagner

Bats: Right **Throws:** Right **Pos:** 3B **Ht:** 6'0" **Wt:** 175 **Born:** 3/4/54 **Age:** 44

Year Team	Lg Org	G	AB	H	2B	3B	HR	TB	R	RBI	TBB	IBB	SO	HBP	SH	SF	SB	CS	SB%	GDP	Avg	OBP	SLG
1997 Chattanooga	AA Cin	2	4	1	0	0	0	1	0	1	0	0	0	0	0	0	0	0	.00	0	.250	.250	.250

Dane Walker

Bats: Left **Throws:** Right **Pos:** 2B **Ht:** 5'10" **Wt:** 180 **Born:** 11/16/69 **Age:** 28

Year Team	Lg Org	G	AB	H	2B	3B	HR	TB	R	RBI	TBB	IBB	SO	HBP	SH	SF	SB	CS	SB%	GDP	Avg	OBP	SLG
1991 Athletics	R Oak	29	118	43	3	0	2	52	37	22	24	1	11	2	1		12	1	.92	5	.364	.479	.441
Modesto	A+ Oak	22	66	18	2	1	0	22	11	5	14	0	9	0	1	1	2	3	.40	2	.273	.395	.333
1992 Madison	A Oak	82	287	85	13	2	3	111	56	23	42	0	57	1	4	2	23	10	.70	6	.296	.386	.387
Reno	A+ Oak	31	122	34	6	0	0	40	24	3	23	1	23	1	0	0	8	7	.53	4	.279	.397	.328
1993 Modesto	A+ Oak	122	443	131	22	1	9	182	94	67	94	0	55	0	7	1	16	16	.50	6	.296	.418	.411
1994 Modesto	A+ Oak	9	27	11	4	0	1	18	6	16	10	0	5	0	1	1	0	0	.00	2	.407	.553	.667
Huntsville	AA Oak	47	153	42	10	0	0	52	21	10	24	0	29	1	6	1	6	7	.46	3	.275	.374	.340
1995 Huntsville	AA Oak	110	370	86	13	2	2	109	46	35	57	6	84	2	2	3	9	7	.56	9	.232	.336	.295
1996 W Michigan	A Oak	127	477	132	25	3	7	184	97	47	112	2	75	3	3	3	14	10	.58	11	.277	.415	.386
1997 Huntsville	AA Oak	106	361	87	17	3	7	131	62	52	68	0	87	0	2	2	7	2	.78	8	.241	.360	.363
7 Min. YEARS		685	2424	669	115	12	31	901	454	280	468	10	435	10	27	14	97	63	.61	56	.276	.393	.372

Mike Walker

Pitches: Right **Bats:** Right **Pos:** P **Ht:** 6'1" **Wt:** 205 **Born:** 10/4/66 **Age:** 31

Year Team	Lg Org	G	GS	CG	GF	IP	BFP	H	R	ER	HR	SH	SF	HB	TBB	IBB	SO	WP	Bk	W	L	Pct.	ShO	Sv	ERA
1986 Burlington	R+ Cle	14	13	1	0	70.1	339	75	65	46	9	2	5	4	45	0	42	1	0	4	6	.400	0	0	5.89
1987 Waterloo	A Cle	23	23	8	0	145.1	637	133	74	58	11	4	3	13	68	1	144	14	0	11	7	.611	1	0	3.59
Kinston	A+ Cle	3	3	0	0	20.2	91	17	7	6	0	0	2	0	14	0	19	2	0	3	0	1.000	0	0	2.61
1988 Williamsprt	AA Cle	28	27	3	1	164.1	717	162	82	68	11	5	3	9	74	1	144	17	2	15	7	.682	0	0	3.72
1989 Colo Spngs	AAA Cle	28	28	4	0	168	772	193	124	108	21	8	7	14	93	0	97	12	0	6	15	.286	0	0	5.79
1990 Colo Spngs	AAA Cle	18	12	0	2	79	374	96	62	49	6	3	9	7	36	5	50	6	0	2	7	.222	0	1	5.58
Canton-Akrn	AA Cle	2	1	0	0	7	29	4	0	0	0	0	0	0	4	0	3	0	0	1	0	1.000	0	0	0.00
1991 Canton-Akrn	AA Cle	45	1	0	34	77.1	347	68	36	24	2	5	1	7	45	6	42	13	0	9	4	.692	0	11	2.79
1992 Toledo	AAA Det	42	1	0	16	78.2	384	102	62	51	5	3	2	8	44	6	44	7	1	2	8	.200	0	4	5.83
1993 Orlando	AA ChN	16	2	0	6	28.1	138	42	26	23	4	3	0	6	9	4	21	5	1	2	3	.400	0	1	7.31
Iowa	AAA ChN	12	0	0	3	23.1	97	22	8	7	1	0	2	2	9	0	11	3	0	1	1	.500	0	0	2.70
1994 Iowa	AAA ChN	56	0	0	37	87.1	367	80	33	29	2	4	3	4	34	8	56	8	1	6	2	.750	0	8	2.99
1995 Iowa	AAA ChN	16	1	0	3	26.1	122	22	13	12	3	1	1	3	19	4	13	0	0	1	1	.500	0	0	4.10
1996 Toledo	AAA Det	28	0	0	14	44.2	194	37	23	19	4	3	0	1	27	1	37	8	0	3	2	.600	0	6	3.83
1997 Indianapols	AAA Cin	55	5	0	19	102.2	431	80	35	34	7	4	1	6	46	4	80	13	0	9	6	.600	0	7	2.98
1988 Cleveland	AL	3	1	0	0	8.2	42	8	7	7	0	1	0	0	10	0	7	0	0	0	1	.000	0	0	7.27
1990 Cleveland	AL	18	11	0	2	75.2	350	82	49	41	6	4	2	6	42	4	34	3	1	2	6	.250	0	0	4.88
1991 Cleveland	AL	5	0	0	3	4.1	22	6	1	1	0	0	1	0	2	1	2	0	0	0	1	.000	0	0	2.08
1995 Chicago	NL	42	0	0	12	44.2	206	42	22	16	2	4	4	0	24	3	20	3	1	1	3	.250	0	1	3.22
1996 Detroit	AL	20	0	0	12	27.2	135	40	26	26	10	1	2	1	17	1	13	2	0	0	0	.000	0	1	8.46
12 Min. YEARS		385	117	16	135	1123.1	5039	1133	650	534	86	45	39	84	567	40	803	109	5	75	69	.521	1	38	4.28
5 Maj. YEARS		88	12	0	29	161	755	181	105	91	18	10	8	8	95	9	76	8	2	3	11	.214	0	2	5.09

Pete Walker

Pitches: Right **Bats:** Right **Pos:** P **Ht:** 6' 2" **Wt:** 195 **Born:** 4/8/69 **Age:** 29

Year Team	Lg Org	G	GS	CG	GF	IP	BFP	H	R	ER	HR	SH	SF	HB	TBB	IBB	SO	WP	Bk	W	L	Pct.	ShO	Sv	ERA
1990 Pittsfield	A- NYN	16	13	1	1	80	346	74	43	37	2	0	4	3	46	0	73	1	0	5	7	.417	0	0	4.16
1991 St. Lucie	A+ NYN	26	25	1	0	151.1	641	145	77	54	9	9	5	4	52	2	95	7	3	10	12	.455	0	0	3.21
1992 Binghamton	AA NYN	24	23	4	1	139.2	605	159	77	64	9	3	2	3	46	0	72	5	2	7	12	.368	0	0	4.12
1993 Binghamton	AA NYN	45	10	0	33	99.1	423	89	45	38	6	6	1	5	46	1	89	5	0	4	9	.308	0	19	3.44
1994 St. Lucie	A+ NYN	3	0	0	2	4	16	3	2	1	1	0	0	0	1	0	5	0	0	0	0	.000	0	0	2.25
Norfolk	AAA NYN	37	0	0	19	47.2	207	48	22	21	3	3	2	0	24	2	42	3	0	2	4	.333	0	3	3.97
1995 Norfolk	AAA NYN	34	1	0	25	48.1	207	51	24	21	4	3	1	1	16	1	39	2	1	5	2	.714	0	8	3.91
1996 Padres	R SD	2	2	0	0	4	17	4	1	1	0	1	0	0	0	0	5	0	0	0	1	.000	0	0	2.25
Las Vegas	AAA SD	26	0	0	8	27.2	129	37	22	21	7	1	4	0	14	2	23	0	0	5	1	.833	0	0	6.83
1997 Red Sox	R Bos	4	3	0	0	9.1	36	5	1	1	0	0	0	1	1	0	14	0	0	0	0	.000	0	0	0.96
Trenton	AA Bos	8	0	0	3	13.1	61	14	6	6	1	3	0	0	7	0	13	0	0	0	0	.000	0	3	4.05
Pawtucket	AAA Bos	7	0	0	2	11.2	57	14	8	7	2	0	0	0	7	1	8	1	0	0	0	.000	0	0	5.40
1995 New York	NL	13	0	0	10	17.2	79	24	9	9	3	0	1	0	5	0	5	0	0	1	0	1.000	0	0	4.58
1996 San Diego	NL	1	0	0	0	0.2	5	0	0	0	0	0	0	0	3	0	1	0	0	0	0	.000	0	0	0.00
8 Min. YEARS		232	77	6	94	636.1	2745	643	328	272	44	29	19	17	260	9	478	24	6	38	48	.442	0	33	3.85
2 Maj. YEARS		14	0	0	10	18.1	84	24	9	9	3	0	1	0	8	0	6	0	0	1	0	1.000	0	0	4.42

Wade Walker

Pitches: Right **Bats:** Right **Pos:** P **Ht:** 6'1" **Wt:** 190 **Born:** 9/18/71 **Age:** 26

Year Team	Lg Org	G	GS	CG	GF	IP	BFP	H	R	ER	HR	SH	SF	HB	TBB	IBB	SO	WP	Bk	W	L	Pct.	ShO	Sv	ERA
1993 Geneva	A- ChN	13	13	1	0	83.2	356	76	38	29	2	4	4	4	36	1	47	15	2	5	2	.714	0	0	3.12
1994 Peoria	A ChN	28	28	4	0	178.1	789	192	108	79	11	6	9	8	72	0	117	17	4	14	12	.538	1	0	3.99
1995 Daytona	A+ ChN	25	24	2	0	135	541	113	50	38	5	3	2	2	36	0	117	8	1	8	6	.571	1	0	2.53
1996 Orlando	AA ChN	29	29	2	0	187.2	833	205	112	92	20	9	4	13	76	2	117	11	1	8	14	.364	0	0	4.41
1997 Orlando	AA ChN	4	4	0	0	16.2	80	19	17	16	0	0	1	1	13	1	11	1	0	2	2	.500	0	0	8.64
5 Min. YEARS		99	98	9	0	601.1	2599	605	325	254	38	22	20	28	233	4	409	52	8	37	36	.507	2	0	3.80

Derek Wallace

Pitches: Right **Bats:** Right **Pos:** P **Ht:** 6' 3" **Wt:** 185 **Born:** 9/1/71 **Age:** 26

Year Team	Lg Org	G	GS	CG	GF	IP	BFP	H	R	ER	HR	SH	SF	HB	TBB	IBB	SO	WP	Bk	W	L	Pct.	ShO	Sv	ERA
1992 Peoria	A ChN	2	0	0	1	3.2	13	3	2	2	0	0	0	0	1	0	2	0	2	0	1	.000	0	0	4.91
1993 Daytona	A+ ChN	14	12	0	1	79.1	342	85	50	37	6	6	2	2	23	2	34	5	11	5	6	.455	0	1	4.20
Iowa	AAA ChN	1	1	0	0	4	20	8	5	5	0	0	1	0	1	0	2	0	0	0	0	.000	0	0	11.25
Orlando	AA ChN	15	15	2	0	96.2	418	105	59	54	12	5	0	10	28	3	69	9	4	5	7	.417	0	0	5.03
1994 Orlando	AA ChN	33	12	1	19	89.1	391	95	61	57	11	3	4	10	31	3	49	6	4	2	9	.182	0	8	5.74
Iowa	AAA ChN	5	0	0	2	4.1	21	4	4	2	0	0	0	0	4	0	3	1	0	0	1	.000	0	1	4.15
1995 Wichita	AA KC	26	0	0	18	43	188	51	23	21	5	1	1	2	13	4	24	3	0	4	3	.571	0	6	4.40
Binghamton	AA NYN	15	0	0	11	15.1	62	11	9	9	1	0	3	1	9	1	8	1	2	0	1	.000	0	2	5.28
1996 Norfolk	AAA NYN	49	0	0	39	57.2	227	37	20	11	4	2	2	1	17	1	52	0	1	5	2	.714	0	26	1.72
1997 Norfolk	AAA NYN	1	0	0	1	1	6	2	2	1	0	0	0	0	1	1	0	0	0	0	1	.000	0	0	9.00
Mets	R NYN	8	5	0	0	8	31	6	3	3	2	0	0	0	1	0	9	0	0	0	1	.000	0	0	3.38
St. Lucie	A+ NYN	5	0	0	3	7	30	7	6	5	0	0	0	0	2	0	8	1	1	0	0	.000	0	0	6.43
1996 New York	NL	19	0	0	11	24.2	115	29	12	11	2	1	0	0	14	2	15	2	0	2	3	.400	0	3	4.01
6 Min. YEARS		174	45	3	95	409.1	1749	414	244	207	41	18	13	26	131	15	260	26	25	21	32	.396	0	44	4.55

Mike Walter

Pitches: Right **Bats:** Right **Pos:** P **Ht:** 6'1" **Wt:** 190 **Born:** 10/23/74 **Age:** 23

Year Team	Lg Org	G	GS	CG	GF	IP	BFP	H	R	ER	HR	SH	SF	HB	TBB	IBB	SO	WP	Bk	W	L	Pct.	ShO	Sv	ERA
1993 Astros	R Hou	17	0	0	16	19.1	88	15	10	6	0	1	1	4	12	0	16	3	0	0	1	.000	0	8	2.79
1994 Quad City	A Hou	23	0	0	10	28.1	134	27	18	13	0	2	2	1	20	1	28	4	1	2	2	.500	0	3	4.13
1995 Kissimmee	A+ Hou	41	0	0	21	71.1	338	78	58	44	4	5	9	10	42	1	42	9	2	4	3	.571	0	0	5.55
1996 Quad City	A Hou	52	0	0	48	61.2	261	37	20	14	3	2	1	7	34	1	85	7	1	3	6	.333	0	21	2.04
1997 Jackson	AA Hou	34	0	0	14	44.2	204	38	20	18	6	4	0	3	30	1	41	4	1	2	3	.400	0	7	3.63
5 Min. YEARS		167	0	0	109	225.1	1025	195	126	95	13	14	13	25	138	4	212	27	5	11	15	.423	0	39	3.79

Brett Walters

Pitches: Right **Bats:** Right **Pos:** P **Ht:** 6'0" **Wt:** 185 **Born:** 9/30/74 **Age:** 23

Year Team	Lg Org	G	GS	CG	GF	IP	BFP	H	R	ER	HR	SH	SF	HB	TBB	IBB	SO	WP	Bk	W	L	Pct.	ShO	Sv	ERA
1994 Spokane	A- SD	2	0	0	1	1.2	9	4	1	1	0	1	0	0	0	0	2	1	0	0	0	.000	0	0	5.40
Padres	R SD	14	6	0	8	45.1	175	28	15	11	1	2	0	0	8	0	45	3	0	2	2	.500	0	6	2.18
1995 Clinton	A SD	32	19	4	4	146	598	133	58	44	9	6	1	10	27	3	122	4	2	8	7	.533	0	1	2.71
1996 Rancho Cuca	A+ SD	24	24	0	0	135.1	575	150	73	65	16	10	6	7	39	0	89	1	0	9	9	.500	0	0	4.32
1997 Mobile	AA SD	31	19	0	1	145	625	169	85	72	17	6	2	11	30	0	98	3	1	10	7	.588	0	0	4.47
4 Min. YEARS		103	68	4	14	473.1	1982	484	232	193	43	25	9	28	104	3	356	12	3	29	25	.537	0	7	3.67

Bryan Ward

Pitches: Left **Bats:** Left **Pos:** P   **Ht:** 6'2" **Wt:** 210 **Born:** 1/28/72 **Age:** 26

		HOW MUCH HE PITCHED						WHAT HE GAVE UP												THE RESULTS					
Year Team	Lg Org	G	GS	CG	GF	IP	BFP	H	R	ER	HR	SH	SF	HB	TBB	IBB	SO	WP	Bk	W	L	Pct.	ShO	Sv	ERA
1993 Elmira	A- Fla	14	11	0	2	61.1	291	82	41	34	6	2	4	4	26	2	63	5	5	2	5	.286	0	0	4.99
1994 Kane County	A Fla	47	0	0	40	55.2	235	46	27	21	4	3	4	2	21	2	62	2	0	3	4	.429	0	11	3.40
1995 Portland	AA Fla	20	11	1	5	72	321	70	42	36	9	1	1	2	31	3	71	7	3	7	3	.700	1	2	4.50
Brevard Cty	A+ Fla	11	11	0	0	72	296	68	27	23	5	4	0	2	17	0	65	1	1	5	1	.833	0	2	2.88
1996 Portland	AA Fla	28	25	2	0	146.2	633	170	97	80	23	9	6	7	32	3	124	0	2	9	9	.500	0	0	4.91
1997 Portland	AA Fla	12	12	0	0	76	316	71	39	33	17	2	2	2	19	1	69	6	0	6	3	.667	0	0	3.91
Charlotte	AAA Fla	15	14	2	0	75.1	349	102	62	58	17	5	4	4	30	4	48	5	1	2	9	.182	0	0	6.93
5 Min. YEARS		147	84	5	47	559	2441	609	335	285	81	26	21	23	176	15	502	26	12	34	34	.500	1	13	4.59

Daryle Ward

Bats: Left **Throws:** Left **Pos:** 1B   **Ht:** 6'2" **Wt:** 230 **Born:** 6/27/75 **Age:** 23

		BATTING														BASERUNNING				PERCENTAGES		
Year Team	Lg Org	G	AB	H	2B	3B	HR	TB	R	RBI	TBB	IBB	SO	HBP	SH	SF	SB	CS	SB%	GDP	Avg	OBP	SLG
1994 Dunedin	R+ Det	48	161	43	6	0	5	64	17	30	19	4	33	0	1	1	5	1	.83	3	.267	.343	.398
1995 Fayetteville	A Det	137	524	149	32	0	14	223	75	106	46	11	111	5	0	7	1	2	.33	13	.284	.344	.426
1996 Toledo	AAA Det	6	23	4	0	0	0	4	1	1	0	0	3	0	0	0	0	0	.00	2	.174	.174	.174
Lakeland	A+ Det	128	464	135	29	4	10	202	65	68	57	6	77	6	0	4	1	1	.50	9	.291	.373	.435
1997 Jackson	AA Hou	114	422	139	25	0	19	221	72	90	46	4	68	3	0	1	4	2	.67	11	.329	.398	.524
New Orleans	AAA Hou	14	48	18	1	0	2	25	4	8	7	1	7	0	0	0	0	0	.00	0	.375	.455	.521
4 Min. YEARS		447	1642	488	93	4	50	739	234	303	175	26	299	14	1	13	11	6	.65	38	.297	.367	.450

Jeff Ware

Pitches: Right **Bats:** Right **Pos:** P   **Ht:** 6'3" **Wt:** 190 **Born:** 11/11/70 **Age:** 27

		HOW MUCH HE PITCHED						WHAT HE GAVE UP												THE RESULTS					
Year Team	Lg Org	G	GS	CG	GF	IP	BFP	H	R	ER	HR	SH	SF	HB	TBB	IBB	SO	WP	Bk	W	L	Pct.	ShO	Sv	ERA
1992 Dunedin	A+ Tor	12	12	1	0	75.1	319	64	26	22	1	3	0	3	30	0	49	7	3	5	3	.625	1	0	2.63
1994 Knoxville	AA Tor	10	10	0	0	38	175	50	32	29	5	0	2	2	16	0	31	1	0	0	7	.000	0	0	6.87
1995 Syracuse	AAA Tor	16	16	0	0	75	319	62	29	25	8	0	1	2	46	0	76	3	0	7	0	1.000	0	0	3.00
1996 Syracuse	AAA Tor	13	13	1	0	77.2	347	83	54	49	6	2	3	6	32	0	59	6	0	3	7	.300	1	0	5.68
1997 Tucson	AAA Mil	25	21	0	1	106	513	127	98	79	16	4	5	2	80	1	69	6	0	5	8	.385	0	0	6.71
1995 Toronto	AL	5	5	0	0	26.1	124	28	18	16	2	1	0	1	21	0	18	2	0	2	1	.667	0	0	5.47
1996 Toronto	AL	13	4	0	6	32.2	163	35	34	33	6	1	0	2	31	1	11	6	1	1	5	.167	0	0	9.09
5 Min. YEARS		76	72	2	1	372	1673	386	239	204	36	9	11	15	204	1	284	23	3	20	25	.444	2	0	4.94
2 Maj. YEARS		18	9	0	6	59	287	63	52	49	8	2	0	3	52	1	29	8	1	3	6	.333	0	0	7.47

Mike Warner

Bats: Left **Throws:** Left **Pos:** OF   **Ht:** 5'10" **Wt:** 170 **Born:** 5/9/71 **Age:** 27

		BATTING														BASERUNNING				PERCENTAGES		
Year Team	Lg Org	G	AB	H	2B	3B	HR	TB	R	RBI	TBB	IBB	SO	HBP	SH	SF	SB	CS	SB%	GDP	Avg	OBP	SLG
1992 Idaho Falls	R+ Atl	10	33	9	3	0	1	15	4	6	3	0	5	0	0	0	1	0	1.00	0	.273	.333	.455
Macon	A Atl	50	180	50	7	2	1	64	40	8	34	0	28	0	3	0	21	4	.84	2	.278	.393	.356
1993 Durham	A+ Atl	77	263	84	18	4	5	125	55	32	50	3	45	2	3	3	29	12	.71	4	.319	.428	.475
Greenville	AA Atl	5	20	7	0	2	0	11	4	3	2	0	4	0	0	0	2	1	.67	0	.350	.409	.550
1994 Durham	A+ Atl	88	321	103	23	8	13	181	80	44	51	1	50	2	1	1	24	10	.71	3	.321	.416	.564
Greenville	AA Atl	16	55	18	5	0	1	26	13	3	9	0	5	1	0	0	3	0	1.00	0	.327	.431	.473
1995 Richmond	AAA Atl	28	97	20	4	1	2	32	10	8	10	0	21	1	2	0	0	3	.00	0	.206	.287	.330
Greenville	AA Atl	53	173	41	12	0	0	53	31	7	47	0	36	1	2	2	12	4	.75	1	.237	.399	.306
1996 Durham	A+ Atl	3	9	1	1	0	0	2	1	2	2	0	2	1	0	0	1	0	1.00	0	.111	.333	.222
Richmond	AAA Atl	7	29	6	1	0	0	7	4	1	1	0	8	0	0	0	1	2	.33	0	.207	.233	.241
Greenville	AA Atl	64	205	53	19	2	6	94	39	33	47	0	45	4	3	0	10	7	.59	4	.259	.406	.459
1997 Greenville	AA Atl	91	303	97	22	3	7	146	58	35	61	6	61	1	3	3	12	9	.57	1	.320	.432	.482
6 Min. YEARS		492	1688	489	115	22	36	756	339	182	317	10	310	13	17	9	116	52	.69	15	.290	.404	.448

Ron Warner

Bats: Right **Throws:** Right **Pos:** OF   **Ht:** 6'3" **Wt:** 185 **Born:** 12/2/68 **Age:** 29

		BATTING														BASERUNNING				PERCENTAGES		
Year Team	Lg Org	G	AB	H	2B	3B	HR	TB	R	RBI	TBB	IBB	SO	HBP	SH	SF	SB	CS	SB%	GDP	Avg	OBP	SLG
1991 Hamilton	A- StL	71	219	66	11	3	1	86	31	20	28	0	43	3	4	1	9	2	.82	4	.301	.386	.393
1992 Savannah	A StL	85	242	53	8	1	0	63	30	12	29	2	63	1	5	2	2	3	.40	5	.219	.303	.260
1993 St. Pete	A+ StL	103	311	90	8	3	4	116	42	37	31	2	39	5	7	4	5	1	.83	9	.289	.359	.373
1994 Arkansas	AA StL	95	233	56	14	1	4	84	28	25	39	5	57	1	2	0	1	1	.50	4	.240	.352	.361
1995 Arkansas	AA StL	47	98	24	3	0	0	27	9	8	16	1	15	1	3	2	0	0	.00	3	.245	.350	.276
1996 Arkansas	AA StL	84	233	70	22	4	6	118	36	39	38	1	25	1	2	2	5	1	.83	4	.300	.398	.506
1997 Louisville	AAA StL	101	276	64	16	0	7	101	43	30	42	0	45	1	6	1	4	1	.80	8	.232	.334	.366
7 Min. YEARS		586	1612	423	82	12	22	595	219	171	223	11	287	13	29	12	26	9	.74	37	.262	.354	.369

Teddy Warrecker

Pitches: Right **Bats:** Left **Pos:** P   **Ht:** 6'6" **Wt:** 215 **Born:** 10/1/72 **Age:** 25

		HOW MUCH HE PITCHED						WHAT HE GAVE UP												THE RESULTS					
Year Team	Lg Org	G	GS	CG	GF	IP	BFP	H	R	ER	HR	SH	SF	HB	TBB	IBB	SO	WP	Bk	W	L	Pct.	ShO	Sv	ERA
1994 Burlington	R+ Cle	12	0	0	5	19.2	99	12	16	12	0	2	2	6	21	2	26	10	1	0	2	.000	0	0	5.49
1995 Columbus	A Cle	24	24	1	0	130.2	559	104	76	60	10	3	3	13	80	1	125	6	0	10	5	.667	1	0	4.13
1996 Kinston	A+ Cle	27	26	1	0	131.1	616	137	105	88	12	3	7	11	88	0	88	14	1	9	11	.450	1	0	6.03

		HOW MUCH HE PITCHED						WHAT HE GAVE UP												THE RESULTS					
Year Team	Lg Org	G	GS	CG	GF	IP	BFP	H	R	ER	HR	SH	SF	HB	TBB	IBB	SO	WP	Bk	W	L	Pct.	ShO	Sv	ERA
1997 Akron	AA Cle	10	7	0	2	32	192	44	50	41	3	1	4	9	40	0	25	4	1	1	5	.167	0	0	11.53
San Berndno	A+ LA	10	3	0	3	29	136	29	28	25	3	0	1	3	20	0	36	10	0	1	5	.167	0	0	7.76
Kinston	A+ Cle	6	4	0	0	24.1	115	19	14	14	1	2	0	6	20	0	26	7	0	1	0	1.000	0	0	5.18
4 Min. YEARS		89	64	2	10	367	1717	345	289	240	29	11	17	48	269	3	326	51	3	22	28	.440	2	0	5.89

Brian Warren

Ht: 6'1" Wt: 165 Born: 4/26/67 Age: 31

Pitches: Right Bats: Right Pos: P

		HOW MUCH HE PITCHED						WHAT HE GAVE UP												THE RESULTS					
Year Team	Lg Org	G	GS	CG	GF	IP	BFP	H	R	ER	HR	SH	SF	HB	TBB	IBB	SO	WP	Bk	W	L	Pct.	ShO	Sv	ERA
1990 Bristol	R+ Det	1	1	0	0	4	17	4	1	1	0	0	0	0	2	0	0	0	1	0	0	.000	0	0	2.25
Niagara Fal	A- Det	12	10	1	2	62.1	258	53	26	15	3	0	2	4	15	0	62	2	0	2	6	.250	0	0	2.17
1991 Fayettevlle	A Det	10	1	0	0	25.2	99	18	6	6	0	0	0	2	5	0	28	3	2	3	1	.750	0	0	2.10
Lakeland	A+ Det	17	16	4	0	103.1	406	86	34	29	3	6	1	1	15	1	75	6	3	8	2	.800	2	0	2.53
1992 London	AA Det	25	25	3	0	147.1	606	146	66	54	10	1	0	5	32	1	83	7	0	7	9	.438	2	0	3.30
1993 London	AA Det	22	1	0	13	29.1	125	36	19	19	6	0	1	0	9	0	21	1	0	3	3	.500	0	5	5.83
Toledo	AA Det	24	1	0	11	36.2	160	40	17	14	3	0	1	2	11	2	26	3	0	2	2	.500	0	1	3.44
1994 Indianapols	AAA Cin	55	0	0	14	80.1	329	82	33	28	4	4	4	3	16	4	56	3	0	5	2	.714	0	1	3.14
1995 Indianapols	AAA Cin	41	0	0	9	56	234	56	18	10	2	1	1	5	9	2	35	2	1	2	1	.667	0	2	1.61
1996 Indianapols	AAA Cin	50	0	0	17	64.2	277	68	30	28	7	2	4	2	25	3	40	4	0	2	3	.400	0	0	3.90
1997 Okla City	AAA Tex	41	0	0	22	69.2	295	73	30	28	6	7	5	7	22	2	39	1	0	5	5	.500	0	6	3.62
8 Min. YEARS		298	55	8	88	679.1	2806	662	280	232	44	21	19	31	161	15	465	32	7	39	34	.534	4	14	3.07

Jarrod Washburn

Ht: 6'1" Wt: 185 Born: 8/13/74 Age: 23

Pitches: Left Bats: Left Pos: P

		HOW MUCH HE PITCHED						WHAT HE GAVE UP												THE RESULTS					
Year Team	Lg Org	G	GS	CG	GF	IP	BFP	H	R	ER	HR	SH	SF	HB	TBB	IBB	SO	WP	Bk	W	L	Pct.	ShO	Sv	ERA
1995 Boise	A- Ana	8	8	0	0	46	185	35	17	17	1	0	1	2	14	0	54	1	0	3	2	.600	0	0	3.33
Cedar Rapds	A Ana	3	3	0	0	18.1	79	17	7	7	1	2	1	3	7	0	20	1	0	1	0	1.000	0	0	3.44
1996 Lk Elsinore	A+ Ana	14	14	3	0	92.2	384	79	38	34	5	2	2	2	33	0	93	8	0	6	3	.667	0	0	3.30
Vancouver	AAA Ana	2	2	0	0	8.1	48	12	16	10	1	0	0	0	12	0	5	1	0	0	2	.000	0	0	10.80
Midland	AA Ana	13	13	1	0	88	361	77	44	43	11	1	2	5	25	0	58	1	1	5	6	.455	0	0	4.40
1997 Midland	AA Ana	29	29	5	0	189.1	818	211	115	101	23	7	4	9	65	0	146	9	1	15	12	.556	1	0	4.80
Vancouver	AAA Ana	1	1	0	0	5	21	4	2	2	0	0	0	0	2	0	6	2	0	0	0	.000	0	0	3.60
3 Min. YEARS		70	70	9	0	447.2	1896	435	239	214	42	12	10	21	158	0	382	23	2	29	26	.527	1	0	4.30

B.J. Waszgis

Ht: 6'2" Wt: 215 Born: 8/24/70 Age: 27

Bats: Right Throws: Right Pos: C

		BATTING															BASERUNNING				PERCENTAGES		
Year Team	Lg Org	G	AB	H	2B	3B	HR	TB	R	RBI	TBB	IBB	SO	HBP	SH	SF	SB	CS	SB%	GDP	Avg	OBP	SLG
1991 Bluefield	R+ Bal	12	35	8	1	0	3	18	8	8	5	0	11	1	0	0	3	0	1.00	1	.229	.341	.514
1992 Kane County	A Bal	111	340	73	18	1	11	126	39	47	54	2	94	4	3	2	3	2	.60	8	.215	.328	.371
1993 Frederick	A+ Bal	31	109	27	4	0	3	40	12	9	9	0	30	2	0	1	1	1	.50	2	.248	.314	.367
Albany	A Bal	86	300	92	25	3	8	147	45	52	27	0	55	6	0	5	4	0	1.00	5	.307	.370	.490
1994 Frederick	A+ Bal	122	426	120	16	3	21	205	76	100	65	2	94	5	3	4	6	1	.86	3	.282	.380	.481
1995 Bowie	AA Bal	130	438	111	22	0	10	163	53	50	70	1	91	9	1	3	2	4	.33	5	.253	.365	.372
1996 Rochester	AAA Bal	96	304	81	16	0	11	130	37	48	41	0	87	4	1	1	2	3	.40	7	.266	.360	.428
1997 Rochester	AAA Bal	100	315	82	15	1	13	138	61	48	56	1	78	9	4	4	1	1	.50	5	.260	.383	.438
7 Min. YEARS		688	2267	594	117	8	80	967	331	362	327	6	540	40	12	20	22	12	.65	39	.262	.362	.427

Dusty Wathan

Ht: 6'5" Wt: 215 Born: 8/22/73 Age: 24

Bats: Both Throws: Right Pos: C

		BATTING															BASERUNNING				PERCENTAGES		
Year Team	Lg Org	G	AB	H	2B	3B	HR	TB	R	RBI	TBB	IBB	SO	HBP	SH	SF	SB	CS	SB%	GDP	Avg	OBP	SLG
1994 Mariners	R Sea	35	86	18	2	0	1	23	14	7	11	0	13	3	0	0	0	0	.00	0	.209	.302	.267
1995 Wisconsin	A Sea	5	11	1	0	0	1	4	1	3	0	0	3	1	0	0	0	0	.00	0	.091	.167	.364
Everett	A- Sea	53	181	49	9	1	6	78	32	25	17	0	26	7	1	0	2	1	.67	4	.271	.356	.431
1996 Lancaster	A+ Sea	74	246	64	10	1	8	100	41	40	26	0	65	6	3	1	1	1	.50	5	.260	.344	.407
1997 Lancaster	A+ Sea	56	202	60	17	0	4	89	27	35	21	0	51	7	1	1	0	1	.00	7	.297	.381	.441
Memphis	AA Sea	49	149	40	4	1	4	58	20	19	19	0	28	5	0	1	1	1	.50	4	.268	.368	.389
4 Min. YEARS		272	875	232	42	3	24	352	135	129	94	0	186	29	5	3	4	4	.50	20	.265	.355	.402

Scott Watkins

Ht: 6'3" Wt: 180 Born: 5/15/70 Age: 28

Pitches: Left Bats: Left Pos: P

		HOW MUCH HE PITCHED						WHAT HE GAVE UP												THE RESULTS					
Year Team	Lg Org	G	GS	CG	GF	IP	BFP	H	R	ER	HR	SH	SF	HB	TBB	IBB	SO	WP	Bk	W	L	Pct.	ShO	Sv	ERA
1992 Kenosha	A Min	27	0	0	11	46.1	196	43	21	19	4	2	1	3	14	0	58	1	0	2	5	.286	0	1	3.69
1993 Ft. Wayne	A Min	15	0	0	8	30.1	124	26	13	11	0	1	2	1	9	0	31	0	1	2	0	1.000	0	1	3.26
Ft. Myers	A+ Min	20	0	0	10	27.2	125	27	14	9	0	2	0	0	12	0	41	2	1	2	2	.500	0	3	2.93
Nashville	AA Min	13	0	0	3	16.2	75	19	15	11	2	0	1	1	7	0	17	2	1	0	1	.000	0	0	5.94
1994 Nashville	AA Min	11	0	0	8	13.2	60	13	9	7	1	1	2	0	4	0	11	1	0	1	0	1.000	0	3	4.61
Salt Lake	AAA Min	46	0	0	26	57.1	269	73	46	43	10	4	5	1	28	5	47	1	1	2	6	.250	0	3	6.75
1995 Salt Lake	AAA Min	45	0	0	33	54.2	217	45	18	17	4	1	3	1	13	1	57	1	0	4	2	.667	0	20	2.80
1996 Salt Lake	AAA Min	47	0	0	29	50.1	244	60	46	43	6	5	3	2	34	5	43	3	1	4	6	.400	0	1	7.69
1997 Omaha	AAA KC	9	0	0	4	15.1	72	19	13	11	4	0	1	1	6	0	15	2	1	0	0	.000	0	0	6.46
New Haven	AA Col	13	0	0	8	15.1	58	9	6	6	1	1	1	1	3	0	8	3	0	2	0	1.000	0	0	3.52

263

Year Team	Lg Org	G	GS	CG	GF	IP	BFP	H	R	ER	HR	SH	SF	HB	TBB	IBB	SO	WP	Bk	W	L	Pct.	ShO	Sv	ERA
1995 Minnesota	AL	27	0	0	7	21.2	94	22	14	13	2	1	3	0	11	1	11	0	0	0	0	.000	0	0	5.40
6 Min. YEARS		246	0	0	140	327.2	1440	334	201	177	32	17	19	10	130	11	328	16	6	19	22	.463	0	32	4.86

Brandon Watts

Pitches: Left Bats: Left Pos: P Ht: 6'3" Wt: 190 Born: 9/13/72 Age: 25

Year Team	Lg Org	G	GS	CG	GF	IP	BFP	H	R	ER	HR	SH	SF	HB	TBB	IBB	SO	WP	Bk	W	L	Pct.	ShO	Sv	ERA
1991 Dodgers	R LA	12	5	0	4	33	148	28	20	17	1	2	0	2	25	0	30	5	1	1	3	.250	0	1	4.64
1992 Great Falls	R+ LA	13	0	0	6	17.2	80	12	11	10	0	0	0	1	14	0	15	1	0	1	1	.500	0	1	5.09
Dodgers	R LA	4	4	0	0	24	95	15	9	8	1	0	1	0	8	0	19	3	0	2	1	.667	1	0	3.00
1993 Vero Beach	A+ LA	8	0	0	1	17.2	81	14	11	8	0	0	1	1	16	0	12	2	0	0	1	.000	0	0	4.08
Yakima	A- LA	2	2	0	0	9	41	8	8	8	3	0	0	0	7	0	12	1	0	0	2	.000	0	0	8.00
1995 Vero Beach	A+ LA	13	8	0	1	49	215	46	29	22	5	0	2	1	22	0	42	4	1	5	3	.625	0	0	4.04
1996 San Antonio	AA LA	22	22	2	0	126	561	136	69	63	21	8	4	2	70	0	79	4	2	6	10	.375	1	0	4.50
1997 San Antonio	AA LA	1	0	0	0	1	5	2	1	1	0	0	0	0	0	0	2	0	0	0	0	.000	0	0	9.00
6 Min. YEARS		75	41	3	12	277.1	1226	261	158	137	31	10	8	7	162	0	211	20	4	15	21	.417	2	2	4.45

Jim Wawruck

Bats: Left Throws: Left Pos: OF Ht: 5'11" Wt: 185 Born: 4/23/70 Age: 28

Year Team	Lg Org	G	AB	H	2B	3B	HR	TB	R	RBI	TBB	IBB	SO	HBP	SH	SF	SB	CS	SB%	GDP	Avg	OBP	SLG
1991 Orioles	R Bal	14	45	17	1	1	0	20	6	6	6	0	4	0	0	0	2	2	.50	0	.378	.451	.444
Frederick	A+ Bal	22	83	23	3	0	0	26	15	7	7	0	14	1	1	0	10	0	1.00	2	.277	.341	.313
1992 Frederick	A+ Bal	102	350	108	18	4	8	158	61	46	47	2	69	2	1	5	11	8	.58	9	.309	.389	.451
1993 Bowie	AA Bal	128	475	141	21	5	4	184	59	44	43	3	66	1	5	2	28	11	.72	7	.297	.355	.387
1994 Rochester	AAA Bal	114	440	132	20	7	9	193	63	53	32	1	77	4	1	2	17	2	.89	6	.300	.351	.439
1995 Bowie	AA Bal	56	212	59	7	1	6	86	29	30	20	2	31	3	1	3	7	3	.70	7	.278	.345	.406
Rochester	AAA Bal	39	149	45	12	3	1	66	21	23	13	0	23	2	1	2	5	4	.56	3	.302	.361	.443
1996 Rochester	AAA Bal	59	204	58	14	6	0	84	31	15	14	1	29	1	4	1	4	2	.67	2	.284	.332	.412
1997 Rochester	AAA Bal	94	339	92	20	3	5	133	47	35	34	1	64	3	1	1	12	6	.67	10	.271	.342	.392
7 Min. YEARS		628	2297	675	116	30	33	950	332	259	216	10	377	17	15	16	96	38	.72	46	.294	.357	.414

Eric Weaver

Pitches: Right Bats: Right Pos: P Ht: 6'5" Wt: 230 Born: 8/4/73 Age: 24

Year Team	Lg Org	G	GS	CG	GF	IP	BFP	H	R	ER	HR	SH	SF	HB	TBB	IBB	SO	WP	Bk	W	L	Pct.	ShO	Sv	ERA
1992 Vero Beach	A+ LA	19	18	1	0	89.2	394	73	52	41	7	5	6	1	57	0	73	17	2	4	11	.267	0	0	4.12
1993 Bakersfield	A+ LA	28	27	0	0	157.2	703	135	89	75	10	2	9	2	118	2	110	16	0	6	11	.353	0	0	4.28
1994 Vero Beach	A+ LA	7	7	0	0	24	109	28	20	18	3	0	0	1	9	1	22	1	0	1	3	.250	0	0	6.75
1995 San Antonio	AA LA	27	26	1	1	141.2	635	147	83	64	10	9	7	7	72	1	105	8	2	8	11	.421	0	0	4.07
1996 San Antonio	AA LA	18	18	0	0	122.2	509	106	51	45	6	7	2	1	44	0	69	2	1	5	5	.667	1	0	3.30
Albuquerque	AAA LA	13	8	0	0	46.2	225	63	39	28	5	2	1	3	22	0	38	3	0	1	4	.200	0	0	5.40
1997 San Antonio	AA LA	13	13	2	0	84.2	363	80	43	34	4	1	4	5	38	0	60	2	0	7	2	.778	1	0	3.61
Albuquerque	AAA LA	21	8	0	5	68.2	335	101	53	49	6	3	4	2	38	1	54	4	0	0	3	.000	0	0	6.42
6 Min. YEARS		146	125	5	6	735.2	3273	733	430	354	51	29	33	24	398	5	531	53	5	37	50	.425	2	0	4.33

Lenny Weber

Pitches: Right Bats: Right Pos: P Ht: 6'1" Wt: 180 Born: 8/6/72 Age: 25

Year Team	Lg Org	G	GS	CG	GF	IP	BFP	H	R	ER	HR	SH	SF	HB	TBB	IBB	SO	WP	Bk	W	L	Pct.	ShO	Sv	ERA
1994 Burlington	R+ Cle	19	0	0	5	27.2	130	29	16	14	2	2	1	1	15	0	35	7	1	0	1	.000	0	1	4.55
1995 Watertown	A- Cle	5	0	0	3	9	37	5	2	2	0	1	0	0	6	1	11	1	0	1	0	1.000	0	0	2.00
Columbus	A Cle	17	0	0	4	29.1	113	19	6	6	0	2	0	0	10	3	32	3	0	4	0	1.000	0	2	1.84
1996 Kinston	A+ Cle	36	0	0	25	59	250	44	12	12	0	6	1	1	36	5	49	2	0	2	4	.333	0	6	1.83
1997 Akron	AA Cle	6	0	0	0	9.1	59	22	17	16	3	0	3	0	9	0	8	0	0	1	0	1.000	0	0	15.43
Madison	IND —	28	0	0	19	42.2	206	47	34	28	3	3	3	2	29	1	28	2	0	2	4	.333	0	1	5.91
4 Min. YEARS		111	0	0	57	177	795	166	87	78	8	14	8	4	105	10	163	15	1	10	9	.526	0	10	3.97

Neil Weber

Pitches: Left Bats: Left Pos: P Ht: 6'5" Wt: 205 Born: 12/6/72 Age: 25

Year Team	Lg Org	G	GS	CG	GF	IP	BFP	H	R	ER	HR	SH	SF	HB	TBB	IBB	SO	WP	Bk	W	L	Pct.	ShO	Sv	ERA
1993 Jamestown	A- Mon	16	16	2	0	94.1	398	84	46	29	3	0	4	4	36	0	80	3	3	6	5	.545	1	0	2.77
1994 Wst Plm Bch	A+ Mon	25	24	1	0	135	566	113	58	48	8	4	4	4	62	0	134	7	5	9	7	.563	0	0	3.20
1995 Harrisburg	AA Mon	28	28	0	0	152.2	696	157	98	85	16	11	7	8	90	1	119	7	1	6	11	.353	0	0	5.01
1996 Harrisburg	AA Mon	18	18	1	0	107	440	90	37	36	8	3	3	5	44	0	74	5	0	7	4	.636	0	0	3.03
1997 Ottawa	AAA Mon	9	9	0	0	39.2	204	46	46	35	7	2	1	2	40	0	27	2	0	5	5	.286	0	0	7.94
Harrisburg	AA Mon	18	18	1	0	112.2	477	93	56	48	17	6	1	8	51	1	121	6	0	7	6	.538	1	0	3.83
5 Min. YEARS		114	113	5	0	641.1	2781	583	341	281	59	26	20	31	323	2	555	30	9	37	38	.493	2	0	3.94

Eric Wedge

Bats: Right **Throws:** Right **Pos:** C | **Ht:** 6'3" **Wt:** 230 **Born:** 1/27/68 **Age:** 30

		BATTING															BASERUNNING				PERCENTAGES		
Year Team	Lg Org	G	AB	H	2B	3B	HR	TB	R	RBI	TBB	IBB	SO	HBP	SH	SF	SB	CS	SB%	GDP	Avg	OBP	SLG
1989 Elmira	A- Bos	41	145	34	6	2	7	65	20	22	15	0	21	0	0	0	1	1	.50	3	.234	.306	.448
New Britain	AA Bos	14	40	8	2	0	0	10	3	2	5	0	10	0	2	0	0	0	.00	1	.200	.289	.250
1990 New Britain	AA Bos	103	339	77	13	1	5	107	36	48	51	2	54	1	0	5	1	3	.25	14	.227	.326	.316
1991 New Britain	AA Bos	2	8	2	0	0	0	2	0	2	0	0	2	0	0	0	0	0	.00	0	.250	.222	.250
Winter Havn	A+ Bos	8	21	5	0	0	1	8	2	1	3	0	7	0	1	0	1	0	1.00	1	.238	.333	.381
Pawtucket	AAA Bos	53	163	38	14	1	5	69	24	18	25	0	26	1	2	5	1	2	.33	3	.233	.330	.423
1992 Pawtucket	AAA Bos	65	211	63	9	0	11	105	28	40	32	3	40	1	0	3	0	0	.00	6	.299	.389	.498
1993 Central Val	A+ Col	6	23	7	0	0	3	16	6	11	2	1	6	0	0	0	0	0	.00	1	.304	.360	.696
Colo Sprngs	AAA Col	38	90	24	6	0	3	39	17	13	16	1	22	2	0	0	0	0	.00	4	.267	.389	.433
1994 Pawtucket	AAA Bos	77	255	73	14	0	19	144	44	59	51	5	48	2	0	2	0	1	.00	6	.286	.406	.565
1995 Pawtucket	AAA Bos	108	376	88	17	1	20	167	52	68	63	4	96	2	0	3	1	3	.25	5	.234	.345	.444
1996 Toledo	AAA Det	96	332	78	25	0	15	148	61	57	43	0	81	0	1	4	2	2	.50	5	.235	.319	.446
1997 Scranton-WB	AAA Phi	47	129	33	8	1	7	64	25	36	22	0	40	0	0	3	0	0	.00	1	.256	.357	.496
1991 Boston	AL	1	1	1	0	0	0	1	0	0	0	0	0	0	0	0	0	0	.00	0	1.000	1.000	1.000
1992 Boston	AL	27	68	17	2	0	5	34	11	11	13	0	18	0	0	0	0	0	.00	0	.250	.370	.500
1993 Colorado	NL	9	11	2	0	0	0	2	2	1	0	0	4	0	0	0	0	0	.00	0	.182	.182	.182
1994 Boston	AL	2	6	0	0	0	0	0	0	0	1	0	3	0	0	0	0	0	.00	0	.000	.143	.000
9 Min. YEARS		658	2132	530	114	6	96	944	318	377	328	16	453	9	6	26	7	12	.37	54	.249	.347	.443
4 Maj. YEARS		39	86	20	2	0	5	37	13	12	14	0	25	0	0	0	0	0	.00	0	.233	.340	.430

Todd Weinberg

Pitches: Left **Bats:** Right **Pos:** P | **Ht:** 6'3" **Wt:** 225 **Born:** 6/13/72 **Age:** 26

		HOW MUCH HE PITCHED						WHAT HE GAVE UP												THE RESULTS					
Year Team	Lg Org	G	GS	CG	GF	IP	BFP	H	R	ER	HR	SH	SF	HB	TBB	IBB	SO	WP	Bk	W	L	Pct.	ShO	Sv	ERA
1994 Sou. Oregon	A- Oak	17	9	0	3	68	306	65	36	27	2	7	3	4	31	3	73	4	0	7	3	.700	0	1	3.57
1995 W Michigan	A Oak	36	9	0	5	87	392	86	52	46	3	2	1	13	56	2	54	19	2	4	5	.444	0	1	4.76
1996 W Michigan	A Oak	43	0	0	16	57.1	253	48	25	22	4	2	1	3	31	4	64	3	0	6	4	.600	0	1	3.45
1997 Visalia	A+ Oak	38	0	0	35	58	166	33	23	18	1	2	4	0	22	2	39	5	0	3	2	.600	0	20	4.26
Huntsville	AA Oak	20	0	0	5	27	114	18	12	7	1	2	2	1	17	0	24	2	0	2	1	.667	0	3	2.33
4 Min. YEARS		154	18	0	64	277.1	1231	250	148	120	11	15	11	21	157	11	254	33	2	22	15	.595	0	26	3.89

Mike Welch

Pitches: Right **Bats:** Left **Pos:** P | **Ht:** 6'2" **Wt:** 207 **Born:** 8/25/72 **Age:** 25

		HOW MUCH HE PITCHED						WHAT HE GAVE UP												THE RESULTS					
Year Team	Lg Org	G	GS	CG	GF	IP	BFP	H	R	ER	HR	SH	SF	HB	TBB	IBB	SO	WP	Bk	W	L	Pct.	ShO	Sv	ERA
1993 Pittsfield	A- NYN	17	0	0	14	31	126	23	9	5	0	2	4	0	6	1	34	3	1	3	1	.750	0	9	1.45
1994 Capital City	A NYN	24	24	5	0	159.2	667	151	81	64	14	7	5	11	33	0	127	5	0	7	11	.389	2	0	3.61
1995 St. Lucie	A+ NYN	44	6	0	33	70	322	96	50	42	7	4	3	6	18	4	51	4	0	4	4	.500	0	15	5.40
Binghamton	AA NYN	1	0	0	1	1	3	0	0	0	0	0	0	0	0	0	2	0	0	0	0	.000	0	0	0.00
1996 Binghamton	AA NYN	46	0	0	37	51	216	55	29	26	4	3	1	3	10-	0	53	0	0	4	2	.667	0	27	4.59
Norfolk	AAA NYN	10	0	0	5	8.2	36	8	4	4	0	0	0	0	2	0	6	0	0	0	1	.000	0	2	4.15
1997 Norfolk	AAA NYN	46	0	0	38	51.2	216	53	21	21	6	2	2	1	16	2	35	0	0	2	2	.500	0	20	3.66
5 Min. YEARS		188	30	5	128	373	1586	386	194	162	31	18	15	21	85	7	308	12	1	20	21	.488	2	73	3.91

Forry Wells

Bats: Left **Throws:** Right **Pos:** 1B | **Ht:** 6'4" **Wt:** 205 **Born:** 3/21/71 **Age:** 27

		BATTING															BASERUNNING				PERCENTAGES		
Year Team	Lg Org	G	AB	H	2B	3B	HR	TB	R	RBI	TBB	IBB	SO	HBP	SH	SF	SB	CS	SB%	GDP	Avg	OBP	SLG
1994 Bend	A- Col	37	117	30	8	0	1	41	19	13	23	2	29	4	0	0	9	1	.90	2	.256	.396	.350
1995 Salem	A+ Col	119	402	102	23	4	18	187	60	67	56	6	105	7	3	1	6	3	.67	2	.254	.354	.465
New Haven	AA Col	4	14	3	0	0	0	3	3	1	1	1	2	1	0	0	0	0	.00	1	.214	.313	.214
1996 New Haven	AA Col	108	304	70	19	1	7	112	44	43	46	4	73	4	2	2	1	2	.33	4	.230	.337	.368
1997 New Haven	AA Col	39	98	22	4	0	2	32	16	7	21	0	37	3	0	1	1	2	.33	2	.224	.374	.327
Salem	A+ Col	93	321	96	27	3	11	162	58	52	48	2	64	9	3	1	19	7	.73	9	.299	.404	.505
4 Min. YEARS		400	1256	323	81	8	39	537	200	183	195	15	310	28	8	5	36	15	.71	20	.257	.368	.428

Bill Wertz

Pitches: Right **Bats:** Right **Pos:** P | **Ht:** 6'6" **Wt:** 220 **Born:** 1/15/67 **Age:** 31

		HOW MUCH HE PITCHED						WHAT HE GAVE UP												THE RESULTS					
Year Team	Lg Org	G	GS	CG	GF	IP	BFP	H	R	ER	HR	SH	SF	HB	TBB	IBB	SO	WP	Bk	W	L	Pct.	ShO	Sv	ERA
1989 Indians	R Cle	12	11	1	0	66	282	57	23	23	0	1	4	4	36	0	56	11	0	4	3	.571	1	0	3.14
1990 Reno	A+ Cle	17	9	0	1	61.1	295	61	58	45	6	3	4	5	52	0	52	12	0	1	3	.250	0	0	6.60
Watertown	A- Cle	14	14	2	0	100.2	431	81	39	32	3	2	3	4	48	0	92	6	0	10	2	.833	0	0	2.86
1991 Columbus	A Cle	49	0	0	31	91	391	81	41	30	6	6	4	6	32	3	95	5	0	6	8	.429	0	9	2.97
1992 Canton-Akrn	AA Cle	57	0	0	24	97.1	382	75	16	13	1	3	2	3	30	6	69	3	0	8	4	.667	0	1	1.20
1993 Charlotte	AAA Cle	28	1	0	9	50.2	207	42	18	11	4	3	0	1	14	4	47	1	0	7	2	.778	0	1	1.95
1994 Charlotte	AAA Cle	44	2	0	8	66	278	53	30	23	5	2	2	1	34	3	60	5	0	4	3	.571	0	1	3.14
1995 Pawtucket	AAA Bos	29	6	0	12	63.2	298	74	47	41	11	4	4	1	31	1	55	0	0	4	5	.444	0	2	5.80
1996 Buffalo	AAA Cle	17	1	0	11	28.2	133	32	16	15	3	1	1	2	19	1	22	0	0	1	2	.333	0	0	4.71
Tacoma	AAA Sea	16	2	0	8	32.1	162	46	21	18	2	0	0	1	23	2	25	3	0	0	3	.000	0	0	5.01
Port City	AA Sea	5	5	1	1	28	120	28	10	8	1	1	1	0	9	0	26	1	0	2	0	.500	0	0	2.57
1997 Akron	AA Cle	11	1	0	2	19.2	105	32	24	21	2	1	0	2	12	0	17	1	0	1	0	1.000	0	0	9.61
1993 Cleveland	AL	34	0	0	7	59.2	262	54	28	24	5	1	1	1	32	2	53	0	0	2	3	.400	0	0	3.62
1994 Cleveland	AL	1	0	0	0	4.1	23	9	5	5	0	0	0	0	1	0	1	0	0	0	0	.000	0	0	10.38

		HOW MUCH HE PITCHED				WHAT HE GAVE UP								THE RESULTS					
Year Team	Lg Org	G GS CG GF	IP BFP	H R ER HR SH SF HB	TBB IBB SO WP Bk	W L Pct. ShO Sv ERA
9 Min. YEARS		300 52 4 107	705.1 3084	662 343 280 44 27 25 30	340 20 606 54 0	48 37 .565 1 20 3.57
2 Maj. YEARS		35 0 0 7	64 285	63 33 29 5 1 1 1	33 2 54 0 0	2 3 .400 0 0 4.08

Jason Wesemann

Bats: Right Throws: Right Pos: 3B   Ht: 6'0" Wt: 180 Born: 3/29/74 Age: 24

		BATTING													BASERUNNING				PERCENTAGES		
Year Team	Lg Org	G	AB	H	2B	3B	HR	TB	R	RBI	TBB	IBB	SO	HBP	SH	SF	SB	CS	SB%	GDP	Avg	OBP	SLG
1996 Batavia	A- Phi	49	156	34	9	0	1	46	21	11	8	0	30	3	4	2	3	1	.75	1	.218	.266	.295
1997 Piedmont	A Phi	44	104	26	1	1	1	32	16	12	8	0	23	0	3	1	1	0	1.00	3	.250	.301	.308
Reading	AA Phi	7	11	2	0	0	0	2	4	1	2	0	2	1	0	0	0	0	.00	1	.182	.357	.182
Clearwater	A+ Phi	38	88	14	1	0	0	15	7	4	10	0	20	0	4	0	1	0	1.00	2	.159	.245	.170
2 Min. YEARS		138	359	76	11	1	2	95	48	28	28	0	75	4	11	3	5	1	.83	7	.212	.274	.265

Destry Westbrook

Pitches: Right Bats: Right Pos: P   Ht: 6'1" Wt: 195 Born: 12/13/70 Age: 27

		HOW MUCH HE PITCHED					WHAT HE GAVE UP							THE RESULTS					
Year Team	Lg Org	G	GS	CG	GF	IP	BFP	H	R	ER	HR	SH	SF	HB	TBB	IBB	SO	WP	Bk	W	L	Pct.	ShO	Sv	ERA
1992 Auburn	A- Hou	12	2	0	5	17	105	29	33	29	5	0	2	4	19	0	19	6	2	0	3	.000	0	0	15.35
1993 Quad City	A Hou	27	0	0	14	36.1	158	29	11	10	3	0	2	0	23	1	41	0	0	3	1	.750	0	2	2.48
1994 Quad City	A Hou	27	0	0	12	46.1	205	48	25	23	3	2	2	2	23	1	50	3	0	0	2	.000	0	1	4.47
1995 Tucson	AAA Hou	5	0	0	2	12.1	60	20	10	10	2	0	0	0	7	0	8	2	0	0	0	.000	0	0	7.30
Kissimmee	A+ Hou	10	0	0	2	19.2	106	34	24	22	2	1	0	0	13	1	22	1	0	0	0	.000	0	1	10.07
Mobile	IND —	8	1	0	1	13	66	13	13	10	1	0	1	0	13	2	11	1	0	0	1	.000	0	0	6.92
1996 Clearwater	A+ Phi	34	0	0	12	43.1	180	35	12	10	3	0	1	1	11	2	35	2	0	3	3	.500	0	3	2.08
Reading	AA Phi	25	0	0	11	34	156	40	19	15	4	3	0	0	14	4	15	1	0	4	3	.571	0	0	3.97
1997 Reading	AA Phi	26	3	0	15	45	226	70	49	41	11	3	3	1	22	1	38	1	0	0	2	.000	0	4	8.20
Arkansas	AA StL	14	0	0	6	23	104	16	11	7	1	3	1	1	17	2	16	2	0	0	2	.000	0	0	2.74
6 Min. YEARS		188	6	0	80	290	1366	334	207	177	35	12	12	9	162	14	255	20	2	10	18	.357	0	8	5.49

Gabe Whatley

Bats: Left Throws: Right Pos: OF-1B   Ht: 6'0" Wt: 180 Born: 12/29/71 Age: 26

		BATTING													BASERUNNING				PERCENTAGES		
Year Team	Lg Org	G	AB	H	2B	3B	HR	TB	R	RBI	TBB	IBB	SO	HBP	SH	SF	SB	CS	SB%	GDP	Avg	OBP	SLG
1993 Huntington	R+ ChN	51	175	46	12	1	5	75	30	25	26	0	32	5	1	1	3	2	.60	3	.263	.372	.429
1994 Williamsprt	A- ChN	71	230	56	9	3	2	77	35	25	36	3	32	4	1	1	10	4	.71	6	.243	.354	.335
1995 Rockford	A ChN	95	339	87	23	2	7	135	54	54	45	3	58	6	0	6	11	3	.79	6	.257	.348	.398
Daytona	A+ ChN	15	42	11	3	0	1	17	8	5	7	0	5	0	0	0	2	0	1.00	0	.262	.367	.405
1996 Daytona	A+ ChN	56	186	42	14	1	2	64	24	25	26	1	27	1	0	2	9	1	.90	2	.226	.321	.344
Durham	A+ Atl	49	160	53	11	0	3	73	29	26	32	1	23	1	2	0	7	6	.54	2	.331	.446	.456
1997 Durham	A+ Atl	43	154	42	16	0	8	82	37	30	28	0	33	3	0	2	9	1	.90	2	.273	.390	.532
Greenville	AA Atl	95	310	94	17	5	15	166	60	57	50	0	42	6	4	6	5	5	.50	9	.303	.403	.535
5 Min. YEARS		475	1596	431	105	12	43	689	277	247	250	8	252	26	8	18	56	22	.72	30	.270	.374	.432

Derrick White

Bats: Right Throws: Right Pos: OF   Ht: 6'1" Wt: 215 Born: 10/12/69 Age: 28

		BATTING													BASERUNNING				PERCENTAGES		
Year Team	Lg Org	G	AB	H	2B	3B	HR	TB	R	RBI	TBB	IBB	SO	HBP	SH	SF	SB	CS	SB%	GDP	Avg	OBP	SLG
1991 Jamestown	A- Mon	72	271	89	10	4	6	125	46	49	40	0	46	7	0	2	8	3	.73	8	.328	.425	.461
1992 Harrisburg	AA Mon	134	495	137	19	2	13	199	63	81	40	3	73	7	0	2	17	3	.85	16	.277	.338	.402
1993 Wst Plm Bch	A+ Mon	6	25	5	0	0	0	5	1	1	1	0	2	0	0	0	2	0	1.00	0	.200	.231	.200
Ottawa	AAA Mon	67	249	70	15	1	4	99	32	29	20	2	52	3	0	1	10	7	.59	10	.281	.341	.398
Harrisburg	AA Mon	21	79	18	1	0	2	25	14	12	5	0	17	2	0	1	2	0	1.00	3	.228	.287	.316
1994 Ottawa	AAA Mon	47	99	21	4	0	0	25	13	9	8	1	25	1	1	1	4	1	.80	3	.212	.275	.253
Portland	AA Fla	74	264	71	13	2	4	100	39	34	28	1	52	3	0	2	14	7	.67	5	.269	.343	.379
1995 Toledo	AAA Det	87	309	82	15	3	14	145	50	49	29	3	65	4	0	4	6	6	.50	12	.265	.332	.469
1996 W Michigan	A Oak	73	263	69	17	0	10	116	49	43	44	2	63	6	0	4	12	3	.80	7	.262	.375	.441
Modesto	A+ Oak	54	197	58	15	1	7	96	45	39	29	1	41	4	0	3	8	3	.73	1	.294	.391	.487
1997 Midland	AA Ana	10	37	7	2	0	0	9	2	3	5	0	6	1	0	0	1	0	1.00	1	.189	.302	.243
Vancouver	AAA Ana	116	414	134	35	2	11	206	64	65	44	2	73	7	1	2	11	7	.61	12	.324	.396	.498
1993 Montreal	NL	17	49	11	3	0	2	20	6	4	2	1	12	1	0	0	2	0	1.00	1	.224	.269	.408
1995 Detroit	AL	39	48	9	2	0	0	11	3	2	0	0	7	0	0	0	1	0	1.00	1	.188	.188	.229
7 Min. YEARS		761	2702	761	146	15	71	1150	418	414	293	15	515	45	2	22	95	40	.70	77	.282	.359	.426
2 Maj. YEARS		56	97	20	5	0	2	31	9	6	2	1	19	1	0	0	3	0	1.00	2	.206	.230	.320

Rick White

Pitches: Right Bats: Right Pos: P   Ht: 6'4" Wt: 215 Born: 12/23/68 Age: 29

		HOW MUCH HE PITCHED					WHAT HE GAVE UP							THE RESULTS					
Year Team	Lg Org	G	GS	CG	GF	IP	BFP	H	R	ER	HR	SH	SF	HB	TBB	IBB	SO	WP	Bk	W	L	Pct.	ShO	Sv	ERA
1990 Pirates	R Pit	7	6	0	0	35.2	142	26	11	2	0	1	1	2	4	0	27	2	1	3	1	.750	0	0	0.50
Welland	A- Pit	9	5	1	1	38.2	165	38	19	14	2	2	2	1	14	2	43	4	0	1	4	.200	0	0	3.26
1991 Augusta	A Pit	34	0	0	18	63	280	68	26	21	2	0	3	1	18	2	52	4	3	4	4	.500	0	6	3.00
Salem	A+ Pit	13	5	1	4	46.1	189	41	27	24	2	3	1	0	9	3	36	2	0	2	3	.400	0	1	4.66
1992 Salem	A+ Pit	18	18	5	0	120.2	490	116	58	51	15	2	4	5	24	1	70	5	0	7	9	.438	0	0	3.80
Carolina	AA Pit	10	10	1	0	57.2	247	59	32	27	8	2	1	3	18	1	45	6	0	1	7	.125	0	0	4.21
1993 Carolina	AA Pit	12	12	1	0	69.1	275	59	29	27	5	2	2	4	12	0	52	4	1	4	3	.571	0	0	3.50

266

		HOW MUCH HE PITCHED						WHAT HE GAVE UP												THE RESULTS					
Year Team	Lg Org	G	GS	CG	GF	IP	BFP	H	R	ER	HR	SH	SF	HB	TBB	IBB	SO	WP	Bk	W	L	Pct	ShO	Sv	ERA
Buffalo	AAA Pit	7	3	0	1	28	117	25	13	11	1	2	0	1	8	0	16	1	0	0	3	.000	0	0	3.54
1995 Calgary	AAA Pit	14	11	1	1	79.1	338	97	40	37	13	0	4	3	10	0	56	2	0	6	4	.600	0	0	4.20
1996 Pirates	R Pit	3	3	0	0	12	43	8	4	3	0	0	1	0	3	0	8	0	0	0	0	.000	0	0	2.25
Carolina	AA Pit	2	1	0	0	6.1	30	9	8	8	2	0	0	1	1	0	7	0	1	0	1	.000	0	0	11.37
1997 Orlando	AA TB	39	8	0	22	86	370	93	55	45	7	4	3	3	22	2	65	6	2	5	7	.417	0	12	4.71
1994 Pittsburgh	NL	43	5	0	23	75.1	317	79	35	32	9	7	5	6	17	3	38	2	2	4	5	.444	0	6	3.82
1995 Pittsburgh	NL	15	9	0	2	55	247	66	33	29	3	3	3	2	18	0	29	2	0	2	3	.400	0	0	4.75
7 Min. YEARS		168	82	10	47	643	2686	639	322	270	57	16	22	25	143	11	477	36	9	33	46	.418	0	19	3.78
2 Maj. YEARS		58	14	0	25	130.1	564	145	68	61	12	10	8	8	35	3	67	4	2	6	8	.429	0	6	4.21

Greg Whiteman

Pitches: Left   Bats: Left   Pos: P   Ht: 6'2" Wt: 185 Born: 6/12/73 Age: 25

		HOW MUCH HE PITCHED						WHAT HE GAVE UP												THE RESULTS					
Year Team	Lg Org	G	GS	CG	GF	IP	BFP	H	R	ER	HR	SH	SF	HB	TBB	IBB	SO	WP	Bk	W	L	Pct	ShO	Sv	ERA
1994 Jamestown	A- Det	15	15	1	0	75.2	328	72	39	34	2	2	0	0	35	0	67	7	2	6	5	.545	1	0	4.04
1995 Lakeland	A+ Det	4	4	0	0	19.1	87	18	16	13	0	0	2	0	15	0	20	1	1	1	2	.333	0	0	6.05
Fayetteville	A Det	23	23	1	0	125.2	547	108	68	59	9	5	4	9	58	0	145	4	1	6	8	.429	1	0	4.23
1996 Lakeland	A+ Det	27	27	1	0	150.1	640	134	66	62	5	4	6	7	89	0	122	8	2	11	10	.524	0	0	3.71
1997 Clearwater	A+ Phi	11	11	0	0	51	228	57	30	26	3	0	2	0	26	0	32	2	1	3	3	.500	0	0	4.59
Reading	AA Phi	9	9	0	0	53.1	226	57	27	24	6	4	1	1	21	0	31	3	0	4	4	.500	0	0	4.05
4 Min. YEARS		89	89	3	0	475.1	2056	446	246	218	25	15	15	17	244	0	417	25	7	31	32	.492	2	0	4.13

Sean Whiteside

Pitches: Left   Bats: Left   Pos: P   Ht: 6'4" Wt: 190 Born: 4/19/71 Age: 27

		HOW MUCH HE PITCHED						WHAT HE GAVE UP												THE RESULTS					
Year Team	Lg Org	G	GS	CG	GF	IP	BFP	H	R	ER	HR	SH	SF	HB	TBB	IBB	SO	WP	Bk	W	L	Pct	ShO	Sv	ERA
1992 Niagara Fal	A- Det	15	11	0	0	69.2	289	54	26	19	2	1	2	0	24	0	72	7	5	8	4	.667	0	0	2.45
1993 Fayetteville	A Det	24	16	0	4	100.2	443	113	68	52	8	0	5	3	41	0	85	18	0	3	5	.375	0	0	4.65
1994 Lakeland	A+ Det	13	0	0	6	31.1	126	21	6	4	0	1	0	0	12	0	39	4	0	0	2	.000	0	2	1.15
Trenton	AA Det	25	0	0	16	36.2	155	26	13	10	2	2	2	1	15	2	31	4	1	2	2	.500	0	5	2.45
1995 Jacksnville	AA Det	27	1	0	4	33.1	148	34	17	14	4	2	3	0	20	4	17	4	0	2	0	1.000	0	0	3.78
1996 Jacksnville	AA Det	8	0	0	3	12.1	54	11	9	8	2	0	0	0	9	0	9	3	0	1	0	1.000	0	0	5.84
Lakeland	A+ Det	19	18	0	0	102.2	432	104	51	44	6	3	3	0	32	0	63	6	0	4	10	.286	0	0	3.86
1997 Memphis	AA Sea	36	0	0	11	57.1	252	57	40	34	7	1	4	2	35	2	40	2	0	3	4	.429	0	0	5.34
1995 Detroit	AL	2	0	0	0	3.2	22	7	6	6	1	0	2	0	4	1	2	1	0	0	0	.000	0	0	14.73
6 Min. YEARS		167	46	0	44	444	1899	420	230	185	31	10	19	6	188	8	356	48	6	23	27	.460	0	7	3.75

Darrell Whitmore

Bats: Left   Throws: Right   Pos: OF   Ht: 6'1" Wt: 210 Born: 11/18/68 Age: 29

		BATTING														BASERUNNING				PERCENTAGES		
Year Team	Lg Org	G	AB	H	2B	3B	HR	TB	R	RBI	TBB	IBB	SO	HBP	SH	SF	SB	CS	SB%	GDP	Avg	OBP	SLG
1990 Burlington	R+ Cle	30	112	27	3	2	0	34	18	13	9	0	30	2	0	1	9	5	.64	0	.241	.306	.304
1991 Watertown	A- Cle	6	19	7	2	1	0	11	2	3	3	0	2	0	0	0	5	0	.00	0	.368	.455	.579
1992 Kinston	A+ Cle	121	443	124	22	2	10	180	71	52	56	5	92	5	0	5	17	9	.65	8	.280	.363	.406
1993 Edmonton	AAA Fla	73	273	97	24	2	9	152	52	62	22	0	53	0	0	3	11	6	.65	12	.355	.399	.557
1994 Edmonton	AAA Fla	115	421	119	24	5	20	213	72	61	41	3	76	2	0	3	14	3	.82	12	.283	.347	.506
1996 Charlotte	AAA Fla	55	204	62	13	0	11	108	27	36	7	2	43	1	0	2	2	5	.29	2	.304	.327	.529
1997 Syracuse	AAA Tor	58	195	50	15	0	4	77	23	21	24	3	54	1	0	2	7	4	.64	6	.256	.338	.395
Carolina	AA Pit	2	9	3	2	0	0	5	1	2	0	0	2	0	0	0	0	0	.00	0	.333	.333	.556
1993 Florida	NL	76	250	51	8	2	4	75	24	19	10	0	72	5	2	4	4	2	.67	8	.204	.249	.300
1994 Florida	NL	9	22	5	1	0	0	6	1	0	3	0	5	0	0	1	1	0	.00	0	.227	.320	.273
1995 Florida	NL	27	58	11	1	0	1	16	6	2	5	0	15	0	1	1	0	0	.00	1	.190	.250	.276
7 Min. YEARS		460	1676	489	105	12	54	780	266	250	162	13	352	11	0	16	60	34	.64	38	.292	.355	.465
3 Maj. YEARS		112	330	67	11	2	5	97	31	21	18	0	92	5	3	1	4	3	.57	9	.203	.254	.294

Casey Whitten

Pitches: Left   Bats: Left   Pos: P   Ht: 6'0" Wt: 175 Born: 5/23/72 Age: 26

		HOW MUCH HE PITCHED						WHAT HE GAVE UP												THE RESULTS					
Year Team	Lg Org	G	GS	CG	GF	IP	BFP	H	R	ER	HR	SH	SF	HB	TBB	IBB	SO	WP	Bk	W	L	Pct	ShO	Sv	ERA
1993 Watertown	A- Cle	14	14	0	0	81.2	331	75	28	22	8	0	4	3	18	0	81	5	0	6	3	.667	0	0	2.42
1994 Kinston	A+ Cle	27	27	0	0	153.1	634	127	78	73	21	4	5	4	64	0	148	9	0	9	10	.474	0	0	4.28
1995 Canton-Akrn	AA Cle	20	20	2	0	114.1	469	100	49	42	10	1	2	3	38	0	91	5	2	9	8	.529	1	0	3.31
1996 Canton-Akrn	AA Cle	8	8	0	0	37.2	150	23	8	7	2	0	0	2	13	0	44	3	0	3	1	.750	0	0	1.67
Buffalo	AAA Cle	12	10	0	0	43.2	209	54	47	39	8	0	3	1	24	0	35	3	0	3	4	.429	0	0	8.04
1997 Buffalo	AAA Cle	2	1	0	0	4	14	1	0	0	0	0	0	0	0	0	0	0	0	0	0	.000	0	0	0.00
Akron	AA Cle	4	4	0	0	15.1	71	20	12	10	1	1	0	0	11	0	14	1	0	1	3	.250	0	0	5.87
5 Min. YEARS		87	83	2	1	447	1868	400	222	193	50	6	14	13	168	0	413	26	2	31	29	.517	1	0	3.89

Scott Wiegandt

Pitches: Left   Bats: Left   Pos: P   Ht: 5'11" Wt: 180 Born: 12/9/67 Age: 30

		HOW MUCH HE PITCHED						WHAT HE GAVE UP												THE RESULTS					
Year Team	Lg Org	G	GS	CG	GF	IP	BFP	H	R	ER	HR	SH	SF	HB	TBB	IBB	SO	WP	Bk	W	L	Pct	ShO	Sv	ERA
1989 Martinsville	R+ Phi	9	9	0	0	45.2	187	44	22	13	4	2	0	1	15	0	47	0	0	2	5	.286	0	0	2.56
1990 Spartanburg	A Phi	10	0	0	8	18.1	66	12	2	2	0	0	0	0	2	0	17	0	0	2	0	1.000	0	0	0.98
Clearwater	A+ Phi	33	4	0	16	75.2	316	70	33	22	4	4	3	3	37	2	52	6	3	4	8	.333	0	4	2.62

267

Year Team	Lg Org	G	GS	CG	GF	IP	BFP	H	R	ER	HR	SH	SF	HB	TBB	IBB	SO	WP	Bk	W	L	Pct.	ShO	Sv	ERA
1991 Clearwater	A+ Phi	11	0	0	5	10.1	47	14	7	4	0	0	0	0	3	0	11	2	0	0	1	.000	0	1	3.48
Reading	AA Phi	48	0	0	5	81	341	66	26	24	4	3	2	1	40	2	50	5	1	2	3	.400	0	1	2.67
1992 Scranton-WB	AAA Phi	1	0	0	1	1	4	0	0	0	0	0	0	0	1	0	2	0	0	0	0	.000	0	0	0.00
Reading	AA Phi	56	0	0	12	81.2	354	66	31	27	3	5	1	1	48	5	65	8	1	6	3	.667	0	2	2.98
1993 Reading	AA Phi	56	0	0	16	73.1	326	75	41	29	3	7	2	0	44	7	60	5	1	6	2	.750	0	0	3.56
1994 Scranton-WB	AAA Phi	6	0	0	1	4.2	30	11	8	7	0	1	1	1	3	0	3	0	0	0	0	.000	0	0	13.50
Reading	AA Phi	52	0	0	16	52.1	219	49	23	18	4	2	3	2	19	1	35	1	1	2	4	.333	0	0	3.10
1995 Scranton-WB	AAA Phi	47	0	0	15	54.1	234	55	19	18	0	1	0	2	27	8	41	5	2	1	3	.250	0	2	2.98
1996 Scranton-WB	AAA Phi	46	0	0	13	63	276	63	21	19	3	4	3	2	33	7	46	1	0	5	6	.455	0	2	2.71
1997 Louisville	AAA StL	40	3	0	10	64.2	280	57	34	32	5	1	2	3	36	0	55	3	0	1	3	.250	0	0	4.45
9 Min. YEARS		415	16	0	118	626	2680	582	267	215	30	30	17	16	308	32	484	36	9	31	38	.449	0	14	3.09

Chris Wilcox

Bats: Left **Throws:** Right **Pos:** OF **Ht:** 6'4" **Wt:** 190 **Born:** 11/15/73 **Age:** 24

Year Team	Lg Org	G	AB	H	2B	3B	HR	TB	R	RBI	TBB	IBB	SO	HBP	SH	SF	SB	CS	SB%	GDP	Avg	OBP	SLG
1995 Oneonta	A- NYA	59	223	73	16	7	1	106	25	28	20	3	28	1	0	2	9	3	.75	4	.327	.382	.475
1996 Tampa	A+ NYA	119	470	133	32	5	11	208	72	76	40	1	71	3	4	6	14	10	.58	14	.283	.339	.443
1997 Tampa	A+ NYA	12	40	12	4	0	0	16	7	4	7	2	6	1	0	1	1	1	.50	0	.300	.408	.400
Norwich	AA NYA	74	300	83	13	1	6	116	45	34	18	1	36	3	1	1	13	3	.81	6	.277	.323	.387
3 Min. YEARS		264	1033	301	65	13	18	446	149	142	85	7	141	8	5	10	37	17	.69	24	.291	.347	.432

Drew Williams

Bats: Left **Throws:** Right **Pos:** 1B **Ht:** 5'11" **Wt:** 200 **Born:** 3/27/72 **Age:** 26

Year Team	Lg Org	G	AB	H	2B	3B	HR	TB	R	RBI	TBB	IBB	SO	HBP	SH	SF	SB	CS	SB%	GDP	Avg	OBP	SLG
1994 Helena	R+ Mil	67	227	55	9	1	12	102	44	53	41	4	55	3	2	1	6	4	.60	3	.242	.364	.449
1995 Beloit	A Mil	135	427	114	21	2	14	181	66	66	81	4	76	6	1	2	8	8	.50	9	.267	.390	.424
1996 Stockton	A+ Mil	112	433	132	28	3	24	238	78	85	64	4	86	4	0	6	8	8	.50	12	.305	.394	.550
1997 El Paso	AA Mil	71	257	61	14	1	9	104	36	36	19	0	49	4	0	2	2	1	.67	4	.237	.298	.405
Stockton	A+ Mil	48	175	45	16	0	3	70	27	23	22	1	37	3	1	4	4	1	.80	4	.257	.343	.400
4 Min. YEARS		433	1519	407	88	7	62	695	251	263	227	13	303	20	4	15	28	22	.56	32	.268	.367	.458

Harold Williams

Bats: Left **Throws:** Right **Pos:** 1B-DH **Ht:** 6'4" **Wt:** 200 **Born:** 2/14/71 **Age:** 27

Year Team	Lg Org	G	AB	H	2B	3B	HR	TB	R	RBI	TBB	IBB	SO	HBP	SH	SF	SB	CS	SB%	GDP	Avg	OBP	SLG
1993 White Sox	R ChA	52	186	52	6	4	1	69	18	21	17	0	40	2	1	2	4	5	.44	6	.280	.343	.371
1994 Hickory	A ChA	137	535	162	27	3	24	267	99	104	53	6	103	11	1	3	1	1	.50	12	.303	.375	.499
1995 Pr William	A+ ChA	129	472	133	30	1	14	207	56	72	48	11	98	11	1	2	4	2	.67	16	.282	.360	.439
1996 Birmingham	AA ChA	14	46	13	4	0	0	17	3	4	4	1	12	2	0	1	1	1	.50	1	.283	.365	.370
Orlando	AA ChN	80	255	67	6	0	10	103	33	36	27	4	55	1	1	1	1	2	.33	9	.263	.335	.404
1997 Iowa	AAA ChN	9	28	5	2	0	1	10	2	2	2	0	8	0	0	0	0	0	.00	0	.179	.233	.357
Orlando	AA ChN	26	88	31	12	0	1	46	13	11	6	1	15	0	0	0	1	1	.50	2	.352	.394	.523
5 Min. YEARS		447	1610	463	87	8	51	719	224	250	157	23	331	27	4	8	12	12	.50	46	.288	.359	.447

Jason Williams

Bats: Right **Throws:** Right **Pos:** 2B **Ht:** NA **Wt:** 180 **Born:** 12/18/73 **Age:** 24

Year Team	Lg Org	G	AB	H	2B	3B	HR	TB	R	RBI	TBB	IBB	SO	HBP	SH	SF	SB	CS	SB%	GDP	Avg	OBP	SLG
1997 Burlington	A Cin	68	256	83	17	1	7	123	49	41	21	0	40	5	6	3	9	6	.60	6	.324	.382	.480
Chattanooga	AA Cin	69	271	84	21	1	5	122	38	28	18	0	35	0	1	3	5	5	.50	7	.310	.349	.450
1 Min. YEARS		137	527	167	38	2	12	245	87	69	39	0	75	5	7	6	14	11	.56	13	.317	.366	.465

Jeff Williams

Pitches: Right **Bats:** Right **Pos:** P **Ht:** 6'4" **Wt:** 230 **Born:** 4/16/69 **Age:** 29

Year Team	Lg Org	G	GS	CG	GF	IP	BFP	H	R	ER	HR	SH	SF	HB	TBB	IBB	SO	WP	Bk	W	L	Pct.	ShO	Sv	ERA
1990 Bluefield	R+ Bal	9	0	0	9	11.1	48	7	3	2	0	0	0	1	5	0	14	1	0	2	0	1.000	0	0	1.59
Frederick	A+ Bal	16	0	0	13	25	115	23	17	13	2	0	2	2	17	0	31	1	0	2	1	.667	0	1	4.68
1991 Frederick	A+ Bal	12	0	0	11	16.2	68	17	6	5	1	1	1	0	6	0	20	0	0	1	2	.333	0	6	2.70
Hagerstown	AA Bal	39	0	0	29	55.1	247	52	23	16	1	2	3	0	32	1	42	6	0	3	5	.375	0	17	2.60
1992 Hagerstown	AA Bal	36	15	3	16	123	579	148	91	66	9	5	6	2	70	0	82	15	1	8	10	.444	0	6	4.83
1993 Rochester	AAA Bal	33	5	0	11	86	389	95	59	55	10	2	7	4	47	3	59	8	1	2	5	.286	0	1	5.76
1994 Albuquerque	AAA LA	3	0	0	0	4.1	21	7	4	4	0	0	0	0	3	0	4	0	0	1	0	1.000	0	0	8.31
Calgary	AAA Sea	43	1	0	16	74	349	95	57	47	4	1	4	2	46	3	34	11	0	3	4	.429	0	0	5.72
1995 Tacoma	AAA Sea	8	3	0	4	23	109	31	21	21	1	0	3	2	12	0	8	0	0	0	3	.000	0	0	8.22
1996 Rochester	AAA Bal	8	0	0	5	8	42	11	7	1	0	0	0	0	4	0	4	2	0	1	1	.500	0	0	1.13
1997 Carolina	AA Pit	3	0	0	1	3.1	21	6	5	4	1	0	0	0	4	0	3	0	0	0	0	.000	0	0	10.80
8 Min. YEARS		210	24	3	115	430	1988	492	293	234	29	11	26	18	246	7	301	44	2	22	32	.407	0	31	4.90

Jeff Williams

Pitches: Left **Bats:** Right **Pos:** P   **Ht:** 6'0" **Wt:** 185 **Born:** 6/6/72 **Age:** 26

Year Team	Lg Org	G	GS	CG	GF	IP	BFP	H	R	ER	HR	SH	SF	HB	TBB	IBB	SO	WP	Bk	W	L	Pct.	ShO	Sv	ERA
1997 San Antonio	AA LA	5	5	0	0	28.1	119	30	17	17	2	2	2	0	7	0	14	3	1	2	1	.667	0	0	5.40
San Berndno	A+ LA	18	18	0	0	116	472	101	52	40	8	4	2	2	34	0	72	7	3	10	4	.714	0	0	3.10
1 Min. YEARS		23	23	0	0	144.1	591	131	69	57	10	6	4	2	41	0	86	10	4	12	5	.706	0	0	3.55

Juan Williams

Bats: Left **Throws:** Right **Pos:** OF   **Ht:** 6'0" **Wt:** 180 **Born:** 10/9/72 **Age:** 25

Year Team	Lg Org	G	AB	H	2B	3B	HR	TB	R	RBI	TBB	IBB	SO	HBP	SH	SF	SB	CS	SB%	GDP	Avg	OBP	SLG
1990 Pulaski	R+ Atl	58	198	54	6	1	0	62	18	22	11	1	45	2	1	0	9	7	.56	6	.273	.318	.313
1991 Macon	A Atl	106	347	81	13	2	1	101	44	32	39	1	100	3	6	2	12	11	.52	5	.233	.315	.291
1992 Macon	A Atl	67	232	54	12	2	2	76	24	14	25	1	77	0	1	1	16	6	.73	2	.233	.307	.328
Pulaski	R+ Atl	47	169	47	6	4	6	79	26	31	13	1	46	0	1	1	9	3	.75	2	.278	.328	.467
1993 Durham	A+ Atl	124	403	93	16	2	11	146	49	44	36	4	120	1	6	1	11	12	.48	9	.231	.295	.362
1994 Durham	A+ Atl	122	394	86	14	0	19	157	55	57	54	1	131	1	0	4	7	10	.41	2	.218	.311	.398
1995 Greenville	AA Atl	62	192	60	14	2	15	123	40	39	19	3	44	0	0	3	4	3	.57	5	.313	.369	.641
Richmond	AAA Atl	45	129	34	5	0	5	54	18	11	17	0	38	0	0	1	1	3	.25	2	.264	.347	.419
1996 Richmond	AAA Atl	119	357	97	22	2	15	168	55	52	51	5	127	0	3	2	5	4	.56	10	.272	.361	.471
1997 Pawtucket	AAA Bos	27	81	16	4	0	3	29	11	10	20	0	35	1	0	1	2	3	.40	1	.198	.359	.358
Trenton	AA Bos	63	200	40	5	1	12	83	34	30	33	2	63	0	1	1	0	4	.00	2	.200	.312	.415
8 Min. YEARS		840	2702	662	117	16	89	1078	374	342	318	19	826	8	18	16	76	66	.54	49	.245	.325	.399

Keith Williams

Bats: Right **Throws:** Right **Pos:** OF   **Ht:** 6'0" **Wt:** 190 **Born:** 4/21/72 **Age:** 26

Year Team	Lg Org	G	AB	H	2B	3B	HR	TB	R	RBI	TBB	IBB	SO	HBP	SH	SF	SB	CS	SB%	GDP	Avg	OBP	SLG
1993 Everett	A- SF	75	288	87	21	5	12	154	57	49	48	4	73	3	2	0	21	7	.75	5	.302	.407	.535
1994 San Jose	A+ SF	128	504	151	30	8	21	260	91	97	66	2	102	4	0	8	4	3	.57	8	.300	.373	.516
1995 Shreveport	AA SF	75	275	84	20	1	9	133	39	55	23	3	39	0	0	7	5	3	.63	5	.305	.351	.484
Phoenix	AAA SF	24	83	25	4	1	2	37	7	14	5	0	11	1	4	2	0	0	.00	4	.301	.341	.446
1996 Phoenix	AAA SF	108	398	109	25	3	13	179	63	63	52	4	96	0	1	5	2	2	.50	7	.274	.354	.450
1997 Phoenix	AAA SF	3	5	1	0	0	0	1	0	0	0	0	2	0	0	0	0	0	.00	0	.200	.200	.200
Shreveport	AA SF	131	493	158	37	7	22	275	83	106	46	3	94	3	0	7	3	0	1.00	12	.320	.377	.558
1996 San Francisco	NL	9	20	5	0	0	0	5	0	0	0	0	6	0	0	0	0	0	.00	0	.250	.250	.250
5 Min. YEARS		544	2046	615	137	25	79	1039	340	384	234	16	417	11	7	29	35	15	.70	43	.301	.371	.508

Reggie Williams

Bats: Both **Throws:** Right **Pos:** OF   **Ht:** 6'1" **Wt:** 189 **Born:** 5/5/66 **Age:** 32

Year Team	Lg Org	G	AB	H	2B	3B	HR	TB	R	RBI	TBB	IBB	SO	HBP	SH	SF	SB	CS	SB%	GDP	Avg	OBP	SLG
1988 Everett	A- SF	60	223	56	8	1	3	75	52	29	47	0	43	3	0	2	36	10	.78	5	.251	.385	.336
1989 Clinton	A SF	68	236	46	9	2	3	68	38	18	29	0	66	3	5	1	14	9	.61	5	.195	.290	.288
Boise	A- —	42	153	41	5	1	3	57	33	14	24	0	29	2	0	1	18	5	.78	2	.268	.372	.373
1990 Quad City	A Ana	58	189	46	11	2	3	70	50	12	39	0	60	4	2	1	24	6	.80	2	.243	.382	.370
1991 Palm Spring	A+ Ana	14	44	13	1	0	1	17	10	2	21	0	15	1	1	0	6	5	.55	0	.295	.530	.386
Midland	AA Ana	83	319	99	12	3	1	120	77	30	62	2	67	0	5	3	21	9	.70	3	.310	.419	.376
1992 Edmonton	AAA Ana	139	519	141	26	9	3	194	96	64	88	1	110	3	7	8	44	14	.76	9	.272	.375	.374
1993 Vancouver	AAA Ana	130	481	132	17	6	2	167	92	53	88	2	99	5	9	6	50	17	.75	7	.274	.388	.347
1994 Albuquerque	AAA LA	104	288	90	15	8	4	133	55	42	33	1	62	0	1	2	21	10	.68	6	.313	.381	.462
1995 Albuquerque	AAA LA	66	234	73	15	5	6	116	44	29	30	0	46	1	1	3	6	4	.60	3	.312	.388	.496
1996 Albuquerque	AAA LA	92	352	101	25	2	6	148	60	42	37	5	72	1	5	1	17	7	.71	6	.287	.355	.420
1997 Vancouver	AAA Ana	12	40	10	3	0	2	19	10	5	6	0	13	0	0	0	3	2	.60	0	.250	.348	.475
1992 California	AL	14	26	6	1	1	0	9	5	2	1	0	10	0	0	0	0	2	.00	0	.231	.259	.346
1995 Los Angeles	NL	15	11	1	0	0	0	1	2	1	2	0	3	0	0	0	0	0	.00	0	.091	.231	.091
10 Min. YEARS		868	3078	848	147	39	37	1184	617	340	504	11	682	23	36	28	260	98	.73	44	.276	.378	.385
2 Maj. YEARS		29	37	7	1	1	0	10	7	3	3	0	13	0	0	0	0	2	.00	0	.189	.250	.270

Todd Williams

Pitches: Right **Bats:** Right **Pos:** P   **Ht:** 6'3" **Wt:** 185 **Born:** 2/13/71 **Age:** 27

Year Team	Lg Org	G	GS	CG	GF	IP	BFP	H	R	ER	HR	SH	SF	HB	TBB	IBB	SO	WP	Bk	W	L	Pct.	ShO	Sv	ERA
1991 Great Falls	R+ LA	28	0	0	14	53	232	50	26	16	1	0	0	1	24	1	59	4	1	5	2	.714	0	8	2.72
1992 Bakersfield	A+ LA	13	0	0	13	15.2	64	11	4	4	1	1	0	0	7	1	11	0	0	0	0	.000	0	9	2.30
San Antonio	AA LA	39	0	0	34	44	196	47	17	16	0	4	1	1	23	6	35	3	0	7	4	.636	0	13	3.27
1993 Albuquerque	AAA LA	65	0	0	50	70.1	321	87	44	39	2	0	1	1	31	6	56	6	0	5	5	.500	0	21	4.99
1994 Albuquerque	AAA LA	59	0	0	36	72.1	299	78	29	25	5	1	3	6	17	3	30	6	1	4	2	.667	0	13	3.11
1995 Albuquerque	AAA LA	25	0	0	5	45.1	203	59	21	17	4	1	1	1	15	4	23	1	2	4	1	.800	0	0	3.38
1996 Edmonton	AAA Oak	35	10	0	9	91.2	427	125	71	56	4	2	5	3	37	3	33	3	0	5	3	.625	0	0	5.50
1997 Chattanooga	AA Cin	48	0	0	44	55.2	231	38	16	13	1	0	2	2	25	2	45	6	0	3	3	.500	0	31	2.10
Indianapolis	AAA Cin	12	0	0	5	12.2	54	11	4	3	0	1	0	1	6	1	11	2	0	2	0	1.000	0	2	2.13
1995 Los Angeles	NL	16	0	0	5	19.1	83	19	11	11	3	3	1	0	7	2	8	0	0	2	2	.500	0	0	5.12
7 Min. YEARS		324	10	0	208	460.2	2027	506	232	189	18	10	11	16	185	27	303	31	4	35	20	.636	0	97	3.69

Brandon Wilson

Bats: Right **Throws:** Right **Pos:** SS **Ht:** 6'1" **Wt:** 175 **Born:** 2/26/69 **Age:** 29

Year Team	Lg Org	G	AB	H	2B	3B	HR	TB	R	RBI	TBB	IBB	SO	HBP	SH	SF	SB	CS	SB%	GDP	Avg	OBP	SLG
1990 White Sox	R ChA	11	41	11	1	0	0	12	4	5	4	0	5	0	1	1	3	1	.75	1	.268	.326	.293
Utica	A- ChA	53	165	41	2	0	0	43	31	14	28	0	45	0	3	2	14	5	.74	1	.248	.354	.261
1991 South Bend	A ChA	125	463	145	18	6	2	181	75	49	61	2	70	2	7	4	41	11	.79	3	.313	.392	.391
Birmingham	AA ChA	2	10	4	1	0	0	5	3	2	0	0	2	0	0	0	0	0	.00	0	.400	.400	.500
1992 Sarasota	A+ ChA	103	399	118	22	6	4	164	68	54	45	2	64	4	5	2	30	16	.65	4	.296	.371	.411
Birmingham	AA ChA	27	107	29	4	0	0	33	10	4	4	0	16	0	0	0	5	0	1.00	1	.271	.297	.308
1993 Birmingham	AA ChA	137	500	135	19	5	2	170	76	48	52	0	77	3	4	3	43	10	.81	7	.270	.341	.340
1994 Nashville	AAA ChA	114	370	83	16	3	5	120	42	26	30	0	67	3	10	4	13	5	.72	4	.224	.286	.324
1995 Nashville	AAA ChA	27	85	25	5	0	1	33	8	10	4	0	11	0	1	0	3	1	.75	3	.294	.326	.388
Indianaplos	AAA Cin	4	12	2	0	0	0	2	3	0	2	0	1	0	0	0	0	0	.00	0	.167	.286	.167
Chattanooga	AA Cin	75	308	101	29	1	9	159	56	50	28	0	52	3	2	2	12	6	.67	7	.328	.387	.516
1996 Indianapolis	AAA Cin	95	305	71	7	3	4	96	48	31	39	0	53	0	1	2	10	6	.63	8	.233	.318	.315
1997 Indianapolis	AAA Cin	68	180	41	3	4	1	55	24	14	18	2	38	1	6	0	5	4	.56	3	.228	.302	.306
Iowa	AAA ChN	19	62	16	2	0	0	18	4	3	2	0	10	0	1	0	3	2	.60	1	.258	.281	.290
8 Min. YEARS		860	3007	822	129	28	28	1091	452	310	317	6	511	16	41	18	182	67	.73	43	.273	.344	.363

Craig Wilson

Bats: Right **Throws:** Right **Pos:** SS **Ht:** 6'1" **Wt:** 190 **Born:** 9/3/70 **Age:** 27

Year Team	Lg Org	G	AB	H	2B	3B	HR	TB	R	RBI	TBB	IBB	SO	HBP	SH	SF	SB	CS	SB%	GDP	Avg	OBP	SLG
1993 South Bend	A ChA	132	455	118	27	2	5	164	56	59	49	2	50	8	7	6	4	4	.50	16	.259	.338	.360
1994 Pr William	A+ ChA	131	496	131	36	4	4	187	70	66	58	2	44	6	5	6	1	2	.33	16	.264	.345	.377
1995 Birmingham	AA ChA	132	471	136	19	1	4	169	56	46	43	0	44	5	10	2	2	2	.50	21	.289	.353	.359
1996 Nashville	AAA ChA	44	123	22	4	1	1	31	13	6	10	0	15	0	5	1	0	0	.00	6	.179	.239	.252
Birmingham	AA ChA	58	202	57	9	0	3	75	36	26	40	1	28	1	6	4	1	1	.50	7	.282	.397	.371
1997 Nashville	AAA ChA	137	453	123	20	2	6	165	71	42	48	1	31	1	12	0	4	4	.50	19	.272	.343	.364
5 Min. YEARS		634	2200	587	115	10	23	791	302	245	248	6	212	21	45	19	12	13	.48	85	.267	.344	.360

Desi Wilson

Bats: Left **Throws:** Left **Pos:** 1B **Ht:** 6'7" **Wt:** 230 **Born:** 5/9/69 **Age:** 29

Year Team	Lg Org	G	AB	H	2B	3B	HR	TB	R	RBI	TBB	IBB	SO	HBP	SH	SF	SB	CS	SB%	GDP	Avg	OBP	SLG
1991 Rangers	R Tex	8	25	4	2	0	0	6	1	7	3	0	2	0	0	1	0	0	.00	0	.160	.241	.240
1992 Butte	R+ Tex	72	253	81	9	4	5	113	45	42	31	1	45	0	0	0	13	11	.54	1	.320	.396	.447
1993 Charlotte	A+ Tex	131	511	156	21	7	3	200	83	70	50	4	90	7	0	2	29	11	.73	18	.305	.374	.391
1994 Tulsa	AA Tex	129	493	142	27	0	6	187	69	55	40	5	115	2	0	1	16	14	.53	14	.288	.343	.379
1995 Shreveport	AA SF	122	482	138	27	3	5	186	77	72	40	2	68	1	0	1	11	9	.55	18	.286	.338	.386
1996 Phoenix	AAA SF	113	407	138	26	7	5	193	56	59	18	3	80	3	0	3	15	4	.79	9	.339	.369	.474
1997 Phoenix	AAA SF	121	451	155	27	6	7	215	76	53	44	5	73	4	0	3	16	3	.84	11	.344	.404	.477
1996 San Francisco	NL	41	118	32	2	0	2	40	10	12	12	2	27	0	0	0	2	2	.00	2	.271	.338	.339
7 Min. YEARS		696	2622	814	139	27	31	1100	407	358	226	20	473	18	0	17	100	52	.66	71	.310	.367	.420

Gary Wilson

Pitches: Right **Bats:** Right **Pos:** P **Ht:** 6'3" **Wt:** 190 **Born:** 1/1/70 **Age:** 28

Year Team	Lg Org	G	GS	CG	GF	IP	BFP	H	R	ER	HR	SH	SF	HB	TBB	IBB	SO	WP	Bk	W	L	Pct.	ShO	Sv	ERA
1992 Welland	A- Pit	13	4	0	5	42.1	170	27	9	5	0	1	0	1	13	1	40	1	0	3	2	.600	0	0	1.06
Augusta	A Pit	7	7	0	0	41.2	177	43	22	17	2	3	3	3	7	0	27	1	1	2	3	.400	0	0	3.67
1993 Salem	A+ Pit	15	15	0	0	78.1	356	102	58	50	15	1	1	2	25	0	54	3	0	5	5	.500	0	0	5.74
Augusta	A Pit	20	6	0	4	51	229	66	35	31	4	1	1	3	11	0	42	3	1	3	7	.300	0	0	5.47
1994 Salem	A+ Pit	6	6	1	0	35	147	41	12	9	2	0	0	0	4	0	26	3	0	3	1	.750	1	0	2.31
Carolina	AA Pit	22	22	7	0	161.2	654	144	55	46	11	8	5	10	37	0	97	2	0	8	5	.615	2	0	2.56
1995 Calgary	AAA Pit	6	4	0	0	16.1	75	19	16	10	1	1	2	0	9	0	12	2	1	1	2	.333	0	0	5.51
Carolina	AA Pit	1	1	0	0	4.2	16	0	0	0	0	0	0	0	3	0	5	0	0	0	0	.000	0	0	0.00
1996 Calgary	AAA Pit	27	27	1	0	161.1	725	209	105	91	18	6	6	9	44	1	88	2	1	6	9	.400	0	0	5.08
1997 Carolina	AA Pit	7	4	0	1	28.2	124	34	19	18	1	2	4	1	5	0	19	0	0	1	2	.333	0	1	5.65
Calgary	AAA Pit	21	11	0	2	84.1	387	115	59	55	10	4	3	5	22	1	54	1	0	6	3	.667	0	0	5.87
1995 Pittsburgh	NL	10	0	0	1	14.1	61	13	8	8	2	0	0	2	5	0	8	1	0	0	1	.000	0	0	5.02
6 Min. YEARS		145	107	9	12	705.1	3060	800	390	332	64	27	25	34	180	3	464	18	4	38	39	.494	3	1	4.24

Pookie Wilson

Bats: Left **Throws:** Left **Pos:** OF **Ht:** 5'10" **Wt:** 185 **Born:** 10/24/69 **Age:** 28

Year Team	Lg Org	G	AB	H	2B	3B	HR	TB	R	RBI	TBB	IBB	SO	HBP	SH	SF	SB	CS	SB%	GDP	Avg	OBP	SLG
1992 Salt Lake	R+ —	66	241	80	5	2	0	89	57	20	26	0	24	4	2	2	24	12	.67	5	.332	.403	.369
1993 Kane County	A Fla	129	469	117	8	2	0	129	74	27	52	0	55	9	10	2	34	15	.69	6	.249	.335	.275
1994 Brevard Cty	A+ Fla	125	483	129	12	4	1	152	81	29	50	1	49	3	8	3	26	14	.65	4	.267	.338	.315
1995 Portland	AA Fla	107	348	95	13	5	3	127	51	44	18	2	51	11	5	4	9	4	.69	9	.273	.325	.365
1996 Portland	AA Fla	113	375	96	16	5	6	140	46	35	33	3	49	8	9	4	7	10	.41	4	.256	.326	.373
1997 Portland	AA Fla	45	115	29	6	0	3	44	15	14	11	1	15	0	2	0	2	3	.40	1	.252	.317	.383
Charlotte	AAA Fla	60	146	37	6	1	2	51	27	13	17	1	26	1	5	0	1	2	.33	2	.253	.335	.349
6 Min. YEARS		645	2177	583	66	19	15	732	351	182	207	8	269	36	41	15	103	60	.63	31	.268	.339	.336

Preston Wilson

Bats: Right Throws: Right Pos: OF Ht: 6'2" Wt: 193 Born: 7/19/74 Age: 23

Year Team	Lg Org	G	AB	H	2B	3B	HR	TB	R	RBI	TBB	IBB	SO	HBP	SH	SF	SB	CS	SB%	GDP	Avg	OBP	SLG
1993 Kingsport	R+ NYN	66	259	60	9	0	16	117	44	48	24	0	75	3	1	1	6	2	.75	6	.232	.303	.452
Pittsfield	A- NYN	8	29	16	5	1	1	26	6	12	2	0	7	1	0	1	1	0	1.00	0	.552	.576	.897
1994 Capital City	A NYN	131	474	108	17	4	14	175	55	58	20	0	135	3	0	3	13	10	.57	4	.228	.262	.369
1995 Capital City	A NYN	111	442	119	26	5	20	215	70	61	19	2	114	9	1	3	20	6	.77	4	.269	.311	.486
1996 St. Lucie	A+ NYN	23	85	15	3	0	1	21	6	7	8	0	21	2	0	0	1	1	.50	3	.176	.263	.247
1997 St. Lucie	A+ NYN	63	245	60	12	1	11	107	32	48	8	0	66	1	0	4	3	4	.43	4	.245	.267	.437
Binghamton	AA NYN	70	259	74	12	1	19	145	37	47	21	0	71	2	0	3	7	1	.88	5	.286	.340	.560
5 Min. YEARS		472	1793	452	84	12	82	806	250	281	102	2	489	21	2	15	51	24	.68	26	.252	.298	.450

Tom Wilson

Bats: Right Throws: Right Pos: C Ht: 6'3" Wt: 185 Born: 12/19/70 Age: 27

Year Team	Lg Org	G	AB	H	2B	3B	HR	TB	R	RBI	TBB	IBB	SO	HBP	SH	SF	SB	CS	SB%	GDP	Avg	OBP	SLG
1991 Oneonta	A- NYA	70	243	59	12	2	4	87	38	42	34	2	71	3	0	5	4	4	.50	6	.243	.337	.358
1992 Greensboro	A NYA	117	395	83	22	0	6	123	50	48	68	0	128	3	1	8	2	1	.67	8	.210	.325	.311
1993 Greensboro	A NYA	120	394	98	20	1	10	150	55	63	91	0	112	4	3	8	2	5	.29	5	.249	.388	.381
1994 Albany-Colo	AA NYA	123	408	100	20	1	7	143	54	42	58	2	100	6	4	4	4	6	.40	6	.245	.345	.350
1995 Columbus	AAA NYA	22	62	16	3	1	0	21	11	9	9	0	10	0	2	0	0	0	.00	0	.258	.352	.339
Tampa	A+ NYA	17	48	8	0	0	0	8	3	2	11	0	13	0	1	1	1	0	1.00	0	.167	.317	.167
Norwich	AA NYA	28	84	12	4	0	0	16	6	4	17	0	22	0	0	0	0	0	.00	0	.143	.287	.190
1996 Columbus	AAA NYA	1	1	0	0	0	0	0	0	0	1	0	0	0	0	0	0	0	.00	0	.000	.500	.000
Buffalo	AAA Cle	72	208	56	14	2	9	101	28	30	35	0	66	6	1	0	0	1	.00	4	.269	.390	.486
1997 Columbus	AAA NYA	1	3	0	0	0	0	0	0	0	1	0	1	0	0	0	0	0	.00	0	.000	.250	.000
Norwich	AA NYA	124	419	124	21	4	21	216	88	80	86	0	126	4	0	5	1	4	.20	8	.296	.416	.516
7 Min. YEARS		695	2265	556	116	11	57	865	333	320	411	4	648	26	12	31	14	21	.40	40	.245	.363	.382

Vance Wilson

Bats: Right Throws: Right Pos: C Ht: 5'11" Wt: 190 Born: 3/17/73 Age: 25

Year Team	Lg Org	G	AB	H	2B	3B	HR	TB	R	RBI	TBB	IBB	SO	HBP	SH	SF	SB	CS	SB%	GDP	Avg	OBP	SLG
1994 Pittsfield	A- NYN	44	166	51	12	0	2	69	22	20	5	2	27	5	0	2	4	1	.80	1	.307	.343	.416
1995 Capital City	A NYN	91	324	81	11	0	6	110	34	32	19	1	45	8	1	2	4	3	.57	6	.250	.306	.340
1996 St. Lucie	A+ NYN	93	311	76	14	2	6	112	29	44	31	2	41	6	0	4	2	4	.33	7	.244	.321	.360
1997 Binghamton	AA NYN	92	322	89	17	0	15	151	46	40	20	0	46	5	3	1	2	5	.29	6	.276	.328	.469
4 Min. YEARS		320	1123	297	54	2	29	442	131	136	75	5	159	24	4	9	12	13	.48	20	.264	.322	.394

Chris Wimmer

Bats: Right Throws: Right Pos: 2B Ht: 5'11" Wt: 170 Born: 9/25/70 Age: 27

Year Team	Lg Org	G	AB	H	2B	3B	HR	TB	R	RBI	TBB	IBB	SO	HBP	SH	SF	SB	CS	SB%	GDP	Avg	OBP	SLG
1993 San Jose	A+ SF	123	493	130	21	4	3	168	76	53	42	1	72	8	7	6	49	12	.80	6	.264	.328	.341
1994 Shreveport	AA SF	126	462	131	21	3	4	170	63	49	25	2	56	8	5	4	21	13	.62	7	.284	.329	.368
1995 Phoenix	AAA SF	132	449	118	23	4	2	155	55	44	31	1	49	13	5	5	11	7	.65	10	.263	.325	.345
1996 Louisville	AAA StL	112	345	86	11	2	2	107	40	23	16	0	41	6	3	2	11	3	.79	11	.249	.293	.310
1997 Louisville	AAA StL	5	12	2	0	0	0	2	0	1	0	0	1	0	0	0	0	0	.00	0	.167	.167	.167
Orlando	AA ChN	102	371	102	15	3	2	129	62	28	23	0	37	10	7	1	23	4	.85	13	.275	.333	.348
5 Min. YEARS		600	2132	569	91	16	13	731	296	198	137	4	256	45	27	18	117	39	.75	47	.267	.322	.343

Mike Windham

Pitches: Right Bats: Right Pos: P Ht: 6'1" Wt: 185 Born: 3/8/72 Age: 26

Year Team	Lg Org	G	GS	CG	GF	IP	BFP	H	R	ER	HR	SH	SF	HB	TBB	IBB	SO	WP	Bk	W	L	Pct.	ShO	Sv	ERA
1993 Glens Falls	A- StL	11	11	0	0	57.2	237	55	24	17	2	3	0	1	16	0	44	5	1	4	5	.444	0	0	2.65
1994 Madison	A StL	21	21	1	0	121.2	526	119	67	58	12	1	3	9	49	0	88	10	3	10	7	.588	0	0	4.29
1995 Savannah	A StL	26	25	0	0	132.2	581	133	73	60	11	2	2	10	60	1	115	16	1	6	9	.400	0	0	4.07
1996 St. Pete	A+ StL	25	25	1	0	143.2	610	153	59	50	4	4	4	6	57	1	87	7	0	7	10	.412	0	0	3.13
1997 Arkansas	AA StL	29	11	1	8	88.2	396	107	61	54	11	1	0	5	37	1	44	4	0	3	3	.500	1	0	5.48
5 Min. YEARS		112	93	3	8	544.1	2350	567	284	239	40	11	9	31	219	3	378	42	5	30	34	.469	1	0	3.95

Ervan Wingate

Bats: Right Throws: Right Pos: DH Ht: 6'0" Wt: 185 Born: 2/4/74 Age: 24

Year Team	Lg Org	G	AB	H	2B	3B	HR	TB	R	RBI	TBB	IBB	SO	HBP	SH	SF	SB	CS	SB%	GDP	Avg	OBP	SLG
1992 Dodgers	R LA	37	126	36	8	1	1	49	22	11	18	0	19	1	1	2	3	2	.60	1	.286	.374	.389
1993 Great Falls	R+ LA	38	126	25	12	1	0	39	13	18	15	0	21	1	0	0	0	0	.00	5	.198	.289	.310
1994 Bakersfield	A+ LA	63	176	44	8	2	3	65	31	15	23	0	39	2	4	3	1	4	.20	5	.250	.338	.369
1995 Bakersfield	A+ LA	121	445	104	23	1	8	153	51	59	42	0	86	6	4	4	5	8	.38	25	.234	.306	.344
1996 San Berndno	A+ LA	115	383	124	16	0	12	176	60	55	32	1	75	6	4	6	7	9	.44	7	.324	.379	.460
1997 Vero Beach	A+ LA	84	224	51	12	1	3	74	26	24	27	0	51	0	3	3	3	2	.60	6	.228	.307	.330
San Antonio	AA LA	1	3	0	0	0	0	0	0	0	0	0	2	0	1	0	0	0	.00	0	.000	.400	.000
6 Min. YEARS		459	1483	384	79	6	27	556	203	182	159	1	292	16	16	18	19	25	.43	49	.259	.334	.375

Randy Winn

Bats: Both **Throws:** Right **Pos:** OF **Ht:** 6'2" **Wt:** 175 **Born:** 6/9/74 **Age:** 24

Year Team	Lg Org	G	AB	H	2B	3B	HR	TB	R	RBI	TBB	IBB	SO	HBP	SH	SF	SB	CS	SB%	GDP	Avg	OBP	SLG
1995 Elmira	A- Fla	51	213	67	7	4	0	82	38	22	15	0	31	3	0	2	19	7	.73	1	.315	.365	.385
1996 Kane County	A Fla	130	514	139	16	3	0	161	90	35	47	0	115	8	11	1	30	18	.63	3	.270	.340	.313
1997 Brevard Cty	A+ Fla	36	143	45	8	2	0	57	26	15	16	1	28	5	2	1	16	8	.67	3	.315	.400	.399
Portland	AA Fla	96	384	112	15	6	8	163	66	36	42	2	92	7	6	1	35	20	.64	4	.292	.371	.424
3 Min. YEARS		313	1254	363	46	15	8	463	220	108	120	3	266	23	19	5	100	53	.65	11	.289	.361	.369

Shannon Withem

Pitches: Right **Bats:** Right **Pos:** P **Ht:** 6'3" **Wt:** 185 **Born:** 9/21/72 **Age:** 25

Year Team	Lg Org	G	GS	CG	GF	IP	BFP	H	R	ER	HR	SH	SF	HB	TBB	IBB	SO	WP	Bk	W	L	Pct.	ShO	Sv	ERA
1990 Bristol	R+ Det	14	13	0	1	62	288	70	43	37	4	0	0	5	35	1	48	12	2	3	9	.250	0	0	5.37
1991 Fayetteville	A Det	11	11	0	0	47.2	241	71	53	45	2	2	0	0	30	0	19	8	0	2	6	.250	0	0	8.50
Niagara Fal	A- Det	8	3	0	2	27	115	26	12	10	0	0	2	2	11	0	17	2	0	1	2	.333	0	0	3.33
1992 Fayetteville	A Det	22	2	0	8	38	173	40	23	20	3	2	2	4	20	0	34	9	0	1	3	.250	0	0	4.74
1993 Lakeland	A+ Det	16	16	2	0	113	462	108	47	43	5	1	5	5	24	0	62	3	0	10	2	.833	1	0	3.42
1994 Trenton	AA Det	25	25	5	0	178	735	190	80	68	10	4	4	4	37	0	135	5	2	7	12	.368	1	0	3.44
1995 Jacksnville	AA Det	19	18	0	1	108	481	142	77	69	17	5	1	5	24	0	80	4	0	5	8	.385	0	0	5.75
1996 St. Lucie	A+ NYN	2	2	0	0	14	53	8	2	2	0	0	0	1	1	0	13	1	0	1	0	1.000	0	0	1.29
Binghamton	AA NYN	12	12	1	0	86	355	86	32	31	8	3	0	3	17	0	59	2	0	6	3	.667	1	0	3.24
Norfolk	AAA NYN	8	8	0	0	42.2	188	56	25	22	6	2	1	0	6	0	30	2	0	3	3	.500	0	0	4.64
1997 Norfolk	AAA NYN	29	27	1	2	155.2	668	167	85	75	21	2	4	4	48	1	109	5	0	9	10	.474	0	1	4.34
8 Min. YEARS		166	137	9	14	872	3759	964	479	422	76	21	19	33	253	3	606	53	6	48	58	.453	3	2	4.36

Kevin Witt

Bats: Left **Throws:** Right **Pos:** 1B **Ht:** 6'4" **Wt:** 185 **Born:** 1/5/76 **Age:** 22

Year Team	Lg Org	G	AB	H	2B	3B	HR	TB	R	RBI	TBB	IBB	SO	HBP	SH	SF	SB	CS	SB%	GDP	Avg	OBP	SLG
1994 Medcne Hat	R+ Tor	60	243	62	10	4	7	101	37	36	15	0	52	1	1	1	4	1	.80	3	.255	.300	.416
1995 Hagerstown	A Tor	119	479	111	35	1	14	190	58	50	28	2	148	4	3	0	1	5	.17	5	.232	.280	.397
1996 Dunedin	A+ Tor	124	446	121	18	6	13	190	63	70	39	3	96	6	2	5	9	4	.69	9	.271	.335	.426
1997 Knoxville	AA Tor	127	501	145	27	4	30	270	76	91	44	7	109	3	1	2	1	0	1.00	13	.289	.349	.539
4 Min. YEARS		430	1669	439	90	15	64	751	234	247	126	12	405	14	7	8	15	10	.60	30	.263	.319	.450

Trey Witte

Pitches: Right **Bats:** Right **Pos:** P **Ht:** 6'1" **Wt:** 190 **Born:** 1/15/70 **Age:** 28

Year Team	Lg Org	G	GS	CG	GF	IP	BFP	H	R	ER	HR	SH	SF	HB	TBB	IBB	SO	WP	Bk	W	L	Pct.	ShO	Sv	ERA
1991 Bellingham	A- Sea	27	0	0	22	45	189	27	12	11	0	1	1	0	31	1	44	5	0	2	2	.500	0	8	2.20
1992 San Berndno	A+ Sea	21	0	0	10	36.2	183	58	36	27	3	3	2	2	11	0	27	3	1	1	1	.500	0	1	6.63
1993 Appleton	A Sea	28	14	1	3	101	425	111	57	48	8	4	8	9	22	0	62	3	0	3	9	.250	0	0	4.28
1994 Riverside	A+ Sea	25	0	0	34	54.1	235	57	29	26	2	1	2	5	15	2	45	3	0	4	3	.571	0	0	4.31
1995 Port City	AA Sea	48	0	0	34	62.1	250	48	17	12	0	6	3	5	14	0	39	0	1	3	2	.600	0	11	1.73
1996 Tacoma	AAA Sea	35	0	0	20	46	191	47	12	11	2	3	3	1	13	2	22	1	0	2	2	.500	0	7	2.15
1997 Tacoma	AAA Sea	32	4	0	7	66.1	304	82	49	39	14	7	3	4	26	0	52	1	0	5	1	.833	0	0	5.29
7 Min. YEARS		216	18	1	100	411.2	1777	430	212	174	29	25	22	26	132	5	291	16	2	20	20	.500	0	27	3.80

Bryan Wolff

Pitches: Right **Bats:** Right **Pos:** P **Ht:** 6'1" **Wt:** 195 **Born:** 3/16/72 **Age:** 26

Year Team	Lg Org	G	GS	CG	GF	IP	BFP	H	R	ER	HR	SH	SF	HB	TBB	IBB	SO	WP	Bk	W	L	Pct.	ShO	Sv	ERA
1993 Spokane	A- SD	25	8	0	7	57	269	52	50	35	4	4	1	5	44	0	48	10	2	3	9	.250	0	1	5.53
1994 Springfield	A SD	60	0	0	33	63.2	298	46	43	38	3	7	1	0	58	4	99	11	4	3	8	.273	0	24	5.37
1995 Rancho Cuca	A+ SD	54	0	0	43	57	262	39	23	21	4	4	3	3	54	0	77	15	0	2	7	.222	0	18	3.32
1996 Wilmington	A+ KC	42	0	0	28	62.1	280	49	35	25	2	3	1	3	38	1	56	6	0	1	2	.333	0	4	3.61
1997 Wichita	AA KC	12	0	0	8	9.2	50	18	7	7	2	1	1	1	5	1	8	1	0	1	1	.500	0	1	6.52
Rancho Cuca	A+ SD	9	2	0	3	33.1	125	19	6	6	2	0	0	3	6	0	39	2	1	3	0	1.000	0	1	1.62
Mobile	AA SD	20	0	0	5	30	141	34	18	16	6	0	1	0	19	1	37	4	1	1	2	.333	0	0	4.80
5 Min. YEARS		222	10	0	141	313	1425	257	182	148	23	19	8	15	224	7	364	49	8	14	29	.326	0	49	4.26

Mike Wolff

Bats: Right **Throws:** Right **Pos:** OF-DH **Ht:** 6'1" **Wt:** 195 **Born:** 12/19/70 **Age:** 27

Year Team	Lg Org	G	AB	H	2B	3B	HR	TB	R	RBI	TBB	IBB	SO	HBP	SH	SF	SB	CS	SB%	GDP	Avg	OBP	SLG
1992 Boise	A- Ana	68	244	66	12	1	11	113	49	39	32	1	60	6	1	2	5	5	.50	0	.270	.366	.463
1993 Cedar Rapds	A Ana	120	407	100	18	5	17	179	63	72	74	1	104	2	5	5	8	8	.50	4	.246	.361	.440
1994 Midland	AA Ana	113	397	115	30	1	13	186	64	58	54	3	91	6	5	6	10	9	.53	4	.290	.378	.469
1995 Midland	AA Ana	127	445	135	28	3	14	211	76	70	65	3	83	3	4	7	10	9	.53	10	.303	.390	.474
1996 Lk Elsinore	A+ Ana	12	42	12	3	0	2	21	12	7	9	0	10	0	0	0	3	0	1.00	1	.286	.412	.500
Vancouver	AAA Ana	71	256	64	15	3	10	115	46	38	34	2	69	4	3	3	6	4	.60	3	.250	.340	.449
1997 Vancouver	AAA Ana	91	266	75	15	0	21	153	58	64	53	3	75	11	4	3	6	4	.60	1	.282	.417	.575
6 Min. YEARS		602	2057	567	121	13	88	978	368	348	321	13	492	32	22	29	48	39	.55	23	.276	.377	.475

272

Jason Wood

Bats: Right **Throws:** Right **Pos:** 3B **Ht:** 6'1" **Wt:** 170 **Born:** 12/16/69 **Age:** 28

		BATTING															BASERUNNING				PERCENTAGES		
Year Team	Lg Org	G	AB	H	2B	3B	HR	TB	R	RBI	TBB	IBB	SO	HBP	SH	SF	SB	CS	SB%	GDP	Avg	OBP	SLG
1991 Sou. Oregon	A- Oak	44	142	44	3	4	3	64	30	23	28	0	30	2	2	3	5	2	.71	0	.310	.423	.451
1992 Modesto	A+ Oak	128	454	105	28	3	6	157	66	49	40	1	106	4	3	5	5	4	.56	15	.231	.296	.346
1993 Huntsville	AA Oak	103	370	85	21	2	3	119	44	36	33	0	97	2	9	3	2	4	.33	7	.230	.294	.322
1994 Huntsville	AA Oak	134	468	128	29	2	6	179	54	84	46	1	83	6	5	15	3	6	.33	9	.274	.336	.382
1995 Edmonton	AAA Oak	127	421	99	20	5	2	135	49	50	29	3	72	3	6	12	1	4	.20	13	.235	.282	.321
1996 Huntsville	AA Oak	133	491	128	21	1	20	211	77	84	72	2	87	1	2	11	2	5	.29	14	.261	.354	.430
Edmonton	AAA Oak	3	12	0	0	0	0	0	0	0	5	0	6	0	0	0	0	1	.00	0	.000	.294	.000
1997 Edmonton	AAA Oak	130	505	162	35	7	19	268	83	87	45	0	74	8	2	4	2	4	.33	21	.321	.383	.531
7 Min. YEARS		802	2863	751	157	24	59	1133	403	413	298	7	555	30	29	53	20	30	.40	79	.262	.333	.396

Kerry Wood

Pitches: Right **Bats:** Right **Pos:** P **Ht:** 6'5" **Wt:** 190 **Born:** 6/16/77 **Age:** 21

		HOW MUCH HE PITCHED						WHAT HE GAVE UP												THE RESULTS					
Year Team	Lg Org	G	GS	CG	GF	IP	BFP	H	R	ER	HR	SH	SF	HB	TBB	IBB	SO	WP	Bk	W	L	Pct.	ShO	Sv	ERA
1995 Cubs	R ChN	1	1	0	0	3	9	0	0	0	0	0	0	0	1	0	2	0	0	0	0	.000	0	0	0.00
Williamsprt	A- ChN	2	2	0	0	4.1	23	5	8	5	0	0	0	0	5	0	5	1	0	0	0	.000	0	0	10.38
1996 Daytona	A+ ChN	22	22	0	0	114.1	495	72	51	37	6	5	4	14	70	0	136	10	7	10	2	.833	0	0	2.91
1997 Orlando	AA ChN	19	19	0	0	94	416	58	49	47	2	0	6	10	79	2	106	10	4	6	7	.462	0	0	4.50
Iowa	AAA ChN	10	10	0	0	57.2	254	35	35	30	2	3	0	6	52	0	80	8	2	4	2	.667	0	0	4.68
3 Min. YEARS		54	54	0	0	273.1	1197	170	143	119	10	8	10	30	207	2	329	29	13	20	11	.645	0	0	3.92

Brad Woodall

Pitches: Left **Bats:** Both **Pos:** P **Ht:** 6'0" **Wt:** 175 **Born:** 6/25/69 **Age:** 29

		HOW MUCH HE PITCHED						WHAT HE GAVE UP												THE RESULTS					
Year Team	Lg Org	G	GS	CG	GF	IP	BFP	H	R	ER	HR	SH	SF	HB	TBB	IBB	SO	WP	Bk	W	L	Pct.	ShO	Sv	ERA
1991 Idaho Falls	R+ Atl	28	0	0	23	39.1	160	29	9	6	1	2	1	0	19	1	57	7	1	4	1	.800	0	11	1.37
Durham	A+ Atl	4	0	0	2	7.1	29	4	3	2	1	0	0	0	4	0	14	0	0	0	0	.000	0	0	2.45
1992 Durham	A+ Atl	24	0	0	16	42.1	163	30	11	10	3	3	1	1	11	1	51	1	2	1	2	.333	0	4	2.13
Greenville	AA Atl	21	1	0	10	39.1	155	26	15	14	1	0	2	0	17	2	45	4	0	3	4	.429	0	1	3.20
1993 Durham	A+ Atl	6	5	1	0	30	120	21	10	10	2	0	1	2	6	1	27	4	0	3	1	.750	1	0	3.00
Greenville	AA Atl	8	7	1	1	53.1	220	43	24	20	1	6	0	2	24	0	38	6	1	2	4	.333	0	0	3.38
Richmond	AAA Atl	10	9	0	0	57.2	246	59	32	27	6	1	2	1	16	0	45	1	0	5	3	.625	0	0	4.21
1994 Richmond	AAA Atl	27	27	4	0	185.2	750	159	62	50	14	7	0	2	49	2	137	7	0	15	6	.714	3	0	2.42
1995 Richmond	AAA Atl	13	11	0	1	65.1	279	70	39	37	5	6	0	3	17	1	44	1	0	4	4	.500	0	0	5.10
1996 Richmond	AAA Atl	21	21	5	0	133.1	555	124	59	50	10	7	3	1	36	1	74	3	0	9	7	.563	1	0	3.38
1997 Richmond	AAA Atl	26	26	1	0	148.2	659	177	100	91	19	9	3	3	52	1	117	6	0	8	11	.421	0	0	5.51
1994 Atlanta	NL	1	1	0	0	6	24	5	3	3	2	0	0	0	2	0	2	0	0	1	0	1.000	0	0	4.50
1995 Atlanta	NL	9	0	0	3	10.1	52	13	10	7	1	1	1	0	8	1	5	1	0	1	1	.500	0	0	6.10
1996 Atlanta	NL	8	3	0	2	19.2	91	28	19	16	4	1	2	0	4	0	20	1	0	2	2	.500	0	0	7.32
7 Min. YEARS		188	107	12	53	802.1	3336	742	364	317	63	41	13	15	251	10	649	40	4	54	43	.557	5	16	3.56
3 Maj. YEARS		18	4	0	5	36	167	46	32	26	7	2	3	0	14	1	27	2	0	3	4	.429	0	0	6.50

Brian Woods

Pitches: Right **Bats:** Right **Pos:** P **Ht:** 6'6" **Wt:** 212 **Born:** 6/7/71 **Age:** 27

		HOW MUCH HE PITCHED						WHAT HE GAVE UP												THE RESULTS					
Year Team	Lg Org	G	GS	CG	GF	IP	BFP	H	R	ER	HR	SH	SF	HB	TBB	IBB	SO	WP	Bk	W	L	Pct.	ShO	Sv	ERA
1993 White Sox	R ChA	2	2	0	0	8	32	4	3	2	0	0	0	0	6	0	6	2	0	0	0	.000	0	0	2.25
Hickory	A ChA	10	10	0	0	61	250	49	20	17	3	0	1	3	31	0	53	2	1	2	5	.286	0	0	2.51
South Bend	A ChA	2	1	0	1	7	31	7	5	3	0	0	1	0	3	0	4	2	0	1	0	1.000	0	0	3.86
1994 South Bend	A ChA	20	18	2	2	115.1	499	108	65	50	9	5	3	5	49	0	107	10	4	4	12	.250	0	0	3.90
1995 Mohawk Vall	IND —	14	13	0	0	81.1	338	75	35	33	5	2	1	3	23	0	69	1	1	7	2	.778	0	0	3.65
Pr William	A+ ChA	27	27	3	0	139.1	632	155	89	80	14	5	4	14	53	1	102	12	3	9	15	.375	0	0	5.17
1996 Birmingham	AA ChA	53	0	0	26	67	301	59	32	28	11	4	0	7	38	2	46	1	0	5	5	.500	0	5	3.76
1997 Birmingham	AA ChA	35	0	0	31	45.2	223	44	41	32	3	6	1	8	28	1	35	4	0	1	5	.167	0	10	6.31
Nashville	AAA ChA	14	1	0	5	23.1	124	34	24	20	2	2	1	1	20	1	22	3	0	1	2	.333	0	0	7.71
5 Min. YEARS		177	72	5	65	548	2430	540	314	265	47	24	11	42	251	5	444	37	9	29	47	.382	0	15	4.35

Ken Woods

Bats: Right **Throws:** Right **Pos:** 2B **Ht:** 5'10" **Wt:** 173 **Born:** 8/2/70 **Age:** 27

		BATTING															BASERUNNING				PERCENTAGES		
Year Team	Lg Org	G	AB	H	2B	3B	HR	TB	R	RBI	TBB	IBB	SO	HBP	SH	SF	SB	CS	SB%	GDP	Avg	OBP	SLG
1992 Everett	A- SF	64	257	65	9	1	0	76	50	31	35	1	46	7	1	0	20	17	.54	2	.253	.358	.296
1993 Clinton	A SF	108	320	90	10	1	4	114	56	44	41	1	55	4	7	2	30	5	.86	13	.281	.368	.356
1994 San Jose	A+ SF	90	336	100	18	3	6	142	58	49	45	0	43	4	3	3	15	7	.68	9	.298	.384	.423
1995 Shreveport	AA SF	89	209	53	11	0	3	73	30	23	23	2	29	1	2	1	4	5	.44	4	.254	.329	.349
1996 Shreveport	AA SF	83	287	80	17	1	1	102	36	29	29	0	35	4	4	6	14	10	.58	11	.279	.347	.355
Phoenix	AAA SF	56	208	58	12	1	2	78	32	13	19	0	29	1	0	3	3	4	.43	6	.279	.338	.375
1997 Phoenix	AAA SF	1	1	1	0	0	0	1	0	1	0	0	0	0	0	0	0	0	.00	0	1.000	1.000	1.000
Shreveport	AA SF	104	293	88	14	2	2	112	41	32	28	0	40	3	4	3	6	4	.60	6	.300	.364	.382
6 Min. YEARS		595	1911	535	91	9	18	698	303	222	220	4	277	24	21	18	92	52	.64	51	.280	.358	.365

Tyrone Woods

Bats: Right **Throws:** Right **Pos:** DH   **Ht:** 6'1" **Wt:** 190 **Born:** 8/19/69 **Age:** 28

Year Team	Lg Org	G	AB	H	2B	3B	HR	TB	R	RBI	TBB	IBB	SO	HBP	SH	SF	SB	CS	SB%	GDP	Avg	OBP	SLG
1988 Expos	R Mon	43	149	18	2	0	2	26	12	12	7	0	47	0	0	2	2	4	.33	3	.121	.158	.174
1989 Jamestown	A- Mon	63	209	55	6	4	9	96	23	29	20	1	59	2	0	3	8	9	.47	5	.263	.329	.459
1990 Rockford	A Mon	123	455	110	27	5	8	171	50	46	45	1	121	1	0	3	5	7	.42	13	.242	.310	.376
1991 Wst Plm Bch	A+ Mon	96	295	65	15	3	5	101	34	31	28	0	85	3	0	3	4	4	.50	5	.220	.292	.342
1992 A Mon	A Mon	101	374	109	22	3	12	173	54	47	34	4	83	1	0	6	15	6	.71	6	.291	.347	.463
Wst Plm Bch	A+ Mon	15	56	16	1	2	1	24	7	7	6	0	15	1	0	1	2	1	.67	1	.286	.359	.429
Harrisburg	AA Mon	4	4	0	0	0	0	0	0	0	0	0	3	0	0	0	0	0	.00	0	.000	.000	.000
1993 Harrisburg	AA Mon	106	318	80	15	1	16	145	51	59	35	0	77	2	2	1	4	1	.80	8	.252	.329	.456
1994 Ottawa	AAA Mon	88	294	66	12	0	6	96	34	30	26	4	76	2	0	3	2	1	.67	8	.224	.289	.327
Harrisburg	AA Mon	38	133	42	16	2	5	77	23	28	13	2	29	1	0	2	2	1	.67	3	.316	.376	.579
1995 Rochester	AAA Bal	70	238	62	17	1	8	105	30	31	24	1	68	1	0	2	3	3	.40	6	.261	.328	.441
1996 Trenton	AA Bos	99	356	111	16	2	25	206	75	71	56	3	66	0	0	2	5	4	.56	6	.312	.403	.579
1997 Pawtucket	AAA Bos	29	105	37	3	1	9	69	16	28	11	0	35	0	0	2	1	1	.50	4	.352	.407	.657
10 Min. YEARS		875	2986	771	152	24	106	1289	409	419	305	16	764	14	2	30	52	42	.55	68	.258	.327	.432

Greg Wooten

Pitches: Right **Bats:** Right **Pos:** P   **Ht:** 6'7" **Wt:** 210 **Born:** 3/30/74 **Age:** 24

		HOW MUCH HE PITCHED						WHAT HE GAVE UP										THE RESULTS					
Year Team	Lg Org	G	GS	CG	GF	IP	BFP	H	R	ER	HR	SH	SF	HB	TBB	IBB	SO	WP	Bk	W	L	Pct.	ShO	Sv	ERA
1996 Wisconsin	A Sea	13	13	3	0	83.2	336	58	27	23	2	1	2	5	29	0	68	4	1	7	1	.875	1	0	2.47
Lancaster	A+ Sea	14	14	1	0	97	408	101	47	41	7	1	2	3	25	1	71	9	0	8	4	.667	0	0	3.80
1997 Memphis	AA Sea	26	26	0	0	155	681	166	91	77	14	5	5	6	59	1	98	12	0	11	10	.524	0	0	4.47
2 Min. YEARS		53	53	4	0	335.2	1425	325	165	141	24	7	9	14	113	2	237	25	1	26	15	.634	1	0	3.78

Steve Worrell

Pitches: Left **Bats:** Left **Pos:** P   **Ht:** 6'2" **Wt:** 190 **Born:** 11/25/69 **Age:** 28

		HOW MUCH HE PITCHED						WHAT HE GAVE UP										THE RESULTS					
Year Team	Lg Org	G	GS	CG	GF	IP	BFP	H	R	ER	HR	SH	SF	HB	TBB	IBB	SO	WP	Bk	W	L	Pct.	ShO	Sv	ERA
1992 White Sox	R ChA	2	0	0	2	3	10	1	0	0	0	0	0	0	0	0	5	0	0	0	0	.000	0	2	0.00
Utica	A- ChA	4	0	0	2	10	45	11	5	4	0	0	1	1	2	0	10	3	0	1	0	1.000	0	1	3.60
South Bend	A ChA	14	0	0	5	22.1	91	17	2	0	0	1	0	0	7	0	21	0	0	1	1	.500	0	2	0.00
1993 South Bend	A ChA	36	0	0	24	59	231	37	12	11	0	7	0	2	23	3	57	2	0	4	2	.667	0	10	1.68
1994 Pr William	A+ ChA	26	0	0	20	48	199	37	23	19	6	1	1	3	19	1	47	2	1	4	2	.667	0	3	3.56
Birmingham	AA ChA	7	0	0	1	10.1	35	2	0	0	0	0	0	0	5	0	6	0	0	1	0	1.000	0	0	0.00
1995 Birmingham	AA ChA	4	0	0	2	4.1	21	5	5	4	2	0	0	0	2	0	2	2	0	0	1	.000	0	0	8.31
Pr William	A+ ChA	29	0	0	18	47.1	180	32	10	8	3	3	1	1	7	2	52	1	0	3	1	.750	0	3	1.52
1996 Birmingham	AA ChA	35	0	0	16	51	200	28	14	12	4	1	0	0	21	0	55	0	0	5	1	.833	0	3	2.12
Nashville	AAA ChA	11	2	0	7	20	84	19	8	7	2	0	0	0	5	1	11	2	0	1	1	.500	0	1	3.15
1997 Birmingham	AA ChA	18	0	0	7	24.2	111	28	16	15	5	0	1	0	12	0	21	2	1	2	2	.500	0	1	5.47
Orlando	AA ChN	26	0	0	8	37.2	146	24	9	9	1	3	2	2	8	1	33	3	0	5	2	.714	0	1	2.15
6 Min. YEARS		212	2	0	112	337.2	1353	241	104	89	23	16	6	9	111	8	320	17	2	27	13	.675	0	26	2.37

Ron Wright

Bats: Right **Throws:** Right **Pos:** 1B   **Ht:** 6'0" **Wt:** 215 **Born:** 1/21/76 **Age:** 22

Year Team	Lg Org	G	AB	H	2B	3B	HR	TB	R	RBI	TBB	IBB	SO	HBP	SH	SF	SB	CS	SB%	GDP	Avg	OBP	SLG
1994 Braves	R Atl	45	169	29	9	0	1	41	10	16	10	0	21	0	0	0	1	0	1.00	5	.172	.218	.243
1995 Macon	A Atl	135	527	143	23	1	32	264	93	104	62	1	118	2	0	3	2	0	1.00	11	.271	.348	.501
1996 Durham	A+ Atl	66	240	66	15	2	20	145	47	62	37	2	71	0	0	7	1	0	1.00	5	.275	.363	.604
Greenville	AA Atl	63	232	59	11	1	16	120	39	52	38	5	73	2	0	3	1	0	1.00	4	.254	.360	.517
Carolina	AA Pit	4	14	2	0	0	0	2	1	0	2	0	7	0	0	0	0	1	.00	0	.143	.250	.143
1997 Calgary	AAA Pit	91	336	102	31	0	16	181	50	63	24	2	81	2	0	6	0	2	.00	4	.304	.348	.539
4 Min. YEARS		404	1518	401	89	4	85	753	240	297	173	10	371	6	0	19	5	3	.63	25	.264	.338	.496

Rick Wrona

Bats: Right **Throws:** Right **Pos:** C   **Ht:** 6'1" **Wt:** 195 **Born:** 12/10/63 **Age:** 34

Year Team	Lg Org	G	AB	H	2B	3B	HR	TB	R	RBI	TBB	IBB	SO	HBP	SH	SF	SB	CS	SB%	GDP	Avg	OBP	SLG
1985 Peoria	A ChN	6	16	4	1	0	0	5	2	2	2	0	5	0	0	0	0	0	.00	2	.250	.333	.313
Winston-Sal	A+ ChN	20	49	11	4	0	0	15	4	2	3	0	15	0	0	0	0	1	.00	1	.224	.269	.306
1986 Winston-Sal	A+ ChN	91	267	68	15	0	4	95	43	32	25	1	37	5	8	0	5	2	.71	9	.255	.330	.356
1987 Pittsfield	AA ChN	70	218	48	10	3	1	67	22	25	7	3	32	1	2	3	5	1	.83	6	.220	.245	.307
1988 Pittsfield	AA ChN	5	6	0	0	0	0	0	0	1	1	1	2	0	1	1	0	0	.00	0	.000	.125	.000
Iowa	AAA ChN	83	193	51	9	0	2	66	28	23	17	1	34	0	0	0	1	1	.50	6	.264	.324	.342
1989 Iowa	AAA ChN	60	189	41	8	3	2	61	15	13	7	2	40	1	0	0	1	1	.50	4	.217	.249	.323
1990 Iowa	AAA ChN	58	146	33	4	0	2	43	16	15	10	1	35	1	3	0	0	2	.00	7	.226	.280	.295
1992 Nashville	AAA Cin	40	118	29	8	2	2	47	16	10	5	0	21	1	1	0	1	1	.50	2	.246	.282	.398
1993 Nashville	AAA ChA	73	184	39	13	0	3	61	24	22	11	0	35	2	4	3	0	1	.00	1	.212	.260	.332
1994 Indianapols	AAA Cin	6	21	6	0	0	0	6	2	0	0	0	6	2	0	0	0	0	.00	1	.286	.348	.286
New Orleans	AAA Mil	53	158	39	8	3	1	56	20	21	7	0	33	2	2	1	2	1	.67	8	.247	.286	.354
1995 Buffalo	AAA Cle	31	93	21	6	0	0	27	9	10	3	0	19	2	2	1	0	0	.00	7	.226	.263	.290
Louisville	AAA StL	16	31	7	1	1	1	13	1	2	2	0	6	0	0	1	0	0	.00	1	.226	.265	.419
1996 Scranton-WB	AAA Phi	61	175	40	8	0	5	63	10	20	7	0	41	3	4	2	1	1	.50	4	.229	.267	.360
1997 Birmingham	AA ChA	29	103	26	7	1	2	41	11	24	3	1	12	2	1	1	0	0	.00	1	.252	.284	.398

Year Team	Lg Org	G	AB	H	2B	3B	HR	TB	R	RBI	TBB	IBB	SO	HBP	SH	SF	SB	CS	SB%	GDP	Avg	OBP	SLG
								BATTING										**BASERUNNING**				**PERCENTAGES**		
Nashville	AAA ChA	70	211	52	15	0	6	85	22	22	3	0	41	3	3	1	1	1	.50	7	.246	.266	.403
1988 Chicago	NL	4	6	0	0	0	0	0	0	0	0	0	1	0	0	0	0	0	.00	0	.000	.000	.000
1989 Chicago	NL	38	92	26	2	1	2	36	11	14	2	1	21	1	0	2	0	0	.00	1	.283	.299	.391
1990 Chicago	NL	16	29	5	0	0	0	5	3	0	2	1	11	0	1	0	1	0	1.00	0	.172	.226	.172
1992 Cincinnati	NL	11	23	4	0	0	0	4	0	0	0	0	3	0	0	0	0	0	.00	2	.174	.174	.174
1993 Chicago	AL	4	8	1	0	0	0	1	0	1	0	0	4	0	0	0	0	0	.00	0	.125	.125	.125
1994 Milwaukee	AL	6	10	5	4	0	1	12	2	3	1	0	1	0	0	1	0	0	.00	0	.500	.545	1.200
12 Min. YEARS		772	2178	515	117	13	31	751	245	244	113	9	414	25	31	14	16	13	.55	64	.236	.280	.345
6 Maj. YEARS		79	168	41	6	1	3	58	16	18	5	2	41	1	2	2	1	0	1.00	3	.244	.267	.345

Ed Yarnall

Pitches: Left **Bats:** Left **Pos:** P   **Ht:** 6'4" **Wt:** 220 **Born:** 12/4/75 **Age:** 22

Year Team	Lg Org	G	GS	CG	GF	IP	BFP	H	R	ER	HR	SH	SF	HB	TBB	IBB	SO	WP	Bk	W	L	Pct.	ShO	Sv	ERA
			HOW MUCH HE PITCHED							**WHAT HE GAVE UP**											**THE RESULTS**			
1997 St. Lucie	A+ NYN	18	18	2	0	105.1	435	93	33	29	5	2	1	2	30	0	114	2	4	5	8	.385	0	0	2.48
Norfolk	AAA NYN	1	1	0	0	5	29	11	8	8	1	0	0	0	7	2	2	0	0	0	1	.000	0	0	14.40
Binghamton	AA NYN	5	5	0	0	32.1	127	20	11	11	2	2	1	0	11	0	32	0	0	3	2	.600	0	0	3.06
1 Min. YEARS		24	24	2	0	142.2	591	124	52	48	8	4	2	2	48	2	148	2	4	8	11	.421	0	0	3.03

Jay Yennaco

Pitches: Right **Bats:** Right **Pos:** P   **Ht:** 6'2" **Wt:** 220 **Born:** 11/17/75 **Age:** 22

Year Team	Lg Org	G	GS	CG	GF	IP	BFP	H	R	ER	HR	SH	SF	HB	TBB	IBB	SO	WP	Bk	W	L	Pct.	ShO	Sv	ERA
			HOW MUCH HE PITCHED							**WHAT HE GAVE UP**											**THE RESULTS**			
1996 Michigan	A Bos	28	28	4	0	169.2	763	195	112	87	13	2	7	6	68	0	117	20	1	10	10	.500	1	0	4.61
1997 Sarasota	A+ Bos	7	7	2	0	44.1	179	30	12	11	3	1	0	1	19	1	41	2	1	4	0	1.000	0	0	2.23
Trenton	AA Bos	21	21	0	0	122.1	557	146	89	86	8	3	10	8	54	0	73	5	0	5	11	.313	0	0	6.33
2 Min. YEARS		56	56	6	0	336.1	1499	371	213	184	24	6	17	15	141	1	231	27	2	19	21	.475	2	0	4.92

Mike York

Pitches: Right **Bats:** Right **Pos:** P   **Ht:** 6'1" **Wt:** 190 **Born:** 9/6/64 **Age:** 33

Year Team	Lg Org	G	GS	CG	GF	IP	BFP	H	R	ER	HR	SH	SF	HB	TBB	IBB	SO	WP	Bk	W	L	Pct.	ShO	Sv	ERA
			HOW MUCH HE PITCHED							**WHAT HE GAVE UP**											**THE RESULTS**			
1984 White Sox	R ChA	5	1	0	0	14.2	70	18	9	6	1	1	0	0	9	0	19	0	0	1	0	1.000	0	0	3.68
1985 Bristol	R+ Det	21	0	0	18	38	168	24	12	10	1	5	2	2	34	2	31	6	1	9	2	.818	0	2	2.37
1986 Lakeland	A+ Det	16	0	0	13	40.2	214	49	42	29	2	1	3	3	43	0	29	9	0	1	3	.250	0	1	6.42
Gastonia	A Det	22	0	0	20	34	153	26	15	13	0	3	6	2	27	1	27	5	0	2	2	.500	0	9	3.44
1987 Macon	A Pit	28	28	3	0	165.2	700	129	71	56	11	5	3	2	88	1	169	9	3	17	6	.739	2	0	3.04
1988 Salem	A+ Pit	13	13	2	0	84	360	65	31	25	3	2	2	1	52	0	77	5	4	9	2	.818	1	0	2.68
Harrisburg	AA Pit	13	13	2	0	82.1	381	92	43	34	5	5	5	1	45	2	61	3	2	0	5	.000	0	0	3.72
1989 Harrisburg	AA Pit	18	18	3	0	121	492	105	37	31	6	1	5	2	40	2	106	8	0	11	5	.688	2	0	2.31
Buffalo	AAA Pit	8	8	0	0	41	193	48	29	27	3	2	0	1	25	0	28	1	0	1	3	.250	0	0	5.93
1990 Buffalo	AAA Pit	27	26	3	0	158.2	707	165	87	74	6	7	2	5	78	2	130	7	5	8	7	.533	1	0	4.20
1991 Buffalo	AAA Pit	7	7	1	0	43.1	181	36	17	14	0	1	2	0	23	0	22	2	0	5	1	.833	0	0	2.91
Colo Sprngs	AAA Cle	5	5	0	0	26	130	40	19	17	2	0	1	1	16	0	13	1	0	0	1	.000	0	0	5.88
1992 Las Vegas	AAA SD	19	17	0	0	88.1	411	96	54	47	5	5	5	8	55	0	54	2	2	5	7	.417	0	0	4.79
Buffalo	AAA Pit	6	6	0	0	32.1	147	31	14	11	2	1	2	1	20	0	20	1	2	4	1	.800	0	0	3.06
1995 Syracuse	AAA Tor	20	5	0	3	45	227	55	50	35	11	0	2	1	27	0	37	5	0	1	4	.200	0	0	7.00
1996 Tri-City	IND —	13	12	0	0	70.2	296	56	31	26	3	2	1	9	26	0	69	4	1	4	3	.571	0	0	3.31
1997 Tulsa	AA Tex	1	1	0	0	5.1	24	7	3	3	0	0	0	2	2	0	2	1	0	0	0	.000	0	0	5.06
Okla City	AAA Tex	4	2	0	0	10	54	12	9	9	0	0	1	1	12	0	1	0	0	0	1	.000	0	0	8.10
1990 Pittsburgh	NL	4	1	0	0	12.2	56	13	5	4	0	2	1	1	5	0	4	0	1	1	1	.500	0	0	2.84
1991 Cleveland	AL	14	4	0	3	34.2	163	45	29	26	2	3	4	2	19	3	19	2	0	1	4	.200	0	0	6.75
12 Min. YEARS		246	162	14	54	1101	4908	1054	573	467	61	41	41	42	622	10	895	68	22	78	53	.595	6	12	3.82
2 Maj. YEARS		18	5	0	3	47.1	219	58	34	30	2	5	5	3	24	3	23	2	1	2	5	.286	0	0	5.70

Joe Young

Pitches: Right **Bats:** Right **Pos:** P   **Ht:** 6'4" **Wt:** 205 **Born:** 4/28/75 **Age:** 23

Year Team	Lg Org	G	GS	CG	GF	IP	BFP	H	R	ER	HR	SH	SF	HB	TBB	IBB	SO	WP	Bk	W	L	Pct.	ShO	Sv	ERA
			HOW MUCH HE PITCHED							**WHAT HE GAVE UP**											**THE RESULTS**			
1993 Blue Jays	R Tor	14	12	1	0	62.1	268	59	34	27	2	1	4	4	31	0	61	1	9	4	5	.444	0	0	3.90
Medicne Hat	R+ Tor	2	2	0	0	11.1	45	6	3	3	0	0	2	0	6	0	7	0	0	0	1	.000	0	0	2.38
1994 Medicne Hat	R+ Tor	15	15	0	0	70.2	331	86	55	42	8	3	1	6	46	0	59	6	1	3	5	.375	0	0	5.35
1995 St. Cathrns	A- Tor	15	15	0	0	83.2	349	72	29	19	4	3	4	3	35	0	73	5	3	6	5	.545	0	0	2.04
1996 Hagerstown	A Tor	21	21	3	0	122	527	101	64	52	7	4	4	11	63	0	157	9	0	9	9	.500	1	0	3.84
Dunedin	A+ Tor	6	6	0	0	33.2	145	30	24	22	3	2	1	2	17	1	36	1	0	3	3	.250	0	0	5.88
1997 Knoxville	AA Tor	19	11	0	2	59	271	52	38	29	4	0	3	5	40	0	62	6	3	5	4	.556	0	0	4.42
5 Min. YEARS		92	82	4	2	442.2	1936	406	243	194	28	13	19	33	238	1	455	30	16	28	32	.467	1	0	3.94

Kevin Young

Bats: Right **Throws:** Right **Pos:** OF   **Ht:** 6'0" **Wt:** 195 **Born:** 1/22/72 **Age:** 26

Year Team	Lg Org	G	AB	H	2B	3B	HR	TB	R	RBI	TBB	IBB	SO	HBP	SH	SF	SB	CS	SB%	GDP	Avg	OBP	SLG
								BATTING										**BASERUNNING**				**PERCENTAGES**		
1994 Boise	A- Ana	63	240	56	7	2	2	73	29	30	15	0	35	7	1	3	8	4	.67	5	.233	.294	.304
1995 Cedar Rapds	A Ana	119	395	115	22	2	2	147	58	46	37	0	42	15	7	4	17	12	.59	7	.291	.370	.372
1996 Lk Elsinore	A+ Ana	114	462	134	17	3	2	163	78	39	50	0	58	4	7	4	24	14	.63	8	.290	.362	.353

275

Year Team	Lg Org	G	AB	H	2B	3B	HR	TB	R	RBI	TBB	IBB	SO	HBP	SH	SF	SB	CS	SB%	GDP	Avg	OBP	SLG
								BATTING										BASERUNNING			PERCENTAGES		
1997 Midland	AA Ana	103	338	96	23	6	6	149	64	53	49	1	40	6	5	3	6	9	.40	5	.284	.381	.441
4 Min. YEARS		399	1435	401	69	13	12	532	229	168	151	1	175	32	20	14	55	39	.59	25	.279	.358	.371

Tim Young

Pitches: Left Bats: Left Pos: P **Tim Young** Ht: 5'9" Wt: 170 Born: 10/15/73 Age: 24

Year Team	Lg Org	G	GS	CG	GF	IP	BFP	H	R	ER	HR	SH	SF	HB	TBB	IBB	SO	WP	Bk	W	L	Pct.	ShO	Sv	ERA
			HOW MUCH HE PITCHED						WHAT HE GAVE UP											THE RESULTS					
1996 Vermont	A- Mon	27	0	0	26	29.1	106	14	1	1	1	2	1	2	4	0	46	0	1	1	0	1.000	0	18	0.31
1997 Cape Fear	A Mon	45	0	0	41	54	214	33	12	9	0	1	2	2	15	0	66	8	0	1	1	.500	0	18	1.50
Wst Plm Bch	A+ Mon	11	0	0	8	15.2	56	8	1	1	0	2	0	1	4	0	13	0	0	0	0	.000	0	5	0.57
Harrisburg	AA Mon	1	0	0	0	2	7	1	0	0	0	0	0	0	0	0	3	0	0	0	0	.000	0	0	0.00
2 Min. YEARS		84	0	0	75	101	383	56	14	11	1	5	3	5	23	0	128	8	1	2	1	.667	0	41	0.98

Dave Zancanaro

Pitches: Left Bats: Both Pos: P **Dave Zancanaro** Ht: 6'1" Wt: 180 Born: 1/8/69 Age: 29

Year Team	Lg Org	G	GS	CG	GF	IP	BFP	H	R	ER	HR	SH	SF	HB	TBB	IBB	SO	WP	Bk	W	L	Pct.	ShO	Sv	ERA
			HOW MUCH HE PITCHED						WHAT HE GAVE UP											THE RESULTS					
1990 Sou. Oregon	A- Oak	10	8	0	0	44.1	188	44	22	19	2	1	0	1	13	0	42	3	4	3	0	1.000	0	0	3.86
Modesto	A+ Oak	4	2	0	0	13	64	13	9	9	1	0	0	1	14	0	7	0	0	1	2	.333	0	0	6.23
1991 Huntsville	AA Oak	29	28	0	1	165	727	151	87	62	7	3	4	6	92	0	104	8	4	5	10	.333	0	0	3.38
1992 Tacoma	AAA Oak	23	19	0	0	105.2	486	108	61	50	3	5	7	2	75	0	47	7	2	2	11	.154	0	0	4.26
1995 W Michigan	A Oak	16	16	0	0	32.2	132	19	8	8	1	2	0	3	15	0	42	1	2	0	2	.000	0	0	2.20
1996 Modesto	A+ Oak	20	3	0	6	77.1	331	61	38	29	9	4	2	3	37	0	66	5	1	7	3	.700	0	3	3.38
Huntsville	AA Oak	10	10	0	0	43.1	206	54	32	27	4	0	1	2	26	1	36	3	0	3	3	.500	0	0	5.61
1997 Las Vegas	AAA SD	3	3	0	0	13.1	77	27	24	23	3	0	0	2	8	0	9	0	0	0	3	.000	0	0	15.53
Mobile	AA SD	27	19	3	3	133.2	581	140	69	66	15	5	3	4	57	0	66	10	1	10	8	.556	0	1	4.44
6 Min. YEARS		142	108	3	10	628.1	2792	617	350	293	45	20	17	23	337	1	419	37	14	31	42	.425	0	4	4.20

Mike Zimmerman

Pitches: Right Bats: Right Pos: P **Mike Zimmerman** Ht: 6'0" Wt: 180 Born: 2/6/69 Age: 29

Year Team	Lg Org	G	GS	CG	GF	IP	BFP	H	R	ER	HR	SH	SF	HB	TBB	IBB	SO	WP	Bk	W	L	Pct.	ShO	Sv	ERA
			HOW MUCH HE PITCHED						WHAT HE GAVE UP											THE RESULTS					
1990 Welland	A- Pit	9	0	0	7	13.1	58	8	4	1	0	1	0	1	9	0	22	1	1	2	0	1.000	0	2	0.68
Salem	A+ Pit	19	0	0	13	25.2	122	28	19	17	1	1	1	1	16	3	24	3	2	1	1	.500	0	8	5.96
1991 Salem	A+ Pit	49	1	0	44	70	344	51	47	34	1	2	1	14	72	2	63	20	0	4	2	.667	0	9	4.37
1992 Carolina	AA Pit	27	27	1	0	153	673	141	82	65	10	8	7	7	75	2	107	13	4	4	15	.211	0	0	3.82
1993 Carolina	AA Pit	33	0	0	23	45	198	40	26	18	2	1	1	4	21	2	30	2	1	2	3	.400	0	9	3.60
Buffalo	AAA Pit	33	0	0	8	46.1	199	45	23	21	5	4	2	0	28	3	32	2	0	3	1	.750	0	1	4.08
1994 Carolina	AA Pit	16	0	0	15	16.1	72	13	6	5	1	1	0	1	8	0	9	2	0	2	2	.500	0	9	2.76
Buffalo	AAA Pit	19	0	0	4	23.1	99	25	10	9	0	2	0	2	13	1	14	3	0	0	1	.000	0	0	3.47
Edmonton	AAA Fla	9	7	0	1	38.2	179	33	19	15	0	1	3	5	29	0	23	7	1	5	1	.833	0	1	3.49
1995 Charlotte	AAA Fla	31	7	0	9	69.2	319	84	46	41	6	3	3	4	41	0	30	10	0	2	2	.500	0	0	5.30
1996 Tacoma	AAA Sea	13	0	0	6	17.2	92	23	19	18	1	0	2	4	13	0	13	2	0	1	1	.500	0	0	9.17
Port City	AA Sea	14	8	0	2	48	231	56	40	37	3	2	2	7	33	0	25	2	0	4	4	.500	0	0	6.94
1997 Rio Grande	IND —	3	3	0	0	16	67	13	11	3	2	0	0	1	5	0	9	2	0	1	1	.500	0	0	1.69
Omaha	AAA KC	7	6	0	1	26.1	110	41	32	31	8	0	0	1	20	0	17	1	1	1	3	.250	0	0	10.59
Wichita	AA KC	11	4	0	3	27	120	21	14	11	2	1	0	7	17	1	11	2	0	1	2	.333	0	0	3.67
8 Min. YEARS		293	63	1	136	636.1	2906	622	398	326	42	27	22	63	400	14	429	72	10	33	39	.458	0	39	4.61

Alan Zinter

Bats: Both Throws: Right Pos: 1B **Alan Zinter** Ht: 6'2" Wt: 190 Born: 5/19/68 Age: 30

Year Team	Lg Org	G	AB	H	2B	3B	HR	TB	R	RBI	TBB	IBB	SO	HBP	SH	SF	SB	CS	SB%	GDP	Avg	OBP	SLG
								BATTING										BASERUNNING			PERCENTAGES		
1989 Pittsfield	A- NYN	12	41	15	2	1	2	25	11	12	12	0	4	0	0	1	0	1	.00	0	.366	.500	.610
St. Lucie	A+ NYN	48	159	38	10	0	3	57	17	32	18	2	31	1	1	5	0	1	.00	5	.239	.311	.358
1990 St. Lucie	A+ NYN	98	333	97	19	6	7	149	63	63	54	1	70	1	0	6	8	1	.89	10	.291	.386	.447
Jackson	AA NYN	6	20	4	1	0	0	5	2	1	3	0	11	0	0	0	1	0	1.00	1	.200	.304	.250
1991 Williamsprt	AA NYN	124	422	93	13	6	9	145	44	54	59	1	106	3	2	2	3	3	.50	10	.220	.319	.344
1992 Binghamton	AA NYN	128	431	96	13	5	16	167	63	50	70	5	117	4	0	0	0	0	.00	7	.223	.337	.387
1993 Binghamton	AA NYN	134	432	113	24	4	24	217	68	87	90	7	105	1	0	5	1	0	1.00	4	.262	.386	.502
1994 Toledo	AAA Det	134	471	112	29	5	21	214	66	58	69	4	185	7	0	0	7	0	1.00	5	.238	.344	.454
1995 Toledo	AAA Det	101	334	74	15	4	13	136	42	48	36	1	102	2	2	5	4	1	.80	5	.222	.297	.407
1996 Pawtucket	AAA Bos	108	357	96	19	5	26	203	78	69	58	2	123	4	0	5	5	1	.83	3	.269	.373	.569
1997 Tacoma	AAA Sea	110	404	116	19	4	20	203	69	70	64	9	113	3	1	1	3	1	.75	7	.287	.388	.502
9 Min. YEARS		1003	3404	854	164	40	141	1521	523	544	533	32	967	26	6	30	38	14	.73	55	.251	.354	.447

Mike Zolecki

Pitches: Right Bats: Right Pos: P **Mike Zolecki** Ht: 6'2" Wt: 195 Born: 12/6/71 Age: 26

Year Team	Lg Org	G	GS	CG	GF	IP	BFP	H	R	ER	HR	SH	SF	HB	TBB	IBB	SO	WP	Bk	W	L	Pct.	ShO	Sv	ERA
			HOW MUCH HE PITCHED						WHAT HE GAVE UP											THE RESULTS					
1993 Bend	A- Col	14	8	1	3	55	247	47	35	27	7	0	3	2	30	1	78	5	1	4	3	.571	0	1	4.42
1994 Central Val	A+ Col	10	4	0	0	35.2	150	27	14	11	0	1	1	1	23	1	30	1	0	0	1	.000	0	0	2.78
1995 Salem	A+ Col	9	0	0	1	15	73	22	15	12	2	0	1	0	7	0	12	4	0	0	1	.000	0	0	7.20
Asheville	A Col	9	9	0	0	42.2	187	34	20	18	3	1	0	3	29	0	33	6	1	3	2	.600	0	0	3.80
New Haven	AA Col	9	7	0	1	55.1	229	56	25	20	2	1	1	1	20	1	32	0	2	3	4	.429	0	0	3.25
1996 New Haven	AA Col	47	10	0	10	91.2	421	82	60	55	13	1	4	5	68	6	84	8	0	2	8	.200	0	2	5.40
1997 Salem	A+ Col	22	0	0	14	34	133	22	10	10	2	1	3	1	11	2	31	3	0	2	2	.500	0	6	2.65

Year Team	Lg Org	HOW MUCH HE PITCHED						WHAT HE GAVE UP												THE RESULTS					
		G	GS	CG	GF	IP	BFP	H	R	ER	HR	SH	SF	HB	TBB	IBB	SO	WP	Bk	W	L	Pct.	ShO	Sv	ERA
New Haven	AA Col	16	7	1	2	56.2	255	64	38	32	10	2	4	1	32	3	32	10	2	3	5	.375	0	0	5.08
5 Min. YEARS		136	49	2	31	386	1695	354	217	185	39	7	17	14	220	14	332	37	6	17	26	.395	0	9	4.31

Julio Zorrilla

Bats: Both **Throws:** Right **Pos:** 2B **Ht:** 5'11" **Wt:** 156 **Born:** 2/20/75 **Age:** 23

Year Team	Lg Org	BATTING															BASERUNNING				PERCENTAGES		
		G	AB	H	2B	3B	HR	TB	R	RBI	TBB	IBB	SO	HBP	SH	SF	SB	CS	SB%	GDP	Avg	OBP	SLG
1994 Mets	R NYN	43	162	46	5	1	0	53	37	10	22	0	19	3	4	1	5	4	.56	2	.284	.378	.327
1995 Capital City	A NYN	133	518	143	15	3	0	164	65	31	31	2	75	0	10	4	42	18	.70	9	.276	.315	.317
1996 St. Lucie	A+ NYN	110	403	100	7	1	0	109	43	27	25	0	72	0	3	1	24	17	.59	10	.248	.291	.270
1997 Binghamton	AA NYN	7	24	3	1	0	0	4	2	0	0	0	5	0	0	0	0	0	.00	0	.125	.125	.167
St. Lucie	A+ NYN	118	418	105	18	3	1	132	41	31	26	3	50	2	16	0	14	12	.54	8	.251	.298	.316
4 Min. YEARS		411	1525	397	46	8	1	462	188	99	104	5	221	5	33	6	85	51	.63	29	.260	.309	.303

Eddie Zosky

Bats: Right **Throws:** Right **Pos:** 3B **Ht:** 6'0" **Wt:** 180 **Born:** 2/10/68 **Age:** 30

Year Team	Lg Org	BATTING															BASERUNNING				PERCENTAGES		
		G	AB	H	2B	3B	HR	TB	R	RBI	TBB	IBB	SO	HBP	SH	SF	SB	CS	SB%	GDP	Avg	OBP	SLG
1989 Knoxville	AA Tor	56	208	46	5	3	2	63	21	14	10	0	32	0	2	1	1	1	.50	4	.221	.256	.303
1990 Knoxville	AA Tor	115	450	122	20	7	3	165	53	45	26	1	73	5	6	3	3	13	.19	7	.271	.316	.367
1991 Syracuse	AAA Tor	119	511	135	18	4	6	179	69	39	35	1	82	5	7	5	9	4	.69	11	.264	.315	.350
1992 Syracuse	AAA Tor	96	342	79	11	6	4	114	31	38	19	0	53	1	7	4	3	4	.43	10	.231	.270	.333
1993 Hagerstown	A Tor	5	20	2	0	0	0	2	2	1	2	0	1	0	0	1	0	0	.00	1	.100	.174	.100
Syracuse	AAA Tor	28	93	20	5	0	0	25	9	8	1	0	20	4	2	3	0	1	.00	1	.215	.248	.269
1994 Syracuse	AAA Tor	85	284	75	15	3	7	117	41	37	9	0	46	2	6	5	3	1	.75	8	.264	.287	.412
1995 Charlotte	AAA Fla	92	312	77	15	2	3	105	27	42	7	0	48	1	5	1	2	3	.40	8	.247	.265	.337
1996 Orioles	R Bal	1	3	1	1	0	0	2	1	0	1	0	0	0	0	0	0	0	.00	0	.333	.500	.667
Rochester	AAA Bal	95	340	87	22	4	3	126	42	34	21	1	40	2	3	6	5	2	.71	8	.256	.298	.371
1997 Phoenix	AAA SF	86	241	67	10	4	9	112	38	45	16	2	38	1	1	2	3	3	.50	5	.278	.323	.465
1991 Toronto	AL	18	27	4	1	1	0	7	2	2	0	0	8	0	1	0	0	0	.00	1	.148	.148	.259
1992 Toronto	AL	8	7	2	0	1	0	4	1	1	0	0	2	0	0	1	0	0	.00	0	.286	.250	.571
1995 Florida	NL	6	5	1	0	0	0	1	0	0	0	0	0	0	0	0	0	0	.00	0	.200	.200	.200
9 Min. YEARS		778	2804	711	122	33	37	1010	334	303	147	5	433	21	39	31	29	32	.48	63	.254	.293	.360
3 Maj. YEARS		32	39	7	1	2	0	12	3	3	0	0	10	0	1	1	0	0	.00	1	.179	.175	.308

Jon Zuber

Bats: Left **Throws:** Left **Pos:** OF **Ht:** 6'0" **Wt:** 190 **Born:** 12/10/69 **Age:** 28

Year Team	Lg Org	BATTING															BASERUNNING				PERCENTAGES		
		G	AB	H	2B	3B	HR	TB	R	RBI	TBB	IBB	SO	HBP	SH	SF	SB	CS	SB%	GDP	Avg	OBP	SLG
1992 Batavia	A- Phi	22	88	30	6	3	1	45	14	21	9	1	11	1	0	1	1	1	.50	1	.341	.404	.511
Spartanburg	A Phi	54	206	59	13	1	3	83	24	36	33	1	31	1	0	1	3	1	.75	6	.286	.386	.403
1993 Clearwater	A+ Phi	129	494	152	37	5	5	214	70	69	49	5	47	0	3	4	6	6	.50	15	.308	.367	.433
1994 Reading	AA Phi	138	498	146	29	5	9	212	81	70	71	4	71	1	1	5	2	4	.33	11	.293	.379	.426
1995 Scranton-WB	AAA Phi	119	418	120	19	5	3	158	53	50	49	2	68	0	1	2	1	2	.33	12	.287	.360	.378
1996 Scranton-WB	AAA Phi	118	412	128	22	5	4	172	62	59	58	3	50	1	2	4	4	2	.67	15	.311	.394	.417
1997 Scranton-WB	AAA Phi	126	435	137	37	2	6	196	85	64	79	0	53	3	1	3	3	4	.43	11	.315	.421	.451
1996 Philadelphia	NL	30	91	23	4	0	1	30	7	10	6	1	11	0	1	1	1	0	1.00	3	.253	.296	.330
6 Min. YEARS		706	2551	772	163	26	31	1080	389	369	348	16	331	7	8	20	20	20	.50	71	.303	.385	.423

277

1997 Class A and Rookie Stats

We don't have the room to give you career stats for every player in the lower echelon of the minor leagues, but we can give you their complete 1997 statistics. They follow on the next several pages.

Baseball officials consider the jump to Double-A the toughest that a prospect will face. In a few years, after they clear that hurdle, several of the players on these pages will become stars. Take some time to acquaint yourself with them, guessing who will emerge from these columns of numbers. Dodgers third baseman Adrian Beltre is a good bet, as is Tigers closer Francisco Cordero. Marvel at the power of Diamondbacks outfielder Mike Stoner. Most of all, enjoy.

The abbreviations are the same as in the career register.

1997 Batting — Single-A and Rookie Leagues

Player	Team	Org	Lg	A	G	AB	H	2B	3B	HR	TB	R	RBI	TBB	IBB	SO	HBP	SH	SF	SB	CS	SB%	GDP	Avg	OBP	SLG
Abbott,Charles	Cedar Rapids	Ana	A	23	133	520	120	21	5	7	172	86	54	62	0	170	3	6	2	31	12	.72	7	.231	.315	.331
Abell,Tony	New Jersey	StL	A-	23	10	40	9	0	0	1	12	11	4	3	0	16	0	1	0	1	1	.50	0	.225	.279	.300
	Peoria	StL	A	23	13	25	4	0	0	0	4	4	2	4	0	12	1	0	0	2	2	.50	0	.160	.300	.160
Abernathy,Micha.	Hagerstown	Tor	A	20	99	379	117	27	2	1	151	69	26	30	0	32	6	6	2	22	13	.63	6	.309	.367	.398
Abreu,Alejandro	Martinsville	Phi	R+	20	15	50	9	1	0	0	10	4	0	1	0	18	0	0	0	1	2	.33	0	.180	.196	.200
Abreu,Dennis	Rockford	ChN	A	20	126	483	155	19	3	1	183	71	37	45	2	99	7	5	1	36	26	.58	8	.321	.386	.379
Abreu,Miguel	Marlins	Fla	R	19	37	94	20	2	1	0	24	10	6	4	0	28	1	0	2	2	2	.50	1	.213	.248	.255
Abreu,Nelson	Rockford	ChN	A	21	63	179	43	4	5	2	63	27	20	19	0	52	0	6	1	9	6	.60	6	.240	.312	.352
	Williamsprt	ChN	A-	21	14	49	15	1	2	0	20	8	3	9	0	17	1	2	0	6	3	.67	0	.306	.424	.408
Acevedo,Luis	Rangers	Tex	R	20	51	155	28	3	0	1	34	16	7	13	0	46	3	0	3	8	3	.73	3	.181	.253	.219
	Charlotte	Tex	A+	20	1	3	0	0	0	0	0	0	0	0	0	2	0	0	0	0	0	.00	0	.000	.000	.000
Aceves,Jonathan	White Sox	ChA	R	20	30	76	14	4	0	0	18	9	4	9	0	18	2	0	0	0	0	.00	5	.184	.287	.237
Ackerman,Scott	Expos	Mon	R	19	43	142	34	6	1	2	48	17	18	14	0	26	1	2	0	3	4	.43	1	.239	.312	.338
Adams,Jason	Kissimmee	Hou	A+	25	31	95	20	6	0	0	26	9	9	11	0	13	1	1	1	0	0	.00	2	.211	.296	.274
Adams,John	South Bend	Ari	A	21	60	216	56	7	1	10	95	22	36	5	1	71	1	0	1	3	0	1.00	8	.259	.278	.440
Adams,Lawrence	Medcne Hat	Tor	R+	21	47	117	21	7	0	1	31	9	13	11	0	44	4	0	1	1	3	.25	2	.179	.271	.265
Adams,Timothy	Butte	Ana	R+	23	38	131	34	4	1	1	43	20	17	8	0	43	4	0	1	0	1	.00	4	.260	.319	.328
Adolfo,Carlos	Wst Plm Bch	Mon	A+	22	120	448	101	15	2	11	153	62	50	38	1	91	2	3	0	9	18	.33	8	.225	.289	.342
Adorno,Wilson	Pirates	Pit	R	20	15	39	7	0	0	0	7	7	4	4	0	12	1	0	0	0	0	.00	2	.179	.273	.179
Agnoly,Earl	Kane County	Fla	A	22	34	100	21	0	1	2	29	9	10	6	0	23	4	3	0	3	1	.75	0	.210	.282	.290
Aguila,Chris	Marlins	Fla	R	19	46	157	34	7	0	1	44	12	17	21	0	49	1	2	2	2	1	.67	3	.217	.309	.280
Ahumada,Alejan.	Michigan	Bos	A	19	3	12	3	1	1	0	6	1	1	0	0	3	0	0	0	0	0	.00	0	.250	.250	.500
	Lowell	Bos	A-	19	57	203	45	4	1	1	54	25	13	15	0	49	4	1	2	5	1	.83	5	.222	.286	.266
Airoso,Kurt	Lakeland	Det	A+	23	22	62	12	1	2	0	17	12	7	11	0	23	1	1	0	0	0	.00	2	.194	.324	.274
	Tigers	Det	R	23	4	10	0	0	0	0	0	1	0	3	0	3	1	0	0	0	0	.00	0	.000	.286	.000
	W Michigan	Det	A	23	14	37	11	5	0	0	16	6	2	6	0	15	0	0	1	0	0	.00	0	.297	.386	.432
Akins,Carlos	Frederick	Bal	A+	23	110	335	71	16	0	2	93	53	30	54	0	79	7	4	3	14	4	.78	2	.212	.331	.278
Alaimo,Jason	Kane County	Fla	A	22	36	90	22	5	0	2	33	7	10	5	1	25	2	0	2	1	2	.33	0	.244	.293	.367
Alamo,Efrain	Asheville	Col	A	21	34	125	29	9	0	1	41	17	14	6	0	49	1	2	0	2	3	.40	3	.232	.273	.328
	Portland	Col	A-	21	69	255	55	13	2	2	78	27	33	22	0	88	2	3	6	12	4	.75	4	.216	.277	.306
Alayon,Elvis	Lowell	Bos	A-	23	32	111	23	4	1	1	32	12	7	5	0	16	1	4	0	1	2	.33	1	.207	.248	.288
Albaral,Randy	St. Cathrns	Tor	A-	21	56	218	49	5	1	0	56	39	23	20	0	27	2	3	2	14	3	.82	1	.225	.293	.257
Albert,Rashad	Bristol	ChA	R+	22	4	17	4	0	0	1	7	2	2	1	0	7	0	0	0	2	0	1.00	0	.235	.278	.412
	Winston-Sal	ChA	A+	22	24	72	13	1	1	4	28	10	9	8	0	25	0	2	0	3	5	.38	0	.181	.263	.389
Alcala,Juan	Mariners	Sea	R	20	29	92	21	5	0	1	29	15	7	7	0	26	0	2	0	5	0	1.00	1	.228	.283	.315
	Everett	Sea	A-	20	9	33	5	1	0	0	6	3	1	1	0	15	0	0	0	1	0	1.00	1	.152	.176	.182
Aldridge,Cory	Braves	Atl	R	19	46	169	47	8	1	3	66	26	37	14	0	37	1	0	0	1	0	1.00	1	.278	.337	.391
Aldrup,Morey	Cubs	ChN	R	19	36	125	24	6	0	1	33	13	12	8	0	43	3	2	0	4	3	.57	2	.192	.257	.264
Alevras,Chad	Lowell	Bos	A-	23	22	55	8	2	0	1	13	8	5	10	0	13	1	1	0	1	1	.50	0	.145	.288	.236
Alexander,Chad	Kissimmee	Hou	A+	24	129	469	127	31	6	4	182	67	46	56	1	91	4	2	3	11	8	.58	15	.271	.352	.388
Alfano,Jeff	Beloit	Mil	A	21	37	121	28	3	2	2	41	14	16	9	0	32	7	1	1	3	1	.75	4	.231	.319	.339
	Ogden	Mil	R+	21	46	175	63	12	4	7	104	39	29	17	1	31	4	0	1	9	4	.69	4	.360	.424	.594
Alfaro,Jason	Astros	Hou	R	20	34	102	27	5	0	2	38	8	13	8	0	14	1	2	0	6	0	1.00	2	.265	.324	.373
Alfonso,Eliezer	Johnson Cty	StL	R+	19	38	120	33	11	1	2	52	15	15	7	0	34	6	0	0	1	0	1.00	1	.275	.346	.433
Alguacil,Jose	San Jose	SF	A+	25	122	392	81	15	2	7	121	53	42	32	2	98	10	10	1	13	13	.50	4	.207	.283	.309
Allen,Jake	Great Falls	LA	R+	19	1	1	0	0	0	0	0	0	0	0	1	0	0	0	0	0	0	.00	0	.000	.000	.000
Allen,Shane	Great Falls	LA	R+	19	24	31	6	0	0	0	6	5	2	1	0	14	1	0	0	0	0	.00	0	.194	.242	.194
	Yakima	LA	A-	19	12	26	0	0	0	0	0	2	0	5	0	13	0	0	0	1	0	1.00	0	.000	.161	.000
Allen,Lucas	Great Falls	LA	R+	19	67	258	89	12	6	7	134	50	40	19	1	53	0	1	2	12	11	.52	3	.345	.390	.519
Allen,Troy	Danville	Atl	R+	22	43	131	28	5	0	2	39	16	12	19	2	44	1	1	0	1	1	.50	2	.214	.312	.298
Alley,Chip	Delmarva	Bal	A	21	82	250	59	17	1	3	87	19	32	34	3	45	8	1	2	7	2	.78	5	.236	.344	.348
Alleyne,Roberto	Astros	Hou	R	21	3	13	5	1	1	0	8	1	3	1	0	0	0	0	0	3	0	1.00	0	.385	.429	.615
	Quad City	Hou	A	21	63	215	56	10	0	5	81	24	30	12	0	55	2	1	0	1	3	.25	6	.260	.306	.377
Allison,Brad	South Bend	Ari	A	24	55	166	22	3	0	0	25	5	9	11	0	52	3	0	0	1	0	1.00	9	.133	.200	.151
Allison,Cody	Watertown	Cle	A-	23	51	181	48	10	0	1	61	25	23	20	2	34	0	1	3	7	3	.70	4	.265	.338	.337
Almonte,Claudio	Twins	Min	R	19	57	188	54	7	2	1	68	19	25	12	0	36	2	0	2	16	5	.76	0	.287	.333	.362
Almonte,Erick	Yankees	NYA	R	20	52	180	51	4	4	3	72	32	31	21	1	27	0	1	0	8	2	.80	5	.283	.355	.400
Alvarez,Carlos	Watertown	Cle	A-	22	22	80	24	5	0	6	47	15	17	2	0	21	5	0	1	3	2	.60	0	.300	.352	.588
Alvarez,Jimmy	Twins	Min	R	18	52	185	46	5	4	0	59	25	14	21	0	46	1	1	1	12	5	.71	4	.249	.327	.319
Alvarez,Julio	Tigers	Det	R	19	6	18	3	0	0	0	3	1	0	2	0	5	0	0	0	0	0	.00	0	.167	.250	.167
Alvarez,Nell	Tigers	Det	R	19	34	85	21	0	1	0	27	21	10	12	0	16	3	0	1	4	3	.57	8	.247	.356	.318
Alviso,Jerome	Portland	Col	A-	22	69	270	86	15	3	2	113	48	45	19	1	46	7	6	6	12	5	.71	3	.319	.371	.419
Amado,Jose	Lansing	KC	A	23	61	234	80	25	1	4	119	49	45	24	1	18	4	0	6	10	2	.83	8	.342	.403	.509
Amerson,Gordie	Clinton	SD	A	21	34	102	24	7	3	0	37	13	16	25	0	31	1	0	2	6	2	.75	0	.235	.385	.363
Ametller,Jesus	Pr William		R	23	58	188	45	10	2	3	81	26	26	15	1	12	0	4	0	3	1	.75	5	.270	.317	.377
Amezcua,Adan	Kissimmee	Hou	A+	24	9	20	8	3	0	0	11	3	5	3	1	3	0	0	0	2	3	.40	0	.400	.458	.550
Amrhein,Michael	Williamsprt	ChN	A-	23	62	237	66	11	1	1	82	17	31	10	1	19	2	0	4	2	0	1.00	11	.278	.308	.346
Andersen,Ryan	Rockford	ChN	A	24	19	53	14	3	0	0	17	2	4	6	0	10	0	1	0	1	0	1.00	1	.264	.339	.321
Anderson,Christ.	Chston-SC	TB	A	23	68	223	42	7	0	4	71	27	28	13	1	87	2	2	1	3	1	.75	5	.188	.238	.318
Anderson,Cliff	San Berndno	LA	A+	27	132	458	125	40	5	21	238	77	79	31	2	137	20	6	7	3	11	.21	7	.273	.341	.520
Anderson,Blake	Asheville	Col	A	24	73	247	66	9	2	7	100	30	31	32	2	50	0	1	0	2	5	.29	7	.267	.351	.405
Ankrum,C.J.	Salem-Keizr	SF	A-	22	74	263	70	14	1	5	101	44	64	49	1	44	11	0	7	6	5	.55	6	.266	.394	.384
Antczak,Chuck	Hickory	ChA	A	24	1	1	1	0	0	0	1	0	1	0	0	0	0	0	0	0	0	.00	0	1.000	.500	1.000
	Winston-Sal	ChA	A+	24	5	14	2	0	0	0	2	0	0	3	0	9	0	0	0	0	0	.00	0	.143	.143	.143
Anthony,Brian	Asheville	Col	A	24	83	296	76	17	1	12	131	41	49	23	0	75	2	1	0	4	4	.50	6	.257	.315	.443
Antigua,Nilson	Lynchburg	Pit	A+	20	46	148	36	5	0	1	44	18	17	5	0	24	2	1	0	2	2	.50	5	.243	.277	.297
Antrim,Patrick	Greensboro	NYA	A	24	68	173	39	3	0	0	42	23	13	7	0	40	0	0	0	3	2	.60	1	.225	.256	.243

1997 Batting — Single-A and Rookie Leagues

					BATTING															BASERUNNING				PERCENTAGES		
Player	Team	Org	Lg	A	G	AB	H	2B	3B	HR	TB	R	RBI	TBB	IBB	SO	HBP	SH	SF	SB	CS	SB%	GDP	Avg	OBP	SLG
Araujo,Danilo	Johnson Cty	StL	R+	21	54	187	47	7	3	1	63	33	24	32	0	42	3	5	0	8	7	.53	2	.251	.369	.337
Arias,Jeison	Princeton	TB	R+	19	5	18	3	0	0	0	3	5	0	1	0	5	1	0	0	0	0	.00	0	.167	.250	.167
	Devil Rays	TB	R	19	39	126	24	4	4	2	42	14	10	16	0	41	2	0	0	7	4	.64	2	.190	.292	.333
Arias,Rogelio	Asheville	Col	A	22	72	251	60	4	0	2	70	23	19	10	0	21	1	5	0	4	2	.67	6	.239	.271	.279
Armenta,Jason	Billings	Cin	R+	21	44	97	23	5	0	0	28	17	5	7	0	27	1	0	0	2	2	.50	3	.237	.295	.289
Arnold,John	Macon	Atl	A	23	2	7	3	0	0	1	6	2	1	1	0	0	0	0	0	0	0	.00	0	.429	.500	.857
	Eugene	Atl	A-	23	50	159	39	9	1	5	65	25	30	28	0	50	2	0	2	0	1	.00	4	.245	.361	.409
Arrendondo,Her.	Chston-SC	TB	A	20	6	17	4	1	0	0	5	0	0	0	0	0	0	0	0	0	0	.00	1	.235	.235	.294
	Hudson Vall	TB	A-	20	50	200	55	14	1	1	74	24	27	15	0	44	3	0	1	1	3	.25	5	.275	.333	.370
Ashley,Steve	Eugene	Atl	A-	24	4	15	4	1	0	0	5	3	0	2	0	3	0	0	0	0	0	.00	1	.267	.353	.333
	Danville	Atl	R+	24	26	74	12	2	0	1	17	7	5	5	0	15	1	1	0	1	0	1.00	4	.162	.225	.230
August,Brian	Yankees	NYA	R	22	17	47	13	2	2	3	28	8	7	5	0	7	0	0	0	0	1	.00	0	.277	.346	.596
	Tampa	NYA	A+	22	23	67	14	4	0	1	21	5	11	5	0	14	0	1	2	0	2	.00	0	.209	.257	.313
Austin,Peter	Erie	Pit	A-	23	5	13	2	0	0	0	2	1	1	1	0	4	2	0	0	0	0	.00	0	.154	.313	.154
	Pirates	Pit	R	23	17	53	13	2	0	0	15	3	6	4	0	10	0	0	1	2	3	.40	3	.245	.293	.283
Auterson,Jeffrey	Great Falls	LA	R+	20	60	156	27	8	1	3	46	28	17	21	0	58	4	3	0	6	6	.50	3	.173	.287	.295
Aversa,Joe	Kane County	Fla	A	30	63	203	41	3	2	0	48	17	17	30	1	58	1	6	3	3	1	.75	1	.202	.304	.236
Avila,Rolo	San Berndno	LA	A+	24	134	507	147	25	3	6	196	94	47	63	4	63	5	7	7	52	24	.68	7	.290	.369	.387
Aybar,Ramon	Jamestown	Det	A-	22	40	125	25	0	0	0	25	20	13	13	2	32	3	3	1	5	2	.71	3	.200	.289	.200
Aylor,Brian	Greensboro	NYA	A	24	61	181	29	7	4	9	71	25	28	16	0	90	0	0	4	3	0	1.00	2	.160	.224	.392
Ayuso,Julio	Elizabethtn	Min	R+	21	39	107	24	8	0	1	35	13	12	17	0	39	1	0	0	0	1	.00	0	.224	.336	.327
Baderdeen,Kevin	Burlington	Cin	A	21	39	127	28	3	0	3	40	18	8	14	0	61	2	2	0	3	1	.75	0	.220	.308	.315
Baez,Juan	Ogden	Mil	R+	20	52	128	37	7	0	3	53	19	21	15	0	45	1	0	1	2	2	.50	2	.289	.366	.414
Baeza,Art	Salem-Keizr	SF	A-	24	6	16	5	1	0	2	12	5	5	2	0	3	1	0	0	0	0	.00	1	.313	.421	.750
	Bakersfield	SF	A+	24	86	310	80	18	3	16	152	51	60	18	0	73	3	3	0	2	3	.40	8	.258	.305	.490
Bagley,Lorenzo	St. Cathrns	Tor	A-	22	58	197	52	10	1	5	79	25	21	12	0	55	2	0	1	3	4	.43	5	.264	.311	.401
Bagley,Sean	Vermont	Mon	A-	22	39	121	22	2	0	1	27	17	9	9	0	36	2	0	1	7	3	.70	3	.182	.248	.223
Bailey,Jeff	Marlins	Fla	R	19	4	7	1	0	0	0	1	0	0	0	0	2	0	0	0	0	0	.00	1	.143	.143	.143
Bain,Tyler	Chston-SC	TB	A	23	118	429	104	17	2	3	134	56	42	66	4	79	3	5	1	33	19	.63	2	.242	.347	.312
Bair,Rod	Salem	Col	A+	23	16	41	9	3	0	1	15	5	6	0	0	6	2	3	1	2	0	1.00	1	.273	.298	.341
	Asheville	Col	A	23	91	356	100	20	1	8	146	50	51	13	1	51	11	3	1	9	6	.60	11	.281	.325	.410
Baker,Derek	Rangers	Tex	R	22	12	44	16	4	0	2	26	7	7	2	0	10	1	0	0	0	1	.00	1	.364	.404	.591
	Charlotte	Tex	A+	22	8	32	11	1	0	1	15	2	5	1	0	7	0	0	0	0	0	.00	0	.344	.364	.469
Baksh,Ray	Greensboro	NYA	A	23	6	6	1	0	0	0	1	1	2	0	0	2	0	0	0	0	0	.00	0	.167	.167	.167
Balbuena,Micha.	Great Falls	LA	R+	19	18	53	8	1	0	0	9	5	4	2	0	3	0	0	0	1	1	.50	2	.151	.182	.170
	Yakima	LA	A-	19	15	48	10	1	1	0	13	2	4	3	0	15	1	0	0	1	0	1.00	0	.208	.269	.271
Balfe,Ryan	Tigers	Det	R	22	2	7	4	0	1	0	7	2	1	1	0	1	0	0	0	0	0	.00	0	.571	.625	1.000
	Lakeland	Det	A+	22	86	312	84	13	2	13	140	40	48	24	3	75	3	1	6	1	1	.50	7	.269	.322	.449
Baltzell,Beau	High Desert	Ari	A+	22	8	20	2	0	0	1	5	3	4	3	0	10	0	0	0	0	0	.00	3	.100	.217	.250
Banks,Tony	Williamsprt	ChN	A-	26	37	116	30	11	3	2	53	21	11	27	1	23	0	0	0	4	1	.80	2	.259	.399	.457
Barajas,Rodrigo	High Desert	Ari	A+	22	57	199	53	11	0	7	85	24	30	8	0	41	1	0	1	0	2	.00	7	.266	.297	.427
Barlok,Todd	San Berndno	LA	A+	26	44	116	35	6	3	5	62	25	19	17	0	32	3	0	2	7	5	.58	2	.302	.399	.534
	Lk Elsinore	Ana	A+	26	49	170	36	5	4	1	52	21	15	17	0	51	7	2	2	10	4	.71	2	.212	.306	.306
Barner,Doug	Chston-SC	TB	A	23	93	302	67	17	1	7	107	35	40	43	0	87	7	1	2	1	3	.25	4	.222	.331	.354
Barnes,John	Michigan	Bos	A	22	130	490	149	19	5	6	196	80	73	65	3	42	5	0	6	19	5	.79	7	.304	.387	.400
Barnes,Kelvin	Daytona	ChN	A+	23	123	433	113	26	7	4	165	64	51	25	1	82	2	2	1	22	8	.73	12	.261	.304	.381
Barnes,Larry	Lk Elsinore	Ana	A+	23	115	446	128	32	2	13	203	68	71	43	4	84	5	1	5	3	4	.43	4	.287	.353	.455
Barnett,Brian	St. Cathrns	Tor	A-	22	45	122	28	9	1	0	39	18	8	22	0	36	0	0	0	3	3	.50	0	.230	.347	.320
Barr,Tucker	Quad City	Hou	A	23	93	309	64	10	1	10	106	42	36	39	0	91	4	0	1	2	0	.00	4	.207	.303	.343
Barrett,Andrew	Medcine Hat	Tor	R+	18	43	103	24	3	0	2	33	4	14	6	0	30	1	0	1	1	1	.50	1	.233	.282	.262
Barrett,Michael	Wst Plm Bch	Mon	A+	21	119	423	120	30	0	8	174	52	61	36	1	49	5	2	10	7	4	.64	11	.284	.340	.411
Basabe,Jesus	Athletics	Oak	R	21	55	201	63	11	4	11	115	51	43	40	0	76	7	1	1	6	2	.75	1	.313	.442	.572
Bass,Jayson	Lakeland	Det	A+	24	108	376	97	18	4	13	162	58	53	41	5	130	2	0	4	17	7	.71	4	.258	.331	.431
Bass,Jayson	Durham	Atl	A+	22	75	277	71	20	4	4	111	48	34	29	1	57	2	2	0	4	2	.67	6	.256	.331	.401
Baston,Stanley	Hagerstown	Tor	A	21	19	66	14	2	1	0	18	8	9	8	0	17	1	1	0	3	1	.75	0	.212	.299	.273
	St. Cathrns	Tor	A-	21	44	137	22	2	0	0	24	10	14	11	0	32	1	1	4	1	3	.25	1	.161	.222	.175
Batista,Angel	Devil Rays	TB	R	18	37	117	24	4	0	0	28	14	11	9	0	35	0	1	0	2	2	.50	1	.205	.262	.239
Battle,Rohn	Butte	Ana	R+	23	2	8	2	0	0	0	2	4	1	0	0	4	0	0	0	0	0	.00	0	.250	.250	.500
Batts,Rodney	Piedmont	Phi	A	24	24	67	15	3	1	1	23	8	7	11	0	19	0	1	1	1	1	.50	0	.224	.329	.343
Baugh,Darren	Winston-Sal	ChA	A+	22	101	325	73	11	4	3	101	41	22	22	0	100	2	9	2	13	3	.81	4	.225	.287	.311
Baughman,Justin	Lk Elsinore	Ana	A+	22	134	478	131	14	3	2	157	71	48	40	3	79	13	11	5	68	15	.82	5	.274	.343	.328
Bautista,Francis.	Spokane	KC	A-	22	26	36	10	3	1	0	15	11	2	5	0	14	0	0	2	4	1	.80	1	.278	.366	.417
Bautista,Jorge	Kane County	Fla	A	21	20	67	10	3	0	0	13	9	7	5	0	18	1	1	2	2	2	.50	2	.149	.213	.194
	Brevard Cty	Fla	A+	21	10	15	0	0	0	0	0	1	0	1	0	7	1	0	2	0	0	.00	0	.000	.118	.000
	Utica	Fla	A-	21	58	201	49	10	1	3	70	19	27	25	1	55	1	2	0	5	3	.63	3	.244	.328	.348
Bautista,Jose	Twins	Min	R	19	14	28	3	0	0	0	3	2	0	8	0	9	0	0	0	2	2	.50	0	.107	.306	.107
Bautista,Juan	South Bend	Ari	A	19	32	92	12	1	1	0	15	12	4	6	0	32	3	1	0	1	0	1.00	1	.130	.208	.163
	Lethbridge	Ari	R+	19	43	136	28	3	1	1	36	23	14	12	0	35	4	2	2	4	1	.80	4	.206	.286	.265
Bautista,Rayner	Tigers	Det	R	18	43	164	49	11	2	1	67	33	17	11	0	33	1	3	0	7	1	.88	2	.299	.347	.409
	Lakeland	Det	A+	18	6	12	2	0	0	0	2	1	0	0	0	1	0	0	0	0	0	.00	1	.167	.167	.167
Bazzani,Matt	Sarasota	Bos	A+	24	58	169	33	5	0	6	56	21	18	11	0	51	8	5	2	4	2	.67	0	.195	.274	.331
Bearden,Doug	Beloit	Mil	A	22	48	163	36	3	1	0	41	15	14	2	0	37	3	4	0	1	1	.50	4	.221	.244	.252
Beatriz,Ramy	Helena	Mil	R+	19	55	187	50	12	3	4	80	35	27	24	1	43	3	1	2	9	7	.56	4	.267	.356	.428
Becker,Brian	Chston-SC	TB	A	23	135	494	116	31	2	11	184	55	70	53	3	120	4	0	9	12	1	.92	12	.235	.309	.372
Bejarano,Brian	Medcine Hat	Tor	R+	23	53	193	56	8	0	6	82	26	29	18	0	38	0	0	0	1	3	.25	2	.290	.351	.425
Bell,Rick	Yakima	LA	A-	19	66	264	68	15	1	2	91	42	24	15	0	52	4	3	3	9	0	1.00	7	.258	.304	.345
Bellenger,Butch	Augusta	Pit	A	24	4	12	2	1	0	0	3	1	0	1	0	4	0	0	0	0	0	.00	0	.167	.231	.250

1997 Batting — Single-A and Rookie Leagues

Player	Team	Org	Lg	A	G	AB	H	2B	3B	HR	TB	R	RBI	TBB	IBB	SO	HBP	SH	SF	SB	CS	SB%	GDP	Avg	OBP	SLG
Bello,Jilberto	Orioles	Bal	R	21	33	102	25	5	1	0	32	8	14	8	1	29	0	0	0	2	2	.50	0	.245	.300	.314
	Frederick	Bal	A+	21	2	7	2	1	0	0	3	0	1	1	0	2	0	0	0	0	0	.00	0	.286	.375	.429
Beltran,Carlos	Wilmington	KC	A+	21	120	419	96	15	4	11	152	57	46	46	3	96	4	3	1	17	7	.71	10	.229	.311	.363
Beltre,Adrian	Vero Beach	LA	A+	20	123	435	138	24	2	26	244	95	104	67	12	66	6	0	11	25	9	.74	9	.317	.407	.561
Beltres,Manuel	Yankees	NYA	R	20	29	103	23	1	0	0	24	13	11	13	0	27	1	5	0	9	4	.69	1	.223	.316	.233
Benavidez,Eric	Princeton	TB	R+	22	52	206	64	12	4	0	84	50	27	11	0	25	8	3	1	14	5	.74	5	.311	.367	.408
Bender,Heath	Watertown	Cle	A-	23	62	186	43	6	0	2	55	19	20	10	1	38	8	1	1	1	1	.50	2	.231	.298	.296
Benefield,Brian	Watertown	Cle	A-	21	69	265	76	9	1	4	99	47	19	49	3	40	1	2	1	23	7	.77	3	.287	.399	.374
Benes,Richard	Royals	KC	R	20	34	39	8	0	1	0	10	15	1	3	0	11	0	0	0	3	1	.75	0	.205	.262	.256
Benjamin,Al	Pirates	Pit	R	20	39	152	49	14	2	2	73	18	21	4	0	26	1	1	2	7	1	.88	3	.322	.340	.480
	Augusta	Pit	A	20	5	14	2	0	0	0	2	2	1	0	0	3	0	1	0	1	0	1.00	0	.143	.143	.143
Bennett,Ryan	St. Lucie	NYN	A+	23	2	2	0	0	0	0	0	0	0	0	0	0	0	0	0	0	0	.00	0	.000	.000	.000
	Capital City	NYN	A	23	19	42	8	1	0	0	9	6	3	5	0	15	0	0	0	0	0	.00	1	.190	.277	.214
Bentley,Kevin	Daytona	ChN	A+	23	26	79	18	2	1	2	28	12	14	8	0	26	1	0	1	1	2	.33	1	.228	.303	.354
Berger,Brandon	Lansing	KC	A	23	107	393	115	22	6	12	185	64	73	42	1	79	7	0	4	13	1	.93	8	.293	.368	.471
Berger,Matt	Bristol	ChA	R+	23	66	232	67	11	1	18	134	51	56	40	1	72	3	0	4	1	0	1.00	7	.289	.394	.578
Bergeron,Peter	Savannah	LA	A	20	131	492	138	18	5	5	181	89	36	67	3	110	2	5	3	32	21	.60	5	.280	.367	.368
	San Berndno	LA	A+	20	2	8	2	0	0	0	2	1	1	0	0	2	0	0	0	2	0	1.00	0	.250	.250	.250
Berkman,Lance	Kissimmee	Hou	A+	22	53	184	54	10	0	12	100	31	35	37	4	38	2	0	0	2	1	.67	2	.293	.417	.543
Bernhardt,Jose	Medicne Hat	Tor	R+	17	60	199	35	2	0	1	40	20	13	8	0	55	1	5	1	3	2	.60	4	.176	.211	.201
Bernhardt,Thom.	Cubs	ChN	A-	23	8	30	8	3	1	0	13	11	5	6	0	6	0	0	0	2	1	.67	0	.267	.410	.433
	Williamsprt	ChN	A-	23	38	122	25	3	4	1	39	8	8	10	1	39	0	1	1	2	1	.67	3	.205	.263	.320
Berns,Robert	Princeton	TB	R+	23	64	245	80	34	1	9	143	53	61	34	0	44	5	0	3	2	4	.33	1	.327	.415	.584
Betances,Junior	Kinston	Cle	A+	23	74	230	64	10	2	4	90	34	26	24	0	34	3	3	3	8	4	.67	5	.278	.350	.391
Betancourt,Oscar	Boise	Ana	A-	22	68	266	76	16	1	9	121	47	46	30	0	70	3	1	1	2	2	.50	8	.286	.363	.455
Betemit,Wilson	Braves	Atl	R	17	32	113	24	6	1	0	32	12	15	9	0	32	0	0	0	0	0	.00	0	.212	.270	.283
Bethea,Larry	Orioles	Bal	R	21	36	116	19	3	2	0	26	6	15	11	0	32	4	0	0	2	1	.67	6	.164	.260	.224
Beverly,Shomari	Martinsvlle	Phi	R+	20	34	125	32	5	0	2	43	13	13	5	0	37	1	0	0	9	5	.64	2	.256	.290	.344
Bevins,Andy	New Jersey	StL	A-	22	65	235	64	9	5	9	110	35	44	18	1	66	3	0	3	2	1	.67	3	.272	.328	.468
Bishop,Tim	Capital City	NYN	A	*	14	49	10	2	0	0	12	4	2	6	0	16	1	1	0	1	0	.78	0	.204	.304	.245
Blake,William	Dunedin	Tor	A+	24	129	449	107	21	0	7	149	56	39	48	2	91	6	2	2	19	9	.68	5	.238	.319	.332
Blakeney,Mo	Cape Fear	Mon	A-	25	17	49	13	1	0	4	26	10	7	3	0	12	0	0	0	3	1	.75	2	.265	.308	.531
	Vermont	Mon	A-	25	32	116	33	3	2	3	49	9	11	8	1	25	2	1	1	4	4	.50	2	.284	.339	.422
Blanco,Dany	San Jose	SF	A+	22	33	73	12	2	1	0	16	8	4	4	0	25	0	0	0	0	0	.00	2	.164	.208	.219
Blandford,Paul	Cape Fear	Mon	A-	24	113	398	115	23	4	5	161	63	40	40	1	50	2	4	3	20	13	.61	11	.289	.354	.405
Blosser,Doug	Lansing	KC	A-	21	38	103	22	3	0	3	34	13	17	20	3	29	0	1	4	0	0	.00	2	.214	.331	.330
	Spokane	KC	A-	21	65	213	63	14	1	12	115	43	50	47	2	61	1	0	3	2	1	.67	5	.296	.420	.540
Bly,Derrick	Rockford	ChA	A-	23	109	392	95	19	5	8	148	48	43	35	0	131	6	2	2	6	3	.67	7	.242	.313	.378
	Williamsprt	ChN	A-	23	13	47	7	2	0	0	9	2	3	5	0	20	1	0	0	0	0	.00	0	.149	.245	.191
Bolivar,Papo	Ft. Wayne	Min	A	19	91	324	85	12	6	7	130	30	42	11	0	82	3	2	3	18	9	.67	7	.262	.290	.401
Bonilla,Elin	Martinsvlle	Phi	R+	20	36	121	25	4	2	2	39	16	20	6	0	46	0	2	0	1	1	.50	0	.207	.244	.322
Boone,Matthew	Tigers	Det	R	18	48	152	31	11	0	0	42	13	15	13	0	37	3	0	2	2	1	.67	7	.204	.276	.276
Borges,Alex	Macon	Atl	A	23	39	118	23	2	0	3	34	14	14	8	0	45	2	4	0	1	0	1.00	3	.195	.258	.288
Borges,Elio	White Sox	ChA	R	20	28	80	23	6	1	0	31	9	15	12	0	14	1	1	2	4	0	1.00	1	.288	.379	.388
Borrego,Ramon	Elizabethtn	Min	R+	20	55	211	59	12	0	4	83	43	34	26	0	44	4	5	2	7	5	.58	3	.280	.366	.393
Boscan,Jean	Braves	Atl	R	18	36	104	21	5	0	1	29	7	12	16	0	21	2	0	1	0	0	.00	2	.202	.317	.279
Bosch,Bryon	Burlington	Cle	R+	20	13	30	2	1	0	0	3	1	0	1	0	17	0	0	0	0	0	.00	2	.067	.097	.100
Boughton,Micha.	High Desert	Ari	A+	23	20	45	8	3	1	0	13	6	2	2	0	11	0	0	0	1	0	1.00	0	.178	.213	.289
	South Bend	Ari	A	23	15	51	5	2	0	0	7	2	2	4	0	11	0	0	0	0	0	.00	0	.098	.164	.137
	Diamondback	Ari	R	23	15	0	0	0	0	0	0	0	0	0	0	0	0	0	0	0	0	.00	0	.000	.000	.000
Boulware,Ben	Winston-Sal	ChA	A+	26	43	176	45	12	3	2	70	24	16	7	0	29	5	0	1	9	8	.53	2	.256	.302	.398
Bovender,Andy	Kissimmee	Hou	A+	25	52	177	38	8	1	3	57	16	16	16	0	56	2	0	0	3	0	1.00	3	.215	.287	.322
	Quad City	Hou	A	25	15	55	12	3	0	1	18	10	8	2	0	15	1	0	2	1	0	1.00	0	.218	.250	.327
Bowers,R.J.	Kissimmee	Hou	A+	24	10	34	7	1	0	0	8	3	3	5	0	7	0	0	1	0	0	.00	2	.206	.300	.235
Bowles,Justin	Modesto	Oak	A+	24	107	394	129	39	9	7	207	66	51	56	2	85	5	5	5	6	3	.67	3	.327	.413	.525
Bowring,Jason	Kingsport	NYN	R+	21	61	218	54	10	1	6	84	32	35	12	0	43	4	0	1	8	3	.73	3	.248	.298	.385
Boyette,Tony	Burlington	Cin	A	22	4	11	3	0	1	0	6	1	4	1	0	4	0	0	2	0	0	.00	0	.273	.286	.545
Bradley,Milton	Vermont	Mon	A-	20	50	200	60	7	5	3	86	29	30	17	1	34	0	1	2	7	7	.50	6	.300	.352	.430
	Expos	Mon	R	20	9	25	5	2	0	1	10	6	2	4	0	4	1	0	0	2	2	.50	0	.200	.333	.400
Brambilla,Micha.	Spokane	KC	A-	22	36	115	26	5	1	4	45	16	21	12	0	34	3	1	1	1	2	.33	2	.226	.313	.391
Bramlett,Jeff	Savannah	LA	A	22	102	326	61	11	6	14	126	49	42	49	1	122	12	0	3	2	1	.67	7	.187	.313	.387
Braughler,Matt	Brevard Cty	Fla	A+	25	26	75	18	2	0	1	23	5	10	6	0	17	1	0	1	0	0	.00	2	.240	.301	.307
Bravo,Danny	Wst Plm Bch	Mon	A+	21	15	37	6	1	1	0	9	3	0	2	0	5	0	0	0	0	0	.00	1	.162	.205	.243
	Cape Fear	Mon	A-	21	73	253	68	9	1	3	88	28	34	9	0	31	4	3	3	3	4	.43	4	.269	.301	.348
Brett,Jason	Kingsport	NYN	R+	21	49	170	46	3	1	3	55	25	18	20	0	42	0	6	1	6	2	.75	2	.271	.347	.324
Brewer,Brad	Butte	Ana	R+	22	19	67	16	2	0	0	18	14	8	14	0	17	2	0	2	4	0	.00	2	.239	.361	.269
Brignac,Junior	Danville	Atl	R+	20	30	225	55	10	0	4	77	47	25	29	0	70	7	1	4	2	0	.75	2	.244	.349	.342
Brito,Alen	Royals	KC	R	21	11	24	6	0	0	0	6	3	3	1	0	7	0	0	0	1	0	1.00	0	.250	.269	.250
Brito,Juan	Royals	KC	R	18	25	70	22	4	0	3	35	14	15	5	1	15	1	1	0	0	0	.00	0	.314	.368	.500
Britt,Bryan	Peoria	StL	A	23	123	413	93	23	1	16	166	58	59	39	3	104	8	0	4	5	3	.63	9	.225	.302	.402
Brock,Tarrik	Lancaster	Sea	A+	24	132	402	108	21	12	7	174	88	47	78	1	106	6	6	0	40	8	.83	7	.269	.395	.433
Bronikowski,Willi.	Oneonta	NYA	A-	23	1	2	0	0	0	0	0	0	0	0	0	2	0	0	0	0	0	.00	0	.000	.000	.000
Bronson,Ben	Wilmington	KC	A+	25	34	57	10	3	0	0	13	9	4	11	1	17	3	3	1	2	2	.50	0	.175	.333	.228
Brooks,Ali	Erie	Pit	A-	22	6	11	0	0	0	0	0	2	0	2	0	1	0	0	0	1	0	1.00	1	.000	.154	.000
Brooks,Anthony	Danville	Atl	R+	21	67	229	62	12	1	4	88	43	24	8	0	59	5	3	3	15	5	.75	5	.271	.306	.384
Brooks,Eddie	St. Lucie	NYN	A+	25	41	119	23	3	0	2	32	12	9	10	1	39	2	1	1	1	3	.25	3	.193	.265	.269
Brooks,Jeffrey	Diamondback	Ari	R	18	54	204	46	9	0	0	55	22	27	12	0	50	4	3	1	3	1	.75	5	.225	.281	.270

* Tim Bishop died 4/18/97

1997 Batting — Single-A and Rookie Leagues

					BATTING															BASERUNNING				PERCENTAGES		
Player	Team	Org	Lg	A	G	AB	H	2B	3B	HR	TB	R	RBI	TBB	IBB	SO	HBP	SH	SF	SB	CS	SB%	GDP	Avg	OBP	SLG
Brosam,Eric	Twins	Min	R	20	44	141	34	3	2	0	41	13	9	14	0	31	3	1	1	3	0	1.00	0	.241	.321	.291
Brown,Dermal	Spokane	KC	A-	20	73	298	97	20	6	13	168	67	73	38	5	65	2	0	1	17	4	.81	5	.326	.404	.564
Brown,Eric	Savannah	LA	A	21	61	211	51	10	3	7	88	26	22	17	0	74	1	0	3	12	1	.92	3	.242	.297	.417
Brown,Gavin	Macon	Atl	A	23	66	227	53	7	2	3	73	27	25	30	0	40	3	0	2	8	4	.67	11	.233	.328	.322
Brown,Jason	Yakima	LA	A-	24	18	59	12	0	0	1	15	6	5	6	0	13	4	1	0	0	0	.00	0	.203	.319	.254
	San Berndno	LA	A+	24	30	102	26	10	0	0	36	15	13	3	0	26	4	3	2	0	3	.00	2	.255	.297	.353
Brown,Kent	Idaho Falls	SD	R+	24	36	126	34	4	0	0	38	22	19	22	0	29	1	0	0	10	7	.59	1	.270	.383	.302
Brown,Nate	Wst Plm Bch	Mon	A+	27	15	40	9	1	0	1	13	7	5	3	2	16	1	0	0	2	0	1.00	0	.225	.295	.325
Brown,Richard	Yankees	NYA	R	21	10	30	11	3	0	0	14	7	3	5	0	6	0	0	1	0	0	.00	2	.367	.444	.467
Brown,Bobby	Spokane	KC	A-	24	14	17	1	0	0	0	1	1	1	2	0	9	0	0	0	0	0	.00	0	.059	.158	.059
Brown,Roosevelt	Kane County	Fla	A	22	61	211	50	7	1	4	71	29	30	22	2	52	1	0	0	5	4	.56	5	.237	.312	.336
	Brevard Cty	Fla	A+	22	33	114	28	7	1	1	40	8	12	7	0	31	0	1	1	0	3	.00	4	.246	.287	.351
Brown,Vick	Tampa	NYA	A+	25	123	463	135	19	4	2	168	77	42	38	0	78	11	6	5	55	13	.81	6	.292	.356	.363
Brown,Billy	Medcne Hat	Tor	R+	22	70	272	78	16	4	8	126	63	39	36	1	66	0	1	3	22	4	.85	2	.287	.367	.463
Bruce,Maurice	Kingsport	NYN	R+	23	34	128	47	8	3	3	70	35	21	16	0	20	2	0	0	14	4	.78	1	.367	.445	.547
	Pittsfield	NYN	A-	23	29	115	40	7	3	4	65	26	14	11	0	23	2	0	0	12	2	.86	4	.348	.408	.565
Bruce,Robert	Columbus	Cle	A	23	69	234	58	8	1	11	101	42	36	33	0	69	10	3	1	6	0	1.00	5	.248	.363	.432
Brumbaugh,Cliff	Charlotte	Tex	A+	25	139	522	136	27	4	15	216	78	70	47	2	99	6	0	4	13	11	.54	7	.261	.326	.414
Bryant,Chris	Frederick	Bal	A+	25	91	317	87	17	1	7	127	53	36	47	2	65	4	3	1	6	3	.67	1	.274	.374	.401
Bryant,Clint	Salem	Col	A+	24	52	185	42	9	0	2	57	15	18	14	0	36	2	2	0	4	4	.50	2	.227	.289	.308
	Asheville	Col	A	24	63	220	59	12	0	2	77	30	25	19	0	62	5	4	3	9	3	.75	0	.268	.336	.350
Buccheri,Jim	St. Pete	TB	A+	29	58	204	50	9	0	0	59	29	13	27	0	20	1	3	3	25	7	.78	2	.245	.332	.289
Buchman,Tom	Ft. Wayne	Min	A	23	13	42	6	1	0	0	7	7	5	4	0	14	0	0	1	0	0	.00	0	.143	.213	.167
Budzinski,Mark	Kinston	Cle	A+	24	68	241	69	13	3	7	109	43	39	48	1	61	1	2	0	6	4	.60	3	.286	.407	.452
Buhner,Shawn	Lancaster	Sea	A+	25	111	397	102	22	1	11	159	66	53	49	3	126	7	0	3	4	1	.80	5	.257	.346	.401
Bunkley,Antuan	Helena	Mil	R+	22	70	270	103	23	0	17	177	52	67	32	5	37	4	0	3	2	4	.33	9	.381	.450	.656
Burford,Kevin	Padres	SD	R	20	47	167	65	15	2	4	96	42	50	49	1	25	4	0	5	12	5	.71	3	.389	.524	.575
	Idaho Falls	SD	R+	20	7	29	6	0	1	1	11	2	3	1	0	5	0	0	0	0	0	.00	0	.207	.233	.379
Burke,Mark	Braves	Atl	R	23	9	30	13	3	0	3	25	9	7	4	0	2	0	0	0	1	0	1.00	2	.433	.500	.833
	Eugene	Atl	A-	23	62	236	72	17	0	7	110	37	45	36	3	41	5	1	2	1	1	.50	4	.305	.405	.466
Burkhart,Lance	Vermont	Mon	A-	23	38	143	24	6	1	0	32	15	12	17	0	40	1	0	0	3	3	.50	3	.168	.261	.224
Burnham,Gary	Batavia	Phi	A-	23	73	289	94	22	4	5	139	44	45	30	0	47	5	1	3	1	1	.75	8	.325	.396	.481
Burns,Kevin	Quad City	Hou	A	22	131	477	129	28	1	20	219	72	86	53	8	114	6	0	4	1	2	.33	12	.270	.348	.459
Burns,Patrick	Kingsport	NYN	R+	20	60	224	55	11	3	0	72	32	30	17	1	67	1	5	1	7	4	.64	2	.246	.300	.321
Burns,Xavier	Erie	Pit	A-	21	63	226	62	13	2	7	100	33	27	18	0	62	6	0	1	4	4	.50	5	.274	.343	.442
Burress,Andy	Chston-WV	Cin	A	20	38	87	18	0	0	2	24	12	14	4	0	26	0	0	2	1	0	1.00	3	.207	.237	.276
	Billings	Cin	R+	20	27	102	31	7	0	5	53	13	18	6	0	20	0	0	1	5	1	.50	4	.304	.343	.520
Burrows,Mike	Wisconsin	Sea	A	22	102	389	97	24	8	12	173	55	54	21	3	91	6	1	2	17	14	.55	8	.249	.297	.445
Bushman,Jonath.	Martinsville	Phi	R+	19	12	19	4	1	0	0	5	3	0	0	0	8	0	0	0	0	0	.00	0	.211	.211	.263
Bustos,Saul	Wst Plm Bch	Mon	A+	25	39	106	28	5	1	0	35	10	12	6	0	23	0	2	1	1	3	.25	2	.264	.301	.330
Butler,Allen	Oneonta	NYA	A-	22	68	214	60	11	4	3	88	40	30	46	2	57	3	2	2	4	3	.57	4	.280	.411	.411
Butler,Garrett	Greensboro	NYA	A	22	82	237	46	14	1	1	65	31	14	11	0	58	4	4	1	11	5	.69	4	.194	.241	.274
Butler,Brent	Peoria	StL	A	20	129	480	147	37	2	15	233	81	71	63	6	69	4	0	5	6	4	.60	9	.306	.388	.485
Byas,Michael	Salem-Keizr	SF	A-	21	71	290	80	9	1	0	91	68	16	48	0	44	2	1	0	51	9	.85	4	.276	.382	.314
Byers,MacGregor	Visalia	Oak	A+	23	18	53	12	5	1	0	19	8	9	6	0	15	0	0	0	2	1	.67	1	.226	.305	.358
Byrd,Tony	Wst Plm Bch	Mon	A+	27	6	18	2	0	0	0	2	2	1	4	0	5	0	0	0	1	0	1.00	0	.111	.273	.111
Byrd,Brandon	Astros	Hou	R	20	45	146	28	5	0	5	48	12	18	14	0	49	2	0	2	2	2	.50	2	.192	.268	.329
Bystrowski,Robb.	Astros	Hou	R	21	51	177	40	8	0	3	57	28	22	22	0	47	6	0	1	5	6	.45	4	.226	.330	.322
Caceres,Wilmy	Billings	Cin	R+	19	15	38	10	2	0	0	12	10	9	2	0	3	1	0	0	1	1	.50	0	.263	.317	.316
Caiazzo,Nicholas	Helena	Mil	R+	23	63	234	63	15	1	3	89	31	37	16	1	34	4	0	2	2	0	1.00	5	.269	.324	.380
Caines,Franklyn	Martinsville	Phi	R+	21	53	197	54	17	0	4	78	26	30	17	0	58	1	0	0	6	0	1.00	3	.274	.335	.396
Calderon,Henry	Royals	KC	R	20	43	139	34	5	3	1	48	17	15	10	0	31	2	2	1	3	1	.75	3	.245	.301	.345
Calloway,Ronald	Lethbridge	Ari	R+	21	43	148	37	5	0	0	42	23	9	14	0	29	3	0	2	5	8	.38	4	.250	.323	.284
	South Bend	Ari	A	21	9	25	7	1	0	0	8	3	1	2	0	8	0	0	0	1	0	1.00	1	.280	.333	.320
Cameron,Ken	Peoria	StL	A	22	105	323	84	20	4	2	118	51	27	35	1	50	5	6	3	21	8	.72	6	.260	.339	.365
Cameron,Stanton	High Desert	Ari	A+	28	139	514	154	31	3	33	290	103	113	93	1	127	7	0	9	1	0	1.00	13	.300	.408	.564
Cameron,Troy	Danville	Atl	R+	19	56	208	45	5	2	6	72	28	24	25	1	80	3	0	0	1	3	.25	3	.216	.309	.346
Camilli,Jason	Cape Fear	Mon	A	22	98	396	118	35	2	3	166	57	43	31	0	64	5	7	2	22	11	.67	7	.298	.355	.419
	Wst Plm Bch	Mon	A+	22	15	47	6	3	0	0	9	1	1	2	0	12	0	1	0	0	0	.00	1	.128	.163	.191
Camilo,Jose	Brevard Cty	Fla	A+	21	107	371	87	12	2	8	127	53	51	46	3	62	1	1	6	20	9	.69	5	.235	.316	.342
Camilo,Juan	Athletics	Oak	R	20	50	191	66	11	5	8	111	48	47	41	0	41	2	0	0	12	2	.86	6	.346	.466	.581
	Sou. Oregon	Oak	A-	20	4	13	3	0	0	0	3	2	1	0		4	0	0	0	0	0	.00	0	.231	.286	.231
Campbell,Wylie	Chston-WV	Cin	A	23	121	453	123	18	4	0	149	73	36	41	0	80	8	10	3	34	12	.74	7	.272	.341	.329
Campusano,Carl.	Bakersfield	SF	A+	22	61	191	38	8	3	1	55	17	15	7	0	49	4	3	2	2	0	1.00	6	.199	.240	.288
Canaguacan,Os.	Yankees	NYA	R	18	7	16	5	1	0	0	6	3	2	2	0	3	0	0	0	1	0	1.00	0	.313	.389	.375
Cancel,Robinson	Beloit	Mil	A	22	17	50	15	3	0	0	18	9	4	7	0	9	3	0	0	0	2	.00	0	.300	.417	.360
	Stockton	Mil	A+	22	63	211	59	11	0	1	73	25	16	13	0	40	2	7	1	9	3	.75	6	.280	.326	.346
Candela,Frank	Ogden	Mil	R+	19	25	75	20	0	1	1	25	9	10	4	0	17	1	2	0	3	1	.75	1	.267	.313	.333
Candelaria,Vidal	Yankees	NYA	R	20	25	114	30	3	0	0	33	12	16	8	0	28	2	2	3	3	0	1.00	4	.263	.317	.289
Capellan,Rene	W Michigan	Det	A	20	100	383	110	26	4	4	156	61	48	25	0	60	11	4	1	9	11	.44	13	.287	.348	.407
Capista,Aaron	Red Sox	Bos	R	19	36	134	32	6	1	0	40	16	14	16	1	17	0	0	2	6	2	.75	3	.239	.316	.299
Caracciolo,Anth.	Expos	Mon	R	18	40	156	31	4	0	1	38	17	10	14	0	35	0	2	0	16	9	.64	0	.199	.265	.244
Caradonna,Brett	White Sox	ChA	R	19	36	123	34	5	3	2	51	15	16	11	1	21	1	0	0	3	2	.60	3	.276	.333	.415
	Bristol	ChA	R	19	28	80	25	3	0	1	31	16	12	13	1	16	1	0	0	2	2	.60	3	.313	.415	.388
Cardona,Javier	Lakeland	Det	A+	22	85	284	82	15	0	7	118	28	38	25	1	51	1	2	2	1	3	.25	8	.289	.346	.415
Cardona,Luis	Mets	NYN	R	20	2	7	1	0	0	0	1	0	0	0	0	1	0	0	0	0	0	.00	0	.143	.143	.143
Carey,Orlando	Oneonta	NYA	A-	22	71	238	59	4	4	2	77	40	17	23	1	59	1	2	2	20	6	.77	4	.248	.314	.324

1997 Batting — Single-A and Rookie Leagues

Player	Team	Org	Lg	A	G	AB	H	2B	3B	HR	TB	R	RBI	TBB	IBB	SO	HBP	SH	SF	SB	CS	SB%	GDP	Avg	OBP	SLG
Carmona,Cesarin	Clinton	SD	A	21	65	234	59	7	2	11	103	33	32	14	0	69	2	0	1	15	5	.75	4	.252	.299	.440
Carr,Dustin	Hudson Vall	TB	A-	23	74	281	81	12	2	5	112	46	47	42	2	42	2	0	3	4	2	.67	10	.288	.381	.399
Carrion,Jorge	Pulaski	Tex	R+	21	43	111	22	7	0	1	32	19	10	12	0	26	0	1	0	8	0	1.00	2	.198	.272	.288
Carroll,Doug	St. Pete	TB	A+	24	73	222	55	14	2	2	79	17	31	13	0	25	0	1	1	0	2	.00	4	.248	.288	.356
Carroll,Jamey	Wst Plm Bch	Mon	A+	23	121	407	99	19	1	0	120	56	38	43	0	48	4	8	4	17	11	.61	4	.243	.319	.295
Carroll,Mark	Mariners	Sea	R	19	36	121	37	4	0	0	41	15	26	27	0	30	6	0	1	3	1	.75	1	.306	.452	.339
Carter,Bart	Hudson Vall	TB	A-	22	10	28	6	1	0	0	7	2	2	1	0	7	3	1	0	0	0	.00	1	.214	.313	.250
	St. Pete	TB	A+	22	6	11	2	0	0	0	2	3	1	2	0	3	2	0	0	0	0	.00	0	.182	.400	.182
Carter,Quincy	Rockford	ChN	A	20	105	388	82	26	2	2	118	61	34	48	0	100	4	1	4	17	10	.63	3	.211	.302	.304
Carter,Shannon	Orioles	Bal	R	19	50	159	31	3	2	0	38	22	11	12	0	45	4	0	0	13	5	.72	1	.195	.269	.239
Caruso,Joe	Spokane	KC	A-	23	57	194	58	12	3	5	91	48	36	29	1	30	6	8	0	10	4	.71	1	.299	.406	.469
Caruso,Michael	San Jose	SF	A+	21	108	441	147	24	11	2	199	76	50	38	3	19	6	4	3	11	16	.41	3	.333	.391	.451
	Winston-Sal	ChA	A+	21	28	119	27	3	2	0	34	12	14	4	0	8	2	0	0	3	0	1.00	0	.227	.264	.286
Casillas,Uriel	Martinsville	Phi	R+	22	60	220	59	12	1	1	76	42	26	23	0	29	12	3	2	5	3	.63	6	.268	.366	.345
Casimiro,Carlos	Delmarva	Bal	A	21	122	457	111	21	8	9	175	54	51	26	1	108	5	4	2	20	13	.61	11	.243	.290	.383
Casper,Brett	Salem-Keizr	SF	A-	22	61	229	51	14	1	7	88	31	34	31	0	86	3	0	1	17	3	.85	2	.223	.322	.384
Castillo,Alex	Helena	Mil	R+	20	5	14	3	2	0	0	5	0	0	1	0	5	0	0	0	0	0	.00	0	.214	.267	.357
Castillo,Geramel	Rangers	Tex	A	20	44	139	33	2	3	2	47	20	10	4	0	33	1	0	1	11	2	.85	3	.237	.262	.338
Castillo,Miguel	Yankees	NYA	R	19	36	123	28	6	1	1	39	19	12	5	0	31	0	2	2	4	2	.67	0	.228	.254	.317
Castro,Al	Eugene	Atl	A-	18	71	226	45	8	3	1	62	20	23	24	0	56	6	4	3	7	1	.88	5	.199	.290	.274
Castro,Juan	Rockies	Col	R	23	33	129	22	4	1	3	37	13	13	5	0	42	2	2	1	3	3	.50	1	.171	.212	.287
Castro,Martires	Pulaski	Tex	R+	20	53	211	54	13	1	3	78	33	27	23	1	53	2	1	0	7	2	.78	4	.256	.335	.370
Castro,Nelson	Boise	Ana	A-	22	69	293	86	16	1	7	125	74	37	38	1	53	4	1	1	26	6	.81	1	.294	.381	.427
Castro,Ramon	Kissimmee	Hou	A+	22	115	410	115	22	1	8	163	53	65	53	3	73	2	0	11	1	0	1.00	17	.280	.357	.398
Cathey,Joseph	Auburn	Hou	A-	22	70	269	72	7	3	0	85	36	13	30	2	56	4	4	1	13	6	.68	6	.268	.349	.316
Catlett,David	Rockford	ChN	A	24	42	132	33	11	3	1	53	21	21	17	0	37	6	1	0	4	2	.67	2	.250	.361	.402
Cedeno,Jesus	W Michigan	Det	A	22	110	429	116	24	3	8	170	42	63	18	0	77	3	2	6	13	5	.72	9	.270	.300	.396
Cepeda,Jose	Wilmington	KC	A+	23	28	71	20	0	0	0	20	9	3	12	0	10	0	3	0	1	0	1.00	1	.282	.386	.282
	Lansing	KC	A	23	89	326	91	17	1	2	116	40	35	42	0	35	3	5	4	4	2	.67	10	.279	.363	.356
Cesar,Dionys	Visalia	Oak	A+	21	97	285	68	16	2	1	91	60	11	43	1	79	1	6	0	10	12	.45	5	.239	.340	.319
Cey,Dan	Ft. Myers	Min	A+	22	127	521	148	34	5	7	213	84	60	34	1	85	5	3	4	23	9	.72	11	.284	.332	.409
Chabot,Kevin	New Jersey	StL	A-	22	12	39	6	0	0	1	9	2	4	1	0	14	0	0	0	0	0	.00	0	.154	.175	.231
Chaidez,Juan	Red Sox	Bos	R	21	14	34	5	0	0	0	5	1	2	5	0	16	0	0	1	0	0	.00	0	.147	.250	.147
Chamblee,James	Michigan	Bos	A	23	133	487	146	29	5	22	251	112	73	53	3	107	17	0	5	18	4	.82	8	.300	.384	.515
Chambliss,Russ.	Oneonta	NYA	A-	23	29	53	7	1	0	0	8	4	2	4	0	24	1	0	1	4	0	1.00	1	.132	.203	.151
Chancey,Bailey	Capital City	NYN	A	23	30	85	21	0	0	0	21	12	7	13	0	19	1	4	1	5	2	.71	0	.247	.350	.247
Chapman,Scott	Kissimmee	Hou	A+	20	2	7	2	0	0	0	2	1	0	0	0	3	0	0	0	0	0	.00	0	.286	.286	.286
	Auburn	Hou	A-	20	53	205	67	11	0	6	96	32	39	6	0	23	0	0	1	1	2	.33	14	.327	.344	.468
Charles,Curtis	Orioles	Bal	R	22	6	20	5	1	0	1	9	4	3	2	0	5	0	0	0	0	0	.00	1	.250	.318	.450
	Delmarva	Bal	A	22	95	244	47	12	2	3	72	29	8	16	0	104	2	2	0	20	10	.67	0	.193	.248	.295
Chatman,Karl	Cape Fear	Mon	A	23	121	443	103	19	6	6	152	65	50	41	0	131	6	0	5	26	4	.87	9	.233	.303	.343
Chavera,Arnoldo	Quad City	Hou	A	20	80	263	69	14	1	14	127	35	44	36	3	69	1	0	5	2	0	1.00	3	.262	.348	.483
Chavez,Endy	Mets	NYN	R	20	33	119	33	6	3	0	45	26	15	20	0	10	0	0	2	1	2	.33	2	.277	.379	.378
	Kingsport	NYN	R+	20	19	73	22	4	0	0	26	16	4	13	0	10	0	2	0	5	2	.71	2	.301	.407	.356
Chavez,Eric	Visalia	Oak	A+	20	134	520	141	30	3	18	231	67	100	37	1	91	2	3	2	13	7	.65	20	.271	.321	.444
Chavez,Steven	Rancho Cuca	SD	A+	24	85	274	54	17	0	5	86	34	30	28	0	77	5	5	4	1	0	1.00	7	.197	.280	.314
Chevalier,Virgil	Sarasota	Bos	A+	24	94	289	60	13	1	6	93	31	37	19	0	43	3	2	3	8	7	.53	6	.208	.261	.322
Chiaffredo,Paul	St. Cathrns	Tor	A-	22	48	163	39	8	1	2	55	20	15	9	0	42	9	1	1	5	2	.71	1	.239	.313	.337
Chiaramonte,Giu.	San Jose	SF	A+	22	64	223	51	11	1	12	100	29	44	25	1	58	4	0	3	0	0	.00	5	.229	.314	.448
Child,Casey	Boise	Ana	A-	22	68	274	89	26	2	11	152	69	57	34	0	47	8	1	5	18	2	.90	7	.325	.408	.555
Choi,Kyung	Sarasota	Bos	A+	26	85	228	53	9	1	3	73	26	25	23	1	35	0	3	4	4	3	.57	5	.232	.298	.320
Christensen,Mc.	Hickory	ChA	A	22	127	503	141	12	12	5	192	95	47	52	0	61	11	4	6	28	20	.58	2	.280	.357	.382
Cintron,Alexand.	Diamondback	Ari	R	19	43	152	30	6	1	0	38	23	20	21	0	32	2	3	1	1	4	.20	3	.197	.301	.250
	Lethbridge	Ari	R+	19	1	3	1	0	0	0	1	0	0	0	0	1	0	0	0	0	0	.00	0	.333	.333	.333
Clapp,Stubby	Pr William	StL	A+	24	78	267	85	21	6	4	130	51	46	52	2	41	6	4	4	9	4	.69	2	.318	.435	.487
Clark,Brady	Burlington	Cin	A	25	126	459	149	29	7	11	225	108	63	76	3	71	4	1	3	31	18	.63	10	.325	.423	.490
Clark,Christopher	Erie	Pit	A-	22	28	90	23	4	0	3	36	14	12	6	0	13	2	1	0	0	0	.00	0	.256	.316	.400
Clark,Chris	Utica	Fla	A-	24	6	16	1	1	0	0	2	1	1	2	0	8	0	0	0	0	0	.00	0	.063	.167	.125
	Kane County	Fla	A	24	21	47	8	3	0	0	11	7	2	6	0	12	2	0	0	2	1	.67	0	.170	.291	.234
Clark,Jason	Hudson Vall	TB	A-	23	62	216	50	12	2	1	69	25	28	4	0	47	4	0	4	10	3	.77	5	.231	.267	.319
Clark,Jermaine	Everett	Sea	A-	21	59	199	67	13	2	3	93	42	29	34	1	31	3	3	2	22	3	.88	3	.337	.437	.467
Clark,John	Portland	Col	A-	25	17	54	11	3	1	0	16	8	3	9	0	16	0	1	0	0	0	.00	0	.204	.317	.296
Clark,Kevin	Sarasota	Bos	A+	25	3	5	3	0	0	0	3	0	1	0	0	2	1	0	0	0	0	.00	0	.600	.667	.600
	High Desert	Ari	A+	25	13	47	11	4	0	1	18	4	3	1	0	13	0	1	0	0	0	.00	0	.234	.280	.383
Clark,Kirby	Piedmont	Phi	A	22	42	143	25	8	0	0	33	18	10	10	0	50	0	1	0	0	1	.00	0	.175	.227	.231
Claybrook,Steve	Chston-WV	Cin	A	25	95	249	60	6	3	1	75	38	21	28	1	68	2	3	0	22	10	.69	4	.241	.323	.301
Cleto,Ambioris	Pirates	Pit	R	18	35	101	19	4	0	1	26	9	3	15	0	27	5	1	0	1	7	.13	1	.188	.322	.257
	Erie	Pit	A-	18	8	22	4	0	0	0	4	3	0	2	0	11	1	1	0	0	0	.00	0	.182	.308	.182
Clifford,Jim	Lancaster	Sea	A+	28	122	453	105	20	3	25	206	73	82	60	4	109	22	0	6	0	0	.00	10	.232	.346	.455
Clifford,John	Salem	Col	A+	23	17	34	8	0	0	0	8	3	3	1	0	1	0	0	0	0	0	.00	1	.235	.278	.235
	Portland	Col	A-	24	6	17	1	0	0	0	1	2	1	0	0	3	0	1	0	0	0	.00	0	.059	.059	.059
Clifton,Rodney	Sou. Oregon	Oak	A-	21	69	256	69	13	5	5	107	66	31	54	0	76	5	2	3	14	3	.82	2	.270	.403	.418
Cochran,Edwin	White Sox	ChA	R	20	28	69	8	1	0	0	9	12	5	4	1	14	1	1	0	2	0	1.00	3	.116	.176	.130
Cochrane,Chris	Athletics	Oak	R	20	2	8	0	0	0	0	0	1	0	0	0	1	0	0	0	0	0	.00	0	.000	.000	.000
Cody,Ryan	Martinsville	Phi	R+	20	26	76	18	4	0	1	25	9	8	8	0	21	1	0	0	0	1	.00	2	.237	.318	.329
Coe,Ryan	Kissimmee	Hou	A+	25	52	161	35	6	0	3	50	21	19	14	0	36	3	1	0	0	1	.00	4	.217	.292	.311
Coffee,Gary	Wilmington	KC	A+	23	120	427	95	11	1	11	141	58	56	55	0	157	7	0	4	6	4	.60	13	.222	.318	.330

1997 Batting — Single-A and Rookie Leagues

Player	Team	Org	Lg	A	G	AB	H	2B	3B	HR	TB	R	RBI	TBB	IBB	SO	HBP	SH	SF	SB	CS	SB%	GDP	Avg	OBP	SLG
Coffie,Evanon	Delmarva	Bal	A	21	90	305	84	14	5	3	117	41	48	23	1	45	4	1	6	19	10	.66	5	.275	.328	.384
Cole,Eric	Auburn	Hou	A-	22	71	222	61	20	3	8	111	29	34	19	1	46	5	2	3	4	4	.50	3	.275	.341	.500
Colina,Roberto	Devil Rays	TB	R	27	1	2	0	0	0	0	0	0	0	1	0	0	0	0	0	0	0	.00	0	.000	.333	.000
	St. Pete	TB	A+	27	96	351	87	13	3	5	121	48	49	45	3	40	5	1	2	4	5	.44	9	.248	.340	.345
Collier,Lamonte	Martinsville	Phi	R+	23	62	222	56	7	2	2	73	49	23	47	0	50	2	3	1	14	9	.61	2	.252	.386	.329
Collier,Marc	Butte	Ana	R+	20	5	14	1	0	0	0	1	0	0	1	0	6	0	1	0	0	0	.00	0	.071	.133	.071
	Orioles	Bal	R	20	25	71	13	2	0	0	15	10	6	10	0	16	1	1	3	2	0	1.00	1	.183	.282	.211
Collins,Francis	Batavia	Phi	A-	24	63	206	55	5	2	0	64	35	16	23	0	46	3	5	1	16	4	.80	4	.267	.348	.311
Colon,Jose	Daytona	ChN	A+	22	52	100	21	4	1	0	27	11	7	8	0	31	3	0	1	1	2	.33	1	.210	.288	.270
	Rockford	ChN	A	22	56	195	48	14	1	2	70	16	28	21	2	35	2	1	2	1	3	.25	6	.246	.323	.359
Colson,Julian	Astros	Hou	R	21	7	10	1	1	0	0	2	1	0	1	0	4	0	0	0	0	0	.00	1	.100	.182	.200
Condon,Michael	Butte	Ana	R+	24	49	181	55	12	1	1	72	38	19	14	0	19	4	0	0	4	1	.80	7	.304	.367	.398
Connacher,Kevin	Winston-Sal	ChA	A+	23	70	243	70	16	2	3	99	32	27	28	0	50	2	2	3	12	8	.60	2	.288	.362	.407
Connell,Jerry	Williamsprt	ChN	A-	20	55	203	57	7	6	3	85	25	18	20	0	55	4	0	1	4	3	.57	2	.281	.355	.419
Connors,Greg	Everett	Sea	A-	23	54	230	67	18	1	6	105	41	43	16	0	44	3	0	4	6	2	.75	3	.291	.340	.457
	Lancaster	Sea	A+	23	10	37	9	2	0	1	14	5	5	4	0	10	0	0	0	1	0	1.00	0	.243	.317	.378
Conti,Jason	South Bend	Ari	A	23	117	458	142	22	10	3	193	78	43	45	2	99	11	4	3	30	18	.63	10	.310	.383	.421
	High Desert	Ari	A+	23	14	59	21	5	1	2	34	15	8	10	0	12	1	0	0	1	2	.33	0	.356	.457	.576
Conway,Scott	Marlins	Fla	R	19	2	4	0	0	0	0	0	0	1	1	0	1	0	0	0	0	0	.00	1	.000	.167	.000
Cook,Josh	Astros	Hou	R	21	4	9	2	1	0	0	3	0	1	1	0	3	0	0	0	0	0	.00	0	.222	.273	.333
	Kingsport	NYN	R+	22	9	20	3	0	0	0	3	0	2	5	0	10	1	0	0	0	1	.00	0	.150	.346	.150
Cooley,Shannon	Piedmont	Phi	A	24	90	304	81	16	1	1	102	35	28	10	1	57	2	2	1	5	4	.56	4	.266	.293	.336
Cooper,Tim	Bakersfield	SF	A+	27	38	112	25	5	0	2	36	15	18	24	0	38	1	0	2	2	2	.50	0	.223	.365	.321
Copeland,Brand.	Kingsport	NYN	R+	21	41	148	50	10	1	7	83	31	37	23	0	33	5	1	2	6	3	.67	1	.338	.438	.561
	Pittsfield	NYN	A-	21	27	90	23	6	0	1	32	24	7	13	0	30	2	0	0	0	0	.00	1	.256	.352	.356
Cordero,Ellery	White Sox	ChA	R	19	29	81	21	5	1	1	31	12	6	5	1	18	3	0	0	2	1	.67	1	.259	.326	.383
Cordero,Willy	Rangers	Tex	A	19	26	66	15	2	0	0	17	6	8	8	0	12	0	1	1	7	2	.78	1	.227	.307	.258
Cornelius,Jon	Clearwater	Phi	A+	24	33	71	10	1	0	1	14	4	4	3	0	29	1	1	1	2	0	1.00	1	.141	.184	.197
Corps,Erick	Chston-SC	TB	A	23	57	188	43	9	0	1	55	28	22	42	0	49	2	4	1	14	6	.70	0	.229	.373	.293
	St. Pete	TB	A+	23	39	121	29	5	1	0	36	16	14	23	1	29	1	2	1	0	2	.00	5	.240	.363	.298
Corujo,Rey	San Jose	SF	A+	26	30	94	19	6	1	2	33	10	11	10	0	19	0	0	0	0	0	.00	1	.202	.276	.351
Cosentino,Antho.	Padres	SD	R	19	33	106	29	3	1	1	37	11	14	18	0	20	1	0	0	1	0	1.00	6	.274	.384	.349
Cosme,Caonabo	Athletics	Oak	R	19	37	130	28	6	1	1	39	28	17	19	0	28	2	1	7	1	0	.88	2	.215	.322	.300
Cota,Humberto	Devil Rays	TB	R	19	44	133	32	6	1	2	46	14	20	17	0	27	3	1	3	3	1	.75	1	.241	.333	.346
	Hudson Vall	Fla	A-	19	3	9	2	0	0	0	2	0	2	0	0	1	0	0	0	0	0	.00	0	.222	.222	.222
Craig,Benny	Burlington	Cin	A	23	61	240	66	16	3	10	104	43	45	22	1	70	0	0	1	6	3	.67	3	.275	.335	.492
Crane,Todd	Piedmont	Phi	A	22	80	314	91	13	0	5	119	50	35	30	1	57	4	6	3	26	6	.81	4	.290	.356	.379
	Clearwater	Phi	A+	24	2	7	1	1	0	0	2	0	1	0	0	1	0	0	0	0	0	.00	1	.143	.250	.286
Cranford,Joseph	Ft. Myers	Min	A	23	112	355	71	9	1	1	85	39	22	21	0	90	1	3	1	4	6	.40	4	.200	.246	.239
Crawford,Marty	Piedmont	Phi	A	24	108	389	88	15	1	4	117	37	51	30	3	51	4	2	4	3	1	.75	10	.226	.286	.301
Crede,Bradley	Piedmont	Phi	A	23	110	402	86	18	1	10	136	52	47	32	1	145	12	1	3	0	0	.00	3	.214	.290	.338
Crede,Joseph	Hickory	ChA	A	23	113	402	109	25	0	5	149	45	62	24	0	83	5	0	2	3	1	.75	6	.271	.319	.371
Crespo,Jesse	Braves	Atl	R	20	16	52	17	2	0	1	22	5	8	3	0	5	0	0	1	2	0	1.00	1	.327	.357	.423
	Danville	Atl	R+	20	14	42	12	0	0	3	21	11	7	3	0	8	0	0	2	0	0	.00	1	.286	.333	.500
Cripps,Bobby	Great Falls	LA	R+	21	47	145	45	6	5	4	73	19	25	7	1	26	3	1	2	4	4	.50	3	.310	.350	.503
	St. Cathrns	Tor	A-	21	14	40	5	0	1	1	10	4	3	4	0	11	2	0	0	0	0	.00	1	.125	.239	.250
Cronin,Shane	Clinton	SD	A	22	69	230	55	1	1	5	73	21	33	25	0	37	6	1	5	4	0	1.00	6	.239	.323	.317
	Idaho Falls	SD	R+	22	42	128	43	10	1	2	61	21	24	11	1	18	4	0	0	4	0	.00	2	.336	.406	.477
Cross,Adam	Clinton	SD	A	24	59	155	35	5	2	0	44	22	16	14	0	28	5	3	1	9	7	.56	2	.226	.309	.284
Cruz,Alain	Yankees	NYA	R	20	1	1	0	0	0	0	0	0	0	0	0	0	0	0	0	0	0	.00	0	.000	.000	.000
	Tampa	NYA	A+	22	10	27	3	2	0	0	5	3	2	2	0	13	0	1	0	0	0	.00	1	.111	.172	.185
Cruz,Andres	Princeton	TB	R+	21	3	13	3	1	0	0	4	3	4	0	0	2	0	1	0	0	0	.00	0	.231	.231	.308
	Devil Rays	TB	R	21	28	83	23	4	1	0	29	7	6	6	0	16	0	0	0	3	2	.60	5	.277	.326	.349
Cruz,Cirilo	Wisconsin	Sea	A	23	69	241	72	12	1	0	86	26	19	21	1	50	4	13	1	1	6	.14	7	.299	.363	.357
	Lancaster	Sea	A+	23	43	152	41	10	1	1	56	22	25	24	0	33	6	0	1	0	3	.00	2	.270	.388	.368
Cruz,Edgar	Burlington	Cle	R+	19	45	171	36	7	0	5	58	18	29	14	1	54	1	0	0	0	1	.00	4	.211	.274	.339
Cruz,Geronimo	Rangers	Tex	R	20	27	70	17	3	2	0	24	6	6	10	0	23	0	0	4	2	1	.67	1	.243	.333	.343
Cruz,Luis	Devil Rays	TB	R	21	34	116	42	8	2	4	66	25	20	16	0	26	1	0	0	17	4	.81	3	.362	.433	.569
	Princeton	TB	R+	21	18	78	22	2	0	3	33	16	14	5	0	16	0	0	3	2	2	.50	2	.282	.314	.423
Cuevas,Trent	Savannah	LA	A	21	90	313	73	10	3	10	119	42	41	13	1	59	5	1	2	3	1	.75	10	.233	.273	.380
Cuntz,Casey	South Bend	Ari	A	23	49	169	46	11	0	1	60	19	14	27	2	34	2	4	0	3	4	.43	4	.272	.379	.355
Curry,Jesse	Padres	SD	R	19	39	145	34	9	1	2	51	17	21	19	0	62	2	1	1	1	1	.50	1	.234	.329	.352
Curtis,Matt	Cedar Rapds	Ana	A	23	34	113	28	8	1	4	50	21	18	17	0	16	2	0	0	0	0	.00	3	.248	.351	.442
	Lk Elsinore	Ana	A+	23	74	264	87	25	8	17	179	58	55	25	1	54	2	0	1	3	1	.75	2	.330	.390	.678
Cust,Jack	Diamondback	Ari	R	19	35	121	37	11	1	3	59	26	33	31	0	39	0	0	0	2	0	1.00	4	.306	.447	.488
Cutshall,Patrick	Auburn	Hou	A-	23	76	273	81	23	1	8	130	54	34	31	1	88	8	3	2	5	6	.45	11	.297	.382	.476
Dallimore,Brian	Quad City	Hou	A	23	130	492	128	23	6	6	175	80	48	38	0	76	20	6	5	24	8	.75	19	.260	.335	.356
	Kissimmee	Hou	A+	24	1	3	0	0	0	0	0	0	0	0	0	0	0	0	0	0	0	.00	0	.000	.000	.000
Dampeer,Kelly	Burlington	Cle	A+	23	53	212	54	10	9	3	85	37	24	15	0	32	4	1	2	9	3	.75	2	.255	.313	.387
Dandridge,Brad	Vero Beach	LA	A+	26	112	388	101	21	1	8	148	45	65	33	4	42	7	1	5	4	6	.40	10	.260	.326	.381
Darden,Tony	Brevard Cty	Fla	A+	20	107	392	112	32	4	6	170	50	48	32	0	72	4	1	7	7	3	.70	12	.286	.343	.434
Darjean,John	Oneonta	NYA	A-	22	58	189	55	4	3	0	65	30	13	8	0	36	3	5	0	27	11	.71	1	.291	.330	.344
Darr,Mike	Rancho Cuca	SD	A+	22	134	521	179	32	11	15	278	104	94	57	1	90	4	0	5	23	7	.77	19	.344	.409	.534
Darr,Ryan	Johnson Cty	StL	R+	22	54	192	57	22	2	10	113	35	33	27	1	51	5	0	0	1	0	1.00	5	.297	.382	.589
Darula,Robert	Ogden	Mil	R+	23	69	262	87	26	4	6	139	61	52	42	0	23	5	1	4	11	2	.85	5	.332	.428	.531
Dasher,Melvin	Royals	KC	R	21	49	154	31	8	0	1	42	20	10	11	0	47	3	0	2	3	1	.75	2	.201	.265	.273
Davanon,Jeff	Visalia	Oak	A+	24	119	408	104	17	3	6	145	70	38	81	1	101	0	10	2	23	14	.62	7	.255	.377	.355

1997 Batting — Single-A and Rookie Leagues

Player	Team	Org	Lg	A	G	AB	H	2B	3B	HR	TB	R	RBI	TBB	IBB	SO	HBP	SH	SF	SB	CS	SB%	GDP	Avg	OBP	SLG
Davidson,Cleatus	Ft. Wayne	Min	A	21	124	478	122	16	8	6	172	80	52	52	1	100	1	5	4	39	9	.81	7	.255	.327	.360
Davila,Angel	Mets	NYN	R	23	5	13	3	0	1	0	5	4	1	5	0	1	0	0	1	0	0	.00	1	.231	.421	.385
Davis,Albert	Augusta	Pit	A	21	77	279	67	13	3	6	104	51	40	49	1	67	5	5	1	27	8	.77	2	.240	.362	.373
	Lynchburg	Pit	A+	21	18	60	10	2	0	1	15	9	3	7	0	13	0	2	1	2	1	.67	2	.167	.250	.250
Davis,Monty	Athletics	Oak	R	20	47	173	57	12	0	5	84	34	34	25	0	25	7	1	1	5	2	.71	2	.329	.432	.486
Davis,Glenn	San Berndno	LA	A+	22	64	228	56	16	0	9	99	44	36	46	0	77	2	0	0	7	3	.70	3	.246	.377	.434
Davis,James	Burlington	Cin	A	25	91	319	93	18	1	5	128	37	46	17	1	46	4	4	2	3	0	1.00	8	.292	.333	.401
Davis,Jerry	Pirates	Pit	R	19	45	165	42	10	2	1	59	19	18	14	2	44	2	0	3	0	0	.00	4	.255	.315	.358
	Erie	Pit	A-	19	4	13	1	0	0	0	1	0	0	0	0	4	0	0	0	0	0	.00	0	.077	.077	.077
Davis,Josh	Clinton	SD	A	22	60	180	34	5	1	0	41	13	18	13	0	45	1	0	2	4	3	.57	4	.189	.241	.228
Davis,Ben	Rancho Cuca	SD	A+	21	122	474	132	30	1	17	215	67	76	28	2	107	2	2	3	3	1	.75	11	.278	.323	.454
Davis,Reginald	High Desert	Ari	A+	23	44	154	41	8	0	8	73	24	35	12	0	26	1	0	2	0	2	.00	3	.266	.323	.474
Davis,Tim	Johnson City	StL	R+	20	13	34	2	0	0	0	2	4	0	1	0	12	1	0	0	2	0	1.00	1	.059	.111	.059
Davison,Ashanti	Bluefield	Bal	R+	19	49	162	40	10	4	2	64	31	25	17	1	29	7	0	2	8	2	.80	3	.247	.340	.395
Dawkins,Travis	Billings	Cin	R+	19	70	253	61	5	0	4	78	47	37	30	0	38	0	3	6	16	6	.73	6	.241	.315	.308
de la Cruz,Henr.	Cubs	ChN	R	21	25	80	11	2	0	0	13	11	3	16	0	32	2	0	0	5	3	.63	0	.138	.296	.163
de la Cruz,Raul	Pirates	Pit	R	21	28	92	22	0	1	2	30	6	11	3	1	25	1	0	1	5	0	1.00	4	.239	.268	.326
Dean,Aaron	Great Falls	LA	R+	21	60	179	59	14	1	4	87	28	27	13	0	41	2	0	0	4	4	.50	1	.330	.381	.486
Deardorff,Jeffrey	Ogden	Mil	R+	19	63	222	61	17	3	2	90	33	27	24	0	74	5	1	0	2	2	.50	1	.275	.359	.405
DeArmas,Franci.	White Sox	ChA	R	20	17	49	11	3	1	0	16	5	2	4	0	12	0	1	0	0	0	.00	2	.224	.283	.327
DeCelle,Michael	Chston-SC	TB	A	23	48	157	35	7	1	1	47	23	17	21	2	39	4	0	4	8	8	.50	6	.223	.323	.299
	Hudson Vall	TB	A-	23	73	270	70	18	7	3	111	41	28	25	1	69	4	0	1	3	4	.43	5	.259	.330	.411
DeCinces,Tim	Delmarva	Bal	A	24	127	416	107	20	0	13	166	65	70	97	1	117	0	1	3	3	4	.43	10	.257	.395	.399
Deck,Billy	Peoria	StL	A	21	114	383	103	30	0	3	142	51	53	51	2	89	4	1	2	2	5	.29	11	.269	.359	.371
Declet,Miguel	Athletics	Oak	R	18	13	30	9	2	0	0	11	7	4	2	0	6	4	0	1	0	2	.00	1	.300	.405	.367
DeHaan,Korwin	Erie	Pit	A-	21	58	205	49	8	6	1	72	43	18	38	2	43	2	6	4	14	9	.61	4	.239	.357	.351
DeJesus,Eddie	Butte	Ana	R+	21	57	219	65	14	1	4	93	38	35	23	0	58	3	0	5	4	4	.50	0	.297	.364	.425
DeJesus,Wilmer	Expos	Mon	R	20	13	34	10	1	0	0	11	5	5	4	0	6	0	1	0	1	0	1.00	2	.294	.368	.324
de La Cruz,Rud.	Mets	NYN	R	18	38	129	22	3	1	0	27	16	6	8	0	25	4	0	0	3	2	.60	0	.171	.241	.209
de La Espada,M.	Astros	Hou	R	21	49	162	33	7	0	3	49	20	14	9	0	45	5	0	1	8	2	.80	1	.204	.266	.302
Delaney,Donnie	Wilmington	KC	A+	24	124	434	102	25	4	5	150	53	60	24	0	112	1	6	6	15	7	.68	4	.235	.273	.346
de la Rosa,Mig.	Pulaski	Tex	R+	21	22	58	10	1	0	3	20	9	8	7	0	28	1	0	1	1	1	.50	2	.172	.269	.345
de la Rosa,Tom.	Wst Plm Bch	Mon	A+	20	4	9	2	0	0	0	2	1	0	2	0	3	0	0	0	2	0	1.00	0	.222	.364	.222
	Vermont	Mon	A-	20	69	271	72	14	6	2	104	46	40	32	0	47	2	3	4	19	6	.76	1	.266	.343	.384
DeLeon,Jorge	Lowell	Bos	A-	23	3	12	4	0	0	0	4	1	2	0	0	6	0	0	0	0	0	.00	0	.333	.333	.333
	Michigan	Bos	A	23	20	59	16	3	0	0	19	10	4	0	0	19	0	1	3	2	0	1.00	3	.271	.258	.322
Delgado,Ariel	Boise	Ana	A-	21	60	207	50	10	1	1	65	37	22	16	3	43	0	0	1	6	1	.86	1	.242	.295	.314
Delgado,Christo.	White Sox	ChA	R	20	51	189	52	12	1	0	66	24	19	7	0	40	1	0	1	0	1	.00	4	.275	.303	.349
Delgado,Jose	Durham	Atl	A+	23	129	492	130	27	1	2	165	72	45	39	1	72	1	6	4	8	10	.44	11	.264	.317	.335
Delgado,Reymu	Bakersfield	SF	A+	22	50	166	44	8	1	5	69	21	29	15	1	27	0	1	3	3	4	.43	3	.265	.324	.416
Dellaero,Jason	White Sox	ChA	R	21	5	15	3	2	0	0	5	1	1	0	0	2	0	0	1	0	0	.00	1	.200	.235	.333
	Hickory	ChA	A	21	55	191	53	10	3	6	87	37	29	17	0	49	3	0	3	3	1	.75	6	.277	.341	.455
de los Santos,E.	Chston-SC	TB	A	19	127	432	101	11	2	2	122	46	40	20	0	101	2	5	4	8	9	.47	3	.234	.269	.282
DeMarco,Joseph	Padres	SD	R	22	7	26	4	2	0	0	6	7	2	5	0	6	1	0	0	1	0	1.00	0	.154	.313	.231
	Idaho Falls	SD	R+	22	32	125	35	5	1	1	45	21	20	16	0	14	0	0	0	9	3	.75	2	.280	.362	.360
Dempsey,Nichol.	Great Falls	LA	R+	19	6	8	0	0	0	0	0	0	0	1	0	2	0	0	0	0	0	.00	1	.000	.111	.000
Denbow,Don	San Jose	SF	A+	25	107	339	84	20	1	10	136	58	50	86	0	138	5	1	4	19	12	.61	6	.248	.403	.401
Denning,Wes	Cape Fear	Mon	A	25	137	557	138	24	10	5	197	77	50	31	0	97	10	5	1	34	13	.72	5	.248	.299	.354
Dent,Darrell	Delmarva	Bal	A	21	128	441	103	17	4	1	131	69	37	63	2	110	4	7	6	60	15	.80	2	.234	.331	.297
DeRosa,Mark	Durham	Atl	A+	23	92	346	93	11	3	8	134	51	37	25	2	73	10	2	4	6	8	.43	12	.269	.332	.387
Deshazer,Jeremy	Kissimmee	Hou	A+	21	2	5	1	0	0	0	1	2	0	2	0	2	0	0	0	0	0	.00	0	.200	.429	.200
	Astros	Hou	R	21	46	164	41	11	2	1	59	23	18	11	1	23	0	1	0	3	4	.43	1	.250	.297	.360
Dewey,Jason	Boise	Ana	A-	21	68	272	88	17	2	13	148	55	64	41	4	70	2	1	2	5	2	.71	2	.324	.413	.544
Diaz,Christian	Royals	KC	R	20	9	15	3	1	0	0	4	3	2	1	0	3	2	0	0	0	0	.00	1	.200	.333	.267
Diaz,Diogenes	Pirates	Pit	R	19	34	111	32	7	0	4	51	19	20	9	0	30	2	2	2	0	0	.00	3	.288	.347	.459
	Erie	Pit	A-	19	10	28	5	3	0	0	8	4	4	4	0	12	0	0	1	0	0	.00	1	.179	.273	.286
Diaz,Jose	Vero Beach	LA	A+	18	1	4	1	0	0	0	1	0	0	0	0	3	0	0	0	0	0	.00	0	.250	.250	.250
Diaz,Juan	Savannah	LA	A	22	127	460	106	24	2	25	209	63	83	48	2	155	4	1	4	2	2	.50	10	.230	.306	.454
	Vero Beach	LA	A+	22	1	3	2	0	0	1	5	2	3	0	0	1	0	0	0	0	0	.00	0	.667	.750	1.667
Diaz,Maikell	Orioles	Bal	R	19	46	137	35	5	2	1	47	19	15	20	0	30	0	3	1	18	2	.90	1	.255	.348	.343
	Frederick	Bal	A+	19	7	15	0	0	0	0	0	2	0	3	0	3	0	1	0	0	1	.00	0	.000	.167	.000
Diaz,Miguel	Johnson Cty	StL	R+	19	59	223	63	17	1	4	94	33	28	7	0	32	2	0	4	1	3	.25	7	.283	.305	.422
Dillon,Joe	Spokane	KC	A-	22	19	70	15	3	0	2	24	6	6	5	0	13	1	0	0	1	0	1.00	2	.214	.276	.343
Dilone,Juan	Modesto	Oak	A+	25	97	325	73	15	6	19	157	54	51	44	1	112	0	3	0	7	1	.88	6	.225	.317	.483
Dishington,Nate	Pr William	StL	A+	23	133	448	122	20	6	28	238	75	106	81	11	121	7	1	6	8	5	.62	3	.272	.387	.531
Doezie,Troy	Lansing	KC	A	24	19	51	8	2	0	0	10	3	1	2	0	14	0	1	1	0	0	.00	2	.157	.185	.196
Doherty,Steven	Lethbridge	Ari	R+	22	53	185	53	12	1	5	82	38	29	22	0	28	2	1	1	5	4	.56	4	.286	.368	.443
Dominique,Andy	Batavia	Phi	A-	22	72	277	77	17	0	14	136	52	48	26	0	60	10	0	5	4	1	.80	6	.278	.355	.491
Donaldson,Rhod.	Utica	Fla	A-	22	70	269	71	3	2	1	81	49	16	37	0	42	2	3	2	21	6	.78	5	.264	.355	.301
Donati,John	Lancaster	Sea	A+	25	4	14	0	0	0	0	0	0	0	0	0	4	0	0	0	0	0	.00	0	.000	.000	.000
Dougherty,Jeb	Boise	Ana	A-	22	25	92	28	5	1	0	35	20	8	8	0	10	3	0	1	3	0	1.00	2	.304	.379	.380
	Lk Elsinore	Ana	A+	22	12	26	6	0	0	0	6	2	1	1	0	5	0	0	0	2	0	.00	2	.231	.259	.231
Downing,Lance	Diamondback	Ari	R	19	55	215	82	12	1	2	102	48	40	37	0	26	1	0	1	10	4	.71	3	.381	.472	.474
Dransfeldt,Kelly	Charlotte	Tex	A+	24	106	366	106	20	7	6	158	64	58	42	0	115	3	4	3	25	16	.61	8	.227	.294	.339
Drizos,Justin	Salem	Col	A+	24	57	151	28	7	1	5	52	13	19	15	2	56	1	2	1	1	1	.50	2	.185	.262	.344
	Hudson Vall	TB	A-	24	43	149	32	8	1	5	57	23	26	21	0	39	2	0	1	0	0	.00	1	.215	.318	.383
DuBose,Brian	W Michigan	Det	A	27	105	358	96	12	7	15	167	72	79	66	3	87	3	3	2	17	2	.89	7	.268	.385	.466

1997 Batting — Single-A and Rookie Leagues

Player	Team	Org	Lg	A	G	AB	H	2B	3B	HR	TB	R	RBI	TBB	IBB	SO	HBP	SH	SF	SB	CS	SB%	GDP	Avg	OBP	SLG
Duffy,James	Kissimmee	Hou	A+	23	19	41	6	1	0	0	7	1	4	4	0	9	0	1	0	0	2	.00	2	.146	.222	.171
	Quad City	Hou	A	23	12	44	11	3	0	0	14	4	7	3	0	9	0	0	1	0	0	.00	1	.250	.292	.318
	Auburn	Hou	A-	23	48	185	51	9	1	9	89	28	25	14	0	47	2	0	0	4	4	.50	4	.276	.333	.481
Dunaway,Micha.	Padres	SD	R	21	44	177	46	14	0	0	60	30	21	19	0	38	5	1	1	8	2	.80	4	.260	.347	.339
Duncan,Jan	Martinsvlle	Phi	R+	21	54	204	53	8	4	13	108	38	33	14	0	62	2	0	0	11	5	.69	3	.260	.311	.529
Dunham,Trey	Idaho Falls	SD	R+	20	1	5	2	0	0	0	2	0	0	0	0	2	0	0	0	0	0	.00	0	.400	.400	.400
	Padres	SD	R	20	35	139	44	13	1	2	65	20	32	17	0	42	1	0	0	0	2	.00	1	.317	.395	.468
Dunn,Nathan	Clinton	SD	A	23	104	399	107	22	7	7	164	58	48	54	1	112	2	5	2	8	11	.42	11	.268	.357	.411
Dunn,Ryan	Auburn	Hou	A-	21	60	142	26	9	2	2	45	16	15	26	0	58	6	1	2	2	1	.67	2	.183	.330	.317
Durham,Chad	White Sox	ChA	R	20	49	189	62	5	3	1	76	24	17	12	1	17	3	3	1	22	3	.88	2	.328	.376	.402
Durick,Chad	Mets	NYN	R	21	25	88	28	10	1	3	49	13	24	2	0	15	1	0	2	3	1	.75	2	.318	.333	.557
	Kingsport	NYN	R+	21	31	126	38	13	0	5	66	23	25	7	0	35	2	0	1	1	0	1.00	1	.302	.346	.524
Durkac,Bo	High Desert	Ari	A+	25	137	510	144	27	4	8	203	76	71	63	2	70	1	2	2	1	0	1.00	10	.282	.361	.398
Durrington,Trent	Lk Elsinore	Ana	A+	22	123	409	101	21	3	3	137	60	36	51	1	90	11	17	3	52	18	.74	8	.247	.344	.335
Duverge,Salvad.	Asheville	Col	A	22	28	94	21	3	1	2	32	7	8	13	0	23	6	1	0	4	1	.80	2	.223	.354	.340
	Salem	Col	A	22	42	113	21	5	0	0	26	9	9	9	0	32	2	1	1	1	4	.20	6	.186	.254	.230
Eaddy,Deon	Cubs	ChN	R	21	53	221	62	5	1	1	72	43	25	18	0	17	2	2	5	2	3	.40	4	.281	.333	.326
Eady,Gerald	Everett	Sea	A-	22	67	248	58	11	2	3	82	32	33	22	0	89	3	1	4	13	4	.76	10	.234	.300	.331
Eckelman,Alex	Johnson Cty	StL	R+	23	49	165	53	13	1	7	89	30	27	10	0	23	7	1	2	3	1	.75	3	.321	.380	.539
Eckstein,David	Lowell	Bos	A-	23	68	249	75	11	4	4	106	43	39	33	1	29	12	8	1	21	5	.81	2	.301	.407	.426
Edge,Michael	Expos	Mon	R	18	50	144	20	1	0	0	21	17	4	28	0	42	0	1	1	20	1	.95	1	.139	.277	.146
Edmondson,Tra.	Capital City	NYN	A	23	50	131	25	6	1	1	36	16	12	16	0	38	1	1	1	1	1	.50	0	.191	.282	.275
Edwards,Lamont	Piedmont	Phi	A	24	106	386	96	16	3	2	124	48	53	29	0	68	1	7	1	18	7	.72	9	.249	.302	.321
Edwards,Michael	Burlington	Cle	R+	21	60	236	68	16	2	4	100	50	41	38	1	53	1	0	2	10	5	.67	2	.288	.386	.424
Edwards,Randy	Pirates	Pit	R	24	4	11	5	3	0	0	8	3	1	5	0	4	1	0	0	0	0	.00	0	.455	.647	.727
	Augusta	Pit	A	24	6	15	1	0	0	0	1	2	0	4	0	2	0	0	0	0	0	.00	1	.067	.263	.067
Ehmann,Kurt	San Jose	SF	A+	27	50	147	35	0	0	1	38	15	13	20	2	33	2	2	0	3	2	.60	5	.238	.337	.259
Elam,Brett	Salem	Col	A+	25	6	15	3	0	0	0	3	0	0	1	0	1	0	0	0	0	2	.00	1	.200	.250	.200
	Asheville	Col	A	25	96	337	82	12	1	2	102	44	30	35	0	58	2	9	3	8	5	.62	8	.243	.316	.303
Elliott,Dave	Stockton	Mil	A+	24	32	82	16	5	1	1	26	8	12		0	18	1	0	1	5	1	.50	6	.195	.305	.317
	Beloit	Mil	A	24	76	267	74	12	2	12	126	44	48	30	3	60	6	1	2	13	7	.65	3	.277	.361	.472
Elliott,Dawan	Erie	Pit	A-	24	57	172	43	13	0	2	62	14	18	9	2	32	1	0	2	1	1	.50	1	.250	.288	.360
Elliott,Zach	Clearwater	Phi	A+	24	129	448	118	21	3	4	157	65	45	46	1	63	6	6	4	7	6	.54	11	.263	.337	.350
Ellis,John	Charlotte	Tex	A+	22	1	2	0	0	0	0	0	0	0	1	0	0	0	0	0	0	0	.00	0	.000	.000	.000
	Pulaski	Tex	R+	22	37	128	37	6	2	1	50	19	21	8	0	22	1	2	1	1	1	.50	2	.289	.336	.391
Ellison,Tony	Rockford	ChN	A	23	34	118	23	5	2	5	47	21	13	14	0	25	1	1	1	1	1	.50	2	.195	.284	.398
Emmons,Scott	Tampa	NYA	A+	24	51	118	21	5	0	2	32	19	14	9	0	28	6	2	1	0	0	.00	2	.178	.269	.271
	Greensboro	NYA	A	24	3	7	2	1	0	0	3	1	0	1	0	1	0	0	0	0	0	.00	0	.286	.375	.429
Encarnacion,Ber.	Rockies	Col	R	20	42	140	36	9	0	3	54	27	22	19	0	37	7	0	1	2	1	.67	2	.257	.371	.386
Encarnacion,Bie.	Butte	Ana	R+	20	26	81	21	5	0	0	26	11	9	2	0	14	1	2	0	5	1	.83	2	.259	.286	.321
Encarnacion,Mar.	Modesto	Oak	A+	20	111	364	108	17	9	18	197	70	78	42	1	121	6	0	1	14	11	.56	7	.297	.378	.541
Engle,Beau	Capital City	NYN	A	23	6	10	3	0	0	0	3	0	2	2	0	3	1	0	0	0	0	.00	0	.300	.462	.300
	St. Lucie	NYN	A+	23	28	78	15	6	0	1	24	3	3	5	0	22	4	0	0	1	1	.50	1	.192	.276	.308
Erickson,Corey	St. Lucie	NYN	A+	21	46	134	27	3	0	3	39	10	11	22	0	43	3	1	2	2	0	1.00	1	.201	.323	.291
	Capital City	NYN	A	21	49	173	37	11	2	2	58	18	16	11	0	49	1	1	3	3	1	.75	2	.214	.261	.335
Erickson,Matt	Utica	Fla	A	21	69	238	78	10	0	5	103	44	44	48	3	36	11	2	4	9	3	.75	7	.328	.455	.433
Escalante,Jaime	Orioles	Bal	R	21	50	143	39	9	1	0	50	12	17	18	2	34	1	2	1	0	1	.00	4	.273	.356	.350
Escalona,Felix	Kissimmee	Hou	A+	19	3	9	2	0	0	0	2	6	0	1	0	2	3	0	0	0	0	.00	0	.222	.462	.222
	Astros	Hou	R	19	51	189	39	9	0	1	51	27	9	20	0	49	3	4	0	11	3	.79	1	.206	.292	.270
Escamilla,Roman	Wilmington	KC	A+	24	57	167	42	7	0	1	52	19	21	28	0	30	0	4	1	0	6	.00	4	.251	.357	.311
Escandon,Emilia.	Wilmington	KC	A+	24	80	238	65	9	3	2	86	40	32	57	3	54	1	5	2	9	4	.69	3	.273	.413	.361
Escobar,Alexand.	Kingsport	NYN	R+	19	10	36	7	3	0	0	10	6	3	3	1	8	0	0	1	1	0	1.00	1	.194	.250	.278
	Mets	NYN	R	19	26	73	18	4	1	1	27	12	11	10	0	17	1	0	1	0	0	.00	0	.247	.341	.370
Espada,Angel	Pittsfield	NYN	A-	22	20	82	25	1	0	0	26	15	7	5	0	5	1	1	1	7	3	.70	2	.305	.348	.317
	Capital City	NYN	A	22	30	102	33	6	0	0	39	17	9	9	0	9	0	5	1	8	4	.67	0	.324	.378	.382
Espada,Josue	Visalia	Oak	A+	22	118	445	122	7	3	3	144	90	39	72	1	69	9	7	3	46	17	.73	6	.274	.384	.324
Espinal,Juan	Sarasota	Bos	A+	23	109	322	80	20	2	7	125	49	45	51	0	79	6	2	3	4	5	.44	2	.248	.359	.388
Espino,Fernando	Everett	Sea	A-	21	64	256	86	17	3	6	127	48	36	33	2	44	4	1	2	9	4	.69	7	.336	.417	.496
	Wisconsin	Sea	A	21	3	8	2	0	0	0	2	2	5	2	0	2	0	0	0	0	0	.00	0	.250	.400	1.000
Estrada,Johnny	Batavia	Phi	A-	22	70	223	70	17	2	6	109	28	43	9	1	15	1	2	5	0	0	.00	9	.314	.336	.489
Estrella,Gorky	Mariners	Sea	R	21	54	188	47	6	0	6	71	40	34	41	0	57	3	0	5	6	4	.60	2	.250	.384	.378
Evans,Lee	Augusta	Pit	A	20	54	186	36	9	2	5	55	19	23	14	1	52	1	0	1	6	3	.67	5	.194	.252	.296
	Erie	Pit	A-	20	40	141	42	6	0	5	63	20	16	11	1	30	2	1	1	1	2	.33	4	.298	.355	.447
Evans,Mick	Wilmington	KC	A+	25	108	352	80	14	1	17	147	55	55	54	2	97	1	1	3	2	2	.60	3	.227	.329	.418
Evans,Pat	Columbus	Cle	A	25	32	83	15	1	0	2	22	13	6	17	0	19	0	3	1	0	0	.00	2	.181	.317	.241
	Kinston	Cle	A+	25	26	69	14	3	0	0	17	5	2	8	0	17	1	1	1	0	0	.00	1	.203	.291	.246
Ewan,Benjamin	Braves	Atl	R	19	36	127	39	3	2	1	53	9	15	12	0	33	1	0	2	5	2	.50	4	.307	.369	.417
Fafard,Mathias	Mets	NYN	R	21	23	69	11	3	2	0	18	11	2	11	0	17	3	0	0	1	0	1.00	3	.159	.301	.261
Failla,Paul	Lk Elsinore	Ana	A+	23	103	360	82	20	1	1	107	43	42	55	3	89	1	11	4	21	10	.68	9	.228	.329	.297
Faircloth,Chad	Salem-Keizr	SF	A-	23	31	102	29	5	2	0	38	13	13	14	0	30	1	0	2	1	0	1.00	1	.284	.373	.373
	Bakersfield	SF	A+	23	19	73	19	5	0	1	27	8	7	6	0	22	0	3	0	1	0	1.00	1	.260	.316	.370
Faircloth,Kevin	San Berndno	LA	A+	23	63	159	36	9	2	1	53	28	16	6	1	49	9	5	0	10	4	.71	3	.226	.293	.333
Fajardo,Alejandr.	Batavia	Phi	A-	22	52	200	54	7	4	2	75	35	29	7	1	34	3	3	1	9	2	.82	5	.270	.303	.375
Falciglia,Tony	Pr William	StL	A+	25	64	147	29	8	0	2	43	16	17	9	1	31	2	1	1	1	1	.50	7	.197	.252	.293
Falcon,Edwin	Great Falls	LA	R+	19	50	133	32	6	1	5	55	20	22	15	0	39	0	1	1	0	0	.00	2	.241	.311	.414
Farley,Cordell	New Jersey	StL	A-	25	6	19	7	0	0	0	7	6	1	2	0	6	1	0	0	1	0	1.00	0	.368	.455	.368
	Pr William	StL	A+	25	61	211	55	9	3	3	79	34	32	15	1	46	1	3	1	24	7	.77	2	.261	.311	.374

287

1997 Batting — Single-A and Rookie Leagues

					BATTING															**BASERUNNING**				**PERCENTAGES**		
Player	Team	Org	Lg	A	G	AB	H	2B	3B	HR	TB	R	RBI	TBB	IBB	SO	HBP	SH	SF	SB	CS	SB%	GDP	Avg	OBP	SLG
Farraez,Jesus	Quad City	Hou	A	25	80	228	50	6	1	5	73	30	24	19	0	61	6	0	1	9	8	.53	10	.219	.295	.320
Farris,Ed	Sou. Oregon	Oak	A-	24	66	255	68	19	2	5	106	33	56	22	3	76	2	0	3	4	1	.80	6	.267	.326	.416
Farris,Mark	Lynchburg	Pit	A+	23	116	367	85	17	3	4	120	40	39	26	5	71	4	0	5	4	1	.80	8	.232	.286	.327
Fatheree,Danny	Astros	Hou	R	19	21	38	9	1	0	0	10	4	3	3	0	0	1	1	0	1	1	.00	0	.237	.286	.263
Faurot,Adam	Beloit	Mil	A	23	100	298	71	11	1	1	87	38	19	17	0	56	10	14	0	9	11	45	4	.238	.302	.292
Fauske,Joshua	Hickory	ChA	A	24	98	344	81	24	0	15	150	56	60	38	0	76	10	0	5	1	0	1.00	4	.235	.325	.436
Febles,Carlos	Wilmington	KC	A+	22	122	438	104	27	6	3	152	78	29	51	2	95	12	3	0	49	11	.82	13	.237	.333	.347
Fefee,Theo	Cedar Rapds	Ana	A	24	110	367	88	13	6	3	122	40	35	18	1	90	1	0	1	10	9	.53	9	.240	.276	.332
Felix,Pedro	Bakersfield	SF	A+	21	135	515	140	25	4	14	215	59	56	23	0	90	7	3	3	5	7	.42	15	.272	.310	.417
Feliz,Joselyn	Marlins	Fla	R	22	34	102	30	4	0	0	34	9	9	6	0	17	0	0	0	0	1	.00	1	.294	.333	.333
Felston,Anthony	Ft. Wayne	Min	A	23	94	338	94	10	2	2	114	63	29	55	1	53	4	11	1	45	15	.75	6	.278	.384	.337
Fennell,Jason	Bristol	ChA	R+	20	48	190	54	9	0	5	78	39	36	18	1	38	4	1	2	6	3	.67	6	.284	.355	.411
Feramisco,Derek	Johnson Cty	StL	R+	23	53	184	63	12	3	6	99	34	36	16	0	37	4	0	0	8	2	.80	2	.342	.407	.538
Fereday,Todd	Cubs	ChN	R	23	24	91	34	12	3	1	55	19	23	8	0	14	0	0	4	5	1	.83	3	.374	.408	.604
	Williamsprt	ChN	A-	23	32	115	24	5	1	2	37	13	11	7	0	20	2	0	1	4	2	.67	4	.209	.264	.322
Ferguson,Dwight	Red Sox	Bos	R	21	33	95	24	5	1	0	31	13	9	5	0	33	5	1	0	8	1	.89	1	.253	.324	.326
Fernandez,Anto.	Stockton	Mil	A+	25	118	412	97	24	0	4	133	46	49	35	0	83	5	5	5	2	4	.33	7	.235	.300	.323
Fernandez,Ram.	Helena	Mil	R+	20	54	196	52	8	1	4	74	36	28	19	0	53	0	1	2	2	1	.67	2	.265	.327	.378
Fernandez,Winst.	Rangers	Tex	R	20	18	58	18	5	1	0	25	10	2	7	0	14	0	0	0	7	2	.78	0	.310	.385	.431
Fick,Robert	W Michigan	Det	A	24	122	463	158	40	3	16	262	100	90	75	11	74	1	0	7	13	4	.76	10	.341	.439	.566
Figgins,Chone	Rockies	Col	R	19	53	210	59	5	6	1	79	41	23	34	0	50	3	0	2	30	12	.71	2	.281	.386	.376
Figueroa,Francis.	Delmarva	Bal	A	21	7	28	5	1	0	0	6	2	3	0	0	3	0	0	0	0	0	.00	2	.179	.179	.214
	Bluefield	Bal	R+	21	63	243	65	14	1	8	105	32	41	14	0	70	2	0	1	4	2	.67	3	.267	.312	.432
Figueroa,Jose	Modesto	Oak	A+	20	7	11	2	0	0	0	2	5	2	3	0	3	1	0	0	1	0	1.00	0	.182	.438	.455
	Sou. Oregon	Oak	A-	20	41	131	31	8	1	2	47	16	16	11	0	40	1	0	0	3	0	1.00	3	.237	.313	.359
Figueroa,Luis	Wisconsin	Sea	A	21	125	482	138	27	2	3	178	56	60	33	1	21	6	2	1	3	3	.50	18	.286	.339	.369
Figueroa,Luis	Augusta	Pit	A	24	71	248	56	8	0	0	64	38	21	35	0	29	1	9	2	22	6	.79	2	.226	.322	.258
	Lynchburg	Pit	A+	24	26	89	25	5	0	0	30	12	2	7	0	6	0	0	1	1	2	.33	5	.281	.333	.337
Filchner,Duane	Visalia	Oak	A+	24	126	432	111	30	3	11	180	59	55	66	1	76	3	3	4	6	3	.67	6	.257	.356	.417
Fink,Marc	Beloit	Mil	A	21	10	27	4	0	0	2	10	4	3	6	1	10	0	0	0	0	0	.00	0	.148	.303	.370
Fischer,Mark	Lowell	Bos	A-	22	48	179	59	15	1	5	91	25	25	15	0	38	3	0	1	13	2	.87	0	.330	.389	.508
Fisher,Anthony	Rangers	Tex	R	23	22	70	22	5	1	1	32	11	12	15	0	17	0	1	1	4	1	.80	2	.314	.435	.457
	Pulaski	Tex	R+	23	30	109	21	5	2	2	36	23	13	14	0	43	0	0	1	6	2	.75	1	.193	.285	.330
Fitzgerald,Jason	Watertown	Cle	A-	22	34	112	22	8	0	1	33	11	13	17	0	31	0	1	0	2	0	1.00	4	.196	.298	.295
Fitzpatrick,Eddie	Batavia	Phi	A-	23	25	63	9	0	0	0	9	5	7	2	0	23	0	0	0	0	0	.00	1	.143	.169	.143
Flaherty,Timothy	Salem-Keizr	SF	A-	21	32	110	25	6	0	4	43	16	17	15	0	44	1	1	0	1	0	1.00	1	.227	.320	.391
Flores,Eric	Savannah	LA	A	21	6	13	1	0	0	0	1	0	0	4	0	7	0	0	0	0	0	.00	0	.077	.294	.077
	Yakima	LA	A-	21	33	104	23	5	2	6	50	17	17	10	0	48	0	1	0	1	1	.50	1	.221	.289	.481
Flores,Javier	Sou. Oregon	Oak	A-	22	45	160	53	11	3	1	73	25	25	17	0	22	9	1	3	2	1	.67	2	.331	.418	.456
Flores,Jose	Red Sox	Bos	R	20	29	90	26	4	3	1	39	18	8	13	0	20	1	2	2	9	6	.60	1	.289	.377	.433
	Lowell	Bos	A-	20	37	122	27	4	0	1	34	13	9	6	0	36	1	0	0	4	1	.80	4	.221	.264	.279
Folkers,Brandon	Johnson Cty	StL	R+	22	53	150	44	8	2	3	65	20	20	25	3	62	3	0	1	3	2	.60	1	.293	.402	.433
Folmar,Ryan	Rockies	Col	R	23	11	46	14	6	0	0	20	5	7	3	0	2	1	0	0	2	0	.00	4	.304	.360	.435
	Portland	Col	A-	23	19	61	11	5	0	1	19	8	9	9	0	19	1	0	0	2	1	.67	4	.180	.296	.311
Foote,Derek	Durham	Atl	A+	23	68	217	52	10	0	6	80	28	33	18	3	73	6	0	1	0	1	.00	2	.240	.314	.369
Forbes,Kevin	Vermont	Mon	A-	22	30	100	20	1	0	0	21	13	8	5	0	22	3	3	0	8	1	.89	2	.200	.259	.210
	Expos	Mon	R	22	22	77	18	3	3	1	30	8	10	8	0	26	2	0	0	1	2	.33	1	.234	.322	.390
Fortin,Blaine	Medicne Hat	Tor	R+	22	55	164	54	5	0	7	80	21	26	5	0	12	2	0	1	3	1	.25	3	.329	.355	.488
Foster,Quincy	Brevard Cty	Fla	A+	23	61	186	46	8	2	1	61	25	11	14	0	47	3	2	0	12	4	.75	0	.247	.310	.328
Foulks,Brian	Savannah	LA	A	24	20	57	6	2	0	1	11	2	3	2	0	21	0	0	0	1	1	.50	0	.105	.136	.193
Fowler,Ben	Columbus	Cle	A	21	19	60	11	1	0	1	15	5	7	2	0	26	1	0	0	1	0	1.00	0	.183	.222	.250
Fowler,Maleke	Delmarva	Bal	A	22	105	339	78	9	2	0	91	49	18	20	0	69	4	4	0	36	16	.69	0	.230	.281	.268
Fox,Brian	Lethbridge	Ari	R+	22	64	220	65	9	2	9	105	30	44	34	1	45	3	0	3	1	0	1.00	6	.295	.392	.477
Francia,David	Piedmont	Phi	A	23	112	424	127	24	7	9	192	72	65	25	2	61	19	4	8	39	12	.76	5	.300	.359	.453
	Clearwater	Phi	A+	23	21	75	21	3	1	0	26	5	10	6	0	7	1	3	0	5	2	.71	1	.280	.341	.347
Franco,Raul	Utica	Fla	A-	22	72	293	103	19	0	3	131	41	38	17	3	24	2	2	5	10	4	.71	11	.352	.385	.447
Frank,Stephen	Billings	Cin	R+	21	69	266	100	22	6	10	164	62	62	35	5	24	2	0	3	18	8	.69	7	.376	.448	.617
Franklin,Jason	Portland	Col	A-	21	63	211	50	13	1	6	83	37	37	37	2	60	5	2	4	4	1	.80	5	.237	.358	.393
Franklin,Toby	Twins	Min	R	21	3	11	1	0	0	0	1	0	0	0	0	6	0	0	0	0	0	.00	0	.091	.091	.091
Fracoccia,Dan	St. Pete	TB	A+	27	129	463	137	34	3	1	180	67	63	53	0	50	14	5	6	7	7	.50	11	.296	.381	.389
Frawley,Scott	Braves	Atl	R	20	26	77	8	0	0	0	8	6	2	11	0	30	1	0	0	0	0	.00	1	.104	.225	.104
Freeman,Sean	Lakeland	Det	A+	26	13	53	12	0	0	1	15	3	5	3	0	12	0	0	0	0	0	.00	2	.226	.268	.283
Freeman,Terran.	Pirates	Pit	R	23	3	11	5	0	0	0	5	1	4	2	0	1	0	0	0	1	1	.50	0	.455	.538	.455
	Erie	Pit	A-	23	63	217	68	9	2	2	87	56	19	38	1	38	11	5	1	46	11	.81	2	.313	.438	.401
Freire,Alejandro	Lakeland	Det	A+	23	130	477	154	30	2	24	260	85	92	50	1	84	12	0	7	13	4	.76	10	.323	.396	.545
Freitas,Joseph	Peoria	StL	A	24	122	436	109	16	1	33	226	78	86	58	1	148	7	0	3	6	1	.86	6	.250	.345	.518
Frias,Ovidio	Hickory	ChA	A	21	13	30	25	3	1	0	30	10	11	6	0	20	1	1	2	1	2	.33	3	.231	.274	.278
	Bristol	ChA	R+	21	35	117	35	7	0	1	45	15	20	7	0	12	2	1	1	3	2	.60	1	.299	.346	.385
Fritz,James	Batavia	Phi	A-	23	35	90	24	8	1	1	37	10	13	14	0	25	5	1	1	4	1	.80	1	.267	.391	.411
Fuentes,Javier	Michigan	Bos	A	23	30	77	13	1	0	0	16	10	8	7	0	18	4	2	0	1	1	.50	2	.169	.273	.208
	Sarasota	Bos	A+	23	47	147	42	6	2	2	58	16	22	12	0	19	1	2	0	4	6	.40	2	.286	.344	.395
Fuentes,Joel	San Jose	SF	A+	22	5	5	1	0	0	0	1	1	1	2	0	2	0	0	0	0	0	.00	GDP	.200	.429	.200
	Salem-Keizr	SF	A-	22	20	55	12	2	0	0	14	7	2	17	0	12	1	0	0	1	1	.50	2	.218	.403	.255
Fuentes,Omar	Yankees	NYA	R	20	33	90	19	5	0	0	24	8	11	11	0	16	5	0	0	1	0	.00	4	.211	.321	.267
Fuller,Brian	Lakeland	Det	A+	25	45	129	28	2	1	2	38	13	18	7	0	26	3	3	2	0	0	.00	5	.217	.270	.295
Funaro,Joe	Brevard Cty	Fla	A+	25	125	470	150	16	6	4	190	67	53	49	3	65	7	3	6	9	5	.64	8	.319	.387	.404
Furcal,Rafael	Braves	Atl	R	17	50	190	49	5	4	1	65	31	9	20	0	21	4	0	0	15	2	.88	1	.258	.335	.342

288

1997 Batting — Single-A and Rookie Leagues

BATTING																				BASERUNNING				PERCENTAGES		
Player	Team	Org	Lg	A	G	AB	H	2B	3B	HR	TB	R	RBI	TBB	IBB	SO	HBP	SH	SF	SB	CS	SB%	GDP	Avg	OBP	SLG
Gainey,Bryon	St. Lucie	NYN	A+	22	117	405	97	22	0	13	158	33	51	18	2	133	6	0	3	0	2	.00	7	.240	.280	.390
Gallagher,Shawn	Charlotte	Tex	A+	21	27	99	14	4	0	0	18	7	8	5	0	35	1	0	1	0	0	.00	0	.141	.189	.182
	Pulaski	Tex	R+	21	50	199	64	13	3	15	128	41	52	10	0	49	4	0	4	2	0	1.00	1	.322	.359	.643
Gallo,Ismael	Great Falls	LA	R+	21	61	199	50	9	5	1	72	31	34	16	0	14	0	3	2	4	3	.57	5	.251	.304	.362
Gambill,Chad	Salem	Col	A+	23	124	450	111	18	2	11	166	61	73	37	4	125	4	0	4	6	11	.35	7	.247	.307	.369
Gancasz,Michael	Lowell	Bos	A-	24	34	81	17	4	0	0	21	10	6	13	0	25	3	1	0	0	0	.00	2	.210	.340	.259
Gann,Jamie	South Bend	Ari	A	23	12	36	6	1	0	0	7	4	3	1	0	9	0	1	0	0	1	.00	0	.167	.189	.194
	High Desert	Ari	A+	23	91	267	60	12	2	6	94	33	32	17	2	71	1	2	2	2	1	.67	6	.225	.272	.352
Garavito,Eddy	Delmarva	Bal	A	19	2	4	0	0	0	0	0	0	0	0	0	0	0	0	0	0	0	.00	0	.000	.000	.000
	Bluefield	Bal	R+	19	61	231	70	12	3	5	103	47	44	21	0	30	3	2	7	26	9	.74	5	.303	.359	.446
Garcia,Alexander	Padres	SD	R	19	21	78	21	3	0	1	27	10	10	9	0	14	1	0	1	1	1	.50	3	.269	.348	.346
Garcia,Amaury	Brevard Cty	Fla	A+	23	124	479	138	30	2	7	193	77	44	49	2	97	5	14	3	45	11	.80	4	.288	.358	.403
Garcia,Carlos	Ft. Myers	Min	A+	22	69	147	20	3	0	0	23	11	2	11	0	31	0	7	0	8	6	.57	4	.136	.196	.156
Garcia,Cipriano	Mariners	Sea	R	19	41	156	32	9	1	2	49	29	21	19	1	43	3	0	1	3	1	.75	1	.205	.302	.314
Garcia,Douglas	Rangers	Tex	R	19	35	119	31	6	0	0	37	11	12	2	0	21	0	1	0	4	3	.57	2	.261	.273	.311
Garcia,Juan	High Desert	Ari	A+	19	3	3	0	0	0	0	0	0	0	0	0	1	0	0	0	0	0	.00	0	.000	.000	.000
Garcia,Luis	Winston-Sal	ChA	A+	22	130	498	128	29	7	13	210	55	81	16	0	93	0	4	5	4	8	.33	9	.257	.277	.422
Garcia,Neil	St. Pete	TB	A+	25	75	195	44	10	2	0	58	33	21	31	3	20	2	5	5	2	3	.40	7	.226	.330	.297
Garcia,Ozzie	Pr William	StL	A+	24	104	247	59	12	3	0	77	38	20	25	0	41	3	6	2	10	5	.67	9	.239	.314	.312
Garcia,Rafael	Royals	KC	R	18	37	115	29	1	0	0	30	19	10	11	0	33	0	2	3	9	4	.69	1	.252	.310	.261
Garcia,Sandro	Padres	SD	R	20	28	103	22	8	2	0	34	22	16	16	0	10	3	0	2	4	0	1.00	5	.214	.331	.330
Garcia,Sandy	Princeton	TB	R+	19	58	216	55	14	2	4	85	38	28	11	0	75	9	1	1	13	2	.87	1	.255	.316	.394
Gargiulo,Jimmy	Peoria	StL	A	22	96	305	73	14	0	2	93	39	29	31	0	54	2	6	1	1	3	.25	4	.239	.313	.305
Gargiulo,Mike	St. Lucie	NYN	A+	23	19	49	11	0	0	1	14	4	5	2	0	10	2	0	0	0	0	.00	1	.224	.283	.286
Garland,Tim	San Jose	SF	A+	29	135	577	172	28	9	3	227	106	39	34	1	88	14	3	3	65	15	.81	6	.298	.350	.393
Garrett,Jason	Kane County	Fla	A	25	128	476	131	28	3	5	180	72	68	35	2	101	5	3	9	3	2	.60	11	.275	.326	.378
Garrett,Scott	Chston-WV	Cin	A	24	33	101	26	4	0	0	30	9	14	4	0	39	1	2	0	1	1	.50	0	.257	.292	.297
Garrick,Matthew	Boise	Ana	A-	21	5	20	6	0	0	0	6	1	4	3	0	2	0	0	0	0	0	.00	1	.300	.391	.300
	Cedar Rapds	Ana	A	21	28	95	21	6	1	0	29	11	14	12	0	23	2	1	0	1	0	1.00	7	.221	.321	.305
Garza,Rolando	White Sox	ChA	R	18	36	109	27	5	1	0	34	2	10	7	0	22	1	0	0	2	1	.67	2	.248	.299	.312
Gentry,Aaron	New Jersey	StL	A-	23	64	225	56	8	6	3	85	30	32	20	1	58	6	1	2	4	7	.36	4	.249	.324	.378
German,Franklin	Cubs	ChN	R	18	35	116	20	3	1	1	28	22	22	16	0	40	3	3	1	8	3	.73	2	.172	.287	.241
German,Manuel	Diamondback	Ari	R	20	34	112	25	5	2	1	37	21	11	16	0	36	2	1	0	2	2	.50	4	.223	.331	.330
Germosen,Julio	Erie	Pit	A-	21	42	115	23	3	3	3	41	21	16	7	0	34	1	1	1	2	3	.40	1	.200	.250	.357
	Lynchburg	Pit	A+	21	3	6	1	0	0	0	1	0	0	1	0	2	0	0	0	0	0	.00	0	.167	.286	.167
Geronimo,Cesar	Cedar Rapds	Ana	A	22	17	42	7	0	0	0	7	5	1	2	0	10	1	1	0	1	0	1.00	0	.167	.222	.167
	Lk Elsinore	Ana	A+	22	3	7	4	0	0	0	4	1	2	0	0	0	1	0	0	0	0	.00	1	.571	.625	.571
	Boise	Ana	A-	22	54	192	55	11	2	2	76	32	29	15	0	29	1	1	2	3	2	.60	5	.286	.338	.396
Gick,Brady	New Jersey	StL	A-	24	32	102	22	4	0	1	29	9	20	8	0	8	1	0	1	0	1	.00	4	.216	.277	.284
Gil,Geronimo	Vero Beach	LA	A+	22	66	213	53	13	1	6	86	30	24	15	0	41	4	1	0	3	0	1.00	5	.249	.310	.404
Giles,Marcus	Danville	Atl	R+	20	55	207	72	13	3	8	115	53	45	32	0	47	3	1	3	5	2	.71	4	.348	.437	.556
Giles,Tim	Hagerstown	Tor	A	22	112	380	127	32	0	12	195	54	56	46	4	95	2	0	7	2	2	.50	8	.334	.402	.513
Gillespie,Eric	Cedar Rapds	Ana	A	23	122	421	107	26	7	18	201	78	72	55	0	80	4	0	4	8	0	1.00	7	.254	.343	.477
Giron,Alejandro	Martinsvlle	Phi	R+	19	54	202	61	15	1	1	81	26	27	11	0	40	3	2	3	6	5	.55	3	.302	.342	.401
Gjerde,Jeffrey	South Bend	Ari	A	23	31	104	21	0	0	0	21	9	3	12	0	34	0	1	1	0	1	.00	1	.202	.282	.202
Glasser,Scott	High Desert	Ari	A+	22	57	121	30	5	0	1	38	23	11	14	0	19	0	0	1	3	4	.43	2	.248	.324	.314
Glassey,Joshua	Savannah	LA	A	21	73	207	38	5	0	0	43	17	20	35	0	72	0	3	1	3	1	.75	3	.184	.300	.208
Glavine,Mike	Columbus	Cle	A	25	114	397	95	16	0	28	195	62	75	80	1	127	3	0	1	0	1	.00	9	.239	.370	.491
Glendenning,Mik.	Bakersfield	SF	A+	21	134	503	130	27	0	33	256	95	100	63	1	150	4	0	7	1	4	.20	15	.258	.341	.509
Gload,Ross	Utica	Fla	A-	22	68	245	64	15	2	3	92	28	43	28	0	57	2	0	5	1	1	.50	5	.261	.336	.376
Glozier,Larry	Kane County	Fla	A	24	55	159	28	5	0	0	33	21	16	16	1	29	6	0	1	2	2	.50	8	.176	.275	.208
Goligoski,Jason	High Desert	Ari	A+	26	123	437	131	17	3	3	163	92	58	76	0	91	3	5	2	15	6	.71	2	.300	.405	.373
Gomera,Rafael	Great Falls	LA	R+	20	59	209	54	11	3	6	89	36	29	16	0	67	3	1	2	13	5	.72	3	.258	.317	.426
Gomez,Erick	Royals	KC	R	22	50	169	54	16	0	3	79	18	29	16	0	36	0	0	2	0	0	.00	6	.320	.374	.467
Gomez,Ramon	Winston-Sal	ChA	A+	22	118	477	132	23	12	2	185	78	42	42	0	132	3	8	2	53	21	.72	9	.277	.338	.388
Gonzales,Jose	Portland	Col	A-	23	48	166	40	9	0	3	58	18	16	25	0	30	3	0	1	1	1	.50	3	.241	.349	.349
Gonzalez,Ender	Bristol	ChA	R+	20	24	85	26	5	1	0	33	10	8	8	0	19	1	1	0	1	1	.50	1	.306	.372	.388
Gonzalez,Frankli.	Padres	SD	R	20	24	99	27	4	0	1	34	12	9	5	0	22	1	1	0	7	4	.64	4	.273	.314	.343
Gonzalez,Manuel	Hickory	ChA	A	22	116	469	129	21	2	11	187	70	54	28	1	78	1	7	5	31	12	.72	11	.275	.314	.399
Gonzalez,Richar.	Kinston	Cle	A+	23	44	142	36	6	0	2	48	17	17	13	0	25	1	2	3	0	0	.00	2	.254	.314	.338
Gonzalez,Santos	Rancho Cuca	SD	A+	21	6	18	2	0	0	0	2	3	1	1	0	7	0	0	1	0	1	.00	0	.111	.150	.111
	Idaho Falls	SD	R+	21	46	192	57	9	6	5	93	41	34	19	0	44	4	1	1	17	7	.71	3	.297	.370	.484
Goodell,Steve	Brevard Cty	Fla	A+	23	117	381	103	18	2	11	158	48	61	60	0	67	14	6	7	1	1	.50	7	.270	.383	.415
Gooden,Carl	Johnson Cty	StL	R+	19	43	107	25	5	0	4	42	17	12	16	0	38	3	1	0	7	2	.78	3	.234	.349	.393
Goodhart,Steve	Burlington	Cin	A	25	19	54	10	3	0	0	13	11	4	16	0	13	1	5	0	3	0	1.00	1	.185	.380	.241
	Chston-WV	Cin	A	25	81	252	57	5	2	1	69	26	28	32	0	66	2	8	5	7	3	.70	4	.226	.313	.274
Goodwin,Joseph	Charlotte	Tex	A+	24	61	185	44	9	1	2	61	18	22	20	0	18	5	2	0	2	2	.50	6	.238	.329	.330
Goodwin,Keith	Lowell	Bos	A-	23	67	241	55	11	0	2	72	23	25	14	0	50	5	4	1	4	0	1.00	5	.228	.284	.299
Gordon,Brian	Diamondback	Ari	R	19	54	219	54	18	4	4	92	27	46	9	1	62	0	0	4	8	3	.73	4	.247	.272	.420
Gordon,Gary	Asheville	Col	A	21	79	231	46	5	1	0	53	34	18	32	0	73	8	11	0	21	10	.68	6	.199	.317	.229
Gorecki,Ryan	Charlotte	Tex	A+	24	101	388	106	13	2	0	123	52	24	28	3	12	9	5	1	6	7	.46	8	.273	.336	.317
Goris,Braulio	Sou. Oregon	Oak	A-	21	5	15	1	1	0	0	2	3	0	4	0	11	0	0	0	0	0	.00	0	.067	.263	.133
Gorrie,Bradford	Sou. Oregon	Oak	A-	23	59	205	62	11	2	3	86	48	29	28	0	50	2	1	1	19	3	.86	2	.302	.390	.420
Goudie,Jaime	Yakima	LA	A-	19	56	230	55	10	6	0	77	33	16	16	0	38	2	1	0	21	5	.81	2	.239	.294	.335
Grabowski,Jason	Pulaski	Tex	R+	22	50	174	51	14	0	4	77	36	24	40	2	32	0	1	1	6	1	.86	2	.293	.423	.443
Graham,Bashaw.	Royals	KC	R	18	28	42	6	0	1	0	8	10	4	20	0	25	4	3	0	1	2	.33	0	.143	.455	.190
Graves,Bryan	Cedar Rapds	Ana	A	23	68	191	39	12	0	1	54	14	17	32	0	32	3	0	0	1	2	.33	4	.204	.327	.283

1997 Batting — Single-A and Rookie Leagues

Player	Team	Org	Lg	A	G	AB	H	2B	3B	HR	TB	R	RBI	TBB	IBB	SO	HBP	SH	SF	SB	CS	SB%	GDP	Avg	OBP	SLG
Gray,Travis	Red Sox	Bos	R	23	8	23	6	2	0	0	8	0	4	5	0	4	0	0	0	0	0	.00	0	.261	.393	.348
	Lowell	Bos	A-	23	45	116	23	3	0	3	35	18	12	21	1	41	3	2	1	2	1	.67	0	.198	.333	.302
Green,Chad	Stockton	Mil	A+	23	127	513	128	26	14	2	188	78	43	37	2	138	2	11	4	37	16	.70	3	.250	.300	.366
Green,Kevin	Utica	Fla	A-	22	10	21	5	0	0	0	5	2	2	4	0	6	0	0	0	2	0	1.00	3	.238	.360	.238
Greene,Clay	Salem-Keizr	SF	A-	23	33	89	20	4	1	0	26	11	5	7	0	19	0	0	0	21	3	.88	1	.225	.281	.292
Griffis,Cade	Spokane	KC	A-	23	24	28	3	0	0	0	3	1	2	5	0	13	0	0	0	0	0	.00	0	.107	.242	.107
	Lansing	KC	A	23	10	30	9	3	0	0	12	4	5	4	0	8	0	0	1	2	1	.67	0	.300	.371	.400
Grimmett,Ryan	Jamestown	Det	A-	23	17	68	22	5	1	2	35	14	9	11	0	9	1	0	0	11	2	.85	4	.324	.425	.515
Grubbs,Christop.	Williamsprt	ChN	A-	22	23	54	11	1	0	0	12	5	2	11	0	17	0	0	0	0	0	.00	1	.204	.338	.222
Guerrero,Francis	Devil Rays	TB	R	18	34	100	21	4	1	0	27	10	6	5	0	24	1	2	2	5	2	.71	3	.210	.250	.270
Guerrero,Jason	Devil Rays	TB	R	19	28	72	8	1	0	0	9	3	3	11	0	22	1	0	0	2	0	1.00	4	.111	.238	.125
Guerrero,Joel	Padres	SD	R	19	41	140	37	2	1	0	41	25	10	28	0	35	1	0	0	22	5	.81	3	.264	.391	.293
Guerrero,Sergio	Stockton	Mil	A+	23	76	241	53	6	1	0	61	23	25	14	0	31	6	6	3	1	6	.14	6	.220	.277	.253
Guiel,Jeff	Cedar Rapds	Ana	A	24	41	132	42	7	0	10	79	32	26	35	5	28	3	0	2	13	2	.87	0	.318	.465	.598
Guillen,Jose	Helena	Mil	R+	18	25	51	11	0	0	1	14	6	6	9	0	17	2	1	0	4	2	.67	0	.216	.355	.275
Gulseth,Mark	San Jose	SF	A+	26	95	325	103	8	3	10	164	47	58	46	5	49	1	2	3	1	0	1.00	11	.317	.400	.505
Gunner,Chie	Devil Rays	TB	R	19	46	144	41	3	3	2	56	18	23	22	0	34	1	0	0	3	2	.60	3	.285	.383	.389
Guse,Bryan	Bakersfield	SF	A+	23	26	87	22	3	0	1	28	7	6	12	0	16	2	0	0	0	1	.00	3	.253	.356	.322
Guthrie,David	Chston-WV	Cin	A	24	73	233	50	7	2	3	70	27	26	20	0	75	7	3	1	6	2	.75	5	.215	.295	.300
Guthrie,Kendal	Ogden	Mil	R+	22	63	239	66	19	1	1	90	38	34	20	1	57	5	5	1	4	5	.44	2	.276	.343	.377
Gutierrez,Victor	Pirates	Pit	R	20	43	156	37	1	1	1	43	28	12	20	0	27	2	1	2	10	3	.77	2	.237	.328	.276
Guzman,Cristian	Tampa	NYA	A+	20	4	14	4	0	0	0	4	4	1	1	0	1	0	0	0	0	1	.00	0	.286	.333	.286
	Greensboro	NYA	A	20	124	495	135	21	4	4	176	66	52	17	0	105	10	4	2	23	12	.66	3	.273	.309	.356
Guzman,Elpidio	Butte	Ana	R+	19	17	43	13	2	1	3	26	12	13	5	0	5	0	0	0	3	0	1.00	0	.302	.375	.605
Guzman,Juan	Orioles	Bal	R	20	15	47	7	1	0	0	8	1	4	1	0	18	0	0	0	0	0	.00	1	.149	.167	.170
Guzman,Julio	Diamondback	Ari	R	22	12	36	8	0	0	1	11	4	5	4	0	11	0	0	0	1	0	1.00	1	.222	.300	.306
	Lethbridge	Ari	R+	22	22	60	13	3	2	1	23	11	12	2	0	23	3	0	1	2	0	1.00	1	.217	.273	.383
Guzman,Martin	Devil Rays	TB	R	21	18	38	10	1	1	1	16	10	6	11	0	7	0	0	0	3	1	.75	1	.263	.429	.421
	Princeton	TB	R+	21	21	74	24	7	1	3	42	22	15	10	0	20	0	0	0	2	1	1.00	0	.324	.405	.568
Haad,Yamid	Erie	Pit	A-	22	43	155	45	7	3	1	61	27	19	7	0	27	0	1	6	3	3	.50	5	.290	.310	.394
Haas,Chris	Peoria	StL	A	21	36	115	36	11	0	5	62	23	22	22	1	38	3	0	2	3	0	1.00	4	.313	.430	.539
	Pr William	StL	A+	21	100	361	86	10	2	14	142	58	54	42	2	144	4	1	2	1	1	.50	7	.238	.323	.393
Haas,Danny	Lowell	Bos	A-	22	9	28	5	3	0	0	8	6	0	2	0	8	1	0	2	0	0	.00	0	.179	.258	.286
Hacker,Steve	Macon	Atl	A	23	117	460	149	35	1	33	285	80	119	34	7	91	5	0	9	1	0	1.00	1	.324	.370	.620
Hafner,Travis	Rangers	Tex	R	21	55	189	54	14	0	5	83	38	24	24	1	45	3	0	0	7	2	.78	3	.286	.375	.439
Hagins,Stephen	Butte	Ana	R+	23	64	268	94	20	1	17	167	59	56	17	2	53	10	1	1	13	3	.81	5	.351	.409	.623
Hahn,Cameron	Astros	Hou	R	19	31	72	14	2	0	1	19	8	7	7	0	22	1	0	0	1	1	.50	1	.194	.275	.264
Hairston,Jason	Danville	Atl	R+	22	52	177	43	4	3	6	71	21	33	19	0	42	9	1	1	7	3	.70	3	.243	.345	.401
Hairston,Jerry	Bluefield	Bal	R+	22	59	221	73	13	4	2	100	44	36	21	0	29	10	4	2	13	9	.59	4	.330	.409	.452
Haley,Ryan	Burlington	Cle	R+	22	8	24	6	1	0	0	7	4	2	1	0	5	0	0	1	2	0	1.00	1	.250	.269	.292
	Watertown	Cle	A-	22	12	13	0	0	0	0	0	4	0	2	0	4	0	0	0	1	1	.50	1	.000	.133	.000
Hall,Andy	Pr William	StL	A-	24	23	83	16	1	2	1	24	13	7	10	0	22	1	3	0	4	1	.80	2	.193	.287	.289
Hall,Douglas	Rockford	ChN	A	23	115	407	118	19	2	3	150	49	46	33	0	106	2	2	2	26	13	.67	0	.290	.345	.369
Hall,Noah	Wst Plm Bch	Mon	A+	21	1	1	0	0	0	0	0	0	0	0	0	1	0	0	0	0	0	.00	0	.000	.000	.000
	Vermont	Mon	A-	21	73	266	73	12	8	2	107	43	45	45	2	48	3	0	2	22	5	.81	1	.274	.383	.402
Hall,Ron	Daytona	ChN	A+	22	125	450	122	23	3	11	184	65	78	47	1	80	18	0	3	21	14	.60	6	.271	.361	.409
Hall,Toby	Hudson Vall	TB	A-	22	55	200	50	3	0	1	56	25	27	13	1	33	1	1	3	0	0	.00	3	.250	.295	.280
Hallmark,Patrick	Lansing	KC	A	24	88	306	87	13	6	0	112	49	39	28	0	43	7	1	5	22	5	.81	4	.284	.353	.366
	Wilmington	KC	A+	24	27	100	30	5	0	2	41	22	11	12	0	16	3	1	2	8	3	.73	0	.300	.385	.410
Halloran,Matthew	Clinton	SD	A	20	46	154	31	7	0	1	41	19	22	8	0	37	4	1	2	9	3	.75	2	.201	.256	.266
Halper,Jason	Oneonta	NYA	A-	23	11	16	1	0	0	0	1	0	3	0	0	4	1	0	1	0	0	.00	1	.063	.111	.063
Haltiwanger,Garr.	Capital City	NYN	A	23	125	441	115	19	2	14	180	59	73	45	0	107	10	1	2	20	7	.74	1	.261	.341	.408
Ham,Kevin	Cedar Rapds	Ana	A	23	123	441	124	26	1	15	197	67	73	41	0	127	3	3	6	9	9	.50	15	.281	.342	.447
Haman,Mack	Bluefield	Bal	R+	22	47	133	30	6	0	5	51	28	17	24	0	51	7	1	1	6	5	.55	1	.226	.370	.383
Hamilton,Jon	Burlington	Cle	R+	20	64	247	60	11	3	4	89	50	20	51	0	69	5	1	2	25	5	.83	0	.243	.380	.360
Hamilton,Joe	Sarasota	Bos	A+	23	117	317	88	17	3	12	147	51	52	43	0	89	0	1	1	14	3	.82	8	.278	.363	.464
Hamlin,Mark	Asheville	Col	A	24	134	497	144	31	4	18	229	79	74	55	1	107	15	1	8	6	3	.67	3	.290	.372	.461
Hampton,Michael	Burlington	Cin	A	26	77	228	55	8	3	13	108	52	42	47	1	58	12	1	4	18	4	.82	3	.241	.392	.474
Hampton,Robby	Hagerstown	Tor	A	22	100	337	71	22	1	9	122	32	34	23	0	124	1	0	3	9	3	.75	0	.211	.261	.362
Harding,Todd		Cle	R	20	24	79	14	1	1	1	20	8	4	4	1	33	2	0	0	3	2	.60	1	.177	.235	.253
Hardy,Brett	High Desert	Ari	A+	24	12	35	4	1	0	0	5	3	0	1	0	14	0	0	0	1	0	1.00	2	.114	.139	.143
Hargreaves,Brad	Cubs	ChN	R	20	32	104	25	2	0	0	27	11	12	8	0	26	5	1	2	1	0	1.00	1	.240	.319	.260
Hargrove,Harvey	Everett	Sea	A-	22	69	258	70	21	5	4	113	40	34	30	0	74	9	2	1	8	2	.80	7	.271	.366	.438
Harkrider,Kip	Savannah	LA	A	22	18	71	13	0	0	0	13	8	4	2	0	6	1	0	1	0	0	.00	1	.183	.203	.183
	Vero Beach	LA	A+	22	33	103	29	5	0	0	34	18	14	5	0	13	1	2	0	2	1	.67	2	.282	.321	.330
Harper,Brandon	Marlins	Fla	R	22	2	6	0	0	0	0	0	0	1	0	0	1	0	0	0	0	0	.00	0	.000	.000	.000
	Utica	Fla	A-	22	47	152	39	7	2	2	56	27	22	19	2	32	1	0	2	1	1	.50	9	.257	.339	.368
Harrell,Ken	Oneonta	NYA	A-	23	11	24	4	1	0	0	5	1	2	2	0	8	0	0	0	5	0	1.00	0	.167	.231	.208
Harris,Brian	Batavia	Phi	A-	23	51	148	46	7	1	0	55	31	19	31	0	27	4	3	1	11	6	.65	0	.311	.440	.372
Harris,Kevin	Rangers	Tex	R	21	55	98	16	1	1	0	19	10	8	3	0	31	1	0	1	11	2	.85	1	.163	.194	.194
Harris,Rodger	Peoria	StL	A	22	85	250	57	7	5	1	77	30	15	19	0	62	2	6	1	12	6	.67	1	.228	.287	.308
Harrison,Adonis	Wisconsin	Sea	A	20	125	412	131	26	6	7	190	61	62	55	2	74	6	5	3	25	18	.58	11	.318	.403	.461
Harrison,Jamal	Twins	Min	R	20	39	126	31	6	1	0	39	12	17	15	0	22	3	0	0	5	3	.63	4	.246	.340	.310
Hartman,Ron	South Bend	Ari	A	23	51	197	50	17	2	3	80	25	37	25	1	35	1	0	0	1	0	1.00	12	.254	.338	.406
	High Desert	Ari	A+	23	75	291	85	22	0	14	149	43	65	30	0	57	4	0	8	0	2	.00	3	.292	.357	.512
Harvey,Aaron	Brevard Cty	Fla	A+	25	115	455	123	17	6	6	170	65	47	30	0	78	1	3	4	30	15	.67	5	.270	.314	.374
Hasbun,Andy	Tigers	Det	R	20	21	52	12	2	0	0	14	7	5	8	0	9	6	1	1	2	0	1.00	2	.231	.388	.269

1997 Batting — Single-A and Rookie Leagues

					BATTING															BASERUNNING				PERCENTAGES		
Player	Team	Org	Lg	A	G	AB	H	2B	3B	HR	TB	R	RBI	TBB	IBB	SO	HBP	SH	SF	SB	CS	SB%	GDP	Avg	OBP	SLG
Haverbusch,Kevi.	Erie	Pit	A-	22	67	241	75	15	2	10	124	37	55	13	1	37	4	2	4	4	4	.50	6	.311	.351	.515
Haws,Scott	Clearwater	Phi	A+	26	39	123	25	1	0	0	26	5	5	11	0	13	0	1	0	0	0	.00	6	.203	.269	.211
Hayes,Chris	Dunedin	Tor	A+	24	60	139	32	5	1	2	45	20	20	15	0	27	4	2	0	2	1	.67	4	.230	.323	.324
Hayes,Heath	Kinston	Cle	A+	26	103	378	96	22	0	24	190	54	59	40	3	107	2	0	2	2	3	.40	7	.254	.327	.503
Haynes,Larry	Mariners	Sea	R	20	45	136	28	6	2	3	47	26	13	20	0	66	0	6	1	10	3	.77	0	.206	.306	.346
Haynes,Nathan	Athletics	Oak	R	18	17	54	15	1	0	0	16	8	6	7	0	9	2	1	0	5	1	.83	3	.278	.381	.296
	Sou. Oregon	Oak	A-	18	24	82	23	1	1	0	26	18	9	26	0	21	2	0	1	19	3	.86	1	.280	.459	.317
Hazelton,Justin	Tigers	Det	R	19	35	105	27	3	2	0	40	21	17	25	0	36	1	0	1	3	1	.75	1	.257	.402	.381
Heffernan,Christi.	Braves	Atl	R	20	36	121	21	1	1	0	24	7	9	6	0	52	1	0	0	3	3	.50	1	.174	.219	.198
Heinrichs,Jon	Kane County	Fla	A	23	60	235	63	12	2	1	82	35	36	19	1	34	0	3	1	8	5	.62	7	.268	.322	.349
Heintz,Chris	Hickory	ChA	A	23	107	388	110	28	1	2	146	57	54	28	0	57	9	2	5	1	3	.25	6	.284	.342	.376
Hemmings,Bran.	Padres	SD	R	21	28	104	21	8	2	1	36	18	11	8	0	33	2	1	1	4	0	1.00	1	.202	.270	.346
Hendricks,Ryan	Frederick	Bal	A+	25	77	222	43	9	0	6	70	21	25	30	0	71	2	1	3	1	4	.20	4	.194	.292	.315
Hernaiz,Juan	Lakeland	Det	A+	23	118	438	122	13	6	12	183	58	56	22	1	107	3	1	1	29	13	.69	0	.279	.317	.418
Hernandez,Alex.	Lynchburg	Pit	A+	21	131	520	151	37	4	5	211	75	68	27	2	140	2	2	7	13	8	.62	6	.290	.324	.406
Hernandez,Jesus	Watertown	Cle	A-	21	16	45	10	4	0	0	14	4	3	6	0	10	0	0	2	1	0	1.00	1	.222	.302	.311
	Burlington	Cle	R+	21	50	192	58	12	0	7	91	37	40	25	1	36	4	0	0	7	2	.78	1	.302	.387	.474
Hernandez,John	Yakima	LA	A-	18	29	77	14	3	0	1	20	7	8	9	0	22	1	1	0	1	1	.50	3	.182	.276	.260
Hernandez,Rafa.	Expos	Mon	R	22	29	82	31	10	0	3	50	17	20	9	0	12	0	2	0	0	2	.00	1	.378	.440	.610
	Vermont	Mon	A-	22	22	77	18	1	0	1	22	8	5	4	0	18	0	0	0	2	2	.00	3	.234	.272	.286
Hernandez,Victor	Sou. Oregon	Oak	A-	21	43	121	18	5	1	0	25	14	18	12	0	43	3	3	0	5	0	1.00	2	.149	.243	.207
Herrera,Pedro	Royals	KC	R	19	36	101	30	2	0	0	32	15	7	7	0	22	0	6	1	2	1	.67	1	.297	.339	.317
Hervey,Brennan	Jamestown	Det	A-	23	58	222	54	10	0	4	76	24	29	17	0	62	0	0	3	1	2	.33	9	.243	.293	.342
Hessman,Micha.	Macon	Atl	A	20	122	459	108	25	0	21	196	69	74	41	0	167	6	0	2	0	0	.00	6	.235	.305	.427
Hill,Bobby	Mets	NYN	R	19	41	144	42	9	2	3	64	27	24	17	0	37	7	1	1	3	5	.38	2	.292	.391	.444
Hill,Jason	Astros	Hou	R	21	8	24	5	0	0	0	5	7	5	5	0	5	1	0	0	3	0	1.00	1	.208	.367	.208
Hill,Jeremy	Spokane	KC	A-	20	60	187	53	12	1	3	76	35	29	25	0	53	1	0	3	1	0	1.00	6	.283	.366	.406
Hill,Michael	White Sox	ChA	R	23	46	134	19	3	1	1	27	16	15	21	0	47	2	2	2	5	2	.71	2	.142	.264	.201
Hillenbrand,Shea	Michigan	Bos	A	22	64	224	65	13	3	3	93	28	39	9	1	20	1	0	4	1	3	.25	2	.290	.315	.415
	Sarasota	Bos	A+	22	57	220	65	12	0	2	83	25	28	7	1	29	2	1	2	9	8	.53	4	.295	.320	.377
Hilliker,Tracey	Great Falls	LA	R+	20	38	99	21	2	0	2	29	14	10	15	0	29	2	0	1	3	2	.60	2	.212	.262	.293
Hines,Pooh	Macon	Atl	A	20	32	104	17	3	2	0	24	19	7	16	0	29	2	0	0	3	2	.60	2	.163	.287	.231
	Eugene	Atl	A-	20	69	266	73	10	4	3	100	40	35	40	1	52	3	3	4	5	6	.45	2	.274	.371	.376
Hodges,Scott	Expos	Mon	R	19	57	198	47	13	2	2	70	27	23	24	1	48	2	1	3	2	2	.50	2	.237	.322	.354
Hogan,Todd	Peoria	StL	A	22	112	449	111	18	3	6	153	57	37	26	2	104	11	3	3	28	16	.64	7	.247	.303	.341
Hollins,Darontay	Hickory	ChA	A	23	42	115	27	9	0	4	48	22	13	15	0	37	1	1	2	3	1	.75	1	.235	.323	.417
	Bristol	ChA	R+	23	54	196	47	10	1	3	68	42	18	20	1	47	4	5	2	21	7	.75	3	.240	.320	.347
Hooper,Daren	Bluefield	Bal	R+	21	10	32	4	1	0	1	8	4	4	6	0	11	0	0	0	0	0	1.00	0	.125	.263	.250
	Delmarva	Bal	A	21	7	15	0	0	0	0	0	1	0	1	0	7	1	0	0	1	1	.00	0	.000	.118	.000
	Orioles	Bal	R	21	19	62	20	5	1	0	30	7	5	9	0	20	1	0	0	1	1	.50	1	.323	.417	.484
Hoover,Paul	Princeton	TB	R+	22	66	251	76	16	4	4	112	55	37	20	0	37	6	3	4	7	4	.64	3	.303	.363	.446
Horne,Tyrone	Kane County	Fla	A	27	133	468	143	24	2	21	234	89	91	104	18	88	3	0	7	18	7	.72	13	.306	.434	.500
Horner,Jim	Wisconsin	Sea	A	24	47	161	40	10	1	5	67	19	24	17	0	53	.5	1	1	2	0	1.00	4	.248	.337	.416
	Lancaster	Sea	A+	24	45	163	42	6	0	9	75	26	27	16	0	48	2	0	1	9	2	.82	8	.258	.330	.460
Horsman,Brent	Idaho Falls	SD	R+	21	52	213	65	9	2	1	81	36	24	10	1	35	1	1	1	2	2	.50	0	.305	.338	.380
Horton,Conan	Yakima	LA	A-	24	1	3	1	1	0	0	2	0	0	1	0	0	0	0	0	0	0	.00	0	.333	.500	.667
	San Berndno	LA	A+	24	14	30	3	0	0	0	3	3	0	2	0	10	4	0	0	1	0	1.00	0	.100	.250	.100
Hoshina,Koji	Expos	Mon	R	18	18	57	18	0	0	0	18	7	5	3	0	6	0	1	0	1	0	1.00	0	.316	.350	.316
Houser,Jeremy	Salem	Col	A+	23	110	383	83	11	1	0	103	36	28	33	1	61	2	10	4	11	8	.58	6	.217	.280	.269
Howard,Marcus	Lowell	Bos	A-	22	70	221	46	10	1	9	85	38	25	29	1	78	6	0	2	2	5	.29	2	.208	.314	.385
Hubbard,Jeremy	Williamsprt	ChN	A-	21	6	8	1	1	0	0	2	0	1	0	0	2	0	0	0	0	0	.00	0	.125	.125	.250
Hubbel,Travis	Medicne Hat	Tor	R+	19	42	119	19	3	1	0	24	10	10	10	0	43	1	1	2	1	2	.33	4	.147	.188	.168
Hudson,Bert	South Bend	Ari	A	20	28	95	14	2	0	0	16	5	9	5	0	36	0	0	1	3	2	.60	4	.256	.321	.429
	Lethbridge	Ari	R+	20	60	219	56	11	0	9	94	28	34	19	1	57	3	0	2	5	3	.63	5	.246	.301	.325
Huelsmann,Mike	Kinston	Cle	A+	23	90	289	71	9	4	2	94	50	19	48	0	56	2	4	0	12	4	.75	8	.246	.357	.325
Huff,B.J.	Capital City	NYN	A	22	99	363	92	20	5	7	143	49	41	19	1	78	4	1	2	11	3	.79	8	.253	.296	.394
Huffman,Ryan	Greensboro	NYA	A	24	4	8	1	0	0	0	1	0	0	2	0	3	0	1	0	0	1	.00	0	.125	.300	.125
Huls,Steve	Ft. Wayne	Min	A	23	56	158	30	7	0	0	37	20	16	12	0	37	0	2	1	2	1	.67	2	.190	.246	.234
Hundt,Bo	Augusta	Pit	A	23	111	407	100	21	2	6	143	56	42	24	3	109	10	3	4	18	7	.72	6	.246	.301	.351
Hunter,Andy	Padres	SD	R	21	5	22	6	1	0	0	9	3	4	2	1	5	0	0	0	0	0	.00	1	.273	.333	.409
Hunter,John	Idaho Falls	SD	R+	21	21	67	18	4	0	4	34	19	15	12	0	24	1	0	1	1	0	1.00	3	.269	.383	.507
Hunter,Travis	Utica	Fla	A-	18	19	53	12	4	0	0	16	3	4	4	0	12	0	0	0	0	0	.00	0	.226	.276	.302
Hutchins,Norm	Lk Elsinore	Ana	A+	21	132	564	163	31	12	15	263	82	69	23	4	147	6	5	6	39	17	.70	2	.289	.321	.466
Hutchison,Berna.	Asheville	Col	A	24	108	419	97	10	2	0	111	59	30	35	0	91	2	16	0	81	18	.82	3	.232	.294	.265
Hyde,Brandon	White Sox	ChA	R	24	28	77	15	4	0	1	22	10	14	11	0	24	2	1	0	0	0	.00	0	.195	.308	.286
Hyers,Matt	Quad City	Hou	A	22	81	270	67	8	3	0	81	32	18	25	1	46	3	2	0	7	6	.54	4	.248	.319	.300
Ide,Antoine	Orioles	Bal	R	19	33	92	19	0	0	0	19	13	6	8	0	21	4	1	3	2	2	.50	2	.207	.290	.207
Iglesias,Rigobert.	White Sox	ChA	R	22	48	159	35	8	4	2	57	20	20	19	0	24	0	1	4	3	1	.75	3	.220	.297	.358
Illig,Brett	Savannah	LA	A	22	51	158	32	4	0	2	42	16	11	20	0	49	5	0	2	1	3	.25	3	.203	.308	.266
	Yakima	LA	A-	22	0	0	0	0	0	0	0	0	0	0	0	2	0	0	0	0	0	.00	0	.000	.000	.000
Infante,Danny	Rangers	Tex	R	20	41	148	45	7	0	2	58	18	24	5	0	34	0	1	2	7	2	.78	6	.304	.323	.392
Inglin,Jeff	Hickory	ChA	A	22	135	536	179	34	6	16	273	100	102	49	4	87	4	0	9	31	8	.79	12	.334	.388	.509
Ingram,Darron	Burlington	Cin	A	23	134	510	135	25	4	29	255	74	97	46	1	195	0	1	3	8	5	.62	9	.265	.324	.500
Izturis,Cesar	St. Cathrns	Tor	A-	18	70	231	44	3	0	1	50	32	11	15	0	27	1	8	2	6	3	.67	3	.190	.241	.216
Jackson,Jeremy	Portland	Col	A-	22	68	289	82	12	4	1	105	45	26	20	1	70	5	3	3	13	4	.76	4	.284	.341	.363
Jackson,Quanta	Marlins	Fla	R	20	41	126	29	8	0	2	43	17	13	8	0	52	3	0	0	6	1	.86	3	.230	.292	.341
Jacobsen,Larry	Ogden	Mil	R+	22	67	238	78	17	2	8	123	57	52	41	0	44	3	0	4	6	6	.50	4	.328	.427	.517

291

1997 Batting — Single-A and Rookie Leagues

Player	Team	Org	Lg	A	G	AB	H	2B	3B	HR	TB	R	RBI	TBB	IBB	SO	HBP	SH	SF	SB	CS	SB%	GDP	Avg	OBP	SLG
Jacomino,Mandy	Jamestown	Det	A-	24	62	229	69	9	0	4	90	32	26	24	0	44	0	1	0	0	1	.00	9	.301	.368	.393
James,Brandon	Ogden	Mil	R+	23	72	267	76	14	2	10	124	51	58	29	2	79	3	2	3	8	3	.73	3	.285	.358	.464
James,Kenny	Vermont	Mon	A-	21	71	301	70	4	5	2	90	61	23	13	1	52	11	2	1	37	4	.90	0	.233	.288	.299
Jaramillo,Francis.	Pulaski	Tex	R+	23	46	156	46	14	0	4	72	26	22	25	0	44	3	3	1	8	4	.67	1	.295	.400	.462
Jaroncyk,Ryan	Capital City	NYN	A	21	29	86	15	1	2	0	20	5	7	11	0	25	0	1	3	4	4	.50	1	.174	.260	.233
Jasco,Elinton	Daytona	ChN	A+	23	84	281	94	10	4	1	115	50	22	31	0	61	3	4	2	32	11	.74	2	.335	.404	.409
Jaworowski,Aaro.	Elizabethtn	Min	R+	22	64	264	77	18	0	13	134	46	66	14	2	65	5	0	5	1	0	1.00	1	.292	.333	.508
Jefferies,Daryl	Williamsprt	ChN	A-	24	10	38	11	2	0	0	13	7	2	2	0	6	1	0	0	1	0	1.00	1	.289	.341	.342
Jefferson,Dave	Rockford	ChN	A	23	18	55	11	2	1	0	15	7	2	3	0	12	1	1	0	3	1	.75	0	.200	.254	.273
	Cape Fear	Mon	A	23	28	87	17	1	0	2	24	12	6	7	0	14	0	1	1	6	2	.75	3	.195	.253	.276
Jenkins,Brian	Mets	NYN	R	19	36	109	38	6	1	1	49	17	15	4	0	16	0	0	1	1	1	.50	3	.349	.368	.450
Jenkins,Corey	Michigan	Bos	A	21	111	426	102	17	4	18	181	68	62	28	1	129	11	0	3	5	5	.50	9	.239	.301	.425
Jergenson,Brian	Idaho Falls	SD	R+	23	54	196	51	8	1	2	67	34	32	23	2	49	4	0	3	6	1	.86	4	.260	.345	.342
Jimenez,Felipe	Williamsprt	ChN	A-	21	10	26	3	0	0	0	3	3	0	1	0	8	0	0	0	0	0	.00	1	.115	.148	.115
	Cubs	ChN	R	21	41	137	34	3	4	1	48	23	22	7	0	37	8	2	2	17	1	.94	1	.248	.318	.350
Jimenez,Ruben	Pr William	StL	A+	22	17	41	6	1	0	0	7	5	1	6	0	7	0	1	0	2	0	1.00	0	.146	.250	.171
Joffrion,Jack	Hudson Vall	TB	A-	22	73	258	62	13	2	9	106	41	37	13	0	61	2	2	3	2	1	.67	2	.240	.279	.411
Johns,Mike	Portland	Col	A-	22	62	220	51	4	3	3	70	28	27	11	0	66	0	6	5	2	2	.50	5	.232	.263	.318
Johnson,Adam	Durham	Atl	A+	22	133	502	141	39	3	26	264	80	92	50	9	94	4	0	16	18	8	.69	10	.281	.341	.526
Johnson,A.J.	Kingsport	NYN	R+	25	15	45	15	3	0	3	27	10	9	9	0	17	0	0	0	1	1	.50	1	.333	.444	.600
Johnson,Damon	Hagerstown	Tor	A	22	84	302	98	21	5	10	159	44	55	13	0	65	5	0	0	11	6	.65	1	.325	.363	.526
Johnson,Douglas	Princeton	TB	R+	20	34	139	28	7	2	4	51	19	19	8	0	56	4	0	1	2	0	1.00	2	.201	.263	.367
Johnson,Duane	Martinsvlle	Phi	R+	19	35	79	11	0	0	0	11	9	3	5	0	35	0	0	0	5	2	.71	0	.139	.190	.139
Johnson,Gary	Cubs	ChN	R	21	52	198	57	14	5	1	84	40	31	23	0	26	14	0	1	9	3	.75	4	.288	.398	.424
	Rockford	ChN	A	21	1	3	0	0	0	0	0	0	0	0	0	1	0	0	0	0	1	.00	0	.000	.250	.000
Johnson,Heath	Ft. Wayne	Min	A	21	22	67	14	4	0	3	27	10	11	13	0	29	0	1	0	1	0	.00	0	.209	.333	.403
Johnson,Jason	Batavia	Phi	A-	20	60	238	70	11	5	0	91	40	28	17	0	26	3	3	5	20	7	.74	3	.294	.342	.382
Johnson,J.J.	Erie	Pit	A-	22	28	103	33	7	1	2	48	19	19	11	0	21	1	0	2	2	2	.50	1	.320	.385	.466
	Augusta	Pit	A	22	20	57	13	1	0	1	17	9	7	12	0	17	0	0	0	4	0	1.00	0	.228	.362	.298
Johnson,Duan	Everett	Sea	A-	22	46	171	43	4	3	0	53	31	14	12	0	26	1	1	0	10	1	.91	4	.251	.303	.310
Johnson,Mark	Winston-Sal	ChA	A+	22	120	375	95	27	4	4	142	59	46	106	2	85	5	0	5	4	2	.67	7	.253	.420	.379
Johnson,Nick	Greensboro	NYA	A	19	127	433	118	23	1	16	191	77	75	76	1	99	18	0	6	16	3	.84	5	.273	.398	.441
Johnson,Patrick	Butte	Ana	R+	23	47	160	40	9	0	3	58	31	21	24	0	32	3	1	2	1	1	.50	3	.250	.354	.363
Johnson,Ric	Kissimmee	Hou	A+	24	121	453	127	11	4	1	149	47	40	21	0	67	6	3	4	21	8	.72	8	.280	.318	.329
Johnson,Rontrez	Michigan	Bos	A	21	118	411	99	10	6	5	136	87	40	65	0	96	9	6	3	29	12	.71	2	.241	.355	.331
Johnson,Thomas	Pittsfield	NYN	A-	22	57	209	49	15	0	5	79	28	38	14	1	51	4	0	1	12	3	.80	3	.234	.294	.378
Johnson,T.J.	Ft. Myers	Min	A+	24	73	227	55	16	1	7	94	29	36	30	2	77	4	0	1	2	1	.67	4	.242	.338	.414
Jones,Aaron	Oneonta	NYA	A-	22	63	166	40	8	2	0	52	25	17	43	3	40	2	1	2	4	6	.40	5	.241	.403	.313
Jones,Jack	San Berndno	LA	A+	19	29	91	20	1	0	0	21	9	6	11	0	21	1	1	0	3	4	.43	2	.220	.311	.231
Jones,Jack	San Berndno	LA	A+	23	123	388	88	21	3	11	148	53	52	40	0	112	6	11	4	10	7	.59	4	.227	.306	.381
Jones,Jacque	Ft. Myers	Min	A+	23	131	539	160	33	6	15	250	84	82	33	3	110	3	0	2	24	12	.67	9	.297	.340	.464
Jones,Jaime	Brevard Cty	Fla	A+	21	95	373	101	27	4	10	166	63	60	44	2	86	1	0	4	6	1	.86	7	.271	.346	.445
Jones,Jay	Kane County	Fla	A	23	64	210	62	6	0	4	80	20	31	8	1	29	3	1	0	2	0	.00	7	.295	.330	.381
Jones,Keith	Lethbridge	Ari	R+	22	58	214	55	18	1	5	80	27	28	15	1	76	2	0	2	3	3	.50	4	.257	.309	.374
Jones,Timothy	Modesto	Oak	A	20	119	309	74	18	3	8	122	45	47	46	2	120	2	1	2	8	3	.73	1	.239	.340	.395
Jordan,Yustin	Pirates	Pit	R	19	30	93	25	6	0	0	31	15	7	14	0	24	1	1	0	3	1	.75	1	.269	.370	.333
Jorgensen,Timot.	Kinston	Cle	A+	19	91	334	95	19	2	18	172	49	65	28	0	47	1	0	6	0	1	.00	9	.284	.336	.515
Kalcounos,Andy	Johnson Cty	StL	R+	22	9	23	3	1	0	0	4	4	2	7	0	10	0	0	0	0	0	.00	0	.130	.333	.174
Kane,Kevin	Oneonta	NYA	A-	24	4	8	1	0	0	0	1	1	0	1	0	4	0	0	0	0	0	.00	0	.125	.222	.125
Kane,Ryan	Tampa	NYA	A+	24	95	303	68	8	2	5	95	36	20	37	1	66	7	2	1	1	1	.50	7	.224	.322	.314
Kaplan,Brett	Pirates	Pit	R	19	57	3	1	0	0	4	5	4	3	0	20	0	0	1	1	0	.00	2	.053	.098	.070
Kapler,Gabe	Lakeland	Det	A+	22	137	519	153	40	6	19	262	87	87	54	4	68	5	0	10	8	6	.57	8	.295	.361	.505
Kastelic,Matthew	Chston-SC	TB	A	24	50	183	55	10	1	0	67	19	14	18	1	19	0	2	1	13	10	.57	1	.301	.361	.366
Katz,Jason	Macon	Atl	A	24	74	222	52	9	0	6	79	36	24	32	0	41	3	4	2	11	4	.73	5	.234	.336	.356
Keaveney,Jeffrey	Lowell	Bos	A-	22	51	191	39	12	0	7	72	26	29	18	0	58	3	0	0	0	0	.00	4	.204	.283	.377
Keck,Brian	Asheville	Col	A	24	37	124	29	3	0	0	32	8	8	9	0	22	0	7	0	5	2	.71	5	.234	.286	.258
	Salem	Col	A+	24	48	121	34	4	0	0	38	22	11	11	1	21	1	3	2	17	3	.85	3	.281	.350	.314
Keech,Erik	Greensboro	NYA	A	23	26	72	18	1	0	2	25	5	9	3	0	15	0	0	1	0	0	.00	1	.250	.276	.347
	Oneonta	NYA	A-	23	12	37	10	1	0	0	11	3	5	0	0	9	0	0	0	0	1	.00	1	.270	.270	.297
Keel,David	Tampa	NYA	A+	25	92	300	80	15	0	16	143	50	48	39	2	57	2	1	1	9	3	.75	4	.267	.354	.477
Kehoe,John	Hagerstown	Tor	A	23	14	58	10	3	1	0	15	9	4	4	0	19	0	0	0	2	0	1.00	1	.172	.226	.259
Kelleher,Patrick	Great Falls	LA	R+	21	57	145	42	8	0	0	50	22	10	19	0	27	1	5	0	6	10	.38	2	.290	.376	.345
Keller,Jeremy	Cin	A	21	117	386	101	19	1	9	149	55	66	48	0	93	3	0	3	2	0	1.00	4	.262	.345	.386
Kelley,Erskine	Lynchburg	Pit	A+	27	39	112	24	8	2	4	48	19	16	9	0	31	1	2	0	2	2	.33	7	.214	.279	.429
	Daytona	ChN	A+	27	35	113	29	6	0	5	50	24	19	11	1	38	1	0	0	2	1	.67	3	.257	.328	.442
Kelly,Kenny	Devil Rays	TB	R	19	27	99	21	2	1	2	31	21	7	11	0	24	2	3	0	6	3	.67	1	.212	.304	.313
Kenna,David	Salem-Keizr	SF	A-	20	64	242	48	8	2	7	81	23	33	17	1	86	3	0	0	1	1	.50	8	.198	.260	.335
Kennedy,Adam	New Jersey	StL	A-	22	29	114	39	6	3	0	51	20	19	13	0	10	2	1	2	9	1	.90	3	.342	.412	.447
	Pr William	StL	A+	22	35	154	48	9	3	1	66	24	27	6	1	17	2	1	0	4	3	.57	3	.312	.346	.429
Kennedy,Brian	Elizabethtn	Min	R+	20	55	191	56	9	0	1	68	26	25	22	2	43	4	1	1	3	4	.43	2	.293	.371	.356
Kennedy,Gus	Daytona	ChN	A+	24	113	368	96	20	0	14	158	63	57	46	1	89	0	0	5	15	8	.65	6	.261	.347	.429
Kent,Robbie	Rancho Cuca	SD	A+	24	78	295	73	18	0	4	103	35	32	22	0	65	4	0	3	0	2	.00	4	.247	.305	.349
Kent,Troy	Columbus	Cle	A	24	117	463	127	22	6	14	203	61	71	31	0	91	2	5	4	15	9	.63	9	.274	.327	.438
Key,Jeffrey	Clearwater	Phi	A+	23	136	522	147	37	11	17	257	85	87	29	5	112	6	1	1	15	9	.63	9	.282	.325	.492
Kidd,Scott	Oneonta	NYA	A-	24	55	181	74	14	3	5	109	38	45	18	2	62	2	2	3	7	2	.78	6	.263	.309	.388
Kiefer,Dax	Williamsprt	ChN	A-	24	70	234	57	5	1	4	76	28	18	28	1	61	0	4	2	7	1	.88	7	.244	.322	.325
Kiil,Harry	Piedmont	Phi	A	24	82	261	59	15	3	7	101	48	34	35	0	74	13	3	0	13	2	.87	0	.226	.343	.387

292

1997 Batting — Single-A and Rookie Leagues

Player	Team	Org	Lg	A	G	AB	H	2B	3B	HR	TB	R	RBI	TBB	IBB	SO	HBP	SH	SF	SB	CS	SB%	GDP	Avg	OBP	SLG
Kilburg,Joe	Burlington	Cle	R+	22	52	182	61	8	7	3	92	59	30	39	0	46	7	3	2	29	5	.85	1	.335	.465	.505
	Kinston	Cle	A+	22	9	30	7	2	0	1	12	5	5	5	0	6	0	0	0	1	0	1.00	0	.233	.343	.400
Kim,David	New Jersey	StL	A-	22	58	205	57	16	2	5	92	38	35	17	0	39	11	0	1	5	2	.71	3	.278	.363	.449
Kim,Yuni	Lancaster	Sea	A+	27	89	289	70	12	6	15	139	52	58	28	0	93	13	0	1	3	1	.75	10	.242	.335	.481
King,Andre	St. Pete	TB	A+	24	48	114	22	2	1	1	29	16	11	10	0	29	2	3	1	8	3	.73	1	.193	.268	.254
King,Bradford	Rockford	ChN	A	23	68	204	51	14	1	7	88	31	29	19	2	35	8	2	4	4	4	.50	5	.250	.332	.431
King,Michael	Chston-SC	TB	A	24	60	199	39	7	0	3	55	16	16	7	0	36	1	3	0	6	1	.86	4	.196	.227	.276
King,William	Yakima	LA	A-	20	50	155	34	4	1	4	52	14	20	27	0	43	1	1	1	1	1	.50	5	.219	.335	.335
Kingsbury,Willy	Lowell	Bos	A-	24	23	77	13	4	0	1	20	6	5	4	0	32	2	3	0	0	0	.00	1	.169	.229	.260
Kirby,Scott	Helena	Mil	R+	20	68	248	65	10	1	11	110	65	47	53	0	65	7	0	4	8	6	.57	5	.262	.401	.444
Kirkpatrick,Brian	Rockies	Col	R	21	45	173	44	5	1	3	60	23	25	9	0	28	2	3	0	2	1	.67	4	.254	.299	.347
	Portland	Col	A-	21	2	7	2	0	0	0	2	1	0	0	0	3	1	0	0	0	0	.00	0	.286	.375	.286
Kirkpatrick,Mich.	Orioles	Bal	R	20	38	115	29	6	3	1	44	18	12	9	0	22	5	1	2	7	0	1.00	1	.252	.328	.383
Klee,Charles	Hickory	ChA	A	21	119	400	108	18	3	1	135	55	48	31	1	78	8	8	3	5	8	.38	8	.270	.333	.338
Kleinz,Larry	Kane County	Fla	A	24	107	364	88	16	1	11	139	50	44	48	2	63	4	2	3	1	2	.33	8	.242	.334	.382
Klimek,Joshua	Beloit	Mil	A	24	121	443	118	31	3	12	191	62	66	39	1	56	5	2	6	4	8	.33	8	.266	.329	.431
Knauss,Tom	Ft. Wayne	Min	A	24	14	58	11	1	0	1	15	3	7	6	0	18	0	0	0	1	0	1.00	1	.190	.266	.259
Knight,Marcus	Butte	Ana	R+	19	72	293	86	15	5	8	135	51	43	44	2	62	8	1	3	8	3	.73	4	.294	.397	.461
Knupfer,Jason	Clearwater	Phi	A+	23	108	365	94	15	0	1	112	56	40	49	1	70	4	7	5	5	6	.45	7	.258	.348	.307
Koehler,Jason	Dunedin	Tor	A+	23	1	1	0	0	0	0	0	1	0	1	0	0	0	0	0	0	0	.00	0	.000	.500	.000
	St. Cathrns	Tor	A-	23	10	39	9	4	0	1	16	4	7	4	0	11	0	0	0	0	1	.00	1	.231	.302	.410
	Hagerstown	Tor	A	23	26	69	14	0	0	3	23	7	12	3	0	19	1	2	0	1	3	.25	1	.203	.247	.333
Koerner,Michael	Sou. Oregon	Oak	A-	22	24	106	36	12	1	2	56	21	19	11	2	30	0	0	0	7	3	.70	1	.340	.402	.528
	Visalia	Oak	A+	22	32	85	16	3	2	2	29	13	12	8	0	27	3	3	1	2	3	.40	2	.188	.278	.341
Kofler,Eric	Greensboro	NYA	A	22	73	262	72	17	2	5	108	23	39	7	0	54	0	3	2	3	2	.60	1	.275	.288	.412
	Tampa	NYA	A+	22	39	151	35	8	1	2	51	12	22	5	0	25	0	0	2	4	4	.00	4	.232	.253	.338
Kokinda,Stephen	Everett	Sea	A-	23	34	98	28	3	1	2	39	18	14	15	1	27	0	3	0	1	1	.50	2	.286	.381	.398
Kominek,Toby	Stockton	Mil	A+	25	128	476	143	28	7	15	230	83	72	50	3	107	24	1	2	22	14	.61	8	.300	.393	.483
Konrady,Dennis	Columbus	Cle	A	23	107	365	110	23	3	2	145	60	43	62	0	60	5	7	5	15	7	.68	6	.301	.405	.397
Kratochvil,Tim	Michigan	Bos	A	24	44	129	34	4	1	0	40	11	19	9	0	35	2	0	0	0	0	.00	4	.264	.317	.310
Kraus,Jake	Ogden	Mil	R+	24	18	63	23	5	0	4	40	16	21	10	0	4	6	0	2	3	0	1.00	2	.365	.481	.635
	Helena	Mil	R+	24	51	183	73	17	1	6	110	35	48	28	3	11	6	0	2	5	4	.56	10	.399	.489	.601
Kurilla,Kevin	Batavia	Phi	A-	23	60	209	50	7	1	5	74	27	36	17	3	59	1	3	1	7	1	.88	3	.239	.296	.354
Kurtz,Tony	Frederick	Bal	A+	24	81	262	57	11	4	3	85	35	17	38	2	90	1	1	5	7	2	.78	1	.218	.318	.324
	Delmarva	Bal	A	24	38	119	29	6	4	0	43	13	9	11	0	49	1	2	2	4	0	1.00	0	.244	.308	.361
LaForest,Pierre	Devil Rays	TB	R	20	34	107	28	7	2	3	48	21	21	10	0	18	1	1	0	4	3	.57	1	.262	.328	.449
Lamb,Michael	Pulaski	Tex	R+	22	60	233	78	19	3	9	130	59	47	31	2	18	4	2	6	7	2	.78	5	.335	.412	.558
Lambert,Clark	Mets	NYN	R	23	35	114	26	5	0	0	31	12	11	12	0	18	1	0	0	0	0	.00	2	.228	.307	.272
	St. Lucie	NYN	A+	23	2	2	0	0	0	0	0	0	0	0	0	0	0	0	0	0	0	.00	0	.000	.000	.000
Landaeta,Luis	Rockies	Col	R	21	37	144	42	6	3	0	54	24	13	7	0	9	1	1	0	4	3	.57	5	.292	.329	.375
Landingham,Ja.	Medicne Hat	Tor	R+	21	21	43	13	3	1	0	18	10	3	3	0	5	0	2	0	3	3	.50	0	.302	.348	.419
Landry,Jacques	W Michigan	Det	A	24	103	369	101	18	5	16	177	51	52	21	1	99	8	0	5	15	3	.83	6	.274	.323	.480
Landstad,Rob	Columbus	Cle	A	25	96	331	74	12	7	13	139	41	56	27	0	91	3	1	2	5	3	.63	7	.224	.287	.420
Langaigne,Selw.	Dunedin	Tor	A+	22	42	90	17	3	0	1	23	9	7	10	0	26	0	4	1	4	1	.80	4	.189	.270	.256
	St. Cathrns	Tor	A-	22	74	266	85	15	4	1	111	50	39	48	1	46	2	0	3	19	9	.68	1	.320	.423	.417
Langdon,Trajan	Idaho Falls	SD	R+	22	22	90	17	7	0	2	30	11	10	11	0	36	1	0	1	0	1	.00	1	.189	.282	.333
Lankford,Derrick	Erie	Pit	A-	23	58	195	60	11	3	10	107	36	55	33	4	57	1	0	2	2	0	1.00	1	.308	.407	.549
Lara,Balmes	Tigers	Det	R	20	43	151	36	4	3	6	64	26	29	20	0	51	2	0	2	0	3	.00	1	.238	.331	.424
Lara,Edward	Visalia	Oak	A+	20	13	45	10	4	0	1	17	10	3	4	0	9	1	0	0	1	1	.50	0	.222	.300	.378
	Modesto	Oak	A+	20	2	2	0	0	0	0	0	0	0	0	0	2	0	0	0	0	0	.00	0	.000	.000	.000
	Sou. Oregon	Oak	A-	22	65	252	69	12	5	2	97	45	43	32	0	28	4	3	5	25	7	.78	3	.274	.358	.385
Lara,Felix	Erie	Pit	A-	22	50	165	41	8	1	1	54	24	16	17	0	55	0	2	0	8	8	.50	1	.248	.319	.327
Larkin,Stephen	Chston-WV	Cin	A	24	129	464	129	23	10	13	211	88	79	52	1	83	5	0	5	28	9	.76	6	.278	.354	.455
LaRue,Jason	Chston-WV	Cin	A	24	132	473	149	50	3	8	229	78	81	47	0	90	5	1	8	14	4	.78	8	.315	.377	.484
Lauterhahn,Dani.	Jamestown	Det	A-	22	53	186	46	7	1	1	56	18	14	14	0	39	2	2	1	2	4	.33	2	.247	.305	.301
Lawler,Scott	Astros	Hou	R	23	1	4	2	1	0	0	3	2	2	1	0	0	0	0	0	2	0	1.00	0	.500	.500	.750
	Auburn	Hou	A-	23	39	106	25	3	0	3	37	16	10	9	0	35	0	0	4	2	0	1.00	3	.236	.305	.349
Lawrence,Joseph	Hagerstown	Tor	A	21	116	446	102	24	1	8	152	63	38	49	0	107	5	3	2	10	12	.45	3	.229	.311	.341
Lawrence,Mike	Butte	Ana	R+	22	69	263	68	10	2	2	88	43	46	36	0	40	1	4	4	4	2	.67	9	.259	.345	.335
Lawrence,Tony	Idaho Falls	SD	R+	23	56	210	56	8	2	7	89	40	36	34	3	48	2	0	4	7	3	.70	2	.267	.369	.424
Layne,Jason	Lansing	KC	A	25	98	337	93	22	3	9	148	54	68	54	3	85	9	0	3	0	0	.00	5	.276	.387	.439
Leach,Nicholas	Savannah	LA	A	20	37	131	35	6	0	0	41	14	13	14	0	23	4	0	0	1	2	.33	2	.267	.356	.313
	Yakima	LA	A-	20	54	192	60	18	1	7	101	33	47	32	4	37	6	0	1	5	0	1.00	1	.313	.424	.526
	San Berndno	LA	A+	20	16	60	22	6	1	4	42	11	12	5	0	11	2	0	0	1	0	1.00	1	.367	.433	.700
Lebron,Hector	Devil Rays	TB	R	20	40	98	25	4	0	0	29	7	19	7	0	16	1	1	0	2	1	.67	5	.255	.305	.296
LeBron,Juan	Lansing	KC	A	21	35	113	24	7	0	3	40	12	20	7	0	32	1	0	0	0	0	.00	4	.212	.216	.354
	Spokane	KC	A-	21	69	288	88	27	1	7	138	49	45	17	2	74	1	0	7	8	4	.67	5	.306	.347	.479
LeBron,Ruben	Lowell	Bos	A-	21	51	167	51	9	1	1	65	25	24	6	0	30	1	7	1	13	3	.81	4	.305	.331	.389
Ledbetter,Blake	Johnson Cty	StL	R+	21	16	42	5	1	0	0	6	2	2	0	0	15	0	0	0	0	0	.00	0	.119	.140	.143
Lee,Carlos	Winston-Sal	ChA	A	22	139	546	172	50	4	17	282	81	82	36	2	65	2	2	7	11	5	.69	12	.317	.357	.516
Lee,David	New Jersey	StL	A-	22	60	226	54	10	0	5	79	34	37	21	0	69	3	0	0	8	2	.80	6	.239	.312	.350
Leggett,Adam	Boise	Ana	A-	22	62	219	49	16	2	1	72	47	32	34	1	54	6	0	3	8	1	.89	7	.224	.340	.329
Lehr,Ryan	Braves	Atl	R	19	54	207	62	15	2	4	93	30	34	9	0	32	0	0	2	1	0	1.00	6	.300	.326	.449
Leidens,Enrique	Expos	Mon	R	20	19	41	13	5	0	0	18	6	3	3	0	9	0	0	1	2	2	.50	0	.317	.364	.439
	Wst Plm Bch	Mon	A+	20	1	7	1	0	0	0	1	0	0	0	0	0	0	0	0	0	0	.00	0	.143	.143	.143
Lemonis,Chris	W Michigan	Det	A	24	48	158	48	10	1	3	69	27	30	9	1	31	1	0	0	2	5	.29	3	.304	.345	.437
Leon,Carlos	Red Sox	Bos	R	18	44	126	31	5	3	0	42	18	15	14	0	25	1	3	0	10	3	.77	4	.246	.326	.333

1997 Batting — Single-A and Rookie Leagues

Player	Team	Org	Lg	A	G	AB	H	2B	3B	HR	TB	R	RBI	TBB	IBB	SO	HBP	SH	SF	SB	CS	SB%	GDP	Avg	OBP	SLG
Leon,Jose	Peoria	StL	A	21	118	399	92	21	2	20	177	50	54	32	1	122	9	2	2	6	5	.55	10	.231	.301	.444
Leon,Donny	Greensboro	NYA	A	22	137	516	131	32	1	12	201	45	74	15	2	106	5	2	7	6	4	.60	13	.254	.278	.390
Lewis,Jeremy	Daytona	ChN	A+	25	72	233	65	15	3	4	98	31	30	9	0	45	1	1	2	2	1	.67	1	.279	.306	.421
Lewis,Keith	Rockford	ChN	A	23	15	41	7	2	0	0	9	5	5	3	0	9	1	1	0	1	0	1.00	1	.171	.244	.220
	Daytona	ChN	A+	23	62	94	20	4	0	1	27	11	10	8	0	25	1	3	1	1	1	.50	1	.213	.279	.287
Lignitz,Jeremiah	Jamestown	Det	A-	21	41	150	42	7	1	2	57	16	27	9	0	47	3	0	0	0	2	.00	6	.280	.333	.380
Ligons,Merrell	Spokane	KC	A-	21	44	143	32	2	0	2	40	25	11	32	0	54	0	1	0	12	2	.86	4	.224	.366	.280
Lina,Donald	Rockies	Col	R	20	28	86	18	1	0	0	19	12	6	7	0	26	1	0	0	8	2	.80	3	.209	.277	.221
Lina,Estivinson	Pulaski	Tex	R+	21	14	51	9	1	0	1	13	5	4	5	0	19	1	0	1	1	0	1.00	3	.176	.263	.255
Linares,Rodney	Tigers	Det	R	20	25	57	13	0	1	0	15	5	10	6	0	23	0	1	0	2	0	.00	1	.228	.288	.263
Lindsey,John	Asheville	Col	A	21	110	399	94	20	2	12	154	54	67	29	1	110	11	1	3	3	2	.60	14	.236	.303	.386
Lindsey,Rod	Clinton	SD	A	22	130	502	107	15	8	6	156	80	49	62	0	161	7	3	2	70	23	.75	8	.213	.307	.311
Lindstrom,David	Lakeland	Det	A+	23	76	213	44	8	0	3	61	25	14	24	0	25	3	5	2	1	0	1.00	9	.207	.293	.286
Little,Josh	Devil Rays	TB	R	19	28	63	13	0	1	0	15	8	4	6	0	22	2	3	0	1	2	.33	4	.206	.296	.238
Liverziani,Claudi	Wisconsin	Sea	A	23	108	346	88	22	4	5	133	73	31	68	0	93	3	2	0	11	4	.73	7	.254	.381	.384
Livingston,Doug	Asheville	Col	A	24	128	468	123	30	3	3	168	53	61	45	1	82	5	15	0	8	5	.62	12	.263	.334	.359
Llanos,Alexis	Butte	Ana	R+	20	49	179	60	9	2	8	97	41	43	17	1	30	3	1	1	3	1	.75	6	.335	.400	.542
Llibre,Brian	Johnson Cty	StL	R+	20	33	105	28	10	4	0	50	17	22	7	0	25	2	0	1	1	1	.50	2	.267	.322	.476
Locurto,Gary	Michigan	Bos	A	20	120	419	99	27	0	4	138	64	63	63	2	93	2	3	2	8	5	.62	13	.236	.337	.329
Lofton,James	Burlington	Cin	A	24	129	483	128	18	3	4	164	83	45	54	1	89	4	9	3	20	12	.63	9	.265	.342	.340
Logan,Kyle	Auburn	Hou	A-	22	71	260	76	16	4	0	100	27	29	20	3	60	1	0	0	5	10	.33	3	.292	.345	.385
Lomasney,Steve	Michigan	Bos	A	20	102	324	89	27	3	12	158	50	51	32	0	98	9	3	3	4	4	.43	8	.275	.353	.488
Lombard,George	Durham	Atl	A+	22	131	462	122	25	7	14	203	65	72	66	9	145	9	2	2	35	7	.83	6	.264	.365	.439
Long,Garrett	Augusta	Pit	A	21	83	280	84	10	2	7	119	50	41	61	2	78	1	0	1	5	2	.71	3	.300	.426	.425
	Lynchburg	Pit	A+	21	9	29	6	3	0	1	12	1	5	3	0	10	0	0	0	0	0	.00	1	.207	.281	.414
Long,Terrence	St. Lucie	NYN	A+	22	126	470	118	29	7	8	185	52	61	40	4	102	2	0	4	24	8	.75	6	.251	.310	.394
Longmire,Marcel	Rockford	ChN	A	20	84	266	58	7	2	3	78	20	21	14	0	77	2	1	1	6	5	.55	13	.218	.261	.293
Longueira,Tony	Wilmington	KC	A+	23	62	195	47	7	0	2	60	27	23	21	0	34	3	3	0	2	3	.40	1	.241	.324	.308
Lopes,Omar	Bristol	ChA	R+	21	49	170	47	4	0	3	60	29	23	24	1	22	2	1	0	7	3	.70	9	.276	.369	.353
Lopez,Henry	Ft. Wayne	Min	A	20	87	327	80	13	4	5	116	43	29	29	1	76	4	4	0	10	9	.53	11	.245	.314	.355
Lopez,Jose	Diamondback	Ari	R	19	41	155	41	7	2	1	55	17	22	7	0	22	1	1	2	1	4	.20	5	.265	.297	.355
Lopez,Luis	Hagerstown	Tor	A	24	136	503	180	47	4	11	268	96	99	60	4	45	8	0	6	5	8	.38	14	.358	.430	.533
Lopez,Luis	Salem-Keizr	SF	A-	20	1	4	0	0	0	0	0	0	1	0	0	1	0	0	0	0	0	.00	1	.000	.000	.000
Lopez,Pee Wee	St. Lucie	NYN	A+	21	113	375	93	19	0	3	121	40	30	39	3	56	0	1	1	3	2	.60	10	.248	.318	.323
Lopez-Cao,Mike	Hudson Vall	TB	A-	22	14	44	13	3	0	1	19	6	7	3	0	10	0	1	0	2	0	1.00	2	.295	.333	.432
	Princeton	TB	R+	22	17	53	12	0	1	1	17	7	7	5	0	8	0	0	0	0	0	.00	2	.226	.288	.321
Lopiccolo,Jamie	Beloit	Mil	A	25	112	410	136	27	3	17	220	72	80	38	2	76	9	1	4	5	6	.45	10	.332	.397	.537
Lorenzana,Luis	Augusta	Pit	A	19	92	288	68	11	1	0	81	36	20	31	0	66	2	4	1	4	5	.44	5	.236	.314	.281
Lorenzo,Juan	Ft. Wayne	Min	A	20	4	7	1	0	0	0	1	0	0	1	0	1	1	0	0	0	0	.00	0	.143	.250	.143
	Elizabethtn	Min	R+	20	22	210	63	10	2	7	98	41	34	12	1	38	6	3	0	4	2	.67	4	.300	.355	.467
Loyd,Brian	Clinton	SD	A	24	73	259	71	10	0	2	87	35	33	25	2	41	8	4	5	6	4	.60	12	.274	.350	.336
Luderer,Brian	Athletics	Oak	R	19	39	123	33	4	0	3	46	21	26	17	0	12	6	1	1	3	4	.43	6	.268	.381	.374
Lugo,Julio	Kissimmee	Hou	A+	22	125	505	135	22	14	7	206	89	61	46	1	99	2	8	4	35	8	.81	8	.267	.329	.408
Lugo,Ursino	Burlington	Cle	R+	23	13	48	13	2	0	0	15	8	5	5	0	7	0	0	0	9	4	.69	0	.271	.340	.313
Lunar,Fernando	Macon	Atl	A	21	105	380	99	26	2	7	150	41	37	18	1	42	5	2	1	0	0	.00	11	.261	.302	.395
Lutz,Manuel	Bristol	ChA	R+	22	65	249	81	11	3	13	137	50	61	19	0	71	4	0	3	6	3	.67	3	.325	.378	.550
Macalutas,Jon	Beloit	Mil	A	23	59	211	66	13	1	10	111	45	36	24	1	19	11	1	1	6	5	.55	6	.313	.409	.526
	Stockton	Mil	A+	23	42	164	44	10	2	4	70	18	35	9	0	13	3	0	2	2	2	.50	6	.268	.315	.427
Macias,Jose	Lakeland	Det	A+	24	122	424	113	18	2	2	141	54	21	51	3	33	2	8	2	10	14	.42	10	.267	.348	.333
MacKay,Tripp	Cape Fear	Mon	A	24	68	189	45	6	1	0	53	25	12	29	0	20	2	7	1	5	9	.36	2	.238	.344	.280
Mackowiak,Rob.	Erie	Pit	A-	21	61	203	58	14	2	1	79	26	25	21	0	47	7	3	1	1	7	.13	5	.286	.371	.389
Macrory,Robert	New Jersey	StL	A-	23	67	248	76	9	2	1	92	52	26	18	0	27	2	3	2	23	3	.88	3	.306	.356	.371
Maddox,Garry	High Desert	Ari	A+	23	101	409	125	22	12	7	192	89	44	52	2	94	0	3	0	25	8	.76	8	.306	.384	.469
Madera,Wil	Lethbridge	Ari	R+	21	33	101	30	4	0	3	43	15	11	4	0	29	1	1	0	5	0	1.00	2	.297	.330	.426
	South Bend	Ari	A	21	70	210	52	8	4	1	71	22	20	16	0	66	1	1	0	6	3	.67	2	.248	.301	.338
Maduro,Remy	Utica	Fla	A-	21	49	157	34	5	3	0	45	16	12	15	0	27	1	1	0	2	5	.29	2	.217	.287	.287
Mahoney,Ricardo	Rockies	Col	R	19	31	121	33	3	0	0	36	14	17	5	0	19	1	1	0	6	2	.62	3	.273	.307	.298
Maier,T.J.	New Jersey	StL	A-	23	55	155	33	9	1	2	50	19	22	20	0	30	2	1	1	6	2	.75	2	.213	.309	.323
Majcherek,Matth.	Pulaski	Tex	R+	23	24	62	12	1	0	1	13	11	2	5	0	17	0	0	0	5	0	1.00	1	.194	.351	.210
Malave,Jaime	Savannah	LA	A	23	58	206	52	11	1	9	92	23	32	4	0	54	1	1	1	2	1	.67	1	.252	.269	.447
	San Berndno	LA	A	23	4	4	1	0	0	0	1	0	0	0	0	0	0	0	0	0	0	.00	0	.250	.250	.250
Maldonado,Carl.	Wisconsin	Sea	A	19	97	316	60	8	2	0	72	15	25	17	1	33	3	8	3	2	3	.40	8	.190	.236	.228
Maloney,Jeffrey	Hagerstown	Tor	A	21	101	395	102	19	2	7	146	49	38	23	2	98	2	3	1	19	9	.68	7	.258	.300	.370
Manfredi,Joel	Vero Beach	LA	A+	22	6	3	0	0	0	0	0	1	0	0	0	0	0	0	0	0	0	.00	0	.000	.000	.000
Mann,Derek	Devil Rays	TB	R	20	50	168	48	2	1	1	55	34	17	29	0	24	1	2	0	8	11	.42	1	.286	.406	.327
Manning,Brian	Bakersfield	SF	A+	23	105	394	111	21	3	8	162	56	41	34	2	74	3	1	3	6	5	.55	10	.282	.347	.411
	Winston-Sal	ChA	A+	23	28	106	31	6	0	2	43	13	12	8	1	14	0	2	1	2	4	.33	3	.292	.353	.406
Manning,Nate	Daytona	ChN	A+	24	120	454	111	29	0	7	161	51	54	14	0	93	6	0	6	5	4	.56	12	.244	.273	.355
Mansavage,Jay	Kissimmee	Hou	A+	22	9	33	9	0	1	1	14	4	1	2	0	6	1	0	0	1	0	1.00	0	.273	.333	.424
	Auburn	Hou	A-	22	13	40	13	3	1	0	18	7	2	5	0	2	0	0	0	1	1	.50	0	.325	.400	.450
Marchant,Nick	Martinsvlle	Phi	R+	19	23	75	7	0	0	0	7	3	3	3	0	32	1	1	0	1	0	1.00	0	.093	.138	.093
Marchiano,Mich.	Everett	Sea	A-	23	63	257	75	20	0	15	140	52	64	22	2	42	5	0	1	6	4	.60	6	.292	.358	.545
	Wisconsin	Sea	A	23	3	9	1	0	0	0	1	0	1	0	0	0	0	0	0	0	0	.00	0	.111	.273	.111
Marcinczyk,T.R.	Modesto	Oak	A+	24	133	463	128	41	2	23	242	89	91	71	5	107	11	1	6	4	4	.50	7	.276	.381	.523
Marino,Lawrence	Red Sox	Bos	R	23	47	145	41	7	0	1	51	15	19	15	0	19	2	1	2	0	0	.00	3	.283	.354	.352
	Sarasota	Bos	A+	23	4	11	1	0	0	0	1	0	0	1	0	2	0	0	0	0	0	.00	0	.091	.167	.182
Markray,Thaddi.	Billings	Cin	R+	18	46	119	17	1	0	0	20	11	5	15	0	44	1	0	0	3	0	1.00	3	.143	.255	.168

1997 Batting — Single-A and Rookie Leagues

Player	Team	Org	Lg	A	G	AB	H	2B	3B	HR	TB	R	RBI	TBB	IBB	SO	HBP	SH	SF	SB	CS	SB%	GDP	Avg	OBP	SLG
Marnell,Dean	Portland	Col	A-	22	19	70	21	1	0	0	22	13	9	7	0	8	2	2	1	1	1	.50	1	.300	.375	.314
	Salem	Col	A+	22	17	52	10	2	0	0	12	4	7	3	0	1	1	2	0	0	0	.00	0	.192	.250	.231
Marsh,Roy	Sarasota	Bos	A+	24	107	230	53	4	4	1	68	47	14	23	0	44	1	8	4	19	8	.70	2	.230	.298	.296
Marshall,Monte	Vero Beach	LA	A+	24	18	26	7	1	0	0	8	4	2	1	0	4	0	0	0	0	0	.00	0	.269	.296	.308
	Great Falls	LA	R+	24	58	184	53	8	3	0	67	29	21	8	0	34	1	6	1	12	6	.67	0	.288	.320	.364
Marsters,Brando.	Piedmont	Phi	A	23	61	212	43	8	0	2	57	25	20	22	2	51	2	1	0	0	0	.00	4	.203	.278	.269
	Clearwater	Phi	A+	23	44	141	26	3	0	0	29	10	18	15	0	26	4	1	2	1	0	1.00	3	.184	.278	.206
Martin,Casey	Boise	Ana	A-	22	50	181	61	14	0	8	99	30	48	23	0	45	1	0	3	1	0	1.00	4	.337	.409	.547
Martin,Chris	St. Pete	TB	A+	30	105	393	102	20	0	9	149	72	49	62	1	66	7	5	4	23	7	.77	13	.260	.367	.379
Martin,Jared	Lethbridge	Ari	A-	23	25	78	18	3	3	0	27	12	5	15	1	19	2	0	1	1	0	1.00	1	.231	.365	.346
	South Bend	Ari	A	23	34	97	24	6	1	0	32	13	10	9	0	30	1	2	2	2	1	.67	0	.247	.312	.330
Martin,Tommy	Bluefield	Bal	R+	22	40	90	26	3	1	1	34	17	9	8	0	31	1	0	1	9	3	.75	0	.289	.350	.378
Martin,Mike	Lancaster	Sea	A+	25	34	110	26	5	0	1	34	17	16	25	0	15	1	1	1	1	1	.50	3	.236	.380	.309
Martine,Chris	New Jersey	StL	A-	22	47	142	30	5	0	0	35	22	12	22	0	37	2	0	3	0	0	.00	3	.211	.320	.246
Martinez,Andres	Mets	NYN	R	21	31	96	23	8	4	0	39	18	7	9	0	33	0	2	1	2	0	1.00	0	.240	.302	.406
Martinez,Tony	South Bend	Ari	A	24	108	404	110	21	1	6	151	54	62	37	1	85	3	3	8	1	3	.25	15	.272	.332	.374
Martinez,Belvani	Diamondback	Ari	R	19	30	134	43	11	2	0	58	25	11	3	0	18	3	2	2	7	2	.78	3	.321	.345	.433
	Lethbridge	Ari	R+	19	25	90	31	4	1	6	55	21	13	5	0	13	4	1	1	4	1	.80	2	.344	.400	.611
Martinez,David	Beloit	Mil	A	22	30	88	19	1	1	0	22	10	5	5	0	33	0	1	0	1	3	.25	0	.216	.258	.250
Martinez,Hipolito	Sou. Oregon	Oak	A-	21	65	222	72	13	4	9	120	45	44	34	2	65	2	1	1	3	2	.60	2	.324	.417	.541
Martinez,Luis	Savannah	LA	A	21	75	294	68	7	3	2	87	26	23	5	0	48	3	3	2	1	0	1.00	6	.231	.250	.296
Martinez,Rafael	St. Lucie	NYN	A+	22	66	204	40	11	2	1	58	24	13	15	1	54	2	1	2	0	1	.00	5	.196	.256	.284
	Capital City	NYN	A	22	44	149	40	7	2	5	66	20	25	17	2	44	1	0	0	10	2	.83	1	.268	.347	.443
Martinez,Victor	Everett	Sea	A-	20	20	58	14	2	1	0	18	10	9	8	0	16	0	1	0	1	0	1.00	2	.241	.333	.310
	Wisconsin	Sea	A	20	30	95	19	2	1	0	23	9	6	4	0	19	1	6	0	3	3	.50	0	.200	.240	.242
Marval,Raul	Bakersfield	SF	A+	22	115	437	112	15	3	2	139	41	42	11	0	66	2	6	3	8	6	.57	8	.256	.276	.318
Mateo,Henry	Vermont	Mon	A-	21	67	228	56	9	3	1	74	32	31	30	1	44	7	3	2	21	11	.66	4	.246	.348	.325
Mateo,Ruben	Charlotte	Tex	A+	20	99	385	121	23	8	12	196	63	67	22	0	55	6	1	2	20	5	.80	16	.314	.359	.509
Mateo,Victor	Yankees	NYA	R	21	26	93	25	3	0	0	28	18	10	6	0	14	1	0	1	4	0	1.00	1	.269	.317	.301
Mathis,Jared	Ogden	Mil	R+	22	54	197	55	14	0	0	69	30	29	6	0	20	4	4	1	7	3	.70	3	.279	.313	.350
Mathis,Joe	Lancaster	Sea	A+	23	134	562	159	28	15	14	259	94	82	38	1	94	7	3	5	25	16	.61	3	.283	.333	.461
Matos,Luis	Delmarva	Bal	A	19	36	119	25	1	2	0	30	10	13	9	0	21	2	2	1	8	5	.62	2	.210	.275	.252
	Bluefield	Bal	R+	19	61	240	66	7	3	2	85	37	35	20	0	36	4	1	1	26	4	.87	5	.275	.340	.354
Matos,Pascual	Durham	Atl	A+	23	117	430	104	18	3	18	182	51	50	14	3	122	2	0	1	4	5	.44	12	.242	.268	.423
Mauck,Matt	Cubs	ChN	R	19	40	144	41	8	4	1	60	28	19	21	0	46	4	0	2	8	3	.73	5	.285	.386	.417
Maxwell,Keith	Erie	Pit	A-	23	42	134	28	3	1	6	51	23	24	10	0	38	7	0	3	1	1	.50	4	.209	.292	.381
Maxwell,Vernon	Oneonta	NYA	A-	21	50	148	29	6	2	0	39	14	22	13	0	49	1	0	4	7	2	.78	3	.196	.256	.264
May,Freddie	Augusta	Pit	A	22	107	358	84	13	7	4	123	51	33	43	1	84	0	6	1	16	18	.47	6	.235	.316	.344
May,Scott	Augusta	Pit	A	25	19	44	11	3	0	0	14	5	2	3	0	8	0	2	0	1	2	.33	0	.250	.298	.318
Mazurek,Brian	Pr William	StL	A+	24	97	324	91	17	1	9	137	39	47	21	0	53	3	1	3	0	2	.00	12	.281	.328	.423
McAffee,Josh	South Bend	Ari	A	20	50	168	33	9	1	4	56	16	17	12	0	67	6	0	0	0	1	.00	6	.196	.274	.333
	Lethbridge	Ari	R+	20	36	101	20	5	2	4	41	26	18	13	0	32	5	2	1	0	1	.00	3	.198	.317	.406
McCain,Marcus	St. Pete	TB	A+	24	84	306	87	13	3	0	106	47	36	10	1	30	8	4	4	19	7	.73	4	.284	.320	.346
	Chston-SC	TB	A	24	9	18	4	0	0	0	4	3	2	0	0	1	0	1	1	7	1	.88	0	.222	.286	.222
McCarthy,Kevin	Capital City	NYN	A	21	31	98	19	1	0	1	23	6	9	8	0	21	0	0	0	1	1	.50	0	.194	.255	.235
	Pittsfield	NYN	A-	21	57	201	41	9	2	0	54	20	20	14	2	55	1	1	0	4	2	.67	1	.204	.259	.269
McCartney,Som.	Brevard Cty	Fla	A+	25	16	53	13	2	0	1	18	3	12	3	1	19	1	0	0	0	0	.00	0	.245	.293	.340
McCarty,Matt	San Berndno	LA	A+	22	12	23	2	0	0	0	2	5	1	5	1	5	1	0	0	3	0	1.00	0	.087	.310	.087
McCladdie,Tony	Pittsfield	NYN	A-	22	52	178	42	9	1	0	53	30	22	25	0	30	1	0	2	11	4	.73	2	.236	.330	.298
McClendon,Trav	Peoria	StL	A	25	6	14	3	0	0	0	3	1	2	3	0	4	0	0	0	0	0	.00	0	.214	.353	.214
McClure,Brian	Clinton	SD	A	23	118	416	115	18	11	4	167	75	55	90	4	64	1	3	6	12	11	.52	7	.276	.402	.401
McCorvey,Kenn.	Twins	Min	R	19	42	134	39	6	1	3	56	19	11	5	0	24	2	1	0	10	6	.63	3	.291	.326	.418
McCrotty,William	Yakima	LA	A-	19	43	135	27	2	0	1	32	12	10	9	0	19	3	2	1	2	0	1.00	3	.200	.264	.237
McDaniel,Ryan	Idaho Falls	SD	R+	23	22	74	14	4	1	1	23	5	7	7	0	31	2	0	1	0	1	.00	0	.189	.274	.311
McDonald,Donz.	Tampa	NYA	A+	23	77	297	88	23	8	3	136	69	23	48	0	75	4	1	1	39	18	.68	3	.296	.400	.458
McDonald,John	Kinston	Cle	A+	23	130	541	140	27	3	5	188	77	53	51	0	75	2	7	2	6	5	.55	12	.259	.324	.348
McDonald,Ryan	Royals	KC	R	22	26	57	16	1	1	0	22	9	9	10	0	8	2	0	0	1	0	1.00	1	.281	.406	.386
McGee,Thomas	Bluefield	Bal	R+	22	27	86	21	5	0	1	29	14	8	11	0	22	5	0	0	2	1	.67	1	.244	.363	.337
McGehee,Mike	Princeton	TB	R+	22	33	107	23	5	0	4	40	16	9	20	0	33	4	0	0	0	1	.00	0	.215	.359	.374
McGrath,Sean	Kingsport	NYN	R+	22	26	78	20	4	0	0	24	18	6	7	0	26	5	3	2	4	4	.50	2	.256	.348	.308
McHenry,Joe	Elizabethtn	Min	R+	22	51	168	54	6	0	6	78	40	31	22	0	48	1	2	3	5	3	.63	1	.321	.397	.464
McHugh,Ryan	Pr William	StL	A+	24	116	442	117	27	2	8	172	68	61	32	4	117	3	1	7	4	7	.36	11	.265	.314	.389
McIntyre,Remer	Johnson Cty	StL	R+	19	39	107	20	3	2	0	27	11	3	7	0	38	1	2	0	2	0	.00	2	.187	.243	.252
McKay,Cody	Modesto	Oak	A+	24	125	390	97	20	1	7	140	47	50	46	2	69	16	3	4	4	2	.67	9	.249	.349	.359
McKinley,Michael	Red Sox	Bos	R	23	22	56	15	3	0	0	18	5	6	3	0	8	1	2	1	1	1	.50	2	.268	.317	.321
McKinney,Antoni.	Tigers	Det	R	20	18	65	16	3	0	3	28	16	12	10	0	13	0	1	1	5	2	.71	0	.246	.347	.431
	Jamestown	Det	A-	20	35	116	18	6	1	0	26	12	3	10	0	41	3	0	0	3	1	.75	0	.155	.240	.224
McKinnis,Leroy	Frederick	Bal	A+	25	88	319	92	24	1	4	130	36	39	20	0	62	5	1	0	3	3	.50	14	.288	.340	.408
McKinnon,Tom	Chston-SC	TB	A	25	108	412	94	19	4	11	154	52	53	26	3	100	1	0	3	13	7	.65	7	.228	.274	.374
McLaughlin,Erik	Braves	Atl	R	19	10	21	6	1	0	2	13	5	6	6	0	6	2	0	0	0	0	.00	0	.286	.467	.619
McMullen,Jon	Clearwater	Phi	A+	24	21	77	15	3	0	0	18	7	8	5	1	19	2	0	0	0	0	.00	1	.195	.262	.234
McNally,Shawn	Pr William	StL	A+	25	47	138	30	7	1	0	39	12	18	27	3	22	2	1	1	3	2	.60	6	.217	.353	.283
McNamara,Jam.	Batavia	Phi	A-	23	72	295	92	17	0	6	127	55	54	15	0	33	10	0	6	3	3	.50	4	.312	.359	.431
McNeal,Aaron	Auburn	Hou	A-	20	12	40	10	3	0	0	13	5	3	4	0	10	0	0	0	1	0	1.00	1	.250	.318	.325
	Astros	Hou	R	20	46	164	48	12	0	3	69	22	26	11	0	28	0	0	2	0	5	.00	4	.293	.333	.421
McNeal,Pepe	Peoria	StL	A	22	56	142	35	9	0	5	59	18	25	18	1	32	1	3	1	0	1	.00	4	.246	.325	.415

1997 Batting — Single-A and Rookie Leagues

Player	Team	Org	Lg	A	G	AB	H	2B	3B	HR	TB	R	RBI	TBB	IBB	SO	HBP	SH	SF	SB	CS	SB%	GDP	Avg	OBP	SLG
Meadows,Mike	Mets	NYN	R	19	43	134	39	12	2	3	64	28	22	16	0	35	2	0	1	0	0	.00	2	.291	.373	.478
Medina,Robert	St. Cathrns	Tor	A-	22	34	123	28	5	1	2	41	18	16	7	0	32	1	0	0	1	0	1.00	4	.228	.269	.333
Medosch,Keith	Boise	Ana	A-	23	45	132	29	5	0	0	34	25	9	26	0	31	3	0	0	5	3	.63	5	.220	.360	.258
Medrano,Jesus	Marlins	Fla	R	19	40	111	31	4	0	0	35	20	16	19	0	18	2	1	1	16	3	.84	0	.279	.391	.315
Medrano,Richar.	White Sox	ChA	R	20	29	91	21	4	1	0	27	10	8	8	1	21	2	0	0	2	1	.67	3	.231	.307	.297
Medrano,Steve	Lansing	KC	A	20	97	321	71	7	5	0	88	35	29	34	0	39	3	3	3	10	5	.67	8	.221	.299	.274
Meier,Rob	Yankees	NYA	R	19	5	5	2	0	0	0	2	1	0	1	0	2	0	0	0	0	0	.00	1	.400	.500	.400
Mejia,Juan	Clearwater	Phi	A+	22	26	78	14	0	1	0	16	9	6	6	0	16	0	7	0	3	1	.75	1	.179	.238	.205
	Piedmont	Phi	A	22	36	112	28	6	2	0	38	15	12	0	0	32	1	1	2	7	0	1.00	3	.250	.252	.339
Mejia,Marlon	Auburn	Hou	A-	23	9	23	7	1	0	0	8	5	2	2	0	5	0	0	0	1	1	.50	0	.304	.360	.348
	Quad City	Hou	A	23	21	54	13	1	0	0	14	4	2	3	0	7	2	0	0	0	0	.00	2	.241	.305	.259
Mejia,Miguel	Pr William	StL	A+	23	39	136	29	2	0	0	31	17	9	10	0	25	1	0	0	7	8	.47	3	.213	.272	.228
	New Jersey	StL	A-	23	30	124	41	8	1	0	51	22	14	6	0	27	0	0	2	11	3	.79	2	.331	.356	.411
Mejia,Oliver	Pirates	Pit	R	21	44	157	46	12	1	0	60	20	9	7	0	26	0	2	2	8	7	.53	2	.293	.319	.382
Mejia,Renato	Marlins	Fla	R	21	35	109	25	9	0	1	37	15	8	14	2	27	1	0	0	2	1	.67	2	.229	.339	.339
Melconian,Alex	Utica	Fla	A-	23	62	215	60	6	2	2	76	37	22	18	0	48	15	4	1	6	6	.50	5	.279	.373	.353
	Kane County	Fla	A	23	3	10	1	0	0	0	1	0	1	0	1	2	1	0	0	0	0	.00	1	.100	.250	.100
Melendez,Angel	San Jose	SF	A+	22	62	203	42	11	2	3	66	16	15	14	0	58	3	1	0	0	1	.00	6	.207	.268	.325
Melendez,Jorge	Columbus	Cle	A	24	57	146	34	9	1	0	45	15	12	11	0	37	1	8	1	0	0	.00	1	.233	.289	.308
Melian,Jackson	Yankees	NYA	R	18	57	213	56	11	2	3	80	32	36	20	0	52	0	0	0	9	1	.90	8	.263	.323	.376
Melson,Bryant	Elizabethtn	Min	R+	23	28	80	21	3	1	0	26	18	9	7	0	21	1	3	1	1	0	1.00	3	.263	.326	.325
Mendez,Donaldo	Kissimmee	Hou	A+	20	5	16	3	0	0	0	3	0	1	0	4	0	0	0	1	1	.50	0	.188	.333	.188
	Astros	Hou	R	20	48	150	29	4	0	1	36	16	13	13	0	32	2	3	3	9	6	.60	0	.193	.262	.240
Mendoza,Angel	Red Sox	Bos	R	19	49	170	46	6	4	0	60	18	17	9	0	36	1	0	0	13	1	.93	4	.271	.311	.353
Mendoza,Carlos	Salem-Keizr	SF	A-	18	33	106	22	0	0	0	22	10	6	11	0	19	1	4	0	6	0	1.00	1	.208	.288	.208
Mensik,Todd	Visalia	Oak	A+	23	15	45	9	1	0	1	13	3	6	6	0	11	1	0	1	0	0	.00	2	.200	.302	.289
Meran,Jorge	Jamestown	Det	A-	23	51	183	32	11	0	4	55	21	15	11	1	50	0	0	1	2	1	.67	3	.175	.221	.301
Messner,Jake	Burlington	Cle	R+	21	49	179	45	10	0	9	82	28	26	8	1	47	1	0	3	7	3	.70	3	.251	.283	.458
Metcalfe,Mike	San Berndno	LA	A+	23	132	519	147	28	7	3	198	83	47	55	0	79	4	6	1	67	32	.68	5	.283	.356	.382
Metzger,Erik	Lowell	Bos	A-	23	41	128	25	7	0	2	38	15	21	11	0	40	6	3	4	0	1	.00	0	.195	.282	.297
Metzler,Rod	Spokane	KC	A-	23	62	224	51	5	5	3	75	37	31	18	0	48	1	5	2	9	2	.82	1	.228	.286	.335
Meyer,Brad	Twins	Min	R	22	16	39	10	1	1	0	13	6	4	6	1	5	1	1	0	0	0	.00	0	.256	.370	.333
	Ft. Wayne	Min	A	22	12	20	6	1	1	0	9	5	3	4	0	6	0	3	0	1	0	1.00	0	.300	.417	.450
Meyer,Travis	Savannah	LA	A	24	13	45	13	2	0	0	15	4	2	1	0	6	1	0	0	1	1	.50	2	.289	.319	.333
Meyers,Chad	Rockford	ChN	A	21	125	439	132	28	4	4	180	89	58	74	5	72	10	6	7	54	16	.77	4	.301	.408	.410
Mikesell,Steve	San Berndno	LA	A+	24	2	1	0	0	0	0	0	0	0	1	0	0	0	0	0	0	0	.00	0	.000	.500	.000
Miles,Aaron	Quad City	Hou	A	21	97	370	97	13	2	1	117	55	35	30	0	45	2	7	4	18	11	.62	8	.262	.318	.316
Miller,Kendrick	Pittsfield	NYN	A-	21	26	93	21	3	0	0	24	16	14	6	0	13	2	1	2	4	1	.80	1	.226	.282	.258
Miller,Travis	Hudson Vall	TB	A-	22	37	120	20	7	0	0	27	16	7	6	0	44	1	0	0	1	2	.33	1	.167	.213	.225
Milton,Prinz	Braves	Atl	R	20	26	83	21	5	0	1	29	12	8	7	0	29	4	0	1	1	1	.50	3	.253	.337	.349
Miner,Tony	Watertown	Cle	A-	23	49	164	45	8	1	4	67	26	23	15	0	30	0	1	1	2	1	.33	2	.274	.333	.409
Minor,Damon	Bakersfield	SF	A+	24	140	532	154	34	1	31	283	98	99	87	8	143	5	0	5	2	1	.67	6	.289	.391	.532
Minor,Damon	Padres	SD	R	23	42	146	43	2	2	0	49	46	18	52	0	36	4	0	2	12	10	.55	0	.295	.485	.336
Minor,Ryan	Delmarva	Bal	A	24	134	488	150	42	1	24	266	83	97	51	2	102	15	0	4	7	3	.70	8	.307	.387	.545
Miranda,Alex	Visalia	Oak	A+	21	11	23	4	1	0	1	7	2	4	3	0	9	0	0	0	1	1	.00	0	.174	.269	.304
Miranda,Tony	Lansing	KC	A	25	104	387	132	35	5	5	192	85	72	54	2	62	10	0	5	11	10	.52	10	.341	.430	.496
Mirizzi,Marc	Oneonta	NYA	A-	23	74	245	64	5	1	1	74	40	33	38	0	36	3	3	3	12	7	.63	4	.261	.363	.302
Mitchell,Andres	Portland	Col	A-	22	69	265	61	5	6	4	90	57	20	36	0	102	6	5	2	21	8	.72	2	.230	.333	.340
Mitchell,Derek	W Michigan	Det	A	24	110	353	70	14	2	1	91	47	31	50	1	91	5	8	3	11	8	.58	5	.198	.304	.258
Mitchell,Mike	Rancho Cuca	SD	A+	25	109	440	154	36	1	17	243	78	106	35	0	83	6	0	5	2	0	1.00	8	.350	.401	.552
Moeller,Chad	Ft. Wayne	Min	A	23	108	384	111	18	3	9	162	58	39	48	0	76	13	2	1	11	8	.58	8	.289	.386	.422
Mohr,Dustan	Watertown	Cle	A-	22	74	275	80	20	2	7	125	52	53	31	1	76	4	0	4	3	6	.33	1	.291	.366	.455
Molina,Luis	Lancaster	Sea	A+	24	105	328	75	11	4	0	115	47	46	26	0	63	4	2	7	0	5	.00	4	.229	.288	.351
Monroe,Craig	Charlotte	Tex	A+	21	92	328	77	23	1	7	123	54	41	44	1	80	0	0	6	24	1	.96	5	.235	.320	.375
Montas,Ricardo	Lansing	KC	A	21	4	10	3	0	0	0	3	0	1	0	0	2	0	0	0	0	0	.00	0	.300	.273	.300
	Spokane	KC	A-	21	66	217	65	5	3	2	82	42	20	35	1	39	2	2	2	5	3	.63	3	.300	.398	.378
	Rangers	Tex	R	19	15	28	11	0	1	1	16	5	6	9	0	5	0	0	0	2	0	1.00	2	.393	.550	.571
	Charlotte	Tex	A+	19	1	0	0	0	0	0	0	0	0	0	0	0	0	0	0	0	0	.00	0	.000	.000	.000
Montgomery,An.	Chston-WV	Cin	A	21	20	58	11	3	0	0	14	6	5	2	0	23	1	1	0	7	2	.78	1	.190	.230	.241
	Billings	Cin	R+	21	51	207	65	18	2	4	99	43	31	15	2	47	2	0	3	6	4	.60	1	.314	.361	.478
Montilla,Alvin	Diamondback	Ari	R	20	20	54	10	1	0	0	11	4	3	7	0	20	1	0	0	0	0	.00	2	.185	.290	.204
Moon,Brian	Helena	Mil	R+	20	49	170	48	5	0	0	53	15	22	8	0	23	5	4	2	2	1	.67	4	.282	.330	.312
Moore,Donnie	Beloit	Mil	A	22	47	157	35	3	0	0	38	19	11	13	0	53	6	2	1	8	4	.67	0	.223	.305	.242
Moore,Jason	South Bend	Ari	A	22	59	196	28	5	0	8	57	21	16	19	3	80	2	1	5	2	0	.50	6	.143	.223	.291
Moore,Kenderick	Lansing	KC	A	25	112	456	130	16	8	6	180	105	42	45	0	78	19	2	5	43	14	.75	5	.285	.370	.395
Moore,Vince	Rancho Cuca	SD	A+	26	100	325	76	23	1	9	128	43	38	30	1	108	3	1	2	13	3	.81	5	.234	.303	.394
Mora,Juan	Tigers	Det	R	20	43	155	54	9	5	4	85	26	31	18	0	43	0	0	2	9	2	.82	3	.348	.411	.548
Morales,Domingo	Bluefield	Bal	R+	21	4	6	0	0	0	0	0	2	0	1	0	2	0	0	0	0	0	.00	0	.000	.000	.000
	Orioles	Bal	R	21	33	98	25	4	0	0	29	8	6	9	0	11	3	0	1	5	2	.71	3	.255	.333	.296
Morales,Erick	St. Lucie	NYN	A+	24	38	101	24	7	0	0	31	12	6	14	2	24	1	0	1	1	2	.33	2	.238	.333	.307
Morales,Alex	San Jose	SF	A+	24	29	83	18	2	0	0	20	8	6	4	0	20	1	1	1	4	5	.44	2	.217	.258	.241
Morales,Stephen	Marlins	Fla	R	20	20	62	13	1	0	2	20	7	13	6	0	10	1	0	0	1	1	.50	3	.210	.282	.323
Moreno,Juan	Mariners	Sea	R	20	51	190	69	12	0	0	81	56	36	25	0	18	2	4	2	31	10	.76	2	.363	.438	.426
Moreno,Juan	Pittsfield	NYN	A-	22	71	287	83	17	4	2	114	35	41	12	2	60	0	1	0	19	6	.76	6	.289	.317	.397
Morenz,Shea	Tampa	NYA	A+	24	114	403	95	14	1	7	132	43	44	18	3	101	7	5	4	12	3	.80	7	.236	.277	.328
Moreta,Juan	Great Falls	LA	R+	22	68	265	89	6	2	1	102	45	20	18	0	38	1	6	0	29	17	.63	5	.336	.380	.385
Morgan,James	Diamondback	Ari	R	23	4	9	0	0	0	0	0	1	0	1	0	4	0	0	0	0	0	.00	0	.000	.100	.000

1997 Batting — Single-A and Rookie Leagues

					BATTING															BASERUNNING				PERCENTAGES		
Player	Team	Org	Lg	A	G	AB	H	2B	3B	HR	TB	R	RBI	TBB	IBB	SO	HBP	SH	SF	SB	CS	SB%	GDP	Avg	OBP	SLG
	South Bend	Ari	A	23	5	6	0	0	0	0	0	0	0	1	0	1	0	0	0	0	0	.00	0	.000	.143	.000
Morgan,Todd	Orioles	Bal	R	20	9	16	0	0	0	0	0	1	0	1	0	11	0	0	0	0	0	.00	0	.000	.059	.000
Morillo,Luis	Medicne Hat	Tor	R+	20	8	35	11	3	0	0	14	5	4	4	0	6	0	0	0	6	1	.86	0	.314	.385	.400
Morimoto,Ken	Vero Beach	LA	A+	23	34	85	15	1	0	0	16	13	5	11	0	29	0	2	1	11	1	.92	0	.176	.268	.188
Morris,Greg	Lk Elsinore	Ana	A+	26	74	278	80	26	1	3	117	38	30	29	0	47	2	1	1	3	3	.25	5	.288	.358	.421
Morris,Jeremy	Oneonta	NYA	A-	23	68	239	67	19	1	2	94	44	28	29	0	47	5	0	3	10	3	.77	0	.280	.366	.393
Morrison,Greg	Medicne Hat	Tor	R+	22	69	241	108	16	3	23	199	63	88	14	1	29	3	0	6	2	3	.40	3	.448	.473	.826
Morrison,Scott	Savannah	LA	A	25	61	219	51	13	3	4	82	30	34	17	0	45	4	5	1	4	1	.80	2	.233	.299	.374
Morrow,Alvin	Ogden	Mil	R+	20	2	4	1	0	0	0	1	1	1	1	0	2	0	0	0	0	0	.00	0	.250	.400	.250
Morrow,Nick	St. Pete	TB	A+	26	108	379	102	23	5	11	168	51	53	43	5	78	3	5	3	20	7	.74	2	.269	.346	.443
Mortimer,Mark	Danville	Atl	R+	22	5	13	1	0	0	0	1	1	3	4	0	1	0	1	1	0	0	.00	1	.077	.278	.077
	Eugene	Atl	A-	22	53	174	53	7	2	2	70	25	21	16	0	24	2	0	2	1	1	.50	3	.305	.364	.402
Mosier,Mark	Salem-Keizr	SF	A-	24	19	62	19	2	0	0	21	10	7	9	0	13	1	1	2	0	2	.00	1	.306	.392	.339
	San Jose	SF	A+	24	25	84	22	2	0	1	27	8	13	10	0	13	1	1	1	1	0	1.00	4	.262	.344	.321
Moss,Rick	Ft. Wayne	Min	A	22	133	508	141	28	4	3	186	76	77	61	4	57	2	2	8	3	3	.50	10	.278	.352	.366
Mota,Antonio	San Berndno	LA	A+	20	111	420	101	14	13	4	153	53	49	30	2	97	4	6	2	11	8	.58	9	.240	.296	.364
Mota,Cristian	Watertown	Cle	A-	20	75	311	74	21	2	2	105	51	33	18	1	67	3	0	1	13	4	.76	5	.238	.285	.338
Mota,Gary	High Desert	Ari	A+	27	31	107	27	3	0	5	45	23	16	15	0	25	1	0	0	2	3	.40	2	.252	.350	.421
Mota,Pedro	San Jose	SF	A+	20	13	31	5	1	0	0	6	2	2	1	0	13	0	0	0	1	1	.50	0	.161	.188	.194
Motley,Brittan	Padres	SD	R	19	39	150	36	4	2	0	44	27	14	10	0	38	0	2	1	9	5	.64	2	.240	.286	.293
Motley,Mel	Kinston	Cle	A+	24	7	19	4	1	0	1	8	3	1	0	0	5	0	0	0	0	0	.00	0	.211	.211	.421
	Columbus	Cle	A+	24	28	92	20	4	1	3	35	18	10	14	0	29	0	1	0	4	2	.67	1	.217	.321	.380
Mounts,Alfonso	White Sox	ChA	R	19	41	145	35	5	0	5	55	18	22	15	0	54	5	2	3	9	4	.69	4	.241	.327	.379
Moye,Melvin	Diamondback	Ari	R	19	28	79	16	1	0	1	20	10	5	14	0	16	3	0	1	2	1	.67	2	.203	.340	.253
Mucker,Kelcey	Ft. Myers	Min	A+	23	114	389	93	26	3	3	134	43	48	33	1	80	4	4	7	1	5	.17	5	.239	.300	.344
Mulvehill,Chase	Mets	NYN	R	20	49	169	44	7	0	1	54	20	19	13	0	30	5	1	3	7	2	.78	3	.260	.326	.320
	St. Lucie	NYN	A+	20	2	6	0	0	0	0	0	0	0	0	0	2	0	0	0	0	0	.00	0	.000	.000	.000
Munson,Michael	Greensboro	NYA	A	22	1	0	0	0	0	0	0	0	0	0	0	0	0	0	0	0	0	.00	0	.000	.000	.000
Murphy,Nathan	Cedar Rapds	Ana	A	23	51	149	33	4	2	0	41	21	13	19	1	43	1	0	1	4	2	.67	2	.221	.312	.275
Murphy,Robby	Chston-WV	Cin	A	25	53	174	32	10	0	0	42	19	7	7	0	38	0	3	1	7	2	.78	0	.184	.214	.241
Murray,Doug	Auburn	Hou	A-	23	34	79	13	1	0	0	14	4	5	8	0	18	4	3	1	0	1	.00	6	.165	.272	.177
Myers,Aaron	Asheville	Col	A	22	12	40	3	1	0	0	4	3	4	0	0	8	1	1	0	0	0	.00	0	.075	.174	.100
Myers,	Charlotte	Tex	A+	23	90	287	71	7	4	0	86	40	21	36	0	73	3	1	1	18	15	.55	5	.247	.336	.300
Myers,Tootie	Expos	Mon	R	19	54	217	50	9	2	0	63	26	13	11	0	58	4	1	0	24	8	.75	3	.230	.280	.290
Myers,Mickey	Everett	Sea	A-	23	4	7	1	0	0	0	1	1	0	0	0	2	0	0	0	0	0	.00	0	.143	.143	.143
	Wisconsin	Sea	A	23	20	55	11	3	1	1	19	4	4	3	0	18	0	0	1	0	1	.00	0	.200	.241	.345
Myles,Dion	Devil Rays	TB	R	20	5	11	1	0	0	0	1	0	1	2	0	5	0	0	0	1	0	1.00	0	.091	.231	.091
Nanita,Emmanu.	Twins	Min	R	18	22	62	16	2	0	0	18	4	2	5	0	14	0	1	0	2	0	1.00	1	.258	.313	.290
Ndungidi,Ntema	Orioles	Bal	R	19	18	54	10	2	1	2	20	10	7	12	0	15	1	0	0	4	0	1.00	1	.185	.343	.370
Nelson,Brian	Everett	Sea	A-	22	13	37	10	2	0	0	12	5	3	3	0	15	1	0	0	0	0	.00	0	.270	.341	.324
Nelson,Charlie	Vero Beach	LA	A+	26	113	417	117	12	1	6	149	73	42	50	0	62	1	11	3	53	16	.77	5	.281	.357	.357
Neubart,Garrett	Salem	Col	A+	24	133	527	135	23	3	0	164	66	34	39	0	90	12	10	2	50	18	.74	3	.256	.321	.311
Neuberger,Scott	Princeton	TB	R+	20	67	254	70	11	2	9	112	46	53	30	0	59	2	0	2	7	1	.88	5	.276	.353	.441
Newkirk,Jeffrey	Bristol	ChA	R+	22	48	188	56	14	3	7	97	46	24	28	2	29	2	1	0	6	4	.60	2	.298	.394	.516
Newman,Howard	Billings	Cin	R+	22	17	44	13	3	0	1	19	7	7	0	0	14	1	0	1	0	0	.00	1	.295	.304	.432
	Chston-WV	Cin	A	22	12	31	5	1	0	1	9	3	4	6	0	10	1	0	0	2	0	1.00	1	.161	.308	.290
Newton,Kimani	Yakima	LA	A-	19	56	201	54	7	1	3	72	34	14	23	1	63	4	1	1	20	6	.77	0	.269	.354	.358
Nichols,Kevin	Piedmont	Phi	A	22	81	321	94	16	2	5	129	21	46	9	0	46	0	0	3	1	1	.50	7	.293	.309	.402
	Clearwater	Phi	A+	22	4	13	0	0	0	0	0	0	0	0	0	5	0	0	0	0	0	.00	0	.000	.000	.000
Nicholson,Kevin	Padres	SD	R	22	7	34	9	1	0	2	16	7	8	2	0	5	0	0	0	2	0	.00	2	.265	.306	.471
	Rancho Cuca	SD	A+	22	17	65	21	5	0	1	29	7	9	4	0	15	2	2	0	2	1	.67	1	.323	.380	.446
Nicley,Dru	Astros	Hou	R	20	26	59	7	0	0	0	7	5	3	4	0	30	0	3	0	0	0	.00	2	.119	.175	.119
Nicolas,Jose	Pirates	Pit	R	19	40	141	34	6	3	0	46	17	11	13	0	44	1	0	0	3	2	.60	2	.241	.310	.326
Nielsen,Bret	Mariners	Sea	R	19	48	163	40	8	2	2	58	23	29	30	0	64	1	0	3	10	3	.77	5	.245	.360	.356
Nieves,Jose	Daytona	ChN	A+	23	85	331	91	20	1	4	125	51	42	17	0	55	4	4	6	16	6	.73	7	.275	.313	.378
Nieves,Juan	St. Cathrns	Tor	A-	21	64	243	56	14	0	2	76	29	30	7	1	41	2	1	1	3	5	.38	3	.230	.257	.313
Nieves,Wilbert	Clinton	SD	A	20	18	55	12	1	1	1	18	6	7	6	0	10	0	1	1	2	1	.67	0	.218	.290	.327
	Padres	SD	R	20	8	27	8	2	0	0	10	2	2	5	0	5	0	0	1	1	0	1.00	0	.296	.406	.370
Nizov,Alexander	Butte	Ana	R+	18	24	87	24	5	1	1	34	12	8	8	0	21	2	1	0	1	2	.33	1	.276	.351	.391
Nolasco,Regino	Orioles	Bal	R	18	58	165	37	10	0	1	50	17	18	21	0	33	1	3	6	3	7	.30	3	.224	.306	.303
Nolte,Bruce	Pittsfield	NYN	A-	24	47	161	37	3	4	0	48	22	18	11	0	37	2	2	1	4	0	1.00	2	.230	.286	.298
Norrell,Troy	Martinsville	Phi	R+	21	36	120	23	6	0	5	44	17	18	15	0	55	3	0	1	4	3	.57	2	.192	.297	.367
Nova,Fernando	Bristol	ChA	R+	22	42	143	38	9	1	2	55	29	23	14	0	35	6	1	1	8	3	.73	3	.266	.354	.385
Nova,Geraldo	Red Sox	Bos	R	20	40	122	35	5	2	0	44	8	17	18	0	33	0	0	2	1	3	.25	6	.287	.373	.361
Nova,Kelvin	Athletics	Oak	R	21	33	123	30	1	3	1	40	19	20	19	0	27	0	0	3	18	4	.82	1	.244	.347	.325
Nunez,Abraham	Diamondback	Ari	R	18	54	213	65	17	4	0	90	52	21	26	0	40	2	2	3	5	5	.50	4	.305	.384	.423
	Lethbridge	Ari	R+	18	2	6	1	0	0	0	1	2	1	1	0	0	0	0	0	0	0	.00	0	.167	.286	.167
Nunez,Jose	South Bend	Ari	A	22	108	351	97	16	11	1	138	55	45	59	0	67	3	7	3	4	1	.80	7	.276	.382	.393
Nunez,Jose	Rockies	Col	R	19	51	204	75	17	3	3	107	30	32	18	2	29	4	1	5	12	2	.86	4	.368	.420	.525
Nunez,Jose	Royals	KC	R	21	51	174	36	7	4	3	60	23	23	21	1	51	2	2	1	2	0	1.00	5	.207	.298	.345
Nunez,Jose	Athletics	Oak	R	21	51	181	51	10	3	6	85	39	42	47	0	47	2	0	2	2	2	.50	6	.282	.431	.470
Nunez,Jose	Mets	NYN	R	21	5	15	5	1	0	0	6	3	2	1	0	4	0	0	0	1	0	1.00	0	.333	.375	.400
	Kingsport	NYN	R+	21	2	6	0	0	0	0	0	1	0	0	0	2	0	0	0	0	0	.00	0	.000	.000	.000
Nunez,Juan	Charlotte	Tex	A+	21	21	61	12	1	1	0	15	7	6	8	0	18	1	3	1	5	7	.42	1	.197	.315	.246
	Pulaski	Tex	R+	21	37	122	23	1	0	2	36	19	14	21	0	39	1	3	1	21	4	.84	0	.189	.310	.295
Nunley,James	Boise	Ana	A-	23	60	216	61	16	1	5	94	34	39	26	0	37	4	1	2	5	3	.63	8	.282	.367	.435
Nunnari,Talmad.	Vermont	Mon	A-	23	62	236	75	11	3	4	104	30	42	31	4	37	3	0	4	6	3	.67	4	.318	.398	.441

1997 Batting — Single-A and Rookie Leagues

Player	Team	Org	Lg	A	G	AB	H	2B	3B	HR	TB	R	RBI	TBB	IBB	SO	HBP	SH	SF	SB	CS	SB%	GDP	Avg	OBP	SLG
	Cape Fear	Mon	A	23	9	35	13	1	1	1	19	8	6	1	0	5	0	0	0	2	0	1.00	0	.371	.389	.543
O'Hearn,Brandon	Chston-WV	Cin	A	23	65	215	52	13	3	6	89	27	32	23	1	69	1	1	2	6	2	.75	0	.242	.315	.414
O'Toole,Bobby	Delmarva	Bal	A	24	1	0	0	0	0	0	0	0	0	0	0	0	0	0	0	0	0	.00	0	.000	.000	.000
	Orioles	Bal	R	24	6	21	6	0	0	1	9	1	3	1	0	5	0	0	0	0	0	.00	0	.286	.318	.429
	Frederick	Bal	A+	24	12	29	8	2	0	1	13	5	4	7	0	4	0	1	0	0	0	.00	0	.276	.417	.448
Ochoa,Javier	Astros	Hou	R	19	30	81	16	2	1	0	20	7	14	7	0	13	2	1	0	1	1	.50	1	.198	.278	.247
Olivares,Teuris	Yankees	NYA	R	19	38	153	40	4	7	0	58	33	17	14	0	40	1	0	0	7	2	.78	1	.261	.327	.379
Oliver,John	Billings	Cin	R+	20	6	11	1	0	0	0	1	1	0	1	0	3	1	0	0	0	0	.00	0	.091	.231	.091
Oliveros,Leonar.	Piedmont	Phi	A	22	38	129	22	3	0	0	25	6	5	5	0	18	1	2	0	0	0	.00	6	.171	.207	.194
Olmeda,Jose	Michigan	Bos	A	20	61	194	37	7	0	1	47	24	21	11	0	63	1	1	0	5	0	1.00	3	.191	.238	.242
	Lowell	Bos	A-	20	54	187	54	8	2	4	78	24	27	16	0	42	1	1	0	2	2	.50	4	.289	.351	.417
Olsen,D.C.	Cape Fear	Mon	A	26	51	160	41	9	2	5	69	18	29	9	0	37	1	0	1	2	1	.67	1	.256	.298	.431
Olson,Dan	Hickory	ChA	A	23	98	350	100	31	3	9	164	59	47	36	1	120	3	1	5	4	1	.80	4	.286	.353	.469
Oquendo,Nelvin	Salem-Keizr	SF	A-	18	4	5	1	0	0	0	1	1	0	1	0	2	0	0	0	0	0	.00	0	.200	.333	.200
Orndorff,Dave	Elizabethtn	Min	R+	20	55	228	84	15	1	11	134	62	42	22	0	25	6	2	2	18	4	.82	1	.368	.434	.588
Oropeza,Asdrub.	Braves	Atl	R	17	50	167	38	8	0	4	58	38	22	37	0	27	4	1	1	3	0	1.00	1	.228	.378	.347
Oropeza,Willie	Cape Fear	Mon	A	22	78	270	63	9	0	7	93	28	32	8	0	46	2	3	5	1	2	.33	10	.233	.256	.344
Ortega,William	Pr William	StL	A+	22	73	249	57	14	0	0	71	23	15	21	1	42	0	1	0	2	1	.33	10	.229	.289	.285
Ortiz,Asbel	Michigan	Bos	A	22	43	143	40	8	1	3	59	19	6	3	0	32	1	1	0	1	0	1.00	2	.280	.299	.413
Ortiz,Carlos	Medcine Hat	Tor	R+	18	31	70	14	2	0	0	16	5	4	6	0	17	1	0	0	0	0	.00	1	.200	.273	.229
Ortiz,Jose	Modesto	Oak	A+	21	128	497	122	25	7	16	209	92	58	60	2	107	6	3	4	22	14	.61	7	.245	.332	.421
Osilka,Garret	Ogden	Mil	R+	20	64	231	59	9	2	0	72	41	19	32	1	50	6	5	0	10	4	.71	0	.255	.361	.312
Otero,Oscar	Williamsprt	ChN	A-	21	19	62	10	1	0	0	11	3	7	3	0	10	1	0	0	0	0	.00	0	.161	.209	.177
Otero,William	Salem-Keizr	SF	A-	21	46	147	35	9	3	0	50	22	12	17	1	32	4	0	1	2	1	.67	4	.238	.331	.340
Ovalles,Homy	Wst Plm Bch	Mon	A+	21	2	1	0	0	0	0	0	2	0	0	0	0	0	0	0	0	0	.00	0	.000	.000	.000
	Vermont	Mon	A-	21	29	84	18	4	0	1	25	6	12	9	0	23	1	4	0	3	2	.60	0	.214	.298	.298
Owen,Andy	San Berndno	LA	A+	24	112	357	96	30	5	10	166	46	49	26	1	77	3	0	1	11	13	.46	1	.269	.323	.465
Owens,Billy	Kissimmee	Hou	A+	27	96	381	108	18	2	10	160	51	60	18	5	68	3	0	3	4	2	.67	10	.283	.319	.420
Owens-Bragg,Lu.	Chston-SC	TB	A	24	53	164	37	6	0	1	46	29	14	21	0	37	1	4	0	14	2	.88	2	.226	.317	.280
Ozarowski,Richa.	Jamestown	Det	A-	23	7	28	8	2	1	0	12	5	2	1	0	8	2	1	0	0	0	.00	1	.286	.355	.429
	W Michigan	Det	A	23	36	134	29	7	1	0	38	14	13	8	0	35	1	2	1	2	1	.67	2	.216	.264	.284
Ozuna,Pablo	Johnson Cty	StL	R+	19	56	232	75	13	1	5	105	40	24	10	0	24	1	6	2	23	5	.82	2	.323	.351	.453
Pacheco,Domin.	Mariners	Sea	R	19	26	105	32	4	4	0	44	16	12	2	0	17	4	1	0	6	3	.67	1	.305	.342	.419
Pacheco,Juan	Bluefield	Bal	R+	21	47	132	26	3	1	1	34	21	12	11	0	32	2	2	1	2	4	.33	2	.197	.267	.258
Paciorek,Pete	Clinton	SD	A	22	126	435	102	19	11	7	164	70	52	70	5	113	4	1	5	10	4	.71	6	.234	.342	.377
Padilla,Roy	Sarasota	Bos	A+	22	130	463	114	16	4	2	144	66	38	41	1	80	5	4	0	24	19	.56	14	.246	.314	.311
Paez,Israel	Ft. Myers	Min	A+	21	135	478	121	11	1	1	137	56	39	35	1	66	1	5	3	26	16	.62	18	.253	.304	.287
Pagan,Carlos	Spokane	KC	A-	22	26	68	19	2	0	1	24	13	10	4	0	13	1	0	0	0	0	.00	0	.279	.329	.353
Pagan,Felix	Elizabethtn	Min	R+	23	59	227	66	18	1	9	113	48	41	31	2	59	2	1	5	4	1	.80	4	.291	.374	.498
Panaro,Carmen	High Desert	Ari	A+	22	11	25	7	3	1	0	25	7	3	1	0	31	0	0	0	0	0	.00	4	.212	.219	.240
Pandolfini,Ryan	Hudson Vall	TB	A-	22	40	130	31	4	0	0	37	12	9	13	0	28	0	0	1	2	4	.33	2	.238	.306	.285
Parent,Jerry	Clinton	SD	A	24	87	304	79	13	1	0	94	37	38	50	3	75	1	2	1	5	4	.56	8	.260	.365	.309
	Padres	SD	R	24	5	0	0	0	0	0	0	0	0	0	0	0	0	0	0	0	0	.00	0	.000	.000	.000
Parker,Chris	Tigers	Det	R	18	31	87	14	1	0	0	15	6	7	10	0	33	4	0	2	1	0	.00	1	.161	.272	.172
Parker,Clark	Jamestown	Det	A-	22	9	25	2	0	0	0	2	1	0	2	0	1	0	0	0	0	0	.00	0	.080	.179	.080
Parker,Allan	Lk Elsinore	Ana	A+	26	8	11	2	0	0	1	5	2	3	0	0	3	1	0	0	0	0	.00	0	.182	.250	.455
	Cedar Rapds	Ana	A	26	15	48	12	2	0	0	14	4	5	3	0	10	0	0	0	3	3	.50	0	.250	.294	.292
Parker,Hubert	Mariners	Sea	R	19	38	123	39	6	0	0	45	23	17	26	1	21	0	2	3	5	2	.71	1	.317	.428	.366
Parra,Jose	Charlotte	Tex	A+	21	15	26	3	0	0	0	3	3	1	3	0	14	0	0	0	2	0	.00	0	.115	.207	.115
	Pulaski	Tex	R+	21	51	161	26	3	1	1	34	18	19	26	0	44	2	4	1	8	3	.73	5	.161	.284	.211
Parsons,Jason	Chston-WV	Cin	A	25	131	460	143	34	0	20	237	87	102	62	5	99	14	0	5	5	1	.83	5	.311	.405	.515
Parsons,Jeff	Capital City	NYN	A	24	52	152	41	2	0	0	43	25	11	26	0	41	1	4	0	16	2	.89	1	.270	.380	.283
	St. Lucie	NYN	A+	24	45	134	28	0	0	0	28	13	5	18	0	31	0	0	0	7	6	.54	1	.209	.301	.209
Pascual,Edison	Billings	Cin	R+	20	10	14	1	0	0	0	1	2	0	2	0	5	0	0	0	0	0	.00	0	.071	.188	.071
Pasqual,Edison	Pirates	Pit	R	21	6	21	9	2	0	0	11	1	1	0	0	3	0	0	0	1	0	1.00	0	.429	.429	.524
Pass,Patrick	Marlins	Fla	R	20	19	45	10	1	0	1	14	7	8	10	0	16	0	0	2	3	1	.75	0	.222	.351	.311
Patel,Manny	St. Pete	TB	A+	26	129	505	135	17	7	4	178	66	54	61	0	51	6	7	4	24	15	.62	10	.267	.351	.352
Paterson,Joe	Yakima	LA	A-	19	47	156	36	12	1	0	50	13	15	5	0	51	4	0	2	2	2	.50	2	.231	.257	.321
Patten,Chris	Ogden	Mil	R+	19	8	26	6	0	0	0	6	2	3	3	0	5	0	0	0	1	0	.00	1	.231	.310	.231
	Helena	Mil	R+	19	41	163	45	6	2	0	55	25	16	12	1	33	1	0	0	4	2	.67	1	.276	.330	.337
Patterson,Jake	Ft. Wayne	Min	A	21	121	469	101	16	2	20	181	61	80	38	1	131	12	2	3	11	2	.85	10	.215	.289	.386
Patterson,Martin	Helena	Mil	R+	23	51	169	40	9	0	3	58	24	23	13	0	56	4	0	3	4	2	.67	3	.237	.302	.343
Patton,Cory	Pittsfield	NYN	A-	21	56	199	42	2	3	1	53	27	18	14	0	51	2	4	1	16	1	.94	0	.211	.269	.266
Patton,Greg	Sarasota	Bos	A+	26	4	16	4	1	0	0	5	2	1	2	1	2	0	0	0	0	0	.00	0	.250	.333	.313
Paulino,Arturo	Modesto	Oak	A+	21	76	217	45	12	0	2	63	26	22	17	0	70	3	4	2	1	5	.17	2	.207	.272	.290
Payne,Ronald	Cubs	ChN	R	22	53	179	50	6	1	1	61	28	31	37	0	71	1	0	4	16	10	.62	3	.279	.408	.341
Paz,Richard	Delmarva	Bal	A	20	111	389	94	14	4	2	122	60	48	38	1	60	5	15	4	15	5	.75	3	.242	.314	.314
Pearson,Ryan	Helena	Mil	R+	23	44	134	28	5	1	2	41	17	14	9	0	33	1	0	1	2	3	.40	3	.209	.262	.306
Peck,Tom	Dunedin	Tor	A+	23	50	105	20	4	1	0	26	12	4	14	0	21	1	1	0	0	0	.00	2	.190	.289	.248
Peckham,Chris	Boise	Ana	A-	22	7	35	9	0	0	0	12	7	6	10	0	10	0	0	0	0	0	.00	1	.257	.413	.343
Pedersoli,Bernar.	Jamestown	Det	A-	23	32	105	17	2	0	0	19	11	6	7	0	28	3	1	1	1	0	1.00	1	.162	.233	.181
Peeples,Michael	Dunedin	Tor	A+	21	129	417	107	29	2	2	161	73	42	54	1	83	3	9	7	26	16	.62	8	.256	.331	.338
Pena,Alex	Augusta	Pit	A	21	111	356	87	12	2	5	118	34	40	18	0	81	3	0	1	11	10	.52	8	.244	.286	.331
Pena,Angel	San Berndno	LA	A+	23	86	322	89	22	4	16	167	53	64	32	4	84	2	1	6	3	5	.38	4	.276	.344	.519
Pena,Elvis	Salem	Col	A+	21	93	279	62	9	2	1	78	41	30	37	0	53	2	14	3	16	6	.73	1	.222	.315	.280
Pena,Frank	Elizabethtn	Min	R+	21	37	131	34	4	1	6	58	21	25	14	0	27	1	0	0	0	0	.00	6	.260	.336	.443
Pena,Jose	Pulaski	Tex	R+	21	51	204	68	14	3	3	97	45	31	12	0	40	1	0	0	17	6	.74	5	.333	.374	.475

1997 Batting — Single-A and Rookie Leagues

Player	Team	Org	Lg	A	G	AB	H	2B	3B	HR	TB	R	RBI	TBB	IBB	SO	HBP	SH	SF	SB	CS	SB%	GDP	Avg	OBP	SLG
Pena,Rodolfo	Red Sox	Bos	R	19	44	124	38	5	1	0	45	7	12	10	0	21	3	0	0	1	2	.33	2	.306	.372	.363
Penacruz,Jose	Devil Rays	TB	R	19	36	87	11	3	1	1	19	12	3	12	0	41	5	0	0	0	0	.00	1	.126	.269	.218
Penalver,Juan	Kingsport	NYN	R+	22	51	180	57	8	1	2	73	37	28	32	1	32	5	2	1	7	6	.54	1	.317	.431	.406
	Capital City	NYN	A	22	9	22	6	1	0	0	7	1	1	3	0	3	0	2	0	0	1	.00	1	.273	.360	.318
Pender,Darrell	Tigers	Det	R	19	37	101	18	2	0	0	20	16	4	9	0	38	0	2	0	1	0	1.00	1	.178	.245	.198
Pendergrass,Tyr.	Macon	Atl	A	21	127	489	127	16	5	6	171	81	37	60	0	101	4	8	3	70	15	.82	5	.260	.344	.350
Peniche,Fray	Tigers	Det	R	21	35	106	28	4	0	0	32	19	9	14	0	16	0	1	1	7	3	.70	2	.264	.347	.302
Penix,Troy	Modesto	Oak	A+	26	58	160	36	8	0	3	53	12	18	10	1	40	2	2	1	0	0	.00	0	.225	.277	.331
	Visalia	Oak	A+	26	49	154	32	7	0	5	54	13	23	9	0	46	1	0	2	2	0	.00	1	.208	.253	.351
Peoples,Danny	Kinston	Cle	A+	23	121	409	102	21	1	34	227	82	84	84	4	145	6	0	6	8	1	.89	6	.249	.380	.555
Peoples,Derrick	Yakima	LA	A-	20	47	144	33	7	2	0	44	14	16	13	0	44	2	2	0	7	0	1.00	5	.229	.302	.306
Perez,Alejandro	Red Sox	Bos	R	19	48	151	41	12	3	3	68	19	10	8	0	33	1	1	1	1	2	.33	2	.272	.311	.450
Perez,Angelo	Medicne Hat	Tor	R+	21	70	269	64	15	5	6	107	37	33	19	0	62	3	5	2	8	3	.73	0	.238	.294	.398
Perez,Edwin	Columbus	Cle	A	23	52	187	52	10	1	5	79	30	24	17	0	41	1	1	0	2	2	.50	4	.278	.341	.422
Perez,Jersen	Kingsport	NYN	R+	22	65	258	69	10	2	3	92	45	29	7	0	41	3	0	2	12	7	.63	4	.267	.293	.357
	Capital City	NYN	A	22	2	6	4	3	0	0	7	3	2	0	0	0	1	0	0	1	0	1.00	0	.667	.714	1.167
Perez,Jesse	Orioles	Bal	R	19	35	110	25	5	1	0	28	12	7	7	0	39	3	1	0	1	4	.20	2	.227	.292	.255
Perez,Richard	Delmarva	Bal	A	20	27	68	16	5	2	0	25	9	8	9	0	21	1	1	0	5	2	.71	3	.235	.333	.368
	Bluefield	Bal	R+	20	20	52	9	3	0	0	12	11	5	6	0	17	0	0	0	6	0	1.00	0	.173	.259	.231
Perez,Santiago	Lakeland	Det	A+	22	111	445	122	20	12	4	178	66	46	20	1	98	2	8	5	21	9	.70	6	.274	.305	.400
Perini,Michael	Red Sox	Bos	R	20	39	118	26	4	1	0	32	12	9	14	0	33	0	2	0	2	0	1.00	1	.220	.303	.271
Pernalete,Marco	Bakersfield	SF	A+	19	17	37	10	0	0	0	10	6	2	2	0	7	1	1	0	0	1	.00	0	.270	.325	.270
Pernell,Brandon	Clinton	SD	A	21	95	340	96	26	3	12	164	63	41	44	1	77	5	2	1	15	5	.75	5	.282	.372	.482
Persails,Michael	Red Sox	Bos	R	20	10	21	4	0	0	1	7	3	4	4	0	7	1	0	1	1	0	1.00	0	.190	.333	.333
Peterman,Thom.	Ft. Wayne	Min	A	23	113	417	122	22	0	7	165	46	57	28	4	69	1	1	5	0	0	.00	9	.293	.335	.396
Peters,Tony	Beloit	Mil	A	23	113	375	88	16	6	9	143	50	43	31	0	110	1	5	1	21	7	.75	8	.235	.294	.381
Petersen,Mike	Portland	Col	A-	21	13	51	12	2	0	0	14	8	5	4	0	12	1	0	0	0	1	.00	0	.235	.304	.275
	Rockies	Col	R	21	32	114	25	7	1	0	34	18	12	7	0	19	3	0	1	2	1	.67	1	.219	.280	.298
Petke,Jonathan	Kinston	Cle	A+	20	41	101	17	6	0	0	23	8	10	9	0	24	1	1	0	1	0	.00	3	.168	.243	.228
Petrick,Ben	Salem	Col	A+	21	121	412	102	23	3	15	176	68	56	62	2	100	2	4	2	30	11	.73	6	.248	.347	.427
Petru,Rich	Royals	KC	R	23	1	1	0	0	0	0	0	0	1	0	0	1	0	0	0	0	0	.00	0	.000	.000	.000
	Spokane	KC	A-	23	33	99	27	5	2	3	45	25	17	11	0	15	2	1	0	2	1	.67	5	.273	.354	.454
Phair,Kelly	Stockton	Mil	A+	23	121	415	107	21	2	1	135	48	31	42	0	84	4	5	2	6	10	.38	10	.258	.330	.325
Phelps,Josh	Hagerstown	Tor	A	20	68	233	49	9	1	7	81	26	24	15	0	72	8	0	3	3	2	.60	6	.210	.279	.348
Philip-Guide,She.	Butte	Ana	R+	20	17	50	13	2	0	0	15	10	2	11	0	17	0	0	0	0	1	.00	1	.260	.383	.300
	Boise	Ana	A-	24	19	51	12	4	0	0	16	7	5	7	0	16	1	1	0	2	0	1.00	1	.235	.339	.314
Phillips,Blaine	Oneonta	NYA	A-	25	31	46	5	0	1	0	7	6	1	5	0	12	1	1	0	1	0	1.00	2	.109	.212	.152
Phillips,Jason	Pittsfield	NYN	A-	21	48	155	32	9	0	2	47	15	17	13	0	24	4	1	2	4	0	1.00	1	.206	.282	.303
Phoenix,Wynter	Yakima	LA	A-	23	56	186	47	14	2	3	74	29	17	23	2	36	3	1	4	11	4	.73	1	.253	.343	.398
Piatt,Adam	Sou. Oregon	Oak	A-	21	57	216	63	9	1	13	113	63	35	35	1	58	1	0	1	19	4	.83	4	.292	.391	.523
Pichardo,Gilberto	Butte	Ana	R+	19	8	23	5	1	0	1	9	7	5	5	0	10	0	0	0	0	1	.00	0	.217	.357	.391
Pickering,Calvin	Delmarva	Bal	A	21	122	444	138	31	1	25	246	88	79	53	2	139	9	0	1	6	3	.67	14	.311	.394	.554
Pierce,Brett	Eugene	Atl	A-	21	57	176	49	7	1	1	61	23	19	22	2	25	4	1	3	3	3	.50	4	.278	.366	.347
Pierce,Kirk	Clearwater	Phi	A+	25	24	68	18	1	1	1	24	9	5	3	0	13	3	1	0	1	0	.00	3	.265	.324	.353
Pierzynski,A.J.	Ft. Myers	Min	A+	21	118	412	115	23	1	9	167	49	64	16	1	59	6	1	4	0	1	.00	9	.279	.313	.405
Pigott,Anthony	Hudson Vall	TB	A-	22	1	4	0	0	0	0	0	0	1	0	0	1	0	0	0	0	0	.00	0	.000	.000	.000
	Princeton	TB	R	22	46	151	35	4	1	0	41	20	14	8	0	34	1	1	1	2	1	.67	4	.232	.273	.272
Pimentel,Baez	Athletics	Oak	R	19	41	123	26	2	0	0	28	17	13	21	0	21	0	0	2	4	1	.80	4	.211	.322	.228
Pimentel,Jose	Vero Beach	LA	A+	23	121	344	89	13	1	5	119	56	40	17	0	67	2	2	1	41	19	.68	8	.259	.297	.346
Pimentel,Marino	Marlins	Fla	R	20	44	133	34	7	2	0	45	23	17	10	0	39	1	4	0	8	3	.73	2	.256	.313	.338
Piniella,Juan	Pulaski	Tex	R+	20	33	126	34	4	3	1	47	20	17	8	0	22	0	3	2	9	4	.69	1	.270	.309	.373
Pinson,Brian	Mariners	Sea	R	20	32	100	20	3	1	1	28	16	7	9	0	20	0	1	0	1	1	.86	3	.200	.264	.280
Pinto,Rene	Greensboro	NYA	A	20	35	105	30	9	1	2	47	20	10	3	0	34	1	0	2	0	0	.00	1	.286	.306	.448
	Oneonta	NYA	A-	20	52	187	54	8	2	4	78	31	29	11	1	37	5	1	4	1	3	.25	5	.289	.338	.417
Pittman,Thomas	Expos	Mon	R	18	15	46	7	2	0	0	9	7	2	6	0	19	1	0	0	0	0	.00	1	.152	.264	.196
Pitts,Rick	Lansing	KC	A	22	35	58	9	3	1	0	14	7	6	8	0	16	2	1	0	2	0	1.00	3	.155	.279	.241
	Wilmington	KC	A+	22	15	37	8	1	0	2	15	6	5	3	0	14	0	1	0	3	1	.75	0	.216	.275	.405
Podsednik,Scott	Kane County	Fla	A	22	135	531	147	23	4	3	187	80	49	60	2	72	3	14	3	28	11	.72	5	.277	.352	.352
Poepard,Scott	Ft. Wayne	Min	A	23	36	103	24	9	0	1	36	16	8	10	0	30	1	1	0	1	1	.75	4	.233	.307	.350
Pointer,Corey	Augusta	Pit	A	22	84	248	47	9	0	7	77	38	26	26	0	116	9	3	3	23	3	.88	1	.190	.287	.310
	Erie	Pit	A-	22	18	43	5	0	0	2	11	5	7	3	0	22	4	0	1	1	0	.75	0	.116	.235	.256
Polanco,Juan	Modesto	Oak	A+	23	68	137	32	3	2	6	57	19	19	21	1	39	1	0	1	7	2	.78	0	.234	.338	.416
Polonia,Isreal	Utica	Fla	A-	20	37	110	19	7	0	1	29	13	8	15	0	51	3	3	1	1	1	.50	3	.173	.287	.264
Pomierski,Joe	St. Pete	TB	A+	24	119	422	112	25	5	11	180	64	49	43	4	78	4	2	3	4	3	.57	5	.265	.337	.427
Pond,Simon	Cape Fear	Mon	A	21	118	444	120	11	0	3	140	48	47	37	1	46	2	1	4	12	8	.60	22	.270	.326	.315
Poor,Jeff	San Jose	SF	A+	24	52	118	22	7	0	0	29	11	14	28	0	18	0	0	0	0	0	.00	0	.186	.342	.246
Porter,Jamie	Athletics	Oak	R	22	33	95	24	11	1	0	40	23	11	11	0	31	0	0	5	5	1	.83	1	.253	.357	.421
Prada,Nelson	Ft. Wayne	Min	A	22	29	98	24	5	0	3	38	8	11	3	0	24	1	0	0	1	0	1.00	1	.245	.265	.388
Pratt,Wes	Quad City	Hou	A	25	124	435	112	26	4	12	174	65	51	35	2	56	4	2	4	10	5	.67	7	.257	.316	.400
Preciado,Victor	Yankees	NYA	R	19	54	187	47	9	5	3	75	21	29	15	1	37	4	0	2	6	1	.86	2	.251	.317	.401
Pressley,Kasey	Williamsprt	ChN	A-	21	44	140	27	7	0	3	43	15	13	8	2	56	1	0	0	1	2	.33	4	.193	.242	.307
Priess,Matthew	Salem-Keizr	SF	A-	23	46	172	47	8	2	3	68	22	31	12	0	30	1	0	3	0	1	.00	3	.273	.319	.395
Prieto,Alejandro	Rancho Cuca	SD	A+	25	129	437	94	13	3	3	122	52	38	41	1	59	2	11	6	20	8	.71	6	.215	.282	.279
Prieto,Rick	Rancho Cuca	SD	A+	25	68	281	82	12	3	5	115	47	31	44	0	45	6	2	0	11	6	.65	0	.292	.399	.409
Proctor,Murph	San Berndno	SD	A+	29	107	381	116	33	2	13	192	66	70	65	1	66	4	0	5	1	7	.13	0	.304	.407	.504
Proctor,Jerry	Diamondback	Ari	R	20	3	12	1	0	1	0	3	2	0	0	0	6	0	0	0	1	0	1.00	1	.083	.083	.250
Proctor,Mark	Mets	NYN	R	18	16	45	12	3	0	0	15	7	3	3	0	14	1	0	0	1	0	.50	0	.267	.327	.333

1997 Batting — Single-A and Rookie Leagues

							BATTING													BASERUNNING				PERCENTAGES		
Player	Team	Org	Lg	A	G	AB	H	2B	3B	HR	TB	R	RBI	TBB	IBB	SO	HBP	SH	SF	SB	CS	SB%	GDP	Avg	OBP	SLG
Prodanov,Peter	Michigan	Bos	A	24	55	141	26	5	1	5	48	24	21	18	1	30	3	2	1	1	1	.50	3	.184	.288	.340
Prokopec,Luke	Savannah	LA	A	20	61	164	38	7	3	2	57	11	20	12	1	49	2	0	1	3	1	.75	2	.232	.291	.348
Prosper,Gerard	Mets	NYN	R	20	39	120	34	8	3	0	48	26	13	30	0	22	2	1	0	7	5	.58	3	.283	.434	.400
Prospero,Teo	San Jose	SF	A+	21	29	65	17	2	1	2	27	6	11	3	0	23	0	1	0	1	0	1.00	1	.262	.294	.415
Pryor,Pete	Winston-Sal	ChA	A+	24	124	391	82	15	0	8	121	51	44	71	4	97	9	3	5	3	0	1.00	11	.210	.340	.309
Pugh,Josh	Eugene	Atl	A-	20	30	88	13	3	0	0	16	10	5	4	1	23	2	0	0	0	0	.00	1	.148	.202	.182
Purkiss,Matt	Oneonta	NYA	A-	22	65	213	59	14	0	6	91	31	41	21	2	53	6	0	2	0	2	.00	3	.277	.355	.427
Quaccia,Luke	New Jersey	StL	A-	23	60	204	47	5	0	5	67	27	23	15	1	52	11	0	3	2	3	.40	4	.230	.313	.328
Quatraro,Matthe.	Chston-SC	TB	A	24	78	294	88	18	2	7	131	35	42	18	0	55	2	1	5	15	5	.75	7	.299	.339	.446
Quero,Pedro	Wst Plm Bch	Mon	A+	20	1	2	0	0	0	0	0	0	0	0	0	0	0	0	0	0	0	.000	0	.000	.000	.000
	Expos	Mon	R	20	56	190	59	14	4	1	84	28	21	12	0	31	1	3	3	6	0	1.00	6	.311	.350	.442
	Vermont	Mon	A-	20	13	40	11	1	0	0	12	2	3	3	0	14	0	1	0	1	0	1.00	0	.275	.326	.300
Quire,Jeremy	Lethbridge	Ari	R+	23	30	58	17	5	0	0	22	11	7	3	0	8	1	0	0	0	0	.00	1	.293	.339	.379
Quittner,Peter	Butte	Ana	R+	23	36	134	38	2	1	3	51	21	13	2	0	26	0	2	1	3	1	.75	2	.284	.292	.381
Radcliff,Vic	Lansing	KC	A	21	81	253	68	25	3	3	108	40	33	19	0	56	9	2	6	3	0	1.00	5	.269	.334	.427
Raifstanger,John	Sarasota	Bos	A+	25	95	256	59	8	1	4	81	26	28	27	0	51	1	3	2	7	9	.44	2	.230	.304	.316
Rains,Nick	Mets	NYN	R	19	30	100	22	4	1	0	28	11	8	7	0	39	0	1	0	4	1	.80	3	.220	.271	.280
Rakers,Jason	Idaho Falls	SD	R+	22	5	20	4	1	0	0	5	3	3	3	0	5	0	0	0	0	0	.00	1	.200	.304	.250
Ramirez,Joel	Lancaster	Sea	A+	24	91	328	92	26	4	2	132	41	39	12	0	51	7	8	5	1	3	.25	6	.280	.315	.402
Ramirez,Aramis	Lynchburg	Pit	A+	20	137	482	134	24	2	29	249	85	114	80	9	103	12	0	5	5	3	.63	12	.278	.390	.517
Ramirez,Daniel	Capital City	NYN	A	20	130	478	146	24	4	1	181	82	42	44	0	104	4	3	3	51	25	.67	4	.305	.367	.379
Ramirez,Edgar	Devil Rays	TB	R	18	42	128	29	8	1	0	39	15	8	22	0	31	3	1	0	2	2	.50	0	.227	.333	.305
Ramirez,Juan	Royals	KC	R	20	46	133	27	5	0	2	38	11	14	6	0	18	0	2	1	0	1	.00	11	.203	.236	.286
Ramirez,Julio	Kane County	Fla	A	20	99	376	96	18	7	14	170	70	53	37	1	122	5	14	2	41	6	.87	1	.255	.329	.452
Ramirez,Luis	Orioles	Bal	R	19	45	156	37	1	0	1	55	24	24	12	1	49	3	1	0	5	2	.71	4	.237	.304	.353
Ramon,Ricardo	White Sox	ChA	R	20	38	136	37	2	0	0	39	10	6	10	0	16	0	1	0	4	5	.44	1	.272	.322	.287
Ramos,Kelly	Kingsport	NYN	R+	21	50	170	38	3	1	7	64	25	32	17	3	33	1	4	0	2	3	.40	5	.224	.298	.376
Ramsey,Brad	Cubs	ChN	R	21	51	200	63	10	3	8	103	50	34	22	0	33	13	0	2	8	0	1.00	3	.315	.414	.515
Rand,Ian	Bakersfield	SF	A+	21	29	82	19	4	0	1	26	9	7	4	0	28	2	1	0	2	2	.50	2	.232	.284	.317
Randolph,Ed	Winston-Sal	ChA	A+	23	72	241	53	12	1	4	79	21	27	13	1	68	2	3	2	0	1	.00	2	.220	.264	.328
Randolph,Jaisen	Cubs	ChN	R	19	53	218	58	1	4	0	67	42	26	26	0	45	5	0	2	24	5	.83	3	.266	.355	.307
Rapp,Travis	Bristol	ChA	R+	23	26	81	15	4	0	2	25	9	12	9	0	33	1	1	2	0	1	.00	1	.185	.269	.309
Rauer,Troy	Visalia	Oak	A+	25	90	299	66	14	3	7	107	37	31	25	0	100	1	4	2	5	5	.50	4	.221	.281	.358
Raynor,Mark	Clearwater	Phi	A+	25	136	469	110	12	2	3	135	54	45	60	1	58	9	3	2	8	6	.57	10	.235	.331	.288
Ready,Randy	Lk Elsinore	Ana	A+	38	7	22	4	1	0	2	11	6	4	8	0	6	1	0	0	0	0	.00	0	.182	.419	.500
Reding,Joshua	Expos	Mon	R	21	56	196	50	11	1	2	69	34	19	22	0	31	4	2	2	14	3	.82	3	.255	.339	.352
	Vermont	Mon	A-	21	8	24	4	2	1	0	8	2	0	3	0	11	0	0	0	0	0	.00	0	.167	.259	.333
Redman,Julian	Lynchburg	Pit	A+	21	125	415	104	18	5	4	144	55	45	45	0	82	7	8	1	21	8	.72	8	.251	.333	.347
Reed,Brian	Marlins	Fla	R	20	48	166	33	3	2	0	40	22	10	27	0	48	6	3	1	16	5	.76	3	.199	.330	.241
Reeder,James	Quad City	Hou	A	23	92	312	76	12	2	2	98	35	21	20	3	29	2	1	1	2	4	.33	11	.244	.293	.314
Reese,Nate	Marlins	Fla	R	23	11	29	7	1	0	0	8	3	3	3	0	9	1	0	0	0	1	.00	1	.241	.333	.276
	Utica	Fla	A-	23	13	44	9	2	0	1	15	5	2	0	0	14	0	0	1	0	0	.00	1	.205	.234	.250
Regan,Jason	Wisconsin	Sea	A	22	51	177	45	14	1	9	88	31	23	23	0	55	4	0	3	2	0	1.00	1	.254	.348	.497
	Lancaster	Sea	A+	22	69	260	73	20	2	22	163	50	54	45	2	79	6	0	2	2	2	.50	2	.281	.399	.627
Rexrode,Jackie	South Bend	Ari	A	19	92	330	93	10	5	2	119	60	27	55	0	47	2	5	3	15	5	.75	3	.282	.385	.361
	Lethbridge	Ari	R+	19	26	89	30	2	1	1	39	29	14	29	0	17	1	2	1	7	3	.70	0	.337	.500	.438
Reyes,Deurys	Tigers	Det	R	18	38	113	29	8	1	1	42	24	14	25	1	32	2	0	2	7	1	.88	1	.257	.394	.372
Reyes,Freddy	Ft. Wayne	Min	A	22	85	306	80	19	2	8	127	37	45	12	1	79	11	1	0	0	0	.00	11	.261	.313	.415
Reyes,Jose	Erie	Pit	A-	25	10	33	5	0	0	1	8	3	3	2	0	6	0	0	0	0	0	.00	1	.152	.200	.242
	Pirates	Pit	R	25	12	32	11	2	1	0	15	4	4	1	0	5	0	0	0	1	0	1.00	1	.344	.353	.469
	Lynchburg	Pit	A+	25	2	5	0	0	0	0	0	0	0	0	0	2	0	0	0	0	0	.00	0	.000	.000	.000
Reynoso,Benja.	Rancho Cuca	SD	A+	23	120	407	78	13	2	1	98	48	35	41	0	92	9	18	1	6	2	.75	10	.192	.279	.241
Reynoso,Ismael	Brevard Cty	Fla	A+	20	2	3	0	0	0	0	0	0	0	1	0	2	0	0	0	0	0	.00	0	.000	.250	.000
	Kane County	Fla	A	20	34	91	12	0	0	0	12	4	10	8	0	21	1	2	0	1	2	.33	5	.132	.210	.132
	Marlins	Fla	R	20	48	162	46	11	0	2	63	19	19	23	0	30	1	2	1	8	2	.80	1	.284	.374	.389
Ribaudo,Mike	Williamsprt	ChN	A-	23	30	88	15	2	0	3	26	6	8	2	1	25	0	2	0	1	0	1.00	4	.170	.189	.295
Rice,Charles	Lynchburg	Pit	A+	22	33	95	20	2	1	2	30	10	13	10	0	28	2	0	1	0	0	.00	3	.211	.296	.316
	Augusta	Pit	A	22	51	156	39	6	1	10	77	24	30	16	2	37	2	0	1	3	1	.75	0	.250	.326	.494
Richey,Mikal	Great Falls	LA	R+	19	32	65	14	0	1	1	19	10	10	1	0	29	1	2	0	1	1	.50	0	.215	.239	.292
Riggio,Bob	Ogden	Mil	R+	22	29	73	13	2	0	0	15	13	10	7	0	9	0	0	0	5	0			.178	.250	.205
Rigoli,David	Cape Fear	Mon	A	22	17	48	9	2	0	0	13	5	3	8	0	6	0	0	1	1	0	1.00	1	.188	.298	.271
Rijo-Berger,Jose	Pittsfield	NYN	A-	23	36	135	40	5	0	0	45	20	9	19	1	11	2	3	1	7	2	.78	2	.296	.389	.333
	Capital City	NYN	A	23	17	48	11	2	0	0	13	4	1	6	0	12	0	1	0	2	1	.67	0	.229	.315	.271
Riley,William	Savannah	LA	A	21	27	87	18	3	3	0	27	6	3	3	0	27	2	0	0	4	2	.67	4	.207	.250	.310
	Yakima	LA	A-	21	65	253	67	12	7	7	114	36	43	21	0	77	5	0	0	14	3	.82	7	.265	.333	.451
Rios,Brian	Jamestown	Det	A-	23	45	167	44	6	1	4	64	23	23	14	0	22	4	0	2	3	0	1.00	6	.263	.332	.383
Rios,Fernando	Billings	Cin	R+	19	41	153	51	8	1	0	61	19	18	11	0	22	3	0	1	1	5	.17	1	.333	.387	.399
Rivas,Luis	Ft. Wayne	Min	A	18	121	419	100	20	6	1	135	61	30	33	1	90	5	6	2	28	18	.61	5	.239	.301	.322
Rivera,Carlos	Augusta	Pit	A	20	120	415	113	16	5	9	166	52	65	19	2	82	10	0	6	4	1	.80	9	.272	.316	.400
Rivera,Francisco	Billings	Cin	R+	18	26	46	11	2	1	0	16	4	5	6	0	13	0	0	2	0	0	.00	0	.239	.315	.348
Rivera,Luis	Expos	Mon	R	23	49	161	34	7	1	0	43	15	7	13	0	33	3	1	0	0	0	.00	3	.211	.282	.267
	Vermont	Mon	A-	23	40	135	34	12	2	0	50	17	13	10	0	37	3	0	3	1	1	.50	2	.252	.311	.370
Rivera,Luis	Wst Plm Bch	Mon	A+	23	1	1	0	0	0	0	0	0	0	0	0	0	0	0	0	0	0	.00	0	.000	.000	.000
Rivera,Michael	Tigers	Det	R	21	47	154	44	9	2	10	87	34	36	18	2	25	3	0	2	0	0	.00	6	.286	.367	.565
Rivera,Micky	Peoria	StL	A	24	49	114	17	0	1	0	19	8	13	7	0	20	1	1	0	1	2	.33	0	.149	.205	.167
Rivera,Roberto	Delmarva	Bal	A	21	17	59	9	0	1	2	17	6	5	1	0	20	0	0	0	1	2	.33	0	.153	.167	.288
	Frederick	Bal	A+	21	16	53	12	1	0	1	16	8	8	3	0	16	1	0	0	1	1	.50	0	.226	.281	.302

1997 Batting — Single-A and Rookie Leagues

																				BASERUNNING				PERCENTAGES		
Player	Team	Org	Lg	A	G	AB	H	2B	3B	HR	TB	R	RBI	TBB	IBB	SO	HBP	SH	SF	SB	CS	SB%	GDP	Avg	OBP	SLG
	Bluefield	Bal	R+	21	50	192	61	20	2	3	94	28	27	13	1	43	1	2	1	6	6	.50	3	.318	.362	.490
Rivero,Eddie	Clearwater	Phi	A+	24	132	455	131	30	2	15	210	61	74	49	4	107	4	1	7	1	2	.33	8	.288	.357	.462
Rivers,Jonathan	Dunedin	Tor	A+	23	132	457	123	21	3	13	189	62	75	53	0	107	5	0	7	24	8	.75	8	.269	.347	.414
Roach,Jason	Pittsfield	NYN	A-	22	64	235	50	11	0	6	79	26	28	8	0	70	5	1	3	0	0	.00	1	.213	.251	.336
Robertson,Ryan	Kane County	Fla	A	25	116	376	107	22	1	11	164	64	71	85	4	69	3	0	7	0	3	.00	9	.285	.414	.436
Robinson,Adam	Sou. Oregon	Oak	A-	23	68	250	68	13	2	3	94	41	27	28	0	68	6	2	3	13	11	.54	8	.272	.355	.376
Robinson,Tony	Augusta	Pit	A	22	18	62	13	4	1	0	19	11	8	5	0	6	2	1	1	3	2	.60	2	.210	.286	.306
	Lynchburg	Pit	A+	22	77	254	75	16	3	2	103	40	33	28	0	37	7	5	3	12	6	.67	3	.295	.377	.406
Robinson,Joey	Auburn	Hou	A-	23	39	75	17	1	1	0	20	6	3	4	0	30	1	0	0	1	2	.33	2	.227	.275	.267
Robles,Juan	Lansing	KC	A	26	51	145	30	6	1	2	44	11	17	14	0	40	1	0	1	1	2	.33	1	.207	.280	.303
Rocha,Juan	Wilmington	KC	A+	24	97	340	87	16	1	10	135	43	42	27	1	67	5	0	1	6	3	.67	3	.256	.319	.397
Roche,Marlon	Quad City	Hou	A	23	72	233	51	5	1	3	67	30	36	21	0	57	2	1	3	7	3	.70	9	.219	.286	.288
Rockow,Jeremy	Pirates	Pit	R	20	23	73	17	5	0	3	31	7	15	7	0	18	2	0	0	0	2	.00	1	.233	.317	.425
Rodriguez,Aureli.	Watertown	Cle	A-	24	51	203	62	11	1	2	81	34	22	16	0	32	0	3	2	5	1	.83	2	.305	.353	.399
Rodriguez,Chris	Asheville	Col	A	22	4	0	0	0	0	0	0	0	0	0	0	0	0	0	0	0	0	.00	0	.000	.000	.000
	Portland	Col	A-	22	23	72	19	1	1	0	22	7	4	6	0	12	2	1	0	0	1	.00	0	.264	.338	.306
Rodriguez,Felipe	Medicne Hat	Tor	R+	20	54	190	48	7	0	0	55	48	12	29	0	38	3	3	0	18	6	.75	1	.253	.360	.289
Rodriguez,Guille.	Salem-Keizr	SF	A-	20	11	39	9	3	0	0	12	3	3	5	0	12	0	0	0	0	1	.00	1	.231	.318	.308
	San Jose	SF	A+	20	13	27	4	3	1	0	9	2	2	0	0	9	0	2	0	0	0	.00	0	.148	.148	.333
Rodriguez,John		NYA	R	19	45	153	47	10	2	3	70	31	23	30	1	31	0	0	3	7	0	1.00	3	.307	.414	.458
Rodriguez,John	Idaho Falls	SD	R+	22	32	115	34	5	0	0	39	17	11	10	0	26	2	2	0	1	4	.20	2	.296	.362	.339
Rodriguez,Juan	Cedar Rapds	Ana	A	23	111	416	117	18	3	12	187	66	55	43	0	106	1	18	3	11	12	.48	4	.281	.348	.450
Rodriguez,Liubie.	Hickory	ChA	A	21	129	450	130	21	6	1	166	72	62	65	0	56	5	10	7	12	13	.48	13	.289	.380	.369
Rodriguez,Mark	Kingsport	NYN	R+	24	26	87	13	1	0	3	23	12	14	8	0	25	0	5	0	0	0	.00	1	.149	.221	.264
Rodriguez,Miguel	Johnson Cty	StL	R+	21	8	19	2	0	0	0	2	1	0	0	0	8	0	0	0	0	0	.00	0	.105	.105	.105
Rodriguez,Miguel	Stockton	Mil	A+	23	95	346	95	16	2	8	139	41	35	17	2	68	6	3	1	16	5	.76	13	.275	.319	.402
Rodriguez,Mike	Hagerstown	Tor	A	23	43	123	28	3	0	0	31	17	12	18	0	25	1	3	0	0	0	.00	0	.228	.324	.252
	St. Cathrns	Tor	A-	23	2	7	2	1	0	0	3	0	1	0	0	1	0	0	0	0	0	.00	0	.286	.286	.429
Rodriguez,Sam.	Pittsfield	NYN	A-	22	36	110	27	6	2	5	52	15	20	21	1	33	2	1	2	2	1	.67	1	.245	.370	.473
Rodrigues,Cecil	Wst Plm Bch	Mon	A+	26	15	41	6	1	0	1	10	9	3	3	1	14	0	0	0	2	0	1.00	3	.146	.205	.244
Rodriguez,Gary	Columbus	Cle	A	23	116	482	124	12	5	1	149	73	37	46	1	94	4	11	2	22	8	.73	5	.257	.326	.309
Rojas,Christian	Burlington	Cin	A	23	101	348	83	17	3	16	154	53	56	33	0	106	1	3	3	7	3	.70	4	.239	.304	.443
Rojas,Clara	Helena	Mil	R+	19	47	149	40	3	0	1	46	26	16	8	0	19	1	2	0	5	2	.71	3	.268	.310	.309
Rojas,Mo	Red Sox	Bos	R	21	39	112	32	7	3	0	45	16	6	7	0	16	2	0	1	1	1	.50	1	.286	.336	.402
Rolison,Nate	Brevard Cty	Fla	A+	21	122	473	121	22	0	16	191	59	65	38	1	143	2	0	3	1	3	.25	16	.256	.313	.404
Rollins,Jimmy	Piedmont	Phi	A	19	139	560	151	22	8	6	207	94	59	52	2	80	0	9	3	46	6	.88	4	.270	.330	.370
Rolls,Damian	Savannah	LA	A	20	130	475	100	17	5	5	142	57	47	38	0	83	5	3	4	11	3	.79	9	.211	.274	.299
Roman,Junior	White Sox	ChA	R	19	37	128	31	1	0	0	32	18	9	6	0	23	3	5	1	8	4	.67	3	.242	.290	.250
Romano,Jason	Rangers	Tex	R	19	34	109	28	5	3	2	45	27	11	13	0	19	3	1	1	13	4	.76	1	.257	.349	.413
Romano,Scott	St. Pete	TB	A	26	99	359	107	25	1	7	155	54	67	42	1	55	7	3	3	5	3	.63	8	.298	.380	.432
Romans,Billy	Martinsvlle	Phi	R+	22	19	68	12	4	0	0	16	7	3	3	0	16	0	0	0	3	2	.60	2	.176	.211	.235
Romero,Marty	Bristol	ChA	R+	21	2	2	1	0	0	0	1	0	1	1	0	1	0	0	0	0	0	.00	0	.500	.667	.500
Roneberg,Brett	Marlins	Fla	R	19	53	185	49	11	2	0	64	25	13	28	1	35	0	1	5	5	5	.55	7	.265	.360	.346
Roney,Chad	Vero Beach	LA	A+	23	18	35	6	3	0	0	9	2	2	2	0	7	0	1	0	0	0	.00	0	.171	.216	.257
Roper,Chad	Ft. Myers	Min	A+	24	66	148	30	3	0	3	42	19	9	22	1	23	0	0	0	1	0	1.00	7	.203	.306	.284
Rosa,Erick	Watertown	Cle	A-	23	28	85	16	2	1	0	20	6	7	7	0	22	1	3	0	0	2	.00	1	.188	.258	.235
Rosario,Carlos	Rockies	Col	R	21	45	164	46	7	0	1	56	28	16	10	0	21	1	2	1	14	3	.82	5	.280	.324	.341
Rosario,Felix	Mariners	Sea	R	18	24	62	17	0	2	0	21	15	4	6	0	19	1	0	0	5	5	.50	1	.274	.348	.339
Rosario,Omar	Athletics	Oak	R	20	56	216	52	9	3	0	67	48	28	38	0	51	7	1	3	40	3	.93	1	.241	.367	.310
Rose,Mike	Quad City	Hou	A	21	79	234	60	6	1	3	77	22	27	28	0	62	4	8	3	3	1	.75	1	.256	.342	.329
Ross,Tony	Kissimmee	Hou	A+	23	74	215	55	6	3	1	70	30	19	18	2	40	1	4	0	11	7	.61	5	.256	.316	.326
Ross,Jason	Macon	Atl	A	24	112	430	111	20	5	9	168	70	59	37	0	121	9	0	3	16	7	.70	7	.258	.328	.391
Rowan,Chris	Ogden	Mil	R+	19	55	211	53	10	3	9	96	46	34	27	0	65	4	2	0	2	5	.29	3	.251	.347	.455
Rowson,James	Oneonta	NYA	A-	21	12	41	8	2	0	0	14	8	4	4	0	17	0	0	1	1	0	1.00	2	.195	.267	.341
	Greensboro	NYA	A	21	8	21	6	1	0	0	7	1	2	5	0	8	0	1	0	0	0	.00	0	.286	.423	.333
	Tampa	NYA	A+	21	25	50	3	2	0	0	5	2	4	4	1	29	1	1	0	2	1	.67	0	.060	.145	.100
Ruecker,Dion	Lowell	Bos	A-	22	50	160	35	6	1	1	46	16	11	4	0	32	1	4	0	0	0	.00	2	.219	.242	.288
Ruiz,Willy	Royals	KC	R	19	54	197	71	4	0	0	75	33	14	9	0	19	6	4	0	20	11	.65	6	.360	.406	.381
Runnells,T.J.	Tigers	Det	R	21	48	159	36	5	1	0	43	19	23	17	0	28	3	2	3	7	1	.88	3	.226	.308	.270
Ruotsinoja,Jacob	Clinton	SD	A	21	54	188	35	10	1	0	47	19	16	24	2	51	2	0	2	2	2	.50	4	.186	.282	.255
	Idaho Falls	SD	R+	21	31	109	33	10	1	2	51	20	17	29	1	21	1	0	0	5	0	1.00	1	.303	.450	.468
Rupcich,Larry	Kane County	Fla	A	23	33	111	24	1	0	0	25	13	8	17	0	21	2	5	0	2	0	1.00	1	.216	.331	.225
Russell,Jake	Burlington	Cle	R+	24	27	86	22	2	0	3	33	20	17	14	0	21	4	0	0	0	0	.00	4	.256	.377	.384
	Watertown	Cle	A-	24	2	2	0	0	0	0	0	0	0	2	0	0	0	0	0	0	0	.00	0	.000	.000	.000
Russoniello,Mich.	Boise	Ana	A-	21	2	3	0	0	0	0	0	1	1	0	0	0	2	0	0	0	0	.00	0	.000	.400	.000
Rust,Brian	Durham	Atl	A	22	122	430	111	29	2	12	180	67	71	43	0	104	3	1	5	10	4	.71	8	.258	.326	.419
Rutherford,Daryl	Idaho Falls	SD	R+	22	15	64	24	4	3	0	34	13	10	3	0	14	0	0	0	8	1	.89	0	.375	.391	.531
	Clinton	SD	A	22	21	59	13	3	0	1	19	9	5	4	0	19	0	0	0	2	1	.67	1	.220	.270	.322
Ryan,Mike	Elizabethtn	Min	R+	20	62	220	66	10	0	3	85	44	29	38	3	39	3	1	4	2	2	.50	8	.300	.404	.386
Ryan,Robert	South Bend	Ari	A	25	121	421	132	35	5	8	201	71	73	89	5	58	2	0	5	12	1	.92	7	.314	.431	.477
Ryden,Karl	Idaho Falls	SD	R+	22	57	198	52	6	3	1	67	48	19	45	2	38	4	0	3	9	6	.60	3	.263	.404	.338
Sachse,Matt	Wisconsin	Sea	A	22	110	373	100	21	3	6	145	37	51	26	1	110	2	1	5	3	3	.63	10	.268	.318	.389
Saenz,Olmedo	White Sox	ChA	R	27	2	10	2	0	0	0	2	0	0	0	0	0	0	0	0	0	0	.00	0	1.000	1.000	2.000
Saffer,Jeff	Greensboro	NYA	A	23	90	267	55	13	1	12	106	40	39	35	0	79	6	2	3	0	3	.00	6	.206	.309	.397
Saitta,Rich	Yakima	LA	A-	22	44	183	57	11	1	1	77	37	15	14	0	27	2	1	1	6	2	.75	2	.311	.365	.421
	Great Falls	LA	R+	22	16	58	14	3	0	0	17	4	4	2	0	9	0	0	1	0	2	.00	0	.241	.267	.293
Salazar,Juan	Williamsport	ChN	A-	20	29	105	21	6	0	1	30	12	11	8	1	20	1	0	1	1	0	1.00	2	.200	.261	.286

1997 Batting — Single-A and Rookie Leagues

Player	Team	Org	Lg	A	G	AB	H	2B	3B	HR	TB	R	RBI	TBB	IBB	SO	HBP	SH	SF	SB	CS	SB%	GDP	Avg	OBP	SLG
	Rockford	ChN	A	20	54	161	43	9	0	3	61	16	17	13	0	36	1	1	0	2	1	.67	3	.267	.326	.379
Salinas,Hector	Chston-SC	TB	A	23	90	322	89	19	3	4	126	33	44	24	0	52	1	3	4	4	6	.40	6	.276	.329	.391
Salzano,Jerry	Lakeland	Det	A+	23	40	135	30	4	1	2	42	20	8	22	2	27	2	1	0	1	1	.50	1	.222	.340	.311
	Durham	Atl	A+	23	68	226	63	20	0	1	86	29	24	26	2	42	12	2	1	6	4	.60	10	.279	.381	.381
Samboy,Nelson	Kissimmee	Hou	A+	21	48	190	60	9	2	1	76	20	13	7	0	34	1	0	0	9	6	.60	5	.316	.347	.400
	Astros	Hou	R	21	2	5	2	0	0	0	2	1	1	1	0	0	0	0	0	0	0	.00	0	.400	.500	.400
	Quad City	Hou	A	21	14	51	18	3	0	0	21	2	8	2	0	8	0	1	0	1	1	.50	0	.353	.377	.412
Samuel,Quiva	Tampa	NYA	A+	24	92	323	75	15	3	16	144	39	61	32	2	121	9	1	6	2	0	1.00	5	.232	.314	.446
Sanchez,Alexis	Chston-SC	TB	A	23	131	537	155	15	6	0	182	73	34	37	2	72	3	12	4	92	40	.70	7	.289	.336	.339
Sanchez,Tino	Rockies	Col	R	19	35	113	30	2	1	0	34	13	13	15	0	23	1	4	1	15	0	1.00	1	.265	.350	.301
Sanchez,Manuel	Eugene	Atl	A-	21	58	229	66	6	4	3	89	46	27	12	0	39	9	4	2	14	5	.74	2	.288	.345	.389
Sanchez,Marcos	Clinton	SD	A	23	63	206	60	6	5	4	88	42	39	42	3	53	3	1	2	4	4	.69	5	.291	.415	.427
Sanchez,Orlando	Sarasota	Bos	A+	19	41	99	18	3	1	0	23	10	9	6	0	29	0	1	0	2	1	.67	2	.182	.229	.232
	Michigan	Bos	A	19	21	61	11	2	1	1	18	3	10	9	0	15	0	0	0	0	0	.00	0	.180	.286	.295
Sanchez,Toby	Billings	Cin	R+	23	62	178	39	5	0	5	59	37	35	39	2	76	0	0	2	4	6	.40	5	.219	.382	.331
Sanchez,Welling	Helena	Mil	A-	21	61	236	64	13	0	2	83	46	20	14	0	47	1	3	0	10	7	.59	3	.271	.315	.352
Sanchez,Yuri	Burlington	Cin	A	24	101	364	93	12	12	13	168	66	48	35	0	116	0	2	1	7	3	.70	9	.255	.320	.462
Sandberg,Jared	St. Pete	TB	A+	20	2	3	1	0	0	0	1	1	2	2	0	2	0	1	0	0	0	.00	0	.333	.600	.333
	Princeton	TB	R+	20	67	268	81	15	5	17	157	61	68	42	5	94	2	0	0	12	3	.80	4	.302	.401	.586
Sanderson,David	St. Lucie	NYN	A+	25	97	267	61	8	2	0	73	41	14	54	0	76	1	8	0	11	3	.79	5	.228	.360	.273
Sandoval,Jhensy	South Bend	Ari	A	19	19	72	19	3	0	1	25	9	4	2	0	19	1	0	0	4	3	.57	0	.264	.293	.347
	Lethbridge	Ari	R+	19	40	160	60	14	1	8	100	33	37	8	1	36	3	1	1	7	3	.70	1	.375	.413	.625
Sankey,Brian	San Berndno	LA	A+	24	55	179	46	10	1	2	64	21	22	16	0	28	2	1	1	3	10	.23	1	.257	.323	.358
	Savannah	LA	A	24	63	210	56	11	0	5	82	25	27	24	1	37	2	0	1	5	2	.71	6	.267	.346	.390
Santana,Pedro	W Michigan	Det	A	21	74	287	75	10	6	3	106	36	28	14	0	55	6	3	0	20	3	.87	8	.261	.309	.369
Santiago,Jorge	Pittsfield	NYN	A-	22	48	145	37	3	1	0	42	16	17	8	0	24	6	3	1	5	3	.63	2	.255	.319	.290
Santo,Jose	Rangers	Tex	R	20	28	93	25	5	1	1	35	17	10	21	0	30	1	0	0	12	1	.92	3	.269	.409	.376
	Charlotte	Tex	A+	20	2	6	0	0	0	0	0	0	0	0	0	4	0	0	0	0	0	.00	0	.000	.000	.000
Santos,Ramon	Red Sox	Bos	R	18	17	60	11	1	0	0	12	8	7	7	0	11	0	1	0	8	3	.73	0	.183	.261	.200
Santos,Jose	Butte	Ana	R+	21	21	70	16	3	0	1	22	11	9	9	0	20	1	0	1	1	1	.50	1	.229	.313	.314
Sassanella,Jere.	Tigers	Det	R	19	32	113	25	4	0	1	32	12	17	5	0	24	1	0	3	3	0	1.00	1	.221	.258	.283
Sasser,Rob	Cedar Rapds	Ana	A	23	134	497	135	26	5	17	222	103	77	69	6	92	8	0	3	37	13	.74	11	.272	.367	.447
Saturria,Luis	Peoria	StL	A	21	122	445	122	19	5	11	184	81	51	44	3	95	3	3	3	23	10	.70	5	.274	.341	.413
Sawai,Ryosuke	Padres	SD	R	20	3	10	1	0	0	0	1	3	1	4	0	3	0	0	0	1	0	1.00	0	.100	.357	.100
Schafer,Brett	Lansing	KC	A	24	21	47	9	3	1	0	14	16	6	15	0	8	3	0	1	1	0	1.00	2	.191	.409	.298
Schaffer,Jake	Tigers	Det	R	23	6	21	7	1	1	0	10	5	4	5	0	2	0	0	0	0	0	.00	0	.333	.462	.476
	Jamestown	Det	A-	22	55	215	63	14	4	6	103	39	26	21	0	35	0	0	2	5	2	.71	0	.293	.353	.479
Scharrer,Jim	Macon	Atl	A	21	121	444	109	19	2	20	192	67	57	37	1	136	2	0	1	0	3	.00	1	.245	.306	.432
Schaub,Greg	Beloit	Mil	A	21	108	394	89	18	4	8	139	35	45	17	1	90	4	0	4	5	3	.63	13	.226	.263	.353
Schesser,Heath	Jamestown	Det	A-	22	67	271	77	12	2	3	102	30	39	21	0	40	4	1	3	3	2	.60	2	.284	.342	.376
Schifano,Anthony	Brevard Cty	Fla	A+	23	1	1	0	0	0	0	0	0	0	0	0	1	0	0	0	0	0	.00	0	.000	.000	.000
	Utica	Fla	A-	23	7	0	1	0	0	1	50	26	14	11	0	28	2	8	1	5	5	.50	3	.261	.317	.327
Schlicher,Blair	Martinsville	Phi	R+	20	58	217	64	16	0	5	95	33	34	28	2	59	0	0	0	5	5	.50	3	.295	.376	.438
Schmidt,Dave	Pr William	StL	A+	23	82	231	45	9	0	0	54	23	19	28	0	66	1	3	1	2	2	.50	6	.195	.305	.234
Schmidt,Todd	New Jersey	StL	A-	23	15	38	8	2	0	0	10	2	2	1	0	12	0	0	0	0	0	.00	0	.211	.318	.263
	Peoria	StL	A	23	1	0	1	0	0	0	0	1	0	1	0	0	0	0	0	0	1	.00	0	.000	1.000	.000
Schnabel,Matt	Utica	Fla	A-	23	67	225	43	6	0	2	55	23	22	37	5	46	2	3	5	5	4	.56	5	.191	.305	.244
Schneider,Brian	Cape Fear	Mon	A	21	113	381	96	20	1	4	130	46	49	53	2	45	4	6	5	3	6	.33	5	.252	.345	.341
Schramm,Kevin	Charlotte	Tex	A+	23	88	284	64	18	0	6	100	37	45	33	0	80	2	1	5	5	1	.83	6	.225	.306	.352
Schreiber,Stanle.	Augusta	Pit	A	22	115	345	74	10	1	1	89	51	26	65	0	83	3	10	4	40	11	.78	7	.214	.341	.258
Schwab,Chris	Cape Fear	Mon	A	23	54	209	56	19	2	11	112	29	42	26	2	70	1	0	2	3	3	.50	3	.268	.349	.536
	Wst Plm Bch	Mon	A+	23	58	207	39	7	0	9	73	22	28	22	0	82	1	0	3	3	1	.75	1	.188	.266	.353
Schwartzbauer,.	Portland	Col	A-	23	50	156	40	7	2	3	60	22	29	37	1	47	5	0	2	2	2	.50	1	.256	.410	.385
Scioneaux,Dami.	Hudson Vall	TB	A-	23	70	273	82	13	4	0	103	48	23	31	0	45	5	3	0	22	10	.69	2	.300	.382	.377
Scott,Tom	Chston-WV	Cin	A	25	60	212	53	14	2	8	95	27	28	17	0	82	1	0	1	6	6	.50	1	.250	.307	.448
	Burlington	Cin	A	25	50	183	55	16	1	6	91	30	34	9	0	57	0	2	1	10	1	.91	2	.301	.332	.497
Seabol,Scott	Greensboro	NYA	A	23	48	136	36	12	2	2	58	11	15	9	0	26	4	0	2	3	1	.75	1	.265	.325	.426
Seal,Scott	Idaho Falls	SD	R+	23	30	120	43	8	3	3	66	18	30	22	1	24	1	0	0	0	3	.00	0	.358	.458	.550
	Clinton	SD	A	23	29	114	29	6	0	5	50	20	23	10	0	37	0	2	1	2	1	.67	3	.254	.323	.439
Sears,Todd	Portland	Col	A-	22	59	200	54	13	1	2	75	37	29	41	7	49	0	1	0	2	1	1.00	4	.270	.393	.375
Secoda,Joe	Johnson Cty	StL	R+	20	52	187	47	5	0	3	61	21	16	17	0	56	3	1	1	4	3	.50	3	.251	.322	.326
Seguignol,Ferna.	Wst Plm Bch	Mon	A+	23	124	456	116	27	5	18	207	70	83	30	3	129	5	0	14	5	5	.50	1	.254	.299	.454
Sell,Chip	Vero Beach	LA	A+	23	111	342	97	21	7	7	153	50	46	29	2	67	4	2	3	25	8	.76	4	.284	.344	.447
Sencion,Pablo	St. Cathrns	Tor	A-	22	51	173	38	7	0	8	69	18	36	24	1	47	2	0	0	0	0	.00	0	.220	.315	.399
Sergio,Thomas	Pulaski	Tex	R+	22	58	226	74	14	4	9	123	57	40	38	0	42	4	1	1	25	6	.81	5	.327	.431	.544
Sevillano,Jose	Pirates	Pit	R	22	1	1	0	0	0	0	0	0	0	0	0	0	0	0	0	0	0	.00	1	.000	.000	.000
Sharp,Scott	Burlington	Cin	A	25	30	87	13	2	0	0	15	9	10	12	1	36	2	1	0	0	0	.00	1	.149	.267	.172
Sharpe,Grant	Columbus	Cle	A	23	33	108	14	4	0	2	24	10	9	15	0	46	0	1	0	0	0	.00	0	.130	.234	.222
	Burlington	Cle	R+	20	64	245	62	12	1	10	106	29	51	29	2	86	2	0	0	0	0	.00	0	.253	.336	.433
Shatley,Andy	Hagerstown	Tor	A	22	117	401	97	28	2	10	161	51	46	17	0	114	9	4	3	6	3	.67	6	.242	.286	.401
Sheppard,Grego.	Hickory	ChA	A	23	102	342	105	27	2	12	172	54	62	46	1	81	6	2	4	4	2	.67	2	.307	.394	.503
Shipp,Skip	Augusta	Pit	A	22	81	254	64	15	2	0	83	29	23	26	0	53	4	2	0	12	5	.71	0	.252	.331	.327
Shockey,Greg	Rancho Cuca	SD	A+	28	103	401	136	28	4	14	214	60	78	36	0	67	3	0	7	6	3	.67	2	.339	.394	.534
Shores,Scott	Clearwater	Phi	A+	25	97	276	74	7	0	3	42	20	7	11	0	23	0	0	0	3	6	.67	2	.268	.343	.433
Short,Rick	Frederick	Bal	A+	25	126	480	153	29	1	10	214	73	72	38	2	44	12	7	1	10	7	.59	20	.319	.382	.446
Shuck,Jason	Mets	NYN	R	20	25	73	20	6	1	0	28	10	8	12	0	13	2	1	0	2	1	.67	1	.274	.386	.384
Shumpert,Derek	Tampa	NYA	A+	22	44	169	44	6	1	1	55	24	6	20	0	49	3	3	0	6	8	.43	1	.260	.349	.325

1997 Batting — Single-A and Rookie Leagues

Player	Team	Org	Lg	A	G	AB	H	2B	3B	HR	TB	R	RBI	TBB	IBB	SO	HBP	SH	SF	SB	CS	SB%	GDP	Avg	OBP	SLG
	Greensboro	NYA	A	22	86	322	97	22	6	6	149	49	39	27	1	91	7	0	1	12	6	.67	3	.301	.367	.463
Simpson,Jeramie	Capital City	NYN	A	23	10	29	7	0	1	0	9	4	2	1	0	15	0	0	0	1	1	.50	0	.241	.267	.310
Skeels,David	Lancaster	Sea	A+	25	59	180	50	7	1	0	59	26	21	9	0	40	3	3	0	0	2	.00	10	.278	.323	.328
Skeens,Jeremy	Billings	Cin	R+	20	23	49	10	0	0	1	13	12	9	12	0	15	0	1	1	2	0	1.00	0	.204	.355	.265
Slater,Wayne	Yakima	LA	A-	22	29	68	16	3	0	1	22	11	7	11	2	11	0	0	0	2	0	1.00	2	.235	.342	.324
Slemmer,Dave	Visalia	Oak	A+	25	115	404	113	25	1	10	170	70	64	44	1	83	3	1	1	11	3	.79	9	.280	.354	.421
Smith,Brian	Everett	Sea	A-	21	33	95	22	3	1	1	30	9	7	12	0	29	2	1	0	6	4	.60	0	.232	.318	.316
Smith,Casey	Burlington	Cle	R+	21	19	77	27	2	0	2	35	8	9	3	0	22	2	0	1	1	0	1.00	0	.351	.386	.455
	Columbus	Cle	A	21	13	36	12	0	0	1	15	6	3	8	0	15	1	0	0	0	0	.00	0	.333	.467	.417
Smith,Jason	Williamsprt	ChN	A-	20	51	205	59	5	2	0	68	25	11	10	0	44	0	0	0	9	2	.82	0	.288	.321	.332
	Rockford	ChN	A	20	9	33	6	0	1	0	8	4	3	2	0	11	0	0	0	1	0	1.00	1	.182	.229	.242
Smith,Marcus	Twins	Min	R	22	6	14	1	0	0	0	1	0	1	3	0	8	0	0	0	1	0	1.00	0	.071	.235	.071
	Elizabethtn	Min	R+	22	44	145	33	1	2	5	53	22	15	12	1	32	2	4	3	4	2	.67	0	.228	.290	.366
Smith,Rod	Greensboro	NYA	A	22	137	528	131	25	6	13	207	96	50	69	0	148	5	2	1	54	20	.73	5	.248	.340	.392
Smith,Sam	Rockies	Col	R	19	52	200	47	9	2	1	63	27	18	24	0	38	7	0	0	6	1	.86	2	.235	.338	.315
Smith,Shane	Kingsport	NYN	R+	23	37	113	25	7	0	3	41	15	13	15	0	22	4	3	0	2	1	.67	2	.221	.333	.363
Smothers,Stewa.	Eugene	Atl	A-	22	101	318	64	11	6	2	93	31	27	21	0	57	1	3	0	12	4	.75	5	.275	.337	.399
Snellgrove,Clayt.	Idaho Falls	SD	R+	23	66	281	97	19	7	2	136	52	48	18	2	39	3	2	6	3	2	.60	7	.345	.383	.484
Snow,Casey	San Berndno	LA	A+	23	43	132	26	5	3	1	40	10	10	4	0	35	2	1	0	2	3	.40	1	.197	.232	.303
	Great Falls	LA	R+	23	17	53	17	3	0	2	26	5	9	8	1	10	1	3	0	2	0	1.00	0	.321	.419	.491
Snusz,Chris	Clearwater	Phi	A+	25	36	105	21	7	0	0	28	12	3	2	0	22	0	3	0	0	0	.00	3	.200	.215	.267
Solano,Angel	Hickory	ChA	A	21	11	21	2	1	0	0	3	0	3	3	0	7	0	0	0	0	0	.00	0	.095	.091	.143
Solano,Manuel	Billings	Cin	R+	20	42	98	22	3	1	1	30	14	9	9	0	15	1	0	0	0	3	.00	4	.224	.296	.306
Sollmann,Scott	W Michigan	Det	A	23	121	460	144	13	4	0	165	89	33	79	5	81	11	8	3	40	14	.74	1	.313	.423	.359
Sorg,Jay	Burlington	Cin	A	25	112	399	113	18	2	13	174	62	72	56	3	65	4	2	2	13	7	.65	10	.283	.375	.436
Soriano,Carlos	Capital City	NYN	A	23	131	318	66	14	0	4	92	37	41	24	1	52	1	3	7	5	2	.71	8	.208	.260	.289
Soriano,Jose	Modesto	Oak	A+	24	124	360	82	13	3	5	116	51	44	37	0	95	5	6	7	28	11	.72	5	.228	.303	.322
Soriano,Rafael	Mariners	Sea	R	18	38	119	32	3	2	0	39	19	12	14	0	31	1	3	0	7	4	.64	6	.269	.351	.328
Sosa,Franklin	W Michigan	Det	A	22	57	195	50	4	0	0	54	24	16	10	1	24	9	2	2	2	3	.40	0	.256	.319	.277
Sosa,Jorge	Rockies	Col	R	20	28	91	12	1	2	0	17	13	6	13	0	35	4	1	0	6	0	1.00	0	.132	.269	.187
Sosa,Juan	Vero Beach	LA	A+	22	92	250	55	5	2	5	79	32	29	14	0	39	2	3	3	20	8	.71	6	.220	.264	.316
Sosa,Nicolas	Sou. Oregon	Oak	A-	20	62	196	45	7	2	2	62	29	26	55	0	80	2	0	3	0	3	.00	3	.230	.398	.316
Sotelo,Danilo	Vero Beach	LA	A+	23	25	56	11	1	0	2	18	13	11	10	0	17	0	1	3	1	1	.50	2	.196	.304	.321
Soto,Luis	Padres	SD	R	23	35	140	40	12	1	4	66	20	32	15	0	33	0	0	2	0	2	.00	3	.286	.350	.471
Southward,Marq.	Twins	Min	R	22	57	154	40	2	0	0	42	24	6	29	1	43	0	0	2	14	4	.78	3	.260	.377	.273
Soverel,Bret	Everett	Sea	A-	22	13	36	4	1	0	0	7	1	3	3	1	13	1	0	0	1	1	.50	1	.111	.200	.194
Spear,Chad	Princeton	TB	R+	22	9	17	3	1	0	0	4	8	3	4	0	6	3	0	1	0	0	.00	2	.176	.400	.235
	Hudson Vall	TB	A-	22	18	57	17	5	1	2	30	13	13	8	0	13	0	0	1	1	0	1.00	0	.298	.379	.526
Speckhardt,Mike	New Jersey	StL	A-	22	51	135	25	5	1	0	32	15	6	12	0	39	2	2	1	3	5	.38	4	.185	.260	.237
Speed,Dorian	Rockford	ChN	A	24	71	157	39	7	1	1	51	27	18	18	0	45	4	3	1	18	4	.82	5	.248	.339	.325
Spencer,Jeffrey	Eugene	Atl	A-	21	67	275	72	14	2	12	126	46	54	27	1	83	1	0	5	4	2	.67	0	.262	.325	.458
Spivey,Ernest	High Desert	Ari	A+	23	136	491	134	24	6	6	188	88	53	69	2	115	11	2	3	14	9	.61	9	.273	.373	.383
Springfield,Bo	Augusta	Pit	A	22	12	33	8	0	0	0	8	7	2	7	0	5	0	1	1	5	1	.83	0	.242	.366	.242
St. Pierre,Maxim	Tigers	Det	R	18	20	41	10	1	0	0	11	3	3	3	0	8	3	0	0	2	0	1.00	3	.244	.340	.268
Stanton,Rob	Watertown	Cle	A-	19	57	189	51	11	4	5	85	21	34	20	0	72	1	0	1	4	2	.67	5	.270	.341	.450
Stanton,Thomas	Capital City	NYN	A	22	60	190	36	10	0	7	67	29	31	24	0	79	7	0	2	0	1	.00	2	.189	.300	.353
Staubach,Jeff	Greensboro	NYA	A	23	1	4	0	0	0	0	0	0	0	0	0	1	0	0	0	0	0	.00	0	.000	.000	.000
Stearns,Randy	Savannah	LA	A	23	94	301	68	10	3	2	90	41	18	31	1	96	2	2	0	21	14	.60	1	.226	.302	.299
Steele,Alexander	Jamestown	Det	A-	22	72	257	80	15	4	14	145	51	43	37	2	61	9	0	1	6	3	.67	5	.311	.414	.564
Steelmon,Wyley	Lethbridge	Ari	R+	22	53	166	45	5	1	8	76	29	26	41	1	50	0	0	0	3	0	1.00	1	.271	.415	.458
Steinmann,Scott	Wisconsin	Sea	A	24	72	225	48	7	0	0	55	26	20	24	1	60	4	5	0	5	3	.63	5	.213	.300	.244
Stenson,Dernell	Michigan	Bos	A	19	131	471	137	35	2	15	221	79	80	72	6	105	19	0	8	6	4	.60	10	.291	.400	.469
Stephens,Joel	Bluefield	Bal	R+	22	6	18	3	0	0	0	3	3	1	2	0	2	0	0	0	2	1	.67	1	.167	.250	.167
	Delmarva	Bal	A	22	36	76	17	4	0	2	27	14	4	12	2	26	7	1	0	4	1	.80	0	.224	.379	.355
Stevens,Nathan	Twins	Min	R	19	47	170	41	3	0	1	47	23	17	9	0	21	2	1	2	9	2	.82	8	.241	.284	.276
Stevenson,Chad	W Michigan	Det	A	22	72	259	57	10	1	7	90	32	32	20	1	77	1	2	1	2	4	.33	3	.220	.278	.347
Steverson,Todd	High Desert	Ari	A+	26	24	83	19	4	0	4	35	16	15	19	0	34	3	0	2	0	1	.00	1	.229	.383	.422
Stewart,Courten.	Williamsprt	ChN	A-	22	54	181	44	5	0	0	49	13	26	11	0	50	0	0	0	8	5	.62	3	.243	.286	.271
Stewart,Keith	Wisconsin	Sea	A	24	4	14	2	1	0	0	3	2	0	2	0	4	0	0	0	0	0	.00	0	.143	.143	.214
	Everett	Sea	A-	24	38	127	34	3	2	1	44	19	11	16	0	46	0	0	0	15	3	.83	0	.268	.350	.346
Stewart,Paxton	Boise	Ana	A-	22	85	282	94	16	2	7	135	59	45	41	3	55	2	1	3	8	5	.62	6	.333	.418	.479
Stone,Craig	Dunedin	Tor	A+	22	113	404	95	28	1	14	167	56	59	25	1	109	8	0	2	1	2	.33	9	.235	.292	.413
Stoner,Michael	High Desert	Ari	A+	25	136	567	203	44	5	33	356	115	142	36	4	91	3	1	11	6	4	.60	17	.358	.392	.628
Strangfeld,Aaron	Eugene	Atl	A-	20	11	44	3	1	0	1	7	4	0	4	0	13	0	0	0	0	0	.00	0	.068	.109	.091
	Braves	Atl	R	20	11	38	9	1	0	1	13	4	4	4	0	10	0	0	0	2	0	1.00	0	.237	.310	.342
Stratton,Robert	Kingsport	NYN	R+	20	63	245	61	11	5	15	127	51	50	19	1	94	6	0	0	11	6	.65	2	.249	.319	.518
Streicher,Robert	Cape Fear	Mon	A	24	15	45	5	0	0	0	5	0	4	6	0	10	0	0	0	0	0	.00	2	.111	.216	.111
Strickland,Grego.	Eugene	Atl	A-	22	36	204	58	8	3	0	72	33	16	14	0	62	0	5	3	9	2	.82	0	.284	.326	.353
Stricklin,Scott	St. Pete	TB	A+	26	85	243	63	6	0	0	69	28	29	52	0	32	2	7	1	0	3	.00	4	.259	.393	.284
Stromsborg,Ryan	Hagerstown	Tor	A	23	56	184	53	10	0	3	72	25	24	13	0	37	2	1	1	5	1	.83	2	.288	.337	.408
Stuart,Rich	Lk Elsinore	Ana	A+	21	45	165	38	11	6	6	79	25	33	13	0	50	3	1	5	6	4	.60	3	.230	.290	.479
Stckenschneider.	Vero Beach	LA	A+	26	131	452	126	25	3	6	175	100	45	101	1	79	12	4	5	40	11	.78	4	.279	.419	.387
Stumberger,Darr.	Kinston	Cle	A+	25	133	502	142	30	0	15	217	72	79	60	6	88	3	0	5	1	0	1.00	13	.283	.360	.432
Suarez,Marc	Billings	Cin	R+	20	64	219	76	17	0	9	120	42	37	33	0	51	5	0	2	2	1	.67	5	.347	.440	.548
Suero,Ignacio	Beloit	Mil	A	24	85	297	67	14	1	7	104	32	41	14	0	49	8	0	4	1	3	.25	12	.226	.276	.350
Suplee,Ray	St. Pete	TB	A+	27	4	13	1	0	0	0	1	0	0	0	0	5	0	0	0	0	0	.00	0	.077	.077	.077
Suriel,Miguel	Chston-SC	TB	A	21	26	85	13	2	0	0	15	7	4	5	0	9	1	0	2	0	1	1.00	1	.153	.204	.176

1997 Batting — Single-A and Rookie Leagues

Player	Team	Org	Lg	A	G	AB	H	2B	3B	HR	TB	R	RBI	TBB	IBB	SO	HBP	SH	SF	SB	CS	SB%	GDP	Avg	OBP	SLG
	Princeton	TB	R+	21	58	202	55	3	2	9	89	40	38	21	0	29	1	2	2	2	2	.50	7	.272	.341	.441
Sutton,Joe	Bristol	ChA	R+	23	56	190	63	18	2	11	118	46	43	35	2	51	1	0	1	7	0	1.00	4	.332	.436	.621
Sutton,Bruce	Twins	Min	R	21	35	96	23	5	0	0	28	13	4	13	0	31	5	1	1	1	2	.33	0	.240	.357	.292
Swafford,Derek	Pirates	Pit	R	23	1	5	1	0	0	1	4	1	1	0	0	0	0	0	0	0	0	.00	0	.200	.200	.800
	Lynchburg	Pit	A+	23	38	112	28	5	0	0	33	16	5	25	0	28	1	3	0	8	3	.73	1	.250	.391	.295
	Augusta	Pit	A	23	21	69	15	2	0	1	20	12	9	8	0	20	3	4	2	6	2	.75	0	.217	.317	.290
Sweeney,Kevin	South Bend	Ari	A	24	68	232	61	16	1	4	91	36	37	39	1	56	4	0	2	1	0	1.00	9	.263	.375	.392
Swinton,Jermain	Stockton	Mil	A+	25	93	352	78	14	2	12	132	41	41	32	0	152	2	0	1	2	5	.29	6	.222	.289	.375
Sykes,James	Lethbridge	Ari	R+	23	58	223	68	8	6	4	100	45	37	25	0	40	3	1	0	9	2	.82	6	.305	.382	.448
Taft,Brett	Lansing	KC	A	24	85	269	67	21	0	4	100	41	30	47	0	60	4	5	2	5	4	.56	9	.249	.366	.372
Talbott,Benjamin	Butte	Ana	R+	23	22	65	13	1	0	1	17	13	13	12	1	29	1	0	1	0	0	.00	0	.200	.329	.262
Tamargo,John	Capital City	NYN	A	23	113	393	98	17	2	1	122	44	47	45	2	72	2	5	1	13	7	.65	9	.249	.329	.310
Tancred,Lachlan	Expos	Mon	R	20	22	52	12	3	0	0	15	4	4	10	0	8	1	0	1	1	4	.20	0	.231	.365	.288
Tanner,Paul	Peoria	StL	A	23	104	318	74	19	3	1	102	31	33	19	1	76	2	1	1	9	3	.75	9	.233	.280	.321
Taveras,Franklin	Burlington	Cle	R+	22	56	194	51	10	3	2	73	29	34	16	0	56	0	1	4	11	8	.58	1	.263	.313	.376
Taveras,Jose	South Bend	Ari	A	19	15	43	8	0	0	1	11	5	2	2	0	11	0	0	0	2	1	.67	0	.186	.222	.256
	Lethbridge	Ari	R+	19	67	235	55	6	2	8	89	36	38	19	1	65	3	1	3	5	4	.56	7	.234	.296	.379
Taveras,Jose	Royals	KC	R	21	57	205	67	14	4	7	110	46	39	24	1	42	3	4	1	14	4	.78	1	.327	.403	.537
Taveras,Luis	Rangers	Tex	R	20	37	83	20	3	0	1	26	10	10	9	1	21	0	0	1	1	0	1.00	2	.241	.312	.313
Taylor,Adam	Columbus	Cle	A	24	47	123	23	3	3	1	35	14	16	24	1	66	6	0	2	1	0	1.00	0	.187	.342	.285
	Watertown	Cle	A-	24	50	149	33	8	2	7	66	27	33	25	0	54	4	3	1	1	0	1.00	1	.221	.346	.443
Taylor,Greg	Piedmont	Phi	A	24	41	115	32	7	1	0	41	15	14	15	0	11	2	4	0	1	2	.33	8	.278	.351	.357
	Clearwater	Phi	A+	24	32	83	16	4	0	0	20	7	6	11	0	16	1	2	0	0	0	.00	2	.193	.302	.241
Taylor,Kirk	Spokane	KC	A-	23	23	59	15	3	1	3	29	9	13	4	0	12	1	0	1	0	1	.00	2	.254	.333	.492
Taylor,Reggie	Clearwater	Phi	A+	21	134	545	133	18	6	12	199	73	47	30	4	130	4	5	6	40	23	.63	3	.244	.285	.365
Tegland,Ron	Sou. Oregon	Oak	A-	24	37	108	25	6	1	3	42	17	19	8	0	37	4	1	1	0	1	.00	2	.231	.306	.389
Terhune,Mike	Eugene	Atl	A-	22	14	61	13	1	0	0	14	4	3	4	1	6	0	2	0	0	0	.00	0	.213	.262	.230
	Macon	Atl	A	22	92	328	74	11	4	1	96	33	28	25	0	45	5	6	2	8	3	.73	4	.226	.289	.293
Terni,Charles	Red Sox	Bos	R	19	27	76	14	3	0	0	17	12	4	7	0	23	1	2	0	1	0	1.00	3	.184	.262	.224
Terrell,James	Bristol	ChA	R+	20	47	176	38	4	1	1	47	30	22	17	0	40	1	1	1	5	0	1.00	5	.216	.286	.267
Terrell,Jeffrey	Batavia	Phi	A-	23	52	159	35	4	1	0	41	20	17	16	0	38	1	5	1	3	1	.75	3	.220	.294	.258
Terry,Tony	Auburn	Hou	A-	22	53	157	28	1	0	2	36	14	17	11	0	56	0	3	2	3	4	.43	4	.178	.229	.229
Tessmar,Tim	Capital City	NYN	A	24	120	430	105	14	4	8	151	53	55	36	1	93	2	0	4	10	3	.77	7	.244	.303	.351
Thames,Marcus	Yankees	NYA	R	21	57	195	67	17	4	7	113	51	36	16	0	26	3	1	4	6	4	.60	3	.344	.394	.579
	Greensboro	NYA	A	21	4	16	5	1	0	0	6	2	2	0	0	3	0	0	0	1	0	1.00	0	.313	.313	.375
t'Hoen,E.J.	Cedar Rapds	Ana	A	22	123	384	78	19	3	3	112	41	46	31	0	114	7	7	3	2	3	.40	7	.203	.273	.292
Thomas,Allen	Winston-Sal	ChA	A+	24	31	77	13	4	0	1	20	11	11	13	0	27	1	0	1	1	3	.25	2	.169	.293	.260
	Hickory	ChA	A	24	27	49	4	2	0	0	6	4	2	4	0	19	1	0	1	0	1	.00	1	.082	.164	.122
Thomas,Gary	Athletics	Oak	R	18	28	92	21	2	2	1	30	17	7	9	0	25	3	1	0	6	2	.75	2	.228	.317	.326
Thomas,James	Auburn	Hou	A-	22	66	211	56	15	0	3	80	29	31	30	1	72	6	1	1	4	6	.40	7	.265	.373	.379
Thompson,Nick	Batavia	Phi	A-	23	4	15	3	2	0	0	5	4	4	3	0	3	1	0	0	0	0	.00	0	.200	.368	.333
	Piedmont	Phi	A	23	58	225	58	8	3	3	81	32	21	8	0	33	4	2	1	1	1	.50	4	.258	.294	.360
Thorpe,A.D.	Macon	Atl	A	21	97	350	87	9	4	2	104	52	29	42	0	46	4	4	1	29	17	.63	5	.249	.331	.297
Thrower,Jake	Idaho Falls	SD	R+	22	35	141	48	10	4	3	75	37	28	31	2	16	4	0	1	10	1	.91	2	.340	.469	.532
	Clinton	SD	A	22	19	63	16	3	0	0	19	8	12	13	0	15	2	1	0	1	3	.25	0	.254	.397	.302
Tidwell,David	Chston-WV	Cin	A	23	65	258	68	8	3	2	88	40	26	25	0	47	2	3	0	15	9	.63	6	.264	.333	.341
Tiller,Brad	Watertown	Cle	A-	22	29	98	24	6	0	2	36	15	10	12	0	25	2	0	1	6	2	.75	1	.245	.336	.367
Tillis,Rashad	Royals	KC	R	21	34	102	23	2	2	1	32	14	12	12	0	28	1	1	0	4	1	.80	2	.225	.313	.314
Tinoco,Luis	Lancaster	Sea	A+	23	12	43	7	2	0	2	15	9	5	5	0	12	1	0	0	1	0	1.00	3	.163	.265	.349
Tolbert,Ernest	Mariners	Sea	R	22	5	19	7	0	0	0	7	1	3	0	0	7	0	0	0	0	0	.00	0	.368	.368	.368
Tolbert,William	Pirates	Pit	R	23	31	94	23	3	0	0	26	10	7	12	1	23	1	0	1	1	1	.50	2	.245	.333	.277
Tolentino,Juan	Butte	Ana	R+	22	61	213	64	16	4	10	118	44	53	24	0	53	2	0	4	21	2	.91	2	.300	.370	.554
Tomlinson,Goefr.	Spokane	KC	A-	21	58	210	71	16	0	4	99	49	28	32	0	20	8	4	2	19	1	.95	1	.338	.440	.471
Torrealba,Steve	Danville	Atl	R+	20	44	150	34	9	2	2	49	17	18	15	0	27	2	2	0	1	0	1.00	6	.227	.302	.327
Torrealba,Yorvit	Bakersfield	SF	A+	19	119	446	122	15	3	4	155	52	40	31	0	58	5	1	3	4	2	.67	8	.274	.326	.348
Torres,Benardino	Great Falls	LA	R+	18	57	175	44	4	3	1	57	23	23	12	0	27	2	5	2	6	4	.60	2	.251	.304	.326
Torres,Franklin	Twins	Min	R	18	48	155	40	7	1	1	52	18	18	17	0	31	2	2	3	7	3	.70	1	.258	.333	.335
Torres,Gabriel	Twins	Min	R	20	45	152	39	5	1	0	46	17	16	19	0	21	6	3	2	18	3	.86	7	.257	.358	.303
Torres,Jaime	Tampa	NYA	A+	24	115	408	120	28	0	10	178	46	56	28	2	30	10	2	1	1	0	.00	13	.294	.353	.436
Torres,Jason	Rangers	Tex	R	19	31	82	18	5	3	0	29	13	17	8	0	10	1	1	1	1	2	.33	1	.220	.293	.354
Torres,Rafael	Royals	KC	R+	18	43	155	47	2	0	3	58	20	32	7	1	15	6	0	3	1	2	.67	1	.303	.351	.374
Torres,Reynaldo	Johnson Cty	StL	R+	19	34	107	15	1	0	1	19	4	4	6	0	58	0	0	0	0	1	.00	6	.140	.186	.178
Torti,Michael	Clearwater	Phi	A+	23	70	232	51	12	1	4	77	29	27	26	0	57	0	0	1	1	0	1.00	9	.220	.297	.332
	Piedmont	Phi	A	23	49	176	44	12	1	6	76	19	31	28	0	47	4	1	0	1	0	1.00	3	.250	.365	.432
Tracy,Andrew	Cape Fear	Mon	A	23	59	210	63	9	2	8	100	31	43	21	4	47	3	0	2	6	1	.86	4	.300	.369	.476
Treanor,Matt	Wilmington	KC	A+	22	80	257	51	4	1	5	74	22	25	25	0	59	2	6	0	1	6	.14	4	.198	.275	.288
	Brevard Cty	Fla	A+	22	23	70	15	4	1	0	21	11	3	12	0	14	2	0	0	0	0	.00	1	.214	.345	.300
Tripp,Terry	Padres	SD	R	23	28	100	13	0	0	0	13	9	2	8	0	19	2	0	1	1	0	1.00	1	.130	.209	.130
Trippy,Joe	Durham	Atl	A+	24	120	437	119	24	4	4	163	62	45	61	0	76	9	10	4	34	20	.63	8	.272	.370	.373
Truby,Chris	Quad City	Hou	A	24	68	268	75	14	1	7	112	34	46	22	0	32	1	1	2	13	4	.76	8	.280	.334	.418
	Kissimmee	Hou	A+	24	57	199	49	11	0	2	66	23	29	8	0	40	2	4	3	8	3	.73	4	.246	.278	.332
Tucci,Peter	Hagerstown	Tor	A	22	127	466	123	28	5	10	191	60	75	35	1	95	5	1	6	5	3	.64	9	.264	.318	.410
Tucent,Francisco	Ogden	Mil	R+	22	42	117	29	4	0	0	33	22	16	9	0	23	4	1	1	2	0	1.00	1	.248	.321	.282
Tucker,Jon	Vero Beach	LA	A+	21	121	422	123	27	0	13	189	59	78	35	1	85	3	0	10	5	3	.63	7	.291	.343	.448
Turlais,John	Lynchburg	Pit	A+	24	14	30	5	1	0	1	9	5	6	5	0	9	0	0	0	1	1	.50	0	.167	.286	.300
	Augusta	Pit	A	24	33	106	31	5	0	4	48	8	18	10	1	20	0	0	0	2	1	.67	3	.292	.345	.453
Twist,Jeff	Bakersfield	SF	A+	25	18	51	7	2	0	0	9	4	1	4	0	18	1	0	0	0	0	.00	1	.137	.214	.176

1997 Batting — Single-A and Rookie Leagues

Player	Team	Org Lg	A	G	AB	H	2B	3B	HR	TB	R	RBI	TBB	IBB	SO	HBP	SH	SF	SB	CS	SB%	GDP	Avg	OBP	SLG
Twombley,Denni.	Tampa	NYA A+	23	4	9	3	0	0	0	3	1	0	0	0	4	0	0	0	1	0	1.00	0	.333	.333	.333
	Greensboro	NYA A	23	15	36	7	0	0	1	10	4	2	3	0	12	0	0	1	0	0	.00	1	.194	.250	.278
	Oneonta	NYA A-	23	15	37	9	1	0	1	13	3	7	10	0	12	1	0	0	0	1	.00	1	.243	.417	.351
Ullery,David	Spokane	KC A-	23	12	23	5	0	0	1	8	1	4	5	1	5	1	0	0	0	0	.00	1	.217	.379	.348
	Lansing	KC A	23	18	44	7	1	2	1	15	5	10	13	0	16	1	0	0	0	0	.00	2	.159	.356	.341
Umbria,Jose	Medcne Hat	Tor R+	20	49	126	22	2	0	0	24	4	15	6	0	24	0	1	3	2	1	.67	2	.175	.207	.190
Underwood,Jaco.	Mariners	Sea R	19	22	69	22	4	2	0	30	10	11	7	0	16	5	1	1	0	2	.00	2	.319	.415	.435
	Everett	Sea A-	19	12	29	3	0	0	0	3	4	3	3	0	9	3	1	2	0	0	.00	1	.103	.243	.103
Upshaw,Ryan	Watertown	Cle A-	23	41	132	32	7	1	3	50	26	21	27	0	31	1	0	2	3	0	1.00	1	.242	.370	.379
Urquiola,Carlos	Diamondback	Ari R	18	2	2	0	0	0	0	0	1	0	0	0	1	0	1	0	1	0	1.00	0	.000	.000	.000
Urso,Joe	Lk Elsinore	Ana A+	27	2	1	0	0	0	0	0	0	0	0	0	0	0	0	0	0	0	.00	0	.000	.000	.000
Ussery,Brian	Cedar Rapds	Ana A	24	1	1	0	0	0	0	0	0	0	0	0	0	0	0	0	0	0	.00	0	.000	.000	.000
	Boise	Ana A-	24	15	42	11	0	0	0	11	5	5	11	0	11	0	1	0	0	0	.00	0	.262	.415	.262
	Lk Elsinore	Ana A+	24	10	29	7	1	0	0	8	1	4	2	0	11	0	0	0	0	0	.00	0	.241	.281	.276
Utting,Andrew	Bluefield	Bal R+	20	51	152	35	7	1	4	56	22	18	30	2	41	1	3	0	2	4	.33	1	.230	.361	.368
Utting,Ben	Durham	Atl A+	22	67	148	32	5	0	0	37	18	5	20	0	26	0	4	1	6	4	.60	2	.216	.308	.250
Valderrama,Carl.	Salem-Keizr	SF A-	20	41	138	44	7	3	3	66	21	28	12	0	29	0	0	2	22	0	1.00	2	.319	.368	.478
Valdez,Angel	Yankees	NYA R	20	41	100	26	1	2	1	34	19	10	13	0	21	5	0	1	6	0	1.00	1	.260	.370	.340
Valdez,Jerry	Martinsvlle	Phi R+	24	34	125	34	7	0	1	44	21	11	7	0	27	4	0	0	2	0	.00	2	.272	.331	.352
Valencia,Victor	Greensboro	NYA A	21	107	353	78	12	1	13	131	42	43	43	0	116	7	2	1	2	1	.67	6	.221	.317	.371
Valenti,Jon	Modesto	Oak A+	24	105	283	83	17	1	5	117	43	43	39	2	55	2	2	2	0	3	.00	5	.293	.380	.413
Valentine,Anthon.	Mets	NYN R	23	30	92	30	7	1	0	39	19	14	15	0	12	1	0	2	3	0	1.00	1	.326	.418	.424
	Pittsfield	NYN A-	23	17	62	11	2	0	0	13	8	3	4	0	19	3	1	0	0	0	.00	1	.177	.261	.210
Valera,Gregori	South Bend	Ari A	19	8	27	5	2	0	0	7	2	2	0	0	7	0	1	0	0	0	.00	1	.185	.185	.259
Valera,Ramon	Wisconsin	Sea A	22	13	34	6	2	0	0	8	6	2	4	0	6	0	2	0	1	4	.20	1	.176	.263	.235
	Everett	Sea A-	22	58	221	70	12	3	2	94	43	23	37	2	65	1	5	1	24	6	.80	2	.317	.415	.425
Valera,Willy	Columbus	Cle A	22	117	431	115	15	6	8	166	47	40	20	0	91	0	5	3	8	4	.67	10	.267	.297	.385
Valera,Yohanny	Capital City	NYN A	21	94	293	56	14	0	8	94	32	33	21	0	101	5	2	1	2	0	1.00	4	.191	.256	.321
Valerio,Denny	Twins	Min R	19	28	44	8	2	0	0	10	8	1	4	0	13	0	1	0	6	1	.86	2	.182	.250	.227
Valette,Ramon	Daytona	ChN A+	26	106	371	123	25	2	6	170	54	50	20	1	49	6	5	4	20	6	.77	6	.332	.372	.458
Vallone,Gar	Cedar Rapds	Ana A	25	41	89	21	1	0	1	25	13	8	18	0	20	0	2	1	0	2	.00	3	.236	.361	.281
Van Iten,Robert	Martinsvlle	Phi R+	20	55	204	63	9	0	5	87	29	35	5	0	27	3	0	3	3	2	.60	1	.309	.330	.426
Van Rossum,Ch.	Bakersfield	SF A+	24	125	441	115	17	5	2	148	72	40	57	1	98	15	5	3	9	12	.43	6	.261	.362	.336
Vanasselberg,Ri.	Bluefield	Bal R+	24	27	62	13	2	0	1	18	5	7	6	0	9	0	0	1	0	1	1.00	0	.210	.279	.290
Vandergriend,Jo.	Lk Elsinore	Ana A+	26	118	402	73	17	2	14	136	45	45	32	0	153	10	3	3	19	5	.79	4	.182	.257	.338
Vasquez,Alejand.	Astros	Hou R	20	53	186	50	9	1	2	67	30	20	18	2	23	5	0	2	8	3	.73	5	.269	.346	.360
Vaughn,Lateef	Elizabethtn	Min R+	22	10	40	12	3	0	0	15	10	5	3	0	5	0	1	0	1	1	.50	1	.300	.349	.375
	Ft. Myers	Min A+	22	36	93	25	2	0	0	27	15	8	6	0	18	1	5	0	2	0	1.00	0	.269	.320	.290
Vaz,Roberto	Sou. Oregon	Oak A-	23	22	78	25	6	0	3	40	11	15	7	1	4	1	0	1	5	3	.63	8	.321	.379	.513
	Visalia	Oak A+	23	19	73	26	5	0	3	40	9	13	8	0	10	0	0	2	2	5	.29	4	.356	.420	.548
Vazquez,Alex	Rangers	Tex R	21	4	10	1	1	0	0	2	2	0	3	0	3	1	0	0	1	0	1.00	0	.100	.357	.200
Vazquez,Carlos	Devil Rays	TB R	19	46	152	39	12	0	1	54	22	17	9	0	28	0	0	0	2	0	1.00	1	.257	.298	.355
Vazquez,Manny	Chston-SC	TB A	23	61	176	41	6	1	0	49	20	11	17	1	26	1	4	0	9	6	.60	2	.233	.304	.278
Vazquez,Ramon	Wisconsin	Sea A	21	131	479	129	25	5	8	188	79	49	78	2	93	3	4	3	16	10	.62	8	.269	.373	.392
Vazquez,Roberto	New Jersey	StL A-	21	19	49	6	1	0	1	10	3	4	4	0	13	0	0	2	0	0	.00	0	.122	.189	.204
Velaquez,Juan	Braves	Atl R	19	30	96	21	3	0	0	24	14	4	18	0	26	0	1	0	2	2	.50	1	.219	.342	.250
Velazquez,Jose	Greensboro	NYA A	22	137	489	137	19	3	9	189	77	62	42	1	71	1	2	5	10	8	.56	15	.280	.335	.387
Venghaus,Jeff	Kane County	Fla A	23	128	416	98	20	3	0	124	71	43	86	1	105	6	15	6	17	11	.61	12	.236	.370	.298
Ventura,Francis.	Burlington	Cle R+	21	35	117	30	6	1	0	38	17	18	13	0	26	3	1	1	3	3	.50	0	.256	.343	.325
Ventura,Wilfredo	Visalia	Oak A+	21	62	184	36	5	0	6	59	23	23	9	0	64	1	1	2	1	0	1.00	1	.196	.235	.321
Veras,Wilton	Michigan	Bos A	20	131	489	141	21	3	8	192	51	68	31	0	51	6	1	3	3	2	.60	19	.288	.336	.393
Verrall,Jared	Chston-SC	TB A	24	8	30	5	1	0	1	9	1	4	0	0	9	0	0	0	2	0	1.00	0	.167	.167	.300
	Hudson Vall	TB A-	24	7	29	4	1	0	1	8	4	4	0	0	14	1	0	0	0	0	.00	0	.138	.161	.276
Vickers,Randy	Capital City	NYN A	22	72	245	42	10	1	10	84	22	26	9	0	99	2	0	1	1	4	.20	5	.171	.206	.343
Vidal,Carlos	Salem	Col A+	23	80	226	54	21	0	6	93	20	30	19	1	54	0	2	5	1	2	.33	4	.239	.292	.412
Vieira,Scott	Daytona	ChN A+	24	134	476	131	27	3	18	218	84	80	70	1	125	17	1	7	9	7	.56	5	.275	.382	.458
Viera,Rob	Pirates	Pit R	25	10	20	4	3	0	0	7	2	1	0	0	5	0	0	0	0	1	.00	0	.200	.238	.350
Villalobos,Carlos	Lancaster	Sea A+	24	86	296	101	22	2	11	160	71	53	60	0	42	7	2	0	4	6	.40	7	.341	.463	.541
	Lakeland	Det A+	24	39	147	37	5	0	1	45	19	15	11	0	25	2	1	0	1	0	1.00	4	.252	.313	.306
Villar,Jose	Danville	Atl R+	19	54	203	45	10	4	2	69	34	16	12	0	69	1	0	2	16	5	.76	3	.222	.266	.340
Vilorio,Leonel	Twins	Min R	20	50	169	33	6	0	0	39	8	6	6	0	31	2	0	1	3	4	.43	4	.195	.230	.231
Voita,Sam	St. Pete	TB A+	24	14	24	6	2	0	1	11	3	6	5	0	6	1	0	0	0	0	.00	0	.250	.400	.458
	Hudson Vall	TB A-	24	32	117	34	10	0	1	47	19	16	11	0	20	0	0	2	1	1	.67	1	.291	.352	.402
Wade,Lloyd	Twins	Min R	23	33	102	17	2	0	1	22	8	14	13	0	26	1	1	2	1	1	.50	2	.167	.263	.216
Wakeland,Christ.	W Michigan	Det A	24	111	414	118	38	3	7	181	64	75	43	5	120	4	0	7	20	6	.77	3	.285	.353	.437
Walker,Javon	Marlins	Fla R	19	16	47	5	0	0	1	7	1	8	0	0	21	0	0	0	0	0	.00	2	.106	.236	.106
Walker,Morgan	Lynchburg	Pit A+	23	29	89	24	6	0	3	39	15	8	6	1	19	0	0	0	0	0	.00	2	.270	.316	.438
	Augusta	Pit A	23	76	295	81	17	2	14	144	40	64	17	2	70	3	3	2	3	2	.60	7	.275	.318	.488
Walker,Ronald	Williamsprt	ChN A-	22	54	189	66	10	1	9	105	30	39	17	7	48	5	0	2	0	1	.00	0	.349	.413	.556
	Rockford	ChN A	22	4	15	5	0	0	1	8	1	5	2	0	8	0	0	0	0	0	.00	0	.333	.444	.533
Walker,Shon	Lynchburg	Pit A+	24	100	303	79	15	6	15	151	59	48	77	3	131	1	1	4	2	3	.40	1	.261	.408	.498
Wallace,Derek	Bristol	ChA R+	21	50	186	45	12	2	7	82	26	29	11	1	65	4	2	2	8	2	.80	3	.242	.296	.441
Walther,Chris	Beloit	Mil A	21	113	437	131	25	4	0	164	55	38	28	0	41	5	3	1	5	7	.42	16	.300	.348	.375
Ward,Gregory	Braves	Atl R	20	48	163	35	7	0	0	42	20	10	16	0	46	0	0	2	0	0	.00	3	.215	.282	.258
Ware,Jeremy	Cape Fear	Mon A	22	138	529	139	32	5	16	229	84	77	43	2	114	6	0	6	32	7	.82	8	.263	.322	.433
Ware,Ryan	Hudson Vall	TB A-	22	44	147	30	6	2	0	40	18	13	14	0	40	2	1	2	7	1	.88	2	.204	.279	.272
Warren,Lance	Great Falls	LA R+	19	3	5	1	0	0	0	1	0	0	0	0	3	0	0	0	0	0	.00	0	.200	.333	.200

1997 Batting — Single-A and Rookie Leagues

BATTING																				BASERUNNING				PERCENTAGES		
Player	Team	Org	Lg	A	G	AB	H	2B	3B	HR	TB	R	RBI	TBB	IBB	SO	HBP	SH	SF	SB	CS	SB%	GDP	Avg	OBP	SLG
	Yakima	LA	A-	19	2	5	2	0	0	0	2	0	1	1	0	1	0	0	0	0	0	.00	0	.400	.500	.400
	Savannah	LA	A	19	11	25	6	1	1	0	9	5	1	3	0	5	0	0	0	2	0	1.00	0	.240	.321	.360
Warren,Thomas	Helena	Mil	R+	18	33	97	27	3	0	0	30	21	8	20	0	30	1	2	0	4	3	.57	1	.278	.407	.309
Warriax,Brandon	Charlotte	Tex	A+	19	1	4	0	0	0	0	0	0	0	0	0	1	0	0	0	0	0	.00	1	.000	.000	.000
	Rangers	Tex	R	19	47	166	36	5	2	0	45	21	14	13	0	47	1	4	2	6	3	.67	6	.217	.275	.271
Washam,Jason	Beloit	Mil	A	23	88	276	78	15	3	8	123	44	46	33	0	31	16	0	3	4	2	.67	5	.283	.387	.446
Washington,Cory	Marlins	Fla	R	20	28	78	17	3	2	1	27	14	10	12	0	20	0	0	0	3	1	.75	2	.218	.322	.346
Washington,Dion	Yankees	NYA	R	21	52	165	50	10	1	3	71	35	33	36	0	39	6	0	2	2	0	1.00	1	.303	.440	.430
Washington,Enri.	Pirates	Pit	R	20	28	98	24	6	0	1	33	12	11	4	1	13	4	0	1	1	0	1.00	2	.245	.299	.337
Washington,Kelly	Marlins	Fla	R	18	34	101	11	0	1	0	13	8	6	10	0	31	3	3	1	2	1	.67	3	.109	.209	.129
Washington,Mau.	Pirates	Pit	R	19	31	94	19	2	1	0	23	8	7	11	0	34	0	1	0	1	1	.50	6	.202	.286	.245
Watkins,Sean	Clinton	SD	A	23	10	27	4	0	0	1	7	1	2	9	0	10	0	0	1	0	2	.00	0	.148	.351	.259
	Charlotte	Tex	A+	23	21	72	16	3	1	0	21	5	10	6	1	25	1	0	0	0	0	.00	1	.222	.291	.292
Watley,Clarence	Medicne Hat	Tor	R+	20	10	33	10	2	0	0	12	3	6	4	0	13	0	0	0	3	0	1.00	0	.303	.378	.364
Watson,Al	Williamsprt	ChN	A-	24	45	136	34	0	0	0	34	21	11	19	1	21	0	5	0	10	5	.67	2	.250	.342	.250
Watson,Jon	Bakersfield	SF	A+	24	119	448	116	22	2	2	148	67	36	30	0	66	5	7	0	14	10	.58	10	.259	.313	.330
Watts,Josh	Wisconsin	Sea	A	23	51	162	45	10	2	8	83	37	24	33	3	55	0	0	1	3	7	.30	5	.278	.398	.512
	Lancaster	Sea	A+	23	56	159	35	5	0	6	58	18	25	23	0	71	1	0	1	1	3	.25	3	.220	.321	.365
Weekley,Jason	San Berndno	LA	A+	24	101	313	88	15	5	16	161	58	59	41	0	102	3	1	5	3	6	.33	5	.281	.365	.514
Weichard,Paul	Diamondback	Ari	R	18	36	115	21	3	1	0	26	27	7	30	0	54	1	1	0	4	3	.57	1	.183	.356	.226
Welles,Robby	Cedar Rapds	Ana	A	25	20	64	17	2	0	2	25	10	8	5	0	18	1	1	0	2	0	1.00	2	.266	.329	.391
	Lk Elsinore	Ana	A+	25	3	5	0	0	0	0	0	0	0	1	0	2	0	0	0	0	0	.00	0	.000	.167	.000
Wells,Vernon	St. Cathrns	Tor	A-	19	66	264	81	20	1	10	133	52	31	30	1	44	1	0	2	8	6	.57	2	.307	.377	.504
Wells,Zachary	Salem-Keizr	SF	A-	21	62	218	62	9	2	10	105	47	43	48	2	57	3	1	4	3	1	.75	3	.284	.414	.482
Welsh,Eric	Billings	Cin	R+	21	67	260	82	13	2	11	132	41	54	18	1	38	2	0	3	2	4	.33	3	.315	.360	.508
Werth,Jayson	Orioles	Bal	R	19	32	88	26	6	0	1	35	16	8	22	0	22	0	0	1	7	1	.88	0	.295	.432	.398
Wesson,Barry	Auburn	Hou	A-	21	58	208	54	7	3	3	76	24	26	10	0	45	1	1	1	8	4	.67	1	.260	.295	.365
Wetmore,Mike	Beloit	Mil	A	23	114	407	103	20	2	2	133	67	27	48	2	83	8	6	3	9	10	.47	7	.253	.341	.327
Wheeler,Michael	Astros	Hou	R	20	41	130	27	4	1	1	36	13	6	8	0	41	1	1	0	5	3	.63	3	.208	.259	.277
	Kissimmee	Hou	A+	20	8	12	5	0	0	0	5	2	2	1	0	3	0	0	0	1	0	1.00	0	.417	.462	.417
Whipple,Boomer	Augusta	Pit	A	25	40	108	24	7	0	0	31	16	13	23	0	19	4	3	3	2	1	.67	2	.222	.370	.287
Whitaker,Chad	Columbus	Cle	A	21	109	432	118	25	2	12	183	48	72	23	3	144	5	0	2	3	0	1.00	6	.273	.316	.424
White,John	Cape Fear	Mon	A	23	3	9	0	0	0	0	0	0	1	1	0	3	1	0	1	0	0	.00	0	.000	.167	.000
White,Walt	Brevard Cty	Fla	A+	26	54	163	33	8	0	1	44	18	15	14	1	41	1	0	1	0	0	.00	4	.202	.268	.270
Whitehead,Braxt.	Burlington	Cin	A	22	36	123	23	6	0	0	29	11	13	9	0	27	1	1	1	2	2	.50	5	.187	.246	.236
Whitley,Matt	Asheville	Col	A	26	129	461	107	21	0	1	131	67	43	77	2	57	8	11	4	14	9	.61	11	.232	.349	.284
Whitlock,Brian	Columbus	Cle	A	23	92	327	86	14	7	11	147	56	41	28	0	92	6	6	2	5	4	.56	5	.263	.331	.450
Whitlock,Michael	Dunedin	Tor	A+	21	107	322	62	14	0	11	109	41	48	69	1	132	9	0	5	1	1	.50	3	.193	.346	.339
Whitner,Keith	Jamestown	Det	A-	22	46	156	37	5	2	0	46	19	12	7	0	40	2	0	2	0	0	.00	5	.237	.275	.295
Whittaker,Jerry	Winston-Sal	ChA	A+	24	52	170	46	17	2	5	82	24	20	14	0	62	0	2	0	3	1	.75	2	.271	.326	.482
Wilder,Paul	Princeton	TB	R+	20	44	155	32	6	2	6	60	25	23	33	0	63	2	0	2	3	2	.60	1	.206	.349	.387
Wilhelm,Brent	Winston-Sal	ChA	A+	25	48	155	32	8	1	3	51	22	26	21	0	33	1	2	1	1	0	1.00	5	.206	.303	.329
Williams,Ricky	Piedmont	Phi	A	21	37	136	28	5	0	1	36	12	6	9	0	44	3	0	1	10	4	.71	0	.206	.268	.265
Williams,Glenn	Macon	Atl	A	20	77	297	79	18	2	14	143	52	52	24	1	105	5	1	4	9	6	.60	4	.266	.327	.481
Williams,Jewell	Columbus	Cle	A	21	113	399	75	20	3	10	131	57	40	33	0	140	10	3	1	14	6	.70	9	.188	.266	.328
Williams,Jovany	Johnson Cty	StL	R+	21	41	142	35	10	1	7	68	25	23	2	0	29	2	2	1	2	1	.67	4	.246	.265	.479
Williams,Micah	Lansing	KC	A	23	65	249	83	13	3	0	102	34	30	9	0	34	9	8	0	22	3	.88	6	.333	.378	.410
Williams,Patrick	Mariners	Sea	R	20	47	177	54	9	1	0	65	28	27	15	0	43	0	0	3	17	2	.89	1	.305	.354	.367
	Everett	Sea	A-	20	64	255	68	7	0	12	111	38	48	19	0	93	3	0	3	1	0	1.00	6	.267	.321	.435
Willis,David	Spokane	KC	A-	23	65	252	72	15	3	5	108	36	36	11	1	54	5	3	1	5	2	.71	3	.286	.327	.429
Willis,Symmion	Hagerstown	Tor	A	25	25	61	15	3	0	0	18	6	11	7	0	21	0	1	0	0	1	.00	1	.246	.324	.295
	Dunedin	Tor	A+	25	56	164	36	5	1	2	49	18	16	10	0	37	0	1	0	2	1	.67	1	.220	.264	.299
Wilson,Steve	Vero Beach	LA	A+	24	84	233	49	14	1	3	74	21	21	11	0	63	3	1	3	4	0	1.00	3	.210	.252	.318
Wilson,Cliff	Bluefield	Bal	R+	21	46	129	31	2	2	1	40	16	14	15	1	35	1	1	1	3	1	.75	1	.240	.322	.310
Wilson,Craig	Lynchburg	Pit	A+	21	117	401	106	26	1	19	191	54	69	39	6	98	15	1	2	6	5	.55	3	.264	.350	.476
Wilson,Heath	Braves	Atl	R	19	21	57	11	2	0	0	13	7	5	13	0	22	1	0	0	0	1	.00	0	.193	.352	.228
Wilson,Keith	High Desert	Ari	A+	24	60	148	34	8	0	5	57	22	25	14	0	40	7	1	4	1	0	1.00	5	.230	.318	.385
Wilson,Scott	New Jersey	StL	A-	23	44	141	35	9	1	6	64	28	21	24	0	36	2	2	2	0	2	.00	4	.248	.361	.454
Wilson,Todd	San Jose	SF	A+	28	130	502	173	35	3	5	229	66	88	32	2	60	9	1	3	7	3	.70	23	.345	.392	.456
Wilson,Travis	Danville	Atl	R+	20	61	233	50	14	6	0	76	29	27	14	0	60	8	1	0	4	1	.80	5	.215	.282	.326
Wise,Dewayne	Billings	Cin	R+	20	62	268	84	13	9	7	136	53	41	9	0	47	2	1	3	18	8	.69	2	.313	.337	.507
Wissen,Collin	Eugene	Atl	A-	22	73	260	53	8	1	1	66	40	22	23	1	75	3	3	3	2	2	.50	4	.204	.273	.254
Wolff,Mike	Frederick	Bal	A+	25	112	321	81	12	0	8	117	50	34	45	4	47	6	11	2	4	4	.50	10	.252	.353	.364
Wong,Jerrod	Macon	Atl	A	24	118	439	122	22	5	15	199	46	60	18	0	92	4	2	4	6	5	.55	3	.278	.310	.453
Woods,Taco	Royals	KC	R	20	2	5	0	0	0	0	0	0	0	1	0	5	1	0	0	0	0	.00	0	.000	.286	.000
Woodward,Chris	Dunedin	Tor	A+	22	91	314	92	13	4	1	116	38	38	52	0	52	5	3	4	4	8	.33	3	.293	.397	.369
Woolf,Jay	Pr William	StL	A+	21	70	251	62	11	3	6	97	59	18	55	1	75	5	1	1	26	5	.84	0	.247	.391	.386
Wooten,Shawn	Cedar Rapds	Ana	A	25	108	353	102	23	1	15	172	43	75	49	0	71	6	3	6	0	1	.00	8	.289	.379	.487
Worthy,Tommy	Batavia	Phi	A-	21	56	141	34	3	0	1	40	28	9	15	0	36	1	0	0	9	3	.75	0	.241	.318	.284
Wright,Corey	Rangers	Tex	R	18	43	145	36	2	3	0	44	19	11	22	0	25	1	3	0	14	11	.56	1	.248	.351	.303
Yancy,Michael	Mets	NYN	R	19	38	131	33	3	4	1	47	22	20	12	0	26	4	0	3	5	2	.71	1	.252	.327	.359
Yard,Bruce	Vero Beach	LA	A+	26	71	236	73	14	1	4	101	37	44	24	0	19	1	1	6	3	2	.60	3	.309	.367	.428
Yedo,Carlos	Tampa	NYA	A+	24	131	446	108	26	1	13	175	51	54	46	3	126	1	3	3	1	0	1.00	10	.242	.313	.392
Yoshida,Kota	Athletics	Oak	R	20	48	181	43	8	1	0	53	47	22	36	0	39	3	5	1	22	6	.79	2	.238	.371	.293
Young,Michael	St. Cathrns	Tor	A-	21	74	276	85	18	3	9	136	49	48	33	1	59	7	0	3	9	5	.64	6	.308	.392	.493
Young,Travis	Salem-Keizr	SF	A-	23	76	320	107	11	6	1	133	80	34	30	0	50	5	1	3	40	8	.83	3	.334	.397	.416
Zachmann,Robe.	Wisconsin	Sea	A	24	107	358	93	24	1	12	155	59	61	37	2	87	3	6	3	5	6	.45	7	.260	.332	.433

1997 Batting — Single-A and Rookie Leagues

Player	Team	Org	Lg	A	G	AB	H	2B	3B	HR	TB	R	RBI	TBB	IBB	SO	HBP	SH	SF	SB	CS	SB%	GDP	Avg	OBP	SLG
Zamora,Junior	Capital City	NYN	A	22	36	124	31	5	0	8	60	16	19	10	0	29	0	0	0	0	1	.00	2	.250	.306	.484
Zapata,Alexis	W Michigan	Det	A	21	64	206	46	8	3	6	78	33	27	11	0	54	2	2	2	4	0	1.00	8	.223	.267	.379
Zapata,Wilson	Red Sox	Bos	R	19	47	109	12	2	1	1	19	16	8	12	0	45	0	2	1	3	1	.75	1	.110	.197	.174
Zapp,A.J.	Danville	Atl	R+	20	65	234	79	23	2	7	127	34	56	35	0	78	7	0	1	0	1	.00	3	.338	.437	.543
Zaun,Brian	Yakima	LA	A-	24	46	186	58	12	1	1	75	23	37	8	0	45	0	1	1	3	1	.75	4	.312	.338	.403
	Savannah	LA	A	24	13	42	10	2	1	1	17	6	6	1	0	16	0	0	0	0	0	.00	0	.238	.256	.405
Zeber,Ryan	Medicne Hat	Tor	R+	20	43	101	20	2	0	1	25	11	7	12	0	26	0	0	0	1	2	.33	2	.198	.283	.248
Zech,Scott	Vermont	Mon	A-	24	63	204	54	11	0	1	68	31	20	27	1	36	7	5	6	17	7	.71	4	.265	.361	.333
Zepeda,Jesse	Medicne Hat	Tor	R+	24	64	216	57	14	1	1	76	39	23	42	0	29	3	2	0	6	5	.55	1	.264	.391	.352
Ziths,Deshawn	Orioles	Bal	R	22	17	33	5	0	0	0	5	7	3	3	0	16	0	0	0	1	0	1.00	0	.152	.222	.152
Zucha,Jason	Idaho Falls	SD	R+	22	13	48	10	1	1	0	13	5	5	3	0	10	0	1	1	0	0	.00	4	.208	.250	.271
Zuleta,Julio	Rockford	ChN	A	23	119	430	124	30	5	6	182	59	77	35	6	88	12	3	8	5	5	.50	7	.288	.353	.423
Zuniga,Tony	San Jose	SF	A+	23	97	289	53	10	0	1	66	24	32	33	0	48	11	6	2	3	3	.50	11	.183	.290	.228
Zweifel,Kent	Portland	Col	A-	21	57	198	57	14	2	4	87	28	44	29	2	50	5	2	3	7	2	.78	1	.288	.387	.439
Zydowsky,John	Danville	Atl	R+	20	43	151	35	6	0	1	44	19	15	20	0	42	3	3	1	2	4	.33	7	.232	.331	.291
Zywica,Michael	Charlotte	Tex	A+	22	126	462	119	25	5	12	190	75	64	50	0	116	12	0	6	19	19	.50	10	.258	.342	.411

1997 Pitching — Single-A and Rookie Leagues

HOW MUCH HE PITCHED											WHAT HE GAVE UP												THE RESULTS					
Player	Team	Org	Lg	A	G	GS	CG	GF	IP	BFP	H	R	ER	HR	SH	SF	HB	TBB	IBB	SO	WP	Bk	W	L	Pct.	ShO	Sv	ERA
Abbott,Todd	Visalia	Oak	A+	24	31	20	0	1	121.1	575	146	100	80	17	4	5	3	63	2	70	11	0	11	10	.524	0	0	5.93
Abeyta,Scott	Diamondback	Ari	R	21	17	0	0	6	27.1	110	29	12	10	1	1	0	0	9	0	25	0	1	1	1	.500	0	1	3.29
Abreu,Oscar	Visalia	Oak	A+	22	5	2	0	0	11.2	65	19	23	19	6	0	0	0	10	0	14	1	0	0	1	.000	0	0	14.66
	Sou. Oregon	Oak	A-	22	20	0	0	9	26	133	26	28	24	6	0	1	1	25	0	47	9	1	2	2	.500	0	1	8.31
Acevedo,Jose	Chston-WV	Cin	A	20	15	8	0	3	57.1	245	61	29	25	8	2	1	5	9	0	34	4	1	3	3	.500	0	0	3.92
Achilles,Matthew	Delmarva	Bal	A	21	3	0	0	1	5.2	36	11	9	6	0	0	0	2	3	0	2	0	0	0	0	.000	0	1	9.53
	Bluefield	Bal	R+	21	14	13	0	0	73	301	60	37	32	9	1	2	2	33	0	68	7	2	7	2	.778	0	0	3.95
Acosta,Alberto	Yankees	NYA	R	20	9	3	0	2	24.2	105	24	14	9	1	0	0	0	10	0	11	3	0	1	1	.500	0	0	3.28
Acosta,Jhon	Cubs	ChN	R	18	14	0	0	5	21.1	96	27	10	6	1	2	0	0	6	0	15	2	1	1	0	1.000	0	1	2.53
Adair,Derek	Batavia	Phi	A-	22	13	12	1	0	76.2	308	71	29	18	4	0	3	2	4	0	53	0	0	7	3	.700	0	0	2.11
Adkins,Tim	Dunedin	Tor	A+	24	39	0	0	10	49.2	252	52	43	26	1	2	3	3	58	0	55	9	2	1	1	.500	0	3	4.71
Affeldt,Jeremy	Royals	KC	R	19	10	9	0	0	40	171	34	24	20	3	2	3	5	21	0	36	4	2	2	0	1.000	0	0	4.50
Agosto,Stevenso.	Lk Elsinore	Ana	A+	22	24	21	1	0	137	603	155	91	81	23	2	2	3	50	0	91	11	3	5	8	.385	1	0	5.32
	Rancho Cuca	SD	A+	22	3	3	1	0	22	89	18	7	7	2	3	0	0	6	0	18	1	0	2	0	1.000	1	0	2.86
Aguiar,Douglas	Clearwater	Phi	A+	21	1	1	0	0	4	17	4	3	3	1	0	0	0	1	0	2	0	0	0	1	.000	0	0	6.75
	Batavia	Phi	A-	21	7	3	0	1	22.2	108	24	15	9	1	1	0	2	15	1	15	3	1	1	0	1.000	0	0	3.57
Ah Yat,Paul	Augusta	Pit	A	24	29	9	0	5	90	366	82	34	29	7	3	0	3	16	1	119	4	0	5	1	.833	0	0	2.90
	Lynchburg	Pit	A+	24	6	6	3	0	48	182	37	8	7	2	2	0	1	4	0	38	1	0	5	1	.833	1	0	1.31
Akin,Aaron	Marlins	Fla	R	21	4	4	0	0	11.2	52	13	5	3	0	0	0	2	3	0	5	1	0	0	0	.000	0	0	2.31
Akin,Jay	Helena	Mil	R+	23	5	5	1	0	27	99	16	5	3	1	0	0	0	5	0	19	1	0	2	0	1.000	0	0	1.00
	Beloit	Mil	A	23	9	9	0	0	48.1	211	52	32	17	3	4	2	3	11	0	25	0	1	1	5	.167	0	0	3.17
Albaugh,Chad	Martinsvlle	Phi	R+	23	20	0	0	4	32.2	154	38	27	21	3	1	3	4	15	1	27	0	0	1	2	.333	0	1	5.79
Alejo,Nigel	Brevard Cty	Fla	A+	23	7	0	0	0	12.2	47	8	4	3	1	0	2	2	1	0	11	0	0	1	0	1.000	0	0	2.13
Alexander,Jordy	Spokane	KC	A-	21	16	12	0	2	86.1	366	82	59	44	10	0	4	6	18	2	83	4	0	7	3	.700	0	1	4.59
Alkire,John	Jamestown	Det	A-	23	9	7	1	1	37	185	61	42	35	2	1	2	4	14	0	33	5	0	0	3	.000	0	0	8.51
Allen,Brandon	Piedmont	Phi	A	23	25	24	4	1	152.2	631	153	78	60	12	9	2	11	38	0	91	4	1	11	8	.579	2	0	3.54
Allen,Craig	Savannah	LA	A	25	10	0	0	6	14.1	71	13	14	12	1	0	0	1	13	0	14	5	0	0	1	.000	0	2	7.53
Allen,Rodney	Eugene	Atl	A-	24	20	1	0	7	43	213	56	35	30	4	1	1	0	27	2	29	5	0	1	1	.500	0	2	6.28
Almanza,Arman.	Pr William	StL	A+	25	58	0	0	47	64.2	259	38	18	12	3	1	4	1	32	1	83	8	1	2	3	.400	0	36	1.67
Almonte,Hector	Marlins	Fla	R	22	8	0	0	7	23.2	89	12	3	2	0	0	1	2	6	0	25	1	0	2	0	1.000	0	3	0.76
	Kane County	Fla	A	22	8	1	0	3	14	59	11	6	6	1	1	2	1	6	0	10	2	0	0	1	.000	0	1	3.86
Altman,Gene	Chston-WV	Cin	A	19	17	1	0	5	32.1	156	45	31	28	1	2	2	3	10	0	35	4	6	1	4	.200	0	0	7.79
	Billings	Cin	R+	19	20	5	0	9	33.1	163	48	36	29	2	0	2	4	19	0	34	2	1	3	2	.600	0	3	7.83
Alvarado,David	Pirates	Pit	R	20	12	6	0	0	47.1	213	51	32	20	4	2	3	3	23	0	34	3	0	1	6	.143	0	0	3.80
Alvarado,Carlos	Augusta	Pit	A	20	29	20	0	2	113	499	114	58	41	4	3	8	11	45	0	109	9	4	6	5	.545	0	0	3.27
Alvarez,Danny	Burlington	Cle	R+	22	3	1	0	0	6.2	33	10	6	5	0	2	1	0	4	0	6	0	0	0	2	.000	0	0	6.75
	Watertown	Cle	A-	22	3	0	0	2	3.1	20	9	6	5	2	0	0	0	0	0	2	0	1	0	0	.000	0	0	13.50
Alvarez,Victor	Great Falls	LA	R+	22	12	8	0	3	48.1	212	49	30	18	0	0	4	3	17	0	50	2	3	4	1	.800	0	0	3.35
Alvord,Aaron	Tigers	Det	R	21	9	5	0	0	29.1	141	36	28	14	4	1	0	0	13	0	24	4	0	0	3	.000	0	0	4.30
	Lakeland	Det	A+	21	5	0	0	2	9.1	39	9	3	3	0	0	0	0	2	0	4	0	0	0	0	.000	0	0	2.89
Ambrose,John	Winston-Sal	ChA	A+	23	27	27	1	0	149.2	688	136	102	91	17	5	9	8	117	2	137	16	5	8	13	.381	1	0	5.47
Anderson,Dallas	Lethbridge	Ari	R+	24	10	0	0	3	11	52	10	12	11	0	0	0	0	11	0	11	3	1	0	0	.000	0	0	9.00
Anderson,Eric	Wilmington	KC	A+	23	14	6	0	2	38.2	169	37	25	21	3	2	4	1	16	0	11	2	0	1	2	.333	0	0	4.89
Anderson,Jason	Boise	Ana	A-	23	5	0	0	2	5	37	15	13	11	1	0	1	0	6	0	3	0	0	1	0	1.000	0	0	19.80
Anderson,Jason	Sou. Oregon	Oak	A-	22	14	9	0	1	52.1	238	63	38	29	4	3	0	5	19	0	38	8	2	3	3	.500	0	0	4.99
Andra,Jeff	Salem-Keizr	SF	A-	22	8	8	0	0	44.1	185	39	21	10	3	1	1	1	10	0	58	4	0	3	1	.750	0	0	2.03
	San Jose	SF	A+	22	6	6	0	0	29.2	142	36	25	23	2	3	0	4	11	0	29	2	2	1	4	.200	0	0	6.98
Andrade,Jancy	Bluefield	Bal	R+	20	4	4	0	0	14.1	62	9	5	4	1	0	0	0	11	0	13	1	1	0	0	.000	0	0	2.51
Andrews,Clayton	Hagerstown	Tor	A	20	28	15	0	7	114.2	512	120	70	58	8	4	4	5	47	1	112	4	2	7	7	.500	0	0	4.55
Andrews,Jeffrey	South Bend	Ari	A	23	23	4	0	7	55	237	52	37	32	4	2	1	2	27	1	32	3	0	1	5	.167	0	0	5.24
	Lethbridge	Ari	R+	23	9	9	1	0	49.2	219	55	27	18	3	1	0	3	10	0	50	3	0	3	3	.500	0	0	3.26
Andujar,Jesse	Expos	Mon	R	18	17	0	0	6	23.2	134	27	25	21	1	0	0	6	30	0	18	4	0	1	2	.333	0	2	7.99
Aquino,Julio	St. Pete	TB	A+	25	50	0	0	8	60	240	53	21	19	3	2	2	3	8	0	39	3	1	3	5	.375	0	1	2.85
Aracena,Juan	Burlington	Cle	R+	21	19	0	0	8	38.2	176	45	32	21	4	1	1	0	16	0	31	3	2	1	4	.200	0	2	4.89
Arias,Rafael	Red Sox	Bos	R	21	11	5	2	3	50	216	65	26	22	1	4	2	0	7	1	37	1	1	3	3	.500	0	2	3.96
Arias,Wagner	Stockton	Mil	A+	23	20	14	0	1	86.2	402	89	63	59	18	3	6	7	64	1	74	10	0	2	6	.250	0	0	6.13
Armas,Tony	Greensboro	NYA	A	20	9	9	2	0	51.2	207	36	13	6	3	1	1	3	13	0	64	1	1	5	2	.714	1	0	1.05
	Tampa	NYA	A+	20	9	9	0	0	46	191	43	23	17	1	3	4	1	16	3	26	2	0	3	1	.750	0	0	3.33
	Sarasota	Bos	A+	20	3	3	0	0	17.2	81	18	13	13	2	2	1	2	12	0	9	3	0	2	1	.667	0	0	6.62
Arminio,Sam	Chston-WV	Cin	A	25	46	2	0	15	90	392	113	45	38	6	1	2	3	20	3	58	5	1	2	3	.400	0	6	3.80
Arnold,Neal	New Jersey	StL	A-	23	23	0	0	4	36.2	154	35	21	16	2	4	1	3	9	0	27	4	0	0	2	.000	0	0	3.93
Arrojo,Rolando	St. Pete	TB	A+	29	16	16	4	0	89.1	349	73	40	34	6	1	3	10	13	0	73	5	1	5	6	.455	1	0	3.43
Arroyo,Bronson	Lynchburg	Pit	A+	21	24	24	3	0	160.1	658	154	69	59	17	7	0	3	33	0	121	9	0	12	4	.750	1	0	3.31
Arroyo,Joel	Ogden	Mil	R+	21	16	0	0	9	20.2	127	33	37	25	1	0	1	8	21	0	18	2	0	0	1	.000	0	0	10.89
Arteaga,Juan	Pittsfield	NYN	A-	23	12	3	0	2	30.1	129	32	15	9	0	1	0	1	4	0	29	1	0	4	2	.667	0	0	2.67
	Capital City	NYN	A	23	1	1	0	0	6	20	3	0	0	0	0	0	0	0	0	4	0	0	1	0	1.000	0	0	0.00
Arthurs,Shane	Expos	Mon	R	18	8	7	0	0	25.2	128	37	31	28	1	0	3	2	14	0	12	1	1	0	3	.000	0	0	9.82
Ashworth,Kym	Yakima	LA	A-	21	4	4	0	0	17.1	73	13	7	7	2	1	1	1	10	0	15	2	0	0	1	.000	0	0	3.63
	San Berndno	LA	A+	21	9	5	0	2	30.2	146	34	27	22	4	0	1	3	24	0	26	8	0	0	3	.000	0	0	6.46
Atkins,Dannon	Kinston	Cle	A+	24	27	16	0	3	117	501	98	53	47	10	2	3	2	62	2	84	11	2	8	4	.667	0	0	3.62
Austin,Shawn	Salem-Keizr	SF	A-	24	13	0	0	2	17	73	12	7	2	1	0	1	1	6	0	18	0	0	1	1	.500	0	0	1.06
Averette,Robert	Billings	Cin	R+	21	2	1	0	1	2.2	11	3	0	0	0	0	0	0	1	1	3	0	0	0	0	.000	0	0	0.00
	Chston-WV	Cin	A	21	11	3	0	2	26.1	131	42	28	23	3	3	1	0	12	0	20	2	0	2	2	.500	0	1	7.86
Avrard,Corey	Peoria	StL	A	21	20	20	0	0	93.1	437	97	76	66	5	4	4	4	69	1	94	9	0	4	5	.444	0	0	6.36
	Pr William	StL	A+	21	8	8	0	0	40.1	190	30	28	24	1	0	0	2	44	0	50	4	1	0	3	.000	0	0	5.36
Ayala,Julio	Wisconsin	Sea	A	23	36	9	0	13	103	443	114	47	42	4	2	1	4	30	4	81	7	2	11	3	.786	0	0	3.67
Ayers,Michael	Lynchburg	Pit	A+	24	39	0	0	13	63	288	54	38	35	8	4	2	6	44	6	62	4	0	5	4	.556	0	4	5.00

1997 Pitching — Single-A and Rookie Leagues

HOW MUCH HE PITCHED											WHAT HE GAVE UP												THE RESULTS					
Player	Team	Org	Lg	A	G	GS	CG	GF	IP	BFP	H	R	ER	HR	SH	SF	HB	TBB	IBB	SO	WP	Bk	W	L	Pct.	ShO	Sv	ERA
Babineaux,Darrin	Vero Beach	LA	A+	23	18	12	0	0	81.2	350	82	46	40	7	1	3	3	32	0	63	6	1	7	3	.700	0	0	4.41
Bacci,Anthony	Augusta	Pit	A	22	6	6	1	0	28.1	127	31	20	15	3	0	0	0	14	0	24	2	0	1	3	.250	1	0	4.76
	Erie	Pit	A-	22	15	14	0	0	84.1	350	68	34	24	5	0	1	3	36	0	50	2	1	8	3	.727	0	0	2.56
Backlund,Brett	High Desert	Ari	A+	28	17	0	0	4	34.1	137	23	19	14	4	5	0	1	11	1	38	1	0	4	2	.667	0	0	3.67
Backowski,Lance	San Berndno	LA	A+	23	4	0	0	2	6	39	10	11	9	0	0	1	2	9	0	3	0	0	0	0	.000	0	0	13.50
	Yakima	LA	A-	23	15	15	1	0	71.2	357	85	72	51	2	1	3	10	53	0	61	9	0	2	12	.143	0	0	6.40
Bacsik,Mike	Columbus	Cle	A	20	28	28	0	0	139	622	163	94	84	16	7	3	9	47	1	100	12	2	4	14	.222	0	0	5.44
Baez,Miguel	Burlington	Cle	R+	20	19	0	0	15	29.1	131	21	17	7	4	3	4	4	14	0	33	3	0	1	3	.250	0	2	2.15
	Watertown	Cle	A-	20	3	0	0	3	4.2	21	5	2	1	1	1	0	0	1	1	6	0	0	0	1	.000	0	1	1.93
Bailey,Ben	Lakeland	Det	A+	23	15	14	1	0	93	394	102	49	40	5	0	2	3	24	0	61	5	1	4	4	.500	1	0	3.87
Bailey,Phillip	San Jose	SF	A+	24	25	10	0	5	60	273	70	54	49	12	1	2	6	33	0	42	11	1	0	9	.000	0	0	7.35
Bair,Andy	Utica	Fla	A-	21	12	12	0	0	52.2	228	54	42	37	8	3	1	7	17	0	32	2	0	1	6	.143	0	0	6.32
Baird,Brandon	Lansing	KC	A	24	55	0	0	36	77.2	336	74	31	26	2	5	3	5	28	6	83	2	0	10	7	.588	0	7	3.01
Baker,Jason	Expos	Mon	R	23	2	2	0	0	7	28	4	0	0	0	0	0	1	3	0	8	0	0	0	0	.000	0	0	0.00
	Wst Plm Bch	Mon	A+	23	15	14	1	0	72	326	90	55	48	10	4	3	2	31	0	47	11	2	3	4	.429	1	0	6.00
Baker,Jason	Great Falls	LA	R+	24	9	0	0	1	15.1	82	24	10	10	1	2	1	1	12	1	22	3	1	0	0	.000	0	1	5.87
Bale,John	Hagerstown	Tor	A	24	25	25	0	0	140.1	603	130	83	67	11	4	3	1	63	1	155	11	0	7	7	.500	0	0	4.30
Bales,Joseph	Hickory	ChA	A	23	11	0	0	4	25	117	29	19	18	4	0	3	2	16	0	28	0	0	0	0	.000	0	1	6.48
	Bristol	ChA	R+	23	14	14	1	0	83	356	73	50	38	7	0	1	1	49	1	86	4	1	8	3	.727	1	0	4.12
Balfour,Grant	Twins	Min	R	20	13	12	0	0	67	275	73	31	28	1	0	1	4	20	0	43	3	2	2	4	.333	0	0	3.76
Bane,Jaymie	Butte	Ana	R+	23	24	0	0	15	40.1	180	43	33	26	6	0	4	2	16	3	47	4	0	3	2	.600	0	6	5.80
Barber,Andrew	Portland	Col	A-	25	22	0	0	8	32.2	132	23	10	9	0	3	0	1	18	0	39	3	5	6	1	.857	0	1	2.48
Barboza,Carlos	Rockies	Col	R	20	16	0	0	7	29	146	29	23	13	1	2	2	3	25	0	18	6	2	1	1	.500	0	1	4.03
Barksdale,Shane	Kissimmee	Hou	A+	21	3	0	0	1	5	22	5	2	0	1	1	0	1	2	0	3	1	0	0	0	.000	0	0	0.00
	Quad City	Hou	A	21	8	0	0	6	12.1	64	22	12	10	3	0	0	1	5	0	8	1	0	0	0	.000	0	1	7.30
	Auburn	Hou	A-	21	22	1	0	4	35.2	159	49	28	22	3	1	2	1	12	1	22	3	0	3	3	.500	0	0	5.55
Barnes,Keith	Sarasota	Bos	A+	23	28	5	0	9	64.2	306	72	48	40	4	2	4	3	38	0	39	9	0	2	3	.400	0	1	5.57
Barnes,Larry	Beloit	Mil	A	21	13	13	0	0	66	294	61	47	42	4	1	2	4	47	1	58	12	0	3	6	.333	0	0	5.73
Barnett,Marty	Piedmont	Phi	A	24	6	6	0	0	37	154	34	16	13	1	1	2	2	11	0	28	1	0	2	1	.667	0	0	3.16
	Clearwater	Phi	A+	24	17	15	1	0	97.2	411	102	50	40	10	1	1	0	29	0	62	6	2	5	6	.455	0	0	3.69
Barrera,Iran	Medicne Hat	Tor	R+	24	17	0	0	7	18.2	95	27	22	12	2	0	1	2	7	0	15	1	2	3	1	.750	0	0	5.79
Barrett,Scott	Medicne Hat	Tor	R+	23	19	8	0	3	53.2	261	69	42	33	6	2	1	5	16	0	46	6	2	0	6	.000	0	0	5.53
Barry,Shawn	Pittsfield	NYN	A-	23	22	0	0	9	26	105	14	6	5	0	0	0	0	10	1	35	4	1	2	3	.400	0	0	1.73
Bass,Randall	Hudson Vall	TB	A-	22	17	3	0	4	45.1	194	34	22	16	1	2	1	2	27	0	31	3	2	6	1	.857	0	0	3.18
Batts,Nathan	Cubs	ChN	R	20	8	1	0	1	9.2	48	11	9	8	0	2	1	1	10	0	9	2	0	2	0	1.000	0	0	7.45
Bauder,Michael	Ft. Wayne	Min	A	23	40	10	0	5	104	435	94	51	43	5	1	4	1	33	0	96	10	3	6	4	.600	0	0	3.72
Bauer,Chris	Lakeland	Det	A+	24	19	0	0	7	35	164	43	31	18	2	0	0	2	11	1	19	3	2	3	2	.600	0	2	4.63
	W Michigan	Det	A	24	18	0	0	15	24.1	111	30	15	11	1	1	1	3	10	1	11	1	0	0	2	.000	0	1	4.07
Bauer,Richard	Bluefield	Bal	R+	21	13	13	0	0	72.1	294	58	31	23	1	0	4	4	20	0	67	8	0	8	3	.727	0	0	2.86
	Delmarva	Bal	A	21	1	0	0	1	2	7	0	0	0	0	0	0	0	1	0	2	0	0	0	0	.000	0	1	0.00
Bauldree,Joey	Macon	Atl	A	21	39	2	0	13	60.1	271	65	40	31	5	2	5	5	25	0	66	2	0	3	1	.750	0	0	4.62
Bausher,Andrew	Erie	Pit	A-	21	15	10	0	1	65	278	62	32	28	3	2	2	3	19	1	44	2	1	4	3	.571	0	1	3.88
Beale,Charles	Michigan	Bos	A	24	39	9	1	28	89.1	405	111	58	37	5	3	2	2	17	2	86	9	2	2	7	.222	0	12	3.73
Beasley,Raymon.	Macon	Atl	A	22	49	0	0	30	71.1	294	52	28	21	4	4	3	5	26	2	102	2	0	3	4	.429	0	8	2.65
Beck,Matthew	Jamestown	Det	A-	22	17	0	0	6	28.2	141	41	30	22	3	1	3	5	9	0	17	0	0	1	0	1.000	0	0	6.91
Becker,Keith	Red Sox	Bos	R	23	5	0	0	5	7.2	34	7	5	4	0	1	0	1	4	1	7	1	0	0	1	.000	0	0	4.70
Becker,Tom	Tampa	NYA	A+	23	25	0	0	9	43	192	45	29	24	2	1	2	0	26	4	26	6	1	2	1	.667	0	0	5.02
Becks,Ryan	Vermont	Mon	A-	22	15	15	1	0	78.2	368	92	61	51	4	4	2	7	33	0	57	12	1	2	8	.200	0	0	5.83
Bedinger,Doug	Diamondback	Ari	R	23	1	0	0	0	2	6	0	0	0	0	0	0	0	0	0	5	0	0	0	0	.000	0	0	0.00
	South Bend	Ari	A	23	11	0	0	6	21.2	91	19	6	6	3	0	0	0	8	2	26	0	0	0	1	.000	0	1	2.49
	High Desert	Ari	A+	23	1	0	0	0	0.2	8	3	5	3	0	1	0	0	2	0	0	2	0	0	0	.000	0	0	40.50
Beebe,Hans	Capital City	NYN	A	23	6	0	0	1	12.2	64	21	15	14	3	1	2	0	6	0	6	0	0	0	0	.000	0	0	9.95
	Pittsfield	NYN	A-	23	15	15	3	0	90	382	90	49	39	9	4	3	3	22	0	71	1	0	6	6	.500	0	0	3.90
Belitz,Todd	Hudson Vall	TB	A-	22	15	15	0	0	74	315	65	41	29	4	1	2	5	18	0	78	0	0	4	5	.444	0	0	3.53
Bell,Matthew	South Bend	Ari	A	20	14	0	0	4	22.2	111	27	27	17	4	3	1	2	9	3	22	2	2	2	3	.400	0	0	6.75
	Lethbridge	Ari	R+	20	2	0	0	0	4.1	19	4	0	0	0	0	0	0	3	0	5	0	0	1	0	1.000	0	0	0.00
	Diamondback	Ari	R	20	18	0	0	7	34.1	152	31	18	11	1	1	2	2	16	0	36	5	3	3	2	.600	0	2	2.88
Bell,Mike	Wst Plm Bch	Mon	A+	25	41	3	0	15	81.1	328	60	30	28	2	4	2	5	27	0	56	2	0	5	4	.556	0	4	3.10
Bell,Rob	Macon	Atl	A	21	27	27	1	0	146.2	614	144	72	60	15	5	5	3	41	1	140	7	0	14	7	.667	0	0	3.68
Bello,Emerson	Everett	Sea	A-	20	22	3	0	10	44.2	209	52	27	20	9	0	1	3	15	1	65	4	4	2	4	.333	0	1	4.03
Beltran,Francis	Cubs	ChN	R	17	16	0	0	5	23.2	111	27	18	9	1	1	1	3	8	0	17	3	2	0	1	.000	0	1	3.42
Benes,Adam	Pr William	StL	A+	25	33	5	0	9	70.1	326	92	54	49	15	3	2	2	29	0	44	4	0	3	3	.500	0	0	6.27
Benesh,Edward	Chston-SC	TB	A	23	46	0	0	40	50.2	210	44	16	11	2	4	0	1	14	1	39	6	0	4	4	.500	0	15	1.95
Bennett,Thomas	Modesto	Oak	A+	22	25	24	0	0	112	521	118	84	71	8	2	7	5	73	2	116	16	0	6	9	.400	0	0	5.71
Benoit,Joaquin	Rangers	Tex	R	19	10	10	1	0	44	177	40	14	10	0	1	0	1	11	0	38	1	0	3	3	.500	0	0	2.05
Benzing,Skipp	Lowell	Bos	A-	21	2	2	0	0	10.2	45	11	8	7	1	0	0	0	2	1	6	1	0	0	1	.000	0	0	5.91
	Red Sox	Bos	R	21	6	2	0	3	16.1	80	16	16	10	2	1	0	1	9	0	17	2	0	0	3	.000	0	1	5.51
Bergan,Thomas	Hudson Vall	TB	A-	24	27	0	0	11	39.2	193	48	34	28	1	3	1	1	20	0	32	8	1	0	5	.000	0	0	6.35
Bermudez,Manu.	San Jose	SF	A+	21	9	9	2	0	44	208	61	35	33	4	1	3	1	22	1	27	5	2	2	6	.250	0	0	6.75
	Bakersfield	SF	A+	21	19	18	1	0	112	482	121	69	61	12	2	2	4	41	1	71	6	8	8	8	.500	0	0	4.90
Bernal,Manuel	Wilmington	KC	A+	24	45	3	0	25	97.2	424	108	51	47	5	4	2	5	27	10	55	2	2	6	8	.429	0	8	4.33
Berninger,D.J.	Stockton	Mil	A+	25	18	0	0	8	31	143	33	20	15	1	5	1	2	17	1	20	3	2	3	2	.600	0	1	4.35
Berry,Jason	Chston-SC	TB	A	24	8	0	0	5	10	43	11	10	6	1	1	0	0	1	0	2	1	1	1	1	.500	0	0	5.40
	St. Pete	TB	A+	24	35	0	0	16	48.2	225	65	32	27	3	2	2	4	11	1	40	2	2	4	2	.667	0	4	4.99
Betancourt,Rafa.	Michigan	Bos	A	23	27	0	0	22	32.1	125	26	9	7	2	1	0	0	2	0	52	3	1	0	3	.000	0	11	1.95
Bettencourt,Justi.	Lakeland	Det	A+	24	25	25	1	0	143.1	624	143	78	66	10	1	8	4	68	0	112	9	0	7	10	.412	0	0	4.14
Bevel,Bobby	Salem	Col	A+	24	50	0	0	18	66	290	69	37	34	5	2	7	9	17	0	57	3	0	4	7	.364	0	3	4.64

1997 Pitching — Single-A and Rookie Leagues

HOW MUCH HE PITCHED											WHAT HE GAVE UP												THE RESULTS					
Player	Team	Org	Lg	A	G	GS	CG	GF	IP	BFP	H	R	ER	HR	SH	SF	HB	TBB	IBB	SO	WP	Bk	W	L	Pct.	ShO	Sv	ERA
Bice,Justin	High Desert	Ari	A+	23	4	4	0	0	24	95	18	12	11	1	0	0	3	9	0	22	0	1	2	0	1.000	0	0	4.13
Biddle,Lee	Hickory	ChA	A	22	13	0	0	4	21.1	96	22	18	11	2	0	1	2	10	0	25	5	0	0	1	.000	0	1	4.64
Bido,Jose	Diamondback	Ari	R	19	1	1	0	0	1	7	5	3	3	0	0	0	1	0	0	0	0	0	0	1	.000	0	0	27.00
Bierbrodt,Nichol.	South Bend	Ari	A	20	15	15	0	0	75.2	340	77	43	34	4	3	1	9	37	0	64	6	1	2	4	.333	0	0	4.04
Billingsley,Brent	Kane County	Fla	A	23	26	26	3	0	170.2	697	146	67	57	9	7	1	11	50	0	175	13	1	14	7	.667	1	0	3.01
Birrell,Simon	Danville	Atl	R+	20	13	9	0	0	49.2	232	59	36	26	6	1	1	8	27	0	25	8	0	4	3	.571	0	0	4.71
Birsner,Roark	Daytona	ChN	A+	22	8	0	0	6	11.1	52	15	6	6	2	0	0	1	3	0	12	1	0	0	0	.000	0	0	4.76
	Rockford	ChN	A	22	18	0	0	5	31.1	155	33	19	13	3	1	0	3	24	1	33	1	0	0	2	.000	0	2	3.73
Bishop,Joshua	Stockton	Mil	A+	23	11	8	0	0	37	188	56	38	35	6	3	0	5	24	0	39	4	0	2	3	.400	0	0	8.51
	Beloit	Mil	A	23	21	11	1	5	79.2	354	79	62	53	10	1	5	6	34	0	61	8	1	5	7	.417	0	1	5.99
Black,Brett	Batavia	Phi	A-	23	28	0	0	23	41	149	23	7	6	2	1	0	0	2	1	66	0	1	3	0	1.000	0	15	1.32
Blackmore,John	Astros	Hou	R	20	15	4	0	3	38.1	200	35	40	33	1	1	2	9	42	0	32	17	3	4	2	.667	0	0	7.75
Blanco,Pablo	Marlins	Fla	R	20	11	9	1	1	51	231	41	31	23	2	1	2	6	36	0	44	6	6	2	5	.286	0	0	4.06
Blanco,Roger	Durham	Atl	A+	21	36	0	0	11	68.1	336	91	64	58	15	6	3	12	33	1	33	3	0	3	3	.500	0	0	7.64
Blank,Matt	Vermont	Mon	A-	22	16	15	2	0	95.2	375	74	26	18	2	1	3	2	14	0	84	0	0	6	4	.600	0	0	1.69
Bleazard,David	Hagerstown	Tor	A	24	10	10	0	0	59.2	250	52	25	22	1	1	2	5	20	0	58	5	4	5	0	1.000	0	0	3.32
Blevins,Jeremy	Yankees	NYA	R	20	11	9	0	0	55.2	235	50	27	15	1	0	0	4	23	1	46	4	0	5	3	.625	0	0	2.43
Bloomer,Christo.	Lethbridge	Ari	R+	23	27	0	0	23	30.2	130	19	14	7	2	0	0	4	9	1	38	2	0	5	2	.714	0	9	2.05
Bloomfield,Shane	Yakima	LA	A-	25	1	0	0	0	1	3	1	0	0	0	0	0	0	0	0	0	0	0	0	0	.000	0	0	0.00
Blumenstock,Bra.	Visalia	Oak	A+	23	9	0	0	3	11.2	67	22	18	18	1	0	0	0	11	1	3	2	0	0	0	.000	0	0	13.89
	Sou. Oregon	Oak	A-	23	19	7	0	2	45.1	227	61	51	47	4	0	1	3	30	0	28	7	0	0	4	.000	0	0	9.33
Blyleven,Todd	Stockton	Mil	A+	25	1	0	0	0	3.1	13	2	0	0	0	0	0	0	0	0	4	0	0	1	0	1.000	0	0	0.00
Blythe,Billy	Macon	Atl	A	22	35	1	0	13	58.2	279	54	40	34	2	6	1	5	38	1	57	4	0	2	5	.286	0	0	5.22
Bogeajis,Dan	Astros	Hou	R	20	7	0	0	5	10.1	50	14	6	6	1	0	1	2	4	0	6	1	1	1	1	.500	0	1	5.23
Bogle,Sean	Daytona	ChN	A+	24	8	0	0	5	6.2	38	11	7	5	1	0	0	0	7	1	3	3	0	1	1	.500	0	2	6.75
	Chstón-SC	TB	A	24	20	0	0	10	36.1	149	24	11	8	0	1	1	2	17	0	38	2	1	3	0	1.000	0	0	1.98
Bond,Aaron	Pulaski	Tex	R+	21	14	14	0	0	77	311	56	29	21	5	4	1	1	22	0	64	9	2	5	2	.714	0	0	2.45
Bond,Jason	Lancaster	Sea	A+	23	36	9	0	11	110	472	99	54	46	17	1	2	8	45	0	123	5	1	5	7	.417	0	2	3.76
Bonilla,Denys	Lancaster	Sea	A+	24	40	0	0	28	76	307	67	29	24	6	5	2	2	18	4	92	3	3	9	6	.600	0	6	2.84
Booker,Chris	Williamsprt	ChN	A-	21	24	3	0	11	45.2	200	39	20	17	2	3	4	0	25	0	60	9	0	1	5	.167	0	1	3.35
Borges,Reece	Utica	Fla	A-	22	15	15	2	0	80.2	358	92	54	43	6	3	1	3	28	0	58	4	0	7	5	.583	0	0	4.80
Boring,Richard	Lansing	KC	A	22	3	0	0	2	2.2	16	6	6	6	0	0	0	0	4	0	2	0	0	0	2	.000	0	0	20.25
	Spokane	KC	A-	22	26	0	0	19	25.1	121	32	15	9	2	1	1	1	7	0	17	4	1	2	1	.667	0	7	3.20
Borkowski,Dave	W Michigan	Det	A	21	25	25	4	0	164	670	143	79	63	15	3	3	7	31	0	104	7	0	15	3	.833	2	0	3.46
Borkowski,Rob	Kingsport	NYN	R+	21	5	0	0	4	5.1	33	13	10	10	1	0	0	0	2	0	5	0	0	2	0	1.000	0	2	16.88
Bornyk,Matthew	Great Falls	LA	R+	19	13	2	0	6	23.1	105	21	16	15	3	0	0	2	15	0	29	4	0	0	3	.000	0	1	5.79
Bosio,Chris	Red Sox	Bos	R	35	2	2	0	0	5	18	2	0	0	0	0	0	0	2	0	4	0	0	0	0	.000	0	0	0.00
	Sarasota	Bos	A+	35	1	1	0	0	4.2	21	6	2	1	0	0	0	0	0	0	5	0	0	0	0	.000	0	0	1.93
Bost,Ronald	Medicne Hat	Tor	R+	18	14	0	0	3	16.1	84	22	20	14	1	1	0	0	17	1	17	1	0	0	2	.000	0	0	7.71
Bourbakis,Mike	Savannah	LA	A	21	23	13	0	2	58.2	286	70	57	51	9	1	2	6	39	0	47	11	3	0	6	.000	0	0	7.82
Bowers,Cedrick	Chston-SC	TB	A	20	28	28	0	0	157	657	119	74	56	11	4	3	3	78	0	164	15	1	8	10	.444	0	0	3.21
Bowers,Jason	Braves	Atl	R	20	12	0	0	10	29.2	152	40	32	30	3	0	1	0	28	0	21	6	1	2	3	.400	0	0	9.10
Bowles,Brian	Hagerstown	Tor	A	21	4	0	0	1	10.1	49	14	10	8	2	0	1	1	5	0	9	1	0	1	0	1.000	0	0	6.97
	Dunedin	Tor	A+	21	7	1	0	3	14.1	68	20	14	12	2	0	1	0	7	1	9	3	1	0	2	.000	0	0	7.53
	St. Cathrns	Tor	A-	21	16	16	0	0	78.2	351	76	53	44	6	0	3	11	35	0	64	4	1	5	8	.385	0	0	5.03
Box,John	Princeton	TB	R+	23	25	0	0	12	38.1	152	29	15	10	2	1	1	1	10	0	53	1	3	4	1	.800	0	3	2.35
Brackeen,Colin	Medicne Hat	Tor	R+	23	18	0	0	14	19.1	83	11	4	3	0	1	0	4	8	1	20	2	1	1	1	.500	0	5	1.40
	Dunedin	Tor	A+	23	6	0	0	4	10	43	13	4	4	0	0	0	1	3	1	11	0	0	0	2	.000	0	0	3.60
Bradford,Chad	Winston-Sal	ChA	A+	23	46	0	0	41	54.2	247	51	30	24	2	4	0	5	25	5	43	2	0	3	7	.300	0	15	3.95
Bradford,Josh	Dunedin	Tor	A+	24	28	23	2	3	158.2	701	173	104	88	11	0	5	11	65	3	92	18	5	8	8	.500	1	0	4.99
Bradley,Ryan	Oneonta	NYA	A-	22	14	0	0	9	26.2	103	22	5	4	1	0	0	0	5	1	22	0	1	3	1	.750	0	1	1.35
Brammer,John	Columbus	Cle	A	23	28	23	0	1	116.2	542	132	102	91	11	2	7	18	50	0	105	9	4	6	10	.375	0	1	7.02
Brand,Scott	Oneonta	NYA	A-	22	10	2	0	2	19.2	92	24	17	16	1	1	1	2	8	0	18	1	0	4	3	.571	0	0	7.32
	Greensboro	NYA	A	22	8	0	0	6	21	88	21	8	8	2	0	0	0	5	0	22	2	0	2	0	1.000	0	1	3.43
Braswell,Bryan	Quad City	Hou	A	23	19	19	1	0	116.1	495	107	70	49	10	0	4	2	32	0	118	2	5	6	6	.500	0	0	3.79
Bravo,Franklin	Pirates	Pit	R	19	4	4	0	0	9	45	16	10	8	1	0	0	1	5	0	5	1	1	0	1	.000	0	0	8.00
	Augusta	Pit	A	19	7	3	0	0	15.1	67	12	9	4	1	0	1	1	5	0	14	0	1	0	0	.000	0	0	2.35
Bray,Chris	Bluefield	Bal	R+	23	3	0	0	0	4	20	1	7	7	0	0	0	3	4	0	5	0	0	0	0	.000	0	0	15.75
Brazoban,Melvin	Rangers	Tex	R	21	14	0	0	9	30	133	28	16	14	1	1	2	2	14	1	36	1	3	1	3	.250	0	2	4.20
Brea,Lesli	Lancaster	Sea	A+	19	1	0	0	0	2	13	5	5	3	1	0	0	0	1	0	1	1	0	0	0	.000	0	0	13.50
	Everett	Sea	A-	19	23	0	0	14	32.2	162	34	29	29	3	2	1	3	29	4	49	8	0	2	4	.333	0	3	7.99
Brester,Jason	San Jose	SF	A+	21	26	26	0	0	142.1	625	164	80	67	4	4	3	3	52	0	172	10	7	9	9	.500	0	0	4.24
Brewer,Clint	Billings	Cin	R+	19	22	0	0	13	41	180	33	21	15	0	1	2	3	20	2	37	11	1	3	5	.375	0	4	3.29
Brewer,Ryan	Wilmington	KC	A+	24	47	0	0	19	105	439	100	41	39	5	6	0	3	29	4	93	4	0	5	4	.556	0	7	3.34
Bridges,Donald	Expos	Mon	R	19	5	2	0	0	10	49	14	9	7	0	0	1	2	5	0	6	0	0	0	2	.000	0	0	6.30
Brittan,Corey	St. Lucie	NYN	A+	23	51	1	0	18	78	338	91	35	31	5	4	0	1	21	4	57	2	0	3	5	.375	0	3	3.58
Brookens,Casey	Rockford	ChN	A	24	28	0	0	9	51	218	48	20	18	6	1	1	1	21	2	51	2	0	3	2	.600	0	3	3.18
Brooks,Wyatt	Augusta	Pit	A	24	16	4	0	2	51.2	220	49	26	18	3	2	1	1	18	1	49	5	0	5	3	.625	0	1	3.14
Brown,Charlie	Tampa	NYA	A+	24	28	0	0	14	39.2	191	44	24	21	4	3	0	6	25	3	26	5	1	4	3	.571	0	0	4.76
Brown,Derek	Delmarva	Bal	A	21	2	0	0	0	2	9	2	0	0	0	0	0	0	1	0	2	0	0	0	0	.000	0	0	0.00
	Bluefield	Bal	R+	21	17	5	1	2	41.1	180	44	26	23	3	1	1	0	13	0	48	3	1	2	5	.286	0	1	5.01
Brown,Elliot	Chston-SC	TB	A	23	33	16	0	6	118.2	525	117	73	57	11	4	2	8	45	0	86	12	0	5	8	.385	0	3	4.32
Brown,Jamie	Watertown	Cle	A-	21	13	13	1	0	73	303	66	35	25	6	1	2	4	15	0	57	1	1	10	2	.833	0	0	3.08
Brown,Trent	Chston-SC	TB	A	22	33	0	0	13	49	190	36	12	11	2	1	2	2	7	0	43	0	0	3	1	.750	0	1	2.02
Brown,Zay	Billings	Cin	R+	19	8	0	0	3	11	64	22	14	7	0	0	0	1	9	0	12	0	0	0	0	.000	0	0	5.73
Brueggemann,D.	Asheville	Col	A	22	34	12	0	7	110	482	116	62	52	11	6	5	1	44	2	99	6	2	2	8	.200	0	3	4.25
Brummitt,Travis	Danville	Atl	R+	22	12	0	0	4	20	118	34	36	29	4	1	1	7	16	0	24	5	1	0	0	.000	0	0	13.05

1997 Pitching — Single-A and Rookie Leagues

HOW MUCH HE PITCHED											WHAT HE GAVE UP												THE RESULTS					
Player	Team	Org	Lg	A	G	GS	CG	GF	IP	BFP	H	R	ER	HR	SH	SF	HB	TBB	IBB	SO	WP	Bk	W	L	Pct.	ShO	Sv	ERA
Bruner,Clay	W Michigan	Det	A	21	24	24	3	0	166.1	664	134	52	44	11	2	7	4	48	1	135	9	1	15	3	.833	2	0	2.38
Brunette,Justin	New Jersey	StL	A-	22	6	0	0	2	5.2	29	13	6	5	0	0	0	0	0	0	6	1	1	1	0	1.000	0	0	7.94
Bryant,Chris	Daytona	ChN	A+	22	8	1	0	1	11.1	59	20	12	12	5	1	1	0	8	0	10	3	0	0	1	.000	0	0	9.53
	Williamsprt	ChN	A-	22	4	0	0	0	6.2	38	13	8	5	0	0	0	0	5	0	8	3	0	0	0	.000	0	0	6.75
Buckman,Thoma.	Hickory	ChA	A	24	24	19	1	3	112.1	503	140	83	71	12	3	8	14	29	0	64	8	1	5	8	.385	0	0	5.69
Budsky,Pavel	Royals	KC	R	22	6	0	0	0	10.1	47	17	6	6	0	0	0	1	1	0	7	1	0	2	1	.667	0	0	5.23
Bullock,Derek	Lynchburg	Pit	A+	25	15	2	0	2	33.2	152	27	20	18	5	0	1	4	21	0	34	3	1	2	0	1.000	0	0	4.81
	Augusta	Pit	A	25	8	6	0	0	33.2	142	32	21	17	6	1	0	1	8	0	30	2	0	2	4	.333	0	0	4.54
Burchart,Kyle	St. Cathrns	Tor	A-	21	14	14	0	0	69.2	314	75	49	37	6	2	5	7	23	2	56	20	0	3	4	.429	0	0	4.78
Burger,Rob	Clearwater	Phi	A+	22	28	27	1	0	160.2	682	131	79	64	8	2	3	13	93	0	154	17	3	11	9	.550	1	0	3.59
Burnett,A.J.	Mets	NYN	R	21	3	2	0	0	11.1	54	8	8	4	0	0	0	2	8	0	15	3	0	0	1	.000	0	0	3.18
	Pittsfield	NYN	A-	21	9	9	0	0	44	192	28	26	23	3	0	2	6	35	0	48	9	0	3	1	.750	0	0	4.70
Burnside,Adrian	Yakima	LA	A-	21	15	13	0	0	65.2	314	67	53	36	9	1	3	5	49	1	66	4	4	6	3	.667	0	0	4.93
Burton,Jaime	Spokane	KC	A-	23	7	0	0	6	7	31	4	2	1	0	0	0	0	5	0	9	1	0	0	0	.000	0	0	1.29
Byrd,Ben	Ogden	Mil	R+	22	18	0	0	8	38.1	173	42	27	19	4	3	1	2	13	0	35	3	0	3	1	.750	0	1	4.46
Byrdak,Timothy	Wilmington	KC	A+	24	22	2	0	15	41	169	34	17	16	3	5	1	2	12	4	47	4	0	4	3	.571	0	3	3.51
Caddell,Carl	Billings	Cin	R+	22	4	1	0	1	9.2	38	7	1	1	0	1	0	0	3	0	5	1	0	1	1	.500	0	0	0.93
Cafaro,Robert	Devil Rays	TB	R	22	4	4	0	0	11	45	9	2	2	0	1	0	0	2	0	8	1	2	0	0	.000	0	0	1.64
Cain,Travis	St. Pete	TB	A+	22	9	8	0	0	42.2	200	44	33	24	2	1	2	1	30	0	21	2	0	1	4	.200	0	0	5.06
	Devil Rays	TB	R	22	4	0	0	2	6	28	8	6	4	1	0	0	0	4	0	6	2	0	1	2	.333	0	0	6.00
Cairncross,Cam	Rancho Cuca	SD	A+	26	40	0	0	17	64	291	81	46	40	5	4	1	5	15	0	70	4	1	1	3	.250	0	1	5.63
Caldwell,David	Kinston	Cle	A+	23	9	3	0	3	27	127	31	16	13	2	1	1	2	10	0	16	2	0	2	1	.667	0	0	4.33
	Columbus	Cle	A	23	5	5	0	0	23.2	104	25	13	11	0	1	1	1	4	0	22	1	1	2	1	.667	0	0	4.18
Cali,Joseph	Watertown	Cle	A-	23	2	0	0	2	3	13	4	3	3	2	0	0	0	0	0	3	1	0	1	0	1.000	0	0	9.00
	Burlington	Cle	R+	23	14	0	0	8	20.1	120	37	36	25	4	0	1	2	20	0	24	8	2	1	2	.333	0	0	11.07
Callahan,Damon	Burlington	Cin	A	22	11	7	0	0	37.1	155	33	17	16	1	1	1	1	15	0	29	3	0	2	2	.500	0	0	3.86
Callaway,Michael	St. Pete	TB	A+	23	28	28	3	0	170.2	696	162	74	61	9	2	3	5	39	0	109	7	7	11	7	.611	0	0	3.22
Calvert,Klae	Lowell	Bos	A-	21	3	3	0	0	14	64	16	13	13	3	1	1	5	3	0	8	3	0	1	0	1.000	0	0	8.36
	Red Sox	Bos	R	21	12	4	0	5	46.2	191	52	16	12	1	0	1	1	7	0	37	4	0	6	0	1.000	0	1	2.31
Cames,Aaron	Kane County	Fla	A	22	26	26	3	0	149.2	627	143	67	65	11	6	6	15	43	0	157	10	6	8	10	.444	3	0	3.91
Cammack,Eric	Pittsfield	NYN	A-	22	23	0	0	17	31.1	117	9	4	3	1	3	1	1	14	1	32	1	1	0	1	.000	0	8	0.86
Camp,Shawn	Idaho Falls	SD	R+	22	30	0	0	24	32.2	150	41	22	20	3	1	1	2	14	0	41	4	0	2	1	.667	0	12	5.51
Campbell,Tedde	Augusta	Pit	A	25	5	0	0	2	4.2	22	6	3	2	0	1	0	0	2	0	4	0	0	2	1	.667	0	1	3.86
Cana,Nelson	Stockton	Mil	A+	22	44	0	0	14	91.2	396	91	46	35	7	4	2	4	34	0	69	12	0	6	1	.857	0	1	3.44
Canciobello,Anth.	Danville	Atl	R+	21	3	0	0	0	3.2	24	6	6	5	0	0	1	0	6	0	4	2	0	0	0	.000	0	0	12.27
Cannon,Jonatha.	Rockford	ChN	A	23	24	20	1	3	129.1	548	110	53	45	13	2	3	7	50	1	130	16	3	9	6	.600	0	0	3.13
	Daytona	ChN	A+	23	2	2	0	0	13.2	55	7	2	2	1	2	1	0	10	1	13	0	0	1	0	1.000	0	0	1.32
Caravelli,Mike	Brevard Cty	Fla	A+	25	40	0	0	18	61.1	279	81	44	32	3	3	3	2	12	2	35	4	1	3	5	.375	0	3	4.70
Cardona,Steve	Hickory	ChA	A	24	32	0	0	12	60.1	265	62	41	29	5	4	6	5	16	0	40	17	0	4	5	.444	0	1	4.33
Carlyle,Buddy	Chston-WV	Cin	A	20	23	23	4	0	143	579	130	51	44	9	4	4	3	27	0	111	5	1	14	5	.737	1	0	2.77
Carmody,Brian	Rancho Cuca	SD	A+	23	4	3	0	0	14.2	75	18	16	14	4	1	0	1	15	0	7	1	0	0	1	.000	0	0	8.59
	Clinton	SD	A	23	8	1	0	2	17.1	69	14	7	3	0	0	0	0	8	1	19	2	1	0	0	.000	0	1	1.56
Carnes,Matt	Elizabethtn	Min	R+	22	8	7	1	0	38	156	33	17	13	3	2	0	1	5	0	42	7	1	3	0	1.000	0	0	3.08
	Ft. Wayne	Min	A	22	1	1	0	0	4	18	2	4	4	1	0	0	0	5	0	3	1	1	0	1	.000	0	0	9.00
Carpenter,Justin	Oneonta	NYA	A-	21	24	0	0	8	29.1	140	32	17	15	1	1	1	0	20	0	36	4	0	3	1	.750	0	0	4.60
Carrion,Jorge	Pulaski	Tex	R+	21	13	13	0	0	76	356	75	64	40	9	0	0	10	44	0	78	7	1	5	5	.500	0	0	4.74
Carroll,Dave	St. Pete	TB	A+	25	47	0	0	9	50.2	218	50	15	10	1	1	2	2	20	3	34	2	0	4	1	.800	0	0	1.78
Carter,Aaron	Spokane	KC	A-	23	24	0	0	7	35	155	23	12	8	0	1	2	0	27	2	52	11	0	2	1	.667	0	2	2.06
Carter,Chris	Princeton	TB	R+	24	26	0	0	13	35.1	147	40	16	13	1	0	1	0	5	0	24	0	3	2	0	1.000	0	2	3.31
Carter,Roger	Princeton	TB	R+	19	13	13	0	0	56.2	247	61	36	29	6	2	4	5	17	0	50	7	1	5	2	.714	0	0	4.61
Casey,Joseph	St. Cathrns	Tor	A-	19	14	11	0	1	64	279	59	42	31	6	0	1	3	23	0	43	11	0	7	4	.636	0	1	4.36
Casey,Shaw	Utica	Fla	A-	23	9	0	0	4	12	76	28	21	16	1	1	0	6	8	0	11	3	0	0	2	.000	0	0	12.00
Casteel,Ricky	Orioles	Bal	R	20	15	9	0	2	65	287	63	31	20	2	1	1	7	30	1	37	9	0	2	3	.400	0	1	2.77
Castillo,Alberto	San Jose	SF	A+	22	18	1	0	8	33.2	162	41	26	21	2	2	2	4	15	0	30	7	0	2	2	.500	0	0	5.61
Castillo,Jose	Tigers	Det	R	21	12	10	1	1	55.1	224	50	28	20	3	1	1	3	7	0	47	5	4	4	5	.444	0	0	3.25
Cavanagh,Andre.	Helena	Mil	R+	21	18	2	0	7	35.2	155	32	22	17	2	2	0	1	18	1	37	3	0	2	1	.667	0	3	4.29
Ceasar,Donald	Braves	Atl	R	19	10	0	0	7	19	102	27	24	15	1	1	0	0	8	0	12	3	0	1	1	.500	0	2	7.11
Cedeno,Blas	Rockford	ChN	A	25	22	0	0	13	40.1	168	36	19	13	3	1	1	1	14	2	25	0	0	3	3	.500	0	0	2.90
Celta,Nicolas	Astros	Hou	R	20	8	0	0	4	13.2	64	14	13	10	0	2	1	0	9	0	16	3	1	0	1	.000	0	1	6.59
Centeno,Juan	Astros	Hou	R	19	7	6	1	1	26	107	21	18	10	1	1	1	1	6	0	17	1	6	1	5	.167	0	0	3.46
Cepeda,Wellingt.	Diamondback	Ari	R	20	15	1	0	0	38.1	158	31	16	7	1	0	0	0	12	0	32	3	0	4	0	1.000	0	0	1.64
Cervantes,Peter	Savannah	LA	A	23	21	20	1	0	103	438	113	48	44	9	2	3	4	22	0	84	1	0	8	8	.500	0	0	3.84
	San Berndno	LA	A+	23	1	0	0	0	1	3	1	0	0	0	0	0	0	0	0	0	0	0	0	0	.000	0	0	0.00
Chacon,Shawn	Asheville	Col	A	20	28	27	1	0	162	701	155	80	70	13	5	3	14	63	1	149	15	1	11	7	.611	0	0	3.89
Chambers,Scott	Vero Beach	LA	A+	22	56	2	0	16	84.2	359	67	40	31	5	2	1	0	48	0	89	10	1	5	5	.500	0	6	3.30
Chaney,Michael	Augusta	Pit	A	23	31	14	0	2	125.1	525	129	58	49	8	4	4	5	28	1	95	7	0	8	7	.533	0	0	3.52
Chantres,Carlos	Winston-Sal	ChA	A+	22	26	26	2	0	164.2	712	152	94	86	21	6	5	4	71	1	158	10	2	9	11	.450	0	0	4.70
Chapman,Walker	Ft. Myers	Min	A+	22	27	14	0	4	90	405	121	64	58	7	2	5	3	32	0	65	1	1	6	5	.545	0	1	5.80
Chapman,Jake	Wilmington	KC	A+	24	27	26	0	0	154.1	673	163	83	66	7	3	5	5	59	5	122	4	0	8	9	.471	0	0	3.85
Charbonneau,M.	Hagerstown	Tor	A	22	6	1	0	1	10.2	58	18	14	11	2	2	0	0	7	0	13	2	0	1	1	.500	0	0	9.28
	St. Cathrns	Tor	A-	22	6	0	0	2	10	46	9	9	8	1	0	1	1	4	0	15	2	0	0	1	.000	0	1	7.20
Chen,Bruce	Macon	Atl	A	21	28	28	1	0	146.1	602	120	67	57	19	4	5	7	44	0	182	5	1	12	7	.632	1	0	3.51
Childers,Jason	Helena	Mil	R+	23	10	0	0	6	16.1	69	14	9	6	2	2	0	0	7	0	25	0	0	1	1	.500	0	2	3.31
Childers,Matt	Helena	Mil	R+	19	14	10	0	1	61	285	81	49	42	5	2	4	0	24	0	19	1	0	1	4	.200	0	1	6.20
Chivers,Jason	Mets	NYN	R	19	11	0	0	5	12	57	10	7	7	1	0	0	1	11	0	14	2	0	1	0	1.000	0	1	5.25
Choate,Randy	Oneonta	NYA	A-	22	10	10	0	0	62.1	242	49	12	12	1	0	0	2	12	1	61	0	2	5	1	.833	0	0	1.73
Christianson,Ro.	Lancaster	Sea	A+	22	6	0	0	4	10	51	15	12	8	2	0	0	3	4	0	4	1	0	0	1	.000	0	0	7.20
	Everett	Sea	A-	22	20	2	0	1	41.1	195	48	31	26	4	1	1	7	23	1	46	4	0	2	2	.500	0	0	5.66

1997 Pitching — Single-A and Rookie Leagues

HOW MUCH HE PITCHED											WHAT HE GAVE UP												THE RESULTS					
Player	Team	Org	Lg	A	G	GS	CG	GF	IP	BFP	H	R	ER	HR	SH	SF	HB	TBB	IBB	SO	WP	Bk	W	L	Pct.	ShO	Sv	ERA
Christman,Tim	Asheville	Col	A	23	29	0	0	11	63.1	263	55	32	24	8	5	3	3	18	1	87	7	4	7	3	.700	0	3	3.41
Chrysler,Robert	Everett	Sea	A-	22	18	0	0	10	22.2	83	11	3	2	0	0	0	0	7	0	25	3	0	3	0	1.000	0	2	0.79
Cintron,Jose	Cedar Rapds	Ana	A	22	2	0	0	0	5	20	3	3	3	2	0	0	1	0	0	4	0	0	0	0	.000	0	0	5.40
	Lk Elsinore	Ana	A+	22	28	6	0	7	63.1	281	76	44	43	8	1	2	7	22	2	50	3	1	2	3	.400	0	0	6.11
Ciravolo,Jon	Danville	Atl	R+	22	19	0	0	5	37.1	176	48	31	21	4	0	0	4	13	0	42	4	0	4	2	.667	0	1	5.06
Civit,Xavier	Cape Fear	Mon	A	25	39	0	0	17	63.1	270	59	28	25	9	2	4	2	18	0	60	5	0	4	3	.571	0	3	3.55
	Wst Plm Bch	Mon	A+	25	4	0	0	1	11	42	5	2	2	0	1	0	0	4	0	9	2	0	3	0	1.000	0	0	1.64
Clark,Chris	Clinton	SD	A	23	32	11	0	5	89	395	89	50	41	5	0	0	3	46	0	91	15	0	5	5	.500	0	3	4.15
Clark,Greg	Elizabethtn	Min	R+	20	16	0	0	7	28.1	124	34	21	16	5	2	1	0	8	0	22	0	0	1	0	1.000	0	0	5.08
	Ft. Wayne	Min	A	20	6	1	0	1	16.1	69	16	9	8	0	0	2	0	8	1	7	2	0	0	1	.000	0	0	4.41
Clark,Rich	Salem-Keizr	SF	A-	20	6	0	0	2	6	32	6	6	5	0	1	0	0	7	0	5	2	0	0	2	.000	0	0	7.50
Coble,Jason	Greensboro	NYA	A	20	24	23	1	0	120.1	552	93	84	66	6	3	3	3	96	1	99	14	0	2	11	.154	0	0	4.94
Coco,Pasqual	St. Cathrns	Tor	A-	20	10	8	0	1	46	199	48	32	25	5	0	4	2	16	1	44	6	1	1	4	.200	0	0	4.89
Coggin,Dave	Clearwater	Phi	A+	21	27	27	3	0	155	697	160	96	81	12	5	7	9	86	0	110	24	1	11	8	.579	2	0	4.70
Collins,Ed	Brevard Cty	Fla	A+	21	26	1	0	7	45.1	209	49	33	26	2	1	4	4	24	0	29	2	0	2	3	.400	0	2	5.16
	Beloit	Mil	A	21	2	0	0	0	1.2	12	3	3	2	0	0	1	0	3	0	3	3	0	0	0	.000	0	0	10.80
Colmenares,Luis	Salem	Col	A+	21	32	3	0	15	66.2	283	60	34	29	5	6	4	4	30	3	70	6	2	6	1	.857	0	2	3.92
Colon,Roman	Braves	Atl	R	18	14	12	0	1	63	289	68	47	30	2	4	3	2	28	0	44	3	0	3	4	.429	0	0	4.29
Combs,Chris	Erie	Pit	A-	23	21	0	0	19	24.2	92	13	2	2	0	0	0	1	3	0	36	1	0	2	1	.667	0	9	0.73
Comer,Scott	Pittsfield	NYN	A-	21	14	14	1	0	93.1	359	71	25	18	4	1	1	1	12	0	98	0	0	7	1	.875	0	0	1.74
Connell,Brian	Cubs	ChN	R	20	11	8	0	0	35.1	174	41	28	13	0	0	0	3	27	0	32	2	4	3	4	.429	0	0	3.31
Connolly,Sean	White Sox	ChA	R	24	15	0	0	11	22	102	21	12	7	0	3	1	2	15	0	17	3	1	2	1	.667	0	3	2.86
Conway,Keith	Pr William	StL	A+	25	15	0	0	2	19.1	83	18	6	6	2	1	0	1	8	0	22	0	0	1	0	1.000	0	0	2.79
Coogan,Patrick	New Jersey	StL	A-	22	10	10	0	0	56	231	56	27	23	4	1	0	3	14	0	37	0	2	2	5	.286	0	0	3.70
Cook,Aaron	Rockies	Col	R	19	9	8	0	0	46	208	48	27	16	1	2	0	5	17	0	35	3	3	1	3	.250	0	0	3.13
Cook,Derrick	Pulaski	Tex	R+	22	6	6	0	0	33.2	141	32	15	14	1	0	1	2	12	0	32	4	0	2	2	.500	0	0	3.74
	Charlotte	Tex	A+	22	8	8	2	0	58.2	243	54	21	15	5	0	1	2	15	0	35	4	0	5	2	.714	0	0	2.30
Cook,Steven	Martinsvlle	Phi	R+	22	7	0	0	3	9	47	11	6	5	1	0	0	2	7	1	8	2	0	0	0	.000	0	0	5.00
Cooper,Brian	Lk Elsinore	Ana	A+	23	17	17	1	0	117	497	111	56	46	7	6	2	10	27	0	104	6	0	7	3	.700	0	0	3.54
Corcoran,Tim	Mets	NYN	R	20	10	0	0	4	21	94	16	8	7	0	2	0	0	15	0	20	4	0	3	0	1.000	0	3	3.00
	Kingsport	NYN	R+	20	7	0	0	3	17	75	12	10	8	2	0	2	3	8	2	14	2	1	2	0	1.000	0	0	4.24
Cordero,Francis.	W Michigan	Det	A	20	50	0	0	47	54.1	208	36	13	6	2	4	2	0	15	2	67	5	0	6	1	.857	0	35	0.99
Corey,Mark	Chston-WV	Cin	A	23	26	26	1	0	136	602	169	87	69	7	8	5	4	42	3	97	14	0	8	13	.381	0	0	4.57
Coriolan,Roberto	Yankees	NYA	R	21	10	0	0	0	18	83	19	14	7	1	0	1	2	10	0	10	2	0	4	0	1.000	0	0	3.50
Corn,Chris	Lynchburg	Pit	A+	26	28	1	0	11	64.2	265	54	30	23	8	4	2	1	23	2	66	1	0	3	4	.429	0	2	3.20
Corniel,Henry	Athletics	Oak	R	21	20	0	0	11	30.2	142	42	27	22	1	0	2	1	11	0	25	4	3	2	1	.667	0	3	6.46
Corominas,Mike	Astros	Hou	R	23	8	2	0	1	19.2	94	31	16	10	1	0	1	1	4	0	8	2	3	1	1	.500	0	0	4.58
Coronado,Osval.	St. Lucie	NYN	A+	24	5	0	0	2	8.1	42	9	7	4	1	0	0	0	4	0	4	1	0	0	0	.000	0	0	4.32
	Capital City	NYN	A	24	26	0	0	9	47.2	195	42	18	14	5	0	1	0	15	0	42	4	0	2	4	.333	0	0	2.64
Correa,Edwin	Vero Beach	LA	A+	32	5	1	0	2	5.2	23	2	3	2	0	1	0	1	3	0	7	1	1	0	0	.000	0	0	3.18
Correa,Elvis	Great Falls	LA	R+	19	21	0	0	5	28	111	20	8	5	2	0	1	0	8	0	38	3	0	3	0	1.000	0	0	1.61
Correa,Ramser	Vero Beach	LA	A+	27	9	9	0	0	45.2	199	45	19	9	0	0	1	0	18	0	31	2	2	2	3	.400	0	0	1.77
Cosgrove,Micha.	Elizabethtn	Min	R+	22	12	1	0	6	22.2	107	25	16	12	1	1	0	1	6	1	31	1	0	1	1	.500	0	2	4.76
Cotton,Joseph	Batavia	Phi	A-	23	15	15	0	0	96.1	402	90	38	32	10	2	2	7	29	0	74	6	0	7	4	.636	0	0	2.99
Cowsill,Brendon	Cedar Rapds	Ana	A	23	26	0	0	18	36	160	41	24	19	4	0	2	3	16	1	32	2	0	3	5	.375	0	3	4.75
Cox,Rob	Kingsport	NYN	R+	22	21	0	0	11	42	188	49	25	22	2	3	3	3	16	2	24	3	2	1	2	.333	0	2	4.71
Crabtree,Robbie	Bakersfield	SF	A+	25	45	9	1	9	112.1	506	124	77	64	10	1	0	5	59	1	116	12	1	7	7	.500	0	1	5.13
Crafton,Kevin	Peoria	StL	A	24	50	0	0	45	55	219	40	16	12	2	5	2	2	18	7	59	2	1	7	2	.778	0	29	1.96
Crane,Randy	Rockford	ChN	A	22	21	12	0	4	73.2	346	68	51	47	7	2	1	9	55	3	62	8	1	3	6	.333	0	0	5.74
Crawford,Jeremy	Athletics	Oak	R	19	15	0	0	6	22.2	114	29	19	17	3	4	1	3	14	1	20	1	0	1	3	.250	0	2	6.75
Crawford,Paxton	Sarasota	Bos	A+	20	12	11	2	0	65.1	289	69	42	33	6	4	2	1	27	2	56	3	0	4	8	.333	1	0	4.55
Cremer,Richard	Yankees	NYA	R	21	10	9	1	0	38.2	170	30	24	17	4	0	0	1	25	0	47	9	0	4	2	.667	1	0	3.96
Cressend,Jack	Sarasota	Bos	A+	23	28	25	2	1	165.2	718	163	98	70	15	8	6	2	56	1	149	14	4	8	11	.421	1	0	3.80
Crews,Jason	South Bend	Ari	A	24	50	0	0	32	82	354	78	39	29	5	4	3	2	27	7	74	4	1	4	6	.400	0	9	3.18
Crossan,Clay	High Desert	Ari	A+	24	2	1	0	0	6	30	8	8	4	0	0	2	1	2	0	0	0	0	0	0	.000	0	0	6.00
Crowther,John	Dunedin	Tor	A+	24	19	0	0	10	26	130	36	23	17	2	1	2	2	15	0	30	7	0	1	2	.333	0	0	5.88
Crutchley,Rickey	Royals	KC	R	19	11	1	0	3	18.2	84	14	6	5	0	0	0	1	14	0	19	1	0	1	1	.500	0	0	2.41
Cruz,Charlie	Durham	Atl	A+	24	49	0	0	23	85.1	379	80	37	30	5	7	4	5	44	3	76	6	0	5	0	1.000	0	1	3.16
Cruz,Charlie	Orioles	Bal	R	21	15	0	0	10	22	112	36	23	23	4	0	1	1	14	0	7	2	0	2	2	.500	0	1	9.41
Cubillan,Darwin	Yankees	NYA	R	23	1	1	0	0	1.2	7	1	0	0	0	0	0	0	1	0	2	0	0	0	0	.000	0	0	0.00
Cueto,Jose	Mariners	Sea	R	21	17	0	0	15	27	134	40	24	18	4	1	1	6	9	0	28	0	0	1	3	.250	0	1	6.00
Cummings,Ryan	Boise	Ana	A-	22	14	13	0	0	70	297	73	38	24	3	2	1	7	10	0	79	4	2	6	2	.750	0	0	3.09
Cummins,Jon	Hudson Vall	TB	A-	22	21	1	0	4	35	175	37	30	25	3	0	1	0	32	0	35	6	2	1	0	1.000	0	0	6.43
Currens,Timothy	Bristol	ChA	R+	22	20	0	0	12	27.2	130	29	21	15	0	2	0	2	13	1	23	3	2	0	4	.000	0	1	4.88
Curtice,John	Red Sox	Bos	R	18	4	3	0	0	11.1	45	6	2	1	0	0	0	1	5	0	11	0	2	2	0	1.000	0	0	0.79
Curtis,Shaun	Orioles	Bal	R	20	15	4	0	1	41.1	199	54	29	21	1	3	4	0	23	0	28	2	1	1	2	.333	0	1	4.57
Curtis,Mark	St. Cathrns	Tor	A-	20	4	0	0	1	5.2	27	6	4	3	0	0	0	0	5	0	5	2	0	1	0	1.000	0	0	4.76
Cutchins,Todd	Capital City	NYN	A	22	3	1	0	1	6.2	31	7	4	4	1	0	0	0	5	0	6	0	0	0	1	.000	0	0	5.40
D'Alessandro,M.	Asheville	Col	A	22	29	0	0	12	65.2	296	87	47	41	6	2	2	1	19	0	46	3	0	0	2	.000	0	1	5.62
Daneker,Patrick	Bristol	ChA	R+	22	12	12	0	0	63.2	294	83	55	46	5	2	3	5	20	1	53	4	5	3	6	.333	0	0	6.50
Daniels,David	Augusta	Pit	A	24	44	0	0	39	55	231	51	22	16	0	1	0	1	13	3	51	0	1	6	3	.667	0	18	2.62
	Lynchburg	Pit	A+	24	10	0	0	8	10	36	6	2	2	1	0	0	0	1	0	6	1	0	1	1	.500	0	4	1.80
Daniels,John	St. Pete	TB	A+	24	55	0	0	44	61.1	255	53	24	18	4	3	1	3	14	3	72	3	0	4	4	.500	0	29	2.64
Daniels,Ronney	Expos	Mon	R	21	8	0	0	2	12	44	2	0	0	0	0	0	1	5	0	7	0	0	0	0	.000	0	0	0.00
	Vermont	Mon	A-	21	3	0	0	2	5	20	5	2	2	0	0	0	0	2	0	1	0	0	0	0	.000	0	0	3.60
Danner,Andy	Chston-WV	Cin	A	22	22	0	0	9	44	186	38	23	13	2	2	0	2	15	2	35	4	0	1	2	.333	0	2	2.66
Danner,Adam	Kane County	Fla	A	23	10	0	0	2	19.2	92	26	12	9	2	3	1	0	8	4	16	2	2	1	4	.200	0	0	4.12

1997 Pitching — Single-A and Rookie Leagues

HOW MUCH HE PITCHED											WHAT HE GAVE UP												THE RESULTS					
Player	Team	Org	Lg	A	G	GS	CG	GF	IP	BFP	H	R	ER	HR	SH	SF	HB	TBB	IBB	SO	WP	Bk	W	L	Pct.	ShO	Sv	ERA
	Brevard Cty	Fla	A+	23	17	0	0	3	26.2	141	50	28	22	3	3	1	4	11	1	14	1	2	1	1	.500	0	0	7.43
Darr,Jerry	Padres	SD	R	19	14	13	0	0	59.2	292	67	59	43	3	2	3	7	33	0	62	10	1	4	6	.400	0	0	6.49
Darrell,Tom	Cedar Rapds	Ana	A	21	27	26	5	0	191.2	810	212	108	86	18	7	0	6	40	1	106	7	2	12	10	.545	0	0	4.04
Darwin,David	W Michigan	Det	A	24	21	4	0	10	40.1	164	23	7	4	2	0	2	2	20	2	31	0	1	1	0	1.000	0	3	0.89
	Lakeland	Det	A+	24	12	12	1	0	82.2	326	70	23	23	2	3	2	0	18	0	41	1	1	10	1	.909	0	0	2.50
Davenport,Joe	Hagerstown	Tor	A	22	37	0	0	29	51.1	225	43	26	21	0	4	1	4	24	2	43	8	0	4	6	.400	0	10	3.68
Davies,Robert	Elizabethtn	Min	R+	22	1	1	0	0	0.2	7	2	3	3	0	0	0	0	3	0	1	1	0	0	1	.000	0	0	40.50
Davis,Douglas	Rangers	Tex	R	22	4	4	0	0	21	88	14	5	4	0	0	1	2	15	0	27	1	1	3	1	.750	0	0	1.71
	Charlotte	Tex	A+	22	9	8	1	0	49.1	205	29	19	17	2	4	2	0	33	1	52	8	3	5	3	.625	0	0	3.10
Davis,Jason	Piedmont	Phi	A	23	17	0	0	7	29.1	102	10	3	2	1	2	0	0	6	0	34	0	0	1	0	1.000	0	1	0.61
	Clearwater	Phi	A+	23	24	0	0	6	42.1	169	31	11	7	0	2	0	1	17	0	36	4	1	2	1	.667	0	2	1.49
Davis,John	San Berndno	LA	A+	24	17	4	0	3	43.2	214	50	48	38	8	1	4	2	34	1	44	6	0	0	2	.000	0	0	7.83
	Vero Beach	LA	A+	24	11	10	0	0	50	228	50	38	30	6	3	1	5	26	2	39	5	0	3	5	.375	0	0	5.40
Davis,Lance	Burlington	Cin	A	21	30	13	0	8	97	452	121	78	71	6	4	3	1	55	0	51	8	3	4	6	.400	0	0	6.59
Davis,Keith	Rancho Cuca	SD	A+	25	35	14	0	4	125.1	575	141	92	80	13	2	3	15	65	0	103	12	0	8	10	.444	0	0	5.74
Davis,Michael	Pittsfield	NYN	A-	22	24	1	0	16	35	162	31	17	13	0	3	1	7	16	1	20	2	0	1	2	.333	0	4	3.34
Davis,Casey	Devil Rays	TB	R	19	13	2	0	5	24	112	13	15	13	0	0	3	5	24	0	26	8	1	0	1	.000	0	0	4.88
Day,Stephen	Oneonta	NYA	A-	20	14	14	0	0	92	372	82	26	22	2	2	4	1	23	0	92	3	0	7	2	.778	0	0	2.15
Deabreu,Milton	Salem-Keizr	SF	A-	20	7	0	0	2	7.2	45	17	12	12	0	1	0	0	6	1	8	1	0	0	0	.000	0	0	14.09
Deakman,Josh	Lk Elsinore	Ana	A+	24	26	25	1	0	165	723	182	107	87	17	1	4	14	42	0	99	9	3	8	11	.421	0	0	4.75
Deckard,Edward	Devil Rays	TB	R	20	4	2	0	0	8.2	48	15	13	7	1	0	0	1	5	0	3	2	0	0	1	.000	0	0	7.27
DeJesus,Tony	Everett	Sea	A-	20	14	14	0	0	62.2	300	68	51	41	7	1	3	5	48	0	53	6	1	2	6	.250	0	0	5.89
DeJesus,Javier	Daytona	ChN	A+	26	8	5	0	0	31.1	131	32	19	18	4	1	2	1	12	0	21	1	0	3	1	.750	0	0	5.17
de la Cruz,Yno.	Mets	NYN	R	21	6	5	0	1	39	154	31	12	5	0	0	0	0	3	0	42	0	0	3	3	.500	0	0	1.15
	Kingsport	NYN	R+	21	6	6	0	0	31.1	151	46	30	23	4	0	1	4	8	1	31	1	0	2	3	.400	0	0	6.61
Delano,Michael	Cubs	ChN	R	20	8	1	0	1	12.1	69	22	21	17	1	0	0	1	9	0	13	3	1	0	1	.000	0	0	12.41
DeLeon,Jose	Peoria	StL	A	21	60	0	0	28	73.2	329	79	46	41	8	3	3	3	35	5	76	3	0	11	3	.786	0	8	5.01
DeLeon,Julio	Princeton	TB	R+	22	11	0	0	0	25.2	116	26	21	15	0	0	3	0	10	0	15	2	0	1	1	.500	0	0	5.26
Delgado,Daniel	Mariners	Sea	R	20	6	0	0	1	8.2	44	11	5	5	2	0	0	0	7	0	8	0	0	0	0	.000	0	0	5.19
Delgado,Ernesto	Hagerstown	Tor	A	22	32	17	0	5	134.1	618	163	96	78	10	6	6	10	56	0	103	12	0	5	10	.333	0	1	5.23
Dellamano,Anth.	Charlotte	Tex	A+	23	15	0	0	7	22.2	125	23	33	31	3	2	2	6	29	1	15	14	0	2	3	.400	0	4	12.31
Della Ratta,Peter	Modesto	Oak	A+	24	45	0	0	19	83.2	362	73	45	31	5	5	4	6	31	8	81	6	0	6	7	.462	0	3	3.33
Dempster,Ryan	Brevard Cty	Fla	A+	21	28	26	2	0	165.1	721	190	100	90	19	3	4	13	46	1	131	8	1	10	9	.526	1	0	4.90
DePaula,Sean	Watertown	Cle	A-	24	9	0	0	2	19	86	21	6	6	1	1	1	1	8	0	17	0	0	1	1	.500	0	0	2.84
	Columbus	Cle	A	24	29	1	0	7	71	336	71	56	41	4	3	7	4	43	3	75	9	0	4	5	.444	0	0	5.20
Derenches,Albert	Wisconsin	Sea	A	21	29	0	0	12	43.2	214	46	36	22	3	4	3	5	25	4	50	2	0	3	2	.600	0	2	4.53
Deschenes,Marc	Columbus	Cle	A	25	40	0	0	39	42.2	180	31	11	9	2	0	1	1	21	0	69	3	0	2	2	.500	0	19	1.90
	Kinston	Cle	A+	25	20	0	0	19	22.1	79	9	2	2	2	0	0	0	4	0	39	1	0	2	0	1.000	0	10	0.81
Deskins,Casey	San Berndno	LA	A+	26	37	6	1	11	97.2	425	110	56	55	11	4	3	5	34	3	65	11	3	6	5	.545	0	2	5.07
Desrosiers,Erik	White Sox	ChA	R	23	7	6	0	0	21.2	88	19	8	8	1	0	1	0	3	0	18	1	0	0	1	.000	0	0	3.32
DeWitt,Chris	Daytona	ChN	A+	24	38	2	0	14	64.1	302	89	55	42	4	1	2	2	20	4	42	10	0	1	8	.111	0	3	5.88
DeWitt,Matt	Peoria	StL	A	20	27	27	1	0	158.1	672	152	84	72	16	7	8	9	57	2	121	6	1	9	9	.500	0	0	4.09
DeWitt,Scott	Brevard Cty	Fla	A+	23	25	24	0	1	132	585	145	80	61	13	6	3	8	51	0	121	3	1	4	10	.286	0	0	4.16
DeYoung,Dan	Pulaski	Tex	R+	22	19	8	1	9	61.1	250	52	16	13	1	0	1	2	12	0	69	3	0	4	1	.800	0	3	1.91
Diaz,Antonio	Padres	SD	R	19	22	0	0	12	39	172	45	22	13	3	2	0	0	4	0	41	5	3	1	1	.500	0	4	3.00
Diaz,Billy	Rangers	Tex	R	18	9	9	1	0	43	182	49	28	24	4	0	1	0	7	0	31	2	2	2	3	.400	0	0	5.02
Dickey,R.A.	Charlotte	Tex	A+	23	8	6	0	2	35	162	51	32	27	8	0	0	0	12	1	32	5	3	1	4	.200	0	0	6.94
Diebolt,Michael	Jamestown	Det	A-	*	15	13	0	1	81.2	355	87	50	39	12	1	2	4	38	0	63	8	5	3	6	.333	0	0	4.30
Dietrich,Jason	Salem	Col	A+	25	21	0	0	11	30.1	121	15	11	11	2	1	2	0	16	0	38	1	1	3	2	.600	0	2	3.26
Dingman,Craig	Tampa	NYA	A+	24	19	0	0	11	22.1	92	15	14	13	2	1	0	0	14	2	26	3	0	0	4	.000	0	6	5.24
	Greensboro	NYA	A	24	30	0	0	27	33	131	19	7	7	0	2	1	1	12	0	41	3	0	2	0	1.000	0	19	1.91
Dinyar,Eric	Lakeland	Det	A+	24	15	0	0	8	16	78	9	10	10	1	1	0	5	22	1	12	0	0	0	0	.000	0	1	5.63
	Tigers	Det	R	24	7	0	0	1	3.2	30	4	9	8	0	0	2	6	9	0	1	2	0	0	0	.000	0	0	19.64
Dishman,Richard	Eugene	Atl	A-	23	19	1	0	6	51	213	47	19	17	2	1	0	7	13	0	60	5	1	2	2	.500	0	3	3.00
Dixon,Jim	Hickory	ChA	A	25	16	0	0	13	22.1	97	17	12	9	0	2	1	1	7	1	22	6	1	1	3	.250	0	6	3.63
	Winston-Sal	ChA	A+	25	16	0	0	6	33.1	139	29	16	15	2	0	2	1	10	0	29	1	0	0	1	.000	0	0	4.05
Doan,Zak	Marlins	Fla	R	22	1	0	0	1	2	8	1	0	0	0	0	0	0	1	0	1	0	0	0	0	.000	0	0	0.00
	Utica	Fla	A-	22	13	0	0	10	28.2	127	34	18	18	2	0	1	0	13	1	22	3	0	2	2	.500	0	1	5.65
Dobson,Dwayne	Boise	Ana	A-	22	12	0	0	3	22.1	106	28	17	16	1	0	0	1	8	0	17	2	0	0	0	.000	0	0	6.45
Dolby,Lawrence	Braves	Atl	R	23	10	6	0	2	35	166	41	34	25	4	0	2	1	16	0	33	4	0	1	5	.167	0	1	6.43
	Danville	Atl	R+	23	3	0	0	0	7.2	35	7	5	5	2	0	0	0	5	0	6	1	0	0	0	.000	0	0	5.87
Dollar,Toby	Savannah	LA	A	23	20	8	3	7	90	359	78	33	26	7	2	0	5	12	0	67	6	0	7	2	.778	1	1	2.60
	Vero Beach	LA	A+	23	1	0	0	0	1	4	1	0	0	0	0	0	0	0	0	2	0	0	0	0	.000	0	0	0.00
Donaldson,Erne.	Boise	Ana	A-	24	27	0	0	25	52	208	31	10	7	0	3	1	2	20	1	88	10	2	3	1	.750	0	15	1.21
Donnelly,Robert	Pr William	StL	A+	24	37	0	0	12	51.1	232	44	33	20	5	2	0	2	26	0	54	7	0	5	0	1.000	0	0	3.51
Dose,Gary	Ft. Wayne	Min	A	24	45	4	0	25	67	313	52	44	35	3	2	3	5	61	0	73	7	2	1	4	.200	0	3	4.70
Dotel,Melido	Great Falls	LA	R+	21	14	11	0	1	42.1	230	59	54	38	3	1	2	5	39	0	26	5	1	3	7	.300	0	0	8.08
Dougherty,James	Mets	NYN	R	20	11	8	0	1	51.1	214	42	18	11	0	1	1	0	13	0	51	6	0	6	1	.857	0	0	1.93
Douglass,Ryan	Royals	KC	R	19	12	9	1	1	56	237	66	21	19	0	0	0	2	12	0	35	2	0	5	1	.833	1	0	3.05
Douglass,Sean	Orioles	Bal	R	19	9	1	0	5	17.2	80	20	14	12	2	4	0	2	9	0	10	1	0	1	3	.250	0	0	6.11
Downs,Scott	Williamsprt	ChN	A-	22	5	5	0	0	23	93	15	11	7	0	1	1	0	7	0	28	0	2	0	2	.000	0	0	2.74
	Rockford	ChN	A	22	5	5	0	0	36	128	17	5	5	1	1	0	1	8	0	43	2	2	3	0	1.000	0	0	1.25
Drew,Tim	Burlington	Cle	R+	19	4	4	0	0	11.2	63	16	15	8	0	0	0	6	4	0	14	4	1	0	1	.000	0	0	6.17
	Watertown	Cle	A-	19	1	1	0	0	4.2	20	4	1	1	0	0	0	0	3	0	9	0	0	0	0	.000	0	0	1.93
Driscoll,Patrick	Martinsvlle	Phi	R+	23	8	0	0	1	14	55	12	4	4	1	2	0	0	4	2	17	1	0	2	2	.500	0	0	2.57
	Batavia	Phi	A-	23	11	0	0	0	9.2	48	14	5	4	0	0	0	2	4	0	10	0	1	0	0	.000	0	0	3.72
Drumheller,Al	Rancho Cuca	SD	A+	26	38	6	0	8	81	355	76	48	41	5	5	1	0	37	2	107	4	1	5	6	.455	0	1	4.56

* Michael Diebolt died 9/5/97

1997 Pitching — Single-A and Rookie Leagues

HOW MUCH HE PITCHED											WHAT HE GAVE UP												THE RESULTS					
Player	Team	Org	Lg	A	G	GS	CG	GF	IP	BFP	H	R	ER	HR	SH	SF	HB	TBB	IBB	SO	WP	Bk	W	L	Pct.	ShO	Sv	ERA
DuBose,Eric	Sou. Oregon	Oak	A-	22	3	1	0	0	10	39	5	0	0	0	0	0	0	6	0	15	0	0	1	0	1.000	0	0	0.00
	Visalia	Oak	A+	22	10	9	0	0	38.1	194	43	37	30	4	2	0	5	28	0	39	6	3	1	3	.250	0	0	7.04
Duchscherer,Jus.	Red Sox	Bos	R	20	10	8	0	0	44.2	190	34	18	9	0	2	1	3	17	0	59	5	4	2	3	.400	0	0	1.81
	Michigan	Bos	A	20	4	4	0	0	24	109	26	17	15	1	0	1	3	10	0	19	0	0	1	1	.500	0	0	5.63
Dudeck,Dave	Greensboro	NYA	A	25	25	1	0	7	50	221	48	29	20	6	4	1	5	16	1	43	6	0	3	4	.429	0	0	3.60
	Tampa	NYA	A+	25	5	0	0	3	9	36	9	3	3	1	0	0	1	2	0	5	0	0	0	0	.000	0	0	3.00
Duff,Matt	Augusta	Pit	A	23	2	1	0	1	6	26	6	1	1	0	0	0	1	2	0	6	0	0	0	1	.000	0	0	1.50
Duncan,Geoff	Kane County	Fla	A	23	44	2	0	13	86.1	375	85	46	39	7	7	2	5	30	5	96	4	0	7	2	.778	0	1	4.07
Duncan,Sean	Winston-Sal	ChA	A+	25	6	0	0	2	9.1	53	16	12	9	4	0	1	0	7	0	9	1	0	0	1	.000	0	0	8.68
	Quad City	Hou	A	25	34	0	0	14	46.2	193	39	19	15	4	2	1	4	15	5	46	4	0	6	0	1.000	0	3	2.89
Dunham,Patrick	Everett	Sea	A-	22	17	0	0	10	28.1	127	26	19	13	3	1	0	1	12	1	39	5	3	0	3	.000	0	3	4.13
Duprey,Peter	Mariners	Sea	R	19	15	0	0	7	43.1	175	29	10	7	1	0	2	0	20	1	55	4	5	4	2	.667	0	2	1.45
Durbin,Chad	Lansing	KC	A	20	26	26	0	0	144.2	642	157	85	77	15	6	6	11	53	0	116	12	1	5	8	.385	0	0	4.79
Durkovic,Peter	Lakeland	Det	A+	24	40	0	0	25	65.2	263	50	21	18	4	3	2	5	14	1	53	2	0	6	4	.600	0	10	2.47
Durocher,Jayson	Wst Plm Bch	Mon	A+	23	25	17	0	2	87	385	84	58	37	6	3	3	4	39	0	71	10	2	6	4	.600	0	0	3.83
Dyess,Todd	Frederick	Bal	A+	25	10	10	0	0	46.2	195	32	19	17	3	1	1	6	23	1	50	3	3	4	2	.667	0	0	3.28
Eason,Roger	Batavia	Phi	A-	22	20	0	0	9	29.1	119	16	6	3	1	0	1	1	11	0	29	2	1	0	1	.000	0	1	0.92
Eaton,Adam	Piedmont	Phi	A	20	14	14	0	0	71.1	318	81	38	33	2	0	2	4	30	0	57	4	2	5	6	.455	0	0	4.16
Eavenson,Samu.	Yankees	NYA	R	20	10	0	0	7	13.1	64	18	10	10	1	2	0	0	8	0	11	3	0	1	1	.500	0	0	6.75
Eden,Bill	High Desert	Ari	A+	25	6	0	0	3	10.1	45	7	6	6	2	1	0	0	8	0	12	0	1	1	0	1.000	0	0	5.23
Edwards,Jon	Kinston	Cle	A+	25	33	0	0	16	61.1	286	65	48	45	13	3	2	2	38	1	55	3	0	6	4	.600	0	2	6.60
Ehlers,Corey	Marlins	Fla	R	24	2	2	0	0	7.2	38	11	6	4	0	0	0	2	0	0	5	0	2	0	1	.000	0	0	4.70
	Brevard Cty	Fla	A+	24	6	0	0	4	11.1	45	9	3	3	2	0	0	0	3	1	3	0	1	0	0	.000	0	0	2.38
	Utica	Fla	A-	24	9	0	0	5	18.1	70	16	3	3	1	0	1	0	1	0	16	1	0	1	0	1.000	0	1	1.47
Eibey,Scott	Delmarva	Bal	A	24	47	0	0	19	93.1	371	65	25	19	3	7	0	2	33	5	82	4	0	10	4	.714	0	7	1.83
Einerston,Darrell	Tampa	NYA	A+	25	45	0	0	24	71	287	63	24	17	2	5	0	1	19	8	55	1	0	5	4	.556	0	6	2.15
Elder,David	Pulaski	Tex	R+	22	20	0	0	17	32.1	127	18	8	7	2	0	0	0	12	0	57	4	0	2	2	.500	0	6	1.95
Ellison,Jason	Oneonta	NYA	A-	22	11	0	0	3	20.2	82	19	6	4	0	0	1	0	4	0	19	2	0	0	1	.000	0	0	1.74
	Greensboro	NYA	A	22	9	0	0	4	13	60	16	10	7	1	0	0	1	3	0	11	1	0	1	0	1.000	0	1	4.85
Elmore,Jason	Augusta	Pit	A	24	10	1	0	0	15	77	17	17	17	3	0	1	0	14	1	15	3	0	2	1	.667	0	0	10.20
Embry,Byron	Danville	Atl	R+	21	20	1	0	14	32	125	14	7	7	0	3	1	0	15	0	56	4	0	2	1	.667	0	3	1.97
Emerson,Scott	High Desert	Ari	A+	26	3	1	0	1	4	21	4	4	3	0	0	0	2	4	0	6	1	0	0	0	.000	0	0	6.75
Emiliano,Jamie	Asheville	Col	A	23	18	0	0	12	20	96	24	15	13	1	0	0	0	12	0	20	3	0	0	1	.000	0	0	5.85
Encarnacion,Orl.	Mets	NYN	R	19	13	0	0	9	22	93	23	8	6	1	2	0	0	5	1	27	0	0	4	2	.667	0	1	2.45
Enders,Trevor	Chston-SC	TB	A	23	44	0	0	24	67	271	55	18	14	2	2	1	2	17	3	73	2	1	4	3	.571	0	2	1.88
Enloe,Mark	Kingsport	NYN	R+	21	15	4	0	4	44.2	208	57	37	32	7	3	3	2	21	0	36	6	1	1	1	.500	0	0	6.45
Enochs,Christop.	Sou. Oregon	Oak	A-	22	3	3	0	0	10.1	45	12	4	4	0	0	0	1	2	0	10	1	0	0	0	.000	0	0	3.48
	Modesto	Oak	A+	22	10	9	0	1	45.1	203	51	20	14	0	3	2	3	12	0	45	7	0	3	0	1.000	0	0	2.78
Ervin,Kent	Rancho Cuca	SD	A+	24	2	0	0	1	3	14	3	2	2	1	0	0	0	2	0	0	0	0	0	0	.000	0	0	6.00
	Idaho Falls	SD	R+	24	16	14	1	0	82.2	377	107	57	49	10	2	4	5	26	0	59	7	0	5	6	.455	0	0	5.33
Erwin,Dave	Watertown	Cle	A-	23	18	2	0	9	36	163	36	24	21	2	1	1	6	23	2	36	2	0	3	1	.750	0	1	5.25
Espina,Rendy	Twins	Min	R	20	8	7	0	0	34.2	132	24	11	5	0	1	0	2	6	0	34	4	0	2	2	.500	0	0	1.30
	Elizabethtn	Min	R+	20	6	3	0	1	17	86	25	21	15	2	0	0	3	9	0	15	3	1	0	3	.000	0	0	7.94
Espinal,Jose	Rockford	ChN	A	21	24	24	1	0	120.2	545	147	83	66	7	2	4	2	41	1	107	4	7	10	10	.500	0	0	4.92
Estavil,Mauricio	Clearwater	Phi	A+	26	9	2	0	2	20.2	96	23	11	9	1	0	0	1	13	0	6	1	0	1	0	1.000	0	0	3.92
Estes,Eric	Frederick	Bal	A+	23	26	25	1	1	148	608	142	70	57	8	2	2	6	30	0	124	4	0	9	8	.529	0	0	3.47
Estrella,Leoncio	Pittsfield	NYN	A-	23	15	15	0	0	92	395	91	48	31	0	2	1	3	27	0	55	3	2	7	6	.538	0	0	3.03
Estrella,Luis	San Jose	SF	A+	23	42	0	0	15	77	332	84	39	29	3	1	0	2	25	3	59	7	6	5	5	.500	0	2	3.39
Evans,Keith	Cape Fear	Mon	A	22	21	21	3	0	138	551	113	56	40	6	2	4	10	18	0	102	1	0	12	7	.632	1	0	2.61
	Wst Plm Bch	Mon	A+	22	7	7	2	0	43.2	185	42	23	21	4	2	2	5	11	0	20	1	0	2	4	.333	2	0	4.33
Everly,William	Yakima	LA	A-	23	28	1	0	11	58	259	48	26	22	4	2	3	9	33	6	63	5	1	2	3	.400	0	3	3.41
Eversgerd,Randy	Hagerstown	Tor	A	21	5	0	0	3	8	38	13	4	4	0	0	0	0	2	0	2	1	1	0	0	.000	0	0	4.50
	St. Cathrns	Tor	A-	21	13	0	0	4	23.2	107	30	16	7	2	1	0	0	5	1	34	1	1	0	1	.000	0	0	2.66
Eye,Jacob	Ogden	Mil	R+	23	1	1	0	0	3	12	2	1	0	0	0	0	0	1	0	2	0	0	0	0	.000	0	0	0.00
Farizo,Brad	Marlins	Fla	R	19	11	11	2	0	60.2	260	55	34	25	1	1	1	2	21	0	52	2	1	3	6	.333	0	0	3.71
Farley,Joe	Hickory	ChA	A	23	28	27	3	0	173.2	742	190	94	83	16	10	5	3	48	0	94	11	1	14	6	.700	2	0	4.30
Farley,Joseph	Salem-Keizr	SF	A-	19	10	0	0	3	14	68	6	7	7	2	0	0	1	16	1	17	5	2	0	1	.000	0	0	4.50
Farnsworth,Jeff	Lancaster	Sea	A+	22	5	5	0	0	20.2	93	24	20	16	2	1	1	3	8	0	18	2	0	1	1	.500	0	0	6.97
Farnsworth,Kyle	Daytona	ChN	A+	22	27	27	2	0	156.1	684	178	91	71	13	6	2	6	47	1	105	5	1	10	10	.500	0	0	4.09
Farson,Bryan	Pirates	Pit	R	25	8	0	0	3	15.1	78	19	15	13	2	1	2	2	12	0	9	3	0	0	0	.000	0	0	7.63
	Augusta	Pit	A	25	7	0	0	0	10	44	5	6	4	1	0	0	1	8	0	7	1	0	0	0	.000	0	0	3.60
Faulkner,Neal	Daytona	ChN	A+	23	36	0	0	20	55.1	251	65	44	42	7	1	1	1	19	4	40	3	1	3	7	.300	0	5	6.83
Faust,Jason	Sou. Oregon	Oak	A-	22	16	2	0	4	46.1	205	37	22	15	1	2	1	1	25	0	62	5	0	5	0	1.000	0	2	2.91
Fausto,Santana	White Sox	ChA	R	20	13	0	0	12	20	85	16	10	9	0	1	1	1	9	0	10	1	0	3	3	.500	0	2	4.05
Feliciano,Pedro	Savannah	LA	A	21	36	9	1	8	105.2	437	90	45	31	11	3	3	1	39	0	94	6	4	3	7	.300	0	4	2.64
	Vero Beach	LA	A+	21	1	0	0	0	2	7	3	1	1	1	0	0	0	0	0	1	0	0	0	0	.000	0	0	4.50
Felix,Miguel	White Sox	ChA	R	21	3	2	0	1	12	45	10	3	2	0	0	0	0	2	0	10	1	0	0	0	.000	0	0	1.50
	Bristol	ChA	R+	21	11	10	0	0	50.1	256	78	52	42	7	0	4	7	22	0	38	5	2	2	5	.286	0	0	7.51
Feliz,Bienvenido	Columbus	Cle	A	21	6	4	0	0	27.2	110	21	7	7	1	0	0	0	8	0	20	0	0	3	0	1.000	0	0	2.28
Fennell,Barry	Williamsprt	ChN	A-	21	17	10	0	1	66.1	306	92	51	45	5	3	3	3	29	0	50	4	1	2	10	.167	0	0	6.11
Fenus,Justin	Batavia	Phi	A-	23	15	7	0	1	54.2	245	54	34	27	2	2	0	5	30	0	26	6	1	3	5	.375	0	0	4.45
Festa,Christoph.	Michigan	Bos	A	25	37	10	0	11	93.2	418	109	50	42	8	1	3	5	34	1	53	7	2	4	5	.444	0	0	4.04
Fidge,Darren	Ft. Wayne	Min	A	23	8	0	0	5	12.2	61	15	4	4	0	3	1	5	4	1	8	1	0	2	2	.500	0	0	2.84
	Ft. Myers	Min	A+	23	24	0	0	13	38.1	175	44	29	27	3	3	6	2	20	0	25	4	0	0	3	.000	0	0	6.34
Figueroa,Carlos	Rangers	Tex	R	19	5	1	0	1	5.2	27	7	2	2	1	1	0	0	2	0	9	0	1	0	0	.000	0	1	3.18
Figueroa,Claudio	Butte	Ana	R+	19	4	0	0	1	4.2	22	7	3	3	0	0	0	0	2	0	4	0	0	1	0	1.000	0	0	5.79
Figueroa,Juan	White Sox	ChA	R	19	11	10	0	0	64.1	274	66	31	24	4	0	3	7	14	0	43	1	0	1	4	.200	0	0	3.36

1997 Pitching — Single-A and Rookie Leagues

HOW MUCH HE PITCHED											WHAT HE GAVE UP												THE RESULTS					
Player	Team	Org	Lg	A	G	GS	CG	GF	IP	BFP	H	R	ER	HR	SH	SF	HB	TBB	IBB	SO	WP	Bk	W	L	Pct.	ShO	Sv	ERA
Finol,Ricardo	Pirates	Pit	R	24	5	1	0	1	19	83	19	13	7	0	1	1	2	4	0	10	4	0	1	1	.500	0	0	3.32
	Augusta	Pit	A	24	11	0	0	5	21.2	98	21	17	16	2	1	1	2	13	1	16	0	1	1	2	.333	0	0	6.65
Fish,Steven	Boise	Ana	A-	23	24	4	0	2	75	314	69	41	34	4	6	3	3	23	3	79	5	0	5	2	.714	0	0	4.08
Fisher,Louis	Williamsprt	ChN	A-	21	11	9	0	0	40.1	188	41	27	21	2	0	0	2	32	0	31	8	0	1	3	.250	0	0	4.69
Fisher,Ryan	Erie	Pit	A-	24	2	2	0	0	9.1	40	11	7	6	1	0	2	0	2	0	6	1	1	0	0	.000	0	0	5.79
	Augusta	Pit	A	24	4	1	0	0	6.2	38	15	11	11	3	0	0	0	3	0	5	0	0	0	1	.000	0	0	14.85
Fitts,Brian	Twins	Min	R	21	10	3	0	0	28.2	125	29	15	9	0	0	0	1	6	2	31	2	0	4	2	.667	0	0	2.83
Fitzgerald,Brian	Wisconsin	Sea	A	23	41	0	0	28	69.2	281	63	16	15	4	1	0	0	19	2	68	2	1	3	1	.750	0	10	1.94
Fitzpatrick,Ken	Spokane	KC	A-	23	12	0	0	5	17	69	15	8	8	2	0	2	0	6	0	26	3	0	2	1	.667	0	0	4.24
Flach,Jason	Eugene	Atl	A-	24	23	0	0	18	39.1	180	40	18	13	2	4	1	1	24	5	51	2	0	4	3	.571	0	5	2.97
Fleck,William	Danville	Atl	R+	21	23	0	0	18	35.1	158	36	17	14	2	1	1	1	17	3	56	3	1	2	3	.400	0	6	3.57
Fleming,Emar	Pulaski	Tex	R+	21	23	1	0	10	51	206	36	16	12	4	1	0	2	16	0	75	2	3	1	1	.500	0	3	2.12
Fleming,John	South Bend	Ari	A	20	5	0	0	2	9.1	44	11	6	4	0	0	0	0	7	1	5	2	0	0	0	.000	0	0	3.86
	High Desert	Ari	A+	20	1	1	0	0	2.2	17	7	5	5	0	0	0	0	3	0	1	0	0	0	0	.000	0	0	16.88
	Lethbridge	Ari	R+	20	12	12	0	0	64	282	80	37	32	6	2	0	3	25	0	32	3	0	3	6	.333	0	0	4.50
Flock,Richard	Twins	Min	R	20	12	0	0	4	18.2	80	21	9	6	0	1	2	0	6	0	17	2	1	2	1	.667	0	0	2.89
Flores,Pedro	Vero Beach	LA	A+	21	3	0	0	1	4.2	26	10	6	3	1	0	0	0	4	0	1	0	0	0	0	.000	0	0	5.79
	Great Falls	LA	R+	21	22	0	0	9	38	176	36	18	15	2	3	0	2	27	3	51	1	0	2	1	.667	0	1	3.55
Flores,Randy	Oneonta	NYA	A-	22	13	13	2	0	74.2	308	64	32	27	3	0	1	4	23	1	70	5	1	4	4	.500	1	0	3.25
Fontaine,Tom	Bluefield	Bal	R+	23	21	2	0	2	40.1	196	44	31	27	3	0	0	5	28	2	50	6	0	5	1	.833	0	0	6.02
Fontanes,Ruben	Lethbridge	Ari	R+	24	5	0	0	3	6	32	8	6	6	0	0	3	0	7	0	8	0	0	1	0	1.000	0	0	9.00
Foran,John	W Michigan	Det	A	24	29	0	0	6	53.1	242	51	27	22	2	1	2	6	29	0	45	12	0	2	2	.500	0	1	3.71
Forbes,Cameron	Delmarva	Bal	A	21	34	17	1	10	130	557	108	68	54	6	2	6	6	64	0	111	9	0	6	7	.462	0	1	3.74
Forti,Gene	White Sox	ChA	R	20	11	8	0	1	52.2	224	42	21	17	1	3	2	2	30	0	44	9	2	4	1	.800	0	0	2.91
Fortune,Peter	Cape Fear	Mon	A	23	12	0	0	2	22.1	113	23	19	19	1	1	2	5	20	2	21	3	0	1	1	.500	0	0	7.66
Foster,Kris	Vero Beach	LA	A+	23	17	17	2	0	89.2	414	97	69	53	8	3	3	7	44	1	77	5	1	6	3	.667	0	0	5.32
Fowler,Blair	Utica	Fla	A-	23	18	1	0	8	36	160	40	23	16	2	2	1	2	9	1	29	1	0	2	2	.500	0	0	4.00
France,Aaron	Augusta	Pit	A	24	26	17	1	2	107.1	458	98	48	42	5	0	2	8	44	0	89	6	3	7	4	.636	0	0	3.52
Franklin,Wayne	Savannah	LA	A	24	28	7	1	10	82	362	79	41	29	10	1	1	4	35	0	58	2	1	5	3	.625	0	2	3.18
	San Berndno	LA	A+	24	1	0	0	0	2	7	2	0	0	0	0	0	0	0	0	1	0	0	0	0	.000	0	0	0.00
Franks,Lance	Johnson Cty	StL	R+	22	26	0	0	23	30.2	113	16	4	4	1	0	0	0	7	1	40	2	0	0	0	.000	0	12	1.17
	Pr William	StL	A+	22	2	0	0	0	4.1	16	3	1	1	1	0	0	0	1	0	4	0	0	1	0	1.000	0	0	2.08
Fraser,Joe	Vermont	Mon	A-	20	10	3	0	2	17.2	95	22	21	12	1	0	3	2	17	0	7	4	0	0	3	.000	0	0	6.11
	Expos	Mon	R	20	3	1	0	0	9.1	37	8	3	3	0	0	0	0	6	0	9	1	0	0	1	.000	0	0	2.89
Freedberg,Todd	Bluefield	Bal	R+	23	11	1	0	1	27.1	131	29	14	6	0	1	3	2	12	3	29	7	0	2	1	.667	0	0	1.98
	Delmarva	Bal	A	23	9	0	0	3	19.1	93	19	9	7	1	2	0	3	15	1	12	2	0	0	1	.000	0	0	3.26
	Frederick	Bal	A+	23	1	0	0	0	3	11	1	1	1	1	0	0	0	1	0	3	0	0	0	0	.000	0	0	3.00
Fretwell,Joseph	Expos	Mon	R	21	8	0	0	3	16	66	19	8	7	3	1	0	0	2	0	14	0	0	2	0	1.000	0	1	3.94
Frias,Miguel	Diamondback	Ari	R	20	21	0	0	18	32	137	35	11	8	1	3	0	1	5	0	38	1	2	4	2	.667	0	8	2.25
	Lethbridge	Ari	R+	20	1	0	0	1	1.1	5	2	0	0	0	0	0	0	0	0	3	0	0	0	0	.000	0	0	0.00
Frias,Yovany	White Sox	ChA	R	20	7	0	0	5	12.1	56	14	12	5	1	0	0	0	7	0	2	1	1	0	0	.000	0	0	3.65
Frush,James	Batavia	Phi	A-	23	26	0	0	7	41	166	34	14	13	5	1	1	4	6	2	37	3	0	6	1	.857	0	1	2.85
Fry,Jeffrey	Danville	Atl	R+	23	21	0	0	10	19.2	99	19	12	9	3	1	1	3	20	1	16	1	0	1	1	.500	0	1	4.12
Fuduric,Tony	Watertown	Cle	A-	23	2	2	0	0	7.2	37	8	8	7	0	1	2	1	5	0	2	2	0	0	1	.000	0	0	8.22
Fuentes,Brian	Wisconsin	Sea	A	22	22	22	0	0	118.2	486	84	52	47	6	3	3	8	59	0	153	11	3	6	7	.462	0	0	3.56
Fulcher,John	Beloit	Mil	A	23	34	0	0	17	51	236	56	33	23	3	6	4	2	25	2	43	3	4	0	4	.000	0	0	4.06
Gadway,Christo.	Cedar Rapds	Ana	A	24	15	0	0	3	23.2	101	23	12	12	1	0	0	3	9	0	14	3	1	0	1	.000	0	0	4.56
Gaerte,Travis	Pirates	Pit	R	21	18	0	0	12	29.2	129	26	19	9	1	4	3	4	10	2	22	3	1	1	2	.333	0	2	2.73
Gagliano,Steve	Marlins	Fla	R	20	12	12	1	0	56	234	56	28	23	1	2	1	3	16	0	50	4	1	3	4	.429	0	0	3.70
	Utica	Fla	A-	20	1	1	0	0	3.2	20	6	4	4	0	0	1	0	3	0	6	0	1	0	1	.000	0	0	9.82
Gallagher,Bryan	Athletics	Oak	R	21	17	0	0	9	33.2	141	29	14	11	2	1	2	2	10	1	27	3	0	1	3	.250	0	2	2.94
	Sou. Oregon	Oak	A-	21	2	0	0	0	2.1	11	1	2	1	0	0	0	0	3	1	3	0	0	0	1	.000	0	0	3.86
Gallagher,Keith	Peoria	StL	A	24	31	1	0	7	56	269	68	45	36	6	0	2	11	29	1	43	3	0	2	1	.667	0	0	5.79
Galvez,Randy	Great Falls	LA	R+	19	16	1	0	5	29.2	128	29	14	12	0	0	1	3	10	0	29	1	0	3	1	.750	0	0	3.64
Gandy,Josh	Elizabethtn	Min	R+	22	8	6	0	0	35	160	36	26	23	3	1	0	1	19	0	47	0	0	3	0	1.000	0	0	5.91
	Ft. Wayne	Min	A	22	8	5	0	1	20	93	25	19	12	0	1	0	1	12	0	14	2	1	2	4	.333	0	0	5.40
Gangemi,Joseph	Boise	Ana	A-	22	16	16	0	0	79	369	97	56	48	2	3	1	6	31	0	61	0	2	7	2	.778	0	0	5.47
Garcia,Apostol	W Michigan	Det	A	21	33	5	0	10	65.2	275	48	26	22	2	1	0	4	31	0	52	10	2	7	2	.778	0	1	3.02
Garcia,Ariel	Hickory	ChA	A	22	1	1	0	0	2.2	17	6	5	4	0	0	1	0	2	0	0	0	0	0	1	.000	0	0	13.50
	White Sox	ChA	R	22	10	1	0	5	28	117	23	11	8	0	0	2	0	11	0	28	0	0	2	1	.667	0	2	2.57
Garcia,Bryan	Athletics	Oak	R	20	15	7	0	2	46	219	50	36	29	2	2	4	3	34	0	45	4	1	4	2	.667	0	0	5.67
Garcia,Eddy	Burlington	Cin	A	22	22	6	0	7	69.1	321	84	49	43	4	2	2	6	21	0	60	5	5	6	6	.500	0	0	5.58
	Chston-WV	Cin	A	22	6	0	0	0	16	70	16	16	14	0	1	1	0	5	0	10	0	0	1	1	.500	0	0	7.88
Garcia,Expeddy	Athletics	Oak	R	21	8	1	0	0	12.2	65	20	13	11	0	1	3	3	7	0	9	2	2	1	3	.250	0	0	7.82
Garcia,Freddy	Kissimmee	Hou	A+	21	27	27	5	0	179	741	165	63	51	6	4	3	4	49	3	131	3	2	10	8	.556	2	0	2.56
Garcia,Gabe	Quad City	Hou	A	21	26	25	2	0	149.1	668	153	86	73	11	3	0	8	75	4	112	14	0	5	14	.263	0	0	4.40
Garcia,Jose	Beloit	Mil	A	20	27	26	2	0	155.1	682	145	89	69	9	7	3	5	70	1	126	12	4	6	11	.353	0	0	4.00
Garcia,Luis	Red Sox	Bos	R	19	8	1	0	5	15.2	70	12	10	5	0	1	0	0	10	0	18	3	0	1	2	.333	0	1	2.87
Garcia,Miguel	Vero Beach	LA	A+	23	45	5	1	8	111	478	110	53	46	10	2	3	7	36	4	105	3	2	10	3	.769	1	0	3.73
Garcia,Wilson	Johnson Cty	StL	R+	18	25	3	0	3	48.2	258	78	59	36	4	2	3	2	21	1	44	5	3	0	2	.000	0	0	6.66
Garey,Daniel	Mariners	Sea	R	20	7	7	0	0	35	163	46	28	23	1	0	1	6	7	0	16	0	0	2	2	.500	0	0	5.91
Garff,Jeff	Burlington	Cle	R+	22	5	0	0	5	8	34	9	4	4	2	0	0	0	2	0	9	1	0	1	1	.500	0	1	4.50
	Watertown	Cle	A-	22	6	4	0	0	25.2	114	31	12	8	0	0	1	1	7	3	18	1	0	3	0	1.000	0	0	2.81
Garland,Jon	Cubs	ChN	R	18	10	7	0	0	40	161	37	14	12	3	0	0	1	10	0	39	3	3	3	2	.600	0	0	2.70
Garmon,Adam	Kingsport	NYN	R+	20	18	5	0	10	42	200	50	43	36	10	0	0	5	21	1	39	6	0	2	2	.500	0	3	7.71
Garrett,Joshua	Michigan	Bos	A	20	22	22	2	0	138.2	619	164	94	74	13	7	4	13	35	0	64	23	3	8	10	.444	0	0	4.80
Garvin,Robert	Marlins	Fla	R	19	14	0	0	12	33.1	138	28	20	6	4	1	1	1	4	0	27	2	1	4	3	.571	0	1	1.62

1997 Pitching — Single-A and Rookie Leagues

HOW MUCH HE PITCHED											WHAT HE GAVE UP												THE RESULTS					
Player	Team	Org	Lg	A	G	GS	CG	GF	IP	BFP	H	R	ER	HR	SH	SF	HB	TBB	IBB	SO	WP	Bk	W	L	Pct.	ShO	Sv	ERA
Garza,Alberto	Columbus	Cle	A	21	18	18	2	0	95	380	72	34	33	7	0	2	9	32	0	107	5	0	8	3	.727	1	0	3.13
	Kinston	Cle	A+	21	1	1	0	0	8	33	5	3	3	0	0	0	0	4	1	4	1	0	1	0	1.000	0	0	3.38
Garza,Chris	Ft. Wayne	Min	A	22	60	0	0	32	95	385	67	28	21	2	3	2	3	38	1	90	11	0	5	2	.714	0	15	1.99
Gaskill,Derek	Pittsfield	NYN	A-	24	21	3	0	2	45.1	187	41	23	13	3	2	4	2	5	0	39	3	0	3	2	.600	0	0	2.58
Geis,John	Johnson Cty	StL	R+	24	30	0	0	12	40.2	188	44	27	18	4	1	2	1	15	1	57	1	0	3	4	.429	0	0	3.98
	New Jersey	StL	A-	24	3	0	0	0	3	14	2	1	1	0	0	0	0	3	0	3	0	0	0	0	.000	0	0	3.00
Getz,Rodney	Brevard Cty	Fla	A+	22	27	26	4	1	164.1	689	166	84	59	12	6	8	10	39	1	92	8	1	9	12	.429	1	0	3.23
Gholar,Antonio	Elizabethtn	Min	R+	24	24	0	0	7	44.2	225	49	41	30	5	0	5	3	32	0	50	7	0	2	2	.500	0	2	6.04
Gilfillan,Jason	Spokane	KC	A-	21	16	0	0	5	16	82	16	13	9	0	1	0	1	16	1	22	3	0	2	1	.667	0	0	5.06
Gillian,Charles	Ft. Wayne	Min	A	24	22	0	0	7	25.2	114	21	11	9	1	1	0	6	13	0	24	2	0	0	0	.000	0	3	3.16
	Ft. Myers	Min	A+	24	10	0	0	3	15.2	65	10	5	4	1	0	0	5	5	0	11	3	0	1	1	.500	0	0	2.30
Giron,Roberto	Chston-WV	Cin	A	22	7	0	0	1	8.1	45	14	8	8	1	0	0	0	6	0	5	3	0	1	1	.500	0	0	8.64
Gissell,Christoph.	Rockford	ChN	A	20	26	24	3	1	143.2	646	155	89	71	7	5	4	11	62	1	105	11	3	6	11	.353	1	0	4.45
Giuliano,Joe	Burlington	Cin	A	22	32	15	0	7	113.2	503	123	74	62	9	7	5	8	44	2	76	3	0	6	5	.545	0	0	4.91
Glaser,Eric	Red Sox	Bos	R	20	7	6	0	0	22.2	102	29	13	10	0	1	1	0	5	0	22	4	0	1	2	.333	0	0	3.97
Glaze,Randy	Sou. Oregon	Oak	A-	24	21	1	0	6	36.1	174	30	21	17	4	2	3	7	21	0	38	7	3	1	2	.333	0	1	4.21
Glover,Gary	Hagerstown	Tor	A	21	28	28	3	0	173.2	751	165	94	72	9	3	5	10	58	1	155	20	4	6	17	.261	0	0	3.73
Gnirk,Mark	Beloit	Mil	A	23	38	0	0	14	76.2	333	95	46	33	2	2	2	2	18	0	63	9	0	3	2	.600	0	1	3.87
Goedhart,Darrell	Lk Elsinore	Ana	A+	27	8	3	0	3	16	92	29	18	15	1	2	0	1	11	1	12	2	1	0	2	.000	0	0	8.44
Goetz,Geoffrey	Mets	NYN	R	19	8	6	0	1	26.1	112	23	11	8	0	1	2	0	18	0	28	1	2	0	2	.000	0	1	2.73
Gogolin,Al	Modesto	Oak	A+	26	4	0	0	2	4	24	9	8	8	0	0	1	1	2	0	3	4	0	0	0	.000	0	0	18.00
Gomez,Dennys	Bakersfield	SF	A+	27	32	2	0	10	57.1	272	61	52	46	9	3	1	8	34	0	50	7	0	0	4	.000	0	1	7.22
Gomez,Miguel	Dunedin	Tor	A+	24	21	0	0	9	34.2	154	41	26	19	1	0	0	4	10	1	30	6	1	4	3	.571	0	2	4.93
	Hagerstown	Tor	A	24	12	0	0	5	15.2	82	27	19	14	2	0	0	0	9	0	17	4	0	1	1	.500	0	0	8.04
Gomez,Rafael	Mets	NYN	R	20	4	2	0	1	10	41	9	2	1	0	1	0	1	2	0	6	2	0	0	0	.000	0	0	0.90
Gomez,Ricardo	Pirates	Pit	R	20	5	4	0	0	19	97	20	17	13	0	0	1	4	17	0	11	2	1	0	2	.000	0	0	6.16
Gonzalez,Arman.	Rockies	Col	R	20	13	4	0	1	42	171	33	27	12	2	0	3	1	13	0	33	1	1	1	3	.250	0	0	2.57
Gonzalez,Dicky	Capital City	NYN	A	19	10	7	1	2	47.1	204	50	28	26	8	2	1	1	15	0	49	2	0	1	4	.200	0	0	4.94
	Kingsport	NYN	R+	19	12	12	1	0	66	282	70	38	32	7	4	2	4	10	0	76	0	0	3	6	.333	0	0	4.36
Gonzalez,Edwin	Royals	KC	R	20	3	3	1	0	18.2	75	16	8	4	0	2	0	1	3	0	12	4	0	2	1	.667	0	0	1.93
	Lansing	KC	A	20	11	11	0	0	69	283	67	32	28	4	2	4	3	15	0	58	3	0	3	5	.375	0	0	3.65
Gonzalez,Franci.	Padres	SD	R	20	26	2	0	19	47.2	229	55	36	29	4	1	1	5	26	2	40	7	3	4	4	.500	0	2	5.48
Gonzalez,Ignacio	Hudson Vall	TB	A-	23	26	0	0	2	38.1	164	35	16	10	1	2	2	3	16	0	40	2	1	1	5	.167	0	0	2.35
Gonzalez,Jose	Everett	Sea	A-	21	6	6	0	0	30.2	152	35	20	6	3	0	2	2	19	0	38	3	0	1	3	.250	0	0	1.76
	Wisconsin	Sea	A	21	8	7	0	0	39	170	35	15	12	4	0	2	4	15	0	43	2	1	2	2	.500	0	0	2.77
Gonzalez,Lariel	Salem	Col	A+	22	44	0	0	25	57	237	42	19	16	3	2	2	3	23	1	79	4	0	5	0	1.000	0	8	2.53
Gonzalez,Micha.	Pirates	Pit	R	20	7	3	0	0	29	115	21	9	8	0	1	0	1	8	0	33	3	3	2	0	1.000	0	0	2.48
	Augusta	Pit	A	20	4	3	0	1	19.1	76	11	5	4	1	1	0	0	8	0	22	3	0	1	1	.500	0	0	1.86
Gooda,David	Ogden	Mil	R+	21	16	5	0	4	61.2	283	78	49	39	7	2	0	6	20	1	62	4	1	3	2	.600	0	0	5.69
Gooden,Derek	Johnson Cty	StL	R+	23	31	0	0	17	36.1	171	41	22	15	1	1	2	0	21	1	48	2	0	2	2	.500	0	1	3.72
Gooding,Jason	Spokane	KC	A-	23	11	11	0	0	55.2	220	44	16	14	2	0	0	3	11	0	58	3	0	4	0	1.000	0	0	2.26
	Lansing	KC	A	23	1	1	0	0	4.2	24	6	5	3	0	0	1	1	1	0	3	2	0	0	1	.000	0	0	5.79
Gorman,Pat	Mets	NYN	R	20	11	0	0	10	15	57	10	3	3	0	2	0	0	4	1	13	0	0	1	1	.500	0	5	1.80
Gorrell,Chris	Sou. Oregon	Oak	A-	22	18	10	1	0	71.2	326	86	50	37	8	4	1	3	28	0	60	5	2	5	3	.625	0	0	4.65
Goure,Sam	Medicne Hat	Tor	R+	20	15	15	1	0	80.1	360	99	61	42	7	3	2	7	20	0	68	6	1	2	6	.250	0	0	4.71
Gourlay,Matthew	Medicne Hat	Tor	R+	19	14	14	1	0	67.2	298	72	56	43	7	1	1	6	28	1	35	9	0	2	6	.250	1	0	5.72
Grabow,John	Pirates	Pit	R	19	11	8	0	0	45.1	204	57	32	23	0	1	2	0	14	0	28	3	0	2	7	.222	0	0	4.57
Graham,Kyle	Yakima	LA	A-	22	21	3	0	10	46.1	217	46	28	20	3	1	5	1	26	1	52	3	2	0	3	.000	0	0	3.88
Granadillo,Adel	Burlington	Cle	R+	19	15	4	0	2	48	224	55	30	29	5	1	1	10	23	1	44	4	0	6	4	.600	0	0	5.44
Granger,Greg	Columbus	Cle	A	25	5	0	0	0	11	44	8	3	1	0	0	0	1	3	0	6	2	0	2	0	1.000	0	0	0.82
	Kinston	Cle	A+	25	18	0	0	9	30.2	141	39	17	15	0	5	2	1	18	4	18	4	0	4	6	.400	0	0	4.40
Gray,Jason	Bristol	ChA	R+	21	4	3	0	0	10.1	61	22	21	21	4	0	0	0	8	0	11	2	0	0	3	.000	0	0	18.29
	White Sox	ChA	R	21	10	5	0	3	36.2	165	43	20	19	4	2	2	0	12	0	34	3	0	3	2	.600	0	0	4.66
Green,David	Kissimmee	Hou	A+	23	8	0	0	4	8.2	50	11	12	5	0	0	0	0	10	1	3	2	0	0	3	.000	0	0	5.19
	Quad City	Hou	A	23	23	22	1	1	125.2	548	126	79	64	9	5	2	8	53	2	96	12	2	7	12	.368	0	0	4.58
Greene,Danny	Cedar Rapds	Ana	A	25	24	0	0	18	39.2	156	27	7	2	1	1	0	1	11	0	42	1	0	1	1	.500	0	12	0.45
Greene,Joel	Jamestown	Det	A-	22	20	0	0	4	30	135	26	14	8	1	1	1	2	19	0	22	5	1	4	1	.800	0	1	2.40
Greene,Ryan	Eugene	Atl	A-	23	15	15	0	0	84.1	381	96	52	43	2	2	4	6	30	1	72	10	6	3	7	.300	0	0	4.59
Gregg,Kevin	Visalia	Oak	A+	20	25	24	0	0	115.1	534	116	81	73	8	2	3	5	74	0	136	28	0	6	8	.429	0	0	5.70
Gresko,Michael	Erie	Pit	A-	21	7	5	0	0	24.2	119	29	26	21	0	1	0	2	17	0	14	1	0	1	2	.333	0	0	7.66
	Pirates	Pit	R	21	6	2	0	1	19.1	82	22	11	11	2	1	0	1	3	0	21	2	0	1	1	.500	0	1	5.12
	Augusta	Pit	A	21	1	1	0	0	5	23	7	2	2	0	0	0	0	3	0	3	0	0	1	0	1.000	0	0	3.60
Griffiths,Everard	Chston-SC	TB	A	24	30	21	0	2	140	593	138	87	66	9	8	4	7	31	0	107	9	0	6	13	.316	0	1	4.24
Grote,Jason	Bakersfield	SF	A+	23	25	25	0	0	156.1	659	156	77	60	11	1	3	2	59	1	116	15	0	12	8	.600	0	0	3.45
Gryboski,Kevin	Lancaster	Sea	A+	24	21	15	0	4	67.1	332	113	82	74	13	2	8	1	26	0	41	7	0	0	7	.000	0	0	9.89
Guilmet,John	Jamestown	Det	A-	23	17	6	0	5	49.2	235	68	44	29	4	1	4	4	10	0	29	4	3	0	6	.000	0	1	5.26
Gulin,Lindsay	St. Lucie	NYN	A+	21	9	6	0	0	26.1	136	36	31	27	2	0	2	1	21	1	11	6	1	0	3	.000	0	0	9.23
	Capital City	NYN	A	21	17	15	1	2	99	421	77	37	32	2	2	2	5	60	0	118	9	1	8	1	.889	1	0	2.91
Gunther,Kevin	Modesto	Oak	A+	25	42	0	0	35	53.1	223	53	24	20	7	2	1	3	11	2	43	2	0	7	2	.778	0	17	3.38
Gutierrez,Alfredo	Beloit	Mil	A	22	19	6	0	6	62.1	269	64	38	29	6	6	1	2	22	1	35	4	2	4	3	.571	0	0	4.19
Gutierrez,Javier	Wisconsin	Sea	A	23	13	3	0	2	35	149	29	13	11	2	1	0	1	19	1	36	4	2	2	3	.400	0	0	2.83
	Everett	Sea	A-	23	1	1	0	0	3.2	21	4	4	4	1	0	2	1	5	0	4	3	0	0	1	.000	0	0	9.82
	Lancaster	Sea	A+	23	14	8	0	3	52	250	60	39	37	8	0	1	4	36	0	51	7	2	1	1	.500	0	0	6.40
Gutierrez,Jose	Ogden	Mil	R+	19	1	1	0	0	1	6	3	2	2	0	0	0	0	0	0	1	0	0	0	0	.000	0	0	18.00
Guttormson,Rick.	Padres	SD	R	21	5	0	0	4	11	55	17	11	6	3	0	1	0	4	0	19	0	0	1	1	.500	0	1	4.91
	Idaho Falls	SD	R+	21	18	2	0	8	28	129	34	25	20	2	5	2	2	11	2	19	5	0	3	2	.600	0	3	6.43
Guy,Bradley	Erie	Pit	A-	22	25	0	0	6	52.2	201	37	12	11	3	3	0	2	7	0	53	9	1	5	1	.833	0	1	1.88

1997 Pitching — Single-A and Rookie Leagues

HOW MUCH HE PITCHED											WHAT HE GAVE UP												THE RESULTS					
Player	Team	Org	Lg	A	G	GS	CG	GF	IP	BFP	H	R	ER	HR	SH	SF	HB	TBB	IBB	SO	WP	Bk	W	L	Pct.	ShO	Sv	ERA
Guzman,Ambiori.	Rangers	Tex	R	20	5	2	0	3	15	57	10	1	0	0	1	0	0	2	0	15	0	2	2	0	1.000	0	1	0.00
	Pulaski	Tex	R+	20	10	2	0	4	35.2	146	40	10	9	1	0	0	3	3	0	26	2	0	3	1	.750	0	2	2.27
Guzman,Doming.	Clinton	SD	A	23	12	12	5	0	79	320	66	36	28	7	2	2	3	25	0	91	5	2	4	5	.444	0	0	3.19
	Rancho Cuca	SD	A+	23	6	6	0	0	38	168	42	23	23	6	2	1	2	16	0	39	2	0	3	2	.600	0	0	5.45
Guzman,Jonath.	Helena	Mil	R+	20	19	1	0	9	31	146	32	23	9	3	0	1	1	20	0	21	4	0	2	1	.667	0	1	2.61
Guzman,Toribio	Johnson Cty	StL	R+	21	13	13	0	0	64	309	91	75	60	9	1	6	1	26	0	49	7	6	1	7	.125	0	0	8.44
Guzman,Wilson	Pirates	Pit	R	20	9	8	0	0	40.1	173	43	15	13	1	1	2	3	8	0	48	2	1	4	1	.800	0	0	2.90
	Erie	Pit	A-	20	5	5	0	0	26.2	112	26	20	15	4	2	1	1	6	0	25	0	0	1	2	.333	0	0	5.06
Hacen,Abraham	Delmarva	Bal	A	22	23	23	0	0	112.1	481	95	59	53	9	2	4	2	58	1	103	9	3	7	5	.583	0	0	4.25
Hafer,Jeffrey	Capital City	NYN	A	23	37	2	0	18	69.1	284	59	29	23	2	3	1	2	21	3	74	10	1	6	5	.545	0	7	2.99
Haigler,Phillip	Ft. Myers	Min	A+	24	25	25	4	0	158.1	652	172	57	50	7	3	4	2	32	0	80	2	0	11	9	.550	1	0	2.84
Hale,Mark	Chston-SC	TB	A	22	18	0	0	13	30.2	126	26	12	10	2	4	1	1	10	0	39	2	1	1	2	.333	0	4	2.93
Hall,Billy	Astros	Hou	R	24	7	7	0	0	37	159	39	17	11	2	1	2	0	9	0	26	2	1	2	5	.286	0	0	2.68
	Kissimmee	Hou	A+	24	6	0	0	1	7	34	7	5	3	0	0	0	1	5	0	5	1	0	0	0	.000	0	0	3.86
Hall,Yates	Pr William	StL	A+	25	26	21	0	0	109.1	500	89	70	58	13	1	4	4	94	0	75	12	1	6	7	.462	0	0	4.77
Halla,Ryan	Augusta	Pit	A	24	32	0	0	22	46.1	176	26	10	9	2	2	1	2	10	1	51	3	0	1	1	.500	0	8	1.75
Halpin,Jeremy	Bluefield	Bal	R+	23	15	0	0	8	25	108	30	14	9	0	0	2	0	4	0	22	1	1	1	0	1.000	0	0	3.24
Hamilton,Jimmy	Columbus	Cle	A	22	22	22	0	0	123	547	123	68	61	10	3	2	0	66	0	137	11	0	5	7	.417	0	0	4.46
Hamilton,Randy	Kingsport	NYN	R+	22	21	0	0	9	46.1	192	38	18	13	0	3	3	1	15	2	44	1	0	5	3	.625	0	4	2.53
Hamulack,Timot.	Astros	Hou	R	21	23	0	0	17	45	198	56	31	21	3	0	0	0	18	0	38	2	2	1	1	.500	0	9	4.20
Handy,Russell	Wst Plm Bch	Mon	A+	23	2	0	0	1	2	15	6	6	5	2	0	0	1	1	0	1	0	0	0	0	.000	0	0	22.50
	Cape Fear	Mon	A	23	19	1	0	8	27	128	20	22	15	2	0	1	3	29	0	22	7	0	1	0	1.000	0	0	5.00
Hannah,Michael	Great Falls	LA	R+	23	2	0	0	0	2.2	11	2	2	2	1	0	0	0	3	0	3	0	0	1	0	1.000	0	0	6.75
	Yakima	LA	A-	23	22	2	0	4	63	300	84	57	39	4	6	1	3	27	2	44	6	0	2	7	.222	0	0	5.57
Harden,Nathan	Braves	Atl	R	20	11	9	0	1	47	220	46	40	28	1	1	5	3	30	0	36	7	2	1	6	.143	0	0	5.36
Hardwick,Bubba	Stockton	Mil	A+	26	31	18	1	2	133.1	570	138	75	69	10	12	3	7	51	0	80	5	0	8	6	.571	1	0	4.66
Haring,Brett	Billings	Cin	R+	23	14	0	0	4	23.1	106	30	14	12	2	0	0	2	9	0	16	1	0	0	2	.000	0	0	4.63
Harper,David	Lethbridge	Ari	R+	23	8	0	0	3	13.1	64	16	9	9	2	0	0	1	6	0	13	2	0	2	0	1.000	0	0	6.08
Harriger,Mark	Cedar Rapds	Ana	A	23	12	11	1	1	50.2	251	70	50	44	4	3	3	1	33	1	50	10	4	1	6	.143	1	0	7.82
	Boise	Ana	A-	23	13	12	0	0	51	243	51	52	45	2	1	5	1	36	1	42	15	0	3	4	.429	0	0	7.94
Harris,Joshua	Billings	Cin	R+	20	14	14	0	0	85	385	103	51	38	3	2	3	2	26	4	56	1	2	4	6	.400	0	0	4.02
Harrison,Scott	Burlington	Cle	R+	20	12	12	0	0	63	276	62	37	26	6	0	2	3	24	0	50	6	0	3	5	.375	0	0	3.71
	Columbus	Cle	A	20	1	1	0	0	3	19	8	7	7	1	0	1	1	1	0	1	0	0	0	1	.000	0	0	21.00
Hart,Len	Rockford	ChN	A	24	27	0	0	5	47.1	194	30	11	11	0	1	0	2	28	1	55	5	0	2	1	.667	0	0	2.09
	Daytona	ChN	A+	24	8	0	0	0	9.1	44	10	6	6	0	1	0	1	7	0	12	1	0	1	2	.333	0	0	5.79
Hartshorn,Ty	Dunedin	Tor	A+	23	26	24	2	1	160	711	197	102	79	19	3	4	12	40	3	101	1	0	5	13	.278	1	0	4.44
Harvell,Pete	South Bend	Ari	A	26	50	0	0	39	62	276	50	27	20	2	1	0	3	36	6	57	5	0	4	5	.444	0	13	2.90
Harvey,Hally	Devil Rays	TB	R	18	5	0	0	1	12	47	5	6	5	0	0	0	0	5	0	11	3	0	2	0	1.000	0	0	3.75
Harvey,Terry	St. Pete	TB	A+	25	18	3	0	7	35	167	39	33	30	6	1	2	6	26	0	15	5	1	3	2	.600	0	0	7.71
Harville,Chad	Sou. Oregon	Oak	A-	21	3	0	0	1	5	23	3	0	0	0	1	0	2	3	0	6	0	0	1	0	1.000	0	0	0.00
	Visalia	Oak	A+	21	14	0	0	1	18.2	92	25	14	12	2	1	1	0	13	1	24	1	3	0	0	.000	0	0	5.79
Hause,Brendan	Athletics	Oak	R	23	6	0	0	1	11.2	49	13	7	5	1	1	1	0	1	0	11	0	0	3	1	.750	0	0	3.86
	Modesto	Oak	A+	23	2	0	0	0	4.2	20	6	2	2	1	0	0	0	1	0	1	0	0	0	0	.000	0	0	3.86
Haverstick,David	Lethbridge	Ari	R+	22	1	0	0	0	1.2	9	3	3	3	1	0	0	0	2	0	1	1	0	0	1	.000	0	0	16.20
	Diamondback	Ari	R	22	14	14	0	0	56.2	261	71	42	35	3	0	3	4	20	0	39	4	4	2	5	.286	0	0	5.56
Hawkins,Alsharik	Beloit	Mil	A	20	6	6	0	0	24.2	133	46	33	29	8	0	1	5	12	0	17	2	1	1	4	.200	0	0	10.58
	Ogden	Mil	R+	20	14	14	0	0	81	394	113	74	53	8	0	2	4	24	0	47	5	0	2	8	.200	0	0	5.89
Hayden,Terry	Red Sox	Bos	R	23	3	0	0	2	8	32	6	2	2	0	0	0	0	1	0	8	0	0	1	0	1.000	0	0	2.25
	Lowell	Bos	A-	23	16	5	0	4	53.2	216	42	21	19	2	5	0	3	14	5	52	1	0	0	6	.000	0	0	3.19
Haynie,Jason	Augusta	Pit	A	24	14	14	1	0	86.2	360	77	39	33	5	2	2	3	24	1	81	8	2	6	5	.545	0	0	3.43
	Lynchburg	Pit	A+	24	13	13	1	0	83	337	68	42	30	8	1	2	1	23	0	69	6	0	2	5	.286	0	0	3.25
Hazlett,Andrew	Lowell	Bos	A-	22	19	3	0	12	50.1	206	44	16	9	1	0	1	0	7	0	66	0	0	5	0	1.000	0	4	1.61
	Michigan	Bos	A	22	2	2	0	0	12	50	15	7	7	2	0	0	0	1	0	12	0	0	1	0	1.000	0	0	5.25
Heams,Shane	Mariners	Sea	R	22	21	0	0	14	37	168	30	20	7	2	3	0	5	22	0	42	7	0	6	2	.750	0	2	1.70
Heath,Woody	St. Cathrns	Tor	A-	21	15	12	0	1	78	316	63	29	21	4	0	1	5	19	1	72	3	3	7	4	.636	0	0	2.42
Hecht,Brian	Auburn	Hou	A-	22	26	0	0	25	37.1	151	35	10	7	0	1	0	1	8	2	35	1	2	2	2	.500	0	11	1.69
	Quad City	Hou	A	22	5	0	0	4	8.1	32	4	3	2	0	0	0	0	2	0	5	1	0	0	0	.000	0	1	2.16
Heffernan,Greg	New Jersey	StL	A-	23	26	0	0	26	28	115	23	9	8	0	2	2	0	7	1	31	3	2	0	2	.000	0	9	2.57
Helmer,Chad	Helena	Mil	R+	22	14	0	0	4	30.1	132	27	12	7	2	2	2	4	9	0	33	1	0	0	2	.000	0	2	2.08
	Stockton	Mil	A+	22	7	0	0	3	11.2	50	12	4	4	0	0	0	1	4	0	10	2	0	2	0	1.000	0	1	3.09
Henderson,Kenn.	Rancho Cuca	SD	A+	25	7	7	0	0	24.2	106	17	14	12	5	1	0	2	17	0	26	0	0	1	2	.333	0	0	4.38
Henderson,Juan	Lk Elsinore	Ana	A+	24	9	0	0	3	10.1	54	20	13	12	4	0	0	1	2	0	6	1	0	1	1	.500	0	0	10.45
	Cedar Rapds	Ana	A	24	20	7	0	4	45.1	224	70	55	46	9	1	5	4	17	0	21	5	2	1	4	.200	0	1	9.13
Henderson,Scott	Utica	Fla	A-	23	15	1	0	6	39.2	151	28	11	10	1	2	1	1	7	0	51	3	0	5	1	.833	0	4	2.27
Henry,Jason	Oneonta	NYA	A-	21	12	12	0	0	63.1	270	61	27	18	2	1	1	3	23	0	57	6	1	5	4	.556	0	0	2.56
Herbison,Brett	Capital City	NYN	A	21	28	27	2	0	160	690	166	86	71	13	7	2	9	63	0	146	11	2	7	14	.333	0	0	3.99
Heredia,Maximo	Delmarva	Bal	A	21	37	6	0	13	114	441	97	29	27	4	3	3	0	20	0	73	2	0	10	5	.667	0	1	2.13
Hernandez,Pedro	Great Falls	LA	R+	22	15	14	0	1	75.2	333	98	44	40	10	0	3	7	12	1	50	5	0	5	5	.500	0	1	4.76
Herndon,Harry	Padres	SD	R	19	14	14	0	0	77.1	348	80	51	38	2	3	3	5	32	0	65	6	2	3	2	.600	0	0	4.42
	Idaho Falls	SD	R+	19	1	1	0	0	5	20	5	0	0	0	0	0	0	1	0	3	0	0	0	0	.000	0	0	0.00
Herrera,Misael	Idaho Falls	SD	R+	21	6	3	0	0	14.1	78	25	22	18	7	0	0	1	8	0	8	0	0	0	1	.000	0	0	11.30
	Padres	SD	R	21	11	0	0	3	19	97	27	19	17	1	2	2	1	10	0	15	0	1	1	2	.333	0	1	8.05
Hibbard,Billy	Hagerstown	Tor	A	22	11	0	0	5	17.1	75	23	10	10	1	0	0	0	3	0	13	2	0	0	0	.000	0	0	5.19
Hill,Jason	Lk Elsinore	Ana	A+	26	54	0	0	37	66	313	71	43	31	2	10	1	5	34	4	73	4	0	3	7	.300	0	15	4.23
Hill,T.J.	Chston-SC	TB	A	22	7	0	0	0	16	69	15	10	8	0	1	0	1	8	0	15	4	0	0	0	.000	0	0	4.50
	Hudson Vall	TB	A-	22	11	11	0	0	45	216	53	36	25	2	3	0	7	22	0	31	3	2	2	2	.500	0	0	5.00
Hite,Kevin	Clinton	SD	A	23	38	4	1	17	87	354	86	38	32	6	0	4	1	11	0	85	2	1	5	5	.500	0	1	3.31

1997 Pitching — Single-A and Rookie Leagues

HOW MUCH HE PITCHED											WHAT HE GAVE UP												THE RESULTS					
Player	Team	Org	Lg	A	G	GS	CG	GF	IP	BFP	H	R	ER	HR	SH	SF	HB	TBB	IBB	SO	WP	Bk	W	L	Pct.	ShO	Sv	ERA
Hlodan,George	Augusta	Pit	A	22	12	6	0	2	40.1	180	40	31	25	7	3	3	5	15	0	33	3	2	1	2	.333	0	1	5.58
	Pirates	Pit	R	22	3	3	2	0	18.1	69	12	1	1	0	0	0	2	4	0	12	0	1	3	0	1.000	2	0	0.49
	Erie	Pit	A-	22	15	1	1	3	33.2	151	39	24	23	3	2	3	1	11	0	21	3	0	1	0	1.000	0	2	6.15
Hodges,Reid	Bristol	ChA	R+	23	27	0	0	17	26.1	125	30	16	15	2	1	0	0	19	1	32	8	0	0	2	.000	0	2	5.13
Hodges,Kevin	Wilmington	KC	A+	25	28	20	0	4	124.2	563	150	78	62	11	3	6	5	44	7	63	5	2	8	11	.421	0	1	4.48
Hoff,Steve	Clinton	SD	A	20	12	12	1	0	76.1	318	72	28	23	4	2	4	5	18	0	78	5	0	7	1	.875	0	0	2.71
	Rancho Cuca	SD	A+	20	14	13	0	1	66.1	319	73	56	46	6	2	2	2	48	0	59	13	0	4	5	.444	0	0	6.24
Hogge,Shawn	Johnson Cty	StL	R+	20	3	3	0	0	12.1	55	16	9	7	3	0	0	0	6	0	10	0	0	0	1	.000	0	0	5.11
Hohenstein,Andr.	Pirates	Pit	R	20	3	2	0	0	9.2	45	11	10	9	1	0	1	1	6	0	4	0	0	1	1	.500	0	0	8.38
	Padres	SD	R	20	9	0	0	2	11.2	59	15	9	9	0	0	0	2	8	0	13	3	1	0	0	.000	0	0	6.94
Holliday,Hugh	Chston-WV	Cin	A	25	14	0	0	7	15	59	10	4	4	0	0	0	0	6	1	15	2	2	0	0	.000	0	1	2.40
Hollins,Jessie	Yankees	NYA	R	28	4	1	0	0	6	37	13	8	8	0	0	0	0	8	0	5	5	0	2	0	1.000	0	0	12.00
Hollis,Ron	Red Sox	Bos	R	24	4	0	0	2	7	27	7	1	1	0	2	0	0	0	0	7	0	0	0	0	.000	0	1	1.29
	Sarasota	Bos	A+	24	13	0	0	9	19	77	13	8	6	2	1	1	2	7	0	21	2	0	1	1	.500	0	4	2.84
Holmes,Michael	Sou. Oregon	Oak	A-	22	7	0	0	2	14.1	57	14	8	4	2	0	0	0	4	0	16	0	0	2	0	1.000	0	0	2.51
	Visalia	Oak	A+	22	16	0	0	11	28.1	116	28	13	12	5	0	0	0	4	0	20	1	0	2	1	.667	0	3	3.81
Holobinko,Mike	Williamsprt	ChN	A-	21	12	0	0	6	13.2	66	16	6	5	1	1	0	3	7	0	10	3	0	0	0	.000	0	0	3.29
Holzbauer,Josep.	Braves	Atl	R	22	15	0	0	11	25.2	135	30	25	22	1	0	0	0	29	0	22	5	0	2	2	.500	0	1	7.71
Hommel,Brian	Stockton	Mil	A+	25	55	0	0	34	71.1	296	45	25	25	5	4	3	8	39	0	76	6	0	7	2	.778	0	14	3.15
Hooten,David	Ft. Wayne	Min	A	23	28	27	2	0	165.2	675	134	57	48	5	4	2	9	54	0	138	4	6	11	8	.579	2	0	2.61
Hootselle,Jeffrey	Martinsvlle	Phi	R+	22	14	12	1	1	66	286	62	43	37	8	1	1	2	28	0	69	5	2	3	3	.500	1	0	5.05
Hopson,Craig	Johnson Cty	StL	R+	19	15	4	0	0	29	169	44	43	32	8	0	3	5	32	1	23	11	0	1	3	.250	0	0	9.93
Horgan,Joe	Watertown	Cle	A-	21	15	4	0	2	38.1	179	48	31	26	4	2	2	1	18	1	31	4	1	0	1	.000	0	0	6.10
	Kinston	Cle	A+	21	4	2	0	0	17.1	83	23	15	14	1	1	0	1	9	0	9	0	0	1	2	.333	0	0	7.27
Horn,Keith	Kinston	Cle	A+	24	9	0	0	5	15	76	20	16	16	3	0	0	1	8	0	11	1	0	0	0	.000	0	1	9.60
Howard,Benjami.	Padres	SD	R	19	13	12	0	1	54.1	281	54	53	45	3	1	0	2	63	0	59	19	7	1	4	.200	0	0	7.45
Howard,Jason	Jamestown	Det	A-	23	13	1	0	3	22.1	110	21	22	13	1	0	3	7	14	0	21	3	0	4	3	.571	0	0	5.24
Howatt,Jeffrey	St. Lucie	NYN	A+	24	39	0	0	14	64.2	305	78	41	31	4	2	3	8	20	1	41	6	1	1	2	.333	0	2	4.31
Hower,Dan	Charlotte	Tex	A+	25	2	0	0	1	2	9	2	1	1	0	0	0	0	2	0	0	0	0	0	1	.000	0	0	4.50
Huber,John	Auburn	Hou	A-	20	4	4	1	0	18	88	27	20	13	0	2	0	1	5	1	5	1	0	0	4	.000	0	0	6.50
Hudson,Timothy	Sou. Oregon	Oak	A-	22	8	4	0	1	28.2	111	12	8	8	0	0	1	1	15	2	37	3	2	3	1	.750	0	0	2.51
Hueda,Alejandro	Medicne Hat	Tor	R+	22	16	8	0	4	52	240	59	41	33	6	1	0	1	28	2	32	4	0	1	4	.200	0	0	5.71
Hueston,Stephen	Lansing	KC	A	24	34	7	0	5	71.1	345	95	65	59	6	6	3	6	49	1	42	5	2	2	2	.500	0	0	7.44
Huff,Timothy	St. Cathrns	Tor	A-	23	15	0	0	3	32	139	38	20	19	3	0	1	1	13	1	20	1	0	1	1	.500	0	0	5.34
Huffaker,Mike	New Jersey	StL	A-	22	33	0	0	4	45	192	40	17	12	0	1	0	3	16	0	36	3	0	1	4	.200	0	1	2.40
Huggins,David	St. Cathrns	Tor	A-	22	27	2	0	18	35.2	159	33	18	13	1	0	2	4	15	1	42	1	2	0	3	.000	0	11	3.28
Hughes,Mike	Watertown	Cle	A-	22	13	13	2	0	77	325	69	37	30	4	0	3	4	25	2	80	7	0	5	3	.625	0	0	3.51
Hughes,Michael	Boise	Ana	A-	21	11	3	0	3	16.2	81	20	16	14	2	0	0	2	12	0	18	4	0	0	2	.000	0	0	7.56
Humphreys,Kevi.	Cedar Rapds	Ana	A	24	30	0	0	16	65.2	283	75	45	41	9	2	3	7	9	0	40	5	3	5	1	.833	0	2	5.62
	Lk Elsinore	Ana	A+	24	16	0	0	4	18	77	19	9	7	2	1	0	3	2	0	15	1	0	0	1	.000	0	0	3.50
Humphries,Chris.	Martinsvlle	Phi	R+	24	5	0	0	1	9.2	50	14	14	9	1	2	0	0	8	0	7	2	0	1	0	1.000	0	0	8.38
Hunt,Jon	Hickory	ChA	A	24	10	9	0	0	47	234	65	33	22	1	1	2	2	23	0	28	3	0	2	3	.400	0	0	4.21
	Winston-Sal	ChA	A+	24	25	2	0	11	31	143	32	21	15	3	0	2	1	14	0	26	4	0	0	2	.000	0	0	4.35
Hunter,Germaine	Michigan	Bos	A	24	52	0	0	21	71.2	322	65	40	29	8	3	4	2	42	4	68	10	6	5	4	.556	0	1	3.64
Huntsman,Brand.	Orioles	Bal	R	22	2	0	0	1	4.2	19	3	0	0	0	0	0	0	1	0	6	0	1	0	0	.000	0	0	0.00
Hurst,Douglas	Billings	Cin	R+	22	1	0	0	1	2	9	2	1	1	0	1	0	0	1	0	2	0	1	0	0	.000	0	0	4.50
	Burlington	Cin	A	22	22	0	0	9	46	194	44	19	16	4	0	3	2	18	1	23	3	2	2	1	.667	0	1	3.13
Hurtado,Victor	Brevard Cty	Fla	A+	21	17	16	2	0	92	405	102	54	50	9	2	2	7	34	1	58	7	0	4	7	.364	0	0	4.89
Husted,Brent	Yakima	LA	A-	22	10	6	0	1	29.2	145	45	32	23	0	0	0	1	11	3	22	2	0	1	5	.167	0	0	6.98
Hutchings,Mark	Salem-Keizr	SF	A-	21	11	0	0	1	13.2	72	24	15	13	2	1	0	3	8	1	5	1	0	1	0	1.000	0	0	8.56
Hutzler,Jeff	Bakersfield	SF	A+	25	47	3	1	12	88.1	391	92	59	52	7	6	3	5	41	1	70	12	0	2	7	.222	0	1	5.30
Iannacone,Steve	Rockies	Col	R	20	11	0	0	4	19.1	92	24	11	9	1	2	1	1	14	0	13	3	0	1	2	.333	0	1	4.19
Iddon,Brent	Sarasota	Bos	A+	22	37	2	0	19	56.1	260	63	39	31	4	1	0	2	28	3	50	3	0	1	2	.333	0	3	4.95
Iglesias,Mario	Hickory	ChA	A	24	36	0	0	27	68.2	289	64	29	26	4	3	2	1	26	5	64	7	2	8	4	.667	0	10	3.41
Iida,Masashi	Padres	SD	R	21	11	1	0	4	20	106	25	29	25	3	1	2	2	18	0	11	8	2	0	2	.000	0	0	11.25
Incantalupo,Todd	Helena	Mil	R+	22	14	11	0	0	65	295	76	48	37	7	1	1	2	24	1	51	2	2	5	4	.556	0	0	5.12
Ireland,Eric	Auburn	Hou	A-	21	16	16	2	0	107	458	111	55	44	4	2	0	12	21	1	78	3	0	5	7	.417	0	0	3.70
Irvine,Kirk	Hickory	ChA	A	23	29	5	0	13	63.2	282	80	34	24	5	3	2	0	18	0	51	1	0	3	3	.500	0	0	3.39
Ishee,Gabe	Beloit	Mil	A	23	13	0	0	4	28.2	122	20	12	12	3	0	0	3	18	1	24	2	1	3	1	.750	0	1	3.77
	Stockton	Mil	A+	23	21	3	0	6	49.1	232	55	38	36	8	2	2	2	29	0	52	5	2	2	3	.400	0	0	6.57
Ishimaru,Taisuke	Mariners	Sea	R	20	7	0	0	1	7.2	44	3	10	9	0	0	0	2	16	0	5	5	2	1	1	.500	0	0	10.57
Izquierdo,Hansel	White Sox	ChA	R	21	5	0	0	2	10.1	45	9	4	4	0	1	0	0	8	0	15	1	0	0	0	.000	0	0	3.48
	Bristol	ChA	R+	21	9	2	0	2	23	104	25	14	11	5	0	0	4	8	0	24	0	1	2	2	.500	0	0	4.30
Jacobs,Jake	Twins	Min	R	20	23	0	0	20	31.1	128	16	7	1	0	0	0	3	11	1	55	3	0	1	1	.500	0	10	0.29
Jacobs,Dwayne	Durham	Atl	A+	21	25	24	1	0	116.2	527	112	78	65	8	4	5	4	85	0	115	20	0	4	8	.333	1	0	5.01
Jacobs,Frankey	Athletics	Oak	R	20	15	3	0	4	36.2	182	52	37	29	2	1	3	2	17	0	22	7	0	0	2	.000	0	0	7.12
Jacobs,Russell	Wisconsin	Sea	A	23	21	9	0	2	77	339	62	41	38	7	3	4	3	58	1	76	14	1	4	2	.667	0	1	4.44
Jacobson,Andre.	Bristol	ChA	R+	22	14	7	0	1	49	249	57	51	38	1	0	3	2	46	2	47	9	2	1	2	.333	0	0	6.98
Jacobson,Brian	Savannah	LA	A	23	23	0	0	18	35.2	159	36	24	16	2	2	0	2	10	2	35	6	1	1	4	.200	0	3	4.04
Jacquez,Thomas	Batavia	Phi	A-	22	4	4	0	0	22.1	93	20	6	6	0	0	2	3	2	0	20	0	0	2	1	.667	0	0	2.42
	Piedmont	Phi	A	22	8	8	0	0	41.2	183	45	29	23	2	2	3	3	13	0	26	1	0	2	4	.333	0	0	4.97
Jaime,Wilson	Astros	Hou	R	23	18	0	0	9	36.2	177	37	25	19	0	1	3	3	29	0	43	10	2	2	0	1.000	0	0	4.66
James,Delvin	Princeton	TB	R+	20	20	5	0	2	58.1	276	71	57	32	11	1	2	4	24	1	46	4	2	4	4	.500	0	0	4.94
Janssen,Mike	Astros	Hou	R	21	13	0	0	6	25	129	28	27	26	2	0	1	1	23	0	20	5	0	0	1	.000	0	1	9.36
Jensen,Jared	Sou. Oregon	Oak	A-	24	23	0	0	18	26.2	113	27	13	11	1	1	0	0	8	0	34	3	0	4	2	.667	0	6	3.71
Jensen,Jason	Lethbridge	Ari	R+	22	14	14	0	0	63.1	282	73	43	35	3	2	1	3	23	0	46	0	0	4	3	.571	0	0	4.97
Jensen,Ryan	Bakersfield	SF	A+	22	1	1	0	0	1.1	7	3	2	2	1	0	1	0	0	0	2	0	0	0	0	.000	0	0	13.50

1997 Pitching — Single-A and Rookie Leagues

HOW MUCH HE PITCHED											WHAT HE GAVE UP												THE RESULTS					
Player	Team	Org	Lg	A	G	GS	CG	GF	IP	BFP	H	R	ER	HR	SH	SF	HB	TBB	IBB	SO	WP	Bk	W	L	Pct.	ShO	Sv	ERA
	Salem-Keizr	SF	A-	22	16	16	0	0	80.1	353	87	55	46	10	2	2	4	32	0	67	2	1	7	3	.700	0	0	5.15
Jerue,Tristan	New Jersey	StL	A-	22	13	13	0	0	71.2	310	73	35	28	3	2	5	5	21	0	55	4	1	5	4	.556	0	0	3.52
Jimenez,Jason	Hudson Vall	TB	A-	22	19	0	0	5	31.2	121	16	5	1	1	0	0	2	10	0	31	0	1	3	0	1.000	0	0	0.28
Jimenez,Jose	Pr William	StL	A+	24	24	24	2	0	145.2	609	128	73	50	12	2	2	9	42	2	81	10	2	9	7	.563	0	0	3.09
Jimenez,Mario	Mariners	Sea	R	19	7	6	0	0	33	158	44	32	23	0	2	2	2	19	0	18	3	2	3	1	.750	0	0	6.27
Jimenez,Ricardo	Orioles	Bal	R	20	8	6	0	2	39	168	30	22	15	1	0	5	3	21	0	27	1	1	3	1	.750	0	1	3.46
Johannsen,Jeff	Kane County	Fla	A	25	7	0	0	3	11.1	55	13	10	9	2	0	2	0	7	0	10	3	0	0	0	.000	0	0	7.15
Johnson,Craig	Jamestown	Det	A-	22	14	14	3	0	83.1	349	88	59	41	4	1	6	6	10	0	66	1	2	3	10	.231	0	0	4.43
Johnson,D	Portland	Col	A-	23	18	0	0	12	16.2	81	10	8	6	0	2	1	0	20	1	21	7	0	0	1	.000	0	5	3.24
Johnson,Eric	Salem-Keizr	SF	A-	20	10	0	0	1	8.1	49	7	12	11	0	0	0	1	18	0	8	2	2	0	0	.000	0	0	11.88
Johnson,Gregory	Lk Elsinore	Ana	A+	24	34	0	0	8	44.2	197	46	21	17	2	2	3	5	9	2	35	1	0	1	0	1.000	0	0	3.43
Johnson,Jeremi.	Orioles	Bal	R	20	6	0	0	3	6.1	27	4	2	2	0	0	1	0	4	0	4	0	0	2	1	.667	0	1	2.84
Johnson,Mark	Kissimmee	Hou	A+	23	26	26	3	0	155.1	652	150	67	53	8	7	5	6	39	1	127	4	6	8	9	.471	1	0	3.07
Johnston,Charles	Tigers	Det	R	21	18	2	0	4	36	157	37	22	16	2	0	1	3	11	0	29	4	2	1	1	.500	0	0	4.00
Johnston,Doug	Helena	Mil	R+	20	13	13	0	0	74.1	318	64	39	36	5	1	1	6	34	0	66	5	0	6	2	.750	0	0	4.36
Jones,Chauncey	Helena	Mil	R+	22	5	0	0	3	5.2	31	8	6	6	1	1	0	0	7	0	7	0	0	0	0	.000	0	0	9.53
	Ogden	Mil	R+	22	9	0	0	7	9.1	50	10	7	6	2	0	0	0	11	0	10	0	0	0	1	.000	0	0	5.79
Jones,Greg	Boise	Ana	A-	21	21	4	0	4	37.1	172	35	19	15	1	2	4	3	19	1	39	5	1	2	2	.500	0	2	3.62
Jones,Marcus	Sou. Oregon	Oak	A-	23	14	10	0	0	56	246	58	37	28	4	0	3	2	22	0	49	4	0	3	3	.500	0	0	4.50
Jones,Sean	Orioles	Bal	R	20	9	0	0	6	15	66	18	7	5	0	0	0	1	7	0	7	1	1	0	0	.000	0	0	3.00
Jones,Travis	Padres	SD	R	20	21	2	0	3	53.1	238	53	28	18	0	1	1	3	23	0	51	2	3	4	3	.571	0	0	3.04
Jones,William	Diamondback	Ari	R	22	7	0	0	4	12	59	14	12	10	1	1	2	0	8	1	10	1	0	0	1	.000	0	1	7.50
	Lethbridge	Ari	R+	22	16	0	0	4	21.2	108	23	21	15	3	1	1	2	17	0	18	0	0	0	3	.000	0	0	6.23
Jordan,Jason	High Desert	Ari	A+	25	6	4	0	0	14.2	70	16	12	10	0	0	1	0	13	0	10	1	0	2	0	1.000	0	0	6.14
Joseph,Kevin	Salem-Keizr	SF	A-	21	17	6	0	5	45	208	44	35	27	4	1	2	2	26	0	45	10	3	3	5	.375	0	1	5.40
Julio,Jorge	Expos	Mon	R	19	15	8	0	4	55.1	248	57	25	22	0	1	2	1	21	0	42	3	0	5	6	.455	0	1	3.58
	Wst Plm Bch	Mon	A+	19	1	0	0	0	0	2	2	1	1	0	0	0	0	0	0	0	0	0	0	0	.000	0	0	0.00
Jurgena,Matthew	Elizabethtn	Min	R+	22	23	5	0	10	42.2	194	46	28	24	8	1	0	5	18	0	57	7	0	2	4	.333	0	4	5.06
Kalinowski,Josh	Portland	Col	A-	21	6	6	0	0	18.2	78	15	6	5	0	0	0	0	10	0	27	3	0	0	1	.000	0	0	2.41
Karabinus,Christ.	Yakima	LA	A-	23	2	0	0	0	3	19	6	7	5	1	0	0	1	1	0	5	0	0	0	0	.000	0	0	15.00
Karnuth,Jason	New Jersey	StL	A-	22	7	7	0	0	38.2	158	33	8	8	0	1	1	2	9	0	23	2	0	4	1	.800	0	0	1.86
	Peoria	StL	A	22	4	4	0	0	23	102	29	19	17	1	1	1	1	7	1	12	2	1	0	3	.000	0	0	6.65
Kaufman,John	St. Pete	TB	A+	23	26	26	2	0	149.2	649	138	62	56	9	4	3	7	66	1	121	3	1	9	5	.643	1	0	3.37
Kawabata,Kyle	Piedmont	Phi	A	24	44	0	0	41	62.2	242	45	14	10	2	6	0	2	13	2	75	5	0	9	5	.643	0	16	1.44
Kawahara,Orin	Everett	Sea	A-	20	23	0	0	5	45.1	219	50	29	24	3	0	3	1	33	0	52	5	3	0	1	.000	0	0	4.76
Kaye,Justin	Wisconsin	Sea	A	22	28	26	0	2	127	618	129	113	103	13	6	5	16	104	0	115	21	6	8	12	.400	0	0	7.30
Kazmirski,Robert	Visalia	Oak	A+	26	5	0	0	3	4.1	30	11	9	8	3	0	0	0	5	2	6	1	0	1	1	.500	0	1	16.62
Keathley,Davan	Medicne Hat	Tor	R+	20	20	0	0	8	25	121	24	24	18	1	1	1	2	20	0	19	6	1	3	4	.429	0	0	6.48
Keith,Jeff	Bakersfield	SF	A+	26	37	0	0	12	44	205	45	29	28	9	1	3	6	32	0	35	4	0	1	2	.333	0	0	5.73
Keller,Kristopher	Jamestown	Det	A-	20	16	0	0	10	27	143	37	33	26	3	1	3	3	20	0	18	5	2	0	2	.000	0	0	8.67
Kelley,Jason	Rockford	ChN	A	22	22	0	0	12	29	148	29	20	16	2	1	0	1	27	1	20	10	0	1	0	1.000	0	2	4.97
	Williamsprt	ChN	A-	22	27	0	0	18	27.2	144	28	31	22	3	4	1	4	32	0	16	12	1	2	2	.500	0	10	7.16
Kelly,John	Augusta	Pit	A	25	1	0	0	0	0.2	6	4	2	2	0	0	0	0	0	0	2	0	0	0	0	.000	0	0	27.00
Kendall,Philip	Helena	Mil	R+	20	14	14	0	0	76	347	84	55	46	6	2	4	6	37	0	73	8	2	3	4	.429	0	0	5.45
Kennedy,Ryan	Portland	Col	A-	22	6	0	0	0	7.1	40	10	10	10	0	0	1	4	4	0	5	1	1	0	0	.000	0	0	12.27
Kennison,Kyle	Wisconsin	Sea	A	25	40	0	0	18	80.1	324	54	24	19	5	1	2	2	38	1	112	6	4	2	3	.400	0	6	2.13
Keppen,Jeffrey	Vero Beach	LA	A+	24	32	8	0	14	68.2	304	61	37	30	3	2	3	8	43	0	54	7	2	2	3	.400	0	0	3.93
Kern,Brian	Visalia	Oak	A+	24	23	0	0	9	34.1	178	42	38	29	5	1	1	2	28	1	39	7	3	3	0	1.000	0	1	7.60
Kershner,Jason	Clearwater	Phi	A+	21	22	16	0	3	99.1	417	113	49	43	9	2	4	4	21	0	51	2	0	5	10	.333	0	1	3.90
Kertis,John	Pulaski	Tex	R+	23	14	0	0	1	21.1	97	14	9	7	0	0	0	4	11	0	22	4	0	2	0	1.000	0	0	2.95
Kessel,Kyle	Capital City	NYN	A	22	27	27	5	0	168.2	685	131	63	51	8	9	5	9	53	3	151	8	0	11	11	.500	1	0	2.72
Key,Scott	Spokane	KC	A-	21	25	1	0	8	69.2	296	55	33	25	5	0	2	4	31	1	66	9	0	3	3	.500	0	3	3.23
Key,Calvin	Martinsvlle	Phi	R+	23	14	6	0	3	50.1	227	56	35	27	5	0	2	3	13	1	53	5	1	5	2	.714	0	0	4.83
	Piedmont	Phi	A	23	3	1	0	1	14.1	61	19	6	6	3	1	1	0	2	0	9	0	0	0	0	.000	0	0	3.77
Kidd,Jake	Rockies	Col	R	20	19	0	0	11	39	163	37	14	7	0	2	0	1	10	0	27	0	0	5	0	1.000	0	3	1.62
Kiess,Barry	South Bend	Ari	A	24	19	0	0	8	31.2	140	29	19	18	3	3	0	3	19	1	34	5	2	3	4	.429	0	1	5.12
Kimball,Andrew	Sou. Oregon	Oak	A-	22	13	7	0	0	54.2	230	37	29	22	4	1	1	3	17	0	75	8	2	3	2	.600	0	0	3.62
Kimbrell,Michael	Chston-SC	TB	A	24	1	0	0	1	3	10	0	0	0	0	0	0	0	1	0	4	0	0	0	0	.000	0	0	0.00
	St. Pete	TB	A+	24	3	0	0	2	9.1	44	10	8	8	2	1	0	0	7	0	7	1	0	0	0	.000	0	0	7.71
	Hudson Vall	TB	A-	24	26	0	0	12	39.2	177	34	32	20	5	4	2	1	18	0	43	1	1	1	3	.250	0	2	4.54
Kimsey,Keith	Lakeland	Det	A+	25	26	12	0	8	80.1	377	92	57	45	5	4	3	6	42	1	42	6	2	2	5	.286	0	1	5.04
Kinney,Matt	Michigan	Bos	A	21	22	22	2	0	117.1	514	93	59	46	4	5	2	0	78	2	123	6	0	8	5	.615	1	0	3.53
Kirst,Mark	Ogden	Mil	R+	23	16	10	0	1	66.2	307	88	49	37	7	1	4	10	14	1	56	4	0	4	4	.500	0	0	5.00
Klein,Cody	Yankees	NYA	R	19	10	0	0	3	17.2	73	13	1	1	0	0	0	0	9	0	17	2	0	1	0	1.000	0	1	0.51
Knickerbocker,T.	Sou. Oregon	Oak	A-	22	4	4	0	0	16	72	20	7	5	0	0	2	0	6	0	18	0	0	1	0	1.000	0	0	2.81
Knoll,Brian	Bakersfield	SF	A+	24	49	0	0	23	68	323	88	50	43	6	3	1	2	35	3	56	10	0	3	6	.333	0	2	5.69
Knoll,Randy	Clearwater	Phi	A+	21	5	5	0	0	30.1	127	33	18	15	0	0	1	2	7	0	20	3	1	1	2	.333	0	0	4.45
Knott,Eric	Lethbridge	Ari	R+	23	21	3	0	7	47	195	41	21	15	4	2	1	0	9	1	62	2	0	0	4	.000	0	3	2.87
Knotts,Gary	Kane County	Fla	A	21	7	7	0	0	20	113	33	34	29	2	2	0	3	17	0	19	8	1	1	5	.167	0	0	13.05
	Utica	Fla	A-	21	12	12	1	0	69.2	304	70	34	28	3	1	2	8	27	1	65	3	0	3	5	.375	0	0	3.62
Knowles,Michael	Yankees	NYA	R	18	9	8	0	0	39	168	41	30	21	2	4	2	1	14	0	24	3	6	2	2	.500	0	0	4.85
Koch,Jack	Oneonta	NYA	A-	21	1	0	0	0	2	8	1	0	0	0	0	0	0	1	0	2	0	0	0	0	.000	0	0	0.00
	Yankees	NYA	R	21	2	0	0	0	1.2	13	6	3	3	0	0	0	0	2	0	0	0	0	0	0	.000	0	0	16.20
Koch,Bill	Dunedin	Tor	A+	23	3	3	0	0	21.2	88	27	10	5	1	1	1	0	3	0	20	1	1	0	1	.000	0	0	2.08
Koehler,Russ	Wisconsin	Sea	A	23	23	0	0	10	48.1	214	50	30	24	6	1	1	4	15	4	33	1	1	3	2	.600	0	2	4.47
Koehler,P.K.	Macon	Atl	A	24	26	7	0	6	62.1	278	60	44	31	6	3	1	1	24	0	46	3	0	3	7	.300	0	0	4.48
Koeman,Matt	Columbus	Cle	A	24	34	0	0	9	58.1	235	38	17	17	8	0	2	2	23	1	63	4	0	4	5	.444	0	2	2.62

1997 Pitching — Single-A and Rookie Leagues

HOW MUCH HE PITCHED											WHAT HE GAVE UP												THE RESULTS					
Player	Team	Org	Lg	A	G	GS	CG	GF	IP	BFP	H	R	ER	HR	SH	SF	HB	TBB	IBB	SO	WP	Bk	W	L	Pct.	ShO	Sv	ERA
	Kinston	Cle	A+	24	7	0	0	3	15.1	70	20	14	13	3	1	0	0	4	0	12	2	0	1	1	.500	0	0	7.63
Kofler,Edward	Princeton	TB	R+	20	13	13	0	0	63	280	63	46	39	9	1	1	7	28	0	66	5	2	5	6	.455	0	0	5.57
Kohl,Douglas	Diamondback	Ari	R	18	14	14	0	0	61.1	270	62	33	27	5	1	3	5	25	0	46	3	1	1	2	.333	0	0	3.96
Kolb,Brandon	Rancho Cuca	SD	A+	24	10	10	0	0	63	261	60	29	21	0	1	1	2	22	0	49	5	0	3	2	.600	0	0	3.00
Konieczki,Dom	Stockton	Mil	A+	29	12	0	0	5	13	56	11	5	4	0	2	0	1	10	0	16	1	0	1	1	.500	0	1	2.77
Kown,John	Pr William	StL	A+	25	20	10	0	1	66.1	310	83	60	51	10	2	4	3	25	0	32	2	0	2	6	.250	0	0	6.92
Krall,Eric	Greensboro	NYA	A	24	15	1	0	9	35	157	37	23	15	3	1	1	1	14	1	26	2	0	2	2	.500	0	0	3.86
Kramer,Matthew	San Berndno	LA	A+	22	10	0	0	2	16.2	79	18	12	11	1	0	2	0	16	0	16	0	0	0	0	.000	0	0	5.94
	Savannah	LA	A	22	23	8	0	3	64.2	290	62	49	42	7	6	1	1	31	1	62	9	0	6	4	.600	0	0	5.85
Kraus,Timothy	Hickory	ChA	A	25	15	0	0	6	30.2	143	37	22	17	1	0	3	1	13	0	29	0	0	0	2	.000	0	0	4.99
Kringen,Jake	Portland	Col	A-	22	15	15	1	0	83.1	349	84	40	32	6	1	1	2	20	0	72	4	2	6	5	.545	1	0	3.46
Kvasnicka,Jay	Bristol	ChA	R+	30	4	4	0	0	23.2	108	22	18	16	3	1	0	4	12	0	19	0	1	1	2	.333	0	0	6.08
Kvasnicka,Jonat.	White Sox	ChA	R	21	8	7	0	1	36.1	158	43	24	22	2	0	1	0	6	0	44	3	0	2	3	.400	0	1	5.45
Kyzar,Cory	Royals	KC	R	20	3	0	0	0	3.2	14	2	2	1	0	0	0	0	0	0	3	0	0	0	0	.000	0	0	2.45
Labitzke,Jesse	Rockies	Col	R	20	12	4	0	1	23.2	131	41	33	27	3	0	1	2	21	0	22	2	1	0	1	.000	0	0	10.27
Lacefield,Timothy	St. Cathrns	Tor	A-	22	25	0	0	9	39.2	177	52	26	22	5	3	1	5	5	1	33	1	1	2	0	1.000	0	2	4.99
LaChapelle,Yan	Hagerstown	Tor	A	22	26	15	1	8	118.2	503	73	54	43	7	6	6	6	74	0	115	12	1	7	7	.500	1	3	3.26
Lagattuta,Rico	Modesto	Oak	A+	24	3	0	0	2	1	9	3	1	1	0	0	0	0	3	0	1	0	0	0	0	.000	0	0	9.00
	Sou. Oregon	Oak	A-	24	16	0	0	9	29	138	35	21	16	2	2	3	1	14	1	17	7	0	2	1	.667	0	2	4.97
LaGrandeur,Yan	Eugene	Atl	A-	21	21	0	0	10	33	169	41	34	29	2	0	2	3	21	1	35	11	0	1	1	.500	0	0	7.91
Lail,Denny.	Tampa	NYA	A+	23	44	1	0	13	62.1	267	67	38	27	2	1	5	0	23	7	40	4	0	3	5	.375	0	1	3.90
Lakman,Jason	Hickory	ChA	A	21	27	27	3	0	154.2	667	139	82	67	11	5	1	4	70	0	168	24	1	10	9	.526	0	0	3.90
Lamber,Justin	Spokane	KC	A-	22	25	0	0	12	27.1	126	24	14	13	1	0	1	1	20	0	40	10	0	1	1	.500	0	4	4.28
Lambert,Jeremy	Johnson Cty	StL	R+	19	27	0	0	4	32.1	181	46	42	33	3	1	1	5	37	1	29	6	0	1	1	.500	0	1	9.19
Lambert,Kristop.	Erie	Pit	A-	24	15	14	0	0	81	330	59	28	21	5	2	0	2	21	0	94	7	1	11	2	.846	0	0	2.33
Lancaster,Roger	Medicne Hat	Tor	R+	23	18	0	0	3	28	133	33	20	15	1	2	0	1	15	0	18	2	2	1	2	.333	0	1	4.82
Lanfranco,Otoni.	Johnson Cty	StL	R+	21	14	14	0	0	68.1	319	85	60	58	14	1	1	6	31	0	69	1	0	2	8	.200	0	0	7.64
Langston,David	Yankees	NYA	R	19	11	0	0	3	20	89	19	11	8	2	0	1	1	9	0	11	6	0	2	1	.667	0	0	3.60
Lanzetta,Tobin	Vermont	Mon	A-	22	23	5	0	5	43.1	206	60	36	27	5	0	3	2	8	0	43	4	0	1	4	.200	0	1	5.61
Lara,Nelson	Kane County	Fla	A	19	29	0	0	18	38.1	169	37	20	17	1	3	3	1	14	0	43	3	1	1	2	.333	0	3	3.99
Lara,Giovanny	Cape Fear	Mon	A	22	28	27	1	0	170	742	199	107	86	13	9	9	9	45	0	100	13	1	9	12	.429	0	0	4.55
Largusa,Levon	Daytona	ChN	A+	27	14	0	0	4	8.2	51	16	11	8	0	0	1	0	8	2	5	1	0	0	0	.000	0	0	8.31
LaRosa,Thomas	Ft. Myers	Min	A+	23	25	23	3	0	135.2	592	120	73	65	10	1	5	7	66	0	118	6	0	8	6	.571	1	0	4.31
Larreal,Guillermo	Bakersfield	SF	A+	22	32	0	0	12	50	222	63	40	34	9	2	3	4	14	0	37	1	1	2	0	1.000	0	1	6.12
	Salem-Keizr	SF	A-	22	13	0	0	7	16.1	75	23	12	10	1	2	0	0	3	0	16	0	0	1	2	.333	0	1	5.51
Larson,Toby	Mets	NYN	R	25	2	1	0	0	4	16	4	1	1	0	0	0	0	0	0	4	0	0	1	0	1.000	0	0	2.25
	St. Lucie	NYN	A+	25	4	0	0	1	5	25	9	6	4	2	0	0	0	1	0	3	0	0	0	1	.000	0	0	7.20
Lawrence,Clint	Hagerstown	Tor	A	21	27	27	1	0	170.1	718	179	76	67	8	4	4	6	40	0	149	3	1	13	10	.565	1	0	3.54
Laxton,Brett	Visalia	Oak	A+	24	29	22	0	2	138.2	606	141	62	46	7	4	0	11	50	0	121	14	0	11	5	.688	0	0	2.99
Layne,Roger	Burlington	Cle	R+	21	11	11	0	0	59.2	257	55	39	24	5	3	2	1	21	0	52	11	0	1	4	.200	0	0	3.62
Lebejko,David	Eugene	Atl	A-	23	20	0	0	9	32	175	44	32	22	2	2	2	2	31	1	27	6	1	0	3	.000	0	0	6.19
Ledden,Ryan	Devil Rays	TB	R	20	8	0	0	3	11.1	59	11	9	8	0	0	2	0	16	0	4	10	0	1	0	1.000	0	0	6.35
Lee,Chris	Bluefield	Bal	R+	22	23	0	0	10	31	128	24	17	14	4	3	2	2	14	1	32	2	1	2	0	1.000	0	2	4.06
Lee,Corey	Charlotte	Tex	A+	23	23	23	6	0	160.2	654	132	66	62	9	5	3	7	60	0	147	7	0	15	5	.750	2	0	3.47
Lee,David	Asheville	Col	A	25	51	0	0	49	53	239	61	30	24	5	3	1	1	23	0	59	4	0	4	8	.333	0	22	4.08
Lee,Jeremy	Dunedin	Tor	A+	23	28	22	0	3	153.1	678	179	95	79	12	4	6	8	54	0	90	12	1	8	9	.471	0	1	4.64
Lee,Derek	Ogden	Mil	R+	23	14	13	0	0	74.1	325	89	49	32	3	2	6	3	20	0	71	8	1	4	4	.500	0	0	3.87
Lee,Garrett	Danville	Atl	R+	21	14	14	1	0	84	360	87	57	46	8	3	2	7	17	1	72	3	1	5	5	.500	1	0	4.93
Leese,Brandon	San Jose	SF	A+	22	19	19	0	0	112	475	99	44	38	11	1	0	4	46	2	99	15	0	7	5	.583	0	0	3.05
	Kane County	Fla	A	22	7	6	0	0	42.1	171	27	18	18	0	1	2	3	18	0	32	3	1	3	1	.750	0	0	3.83
Leon,Scott	Chston-SC	TB	A	23	27	25	1	1	156.1	654	151	70	55	13	5	8	7	41	0	109	10	1	6	12	.333	0	0	3.17
Leshay,Maney	Helena	Mil	R+	25	5	2	0	0	5.1	35	11	12	11	1	0	0	0	10	0	5	0	0	1	0	1.000	0	0	18.56
Leslie,Sean	Wst Plm Bch	Mon	A+	24	1	0	0	0	0.2	5	2	2	2	0	0	0	0	1	0	0	0	0	0	0	.000	0	0	27.00
	Cape Fear	Mon	A	24	34	1	0	14	61	284	75	40	34	8	5	2	2	27	0	42	6	0	0	5	.000	0	0	5.02
Levan,Matt	Utica	Fla	A-	23	1	1	0	0	4	20	5	3	3	1	0	0	1	1	0	6	1	0	0	0	.000	0	0	6.75
	Kane County	Fla	A	23	11	9	0	0	43.2	183	44	16	15	5	1	0	3	16	0	45	5	2	2	3	.400	0	0	3.09
Levey,Josh	New Jersey	StL	A-	23	18	3	0	3	33.2	149	31	21	20	1	1	3	7	14	0	25	10	0	1	3	.250	0	0	5.35
Levrault,Allen	Beloit	Mil	A	20	24	24	1	0	131.1	561	141	89	77	18	1	2	6	40	1	112	3	12	3	10	.231	0	0	5.28
Levy,Tye	Billings	Cin	R+	20	18	2	0	5	30	131	32	14	12	2	0	0	1	9	1	32	3	2	1	0	1.000	0	0	3.60
Lewis,Derrick	Danville	Atl	R+	22	16	9	0	2	49.2	241	59	48	35	5	1	1	2	31	0	46	8	0	2	4	.333	0	0	6.34
Leyva,Edgar	Cedar Rapds	Ana	A	20	22	21	0	1	121	529	118	73	63	13	3	3	9	58	1	77	3	3	8	6	.571	0	1	4.69
Leyva,Julian	Modesto	Oak	A+	20	28	19	0	6	139	596	148	99	76	21	3	3	6	38	1	90	5	1	4	9	.308	0	2	4.92
Licciardi,Ron	Williamsprt	ChN	A-	22	17	9	0	1	65	305	84	41	36	6	2	2	0	25	1	56	6	1	4	1	.800	0	0	4.98
Lilly,Theodore	San Berndno	LA	A+	22	23	21	2	0	134.2	540	116	52	42	9	5	3	4	32	0	158	7	5	7	8	.467	1	0	2.81
Lima,Cory	Utica	Fla	A-	23	17	2	0	7	40	160	31	11	9	1	0	0	2	11	0	40	2	2	3	1	.750	0	1	2.03
Lincoln,Mike	Ft. Myers	Min	A+	23	20	20	1	0	134	553	130	41	34	4	5	3	4	25	0	75	4	2	13	4	.765	1	0	2.28
Lindberg,Frederi.	Ft. Wayne	Min	A	24	5	0	0	2	12.1	53	16	5	5	0	0	0	0	5	0	8	2	1	0	0	.000	0	0	3.65
Linebrink,Scott	Salem-Keizr	SF	A-	21	3	3	0	0	10	42	7	5	5	1	0	0	0	6	0	6	1	0	0	0	.000	0	0	4.50
	San Jose	SF	A+	21	6	6	0	0	28.1	120	29	11	10	2	0	0	0	10	0	40	2	0	2	1	.667	0	0	3.18
Lineweaver,Aaro.	Lansing	KC	A	24	21	9	0	3	83.2	359	89	38	31	4	2	2	3	28	1	73	6	1	7	1	.875	0	0	3.33
Lisio,Joe	St. Lucie	NYN	A+	24	48	0	0	44	47.1	209	48	27	24	4	4	0	4	19	5	42	3	2	2	6	.250	0	16	4.56
Lister,Martin	South Bend	Ari	A	26	3	0	0	2	3.1	18	6	6	6	1	0	1	0	2	0	1	1	0	0	0	.000	0	0	16.20
Little,Rodney	Rockies	Col	R	19	15	1	0	4	25.2	132	29	26	21	4	0	1	5	19	0	21	2	0	3	1	.750	0	0	7.36
Little,Roger	Rockies	Col	R	19	14	4	0	4	33	156	30	24	20	1	0	1	4	23	0	31	6	1	2	1	.667	0	1	5.45
Lohrman,Dave	Pittsfield	NYN	A-	22	22	0	0	13	34	146	25	18	11	2	0	0	5	12	0	42	3	1	1	2	.333	0	4	2.91
Lohse,Kyle	Cubs	ChN	R	19	12	11	0	0	47.2	210	46	22	16	0	1	1	1	22	0	49	3	0	2	2	.500	0	0	3.02
Loiz,Niuman	Kissimmee	Hou	A+	24	11	3	1	2	33	141	37	19	14	4	1	3	2	8	0	19	2	0	1	1	.500	0	0	3.82

1997 Pitching — Single-A and Rookie Leagues

HOW MUCH HE PITCHED											WHAT HE GAVE UP												THE RESULTS					
Player	Team	Org	Lg	A	G	GS	CG	GF	IP	BFP	H	R	ER	HR	SH	SF	HB	TBB	IBB	SO	WP	Bk	W	L	Pct.	ShO	Sv	ERA
	Quad City	Hou	A	24	18	9	0	4	64.2	282	63	37	35	8	3	3	5	29	1	49	10	0	2	5	.286	0	0	4.87
Loonam,Rick	Ft. Wayne	Min	A	22	34	1	0	6	49.1	245	63	36	31	3	1	2	1	33	0	35	8	2	3	2	.600	0	0	5.66
Lopez,Carlos	Expos	Mon	R	18	14	6	0	2	42.2	195	47	28	16	2	1	1	1	14	0	24	7	0	2	4	.333	0	0	3.38
Lopez,Gustavo	Marlins	Fla	R	19	7	6	1	0	32.2	140	33	20	15	0	3	1	1	10	0	25	3	1	0	3	.000	0	0	4.13
Lopez,Jose	Bristol	ChA	R+	22	20	0	0	6	43.2	213	62	42	34	1	2	4	1	18	0	33	1	0	3	1	.750	0	0	7.01
Lopez,Rodrigo	Clinton	SD	A	22	37	14	2	19	121.2	508	103	49	43	6	7	4	3	42	1	123	3	4	6	8	.429	0	9	3.18
Lora (diaz),Diaz	Rockies	Col	R	20	10	0	0	1	20	99	27	18	14	1	0	2	3	8	0	8	3	0	0	0	.000	0	0	6.30
Loubier,Scott	Wst Plm Bch	Mon	A+	24	4	0	0	3	5	27	10	7	7	1	0	0	1	2	0	3	0	1	0	0	.000	0	0	12.60
	Vermont	Mon	A-	24	7	6	0	0	38	155	32	16	13	3	1	1	1	10	0	29	3	1	3	2	.600	0	0	3.08
	Cape Fear	Mon	A	24	10	2	0	2	28	114	19	9	9	1	1	1	4	12	0	20	2	0	1	1	.500	0	0	2.89
Loux,Shane	Tigers	Det	R	18	10	9	1	0	43	158	19	7	4	0	0	0	1	10	0	33	2	1	4	1	.800	1	0	0.84
Love,Farley	Astros	Hou	R	25	2	0	0	0	3	12	1	0	0	0	0	0	0	2	0	7	0	0	0	0	.000	0	0	0.00
	Auburn	Hou	A-	25	3	0	0	1	3	11	1	0	0	0	1	0	0	1	0	2	0	0	0	0	.000	0	1	0.00
Lovingood,Ray	Kingsport	NYN	R+	20	13	13	0	0	63	294	80	48	41	11	1	1	5	30	2	65	7	0	6	3	.667	0	0	5.86
Lowe,Matthew	Mets	NYN	R	19	5	0	0	2	8	37	4	1	1	0	0	0	0	9	1	15	1	0	2	0	1.000	0	1	1.13
Lundberg,Dave	Rangers	Tex	R	21	14	1	0	11	32.1	115	13	4	3	1	0	1	0	11	0	32	0	1	1	1	.500	0	5	0.84
Lunney,Barry	Elizabethtn	Min	R+	23	22	0	0	12	25	132	30	26	25	3	5	0	3	22	1	21	11	0	1	3	.250	0	1	9.00
Luttig,Christophe.	Pirates	Pit	R	22	12	0	0	8	21.2	102	23	9	6	0	0	0	1	9	0	21	1	0	1	1	.500	0	3	2.49
	Erie	Pit	A-	22	11	0	0	5	19	85	18	12	7	0	0	1	0	8	0	16	1	0	1	2	.333	0	0	3.32
Lynch,Jim	Quad City	Hou	A	22	37	0	0	14	58.1	280	44	37	30	4	1	1	10	46	4	68	5	2	3	3	.500	0	1	4.63
Lynch,Pat	Medicne Hat	Tor	R+	20	12	11	0	0	49.2	231	64	40	29	8	1	2	1	24	0	34	8	0	3	3	.500	0	0	5.26
Lynch,Ryan	Ft. Wayne	Min	A	23	15	2	0	5	34.1	155	38	20	12	2	1	1	3	10	0	39	0	0	2	2	.500	0	0	3.15
Lynde,Jerry	Vermont	Mon	A-	23	12	2	0	4	12.2	74	17	17	13	1	0	1	1	18	0	12	1	0	0	2	.000	0	0	9.24
Lyons,Jonathan	Sarasota	Bos	A+	23	25	14	0	6	96.2	462	125	79	65	11	3	12	1	45	2	47	5	7	3	12	.200	0	0	6.05
Lyons,Michael	Capital City	NYN	A	23	44	0	0	32	58	228	40	15	12	3	4	0	1	20	4	55	2	0	6	2	.750	0	14	1.86
Lyons,Timothy	Braves	Atl	R	23	1	0	0	1	1	5	1	0	0	0	0	0	0	1	0	3	0	0	0	0	.000	0	0	0.00
	Danville	Atl	R+	23	10	0	0	5	8.1	70	14	31	30	0	0	1	12	19	0	13	24	1	0	0	.000	0	0	32.40
Maberry,Mark	Kingsport	NYN	R+	23	22	0	0	13	35	158	36	14	7	3	3	1	0	13	4	51	2	0	2	2	.500	0	5	1.80
Machado,Dougl.	Rangers	Tex	R	18	11	9	1	1	62	271	69	34	26	4	1	2	0	18	1	46	4	3	5	4	.556	0	0	3.77
Mackey,Jason	Columbus	Cle	A	24	18	17	0	1	93.1	411	86	61	52	14	0	4	11	45	1	69	8	2	2	8	.200	0	0	5.01
MacRae,Scott	Burlington	Cin	A	23	27	26	4	0	160.1	694	159	76	68	9	7	4	9	57	0	89	18	1	11	4	.733	1	0	3.82
Madison,Scott	Chston-SC	TB	A	23	2	0	0	0	4	23	7	6	2	0	0	1	0	2	0	4	1	0	0	1	.000	0	0	4.50
	Hudson Vall	TB	A-	23	15	15	1	0	86.2	362	87	43	36	9	1	3	2	28	0	54	5	6	6	4	.600	0	0	3.74
Maestas,Mickey	Yakima	LA	A-	22	21	3	0	6	47.2	239	65	44	35	2	0	2	4	30	1	50	6	0	1	4	.200	0	0	6.61
Magers,Mathew	Williamsprt	ChN	A-	22	27	0	0	14	50.1	231	46	28	20	0	3	5	1	35	3	48	4	1	4	4	.500	0	5	3.58
Mahlberg,John	Asheville	Col	A	21	12	0	0	8	19.2	96	29	15	11	1	0	1	0	8	0	16	2	0	0	0	.000	0	2	5.03
	Portland	Col	A-	21	18	7	0	6	46	225	69	47	34	3	2	3	5	14	1	31	1	0	2	4	.333	0	0	6.65
Mairena,Oswaldo	Tampa	NYA	A+	22	3	0	0	0	4.1	19	6	2	2	1	0	0	0	0	0	6	0	0	0	0	.000	0	0	4.15
	Greensboro	NYA	A	22	49	0	0	20	60.1	241	43	24	17	2	3	1	1	16	3	75	0	3	6	1	.857	0	8	2.54
Maldonado,Este.	Quad City	Hou	A	22	39	4	0	24	68.2	294	51	38	27	3	2	3	2	32	1	56	2	1	4	4	.500	0	9	3.54
Malenfant,David	Tigers	Det	R	23	1	0	0	0	0.2	5	1	2	2	0	0	0	0	2	0	1	0	0	0	0	.000	0	0	27.00
	Lakeland	Det	A+	23	6	0	0	2	6	46	18	12	10	1	1	1	1	7	0	3	1	0	0	0	.000	0	0	15.00
Malerich,William	Salem-Keizr	SF	A-	22	21	0	0	5	26.2	130	26	14	9	2	1	0	3	21	1	43	4	0	2	1	.667	0	0	3.04
Malko,Bryan	Ft. Wayne	Min	A	21	14	13	0	1	64.1	271	68	29	27	2	1	4	2	22	0	59	3	1	4	4	.500	0	0	3.78
Mallard,Randi	Chston-WV	Cin	A	22	13	12	0	0	56.1	238	51	25	24	0	2	3	5	23	0	61	8	0	3	3	.500	0	0	3.83
Mallette,Brian	Helena	Mil	R+	23	23	0	0	13	35.1	156	33	19	17	1	3	2	1	20	2	58	7	0	6	2	.750	0	5	4.33
Mallory,Andrew	Cubs	ChN	R	21	12	10	0	0	51	235	63	38	24	3	0	2	9	22	0	32	8	3	3	4	.429	0	0	4.24
Malloy,Pat	Burlington	Cle	R+	22	17	0	0	6	29	138	35	24	22	3	1	1	5	14	0	26	2	0	0	1	.000	0	1	6.83
Malloy,William	Bakersfield	SF	A+	23	29	29	0	0	167.1	755	184	106	89	11	5	3	7	83	1	124	23	1	7	9	.438	0	0	4.79
Manbeck,Mark	Martinsvlle	Phi	R+	23	9	9	0	0	56.2	227	51	16	14	4	0	0	2	3	0	64	0	0	3	1	.750	0	0	2.22
	Batavia	Phi	A-	23	5	5	0	0	28.1	116	36	16	15	1	0	0	0	4	0	27	1	0	1	2	.333	0	0	4.76
Mancha,Tony	Royals	KC	R	19	13	7	0	4	49.1	216	53	28	18	1	0	1	4	11	0	47	2	0	2	6	.250	0	2	3.28
Maness,Nicholas	Mets	NYN	R	19	11	6	0	2	44.2	205	52	25	15	3	1	1	1	20	0	54	2	2	3	2	.600	0	0	3.02
Mangieri,John	Pittsfield	NYN	A-	21	2	0	0	1	1.1	9	3	3	3	0	0	0	2	0	0	0	0	0	0	0	.000	0	0	20.25
	Mets	NYN	R	21	13	0	0	3	20.1	101	28	16	16	3	0	1	1	14	0	15	2	2	2	0	1.000	0	1	7.08
Mangum,Mark	Rockies	Col	R	19	13	13	0	0	60.2	286	66	45	35	1	0	3	7	35	0	72	9	1	3	6	.333	0	0	5.19
Manias,James	St. Pete	TB	A+	23	28	28	2	0	171.1	710	163	84	72	16	3	4	11	40	0	119	6	0	13	5	.722	2	0	3.78
Mann,Jim	Hagerstown	Tor	A	23	19	0	0	16	26.2	122	35	18	15	4	0	1	1	11	0	30	2	0	0	1	.000	0	4	5.06
	Dunedin	Tor	A+	23	12	0	0	4	18	88	27	12	12	2	0	1	1	6	1	13	1	0	1	0	1.000	0	0	6.00
Manon,Julio	Chston-SC	TB	A	24	27	9	0	4	88.2	392	95	53	44	8	5	3	3	22	1	98	7	0	3	5	.375	0	0	4.47
Manwiller,Tim	Sou. Oregon	Oak	A-	23	12	3	0	5	29	115	19	8	6	0	2	1	0	10	0	30	1	2	2	0	1.000	0	2	1.86
	Modesto	Oak	A+	23	7	0	0	0	20.2	85	21	8	7	1	2	3	0	7	2	18	1	1	1	1	.500	0	0	3.05
Marache,Luis	Orioles	Bal	R	18	11	10	1	0	57.1	232	48	26	20	4	0	1	2	17	0	45	2	2	4	6	.400	1	0	3.14
	Frederick	Bal	A+	18	2	2	0	0	8	44	12	14	9	4	1	0	0	7	0	6	1	0	0	2	.000	0	0	10.13
Marenghi,Matt	High Desert	Ari	A+	25	38	0	0	14	73.1	326	81	38	25	8	0	1	2	23	1	45	4	0	4	3	.571	0	2	3.07
Markey,Barry	Daytona	ChN	A+	21	22	21	2	1	120	537	144	81	74	13	2	5	8	41	1	67	4	2	5	7	.417	0	0	5.55
Markham,Andy	Frederick	Bal	A+	25	20	0	0	9	29.2	130	31	13	10	3	2	1	0	12	1	22	1	0	4	0	1.000	0	1	3.03
Markwell,Diego.	St. Cathrns	Tor	A-	17	16	11	0	1	48.2	240	50	35	27	1	3	0	8	40	0	33	5	1	1	6	.143	0	0	4.99
Marquez,Robert	Cape Fear	Mon	A	25	12	0	0	5	18.1	81	15	6	6	0	0	0	1	12	0	18	0	2	0	0	.000	0	2	2.95
	Wst Plm Bch	Mon	A+	25	21	0	0	13	28	117	28	12	8	3	1	0	0	3	0	22	0	0	1	1	.500	0	6	2.57
Marquis,Jason	Macon	Atl	A	19	28	28	0	0	141.2	627	156	78	69	10	2	7	2	55	1	121	8	2	14	10	.583	0	0	4.38
Marriott,Mike	Utica	Fla	A-	21	7	7	0	0	29.1	134	31	25	18	1	0	1	2	14	0	21	2	0	1	2	.333	0	0	5.52
Marshall,Lee	Elizabethtn	Min	R+	21	14	14	1	0	84	369	93	56	36	6	4	1	5	16	0	41	2	0	5	3	.625	0	0	3.86
Marshall,Gary	Daytona	ChN	A+	24	22	0	0	11	20.2	92	23	13	11	4	0	1	0	8	2	23	1	0	0	0	.000	0	6	4.79
	Rockford	ChN	A	24	29	0	0	7	33	154	34	20	14	3	2	2	2	17	1	21	1	0	4	1	.800	0	2	3.82
Marsonek,Sam	Charlotte	Tex	A+	19	2	2	0	0	8.1	41	14	10	7	3	0	0	1	2	0	7	3	0	0	2	.000	0	0	7.56
	Pulaski	Tex	R+	19	12	11	0	0	71.2	331	90	57	40	4	2	3	3	20	0	65	13	3	7	3	.700	0	0	5.02

1997 Pitching — Single-A and Rookie Leagues

HOW MUCH HE PITCHED											WHAT HE GAVE UP												THE RESULTS					
Player	Team	Org	Lg	A	G	GS	CG	GF	IP	BFP	H	R	ER	HR	SH	SF	HB	TBB	IBB	SO	WP	Bk	W	L	Pct.	ShO	Sv	ERA
Marte,Damaso	Lancaster	Sea	A+	24	25	25	2	0	139.1	609	144	75	64	15	4	4	8	62	1	127	8	4	8	8	.500	1	0	4.13
Martin,Chandler	Salem	Col	A+	24	16	5	0	8	45.1	205	46	25	20	1	1	0	3	25	0	30	7	0	1	5	.167	0	1	3.97
Martin,Trey	Vermont	Mon	A-	21	11	0	0	1	24.2	110	30	19	17	3	1	2	2	7	0	13	1	0	1	0	1.000	0	0	6.20
Martin,Jeff	Lynchburg	Pit	A+	24	24	21	0	1	115.1	527	139	86	74	8	3	2	6	48	1	101	9	2	8	10	.444	0	0	5.77
Martines,Jason	Lethbridge	Ari	R+	22	22	0	0	6	43	180	45	15	15	4	1	1	2	11	0	34	1	0	3	3	.500	0	0	3.14
Martinez,Caleb	Piedmont	Phi	A	21	20	19	0	0	110	487	117	70	57	11	7	5	10	38	0	89	3	3	5	10	.333	0	0	4.66
	Martinsvlle	Phi	R+	21	7	7	0	0	39	167	37	21	16	3	0	2	2	18	0	27	1	3	1	3	.250	0	0	3.69
Martinez,Carlos	Royals	KC	R	19	14	1	1	6	32	128	24	8	7	0	3	2	1	14	1	19	1	1	1	0	1.000	1	4	1.97
Martinez,Francis.	Helena	Mil	R+	20	16	0	0	6	25.2	129	30	26	16	2	0	1	1	18	0	20	1	0	0	2	.000	0	0	5.61
Martinez,Javier	Daytona	ChN	A+	21	9	9	2	0	51.1	238	65	40	33	8	1	3	3	26	0	34	3	2	2	6	.250	0	0	5.79
	Rockford	ChN	A	21	17	17	1	0	79	369	85	61	50	7	3	2	3	50	1	70	10	0	1	7	.125	0	0	5.70
Martinez,Jose	Charlotte	Tex	A+	23	26	0	0	13	57.2	229	52	25	24	6	3	0	0	13	0	48	4	1	3	1	.750	0	2	3.75
Martinez,Dennis	Columbus	Cle	A	24	6	0	0	2	5	32	7	13	13	2	0	0	3	8	0	2	2	0	0	2	.000	0	0	23.40
Martinez,Mark	Red Sox	Bos	R	20	14	4	0	1	47.2	199	35	18	14	1	0	1	1	18	0	78	4	2	4	2	.667	0	0	2.64
Martinez,Ramon	San Berndno	LA	A+	19	4	4	0	0	15.2	58	10	2	2	0	0	0	1	4	0	16	0	0	0	1	.000	0	0	1.15
Martinez,Romulo	W Michigan	Det	A	21	36	0	0	12	79	329	73	28	21	3	6	0	0	21	0	51	4	3	6	4	.600	0	2	2.39
Martinez,William	Kinston	Cle	A+	20	23	23	1	0	137	568	125	61	47	13	4	3	4	42	2	120	4	0	8	2	.800	0	0	3.09
Masaoka,Onan	Vero Beach	LA	A+	20	28	24	2	3	148.2	612	113	72	64	16	6	4	10	55	1	132	10	1	6	8	.429	1	1	3.87
Mason,Chris	Princeton	TB	R+	23	19	1	0	7	42	174	43	17	17	3	2	1	2	5	0	45	4	0	2	1	.667	0	1	3.64
Mastrolonardo,D.	Bluefield	Bal	R+	23	26	0	0	22	33.1	130	15	5	4	3	0	1	0	12	1	45	1	0	4	0	1.000	0	12	1.08
Matcuk,Steve	Asheville	Col	A	22	28	27	3	1	159.2	674	157	86	79	15	2	5	10	55	1	100	2	1	5	12	.294	0	1	4.45
Mateo,Julio	Mariners	Sea	R	18	13	6	0	4	60	254	45	32	22	1	2	2	8	23	0	54	10	1	3	1	.750	0	1	3.30
Matos,Josue	Mariners	Sea	R	20	14	1	0	5	45.1	190	48	27	21	4	1	1	0	6	0	50	3	4	1	0	1.000	0	1	4.17
	Everett	Sea	A-	20	2	0	0	1	4.1	20	5	2	1	0	0	0	0	2	0	6	1	1	0	0	.000	0	0	2.08
Mattes,Troy	Wst Plm Bch	Mon	A+	22	20	16	2	3	102	441	123	61	56	8	3	5	5	20	0	61	11	1	6	9	.400	2	1	4.94
Mattson,Craig	Lynchburg	Pit	A+	24	4	0	0	3	4.1	20	6	3	3	3	1	0	0	2	0	3	1	0	0	0	.000	0	1	6.23
Mattson,John	Kingsport	NYN	R+	21	6	4	0	1	23.1	98	25	12	12	2	1	0	2	5	0	25	3	0	1	0	1.000	0	0	4.63
Matz,Brian	Cape Fear	Mon	A	23	44	5	1	12	96.1	424	102	54	47	9	5	6	8	41	0	64	13	1	4	6	.400	1	0	4.39
Maurer,David	Clinton	SD	A	23	25	0	0	10	34.1	142	24	15	11	1	2	1	0	15	0	43	3	1	0	4	.000	0	3	2.88
Mayer,Aaron	Lk Elsinore	Ana	A+	23	36	0	0	14	58	282	69	57	47	4	3	5	6	41	1	38	6	0	2	3	.400	0	0	7.29
Mayo,Blake	San Berndno	LA	A+	25	20	0	0	5	29.2	141	36	18	17	0	1	1	1	17	2	29	6	0	1	1	.500	0	0	5.16
Mays,Jarrod	Kinston	Cle	A+	23	20	19	0	0	100.1	435	94	53	46	8	1	1	13	42	0	64	5	0	7	5	.583	0	0	4.13
Mays,Joseph	Wisconsin	Sea	A	22	13	13	1	0	81.2	322	62	20	19	3	1	2	6	23	1	79	1	0	9	3	.750	0	0	2.09
	Lancaster	Sea	A+	22	15	15	1	0	96.1	420	108	55	52	9	2	6	5	34	0	82	2	0	7	4	.636	0	0	4.86
McBride,Jason	Oneonta	NYA	A-	22	2	0	0	0	2.2	15	1	1	0	0	0	0	2	3	0	2	0	0	0	0	.000	0	0	0.00
McBride,Rodney	Ft. Wayne	Min	A	23	31	0	0	11	45.2	232	57	40	32	3	0	1	4	32	0	54	7	1	3	4	.429	0	0	6.31
McCall,Travis	South Bend	Ari	A	20	25	22	0	0	121	537	140	74	52	6	2	9	11	35	0	86	6	1	7	6	.538	0	0	3.87
McCarter,Jason	Quad City	Hou	A	21	5	0	0	2	9.1	50	10	7	5	1	2	1	1	9	0	7	4	0	1	0	1.000	0	0	4.82
	Auburn	Hou	A-	21	16	0	0	5	21.2	113	23	12	9	1	0	4	10	17	0	20	3	0	0	0	.000	0	0	3.74
McClaskey,Tim	Utica	Fla	A-	22	1	0	0	1	5	16	1	0	0	0	0	0	0	0	0	8	0	0	1	0	1.000	0	0	0.00
	Kane County	Fla	A	22	18	2	0	7	37	151	29	18	13	3	1	2	3	8	2	38	3	1	2	1	.667	0	1	3.16
McCleary,Marty	Lowell	Bos	A-	23	13	13	0	0	62.1	275	53	38	26	2	3	3	5	36	1	43	6	2	3	6	.333	0	0	3.75
McClellan,Matth.	Medicne Hat	Tor	R+	21	14	6	0	1	39	192	50	36	30	7	0	3	3	24	0	43	2	0	2	5	.286	0	0	6.92
McClellan,Sean	Dunedin	Tor	A+	25	3	0	0	2	3.1	20	5	4	4	0	0	1	0	5	0	4	0	0	0	0	.000	0	0	10.80
	Hagerstown	Tor	A	25	35	0	0	26	65	271	49	21	12	3	5	3	1	26	1	80	4	0	3	2	.600	0	11	1.66
McClinton,Pat	Frederick	Bal	A+	26	1	0	0	1	0.1	5	1	1	1	0	0	0	1	2	0	0	0	1	0	1	.000	0	0	27.00
McConnell,John	Erie	Pit	A-	22	17	10	0	0	58.2	261	56	38	33	7	1	3	3	24	0	45	6	0	2	2	.500	0	0	5.06
McCormack,And.	Devil Rays	TB	R	24	10	9	0	0	43	192	37	26	22	3	1	2	4	24	0	41	7	0	2	5	.286	0	0	4.60
McCrary,Scott	Mets	NYN	R	24	5	0	0	4	9	36	5	3	0	0	0	0	1	2	0	15	2	1	1	0	1.000	0	2	0.00
	Capital City	NYN	A	24	13	0	0	5	28	104	20	4	3	1	1	1	0	5	1	24	2	0	3	2	.600	0	0	0.96
McCutcheon,Mik.	South Bend	Ari	A	20	31	17	0	6	105.2	464	104	55	40	5	3	5	5	49	1	67	9	2	7	5	.583	0	1	3.41
McDade,Neal	Augusta	Pit	A	22	36	12	0	8	112.1	466	105	42	35	4	3	3	5	24	3	104	5	2	10	4	.714	0	3	2.80
	Lynchburg	Pit	A+	22	3	3	0	0	18.2	77	16	8	6	3	1	0	1	6	0	15	2	0	2	0	1.000	0	0	2.89
McDermott,Ryan	Burlington	Cle	R+	20	8	8	0	0	34.2	168	45	29	25	2	0	1	4	25	0	22	7	0	3	3	.500	0	0	6.49
McDermott,Toby	Princeton	TB	R+	22	17	0	0	6	24	97	16	9	6	3	1	1	0	11	0	23	3	0	0	0	.000	0	0	2.25
McDonald,Matt	Vero Beach	LA	A+	24	57	3	0	3	109	484	93	53	45	9	6	4	2	67	2	123	10	1	8	8	.500	0	0	3.72
McDougal,Mike	New Jersey	StL	A-	23	13	11	2	0	68.2	272	62	24	19	1	3	0	2	9	0	63	1	0	4	4	.500	2	0	2.49
McEntire,Ethan	St. Lucie	NYN	A+	22	3	3	0	0	11.2	54	16	9	8	0	0	1	0	7	0	8	0	0	0	1	.000	0	0	6.17
McFerrin,Chris	Quad City	Hou	A	22	37	0	0	18	56	269	55	42	36	7	1	2	11	49	1	47	10	0	1	3	.250	0	3	5.79
McGlinchy,Kevin	Durham	Atl	A+	21	26	26	0	0	139.2	595	145	78	76	14	2	4	9	39	2	113	4	2	3	7	.300	0	0	4.90
McGuire,Brandon	Butte	Ana	R+	20	17	2	0	5	34	185	55	43	37	5	3	1	5	25	0	20	1	0	3	4	.429	0	0	9.79
McHugh,Mike	Charlotte	Tex	A+	25	18	0	0	10	26	137	32	25	22	4	3	3	3	27	2	23	3	0	0	1	.000	0	0	7.62
McKnight,Tony	Quad City	Hou	A	21	20	20	0	0	115.1	504	116	71	60	7	6	3	5	55	5	92	6	3	4	9	.308	0	0	4.68
McLaughlin,Deni.	Durham	Atl	A+	25	11	0	0	8	9	62	23	20	15	4	0	2	1	11	1	4	3	0	0	1	.000	0	0	15.00
McMullen,Jerry	Sarasota	Bos	A+	24	33	0	0	18	51.2	243	61	33	30	5	2	3	3	28	0	37	6	0	2	4	.333	0	2	5.23
McMullen,Mike	San Jose	SF	A+	24	56	0	0	23	91	377	85	37	27	1	9	4	5	33	3	71	6	0	6	4	.600	0	7	2.67
McNally,Andy	Watertown	Cle	A-	24	23	0	0	18	31.1	127	23	10	10	2	2	0	0	13	1	37	2	0	2	3	.400	0	8	2.87
McNatt,Joshua	Delmarva	Bal	A	20	28	11	0	2	96.2	425	97	48	39	4	2	6	1	45	1	73	4	0	6	2	.750	0	1	3.63
McNeely,Mitch	Vero Beach	LA	A+	24	14	1	0	4	27	122	36	18	16	5	2	1	0	7	0	15	0	3	1	1	.500	0	2	5.33
	San Berndno	LA	A+	24	18	0	0	8	39.1	196	61	36	33	9	3	3	0	20	1	28	3	3	1	3	.250	0	0	7.55
McNeill,Kevin	Pr William	StL	A+	27	55	1	0	14	69	303	66	43	38	3	6	0	2	28	1	58	1	0	2	6	.250	0	1	4.96
Meady,Todd	Lansing	KC	A	21	4	2	0	1	13	64	25	10	7	0	1	1	0	6	0	5	2	0	0	1	.000	0	0	4.85
	Spokane	KC	A-	21	21	4	0	4	65.1	283	68	38	27	4	2	4	3	18	1	39	8	0	2	3	.400	0	0	3.72
Mear,Richard	Jamestown	Det	A-	22	8	0	0	2	9.1	62	6	18	13	0	0	1	1	28	0	7	8	0	1	1	.500	0	0	12.54
Mears,Chris	Everett	Sea	A-	20	12	12	0	0	62.1	283	82	47	37	5	3	1	1	20	0	47	3	1	3	5	.375	0	0	5.34
Meche,Gilbert	Everett	Sea	A-	19	12	12	1	0	74.2	316	75	40	33	7	3	2	3	24	0	62	7	0	3	4	.429	0	0	3.98
	Wisconsin	Sea	A	19	2	2	0	0	12	51	12	5	4	1	0	0	1	4	0	14	2	1	0	2	.000	0	0	3.00

1997 Pitching — Single-A and Rookie Leagues

HOW MUCH HE PITCHED											WHAT HE GAVE UP												THE RESULTS					
Player	Team	Org	Lg	A	G	GS	CG	GF	IP	BFP	H	R	ER	HR	SH	SF	HB	TBB	IBB	SO	WP	Bk	W	L	Pct.	ShO	Sv	ERA
Medina,Eleazar	Cubs	ChN	R	18	8	0	0	1	13	67	17	11	9	0	0	1	0	17	0	2	2	3	0	0	.000	0	0	6.23
Medina,Jaime	Rockies	Col	R	18	10	0	0	4	15	82	19	17	12	0	1	1	2	10	0	8	4	1	1	1	.500	0	0	7.20
Medina,Tomas	Auburn	Hou	A-	23	15	0	0	5	22.1	125	33	24	21	5	0	1	7	21	1	19	8	0	0	0	.000	0	0	8.46
Medrano,Juan	Royals	KC	R	19	15	2	0	9	29.2	132	33	21	15	0	3	2	3	9	0	17	7	1	1	3	.250	0	1	4.55
Meeks,Eric	Athletics	Oak	R	19	15	3	0	2	38.2	185	40	30	23	2	0	1	4	26	0	24	6	0	1	2	.333	0	1	5.35
Mejia,Francisco	Clearwater	Phi	A+	23	52	0	0	26	64	276	68	22	22	1	3	2	1	24	0	54	5	0	6	3	.667	0	7	3.09
Mejia,Luis	Yankees	NYA	R	21	13	0	0	9	23.2	88	8	4	3	0	0	1	3	9	1	31	2	1	1	2	.333	0	2	1.14
Melson,Nathan	Twins	Min	R	19	12	7	0	1	38.1	190	52	35	24	1	0	3	2	22	0	29	15	2	0	4	.000	0	0	5.63
Mendes,Jaime	Piedmont	Phi	A	25	42	2	0	10	85	368	103	48	42	7	8	3	2	20	2	47	2	1	4	5	.444	0	0	4.45
Mendoza,Geroni.	White Sox	ChA	R	20	12	8	0	1	54	241	51	32	22	3	5	2	3	28	0	41	4	0	2	7	.222	0	0	3.67
Mendoza,Hatuey	Diamondback	Ari	R	18	17	0	0	5	29.2	151	29	27	25	0	2	0	8	25	1	24	3	0	1	5	.167	0	0	7.58
Mercado,Hector	Tigers	Det	R	21	15	5	0	1	40.1	181	45	23	17	2	3	2	0	12	0	32	4	0	3	3	.500	0	0	3.79
Mercedes,Alexis	Athletics	Oak	R	21	14	12	0	0	57	266	68	43	35	3	3	2	5	30	0	35	1	0	5	1	.833	0	0	5.53
Mercedes,Carlos	Auburn	Hou	A-	22	28	1	0	10	44.1	193	47	26	22	2	4	0	1	19	5	43	4	1	2	4	.333	0	2	4.47
Merrell,Philip	Billings	Cin	R+	20	14	14	0	0	72.2	313	72	51	35	6	3	1	2	27	1	62	2	0	2	6	.250	0	0	4.33
Merrick,Brett	Kinston	Cle	A+	24	8	0	0	4	8.1	39	7	4	1	0	2	0	1	5	0	3	0	1	0	1	.000	0	1	1.08
	Columbus	Cle	A	24	23	0	0	11	31	144	29	24	17	4	1	1	1	21	1	25	2	0	2	2	.500	0	0	4.94
Merrill,Ethan	Sarasota	Bos	A+	26	12	0	0	6	15.2	82	27	11	11	0	3	1	2	8	2	8	1	1	2	0	1.000	0	1	6.32
Messman,Joey	Auburn	Hou	A-	22	25	0	0	10	28	132	26	13	10	1	3	0	6	21	3	31	8	0	1	2	.333	0	1	3.21
Meyer,Jake	Bristol	ChA	R+	23	17	0	0	15	20	84	15	7	5	3	1	0	0	7	0	25	4	0	1	1	.500	0	5	2.25
Meyers,Mike	Cubs	ChN	R	20	12	2	0	4	38.1	166	34	15	6	2	1	1	2	13	0	45	0	0	3	1	.750	0	3	1.41
	Williamsprt	ChN	A-	20	1	1	0	0	4	15	3	0	0	0	1	0	0	1	0	2	0	0	0	0	.000	0	0	0.00
Michalak,Chris	High Desert	Ari	A+	27	49	0	0	17	85	362	76	36	25	4	3	0	9	31	1	74	6	1	3	7	.300	0	4	2.65
Middlebrook,Jas.	Rancho Cuca	SD	A+	23	6	6	0	0	22.1	105	29	15	10	1	1	3	0	12	1	18	2	1	0	2	.000	0	0	4.03
	Clinton	SD	A	23	14	14	2	0	81.1	353	76	46	36	4	3	1	1	39	0	86	6	5	6	4	.600	1	0	3.98
Mikkola,Shaun	Mets	NYN	R	18	14	4	0	3	38.1	154	25	11	5	0	2	1	4	16	0	23	2	2	5	0	1.000	0	0	1.17
Milburn,Robert	Macon	Atl	A	24	46	0	0	18	70	301	71	29	26	6	2	1	3	23	2	51	2	0	4	1	.800	0	4	3.34
Miles,Chad	Brevard Cty	Fla	A+	25	42	0	0	18	64	291	63	46	32	4	2	1	2	31	4	59	6	0	3	4	.429	0	5	4.50
Miller,Aaron	Elizabethtn	Min	R+	21	23	0	0	7	30	140	25	25	21	4	1	0	5	25	0	43	6	0	2	1	.667	0	0	6.30
Miller,Brian	Piedmont	Phi	A	25	29	7	0	6	74.2	338	91	44	41	10	1	2	4	24	1	63	2	1	1	2	.333	0	1	4.94
Miller,Ernest	Butte	Ana	R+	22	20	2	0	7	39.1	204	53	41	35	1	0	2	2	26	0	39	12	0	1	4	.200	0	1	8.01
Miller,Gregory	Red Sox	Bos	R	18	4	4	0	0	9.2	40	8	6	4	0	0	0	0	6	0	6	0	2	0	2	.000	0	0	3.72
Miller,James	Helena	Mil	R+	22	16	13	1	0	70.2	324	88	56	47	9	2	5	2	24	0	51	3	1	5	7	.417	0	0	5.99
Miller,Justin	Portland	Col	A-	20	14	11	0	1	67.1	288	68	26	16	3	2	2	4	20	0	54	6	0	4	2	.667	0	0	2.14
Miller,Matt	Johnson Cty	StL	R+	24	20	3	0	2	40	200	62	43	35	4	0	1	2	16	2	32	3	1	2	2	.500	0	0	7.88
Miller,Thomas	Red Sox	Bos	R	23	1	0	0	0	1.1	8	2	1	1	0	1	0	0	2	0	3	0	0	0	1	.000	0	0	6.75
	Lowell	Bos	A-	23	24	0	0	9	39	183	38	24	12	2	3	3	3	20	3	42	2	0	1	3	.250	0	1	2.77
Miller,Wade	Quad City	Hou	A	21	10	8	2	1	59	235	45	27	22	7	0	1	0	10	0	50	4	0	5	3	.625	0	0	3.36
	Kissimmee	Hou	A+	21	14	14	4	0	100	395	79	28	20	3	3	5	4	14	1	76	4	1	10	2	.833	1	0	1.80
Minaya,Pedro	Marlins	Fla	R	20	12	6	0	4	38.1	164	30	14	8	0	0	0	6	15	0	39	1	0	3	1	.750	0	0	1.88
Minter,Matt	Watertown	Cle	A-	25	7	0	0	5	7.2	35	6	4	4	0	0	2	1	5	0	12	3	0	0	0	.000	0	0	4.70
	Columbus	Cle	A	25	30	0	0	13	57	242	57	29	27	6	3	3	2	18	0	49	3	0	5	3	.625	0	2	4.26
Miranda,Javier	Butte	Ana	R+	19	18	0	0	10	26.2	144	47	36	21	2	3	2	3	16	1	18	2	0	0	2	.000	0	0	7.09
Miranda,Walter	Brevard Cty	Fla	A+	23	10	9	0	0	34.2	170	45	32	20	2	0	1	2	26	0	15	4	0	2	3	.400	0	0	5.19
Mitchell,Courtney	Piedmont	Phi	A	25	47	0	0	29	78.1	306	60	25	21	3	0	2	1	19	0	68	7	1	7	4	.636	0	3	2.41
Mitchell,Ken	White Sox	ChA	R	24	4	0	0	0	8.2	36	3	0	0	0	0	0	0	6	0	12	2	0	0	0	.000	0	0	0.00
	Winston-Sal	ChA	A+	24	5	0	0	5	6	28	7	3	3	0	0	0	2	2	0	5	2	0	0	0	.000	0	0	4.50
Mitchell,Dean	Savannah	LA	A	24	52	7	1	38	122	499	110	50	39	6	5	3	1	25	1	118	2	1	11	5	.688	0	16	2.88
	San Berndno	LA	A+	24	1	0	0	1	1	4	0	0	0	0	0	0	0	1	0	1	0	0	0	0	.000	0	0	0.00
Mlodik,Kevin	Visalia	Oak	A+	23	35	19	0	3	129	580	164	86	78	17	3	5	5	42	1	91	7	2	8	9	.471	0	0	5.44
Mobley,Kevin	Jamestown	Det	A-	23	18	0	0	9	25.2	115	27	10	9	1	4	2	1	11	1	24	0	0	2	1	.667	0	0	3.16
Molina,Gabe	Delmarva	Bal	A	23	46	0	0	31	91	364	59	24	22	3	6	1	3	32	5	119	7	2	8	6	.571	0	7	2.18
Molina,Primitivo	Red Sox	Bos	R	20	15	0	0	11	19.2	72	12	0	0	0	1	0	1	2	0	22	0	0	2	0	1.000	0	4	0.00
Molta,Salvatore	Martinsvlle	Phi	R+	20	13	0	0	10	17	89	25	18	18	2	1	2	3	13	0	12	7	0	0	2	.000	0	0	9.53
Mondello,Peter	Batavia	Phi	A-	23	27	0	0	13	34	157	32	20	14	5	1	0	3	17	1	41	3	0	0	1	.000	0	0	3.71
Montada,Joaquin	Kingsport	NYN	R+	20	13	11	0	0	60	282	78	55	46	11	2	1	6	22	1	52	5	1	3	2	.600	0	0	6.90
Montanez,Jorge	Red Sox	Bos	R	21	5	0	0	2	5	20	5	2	1	0	1	0	0	2	1	1	0	0	0	1	.000	0	0	1.80
Montemayor,Hu.	Lowell	Bos	A-	20	1	0	0	1	0.2	6	2	1	1	0	1	0	1	1	1	0	0	0	0	1	.000	0	0	13.50
	Red Sox	Bos	R	20	9	0	0	4	19.1	87	29	13	9	1	3	2	0	2	1	19	0	1	1	0	1.000	0	1	4.19
Montero,Agustin	Athletics	Oak	R	20	14	13	0	1	72.2	327	72	38	29	3	0	0	8	31	0	88	9	9	3	2	.600	0	0	3.59
	Sou. Oregon	Oak	A-	20	2	0	0	1	2.2	15	4	2	2	0	0	0	2	3	0	1	0	0	0	0	.000	0	0	6.75
Montero,Francis.	Martinsvlle	Phi	R+	22	14	14	0	0	77	342	79	49	35	4	5	2	3	22	0	47	2	1	3	5	.375	0	0	4.09
Montgomery,Gre.	Peoria	StL	A	23	40	11	0	5	82.1	424	103	89	78	6	1	5	8	69	4	68	27	3	2	8	.200	0	1	8.53
Montgomery,Mat.	Yakima	LA	A-	22	11	9	0	0	55.1	229	48	23	15	3	2	0	1	17	0	38	2	2	2	2	.500	0	0	2.44
	Great Falls	LA	R+	22	4	4	0	0	23	92	24	11	10	1	0	0	0	3	0	6	1	0	1	1	.500	0	0	3.91
Moon,Jared	Yakima	LA	A-	19	11	6	0	0	37.1	168	45	29	24	4	0	3	1	17	0	32	3	0	2	2	.500	0	0	5.79
Moore,Christoph.	Marlins	Fla	R	19	10	9	1	0	54.1	225	39	23	16	1	1	3	2	29	0	40	1	0	3	2	.600	1	0	2.65
Moraga,David	Wst Plm Bch	Mon	A+	22	13	7	0	3	47.2	207	50	27	26	3	1	2	1	18	0	37	6	0	1	4	.200	0	0	4.91
Morales,Johnny	Orioles	Bal	R	21	18	1	0	7	38.1	169	40	21	18	2	2	2	5	12	0	47	7	6	3	4	.429	0	1	4.23
Morel,Jose	Pirates	Pit	R	22	7	0	0	3	15.1	60	11	5	5	2	2	1	0	6	0	10	1	0	2	0	1.000	0	0	2.93
Moreno,Orber	Lansing	KC	A	21	27	25	0	0	138.1	603	150	83	74	15	6	4	8	45	0	128	9	0	4	8	.333	0	0	4.81
Morgan,Eric	Lancaster	Sea	A+	25	24	13	0	3	89.2	413	98	59	54	9	6	3	7	56	2	56	12	0	4	3	.571	0	0	5.42
Morris,Alexander	Kane County	Fla	A	21	19	0	0	5	32	149	39	24	19	3	2	1	1	19	2	22	6	1	4	0	1.000	0	0	5.34
	Brevard Cty	Fla	A+	21	2	0	0	2	3	12	1	1	0	0	0	0	2	0	0	2	0	0	0	0	.000	0	0	0.00
Morrison,Chris	Visalia	Oak	A+	26	48	0	0	21	79.2	366	92	46	34	2	6	4	6	39	4	43	8	0	3	3	.500	0	2	3.84
Morrobel,Juan	Pirates	Pit	R	20	3	0	0	1	8	33	7	1	0	0	0	0	0	2	0	4	0	0	1	0	1.000	0	0	0.00
Morseman,Bob	Delmarva	Bal	A	24	7	0	0	3	13.1	65	13	11	7	2	0	0	0	11	0	18	1	2	0	1	.000	0	0	4.72

1997 Pitching — Single-A and Rookie Leagues

HOW MUCH HE PITCHED											WHAT HE GAVE UP												THE RESULTS					
Player	Team	Org	Lg	A	G	GS	CG	GF	IP	BFP	H	R	ER	HR	SH	SF	HB	TBB	IBB	SO	WP	Bk	W	L	Pct.	ShO	Sv	ERA
	Frederick	Bal	A+	24	38	0	0	23	63.2	303	61	37	34	4	6	2	6	46	3	61	3	0	0	5	.000	0	2	4.81
Mota,Daniel	Greensboro	NYA	A	22	20	0	0	9	29.2	111	17	6	6	1	0	0	0	11	1	30	0	0	2	0	1.000	0	1	1.82
	Oneonta	NYA	A-	22	27	0	0	25	28.1	119	21	8	7	0	1	0	0	16	0	40	0	0	1	0	1.000	0	17	2.22
Mota,Guillermo	Cape Fear	Mon	A	24	25	23	0	0	126	528	135	65	61	8	2	3	4	33	0	112	1	2	5	10	.333	0	0	4.36
Mota,Henry	Charlotte	Tex	A+	20	31	3	0	11	74	330	84	51	43	14	2	2	5	29	2	45	4	0	2	5	.286	0	2	5.23
Moylan,Peter	Twins	Min	R	19	12	7	0	2	40	178	46	21	18	0	0	1	4	10	0	40	3	0	4	2	.667	0	0	4.05
Mudd,Scott	Charlotte	Tex	A+	25	4	0	0	2	3.2	19	5	2	2	0	0	0	0	4	0	3	1	0	0	1	.000	0	0	4.91
Mullen,Scott	Lansing	KC	A	23	16	16	0	0	92.1	391	90	46	38	14	0	3	4	31	0	78	2	1	5	2	.714	0	0	3.70
	Wilmington	KC	A+	23	11	11	0	0	59.1	260	64	35	30	5	1	2	1	26	4	43	5	2	4	4	.500	0	0	4.55
Mundine,John	Twins	Min	R	20	15	0	0	7	32	125	20	7	6	1	2	0	1	9	2	32	1	0	1	1	.500	0	0	1.69
Murphy,Darren	Bluefield	Bal	R+	21	23	1	0	6	38.2	182	48	28	25	8	1	0	3	18	2	42	3	0	1	3	.250	0	0	5.82
Murphy,Sean	Salem	Col	A+	25	15	0	0	5	19.2	93	21	16	10	0	1	3	2	12	0	11	5	0	1	3	.250	0	0	4.58
Murray,Dan	St. Lucie	NYN	A+	24	30	24	4	3	156.1	682	150	75	60	4	5	3	10	55	3	91	13	0	12	10	.545	2	0	3.45
Musachio,John	Hickory	ChA	A	24	11	0	0	5	19.2	82	21	8	8	1	1	0	1	4	0	19	0	0	1	0	1.000	0	1	3.66
Musgrave,Scott	Michigan	Bos	A	24	15	11	0	2	78.2	357	96	59	49	11	4	2	5	17	2	51	3	1	4	5	.444	0	0	5.61
Myers,Rob	Twins	Min	R	22	9	0	0	6	14.1	53	5	2	1	0	0	0	2	5	0	13	0	0	1	1	.500	0	0	0.63
	Elizabethtn	Min	R+	22	3	0	0	0	4.2	35	9	11	8	0	0	0	1	11	1	6	4	1	0	1	.000	0	0	15.43
Myers,Robert	Helena	Mil	R+	21	18	0	0	6	27.2	155	43	42	29	4	2	4	1	24	1	24	6	0	1	3	.250	0	0	9.43
Myers,Taylor	Lansing	KC	A	20	8	2	0	3	23.1	116	29	24	24	10	1	1	4	13	0	19	0	0	1	1	.500	0	1	9.26
	Royals	KC	R	20	11	10	2	1	59.2	248	48	21	16	3	2	1	5	20	0	48	6	0	5	4	.556	2	0	2.41
Myette,Aaron	Bristol	ChA	R+	20	9	8	1	0	47.1	215	39	28	19	9	0	0	7	20	0	50	2	1	4	3	.571	0	0	3.61
	Hickory	ChA	A	20	5	5	0	0	31.2	121	19	6	4	1	1	0	2	11	0	27	2	2	3	1	.750	0	0	1.14
Naff,Todd	Idaho Falls	SD	R+	23	24	0	0	5	38	180	43	31	23	5	0	0	1	25	2	29	6	0	3	3	.500	0	1	5.45
Nakashima,Tony	Vero Beach	LA	A+	20	10	0	0	2	15.2	80	23	19	19	2	0	1	0	11	1	17	2	1	1	0	1.000	0	0	10.91
Narcisse,Tyrone	Rancho Cuca	SD	A+	26	22	0	0	9	34.1	140	21	13	13	3	2	2	2	22	0	38	4	0	2	0	1.000	0	0	3.41
Nash,Damond	Rancho Cuca	SD	A+	22	1	0	0	0	0	3	1	1	1	0	0	0	0	2	0	0	1	0	0	0	.000	0	0	0.00
	Clinton	SD	A	22	4	0	0	1	7	33	5	3	3	0	0	0	2	5	0	6	2	0	1	1	.500	0	0	3.86
	Idaho Falls	SD	R+	22	14	10	0	0	60	279	79	48	44	9	0	1	3	29	0	65	4	0	3	2	.600	0	0	6.60
Nathan,Joe	Salem-Keizr	SF	A-	23	18	5	0	4	62	254	53	22	17	7	4	2	4	26	0	44	2	0	2	1	.667	0	2	2.47
Nation,Joseph	Danville	Atl	R+	19	8	8	0	0	26.1	107	24	11	8	1	0	0	1	5	0	41	1	0	1	2	.333	0	0	2.73
Navarro,Jason	New Jersey	StL	A-	22	10	10	1	0	44.2	211	60	40	34	4	0	1	1	22	0	41	7	3	1	6	.143	0	0	6.85
Neal,Blaine	Marlins	Fla	R	20	10	0	0	5	22.1	102	24	11	9	1	0	0	1	11	0	19	2	0	4	1	.800	0	1	3.63
Needham,Kevin	Chston-WV	Cin	A	23	35	11	0	13	78.2	354	93	58	42	5	4	4	3	28	0	51	8	1	4	3	.571	0	2	4.81
Needle,Chad	Medicne Hat	Tor	R+	19	10	0	0	7	16.2	68	17	6	5	1	1	0	0	5	0	17	1	0	0	1	.000	0	0	2.70
Negrette,Richard	Columbus	Cle	A	22	16	0	0	8	36.1	155	24	23	18	2	2	1	6	16	0	21	5	0	2	1	.667	0	1	4.46
	Watertown	Cle	A-	22	17	0	0	7	39.1	171	25	17	16	0	5	2	3	29	2	30	6	1	2	3	.400	0	1	3.66
Neiman,Josh	Clinton	SD	A	23	5	0	0	2	7.2	44	16	11	11	2	1	1	1	4	1	5	1	0	0	0	.000	0	0	12.91
Nelson,Joseph	Durham	Atl	A+	23	25	24	0	0	124.2	543	114	74	66	17	5	4	12	61	1	99	5	0	10	6	.625	0	0	4.76
Nestor,Joe	Pr William	StL	A+	24	58	0	0	27	76.2	339	77	39	33	10	6	1	3	29	1	63	6	0	3	7	.300	0	3	3.87
Newell,Brett	Eugene	Atl	A-	25	19	0	0	11	34.1	140	17	12	10	1	1	0	1	18	1	46	3	0	2	1	.667	0	4	2.62
Newman,Eric	Rancho Cuca	SD	A+	25	35	15	0	3	123.2	542	104	64	57	12	1	3	7	73	1	141	12	0	13	6	.684	0	0	4.15
Newton,Geronim.	Mariners	Sea	R	24	4	0	0	3	4	12	0	0	0	0	0	0	0	0	0	6	0	0	0	0	.000	0	3	0.00
Nichols,Jamie	Hickory	ChA	A	22	28	27	1	1	158.2	681	161	85	73	12	8	8	6	49	0	112	7	0	12	6	.667	0	0	4.14
Nicholson,John	Asheville	Col	A	20	25	25	0	0	135.2	570	128	70	57	13	8	7	7	36	0	115	4	3	8	9	.471	0	0	3.78
Nickle,Douglas	Boise	Ana	A-	23	17	2	0	7	19.2	96	27	17	14	3	0	2	1	8	1	22	0	0	0	1	.000	0	0	6.41
Nielsen,Thomas	Salem-Keizr	SF	A-	21	7	0	0	4	9.1	42	10	5	5	0	0	0	0	4	1	12	2	1	1	1	.500	0	0	4.82
Niles,Randall	Sou. Oregon	Oak	A-	22	7	4	0	0	22.2	98	14	12	5	0	1	1	4	12	0	15	4	5	0	1	.000	0	0	1.99
	Modesto	Oak	A+	22	7	5	0	0	34.2	148	32	13	10	3	1	0	6	9	0	20	0	0	4	0	1.000	0	0	2.60
Nina,Elvin	Sou. Oregon	Oak	A-	22	18	2	0	8	31	150	36	24	18	4	0	0	2	18	1	26	2	2	1	3	.250	0	1	5.23
Nix,Wayne	Athletics	Oak	R	21	15	4	0	1	32.1	162	32	28	21	2	0	1	2	29	1	32	8	4	1	3	.250	0	0	5.85
Noe,Matt	Everett	Sea	A-	21	23	0	0	7	36.1	170	38	20	11	4	1	1	1	18	1	35	8	0	0	1	.000	0	1	2.72
Noel,Todd	Cubs	ChN	R	19	12	11	0	1	59	245	39	27	13	1	2	1	1	30	0	63	6	1	5	1	.833	0	1	1.98
Nogowski,Brand.	Everett	Sea	A-	22	16	9	0	0	59.2	313	67	67	44	8	5	5	2	57	2	60	7	0	4	5	.444	0	0	6.64
Noriega,Raymun.	Modesto	Oak	A+	24	28	28	0	0	156	698	161	101	70	17	8	2	4	69	1	119	10	3	5	8	.385	0	0	4.04
Norris,Ben	South Bend	Ari	A	20	14	13	0	0	60.1	291	69	44	27	7	2	2	6	31	0	40	2	1	1	8	.111	0	0	4.03
	Lethbridge	Ari	R+	20	14	14	0	0	83.1	373	93	61	45	6	1	3	8	23	0	54	4	0	7	3	.700	0	0	4.86
Norris,Mac	Beloit	Mil	A	22	4	4	0	0	15.2	81	20	18	15	0	0	0	2	13	0	10	2	0	1	1	.500	0	0	8.62
Norris,Stephen	Johnson Cty	StL	R+	22	14	14	0	0	71.2	340	84	64	47	8	0	4	9	42	0	72	7	2	4	7	.364	0	0	5.90
Nunez,Vladimir	High Desert	Ari	A+	23	28	28	1	0	158.1	682	169	102	91	36	1	3	14	40	1	142	10	2	8	5	.615	1	0	5.17
Nussbeck,Mark	Peoria	StL	A	24	27	27	2	0	151.1	683	181	92	77	14	4	8	3	56	3	132	6	4	8	12	.400	2	0	4.58
Nyari,Pete	Clearwater	Phi	A+	26	31	0	0	18	43.1	181	29	20	13	1	2	0	2	21	2	35	3	1	0	4	.000	0	5	2.70
O'Connor,Brian	Augusta	Pit	A	21	25	14	0	3	85.2	385	90	54	42	6	4	1	2	39	1	91	11	0	2	7	.222	0	0	4.41
	Lynchburg	Pit	A+	21	11	0	0	6	13	55	11	5	5	0	0	0	1	6	1	14	3	0	2	1	.667	0	2	3.46
O'Dell,Jacob	Visalia	Oak	A+	24	27	27	1	0	150.2	648	159	86	76	17	4	2	11	47	0	117	10	0	8	5	.615	1	0	4.54
O'Dette,Richard	Red Sox	Bos	R	22	3	0	0	0	8	31	6	3	2	0	0	0	0	1	0	6	0	0	0	1	.000	0	0	2.25
	Lowell	Bos	A-	22	13	10	1	1	59.2	268	64	30	23	1	1	1	0	28	3	61	4	2	5	3	.625	0	0	3.47
O'Quinn,Jimmy	Cedar Rapds	Ana	A	24	14	0	0	7	15.1	71	17	14	14	4	1	1	0	11	1	17	1	0	0	1	.000	0	0	8.22
O'Reilly,John	Beloit	Mil	A	23	36	7	0	16	101.1	433	95	51	41	4	3	2	5	43	0	106	6	2	9	2	.818	0	2	3.64
O'Shaughnessy	Savannah	LA	A	23	27	24	0	1	115.2	509	87	64	57	10	2	1	2	83	0	150	13	1	6	12	.333	0	0	4.44
O'Toole,Ryan	Billings	Cin	R+	22	11	1	0	4	19	84	20	12	5	1	1	1	0	7	0	6	0	1	1	0	1.000	0	1	2.37
	Burlington	Cin	A	22	3	0	0	1	9.1	41	9	4	2	1	0	1	0	3	0	4	0	0	1	1	.500	0	0	1.93
Oakley,Matt	Lakeland	Det	A+	24	27	0	0	8	43.2	211	54	35	29	2	2	3	2	26	1	34	3	0	1	2	.333	0	0	5.98
Obando,Omar	Greensboro	NYA	A	21	45	0	0	23	60	267	61	36	31	5	2	1	4	26	2	41	8	0	5	7	.417	0	7	4.65
Ochsenfeld,Chris	Yakima	LA	A-	21	12	0	0	7	21.2	89	13	6	5	0	1	0	2	13	0	18	3	1	2	0	1.000	0	3	2.08
	San Berndno	LA	A+	21	13	0	0	7	15.1	80	18	13	10	0	1	1	0	14	1	12	4	0	1	1	.500	0	1	5.87
Oiseth,Jon	Idaho Falls	SD	R+	23	18	0	0	2	26.2	113	22	15	13	2	0	1	1	13	2	27	4	0	3	1	.750	0	1	4.39
Ojeda,Erick	Capital City	NYN	A	22	7	0	0	4	14	58	14	10	9	2	3	1	1	4	0	13	1	1	0	2	.000	0	0	5.79

1997 Pitching — Single-A and Rookie Leagues

HOW MUCH HE PITCHED											WHAT HE GAVE UP												THE RESULTS					
Player	Team	Org	Lg	A	G	GS	CG	GF	IP	BFP	H	R	ER	HR	SH	SF	HB	TBB	IBB	SO	WP	Bk	W	L	Pct.	ShO	Sv	ERA
	Augusta	Pit	A	22	37	0	0	14	61	260	63	36	31	2	3	2	2	16	5	53	5	0	3	6	.333	0	1	4.57
Oleksik,George	High Desert	Ari	A+	24	17	0	0	3	24	128	32	28	23	3	1	0	3	22	0	13	1	0	2	2	.500	0	0	8.63
	South Bend	Ari	A	24	24	0	0	6	50	223	52	26	14	3	2	4	2	29	1	44	3	0	3	2	.600	0	1	2.52
Olivier,Rich	Greensboro	NYA	A	23	35	13	0	6	106.2	471	111	61	49	8	4	2	8	51	1	79	6	0	8	5	.615	0	2	4.13
Olivo,Gary	Salem-Keizr	SF	A-	24	3	0	0	3	3	21	4	11	8	2	1	0	1	6	0	3	0	0	0	0	.000	0	0	24.00
Olson,Phil	St. Lucie	NYN	A+	24	47	0	0	16	71	307	74	32	26	4	4	3	7	26	4	57	10	0	3	3	.500	0	1	3.30
Olszewski,Timot.	Delmarva	Bal	A	24	3	0	0	0	5.2	21	4	3	2	1	0	0	0	0	0	7	0	0	0	0	.000	0	0	3.18
	Frederick	Bal	A+	24	34	0	0	7	64.2	293	75	48	39	14	2	4	4	29	2	41	2	0	3	1	.750	0	1	5.43
Onley,Shawn	Durham	Atl	A+	23	27	27	0	0	133.2	614	158	86	73	11	2	7	4	59	5	112	6	1	5	11	.313	0	0	4.92
Onofrei,Tim	Peoria	StL	A	23	42	9	0	4	98	442	111	66	52	6	4	5	5	45	1	69	4	0	5	5	.500	0	0	4.78
Ontiveros,Steve	Lk Elsinore	Ana	A+	37	1	1	0	0	0.1	2	0	1	1	0	0	0	0	1	0	0	0	0	0	1	.000	0	0	27.00
Opipari,Mario	Ft. Wayne	Min	A	23	53	2	0	27	70.2	307	71	45	27	2	5	3	3	24	3	61	7	1	6	7	.462	0	8	3.44
Orta,Juan	Expos	Mon	R	20	19	0	0	16	29	118	27	12	10	0	1	2	2	7	0	12	1	1	0	4	.000	0	4	3.10
	Wst Plm Bch	Mon	A+	20	1	0	0	1	0.2	4	2	0	0	0	0	1	0	0	0	0	0	0	0	0	.000	0	0	0.00
Ortega,Franklin	Johnson Cty	StL	R+	24	18	7	1	1	49.1	241	62	46	40	6	1	3	2	39	1	46	2	4	3	4	.429	0	0	7.30
Ortega,Pablo	Chston-SC	TB	A	21	29	29	3	0	188.2	778	173	87	60	10	7	6	10	30	0	142	4	1	12	10	.545	0	0	2.86
Ortiz,Ramon	Cedar Rapds	Ana	A	22	27	27	8	0	181	740	156	78	72	22	2	1	7	53	0	225	14	5	11	10	.524	4	0	3.58
Osting,Jimmy	Macon	Atl	A	21	15	15	0	0	57.2	251	54	28	21	3	1	0	2	29	0	62	5	0	2	3	.400	0	0	3.28
Oswalt,Roy	Astros	Hou	R	20	5	5	0	0	28.1	117	25	7	2	2	0	0	0	7	0	28	0	0	1	1	.500	0	0	0.64
	Auburn	Hou	A-	20	9	9	1	0	51.2	220	50	29	26	1	0	1	6	15	1	44	3	1	2	4	.333	1	0	4.53
Ovalle,Bonelly	Charlotte	Tex	A+	19	14	0	0	7	23	108	26	20	15	3	1	1	1	15	0	16	5	0	2	2	.500	0	2	5.87
	Pulaski	Tex	R+	19	26	0	0	17	33	149	27	23	18	4	0	1	3	15	0	39	4	0	3	4	.429	0	1	4.91
Pacheco,Delvis	Macon	Atl	A	20	35	4	0	7	80	335	77	39	36	8	1	2	3	23	0	74	1	0	1	3	.250	0	2	4.05
Padilla,Charly	Butte	Ana	R+	19	20	0	0	6	34	155	44	31	25	2	1	1	1	12	0	24	8	1	0	2	.000	0	0	6.62
Padua,Geraldo	Yankees	NYA	R	21	11	8	1	1	61.2	237	46	24	20	5	2	0	1	8	0	36	5	1	8	0	1.000	1	0	2.92
Pageler,Michael	Bakersfield	SF	A+	22	61	0	0	53	65.1	291	69	39	34	8	2	1	5	26	3	68	4	0	2	5	.286	0	29	4.68
Paige,Carey	Dunedin	Tor	A+	24	12	9	0	2	44.2	191	36	21	15	3	2	2	0	22	1	39	1	0	1	3	.250	0	1	3.02
Pailthorpe,Rob	Brevard Cty	Fla	A+	25	35	3	0	13	74	327	88	50	40	6	2	2	2	24	1	53	4	1	6	4	.600	0	1	4.86
Palki,Jeromy	Wisconsin	Sea	A	22	44	0	0	35	64.2	255	50	22	20	2	5	2	2	18	2	75	2	0	9	3	.750	0	8	2.78
Palma,Ricardo	Williamsprt	ChN	A-	18	14	14	1	0	77.2	336	77	36	30	6	1	3	2	36	1	47	2	5	4	7	.364	0	0	3.48
Paluk,Brian	Savannah	LA	A	22	27	20	1	0	118.1	527	141	82	76	10	7	1	9	35	0	61	11	0	3	8	.273	1	0	5.78
Paluk,Jeff	San Berndno	LA	A+	25	28	0	0	10	44	218	63	39	37	6	0	4	1	25	1	38	6	0	1	3	.250	0	0	7.57
Paraqueima,Jes.	Yankees	NYA	R	20	3	0	0	0	5.1	32	14	11	5	1	1	1	1	0	0	2	1	0	0	1	.000	0	0	8.44
Paredes,Carlos	Wilmington	KC	A+	22	23	21	0	0	112	511	130	90	77	10	3	3	6	49	2	93	7	1	5	9	.357	0	0	6.19
	Lansing	KC	A	22	5	0	0	3	7	36	8	7	7	0	0	0	1	8	0	9	3	0	0	1	.000	0	0	9.00
Paredes,Roberto	Beloit	Mil	A	24	46	0	0	44	50.1	225	36	19	16	2	2	4	4	33	2	49	5	0	5	4	.556	0	15	2.86
Paredes,Vladimir	Diamondback	Ari	R	20	12	0	0	5	16.2	69	18	10	7	0	0	3	0	7	0	12	0	0	2	0	1.000	0	0	3.78
Parker,Beau	Yakima	LA	A-	19	15	12	0	1	51	252	63	59	53	4	3	3	4	32	1	44	10	4	0	8	.000	0	0	9.35
Parker,Brandon	Everett	Sea	A-	22	2	1	0	0	3	16	7	3	3	1	0	0	0	0	0	5	1	2	0	0	.000	0	0	9.00
Parker,Christian	Cape Fear	Mon	A	22	25	25	0	0	153	640	146	72	53	5	9	6	7	49	0	106	9	2	11	10	.524	0	0	3.12
	Wst Plm Bch	Mon	A+	22	3	3	0	0	19	81	22	7	7	0	0	0	0	5	0	10	2	0	0	1	.000	0	0	3.32
Parker,Eric	Lowell	Bos	A-	24	23	0	0	11	41.2	180	32	20	15	3	4	1	1	23	0	41	6	0	3	0	1.000	0	1	3.24
Parkerson,Micha.	Pirates	Pit	R	19	14	0	0	9	27.1	124	27	15	13	1	5	3	4	10	0	25	7	3	2	3	.400	0	3	4.28
Paronto,Chad	Delmarva	Bal	A	22	28	23	0	2	127.1	569	133	95	67	9	5	5	1	56	1	93	6	0	6	9	.400	0	0	4.74
Parotte,Frisco	Greensboro	NYA	A	22	18	0	0	11	38.2	174	48	27	18	6	0	3	0	14	2	28	5	0	1	1	.500	0	2	4.19
	Daytona	ChN	A+	22	5	0	0	5	5.1	20	1	0	0	0	0	1	0	4	1	4	2	0	0	0	.000	0	0	0.00
Partenheimer,Bri.	Lowell	Bos	A-	23	5	0	0	3	13.1	51	9	1	1	0	1	0	0	1	0	11	0	0	2	1	.667	0	1	0.68
	Michigan	Bos	A	23	17	0	0	4	21.2	104	32	16	16	1	0	2	3	9	3	16	4	0	1	1	.500	0	0	6.65
Pascarella,Josh.	Astros	Hou	R	21	10	6	1	2	42.1	178	37	19	12	3	1	2	3	15	0	33	5	0	2	2	.500	0	1	2.55
	Auburn	Hou	A-	21	1	1	0	0	6	27	8	5	2	1	0	0	2	1	0	2	0	0	0	0	.000	0	0	3.00
Pasqualicchio,Mi.	Stockton	Mil	A+	23	17	15	1	1	85.1	389	93	67	61	10	4	3	7	44	0	58	12	3	1	10	.091	0	1	6.43
Passini,Brian	Beloit	Mil	A	23	19	19	1	0	123	505	114	48	44	14	2	1	4	35	0	116	3	3	9	5	.643	0	0	3.22
	Stockton	Mil	A+	23	8	8	1	0	45.1	185	40	28	24	7	3	1	3	21	0	34	1	0	1	5	.167	0	0	4.76
Patino,Leonardo	Lakeland	Det	A+	24	40	3	0	23	72	289	61	25	21	3	4	2	0	20	0	75	3	3	6	4	.600	0	8	2.63
Patterson,John	South Bend	Ari	A	20	18	18	0	0	78	327	63	32	28	3	1	2	5	34	0	95	8	0	1	9	.100	0	0	3.23
Paulino,Jose	Visalia	Oak	A+	21	39	0	0	7	83.1	363	89	48	42	7	1	2	1	32	1	67	6	0	3	2	.600	0	2	4.54
Payne,Tony	Kingsport	NYN	R+	20	10	0	0	2	25.2	120	31	17	15	3	4	0	4	14	0	28	2	0	3	0	1.000	0	0	5.26
Pearsall,J.J.	San Berndno	LA	A+	24	31	28	0	1	160.2	696	145	91	81	12	4	4	8	93	0	112	9	2	14	11	.560	0	0	4.54
Pederson,Justin	Spokane	KC	A-	23	15	13	0	0	65.1	280	61	34	25	4	0	2	4	24	0	84	2	2	5	3	.625	0	0	3.44
Peguero,Americo	Delmarva	Bal	A	21	27	26	1	0	142.1	631	152	97	77	14	2	6	8	53	1	133	7	2	11	10	.524	0	0	4.87
Peguero,Darwin	Astros	Hou	R	19	9	8	0	0	32.1	155	30	26	20	1	0	0	4	23	0	36	6	1	0	4	.000	0	0	5.57
Peguero,Radha.	Devil Rays	TB	R	20	3	2	0	0	11.1	55	19	11	11	2	1	0	1	3	0	9	0	3	1	1	.500	0	0	8.74
Pelton,Brad	Watertown	Cle	A-	23	9	9	0	0	47.2	211	54	31	27	2	0	0	0	18	1	29	3	1	1	5	.167	0	0	5.10
Pena,Alex	High Desert	Ari	A+	25	33	3	0	7	69.1	310	80	56	50	15	1	2	3	30	0	39	6	1	2	1	.667	0	0	6.49
Pena,Jesus	Hickory	ChA	A	23	43	0	0	32	65	263	55	24	16	3	4	3	0	19	1	57	3	0	5	3	.625	0	8	2.22
Pena,Juan	Athletics	Oak	R	19	14	13	0	0	65	290	54	38	21	0	5	0	2	33	0	67	5	5	6	2	.750	0	0	2.91
Penny,Brad	South Bend	Ari	A	20	25	25	0	0	118.2	489	91	44	36	4	5	0	4	43	2	116	10	2	10	5	.667	0	0	2.73
Penny,Tony	Lansing	KC	A	22	22	2	0	6	38	179	46	30	22	8	3	0	0	15	1	25	5	1	4	1	.800	0	0	5.21
Perez,Elvis	White Sox	ChA	R	20	12	8	1	1	58	281	57	41	27	0	3	1	5	44	0	50	2	5	3	7	.300	0	0	4.19
Perez,Juan	Visalia	Oak	A+	25	53	0	0	25	64.2	266	47	30	20	6	2	6	1	24	4	66	7	1	3	6	.333	0	8	2.78
Perez,Julio	Expos	Mon	R	19	10	9	0	1	50	205	38	18	16	0	1	2	4	13	0	38	1	0	3	2	.600	0	0	2.88
	Vermont	Mon	A-	19	3	1	0	0	6.1	35	12	8	4	1	0	0	0	2	0	5	1	0	0	1	.000	0	0	5.68
Perez,Norberto	Bluefield	Bal	R+	20	10	10	0	0	54.2	231	52	29	21	5	0	2	2	16	0	58	5	1	3	5	.375	0	0	3.46
Perez,Odaliz	Macon	Atl	A	20	36	0	0	12	87.1	358	67	31	16	4	4	1	5	27	1	100	3	0	4	5	.444	0	5	1.65
Perez,Pablo	Elizabethtn	Min	R+	24	17	10	0	3	79.1	327	79	37	31	10	3	1	1	12	0	69	4	0	10	0	1.000	0	0	3.52
Perez,Sam	Burlington	Cle	R+	21	16	1	0	9	22.2	100	26	19	15	3	1	0	1	10	0	14	2	1	1	1	.500	0	0	5.96
Perozo,Felix	Butte	Ana	R+	24	14	14	2	0	79	374	106	63	51	5	2	2	8	35	1	54	7	2	1	6	.143	0	0	5.81

1997 Pitching — Single-A and Rookie Leagues

HOW MUCH HE PITCHED											WHAT HE GAVE UP												THE RESULTS					
Player	Team	Org	Lg	A	G	GS	CG	GF	IP	BFP	H	R	ER	HR	SH	SF	HB	TBB	IBB	SO	WP	Bk	W	L	Pct.	ShO	Sv	ERA
Perry,Tim	Clinton	SD	A	20	6	0	0	3	8.1	47	9	7	4	0	1	1	1	10	0	13	2	1	1	0	1.000	0	0	4.32
	Idaho Falls	SD	R+	20	15	14	1	0	78.1	356	84	52	47	6	1	1	7	38	1	84	6	0	5	3	.625	1	0	5.40
Persails,Mark	Jamestown	Det	A-	22	15	14	2	1	84.2	384	103	64	54	5	1	3	3	33	1	56	13	0	3	7	.300	0	0	5.74
Petcka,Joe	Visalia	Oak	A+	27	4	0	0	0	2.2	22	8	8	7	1	1	0	0	6	0	1	1	0	0	1	.000	0	0	23.63
Peters,Don	South Bend	Ari	A	28	13	0	0	5	15.1	65	19	7	5	0	1	0	1	4	0	8	1	0	0	2	.000	0	0	2.93
	High Desert	Ari	A+	28	21	0	0	15	33.1	134	20	10	6	2	1	0	1	13	0	25	3	0	1	2	.333	0	7	1.62
Peterson,Jay	Burlington	Cin	A	22	26	26	0	0	144.2	646	139	88	72	12	3	2	4	79	0	112	10	0	14	6	.700	0	0	4.48
Peterson,Kyle	Ogden	Mil	R+	22	3	3	0	0	10.1	40	5	2	1	1	0	0	1	4	0	11	0	0	0	0	.000	0	0	0.87
Petique,Marino	Devil Rays	TB	R	22	22	0	0	13	39	180	48	21	18	2	1	3	5	11	0	38	2	0	2	2	.500	0	3	4.15
Petrosian,Ara	Portland	Col	A-	23	29	0	0	21	45	190	42	18	12	1	0	1	3	14	0	37	3	1	3	1	.750	0	13	2.40
Phelps,Travis	Princeton	TB	R+	20	14	13	1	0	62.2	279	73	42	34	4	3	1	2	23	0	60	4	1	4	3	.571	0	0	4.88
Phillips,Ben	Tampa	NYA	A+	22	25	25	0	0	136.2	608	135	83	67	9	4	5	4	79	0	97	11	1	8	11	.421	0	0	4.41
Phillips,Jon	Burlington	Cin	A	23	37	1	0	14	70.2	306	63	33	31	3	3	5	6	33	1	66	2	0	4	5	.444	0	0	3.95
Phillips,Marc	Wilmington	KC	A+	26	40	0	0	21	60.2	276	72	39	35	5	4	3	3	23	3	44	8	0	0	3	.000	0	1	5.19
Phillips,Randy	Braves	Atl	R	21	4	0	0	3	4	19	6	3	2	0	0	1	0	2	0	4	0	1	0	1	.000	0	0	4.50
Phipps,Jeff	Bluefield	Bal	R+	23	4	2	0	1	10	50	12	13	12	2	0	2	1	8	0	6	1	0	0	2	.000	0	0	10.80
Pidgeon,Matt	Marlins	Fla	R	21	16	0	0	13	25.2	126	25	21	13	1	2	0	5	15	0	21	1	0	2	1	.667	0	4	4.56
Piersoll,Christop.	Cubs	ChN	R	20	14	0	0	3	31.2	130	21	11	8	0	0	0	2	9	0	35	2	4	4	0	1.000	0	2	2.27
Pincavitch,Kevin	San Berndno	LA	A+	27	28	27	0	1	135.1	665	135	128	102	18	3	6	19	112	0	130	27	1	6	9	.400	0	0	6.78
Pineiro,Joel	Mariners	Sea	R	19	1	0	0	0	3	11	1	0	0	0	0	0	1	0	0	4	0	0	1	0	1.000	0	0	0.00
	Everett	Sea	A-	19	18	6	0	9	49	223	54	33	29	2	0	0	3	18	1	59	3	2	4	2	.667	0	2	5.33
Pitt,Jye	Williamsprt	ChN	A-	20	4	0	0	0	6.1	37	9	11	3	1	0	0	0	5	0	9	0	0	0	1	.000	0	0	4.26
	Cubs	ChN	R	20	13	1	0	1	23.2	105	14	9	7	1	0	0	1	17	0	28	2	0	3	0	1.000	0	1	2.66
Plummer,Raymo.	Vermont	Mon	A-	22	28	0	0	4	39.1	179	39	28	23	5	3	4	3	17	0	28	3	1	4	3	.571	0	0	5.26
Pohl,Jeff	Salem-Keizr	SF	A-	22	18	8	0	3	71.2	329	88	51	37	8	3	3	6	20	0	47	6	2	5	4	.556	0	0	4.65
Polanco,Elvis	Rockford	ChN	A	20	16	5	0	4	45	235	66	53	43	4	1	5	1	36	2	34	7	0	2	5	.286	0	0	8.60
	Williamsprt	ChN	A-	20	15	15	0	0	83.2	364	71	45	30	5	4	1	9	46	0	64	6	1	2	5	.286	0	0	3.23
Poland,Robert	Pulaski	Tex	R+	23	13	13	3	0	85.1	333	57	29	19	9	2	0	3	18	0	106	4	3	7	3	.700	2	0	2.00
Porter,Aaron	Butte	Ana	R+	23	13	4	0	3	37.1	181	53	34	31	3	1	2	7	15	0	25	12	1	2	2	.500	0	0	7.47
Porter,Bobby	Braves	Atl	R	21	7	0	0	1	15.2	94	23	20	16	1	0	0	0	15	0	20	4	3	0	1	.000	0	0	9.19
Poupart,Melvin	Pittsfield	NYN	A-	23	8	1	0	0	10	56	10	8	3	2	0	0	3	14	0	9	2	1	0	0	.000	0	0	2.70
Powalski,Richard	Cubs	ChN	R	20	6	0	0	0	11.1	51	11	4	2	0	0	0	0	7	0	13	0	0	0	0	.000	0	0	1.59
Powell,Jeremy	Wst Plm Bch	Mon	A+	22	26	26	1	0	155	675	162	75	52	3	9	5	12	62	0	121	12	2	9	10	.474	0	0	3.02
Powell,Brian	Lakeland	Det	A+	24	27	27	8	0	183.1	732	153	70	51	9	4	5	6	35	2	122	5	0	13	9	.591	2	0	2.50
Pozo,Jay	Ogden	Mil	R+	22	2	0	0	1	3	19	7	7	7	1	0	2	0	3	0	2	1	0	0	0	.000	0	0	21.00
Prater,Andrew	Augusta	Pit	A	20	6	3	0	1	12.1	64	21	16	15	3	0	0	1	6	0	9	2	0	0	0	.000	0	0	10.95
	Erie	Pit	A-	20	15	14	0	0	73.2	320	82	37	36	6	2	2	7	26	0	40	4	0	3	2	.600	0	0	4.40
Precinal,Huilbert.	Padres	SD	R	20	13	0	0	2	15	105	27	37	35	1	0	3	2	34	0	11	4	2	0	2	.000	0	0	21.00
Prempas,Lyle	Michigan	Bos	A	23	13	1	0	4	17.1	98	27	17	15	2	3	0	3	20	2	15	5	0	2	1	.667	0	0	7.79
	Lowell	Bos	A-	23	3	0	0	2	3.1	15	1	4	4	1	0	0	0	4	0	2	1	0	0	0	.000	0	0	10.80
Presley,Kirk	Capital City	NYN	A	23	2	0	0	0	3.1	15	5	4	4	0	0	1	0	0	0	5	0	0	0	1	.000	0	0	10.80
Price,Chris	Portland	Col	A-	23	26	0	0	18	32.2	146	41	25	22	4	0	1	2	5	0	22	1	0	3	1	.750	0	1	6.06
Price,Ryan	Rockies	Col	R	20	14	14	0	0	77	338	69	49	30	2	1	2	5	28	0	98	10	4	2	7	.222	0	0	3.51
Price,Thomas	Devil Rays	TB	R	19	15	4	0	2	39	167	31	16	12	0	1	2	3	17	0	29	3	3	3	3	.500	0	0	2.77
Priebe,Kevin	Helena	Mil	R+	23	19	0	0	12	28	115	24	7	5	0	2	0	0	9	0	25	0	0	2	1	.667	0	6	1.61
Prouty,Scott	Mariners	Sea	R	19	3	0	0	0	5	35	11	10	10	1	0	0	1	9	0	3	2	0	0	1	.000	0	0	18.00
Pruett,Matt	Princeton	TB	R+	23	24	0	0	19	24.2	111	26	19	12	1	1	1	1	10	1	22	2	0	3	2	.600	0	4	4.38
Puffer,Brandon	Boise	Ana	A-	22	6	0	0	2	15.1	63	10	5	4	0	0	1	1	2	0	15	1	0	0	0	.000	0	1	2.35
	Cedar Rapds	Ana	A	22	10	0	0	2	17.1	66	8	6	5	0	0	0	0	10	0	11	3	1	0	0	.000	0	0	2.60
Pugmire,Robert	Burlington	Cle	R+	19	14	14	0	0	66.2	302	72	42	29	4	3	4	4	29	0	62	7	2	1	2	.333	0	0	3.92
Pujals,Denis	St. Pete	TB	A+	25	24	24	2	0	140.1	588	156	74	69	14	6	8	8	27	1	69	1	0	9	4	.692	1	0	4.43
Pumphrey,Kenny	Capital City	NYN	A	21	27	27	3	0	165.2	708	137	70	57	11	7	3	20	72	0	133	11	1	12	6	.667	2	0	3.10
Puorto,Jamie	Lethbridge	Ari	R+	23	20	6	0	4	59.1	236	44	26	16	5	0	1	3	9	0	58	0	0	4	2	.667	0	2	2.43
Putnicki,Billy	Utica	Fla	A-	24	21	0	0	13	43.2	184	44	17	12	3	1	2	3	10	1	33	2	1	3	4	.429	0	4	2.47
Pyrtle,Joe	Pittsfield	NYN	A-	24	23	0	0	9	36	137	13	7	3	0	1	0	3	8	0	44	3	0	3	2	.600	0	4	0.75
Queen,Mike	Pittsfield	NYN	A-	20	13	13	1	0	75	326	86	33	27	3	3	0	2	13	0	63	3	3	5	4	.556	1	0	3.24
Quevedo,Ruben	Danville	Atl	R+	19	13	11	0	0	68.1	286	46	37	27	6	3	5	4	27	0	78	3	1	1	5	.167	0	0	3.56
Quezada,Edward	Cape Fear	Mon	A	23	30	19	0	5	141.1	589	143	73	67	12	1	1	11	31	0	87	4	0	8	6	.571	0	2	4.27
Quigley,Donald	Spokane	KC	A-	23	22	1	0	6	45	212	56	35	27	5	2	0	0	21	0	21	2	1	4	2	.667	0	0	5.40
Quintal,Craig	W Michigan	Det	A	23	23	23	3	0	156.1	634	133	48	34	3	4	6	13	31	0	88	2	0	11	6	.647	2	0	1.96
Quintana,Urbano	Batavia	Phi	A-	23	6	0	0	2	8.1	36	9	5	2	0	0	0	1	1	0	5	0	0	1	0	1.000	0	0	2.16
	Piedmont	Phi	A	23	3	0	0	2	6.1	34	12	13	13	2	0	2	1	3	0	2	1	0	0	0	.000	0	0	18.47
Quintero,Jose	Rangers	Tex	R	18	12	9	0	1	59.1	245	49	29	24	1	1	1	2	26	0	45	1	2	4	4	.500	0	1	3.64
Quiros,Miguel	Pirates	Pit	R	21	13	3	0	7	37	172	42	20	15	0	3	1	6	14	0	24	6	2	2	4	.333	0	0	3.65
Radlosky,Rob	Ft. Myers	Min	A+	24	23	22	3	1	128.1	510	87	42	37	10	5	4	5	37	0	109	2	0	9	5	.643	1	0	2.59
Rahilly,Michael	Expos	Mon	R	21	12	0	0	4	28.1	119	25	11	10	0	1	2	3	7	0	19	3	0	4	0	1.000	0	2	3.18
	Vermont	Mon	A-	21	9	0	0	5	15.2	60	9	4	4	1	0	0	0	4	0	18	2	1	2	0	1.000	0	1	2.30
Raino,Bryan	Pirates	Pit	R	24	1	0	0	0	0.2	6	3	3	3	0	0	0	0	1	0	2	0	0	0	0	.000	0	0	40.50
Rama,Shelby	St. Pete	TB	A+	26	1	0	0	0	1	5	1	2	2	0	0	0	0	1	0	1	0	0	0	0	.000	0	0	18.00
Ramagli,Matt	Delmarva	Bal	A	23	4	0	0	0	8	40	13	6	5	1	1	0	1	5	0	6	0	0	1	1	.500	0	0	5.63
Ramirez,Horacio	Braves	Atl	R	18	11	8	0	2	44	175	30	13	11	1	0	1	0	18	0	61	4	0	3	3	.500	0	0	2.25
Ramirez,Jose	Jamestown	Det	A-	22	15	15	1	0	94.2	398	84	49	41	4	4	4	4	38	0	75	5	2	3	4	.429	0	0	3.90
Ramos,Fernando	Martinsvlle	Phi	R+	22	24	0	0	21	26.1	106	13	8	6	0	2	0	1	12	3	25	1	0	2	3	.400	0	9	2.05
Ramsay,Robert	Sarasota	Bos	A+	24	23	22	1	0	135.2	603	134	90	72	16	1	3	5	63	0	115	7	0	9	9	.500	0	0	4.78
Randall,Scott	Salem	Col	A+	22	27	26	2	1	176	763	167	93	75	8	8	6	11	66	3	128	14	0	9	10	.474	1	0	3.84
Randolph,Steph.	Tampa	NYA	A+	24	34	13	1	6	95.1	417	74	55	41	8	7	3	3	63	5	108	4	1	4	7	.364	0	1	3.87
Rangel,Julio	Greensboro	NYA	A	22	26	26	4	0	163.2	681	147	80	65	17	7	5	6	49	0	122	9	5	12	9	.571	1	0	3.57

1997 Pitching — Single-A and Rookie Leagues

HOW MUCH HE PITCHED											WHAT HE GAVE UP												THE RESULTS					
Player	Team	Org	Lg	A	G	GS	CG	GF	IP	BFP	H	R	ER	HR	SH	SF	HB	TBB	IBB	SO	WP	Bk	W	L	Pct.	ShO	Sv	ERA
Ratliff,Craig	Orioles	Bal	R	20	12	12	0	0	59	260	60	26	18	2	2	3	0	32	0	50	10	3	2	5	.286	0	0	2.75
Rawls,Mike	Yakima	LA	A-	23	22	2	0	9	38	176	38	27	22	4	2	4	3	28	2	27	6	1	0	2	.000	0	2	5.21
Rayborn,Kenny	Lowell	Bos	A-	23	11	7	0	1	46	197	39	18	14	0	1	2	6	15	0	35	8	0	2	2	.500	0	1	2.74
Reames,Jim	Peoria	StL	A	23	27	24	2	1	133.1	599	132	77	59	6	9	6	5	86	3	83	12	0	6	9	.400	1	0	3.98
Reed,Aaron	Tigers	Det	R	20	13	0	0	5	23.2	98	18	7	7	2	0	0	1	6	1	24	3	0	2	2	.500	0	0	2.66
Reed,Daniel	Frederick	Bal	A+	23	28	27	2	0	173.1	772	189	104	81	14	4	3	1	75	2	108	2	0	10	10	.500	0	0	4.21
Reed,Steve	Peoria	StL	A	22	38	6	0	7	75.2	349	107	56	50	7	4	1	5	16	0	64	4	2	4	3	.571	0	0	5.95
	Pr William	StL	A+	22	7	7	0	0	39.2	176	45	24	19	6	0	1	0	12	0	25	2	2	2	2	.500	0	0	4.31
Regalado,Frank	Devil Rays	TB	R	21	18	1	0	10	30.2	132	31	15	6	0	1	1	0	11	0	31	4	0	2	3	.400	0	3	1.76
	Hudson Vall	Fla	A-	21	5	0	0	5	4.1	16	5	1	1	0	0	0	0	0	0	3	0	0	0	0	.000	0	0	2.08
Regalado,Maxi.	Great Falls	LA	R+	25	9	6	0	0	36.2	158	27	12	8	0	1	1	2	21	0	24	1	0	2	1	.667	0	0	1.96
Reichert,Dan	Spokane	KC	A-	21	9	9	0	0	38	178	40	25	12	2	0	2	3	16	0	39	2	2	3	4	.429	0	0	2.84
Reichow,Bob	Columbus	Cle	A	24	20	2	0	4	61	254	54	32	23	4	1	2	4	11	5	50	5	0	3	2	.600	0	2	3.39
Reimers,Tom	Bristol	ChA	R+	23	12	4	0	1	42.1	212	47	35	30	3	5	2	4	28	0	47	18	0	3	2	.600	0	0	6.38
Reith,Brian	Yankees	NYA	R	20	12	11	1	0	63	270	70	28	20	1	2	2	3	14	0	40	8	0	4	2	.667	0	0	2.86
Reitsma,Christo.	Michigan	Bos	A	20	9	9	0	0	49.2	217	57	23	16	4	0	2	2	13	0	41	3	0	4	1	.800	0	0	2.90
Remington,Jake	Rancho Cuca	SD	A+	22	6	0	0	2	9.2	43	12	9	8	1	0	0	0	3	1	9	2	0	2	1	.667	0	0	7.45
Reyes,Arquimed.	Martinsvlle	Phi	R+	19	20	0	0	7	39	170	32	17	10	3	1	2	1	15	1	39	8	0	4	1	.800	0	0	2.31
Reyes,Eddy	Hudson Vall	TB	A-	22	31	0	0	29	32.2	144	24	12	10	1	2	0	4	18	0	29	0	5	0	2	.000	0	14	2.76
Reyes,Natanahel	Great Falls	LA	R+	19	24	0	0	22	28.2	120	26	9	8	1	1	0	0	15	1	30	2	0	3	3	.500	0	8	2.51
Reynolds,Christ.	Princeton	TB	R+	22	12	0	0	3	19.2	88	21	13	12	2	0	2	0	6	0	18	4	0	1	0	1.000	0	0	5.49
	Devil Rays	TB	R	22	8	0	0	5	14.1	61	12	9	8	2	2	1	0	4	1	16	1	1	0	1	.000	0	2	5.02
Rhodes,Joey	Frederick	Bal	A+	23	28	22	0	2	117.1	530	130	86	71	16	8	7	4	61	3	75	5	1	7	11	.389	0	0	5.45
Ricabal,Dan	Vero Beach	LA	A+	25	75	0	0	71	84.2	373	78	44	40	1	4	4	7	39	5	79	5	2	4	5	.444	0	28	4.25
Rice,Nathan	Salem-Keizr	SF	A-	24	13	0	0	4	18.1	85	22	13	11	0	0	1	2	7	0	26	5	0	1	2	.333	0	0	5.40
	Bakersfield	SF	A+	24	8	1	0	4	18.1	77	13	4	4	0	0	0	1	9	0	9	0	0	2	0	1.000	0	0	1.96
Richards,Mark	Utica	Fla	A-	24	2	0	0	2	2	7	1	0	0	0	0	0	0	0	0	3	0	0	0	0	.000	0	0	0.00
	Kane County	Fla	A	24	18	0	0	5	34	142	34	13	9	3	2	0	1	7	3	27	1	0	1	1	.500	0	1	2.38
Richardson,Kas.	Ft. Wayne	Min	A	21	19	19	1	0	114.1	476	100	47	39	5	4	3	4	46	0	84	10	0	7	5	.583	1	0	3.07
	Ft. Myers	Min	A+	21	7	7	0	0	34.1	156	35	23	17	1	3	3	3	18	0	17	5	0	1	3	.250	0	0	4.46
Ricks,Ronald	Butte	Ana	R+	23	17	8	2	7	62	301	80	48	36	2	3	1	5	22	1	48	9	0	5	3	.625	0	0	5.23
Ridenour,Jeffrey	Rangers	Tex	R	21	12	0	0	5	31.2	134	26	10	9	2	0	0	1	14	1	30	2	0	3	1	.750	0	2	2.56
Riedling,John	Burlington	Cin	A	22	35	16	0	11	102.2	461	101	70	60	8	3	5	7	47	0	104	10	0	7	6	.538	0	0	5.26
Riegert,Tim	Peoria	StL	A	24	55	0	0	19	75.1	324	79	35	26	5	0	5	1	31	0	69	2	4	4	2	.667	0	0	3.11
Riggan,Jerrod	Lk Elsinore	Ana	A+	24	8	8	0	0	43	202	60	36	29	1	4	2	4	16	0	31	6	2	2	5	.286	0	0	6.07
	Cedar Rapds	Ana	A	24	19	19	3	0	116	506	132	70	63	15	3	7	2	36	2	65	12	2	9	8	.529	1	0	4.89
Rijo,Jose	Quad City	Hou	A	22	35	0	0	19	59.1	275	63	43	29	6	2	3	7	27	6	41	3	2	3	6	.333	0	2	4.40
Riley,Michael	Bakersfield	SF	A+	23	6	4	0	0	20.1	94	25	20	19	4	0	1	0	8	0	17	0	0	1	2	.333	0	0	8.41
	Salem-Keizr	SF	A-	23	15	15	1	0	88.1	375	76	39	34	9	2	2	4	28	0	96	6	1	9	2	.818	0	0	3.46
Rincon,Juan	Twins	Min	R	19	11	10	1	1	58	245	55	21	19	0	2	3	4	24	0	46	7	1	3	3	.500	0	0	2.95
	Elizabethtn	Min	R+	19	2	1	0	0	9.1	41	11	4	4	0	0	0	0	3	0	7	2	0	0	1	.000	0	0	3.86
Rincones,Gabriel	Mariners	Sea	R	21	13	11	1	2	68.1	302	60	37	29	4	2	2	9	36	0	67	6	1	5	4	.556	0	0	3.82
Rios,Romualdo	Rangers	Tex	R	18	10	2	0	6	28.1	131	31	24	18	0	2	2	2	15	0	31	4	1	1	2	.333	0	1	5.72
Riske,David	Kinston	Cle	A+	21	39	0	0	23	72	299	58	22	18	3	6	1	2	33	4	90	0	0	4	4	.500	0	2	2.25
Rivera,Alvin	Asheville	Col	A	19	1	1	0	0	2.1	13	2	1	0	0	0	0	0	4	0	0	0	0	0	1	.000	0	0	0.00
	Portland	Col	A-	19	13	6	0	0	39.2	171	41	23	22	3	1	1	1	13	0	19	3	1	3	0	1.000	0	0	4.99
Rivera,Homero	Tigers	Det	R	19	15	9	0	1	51	231	67	36	28	3	1	0	3	10	0	47	6	1	4	4	.500	0	0	4.94
Rivera,Luis	Danville	Atl	R+	20	9	9	0	0	41	169	28	15	11	2	1	1	1	17	0	57	5	0	3	1	.750	0	0	2.41
	Macon	Atl	A	20	4	4	0	0	21	81	13	4	3	1	0	1	1	7	0	27	2	0	2	0	1.000	0	0	1.29
Rivera,Marcos	Expos	Mon	R	21	19	0	0	11	28	116	28	10	7	1	1	0	0	6	0	17	2	0	1	4	.200	0	0	2.25
	Wst Plm Bch	Mon	A+	21	2	0	0	1	2	11	4	5	5	0	1	0	0	2	0	1	0	0	0	1	.000	0	0	22.50
Rivera,Raul	Tigers	Det	R	21	15	2	0	7	29.2	130	20	15	9	2	0	0	3	21	1	36	4	0	2	1	.667	0	2	2.73
Rizzo,Nick	Utica	Fla	A-	24	15	10	0	3	68.2	278	64	30	18	3	0	5	1	12	1	54	3	0	4	1	.800	0	1	2.36
Robbins,Jason	South Bend	Ari	A	25	5	4	0	0	20.2	78	7	2	2	1	1	0	3	10	0	26	1	0	2	0	1.000	0	0	0.87
	High Desert	Ari	A+	25	23	23	1	0	128.1	549	125	74	63	15	1	2	8	42	0	127	6	1	7	5	.583	0	0	4.42
Robbins,Mike	Wilmington	KC	A+	24	20	0	0	9	31.1	146	41	26	25	3	1	3	1	14	1	24	2	0	0	0	.000	0	0	7.18
Robbins,Jacob	Greensboro	NYA	A	22	20	19	0	0	101.1	462	114	81	65	6	2	3	2	55	1	72	7	0	6	4	.600	0	0	5.77
	Tampa	NYA	A+	22	3	3	0	0	16	73	18	14	9	2	0	2	0	10	1	5	2	0	1	1	.500	0	0	5.06
Roberson,Charl.	Columbus	Cle	A	23	1	0	0	0	2	7	1	1	1	0	0	0	0	1	0	2	1	0	0	0	.000	0	0	4.50
	Watertown	Cle	A-	23	18	2	0	6	43.2	183	39	18	15	4	0	2	0	17	2	35	4	0	3	1	.750	0	2	3.09
Roberts,Grant	Capital City	NYN	A	20	22	22	2	0	129.2	530	98	37	34	1	3	3	8	44	0	122	5	0	11	3	.786	1	0	2.36
Roberts,Mark	Hickory	ChA	A	22	4	4	0	0	22	96	23	12	9	3	1	1	0	9	0	14	1	0	0	2	.000	0	0	3.68
	Winston-Sal	ChA	A+	22	14	14	3	0	91.1	379	78	48	41	10	1	3	3	45	0	64	4	0	5	9	.357	0	0	4.04
Roberts,Marquis	Devil Rays	TB	R	18	12	10	0	1	53.1	206	27	8	3	1	2	0	1	19	0	68	2	0	6	1	.857	0	0	0.51
	Princeton	TB	R+	18	3	3	0	0	18.1	78	20	10	10	2	0	0	1	4	0	15	2	0	2	0	1.000	0	0	4.91
Roberts,Michael	Eugene	Atl	A-	22	15	15	0	0	75	359	104	63	59	7	2	6	7	33	2	33	3	3	7	6	.538	0	0	7.08
Roberts,Richard	Tigers	Det	R	19	11	10	0	0	34	159	35	22	16	0	0	1	1	19	0	40	9	2	2	2	.500	0	0	4.24
Robertson,Dougl.	Modesto	Oak	A+	23	1	0	0	0	1	4	1	0	0	0	0	0	0	0	0	0	0	0	0	0	.000	0	0	0.00
Robertson,Jero.	Quad City	Hou	A	21	26	25	2	1	146	647	151	86	66	12	1	4	8	56	1	135	5	3	11	8	.579	1	1	4.07
Robinson,Dustin	Billings	Cin	R+	22	16	9	2	5	73.1	311	91	38	30	5	3	1	1	6	0	48	6	0	6	2	.750	0	4	3.68
Rodgers,Marcus	Bristol	ChA	R+	21	6	4	0	0	21	113	35	26	22	1	1	4	0	16	0	14	3	1	0	1	.000	0	0	9.43
Rodgers,Bobby	Kane County	Fla	A	23	27	27	2	0	165.2	699	154	81	71	9	6	4	14	61	0	138	7	1	8	10	.444	0	0	3.86
Rodriguez,Chad	Lansing	KC	A	24	48	0	0	37	60.2	256	66	29	27	5	4	1	4	11	0	48	3	0	5	3	.625	0	12	4.01
Rodriguez,Cristo.	Expos	Mon	R	19	13	10	0	3	54.2	220	45	15	10	1	0	2	1	16	0	61	2	1	3	3	.500	0	1	1.65
Rodriguez,Frank	Medicne Hat	Tor	R+	21	7	0	0	1	9.2	56	22	13	11	1	0	1	0	7	0	9	2	3	0	0	.000	0	0	10.24
Rodriguez,Hector	Cedar Rapds	Ana	A	23	9	0	0	4	10.1	58	14	15	14	4	0	1	0	13	0	15	1	0	1	0	1.000	0	0	12.19
	Butte	Ana	R+	23	2	0	0	0	4.2	24	5	1	1	1	0	0	0	4	0	7	0	0	1	0	1.000	0	0	1.93

1997 Pitching — Single-A and Rookie Leagues

HOW MUCH HE PITCHED											WHAT HE GAVE UP												THE RESULTS					
Player	Team	Org	Lg	A	G	GS	CG	GF	IP	BFP	H	R	ER	HR	SH	SF	HB	TBB	IBB	SO	WP	Bk	W	L	Pct.	ShO	Sv	ERA
	Boise	Ana	A-	23	25	0	0	6	41.2	194	35	16	11	0	0	3	3	30	1	55	9	0	5	1	.833	0	2	2.38
Rodriguez,Jorge	Yankees	NYA	R	21	17	0	0	11	25.2	117	31	19	14	2	1	2	2	8	1	12	1	2	0	3	.000	0	4	4.91
Rodriguez,Jose	Johnson Cty	StL	R+	23	4	0	0	1	6.2	27	4	3	3	1	1	0	1	3	1	8	1	0	0	0	.000	0	0	4.05
Rodriguez,Larry	South Bend	Ari	A	23	19	19	1	0	104.1	458	102	56	42	6	6	6	8	37	3	72	10	0	4	11	.267	0	0	3.62
Rodriguez,Wilfre.	Astros	Hou	R	19	12	12	1	0	68	279	54	30	23	1	1	1	2	32	0	71	6	4	8	2	.800	1	0	3.04
Roeder,Jason	Spokane	KC	A-	24	9	0	0	2	18.2	93	29	20	15	3	2	1	0	6	1	14	1	0	2	1	.667	0	0	7.23
Rogers,Jason	Frederick	Bal	A+	25	36	5	0	8	70.2	320	68	46	45	6	1	2	5	48	1	57	2	3	5	3	.625	0	0	5.73
Rojas,Cesar	Rangers	Tex	R	22	10	0	0	5	20.1	85	20	8	5	1	0	1	0	2	0	15	0	1	2	0	1.000	0	3	2.21
Rojas,Francisco	Johnson Cty	StL	R+	21	6	0	0	0	10	49	11	8	6	2	0	0	0	8	0	9	2	1	1	1	.500	0	0	5.40
Rojas,Renney	Butte	Ana	R+	19	15	15	5	0	110.1	454	113	54	43	7	2	5	1	19	0	65	5	0	8	4	.667	0	0	3.51
Roller,Adam	Red Sox	Bos	R	20	10	0	0	2	17	78	7	9	6	0	1	1	6	14	0	21	5	0	1	1	.500	0	0	3.18
Rolocut,Brian	Rockford	ChN	A	24	14	0	0	1	30.2	148	43	23	21	2	3	1	1	15	0	20	8	0	0	1	.000	0	1	6.16
	Devil Rays	TB	R	24	3	0	0	2	7	27	5	0	0	0	0	0	0	1	0	10	0	0	1	0	1.000	0	0	0.00
	Chston-SC	TB	A	24	10	1	0	4	17.1	85	23	20	14	3	0	1	2	7	0	14	3	0	0	1	.000	0	0	7.27
Romboli,Curtis	Michigan	Bos	A	25	46	1	0	20	69	293	60	29	23	3	5	5	3	25	2	69	6	0	5	2	.714	0	1	3.00
Romero,Alejandr.	Savannah	LA	A	20	5	0	0	2	4.1	28	12	10	5	0	0	0	0	1	0	5	0	0	0	1	.000	0	0	10.38
	Great Falls	LA	R+	20	25	0	0	9	42.2	193	50	28	19	7	0	3	1	11	0	27	3	1	2	1	.667	0	0	4.01
Romero,John	Butte	Ana	R+	22	15	1	0	7	22.1	122	33	34	25	3	2	2	3	22	0	17	5	0	0	3	.000	0	0	10.07
Romero,Jordan	Bluefield	Bal	R+	21	12	5	0	3	27.2	131	31	20	20	0	0	3	1	17	0	38	6	0	1	3	.250	0	0	6.51
Romero,Juan	Elizabethtn	Min	R+	22	18	0	0	12	24	110	27	16	13	4	1	0	4	7	0	29	0	4	3	2	.600	0	3	4.88
	Ft. Myers	Min	A+	22	7	1	0	3	12.1	50	11	6	6	1	0	0	1	4	0	9	0	0	1	1	.500	0	0	4.38
Romine,Jason	Asheville	Col	A	23	28	0	0	15	47	201	45	23	21	6	0	3	4	14	0	53	4	0	4	2	.667	0	1	4.02
Romo,Gregory	W Michigan	Det	A	23	24	24	0	0	139.2	595	128	65	55	7	3	5	0	51	0	124	14	3	12	6	.667	0	0	3.54
Rooney,Michael	Lethbridge	Ari	R+	22	13	13	1	0	62.1	282	72	42	38	4	2	3	5	24	0	40	3	0	5	2	.714	0	0	5.49
Root,Derek	Kissimmee	Hou	A+	23	26	22	2	0	129	555	131	76	60	10	4	7	7	42	1	68	7	5	4	14	.222	0	0	4.19
Rosa,Cristy	Portland	Col	A-	20	21	0	0	2	43.2	200	54	32	27	4	3	0	2	14	0	35	2	0	4	2	.667	0	1	5.56
Rosario,Rafael	Tigers	Det	R	21	23	0	0	12	37.1	168	37	19	13	3	1	1	4	18	0	29	3	1	1	1	.500	0	0	3.13
Rosario,Reynald.	Tigers	Det	R	21	20	0	0	11	31	132	32	15	14	3	1	0	0	13	0	38	3	0	2	2	.500	0	4	4.06
Rosario,Ruben	New Jersey	StL	A-	23	14	14	1	0	73.2	315	64	42	35	3	0	5	2	37	0	66	11	1	5	5	.500	0	0	4.28
Rose,Ted	Chston-WV	Cin	A	24	38	13	2	9	129.1	525	108	44	36	7	9	3	6	27	0	132	3	2	11	6	.647	2	4	2.51
Roundtree,Monte	Billings	Cin	R+	20	13	5	0	2	37.1	186	37	38	21	5	1	1	0	33	0	40	5	0	1	2	.333	0	1	5.06
Royer,Jason	Diamondback	Ari	R	19	13	13	0	0	51	222	53	29	21	2	1	2	3	22	0	40	3	2	3	0	1.000	0	0	3.71
Ruiz,Rafael	Winston-Sal	ChA	A+	23	10	0	0	5	8.2	54	16	10	8	2	0	1	2	10	1	9	1	1	0	1	.000	0	0	8.31
	Bristol	ChA	R+	23	23	0	0	10	38	169	34	21	18	0	0	2	6	18	1	56	1	0	2	1	.667	0	1	4.26
Runk,David	Billings	Cin	R+	19	10	0	0	4	13.1	69	13	14	12	3	0	1	1	16	0	8	6	0	0	0	.000	0	0	8.10
Rupp,Michael	Red Sox	Bos	R	20	11	9	3	0	59	246	51	23	8	0	2	0	3	17	1	56	4	0	1	4	.200	0	0	1.22
	Lowell	Bos	A-	20	2	2	0	0	12.2	49	8	5	5	1	0	0	0	3	0	10	0	0	0	1	.000	0	0	3.55
Rutherford,Mark	Batavia	Phi	A-	23	3	2	0	0	12	47	10	5	1	0	0	1	0	3	0	11	3	0	2	1	.667	0	0	0.75
	Piedmont	Phi	A	23	9	9	0	0	58.1	225	42	17	16	4	2	0	1	9	0	47	3	0	1	4	.200	0	0	2.47
Ryan,Jay	Daytona	ChN	A+	22	27	27	5	0	170.1	740	168	105	84	22	3	10	6	55	2	140	12	0	9	8	.529	0	0	4.44
Ryan,Patrick	Idaho Falls	SD	R+	23	14	10	0	0	60.1	260	64	42	32	8	2	8	2	17	0	47	3	0	2	1	.667	0	0	4.77
Ryba,Jason	Orioles	Bal	R	19	14	8	1	3	43	200	51	33	22	3	0	3	4	19	0	30	10	1	3	4	.429	0	1	4.60
Sabel,Erik	High Desert	Ari	A+	23	31	22	0	4	143.2	646	174	101	85	21	10	6	10	40	0	86	6	0	11	11	.500	0	1	5.32
Sadler,Carl	Expos	Mon	R	21	9	3	0	0	20.2	91	26	11	10	0	0	1	2	5	0	14	2	0	0	2	.000	0	0	4.35
	Vermont	Mon	A-	21	7	6	0	0	36.1	167	33	20	17	2	1	2	2	23	0	27	4	1	2	2	.500	0	0	4.21
Sak,Jim	Rancho Cuca	SD	A+	24	57	3	0	50	70.2	286	42	28	23	5	1	3	5	30	2	113	4	1	6	3	.667	0	27	2.93
Salley,Anthony	Medicne Hat	Tor	R+	22	24	0	0	8	36.1	165	32	27	18	5	0	4	3	24	0	28	5	1	2	2	.500	0	1	4.46
Salyers,Jeremy	Vermont	Mon	A-	22	16	14	0	0	77.1	346	87	53	43	4	3	6	5	31	0	32	6	2	3	4	.429	0	0	5.00
Sanchez,Martin	Kane County	Fla	A	21	51	0	0	44	54	237	40	31	27	2	4	0	5	32	2	57	11	0	3	5	.375	0	22	4.50
Sanchez,Simon	Diamondback	Ari	R	20	14	12	0	0	57	266	66	45	32	2	1	3	6	25	0	44	2	0	3	5	.375	0	0	5.05
Sanchez,Mike	Savannah	LA	A	22	40	0	0	16	75	321	72	43	39	10	6	5	3	32	2	74	21	1	1	5	.167	0	0	4.68
Sanders,Frankie	Kinston	Cle	A+	22	25	25	2	0	146.1	611	130	72	66	10	6	2	2	66	1	127	8	0	11	5	.688	0	0	4.06
Sanders,Allen	Lansing	KC	A	23	32	18	2	7	140.1	594	143	72	59	15	3	6	2	32	0	79	8	1	12	7	.632	1	2	3.78
Santa,Jeffrey	Lethbridge	Ari	R+	23	18	1	0	6	25	113	27	19	13	2	2	1	1	8	1	28	2	0	0	0	.000	0	0	4.68
Santamaria,Juan	Jamestown	Det	A-	21	8	4	0	0	24.2	123	28	29	26	5	0	2	6	18	0	11	6	1	0	2	.000	0	0	9.49
Santamaria,Bill	Capital City	NYN	A	22	14	0	0	8	24.1	109	22	11	9	0	0	1	2	16	1	18	1	1	2	1	.667	0	0	3.33
Santana,Alfredo	Tigers	Det	R	20	19	0	0	13	36.2	166	37	20	14	3	1	2	2	11	1	20	10	1	3	3	.500	0	3	3.44
Santana,Humber.	Kingsport	NYN	R+	21	13	13	1	0	76.2	329	87	51	45	9	3	1	6	16	4	71	10	2	3	6	.333	0	0	5.28
Santana,Johan	Auburn	Hou	A-	19	1	1	0	0	4	19	1	1	1	0	0	1	0	6	0	5	0	0	0	0	.000	0	0	2.25
	Astros	Hou	R	19	9	5	1	0	36.1	176	49	36	32	2	3	1	2	18	0	25	5	1	0	4	.000	0	0	7.93
Santana,Pedro	Lowell	Bos	A-	20	15	15	2	0	88	364	90	47	40	6	0	5	6	17	1	65	3	1	6	3	.667	0	0	4.09
Santiago,Antonio	Williamsprt	ChN	A-	21	26	0	0	13	46.1	204	41	15	8	1	5	1	3	21	1	33	5	0	3	1	.750	0	1	1.55
Santiago,Derek	Kane County	Fla	A	22	12	8	0	0	46	224	72	46	41	6	1	3	2	18	0	30	3	1	1	6	.143	0	0	8.02
	Brevard Cty	Fla	A+	22	10	1	0	4	28.1	123	20	14	14	2	2	0	4	19	4	17	2	0	3	2	.600	0	0	4.45
Santoro,Gary	Brevard Cty	Fla	A+	25	20	0	0	16	26.2	112	32	11	10	2	1	0	2	3	0	14	3	0	0	0	.000	0	2	3.38
Santos,Juan	Orioles	Bal	R	22	3	0	0	1	6	28	6	4	1	0	0	1	0	2	0	5	0	0	0	1	.000	0	0	1.50
Santos,Victor	Lakeland	Det	A+	21	26	26	4	0	145	623	136	74	52	10	4	6	6	59	1	108	12	1	10	5	.667	2	0	3.23
Sasaki,Junichi	Expos	Mon	R	23	11	0	0	6	17.1	67	15	2	1	0	0	0	0	3	0	13	0	1	1	0	1.000	0	2	0.52
	Wst Plm Bch	Mon	A+	23	1	0	0	1	0.1	2	1	0	0	0	0	0	0	0	0	0	0	0	0	0	.000	0	0	0.00
	Vermont	Mon	A-	23	11	0	0	6	16.2	70	14	7	6	0	1	1	1	4	0	19	2	1	1	0	1.000	0	1	3.24
Satterfield,Jerem.	Medicne Hat	Tor	R+	22	16	0	0	5	22.1	127	29	29	21	2	1	1	2	27	0	26	7	0	0	1	.000	0	0	8.46
Saylor,Ryan	Vermont	Mon	A-	23	16	0	0	14	19	82	17	7	5	0	1	1	1	8	0	29	2	0	3	0	1.000	0	2	2.37
	Cape Fear	Mon	A	23	10	0	0	7	14.2	70	17	9	7	2	1	0	0	9	0	19	2	0	2	1	.667	0	1	4.30
Schaffner,Eric	Greensboro	NYA	A	23	28	7	0	9	78.1	329	73	35	30	1	1	5	4	23	0	73	3	2	5	2	.714	0	0	3.45
Scheffer,Aaron	Lancaster	Sea	A+	22	37	3	0	9	92.2	410	93	58	56	17	4	3	7	42	1	103	10	0	11	3	.786	0	4	5.44
Schmack,Brian	Winston-Sal	ChA	A+	24	42	0	0	18	75.1	325	65	32	23	0	5	3	2	36	4	71	6	1	2	5	.286	0	6	2.75
Schmalz,Darin	Yakima	LA	A-	23	22	0	0	14	33.1	163	45	27	19	2	2	2	1	12	1	29	2	2	3	1	.750	0	1	5.13

1997 Pitching — Single-A and Rookie Leagues

HOW MUCH HE PITCHED											WHAT HE GAVE UP												THE RESULTS					
Player	Team	Org	Lg	A	G	GS	CG	GF	IP	BFP	H	R	ER	HR	SH	SF	HB	TBB	IBB	SO	WP	Bk	W	L	Pct.	ShO	Sv	ERA
Schmidt,Don	Portland	Col	A-	23	22	0	0	5	41.2	189	47	24	23	0	1	0	5	23	0	32	6	0	4	2	.667	0	2	4.97
Schmidt,Patrick	Braves	Atl	R	19	12	1	0	5	38	182	52	29	17	0	0	2	2	20	0	23	2	0	2	3	.400	0	0	4.03
Schnautz,Bradley	Oneonta	NYA	A-	22	4	0	0	1	7.2	43	16	14	8	1	0	0	0	2	0	9	1	0	0	1	.000	0	0	9.39
Schroeffel,Scott	Salem	Col	A+	24	16	3	0	6	28.2	140	34	27	26	3	1	2	5	17	1	24	0	0	1	4	.200	0	0	8.16
	Asheville	Col	A	24	19	2	0	5	45.2	185	31	23	19	5	2	1	4	20	1	40	5	0	2	3	.400	0	0	3.74
Schubmehl,Brian	Ogden	Mil	R+	23	19	0	0	17	30	139	32	23	18	6	3	1	0	15	2	38	4	0	4	3	.571	0	4	5.40
Schurman,Ryan	Eugene	Atl	A-	21	16	15	0	0	86.1	379	75	46	31	8	1	2	5	43	0	95	2	1	4	6	.400	0	0	3.23
Scott,Brian	Hickory	ChA	A	22	13	13	1	0	83.1	321	57	26	20	4	4	0	1	23	0	69	2	3	6	3	.667	0	0	2.16
Scutero,Brian	Cedar Rapds	Ana	A	24	10	0	0	9	10.1	54	14	5	1	0	1	0	0	6	3	11	1	0	0	1	.000	0	1	0.87
	Lk Elsinore	Ana	A+	24	5	0	0	2	8	42	16	11	10	2	0	0	0	6	1	8	1	0	0	1	.000	0	0	11.25
Seabury,Jaron	St. Cathrns	Tor	A-	22	8	0	0	7	8	37	7	4	4	0	0	0	0	6	1	11	1	0	2	0	1.000	0	4	4.50
Seale,Dustin	Medicne Hat	Tor	R+	20	10	0	0	2	15.2	68	21	8	4	0	1	0	0	3	0	24	1	1	0	1	.000	0	0	2.30
Seaver,Mark	Frederick	Bal	A+	23	11	10	0	0	62	258	57	29	21	6	2	0	6	17	0	68	6	1	3	2	.600	0	0	3.05
Seay,Robert	Chston-SC	TB	A	20	13	13	0	0	61.1	269	56	35	31	2	2	2	3	37	0	64	6	0	3	4	.429	0	0	4.55
Seberino,Ronni	Princeton	TB	R+	19	14	14	0	0	65.1	292	71	39	23	3	0	1	1	28	0	57	6	2	4	4	.500	0	0	3.17
Sebring,Jeff	Portland	Col	A-	23	13	0	0	0	25.1	110	28	10	9	1	0	0	1	8	0	27	1	0	2	0	1.000	0	0	3.20
Secoda,Jason	Winston-Sal	ChA	A+	23	29	15	1	5	119.2	525	118	67	55	11	3	5	4	57	1	85	16	1	7	4	.636	0	2	4.14
Seifert,Ryan	Portland	Col	A-	22	16	15	0	0	74.1	337	89	49	40	8	0	4	4	31	0	52	3	0	1	7	.125	0	0	4.84
Sekany,Jason	Michigan	Bos	A	22	16	16	3	0	106	448	92	55	48	5	2	4	4	41	1	103	14	0	5	6	.455	0	0	4.08
	Sarasota	Bos	A+	22	10	9	0	1	64.2	290	56	43	40	8	2	2	2	41	0	32	3	2	4	4	.500	0	0	5.57
Sellers,Justin	Idaho Falls	SD	R+	21	24	0	0	6	43.2	194	58	28	27	7	1	2	2	9	1	32	0	0	5	1	.833	0	4	5.56
Serrano,Elio	Martinsvlle	Phi	R+	19	21	0	0	8	41	187	46	34	27	10	2	1	2	16	0	40	3	1	1	5	.167	0	1	5.93
Serrano,Wascar	Idaho Falls	SD	R+	20	2	2	0	0	8.1	43	13	12	11	2	0	0	1	4	0	13	0	0	0	1	.000	0	0	11.88
	Padres	SD	R	20	12	11	0	1	70.2	301	60	43	25	4	0	4	4	22	0	75	8	3	6	3	.667	0	1	3.18
	Clinton	SD	A	20	1	1	1	0	6	24	6	5	4	0	0	0	0	2	1	2	1	0	0	1	.000	0	0	6.00
Shaffer,Trevor	Rockford	ChN	A	24	46	0	0	42	47.1	206	44	16	13	3	2	0	5	19	2	46	7	0	2	3	.400	0	21	2.47
Shanklin,Paul	Danville	Atl	R+	22	17	0	0	5	43.2	195	51	27	24	2	0	0	4	9	0	44	9	3	4	3	.571	0	3	4.95
Shearn,Thomas	Auburn	Hou	A-	20	14	14	2	0	82.1	349	79	42	32	4	1	4	9	26	3	59	7	1	4	6	.400	2	0	3.50
Sheets,Matthew	Twins	Min	R	20	15	5	0	5	53	215	49	17	14	1	1	2	4	10	1	24	2	0	2	2	.500	0	2	2.38
Shelby,Anthony	Tampa	NYA	A+	24	48	0	0	11	69.1	285	68	23	20	4	4	4	0	16	5	57	3	1	4	3	.571	0	2	2.60
Shepard,David	Chston-WV	Cin	A	24	18	10	0	8	67.1	292	82	46	37	11	2	1	2	17	3	45	1	0	5	2	.714	0	3	4.95
Shields,Drew	Marlins	Fla	R	19	10	0	0	5	30.1	143	42	24	20	3	2	0	3	10	0	27	2	1	3	1	.750	0	0	5.93
Shields,Robert	Boise	Ana	A-	22	30	0	0	13	52	225	45	20	17	1	3	2	3	24	4	61	9	1	7	2	.778	0	2	2.94
Shiell,Jason	Macon	Atl	A	21	27	24	0	0	129	523	113	53	41	12	3	5	8	32	0	101	6	0	10	5	.667	0	0	2.86
Shipp,Kevin	Batavia	Phi	A-	23	13	7	0	4	47.2	188	44	17	15	1	1	0	2	6	0	41	1	2	5	3	.625	0	0	2.83
Shockley,Keith	Batavia	Phi	A-	21	27	2	0	12	31.2	146	48	30	24	3	1	2	3	6	0	10	3	1	1	3	.250	0	2	6.82
Shourds,Anthony	Rangers	Tex	R	21	13	1	0	10	34.1	134	25	7	4	0	1	0	2	5	1	24	0	1	3	1	.750	0	1	1.05
Shumaker,Antho.	Clearwater	Phi	A+	25	61	0	0	28	72	295	64	22	17	1	2	0	2	17	1	77	5	0	5	4	.556	0	9	2.13
Shumate,Jacob	Eugene	Atl	A-	22	19	0	0	7	20.2	126	19	32	25	1	0	0	2	43	0	23	7	0	0	2	.000	0	0	10.89
Siciliano,Jess	Erie	Pit	A-	21	16	0	0	8	23.1	107	22	16	11	2	3	1	2	10	0	20	6	1	2	0	1.000	0	3	4.24
	Augusta	Pit	A	21	11	0	0	6	19.1	88	22	12	10	2	1	1	2	5	0	9	1	0	0	0	.000	0	1	4.66
Siegel,Justin	Rangers	Tex	R	22	4	0	0	3	7.2	36	6	5	1	0	0	0	0	6	0	6	1	0	0	1	.000	0	1	1.17
Sikes,Jason	Piedmont	Phi	A	22	27	11	0	7	96	432	124	67	60	16	1	2	5	31	0	63	5	0	4	5	.444	0	0	5.63
Silva,Carlos	Martinsvlle	Phi	R+	19	11	11	0	0	57.2	252	66	46	33	9	3	2	1	14	0	31	6	3	2	2	.500	0	0	5.15
Silva,Troy	Burlington	Cle	R+	22	20	0	0	9	40.2	181	35	22	16	4	2	1	4	18	0	50	5	2	1	1	.500	0	3	3.54
Simon,Benjamin	Savannah	LA	A	23	18	17	2	1	93.1	398	84	35	32	2	6	4	7	27	0	93	3	0	7	5	.583	1	0	3.09
Simontacchi,Jas.	Lansing	KC	A	24	29	1	0	11	60.2	295	93	56	47	7	3	4	4	15	1	38	1	2	3	7	.300	0	2	6.97
Simpson,Cory	Braves	Atl	R	20	12	2	0	8	26.2	133	29	20	14	2	0	0	1	22	0	27	1	0	1	3	.250	0	1	4.72
Simpson,Allan	Everett	Sea	A-	20	16	0	0	6	26.1	127	26	23	20	1	1	1	2	24	1	26	3	0	0	3	.000	0	0	6.84
Sims,Ken	Bluefield	Bal	R+	22	18	2	0	10	35.1	158	30	18	12	2	0	1	3	22	0	33	1	1	1	2	.333	0	1	3.06
Slamka,John	Asheville	Col	A	24	26	2	0	8	57.2	250	61	31	24	7	3	2	5	27	0	48	8	0	1	3	.250	0	0	3.75
Smith,Andy	Oneonta	NYA	A-	22	26	0	0	11	40	164	30	13	13	0	1	2	1	13	1	55	1	1	3	2	.600	0	1	2.93
Smith,Andy	Visalia	Oak	A+	23	42	0	0	14	70.2	330	77	40	30	7	4	1	4	39	6	67	9	1	3	7	.300	0	1	3.82
Smith,Dan	Charlotte	Tex	A+	22	26	25	2	0	160.2	705	169	93	79	17	6	4	11	66	1	113	9	0	8	10	.444	0	0	4.43
Smith,Eric	Kissimmee	Hou	A+	24	32	6	0	10	79.2	347	84	44	39	5	3	2	2	29	3	59	6	1	2	2	.500	0	1	4.41
Smith,Josh	Idaho Falls	SD	R+	20	26	0	0	10	26.2	146	35	33	30	1	1	0	0	31	4	24	9	1	2	2	.500	0	0	10.13
Smith,Keilan	Lakeland	Det	A+	24	40	3	0	24	77	314	65	23	22	2	4	3	2	27	2	46	7	0	9	2	.818	0	7	2.57
Smith,Ottis	Charlotte	Tex	A+	27	27	0	0	21	48	204	34	21	21	2	2	0	4	27	0	34	12	0	2	3	.400	0	5	3.94
Smith,Ryan	Pulaski	Tex	R+	23	15	0	0	6	22.1	128	41	33	22	3	1	0	0	14	0	30	9	3	2	1	.667	0	0	8.87
Sneed,John	Medicne Hat	Tor	R+	22	15	10	2	1	69.2	275	42	19	10	5	2	1	7	20	0	79	2	0	6	1	.857	0	0	1.29
Snellings,William	Boise	Ana	A-	21	12	6	0	1	29.2	147	44	28	21	5	1	1	0	11	1	27	5	1	1	2	.333	0	1	6.37
Snyder,Bill	Jamestown	Det	A-	23	25	0	0	25	29	126	19	8	7	1	2	0	2	20	2	42	1	1	1	3	.250	0	9	2.17
Sobik,Trad	Lakeland	Det	A+	22	2	0	0	0	0.2	9	4	3	3	0	0	0	0	3	0	1	1	0	0	1	.000	0	0	40.50
Sobkoviak,Jeff	High Desert	Ari	A+	26	28	28	0	0	160	683	167	88	76	12	6	4	11	37	0	101	9	1	14	6	.700	0	0	4.28
Sokol,Trad	Ogden	Mil	R+	21	17	0	0	6	38.2	177	44	18	18	6	1	1	1	16	0	43	2	1	2	0	1.000	0	3	4.19
Solano,Francisco	Royals	KC	R	18	12	7	1	4	49.2	213	53	25	21	2	2	0	4	9	0	30	1	0	4	1	.800	1	0	3.81
Sordo,Fernando	Mets	NYN	R	21	11	3	0	3	27.2	116	26	12	11	2	1	0	2	7	0	12	3	0	3	1	.750	0	0	3.58
Soriano,Jacobo	Boise	Ana	A-	23	3	0	0	3	4	20	3	3	3	0	0	0	1	4	0	3	0	0	0	0	.000	0	0	6.75
	Cedar Rapds	Ana	A	23	25	0	0	12	33.2	169	43	33	29	5	2	0	4	23	1	28	6	1	1	4	.200	0	1	7.75
Soto,Seferino	Savannah	LA	A	22	26	0	0	9	54.2	244	57	29	23	2	3	3	1	28	0	59	11	1	2	2	.500	0	3	3.79
Sparks,Eric	Vermont	Mon	A-	24	28	0	0	10	42	189	34	22	20	2	2	4	3	26	0	46	3	0	0	4	.000	0	2	4.29
Sparks,Jeff	Burlington	Cin	A	26	22	9	0	5	61.1	281	61	49	39	7	2	3	0	39	1	72	6	1	2	5	.286	0	0	5.72
Spear,Russell	W Michigan	Det	A	20	23	23	1	0	139.2	605	126	63	46	9	3	3	11	61	0	112	9	0	11	6	.647	1	0	2.96
Spence,Cam	Tampa	NYA	A+	23	15	5	0	2	49.1	191	42	16	13	2	2	0	1	10	0	31	1	2	1	2	.333	0	0	2.37
	Greensboro	NYA	A	23	8	7	0	0	48	195	43	23	18	4	3	3	3	10	0	35	0	0	2	2	.500	0	0	3.38
Spencer,Sean	Lancaster	Sea	A+	23	39	0	0	32	60.1	227	41	12	11	4	4	1	2	15	0	72	2	0	2	3	.400	0	18	1.64
Spiegel,Mike	Columbus	Cle	A	22	2	2	0	0	10	39	6	4	4	1	0	0	1	5	0	6	0	0	0	0	.000	0	0	3.60

1997 Pitching — Single-A and Rookie Leagues

HOW MUCH HE PITCHED											WHAT HE GAVE UP												THE RESULTS					
Player	Team	Org	Lg	A	G	GS	CG	GF	IP	BFP	H	R	ER	HR	SH	SF	HB	TBB	IBB	SO	WP	Bk	W	L	Pct.	ShO	Sv	ERA
Spiers,Corey	Ft. Wayne	Min	A	23	24	23	0	0	120.1	530	154	83	65	5	4	5	2	33	0	94	12	1	5	9	.357	0	0	4.86
Spinelli,Mike	Red Sox	Bos	R	21	3	3	0	0	6.1	42	15	16	8	0	1	0	1	4	0	15	1	1	0	2	.000	0	0	11.37
	Sarasota	Bos	A+	21	5	5	0	0	26.2	127	34	22	16	3	0	3	1	12	0	11	4	0	0	4	.000	0	0	5.40
Splawn,Matt	Capital City	NYN	A	25	7	0	0	5	9.2	40	7	4	1	1	0	0	1	1	0	10	0	0	0	0	.000	0	0	0.93
Splittorff,Jamie	Twins	Min	R	24	2	0	0	2	4.1	19	2	1	1	0	0	0	1	4	0	6	0	0	0	1	.000	0	0	2.08
	Ft. Myers	Min	A+	24	2	2	0	0	5.2	29	11	6	6	0	0	0	0	1	0	3	0	0	0	0	.000	0	0	9.53
Spurgeon,Jay	Bluefield	Bal	R+	21	9	7	0	1	35	146	35	13	13	4	0	1	1	14	1	32	1	1	1	1	.500	0	0	3.34
Spykstra,Dave	Vero Beach	LA	A+	24	25	14	0	7	70	335	79	54	46	5	1	4	4	51	1	48	19	1	2	6	.250	0	0	5.91
St. Pierre,Bobby	Tampa	NYA	A+	24	27	3	0	7	51.1	225	66	27	22	5	3	1	1	18	4	37	0	0	3	5	.375	0	1	3.86
Stabile,Paul	Erie	Pit	A-	22	22	0	0	5	43	174	32	17	13	1	2	1	3	16	0	50	1	0	4	4	.500	0	1	2.72
Stachler,Eric	Kissimmee	Hou	A+	25	48	0	0	22	65.1	291	76	38	30	2	1	2	3	21	3	43	2	0	4	4	.500	0	4	4.13
Standridge,Jason	Devil Rays	TB	R	19	13	13	0	0	57.2	246	56	30	23	3	2	5	2	13	1	55	2	2	0	6	.000	0	0	3.59
Stark,Dennis	Wisconsin	Sea	A	23	16	15	1	0	91.1	361	52	27	20	3	4	1	2	33	0	105	5	1	6	3	.667	0	0	1.97
	Lancaster	Sea	A+	23	3	3	0	0	16.2	71	13	7	6	1	1	0	2	10	0	17	0	0	1	1	.500	0	0	3.24
Stechschulte,Ge.	New Jersey	StL	A-	24	30	0	0	9	36.1	164	45	16	13	2	0	2	1	16	0	28	3	0	1	1	.500	0	1	3.22
Steed,Rick	High Desert	Ari	A+	27	46	0	0	21	77.1	325	58	28	24	5	3	2	6	31	7	64	10	0	6	1	.857	0	1	2.79
Steele,Brandon	Butte	Ana	R+	19	13	13	1	0	69.2	326	83	53	35	8	2	2	4	42	0	55	9	1	3	4	.429	0	0	4.52
Stein,Ethan	Lansing	KC	A	23	39	10	1	13	124.2	549	150	83	65	19	8	1	8	24	1	72	4	1	6	10	.375	0	2	4.69
Steinmetz,Earl	Kissimmee	Hou	A+	27	4	0	0	2	6	28	8	8	8	0	0	1	0	3	0	4	1	0	0	0	.000	0	0	12.00
Stenger,Patrick	Twins	Min	R	19	15	2	0	3	35.2	155	41	21	18	3	0	3	3	10	1	22	6	3	0	2	.000	0	0	4.54
Stentz,Brent	Ft. Myers	Min	A+	22	49	1	0	30	69.1	285	53	20	19	4	2	3	2	24	3	70	5	2	7	2	.778	0	17	2.47
Stephens,Jason	Lk Elsinore	Ana	A+	22	24	22	1	1	126.2	569	149	86	76	14	1	2	16	42	2	101	4	1	7	11	.389	0	0	5.40
Stephens,John	Orioles	Bal	R	18	9	3	0	3	33	121	15	3	3	1	3	2	0	9	0	43	0	0	3	0	1.000	0	1	0.82
	Bluefield	Bal	R+	18	4	4	0	0	24	93	17	6	6	4	0	0	1	5	0	34	1	1	2	0	1.000	0	0	2.25
Stephens,Shann.	Brevard Cty	Fla	A+	24	27	25	2	0	149.2	647	162	93	80	11	7	10	14	34	2	90	5	0	8	13	.381	2	0	4.81
Stepka,Tom	Salem	Col	A+	22	28	28	4	0	182.1	766	205	100	84	25	2	5	9	28	0	120	3	0	11	14	.440	3	0	4.15
Stevens,Kris	Piedmont	Phi	A	20	14	14	3	0	89.1	361	66	30	22	2	1	1	3	31	0	72	4	0	6	4	.600	3	0	2.22
	Clearwater	Phi	A+	20	13	13	0	0	71	319	80	42	36	4	3	4	3	30	0	53	3	0	6	3	.667	0	0	4.56
Stewart,Paul	Ogden	Mil	R+	19	15	15	1	0	81.1	370	88	59	48	13	1	3	6	30	0	82	3	2	5	6	.455	1	0	5.31
Stewart,Scott	St. Lucie	NYN	A+	22	22	18	4	1	123.1	496	114	62	55	8	3	7	4	18	1	64	4	7	5	10	.333	0	0	4.01
Stinson,Kevin	White Sox	ChA	R	22	10	0	0	6	13.2	64	21	10	10	0	0	1	1	8	0	12	0	1	1	2	.333	0	0	6.59
Stockstill,Jason	Cedar Rapds	Ana	A	21	27	27	1	0	160.2	706	167	111	96	25	3	5	5	86	1	116	10	4	7	14	.333	0	0	5.38
Stoops,Jim	San Jose	SF	A+	26	50	0	0	16	91.2	401	92	56	53	3	2	3	7	45	2	114	7	1	2	5	.286	0	4	5.20
Stover,C.D.	Great Falls	LA	R+	22	12	12	1	0	77.1	324	71	36	22	4	1	3	2	14	0	61	3	1	7	2	.778	0	0	2.56
Stowe,Chris	Expos	Mon	R	19	9	9	0	0	39	163	32	19	14	5	1	0	1	20	0	36	0	0	2	1	.667	0	0	3.23
Strickland,Scott	Vermont	Mon	A-	22	15	9	1	5	61.1	255	56	27	26	5	3	2	6	20	0	69	3	1	5	2	.714	0	0	3.82
	Cape Fear	Mon	A	22	3	1	0	2	5.2	26	8	7	4	0	0	0	0	1	0	8	1	0	0	1	.000	0	1	6.35
Stumbo,Wesley	Billings	Cin	R+	22	15	2	0	4	34.1	157	33	21	16	0	0	2	4	22	2	40	7	0	3	2	.600	0	1	4.19
Stumpf,Brian	Clearwater	Phi	A+	26	17	0	0	6	24.1	112	31	18	16	7	1	1	0	9	1	23	3	0	0	0	.000	0	0	5.92
Sturdy,Timothy	Twins	Min	R	19	9	2	1	3	24	88	12	4	2	0	0	0	0	6	0	14	0	2	1	1	.500	1	0	0.75
Stutz,Shawn	Hudson Vall	TB	A-	23	6	0	0	1	13.1	83	16	21	12	1	1	2	4	21	0	9	8	1	1	0	1.000	0	1	8.10
	Devil Rays	TB	R	23	2	0	0	0	4	16	3	2	2	0	0	0	2	1	0	2	1	0	0	0	.000	0	0	4.50
Suggs,Willie	Mets	NYN	R	19	10	8	1	1	50.2	200	34	21	14	1	1	1	4	22	0	32	5	0	5	3	.625	0	0	2.49
Sullivan,Brendan	Clinton	SD	A	23	47	0	0	35	62.1	283	55	33	27	1	4	3	7	34	2	54	2	0	7	5	.583	0	6	3.90
Sullivan,Peter	Astros	Hou	R	23	14	3	0	2	23.2	141	39	35	25	0	0	3	3	26	0	14	4	1	0	6	.000	0	0	9.51
Sullivan,Shane	Cubs	ChN	R	20	21	0	0	20	23.1	99	21	11	7	1	0	1	0	8	0	22	0	1	1	2	.333	0	9	2.70
Sweeney,Brian	Lancaster	Sea	A+	24	40	0	0	13	85.1	358	83	39	36	11	2	4	2	21	1	73	8	0	6	3	.667	0	1	3.80
Swinburnson,Tyl.	Watertown	Cle	A-	22	25	0	0	12	39	176	40	26	20	1	3	1	2	24	5	38	1	4	3	2	.600	0	5	4.62
Sylvesterjr,Willia.	Braves	Atl	R	21	12	9	0	1	53	225	45	25	23	2	0	0	3	28	0	58	6	0	3	4	.429	0	0	3.91
Szymborski,Tom	Clinton	SD	A	23	22	22	1	0	134.2	591	141	67	58	11	3	4	12	46	0	74	7	1	5	7	.417	1	0	3.88
Taczy,Craig	Great Falls	LA	R+	21	18	4	0	6	53.2	242	65	29	24	2	2	0	2	15	0	44	4	0	2	1	.667	0	3	4.02
Taglienti,Jeffrey	Lowell	Bos	A-	22	17	4	0	11	36.2	150	30	22	20	2	0	0	0	13	0	34	3	2	3	4	.429	0	6	4.91
Takahashi,Kurt	Salem-Keizr	SF	A-	24	10	1	0	2	17	82	22	9	7	1	1	0	1	8	1	19	1	0	0	1	.000	0	0	3.71
	San Jose	SF	A+	24	10	0	0	6	19.2	90	20	17	13	1	1	3	4	8	1	21	2	0	1	1	.500	0	1	5.95
Tank,Travis	Beloit	Mil	A	23	41	0	0	18	79	339	80	42	34	6	3	1	3	33	0	45	7	0	6	3	.667	0	1	3.87
Tanksley,Scott	Twins	Min	R	24	4	0	0	0	8.2	31	5	2	2	0	0	0	0	1	0	7	1	0	0	2	.000	0	0	2.08
	Ft. Wayne	Min	A	24	5	0	0	1	6.2	28	4	5	3	0	2	0	1	4	0	2	0	0	0	1	.000	0	0	4.05
Tate,Seth	Diamondback	Ari	R	21	11	0	0	4	22.2	107	25	21	12	0	1	0	1	11	0	12	4	0	0	2	.000	0	1	4.76
Taylor,Aaron	Danville	Atl	R+	20	15	7	0	2	55.1	261	65	49	34	4	1	1	2	31	0	38	11	1	1	8	.111	0	0	5.53
Taylor,Brien	Greensboro	NYA	A	26	8	7	0	1	27	162	31	47	43	6	3	2	0	52	0	20	13	0	1	4	.200	0	0	14.33
Taylor,Mark	Columbus	Cle	A	23	20	0	0	11	30	147	37	29	25	1	1	4	1	26	0	28	7	0	1	1	.500	0	0	7.50
	Watertown	Cle	A-	23	15	13	1	1	71.1	320	68	45	37	5	2	6	2	45	2	58	6	1	3	7	.300	1	0	4.67
Tejera,Michael	Utica	Fla	A-	21	12	12	0	0	69.1	279	65	36	29	8	3	1	2	11	0	67	6	0	3	3	.500	0	0	3.76
Tellez,Eloy	White Sox	ChA	R	22	2	2	0	0	4	19	2	2	1	0	0	0	2	3	0	2	0	1	0	0	.000	0	0	2.25
Temple,Jason	Augusta	Pit	A	23	11	5	0	1	37.1	185	46	29	23	2	0	3	1	22	0	38	7	1	0	4	.000	0	0	5.54
	Lynchburg	Pit	A+	23	28	0	0	15	37	171	39	21	17	4	1	1	2	24	0	34	7	0	2	0	1.000	0	1	4.14
Tetz,Kristofer	Expos	Mon	R	19	3	0	0	0	4.1	17	2	2	2	0	0	0	0	3	0	5	1	0	0	0	.000	0	0	4.15
Teut,Nathan	Williamsprt	ChN	A-	22	9	9	0	0	49	203	55	23	14	0	1	2	0	6	1	37	2	1	3	4	.429	0	0	2.57
	Rockford	ChN	A	22	2	2	0	0	10.2	52	18	12	12	1	0	0	1	2	0	6	0	0	0	1	.000	0	0	10.13
Theodile,Simeon	Orioles	Bal	R	21	15	0	0	13	22.2	95	22	6	5	0	0	0	0	7	0	17	1	2	0	1	.000	0	6	1.99
	Bluefield	Bal	R+	21	4	0	0	0	7	49	21	20	17	1	0	1	0	4	0	6	0	3	0	0	.000	0	0	21.86
Thieme,Richard	Eugene	Atl	A-	22	14	14	0	0	69.2	332	92	50	45	8	1	3	2	39	0	51	4	0	5	3	.625	0	0	5.81
Thomas,Benjami.	Elizabethtn	Min	R+	22	7	7	0	0	26.2	127	37	25	22	6	3	2	1	12	0	28	0	1	2	4	.333	0	0	7.43
Thomas,Bradley	Elizabethtn	Min	R+	20	14	13	0	0	70.1	307	78	43	35	5	3	0	3	21	0	53	8	2	3	4	.429	0	0	4.48
Thomas,Don	Auburn	Hou	A-	22	15	15	1	0	87.1	374	93	50	44	5	5	0	6	21	1	72	9	0	6	4	.600	0	0	4.53
Thomas,Gaige	Marlins	Fla	R	19	12	0	0	4	23	109	18	16	9	2	0	0	3	17	0	30	5	0	2	0	1.000	0	0	3.52
Thomas,Joseph	Lowell	Bos	A-	23	18	11	0	6	75	327	71	43	32	3	3	8	6	19	1	61	3	0	4	5	.444	0	2	3.84

1997 Pitching — Single-A and Rookie Leagues

HOW MUCH HE PITCHED											WHAT HE GAVE UP												THE RESULTS					
Player	Team	Org	Lg	A	G	GS	CG	GF	IP	BFP	H	R	ER	HR	SH	SF	HB	TBB	IBB	SO	WP	Bk	W	L	Pct.	ShO	Sv	ERA
Thompson,Chris.	Michigan	Bos	A	25	8	0	0	3	15.2	62	11	7	2	1	1	0	0	1	1	13	1	0	0	1	.000	0	0	1.15
	Sarasota	Bos	A+	25	29	6	0	8	61	289	68	35	25	7	1	3	1	29	2	36	6	0	5	2	.714	0	0	3.69
Thompson,Frank	San Berndno	LA	A+	25	39	0	0	12	55.1	258	58	39	35	6	1	3	3	35	2	40	5	1	5	2	.714	0	2	5.69
Thompson,Travis	Portland	Col	A-	23	18	11	0	2	74	328	88	51	37	6	2	2	6	16	0	51	2	0	5	5	.500	0	0	4.50
Thorn,Todd	Wilmington	KC	A+	21	27	21	1	4	132.2	584	163	89	76	14	3	6	7	30	3	71	7	5	6	10	.375	0	0	5.16
Thurman,Corey	Royals	KC	R	19	8	8	1	0	34	149	28	12	9	1	1	0	2	22	0	42	1	0	2	1	.667	0	0	2.38
	Spokane	KC	A-	19	5	5	0	0	22.2	106	23	19	13	2	0	2	2	13	0	24	2	1	1	2	.333	0	0	5.16
Tilton,Ira	Piedmont	Phi	A	23	28	27	3	0	152.2	674	171	100	81	10	2	0	17	50	0	103	14	0	7	13	.350	1	0	4.78
Timm,Dan	Billings	Cin	R+	22	20	4	0	11	38.2	190	47	24	20	2	0	0	6	26	2	36	9	0	4	1	.800	0	4	4.66
Timmerman,Hea.	Butte	Ana	R+	20	7	6	0	0	17	88	26	21	12	3	1	0	0	10	0	10	2	0	0	2	.000	0	0	6.35
Tisone,Jason	Oneonta	NYA	A-	23	18	0	0	5	31	150	42	27	22	2	0	2	3	13	0	27	6	0	1	0	1.000	0	2	6.39
Tober,David	Piedmont	Phi	A	24	46	0	0	27	81.2	333	65	34	31	6	4	0	3	25	0	55	5	1	5	1	.833	0	10	3.42
Tokarse,Brian	Butte	Ana	R+	23	8	7	0	0	36.2	162	44	33	28	3	1	4	2	8	0	34	2	0	2	4	.333	0	0	6.87
Torrealba,Aquiles	Butte	Ana	R+	19	2	0	0	1	2.1	11	2	1	1	0	0	1	1	1	0	3	0	0	0	0	.000	0	0	3.86
Torres,Luis	Clinton	SD	A	22	5	0	0	1	7.2	39	3	5	1	0	2	1	2	9	1	8	5	0	1	0	1.000	0	0	1.17
	Rancho Cuca	SD	A+	22	31	0	0	16	56	239	53	30	27	7	2	0	4	24	1	46	7	1	2	2	.500	0	2	4.34
Torres,Melqui	Mariners	Sea	R	21	13	10	0	2	54.2	266	60	53	40	1	1	0	11	38	0	42	9	4	2	6	.250	0	1	6.59
Torres,Michael	Royals	KC	R	20	15	0	0	8	35.2	155	32	19	14	0	2	1	4	12	0	27	10	1	1	1	.500	0	1	3.53
Towers,Joshua	Delmarva	Bal	A	21	9	1	0	5	18.1	73	18	8	7	1	1	1	0	2	0	16	0	0	0	0	.000	0	1	3.44
	Frederick	Bal	A+	21	25	3	0	8	53.2	252	74	36	29	4	1	1	3	18	0	64	2	1	6	2	.750	0	1	4.86
Tranbarger,Mark	High Desert	Ari	A+	28	5	0	0	2	7.2	36	9	4	4	1	1	1	0	5	0	4	1	0	1	0	1.000	0	0	4.70
	South Bend	Ari	A	28	32	0	0	9	54.1	239	56	29	25	3	3	1	4	27	4	39	6	1	2	2	.500	0	0	4.14
Travis,Jesse	Salem-Keizr	SF	A-	23	28	0	0	27	29.1	125	24	9	8	3	0	1	0	12	0	19	5	0	0	1	.000	0	16	2.45
Tribe,Byron	Daytona	ChN	A+	23	18	0	0	7	19.2	102	21	20	16	0	1	3	1	22	0	19	7	0	0	0	.000	0	0	7.32
	Rockford	ChN	A	23	13	0	0	4	21.2	100	20	14	13	1	3	2	1	20	1	30	1	3	2	2	.500	0	0	5.40
Trumpour,Andy	St. Lucie	NYN	A+	24	27	27	0	0	144.2	632	159	75	66	12	2	5	3	57	2	86	8	2	8	10	.444	0	0	4.11
Tucker,Julien	Kissimmee	Hou	A+	25	33	8	0	7	69	324	79	48	40	1	0	3	5	42	3	49	2	1	8	7	.533	0	0	5.22
	Hickory	ChA	A	25	4	0	0	1	7.1	35	11	7	3	1	0	1	1	2	0	7	0	0	0	0	.000	0	0	3.68
Tucker,Thomas	Expos	Mon	R	19	3	2	0	0	4.2	19	5	1	1	0	0	0	0	1	0	11	0	0	1	0	1.000	0	0	1.93
Turman,Jimmy	Cape Fear	Mon	A	22	19	15	1	1	88.1	374	84	45	41	4	1	1	6	35	0	72	8	0	5	7	.417	0	0	4.18
Turnbow,Jonath.	Burlington	Cle	R+	19	13	13	0	0	74.1	297	49	25	23	1	4	2	4	18	0	53	2	0	8	2	.800	0	0	2.78
Turnbow,Thomas	Martinsvlle	Phi	R+	20	7	7	0	0	24.1	121	34	29	20	5	0	6	3	16	1	7	5	0	1	3	.250	0	0	7.40
Tuttle,Dave	High Desert	Ari	A+	28	50	0	0	42	63	262	54	22	17	4	3	3	0	23	3	57	5	0	4	3	.571	0	19	2.43
Tuttle,John	Johnson Cty	StL	R+	20	7	7	0	0	32	148	35	30	28	9	2	2	2	15	0	24	4	0	2	3	.400	0	0	7.88
Tynan,Christoph.	Rangers	Tex	R	19	11	10	1	1	58.1	233	46	27	19	3	2	3	1	23	2	39	6	3	4	2	.667	0	0	2.93
Tyrrell,Jim	Red Sox	Bos	R	25	3	0	0	0	3.1	16	5	3	2	0	0	0	0	1	0	6	1	0	0	0	.000	0	0	5.40
Vael,Rob	Watertown	Cle	A-	22	12	12	1	0	62.1	279	63	38	32	5	6	3	0	30	2	47	4	1	1	4	.200	0	0	4.62
Valle,Yoiset	Yankees	NYA	R	20	11	0	0	6	20	76	8	1	1	1	0	0	1	4	0	20	0	0	1	1	.500	0	0	0.45
Vallis,Jamie	Twins	Min	R	21	14	3	0	3	34	147	30	20	18	0	1	1	1	14	1	34	3	0	5	3	.625	0	0	4.76
Van Gilder,Ryan	Vermont	Mon	A-	22	19	0	0	11	20.2	88	17	9	6	0	0	2	1	9	0	19	1	0	2	1	.667	0	8	2.61
	Cape Fear	Mon	A	22	4	0	0	2	5.2	31	8	3	2	0	0	0	3	4	0	8	0	0	1	2	.333	0	0	3.18
Vandemark,John	Clearwater	Phi	A+	26	14	0	0	4	25	106	21	11	8	2	3	1	0	12	1	22	1	1	2	1	.667	0	0	2.88
Vanderhorst,Fra.	Royals	KC	R	20	18	1	0	13	43	179	35	20	13	1	1	3	1	17	0	34	5	1	8	4	.667	0	2	2.72
Van Wormer,Ma.	South Bend	Ari	A	20	39	0	0	7	76.1	356	90	63	47	7	0	5	5	45	1	56	23	1	0	5	.000	0	1	5.54
Vargas,Derrick	Rockies	Col	R	21	11	7	0	2	31.1	159	40	33	21	0	1	0	0	23	0	28	9	3	0	3	.000	0	0	6.03
Vasquez,Antonio	Burlington	Cle	R+	21	12	0	0	5	25.2	118	23	13	8	1	2	0	2	13	1	20	1	2	2	0	1.000	0	1	2.81
	Watertown	Cle	A-	21	3	0	0	1	8	45	13	7	6	0	0	0	0	6	2	6	1	0	1	1	.500	0	0	6.75
Verdin,Cesar	Tampa	NYA	A+	21	8	8	0	0	43.1	180	41	27	26	3	1	2	4	13	0	37	1	2	3	4	.429	0	0	5.40
	Yankees	NYA	R	21	3	3	0	0	12	42	5	2	2	0	0	1	0	2	0	17	1	1	1	0	1.000	0	0	1.50
	Greensboro	NYA	A	21	1	1	0	0	5	21	5	3	1	2	0	0	0	1	0	8	0	0	0	1	.000	0	0	1.80
Verdugo,Jason	Salem-Keizr	SF	A-	23	16	14	0	0	78.1	347	85	48	42	7	5	1	6	25	1	82	1	1	4	8	.333	0	0	4.83
Verigood,Stephe.	Yakima	LA	A-	22	21	0	0	12	33.2	164	46	26	20	2	2	1	1	13	2	33	2	1	0	0	.000	0	0	5.35
Verplancke,Jose.	South Bend	Ari	A	23	2	0	0	0	4.2	20	3	1	1	0	0	0	0	3	0	3	1	0	1	0	1.000	0	0	1.93
	High Desert	Ari	A+	23	17	17	0	0	74.1	345	91	53	48	15	1	2	12	30	0	64	4	2	7	2	.778	0	0	5.81
Viano,Jake	St. Pete	TB	A+	24	31	2	0	14	60	253	62	23	21	2	1	2	0	18	0	68	2	1	3	4	.429	0	1	3.15
Viator,Dustin	Idaho Falls	SD	R+	22	23	5	0	6	50.1	236	57	34	28	7	1	0	2	24	1	42	3	0	2	2	.500	0	1	5.01
Victery,Joe	Lancaster	Sea	A+	23	28	14	0	5	102.1	460	98	70	55	9	5	7	7	53	3	86	9	1	5	4	.556	0	0	4.84
Viegas,Randy	Idaho Falls	SD	R+	22	5	0	0	2	7.2	39	2	4	2	0	0	1	1	11	0	12	4	1	1	1	.500	0	0	2.35
	Clinton	SD	A	22	18	0	0	6	26.2	120	18	11	8	1	1	1	1	24	0	21	7	0	1	1	.500	0	2	2.70
Villafana,Jose	New Jersey	StL	A-	24	5	5	0	0	27.1	109	20	10	8	1	0	0	0	9	0	20	2	0	4	0	1.000	0	0	2.63
	Peoria	StL	A	24	10	10	1	0	60.2	260	59	22	19	5	2	2	1	26	2	28	8	2	5	3	.625	0	0	2.82
Villafuerte,Brand.	Capital City	NYN	A	22	47	3	0	31	75.2	308	58	23	20	6	2	1	4	33	0	88	12	0	3	1	.750	0	7	2.38
Villalobos,Noe	Lowell	Bos	A-	22	24	0	0	12	48.2	218	58	30	23	5	1	1	1	13	4	51	6	1	3	2	.600	0	3	4.25
Villegas,Ismael	Durham	Atl	A+	21	30	1	0	5	55	255	60	33	31	5	2	2	4	32	0	44	5	0	2	5	.286	0	1	5.07
Vining,Ken	San Jose	SF	A+	23	23	23	1	0	136.2	592	140	77	64	9	1	6	5	60	0	142	3	1	9	6	.600	1	0	4.21
	Winston-Sal	ChA	A+	23	5	5	0	0	34.2	153	36	17	11	2	3	0	0	11	0	38	2	0	2	2	.500	0	0	2.86
Virchis,Adam	Winston-Sal	ChA	A+	24	14	9	1	1	58.1	265	62	44	31	12	1	2	2	19	1	42	6	2	3	7	.300	0	0	4.78
	Hickory	ChA	A	24	15	2	0	4	44.1	183	42	20	19	3	0	1	3	11	0	34	3	1	2	3	.400	0	1	3.86
Vizcaino,Ed	Williamsprt	ChN	A-	21	11	0	0	5	19.2	78	15	13	6	1	0	1	0	4	0	14	0	0	1	1	.500	0	0	2.75
Vizcaino,Luis	Modesto	Oak	A+	21	7	0	0	3	14.1	76	24	24	21	4	1	0	0	13	4	15	0	2	0	3	.000	0	0	13.19
	Sou. Oregon	Oak	A-	21	22	5	0	7	47.2	237	62	51	42	5	1	5	3	27	0	42	14	0	1	6	.143	0	0	7.93
Vogt,Robert	Erie	Pit	A-	19	1	1	0	0	3.1	17	3	4	4	0	0	0	0	4	0	0	0	0	0	0	.000	0	0	10.80
	Pirates	Pit	R	19	12	4	0	4	34	142	23	17	15	1	1	2	0	19	0	40	2	1	2	2	.500	0	0	3.97
Volkert,Rusty	Hagerstown	Tor	A	23	34	0	0	19	51.1	220	42	22	21	2	3	1	7	22	1	45	1	0	4	4	.500	0	1	3.68
Volkman,Keith	Cedar Rapds	Ana	A	22	38	0	0	20	51.1	218	36	18	14	7	1	3	7	27	1	43	6	0	2	2	.500	0	5	2.45
Vracar,Paul	Cubs	ChN	R	18	6	2	0	1	8.2	48	13	8	8	0	0	3	1	9	0	6	2	2	0	1	.000	0	0	8.31
Wagner,Denny	Sou. Oregon	Oak	A-	21	10	4	0	1	14	86	29	27	24	3	0	0	1	14	0	11	8	1	1	1	.500	0	0	15.43

1997 Pitching — Single-A and Rookie Leagues

HOW MUCH HE PITCHED											WHAT HE GAVE UP												THE RESULTS					
Player	Team	Org	Lg	A	G	GS	CG	GF	IP	BFP	H	R	ER	HR	SH	SF	HB	TBB	IBB	SO	WP	Bk	W	L	Pct.	ShO	Sv	ERA
Wagner,Ken	Columbus	Cle	A	23	47	0	0	25	85.1	373	80	50	47	8	2	5	2	37	3	92	7	0	6	4	.600	0	11	4.96
Wagner,Matt	Wst Plm Bch	Mon	A+	26	1	1	0	0	0.2	8	4	4	4	0	0	1	1	1	0	0	2	0	0	0	.000	0	0	54.00
Waites,David	Athletics	Oak	R	22	21	0	0	17	23.1	109	24	14	8	1	0	1	2	11	0	35	5	1	1	2	.333	0	5	3.09
	Sou. Oregon	Oak	A-	22	1	0	0	0	1.1	8	3	1	1	0	0	0	0	2	0	0	0	0	0	0	.000	0	0	6.75
Waldrum,Kevin	Cubs	ChN	R	19	8	0	0	0	7.1	47	10	15	6	0	0	0	1	13	0	6	1	1	1	1	.500	0	0	7.36
Waligora,Thomas	Cubs	ChN	R	21	16	0	0	11	22.2	110	25	16	13	0	1	0	2	15	0	29	1	0	3	0	1.000	0	2	5.16
Walker,Adam	Martinsvlle	Phi	R+	22	21	2	0	8	28.2	131	32	28	20	1	1	3	4	11	0	30	5	0	0	5	.000	0	2	6.28
Walker,Kevin	Clinton	SD	A	21	19	19	3	0	110.2	495	133	80	60	9	2	5	4	37	0	80	5	2	6	10	.375	1	0	4.88
Walker,Tyler	Mets	NYN	R	22	5	0	0	5	9	37	8	1	1	0	1	0	0	2	1	9	0	0	0	0	.000	0	3	1.00
	Pittsfield	NYN	A-	22	1	0	0	0	0.2	6	2	2	1	1	0	0	0	1	0	1	1	0	0	0	.000	0	0	13.50
Wallace,Christop.	Oneonta	NYA	A-	22	10	2	0	1	22.1	98	22	13	9	2	1	1	2	8	0	13	0	0	2	1	.667	0	0	3.63
Wallace,Flint	Modesto	Oak	A+	23	35	8	0	9	99	437	105	53	41	12	6	6	3	34	9	59	4	2	10	4	.714	0	1	3.73
Wallace,Jim	Auburn	Hou	A-	22	14	14	0	0	65.2	328	98	64	52	2	5	2	3	37	1	47	8	3	3	8	.273	0	0	7.13
Walls,Doug	Portland	Col	A-	24	5	5	0	0	22	92	19	3	3	0	0	0	1	10	0	23	1	0	1	0	1.000	0	0	1.23
	Asheville	Col	A	24	10	9	0	1	51.2	227	50	23	17	4	0	1	2	22	0	62	2	1	4	2	.667	0	0	2.96
Walsh,Steven	Royals	KC	R	20	4	0	0	3	3.2	18	2	3	2	0	0	0	1	4	0	1	0	0	0	0	.000	0	0	4.91
Walton,Samuel	Mariners	Sea	R	19	13	12	0	0	49.1	249	54	49	32	1	2	4	5	46	0	46	19	3	1	3	.250	0	0	5.84
Ward,Brandon	Rockford	ChN	A	22	9	3	0	1	20.1	116	30	33	27	4	0	2	4	24	0	18	6	3	1	2	.333	0	0	11.95
	Williamsprt	ChN	A-	22	19	0	0	5	21	99	11	12	9	1	1	1	4	24	0	16	7	0	2	0	1.000	0	0	3.86
Wasinger,Mark	Idaho Falls	SD	R+	36	1	0	0	0	3	14	2	2	1	0	0	1	0	2	0	1	0	0	0	0	.000	0	0	3.00
Watson,Mark	Beloit	Mil	A	24	8	7	0	0	32.1	153	40	33	24	3	0	3	1	20	0	33	3	0	0	3	.000	0	0	6.68
	Ogden	Mil	R+	24	10	10	1	0	47.2	202	44	26	22	4	1	2	0	19	0	49	2	0	4	3	.571	0	0	4.15
Webb,Alan	Tigers	Det	R	18	9	8	0	0	33.2	139	27	17	14	3	1	0	2	11	0	46	4	4	3	1	.750	0	0	3.74
Weibl,Clint	Pr William	StL	A+	23	29	29	0	0	163	718	185	90	84	18	5	2	9	62	2	135	3	1	12	11	.522	0	0	4.64
Weidert,Chris	Wst Plm Bch	Mon	A+	24	4	0	0	0	6	26	5	1	0	0	0	1	0	3	0	7	0	0	0	1	.000	0	0	0.00
Weimer,Matthew	St. Cathrns	Tor	A-	23	23	0	0	15	35.1	150	35	21	14	1	1	2	3	4	0	22	3	0	2	2	.500	0	0	3.57
Welch,Robb	Michigan	Bos	A	22	26	26	3	0	153.2	678	142	88	72	8	3	4	17	80	2	158	19	1	13	10	.565	1	0	4.22
Welch,Travis	Pr William	StL	A+	24	58	0	0	20	79.1	369	82	48	43	11	4	2	1	53	0	69	6	1	4	5	.444	0	2	4.88
Wells,Matt	Bakersfield	SF	A+	23	29	25	0	2	143.2	654	154	87	71	10	6	7	6	81	2	109	8	0	8	12	.400	0	0	4.45
West,Adam	Peoria	StL	A	24	62	0	0	16	65.2	274	46	23	22	2	3	2	3	33	4	83	3	0	3	4	.429	0	0	3.02
Westbrook,Jake	Asheville	Col	A	20	28	27	3	0	170	736	176	93	81	16	5	6	15	55	0	92	3	0	14	11	.560	2	0	4.29
Westfall,Allan	Lancaster	Sea	A+	23	15	0	0	8	19	88	23	17	13	4	1	0	2	8	0	14	1	0	0	3	.000	0	3	6.16
	Wisconsin	Sea	A	23	18	0	0	10	32.1	142	26	14	13	2	0	2	1	20	2	41	4	0	0	2	.000	0	3	3.62
Westover,Richar.	Wst Plm Bch	Mon	A+	23	3	0	0	3	3	21	10	7	5	1	1	0	0	2	0	2	1	0	0	0	.000	0	0	15.00
	Vermont	Mon	A-	23	7	0	0	3	8.1	51	19	18	14	2	0	0	3	6	0	8	0	0	0	1	.000	0	0	15.12
Weymouth,Marty	Wisconsin	Sea	A	20	23	19	0	0	110.1	484	116	75	62	14	2	3	3	33	1	83	5	2	5	7	.417	0	0	5.06
Wheeler,Daniel	Hudson Vall	TB	A-	20	15	15	0	0	84	351	75	38	28	2	1	1	3	17	0	81	4	2	6	7	.462	0	0	3.00
Wheeler,Johnnie	Burlington	Cle	R+	20	6	0	0	1	13	56	10	3	3	0	0	0	2	6	0	12	1	0	2	0	1.000	0	0	2.08
White,Matthew	Hudson Vall	TB	A-	19	15	15	0	0	84	369	78	44	38	3	3	2	11	29	0	82	11	1	4	6	.400	0	0	4.07
White,Samuel	Oneonta	NYA	A-	24	17	8	0	6	52.1	231	52	32	26	3	0	3	1	30	1	43	1	1	5	2	.714	0	0	4.47
Whiteman,Trevor	Auburn	Hou	A-	25	30	0	0	9	36.1	173	36	26	17	3	2	0	0	18	4	50	3	0	1	3	.250	0	0	4.21
Whitesides,John	Billings	Cin	R+	20	9	0	0	0	11	59	16	14	9	2	1	2	1	7	1	10	3	0	2	1	.667	0	0	7.36
Whitley,Garry	White Sox	ChA	R	24	3	0	0	1	4.1	21	7	4	3	0	0	0	0	2	0	6	0	0	1	1	.500	0	0	6.23
	Hickory	ChA	A	24	9	0	0	6	12.1	58	11	7	5	1	0	0	1	5	0	8	2	0	0	1	.000	0	0	3.65
Whitson,Eric	Chston-SC	TB	A	25	30	0	0	15	48.1	204	46	23	22	5	2	2	5	13	2	47	2	2	1	7	.125	0	1	4.10
Widerski,Jon	Kane County	Fla	A	21	17	10	0	0	64.2	307	76	46	41	5	1	1	14	30	0	45	5	0	2	4	.333	0	0	5.71
Wiggins,Scott	Oneonta	NYA	A-	22	13	13	1	0	63.1	261	58	25	18	1	0	0	2	22	0	44	0	0	6	2	.750	1	0	2.56
Williams,Brad	Yankees	NYA	R	21	11	2	0	1	20.1	97	16	19	13	2	1	2	1	19	0	27	9	1	1	0	1.000	0	0	5.75
Williams,Henry	Utica	Fla	A-	23	18	0	0	10	24.2	130	38	24	21	1	1	2	2	18	1	26	2	0	0	3	.000	0	2	7.66
Williams,Kristop.	Boise	Ana	A-	21	19	1	0	5	39.1	186	47	33	15	0	4	1	2	14	1	35	12	0	2	3	.400	0	0	3.43
Williams,Matt	St. Pete	TB	A+	27	43	0	0	15	63.2	267	57	26	21	4	2	0	2	24	3	50	3	3	9	5	.643	0	1	2.97
Williams,Thomas	Bristol	ChA	R+	22	4	0	0	2	4.2	26	4	8	7	1	0	0	0	8	0	2	3	0	0	0	.000	0	0	13.50
	White Sox	ChA	R	22	11	0	0	8	20.2	97	22	16	9	1	1	1	0	9	0	15	0	1	2	1	.667	0	2	3.92
Williamson,Jere.	Lansing	KC	A	23	8	7	0	1	32	141	31	22	15	3	0	1	0	16	0	24	0	0	1	1	.500	0	0	4.22
Williamson,Scott	Billings	Cin	R+	22	13	13	2	0	86	346	66	25	17	5	1	2	4	23	0	101	12	2	8	2	.800	1	0	1.78
Willoughby,Justin	Braves	Atl	R	20	13	6	0	5	42	177	40	24	19	0	0	3	1	12	0	45	1	0	0	2	.000	0	1	4.07
Wilson,Jeffrey	Lethbridge	Ari	R+	22	22	0	0	9	36.1	157	35	22	18	4	2	1	0	12	0	49	5	0	1	1	.500	0	0	4.46
Wilson,Kris	Spokane	KC	A-	21	15	15	0	0	73.2	345	101	50	37	6	0	3	5	21	1	72	1	2	5	3	.625	0	0	4.52
Wilson,Paul	St. Lucie	NYN	A+	25	1	1	0	0	7	26	6	2	2	1	0	0	0	0	0	6	0	0	0	0	.000	0	0	2.57
	Mets	NYN	R	25	4	3	0	1	18.2	77	14	7	3	0	1	0	3	4	0	18	0	0	1	0	1.000	0	1	1.45
Wimberly,Larry	Red Sox	Bos	R	22	1	0	0	0	3	10	2	1	1	0	0	0	1	0	0	1	0	0	1	0	1.000	0	0	3.00
	Michigan	Bos	A	22	13	4	0	4	31.1	138	34	25	24	4	0	0	2	9	0	27	3	0	1	3	.250	0	1	6.89
Wingerd,Josh	New Jersey	StL	A-	22	20	1	0	2	28	130	43	23	20	3	3	0	0	6	0	20	4	3	4	1	.800	0	0	6.43
Winkelsas,Josep.	Macon	Atl	A	24	38	0	0	15	62.2	242	44	17	14	1	3	0	4	13	0	45	4	2	3	2	.600	0	5	2.01
	Durham	Atl	A+	24	13	0	0	8	19	93	24	18	15	0	5	2	4	11	1	17	1	0	1	4	.200	0	1	7.11
Winkleman,Greg	Modesto	Oak	A+	24	39	1	0	19	60	284	71	44	38	4	3	3	2	37	2	54	7	1	2	2	.500	0	0	5.70
Winslett,Dax	Daytona	ChN	A+	26	9	7	0	1	36.1	164	51	27	25	4	2	4	1	7	0	16	3	2	4	3	.571	0	0	6.19
Wise,Jamie	Eugene	Atl	A-	22	22	0	0	7	43	210	59	34	18	3	2	0	3	20	0	31	4	1	2	0	1.000	0	2	3.77
Wise,Matthew	Boise	Ana	A-	22	15	15	0	0	83	342	62	37	30	5	0	1	2	34	0	86	7	3	9	1	.900	0	0	3.25
Witte,Dominic	Clinton	SD	A	24	40	1	0	16	65.1	295	77	44	26	7	6	0	5	10	1	55	0	0	1	4	.200	0	1	3.58
Wolf,Randy	Batavia	Phi	A-	21	7	7	0	0	40	153	29	8	7	1	0	1	2	8	0	53	0	0	4	0	1.000	0	0	1.58
Wood,Stanton	Yankees	NYA	R	21	17	0	0	14	25.2	99	18	7	7	3	0	1	0	7	0	21	1	0	2	0	1.000	0	8	2.45
Woodard,Brad	Rockies	Col	R	20	18	0	0	15	27	130	31	24	8	0	2	2	2	7	0	29	2	0	1	5	.167	0	6	2.67
Woodards,Orlan.	St. Cathrns	Tor	A-	20	21	0	0	6	36.2	174	41	23	21	2	0	3	1	24	0	32	5	2	2	2	.500	0	2	5.15
Woodring,Jason	Wst Plm Bch	Mon	A+	24	16	0	0	14	16.1	67	12	6	5	0	0	1	3	5	0	8	4	0	1	1	.500	0	5	2.76
Woodward,Finley	New Jersey	StL	A-	22	29	0	0	20	32.1	137	30	14	12	3	0	1	2	10	1	39	3	1	2	1	.667	0	1	3.34
Wooten,Brandon	Ogden	Mil	R+	23	18	0	0	10	34	164	43	33	20	3	2	4	2	14	1	27	1	0	4	1	.800	0	1	5.29

1997 Pitching — Single-A and Rookie Leagues

					HOW MUCH HE PITCHED						WHAT HE GAVE UP												THE RESULTS					
Player	Team	Org	Lg	A	G	GS	CG	GF	IP	BFP	H	R	ER	HR	SH	SF	HB	TBB	IBB	SO	WP	Bk	W	L	Pct.	ShO	Sv	ERA
Workman,Widd	Clinton	SD	A	24	25	25	1	0	144	663	161	91	79	17	1	8	12	72	0	107	17	5	9	10	.474	0	0	4.94
Wright,Barrett	Devil Rays	TB	R	19	13	11	0	1	49.1	215	40	27	19	0	3	3	3	22	0	33	3	1	2	5	.286	0	0	3.47
Wright,Christoph.	Princeton	TB	R+	21	14	7	0	0	43.1	203	62	39	35	7	2	0	1	20	0	35	6	2	2	4	.333	0	0	7.27
Wright,Jason	Devil Rays	TB	R	21	14	1	0	3	24	117	27	21	18	2	0	1	3	18	1	31	1	0	1	2	.333	0	0	6.75
Wright,Scott	Burlington	Cin	A	25	42	1	0	20	84	351	74	39	29	5	3	1	1	34	3	75	8	1	5	7	.417	0	5	3.11
Wunsch,Kelly	Stockton	Mil	A+	25	24	22	2	0	143	627	141	65	55	11	10	4	14	62	0	98	9	2	7	9	.438	2	0	3.46
Wyatt,Ben	Eugene	Atl	A-	21	15	15	0	0	59	311	88	65	46	10	0	4	1	42	1	47	13	1	0	10	.000	0	0	7.02
Wyckoff,Travis	Kane County	Fla	A	24	40	0	0	14	50.1	226	50	23	15	2	3	0	5	22	1	36	3	0	4	2	.667	0	0	2.68
Yanez,Luis	Quad City	Hou	A	20	27	2	0	18	39.1	174	46	25	21	8	1	0	0	14	2	33	1	0	1	2	.333	0	7	4.81
Yanz,Eric	Spokane	KC	A-	23	8	5	0	0	17	92	28	27	23	2	3	1	3	12	0	17	4	1	0	2	.000	0	0	12.18
Ybarra,Jamie	St. Pete	TB	A+	27	3	0	0	0	5.1	23	8	3	3	0	0	2	1	0	0	3	1	0	1	0	1.000	0	0	5.06
Yeager,Gary	Clearwater	Phi	A+	24	39	6	0	9	73.2	334	91	55	50	5	5	2	3	25	0	42	4	1	5	5	.500	0	0	6.11
Yeskie,Nate	Ft. Wayne	Min	A	23	27	27	2	0	165.1	718	190	99	89	12	3	3	5	41	1	111	7	3	11	7	.611	0	0	4.84
Young,Danny	Lynchburg	Pit	A+	26	15	0	0	8	24.1	113	27	17	16	2	1	1	1	14	0	22	0	0	0	0	.000	0	0	5.92
	Augusta	Pit	A	26	3	2	0	0	7.1	42	16	15	8	1	0	0	2	2	0	5	0	0	0	2	.000	0	0	9.82
Young,Douglas	Idaho Falls	SD	R+	22	15	10	0	3	59.2	274	69	41	37	2	0	1	2	27	0	44	7	1	3	4	.429	0	1	5.58
Young,Spencer	Devil Rays	TB	R	20	14	1	0	7	24	105	20	14	11	2	0	1	3	9	0	27	4	1	1	1	.500	0	1	4.13
Zaleski,Kevin	Kane County	Fla	A	24	21	0	0	13	24.2	124	37	20	15	4	4	0	1	12	4	19	1	0	2	3	.400	0	0	5.47
	Brevard Cty	Fla	A+	24	3	0	0	3	4	15	3	0	0	0	0	0	0	0	0	3	0	0	1	0	1.000	0	0	0.00
Zamarripa,Mark	W Michigan	Det	A	23	20	0	0	9	29.2	128	13	17	7	0	2	1	2	18	2	41	3	4	3	1	.750	0	2	2.12
	Lakeland	Det	A+	23	11	0	0	8	12.1	59	16	12	11	0	0	0	0	11	0	9	1	0	2	1	.667	0	1	8.03
	Tigers	Det	R	23	4	0	0	1	8.1	35	6	6	6	2	0	0	0	6	0	11	2	1	0	0	.000	0	0	6.48
Zambrano,Victor	Devil Rays	TB	R	23	2	0	0	0	3	10	1	0	0	0	0	0	0	0	2	0	0	0	0	.000	0	0	1.82
	Princeton	TB	R+	23	20	0	0	6	29.2	126	18	13	6	1	0	0	4	9	1	36	2	1	0	2	.000	0	0	1.82
Zamora,Peter	Great Falls	LA	R+	22	13	10	1	2	69.2	289	59	27	20	3	1	1	3	30	0	73	3	1	2	5	.286	0	2	2.58
Zapata,Juan	Ogden	Mil	R+	22	8	0	0	6	22	93	11	5	3	1	1	0	1	13	2	19	2	0	2	1	.667	0	2	1.23
	Beloit	Mil	A	22	12	0	0	4	21	98	26	20	16	5	1	2	2	9	0	14	4	0	1	2	.333	0	0	6.86
Zawatski,Geoff	Batavia	Phi	A-	22	15	10	0	1	55.1	259	87	41	31	6	0	1	2	8	0	33	4	0	4	2	.667	0	0	5.04
Zerbe,Chad	High Desert	Ari	A+	26	9	8	0	0	36.1	192	61	49	30	7	0	3	1	15	0	26	1	0	1	6	.143	0	0	7.43
Zimmerman,Jord.	Everett	Sea	A-	23	11	9	0	1	39	177	37	27	18	2	0	3	3	23	0	54	1	2	2	3	.400	0	0	4.15
	Wisconsin	Sea	A	23	3	3	0	0	17	75	18	11	11	0	0	1	0	10	0	18	2	0	0	1	.000	0	0	5.82
Zwirchitz,Andy	Durham	Atl	A+	22	33	13	0	6	107.2	483	107	59	51	10	7	5	7	59	4	100	3	2	7	5	.583	0	0	4.26

Team Stats

American Association Batting - AAA

Team	Org	G	AB	H	2B	3B	HR	TB	R	RBI	TBB	IBB	SO	HBP	SH	SF	SB	CS	SB%	GDP	Avg	OBP	SLG
Buffalo	Cle	144	4804	1286	242	21	182	2116	711	656	509	23	910	57	39	50	99	66	.60	110	.268	.342	.440
Nashville	ChA	143	4797	1292	246	23	153	2043	706	659	454	19	859	43	45	36	81	49	.62	120	.269	.336	.426
Indianapolis	Cin	144	4758	1257	233	35	150	2010	669	621	515	26	928	26	35	47	122	70	.64	101	.264	.336	.422
Iowa	ChN	143	4779	1265	254	21	150	2011	666	627	453	29	893	47	34	36	91	52	.64	116	.265	.332	.421
Omaha	KC	144	4738	1235	232	16	178	2033	663	622	434	16	1014	48	33	35	75	41	.65	115	.261	.327	.429
New Orleans	Hou	144	4855	1253	242	32	77	1790	639	595	536	30	814	36	49	52	58	50	.54	131	.258	.333	.369
Oklahoma City	Tex	143	4881	1278	266	32	138	2022	622	577	486	18	1055	36	29	38	134	62	.68	119	.262	.331	.414
Louisville	StL	143	4724	1195	220	39	130	1883	611	560	479	15	953	41	37	34	93	65	.59	117	.253	.325	.399
Total		574	38336	10061	1935	219	1158	15908	5287	4917	3866	176	7426	334	301	328	753	455	.62	929	.262	.333	.415

American Association Pitching - AAA

Team	Org	G	GS	CG	GF	IP	BFP	H	R	ER	HR	SH	SF	HB	TBB	IBB	SO	WP	Bk	W	L	Pct.	ShO	Sv	ERA
New Orleans	Hou	144	144	6	138	1287	5349	1231	560	494	103	59	49	29	387	30	1073	48	6	74	70	.514	12	27	3.45
Indianapolis	Cin	144	144	8	136	1249	5298	1171	567	495	126	43	32	44	438	20	959	64	9	85	59	.590	12	48	3.57
Buffalo	Cle	144	144	18	126	1255.2	5327	1197	593	510	156	30	38	27	469	8	900	63	7	87	57	.604	9	28	3.66
Iowa	ChN	143	143	13	130	1242	5291	1201	645	567	155	42	36	31	472	24	969	75	6	74	69	.517	11	33	4.11
Louisville	StL	143	143	9	134	1243	5371	1260	651	586	139	40	37	56	465	28	944	54	8	58	85	.406	3	30	4.24
Nashville	ChA	143	143	11	132	1233.1	5456	1287	718	636	156	31	45	37	554	19	881	90	14	74	69	.517	4	41	4.64
Oklahoma City	Tex	143	143	10	133	1265.2	5598	1398	746	657	129	34	46	58	483	32	794	44	13	61	82	.427	8	34	4.67
Omaha	KC	144	144	8	136	1215.2	5486	1316	807	724	194	22	45	52	598	15	906	62	9	61	83	.424	7	35	5.36
Total		574	574	83	491	9991.1	43176	10061	5287	4669	1158	301	328	334	3866	176	7426	500	72	574	574	.500	66	276	4.21

International League Batting - AAA

Team	Org	G	AB	H	2B	3B	HR	TB	R	RBI	TBB	IBB	SO	HBP	SH	SF	SB	CS	SB%	GDP	Avg	OBP	SLG
Columbus	NYA	142	4751	1274	266	46	159	2109	768	728	587	24	920	54	25	33	124	70	.64	109	.268	.353	.444
Charlotte	Fla	141	4529	1214	268	28	169	2045	720	676	508	35	1013	41	54	38	125	52	.71	94	.268	.345	.452
Scranton-WB	Phi	142	4714	1304	303	36	118	2033	715	664	496	17	867	53	35	48	70	43	.62	113	.277	.349	.431
Rochester	Bal	141	4750	1295	248	39	103	1930	702	621	485	15	879	56	38	38	116	46	.72	136	.273	.345	.406
Pawtucket	Bos	141	4692	1200	212	19	161	1933	692	632	529	15	974	38	33	33	105	60	.64	119	.256	.334	.412
Richmond	Atl	142	4735	1284	266	36	110	1952	680	625	472	22	963	38	60	37	70	50	.58	114	.271	.340	.412
Norfolk	NYN	142	4727	1260	245	21	131	1940	659	610	544	27	993	48	48	38	91	58	.61	104	.267	.346	.410
Ottawa	Mon	140	4530	1177	240	30	112	1813	636	592	483	31	915	42	51	47	131	65	.67	126	.260	.334	.400
Syracuse	Tor	142	4695	1191	245	24	128	1868	617	566	537	25	1008	62	45	32	81	58	.58	85	.254	.336	.398
Toledo	Det	141	4615	1132	224	31	121	1781	596	552	453	18	1030	40	44	41	107	56	.66	91	.245	.316	.386
Total		707	46738	12331	2517	310	1312	19404	6785	6266	5094	229	9562	472	433	385	1020	558	.65	1091	.264	.340	.415

International League Pitching - AAA

Team	Org	G	GS	CG	GF	IP	BFP	H	R	ER	HR	SH	SF	HB	TBB	IBB	SO	WP	Bk	W	L	Pct.	ShO	Sv	ERA
Rochester	Bal	141	141	13	128	1226	5173	1112	605	535	134	33	40	49	441	9	1108	51	14	83	58	.589	13	43	3.93
Norfolk	NYN	142	142	7	135	1232.1	5329	1238	616	515	105	49	37	49	509	25	952	48	14	75	67	.528	9	37	3.76
Pawtucket	Bos	141	141	11	130	1242.1	5342	1198	636	562	135	38	40	53	491	32	991	65	5	81	60	.574	7	38	4.07
Columbus	NYA	142	142	9	133	1234.2	5304	1288	654	571	108	40	37	38	426	10	975	60	11	79	63	.556	9	45	4.16
Richmond	Atl	142	142	6	136	1234	5302	1252	671	594	143	51	34	24	470	20	922	59	2	70	72	.493	10	34	4.33
Toledo	Det	141	141	6	135	1223	5398	1211	689	600	129	52	41	59	581	22	979	58	10	68	73	.482	10	38	4.42
Scranton-WB	Phi	142	142	20	122	1208.2	5289	1248	700	617	142	44	32	31	488	38	964	60	6	66	76	.465	7	32	4.59
Syracuse	Tor	142	142	9	133	1218.2	5352	1218	720	638	135	36	45	52	582	11	902	68	11	55	87	.387	11	23	4.71
Charlotte	Fla	141	141	6	135	1190	5289	1278	744	655	150	40	39	55	535	32	895	68	7	76	65	.539	4	43	4.95
Ottawa	Mon	140	140	5	135	1197.1	5354	1288	750	669	131	50	40	62	571	30	874	73	3	54	86	.386	5	28	5.03
Total		707	707	92	615	12207	53132	12331	6785	5956	1312	433	385	472	5094	229	9562	610	83	707	707	.500	85	361	4.39

Pacific Coast League Batting - AAA

Team	Org	G	AB	H	2B	3B	HR	TB	R	RBI	TBB	IBB	SO	HBP	SH	SF	SB	CS	SB%	GDP	Avg	OBP	SLG
Col. Springs	Col	140	4937	1506	326	39	160	2390	924	863	527	32	986	60	48	43	93	34	.73	99	.305	.376	.484
Salt Lake	Min	143	4998	1482	295	54	162	2371	889	835	547	18	1034	56	27	49	117	57	.67	106	.297	.369	.474
Edmonton	Oak	144	4733	1433	305	44	166	2324	878	826	692	26	922	52	41	40	95	49	.66	133	.303	.395	.491
Tucson	Mil	142	4911	1433	361	43	131	2273	829	780	557	14	936	69	25	41	58	39	.60	134	.292	.368	.463
Albuquerque	LA	141	4815	1379	246	51	182	2273	820	770	505	22	853	43	44	35	121	65	.65	103	.286	.357	.472
Phoenix	SF	143	4918	1445	296	46	127	2214	816	752	530	40	928	49	38	34	134	57	.70	114	.294	.366	.450
Calgary	Pit	138	4677	1375	340	38	139	2208	787	731	465	34	888	44	36	38	111	55	.67	118	.294	.361	.472
Tacoma	Sea	141	4853	1430	316	28	155	2267	770	731	453	28	864	42	30	44	42	42	.50	117	.295	.357	.467
Vancouver	Ana	143	4839	1396	293	42	136	2181	766	703	445	34	855	62	68	36	124	72	.63	125	.288	.354	.451
Las Vegas	SD	141	4888	1376	290	34	110	2064	686	618	473	29	971	46	48	37	113	54	.68	117	.282	.348	.422
Total		708	48569	14255	3068	419	1468	22565	8165	7609	5194	277	9237	523	405	407	1008	524	.66	1171	.294	.365	.465

Pacific Coast League Pitching - AAA

Team	Org	G	GS	CG	GF	IP	BFP	H	R	ER	HR	SH	SF	HB	TBB	IBB	SO	WP	Bk	W	L	Pct.	ShO	Sv	ERA
Tacoma	Sea	141	141	9	132	1211.1	5358	1294	694	626	134	44	29	57	512	19	1017	54	12	75	66	.532	8	33	4.65
Phoenix	SF	143	143	3	140	1241.2	5494	1405	721	657	128	43	32	47	493	17	926	58	11	88	55	.615	3	46	4.76
Vancouver	Ana	143	143	16	127	1237	5534	1331	767	676	134	37	44	59	591	17	836	85	7	75	68	.524	6	36	4.92
Edmonton	Oak	144	144	8	136	1193	5502	1400	783	709	158	33	48	32	402	33	866	64	7	80	64	.556	7	45	5.35
Calgary	Pit	138	138	2	136	1173.2	5461	1479	844	738	135	50	43	55	507	43	909	56	12	60	78	.435	1	27	5.66
Albuquerque	LA	141	141	7	134	1221	5611	1518	849	751	143	52	48	46	527	23	992	76	3	62	79	.440	6	30	5.54
Salt Lake	Min	143	143	7	136	1251	5651	1511	855	757	141	36	36	52	472	30	893	79	7	72	71	.503	5	34	5.45
Tucson	Mil	142	142	1	141	1229.1	5582	1444	869	748	148	45	44	51	541	33	843	81	12	64	78	.451	4	31	5.48
Col. Springs	Col	140	140	6	134	1203	5475	1406	881	791	186	24	37	66	584	24	962	73	6	76	64	.543	3	27	5.92
Las Vegas	SD	141	141	6	135	1230	5635	1467	902	806	161	42	42	58	565	38	993	77	9	56	85	.397	3	30	5.90
Total		708	708	65	643	12191	55103	14255	8165	7259	1468	405	407	523	5194	277	9237	703	86	708	708	.500	46	339	5.36

Eastern League Batting - AA

Team	Org	G	AB	H	2B	3B	HR	TB	R	RBI	TBB	IBB	SO	HBP	SH	SF	SB	CS	SB%	GDP	Avg	OBP	SLG
Portland	Fla	142	4890	1407	262	31	191	2304	824	765	510	28	971	41	47	34	103	79	.57	110	.288	.358	.471
Norwich	NYA	142	4806	1359	234	30	129	2040	784	718	576	9	917	71	32	39	109	64	.63	112	.283	.365	.424
Trenton	Bos	141	4726	1274	236	33	142	2002	766	697	578	19	977	76	55	38	125	70	.64	93	.270	.356	.424
Akron	Cle	141	4671	1254	245	28	143	1984	758	717	593	20	936	66	39	40	73	57	.56	114	.268	.356	.425
Bowie	Bal	142	4809	1283	259	16	134	1976	701	644	540	14	1001	59	53	38	72	47	.61	103	.267	.346	.411
Harrisburg	Mon	142	4721	1274	227	35	145	2006	692	631	431	27	829	65	52	39	143	69	.67	87	.270	.337	.425
New Britain	Min	142	4543	1137	242	29	105	1752	670	616	585	22	914	48	53	41	121	67	.64	92	.250	.339	.386
New Haven	Col	142	4637	1216	211	22	119	1828	663	612	482	24	957	47	78	47	77	69	.53	95	.262	.335	.394
Reading	Phi	142	4721	1182	201	35	119	1810	658	595	493	27	965	77	69	32	86	63	.58	103	.250	.329	.383
Binghamton	NYN	142	4662	1197	223	18	182	2002	654	608	464	29	1097	56	59	36	139	71	.66	89	.257	.329	.429
Total		709	47186	12583	2340	277	1409	19704	7170	6603	5252	219	9564	606	537	384	1048	656	.62	997	.267	.345	.418

Eastern League Pitching - AA

Team	Org	G	GS	CG	GF	IP	BFP	H	R	ER	HR	SH	SF	HB	TBB	IBB	SO	WP	Bk	W	L	Pct.	ShO	Sv	ERA
Harrisburg	Mon	142	142	5	137	1243.2	5359	1135	644	522	145	64	37	68	513	11	1087	49	3	86	56	.606	8	42	3.78
New Britain	Min	142	142	10	132	1209.2	5220	1196	666	581	125	49	41	50	521	13	888	102	6	70	72	.493	6	38	4.32
Norwich	NYA	142	142	9	133	1222.1	5351	1235	681	562	107	32	39	50	490	9	999	82	17	73	69	.514	11	29	4.14
Bowie	Bal	142	142	5	137	1250.2	5391	1215	681	576	156	41	41	71	553	42	1029	77	14	75	67	.528	5	37	4.14
New Haven	Col	142	142	11	131	1214.2	5273	1200	696	598	143	59	37	64	515	29	949	75	11	64	78	.451	9	31	4.43
Portland	Fla	142	142	7	135	1245	5479	1365	728	621	164	61	34	66	426	33	919	75	6	79	63	.556	5	41	4.49
Binghamton	NYN	142	142	11	131	1227.2	5392	1258	732	615	136	58	32	37	553	16	983	62	11	66	76	.465	8	28	4.51
Reading	Phi	142	142	3	139	1257.1	5528	1309	741	643	169	67	34	69	538	27	959	48	9	74	68	.521	4	42	4.60
Trenton	Bos	141	141	6	135	1229.1	5487	1313	760	672	132	42	43	52	555	15	900	66	9	71	70	.504	5	36	4.92
Akron	Cle	141	141	16	125	1197	5503	1357	841	700	132	64	46	79	588	24	851	69	17	51	90	.362	5	19	5.26
Total		709	709	83	626	12297.1	53983	12583	7170	6090	1409	537	384	606	5252	219	9564	705	103	709	709	.500	66	343	4.46

Southern League Batting - AA

Team	Org	G	AB	H	2B	3B	HR	TB	R	RBI	TBB	IBB	SO	HBP	SH	SF	SB	CS	SB%	GDP	Avg	OBP	SLG
Huntsville	Oak	139	4818	1380	281	34	164	2221	942	871	664	12	1036	54	19	50	121	59	.67	108	.286	.376	.461
Birmingham	ChA	139	4761	1330	287	40	124	2069	793	729	540	25	1015	60	47	44	70	45	.61	104	.279	.357	.435
Mobile	SD	137	4676	1297	255	39	108	1954	768	702	596	23	887	52	28	48	126	62	.67	109	.277	.362	.418
Chattanooga	Cin	139	4766	1354	274	33	128	2078	744	677	484	22	826	37	40	47	94	71	.57	98	.284	.352	.436
Orlando	ChN	138	4670	1242	244	37	123	1929	733	651	500	33	846	69	37	41	123	76	.62	114	.272	.350	.422
Knoxville	Tor	139	4669	1269	255	42	153	2067	727	661	466	23	933	56	28	40	76	73	.51	107	.272	.342	.443
Greenville	Atl	140	4701	1283	225	22	147	1993	711	640	478	26	832	61	69	35	92	84	.52	126	.273	.345	.424
Jacksonville	Det	139	4730	1263	245	29	127	1947	699	630	467	16	918	57	45	36	115	38	.75	111	.267	.338	.412
Carolina	Pit	137	4745	1255	253	44	129	1983	688	631	456	25	1024	58	43	35	112	66	.63	81	.264	.334	.418
Memphis	Sea	139	4563	1239	229	36	84	1792	672	603	495	18	853	63	22	40	109	68	.62	108	.272	.348	.393
Total		693	46999	12912	2548	356	1287	20033	7477	6795	5146	223	9170	567	378	416	1038	642	.62	1066	.275	.351	.426

Southern League Pitching - AA

Team	Org	G	GS	CG	GF	IP	BFP	H	R	ER	HR	SH	SF	HB	TBB	IBB	SO	WP	Bk	W	L	Pct.	ShO	Sv	ERA
Memphis	Sea	139	139	13	126	1171	5089	1187	657	577	130	24	40	63	486	14	910	79	6	67	72	.482	8	28	4.43
Mobile	SD	137	137	8	129	1197.2	5303	1261	687	602	116	45	32	57	507	19	975	81	8	69	68	.504	3	33	4.52
Knoxville	Tor	139	139	9	130	1202.1	5351	1307	723	615	113	43	35	67	480	26	980	89	14	75	63	.543	6	40	4.60
Jacksonville	Det	139	139	14	125	1218.2	5352	1270	741	643	161	33	57	52	482	4	869	70	9	66	73	.475	7	29	4.75
Birmingham	ChA	139	139	6	133	1211	5407	1266	744	604	95	34	39	67	559	15	941	79	11	76	62	.551	8	36	4.49
Greenville	Atl	140	140	1	139	1228.1	5433	1283	755	667	157	38	43	43	531	17	994	104	10	74	66	.529	4	49	4.89
Orlando	ChN	138	138	2	136	1184	5239	1255	759	646	122	40	45	42	515	34	927	90	20	63	75	.457	9	34	4.91
Carolina	Pit	137	137	3	134	1205	5464	1281	786	639	116	50	40	73	569	36	933	80	8	55	82	.401	3	27	4.77
Chattanooga	Cin	139	139	2	137	1205.1	5433	1359	809	704	143	36	44	51	540	36	814	71	7	70	69	.504	2	41	5.26
Huntsville	Oak	139	139	3	136	1209	5445	1443	816	693	134	35	47	47	477	22	827	78	8	77	62	.554	1	36	5.16
Total		693	693	61	632	12032.1	53516	12912	7477	6390	1287	378	416	567	5146	223	9170	821	101	692	692	.500	51	353	4.78

Texas League Batting - AA

Team	Org	G	AB	H	2B	3B	HR	TB	R	RBI	TBB	IBB	SO	HBP	SH	SF	SB	CS	SB%	GDP	Avg	OBP	SLG
El Paso	Mil	140	4822	1489	300	76	111	2274	851	777	410	10	881	72	46	56	139	59	.70	117	.309	.368	.472
Midland	Ana	139	4687	1324	315	43	134	2127	792	728	515	13	841	56	49	39	70	60	.54	112	.282	.358	.454
San Antonio	LA	139	4548	1289	245	49	105	1947	736	679	452	20	773	60	59	41	161	85	.65	100	.283	.353	.428
Shreveport	SF	138	4610	1282	249	47	111	1958	735	673	518	20	821	31	44	50	133	54	.71	111	.278	.352	.425
Wichita	KC	140	4658	1282	240	21	111	1897	723	665	465	14	824	58	37	51	121	70	.63	108	.275	.345	.407
Tulsa	Tex	139	4619	1237	272	24	149	2004	712	652	532	19	1025	53	22	33	66	49	.57	96	.268	.348	.434
Arkansas	StL	140	4565	1238	208	35	61	1699	643	581	447	14	753	29	62	38	111	79	.58	103	.271	.337	.372
Jackson	Hou	139	4583	1220	210	18	112	1802	638	586	488	20	844	46	63	30	85	59	.59	95	.266	.341	.393
Total		557	37092	10361	2039	313	894	15708	5830	5341	3827	130	6762	405	382	338	886	515	.63	842	.279	.350	.423

Texas League Pitching - AA

Team	Org	G	GS	CG	GF	IP	BFP	H	R	ER	HR	SH	SF	HB	TBB	IBB	SO	WP	Bk	W	L	Pct.	ShO	Sv	ERA
San Antonio	LA	139	139	11	128	1183.1	5039	1166	592	522	88	49	33	40	438	5	901	85	11	84	55	.604	11	34	3.97
Arkansas	StL	140	140	5	135	1184.1	5138	1221	639	541	120	56	29	44	469	21	868	63	11	68	72	.486	9	35	4.11
Shreveport	SF	138	138	5	133	1187.2	5147	1195	651	558	106	51	40	37	514	7	743	68	21	76	62	.551	7	39	4.23
Jackson	Hou	139	139	3	136	1205.2	5379	1282	722	610	112	54	33	60	523	34	939	69	10	66	73	.475	0	37	4.55
Tulsa	Tex	139	139	14	125	1175	5163	1252	727	606	108	40	62	33	445	7	850	79	13	61	78	.439	5	16	4.64
Wichita	KC	140	140	5	135	1190	5362	1370	781	681	136	48	36	64	477	35	815	58	9	64	76	.457	3	32	5.15
El Paso	Mil	140	140	14	126	1195	5398	1439	797	662	94	48	46	52	455	14	800	93	15	74	66	.529	7	29	4.99
Midland	Ana	139	139	18	121	1192	5432	1436	921	801	130	36	59	75	506	7	846	98	19	64	75	.460	2	35	6.05
Total		557	557	75	482	9513	42058	10361	5830	4981	894	382	338	405	3827	130	6762	613	109	557	557	.500	44	257	4.71

California League Batting - A+

Team	Org	G	AB	H	2B	3B	HR	TB	R	RBI	TBB	IBB	SO	HBP	SH	SF	SB	CS	SB%	GDP	Avg	OBP	SLG
High Desert	Ari	140	4933	1411	274	40	165	2260	890	808	606	20	1055	49	19	50	79	46	.63	108	.286	.366	.458
Lancaster	Sea	141	4873	1319	282	60	161	2204	842	759	584	17	1146	10	30	36	101	77	.57	97	.271	.348	.452
Rancho Cuca	SD	140	4914	1354	298	37	124	2098	783	718	516	10	1077	67	45	39	95	45	.68	96	.276	.350	.427
Modesto	Oak	141	4704	1218	277	50	148	2039	769	692	609	26	1238	76	48	41	137	76	.64	68	.259	.350	.433
Visalia	Oak	140	4772	1264	246	36	116	1930	763	670	615	11	1065	46	47	36	157	96	.62	94	.265	.352	.404
San Bernardino	LA	140	4727	1256	290	57	123	2029	748	648	489	17	1098	80	47	36	195	143	.58	63	.266	.342	.429
Lake Elsinore	Ana	140	4759	1250	265	57	104	1941	703	635	460	24	1105	80	63	47	250	99	.72	66	.263	.335	.408
Bakersfield	SF	140	4825	1264	229	28	123	1918	678	599	428	13	1023	64	35	30	61	60	.50	99	.262	.328	.398
San Jose	SF	140	4736	1258	241	40	79	1816	656	610	530	23	964	76	40	31	150	85	.64	115	.266	.347	.383
Stockton	Mil	140	4762	1272	251	48	72	1835	622	543	393	13	1000	82	55	34	151	101	.60	104	.267	.331	.385
Total		701	48005	12866	2653	453	1215	20070	7454	6682	5230	174	10771	630	429	383	1376	828	.62	910	.268	.345	.418

California League Pitching - A+

Team	Org	G	GS	CG	GF	IP	BFP	H	R	ER	HR	SH	SF	HB	TBB	IBB	SO	WP	Bk	W	L	Pct.	ShO	Sv	ERA
Stockton	Mil	140	140	9	131	1243.1	5426	1207	672	591	116	63	35	97	576	6	953	99	11	70	70	.500	9	38	4.28
Rancho Cuca	SD	140	140	3	137	1247	5405	1156	683	566	105	42	31	71	556	11	1292	102	9	77	63	.550	12	35	4.09
San Jose	SF	140	140	4	136	1231.2	5389	1314	706	608	95	38	37	59	483	19	1210	96	23	60	80	.429	8	35	4.44
Modesto	Oak	141	141	3	138	1233.2	5444	1309	737	568	114	46	46	60	466	36	1076	91	14	74	67	.525	4	33	4.14
Lake Elsinore	Ana	140	140	6	134	1248.1	5498	1327	758	628	113	45	32	99	437	18	998	78	19	61	79	.436	4	29	4.53
San Bernardino	LA	140	140	3	137	1238.2	5482	1218	760	652	114	37	48	65	630	14	1097	127	19	68	72	.486	9	35	4.74
High Desert	Ari	140	140	2	138	1251	5485	1300	766	629	156	39	32	87	438	14	984	80	10	83	57	.593	5	34	4.53
Lancaster	Sea	141	141	3	138	1255.2	5549	1341	773	661	153	46	51	77	518	17	1130	97	12	75	66	.532	4	37	4.74
Bakersfield	SF	140	140	3	137	1233.2	5483	1339	790	671	124	35	33	58	554	14	973	107	12	62	78	.443	10	35	4.90
Visalia	Oak	140	140	2	138	1244	5627	1355	809	676	125	38	38	57	572	25	1058	126	14	71	69	.507	3	38	4.89
Total		701	701	38	663	12427	54788	12866	7454	6250	1215	429	383	730	5230	174	10771	1003	143	701	701	.500	68	349	4.53

Carolina League Batting - A+

Team	Org	G	AB	H	2B	3B	HR	TB	R	RBI	TBB	IBB	SO	HBP	SH	SF	SB	CS	SB%	GDP	Avg	OBP	SLG
Kinston	Cle	140	4715	1265	270	26	185	2142	775	715	588	21	1037	48	25	43	92	46	.67	99	.268	.352	.454
Prince William	StL	139	4700	1221	246	45	91	1830	689	631	526	35	1020	53	33	40	116	61	.66	112	.260	.338	.389
Lynchburg	Pit	140	4670	1215	253	38	110	1874	683	625	500	27	1061	66	42	39	147	66	.69	87	.260	.338	.401
Frederick	Bal	140	4665	1194	248	19	111	1813	670	597	534	25	964	75	70	30	94	57	.62	119	.256	.340	.389
Durham	Atl	139	4642	1199	270	27	112	1859	657	599	468	32	1015	69	31	47	154	85	.64	98	.258	.332	.400
Wilmington	KC	140	4591	1109	203	29	107	1691	652	589	549	21	1062	54	53	34	147	70	.68	86	.242	.337	.368
Winston-Salem	ChA	140	4595	1168	268	45	92	1802	615	552	465	11	1045	42	39	37	128	71	.64	83	.254	.326	.392
Salem	Col	138	4439	1084	227	22	72	1571	588	522	467	20	980	59	73	35	191	92	.67	77	.244	.322	.354
Total		558	37017	9455	1985	251	880	14582	5329	4830	4097	192	8184	466	366	305	1069	548	.66	761	.255	.335	.394

Carolina League Pitching - A+

Team	Org	G	GS	CG	GF	IP	BFP	H	R	ER	HR	SH	SF	HB	TBB	IBB	SO	WP	Bk	W	L	Pct.	ShO	Sv	ERA
Kinston	Cle	140	140	5	135	1218.2	5157	1114	597	514	107	46	22	49	470	18	1046	68	7	87	53	.621	8	47	3.80
Lynchburg	Pit	140	140	9	131	1224.2	5187	1154	607	523	103	50	23	56	410	22	1093	83	6	82	58	.586	7	45	3.84
Salem	Col	138	138	11	127	1190.1	5112	1143	612	515	99	41	53	81	431	12	985	71	7	63	75	.457	12	26	3.89
Winston-Salem	ChA	140	140	9	131	1198.1	5200	1081	653	537	115	37	45	51	567	23	1075	91	16	63	77	.450	5	34	4.03
Prince William	StL	139	139	2	137	1224	5377	1189	698	579	132	34	28	45	559	7	1007	73	13	69	70	.496	7	42	4.26
Wilmington	KC	140	140	1	139	1216.1	5337	1317	701	589	86	51	46	49	435	57	856	66	12	62	78	.443	9	30	4.36
Frederick	Bal	140	140	4	136	1220.1	5386	1195	706	583	122	47	38	59	605	23	1096	66	14	69	71	.493	7	35	4.30
Durham	Atl	139	139	1	138	1218.2	5504	1262	755	649	116	60	50	76	620	30	1026	85	8	63	76	.453	3	30	4.79
Total		558	558	42	516	9711.1	42260	9455	5329	4489	880	366	305	466	4097	192	8184	603	83	558	558	.500	58	289	4.16

Florida State League Batting - A+

Team	Org	G	AB	H	2B	3B	HR	TB	R	RBI	TBB	IBB	SO	HBP	SH	SF	SB	CS	SB%	GDP	Avg	OBP	SLG
Vero Beach	LA	137	4551	1220	225	24	107	1814	728	644	500	17	796	49	37	61	245	89	.73	82	.268	.343	.399
Daytona	ChN	138	4601	1262	247	33	95	1860	698	628	405	8	979	73	28	43	177	89	.67	83	.274	.340	.404
Dunedin	Tor	139	4644	1160	229	24	111	1770	662	590	567	17	1109	81	48	42	168	88	.66	72	.250	.339	.381
St. Petersburg	TB	137	4517	1201	227	35	64	1690	655	580	559	24	661	65	53	43	148	83	.64	93	.266	.352	.374
Charlotte	Tex	139	4598	1193	228	48	82	1763	653	583	466	11	968	62	24	36	167	100	.63	88	.259	.333	.383
Lakeland	Det	138	4608	1251	216	44	112	1891	650	583	412	21	926	42	44	45	123	67	.65	82	.271	.334	.410
Fort Myers	Min	139	4636	1239	231	23	81	1759	635	581	377	16	834	39	36	39	132	79	.63	101	.267	.325	.379
Tampa	NYA	136	4543	1159	210	29	91	1700	621	531	471	27	1003	68	40	43	136	85	.62	83	.255	.331	.374
Brevard County	Fla	138	4632	1220	234	34	75	1747	617	544	442	14	956	56	39	42	149	63	.70	101	.263	.332	.377
Kissimmee	Hou	137	4618	1230	214	43	62	1716	615	533	415	17	823	43	40	40	122	66	.65	108	.266	.330	.372
Sarasota	Bos	138	4506	1171	199	39	69	1655	608	545	422	17	861	44	49	35	164	113	.59	90	.260	.327	.367
W. Palm Beach	Mon	135	4402	1112	218	30	85	1645	583	508	372	22	870	47	28	41	154	105	.59	56	.253	.315	.374
Clearwater	Phi	138	4503	1104	199	32	78	1601	583	507	401	17	906	54	49	36	105	63	.63	87	.245	.312	.356
St. Lucie	NYN	135	4400	1059	214	34	70	1551	512	460	399	22	996	40	35	27	122	78	.61	77	.241	.308	.353
Total		962	63759	16581	3091	472	1182	24162	8820	7817	6208	250	12688	763	550	573	2112	1165	.64	1193	.260	.330	.379

Florida State League Pitching - A+

Team	Org	G	GS	CG	GF	IP	BFP	H	R	ER	HR	SH	SF	HB	TBB	IBB	SO	WP	Bk	W	L	Pct.	ShO	Sv	ERA
Kissimmee	Hou	137	137	16	121	1192	5061	1134	562	445	54	36	43	57	385	25	862	46	24	71	66	.518	15	36	3.36
Fort Myers	Min	139	139	12	127	1204	5069	1138	563	473	71	42	52	40	384	11	911	54	6	81	58	.583	16	39	3.54
St. Petersburg	TB	137	137	13	124	1200.2	5055	1169	564	484	81	32	37	63	349	13	869	47	18	81	56	.591	8	36	3.63
Lakeland	Det	138	138	17	121	1192.2	5064	1122	569	454	63	32	42	49	430	11	829	63	13	81	57	.587	9	30	3.43
St. Lucie	NYN	135	135	12	123	1151.2	4961	1137	574	483	69	34	33	51	411	23	829	80	28	54	81	.400	11	24	3.77
W. Palm Beach	Mon	135	135	8	131	1159.1	4956	1162	583	478	75	45	36	63	376	1	883	99	11	69	66	.511	13	29	3.71
Clearwater	Phi	138	138	7	131	1193.2	5101	1156	584	486	72	38	30	44	476	6	957	96	17	70	68	.507	7	37	3.66
Tampa	NYA	136	136	3	133	1207	5103	1145	594	495	81	48	39	43	458	45	939	64	17	70	66	.515	5	35	3.69
Vero Beach	LA	137	137	6	131	1178.1	5159	1113	653	549	92	40	39	56	566	18	1064	94	20	70	67	.511	11	37	4.19
Charlotte	Tex	139	139	24	115	1202.2	5211	1198	666	574	115	48	38	55	502	10	937	103	10	68	71	.489	7	30	4.30
Daytona	ChN	138	138	15	123	1173.2	5170	1250	696	565	109	39	49	51	440	27	913	88	13	65	73	.471	3	28	4.33
Sarasota	Bos	138	138	10	128	1184.2	5277	1213	721	580	110	43	52	34	521	15	939	82	20	63	75	.457	5	24	4.41
Brevard County	Fla	138	138	10	128	1197.2	5255	1312	731	583	102	41	44	85	388	19	835	65	10	62	76	.449	11	26	4.38
Dunedin	Tor	139	139	5	134	1216	5432	1332	760	580	88	32	39	72	522	26	921	105	22	57	82	.410	4	22	4.29
Total		962	962	158	804	16654	71874	16581	8820	7229	1182	550	573	763	6208	250	12688	1084	229	962	962	.500	125	433	3.91

Midwest League Batting - A

Team	Org	G	AB	H	2B	3B	HR	TB	R	RBI	TBB	IBB	SO	HBP	SH	SF	SB	CS	SB%	GDP	Avg	OBP	SLG
Burlington	Cin	140	4646	1255	238	42	143	2006	785	699	527	14	1158	44	43	32	162	76	.68	89	.270	.348	.432
Lansing	KC	137	4731	1316	276	52	74	1918	772	685	542	14	889	0	29	62	162	52	.76	106	.278	.348	.405
Michigan	Bos	137	4591	1212	231	37	103	1826	725	640	481	17	965	91	20	44	103	46	.69	97	.264	.343	.398
West Michigan	Det	131	4505	1229	249	42	86	1820	698	619	455	29	980	66	36	41	168	67	.71	76	.273	.345	.404
Cedar Rapids	Ana	138	4520	1135	220	40	112	1771	685	619	531	14	1080	50	44	35	135	71	.66	99	.251	.334	.392
Kane County	Fla	138	4541	1152	196	27	78	1636	667	596	598	37	944	53	69	40	137	64	.68	102	.254	.345	.360
Peoria	StL	139	4611	1160	244	27	120	1818	662	579	472	22	1079	63	36	34	125	69	.64	87	.252	.327	.394
Clinton	SD	136	4422	1084	184	56	68	1584	644	557	602	21	1085	55	28	42	191	96	.67	91	.245	.340	.358
Fort Wayne	Min	135	4568	1164	203	38	76	1671	627	548	422	14	973	58	45	32	173	82	.68	96	.255	.324	.366
Wisconsin	Sea	139	4585	1187	250	39	79	1752	625	541	480	17	972	52	58	23	102	90	.53	109	.259	.334	.382
Beloit	Mil	133	4480	1170	218	34	90	1726	619	550	367	12	853	2	41	31	95	81	.54	102	.261	.315	.385
Rockford	ChN	132	4339	1133	228	38	49	1584	594	503	438	17	1025	72	39	38	197	103	.66	84	.261	.336	.365
South Bend	Ari	137	4499	1131	223	45	61	1627	591	527	526	17	1113	47	34	37	92	49	.65	107	.251	.334	.362
Quad City	Hou	134	4371	1103	190	17	89	1594	586	529	399	18	848	60	32	36	102	60	.63	105	.252	.321	.365
Total		953	63409	16431	3150	534	1228	24333	9280	8192	6840	263	13964	713	554	527	1944	1006	.66	1350	.259	.335	.384

Midwest League Pitching - A

Team	Org	G	GS	CG	GF	IP	BFP	H	R	ER	HR	SH	SF	HB	TBB	IBB	SO	WP	Bk	W	L	Pct.	ShO	Sv	ERA
West Michigan	Det	131	131	11	120	1169.1	4861	984	456	347	57	31	33	53	386	10	916	79	15	92	39	.702	13	47	2.67
Wisconsin	Sea	139	139	2	137	1217.2	5236	1084	612	524	82	35	34	64	555	23	1220	106	27	76	63	.547	13	32	3.87
Kane County	Fla	138	138	10	128	1192	5148	1164	620	534	82	56	32	96	439	23	1090	98	19	70	68	.507	10	29	4.03
Clinton	SD	136	136	17	119	1168.1	5101	1154	626	497	81	37	40	63	459	8	1042	90	23	65	71	.478	5	26	3.83
Fort Wayne	Min	135	135	5	130	1195.2	5189	1191	638	516	51	36	36	55	480	7	1003	96	23	68	67	.504	12	29	3.88
South Bend	Ari	137	137	1	136	1178.2	5195	1158	653	493	72	42	41	76	524	33	972	109	14	54	83	.394	6	27	3.76
Rockford	ChN	132	132	9	123	1142	5106	1133	665	547	79	35	33	58	572	23	1031	112	23	66	66	.500	9	34	4.31
Michigan	Bos	137	137	11	126	1168	5149	1195	672	533	83	40	39	67	448	22	1018	119	16	70	67	.511	5	28	4.11
Quad City	Hou	134	134	8	126	1134.2	5010	1095	682	544	100	29	28	72	509	32	963	84	18	59	75	.440	4	28	4.31
Burlington	Cin	140	140	4	136	1199.2	5325	1230	709	598	80	46	43	59	529	14	924	82	14	72	68	.514	2	28	4.49
Beloit	Mil	133	133	5	128	1151.1	5051	1173	715	576	100	39	36	59	487	9	947	88	31	60	73	.451	5	21	4.50
Lansing	KC	137	137	3	134	1197	5286	1335	730	618	127	50	42	64	400	12	910	67	10	69	68	.504	5	27	4.65
Peoria	StL	139	139	6	133	1202.2	5387	1284	746	627	89	47	54	61	578	34	1001	91	18	70	69	.504	10	38	4.69
Cedar Rapids	Ana	138	138	18	120	1189	5214	1251	756	646	145	31	36	66	474	13	927	93	28	62	76	.449	7	27	4.89
Total		953	953	110	843	16506	72258	16431	9280	7600	1228	554	527	913	6840	263	13964	1314	279	953	953	.500	106	421	4.14

Northwest League Batting - A-

Team	Org	G	AB	H	2B	3B	HR	TB	R	RBI	TBB	IBB	SO	HBP	SH	SF	SB	CS	SB%	GDP	Avg	OBP	SLG
Boise	Ana	76	2777	804	172	15	65	1201	550	457	363	12	585	40	9	24	92	27	.77	63	.290	.377	.432
Spokane	KC	76	2741	771	149	28	70	1186	514	435	341	14	628	36	26	19	97	27	.78	50	.281	.366	.433
South. Oregon	Oak	76	2675	736	147	31	53	1104	496	416	387	10	714	47	14	28	138	46	.75	47	.275	.373	.413
Everett	Sea	76	2755	761	143	25	61	1137	457	397	295	9	729	39	21	22	127	36	.78	49	.276	.352	.413
Salem-Keizer	SF	76	2607	686	112	24	42	972	434	354	345	9	613	37	9	26	173	36	.83	49	.263	.354	.373
Portland	Col	76	2562	653	117	26	31	915	394	337	312	14	681	45	33	31	80	35	.70	38	.255	.342	.357
Eugene	Atl	76	2649	677	111	27	37	953	383	328	275	10	610	38	27	29	58	28	.67	47	.256	.331	.360
Yakima	LA	76	2678	674	139	28	38	983	365	316	251	9	658	41	20	15	107	26	.80	48	.252	.324	.367
Total		304	21444	5762	1090	204	397	8451	3593	3040	2569	83	5218	323	159	194	872	261	.77	391	.269	.353	.394

Northwest League Pitching - A-

Team	Org	G	GS	CG	GF	IP	BFP	H	R	ER	HR	SH	SF	HB	TBB	IBB	SO	WP	Bk	W	L	Pct.	ShO	Sv	ERA
Portland	Col	76	76	1	75	670.1	2956	728	382	307	39	17	17	41	240	2	547	47	10	44	32	.579	3	23	4.12
Salem-Keizer	SF	76	76	1	75	666.2	2992	682	408	322	63	26	16	40	295	7	644	60	13	40	36	.526	1	20	4.35
Spokane	KC	76	76	0	75	685	3055	701	420	306	50	12	27	36	272	9	683	70	10	45	31	.592	2	17	4.02
Boise	Ana	76	76	0	76	693	3100	692	421	329	30	25	27	38	292	14	730	88	12	51	25	.671	0	23	4.27
South. Oregon	Oak	76	76	1	75	679.1	3097	694	464	366	52	20	24	42	334	5	678	96	22	41	35	.539	2	15	4.85
Everett	Sea	76	76	1	75	672.2	3142	726	480	365	64	18	27	38	380	12	735	75	19	29	47	.382	3	12	4.88
Eugene	Atl	76	76	1	75	671.2	3194	781	495	391	53	17	25	40	384	14	602	76	14	31	45	.408	3	16	5.24
Yakima	LA	76	76	1	75	673.2	3167	758	523	396	46	24	31	48	372	20	599	65	18	23	53	.303	0	9	5.29
Total		304	304	5	299	5412.1	24703	5762	3593	2782	397	159	194	323	2569	83	5218	577	118	304	304	.500	14	135	4.63

New York-Penn League Batting - A-

Team	Org	G	AB	H	2B	3B	HR	TB	R	RBI	TBB	IBB	SO	HBP	SH	SF	SB	CS	SB%	GDP	Avg	OBP	SLG
Batavia	Phi	74	2553	713	127	21	40	1002	414	368	225	5	472	48	26	29	89	30	.75	48	.279	.345	.392
Erie	Pit	76	2525	672	124	26	57	1019	410	356	254	10	595	52	23	30	93	59	.61	44	.266	.342	.404
Watertown	Cle	75	2491	640	136	15	46	944	383	331	277	8	588	30	15	20	74	33	.69	37	.257	.336	.379
New Jersey	StL	74	2441	615	106	22	40	885	375	326	230	4	559	48	13	23	75	34	.69	46	.252	.326	.363
St. Catharines	Tor	75	2499	623	121	14	42	898	368	303	246	5	511	31	14	23	72	44	.62	37	.249	.322	.359
Hudson Valley	TB	75	2532	639	130	23	30	905	363	317	224	4	558	30	8	22	57	31	.65	43	.252	.318	.357
Vermont	Mon	76	2546	644	100	36	21	879	361	304	263	11	524	45	23	26	156	59	.73	35	.253	.331	.345
Oneonta	NYA	74	2384	606	99	25	24	827	359	299	276	11	568	35	17	27	103	47	.69	42	.254	.337	.347
Pittsfield	NYN	74	2457	600	108	20	26	826	343	293	198	7	536	39	21	23	107	28	.79	31	.244	.308	.336
Jamestown	Det	74	2503	636	111	17	44	913	336	287	219	5	565	37	11	16	42	23	.65	61	.254	.321	.365
Utica	Fla	74	2392	627	102	12	23	822	334	280	282	14	486	42	26	31	68	39	.64	59	.262	.346	.344
Lowell	Bos	76	2529	604	117	12	43	874	334	285	222	3	618	55	41	13	71	24	.75	46	.239	.313	.346
Auburn	Hou	76	2503	658	129	20	44	959	332	289	230	6	586	40	20	15	55	52	.51	67	.263	.333	.383
Williamsport	ChN	75	2490	625	91	23	29	849	275	246	215	17	581	21	15	15	68	32	.68	57	.251	.314	.341
Total		524	34845	8902	1601	286	509	12602	4987	4284	3361	112	7747	553	273	313	1130	535	.68	653	.255	.328	.362

New York-Penn League Pitching - A-

Team	Org	G	GS	CG	GF	IP	BFP	H	R	ER	HR	SH	SF	HB	TBB	IBB	SO	WP	Bk	W	L	Pct.	ShO	Sv	ERA
Oneonta	NYA	74	74	3	71	638.1	2698	596	275	221	20	8	17	23	226	5	610	30	7	49	25	.662	8	21	3.12
Pittsfield	NYN	74	74	5	69	644.1	2708	546	284	202	28	20	13	39	193	3	586	36	9	42	32	.568	3	20	2.82
Batavia	Phi	74	74	1	73	651	2740	641	296	227	42	10	14	39	156	5	551	35	8	47	27	.635	9	19	3.14
New Jersey	StL	74	74	4	70	629.1	2690	630	314	262	27	18	21	31	202	2	520	58	14	35	39	.473	5	12	3.75
Erie	Pit	76	76	1	75	663.1	2810	595	323	264	42	20	17	30	230	1	558	51	6	50	26	.658	7	27	3.58
Lowell	Bos	76	76	3	73	658.2	2824	609	341	262	33	24	26	37	219	20	590	47	8	38	38	.500	5	19	3.58
Utica	Fla	74	74	3	71	629.1	2713	653	359	288	42	17	21	40	192	6	549	38	4	36	38	.486	4	14	4.12
Watertown	Cle	75	75	5	70	642.2	2828	632	361	300	41	25	28	26	292	26	553	48	11	39	36	.520	3	18	4.20
Williamsport	ChN	75	75	1	74	646.1	2907	656	378	277	34	30	25	31	340	7	529	71	13	29	46	.387	4	17	3.86
Hudson Valley	TB	75	75	1	74	654.2	2889	610	379	279	34	23	17	46	277	0	579	51	25	35	40	.467	4	17	3.84
St. Catharines	Tor	75	75	0	75	645.1	2854	652	399	306	47	12	26	52	244	9	558	69	12	35	40	.467	1	21	4.27
Vermont	Mon	76	76	4	72	658.2	2925	669	401	321	41	21	37	42	259	0	546	52	9	35	41	.461	1	15	4.39
Auburn	Hou	76	76	7	69	650.2	2920	717	405	322	32	27	15	65	249	24	534	61	8	29	47	.382	5	15	4.45
Jamestown	Det	74	74	7	67	627.2	2861	696	472	363	46	18	36	52	282	4	484	64	17	25	49	.338	2	11	5.20
Total		524	524	45	479	9040.1	39367	8902	4987	3894	509	273	313	553	3361	112	7747	711	151	524	524	.500	61	246	3.88

South Atlantic League Batting - A

Team	Org	BATTING																BASERUNNING				PERCENTAGES		
		G	AB	H	2B	3B	HR	TB	R	RBI	TBB	IBB	SO	HBP	SH	SF	SB	CS	SB%	GDP	Avg	OBP	SLG
Hickory	ChA	140	4771	1327	272	39	91	1950	748	666	446	8	940	68	37	61	127	73	.64	84	.278	.344	.409
Charleston-WV	Cin	138	4533	1198	235	35	77	1734	695	631	465	8	1074	61	44	47	192	69	.74	55	.264	.338	.383
Macon	Atl	140	4757	1213	222	31	141	1920	689	623	423	10	1101	56	31	33	162	69	.70	72	.255	.321	.404
Delmarva	Bal	142	4729	1182	241	38	91	1772	668	589	510	18	1148	70	48	37	232	97	.71	89	.250	.330	.375
Columbus	Cle	138	4696	1163	201	47	123	1827	658	598	491	6	1278	64	52	29	99	43	.70	80	.248	.325	.389
Hagerstown	Tor	138	4617	1254	293	23	96	1881	644	583	371	11	1032	59	28	44	118	73	.62	83	.272	.331	.407
Augusta	Pit	142	4635	1120	193	31	77	1606	642	554	517	15	1111	63	54	39	218	91	.71	79	.242	.324	.346
Greensboro	NYA	141	4667	1174	233	33	107	1794	641	570	391	5	1162	68	19	42	147	68	.68	67	.252	.316	.384
Cape Fear	Mon	140	4712	1222	230	38	83	1777	634	575	404	12	848	49	37	43	181	85	.68	101	.259	.322	.377
Piedmont	Phi	142	4786	1195	216	35	63	1670	624	556	369	12	967	70	52	36	173	51	.77	77	.250	.311	.349
Asheville	Col	139	4569	1136	207	14	70	1581	599	531	437	8	940	78	89	23	180	78	.70	114	.249	.323	.346
Columbia	NYN	140	4457	1067	190	26	77	1540	564	515	411	7	1124	45	35	31	172	75	.70	60	.239	.308	.346
Charleston-SC	TB	142	4662	1132	213	25	56	1563	563	498	433	17	977	37	45	42	255	125	.67	70	.243	.310	.335
Savannah	LA	140	4507	1034	174	42	94	1574	560	488	410	10	1164	55	25	29	111	58	.66	78	.229	.300	.349
Total		981	65098	16417	3120	457	1246	24189	8929	7977	6078	147	14866	843	596	536	2367	1055	.69	1109	.252	.322	.372

South Atlantic League Pitching - A

Team	Org	HOW MUCH THEY PITCHED						WHAT THEY GAVE UP												THE RESULTS					
		G	GS	CG	GF	IP	BFP	H	R	ER	HR	SH	SF	HB	TBB	IBB	SO	WP	Bk	W	L	Pct.	ShO	Sv	ERA
Columbia	NYN	140	140	14	126	1181.2	4944	1020	495	416	71	45	27	66	455	13	1113	85	8	77	63	.550	19	29	3.17
Macon	Atl	140	140	2	138	1226.1	5170	1106	573	462	96	42	38	56	411	8	1206	54	5	80	60	.571	14	39	3.39
Charleston-SC	TB	142	142	4	138	1243	5248	1136	617	475	81	51	37	57	381	7	1088	86	9	60	82	.423	9	27	3.44
Delmarva	Bal	142	142	2	140	1261	5343	1129	625	507	79	40	39	45	495	21	1139	79	10	77	65	.542	12	46	3.62
Cape Fear	Mon	140	140	6	134	1231	5251	1208	630	522	80	40	42	77	405	3	947	84	8	66	74	.471	8	32	3.82
Piedmont	Phi	142	142	10	132	1242.1	5252	1238	632	531	94	47	27	69	363	5	929	61	10	70	72	.493	10	31	3.85
Hagerstown	Tor	138	138	5	133	1187.1	5172	1159	646	523	70	42	37	58	472	7	1119	94	13	65	73	.471	8	32	3.96
Charleston-WV	Cin	138	138	9	129	1182.2	5083	1262	650	535	83	46	42	50	325	15	934	81	16	76	62	.551	6	37	4.07
Asheville	Col	139	139	8	131	1215	5249	1225	651	549	112	41	41	70	445	6	1022	69	12	62	76	.449	5	33	4.07
Augusta	Pit	142	142	3	139	1249.2	5388	1225	656	531	84	37	34	60	417	20	1174	88	18	71	71	.500	9	42	3.82
Savannah	LA	140	140	10	130	1195.1	5181	1162	660	556	104	48	30	50	451	6	1079	112	13	63	77	.450	6	31	4.19
Hickory	ChA	140	140	9	131	1229.2	5305	1255	669	540	90	50	49	50	411	7	962	102	12	76	64	.543	3	29	3.95
Greensboro	NYA	141	141	9	132	1216	5266	1125	683	530	88	41	40	53	516	14	1026	87	13	75	65	.536	7	41	3.92
Columbus	Cle	138	138	2	136	1213	5335	1167	742	645	114	26	53	82	531	15	1128	104	9	62	76	.449	8	38	4.79
Total		981	981	93	888	17074	73187	16417	8929	7322	1246	596	536	843	6078	147	14866	1186	156	980	980	.500	124	487	3.86

Appalachian League Batting - R+

Team	Org	G	AB	H	2B	3B	HR	TB	R	RBI	TBB	IBB	SO	HBP	SH	SF	SB	CS	SB%	GDP	Avg	OBP	SLG
Princeton	TB	69	2447	666	138	27	73	1077	484	420	263	5	606	48	11	23	70	27	.72	47	.272	.351	.440
Elizabethton	Min	68	2387	704	130	8	72	1066	469	402	273	14	518	40	23	31	50	26	.66	45	.295	.372	.447
Bristol	ChA	68	2302	642	121	15	75	1018	440	389	265	10	558	36	17	22	84	31	.73	51	.279	.359	.442
Pulaski	Tex	68	2331	629	130	25	59	986	440	351	295	5	538	25	22	21	132	36	.79	36	.270	.355	.423
Kingsport	NYN	68	2327	621	109	20	57	941	414	356	230	7	560	39	32	11	87	47	.65	36	.267	.341	.404
Burlington	Cle	68	2320	609	120	18	53	924	403	350	276	10	611	36	8	25	116	41	.74	26	.263	.347	.398
Bluefield	Bal	69	2325	615	120	22	42	905	389	334	247	9	520	48	16	19	116	53	.69	42	.265	.345	.389
Danville	Atl	68	2277	573	113	21	46	866	360	310	240	3	642	50	14	17	64	30	.68	50	.252	.334	.380
Johnson City	StL	68	2326	617	139	17	57	961	346	291	197	4	598	39	18	13	62	30	.67	42	.265	.331	.413
Martinsville	Phi	68	2324	585	111	10	42	842	345	287	198	2	620	33	10	12	72	45	.62	35	.252	.318	.362
Total		341	23366	6261	1231	183	576	9586	4090	3490	2484	69	5771	394	171	194	853	366	.70	410	.268	.346	.410

Appalachian League Pitching - R+

Team	Org	G	GS	CG	GF	IP	BFP	H	R	ER	HR	SH	SF	HB	TBB	IBB	SO	WP	Bk	W	L	Pct.	ShO	Sv	ERA
Pulaski	Tex	68	68	4	64	600.2	2575	538	309	222	43	10	7	33	199	0	663	65	15	43	25	.632	4	15	3.33
Bluefield	Bal	69	69	1	68	595.2	2598	564	337	278	51	7	25	30	255	10	628	55	13	40	29	.580	4	16	4.20
Princeton	TB	68	68	1	68	607	2666	640	392	293	55	14	19	29	210	3	565	52	17	39	30	.565	4	10	4.34
Burlington	Cle	68	68	0	68	592	2674	605	393	290	48	23	21	52	261	2	522	67	12	32	36	.471	5	10	4.41
Martinsville	Phi	68	68	1	67	588.1	2611	608	395	302	60	21	26	33	215	10	503	53	11	29	39	.426	3	13	4.62
Elizabethton	Min	68	68	2	66	582.2	2648	639	416	331	65	27	10	37	229	3	562	63	10	38	30	.559	3	12	5.11
Kingsport	NYN	68	68	2	66	592	2670	683	418	350	75	27	18	45	208	19	578	50	7	37	31	.544	1	16	5.32
Danville	Atl	68	68	1	67	583.2	2666	601	428	333	49	16	17	56	275	5	621	92	9	30	38	.441	3	14	5.13
Bristol	ChA	68	68	2	66	574	2715	655	465	377	52	15	23	43	312	7	560	67	16	30	38	.441	4	9	5.91
Johnson City	StL	68	68	1	67	578.1	2796	728	537	424	78	11	28	36	320	10	569	57	17	23	45	.338	0	14	6.60
Total		341	341	15	326	5894.1	26619	6261	4090	3200	576	171	194	394	2484	69	5771	621	127	341	341	.500	31	129	4.89

Arizona League Batting - R

Team	Org	G	AB	H	2B	3B	HR	TB	R	RBI	TBB	IBB	SO	HBP	SH	SF	SB	CS	SB%	GDP	Avg	OBP	SLG
Athletics	Oak	56	1931	520	91	23	37	768	407	321	332	0	442	52	13	17	137	31	.82	41	.269	.388	.398
Mariners	Sea	56	1956	543	90	20	22	739	364	295	264	3	510	28	19	24	114	43	.73	29	.278	.368	.378
Cubs	ChN	54	1852	488	75	27	16	665	342	265	218	0	404	67	13	28	109	36	.75	31	.263	.357	.359
Padres	SD	55	1939	513	106	16	18	705	335	280	296	3	464	28	8	16	85	41	.67	41	.265	.367	.364
Diamondbacks	Ari	56	1937	507	105	21	15	699	324	260	226	1	469	22	14	13	47	27	.64	45	.262	.343	.361
Rockies	Col	55	1940	505	82	20	15	672	290	225	176	2	379	38	15	12	112	36	.76	36	.260	.332	.346
Total		166	11555	3076	549	127	123	4248	2062	1646	1512	9	2668	235	82	110	604	214	.74	223	.266	.360	.368

Arizona League Pitching - R

Team	Org	G	GS	CG	GF	IP	BFP	H	R	ER	HR	SH	SF	HB	TBB	IBB	SO	WP	Bk	W	L	Pct.	ShO	Sv	ERA
Cubs	ChN	54	54	0	54	480	2172	479	287	183	14	10	12	29	252	0	455	42	26	34	20	.630	4	20	3.43
Diamondbacks	Ari	56	56	0	56	494.1	2210	530	309	229	21	14	20	38	200	3	399	33	15	27	29	.482	1	13	4.17
Mariners	Sea	56	56	1	55	492	2249	485	344	252	22	14	16	56	268	1	458	71	22	30	26	.536	1	11	4.61
Athletics	Oak	56	56	0	56	484.1	2263	526	349	262	22	18	21	38	260	3	441	55	25	29	27	.518	1	13	4.87
Rockies	Col	55	55	0	55	490	2300	525	373	247	17	13	20	41	254	0	443	60	17	21	34	.382	0	12	4.54
Padres	SD	55	55	0	55	487.1	2316	531	400	304	27	13	21	33	278	2	472	74	29	25	30	.455	0	9	5.61
Total		166	166	1	165	2928	13510	3076	2062	1477	123	82	110	235	1512	9	2668	335	134	166	166	.500	7	78	4.54

Gulf Coast League Batting - R

Team	Org	G	AB	H	2B	3B	HR	TB	R	RBI	TBR	IBB	SO	HBP	SH	SF	SB	CS	SB%	GDP	Avg	OBP	SLG
Yankees	NYA	60	2002	550	91	30	28	785	349	293	225	4	414	29	12	25	74	18	.80	38	.275	.352	.392
Tigers	Det	60	1916	477	81	18	30	684	310	264	235	3	476	33	11	23	69	21	.77	41	.249	.338	.357
Mets	NYN	60	1862	491	105	28	15	697	308	234	210	0	392	34	8	18	43	25	.63	30	.264	.346	.374
Royals	KC	60	1916	516	73	17	25	698	293	241	175	4	411	34	27	18	67	28	.71	46	.269	.338	.364
Rangers	Tex	60	1872	470	78	21	18	644	267	199	191	2	446	19	13	15	120	43	.74	37	.251	.324	.344
Devil Rays	TB	60	1850	440	73	20	19	610	255	202	232	0	443	27	11	9	71	40	.64	45	.238	.330	.330
Braves	Atl	58	1819	443	75	10	25	613	244	208	206	0	432	19	2	10	31	12	.72	29	.244	.325	.337
Expos	Mon	59	1822	439	91	14	13	597	241	166	185	1	385	20	17	9	92	40	.70	23	.241	.316	.328
Astros	Hou	60	1895	427	83	6	23	591	236	198	165	3	429	29	16	13	65	37	.64	31	.225	.295	.312
Pirates	Pit	59	1883	472	91	12	17	638	226	187	166	5	445	25	11	17	49	34	.59	46	.251	.317	.339
Orioles	Bal	60	1856	427	70	19	12	571	226	187	201	4	481	35	13	18	85	33	.72	33	.230	.314	.308
Marlins	Fla	59	1779	414	75	10	10	539	225	176	220	3	459	27	16	14	77	29	.73	35	.233	.324	.303
Twins	Min	60	1970	476	62	13	7	585	220	165	199	2	418	30	17	15	110	41	.73	39	.242	.318	.297
White Sox	ChA	60	1865	455	76	18	13	606	218	189	163	5	390	28	19	19	66	24	.73	40	.244	.311	.325
Red Sox	Bos	59	1818	456	82	23	8	608	213	181	176	1	404	19	16	16	68	26	.72	36	.251	.321	.334
Total		447	28125	6953	1206	259	263	9466	3831	3090	2949	37	6425	408	209	239	1087	451	.71	552	.247	.325	.337

Gulf Coast League Pitching - R

Team	Org	G	GS	CG	GF	IP	BFP	H	R	ER	HR	SH	SF	HB	TBB	IBB	SO	WP	Bk	W	L	Pct.	ShO	Sv	ERA
Mets	NYN	60	60	1	59	479.1	2019	406	189	133	14	16	7	21	183	4	462	38	11	42	18	.700	8	21	2.50
Red Sox	Bos	59	59	5	54	484	2040	437	213	138	7	22	9	23	146	5	522	37	13	31	28	.525	5	12	2.57
Rangers	Tex	60	60	4	56	500	2077	441	215	163	19	11	14	13	171	6	429	23	21	34	26	.567	7	18	2.93
Royals	KC	60	60	7	53	493	2094	461	225	171	11	18	13	36	170	1	385	45	8	36	24	.600	9	10	3.12
Twins	Min	60	60	2	58	527	2203	482	225	173	7	8	17	32	168	8	450	52	11	28	32	.467	7	12	2.95
Expos	Mon	59	59	0	59	478.2	2070	462	231	186	14	8	16	27	181	0	366	28	4	25	35	.417	4	13	3.50
Orioles	Bal	60	60	2	58	496.1	2155	489	251	188	22	15	24	26	210	1	394	46	18	27	33	.450	5	15	3.41
Marlins	Fla	59	59	6	53	473.1	2061	428	256	176	16	13	10	39	194	0	410	31	13	31	28	.525	5	9	3.35
Devil Rays	TB	60	60	0	60	491.1	2145	436	258	198	20	16	26	35	214	4	460	58	14	25	35	.417	4	9	3.63
White Sox	ChA	60	60	1	59	487.2	2144	473	261	197	17	19	18	23	217	0	412	32	12	26	34	.433	1	11	3.64
Yankees	NYA	60	60	3	57	505	2164	468	266	192	27	13	14	21	191	3	405	65	12	40	20	.667	4	15	3.42
Pirates	Pit	59	59	3	56	493.1	2165	489	273	207	17	23	23	37	189	2	403	46	16	27	32	.458	4	10	3.78
Tigers	Det	60	60	2	58	495.2	2163	474	278	204	33	10	10	29	180	3	459	65	17	31	29	.517	5	10	3.70
Braves	Atl	58	58	0	58	462.2	2148	491	342	258	19	6	18	13	263	0	430	46	7	21	38	.356	0	6	5.02
Astros	Hou	60	60	4	56	498.2	2290	516	348	261	20	11	20	33	272	0	438	70	26	24	36	.400	4	13	4.71
Total		447	447	40	407	7366	31938	6953	3831	2845	263	209	239	408	2949	37	6425	682	203	448	448	.500		72	184	3.48

Pioneer League Batting - R+

Team	Org	G	AB	H	2B	3B	HR	TB	R	RBI	TBB	IBB	SO	HBP	SH	SF	SB	CS	SB%	GDP	Avg	OBP	SLG
Ogden	Mil	72	2528	727	156	22	51	1080	478	416	287	5	548	51	23	18	69	38	.64	33	.288	.369	.427
Butte	Ana	72	2549	728	132	21	64	1094	478	414	276	6	558	43	16	28	71	27	.72	50	.286	.362	.429
Idaho Falls	SD	72	2552	743	132	37	37	1060	465	395	330	15	524	35	7	26	95	46	.67	58	.291	.376	.415
Billings	Cin	71	2482	713	127	21	59	1059	446	390	257	10	516	33	7	31	76	50	.60	51	.287	.358	.427
Lethbridge	Ari	72	2492	683	107	25	72	1056	439	377	281	7	603	43	13	20	66	33	.67	52	.274	.355	.424
Helena	Mil	71	2501	712	131	10	54	1025	434	379	266	11	506	40	14	21	63	44	.59	52	.285	.360	.410
Medicine Hat	Tor	72	2492	654	110	15	54	956	378	339	233	2	538	22	20	19	79	43	.65	32	.262	.329	.384
Great Falls	LA	72	2441	669	101	31	37	943	376	307	188	3	527	22	37	13	103	76	.58	36	.274	.330	.386
Total		287	20037	5629	996	182	428	8273	3494	3017	2118	59	4320	289	137	176	622	357	.64	364	.281	.355	.413

Pioneer League Pitching - R+

Team	Org	G	GS	CG	GF	IP	BFP	H	R	ER	HR	SH	SF	HB	TBB	IBB	SO	WP	Bk	W	L	Pct.	ShO	Sv	ERA
Great Falls	LA	72	72	2	70	635	2806	660	348	266	40	12	20	33	252	6	563	41	8	40	32	.556	5	17	3.77
Lethbridge	Ari	72	72	2	70	624.1	2745	652	379	294	49	16	16	35	209	3	550	31	1	39	33	.542	3	14	4.24
Billings	Cin	71	71	4	67	623.2	2802	675	389	279	38	15	18	32	264	14	548	69	10	39	32	.549	3	18	4.03
Helena	Mil	71	71	2	69	616.2	2799	664	430	334	51	22	25	25	292	5	536	42	5	37	34	.521	2	20	4.87
Ogden	Mil	72	72	2	70	623.1	2882	732	468	350	67	17	27	44	238	7	573	41	5	37	35	.514	1	11	5.05
Medicine Hat	Tor	72	72	4	68	621	2863	696	469	342	60	18	18	44	294	5	530	65	14	26	46	.361	1	7	4.96
Idaho Falls	SD	72	72	2	70	632	2931	756	482	416	72	16	23	32	294	13	550	62	3	39	33	.542	2	24	5.92
Butte	Ana	72	72	10	62	620.1	2933	794	529	409	51	21	29	44	275	6	470	78	5	30	42	.417	1	7	5.93
Total		287	287	28	259	4996.1	22761	5629	3494	2690	428	137	176	289	2118	59	4320	429	51	287	287	.500	18	118	4.85

1997 Leader Boards

We list the top Double-A and Triple-A players in a variety of statistical categories, ranging from the standard (home runs) to the more esoteric (switch-hitter batting average). Oakland outfield prospect Ben Grieve shows up prominently, leading in RBI (136), on-base percentage (.461) and slugging percentage (.640), as well as making the top 10 on several other leader boards.

If a player appeared in both Double-A and Triple-A, we present his combined statistics. To qualify for leadership, he must have had 385 plate appearances or 115 innings.

Triple-A League Abbreviations	Double-A League Abbreviations
AMAS—American Association	EAST—Eastern League
INT—International League	SOU—Southern League
PCL—Pacific Coast League	TEX—Texas League

Triple-A/Double-A Batting Leaders

Batting Average

Player, Team	Lg	Org	Avg
Mike Kinkade, El Paso	**TEX**	**Mil**	**.385**
Jacob Cruz, Phoenix	PCL	SF	.361
Scott Krause, El Paso	TEX	Mil	.361
Dave McCarty, Phoenix	PCL	SF	.353
Todd Helton, Colorado Springs	PCL	Col	.352
Brian Raabe, Tacoma	PCL	Sea	.352
Ben Grieve, Edmonton	PCL	Oak	.350
Desi Wilson, Phoenix	PCL	SF	.344
Kevin Millar, Portland	EAST	Fla	.342
Luis Raven, Birmingham	SOU	ChA	.336
Kevin Gibbs, San Antonio	TEX	LA	.335
Craig Counsell, Colorado Springs	PCL	Col	.335
Daryle Ward, New Orleans	AMAS	Hou	.334
Mike Neill, Huntsville	SOU	Oak	.333
Aaron Guiel, Mobile	SOU	SD	.333

On-Base Percentage

Player, Team	Lg	Org	OBP
Ben Grieve, Edmonton	**PCL**	**Oak**	**.461**
Mike Kinkade, El Paso	TEX	Mil	.455
Kevin Gibbs, San Antonio	TEX	LA	.451
Aaron Guiel, Mobile	SOU	SD	.435
Frankie Menechino, Birmingham	SOU	ChA	.434
Jacob Cruz, Phoenix	PCL	SF	.434
Todd Helton, Colorado Springs	PCL	Col	.434
Roberto Petagine, Norfolk	INT	NYN	.430
Trey Beamon, Las Vegas	PCL	SD	.425
Mike Neill, Huntsville	SOU	Oak	.425
Kevin Millar, Portland	EAST	Fla	.423
Jon Zuber, Scranton/Wilkes-Barre	INT	Phi	.421
David Dellucci, Bowie	EAST	Bal	.421
Dave McCarty, Phoenix	PCL	SF	.419
Chris Prieto, Mobile	SOU	SD	.418

Slugging Percentage

Player, Team	Lg	Org	Slg
Ben Grieve, Edmonton	**PCL**	**Oak**	**.640**
Russ Morman, Charlotte	INT	Fla	.623
Paul Konerko, Albuquerque	PCL	LA	.621
Dan Rohrmeier, Tacoma	PCL	Sea	.616
Luis Raven, Birmingham	SOU	ChA	.612
Aaron Guiel, Mobile	SOU	SD	.607
Roberto Petagine, Norfolk	INT	NYN	.605
Kevin Millar, Portland	EAST	Fla	.605
Dave McCarty, Phoenix	PCL	SF	.590
Mike Kinkade, El Paso	TEX	Mil	.588
Scott Krause, El Paso	TEX	Mil	.578
Fernando Tatis, Tulsa	TEX	Tex	.576
Chad Rupp, Salt Lake	PCL	Min	.575
David Dellucci, Bowie	EAST	Bal	.574
Tate Seefried, Norfolk	INT	NYN	.573

Home Runs

Player, Team	Lg	Org	HR
Paul Konerko, Albuquerque	**PCL**	**LA**	**37**
Matt Raleigh, Binghamton	**EAST**	**NYN**	**37**
Dan Rohrmeier, Tacoma	PCL	Sea	33
Russ Morman, Charlotte	INT	Fla	33
Chad Rupp, Salt Lake	PCL	Min	32
Tate Seefried, Norfolk	INT	NYN	32
Kevin Millar, Portland	EAST	Fla	32
Richie Sexson, Buffalo	AMAS	Cle	31
Ben Grieve, Edmonton	PCL	Oak	31
Roberto Petagine, Norfolk	INT	NYN	31
Luis Raven, Birmingham	SOU	ChA	30
Shane Spencer, Columbus	INT	NYA	30
Mike Lowell, Columbus	INT	NYA	30
Mike Coolbaugh, Huntsville	SOU	Oak	30
Kevin Witt, Knoxville	SOU	Tor	30

Runs Batted In

Player, Team	Lg	Org	RBI
Ben Grieve, Edmonton	**PCL**	**Oak**	**136**
Mike Coolbaugh, Huntsville	SOU	Oak	132
Kevin Millar, Portland	EAST	Fla	131
Paul Konerko, Albuquerque	PCL	LA	127
D.T. Cromer, Huntsville	SOU	Oak	121
Dan Rohrmeier, Tacoma	PCL	Sea	120
Tom Quinlan, Colorado Springs	PCL	Col	113
Luis Raven, Birmingham	SOU	ChA	112
Mike Kinkade, El Paso	TEX	Mil	109
Keith Williams, Shreveport	TEX	SF	106
J.P. Roberge, San Antonio	TEX	LA	105
Jeff Ball, Phoenix	PCL	SF	103
Randall Simon, Richmond	INT	Atl	102
Roberto Petagine, Norfolk	INT	NYN	100
Several tied at			99

Stolen Bases

Player, Team	Lg	Org	SB
Calvin Murray, Shreveport	**TEX**	**SF**	**52**
Jeremy Carr, Omaha	AMAS	KC	51
Kevin Gibbs, San Antonio	TEX	LA	49
Earl Johnson, Jacksonville	SOU	Det	42
Demond Smith, Huntsville	SOU	Oak	41
Aaron Fuller, Trenton	EAST	Bos	40
Miguel Cairo, Iowa	AMAS	ChN	40
Kerry Robinson, Louisville	AMAS	StL	40
Greg Martinez, Tucson	PCL	Mil	39
Lou Frazier, Rochester	INT	Bal	37
Terry Jones, Colorado Springs	PCL	Col	36
Hanley Frias, Oklahoma City	AMAS	Tex	35
Randy Winn, Portland	EAST	Fla	35
Dante Powell, Phoenix	PCL	SF	34
Kimera Bartee, Toledo	INT	Det	33

Triple-A/Double-A Batting Leaders

Catchers Batting Average

Player, Team	Lg	Org	Avg
Jamie Burke, Vancouver	**PCL**	**Ana**	**.327**
Paul LoDuca, San Antonio	TEX	LA	.327
Justin Towle, Chattanooga	SOU	Cin	.309
Johnny Roskos, Portland	EAST	Fla	.308
Mitch Meluskey, New Orleans	AMAS	Hou	.303
Tom Wilson, Norwich	EAST	NYA	.294
Eli Marrero, Louisville	AMAS	StL	.273
Doug Mirabelli, Phoenix	PCL	SF	.265
Mel Rosario, Bowie	EAST	Bal	.263
Mark Dalesandro, Iowa	AMAS	ChN	.262
B.J. Waszgis, Rochester	INT	Bal	.260
Jimmy Gonzalez, Jackson	TEX	Hou	.254
Pat Cline, Orlando	SOU	ChN	.246
Jason Varitek, Pawtucket	INT	Bos	.244
Mike Figga, Columbus	INT	NYA	.244

First Basemen Batting Average

Player, Team	Lg	Org	Avg
Dave McCarty, Phoenix	**PCL**	**SF**	**.353**
Todd Helton, Colorado Springs	PCL	Col	.352
Desi Wilson, Phoenix	PCL	SF	.344
Kevin Millar, Portland	EAST	Fla	.342
Daryle Ward, New Orleans	AMAS	Hou	.334
Carlos Mendez, Wichita	TEX	KC	.325
Derrek Lee, Las Vegas	PCL	SD	.324
David Cromer, Huntsville	SOU	Oak	.323
Russ Morman, Charlotte	INT	Fla	.319
Roberto Petagine, Norfolk	INT	NYN	.317
Chan Perry, Akron	EAST	Cle	.315
Randall Simon, Richmond	INT	Atl	.308
Brad Fullmer, Ottawa	INT	Mon	.308
Tommy Davis, Rochester	INT	Bal	.304
Tim Costo, Louisville	AMAS	StL	.303

Second Basemen Batting Average

Player, Team	Lg	Org	Avg
Brian Raabe, Tacoma	**PCL**	**Sea**	**.352**
Craig Counsell, Colorado Springs	PCL	Col	.335
Francisco Matos, Rochester	INT	Bal	.324
David Doster, Scranton/Wilkes-Barre	INT	Phi	.315
Lou Merloni, Pawtucket	INT	Bos	.305
Tim Florez, Phoenix	PCL	SF	.301
Rudy Gomez, Norwich	EAST	NYA	.300
Mickey Lopez, El Paso	TEX	Mil	.300
Frank Catalanotto, Toledo	INT	Det	.300
Garey Ingram, San Antonio	TEX	LA	.299
Mitch Simons, Salt Lake	PCL	Min	.299
Kary Bridges, Calgary	PCL	Pit	.296
Carlos Hernandez, Jackson	TEX	Hou	.292
Placido Polanco, Arkansas	TEX	StL	.291
Webster Garrison, Edmonton	PCL	Oak	.289

Third Basemen Batting Average

Player, Team	Lg	Org	Avg
Mike Kinkade, El Paso	**TEX**	**Mil**	**.385**
Eddy Diaz, Tucson	PCL	Mil	.329
Paul Torres, Tacoma	PCL	Sea	.323
Paul Konerko, Albuquerque	PCL	LA	.323
Jeff Ball, Phoenix	PCL	SF	.321
Jason Wood, Edmonton	PCL	Oak	.321
Mike Lowell, Columbus	INT	NYA	.315
Fernando Tatis, Tulsa	TEX	Tex	.314
Mike Coolbaugh, Huntsville	SOU	Oak	.308
Pete Rose Jr, Chattanooga	SOU	Cin	.301
Gabe Alvarez, Mobile	SOU	SD	.300
Brian Richardson, San Antonio	TEX	LA	.298
Ed Giovanola, Richmond	INT	Atl	.291
Brad Seitzer, Memphis	SOU	Sea	.291
Aaron Boone, Indianapolis	AMAS	Cin	.290

Shortstops Batting Average

Player, Team	Lg	Org	Avg
Danny Klassen, El Paso	**TEX**	**Mil**	**.331**
Lou Collier, Calgary	PCL	Pit	.330
Jon Shave, Salt Lake	PCL	Min	.329
Scott Sheldon, Edmonton	PCL	Oak	.315
Ramon Martinez, Shreveport	TEX	SF	.315
Matt Howard, Columbus	INT	NYA	.312
Robert Eenhoorn, Vancouver	PCL	Ana	.308
Enrique Wilson, Buffalo	AMAS	Cle	.306
Dave Berg, Charlotte	INT	Fla	.295
Manny Jimenez, Greenville	SOU	Atl	.291
Chris Sexton, Colorado Springs	PCL	Col	.290
Wilson Delgado, Phoenix	PCL	SF	.288
Luis Ordaz, Arkansas	TEX	StL	.287
Juan Melo, Mobile	SOU	SD	.286
Jason Maxwell, Orlando	SOU	ChN	.279

Outfielders Batting Average

Player, Team	Lg	Org	Avg
Jacob Cruz, Phoenix	**PCL**	**SF**	**.361**
Scott Krause, El Paso	TEX	Mil	.361
Ben Grieve, Edmonton	PCL	Oak	.350
Kevin Gibbs, San Antonio	TEX	LA	.335
Mike Neill, Huntsville	SOU	Oak	.333
Aaron Guiel, Mobile	SOU	SD	.333
Tommy Gregg, Richmond	INT	Atl	.332
Derrick Gibson, Colorado Springs	PCL	Col	.332
Manny Martinez, Calgary	PCL	Pit	.331
Eddie Christian, Tacoma	PCL	Sea	.330
Magglio Ordonez, Nashville	AMAS	ChA	.329
Trey Beamon, Las Vegas	PCL	SD	.328
David Dellucci, Bowie	EAST	Bal	.327
Jeff Abbott, Nashville	AMAS	ChA	.327
Several tied at			.323

Triple-A/Double-A Batting Leaders

Hits

Player, Team	Lg	Org	H
Brian Raabe, Tacoma	**PCL**	**Sea**	**191**
Mike Kinkade, El Paso	TEX	Mil	180
Derrick Gibson, Colorado Springs	PCL	Col	179
Jacob Cruz, Phoenix	PCL	SF	178
David Cromer, Huntsville	SOU	Oak	176
Kevin Millar, Portland	EAST	Fla	175
Magglio Ordonez, Nashville	AMAS	ChA	172
Danny Klassen, El Paso	TEX	Mil	172
Mike Coolbaugh, Huntsville	SOU	Oak	172
Scott Krause, El Paso	TEX	Mil	171
Mike Neill, Huntsville	SOU	Oak	169
Kerry Robinson, Louisville	AMAS	StL	169
Ben Grieve, Edmonton	PCL	Oak	168
J.P. Roberge, San Antonio	TEX	LA	166
Carlos Mendez, Wichita	TEX	KC	165

Doubles

Player, Team	Lg	Org	2B
Darrell Nicholas, El Paso	**TEX**	**Mil**	**47**
Jamie Burke, Vancouver	PCL	Ana	45
Randall Simon, Richmond	INT	Atl	45
Jacob Cruz, Phoenix	PCL	SF	45
Dan Rohrmeier, Tacoma	PCL	Sea	43
Danny Buxbaum, Midland	TEX	Ana	42
D.T. Cromer, Huntsville	SOU	Oak	40
Ben Grieve, Edmonton	PCL	Oak	40
Brian Daubach, Charlotte	INT	Fla	40
Aaron Guiel, Mobile	SOU	SD	39
Scott Sheldon, Edmonton	PCL	Oak	39
Jeff Ball, Phoenix	PCL	SF	38
Several tied at			37

Triples

Player, Team	Lg	Org	3B
Jovino Carvajal, Vancouver	**PCL**	**Ana**	**20**
Brian Richardson, San Antonio	TEX	LA	13
Brian Simmons, Birmingham	SOU	ChA	12
Mike Kinkade, El Paso	TEX	Mil	12
Scott Krause, El Paso	TEX	Mil	11
Terry Joseph, Orlando	SOU	ChN	11
Chance Sanford, Calgary	PCL	Pit	11
Brad Tyler, Richmond	INT	Atl	10
Michael Coleman, Pawtucket	INT	Bos	10
Greg Martinez, Tucson	PCL	Mil	10
Mickey Lopez, El Paso	TEX	Mil	10
Mitch Simons, Salt Lake	PCL	Min	10
Demond Smith, Huntsville	SOU	Oak	10
Chris Singleton, Shreveport	TEX	SF	10
Edgard Velazquez, Colorado Springs	PCL	Col	10

Extra Base Hits

Player, Team	Lg	Org	XBH
Dan Rohrmeier, Tacoma	**PCL**	**Sea**	**80**
Ben Grieve, Edmonton	PCL	Oak	74
Aaron Guiel, Mobile	SOU	SD	69
Mike Coolbaugh, Huntsville	SOU	Oak	69
Paul Konerko, Albuquerque	PCL	LA	69
Shane Spencer, Columbus	INT	NYA	68
Kevin Millar, Portland	EAST	Fla	68
Darrell Nicholas, El Paso	TEX	Mil	66
Keith Williams, Shreveport	TEX	SF	66
Scott Sheldon, Edmonton	PCL	Oak	64
Roberto Petagine, Norfolk	INT	NYN	64
Luis Raven, Birmingham	SOU	ChA	63
Rich Butler, Syracuse	INT	Tor	63
Brian Daubach, Charlotte	INT	Fla	63
Chance Sanford, Calgary	PCL	Pit	63

Plate Appearances per Strikeout

Player, Team	Lg	Org	PA/K
Brian Raabe, Tacoma	**PCL**	**Sea**	**30.35**
Kary Bridges, Calgary	PCL	Pit	18.84
Dave Hajek, Las Vegas	PCL	SD	18.71
Matt Howard, Columbus	INT	NYA	16.61
Craig Wilson, Nashville	AMAS	ChA	16.58
Paul Loduca, San Antonio	TEX	LA	16.41
Eddy Diaz, Tucson	PCL	Mil	16.08
Chris Stynes, Indianapolis	AMAS	Cin	14.97
Brad Fullmer, Ottawa	INT	Mon	14.26
Carlos Mendez, Wichita	TEX	KC	12.47
Enrique Wilson, Buffalo	AMAS	Cle	12.34
Tony Medrano, Omaha	AMAS	KC	12.30
Craig Counsell, Colorado Springs	PCL	Col	11.58
P.J. Forbes, Rochester	INT	Bal	11.57
Doug Dascenzo, Las Vegas	PCL	SD	11.57

Switch-Hitters Batting Average

Player, Team	Lg	Org	Avg
Kevin Gibbs, San Antonio	**TEX**	**LA**	**.335**
Eddie Christian, Tacoma	PCL	Sea	.330
Fernando Tatis, Tulsa	TEX	Tex	.314
Adrian Brown, Calgary	PCL	Pit	.313
Frank Bolick, Vancouver	PCL	Ana	.309
Chris Latham, Salt Lake	PCL	Min	.309
Enrique Wilson, Buffalo	AMAS	Cle	.306
Mitch Meluskey, New Orleans	AMAS	Hou	.303
Mickey Lopez, El Paso	TEX	Mil	.300
Eddie Pearson, Nashville	AMAS	ChA	.298
Brian Banks, Tucson	PCL	Mil	.296
Jason Evans, Nashville	AMAS	ChA	.295
Greg Martinez, Tucson	PCL	Mil	.295
Randy Winn, Portland	EAST	Fla	.292
Several tied at			.288

Triple-A/Double-A Pitching Leaders

Earned Run Average

Player, Team	Lg	Org	ERA
Troy Brohawn, Shreveport	**TEX**	**SF**	**2.56**
Mike Vavrek, New Haven	EAST	Col	2.57
John Halama, New Orleans	AMAS	Hou	2.58
Frank Lankford, Columbus	INT	NYA	2.78
Dave Swartzbaugh, Iowa	AMAS	ChN	2.82
Gabe White, Indianapolis	AMAS	Cin	2.82
Brian Keyser, Nashville	AMAS	ChA	2.87
Roland Delamaza, Buffalo	AMAS	Cle	2.90
Steve Woodard, Tucson	PCL	Mil	3.01
Brian Rose, Pawtucket	INT	Bos	3.02
Kevin Millwood, Richmond	INT	Atl	3.02
Esteban Yan, Rochester	INT	Bal	3.10
Carl Pavano, Pawtucket	INT	Bos	3.12
Mike Jerzembeck, Columbus	INT	NYA	3.13
Joel Bennett, Bowie	EAST	Bal	3.18

Wins

Player, Team	Lg	Org	W
Brian Rose, Pawtucket	**INT**	**Bos**	**17**
Reid Cornelius, Charlotte	**INT**	**Fla**	**17**
Travis Smith, El Paso	TEX	Mil	16
Giovanni Carrara, Indianapolis	AMAS	Cin	16
Jarrod Washburn, Vancouver	PCL	Ana	15
Steve Woodard, Tucson	PCL	Mil	15
Nate Minchey, Colorado Springs	PCL	Col	15
Rick Krivda, Rochester	INT	Bal	14
Geoff Edsell, Vancouver	PCL	Ana	14
Willie Banks, Columbus	INT	NYA	14
Dennis Reyes, Albuquerque	PCL	LA	14
Several tied at			13

Saves

Player, Team	Lg	Org	Sv
Todd Williams, Indianapolis	**AMAS**	**Cin**	**33**
Ben Fleetham, Harrisburg	EAST	Mon	31
Eddie Gaillard, Toledo	INT	Det	28
Todd Erdos, Mobile	SOU	SD	27
John Johnstone, Phoenix	PCL	SF	24
Scott Service, Omaha	AMAS	KC	24
Bob Howry, Birmingham	SOU	ChA	24
Jeff Darwin, Nashville	AMAS	ChA	22
Adam Butler, Greenville	SOU	Atl	22
Marc Pisciotta, Iowa	AMAS	ChN	22
Anthony Chavez, Vancouver	PCL	Ana	21
Mike Welch, Norfolk	INT	NYN	20
Ryan Brannan, Reading	EAST	Phi	20
Heath Bost, New Haven	EAST	Col	20
Several tied at			19

Games Pitched

Player, Team	Lg	Org	GP
Steve Prihoda, Wichita	**TEX**	**KC**	**70**
Matt Snyder, Bowie	EAST	Bal	67
Gabe Gonzalez, Charlotte	INT	Fla	66
Tom Doyle, Chattanooga	SOU	Cin	65
Keith Glauber, Louisville	AMAS	StL	65
Robert Dodd, Reading	EAST	Phi	63
Brendan Donnelly, Chattanooga	SOU	Cin	62
Dale Polley, Columbus	INT	NYA	62
Dan Hubbs, Albuquerque	PCL	LA	62
Anthony Chavez, Vancouver	PCL	Ana	61
Rich Turrentine, Binghamton	EAST	NYN	61
Scott Brow, Richmond	INT	Atl	61
Ricky Pickett, Phoenix	PCL	SF	61
Jason Bullard, Bowie	EAST	Bal	61
Several tied at			60

Complete Games

Player, Team	Lg	Org	CG
Rick Krivda, Rochester	**INT**	**Bal**	**6**
Geoff Edsell, Vancouver	**PCL**	**Ana**	**6**
Steve Woodard, Tucson	**PCL**	**Mil**	**6**
Jarrod Washburn, Vancouver	PCL	Ana	5
Maximo de la Rosa, Akron	EAST	Cle	5
Travis Smith, El Paso	TEX	Mil	5
Brett Hinchliffe, Memphis	SOU	Sea	5
Jonathan Johnson, Tulsa	TEX	Tex	5
Edwin Hurtado, Tacoma	PCL	Sea	5
Mike Saipe, Colorado Springs	PCL	Col	5
Several tied at			4

Shutouts

Player, Team	Lg	Org	ShO
Rick Krivda, Rochester	**INT**	**Bal**	**3**
Edwin Hurtado, Tacoma	**PCL**	**Sea**	**3**
Several tied at			2

349

Triple-A/Double-A Pitching Leaders

Strikeouts

Player, Team	Lg	Org	K
Scott Elarton, New Orleans	**AMAS**	**Hou**	**191**
Kerry Wood, Iowa	AMAS	ChN	186
Jesus Sanchez, Binghamton	EAST	NYN	176
Mark Brownson, New Haven	EAST	Col	170
Mike Saipe, Colorado Springs	PCL	Col	163
Nerio Rodriguez, Rochester	INT	Bal	160
Mike Jerzembeck, Columbus	INT	NYA	160
Giovanni Carrara, Indianapolis	AMAS	Cin	153
Jarrod Washburn, Vancouver	PCL	Ana	152
Carlton Loewer, Scranton/Wilkes-Barre	INT	Phi	152
Neil Weber, Harrisburg	EAST	Mon	148
Carl Pavano, Pawtucket	INT	Bos	147
Joel Bennett, Bowie	EAST	Bal	146
Jason Bell, New Britain	EAST	Min	142
C.J. Nitkowski, New Orleans	AMAS	Hou	141

Strikeouts per 9 IP — Starters

Player, Team	Lg	Org	K/9
Kerry Wood, Iowa	**AMAS**	**ChN**	**11.04**
Steve Shoemaker, Colorado Springs	PCL	Col	10.74
Jesus Sanchez, Binghamton	EAST	NYN	9.58
Doug Creek, Phoenix	PCL	SF	9.51
Jimmy Haynes, Edmonton	PCL	Oak	9.36
Damian Moss, Greenville	SOU	Atl	9.27
Scott Elarton, New Orleans	AMAS	Hou	9.18
Kevin Lomon, Norwich	EAST	NYA	9.12
Scott Eyre, Birmingham	SOU	ChA	9.02
Earl Byrne, Orlando	SOU	ChN	8.86
Neil Weber, Harrisburg	EAST	Mon	8.74
Marcus Moore, Buffalo	AMAS	Cle	8.56
Nerio Rodriguez, Rochester	INT	Bal	8.55
Silvio Censale, Reading	EAST	Phi	8.55
Peter Munro, Trenton	EAST	Bos	8.43

Strikeouts per 9 IP — Relievers

Player, Team	Lg	Org	K/9
Roberto Duran, Jacksonville	**SOU**	**Det**	**14.09**
Scott Service, Omaha	AMAS	KC	12.76
Ben Fleetham, Harrisburg	EAST	Mon	12.59
Kerry Ligtenberg, Richmond	INT	Atl	11.64
Fernando Hernandez, Toledo	INT	Det	11.50
Marc Kroon, Las Vegas	PCL	SD	11.45
Andy Croghan, Norwich	EAST	NYA	11.31
Ricky Pickett, Phoenix	PCL	SF	11.31
Robbie Beckett, Colorado Springs	PCL	Col	11.10
Ken Robinson, Syracuse	INT	Tor	10.67
Jeff Tabaka, Indianapolis	AMAS	Cin	10.61
Robert Dodd, Reading	EAST	Phi	10.53
Bubba Dixon, Mobile	SOU	SD	10.47
Jason Brosnan, Memphis	SOU	Sea	10.46
Adam Butler, Greenville	SOU	Atl	10.29

Innings Pitched

Player, Team	Lg	Org	IP
Mike Saipe, Colorado Springs	**PCL**	**Col**	**197.0**
Jarrod Washburn, Vancouver	PCL	Ana	194.1
Mike Bovee, Vancouver	PCL	Ana	191.0
Brian Rose, Pawtucket	INT	Bos	190.2
Scott Elarton, New Orleans	AMAS	Hou	187.1
Mark Brownson, New Haven	EAST	Col	184.2
Travis Smith, El Paso	TEX	Mil	184.1
Carlton Loewer, Scranton/Wilkes-Barre	INT	Phi	184.0
Geoff Edsell, Vancouver	PCL	Ana	183.1
Jared Fernandez, Trenton	EAST	Bos	182.0
Brian Barkley, Trenton	EAST	Bos	178.2
Brian Harrison, Omaha	AMAS	KC	178.1
Scott Klingenbeck, Indianapolis	AMAS	Cin	177.2
Several tied at			176.0

Opponent Batting Average — Starters

Player, Team	Lg	Org	OAvg
Kerry Wood, Iowa	**AMAS**	**ChN**	**.181**
Nerio Rodriguez, Rochester	INT	Bal	.203
Steve Shoemaker, Colorado Springs	PCL	Col	.214
Kevin Millwood, Richmond	INT	Atl	.216
Earl Byrne, Orlando	SOU	ChN	.217
Scott Elarton, New Orleans	AMAS	Hou	.221
Rick Krivda, Rochester	INT	Bal	.223
Chris Brock, Richmond	INT	Atl	.224
Silvio Censale, Reading	EAST	Phi	.225
Mike Jerzembeck, Columbus	INT	NYA	.229
Scott Eyre, Birmingham	SOU	ChA	.231
Mike Bertotti, Nashville	AMAS	ChA	.233
Frank Lankford, Columbus	INT	NYA	.235
Russ Herbert, Birmingham	SOU	ChA	.235
Several tied at			.236

Opponent Batting Average — Relievers

Player, Team	Lg	Org	OAvg
Ben Fleetham, Harrisburg	**EAST**	**Mon**	**.146**
Ken Robinson, Syracuse	INT	Tor	.158
Matt Ryan, Carolina	SOU	Pit	.167
Marc Pisciotta, Iowa	AMAS	ChN	.175
Roberto Duran, Jacksonville	SOU	Det	.188
Archie Corbin, Rochester	INT	Bal	.191
Kirk Bullinger, Ottawa	INT	Mon	.191
Brian Shouse, Rochester	INT	Bal	.191
Kerry Ligtenberg, Richmond	INT	Atl	.192
Todd Williams, Indianapolis	AMAS	Cin	.196
Rick Greene, Toledo	INT	Det	.201
Alan Newman, Birmingham	SOU	ChA	.205
Todd Erdos, Mobile	SOU	SD	.205
Robert Dodd, Reading	EAST	Phi	.212
Several tied at			.213

1997 Park Data

Thanks to Coors Field, baseball watchers are becoming more knowledgable about the effect a major league ballpark can have on a player's statistics. Here at STATS, we're naturally curious about minor league ballpark effects as well. For instance, the Rockies' Triple-A park in Colorado Springs is also a launching pad.

In order to avoid a one-year aberration presenting a misleading picture of a ballpark, we present four-year data wherever possible. If a park was built or had its dimensions altered significantly during the last four years, we only use the numbers from the years the stadium existed in its current configuration. A single asterisk next to the minor league team means we used data from 1997 only, two asterisks means we used data from 1996-97 and three means we used data from 1995-97.

Last year, we used four-year data for all Double-A and Triple-A ballparks. In our never-ending quest to make this book better, we used four-year numbers all the way down through Class-A this time around. Similarly, we indicate whether all parks use grass, artificial turf or a mixture.

How exactly can park data be used? It expresses the characteristics of a stadium as an index, with 100 being neutral. If a park has a home-run index of 110, that means 10 percent more homers were hit in the team's home games than were during its road games. If 10 percent fewer homers were hit in the team's home games compared to its road games, the home-run index would be 90.

One thing to bear in mind is to be careful how you use the index. If Joe Slugger hit 40 homers while playing his home games in a stadium with a home-run index of 150, don't just lop off half of his homers. Remember, he plays half of his games on the road. So reducing his homers by 25 instead of 50 percent would be more realistic.

American Association — AAA

Buffalo** — Cleveland Indians — Surface: Grass

	G	Avg	AB	R	H	2B	3B	HR	SO
Home	144	.250	9246	1205	2314	404	22	306	1716
Road	144	.271	9951	1454	2697	530	62	321	1914
Index	—	92	93	83	86	82	38	103	96

Indianapolis* — Cincinnati Reds — Surface: Grass

	G	Avg	AB	R	H	2B	3B	HR	SO
Home	72	.250	4760	594	1192	231	26	110	969
Road	72	.261	4739	642	1236	225	28	166	918
Index	—	96	100	93	96	102	92	66	105

Iowa — Chicago Cubs — Surface: Grass

	G	Avg	AB	R	H	2B	3B	HR	SO
Home	287	.261	18974	2527	4946	1074	109	558	3488
Road	284	.270	18948	2622	5111	975	118	529	3359
Index	—	97	99	95	96	110	92	105	104

Louisville — St. Louis Cardinals — Surface: Turf

	G	Avg	AB	R	H	2B	3B	HR	SO
Home	287	.262	19161	2702	5014	1014	177	547	3849
Road	286	.260	18801	2515	4879	1027	134	474	3434
Index	—	101	102	107	102	97	130	113	110

Nashville — Chicago White Sox — Surface: Grass

	G	Avg	AB	R	H	2B	3B	HR	SO
Home	286	.261	19371	2676	5047	960	123	544	3630
Road	289	.261	19161	2520	5003	974	124	519	3438
Index	—	100	102	107	102	97	98	104	104

New Orleans* — Houston Astros — Surface: Grass

	G	Avg	AB	R	H	2B	3B	HR	SO
Home	71	.250	4795	543	1200	223	32	61	924
Road	73	.263	4884	656	1284	245	23	119	963
Index	—	95	101	86	96	93	142	52	98

Oklahoma City — Texas Rangers — Surface: Grass

	G	Avg	AB	R	H	2B	3B	HR	SO
Home	287	.274	19360	2677	5300	1083	172	392	3610
Road	287	.263	19243	2636	5052	976	124	541	3650
Index	—	104	101	102	105	110	138	72	98

Omaha — Kansas City Royals — Surface: Grass

	G	Avg	AB	R	H	2B	3B	HR	SO
Home	289	.279	19350	3030	5402	954	112	755	3242
Road	287	.262	18891	2638	4949	956	141	499	3786
Index	—	107	102	114	108	97	78	148	84

International League — AAA

Charlotte — Florida Marlins — Surface: Grass

	G	Avg	AB	R	H	2B	3B	HR	SO
Home	288	.278	19304	3043	5376	948	86	711	3360
Road	277	.268	18088	2679	4852	984	128	437	3334
Index	—	104	103	109	107	90	63	152	94

Columbus — New York Yankees — Surface: Turf

	G	Avg	AB	R	H	2B	3B	HR	SO
Home	286	.265	18961	2826	5023	1063	218	457	3627
Road	280	.266	18560	2649	4930	935	119	500	3567
Index	—	100	100	104	100	111	179	89	100

Norfolk — New York Mets — Surface: Grass

	G	Avg	AB	R	H	2B	3B	HR	SO
Home	279	.254	18416	2260	4676	873	128	325	3446
Road	288	.261	19118	2553	4983	961	139	496	3658
Index	—	97	99	91	97	94	96	68	98

Ottawa — Montreal Expos — Surface: Grass

	G	Avg	AB	R	H	2B	3B	HR	SO
Home	282	.261	18594	2526	4848	1027	135	359	3395
Road	284	.271	18652	2801	5062	1002	134	530	3381
Index	—	96	100	91	96	103	101	68	101

Pawtucket — Boston Red Sox — Surface: Grass

	G	Avg	AB	R	H	2B	3B	HR	SO
Home	284	.267	19088	2922	5098	985	52	783	3732
Road	283	.260	19090	2649	4968	968	172	473	3689
Index	—	103	100	110	102	102	30	166	101

Richmond — Atlanta Braves — Surface: Grass

	G	Avg	AB	R	H	2B	3B	HR	SO
Home	282	.262	18671	2329	4900	879	119	336	3473
Road	284	.261	18998	2575	4956	999	151	481	3642
Index	—	101	99	91	100	90	80	71	97

Rochester* — Baltimore Orioles — Surface: Grass

	G	Avg	AB	R	H	2B	3B	HR	SO
Home	71	.258	4667	672	1205	264	34	119	1032
Road	70	.256	4690	635	1202	246	36	118	955
Index	—	101	98	104	99	108	95	101	109

Scranton-WB — Philadelphia Phillies — Surface: Turf

	G	Avg	AB	R	H	2B	3B	HR	SO
Home	283	.266	18854	2698	5016	1121	215	386	3378
Road	285	.263	18908	2668	4981	1006	118	503	3526
Index	—	101	100	102	101	112	183	77	96

Syracuse* — Toronto Blue Jays — Surface: Turf

	G	Avg	AB	R	H	2B	3B	HR	SO
Home	71	.251	4755	670	1193	259	21	129	936
Road	71	.266	4577	667	1216	220	28	134	974
Index	—	94	104	100	98	113	72	93	93

Toledo — Detroit Tigers — Surface: Grass

	G	Avg	AB	R	H	2B	3B	HR	SO
Home	283	.256	18662	2556	4775	853	125	561	3501
Road	284	.264	19062	2676	5040	999	164	461	3853
Index	—	97	98	96	95	87	78	124	103

Pacific Coast League — AAA

Albuquerque — Los Angeles Dodgers — Surface: Grass

	G	Avg	AB	R	H	2B	3B	HR	SO
Home	285	.299	19911	3413	5958	1032	182	539	3761
Road	282	.281	19248	2879	5405	1054	180	504	3576
Index	—	107	102	117	109	95	98	103	102

Calgary** — Pittsburgh Pirates — Surface: Grass

	G	Avg	AB	R	H	2B	3B	HR	SO
Home	140	.301	9541	1604	2872	661	56	276	1630
Road	141	.288	9693	1482	2792	540	95	208	1799
Index	—	105	99	109	104	124	60	135	92

Colorado Springs*** — Colorado Rockies — Surface: Grass

	G	Avg	AB	R	H	2B	3B	HR	SO
Home	210	.297	14455	2636	4292	926	132	498	2642
Road	215	.287	14528	2311	4163	846	130	369	2726
Index	—	104	102	117	106	110	102	136	97

Edmonton*** — Oakland Athletics — Surface: Mixed

	G	Avg	AB	R	H	2B	3B	HR	SO
Home	215	.282	14298	2314	4039	871	131	371	2438
Road	215	.284	14355	2309	4083	844	130	395	2672
Index	—	99	100	100	99	104	101	94	92

Las Vegas — San Diego Padres — Surface: Grass

	G	Avg	AB	R	H	2B	3B	HR	SO
Home	287	.286	20018	3208	5727	1167	170	554	3859
Road	282	.277	18790	2835	5202	1068	162	440	3531
Index	—	103	105	111	108	103	99	118	103

Phoenix — San Francisco Giants — Surface: Grass

	G	Avg	AB	R	H	2B	3B	HR	SO
Home	287	.282	19843	2922	5595	1039	253	457	3569
Road	287	.285	19486	2958	5559	1181	159	423	3277
Index	—	99	99	99	101	86	156	106	107

Salt Lake — Minnesota Twins — Surface: Grass

	G	Avg	AB	R	H	2B	3B	HR	SO
Home	288	.300	20283	3434	6091	1220	201	607	3393
Road	287	.296	19976	3342	5908	1210	189	501	3502
Index	—	102	101	102	103	99	105	119	95

Tacoma — Seattle Mariners — Surface: Grass

	G	Avg	AB	R	H	2B	3B	HR	SO
Home	286	.261	18999	2461	4958	966	99	451	3638
Road	283	.297	19760	3210	5876	1179	180	543	3247
Index	—	88	95	76	83	85	57	86	117

Tucson — Milwaukee Brewers — Surface: Grass

	G	Avg	AB	R	H	2B	3B	HR	SO
Home	289	.296	19981	3151	5916	1245	261	313	3447
Road	284	.284	19405	3118	5512	1087	174	543	3577
Index	—	104	101	99	105	111	146	56	94

Vancouver*** — Anaheim Angels — Surface: Grass

	G	Avg	AB	R	H	2B	3B	HR	SO
Home	207	.256	13496	1682	3451	684	81	217	2366
Road	215	.291	14845	2510	4325	938	128	399	2477
Index	—	88	94	70	83	80	70	60	105

Eastern League — AA

Akron* — Cleveland Indians — Surface: Grass

	G	Avg	AB	R	H	2B	3B	HR	SO
Home	70	.277	4738	781	1313	251	24	137	874
Road	71	.279	4659	818	1298	228	20	138	913
Index	—	99	103	97	103	108	118	98	94

Binghamton — New York Mets — Surface: Grass

	G	Avg	AB	R	H	2B	3B	HR	SO
Home	284	.266	18904	2737	5024	987	142	448	3655
Road	283	.254	18806	2488	4784	932	100	465	3652
Index	—	104	100	110	105	105	141	96	100

Bowie — Baltimore Orioles — Surface: Grass

	G	Avg	AB	R	H	2B	3B	HR	SO
Home	283	.261	18704	2644	4878	917	69	526	3618
Road	285	.265	19070	2727	5049	996	135	456	3813
Index	—	99	99	98	97	94	52	118	97

Harrisburg — Montreal Expos — Surface: Grass

	G	Avg	AB	R	H	2B	3B	HR	SO
Home	279	.254	18152	2554	4603	800	116	547	3695
Road	285	.254	18835	2558	4793	913	121	397	3794
Index	—	100	98	102	98	91	99	143	101

New Britain** — Minnesota Twins — Surface: Grass

	G	Avg	AB	R	H	2B	3B	HR	SO
Home	142	.254	9090	1181	2305	502	65	174	1794
Road	142	.266	9335	1498	2480	474	67	297	1844
Index	—	95	97	79	93	109	100	60	100

New Haven — Colorado Rockies — Surface: Grass

	G	Avg	AB	R	H	2B	3B	HR	SO
Home	285	.252	18711	2560	4723	893	106	356	3949
Road	280	.254	18182	2424	4626	843	121	437	3660
Index	—	99	101	104	100	103	85	79	105

Norwich*** — New York Yankees — Surface: Grass

	G	Avg	AB	R	H	2B	3B	HR	SO
Home	211	.254	13957	1899	3544	680	93	221	2928
Road	213	.272	14233	2226	3868	743	105	393	2929
Index	—	93	99	86	92	93	90	57	102

Portland — Florida Marlins — Surface: Grass

	G	Avg	AB	R	H	2B	3B	HR	SO
Home	286	.271	19542	3002	5289	998	141	614	3986
Road	280	.263	18605	2508	4900	883	107	388	3473
Index	—	103	104	117	106	108	125	151	109

Reading — Philadelphia Phillies — Surface: Grass

	G	Avg	AB	R	H	2B	3B	HR	SO
Home	284	.262	19175	2938	5030	900	140	631	3869
Road	281	.252	18597	2484	4688	865	113	377	3758
Index	—	104	102	117	106	101	120	162	100

Trenton — Boston Red Sox — Surface: Grass

	G	Avg	AB	R	H	2B	3B	HR	SO
Home	279	.255	18512	2539	4727	906	128	396	3534
Road	286	.262	18957	2806	4976	954	116	532	3721
Index	—	97	100	93	97	97	113	76	97

Southern League — AA

Birmingham — Chicago White Sox — Surface: Grass

	G	Avg	AB	R	H	2B	3B	HR	SO
Home	283	.258	18809	2581	4846	947	110	287	3627
Road	278	.267	18626	2736	4964	942	125	476	3669
Index	—	97	99	93	96	100	87	60	98

Carolina — Pittsburgh Pirates — Surface: Grass

	G	Avg	AB	R	H	2B	3B	HR	SO
Home	281	.264	19007	2640	5013	1075	157	337	3835
Road	279	.263	19163	2653	5045	898	142	434	3560
Index	—	100	98	99	99	121	111	78	109

Chattanooga** — Cincinnati Reds — Surface: Grass

	G	Avg	AB	R	H	2B	3B	HR	SO
Home	138	.278	9204	1396	2557	492	64	214	1679
Road	141	.270	9592	1481	2593	568	67	272	1871
Index	—	103	98	96	101	90	100	82	94

Greenville — Atlanta Braves — Surface: Grass

	G	Avg	AB	R	H	2B	3B	HR	SO
Home	282	.274	18917	2855	5182	957	112	544	3592
Road	276	.259	18272	2520	4729	925	131	422	3564
Index	—	106	101	111	107	100	83	125	97

Huntsville — Oakland Athletics — Surface: Grass

	G	Avg	AB	R	H	2B	3B	HR	SO
Home	280	.266	18776	2801	4986	941	138	447	3727
Road	281	.267	18710	2877	4992	970	120	442	3689
Index	—	100	101	98	100	97	115	101	101

Jacksonville — Detroit Tigers — Surface: Grass

	G	Avg	AB	R	H	2B	3B	HR	SO
Home	277	.255	18625	2618	4748	963	66	618	3606
Road	281	.270	18677	2726	5051	964	147	446	3562
Index	—	94	101	97	95	100	45	139	102

Knoxville — Toronto Blue Jays — Surface: Grass

	G	Avg	AB	R	H	2B	3B	HR	SO
Home	280	.277	18972	2957	5263	1040	204	430	3727
Road	283	.252	18238	2470	4596	850	123	387	3876
Index	—	110	105	121	116	118	159	107	92

Memphis — Seattle Mariners — Surface: Mixed

	G	Avg	AB	R	H	2B	3B	HR	SO
Home	275	.255	18007	2533	4594	886	114	478	3895
Road	282	.261	18773	2613	4895	973	147	390	3713
Index	—	98	98	96	96	95	81	128	109

Mobile* — San Diego Padres — Surface: Grass

	G	Avg	AB	R	H	2B	3B	HR	SO
Home	72	.271	4894	758	1326	264	37	124	950
Road	65	.277	4443	697	1232	264	30	100	912
Index	—	98	99	98	97	91	112	113	95

Orlando — Chicago Cubs — Surface: Grass

	G	Avg	AB	R	H	2B	3B	HR	SO
Home	276	.261	18086	2423	4724	820	149	397	3155
Road	281	.262	18617	2641	4873	1006	129	414	3607
Index	—	100	98	99	99	84	119	99	90

Texas League — AA

Arkansas — St. Louis Cardinals — Surface: Grass

	G	Avg	AB	R	H	2B	3B	HR	SO
Home	273	.261	17372	2397	4536	934	125	379	3132
Road	277	.258	18348	2369	4726	879	151	347	3477
Index	—	101	96	103	97	112	87	115	95

El Paso** — Milwaukee Brewers — Surface: Grass

	G	Avg	AB	R	H	2B	3B	HR	SO
Home	140	.312	9729	1739	3033	696	174	164	1717
Road	139	.279	9319	1464	2604	498	83	250	1707
Index	—	112	118	116	134	201	63	96	

Jackson — Houston Astros — Surface: Grass

	G	Avg	AB	R	H	2B	3B	HR	SO
Home	276	.257	18144	2325	4660	741	93	397	3523
Road	273	.267	18083	2558	4824	948	132	368	3212
Index	—	96	99	90	96	78	70	108	109

Midland* — Anaheim Angels — Surface: Grass

	G	Avg	AB	R	H	2B	3B	HR	SO
Home	69	.303	4754	952	1441	325	54	161	839
Road	70	.281	4688	761	1319	288	33	103	848
Index	—	108	103	127	111	111	161	154	98

San Antonio — Los Angeles Dodgers — Surface: Grass

	G	Avg	AB	R	H	2B	3B	HR	SO
Home	277	.254	18232	2118	4623	857	143	230	3447
Road	273	.277	18038	2741	4999	970	188	427	3245
Index	—	91	100	76	91	87	75	53	105

Shreveport — San Francisco Giants — Surface: Grass

	G	Avg	AB	R	H	2B	3B	HR	SO
Home	273	.252	17877	2309	4507	852	133	320	3025
Road	275	.278	18576	2751	5155	957	124	461	3162
Index	—	91	97	85	88	93	111	72	99

Tulsa — Texas Rangers — Surface: Grass

	G	Avg	AB	R	H	2B	3B	HR	SO
Home	277	.266	18666	2606	4968	899	108	526	3515
Road	272	.270	17943	2616	4840	1004	137	423	3246
Index	—	99	102	98	101	86	76	120	104

Wichita — Kansas City Royals — Surface: Mixed

	G	Avg	AB	R	H	2B	3B	HR	SO
Home	275	.281	18729	2882	5263	926	122	549	3084
Road	277	.272	18735	2736	5102	1038	202	364	3439
Index	—	103	101	106	104	89	60	151	90

California League — A+

Bakersfield — San Francisco Giants — Surface: Grass

	G	Avg	AB	R	H	2B	3B	HR	SO
Home	278	.273	19170	3025	5231	1012	39	502	3999
Road	278	.268	18843	2910	5054	957	166	412	3989
Index	—	102	102	104	104	104	23	120	99

High Desert** — Arizona Diamondbacks — Surface: Grass

	G	Avg	AB	R	H	2B	3B	HR	SO
Home	140	.292	9947	1916	2903	582	116	395	2009
Road	140	.271	9680	1545	2626	527	73	225	2029
Index	—	108	103	124	111	107	155	171	96

Lake Elsinore — Anaheim Angels — Surface: Grass

	G	Avg	AB	R	H	2B	3B	HR	SO
Home	278	.266	18988	2832	5044	1117	172	341	3894
Road	277	.272	19035	2996	5177	1007	155	524	4091
Index	—	98	99	94	97	111	111	65	95

Lancaster — Seattle Mariners — Surface: Grass

	G	Avg	AB	R	H	2B	3B	HR	SO
Home	140	.288	9959	1801	2868	548	106	347	2115
Road	142	.259	9494	1413	2455	473	81	206	2250
Index	—	111	106	129	118	110	125	161	90

Modesto** — Oakland Athletics — Surface: Grass

	G	Avg	AB	R	H	2B	3B	HR	SO
Home	141	.271	9487	1610	2575	547	83	274	2309
Road	140	.272	9772	1597	2656	497	79	275	2245
Index	—	100	96	100	96	113	108	103	106

Rancho Cucamonga — San Diego Padres — Surface: Grass

	G	Avg	AB	R	H	2B	3B	HR	SO
Home	278	.269	19032	2947	5115	959	174	419	4325
Road	277	.268	18805	2979	5043	998	143	437	4408
Index	—	100	101	99	101	95	120	95	97

San Bernardino** — Los Angeles Dodgers — Surface: Grass

	G	Avg	AB	R	H	2B	3B	HR	SO
Home	140	.259	9497	1521	2462	504	90	222	2297
Road	140	.275	9626	1658	2643	553	83	276	2137
Index	—	94	99	92	93	92	110	82	109

San Jose** — San Francisco Giants — Surface: Grass

	G	Avg	AB	R	H	2B	3B	HR	SO
Home	140	.255	9436	1167	2405	434	90	101	2233
Road	140	.282	9764	1560	2754	528	84	231	2079
Index	—	90	97	75	87	85	111	45	111

Stockton — Milwaukee Brewers — Surface: Grass

	G	Avg	AB	R	H	2B	3B	HR	SO
Home	279	.265	18622	2557	4927	816	148	290	3559
Road	278	.275	18957	2912	5216	963	155	435	3809
Index	—	96	98	87	94	86	97	68	95

Visalia — Oakland Athletics — Surface: Grass

	G	Avg	AB	R	H	2B	3B	HR	SO
Home	210	.277	14613	2374	4044	801	122	330	3162
Road	210	.264	14371	2212	3791	720	102	333	3145
Index	—	105	102	107	107	109	118	97	99

Carolina League — A+

Durham*** — Atlanta Braves — Surface: Grass

	G	Avg	AB	R	H	2B	3B	HR	SO
Home	210	.263	13955	2047	3669	711	82	388	2943
Road	207	.257	13627	1911	3500	695	91	309	2991
Index	—	102	101	106	103	100	88	123	96

Frederick*** — Baltimore Orioles — Surface: Grass

	G	Avg	AB	R	H	2B	3B	HR	SO
Home	207	.255	13666	1933	3485	681	70	367	3075
Road	209	.253	13794	1925	3486	721	87	245	2905
Index	—	101	100	101	101	95	81	151	107

Kinston — Cleveland Indians — Surface: Grass

	G	Avg	AB	R	H	2B	3B	HR	SO
Home	279	.243	18056	2370	4386	801	79	448	3922
Road	274	.259	18164	2608	4706	960	111	458	3729
Index	—	94	98	89	92	84	72	98	106

Lynchburg — Pittsburgh Pirates — Surface: Grass

	G	Avg	AB	R	H	2B	3B	HR	SO
Home	277	.265	18528	2688	4910	1011	124	431	3838
Road	279	.264	18592	2699	4915	937	130	441	3846
Index	—	100	100	100	101	108	96	98	100

Prince William — St. Louis Cardinals — Surface: Grass

	G	Avg	AB	R	H	2B	3B	HR	SO
Home	276	.259	18213	2563	4712	956	172	357	3618
Road	277	.256	18543	2624	4743	855	118	471	3830
Index	—	101	99	98	100	114	148	77	96

Salem*** — Colorado Rockies — Surface: Grass

	G	Avg	AB	R	H	2B	3B	HR	SO
Home	210	.262	13850	1941	3624	772	80	275	2690
Road	206	.248	13559	1785	3359	626	61	284	2943
Index	—	106	100	107	106	121	128	95	89

Wilmington — Kansas City Royals — Surface: Grass

	G	Avg	AB	R	H	2B	3B	HR	SO
Home	281	.247	18519	2277	4579	834	145	229	3722
Road	275	.257	18415	2543	4725	921	118	486	3611
Index	—	96	98	88	95	90	122	47	102

Winston-Salem** — Chicago White Sox — Surface: Grass

	G	Avg	AB	R	H	2B	3B	HR	SO
Home	138	.249	9122	1286	2271	433	59	249	2046
Road	141	.259	9111	1266	2364	470	64	222	1890
Index	—	102	104	98	92	92	112	108	

Florida State League — A+

Brevard County — Florida Marlins — Surface: Grass

	G	Avg	AB	R	H	2B	3B	HR	SO
Home	277	.246	18192	2219	4470	804	97	237	3553
Road	274	.266	18411	2568	4897	873	147	289	3271
Index	—	92	98	85	90	93	67	83	110

Charlotte*** — Florida Marlins — Surface: Grass

	G	Avg	AB	R	H	2B	3B	HR	SO
Home	208	.254	13772	1820	3499	671	117	246	2802
Road	203	.266	13585	1894	3620	678	111	231	2434
Index	—	95	99	94	94	98	104	105	114

Clearwater — Philadelphia Phillies — Surface: Grass

	G	Avg	AB	R	H	2B	3B	HR	SO
Home	276	.260	18418	2489	4780	922	134	285	3294
Road	272	.252	17811	2280	4480	801	133	283	3514
Index	—	103	102	108	105	111	97	97	91

Daytona — Chicago Cubs — Surface: Grass

	G	Avg	AB	R	H	2B	3B	HR	SO
Home	273	.261	17962	2619	4686	860	149	327	3602
Road	271	.256	17784	2357	4552	827	128	276	3384
Index	—	102	100	110	102	103	115	117	105

Dunedin — Toronto Blue Jays — Surface: Grass

	G	Avg	AB	R	H	2B	3B	HR	SO
Home	274	.262	18644	2688	4885	959	128	400	3828
Road	273	.255	17906	2451	4564	842	136	278	3695
Index	—	103	104	109	107	109	90	138	99

Fort Myers — Minnesota Twins — Surface: Grass

	G	Avg	AB	R	H	2B	3B	HR	SO
Home	269	.252	17441	2118	4387	760	105	217	3345
Road	273	.255	18138	2424	4630	847	149	295	3522
Index	—	99	98	89	96	93	73	76	99

Kissimmee — Houston Astros — Surface: Grass

	G	Avg	AB	R	H	2B	3B	HR	SO
Home	205	.251	13497	1663	3389	570	106	128	2445
Road	203	.260	13447	1854	3499	638	96	192	2447
Index	—	96	99	89	96	89	110	66	100

Lakeland — Detroit Tigers — Surface: Grass

	G	Avg	AB	R	H	2B	3B	HR	SO
Home	263	.261	16989	2270	4427	761	196	259	3169
Road	280	.253	18490	2297	4673	885	126	264	3954
Index	—	103	100	105	101	94	169	107	87

St. Lucie — New York Mets — Surface: Grass

	G	Avg	AB	R	H	2B	3B	HR	SO
Home	270	.252	17479	2159	4401	724	121	216	3341
Road	270	.247	17494	2059	4319	775	126	219	3506
Index	—	102	100	105	102	93	96	99	95

St. Petersburg — Tampa Bay Devil Rays — Surface: Grass

	G	Avg	AB	R	H	2B	3B	HR	SO
Home	275	.246	17871	2067	4394	783	138	184	3287
Road	271	.250	17824	2187	4464	823	122	279	3404
Index	—	98	99	93	97	95	113	66	96

Sarasota — Boston Red Sox — Surface: Grass

	G	Avg	AB	R	H	2B	3B	HR	SO
Home	276	.270	18433	2673	4972	920	144	272	3597
Road	265	.255	17351	2273	4431	769	126	263	3369
Index	—	106	102	113	108	113	108	97	101

Tampa** — New York Yankees — Surface: Grass

	G	Avg	AB	R	H	2B	3B	HR	SO
Home	134	.251	9006	1105	2264	372	59	156	1897
Road	136	.257	8938	1219	2294	433	71	153	1849
Index	—	98	102	92	100	85	82	101	102

Vero Beach — Los Angeles Dodgers — Surface: Grass

	G	Avg	AB	R	H	2B	3B	HR	SO
Home	268	.260	17568	2575	4573	842	103	413	3556
Road	268	.249	17353	2266	4313	746	131	192	3485
Index	—	105	101	114	106	111	78	212	101

West Palm Beach — Montreal Expos — Surface: Grass

	G	Avg	AB	R	H	2B	3B	HR	SO
Home	267	.263	17357	2194	4384	808	137	173	3504
Road	271	.255	17590	2263	4484	779	111	278	3319
Index	—	99	100	98	99	105	125	63	107

Midwest League — A

Beloit — Milwaukee Brewers — Surface: Grass

	G	Avg	AB	R	H	2B	3B	HR	SO
Home	275	.261	17901	2744	4665	859	96	380	3849
Road	273	.253	17923	2516	4543	855	135	302	3796
Index	—	103	99	108	102	101	71	126	102

Burlington* — Cincinnati Reds — Surface: Grass

	G	Avg	AB	R	H	2B	3B	HR	SO
Home	68	.266	4507	736	1197	209	48	99	1040
Road	72	.269	4787	758	1288	252	27	124	1042
Index	—	99	100	103	98	88	189	85	106

Cedar Rapids — Anaheim Angels — Surface: Grass

	G	Avg	AB	R	H	2B	3B	HR	SO
Home	275	.262	18172	2756	4766	912	112	479	3842
Road	275	.257	18186	2675	4667	874	149	352	3783
Index	—	102	100	103	102	104	75	136	102

Clinton — San Diego Padres — Surface: Grass

	G	Avg	AB	R	H	2B	3B	HR	SO
Home	268	.250	17646	2504	4420	769	140	255	4029
Road	278	.252	17808	2604	4496	827	137	325	3882
Index	—	99	100	100	102	94	103	79	105

Fort Wayne — Minnesota Twins — Surface: Grass

	G	Avg	AB	R	H	2B	3B	HR	SO
Home	278	.261	19079	2567	4980	961	150	284	4051
Road	272	.257	17916	2561	4602	849	155	315	3786
Index	—	102	104	98	106	106	91	85	100

Kane County — Florida Marlins — Surface: Grass

	G	Avg	AB	R	H	2B	3B	HR	SO
Home	284	.254	18619	2636	4725	857	131	314	3946
Road	264	.254	17339	2497	4404	846	108	314	3844
Index	—	100	100	98	100	94	113	93	100

Lansing** — Kansas City Royals — Surface: Grass

	G	Avg	AB	R	H	2B	3B	HR	SO
Home	140	.260	9669	1590	2731	545	113	185	1685
Road	136	.270	9401	1378	2541	470	80	169	1813
Index	—	104	100	112	104	113	137	106	90

Michigan* — Boston Red Sox — Surface: Grass

	G	Avg	AB	R	H	2B	3B	HR	SO
Home	66	.260	4420	664	1147	219	46	94	960
Road	71	.267	4726	733	1260	241	38	92	1023
Index	—	97	101	97	98	97	129	109	100

Peoria — St. Louis Cardinals — Surface: Grass

	G	Avg	AB	R	H	2B	3B	HR	SO
Home	279	.260	18363	2666	4770	994	171	285	3952
Road	268	.253	17458	2505	4422	832	104	317	3715
Index	—	103	101	102	104	114	156	85	101

Quad City — Houston Astros — Surface: Grass

	G	Avg	AB	R	H	2B	3B	HR	SO
Home	268	.247	17329	2387	4287	810	101	338	3519
Road	272	.262	18128	2616	4747	862	139	331	3786
Index	—	94	97	93	92	98	76	107	97

Rockford* — Chicago Cubs — Surface: Grass

	G	Avg	AB	R	H	2B	3B	HR	SO
Home	64	.264	4240	591	1118	230	35	62	976
Road	68	.255	4505	668	1148	235	43	66	1080
Index	—	103	100	94	103	104	86	100	96

South Bend — Arizona Diamondbacks — Surface: Grass

	G	Avg	AB	R	H	2B	3B	HR	SO
Home	272	.259	18054	2526	4685	885	168	247	3593
Road	275	.252	18342	2520	4631	867	130	317	3869
Index	—	103	100	101	102	104	131	79	94

West Michigan — Detroit Tigers — Surface: Grass

	G	Avg	AB	R	H	2B	3B	HR	SO
Home	275	.234	18072	2270	4204	773	106	200	3887
Road	269	.257	17985	2612	4629	873	154	334	3902
Index	—	91	98	85	89	89	69	60	100

Wisconsin — Seattle Mariners — Surface: Grass

	G	Avg	AB	R	H	2B	3B	HR	SO
Home	208	.250	13460	1934	3364	722	109	229	3050
Road	204	.251	13591	1935	3414	747	97	207	2884
Index	—	99	97	98	98	98	113	112	107

South Atlantic League — A

Asheville — Colorado Rockies — Surface: Grass

	G	Avg	AB	R	H	2B	3B	HR	SO
Home	273	.261	18072	2539	4718	922	48	413	3878
Road	275	.236	17844	2185	4213	747	105	281	4055
Index	—	111	102	117	113	122	45	145	94

Augusta — Pittsburgh Pirates — Surface: Grass

	G	Avg	AB	R	H	2B	3B	HR	SO
Home	277	.242	18207	2321	4398	780	135	183	4223
Road	281	.250	18739	2586	4679	872	161	322	4251
Index	—	97	99	91	95	92	86	58	102

Cape Fear — Montreal Expos — Surface: Grass

	G	Avg	AB	R	H	2B	3B	HR	SO
Home	71	.268	4820	640	1291	227	39	85	883
Road	69	.249	4578	624	1139	241	24	78	912
Index	—	108	102	100	110	89	154	104	92

Charleston-SC* — Tampa Bay Devil Rays — Surface: Grass

	G	Avg	AB	R	H	2B	3B	HR	SO
Home	72	.237	4756	549	1126	206	35	49	1046
Road	70	.247	4622	631	1142	216	32	88	1019
Index	—	96	100	85	96	93	106	54	100

Charleston-WV — Cincinnati Reds — Surface: Grass

	G	Avg	AB	R	H	2B	3B	HR	SO
Home	281	.254	18205	2477	4633	940	154	171	3910
Road	281	.254	18461	2557	4683	899	136	363	4108
Index	—	100	99	97	99	106	115	48	97

Columbia* — New York Mets — Surface: Grass

	G	Avg	AB	R	H	2B	3B	HR	SO
Home	70	.239	4342	525	1036	202	19	82	1173
Road	70	.235	4465	534	1051	197	23	66	1064
Index	—	101	97	98	99	105	85	128	113

Columbus — New York Yankees — Surface: Grass

	G	Avg	AB	R	H	2B	3B	HR	SO
Home	281	.255	18627	2786	4757	810	187	514	4083
Road	279	.239	18418	2442	4409	801	140	341	4501
Index	—	107	100	113	107	100	132	149	90

Delmarva** — Baltimore Orioles — Surface: Grass

	G	Avg	AB	R	H	2B	3B	HR	SO
Home	142	.224	9257	1194	2078	433	71	152	2184
Road	142	.253	9403	1306	2380	454	64	176	2122
Index	—	89	98	91	87	97	113	88	105

Greensboro — New York Yankees — Surface: Grass

	G	Avg	AB	R	H	2B	3B	HR	SO
Home	282	.241	18538	2513	4459	840	124	346	4528
Road	281	.252	18604	2604	4682	875	139	337	4338
Index	—	96	99	96	95	96	90	103	105

Hagerstown — Toronto Blue Jays — Surface: Grass

	G	Avg	AB	R	H	2B	3B	HR	SO
Home	281	.259	18544	2682	4811	968	117	382	4279
Road	275	.249	18089	2412	4498	902	134	299	4178
Index	—	104	100	109	105	105	85	125	100

Hickory	Chicago White Sox						Surface: Grass	
	G	Avg	AB	R	H	2B	3B	HR	SO
Home	281	.261	19271	2706	5025	900	153	409	4024
Road	277	.256	18490	2544	4737	916	129	296	3900
Index	—	102	103	105	105	94	114	133	99

Macon	Atlanta Braves						Surface: Grass	
	G	Avg	AB	R	H	2B	3B	HR	SO
Home	278	.245	18604	2582	4550	834	112	421	4347
Road	280	.248	18607	2611	4612	879	145	377	4431
Index	—	99	101	99	95	77	112	98

Piedmont***	Philadelphia Phillies						Surface: Grass	
	G	Avg	AB	R	H	2B	3B	HR	SO
Home	207	.243	13575	1742	3301	627	103	167	2993
Road	213	.249	14240	1872	3543	651	91	221	3041
Index	—	98	98	98	96	101	119	79	103

Savannah***	Los Angeles Dodgers						Surface: Grass	
	G	Avg	AB	R	H	2B	3B	HR	SO
Home	211	.227	13966	1733	3172	476	116	290	3599
Road	209	.243	13682	1851	3330	589	103	233	3304
Index	—	93	101	93	94	79	110	122	107

New York - Penn League — A-

Auburn***	Houston Astros						Surface: Grass	
	G	Avg	AB	R	H	2B	3B	HR	SO
Home	112	.261	7373	1070	1921	343	53	77	1477
Road	114	.260	7541	1095	1962	338	57	122	1525
Index	—	100	100	99	100	104	95	65	99

Batavia	Philadelphia Phillies						Surface: Grass	
	G	Avg	AB	R	H	2B	3B	HR	SO
Home	147	.257	9796	1335	2520	436	120	86	1916
Road	151	.261	10208	1427	2664	450	90	158	2078
Index	—	99	99	96	97	101	139	57	96

Erie***	Pittsburgh Pirates						Surface: Grass	
	G	Avg	AB	R	H	2B	3B	HR	SO
Home	115	.262	7773	1157	2037	398	62	139	1561
Road	112	.252	7351	1001	1856	314	72	109	1611
Index	—	104	103	113	107	120	81	121	92

Hudson Valley	Tampa Bay Devil Rays						Surface: Grass	
	G	Avg	AB	R	H	2B	3B	HR	SO
Home	150	.245	10172	1398	2492	453	95	117	2256
Road	149	.250	10029	1477	2510	462	96	117	2274
Index	—	98	101	94	99	97	98	99	98

Jamestown	Detroit Tigers						Surface: Grass	
	G	Avg	AB	R	H	2B	3B	HR	SO
Home	147	.261	9819	1506	2559	472	121	196	2056
Road	153	.250	10145	1463	2535	470	77	130	2154
Index	—	104	101	107	105	104	162	156	99

Lowell**	Boston Red Sox						Surface: Grass	
	G	Avg	AB	R	H	2B	3B	HR	SO
Home	75	.241	5032	729	1212	239	24	86	1238
Road	75	.242	4925	624	1190	192	42	59	1137
Index	—	100	102	117	102	122	56	143	107

New Jersey**	St. Louis Cardinals						Surface: Grass	
	G	Avg	AB	R	H	2B	3B	HR	SO
Home	77	.258	5195	739	1341	220	80	56	1197
Road	72	.259	4746	696	1230	212	47	74	1094
Index	—	100	102	99	102	95	156	69	100

Oneonta	New York Yankees						Surface: Grass	
	G	Avg	AB	R	H	2B	3B	HR	SO
Home	149	.243	9601	1252	2335	373	124	52	2289
Road	151	.241	9901	1379	2388	426	80	103	2423
Index	—	101	98	92	99	90	160	52	97

Pittsfield	New York Mets						Surface: Grass	
	G	Avg	AB	R	H	2B	3B	HR	SO
Home	150	.247	9774	1262	2412	427	88	63	2033
Road	150	.251	10074	1391	2528	440	112	130	2144
Index	—	98	97	91	95	100	81	50	98

St. Catharines*	Toronto Blue Jays						Surface: Grass	
	G	Avg	AB	R	H	2B	3B	HR	SO
Home	38	.261	2548	407	666	111	10	61	556
Road	37	.246	2471	360	609	129	24	28	513
Index	—	105	100	110	106	83	40	211	105

Utica	Florida Marlins						Surface: Grass	
	G	Avg	AB	R	H	2B	3B	HR	SO
Home	149	.258	9804	1403	2527	462	92	125	2131
Road	146	.252	9521	1298	2398	411	75	95	2060
Index	—	102	101	106	103	109	119	128	100

Vermont*	Montreal Expos						Surface: Grass	
	G	Avg	AB	R	H	2B	3B	HR	SO
Home	38	.244	2584	395	630	102	26	31	540
Road	38	.271	2524	367	683	118	30	31	530
Index	—	90	102	108	92	84	85	98	100

Watertown	Cleveland Indians						Surface: Grass	
	G	Avg	AB	R	H	2B	3B	HR	SO
Home	148	.252	9719	1366	2448	423	60	183	2276
Road	149	.247	9897	1404	2445	446	85	107	2125
Index	—	102	99	98	101	97	72	174	109

Williamsport	Chicago Cubs						Surface: Grass	
	G	Avg	AB	R	H	2B	3B	HR	SO
Home	151	.253	10062	1437	2547	424	103	107	2086
Road	151	.254	9946	1402	2528	449	90	118	2111
Index	—	100	101	102	101	93	113	90	98

Northwest League — A-

Boise	Anaheim Angels						Surface: Grass	
	G	Avg	AB	R	H	2B	3B	HR	SO
Home	151	.265	10489	1698	2782	488	86	180	2290
Road	152	.258	10573	1724	2726	541	81	188	2469
Index	—	103	100	99	103	91	107	97	93

Eugene	Atlanta Braves						Surface: Grass	
	G	Avg	AB	R	H	2B	3B	HR	SO
Home	152	.246	10479	1478	2579	467	90	181	2642
Road	152	.258	10511	1655	2714	506	96	200	2451
Index	—	95	100	89	95	93	94	91	108

Everett	Seattle Mariners						Surface: Grass	
	G	Avg	AB	R	H	2B	3B	HR	SO
Home	152	.253	10474	1630	2654	521	51	264	3019
Road	151	.254	10363	1503	2636	462	91	173	2448
Index	—	100	100	108	100	107	55	151	122

Portland***	Florida Marlins						Surface: Grass	
	G	Avg	AB	R	H	2B	3B	HR	SO
Home	114	.243	7644	1038	1859	333	91	95	1728
Road	113	.248	7640	1091	1898	333	54	119	1732
Index	—	99	94	97	100	168	80	100

Salem-Keizer*	San Francisco Giants						Surface: Grass	
	G	Avg	AB	R	H	2B	3B	HR	SO
Home	38	.262	2573	429	675	112	26	54	612
Road	38	.262	2649	413	693	132	13	51	645
Index	—	100	97	104	97	87	206	109	98

Southern Oregon***	Oakland Athletics						Surface: Grass	
	G	Avg	AB	R	H	2B	3B	HR	SO
Home	114	.271	7972	1395	2160	429	74	168	1791
Road	114	.246	7731	1169	1902	384	59	144	1836
Index	—	110	103	119	114	108	122	113	95

Spokane	Kansas City Royals						Surface: Grass	
	G	Avg	AB	R	H	2B	3B	HR	SO
Home	152	.263	10502	1628	2763	539	58	175	2283
Road	152	.252	10548	1538	2660	455	83	208	2495
Index	—	104	100	106	104	119	70	85	92

Yakima	Los Angeles Dodgers						Surface: Grass	
	G	Avg	AB	R	H	2B	3B	HR	SO
Home	152	.248	10513	1483	2602	538	101	108	2485
Road	152	.253	10329	1556	2615	488	74	176	2561
Index	—	98	102	95	100	108	134	60	95

1997 Triple-A Splits

Here's yet another section that we've improved this year. Last year, we gave you lefty/righty splits for all Triple-A hitters with 200 at-bats and Triple-A pitchers with 200 batters faced.

This year we offer much more detail. We offer home/road splits as well, and we do so for all hitters with 100 at-bats in Triple-A and all pitchers with 100 at-bats against (lefty/righty) or 80 innings (home/road).

These numbers will help you identify which prospects can handle all kinds of pitching and which may need to be platooned. They'll also separate the true stars of tomorrow from players whose numbers are pumped up by their ballparks.

AAA Batting vs. Lefthanded and Righthanded Pitchers

			vs Left					vs Right				
Player	Team	Org	AB	H	HR	RBI	Avg	AB	H	HR	RBI	Avg
Andy Abad	Pawtucket	Bos	42	9	1	6	.214	185	53	8	26	.286
Jeff Abbott	Nashville	ChA	122	39	4	20	.320	343	113	7	43	.329
Benny Agbayani	Norfolk	NYN	89	34	5	12	.382	379	111	6	39	.293
Doug Angeli	Scrnton-WB	Phi	54	15	1	8	.278	187	39	1	11	.209
George Arias	Vancouver	Cal	140	37	2	14	.264	291	85	10	51	.292
Rich Aude	Syracuse	Tor	79	19	4	10	.241	271	80	11	49	.295
Bruce Aven	Buffalo	Cle	117	44	6	23	.376	318	81	11	54	.255
Kevin Baez	Salt Lake	Min	106	25	2	15	.236	277	80	3	39	.289
Paul Bako	Indianapolis	Cin	60	14	1	8	.233	261	64	7	35	.245
Jeff Ball	Phoenix	SF	149	46	2	27	.309	321	105	16	76	.327
Brian Banks	Tucson	Mil	101	36	3	15	.356	270	75	7	48	.278
Tim Barker	Columbus	NYA	66	17	0	6	.258	142	41	5	24	.289
Tony Barron	Scrnton-WB	Phi	96	34	8	27	.354	233	74	10	51	.318
Jeff Barry	Col. Springs	Col	69	22	1	15	.319	204	60	12	55	.294
Kimera Bartee	Toledo	Det	108	31	2	11	.287	393	78	1	22	.198
Trey Beamon	Las Vegas	SD	86	23	0	10	.267	243	85	5	39	.350
Tony Beasley	Calgary	Pit	64	16	1	4	.250	156	44	0	24	.282
Tim Belk	Indianapolis	Cin	80	26	4	13	.325	175	48	4	25	.274
Mike Bell	Oklahoma City	Tex	98	30	2	12	.306	230	47	3	26	.204
Mark Bellhorn	Edmonton	Oak	78	31	4	14	.397	163	48	7	32	.294
Ronnie Belliard	Tucson	Mil	92	33	0	13	.359	345	92	4	42	.267
Clay Bellinger	Columbus	NYA	110	32	4	15	.291	306	82	8	44	.268
Yamil Benitez	Omaha	KC	83	26	5	15	.313	246	71	16	56	.289
Gary Bennett	Pawtucket	Bos	57	11	3	12	.193	167	37	1	10	.222
Jeff Berblinger	Louisville	StL	144	44	5	23	.306	373	91	6	35	.244
Dave Berg	Charlotte	Fla	106	34	4	16	.321	318	91	5	31	.286
Henry Blanco	Albuquerque	LA	74	20	0	6	.270	220	72	6	41	.327
Geoff Blum	Ottawa	Mon	84	22	0	7	.262	323	79	3	28	.245
Frank Bolick	Vancouver	Cal	108	41	5	22	.380	254	69	11	44	.272
Aaron Boone	Indianapolis	Cin	116	33	6	17	.284	360	105	16	58	.292
Terry Bradshaw	Louisville	StL	120	29	2	11	.242	337	85	7	33	.252
Doug Brady	Nashville	ChA	73	11	1	5	.151	297	77	6	31	.259
Brent Brede	Salt Lake	Min	102	36	2	23	.353	226	80	7	53	.354
Stoney Briggs	Las Vegas	SD	130	30	3	12	.231	305	87	8	45	.285
Adrian Brown	Calgary	Pit	61	20	1	10	.328	187	59	0	9	.316
Brant Brown	Iowa	ChN	106	29	6	20	.274	150	48	10	31	.320
Jarvis Brown	Tucson	Mil	101	33	1	6	.327	284	69	5	29	.243
Kevin Brown	Oklahoma City	Tex	97	28	5	13	.289	306	69	14	37	.225
Scott Bullett	Rochester	Bal	110	24	1	14	.218	402	104	8	44	.259
Darren Burton	Scranton-WB	Phi	79	23	3	15	.291	174	40	5	24	.230
Homer Bush	Columbus	NYA	73	15	1	7	.205	202	53	1	19	.262
Rich Butler	Syracuse	Tor	128	32	4	17	.250	409	129	20	70	.315
Edgar Caceres	Vancouver	Cal	79	27	1	12	.342	172	49	1	25	.285
Miguel Cairo	Iowa	ChN	199	53	3	21	.266	370	106	2	25	.286
Casey Candaele	Buffalo	Cle	105	24	2	17	.229	209	47	5	22	.225
Todd Carey	Pawtucket	Bos	56	10	1	11	.179	324	72	11	47	.222
Bubba Carpenter	Columbus	NYA	55	17	0	7	.309	216	59	6	32	.273
Jovino Carvajal	Vancouver	Cal	150	39	0	11	.260	324	97	2	39	.299
Frank Catalanotto	Toledo	Det	122	25	0	13	.205	378	125	16	55	.331
Wes Chamberlain	Norfolk	NYN	74	29	3	18	.392	262	63	4	32	.240
Raul Chavez	Ottawa	Mon	81	23	2	17	.284	229	53	2	29	.231
Chris Clapinski	Charlotte	Fla	80	22	1	9	.275	260	67	11	43	.258
Danny Clyburn	Rochester	Bal	115	37	3	13	.322	405	119	17	63	.294
Lou Collier	Calgary	Pit	116	44	1	17	.379	281	87	0	31	.310
Dennis Colon	New Orleans	Hou	113	27	1	20	.239	287	81	5	44	.282
Tim Costo	Louisville	StL	119	42	4	12	.353	284	81	10	42	.285
John Cotton	Nashville	ChA	61	17	0	9	.279	262	70	11	41	.267
Craig Counsell	Col. Springs	Col	121	40	0	20	.331	255	86	5	43	.337
Steve Cox	Edmonton	Oak	140	40	3	31	.286	327	88	12	62	.269
Felipe Crespo	Syracuse	Tor	75	21	3	6	.280	215	54	9	20	.251
Brandon Cromer	Calgary	Pit	56	11	1	9	.196	172	42	7	27	.244
Fausto Cruz	Vancouver	Cal	132	41	6	31	.311	274	75	5	36	.274
Ivan Cruz	Columbus	NYA	135	34	6	26	.252	282	91	18	69	.323
Jacob Cruz	Phoenix	SF	156	61	3	36	.391	337	117	9	59	.347
Mark Dalesandro	Iowa	ChN	147	38	2	18	.259	258	68	6	30	.264
Doug Dascenzo	Las Vegas	SD	128	42	6	23	.328	305	78	3	22	.256
Brian Daubach	Charlotte	Fla	127	37	6	29	.291	334	91	15	64	.272
Tommy Davis	Rochester	Bal	95	27	3	15	.284	343	106	12	47	.309
Steve Decker	Tacoma	Sea	123	30	4	18	.244	227	74	6	34	.326
Wilson Delgado	Phoenix	SF	104	29	0	13	.279	312	91	9	46	.292
Alex Diaz	Oklahoma City	Tex	104	37	4	16	.356	322	85	8	33	.264
Eddy Diaz	Tucson	Mil	89	22	0	12	.247	263	93	9	58	.354
Einar Diaz	Buffalo	Cle	89	22	1	9	.247	248	64	2	22	.258
David Doster	Scranton-WB	Phi	89	28	3	15	.315	321	101	13	64	.315
Todd Dunn	Tucson	Mil	88	25	3	12	.284	238	74	15	54	.311
Todd Dunwoody	Charlotte	Fla	113	30	5	13	.265	288	75	18	49	.260
Mike Durant	Salt Lake	Min	64	15	1	13	.234	159	31	7	23	.195
Angel Echevarria	Col. Springs	Col	89	33	2	20	.371	206	62	11	60	.301
Robert Eenhoorn	Vancouver	Cal	132	48	3	17	.364	317	91	8	40	.287
Angel. Encarnacion	Las Vegas	SD	73	16	0	8	.219	180	46	3	15	.256
Bobby Estalella	Scranton-WB	Phi	97	25	8	22	.258	336	76	8	43	.226
Osmani Estrada	Oklahoma City	Tex	76	20	0	7	.263	212	45	1	13	.212
Tom Evans	Syracuse	Tor	79	16	5	12	.203	297	83	10	53	.279
Jeff Ferguson	Salt Lake	Min	79	27	3	14	.342	162	41	5	21	.253
Mike Figga	Columbus	NYA	110	29	4	19	.264	280	66	8	35	.236
Jose Flores	Scranton-WB	Phi	65	20	1	8	.308	139	31	0	10	.223
Tim Florez	Phoenix	SF	142	47	3	21	.331	260	74	4	40	.285
Chad Fonville	Albuquerque	LA	96	25	0	7	.260	275	56	0	15	.204
P.J. Forbes	Rochester	Bal	92	27	1	11	.293	342	91	7	43	.266
Andy Fox	Columbus	NYA	85	20	2	8	.235	233	67	4	25	.288
Eric Fox	Scranton-WB	Phi	67	23	0	5	.343	197	51	3	21	.259
Micah Franklin	Louisville	StL	94	20	1	9	.213	236	52	11	39	.220
Lou Frazier	Rochester	Bal	78	15	1	8	.192	224	60	1	31	.268
Hanley Frias	Oklahoma City	Tex	121	32	1	10	.264	363	96	4	36	.264
Karim Garcia	Albuquerque	LA	70	18	4	15	.257	192	62	16	51	.323
Webster Garrison	Edmonton	Oak	133	37	4	24	.278	296	87	11	56	.294

			vs Left					vs Right				
Player	Team	Org	AB	H	HR	RBI	Avg	AB	H	HR	RBI	Avg
Phil Geisler	Norfolk	NYN	50	12	0	7	.240	286	74	9	50	.259
Shawn Gilbert	Norfolk	NYN	63	10	1	4	.159	225	66	7	29	.293
Ed Giovanola	Richmond	Atl	84	25	0	7	.298	311	90	2	39	.289
Rene Gonzales	Las Vegas	SD	122	35	1	11	.287	217	61	2	31	.281
Scarb. Green	Louisville	StL	61	14	1	5	.230	152	39	2	8	.257
Charles Greene	Norfolk	NYN	51	7	1	5	.137	187	42	7	23	.225
Todd Greene	Vancouver	Cal	82	26	10	26	.317	178	66	15	49	.371
Tommy Gregg	Richmond	Atl	91	34	3	18	.374	294	94	6	36	.320
Creight. Gubanich	Tucson	Mil	84	29	6	23	.345	146	48	6	28	.329
Mike Gulan	Louisville	StL	114	36	3	15	.316	302	75	11	47	.248
Dave Hajek	Toledo	Det	49	12	1	4	.245	204	43	3	28	.211
Chip Hale	Albuquerque	LA	39	4	0	7	.103	208	62	2	23	.298
Joe Hall	Toledo	Det	58	18	2	9	.310	213	50	4	21	.235
Todd Haney	New Orleans	Hou	108	32	0	19	.296	346	96	2	44	.277
Jed Hansen	Omaha	KC	104	28	3	10	.269	276	74	8	34	.268
Jason Hardtke	Norfolk	NYN	68	22	1	9	.324	320	85	10	36	.266
Chris Hatcher	Omaha	KC	70	16	3	5	.229	152	35	8	19	.230
Eric Helfand	Las Vegas	SD	53	14	2	7	.264	185	61	4	26	.330
Todd Helton	Col. Springs	Col	141	43	2	28	.305	251	95	14	60	.378
Jose Herrera	Edmonton	Oak	102	27	0	6	.265	319	98	4	35	.307
Richard Hidalgo	New Orleans	Hou	136	35	3	19	.257	390	112	8	59	.287
Aaron Holbert	Louisville	StL	77	18	0	6	.234	240	63	4	26	.262
Ray Holbert	Toledo	Det	86	18	1	6	.209	286	72	6	31	.252
Damon Hollins	Richmond	Atl	98	30	4	18	.306	400	102	16	45	.255
Matt Howard	Columbus	NYA	119	35	2	19	.294	359	114	4	48	.318
Dann Howitt	Col. Springs	Col	48	13	1	8	.271	268	92	13	54	.343
Trenidad Hubbard	Buffalo	Cle	112	37	5	17	.330	267	81	11	44	.303
Ken Huckaby	Albuquerque	LA	59	8	0	2	.136	142	32	0	16	.225
Bobby Hughes	Tucson	Mil	79	21	1	13	.266	211	69	6	38	.327
Brian Hunter	Indianapolis	Cin	132	39	6	25	.295	374	103	15	60	.275
Jimmy Hurst	Toledo	Det	72	20	3	8	.278	306	82	15	50	.268
Tim Hyers	Toledo	Det	76	16	1	11	.211	348	100	11	44	.287
Adam Hyzdu	Pawtucket	Bos	85	29	7	26	.341	328	85	16	58	.259
Raul Ibanez	Tacoma	Sea	130	35	2	23	.269	308	98	13	61	.318
Damian Jackson	Indianapolis	Cin	86	21	2	7	.244	251	76	2	13	.303
Geoff Jenkins	Tucson	Mil	57	11	1	8	.193	283	70	9	48	.247
Robin Jennings	Iowa	ChN	159	50	4	25	.314	305	78	16	46	.256
Keith Johns	Tucson	Mil	83	24	3	12	.289	249	64	2	24	.257
Russ Johnson	Nw Orleans	Hou	114	28	2	16	.246	331	95	2	33	.287
Dax Jones	Phoenix	SF	103	31	2	14	.301	168	38	1	14	.226
Terry Jones	Col. Springs	Col	122	41	1	10	.336	241	57	0	15	.237
Frank Kellner	Tucson	Mil	68	21	0	5	.309	162	45	0	20	.278
Brooks Kieschnick	Iowa	ChN	135	26	3	18	.193	225	67	18	48	.298
Wayne Kirby	Albuquerque	LA	64	22	1	10	.344	205	68	9	33	.332
Randy Knorr	New Orleans	Hou	55	15	1	7	.273	189	43	4	20	.228
Paul Konerko	Albuquerque	LA	133	42	9	30	.316	350	114	28	97	.326
Kevin Koslofski	Louisville	StL	79	16	3	13	.203	206	44	6	14	.214
Tim Laker	Rochester	Bal	69	15	3	7	.217	221	60	8	30	.271
Chris Latham	Salt Lake	Min	134	45	2	19	.336	358	107	6	39	.299
Jalal Leach	Tacoma	Sea	93	28	2	14	.301	322	100	7	41	.311
Aaron Ledesma	Rochester	Bal	67	25	1	16	.373	259	81	2	27	.313
Derek Lee	Las Vegas	SD	57	13	1	5	.228	174	55	4	30	.316
Derrek Lee	Las Vegas	SD	122	42	5	16	.344	350	111	8	48	.317
Travis Lee	Tucson	Ari	76	14	6	12	.184	151	54	8	34	.358
Brian Lesher	Edmonton	Oak	125	38	9	23	.304	290	96	12	55	.331
T.R. Lewis	Richmond	Atl	98	31	3	17	.316	265	76	4	41	.287
Mark Little	Oklahoma City	Tex	103	27	2	11	.262	312	82	13	34	.263
Ryan Long	Omaha	KC	119	33	7	20	.277	292	76	12	36	.260
Luis Lopez	Norfolk	NYN	48	12	0	4	.250	155	55	4	15	.355
Billy Lott	Calgary	Pit	67	22	2	12	.328	172	53	13	43	.308
Torey Lovullo	Buffalo	Cle	97	26	0	7	.268	228	48	12	33	.211
Mike Lowell	Columbus	NYA	52	18	4	11	.346	158	40	11	34	.253
Terrell Lowery	Iowa	ChN	145	47	6	28	.324	241	69	11	43	.286
Lou Lucca	Charlotte	Fla	72	19	6	15	.264	220	64	12	36	.291
Rob Lukachyk	Ottawa	Mon	60	9	1	6	.150	226	62	11	33	.274
Matt Luke	Columbus	NYA	100	25	2	12	.250	237	52	6	33	.219
Kevin Maas	New Orleans	Hou	54	12	2	11	.222	206	45	5	23	.218
Robert Machado	Nashville	ChA	95	28	4	13	.295	213	55	4	17	.258
Wendell Magee	Scrnton-WB	Phi	78	21	2	9	.269	216	51	8	30	.236
Scott Makarewicz	Toledo	Det	79	21	4	16	.266	261	59	3	22	.226
Jose Malave	Pawtucket	Bos	80	20	5	14	.250	347	107	12	56	.308
Marty Malloy	Richmond	Atl	54	12	0	3	.222	360	106	2	22	.294
Eli Marrero	Louisville	StL	111	35	7	19	.315	284	73	13	49	.257
Oreste Marrero	Albuquerque	LA	29	5	1	5	.172	234	64	8	37	.274
Felix Martinez	Omaha	KC	129	27	0	8	.209	281	77	2	28	.274
Manny Martinez	Calgary	Pit	116	38	8	18	.328	304	101	8	48	.332
Pablo Martinez	Richmond	Atl	93	30	2	8	.323	203	46	2	12	.227
Sandy Martinez	Syracuse	Tor	56	9	1	6	.161	265	63	3	23	.238
Tim Marx	Calgary	Pit	82	23	1	8	.280	218	52	2	32	.239
Francisco Matos	Rochester	Bal	89	28	2	13	.315	300	98	2	38	.327
Ron Maurer	Albuquerque	LA	112	31	2	13	.277	237	65	6	37	.274
Rod McCall	Iowa	ChN	51	8	1	5	.157	204	59	19	50	.289
Dave McCarty	Phoenix	SF	139	53	7	36	.381	295	100	15	56	.339
Scott McClain	Norfolk	NYN	89	29	5	17	.326	340	91	16	47	.268
Jason McDonald	Edmonton	Oak	82	21	1	6	.256	194	52	3	24	.268
Walt McKeel	Pawtucket	Bos	61	18	2	13	.295	176	42	4	17	.239
Billy McMillon	Scrnton-WB	Phi	77	22	6	18	.286	219	62	6	29	.283
Hensley Meulens	Ottawa	Mon	107	26	5	19	.243	316	90	19	56	.285
Damian Miller	Salt Lake	Min	86	36	5	33	.419	228	70	6	49	.307
Doug Mirabelli	Phoenix	SF	99	22	2	13	.222	233	66	6	35	.283
Keith Mitchell	Indianapolis	Cin	99	31	7	17	.313	308	77	8	43	.250
Izzy Molina	Edmonton	Oak	69	17	1	12	.246	149	40	5	22	.268
Melvin Mora	New Orleans	Hou	103	31	1	13	.301	267	64	1	25	.240
Kevin Morgan	Norfolk	NYN	38	11	1	4	.289	218	59	1	16	.271
Russ Morman	Charlotte	Fla	98	35	11	32	.357	297	91	22	67	.306
Chad Mottola	Indianapolis	Cin	63	17	2	7	.270	221	65	5	38	.294

AAA Batting vs. Lefthanded and Righthanded Pitchers

Player	Team	Org	vs Left AB	H	HR	RBI	Avg	vs Right AB	H	HR	RBI	Avg
Rob Mummau	Syracuse	Tor	93	23	3	10	.247	240	62	5	30	.258
Mike Murphy	Okla. City	Tex	62	22	2	5	.355	181	58	3	20	.320
Bob Natal	Charlotte	Fla	70	22	2	14	.314	181	45	9	35	.249
Lipso Nava	Iowa	ChN	108	32	6	12	.296	211	53	3	24	.251
Tom Nevers	Louisville	StL	68	18	1	6	.265	159	35	7	21	.220
Trot Nixon	Pawtucket	Bos	96	22	4	11	.229	379	94	16	50	.248
Les Norman	Buffalo	Cle	127	41	9	24	.323	301	70	8	32	.233
Greg Norton	Nashville	ChA	122	30	9	28	.246	292	84	17	48	.288
Jon Nunnally	Omaha	KC	61	18	2	8	.295	169	46	13	25	.272
Jamie Ogden	Salt Lake	Min	90	27	3	14	.300	277	78	11	39	.282
Jose Olmeda	Charlotte	Fla	54	18	0	10	.333	188	32	1	19	.170
Magglio Ordonez	Nashville	ChA	141	53	5	26	.376	382	119	9	64	.312
Eric Owens	Indianapolis	Cin	91	27	1	8	.297	300	85	10	36	.283
Jayhawk Owens	Col. Springs	Col	78	19	3	11	.244	211	56	7	23	.265
Jeff Patzke	Syracuse	Tor	65	8	0	4	.123	251	82	2	25	.327
Will. Pennyfeather	Albuquerque	LA	113	30	6	17	.265	289	72	11	37	.249
Neifi Perez	Col. Springs	Col	84	38	4	16	.452	219	72	4	30	.329
Tomas Perez	Syracuse	Tor	78	15	1	8	.192	225	53	0	12	.236
Roberto Petagine	Norfolk	NYN	93	30	7	25	.323	348	110	24	75	.316
Chris Petersen	Iowa	ChN	130	30	2	18	.231	261	64	1	15	.245
J.R. Phillips	New Orleans	Hou	121	36	2	11	.298	290	83	19	60	.286
Scott Pose	Columbus	NYA	72	19	1	9	.264	146	47	1	22	.322
Chop Pough	Omaha	KC	130	30	8	13	.231	303	79	14	46	.261
Dante Powell	Phoenix	SF	129	30	4	12	.233	323	79	7	30	.245
Arquimedez Pozo	Pawtucket	Bos	73	24	7	19	.329	304	83	15	51	.273
Todd Pratt	Norfolk	NYN	48	15	3	12	.313	158	47	6	22	.297
Chris Pritchett	Vancouver	Cal	113	29	3	14	.257	264	77	4	33	.292
Tom Quinlan	Col. Springs	Col	160	41	6	32	.256	349	104	17	81	.298
Brian Raabe	Tacoma	Sea	172	57	6	26	.331	371	134	8	54	.361
Ry. Radmanovich	Salt Lake	Min	132	38	12	25	.288	353	90	16	53	.255
Alex Ramirez	Buffalo	Cle	129	42	3	14	.326	287	77	8	30	.268
Ken Ramos	New Orleans	Hou	38	8	0	3	.211	215	65	0	19	.302
Desi Relaford	Scrntn-WB	Phi	134	41	3	14	.306	383	97	6	39	.253
Adam Riggs	Albuquerque	LA	67	22	3	10	.328	160	47	10	18	.294
Marquis Riley	Vancouver	Cal	61	16	0	3	.262	175	48	0	5	.274
Luis Rivera	New Orleans	Hou	103	32	1	18	.311	279	59	2	27	.211
Kevin Roberson	Phoenix	SF	100	28	3	19	.280	249	72	11	48	.289
Mike Robertson	Scrntn-WB	Phi	90	24	2	15	.267	326	100	10	57	.307
Steve Rodriguez	Toledo	Det	79	23	1	13	.291	346	76	3	25	.220
Tony Rodriguez	Pawtucket	Bos	77	20	0	1	.260	208	51	2	18	.245
Dan Rohrmeier	Tacoma	Sea	149	43	6	28	.289	322	97	27	92	.301
Rico Rossy	Ottawa	Mon	96	29	3	15	.302	279	85	7	37	.233
Chad Rupp	Salt Lake	Min	113	27	7	21	.239	313	89	25	73	.284
Donnie Sadler	Pawtucket	Bos	100	14	3	8	.140	381	88	8	28	.231
Jon Saffer	Ottawa	Mon	127	35	2	17	.276	356	94	13	43	.264
Marc Sagmoen	Oklahoma City	Tex	83	21	0	5	.253	335	89	5	39	.266
Chance Sanford	Calgary	Pit	86	26	2	17	.302	239	69	4	43	.289
Steve Scarsone	Las Vegas	SD	71	18	5	14	.254	180	40	6	21	.222
Brad Seitzer	Tucson	Mil	56	23	3	16	.411	173	50	6	26	.289
Richie Sexson	Buffalo	Cle	122	32	11	23	.262	316	82	20	65	.259
Jon Shave	Salt Lake	Min	101	33	2	16	.327	294	97	5	44	.330
Andy Sheets	Tacoma	Sea	128	30	6	19	.234	273	74	8	34	.271
Chris Sheff	Charlotte	Fla	87	21	3	9	.241	235	61	8	34	.260
Scott Sheldon	Edmonton	Oak	112	40	6	17	.357	310	93	13	60	.300
Dave Silvestri	Oklahoma City	Tex	113	26	2	12	.230	354	86	15	56	.243
Randall Simon	Richmond	Atl	132	40	1	25	.303	387	120	13	77	.310
Mitch Simons	Salt Lake	Min	93	24	0	6	.258	369	114	5	53	.309
Duane Singleton	Vancouver	Cal	117	22	2	9	.188	266	57	3	27	.214
Bubba Smith	Okla. City	Tex	122	43	7	37	.352	392	88	20	57	.224
Bobby Smith	Richmond	Atl	80	16	4	11	.200	277	72	8	36	.260
Shane Spencer	Columbus	NYA	124	28	6	22	.226	328	81	24	64	.247
Mike Stefanski	Louisville	StL	57	15	0	3	.263	144	46	6	19	.319
Andy Stewart	Omaha	KC	90	28	4	12	.311	198	51	2	12	.258
Shannon Stewart	Syracuse	Tor	34	17	0	3	.500	174	55	5	21	.316
Kelly Stinnett	Tucson	Mil	45	12	2	8	.267	161	52	8	35	.323
Darond Stovall	Ottawa	Mon	79	17	0	6	.215	263	66	4	42	.251
Chris Stynes	Omaha	KC	102	37	1	10	.363	316	82	8	51	.259
Larry Sutton	Omaha	KC	106	33	4	21	.311	274	81	15	51	.296
Jeff Tackett	Okla. City	Tex	65	16	1	6	.246	144	41	4	13	.285
Jesus Tavarez	Pawtucket	Bos	71	21	1	4	.296	158	40	2	16	.253
Fausto Tejero	Richmond	Atl	43	6	1	3	.140	182	46	5	25	.253
Ryan Thompson	Syracuse	Tor	82	25	7	19	.305	248	70	9	39	.282
Ozzie Timmons	Indianapolis	Cin	96	21	2	12	.219	311	82	12	43	.264
Jose Tolentino	Calgary	Pit	75	25	3	21	.333	230	69	13	48	.300
Paul Torres	Tacoma	Sea	68	17	0	3	.250	141	46	5	19	.326
Bubba Trammell	Toledo	Det	67	16	5	10	.239	252	64	23	65	.254
Chad Tredaway	Las Vegas	SD	88	22	0	8	.250	321	83	7	42	.259
Brad Tyler	Richmond	Atl	67	18	2	12	.269	316	83	16	65	.263
Tim Unroe	Tucson	Mil	59	17	0	10	.288	169	49	9	35	.290
Pedro Valdes	Iowa	ChN	176	54	3	20	.307	288	78	11	40	.271
Mario Valdez	Nashville	ChA	65	13	1	11	.200	217	66	14	50	.304
Jason Varitek	Tacoma	Sea	80	23	6	17	.287	227	55	9	31	.242
Jorge Velandia	Las Vegas	SD	108	36	1	14	.333	297	74	2	21	.249
Edgard Velazquez	Col. Spmgs	Col	137	37	2	20	.270	301	86	15	53	.286
Jose Vidro	Ottawa	Mon	74	27	6	13	.365	205	63	7	34	.307
Julio Vinas	Nashville	ChA	103	21	2	8	.204	211	52	9	33	.246
Jack Voigt	Tucson	Mil	50	14	0	9	.280	185	50	5	31	.270
Todd Walker	Salt Lake	Min	98	36	3	18	.367	224	75	9	35	.335
Turner Ward	Calgary	Pit	62	20	5	16	.323	147	51	4	28	.347
Ron Warner	Louisville	StL	101	25	3	10	.248	175	39	4	20	.223
B.J. Waszgis	Rochester	Bal	75	17	3	12	.227	240	65	10	36	.271
Pat Watkins	Indianapolis	Cin	84	22	2	11	.262	241	69	7	24	.286
Jim Wawruck	Rochester	Bal	41	10	0	3	.244	298	82	5	32	.275
Derrick White	Vancouver	Cal	127	36	3	18	.283	281	97	8	47	.345
Eddie Williams	Albuquerque	LA	75	30	9	24	.400	204	72	20	52	.353
Antone Williamson	Tucson	Mil	82	24	1	16	.293	215	63	4	25	.293

Player	Team	Org	vs Left AB	H	HR	RBI	Avg	vs Right AB	H	HR	RBI	Avg
Brandon Wilson	Iowa	ChN	78	17	0	1	.218	164	40	1	16	.244
Craig Wilson	Nashville	ChA	125	32	0	8	.256	328	91	6	34	.277
Desi Wilson	Phoenix	SF	112	29	0	10	.259	339	126	7	43	.372
Enrique Wilson	Buffalo	Cle	130	39	5	17	.300	322	99	6	23	.307
Mike Wolff	Vancouver	Cal	89	28	8	22	.315	172	45	13	41	.262
Jason Wood	Edmonton	Oak	145	45	2	18	.310	360	117	17	69	.325
Ron Wright	Calgary	Pit	95	30	5	21	.316	241	72	11	42	.299
Rick Wrona	Nashville	ChA	62	17	3	7	.274	149	35	3	15	.235
Alan Zinter	Tacoma	Sea	127	39	3	23	.307	277	77	17	47	.278
Eddie Zosky	Phoenix	SF	99	27	4	12	.273	142	40	5	33	.282
Jon Zuber	Scranton-WB	Phi	106	37	1	17	.349	329	100	5	47	.304

AAA Batting at Home and on the Road

			Home					Road				
Player	Team	Org	AB	H	HR	RBI	Avg	AB	H	HR	RBI	Avg
Andy Abad	Pawtucket	Bos	106	33	9	23	.311	121	29	0	9	.240
Jeff Abbott	Nashville	ChA	241	81	8	39	.336	224	71	3	24	.317
Benny Agbayani	Norfolk	NYN	228	79	6	28	.346	240	66	5	23	.275
Doug Angeli	Scranton-WB	Phi	104	25	0	11	.240	137	29	2	8	.212
George Arias	Vancouver	Cal	192	46	5	22	.240	239	76	7	43	.318
Rich Aude	Syracuse	Tor	166	42	8	26	.253	184	57	7	33	.310
Bruce Aven	Buffalo	Cle	189	57	11	37	.302	243	67	6	40	.276
Kevin Baez	Salt Lake	Min	189	57	4	23	.302	194	48	1	31	.247
Paul Bako	Indianapolis	Cin	168	44	5	26	.262	153	34	3	17	.222
Jeff Ball	Phoenix	SF	216	75	13	54	.347	254	76	5	49	.299
Brian Banks	Tucson	Mil	183	59	5	35	.322	195	53	5	28	.272
Tim Barker	Columbus	NYA	84	17	1	9	.202	124	41	4	21	.331
Tony Barron	Scranton-WB	Phi	168	55	10	38	.327	161	53	8	40	.329
Jeff Barry	Col. Springs	Col	135	45	7	43	.333	138	37	6	27	.268
Kimera Bartee	Toledo	Det	254	52	2	16	.205	247	57	1	17	.231
Trey Beamon	Las Vegas	SD	177	62	2	24	.350	152	46	3	25	.303
Tony Beasley	Calgary	Pit	116	32	1	19	.276	104	28	0	9	.269
Tim Belk	Indianapolis	Cin	122	38	6	25	.311	133	36	2	13	.271
Mike Bell	Oklahoma City	Tex	177	47	2	24	.266	151	30	3	14	.199
Mark Bellhorn	Edmonton	Oak	112	38	7	27	.339	129	41	4	19	.318
Ronnie Belliard	Tucson	Mil	226	69	0	31	.305	217	56	4	24	.258
Clay Bellinger	Columbus	NYA	205	65	6	35	.317	211	49	6	24	.232
Yamil Benitez	Omaha	KC	177	61	16	53	.345	152	36	5	18	.237
Gary Bennett	Pawtucket	Bos	104	19	2	9	.183	120	29	2	13	.242
Jeff Berblinger	Louisville	StL	245	71	5	36	.290	268	64	6	22	.239
Dave Berg	Charlotte	Fla	206	54	5	22	.262	218	71	4	25	.326
Henry Blanco	Albuquerque	LA	149	53	4	30	.356	145	39	2	17	.269
Geoff Blum	Ottawa	Mon	189	47	1	22	.249	218	54	2	13	.248
Frank Bolick	Vancouver	Cal	172	59	7	33	.343	190	51	9	33	.268
Aaron Boone	Indianapolis	Cin	232	65	8	33	.280	244	73	14	42	.299
Terry Bradshaw	Louisville	StL	228	60	5	27	.263	225	53	3	16	.236
Doug Brady	Nashville	ChA	162	37	3	16	.228	208	51	4	20	.245
Brent Brede	Salt Lake	Min	159	54	5	38	.340	169	62	4	38	.367
Stoney Briggs	Las Vegas	SD	197	56	6	28	.284	238	61	5	29	.256
Adrian Brown	Calgary	Pit	117	34	0	7	.291	131	45	1	12	.344
Brant Brown	Iowa	ChN	119	36	11	30	.303	137	41	5	21	.299
Jarvis Brown	Tucson	Mil	199	54	2	20	.271	186	48	4	15	.258
Kevin Brown	Oklahoma City	Tex	209	57	8	28	.273	194	40	11	22	.206
Scott Bullett	Rochester	Bal	248	67	6	35	.270	264	61	3	23	.231
Darren Burton	Scranton-WB	Phi	147	37	4	21	.252	106	26	4	18	.245
Homer Bush	Columbus	NYA	133	37	0	20	.278	142	31	2	6	.218
Rich Butler	Syracuse	Tor	273	79	15	44	.289	264	82	9	43	.311
Edgar Caceres	Vancouver	Cal	132	39	2	14	.295	126	41	0	23	.325
Miguel Cairo	Iowa	ChN	278	76	3	27	.273	291	83	2	19	.285
Casey Candaele	Buffalo	Cle	139	34	4	18	.245	172	37	3	20	.215
Todd Carey	Pawtucket	Bos	185	47	8	34	.254	195	35	4	24	.179
Bubba Carpenter	Columbus	NYA	111	37	4	24	.333	160	39	2	15	.244
Jovino Carvajal	Vancouver	Cal	232	63	1	23	.272	248	74	1	28	.298
Frank Catalanotto	Toledo	Det	245	71	10	37	.290	255	79	6	31	.310
Wes Chamberlain	Norfolk	NYN	178	54	5	30	.303	158	38	2	20	.241
Raul Chavez	Ottawa	Mon	159	39	2	23	.245	151	37	2	23	.245
Chris Clapinski	Charlotte	Fla	146	40	8	24	.274	194	49	4	28	.253
Danny Clyburn	Rochester	Bal	254	86	15	55	.339	266	70	5	21	.263
Lou Collier	Calgary	Pit	191	70	0	24	.366	206	61	1	24	.296
Dennis Colon	New Orleans	Hou	188	49	1	25	.261	212	59	5	39	.278
Tim Costo	Louisville	StL	196	53	5	26	.270	204	68	9	28	.333
John Cotton	Nashville	ChA	158	43	7	29	.272	165	44	4	21	.267
Craig Counsell	Col. Springs	Col	192	70	5	38	.365	184	56	0	25	.304
Steve Cox	Edmonton	Oak	237	71	12	59	.300	230	57	3	34	.248
Felipe Crespo	Syracuse	Tor	144	36	6	14	.250	146	39	6	12	.267
Brandon Cromer	Calgary	Pit	127	34	8	30	.268	101	19	0	6	.188
Fausto Cruz	Vancouver	Cal	209	65	5	36	.311	204	54	6	31	.265
Ivan Cruz	Columbus	NYA	227	72	13	61	.317	190	53	11	34	.279
Jacob Cruz	Phoenix	SF	239	91	7	44	.381	254	87	5	51	.343
Mark Dalesandro	Iowa	ChN	188	52	4	23	.277	217	54	4	25	.249
Doug Dascenzo	Las Vegas	SD	225	55	3	21	.244	208	65	6	24	.313
Brian Daubach	Charlotte	Fla	238	64	13	47	.269	223	64	8	46	.287
Tommy Davis	Rochester	Bal	209	59	7	36	.282	229	74	8	26	.323
Steve Decker	Tacoma	Sea	156	44	6	18	.282	194	60	4	34	.309
Wilson Delgado	Phoenix	SF	212	58	7	32	.274	204	62	2	27	.304
Alex Diaz	Oklahoma City	Tex	198	62	6	25	.313	228	60	6	24	.263
Eddy Diaz	Tucson	Mil	173	53	2	30	.306	183	64	7	40	.350
Einar Diaz	Buffalo	Cle	145	33	1	12	.228	191	53	2	19	.277
David Doster	Scranton-WB	Phi	190	56	4	33	.295	220	73	12	46	.332
Todd Dunn	Tucson	Mil	161	49	7	31	.304	171	52	11	35	.304
Todd Dunwoody	Charlotte	Fla	225	65	18	39	.289	176	40	5	23	.227
Mike Durant	Salt Lake	Min	105	23	6	18	.219	118	23	2	18	.195
Angel Echevarria	Col. Springs	Col	139	45	6	35	.324	156	50	7	45	.321
Robert Eenhoorn	Vancouver	Cal	232	67	6	34	.289	223	73	6	24	.327
Angel Encarnacion	Las Vegas	SD	115	28	2	15	.243	138	34	1	8	.246
Bobby Estalella	Scranton-WB	Phi	224	52	11	34	.232	209	49	5	31	.234
Osmani Estrada	Oklahoma City	Tex	126	37	0	12	.294	162	28	1	8	.173
Tom Evans	Syracuse	Tor	171	41	5	26	.240	205	58	10	39	.283
Jeff Ferguson	Salt Lake	Min	136	36	5	18	.265	105	32	3	17	.305
Mike Figga	Columbus	NYA	194	49	5	28	.253	196	46	7	26	.235
Jose Flores	Scranton-WB	Phi	97	27	1	8	.278	107	24	0	10	.224
Tim Florez	Phoenix	SF	186	47	3	32	.253	216	74	4	29	.343
Chad Fonville	Albuquerque	LA	171	35	0	10	.205	200	46	0	12	.230
P.J. Forbes	Rochester	Bal	241	70	3	31	.290	193	48	5	23	.249
Andy Fox	Columbus	NYA	164	46	1	15	.280	154	41	5	18	.266
Eric Fox	Scranton-WB	Phi	93	32	0	11	.344	153	38	3	15	.248
Micah Franklin	Louisville	StL	158	36	5	19	.228	168	36	7	29	.214
Lou Frazier	Rochester	Bal	154	41	1	20	.266	148	34	1	19	.230
Hanley Frias	Oklahoma City	Tex	260	74	2	25	.285	224	54	3	21	.241
Karim Garcia	Albuquerque	LA	137	49	13	40	.358	125	31	7	26	.248
Webster Garrison	Edmonton	Oak	211	56	6	32	.265	218	68	9	48	.312

			Home					Road				
Player	Team	Org	AB	H	HR	RBI	Avg	AB	H	HR	RBI	Avg
Phil Geisler	Norfolk	NYN	169	45	3	22	.266	167	41	6	35	.246
Shawn Gilbert	Norfolk	NYN	139	33	3	13	.237	149	43	5	20	.289
Ed Giovanola	Richmond	Atl	192	59	0	19	.307	203	56	2	27	.276
Rene Gonzales	Las Vegas	SD	138	35	1	22	.254	201	61	2	20	.303
Scarb. Green	Louisville	StL	90	21	2	7	.233	119	32	1	6	.269
Charles Greene	Norfolk	NYN	117	22	4	12	.188	121	27	4	16	.223
Todd Greene	Vancouver	Cal	114	42	11	32	.368	146	50	14	43	.342
Tommy Gregg	Richmond	Atl	192	71	6	30	.370	193	57	3	24	.295
Creight. Gubanich	Tucson	Mil	123	45	7	30	.366	107	32	5	21	.299
Mike Gulan	Louisville	StL	196	58	13	39	.296	216	52	1	22	.241
Dave Hajek	Toledo	Det	140	28	2	16	.200	113	27	2	16	.239
Chip Hale	Albuquerque	LA	138	38	1	16	.275	109	28	1	14	.257
Joe Hall	Toledo	Det	147	39	4	20	.265	124	29	2	10	.234
Todd Haney	New Orleans	Hou	221	59	0	28	.267	233	69	2	35	.296
Jed Hansen	Omaha	KC	204	65	9	32	.319	176	37	2	12	.210
Jason Hardtke	Norfolk	NYN	175	53	3	25	.303	213	54	8	20	.254
Chris Hatcher	Omaha	KC	122	33	9	18	.270	100	18	2	6	.180
Eric Helfand	Las Vegas	SD	133	43	5	19	.323	105	32	1	14	.305
Todd Helton	Col. Springs	Col	171	63	8	45	.368	221	75	8	43	.339
Jose Herrera	Edmonton	Oak	194	53	1	19	.273	227	72	3	22	.317
Richard Hidalgo	New Orleans	Hou	258	78	4	28	.302	268	69	7	50	.257
Aaron Holbert	Louisville	StL	142	40	0	19	.282	172	40	4	13	.233
Ray Holbert	Toledo	Det	174	39	1	9	.224	198	51	6	28	.258
Damon Hollins	Richmond	Atl	257	78	12	37	.304	241	54	8	26	.224
Matt Howard	Columbus	NYA	253	78	3	32	.308	225	71	3	35	.316
Dann Howitt	Col. Springs	Col	145	50	9	33	.345	171	55	5	29	.322
Trenidad Hubbard	Buffalo	Cle	185	54	9	31	.292	190	63	7	29	.332
Ken Huckaby	Albuquerque	LA	111	26	0	12	.234	90	14	0	6	.156
Bobby Hughes	Tucson	Mil	158	45	1	26	.285	132	45	6	25	.341
Brian Hunter	Indianapolis	Cin	243	62	7	33	.255	263	80	14	52	.304
Jimmy Hurst	Toledo	Det	161	35	7	22	.217	216	67	11	36	.310
Tim Hyers	Toledo	Det	201	54	3	21	.269	223	62	9	34	.278
Adam Hyzdu	Pawtucket	Bos	214	61	16	47	.285	199	53	7	37	.266
Raul Ibanez	Tacoma	Sea	192	58	7	43	.302	246	75	8	41	.305
Damian Jackson	Indianapolis	Cin	154	40	2	7	.260	183	57	2	13	.311
Geoff Jenkins	Tucson	Mil	147	36	3	20	.245	200	46	7	36	.230
Robin Jennings	Iowa	ChN	233	72	13	48	.309	231	56	7	23	.242
Keith Johns	Tucson	Mil	153	37	1	13	.242	180	51	4	23	.283
Russ Johnson	New Orleans	Hou	203	54	1	18	.266	242	69	3	31	.285
Dax Jones	Phoenix	SF	119	30	2	18	.252	152	39	1	10	.257
Terry Jones	Col. Springs	Col	185	49	1	10	.265	178	49	0	15	.275
Frank Kellner	Tucson	Mil	107	30	0	14	.280	123	36	0	11	.293
Brooks Kieschnick	Iowa	ChN	167	42	5	21	.251	193	51	16	45	.264
Wayne Kirby	Albuquerque	LA	122	36	5	24	.295	147	54	5	19	.367
Randy Knorr	New Orleans	Hou	125	32	1	13	.256	119	26	4	14	.218
Paul Konerko	Albuquerque	LA	229	90	23	76	.393	254	66	14	51	.260
Kevin Koslofski	Louisville	StL	147	33	5	16	.224	138	27	4	11	.196
Tim Laker	Rochester	Bal	149	36	6	21	.242	141	39	5	16	.277
Chris Latham	Salt Lake	Min	232	77	6	29	.332	260	75	2	29	.288
Jalal Leach	Tacoma	Sea	195	56	7	30	.287	220	72	2	25	.327
Aaron Ledesma	Rochester	Bal	168	55	2	20	.327	158	51	1	23	.323
Derek Lee	Las Vegas	SD	106	32	1	14	.302	125	36	4	21	.288
Derrek Lee	Las Vegas	SD	246	85	8	38	.346	226	68	5	26	.301
Travis Lee	Tucson	Ari	119	38	7	25	.319	108	30	7	21	.278
Brian Lesher	Edmonton	Oak	221	77	11	52	.348	194	57	10	26	.294
T.R. Lewis	Richmond	Atl	164	48	2	32	.293	199	59	5	26	.296
Mark Little	Oklahoma City	Tex	191	55	7	26	.288	224	54	8	19	.241
Ryan Long	Omaha	KC	202	61	8	27	.302	209	48	11	29	.230
Luis Lopez	Norfolk	NYN	98	39	0	7	.398	105	28	4	12	.267
Billy Lott	Calgary	Pit	120	40	8	31	.333	119	35	7	24	.294
Torey Lovullo	Buffalo	Cle	134	27	5	13	.201	187	46	7	27	.246
Mike Lowell	Columbus	NYA	74	16	5	19	.216	136	42	10	26	.309
Terrell Lowery	Iowa	ChN	195	56	8	32	.287	191	60	9	39	.314
Lou Lucca	Charlotte	Fla	165	51	10	28	.309	127	32	8	23	.252
Rob Lukachyk	Ottawa	Mon	142	36	7	22	.254	144	35	5	17	.243
Matt Luke	Columbus	NYA	166	35	5	23	.211	171	42	3	22	.246
Kevin Maas	New Orleans	Hou	136	35	3	23	.257	124	22	4	11	.177
Robert Machado	Nashville	ChA	147	43	4	11	.293	161	40	4	19	.248
Wendell Magee	Scranton-WB	Phi	162	48	4	18	.296	132	24	6	21	.182
Scott Makarewicz	Toledo	Det	161	43	4	17	.267	179	37	3	21	.207
Jose Malave	Pawtucket	Bos	199	57	9	35	.286	228	70	8	35	.307
Marty Malloy	Richmond	Atl	206	54	1	13	.262	208	64	1	12	.308
Eli Marrero	Louisville	StL	190	52	7	31	.274	205	56	13	37	.273
Oreste Marrero	Albuquerque	LA	156	42	5	29	.269	107	27	4	13	.252
Felix Martinez	Omaha	KC	230	58	2	22	.252	180	46	0	14	.256
Manny Martinez	Calgary	Pit	202	72	10	41	.356	218	67	6	25	.307
Pablo Martinez	Richmond	Atl	132	37	1	9	.280	164	39	3	11	.238
Sandy Martinez	Syracuse	Tor	164	32	2	15	.195	158	40	2	14	.253
Tim Marx	Calgary	Pit	133	38	3	25	.286	167	37	0	15	.222
Francisco Matos	Rochester	Bal	183	59	3	31	.322	206	67	1	20	.325
Ron Maurer	Albuquerque	LA	187	56	5	30	.299	162	40	3	20	.247
Rod McCall	Iowa	ChN	123	33	9	22	.268	132	34	11	33	.258
Dave McCarty	Phoenix	SF	206	76	13	51	.369	228	77	9	41	.338
Scott McClain	Norfolk	NYN	192	50	6	21	.260	237	70	15	43	.295
Jason McDonald	Edmonton	Oak	125	31	3	19	.248	151	42	1	11	.278
Walt McKeel	Pawtucket	Bos	99	24	2	11	.242	138	36	4	19	.261
Billy McMillon	Scranton-WB	Phi	174	53	9	28	.305	122	31	3	19	.254
Hensley Meulens	Ottawa	Mon	185	52	9	36	.281	238	64	15	39	.269
Damian Miller	Salt Lake	Min	149	62	6	49	.416	165	44	5	33	.267
Doug Mirabelli	Phoenix	SF	171	45	5	24	.263	161	43	3	24	.267
Keith Mitchell	Indianapolis	Cin	200	55	4	34	.275	207	53	11	26	.256
Izzy Molina	Edmonton	Oak	92	25	1	10	.272	126	32	5	24	.254
Melvin Mora	New Orleans	Hou	190	48	0	17	.253	180	47	2	21	.261
Kevin Morgan	Norfolk	NYN	112	28	1	7	.250	144	42	1	13	.292
Russ Morman	Charlotte	Fla	216	74	24	64	.343	179	52	9	35	.291
Chad Mottola	Indianapolis	Cin	147	47	3	22	.320	137	35	4	23	.255

AAA Batting at Home and on the Road

Player	Team	Org	Home AB	H	HR	RBI	Avg	Road AB	H	HR	RBI	Avg
Rob Mummau	Syracuse	Tor	165	45	5	22	.273	168	40	3	18	.238
Mike Murphy	Oklahoma City	Tex	135	49	3	12	.363	108	31	2	13	.287
Bob Natal	Charlotte	Fla	133	41	8	34	.308	118	26	3	15	.220
Lipso Nava	Iowa	ChN	151	39	3	22	.258	168	46	6	14	.274
Tom Nevers	Louisville	StL	98	19	4	13	.194	129	34	4	14	.264
Trot Nixon	Pawtucket	Bos	229	66	15	39	.288	246	50	5	22	.203
Les Norman	Buffalo	Cle	199	58	8	28	.291	229	53	9	28	.231
Greg Norton	Nashville	ChA	199	53	11	34	.266	215	61	15	42	.284
Jon Nunnally	Omaha	KC	126	42	10	20	.333	104	22	5	13	.212
Jamie Ogden	Salt Lake	Min	180	55	8	29	.306	187	50	6	24	.267
Jose Olmeda	Charlotte	Fla	107	26	1	11	.243	135	24	0	18	.178
Magglio Ordonez	Nashville	ChA	263	85	9	50	.323	260	87	5	40	.335
Eric Owens	Indianapolis	Cin	196	59	7	27	.301	195	53	4	17	.272
Jayhawk Owens	Col. Springs	Col	139	37	8	18	.266	150	38	2	16	.253
Jeff Patzke	Syracuse	Tor	176	45	1	18	.256	140	45	1	11	.321
Will. Pennyfeather	Albuquerque	LA	202	48	12	39	.238	200	54	5	15	.270
Neifi Perez	Col. Springs	Col	134	46	3	20	.343	169	64	5	26	.379
Tomas Perez	Syracuse	Tor	161	36	0	4	.224	142	32	1	16	.225
Roberto Petagine	Norfolk	NYN	199	71	15	53	.357	242	69	16	47	.285
Chris Petersen	Iowa	ChN	207	47	2	23	.227	184	47	1	10	.255
J.R. Phillips	New Orleans	Hou	190	49	6	25	.258	221	70	15	46	.317
Scott Pose	Columbus	NYA	125	38	1	15	.304	102	32	1	17	.314
Chop Pough	Omaha	KC	216	56	17	34	.259	217	53	5	25	.244
Dante Powell	Phoenix	SF	203	51	8	24	.251	249	58	3	18	.233
Arquimedez Pozo	Pawtucket	Bos	202	49	12	35	.243	175	58	10	35	.331
Todd Pratt	Norfolk	NYN	94	26	2	10	.277	112	36	7	24	.321
Chris Pritchett	Vancouver	Cal	184	47	2	15	.255	199	60	5	32	.302
Tom Quinlan	Col. Springs	Col	247	74	17	61	.300	262	71	6	52	.271
Brian Raabe	Tacoma	Sea	253	86	3	27	.340	290	105	11	53	.362
Ry. Radmanovich	Salt Lake	Min	221	51	12	38	.231	264	77	16	40	.292
Alex Ramirez	Buffalo	Cle	198	57	7	17	.288	218	62	4	27	.284
Ken Ramos	New Orleans	Hou	135	38	0	13	.281	118	35	0	9	.297
Desi Relaford	Scranton-WB	Phi	254	66	7	33	.260	263	72	2	20	.274
Adam Riggs	Albuquerque	LA	97	29	3	11	.299	130	40	10	17	.308
Marquis Riley	Vancouver	Cal	123	35	0	3	.285	119	29	0	5	.244
Luis Rivera	New Orleans	Hou	187	46	1	19	.246	195	45	2	26	.231
Kevin Roberson	Phoenix	SF	166	48	9	39	.289	183	52	5	28	.284
Mike Robertson	Scranton-WB	Phi	204	57	3	29	.279	212	67	9	43	.316
Tony Rodriguez	Pawtucket	Bos	123	23	0	4	.187	162	48	2	15	.296
Steve Rodriguez	Toledo	Det	206	62	3	23	.301	219	37	1	15	.169
Dan Rohrmeier	Tacoma	Sea	213	61	14	42	.286	258	79	19	78	.306
Rico Rossy	Ottawa	Mon	195	51	5	34	.262	180	43	5	18	.239
Chad Rupp	Salt Lake	Min	202	54	14	38	.267	224	62	18	56	.277
Donnie Sadler	Pawtucket	Bos	223	52	7	21	.233	258	50	4	15	.194
Jon Saffer	Ottawa	Mon	234	65	5	20	.278	249	64	10	40	.257
Marc Sagmoen	Oklahoma City	Tex	216	57	1	26	.264	202	53	4	18	.262
Chance Sanford	Calgary	Pit	170	50	6	34	.294	155	45	0	26	.290
Steve Scarsone	Las Vegas	SD	101	25	6	18	.248	150	33	5	17	.220
Brad Seitzer	Tucson	Mil	117	35	3	16	.299	117	39	6	20	.333
Richie Sexson	Buffalo	Cle	207	56	21	52	.271	227	57	10	36	.251
Jon Shave	Salt Lake	Min	189	60	2	23	.317	206	70	5	37	.340
Andy Sheets	Tacoma	Sea	196	44	5	19	.224	205	60	9	34	.293
Chris Sheff	Charlotte	Fla	170	45	8	28	.265	152	37	3	15	.243
Scott Sheldon	Edmonton	Oak	201	59	7	44	.294	221	74	12	33	.335
Dave Silvestri	Oklahoma City	Tex	241	61	9	39	.253	226	51	9	29	.226
Randall Simon	Richmond	Atl	255	77	6	51	.302	264	83	8	51	.314
Mitch Simons	Salt Lake	Min	239	84	2	31	.351	223	54	3	28	.242
Duane Singleton	Vancouver	Cal	186	36	0	12	.194	197	43	5	24	.218
Bubba Smith	Oklahoma City	Tex	260	71	18	59	.273	254	60	9	35	.236
Bobby Smith	Richmond	Atl	181	44	4	22	.243	176	44	8	25	.250
Shane Spencer	Columbus	NYA	207	44	8	34	.213	245	65	22	52	.265
Andy Stewart	Omaha	KC	162	53	5	20	.327	126	26	1	4	.206
Shannon Stewart	Syracuse	Tor	93	32	2	8	.344	115	40	3	16	.348
Kelly Stinnett	Tucson	Mil	125	45	4	25	.360	84	22	6	18	.262
Darond Stovall	Ottawa	Mon	168	38	2	19	.226	174	45	2	29	.259
Chris Stynes	Omaha	KC	184	58	6	31	.315	234	61	3	30	.261
Larry Sutton	Omaha	KC	194	64	13	46	.330	186	50	6	26	.269
Jeff Tackett	Oklahoma City	Tex	90	25	1	6	.278	119	32	4	13	.269
Jesus Tavarez	Pawtucket	Bos	114	31	2	13	.272	115	30	1	7	.261
Fausto Tejero	Richmond	Atl	93	24	1	9	.258	132	28	5	19	.212
Ryan Thompson	Syracuse	Tor	154	45	8	26	.292	176	50	8	32	.284
Ozzie Timmons	Indianapolis	Cin	205	45	3	21	.220	202	58	11	34	.287
Jose Tolentino	Calgary	Pit	156	48	8	33	.308	149	46	8	36	.309
Paul Torres	Tacoma	Sea	101	27	1	6	.267	108	36	4	16	.333
Bubba Trammell	Toledo	Det	136	34	16	34	.250	183	46	12	41	.251
Chad Tredaway	Las Vegas	SD	193	50	5	29	.259	216	55	2	21	.255
Brad Tyler	Richmond	Atl	172	49	8	38	.285	211	52	10	39	.246
Tim Unroe	Tucson	Mil	105	30	1	18	.286	129	38	8	28	.295
Pedro Valdes	Iowa	ChN	227	67	9	28	.295	237	65	5	32	.274
Mario Valdez	Nashville	ChA	150	45	7	31	.300	132	34	8	30	.258
Jason Varitek	Tacoma	Sea	153	36	8	19	.235	154	42	7	29	.273
Jorge Velandia	Las Vegas	SD	204	56	3	20	.275	201	54	7	33	.269
Edgard Velazquez	Col. Springs	Col	226	68	10	41	.301	212	55	7	32	.259
Jose Vidro	Ottawa	Mon	123	36	2	19	.293	156	54	11	28	.346
Julio Vinas	Nashville	ChA	147	33	6	21	.224	167	40	5	20	.240
Jack Voigt	Tucson	Mil	119	36	1	21	.303	116	28	4	19	.241
Todd Walker	Salt Lake	Min	151	48	6	26	.318	171	63	5	27	.368
Turner Ward	Calgary	Pit	95	36	5	25	.379	114	35	4	19	.307
Ron Warner	Louisville	StL	132	32	3	13	.242	144	32	4	17	.222
B.J. Waszgis	Rochester	Bal	152	41	6	23	.270	163	41	7	25	.252
Pat Watkins	Indianapolis	Cin	192	58	3	19	.302	133	33	6	16	.248
Jim Wawruck	Rochester	Bal	172	38	0	13	.221	167	54	5	22	.323
Derrick White	Vancouver	Cal	212	67	7	35	.316	202	67	4	30	.332
Eddie Williams	Albuquerque	LA	134	49	14	40	.366	145	53	15	36	.366
Antone Williamson	Tucson	Mil	135	43	2	21	.319	169	44	3	20	.260
Brandon Wilson	Iowa	ChN	134	32	0	8	.239	108	25	1	9	.231
Craig Wilson	Nashville	ChA	235	67	4	24	.285	218	56	2	18	.257
Desi Wilson	Phoenix	SF	234	80	5	27	.342	217	75	2	26	.346
Enrique Wilson	Buffalo	Cle	215	58	2	18	.270	236	80	9	21	.339
Mike Wolff	Vancouver	Cal	101	24	6	25	.238	165	51	15	39	.309
Jason Wood	Edmonton	Oak	253	86	8	46	.340	252	76	11	41	.302
Ron Wright	Calgary	Pit	175	51	9	32	.291	161	51	7	31	.317
Rick Wrona	Nashville	ChA	119	29	4	15	.244	92	23	2	7	.250
Alan Zinter	Tacoma	Sea	187	40	8	27	.214	217	76	12	43	.350
Eddie Zosky	Phoenix	SF	108	37	2	18	.343	133	30	7	27	.226
Jon Zuber	Scranton-WB	Phi	209	69	2	35	.330	226	68	4	29	.301

AAA Pitching vs. Lefthanded and Righthanded Batters

			vs Left					vs Right				
Player	Team	Org	AB	H	HR	RBI	Avg	AB	H	HR	RBI	Avg
Paul Abbott	Tacoma	Sea	127	28	3	41	.220	224	52	8	76	.232
Juan Acevedo	Norfolk	NYN	217	57	5	48	.263	225	54	2	51	.240
Willie Adams	Edmonton	Oak	138	45	2	29	.326	180	60	11	29	.333
Pat Aheame	Albuquerque	LA	98	34	2	13	.347	155	48	7	31	.310
Jose Alberro	Oklahoma City	Tex	119	26	2	22	.218	232	64	4	37	.276
Antonio Alfonseca	Charlotte	Fla	84	27	2	14	.321	136	31	6	31	.228
Tavo Alvarez	Ottawa	Mon	182	53	6	44	.291	234	70	5	42	.299
Brian Anderson	Buffalo	Cle	57	19	4	8	.333	271	59	9	52	.218
Jimmy Anderson	Calgary	Pit	61	17	0	16	.279	345	107	9	55	.310
Rene Arocha	Phoenix	SF	178	54	7	33	.303	256	67	10	35	.262
Matt Arrandale	Louisville	StL	88	28	1	9	.318	224	56	8	23	.250
Manuel Aybar	Louisville	StL	180	44	6	34	.244	345	87	4	80	.252
Willie Banks	Columbus	NYA	296	81	7	61	.274	311	83	11	69	.267
Brian Barber	Louisville	StL	114	29	6	27	.254	264	82	14	47	.311
Brian Barnes	Toledo	Det	127	33	1	29	.260	339	110	15	57	.324
Manuel Barrios	New Orleans	Hou	89	22	1	14	.247	212	48	4	63	.226
Miguel Batista	Iowa	ChN	144	38	5	31	.264	321	79	14	64	.246
Robbie Beckett	Col. Springs	Col	62	17	1	26	.274	152	44	11	41	.289
Rigo Beltran	Louisville	StL	18	4	0	5	.222	186	41	7	41	.220
Mike Bertotti	Nashville	ChA	66	13	1	14	.197	324	78	16	73	.241
Andres Berumen	Tacoma	Sea	185	49	5	51	.265	268	78	8	63	.291
Ben Blomdahl	Buffalo	Cle	143	48	9	23	.336	264	62	11	37	.235
Joe Boever	Edmonton	Oak	131	41	3	28	.313	246	71	10	53	.289
Brian Bohanon	Norfolk	NYN	63	18	1	14	.286	303	70	8	70	.231
Rodney Bolton	Indianapolis	Cin	253	70	8	31	.277	417	115	13	77	.276
Tom Bolton	Tucson	Mil	109	38	3	22	.349	293	104	8	49	.355
Steve Bourgeois	Col. Springs	Col	212	61	6	45	.288	283	93	12	41	.329
Mike Bovee	Vancouver	Cal	127	38	2	22	.299	212	54	5	49	.255
Shane Bowers	Salt Lake	Min	108	32	4	19	.296	117	32	8	27	.274
Marshall Boze	Las Vegas	SD	85	24	4	12	.282	132	44	7	32	.333
Derek Brandow	Syracuse	Tor	239	67	5	57	.280	319	94	9	63	.295
Chris Brock	Richmond	Atl	201	49	3	37	.244	232	48	6	46	.207
Scott Brow	Richmond	Atl	129	33	7	29	.256	201	56	5	33	.279
Alvin Brown	Albuquerque	LA	115	36	5	19	.313	134	38	4	24	.284
Jim Bruske	Las Vegas	SD	113	29	4	26	.257	153	44	4	41	.288
Travis Buckley	Vancouver	Cal	286	77	11	45	.269	418	142	14	73	.340
Mike Buddie	Columbus	NYA	113	38	3	24	.336	172	47	1	43	.273
Melvin Bunch	Ottawa	Mon	141	45	8	36	.319	173	57	5	22	.329
Terry Burrows	Las Vegas	SD	68	19	1	11	.279	180	60	4	39	.333
Mike Busby	Louisville	StL	146	33	4	32	.226	231	65	8	37	.281
Jose Cabrera	New Orleans	Hou	72	9	3	24	.125	142	30	1	35	.211
Tim Cain	Syracuse	Tor	78	26	3	9	.333	127	34	7	18	.268
Dan Carlson	Phoenix	SF	167	52	5	34	.311	240	50	7	74	.208
Ken Carlyle	Richmond	Atl	109	33	2	18	.303	153	36	2	30	.235
Rafael Carmona	Tacoma	Sea	85	22	1	18	.259	138	30	6	38	.217
Chris Carpenter	Syracuse	Tor	197	55	5	35	.279	243	58	11	62	.239
Giovanni Carrara	Indianapolis	Cin	178	42	6	35	.236	272	69	6	70	.254
Marino Castillo	Las Vegas	SD	243	70	4	47	.288	273	76	14	55	.278
Robinson Checo	Pawtucket	Bos	101	19	6	29	.188	102	22	2	27	.216
Bobby Chouinard	Edmonton	Oak	185	58	10	28	.314	233	71	9	30	.305
Terry Clark	Buffalo	Cle	123	30	3	25	.244	229	56	5	38	.245
Chris Clemons	Nashville	ChA	150	38	4	23	.253	319	77	11	47	.241
Bartolo Colon	Buffalo	Cle	66	16	1	16	.242	138	29	3	38	.210
Archie Corbin	Rochester	Bal	107	17	1	29	.159	139	30	4	37	.216
Reid Cornelius	Charlotte	Fla	206	57	8	34	.277	289	77	11	46	.266
Carlos Crawford	Calgary	Pit	84	20	4	10	.238	120	40	4	16	.333
Joe Crawford	Norfolk	NYN	111	34	3	20	.306	278	75	3	52	.270
Doug Creek	Phoenix	SF	97	19	1	34	.196	410	121	14	103	.295
Nelson Cruz	Nashville	ChA	173	51	10	26	.295	315	88	10	67	.279
Jeff Darwin	Nashville	ChA	52	12	1	9	.231	162	48	7	35	.296
Clint Davis	Oklahoma City	Tex	72	16	2	13	.222	183	39	2	40	.213
Rick DeHart	Ottawa	Mon	77	23	0	9	.299	158	37	6	48	.234
Roland de la Maza	Buffalo	Cle	150	41	6	24	.273	283	63	6	49	.223
Glenn Dishman	Toledo	Det	98	25	2	14	.255	329	87	10	63	.264
Jim Dougherty	Norfolk	NYN	78	20	3	26	.256	130	25	0	33	.192
Travis Driskill	Buffalo	Cle	217	57	10	35	.263	356	102	12	67	.287
Mike Drumright	Toledo	Det	238	67	8	54	.282	263	67	14	61	.255
Brian Edmondson	Norfolk	NYN	93	24	3	24	.258	156	38	2	41	.244
Geoff Edsell	Vancouver	Cal	266	70	3	39	.263	441	126	8	56	.286
Dave Eiland	Columbus	NYA	144	49	6	19	.340	119	31	2	24	.261
Scott Elarton	New Orleans	Hou	69	18	2	23	.261	136	33	3	27	.243
Robert Ellis	Vancouver	Cal	235	68	6	27	.289	361	117	9	43	.324
Vaughn Eshelman	Pawtucket	Bos	42	8	0	15	.190	201	55	4	42	.274
Bryan Eversgerd	Oklahoma City	Tex	56	20	2	12	.357	251	71	10	31	.283
Steve Falteisek	Ottawa	Mon	198	56	7	24	.283	284	79	3	32	.278
Mike Farmer	Col. Springs	Col	43	13	3	8	.302	173	57	11	21	.329
Ramon Fermin	Toledo	Det	141	47	4	12	.333	187	56	6	34	.299
Jared Fernandez	Pawtucket	Bos	129	34	3	16	.264	115	42	4	17	.365
Tony Fiore	Scranton-WB	Phi	94	25	1	29	.266	144	35	2	27	.243
Huck Flener	Syracuse	Tor	108	29	1	9	.269	365	97	13	49	.266
Paul Fletcher	Iowa	ChN	68	16	1	19	.235	217	47	10	48	.217
Tom Fordham	Nashville	ChA	82	26	1	17	.317	351	87	13	73	.248
Keith Foulke	Phoenix	SF	114	33	6	23	.289	179	46	5	31	.257
Ryan Franklin	Tacoma	Sea	150	44	1	20	.293	195	53	10	39	.272
Eddie Gaillard	Toledo	Det	96	23	5	24	.240	109	29	2	30	.266
Steve Gajkowski	Tacoma	Sea	146	43	6	20	.295	216	57	5	28	.264
Mike Gardiner	Columbus	NYA	146	39	6	35	.267	168	44	4	30	.262
Jeremi Gonzalez	Iowa	ChN	75	16	4	15	.213	150	31	4	43	.207
Mike Grace	Scranton-WB	Phi	125	38	0	21	.304	168	46	0	34	.274
Jeff Granger	Calgary	Pit	65	19	1	20	.292	282	92	6	48	.326
Danny Graves	Indianapolis	Cin	71	21	2	9	.296	130	31	2	17	.238
Tyler Green	Scranton-WB	Phi	129	32	8	18	.248	162	48	5	22	.296
Tommy Greene	New Orleans	Hou	95	23	6	25	.242	178	36	6	50	.202
Rick Greene	Toledo	Det	92	18	1	16	.196	151	31	3	35	.205
Jason Grimsley	Tucson	Mil	148	41	1	22	.277	183	54	5	39	.295
Matt Grott	Tucson	Mil	103	29	3	17	.282	243	62	8	40	.255

			vs Left					vs Right				
Player	Team	Org	AB	H	HR	RBI	Avg	AB	H	HR	RBI	Avg
John Halama	New Orleans	Hou	67	17	2	18	.254	562	133	7	108	.237
Roy Halladay	Syracuse	Tor	207	48	3	32	.232	271	84	10	32	.310
Ryan Hancock	Vancouver	Cal	120	27	2	22	.225	188	54	3	41	.287
Greg Hansell	Tucson	Mil	137	42	6	29	.307	197	55	9	44	.279
Tim Harikkala	Tacoma	Sea	199	74	5	37	.372	277	86	6	49	.310
Mike Harkey	Albuquerque	LA	70	12	2	24	.171	134	38	2	33	.284
Denny Harriger	Toledo	Det	314	72	7	55	.229	329	87	12	54	.264
Brian Harrison	Omaha	KC	267	80	11	22	.300	442	128	9	61	.290
Tommy Harrison	Richmond	Atl	198	52	7	37	.263	270	66	14	55	.244
Dean Hartgraves	Richmond	Atl	81	22	1	14	.272	190	54	5	42	.284
Chad Hartvigson	Phoenix	SF	41	7	0	16	.171	176	56	4	36	.318
Ryan Hawblitzel	Scranton-WB	Phi	198	66	2	25	.333	256	66	14	55	.258
LaTroy Hawkins	Salt Lake	Min	135	43	1	22	.319	187	57	3	31	.305
Jimmy Haynes	Rochester	Bal	171	43	8	55	.251	201	46	1	58	.229
Rod Henderson	Ottawa	Mon	212	63	7	57	.297	269	73	11	46	.271
Oscar Henriquez	New Orleans	Hou	79	20	0	20	.253	193	45	4	60	.233
Wilson Heredia	Oklahoma City	Tex	207	52	7	38	.251	440	115	15	75	.261
Matt Herges	Albuquerque	LA	126	49	7	23	.389	227	71	6	38	.313
Fern. Hernandez	Toledo	Det	122	29	2	40	.238	169	42	3	58	.249
Livan Hernandez	Charlotte	Fla	136	33	5	28	.243	172	43	0	30	.250
Craig Holman	Scranton-WB	Phi	117	48	1	31	.410	194	52	6	44	.268
Chris Hook	Las Vegas	SD	106	37	3	13	.349	129	43	6	22	.333
John Hope	Col. Springs	Col	153	44	5	24	.288	241	71	10	43	.295
Dan Hubbs	Albuquerque	LA	134	36	6	22	.269	226	67	5	65	.296
Jeff Huber	Tucson	Mil	75	22	4	11	.293	168	45	7	26	.268
Rick Huisman	Omaha	KC	79	20	0	24	.253	147	39	7	33	.265
Edwin Hurtado	Tacoma	Sea	226	69	2	28	.305	294	70	7	72	.238
Marty Janzen	Syracuse	Tor	102	26	5	22	.255	157	50	7	34	.318
Mike Jerzembeck	Columbus	NYA	214	38	5	63	.178	278	87	9	55	.313
Doug Johns	Rochester	Bal	46	10	0	8	.217	170	47	5	34	.276
Barry Johnson	Calgary	Pit	68	14	0	19	.206	151	41	7	32	.272
Jonathan Johnson	Oklahoma City	Tex	75	29	1	10	.387	167	54	5	23	.323
Bobby Jones	Col. Springs	Col	107	25	3	29	.234	397	110	13	75	.277
Jarod Juelsgaard	Charlotte	Fla	85	28	2	8	.329	122	37	3	23	.303
Ryan Karp	Scranton-WB	Phi	82	21	2	21	.256	195	51	7	34	.262
Greg Keagle	Toledo	Det	273	62	5	82	.227	295	74	3	58	.251
Brian Keyser	Nashville	ChA	117	26	0	17	.222	327	88	10	51	.269
Steve Kline	Buffalo	Cle	49	11	1	18	.224	151	42	3	23	.278
Scott Klingenbeck	Indianapolis	Cin	258	68	10	41	.264	412	112	13	78	.272
Tommy Kramer	Col. Springs	Col	96	28	7	26	.292	134	29	3	30	.216
Rick Krivda	Rochester	Bal	121	37	2	28	.306	425	85	11	100	.200
Tim Kubinski	Edmonton	Oak	80	21	2	12	.262	193	43	6	41	.223
Frank Lankford	Columbus	NYA	167	44	1	14	.263	179	40	1	26	.223
Andy Larkin	Charlotte	Fla	243	74	13	34	.305	329	92	10	69	.280
Sean Lawrence	Calgary	Pit	103	32	4	25	.311	463	122	13	91	.263
Mark Lee	Col. Springs	Col	68	23	1	20	.338	214	70	14	43	.327
Keith Linebarger	Salt Lake	Min	168	59	1	28	.351	248	76	9	31	.306
Carlton Loewer	Scranton-WB	Phi	315	89	11	78	.283	413	109	9	74	.264
Andrew Lorraine	Edmonton	Oak	80	26	2	12	.325	394	117	10	63	.297
Derek Lowe	Tacoma	Sea	92	20	0	27	.217	127	33	3	22	.260
Sean Lowe	Louisville	StL	194	49	4	58	.253	318	93	9	59	.292
Eric Ludwick	Louisville	StL	93	29	5	19	.312	200	38	2	66	.190
Larry Luebbers	Richmond	Atl	237	75	8	41	.316	342	105	12	50	.307
Calvin Maduro	Scranton-WB	Phi	130	42	5	22	.323	159	29	5	31	.182
Barry Manuel	Norfolk	NYN	102	27	2	24	.265	128	33	7	28	.258
Jesus Martinez	Albuquerque	LA	70	14	1	20	.200	277	98	7	60	.354
Pedro Martinez	Indianapolis	Cin	66	9	1	18	.136	236	61	8	18	.258
Jeff Matranga	Louisville	StL	72	23	2	8	.319	157	52	3	22	.331
Darrell May	Vancouver	Cal	68	19	2	17	.279	224	46	8	45	.205
Jamie McAndrew	Tucson	Mil	206	55	3	27	.267	236	77	7	36	.326
Allen McDill	Omaha	KC	52	12	0	17	.231	208	68	10	34	.327
Rafael Medina	Las Vegas	SD	132	36	3	29	.273	146	54	9	21	.370
Reynol Mendoza	Charlotte	Fla	198	57	6	37	.288	261	77	8	56	.295
Paul Menhart	Tacoma	Sea	215	73	7	32	.340	289	81	11	63	.280
Travis Miller	Salt Lake	Min	86	26	2	13	.302	404	114	9	73	.282
Trever Miller	New Orleans	Hou	83	20	1	18	.241	542	157	14	81	.290
Kevin Millwood	Richmond	Atl	96	24	1	21	.250	117	14	1	25	.120
Mark Mimbs	Pawtucket	Bos	84	26	3	15	.310	251	71	8	66	.283
Nate Minchey	Col. Springs	Col	298	76	9	59	.255	312	96	8	48	.308
Mike Misuraca	Tucson	Mil	190	58	6	23	.305	227	60	9	39	.264
Norm Montoya	Tucson	Mil	112	40	2	15	.357	426	135	14	60	.317
Eric Moody	Oklahoma City	Tex	168	46	5	26	.274	270	68	8	46	.252
Marcus Moore	Buffalo	Cle	92	25	3	24	.272	167	29	3	48	.174
Ramon Morel	Calgary	Pit	172	58	6	22	.337	243	73	7	50	.300
Bobby Munoz	Las Vegas	SD	85	29	1	15	.341	139	44	3	18	.317
Heath Murray	Las Vegas	SD	85	23	2	22	.271	359	119	8	77	.331
Jimmy Myers	Norfolk	NYN	81	19	0	7	.235	167	38	1	24	.228
Rod Myers	Iowa	ChN	199	48	6	36	.241	337	92	12	43	.273
Chris Nichting	Edmonton	Oak	223	68	9	41	.305	323	102	12	49	.316
C.J. Nitkowski	New Orleans	Hou	91	24	0	23	.264	571	159	10	118	.278
Ryan Nye	Scranton-WB	Phi	192	58	7	33	.302	235	59	13	52	.251
Kevin Ohme	Salt Lake	Min	69	16	1	12	.232	209	54	5	33	.258
Kirt Ojala	Charlotte	Fla	118	27	4	34	.229	446	121	9	85	.271
Steve Olsen	Omaha	KC	124	42	4	14	.339	221	54	7	29	.244
Mike Oquist	Edmonton	Oak	92	31	1	12	.337	114	26	2	25	.228
Rafael Orellano	Pawtucket	Bos	60	14	0	17	.233	197	51	12	29	.259
Russ Ortiz	Phoenix	SF	156	48	5	33	.308	179	48	6	37	.268
Donn Pall	Charlotte	Fla	121	33	4	27	.273	194	49	6	43	.253
Jose Paniagua	Ottawa	Mon	244	76	4	38	.311	312	88	9	49	.282
Jose Parra	Salt Lake	Min	153	42	2	25	.275	241	84	6	36	.349
Bronswell Patrick	New Orleans	Hou	111	37	3	19	.333	277	71	7	69	.256
Carl Pavano	Pawtucket	Bos	278	60	4	79	.216	341	88	9	68	.258
Matt Perisho	Vancouver	Cal	35	11	0	9	.314	182	57	3	38	.313
Chris Peters	Calgary	Pit	37	8	1	14	.216	169	44	4	41	.260
Tony Phillips	Tucson	Mil	115	39	3	22	.339	195	52	7	24	.267
Ricky Pickett	Phoenix	SF	77	17	1	27	.221	167	35	1	58	.210

AAA Pitching vs. Lefthanded and Righthanded Batters

Player	Team	Org	vs Left AB	H	HR	RBI	Avg	vs Right AB	H	HR	RBI	Avg
Rich Pratt	Nashville	ChA	86	26	3	12	.302	497	139	19	59	.280
Tim Pugh	Toledo	Det	212	58	6	43	.274	210	57	12	54	.271
Carlos Pulido	Ottawa	Mon	74	18	2	11	.243	230	66	8	33	.287
Shawn Purdy	Phoenix	SF	129	37	3	19	.287	199	66	5	23	.332
Dave Pyc	Albuquerque	LA	135	31	5	30	.230	475	150	13	76	.316
Brady Raggio	Louisville	StL	170	56	13	18	.329	360	89	5	73	.247
Hector Ramirez	Rochester	Bal	192	55	6	26	.286	210	59	5	24	.281
Gary Rath	Albuquerque	LA	116	37	5	25	.319	435	140	12	75	.322
Ken Ray	Omaha	KC	163	43	7	34	.264	279	88	14	62	.315
Mark Redman	Salt Lake	Min	122	40	3	22	.328	524	164	16	103	.313
Bryan Rekar	Col. Springs	Col	245	75	6	37	.306	338	94	15	79	.278
Alberto Reyes	Tucson	Mil	80	22	1	20	.275	129	30	11	49	.233
Dennis Reyes	Albuquerque	LA	39	13	1	12	.333	192	57	3	33	.297
Ray Ricken	Columbus	NYA	259	79	8	33	.305	349	93	4	66	.266
Brad Rigby	Edmonton	Oak	161	52	5	20	.323	174	43	5	29	.247
Danny Rios	Columbus	NYA	145	29	2	23	.200	167	44	6	30	.263
Todd Rizzo	Nashville	ChA	54	12	3	8	.222	224	51	3	52	.228
Brett Roberts	Salt Lake	Min	106	41	3	17	.387	143	48	8	16	.336
Ken Robinson	Syracuse	Tor	103	15	1	34	.146	174	29	5	62	.167
Nerio Rodriguez	Rochester	Bal	288	52	11	80	.181	324	72	12	80	.222
Mike Romano	Syracuse	Tor	176	53	4	39	.301	227	47	6	44	.207
Brian Rose	Pawtucket	Bos	355	94	9	62	.265	373	94	12	54	.252
John Rosengren	Toledo	Det	85	21	1	16	.247	121	23	0	37	.190
Tim Rumer	Columbus	NYA	52	17	3	12	.327	216	62	5	34	.287
Mike Saipe	Col. Springs	Col	109	36	4	19	.330	140	38	6	21	.271
Roger Salkeld	Indianapolis	Cin	129	38	6	27	.295	223	53	10	61	.238
Todd Schmitt	Las Vegas	SD	72	20	4	23	.278	132	35	3	36	.265
Steve Schrenk	Rochester	Bal	227	60	8	40	.264	267	67	13	59	.251
Carl Schutz	Richmond	Atl	77	22	3	18	.286	233	61	9	48	.262
Darryl Scott	Buffalo	Cle	79	15	2	12	.190	160	37	8	17	.231
Chris Seelbach	Charlotte	Fla	96	30	2	20	.313	104	28	5	30	.269
Dan Serafini	Salt Lake	Min	107	28	1	25	.262	482	138	17	93	.286
Keith Shepherd	Norfolk	NYN	172	55	6	27	.320	246	64	4	51	.260
Brian Shouse	Rochester	Bal	88	13	2	31	.148	163	35	4	50	.215
Jose Silva	Calgary	Pit	107	33	1	19	.308	152	41	2	35	.270
Mike Sirotka	Nashville	ChA	61	13	0	17	.213	380	102	13	75	.268
Danny Smith	Oklahoma City	Tex	91	23	1	21	.253	429	131	10	46	.305
Brian Smith	Syracuse	Tor	241	76	5	27	.315	311	93	7	46	.299
Steve Soderstrom	Phoenix	SF	180	54	6	28	.300	256	87	6	50	.340
Kennie Steenstra	Iowa	ChN	188	44	4	38	.234	421	117	11	73	.278
Dave Stevens	Salt Lake	Min	159	41	5	30	.258	198	52	5	41	.263
Everett Stull	Ottawa	Mon	256	65	7	66	.254	347	101	18	64	.291
Tanyon Sturtze	Oklahoma City	Tex	139	43	2	25	.309	312	90	8	54	.288
Jeff Suppan	Pawtucket	Bos	104	22	3	23	.212	115	29	4	17	.252
Mac Suzuki	Tacoma	Sea	144	38	8	25	.264	173	41	5	38	.237
Dave Swartzbaugh	Iowa	ChN	172	38	4	40	.221	331	91	8	57	.275
Jeff Tabaka	Indianapolis	Cin	69	14	1	25	.203	136	30	4	43	.221
Jeff Tam	Norfolk	NYN	200	64	4	31	.320	249	73	5	38	.293
Kerry Taylor	Las Vegas	SD	249	76	8	41	.305	297	74	7	62	.249
Scott Taylor	Las Vegas	SD	106	28	3	22	.264	180	41	3	31	.228
Amaury Telemaco	Iowa	ChN	152	39	1	32	.257	301	82	19	43	.272
Tom Thobe	Richmond	Atl	65	17	2	11	.262	204	53	7	25	.260
Brett Tomko	Indianapolis	Cin	82	23	4	20	.280	146	30	3	40	.205
Bobby Toth	Omaha	KC	83	19	3	16	.229	121	31	3	14	.256
Jody Treadwell	Albuquerque	LA	217	54	5	43	.249	294	89	11	65	.303
Carlos Valdez	Pawtucket	Bos	126	41	6	14	.325	166	32	1	50	.193
Doug Vanderweele	Phoenix	SF	100	36	2	8	.360	185	63	4	27	.341
Ben VanRyn	Iowa	ChN	66	15	2	14	.227	243	73	8	50	.300
Mike Villano	Phoenix	SF	136	39	5	25	.287	139	36	2	16	.259
Mike Walker	Indianapolis	Cin	118	25	3	24	.212	256	55	4	56	.215
Donne Wall	New Orleans	Hou	134	29	4	40	.216	279	80	9	44	.287
Bryan Ward	Charlotte	Fla	59	18	2	9	.305	247	84	15	39	.340
Jeff Ware	Tucson	Mil	186	58	9	28	.312	236	69	7	41	.292
Brian Warren	Oklahoma City	Tex	74	18	2	10	.243	180	55	4	29	.306
Dave Weathers	Buffalo	Cle	76	22	2	10	.289	191	49	5	41	.257
Eric Weaver	Albuquerque	LA	115	48	3	17	.417	173	53	3	37	.306
Gabe White	Indianapolis	Cin	87	20	1	16	.230	376	99	9	46	.263
Scott Wiegandt	Louisville	StL	38	8	2	13	.211	200	49	3	42	.245
Brian Williams	Rochester	Bal	127	31	3	38	.244	140	37	5	40	.264
Mike Williams	Omaha	KC	123	31	5	28	.252	197	46	6	48	.234
Shad Williams	Vancouver	Cal	138	34	5	22	.246	230	62	8	30	.270
Gary Wilson	Calgary	Pit	146	45	5	28	.308	207	70	5	26	.338
Darrin Winston	Scranton-WB	Phi	88	15	1	25	.170	236	59	8	41	.250
Shannon Withem	Norfolk	NYN	275	77	7	43	.280	335	90	14	66	.269
Trey Witte	Tacoma	Sea	104	31	4	20	.298	160	51	10	32	.319
St. Wojciechowski	Edmonton	Oak	68	16	1	12	.235	191	52	5	37	.272
Brad Woodall	Richmond	Atl	129	43	4	29	.333	463	134	15	88	.289
Esteban Yan	Rochester	Bal	215	49	5	59	.228	226	58	8	72	.257

AAA Pitching at Home and on the Road

			Home					Road				
Player	Team	Org	G	IP	W	L	ERA	G	IP	W	L	ERA
Paul Abbott	Tacoma	Sea	9	48.0	3	3	3.56	8	45.2	5	1	4.78
Juan Acevedo	Norfolk	NYN	9	56.1	3	3	4.33	9	60.1	3	3	3.44
Jose Alberro	Oklahoma City	Tex	8	48.1	2	1	3.74	8	43.1	3	5	4.80
Tavo Alvarez	Ottawa	Mon	18	54.2	2	2	4.65	19	51.2	2	6	5.10
Brian Anderson	Buffalo	Cle	8	46.1	3	0	2.54	7	39.1	4	1	3.68
Jimmy Anderson	Calgary	Pit	11	58.1	4	2	5.89	10	44.2	3	4	5.50
Rene Arocha	Phoenix	SF	9	51.1	3	1	5.99	9	60.1	4	2	3.74
Matt Arrandale	Louisville	StL	27	37.2	2	4	3.87	29	45.2	0	2	3.58
Manuel Aybar	Louisville	StL	14	83.2	2	4	3.25	8	53.1	3	4	3.90
Willie Banks	Columbus	NYA	16	74.1	7	4	5.10	17	79.2	7	1	3.52
Brian Barber	Louisville	StL	9	40.2	2	4	10.52	9	52.0	2	4	4.15
Brian Barnes	Toledo	Det	15	51.1	3	6	8.63	17	64.0	4	4	5.20
Manuel Barrios	New Orleans	Hou	30	46.1	3	2	2.54	27	36.1	1	6	4.24
Miguel Batista	Iowa	ChN	15	62.1	4	2	3.19	16	59.2	5	2	5.32
Mike Bertotti	Nashville	ChA	10	48.0	1	4	6.56	11	59.2	4	5	4.41
Andres Berumen	Tacoma	Sea	20	74.1	7	2	4.74	14	39.1	2	2	5.29
Ben Blomdahl	Buffalo	Cle	11	42.1	3	3	4.28	18	61.2	4	5	5.15
Joe Boever	Edmonton	Oak	27	46.0	7	4	5.09	26	46.0	3	4	4.89
Brian Bohanon	Norfolk	NYN	7	46.0	3	3	3.33	8	50.0	6	0	1.98
Rodney Bolton	Indianapolis	Cin	14	84.2	4	4	3.74	14	85.0	5	4	4.87
Tom Bolton	Tucson	Mil	12	49.0	2	6	7.71	11	45.3	3	4	6.16
Steve Bourgeois	Col. Springs	Col	17	62.1	4	4	6.81	16	59.1	5	3	5.18
Mike Bovee	Vancouver	Cal	6	48.2	3	1	3.17	6	40.1	1	2	3.82
Derek Brandow	Syracuse	Tor	10	54.1	1	4	4.49	21	88.2	6	7	6.02
Chris Brock	Richmond	Atl	8	48.0	4	2	2.81	12	70.2	6	4	3.72
Scott Brow	Richmond	Atl	28	41.1	5	3	4.16	33	41.2	0	6	4.81
Travis Buckley	Vancouver	Cal	17	99.0	3	5	5.00	15	77.0	4	6	5.26
Mike Busby	Louisville	StL	8	51.2	4	3	3.69	7	42.0	0	5	5.79
Dan Carlson	Phoenix	SF	11	40.2	4	1	3.13	18	68.1	9	2	4.36
Chris Carpenter	Syracuse	Tor	12	80.0	0	7	5.06	7	40.0	4	2	3.38
Giovanni Carrara	Indianapolis	Cin	10	62.1	6	3	3.48	9	58.1	6	2	3.56
Marino Castillo	Las Vegas	SD	14	63.2	3	2	5.55	16	62.1	3	3	4.78
Bobby Chouinard	Edmonton	Oak	12	49.1	4	2	5.68	13	50.2	2	4	6.45
Terry Clark	Buffalo	Cle	12	38.2	3	2	1.88	13	56.0	4	1	3.54
Chris Clemons	Nashville	ChA	12	66.1	3	3	5.17	10	58.1	2	2	3.87
Reid Cornelius	Charlotte	Fla	12	75.0	6	2	4.68	10	55.2	6	3	5.71
Joe Crawford	Norfolk	NYN	7	43.2	3	0	3.96	9	56.0	5	2	3.21
Doug Creek	Phoenix	SF	15	79.2	4	3	3.86	10	50.0	4	3	6.66
Nelson Cruz	Nashville	ChA	14	78.0	6	6	5.31	7	45.1	5	1	4.79
Roland de la Maza	Buffalo	Cle	16	61.0	6	2	2.07	18	54.0	3	2	3.83
Glenn Dishman	Toledo	Det	9	52.2	5	2	2.59	12	61.1	2	4	5.01
Travis Driskill	Buffalo	Cle	15	80.0	4	2	3.94	14	67.0	4	5	5.51
Mike Drumright	Toledo	Det	8	48.0	1	5	4.13	15	85.1	4	5	5.61
Geoff Edsell	Vancouver	Cal	15	93.0	8	5	5.13	15	90.1	6	6	5.19
Robert Ellis	Vancouver	Cal	13	60.2	5	3	3.59	16	88.1	4	7	7.56
Steve Falteisek	Ottawa	Mon	11	57.1	3	6	5.52	11	67.2	3	3	2.68
Ramon Fermin	Toledo	Det	24	49.2	3	1	5.67	17	30.2	1	1	3.87
Huck Flener	Syracuse	Tor	10	65.1	5	1	4.01	10	58.2	1	5	4.33
Tom Fordham	Nashville	ChA	11	58.2	4	3	5.26	10	55.1	2	4	4.25
Ryan Franklin	Tacoma	Sea	8	51.1	1	4	3.52	6	39.0	4	1	5.08
Steve Gajkowski	Tacoma	Sea	19	43.2	4	0	2.50	25	49.1	1	3	5.13
Mike Gardiner	Columbus	NYA	7	42.2	3	1	2.35	7	42.1	2	3	5.56
Jeff Granger	Calgary	Pit	12	34.1	0	4	8.18	18	48.1	1	3	3.74
Jason Grimsley	Tucson	Mil	17	45.2	4	5	3.98	19	39.2	1	5	7.81
Matt Grott	Tucson	Mil	30	47.2	2	0	4.77	25	40.2	1	1	4.93
John Halama	New Orleans	Hou	13	87.2	6	2	1.75	13	83.1	7	1	3.47
Roy Halladay	Syracuse	Tor	9	52.1	2	3	4.84	13	73.1	5	7	4.43
Greg Hansell	Tucson	Mil	20	45.2	2	1	4.18	20	41.2	0	2	5.24
Tim Harikkala	Tacoma	Sea	11	62.1	3	4	5.07	10	51.0	3	4	8.12
Denny Harriger	Toledo	Det	15	95.1	8	3	2.56	12	71.2	3	5	5.94
Brian Harrison	Omaha	KC	13	80.1	6	3	5.17	17	98.0	4	9	4.96
Tommy Harrison	Richmond	Atl	10	58.1	3	3	3.56	12	63.2	6	4	4.84
Ryan Hawblitzel	Scranton-WB	Phi	16	55.1	4	2	2.45	18	60.0	2	7	7.35
Jimmy Haynes	Rochester	Bal	5	32.1	1	1	3.64	11	69.2	4	3	3.38
Rod Henderson	Ottawa	Mon	15	75.2	5	2	3.23	11	48.0	0	7	7.69
Wilson Heredia	Oklahoma City	Tex	15	88.2	3	7	5.61	12	79.2	4	5	4.32
Matt Herges	Albuquerque	LA	16	40.2	0	3	9.40	15	44.1	0	5	8.57
Livan Hernandez	Charlotte	Fla	5	31.0	2	2	3.77	9	50.1	3	1	4.13
John Hope	Col. Springs	Col	22	52.1	2	2	7.26	21	47.1	2	1	7.26
Dan Hubbs	Albuquerque	LA	30	49.2	4	3	3.48	32	45.0	2	1	4.40
Edwin Hurtado	Tacoma	Sea	7	51.0	4	2	3.00	13	81.1	6	4	4.44
Mike Jerzembeck	Columbus	NYA	8	52.2	4	2	3.28	12	77.2	3	3	3.85
Bobby Jones	Col. Springs	Col	14	73.1	5	4	4.19	11	59.2	2	7	6.39
Greg Keagle	Toledo	Det	12	84.0	7	4	3.00	11	67.1	4	3	4.83
Brian Keyser	Nashville	ChA	22	60.0	3	1	3.30	22	59.0	4	4	2.44
Scott Klingenbeck	Indianapolis	Cin	14	91.2	7	2	2.86	13	79.0	5	6	5.24
Rick Krivda	Rochester	Bal	14	101.2	9	0	3.20	8	44.1	5	2	3.88
Frank Lankford	Columbus	NYA	8	49.2	6	0	1.10	7	44.0	1	4	4.50
Andy Larkin	Charlotte	Fla	16	83.0	3	6	6.51	12	61.1	3	5	5.45
Sean Lawrence	Calgary	Pit	14	79.2	5	3	3.98	12	63.2	3	6	4.56
Keith Linebarger	Salt Lake	Min	21	50.1	3	2	6.65	20	47.1	1	4	6.69
Carlton Loewer	Scranton-WB	Phi	13	87.2	4	4	5.16	16	96.1	1	9	4.12
Andrew Lorraine	Edmonton	Oak	9	50.1	4	3	6.65	14	67.1	4	3	3.35
Sean Lowe	Louisville	StL	10	60.1	4	2	2.85	16	71.1	2	8	5.70
Eric Ludwick	Louisville	StL	16	53.0	4	4	2.38	8	27.0	2	4	4.00
Larry Luebbers	Richmond	Atl	13	67.2	1	6	5.09	14	76.1	2	8	5.68
Jesus Martinez	Albuquerque	LA	15	53.1	5	1	6.10	11	30.2	2	0	6.56
Pedro Martinez	Indianapolis	Cin	13	38.1	1	2	4.02	15	42.0	3	1	3.00
Darrell May	Vancouver	Cal	7	50.2	5	1	1.25	6	29.1	2	4	6.80
Jamie McAndrew	Tucson	Mil	12	59.2	4	4	6.69	10	49.0	3	4	6.98
Reynol Mendoza	Charlotte	Fla	25	75.1	7	6	4.55	21	39.1	0	2	7.37
Paul Menhart	Tacoma	Sea	14	65.0	1	10	6.51	12	62.2	3	4	5.64
Travis Miller	Salt Lake	Min	12	75.2	8	3	4.31	9	50.0	2	3	5.40
Trever Miller	New Orleans	Hou	17	94.2	4	5	3.15	12	69.0	2	2	3.52
Mark Mimbs	Pawtucket	Bos	5	28.0	1	1	3.54	10	55.2	2	7	5.87
Nate Minchey	Col. Springs	Col	13	77.0	9	0	4.09	14	80.2	6	6	4.94

			Home					Road				
Player	Team	Org	G	IP	W	L	ERA	G	IP	W	L	ERA
Mike Misuraca	Tucson	Mil	15	52.1	5	1	2.59	18	56.0	3	6	7.23
Norm Montoya	Tucson	Mil	14	75.2	5	5	4.79	13	55.1	1	5	8.33
Eric Moody	Oklahoma City	Tex	19	62.0	1	3	3.48	16	50.0	4	3	3.42
Ramon Morel	Calgary	Pit	14	54.1	4	1	4.49	13	47.1	2	6	7.26
Heath Murray	Las Vegas	SD	11	65.2	3	5	5.80	8	43.1	3	3	5.01
Rod Myers	Iowa	ChN	11	68.2	2	4	3.96	13	72.0	5	4	4.25
Chris Nichting	Edmonton	Oak	17	72.0	6	4	6.00	16	59.0	1	9	9.92
C.J. Nitkowski	New Orleans	Hou	14	89.2	5	4	3.13	14	84.2	3	6	4.92
Ryan Nye	Scranton-WB	Phi	8	55.1	2	5	4.25	9	54.0	2	5	6.83
Kirt Ojala	Charlotte	Fla	12	72.1	4	3	3.25	13	76.2	4	4	3.78
Steve Olsen	Omaha	KC	10	39.1	1	3	4.14	12	45.0	3	2	7.20
Russ Ortiz	Phoenix	SF	8	51.2	3	1	4.75	6	33.1	1	2	6.80
Donn Pall	Charlotte	Fla	32	41.0	3	2	2.63	27	38.2	1	5	4.24
Jose Paniagua	Ottawa	Mon	12	76.1	5	5	5.20	10	61.1	3	5	3.98
Jose Parra	Salt Lake	Min	28	57.0	1	3	5.37	22	37.0	1	5	7.05
Bronswell Patrick	New Orleans	Hou	12	44.2	2	2	3.26	18	56.0	4	3	3.21
Carl Pavano	Pawtucket	Bos	12	85.2	7	3	2.75	11	76.0	4	3	3.55
Tony Phillips	Tucson	Mil	21	40.3	2	1	5.14	19	40.0	2	1	5.85
Rich Pratt	Nashville	ChA	15	77.1	4	7	5.49	14	72.0	5	1	3.63
Tim Pugh	Toledo	Det	11	67.2	2	3	4.02	8	41.1	1	2	4.82
Shawn Purdy	Phoenix	SF	26	40.1	6	0	3.59	30	42.0	4	3	5.14
Dave Pyc	Albuquerque	LA	18	98.2	8	6	5.50	13	53.1	4	6	5.08
Brady Raggio	Louisville	StL	10	66.2	6	3	3.40	12	71.1	2	8	4.94
Hector Ramirez	Rochester	Bal	21	56.0	4	5	4.98	18	46.2	4	2	4.87
Gary Rath	Albuquerque	LA	10	52.0	3	3	5.19	14	80.1	4	8	6.63
Ken Ray	Omaha	KC	10	39.0	1	5	10.38	15	74.0	4	7	4.26
Mark Redman	Salt Lake	Min	15	79.1	5	6	6.60	14	79.0	3	9	6.04
Bryan Rekar	Col. Springs	Col	12	59.2	2	5	6.54	16	85.1	8	4	4.76
Ray Ricken	Columbus	NYA	13	78.1	5	3	6.34	13	74.1	6	4	4.74
Brad Rigby	Edmonton	Oak	8	44.1	5	2	4.69	7	38.0	3	2	4.03
Danny Rios	Columbus	NYA	30	43.0	3	3	3.77	28	41.2	4	1	2.40
Ken Robinson	Syracuse	Tor	30	41.2	3	4	2.62	26	39.1	4	3	2.53
Nerio Rodriguez	Rochester	Bal	13	88.2	7	3	2.96	14	79.2	4	7	5.00
Mike Romano	Syracuse	Tor	21	61.0	2	2	4.57	19	47.0	0	2	3.83
Brian Rose	Pawtucket	Bos	16	113.2	9	4	3.26	11	77.0	8	1	2.69
Roger Salkeld	Indianapolis	Cin	20	45.0	3	3	6.60	16	43.0	1	5	6.91
Steve Schrenk	Rochester	Bal	12	65.0	1	3	4.43	13	60.2	3	4	4.93
Carl Schutz	Richmond	Atl	13	39.1	2	3	5.75	14	40.0	2	3	4.95
Dan Serafini	Salt Lake	Min	14	82.1	6	3	4.49	14	69.2	3	4	5.59
Keith Shepherd	Norfolk	NYN	8	45.0	3	2	4.60	11	62.0	5	6	4.21
Mike Sirotka	Nashville	ChA	7	43.2	2	3	2.92	12	68.2	5	2	3.56
Danny Smith	Oklahoma City	Tex	11	64.2	2	6	5.61	12	64.2	1	8	5.75
Brian Smith	Syracuse	Tor	18	81.1	4	7	4.44	13	56.0	3	4	6.75
Steve Soderstrom	Phoenix	SF	12	43.0	2	4	6.91	19	62.2	2	4	6.22
Kennie Steenstra	Iowa	ChN	13	87.2	4	4	2.99	12	73.0	1	6	5.05
Dave Stevens	Salt Lake	Min	6	32.2	3	1	4.75	10	57.1	6	2	4.10
Everett Stull	Ottawa	Mon	11	68.1	5	3	4.49	16	91.0	3	7	6.82
Tanyon Sturtze	Oklahoma City	Tex	12	52.2	4	3	6.21	13	62.0	4	3	4.21
Mac Suzuki	Tacoma	Sea	16	36.1	1	4	4.49	16	47.0	3	5	7.09
Dave Swartzbaugh	Iowa	ChN	14	76.0	7	3	2.61	10	58.0	1	4	3.10
Jeff Tam	Norfolk	NYN	20	60.0	3	4	4.50	20	51.2	4	1	4.92
Kerry Taylor	Las Vegas	SD	11	74.0	6	2	3.65	11	70.0	1	7	5.01
Amaury Telemaco	Iowa	ChN	9	58.2	2	5	4.64	9	55.0	3	4	4.42
Jody Treadwell	Albuquerque	LA	11	51.0	3	2	5.12	16	77.1	7	3	5.14
Ben VanRyn	Iowa	ChN	23	46.1	1	2	3.51	28	34.0	1	0	6.09
Mike Walker	Indianapolis	Cin	33	56.2	6	3	2.40	22	46.0	3	3	3.72
Donne Wall	New Orleans	Hou	9	57.0	4	4	3.79	8	53.0	4	3	3.91
Jeff Ware	Tucson	Mil	12	52.1	1	3	6.74	13	53.2	4	5	6.77
Gabe White	Indianapolis	Cin	10	55.1	4	1	3.10	10	62.2	3	3	2.60
Shad Williams	Vancouver	Cal	20	57.0	5	1	3.47	20	42.0	1	1	4.29
Gary Wilson	Calgary	Pit	9	37.1	4	1	5.09	12	47.0	2	2	6.51
Darrin Winston	Scranton-WB	Phi	19	51.2	4	2	3.34	20	37.2	3	2	3.63
Shannon Withem	Norfolk	NYN	14	78.2	4	5	3.91	15	77.0	5	5	4.79
Brad Woodall	Richmond	Atl	12	70.2	3	6	6.79	14	78.0	5	5	4.38
Esteban Yan	Rochester	Bal	18	70.0	9	1	2.70	16	49.0	2	4	3.67

1997 Major League Equivalencies

When Bill James introduced Major League Equivalencies 12 years ago, he said it was easily the most important research he had ever done. When you consider how much he's illuminated the game of baseball for the rest of us, that's quite a statement.

What the MLE does is translate a Double-A or Triple-A hitter's numbers into major league numbers. It does this by making a series of adjustments for a player's home ballpark, his league and his future major league home park. If he plays in the Pacific Coast League, his numbers get knocked down a peg. If he played his home games at New Britain Stadium, where homers go to die, he gets extra credit. If he's a Rockies prospect, his numbers will be inflated by Coors Field. If he's an Astros prospect, his numbers will be deflated by the Astrodome. The MLE also accounts for level of competition, taking into account how much more difficult pitchers become as a hitter climbs the minor league ladder.

What we wind up with is a reasonable estimation of what the hitter would have done had he been in the major leagues with his parent club in 1997. These are not projections. Just because a player's MLE shows him with 30 homers, that doesn't mean he'll hit 30 homers in the majors if given a chance in 1998. Treat the MLEs as if they were single seasons in players' major league careers.

We can't tell you who's going to get the opportunity to play in the major leagues. But the MLEs can give you a good idea of what they would have done had they gotten that chance last year.

Major League Equivalencies for 1997 AAA/AA Batters

ANAHEIM ANGELS		Age	Avg	G	AB	R	H	2B	3B	HR	RBI	BB	SO	SB	CS	OBP	SLG
Betten,Randy	OF	26	.251	80	267	35	67	13	1	2	26	18	71	4	4	.298	.330
Bolick,Frank	DH	32	.280	130	440	68	123	26	2	21	73	52	94	2	1	.356	.491
Burke,Jamie	3B	26	.285	124	428	59	122	36	1	4	54	26	52	1	3	.326	.402
Buxbaum,Danny	1B	25	.248	130	487	56	121	34	1	7	51	31	99	0	1	.293	.366
Caceres,Edgar	2B	34	.282	82	248	24	70	11	0	1	30	15	24	4	6	.323	.339
Carvajal,Jovino	OF	29	.256	131	461	66	118	17	10	1	42	17	92	19	8	.282	.343
Cruz,Fausto	2B	26	.263	118	399	43	105	24	0	9	55	14	86	3	8	.288	.391
Dalton,Jed	OF	25	.194	94	346	45	67	14	1	8	35	21	63	4	12	.240	.309
Eenhoorn,Robert	SS	30	.281	120	438	64	123	25	3	10	48	20	63	0	4	.312	.420
Encarnacion,Ang.	C	25	.214	79	243	20	52	9	0	2	17	11	33	0	4	.248	.276
Greene,Todd	C	27	.328	64	250	42	82	19	0	22	62	16	33	3	1	.368	.668
Harkrider,Tim	SS	26	.248	69	238	28	59	9	1	0	17	13	18	0	2	.287	.294
Hemphill,Bret	C	26	.270	78	252	33	68	11	1	8	45	28	61	0	2	.343	.417
Herrick,Jason	OF	24	.219	118	398	43	87	22	2	15	48	20	154	5	6	.256	.397
Luuloa,Keith	2B	23	.235	120	400	48	94	23	2	7	43	22	64	4	4	.275	.355
Pritchett,Chris	1B	28	.254	109	370	49	94	26	1	6	39	34	77	3	3	.317	.378
Riley,Marquis	OF	27	.239	65	234	27	56	5	0	0	6	29	29	18	8	.323	.261
Singleton,Duane	OF	25	.195	121	425	56	83	18	1	5	34	33	92	12	12	.253	.278
White,Derrick	OF	28	.284	126	433	54	123	31	1	9	56	39	84	7	7	.343	.423
Wolff,Mike	OF-DH	27	.260	91	258	48	67	13	0	18	53	43	80	4	4	.365	.519
Young,Kevin	OF	26	.244	103	320	46	78	18	3	4	38	30	43	3	9	.309	.356
ARI DIAMONDBACKS		**Age**	**Avg**	**G**	**AB**	**R**	**H**	**2B**	**3B**	**HR**	**RBI**	**BB**	**SO**	**SB**	**CS**	**OBP**	**SLG**
Lee,Travis	1B	23	.257	59	214	29	55	13	1	9	32	21	48	1	0	.323	.453
ATLANTA BRAVES		**Age**	**Avg**	**G**	**AB**	**R**	**H**	**2B**	**3B**	**HR**	**RBI**	**BB**	**SO**	**SB**	**CS**	**OBP**	**SLG**
Benbow,Lou	1B	27	.193	117	300	26	58	11	0	5	22	19	85	2	8	.241	.280
Brito,Luis	SS	27	.244	97	316	23	77	9	0	0	24	8	26	2	5	.262	.272
Eaglin,Mike	2B	25	.244	126	373	41	91	12	2	3	31	23	70	9	10	.288	.311
Giovanola,Ed	3B	29	.261	116	379	50	99	20	3	1	35	49	58	1	2	.346	.338
Gregg,Tommy	OF	34	.300	115	367	40	110	31	0	6	41	35	67	2	3	.361	.433
Grijak,Kevin	1B	27	.207	72	227	23	47	9	0	8	32	10	37	0	1	.241	.352
Helms,Wes	3B	22	.229	118	402	41	92	14	0	9	40	25	88	1	5	.274	.331
Hollins,Damon	OF	24	.236	134	479	56	113	27	2	15	48	34	88	5	2	.287	.395
Jimenez,Manny	SS	26	.247	115	405	39	100	19	1	3	30	12	74	1	10	.269	.321
Lewis,Marc	OF	23	.231	135	484	43	112	13	2	11	45	14	89	13	5	.253	.335
Lewis,T.R.	OF	27	.264	117	348	50	92	17	3	5	45	28	74	5	3	.319	.374
Mahoney,Mike	C	25	.190	87	284	30	54	13	0	5	30	16	80	0	0	.233	.289
Malloy,Marty	2B	25	.254	108	397	51	101	16	3	1	19	31	64	12	7	.308	.317
Martinez,Pablo	2B	29	.228	96	285	24	65	12	0	3	15	20	80	6	11	.279	.302
Rodarte,Raul	OF	28	.192	96	255	29	49	9	0	4	21	21	55	7	8	.254	.275
Simon,Randall	1B	23	.276	133	496	48	137	39	0	10	79	13	79	0	6	.295	.415
Smith,Bobby	SS	24	.218	100	344	36	75	8	1	9	36	34	114	4	5	.288	.326
Swann,Pedro	OF	27	.242	124	438	52	106	23	1	15	55	28	80	3	5	.288	.402
Tejero,Fausto	C	29	.203	76	217	24	44	9	0	4	21	17	43	0	1	.261	.300
Toth,Dave	C	28	.196	72	219	19	43	9	0	4	19	17	45	1	2	.254	.292
Tyler,Brad	OF	29	.234	129	368	53	86	13	7	13	59	42	115	9	6	.312	.413
Warner,Mike	OF	27	.272	91	283	39	77	17	2	4	23	34	65	7	9	.350	.389
Whatley,Gabe	OF-1B	26	.258	95	291	40	75	13	3	9	38	28	44	3	5	.323	.416
BALTIMORE ORIOLES		**Age**	**Avg**	**G**	**AB**	**R**	**H**	**2B**	**3B**	**HR**	**RBI**	**BB**	**SO**	**SB**	**CS**	**OBP**	**SLG**
Almonte,Wady	OF	23	.189	69	217	21	41	6	1	5	21	19	69	1	4	.254	.295
Berry,Mike	3B	27	.241	107	370	49	89	17	2	7	42	28	89	0	2	.294	.354

Major League Equivalencies for 1997 AAA/AA Batters

BALTIMORE ORIOLES		Age	Avg	G	AB	R	H	2B	3B	HR	RBI	BB	SO	SB	CS	OBP	SLG
Bogle, Bryan	OF	25	.237	102	375	43	89	15	0	12	50	19	99	2	4	.274	.373
Bullett, Scott	OF	29	.232	136	500	64	116	21	5	8	50	39	118	14	11	.288	.342
Clark, Howie	3B	24	.268	105	306	34	82	14	0	8	32	23	41	1	2	.319	.392
Clyburn, Danny	OF	24	.279	137	505	79	141	29	3	18	66	46	113	10	4	.339	.455
Davis, Tommy	1B	25	.282	119	425	64	120	19	1	13	54	37	95	4	1	.340	.424
Dellucci, David	OF	24	.307	107	374	62	115	25	2	18	48	42	74	8	4	.377	.529
Forbes, P.J.	2B-3B	30	.251	116	422	58	106	19	1	7	47	30	44	11	4	.301	.351
Foster, Jim	C	26	.263	66	213	34	56	11	0	6	38	28	33	0	2	.349	.399
Frazier, Lou	OF	33	.223	109	394	52	88	13	3	1	41	46	93	27	8	.305	.279
Garcia, Jesse	2B	24	.218	141	427	45	93	16	0	4	36	28	76	5	7	.266	.283
Greene, Charlie	C	27	.185	76	232	23	43	6	0	6	24	7	56	0	0	.209	.289
Isom, Johnny	OF	24	.254	135	504	61	128	24	2	18	79	32	130	0	5	.299	.417
Johns, Keith	SS	26	.234	113	321	33	75	18	2	3	26	31	63	2	1	.301	.330
Kirgan, Chris	1B	25	.213	139	493	63	105	22	0	17	62	44	152	0	0	.277	.361
Laker, Tim	DH-C	28	.240	79	283	39	68	9	0	10	32	29	51	0	2	.311	.378
Lamb, David	2B-SS	23	.308	73	260	40	80	17	1	3	33	24	38	0	0	.366	.415
Ledesma, Aaron	SS	27	.302	85	315	35	95	23	0	2	37	30	50	9	2	.362	.394
Luzinski, Ryan	C	24	.219	72	201	20	44	9	0	5	27	23	69	2	1	.299	.338
Matos, Francisco	2B	28	.301	101	376	44	113	15	2	3	44	7	44	6	2	.313	.375
Ojeda, Augie	SS	23	.259	73	243	32	63	9	0	1	25	28	22	5	2	.336	.309
Otanez, Willis	3B	25	.226	68	239	28	54	16	0	6	32	19	57	0	1	.283	.368
Rosario, Mel	C	25	.243	123	419	59	102	22	0	11	52	19	115	3	7	.276	.375
Wawruck, Jim	OF	28	.254	94	331	41	84	17	2	4	30	29	67	9	6	.314	.353
BOSTON RED SOX		Age	Avg	G	AB	R	H	2B	3B	HR	RBI	BB	SO	SB	CS	OBP	SLG
Abad, Andy	1B-OF	25	.273	113	385	55	105	20	0	13	48	55	77	3	4	.364	.426
Bennett, Gary	C	26	.204	71	221	14	45	7	0	3	19	15	40	0	0	.254	.276
Borrero, Richie	C	25	.240	72	250	29	60	13	0	3	24	9	66	1	1	.266	.328
Bryant, Pat	OF	25	.274	113	405	64	111	22	2	16	69	43	92	13	6	.344	.457
Carey, Todd	1B	26	.207	113	376	31	78	16	0	10	51	30	119	0	1	.266	.330
Coleman, Michael	OF	22	.291	130	488	71	142	26	7	17	65	40	123	15	6	.345	.477
Correia, Rod	2B	30	.248	102	371	49	92	22	0	5	41	20	48	4	1	.286	.348
DePastino, Joe	C	24	.240	79	271	43	65	14	0	14	47	23	67	0	1	.299	.446
DeRosso, Tony	3B	22	.205	102	352	43	72	18	0	11	34	19	100	8	0	.245	.349
Fuller, Aaron	OF	26	.247	128	473	74	117	18	4	4	39	69	89	25	10	.343	.328
Gibralter, David	1B	23	.262	123	470	60	123	25	0	11	74	32	110	2	4	.309	.385
Hyzdu, Adam	OF	26	.265	119	407	68	108	21	0	19	74	63	118	7	5	.364	.457
Jackson, Gavin	SS	24	.260	100	296	39	77	12	0	0	39	35	38	1	5	.338	.301
Malave, Jose	OF	27	.287	115	421	77	121	25	1	14	62	48	81	8	3	.360	.451
McKeel, Walt	C	26	.233	73	258	30	60	17	0	5	29	30	42	0	0	.313	.357
Merloni, Lou	3B-2B	27	.291	118	412	63	120	27	3	8	52	34	67	2	2	.345	.430
Nixon, Trot	OF	24	.235	130	469	70	110	18	2	17	54	55	90	7	3	.315	.390
Ortiz, Nicky	2B	24	.269	87	283	40	76	17	1	6	45	19	58	2	1	.315	.399
Pozo, Arquimedez	3B	24	.272	101	371	54	101	18	0	19	62	32	57	2	3	.330	.474
Rodriguez, Tony	SS	27	.238	82	281	23	67	12	0	1	16	7	49	3	1	.257	.292
Sadler, Donnie	2B-SS	23	.204	125	476	65	97	18	1	9	31	50	127	14	5	.279	.303
Tavarez, Jesus	OF	27	.257	59	226	38	58	6	2	2	17	23	32	15	6	.325	.327
Varitek, Jason	C	26	.234	107	368	55	86	18	0	14	48	39	91	0	0	.307	.397
Waszgis, B.J.	C	27	.241	100	307	53	74	13	0	12	42	48	82	0	1	.344	.401
Williams, Juan	OF	25	.188	90	277	38	52	9	0	11	33	41	103	1	5	.292	.339

Major League Equivalencies for 1997 AAA/AA Batters

CHICAGO CUBS		Age	Avg	G	AB	R	H	2B	3B	HR	RBI	BB	SO	SB	CS	OBP	SLG
Brown,Brant	OF	27	.278	71	248	42	69	16	2	13	42	25	46	4	6	.344	.516
Cairo,Miguel	2B	24	.255	135	550	68	140	31	3	4	38	20	56	30	11	.281	.344
Cline,Pat	C	23	.214	105	351	33	75	16	0	7	35	24	108	1	3	.264	.319
Dalesandro,Mark	C	30	.239	115	393	40	94	12	0	7	40	27	53	0	0	.288	.323
Dowler,Dee	OF	26	.213	94	267	34	57	6	0	3	23	21	40	9	5	.271	.270
Ellis,Kevin	OF	26	.222	104	316	29	70	12	2	6	29	15	70	4	1	.257	.329
Freeman,Ricky	1B	26	.248	112	367	47	91	15	1	12	56	24	75	5	5	.294	.392
Gazarek,Marty	OF	25	.292	76	274	40	80	19	0	8	37	12	33	6	3	.322	.449
Hightower,Vee	OF	26	.202	87	272	25	55	6	1	4	21	26	70	10	11	.272	.276
Jennings,Robin	OF	26	.255	126	451	55	115	22	3	16	59	46	76	3	3	.324	.424
Joseph,Terry	OF	24	.241	134	431	58	104	18	7	8	49	36	93	11	16	.300	.371
Kieschnick,Brooks	1B	26	.237	97	350	47	83	18	0	17	55	30	93	0	2	.297	.434
Lowery,Terrell	OF	27	.276	110	373	57	103	24	2	15	59	54	101	6	8	.368	.472
Maxwell,Jason	SS	26	.244	122	390	63	95	18	4	11	42	50	77	7	9	.330	.395
McCall,Rod	1B-DH	26	.245	104	314	40	77	9	0	20	61	32	118	0	0	.315	.465
Nava,Lipso	3B	29	.243	109	309	30	75	15	0	8	30	18	55	1	3	.284	.369
Nelson,Bry	3B	24	.251	110	363	37	91	26	1	6	42	27	46	3	7	.303	.377
Nunez,Ramon	3B	25	.260	106	334	43	87	10	2	12	47	9	69	0	2	.280	.410
Pegues,Steve	OF	30	.271	72	203	16	55	12	0	1	20	6	33	2	3	.292	.345
Petersen,Chris	SS	27	.218	119	380	40	83	13	1	2	27	26	93	0	6	.268	.274
Valdes,Pedro	OF	25	.262	125	450	54	118	26	0	11	50	40	70	6	2	.322	.393
Wilson,Brandon	SS	29	.213	87	235	23	50	3	3	0	14	17	48	5	5	.266	.251
Wimmer,Chris	2B	27	.234	107	364	45	85	12	2	1	20	14	40	15	6	.262	.286
CHICAGO WHITE SOX		Age	Avg	G	AB	R	H	2B	3B	HR	RBI	BB	SO	SB	CS	OBP	SLG
Abbott,Jeff	OF	25	.311	118	454	80	141	32	2	9	57	37	54	9	7	.363	.449
Alvarez,Clemente	C	30	.182	79	236	23	43	8	0	2	18	18	52	0	0	.240	.242
Brady,Doug	2B	28	.223	106	363	39	81	10	2	5	32	16	49	10	4	.256	.303
Coolbaugh,Scott	3B	32	.261	68	226	28	59	15	0	8	40	25	64	0	0	.335	.434
Cotton,John	OF	27	.252	127	433	59	109	20	3	14	66	27	133	6	4	.296	.409
Evans,Jason	OF	27	.270	128	403	60	109	22	0	3	44	62	101	5	5	.368	.347
Finn,John	3B	30	.249	73	237	39	59	13	0	0	21	26	29	8	2	.323	.304
Fonville,Chad	OF	27	.171	102	350	30	60	3	0	0	13	17	40	15	5	.210	.180
Liefer,Jeffrey	OF	23	.212	119	458	54	97	20	7	10	57	26	123	1	0	.254	.352
Machado,Robert	C	25	.255	84	302	39	77	16	0	7	27	10	64	3	0	.279	.377
McKinnon,Sandy	OF	24	.244	96	320	47	78	17	0	3	25	21	72	9	6	.290	.325
Menechino,Franki	2B	27	.257	127	417	81	107	27	3	12	58	77	114	6	5	.372	.422
Moore,Brandon	SS	25	.232	125	401	47	93	13	0	0	38	30	51	2	7	.285	.264
Norton,Greg	3B	25	.257	114	404	74	104	24	0	21	69	51	106	2	5	.341	.473
Ordonez,Magglio	OF	24	.313	135	511	59	160	26	2	12	82	28	64	11	10	.349	.442
Pearson,Eddie	1B	24	.271	136	510	63	138	31	0	6	62	20	77	0	2	.298	.367
Raven,Luis	DH	29	.307	117	437	71	134	26	2	23	91	31	134	2	3	.353	.533
Simmons,Brian	OF	24	.237	138	528	87	125	24	9	10	58	59	132	10	12	.313	.373
Thomas,Juan	1B-DH	26	.274	80	299	40	82	13	1	7	44	15	98	0	2	.309	.395
Valdez,Mario	1B	23	.259	81	274	40	71	18	0	12	55	38	80	0	1	.349	.456
Vinas,Julio	DH	25	.218	91	308	35	67	11	1	9	37	22	75	3	4	.270	.347
Wilson,Craig	SS	27	.257	137	444	64	114	18	1	5	38	43	32	3	4	.322	.336
Wrona,Rick	C	34	.229	99	306	28	70	19	0	6	39	4	55	0	1	.239	.350
CINCINNATI REDS		Age	Avg	G	AB	R	H	2B	3B	HR	RBI	BB	SO	SB	CS	OBP	SLG
Bako,Paul	C	26	.229	104	315	29	72	13	0	7	37	30	82	0	4	.296	.337
Belk,Tim	1B	28	.270	90	248	31	67	17	0	6	32	23	45	3	2	.332	.411

Major League Equivalencies for 1997 AAA/AA Batters

CINCINNATI REDS		Age	Avg	G	AB	R	H	2B	3B	HR	RBI	BB	SO	SB	CS	OBP	SLG
Boone,Aaron	3B	25	.270	131	463	68	125	28	3	18	64	35	82	9	3	.321	.460
Broach,Donald	OF	26	.238	105	383	44	91	13	2	0	22	22	48	8	14	.279	.282
Coughlin,Kevin	OF	27	.254	92	279	28	71	11	0	2	17	15	39	0	2	.293	.315
Eddie,Steve	3B	27	.249	118	374	40	93	22	2	5	35	13	66	2	1	.274	.358
Garcia,Guillermo	C	26	.226	75	217	20	49	1	0	10	30	13	59	0	1	.270	.369
Griffey,Craig	OF	27	.198	93	293	39	58	7	0	0	14	25	66	9	6	.261	.222
Hunter,Brian	1B-OF	30	.262	139	493	63	129	34	3	17	73	37	77	7	5	.313	.446
Jackson,Damian	SS	24	.275	92	331	57	91	16	0	3	18	42	64	19	6	.357	.350
Koelling,Brian	2B	29	.242	73	265	35	64	7	2	2	15	17	50	12	8	.287	.306
Maas,Kevin	DH	33	.198	86	253	32	50	20	0	4	29	40	60	0	0	.307	.324
Magdaleno,Ricky	SS	23	.209	117	330	40	69	21	0	8	36	40	100	0	0	.295	.345
Mitchell,Keith	OF	28	.247	124	397	62	98	23	0	12	51	64	66	7	3	.351	.395
Mottola,Chad	OF	26	.287	129	439	53	126	16	6	8	61	24	66	13	3	.324	.405
Murray,Glenn	OF	27	.238	101	323	47	77	14	1	18	52	36	97	4	4	.315	.455
Nunnally,Jon	OF	26	.249	68	221	27	55	9	0	11	26	30	66	5	3	.339	.439
Owens,Eric	2B	27	.266	104	380	48	101	14	3	9	38	37	56	17	6	.331	.389
Rose Jr,Pete	3B	28	.268	124	463	54	124	28	0	19	70	22	76	0	0	.301	.451
Rumfield,Toby	1B	25	.251	101	315	25	79	19	0	3	27	11	33	0	0	.276	.340
Stynes,Chris	2B	25	.258	103	403	54	104	23	0	5	49	16	29	5	1	.286	.352
Timmons,Ozzie	OF	27	.234	125	397	39	93	13	0	11	47	53	101	0	3	.324	.350
Towle,Justin	C	24	.270	119	396	44	107	32	3	7	50	34	79	3	4	.328	.419
Watkins,Pat	OF	25	.276	130	482	64	133	26	5	11	51	30	72	16	10	.318	.419
Williams,Jason	2B	24	.270	69	256	27	69	18	0	3	20	11	36	3	4	.300	.375
CLEVELAND INDIANS		**Age**	**Avg**	**G**	**AB**	**R**	**H**	**2B**	**3B**	**HR**	**RBI**	**BB**	**SO**	**SB**	**CS**	**OBP**	**SLG**
Aven,Bruce	OF	26	.275	121	425	64	117	26	2	15	72	46	103	8	3	.346	.452
Betts,Todd	3B	25	.216	128	422	49	91	21	0	14	52	46	103	0	3	.293	.365
Betzsold,Jim	OF	25	.233	118	416	57	97	18	3	13	59	38	127	2	5	.297	.385
Candaele,Casey	2B	37	.218	79	307	36	67	20	0	6	35	29	45	0	6	.286	.342
Casey,Sean	1B	23	.347	82	297	39	103	22	0	11	65	22	47	0	1	.392	.532
Diaz,Einar	C	25	.245	109	331	37	81	17	1	2	29	16	35	1	6	.280	.320
Glass,Chip	OF	27	.228	113	378	55	86	14	2	3	27	35	65	10	10	.293	.299
Hubbard,Trent	OF	32	.299	103	368	66	110	21	0	14	56	53	54	20	8	.387	.470
Lovullo,Torey	3B	32	.201	125	379	41	76	19	0	10	41	51	80	0	5	.295	.330
Manto,Jeff	DH-3B	33	.254	94	311	47	79	14	0	20	58	45	76	0	3	.348	.492
Mercedes,Guiller.	SS	24	.183	97	279	27	51	6	0	0	20	17	40	1	3	.230	.204
Miller,David	OF	24	.267	134	486	63	130	23	6	2	46	30	82	14	5	.310	.352
Moyle,Mike	C	26	.203	104	330	42	67	13	0	11	40	34	76	1	0	.277	.342
Neal,Mike	2B-SS	26	.249	126	437	58	109	21	1	12	52	35	110	5	7	.305	.384
Norman,Les	OF	29	.249	118	422	66	105	19	0	15	52	40	84	5	6	.314	.400
Perry,Chan	1B-DH	25	.280	119	453	55	127	29	1	14	72	17	65	2	3	.306	.442
Ramirez,Alex	OF	23	.274	119	409	55	112	18	6	10	41	12	99	8	5	.311	.421
Sexson,Richie	1B	23	.248	115	427	53	106	19	1	28	82	25	91	4	1	.290	.494
Thomas,Greg	1B	25	.204	78	245	20	50	11	1	5	32	20	59	1	1	.264	.318
Wilson,Enrique	SS-2B	22	.293	118	443	73	130	19	2	9	36	39	43	7	8	.351	.406
COLORADO ROCKIES		**Age**	**Avg**	**G**	**AB**	**R**	**H**	**2B**	**3B**	**HR**	**RBI**	**BB**	**SO**	**SB**	**CS**	**OBP**	**SLG**
Barry,Jeff	OF	29	.282	121	425	58	120	19	3	22	67	26	76	5	2	.324	.496
Barthol,Blake	C	25	.274	109	339	45	93	13	2	9	41	28	77	4	3	.330	.404
Bernhardt,Steve	2B	27	.239	101	326	37	78	16	0	9	40	24	46	1	2	.291	.371
Boston,D.J.	1B	26	.308	85	308	56	95	16	2	8	52	44	66	0	5	.395	.451
Curtis,Kevin	OF	25	.300	127	446	68	134	32	0	25	84	35	106	0	3	.351	.540

Major League Equivalencies for 1997 AAA/AA Batters

COLORADO ROCKIES		Age	Avg	G	AB	R	H	2B	3B	HR	RBI	BB	SO	SB	CS	OBP	SLG
Echevarria,Angel	OF	27	.324	77	296	46	96	23	0	14	63	22	46	4	2	.371	.544
Gibson,Derrick	OF	23	.366	140	568	108	208	33	2	37	89	35	109	16	8	.403	.627
Giudice,John	OF	27	.280	63	225	27	63	9	2	7	32	14	49	4	1	.322	.431
Gonzales,Rene	2B	36	.279	98	337	39	94	19	0	3	33	33	48	1	4	.343	.362
Grunewald,Keith	2B	26	.266	103	320	43	85	13	1	0	25	22	76	5	3	.313	.313
Gubanich,Creight.	C	26	.282	81	266	30	75	15	0	11	43	14	79	0	2	.318	.462
Hall,Billy	2B	29	.226	98	336	36	76	5	4	3	26	23	59	15	9	.276	.292
Helton,Todd	1B	24	.345	99	388	69	134	30	2	14	70	48	67	2	1	.417	.541
Howitt,Dann	DH	34	.326	102	313	45	102	28	0	12	49	25	70	1	2	.376	.530
Jarrett,Link	SS	26	.331	88	272	20	90	11	1	1	28	16	29	1	2	.368	.390
Jones,Terry	OF	27	.268	92	362	55	97	13	3	1	19	19	48	26	10	.304	.329
Newstrom,Doug	C	26	.290	95	252	31	73	11	1	1	46	35	32	7	5	.376	.353
Owens,Jayhawk	C	29	.262	95	290	45	76	16	0	11	27	43	97	2	1	.357	.431
Perez,Neifi	SS	23	.363	68	303	54	110	25	3	9	36	13	26	5	2	.389	.554
Pledger,Kinnis	OF	29	.246	73	244	39	60	11	2	12	27	30	67	1	2	.328	.455
Quinlan,Tom	3B	30	.289	134	512	67	148	35	1	25	89	39	116	0	1	.339	.508
Raabe,Brian	2B	30	.340	135	533	93	181	35	2	12	74	35	21	0	5	.380	.480
Sexton,Chris	SS	26	.315	131	489	83	154	27	4	2	46	68	57	6	17	.399	.399
Taylor,Jamie	3B	27	.351	104	342	46	120	19	1	9	43	31	49	1	3	.405	.491
Velazquez,Edgard	OF	22	.286	120	441	55	126	23	9	18	58	27	118	4	3	.327	.501
DETROIT TIGERS		Age	Avg	G	AB	R	H	2B	3B	HR	RBI	BB	SO	SB	CS	OBP	SLG
Almanzar,Richard	2B	22	.219	103	375	46	82	17	1	4	29	26	46	14	5	.269	.301
Barker,Glen	OF	27	.241	90	294	47	71	7	3	5	26	24	92	16	8	.299	.337
Bartee,Kimera	OF	25	.202	136	491	60	99	11	5	3	29	46	161	25	9	.270	.263
Bruno,Julio	3B	25	.241	120	424	42	102	19	2	5	47	27	74	4	2	.286	.330
Catalanotto,Frank	2B	24	.281	134	487	67	137	29	2	16	61	42	84	9	10	.338	.448
Encarnacion,Juan	OF	22	.297	131	475	76	141	27	3	23	75	30	92	12	2	.339	.512
Garcia,Luis	SS	23	.243	126	441	46	107	16	0	4	40	7	63	2	1	.254	.306
Hall,Joe	OF	32	.234	75	265	31	62	16	1	5	26	19	50	1	0	.285	.358
Holbert,Ray	SS	27	.225	109	364	38	82	16	5	6	33	28	114	12	6	.281	.346
Hurst,Jimmy	OF	26	.262	115	385	49	101	11	2	18	57	44	126	10	4	.338	.442
Hyers,Tim	1B	26	.256	121	414	54	106	20	2	12	49	36	68	0	1	.316	.401
Ibarra,Jesse	1B	25	.262	115	428	61	112	20	0	24	76	39	91	2	1	.323	.477
Johnson,Earl	OF	26	.216	114	436	58	94	10	1	1	26	18	79	27	9	.247	.250
Makarewicz,Scott	C	31	.219	100	333	30	73	13	0	6	34	12	71	0	4	.246	.312
Marine,Del	C	26	.216	99	319	37	69	19	0	10	36	34	98	0	0	.292	.370
Marquez,Jesus	OF	25	.244	114	451	47	110	21	3	11	62	15	82	6	4	.268	.377
Roberts,David	DH	26	.270	105	400	63	108	21	1	3	34	32	66	16	6	.324	.350
Rodriguez,Steve	3B	27	.214	107	415	51	89	27	0	3	34	23	60	14	4	.256	.301
Schmidt,Tom	3B	25	.234	82	282	31	66	14	0	8	37	20	86	1	0	.285	.369
Smith,Ira	OF-DH	30	.252	92	309	41	78	19	1	4	27	34	62	0	0	.327	.359
Trammell,Bubba	OF	26	.239	90	314	50	75	13	0	27	67	34	95	1	1	.313	.538
FLORIDA MARLINS		Age	Avg	G	AB	R	H	2B	3B	HR	RBI	BB	SO	SB	CS	OBP	SLG
Berg,Dave	SS	27	.251	117	399	50	100	20	4	5	31	37	74	10	6	.314	.358
Booty,Josh	3B	23	.177	122	430	29	76	15	1	13	47	16	177	1	1	.206	.307
Clapinski,Chris	2B	26	.218	110	321	41	70	18	1	7	34	32	67	8	1	.289	.346
Counsell,Craig	2B	27	.330	96	373	61	123	30	6	4	50	35	37	8	2	.387	.475
Daubach,Brian	1B	26	.231	136	433	44	100	31	1	12	62	43	132	0	7	.300	.390
Dunwoody,Todd	OF	23	.217	107	378	49	82	12	5	13	41	26	135	16	6	.267	.378
Gonzalez,Alex	SS	21	.217	133	428	47	93	12	3	12	45	16	88	2	6	.245	.343

Major League Equivalencies for 1997 AAA/AA Batters

FLORIDA MARLINS		Age	Avg	G	AB	R	H	2B	3B	HR	RBI	BB	SO	SB	CS	OBP	SLG
Hastings,Lionel	2B	25	.299	93	261	38	78	16	0	6	24	23	56	3	2	.356	.429
Jackson,Ryan	OF	26	.265	134	460	60	122	22	3	16	67	30	91	1	4	.310	.430
Koeyers,Ramsey	C	23	.221	83	272	25	60	11	0	8	34	8	71	0	2	.243	.349
Kotsay,Mark	OF	22	.260	114	411	71	107	21	1	12	53	44	69	10	4	.332	.404
Lucca,Lou	3B	27	.240	96	275	26	66	17	0	11	34	14	58	3	3	.277	.422
Millar,Kevin	1B	26	.297	135	478	65	142	27	1	21	90	39	56	1	2	.350	.490
Morman,Russ	1B-OF	36	.271	117	369	54	100	13	1	21	66	39	93	1	1	.341	.482
Natal,Bob	C	32	.224	78	237	22	53	13	1	7	32	12	38	1	1	.261	.376
Olmeda,Jose	OF	30	.172	83	232	16	40	8	0	0	19	14	43	1	1	.220	.207
Reeves,Glenn	OF	24	.304	66	207	36	63	11	1	4	24	23	46	5	3	.374	.425
Rodriguez,Victor	2B	21	.239	113	381	43	91	14	3	2	26	17	46	8	6	.271	.307
Roskos,John	C	23	.266	123	425	45	113	25	0	16	58	29	86	2	5	.313	.438
Sheff,Chris	OF	27	.213	120	305	36	65	18	0	7	28	29	79	10	3	.281	.341
Wilson,Pookie	OF	27	.211	105	247	28	52	8	0	2	17	17	43	1	3	.261	.267
Winn,Randy	OF	24	.251	96	363	45	91	11	5	4	24	25	98	22	8	.299	.342
HOUSTON ASTROS		**Age**	**Avg**	**G**	**AB**	**R**	**H**	**2B**	**3B**	**HR**	**RBI**	**BB**	**SO**	**SB**	**CS**	**OBP**	**SLG**
Colon,Dennis	1B	24	.247	129	388	42	96	21	0	4	54	34	52	1	2	.308	.332
Forkner,Tim	3B	25	.230	116	382	40	88	20	0	4	36	38	76	2	0	.300	.314
Gonzalez,Jimmy	C	25	.223	97	328	38	73	15	0	9	45	23	102	1	1	.274	.351
Guillen,Carlos	SS	22	.225	118	387	39	87	14	0	6	30	23	94	4	5	.268	.307
Haney,Todd	2B	32	.261	119	456	56	119	27	0	1	55	36	57	3	2	.315	.327
Hernandez,Carlos	2B	22	.259	92	347	49	90	10	0	2	26	21	66	12	8	.302	.305
Hidalgo,Richard	OF	22	.255	134	509	63	130	34	3	8	66	28	62	4	10	.294	.381
Johnson,Russ	3B	25	.253	122	431	61	109	14	4	3	42	54	85	5	4	.336	.325
Knorr,Randy	C	29	.215	72	237	18	51	9	0	3	23	18	41	0	0	.271	.291
Martin,Jim	OF	27	.224	112	299	32	67	7	1	12	43	26	132	11	10	.286	.375
McNabb,Buck	OF	25	.224	123	398	52	89	14	1	0	23	27	71	6	9	.273	.264
Meluskey,Mitch	C	24	.271	124	395	56	107	21	0	11	54	39	88	0	3	.336	.408
Mitchell,Donovan	OF	28	.225	128	458	50	103	15	4	3	34	39	63	15	6	.286	.295
Mora,Melvin	OF	26	.234	119	359	47	84	13	2	1	32	38	57	5	7	.307	.290
Phillips,J.R.	OF-1B	28	.263	104	396	50	104	25	0	15	60	32	123	0	1	.318	.439
Ramos,Ken	OF	31	.265	92	245	27	65	8	0	0	18	37	16	1	7	.362	.298
Rivera,Luis	SS	34	.218	124	372	39	81	21	2	2	38	28	56	3	4	.273	.301
Trammell,Gary	OF	25	.233	110	301	29	70	8	0	1	22	15	59	0	4	.269	.269
Ward,Daryle	1B	23	.297	128	445	59	132	22	0	14	76	34	83	2	2	.347	.440
KANSAS CITY ROYALS		**Age**	**Avg**	**G**	**AB**	**R**	**H**	**2B**	**3B**	**HR**	**RBI**	**BB**	**SO**	**SB**	**CS**	**OBP**	**SLG**
Benitez,Yamil	OF	25	.266	92	316	48	84	12	0	15	56	18	81	8	3	.305	.446
Carr,Jeremy	OF	27	.262	126	439	69	115	18	1	6	36	42	69	33	12	.326	.349
Diaz,Lino	3B	27	.250	92	276	26	69	22	2	1	37	14	27	1	6	.286	.355
Fasano,Sal	C	26	.168	89	273	32	46	10	0	11	30	21	87	0	2	.228	.326
Giambi,Jeremy	OF	23	.283	74	254	36	72	12	0	7	38	27	47	2	4	.352	.413
Gonzalez,Raul	OF	24	.251	129	431	48	108	25	3	9	54	22	52	7	8	.287	.385
Hansen,Jed	2B	25	.243	114	367	34	89	17	1	8	35	25	77	5	1	.291	.360
Hatcher,Chris	OF-DH	29	.208	79	255	32	53	8	0	11	24	15	83	0	1	.252	.369
Long,Ryan	OF	25	.237	113	396	38	94	23	0	14	44	14	97	1	4	.263	.402
Lopez,Mendy	SS	23	.203	118	394	45	80	14	2	3	35	28	91	4	5	.256	.272
Martinez,Felix	SS	24	.229	112	397	43	91	16	4	1	28	22	82	14	5	.270	.297
Medrano,Tony	2B	23	.209	125	392	40	82	7	0	4	38	19	36	5	3	.246	.258
Mendez,Carlos	1B	24	.288	129	480	53	138	27	0	8	66	11	43	2	7	.303	.394
Ortiz,Hector	C	28	.202	80	233	19	47	4	0	0	20	23	29	0	2	.273	.219

371

Major League Equivalencies for 1997 AAA/AA Batters

KANSAS CITY ROYALS		Age	Avg	G	AB	R	H	2B	3B	HR	RBI	BB	SO	SB	CS	OBP	SLG
Pellow,Kit	3B	24	.216	68	231	29	50	10	0	6	30	13	73	3	2	.258	.338
Pough,Chop	3B	28	.225	124	418	50	94	17	0	16	47	41	112	0	1	.294	.380
Shirley,Al	OF	24	.236	81	229	22	54	8	0	2	18	13	93	5	7	.277	.297
Sisco,Steve	2B	28	.242	109	355	43	86	13	1	4	26	20	62	2	2	.283	.318
Stewart,Andy	C	27	.248	86	278	30	69	8	0	4	19	14	42	0	1	.284	.320
Sutton,Larry	1B	28	.271	106	365	48	99	24	0	14	57	48	56	0	0	.356	.452
LA DODGERS		Age	Avg	G	AB	R	H	2B	3B	HR	RBI	BB	SO	SB	CS	OBP	SLG
Blanco,Henry	C	26	.249	91	269	23	67	13	0	3	29	22	66	4	4	.306	.331
Cooney,Kyle	C	25	.242	72	236	28	57	12	1	5	36	4	47	2	2	.254	.364
Cora,Alex	SS	22	.195	127	426	38	83	15	2	2	35	15	64	8	9	.222	.254
Garcia,Karim	OF	22	.238	71	239	32	57	11	3	11	40	13	73	7	5	.278	.448
Gibbs,Kevin	OF	24	.285	101	333	66	95	14	2	1	25	43	51	33	12	.367	.348
Hale,Chip	1B	33	.210	88	229	26	48	11	0	1	18	35	27	1	3	.314	.271
Ingram,Garey	2B	27	.249	92	325	50	81	21	3	8	38	22	53	11	6	.297	.406
Johnson,Keith	2B	27	.227	96	282	31	64	6	1	6	38	10	51	4	6	.253	.319
Kirby,Wayne	OF	34	.266	68	244	35	65	11	2	5	26	15	34	11	5	.309	.389
Kirkpatrick,Jay	1B-DH	28	.217	62	203	16	44	6	0	5	31	4	56	0	1	.232	.320
Konerko,Paul	3B	22	.257	130	440	60	113	21	0	21	78	38	64	1	3	.316	.448
LoDuca,Paul	C	26	.279	105	359	46	100	21	1	4	51	28	28	11	8	.331	.376
Marrero,Oreste	OF	28	.202	96	243	23	49	13	0	5	26	14	73	0	1	.245	.317
Maurer,Ron	SS	30	.214	114	322	37	69	14	2	4	30	23	61	1	3	.267	.307
Melendez,Dan	1B	27	.213	87	244	29	52	14	0	1	17	27	44	2	2	.292	.283
Pennyfeather,Willi.	OF	30	.196	115	373	36	73	14	2	9	33	15	76	7	11	.227	.316
Richardson,Brian	3B	22	.249	133	453	54	113	17	7	8	66	25	103	2	6	.289	.371
Richardson,Scott	OF	27	.238	92	286	36	68	11	0	4	28	28	57	4	5	.306	.318
Riggs,Adam	2B	25	.240	57	208	36	50	5	1	7	17	17	40	7	2	.298	.375
Roberge,J.P.	OF	25	.274	134	482	69	132	19	2	11	77	24	74	12	9	.308	.390
Spearman,Vernon	OF	28	.206	71	214	30	44	4	1	0	9	19	37	9	4	.270	.234
MILWAUKEE BREWERS		Age	Avg	G	AB	R	H	2B	3B	HR	RBI	BB	SO	SB	CS	OBP	SLG
Banks,Brian	OF	27	.263	98	361	39	95	23	2	6	46	26	85	5	2	.313	.388
Barker,Kevin	1B	22	.239	65	226	25	54	12	4	6	44	16	42	2	2	.289	.407
Belliard,Ron	2B	23	.252	118	425	58	107	30	3	2	40	45	71	7	6	.323	.351
Brown,Jarvis	OF	31	.235	112	370	47	87	18	2	4	25	38	87	10	5	.306	.327
Diaz,Eddy	3B	26	.293	94	338	47	99	21	2	6	51	19	25	0	0	.331	.420
Dobrolsky,Bill	C	28	.228	102	289	30	66	19	0	3	31	22	66	0	2	.283	.325
Dunn,Todd	OF	27	.269	93	316	48	85	27	3	12	48	28	86	3	4	.328	.487
Hughes,Bobby	C	27	.275	89	276	31	76	25	1	4	37	17	47	0	0	.317	.417
Jenkins,Geoff	OF	23	.207	93	334	32	69	21	2	6	41	24	90	0	1	.260	.335
Kellner,Frank	SS	31	.255	67	220	22	56	12	3	0	18	11	39	1	0	.290	.336
Kinkade,Mike	3B	25	.342	125	438	78	150	29	8	8	76	31	69	11	3	.386	.500
Klassen,Danny	SS	22	.292	135	490	78	143	25	4	9	56	28	110	11	8	.330	.414
Krause,Scott	OF	24	.319	125	445	68	142	28	8	10	61	12	114	9	3	.337	.485
Landry,Todd	1B	25	.277	106	328	30	91	20	2	4	48	9	55	3	4	.297	.387
Lopez,Mickey	2B	24	.264	134	459	55	121	18	7	1	40	29	63	14	4	.307	.340
Martinez,Greg	OF	26	.259	98	374	53	97	9	7	0	22	19	58	27	9	.295	.321
Nicholas,Darrell	OF	26	.277	127	491	55	136	40	3	9	47	16	122	11	5	.300	.426
Rennhack,Mike	OF	23	.241	106	352	41	85	24	5	5	44	23	85	2	2	.288	.381
Unroe,Tim	3B	27	.256	63	223	33	57	14	0	6	33	6	64	2	2	.275	.399
Voigt,Jack	OF	32	.240	66	225	26	54	17	0	3	29	31	59	2	2	.332	.356
Williams,Drew	1B	26	.203	71	246	25	50	11	0	5	25	11	51	1	0	.237	.309

Major League Equivalencies for 1997 AAA/AA Batters

MILWAUKEE BREWERS		Age	Avg	G	AB	R	H	2B	3B	HR	RBI	BB	SO	SB	CS	OBP	SLG
Williamson, Antone	1B	24	.254	83	291	39	74	17	3	3	30	36	42	2	0	.336	.364
MINNESOTA TWINS		Age	Avg	G	AB	R	H	2B	3B	HR	RBI	BB	SO	SB	CS	OBP	SLG
Baez, Kevin	SS	31	.240	112	366	27	88	21	2	3	39	21	80	2	4	.282	.333
Brede, Brent	OF-1B	26	.314	84	309	59	97	23	3	6	55	34	67	2	2	.382	.466
Durant, Mike	C	28	.177	66	215	24	38	11	0	6	26	15	45	2	1	.230	.312
Ferguson, Jeff	2B	25	.240	101	362	54	87	19	1	6	43	26	85	2	3	.291	.348
Fraser, Joe	OF	23	.226	79	234	29	53	10	0	0	14	22	55	8	6	.293	.269
Horn, Jeff	C	27	.256	79	254	26	65	14	0	3	32	22	49	1	4	.315	.346
Hunter, Torii	OF	22	.220	127	464	51	102	21	1	7	50	36	103	6	8	.276	.315
Johnson, J.J.	OF	24	.205	129	430	58	88	10	2	2	40	31	128	10	3	.258	.251
Koskie, Corey	3B	25	.273	131	429	79	117	25	5	21	71	69	116	6	5	.373	.501
Lane, Ryan	2B	23	.245	128	436	56	107	25	1	4	50	33	87	13	7	.299	.335
Latham, Chris	OF	25	.272	118	467	56	127	19	3	6	42	42	121	14	5	.332	.364
Legree, Keith	OF	26	.228	113	337	41	77	18	1	8	52	43	77	7	4	.316	.359
Mientkiewicz, Dou.	1B	24	.242	132	459	78	111	27	1	13	55	76	73	15	5	.350	.390
Miller, Damian	C	28	.300	85	297	34	89	16	2	8	59	21	67	4	1	.346	.448
Moriarty, Mike	SS	24	.210	135	415	54	87	21	4	5	43	41	75	9	5	.281	.316
Ogden, Jamie	OF	26	.251	97	350	48	88	15	3	10	38	25	107	9	3	.301	.397
Ortiz, David	1B	22	.290	79	293	39	85	21	1	16	57	17	97	1	7	.329	.532
Radmanovich, Ry.	OF	26	.232	133	465	67	108	21	3	21	56	49	149	7	4	.305	.426
Rupp, Chad	1B-DH	26	.240	117	408	56	98	16	5	24	68	36	121	1	1	.302	.480
Shave, Jon	SS	30	.291	103	374	54	109	23	2	5	43	28	67	4	6	.341	.404
Simons, Mitch	2B	29	.264	115	440	63	116	29	7	3	43	34	51	18	6	.316	.382
Valentin, Javier	C	22	.231	102	364	37	84	16	0	7	45	23	68	1	3	.276	.332
Walker, Todd	3B	25	.306	83	304	50	93	17	0	8	38	33	52	3	5	.374	.441
MONTREAL EXPOS		Age	Avg	G	AB	R	H	2B	3B	HR	RBI	BB	SO	SB	CS	OBP	SLG
Alcantara, Israel	3B	25	.250	89	288	37	72	8	1	19	53	20	89	2	4	.299	.483
Bady, Edward	OF	25	.188	97	260	28	49	7	3	0	17	14	66	10	4	.230	.238
Blum, Geoff	2B	25	.219	118	392	43	86	20	1	2	25	40	76	10	5	.292	.291
Bocachica, Hiram	SS	22	.251	119	427	64	107	18	2	7	27	28	104	20	7	.297	.351
Cabrera, Jolbert	3B	25	.239	116	348	42	83	17	3	1	16	27	61	13	7	.293	.313
Cabrera, Orlando	SS	24	.257	66	245	38	63	16	2	4	25	15	35	10	1	.300	.388
Campos, Jesus	OF	24	.280	82	275	26	77	11	0	3	28	5	25	4	7	.293	.353
Carvajal, Jhonny	3B-SS	23	.235	116	366	28	86	11	0	0	24	18	70	7	6	.271	.265
Chavez, Raul	C	25	.215	92	298	22	64	15	0	2	33	13	44	0	2	.248	.285
Coquillette, Trace	2B	24	.233	81	283	36	66	16	2	7	40	17	42	6	3	.277	.378
Fullmer, Brad	1B	23	.281	118	431	56	121	28	1	16	61	22	36	4	3	.316	.462
Henley, Bob	C	25	.275	79	269	32	74	18	0	8	38	22	42	3	0	.330	.431
Lukachyk, Rob	OF	29	.231	124	424	48	98	19	2	13	48	31	99	15	6	.284	.377
Meulens, Hensley	3B	31	.240	121	404	59	97	18	1	15	55	47	124	13	4	.319	.401
Pachot, John	C	23	.253	94	312	31	79	21	2	4	39	15	44	4	5	.287	.372
Peterson, Nate	OF	26	.243	101	272	27	66	12	1	5	32	21	51	1	2	.297	.349
Rossy, Rico	SS	34	.219	117	360	41	79	21	0	6	38	28	67	3	0	.276	.328
Saffer, Jon	OF	24	.239	134	465	59	111	18	7	10	44	57	77	9	5	.322	.372
Samuels, Scott	OF	27	.270	118	389	50	105	25	2	5	42	39	94	13	7	.336	.383
Stovall, Darond	OF	25	.228	143	492	51	112	25	1	8	65	40	151	9	11	.286	.331
Vidro, Jose	3B	23	.287	73	265	29	76	16	0	8	34	17	42	1	0	.330	.438
NEW YORK METS		Age	Avg	G	AB	R	H	2B	3B	HR	RBI	BB	SO	SB	CS	OBP	SLG
Agbayani, Benny	OF	26	.284	127	451	78	128	21	1	8	44	58	111	21	9	.365	.388
Azuaje, Jesus	2B	25	.250	122	364	48	91	14	0	4	34	36	52	7	9	.318	.321

Major League Equivalencies for 1997 AAA/AA Batters

NEW YORK METS		Age	Avg	G	AB	R	H	2B	3B	HR	RBI	BB	SO	SB	CS	OBP	SLG
Bates,Fletcher	OF	24	.226	68	235	35	53	11	1	9	27	17	76	5	3	.278	.396
Chamberlain,Wes	OF	32	.252	115	381	32	96	17	1	6	49	20	74	5	2	.289	.349
Espinosa,Ramon	OF	26	.253	113	387	38	98	8	0	8	43	10	67	7	3	.272	.336
Geisler,Phil	OF	28	.235	109	327	24	77	21	0	8	49	20	94	1	5	.280	.373
Gilbert,Shawn	SS-OF	33	.240	78	279	46	67	11	0	6	28	37	67	11	4	.329	.344
Hardtke,Jason	2B	26	.258	103	400	42	103	20	2	9	42	35	58	2	6	.317	.385
Hunter,Scott	OF	22	.224	80	277	35	62	10	1	7	24	16	55	16	6	.266	.343
Lopez,Jose	DH-3B	22	.216	68	204	24	44	8	0	8	20	8	69	2	2	.245	.373
Maness,Dwight	OF	24	.163	74	251	26	41	10	2	3	24	16	78	2	4	.213	.255
McClain,Scott	3B	26	.254	127	414	62	105	25	1	17	56	55	97	0	3	.341	.442
Mendoza,Carlos	OF	23	.316	69	250	30	79	10	1	0	10	11	30	9	12	.345	.364
Moore,Mike	OF	27	.245	84	204	23	50	12	0	2	15	19	84	4	3	.309	.333
Morgan,Kevin	SS	28	.215	122	433	41	93	14	0	1	24	35	53	11	7	.274	.254
Petagine,Roberto	1B	27	.297	129	428	78	127	28	0	27	87	73	96	0	1	.399	.551
Polanco,Enohel	SS	22	.267	82	251	27	67	10	3	2	25	11	63	4	5	.298	.355
Raleigh,Matt	3B-1B	27	.167	122	384	56	64	12	0	27	59	53	180	0	2	.268	.409
Saunders,Chris	3B	27	.249	98	273	33	68	17	0	2	38	40	59	3	3	.345	.333
Seefried,Tate	1B	26	.266	129	414	56	110	18	0	25	74	47	138	6	4	.341	.490
Wilson,Preston	OF	23	.251	70	247	29	62	10	0	14	37	14	76	4	1	.291	.462
Wilson,Vance	C	25	.244	92	308	36	75	14	0	11	31	13	49	1	5	.274	.396
NEW YORK YANKEES		**Age**	**Avg**	**G**	**AB**	**R**	**H**	**2B**	**3B**	**HR**	**RBI**	**BB**	**SO**	**SB**	**CS**	**OBP**	**SLG**
Ashby,Chris	1B	23	.226	136	443	75	100	17	0	19	67	55	99	6	7	.311	.393
Barker,Tim	2B	30	.254	65	201	29	51	8	1	4	24	25	42	10	6	.336	.363
Bellinger,Clay	3B	29	.249	111	402	45	100	27	2	9	48	27	76	7	4	.296	.393
Bierek,Kurt	OF	25	.250	133	460	63	115	28	1	15	64	38	93	2	4	.307	.413
Brown,Randy	SS	28	.235	116	388	51	91	12	3	8	48	33	132	7	7	.295	.343
Brown,Ron	OF	28	.254	110	382	41	97	15	2	4	41	25	64	3	7	.300	.335
Buchanan,Brian	OF	24	.279	134	512	67	143	22	1	11	61	25	100	8	10	.313	.391
Bush,Homer	2B	25	.231	112	415	47	96	16	2	3	31	25	98	11	7	.275	.301
Carpenter,Bubba	OF	29	.259	85	263	38	68	10	2	5	32	38	47	2	8	.352	.369
Cruz,Ivan	1B	30	.277	116	404	57	112	31	0	20	78	52	80	2	5	.360	.502
Donato,Dan	3B	25	.254	96	339	36	86	14	0	4	35	17	46	4	4	.289	.330
Figga,Mike	C	27	.220	110	378	39	83	12	2	9	44	14	107	2	3	.247	.333
Fithian,Grant	C	26	.254	79	244	31	62	14	0	6	42	28	54	0	1	.331	.385
Fox,Andy	3B	27	.252	95	309	54	78	9	2	5	27	43	65	19	8	.344	.343
Gomez,Rudy	2B	23	.274	102	379	53	104	16	4	4	42	41	67	7	7	.345	.369
Howard,Matt	SS	30	.285	122	460	74	131	24	4	4	55	43	33	15	6	.346	.380
Lowell,Mike	3B	24	.288	135	476	78	137	26	0	24	75	51	65	2	5	.357	.494
Luke,Matt	OF	27	.210	87	329	34	69	16	2	6	37	23	65	0	4	.261	.325
Martinez,Gabby	SS	24	.293	77	300	40	88	10	3	4	44	7	46	15	6	.309	.387
Pose,Scott	OF	31	.283	57	219	41	62	8	4	1	26	25	29	9	5	.357	.370
Ramirez,Angel	OF	25	.261	94	372	42	97	20	5	3	26	6	59	7	5	.272	.366
Spencer,Shane	OF	26	.217	125	438	64	95	30	2	24	71	57	108	0	2	.307	.459
Wilcox,Chris	OF	24	.254	74	291	37	74	11	0	5	28	12	37	9	3	.284	.344
Wilson,Tom	C	27	.268	125	407	72	109	18	2	16	66	59	132	0	4	.361	.440
OAKLAND ATHLETICS		**Age**	**Avg**	**G**	**AB**	**R**	**H**	**2B**	**3B**	**HR**	**RBI**	**BB**	**SO**	**SB**	**CS**	**OBP**	**SLG**
Ardoin,Danny	C	23	.200	57	200	19	40	8	0	2	17	10	40	1	3	.238	.270
Bellhorn,Mark	2B	23	.299	70	231	44	69	16	2	8	37	50	60	4	6	.423	.489
Coolbaugh,Mike	3B	26	.271	139	531	74	144	31	1	21	98	32	111	5	3	.313	.452
Cox,Steven	1B	23	.248	131	451	68	112	30	0	11	76	70	93	0	3	.349	.388

Major League Equivalencies for 1997 AAA/AA Batters

OAKLAND ATHLETICS		Age	Avg	G	AB	R	H	2B	3B	HR	RBI	BB	SO	SB	CS	OBP	SLG
Cromer,D.T.	1B	27	.286	134	517	74	148	34	4	10	90	37	108	8	7	.334	.426
DeBoer,Rob	DH-C	27	.210	91	276	40	58	13	0	13	35	37	117	5	5	.304	.399
Garrison,Webster	2B	32	.263	125	414	57	109	21	1	11	65	45	94	3	3	.336	.399
Grieve,Ben	OF	22	.313	127	454	96	142	34	1	22	102	59	95	3	2	.392	.537
Herrera,Jose	OF	25	.271	122	406	52	110	18	1	3	33	33	66	5	5	.326	.342
Hughes,Troy	OF	27	.181	72	249	27	45	10	0	3	24	14	53	1	1	.224	.257
Lesher,Brian	OF	27	.296	110	399	69	118	24	3	16	63	51	89	10	3	.376	.491
Martins,Eric	2B	25	.233	88	275	37	64	14	2	2	29	22	51	1	1	.290	.320
McDonald,Jason	OF	26	.240	79	267	60	64	12	4	3	24	58	59	22	9	.375	.348
Molina,Izzy	C	27	.237	61	211	26	50	9	2	4	27	9	28	1	0	.268	.355
Morales,Willie	C	25	.252	92	302	32	76	19	0	5	45	18	53	0	2	.294	.364
Neill,Mike	OF	28	.296	129	480	98	142	25	1	10	61	49	126	10	8	.361	.415
Newhan,David	2B	24	.279	57	201	29	56	11	1	3	26	17	62	3	5	.335	.388
Sheldon,Scott	SS	29	.288	118	406	72	117	35	4	15	62	47	108	3	2	.362	.505
Smith,Demond	OF	25	.227	129	454	75	103	19	6	8	46	57	112	26	11	.313	.348
Tejada,Miguel	SS	22	.242	128	480	63	116	17	2	15	72	31	104	10	11	.288	.379
Walker,Dane	2B	28	.210	106	347	46	73	14	2	5	38	42	92	4	2	.296	.305
Wood,Jason	3B	28	.293	130	485	67	142	31	5	15	71	36	76	1	4	.342	.470
PHIL. PHILLIES		**Age**	**Avg**	**G**	**AB**	**R**	**H**	**2B**	**3B**	**HR**	**RBI**	**BB**	**SO**	**SB**	**CS**	**OBP**	**SLG**
Amador,Manuel	3B	22	.240	86	229	21	55	12	0	1	22	16	43	0	0	.290	.306
Anderson,Marlon	2B	24	.235	137	531	65	125	16	4	7	46	26	84	18	7	.271	.320
Angeli,Doug	SS-3B	27	.199	120	377	36	75	14	1	4	28	30	86	0	5	.258	.273
Barron,Tony	OF	31	.298	92	315	39	94	19	2	14	59	20	68	2	4	.340	.505
Burton,Darren	OF	25	.248	115	420	43	104	25	4	11	54	19	86	2	1	.280	.405
Carver,Steve	OF	25	.232	79	271	30	63	10	2	10	32	22	75	1	2	.290	.395
Dawkins,Walt	OF	25	.210	106	319	35	67	12	0	6	29	22	98	2	5	.261	.304
Doster,David	2B	27	.287	108	394	53	113	30	1	12	60	22	64	3	5	.325	.459
Estalella,Bobby	C	23	.211	123	421	48	89	30	0	12	49	42	116	2	0	.283	.368
Fox,Eric	OF	34	.252	92	254	30	64	15	2	2	19	15	54	1	3	.294	.350
Guiliano,Matt	SS	26	.200	119	355	28	71	13	2	5	27	21	108	4	6	.245	.290
Held,Dan	1B	27	.244	138	505	59	123	28	2	19	64	26	126	0	3	.281	.420
Huff,Larry	3B	26	.235	124	409	43	96	19	2	3	30	22	62	16	6	.274	.313
Magee,Wendell	OF	25	.221	83	285	29	63	18	0	7	29	22	59	2	7	.277	.358
McMillon,Billy	OF	26	.240	83	279	35	67	21	0	7	33	30	78	6	0	.314	.391
Millan,Adam	C	26	.214	96	257	32	55	9	0	6	32	27	56	0	0	.289	.319
Pagano,Scott	OF	27	.243	117	449	57	109	15	2	2	32	30	68	11	13	.290	.298
Relaford,Desi	SS	24	.240	131	499	62	120	33	2	6	40	32	83	20	8	.286	.351
Robertson,Mike	1B	27	.268	121	399	46	107	16	2	9	55	44	71	0	2	.341	.386
Royster,Aaron	OF	25	.229	112	397	43	91	16	3	11	46	33	113	1	3	.288	.368
Tremie,Chris	C	28	.178	97	286	14	51	10	0	1	23	22	66	0	5	.237	.224
Zuber,Jon	OF	28	.285	126	417	65	119	34	1	4	49	60	56	2	4	.375	.400
PITTSBURGH PIRATES		**Age**	**Avg**	**G**	**AB**	**R**	**H**	**2B**	**3B**	**HR**	**RBI**	**BB**	**SO**	**SB**	**CS**	**OBP**	**SLG**
Beasley,Tony	2B	31	.239	106	322	36	77	10	3	0	28	21	41	8	5	.286	.289
Bridges,Kary	2B	26	.265	122	423	44	112	18	1	2	28	13	25	6	4	.287	.326
Brown,Adrian	OF	24	.276	99	373	59	103	12	3	1	24	30	51	20	9	.330	.332
Collier,Lou	SS	24	.291	112	375	46	109	27	3	0	34	26	49	8	6	.337	.379
Cromer,Brandon	SS	24	.202	123	406	38	82	24	4	8	35	32	101	2	4	.260	.340
Garcia,Freddy	3B	25	.245	108	387	50	95	20	3	17	56	17	80	0	0	.277	.444
Hazlett,Steve	OF	28	.228	82	237	29	54	16	3	3	23	17	52	0	5	.280	.359
Hermansen,Chad	OF	20	.249	129	470	67	117	28	3	15	54	45	145	12	5	.315	.417

Major League Equivalencies for 1997 AAA/AA Batters

PITTSBURGH PIRATES		Age	Avg	G	AB	R	H	2B	3B	HR	RBI	BB	SO	SB	CS	OBP	SLG
Lott,Billy	OF	27	.248	103	330	40	82	19	0	11	52	30	81	4	0	.311	.406
Martinez,Manny	OF	27	.292	109	397	55	116	30	0	11	47	23	84	11	8	.331	.451
Marx,Tim	C	29	.216	90	287	29	62	15	1	2	28	16	44	6	0	.257	.296
Peterson,Charles	OF	24	.227	126	428	46	97	24	3	5	53	26	112	14	5	.271	.332
Sanders,Tracy	1B	28	.245	116	363	60	89	21	0	16	60	49	94	4	5	.335	.435
Sanford,Chance	3B	26	.251	133	454	64	114	32	7	11	70	40	127	8	6	.312	.425
Staton,T.J.	OF	23	.233	123	390	46	91	22	1	5	40	22	117	7	5	.274	.333
Sweet,Jon	C	26	.220	82	264	17	58	13	0	0	21	9	21	0	0	.245	.269
Thobe,Steve	3B	26	.247	87	271	27	67	16	0	8	34	18	81	3	0	.294	.395
Tolentino,Jose	1B	37	.258	108	345	42	89	22	0	11	56	34	62	1	4	.325	.417
Williams,Eddie	DH-1B	33	.295	76	251	45	74	11	0	16	47	22	47	0	2	.352	.530
Wright,Ron	1B	22	.266	91	319	35	85	27	0	11	44	17	85	0	1	.304	.455
SAN DIEGO PADRES		Age	Avg	G	AB	R	H	2B	3B	HR	RBI	BB	SO	SB	CS	OBP	SLG
Allen,Dusty	1B-OF	25	.221	131	456	62	101	22	2	14	55	49	122	0	3	.297	.371
Alvarez,Gabe	3B	24	.265	114	407	52	108	22	1	11	57	31	67	0	0	.317	.405
Arias,George	3B	26	.255	115	415	62	106	27	1	9	52	34	62	2	4	.312	.390
Beamon,Trey	OF	24	.289	90	311	48	90	15	2	3	37	35	60	9	5	.361	.379
Briggs,Stoney	OF	26	.239	119	418	43	100	17	3	9	43	20	126	12	11	.274	.359
Brinkley,Darryl	OF	29	.270	55	204	30	55	11	0	4	24	16	31	6	8	.323	.382
Brown,Ray	1B-OF	25	.267	98	300	29	80	22	0	4	33	28	63	0	0	.329	.380
Dascenzo,Doug	OF	34	.244	109	414	46	101	18	2	7	34	32	43	10	7	.298	.348
Gama,Rick	2B	25	.253	88	281	41	71	12	1	5	31	31	43	5	2	.327	.356
Guiel,Aaron	OF	25	.291	124	419	72	122	31	4	17	68	39	106	8	10	.352	.506
Hajek,Dave	3B-2B	30	.238	113	395	42	94	23	1	3	46	28	24	4	2	.288	.324
Helfand,Eric	C	29	.276	80	225	23	62	17	0	4	24	20	48	0	0	.335	.404
Hills,Rich	3B	24	.217	71	207	27	45	9	0	4	22	15	36	1	0	.270	.319
LaRocca,Greg	2B	25	.233	76	287	32	67	12	1	2	22	16	48	5	2	.274	.303
Lee,Derek	OF	31	.256	75	219	16	56	13	0	3	26	23	36	2	0	.326	.356
Lee,Derrek	1B	22	.290	125	449	65	130	23	1	11	48	44	120	11	2	.353	.419
Mashore,Justin	OF	26	.207	90	270	39	56	8	3	9	30	19	74	6	7	.260	.359
Melo,Juan	SS	21	.248	125	479	42	119	20	1	5	53	17	104	4	8	.274	.326
Poe,Charles	OF	26	.253	107	356	43	90	12	3	8	50	22	78	3	1	.296	.371
Prieto,Chris	OF	25	.277	109	365	59	101	17	5	1	42	36	58	16	6	.342	.359
Romero,Mandy	C	30	.277	94	296	50	82	20	0	12	47	31	51	0	0	.346	.466
Tredaway,Chad	3B	26	.218	120	403	44	88	18	0	5	37	25	66	3	3	.264	.300
Velandia,Jorge	SS	23	.240	114	388	34	93	12	1	2	26	21	64	8	2	.279	.291
SF GIANTS		Age	Avg	G	AB	R	H	2B	3B	HR	RBI	BB	SO	SB	CS	OBP	SLG
Ball,Jeff	3B	29	.283	126	445	70	126	32	1	13	80	45	89	7	4	.349	.447
Canizaro,Jay	2B	24	.206	73	247	38	51	12	0	9	39	25	72	2	4	.279	.364
Cruz,Jacob	OF	25	.321	127	464	75	149	38	1	9	74	50	67	12	3	.387	.466
Delgado,Wilson	SS	22	.253	119	396	36	100	18	2	6	46	19	74	6	3	.287	.354
Florez,Tim	2B	28	.264	114	382	44	101	20	2	5	47	25	72	4	3	.310	.366
Guzman,Edwards	3B	21	.255	118	365	42	93	12	2	2	34	23	61	2	1	.299	.315
Jones,Dax	OF	27	.220	93	259	37	57	5	3	2	21	30	41	6	10	.301	.286
Martinez,Ramon	SS	25	.280	123	439	62	123	28	2	3	48	30	60	2	5	.326	.374
Mayes,Craig	C	28	.229	93	301	22	69	6	3	1	30	9	36	0	0	.252	.279
McCarty,Dave	1B	28	.311	121	408	66	127	22	3	16	71	38	79	6	4	.370	.498
Mirabelli,Doug	C	27	.230	100	317	38	73	19	1	6	37	45	73	0	2	.326	.353
Murray,Calvin	OF	26	.241	122	402	67	97	21	2	7	45	46	78	35	14	.319	.356
Powell,Dante	OF	24	.210	108	434	70	91	20	2	8	32	40	111	24	9	.276	.320

Major League Equivalencies for 1997 AAA/AA Batters

SF GIANTS		Age	Avg	G	AB	R	H	2B	3B	HR	RBI	BB	SO	SB	CS	OBP	SLG
Rios,Armando	OF	26	.258	127	442	70	114	25	4	11	64	44	91	11	7	.325	.407
Roberson,Kevin	OF	30	.250	109	332	46	83	15	3	10	52	29	104	6	5	.310	.404
Sbrocco,Jon	2B	27	.234	97	261	26	61	12	2	1	21	27	22	4	8	.306	.307
Simonton,Benji	1B	26	.226	116	372	59	84	12	1	15	64	56	129	4	5	.327	.384
Singleton,Chris	OF	25	.284	126	443	69	126	22	6	7	49	15	54	19	7	.308	.409
Williams,Keith	OF	26	.283	134	473	67	134	32	4	17	86	32	103	2	0	.329	.476
Wilson,Desi	1B	30	.305	121	426	59	130	22	3	5	41	34	77	11	3	.357	.406
Woods,Ken	2B	27	.268	105	280	33	75	12	1	1	26	19	43	4	4	.314	.329
Zosky,Eddie	3B	30	.240	86	229	29	55	8	2	6	35	12	40	2	3	.278	.371
SEATTLE MARINERS		Age	Avg	G	AB	R	H	2B	3B	HR	RBI	BB	SO	SB	CS	OBP	SLG
Christian,Eddie	OF-DH	26	.321	103	368	62	118	26	0	4	45	43	53	8	3	.392	.424
Correa,Miguel	OF	26	.254	68	248	31	63	14	0	6	29	13	56	1	1	.291	.383
Dean,Chris	2B	24	.247	67	235	23	58	11	3	3	17	21	42	2	4	.309	.357
Decker,Steve	C	32	.287	99	345	40	99	25	0	9	48	20	40	0	0	.326	.438
Gipson,Charles	3B	25	.245	99	351	57	86	11	3	0	30	31	82	25	9	.306	.293
Guevara,Giomar	SS-2B	25	.244	119	398	54	97	15	3	4	38	20	88	6	10	.280	.327
Ibanez,Raul	OF	26	.294	111	432	77	127	30	3	14	77	30	81	5	4	.340	.475
Jorgensen,Randy	1B	26	.285	129	473	63	135	29	2	11	67	31	64	0	1	.329	.425
Leach,Jalal	OF	29	.298	115	409	51	122	26	2	8	50	30	80	4	5	.346	.430
Millette,Joe	SS	31	.258	103	310	45	80	13	0	2	25	18	63	1	4	.299	.319
Monahan,Shane	OF	23	.292	128	480	63	140	28	4	13	84	29	133	15	6	.332	.448
Rohrmeier,Dan	OF	32	.288	125	465	79	134	43	2	30	111	42	88	0	0	.347	.583
Saunders,Doug	3B	28	.252	73	230	31	58	15	0	1	26	38	49	0	2	.358	.330
Seitzer,Brad	3B-1B	28	.261	118	406	54	106	21	2	7	50	30	68	0	1	.312	.374
Sheets,Andy	SS	26	.250	113	396	52	99	23	0	12	49	43	105	5	1	.323	.399
Smith,Scott	OF	26	.243	123	449	55	109	19	1	13	64	36	147	3	6	.299	.376
Sturdivant,Jack	OF	24	.264	112	428	68	113	18	3	2	33	52	67	16	6	.344	.334
Torres,Paul	3B	27	.314	121	421	60	132	27	2	9	72	44	66	2	0	.378	.451
Zinter,Alan	1B	30	.276	110	398	63	110	20	2	19	64	61	126	2	0	.373	.480
ST. LOUIS CARDINALS		Age	Avg	G	AB	R	H	2B	3B	HR	RBI	BB	SO	SB	CS	OBP	SLG
Berblinger,Jeff	2B	27	.238	133	496	50	118	17	4	8	46	44	102	17	6	.300	.337
Bradshaw,Terry	OF	29	.226	130	439	63	99	15	4	6	34	49	82	18	7	.303	.319
Costo,Tim	1B	29	.275	121	385	41	106	24	1	11	43	32	75	2	4	.331	.429
Dalton,Dee	3B	26	.206	116	350	41	72	14	0	3	34	25	70	1	5	.259	.271
Franklin,Micah	OF	26	.199	99	317	39	63	13	0	9	38	40	77	1	0	.289	.325
Green,Scarborou.	OF	24	.255	128	443	56	113	23	3	3	33	41	108	14	12	.318	.341
Gulan,Mike	3B	27	.241	116	398	40	96	18	4	11	49	22	127	3	2	.281	.389
Holbert,Aaron	SS	25	.230	93	304	25	70	12	2	3	25	12	58	6	5	.259	.313
Koslofski,Kevin	OF	31	.188	106	277	29	52	12	2	7	21	34	81	0	9	.277	.321
LaRiviere,Jason	OF	24	.248	118	359	40	89	22	3	4	48	22	73	2	3	.291	.359
Marrero,Eli	C	24	.247	112	381	48	94	19	4	15	54	20	55	2	4	.284	.436
McDonald,Keith	C	25	.217	79	226	25	49	14	0	3	24	21	59	0	1	.283	.319
McEwing,Joe	OF	25	.232	103	254	26	59	5	2	3	28	12	41	1	4	.267	.303
Munoz,Juan	OF	24	.251	58	207	22	52	8	1	4	24	10	27	4	10	.286	.357
Nevers,Tom	SS	26	.209	71	220	17	46	8	0	6	21	9	50	0	3	.240	.327
Ordaz,Luis	SS	22	.261	115	376	35	98	18	4	3	46	15	41	7	10	.289	.354
Polanco,Placido	2B	22	.265	129	490	57	130	14	2	1	41	19	54	13	5	.293	.308
Richard,Chris	1B	24	.244	113	377	49	92	22	2	8	46	41	63	4	4	.318	.377
Robinson,Kerry	OF	24	.288	138	510	64	147	14	2	1	49	36	69	28	11	.335	.329
Rupp,Brian	3B-1B	26	.254	95	299	27	76	14	1	0	24	23	54	0	4	.307	.308

Major League Equivalencies for 1997 AAA/AA Batters

ST. LOUIS CARDINALS		Age	Avg	G	AB	R	H	2B	3B	HR	RBI	BB	SO	SB	CS	OBP	SLG
Scarsone,Steve	2B	32	.198	92	268	31	53	10	0	9	28	33	91	1	1	.286	.336
Warner,Ron	OF	29	.209	101	268	34	56	14	0	5	24	33	47	2	1	.296	.317
TEXAS RANGERS		**Age**	**Avg**	**G**	**AB**	**R**	**H**	**2B**	**3B**	**HR**	**RBI**	**BB**	**SO**	**SB**	**CS**	**OBP**	**SLG**
Barkett,Andy	1B	23	.278	130	457	67	127	30	7	7	53	44	91	0	2	.341	.420
Bell,Mike	3B-2B	23	.231	126	441	46	102	25	1	10	54	37	110	3	1	.291	.361
Blair,Brian	OF	26	.241	86	253	38	61	7	2	3	23	34	67	7	1	.331	.320
Bokemeier,Matt	SS	25	.211	105	384	42	81	15	2	4	35	26	76	0	5	.261	.292
Brown,Kevin L.	C	25	.229	116	397	52	91	16	1	16	46	35	115	1	1	.292	.395
Charles,Frank	C	29	.209	95	326	31	68	15	1	7	40	17	85	1	1	.248	.325
Collier,Dan	DH-OF	27	.233	115	377	49	88	17	0	20	65	31	142	0	1	.292	.438
Diaz,Alex	OF	29	.261	112	444	60	116	22	2	11	45	32	57	20	7	.311	.394
Diaz,Edwin	2B	23	.229	125	498	58	114	29	0	11	41	24	136	4	8	.264	.353
Estrada,Osmani	2B	29	.215	91	284	20	61	8	0	0	18	18	38	5	1	.262	.243
Frias,Hanley	SS	24	.254	132	477	59	121	15	4	4	42	52	74	27	10	.327	.327
Little,Mark	OF	25	.250	121	408	66	102	21	3	13	41	36	103	16	6	.311	.412
Morillo,Cesar	SS	24	.240	84	279	31	67	15	0	0	19	20	55	0	3	.291	.294
Murphy,Mike	OF	26	.285	119	390	58	111	20	4	7	38	59	115	14	6	.379	.410
O'Neill,Doug	OF	28	.245	129	428	58	105	20	0	15	53	36	139	8	3	.304	.397
Sagmoen,Marc	OF	27	.252	111	412	43	104	29	5	4	40	24	98	3	2	.294	.376
Silvestri,Dave	3B	30	.228	124	460	50	105	23	2	15	63	51	108	3	5	.305	.385
Smith,Bubba	1B-DH	28	.242	140	505	55	122	28	0	23	87	49	144	1	1	.309	.434
Tackett,Jeff	C	32	.259	64	205	21	53	14	0	4	17	24	50	3	0	.336	.385
Tatis,Fernando	3B	23	.288	102	368	60	106	22	0	20	50	32	75	11	7	.345	.511
Vessel,Andrew	OF	23	.238	138	501	64	119	30	0	9	62	29	92	2	0	.279	.351
TORONTO BLUE JAYS		**Age**	**Avg**	**G**	**AB**	**R**	**H**	**2B**	**3B**	**HR**	**RBI**	**BB**	**SO**	**SB**	**CS**	**OBP**	**SLG**
Adriana,Sharnol	2B	27	.203	99	301	36	61	9	0	4	28	28	70	5	6	.271	.272
Aude,Rich	1B	26	.253	100	336	36	85	20	1	11	45	19	92	2	0	.293	.417
Butler,Rich	OF	25	.267	137	513	71	137	26	7	18	66	46	112	14	5	.327	.450
Candelaria,Benja.	OF	23	.255	120	447	58	114	27	3	10	48	25	95	2	2	.294	.396
Cradle,Rickey	OF	25	.173	95	271	39	47	13	0	7	26	26	80	3	5	.246	.299
Crespo,Felipe	OF-2B	25	.229	80	279	40	64	10	0	9	19	35	39	5	6	.315	.362
de la Cruz,Lorenz.	DH	26	.242	78	260	31	63	9	1	8	27	12	76	1	2	.276	.377
Evans,Tom	3B	23	.233	107	361	46	84	15	0	11	49	40	109	0	1	.309	.366
Henry,Santiago	SS-2B	25	.238	96	298	29	71	12	0	4	30	3	59	5	1	.246	.319
Jones,Ryan	1B	23	.194	127	434	35	84	20	2	10	48	27	96	0	1	.241	.318
Martinez,Sandy	C	25	.196	96	311	21	61	10	0	3	22	20	79	5	1	.245	.257
Mosquera,Julio	C	26	.245	97	326	36	80	19	0	3	36	14	64	2	3	.276	.331
Mummau,Rob	2B	26	.225	103	320	36	72	15	1	6	30	26	62	1	2	.283	.334
Patzke,Jeff	2B	24	.254	96	303	29	77	22	1	1	22	39	69	0	2	.339	.343
Perez,Tomas	SS	24	.195	89	292	24	57	11	0	0	15	28	70	2	3	.266	.233
Sanders,Anthony	OF	24	.232	111	410	48	95	17	3	18	49	26	129	13	4	.278	.420
Solano,Fausto	SS	24	.230	115	361	37	83	20	3	7	40	22	50	5	13	.274	.360
Thompson,Andy	3B	22	.249	124	426	54	106	21	2	10	51	38	81	0	4	.310	.378
Thompson,Ryan	OF	30	.252	107	381	37	96	20	0	12	49	20	77	3	2	.289	.399
Witt,Kevin	1B	22	.251	127	475	54	119	23	3	21	65	26	116	0	0	.289	.444

Appendix

Minor League Team	Organization	League	Level	Minor League Team	Organization	League	Level
Akron Aeros	Indians	EL	AA	Dunedin Blue Jays	Blue Jays	FSL	A+
Albuquerque Dukes	Dodgers	PCL	AAA	Durham Bulls	Braves	CL	A+
Arkansas Travelers	Cardinals	TL	AA	Edmonton Trappers	Athletics	PCL	AAA
Asheville Tourists	Rockies	SAL	A	El Paso Diablos	Brewers	TL	AA
Astros (Kissimmee)	Astros	GCL	R	Elizabethton Twins	Twins	APPY	R+
Athletics (Phoenix)	Athletics	AZL	R	Erie SeaWolves	Pirates	NY-P	A-
Auburn Doubledays	Astros	NY-P	A-	Eugene Emeralds	Braves	NWL	A-
Augusta GreenJackets	Pirates	SAL	A	Everett AquaSox	Mariners	NWL	A-
Bakersfield Blaze	Giants	CAL	A+	Expos (West Palm Beach)	Expos	GCL	R
Batavia Clippers	Phillies	NY-P	A-	Frederick Keys	Orioles	CL	A+
Beloit Snappers	Brewers	MWL	A	Fort Myers Miracle	Twins	FSL	A+
Billings Mustangs	Reds	PIO	R+	Fort Wayne Wizards	Twins	MWL	A
Binghamton Mets	Mets	EL	AA	Great Falls Dodgers	Dodgers	PIO	R+
Birmingham Barons	White Sox	SL	AA	Greensboro Bats	Yankees	SAL	A
Bluefield Orioles	Orioles	APPY	R+	Greenville Braves	Braves	SL	AA
Boise Hawks	Angels	NWL	A-	Hagerstown Suns	Blue Jays	SAL	A
Bowie Baysox	Orioles	EL	AA	Harrisburg Senators	Expos	EL	AA
Braves (Orlando)	Braves	GCL	R	Helena Brewers	Brewers	PIO	R+
Brevard County Manatees	Marlins	FSL	A+	Hickory Crawdads	White Sox	SAL	A
Bristol Sox	White Sox	APPY	R+	High Desert Mavericks	Diamondbacks	CAL	A+
Buffalo Bisons	Indians	AA	AAA	Hudson Valley Renegades	Devil Rays	NY-P	A-
Burlington Bees	Reds	MWL	A	Huntsville Stars	Athletics	SL	AA
Burlington Indians	Indians	APPY	R+	Idaho Falls Braves	Padres	PIO	R+
Butte Copper Kings	Angels	PIO	R+	Indianapolis Indians	Reds	AA	AAA
Calgary Cannons	Pirates	PCL	AAA	Iowa Cubs	Cubs	AA	AAA
Cape Fear Crocs	Expos	SAL	A	Jackson Generals	Astros	TL	AA
Capital City Bombers	Mets	SAL	A	Jacksonville Suns	Tigers	SL	AA
Carolina Mudcats	Pirates	SL	AA	Jamestown Jammers	Tigers	NY-P	A-
Cedar Rapids Kernels	Angels	MWL	A	Johnson City Cardinals	Cardinals	APPY	R+
Charleston (S.C.) River Dogs	Devil Rays	SAL	A	Kane County Cougars	Marlins	MWL	A
Charleston (W.Va.) Alley Cats	Reds	SAL	A	Kingsport Mets	Mets	APPY	R+
Charlotte Knights	Marlins	IL	AAA	Kinston Indians	Indians	CL	A+
Charlotte Rangers	Rangers	FSL	A+	Kissimmee Cobras	Astros	FSL	A+
Chattanooga Lookouts	Reds	SL	AA	Knoxville Smokies	Blue Jays	SL	AA
Clearwater Phillies	Phillies	FSL	A+	Lake Elsinore Storm	Angels	CAL	A+
Clinton Lumber Kings	Padres	MWL	A	Lakeland Tigers	Tigers	FSL	A+
Colorado Springs Sky Sox	Rockies	PCL	AAA	Lancaster Jet Hawks	Mariners	CAL	A+
Columbus Clippers	Yankees	IL	AAA	Lansing Lugnuts	Royals	MWL	A
Columbus RedStixx	Indians	SAL	A	Las Vegas Stars	Padres	PCL	AAA
Cubs (Mesa)	Cubs	AZL	R	Lethbridge Black Diamonds	Diamondbacks	PIO	R+
Danville Braves	Braves	APPY	R+	Louisville Redbirds	Cardinals	AA	AAA
Daytona Cubs	Cubs	FSL	A+	Lowell Spinners	Red Sox	NY-P	A-
Delmarva Shorebirds	Orioles	SAL	A	Lynchburg Hillcats	Pirates	CL	A+
Devil Rays (St. Petersburg)	Devil Rays	GCL	R	Macon Braves	Braves	SAL	A
Diamondbacks (Peoria)	Diamondbacks	AZL	R	Mariners (Peoria)	Mariners	AZL	R

Minor League Team	Organization	League	Level	Minor League Team	Organization	League	Level
Marlins (Melbourne)	Marlins	GCL	R	Salem Avalanche	Rockies	CL	A+
Martinsville Phillies	Phillies	APPY	R+	Salem-Keizer Volcanoes	Giants	NWL	A-
Medicine Hat Blue Jays	Blue Jays	PIO	R+	Salt Lake Buzz	Twins	PCL	AAA
Memphis Chicks	Mariners	SL	AA	San Antonio Missions	Dodgers	TL	AA
Mets (Port St. Lucie)	Mets	GCL	R	San Bernardino Stampede	Dodgers	CAL	A+
Michigan Battle Cats	Red Sox	MWL	A	San Jose Giants	Giants	CAL	A+
Midland Angels	Angels	TL	AA	Sarasota Red Sox	Red Sox	FSL	A+
Mobile BayBears	Padres	SL	AA	Savannah Sand Gnats	Dodgers	SAL	A
Modesto A's	Athletics	CAL	A+	Scranton/Wilkes-Barre Red Barons	Phillies	IL	AAA
Nashville Sounds	White Sox	AA	AAA	Shreveport Captains	Giants	TL	AA
New Britain Rock Cats	Twins	EL	AA	South Bend Silver Hawks	Diamondbacks	MWL	A
New Haven Ravens	Rockies	EL	AA	Southern Oregon Timberjacks	Athletics	NWL	A-
New Jersey Cardinals	Cardinals	NY-P	A-	Spokane Indians	Royals	NWL	A-
New Orleans Zephyrs	Astros	AA	AAA	St. Catharines Stompers	Blue Jays	NY-P	A-
Norfolk Tides	Mets	IL	AAA	St. Lucie Mets	Mets	FSL	A+
Norwich Navigators	Yankees	EL	AA	St. Petersburg Devil Rays	Devil Rays	FSL	A+
Ogden Raptors	Brewers	PIO	R+	Stockton Ports	Brewers	CAL	A+
Oklahoma City 89ers	Rangers	AA	AAA	Syracuse SkyChiefs	Blue Jays	IL	AAA
Omaha Royals	Royals	AA	AAA	Tacoma Rainiers	Mariners	PCL	AAA
Oneonta Yankees	Yankees	NY-P	A-	Tampa Yankees	Yankees	FSL	A+
Orioles (Sarasota)	Orioles	GCL	R	Tigers (Lakeland)	Tigers	GCL	R
Orlando Rays	Cubs	SL	AA	Toledo Mud Hens	Tigers	IL	AAA
Ottawa Lynx	Expos	IL	AAA	Tucson Toros	Brewers	PCL	AAA
Padres (Peoria)	Padres	AZL	R	Trenton Thunder	Red Sox	EL	AA
Pawtucket Red Sox	Red Sox	IL	AAA	Tulsa Drillers	Rangers	TL	AA
Peoria Chiefs	Cardinals	MWL	A	Twins (Fort Myers)	Twins	GCL	R
Phoenix Firebirds	Giants	PCL	AAA	Utica Blue Sox	Marlins	NY-P	A-
Piedmont Boll Weevils	Phillies	SAL	A	Vancouver Canadians	Angels	PCL	AAA
Pirates (Bradenton)	Pirates	GCL	R	Vermont Expos	Expos	NY-P	A-
Pittsfield Mets	Mets	NY-P	A-	Vero Beach Dodgers	Dodgers	FSL	A+
Portland Sea Dogs	Marlins	EL	AA	Visalia Oaks	Athletics	CAL	A+
Portland Rockies	Rockies	NWL	A-	Watertown Indians	Indians	NY-P	A-
Prince William Cannons	Cardinals	CL	A+	West Michigan Whitecaps	Tigers	MWL	A
Princeton Devil Rays	Devil Rays	APPY	R+	West Palm Beach Expos	Expos	FSL	A+
Pulaski Rangers	Rangers	APPY	R+	White Sox (Sarasota)	White Sox	GCL	R
Quad City River Bandits	Astros	MWL	A	Wichita Wranglers	Royals	TL	AA
Rancho Cucamonga Quakes	Padres	CAL	A+	Williamsport Cubs	Cubs	NY-P	A-
Rangers (Port Charlotte)	Rangers	GCL	R	Wilmington Blue Rocks	Royals	CL	A+
Reading Phillies	Phillies	EL	AA	Winston-Salem Warthogs	White Sox	CL	A+
Red Sox (Fort Myers)	Red Sox	GCL	R	Wisconsin Timber Rattlers	Mariners	MWL	A
Richmond Braves	Braves	IL	AAA	Yakima Bears	Dodgers	NWL	A-
Rochester Red Wings	Orioles	IL	AAA	Yankees (Tampa)	Yankees	GCL	R
Rockford Cubbies	Cubs	MWL	A				
Rockies (Chandler)	Rockies	AZL	R				
Royals (Fort Myers)	Royals	GCL	R				

About STATS, Inc. & Howe Sportsdata

About STATS, Inc.

STATS, Inc. is the nation's leading independent sports information and statistical analysis company, providing detailed sports services for a wide array of commercial clients.

As one of the fastest-growing sports companies—in 1994, we ranked 144th on the "Inc. 500" list of fastest-growing privately held firms—STATS provides the most up-to-the-minute sports information to professional teams, print and broadcast media, software developers and interactive service providers around the country. Some of our major clients are ESPN, the Associated Press, Fox Sports, Electronic Arts, MSNBC, SONY and Topps. Much of the information we provide is available to the public via STATS On-Line. With a computer and a modem, you can follow action in the four major professional sports, as well as NCAA football and basketball. . . as it happens!

STATS Publishing, a division of STATS, Inc., produces 12 annual books, including the *Major League Handbook*, *The Scouting Notebook*, the *Pro Football Handbook*, the *Pro Basketball Handbook* and the *Hockey Handbook* as well as the *STATS Fantasy Insider* magazine. These publications deliver STATS' expertise to fans, scouts, general managers and media around the country.

In addition, STATS offers the most innovative—and fun—fantasy sports games and support products around, from *Bill James Fantasy Baseball* and *Bill James Classic Baseball* to *STATS Fantasy Football* and *STATS Fantasy Hoops*. Check out the latest STATS and Bill James fantasy game, *Stock Market Baseball* and our immensely popular Fantasy Portfolios.

Information technology has grown by leaps and bounds in the last decade, and STATS will continue to be at the forefront as a supplier of the most up-to-date, in-depth sports information available. For those of you on the information superhighway, you can always catch STATS in our area on America Online or at our Internet site.

For more information on our products, or on joining our reporter network, contact us on:

America On-Line — (Keyword: STATS)

Internet — www.stats.com

Toll Free in the USA at 1-800-63-STATS (1-800-637-8287)

Outside the USA at 1-847-676-3383

Or write to:

STATS, Inc.
8131 Monticello Ave.
Skokie, IL 60076-3300

About Howe Sportsdata

Howe Sportsdata International has been keeping statistics on professional baseball since 1910. Currently, Howe is the official statistician for all 17 U.S.-based National Association professional baseball leagues. Howe also compiles statistics for the Arizona Fall League, the Hawaiian Winter League and winter leagues located in Mexico, Puerto Rico, the Dominican Republic, Venezuela and Australia. In addition, Howe keeps the official statistics of the Continental Basketball Association, all professional minor hockey leagues and the National Professional Soccer League.

Originally based in Chicago, Howe Sportsdata International is now located in Boston, Massachusetts on the historic Fish Pier, maintaining a 24-hour/seven-days-per-week operation during the baseball season. Howe also maintains a satellite office in San Mateo, California. Howe is responsible for maintaining statistics for more than 250 teams who collectively play more than 13,000 games per year.

Howe also provides statistical information to all 30 major league teams and to major media outlets such as *USA Today*, *The Sporting News*, *Baseball America*, the *Associated Press* and *Sports Illustrated*. Howe also counts as its customers many leading newspapers, of which the following are a small representative sample: *The Los Angeles Times*, *The Detroit Free Press*, *The Miami Herald* and both the *Chicago Sun-Times* and *Chicago Tribune*. For more information about Howe, write to:

Howe Sportsdata International
Boston Fish Pier, West Building #2, Suite 306
Boston, Massachusetts 02110

Remembering Baseball

MORE OF STATS' STARTING LINEUP...

STATS Scouting Notebook: 1998

- Extensive scouting reports on over 700 major league players
- Evaluations of nearly 200 minor league prospects
- Expert analysis from nationally-known writers
- Manager profiles section evaluates skipper style and strategy

"*A phenomenal resource!* " Jayson Stark, Baseball America

- **Item #SN98, $19.95, Available 1/1/98**

STATS Minor League Scouting Notebook 1998

- Evaluation of each organization's top prospects
- Essays, stat lines and grades for more than 400 prospects
- Author John Sickels' exclusive list of baseball's top 50 prospects
- Each prospect rated with a grade from A to C-minus
- "*John Sickels knows the minor leagues like no one else.*" John Benson, Baseball Weekly
- **Item #MH98, $19.95, Available 1/15/98**

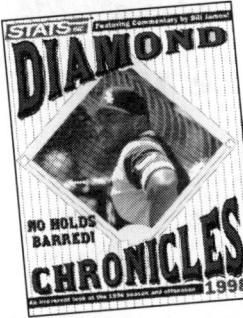

STATS analyzes baseball like nobody else!

STATS Diamond Chronicles 1998

- Essays, debates and discussions from the 1997 season and offseason
- In-depth, often heated dialogue between well-known baseball analysts
- Learn what experts think of trades, managerial styles, realignment, etc.
- Featuring commentary by Bill James, Don Zminda, Steve Moyer and John Dewan
- **Item #CH98, $19.95, Available 2/15/98**

STATS Baseball Scoreboard 1998

- Oh Yeah? Prove It! STATS' experts answer all the tough questions about baseball today
- Easy-to-understand charts and graphs answer the questions fans always ask
- In-depth coverage for each major league team
- Equal measures informative and entertaining
- **Item #SB98, $19.95, Available 3/1/98**

Order from STATS™ INC. Today!

Use Order Form in This Book, or Call 1-800-63-STATS or 847-676-3383 or visit www.stats.com

ROUNDING OUT THE STARTING LINEUP...

STATS Pro Football Handbook 1997

- A complete season-by-season register for every active NFL player
- Numerous statistical breakdowns for hundreds of NFL players
- Leader boards in a number of innovative and traditional categories
- Exclusive evaluations of offensive linemen
- **Item #FH97, $19.95, Available NOW!** *1998 Edition Available 2/1/98!*

STATS Pro Football Revealed 1997
The 100-Yard War

- Profiles each team, complete with essays, charts and play diagrams
- Detailed statistical breakdowns on players, teams and coaches
- Essays about NFL trends and happenings by leading experts
- Same data as seen on ESPN's *Sunday Night Football* broadcasts
- **Item #PF97, $18.95, Available NOW!** *1998 Edition Available 7/1/98!*

STATS Pro Basketball Handbook 1997-98

- Career stats for every player who logged minutes during 1996-97
- Team game logs with points, rebounds, assists and much more
- Leader boards from points per game to triple doubles
- Essays cover the hottest topics facing the NBA. Foreword by Bill Walton
- **Item #BH98, $19.95, Available Now!**

STATS Hockey Handbook 1997-98

- Complete career register for every 1996-97 NHL player and goalie
- Exclusive breakdowns identify player strengths and weaknesses
- Specific coverage for each team, plus league profiles
- Standard and exclusive leader boards
- **Item #HH98, $19.95, Available Now!**

Order from STATS INC. Today!

Use Order Form in This Book, or Call 1-800-63-STATS or 847-676-3383 or visit www.stats.com

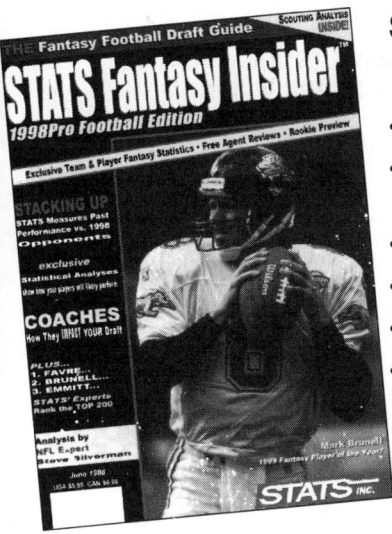

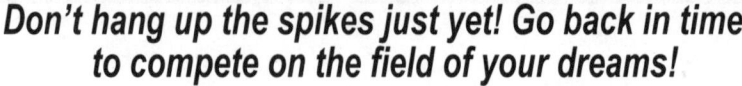 

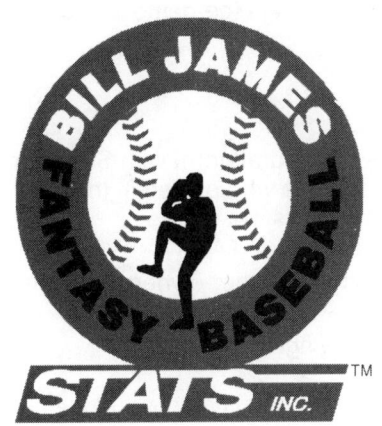

Get Into STATS Fantasy Hoops!

Soar into the 1997-98 season with STATS Fantasy Hoops! SFH puts YOU in charge. Don't just sit back and watch Grant Hill, Shawn Kemp and Michael Jordan — get in the game and coach your team to the top!

How to Play SFH:
1. Sign up to coach a team
2. You'll receive a full set of rules and a draft form with SFH point values for all eligible players - anyone who played in the NBA in 1996-97, plus all 1997 NBA draft picks
3. Complete the draft form and return it to STATS
4. You will take part in the draft with nine other owners, and we will send you league rosters
5. You make unlimited weekly transactions including trades, free agent signings, activations, and benchings
6. Six of the 10 teams in your league advance to postseason play, with two teams ultimately advancing to the Finals

SFH point values are based on actual NBA results, mirroring the real thing. Weekly reports will tell you everything you need to know to lead your team to the SFH Championship!

PLAY STATS Fantasy Football!

STATS Fantasy Football puts YOU in charge! You draft, trade, cut, bench, activate players and even sign free agents each week. SFF pits you head-to-head against 11 other owners.

STATS' scoring system applies realistic values, tested against actual NFL results. Each week, you'll receive a superb in-depth report telling you all about both team and league performances.

How to Play SFF:
1. Sign up today!
2. STATS sends you a draft form listing all eligible NFL players
3. Fill out the draft form and return it to STATS, and you will take part in the draft along with 11 other team owners
4. Go head-to-head against the other owners in your league. You'll make week-by-week roster moves and transactions through STATS' Fantasy Football experts, via phone, fax, or on-line!

STATS Fantasy Football on the Web? Check it out! www.stats.com

Order from STATS INC. Today!

Use Order Form in This Book, or Call 1-800-63-STATS or 847-676-3383 or visit www.stats.com

STATS, Inc. Order Form

Name_____

Address_____

City_____ State_____ Zip_____

Phone_____Fax_____E-mail Address_____

Method of Payment (U.S. Funds Only):
❏ Check   ❏ Money Order   ❏ Visa   ❏ MasterCard

Credit Card Information:

Cardholder Name_____

Credit Card Number_____ Exp. Date_____

Signature_____

PUBLICATIONS (STATS books now include FREE first class shipping; magazines — add $2)

Qty.	Product Name	Item #	Price	Total
	STATS All-Time Major League Handbook	ATHA	$54.95	
	STATS All-Time Baseball Sourcebook	ATSA	$54.95	
	STATS All-Time Major League COMBO (BOTH books!)	ATCA	$99.95	
	STATS Major League Handbook 1998	HB98	$19.95	
	STATS Major League Handbook 1998 (Comb-bound)	HC98	$21.95	
	STATS Projections Update 1998 (MAGAZINE)	PJUP	$9.95	
	The Scouting Notebook: 1998	SN98	$19.95	
	The Scouting Notebook: 1998 (Comb-bound)	SC98	$21.95	
	STATS Minor League Scouting Notebook 1998	MN98	$19.95	
	STATS Minor League Handbook 1998	MH98	$19.95	
	STATS Minor League Handbook 1998 (Comb-bound)	MC98	$21.95	
	STATS Player Profiles 1998	PP98	$19.95	
	STATS Player Profiles 1998 (Comb-bound)	PC98	$21.95	
	STATS 1998 BVSP Match-Ups!	BP98	$19.95	
	STATS Baseball Scoreboard 1998	SB98	$19.95	
	STATS Diamond Chronicles 1998	CH98	$19.95	
	Pro Football Revealed: The 100 Yard War (1997 Edition)	PF97	$18.95	
	STATS Pro Football Handbook 1997	FH97	$19.95	
	STATS Basketball Handbook 1997-98	BH98	$19.95	
	STATS Hockey Handbook 1997-98	HH98	$19.95	
	STATS Fantasy Insider: 1998 Major League Baseball Edition (MAGAZINE)	IB98	$5.95	
	STATS Fantasy Insider: 1998 Pro Football Edition (MAGAZINE)	IF98	$5.95	
	Prior Editions (Please circle appropriate year)			
	STATS Major League Handbook '90 '91 '92 '93 '94 '95 '96 '97		$9.95	
	The Scouting Report/Notebook '94 '95 '96 '97		$9.95	
	STATS Player Profiles '93 '94 '95 '96 '97		$9.95	
	STATS Minor League Handbook '92 '93 '94 '95 '96 '97		$9.95	
	STATS BVSP Match-Ups! '94 '95 '96 '97		$5.95	
	STATS Baseball Scoreboard '92 '93 '94 '95 '96 '97		$9.95	
	STATS Basketball Scoreboard/Handbook '93-'94 '94-'95 '95-'96 '96-'97		$9.95	
	Pro Football Revealed: The 100 Yard War '94 '95 '96		$9.95	
	STATS Pro Football Handbook '95 '96		$9.95	
	STATS Minor League Scouting Notebook '95 '96 '97		$9.95	
	STATS Hockey Handbook '96-'97		$9.95	

FANTASY GAMES

Qty.	Product Name	Item Number	Price	Total
	Bill James Classic Baseball	BJCB	$129.00	
	STATS Fantasy Hoops	SFH	$79.00	
	STATS Fantasy Football	SFF	$69.00	
	Bill James Fantasy Baseball	BJFB	$89.00	

1st Fantasy Team Name (ex. Colt 45's):_____ _____

   What Fantasy Game is this team for?_____

2nd Fantasy Team Name (ex. Colt 45's):_____ _____

   What Fantasy Game is this team for?_____

        NOTE: $1.00/player is charged for all roster moves and transactions.

For Bill James Fantasy Baseball:

Would you like to play in a league drafted by Bill James?   ❑ Yes   ❑ No

MULTIMEDIA PRODUCTS (Prices include shipping & handling charges)

Qty.	Product Name	Item Number	Price	Total
	Bill James Encyclopedia CD-Rom	BJCD	$49.95	

TOTALS

	Price	Total
Product Total (excl. Fantasy Games)		
Canada—all orders—add:	$2.50/book	
Magazines—shipping—add:	$2.00/each	
Order 2 or more books—subtract:	$1.00/book	
(**NOT** to be combined with other specials)		
Subtotal		
Fantasy Games Total		
IL residents add 8.5% sales tax		
GRAND TOTAL		

For Faster Service, Please Call 800-63-STATS or 847-676-3383
Visit STATS on the World Wide Web at www.stats.com
Fax Your Order to 847-676-0821
STATS, Inc • 8131 Monticello Avenue • Skokie, Illinois 60076-3300

NOTE: *Orders for shipments outside of the USA or Canada are Credit Card only.*
Actual shipping charges will be added to the product cost.